The Bill James Handbook 2013

Baseball Info Solutions

www.baseballinfosolutions.com

Published by ACTA Sports

A Division of ACTA Publications

ACTA SPORTS

Cover by Tom A. Wright
Cover Photo by Jeff Curry
Back Cover Photo by Jayne Kamin-Oncea

First Edition: November 2012

Published by:
ACTA Sports, a division of ACTA Publications
4848 North Clark Street
Chicago, IL 60640
(800) 397-2282
www.actasports.com www.actapublications.com

ISBN: 978-0-87946-496-7
ISSN: 1940-8668

Printed in the United States of America by McNaughton & Gunn

Dedication

This book is dedicated to my dad, who taught me to play, understand, and appreciate this great game. It is also dedicated to my family and friends who I do not get to see often enough during the baseball season, and to all of my co-workers, past and present, whose tireless efforts have made the publication of this book possible.

Mike Piekarski

Table of Contents

Introduction

"The times they are a-changin'"
-Bob Dylan (1964)

We broke from our traditional cover photo selection this year to pay homage to an all time great. Having grown up in the South in the 1990's, I know there's an entire generation of young men and women, baseball fans and non-fans alike, who appreciated what Chipper Jones brought to baseball. And in this day and age, it's increasingly rare for a player to retire a sure-fire Hall of Famer with nary a hint of suspicion around him.

The back cover paints the other half of our theme. Mike Trout turned in maybe the most exciting rookie season, ever. And he did it at the tender age of 20. Think Frank Robinson, Mickey Mantle and Ted Williams. This is the caliber of player who has a season like that at age 20. But Trout was not the only incredibly young rookie capturing our attention. A year younger than Trout, teenager Bryce Harper began his major league career with expectations through the roof. Amazingly enough, he's lived up to every single one of them. After Cole Hamels beaned the Nationals' youngster in early May, Harper handled the situation with the professionalism of a veteran, even stealing home later in the inning as a peaceful (and thrilling!) dose of retaliation. Here's to hoping we put Harper on our front cover in 20 years and look back at his career as we do Chipper's.

There was plenty more to the 2012 season. We witnessed seven no-hitters, including (for the first time ever) three perfect games. Miguel Cabrera completed the Triple Crown, the first hitter to do so in 45 years, among the rarest and most impressive feats in sports. Yet, as we've grown to understand more about the

1

game, we might now argue that Cabrera's historic performance might not have been the most valuable season in the American League.

And for the second time in two decades, Bud Selig gave us another round of playoff baseball, this time in a single life-or-death wild card game.

We've made some changes of our own at Baseball Info Solutions, saying goodbye to some old friends and hello to some new ones. This year's crew is thrilled to bring you the 2013 Handbook, which we're proud to say is our best ever. This is the 24th Handbook for John and Bill, and I'm sure they'll tell you that each one has been at least one step stronger than the previous. Knowing them, I'm sure they wouldn't settle for anything less.

After all, the more things change, the more they stay the same.

Ben Jedlovec
Coplay, PA
October 10, 2012

2012 Team Statistics

This section contains all of the team-level stats you would expect to find in any standard publication or website, but it goes way beyond. For example, Final Standings for the 2012 season, as well as several different splits such as day-night records or grass-turf records, can be found in the first group of pages. We've also included postseason clinch dates and a team-by-team breakdown. The San Francisco Giants and the Cincinnati Reds were the first teams to clinch their playoff spots in 2012.

In addition to the traditional team batting, pitching, and fielding stats, a team breakdown of Runs Saved by position can be found following the standings. Also included is a pitching staff summary, so you can easily see that the Tampa Bay Rays had 2012's best starting rotation while the Reds featured the major's top bullpen.

2012 American League Standings

Overall

EAST							CENTRAL							WEST						
Team	W-L	Pct	GB	D1	LD1	LLd	Team	W-L	Pct	GB	D1	LD1	LLd	Team	W-L	Pct	GB	D1	LD1	LLd
New York Yankees	95-67	.586	0.0	122	10/3	10.0	Detroit Tigers	88-74	.543	0.0	33	10/3	3.0	Oakland Athletics	94-68	.580	0.0	10	10/3	1.0
Baltimore Orioles	93-69	.574	2.0	54	9/30	2.0	Chicago White Sox	85-77	.525	3.0	114	9/25	3.5	Texas Rangers	93-69	.574	1.0	178	10/2	6.5
Tampa Bay Rays	90-72	.556	5.0	42	6/11	1.5	Kansas City Royals	72-90	.444	16.0	0	-	0.0	Los Angeles Angels	89-73	.549	5.0	1	4/6	0.0
Toronto Blue Jays	73-89	.451	22.0	9	4/24	1.0	Cleveland Indians	68-94	.420	20.0	40	6/23	4.0	Seattle Mariners	75-87	.463	19.0	11	4/8	1.0
Boston Red Sox	69-93	.426	26.0	0	-	0.0	Minnesota Twins	66-96	.407	22.0	0	-	0.0							

Wild Card Clinch Dates: Texas 9/30, Baltimore 9/30. Division Clinch Dates: Detroit 10/1, Oakland 10/3, New York 10/3.
D1 = Number of days a team had at least a share of first place of their division; LD1 = Last date the team had at least a share of first place; LLd = The largest number of games that a team led their division by.

East Division

	AT		VERSUS					CONDITIONS				GAME			MONTHLY						ALL-STAR	
Tm	Home	Road	East	Cent	West	NL	LHS	RHS	Day	Night	Grass	Turf	1-Rn	5+Rn	XInn	April	May	June	July	Aug	S/O	Pre	Post
NYY	51-30	44-37	41-31	21-16	20-15	13-5	37-24	58-43	33-20	62-47	89-55	6-12	22-25	24-12	6-3	13-9	14-14	20-7	13-13	15-13	20-11	52-33	43-34
Bal	47-34	46-35	43-29	23-15	16-18	11-7	26-18	67-51	30-15	63-54	85-59	8-10	29-9	25-23	16-2	14-9	15-13	13-13	13-14	18-9	20-11	45-40	48-29
TB	46-35	44-37	41-31	16-18	24-14	9-9	27-23	63-49	30-24	60-48	38-34	52-38	21-27	24-11	5-7	15-8	14-14	12-15	13-13	17-11	19-11	45-41	45-31
Tor	41-40	32-49	29-43	21-16	14-21	9-9	21-27	52-62	29-30	44-59	31-41	42-48	15-25	19-26	7-6	12-11	15-13	13-14	11-14	9-19	13-18	43-43	30-46
Bos	34-47	35-46	26-46	24-16	8-24	11-7	26-25	43-68	21-25	48-68	59-85	10-8	17-22	20-22	2-10	11-11	15-14	15-12	12-14	9-20	7-22	43-43	26-50

Central Division

	AT		VERSUS					CONDITIONS				GAME			MONTHLY						ALL-STAR	
Tm	Home	Road	East	Cent	West	NL	LHS	RHS	Day	Night	Grass	Turf	1-Rn	5+Rn	XInn	April	May	June	July	Aug	S/O	Pre	Post
Det	50-31	38-43	21-18	43-29	13-20	11-7	26-25	62-49	38-26	50-48	84-71	4-3	21-27	16-14	4-5	11-11	13-16	14-13	16-10	16-11	18-13	44-42	44-32
CWS	45-36	40-41	19-21	37-35	20-12	9-9	23-24	62-53	31-23	54-54	79-76	6-1	26-21	26-16	5-9	11-11	18-11	13-14	14-11	16-12	13-18	47-38	38-39
KC	37-44	35-46	16-21	34-38	14-21	8-10	24-28	48-62	16-36	56-54	69-86	3-4	27-26	14-21	8-7	6-15	15-13	14-13	7-19	17-11	13-19	37-47	35-43
Cle	37-44	31-50	14-22	31-41	15-21	8-10	18-35	50-59	22-34	46-60	65-90	3-4	24-12	12-32	5-8	11-9	16-14	12-15	11-15	5-24	13-17	44-41	24-53
Min	31-50	35-46	11-23	35-37	11-27	9-9	22-29	44-67	20-37	46-59	65-91	1-5	26-28	16-29	8-5	6-16	12-16	14-13	12-14	9-19	13-18	36-49	30-47

West Division

	AT		VERSUS					CONDITIONS				GAME			MONTHLY						ALL-STAR	
Tm	Home	Road	East	Cent	West	NL	LHS	RHS	Day	Night	Grass	Turf	1-Rn	5+Rn	XInn	M/Al	May	June	July	Aug	S/O	Pre	Post
Oak	50-31	44-37	28-18	23-18	33-24	10-8	30-29	64-39	30-27	64-41	87-64	7-4	25-18	27-21	11-5	11-13	11-16	15-13	19-5	18-10	20-11	43-43	51-25
Tex	50-31	43-38	24-16	28-19	27-30	14-4	28-19	65-50	26-15	67-54	89-64	4-5	24-22	30-18	8-5	17-6	14-14	19-9	9-14	19-10	15-16	52-34	41-35
LAA	46-35	43-38	22-20	25-20	30-27	12-6	27-22	62-51	25-25	64-48	87-68	2-5	18-18	27-23	3-4	8-15	18-11	17-9	14-12	13-15	19-11	48-38	41-35
Sea	40-41	35-46	18-28	25-16	24-33	8-10	25-32	50-55	23-30	52-57	69-78	6-9	25-28	15-20	5-10	11-13	12-17	11-16	15-11	15-12	11-18	36-51	39-36

Team vs. Team Breakdown

	EAST					CENTRAL					WEST			
	NYY	Bal	TB	Tor	Bos	Det	CWS	KC	Cle	Min	Oak	Tex	LAA	Sea
New York Yankees	-	9	8	11	13	6	2	4	5	4	5	4	5	6
Baltimore Orioles	9	-	10	11	13	3	6	5	4	5	4	2	2	8
Tampa Bay Rays	10	8	-	14	9	2	3	2	4	5	4	5	9	6
Toronto Blue Jays	7	7	4	-	11	2	4	6	4	5	4	3	4	3
Boston Red Sox	5	5	9	7	-	5	6	4	5	4	1	2	0	5
Detroit Tigers	4	3	5	4	5	-	12	13	8	10	4	3	5	1
Chicago White Sox	5	2	4	6	2	6	-	6	11	14	3	6	3	8
Kansas City Royals	3	4	4	2	3	5	12	-	10	7	5	4	4	1
Cleveland Indians	1	4	4	2	3	10	7	8	-	6	2	4	5	4
Minnesota Twins	3	2	1	2	3	8	4	11	12	-	4	2	3	2
Oakland Athletics	5	5	5	5	8	3	3	4	8	5	-	11	10	12
Texas Rangers	3	5	4	6	6	7	3	5	5	8	8	-	9	10
Los Angeles Angels	4	7	1	4	6	5	5	5	4	6	9	10	-	11
Seattle Mariners	3	1	4	6	4	5	1	7	4	8	7	9	8	-

2012 National League Standings

Overall

EAST						CENTRAL						WEST					
Team	W-L	Pct	GB	D1	LD1	LLd	Team	W-L	Pct	GB	D1	LD1	LLd	Team	W-L	Pct	GB	D1	LD1	LLd
Washington Nationals	98-64	.605	0.0	172	10/3	8.5	Cincinnati Reds	97-65	.599	0.0	125	10/3	11.5	San Francisco Giants	94-68	.580	0.0	86	10/3	11.0
Atlanta Braves	94-68	.580	4.0	8	5/21	1.5	St Louis Cardinals	88-74	.543	9.0	50	5/23	4.5	Los Angeles Dodgers	86-76	.531	8.0	97	8/19	7.5
Philadelphia Phillies	81-81	.500	17.0	2	4/6	0.0	Milwaukee Brewers	83-79	.512	14.0	0	-	0.0	Arizona Diamondbacks	81-81	.500	13.0	3	4/10	0.5
New York Mets	74-88	.457	24.0	7	4/11	2.0	Pittsburgh Pirates	79-83	.488	18.0	15	7/18	2.0	San Diego Padres	76-86	.469	18.0	0	-	0.0
Miami Marlins	69-93	.426	29.0	1	4/4	0.0	Chicago Cubs	61-101	.377	36.0	0	-	0.0	Colorado Rockies	64-98	.395	30.0	0	-	0.0
							Houston Astros	55-107	.340	42.0	0	-	0.0							

Wild Card Clinch Dates: Atlanta 9/25, St Louis 10/2. Division Clinch Dates: San Francisco 9/22, Cincinnati 9/22, Washington 10/1.
D1 = Number of days a team had at least a share of first place of their division; LD1 = Last date the team had at least a share of first place; LLd = The largest number of games that a team led their division

East Division

	AT		VERSUS					CONDITIONS				GAME			MONTHLY						ALL-STAR	
Tm	Home	Road	East	Cent	West	AL	LHS	RHS	Day	Night	Grass	Turf	1-Rn	5+Rn	XInn	April	May	June	July	Aug	S/O	Pre	Post
Was	50-31	48-33	42-30	29-13	17-15	10-8	29-19	69-45	30-23	68-41	95-64	3-0	27-21	21-11	13-7	14-8	15-13	15-11	17-9	19-10	18-13	49-34	49-30
Atl	48-33	46-35	46-26	19-19	21-13	8-10	30-31	64-37	28-18	66-50	92-67	2-1	25-13	31-17	7-4	14-9	14-15	13-12	18-8	15-14	20-10	46-39	48-29
Phi	40-41	41-40	33-39	24-16	19-16	5-10	23-30	58-51	23-28	58-53	81-78	0-3	25-27	14-14	7-10	11-12	16-13	9-19	10-13	17-12	18-12	37-50	44-31
NYM	36-45	38-43	32-40	17-22	17-19	8-7	21-38	53-50	33-26	41-62	70-86	4-2	20-22	20-24	3-7	13-10	15-13	15-13	7-18	12-16	12-18	46-40	28-48
Mia	38-43	31-50	27-45	18-20	19-15	5-13	24-29	45-64	22-32	47-61	68-91	1-2	26-26	8-22	12-5	8-14	21-8	8-18	10-16	12-17	10-20	41-44	28-49

Central Division

	AT		VERSUS					CONDITIONS				GAME			MONTHLY						ALL-STAR	
Tm	Home	Road	East	Cent	West	AL	LHS	RHS	Day	Night	Grass	Turf	1-Rn	5+Rn	XInn	April	May	June	July	Aug	S/O	Pre	Post
Cin	50-31	47-34	19-15	49-30	22-12	7-8	32-18	65-47	39-17	58-48	97-65	0-0	31-21	20-13	7-7	11-11	17-11	15-12	19-7	19-11	16-13	47-38	50-27
StL	50-31	38-43	14-20	45-32	21-15	8-7	31-17	57-57	33-24	55-50	88-74	0-0	21-26	31-17	6-12	14-8	13-16	13-14	15-10	16-13	17-13	46-40	42-34
Mil	49-32	34-47	15-19	45-32	21-15	6-9	26-21	57-58	25-35	58-44	83-79	0-0	24-32	22-19	7-11	11-12	12-16	12-14	12-14	16-12	20-11	40-45	43-34
Pit	45-36	34-47	17-14	39-42	13-19	10-8	22-19	57-64	29-26	50-57	79-83	0-0	28-29	14-21	4-2	10-12	15-13	17-10	17-9	11-17	9-22	48-37	31-46
ChC	38-43	23-58	13-19	31-50	12-22	5-10	18-26	43-75	35-46	26-55	61-101	0-0	15-27	15-27	4-6	8-15	10-17	10-15	15-10	8-21	10-21	33-52	28-49
Hou	35-46	20-61	12-20	29-50	8-28	6-9	15-27	40-80	15-32	40-75	55-107	0-0	17-27	13-32	1-11	9-14	13-15	10-17	3-24	5-22	15-15	33-53	22-54

West Division

	AT		VERSUS					CONDITIONS				GAME			MONTHLY						ALL-STAR	
Tm	Home	Road	East	Cent	West	AL	LHS	RHS	Day	Night	Grass	Turf	1-Rn	5+Rn	XInn	April	May	June	July	Aug	S/O	Pre	Post
SF	48-33	46-35	15-19	27-14	45-27	7-8	40-19	54-49	32-32	62-36	94-68	0-0	30-20	24-18	8-5	12-10	15-14	17-11	12-12	18-11	20-10	46-40	48-28
LAD	45-36	41-40	20-12	25-18	35-37	6-9	36-26	50-50	28-19	58-57	86-76	0-0	29-27	24-14	8-7	16-7	16-12	11-17	13-13	14-14	16-13	47-40	39-36
Ari	41-40	40-41	14-20	20-21	38-34	9-6	32-31	49-50	24-24	57-57	81-81	0-0	15-27	28-21	3-4	12-11	11-17	16-10	14-13	13-16	15-14	42-43	39-38
SD	42-39	34-47	12-20	22-21	34-38	8-7	24-31	52-55	26-26	50-60	76-86	0-0	26-21	17-22	4-6	7-17	10-18	12-15	15-11	18-10	14-15	34-53	42-33
Col	35-46	29-52	15-22	19-19	28-44	2-13	15-35	49-63	16-37	48-61	64-98	0-0	18-23	14-31	5-2	11-11	10-18	9-18	7-17	16-13	11-21	33-52	31-46

Team vs. Team Breakdown

	EAST					CENTRAL						WEST				
	Was	Atl	Phi	NYM	Mia	Cin	StL	Mil	Pit	ChC	Hou	SF	LAD	Ari	SD	Col
Washington Nationals	-	10	9	14	9	5	4	5	2	6	7	5	2	4	3	3
Atlanta Braves	8	-	12	12	14	1	5	3	3	3	4	3	3	5	4	6
Philadelphia Phillies	9	6	-	8	10	4	5	5	3	4	3	2	2	4	4	7
New York Mets	4	6	10	-	12	2	4	2	5	2	2	4	3	4	4	2
Miami Marlins	9	4	8	6	-	3	2	4	1	4	4	5	2	3	5	4
Cincinnati Reds	2	5	3	6	3	-	7	9	11	12	10	4	2	5	6	5
St Louis Cardinals	3	1	2	3	5	8	-	9	7	10	11	3	5	5	3	5
Milwaukee Brewers	3	3	2	3	4	6	6	-	11	13	9	2	6	3	5	1
Pittsburgh Pirates	3	4	4	2	4	7	8	4	-	8	12	3	1	4	1	4
Chicago Cubs	1	4	2	4	2	4	7	4	8	-	8	1	2	4	3	2
Houston Astros	1	2	3	4	2	5	4	8	5	7	-	1	2	0	3	2
San Francisco Giants	1	4	4	4	2	3	3	4	3	6	8	-	10	9	12	14
Los Angeles Dodgers	4	3	5	4	4	4	6	1	6	4	4	8	-	6	11	10
Arizona Diamondbacks	2	2	2	3	5	2	1	3	3	5	6	9	12	-	7	10
San Diego Padres	2	3	3	3	1	2	3	4	5	3	5	6	7	11	-	10
Colorado Rockies	4	1	2	5	3	1	2	5	2	4	5	4	8	8	8	-

American League Batting

							BATTING													BASERUNNING					PERCENTAGES		
Tm	G	AB	H	2B	3B	HR	(Hm Rd)	TB	R	RBI	TBB	IBB	SO	HBP	SH	SF	ShO	SB	CS	SB%	GDP	LOB	Avg	OBP	Slg
Tex	162	5590	1526	303	32	200	(108 92)	2493	808	780	478	44	1103	57	36	53	5	91	44	.67	121	1700	.273	.334	.446
NYY	162	5524	1462	280	13	245	(138 107)	2503	804	774	565	31	1176	62	31	49	6	93	27	.78	136	1732	.265	.337	.453
LAA	162	5536	1518	273	22	187	(82 105)	2396	767	732	449	29	1113	47	47	41	13	134	33	.80	138	1665	.274	.332	.433
CWS	162	5518	1409	228	29	211	(120 91)	2328	748	726	461	24	1203	65	31	36	11	109	43	.72	113	1573	.255	.318	.422
Bos	162	5604	1459	339	16	165	(88 77)	2325	734	695	428	27	1197	45	34	55	7	97	31	.76	105	1650	.260	.315	.415
Det	162	5476	1467	279	39	163	(92 71)	2313	726	698	511	46	1103	57	36	39	2	59	23	.72	156	1713	.268	.335	.422
Tor	162	5487	1346	247	22	198	(102 96)	2231	716	677	473	29	1251	55	33	45	9	123	41	.75	109	1539	.245	.309	.407
Oak	162	5527	1315	267	32	195	(92 103)	2231	713	676	550	29	1387	45	27	34	16	122	32	.79	97	1613	.238	.310	.404
Bal	162	5560	1375	270	16	214	(127 87)	2319	712	677	480	24	1315	50	38	30	9	58	29	.67	152	1557	.247	.311	.417
Min	162	5562	1448	270	30	131	(69 62)	2171	701	667	505	28	1069	53	33	56	11	135	37	.78	149	1748	.260	.325	.390
TB	162	5398	1293	250	30	175	(82 93)	2128	697	665	571	26	1323	58	34	42	10	134	44	.75	133	1590	.240	.317	.394
KC	162	5636	1492	295	37	131	(62 69)	2254	676	643	404	35	1032	42	26	41	7	132	38	.78	130	1678	.265	.317	.400
Cle	162	5525	1385	266	24	136	(64 72)	2107	667	635	555	28	1087	59	17	39	12	110	44	.71	142	1784	.251	.324	.381
Sea	162	5494	1285	241	27	149	(56 93)	2027	619	584	466	21	1259	30	32	35	12	104	35	.75	95	1595	.234	.296	.369
AL	1134	77437	19780	3808	369	2500	(1282 1218)	31826	10088	9629	6896	421	16618	725	455	595	130	1501	501	.75	1776	23137	.255	.320	.411

American League Pitching

HOW MUCH THEY PITCHED					WHAT THEY GAVE UP												THE RESULTS									
Tm	G	CG	Rel	IP	BFP	H	R	ER	HR	SH	SF	HB	TBB	IBB	SO	WP	Bk	W	L	Pct.	ShO	Sv-Op	Hld	OAvg	OOBP	OSlg	ERA
TB	162	7	472	1459.2	6000	1233	577	518	139	26	33	54	469	35	1383	59	4	90	72	.556	15	50-58	77	.228	.294	.352	3.19
Oak	162	1	462	1470.0	6131	1360	614	569	147	36	47	46	462	34	1136	40	5	94	68	.580	13	47-64	79	.245	.306	.378	3.48
Sea	162	8	451	1456.2	6062	1359	651	608	166	35	45	49	449	39	1166	61	5	75	87	.463	11	43-62	61	.248	.308	.394	3.76
NYY	162	6	485	1445.1	6085	1401	668	618	190	31	32	49	431	32	1318	53	9	95	67	.586	9	51-64	87	.253	.311	.419	3.85
Det	162	9	420	1430.2	6045	1409	670	596	151	33	35	42	438	35	1318	46	6	88	74	.543	8	40-56	73	.256	.314	.402	3.75
CWS	162	6	466	1445.2	6098	1365	676	646	186	24	33	68	503	29	1246	66	9	85	77	.525	11	37-58	65	.250	.319	.405	4.02
LAA	162	6	444	1433.1	6034	1339	699	640	186	31	45	40	483	20	1157	38	2	89	73	.549	16	38-60	80	.246	.310	.403	4.02
Bal	162	1	492	1483.0	6278	1433	705	642	184	30	38	53	481	36	1177	34	6	93	69	.574	10	55-73	67	.252	.315	.403	3.90
Tex	162	7	428	1442.0	6067	1378	707	639	175	22	40	41	446	15	1286	53	8	93	69	.574	10	43-52	61	.250	.309	.408	3.99
KC	162	2	500	1451.1	6251	1504	746	693	163	40	42	60	542	14	1177	49	8	72	90	.444	12	44-64	78	.270	.339	.423	4.30
Tor	162	5	495	1443.2	6216	1439	784	745	204	35	35	55	574	20	1142	56	7	73	89	.451	11	29-44	72	.261	.335	.438	4.64
Bos	162	6	489	1443.0	6209	1449	806	754	190	27	64	66	529	33	1176	42	11	69	93	.426	4	35-57	76	.262	.331	.428	4.70
Min	162	3	499	1438.2	6214	1536	832	762	198	34	48	57	441	43	943	60	2	66	96	.407	6	35-49	63	.274	.333	.442	4.77
Cle	162	2	494	1442.0	6283	1503	845	766	174	25	57	55	543	27	1086	67	6	68	94	.420	6	43-56	81	.268	.336	.430	4.78
AL	1134	69	6597	20285.0	85973	19708	9980	9196	2453	429	594	735	6815	442	16711	724	88	1150	1118	.507	142	590-817	1020	.255	.319	.409	4.08

American League Fielding

Team	G	Inn	PO	Ast	OFAst	E	(Throw Field)	TC	DP	GDP	SB	CS	SB%	CPkof	PPkof	PB	UER	UERA	FPct
Chicago	162	1445.2	4337	1578	28	70	(33 37)	5985	154	129	104	41	.72	1	5	9	30	0.19	.988
Seattle	162	1456.2	4370	1570	19	72	(36 36)	6012	155	137	128	39	.77	1	1	20	43	0.27	.988
New York	162	1445.1	4372	1472	17	74	(30 44)	5882	135	115	90	28	.76	3	5	17	50	0.31	.987
Texas	162	1442.0	4326	1496	26	85	(36 49)	5907	136	115	106	27	.80	0	3	13	68	0.42	.986
Cleveland	162	1442.0	4326	1665	25	96	(54 42)	6087	157	137	140	37	.79	1	2	13	79	0.49	.984
Toronto	162	1443.2	4331	1736	32	101	(49 52)	6168	168	143	87	43	.67	3	0	15	39	0.24	.984
Los Angeles	162	1433.1	4300	1577	23	98	(47 51)	5975	141	112	127	41	.76	0	11	11	59	0.37	.984
Boston	162	1443.0	4329	1687	26	101	(49 52)	6117	159	139	127	31	.80	1	7	11	52	0.32	.983
Detroit	162	1430.2	4292	1481	20	99	(52 47)	5872	127	112	131	45	.74	1	4	14	74	0.47	.983
Baltimore	162	1483.0	4449	1680	20	106	(44 62)	6235	151	131	63	36	.64	1	0	10	66	0.38	.983
Minnesota	162	1438.2	4316	1785	30	107	(45 62)	6208	188	159	111	24	.82	1	3	8	70	0.44	.983
Oakland	162	1470.0	4410	1568	37	111	(48 63)	6089	135	112	99	45	.69	2	4	12	45	0.28	.982
Kansas City	162	1451.1	4354	1624	51	113	(50 63)	6091	171	137	113	51	.69	6	6	11	53	0.33	.981
Tampa Bay	162	1459.2	4379	1641	24	114	(54 60)	6134	155	126	101	33	.75	1	6	6	59	0.36	.981
American League	1134	20285.0	60855	22560	378	1347	(627 720)	84762	2132	1804	1527	521	.75	22	57	170	784	0.35	.984

National League Batting

	BATTING																		BASERUNNING					PERCENTAGES		
Tm	G	AB	H	2B	3B	HR	(Hm	Rd)	TB	R	RBI	TBB	IBB	SO	HBP	SH	SF	ShO	SB	CS	SB%	GDP	LOB	Avg	OBP	Slg
Mil	162	5557	1442	300	39	202	(119	83)	2426	776	741	466	35	1240	90	76	35	11	158	39	.80	111	1653	.259	.325	.437
StL	162	5622	1526	290	37	159	(76	83)	2367	765	732	533	45	1192	53	69	49	11	91	37	.71	135	1797	.271	.338	.421
Col	162	5577	1526	306	52	166	(100	66)	2434	758	716	450	34	1213	36	74	39	11	100	40	.71	132	1671	.274	.330	.436
Ari	162	5462	1416	307	33	165	(84	81)	2284	734	710	539	47	1266	41	61	45	9	93	51	.65	108	1671	.259	.328	.418
Was	162	5615	1468	301	25	194	(101	93)	2401	731	688	479	43	1325	41	50	36	8	105	35	.75	111	1687	.261	.322	.428
SF	162	5558	1495	287	57	103	(31	72)	2205	718	675	483	44	1097	29	69	61	6	118	39	.75	115	1778	.269	.327	.397
Atl	162	5425	1341	263	30	149	(70	79)	2111	700	660	567	37	1289	34	53	46	13	101	32	.76	109	1687	.247	.320	.389
Phi	162	5544	1414	271	28	158	(82	76)	2215	684	659	454	41	1094	63	72	39	6	116	23	.83	115	1723	.255	.317	.400
Cin	162	5477	1377	296	30	172	(103	69)	2249	669	636	481	54	1266	47	73	37	4	87	27	.76	100	1698	.251	.315	.411
SD	162	5422	1339	272	43	121	(47	74)	2060	651	610	539	36	1238	54	63	34	12	155	46	.77	100	1733	.247	.319	.380
Pit	162	5412	1313	241	37	170	(67	103)	2138	651	620	444	32	1354	51	62	45	15	73	52	.58	98	1552	.243	.304	.395
NYM	162	5450	1357	286	21	139	(67	72)	2102	650	625	503	43	1250	42	64	30	12	79	38	.68	118	1695	.249	.316	.386
LAD	162	5438	1369	269	23	116	(59	57)	2032	637	607	481	49	1156	52	82	38	15	104	44	.70	139	1689	.252	.317	.374
ChC	162	5411	1297	265	36	137	(65	72)	2045	613	590	447	29	1235	44	54	24	16	94	45	.68	125	1586	.240	.302	.378
Mia	162	5437	1327	261	39	137	(55	82)	2077	609	576	484	46	1228	35	60	40	17	149	41	.78	114	1638	.244	.308	.382
Hou	162	5407	1276	238	28	146	(79	67)	2008	583	545	463	19	1365	58	54	30	14	105	46	.70	114	1623	.236	.302	.371
NL	1296	87814	22283	4453	558	2434	(1205	1229)	35154	10929	10370	7813	634	19808	769	1024	628	180	1728	635	.73	1844	26881	.254	.318	.400

National League Pitching

HOW MUCH THEY PITCHED					WHAT THEY GAVE UP												THE RESULTS									
Tm	G	CG	Rel	IP	BFP	H	R	ER	HR	SH	SF	HB	TBB	IBB	SO	WP	Bk	W	L	Pct.	ShO	Sv-Op	Hld	OAvg	OOBP	OSlg	ERA
Cin	162	9	425	1453.0	6056	1356	588	540	152	44	41	51	427	33	1248	34	7	97	65	.599	12	56-74	73	.247	.305	.390	3.34
Was	162	3	482	1468.1	6133	1296	594	543	129	69	46	47	497	32	1325	62	4	98	64	.605	9	51-68	105	.237	.303	.373	3.33
LAD	162	2	506	1449.2	6068	1277	597	538	122	73	38	45	539	62	1276	46	2	86	76	.531	10	40-59	81	.238	.310	.364	3.34
Atl	162	5	460	1445.1	5991	1310	600	549	145	62	26	41	464	40	1232	54	3	94	68	.580	16	47-60	81	.243	.306	.378	3.42
StL	162	4	506	1462.2	6158	1420	648	603	134	66	35	50	436	28	1218	46	4	88	74	.543	10	42-64	105	.255	.313	.387	3.71
SF	162	5	526	1451.0	6138	1361	649	593	142	66	36	51	489	42	1237	54	4	94	68	.580	14	53-66	102	.248	.313	.393	3.68
Pit	162	2	483	1433.1	6097	1357	674	615	153	67	40	45	490	30	1192	45	3	79	83	.488	10	45-59	92	.249	.314	.390	3.86
Phi	162	5	440	1451.1	6072	1387	680	618	178	60	32	44	409	33	1385	30	3	81	81	.500	11	42-61	78	.251	.306	.407	3.83
Ari	162	4	461	1433.2	6063	1432	688	626	155	67	37	51	417	18	1200	52	10	81	81	.500	9	39-59	68	.261	.317	.415	3.93
NYM	162	7	505	1434.0	6086	1368	709	651	161	64	43	40	488	29	1240	40	3	74	88	.457	13	36-55	66	.251	.315	.401	4.09
SD	162	4	529	1434.2	6151	1356	710	640	162	62	38	48	539	48	1205	49	8	76	86	.469	11	43-60	98	.248	.319	.398	4.01
Mia	162	5	483	1440.2	6186	1448	724	655	133	75	55	55	495	61	1113	36	4	69	93	.426	7	38-60	88	.263	.327	.399	4.09
Mil	162	0	512	1453.2	6245	1458	733	682	169	61	34	31	525	20	1402	57	5	83	79	.512	9	44-73	81	.261	.326	.414	4.22
ChC	162	1	493	1413.2	6140	1399	759	708	175	58	42	65	573	36	1128	44	5	61	101	.377	9	28-49	56	.259	.335	.424	4.51
Hou	162	3	541	1423.1	6238	1493	794	721	173	44	51	48	540	40	1170	75	6	55	107	.340	11	31-50	70	.270	.337	.427	4.56
Col	162	0	575	1422.0	6384	1637	890	824	198	87	45	47	566	61	1144	94	6	64	98	.395	7	36-63	73	.290	.357	.470	5.22
NL	1296	59	7927	23070.1	98206	22355	11037	10106	2481	1050	629	759	7894	613	19715	818	77	1280	1312	.494	168	671-980	1317	.254	.319	.402	3.94

National League Fielding

							Fielding													
Team	G	Inn	PO	Ast	OFAst	E	(Throw	Field)	TC	DP	GDP	SB	CS	SB%	CPkof	PPkof	PB	UER	UERA	FPct
Atlanta	162	1445.1	4336	1654	27	86	42	44	6076	147	123	98	39	.72	1	7	10	51	0.32	.986
Cincinnati	162	1453.0	4359	1602	19	89	43	46	6050	113	102	78	43	.64	1	9	7	48	0.30	.985
Arizona	162	1433.2	4301	1676	34	90	37	53	6067	146	126	48	37	.56	2	1	9	62	0.39	.985
Washington	162	1468.1	4405	1632	25	94	47	47	6131	134	120	111	22	.83	0	1	15	51	0.31	.985
Los Angeles	162	1449.2	4349	1669	26	98	49	49	6116	138	114	92	43	.68	1	9	11	59	0.37	.984
Milwaukee	162	1453.2	4361	1532	25	99	48	51	5992	123	104	123	39	.76	3	5	5	51	0.32	.983
Philadelphia	162	1451.1	4354	1560	31	101	37	64	6015	118	98	99	56	.64	3	1	9	62	0.38	.983
Miami	162	1440.2	4322	1648	19	103	42	61	6073	154	135	88	28	.76	0	4	14	69	0.43	.983
New York	162	1434.0	4302	1502	18	101	44	57	5905	135	117	97	30	.76	1	5	32	58	0.36	.983
St Louis	162	1462.2	4388	1754	24	107	44	63	6249	149	130	56	43	.57	3	6	9	45	0.28	.983
Chicago	162	1413.2	4241	1583	26	105	45	60	5929	148	121	125	36	.78	1	4	9	51	0.32	.982
Pittsburgh	162	1433.1	4300	1656	20	112	53	59	6068	126	111	154	19	.89	0	4	9	59	0.37	.982
San Francisco	162	1451.0	4353	1638	21	115	49	66	6106	134	110	129	53	.71	2	3	5	56	0.35	.981
Houston	162	1423.1	4270	1729	32	118	55	63	6117	132	108	131	37	.78	1	2	13	73	0.46	.981
San Diego	162	1434.2	4304	1655	18	121	62	59	6080	97	78	152	47	.76	3	5	18	70	0.44	.980
Colorado	162	1422.0	4266	1718	32	122	66	56	6106	139	119	121	43	.74	1	9	22	66	0.42	.980
National League	1296	23070.1	69211	26208	397	1661	763	898	97080	2143	1816	1702	615	.73	23	75	197	931	0.36	.983

Team Pitching Staff Summary

Team	Starters				Bullpen					
	IP	ERA	ERA Rank	W-L	IP	ERA	ERA Rank	W-L	Sv-Opp	Sv Pct
Arizona Diamondbacks	967.0	4.26	19	64-61	466.2	3.28	10	17-20	39-59	66%
Atlanta Braves	959.0	3.75	7	69-54	486.1	2.76	2	25-14	47-60	78%
Baltimore Orioles	937.2	4.42	21	61-58	545.1	3.00	5	32-11	55-73	75%
Boston Red Sox	928.1	5.19	27	48-72	514.2	3.88	19	21-21	35-57	61%
Chicago Cubs	922.2	4.52	23	42-76	491.0	4.49	27	19-25	28-49	57%
Chicago White Sox	980.0	4.15	17	60-52	465.2	3.75	16	25-25	37-58	64%
Cincinnati Reds	1018.2	3.64	5	66-43	434.1	2.65	1	31-22	56-74	76%
Cleveland Indians	913.2	5.25	28	48-76	528.1	3.99	23	20-18	43-56	77%
Colorado Rockies	765.0	5.81	30	29-68	657.0	4.52	28	35-30	36-65	55%
Detroit Tigers	972.0	3.76	8	63-51	458.2	3.79	18	25-23	40-57	70%
Houston Astros	918.2	4.62	24	43-76	504.2	4.46	26	12-31	31-51	61%
Kansas City Royals	890.0	5.01	26	47-69	561.1	3.17	6	25-21	44-64	69%
Los Angeles Angels	984.1	4.04	14	70-53	449.0	3.97	22	19-20	38-60	63%
Los Angeles Dodgers	987.2	3.41	3	56-56	462.0	3.23	7	30-20	40-59	68%
Miami Marlins	982.1	4.12	16	48-73	458.1	4.06	24	21-20	38-60	63%
Milwaukee Brewers	941.1	3.99	13	55-46	512.1	4.66	30	28-33	44-73	60%
Minnesota Twins	880.0	5.40	29	39-75	558.2	3.77	17	27-21	35-49	71%
New York Mets	975.1	3.83	11	58-59	458.2	4.65	29	16-29	36-55	65%
New York Yankees	1001.1	4.05	15	71-50	444.0	3.43	14	24-17	51-65	78%
Oakland Athletics	958.0	3.80	9	64-54	512.0	2.94	4	30-14	47-64	73%
Philadelphia Phillies	1033.0	3.82	10	59-54	418.1	3.94	21	22-27	42-61	69%
Pittsburgh Pirates	934.2	4.21	18	61-64	498.2	3.36	11	18-19	45-59	76%
San Diego Padres	929.1	4.44	22	54-65	505.1	3.24	9	22-21	43-60	72%
San Francisco Giants	998.1	3.73	6	71-49	452.2	3.56	15	23-19	53-67	79%
Seattle Mariners	1002.2	3.93	12	55-62	454.0	3.39	12	20-25	43-62	69%
St Louis Cardinals	989.1	3.62	4	71-47	473.1	3.90	20	17-27	42-64	66%
Tampa Bay Rays	993.2	3.34	1	70-51	466.0	2.88	3	20-21	50-58	86%
Texas Rangers	984.2	4.30	20	72-55	457.1	3.42	13	21-14	43-52	83%
Toronto Blue Jays	916.0	4.82	25	52-69	527.2	4.33	25	21-20	29-44	66%
Washington Nationals	953.0	3.40	2	72-45	515.1	3.23	7	26-19	51-68	75%

Team Defense
Defensive Runs Saved by Position and Team

Team	P	C	1B	2B	3B	SS	LF	CF	RF	Shifts	Total
Toronto Blue Jays	10	6	-3	5	21	18	-4	10	-4	12	71
Atlanta Braves	-5	-1	4	6	3	9	13	24	18	0	71
Los Angeles Angels	2	2	8	3	4	-7	7	30	9	-3	55
Boston Red Sox	-3	-6	14	13	-7	25	3	0	4	7	50
Cincinnati Reds	23	3	1	7	2	9	-7	-1	-5	6	38
Tampa Bay Rays	10	-3	-1	-1	9	-4	10	-6	8	10	32
Minnesota Twins	-6	-10	-4	23	-6	11	-11	17	15	1	30
Arizona Diamondbacks	16	-3	2	-2	2	-8	-2	10	8	1	24
Seattle Mariners	-3	-6	1	13	-4	28	-1	-20	9	1	18
Oakland Athletics	-5	1	-8	0	12	-3	2	-14	29	2	16
Milwaukee Brewers	8	6	1	-28	4	-2	7	9	8	1	14
St Louis Cardinals	15	14	-4	-9	3	-8	-3	0	4	1	13
Kansas City Royals	1	14	-8	-15	14	-5	25	-1	-13	-3	9
Chicago White Sox	1	0	-13	1	5	12	4	-7	5	0	8
Los Angeles Dodgers	10	1	4	1	12	-21	8	-15	4	1	5
Chicago Cubs	-9	-3	-6	25	1	4	-4	-11	-4	5	-2
San Francisco Giants	1	0	7	-18	-9	3	4	-7	12	2	-5
Baltimore Orioles	7	2	-7	-3	-7	18	-1	-15	-7	8	-5
Texas Rangers	-3	-16	-1	-3	9	8	9	4	-13	0	-6
Philadelphia Phillies	-8	8	-7	16	1	-5	-1	-5	-7	1	-7
Washington Nationals	-1	0	8	2	1	-3	-17	4	-7	-1	-14
San Diego Padres	-16	11	3	-17	-3	-5	-6	8	1	5	-19
New York Yankees	-14	-2	23	16	-6	-21	-2	-11	-5	0	-22
Pittsburgh Pirates	-17	-12	-1	-2	-3	10	9	-5	-4	0	-25
Detroit Tigers	0	0	-5	-8	-3	-3	4	0	-17	5	-27
New York Mets	-2	0	-1	-16	15	-5	-8	-3	-24	2	-42
Cleveland Indians	-13	-6	-4	6	-6	-12	-2	1	-15	8	-43
Miami Marlins	6	-1	4	7	-24	-17	-17	-10	6	-2	-48
Houston Astros	-15	-1	-8	-22	-14	-9	-9	10	-2	4	-66
Colorado Rockies	-7	-11	1	1	-32	-24	-8	3	-11	1	-87

Team Efficiency Summary

Certain teams seem to squeeze out more wins than you might expect looking at their production on paper. It's not always predictable or explainable even after the fact, but a little efficiency can make a sizable difference in a team's record.

Given their component offensive production (singles, doubles, triples, etc.) we can predict with reasonable accuracy the number of runs a team will score. If a team scores more or fewer runs than expected by their components, we chalk up the difference as "Hitting Efficiency" (labeled "Hit Eff" in the below charts). We make a similar comparison for each team's pitching staff, naming it "Pitching Efficiency" ("Pit Eff" in the charts). Similarly, a team's winning percentage can be approximated with the number of runs scored and allowed over the course of the season. If a team scores and allows their runs efficiently, they can beat their expected win/loss record. We call this "Runs Efficiency" ("Runs Eff"). We combine these three measures of efficiency into "Overall Efficiency".

Baltimore set a new standard for team efficiency in 2012. Assembled by Bill James Handbook reader Dan Duquette and managed by Buck Showalter, the Orioles posted an Overall Efficiency rating of 119, the highest team rating since we began tracking the statistic in 2003. The Orioles had an unspectacular but efficient offense and a pitching staff with roughly neutral efficiency. In other words, the Orioles scored a few more runs than they should have, but the pitching staff allowed about as many as they should have. Baltimore was especially efficient with their runs, thanks to a 29-9 record in one run games and a 16-2 record in extra inning games. Essentially, the Orioles used their runs when they needed them the most.

This is the seventh year of The Fielding Bible Awards. Among our winners at each of the nine positions this year, we have six first-time winners. The fact that Mark Teixeria is a first-time winner is a bit of a surprise. Everyone knows that he has always been a good fielder at first base. Brendan Ryan's first award at shortstop is overdue as well. The other first timers are Darwin Barney, Alex Gordon, Mike Trout and Jason Heyward.

The repeat winners in 2012 have all been elite defenders over a long period of time and have all now won at least four awards: Yadier Molina (his fifth award), Mark Buehrle (fourth in a row), and Adrian Beltre (four).

Here's a short refresher course on how the awards are determined: We asked our panel of ten experts to rank 10 players at each position on a scale from one to ten. We then use the same voting technique as the Major League Baseball MVP voting. A first place vote gets 10 points, second place 9 points, third place 8 points, etc. Total up the points for each player and the player with the most points wins the award. A perfect score is 100.

One important distinction that differentiates our award from most other baseball awards, including the Gold Gloves, is that we only have one winner for all of Major League Baseball, instead of separate winners for each league. Our intention is to continue to stand up and say, "This is the best fielder at this position in the major leagues last season."

Here are the Fielding Bible Awards for the 2012 season:

First Base – Mark Teixeira, New York Yankees

Mark Teixeira finally wins his first Fielding Bible Award at first base. Always well known for his defense, Teixeira broke through for another one of his huge defensive years in 2012 as he has done before from time to time. In 2003 and 2005, before the Fielding Bible Award began, he had seasons of 19 runs saved and 13 runs saved respectively. In 2008 he had his best season with 21 Defensive Runs Saved, but lost the Fielding Bible Award in a close vote to Albert Pujols. In 2012 he notched 17 runs and earned his first Fielding Bible Award. But it's not that his defense has been poor in his other seasons. In the last decade Mark has never cost his team runs in any single year. But in his four best seasons he has saved 70 runs, while only saving a total of 24 runs in the other six.

Previous Winners:

2011   Albert Pujols
2010   Daric Barton
2009   Albert Pujols
2008   Albert Pujols
2007   Albert Pujols
2006   Albert Pujols

Second Base – Darwin Barney, Chicago Cubs

Darwin Barney's defense is a shining star in an otherwise cloudy season for the 2012 Chicago Cubs. After a nondescript debut at second base in 2011, when he saved only one run defensively, Barney led all second basemen in 2012 with 28 runs saved. This total led by a wide margin. He had a lot more runs saved than defending Fielding Bible Award winner Dustin Pedroia's total of 11, a lot more than Robinson Cano's 15, and a lot more than Brandon Phillips' 11. Those three came in second, third and fourth in a vote that wasn't close; Barney received eight of ten first-place votes. Barney's vote tabulation of 96 points was only four short of perfection.

Previous Winners:

2011	Dustin Pedroia
2010	Chase Utley
2009	Aaron Hill
2008	Brandon Phillips
2007	Aaron Hill
2006	Orlando Hudson

Third Base – Adrian Beltre, Texas

Adrian Beltre has been the best defensive third baseman of our generation, and he now has his fourth Fielding Bible Award to prove it. But he has had competition. When Beltre won his first award in 2006, he barely beat out Scott Rolen and Joe Crede for the award. He won the award pretty easily in 2008 over Evan Longoria, but Longoria gave him a much tougher battle in 2011 when Beltre beat him by a 98-90 score in the voting. This year it was Mike Moustakas on Beltre's heels. Third base was 2012's slimmest margin of victory, with Beltre winning 90 to 86 in the tabulation. Brett Lawrie was a close third with 83 points. Both Lawrie and Moustakas had a few more runs saved than Beltre this year (20 and 14, respectively, compared to 13 Defensive Runs Saved for Beltre), but it is Beltre's long time excellence year after year that allowed him to retain the award this year. He has saved the most runs at third base in baseball over the last three years with 45. But if Lawrie or Moustakas repeat next year what they did this year, one of them will no doubt unseat Beltre.

Previous Winners:

2011	Adrian Beltre
2010	Evan Longoria
2009	Ryan Zimmerman
2008	Adrian Beltre
2007	Pedro Feliz
2006	Adrian Beltre

Shortstop – Brendan Ryan, Seattle

Brendan Ryan is the best defender in baseball. Period. Make that double period. His has saved 67 runs for his teams defensively over the last three years, the highest total among all players. The next highest runs saved total is not even close (Michael Bourn, 51). Ryan led all shortstops in 2012 with 27 runs saved, led in 2011 with 18, and finished second in both 2010 and 2009 with 22 runs saved each year. Seattle recognizes the value of Ryan's defense, and that's why they keep putting him out there day after day despite his .194 batting average during the 2012 season. It will be interesting to see if the American League coaches and managers, who vote for the Gold Glove Awards, can look past Ryan's offense and base their ballot on his defense alone. This has been one of the problems with the Gold Glove voting—a certain amount of offense has always been required for what should be a defense-only award. Gold Glove voting has never allowed for a position player hitting below the Mendoza line to win a Gold Glove. Hopefully Ryan will be the first.

Previous Winners:

2011	Troy Tulowitzki
2010	Troy Tulowitzki
2009	Jack Wilson
2008	Jimmy Rollins
2007	Troy Tulowitzki
2006	Adam Everett

Left Field – Alex Gordon, Kansas City

In the history of the Fielding Bible Awards, Carl Crawford and Brett Gardner have won every award given out to left fielders except one. But this year both Crawford and Gardner were injured, opening the door for Alex Gordon. Gordon didn't stroll through that door—he tore it off its hinges and burst through the other side. He lapped the field with his 24 runs saved defensively, his nearest competitors being Martin Prado of Atlanta with 12 and Tampa Bay's Desmond Jennings with 9 runs saved. Gordon was a unanimous choice for the 2012 Fielding Bible Award, finishing first on every single ballot cast by the panelists.

Previous Winners:

2011	Brett Gardner
2010	Brett Gardner
2009	Carl Crawford
2008	Carl Crawford
2007	Eric Byrnes
2006	Carl Crawford

Center Field – Mike Trout, Los Angeles Angels

Can Mike Trout win every single award in his rookie season? In 1975 another rookie center fielder, Fred Lynn, won the MVP award, the Rookie of the Year award, and a Gold Glove. It was the first and last time this has ever been done. (Technically, Ichiro also won the same three awards in 2001, but he wasn't really a rookie at age 27 having played many years of professional baseball in Japan, was he?) Mike Trout can now top that. Trout wins his first award in a possible Grand Slam of Awards with a Fielding Bible Award for his play defensively. He has incredible range, especially on balls hit deep, where he saved many a run, converting possible doubles and triples into outs. He made 23 more plays on balls hit deep than an average center fielder would have made on the identical type of batted balls. The other thing that set him apart was his four home-run saving catches in 2012. Cameron Maybin was second with three, and no one else had more than two.

Previous Winners:

- 2011 Austin Jackson
- 2010 Michael Bourn
- 2009 Franklin Gutierrez
- 2008 Carlos Beltran
- 2007 Andruw Jones
- 2006 Carlos Beltran

Right Field – Jason Heyward, Atlanta

After finishing second to Justin Upton in 2011, Jason Heyward wins his first Fielding Bible Award in 2012. Heyward demonstrated that his superlative performance in 2011 was no fluke. And neither was 2010. In 2011 he led all right fielders with 15 runs saved defensively. He saved 15 runs in 2010 as well. He topped both those years in 2012 with 20 runs saved, just two behind Josh Reddick's total of 22. How does he do it? He covers a ton of ground in right field, whether the ball is hit shallow, medium, or deep. In each of the last three years he has made between 30 and 40 more plays than an average right fielder would have made. All those extra plays more than make up for what is a slightly below average throwing arm for a right fielder.

Previous Winners:

- 2011 Justin Upton
- 2010 Ichiro Suzuki
- 2009 Ichiro Suzuki
- 2008 Franklin Gutierrez
- 2007 Alex Rios
- 2006 Ichiro Suzuki

Catcher – Yadier Molina, St. Louis

Yadier is back. After a one-year hiatus when he came in second to Matt Wieters, Molina wins his fifth Fielding Bible Award, tying him with Albert Pujols for the most awards won in the seven-year history of The Fielding Bible Awards. In 2011 Molina dropped to his all-time low only throwing out 25% of baserunners attempting to steal. In 2012 he threw out 46%, an MLB leading percentage in line with the rest of his career. On top of that he was superlative handling bunts, saving four runs in the process and giving him 16 Defensive Runs Saved on the season, the most among catchers in baseball last year.

Molina was another unanimous selection among the ten Fielding Bible Award panelists.

Previous Winners:

2011   Matt Wieters
2010   Yadier Molina
2009   Yadier Molina
2008   Yadier Molina
2007   Yadier Molina
2006   Ivan Rodriguez

Pitcher – Mark Buehrle, Chicago White Sox

Mark Buehrle wins his fourth consecutive Fielding Bible Award. His 12 Defensive Runs Saved was the highest total among pitchers. As a player who only plays once every five games compared to those in other positions, it is Buehrle's consistency defensively that really stands out. In the last nine years, he has ranked no worse than number 11 in Defensive Runs Saved among the 175 pitchers we rank each year. In seven of those nine years he was no worse than fifth. In that time span, only 42 runners have stolen a base on him, while 48 have been thrown out and another 31 have been picked off by Buehrle. That comes out to 32 runs saved for Buehrle preventing stolen bases when we do our calculations. On top of that, he has saved another 36 runs with the way he has fielded his position in those nine years. Buehrle joins Alex Gordon and Yadier Molina as the third player in 2012 to receive a perfect total of 100 points in the balloting. The Fielding Bible Awards have never had more than one unanimous selection in any other year.

Previous Winners:

2011   Mark Buehrle
2010   Mark Buehrle
2009   Mark Buehrle
2008   Kenny Rogers
2007   Johan Santana
2006   Greg Maddux

Background of the Fielding Bible Awards

While the first *The Fielding Bible*, *The Fielding Bible—Volume II*, and *The Fielding Bible—Volume III* put a lot of emphasis on the numbers, especially Defensive Runs Saved and the Plus-Minus system, I feel that visual observation and subjective judgment are still very important parts of determining the best defensive players. Also, I think people have a right to know who is voting and all the players they are voting for. Therefore, in setting up the Fielding Bible Awards, we took the following steps:

1. *We appointed a panel of experts to vote.* We have a panel of ten experts plus three "tie-breaker" ballots. (See below.)

2. *We rate everybody in one group.* The Gold Glove vote is divided into National League and American League. We make ours different by putting everybody together. Besides, is playing shortstop in the American League one thing and playing shortstop in the National League a different thing, or are they really very much the same thing? A couple of years ago we had a great example of this rule. Without the Fielding Bible Award, Jack Wilson wins nada, because he switched teams in mid-year. According to our panelists (and unlike the Gold Glove voters), Jack was the best fielding shortstop in baseball in 2009. Period. He deserved to be recognized for that.

3. *We use a ten-man ballot and a ten-point scale.* We use a ten-man ballot (I'm referring to the players listed, not the panel of experts). We give ten points for first place, nine points for second place, etc, down to one point for tenth place. We feel strongly that a ten-man ballot with weighted positions leads to more accurate outcomes.

4. *We defined the list of candidates.* Only players who actually were regulars at the position are candidates. This eliminates the possibility of a vote going to somebody who wasn't really playing the position.

5. *We are publishing the balloting.* We summarize the voting at each position, clearly identifying whom everybody voted for. Publishing the actual vote totals encourages the voters to take their votes more seriously. Also, we feel the public will have more respect for the voting if they have more insight into the process.

There is something cool about having 10 experts and a 10-man ballot and a 10-point scale, because that gives each position 100 possible points. If all 10 voters place one player first on their ballot, he scores 100. Three players had perfect scores of 100 this year, Alex Gordon, Yadier Molina and Mark Buehrle.

Here are the tie-breaker rules (which came into play in our very first year and did so again in 2010). They are applied one at a time until we have a winner:
  1. Most first-place votes wins.
  2. Count the tie-breaker ballots, highest point tally wins.

The Fielding Bible Awards

Below we show the final point tally for The 2012 Fielding Bible Awards. We asked a panel of experts to complete a ten-man ballot ranking players from 1 to 10 based on their defensive abilities. We show the ranks in the tables below. We then awarded points in the same way as Major League Baseball's MVP voting: ten points for a first place vote, nine for second, etc., down to one point for tenth place. We cover all nine positions, looking at the 2012 season. Non-pitchers are eligible if they played at least 500 innings by the time the ballot was prepared in early September. Pitchers require a minimum of 100 innings pitched.

First Basemen

First Basemen	Bill James	BIS Video Scouts	Doug Glanville	Hal Richman	Joe Posnanski	John Dewan	Mark Simon	Peter Gammons	Rob Neyer	Tango Fan Poll	Total Points
Mark Teixeira	1	1	1	1	2	1	1	1	2	4	95
Adrian Gonzalez	3	2	2	2	1	2	2	2	1	9	84
Albert Pujols	2	4	3	4	4	3	3	9	5	1	72
Joey Votto	5	3		3	3	4	4		3	5	58
James Loney	6	5	4	8	5	6	5		4	10	46
Adam LaRoche	4	6		7	6	5	6	3	6		45
Brandon Belt	7	8		9		7		5	10	2	29
Freddie Freeman	8	7	5				7	8	9		22
Casey Kotchman	9			5				6		3	21
Carlos Pena			6	6			9	4			19
Others receiving points: Yonder Alonso 15, Gaby Sanchez 13, Anthony Rizzo 6, Todd Helton 6, Ike Davis 4, Allen Craig 4, Paul Goldschmidt 3, Justin Smoak 3, Michael Young 3, Eric Hosmer 1, Justin Morneau 1											

Second Basemen

Second Basemen	Bill James	BIS Video Scouts	Doug Glanville	Hal Richman	Joe Posnanski	John Dewan	Mark Simon	Peter Gammons	Rob Neyer	Tango Fan Poll	Total Points
Darwin Barney	1	1	1	2	1	1	1	2	1	3	96
Dustin Pedroia	2	2	2	4	3	3	3	4	3	2	82
Robinson Cano	3	3	3	3	2	2	2	6	2	5	79
Brandon Phillips	8	6	7	1	8	4	4		7	1	53
Alexi Casilla	4	4	5	9	6	8	6	5	6		46
Dustin Ackley	5	5	4	8	4	6	7	10	5		45
Mark Ellis	6	7	9		7	5	5		4	10	35
Omar Infante	9		6	7	5	9	10		9	4	29
Danny Espinosa		9	8	10	9			3		6	21
Chase Utley					10	7	8		8	8	14
Others receiving points: Gordon Beckham 13, Aaron Hill 12, Robert Andino 6, Ian Kinsler 4, Jason Kipnis 4, Marco Scutaro 4, Jose Altuve 3, Howie Kendrick 2, Neil Walker 2											

Third Basemen

Third Basemen	Bill James	BIS Video Scouts	Doug Glanville	Hal Richman	Joe Posnanski	John Dewan	Mark Simon	Peter Gammons	Rob Neyer	Tango Fan Poll	Total Points
Adrian Beltre	2	2	4	1	2	1	2	4	1	1	90
Mike Moustakas	3	1	1	6	1	3	4	1	2	2	86
Brett Lawrie	1	3	2	5	3	2	1	2	3	5	83
David Wright	4	4	3	4	4	6	3	3	4	8	67
Ryan Zimmerman	7	5	5	2	7	10	7	8		4	44
Alberto Callaspo		6	6	7	5	4	6	6	5		43
Brandon Inge	5	7	9	10		8	5		8	9	27
Scott Rolen			3		9	9	10	10		3	22
Ryan Roberts	6	8	7		8				6		20
Jack Hannahan	8	9	8	8		5				10	18
Others receiving points: Placido Polanco 15, Chase Headley 11, Aramis Ramirez 10, Hanley Ramirez 5, Chipper Jones 3, David Freese 2, Will Middlebrooks 2, Kyle Seager 2											

Shortstops

Shortstops	Bill James	BIS Video Scouts	Doug Glanville	Hal Richman	Joe Posnanski	John Dewan	Mark Simon	Peter Gammons	Rob Neyer	Tango Fan Poll	Total Points
Brendan Ryan	1	1	1	1	1	1	1	2	1	1	99
J.J. Hardy	2	2	2	6	2	5	2	1	2	8	78
Elvis Andrus	9	4	9	2	7	9	5	5	8	2	50
Zack Cozart	5	3	6	9	8	7	4	3	7	10	48
Clint Barmes	10	5	3	8	3	4	3		5		47
Alexei Ramirez	7	6	8		6	2	6	8	4	6	46
Yunel Escobar	4	7	5		4	3			3		40
Mike Aviles	3	10	4		5	6	7	6	9		38
Brandon Crawford		8	7	7	9	8	9	7	6	3	35
Alcides Escobar	6			4			8			7	19

Others receiving points: Erick Aybar 16, Jimmy Rollins 13, Ruben Tejada 10, Cliff Pennington 8, Starlin Castro 2, Ian Desmond 1

Left Fielders

Left Fielders	Bill James	BIS Video Scouts	Doug Glanville	Hal Richman	Joe Posnanski	John Dewan	Mark Simon	Peter Gammons	Rob Neyer	Tango Fan Poll	Total Points
Alex Gordon	1	1	1	1	1	1	1	1	1	1	100
Martin Prado	4	3	5	4	2	2	2	3	2	3	80
Desmond Jennings	2	2	4	3	3	4	3	2	3	4	80
Ryan Braun	5	5	2	10	4	3	5	4	4	7	61
David Murphy	3	4	3	9	5	5	4	5	5	8	59
Rajai Davis	6	6	6	5	8	8	6	6	6		42
Casper Wells	7			6	9	6			7	6	25
Carlos Gonzalez				2						2	18
Dayan Viciedo	9	10	9		7	10	7	7			18
Mark Trumbo		7			10	7	8				12

Others receiving points: Alex Presley 11, Alfonso Soriano 8, Melky Cabrera 8, Matt Holliday 7, Juan Pierre 7, Quintin Berry 6, Chris Heisey 3, J.D. Martinez 3, John Mayberry 2

Center Fielders

Center Fielders	Bill James	BIS Video Scouts	Doug Glanville	Hal Richman	Joe Posnanski	John Dewan	Mark Simon	Peter Gammons	Rob Neyer	Tango Fan Poll	Total Points
Mike Trout	1	1	2	1	2	2	1	1	1	2	96
Michael Bourn	2	2	1	2	1	1	2	2	2	5	90
Denard Span	3	3	3	6	3	3	3	4	3		68
Craig Gentry	6	4	6	9	7	4	4		4	4	51
Austin Jackson	5	5	9	4	8	7	8	3		1	49
Cameron Maybin	7	7	4		5	6	7	5	5	9	44
Bryce Harper	4	6	5		4	9	9	7	6		38
Chris Young	8		10	8	6	5	5		8	10	28
Carlos Gomez		10		3	9	10	10			3	21
Andrew McCutchen		8	7	5							13

Others receiving points: Gerardo Parra 9, Shane Victorino 6, Michael Brantley 6, Drew Stubbs 5, Coco Crisp 5, Jarrod Dyson 4, Adam Jones 4, Matt Kemp 3, Justin Maxwell 3, Tony Gwynn 2, Jon Jay 2, Dexter Fowler 1, Nyjer Morgan 1, Colby Rasmus 1

Right Fielders

Right Fielders	Bill James	BIS Video Scouts	Doug Glanville	Hal Richman	Joe Posnanski	John Dewan	Mark Simon	Peter Gammons	Rob Neyer	Tango Fan Poll	Total Points
Jason Heyward	4	1	1	2	1	1	1	1	1	1	96
Josh Reddick	3	2	3	3	2	2	2	3	2	4	84
Torii Hunter	1	4	5	4	4	3	3	4	3	3	76
Ben Revere	5	3	4	1	8	6	4	2	6		60
Ichiro Suzuki		5	2	8	3	7	5	6	4	2	57
Ben Zobrist	2	8	8		9	5	6		7	6	37
Giancarlo Stanton	9	7			5	4	8	5	5	8	37
Alex Rios	6	9	9		6	8	7	9	8		26
Norichika Aoki		6	7		10	10		8	9		16
Carlos Beltran	7	10	10		7				10		11

Others receiving points: Jay Bruce 10, Justin Upton 8, Gregor Blanco 7, Nick Markakis 7, Lucas Duda 5, Brian Bogusevic 4, Shin-Soo Choo 4, Jeff Francoeur 4, David DeJesus 1

Catchers

Catchers	Bill James	BIS Video Scouts	Doug Glanville	Hal Richman	Joe Posnanski	John Dewan	Mark Simon	Peter Gammons	Rob Neyer	Tango Fan Poll	Total Points
Yadier Molina	1	1	1	1	1	1	1	1	1	1	100
Matt Wieters	5	2	3	2	2	2	3	2	6	2	81
Ryan Hanigan	2	3	4	7	3	3	2	5	2	4	75
Carlos Ruiz	3	4	2	3	4	4	4	3		5	67
Buster Posey	7	9		6		5		4	10	3	33
Jose Molina		7	7	4			5		5	10	28
Kurt Suzuki		5	8	5		6	10	6	9		28
Jonathan Lucroy	9	8	10			7	6		4	8	25
Alex Avila		6	6		6	8	8			9	23
Josh Thole	10		9		5	10			3		18

Others receiving points: J.P. Arencibia 17, A.J. Ellis 11, Miguel Montero 8, Joe Mauer 8, Miguel Olivo 7, A.J. Pierzynski 7, Russell Martin 6, John Buck 4, Brian McCann 2, Carlos Santana 2

Pitchers

Pitchers	Bill James	BIS Video Scouts	Doug Glanville	Hal Richman	Joe Posnanski	John Dewan	Mark Simon	Peter Gammons	Rob Neyer	Ben Jedlovec	Total Points
Mark Buehrle	1	1	1	1	1	1	1	1	1	1	100
Jake Westbrook	3	3	10	2	2	2	2	6	3	2	75
Zack Greinke	2	5	2		3	5	3	5	5	5	64
R.A. Dickey		2	8	8	4	3	4	3	2	4	61
Johnny Cueto	4	4		7	7	6	5	9		3	43
Ricky Romero		7	5		6	4	8	7	4	9	38
Mike Leake		9	9	6		7		2	6		27
Clayton Kershaw	8	8		3	10	8	6			8	26
Bronson Arroyo	5			4	8			8	7		23
Randy Wolf		10	3			9	7			7	19

Others receiving points: Justin Verlander 16, Kris Medlen 12, David Price 11, Joe Saunders 9, Tommy Hunter 8, Jason Vargas 5, Jordan Zimmermann 5, Clay Buchholz 2, Alex Cobb 2, Hiroki Kuroda 2, Justin Masterson 2

Runs Saved and Plus/Minus Leaders

The Runs Saved and Plus/Minus leaders showcase baseball's best fielders from 2012 and over the past three seasons. The three-year leaders identify the best defensive players in baseball. Take a look at the top five at each position on the 3-Year Runs Saved and Plus/Minus Leaderboards and you get an excellent idea of the best defenders at each position.

The Plus/Minus System is a way to evaluate defensive range by measuring how often defenders turn grounders and fly balls into outs. A number greater than zero (plus "+") is above average. Below zero (minus "-") is below average. In 2012, J.J. Hardy had a plus/minus figure of +19, which means he made 19 more plays than an average shortstop would have made on the same types of batted balls. Run Saved is an estimate of the number of runs each fielder saves with his defense. It combines Plus/Minus with our analysis of bunts, double plays, outfield arms, catchers' earned runs, catchers' stolen bases allowed, pitchers' stolen bases allowed, and good plays/misplays to form a complete evaluation of a fielder.

Please see the Glossary for a more complete description of Runs Saved and Plus/Minus.

Pitcher/Catcher Runs Saved Leaders

Pitchers 3-Year Leaders

Westbrook,Jake	31
Buehrle,Mark	31
Dickey,R.A.	24
Romero,Ricky	21
Greinke,Zack	19
Arroyo,Bronson	16
Saunders,Joe	15
Kershaw,Clayton	14
Cueto,Johnny	13
Verlander,Justin	12

Catchers 3-Year Leaders

Molina,Yadier	32
Wieters,Matt	29
Quintero,Humberto	18
Mathis,Jeff	17
Stewart,Chris	16
Hanigan,Ryan	11
Posey,Buster	11
Perez,Salvador	10
Ruiz,Carlos	10
2 tied with	9

Pitchers 3-Year Trailers

Hanson,Tommy	-16
Garcia,Freddy	-14
Santana,Ervin	-14
Burnett,A.J.	-14
Beckett,Josh	-11
Humber,Philip	-10

Catchers 3-Year Trailers

Hernandez,Ramon	-18
Doumit,Ryan	-16
Buck,John	-14
Pierzynski,A.J.	-14
Barajas,Rod	-13
Soto,Geovany	-12

Pitchers 2012 Leaders

Buehrle,Mark	12
Westbrook,Jake	11
Cueto,Johnny	8
Wolf,Randy	7
Dickey,R.A.	6
Leake,Mike	6
Greinke,Zack	6
Romero,Ricky	6
Kershaw,Clayton	6
Cobb,Alex	5

Catchers 2012 Leaders

Molina,Yadier	16
Perez,Salvador	9
Hanigan,Ryan	7
Avila,Alex	6
Wieters,Matt	5
Mathis,Jeff	5
Lucroy,Jonathan	4
Maldonado,Martin	4
Thole,Josh	4
3 tied with	3

Pitchers 2012 Trailers

Lowe,Derek	-8
McAllister,Zach	-6
Hanson,Tommy	-6
Rodriguez,Wandy	-6
Humber,Philip	-5
Young,Chris	-5

Catchers 2012 Trailers

Barajas,Rod	-12
Marson,Lou	-8
Soto,Geovany	-8
Mauer,Joe	-6
Martin,Russell	-6

Infield Plus/Minus Leaders

First Basemen 3-Year Leaders		Second Basemen 3-Year Leaders		Third Basemen 3-Year Leaders		Shortstops 3-Year Leaders	
Barton,Daric	+32	Cano,Robinson	+42	Beltre,Adrian	+50	Ryan,Brendan	+73
Teixeira,Mark	+30	Utley,Chase	+38	Lawrie,Brett	+48	Barmes,Clint	+47
Pujols,Albert	+22	Ellis,Mark	+34	Longoria,Evan	+37	Ramirez,Alexei	+46
Gonzalez,Adrian	+20	Zobrist,Ben	+34	Moustakas,Mike	+25	Escobar,Yunel	+42
Votto,Joey	+19	Kinsler,Ian	+32	Headley,Chase	+20	Gonzalez,Alex	+33
Loney,James	+17	Barney,Darwin	+32	Rolen,Scott	+20	Hardy,J.J.	+24
LaRoche,Adam	+17	Phillips,Brandon	+31	Sandoval,Pablo	+19	Aviles,Mike	+22
Davis,Ike	+13	Pedroia,Dustin	+30	Rodriguez,Alex	+19	Cozart,Zack	+21
Trumbo,Mark	+11	Rodriguez,Sean	+26	Polanco,Placido	+17	McDonald,John	+20
Youkilis,Kevin	+10	Ackley,Dustin	+23	Inge,Brandon	+17	Simmons,Andrelton	+20

First Basemen 3-Year Trailers		Second Basemen 3-Year Trailers		Third Basemen 3-Year Trailers		Shortstops 3-Year Trailers	
Konerko,Paul	-42	Weeks,Rickie	-53	Johnson,Chris	-50	Jeter,Derek	-54
Howard,Ryan	-33	Keppinger,Jeff	-28	Reynolds,Mark	-36	Ramirez,Hanley	-43
Fielder,Prince	-32	Weeks,Jemile	-25	Ramirez,Aramis	-33	Reyes,Jose	-41
Hosmer,Eric	-19	Walker,Neil	-25	Betemit,Wilson	-29	Betancourt,Yuniesky	-40
Dunn,Adam	-13	Schumaker,Skip	-24	Dobbs,Greg	-27	Rollins,Jimmy	-25
Cabrera,Miguel	-13	Uggla,Dan	-19	Young,Michael	-27	Plouffe,Trevor	-19

First Basemen 2012 Leaders		Second Basemen 2012 Leaders		Third Basemen 2012 Leaders		Shortstops 2012 Leaders	
Teixeira,Mark	+17	Barney,Darwin	+29	Lawrie,Brett	+28	Ryan,Brendan	+27
Gonzalez,Adrian	+15	Cano,Robinson	+22	Moustakas,Mike	+20	Escobar,Yunel	+22
Sanchez,Gaby	+12	Casilla,Alexi	+14	Wright,David	+19	Simmons,Andrelton	+20
Votto,Joey	+9	Phillips,Brandon	+13	Beltre,Adrian	+12	Hardy,J.J.	+19
Pujols,Albert	+8	Utley,Chase	+13	Callaspo,Alberto	+8	Aviles,Mike	+19
Loney,James	+8	Ackley,Dustin	+12	Frazier,Todd	+8	Ramirez,Alexei	+17
LaRoche,Adam	+5	Johnson,Kelly	+11	Machado,Manny	+8	Cozart,Zack	+16
Pena,Carlos	+5	Ellis,Mark	+11	Donaldson,Josh	+6	Barmes,Clint	+14
Belt,Brandon	+4	LeMahieu,DJ	+11	Roberts,Ryan	+6	Crawford,Brandon	+13
Rizzo,Anthony	+3	Infante,Omar	+8	Valbuena,Luis	+6	Castro,Starlin	+12

First Basemen 2012 Trailers		Second Basemen 2012 Trailers		Third Basemen 2012 Trailers		Shortstops 2012 Trailers	
Konerko,Paul	-14	Weeks,Rickie	-34	Nelson,Chris	-22	Jeter,Derek	-26
Hosmer,Eric	-10	Altuve,Jose	-19	Pacheco,Jordan	-19	Reyes,Jose	-18
Reynolds,Mark	-8	Weeks,Jemile	-16	Ramirez,Hanley	-17	Gordon,Dee	-14
Hart,Corey	-7	Theriot,Ryan	-14	Plouffe,Trevor	-12	Rollins,Jimmy	-14
LaHair,Bryan	-6	Beckham,Gordon	-12	Johnson,Chris	-12	Bloomquist,Willie	-11
Craig,Allen	-6	Forsythe,Logan	-11	Cabrera,Miguel	-11	Rutledge,Josh	-11

Outfield Plus/Minus Leaders

Left Fielders 3-Year Leaders		Center Fielders 3-Year Leaders		Right Fielders 3-Year Leaders	
Gardner,Brett	+64	Bourn,Michael	+91	Heyward,Jason	+105
Braun,Ryan	+49	Young,Chris	+81	Upton,Justin	+58
Parra,Gerardo	+37	Jackson,Austin	+78	Stanton,Giancarlo	+45
Murphy,David	+32	Maybin,Cameron	+60	Reddick,Josh	+39
Gordon,Alex	+29	Span,Denard	+49	Venable,Will	+37
Tabata,Jose	+28	Trout,Mike	+37	Bruce,Jay	+24
Jennings,Desmond	+25	Ellsbury,Jacoby	+33	Hart,Corey	+24
Hamilton,Josh	+24	Bourjos,Peter	+31	Zobrist,Ben	+24
Gwynn,Tony	+22	Gentry,Craig	+31	Revere,Ben	+20
Dirks,Andy	+22	Gomez,Carlos	+28	DeJesus,David	+18

Left Fielders 3-Year Trailers		Center Fielders 3-Year Trailers		Right Fielders 3-Year Trailers	
Morrison,Logan	-57	Kemp,Matt	-105	Cuddyer,Michael	-60
Ibanez,Raul	-42	Jones,Adam	-66	Bautista,Jose	-56
Soriano,Alfonso	-32	Upton,B.J.	-38	Markakis,Nick	-41
Young,Delmon	-31	McLouth,Nate	-36	Duda,Lucas	-36
Gomes,Jonny	-29	Brantley,Michael	-30	Werth,Jayson	-36
Abreu,Bobby	-21	Coghlan,Chris	-24	Choo,Shin-Soo	-34

Left Fielders 2012 Leaders		Center Fielders 2012 Leaders		Right Fielders 2012 Leaders	
Jennings,Desmond	+17	Bourn,Michael	+37	Heyward,Jason	+40
Braun,Ryan	+16	Trout,Mike	+34	Reddick,Josh	+22
Gordon,Alex	+14	Span,Denard	+31	Stanton,Giancarlo	+19
Murphy,David	+14	Maxwell,Justin	+21	Revere,Ben	+18
Victorino,Shane	+13	Harper,Bryce	+17	Suzuki,Ichiro	+15
Presley,Alex	+11	Maybin,Cameron	+15	Venable,Will	+15
Dirks,Andy	+10	Gentry,Craig	+14	Upton,Justin	+13
Wells,Vernon	+9	Young,Chris	+13	Aoki,Norichika	+12
Prado,Martin	+7	Bourjos,Peter	+13	Ethier,Andre	+11
Trumbo,Mark	+7	Ruggiano,Justin	+13	Blanco,Gregor	+11

Left Fielders 2012 Trailers		Center Fielders 2012 Trailers		Right Fielders 2012 Trailers	
Kubel,Jason	-20	Kemp,Matt	-32	Francoeur,Jeff	-34
Gonzalez,Carlos	-13	Saunders,Michael	-23	Duda,Lucas	-21
Davis,Rajai	-11	Jones,Adam	-23	Cruz,Nelson	-20
Quentin,Carlos	-10	Cespedes,Yoenis	-17	Choo,Shin-Soo	-20
Holliday,Matt	-10	Granderson,Curtis	-17	Cuddyer,Michael	-17
Ludwick,Ryan	-9	Hamilton,Josh	-13	Pence,Hunter	-17

Pitcher Plus/Minus Leaders

Pitchers
3-Year Leaders

Westbrook,Jake	+30
Buehrle,Mark	+22
Dickey,R.A.	+20
Romero,Ricky	+16
Arroyo,Bronson	+15
Cahill,Trevor	+14
Wolf,Randy	+13
Verlander,Justin	+12
Hernandez,Roberto	+12
Chacin,Jhoulys	+12

Pitchers
3-Year Trailers

Scherzer,Max	-15
Marquis,Jason	-10
Lee,Cliff	-10
Morrow,Brandon	-9
Rodriguez,Francisco	-8
Humber,Philip	-8

Pitchers
2012 Leaders

Westbrook,Jake	+9
Cobb,Alex	+9
Buehrle,Mark	+8
Dempster,Ryan	+6
Masterson,Justin	+5
Wolf,Randy	+5
Billingsley,Chad	+5
Hochevar,Luke	+5
Bailey,Homer	+5
Price,David	+5

Pitchers
2012 Trailers

Lowe,Derek	-8
Scherzer,Max	-7
Volquez,Edinson	-6
Matusz,Brian	-5
Young,Chris	-4
McAllister,Zach	-4

2012 Career Register

This section contains the complete up-to-date career statistics for every major league player in the 2012 season. For players who have appeared in fewer than three major league seasons, we have included their full minor league statistics. For those players with three or more years in the big leagues who also spent time in the minor leagues in 2012 (for example, if they had a rehab assignment) we included only their 2012 minor league statistics—indicated by an asterisk. Those players who split time between the majors and the minors last season but have fewer than three years of major league experience will still have their full minor league stats included.

If a player led either the American or National League in a particular category, that number will appear in **boldface.**

Age is seasonal as of June 30, 2013.

For pitchers, BFP is Batters Facing Pitcher; TBB is Total Bases on Balls (or, Total Walks, intentional and unintentional); Op is Save Opportunities; Hld is Holds.

For the various levels of Class-A ball, we have used "A+" to indicate High A and "A-" to indicate Low A. To help readers decode our minor league team abbreviations, we added a legend in the back of the book. Thank you for the suggestion, David G. Barlow.

Regardless of whether their name at the time was Los Angeles, Anaheim, California, or Los Angeles of Anaheim, the abbreviation LAA denotes a reference to the Angels franchise.

A pronunciation guide is provided underneath the name of select players.

The Register also features Runs Created (RC) for hitters and Component ERA (ERC) for pitchers, in addition to the more traditional statistics. Developed by Bill James, Runs Created is a method of measuring every facet of a hitter's strengths and weaknesses, combining those factors into one number, indicative of a player's production. Component ERA estimates what a pitcher's ERA should have been based upon his raw pitching statistics and gives us a good indication of whether or not a pitcher actually deserved his ERA. An explanation of Bill's most-current formulas for both RC and ERC can be found in the Baseball Glossary at the end of the Handbook.

A player's total career numbers in the postseason appear on one line above his total regular season career numbers. Since we work hard to bring you this publication by November 1, 2012, postseason data from 2012 is not included.

David Aardsma

Pitches: R **Bats:** R **Pos:** RP-1   ARDZ-muh   **Ht:** 6'3" **Wt:** 205 **Born:** 12/27/1981 **Age:** 31

			HOW MUCH HE PITCHED						WHAT HE GAVE UP											THE RESULTS						
Year	Team	Lg	G	GS	CG	GF	IP	BFP	H	R	ER	HR	SH	SF	HB	TBB	IBB	SO	WP	Bk	W	L	Pct	Sh	Sv-Op	Hld	ERC	ERA
2012	Yanks*	R	3	3	0	0	5.0	20	3	1	0	0	0	0	0	1	0	7	1	0	0	0	-	0	0--	-	1.06	0.00
2012	Tampa*	A+	1	1	0	0	1.0	4	0	0	0	0	0	0	0	1	0	1	0	0	0	0	-	0	0--	-	0.95	0.00
2012	StsInd*	A-	1	1	0	0	0.2	9	4	4	2	1	0	0	0	1	0	1	0	0	0	1	.000	0	0--	-	55.47	27.00
2004	SF	NL	11	0	0	5	10.2	61	20	8	8	1	0	1	2	10	0	5	0	0	1	0	1.000	0	0-1	1	13.38	6.75
2006	ChC	NL	45	0	0	9	53.0	225	41	25	24	9	1	3	1	28	0	49	1	0	3	0	1.000	0	0-0	5	3.88	4.08
2007	CWS	AL	25	0	0	7	32.1	151	39	24	23	4	2	1	1	17	3	36	2	0	2	1	.667	0	0-3	3	5.93	6.40
2008	Bos	AL	47	0	0	7	48.2	228	49	32	30	4	3	2	5	35	2	49	3	0	4	2	.667	0	0-1	4	5.63	5.55
2009	Sea	AL	73	0	0	53	71.1	296	49	23	20	4	3	2	5	34	3	80	2	0	3	6	.333	0	38-42	6	2.34	2.52
2010	Sea	AL	53	0	0	43	49.2	202	33	19	19	5	7	1	2	25	5	49	2	0	0	6	.000	0	31-36	5	2.74	3.44
2012	NYY	AL	1	0	0	1	1.0	5	1	1	1	1	0	0	0	1	0	1	0	0	0	0	-	0	0-0	0	14.27	9.00
	7 ML YEARS		255	0	0	125	266.2	1168	232	132	125	28	15	9	11	150	13	269	10	0	13	15	.464	0	69-83	19	4.10	4.22

Fernando Abad

Pitches: L **Bats:** L **Pos:** RP-31; SP-6   ah-BAHD   **Ht:** 6'2" **Wt:** 215 **Born:** 12/17/1985 **Age:** 27

			HOW MUCH HE PITCHED						WHAT HE GAVE UP											THE RESULTS						
Year	Team	Lg	G	GS	CG	GF	IP	BFP	H	R	ER	HR	SH	SF	HB	TBB	IBB	SO	WP	Bk	W	L	Pct	Sh	Sv-Op	Hld	ERC	ERA
2012	OKCity*	AAA	13	3	0	3	27.2	121	33	12	12	3	2	2	1	7	1	28	0	2	2	0	1.000	0	2--	-	4.74	3.90
2010	Hou	NL	22	0	0	6	19.0	76	14	6	6	3	0	1	0	5	0	12	0	0	1	0	1.000	0	0-0	6	2.49	2.84
2011	Hou	NL	29	0	0	1	19.2	99	28	18	16	5	1	2	1	9	0	15	0	0	1	4	.200	0	0-2	7	8.06	7.32
2012	Hou	NL	37	6	0	8	46.0	208	57	27	26	6	2	1	3	19	1	38	4	0	0	6	.000	0	0-0	3	6.13	5.09
	3 ML YEARS		88	6	0	15	84.2	383	99	51	48	14	3	4	4	33	1	65	4	0	1	11	.083	0	0-2	16	5.67	5.10

Bobby Abreu

Bats: L **Throws:** R **Pos:** LF-52; PH-44; DH-4; RF-2; PR-1   **Ht:** 6'0" **Wt:** 210 **Born:** 3/11/1974 **Age:** 39

			BATTING																	BASERUNNING				AVERAGES		
Year	Team	Lg	G	AB	H	2B	3B	HR	(Hm	Rd)	TB	R	RBI	RC	TBB	IBB	SO	HBP	SH	SF	SB	CS	SB%	GDP	Avg	OBP	Slg
2012	Albq*	AAA	5	17	6	1	0	0	(-	-)	7	2	0	3	3	0	4	0	0	0	0	0	-	0	.353	.450	.412
1996	Hou	NL	15	22	5	1	0	0	(0	0)	6	1	1	1	2	0	3	0	0	0	0	0	-	1	.227	.292	.273
1997	Hou	NL	59	188	47	10	2	3	(3	0)	70	22	26	25	21	0	48	1	0	0	7	2	.78	0	.250	.329	.372
1998	Phi	NL	151	497	155	29	6	17	(10	7)	247	68	74	101	84	14	133	0	0	4	19	10	.66	6	.312	.409	.497
1999	Phi	NL	152	546	183	35	11	20	(13	7)	300	118	93	131	109	8	113	3	0	4	27	9	.75	13	.335	.446	.549
2000	Phi	NL	154	576	182	42	10	25	(14	11)	319	103	79	130	100	9	116	1	0	3	28	8	.78	12	.316	.416	.554
2001	Phi	NL	162	588	170	48	4	31	(13	18)	319	118	110	125	106	11	137	1	0	9	36	14	.72	13	.289	.393	.543
2002	Phi	NL	157	572	176	50	6	20	(8	12)	298	102	85	112	104	9	117	3	0	6	31	12	.72	11	.308	.413	.521
2003	Phi	NL	158	577	173	35	1	20	(11	9)	270	99	101	120	109	13	126	2	0	7	22	9	.71	13	.300	.409	.468
2004	Phi	NL	159	574	173	47	1	30	(13	17)	312	118	105	139	127	10	116	5	0	7	40	5	.89	5	.301	.428	.544
2005	Phi	NL	162	588	168	37	1	24	(15	9)	279	104	102	116	117	15	134	6	0	8	31	9	.78	7	.286	.405	.474
2006	2 Tms		156	548	163	41	2	15	(8	7)	253	98	107	123	124	6	138	3	2	9	30	6	.83	13	.297	.424	.462
2007	NYY	AL	158	605	171	40	5	16	(10	6)	269	123	101	101	84	0	115	3	0	7	25	8	.76	11	.283	.369	.445
2008	NYY	AL	156	609	180	39	4	20	(14	6)	287	100	100	108	73	2	109	1	0	1	22	11	.67	14	.296	.371	.471
2009	LAA	AL	152	563	165	29	3	15	(7	8)	245	96	103	109	94	7	113	1	0	9	30	8	.79	15	.293	.390	.435
2010	LAA	AL	154	573	146	41	1	20	(11	9)	249	88	78	91	87	3	132	2	0	5	24	10	.71	13	.255	.352	.435
2011	LAA	AL	142	502	127	30	1	8	(3	5)	183	54	60	74	78	5	113	1	1	3	21	5	.81	8	.253	.353	.365
2012	2 Tms		100	219	53	11	1	3	(1	2)	75	29	24	29	37	3	56	0	0	1	6	2	.75	7	.242	.350	.342
06	Phi	NL	98	339	94	25	2	8	(5	3)	147	61	65	76	91	5	86	2	0	6	20	4	.83	8	.277	.427	.434
06	NYY	AL	58	209	69	16	0	7	(3	4)	106	37	42	47	33	1	52	1	2	3	10	2	.83	5	.330	.419	.507
12	LAA	AL	8	24	5	3	0	0	(1	0)	8	1	5	4	2	0	5	0	0	1	0	0	-	1	.208	.259	.333
12	LAD	NL	92	195	48	8	1	3	(1	2)	67	28	19	25	35	3	51	0	0	0	6	2	.75	6	.246	.361	.344
	Postseason		20	67	19	6	0	1	(1	0)	28	9	9	11	12	3	15	0	0	0	2	1	.67	0	.284	.392	.418
	17 ML YEARS		2347	8347	2437	565	59	287	(154	133)	3981	1441	1349	1635	1456	115	1819	33	7	83	399	128	.76	162	.292	.396	.477

Tony Abreu

Bats: B **Throws:** R **Pos:** 2B-11; 3B-6; SS-4; DH-2; PH-2; PR-1   **Ht:** 5'9" **Wt:** 200 **Born:** 11/13/1984 **Age:** 28

			BATTING																	BASERUNNING				AVERAGES		
Year	Team	Lg	G	AB	H	2B	3B	HR	(Hm	Rd)	TB	R	RBI	RC	TBB	IBB	SO	HBP	SH	SF	SB	CS	SB%	GDP	Avg	OBP	Slg
2012	Omha*	AAA	103	429	138	36	5	9	(-	-)	211	60	73	73	14	2	69	4	4	2	7	2	.78	7	.322	.347	.492
2007	LAD	NL	59	166	45	14	1	2	(0	2)	67	19	17	18	7	1	21	3	0	2	0	0	-	5	.271	.309	.404
2009	LAD	NL	6	8	2	0	0	0	(0	0)	2	0	1	2	3	0	2	0	0	0	0	1	.00	0	.250	.455	.250
2010	Ari	NL	81	193	45	11	1	1	(1	0)	61	16	13	12	4	0	47	0	0	4	2	1	.67	8	.233	.244	.316
2012	KC	AL	22	70	18	2	1	1	(1	0)	25	5	15	13	2	0	13	1	0	1	0	0	-	1	.257	.284	.357
	4 ML YEARS		168	437	110	27	3	4	(2	2)	155	40	46	45	16	1	83	4	0	7	2	2	.50	14	.252	.280	.355

Jeremy Accardo

Pitches: R **Bats:** R **Pos:** RP-27   uh-CAR-doe   **Ht:** 6'1" **Wt:** 200 **Born:** 12/8/1981 **Age:** 31

			HOW MUCH HE PITCHED						WHAT HE GAVE UP											THE RESULTS						
Year	Team	Lg	G	GS	CG	GF	IP	BFP	H	R	ER	HR	SH	SF	HB	TBB	IBB	SO	WP	Bk	W	L	Pct	Sh	Sv-Op	Hld	ERC	ERA
2012	Clmbs*	AAA	13	0	0	9	16.1	67	12	7	5	0	0	1	1	7	2	16	1	0	0	2	.000	0	4--	-	2.20	2.76
2012	Scrmto*	AAA	7	0	0	4	7.2	34	7	1	1	0	0	0	1	3	0	4	0	0	1	0	1.000	0	2--	-	3.26	1.17
2005	SF	NL	28	0	0	7	29.2	124	26	13	13	2	1	1	1	9	1	16	1	0	1	5	.167	0	0-1	4	2.87	3.94
2006	2 Tms		65	0	0	27	69.0	297	76	42	41	7	1	4	1	20	5	54	4	1	2	4	.333	0	3-8	10	4.17	5.35
2007	Tor	AL	64	0	0	48	67.1	275	51	19	16	4	0	1	2	24	2	57	0	1	4	4	.500	0	30-35	2	2.44	2.14
2008	Tor	AL	16	0	0	6	12.1	56	15	10	9	1	0	1	1	4	2	5	1	0	0	3	.000	0	4-6	2	4.88	6.57
2009	Tor	AL	26	0	0	5	24.2	107	23	8	7	2	0	2	2	17	1	18	0	0	0	0	-	0	1-1	4	5.26	2.55
2010	Tor	AL	5	0	0	2	6.2	34	12	6	6	0	0	0	1	3	0	3	2	0	0	1	.000	0	0-0	0	9.38	8.10

Year	Team	Lg	G	GS	CG	GF	IP	BFP	H	R	ER	HR	SH	SF	HB	TBB	IBB	SO	WP	Bk	W	L	Pct	Sh	Sv-Op	Hld	ERC	ERA
2011	Bal	AL	31	0	0	7	37.2	167	43	24	24	5	2	0	1	18	4	23	0	0	3	3	.500	0	0-1	2	5.53	5.73
2012	2 Tms	AL	27	0	0	13	37.1	162	42	21	20	3	1	4	0	16	1	29	2	0	0	0	-	0	0-0	0	4.85	4.82
06	SF	NL	38	0	0	16	40.1	170	38	23	22	2	0	4	1	11	3	40	2	0	1	3	.250	0	3-6	8	2.88	4.91
06	Tor	AL	27	0	0	11	28.2	127	38	19	19	5	1	0	0	9	2	14	2	1	1	1	.500	0	0-2	6	2.65	5.97
12	Cle	AL	26	0	0	13	35.1	152	38	19	18	3	1	3	0	16	1	28	2	0	0	0	-	0	0-0	0	4.70	4.58
12	Oak	AL	1	0	0	0	2.0	10	4	2	2	0	0	1	0	0	0	1	0	0	0	0	-	0	0-0	0	7.48	9.00
8 ML YEARS			262	0	0	115	284.2	1222	288	143	136	24	5	13	9	111	16	205	10	2	10	20	.333	0	38-52	24	4.07	4.30

Alfredo Aceves

Pitches: R **Bats:** R **Pos:** RP-69   ah-SEVV-us   **Ht:** 6'3" **Wt:** 220 **Born:** 12/8/1981 **Age:** 31

Year	Team	Lg	G	GS	CG	GF	IP	BFP	H	R	ER	HR	SH	SF	HB	TBB	IBB	SO	WP	Bk	W	L	Pct	Sh	Sv-Op	Hld	ERC	ERA
2008	NYY	AL	6	4	0	1	30.0	120	25	8	8	4	0	0	0	10	0	16	1	0	1	0	1.000	0	0-0	0	3.23	2.40
2009	NYY	AL	43	1	0	10	84.0	337	69	36	33	10	1	2	5	16	2	69	0	0	10	1	.909	0	1-2	5	2.65	3.54
2010	NYY	AL	10	0	0	2	12.0	53	10	5	4	1	0	0	1	4	1	2	0	0	3	0	1.000	0	1-1	1	2.80	3.00
2011	Bos	AL	55	4	0	15	114.0	474	84	37	33	8	3	3	15	42	1	80	1	2	10	2	.833	0	2-5	11	2.84	2.61
2012	Bos	AL	69	0	0	55	84.0	361	80	51	50	11	2	7	6	31	2	75	3	1	2	10	.167	0	25-33	0	4.16	5.36
Postseason			4	0	0	1	4.1	20	5	2	2	0	1	0	0	3	1	2	1	0	0	1	.000	0	0-0	0	5.01	4.15
5 ML YEARS			183	9	0	83	324.0	1345	268	137	128	34	6	12	27	103	6	242	5	3	26	13	.667	0	29-41	17	3.15	3.56

Dustin Ackley

Bats: L **Throws:** R **Pos:** 2B-142; 1B-11; DH-4; PH-2   **Ht:** 6'1" **Wt:** 190 **Born:** 2/26/1988 **Age:** 25

Year	Team	Lg	G	AB	H	2B	3B	HR	(Hm	Rd)	TB	R	RBI	RC	TBB	IBB	SO	HBP	SH	SF	SB	CS	SB%	GDP	Avg	OBP	Slg
2010	WTenn	AA	82	289	76	21	4	2	(-	-)	111	42	28	49	55	0	41	5	0	1	8	2	.80	5	.263	.389	.384
2010	Tacom	AAA	52	212	58	12	4	5	(-	-)	93	37	23	32	20	1	38	2	0	3	2	1	.67	3	.274	.338	.439
2011	Tacom	AAA	66	271	82	17	3	9	(-	-)	132	57	35	58	55	2	38	1	3	1	7	3	.70	3	.303	.421	.487
2011	Sea	AL	90	333	91	16	7	6	(3	3)	139	39	36	53	40	1	79	0	0	3	6	0	1.00	3	.273	.348	.417
2012	Sea	AL	153	607	137	22	2	12	(2	10)	199	84	50	62	59	7	124	0	1	1	13	3	.81	3	.226	.294	.328
2 ML YEARS			243	940	228	38	9	18	(5	13)	338	123	86	115	99	8	203	0	1	4	19	3	.86	6	.243	.314	.360

Manny Acosta

Pitches: R **Bats:** B **Pos:** RP-45   **Ht:** 6'4" **Wt:** 215 **Born:** 5/1/1981 **Age:** 32

Year	Team	Lg	G	GS	CG	GF	IP	BFP	H	R	ER	HR	SH	SF	HB	TBB	IBB	SO	WP	Bk	W	L	Pct	Sh	Sv-Op	Hld	ERC	ERA
2012	Buffalo*	AAA	17	0	0	4	28.0	111	24	12	7	1	2	2	0	4	0	25	2	0	1	0	1.000	0	0--	-	1.99	2.25
2007	Atl	NL	21	0	0	5	23.2	93	13	6	6	2	0	0	0	14	1	22	1	0	1	1	.500	0	0-0	4	2.39	2.28
2008	Atl	NL	46	0	0	22	53.0	226	48	25	21	7	4	1	1	26	5	31	5	0	3	5	.375	0	3-5	4	4.12	3.57
2009	Atl	NL	36	0	0	17	37.1	174	45	19	18	4	3	0	2	19	2	32	3	0	1	1	.500	0	0-0	5	5.90	4.34
2010	NYM	NL	41	0	0	12	39.2	157	30	13	13	4	1	1	0	18	1	42	3	0	3	2	.600	0	1-3	2	3.10	2.95
2011	NYM	NL	44	0	0	15	47.0	204	50	21	18	6	0	1	2	15	0	46	0	0	4	1	.800	0	4-7	7	4.47	3.45
2012	NYM	NL	45	0	0	7	47.1	216	48	38	34	7	1	2	3	25	1	46	2	0	1	3	.250	0	1-2	4	5.18	6.46
6 ML YEARS			233	0	0	78	248.0	1070	234	122	110	30	9	5	8	117	10	219	14	0	13	13	.500	0	9-17	23	4.30	3.99

Matt Adams

Bats: L **Throws:** R **Pos:** 1B-24; PH-3   **Ht:** 6'3" **Wt:** 230 **Born:** 8/31/1988 **Age:** 24

Year	Team	Lg	G	AB	H	2B	3B	HR	(Hm	Rd)	TB	R	RBI	RC	TBB	IBB	SO	HBP	SH	SF	SB	CS	SB%	GDP	Avg	OBP	Slg
2009	JhsCty	R+	32	115	42	6	0	6	(-	-)	66	15	25	26	9	0	20	1	0	3	0	0	-	3	.365	.406	.574
2009	Batvia	A-	31	130	45	11	0	4	(-	-)	68	16	27	26	11	3	21	0	0	1	0	0	-	4	.346	.394	.523
2010	QuadC	A	121	464	144	41	0	22	(-	-)	251	71	88	90	33	3	78	4	0	9	5	1	.83	11	.310	.355	.541
2011	Sprgfld	AA	115	463	139	23	2	32	(-	-)	262	80	101	92	40	7	90	4	0	6	1	0	1.00	12	.300	.357	.566
2012	Memp	AAA	67	258	85	22	0	18	(-	-)	161	41	50	56	15	1	57	0	0	3	3	1	.75	5	.329	.362	.624
2012	StL	NL	27	86	21	6	0	2	(1	1)	33	8	13	9	5	0	24	0	0	0	0	0	-	3	.244	.286	.384

Mike Adams

Pitches: R **Bats:** R **Pos:** RP-61   **Ht:** 6'5" **Wt:** 195 **Born:** 7/29/1978 **Age:** 34

Year	Team	Lg	G	GS	CG	GF	IP	BFP	H	R	ER	HR	SH	SF	HB	TBB	IBB	SO	WP	Bk	W	L	Pct	Sh	Sv-Op	Hld	ERC	ERA
2004	Mil	NL	46	0	0	13	53.0	225	50	21	20	5	5	2	2	14	2	39	2	0	2	3	.400	0	0-5	12	3.22	3.40
2005	Mil	NL	13	0	0	7	13.1	61	12	4	4	2	0	0	0	10	1	14	1	0	0	1	.000	0	1-2	2	5.12	2.70
2006	Mil	NL	2	0	0	0	2.1	13	4	3	3	1	0	0	0	2	0	1	0	0	0	0	-	0	0-0	0	13.74	11.57
2008	SD	NL	54	0	0	11	65.1	259	49	18	18	7	2	3	0	19	2	74	0	0	2	3	.400	0	0-2	10	2.38	2.48
2009	SD	NL	37	0	0	5	37.0	136	14	9	3	1	2	0	0	8	1	45	1	0	0	0	-	0	0-1	15	0.65	0.73
2010	SD	NL	70	0	0	3	66.2	268	48	14	13	2	0	0	0	23	2	73	0	0	4	1	.800	0	0-4	38	1.95	1.76
2011	2 Tms	NL	76	0	0	11	73.2	277	44	13	12	5	2	1	0	14	2	74	0	0	5	4	.556	0	2-5	32	1.31	1.47
2012	Tex	AL	61	0	0	7	52.1	228	56	21	19	4	0	0	3	17	1	45	2	0	5	3	.625	0	1-2	27	4.20	3.27
11	SD	NL	49	0	0	6	48.0	179	26	7	6	2	1	1	0	9	1	49	0	0	3	1	.750	0	1-3	23	1.06	1.13
11	Tex	AL	27	0	0	5	25.2	98	18	6	6	3	1	0	0	5	1	25	0	0	2	3	.400	0	1-2	9	1.88	2.10
Postseason			11	0	0	2	8.1	39	11	3	3	2	0	0	0	6	1	6	0	0	2	0	1.000	0	0-0	5	8.84	3.24
8 ML YEARS			359	0	0	57	363.2	1467	277	103	92	27	11	6	5	107	11	365	6	0	18	15	.545	0	4-21	136	2.27	2.28

Nathan Adcock

Pitches: R Bats: R Pos: RP-10; SP-2   Ht: 6'4" Wt: 225 Born: 2/25/1988 Age: 25

Year	Team	Lg	G	GS	CG	GF	IP	BFP	H	R	ER	HR	SH	SF	HB	TBB	IBB	SO	WP	Bk	W	L	Pct	Sh	Sv-Op	Hld	ERC	ERA
2006	Ms	R	10	6	0	0	35.1	159	33	21	13	1	2	0	5	16	0	31	5	0	0	2	.000	0	0--	-	3.86	3.31
2007	Wisc	A	17	16	0	0	87.2	392	85	60	36	7	1	4	5	38	0	66	13	0	2	8	.200	0	0--	-	4.00	3.70
2007	Hi Dsrt	A+	5	5	0	0	18.1	98	20	26	18	0	0	2	2	22	0	11	2	0	1	3	.250	0	0--	-	7.33	8.84
2008	Wisc	A	15	14	0	0	77.1	339	81	45	32	3	3	1	5	29	0	82	13	0	2	5	.286	0	0--	-	4.05	3.72
2009	Hi Dsrt	A+	21	19	1	0	102.0	457	103	72	60	10	5	4	6	54	0	71	6	0	5	7	.417	0	0--	-	4.89	5.29
2009	Lynbrg	A+	7	4	0	1	24.0	109	29	17	14	5	0	2	2	7	0	15	3	0	3	2	.600	0	0--	-	5.93	5.25
2010	Bradtn	A+	27	26	0	0	141.1	593	131	66	53	8	3	5	7	38	0	113	12	0	11	7	.611	0	0--	-	3.05	3.38
2012	Omha	AAA	19	18	0	0	99.1	435	116	67	61	5	3	3	7	30	0	60	9	0	8	6	.571	0	0--	-	4.62	5.53
2011	KC	AL	24	3	0	5	60.1	265	63	34	31	5	3	1	3	26	3	36	4	1	1	1	.500	0	1-2	0	4.47	4.62
2012	KC	AL	12	2	0	3	34.2	148	37	13	9	4	1	2	1	13	2	22	0	0	0	3	.000	0	0-0	1	4.61	2.34
	2 ML YEARS		36	5	0	8	95.0	413	100	47	40	9	4	3	4	39	5	58	4	1	1	4	.200	0	1-2	1	4.52	3.79

Jeremy Affeldt

Pitches: L Bats: L Pos: RP-67   AFF-felt   Ht: 6'4" Wt: 230 Born: 6/6/1979 Age: 34

Year	Team	Lg	G	GS	CG	GF	IP	BFP	H	R	ER	HR	SH	SF	HB	TBB	IBB	SO	WP	Bk	W	L	Pct	Sh	Sv-Op	Hld	ERC	ERA
2002	KC	AL	34	7	0	4	77.2	353	85	41	40	8	2	1	3	37	4	67	5	2	3	4	.429	0	0-1	1	4.97	4.64
2003	KC	AL	36	18	0	5	126.0	533	126	58	55	12	2	5	5	38	1	98	2	2	7	6	.538	0	4-4	3	3.82	3.93
2004	KC	AL	38	8	0	26	76.1	344	91	49	42	6	4	4	3	32	2	49	4	3	4	4	.429	0	13-17	0	5.26	4.95
2005	KC	AL	49	0	0	13	49.2	232	56	35	29	3	0	1	0	29	2	39	5	0	0	2	.000	0	0-0	12	5.08	5.26
2006	2 Tms		54	9	0	12	97.1	448	102	74	67	13	4	4	2	55	3	48	2	0	8	8	.500	0	1-3	5	5.21	6.20
2007	Col	NL	75	0	0	11	59.0	253	47	26	23	3	3	6	3	33	9	46	6	1	4	3	.571	0	0-4	9	3.19	3.51
2008	Cin	NL	74	0	0	20	78.1	335	78	36	29	9	7	0	3	25	0	80	6	0	1	1	.500	0	0-1	5	3.98	3.33
2009	SF	NL	74	0	0	8	62.1	248	42	14	12	3	0	1	3	31	3	55	5	0	2	2	.500	0	0-0	33	2.61	1.73
2010	SF	NL	53	0	0	14	50.0	228	56	25	23	4	7	1	3	24	5	44	4	0	4	3	.571	0	4-7	7	4.99	4.14
2011	SF	NL	67	0	0	12	61.2	259	47	22	18	5	4	0	4	24	3	54	4	0	3	2	.600	0	3-6	13	2.77	2.63
2012	SF	NL	67	0	0	10	63.1	267	57	23	19	1	4	0	3	23	1	57	5	0	1	2	.333	0	3-4	16	2.98	2.70
06	KC	AL	27	9	0	3	70.0	320	71	51	46	9	3	3	1	42	0	28	2	0	4	6	.400	0	0-0	2	5.18	5.91
06	Col	NL	27	0	0	9	27.1	128	31	23	21	4	1	1	1	13	3	20	0	0	4	2	.667	0	1-3	3	5.29	6.91
	Postseason		12	0	0	1	9.1	33	4	3	3	1	0	0	0	3	1	8	1	0	0	0	-	0	0-0	2	1.23	2.89
	11 ML YEARS		621	42	0	135	801.2	3500	787	403	357	67	37	23	32	351	33	637	48	8	36	37	.493	0	28-47	104	4.09	4.01

Jonathan Albaladejo

Pitches: R Bats: R Pos: RP-3   ahl-bah-lah-DAY-hoe   Ht: 6'5" Wt: 255 Born: 10/30/1982 Age: 30

Year	Team	Lg	G	GS	CG	GF	IP	BFP	H	R	ER	HR	SH	SF	HB	TBB	IBB	SO	WP	Bk	W	L	Pct	Sh	Sv-Op	Hld	ERC	ERA
2012	Reno*	AAA	49	0	0	42	56.2	234	46	23	23	8	2	1	3	23	2	60	2	1	5	3	.625	0	25--	-	3.56	3.65
2007	Was	NL	14	0	0	1	14.1	51	7	3	3	1	0	1	1	2	0	12	0	0	1	1	.500	0	0-1	2	1.10	1.88
2008	NYY	AL	7	0	0	2	13.2	58	15	6	6	1	1	0	0	6	0	13	0	0	0	1	.000	0	0-0	1	4.82	3.95
2009	NYY	AL	32	0	0	5	34.1	158	41	23	20	6	1	4	3	16	2	21	0	0	5	1	.833	0	0-1	5	6.41	5.24
2010	NYY	AL	10	0	0	5	11.1	50	9	5	5	1	1	0	2	8	1	8	0	0	0	0	-	0	0-0	4	4.73	3.97
2012	Ari	NL	3	0	0	0	3.0	15	5	3	3	1	0	1	1	0	0	2	0	1	0	0	-	0	0-0	0	9.75	9.00
	5 ML YEARS		66	0	0	13	76.2	332	77	40	37	10	2	7	7	32	3	56	0	1	6	3	.667	0	0-2	4	4.80	4.34

Matt Albers

Pitches: R Bats: L Pos: RP-63   Ht: 6'0" Wt: 225 Born: 1/20/1983 Age: 30

Year	Team	Lg	G	GS	CG	GF	IP	BFP	H	R	ER	HR	SH	SF	HB	TBB	IBB	SO	WP	Bk	W	L	Pct	Sh	Sv-Op	Hld	ERC	ERA
2006	Hou	NL	4	2	0	0	15.0	68	17	10	10	1	2	0	0	7	0	11	0	0	0	2	.000	0	0-0	0	4.97	6.00
2007	Hou	NL	31	18	0	2	110.2	508	127	77	72	16	6	8	7	50	6	71	7	0	4	11	.267	0	0-0	0	5.76	5.86
2008	Bal	AL	28	3	0	5	49.0	208	43	21	19	4	1	3	2	22	1	26	1	0	3	3	.500	0	0-2	6	3.62	3.49
2009	Bal	AL	56	0	0	13	67.0	309	80	43	41	3	5	2	2	36	3	49	3	0	3	6	.333	0	0-4	10	5.41	5.51
2010	Bal	AL	62	0	0	19	75.2	329	78	41	38	6	3	0	2	34	5	49	2	0	5	3	.625	0	0-2	7	4.35	4.52
2011	Bos	AL	56	0	0	10	64.2	289	62	35	34	7	4	2	5	31	1	68	2	0	4	4	.500	0	0-3	10	4.44	4.73
2012	2 Tms		63	0	0	12	60.1	241	46	21	16	9	1	2	2	22	3	44	1	0	3	1	.750	0	0-6	9	3.13	2.39
12	Bos	AL	40	0	0	8	39.1	157	30	14	10	6	0	1	0	15	3	25	0	0	2	0	1.000	0	0-4	7	3.16	2.29
12	Ari	NL	23	0	0	4	21.0	84	16	7	6	3	1	0	1	7	0	19	1	0	1	1	.500	0	0-2	3	3.07	2.57
	7 ML YEARS		300	23	0	61	442.1	1950	453	248	230	48	22	17	20	202	19	318	16	0	22	30	.423	0	0-17	42	4.63	4.68

Al Alburquerque

Pitches: R Bats: R Pos: RP-8   Ht: 6'0" Wt: 195 Born: 6/10/1986 Age: 27

Year	Team	Lg	G	GS	CG	GF	IP	BFP	H	R	ER	HR	SH	SF	HB	TBB	IBB	SO	WP	Bk	W	L	Pct	Sh	Sv-Op	Hld	ERC	ERA
2006	Cubs	R	8	5	0	0	12.2	56	10	8	8	1	1	2	0	10	0	15	1	0	0	2	.000	0	0--	-	4.32	5.68
2007	Peoria	A	11	4	0	0	25.1	123	36	29	26	5	0	1	0	12	1	20	4	0	1	4	.200	0	0--	-	7.56	9.24
2007	Boise	A-	10	6	0	0	41.0	180	42	20	17	2	2	0	3	17	0	49	3	0	3	2	.600	0	1--	-	4.20	3.73
2009	Dytona	A+	24	0	0	11	34.2	144	26	11	8	4	0	1	4	14	0	44	3	2	1	0	1.000	0	2--	-	2.93	2.08
2009	Tulsa	AA	23	0	0	7	26.1	113	23	13	11	0	2	0	2	13	0	31	1	0	1	3	.250	0	0--	-	3.36	3.76
2010	Tulsa	AA	25	0	0	9	34.1	149	32	23	19	1	4	0	2	19	0	32	4	4	2	4	.333	0	3--	-	4.10	4.98
2011	Toledo	AAA	4	0	0	3	4.2	22	5	1	1	0	0	0	1	2	0	10	0	0	0	0	-	0	0--	-	4.53	1.93
2012	Lkland	A+	4	3	0	0	3.1	16	5	2	2	1	0	0	0	1	0	9	0	1	0	0	-	0	0--	-	8.14	5.40
2012	Toledo	AAA	9	0	0	1	10.2	46	9	2	2	1	1	0	0	4	0	18	0	0	1	0	1.000	0	0--	-	3.37	1.69

Year	Team	Lg	G	GS	CG	GF	IP	BFP	H	R	ER	HR	SH	SF	HB	TBB	IBB	SO	WP	Bk	W	L	Pct	Sh	Sv-Op	Hld	ERC	ERA
2011	Det	AL	41	0	0	11	43.1	182	21	9	9	0	2	1	2	29	4	67	4	0	6	1	.857	0	0-0	6	1.73	1.87
2012	Det	AL	8	0	0	12	13.1	53	6	1	1	0	0	0	0	8	0	18	0	1	0	0	-	0	0-0	1	1.50	0.68
	Postseason		4	0	0	1	2.0	11	2	3	3	1	0	0	0	3	0	2	1	1	0	0	-	0	0-0	0	12.44	13.50
	2 ML YEARS		49	0	0	11	56.2	235	27	10	10	0	2	1	2	37	4	85	4	1	6	1	.857	0	0-0	7	1.66	1.59

Brandon Allen

Bats: L Throws: R Pos: PH-4; 1B-3; LF-3; PR-1 **Ht: 6'2" Wt: 235 Born: 2/12/1986 Age: 27**

Year	Team	Lg	G	AB	H	2B	3B	HR	(Hm	Rd)	TB	R	RBI	RC	TBB	IBB	SO	HBP	SH	SF	SB	CS	SB%	GDP	Avg	OBP	Slg
2012	Charltt*	A+	14	51	13	3	0	2	(-	-)	22	8	4	8	9	0	14	0	0	1	0	0	-	0	.255	.361	.431
2012	Drham*	AAA	29	122	32	9	1	4	(-	-)	55	17	14	16	4	1	32	2	0	1	0	0	-	1	.262	.295	.451
2012	Sbank*	Jap	12	35	6	1	0	0	(-	-)	7	4	1	0	1	0	13	0	0	0	0	0	-	0	.171	.194	.200
2009	Ari	NL	32	104	21	7	0	4	(1	3)	40	13	14	12	12	2	40	0	0	0	0	0	-	4	.202	.284	.385
2010	Ari	NL	22	45	12	3	0	1	(1	0)	18	5	6	7	10	1	20	0	0	1	0	0	-	0	.267	.393	.400
2011	2 Tms		52	175	35	9	2	6	(2	4)	66	23	18	18	18	3	68	1	0	1	3	0	1.00	0	.200	.277	.377
2012	2 Tms	AL	10	20	2	0	0	1	(1	0)	5	3	3	2	2	0	9	0	0	0	0	0	-	0	.100	.182	.250
11	Ari	NL	11	29	5	0	0	3	(2	1)	14	5	7	6	7	2	13	1	0	0	1	0	1.00	0	.172	.351	.483
11	Oak	AL	41	146	30	9	2	3	(0	3)	52	18	11	12	11	1	55	0	0	1	2	0	1.00	0	.205	.259	.356
12	Oak	AL	3	7	0	0	0	0	(0	0)	0	0	0	0	0	0	5	0	0	0	0	0	-	0	.000	.000	.000
12	TB	AL	7	13	2	0	0	1	(1	0)	5	3	3	2	2	0	4	0	0	0	0	0	-	0	.154	.267	.385
	4 ML YEARS		116	344	70	19	2	12	(5	7)	129	44	41	39	42	6	137	1	0	2	3	0	1.00	4	.203	.290	.375

Cody Allen

Pitches: R Bats: R Pos: RP-27 **Ht: 6'1" Wt: 210 Born: 11/20/1988 Age: 24**

Year	Team	Lg	G	GS	CG	GF	IP	BFP	H	R	ER	HR	SH	SF	HB	TBB	IBB	SO	WP	Bk	W	L	Pct	Sh	Sv-Op	Hld	ERC	ERA
2011	MhVlly	A-	14	0	0	3	33.2	133	21	9	8	1	3	3	3	9	0	42	1	2	3	1	.750	0	0--	-	1.62	2.14
2011	Lk Cty	A	7	0	0	1	17.0	66	10	0	0	0	0	0	0	5	0	28	2	0	2	0	1.000	0	0--	-	1.26	0.00
2011	Akron	AA	1	0	0	1	1.0	6	3	2	2	0	0	0	0	0	0	2	0	0	0	0	-	0	0--	-	14.52	18.00
2011	Knstn	A+	1	0	0	0	3.0	10	1	0	0	0	0	0	0	0	0	3	0	0	0	0	-	0	0--	-	0.25	0.00
2012	Carlina	AA	2	0	0	1	4.0	13	1	0	0	0	0	0	0	0	0	8	0	0	0	0	-	0	0--	-	0.14	0.00
2012	Akron	AA	5	0	0	2	7.2	25	2	1	1	1	0	0	0	0	0	10	0	0	0	0	-	0	1--	-	0.33	1.17
2012	Clmbs	AAA	24	0	0	10	31.2	125	22	8	8	3	3	0	0	9	1	35	0	0	3	2	.600	0	2--	-	2.00	2.27
2012	Cle	AL	27	0	0	9	29.0	126	29	12	12	2	1	1	0	15	0	27	0	0	0	1	.000	0	0-1	1	4.39	3.72

Yonder Alonso

Bats: L Throws: R Pos: 1B-149; PH-9 YONN-dur ah-LONN-zo **Ht: 6'2" Wt: 240 Born: 4/8/1987 Age: 26**

Year	Team	Lg	G	AB	H	2B	3B	HR	(Hm	Rd)	TB	R	RBI	RC	TBB	IBB	SO	HBP	SH	SF	SB	CS	SB%	GDP	Avg	OBP	Slg
2010	Cin	NL	22	29	6	2	0	0	(0	0)	8	2	3	0	0	0	10	0	0	0	0	0	-	1	.207	.207	.276
2011	Cin	NL	47	88	29	4	0	5	(2	3)	48	9	15	16	10	0	21	0	0	0	0	0	-	2	.330	.398	.545
2012	SD	NL	155	549	150	39	0	9	(3	6)	216	47	62	71	62	9	101	3	1	4	3	0	1.00	14	.273	.348	.393
	3 ML YEARS		224	666	185	45	0	14	(5	9)	272	58	80	87	72	9	132	3	1	4	3	0	1.00	17	.278	.349	.408

Jose Altuve

Bats: R Throws: R Pos: 2B-147; PH-2 al-TOO-vay **Ht: 5'5" Wt: 170 Born: 5/6/1990 Age: 23**

Year	Team	Lg	G	AB	H	2B	3B	HR	(Hm	Rd)	TB	R	RBI	RC	TBB	IBB	SO	HBP	SH	SF	SB	CS	SB%	GDP	Avg	OBP	Slg
2008	Grnville	R	40	141	40	9	3	2	(-	-)	61	26	21	20	8	0	26	0	2	1	8	2	.80	2	.284	.320	.433
2009	Grnville	R	45	179	58	20	2	3	(-	-)	91	45	18	40	26	0	16	0	2	1	21	4	.84	6	.324	.408	.508
2009	TriCity	A-	21	76	19	5	0	0	(-	-)	24	13	7	9	8	0	10	2	1	0	7	2	.78	0	.250	.337	.316
2010	Lxngtn	A+	94	393	121	15	3	11	(-	-)	175	75	45	67	33	0	49	2	5	1	39	14	.74	7	.308	.364	.445
2010	Lancst	A+	31	116	32	5	2	4	(-	-)	53	18	22	15	9	0	17	1	1	0	3	4	.43	7	.276	.333	.457
2011	Lancst	A+	52	213	87	13	7	5	(-	-)	129	38	34	54	19	1	26	0	3	3	19	9	.68	5	.408	.451	.606
2011	CpChr	AA	35	144	52	9	3	5	(-	-)	82	21	25	29	7	0	14	0	1	1	5	5	.50	5	.361	.388	.569
2011	Hou	NL	57	221	61	10	1	2	(2	0)	79	26	12	18	5	0	29	2	5	1	7	3	.70	5	.276	.297	.357
2012	Hou	NL	147	576	167	34	4	7	(4	3)	230	80	37	76	40	0	74	6	4	4	33	11	.75	8	.290	.340	.399
	2 ML YEARS		204	797	228	44	5	9	(6	3)	309	106	49	94	45	0	103	8	9	5	40	14	.74	13	.286	.329	.388

Henderson Alvarez

Pitches: R Bats: R Pos: SP-31 **Ht: 6'1" Wt: 210 Born: 4/18/1990 Age: 23**

Year	Team	Lg	G	GS	CG	GF	IP	BFP	H	R	ER	HR	SH	SF	HB	TBB	IBB	SO	WP	Bk	W	L	Pct	Sh	Sv-Op	Hld	ERC	ERA
2008	B Jays	R	12	11	0	0	46.1	218	63	41	29	3	0	3	6	6	0	34	3	1	1	4	.200	0	0--	-	5.08	5.63
2009	Lnsng	A	23	23	1	0	124.1	515	121	54	48	1	2	4	6	19	0	92	4	3	9	6	.600	0	0--	-	2.55	3.47
2010	Dnedin	A+	23	21	0	0	112.1	498	137	65	54	10	4	3	7	27	0	78	5	0	8	7	.533	0	0--	-	4.85	4.33
2011	Dnedin	A+	2	2	0	0	8.1	39	11	9	6	0	0	0	2	1	0	4	0	1	1	0	1.000	0	0--	-	4.85	6.48
2011	NHam	AA	15	14	1	0	88.0	353	81	31	28	7	0	1	4	17	0	66	1	0	8	4	.667	0	0--	-	2.97	2.86
2011	Tor	AL	10	10	0	0	63.2	259	64	26	25	8	1	2	4	8	0	40	2	0	1	3	.250	0	0-0	0	3.49	3.53
2012	Tor	AL	31	31	0	0	187.1	807	216	110	101	29	2	4	3	54	2	79	3	1	9	14	.391	1	0-0	0	5.01	4.85
	2 ML YEARS		41	41	1	0	251.0	1066	280	136	126	37	3	6	7	62	2	119	5	1	10	17	.370	1	0-0	0	4.61	4.52

Pedro Alvarez

Bats: L Throws: R Pos: 3B-145; PH-4; DH-1 **Ht: 6'3" Wt: 235 Born: 2/6/1987 Age: 26**

Year	Team	Lg	G	AB	H	2B	3B	HR	(Hm	Rd)	TB	R	RBI	RC	TBB	IBB	SO	HBP	SH	SF	SB	CS	SB%	GDP	Avg	OBP	Slg
2010	Pit	NL	95	347	89	21	1	16	(12	4)	160	42	64	50	37	1	119	0	0	2	0	0		8	.256	.326	.461
2011	Pit	NL	74	235	45	9	1	4	(0	4)	68	18	19	14	24	1	80	2	1	0	1	0	1.00	11	.191	.272	.289
2012	Pit	NL	149	525	128	25	1	30	(12	18)	245	64	85	77	57	6	180	1	0	3	1	0	1.00	10	.244	.317	.467
	3 ML YEARS		318	1107	262	55	3	50	(24	26)	473	124	168	141	118	8	379	3	1	5	2	0	1.00	29	.237	.311	.427

Alexi Amarista

ah-mah-REE-stah

Bats: L Throws: R Pos: 2B-52; LF-27; PH-26; SS-12; CF-11; RF-4; PR-4; 3B-1; DH-1 **Ht: 5'7" Wt: 150 Born: 4/6/1989 Age: 24**

Year	Team	Lg	G	AB	H	2B	3B	HR	(Hm	Rd)	TB	R	RBI	RC	TBB	IBB	SO	HBP	SH	SF	SB	CS	SB%	GDP	Avg	OBP	Slg
2008	Angels	R	51	202	67	6	4	2	(-	-)	87	46	21	37	29	0	20	1	3	1	22	14	.61	3	.332	.416	.431
2008	CRpds	A	1	2	0	0	0	0	(-	-)	0	0	0	0	0	0	1	0	0	0	0	0		0	.000	.000	.000
2009	CRpds	A	125	477	152	39	10	4	(-	-)	223	84	49	89	50	0	61	8	18	4	38	20	.66	10	.319	.390	.468
2010	RCuca	A+	72	297	90	19	6	4	(-	-)	133	39	39	46	19	2	42	3	2	2	17	10	.63	1	.303	.349	.448
2010	Salt Lk	AAA	15	65	26	6	3	0	(-	-)	38	13	9	14	1	0	4	1	2	1	4	2	.67	1	.400	.412	.585
2010	Ark	AA	48	191	55	2	1	1	(-	-)	62	25	20	23	13	0	15	2	2	5	4	1	.80	8	.288	.332	.325
2011	Salt Lk	AAA	86	363	106	24	5	4	(-	-)	152	49	50	52	22	0	56	4	4	3	15	8	.65	4	.292	.337	.419
2012	Salt Lk	AAA	18	77	21	6	2	0	(-	-)	31	11	12	9	3	0	6	0	0	3	1	0	1.00	0	.273	.289	.403
2012	Tucsn	AAA	11	49	14	1	0	1	(-	-)	18	6	6	6	1	0	6	1	0	0	3	0	1.00	0	.286	.300	.367
2011	LAA	AL	23	52	8	3	1	0	(0	0)	13	2	5	1	2	0	8	0	1	1	0	0		1	.154	.182	.250
2012	2 Tms		106	275	66	15	5	5	(0	5)	106	36	32	31	17	1	42	0	6	2	8	4	.67	2	.240	.282	.385
12	LAA	AL	1	0	0	0	0	0	(0	0)	0	1	0	0	0	0	0	0	0	0	0	0		-	-	-	-
12	SD	NL	105	275	66	15	5	5	(0	5)	106	35	32	31	17	1	42	0	6	2	8	4	.67	2	.240	.282	.385
	2 ML YEARS		129	327	74	18	6	5	(0	5)	119	38	37	32	19	1	50	0	7	3	8	4	.67	3	.226	.266	.364

Hector Ambriz

AMM-brizz

Pitches: R Bats: L Pos: RP-18 **Ht: 6'2" Wt: 235 Born: 5/24/1984 Age: 29**

Year	Team	Lg	G	GS	CG	GF	IP	BFP	H	R	ER	HR	SH	SF	HB	TBB	IBB	SO	WP	Bk	W	L	Pct	Sh	Sv-Op	Hld	ERC	ERA
2006	Msoula	R+	15	4	0	3	42.1	165	29	10	9	1	1	0	2	11	0	52	6	0	1	3	.250	0	3--	-	1.72	1.91
2007	Visalia	A+	28	26	2	1	150.0	640	137	79	68	12	3	12	6	50	1	133	14	0	10	8	.556	0	0--	-	3.30	4.08
2008	Mobile	AA	27	26	2	1	152.2	651	155	91	83	22	4	4	3	47	0	118	10	0	5	13	.278	0	0--	-	4.17	4.89
2009	Mobile	AA	5	5	0	0	29.0	109	18	7	7	1	3	0	0	6	0	32	0	0	3	2	.600	0	0--	-	1.33	2.17
2009	Reno	AAA	23	22	0	0	127.2	578	164	88	79	12	9	2	2	40	1	103	4	1	9	9	.500	0	0--	-	5.36	5.57
2010	Clmbs	AAA	7	0	0	0	8.0	35	9	1	1	0	0	1	0	1	0	15	1	0	0	0		0	0--	-	2.85	1.13
2012	Clmbs	AAA	20	1	0	7	33.0	140	29	14	13	3	2	0	0	17	1	25	6	0	0	1	.000	0	1--	-	3.80	3.55
2012	OKCity	AAA	18	0	0	7	24.1	108	28	9	9	1	2	2	1	11	3	18	1	0	1	1	.500	0	2--	-	4.75	3.33
2010	Cle	AL	34	0	0	20	48.1	224	68	31	30	10	2	3	1	17	1	37	4	0	0	2	.000	0	0-0	0	7.30	5.59
2012	Hou	NL	18	0	0	2	19.1	83	14	9	9	0	2	0	2	11	2	22	4	0	1	1	.500	0	0-0	3	2.74	4.19
	2 ML YEARS		52	0	0	22	67.2	307	82	40	39	10	4	3	3	28	3	59	8	0	1	3	.250	0	0-0	3	5.89	5.19

Brett Anderson

Pitches: L Bats: L Pos: SP-6 **Ht: 6'4" Wt: 235 Born: 2/1/1988 Age: 25**

Year	Team	Lg	G	GS	CG	GF	IP	BFP	H	R	ER	HR	SH	SF	HB	TBB	IBB	SO	WP	Bk	W	L	Pct	Sh	Sv-Op	Hld	ERC	ERA
2012	Stcktn*	A+	1	1	0	0	2.0	11	4	2	2	0	0	0	1	0	0	0	0	0	0	0	-	0	0--	-	9.72	9.00
2012	Scrmto*	AAA	5	5	0	0	23.1	99	27	12	11	4	0	0	1	5	0	18	1	1	1	1	.500	0	0--	-	5.01	4.24
2009	Oak	AL	30	30	1	0	175.1	735	180	94	79	20	4	4	3	45	1	150	0	1	11	11	.500	1	0-0	0	3.84	4.06
2010	Oak	AL	19	19	0	0	112.1	470	112	41	35	6	3	2	7	22	2	75	4	2	7	6	.538	0	0-0	0	3.16	2.80
2011	Oak	AL	13	13	1	0	83.1	356	86	40	37	8	4	1	7	25	1	61	0	1	3	6	.333	0	0-0	0	4.20	4.00
2012	Oak	AL	6	6	0	0	35.0	137	29	11	10	1	0	0	1	7	1	25	1	0	4	2	.667	1	0-0	0	2.13	2.57
	4 ML YEARS		68	68	2	0	406.0	1698	407	186	161	35	11	7	18	99	5	311	5	4	25	25	.500	1	0-0	0	3.56	3.57

Bryan Anderson

Bats: L Throws: R Pos: PH-7; C-2; 1B-1 **Ht: 6'1" Wt: 200 Born: 12/16/1986 Age: 26**

Year	Team	Lg	G	AB	H	2B	3B	HR	(Hm	Rd)	TB	R	RBI	RC	TBB	IBB	SO	HBP	SH	SF	SB	CS	SB%	GDP	Avg	OBP	Slg
2005	JhsCty	R+	51	154	51	8	1	6	(-	-)	79	28	36	31	15	1	29	1	1	5	6	1	.86	3	.331	.383	.513
2006	QuadC	A	109	381	115	29	3	3	(-	-)	159	50	51	61	42	2	66	5	1	7	2	6	.25	13	.302	.377	.417
2007	Sprgfld	AA	103	389	116	15	1	6	(-	-)	151	51	53	55	32	1	77	2	2	6	0	1	.00	9	.298	.350	.388
2008	Sprgfld	AA	19	80	31	5	0	2	(-	-)	42	12	14	16	4	0	12	0	1	1	0	0	-	3	.388	.412	.525
2008	Memp	AAA	73	235	66	13	2	2	(-	-)	89	27	27	36	32	3	46	1	5	2	2	0	1.00	5	.281	.367	.379
2009	Memp	AAA	53	163	40	7	3	4	(-	-)	65	22	11	19	10	1	42	1	0	1	1	0	1.00	1	.245	.293	.399
2009	Cards	R	5	16	5	0	0	1	(-	-)	8	3	2	3	4	0	4	0	0	0	1	0	1.00	0	.313	.450	.500
2010	Memp	AAA	82	270	73	12	0	12	(-	-)	121	39	42	42	27	1	54	3	0	2	0	0	-	5	.270	.341	.448
2011	Memp	AAA	98	335	94	19	0	8	(-	-)	137	39	37	51	36	3	76	5	0	2	1	1	.50	8	.281	.357	.409
2012	Memp	AAA	100	347	78	12	1	6	(-	-)	110	35	35	35	36	4	89	4	1	4	0	0	-	7	.225	.302	.317
2010	StL	NL	15	32	9	2	0	0	(0	0)	11	1	4	5	1	0	7	1	0	1	0	0	-	0	.281	.314	.344
2012	StL	NL	10	12	3	1	0	0	(0	0)	4	2	0	2	1	0	6	1	0	0	1	0	1.00	0	.250	.357	.333
	2 ML YEARS		25	44	12	3	0	0	(0	0)	15	3	4	7	2	0	13	2	0	1	1	0	1.00	0	.273	.327	.341

Lars Anderson

Bats: L **Throws:** L **Pos:** LF-4; PH-3; 1B-2   **Ht:** 6'4" **Wt:** 215 **Born:** 9/25/1987 **Age:** 25

Year	Team	Lg	G	AB	H	2B	3B	HR	(Hm	Rd)	TB	R	RBI	RC	TBB	IBB	SO	HBP	SH	SF	SB	CS	SB%	GDP	Avg	OBP	Slg
2012	Pwtckt*	AAA	93	340	88	22	2	9	(-	-)	141	49	52	55	56	3	89	0	0	5	1	0	1.00	10	.259	.359	.415
2012	Clmbs*	AAA	18	56	11	5	0	0	(-	-)	16	4	7	6	9	0	18	2	0	2	0	0	-	0	.196	.319	.286
2010	Bos	AL	18	35	7	1	0	0	(0	0)	8	4	4	4	7	0	8	0	0	1	0	0	-	1	.200	.326	.229
2011	Bos	AL	6	5	0	0	0	0	(0	0)	0	2	0	0	0	0	3	0	0	0	0	0	-	0	.000	.000	.000
2012	Bos	AL	6	8	1	0	0	0	(0	0)	1	1	0	0	0	0	3	0	0	0	0	0	-	0	.125	.125	.125
	3 ML YEARS		30	48	8	1	0	0	(0	0)	9	7	4	4	7	0	14	0	0	1	0	0	-	1	.167	.268	.188

Robert Andino

Bats: R **Throws:** R **Pos:** 2B-108; 3B-15; PH-6; PR-4; SS-2; LF-1; CF-1   ann-DEE-no   **Ht:** 6'0" **Wt:** 195 **Born:** 4/25/1984 **Age:** 29

Year	Team	Lg	G	AB	H	2B	3B	HR	(Hm	Rd)	TB	R	RBI	RC	TBB	IBB	SO	HBP	SH	SF	SB	CS	SB%	GDP	Avg	OBP	Slg
2012	Norfolk*	AAA	2	9	3	0	0	0	(-	-)	3	1	2	1	1	0	1	0	0	0	0	0	-	0	.333	.400	.333
2005	Fla	NL	17	44	7	4	0	0	(0	0)	11	4	1	1	5	1	8	0	1	0	1	0	1.00	2	.159	.245	.250
2006	Fla	NL	11	24	4	1	0	0	(0	0)	5	0	2	0	1	0	6	0	1	2	1	0	1.00	1	.167	.185	.208
2007	Fla	NL	7	13	5	1	0	0	(0	0)	6	0	0	1	0	0	2	0	0	0	0	0	-	0	.385	.385	.462
2008	Fla	NL	44	63	13	2	0	2	(1	1)	21	7	9	7	4	0	23	0	1	0	0	0	-	1	.206	.254	.333
2009	Bal	AL	78	198	44	7	0	2	(1	1)	57	31	10	11	15	1	47	0	0	2	3	3	.50	6	.222	.274	.288
2010	Bal	AL	16	61	18	4	0	2	(2	0)	28	6	6	4	3	0	13	1	0	1	1	1	.50	3	.295	.333	.459
2011	Bal	AL	139	457	120	22	0	5	(2	3)	157	63	36	52	41	0	83	3	9	1	13	3	.81	14	.263	.327	.344
2012	Bal	AL	127	384	81	13	1	7	(4	3)	117	41	28	31	37	0	100	2	7	1	5	5	.50	13	.211	.283	.305
	8 ML YEARS		439	1244	292	54	1	18	(10	8)	402	152	92	107	106	2	282	6	19	7	24	12	.67	39	.235	.296	.323

Elvis Andrus

Bats: R **Throws:** R **Pos:** SS-153; DH-4; PH-2   AHN-drews   **Ht:** 6'0" **Wt:** 200 **Born:** 8/26/1988 **Age:** 24

Year	Team	Lg	G	AB	H	2B	3B	HR	(Hm	Rd)	TB	R	RBI	RC	TBB	IBB	SO	HBP	SH	SF	SB	CS	SB%	GDP	Avg	OBP	Slg
2009	Tex	AL	145	480	128	17	8	6	(3	3)	179	72	40	65	40	0	77	6	12	3	33	6	.85	4	.267	.329	.373
2010	Tex	AL	148	588	156	15	3	0	(0	0)	177	88	35	79	64	0	96	5	17	0	32	15	.68	6	.265	.342	.301
2011	Tex	AL	150	587	164	27	3	5	(2	3)	212	96	60	76	56	0	74	5	16	1	37	12	.76	17	.279	.347	.361
2012	Tex	AL	158	629	180	31	9	3	(1	2)	238	85	62	92	57	0	96	5	17	3	21	10	.68	15	.286	.349	.378
	Postseason		33	136	36	4	0	0	(0	0)	40	18	5	13	12	0	20	1	4	1	9	3	.75	5	.265	.327	.294
	4 ML YEARS		601	2284	628	90	23	14	(6	8)	806	341	197	312	217	0	343	21	62	7	123	43	.74	42	.275	.342	.353

Rick Ankiel

Bats: L **Throws:** L **Pos:** CF-62; PH-13   ANN-keel   **Ht:** 6'1" **Wt:** 210 **Born:** 7/19/1979 **Age:** 33

Year	Team	Lg	G	AB	H	2B	3B	HR	(Hm	Rd)	TB	R	RBI	RC	TBB	IBB	SO	HBP	SH	SF	SB	CS	SB%	GDP	Avg	OBP	Slg
2012	Hrsbrg*	AA	4	9	3	0	0	2	(-	-)	9	3	3	3	2	0	2	0	0	0	0	0	-	0	.333	.455	1.000
2012	Hgrstn*	A	3	8	4	1	0	1	(-	-)	8	2	4	4	3	0	2	0	0	0	0	0	-	0	.500	.636	1.000
2012	Syrcse*	AAA	1	3	1	0	0	0	(-	-)	1	1	0	0	0	0	2	1	0	0	0	0	-	0	.333	.500	.333
1999	StL	NL	9	10	1	0	0	0	(0	0)	1	0	0	0	0	0	3	0	1	0	0	0	-	0	.100	.100	.100
2000	StL	NL	33	68	17	1	1	2	(2	0)	26	8	9	9	4	0	20	0	1	0	0	0	-	1	.250	.292	.382
2001	StL	NL	6	8	0	0	0	0	(0	0)	0	1	0	0	1	0	5	0	1	0	0	0	-	0	.000	.111	.000
2004	StL	NL	5	1	0	0	0	0	(0	0)	0	0	0	0	0	0	1	0	0	0	0	0	-	0	.000	.500	.000
2007	StL	NL	47	172	49	8	1	11	(9	2)	92	31	39	32	13	0	41	0	1	4	1	0	1.00	3	.285	.328	.535
2008	StL	NL	120	413	109	21	2	25	(11	14)	209	65	71	60	42	3	100	5	0	3	2	1	.67	8	.264	.337	.506
2009	StL	NL	122	372	86	21	2	11	(4	7)	144	50	38	32	26	4	99	3	0	3	4	3	.57	5	.231	.285	.387
2010	2 Tms		74	211	49	13	1	6	(1	5)	82	31	24	22	26	2	71	2	0	1	3	1	.75	3	.232	.321	.389
2011	Was	NL	122	380	91	20	0	9	(8	1)	138	46	37	35	29	1	96	2	3	1	10	3	.77	7	.239	.296	.363
2012	Was	NL	68	158	36	10	2	5	(2	3)	65	15	15	14	12	3	59	0	1	0	1	3	.25	3	.228	.282	.411
10	KC	AL	27	92	24	7	0	4	(1	3)	43	14	15	11	7	0	29	1	0	1	1	0	1.00	2	.261	.317	.467
10	Atl	NL	47	119	25	6	1	2	(0	2)	39	17	9	11	19	2	42	1	0	0	2	1	.67	1	.210	.324	.328
	Postseason		9	15	2	0	0	1	(0	1)	5	1	1	1	2	0	6	0	0	0	0	0	-	0	.133	.235	.333
	10 ML YEARS		606	1793	438	94	9	69	(37	32)	757	247	233	195	154	13	495	12	8	12	21	11	.66	30	.244	.306	.422

Norichika Aoki

Bats: L **Throws:** R **Pos:** RF-107; PH-24; CF-19; LF-13   no-ree-CHEE-kah AH-oh-kee   **Ht:** 5'9" **Wt:** 182 **Born:** 1/5/1982 **Age:** 31

Year	Team	Lg	G	AB	H	2B	3B	HR	(Hm	Rd)	TB	R	RBI	RC	TBB	IBB	SO	HBP	SH	SF	SB	CS	SB%	GDP	Avg	OBP	Slg
2004	Yakult	Jap	10	15	3	0	0	0	(-	-)	3	1	0	0	1	-	6	0	0	0	1	0	1.00	-	.200	.250	.200
2005	Yakult	Jap	144	588	202	26	4	3	(-	-)	245	100	28	97	37	-	113	5	18	1	29	7	.81	-	.344	.387	.417
2006	Yakult	Jap	146	599	192	26	3	13	(-	-)	263	112	62	111	68	-	78	8	4	1	41	12	.77	-	.321	.396	.439
2007	Yakult	Jap	143	557	193	26	2	20	(-	-)	283	114	58	125	80	-	66	8	4	3	17	6	.74	-	.346	.434	.508
2008	Yakult	Jap	112	444	154	29	5	14	(-	-)	235	85	64	98	42	-	47	10	1	3	31	9	.78	-	.347	.413	.529
2009	Yakult	Jap	142	531	161	23	2	16	(-	-)	236	87	66	100	75	-	65	13	1	4	18	10	.64	-	.303	.400	.444
2010	Yakult	Jap	144	583	209	44	1	14	(-	-)	297	92	63	131	63	-	61	18	0	3	19	4	.83	-	.358	.435	.509
2011	Yakult	Jap	144	583	170	18	5	4	(-	-)	210	73	44	81	51	-	55	9	0	0	8	3	.73	-	.292	.358	.360
2012	Mil	NL	151	520	150	37	4	10	(4	6)	225	81	50	80	43	1	55	13	7	5	30	8	.79	6	.288	.355	.433

Chris Archer

Pitches: R **Bats:** R **Pos:** SP-4; RP-2   **Ht:** 6'3" **Wt:** 200 **Born:** 9/26/1988 **Age:** 24

Year Team	Lg	G	GS	CG	GF	IP	BFP	H	R	ER	HR	SH	SF	HB	TBB	IBB	SO	WP	Bk	W	L	Pct	Sh	Sv-Op	Hld	ERC	ERA
2006 Indns	R	7	6	0	1	19.1	97	17	22	16	1	0	1	3	17	0	21	6	1	0	3	.000	0	0--	-	5.23	7.45
2006 Burlgtn	R	1	0	0	0	1.2	8	2	2	2	1	0	0	1	1	0	1	1	0	0	0	-	0	0--	-	15.09	10.80
2007 Indns	R	12	11	0	0	52.2	237	56	36	33	4	1	0	8	21	0	48	9	0	1	7	.125	0	0--	-	4.87	5.64
2007 Lk Cty	A	1	0	0	1	4.0	21	5	4	4	0	0	2	1	3	0	5	1	0	0	0	-	0	0--	-	6.99	9.00
2008 Lk Cty	A	27	27	0	0	115.1	521	92	64	55	8	3	4	11	84	0	106	18	0	4	8	.333	0	0--	-	4.36	4.29
2009 Peoria	A	27	26	0	0	109.0	463	78	41	34	0	2	2	7	66	0	119	10	1	6	4	.600	0	0--	-	2.89	2.81
2010 Dytona	A+	15	14	0	1	72.1	299	54	27	23	4	1	2	3	26	1	82	1	0	7	1	.875	0	0--	-	2.40	2.86
2010 Tenn	AA	13	13	0	0	70.0	291	48	19	14	2	1	4	2	39	1	67	5	0	8	2	.800	0	0--	-	2.62	1.80
2011 Mont	AA	25	25	0	0	134.1	612	136	76	66	11	7	4	10	80	1	118	18	0	8	7	.533	0	0--	-	5.10	4.42
2011 Drham	AAA	2	2	0	0	13.0	55	11	1	1	0	0	0	6	6	0	12	0	0	1	0	1.000	0	0--	-	2.79	0.69
2012 Drham	AAA	25	25	0	0	128.0	531	99	54	52	8	6	2	7	62	0	139	12	1	7	9	.438	0	0--	-	3.09	3.66
2012 TB	AL	6	4	0	1	29.1	122	23	17	15	3	1	0	1	13	0	36	2	0	1	3	.250	0	0-0	0	3.24	4.60

J.P. Arencibia

Bats: R **Throws:** R **Pos:** C-94; PH-5; DH-4   air-en-SEE-bee-uh   **Ht:** 6'0" **Wt:** 205 **Born:** 1/5/1986 **Age:** 27

Year Team	Lg	G	AB	H	2B	3B	HR	(Hm	Rd)	TB	R	RBI	RC	TBB	IBB	SO	HBP	SH	SF	SB	CS	SB%	GDP	Avg	OBP	Slg
2012 Dnedin*	A+	1	5	1	1	0	0	(-	-)	2	0	0	0	1	0	0	0	0	0	0	0	-	0	.200	.333	.400
2010 Tor	AL	11	35	5	1	0	2	(2	0)	12	3	4	4	2	0	11	0	0	0	0	0	-	0	.143	.189	.343
2011 Tor	AL	129	443	97	20	4	23	(13	10)	194	47	78	58	36	3	133	4	0	3	1	1	.50	6	.219	.282	.438
2012 Tor	AL	102	347	81	16	0	18	(9	9)	151	45	56	47	18	1	108	3	1	3	1	0	1.00	4	.233	.275	.435
3 ML YEARS		242	825	183	37	4	43	(24	19)	357	95	138	109	56	4	252	7	1	6	2	1	.67	10	.222	.275	.433

Joaquin Arias

Bats: R **Throws:** R **Pos:** 3B-74; SS-50; PH-14; 2B-4; PR-2   wah-KEEN AH-ree-us   **Ht:** 6'1" **Wt:** 170 **Born:** 9/21/1984 **Age:** 28

Year Team	Lg	G	AB	H	2B	3B	HR	(Hm	Rd)	TB	R	RBI	RC	TBB	IBB	SO	HBP	SH	SF	SB	CS	SB%	GDP	Avg	OBP	Slg
2012 Fresno*	AAA	18	70	28	5	0	2	(-	-)	39	14	17	15	3	0	11	1	0	0	0	1	.00	1	.400	.432	.557
2006 Tex	AL	6	11	6	1	0	0	(0	0)	7	4	1	3	1	0	0	0	0	0	1	0	1.00	0	.545	.583	.636
2008 Tex	AL	32	110	32	7	3	0	(0	0)	45	15	9	15	7	0	12	2	1	0	4	1	.80	4	.291	.345	.409
2009 Tex	AL	3	8	0	0	0	0	(0	0)	0	0	0	0	0	0	3	0	1	0	0	0	-	0	.000	.000	.000
2010 2 Tms		72	128	33	6	1	0	(0	0)	41	23	13	10	4	0	23	0	2	0	1	0	1.00	2	.258	.280	.320
2012 SF	NL	112	319	86	13	5	5	(0	5)	124	30	34	32	13	4	44	5	2	5	5	1	.83	12	.270	.304	.389
10 Tex	AL	50	98	27	5	1	0	(0	0)	34	18	9	8	2	0	17	0	1	0	1	0	1.00	2	.276	.290	.347
10 NYM	NL	22	30	6	1	0	0	(0	0)	7	5	4	2	2	0	6	0	1	0	0	0	-	0	.200	.250	.233
5 ML YEARS		225	576	157	27	9	5	(0	5)	217	72	57	60	25	4	82	7	6	5	10	3	.77	18	.273	.308	.377

Jose Arredondo

Pitches: R **Bats:** R **Pos:** RP-66   air-eh-DON-doe   **Ht:** 6'0" **Wt:** 190 **Born:** 3/12/1984 **Age:** 29

Year Team	Lg	G	GS	CG	GF	IP	BFP	H	R	ER	HR	SH	SF	HB	TBB	IBB	SO	WP	Bk	W	L	Pct	Sh	Sv-Op	Hld	ERC	ERA
2008 LAA	AL	52	0	0	10	61.0	244	42	15	11	3	0	0	1	22	0	55	1	0	10	2	.833	0	0-7	16	2.08	1.62
2009 LAA	AL	43	0	0	15	45.0	202	47	30	30	6	3	1	0	23	2	47	5	1	2	3	.400	0	0-1	16	4.91	6.00
2011 Cin	NL	53	0	0	10	53.0	226	43	21	19	5	3	0	2	31	5	48	4	2	4	4	.500	0	0-1	4	3.78	3.23
2012 Cin	NL	66	0	0	17	61.0	263	50	26	20	7	2	4	1	34	2	62	0	2	6	2	.750	0	1-2	12	3.80	2.95
Postseason		3	0	0	1	3.2	15	2	0	0	0	0	0	0	2	0	4	0	0	0	0	-	0	0-0	0	1.65	0.00
4 ML YEARS		214	0	0	52	220.0	935	182	92	80	21	8	5	4	110	9	212	10	5	22	11	.667	0	1-11	48	3.50	3.27

Jake Arrieta

Pitches: R **Bats:** R **Pos:** SP-18; RP-6   air-ee-ETT-uh   **Ht:** 6'4" **Wt:** 225 **Born:** 3/6/1986 **Age:** 27

Year Team	Lg	G	GS	CG	GF	IP	BFP	H	R	ER	HR	SH	SF	HB	TBB	IBB	SO	WP	Bk	W	L	Pct	Sh	Sv-Op	Hld	ERC	ERA
2012 Norfolk*	AAA	10	10	1	0	56.0	239	46	25	25	3	0	1	4	28	0	54	4	0	5	4	.556	1	0--	-	3.46	4.02
2010 Bal	AL	18	18	0	0	100.1	449	106	57	52	9	4	4	8	48	3	52	5	0	6	6	.500	0	0--	-	4.74	4.66
2011 Bal	AL	22	22	0	0	119.1	523	115	70	67	21	3	2	4	59	2	93	0	0	10	8	.556	0	0--	-	4.93	5.05
2012 Bal	AL	24	18	0	1	114.2	496	122	82	79	16	3	4	5	35	3	109	4	0	3	9	.250	0	0-0	1	4.47	6.20
3 ML YEARS		64	58	0	1	334.1	1468	343	209	198	46	10	8	13	142	8	254	9	0	19	23	.452	0	0-0	1	4.72	5.33

Bronson Arroyo

Pitches: R **Bats:** R **Pos:** SP-32   uh-ROY-oh   **Ht:** 6'4" **Wt:** 195 **Born:** 2/24/1977 **Age:** 36

Year Team	Lg	G	GS	CG	GF	IP	BFP	H	R	ER	HR	SH	SF	HB	TBB	IBB	SO	WP	Bk	W	L	Pct	Sh	Sv-Op	Hld	ERC	ERA
2000 Pit	NL	20	12	0	1	71.2	338	88	61	51	10	5	2	4	36	6	50	3	1	2	6	.250	0	0-0	0	6.18	6.40
2001 Pit	NL	24	13	1	1	88.1	390	99	54	50	12	4	6	4	34	6	39	4	1	5	7	.417	0	0-0	2	5.09	5.09
2002 Pit	NL	9	4	0	1	27.0	123	30	14	12	1	1	1	0	15	3	22	0	0	2	1	.667	0	0-0	0	4.64	4.00
2003 Bos	AL	6	0	0	2	17.1	66	10	5	4	0	0	0	1	4	2	14	0	0	0	0	-	0	1-1	0	1.14	2.08
2004 Bos	AL	32	29	0	0	178.2	764	171	99	80	17	5	4	20	47	3	142	5	0	10	9	.526	0	0-0	0	3.65	4.03
2005 Bos	AL	35	32	0	1	205.1	870	213	116	103	22	4	4	14	54	3	100	5	1	14	10	.583	0	0-0	0	4.04	4.51
2006 Cin	NL	35	35	3	0	240.2	992	222	98	88	31	9	2	5	64	7	184	6	0	14	11	.560	1	0-0	0	3.37	3.29
2007 Cin	NL	34	34	1	0	210.2	921	232	109	99	28	10	7	13	63	6	156	4	0	9	15	.375	0	0-0	0	4.68	4.23
2008 Cin	NL	34	34	1	0	200.0	871	219	116	106	29	13	6	6	68	2	163	6	0	15	11	.577	0	0-0	0	4.83	4.77
2009 Cin	NL	33	33	3	0	220.1	923	214	101	94	31	9	5	8	65	6	127	1	0	15	13	.536	2	0-0	0	3.94	3.84

Year Team	Lg	G	GS	CG	GF	IP	BFP	H	R	ER	HR	SH	SF	HB	TBB	IBB	SO	WP	Bk	W	L	Pct	Sh	Sv-Op	Hld	ERC	ERA
				HOW MUCH HE PITCHED							WHAT HE GAVE UP											THE RESULTS					
2010 Cin	NL	33	33	2	0	215.2	880	188	95	93	29	6	5	6	59	5	121	1	1	17	10	.630	4	0-0	0	3.21	3.88
2011 Cin	NL	32	32	1	0	199.0	855	227	119	112	46	6	5	6	45	5	108	0	0	9	12	.429	1	0-0	0	5.20	5.07
2012 Cin	NL	32	32	1	0	202.0	835	209	86	84	26	7	6	5	35	1	129	3	0	12	10	.545	1	0-0	0	3.68	3.74
Postseason		11	3	0	3	22.1	104	23	17	15	5	0	0	2	12	0	22	0	0	0	0	-	0	0-0	2	6.00	6.04
13 ML YEARS		359	323	13	6	2076.2	8836	2122	1073	976	282	79	53	93	589	55	1355	38	4	124	115	.519	5	1-1	3	4.13	4.23

Jairo Asencio

Pitches: R **Bats:** R **Pos:** RP-30   HIGH-row ahh-SEN-cee-oh   **Ht:** 6'2" **Wt:** 180 **Born:** 5/5/1984 **Age:** 29

Year Team	Lg	G	GS	CG	GF	IP	BFP	H	R	ER	HR	SH	SF	HB	TBB	IBB	SO	WP	Bk	W	L	Pct	Sh	Sv-Op	Hld	ERC	ERA
				HOW MUCH HE PITCHED							WHAT HE GAVE UP											THE RESULTS					
2012 Iowa*	AAA	13	0	0	12	13.1	51	6	4	2	1	1	0	0	4	0	13	1	0	0	1	.000	0	5--	-	1.13	1.35
2009 Atl	NL	3	0	0	2	2.2	13	3	1	1	0	0	0	0	2	0	0	0	0	0	1	.000	0	0-0	0	5.24	3.38
2011 Atl	NL	6	0	0	3	10.1	52	16	11	8	1	0	0	0	5	2	8	0	0	0	0	-	0	0-1	0	7.18	6.97
2012 2 Tms		30	0	0	13	40.1	175	39	23	22	5	0	0	1	19	1	29	3	0	1	1	.500	0	0-0	0	4.44	4.91
12 Cle	AL	18	0	0	9	25.2	108	27	17	17	4	0	0	1	8	0	21	3	0	1	1	.500	0	0-0	0	4.70	5.96
12 ChC	NL	12	0	0	4	14.2	67	12	6	5	1	0	0	0	11	1	8	0	0	0	0	-	0	0-0	0	3.96	3.07
3 ML YEARS		39	0	0	18	53.1	240	58	35	31	6	0	0	1	26	3	37	3	0	1	2	.333	0	0-1	0	4.99	5.23

Scott Atchison

Pitches: R **Bats:** R **Pos:** RP-42   **Ht:** 6'2" **Wt:** 200 **Born:** 3/29/1976 **Age:** 37

Year Team	Lg	G	GS	CG	GF	IP	BFP	H	R	ER	HR	SH	SF	HB	TBB	IBB	SO	WP	Bk	W	L	Pct	Sh	Sv-Op	Hld	ERC	ERA
				HOW MUCH HE PITCHED							WHAT HE GAVE UP											THE RESULTS					
2012 Pwtckt*	AAA	2	1	0	0	2.0	9	3	3	3	1	0	0	0	0	0	2	0	0	0	0	-	0	0--	-	8.13	13.50
2004 Sea	AL	25	0	0	8	30.2	133	29	12	12	4	2	1	0	14	2	36	2	0	2	3	.400	0	0-0	2	4.08	3.52
2005 Sea	AL	6	0	0	2	6.2	27	7	5	5	1	0	0	0	1	0	9	0	0	0	0	-	0	0-0	0	3.77	6.75
2007 SF	NL	22	0	0	4	30.2	131	32	14	14	5	1	2	1	10	0	25	2	0	0	0	-	0	0-1	5	4.65	4.11
2010 Bos	AL	43	1	0	8	60.0	253	58	37	30	9	1	2	1	19	2	41	4	0	2	3	.400	0	0-0	7	3.92	4.50
2011 Bos	AL	17	0	0	4	30.1	122	31	11	11	0	1	2	2	6	0	17	2	0	1	0	1.000	0	1-1	5	3.15	3.26
2012 Bos	AL	42	0	0	7	51.1	200	42	10	9	2	1	2	0	9	3	36	2	0	2	1	.667	0	0-1	5	1.91	1.58
6 ML YEARS		155	1	0	33	209.2	866	199	89	81	21	6	9	4	59	7	164	12	0	7	7	.500	0	1-3	19	3.40	3.48

Phillippe Aumont

Pitches: R **Bats:** L **Pos:** RP-18   fih-LEEP ah-MOHNT   **Ht:** 6'7" **Wt:** 260 **Born:** 1/7/1989 **Age:** 24

Year Team	Lg	G	GS	CG	GF	IP	BFP	H	R	ER	HR	SH	SF	HB	TBB	IBB	SO	WP	Bk	W	L	Pct	Sh	Sv-Op	Hld	ERC	ERA
				HOW MUCH HE PITCHED							WHAT HE GAVE UP											THE RESULTS					
2008 Wisc	A	15	8	0	4	55.2	231	46	22	17	4	2	1	4	19	0	50	9	1	4	4	.500	0	2--	-	3.02	2.75
2009 Hi Dsrt	A+	29	0	0	21	33.1	137	24	14	12	3	0	0	2	12	0	35	5	0	1	2	.333	0	12--	-	2.58	3.24
2009 WTenn	AA	15	0	0	11	17.2	88	21	15	10	1	1	1	3	11	1	24	6	2	1	4	.200	0	4--	-	6.16	5.09
2010 Rdng	AA	11	11	0	0	49.2	240	55	45	41	4	1	1	6	38	0	38	6	1	1	6	.143	0	0--	-	6.60	7.43
2010 Clrwtr	A+	16	10	1	2	72.1	325	74	41	36	6	0	3	4	42	0	77	11	1	2	5	.286	0	1--	-	5.24	4.48
2011 Rdng	AA	25	0	0	21	31.0	134	23	16	8	2	4	0	1	11	1	41	1	0	1	5	.167	0	4--	-	2.23	2.32
2011 LV	AAA	18	0	0	9	22.2	104	21	9	8	0	1	1	2	14	1	37	2	1	1	0	1.000	0	3--	-	3.94	3.18
2012 LV	AAA	41	0	0	26	44.1	203	34	23	21	3	1	0	5	34	1	59	15	1	3	1	.750	0	15--	-	4.30	4.26
2012 Phi	NL	18	0	0	3	14.2	65	10	6	6	0	2	0	1	9	1	14	2	0	0	1	.000	0	2-3	5	2.50	3.68

Xavier Avery

Bats: L **Throws:** L **Pos:** LF-27; PR-4; DH-2; PH-2; CF-1   **Ht:** 6'0" **Wt:** 190 **Born:** 1/1/1990 **Age:** 23

Year Team	Lg	G	AB	H	2B	3B	HR	(Hm	Rd)	TB	R	RBI	RC	TBB	IBB	SO	HBP	SH	SF	SB	CS	SB%	GDP	Avg	OBP	Slg
				BATTING																BASERUNNING				AVERAGES		
2008 Orioles	R	47	175	49	8	1	0	(-	-)	59	27	7	22	10	0	51	4	3	0	13	3	.81	1	.280	.333	.337
2009 Dlmrva	A	129	473	124	15	8	2	(-	-)	161	55	36	52	27	0	111	4	3	2	30	10	.75	3	.262	.306	.340
2010 Frdrck	A+	109	447	125	25	6	4	(-	-)	174	73	48	64	42	1	96	6	2	1	28	14	.67	5	.280	.349	.389
2010 Bowie	AA	27	107	25	6	0	3	(-	-)	40	10	18	14	7	0	34	2	2	2	10	0	1.00	0	.234	.288	.374
2011 Bowie	AA	138	557	144	31	2	4	(-	-)	191	72	26	67	49	0	156	5	14	1	36	14	.72	4	.259	.324	.343
2012 Norfolk	AAA	102	390	92	13	5	8	(-	-)	139	57	34	52	51	0	106	5	9	3	22	7	.76	4	.236	.330	.356
2012 Bal	AL	32	94	21	6	1	1	(1	0)	32	14	6	8	11	0	23	0	2	0	6	3	.67	2	.223	.305	.340

Alex Avila

Bats: L **Throws:** R **Pos:** C-113; PH-8   ah-VEE-lah   **Ht:** 5'11" **Wt:** 210 **Born:** 1/29/1987 **Age:** 26

Year Team	Lg	G	AB	H	2B	3B	HR	(Hm	Rd)	TB	R	RBI	RC	TBB	IBB	SO	HBP	SH	SF	SB	CS	SB%	GDP	Avg	OBP	Slg
				BATTING																BASERUNNING				AVERAGES		
2012 Toledo*	AAA	3	7	3	0	0	0	(-	-)	3	0	1	1	1	0	3	0	0	0	0	0	-	0	.429	.500	.429
2009 Det	AL	29	61	17	4	0	5	(4	1)	36	9	14	12	10	0	18	0	0	1	0	0	-	0	.279	.375	.590
2010 Det	AL	104	294	67	12	0	7	(4	3)	100	28	31	26	36	0	71	2	1	0	2	2	.50	12	.228	.316	.340
2011 Det	AL	141	464	137	33	4	19	(10	9)	235	63	82	86	73	9	131	3	3	8	3	1	.75	8	.295	.389	.506
2012 Det	AL	116	367	89	21	2	9	(7	2)	141	42	48	53	61	2	104	2	2	2	2	0	1.00	12	.243	.352	.384
Postseason		11	41	3	0	0	1	(1	0)	6	1	2	2	2	0	16	0	1	0	0	0	-	1	.073	.116	.146
4 ML YEARS		390	1186	310	70	6	40	(25	15)	512	142	175	177	180	11	324	7	6	11	7	3	.70	32	.261	.359	.432

Luis Avilan

Pitches: L **Bats:** L **Pos:** RP-31   ah-VEE-lan   **Ht:** 6'2" **Wt:** 220 **Born:** 7/19/1989 **Age:** 23

Year	Team	Lg	G	GS	CG	GF	IP	BFP	H	R	ER	HR	SH	SF	HB	TBB	IBB	SO	WP	Bk	W	L	Pct	Sh	Sv-Op	Hld	ERC	ERA
2008	Braves	R	10	4	0	1	38.1	163	31	14	11	2	0	2	3	15	1	49	1	0	0	3	.000	0	0--	-	2.90	2.58
2009	Danvle	R	14	3	0	7	38.1	157	25	14	13	1	1	0	4	17	0	34	0	0	0	2	.000	0	2--	-	2.34	3.05
2010	Rome	A	10	0	0	2	20.2	87	15	8	6	1	1	2	1	9	0	21	0	0	2	1	.667	0	0--	-	2.54	2.61
2010	MrtlBh	A+	31	0	0	21	48.0	203	42	25	21	5	4	3	2	18	4	37	3	1	4	3	.571	0	9--	-	3.43	3.94
2011	Missi	AA	36	13	0	5	105.1	472	113	66	54	10	4	5	8	36	4	77	5	3	4	8	.333	0	1--	-	4.36	4.61
2012	Missi	AA	16	12	0	2	61.1	260	50	27	22	7	4	1	1	31	0	55	5	0	3	6	.333	0	1--	-	3.65	3.23
2012	Atl	NL	31	0	0	2	36.0	142	27	9	8	1	3	0	1	10	1	33	3	1	1	0	1.000	0	0-0	5	2.00	2.00

Mike Aviles

Bats: R **Throws:** R **Pos:** SS-128; DH-5; 2B-2; PR-2; 3B-1; PH-1   uh-VEE-less   **Ht:** 5'10" **Wt:** 205 **Born:** 3/13/1981 **Age:** 32

										BATTING											BASERUNNING				AVERAGES		
Year	Team	Lg	G	AB	H	2B	3B	HR	(Hm	Rd)	TB	R	RBI	RC	TBB	IBB	SO	HBP	SH	SF	SB	CS	SB%	GDP	Avg	OBP	Slg
2008	KC	AL	102	419	136	27	4	10	(4	6)	201	68	51	62	18	4	58	2	0	2	8	3	.73	12	.325	.354	.480
2009	KC	AL	36	120	22	3	1	1	(1	0)	30	10	8	4	4	0	26	0	2	1	1	0	1.00	3	.183	.208	.250
2010	KC	AL	110	424	129	16	3	8	(4	4)	175	63	32	47	20	0	49	1	0	3	14	5	.74	13	.304	.335	.413
2011	2 Tms	AL	91	286	73	17	3	7	(4	3)	117	31	39	31	13	0	44	2	4	4	14	4	.78	8	.255	.289	.409
2012	Bos	AL	136	512	128	28	0	13	(7	6)	195	57	60	57	23	0	77	2	3	6	14	6	.70	6	.250	.282	.381
11	KC	AL	53	185	41	11	3	5	(2	3)	73	14	31	18	9	0	27	2	3	3	10	2	.83	5	.222	.261	.395
11	Bos	AL	38	101	32	6	0	2	(2	0)	44	17	8	13	4	0	17	0	1	1	4	2	.67	3	.317	.340	.436
5 ML YEARS			475	1761	488	91	11	39	(20	19)	718	229	190	201	78	4	254	7	9	16	51	18	.74	42	.277	.308	.408

Dylan Axelrod

Pitches: R **Bats:** R **Pos:** SP-7; RP-7   **Ht:** 6'0" **Wt:** 195 **Born:** 7/30/1985 **Age:** 27

Year	Team	Lg	G	GS	CG	GF	IP	BFP	H	R	ER	HR	SH	SF	HB	TBB	IBB	SO	WP	Bk	W	L	Pct	Sh	Sv-Op	Hld	ERC	ERA
2007	Padres	R	11	0	0	9	11.2	55	15	11	7	0	0	0	0	4	0	15	1	0	0	2	.000	0	2--	-	4.50	5.40
2007	FtWyn	A	10	0	0	3	21.1	81	18	4	3	0	1	0	0	4	0	15	1	0	2	1	.667	0	0--	-	2.00	1.27
2008	Lk Els	A+	32	0	0	5	49.1	224	51	36	29	4	0	5	2	19	0	55	9	0	2	1	.667	0	0--	-	4.04	5.29
2008	FtWyn	A	23	0	0	8	27.1	115	26	12	11	2	1	1	0	7	0	25	4	0	1	1	.500	0	0--	-	3.02	3.62
2009	Lk Els	A+	11	0	0	4	12.0	54	12	6	6	0	0	0	0	5	0	6	0	0	0	0	-	0	0--	-	3.27	4.50
2009	Knapol	A	2	0	0	1	4.1	20	3	2	1	0	0	0	0	1	0	3	1	0	0	0	-	0	0--	-	1.22	2.08
2009	WinSa	A+	5	5	0	0	28.1	114	29	7	6	2	4	0	0	4	1	17	1	0	2	1	.667	0	0--	-	3.02	1.91
2010	WinSa	A+	23	13	1	2	99.1	397	95	30	22	2	3	3	2	12	0	84	5	0	8	3	.727	1	0--	-	2.40	1.99
2010	Brham	AA	2	2	0	0	10.0	41	8	3	3	0	0	1	0	3	0	8	0	0	1	0	1.000	0	0--	-	2.00	2.70
2011	Brham	AA	11	9	0	0	59.1	238	52	23	22	1	2	0	3	14	0	57	4	1	3	2	.600	0	0--	-	2.52	3.34
2011	Charltt	AAA	15	15	0	0	91.1	367	74	27	23	2	1	4	4	21	0	75	0	0	6	1	.857	0	0--	-	2.14	2.27
2012	Charltt	AAA	16	16	1	0	97.0	391	81	34	31	8	4	2	2	30	0	92	3	1	7	5	.583	0	0--	-	2.92	2.88
2011	CWS	AL	4	3	0	1	18.2	82	18	6	6	1	0	2	1	9	2	19	0	0	1	0	1.000	0	0-0	0	3.89	2.89
2012	CWS	AL	14	7	0	4	51.0	231	56	32	31	8	0	2	4	21	0	40	1	0	2	2	.500	0	0-0	0	5.39	5.47
2 ML YEARS			18	10	0	5	69.2	313	74	38	37	9	0	4	5	30	2	59	1	0	3	2	.600	0	0-0	0	4.98	4.78

John Axford

Pitches: R **Bats:** R **Pos:** RP-75   **Ht:** 6'5" **Wt:** 210 **Born:** 4/1/1983 **Age:** 30

Year	Team	Lg	G	GS	CG	GF	IP	BFP	H	R	ER	HR	SH	SF	HB	TBB	IBB	SO	WP	Bk	W	L	Pct	Sh	Sv-Op	Hld	ERC	ERA
2009	Mil	NL	7	0	0	6	7.2	34	5	3	3	0	0	0	0	6	1	9	1	0	0	0	-	0	1-1	0	2.62	3.52
2010	Mil	NL	50	0	0	43	58.0	238	42	17	16	1	2	2	1	27	3	76	4	0	8	2	.800	0	24-27	3	2.33	2.48
2011	Mil	NL	74	0	0	63	73.2	305	59	19	16	4	1	1	0	25	1	86	8	0	2	2	.500	0	46-48	3	2.44	1.95
2012	Mil	NL	75	0	0	54	69.1	310	61	42	36	10	1	2	2	39	2	93	10	0	5	8	.385	0	35-44	3	4.33	4.67
Postseason			6	0	0	6	7.0	28	5	1	1	0	0	0	0	2	0	9	0	0	1	0	1.000	0	3-4	0	1.62	1.29
4 ML YEARS			206	0	0	166	208.2	887	167	81	71	15	4	5	3	97	7	264	23	0	15	12	.556	0	106-120	6	3.01	3.06

Luis Ayala

Pitches: R **Bats:** R **Pos:** RP-66   **Ht:** 6'2" **Wt:** 175 **Born:** 1/12/1978 **Age:** 35

Year	Team	Lg	G	GS	CG	GF	IP	BFP	H	R	ER	HR	SH	SF	HB	TBB	IBB	SO	WP	Bk	W	L	Pct	Sh	Sv-Op	Hld	ERC	ERA
2003	Mon	NL	65	0	0	24	71.0	288	65	27	23	8	3	5	5	13	3	46	1	0	10	3	.769	0	5-8	19	3.11	2.92
2004	Mon	NL	81	0	0	28	90.1	367	92	30	27	6	2	2	5	15	2	63	3	1	6	12	.333	0	2-7	21	3.32	2.69
2005	Was	NL	68	0	0	18	71.0	293	75	23	21	7	3	3	6	14	4	40	0	0	8	7	.533	0	1-3	22	3.95	2.66
2007	Was	NL	44	0	0	11	42.1	181	43	16	15	5	3	4	1	12	0	28	1	0	2	2	.500	0	1-2	6	3.88	3.19
2008	2 Tms	NL	81	0	0	25	75.2	335	86	53	48	9	4	3	4	24	4	50	1	0	2	10	.167	0	9-15	19	4.76	5.71
2009	2 Tms	NL	38	0	0	13	40.0	180	50	28	25	5	3	2	4	13	3	28	0	0	1	5	.167	0	0-4	3	5.94	5.63
2011	NYY	AL	52	0	0	20	56.0	233	51	17	13	5	4	4	6	20	3	39	2	1	2	2	.500	0	0-1	4	3.80	2.09
2012	Bal	AL	66	0	0	15	75.0	320	81	27	22	7	2	2	4	14	3	51	2	0	5	5	.500	0	1-3	11	3.75	2.64
08	Was	NL	62	0	0	12	57.2	257	63	41	37	6	4	2	4	22	4	36	1	0	1	8	.111	0	0-4	19	4.70	5.77
08	NYM	NL	19	0	0	13	18.0	78	23	12	11	3	0	1	0	2	0	14	0	0	1	2	.333	0	9-11	0	4.91	5.50
09	Min	AL	28	0	0	11	32.1	138	38	18	15	4	1	2	3	8	0	21	0	0	1	2	.333	0	0-3	1	5.21	4.18
09	Fla	NL	10	0	0	2	7.2	42	12	10	10	1	2	0	1	6	3	7	0	0	0	3	.000	0	0-1	2	9.04	11.74
Postseason			2	0	0	1	1.1	8	3	1	1	0	1	0	1	0	0	0	0	0	0	0	-	0	0-0	0	12.64	6.75
8 ML YEARS			495	0	0	154	521.1	2197	543	221	194	52	29	21	35	126	22	345	10	2	36	46	.439	0	19-43	105	3.93	3.35

Erick Aybar

Bats: B **Throws:** R **Pos:** SS-139; PH-3   EYE-barr   **Ht:** 5'10" **Wt:** 180 **Born:** 1/14/1984 **Age:** 29

Year	Team	Lg	G	AB	H	2B	3B	HR	(Hm	Rd)	TB	R	RBI	RC	TBB	IBB	SO	HBP	SH	SF	SB	CS	SB%	GDP	Avg	OBP	Slg
2006	LAA	AL	34	40	10	1	1	0	(0	0)	13	5	2	4	0	0	8	0	0	0	1	0	1.00	1	.250	.250	.325
2007	LAA	AL	79	194	46	5	1	1	(0	1)	56	18	19	16	10	0	32	2	3	2	4	4	.50	8	.237	.279	.289
2008	LAA	AL	98	346	96	18	5	3	(2	1)	133	53	39	49	14	0	45	5	9	1	7	2	.78	2	.277	.314	.384
2009	LAA	AL	137	504	157	23	9	5	(2	3)	213	70	58	73	30	1	54	5	12	5	14	7	.67	9	.312	.353	.423
2010	LAA	AL	138	534	135	18	4	5	(3	2)	176	69	29	51	35	1	81	7	11	2	22	8	.73	7	.253	.306	.330
2011	LAA	AL	143	556	155	33	8	10	(2	8)	234	71	59	72	31	1	68	6	9	3	30	6	.83	13	.279	.322	.421
2012	LAA	AL	141	517	150	31	5	8	(4	4)	215	67	45	63	22	1	61	5	7	2	20	4	.83	11	.290	.324	.416
	Postseason		14	50	11	2	1	0	(0	0)	15	4	4	4	1	0	4	0	2	0	3	0	1.00	1	.220	.235	.300
	7 ML YEARS		770	2691	749	129	33	32	(13	19)	1040	353	251	328	142	4	349	30	51	15	98	31	.76	51	.278	.320	.386

Burke Badenhop

Pitches: R **Bats:** R **Pos:** RP-66   BADE-en-hopp   **Ht:** 6'5" **Wt:** 220 **Born:** 2/8/1983 **Age:** 30

Year	Team	Lg	G	GS	CG	GF	IP	BFP	H	R	ER	HR	SH	SF	HB	TBB	IBB	SO	WP	Bk	W	L	Pct	Sh	Sv-Op	Hld	ERC	ERA
2008	Fla	NL	13	8	0	2	47.1	218	55	34	32	7	2	2	3	21	1	35	2	0	2	3	.400	0	0-0	0	5.74	6.08
2009	Fla	NL	35	2	0	7	72.0	303	71	32	30	5	3	2	1	24	4	57	1	0	7	4	.636	0	0-1	2	3.53	3.75
2010	Fla	NL	53	0	0	16	67.2	281	62	33	30	5	5	1	2	21	5	47	1	0	2	5	.286	0	1-3	8	3.12	3.99
2011	Fla	NL	50	0	0	15	63.2	276	65	29	29	1	1	2	4	24	4	51	4	0	2	3	.400	0	1-1	5	3.65	4.10
2012	TB	AL	66	0	0	14	62.1	262	63	24	21	6	2	4	1	12	5	42	1	0	3	2	.600	0	0-0	5	3.19	3.03
	5 ML YEARS		217	10	0	54	313.0	1340	316	152	142	24	13	11	11	102	19	232	9	0	16	17	.485	0	2-5	20	3.71	4.08

Andrew Bailey

Pitches: R **Bats:** R **Pos:** RP-19   **Ht:** 6'3" **Wt:** 240 **Born:** 5/31/1984 **Age:** 29

Year	Team	Lg	G	GS	CG	GF	IP	BFP	H	R	ER	HR	SH	SF	HB	TBB	IBB	SO	WP	Bk	W	L	Pct	Sh	Sv-Op	Hld	ERC	ERA
2012	RedSx*	R	2	2	0	0	2.0	9	2	0	0	0	0	0	1	1	0	4	0	0	0	0	-	0	0--	-	6.15	0.00
2012	Portlnd*	AA	1	0	0	0	1.0	6	3	1	1	0	0	0	0	0	0	2	0	0	0	0	-	0	0--	-	14.52	9.00
2012	Pwtckt*	AAA	3	0	0	1	3.1	11	1	0	0	0	0	0	0	0	0	4	0	0	0	0	-	0	0--	-	0.21	0.00
2009	Oak	AL	68	0	0	54	83.1	323	49	17	17	5	3	2	0	24	3	91	6	0	6	3	.667	0	26-30	2	1.44	1.84
2010	Oak	AL	47	0	0	42	49.0	189	34	8	8	3	2	3	0	13	1	42	0	0	1	3	.250	0	25-28	0	1.82	1.47
2011	Oak	AL	42	0	0	37	41.2	170	34	18	15	3	1	1	0	12	2	41	0	0	0	4	.000	0	24-26	1	2.42	3.24
2012	Bos	AL	19	0	0	13	15.1	74	21	12	12	2	0	0	0	8	2	14	0	1	1	1	.500	0	6-9	1	6.73	7.04
	4 ML YEARS		176	0	0	146	189.1	756	138	55	52	13	6	6	0	57	8	188	6	1	8	11	.421	0	81-93	4	2.06	2.47

Homer Bailey

Pitches: R **Bats:** R **Pos:** SP-33   **Ht:** 6'3" **Wt:** 225 **Born:** 5/3/1986 **Age:** 27

Year	Team	Lg	G	GS	CG	GF	IP	BFP	H	R	ER	HR	SH	SF	HB	TBB	IBB	SO	WP	Bk	W	L	Pct	Sh	Sv-Op	Hld	ERC	ERA
2007	Cin	NL	9	9	0	0	45.1	205	43	32	29	3	1	6	3	28	1	28	1	1	4	2	.667	0	0-0	0	4.61	5.76
2008	Cin	NL	8	8	0	0	36.1	180	59	36	32	8	5	2	0	17	1	18	4	1	0	6	.000	0	0-0	0	9.31	7.93
2009	Cin	NL	20	20	0	0	113.1	496	115	61	57	12	4	4	3	52	1	86	6	0	8	5	.615	0	0-0	0	4.56	4.53
2010	Cin	NL	19	19	1	0	109.0	465	109	55	54	11	2	1	3	40	6	100	3	1	4	3	.571	1	0-0	0	4.01	4.46
2011	Cin	NL	22	22	0	0	132.0	561	136	68	65	18	4	4	5	33	2	106	4	0	9	7	.563	0	0-0	0	4.01	4.43
2012	Cin	NL	33	33	2	0	208.0	874	206	97	86	26	5	5	8	52	3	168	3	0	13	10	.565	1	0-0	0	3.73	3.68
	Postseason		1	0	0	0	2.0	8	2	0	0	0	0	0	0	0	0	2	0	0	0	0	-	0	0-0	0	1.95	0.00
	6 ML YEARS		111	111	3	0	644.0	2781	668	349	322	78	21	22	22	222	14	506	21	3	38	33	.535	2	0-0	0	4.32	4.50

Jeff Baker

Bats: R **Throws:** R **Pos:** PH-30; RF-26; 1B-20; 2B-9; LF-5; 3B-4; PR-2   **Ht:** 6'2" **Wt:** 210 **Born:** 6/21/1981 **Age:** 32

Year	Team	Lg	G	AB	H	2B	3B	HR	(Hm	Rd)	TB	R	RBI	RC	TBB	IBB	SO	HBP	SH	SF	SB	CS	SB%	GDP	Avg	OBP	Slg
2005	Col	NL	12	38	8	4	0	1	(1	0)	15	6	4	4	5	0	12	0	0	0	0	0	-	1	.211	.302	.395
2006	Col	NL	18	57	21	7	2	5	(4	1)	47	13	21	17	1	0	14	0	0	0	2	0	1.00	0	.368	.379	.825
2007	Col	NL	85	144	32	2	2	4	(4	0)	50	17	12	8	13	1	40	2	0	0	0	0	-	7	.222	.296	.347
2008	Col	NL	104	299	80	22	1	12	(8	4)	140	55	48	40	26	2	85	1	1	6	4	0	1.00	5	.268	.322	.468
2009	2 Tms		81	226	65	15	2	4	(3	1)	96	27	24	28	18	0	53	2	0	2	1	0	1.00	8	.288	.343	.425
2010	ChC	NL	79	206	56	13	2	4	(3	1)	85	29	21	21	16	0	50	1	0	1	1	0	1.00	6	.272	.326	.413
2011	ChC	NL	81	201	54	12	1	3	(1	2)	77	20	23	20	10	0	46	0	0	1	0	0	-	8	.269	.302	.383
2012	3 Tms		83	188	45	12	1	4	(1	3)	71	18	25	18	11	1	48	0	0	2	4	1	.80	7	.239	.279	.378
09	Col	NL	12	23	3	0	1	0	(0	0)	5	0	3	0	1	0	7	0	0	0	1	0	1.00	3	.130	.167	.217
09	ChC	NL	69	203	62	15	1	4	(3	1)	91	27	21	28	17	0	46	2	0	2	0	0	-	5	.305	.362	.448
12	ChC	NL	54	134	36	10	1	4	(1	3)	60	16	20	17	8	0	28	0	0	2	4	1	.80	4	.269	.306	.448
12	Det	AL	15	35	7	2	0	0	(0	0)	9	1	4	1	2	0	10	0	0	0	0	0	-	0	.200	.243	.257
12	Atl	NL	14	19	2	0	0	0	(0	0)	2	1	1	0	1	1	10	0	0	0	0	0	-	3	.105	.150	.105
	Postseason		4	4	2	0	0	0	(0	0)	2	0	1	0	0	0	1	0	0	0	0	0	-	0	.500	.500	.500
	8 ML YEARS		543	1359	361	87	11	37	(25	12)	581	185	178	156	100	4	348	6	1	12	12	1	.92	42	.266	.316	.428

43

John Baker

Bats: L **Throws:** R **Pos:** C-56; PH-9   **Ht:** 6'1" **Wt:** 220 **Born:** 1/20/1981 **Age:** 32

							BATTING																BASERUNNING				AVERAGES		
Year	Team	Lg	G	AB	H	2B	3B	HR	(Hm	Rd)	TB	R	RBI	RC	TBB	IBB	SO	HBP	SH	SF		SB	CS	SB%	GDP		Avg	OBP	Slg
2008	Fla	NL	61	197	59	14	0	5	(3	2)	88	32	32	36	30	4	48	2	1	3		0	0	-	6		.299	.392	.447
2009	Fla	NL	112	373	101	25	0	9	(3	6)	153	59	50	54	41	5	89	5	2	2		0	0	-	10		.271	.349	.410
2010	Fla	NL	23	78	17	3	1	0	(0	0)	22	7	6	4	9	1	18	1	0	0		0	0	-	5		.218	.307	.282
2011	Fla	NL	16	13	2	0	0	0	(0	0)	2	0	1	0	2	0	3	0	1	0		0	0	-	-		.154	.267	.154
2012	SD	NL	63	193	46	8	0	0	(0	0)	54	17	14	19	20	2	41	0	1	0		2	1	.67	4		.238	.310	.280
	5 ML YEARS		275	854	225	50	1	14	(6	8)	319	115	103	113	102	12	199	8	5	5		2	1	.67	25		.263	.346	.374

Scott Baker

Pitches: R **Bats:** R **Pos:** P   **Ht:** 6'4" **Wt:** 215 **Born:** 9/19/1981 **Age:** 31

			HOW MUCH HE PITCHED						WHAT HE GAVE UP												THE RESULTS							
Year	Team	Lg	G	GS	CG	GF	IP	BFP	H	R	ER	HR	SH	SF	HB	TBB	IBB	SO	WP	Bk	W	L	Pct	Sh	Sv-Op	Hld	ERC	ERA
2012	FtMyrs*	A+	1	1	0	0	0.1	3	2	2	2	0	0	0	0	0	0	0	0	0	0	0	-	0	0--	-	39.65	54.00
2005	Min	AL	10	9	0	0	53.2	217	48	21	20	5	2	2	0	14	0	32	0	0	3	3	.500	0	0-0	1	2.97	3.35
2006	Min	AL	16	16	0	0	83.1	377	114	63	59	17	2	4	3	16	1	62	0	0	5	8	.385	0	0-0	0	6.26	6.37
2007	Min	AL	24	23	2	0	143.2	606	162	70	68	15	6	2	5	29	4	102	0	0	9	9	.500	1	0-0	1	4.19	4.26
2008	Min	AL	28	28	0	0	172.1	703	161	66	66	20	2	3	3	42	2	141	6	0	11	4	.733	0	0-0	0	3.31	3.45
2009	Min	AL	33	33	1	0	200.0	828	190	99	97	28	1	6	4	48	1	162	4	0	15	9	.625	1	0-0	0	3.51	4.37
2010	Min	AL	29	29	0	0	170.1	725	186	87	85	23	1	4	6	43	0	148	7	0	12	9	.571	0	0-0	0	4.43	4.49
2011	Min	AL	23	21	1	2	134.2	548	126	50	47	15	1	4	2	32	2	123	4	0	8	6	.571	0	0-0	0	3.32	3.14
	Postseason		1	0	0	0	2.1	10	3	1	1	1	0	0	0	0	0	2	0	0	0	0	-	0	0-0	0	6.14	3.86
	7 ML YEARS		163	159	4	2	958.0	4004	987	456	442	123	15	23	25	224	10	770	21	0	63	48	.568	2	0-0	2	3.90	4.15

Collin Balester

Pitches: R **Bats:** R **Pos:** RP-11   BAL-iss-ster   **Ht:** 6'5" **Wt:** 200 **Born:** 6/6/1986 **Age:** 27

			HOW MUCH HE PITCHED						WHAT HE GAVE UP												THE RESULTS							
Year	Team	Lg	G	GS	CG	GF	IP	BFP	H	R	ER	HR	SH	SF	HB	TBB	IBB	SO	WP	Bk	W	L	Pct	Sh	Sv-Op	Hld	ERC	ERA
2012	Toledo*	AAA	31	0	0	13	47.0	188	38	20	19	7	1	2	3	12	2	45	1	1	1	1	.500	0	1--	-	3.05	3.64
2008	Was	NL	15	15	0	0	80.0	358	92	53	49	12	2	3	6	28	1	50	4	0	3	7	.300	0	0-0	0	5.40	5.51
2009	Was	NL	7	7	0	0	30.1	135	34	24	23	10	0	0	0	14	0	20	0	0	1	4	.200	0	0-0	0	6.85	6.82
2010	Was	NL	17	0	0	8	21.0	89	15	6	6	2	2	0	2	11	1	28	4	0	0	1	.000	0	0-0	0	3.26	2.57
2011	Was	NL	23	0	0	9	35.2	159	38	21	18	7	1	1	1	14	0	34	2	1	1	4	.200	0	0-1	2	5.16	4.54
2012	Det	AL	11	0	0	2	18.0	83	14	14	13	5	0	2	3	11	1	12	4	0	2	0	1.000	0	0-0	0	5.37	6.50
	5 ML YEARS		73	22	0	19	185.0	824	193	118	109	36	5	6	12	78	3	144	14	1	7	16	.304	0	0-1	2	5.33	5.30

Grant Balfour

Pitches: R **Bats:** R **Pos:** RP-75   BAL-fore   **Ht:** 6'2" **Wt:** 200 **Born:** 12/30/1977 **Age:** 35

			HOW MUCH HE PITCHED						WHAT HE GAVE UP												THE RESULTS							
Year	Team	Lg	G	GS	CG	GF	IP	BFP	H	R	ER	HR	SH	SF	HB	TBB	IBB	SO	WP	Bk	W	L	Pct	Sh	Sv-Op	Hld	ERC	ERA
2001	Min	AL	2	0	0	1	2.2	14	3	4	4	2	1	1	0	3	0	2	0	0	0	0	-	0	0-0	0	13.78	13.50
2003	Min	AL	17	1	0	6	26.0	115	23	12	12	4	2	1	0	14	2	30	0	0	1	0	1.000	0	0-1	1	4.14	4.15
2004	Min	AL	36	0	0	14	39.1	172	35	19	19	4	2	0	2	21	1	42	3	0	4	1	.800	0	0-1	4	4.16	4.35
2007	2 Tms	AL	25	0	0	4	24.2	121	30	21	21	2	2	3	1	20	0	30	0	0	1	2	.333	0	0-0	1	7.15	7.66
2008	TB	AL	51	0	0	12	58.1	224	28	10	10	3	1	3	0	24	1	82	2	0	6	2	.750	0	4-5	14	1.38	1.54
2009	TB	AL	73	0	0	15	67.1	289	59	38	36	6	1	2	2	33	0	69	1	0	5	4	.556	0	4-9	18	3.79	4.81
2010	TB	AL	57	0	0	15	55.1	222	43	16	14	3	2	4	0	17	2	56	4	1	2	1	.667	0	0-1	16	2.24	2.28
2011	Oak	AL	62	0	0	15	62.0	242	44	17	17	8	1	0	0	20	1	59	0	0	5	2	.714	0	2-7	26	2.49	2.47
2012	Oak	AL	75	0	0	34	74.2	289	41	21	21	4	0	3	1	28	2	72	2	0	3	2	.600	0	24-26	15	1.55	2.53
07	Mil	NL	3	0	0	2	2.2	18	4	6	6	1	1	0	1	4	0	3	0	0	0	2	.000	0	0-0	0	15.83	20.25
07	TB	AL	22	0	0	6	22.0	103	26	15	15	1	1	3	0	16	0	27	0	0	1	0	1.000	0	0-0	1	6.19	6.14
	Postseason		15	0	0	3	15.0	65	13	6	6	2	1	0	1	8	3	10	1	0	0	0	-	0	0-0	2	4.06	3.60
	9 ML YEARS		398	1	0	113	410.1	1688	306	158	154	36	12	17	6	180	9	442	12	1	27	14	.659	0	34-50	95	2.82	3.38

Rod Barajas

Bats: R **Throws:** R **Pos:** C-99; PH-6; 1B-1   bah-RAH-hahss   **Ht:** 6'2" **Wt:** 250 **Born:** 9/5/1975 **Age:** 37

							BATTING																BASERUNNING				AVERAGES		
Year	Team	Lg	G	AB	H	2B	3B	HR	(Hm	Rd)	TB	R	RBI	RC	TBB	IBB	SO	HBP	SH	SF		SB	CS	SB%	GDP		Avg	OBP	Slg
1999	Ari	NL	5	16	4	1	0	1	(1	0)	8	3	3	2	1	0	1	0	1	0		0	0	-	0		.250	.294	.500
2000	Ari	NL	5	13	3	0	0	1	(1	0)	6	1	3	1	0	0	4	0	1	0		0	0	-	0		.231	.231	.462
2001	Ari	NL	51	106	17	3	0	3	(2	1)	29	9	9	4	4	0	26	0	0	0		0	0	-	0		.160	.191	.274
2002	Ari	NL	70	154	36	10	0	3	(1	2)	55	12	23	15	10	4	25	3	2	3		1	0	1.00	0		.234	.288	.357
2003	Ari	NL	80	220	48	15	0	3	(3	0)	72	19	28	19	14	7	43	1	1	3		0	0	-	6		.218	.265	.327
2004	Tex	AL	108	358	89	26	1	15	(8	7)	162	50	58	43	13	0	63	3	8	7		0	1	.00	3		.249	.276	.453
2005	Tex	AL	120	410	104	24	0	21	(7	14)	191	53	60	56	26	0	70	6	4	3		0	0	-	6		.254	.306	.466
2006	Tex	AL	97	344	88	20	0	11	(6	5)	141	49	41	36	17	0	51	4	5	1		0	0	-	9		.256	.298	.410
2007	Phi	NL	48	122	28	8	0	4	(1	3)	48	16	10	12	21	3	24	2	1	0		0	1	.00	6		.230	.332	.393
2008	Tor	AL	104	349	87	23	0	11	(4	7)	143	44	49	37	17	0	61	7	0	4		0	0	-	9		.249	.294	.410
2009	Tor	AL	125	429	97	19	0	19	(8	11)	173	43	71	50	20	2	76	1	3	7		1	0	1.00	4		.226	.258	.403
2010	2 Tms	NL	99	313	75	14	0	17	(7	10)	140	39	47	42	13	6	54	8	1	4		0	0	-	5		.240	.284	.447
2011	LAD	NL	98	305	70	13	0	16	(3	13)	131	29	47	31	22	4	71	4	2	4		0	0	-	4		.230	.287	.430
2012	Pit	NL	104	321	66	11	0	11	(3	8)	110	29	31	32	29	5	69	7	0	4		0	0	-	4		.206	.283	.343
10	NYM	NL	74	249	56	11	0	12	(5	7)	103	30	34	27	8	3	39	6	1	3		0	0	-	9		.225	.263	.414
10	LAD	NL	25	64	19	3	0	5	(2	3)	37	9	13	15	5	3	15	2	0	1		0	0	-	5		.297	.361	.578
	Postseason		5	9	3	0	0	2	(0	2)	9	2	2	2	0	0	1	0	0	0		0	0	-	0		.333	.333	1.000
	14 ML YEARS		1114	3460	812	187	1	136	(55	81)	1409	396	480	380	207	31	638	46	28	39		2	2	.50	61		.235	.284	.407

Daniel Bard

Pitches: R Bats: R Pos: SP-10; RP-7 Ht: 6'4" Wt: 215 Born: 6/25/1985 Age: 28

			HOW MUCH HE PITCHED						WHAT HE GAVE UP										THE RESULTS						
Year	Team	Lg	G	GS	CG	GF	IP	BFP	H	R	ER	HR	SH	SF	HB	TBB	IBB	SO	WP	Bk	W	L	Pct	Sh	Sv-Op Hld	ERC	ERA
2012	Pwtckt*	AAA	31	1	0	1	32.0	163	31	29	25	2	2	0	10	29	0	32	9	0	3	2	.600	0	0- -	6.85	7.03
2009	Bos	AL	49	0	0	12	49.1	212	41	24	20	5	4	3	3	22	3	63	1	1	2	2	.500	0	1-4 13	3.43	3.65
2010	Bos	AL	73	0	0	12	74.2	295	45	18	16	6	2	5	2	30	3	76	2	0	1	2	.333	0	3-10 32	1.99	1.93
2011	Bos	AL	70	0	0	10	73.0	288	46	29	27	5	5	0	2	24	3	74	2	1	2	9	.182	0	1-6 34	1.80	3.33
2012	Bos	AL	17	10	0	2	59.1	277	60	42	41	9	2	3	8	43	1	38	1	2	5	6	.455	0	0-0 0	6.55	6.22
	Postseason		2	0	0	1	3.0	8	0	0	0	0	0	0	0	0	0	4	0	0	0	0	-	0	0-0 1	0.00	0.00
	4 ML YEARS		209	10	0	36	256.1	1072	192	113	104	25	13	11	15	119	10	251	6	4	10	19	.345	0	5-20 79	3.12	3.65

Clint Barnes

Bats: R Throws: R Pos: SS-142; PH-2; 1B-1; PR-1   BAR-mess Ht: 6'1" Wt: 205 Born: 3/6/1979 Age: 34

						BATTING																	BASERUNNING				AVERAGES		
Year	Team	Lg	G	AB	H	2B	3B	HR	(Hm	Rd)	TB	R	RBI	RC	TBB	IBB	SO	HBP	SH	SF	SB	CS	SB%	GDP	Avg	OBP	Slg
2003	Col	NL	12	25	8	2	0	0	(0	0)	10	2	2	3	0	0	10	2	0	1	0	0	-	0	.320	.357	.400
2004	Col	NL	20	71	20	3	1	2	(0	2)	31	14	10	12	3	0	10	1	2	0	0	1	.00	2	.282	.320	.437
2005	Col	NL	81	350	101	19	1	10	(7	3)	152	55	46	49	16	1	36	6	4	1	6	4	.60	4	.289	.330	.434
2006	Col	NL	131	478	105	26	4	7	(3	4)	160	57	56	47	22	6	72	9	19	7	5	4	.56	2	.220	.264	.335
2007	Col	NL	27	37	8	3	0	0	(0	0)	11	5	1	1	1	1	13	0	1	0	0	0	-	1	.216	.237	.297
2008	Col	NL	107	393	114	25	6	11	(8	3)	184	47	44	54	17	0	69	2	4	1	13	4	.76	9	.290	.322	.468
2009	Col	NL	154	550	135	32	3	23	(13	10)	242	69	76	63	31	2	121	10	6	7	12	10	.55	6	.245	.294	.440
2010	Col	NL	133	387	91	21	0	8	(4	4)	136	43	50	43	35	10	66	5	2	3	2	2	.60	5	.235	.305	.351
2011	Hou	NL	123	446	109	27	0	12	(5	7)	172	47	39	46	38	2	88	7	2	2	3	1	.75	9	.244	.312	.386
2012	Pit	NL	144	455	104	16	1	8	(3	5)	146	34	45	38	20	3	106	8	8	2	0	2	.00	9	.229	.272	.321
	Postseason		4	14	0	0	0	0	(0	0)	0	0	0	0	0	0	2	0	1	0	0	0	-	0	.000	.000	.000
	10 ML YEARS		932	3192	795	174	16	81	(43	38)	1244	373	369	356	183	25	591	50	48	24	42	28	.60	47	.249	.298	.390

Brandon Barnes

Bats: R Throws: R Pos: CF-32; PH-9; RF-5; LF-1 Ht: 6'2" Wt: 205 Born: 5/15/1986 Age: 27

						BATTING																	BASERUNNING				AVERAGES		
Year	Team	Lg	G	AB	H	2B	3B	HR	(Hm	Rd)	TB	R	RBI	RC	TBB	IBB	SO	HBP	SH	SF	SB	CS	SB%	GDP	Avg	OBP	Slg
2005	Grnsvle	R+	39	145	29	5	2	2	(-	-)	44	21	13	12	10	1	36	5	0	1	3	2	.60	1	.200	.273	.303
2006	Grnsvle	R+	52	173	38	11	1	2	(-	-)	57	19	14	17	16	1	47	2	0	0	5	3	.63	4	.220	.293	.329
2007	TriCity	A-	63	231	58	16	1	10	(-	-)	106	34	41	37	31	1	71	0	0	3	5	3	.63	4	.251	.336	.459
2008	Lxngtn	A	87	311	75	19	1	2	(-	-)	102	27	19	29	18	0	96	2	3	2	7	3	.70	3	.241	.285	.328
2009	Lxngtn	A	57	197	52	11	3	5	(-	-)	84	23	25	25	10	1	52	4	2	2	3	6	.33	3	.264	.310	.426
2009	Lancst	A+	68	266	78	19	3	12	(-	-)	139	51	52	46	15	0	74	5	3	2	1	2	.33	5	.293	.340	.523
2009	CpChr	AA	7	21	2	0	0	1	(-	-)	5	2	1	0	3	0	7	0	0	0	0	0	-	0	.095	.208	.238
2010	RdRck	AAA	6	21	6	1	0	1	(-	-)	10	2	1	3	1	0	6	0	0	0	1	0	1.00	0	.286	.318	.476
2011	CpChr	AA	54	203	58	13	0	7	(-	-)	92	25	27	31	14	0	42	2	3	2	8	3	.67	4	.286	.335	.453
2011	OKCity	AAA	71	229	45	13	5	8	(-	-)	92	34	27	29	29	0	69	3	1	1	5	1	.83	6	.197	.294	.402
2012	CpChr	AA	44	164	52	20	0	7	(-	-)	93	30	31	35	14	0	42	3	0	2	7	2	.78	8	.317	.377	.567
2012	OKCity	AAA	62	235	76	19	1	5	(-	-)	112	51	38	44	23	0	49	1	2	2	14	4	.78	4	.323	.383	.477
2012	Hou	NL	43	98	20	3	0	1	(0	1)	26	8	7	4	5	0	29	1	1	0	1	1	.50	1	.204	.250	.265

Scott Barnes

Pitches: L Bats: L Pos: RP-16 Ht: 6'4" Wt: 200 Born: 9/5/1987 Age: 25

			HOW MUCH HE PITCHED						WHAT HE GAVE UP										THE RESULTS						
Year	Team	Lg	G	GS	CG	GF	IP	BFP	H	R	ER	HR	SH	SF	HB	TBB	IBB	SO	WP	Bk	W	L	Pct	Sh	Sv-Op Hld	ERC	ERA
2008	Giants	R	3	0	0	0	5.1	22	3	2	2	0	0	0	0	4	0	11	1	0	0	1	.000	0	0- -	2.44	3.38
2008	SlmKzr	A-	2	1	0	0	5.2	25	6	3	3	0	0	0	0	1	0	11	0	0	0	0	-	0	0- -	2.67	4.76
2008	Augsta	A	6	6	0	0	32.2	121	15	6	5	0	0	1	0	7	0	41	1	0	3	2	.600	0	0- -	0.78	1.38
2009	SnJos	A+	18	18	0	0	98.0	401	82	36	31	7	1	1	9	29	0	99	5	0	12	3	.800	0	0- -	3.01	2.85
2009	Knstn	A+	3	3	0	0	12.2	56	14	3	3	1	0	0	0	6	0	10	1	0	0	0	-	0	0- -	4.88	2.13
2009	Akron	AA	6	6	0	0	31.2	140	35	22	20	7	2	2	2	14	0	29	3	0	2	2	.500	0	0- -	6.19	5.68
2010	Akron	AA	26	26	0	0	138.0	599	126	90	80	15	2	8	8	58	0	127	1	1	6	11	.353	0	0- -	3.96	5.22
2011	Akron	AA	2	2	0	0	11.0	39	5	2	2	0	1	0	0	2	0	17	0	0	1	0	1.000	0	0- -	0.74	1.64
2011	Clmbs	AAA	16	15	0	1	88.0	372	80	41	36	12	1	0	3	34	0	90	3	1	7	4	.636	0	0- -	3.92	3.68
2012	Clmbs	AAA	31	3	0	8	52.0	220	37	26	23	1	1	3	4	23	0	67	3	0	2	3	.400	0	2- -	2.41	3.98
2012	Cle	AL	16	0	0	3	19.0	82	17	9	9	1	0	0	3	7	0	16	2	0	0	0	-	0	0-0 1	3.66	4.26

Darwin Barney

Bats: R Throws: R Pos: 2B-155; PH-4; SS-3; PR-1 Ht: 5'10" Wt: 185 Born: 11/8/1985 Age: 27

						BATTING																	BASERUNNING				AVERAGES		
Year	Team	Lg	G	AB	H	2B	3B	HR	(Hm	Rd)	TB	R	RBI	RC	TBB	IBB	SO	HBP	SH	SF	SB	CS	SB%	GDP	Avg	OBP	Slg
2010	ChC	NL	30	79	19	4	0	0	(0	0)	23	12	2	6	6	0	12	0	0	0	0	0	-	0	.241	.294	.291
2011	ChC	NL	143	529	146	23	4	2	(2	0)	187	66	43	60	22	2	67	8	7	4	9	2	.82	14	.276	.313	.353
2012	ChC	NL	156	548	139	26	4	7	(7	0)	194	73	44	60	33	1	58	3	3	1	6	1	.86	11	.254	.299	.354
	3 ML YEARS		329	1156	304	53	10	9	(9	0)	404	151	89	126	61	3	137	11	10	5	15	3	.83	25	.263	.305	.349

Jason Bartlett

Bats: R **Throws:** R **Pos:** SS-27; PH-1; PR-1   **Ht:** 6'0" **Wt:** 190 **Born:** 10/30/1979 **Age:** 33

										BATTING												BASERUNNING				AVERAGES		
Year	Team	Lg	G	AB	H	2B	3B	HR	(Hm	Rd)	TB	R	RBI	RC	TBB	IBB	SO	HBP	SH	SF	SB	CS	SB%	GDP	Avg	OBP	Slg
2004	Min	AL	8	12	1	0	0	0	(0	0)	1	2	1	1	1	0	1	0	1	0	2	0	1.00	0	.083	.154	.083
2005	Min	AL	74	224	54	10	1	3	(2	1)	75	33	16	22	21	0	37	4	2	1	4	0	1.00	6	.241	.316	.335
2006	Min	AL	99	333	103	18	2	2	(0	2)	131	44	32	50	22	1	46	11	1	5	10	5	.67	8	.309	.367	.393
2007	Min	AL	140	510	135	20	7	5	(2	3)	184	75	43	65	50	3	73	8	0	2	23	3	.88	8	.265	.339	.361
2008	TB	AL	128	454	130	25	3	1	(1	0)	164	48	37	56	22	1	69	9	5	4	20	6	.77	9	.286	.329	.361
2009	TB	AL	137	500	160	29	7	14	(3	11)	245	90	66	97	54	2	89	5	4	4	30	7	.81	5	.320	.389	.490
2010	TB	AL	135	468	119	27	3	4	(1	3)	164	71	47	62	45	1	83	5	11	3	11	6	.65	6	.254	.308	.350
2011	SD	NL	139	554	136	22	3	2	(1	1)	170	61	40	50	48	0	98	5	5	6	23	10	.70	13	.245	.308	.307
2012	SD	NL	29	83	11	5	0	0	(0	0)	16	8	4	1	12	0	27	0	2	1	0	0	-	6	.133	.240	.193
	Postseason		24	77	21	3	1	1	(1	0)	29	8	3	6	5	0	13	3	1	0	2	0	1.00	2	.273	.341	.377
	9 ML YEARS		889	3138	849	156	26	31	(10	21)	1150	432	286	404	275	8	523	47	31	26	123	37	.77	61	.271	.336	.366

Daric Barton

Bats: L **Throws:** R **Pos:** 1B-43; PH-5   DARE-ick   **Ht:** 6'0" **Wt:** 205 **Born:** 8/16/1985 **Age:** 27

										BATTING												BASERUNNING				AVERAGES		
Year	Team	Lg	G	AB	H	2B	3B	HR	(Hm	Rd)	TB	R	RBI	RC	TBB	IBB	SO	HBP	SH	SF	SB	CS	SB%	GDP	Avg	OBP	Slg
2012	Scrmto*	AAA	74	259	66	14	3	8	(-	-)	110	49	35	53	66	1	53	6	0	5	7	1	.88	9	.255	.411	.425
2007	Oak	AL	18	72	25	9	0	4	(2	2)	46	16	8	14	10	0	11	1	0	1	1	0	1.00	2	.347	.429	.639
2008	Oak	AL	140	446	101	17	5	9	(1	8)	155	59	47	56	65	5	99	3	6	3	2	1	.67	6	.226	.327	.348
2009	Oak	AL	54	160	43	12	1	3	(2	1)	66	31	24	28	26	0	25	2	1	3	0	2	.00	1	.269	.372	.413
2010	Oak	AL	159	556	152	33	5	10	(1	9)	225	79	57	92	110	2	102	3	12	5	7	3	.70	8	.273	.393	.405
2011	Oak	AL	67	236	50	13	0	0	(0	0)	63	27	21	24	39	3	47	2	0	3	2	1	.67	6	.212	.325	.267
2012	Oak	AL	46	113	23	7	0	1	(0	1)	33	8	6	14	22	0	32	1	0	0	1	0	1.00	1	.204	.338	.292
	6 ML YEARS		484	1583	394	91	11	27	(6	21)	588	220	163	228	272	10	316	12	19	15	13	7	.65	24	.249	.360	.371

Anthony Bass

Pitches: R **Bats:** R **Pos:** SP-15; RP-9   **Ht:** 6'2" **Wt:** 190 **Born:** 11/1/1987 **Age:** 25

			HOW MUCH HE PITCHED						WHAT HE GAVE UP										THE RESULTS						
Year	Team	Lg	G	GS	CG	GF	IP	BFP	H	R	ER	HR	SH	SF	HB	TBB	IBB	SO	WP	Bk	W	L	Pct	Sh	Sv-Op Hld	ERC	ERA
2008	Eugene	A-	25	0	0	21	34.1	145	25	12	8	3	2	1	1	14	0	41	6	0	2	2	.500	0	7- - -	2.60	2.10
2009	FtWyn	A	18	18	0	0	90.1	369	79	31	22	5	4	1	3	25	0	69	3	1	9	3	.750	0	0- - -	2.80	2.19
2009	Lk Els	A+	10	8	0	1	33.1	143	33	17	13	3	2	1	2	14	0	20	3	0	3	0	1.000	0	0- - -	4.36	3.51
2010	Lk Els	A+	27	27	0	0	132.1	528	124	59	46	9	3	3	1	20	0	109	3	0	8	7	.533	0	0- - -	2.66	3.13
2010	Portlnd	AAA	1	1	0	0	5.2	27	7	5	5	1	0	2	1	3	0	3	0	1	0	1	.000	0	0- - -	7.53	7.94
2011	SnAnt	AA	13	13	0	0	69.2	282	62	31	29	6	2	3	0	21	0	62	3	0	6	4	.600	0	0- - -	3.08	3.75
2011	Tucsn	AAA	1	1	0	0	5.0	21	6	1	1	0	0	1	0	3	0	3	1	0	1	0	1.000	0	0- - -	3.80	1.80
2012	Tucsn	AAA	3	3	0	0	8.0	33	8	6	5	0	0	1	0	0	0	9	0	0	0	0	-	0	0- - -	1.88	5.63
2011	SD	NL	27	3	0	6	48.1	198	41	9	9	3	2	0	1	21	1	24	1	0	2	0	1.000	0	4 3- -	3.28	1.68
2012	SD	NL	24	15	1	3	97.0	411	89	59	51	10	2	2	1	39	3	80	5	1	2	8	.200	0	1-1 -	3.65	4.73
	2 ML YEARS		51	18	1	9	145.1	609	130	68	60	13	4	2	2	60	4	104	6	1	4	8	.333	0	1-1 5	3.53	3.72

Antonio Bastardo

Pitches: L **Bats:** R **Pos:** RP-65   bah-STAHR-doh   **Ht:** 5'11" **Wt:** 197 **Born:** 9/21/1985 **Age:** 27

			HOW MUCH HE PITCHED						WHAT HE GAVE UP										THE RESULTS						
Year	Team	Lg	G	GS	CG	GF	IP	BFP	H	R	ER	HR	SH	SF	HB	TBB	IBB	SO	WP	Bk	W	L	Pct	Sh	Sv-Op Hld	ERC	ERA
2009	Phi	NL	6	5	0	0	23.2	106	26	18	17	4	0	0	2	9	0	19	0	0	2	3	.400	0	0-0 0	5.41	6.46
2010	Phi	NL	25	0	0	2	18.2	86	19	9	9	1	0	0	2	9	0	26	0	0	2	0	1.000	0	0-1 2	4.46	4.34
2011	Phi	NL	64	0	0	15	58.0	225	28	17	17	6	2	2	0	26	0	70	4	0	6	1	.857	0	8-9 17	1.69	2.64
2012	Phi	NL	65	0	0	10	52.0	224	40	26	25	7	1	2	2	26	3	81	5	0	2	5	.286	0	1-5 26	3.42	4.33
	Postseason		5	0	0	0	1.2	8	2	0	0	0	1	0	0	1	0	2	0	0	0	0	-	0	0-0 1	5.10	0.00
	4 ML YEARS		160	5	0	27	152.1	641	113	70	68	18	3	4	6	70	3	196	9	0	12	9	.571	0	9-15 45	3.12	4.02

Miguel Batista

Pitches: R **Bats:** R **Pos:** RP-30; SP-5   **Ht:** 6'1" **Wt:** 210 **Born:** 2/19/1971 **Age:** 42

			HOW MUCH HE PITCHED						WHAT HE GAVE UP										THE RESULTS						
Year	Team	Lg	G	GS	CG	GF	IP	BFP	H	R	ER	HR	SH	SF	HB	TBB	IBB	SO	WP	Bk	W	L	Pct	Sh	Sv-Op Hld	ERC	ERA
2012	Bnghtn*	AA	1	1	0	0	7.0	28	4	5	4	1	0	2	0	4	0	3	2	0	0	1	.000	0	0- - -	2.80	5.14
2012	Gwnntt*	AAA	6	4	0	0	24.0	99	19	9	9	2	0	0	1	10	0	21	1	0	1	1	.500	0	0- - -	3.11	3.38
1992	Pit	NL	1	0	0	1	2.0	13	4	2	2	1	0	0	0	3	0	1	0	0	0	0	-	0	0-0 0	20.26	9.00
1996	Fla	NL	9	0	0	4	11.1	49	9	8	7	0	3	0	0	7	2	6	1	0	0	0	-	0	0-0 0	2.77	5.56
1997	ChC	NL	11	6	0	2	36.1	168	36	24	23	4	4	4	1	24	2	27	2	0	0	5	.000	0	0-0 0	5.09	5.70
1998	Mon	NL	56	13	0	12	135.0	598	141	66	57	12	7	5	6	65	7	92	6	1	3	5	.375	0	0-0 3	4.70	3.80
1999	Mon	NL	39	17	2	3	134.2	606	146	88	73	10	8	11	7	58	2	95	6	0	8	7	.533	1	1-1 0	4.62	4.88
2000	2 Tms		18	9	0	2	65.1	310	85	68	62	19	1	2	2	37	2	37	4	0	2	7	.222	0	0-2 0	8.37	8.54
2001	Ari	NL	48	18	0	6	139.1	581	113	57	52	13	9	3	10	60	2	90	6	0	11	8	.579	0	0-0 4	3.43	3.36
2002	Ari	NL	36	29	1	2	184.2	790	172	99	88	12	5	8	8	70	3	112	9	2	8	9	.471	0	0-0 0	3.45	4.29
2003	Ari	NL	36	29	2	5	193.1	822	197	85	76	13	10	6	8	60	3	142	7	0	10	9	.526	1	0-0 0	3.77	3.54
2004	Tor	AL	38	31	2	7	198.2	867	206	115	106	22	7	6	3	96	1	104	12	0	10	13	.435	1	0-0 0	4.84	4.80
2005	Tor	AL	71	0	0	62	74.2	331	80	39	34	9	2	2	2	27	5	54	3	0	5	8	.385	0	31-39 0	4.39	4.10
2006	Ari	NL	34	33	3	0	206.1	910	231	116	105	18	12	5	6	84	5	110	14	1	11	8	.579	1	0-0 0	4.82	4.58
2007	Sea	AL	33	32	0	0	193.0	860	209	101	92	18	5	5	8	85	3	133	15	2	16	11	.593	0	0-0 0	4.81	4.29
2008	Sea	AL	44	20	0	9	115.0	556	135	89	80	19	3	11	6	79	6	73	5	0	4	14	.222	0	1-4 0	6.92	6.26
2009	Sea	AL	56	0	0	18	71.1	326	79	37	32	7	4	1	2	39	1	52	4	0	7	4	.636	0	1-5 14	5.37	4.04
2010	Was	NL	58	1	0	18	82.2	350	71	36	34	9	1	2	5	39	8	55	4	0	1	2	.333	0	2-2 1	3.78	3.70

Year Team	Lg	G	GS	CG	GF	IP	BFP	H	R	ER	HR	SH	SF	HB	TBB	IBB	SO	WP	Bk	W	L	Pct	Sh	Sv-Op	Hld	ERC	ERA
						HOW MUCH HE PITCHED						WHAT HE GAVE UP												THE RESULTS				
2011 2 Tms	NL	35	5	1	2	60.0	262	49	29	24	2	4	1	6	33	5	31	3	0	5	2	.714	1	0-1	7	3.40	3.60
2012 2 Tms	NL	35	5	0	11	52.2	244	58	30	27	6	3	2	1	33	1	36	1	0	1	3	.250	0	0-0	0	5.75	4.61
00 Mon	NL	4	0	0	0	8.1	49	19	14	13	2	1	1	2	3	0	7	0	0	0	1	.000	0	0-2	0	14.73	14.04
00 KC	AL	14	9	0	2	57.0	261	66	54	49	17	0	1	0	34	2	30	4	0	2	6	.250	0	0-0	0	7.50	7.74
11 StL	NL	26	1	0	2	29.1	137	27	20	15	2	2	0	4	19	4	16	2	0	3	2	.600	0	0-1	6	4.56	4.60
11 NYM	NL	9	4	1	0	30.2	125	22	9	9	0	2	1	2	14	1	15	1	0	2	0	1.000	1	0-0	1	2.38	2.64
12 NYM	NL	30	5	0	7	46.2	220	53	28	25	5	3	2	1	31	0	34	1	0	1	3	.250	0	0-0	0	6.10	4.82
12 Atl	NL	5	0	0	4	6.0	24	5	2	2	1	0	0	0	2	1	2	0	0	-	-	-	0	0-0	0	3.20	3.00
Postseason		7	4	0	1	25.1	104	18	10	10	3	3	0	1	11	0	14	1	0	1	2	.333	0	0-0	0	2.94	3.55
18 ML YEARS		658	248	11	164	1956.1	8643	2021	1089	974	194	88	74	79	899	58	1250	102	6	102	115	.470	5	41-59	35	4.62	4.48

Trevor Bauer

Pitches: R Bats: R Pos: SP-4   BOU-wur   **Ht: 6'1" Wt: 185 Born: 1/17/1991 Age: 22**

Year Team	Lg	G	GS	CG	GF	IP	BFP	H	R	ER	HR	SH	SF	HB	TBB	IBB	SO	WP	Bk	W	L	Pct	Sh	Sv-Op	Hld	ERC	ERA
						HOW MUCH HE PITCHED						WHAT HE GAVE UP												THE RESULTS				
2011 Visalia	A+	3	3	0	0	9.0	39	7	3	3	1	0	0	0	4	0	17	1	0	0	1	.000	0	0--	-	2.97	3.00
2011 Mobile	AA	4	4	0	0	16.2	80	20	14	14	2	0	0	2	8	0	26	5	0	1	1	.500	0	0--	-	6.09	7.56
2012 Mobile	AA	8	8	0	0	48.1	201	33	12	9	1	1	0	2	26	0	60	8	0	7	1	.875	0	0--	-	2.55	1.68
2012 Reno	AAA	14	14	1	0	82.0	347	74	28	26	8	3	2	0	35	0	97	12	0	5	1	.833	0	0--	-	3.64	2.85
2012 Ari	NL	4	4	0	0	16.1	77	14	13	11	2	1	1	1	13	0	17	2	0	1	2	.333	0	0-0	0	5.12	6.06

Jose Bautista

Bats: R Throws: R Pos: RF-90; 1B-4; DH-2; 3B-1   bah-TEE-stah   **Ht: 6'0" Wt: 190 Born: 10/19/1980 Age: 32**

Year Team	Lg	G	AB	H	2B	3B	HR	(Hm	Rd)	TB	R	RBI	RC	TBB	IBB	SO	HBP	SH	SF	SB	CS	SB%	GDP	Avg	OBP	Slg
								BATTING												BASERUNNING				AVERAGES		
2012 B Jays*	R	1	3	0	0	0	0	(-	-)	0	0	0	0	1	0	1	0	0	0	0	0	-	0	.000	.250	.000
2012 NHam*	AA	1	4	2	0	0	2	(-	-)	8	2	5	3	1	0	1	0	0	0	0	0	-	0	.500	.600	2.000
2004 4 Tms		64	88	18	3	0	0	(0	0)	21	6	2	2	7	0	40	0	1	0	0	1	.00	1	.205	.263	.239
2005 Pit	NL	11	28	4	1	0	0	(0	0)	5	3	1	0	3	0	7	0	0	0	1	0	1.00	2	.143	.226	.179
2006 Pit	NL	117	400	94	20	3	16	(11	5)	168	58	51	55	46	2	110	16	3	4	2	4	.33	12	.235	.335	.420
2007 Pit	NL	142	532	135	36	2	15	(8	7)	220	75	63	71	68	1	101	4	4	6	6	3	.67	16	.254	.339	.414
2008 2 Tms		128	370	88	17	0	15	(5	10)	150	45	54	43	40	5	91	2	8	4	1	1	.50	12	.238	.313	.405
2009 Tor	AL	113	336	79	13	3	13	(5	8)	137	54	40	42	56	1	85	4	6	2	4	0	1.00	9	.235	.349	.408
2010 Tor	AL	161	569	148	35	3	54	(33	21)	351	109	124	132	100	2	116	10	0	4	9	2	.82	10	.260	.378	.617
2011 Tor	AL	149	513	155	24	2	43	(20	23)	312	105	103	133	132	24	111	6	0	4	9	5	.64	8	.302	.447	.608
2012 Tor	AL	92	332	80	14	0	27	(11	16)	175	64	65	58	59	2	63	4	0	4	5	2	.71	11	.241	.358	.527
04 Bal	AL	16	11	3	0	0	0	(0	0)	3	3	0	1	1	0	3	0	0	0	0	0	-	0	.273	.333	.273
04 TB	AL	12	12	2	0	0	0	(0	0)	2	1	1	0	3	0	7	0	0	0	0	1	.00	0	.167	.333	.167
04 KC	AL	13	25	5	1	0	0	(0	0)	6	1	1	0	1	0	12	0	0	0	0	0	-	0	.200	.231	.240
04 Pit	NL	23	40	8	2	0	0	(0	0)	10	1	0	1	2	0	18	0	1	0	0	0	-	1	.200	.238	.250
08 Pit	NL	107	314	76	15	0	12	(3	9)	127	38	44	39	38	4	77	2	6	3	1	1	.50	10	.242	.325	.404
08 Tor	AL	21	56	12	2	0	3	(2	1)	23	7	10	4	2	1	14	0	2	1	0	0	-	2	.214	.237	.411
9 ML YEARS		977	3168	801	163	13	183	(93	90)	1539	519	503	536	511	37	724	46	22	28	37	18	.67	81	.253	.362	.486

Mike Baxter

Bats: L Throws: R Pos: RF-45; PH-35; LF-18; CF-1; DH-1; PR-1   **Ht: 6'0" Wt: 195 Born: 12/7/1984 Age: 28**

Year Team	Lg	G	AB	H	2B	3B	HR	(Hm	Rd)	TB	R	RBI	RC	TBB	IBB	SO	HBP	SH	SF	SB	CS	SB%	GDP	Avg	OBP	Slg
								BATTING												BASERUNNING				AVERAGES		
2012 StLuci*	A+	4	15	4	3	0	0	(-	-)	7	1	4	2	1	0	4	1	0	0	0	0	-	0	.267	.353	.467
2012 Bnghtn*	AA	3	10	3	0	0	0	(-	-)	3	1	1	1	1	0	2	1	0	1	0	0	-	0	.300	.385	.300
2012 Buffalo*	AAA	6	24	9	1	0	0	(-	-)	10	2	3	4	2	0	7	1	0	0	0	0	-	0	.375	.444	.417
2010 SD	NL	9	8	1	0	0	0	(0	0)	1	0	1	0	0	0	2	0	0	0	0	0	-	1	.125	.111	.125
2011 NYM	NL	22	34	8	2	1	1	(1	0)	15	6	4	5	5	0	9	1	0	0	0	0	-	1	.235	.350	.441
2012 NYM	NL	89	179	47	14	2	3	(1	2)	74	26	17	30	25	4	45	5	0	2	5	3	.63	0	.263	.365	.413
3 ML YEARS		120	221	56	16	3	4	(2	2)	90	32	22	35	30	4	56	6	0	3	5	3	.63	2	.253	.354	.407

Jason Bay

Bats: R Throws: R Pos: LF-65; PH-7; PR-2   **Ht: 6'2" Wt: 210 Born: 9/20/1978 Age: 34**

Year Team	Lg	G	AB	H	2B	3B	HR	(Hm	Rd)	TB	R	RBI	RC	TBB	IBB	SO	HBP	SH	SF	SB	CS	SB%	GDP	Avg	OBP	Slg
								BATTING												BASERUNNING				AVERAGES		
2012 StLuci*	A+	5	15	2	0	0	0	(-	-)	2	0	1	1	4	0	6	0	0	1	1	0	1.00	1	.133	.300	.133
2012 Buffalo*	AAA	3	10	3	0	0	0	(-	-)	3	2	0	2	4	0	3	0	0	0	1	0	1.00	0	.300	.500	.300
2003 2 Tms	NL	30	87	25	7	1	4	(2	2)	46	15	14	19	19	0	29	1	0	0	3	1	.75	0	.287	.421	.529
2004 Pit	NL	120	411	116	24	4	26	(15	11)	226	61	82	75	41	2	129	10	5	5	4	6	.40	9	.282	.358	.550
2005 Pit	NL	162	599	183	44	6	32	(9	23)	335	110	101	128	95	9	142	6	0	7	21	1	.95	12	.306	.402	.559
2006 Pit	NL	159	570	163	29	3	35	(13	22)	303	101	109	103	102	9	156	8	0	9	11	2	.85	15	.286	.396	.532
2007 Pit	NL	145	538	133	25	2	21	(7	14)	225	78	84	74	59	3	141	9	0	1	4	1	.80	8	.247	.327	.418
2008 2 Tms		155	577	165	35	4	31	(18	13)	301	111	101	104	81	4	137	4	0	8	10	0	1.00	7	.286	.373	.522
2009 Bos	NL	151	531	142	29	3	36	(15	21)	285	103	119	122	94	4	162	9	0	4	13	3	.81	9	.267	.384	.537
2010 NYM	NL	95	348	90	20	6	6	(3	3)	140	48	47	50	44	3	91	5	0	4	10	0	1.00	7	.259	.347	.402
2011 NYM	NL	123	444	109	19	1	12	(6	6)	166	59	57	50	56	3	109	2	1	6	11	1	.92	8	.245	.329	.374
2012 NYM	NL	70	194	32	2	0	8	(2	6)	58	21	20	11	19	0	58	0	0	2	5	1	.83	3	.165	.237	.299
03 SD	NL	3	8	2	1	0	1	(0	1)	6	2	2	2	1	0	1	1	0	0	0	0	-	0	.250	.400	.750
03 Pit	NL	27	79	23	6	1	3	(2	1)	40	13	12	17	18	0	28	0	0	0	3	1	.75	0	.291	.423	.506

Year	Team	Lg	G	AB	H	2B	3B	HR	(Hm	Rd)	TB	R	RBI	RC	TBB	IBB	SO	HBP	SH	SF	SB	CS	SB%	GDP	Avg	OBP	Slg
									BATTING												**BASERUNNING**				**AVERAGES**		
08	Pit	NL	106	393	111	23	2	22	(15	7)	204	72	64	73	59	2	86	2	0	5	7	0	1.00	3	.282	.375	.519
08	Bos	AL	49	184	54	12	2	9	(3	6)	97	39	37	31	22	2	51	2	0	3	3	0	1.00	4	.293	.370	.527
	Postseason		14	49	15	3	0	3	(0	3)	27	6	9	11	12	1	15	1	0	0	0	0	-	0	.306	.452	.551
10 ML YEARS			1210	4299	1158	234	30	211	(90	121)	2085	707	734	736	610	37	1154	54	6	53	92	16	.85	78	.269	.363	.485

Brandon Beachy

Pitches: R Bats: R Pos: SP-13   **Ht: 6'3" Wt: 215 Born: 9/3/1986 Age: 26**

Year	Team	Lg	G	GS	CG	GF	IP	BFP	H	R	ER	HR	SH	SF	HB	TBB	IBB	SO	WP	Bk	W	L	Pct	Sh	Sv-Op	Hld	ERC	ERA
												HOW MUCH HE PITCHED · **WHAT HE GAVE UP** · **THE RESULTS**																
2010	Atl	NL	3	3	0	0	15.0	67	16	9	5	0	0	0	0	7	3	15	1	0	0	2	.000	0	0-0	0	3.58	3.00
2011	Atl	NL	25	25	0	0	141.2	591	125	62	58	16	6	5	5	46	9	169	11	1	7	3	.700	0	0-0	0	3.27	3.68
2012	Atl	NL	13	13	1	0	81.0	319	49	24	18	6	1	2	1	29	1	68	4	0	5	5	.500	1	0-0	0	1.80	2.00
3 ML YEARS			41	41	1	0	237.2	977	190	95	81	22	7	7	6	82	13	252	16	1	12	10	.545	1	0-0	0	2.76	3.07

Pedro Beato

Pitches: R Bats: R Pos: RP-11   bay-AHH-toe   **Ht: 6'4" Wt: 220 Born: 10/27/1986 Age: 26**

Year	Team	Lg	G	GS	CG	GF	IP	BFP	H	R	ER	HR	SH	SF	HB	TBB	IBB	SO	WP	Bk	W	L	Pct	Sh	Sv-Op	Hld	ERC	ERA
2006	Abrdn	A-	14	10	0	1	57.0	240	47	31	23	6	5	0	4	23	0	52	3	1	3	2	.600	0	0- -		3.13	3.63
2007	Dlmrva	A	27	27	0	0	142.1	620	139	75	64	10	6	8	3	59	0	106	12	1	7	8	.467	0	0- -		3.84	4.05
2008	Frdrck	A+	19	19	0	0	97.0	438	119	74	63	11	3	5	7	33	0	51	3	1	4	10	.286	0	0- -		5.58	5.85
2008	Orioles	R	2	2	0	0	10.2	44	10	3	3	1	1	0	1	1	0	3	1	0	0	0	-	0	0- -		2.83	2.53
2009	Frdrck	A+	20	20	1	0	105.1	475	125	60	53	12	2	3	9	40	0	70	6	1	5	7	.417	0	0- -		5.59	4.53
2009	Bowie	AA	6	5	0	0	32.0	133	33	16	16	6	2	1	0	7	0	18	1	0	1	3	.250	0	0- -		4.13	4.50
2010	Bowie	AA	43	0	0	33	59.2	242	49	14	14	4	2	0	3	19	0	50	4	0	4	0	1.000	0	16- -		2.84	2.11
2011	Buffalo	AAA	1	0	0	0	1.1	7	2	0	0	0	1	0	0	1	0	0	0	0	1	0	1.000	0	0- -		7.52	0.00
2012	StLuci	A+	3	0	0	0	4.0	14	2	0	0	0	0	0	0	1	0	4	0	0	0	0	-	0	0- -		1.01	0.00
2012	Buffalo	AAA	24	1	0	8	37.0	151	32	21	17	7	0	1	2	11	3	27	1	2	4	4	.500	0	0- -		3.68	4.14
2012	Pwtckt	AAA	4	0	0	2	5.0	19	1	1	0	0	0	0	0	4	0	7	2	0	0	0	-	0	1- -		1.19	0.00
2011	NYM	NL	60	0	0	7	67.0	283	59	41	32	5	2	4	4	27	3	39	1	0	2	1	.667	0	0-1	11	3.45	4.30
2012	2 Tms		11	0	0	2	12.0	51	11	9	9	1	0	0	1	5	0	12	1	0	1	0	1.000	0	0-0	1	3.96	6.75
12	NYM	NL	7	0	0	2	4.1	20	5	5	5	1	0	0	0	2	0	5	1	0	0	0	-	0	0-0	1	6.09	10.38
12	Bos	AL	4	0	0	0	7.2	31	6	4	4	0	0	0	1	3	0	7	0	0	1	0	1.000	0	0-0	0	2.83	4.70
2 ML YEARS			71	0	0	9	79.0	334	70	50	41	6	2	4	5	32	3	51	2	0	3	1	.750	0	0-1	12	3.52	4.67

Blake Beavan

Pitches: R Bats: R Pos: SP-26   BEV-uhn   **Ht: 6'7" Wt: 240 Born: 1/17/1989 Age: 24**

Year	Team	Lg	G	GS	CG	GF	IP	BFP	H	R	ER	HR	SH	SF	HB	TBB	IBB	SO	WP	Bk	W	L	Pct	Sh	Sv-Op	Hld	ERC	ERA
2008	Clinton	A	23	23	0	0	121.2	479	105	42	32	12	1	5	4	20	0	73	2	0	10	6	.625	0	0- -		2.63	2.37
2009	Bkrsfld	A+	12	12	1	0	73.1	310	75	44	35	6	1	4	5	16	0	51	2	2	5	4	.556	0	0- -		3.63	4.30
2009	Frisco	AA	15	15	0	0	89.2	390	113	47	40	4	3	7	1	13	0	34	6	0	4	4	.500	0	0- -		4.14	4.01
2010	Frisco	AA	17	17	0	0	110.0	432	100	37	34	6	3	3	1	12	0	68	2	0	10	5	.667	0	0- -		2.30	2.78
2010	WTenn	AA	3	3	0	0	18.0	73	18	11	10	1	1	4	2	1	0	11	1	0	2	1	.667	0	0- -		2.92	5.00
2010	Tacom	AAA	7	7	0	0	40.1	180	56	31	29	6	1	0	2	8	0	22	3	0	2	2	.500	0	0- -		6.22	6.47
2011	Tacom	AAA	16	16	0	0	93.0	413	118	52	46	10	2	2	1	20	0	64	3	0	5	3	.625	0	0- -		4.91	4.45
2012	Tacom	AAA	6	6	0	0	38.0	159	39	12	11	3	0	1	2	9	0	15	5	0	4	0	1.000	0	0- -		3.69	2.61
2011	Sea	AL	15	15	0	0	97.0	405	106	46	46	13	1	5	3	15	0	42	4	0	5	6	.455	0	0-0	0	3.99	4.27
2012	Sea	AL	26	26	0	0	152.1	638	168	76	75	23	1	5	10	24	0	67	3	0	11	11	.500	0	0-0	0	4.36	4.43
2 ML YEARS			41	41	0	0	249.1	1043	274	122	121	36	2	10	13	39	0	109	7	0	16	17	.485	0	0-0	0	4.21	4.37

Chad Beck

Pitches: R Bats: R Pos: RP-14   **Ht: 6'4" Wt: 255 Born: 1/17/1985 Age: 28**

Year	Team	Lg	G	GS	CG	GF	IP	BFP	H	R	ER	HR	SH	SF	HB	TBB	IBB	SO	WP	Bk	W	L	Pct	Sh	Sv-Op	Hld	ERC	ERA
2006	Yakima	A-	16	2	0	1	40.1	186	47	37	28	8	4	3	2	18	0	45	3	1	1	5	.167	0	0- -		6.13	6.25
2007	Sbend	A	31	0	0	14	52.0	227	53	27	25	5	3	0	3	20	1	48	5	0	1	2	.333	0	1- -		4.29	4.33
2008	Sbend	A	7	0	0	3	17.2	73	13	7	4	0	0	0	0	3	0	19	2	1	2	0	1.000	0	0- -		1.36	2.04
2008	Visalia	A+	25	15	0	8	95.0	392	86	45	42	8	1	1	5	25	0	89	10	0	6	5	.545	0	1- -		3.15	3.98
2009	Dnedin	A+	6	0	0	2	10.1	51	12	9	5	1	1	0	1	6	1	14	2	0	0	0	-	0	0- -		5.67	4.35
2009	Lnsng	A	20	20	1	0	110.2	501	135	78	73	10	4	5	9	29	0	85	7	1	6	8	.429	0	0- -		4.96	5.94
2010	Dnedin	A+	41	11	0	6	101.2	432	97	44	42	5	3	0	1	31	0	79	6	0	3	6	.333	0	0- -		3.10	3.72
2011	Dnedin	A+	1	1	0	0	5.1	20	4	1	1	1	0	0	1	1	0	7	0	0	0	0	-	0	0- -		3.51	1.69
2011	NHam	AA	22	14	0	5	95.0	393	92	41	39	7	1	4	3	28	0	70	2	0	7	4	.636	0	0- -		3.51	3.69
2011	LsVgs	AAA	8	8	0	0	41.2	209	61	36	31	7	0	2	2	26	0	23	3	0	2	4	.333	0	0- -		8.72	6.70
2012	LsVgs	AAA	43	0	0	38	48.0	193	39	7	7	2	0	0	1	13	1	24	2	0	2	0	1.000	0	18- -		2.31	1.31
2011	Tor	AL	3	0	0	3	2.1	8	1	0	0	0	0	0	0	0	0	3	0	0	0	0	-	0	0-0	0	0.40	0.00
2012	Tor	AL	14	0	0	2	15.2	72	21	12	11	2	0	1	0	5	0	9	1	1	0	0	-	0	0-0	0	5.90	6.32
2 ML YEARS			17	0	0	5	18.0	80	22	12	11	2	0	1	0	5	0	12	1	1	0	0	-	0	0-0	0	4.88	5.50

Josh Beckett

Pitches: R **Bats:** R **Pos:** SP-28   **Ht:** 6'5" **Wt:** 225 **Born:** 5/15/1980 **Age:** 33

Year	Team	Lg	G	GS	CG	GF	IP	BFP	H	R	ER	HR	SH	SF	HB	TBB	IBB	SO	WP	Bk	W	L	Pct	Sh	Sv-Op	Hld	ERC	ERA
2001	Fla	NL	4	4	0	0	24.0	99	14	9	4	3	0	0	1	11	0	24	1	0	2	2	.500	0	0-0	0	2.36	1.50
2002	Fla	NL	23	21	0	0	107.2	454	93	56	49	13	5	3	1	44	2	113	5	0	6	7	.462	0	0-0	0	3.50	4.10
2003	Fla	NL	24	23	0	1	142.0	601	132	54	48	9	5	1	2	56	4	152	6	1	9	8	.529	0	0-0	0	3.44	3.04
2004	Fla	NL	26	26	1	0	156.2	654	137	72	66	16	9	3	6	54	3	152	5	0	9	9	.500	1	0-0	0	3.32	3.79
2005	Fla	NL	29	29	2	0	178.2	728	153	75	67	14	8	2	7	58	2	166	5	0	15	8	.652	1	0-0	0	3.07	3.38
2006	Bos	AL	33	33	0	0	204.2	869	191	120	114	36	2	3	10	74	1	158	11	1	16	11	.593	0	0-0	0	4.28	5.01
2007	Bos	AL	30	30	1	0	200.2	822	189	76	73	17	3	2	5	40	0	194	3	0	20	7	.741	0	0-0	0	2.99	3.27
2008	Bos	AL	27	27	1	0	174.1	725	173	80	78	18	4	3	9	34	1	172	5	0	12	10	.545	0	0-0	0	3.45	4.03
2009	Bos	AL	32	32	4	0	212.1	883	198	99	91	25	5	5	7	55	1	199	3	1	17	6	.739	2	0-0	0	3.39	3.86
2010	Bos	AL	21	21	0	0	127.2	577	151	89	82	20	4	2	8	45	3	116	3	0	6	6	.500	0	0-0	0	5.56	5.78
2011	Bos	AL	30	30	1	0	193.0	767	146	65	62	21	8	5	9	52	1	175	6	0	13	7	.650	1	0-0	0	2.56	2.89
2012	2 Tms		28	28	0	0	170.1	730	174	91	88	21	5	8	5	52	6	132	5	0	7	14	.333	0	0-0	0	4.02	4.65
12	Bos	AL	21	21	0	0	127.1	547	131	75	74	16	3	8	5	38	2	94	4	0	5	11	.313	0	0-0	0	4.12	5.23
12	LAD	NL	7	7	0	0	43.0	183	43	16	14	5	2	0	0	14	4	38	1	0	2	3	.400	0	0-0	0	3.73	2.93
	Postseason		14	13	3	0	93.2	366	67	32	32	11	2	1	4	21	1	99	3	0	7	3	.700	3	0-0	1	2.22	3.07
	12 ML YEARS		307	304	10	1	1892.0	7909	1751	886	822	213	58	37	70	575	24	1753	58	3	132	95	.581	5	0-0	0	3.51	3.91

Gordon Beckham

Bats: R **Throws:** R **Pos:** 2B-149; PR-2; DH-1; PH-1   **Ht:** 6'0" **Wt:** 190 **Born:** 9/16/1986 **Age:** 26

						BATTING																	BASERUNNING				AVERAGES		
Year	Team	Lg	G	AB	H	2B	3B	HR	(Hm	Rd)	TB	R	RBI	RC	TBB	IBB	SO	HBP	SH	SF	SB	CS	SB%	GDP	Avg	OBP	Slg
2009	CWS	AL	103	378	102	28	1	14	(4	10)	174	58	63	60	41	0	65	6	1	4	7	4	.64	10	.270	.347	.460
2010	CWS	AL	131	444	112	25	2	9	(7	2)	168	58	49	52	37	0	92	7	6	4	4	6	.40	9	.252	.317	.378
2011	CWS	AL	150	499	115	23	0	10	(7	3)	168	60	44	48	35	0	111	13	7	3	5	3	.63	6	.230	.296	.337
2012	CWS	AL	151	525	123	24	0	16	(12	4)	195	62	60	58	40	0	89	7	8	2	5	4	.56	10	.234	.296	.371
	4 ML YEARS		535	1846	452	100	3	49	(30	19)	705	238	216	218	153	0	357	33	22	13	21	17	.55	35	.245	.312	.382

Erik Bedard

Pitches: L **Bats:** L **Pos:** SP-24   buh-DARD   **Ht:** 6'1" **Wt:** 200 **Born:** 3/5/1979 **Age:** 34

Year	Team	Lg	G	GS	CG	GF	IP	BFP	H	R	ER	HR	SH	SF	HB	TBB	IBB	SO	WP	Bk	W	L	Pct	Sh	Sv-Op	Hld	ERC	ERA
2002	Bal	AL	2	0	0	0	0.2	4	2	1	1	0	0	0	0	0	0	1	0	0	0	0	-	0	0-0	0	14.52	13.50
2004	Bal	AL	27	26	0	0	137.1	633	149	83	70	13	0	4	7	71	1	121	7	2	6	10	.375	0	0-0	0	5.11	4.59
2005	Bal	AL	24	24	0	0	141.2	606	139	66	63	10	3	6	5	57	1	125	4	1	6	8	.429	0	0-0	0	3.95	4.00
2006	Bal	AL	33	33	0	0	196.1	844	196	92	82	16	4	4	5	69	0	171	6	0	15	11	.577	0	0-0	0	3.83	3.76
2007	Bal	AL	28	28	1	0	182.0	733	141	66	64	19	2	4	5	57	0	221	3	0	13	5	.722	1	0-0	0	2.71	3.16
2008	Sea	AL	15	15	0	0	81.0	347	70	38	33	9	1	2	4	37	0	72	3	0	6	4	.600	0	0-0	0	3.82	3.67
2009	Sea	AL	15	15	0	0	83.0	348	65	29	26	8	2	1	4	34	0	90	2	0	5	3	.625	0	0-0	0	3.08	2.82
2011	2 Tms		24	24	0	0	129.1	541	118	63	52	14	1	1	1	48	0	125	5	0	5	9	.357	0	0-0	0	3.60	3.62
2012	Pit	NL	24	24	0	0	125.2	557	129	76	70	14	5	2	3	56	2	118	1	1	7	14	.333	0	0-0	0	4.52	5.01
11	Sea	AL	16	16	0	0	91.1	373	77	41	35	11	1	0	1	30	0	87	5	0	4	7	.364	0	0-0	0	3.16	3.45
11	Bos	AL	8	8	0	0	38.0	168	41	22	17	3	0	1	0	18	0	38	0	0	1	2	.333	0	0-0	0	4.70	4.03
	9 ML YEARS		192	189	1	0	1077.0	4613	1009	514	461	103	20	24	34	429	4	1044	31	4	63	64	.496	1	0-0	0	3.80	3.85

Ronald Belisario

Pitches: R **Bats:** R **Pos:** RP-68   bell-ih-SAR-ee-oh   **Ht:** 6'3" **Wt:** 245 **Born:** 12/31/1982 **Age:** 30

Year	Team	Lg	G	GS	CG	GF	IP	BFP	H	R	ER	HR	SH	SF	HB	TBB	IBB	SO	WP	Bk	W	L	Pct	Sh	Sv-Op	Hld	ERC	ERA
2012	RCuca*	A+	2	1	0	0	3.0	15	6	4	4	0	0	1	0	0	0	1	0	0	0	1	.000	0	0- -	-	7.48	12.00
2012	Albq*	AAA	2	0	0	0	1.2	9	2	2	0	0	0	0	0	2	0	0	0	0	0	0	-	0	0- -	-	7.49	0.00
2009	LAD	NL	69	0	0	13	70.2	299	52	21	16	4	3	2	6	29	7	64	4	0	4	3	.571	0	0-7	12	2.54	2.04
2010	LAD	NL	59	0	0	13	55.1	233	52	31	31	6	3	0	3	19	4	38	4	1	3	1	.750	0	2-4	16	3.72	5.04
2012	LAD	NL	68	0	0	13	71.0	286	47	22	20	3	1	0	4	29	4	69	1	0	8	1	.889	0	1-5	23	2.14	2.54
	Postseason		6	0	0	2	4.2	20	5	4	4	1	0	0	0	1	0	1	0	0	0	0	-	0	0-0	2	4.41	7.71
	3 ML YEARS		196	0	0	39	197.0	818	151	74	67	13	7	2	13	77	15	171	9	1	15	5	.750	0	3-16	51	2.70	3.06

Matt Belisle

Pitches: R **Bats:** R **Pos:** RP-80   bell-EYE-el   **Ht:** 6'4" **Wt:** 225 **Born:** 6/6/1980 **Age:** 33

Year	Team	Lg	G	GS	CG	GF	IP	BFP	H	R	ER	HR	SH	SF	HB	TBB	IBB	SO	WP	Bk	W	L	Pct	Sh	Sv-Op	Hld	ERC	ERA
2003	Cin	NL	6	0	0	2	8.2	39	10	5	5	1	2	1	1	2	0	6	0	0	1	1	.500	0	0-1	0	4.73	5.19
2005	Cin	NL	60	5	0	17	85.2	382	101	49	42	11	4	2	6	26	6	59	3	0	4	8	.333	0	1-4	8	5.08	4.41
2006	Cin	NL	30	2	0	5	40.0	180	43	18	16	5	1	2	3	19	1	26	3	0	2	0	1.000	0	0-1	0	5.29	3.60
2007	Cin	NL	30	30	1	0	177.2	771	212	111	105	26	7	9	7	43	4	125	6	1	8	9	.471	0	0-0	0	5.05	5.32
2008	Cin	NL	6	6	0	0	29.2	142	47	27	24	4	1	2	0	6	0	14	2	0	1	4	.200	0	0-0	0	6.87	7.28
2009	Col	NL	24	0	0	4	31.0	133	35	21	19	6	0	2	1	5	1	22	1	0	3	1	.750	0	0-0	4	4.50	5.52
2010	Col	NL	76	0	0	11	92.0	365	84	34	30	7	4	2	2	16	5	91	3	1	7	5	.583	0	1-2	21	2.67	2.93
2011	Col	NL	74	0	0	10	72.0	301	77	33	26	5	4	0	4	14	3	58	2	0	10	4	.714	0	0-7	14	3.65	3.25
2012	Col	NL	80	0	0	14	80.0	348	91	36	33	5	4	0	3	18	6	69	1	1	3	8	.273	0	3-10	26	3.87	3.71
	Postseason		2	0	0	0	2.0	7	0	0	0	0	0	0	0	1	0	2	0	0	0	0	-	0	0-0	1	0.27	0.00
	9 ML YEARS		386	43	1	65	616.2	2661	700	334	300	70	27	20	27	149	26	470	21	3	39	40	.494	0	5-25	70	4.42	4.38

Jeff Beliveau

Pitches: L Bats: L Pos: RP-22   BELL-iv-oh   Ht: 6'1" Wt: 195 Born: 1/17/1987 Age: 26

			HOW MUCH HE PITCHED						WHAT HE GAVE UP									THE RESULTS						
Year	Team	Lg	G	GS	CG	GF	IP	BFP	H	R	ER	HR	SH	SF	HB	TBB	IBB	SO	WP	Bk	W	L	Pct	Sh	Sv-Op Hld	ERC	ERA
2008	Cubs	R	1	0	0	0	0.2	4	1	1	1	0	0	0	0	1	0	1	1	0	0	0	-	0	0--	10.76	13.50
2008	Boise	A-	13	7	0	0	34.2	157	25	12	10	1	0	0	5	28	0	51	1	0	2	1	.667	0	0--	4.12	2.60
2009	Peoria	A	29	7	0	9	96.2	414	77	40	38	5	2	4	7	45	1	117	7	1	5	4	.556	0	3--	3.12	3.54
2010	Peoria	A	6	0	0	1	11.1	44	6	2	2	1	0	0	1	6	0	23	1	0	0	0	-	0	0--	2.51	1.59
2010	Dytona	A+	40	0	0	14	53.0	225	41	20	17	4	3	0	2	23	3	74	0	0	4	2	.667	0	2--	2.82	2.89
2011	Dytona	A+	12	0	0	3	17.1	69	13	1	1	0	2	1	2	6	2	20	0	0	0	1	.000	0	2--	2.27	0.52
2011	Tenn	AA	41	0	0	9	57.0	220	37	14	12	7	2	2	1	13	3	69	1	0	6	1	.857	0	3--	1.80	1.89
2012	Iowa	AAA	37	0	0	13	44.0	190	44	21	19	4	1	2	0	18	0	52	2	1	4	5	.444	0	2--	4.05	3.89
2012	ChC	NL	22	0	0	4	17.2	86	21	9	9	5	1	0	1	12	1	17	1	1	1	0	1.000	0	0-0 1	7.98	4.58

Heath Bell

Pitches: R Bats: R Pos: RP-73   BELL-iv-oh   Ht: 6'2" Wt: 260 Born: 9/29/1977 Age: 35

			HOW MUCH HE PITCHED						WHAT HE GAVE UP									THE RESULTS						
Year	Team	Lg	G	GS	CG	GF	IP	BFP	H	R	ER	HR	SH	SF	HB	TBB	IBB	SO	WP	Bk	W	L	Pct	Sh	Sv-Op Hld	ERC	ERA
2004	NYM	NL	17	0	0	2	24.1	94	22	9	9	5	1	0	0	6	0	27	0	0	0	2	.000	0	0-1 1	3.86	3.33
2005	NYM	NL	42	0	0	12	46.2	206	56	30	29	3	4	0	1	13	3	43	0	1	1	3	.250	0	0-0 4	4.42	5.59
2006	NYM	NL	22	0	0	6	37.0	166	51	25	21	6	1	0	0	11	2	35	1	0	0	0	-	0	0-0 0	6.40	5.11
2007	SD	NL	81	0	0	16	93.2	363	60	21	21	3	4	1	2	30	1	102	4	0	6	4	.600	0	2-6 34	1.67	2.02
2008	SD	NL	74	0	0	8	78.0	324	66	31	31	5	3	2	3	28	4	71	2	0	6	6	.500	0	0-7 23	2.93	3.58
2009	SD	NL	68	0	0	59	69.2	278	54	21	21	3	0	0	0	24	1	79	4	0	6	4	.600	0	42-48 0	2.36	2.71
2010	SD	NL	67	0	0	57	70.0	287	56	17	15	1	4	1	1	28	3	86	1	0	6	1	.857	0	47-50 0	2.47	1.93
2011	SD	NL	64	0	0	54	62.2	256	51	20	17	4	5	1	0	21	2	51	8	0	3	4	.429	0	43-48 0	2.57	2.44
2012	Mia	NL	73	0	0	41	63.2	286	70	38	36	5	2	4	2	29	3	59	2	0	4	5	.444	0	19-27 13	4.74	5.09
	9 ML YEARS		508	0	0	255	545.2	2260	486	212	200	35	24	9	9	190	19	553	22	1	32	29	.525	0	153-187 75	3.09	3.30

Josh Bell

Bats: B Throws: R Pos: 3B-12; PH-9   Ht: 6'3" Wt: 230 Born: 11/13/1986 Age: 26

			BATTING															BASERUNNING				AVERAGES		
Year	Team	Lg	G	AB	H	2B	3B	HR	(Hm | Rd)	TB	R	RBI	RC	TBB	IBB	SO	HBP	SH	SF	SB	CS	SB%	GDP	Avg	OBP	Slg
2012	Norfolk*	AAA	9	32	3	2	0	1	(- | -)	8	2	3	1	7	1	8	0	0	0	0	1	.00	0	.094	.256	.250
2012	Reno*	AAA	85	328	102	25	2	12	(- | -)	167	60	75	62	33	2	70	3	0	7	3	4	.43	9	.311	.372	.509
2010	Bal	AL	53	159	34	5	0	3	(2 | 1)	48	15	12	10	2	0	53	0	0	1	0	1	.00	4	.214	.224	.302
2011	Bal	AL	26	61	10	0	0	0	(0 | 0)	10	6	4	4	4	0	25	0	0	0	0	0	-	1	.164	.215	.164
2012	Ari	NL	21	52	9	2	0	1	(1 | 0)	14	3	4	3	4	1	14	0	0	0	0	0	-	3	.173	.232	.269
	3 ML YEARS		100	272	53	7	0	4	(3 | 1)	72	24	22	17	10	1	92	0	0	0	0	1	.00	8	.195	.223	.265

Duane Below

Pitches: L Bats: L Pos: RP-26; SP-1   BEE-low   Ht: 6'3" Wt: 220 Born: 11/15/1985 Age: 27

			HOW MUCH HE PITCHED						WHAT HE GAVE UP									THE RESULTS						
Year	Team	Lg	G	GS	CG	GF	IP	BFP	H	R	ER	HR	SH	SF	HB	TBB	IBB	SO	WP	Bk	W	L	Pct	Sh	Sv-Op Hld	ERC	ERA
2006	Tigers	R	15	4	0	2	33.2	136	27	8	6	1	1	0	0	10	0	30	2	0	2	0	1.000	0	0--	2.22	1.60
2006	Oneont	A-	2	2	0	0	9.1	44	11	6	4	0	0	0	0	5	0	8	0	0	0	0	-	0	0--	4.73	3.86
2007	WMich	A	26	26	0	0	145.2	608	128	54	48	6	1	3	3	58	0	160	9	2	13	5	.722	0	0--	3.12	2.97
2008	Lkland	A+	27	26	0	0	133.1	594	144	75	66	10	2	3	2	70	0	126	6	2	8	7	.533	0	0--	4.98	4.46
2009	Lkland	A+	6	6	0	0	28.2	123	22	11	10	4	0	3	0	14	0	38	2	0	1	4	.200	0	0--	3.32	3.14
2009	Erie	AA	2	2	0	0	11.1	48	7	4	2	1	1	1	0	6	0	7	1	0	1	0	1.000	0	0--	2.37	1.59
2010	Erie	AA	28	28	0	0	126.0	544	137	78	69	17	1	4	3	37	0	103	6	2	7	12	.368	0	0--	4.48	4.93
2011	Toledo	AAA	18	18	0	0	115.0	472	99	46	40	12	0	4	5	37	0	83	0	0	9	4	.692	0	0--	3.26	3.13
2012	Toledo	AAA	4	4	0	0	17.1	82	24	12	12	3	1	1	0	12	0	7	1	0	1	2	.333	0	0--	8.75	6.23
2011	Det	AL	14	2	0	4	29.0	127	28	16	14	2	1	3	1	11	2	14	2	0	2	0	.000	0	0-0 0	3.52	4.34
2012	Det	AL	27	1	0	7	46.1	189	49	25	20	6	2	3	1	8	0	29	1	1	2	1	.667	0	0-0 0	3.88	3.88
	2 ML YEARS		41	3	0	11	75.1	316	77	41	34	8	3	6	2	19	2	43	3	1	2	3	.400	0	0-0 0	3.74	4.06

Brandon Belt

Bats: L Throws: L Pos: 1B-139; PH-14; LF-4; PR-3   Ht: 6'5" Wt: 220 Born: 4/20/1988 Age: 25

			BATTING															BASERUNNING				AVERAGES		
Year	Team	Lg	G	AB	H	2B	3B	HR	(Hm | Rd)	TB	R	RBI	RC	TBB	IBB	SO	HBP	SH	SF	SB	CS	SB%	GDP	Avg	OBP	Slg
2010	SnJos	A+	77	269	103	28	4	10	(- | -)	169	62	62	80	58	3	50	3	0	3	18	7	.72	1	.383	.492	.628
2010	Rchmd	AA	46	175	59	11	6	9	(- | -)	109	26	40	43	22	1	34	2	0	2	2	1	.67	1	.337	.413	.623
2010	Fresno	AAA	13	48	11	4	0	4	(- | -)	27	11	10	11	13	0	15	0	0	0	2	0	1.00	0	.229	.393	.563
2011	Fresno	AAA	49	165	51	12	0	8	(- | -)	87	32	32	40	42	2	47	2	0	3	4	4	.50	1	.309	.448	.527
2011	SnJos	A+	4	13	6	1	0	0	(- | -)	7	3	4	4	5	0	1	0	0	0	1	0	1.00	0	.462	.611	.538
2011	SF	NL	63	187	42	6	1	9	(2 | 7)	77	21	18	20	20	1	57	2	0	0	3	2	.60	3	.225	.306	.412
2012	SF	NL	145	411	113	27	6	7	(5 | 2)	173	47	56	63	54	5	106	3	0	4	12	2	.86	3	.275	.360	.421
	2 ML YEARS		208	598	155	33	7	16	(7 | 9)	250	68	74	83	74	6	163	5	0	4	15	4	.79	6	.259	.344	.418

Carlos Beltran

Bats: B **Throws:** R **Pos:** RF-132; PH-15; CF-9; DH-3   BELL-trahn   **Ht:** 6'1" **Wt:** 215 **Born:** 4/24/1977 **Age:** 36

Year	Team	Lg	G	AB	H	2B	3B	HR	(Hm	Rd)	TB	R	RBI	RC	TBB	IBB	SO	HBP	SH	SF	SB	CS	SB%	GDP	Avg	OBP	Slg
1998	KC	AL	14	58	16	5	3	0	(0	0)	27	12	7	9	3	0	12	1	0	1	3	0	1.00	2	.276	.317	.466
1999	KC	AL	156	663	194	27	7	22	(12	10)	301	112	108	100	46	2	123	4	0	10	27	8	.77	17	.293	.337	.454
2000	KC	AL	98	372	92	15	4	7	(4	3)	136	49	44	43	35	2	69	0	2	4	13	0	1.00	12	.247	.309	.366
2001	KC	AL	155	617	189	32	12	24	(7	17)	317	106	101	118	52	2	120	5	1	5	31	1	**.97**	7	.306	.362	.514
2002	KC	AL	162	637	174	44	7	29	(19	10)	319	114	105	117	71	1	135	4	3	7	35	7	.83	12	.273	.346	.501
2003	KC	AL	141	521	160	14	10	26	(10	16)	272	102	100	117	72	4	81	2	0	7	41	4	**.91**	8	.307	.389	.522
2004	2 Tms		159	599	160	36	9	38	(15	23)	328	121	104	124	92	10	101	7	3	7	42	3	.93	8	.267	.367	.548
2005	NYM	NL	151	582	155	34	2	16	(6	10)	241	83	78	88	56	5	96	2	4	6	17	6	.74	9	.266	.330	.414
2006	NYM	NL	140	510	140	38	1	41	(15	26)	303	127	116	121	95	6	99	4	1	7	18	3	.86	6	.275	.388	.594
2007	NYM	NL	144	554	153	33	3	33	(11	22)	291	93	112	97	69	10	111	2	1	10	23	2	.92	8	.276	.353	.525
2008	NYM	NL	161	606	172	40	5	27	(14	13)	303	116	112	116	92	13	96	1	1	6	25	3	.89	11	.284	.376	.500
2009	NYM	NL	81	308	100	22	1	10	(3	7)	154	50	48	54	47	10	43	1	0	1	11	1	.92	9	.325	.415	.500
2010	NYM	NL	64	220	56	11	3	7	(3	4)	94	21	27	31	30	5	39	1	0	4	3	1	.75	4	.255	.341	.427
2011	2 Tms		142	520	156	39	6	22	(14	8)	273	78	84	96	71	7	88	3	0	4	4	2	.67	18	.300	.385	.525
2012	StL	NL	151	547	147	26	4	32	(20	12)	271	83	97	87	65	15	124	2	1	4	13	6	.68	5	.269	.346	.495
04	KC	AL	69	266	74	19	2	15	(8	7)	142	51	51	57	37	7	44	2	1	3	14	3	.82	4	.278	.367	.534
04	Hou	NL	90	333	86	17	7	23	(7	16)	186	70	53	67	55	3	57	5	2	4	28	0	1.00	4	.258	.368	.559
11	NYM	NL	98	353	102	30	2	15	(9	6)	181	61	66	72	60	6	61	2	0	4	3	0	1.00	9	.289	.391	.513
11	SF	NL	44	167	54	9	4	7	(5	2)	92	17	18	24	11	1	27	1	0	0	1	2	.33	9	.323	.369	.551
	Postseason		22	82	30	4	0	11	(4	7)	67	31	19	26	18	1	13	1	0	0	8	0	1.00	1	.366	.485	.817
	15 ML YEARS		1919	7314	2064	416	74	334	(153	181)	3630	1267	1243	1318	896	92	1337	39	17	83	306	47	.87	140	.282	.360	.496

Adrian Beltre

Bats: R **Throws:** R **Pos:** 3B-129; DH-23; PH-4   **Ht:** 5'11" **Wt:** 220 **Born:** 4/7/1979 **Age:** 34

Year	Team	Lg	G	AB	H	2B	3B	HR	(Hm	Rd)	TB	R	RBI	RC	TBB	IBB	SO	HBP	SH	SF	SB	CS	SB%	GDP	Avg	OBP	Slg
1998	LAD	NL	77	195	42	9	0	7	(5	2)	72	18	22	20	14	0	37	3	2	0	3	1	.75	4	.215	.278	.369
1999	LAD	NL	152	538	148	27	5	15	(6	9)	230	84	67	84	61	12	105	6	4	5	18	7	.72	4	.275	.352	.428
2000	LAD	NL	138	510	148	30	2	20	(7	13)	242	71	85	85	56	2	80	2	3	4	12	5	.71	13	.290	.360	.475
2001	LAD	NL	126	475	126	22	4	13	(4	9)	195	59	60	60	28	1	82	5	2	5	13	4	.76	9	.265	.310	.411
2002	LAD	NL	159	587	151	26	5	21	(7	14)	250	70	75	74	37	4	96	4	1	6	7	5	.58	17	.257	.303	.426
2003	LAD	NL	158	559	134	30	2	23	(13	10)	237	50	80	66	37	4	103	5	1	6	2	2	.50	13	.240	.290	.424
2004	LAD	NL	156	598	200	32	0	**48**	(23	25)	376	104	121	120	53	9	87	2	0	4	7	2	.78	15	.334	.388	.629
2005	Sea	AL	156	603	154	36	1	19	(7	12)	249	69	87	75	38	6	108	5	0	4	3	1	.75	15	.255	.303	.413
2006	Sea	AL	156	620	166	39	4	25	(16	9)	288	88	89	85	47	4	118	10	1	3	11	5	.69	15	.268	.328	.465
2007	Sea	AL	149	595	164	41	2	26	(11	15)	287	87	99	79	38	2	104	2	0	4	14	2	.88	18	.276	.319	.482
2008	Sea	AL	143	556	148	29	1	25	(10	15)	254	74	77	71	50	10	90	2	0	4	8	2	.80	11	.266	.327	.457
2009	Sea	AL	111	449	119	27	0	8	(4	4)	170	54	44	48	19	1	74	7	0	2	13	2	.87	19	.265	.304	.379
2010	Bos	AL	154	589	189	**49**	2	28	(13	15)	326	84	102	103	40	10	82	5	0	7	2	1	.67	25	.321	.365	.553
2011	Tex	AL	124	487	144	33	0	32	(23	9)	273	82	105	80	25	0	53	5	0	8	1	1	.50	13	.296	.331	.561
2012	Tex	AL	156	604	194	33	2	36	(20	16)	339	95	102	109	36	8	82	5	0	9	1	0	1.00	18	.321	.359	.561
	Postseason		21	87	23	5	0	5	(1	4)	43	15	10	8	2	1	22	2	0	1	0	0	-	1	.264	.293	.494
	15 ML YEARS		2115	7965	2227	463	30	346	(169	177)	3788	1089	1215	1159	579	73	1301	68	14	71	115	40	.74	199	.280	.331	.476

Joaquin Benoit

Pitches: R **Bats:** R **Pos:** RP-73   ben-WAH   **Ht:** 6'3" **Wt:** 220 **Born:** 7/26/1977 **Age:** 35

			HOW MUCH HE PITCHED					WHAT HE GAVE UP											THE RESULTS							
Year	Team	Lg	G	GS	CG	GF	IP	BFP	H	R	ER	HR	SH	SF	HB	TBB	IBB	SO	WP	Bk	W	L	Pct	Sh	Sv-Op	Hld	ERC	ERA
2001	Tex	AL	1	1	0	0	5.0	26	8	6	6	3	0	1	0	3	0	4	0	0	0	0	-	0	0-0	0	13.11	10.80
2002	Tex	AL	17	13	0	2	84.2	405	91	51	50	6	4	3	5	58	2	59	7	0	4	5	.444	0	1-1	0	5.52	5.31
2003	Tex	AL	25	17	0	1	105.0	462	99	67	64	23	1	4	3	51	0	87	3	1	8	5	.615	0	0-0	0	5.03	5.49
2004	Tex	AL	28	15	0	2	103.0	456	113	67	65	19	2	10	8	31	0	95	3	0	3	5	.375	0	0-0	0	5.10	5.68
2005	Tex	AL	32	9	0	6	87.0	369	69	39	36	9	2	1	2	38	0	78	1	0	4	4	.500	0	0-0	5	3.15	3.72
2006	Tex	AL	56	0	0	7	79.2	347	68	49	43	5	0	3	3	38	4	85	3	0	1	1	.500	0	0-2	7	3.30	4.86
2007	Tex	AL	70	0	0	22	82.0	337	68	28	26	6	3	2	2	28	2	87	3	0	7	4	.636	0	6-13	19	2.83	2.85
2008	Tex	AL	44	0	0	8	45.0	203	40	28	25	6	2	0	0	35	2	43	3	0	3	2	.600	0	1-4	13	5.02	5.00
2010	TB	AL	63	0	0	16	60.1	217	30	10	9	6	0	2	0	11	1	75	1	0	1	2	.333	0	1-4	25	1.14	1.34
2011	Det	AL	66	0	0	13	61.0	241	47	22	20	5	1	5	2	17	1	63	3	0	4	3	.571	0	2-7	29	2.46	2.95
2012	Det	AL	73	0	0	18	71.0	288	59	31	29	14	3	3	1	22	2	84	2	0	5	3	.625	0	2-6	30	3.48	3.68
	Postseason		8	0	0	0	11.1	39	4	1	1	1	0	0	0	3	0	12	0	0	1	0	1.000	0	0-0	3	0.92	0.79
	11 ML YEARS		475	55	0	95	783.2	3357	692	398	373	102	18	34	26	332	14	760	29	1	40	34	.541	0	13-37	128	3.80	4.28

Brad Bergesen

Pitches: R **Bats:** L **Pos:** RP-19   BURR-guess-inn   **Ht:** 6'2" **Wt:** 210 **Born:** 9/25/1985 **Age:** 27

			HOW MUCH HE PITCHED					WHAT HE GAVE UP											THE RESULTS							
Year	Team	Lg	G	GS	CG	GF	IP	BFP	H	R	ER	HR	SH	SF	HB	TBB	IBB	SO	WP	Bk	W	L	Pct	Sh	Sv-Op	Hld	ERC	ERA
2012	Norfolk*	AAA	22	10	0	4	80.1	345	90	42	36	10	4	4	2	23	1	41	1	0	4	3	.571	0	1--	-	4.61	4.03
2012	Reno*	AAA	1	1	0	0	3.2	13	1	0	0	0	1	0	0	1	0	3	0	0	0	0	-	0	0--	-	0.47	0.00
2009	Bal	AL	19	19	1	0	123.1	519	126	52	47	11	3	4	5	32	4	65	2	0	7	5	.583	0	0-0	0	3.70	3.43
2010	Bal	AL	30	28	2	1	170.0	746	193	104	94	26	5	5	7	51	4	81	0	3	8	12	.400	0	0-0	0	4.95	4.98
2011	Bal	AL	34	12	1	3	101.0	451	119	73	64	16	0	3	3	32	3	61	2	0	2	7	.222	1	0-0	0	5.22	5.70
2012	Ari	NL	19	0	0	5	29.2	121	29	14	12	2	3	1	1	7	0	18	2	0	2	1	.667	0	0-1	0	3.31	3.64
	4 ML YEARS		102	59	4	9	424.0	1837	467	243	217	55	11	13	16	122	11	225	6	3	19	25	.432	1	0-1	0	4.52	4.61

Jason Berken

Pitches: R Bats: R Pos: SP-4; RP-1   Ht: 6'0" Wt: 205 Born: 11/27/1983 Age: 29

Year	Team	Lg	G	GS	CG	GF	IP	BFP	H	R	ER	HR	SH	SF	HB	TBB	IBB	SO	WP	Bk	W	L	Pct	Sh	Sv-Op	Hld	ERC	ERA
2012	Norfolk*	AAA	26	26	1	0	144.0	615	160	73	56	10	5	6	5	39	0	98	15	1	5	6	.455	0	0- -	-	4.16	3.50
2009	Bal	AL	24	24	0	0	119.2	560	164	92	87	19	3	5	6	44	2	66	0	1	6	12	.333	0	0-0	0	6.81	6.54
2010	Bal	AL	41	0	0	8	62.1	262	64	24	21	5	4	1	0	19	3	45	3	0	3	3	.500	0	0-4	7	3.68	3.03
2011	Bal	AL	40	0	0	10	47.0	223	63	29	28	10	1	2	1	21	2	41	4	0	1	2	.333	0	0-3	4	7.18	5.36
2012	2 Tms		5	4	0	1	19.2	95	29	21	12	5	1	1	1	7	0	11	1	0	0	3	.000	0	0-0	0	8.19	5.49
12	Bal	AL	1	0	0	1	1.0	10	6	7	2	2	0	0	0	1	0	0	0	0	0	0	-	0	0-0	0	75.97	18.00
12	ChC	NL	4	4	0	0	18.2	85	23	14	10	3	1	1	1	6	0	11	1	0	0	3	.000	0	0-0	0	5.73	4.82
4 ML YEARS			110	28	0	19	248.2	1140	320	166	148	39	9	9	8	91	7	163	8	1	10	20	.333	0	0-7	11	6.15	5.36

Lance Berkman

Bats: B Throws: L Pos: 1B-23; PH-10   Ht: 6'1" Wt: 220 Born: 2/10/1976 Age: 37

Year	Team	Lg	G	AB	H	2B	3B	HR	(Hm	Rd)	TB	R	RBI	RC	TBB	IBB	SO	HBP	SH	SF	SB	CS	SB%	GDP	Avg	OBP	Slg
2012	Memp*	AAA	6	17	4	1	0	0	(-	-)	5	1	1	2	3	0	3	0	0	0	0	0	-	1	.235	.350	.294
1999	Hou	NL	34	93	22	2	0	4	(2	2)	36	10	15	12	12	0	21	0	1	0	5	1	.83	2	.237	.321	.387
2000	Hou	NL	114	353	105	28	1	21	(10	11)	198	76	67	76	56	1	73	1	0	7	6	2	.75	6	.297	.388	.561
2001	Hou	NL	156	577	191	55	5	34	(13	21)	358	110	126	144	92	5	121	13	0	6	7	9	.44	8	.331	.430	.620
2002	Hou	NL	158	578	169	35	2	42	(20	22)	334	106	128	130	107	20	118	4	0	3	8	4	.67	10	.292	.405	.578
2003	Hou	NL	153	538	155	35	6	25	(11	14)	277	110	93	115	107	13	108	9	1	3	5	3	.63	10	.288	.412	.515
2004	Hou	NL	160	544	172	40	3	30	(8	22)	308	104	106	126	127	14	101	10	0	6	9	7	.56	10	.316	.450	.566
2005	Hou	NL	132	468	137	34	1	24	(13	11)	245	76	82	88	91	12	72	4	0	2	4	1	.80	18	.293	.411	.524
2006	Hou	NL	152	536	169	29	0	45	(24	21)	333	95	136	138	98	22	106	4	0	8	3	2	.60	11	.315	.420	.621
2007	Hou	NL	153	561	156	24	2	34	(13	21)	286	95	102	105	94	11	125	8	0	5	7	3	.70	11	.278	.386	.510
2008	Hou	NL	159	554	173	46	4	29	(16	13)	314	114	106	129	99	18	108	7	0	5	18	4	.82	13	.312	.420	.567
2009	Hou	NL	136	460	126	31	1	25	(14	11)	234	73	80	83	97	14	98	1	0	4	7	4	.64	13	.274	.399	.509
2010	2 Tms		122	404	100	23	1	14	(10	4)	167	48	58	61	77	7	85	0	0	3	3	2	.60	18	.248	.368	.413
2011	StL	NL	145	488	147	23	2	31	(9	22)	267	90	94	107	92	17	93	3	0	4	2	6	.25	7	.301	.412	.547
2012	StL	NL	32	81	21	7	1	2	(0	2)	36	12	7	10	14	3	19	2	0	0	2	0	1.00	3	.259	.381	.444
10	Hou	NL	85	298	73	16	1	13	(9	4)	130	39	49	48	60	4	70	0	0	0	3	2	.60	12	.245	.372	.436
10	NYY	AL	37	106	27	7	0	1	(1	0)	37	9	9	13	17	3	15	0	0	0	0	0	-	6	.255	.358	.349
Postseason			52	186	59	11	1	9	(5	4)	99	38	41	46	31	6	41	3	0	3	4	1	.80	4	.317	.417	.532
14 ML YEARS			1806	6235	1843	412	29	360	(163	197)	3393	1119	1200	1324	1163	157	1248	66	1	54	86	48	.64	140	.296	.409	.544

Roger Bernadina

Bats: L Throws: L Pos: LF-57; PH-46; CF-37; PR-8; RF-7   burn-ah-DEEN-ah   Ht: 6'2" Wt: 215 Born: 6/12/1984 Age: 29

Year	Team	Lg	G	AB	H	2B	3B	HR	(Hm	Rd)	TB	R	RBI	RC	TBB	IBB	SO	HBP	SH	SF	SB	CS	SB%	GDP	Avg	OBP	Slg
2008	Was	NL	26	76	16	1	1	0	(0	0)	19	10	2	4	9	0	21	0	1	0	4	3	.57	3	.211	.294	.250
2009	Was	NL	3	4	1	1	0	0	(0	0)	2	1	0	1	1	0	1	0	0	0	1	0	1.00	0	.250	.400	.500
2010	Was	NL	134	414	102	18	3	11	(3	8)	159	52	47	53	35	1	93	4	2	6	16	2	.89	3	.246	.307	.384
2011	Was	NL	91	309	75	12	2	7	(5	2)	112	40	27	34	22	1	63	4	2	0	17	3	.85	7	.243	.301	.362
2012	Was	NL	129	227	66	11	0	5	(1	4)	92	25	25	40	28	3	53	2	3	1	15	3	.83	2	.291	.372	.405
5 ML YEARS			383	1030	260	43	6	23	(9	14)	384	128	101	132	95	5	231	10	8	7	53	11	.83	15	.252	.320	.373

Quintin Berry

Bats: L Throws: L Pos: LF-64; CF-22; PH-9; PR-6; RF-5; DH-3   Ht: 6'1" Wt: 175 Born: 11/21/1984 Age: 28

Year	Team	Lg	G	AB	H	2B	3B	HR	(Hm	Rd)	TB	R	RBI	RC	TBB	IBB	SO	HBP	SH	SF	SB	CS	SB%	GDP	Avg	OBP	Slg
2006	Batvia	A-	62	210	46	2	2	0	(-	-)	52	34	13	21	25	1	51	5	5	2	19	4	.83	0	.219	.314	.248
2007	Lakwd	A	126	487	152	19	4	3	(-	-)	188	86	44	86	61	0	85	12	12	9	55	18	.75	6	.312	.395	.386
2008	Clrwtr	A+	134	511	139	24	1	3	(-	-)	174	63	43	74	65	1	103	6	7	1	51	14	.78	6	.272	.360	.341
2009	Rdng	AA	135	516	137	17	2	5	(-	-)	173	89	28	72	63	2	118	9	10	0	48	14	.77	10	.266	.355	.335
2010	Rdng	AA	66	238	50	10	2	2	(-	-)	70	35	25	27	33	0	50	3	9	2	23	6	.79	6	.210	.312	.294
2010	SnAnt	AA	33	110	23	1	1	1	(-	-)	29	11	8	9	10	0	28	3	1	0	4	2	.67	1	.209	.293	.264
2011	Carlina	AA	93	320	95	16	1	6	(-	-)	131	64	41	61	52	1	83	3	2	1	40	7	.85	4	.297	.399	.409
2011	Lsvlle	AAA	4	18	1	0	0	0	(-	-)	1	2	0	0	0	0	4	0	1	0	2	0	1.00	0	.056	.056	.056
2012	Toledo	AAA	39	159	43	8	0	0	(-	-)	51	18	11	24	22	0	46	3	2	1	19	3	.86	1	.270	.368	.321
2012	Det	AL	94	291	75	10	6	2	(1	1)	103	44	29	44	25	0	80	7	6	1	21	0	1.00	4	.258	.330	.354

Rafael Betancourt

Pitches: R Bats: R Pos: RP-60   BETT-an-court   Ht: 6'2" Wt: 220 Born: 4/29/1975 Age: 38

Year	Team	Lg	G	GS	CG	GF	IP	BFP	H	R	ER	HR	SH	SF	HB	TBB	IBB	SO	WP	Bk	W	L	Pct	Sh	Sv-Op	Hld	ERC	ERA
2003	Cle	AL	33	0	0	13	38.0	154	27	11	9	5	1	1	1	13	2	36	1	0	2	2	.500	0	1-3	4	2.54	2.13
2004	Cle	AL	68	0	0	21	66.2	286	71	32	29	7	1	2	0	18	6	76	5	1	5	6	.455	0	4-11	12	3.77	3.92
2005	Cle	AL	54	0	0	12	67.2	272	57	23	21	5	1	0	0	17	2	73	0	0	4	3	.571	0	1-3	10	2.49	2.79
2006	Cle	AL	50	0	0	11	56.2	231	52	25	24	7	2	2	0	11	5	48	0	0	3	4	.429	0	3-6	7	2.84	3.81
2007	Cle	AL	68	0	0	15	79.1	289	51	13	13	4	0	2	0	9	3	80	0	0	5	1	.833	0	3-6	31	1.24	1.47
2008	Cle	AL	69	0	0	20	71.0	309	76	41	40	11	4	5	0	25	5	64	2	0	3	4	.429	0	4-8	12	5.43	5.07
2009	2 Tms		61	0	0	10	56.0	227	42	20	17	4	2	4	0	20	5	61	0	0	4	3	.571	0	2-6	20	2.30	2.73
2010	Col	NL	72	0	0	18	62.1	248	52	25	25	9	3	1	0	8	2	89	7	0	5	1	.833	0	1-5	23	2.35	3.61
2011	Col	NL	68	0	0	24	62.1	237	46	21	20	7	0	2	0	8	0	73	1	2	2	0	1.000	0	8-12	22	1.84	2.89
2012	Col	NL	60	0	0	53	57.2	236	53	19	18	6	2	0	1	12	4	57	0	1	1	4	.200	0	31-38	1	2.81	2.81

Year	Team	Lg	G	GS	CG	GF	IP	BFP	H	R	ER	HR	SH	SF	HB	TBB	IBB	SO	WP	Bk	W	L	Pct	Sh	Sv-Op	Hld	ERC	ERA
			HOW MUCH HE PITCHED						**WHAT HE GAVE UP**												**THE RESULTS**							
09	Cle	AL	29	0	0	7	30.2	129	25	15	12	3	1	2	0	15	4	32	0	0	1	2	.333	0	1-3	8	3.21	3.52
09	Col	NL	32	0	0	3	25.1	98	17	5	5	1	1	2	0	5	1	29	0	0	3	1	.750	0	1-3	12	1.42	1.78
	Postseason		10	0	0	2	12.1	49	9	8	7	2	1	1	0	2	1	12	0	0	-	0		0	0-0	1	1.98	5.11
	10 ML YEARS		603	0	0	203	617.2	2489	527	230	216	65	16	21	1	141	34	657	16	4	34	28	.548	0	58-98	142	2.60	3.15

Yuniesky Betancourt

Bats: R **Throws:** R **Pos:** 2B-46; 3B-8; PH-5; SS-1; DH-1   yoo-NESS-kee BETT-an-coor   **Ht:** 5'11" **Wt:** 205 **Born:** 1/31/1982 **Age:** 31

Year	Team	Lg	G	AB	H	2B	3B	HR	(Hm	Rd)	TB	R	RBI	RC	TBB	IBB	SO	HBP	SH	SF	SB	CS	SB%	GDP	Avg	OBP	Slg
								BATTING													**BASERUNNING**				**AVERAGES**		
2012	NWArk*	AA	4	15	5	1	0	1	(-	-)	9	1	4	2	0	0	3	0	0	0	0	0	-	0	.333	.333	.600
2012	Omha*	AAA	2	8	5	0	0	1	(-	-)	8	1	2	3	0	0	0	0	0	0	0	0	-	1	.625	.625	1.000
2005	Sea	AL	60	211	54	11	5	1	(0	1)	78	24	15	21	11	0	24	2	2	2	1	3	.25	2	.256	.296	.370
2006	Sea	AL	157	558	161	28	6	8	(2	6)	225	68	47	60	17	0	54	1	7	1	11	8	.58	10	.289	.310	.403
2007	Sea	AL	155	536	155	38	2	9	(6	3)	224	72	67	73	15	3	48	1	3	4	5	4	.56	10	.289	.308	.418
2008	Sea	AL	153	559	156	36	3	7	(3	4)	219	66	51	53	17	0	42	2	6	6	4	4	.50	23	.279	.300	.392
2009	2 Tms	AL	134	470	115	20	6	6	(2	4)	165	40	49	41	21	0	44	0	11	6	3	3	.50	17	.245	.274	.351
2010	KC	AL	151	556	144	29	2	16	(8	8)	225	60	78	56	23	1	64	1	4	4	2	3	.40	13	.259	.288	.405
2011	Mil	NL	152	556	140	27	3	13	(8	5)	212	51	68	47	16	3	63	2	0	10	4	4	.50	16	.252	.271	.381
2012	KC	AL	57	215	49	14	1	7	(4	3)	86	21	36	19	9	0	25	0	1	3	0	1	.00	16	.228	.256	.400
09	Sea	AL	63	224	56	10	1	2	(1	1)	74	15	22	19	10	0	18	0	8	3	3	1	.75	9	.250	.278	.330
09	KC	AL	71	246	59	10	5	4	(1	3)	91	25	27	22	11	0	26	0	3	3	0	2	.00	8	.240	.269	.370
	Postseason		11	42	13	3	1	1	(1	0)	21	7	6	8	1	0	4	0	0	0	0	0	-	1	.310	.326	.500
	8 ML YEARS		1019	3661	974	203	28	67	(34	33)	1434	402	411	370	129	7	364	9	34	36	30	30	.50	101	.266	.290	.392

Wilson Betemit

Bats: B **Throws:** R **Pos:** 3B-75; 1B-15; DH-8; LF-5; PH-5   BETT-uh-meet   **Ht:** 6'2" **Wt:** 220 **Born:** 11/2/1981 **Age:** 31

Year	Team	Lg	G	AB	H	2B	3B	HR	(Hm	Rd)	TB	R	RBI	RC	TBB	IBB	SO	HBP	SH	SF	SB	CS	SB%	GDP	Avg	OBP	Slg
								BATTING													**BASERUNNING**				**AVERAGES**		
2012	Bowie*	AA	2	8	2	0	0	1	(-	-)	5	1	4	1	0	0	1	0	0	0	0	0	-	0	.250	.250	.625
2001	Atl	NL	8	3	0	0	0	0	(0	0)	0	1	0	0	2	0	3	0	0	0	1	0	1.00	0	.000	.400	.000
2004	Atl	NL	22	47	8	0	0	0	(0	0)	8	2	3	0	4	0	16	0	0	1	0	1	.00	0	.170	.231	.170
2005	Atl	NL	115	246	75	12	4	4	(0	4)	107	36	20	36	22	4	55	0	4	2	1	3	.25	5	.305	.359	.435
2006	2 Tms	NL	143	373	98	23	0	18	(7	11)	175	49	53	52	36	6	102	0	1	2	3	1	.75	11	.263	.326	.469
2007	2 Tms		121	240	55	12	0	14	(8	6)	109	33	50	42	38	0	82	1	2	3	0	0	-	2	.229	.333	.454
2008	NYY	AL	87	189	50	13	0	6	(5	1)	81	24	25	17	6	0	56	1	1	1	0	1	.00	7	.265	.289	.429
2009	CWS	AL	20	45	9	5	0	0	(0	0)	14	2	3	3	5	0	13	0	0	0	0	0	-	2	.200	.280	.311
2010	KC	AL	84	276	82	20	0	13	(7	6)	141	36	43	48	36	2	74	1	0	2	0	0	-	3	.297	.378	.511
2011	2 Tms	AL	97	323	92	22	4	8	(6	2)	146	40	46	50	31	6	105	0	0	5	4	1	.80	7	.285	.343	.452
2012	Bal	AL	102	341	89	19	0	12	(7	5)	144	40	40	42	31	0	103	1	0	3	0	1	.00	8	.261	.322	.422
06	Atl	NL	88	199	56	16	0	9	(3	6)	99	30	29	35	19	3	57	0	1	0	2	1	.67	4	.281	.344	.497
06	LAD	NL	55	174	42	7	0	9	(4	5)	76	19	24	17	17	3	45	0	0	2	1	0	1.00	7	.241	.306	.437
07	Atl	NL	84	156	36	8	0	10	(6	4)	74	22	26	26	32	0	49	1	0	3	0	0	-	1	.231	.359	.474
07	NYY	AL	37	84	19	4	0	4	(2	2)	35	11	24	16	6	0	33	0	2	0	0	0	-	1	.226	.278	.417
11	KC	AL	57	203	57	15	1	3	(2	1)	83	29	27	30	20	6	58	0	0	3	3	1	.75	6	.281	.341	.409
11	Det	AL	40	120	35	7	3	5	(4	1)	63	11	19	20	11	0	47	0	0	2	1	0	1.00	1	.292	.346	.525
	Postseason		10	19	5	1	0	1	(0	1)	9	3	1	2	2	1	7	0	0	0	0	0	-	1	.263	.333	.474
	10 ML YEARS		799	2083	558	126	8	75	(40	35)	925	264	283	290	211	18	609	4	8	19	9	8	.53	45	.268	.334	.444

Jeff Bianchi

Bats: R **Throws:** R **Pos:** SS-14; PH-13; 3B-6; 2B-4   bee-YANK-ee   **Ht:** 5'11" **Wt:** 180 **Born:** 10/5/1986 **Age:** 26

Year	Team	Lg	G	AB	H	2B	3B	HR	(Hm	Rd)	TB	R	RBI	RC	TBB	IBB	SO	HBP	SH	SF	SB	CS	SB%	GDP	Avg	OBP	Slg
								BATTING													**BASERUNNING**				**AVERAGES**		
2005	Royals	R	28	98	40	7	4	6	(-	-)	73	29	30	33	16	0	22	3	0	5	5	2	.71	2	.408	.484	.745
2006	Royals	R	12	42	18	4	0	2	(-	-)	28	13	6	14	9	0	3	2	0	1	1	1	.50	0	.429	.537	.667
2007	Burlgtn	A	99	368	91	19	0	2	(-	-)	116	43	36	37	25	3	72	3	1	6	15	4	.79	10	.247	.296	.315
2008	Wilmg	A+	104	396	101	34	5	10	(-	-)	175	57	61	53	20	1	95	3	4	8	13	4	.76	7	.255	.290	.442
2009	Wilmg	A+	60	220	66	12	2	4	(-	-)	94	32	28	36	20	3	47	1	3	1	12	2	.86	3	.300	.360	.427
2009	NWArk	AA	68	270	85	17	1	5	(-	-)	119	42	42	44	19	0	58	1	2	5	10	4	.71	2	.315	.356	.441
2011	NWArk	AA	119	444	115	23	2	2	(-	-)	148	63	48	53	39	0	85	3	9	4	20	5	.80	7	.259	.320	.333
2012	Hntsvl	AA	19	77	27	4	0	0	(-	-)	31	11	6	12	6	1	11	0	2	0	3	1	.75	1	.351	.398	.403
2012	Nashv	AAA	73	249	79	13	1	5	(-	-)	109	33	19	42	22	1	48	1	5	1	11	5	.69	3	.317	.374	.438
2012	Mil	NL	33	69	13	2	0	3	(1	2)	24	8	9	6	4	0	13	0	2	1	0	0	-	1	.188	.230	.348

Chad Billingsley

Pitches: R **Bats:** R **Pos:** SP-25   **Ht:** 6'1" **Wt:** 240 **Born:** 7/29/1984 **Age:** 28

Year	Team	Lg	G	GS	CG	GF	IP	BFP	H	R	ER	HR	SH	SF	HB	TBB	IBB	SO	WP	Bk	W	L	Pct	Sh	Sv-Op	Hld	ERC	ERA
			HOW MUCH HE PITCHED						**WHAT HE GAVE UP**												**THE RESULTS**							
2006	LAD	NL	18	16	0	0	90.0	403	92	43	38	7	4	0	3	58	3	59	5	0	7	4	.636	0	0-0	0	5.22	3.80
2007	LAD	NL	43	20	1	6	147.0	623	131	56	54	15	9	3	3	64	3	141	5	0	12	5	.706	0	0-1	3	3.70	3.31
2008	LAD	NL	35	32	1	1	200.2	859	188	76	70	14	8	5	8	80	6	201	10	0	16	10	.615	1	0-0	1	3.62	3.14
2009	LAD	NL	33	32	0	0	196.1	823	173	94	88	17	9	11	7	86	7	179	14	0	12	11	.522	0	0-0	0	3.63	4.03
2010	LAD	NL	31	31	1	0	191.2	817	176	82	76	8	7	11	10	69	7	171	4	0	12	11	.522	1	0-0	0	3.20	3.57
2011	LAD	NL	32	32	1	0	188.0	829	189	98	88	14	13	8	7	84	4	152	5	0	11	11	.500	0	0-0	0	4.19	4.21
2012	LAD	NL	25	25	0	0	149.2	634	148	66	59	11	6	3	5	45	2	128	5	0	10	9	.526	0	0-0	0	3.55	3.55
	Postseason		6	3	0	0	17.0	78	20	14	13	1	0	0	0	10	2	22	2	0	1	2	.333	0	0-0	0	5.40	6.88
	7 ML YEARS		217	188	4	7	1163.1	4988	1097	515	473	86	56	41	43	486	32	1031	48	0	80	61	.567	2	0-1	4	3.76	3.66

Brian Bixler

Bats: R Throws: R Pos: PH-10; RF-9; SS-6; 2B-5; 3B-4; LF-3; PR-2   Ht: 6'1" Wt: 195 Born: 10/22/1982 Age: 30

						BATTING														BASERUNNING				AVERAGES		
Year	Team	Lg	G	AB	H	2B	3B	HR	(Hm	Rd)	TB	R	RBI	RC	TBB	IBB	SO	HBP	SH	SF	SB	CS	SB%	GDP	Avg	OBP	Slg
2012	OKCity*	AAA	75	249	67	12	1	3	(-	-)	90	43	19	34	27	0	59	3	1	1	11	2	.85	4	.269	.346	.361
2008	Pit	NL	50	108	17	2	1	0	(0	0)	21	16	2	2	6	2	36	4	2	0	1	0	1.00	1	.157	.229	.194
2009	Pit	NL	18	44	10	5	0	0	(0	0)	15	5	3	3	2	0	26	0	0	0	1	0	1.00	0	.227	.261	.341
2011	Was	NL	79	83	17	1	2	0	(0	0)	22	9	2	5	7	3	19	0	4	0	4	3	.57	1	.205	.267	.265
2012	Hou	NL	36	88	17	6	0	2	(2	0)	29	11	7	7	7	0	36	0	1	0	3	0	1.00	0	.193	.253	.330
	4 ML YEARS		183	323	61	14	3	2	(2	0)	87	41	14	17	22	5	117	4	7	0	9	3	.75	2	.189	.249	.269

Nick Blackburn

Pitches: R Bats: R Pos: SP-19   Ht: 6'4" Wt: 240 Born: 2/24/1982 Age: 31

			HOW MUCH HE PITCHED					WHAT HE GAVE UP											THE RESULTS						
Year	Team	Lg	G	GS	CG	GF	IP	BFP	H	R	ER	HR	SH	SF	HB	TBB	IBB	SO	WP	Bk	W	L	Pct	Sh	Sv-Op	Hld	ERC	ERA
2012	Roch*	AAA	7	7	1	0	36.2	151	42	16	11	2	2	1	0	9	0	11	1	0	3	1	.750	0	0--	-	4.15	2.70
2007	Min	AL	6	0	0	3	11.2	54	19	12	10	2	0	0	0	2	0	8	0	0	0	2	.000	0	0-1	1	7.61	7.71
2008	Min	AL	33	33	0	0	193.1	823	224	102	87	23	5	4	7	39	4	96	2	0	11	11	.500	0	0-0	0	4.48	4.05
2009	Min	AL	33	33	3	0	205.2	882	240	103	92	25	5	5	3	41	1	98	2	0	11	11	.500	0	0-0	0	4.42	4.03
2010	Min	AL	28	26	1	2	161.0	692	194	101	97	25	2	3	4	40	1	68	3	1	10	12	.455	0	0-0	0	5.24	5.42
2011	Min	AL	26	26	1	0	148.1	670	183	91	74	19	4	5	4	54	5	76	5	0	7	10	.412	0	0-0	0	5.56	4.49
2012	Min	AL	19	19	0	0	98.2	456	143	81	81	23	2	6	1	26	0	42	2	0	4	9	.308	0	0-0	0	7.30	7.39
	Postseason		1	1	0	0	5.2	22	3	1	1	0	0	0	0	2	0	3	0	0	0	0	-	0	0-0	0	1.21	1.59
	6 ML YEARS		145	137	5	5	818.2	3577	1003	490	441	117	21	23	19	202	11	388	14	1	43	55	.439	0	0-1	1	5.17	4.85

Travis Blackley

Pitches: L Bats: L Pos: SP-15; RP-13   Ht: 6'3" Wt: 205 Born: 11/4/1982 Age: 30

			HOW MUCH HE PITCHED					WHAT HE GAVE UP											THE RESULTS						
Year	Team	Lg	G	GS	CG	GF	IP	BFP	H	R	ER	HR	SH	SF	HB	TBB	IBB	SO	WP	Bk	W	L	Pct	Sh	Sv-Op	Hld	ERC	ERA
2012	Fresno*	AAA	4	3	0	1	23.1	104	13	1	1	0	0	0	0	3	0	19	1	0	3	0	1.000	0	1--	-	1.04	0.39
2004	Sea	AL	6	6	0	0	26.0	134	35	31	29	9	1	1	1	22	0	16	3	1	1	3	.250	0	0-0	0	10.52	10.04
2007	SF	NL	2	2	0	0	8.2	40	10	7	7	2	1	0	0	5	0	5	0	1	0	0	-	0	0-0	0	6.78	7.27
2012	2 Tms		28	15	0	6	107.2	444	98	53	49	10	3	3	3	32	1	71	7	3	6	4	.600	0	0-0	0	3.27	4.10
12	SF	NL	4	0	0	1	5.0	25	7	6	5	0	2	0	0	2	0	2	1	0	0	0	-	0	0-0	0	5.23	9.00
12	Oak	AL	24	15	0	5	102.2	419	91	47	44	10	1	3	3	30	1	69	6	3	6	4	.600	0	0-0	0	3.18	3.86
	3 ML YEARS		36	23	0	6	142.1	618	143	91	85	21	5	4	4	59	1	92	10	5	7	7	.500	0	0-0	0	4.62	5.37

Charlie Blackmon

Bats: L Throws: L Pos: RF-17; LF-15; PH-11; PR-2; CF-1   Ht: 6'3" Wt: 210 Born: 7/1/1986 Age: 26

						BATTING														BASERUNNING				AVERAGES		
Year	Team	Lg	G	AB	H	2B	3B	HR	(Hm	Rd)	TB	R	RBI	RC	TBB	IBB	SO	HBP	SH	SF	SB	CS	SB%	GDP	Avg	OBP	Slg
2008	TriCity	A-	68	290	98	21	5	2	(-	-)	135	42	33	52	16	2	37	10	3	2	13	7	.65	2	.338	.390	.466
2009	Mdest	A+	133	550	169	34	7	7	(-	-)	238	87	69	92	39	1	83	19	3	5	30	13	.70	5	.307	.370	.433
2010	Tulsa	AA	86	337	100	22	4	11	(-	-)	163	53	55	61	32	2	43	4	3	5	19	7	.73	6	.297	.360	.484
2011	ColSpr	AAA	58	243	82	19	4	10	(-	-)	139	49	49	53	19	0	34	5	2	3	12	5	.71	2	.337	.393	.572
2012	ColSpr	AAA	59	228	69	18	4	5	(-	-)	110	55	34	45	29	1	42	3	2	2	10	0	1.00	6	.303	.385	.482
2012	TriCity	A-	17	59	14	5	0	1	(-	-)	22	8	3	9	7	0	10	3	0	0	3	0	1.00	1	.237	.348	.373
2011	Col	NL	27	98	25	1	0	1	(1	0)	29	9	8	10	3	1	8	0	1	0	5	1	.83	2	.255	.277	.296
2012	Col	NL	42	113	32	8	0	2	(1	1)	46	15	9	11	4	0	17	3	1	0	1	2	.33	4	.283	.325	.407
	2 ML YEARS		69	211	57	9	0	3	(2	1)	75	24	17	21	7	1	25	3	2	0	6	3	.67	6	.270	.303	.355

Gregor Blanco

Bats: L Throws: L Pos: RF-54; LF-53; CF-30; PH-21; PR-7; DH-1   Ht: 5'11" Wt: 185 Born: 12/24/1983 Age: 29

						BATTING														BASERUNNING				AVERAGES		
Year	Team	Lg	G	AB	H	2B	3B	HR	(Hm	Rd)	TB	R	RBI	RC	TBB	IBB	SO	HBP	SH	SF	SB	CS	SB%	GDP	Avg	OBP	Slg
2008	Atl	NL	144	430	108	14	4	1	(0	1)	133	52	38	60	74	2	99	6	6	3	13	5	.72	3	.251	.366	.309
2009	Atl	NL	24	43	8	0	1	0	(0	0)	10	5	1	2	4	0	9	0	1	0	2	0	1.00	1	.186	.255	.233
2010	2 Tms		85	237	67	9	4	1	(1	0)	87	31	14	30	29	1	50	0	2	1	11	4	.73	5	.283	.360	.367
2012	SF	NL	141	393	96	14	5	5	(2	3)	135	56	34	50	51	2	104	2	5	2	26	6	.81	6	.244	.333	.344
10	Atl	NL	36	58	18	1	1	0	(0	0)	21	9	3	8	8	1	15	0	0	0	1	2	.33	2	.310	.394	.362
10	KC	AL	49	179	49	8	3	1	(1	0)	66	22	11	22	21	0	35	0	2	1	10	2	.83	3	.274	.348	.369
	4 ML YEARS		394	1103	279	37	14	7	(3	4)	365	144	87	142	158	5	262	8	14	6	52	15	.78	9	.253	.349	.331

Henry Blanco

Bats: R Throws: R Pos: C-21; PH-2   Ht: 5'11" Wt: 220 Born: 8/29/1971 Age: 41

						BATTING														BASERUNNING				AVERAGES		
Year	Team	Lg	G	AB	H	2B	3B	HR	(Hm	Rd)	TB	R	RBI	RC	TBB	IBB	SO	HBP	SH	SF	SB	CS	SB%	GDP	Avg	OBP	Slg
1997	LAD	NL	3	5	2	0	0	1	(0	1)	5	1	1	2	0	0	1	0	0	0	0	0	-	0	.400	.400	1.000
1999	Col	NL	88	263	61	12	3	6	(3	3)	97	30	28	32	34	1	38	1	3	2	1	1	.50	4	.232	.320	.369
2000	Mil	NL	93	284	67	24	0	7	(3	4)	112	29	31	33	36	6	60	0	0	4	0	3	.00	9	.236	.318	.394
2001	Mil	NL	104	314	66	18	3	6	(2	4)	108	33	31	30	34	4	72	2	5	2	3	1	.75	10	.210	.290	.344
2002	Atl	NL	81	221	45	9	1	6	(4	2)	74	17	22	15	20	5	51	1	2	5	0	2	.00	5	.204	.267	.335
2003	Atl	NL	55	151	30	8	0	1	(0	1)	41	11	13	13	10	2	21	1	3	1	0	0	-	3	.199	.252	.272
2004	Min	AL	114	315	65	19	1	10	(4	6)	116	36	37	25	21	0	56	3	11	3	0	0	.00	8	.206	.260	.368
2005	ChC	NL	54	161	39	6	0	6	(2	4)	63	16	25	17	11	1	24	0	4	2	0	0	-	6	.242	.287	.391
2006	ChC	NL	74	241	64	15	2	6	(2	4)	101	23	37	26	14	1	38	0	0	2	0	0	-	8	.266	.304	.419

			BATTING																				BASERUNNING				AVERAGES		
Year	Team	Lg	G	AB	H	2B	3B	HR	(Hm	Rd)	TB	R	RBI	RC	TBB	IBB	SO	HBP	SH	SF	SB	CS	SB%	GDP	Avg	OBP	Slg
2007	ChC	NL	22	54	9	3	0	0	(0	0)	12	3	4	2	2	0	12	0	1	1	0	0	-	0	.167	.193	.222
2008	ChC	NL	58	120	35	3	0	3	(2	1)	47	15	12	11	6	1	22	0	2	0	0	0	-	4	.292	.325	.392
2009	SD	NL	67	204	48	12	0	6	(4	2)	78	21	16	20	26	2	50	0	1	1	0	0	-	5	.235	.320	.382
2010	NYM	NL	50	130	28	5	0	2	(2	0)	39	10	8	7	11	2	26	0	0	3	1	0	1.00	1	.215	.271	.300
2011	Ari	NL	37	100	25	3	1	8	(6	2)	54	12	12	13	12	1	21	0	0	0	1	1	.00	2	.250	.330	.540
2012	Ari	NL	21	64	12	3	0	1	(0	1)	18	6	7	6	3	0	18	0	0	0	1	0	1.00	1	.188	.224	.281
	Postseason		7	15	3	0	0	1	(1	0)	6	1	2	0	0	0	4	0	1	1	0	0	-	1	.200	.188	.400
	15 ML YEARS		921	2627	596	140	11	69	(36	33)	965	263	284	252	240	28	510	8	36	26	6	11	.35	66	.227	.291	.367

Kyle Blanks

Bats: R **Throws:** R **Pos:** PH-3; 1B-1; LF-1   **Ht:** 6'6" **Wt:** 270 **Born:** 9/11/1986 **Age:** 26

			BATTING																				BASERUNNING				AVERAGES		
Year	Team	Lg	G	AB	H	2B	3B	HR	(Hm	Rd)	TB	R	RBI	RC	TBB	IBB	SO	HBP	SH	SF	SB	CS	SB%	GDP	Avg	OBP	Slg
2009	SD	NL	54	148	37	9	0	10	(6	4)	76	24	22	21	18	1	55	6	0	0	1	1	.50	4	.250	.355	.514
2010	SD	NL	33	102	16	6	1	3	(2	1)	33	14	15	10	15	0	46	3	0	0	1	0	1.00	1	.157	.283	.324
2011	SD	NL	55	170	39	7	1	7	(2	5)	69	21	26	16	16	0	51	2	0	2	2	0	1.00	3	.229	.300	.406
2012	SD	NL	4	5	1	0	0	0	(0	0)	1	0	0	0	1	0	2	0	0	0	0	0	-	0	.200	.333	.200
	4 ML YEARS		146	425	93	22	2	20	(10	10)	179	59	63	47	50	1	154	11	0	2	4	1	.80	8	.219	.316	.421

Joe Blanton

Pitches: R **Bats:** R **Pos:** SP-30; RP-1   **Ht:** 6'3" **Wt:** 235 **Born:** 12/11/1980 **Age:** 32

			HOW MUCH HE PITCHED						WHAT HE GAVE UP										THE RESULTS							
Year	Team	Lg	G	GS	CG	GF	IP	BFP	H	R	ER	HR	SH	SF	HB	TBB	IBB	SO	WP	Bk	W	L	Pct	Sh	Sv-Op	Hld	ERC	ERA
2004	Oak	AL	3	0	0	1	8.0	30	6	5	5	1	0	0	0	2	0	6	0	0	0	0	-	0	0-0	0	2.52	5.63
2005	Oak	AL	33	33	2	0	201.1	835	178	86	79	23	2	7	5	67	3	116	4	2	12	12	.500	1	0-0	0	3.37	3.53
2006	Oak	AL	32	31	1	0	194.1	856	241	111	104	17	3	9	5	58	4	107	3	0	16	12	.571	1	0-0	0	5.09	4.82
2007	Oak	AL	34	34	3	0	230.0	950	240	106	101	16	5	8	4	40	4	140	3	1	14	10	.583	1	0-0	0	3.30	3.95
2008	2 Tms		33	33	0	0	197.2	855	211	110	103	22	2	4	4	66	3	111	2	0	9	12	.429	0	0-0	0	4.33	4.69
2009	Phi	NL	31	31	0	0	195.1	837	198	89	88	30	11	4	8	59	4	163	7	0	12	8	.600	0	0-0	0	4.25	4.05
2010	Phi	NL	29	28	0	0	175.2	765	206	104	94	27	5	7	3	43	6	134	2	0	9	6	.600	0	0-0	0	4.81	4.82
2011	Phi	NL	11	8	0	1	41.1	180	52	23	23	5	5	2	1	9	0	35	0	0	1	2	.333	0	0-0	0	5.13	5.01
2012	2 Tms	NL	31	30	2	1	191.0	806	207	106	100	29	8	4	3	34	5	166	5	0	10	13	.435	1	0-0	0	4.00	4.71
08	Oak	AL	20	20	0	0	127.0	550	145	74	70	12	1	2	1	35	3	62	1	0	5	12	.294	0	0-0	0	4.33	4.96
08	Phi	NL	13	13	0	0	70.2	305	66	36	33	10	1	2	3	31	0	49	1	0	4	0	1.000	0	0-0	0	4.33	4.20
12	Phi	NL	21	20	2	1	133.1	560	141	74	68	22	6	3	3	18	2	115	4	0	8	9	.471	1	0-0	0	3.77	4.59
12	LAD	NL	10	10	0	0	57.2	246	66	32	32	7	2	1	0	16	3	51	1	0	2	4	.333	0	0-0	0	4.54	4.99
	Postseason		10	6	0	1	40.1	172	36	19	18	5	1	1	3	13	2	33	2	0	2	0	1.000	0	0-0	0	3.51	4.02
	9 ML YEARS		237	228	8	3	1434.2	6114	1539	740	697	170	41	45	33	378	29	978	26	3	83	75	.525	3	0-0	0	4.14	4.37

Jerry Blevins

Pitches: L **Bats:** L **Pos:** RP-63   **Ht:** 6'6" **Wt:** 175 **Born:** 9/6/1983 **Age:** 29

			HOW MUCH HE PITCHED						WHAT HE GAVE UP										THE RESULTS							
Year	Team	Lg	G	GS	CG	GF	IP	BFP	H	R	ER	HR	SH	SF	HB	TBB	IBB	SO	WP	Bk	W	L	Pct	Sh	Sv-Op	Hld	ERC	ERA
2007	Oak	AL	6	0	0	1	4.2	25	8	6	5	1	0	0	0	2	0	3	0	0	0	1	.000	0	0-0	0	9.08	9.64
2008	Oak	AL	36	0	0	8	37.2	156	32	14	13	2	0	1	3	13	2	35	0	0	1	3	.250	0	0-1	5	3.00	3.11
2009	Oak	AL	20	0	0	5	22.1	90	19	12	12	2	1	0	0	6	1	23	0	0	0	0	-	0	0-0	0	2.68	4.84
2010	Oak	AL	63	0	0	9	48.2	220	54	20	20	7	3	1	1	18	1	46	0	0	2	1	.667	0	1-2	11	4.81	3.70
2011	Oak	AL	26	0	0	11	28.1	122	24	14	9	2	2	3	1	14	1	26	0	0	0	0	-	0	0-0	0	3.45	2.86
2012	Oak	AL	63	0	0	17	65.1	261	45	20	18	7	5	2	5	25	5	54	2	0	5	1	.833	0	1-1	14	2.66	2.48
	6 ML YEARS		214	0	0	51	207.0	874	182	86	77	21	10	8	10	78	10	187	2	0	8	6	.571	0	2-4	30	3.45	3.35

Willie Bloomquist

Bats: R **Throws:** R **Pos:** SS-64; 3B-11; PH-4; 2B-1; LF-1; RF-1; PR-1   **Ht:** 5'11" **Wt:** 185 **Born:** 11/27/1977 **Age:** 35

			BATTING																				BASERUNNING				AVERAGES		
Year	Team	Lg	G	AB	H	2B	3B	HR	(Hm	Rd)	TB	R	RBI	RC	TBB	IBB	SO	HBP	SH	SF	SB	CS	SB%	GDP	Avg	OBP	Slg
2012	DBcks*	R	4	9	3	1	1	0	(-	-)	6	3	4	2	1	0	1	0	0	0	0	0	-	0	.333	.400	.667
2002	Sea	AL	12	33	15	4	0	0	(0	0)	19	11	7	10	5	0	2	0	0	0	3	1	.75	0	.455	.526	.576
2003	Sea	AL	89	196	49	7	2	1	(1	0)	63	30	14	18	19	1	39	1	2	2	4	1	.80	6	.250	.317	.321
2004	Sea	AL	93	188	46	10	2	0	(0	2)	62	27	18	18	10	0	48	0	3	0	13	2	.87	2	.245	.283	.330
2005	Sea	AL	82	249	64	15	2	0	(0	0)	83	27	22	26	11	0	38	1	4	2	14	1	.93	5	.257	.289	.333
2006	Sea	AL	102	251	62	6	2	1	(0	1)	75	36	15	27	24	0	40	4	2	2	16	3	.84	3	.247	.320	.299
2007	Sea	AL	91	173	48	3	0	2	(1	1)	57	28	13	16	10	0	35	1	4	0	7	5	.58	7	.277	.321	.329
2008	Sea	AL	71	165	46	1	0	0	(0	0)	47	32	9	24	25	1	29	1	1	0	14	3	.82	1	.279	.377	.285
2009	KC	AL	125	434	115	11	8	4	(0	4)	154	52	29	45	27	1	73	1	4	2	25	6	.81	7	.265	.308	.355
2010	2 Tms		83	187	50	10	1	3	(2	1)	71	31	17	19	9	0	28	0	2	1	8	5	.62	4	.267	.299	.380
2011	Ari	NL	97	350	93	10	2	4	(2	2)	119	44	26	37	23	3	51	4	2	2	20	10	.67	3	.266	.317	.340
2012	Ari	NL	80	324	98	21	5	0	(0	0)	129	47	23	46	12	0	55	0	0	2	7	10	.41	5	.302	.325	.398
10	KC	AL	72	170	45	10	1	3	(2	1)	66	31	17	18	8	0	25	0	2	1	8	5	.62	4	.265	.296	.388
10	Cin	NL	11	17	5	0	0	0	(0	0)	5	0	0	1	1	0	3	0	0	0	0	0	-	0	.294	.333	.294
	Postseason		5	22	7	0	0	0	(0	0)	7	3	1	3	1	0	3	0	0	0	3	0	1.00	2	.318	.348	.318
	11 ML YEARS		925	2550	686	98	22	17	(6	11)	879	365	193	286	175	6	438	13	24	13	131	47	.74	43	.269	.318	.345

Geoff Blum

Bats: B Throws: R Pos: PH-12; 3B-6   BLUMM   Ht: 6'3" Wt: 221 Born: 4/26/1973 Age: 40

Year	Team	Lg	G	AB	H	2B	3B	HR	(Hm	Rd)	TB	R	RBI	RC	TBB	IBB	SO	HBP	SH	SF	SB	CS	SB%	GDP	Avg	OBP	Slg
2012	Reno*	AAA	12	38	9	3	0	1	(-	-)	15	5	8	7	10	0	5	1	0	0	0	0	-	1	.237	.408	.395
1999	Mon	NL	45	133	32	7	2	8	(0	8)	67	21	18	22	17	3	25	0	3	0	1	0	1.00	3	.241	.327	.504
2000	Mon	NL	124	343	97	20	2	11	(5	6)	154	40	45	50	26	2	60	3	3	4	1	4	.20	4	.283	.335	.449
2001	Mon	NL	148	453	107	25	0	9	(6	3)	159	57	50	49	43	8	94	10	3	5	9	5	.64	12	.236	.313	.351
2002	Hou	NL	130	368	104	20	4	10	(6	4)	162	45	52	62	49	5	70	1	1	2	2	0	1.00	8	.283	.367	.440
2003	Hou	NL	123	420	110	19	0	10	(6	4)	159	51	52	40	20	1	50	2	2	5	0	0	-	15	.262	.295	.379
2004	TB	AL	112	339	73	21	0	8	(2	6)	118	38	35	29	24	1	58	0	4	2	2	3	.40	4	.215	.266	.348
2005	2 Tms		109	319	73	15	2	6	(1	5)	110	32	25	27	28	0	43	3	0	1	3	3	.50	6	.229	.296	.345
2006	SD	NL	109	276	70	17	1	4	(0	4)	101	27	34	26	17	1	51	0	2	4	0	1	.00	5	.254	.293	.366
2007	SD	NL	122	330	83	21	1	5	(1	4)	121	34	33	38	32	4	52	2	3	3	0	0	-	10	.252	.319	.367
2008	Hou	NL	114	325	78	14	1	14	(6	8)	136	36	53	42	21	2	54	3	0	7	1	2	.33	5	.240	.287	.418
2009	Hou	NL	120	381	94	14	1	10	(4	6)	140	34	49	39	33	4	61	7	0	6	0	1	.00	9	.247	.314	.367
2010	Hou	NL	93	202	54	10	1	2	(1	1)	72	22	22	28	15	2	33	1	0	0	0	0	-	3	.267	.321	.356
2011	Ari	NL	23	49	11	3	0	2	(1	1)	20	8	10	3	5	1	9	1	0	0	0	0	-	2	.224	.309	.408
2012	Ari	NL	17	28	4	0	0	0	(0	0)	4	1	1	0	2	0	7	0	0	1	0	0	-	0	.143	.194	.143
05	SD	NL	78	224	54	13	1	5	(1	4)	84	26	22	23	24	0	28	3	0	1	3	2	.60	5	.241	.321	.375
05	CWS	AL	31	95	19	2	1	1	(0	1)	26	6	3	4	4	0	15	0	0	0	0	1	.00	1	.200	.232	.274
	Postseason		8	12	2	1	0	1	(0	1)	6	1	2	1	4	1	3	0	0	1	0	0	-	1	.167	.353	.500
	14 ML YEARS		1389	3966	990	206	15	99	(39	60)	1523	446	479	455	332	34	667	33	21	40	19	19	.50	86	.250	.310	.384

Brennan Boesch

Bats: L Throws: L Pos: RF-121; DH-9; PH-8   BOSH   Ht: 6'5" Wt: 235 Born: 4/12/1985 Age: 28

Year	Team	Lg	G	AB	H	2B	3B	HR	(Hm	Rd)	TB	R	RBI	RC	TBB	IBB	SO	HBP	SH	SF	SB	CS	SB%	GDP	Avg	OBP	Slg
2010	Det	AL	133	464	119	26	3	14	(7	7)	193	49	67	61	40	5	99	5	0	3	7	1	.88	5	.256	.320	.416
2011	Det	AL	115	428	121	25	1	16	(9	7)	196	75	54	56	35	2	83	5	0	4	5	3	.63	7	.283	.341	.458
2012	Det	AL	132	470	113	22	2	12	(9	3)	175	52	54	47	26	1	104	5	0	2	6	3	.67	11	.240	.286	.372
	3 ML YEARS		380	1362	353	73	6	42	(25	17)	564	176	175	164	101	8	286	15	0	9	18	7	.72	23	.259	.315	.414

Mitchell Boggs

Pitches: R Bats: R Pos: RP-78   Ht: 6'4" Wt: 215 Born: 2/15/1984 Age: 29

Year	Team	Lg	G	GS	CG	GF	IP	BFP	H	R	ER	HR	SH	SF	HB	TBB	IBB	SO	WP	Bk	W	L	Pct	Sh	Sv-Op	Hld	ERC	ERA
2008	StL	NL	8	6	0	1	34.0	164	42	29	28	5	1	1	2	22	0	13	2	0	3	2	.600	0	0-0	0	7.17	7.41
2009	StL	NL	16	9	0	2	58.0	268	71	28	27	3	1	2	4	33	0	46	4	1	2	3	.400	0	0-0	1	6.15	4.19
2010	StL	NL	61	0	0	22	67.1	285	60	29	27	5	4	3	4	27	2	52	5	0	2	3	.400	0	0-0	6	3.51	3.61
2011	StL	NL	51	0	0	20	60.2	260	62	27	24	4	2	2	2	21	2	48	5	0	2	3	.400	0	4-8	1	3.84	3.56
2012	StL	NL	78	0	0	12	73.1	296	56	20	18	5	6	0	4	21	3	58	0	0	4	1	.800	0	0-3	34	2.36	2.21
	Postseason		8	0	0	3	8.2	39	10	5	5	2	0	1	0	4	0	6	0	0	0	0	-	0	0-0	1	6.26	5.19
	5 ML YEARS		214	15	0	57	293.1	1273	291	133	124	22	14	8	16	124	7	217	16	1	13	12	.520	0	4-11	42	4.15	3.80

Brian Bogusevic

Bats: L Throws: L Pos: RF-104; PH-36; CF-20; PR-4; LF-1   boe-gah-SEVV-ick   Ht: 6'3" Wt: 220 Born: 2/18/1984 Age: 29

Year	Team	Lg	G	AB	H	2B	3B	HR	(Hm	Rd)	TB	R	RBI	RC	TBB	IBB	SO	HBP	SH	SF	SB	CS	SB%	GDP	Avg	OBP	Slg
2010	Hou	NL	19	28	5	3	0	0	(0	0)	8	5	3	2	3	0	12	0	0	0	1	1	.50	2	.179	.258	.286
2011	Hou	NL	87	164	47	14	1	4	(2	2)	75	22	15	19	15	1	40	1	1	1	4	2	.67	8	.287	.348	.457
2012	Hou	NL	146	355	72	9	2	7	(4	3)	106	39	28	31	41	1	96	7	0	1	15	4	.79	6	.203	.297	.299
	3 ML YEARS		252	547	124	26	3	11	(6	5)	189	66	46	52	59	2	148	8	1	2	20	7	.74	16	.227	.310	.346

Emilio Bonifacio

Bats: B Throws: R Pos: CF-51; 2B-15   bo-knee-FAH-see-oh   Ht: 5'11" Wt: 205 Born: 4/23/1985 Age: 28

Year	Team	Lg	G	AB	H	2B	3B	HR	(Hm	Rd)	TB	R	RBI	RC	TBB	IBB	SO	HBP	SH	SF	SB	CS	SB%	GDP	Avg	OBP	Slg
2012	Jupiter*	A+	9	30	5	1	0	0	(-	-)	6	6	4	2	6	0	9	0	0	0	3	1	.75	1	.167	.306	.200
2007	Ari	NL	11	23	5	1	0	0	(0	0)	6	2	2	4	4	0	3	0	0	0	0	1	.00	0	.217	.333	.261
2008	2 Tms		49	169	41	6	5	0	(0	0)	57	29	14	16	14	0	46	0	0	3	14	4	.64	2	.243	.296	.337
2009	Fla	NL	127	461	116	11	6	1	(1	0)	142	72	27	41	34	0	95	2	8	4	21	9	.70	5	.252	.303	.308
2010	Fla	NL	73	180	47	6	3	0	(0	0)	59	30	10	24	17	0	42	0	1	3	12	0	1.00	1	.261	.320	.328
2011	Fla	NL	152	565	167	26	7	5	(1	4)	222	78	36	83	59	1	129	1	11	5	40	11	.78	4	.296	.360	.393
2012	Mia	NL	64	244	63	3	4	1	(1	0)	77	30	11	30	25	1	52	1	4	0	30	3	.91	3	.258	.330	.316
08	Ari	NL	8	12	2	1	0	0	(0	0)	3	3	2	1	0	0	5	0	0	0	1	0	1.00	0	.167	.167	.250
08	Was	NL	41	157	39	5	5	0	(0	0)	54	26	12	15	14	0	41	0	0	3	6	4	.60	2	.248	.305	.344
	6 ML YEARS		476	1642	439	53	25	7	(3	4)	563	241	100	198	153	2	367	4	24	15	110	28	.80	15	.267	.329	.343

J.C. Boscan

Bats: R Throws: R Pos: C-6; PR-1   BAHS-cann   Ht: 6'2" Wt: 215 Born: 12/26/1979 Age: 33

Year	Team	Lg	G	AB	H	2B	3B	HR	(Hm	Rd)	TB	R	RBI	RC	TBB	IBB	SO	HBP	SH	SF	SB	CS	SB%	GDP	Avg	OBP	Slg
2012	Gwnntt*	AAA	70	222	42	12	0	3	(-	-)	63	22	23	17	19	1	59	4	4	1	1	0	1.00	4	.189	.264	.284
2010	Atl	NL	1	0	0	0	0	0	(0	0)	0	1	0	0	1	0	0	0	0	0	0	0	-	0	-	1.000	-
2011	Atl	NL	4	9	3	0	0	0	(0	0)	3	0	0	0	0	0	5	0	0	0	0	0	-	0	.333	.333	.333
2012	Atl	NL	6	10	2	0	0	0	(0	0)	2	0	2	0	0	0	1	0	0	0	0	0	-	0	.200	.200	.200
	3 ML YEARS		11	19	5	0	0	0	(0	0)	5	1	2	0	1	0	6	0	0	0	0	0	-	0	.263	.300	.263

Jason Bourgeois

Bats: R Throws: R Pos: CF-23; PH-7; PR-6; LF-2; DH-2   boosh-WAH   Ht: 5'9" Wt: 195 Born: 1/4/1982 Age: 31

Year	Team	Lg	G	AB	H	2B	3B	HR	(Hm	Rd)	TB	R	RBI	RC	TBB	IBB	SO	HBP	SH	SF	SB	CS	SB%	GDP	Avg	OBP	Slg
2012	Omha*	AAA	60	222	54	7	1	3	(-	-)	72	41	8	23	21	0	24	2	2	0	7	5	.58	0	.243	.314	.324
2008	CWS	AL	6	3	1	1	0	0	(0	0)	2	0	0	0	0	0	0	0	0	0	0	0	-	0	.333	.333	.667
2009	Mil	NL	24	37	7	0	0	1	(1	0)	10	6	3	1	3	0	7	0	0	0	3	0	1.00	2	.189	.250	.270
2010	Hou	NL	69	123	27	4	1	0	(0	0)	33	16	3	8	13	0	16	0	0	0	12	4	.75	5	.220	.294	.268
2011	Hou	NL	93	238	70	8	2	1	(0	1)	85	30	16	31	10	0	24	0	4	0	31	6	.84	5	.294	.323	.357
2012	KC	AL	30	62	16	2	1	0	(0	0)	20	10	5	5	4	0	4	0	0	0	5	4	.56	1	.258	.303	.323
	5 ML YEARS		222	463	121	15	4	2	(1	1)	150	62	27	45	30	0	51	0	4	0	51	14	.78	13	.261	.306	.324

Peter Bourjos

Bats: R Throws: R Pos: CF-90; PR-17; DH-3; PH-2   BORE-juss   Ht: 6'1" Wt: 185 Born: 3/31/1987 Age: 26

Year	Team	Lg	G	AB	H	2B	3B	HR	(Hm	Rd)	TB	R	RBI	RC	TBB	IBB	SO	HBP	SH	SF	SB	CS	SB%	GDP	Avg	OBP	Slg
2012	Salt Lk*	AAA	7	29	9	1	3	0	(-	-)	16	4	3	5	3	0	6	0	0	0	0	0	-	0	.310	.375	.552
2010	LAA	AL	51	181	37	6	4	6	(1	5)	69	19	15	13	6	0	40	2	3	1	10	3	.77	2	.204	.237	.381
2011	LAA	AL	147	502	136	26	11	12	(7	5)	220	72	43	66	32	0	124	10	7	1	22	9	.71	7	.271	.327	.438
2012	LAA	AL	101	168	37	7	0	3	(1	2)	53	27	19	18	15	0	44	3	6	3	3	1	.75	2	.220	.291	.315
	3 ML YEARS		299	851	210	39	15	21	(9	12)	342	118	77	97	53	0	208	15	16	5	35	13	.73	11	.247	.301	.402

Michael Bourn

Bats: L Throws: R Pos: CF-153; PH-3   BORN   Ht: 5'11" Wt: 180 Born: 12/27/1982 Age: 30

Year	Team	Lg	G	AB	H	2B	3B	HR	(Hm	Rd)	TB	R	RBI	RC	TBB	IBB	SO	HBP	SH	SF	SB	CS	SB%	GDP	Avg	OBP	Slg
2006	Phi	NL	17	8	1	0	0	0	(0	0)	1	2	0	0	1	0	3	0	2	0	1	2	.33	0	.125	.222	.125
2007	Phi	NL	105	119	33	3	3	1	(1	0)	45	29	6	19	13	2	21	0	1	0	18	1	.95	1	.277	.348	.378
2008	Hou	NL	138	467	107	10	4	5	(3	2)	140	57	29	43	37	0	111	2	7	1	41	10	.80	3	.229	.288	.300
2009	Hou	NL	157	606	173	27	12	3	(2	1)	233	97	35	94	63	1	140	2	5	2	61	12	.84	1	.285	.354	.384
2010	Hou	NL	141	535	142	25	6	2	(0	2)	185	84	38	74	59	5	109	3	6	2	52	12	.81	6	.265	.341	.346
2011	2 Tms	NL	158	656	193	34	10	2	(2	0)	253	94	50	92	53	3	140	4	5	4	61	14	.81	6	.294	.349	.386
2012	Atl	NL	155	624	171	26	10	9	(2	7)	244	96	57	102	70	1	155	3	2	4	42	13	.76	2	.274	.348	.391
11	Hou	NL	105	429	130	26	7	1	(1	0)	173	64	32	66	38	2	90	3	2	1	39	7	.85	5	.303	.363	.403
11	Atl	NL	53	227	63	8	3	1	(1	0)	80	30	18	26	15	1	50	1	3	3	22	7	.76	1	.278	.321	.352
	Postseason		2	1	0	0	0	0	(0	0)	0	0	0	0	0	0	0	0	0	0	0	0	-	0	.000	.000	.000
	7 ML YEARS		871	3015	820	125	45	22	(10	12)	1101	459	215	424	296	12	679	14	28	13	276	64	.81	19	.272	.339	.365

Michael Bowden

Pitches: R Bats: R Pos: RP-32   BOE-din   Ht: 6'3" Wt: 215 Born: 9/9/1986 Age: 26

			HOW MUCH HE PITCHED						WHAT HE GAVE UP									THE RESULTS						
Year	Team	Lg	G	GS	CG	GF	IP	BFP	H	R	ER	HR	SH	SF	HB	TBB	IBB	SO	WP	Bk	W	L	Pct	Sh	Sv-Op Hld	ERC	ERA
2012	Iowa*	AAA	23	0	0	11	32.2	133	19	12	10	2	2	0	0	17	2	35	1	2	3	2	.600	0	2- -	2.01	2.76
2008	Bos	AL	1	1	0	0	5.0	22	7	2	2	0	0	0	0	1	0	3	0	0	1	0	1.000	0	0-0	4.92	3.60
2009	Bos	AL	8	1	0	3	16.0	75	23	17	17	3	0	0	0	6	0	12	3	0	1	1	.500	0	0-0	1	7.35	9.56
2010	Bos	AL	14	0	0	7	15.1	66	20	8	8	2	0	0	0	4	0	13	2	0	1	0	.000	0	0-0	5.73	4.70
2011	Bos	AL	14	0	0	9	20.0	90	19	9	9	3	0	0	0	11	0	17	3	0	0	0	-	0	0-0	4.65	4.05
2012	2 Tms		32	0	0	13	39.2	165	32	13	13	5	2	2	1	17	1	32	1	0	0	0	-	0	0-1	2	3.39	2.95
12	Bos	AL	2	0	0	2	3.0	11	2	1	1	1	0	0	0	1	0	3	0	0	0	0	-	0	0-0	3.72	3.00
12	ChC	NL	30	0	0	11	36.2	154	30	12	12	4	2	2	1	16	1	29	1	0	0	0	-	0	0-1	2	3.35	2.95
	5 ML YEARS		69	2	0	32	96.0	418	101	49	49	13	2	2	1	39	1	77	9	0	2	2	.500	0	0-1	3	4.70	4.59

Brad Boxberger

Pitches: R Bats: R Pos: RP-24   Ht: 6'2" Wt: 200 Born: 5/27/1988 Age: 25

			HOW MUCH HE PITCHED						WHAT HE GAVE UP									THE RESULTS						
Year	Team	Lg	G	GS	CG	GF	IP	BFP	H	R	ER	HR	SH	SF	HB	TBB	IBB	SO	WP	Bk	W	L	Pct	Sh	Sv-Op Hld	ERC	ERA
2010	Lynbrg	A+	14	13	0	0	62.0	259	57	30	22	3	3	2	5	20	0	70	1	0	4	6	.400	0	0- -	3.35	3.19
2010	Carlina	AA	22	0	0	6	29.2	148	35	28	28	4	2	0	3	22	1	40	5	1	1	4	.200	0	0- -	7.10	8.49
2011	Carlina	AA	30	0	0	22	34.1	130	16	5	5	2	2	0	0	13	1	57	1	0	1	2	.333	0	4- -	1.29	1.31
2011	Lsville	AAA	25	0	0	12	27.2	113	16	10	9	2	1	1	0	15	0	36	0	1	1	2	.333	0	7- -	2.22	2.93
2012	Tucsn	AAA	37	0	0	15	43.1	183	37	14	13	0	2	1	2	19	0	62	4	0	2	2	.500	0	5- -	2.93	2.70
2012	SD	NL	24	0	0	4	27.2	120	22	12	8	3	0	1	2	18	1	33	0	0	0	0	-	0	0-0	1	4.28	2.60

Brad Brach

Pitches: R **Bats:** R **Pos:** RP-67 — BROCK — **Ht:** 6'6" **Wt:** 210 **Born:** 4/12/1986 **Age:** 27

			HOW MUCH HE PITCHED					WHAT HE GAVE UP											THE RESULTS						
Year	Team	Lg	G	GS	CG	GF	IP	BFP	H	R	ER	HR	SH	SF	HB	TBB	IBB	SO	WP	Bk	W	L	Pct	Sh	Sv-Op Hld	ERC	ERA
2008	Padres	R	18	0	0	11	22.1	94	21	5	5	0	3	0	2	5	0	33	2	0	1	1	.500	0	4-- -	2.73	2.01
2009	FtWyn	A	60	0	0	57	63.2	235	36	10	9	1	0	0	4	11	0	82	3	0	3	3	.500	0	33-- -	1.17	1.27
2010	Lk Els	A+	62	0	0	60	65.2	255	50	20	18	6	2	0	6	11	0	74	2	1	5	2	.714	0	41-- -	1.95	2.47
2011	SnAnt	AA	42	0	0	40	44.0	169	32	11	11	3	0	0	2	5	1	64	3	0	2	2	.500	0	23-- -	1.64	2.25
2011	Tucsn	AAA	25	0	0	22	27.2	118	28	13	12	1	4	0	0	7	1	30	4	0	1	3	.250	0	11-- -	3.02	3.90
2012	Tucsn	AAA	10	0	0	10	9.2	38	10	3	3	0	0	1	0	1	0	5	1	0	2	1	.667	0	3-- -	2.60	2.79
2011	SD	NL	9	0	0	4	7.0	38	9	5	4	0	0	0	1	7	4	11	1	0	0	2	.000	0	0-0 0	6.51	5.14
2012	SD	NL	67	0	0	13	66.2	280	50	28	28	11	1	3	2	33	7	75	4	0	2	4	.333	0	0-1 15	3.47	3.78
	2 ML YEARS		76	0	0	17	73.2	318	59	33	32	11	1	3	3	40	11	86	5	0	2	6	.250	0	0-1 15	3.78	3.91

Dallas Braden

Pitches: L **Bats:** L **Pos:** P — **Ht:** 6'1" **Wt:** 185 **Born:** 8/13/1983 **Age:** 29

			HOW MUCH HE PITCHED					WHAT HE GAVE UP											THE RESULTS						
Year	Team	Lg	G	GS	CG	GF	IP	BFP	H	R	ER	HR	SH	SF	HB	TBB	IBB	SO	WP	Bk	W	L	Pct	Sh	Sv-Op Hld	ERC	ERA
2007	Oak	AL	20	14	0	1	72.1	332	91	59	54	9	4	0	2	26	1	55	6	1	1	8	.111	0	0-0 1	5.63	6.72
2008	Oak	AL	19	10	0	7	71.2	301	77	36	33	8	1	2	2	25	2	41	0	1	5	4	.556	0	0-0 1	4.63	4.14
2009	Oak	AL	22	22	0	0	136.2	589	144	63	59	9	4	4	2	42	2	81	1	0	8	9	.471	0	0-0 0	3.78	3.89
2010	Oak	AL	30	30	5	0	192.2	781	180	83	75	17	6	4	5	43	0	113	2	1	11	14	.440	2	0-0 0	3.11	3.50
2011	Oak	AL	3	3	0	0	18.0	73	18	7	6	2	0	0	0	5	0	15	0	0	1	1	.500	0	0-0 0	3.82	3.00
	5 ML YEARS		94	79	5	8	491.1	2076	510	248	227	45	15	10	11	141	5	305	9	3	26	36	.419	2	0-0 1	3.89	4.16

Michael Brantley

Bats: L **Throws:** L **Pos:** CF-144; PH-4; DH-3; PR-1 — **Ht:** 6'2" **Wt:** 200 **Born:** 5/15/1987 **Age:** 26

			BATTING																		BASERUNNING				AVERAGES		
Year	Team	Lg	G	AB	H	2B	3B	HR	(Hm	Rd)	TB	R	RBI	RC	TBB	IBB	SO	HBP	SH	SF	SB	CS	SB%	GDP	Avg	OBP	Slg
2009	Cle	AL	28	112	35	4	0	0	(0	0)	39	10	11	16	8	0	19	0	1	0	4	4	.50	3	.313	.358	.348
2010	Cle	AL	72	297	73	9	3	3	(2	1)	97	38	22	32	22	0	38	0	4	2	10	2	.83	6	.246	.296	.327
2011	Cle	AL	114	451	120	24	4	7	(4	3)	173	63	46	56	34	2	76	3	3	5	13	5	.72	11	.266	.318	.384
2012	Cle	AL	149	552	159	37	4	6	(3	3)	222	63	60	76	53	12	56	0	0	4	12	9	.57	7	.288	.348	.402
	4 ML YEARS		363	1412	387	74	11	16	(9	7)	531	174	139	180	117	14	189	3	8	11	39	20	.66	27	.274	.329	.376

Rob Brantly

Bats: L **Throws:** R **Pos:** C-28; PH-3 — **Ht:** 6'2" **Wt:** 205 **Born:** 7/14/1989 **Age:** 23

			BATTING																		BASERUNNING				AVERAGES		
Year	Team	Lg	G	AB	H	2B	3B	HR	(Hm	Rd)	TB	R	RBI	RC	TBB	IBB	SO	HBP	SH	SF	SB	CS	SB%	GDP	Avg	OBP	Slg
2010	WMich	A	52	188	48	10	1	1	(-	-)	63	26	21	24	23	0	22	5	1	0	2	2	.50	4	.255	.352	.335
2011	WMich	A	75	284	86	16	1	7	(-	-)	125	42	44	47	24	3	39	5	3	1	2	2	.50	12	.303	.366	.440
2011	Lkland	A+	39	146	32	6	0	3	(-	-)	47	16	18	11	5	0	17	0	0	4	0	0	-	4	.219	.239	.322
2012	Erie	AA	46	180	56	16	1	3	(-	-)	83	16	24	29	12	0	17	2	0	1	0	3	.00	4	.311	.359	.461
2012	Toledo	AAA	36	130	33	4	0	0	(-	-)	37	11	6	11	7	0	25	1	0	0	0	0	-	5	.254	.295	.285
2012	NewOr	AAA	14	52	19	4	0	2	(-	-)	29	7	11	10	1	0	9	1	0	0	0	0	-	0	.365	.389	.558
2012	Mia	NL	31	100	29	8	0	3	(1	2)	46	14	8	14	13	2	16	0	0	0	1	1	.50	1	.290	.372	.460

Ryan Braun

Bats: R **Throws:** R **Pos:** LF-151; DH-2; PH-1 — **Ht:** 6'1" **Wt:** 200 **Born:** 11/17/1983 **Age:** 29

			BATTING																		BASERUNNING				AVERAGES		
Year	Team	Lg	G	AB	H	2B	3B	HR	(Hm	Rd)	TB	R	RBI	RC	TBB	IBB	SO	HBP	SH	SF	SB	CS	SB%	GDP	Avg	OBP	Slg
2007	Mil	NL	113	451	146	26	6	34	(17	17)	286	91	97	94	29	1	112	7	0	5	15	5	.75	13	.324	.370	**.634**
2008	Mil	NL	151	611	174	39	7	37	(23	14)	338	92	106	100	42	4	129	6	0	4	14	4	.78	13	.285	.335	.553
2009	Mil	NL	158	635	**203**	39	6	32	(15	17)	350	113	114	133	57	1	121	13	0	3	20	6	.77	7	.320	.386	.551
2010	Mil	NL	157	619	188	45	1	25	(13	12)	310	101	103	104	56	1	105	6	0	3	14	3	.82	17	.304	.365	.501
2011	Mil	NL	150	563	187	38	6	33	(16	17)	336	109	111	124	58	2	93	5	0	5	33	6	.85	9	.332	.397	**.597**
2012	Mil	NL	154	598	191	36	3	**41**	**(24**	17)	**356**	**108**	112	**125**	63	15	128	11	0	5	30	7	.81	12	.319	.391	.595
	Postseason		15	58	22	9	0	2	(2	0)	37	7	12	13	4	0	13	1	0	1	1	0	1.00	0	.379	.422	.638
	6 ML YEARS		883	3477	1089	223	29	202	(108	94)	1976	614	643	680	305	24	688	48	0	23	126	31	.80	71	.313	.374	.568

Bill Bray

Pitches: L **Bats:** L **Pos:** RP-14 — **Ht:** 6'3" **Wt:** 230 **Born:** 6/5/1983 **Age:** 30

			HOW MUCH HE PITCHED					WHAT HE GAVE UP											THE RESULTS						
Year	Team	Lg	G	GS	CG	GF	IP	BFP	H	R	ER	HR	SH	SF	HB	TBB	IBB	SO	WP	Bk	W	L	Pct	Sh	Sv-Op Hld	ERC	ERA
2012	Lsvlle*	AAA	14	0	0	4	12.0	64	17	14	12	1	0	0	0	12	0	10	0	0	1	0	1.000	0	0-- -	9.01	9.00
2012	Dayton	A	2	0	0	0	2.2	10	0	0	0	0	0	0	0	1	0	4	0	0	1	0	1.000	0	0-- -	0.14	0.00
2006	2 Tms	NL	48	0	0	10	50.2	223	57	27	23	5	2	1	1	18	3	39	0	0	3	2	.600	0	2-3 3	4.58	4.09
2007	Cin	NL	19	0	0	5	14.1	63	16	10	10	1	0	1	0	5	1	14	0	0	3	3	.500	0	1-1 3	4.16	6.28
2008	Cin	NL	63	0	0	11	47.0	215	50	19	15	4	3	1	4	24	5	54	2	0	2	2	.500	0	0-4 9	4.57	2.87
2010	Cin	NL	35	0	0	4	28.1	117	21	13	13	4	1	0	0	10	1	30	2	0	0	0	.000	0	0-0 2	2.66	4.13
2011	Cin	NL	79	0	0	11	48.1	196	35	16	16	3	1	3	2	17	3	44	1	0	5	3	.625	0	0-3 20	2.28	2.98
2012	Cin	NL	14	0	0	2	8.2	43	6	5	5	2	0	2	0	14	0	7	0	0	0	0	-	0	0-2 1	8.82	5.19
	06 Was	NL	19	0	0	4	23.0	100	24	11	10	2	1	1	1	9	2	16	0	0	1	1	.500	0	0-0 1	4.25	3.91
	06 Cin	NL	29	0	0	6	27.2	123	33	16	13	3	1	0	0	9	1	23	0	0	2	1	.667	0	2-3 2	4.85	4.23
	Postseason		2	0	0	1	1.2	5	0	0	0	0	0	0	0	0	0	2	0	0	0	0	-	0	0-0 0	0.00	0.00
	6 ML YEARS		258	0	0	43	197.1	857	185	90	82	19	7	8	4	88	13	188	5	0	13	12	.520	0	3-13 38	3.82	3.74

Craig Breslow

Pitches: L Bats: L Pos: RP-63   BREHZ-loh   Ht: 6'0" Wt: 190 Born: 8/8/1980 Age: 32

			HOW MUCH HE PITCHED					WHAT HE GAVE UP										THE RESULTS							
Year	Team	Lg	G	GS	CG	GF	IP	BFP	H	R	ER	HR	SH	SF	HB	TBB	IBB	SO	WP	Bk	W	L	Pct	Sh	Sv-Op	Hld	ERC	ERA
2005	SD	NL	14	0	0	3	16.1	78	15	6	4	1	0	1	1	13	0	14	1	0	0	0	-	0	0-0	1	4.98	2.20
2006	Bos	AL	13	0	0	3	12.0	55	12	5	5	0	0	2	1	6	1	12	2	1	0	2	.000	0	0-0	3	3.78	3.75
2008	2 Tms	AL	49	0	0	13	47.0	189	34	12	10	1	2	0	0	19	2	39	4	1	0	2	.000	0	1-2	5	2.12	1.91
2009	2 Tms	AL	77	0	0	9	69.2	281	48	31	26	8	4	1	3	29	0	55	3	1	8	7	.533	0	0-2	15	2.79	3.36
2010	Oak	AL	75	0	0	23	74.2	304	53	26	25	9	2	0	0	29	4	71	0	1	4	4	.500	0	5-7	16	2.53	3.01
2011	Oak	AL	67	0	0	10	59.1	261	69	29	25	4	3	2	2	21	1	44	3	0	0	2	.000	0	0-3	8	4.74	3.79
2012	2 Tms		63	0	0	16	63.1	261	52	22	19	5	3	3	2	22	2	61	2	0	3	0	1.000	0	0-1	9	2.86	2.70
08	Cle	AL	7	0	0	3	8.1	40	10	3	1	0	0	0	0	5	0	7	0	0	0	0	-	0	0-0	0	6.09	3.24
08	Min	AL	42	0	0	10	38.2	149	24	9	7	0	2	0	0	14	2	32	4	1	0	2	.000	0	1-2	5	1.49	1.63
09	Min	AL	17	0	0	5	14.1	64	11	11	10	3	2	0	1	11	0	11	3	0	1	2	.333	0	0-0	2	5.38	6.28
09	Oak	AL	60	0	0	4	55.1	217	37	20	16	5	2	1	2	18	0	44	0	1	7	5	.583	0	0-2	13	2.21	2.60
12	Ari	NL	40	0	0	12	43.1	180	38	15	13	5	2	1	0	13	0	42	1	0	2	0	1.000	0	0-0	4	3.19	2.70
12	Bos	AL	23	0	0	4	20.0	81	14	7	6	0	1	2	1	9	2	19	1	0	1	0	1.000	0	0-1	5	2.12	2.70
	7 ML YEARS		358	0	0	77	342.1	1429	283	131	114	28	14	9	9	139	10	296	15	4	15	17	.469	0	6-15	57	3.10	3.00

Reid Brignac

Bats: L Throws: R Pos: SS-11; 3B-4; 2B-1; LF-1; PH-1   BRINN-yak   Ht: 6'3" Wt: 190 Born: 1/16/1986 Age: 27

							BATTING													BASERUNNING				AVERAGES		
Year	Team	Lg	G	AB	H	2B	3B	HR	(Hm	Rd)	TB	R	RBI	RC	TBB	IBB	SO	HBP	SH	SF	SB	CS	SB%	GDP	Avg	OBP	Slg
2012	Drham*	AAA	99	346	80	14	2	8	(-	-)	122	45	46	42	45	0	79	3	4	2	3	3	.50	10	.231	.323	.353
2008	TB	AL	4	10	0	0	0	0	(0	0)	0	1	0	0	1	0	5	0	0	0	0	0	-	0	.000	.091	.000
2009	TB	AL	31	90	25	8	2	1	(0	1)	40	10	6	10	3	0	20	1	0	0	2	2	.50	1	.278	.301	.444
2010	TB	AL	113	301	77	13	1	8	(3	5)	116	39	45	38	20	3	77	3	0	2	3	3	.50	6	.256	.307	.385
2011	TB	AL	92	249	48	4	0	1	(0	1)	55	18	15	8	10	1	63	1	4	0	3	1	.75	2	.193	.227	.221
2012	TB	AL	16	21	2	0	0	0	(0	0)	2	1	1	0	1	0	5	0	0	0	0	0	-	0	.095	.136	.095
	Postseason		5	4	0	0	0	0	(0	0)	0	0	0	0	1	0	3	0	0	0	0	0	-	0	.000	.200	.000
	5 ML YEARS		256	671	152	25	3	10	(3	7)	213	69	67	56	35	4	170	4	4	2	8	6	.57	9	.227	.268	.317

Zach Britton

Pitches: L Bats: L Pos: SP-11; RP-1   Ht: 6'3" Wt: 195 Born: 12/22/1987 Age: 25

			HOW MUCH HE PITCHED					WHAT HE GAVE UP											THE RESULTS						
Year	Team	Lg	G	GS	CG	GF	IP	BFP	H	R	ER	HR	SH	SF	HB	TBB	IBB	SO	WP	Bk	W	L	Pct	Sh	Sv-Op	Hld	ERC	ERA
2006	Bluefld	R	11	11	0	0	34.0	153	35	22	20	4	1	1	2	20	0	21	5	0	0	4	.000	0	0--	-	5.47	5.29
2007	Abrdn	A-	15	15	0	0	63.2	278	64	33	26	1	0	1	5	22	0	45	4	0	6	4	.600	0	0--	-	3.56	3.68
2008	Dlmrva	A	27	27	1	0	147.1	605	118	68	51	9	6	4	6	49	0	114	13	0	12	7	.632	0	0--	-	2.66	3.12
2009	Frdrck	A+	25	24	0	0	140.0	599	123	64	42	6	3	1	6	55	0	131	21	0	9	6	.600	0	0--	-	3.21	2.70
2010	Bowie	AA	15	14	0	0	87.0	363	76	33	24	4	3	0	3	28	1	68	10	0	7	3	.700	0	0--	-	2.84	2.48
2010	Norfolk	AAA	12	12	0	0	66.1	281	63	31	22	3	0	0	1	23	0	56	8	0	3	4	.429	0	0--	-	3.27	2.98
2011	Bowie	AA	3	3	0	0	11.2	52	14	11	7	3	0	0	1	2	0	15	1	1	0	2	.000	0	0--	-	5.66	5.40
2011	Norfolk	AAA	1	1	0	0	5.0	18	3	1	1	0	0	0	0	1	0	3	0	0	0	1	.000	0	0--	-	1.17	1.80
2012	Bowie	AA	2	2	0	0	12.0	48	8	4	1	0	0	1	1	3	0	11	2	0	1	0	1.000	0	0--	-	1.57	0.75
2012	Norfolk	AAA	9	9	0	0	51.1	220	49	29	28	5	3	0	0	20	0	37	7	0	4	2	.667	0	0--	-	3.74	4.91
2011	Bal	AL	28	28	0	0	154.1	666	162	93	79	12	8	7	1	62	3	97	7	0	11	11	.500	0	0-0	0	4.24	4.61
2012	Bal	AL	12	11	0	0	60.1	270	61	37	34	6	0	1	2	32	3	53	4	0	5	3	.625	0	0-0	0	4.70	5.07
	2 ML YEARS		40	39	0	0	214.2	936	223	130	113	18	8	8	3	94	6	150	11	0	16	14	.533	0	0-0	0	4.37	4.74

Rex Brothers

Pitches: L Bats: L Pos: RP-75   Ht: 6'0" Wt: 210 Born: 12/18/1987 Age: 25

			HOW MUCH HE PITCHED					WHAT HE GAVE UP											THE RESULTS						
Year	Team	Lg	G	GS	CG	GF	IP	BFP	H	R	ER	HR	SH	SF	HB	TBB	IBB	SO	WP	Bk	W	L	Pct	Sh	Sv-Op	Hld	ERC	ERA
2009	TriCity	A-	8	0	0	2	10.2	44	10	4	4	0	0	0	0	5	0	18	0	0	2	0	1.000	0	0--	-	3.46	3.38
2009	Ashvll	A	9	0	0	2	10.2	41	6	4	4	1	0	0	2	3	0	10	0	0	0	0	-	0	0--	-	2.14	3.38
2010	Mdest	A+	33	0	0	12	37.0	147	20	14	11	0	4	3	0	19	1	43	8	1	0	2	.000	0	3--	-	1.57	2.68
2010	Tulsa	AA	24	0	0	8	23.0	101	14	13	10	2	2	1	1	18	1	27	2	0	1	2	.667	0	4--	-	3.35	3.91
2011	ColSpr	AAA	25	0	0	9	28.0	126	29	10	9	2	1	1	0	15	1	45	2	0	3	2	.600	0	0--	-	4.50	2.89
2012	ColSpr	AAA	4	0	0	2	5.1	22	3	1	1	0	1	0	0	3	0	13	0	0	0	0	-	0	1--	-	1.76	1.69
2011	Col	NL	48	0	0	6	40.2	172	33	14	13	4	0	0	0	20	2	59	2	0	1	2	.333	0	1-3	16	3.31	2.88
2012	Col	NL	75	0	0	10	67.2	295	63	33	29	5	3	3	1	37	7	83	5	1	8	2	.800	0	0-5	18	3.99	3.86
	2 ML YEARS		123	0	0	16	108.1	467	96	47	42	9	3	3	1	57	9	142	7	1	9	4	.692	0	1-8	34	3.73	3.49

Andrew Brown

Bats: R Throws: R Pos: RF-24; PH-13; LF-12; PR-1   Ht: 6'0" Wt: 185 Born: 9/10/1984 Age: 28

							BATTING													BASERUNNING				AVERAGES		
Year	Team	Lg	G	AB	H	2B	3B	HR	(Hm	Rd)	TB	R	RBI	RC	TBB	IBB	SO	HBP	SH	SF	SB	CS	SB%	GDP	Avg	OBP	Slg
2007	Batvia	A-	66	239	57	14	7	7	(-	-)	106	34	40	36	31	1	52	3	0	3	1	2	.33	6	.238	.330	.444
2008	QuadC	A	34	117	32	10	0	5	(-	-)	57	18	23	21	17	0	30	1	0	1	0	1	.00	3	.274	.368	.487
2008	PlmBh	A+	24	88	29	8	0	4	(-	-)	49	14	15	19	11	0	25	1	0	0	0	0	-	2	.330	.410	.557
2008	Sprgfld	AA	68	247	62	14	0	12	(-	-)	112	36	38	39	30	1	81	4	0	1	1	0	1.00	11	.251	.340	.453
2009	Sprgfld	AA	74	263	75	11	2	13	(-	-)	129	40	42	49	31	2	49	6	0	2	1	0	1.00	5	.285	.371	.490
2009	Cards	R	1	3	2	0	0	0	(-	-)	2	1	0	1	0	0	0	0	0	0	0	0	-	0	.667	.667	.667
2009	PlmBh	A+	4	11	2	1	1	0	(-	-)	5	1	2	1	2	0	4	1	0	0	0	0	-	1	.182	.357	.455
2010	Sprgfld	AA	98	361	105	17	1	22	(-	-)	190	65	63	70	41	3	98	5	0	0	1	2	.33	11	.291	.371	.526
2011	Memp	AAA	107	359	102	12	3	20	(-	-)	180	67	73	71	56	1	105	5	1	7	4	4	.50	6	.284	.382	.501

Year	Team	Lg	G	AB	H	2B	3B	HR	(Hm	Rd)	TB	R	RBI	RC	TBB	IBB	SO	HBP	SH	SF	SB	CS	SB%	GDP	Avg	OBP	Slg
2012	ColSpr	AAA	100	390	120	33	4	24	(-	-)	233	81	98	84	37	3	100	2	1	8	3	1	.75	10	.308	.364	.597
2011	StL	NL	11	22	4	1	0	0	(0	0)	5	1	3	1	0	0	8	0	0	0	0	0	-	1	.182	.182	.227
2012	Col	NL	46	112	26	7	0	5	(3	2)	48	14	11	7	12	0	34	0	0	2	2	2	.50	3	.232	.302	.429
	2 ML YEARS		57	134	30	8	0	5	(3	2)	53	15	14	8	12	0	42	0	0	2	2	2	.50	4	.224	.284	.396

Corey Brown

Bats: L **Throws:** L **Pos:** PH-11; LF-7; CF-2; RF-2   **Ht:** 6'1" **Wt:** 210 **Born:** 11/26/1985 **Age:** 27

								BATTING												BASERUNNING				AVERAGES		
Year	Team	Lg	G	AB	H	2B	3B	HR	(Hm	Rd)	TB	R	RBI	RC	TBB	IBB	SO	HBP	SH	SF	SB	CS	SB%	GDP	Avg	OBP	Slg
2007	Vancvr	A-	59	213	57	18	4	11	(-	-)	116	31	48	45	37	0	77	3	0	3	5	3	.63	2	.268	.379	.545
2008	Kane	A	85	300	81	18	2	14	(-	-)	145	44	49	56	41	1	96	3	3	4	12	0	1.00	0	.270	.359	.483
2008	Stcktn	A+	49	196	51	9	0	16	(-	-)	108	34	34	35	17	0	72	1	0	0	4	1	.80	1	.260	.322	.551
2009	Mdland	AA	66	250	67	20	4	9	(-	-)	122	46	43	43	27	0	69	4	0	0	5	2	.71	5	.268	.349	.488
2010	Scrmto	AAA	41	135	26	4	3	5	(-	-)	51	21	20	13	11	1	36	0	2	0	3	1	.75	1	.193	.253	.378
2010	Mdland	AA	90	331	106	14	8	10	(-	-)	166	63	49	73	52	1	93	2	0	1	19	1	.95	5	.320	.415	.502
2011	Syrcse	AAA	124	396	93	18	3	14	(-	-)	159	50	39	53	47	1	134	7	11	1	4	7	.36	1	.235	.326	.402
2012	Syrcse	AAA	126	484	138	22	9	25	(-	-)	253	83	71	94	59	5	139	4	3	4	18	7	.72	3	.285	.365	.523
2011	Was	NL	3	3	0	0	0	0	(0	0)	0	0	0	0	0	0	2	0	0	0	0	0	-	0	.000	.000	.000
2012	Was	NL	19	25	5	2	0	1	(0	1)	10	4	3	2	1	0	9	0	1	0	0	0	-	0	.200	.231	.400
	2 ML YEARS		22	28	5	2	0	1	(0	1)	10	4	3	2	1	0	11	0	1	0	0	0	-	0	.179	.207	.357

Domonic Brown

Bats: L **Throws:** L **Pos:** RF-38; LF-29; PH-5   **Ht:** 6'5" **Wt:** 205 **Born:** 9/3/1987 **Age:** 25

								BATTING												BASERUNNING				AVERAGES		
Year	Team	Lg	G	AB	H	2B	3B	HR	(Hm	Rd)	TB	R	RBI	RC	TBB	IBB	SO	HBP	SH	SF	SB	CS	SB%	GDP	Avg	OBP	Slg
2012	LV*	AAA	60	220	63	13	2	5	(-	-)	95	33	28	31	17	1	42	0	0	2	4	6	.40	6	.286	.335	.432
2012	Phillies*	R	5	19	11	7	0	0	(-	-)	18	4	4	8	3	1	3	0	0	0	1	0	1.00	1	.579	.636	.947
2010	Phi	NL	35	62	13	3	0	2	(2	0)	22	8	13	5	5	1	24	0	0	3	2	1	.67	1	.210	.257	.355
2011	Phi	NL	56	184	45	10	1	5	(4	1)	72	28	19	21	25	1	35	0	0	1	3	1	.75	2	.245	.333	.391
2012	Phi	NL	56	187	44	11	2	5	(3	2)	74	21	26	25	21	2	34	2	0	2	0	0	-	6	.235	.316	.396
	Postseason		3	3	0	0	0	0	(0	0)	0	1	0	0	0	0	0	0	0	0	0	0	-	0	.000	.000	.000
	3 ML YEARS		147	433	102	24	3	12	(9	3)	168	57	58	51	51	4	93	2	0	6	5	2	.71	9	.236	.315	.388

Barret Browning

Pitches: L **Bats:** L **Pos:** RP-22   **Ht:** 6'2" **Wt:** 205 **Born:** 12/28/1984 **Age:** 28

			HOW MUCH HE PITCHED					WHAT HE GAVE UP											THE RESULTS						
Year	Team	Lg	G	GS	CG	GF	IP	BFP	H	R	ER	HR	SH	SF	HB	TBB	IBB	SO	WP	Bk	W	L	Pct	Sh	Sv-Op Hld	ERC	ERA
2006	Orem	R+	23	0	0	4	41.1	169	33	17	14	3	3	0	3	13	1	40	2	1	3	2	.600	0	1-- -	2.76	3.05
2007	CRpds	A	48	0	0	15	74.0	302	54	25	23	2	2	1	3	26	1	74	6	0	9	4	.692	0	8-- -	2.14	2.80
2008	RCuca	A+	30	0	0	13	33.2	148	35	16	15	2	1	0	2	16	0	39	4	0	2	1	.667	0	6-- -	4.62	4.01
2008	Ark	AA	27	0	0	7	31.2	139	31	21	21	2	1	0	6	14	0	34	0	0	1	1	.500	0	1-- -	4.73	5.97
2009	Ark	AA	48	7	0	12	90.2	408	92	54	42	3	5	2	9	45	3	73	4	0	3	10	.231	0	0-- -	4.36	4.17
2010	Ark	AA	25	1	0	6	46.0	195	38	22	20	3	0	1	3	22	4	44	4	0	5	4	.556	0	0-- -	3.33	3.91
2010	Salt Lk	AAA	26	1	0	5	42.2	204	61	33	31	4	3	2	3	22	1	41	5	0	2	1	.667	0	0-- -	7.56	6.54
2011	Salt Lk	AAA	50	2	0	9	66.1	287	67	38	34	5	4	5	4	35	0	47	6	0	2	1	.667	0	0-- -	4.90	4.61
2012	Memp	AAA	35	0	0	7	41.2	166	28	11	8	1	2	0	2	18	2	38	2	0	2	3	.400	0	1-- -	2.18	1.73
2012	StL	NL	22	0	0	4	19.1	84	18	11	11	2	2	2	0	7	0	11	1	1	1	3	.250	0	0-0 4	3.45	5.12

Jonathan Broxton

Pitches: R **Bats:** R **Pos:** RP-60   **Ht:** 6'4" **Wt:** 300 **Born:** 6/16/1984 **Age:** 29

			HOW MUCH HE PITCHED					WHAT HE GAVE UP											THE RESULTS						
Year	Team	Lg	G	GS	CG	GF	IP	BFP	H	R	ER	HR	SH	SF	HB	TBB	IBB	SO	WP	Bk	W	L	Pct	Sh	Sv-Op Hld	ERC	ERA
2005	LAD	NL	14	0	0	5	13.2	68	13	11	9	0	0	2	1	12	2	22	2	0	1	0	1.000	0	0-1 1	4.65	5.93
2006	LAD	NL	68	0	0	20	76.1	320	61	25	22	7	3	1	1	33	6	97	7	0	4	1	.800	0	3-7 12	2.97	2.59
2007	LAD	NL	83	0	0	18	82.0	334	69	30	26	6	0	1	1	25	3	99	4	0	4	4	.500	0	2-8 32	2.71	2.85
2008	LAD	NL	70	0	0	32	69.0	285	54	29	24	2	3	3	3	27	5	88	3	0	3	5	.375	0	14-22 13	2.48	3.13
2009	LAD	NL	73	0	0	58	76.0	300	44	24	22	4	0	3	1	29	1	114	2	0	7	2	.778	0	36-42 1	1.65	2.61
2010	LAD	NL	64	0	0	46	62.1	271	64	30	28	4	3	1	2	28	5	73	1	0	5	6	.455	0	22-29 3	4.21	4.04
2011	LAD	NL	14	0	0	12	12.2	62	15	10	8	2	0	0	0	9	2	10	0	0	1	2	.333	0	7-8 0	6.47	5.68
2012	2 Tms		60	0	0	39	58.0	238	56	18	16	2	2	1	3	17	0	45	0	0	4	5	.444	0	27-33 10	3.34	2.48
12	KC	AL	35	0	0	32	35.2	151	36	11	9	1	2	1	2	14	0	25	0	0	1	2	.333	0	23-27 0	3.93	2.27
12	Cin	NL	25	0	0	7	22.1	87	20	7	7	1	0	0	1	3	0	20	0	0	3	3	.500	0	4-6 10	2.44	2.82
	Postseason		13	0	0	10	14.1	64	14	7	7	1	0	0	1	6	0	15	0	0	0	2	.000	0	3-5 0	3.97	4.40
	8 ML YEARS		446	0	0	230	450.0	1878	376	177	155	27	11	12	12	180	24	548	19	0	29	25	.537	0	111-150 72	2.95	3.10

Jay Bruce

Bats: L **Throws:** L **Pos:** RF-154; PH-5   **Ht:** 6'3" **Wt:** 225 **Born:** 4/3/1987 **Age:** 26

								BATTING												BASERUNNING				AVERAGES		
Year	Team	Lg	G	AB	H	2B	3B	HR	(Hm	Rd)	TB	R	RBI	RC	TBB	IBB	SO	HBP	SH	SF	SB	CS	SB%	GDP	Avg	OBP	Slg
2008	Cin	NL	108	413	105	17	1	21	(13	8)	187	63	52	49	33	1	110	4	0	2	4	6	.40	8	.254	.314	.453
2009	Cin	NL	101	345	77	15	2	22	(13	9)	162	47	58	47	38	2	75	2	1	1	3	3	.50	5	.223	.303	.470
2010	Cin	NL	148	509	143	23	5	25	(19	6)	251	80	70	71	58	5	136	1	0	5	5	4	.56	12	.281	.353	.493

Year	Team	Lg	G	AB	H	2B	3B	HR	(Hm	Rd)	TB	R	RBI	RC	TBB	IBB	SO	HBP	SH	SF	SB	CS	SB%	GDP	Avg	OBP	Slg
									BATTING												BASERUNNING				AVERAGES		
2011	Cin	NL	157	585	150	27	2	32	(16	16)	277	84	97	96	71	14	158	5	1	2	8	7	.53	8	.256	.341	.474
2012	Cin	NL	155	560	141	35	5	34	(21	13)	288	89	99	85	62	11	155	4	0	7	9	3	.75	5	.252	.327	.514
	Postseason		3	8	2	0	0	1	(0	1)	5	1	1	1	2	0	0	0	0	0	0	0	-	0	.250	.400	.625
	5 ML YEARS		669	2412	616	117	15	134	(82	52)	1165	363	376	348	262	33	634	16	2	17	29	23	.56	38	.255	.330	.483

Tyson Brummett

Pitches: R **Bats:** R **Pos:** RP-1   **Ht:** 6'0" **Wt:** 180 **Born:** 8/15/1984 **Age:** 28

Year	Team	Lg	G	GS	CG	GF	IP	BFP	H	R	ER	HR	SH	SF	HB	TBB	IBB	SO	WP	Bk	W	L	Pct	Sh	Sv-Op	Hld	ERC	ERA
				HOW MUCH HE PITCHED								WHAT HE GAVE UP											THE RESULTS					
2007	Wmspt	A-	15	12	1	2	76.2	317	71	34	29	2	1	2	4	14	0	55	1	0	5	5	.500	0	0- -	-	2.55	3.40
2008	Lakwd	A	6	6	0	0	37.0	146	28	12	8	1	1	3	1	10	0	36	0	0	3	0	1.000	0	0- -	-	2.03	1.95
2008	Clrwtr	A+	8	8	0	0	52.2	221	52	24	21	8	0	1	1	13	1	39	1	0	2	3	.400	0	0- -	-	3.77	3.59
2008	Rdng	AA	14	14	0	0	80.1	383	105	68	65	10	4	1	3	46	2	47	7	0	2	9	.182	0	0- -	-	7.01	7.28
2009	Rdng	AA	26	15	0	5	98.1	435	119	63	57	12	5	5	4	27	0	70	5	0	3	9	.250	0	2- -	-	5.11	5.22
2009	LV	AAA	1	1	0	0	4.0	20	7	6	5	1	0	2	0	1	0	3	0	1	0	1	.000	0	0- -	-	9.18	11.25
2009	Clrwtr	A+	4	0	0	0	5.0	25	5	7	5	0	0	2	0	4	0	3	2	0	0	0	-	0	0- -	-	4.51	9.00
2010	Clrwtr	A+	11	0	0	8	15.1	58	7	1	1	0	0	0	0	4	0	11	1	0	0	0	-	0	2- -	-	0.84	0.59
2010	Rdng	AA	28	2	0	6	55.2	248	66	34	31	2	2	3	2	15	1	34	2	0	1	2	.333	0	1- -	-	4.18	5.01
2011	Rdng	AA	30	11	0	0	91.2	402	103	53	46	11	3	3	2	28	0	72	5	0	4	8	.333	0	0- -	-	4.60	4.52
2011	LV	AAA	7	6	0	0	34.0	147	41	22	22	6	2	0	0	11	0	20	1	0	1	4	.200	0	0- -	-	5.68	5.82
2012	Rdng	AA	10	1	0	2	18.0	63	7	3	3	2	0	0	1	2	0	18	1	0	1	0	1.000	0	1- -	-	0.86	1.50
2012	LV	AAA	34	7	0	9	72.0	302	67	33	29	2	3	2	3	27	1	65	4	1	4	6	.400	0	1- -	-	3.29	3.63
2012	Phi	NL	1	0	0	1	0.2	4	2	0	0	0	0	0	0	0	0	2	0	0	0	0	-	0	0-0	0	14.52	0.00

Brian Bruney

Pitches: R **Bats:** R **Pos:** RP-1   BRUE-nee   **Ht:** 6'3" **Wt:** 235 **Born:** 2/17/1982 **Age:** 31

Year	Team	Lg	G	GS	CG	GF	IP	BFP	H	R	ER	HR	SH	SF	HB	TBB	IBB	SO	WP	Bk	W	L	Pct	Sh	Sv-Op	Hld	ERC	ERA
				HOW MUCH HE PITCHED								WHAT HE GAVE UP											THE RESULTS					
2012	Charltt*	AAA	25	4	0	17	37.0	145	22	7	7	1	2	0	1	13	0	37	2	0	2	3	.400	0	11- -	-	1.58	1.70
2004	Ari	NL	30	0	0	14	31.1	135	20	16	15	2	1	0	1	27	5	34	2	0	3	4	.429	0	0-0	3	3.54	4.31
2005	Ari	NL	47	0	0	21	46.0	230	56	39	38	6	2	1	5	35	2	51	2	0	1	3	.250	0	12-16	4	7.48	7.43
2006	NYY	AL	19	0	0	2	20.2	90	14	2	2	1	0	0	1	15	0	25	2	0	1	1	.500	0	0-0	4	3.37	0.87
2007	NYY	AL	58	0	0	16	50.0	228	44	28	26	5	1	6	3	37	2	39	4	0	3	2	.600	0	0-2	6	4.92	4.68
2008	NYY	AL	32	1	0	5	34.1	137	18	7	7	2	0	2	1	16	0	33	1	0	3	0	1.000	0	1-2	12	1.75	1.83
2009	NYY	AL	44	0	0	6	39.0	175	36	17	17	6	2	1	1	23	3	36	2	0	5	0	1.000	0	0-1	14	4.71	3.92
2010	Was	NL	19	0	0	6	17.2	93	21	18	15	1	3	2	0	20	1	16	1	0	1	2	.333	0	0-0	3	7.65	7.64
2011	CWS	AL	23	0	0	6	19.2	93	26	15	15	4	3	1	0	12	0	16	0	0	1	0	1.000	0	0-0	3	7.95	6.86
2012	CWS	AL	1	0	0	1	1.0	5	0	0	0	0	0	0	0	2	0	2	0	0	1	0	1.000	0	0-0	0	3.47	0.00
	Postseason		4	0	0	1	3.0	13	4	3	3	1	0	1	0	4	0	4	0	0	0	0	-	0	0-0	0	5.82	9.00
	9 ML YEARS		273	1	0	77	259.2	1186	235	142	135	27	12	13	12	187	13	252	14	0	19	12	.613	0	13-22	49	4.93	4.68

Clay Buchholz

Pitches: R **Bats:** L **Pos:** SP-29   BUCK-holtz   **Ht:** 6'3" **Wt:** 190 **Born:** 8/14/1984 **Age:** 28

Year	Team	Lg	G	GS	CG	GF	IP	BFP	H	R	ER	HR	SH	SF	HB	TBB	IBB	SO	WP	Bk	W	L	Pct	Sh	Sv-Op	Hld	ERC	ERA
				HOW MUCH HE PITCHED								WHAT HE GAVE UP											THE RESULTS					
2012	Pwtckt*	AAA	1	1	0	0	2.1	10	1	0	0	0	0	0	0	2	0	3	0	0	0	0	-	0	0- -	-	2.03	0.00
2007	Bos	AL	4	3	1	0	22.2	88	14	6	4	0	0	1	1	10	0	22	0	0	3	1	.750	1	0-0	0	1.90	1.59
2008	Bos	AL	16	15	1	0	76.0	357	93	63	57	11	0	3	2	41	1	72	2	1	2	9	.182	0	0-0	0	6.40	6.75
2009	Bos	AL	16	16	0	0	92.0	399	91	44	43	13	2	3	2	36	1	68	1	0	7	4	.636	0	0-0	0	4.31	4.21
2010	Bos	AL	28	28	1	0	173.2	711	142	55	45	9	5	5	5	67	1	120	7	1	17	7	.708	1	0-0	0	2.88	2.33
2011	Bos	AL	14	14	0	0	82.2	353	76	34	32	10	1	4	2	31	1	60	3	0	6	3	.667	0	0-0	0	3.72	3.48
2012	Bos	AL	29	29	2	0	189.1	802	187	104	96	25	5	9	12	64	2	129	2	2	11	8	.579	1	0-0	0	4.29	4.56
	Postseason		1	1	0	0	5.0	23	6	2	2	1	0	0	1	1	0	3	0	1	0	0	-	0	0-0	0	5.87	3.60
	6 ML YEARS		107	105	5	0	636.1	2710	603	306	277	68	13	25	24	249	6	471	15	4	46	32	.590	3	0-0	0	3.96	3.92

John Buck

Bats: R **Throws:** R **Pos:** C-105; PH-1   **Ht:** 6'2" **Wt:** 230 **Born:** 7/7/1980 **Age:** 32

Year	Team	Lg	G	AB	H	2B	3B	HR	(Hm	Rd)	TB	R	RBI	RC	TBB	IBB	SO	HBP	SH	SF	SB	CS	SB%	GDP	Avg	OBP	Slg
									BATTING												BASERUNNING				AVERAGES		
2004	KC	AL	71	238	56	9	0	12	(6	6)	101	36	30	26	15	0	79	0	4	1	1	1	.50	6	.235	.280	.424
2005	KC	AL	118	401	97	21	1	12	(9	4)	156	40	47	43	23	2	94	3	1	2	2	2	.50	9	.242	.287	.389
2006	KC	AL	114	371	91	21	1	11	(6	5)	147	37	50	43	26	2	84	7	4	1	0	2	.00	7	.245	.306	.396
2007	KC	AL	113	347	77	18	0	18	(6	12)	149	41	48	37	36	0	92	10	0	6	0	1	.00	11	.222	.308	.429
2008	KC	AL	109	370	83	23	1	9	(4	5)	135	48	48	42	38	2	96	6	0	4	0	3	.00	12	.224	.304	.365
2009	KC	AL	59	186	46	12	4	8	(3	5)	90	16	36	30	13	0	55	1	1	1	1	1	.50	2	.247	.299	.484
2010	KC	AL	118	409	115	25	0	20	(9	11)	200	53	66	61	16	1	111	6	0	6	0	0	-	6	.281	.314	.489
2011	Fla	NL	140	466	106	15	1	16	(7	9)	171	41	57	55	54	7	115	7	2	1	0	1	.00	11	.227	.316	.367
2012	Mia	NL	106	343	66	15	1	12	(4	8)	119	29	41	40	49	5	103	3	1	2	0	0	-	8	.192	.297	.347
	9 ML YEARS		948	3131	737	159	9	118	(48	70)	1268	341	423	377	270	19	829	43	13	24	4	11	.27	72	.235	.303	.405

Travis Buck

Bats: L **Throws:** R **Pos:** PH-14; LF-11; RF-10   **Ht:** 6'2" **Wt:** 230 **Born:** 11/18/1983 **Age:** 29

								BATTING												BASERUNNING				AVERAGES		
Year	Team	Lg	G	AB	H	2B	3B	HR	(Hm | Rd)	TB	R	RBI	RC	TBB	IBB	SO	HBP	SH	SF	SB	CS	SB%	GDP	Avg	OBP	Slg
2012	CpChr*	AA	7	21	3	2	0	0	(- | -)	5	3	3	1	4	0	9	0	0	0	0	0	-	1	.143	.280	.238
2012	OKCity*	AAA	22	64	23	4	0	1	(- | -)	30	9	6	12	5	0	8	1	1	0	0	0	-	4	.359	.414	.469
2007	Oak	AL	82	285	82	22	5	7	(3 | 4)	135	41	34	48	39	2	66	4	2	4	4	1	.80	9	.288	.377	.474
2008	Oak	AL	38	155	35	9	1	7	(3 | 4)	67	16	25	22	11	0	38	4	0	2	1	0	1.00	2	.226	.291	.432
2009	Oak	AL	36	105	23	3	0	3	(2 | 1)	35	11	10	10	10	0	20	0	0	0	1	1	.50	0	.219	.287	.333
2010	Oak	AL	14	42	7	2	0	1	(1 | 0)	12	6	2	2	4	0	14	1	1	0	1	0	1.00	0	.167	.255	.286
2011	Cle	AL	50	149	34	11	0	2	(2 | 0)	51	18	18	17	8	0	30	2	0	1	1	1	.50	3	.228	.275	.342
2012	Hou	NL	33	74	16	5	1	0	(0 | 0)	23	7	6	5	6	0	18	1	0	0	0	0	-	0	.216	.284	.311
6 ML YEARS			253	810	197	52	7	20	(11 | 9)	323	99	95	104	78	2	186	12	3	7	8	3	.73	16	.243	.316	.399

Mark Buehrle

Pitches: L **Bats:** L **Pos:** SP-31   BURR-lee   **Ht:** 6'2" **Wt:** 245 **Born:** 3/23/1979 **Age:** 34

			HOW MUCH HE PITCHED					WHAT HE GAVE UP											THE RESULTS							
Year	Team	Lg	G	GS	CG	GF	IP	BFP	H	R	ER	HR	SH	SF	HB	TBB	IBB	SO	WP	Bk	W	L	Pct	Sh	Sv-Op	Hld	ERC	ERA
2000	CWS	AL	28	3	0	6	51.1	225	55	27	24	5	1	0	3	19	1	37	0	0	4	1	.800	0	0-2	3	4.56	4.21
2001	CWS	AL	32	32	4	0	221.1	885	188	89	81	24	9	4	8	48	2	126	1	5	16	8	.667	2	0-0	0	2.79	3.29
2002	CWS	AL	34	34	5	0	239.0	984	236	102	95	25	9	3	3	61	7	134	6	1	19	12	.613	2	0-0	0	3.53	3.58
2003	CWS	AL	35	35	2	0	230.1	978	250	124	106	22	7	7	5	61	2	119	1	0	14	14	.500	2	0-0	0	4.10	4.14
2004	CWS	AL	35	35	4	0	245.1	1016	257	119	106	33	4	6	5	51	2	165	0	0	16	10	.615	1	0-0	0	4.00	3.89
2005	CWS	AL	33	33	3	0	236.2	971	240	99	82	20	7	4	4	40	4	149	2	2	16	8	.667	1	0-0	0	3.21	3.12
2006	CWS	AL	32	32	1	0	204.0	876	247	124	113	36	6	7	6	48	5	98	0	1	12	13	.480	0	0-0	0	5.37	4.99
2007	CWS	AL	30	30	3	0	201.0	835	208	86	81	22	7	5	5	45	5	115	1	0	10	9	.526	1	0-0	0	3.75	3.63
2008	CWS	AL	34	34	1	0	218.2	918	240	106	92	22	2	6	5	52	4	140	4	0	15	12	.556	0	0-0	0	4.12	3.79
2009	CWS	AL	33	33	1	0	213.1	874	222	97	91	27	11	7	5	45	3	105	2	1	13	10	.565	1	0-0	0	3.91	3.84
2010	CWS	AL	33	33	3	0	210.1	897	246	105	100	17	6	7	1	49	1	99	3	5	13	13	.500	0	0-0	0	4.29	4.28
2011	CWS	AL	31	31	0	0	205.1	858	221	93	82	21	6	7	2	45	3	109	1	0	13	9	.591	0	0-0	0	3.86	3.59
2012	Mia	NL	31	31	1	0	202.1	828	197	88	84	26	14	7	4	40	3	125	2	0	13	13	.500	0	0-0	0	3.41	3.74
Postseason			6	4	1	2	30.2	124	32	14	14	3	2	1	1	1	1	16	0	0	2	1	.667	0	1-1	0	2.95	4.11
13 ML YEARS			421	396	28	6	2679.0	11145	2807	1259	1137	300	89	70	59	604	42	1521	23	15	174	132	.569	8	0-2	3	3.85	3.82

Francisley Bueno

Pitches: L **Bats:** L **Pos:** RP-18   fran-SISS-lee BWAY-no   **Ht:** 5'11" **Wt:** 200 **Born:** 3/5/1981 **Age:** 32

			HOW MUCH HE PITCHED					WHAT HE GAVE UP											THE RESULTS							
Year	Team	Lg	G	GS	CG	GF	IP	BFP	H	R	ER	HR	SH	SF	HB	TBB	IBB	SO	WP	Bk	W	L	Pct	Sh	Sv-Op	Hld	ERC	ERA
2006	Missi	AA	17	14	1	0	80.1	335	77	36	32	10	5	4	2	19	1	84	3	1	1	7	.125	1	0- -	-	3.43	3.59
2007	Missi	AA	22	19	0	0	112.2	490	132	55	46	8	8	3	2	26	2	77	5	4	6	4	.600	0	0- -	-	4.22	3.67
2007	Rchmd	AAA	3	3	0	0	19.1	81	19	6	6	3	1	0	0	3	0	19	2	1	1	0	1.000	0	0- -	-	3.26	2.79
2008	Rchmd	AAA	19	14	0	1	84.1	374	100	51	49	8	4	2	2	29	0	59	6	3	2	6	.250	0	0- -	-	4.99	5.23
2009	Gwnntt	AAA	33	5	0	5	54.2	228	47	21	19	1	1	1	4	21	2	33	1	0	4	1	.800	0	1- -	-	2.97	3.13
2012	Omha	AAA	35	0	0	16	55.2	227	43	23	17	5	3	2	3	15	1	54	3	0	1	4	.200	0	6- -	-	2.47	2.75
2008	Atl	NL	1	0	0	0	2.1	13	5	2	2	1	0	0	0	1	0	1	0	0	0	0	-	0	0-0	0	14.73	7.71
2012	KC	AL	18	0	0	6	17.1	69	16	4	3	0	0	1	1	2	1	7	0	0	1	1	.500	0	0-0	4	2.16	1.56
2 ML YEARS			19	0	0	6	19.2	82	21	6	5	1	0	1	1	3	1	8	0	0	1	1	.500	0	0-0	4	3.29	2.29

Madison Bumgarner

Pitches: L **Bats:** R **Pos:** SP-32   **Ht:** 6'5" **Wt:** 235 **Born:** 8/1/1989 **Age:** 23

			HOW MUCH HE PITCHED					WHAT HE GAVE UP											THE RESULTS							
Year	Team	Lg	G	GS	CG	GF	IP	BFP	H	R	ER	HR	SH	SF	HB	TBB	IBB	SO	WP	Bk	W	L	Pct	Sh	Sv-Op	Hld	ERC	ERA
2009	SF	NL	4	1	0	1	10.0	40	8	2	2	2	1	1	0	3	1	10	0	0	0	0	-	0	0-0	0	3.14	1.80
2010	SF	NL	18	18	0	0	111.0	472	119	40	37	11	0	4	5	26	2	86	1	1	7	6	.538	0	0-0	0	3.98	3.00
2011	SF	NL	33	33	0	0	204.2	844	202	82	73	12	12	4	5	46	5	191	0	1	13	13	.500	0	0-0	0	3.14	3.21
2012	SF	NL	32	32	2	0	208.1	849	183	87	78	23	7	4	7	49	6	191	3	2	16	11	.593	1	0-0	0	2.95	3.37
Postseason			4	3	0	0	20.2	83	18	5	5	1	2	1	0	5	1	18	0	0	2	0	1.000	0	0-0	0	2.63	2.18
4 ML YEARS			87	84	2	1	534.0	2205	512	211	190	48	20	13	17	124	14	478	4	4	36	30	.545	1	0-0	0	3.23	3.20

Dylan Bundy

Pitches: R **Bats:** B **Pos:** RP-2   **Ht:** 6'1" **Wt:** 195 **Born:** 11/15/1992 **Age:** 20

			HOW MUCH HE PITCHED					WHAT HE GAVE UP											THE RESULTS							
Year	Team	Lg	G	GS	CG	GF	IP	BFP	H	R	ER	HR	SH	SF	HB	TBB	IBB	SO	WP	Bk	W	L	Pct	Sh	Sv-Op	Hld	ERC	ERA
2012	Dlmrva	A	8	8	0	0	30.0	99	5	2	0	0	0	1	2	2	0	40	1	0	1	0	1.000	0	0- -	-	0.16	0.00
2012	Frdrck	A+	12	12	0	0	57.0	228	48	20	18	5	2	1	1	18	0	66	4	1	6	3	.667	0	0- -	-	2.99	2.84
2012	Bowie	AA	3	3	0	0	16.2	71	14	7	6	1	2	0	0	8	0	13	1	0	2	0	1.000	0	0- -	-	3.21	3.24
2012	Bal	AL	2	0	0	2	1.2	6	1	0	0	0	0	0	0	1	0	0	0	0	0	0	-	0	0-0	0	2.46	0.00

A.J. Burnett

Pitches: R **Bats:** R **Pos:** SP-31   **Ht:** 6'4" **Wt:** 230 **Born:** 1/3/1977 **Age:** 36

			HOW MUCH HE PITCHED					WHAT HE GAVE UP											THE RESULTS							
Year	Team	Lg	G	GS	CG	GF	IP	BFP	H	R	ER	HR	SH	SF	HB	TBB	IBB	SO	WP	Bk	W	L	Pct	Sh	Sv-Op	Hld	ERC	ERA
2012	Bradtn*	A+	2	2	0	0	6.1	30	7	9	6	0	0	0	1	2	0	9	1	0	0	2	.000	0	0- -	-	3.94	8.53
2012	Indy*	AAA	1	1	0	0	4.0	21	7	5	5	2	0	0	0	4	0	0	0	0	0	1	.000	0	0- -	-	17.05	11.25
1999	Fla	NL	7	7	0	0	41.1	182	37	23	16	3	1	3	0	25	2	33	0	0	4	2	.667	0	0-0	0	4.00	3.48
2000	Fla	NL	13	13	0	0	82.2	364	80	46	44	8	6	3	2	44	3	57	2	0	3	7	.300	0	0-0	0	4.45	4.79

Year	Team	Lg	G	GS	CG	GF	IP	BFP	H	R	ER	HR	SH	SF	HB	TBB	IBB	SO	WP	Bk	W	L	Pct	Sh	Sv-Op	Hld	ERC	ERA
2001	Fla	NL	27	27	2	0	173.1	733	145	82	78	20	6	8	7	83	3	128	7	1	11	12	.478	1	0-0	0	3.76	4.05
2002	Fla	NL	31	29	7	0	204.1	844	153	84	75	12	9	4	9	90	5	203	14	0	12	9	.571	5	0-1	0	2.77	3.30
2003	Fla	NL	4	4	0	0	23.0	106	18	13	12	2	2	1	2	18	2	21	0	0	0	2	.000	0	0-0	0	4.36	4.70
2004	Fla	NL	20	19	1	0	120.0	490	102	50	49	9	3	3	4	38	0	113	7	0	7	6	.538	0	0-0	0	2.95	3.68
2005	Fla	NL	32	32	4	0	209.0	873	184	97	80	12	7	5	7	79	1	198	12	0	12	12	.500	2	0-0	0	3.20	3.44
2006	Tor	AL	21	21	2	0	135.2	577	138	67	60	14	4	3	8	39	3	118	6	1	10	8	.556	1	0-0	0	3.97	3.98
2007	Tor	AL	25	25	2	0	165.2	691	131	74	69	23	0	2	12	66	2	176	5	0	10	8	.556	0	0-0	0	3.47	3.75
2008	Tor	AL	35	34	1	1	221.1	957	211	109	100	19	8	5	9	86	2	231	11	2	18	10	.643	0	0-0	0	3.78	4.07
2009	NYY	AL	33	33	1	0	207.0	896	193	99	93	25	2	5	10	97	0	195	17	1	13	9	.591	0	0-0	0	4.34	4.04
2010	NYY	AL	33	33	1	0	186.2	829	204	118	109	25	7	10	19	78	2	145	16	0	10	15	.400	0	0-0	0	5.43	5.26
2011	NYY	AL	33	32	0	0	190.1	837	190	115	109	31	4	10	9	83	2	173	25	0	11	11	.500	0	0-0	0	4.83	5.15
2012	Pit	NL	31	31	1	0	202.1	851	189	86	79	18	5	8	9	62	1	180	10	0	16	10	.615	1	0-0	0	3.44	3.51
	Postseason		7	7	0	0	39.0	173	32	22	22	3	1	0	6	23	3	31	4	0	2	2	.500	0	0-0	0	4.13	5.08
	14 ML YEARS		345	340	22	1	2162.2	9230	1975	1063	973	221	64	70	107	888	28	1971	134	5	137	121	.531	10	0-1	0	3.84	4.05

Alex Burnett

Pitches: R **Bats:** R **Pos:** RP-67 — **Ht:** 6'0" **Wt:** 221 **Born:** 7/26/1987 **Age:** 25

Year	Team	Lg	G	GS	CG	GF	IP	BFP	H	R	ER	HR	SH	SF	HB	TBB	IBB	SO	WP	Bk	W	L	Pct	Sh	Sv-Op	Hld	ERC	ERA
2010	Min	AL	41	0	0	11	47.2	211	52	28	28	6	4	1	2	23	3	37	2	2	2	2	.500	0	0-0	2	5.30	5.29
2011	Min	AL	66	0	0	12	50.2	225	50	32	31	4	2	4	8	21	1	33	2	0	2	5	.286	0	0-2	10	4.51	5.51
2012	Min	AL	67	0	0	18	71.2	309	71	33	28	4	2	2	3	26	5	36	6	0	4	4	.500	0	0-1	10	3.61	3.52
	3 ML YEARS		174	0	0	41	170.0	745	173	93	87	14	8	7	13	70	9	106	10	2	8	11	.421	0	0-3	22	4.33	4.61

Sean Burnett

Pitches: L **Bats:** L **Pos:** RP-70 — **Ht:** 6'1" **Wt:** 180 **Born:** 9/17/1982 **Age:** 30

Year	Team	Lg	G	GS	CG	GF	IP	BFP	H	R	ER	HR	SH	SF	HB	TBB	IBB	SO	WP	Bk	W	L	Pct	Sh	Sv-Op	Hld	ERC	ERA
2004	Pit	NL	13	13	1	0	71.2	318	86	41	40	9	2	1	1	28	2	30	2	0	5	5	.500	1	0-0	0	5.49	5.02
2008	Pit	NL	58	0	0	16	56.2	253	57	31	30	7	4	3	2	34	3	42	4	0	1	1	.500	0	0-0	8	5.23	4.76
2009	2 Tms	NL	71	0	0	8	57.2	237	36	21	20	6	6	1	3	28	8	43	4	0	2	3	.400	0	1-3	11	2.43	3.12
2010	Was	NL	73	0	0	10	63.0	261	52	17	15	3	4	0	1	20	4	62	2	0	1	7	.125	0	3-4	20	2.43	2.14
2011	Was	NL	69	0	0	17	56.2	242	54	24	24	6	3	2	3	21	4	33	2	0	5	5	.500	0	4-11	15	3.85	3.81
2012	Was	NL	70	0	0	16	56.2	239	58	16	15	4	1	2	3	12	3	57	2	0	1	2	.333	0	2-5	31	3.38	2.38
09	Pit	NL	38	0	0	7	32.1	133	22	12	11	3	4	1	3	15	4	23	2	0	1	2	.333	0	1-2	6	2.77	3.06
09	Was	NL	33	0	0	1	25.1	104	14	9	9	3	2	0	0	13	4	20	2	0	1	1	.500	0	0-1	5	2.02	3.20
	6 ML YEARS		354	13	1	67	362.1	1550	343	150	144	35	20	9	13	143	24	267	16	0	15	23	.395	1	10-23	85	3.78	3.58

Cory Burns

Pitches: R **Bats:** R **Pos:** RP-17 — **Ht:** 6'0" **Wt:** 205 **Born:** 10/9/1987 **Age:** 25

Year	Team	Lg	G	GS	CG	GF	IP	BFP	H	R	ER	HR	SH	SF	HB	TBB	IBB	SO	WP	Bk	W	L	Pct	Sh	Sv-Op	Hld	ERC	ERA
2009	MhVlly	A-	22	0	0	21	32.2	124	18	8	7	2	0	1	2	6	0	37	2	0	3	2	.600	0	11--	-	1.28	1.93
2010	Lk Cty	A	14	0	0	14	15.2	61	13	4	4	0	0	0	0	1	0	25	1	0	0	0	-	0	12--	-	1.49	2.30
2010	Knstn	A+	40	0	0	39	39.1	161	30	13	8	2	2	1	2	13	0	56	1	0	1	2	.333	0	30--	-	2.43	1.83
2011	Akron	AA	54	0	0	52	59.2	235	47	15	14	3	5	1	0	15	2	70	7	0	2	5	.286	0	35--	-	2.11	2.11
2012	Tucsn	AAA	54	0	0	15	66.0	261	49	25	23	1	1	0	4	17	3	78	8	0	1	2	.333	0	3--	-	1.90	3.14
2012	SD	NL	17	0	0	9	18.0	92	26	11	11	1	0	0	1	10	1	18	1	0	0	1	.000	0	0-0	0	6.90	5.50

Emmanuel Burriss

Bats: B **Throws:** R **Pos:** 2B-37; PH-10; 3B-6; SS-6; PR-5; RF-1 — **Ht:** 6'0" **Wt:** 205 **Born:** 1/17/1985 **Age:** 28

Year	Team	Lg	G	AB	H	2B	3B	HR	(Hm	Rd)	TB	R	RBI	RC	TBB	IBB	SO	HBP	SH	SF	SB	CS	SB%	GDP	Avg	OBP	Slg
2012	Fresno*	AAA	29	106	29	7	2	0	(-	-)	40	12	3	15	11	2	12	1	0	2	5	0	1.00	0	.274	.342	.377
2008	SF	NL	95	240	68	6	1	1	(0	1)	79	37	18	22	23	1	24	5	5	1	13	5	.72	7	.283	.357	.329
2009	SF	NL	61	202	48	6	0	0	(0	0)	54	18	13	15	14	1	34	2	1	1	11	4	.73	3	.238	.292	.267
2010	SF	NL	7	5	2	0	0	0	(0	0)	2	3	0	1	0	0	1	0	0	0	0	0	-	0	.400	.400	.400
2011	SF	NL	59	137	28	1	0	0	(0	0)	29	14	4	6	6	0	17	3	6	0	11	3	.79	6	.204	.253	.212
2012	SF	NL	60	136	29	1	0	0	(0	0)	30	15	7	4	10	1	25	1	2	1	5	3	.63	6	.213	.270	.221
	5 ML YEARS		282	720	175	14	1	1	(0	1)	194	87	42	48	53	3	101	11	14	3	40	15	.73	18	.243	.304	.269

Sean Burroughs

Bats: L **Throws:** R **Pos:** PH-7; 3B-3; 1B-1; DH-1 — **Ht:** 6'1" **Wt:** 195 **Born:** 9/12/1980 **Age:** 32

Year	Team	Lg	G	AB	H	2B	3B	HR	(Hm	Rd)	TB	R	RBI	RC	TBB	IBB	SO	HBP	SH	SF	SB	CS	SB%	GDP	Avg	OBP	Slg
2012	Roch*	AAA	67	221	60	14	0	1	(-	-)	77	23	18	26	16	1	25	2	0	1	2	0	1.00	8	.271	.326	.348
2002	SD	NL	63	192	52	5	1	1	(0	1)	62	18	11	15	12	1	30	1	1	0	2	0	1.00	5	.271	.317	.323
2003	SD	NL	146	517	148	27	6	7	(2	5)	208	62	58	68	44	4	75	11	2	4	7	2	.78	13	.286	.352	.402
2004	SD	NL	130	523	156	23	3	2	(0	2)	191	76	47	70	31	4	52	9	1	6	5	4	.56	6	.298	.348	.365
2005	SD	NL	93	284	71	7	2	1	(1	0)	85	20	17	24	24	4	41	5	3	1	4	0	1.00	7	.250	.318	.299
2006	TB	AL	8	21	4	1	0	0	(0	0)	5	3	1	2	4	0	7	0	0	0	1	0	1.00	1	.190	.320	.238
2011	Ari	NL	78	110	30	4	0	1	(0	1)	37	8	8	10	3	0	15	0	1	1	1	0	1.00	4	.273	.289	.336
2012	Min	AL	10	17	2	1	0	0	(0	0)	3	0	1	0	1	0	3	0	0	0	0	0	-	1	.118	.167	.176
	Postseason		5	4	1	0	0	0	(0	0)	1	0	0	1	0	0	2	0	0	0	0	0	-	0	.250	.250	.250
	7 ML YEARS		528	1664	463	68	12	12	(3	9)	591	187	143	189	119	13	223	26	8	6	20	6	.77	38	.278	.335	.355

Jared Burton

Pitches: R **Bats:** R **Pos:** RP-64　　　　　　　　　　　　　　　　**Ht:** 6'6" **Wt:** 225 **Born:** 6/2/1981 **Age:** 32

			HOW MUCH HE PITCHED					WHAT HE GAVE UP											THE RESULTS						
Year Team	Lg	G	GS	CG	GF	IP	BFP	H	R	ER	HR	SH	SF	HB	TBB	IBB	SO	WP	Bk	W	L	Pct	Sh	Sv-Op	Hld	ERC	ERA
2007 Cin	NL	47	0	0	12	43.0	176	28	15	12	2	1	1	2	22	4	36	3	1	4	2	.667	0	0-3	11	2.37	2.51
2008 Cin	NL	54	0	0	12	58.2	257	56	24	21	6	2	3	2	25	3	58	2	1	5	1	.833	0	0-2	11	3.93	3.22
2009 Cin	NL	53	0	0	13	59.1	265	61	30	29	5	3	1	4	23	6	45	2	0	1	0	1.000	0	0-0	7	4.08	4.40
2010 Cin	NL	4	0	0	2	3.1	10	0	0	0	0	0	0	0	0	0	1	0	0	0	0	-	0	0-0	1	0.00	0.00
2011 Cin	NL	6	0	0	1	4.2	23	6	2	2	1	1	0	0	3	0	3	0	0	0	0	-	0	0-0	1	7.61	3.86
2012 Min	AL	64	0	0	12	62.0	245	41	21	15	5	2	1	5	16	1	55	0	0	3	2	.600	0	5-9	18	1.98	2.18
6 ML YEARS		228	0	0	52	231.0	976	192	92	79	19	9	6	13	89	14	198	7	2	13	5	.722	0	5-14	49	3.08	3.08

Drew Butera

Bats: R **Throws:** R **Pos:** C-41; PH-3　　　　　　bue-TARE-ah　　　　　　**Ht:** 6'1" **Wt:** 201 **Born:** 8/9/1983 **Age:** 29

								BATTING												BASERUNNING				AVERAGES		
Year Team	Lg	G	AB	H	2B	3B	HR	(Hm	Rd)	TB	R	RBI	RC	TBB	IBB	SO	HBP	SH	SF	SB	CS	SB%	GDP	Avg	OBP	Slg
2012 Roch*	AAA	15	43	12	3	0	1	(-	-)	18	6	5	6	3	0	9	0	1	1	0	0	-	0	.279	.319	.419
2010 Min	AL	49	142	28	6	1	2	(0	2)	42	12	13	7	4	0	25	4	3	2	0	0	-	5	.197	.237	.296
2011 Min	AL	93	234	39	9	1	2	(1	1)	56	19	23	11	11	0	42	2	6	1	0	0	-	7	.167	.210	.239
2012 Min	AL	42	111	22	6	0	1	(1	0)	31	7	5	6	9	0	26	2	0	0	0	0	-	3	.198	.270	.279
3 ML YEARS		184	487	89	21	2	5	(2	3)	129	38	41	24	24	0	93	8	9	3	0	0	-	15	.183	.232	.265

Billy Butler

Bats: R **Throws:** R **Pos:** DH-138; 1B-20; PH-3　　　　　　　　　　**Ht:** 6'1" **Wt:** 240 **Born:** 4/18/1986 **Age:** 27

								BATTING												BASERUNNING				AVERAGES		
Year Team	Lg	G	AB	H	2B	3B	HR	(Hm	Rd)	TB	R	RBI	RC	TBB	IBB	SO	HBP	SH	SF	SB	CS	SB%	GDP	Avg	OBP	Slg
2007 KC	AL	92	329	96	23	2	8	(5	3)	147	38	52	50	27	5	55	2	0	2	0	0	-	8	.292	.347	.447
2008 KC	AL	124	443	122	22	0	11	(4	7)	177	44	55	57	33	0	57	0	0	2	0	1	.00	23	.275	.324	.400
2009 KC	AL	159	608	183	51	1	21	(16	5)	299	78	93	99	58	3	103	2	0	4	1	0	1.00	19	.301	.362	.492
2010 KC	AL	158	595	189	45	0	15	(9	6)	279	77	78	91	69	8	78	5	0	9	0	0	-	32	.318	.388	.469
2011 KC	AL	159	597	174	44	0	19	(9	10)	275	74	95	94	66	15	95	3	0	7	2	1	.67	16	.291	.361	.461
2012 KC	AL	161	614	192	32	1	29	(11	18)	313	72	107	102	54	9	111	7	0	4	2	1	.67	20	.313	.373	.510
6 ML YEARS		853	3186	956	217	4	103	(54	49)	1490	383	480	493	307	40	499	19	0	28	5	3	.63	119	.300	.362	.468

Marlon Byrd

Bats: R **Throws:** R **Pos:** CF-47; RF-2; PH-1　　　　　　　　　　**Ht:** 6'0" **Wt:** 215 **Born:** 8/30/1977 **Age:** 35

								BATTING												BASERUNNING				AVERAGES		
Year Team	Lg	G	AB	H	2B	3B	HR	(Hm	Rd)	TB	R	RBI	RC	TBB	IBB	SO	HBP	SH	SF	SB	CS	SB%	GDP	Avg	OBP	Slg
2002 Phi	NL	10	35	8	2	0	1	(1	0)	13	2	1	0	1	0	8	0	0	0	0	2	.00	0	.229	.250	.371
2003 Phi	NL	135	495	150	28	4	7	(3	4)	207	86	45	72	44	3	94	7	4	3	11	1	.92	8	.303	.366	.418
2004 Phi	NL	106	346	79	13	2	5	(3	2)	111	48	33	35	22	1	68	7	2	1	2	2	.50	10	.228	.287	.321
2005 2 Tms	NL	79	229	61	15	2	2	(0	2)	86	20	26	30	19	1	50	2	5	4	5	1	.83	5	.266	.323	.376
2006 Was	NL	78	197	44	8	1	5	(1	4)	69	28	18	18	22	1	47	6	1	2	3	3	.50	6	.223	.317	.350
2007 Tex	AL	109	414	127	17	8	10	(4	6)	190	60	70	68	29	3	88	5	0	6	5	3	.63	9	.307	.355	.459
2008 Tex	AL	122	403	120	28	4	10	(7	3)	186	70	53	63	46	3	62	9	2	2	7	2	.78	10	.298	.380	.462
2009 Tex	AL	146	547	155	43	2	20	(14	6)	262	66	89	91	32	2	98	10	0	10	8	4	.67	11	.283	.329	.479
2010 ChC	NL	152	580	170	39	2	12	(6	6)	249	84	66	80	31	1	98	17	0	2	5	1	.83	12	.293	.346	.429
2011 ChC	NL	119	446	123	22	2	9	(4	5)	176	51	35	43	25	2	78	8	1	2	3	2	.60	13	.276	.324	.395
2012 2 Tms	NL	48	143	30	2	0	1	(0	1)	35	10	9	8	5	1	31	2	1	2	0	3	.00	2	.210	.243	.245
05 Phi	NL	5	13	4	0	0	0	(0	0)	4	0	0	2	1	0	3	1	0	0	0	0	-	0	.308	.400	.308
05 Was	NL	74	216	57	15	2	2	(0	2)	82	20	26	28	18	1	47	1	5	4	5	1	.83	5	.264	.318	.380
12 ChC	NL	13	43	3	0	0	0	(0	0)	3	1	2	0	3	1	10	1	0	0	0	1	.00	2	.070	.149	.070
12 Bos	AL	35	100	27	2	0	1	(0	1)	32	9	7	8	2	0	21	1	1	2	0	2	.00	1	.270	.286	.320
11 ML YEARS		1104	3835	1067	217	27	82	(43	39)	1584	525	445	508	276	18	722	73	16	34	49	24	.67	87	.278	.336	.413

Tim Byrdak

Pitches: L **Bats:** L **Pos:** RP-56　　　　　　BURR-dack　　　　　　**Ht:** 5'11" **Wt:** 190 **Born:** 10/31/1973 **Age:** 39

			HOW MUCH HE PITCHED					WHAT HE GAVE UP											THE RESULTS						
Year Team	Lg	G	GS	CG	GF	IP	BFP	H	R	ER	HR	SH	SF	HB	TBB	IBB	SO	WP	Bk	W	L	Pct	Sh	Sv-Op	Hld	ERC	ERA
1998 KC	AL	3	0	0	0	1.2	9	5	1	1	1	0	0	0	0	0	1	0	0	0	0	-	0	0-0	0	23.52	5.40
1999 KC	AL	33	0	0	5	24.2	128	32	24	21	5	3	0	1	20	2	17	3	1	0	3	.000	0	1-4	10	8.29	7.66
2000 KC	AL	12	0	0	1	6.1	34	11	8	8	3	0	0	0	4	0	8	1	0	0	1	.000	0	0-2	3	13.14	11.37
2005 Bal	AL	41	0	0	3	26.2	131	27	14	12	1	2	1	1	21	1	31	5	0	0	1	.000	0	1-1	11	5.04	4.05
2006 Bal	AL	16	0	0	2	7.0	42	14	10	10	2	2	0	0	8	1	2	1	0	1	0	1.000	0	0-0	3	15.90	12.86
2007 Det	AL	39	0	0	3	45.0	199	38	23	16	3	2	5	1	26	4	49	3	0	3	0	1.000	0	1-2	8	3.53	3.20
2008 Hou	NL	59	0	0	9	55.1	237	45	24	24	10	2	1	2	29	2	47	0	0	2	1	.667	0	0-0	8	4.18	3.90
2009 Hou	NL	76	0	0	8	61.1	261	39	23	22	10	0	3	3	36	0	58	2	0	1	2	.333	0	0-2	9	3.38	3.23
2010 Hou	NL	64	0	0	9	38.2	170	40	15	15	4	0	3	0	20	0	29	2	0	2	2	.500	0	0-0	11	4.83	3.49
2011 NYM	NL	72	0	0	10	53.2	220	34	20	16	3	4	2	1	19	4	47	1	0	2	1	.667	0	1-4	8	3.61	3.82
2012 NYM	NL	56	0	0	4	30.2	125	18	16	15	2	4	2	1	18	5	34	0	0	2	2	.500	0	0-2	17	2.29	4.40
11 ML YEARS		471	0	0	54	335.0	1504	303	178	160	44	19	17	10	201	19	323	18	1	13	13	.500	0	4-17	88	4.52	4.30

Alberto Cabrera

Pitches: R **Bats:** R **Pos:** RP-25   **Ht:** 6'4" **Wt:** 210 **Born:** 10/25/1988 **Age:** 24

Year	Team	Lg	G	GS	CG	GF	IP	BFP	H	R	ER	HR	SH	SF	HB	TBB	IBB	SO	WP	Bk	W	L	Pct	Sh	Sv-Op	Hld	ERC	ERA
2007	Boise	A-	9	9	0	0	38.1	163	41	24	23	4	0	2	0	18	0	33	3	0	3	3	.500	0	0- -	-	5.02	5.40
2008	Peoria	A	12	11	0	0	52.0	234	55	39	33	7	0	7	1	30	0	37	2	0	4	6	.400	0	0- -	-	5.54	5.71
2009	Peoria	A	27	8	0	2	96.1	434	94	53	48	6	4	3	6	54	2	73	15	3	8	2	.800	0	1- -	-	4.48	4.48
2010	Dytona	A+	18	17	1	0	93.1	391	92	44	34	6	0	1	1	26	1	90	12	1	7	5	.583	1	0- -	-	3.31	3.28
2010	Tenn	AA	10	9	0	0	42.2	213	57	39	30	1	2	3	3	24	0	35	8	1	0	4	.000	0	0- -	-	6.20	6.33
2011	Tenn	AA	9	9	0	0	48.2	225	60	36	29	4	4	3	2	21	0	34	4	0	6	2	.750	0	0- -	-	5.56	5.36
2011	Iowa	AAA	19	17	0	1	88.2	421	118	67	65	11	3	4	3	53	0	67	11	0	3	6	.333	0	0- -	-	7.41	6.60
2012	Tenn	AA	23	0	0	13	35.2	149	30	15	10	2	0	1	0	10	0	45	1	0	2	1	.667	0	5- -	-	2.42	2.52
2012	Iowa	AAA	13	0	0	7	19.1	93	29	13	9	4	0	0	2	4	0	29	2	0	2	0	1.000	0	0- -	-	7.42	4.19
2012	ChC	NL	25	0	0	6	21.2	99	16	15	13	1	1	1	1	18	1	27	5	0	1	1	.500	0	0-0	1	3.90	5.40

Asdrubal Cabrera

Bats: B **Throws:** R **Pos:** SS-136; DH-6; PH-1   azz-DRUE-bull   **Ht:** 6'0" **Wt:** 180 **Born:** 11/13/1985 **Age:** 27

							BATTING														BASERUNNING				AVERAGES		
Year	Team	Lg	G	AB	H	2B	3B	HR	(Hm	Rd)	TB	R	RBI	RC	TBB	IBB	SO	HBP	SH	SF	SB	CS	SB%	GDP	Avg	OBP	Slg
2007	Cle	AL	45	159	45	9	2	3	(1	2)	67	30	22	27	17	0	29	2	5	3	0	0	-	7	.283	.354	.421
2008	Cle	AL	114	352	91	20	0	6	(5	1)	129	48	47	48	46	2	77	4	11	5	4	4	.50	8	.259	.346	.366
2009	Cle	AL	131	523	161	42	4	6	(4	2)	229	81	68	81	44	1	89	1	10	3	17	4	.81	13	.308	.361	.438
2010	Cle	AL	97	381	105	16	1	3	(2	1)	132	39	29	46	25	0	60	5	11	3	6	4	.60	10	.276	.326	.346
2011	Cle	AL	151	604	165	32	3	25	(13	12)	278	87	92	100	44	5	119	11	4	4	17	5	.77	10	.273	.332	.460
2012	Cle	AL	143	555	150	35	1	16	(10	6)	235	70	68	74	52	3	99	6	1	2	9	4	.69	18	.270	.338	.423
	Postseason		11	46	10	0	0	1	(1	0)	13	5	6	5	2	0	12	0	3	1	0	0	-	2	.217	.245	.283
	6 ML YEARS		681	2574	717	154	11	59	(35	24)	1070	355	326	376	228	11	473	29	42	20	53	21	.72	66	.279	.342	.416

Edwar Cabrera

Pitches: L **Bats:** L **Pos:** SP-2   **Ht:** 6'0" **Wt:** 175 **Born:** 10/20/1987 **Age:** 25

Year	Team	Lg	G	GS	CG	GF	IP	BFP	H	R	ER	HR	SH	SF	HB	TBB	IBB	SO	WP	Bk	W	L	Pct	Sh	Sv-Op	Hld	ERC	ERA
2008	Casper	R+	9	5	0	0	30.0	144	38	29	26	7	1	0	3	15	0	38	7	3	0	4	.000	0	0- -	-	7.56	7.80
2009	Casper	R+	9	1	0	1	21.1	97	19	10	8	2	1	1	2	12	0	28	1	0	0	0	-	0	0- -	-	4.31	3.38
2010	TriCity	A-	14	14	0	0	73.1	315	71	34	25	2	0	1	7	24	0	87	9	2	1	8	.111	0	0- -	-	3.48	3.07
2011	Ashvll	A	13	13	0	0	86.0	351	77	33	30	10	1	1	6	18	0	110	4	0	4	2	.667	0	0- -	-	3.17	3.14
2011	Mdest	A+	13	13	0	0	81.0	338	78	33	32	8	3	1	1	23	0	107	8	0	4	1	.800	0	0- -	-	3.47	3.56
2012	Tulsa	AA	15	15	0	0	98.0	378	65	35	32	15	1	1	3	23	1	82	3	2	8	4	.667	0	0- -	-	2.16	2.94
2012	ColSpr	AAA	6	6	1	0	31.2	133	26	18	12	6	2	1	2	12	0	39	1	1	3	1	.750	0	0- -	-	3.85	3.41
2012	Col	NL	2	2	0	0	5.2	33	9	9	7	3	0	0	2	7	1	5	0	0	0	2	.000	0	0-0	0	15.41	11.12

Everth Cabrera

Bats: B **Throws:** R **Pos:** SS-111; 2B-6; PH-2; PR-2; 3B-1   EVV-urth   **Ht:** 5'10" **Wt:** 175 **Born:** 11/17/1986 **Age:** 26

							BATTING														BASERUNNING				AVERAGES		
Year	Team	Lg	G	AB	H	2B	3B	HR	(Hm	Rd)	TB	R	RBI	RC	TBB	IBB	SO	HBP	SH	SF	SB	CS	SB%	GDP	Avg	OBP	Slg
2012	Tucsn*	AAA	34	144	48	9	1	0	(-	-)	59	27	15	26	12	1	28	1	2	0	15	0	1.00	0	.333	.389	.410
2009	SD	NL	103	377	96	18	8	2	(1	1)	136	59	31	48	46	5	88	5	8	2	25	8	.76	3	.255	.342	.361
2010	SD	NL	76	212	44	6	3	1	(0	1)	59	22	22	15	19	3	54	2	8	0	10	6	.63	8	.208	.279	.278
2011	SD	NL	2	8	1	0	0	0	(0	0)	1	1	0	1	1	0	3	0	0	0	2	0	1.00	0	.125	.222	.125
2012	SD	NL	115	398	98	19	3	2	(0	2)	129	49	24	43	43	2	110	3	5	0	44	4	.92	3	.246	.324	.324
	4 ML YEARS		296	995	239	43	14	5	(1	4)	325	131	77	107	109	10	255	10	21	2	81	18	.82	14	.240	.321	.327

Melky Cabrera

Bats: B **Throws:** L **Pos:** LF-106; RF-11; PH-1   **Ht:** 6'0" **Wt:** 200 **Born:** 8/11/1984 **Age:** 28

							BATTING														BASERUNNING				AVERAGES		
Year	Team	Lg	G	AB	H	2B	3B	HR	(Hm	Rd)	TB	R	RBI	RC	TBB	IBB	SO	HBP	SH	SF	SB	CS	SB%	GDP	Avg	OBP	Slg
2005	NYY	AL	6	19	4	0	0	0	(0	0)	4	1	0	0	0	0	2	0	0	0	0	0	-	0	.211	.211	.211
2006	NYY	AL	130	460	129	26	2	7	(3	4)	180	75	50	68	56	3	59	2	5	1	12	5	.71	9	.280	.360	.391
2007	NYY	AL	150	545	149	24	8	8	(4	4)	213	66	73	70	43	0	68	5	10	9	13	5	.72	14	.273	.327	.391
2008	NYY	AL	129	414	103	12	1	8	(4	4)	141	42	37	37	29	5	58	3	4	3	9	2	.82	11	.249	.301	.341
2009	NYY	AL	154	485	133	28	1	13	(9	4)	202	66	68	69	43	4	59	4	4	4	10	2	.83	15	.274	.336	.416
2010	Atl	NL	147	458	117	27	3	4	(1	3)	162	50	42	45	42	11	64	1	5	3	7	1	.88	8	.255	.317	.354
2011	KC	NL	155	658	201	44	5	18	(6	12)	309	102	87	92	35	3	94	1	7	5	20	10	.67	13	.305	.339	.470
2012	SF	NL	113	459	159	25	10	11	(9	2)	237	84	60	83	36	4	63	0	1	5	13	5	.72	8	.346	.390	.516
	Postseason		22	75	16	2	0	1	(0	1)	21	8	7	5	3	0	16	0	2	0	0	0	-	0	.213	.244	.280
	8 ML YEARS		984	3498	995	186	30	69	(29	40)	1448	486	417	464	284	30	467	16	36	30	84	30	.74	78	.284	.338	.414

Miguel Cabrera

Bats: R **Throws:** R **Pos:** 3B-154; DH-7; 1B-2   **Ht:** 6'4" **Wt:** 240 **Born:** 4/18/1983 **Age:** 30

							BATTING														BASERUNNING				AVERAGES		
Year	Team	Lg	G	AB	H	2B	3B	HR	(Hm	Rd)	TB	R	RBI	RC	TBB	IBB	SO	HBP	SH	SF	SB	CS	SB%	GDP	Avg	OBP	Slg
2003	Fla	NL	87	314	84	21	3	12	(7	5)	147	39	62	51	25	3	84	2	4	1	0	2	.00	12	.268	.325	.468
2004	Fla	NL	160	603	177	31	1	33	(14	19)	309	101	112	92	68	5	148	6	0	8	5	2	.71	20	.294	.366	.512
2005	Fla	NL	158	613	198	43	2	33	(11	22)	344	106	116	108	64	12	125	2	0	6	1	0	1.00	20	.323	.385	.561
2006	Fla	NL	158	576	195	50	2	26	(15	11)	327	112	114	132	86	27	108	10	0	4	9	6	.60	18	.339	.430	.568
2007	Fla	NL	157	588	188	38	2	34	(19	15)	332	91	119	122	79	23	127	5	1	7	2	1	.67	17	.320	.401	.565

Year	Team	Lg	G	AB	H	2B	3B	HR	(Hm	Rd)	TB	R	RBI	RC	TBB	IBB	SO	HBP	SH	SF	SB	CS	SB%	GDP	Avg	OBP	Slg
2008	Det	AL	160	616	180	36	2	37	(19	18)	331	85	127	109	56	6	126	3	0	9	1	0	1.00	16	.292	.349	.537
2009	Det	AL	160	611	198	34	0	34	(19	15)	334	96	103	114	68	14	107	5	0	1	6	2	.75	22	.324	.396	.547
2010	Det	AL	150	548	180	45	1	38	(17	21)	341	111	126	122	89	32	95	3	0	8	3	3	.50	17	.328	.420	.622
2011	Det	AL	161	572	197	48	0	30	(15	15)	335	111	105	141	108	22	89	3	0	5	2	1	.67	24	.344	.448	.586
2012	Det	AL	161	622	205	40	0	44	(28	16)	377	109	139	123	66	17	98	3	0	6	4	1	.80	28	.330	.393	.606
	Postseason		28	103	29	6	0	8	(2	6)	59	18	22	19	16	5	30	1	1	0	2	0	1.00	3	.282	.383	.573
10 ML YEARS			1512	5663	1802	386	13	321	(164	157)	3177	961	1123	1114	709	161	1107	42	5	55	33	18	.65	194	.318	.395	.561

Trevor Cahill

Pitches: R **Bats:** R **Pos:** SP-32   KAY-hill   **Ht:** 6'4" **Wt:** 222 **Born:** 3/1/1988 **Age:** 25

Year	Team	Lg	G	GS	CG	GF	IP	BFP	H	R	ER	HR	SH	SF	HB	TBB	IBB	SO	WP	Bk	W	L	Pct	Sh	Sv-Op	Hld	ERC	ERA
2009	Oak	AL	32	32	0	0	178.2	773	185	99	92	27	4	7	4	72	1	90	5	0	10	13	.435	0	0-0	0	4.79	4.63
2010	Oak	AL	30	30	1	0	196.2	783	155	73	65	19	3	6	6	63	1	118	2	2	18	8	.692	1	0-0	0	2.81	2.97
2011	Oak	AL	34	34	0	0	207.2	901	214	102	96	19	8	6	8	82	1	147	15	0	12	14	.462	0	0-0	0	4.34	4.16
2012	Ari	NL	32	32	2	0	200.0	839	184	93	84	16	12	6	11	74	0	156	10	2	13	12	.520	1	0-0	0	3.66	3.78
4 ML YEARS			128	128	3	0	783.0	3296	738	367	337	81	27	25	29	291	3	511	32	4	53	47	.530	2	0-0	0	3.87	3.87

Lorenzo Cain

Bats: R **Throws:** R **Pos:** CF-50; RF-9; PH-4; LF-1; DH-1; PR-1   **Ht:** 6'2" **Wt:** 200 **Born:** 4/13/1986 **Age:** 27

Year	Team	Lg	G	AB	H	2B	3B	HR	(Hm	Rd)	TB	R	RBI	RC	TBB	IBB	SO	HBP	SH	SF	SB	CS	SB%	GDP	Avg	OBP	Slg
2012	NWArk*	AA	7	24	5	1	0	1	(-	-)	9	4	1	1	0	0	6	0	0	0	0	0	-	0	.208	.208	.375
2012	Omha*	AAA	7	28	9	3	0	1	(-	-)	15	4	6	5	2	0	4	0	0	1	0	0	-	0	.321	.355	.536
2010	Mil	NL	43	147	45	11	1	1	(1	0)	61	17	13	23	9	0	28	1	0	1	7	1	.88	1	.306	.348	.415
2011	KC	AL	6	22	6	1	0	0	(0	0)	7	4	1	2	1	0	4	0	0	0	0	0	-	0	.273	.304	.318
2012	KC	AL	61	222	59	9	2	7	(3	4)	93	27	31	32	15	0	56	3	0	4	10	0	1.00	4	.266	.316	.419
3 ML YEARS			110	391	110	21	3	8	(4	4)	161	48	45	57	25	0	88	4	0	5	17	1	.94	5	.281	.327	.412

Matt Cain

Pitches: R **Bats:** R **Pos:** SP-32   **Ht:** 6'3" **Wt:** 230 **Born:** 10/1/1984 **Age:** 28

Year	Team	Lg	G	GS	CG	GF	IP	BFP	H	R	ER	HR	SH	SF	HB	TBB	IBB	SO	WP	Bk	W	L	Pct	Sh	Sv-Op	Hld	ERC	ERA
2005	SF	NL	7	7	1	0	46.1	181	24	12	12	4	2	1	0	19	1	30	1	0	2	1	.667	0	0-0	0	1.61	2.33
2006	SF	NL	32	31	1	1	190.2	818	157	93	88	18	11	6	6	87	1	179	9	2	13	12	.520	1	0-0	0	3.35	4.15
2007	SF	NL	32	32	1	0	200.0	832	173	84	81	14	8	5	5	79	3	163	12	0	7	16	.304	0	0-0	0	3.23	3.65
2008	SF	NL	34	34	1	0	217.2	933	206	95	91	19	7	7	7	91	9	186	7	2	8	14	.364	1	0-0	0	3.84	3.76
2009	SF	NL	33	33	4	0	217.2	886	184	73	70	22	10	6	3	73	6	171	9	0	14	8	.636	0	0-0	0	3.06	2.89
2010	SF	NL	33	33	4	0	223.1	896	181	84	78	22	6	7	4	61	4	177	4	0	13	11	.542	2	0-0	0	2.65	3.14
2011	SF	NL	33	33	1	0	221.2	907	177	82	71	9	11	6	9	63	5	179	4	0	12	11	.522	0	0-0	0	2.31	2.88
2012	SF	NL	32	32	2	0	219.1	876	177	73	68	21	11	9	9	51	1	193	8	0	16	5	.762	2	0-0	0	2.57	2.79
	Postseason		3	3	0	0	21.1	85	13	1	0	0	1	0	2	7	1	13	1	0	2	0	1.000	0	0-0	0	1.56	0.00
8 ML YEARS			236	235	15	1	1536.2	6329	1279	596	559	129	66	47	43	524	30	1278	58	4	85	78	.521	6	0-0	0	2.93	3.27

Miguel Cairo

Bats: R **Throws:** R **Pos:** 1B-24; PH-24; 3B-13; 2B-8; PR-3; DH-1   **Ht:** 6'1" **Wt:** 225 **Born:** 5/4/1974 **Age:** 39

Year	Team	Lg	G	AB	H	2B	3B	HR	(Hm	Rd)	TB	R	RBI	RC	TBB	IBB	SO	HBP	SH	SF	SB	CS	SB%	GDP	Avg	OBP	Slg
2012	Dayton*	A+	3	10	0	0	0	0	(-	-)	0	0	0	0	0	0	2	0	1	0	0	0	-	0	.000	.000	.000
1996	Tor	AL	9	27	6	2	0	0	(0	0)	8	5	1	2	2	0	9	1	0	0	0	0	-	1	.222	.300	.296
1997	ChC	NL	16	29	7	1	0	0	(0	0)	8	7	1	3	2	0	3	1	0	0	0	0	-	0	.241	.313	.276
1998	TB	AL	150	515	138	26	5	5	(3	2)	189	49	46	58	24	0	44	6	11	2	19	8	.70	9	.268	.307	.367
1999	TB	AL	120	465	137	15	5	3	(1	2)	171	61	36	57	24	0	46	7	7	5	22	7	.76	13	.295	.335	.368
2000	TB	AL	119	375	98	18	2	1	(0	1)	123	49	34	42	29	0	34	2	6	5	28	7	.80	7	.261	.314	.328
2001	2 Tms	NL	93	156	46	8	1	3	(2	1)	65	25	16	23	18	1	23	0	7	1	2	1	.67	4	.295	.366	.417
2002	StL	NL	108	184	46	9	2	2	(1	1)	65	28	23	19	13	2	36	3	6	2	1	1	.50	5	.250	.307	.353
2003	StL	NL	92	261	64	15	2	5	(2	3)	98	41	32	25	13	1	30	6	3	7	4	1	.80	6	.245	.289	.375
2004	NYY	AL	122	360	105	17	5	6	(4	2)	150	48	42	50	18	1	49	14	12	4	11	3	.79	7	.292	.346	.417
2005	NYM	NL	100	327	82	18	0	2	(1	1)	106	31	19	29	19	2	31	4	12	5	13	3	.81	5	.251	.296	.324
2006	NYY	AL	81	222	53	12	2	0	(0	0)	71	28	30	26	13	0	31	1	5	3	13	1	.93	4	.239	.280	.320
2007	2 Tms	NL	82	174	44	9	2	0	(0	0)	57	20	15	21	11	1	24	2	5	1	10	2	.83	4	.253	.303	.328
2008	Sea	AL	108	221	55	14	2	0	(0	0)	73	34	23	26	18	0	32	4	6	1	5	2	.71	6	.249	.316	.330
2009	Phi	NL	27	45	12	2	1	1	(1	0)	19	6	2	4	4	1	1	0	0	0	0	0	-	1	.267	.283	.422
2010	Cin	NL	91	200	58	12	0	4	(4	0)	82	30	28	27	17	0	30	4	2	3	4	0	1.00	4	.290	.353	.410
2011	Cin	NL	102	245	65	8	2	6	(8	0)	101	33	33	37	18	1	36	7	3	3	3	4	.43	3	.265	.330	.412
2012	Cin	NL	70	150	28	7	2	1	(1	0)	42	9	13	9	4	0	20	1	0	1	4	0	1.00	4	.187	.212	.280
01	ChC	NL	66	123	35	3	1	2	(1	1)	46	20	9	17	16	1	21	0	7	1	2	1	.67	3	.285	.364	.374
01	StL	NL	27	33	11	5	0	1	(1	0)	19	5	7	6	2	0	2	0	0	0	0	0	-	1	.333	.371	.576
07	NYY	AL	54	107	27	7	0	0	(0	0)	34	12	10	12	8	1	19	1	4	1	8	1	.89	3	.252	.308	.318
07	StL	NL	28	67	17	2	2	0	(0	0)	23	8	5	9	3	0	5	1	1	0	2	1	.67	1	.254	.296	.343
	Postseason		26	69	20	5	0	1	(1	0)	28	11	6	9	4	0	14	5	2	0	2	1	.67	0	.290	.372	.406
17 ML YEARS			1490	3956	1044	193	34	41	(28	13)	1428	504	394	456	243	9	482	64	86	43	139	40	.78	82	.264	.314	.361

Kole Calhoun

Bats: L **Throws:** L **Pos:** RF-14; PH-7; LF-4; DH-1; PR-1   **Ht:** 5'10" **Wt:** 190 **Born:** 10/14/1987 **Age:** 25

								BATTING											BASERUNNING				AVERAGES		
Year	Team	Lg	G	AB	H	2B	3B	HR	(Hm | Rd)	TB	R	RBI	RC	TBB	IBB	SO	HBP	SH	SF	SB	CS	SB%	GDP	Avg	OBP	Slg
2010	Orem	R+	56	202	55	14	4	7	(- | -)	102	43	42	44	39	1	45	3	1	2	3	1	.75	3	.292	.411	.505
2011	InldEm	A+	133	512	166	36	6	22	(- | -)	280	94	99	114	73	3	96	4	1	4	20	10	.67	10	.324	.410	.547
2012	Salt Lk	AAA	105	410	122	30	7	14	(- | -)	208	79	73	79	44	0	88	5	0	4	12	3	.80	9	.298	.369	.507
2012	LAA	AL	21	23	4	1	0	0	(0 | 0)	5	2	1	0	2	1	6	0	0	0	1	0	1.00	0	.174	.240	.217

Alberto Callaspo

Bats: B **Throws:** R **Pos:** 3B-131; PH-10; PR-2   ky-AHS-po   **Ht:** 5'9" **Wt:** 200 **Born:** 4/19/1983 **Age:** 30

								BATTING											BASERUNNING				AVERAGES		
Year	Team	Lg	G	AB	H	2B	3B	HR	(Hm | Rd)	TB	R	RBI	RC	TBB	IBB	SO	HBP	SH	SF	SB	CS	SB%	GDP	Avg	OBP	Slg
2006	Ari	NL	23	42	10	1	1	0	(0 | 0)	13	2	6	5	4	0	6	0	0	1	0	1	.00	0	.238	.298	.310
2007	Ari	NL	56	144	31	8	0	0	(0 | 0)	39	10	7	7	9	0	14	1	1	1	1	1	.50	8	.215	.265	.271
2008	KC	AL	74	213	65	8	3	0	(0 | 0)	79	21	16	25	19	0	14	0	1	1	2	1	.67	6	.305	.361	.371
2009	KC	AL	155	576	173	41	8	11	(5 | 6)	263	79	73	90	52	4	51	1	0	5	2	1	.67	15	.300	.356	.457
2010	2 Tms	AL	146	562	149	27	2	10	(2 | 8)	210	61	56	54	31	3	42	1	1	6	5	3	.63	22	.265	.302	.374
2011	LAA	AL	141	475	137	23	0	6	(1 | 5)	178	54	46	66	58	8	48	1	0	2	8	1	.89	11	.288	.366	.375
2012	LAA	AL	138	457	115	20	0	10	(3 | 7)	165	55	53	60	56	1	59	0	3	4	4	3	.57	6	.252	.331	.361
10	KC	AL	88	349	96	19	2	8	(2 | 6)	143	40	43	38	19	2	29	0	0	5	3	1	.75	14	.275	.308	.410
10	LAA	AL	58	213	53	8	0	2	(0 | 2)	67	21	13	16	12	1	13	1	1	1	2	2	.50	8	.249	.291	.315
	Postseason		2	2	0	0	0	0	(0 | 0)	0	0	0	0	0	0	0	0	0	0	0	0	-	0	.000	.000	.000
	7 ML YEARS		733	2469	680	128	14	37	(12 | 25)	947	282	257	307	229	16	234	4	6	20	22	11	.67	68	.275	.335	.384

Shawn Camp

Pitches: R **Bats:** R **Pos:** RP-80   **Ht:** 6'0" **Wt:** 205 **Born:** 11/18/1975 **Age:** 37

			HOW MUCH HE PITCHED					WHAT HE GAVE UP											THE RESULTS						
Year	Team	Lg	G	GS	CG	GF	IP	BFP	H	R	ER	HR	SH	SF	HB	TBB	IBB	SO	WP	Bk	W	L	Pct	Sh	Sv-Op	Hld	ERC	ERA
2004	KC	AL	42	0	0	12	66.2	286	74	37	29	10	2	3	5	16	1	51	2	1	2	2	.500	0	2-3	5	4.74	3.92
2005	KC	AL	29	0	0	7	49.0	228	69	40	35	4	0	3	4	13	3	28	3	0	1	4	.200	0	0-2	0	6.00	6.43
2006	TB	AL	75	0	0	15	75.0	328	93	43	39	9	2	3	7	19	3	53	4	0	7	4	.636	0	4-6	12	5.48	4.68
2007	TB	AL	50	0	0	8	40.0	198	63	33	32	7	5	1	3	18	6	36	2	0	0	3	.000	0	0-2	11	8.59	7.20
2008	Tor	AL	40	0	0	16	39.1	166	40	18	18	2	0	1	2	11	3	31	0	0	3	1	.750	0	0-0	7	3.47	4.12
2009	Tor	AL	59	0	0	17	79.2	333	73	36	31	7	1	1	4	29	4	58	0	0	2	6	.250	0	1-1	6	3.57	3.50
2010	Tor	AL	70	0	0	13	72.1	298	71	26	24	8	0	2	4	18	5	46	2	0	4	3	.571	0	2-4	13	3.65	2.99
2011	Tor	AL	67	0	0	23	66.1	292	79	36	31	3	2	1	6	22	9	32	0	0	6	3	.667	0	1-4	5	4.72	4.21
2012	ChC	NL	80	0	0	21	77.2	327	79	32	31	7	1	2	0	21	4	54	1	0	3	6	.333	0	2-6	18	3.51	3.59
	9 ML YEARS		512	0	0	132	566.0	2456	641	301	270	57	13	17	35	167	38	389	14	1	28	32	.467	0	12-28	77	4.61	4.29

Tony Campana

Bats: L **Throws:** L **Pos:** CF-55; PH-22; LF-11; PR-11; RF-4   camm-PAH-nah   **Ht:** 5'8" **Wt:** 165 **Born:** 5/30/1986 **Age:** 27

								BATTING											BASERUNNING				AVERAGES		
Year	Team	Lg	G	AB	H	2B	3B	HR	(Hm | Rd)	TB	R	RBI	RC	TBB	IBB	SO	HBP	SH	SF	SB	CS	SB%	GDP	Avg	OBP	Slg
2008	Boise	A-	1	3	0	0	0	0	(- | -)	0	0	0	0	1	0	1	0	0	0	0	1	.00	1	.000	.400	.000
2008	Cubs	R	24	83	23	0	0	0	(- | -)	23	17	10	10	8	0	14	0	1	1	22	2	.92	2	.277	.337	.277
2009	Peoria	A	18	53	15	1	1	0	(- | -)	18	14	5	7	5	0	6	0	0	0	11	2	.85	0	.283	.345	.340
2009	Dytona	A+	108	430	122	8	2	0	(- | -)	134	56	25	52	34	0	78	0	7	2	55	16	.77	2	.284	.335	.312
2010	Tenn	AA	131	489	156	22	5	0	(- | -)	188	76	39	77	44	1	82	5	8	4	47	20	.70	2	.319	.378	.384
2011	Iowa	AAA	30	120	41	8	2	0	(- | -)	53	27	9	21	6	0	23	2	1	0	8	1	.89	0	.342	.383	.442
2012	Iowa	AAA	37	143	40	2	1	1	(- | -)	47	24	4	18	12	0	34	1	8	1	18	7	.72	0	.280	.338	.329
2011	ChC	NL	95	143	37	3	0	1	(1 | 0)	43	24	6	17	8	1	30	1	3	0	24	2	.92	1	.259	.303	.301
2012	ChC	NL	89	174	46	6	0	0	(0 | 0)	52	26	5	20	11	0	43	0	7	0	30	3	.91	0	.264	.308	.299
	2 ML YEARS		184	317	83	9	0	1	(1 | 0)	95	50	11	37	19	1	73	1	10	0	54	5	.92	1	.262	.306	.300

Robinson Cano

Bats: L **Throws:** R **Pos:** 2B-154; DH-9; PH-2   kuh-NOE   **Ht:** 6'0" **Wt:** 212 **Born:** 10/22/1982 **Age:** 30

								BATTING											BASERUNNING				AVERAGES		
Year	Team	Lg	G	AB	H	2B	3B	HR	(Hm | Rd)	TB	R	RBI	RC	TBB	IBB	SO	HBP	SH	SF	SB	CS	SB%	GDP	Avg	OBP	Slg
2005	NYY	AL	132	522	155	34	4	14	(5 | 9)	239	78	62	59	16	1	68	3	7	3	1	3	.25	16	.297	.320	.458
2006	NYY	AL	122	482	165	41	1	15	(9 | 6)	253	62	78	74	18	3	54	2	1	5	5	2	.71	19	.342	.365	.525
2007	NYY	AL	160	617	189	41	7	19	(10 | 9)	301	93	97	94	39	5	85	8	1	4	4	5	.44	19	.306	.353	.488
2008	NYY	AL	159	597	162	35	3	14	(7 | 7)	245	70	72	64	26	3	65	5	1	5	2	4	.33	18	.271	.305	.410
2009	NYY	AL	161	637	204	48	2	25	(14 | 11)	331	103	85	79	30	2	63	3	0	4	5	7	.42	22	.320	.352	.520
2010	NYY	AL	160	626	200	41	3	29	(16 | 13)	334	103	109	118	57	14	77	8	0	5	3	2	.60	19	.319	.381	.534
2011	NYY	AL	159	623	188	46	7	28	(16 | 12)	332	104	118	111	38	11	96	12	0	8	8	2	.80	18	.302	.349	.533
2012	NYY	AL	161	627	196	48	1	33	(22 | 11)	345	105	94	110	61	10	96	7	0	2	3	2	.60	22	.313	.379	.550
	Postseason		42	163	42	8	3	8	(5 | 3)	80	21	29	23	10	2	22	2	0	1	0	2	.00	6	.258	.307	.491
	8 ML YEARS		1214	4731	1459	334	28	177	(99 | 78)	2380	718	715	709	285	49	604	48	10	36	31	27	.53	153	.308	.351	.503

Russ Canzler

Bats: R **Throws:** R **Pos:** LF-11; 1B-8; DH-6; PH-2   **Ht:** 6'2" **Wt:** 220 **Born:** 4/11/1986 **Age:** 27

Year	Team	Lg	G	AB	H	2B	3B	HR	(Hm Rd)	TB	R	RBI	RC	TBB	IBB	SO	HBP	SH	SF	SB	CS	SB%	GDP	Avg	OBP	Slg
2004	Cubs	R	32	105	26	2	3	1	(- -)	37	12	13	11	9	0	35	1	3	1	0	1	.00	2	.248	.310	.352
2005	Cubs	R	49	157	47	11	3	1	(- -)	67	22	20	26	24	1	41	1	2	4	1	5	.17	4	.299	.387	.427
2006	Boise	A-	73	280	74	22	4	16	(- -)	152	49	61	49	22	0	70	3	1	5	7	4	.64	10	.264	.319	.543
2007	Peoria	A	125	460	124	24	2	7	(- -)	173	60	54	57	35	2	88	2	1	5	12	8	.60	11	.270	.321	.376
2008	Dytona	A+	98	326	89	22	2	12	(- -)	151	47	59	50	27	1	70	1	3	4	7	4	.64	12	.273	.327	.463
2009	Dytona	A+	28	100	27	8	1	2	(- -)	43	14	14	14	7	0	24	0	0	1	2	0	1.00	1	.270	.315	.430
2009	Tenn	AA	91	233	60	15	0	6	(- -)	93	27	36	33	31	1	41	1	1	1	2	5	.29	6	.258	.346	.399
2010	Tenn	AA	113	356	102	28	4	21	(- -)	201	68	66	74	46	1	95	5	0	5	4	4	.56	5	.287	.371	.565
2011	Drham	AAA	131	474	149	40	4	18	(- -)	251	78	83	101	67	0	129	4	0	4	5	2	.71	10	.314	.401	.530
2012	Clmbs	AAA	130	487	129	36	3	22	(- -)	237	68	79	78	46	1	128	2	0	4	2	4	.33	12	.265	.328	.487
2011	TB	AL	3	3	1	0	0	0	(0 0)	1	0	1	1	1	0	1	0	0	1	0	0	-	0	.333	.400	.333
2012	Cle	AL	26	93	25	3	0	3	(0 3)	37	9	11	12	4	1	22	0	0	0	0	0	-	0	.269	.299	.398
2 ML YEARS			29	96	26	3	0	3	(0 3)	38	9	12	13	5	1	23	0	0	1	0	0	-	0	.271	.304	.396

Carter Capps

Pitches: R **Bats:** R **Pos:** RP-18   **Ht:** 6'5" **Wt:** 220 **Born:** 8/7/1990 **Age:** 22

Year	Team	Lg	G	GS	CG	GF	IP	BFP	H	R	ER	HR	SH	SF	HB	TBB	IBB	SO	WP	Bk	W	L	Pct	Sh	Sv-Op	Hld	ERC	ERA
2011	Clinton	A	4	4	0	0	18.0	81	19	12	12	1	0	2	2	10	0	21	1	0	1	1	.500	0	0- -	-	5.25	6.00
2012	Jacksn	AA	38	0	0	31	50.0	203	40	8	7	2	1	0	1	12	0	72	1	0	2	3	.400	0	19- -	-	2.11	1.26
2012	Tacom	AAA	1	0	0	0	1.1	4	0	0	0	0	0	0	0	0	0	3	0	0	0	0	-	0	0- -	-	0.00	0.00
2012	Sea	AL	18	0	0	2	25.0	109	25	11	11	0	1	1	0	11	0	28	1	0	0	0	-	0	0-0	2	3.49	3.96

Matt Capps

Pitches: R **Bats:** R **Pos:** RP-30   **Ht:** 6'2" **Wt:** 260 **Born:** 9/3/1983 **Age:** 29

Year	Team	Lg	G	GS	CG	GF	IP	BFP	H	R	ER	HR	SH	SF	HB	TBB	IBB	SO	WP	Bk	W	L	Pct	Sh	Sv-Op	Hld	ERC	ERA
2012	FtMyrs*	A+	2	1	0	0	2.0	8	1	1	0	0	0	1	0	0	0	1	0	0	1	0	1.000	0	0- -	-	0.47	0.00
2005	Pit	NL	4	0	0	0	4.0	16	5	2	2	0	0	1	0	0	0	3	0	0	0	0	-	0	0-0	0	4.62	4.50
2006	Pit	NL	85	0	0	15	80.2	329	81	37	34	12	8	2	3	12	5	56	4	0	9	1	.900	0	1-10	13	3.52	3.79
2007	Pit	NL	76	0	0	47	79.0	315	64	22	20	5	3	2	3	16	10	64	1	0	4	7	.364	0	18-21	15	2.10	2.28
2008	Pit	NL	49	0	0	39	53.2	211	47	20	18	5	2	0	2	5	0	39	0	0	2	3	.400	0	21-26	0	2.39	3.02
2009	Pit	NL	57	0	0	50	54.1	251	73	36	35	10	2	4	3	17	3	46	0	0	4	8	.333	0	27-32	1	6.53	5.80
2010	2 Tms		74	0	0	66	73.0	305	75	27	20	6	5	0	0	17	4	59	1	0	5	3	.625	0	42-48	0	3.37	2.47
2011	Min	AL	69	0	0	35	65.2	274	66	31	31	10	2	3	4	13	1	34	1	0	4	7	.364	0	15-24	7	3.89	4.25
2012	Min	AL	30	0	0	29	29.1	120	28	13	12	5	0	0	0	4	1	18	3	0	1	4	.200	0	14-15	0	3.14	3.68
10	Was	AL	47	0	0	43	46.0	199	51	20	14	5	4	0	0	9	3	38	0	0	3	3	.500	0	26-30	0	3.72	2.74
10	Min	AL	27	0	0	23	27.0	106	24	7	6	1	1	0	0	8	1	21	1	0	2	0	1.000	0	16-18	0	2.78	2.00
Postseason			1	0	0	1	1.0	5	2	1	1	0	0	0	0	0	0	0	0	0	0	0	-	0	0-0	0	7.48	9.00
8 ML YEARS			444	0	0	281	439.2	1821	439	188	172	53	22	11	16	84	24	319	10	0	29	33	.468	0	138-176	36	3.45	3.52

Chris Capuano

Pitches: L **Bats:** L **Pos:** SP-33   capp-ue-AHH-noe   **Ht:** 6'3" **Wt:** 215 **Born:** 8/19/1978 **Age:** 34

Year	Team	Lg	G	GS	CG	GF	IP	BFP	H	R	ER	HR	SH	SF	HB	TBB	IBB	SO	WP	Bk	W	L	Pct	Sh	Sv-Op	Hld	ERC	ERA
2003	Ari	NL	9	5	0	2	33.0	139	27	19	17	3	4	1	6	11	1	23	3	0	2	4	.333	0	0-0	1	3.45	4.64
2004	Mil	NL	17	17	0	0	88.1	385	91	55	49	18	4	1	5	37	1	80	3	1	6	8	.429	0	0-0	0	5.37	4.99
2005	Mil	NL	35	35	0	0	219.0	949	212	105	97	31	14	5	12	91	6	176	3	4	18	12	.600	0	0-0	0	4.44	3.99
2006	Mil	NL	34	34	3	0	221.1	936	229	108	99	29	9	8	9	47	4	174	7	0	11	12	.478	2	0-0	0	3.84	4.03
2007	Mil	NL	29	25	0	0	150.0	669	170	93	85	20	10	3	8	54	2	132	10	0	5	12	.294	0	0-0	0	5.11	5.10
2010	Mil	NL	24	9	0	5	66.0	278	65	29	29	9	3	2	1	21	1	54	5	0	4	4	.500	0	0-0	0	3.98	3.95
2011	NYM	NL	33	31	1	0	186.0	802	198	99	94	27	9	1	5	53	5	168	4	0	11	12	.478	1	0-0	1	4.33	4.55
2012	LAD	NL	33	33	0	0	198.1	817	188	91	82	25	16	4	2	54	4	162	6	0	12	12	.500	0	0-0	0	3.51	3.72
8 ML YEARS			214	189	4	7	1162.0	4975	1180	599	552	162	69	25	48	368	24	969	41	5	69	76	.476	3	0-0	3	4.24	4.28

Adrian Cardenas

Bats: L **Throws:** R **Pos:** PH-33; 2B-12; LF-3; 3B-1   CARD-inn-us   **Ht:** 6'0" **Wt:** 205 **Born:** 10/10/1987 **Age:** 25

Year	Team	Lg	G	AB	H	2B	3B	HR	(Hm Rd)	TB	R	RBI	RC	TBB	IBB	SO	HBP	SH	SF	SB	CS	SB%	GDP	Avg	OBP	Slg
2006	Phillies	R	41	154	49	5	4	2	(- -)	68	22	21	29	17	1	28	2	0	4	13	3	.81	3	.318	.384	.442
2007	Lakwd	A	127	499	147	30	2	9	(- -)	208	70	79	79	47	2	80	4	4	10	20	7	.74	17	.295	.354	.417
2008	Clrwtr	A+	68	261	80	11	6	4	(- -)	115	44	23	47	28	1	42	0	2	2	16	0	1.00	5	.307	.371	.441
2008	Stcktn	A+	15	72	20	1	0	1	(- -)	24	11	10	7	1	0	14	1	0	0	1	0	1.00	4	.278	.297	.333
2008	Mdland	AA	26	86	24	4	0	0	(- -)	28	12	7	12	15	2	10	1	0	0	0	1	.00	4	.279	.392	.326
2009	Mdland	AA	79	325	106	26	2	3	(- -)	145	56	55	59	38	1	44	1	3	6	5	4	.56	16	.326	.394	.446
2009	Scrmto	AAA	51	183	46	15	2	1	(- -)	68	23	24	23	17	0	29	2	2	3	3	2	.60	4	.251	.317	.372
2010	Scrmto	AAA	58	210	56	8	1	1	(- -)	69	30	21	23	17	2	28	0	3	1	2	2	.50	7	.267	.320	.329
2010	Mdland	AA	51	194	67	15	3	0	(- -)	91	36	32	41	33	3	23	3	0	6	4	6	.40	8	.345	.436	.469
2011	Scrmto	AAA	127	491	154	28	4	5	(- -)	205	70	51	80	47	1	56	2	2	3	13	6	.68	10	.314	.374	.418
2012	Iowa	AAA	65	243	73	22	4	3	(- -)	112	30	32	46	33	2	32	1	1	4	5	0	1.00	7	.300	.381	.461
2012	ChC	NL	45	60	11	6	0	0	(0 0)	17	5	2	4	7	1	13	0	0	0	0	0	-	0	.183	.269	.283

Andrew Carignan

Pitches: R Bats: R Pos: RP-11   CARE-uh-gun   Ht: 5'11" Wt: 235 Born: 7/23/1986 Age: 26

		HOW MUCH HE PITCHED						WHAT HE GAVE UP										THE RESULTS							
Year	Team	Lg	G	GS	CG	GF	IP	BFP	H	R	ER	HR	SH	SF	HB	TBB	IBB	SO	WP	Bk	W	L	Pct	Sh	Sv-Op Hld	ERC	ERA
2007	Kane	A	12	0	0	10	13.1	57	6	7	3	0	1	1	0	11	1	19	4	0	1	1	.500	0	4- - -	1.92	2.03
2008	Stcktn	A+	9	0	0	9	10.0	40	5	1	1	0	0	0	1	5	0	17	1	0	1	1	.500	0	4- - -	1.66	0.90
2008	Mdland	AA	46	0	0	42	52.2	230	36	15	13	4	4	0	3	39	1	67	4	0	3	3	.500	0	24- - -	3.67	2.22
2009	Stcktn	A+	2	0	0	2	2.0	10	1	1	1	0	0	1	0	3	0	2	0	0	0	0	-	0	0- - -	4.47	4.50
2010	Stcktn	A+	30	0	0	10	33.0	163	28	31	23	2	1	0	5	34	0	44	7	0	3	3	.500	0	0- - -	5.94	6.27
2011	Scrmto	AAA	13	0	0	5	16.2	68	11	5	4	1	0	1	1	7	0	19	0	0	0	0	-	0	0- - -	2.34	2.16
2011	Stcktn	A+	9	0	0	7	11.0	40	4	1	0	0	0	0	1	2	0	12	1	0	1	0	1.000	0	5- - -	0.66	0.00
2011	Mdland	AA	11	0	0	8	11.1	46	10	4	4	1	0	0	1	3	0	15	0	0	0	0	-	0	3- - -	3.27	3.18
2012	Scrmto	AAA	9	0	0	3	13.1	50	9	4	4	0	0	0	1	1	0	21	0	0	2	0	1.000	0	1- - -	1.07	2.70
2011	Oak	AL	6	0	0	3	6.1	31	8	4	3	1	0	0	0	2	0	5	1	0	0	0	-	0	0-0 0	5.17	4.26
2012	Oak	AL	11	0	0	5	9.2	44	8	5	5	0	1	0	0	10	0	8	1	0	1	1	.500	0	0-0 0	4.98	4.66
	2 ML YEARS		17	0	0	8	16.0	75	16	9	8	1	1	0	0	12	0	13	2	0	1	1	.500	0	0-0 0	5.12	4.50

Luke Carlin

Bats: B Throws: R Pos: C-4   Ht: 5'10" Wt: 195 Born: 12/20/1980 Age: 32

			BATTING																BASERUNNING				AVERAGES		
Year	Team	Lg	G	AB	H	2B	3B	HR	(Hm | Rd)	TB	R	RBI	RC	TBB	IBB	SO	HBP	SH	SF	SB	CS	SB%	GDP	Avg	OBP	Slg
2012	Clmbs*	AAA	62	206	52	10	0	3	(- | -)	71	23	27	28	34	2	26	1	1	2	0	1	.00	7	.252	.358	.345
2008	SD	NL	36	94	14	3	1	1	(0 | 1)	22	12	6	2	10	0	34	1	0	0	0	0	-	3	.149	.238	.234
2009	Ari	NL	10	18	3	0	0	0	(0 | 0)	3	3	1	2	3	0	3	0	0	0	0	0	-	0	.167	.286	.167
2010	Cle	AL	6	14	5	0	0	2	(1 | 1)	11	4	3	3	2	0	5	0	0	0	0	0	-	0	.357	.438	.786
2012	Cle	AL	4	14	3	1	0	0	(0 | 0)	4	2	1	0	0	0	3	0	0	0	1	0	1.00	1	.214	.214	.286
	4 ML YEARS		56	140	25	4	1	3	(1 | 2)	40	21	11	7	15	0	45	1	0	0	1	0	1.00	4	.179	.263	.286

Mike Carp

Bats: L Throws: R Pos: LF-24; 1B-23; PH-11; DH-4   Ht: 6'2" Wt: 210 Born: 6/30/1986 Age: 27

			BATTING																BASERUNNING				AVERAGES		
Year	Team	Lg	G	AB	H	2B	3B	HR	(Hm	Rd)	TB	R	RBI	RC	TBB	IBB	SO	HBP	SH	SF	SB	CS	SB%	GDP	Avg	OBP	Slg
2012	Tacom*	AAA	35	139	31	8	0	2	(-	-)	45	13	17	12	12	0	31	1	0	2	1	3	.25	5	.223	.286	.324
2012	Hi Dsrt*	A+	2	9	6	1	0	1	(-	-)	10	2	4	5	2	0	0	0	0	0	1	0	1.00	0	.667	.727	1.111
2009	Sea	AL	21	54	17	3	1	1	(1	0)	25	7	5	8	8	0	10	2	0	1	0	0	-	1	.315	.415	.463
2010	Sea	AL	14	37	7	2	0	0	(0	0)	9	1	0	2	4	0	8	0	0	0	0	0	-	0	.189	.268	.243
2011	Sea	AL	79	290	80	17	1	12	(5	7)	135	27	46	39	19	0	81	3	0	1	0	2	.00	10	.276	.326	.466
2012	Sea	AL	59	164	35	6	0	5	(2	3)	56	17	20	15	21	1	46	3	0	1	1	0	1.00	7	.213	.312	.341
	4 ML YEARS		173	545	139	28	2	18	(8	10)	225	52	71	64	52	1	145	8	0	3	1	2	.33	18	.255	.327	.413

Andrew Carpenter

Pitches: R Bats: R Pos: RP-6   Ht: 6'3" Wt: 229 Born: 5/18/1985 Age: 28

			HOW MUCH HE PITCHED							WHAT HE GAVE UP											THE RESULTS						
Year	Team	Lg	G	GS	CG	GF	IP	BFP	H	R	ER	HR	SH	SF	HB	TBB	IBB	SO	WP	Bk	W	L	Pct	Sh	Sv-Op Hld	ERC	ERA
2012	LsVgs*	AAA	21	12	0	1	74.2	319	83	31	28	10	2	4	2	19	0	56	2	1	6	3	.667	0	3- - -	4.51	3.38
2012	Bnghtn*	AA	5	0	0	4	5.0	21	4	0	0	0	0	0	0	2	0	10	0	0	0	0	-	0	3- - -	2.31	0.00
2012	Buffalo*	AAA	5	0	0	1	4.2	19	5	1	1	1	0	0	0	0	0	6	1	0	0	0	-	0	0- - -	3.51	1.93
2008	Phi	NL	1	0	0	1	1.0	5	1	0	0	0	1	0	0	1	1	1	0	0	0	0	-	0	0-0 0	3.46	0.00
2009	Phi	NL	3	1	0	0	5.2	32	11	7	7	1	1	0	1	4	0	5	0	0	1	0	1.000	0	0-0 0	13.36	11.12
2010	Phi	NL	1	0	0	0	3.0	14	5	3	3	1	1	0	0	0	0	2	1	0	0	1	.000	0	0-0 0	8.04	9.00
2011	2 Tms	NL	12	0	0	3	14.2	68	19	13	13	3	2	0	0	7	1	16	3	0	0	0	-	0	0-1 0	6.93	7.98
2012	Tor	AL	6	0	0	4	9.0	40	7	5	5	4	0	0	0	6	0	9	1	0	0	0	-	0	0-0 1	6.25	5.00
11	Phi	NL	6	0	0	1	9.1	44	13	8	8	2	1	0	0	4	0	10	0	0	0	0	-	0	0-1 0	7.50	7.71
11	SD	NL	6	0	0	2	5.1	24	6	5	5	1	1	0	0	3	1	6	3	0	0	0	-	0	0-0 0	5.94	8.44
	5 ML YEARS		23	1	0	8	33.1	159	43	28	28	9	5	0	1	18	2	33	5	0	1	1	.500	0	0-1 1	7.81	7.56

Chris Carpenter

Pitches: R Bats: R Pos: SP-3   Ht: 6'6" Wt: 230 Born: 4/27/1975 Age: 38

			HOW MUCH HE PITCHED							WHAT HE GAVE UP											THE RESULTS						
Year	Team	Lg	G	GS	CG	GF	IP	BFP	H	R	ER	HR	SH	SF	HB	TBB	IBB	SO	WP	Bk	W	L	Pct	Sh	Sv-Op Hld	ERC	ERA
1997	Tor	AL	14	13	1	1	81.1	374	108	55	46	7	1	2	2	37	0	55	7	1	3	7	.300	1	0-0 0	6.38	5.09
1998	Tor	AL	33	24	1	4	175.0	742	177	97	85	18	4	5	5	61	1	136	5	0	12	7	.632	1	0-0 0	4.12	4.37
1999	Tor	AL	24	24	4	0	150.0	663	177	81	73	16	4	6	3	48	1	106	9	1	9	8	.529	1	0-0 0	4.90	4.38
2000	Tor	AL	34	27	2	1	175.1	795	204	130	122	30	3	1	5	83	1	113	3	0	10	12	.455	0	0-0 0	6.04	6.26
2001	Tor	AL	34	34	3	0	215.2	930	229	112	98	29	3	1	16	75	5	157	5	0	11	11	.500	2	0-0 0	4.82	4.09
2002	Tor	AL	13	13	1	0	73.1	327	89	45	43	11	1	4	4	27	0	45	3	0	4	5	.444	0	0-0 0	5.91	5.28
2004	StL	NL	28	28	1	0	182.0	746	169	75	70	24	6	3	8	38	2	152	4	0	15	5	.750	0	0-0 0	3.32	3.46
2005	StL	NL	33	33	7	0	241.2	953	204	82	76	18	7	7	3	51	0	213	5	0	21	5	.808	4	0-0 0	2.49	2.83
2006	StL	NL	32	32	5	0	221.2	896	194	81	76	21	12	4	10	43	3	184	3	0	15	8	.652	3	0-0 0	2.75	3.09
2007	StL	NL	1	1	0	0	6.0	29	9	5	5	1	0	1	0	1	0	3	0	0	0	1	.000	0	0-0 0	5.80	7.50
2008	StL	NL	4	3	0	0	15.1	63	16	5	3	0	2	1	0	4	0	7	0	0	0	1	.000	0	0-0 0	3.11	1.76
2009	StL	NL	28	28	3	0	192.2	750	156	49	48	7	10	4	7	38	1	144	1	0	17	4	.810	1	0-0 0	2.14	2.24
2010	StL	NL	35	35	1	0	235.0	969	214	99	84	21	9	7	13	63	4	179	3	0	16	9	.640	0	0-0 0	3.23	3.22
2011	StL	NL	34	34	4	0	237.1	996	243	99	91	16	11	3	6	55	5	191	3	1	11	9	.550	2	0-0 0	3.40	3.45
2012	StL	NL	3	3	0	0	17.0	72	16	7	7	2	1	0	2	3	0	12	0	0	0	2	.000	0	0-0 0	3.39	3.71
	Postseason		15	15	1	0	94.1	392	85	33	32	10	10	3	6	30	1	59	1	0	9	2	.818	1	0-0 0	3.53	3.05
	15 ML YEARS		350	332	33	6	2219.1	9305	2205	1021	927	220	75	48	85	627	23	1697	51	3	144	94	.605	15	0-0 0	3.74	3.76

Chris Carpenter

Pitches: R **Bats:** R **Pos:** RP-8   **Ht:** 6'4" **Wt:** 220 **Born:** 12/26/1985 **Age:** 27

Year Team	Lg	G	GS	CG	GF	IP	BFP	H	R	ER	HR	SH	SF	HB	TBB	IBB	SO	WP	Bk	W	L	Pct	Sh	Sv-Op	Hld	ERC	ERA
2008 Cubs	R	1	1	0	0	1.0	5	2	2	2	0	0	0	0	1	0	1	0	0	0	0	-	0	0- -	-	14.53	18.00
2008 Boise	A-	10	6	0	0	32.0	150	32	21	15	2	1	1	2	22	0	24	2	0	4	2	.667	0	0- -	-	5.12	4.22
2009 Peoria	A	15	15	1	0	73.2	301	55	23	20	4	2	3	1	33	1	60	0	1	4	3	.571	1	0- -	-	2.68	2.44
2009 Dytona	A+	5	5	0	0	25.0	101	15	7	4	1	0	0	1	8	0	33	3	0	2	1	.667	0	0- -	-	1.56	1.44
2009 Tenn	AA	7	7	0	0	32.0	138	30	20	17	0	1	0	4	11	0	25	2	0	0	3	.000	0	0- -	-	3.28	4.78
2010 Tenn	AA	23	23	0	0	119.2	514	117	56	42	5	7	2	7	48	2	100	11	0	8	6	.571	0	0- -	-	3.78	3.16
2010 Iowa	AAA	3	3	0	0	15.0	70	19	9	9	3	0	1	0	9	0	12	1	0	0	0	-	0	0- -	-	7.50	5.40
2011 Iowa	AAA	22	0	0	8	30.1	145	32	25	22	3	4	3	3	23	1	28	6	0	2	3	.400	0	1- -	-	6.21	6.53
2011 Tenn	AA	10	0	0	6	12.1	50	10	6	6	2	1	0	1	4	0	6	1	0	1	1	.500	0	1- -	-	3.57	4.38
2012 RedSx	R	2	1	0	0	2.0	8	1	1	1	0	0	1	0	1	0	1	1	0	0	0	-	0	0- -	-	1.41	4.50
2012 Grnville	A	2	2	0	0	2.0	9	1	1	1	0	0	0	1	1	0	4	1	0	0	0	-	0	0- -	-	2.80	4.50
2012 Portlnd	A+	1	1	0	0	2.0	8	2	1	1	0	0	0	0	0	0	3	0	0	0	0	-	0	0- -	-	1.95	4.50
2012 Pwtckt	AAA	16	0	0	11	15.2	60	7	2	2	1	1	0	0	8	0	17	0	0	1	0	1.000	0	4- -	-	1.59	1.15
2011 ChC	NL	10	0	0	1	9.2	47	12	3	3	1	0	2	0	7	1	8	2	0	0	0	-	0	0-0	0	6.67	2.79
2012 Bos	AL	8	0	0	3	6.0	34	7	6	6	1	2	0	0	10	2	2	2	0	1	0	1.000	0	0-0	0	10.50	9.00
2 ML YEARS		18	0	0	4	15.2	81	19	9	9	2	2	2	0	17	3	10	4	0	1	0	1.000	0	0-0	0	8.11	5.17

David Carpenter

Pitches: R **Bats:** R **Pos:** RP-33   **Ht:** 6'2" **Wt:** 215 **Born:** 7/15/1985 **Age:** 27

Year Team	Lg	G	GS	CG	GF	IP	BFP	H	R	ER	HR	SH	SF	HB	TBB	IBB	SO	WP	Bk	W	L	Pct	Sh	Sv-Op	Hld	ERC	ERA
2008 Cards	R	9	0	0	6	8.2	41	9	6	1	0	2	0	1	6	0	9	1	0	0	0	-	0	3- -	-	5.10	1.04
2008 JhsCty	R	6	0	0	2	6.0	28	7	3	2	1	1	0	1	1	0	8	0	0	0	0	-	0	0- -	-	4.93	3.00
2009 QuadC	A	52	0	0	32	67.1	302	61	34	32	2	1	5	10	36	0	77	1	1	5	3	.625	0	12- -	-	4.12	4.28
2010 PlmBh	A+	49	0	0	44	53.1	219	45	16	14	3	1	1	3	15	1	50	3	0	5	3	.625	0	20- -	-	2.70	2.36
2010 Lancst	A+	6	0	0	5	7.2	34	8	4	3	0	0	0	0	4	2	8	1	0	1	1	.500	0	0- -	-	3.61	3.52
2011 CpChr	AA	14	0	0	14	14.0	59	14	7	7	4	0	0	2	3	1	17	0	0	0	1	.000	0	5- -	-	5.16	4.50
2011 OKCity	AAA	19	0	0	15	19.0	76	15	0	0	0	0	2	0	6	0	21	3	0	0	0	-	0	9- -	-	2.07	0.00
2012 OKCity	AAA	7	0	0	5	8.2	33	7	2	2	1	0	0	0	0	0	6	0	0	1	0	1.000	0	3- -	-	1.70	2.08
2012 LsVgs	AAA	16	0	0	9	17.2	76	15	8	7	1	0	0	1	7	0	19	1	0	0	1	.000	0	1- -	-	3.09	3.57
2011 Hou	NL	34	0	0	12	27.2	125	28	9	9	3	4	1	4	13	7	29	2	1	1	3	.250	0	1-2	3	4.62	2.93
2012 2 Tms		33	0	0	9	32.1	163	51	31	29	5	2	0	2	16	4	31	2	0	0	2	.000	0	0-1	2	8.52	8.07
12 Hou	NL	30	0	0	8	29.2	143	43	21	20	4	2	0	1	14	3	27	2	0	0	2	.000	0	0-1	2	7.38	6.07
12 Tor	AL	3	0	0	1	2.2	20	8	10	9	1	0	0	1	2	1	4	0	0	0	0	-	0	0-0	0	22.64	30.38
2 ML YEARS		67	0	0	21	60.0	288	79	40	38	8	6	1	6	29	11	60	4	1	1	5	.167	0	1-3	5	6.64	5.70

David Carpenter

Pitches: R **Bats:** R **Pos:** RP-28   **Ht:** 6'3" **Wt:** 180 **Born:** 9/1/1987 **Age:** 25

Year Team	Lg	G	GS	CG	GF	IP	BFP	H	R	ER	HR	SH	SF	HB	TBB	IBB	SO	WP	Bk	W	L	Pct	Sh	Sv-Op	Hld	ERC	ERA
2009 Orem	R+	25	0	0	16	34.1	142	26	12	9	2	1	0	1	11	1	42	2	1	2	2	.500	0	8- -	-	2.25	2.36
2010 CRpds	A	37	0	0	28	45.1	193	36	19	13	2	3	4	7	19	2	52	3	0	2	4	.333	0	8- -	-	3.17	2.58
2011 InldEm	A+	25	0	0	18	29.0	118	23	6	3	1	2	1	1	9	2	36	1	0	0	1	.000	0	11- -	-	2.27	0.93
2011 Ark	AA	19	0	0	15	18.2	75	12	0	0	0	2	1	1	5	0	16	2	0	1	0	1.000	0	5- -	-	1.45	0.00
2012 Salt Lk	AAA	15	0	0	6	19.2	77	10	6	6	2	0	1	1	8	0	14	1	0	0	0	-	0	1- -	-	1.82	2.75
2012 LAA	AL	28	0	0	12	39.2	172	42	21	21	6	1	1	0	17	0	28	2	0	1	2	.333	0	0-0	2	4.97	4.76

Matt Carpenter

Bats: L **Throws:** R **Pos:** 1B-44; PH-37; 3B-33; RF-15; LF-7; 2B-5; PR-1   **Ht:** 6'3" **Wt:** 200 **Born:** 11/26/1985 **Age:** 27

Year Team	Lg	G	AB	H	2B	3B	HR	(Hm	Rd)	TB	R	RBI	RC	TBB	IBB	SO	HBP	SH	SF	SB	CS	SB%	GDP	Avg	OBP	Slg
2009 Batvia	A-	9	32	15	3	0	0	(-	-)	18	9	3	8	4	0	2	1	0	0	0	1	.00	0	.469	.541	.563
2009 QuadC	A	29	105	31	6	2	0	(-	-)	41	11	10	19	17	0	13	3	0	1	2	0	1.00	3	.295	.405	.390
2009 PlmBh	A+	32	114	25	6	1	2	(-	-)	39	13	9	12	10	0	24	1	2	1	1	0	1.00	3	.219	.286	.342
2010 PlmBh	A+	28	99	28	5	2	1	(-	-)	40	17	16	20	26	0	14	2	1	0	1	0	1.00	1	.283	.441	.404
2010 Sprgfld	AA	105	396	125	26	3	12	(-	-)	193	76	53	84	64	4	88	4	4	4	11	2	.85	12	.316	.412	.487
2011 Memp	AAA	130	434	130	29	3	12	(-	-)	201	61	70	90	84	1	68	8	3	6	5	4	.56	12	.300	.417	.463
2012 Memp	AAA	3	7	1	0	0	0	(-	-)	1	1	0	0	2	0	2	0	0	2	0	0	-	2	.143	.333	.143
2012 Sprgfld	AA	3	10	3	0	0	1	(-	-)	6	3	3	2	3	0	1	0	0	1	0	0	1.00	0	.300	.462	.600
2011 StL	NL	7	15	1	1	0	0	(0	0)	2	0	0	0	4	0	4	0	0	0	0	0	-	0	.067	.263	.133
2012 StL	NL	114	296	87	22	5	6	(3	3)	137	44	46	46	34	2	63	3	0	7	1	1	.50	10	.294	.365	.463
2 ML YEARS		121	311	88	23	5	6	(3	3)	139	44	46	46	38	2	67	3	0	7	1	1	.50	10	.283	.359	.447

Carlos Carrasco

Pitches: R **Bats:** R **Pos:** P   **Ht:** 6'3" **Wt:** 210 **Born:** 3/21/1987 **Age:** 26

Year Team	Lg	G	GS	CG	GF	IP	BFP	H	R	ER	HR	SH	SF	HB	TBB	IBB	SO	WP	Bk	W	L	Pct	Sh	Sv-Op	Hld	ERC	ERA
2009 Cle	AL	5	5	0	0	22.1	112	40	23	22	6	0	1	0	11	1	11	0	1	0	4	.000	0	0-0	0	11.36	8.87
2010 Cle	AL	7	7	1	0	44.2	188	47	20	19	6	2	1	1	14	1	38	1	0	2	2	.500	0	0-0	0	4.42	3.83
2011 Cle	AL	21	21	1	0	124.2	536	130	68	64	15	3	7	4	40	3	85	3	0	8	9	.471	0	0-0	0	4.24	4.62
3 ML YEARS		33	33	2	0	191.2	836	217	111	105	27	5	9	5	65	5	134	4	1	10	15	.400	0	0-0	0	5.00	4.93

D.J. Carrasco

Pitches: R **Bats:** R **Pos:** RP-4   **Ht:** 6'4" **Wt:** 215 **Born:** 4/12/1977 **Age:** 36

Year	Team	Lg	G	GS	CG	GF	IP	BFP	H	R	ER	HR	SH	SF	HB	TBB	IBB	SO	WP	Bk	W	L	Pct	Sh	Sv-Op	Hld	ERC	ERA
2012	StLuci*	A+	4	2	0	0	6.0	19	1	0	0	0	0	0	0	1	0	4	0	0	1	0	1.000	0	0--	-	0.20	0.00
2012	Buffalo*	AAA	2	0	0	1	3.0	11	2	1	1	1	0	0	0	0	0	1	0	0	0	0	-	0	0--	-	1.99	3.00
2012	Gwnntt*	AAA	5	0	0	3	5.0	30	10	7	7	0	0	2	0	5	0	3	0	0	1	0	1.000	0	0--	-	12.01	12.60
2003	KC	AL	50	2	0	21	80.1	355	82	44	43	8	1	4	7	40	4	57	6	0	6	5	.545	0	2-5	6	4.94	4.82
2004	KC	AL	30	0	0	11	35.1	163	41	22	19	5	1	1	3	15	3	22	2	0	2	2	.500	0	0-3	4	5.56	4.84
2005	KC	AL	21	20	1	0	114.2	511	129	67	61	11	3	5	6	51	2	49	7	3	6	8	.429	0	0-0	0	5.20	4.79
2008	CWS	AL	31	0	0	6	38.2	158	30	17	17	2	1	1	5	14	1	30	0	0	1	0	1.000	0	0-1	7	2.94	3.96
2009	CWS	AL	49	1	0	11	93.1	405	103	42	39	5	2	4	2	29	4	62	3	0	5	1	.833	0	0-1	1	3.98	3.76
2010	2 Tmms	NL	63	0	0	8	78.1	330	68	39	32	5	3	3	5	34	3	65	6	0	3	2	.600	0	0-1	7	3.48	3.68
2011	NYM	NL	42	1	0	15	49.1	225	67	35	33	7	4	0	6	16	4	27	3	1	1	3	.250	0	0-1	2	6.80	6.02
2012	NYM	NL	4	1	0	3	3.2	18	6	3	3	2	0	0	1	0	0	3	1	0	0	0	-	0	0-0	0	11.04	7.36
	10 Pit	NL	45	0	0	6	55.2	232	50	24	24	4	3	1	4	22	1	45	4	0	2	2	.500	0	0-0	5	3.66	3.88
	10 Ari	NL	18	0	0	2	22.2	98	18	15	8	1	0	2	1	12	2	20	2	0	1	0	1.000	0	0-1	2	3.05	3.18
8 ML YEARS			290	24	1	75	493.2	2165	526	269	247	45	15	18	35	199	21	315	28	4	24	21	.533	0	2-12	26	4.67	4.50

Joel Carreno

Pitches: R **Bats:** R **Pos:** RP-9; SP-2   jo-ELL kuh-RAIN-yo   **Ht:** 6'2" **Wt:** 220 **Born:** 3/7/1987 **Age:** 26

Year	Team	Lg	G	GS	CG	GF	IP	BFP	H	R	ER	HR	SH	SF	HB	TBB	IBB	SO	WP	Bk	W	L	Pct	Sh	Sv-Op	Hld	ERC	ERA
2007	B Jays	R	12	12	0	0	65.1	274	60	27	19	4	2	3	9	13	0	64	3	0	6	4	.600	0	0--	-	3.11	2.62
2008	Auburn	A-	15	13	0	0	76.1	318	74	32	29	6	3	1	5	19	0	85	4	0	5	5	.500	0	0--	-	3.46	3.42
2009	Auburn	A-	2	2	0	0	11.0	42	6	2	1	0	0	0	1	3	0	12	0	0	1	0	1.000	0	0--	-	1.31	0.82
2009	Lnsng	A	14	14	0	0	79.2	333	76	36	32	5	0	4	1	29	0	62	3	1	2	4	.333	0	0--	-	3.54	3.62
2010	Dnedin	A+	27	25	1	1	137.2	588	147	65	57	8	6	6	12	30	0	173	6	3	9	6	.600	0	0--	-	3.80	3.73
2011	NHam	AA	24	23	0	0	134.2	563	100	56	51	12	2	1	12	68	0	152	16	3	7	9	.438	0	0--	-	3.41	3.41
2012	LsVgs	AAA	10	8	0	1	36.1	182	50	41	36	7	1	3	2	27	0	30	2	0	2	5	.286	0	0--	-	9.03	8.92
2012	NHam	AA	17	7	0	1	53.2	221	43	25	23	4	0	4	1	19	0	58	3	0	2	4	.333	0	0--	-	2.74	3.86
2011	Tor	AL	11	0	0	3	15.2	59	11	2	2	1	0	0	0	4	0	14	0	0	1	0	1.000	0	0-0	0	1.92	1.15
2012	Tor	AL	11	2	0	3	22.0	97	22	15	15	7	0	0	0	14	0	16	0	0	0	2	.000	0	0-0	0	6.96	6.14
2 ML YEARS			22	2	0	6	37.2	156	33	17	17	8	0	0	0	18	0	30	0	0	1	2	.333	0	0-0	0	4.63	4.06

Ezequiel Carrera

Bats: L **Throws:** L **Pos:** LF-36; CF-15; RF-1; PH-1; PR-1   ee-ZEEK-ee-ull   **Ht:** 5'10" **Wt:** 185 **Born:** 6/11/1987 **Age:** 26

Year	Team	Lg	G	AB	H	2B	3B	HR	(Hm	Rd)	TB	R	RBI	RC	TBB	IBB	SO	HBP	SH	SF	SB	CS	SB%	GDP	Avg	OBP	Slg
2007	Mets	R	45	179	61	8	3	1	(-	-)	78	41	26	36	26	0	29	2	2	0	16	5	.76	1	.341	.430	.436
2007	Bklyn	A-	20	70	21	2	0	0	(-	-)	23	11	6	9	4	0	13	1	2	0	6	1	.86	0	.300	.347	.329
2008	StLuci	A+	114	430	113	11	12	7	(-	-)	169	61	29	63	46	1	86	9	6	3	28	9	.76	6	.263	.344	.393
2009	WTenn	AA	91	329	111	12	4	2	(-	-)	137	68	38	67	59	1	62	4	10	3	27	13	.68	4	.337	.441	.416
2010	Tacom	AAA	64	213	57	6	2	0	(-	-)	67	24	18	24	20	0	32	3	7	0	9	5	.64	2	.268	.339	.315
2010	Clmbs	AAA	41	161	46	7	3	1	(-	-)	62	19	16	23	12	0	34	1	8	1	11	3	.79	5	.286	.337	.385
2010	Indns	R	4	14	6	1	0	0	(-	-)	7	2	4	3	1	0	2	0	0	0	0	0	-	0	.429	.467	.500
2011	Clmbs	AAA	82	328	94	8	3	2	(-	-)	114	63	25	52	39	0	53	5	5	0	35	4	.90	4	.287	.371	.348
2012	Clmbs	AAA	97	394	116	19	6	6	(-	-)	165	65	42	61	29	0	60	3	9	3	26	7	.79	3	.294	.345	.419
2011	Cle	AL	68	202	49	8	3	0	(0	0)	63	27	14	25	16	0	35	1	7	0	10	5	.67	4	.243	.301	.312
2012	Cle	AL	48	147	40	6	3	2	(0	2)	58	20	11	17	8	1	35	1	1	1	8	1	.89	3	.272	.312	.395
2 ML YEARS			116	349	89	14	6	2	(0	2)	121	47	25	42	24	1	70	2	8	1	18	6	.75	7	.255	.306	.347

Brett Carroll

Bats: R **Throws:** R **Pos:** CF-3; PR-3; PH-2   **Ht:** 5'11" **Wt:** 210 **Born:** 10/3/1982 **Age:** 30

Year	Team	Lg	G	AB	H	2B	3B	HR	(Hm	Rd)	TB	R	RBI	RC	TBB	IBB	SO	HBP	SH	SF	SB	CS	SB%	GDP	Avg	OBP	Slg
2012	Syrcse*	AAA	111	364	91	23	2	10	(-	-)	148	55	50	52	44	1	97	3	2	4	7	5	.58	2	.250	.333	.407
2007	Fla	NL	23	49	9	1	0	0	(0	0)	10	10	2	0	3	0	15	0	1	0	0	0	-	1	.184	.231	.204
2008	Fla	NL	26	17	1	0	0	0	(0	0)	3	5	1	0	1	0	6	0	0	0	0	0	-	0	.059	.111	.176
2009	Fla	NL	92	141	33	8	2	3	(1	2)	54	18	18	20	11	1	33	4	1	1	0	0	-	3	.234	.306	.383
2010	Fla	NL	32	76	15	4	0	2	(1	1)	25	13	7	5	6	3	29	7	0	1	2	1	.67	2	.197	.311	.329
2011	Mil	NL	2	3	0	0	0	0	(0	0)	0	0	0	0	0	0	1	0	0	0	0	0	-	0	.000	.000	.000
2012	Was	NL	5	2	0	0	0	0	(0	0)	0	2	0	0	0	0	0	0	0	0	0	0	-	0	.000	.000	.000
6 ML YEARS			180	288	58	13	3	5	(2	3)	92	48	28	25	21	4	84	11	2	2	2	1	.67	5	.201	.280	.319

Jamey Carroll

Bats: R **Throws:** R **Pos:** 2B-66; 3B-44; SS-37; PR-3   **Ht:** 5'11" **Wt:** 175 **Born:** 2/18/1974 **Age:** 39

Year	Team	Lg	G	AB	H	2B	3B	HR	(Hm	Rd)	TB	R	RBI	RC	TBB	IBB	SO	HBP	SH	SF	SB	CS	SB%	GDP	Avg	OBP	Slg
2002	Mon	NL	16	71	22	5	3	1	(1	0)	36	16	6	12	4	0	12	0	4	0	1	0	1.00	1	.310	.347	.507
2003	Mon	NL	105	227	59	10	1	1	(1	0)	74	31	10	18	19	0	39	3	9	2	5	2	.71	10	.260	.323	.326
2004	Mon	NL	102	218	63	14	2	0	(0	0)	81	36	16	28	32	1	21	1	2	3	5	1	.83	3	.289	.378	.372
2005	Was	NL	113	303	76	8	1	0	(0	0)	86	44	22	38	34	1	55	5	13	3	3	4	.43	2	.251	.333	.284
2006	Col	NL	136	463	139	23	5	5	(2	3)	187	84	36	65	56	1	66	3	9	3	10	12	.45	10	.300	.377	.404
2007	Col	NL	108	227	51	9	1	2	(1	1)	68	45	22	24	28	1	34	4	6	3	6	2	.75	2	.225	.317	.300
2008	Cle	AL	113	347	96	13	4	1	(0	1)	120	60	36	48	34	0	65	9	10	2	7	3	.70	2	.277	.355	.346
2009	Cle	AL	93	315	87	10	2	2	(0	2)	107	53	26	43	36	0	63	3	3	1	4	2	.67	8	.276	.355	.340
2010	LAD	NL	133	351	102	15	1	0	(0	0)	119	48	23	48	51	3	64	2	5	5	12	4	.75	3	.291	.379	.339

Year	Team	Lg	G	AB	H	2B	3B	HR	(Hm	Rd)	TB	R	RBI	RC	TBB	IBB	SO	HBP	SH	SF	SB	CS	SB%	GDP	Avg	OBP	Slg
									BATTING												BASERUNNING				AVERAGES		
2011	LAD	NL	146	452	131	14	6	0	(0	0)	157	52	17	55	47	3	58	2	8	1	10	0	1.00	3	.290	.359	.347
2012	Min	AL	138	470	126	18	1	1	(0	1)	149	65	40	62	52	0	65	4	7	4	9	5	.64	9	.268	.343	.317
	Postseason		4	2	0	0	0	0	(0	0)	0	0	0	0	1	0	1	0	0	0	0	0	-	0	.000	.333	.000
11 ML YEARS			1203	3444	952	139	27	13	(5	8)	1184	534	254	441	393	10	542	36	76	27	72	35	.67	58	.276	.354	.344

Matt Carson

Bats: R **Throws:** R **Pos:** LF-15; RF-9; PH-3; DH-2; PR-2   **Ht:** 6'2" **Wt:** 200 **Born:** 7/1/1981 **Age:** 31

Year	Team	Lg	G	AB	H	2B	3B	HR	(Hm	Rd)	TB	R	RBI	RC	TBB	IBB	SO	HBP	SH	SF	SB	CS	SB%	GDP	Avg	OBP	Slg
									BATTING												BASERUNNING				AVERAGES		
2012	Roch*	AAA	115	422	119	28	2	14	(-	-)	193	64	53	68	37	2	106	6	2	2	9	5	.64	7	.282	.347	.457
2009	Oak	AL	10	21	6	0	0	1	(1	0)	9	1	5	4	0	0	7	0	0	1	0	0	-	0	.286	.273	.429
2010	Oak	AL	36	79	14	2	0	4	(2	2)	28	7	9	3	2	0	23	0	0	2	4	0	1.00	0	.177	.193	.354
2012	Min	AL	26	66	15	1	0	0	(0	0)	16	3	4	3	2	0	21	0	0	1	0	0	-	0	.227	.246	.242
3 ML YEARS			72	166	35	3	0	5	(3	2)	53	11	18	10	4	0	51	0	0	4	4	0	1.00	0	.211	.224	.319

Robert Carson

Pitches: L **Bats:** L **Pos:** RP-17   **Ht:** 6'4" **Wt:** 240 **Born:** 1/23/1989 **Age:** 24

Year	Team	Lg	G	GS	CG	GF	IP	BFP	H	R	ER	HR	SH	SF	HB	TBB	IBB	SO	WP	Bk	W	L	Pct	Sh	Sv-Op	Hld	ERC	ERA
			HOW MUCH HE PITCHED						WHAT HE GAVE UP												THE RESULTS						
2007	Mets	R	4	1	0	1	9.0	43	8	7	5	1	0	1	0	5	0	9	2	0	1	0	1.000	0	0--	-	3.73	5.00
2008	Mets	R	5	5	0	0	23.0	84	11	5	4	0	1	0	0	6	0	25	0	0	1	0	1.000	0	0--	-	0.93	1.57
2008	Kngspt	R+	6	6	0	0	30.2	130	29	12	6	1	1	1	4	18	0	21	1	1	2	3	.400	0	0--	-	4.87	1.76
2009	Savann	A	25	25	2	0	131.2	575	139	68	47	4	4	6	5	45	0	90	14	3	8	10	.444	1	0--	-	3.78	3.21
2010	StLuci	A+	17	16	0	0	86.1	385	98	42	40	5	4	2	5	33	0	69	3	1	7	5	.583	0	0--	-	4.70	4.17
2010	Bnghtn	AA	10	10	0	0	48.2	228	68	46	45	7	4	1	2	23	0	30	3	0	1	6	.143	0	0--	-	7.52	8.32
2011	Bnghtn	AA	25	24	0	1	128.1	583	154	88	72	14	5	5	3	55	1	91	7	2	4	11	.267	0	0--	-	5.51	5.05
2012	Bnghtn	AA	31	0	0	22	35.2	168	44	22	18	2	1	2	0	15	1	37	5	1	1	2	.333	0	9--	-	4.92	4.54
2012	Buffalo	AAA	10	0	0	5	15.2	65	16	4	3	1	1	0	0	6	1	15	1	0	0	0	-	0	1--	-	3.93	1.72
2012	NYM	NL	17	0	0	2	13.1	57	13	7	7	2	1	0	2	4	0	5	0	0	0	0	-	0	0-0	1	4.56	4.73

Chris Carter

Bats: R **Throws:** R **Pos:** 1B-55; DH-9; PH-7   **Ht:** 6'4" **Wt:** 245 **Born:** 12/18/1986 **Age:** 26

Year	Team	Lg	G	AB	H	2B	3B	HR	(Hm	Rd)	TB	R	RBI	RC	TBB	IBB	SO	HBP	SH	SF	SB	CS	SB%	GDP	Avg	OBP	Slg
									BATTING												BASERUNNING				AVERAGES		
2012	Scrmto*	AAA	72	276	77	19	1	12	(-	-)	134	48	53	52	38	0	74	4	0	6	5	1	.83	11	.279	.367	.486
2010	Oak	AL	24	70	13	1	0	3	(1	2)	23	8	7	5	7	0	21	0	0	1	1	0	1.00	3	.186	.256	.329
2011	Oak	AL	15	44	6	0	0	0	(0	0)	6	2	0	0	2	0	20	0	0	0	0	0	-	1	.136	.174	.136
2012	Oak	AL	67	218	52	12	0	16	(5	11)	112	38	39	36	39	1	83	0	0	3	0	0	-	4	.239	.350	.514
3 ML YEARS			106	332	71	13	0	19	(6	13)	141	48	46	41	48	1	124	0	0	4	1	0	1.00	8	.214	.310	.425

Andrew Cashner

Pitches: R **Bats:** R **Pos:** RP-28; SP-5   **Ht:** 6'6" **Wt:** 200 **Born:** 9/11/1986 **Age:** 26

Year	Team	Lg	G	GS	CG	GF	IP	BFP	H	R	ER	HR	SH	SF	HB	TBB	IBB	SO	WP	Bk	W	L	Pct	Sh	Sv-Op	Hld	ERC	ERA
			HOW MUCH HE PITCHED						WHAT HE GAVE UP												THE RESULTS						
2012	SnAnt*	AA	3	3	0	0	14.1	56	10	3	3	0	0	0	2	3	0	22	0	0	2	0	1.000	0	0--	-	1.79	1.88
2012	Tucsn*	AAA	3	3	0	0	9.0	36	8	3	3	0	1	0	0	2	0	8	0	0	0	1	.000	0	0--	-	2.23	3.00
2010	ChC	NL	53	0	0	9	54.1	248	55	31	29	8	6	2	4	30	5	50	4	1	2	6	.250	0	0-1	16	5.22	4.80
2011	ChC	NL	7	1	0	0	10.2	39	3	2	2	1	0	0	0	4	0	8	0	0	0	0	-	0	0-0	1	0.91	1.69
2012	SD	NL	33	5	0	5	46.1	196	42	23	22	5	3	1	1	19	1	52	2	0	3	4	.429	0	0-4	6	3.73	4.27
3 ML YEARS			93	6	0	14	111.1	483	100	56	53	14	9	3	5	53	6	110	6	1	5	10	.333	0	0-5	23	4.07	4.28

Alexi Casilla

Bats: B **Throws:** R **Pos:** 2B-96; PR-12; PH-6; 3B-4   cuh-SEE-ya   **Ht:** 5'10" **Wt:** 179 **Born:** 7/20/1984 **Age:** 28

Year	Team	Lg	G	AB	H	2B	3B	HR	(Hm	Rd)	TB	R	RBI	RC	TBB	IBB	SO	HBP	SH	SF	SB	CS	SB%	GDP	Avg	OBP	Slg
									BATTING												BASERUNNING				AVERAGES		
2006	Min	AL	9	4	1	0	0	0	(0	0)	1	1	0	1	2	0	1	0	0	0	0	0	-	0	.250	.500	.250
2007	Min	AL	56	189	42	5	1	0	(0	0)	49	15	9	11	9	0	29	0	5	1	11	1	.92	5	.222	.256	.259
2008	Min	AL	98	385	108	15	0	7	(2	5)	144	58	50	50	31	0	45	2	13	6	7	2	.78	8	.281	.333	.374
2009	Min	AL	80	228	46	7	3	0	(0	0)	59	25	17	20	22	0	36	3	2	1	11	0	1.00	6	.202	.280	.259
2010	Min	AL	69	152	42	7	4	1	(1	0)	60	19	20	23	13	0	17	0	4	1	6	1	.86	5	.276	.331	.395
2011	Min	AL	97	323	84	21	4	2	(1	1)	119	52	21	33	28	0	45	3	8	3	15	4	.79	4	.260	.322	.368
2012	Min	AL	106	299	72	17	2	1	(0	1)	96	33	30	29	16	0	52	3	3	5	21	1	.95	6	.241	.282	.321
7 ML YEARS			515	1580	395	72	14	11	(4	7)	528	210	147	167	121	0	225	11	35	17	71	9	.89	34	.250	.305	.334

Santiago Casilla

Pitches: R **Bats:** R **Pos:** RP-73   cuh-SEE-ya   **Ht:** 6'0" **Wt:** 220 **Born:** 7/25/1980 **Age:** 32

Year	Team	Lg	G	GS	CG	GF	IP	BFP	H	R	ER	HR	SH	SF	HB	TBB	IBB	SO	WP	Bk	W	L	Pct	Sh	Sv-Op	Hld	ERC	ERA
			HOW MUCH HE PITCHED						WHAT HE GAVE UP												THE RESULTS						
2004	Oak	AL	4	0	0	2	5.2	32	5	8	8	3	0	0	1	9	0	5	0	0	0	0	-	0	0-0	0	13.22	12.71
2005	Oak	AL	3	0	0	3	3.0	12	2	1	1	0	0	0	0	1	0	1	1	0	0	0	-	0	0-0	0	1.57	3.00
2006	Oak	AL	2	0	0	1	2.1	10	2	3	3	0	0	0	0	2	0	2	0	0	0	0	-	0	0-0	0	4.61	11.57
2007	Oak	AL	46	0	0	10	50.2	219	43	25	25	6	0	3	1	23	6	52	5	0	3	1	.750	0	2-5	12	3.39	4.44
2008	Oak	AL	51	0	0	9	50.1	229	60	22	22	5	3	2	3	20	2	43	6	0	2	1	.667	0	2-3	7	5.34	3.93

Year	Team	Lg	G	GS	CG	GF	IP	BFP	H	R	ER	HR	SH	SF	HB	TBB	IBB	SO	WP	Bk	W	L	Pct	Sh	Sv-Op	Hld	ERC	ERA
2009	Oak	AL	46	0	0	15	48.1	233	61	36	32	6	1	3	3	25	3	35	5	0	1	2	.333	0	0-0	5	6.32	5.96
2010	SF	NL	52	0	0	13	55.1	225	40	14	12	2	2	1	4	26	4	56	10	0	7	2	.778	0	2-3	11	2.68	1.95
2011	SF	NL	49	0	0	20	51.2	211	33	11	10	1	4	0	2	25	1	45	5	0	2	2	.500	0	6-7	6	2.11	1.74
2012	SF	NL	73	0	0	37	63.1	272	55	24	20	8	2	1	2	22	4	55	1	0	7	6	.538	0	25-31	12	3.24	2.84
	Postseason		4	0	0	0	4.2	20	3	1	1	0	0	0	1	1	1	5	1	0	0	0	-	0	0-0	2	1.41	1.93
	9 ML YEARS		326	0	0	110	330.2	1443	301	144	133	31	12	10	16	153	20	294	33	0	22	14	.611	0	37-49	53	3.83	3.62

Bobby Cassevah

Pitches: R **Bats:** R **Pos:** RP-4   CASS-eh-vah   **Ht:** 6'3" **Wt:** 220 **Born:** 9/11/1985 **Age:** 27

Year	Team	Lg	G	GS	CG	GF	IP	BFP	H	R	ER	HR	SH	SF	HB	TBB	IBB	SO	WP	Bk	W	L	Pct	Sh	Sv-Op	Hld	ERC	ERA
2012	InldEm*	A+	5	0	0	1	5.0	19	4	1	1	1	0	0	0	2	0	4	0	0	0	0	-	0	1--	-	4.00	1.80
2012	Salt Lk*	AAA	44	0	0	17	46.1	215	60	33	32	3	1	1	1	19	0	28	3	0	4	1	.800	0	10--	-	5.62	6.22
2010	LAA	AL	16	0	0	9	20.0	94	23	11	7	0	1	1	0	8	2	8	1	0	1	2	.333	0	0-0	0	3.98	3.15
2011	LAA	AL	30	0	0	6	39.2	157	28	12	12	1	1	1	1	19	2	24	3	0	1	1	.500	0	0-1	6	2.48	2.72
2012	LAA	AL	4	0	0	0	5.0	29	5	4	4	2	1	2	1	6	1	2	0	0	1	0	1.000	0	0-2	0	9.74	7.20
	3 ML YEARS		50	0	0	15	64.2	280	56	27	23	3	3	4	3	33	5	34	4	0	3	3	.500	0	0-3	6	3.43	3.20

Alex Castellanos

Bats: R **Throws:** R **Pos:** LF-11; PR-5; RF-4; PH-3   kah-stay-AH-nos   **Ht:** 5'11" **Wt:** 195 **Born:** 8/4/1986 **Age:** 26

Year	Team	Lg	G	AB	H	2B	3B	HR	(Hm	Rd)	TB	R	RBI	RC	TBB	IBB	SO	HBP	SH	SF	SB	CS	SB%	GDP	Avg	OBP	Slg
2008	JhsCty	R+	49	181	54	14	4	7	(-	-)	97	42	31	37	8	0	45	8	1	1	20	2	.91	1	.298	.354	.536
2008	Batvia	A-	10	26	7	2	2	0	(-	-)	13	6	4	4	2	0	7	1	0	0	0	1	.00	0	.269	.345	.500
2009	QuadC	A	82	311	84	21	4	5	(-	-)	128	51	34	47	20	0	89	12	1	2	21	4	.84	5	.270	.336	.412
2009	PlmBh	A+	21	53	10	1	1	1	(-	-)	16	5	2	2	2	0	19	1	0	0	0	2	.00	0	.189	.232	.302
2010	PlmBh	A+	129	459	124	35	7	13	(-	-)	212	62	58	74	38	3	112	12	4	4	19	9	.68	11	.270	.339	.462
2011	Sprgfld	AA	93	354	113	21	4	19	(-	-)	199	72	62	75	24	3	94	11	0	2	10	1	.91	7	.319	.379	.562
2011	Chatt	AA	32	121	39	14	4	4	(-	-)	73	30	23	29	15	1	24	4	0	3	4	1	.80	3	.322	.406	.603
2012	Albq	AAA	94	344	113	25	7	17	(-	-)	203	74	52	83	46	2	85	11	2	4	16	8	.67	3	.328	.420	.590
2012	LAD	NL	16	23	4	0	1	1	(1	0)	9	3	3	2	0	0	8	1	0	1	0	0	-	0	.174	.200	.391

Lendy Castillo

Pitches: R **Bats:** B **Pos:** RP-13   LENN-dee   **Ht:** 6'1" **Wt:** 170 **Born:** 4/8/1989 **Age:** 24

Year	Team	Lg	G	GS	CG	GF	IP	BFP	H	R	ER	HR	SH	SF	HB	TBB	IBB	SO	WP	Bk	W	L	Pct	Sh	Sv-Op	Hld	ERC	ERA
2010	Phillies	R	13	6	0	1	44.2	180	33	13	11	2	-	-	4	18	0	51	2	1	3	1	.750	0	0--	-	2.77	2.22
2010	Wmspt	A-	1	1	0	0	5.0	20	3	0	0	0	0	0	0	2	0	3	0	0	0	0	-	0	0--	-	1.51	0.00
2011	Lakwd	A	21	2	0	4	46.0	194	37	16	13	1	1	4	5	16	0	46	2	0	4	2	.667	0	0--	-	2.69	2.54
2012	Cubs	R	4	4	0	0	13.0	48	7	1	1	0	0	0	0	3	0	16	2	0	0	0	-	0	0--	-	1.03	0.69
2012	Dytona	A+	1	1	0	0	4.0	16	3	1	1	0	0	0	0	1	0	4	0	0	0	0	-	0	0--	-	1.65	0.00
2012	Tenn	AA	2	2	0	0	3.0	13	3	1	1	0	0	0	0	2	0	2	0	1	0	0	-	0	0--	-	4.60	3.00
2012	ChC	NL	13	0	0	2	16.0	88	24	16	14	2	2	1	3	12	0	13	2	0	0	1	.000	0	0-0	0	9.43	7.88

Welington Castillo

Bats: R **Throws:** R **Pos:** C-49; PH-5; 1B-1   WELL-ing-tunn   **Ht:** 5'10" **Wt:** 210 **Born:** 4/24/1987 **Age:** 26

Year	Team	Lg	G	AB	H	2B	3B	HR	(Hm	Rd)	TB	R	RBI	RC	TBB	IBB	SO	HBP	SH	SF	SB	CS	SB%	GDP	Avg	OBP	Slg
2012	Iowa*	AAA	44	146	38	6	0	6	(-	-)	62	22	22	25	23	0	37	5	0	2	0	0	-	9	.260	.375	.425
2012	Tenn*	AA	5	11	4	0	0	2	(-	-)	10	3	6	5	5	0	3	1	0	0	0	0	-	1	.364	.588	.909
2010	ChC	NL	7	20	6	4	0	1	(0	1)	13	3	5	3	1	0	7	0	0	0	0	0	-	0	.300	.333	.650
2011	ChC	NL	4	13	2	0	0	0	(0	0)	2	0	0	0	0	0	4	0	0	0	0	0	-	1	.154	.154	.154
2012	ChC	NL	52	170	45	11	0	5	(4	1)	71	16	22	22	17	2	51	2	0	1	0	0	-	4	.265	.337	.418
	3 ML YEARS		63	203	53	15	0	6	(4	2)	86	19	27	25	18	2	62	2	0	1	0	0	-	5	.261	.326	.424

Jason Castro

Bats: L **Throws:** R **Pos:** C-79; PH-10   **Ht:** 6'3" **Wt:** 215 **Born:** 6/18/1987 **Age:** 26

Year	Team	Lg	G	AB	H	2B	3B	HR	(Hm	Rd)	TB	R	RBI	RC	TBB	IBB	SO	HBP	SH	SF	SB	CS	SB%	GDP	Avg	OBP	Slg
2008	TriCity	A-	39	138	38	9	0	2	(-	-)	53	10	12	22	22	2	32	2	0	0	2	0	.00	1	.275	.383	.384
2009	Lancst	A+	56	207	64	20	1	7	(-	-)	107	27	44	43	30	2	41	3	0	3	1	1	.50	5	.309	.399	.517
2009	CpChr	AA	63	239	70	11	1	3	(-	-)	92	38	29	35	25	0	35	2	0	2	2	1	.67	5	.293	.362	.385
2010	RdRck	AAA	57	211	56	7	0	4	(-	-)	75	31	26	30	32	0	34	1	0	0	1	1	.50	5	.265	.365	.355
2012	CpChr	AA	3	5	4	2	0	0	(-	-)	6	1	0	3	2	0	0	0	0	0	0	0	-	0	.800	.857	1.200
2012	OKCity	AAA	4	13	6	1	0	1	(-	-)	10	1	2	4	2	0	1	0	0	0	0	0	-	0	.462	.533	.769
2010	Hou	NL	67	195	40	8	1	2	(1	1)	56	26	8	12	22	2	41	0	0	4	0	0	-	4	.205	.286	.287
2012	Hou	NL	87	257	66	15	2	6	(3	3)	103	29	29	33	31	2	61	1	2	4	0	0	-	8	.257	.334	.401
	2 ML YEARS		154	452	106	23	3	8	(4	4)	159	55	37	45	53	4	102	1	2	4	0	0	-	12	.235	.314	.352

Starlin Castro

Bats: R **Throws:** R **Pos:** SS-162   STARR-linn   **Ht:** 6'0" **Wt:** 190 **Born:** 3/24/1990 **Age:** 23

Year Team	Lg	G	AB	H	2B	3B	HR	(Hm	Rd)	TB	R	RBI	RC	TBB	IBB	SO	HBP	SH	SF	SB	CS	SB%	GDP	Avg	OBP	Slg
2010 ChC	NL	125	463	139	31	5	3	(1	2)	189	53	41	56	29	7	71	6	4	4	10	8	.56	14	.300	.347	.408
2011 ChC	NL	158	674	207	36	9	10	(4	6)	291	91	66	93	35	2	96	2	0	4	22	9	.71	20	.307	.341	.432
2012 ChC	NL	162	646	183	29	12	14	(7	7)	278	78	78	91	36	5	100	4	0	5	25	13	.66	15	.283	.323	.430
3 ML YEARS		445	1783	529	96	26	27	(12	15)	758	222	185	240	100	14	267	12	4	13	57	30	.66	49	.297	.336	.425

Brett Cecil

Pitches: L **Bats:** R **Pos:** RP-12; SP-9   **Ht:** 6'1" **Wt:** 215 **Born:** 7/2/1986 **Age:** 26

Year Team	Lg	G	GS	CG	GF	IP	BFP	H	R	ER	HR	SH	SF	HB	TBB	IBB	SO	WP	Bk	W	L	Pct	Sh	Sv-Op	Hld	ERC	ERA
2012 NHam*	AA	9	9	0	0	42.2	184	44	18	16	2	2	1	2	14	0	34	1	0	3	2	.600	0	0- -	-	3.77	3.38
2012 LsVgs*	AAA	6	6	0	0	39.2	154	36	11	11	1	1	0	1	7	0	33	2	0	1	2	.333	0	0- -	-	2.50	2.50
2009 Tor	AL	18	17	0	1	93.1	422	116	59	55	17	0	2	5	38	0	69	0	0	7	4	.636	0	0-0	0	6.53	5.30
2010 Tor	AL	28	28	0	0	172.2	726	175	87	81	18	1	6	1	54	2	117	7	1	15	7	.682	0	0-0	0	3.88	4.22
2011 Tor	AL	20	20	2	0	123.2	532	122	68	65	22	3	5	6	42	1	87	1	0	4	11	.267	1	0-0	0	4.47	4.73
2012 Tor	AL	21	9	0	2	61.1	270	70	40	39	11	3	3	3	23	0	51	0	0	2	4	.333	0	0-0	1	5.68	5.72
4 ML YEARS		87	74	2	3	451.0	1950	483	254	240	68	7	16	15	157	3	324	8	1	28	26	.519	1	0-0	1	4.80	4.79

Jose Ceda

Pitches: R **Bats:** R **Pos:** P   SAY-dah   **Ht:** 6'5" **Wt:** 280 **Born:** 1/28/1987 **Age:** 26

Year Team	Lg	G	GS	CG	GF	IP	BFP	H	R	ER	HR	SH	SF	HB	TBB	IBB	SO	WP	Bk	W	L	Pct	Sh	Sv-Op	Hld	ERC	ERA
2006 Padres	R	8	4	0	0	23.0	100	20	14	13	1	0	1	1	13	0	31	0	0	2	0	1.000	0	0- -	-	3.78	5.09
2006 Cubs	R	5	3	0	0	12.0	47	6	2	1	0	1	0	0	7	0	21	1	0	0	0	-	0	0- -	-	1.65	0.75
2006 Boise	A-	3	3	0	0	11.0	41	5	4	4	1	0	0	3	2	0	11	2	0	1	0	1.000	0	0- -	-	1.62	3.27
2007 Peoria	A	21	6	0	5	46.1	186	14	18	16	1	0	0	2	31	0	66	8	0	2	2	.500	0	0- -	-	1.35	3.11
2007 Cubs	R	2	1	0	0	3.2	15	2	1	1	0	0	1	0	3	0	3	0	0	0	0	-	0	0- -	-	2.64	2.45
2008 Dytona	A+	15	12	0	1	54.1	229	41	29	29	4	0	4	4	28	0	53	3	1	2	2	.500	0	0- -	-	3.32	4.80
2008 Tenn	AA	22	0	0	19	30.1	129	26	8	8	2	3	0	1	14	1	42	3	0	2	1	.667	0	9- -	-	3.38	2.37
2010 Grnsbr	A	7	0	0	0	8.0	33	7	4	4	2	0	0	1	1	0	5	0	0	0	0	-	0	0- -	-	3.68	4.50
2010 Jaxnvl	AA	27	0	0	18	32.1	134	18	5	5	3	2	3	1	20	2	45	0	0	4	1	.800	0	6- -	-	2.57	1.39
2011 NewOr	AAA	36	0	0	34	39.2	165	30	14	6	1	1	1	1	13	0	53	6	1	3	1	.750	0	24- -	-	2.09	1.36
2010 Fla	NL	8	0	0	1	8.2	45	8	5	5	1	0	0	1	11	1	9	0	0	0	0	-	0	0-0	-	7.53	5.19
2011 Fla	NL	17	0	0	9	20.1	88	16	11	10	1	0	0	0	12	0	21	1	0	0	1	.000	0	0-0	-	3.25	4.43
2 ML YEARS		25	0	0	10	29.0	133	24	16	15	2	0	0	1	23	1	30	1	1	0	1	.000	0	0-0	-	4.43	4.66

Ronny Cedeno

Bats: R **Throws:** R **Pos:** 2B-28; SS-27; PH-25; 3B-3; PR-2   **Ht:** 6'0" **Wt:** 195 **Born:** 2/2/1983 **Age:** 30

Year Team	Lg	G	AB	H	2B	3B	HR	(Hm	Rd)	TB	R	RBI	RC	TBB	IBB	SO	HBP	SH	SF	SB	CS	SB%	GDP	Avg	OBP	Slg
2012 StLuci*	A+	1	4	0	0	0	0	(-	-)	0	0	0	0	0	0	0	0	0	0	0	0	-	0	.000	.000	.000
2012 Buffalo*	AAA	7	29	5	0	0	0	(-	-)	5	2	1	0	1	0	6	0	0	0	0	0	-	2	.172	.200	.172
2005 ChC	NL	41	80	24	3	0	1	(0	1)	30	13	6	11	5	1	11	2	2	0	1	0	1.00	4	.300	.356	.375
2006 ChC	NL	151	534	131	18	7	6	(4	2)	181	51	41	41	17	4	109	3	15	3	8	8	.50	10	.245	.271	.339
2007 ChC	NL	38	74	15	2	0	4	(2	2)	29	6	13	8	3	0	18	0	2	1	2	1	.67	2	.203	.231	.392
2008 ChC	NL	99	216	58	12	0	2	(2	0)	76	36	28	23	18	2	41	1	1	0	4	1	.80	6	.269	.328	.352
2009 2 Tms		105	341	71	8	3	10	(7	3)	115	32	38	29	19	3	79	3	13	0	5	2	.71	9	.208	.256	.337
2010 Pit	NL	139	468	120	29	3	8	(4	4)	179	42	38	46	23	4	106	2	7	2	12	3	.80	10	.256	.293	.382
2011 Pit	NL	128	413	103	25	3	2	(0	2)	140	43	32	36	30	7	93	0	6	5	2	5	.29	11	.249	.297	.339
2012 NYM	NL	78	166	43	11	1	4	(3	1)	68	18	22	19	17	0	35	1	2	0	1	0	1.00	10	.259	.332	.410
09 Sea	AL	59	186	31	4	2	5	(2	3)	54	15	17	7	10	1	50	1	9	0	3	2	.60	6	.167	.213	.290
09 Pit	NL	46	155	40	4	1	5	(5	0)	61	17	21	22	9	2	29	2	4	0	2	0	1.00	3	.258	.307	.394
Postseason		3	0	0	0	0	0	(0	0)	0	0	0	0	0	0	0	0	0	0	1	0	1.00	0	-	-	-
8 ML YEARS		779	2292	565	108	17	37	(22	15)	818	241	218	213	132	21	492	12	48	11	34	21	.62	60	.247	.290	.357

Xavier Cedeno

Pitches: L **Bats:** L **Pos:** RP-44   **Ht:** 6'1" **Wt:** 205 **Born:** 8/26/1986 **Age:** 26

Year Team	Lg	G	GS	CG	GF	IP	BFP	H	R	ER	HR	SH	SF	HB	TBB	IBB	SO	WP	Bk	W	L	Pct	Sh	Sv-Op	Hld	ERC	ERA
2005 Casper	R+	12	12	0	0	53.0	236	62	36	32	4	3	1	8	17	0	47	3	0	1	3	.250	0	0- -	-	5.26	5.43
2006 Ashvll	A	27	27	0	0	138.0	615	144	79	62	8	9	4	5	63	0	99	14	0	8	9	.471	0	0- -	-	4.35	4.04
2007 Mdest	A+	23	23	0	0	116.2	530	121	78	66	6	2	7	5	61	0	83	12	0	6	8	.429	0	0- -	-	4.52	5.09
2008 Tulsa	AA	19	19	0	0	102.2	473	126	66	47	10	10	3	4	37	0	52	8	0	7	7	.500	0	0- -	-	5.21	4.12
2009 Tulsa	AA	28	0	0	7	47.0	212	46	30	25	6	1	3	3	22	1	25	2	0	3	2	.600	0	0- -	-	4.54	4.79
2009 Mdest	A+	16	0	0	4	16.2	78	15	10	8	1	0	0	9	0	21	1	0	1	2	.333	0	0- -	-	3.06	4.32
2011 CpChr	AA	23	19	0	1	111.2	478	98	59	49	8	6	5	45	5	110	7	0	5	6	.455	0	0- -	-	3.29	3.95
2011 OKCity	AAA	12	3	0	2	26.0	117	32	20	18	2	1	1	0	8	0	27	1	1	2	3	.400	0	0- -	-	4.78	6.23
2012 OKCity	AAA	22	0	0	5	27.2	122	27	16	7	0	1	2	2	9	2	25	1	0	2	0	1.000	0	1- -	-	3.01	2.28
2011 Hou	NL	3	0	0	1	1.2	11	7	5	5	2	0	0	0	0	0	0	0	0	0	0	-	0	0-0	0	43.10	27.00
2012 Hou	NL	44	0	0	12	31.0	138	30	15	13	3	2	3	1	14	1	36	3	0	0	1	.000	0	1-3	6	4.05	3.77
2 ML YEARS		47	0	0	12	32.2	149	37	20	18	5	2	3	1	14	1	36	3	0	0	1	.000	0	1-3	6	5.34	4.96

Francisco Cervelli

Bats: R Throws: R Pos: C-3   serr-VELL-ee   Ht: 6'1" Wt: 205 Born: 3/6/1986 Age: 27

Year	Team	Lg	G	AB	H	2B	3B	HR	(Hm	Rd)	TB	R	RBI	RC	TBB	IBB	SO	HBP	SH	SF	SB	CS	SB%	GDP	Avg	OBP	Slg
2012	S-WB*	AAA	99	354	87	15	2	2	(-	-)	112	43	39	45	39	1	82	15	3	6	6	0	1.00	14	.246	.341	.316
2008	NYY	AL	3	5	0	0	0	0	(0	0)	0	0	0	0	0	0	3	0	0	0	0	0	-	1	.000	.000	.000
2009	NYY	AL	42	94	28	4	0	1	(0	1)	35	13	11	11	2	0	11	0	4	1	0	3	.00	1	.298	.309	.372
2010	NYY	AL	93	266	72	11	3	0	(0	0)	89	27	38	40	33	1	42	6	8	4	1	1	.50	7	.271	.359	.335
2011	NYY	AL	43	124	33	4	0	4	(2	2)	49	17	22	17	9	0	29	2	1	1	4	1	.80	4	.266	.324	.395
2012	NYY	AL	3	1	0	0	0	0	(0	0)	0	1	0	0	1	0	0	0	0	0	0	0	-	0	.000	.500	.000
	Postseason		3	3	0	0	0	0	(0	0)	0	0	0	0	0	0	2	0	0	0	0	0	-	0	.000	.000	.000
	5 ML YEARS		184	490	133	19	3	5	(2	3)	173	58	71	68	45	1	85	8	13	6	5	5	.50	13	.271	.339	.353

Yoenis Cespedes

Bats: R Throws: R Pos: LF-56; CF-48; DH-26; PR-1   yo-EHN-ess SESS-peh-des   Ht: 5'10" Wt: 210 Born: 10/18/1985 Age: 27

Year	Team	Lg	G	AB	H	2B	3B	HR	(Hm	Rd)	TB	R	RBI	RC	TBB	IBB	SO	HBP	SH	SF	SB	CS	SB%	GDP	Avg	OBP	Slg
2012	Scrmto	AAA	3	9	3	0	0	0	(-	-)	3	1	0	1	1	0	1	1	0	0	0	0	-	0	.333	.455	.333
2012	Oak	AL	129	487	142	25	5	23	(11	12)	246	70	82	90	43	5	102	7	0	3	16	4	.80	9	.292	.356	.505

Jhoulys Chacin

Pitches: R Bats: R Pos: SP-14   joo-LEEZ cha-SEEN   Ht: 6'3" Wt: 225 Born: 1/7/1988 Age: 25

Year	Team	Lg	G	GS	CG	GF	IP	BFP	H	R	ER	HR	SH	SF	HB	TBB	IBB	SO	WP	Bk	W	L	Pct	Sh	Sv-Op Hld	ERC	ERA
2012	Mdest*	A+	1	1	0	0	2.1	13	7	5	5	0	0	1	0	0	0	1	0	0	0	1	.000	0	0--	15.68	19.29
2012	Tulsa*	AA	2	2	0	0	9.0	37	9	6	6	1	0	0	0	2	0	7	0	0	0	1	.000	0	0--	3.49	6.00
2012	ColSpr*	AAA	2	2	0	0	13.2	55	10	4	4	1	2	0	0	5	0	5	0	0	1	1	.500	0	0--	2.39	2.63
2009	Col	NL	9	1	0	3	11.0	48	6	6	6	1	1	0	0	11	0	13	2	0	0	1	.000	0	0-0	3.87	4.91
2010	Col	NL	28	21	0	2	137.1	583	114	64	50	10	6	5	9	61	5	138	4	0	9	11	.450	0	0-0	3.33	3.28
2011	Col	NL	31	31	2	0	194.0	827	168	87	78	20	5	3	4	87	1	150	7	0	11	14	.440	1	0-0	3.61	3.62
2012	Col	NL	14	14	0	0	69.0	314	80	35	34	10	1	1	2	32	0	45	3	0	3	5	.375	0	0-0	5.73	4.43
	4 ML YEARS		82	67	2	5	411.1	1772	368	192	168	41	13	9	15	191	6	346	16	0	23	31	.426	1	0-0	3.86	3.68

Joba Chamberlain

Pitches: R Bats: R Pos: RP-22   JOBB-ah CHAME-berr-linn   Ht: 6'2" Wt: 250 Born: 9/23/1985 Age: 27

Year	Team	Lg	G	GS	CG	GF	IP	BFP	H	R	ER	HR	SH	SF	HB	TBB	IBB	SO	WP	Bk	W	L	Pct	Sh	Sv-Op Hld	ERC	ERA
2012	Yanks*	R	3	3	0	0	4.0	14	0	1	0	0	0	0	0	0	0	6	0	0	0	0	-	0	0--	0.00	0.00
2012	Tampa*	A+	3	3	0	0	4.0	14	3	2	1	0	1	0	1	1	0	1	0	0	0	1	.000	0	0--	3.52	2.25
2012	Trntn*	AA	1	0	0	0	1.1	6	1	0	0	0	0	0	0	0	0	3	0	0	1	0	1.000	0	0--	0.94	0.00
2007	NYY	AL	19	0	0	3	24.0	91	12	2	1	1	1	0	1	6	0	34	1	0	2	0	1.000	0	1-1 8	1.16	0.38
2008	NYY	AL	42	12	0	5	100.1	417	87	32	29	5	2	1	2	39	3	118	4	2	4	3	.571	0	0-1 19	3.04	2.60
2009	NYY	AL	32	31	0	0	157.1	709	167	94	83	21	6	5	12	76	2	133	5	2	9	6	.600	0	0-0 0	5.32	4.75
2010	NYY	AL	73	0	0	18	71.2	305	71	37	35	6	0	1	1	22	2	77	5	1	3	4	.429	0	3-7 26	3.53	4.40
2011	NYY	AL	27	0	0	3	28.2	110	23	10	9	3	0	1	1	7	0	24	1	0	2	0	1.000	0	0-1 12	2.76	2.83
2012	NYY	AL	22	0	0	5	20.2	95	26	11	10	3	0	1	2	6	2	22	0	0	1	0	1.000	0	0-0 4	5.63	4.35
	Postseason		15	0	0	0	13.1	62	16	5	5	1	1	1	1	6	0	14	2	0	1	0	1.000	0	0-2 3	5.51	3.38
	6 ML YEARS		215	43	0	34	402.2	1727	386	186	167	39	9	9	19	156	9	408	16	5	21	13	.618	0	4-10 69	3.94	3.73

Adron Chambers

Bats: L Throws: L Pos: PH-14; PR-11; LF-10; CF-10; RF-8   AID-run   Ht: 5'10" Wt: 185 Born: 10/8/1986 Age: 26

Year	Team	Lg	G	AB	H	2B	3B	HR	(Hm	Rd)	TB	R	RBI	RC	TBB	IBB	SO	HBP	SH	SF	SB	CS	SB%	GDP	Avg	OBP	Slg
2007	JhsCty	R	36	111	31	7	1	0	(-	-)	40	16	10	15	10	0	21	5	2	1	6	5	.55	1	.279	.362	.360
2008	QuadC	A	95	336	80	13	7	3	(-	-)	116	56	25	41	33	0	66	10	2	3	13	8	.62	2	.238	.322	.345
2009	PlmBh	A+	122	448	127	17	16	1	(-	-)	179	66	46	69	47	0	96	16	4	2	21	12	.64	7	.283	.370	.400
2010	Sprgfld	AA	75	252	71	9	5	5	(-	-)	105	52	27	42	31	0	50	7	2	0	8	4	.67	2	.282	.376	.417
2010	Memp	AAA	37	69	20	0	1	1	(-	-)	25	11	8	11	9	0	18	3	1	1	6	1	.86	0	.290	.390	.362
2011	Memp	AAA	128	426	118	19	5	10	(-	-)	177	73	44	69	53	0	90	10	9	3	22	13	.63	9	.277	.368	.415
2012	Memp	AAA	96	357	114	17	2	3	(-	-)	144	60	44	64	51	4	80	4	2	5	13	4	.76	7	.319	.405	.403
2011	StL	NL	18	8	3	0	0	0	(0	0)	5	2	4	3	0	0	1	0	0	0	0	0	-	0	.375	.375	.625
2012	StL	NL	41	54	12	0	2	0	(0	0)	16	4	4	7	5	2	18	1	2	0	2	1	.67	0	.222	.300	.296
	Postseason		10	5	1	0	0	0	(0	0)	1	2	2	1	0	0	4	0	0	1	0	0	-	0	.200	.167	.200
	2 ML YEARS		59	62	15	0	3	0	(0	0)	21	6	8	10	5	2	19	1	2	0	2	1	.67	0	.242	.309	.339

Aroldis Chapman

Pitches: L Bats: L Pos: RP-68   ah-ROLL-diss   Ht: 6'4" Wt: 200 Born: 2/28/1988 Age: 25

Year	Team	Lg	G	GS	CG	GF	IP	BFP	H	R	ER	HR	SH	SF	HB	TBB	IBB	SO	WP	Bk	W	L	Pct	Sh	Sv-Op Hld	ERC	ERA
2010	Cin	NL	15	0	0	3	13.1	51	9	4	3	0	0	0	0	5	0	19	2	0	2	2	.500	0	0-1 4	1.82	2.03
2011	Cin	NL	54	0	0	13	50.0	207	24	21	20	2	1	0	2	41	0	71	4	0	4	1	.800	0	1-3 13	2.69	3.60
2012	Cin	NL	68	0	0	52	71.2	276	35	13	12	4	0	1	4	23	0	122	4	0	5	5	.500	0	38-43 6	1.35	1.51
	Postseason		2	0	0	1	1.2	11	3	3	0	0	0	0	0	0	0	1	0	0	0	1	.000	0	0-1 0	7.12	0.00
	3 ML YEARS		137	0	0	68	135.0	534	68	38	35	6	1	1	6	69	0	212	10	0	11	8	.579	0	39-47 23	1.81	2.33

Jaye Chapman

Pitches: R **Bats:** R **Pos:** RP-14 | JAY | **Ht:** 6'0" **Wt:** 195 **Born:** 5/22/1987 **Age:** 26

				HOW MUCH HE PITCHED			WHAT HE GAVE UP												THE RESULTS						
Year	Team	Lg	G	GS	CG	GF	IP	BFP	H	R	ER	HR	SH	SF	HB	TBB	IBB	SO	WP	Bk	W	L	Pct	Sh	Sv-Op Hld	ERC	ERA
2006	Danvle	R	14	5	0	2	34.1	169	46	25	22	2	5	4	2	21	1	24	1	0	1	2	.333	0	1- -	6.78	5.77
2007	Rome	A	20	0	0	3	37.1	161	31	26	26	4	1	1	2	19	0	42	3	0	3	1	.750	0	0- -	3.81	6.27
2007	Danvle	R	3	0	0	1	7.1	31	6	3	1	1	0	0	0	1	0	13	1	0	0	1	.000	0	1- -	2.13	1.23
2008	Rome	A	8	0	0	1	19.1	86	21	8	8	1	0	1	1	8	0	14	0	0	0	0	-	0	0- -	4.46	3.72
2008	MrtlBh	A+	13	1	0	5	29.2	130	30	13	11	3	0	2	0	12	1	25	0	0	4	2	.667	0	0- -	4.05	3.34
2009	MrtlBh	A+	27	0	0	4	35.1	157	35	19	17	3	0	1	0	20	0	37	4	0	1	2	.333	0	0- -	4.58	4.33
2009	Rome	A	19	0	0	17	22.2	85	9	3	1	0	0	0	1	4	0	29	2	0	1	0	1.000	0	13- -	0.63	0.40
2010	MrtlBh	A+	10	0	0	6	12.2	57	10	8	8	1	1	1	0	7	0	21	6	0	1	0	.000	0	2- -	3.16	5.68
2010	Missi	AA	36	1	0	19	50.1	238	59	35	29	1	2	1	3	25	3	53	4	0	1	4	.200	0	0- -	4.82	5.19
2011	Missi	AA	9	0	0	5	14.0	51	5	1	1	1	0	0	0	5	0	16	0	0	1	0	1.000	0	2- -	1.02	0.64
2011	Gwnntt	AAA	43	1	0	18	54.1	223	40	20	18	5	3	0	0	26	4	61	6	1	2	3	.400	0	2- -	2.83	2.98
2012	Gwnntt	AAA	40	0	0	20	53.2	232	46	31	21	3	3	2	0	29	3	60	1	0	3	6	.333	0	7- -	3.41	3.52
2012	Iowa	AAA	8	0	0	4	9.1	46	11	8	8	0	2	1	0	7	2	10	2	0	0	2	.000	0	0- -	5.13	7.71
2012	Tenn	AA	2	0	0	1	2.0	6	0	0	0	0	0	0	0	0	0	2	0	0	0	0	-	0	0- -	0.00	0.00
2012	ChC	NL	14	0	0	5	12.0	50	8	5	5	0	0	0	0	10	2	12	0	0	0	1	.000	0	0-0 5	3.06	3.75

Tyler Chatwood

Pitches: R **Bats:** R **Pos:** SP-12; RP-7 | | **Ht:** 6'0" **Wt:** 185 **Born:** 12/16/1989 **Age:** 23

				HOW MUCH HE PITCHED			WHAT HE GAVE UP												THE RESULTS						
Year	Team	Lg	G	GS	CG	GF	IP	BFP	H	R	ER	HR	SH	SF	HB	TBB	IBB	SO	WP	Bk	W	L	Pct	Sh	Sv-Op Hld	ERC	ERA
2008	Angels	R	11	11	0	0	38.0	166	25	15	13	1	1	1	0	36	0	48	7	0	1	2	.333	0	0- -	3.84	3.08
2009	CRpds	A	24	24	0	0	116.1	492	99	60	52	3	2	3	3	66	0	106	11	0	8	7	.533	0	0- -	3.58	4.02
2010	RCuca	A+	14	13	0	0	81.1	335	71	18	16	6	1	1	2	36	0	70	5	0	8	3	.727	0	0- -	3.59	1.77
2010	Ark	AA	12	12	1	0	68.1	296	72	38	29	3	2	1	2	27	0	36	7	0	4	6	.400	1	0- -	4.11	3.82
2010	Salt Lk	AAA	1	1	0	0	5.2	26	9	4	4	1	0	0	0	0	0	3	0	0	1	0	1.000	0	0- -	6.31	6.35
2011	Salt Lk	AAA	4	4	0	0	16.0	79	21	11	9	2	1	0	2	11	0	11	1	0	1	2	.333	0	0- -	8.06	5.06
2012	ColSpr	AAA	9	9	0	0	37.1	181	52	26	24	2	0	1	2	19	0	31	1	0	0	2	.000	0	0- -	6.71	5.79
2012	Tulsa	AA	4	4	0	0	24.0	93	17	9	8	2	0	0	0	7	0	22	7	0	1	1	.500	0	0- -	2.13	3.00
2011	LAA	AL	27	25	0	0	142.0	633	166	81	75	14	6	3	6	71	4	74	3	1	6	11	.353	0	0-0 0	5.78	4.75
2012	Col	NL	19	12	0	3	64.2	294	74	43	39	9	4	2	0	33	2	41	4	0	5	6	.455	0	1-1 0	5.62	5.43
	2 ML YEARS		46	37	0	3	206.2	927	240	124	114	23	10	5	6	104	6	115	7	1	11	17	.393	0	1-1 0	5.73	4.96

Endy Chavez

Bats: L **Throws:** L **Pos:** LF-35; RF-21; PH-7; PR-6; CF-3 | EN-dee SHAH-vezz | **Ht:** 6'0" **Wt:** 170 **Born:** 2/7/1978 **Age:** 35

									BATTING													BASERUNNING					AVERAGES		
Year	Team	Lg	G	AB	H	2B	3B	HR	(Hm	Rd)	TB	R	RBI	RC	TBB	IBB	SO	HBP	SH	SF		SB	CS	SB%	GDP		Avg	OBP	Slg
2012	Bowie*	AA	3	10	2	0	0	0	(-	-)	2	3	0	0	2	0	0	0	0	0		0	0	-	0		.200	.333	.200
2012	Orioles*	R	1	4	0	0	0	0	(-	-)	0	0	0	0	0	0	2	0	0	0		0	0	-	0		.000	.000	.000
2012	Dlmrva*	A	3	9	1	0	0	0	(-	-)	1	2	1	0	2	0	1	0	0	0		0	0	-	0		.111	.273	.111
2012	Norfolk*	AAA	15	47	7	3	0	0	(-	-)	10	2	4	1	2	0	6	1	1	2		0	0	-	1		.149	.192	.213
2001	KC	AL	29	77	16	2	0	0	(0	0)	18	4	5	2	3	0	8	0	0	0		0	2	.00	3		.208	.238	.234
2002	Mon	NL	36	125	37	8	5	1	(0	1)	58	20	9	14	5	0	16	0	7	1		3	5	.38	0		.296	.321	.464
2003	Mon	NL	141	483	121	25	5	5	(4	1)	171	66	47	56	31	3	59	0	9	3		18	7	.72	7		.251	.294	.354
2004	Mon	NL	132	502	139	20	6	5	(4	1)	186	65	34	56	30	0	40	1	12	2		32	7	.82	6		.277	.318	.371
2005	2 Tms	NL	98	116	25	4	3	0	(0	0)	35	19	11	8	7	0	14	0	7	0		2	2	.50	3		.216	.260	.302
2006	NYM	NL	133	353	108	22	5	4	(2	2)	152	48	42	54	24	3	44	0	11	2		12	3	.80	7		.306	.348	.431
2007	NYM	NL	71	150	43	7	2	1	(1	0)	57	20	17	20	9	0	16	0	5	1		5	2	.71	5		.287	.325	.380
2008	NYM	NL	133	270	72	10	2	1	(1	0)	89	30	12	21	17	3	22	0	9	2		6	1	.86	6		.267	.308	.330
2009	Sea	AL	54	161	44	3	1	2	(1	1)	55	17	13	15	14	1	22	0	5	2		9	1	.90	4		.273	.328	.342
2011	Tex	AL	83	256	77	11	3	5	(3	2)	109	37	27	32	10	0	30	0	5	3		10	5	.67	7		.301	.323	.426
2012	Bal	AL	64	158	32	6	0	2	(0	2)	44	15	12	10	6	1	24	1	4	0		3	2	.60	2		.203	.236	.278
05	Was	NL	7	9	2	1	0	0	(0	0)	3	2	1	1	3	0	1	0	0	0		0	1	.00	1		.222	.417	.333
05	Phi	NL	91	107	23	3	3	0	(0	0)	32	17	10	7	4	0	13	0	7	0		2	1	.67	2		.215	.243	.299
	Postseason		15	40	8	2	0	0	(0	0)	10	2	0	0	0	0	1	0	0	0		0	0	-	1		.200	.200	.250
	11 ML YEARS		974	2651	714	118	32	26	(16	10)	974	341	229	288	156	11	295	2	74	16		100	37	.73	50		.269	.309	.367

Eric Chavez

Bats: L **Throws:** R **Pos:** 3B-64; PH-36; DH-18; 1B-10 | shah-VEZZ | **Ht:** 6'1" **Wt:** 215 **Born:** 12/7/1977 **Age:** 35

									BATTING													BASERUNNING					AVERAGES		
Year	Team	Lg	G	AB	H	2B	3B	HR	(Hm	Rd)	TB	R	RBI	RC	TBB	IBB	SO	HBP	SH	SF		SB	CS	SB%	GDP		Avg	OBP	Slg
1998	Oak	AL	16	45	14	4	1	0	(0	0)	20	6	6	7	3	1	5	0	0	0		1	1	.50	1		.311	.354	.444
1999	Oak	AL	115	356	88	21	2	13	(8	5)	152	47	50	50	46	4	56	0	0	0		1	1	.50	7		.247	.333	.427
2000	Oak	AL	153	501	139	23	4	26	(15	11)	248	89	86	86	62	6	94	1	0	5		2	2	.50	9		.277	.355	.495
2001	Oak	AL	151	552	159	43	0	32	(14	18)	298	91	114	99	41	9	99	4	0	7		8	2	.80	7		.288	.338	.540
2002	Oak	AL	153	585	161	31	3	34	(17	17)	300	87	109	103	63	17	119	1	0	2		8	3	.73	8		.275	.348	.513
2003	Oak	AL	156	588	166	39	5	29	(12	17)	302	94	101	97	62	10	89	1	0	3		8	3	.73	14		.282	.350	.514
2004	Oak	AL	125	475	131	20	0	29	(15	14)	238	87	77	84	95	10	99	3	0	4		6	3	.67	21		.276	.397	.501
2005	Oak	AL	160	625	168	40	1	27	(12	15)	291	92	101	95	58	4	129	3	0	9		6	0	1.00	9		.269	.329	.466
2006	Oak	AL	137	485	117	24	2	22	(8	14)	211	74	72	70	84	6	100	1	0	6		3	0	1.00	19		.241	.351	.435
2007	Oak	AL	90	341	82	21	2	15	(10	5)	152	43	46	38	34	2	76	0	0	4		2	1	.67	9		.240	.306	.446
2008	Oak	AL	23	89	22	7	0	2	(1	1)	35	10	14	14	6	0	18	0	0	0		0	0	-	2		.247	.295	.393
2009	Oak	AL	8	30	3	1	0	0	(0	0)	4	0	1	0	1	0	7	0	0	0		0	0	-	0		.100	.129	.133
2010	Oak	AL	33	111	26	8	0	1	(0	1)	37	10	10	7	8	0	31	0	0	4		0	0	-	3		.234	.276	.333

							BATTING												BASERUNNING				AVERAGES		
Year	Team	Lg	G	AB	H	2B	3B	HR	(Hm | Rd)	TB	R	RBI	RC	TBB	IBB	SO	HBP	SH	SF	SB	CS	SB%	GDP	Avg	OBP	Slg
2011	NYY	AL	58	160	42	7	1	2	(0 | 2)	57	16	26	26	14	3	34	0	0	1	0	0	-	4	.263	.320	.356
2012	NYY	AL	113	278	78	12	0	16	(7 | 9)	138	36	37	39	30	3	59	1	0	4	0	0	-	10	.281	.348	.496
	Postseason		28	109	24	7	0	3	(3 | 0)	40	11	12	12	7	2	23	0	0	0	1	0	1.00	2	.220	.267	.367
	15 ML YEARS		1491	5221	1396	301	21	248	(122 | 126)	2483	782	850	815	609	73	1015	14	0	49	47	17	.73	123	.267	.343	.476

Jesse Chavez

Pitches: R **Bats:** R **Pos:** RP-11; SP-2   CHAH-vezz   **Ht:** 6'2" **Wt:** 160 **Born:** 8/21/1983 **Age:** 29

			HOW MUCH HE PITCHED							WHAT HE GAVE UP											THE RESULTS						
Year	Team	Lg	G	GS	CG	GF	IP	BFP	H	R	ER	HR	SH	SF	HB	TBB	IBB	SO	WP	Bk	W	L	Pct	Sh	Sv-Op	Hld	ERC	ERA
2012	LsVgs*	AAA	19	17	1	1	95.0	389	90	45	42	10	1	1	1	20	0	86	5	1	8	5	.615	0	1- -		3.14	3.98
2012	Scrmto*	AAA	2	1	0	1	10.0	40	8	2	2	0	0	0	0	2	0	9	0	0	0	0	-	0	1- -		1.70	1.80
2008	Pit	NL	15	0	0	6	15.0	74	20	11	11	2	3	1	0	9	2	16	2	0	0	1	.000	0	0-2	0	6.76	6.60
2009	Pit	NL	73	0	0	24	67.1	286	69	33	30	11	1	1	1	22	3	47	5	0	1	4	.200	0	0-4	15	4.39	4.01
2010	2 Tms		51	0	0	26	62.2	280	69	44	41	11	5	3	1	23	7	45	2	0	5	5	.500	0	0-1	6	4.85	5.89
2011	KC	AL	4	0	0	3	7.2	39	12	9	9	3	0	0	0	5	0	3	0	0	0	0	-	0	0-0	0	11.48	10.57
2012	2 Tms	AL	13	2	0	3	24.2	123	34	29	27	7	0	1	3	11	1	30	1	0	1	1	.500	0	0-0	0	8.32	9.85
10	Atl	NL	28	0	0	16	36.2	162	40	24	24	6	3	2	1	12	3	29	0	0	3	2	.600	0	0-0	4	4.65	5.89
10	KC		23	0	0	10	26.0	118	29	20	17	5	2	1	0	11	4	16	2	0	2	3	.400	0	0-1	6	5.13	5.88
12	Tor	AL	9	2	0	2	21.1	102	25	22	20	6	0	1	2	10	1	27	0	0	1	1	.500	0	0-0	0	6.90	8.44
12	Oak	AL	4	0	0	1	3.1	21	9	7	7	1	0	0	1	1	0	3	1	0	0	0	-	0	0-0	0	18.70	18.90
	5 ML YEARS		156	2	0	62	177.1	802	204	126	118	34	9	6	5	70	13	146	10	0	7	11	.389	0	0-7	21	5.54	5.99

Bruce Chen

Pitches: L **Bats:** L **Pos:** SP-34   **Ht:** 6'2" **Wt:** 201 **Born:** 6/19/1977 **Age:** 36

			HOW MUCH HE PITCHED							WHAT HE GAVE UP											THE RESULTS						
Year	Team	Lg	G	GS	CG	GF	IP	BFP	H	R	ER	HR	SH	SF	HB	TBB	IBB	SO	WP	Bk	W	L	Pct	Sh	Sv-Op	Hld	ERC	ERA
1998	Atl	NL	4	4	0	0	20.1	91	23	9	9	3	1	0	1	9	1	17	0	0	2	0	1.000	0	0-0	0	5.55	3.98
1999	Atl	NL	16	7	0	3	51.0	214	38	32	31	11	1	1	2	27	3	45	0	0	2	2	.500	0	0-0	0	4.07	5.47
2000	2 Tms	NL	37	15	0	4	134.0	559	116	54	49	18	8	3	2	46	4	112	4	1	7	4	.636	0	0-0	3	3.35	3.29
2001	2 Tms	NL	27	27	0	0	146.0	634	146	90	79	29	4	7	1	59	4	126	5	0	7	7	.500	0	0-0	0	4.75	4.87
2002	3 Tms	NL	55	6	0	9	77.2	360	85	53	48	16	2	3	2	43	5	80	4	0	2	5	.286	0	0-0	4	5.99	5.56
2003	2 Tms		16	2	0	4	24.1	110	26	16	15	6	3	3	2	10	1	20	0	0	0	1	.000	0	0-0	1	5.81	5.55
2004	Bal	AL	8	7	1	0	47.2	196	39	19	16	7	2	1	0	16	0	32	0	0	2	1	.667	0	0-0	0	3.13	3.02
2005	Bal	AL	34	32	1	0	197.1	832	187	94	84	33	3	3	9	63	0	133	2	1	13	10	.565	0	0-1	0	4.12	3.83
2006	Bal	AL	40	12	0	16	98.2	453	137	81	76	28	3	5	0	35	3	70	1	0	0	7	.000	0	0-1	1	7.73	6.93
2007	Tex	AL	5	0	0	3	10.0	46	11	11	8	3	0	0	0	6	1	7	0	0	0	0	-	0	0-0	0	6.90	7.20
2009	KC	AL	17	9	0	4	62.1	279	74	42	40	12	2	2	4	25	3	45	4	0	1	6	.143	0	0-0	0	6.18	5.78
2010	KC	AL	33	23	1	4	140.1	608	136	68	65	17	6	7	3	57	4	98	3	0	12	7	.632	1	1-1	0	4.09	4.17
2011	KC	AL	25	25	0	0	155.0	654	152	71	65	18	3	5	7	50	2	97	2	0	12	8	.600	0	0-0	0	3.98	3.77
2012	KC	AL	34	34	0	0	191.2	827	215	114	108	33	3	5	8	47	3	140	5	0	11	14	.440	0	0-0	0	4.80	5.07
00	Atl	NL	22	0	0	0	39.2	176	35	15	11	4	3	2	1	19	2	32	0	1	4	0	1.000	0	0-0	0	3.62	2.50
00	Phi	NL	15	15	0	0	94.1	383	81	39	38	14	5	1	1	27	2	80	4	0	3	4	.429	0	0-0	0	3.22	3.63
01	Phi	NL	16	16	0	0	86.1	381	90	53	48	19	2	4	1	31	4	79	2	0	4	5	.444	0	0-0	0	4.87	5.00
01	NYM	NL	11	11	0	0	59.2	253	56	37	31	10	2	3	0	28	0	47	3	0	3	2	.600	0	0-0	0	4.58	4.68
02	NYM	NL	1	0	0	0	0.2	3	1	0	0	0	0	0	0	0	0	0	0	0	0	0	-	0	0-0	0	4.47	0.00
02	Mon	NL	15	5	0	4	37.1	179	47	29	29	9	0	1	1	23	3	43	3	0	2	3	.400	0	0-0	0	7.69	6.99
02	Cin	NL	39	1	0	5	39.2	178	37	24	19	7	2	3	1	20	2	37	1	0	0	2	.000	0	0-0	1	4.55	4.31
03	Hou	NL	11	0	0	2	12.0	60	14	8	8	2	3	2	2	8	1	8	0	0	0	0	-	0	0-0	1	7.11	6.00
03	Bos	AL	5	2	0	2	12.1	50	12	8	7	4	0	1	0	2	0	12	0	0	0	1	.000	0	0-0	0	4.40	5.11
	14 ML YEARS		351	203	4	47	1356.1	5863	1385	754	693	234	41	45	41	493	34	1022	30	2	71	72	.497	1	1-2	6	4.65	4.60

Wei-Yin Chen

Pitches: L **Bats:** L **Pos:** SP-32   way-ying   **Ht:** 6'0" **Wt:** 195 **Born:** 7/21/1985 **Age:** 27

			HOW MUCH HE PITCHED							WHAT HE GAVE UP											THE RESULTS						
Year	Team	Lg	G	GS	CG	GF	IP	BFP	H	R	ER	HR	SH	SF	HB	TBB	IBB	SO	WP	Bk	W	L	Pct	Sh	Sv-Op	Hld	ERC	ERA
2008	Chnchi	Jap	39	14	1	-	114.2	478	101	40	37	7	-	-	5	33	0	107	5	0	7	6	.538	1	0- -		2.89	2.90
2009	Chnchi	Jap	24	23	5	-	164.0	645	113	32	28	10	-	-	3	40	0	146	2	0	8	4	.667	4	0- -		1.76	1.54
2010	Chnchi	Jap	29	27	3	-	188.0	779	166	63	60	21	-	-	8	49	2	153	5	0	13	10	.565	2	0- -		3.11	2.87
2011	Chnchi	Jap	25	24	4	-	164.2	663	138	57	49	9	-	-	5	31	2	94	2	0	8	10	.444	1	0- -		2.24	2.68
2012	Bal	AL	32	32	0	0	192.2	818	186	97	86	29	5	8	5	57	0	154	2	1	12	11	.522	0	0-0	0	3.88	4.02

Robinson Chirinos

Bats: R **Throws:** R **Pos:** C   chee-REE-nos   **Ht:** 6'1" **Wt:** 205 **Born:** 6/5/1984 **Age:** 29

							BATTING												BASERUNNING				AVERAGES		
Year	Team	Lg	G	AB	H	2B	3B	HR	(Hm	Rd)	TB	R	RBI	RC	TBB	IBB	SO	HBP	SH	SF	SB	CS	SB%	GDP	Avg	OBP	Slg
2001	Cubs	R	47	154	36	12	0	2	(-	-)	54	15	15	16	10	0	42	4	6	3	4	3	.57	0	.234	.292	.351
2002	Boise	A-	62	231	57	15	2	8	(-	-)	100	35	38	32	16	0	66	6	1	1	5	2	.71	2	.247	.311	.433
2003	Lansng	A	108	362	84	27	1	7	(-	-)	134	51	39	43	28	0	82	7	4	2	10	2	.83	11	.232	.298	.370
2004	Lansng	A	84	319	77	18	6	7	(-	-)	128	56	39	42	25	1	70	8	3	0	7	2	.78	4	.241	.303	.401
2005	Dytona	A+	73	227	62	6	0	7	(-	-)	89	29	27	29	16	0	41	3	1	2	3	4	.43	5	.273	.327	.392
2006	Peoria	A	126	433	105	30	2	9	(-	-)	166	74	47	67	69	0	79	14	7	6	19	10	.66	7	.242	.360	.383
2007	Dytona	A+	79	239	62	14	2	3	(-	-)	89	35	20	38	37	0	48	12	5	2	8	5	.62	5	.259	.385	.372
2007	Tenn	AA	42	127	28	4	2	2	(-	-)	42	11	16	13	13	2	31	1	5	0	1	1	.50	1	.220	.298	.331
2008	Tenn	AA	38	103	25	7	3	0	(-	-)	38	12	8	12	10	0	18	0	2	2	0	0	-	2	.243	.304	.369
2008	Cubs	R	4	13	6	1	1	0	(-	-)	9	5	2	6	6	0	1	1	0	0	0	0	1.00	0	.462	.632	.692
2008	Dytona	A+	37	120	34	4	2	5	(-	-)	57	22	18	27	26	0	21	6	3	1	3	1	.75	2	.283	.431	.475
2009	Dytona	A+	69	227	68	13	5	11	(-	-)	124	40	47	49	35	0	40	5	0	3	2	2	.50	4	.300	.400	.546

Year	Team	Lg	G	AB	H	2B	3B	HR	(Hm	Rd)	TB	R	RBI	RC	TBB	IBB	SO	HBP	SH	SF	SB	CS	SB%	GDP	Avg	OBP	Slg
2009	Tenn	AA	12	35	9	3	0	0	(-	-)	12	4	5	4	7	0	4	0	0	1	0	1	1.00	1	.257	.372	.343
2010	Tenn	AA	77	264	84	24	0	15	(-	-)	153	53	64	62	42	4	35	5	0	7	1	5	.17	6	.318	.412	.580
2010	Iowa	AAA	15	55	20	4	0	3	(-	-)	33	10	10	13	2	0	8	5	0	0	0	0	-	3	.364	.435	.600
2011	Drham	AAA	78	282	73	13	1	6	(-	-)	106	24	24	38	29	0	69	7	1	0	1	1	.50	9	.259	.343	.376
2011	TB	AL	20	55	12	2	0	1	(1	0)	17	4	7	5	5	0	13	0	0	0	0	0	-	0	.218	.283	.309

Lonnie Chisenhall

Bats: L **Throws:** R **Pos:** 3B-30; DH-9; PH-6   CHIZZ-en-hall   **Ht:** 6'2" **Wt:** 190 **Born:** 10/4/1988 **Age:** 24

Year	Team	Lg	G	AB	H	2B	3B	HR	(Hm	Rd)	TB	R	RBI	RC	TBB	IBB	SO	HBP	SH	SF	SB	CS	SB%	GDP	Avg	OBP	Slg
2008	MhVlly	A-	68	276	80	20	3	5	(-	-)	121	38	45	45	24	2	32	4	1	0	7	2	.78	6	.290	.355	.438
2009	Knstn	A+	99	388	107	26	2	18	(-	-)	191	59	79	67	37	1	80	5	1	1	2	1	.67	15	.276	.346	.492
2009	Akron	AA	24	93	17	5	1	4	(-	-)	36	13	13	9	7	1	16	0	0	1	1	0	1.00	2	.183	.238	.387
2010	Akron	AA	117	460	128	22	3	17	(-	-)	207	81	84	77	46	1	77	10	0	8	3	0	1.00	12	.278	.351	.450
2011	Clmbs	AAA	66	255	68	16	3	7	(-	-)	111	45	45	41	28	2	47	7	0	2	0	1	.00	9	.267	.353	.435
2012	Clmbs	AAA	30	118	37	12	0	4	(-	-)	61	16	17	20	4	1	22	2	0	2	0	0	-	1	.314	.341	.517
2011	Cle	AL	66	212	54	13	0	7	(2	5)	88	27	22	24	8	1	49	1	1	1	1	0	1.00	3	.255	.284	.415
2012	Cle	AL	43	142	38	6	1	5	(4	1)	61	16	16	18	8	0	27	1	0	0	2	1	.67	2	.268	.311	.430
	2 ML YEARS		109	354	92	19	1	12	(6	6)	149	43	38	42	16	1	76	2	1	1	3	1	.75	5	.260	.295	.421

Randy Choate

Pitches: L **Bats:** L **Pos:** RP-80   CHOTE   **Ht:** 6'1" **Wt:** 203 **Born:** 9/5/1975 **Age:** 37

			HOW MUCH HE PITCHED						WHAT HE GAVE UP										THE RESULTS							
Year	Team	Lg	G	GS	CG	GF	IP	BFP	H	R	ER	HR	SH	SF	HB	TBB	IBB	SO	WP	Bk	W	L	Pct	Sh	Sv-Op	Hld	ERC	ERA
2000	NYY	AL	22	0	0	6	17.0	75	14	10	9	3	0	1	1	8	0	12	1	0	0	1	.000	0	0-0	2	3.99	4.76
2001	NYY	AL	37	0	0	13	48.1	207	34	21	18	0	2	1	9	27	2	35	3	0	3	1	.750	0	0-0	3	3.03	3.35
2002	NYY	AL	18	0	0	11	22.1	101	18	18	15	1	0	0	3	15	0	17	3	0	0	0	-	0	0-0	0	4.13	6.04
2003	NYY	AL	5	0	0	2	3.2	16	7	3	3	0	0	0	0	1	0	0	0	0	0	0	-	0	0-0	0	9.72	7.36
2004	Ari	NL	74	0	0	17	50.2	232	52	26	26	1	0	4	5	28	11	49	1	1	2	4	.333	0	0-2	11	4.18	4.62
2005	Ari	NL	8	0	0	1	7.0	35	8	7	7	0	0	0	1	5	1	4	1	0	0	0	-	0	0-0	2	5.48	9.00
2006	Ari	NL	30	0	0	3	16.0	75	21	9	7	0	0	0	3	3	0	12	0	0	0	1	.000	0	0-0	5	4.87	3.94
2007	Ari	NL	2	0	0	0	0.0	3	3	0	0	0	0	0	0	0	0	0	0	0	0	0	-	0	0-0	0		
2009	TB	AL	61	0	0	13	36.1	142	28	15	14	4	0	0	0	11	3	28	0	0	1	0	1.000	0	5-5	9	2.54	3.47
2010	TB	AL	85	0	0	8	44.2	187	41	23	21	3	2	2	3	17	5	40	4	0	4	3	.571	0	0-2	18	3.48	4.23
2011	Fla	NL	54	0	0	6	24.2	103	13	7	5	3	1	0	2	13	5	31	0	0	1	1	.500	0	0-0	16	2.16	1.82
2012	2 Tms	NL	80	0	0	4	38.2	168	29	18	13	1	2	2	5	18	3	38	2	0	0	0	-	0	1-1	20	2.76	3.03
12	Mia	NL	44	0	0	4	25.1	104	16	11	7	0	1	1	3	9	0	27	2	0	0	0	-	0	1-1	15	1.79	2.49
12	LAD	NL	36	0	0	0	13.1	64	13	7	6	1	1	1	2	9	3	11	0	0	0	0	-	0	0-0	5	4.87	4.05
	Postseason		7	0	0	0	6.1	30	7	5	2	0	0	0	0	2	1	4	0	0	0	0	-	0	0-0	0	3.01	2.84
	12 ML YEARS		476	0	0	83	309.1	1344	268	157	138	16	7	10	32	146	30	266	15	1	11	11	.500	0	6-10	84	3.51	4.02

Shin-Soo Choo

Bats: L **Throws:** L **Pos:** RF-154; PH-2   SHIN-sue CHEW   **Ht:** 5'11" **Wt:** 205 **Born:** 7/13/1982 **Age:** 30

Year	Team	Lg	G	AB	H	2B	3B	HR	(Hm	Rd)	TB	R	RBI	RC	TBB	IBB	SO	HBP	SH	SF	SB	CS	SB%	GDP	Avg	OBP	Slg
2005	Sea	AL	10	18	1	0	0	0	(0	0)	1	1	1	0	3	0	4	0	0	0	0	0	-	0	.056	.190	.056
2006	2 Tms	AL	49	157	44	12	3	3	(2	1)	71	23	22	24	18	2	50	2	1	1	5	3	.63	3	.280	.360	.452
2007	Cle	AL	6	17	5	0	0	0	(0	0)	5	5	5	3	2	1	5	0	0	1	1	0	1.00	0	.294	.350	.294
2008	Cle	AL	94	317	98	28	3	14	(10	4)	174	68	66	72	44	4	78	5	0	4	4	3	.57	5	.309	.397	.549
2009	Cle	AL	156	583	175	38	6	20	(11	9)	285	87	86	111	78	5	151	17	0	7	21	2	.91	9	.300	.394	.489
2010	Cle	AL	144	550	165	31	2	22	(8	14)	266	81	90	106	83	11	118	11	0	2	22	7	.76	11	.300	.401	.484
2011	Cle	AL	85	313	81	11	3	8	(7	1)	122	37	36	38	36	3	78	6	0	3	12	5	.71	7	.259	.344	.390
2012	Cle	AL	155	598	169	43	2	16	(8	8)	264	88	67	96	73	0	150	14	0	1	21	7	.75	11	.283	.373	.441
06	Sea	AL	4	11	1	1	0	0	(0	0)	2	0	0	0	0	0	4	1	0	0	0	0	-	0	.091	.167	.182
06	Cle	AL	45	146	43	11	3	3	(2	1)	69	23	22	24	18	2	46	1	1	1	5	3	.63	2	.295	.373	.473
	8 ML YEARS		699	2553	738	163	19	83	(46	37)	1188	390	373	450	337	26	634	55	1	19	85	28	.75	46	.289	.381	.465

Justin Christian

Bats: R **Throws:** R **Pos:** PH-15; LF-10; RF-8; DH-3; PR-2; CF-1   **Ht:** 6'1" **Wt:** 195 **Born:** 4/3/1980 **Age:** 33

Year	Team	Lg	G	AB	H	2B	3B	HR	(Hm	Rd)	TB	R	RBI	RC	TBB	IBB	SO	HBP	SH	SF	SB	CS	SB%	GDP	Avg	OBP	Slg
2012	Fresno*	AAA	72	303	104	23	3	7	(-	-)	154	58	35	63	28	1	32	6	1	0	12	5	.71	5	.343	.409	.508
2008	NYY	AL	24	40	10	3	0	0	(0	0)	13	6	6	7	3	0	4	0	0	0	7	1	.88	1	.250	.302	.325
2011	SF	NL	18	47	12	5	0	0	(0	0)	17	6	4	5	2	0	8	0	2	0	3	2	.60	0	.255	.286	.362
2012	SF	NL	34	56	7	1	0	0	(0	0)	8	6	2	0	5	0	3	0	0	0	2	1	.67	0	.125	.197	.143
	3 ML YEARS		76	143	29	9	0	0	(0	0)	38	18	12	12	10	0	15	0	2	0	12	4	.75	1	.203	.255	.266

Vinnie Chulk

Pitches: R **Bats:** R **Pos:** RP-7   **Ht:** 6'2" **Wt:** 200 **Born:** 12/19/1978 **Age:** 34

			HOW MUCH HE PITCHED						WHAT HE GAVE UP										THE RESULTS							
Year	Team	Lg	G	GS	CG	GF	IP	BFP	H	R	ER	HR	SH	SF	HB	TBB	IBB	SO	WP	Bk	W	L	Pct	Sh	Sv-Op	Hld	ERC	ERA
2012	Nashv*	AAA	16	0	0	7	25.2	102	17	7	5	2	1	1	0	9	1	25	0	0	3	0	1.000	0	1- --	1	1.97	1.75
2012	Brewrs*	R	2	1	0	0	2.0	6	0	0	0	0	0	0	0	0	0	1	0	0	0	0	-	0	0- --	0	0.00	0.00
2003	Tor	AL	3	0	0	2	5.1	25	6	3	3	0	0	0	0	3	0	2	0	0	0	0	-	0	0-1	4	4.53	5.06
2004	Tor	AL	47	0	0	10	56.0	248	59	30	29	6	1	1	4	27	1	44	2	0	1	3	.250	0	2-5	13	4.83	4.66

Year	Team	Lg	G	GS	CG	GF	IP	BFP	H	R	ER	HR	SH	SF	HB	TBB	IBB	SO	WP	Bk	W	L	Pct	Sh	Sv-Op Hld	ERC	ERA
			HOW MUCH HE PITCHED						**WHAT HE GAVE UP**												**THE RESULTS**						
2005	Tor	AL	62	0	0	10	72.0	301	68	33	31	9	3	4	1	26	3	39	5	0	0	1	.000	0	0-1 13	3.83	3.88
2006	2 Tms		48	0	0	13	46.1	205	46	29	27	6	0	2	3	20	2	43	4	0	1	3	.250	0	0-2 6	4.53	5.24
2007	SF	NL	57	0	0	15	53.0	222	53	22	21	3	1	4	2	14	2	41	2	0	5	4	.556	0	0-2 9	3.37	3.57
2008	SF	NL	27	0	0	9	31.2	139	33	18	17	6	1	1	2	8	2	16	1	0	0	3	.000	0	0-2 2	4.36	4.83
2009	Cle	AL	8	0	0	3	12.0	55	10	6	5	1	2	0	0	10	0	4	0	0	0	1	.000	0	0-1 0	4.68	3.75
2012	Mil	NL	7	0	0	4	9.0	48	17	10	10	0	0	0	0	4	1	10	0	0	1	0	1.000	0	0-0 0	8.48	10.00
06	Tor	AL	20	0	0	8	24.0	107	29	16	14	4	0	1	2	5	0	18	1	0	1	0	1.000	0	0-1 1	5.25	5.25
06	SF	NL	28	0	0	5	22.1	98	17	13	13	2	0	1	1	15	2	25	3	0	0	3	.000	0	0-1 5	3.74	5.24
8 ML YEARS			259	0	0	66	285.1	1243	292	151	143	31	8	12	9	112	11	199	14	0	8	15	.348	0	2-14 43	4.30	4.51

Tony Cingrani

Pitches: L **Bats:** L **Pos:** RP-3   sin-GRAHN-ee   **Ht:** 6'4" **Wt:** 200 **Born:** 7/5/1989 **Age:** 23

Year	Team	Lg	G	GS	CG	GF	IP	BFP	H	R	ER	HR	SH	SF	HB	TBB	IBB	SO	WP	Bk	W	L	Pct	Sh	Sv-Op Hld	ERC	ERA
			HOW MUCH HE PITCHED						**WHAT HE GAVE UP**												**THE RESULTS**						
2011	Billings	R+	13	13	0	0	51.1	191	35	11	10	1	0	0	1	6	0	80	1	0	3	2	.600	0	0- -	1.31	1.75
2012	Bkrsfld	A+	10	10	0	0	56.2	220	39	13	7	2	1	0	0	13	0	71	1	0	5	1	.833	0	0- -	1.57	1.11
2012	Penscla	AA	16	15	1	0	89.1	350	59	24	21	7	3	0	1	39	0	101	1	0	5	3	.625	0	0- -	2.44	2.12
2012	Cin	NL	3	0	0	1	5.0	22	4	1	1	1	0	0	0	2	0	9	0	0	0	0	-	0	0-0 0	3.38	1.80

Pedro Ciriaco

see-ree-AH-koe

Bats: R **Throws:** R **Pos:** 3B-35; 2B-16; SS-12; DH-10; CF-3; PH-3; LF-2; RF-2; PR-2   **Ht:** 6'0" **Wt:** 170 **Born:** 9/27/1985 **Age:** 27

Year	Team	Lg	G	AB	H	2B	3B	HR	(Hm	Rd)	TB	R	RBI	RC	TBB	IBB	SO	HBP	SH	SF	SB	CS	SB%	GDP	Avg	OBP	Slg
			BATTING																		**BASERUNNING**				**AVERAGES**		
2012	Pwtckt*	AAA	64	276	83	13	2	4	(-	-)	112	41	21	35	6	0	49	2	3	2	14	8	.64	3	.301	.318	.406
2010	Pit	NL	8	6	3	1	1	0	(0	0)	6	3	1	3	0	0	3	0	0	0	0	0	-	0	.500	.500	1.000
2011	Pit	NL	23	33	10	2	1	0	(0	0)	14	4	6	5	1	0	6	0	0	0	2	1	.67	1	.303	.324	.424
2012	Bos	AL	76	259	76	15	2	2	(2	0)	101	33	19	32	8	2	47	0	5	0	16	3	.84	2	.293	.315	.390
3 ML YEARS			107	298	89	18	4	2	(2	0)	121	40	26	40	9	2	56	0	5	0	18	4	.82	3	.299	.319	.406

Steve Cishek

Pitches: R **Bats:** R **Pos:** RP-68   SEE-sheck   **Ht:** 6'6" **Wt:** 215 **Born:** 6/18/1986 **Age:** 27

Year	Team	Lg	G	GS	CG	GF	IP	BFP	H	R	ER	HR	SH	SF	HB	TBB	IBB	SO	WP	Bk	W	L	Pct	Sh	Sv-Op Hld	ERC	ERA
			HOW MUCH HE PITCHED						**WHAT HE GAVE UP**												**THE RESULTS**						
2010	Fla	NL	3	0	0	2	4.1	15	1	0	0	0	0	0	0	1	0	3	0	0	0	0	-	0	0-0 0	0.35	0.00
2011	Fla	NL	45	0	0	21	54.2	229	45	18	16	1	3	0	3	19	7	55	5	0	2	1	.667	0	3-3 2	2.38	2.63
2012	Mia	NL	68	0	0	36	63.2	275	54	26	19	3	3	2	6	29	6	68	1	1	5	2	.714	0	15-19 13	3.28	2.69
3 ML YEARS			116	0	0	59	122.2	519	100	44	35	4	6	2	9	49	13	126	6	1	7	3	.700	0	18-22 15	2.72	2.57

Jeff Clement

Bats: L **Throws:** R **Pos:** PH-22; 1B-1   **Ht:** 6'1" **Wt:** 220 **Born:** 8/21/1983 **Age:** 29

Year	Team	Lg	G	AB	H	2B	3B	HR	(Hm	Rd)	TB	R	RBI	RC	TBB	IBB	SO	HBP	SH	SF	SB	CS	SB%	GDP	Avg	OBP	Slg
			BATTING																		**BASERUNNING**				**AVERAGES**		
2012	Indy*	AAA	112	416	115	35	2	16	(-	-)	202	58	57	70	41	4	101	0	0	2	1	0	1.00	9	.276	.340	.486
2007	Sea	AL	9	16	6	1	0	2	(2	0)	13	4	3	6	3	0	3	0	0	0	0	0	-	0	.375	.474	.813
2008	Sea	AL	66	203	46	10	1	5	(2	3)	73	17	23	22	15	0	63	5	0	1	0	1	.00	4	.227	.295	.360
2010	Pit	NL	54	144	29	3	0	7	(1	6)	53	11	12	6	6	3	37	1	1	1	0	0	-	2	.201	.237	.368
2012	Pit	NL	23	22	3	1	0	0	(0	0)	4	1	1	0	2	0	7	0	0	0	0	0	-	2	.136	.208	.182
4 ML YEARS			152	385	84	15	1	14	(5	9)	143	33	39	34	26	3	110	6	1	2	0	1	.00	8	.218	.277	.371

Maikel Cleto

Pitches: R **Bats:** R **Pos:** RP-9   MY-kel CLAY-toe   **Ht:** 6'3" **Wt:** 235 **Born:** 5/1/1989 **Age:** 24

Year	Team	Lg	G	GS	CG	GF	IP	BFP	H	R	ER	HR	SH	SF	HB	TBB	IBB	SO	WP	Bk	W	L	Pct	Sh	Sv-Op Hld	ERC	ERA
			HOW MUCH HE PITCHED						**WHAT HE GAVE UP**												**THE RESULTS**						
2007	Mets	R	11	4	0	2	34.0	157	34	21	19	2	2	2	2	25	0	28	8	0	1	2	.333	0	1- -	5.40	5.03
2008	Savann	A	25	22	1	0	135.2	577	140	78	64	8	5	9	7	34	0	81	25	1	5	11	.313	1	0- -	3.58	4.25
2008	StLuci	A+	1	1	0	0	5.0	21	5	5	5	1	1	0	0	2	0	1	0	0	0	1	.000	0	0- -	4.93	9.00
2009	Ms	R	1	0	0	0	0.2	8	3	6	1	0	0	0	1	1	0	1	0	0	0	1	.000	0	0- -	37.16	13.50
2009	Clinton	A	8	8	0	0	25.1	123	35	20	15	4	0	1	2	11	0	24	2	0	0	3	.000	0	0- -	7.22	5.33
2010	Hi Dsrt	A+	23	21	0	0	102.1	466	125	81	70	10	4	1	7	44	0	83	19	1	4	9	.308	0	0- -	5.84	6.16
2011	PlmBh	A+	5	5	0	0	29.0	119	20	10	8	2	1	1	2	10	0	33	2	0	1	1	.500	0	0- -	2.27	2.48
2011	Sprgfld	AA	7	6	0	0	34.1	154	40	19	15	2	3	1	5	12	1	36	1	0	2	2	.500	0	0- -	5.12	3.93
2011	Memp	AAA	13	13	0	0	71.1	311	57	37	34	6	2	2	3	43	0	66	4	1	5	3	.625	0	0- -	3.79	4.29
2012	Memp	AAA	45	0	0	9	53.2	232	51	35	32	4	3	2	4	22	2	66	6	0	3	2	.600	0	2- -	3.90	5.37
2011	StL	NL	3	0	0	2	4.1	25	7	6	6	2	0	0	0	4	0	6	0	0	0	0	-	0	0-0 0	13.10	12.46
2012	StL	NL	9	0	0	2	9.0	41	13	7	7	4	0	0	1	2	0	15	0	0	0	0	-	0	0-0 1	9.58	7.00
2 ML YEARS			12	0	0	4	13.1	66	20	13	13	6	0	0	1	6	0	21	0	0	0	0	-	0	0-0 1	10.74	8.78

Steve Clevenger

Bats: L **Throws:** R **Pos:** C-51; PH-15; 1B-9; 3B-1 CLEV-en-jer **Ht:** 6'0" **Wt:** 195 **Born:** 4/5/1986 **Age:** 27

									BATTING												BASERUNNING				AVERAGES		
Year	Team	Lg	G	AB	H	2B	3B	HR	(Hm Rd)	TB	R	RBI	RC	TBB	IBB	SO	HBP	SH	SF	SB	CS	SB%	GDP	Avg	OBP	Slg
2006	Boise	A-	63	220	63	8	1	2	(- -)	79	35	21	31	26	0	28	1	1	1	5	2	.71	7	.286	.363	.359
2007	Boise	A-	22	83	31	9	0	0	(- -)	40	10	18	15	4	0	6	0	0	1	0	0	-	6	.373	.398	.482
2007	Dytona	A+	43	164	53	8	1	2	(- -)	69	21	24	26	13	0	5	1	1	4	0	0	-	7	.323	.368	.421
2008	Dytona	A+	84	284	89	20	0	2	(- -)	115	36	39	49	39	3	41	1	1	4	7	3	.70	9	.313	.393	.405
2008	Tenn	AA	29	89	22	5	1	1	(- -)	32	5	15	11	10	1	10	0	2	3	0	0	-	4	.247	.314	.360
2009	Tenn	AA	26	77	28	4	3	1	(- -)	41	12	10	17	10	1	8	1	1	0	0	0	-	3	.364	.443	.532
2009	Iowa	AAA	68	230	61	12	1	0	(- -)	75	21	26	24	15	0	31	1	2	3	4	3	.57	9	.265	.309	.326
2010	Tenn	AA	88	271	86	24	0	5	(- -)	125	37	47	44	20	4	28	2	0	1	0	6	.00	11	.317	.367	.461
2011	Tenn	AA	95	312	92	27	3	5	(- -)	140	42	39	53	35	2	39	0	1	3	1	0	1.00	8	.295	.363	.449
2011	Iowa	AAA	25	86	35	3	1	3	(- -)	49	9	15	21	9	0	7	0	0	2	1	0	1.00	1	.407	.454	.570
2012	Iowa	AAA	5	13	6	2	0	1	(- -)	11	5	3	4	2	0	0	0	0	0	0	0	-	1	.462	.533	.846
2011	ChC	NL	2	4	1	1	0	0	(0 0)	2	1	0	0	0	0	0	1	0	0	0	0	-	0	.250	.400	.500
2012	ChC	NL	69	199	40	12	0	1	(1 0)	55	16	16	12	16	0	39	0	0	0	0	1	.00	10	.201	.260	.276
2 ML YEARS			71	203	41	13	0	1	(1 0)	57	17	16	12	16	0	39	1	0	0	0	1	.00	10	.202	.264	.281

Tyler Clippard

Pitches: R **Bats:** R **Pos:** RP-74 **Ht:** 6'3" **Wt:** 200 **Born:** 2/14/1985 **Age:** 28

			HOW MUCH HE PITCHED						WHAT HE GAVE UP												THE RESULTS					
Year	Team	Lg	G	GS	CG	GF	IP	BFP	H	R	ER	HR	SH	SF	HB	TBB	IBB	SO	WP	Bk	W	L	Pct	Sh	Sv-Op	Hld	ERC	ERA
2007	NYY	AL	6	6	0	0	27.0	124	29	19	19	6	0	0	0	17	1	18	2	1	3	1	.750	0	0-0	0	6.37	6.33
2008	Was	NL	2	2	0	0	10.1	48	12	5	5	2	0	0	0	7	1	8	1	0	1	1	.500	0	0-0	0	6.90	4.35
2009	Was	NL	41	0	0	8	60.1	246	36	20	18	9	3	1	1	32	1	67	1	1	4	2	.667	0	0-1	3	2.79	2.69
2010	Was	NL	78	0	0	18	91.0	378	69	33	31	8	3	7	2	41	4	112	1	1	11	8	.579	0	1-11	23	2.91	3.07
2011	Was	NL	72	0	0	8	88.1	329	48	18	18	11	4	3	0	26	2	104	1	0	3	0	1.000	0	0-7	38	1.61	1.83
2012	Was	NL	74	0	0	42	72.2	307	55	32	30	7	3	4	2	29	2	84	5	0	2	6	.250	0	32-37	13	2.73	3.72
6 ML YEARS			273	8	0	76	349.2	1432	249	127	121	43	13	15	5	152	11	393	11	3	24	18	.571	0	33-56	77	2.83	3.11

Tyler Cloyd

Pitches: R **Bats:** R **Pos:** SP-6 CLOID **Ht:** 6'3" **Wt:** 210 **Born:** 5/16/1987 **Age:** 26

			HOW MUCH HE PITCHED						WHAT HE GAVE UP												THE RESULTS					
Year	Team	Lg	G	GS	CG	GF	IP	BFP	H	R	ER	HR	SH	SF	HB	TBB	IBB	SO	WP	Bk	W	L	Pct	Sh	Sv-Op	Hld	ERC	ERA
2008	Phillies	R	2	1	0	0	11.0	38	5	0	0	0	0	0	0	1	0	11	0	0	2	0	1.000	0	0- -	-	0.76	0.00
2008	Wmspt	A-	12	12	0	0	65.0	283	76	35	33	8	2	2	3	21	0	58	2	1	5	4	.556	0	0- -	-	5.21	4.57
2009	Lakwd	A	14	14	1	0	88.2	362	90	32	30	3	4	1	2	19	2	77	1	0	7	3	.700	0	0- -	-	3.13	3.05
2009	Clrwtr	A+	13	12	0	0	76.2	337	83	43	35	4	0	5	6	23	1	39	1	0	5	6	.455	0	0- -	-	4.05	4.11
2010	Clrwtr	A+	35	4	0	8	69.1	310	85	45	41	8	3	5	2	16	0	67	5	0	4	3	.571	0	0- -	-	4.81	5.32
2010	Rdng	AA	2	1	0	1	9.0	34	5	4	4	3	0	0	0	1	0	6	0	0	1	1	.500	0	0- -	-	1.82	4.00
2011	Clrwtr	A+	13	5	0	3	39.1	154	31	12	12	3	0	0	1	7	0	39	2	0	3	1	.750	0	0- -	-	2.13	2.75
2011	Rdng	AA	18	17	0	0	106.2	430	101	35	33	7	2	2	7	15	0	99	2	0	6	3	.667	0	0- -	-	2.87	2.78
2012	LV	AAA	22	22	1	0	142.0	552	105	39	37	14	6	3	4	38	3	93	1	0	12	1	.923	1	0- -	-	2.37	2.35
2012	Rdng	AA	4	4	0	0	25.0	97	22	5	5	1	0	1	1	3	0	20	0	0	3	0	1.000	0	0- -	-	2.26	1.80
2012	Phi	NL	6	6	0	0	33.0	138	33	18	18	8	2	0	2	7	0	30	0	0	2	2	.500	0	0-0	-	4.54	4.91

Alex Cobb

Pitches: R **Bats:** R **Pos:** SP-23 **Ht:** 6'2" **Wt:** 195 **Born:** 10/7/1987 **Age:** 25

			HOW MUCH HE PITCHED						WHAT HE GAVE UP												THE RESULTS					
Year	Team	Lg	G	GS	CG	GF	IP	BFP	H	R	ER	HR	SH	SF	HB	TBB	IBB	SO	WP	Bk	W	L	Pct	Sh	Sv-Op	Hld	ERC	ERA
2006	Princtn	R	6	1	0	1	8.2	38	9	7	5	3	0	1	0	3	0	8	1	0	0	0	-	0	0- -	-	5.69	5.19
2007	HudVal	A-	16	16	0	0	81.1	345	78	36	32	4	5	4	4	31	0	62	2	1	5	6	.455	0	0- -	-	3.66	3.54
2008	Clmbs	A	25	25	0	0	139.2	560	113	59	51	16	2	3	16	35	0	97	3	2	9	7	.563	0	0- -	-	3.10	3.29
2009	Charltt	A+	24	23	0	0	124.2	515	116	49	42	6	3	6	9	31	1	107	8	2	8	5	.615	0	0- -	-	3.07	3.03
2010	Mont	AA	23	22	0	0	119.2	503	119	46	35	7	2	5	4	35	1	128	5	0	7	5	.583	0	0- -	-	3.49	2.63
2011	Drham	AAA	12	12	0	0	67.1	264	61	19	14	4	2	1	2	16	0	70	1	0	5	1	.833	0	0- -	-	2.96	1.87
2012	Drham	AAA	8	8	0	0	41.1	186	44	21	19	1	0	1	2	18	1	44	2	0	1	4	.200	0	0- -	-	4.10	4.14
2011	TB	AL	9	9	0	0	52.2	224	49	21	20	3	0	1	1	21	1	37	2	0	3	2	.600	0	0-0	-	3.44	3.42
2012	TB	AL	23	23	2	0	136.1	569	130	67	61	11	3	6	9	40	2	106	8	1	11	9	.550	1	0-0	-	3.56	4.03
2 ML YEARS			32	32	2	0	189.0	793	179	88	81	14	3	7	10	61	3	143	10	1	14	11	.560	1	0-0	-	3.53	3.86

Robert Coello

Pitches: R **Bats:** R **Pos:** RP-6 koe-AY-oh **Ht:** 6'5" **Wt:** 250 **Born:** 11/23/1984 **Age:** 28

			HOW MUCH HE PITCHED						WHAT HE GAVE UP												THE RESULTS					
Year	Team	Lg	G	GS	CG	GF	IP	BFP	H	R	ER	HR	SH	SF	HB	TBB	IBB	SO	WP	Bk	W	L	Pct	Sh	Sv-Op	Hld	ERC	ERA
2007	Angels	R	20	0	0	6	26.1	111	23	9	4	0	1	0	4	7	0	26	4	2	1	1	.500	0	0- -	-	2.77	1.37
2008	Calgary	IND	12	0	0	5	15.2	74	19	12	10	2	2	0	1	7	1	18	0	1	1	1	.500	0	0- -	-	5.73	5.74
2008	Edmtn	IND	20	0	0	9	25.1	114	18	6	5	2	0	1	2	17	1	29	3	0	2	0	1.000	0	0- -	-	3.48	1.78
2009	Pwtckt	AAA	1	0	0	1	1.1	5	1	0	0	0	0	0	0	0	0	1	0	0	0	0	-	0	0- -	-	1.13	0.00
2009	Salem	A+	33	0	0	13	66.0	274	38	22	15	4	3	2	7	34	0	82	2	1	5	3	.625	0	2- -	-	2.40	2.05
2010	Portlnd	AA	14	0	0	4	43.1	180	37	16	16	4	2	0	1	14	0	51	2	0	4	1	.800	0	1- -	-	3.01	3.32
2010	Pwtckt	AAA	18	9	0	1	64.0	269	44	33	30	10	1	3	6	30	0	79	1	2	3	5	.375	0	1- -	-	3.36	4.22
2011	Iowa	AAA	30	11	0	7	95.0	407	85	48	47	11	7	2	3	41	0	94	1	2	6	6	.500	0	1- -	-	3.84	4.45
2011	Tenn	AA	4	4	0	0	21.0	88	19	7	7	2	1	0	7	7	0	16	1	0	1	2	.333	0	0- -	-	2.93	3.00

Year	Team	Lg	G	GS	CG	GF	IP	BFP	H	R	ER	HR	SH	SF	HB	TBB	IBB	SO	WP	Bk	W	L	Pct	Sh	Sv-Op	Hld	ERC	ERA
			HOW MUCH HE PITCHED						WHAT HE GAVE UP												THE RESULTS							
2012	LsVgs	AAA	19	3	0	3	42.0	169	31	16	14	4	0	2	0	18	0	43	1	0	4	1	.800	0	0- -	-	2.82	3.00
2010	Bos	AL	6	0	0	2	5.2	26	4	3	3	0	0	0	0	5	0	5	1	0	0	0	-	0	0-0	-	3.44	4.76
2012	Tor	AL	6	0	0	1	6.1	33	10	9	9	2	0	0	1	4	0	11	0	0	0	1	.000	0	0-0	1	11.62	12.79
2 ML YEARS			12	0	0	3	12.0	59	14	12	12	2	0	0	1	9	0	16	1	0	0	1	.000	0	0-0	1	7.41	9.00

Todd Coffey

Pitches: R Bats: R Pos: RP-23   Ht: 6'4" Wt: 240 Born: 9/9/1980 Age: 32

Year	Team	Lg	G	GS	CG	GF	IP	BFP	H	R	ER	HR	SH	SF	HB	TBB	IBB	SO	WP	Bk	W	L	Pct	Sh	Sv-Op	Hld	ERC	ERA
			HOW MUCH HE PITCHED						WHAT HE GAVE UP												THE RESULTS							
2012	RCuca*	A+	2	2	0	0	2.0	8	3	1	1	0	0	0	0	0	0	1	0	0	0	1	.000	0	0- -	-	5.09	4.50
2005	Cin	NL	57	0	0	14	58.0	265	84	33	29	5	3	2	5	11	2	26	1	0	4	1	.800	0	1-2	3	6.11	4.50
2006	Cin	NL	81	0	0	28	78.0	340	85	34	31	7	0	1	2	27	5	60	4	0	6	7	.462	0	8-12	15	4.29	3.58
2007	Cin	NL	58	0	0	8	51.0	242	70	36	33	12	1	0	5	19	4	43	4	0	2	1	.667	0	0-3	7	7.58	5.82
2008	2 Tms		26	0	0	9	26.2	116	31	13	13	4	2	1	1	8	0	15	0	0	1	0	1.000	0	0-0	1	5.19	4.39
2009	Mil	NL	78	0	0	17	83.2	336	76	28	27	8	2	2	3	21	3	65	1	0	4	4	.500	0	2-6	27	3.16	2.90
2010	Mil	NL	69	0	0	12	62.1	274	65	40	33	8	2	5	3	23	5	56	6	0	2	4	.333	0	0-2	13	4.42	4.76
2011	Was	NL	69	0	0	15	59.2	254	55	25	24	4	5	3	1	20	3	46	1	0	5	1	.833	0	0-2	10	3.11	3.62
2012	LAD	NL	23	0	0	5	19.1	83	17	11	10	1	0	1	2	9	1	18	1	0	1	0	1.000	0	0-0	2	3.69	4.66
08	Cin	NL	17	0	0	6	19.1	87	25	13	13	4	1	1	1	6	0	8	0	0	0	0	-	0	0-0	0	6.57	6.05
08	Mil	NL	9	0	0	3	7.1	29	6	0	0	0	1	0	0	2	0	7	0	0	1	0	1.000	0	0-0	1	2.09	0.00
8 ML YEARS			461	0	0	108	438.2	1910	483	220	200	49	15	15	22	138	23	329	18	0	25	18	.581	0	11-27	78	4.52	4.10

Chris Coghlan

Bats: L Throws: R Pos: LF-21; CF-13; PH-8; RF-2; PR-2   COGG-lan   Ht: 6'0" Wt: 190 Born: 6/18/1985 Age: 28

Year	Team	Lg	G	AB	H	2B	3B	HR	(Hm	Rd)	TB	R	RBI	RC	TBB	IBB	SO	HBP	SH	SF	SB	CS	SB%	GDP	Avg	OBP	Slg
								BATTING													BASERUNNING				AVERAGES		
2012	NewOr*	AAA	84	317	90	21	3	7	(-	-)	138	42	31	56	46	1	44	2	0	3	10	2	.83	4	.284	.375	.435
2009	Fla	NL	128	504	162	31	6	9	(5	4)	232	84	47	91	53	2	77	4	3	1	8	5	.62	3	.321	.390	.460
2010	Fla	NL	91	358	96	20	3	5	(5	0)	137	60	28	43	33	1	84	4	3	2	10	3	.77	3	.268	.335	.383
2011	Fla	NL	65	269	62	20	1	5	(4	1)	99	33	22	23	22	3	49	4	1	2	7	6	.54	3	.230	.296	.368
2012	Mia	NL	39	93	13	1	0	1	(1	0)	17	10	10	2	9	1	12	0	1	2	0	2	.00	4	.140	.212	.183
4 ML YEARS			323	1224	333	72	10	20	(15	5)	485	187	107	159	117	7	222	12	8	7	25	16	.61	13	.272	.340	.396

Phil Coke

Pitches: L Bats: L Pos: RP-66   Ht: 6'1" Wt: 210 Born: 7/19/1982 Age: 30

Year	Team	Lg	G	GS	CG	GF	IP	BFP	H	R	ER	HR	SH	SF	HB	TBB	IBB	SO	WP	Bk	W	L	Pct	Sh	Sv-Op	Hld	ERC	ERA
			HOW MUCH HE PITCHED						WHAT HE GAVE UP												THE RESULTS							
2008	NYY	AL	12	0	0	0	14.2	52	8	1	1	0	0	0	0	2	0	14	1	0	1	0	1.000	0	0-0	5	0.89	0.61
2009	NYY	AL	72	0	0	13	60.0	238	44	34	30	10	1	5	1	20	4	49	7	0	4	3	.571	0	2-7	21	2.84	4.50
2010	Det	AL	74	1	0	18	64.2	279	67	29	27	2	2	3	4	26	4	53	3	0	7	5	.583	0	2-4	17	4.00	3.76
2011	Det	AL	48	14	0	6	108.2	474	118	64	54	5	4	3	4	40	5	69	4	0	3	9	.250	0	1-2	8	4.13	4.47
2012	Det	AL	66	0	0	11	54.0	245	71	28	24	5	5	2	1	18	4	51	3	0	2	3	.400	0	1-3	20	5.56	4.00
Postseason			11	0	0	3	7.0	32	10	6	6	2	0	0	0	3	0	6	0	0	0	0	-	0	1-1	0	8.70	7.71
5 ML YEARS			272	15	0	48	302.0	1288	308	156	136	22	12	13	10	106	17	236	18	0	17	20	.459	0	6-16	71	3.89	4.05

Casey Coleman

Pitches: R Bats: L Pos: RP-16; SP-1   Ht: 6'0" Wt: 185 Born: 7/3/1987 Age: 25

Year	Team	Lg	G	GS	CG	GF	IP	BFP	H	R	ER	HR	SH	SF	HB	TBB	IBB	SO	WP	Bk	W	L	Pct	Sh	Sv-Op	Hld	ERC	ERA
			HOW MUCH HE PITCHED						WHAT HE GAVE UP												THE RESULTS							
2012	Iowa*	AAA	13	11	0	1	58.0	247	53	29	28	4	4	1	2	25	2	52	0	0	2	4	.333	0	0- -	-	3.61	4.34
2010	ChC	NL	12	8	0	0	57.0	248	56	27	26	3	2	4	2	25	2	27	3	0	4	2	.667	0	0-0	0	3.87	4.11
2011	ChC	NL	19	17	0	1	84.1	398	102	62	60	10	6	2	4	46	3	75	3	1	3	9	.250	0	0-0	0	6.15	6.40
2012	ChC	NL	17	1	0	5	24.1	119	37	20	20	5	1	0	0	12	0	16	1	0	0	2	.000	0	0-1	0	8.62	7.40
3 ML YEARS			48	26	0	6	165.2	765	195	109	106	18	9	6	6	83	5	118	7	1	7	13	.350	0	0-1	0	5.67	5.76

Louis Coleman

Pitches: R Bats: R Pos: RP-42   Ht: 6'4" Wt: 205 Born: 4/4/1986 Age: 27

Year	Team	Lg	G	GS	CG	GF	IP	BFP	H	R	ER	HR	SH	SF	HB	TBB	IBB	SO	WP	Bk	W	L	Pct	Sh	Sv-Op	Hld	ERC	ERA
			HOW MUCH HE PITCHED						WHAT HE GAVE UP												THE RESULTS							
2009	Burlgtn	A	4	0	0	2	7.1	24	2	2	2	0	0	0	1	1	0	6	0	0	1	0	1.000	0	1- -	-	0.51	2.45
2009	Wilmg	A+	10	0	0	4	14.1	54	8	3	2	0	0	0	1	3	0	16	1	0	3	1	.750	0	1- -	-	1.02	1.26
2010	NWArk	AA	21	1	0	13	51.2	198	31	13	12	5	1	0	2	14	1	55	4	0	2	1	.667	0	6- -	-	1.72	2.09
2010	Omha	AAA	21	0	0	5	40.1	164	31	11	10	2	2	2	5	11	1	48	1	0	5	2	.714	0	1- -	-	2.50	2.23
2011	Omha	AAA	6	0	0	5	7.0	30	4	4	3	0	0	1	0	4	0	16	1	0	1	0	1.000	0	2- -	-	1.74	3.86
2012	Omha	AAA	11	1	0	7	19.2	80	13	7	7	1	1	0	0	8	1	26	1	0	0	2	.000	0	3- -	-	1.95	3.20
2011	KC	AL	48	0	0	11	59.2	244	44	20	19	9	1	1	3	26	6	64	4	0	1	4	.200	0	1-2	11	3.23	2.87
2012	KC	AL	42	0	0	18	51.0	217	41	23	21	10	3	0	1	26	3	65	1	0	0	0	-	0	0-2	2	4.07	3.71
2 ML YEARS			90	0	0	29	110.2	461	85	43	40	19	4	1	4	52	9	129	5	0	1	4	.200	0	1-2	13	3.61	3.25

Tim Collins

Pitches: L **Bats:** L **Pos:** RP-72 **Ht:** 5'7" **Wt:** 165 **Born:** 8/21/1989 **Age:** 23

Year	Team	Lg	G	GS	CG	GF	IP	BFP	H	R	ER	HR	SH	SF	HB	TBB	IBB	SO	WP	Bk	W	L	Pct	Sh	Sv-Op	Hld	ERC	ERA
2007	B Jays	R	7	0	0	1	6.0	24	6	3	3	0	0	0	0	2	0	7	0	0	0	0	-	0	0--	-	3.35	4.50
2008	Lnsng	A	39	0	0	28	68.1	267	36	13	12	3	1	1	2	32	1	98	5	2	4	2	.667	0	14--	-	1.72	1.58
2009	Dnedin	A+	40	0	0	15	64.2	270	47	21	17	2	2	1	3	28	1	99	2	0	7	4	.636	0	3--	-	2.42	2.37
2009	NHam	AA	9	0	0	2	12.2	56	12	9	8	1	2	0	0	7	0	17	2	0	2	3	.400	0	0--	-	4.21	5.68
2010	NHam	AA	35	0	0	18	43.0	171	27	12	12	4	0	0	0	16	0	73	2	1	1	0	1.000	0	9--	-	2.01	2.51
2010	Missi	AA	6	0	0	4	8.0	29	4	1	1	1	0	0	0	3	0	14	0	0	0	0	-	0	2--	-	1.77	1.13
2010	Omha	AAA	15	0	0	8	20.1	79	9	3	3	0	0	0	0	8	0	21	0	0	2	1	.667	0	4--	-	1.04	1.33
2011	KC	AL	68	0	0	18	67.0	295	52	28	27	5	3	1	2	48	2	60	3	0	4	4	.500	0	0-1	11	3.95	3.63
2012	KC	AL	72	0	0	9	69.2	295	55	29	26	8	3	1	2	34	8	93	3	0	5	4	.556	0	0-4	11	3.29	3.36
	2 ML YEARS		140	0	0	27	136.2	590	107	57	53	13	6	2	4	82	10	153	6	0	9	8	.529	0	0-5	22	3.62	3.49

Josh Collmenter

Pitches: R **Bats:** R **Pos:** RP-17; SP-11 COLE-men-ter **Ht:** 6'2" **Wt:** 235 **Born:** 2/7/1986 **Age:** 27

Year	Team	Lg	G	GS	CG	GF	IP	BFP	H	R	ER	HR	SH	SF	HB	TBB	IBB	SO	WP	Bk	W	L	Pct	Sh	Sv-Op	Hld	ERC	ERA
2007	Yakima	A-	14	12	0	1	66.1	275	60	22	20	4	2	4	2	21	0	57	2	1	6	3	.667	0	0--	-	3.11	2.71
2008	Sbend	A	27	27	0	0	145.1	606	126	62	55	8	2	4	6	47	0	123	3	0	12	8	.600	0	0--	-	2.91	3.41
2009	Visalia	A+	27	27	1	0	145.1	612	127	76	67	8	9	6	8	55	0	152	9	0	8	10	.444	0	0--	-	3.22	4.15
2010	Visalia	A+	3	3	0	0	15.0	59	11	4	4	2	1	0	1	3	0	21	0	0	2	0	1.000	0	0--	-	2.40	2.40
2010	Reno	AAA	10	10	0	0	57.2	258	64	40	37	8	2	1	1	26	1	39	3	0	4	3	.571	0	0--	-	5.25	5.77
2010	Mobile	AA	12	12	2	0	79.1	315	61	18	16	3	3	2	1	22	0	73	4	0	8	3	.727	1	0--	-	2.11	1.82
2011	Reno	AAA	1	1	0	0	6.0	21	2	2	1	1	0	0	0	2	0	7	1	0	1	0	1.000	0	0--	-	1.24	1.50
2012	DBcks	R	3	3	0	0	8.0	28	5	0	0	0	0	0	0	0	0	11	0	0	0	0	-	0	0--	-	0.84	0.00
2011	Ari	NL	31	24	0	3	154.1	621	137	61	58	17	9	2	5	28	2	100	1	1	10	10	.500	0	0-0	0	2.82	3.38
2012	Ari	NL	28	11	0	7	90.1	375	92	39	37	13	5	0	0	22	2	80	1	0	5	3	.625	0	0-0	0	3.85	3.69
	Postseason		1	1	0	0	7.0	26	2	1	1	1	0	0	1	2	0	6	0	0	1	0	1.000	0	0-0	0	1.18	1.29
	2 ML YEARS		59	35	0	10	244.2	996	229	100	95	30	14	2	5	50	4	180	2	1	15	13	.536	0	0-0	0	3.19	3.49

Bartolo Colon

Pitches: R **Bats:** R **Pos:** SP-24 co-LONE **Ht:** 5'11" **Wt:** 265 **Born:** 5/24/1973 **Age:** 40

Year	Team	Lg	G	GS	CG	GF	IP	BFP	H	R	ER	HR	SH	SF	HB	TBB	IBB	SO	WP	Bk	W	L	Pct	Sh	Sv-Op	Hld	ERC	ERA
1997	Cle	AL	19	17	1	0	94.0	427	107	66	59	12	4	1	3	45	1	66	5	0	4	7	.364	0	0-0	0	5.53	5.65
1998	Cle	AL	31	31	6	0	204.0	883	205	91	84	15	10	2	3	79	5	158	4	0	14	9	.609	2	0-0	0	3.87	3.71
1999	Cle	AL	32	32	1	0	205.0	858	185	97	90	24	5	4	7	76	5	161	4	0	18	5	.783	1	0-0	0	3.68	3.95
2000	Cle	AL	30	30	2	0	188.0	807	163	86	81	21	2	3	4	98	4	212	4	0	15	8	.652	1	0-0	0	3.97	3.88
2001	Cle	AL	34	34	1	0	222.1	947	220	106	101	26	8	4	2	90	2	201	4	1	14	12	.538	0	0-0	0	4.24	4.09
2002	2 Tms		33	33	8	0	233.1	966	219	85	76	20	19	6	2	70	5	149	4	0	20	8	.714	3	0-0	0	3.29	2.93
2003	CWS	AL	34	34	9	0	242.0	984	223	107	104	30	5	8	5	67	3	173	8	3	15	13	.536	0	0-0	0	3.47	3.87
2004	LAA	AL	34	34	0	0	208.1	897	215	122	116	38	5	8	3	71	1	158	1	0	18	12	.600	0	0-0	0	4.64	5.01
2005	LAA	AL	33	33	2	0	222.2	906	215	93	86	26	9	4	3	43	0	157	2	1	21	8	.724	0	0-0	0	3.28	3.48
2006	LAA	AL	10	10	1	0	56.1	251	71	39	32	11	4	1	3	11	0	31	1	0	1	5	.167	0	0-0	0	5.61	5.11
2007	LAA	AL	19	18	0	0	99.1	453	132	74	70	15	4	3	5	29	1	76	1	0	6	8	.429	0	0-0	0	6.17	6.34
2008	Bos	AL	7	7	0	0	39.0	173	44	23	17	5	3	2	2	10	0	27	0	0	4	2	.667	0	0-0	0	4.53	3.92
2009	CWS	AL	12	12	0	0	62.1	276	69	42	29	13	4	3	2	21	3	38	1	0	3	6	.333	0	0-0	0	5.22	4.19
2011	NYY	AL	29	26	1	0	164.1	694	172	85	73	21	2	6	3	40	3	135	0	0	8	10	.444	1	0-0	0	3.95	4.00
2012	Oak	AL	24	24	0	0	152.1	636	161	62	58	17	3	4	1	23	3	91	0	0	10	9	.526	0	0-0	0	3.45	3.43
02	Cle	AL	16	16	4	0	116.1	467	104	37	33	11	6	3	2	31	1	75	3	0	10	4	.714	2	0-0	0	3.09	2.55
02	Mon	NL	17	17	4	0	117.0	499	115	48	43	9	13	3	0	39	4	74	1	0	10	4	.714	1	0-0	0	3.48	3.31
	Postseason		9	9	1	0	52.1	215	49	21	21	5	1	1	1	22	1	41	0	0	2	3	.400	0	0-0	0	4.01	3.61
	15 ML YEARS		381	375	32	0	2393.1	10158	2401	1178	1076	294	87	59	48	773	36	1833	39	5	171	122	.584	9	0-0	1	4.02	4.05

Roman Colon

Pitches: R **Bats:** R **Pos:** RP-3 row-MAHN ko-LONE **Ht:** 6'5" **Wt:** 245 **Born:** 8/13/1979 **Age:** 33

Year	Team	Lg	G	GS	CG	GF	IP	BFP	H	R	ER	HR	SH	SF	HB	TBB	IBB	SO	WP	Bk	W	L	Pct	Sh	Sv-Op	Hld	ERC	ERA
2012	Omha*	AAA	40	1	0	18	67.0	290	66	31	23	7	2	2	1	28	4	59	8	0	4	2	.667	0	7--	-	4.05	3.09
2004	Atl	NL	18	0	0	7	19.0	82	18	9	7	0	1	2	0	8	1	15	0	0	2	1	.667	0	0-1	1	3.05	3.32
2005	2 Tms		35	7	0	7	69.1	306	82	45	43	17	2	3	0	21	1	47	4	1	2	6	.250	0	0-1	3	5.75	5.58
2006	Det	AL	20	1	0	4	38.2	170	46	21	21	6	1	2	1	14	2	25	6	0	2	0	1.000	0	1-1	3	5.56	4.89
2009	KC	AL	43	0	0	13	50.1	220	50	27	27	7	1	0	2	22	1	29	1	2	2	3	.400	0	0-3	6	4.60	4.83
2010	KC	AL	5	0	0	2	2.0	14	5	4	4	0	0	0	1	2	0	1	0	0	0	0	-	0	0-0	0	18.12	18.00
2012	KC	AL	3	0	0	0	8.0	37	12	6	6	0	0	0	0	3	0	3	1	0	0	0	-	0	0-0	1	6.32	6.75
05	Atl	NL	23	4	0	6	44.1	191	47	28	26	10	2	2	0	14	1	30	2	1	1	5	.167	0	0-0	2	4.90	5.28
05	Det	AL	12	3	0	1	25.0	115	35	17	17	7	0	1	0	7	0	17	2	0	1	1	.500	0	0-1	1	7.34	6.12
	6 ML YEARS		124	8	0	33	187.1	829	213	112	108	30	5	7	4	70	5	120	12	3	8	10	.444	0	1-6	13	5.26	5.19

Tyler Colvin

Bats: L Throws: L Pos: RF-59; CF-38; 1B-31; PH-23; LF-10   Ht: 6'3" Wt: 210 Born: 9/5/1985 Age: 27

Year	Team	Lg	G	AB	H	2B	3B	HR	(Hm	Rd)	TB	R	RBI	RC	TBB	IBB	SO	HBP	SH	SF	SB	CS	SB%	GDP	Avg	OBP	Slg
2009	ChC	NL	6	17	3	0	0	0	(0	0)	3	1	2	1	2	0	5	0	0	1	0	0	-	0	.176	.176	.176
2010	ChC	NL	135	358	91	18	5	20	(9	11)	179	60	56	46	30	2	100	3	1	2	6	1	.86	6	.254	.316	.500
2011	ChC	NL	80	206	31	8	3	6	(2	4)	63	17	20	9	14	3	58	0	1	1	0	0	-	2	.150	.204	.306
2012	Col	NL	136	420	122	27	10	18	(11	7)	223	62	72	73	21	0	117	2	2	1	7	3	.70	6	.290	.327	.531
4 ML YEARS			357	1001	247	53	18	44	(22	22)	468	140	150	129	67	5	280	5	4	5	13	4	.76	14	.247	.296	.468

Hank Conger

Bats: B Throws: R Pos: C-7   KONG-gerr   Ht: 6'1" Wt: 220 Born: 1/29/1988 Age: 25

Year	Team	Lg	G	AB	H	2B	3B	HR	(Hm	Rd)	TB	R	RBI	RC	TBB	IBB	SO	HBP	SH	SF	SB	CS	SB%	GDP	Avg	OBP	Slg
2012	Salt Lk*	AAA	67	264	78	17	0	10	(-	-)	125	48	42	44	19	2	49	3	0	2	2	0	1.00	4	.295	.347	.473
2010	LAA	AL	13	29	5	1	1	0	(0	0)	8	2	5	3	5	0	9	0	0	0	0	0	-	1	.172	.294	.276
2011	LAA	AL	59	177	37	8	0	6	(2	4)	63	14	19	18	17	2	37	1	2	0	0	0	-	2	.209	.282	.356
2012	LAA	AL	7	18	3	0	0	0	(0	0)	3	0	1	1	1	0	1	1	1	0	0	0	-	0	.167	.238	.167
3 ML YEARS			79	224	45	9	1	6	(2	4)	74	16	25	22	23	2	46	2	3	1	0	0	-	4	.201	.280	.330

Brooks Conrad

Bats: B Throws: R Pos: PH-23; 3B-16; 2B-13; 1B-7; SS-1; DH-1   Ht: 5'10" Wt: 190 Born: 1/16/1980 Age: 33

Year	Team	Lg	G	AB	H	2B	3B	HR	(Hm	Rd)	TB	R	RBI	RC	TBB	IBB	SO	HBP	SH	SF	SB	CS	SB%	GDP	Avg	OBP	Slg
2012	Nashv*	AAA	21	74	30	5	1	10	(-	-)	67	17	28	26	11	2	15	0	0	0	0	1	.00	0	.405	.482	.905
2012	Drhm*	AAA	25	83	22	5	0	4	(-	-)	39	10	12	15	18	1	34	0	0	1	0	3	.00	1	.265	.392	.470
2008	Oak	AL	6	19	3	1	0	0	(0	0)	4	0	2	1	0	0	9	0	0	0	0	0	-	1	.158	.158	.211
2009	Atl	NL	30	54	11	1	2	2	(0	2)	22	7	8	6	3	1	14	1	0	0	0	0	-	1	.204	.259	.407
2010	Atl	NL	103	156	39	11	1	8	(4	4)	76	31	33	32	16	0	45	1	4	0	5	1	.83	0	.250	.324	.487
2011	Atl	NL	92	103	23	5	0	4	(2	2)	40	11	13	12	15	2	41	1	2	1	2	0	1.00	0	.223	.325	.388
2012	2 Tms		49	98	13	5	0	4	(2	2)	30	6	15	5	6	0	43	0	0	1	0	0	-	2	.133	.181	.306
12	Mil	NL	25	40	3	0	0	2	(2	0)	9	2	6	0	3	0	16	0	0	1	0	0	-	0	.075	.136	.225
12	TB	AL	24	58	10	5	0	2	(0	2)	21	4	9	5	3	0	27	0	0	0	0	0	-	2	.172	.213	.362
Postseason			4	11	1	0	0	0	(0	0)	1	0	0	0	0	0	4	0	1	0	0	0	-	0	.091	.091	.091
5 ML YEARS			280	430	89	23	3	18	(8	10)	172	55	71	56	40	3	152	3	6	2	7	1	.88	4	.207	.278	.400

Jose Constanza

Bats: L Throws: L Pos: LF-21; PH-9; CF-5; PR-3   cohn-STAHN-zah   Ht: 5'9" Wt: 150 Born: 9/1/1983 Age: 29

Year	Team	Lg	G	AB	H	2B	3B	HR	(Hm	Rd)	TB	R	RBI	RC	TBB	IBB	SO	HBP	SH	SF	SB	CS	SB%	GDP	Avg	OBP	Slg
2005	Lk Cty	A	23	72	17	0	0	0	(-	-)	17	9	4	8	15	0	13	0	1	0	2	1	.67	2	.236	.368	.236
2005	MhVlly	A-	64	270	71	5	5	0	(-	-)	86	30	20	34	28	1	39	4	1	1	24	6	.80	6	.263	.340	.319
2006	Lk Cty	A	44	159	44	5	3	1	(-	-)	58	31	9	28	30	0	30	1	1	0	19	4	.83	1	.277	.395	.365
2006	Knstn	A+	76	275	90	15	6	1	(-	-)	120	55	27	55	42	0	50	2	1	1	20	4	.83	5	.327	.419	.436
2007	Knstn	A+	112	445	122	13	4	2	(-	-)	149	71	34	57	39	0	80	2	10	2	39	9	.81	1	.274	.334	.335
2008	Akron	AA	95	338	94	12	6	0	(-	-)	118	44	34	44	28	1	42	2	5	3	24	6	.80	7	.278	.334	.349
2009	Akron	AA	130	486	137	15	7	0	(-	-)	166	98	46	75	75	1	65	1	11	2	49	14	.78	3	.282	.378	.342
2010	Clmbs	AAA	113	404	129	11	8	1	(-	-)	159	69	32	66	35	1	54	0	8	1	34	6	.85	7	.319	.373	.394
2011	Gwnntt	AAA	86	333	104	2	4	1	(-	-)	117	47	25	46	25	3	41	1	3	1	23	8	.74	7	.312	.361	.351
2012	Gwnntt	AAA	88	344	108	10	4	1	(-	-)	129	54	27	49	36	3	43	2	8	2	14	6	.70	5	.314	.380	.375
2011	Atl	NL	42	109	33	1	1	2	(1	1)	42	21	10	12	6	0	14	0	4	0	7	4	.64	1	.303	.339	.385
2012	Atl	NL	37	76	19	2	0	0	(0	0)	21	8	4	9	8	2	21	0	2	0	5	2	.71	0	.250	.321	.276
2 ML YEARS			79	185	52	3	1	2	(1	1)	63	29	14	21	14	2	35	0	6	0	12	6	.67	1	.281	.332	.341

Jose Contreras

Pitches: R Bats: R Pos: RP-17   conn-TRAIR-us   Ht: 6'4" Wt: 255 Born: 12/6/1971 Age: 41

			HOW MUCH HE PITCHED						WHAT HE GAVE UP												THE RESULTS						
Year	Team	Lg	G	GS	CG	GF	IP	BFP	H	R	ER	HR	SH	SF	HB	TBB	IBB	SO	WP	Bk	W	L	Pct	Sh	Sv-Op	Hld	ERC	ERA
2012	Clrwtr*	A+	5	1	0	0	4.1	20	5	4	4	1	0	0	0	1	0	7	2	0	0	1	.000	0	0- -	-	4.79	8.31
2003	NYY	AL	18	9	0	2	71.0	293	52	27	26	4	0	1	5	30	1	72	2	0	7	2	.778	0	0-1	1	2.71	3.30
2004	2 Tms	AL	31	31	0	0	170.1	758	166	114	104	31	3	6	8	84	1	150	17	0	13	9	.591	0	0-0	0	5.05	5.50
2005	CWS	AL	32	32	1	0	204.2	857	177	91	82	23	7	2	9	75	2	154	20	2	15	7	.682	0	0-0	0	3.46	3.61
2006	CWS	AL	30	30	1	0	196.0	833	194	101	93	20	2	8	10	55	4	134	16	0	13	9	.591	1	0-0	0	3.72	4.27
2007	CWS	AL	32	30	2	0	189.0	858	232	134	117	21	8	10	15	62	1	113	3	0	10	17	.370	2	0-0	0	5.49	5.57
2008	CWS	AL	20	20	1	0	121.0	522	130	64	61	12	4	2	3	35	0	70	6	0	7	6	.538	0	0-0	0	4.13	4.54
2009	2 Tms	AL	28	23	0	0	131.2	589	141	86	72	13	10	2	6	53	4	106	8	0	6	13	.316	0	0-1	1	4.55	4.92
2010	Phi	NL	67	0	0	21	56.2	233	53	22	21	5	4	1	6	16	2	57	0	0	6	4	.600	0	4-5	13	3.50	3.34
2011	Phi	NL	17	0	0	8	14.0	60	11	6	6	1	0	1	0	8	0	13	0	0	0	0	-	0	5-5	4	3.15	3.86
2012	Phi	NL	17	0	0	3	13.2	56	13	10	8	1	0	1	1	3	0	15	0	0	1	0	1.000	0	0-0	4	3.28	5.27
04	NYY	AL	18	18	0	0	95.2	425	93	66	60	22	1	4	6	42	1	82	10	0	8	5	.615	0	0-0	0	5.18	5.64
04	CWS	AL	13	13	0	0	74.2	333	73	48	44	9	2	2	2	42	0	68	7	0	5	4	.556	0	0-0	0	4.87	5.30
09	CWS	AL	21	21	0	0	114.2	513	121	83	69	11	7	2	6	45	3	89	8	0	5	13	.278	0	0-0	0	4.41	5.42
09	Col	NL	7	2	0	0	17.0	76	20	3	3	2	3	0	0	8	1	17	0	0	1	0	1.000	0	0-1	1	5.51	1.59
Postseason			18	4	1	4	49.0	199	41	19	19	2	5	1	3	11	0	38	4	0	4	3	.571	0	0-1	4	2.41	3.49
10 ML YEARS			292	175	5	36	1168.0	5059	1169	655	590	130	39	33	62	421	15	884	72	2	78	67	.538	3	9-12	23	4.18	4.55

Aaron Cook

Pitches: R **Bats:** R **Pos:** SP-18   **Ht:** 6'3" **Wt:** 215 **Born:** 2/8/1979 **Age:** 34

			HOW MUCH HE PITCHED						WHAT HE GAVE UP											THE RESULTS					
Year	Team	Lg	G	GS	CG	GF	IP	BFP	H	R	ER	HR	SH	SF	HB	TBB	IBB	SO	WP	Bk	W	L	Pct	Sh	Sv-Op Hld	ERC	ERA
2012 Pwtckt*	AAA		6	6	2	0	37.1	153	33	12	10	1	1	1	0	12	1	16	3	0	3	0	1.000	0	0- -	2.66	2.41
2002 Col	NL		9	5	0	1	35.2	154	41	18	18	4	0	0	2	13	0	14	0	0	2	1	.667	0	0-0	5.31	4.54
2003 Col	NL		43	16	1	4	124.0	579	160	89	83	8	4	6	8	57	7	43	10	0	4	6	.400	0	0-0	1	5.95	6.02
2004 Col	NL		16	16	1	0	96.2	433	112	47	46	7	5	1	7	39	5	40	6	1	6	4	.600	0	0-0	5.05	4.28
2005 Col	NL		13	13	2	0	83.1	357	101	38	34	8	1	3	2	16	2	24	3	0	7	2	.778	0	0-0	4.53	3.67
2006 Col	NL		32	32	0	0	212.2	915	242	107	100	17	8	5	7	55	11	92	2	0	9	15	.375	0	0-0	4.23	4.23
2007 Col	NL		25	25	2	0	166.0	698	178	87	76	15	6	3	6	44	6	61	0	0	8	7	.533	0	0-0	4.05	4.12
2008 Col	NL		32	32	2	0	211.1	886	236	102	93	13	9	4	4	48	2	96	6	0	16	9	.640	1	0-0	3.92	3.96
2009 Col	NL		27	27	1	0	158.0	675	175	76	73	19	3	6	2	47	2	78	2	0	11	6	.647	1	0-0	4.51	4.16
2010 Col	NL		23	23	2	0	127.2	572	147	77	72	11	3	6	4	52	4	62	3	1	6	8	.429	0	0-0	4.95	5.08
2011 Col	NL		18	17	0	0	97.0	441	127	67	65	9	1	8	5	37	5	48	3	0	3	10	.231	0	0-0	6.00	6.03
2012 Bos	AL		18	18	1	0	94.0	411	117	68	59	15	2	2	1	21	1	20	2	0	4	11	.267	1	0-0	5.24	5.65
Postseason			2	2	0	0	11.0	45	13	6	6	1	0	0	0	2	0	6	0	0	1	1	.500	0	0-0	4.37	4.91
11 ML YEARS			256	224	12	5	1406.1	6121	1636	776	719	126	42	44	48	429	45	578	37	2	76	79	.490	3	0-0	2	4.69	4.60

Ryan Cook

Pitches: R **Bats:** R **Pos:** RP-71   **Ht:** 6'2" **Wt:** 215 **Born:** 6/30/1987 **Age:** 26

			HOW MUCH HE PITCHED						WHAT HE GAVE UP											THE RESULTS					
Year	Team	Lg	G	GS	CG	GF	IP	BFP	H	R	ER	HR	SH	SF	HB	TBB	IBB	SO	WP	Bk	W	L	Pct	Sh	Sv-Op Hld	ERC	ERA
2008 Yakima	A-		7	7	0	0	33.0	152	37	25	17	4	0	0	5	11	0	23	1	0	2	2	.500	0	0- -	5.15	4.64
2009 Sbend	A		25	25	0	0	142.2	590	140	71	58	5	2	6	10	44	0	103	7	1	11	11	.500	0	0- -	3.56	3.66
2010 Visalia	A+		20	20	0	0	108.1	475	110	62	51	3	3	4	13	36	0	100	8	1	4	7	.364	0	0- -	3.82	4.24
2010 Reno	AAA		1	1	0	0	5.0	25	7	6	6	1	0	0	2	2	0	5	0	1	0	0	-	0	0- -	9.34	10.80
2010 Mobile	AA		3	3	0	0	18.2	77	13	7	6	1	1	0	1	10	0	12	1	0	1	1	.500	0	0- -	2.91	2.89
2011 Mobile	AA		34	0	0	21	44.0	174	28	12	11	2	1	1	2	14	2	50	3	0	1	4	.200	0	13- -	1.72	2.25
2011 Reno	AAA		14	0	0	9	17.0	67	13	6	4	0	0	0	1	8	1	12	4	0	0	1	.000	0	6- -	2.74	2.12
2011 Ari	NL		12	0	0	5	7.2	41	11	6	6	0	0	0	0	8	0	7	1	1	0	1	.000	0	0-0	1	8.56	7.04
2012 Oak	AL		71	0	0	23	73.1	288	42	18	17	4	3	1	4	27	4	80	4	0	6	2	.750	0	14-21	21	1.68	2.09
2 ML YEARS			83	0	0	28	81.0	329	53	24	23	4	3	1	4	35	4	87	5	1	6	3	.667	0	14-21	22	2.19	2.56

David Cooper

Bats: L **Throws:** L **Pos:** 1B-29; DH-9; PH-8   **Ht:** 6'0" **Wt:** 200 **Born:** 2/12/1987 **Age:** 26

			BATTING																				BASERUNNING				AVERAGES		
Year	Team	Lg	G	AB	H	2B	3B	HR	(Hm	Rd)	TB	R	RBI	RC	TBB	IBB	SO	HBP	SH	SF	SB	CS	SB%	GDP	Avg	OBP	Slg
2008 Auburn	A-		21	85	29	10	1	2	(-	-)	47	10	21	18	10	2	16	0	0	0	0	1	.00	5	.341	.411	.553
2008 Lnsng	A		24	96	34	10	0	2	(-	-)	50	15	17	20	10	0	14	0	0	0	0	0	-	3	.354	.415	.521
2008 Dnedin	A+		24	92	28	9	0	1	(-	-)	40	10	13	15	10	1	16	0	0	0	0	0	-	3	.304	.373	.435
2009 NHam	AA		128	473	122	32	0	10	(-	-)	184	62	66	67	59	3	92	2	0	4	0	0	-	17	.258	.340	.389
2010 NHam	AA		132	498	128	30	1	20	(-	-)	220	59	78	75	52	1	74	1	0	2	0	0	-	9	.257	.327	.442
2011 LsVgs	AAA		120	467	170	51	1	9	(-	-)	250	77	96	109	67	6	43	2	0	9	1	3	.25	14	.364	.439	.535
2012 LsVgs	AAA		68	261	82	27	1	10	(-	-)	141	45	52	56	37	4	34	1	0	5	0	1	.00	13	.314	.395	.540
2011 Tor	AL		27	71	15	7	0	2	(2	0)	28	9	12	10	7	0	14	1	0	2	0	0	-	2	.211	.284	.394
2012 Tor	AL		45	140	42	11	0	4	(1	3)	65	16	11	15	4	0	22	1	0	1	0	1	.00	1	.300	.324	.464
2 ML YEARS			72	211	57	18	0	6	(3	3)	93	25	23	25	11	0	36	2	0	3	0	1	.00	3	.270	.310	.441

Patrick Corbin

Pitches: L **Bats:** L **Pos:** SP-17; RP-5   **Ht:** 6'2" **Wt:** 187 **Born:** 7/19/1989 **Age:** 23

			HOW MUCH HE PITCHED						WHAT HE GAVE UP											THE RESULTS					
Year	Team	Lg	G	GS	CG	GF	IP	BFP	H	R	ER	HR	SH	SF	HB	TBB	IBB	SO	WP	Bk	W	L	Pct	Sh	Sv-Op Hld	ERC	ERA
2009 Orem	R+		13	12	0	0	46.1	214	59	34	26	6	0	0	1	11	0	46	6	1	4	2	.667	0	0- -	4.95	5.05
2010 CRpds	A		9	9	0	0	58.1	230	52	28	25	2	2	3	3	10	0	42	4	1	8	0	1.000	0	0- -	2.50	3.86
2010 RCuca	A+		11	11	0	0	60.1	253	57	29	26	7	1	2	1	18	0	64	6	0	5	3	.625	0	0- -	3.54	3.88
2010 Visalia	A+		8	8	0	0	26.0	99	17	4	4	1	0	0	0	9	0	30	0	0	1	0	1.000	0	0- -	1.85	1.38
2011 Mobile	AA		26	26	1	0	160.1	688	172	78	75	15	7	3	12	40	0	142	16	1	9	8	.529	1	0- -	4.15	4.21
2012 Mobile	AA		4	4	0	0	27.0	106	22	5	5	0	3	0	1	8	0	25	2	0	2	0	1.000	0	0- -	2.33	1.67
2012 Reno	AAA		9	9	0	0	52.1	227	57	24	20	4	1	2	1	15	1	55	1	0	3	2	.600	0	0- -	3.97	3.44
2012 Ari	NL		22	17	0	3	107.0	454	117	56	54	14	2	5	4	25	2	86	1	0	6	8	.429	0	1-1	0	4.31	4.54

Francisco Cordero

Pitches: R **Bats:** R **Pos:** RP-47   **Ht:** 6'3" **Wt:** 245 **Born:** 5/11/1975 **Age:** 38

			HOW MUCH HE PITCHED						WHAT HE GAVE UP											THE RESULTS					
Year	Team	Lg	G	GS	CG	GF	IP	BFP	H	R	ER	HR	SH	SF	HB	TBB	IBB	SO	WP	Bk	W	L	Pct	Sh	Sv-Op Hld	ERC	ERA
1999 Det	AL		20	0	0	4	19.0	91	19	7	7	2	2	4	0	18	2	19	1	0	2	2	.500	0	0-3	6.19	3.32
2000 Tex	AL		56	0	0	13	77.1	365	87	51	46	11	2	6	4	48	3	49	7	0	1	2	.333	0	0-3	4	6.15	5.35
2001 Tex	AL		3	0	0	2	2.1	12	3	1	1	0	0	0	0	2	1	1	1	0	0	1	.000	0	0-0	1	5.73	3.86
2002 Tex	AL		39	0	0	25	45.1	177	33	12	9	2	0	0	2	13	1	41	1	0	2	0	1.000	0	10-12	5	2.11	1.79
2003 Tex	AL		73	0	0	36	82.2	352	70	33	27	4	3	4	2	38	6	90	1	0	5	8	.385	0	15-25	18	3.08	2.94
2004 Tex	AL		67	0	0	63	71.2	304	60	19	17	1	5	1	1	32	2	79	3	2	3	4	.429	0	49-54	0	2.78	2.13
2005 Tex	AL		69	0	0	60	69.0	302	61	28	26	5	4	3	4	30	2	79	0	0	3	1	.750	0	37-45	0	3.47	3.39
2006 2 Tms			77	0	0	47	75.1	322	69	32	31	7	3	5	3	32	2	84	4	0	10	5	.667	0	22-33	16	3.79	3.70
2007 Mil	NL		66	0	0	58	63.1	261	52	23	21	4	2	1	1	18	1	86	2	0	0	4	.000	0	44-51	0	2.45	2.98
2008 Cin	NL		72	0	0	63	70.1	307	61	28	26	6	3	3	3	38	3	78	3	0	5	4	.556	0	34-40	0	3.86	3.33
2009 Cin	NL		68	0	0	59	66.2	276	58	21	16	2	3	4	0	30	2	58	0	0	2	6	.250	0	39-43	0	3.11	2.16
2010 Cin	NL		75	0	0	64	72.2	316	68	32	31	4	4	5	1	36	1	59	2	0	6	5	.545	0	40-48	1	3.96	3.84

Year	Team	Lg	G	GS	CG	GF	IP	BFP	H	R	ER	HR	SH	SF	HB	TBB	IBB	SO	WP	Bk	W	L	Pct	Sh	Sv-Op	Hld	ERC	ERA
2011	Cin	NL	68	0	0	63	69.2	274	49	20	19	6	1	1	3	22	0	42	4	1	5	3	.625	0	37-43	0	2.35	2.45
2012	2 Tms		47	0	0	18	39.1	192	61	35	33	9	4	0	2	18	4	31	5	0	3	8	.273	0	2-8	6	9.00	7.55
06	Tex	AL	49	0	0	21	48.2	210	49	27	26	5	1	5	3	16	1	54	3	0	7	4	.636	0	6-15	15	4.05	4.81
06	Mil		28	0	0	26	26.2	112	20	5	5	2	2	0	0	16	1	30	1	0	3	1	.750	0	16-18	1	3.30	1.69
12	Tor	AL	41	0	0	17	34.1	160	48	24	22	7	4	0	1	14	3	26	4	0	3	5	.375	0	2-5	6	7.43	5.77
12	Hou	NL	6	0	0	1	5.0	32	13	11	11	2	0	0	1	4	1	5	1	0	0	3	.000	0	0-3	0	21.36	19.80
14 ML YEARS			800	0	0	575	824.2	3551	751	342	310	64	33	33	27	375	30	796	37	3	47	53	.470	0	329-405	53	3.70	3.38

Manuel Corpas

Pitches: R Bats: R Pos: RP-48   mann-WELL   Ht: 6'3" Wt: 210 Born: 12/3/1982 Age: 30

Year	Team	Lg	G	GS	CG	GF	IP	BFP	H	R	ER	HR	SH	SF	HB	TBB	IBB	SO	WP	Bk	W	L	Pct	Sh	Sv-Op	Hld	ERC	ERA
2012	Iowa*	AAA	19	0	0	5	33.2	145	30	16	15	4	4	2	4	9	1	19	2	0	0	2	.000	0	0--	-	3.40	4.01
2006	Col	NL	35	0	0	3	32.1	136	36	13	13	3	0	0	2	8	1	27	2	0	1	2	.333	0	0-2	7	4.39	3.62
2007	Col	NL	78	0	0	46	78.0	306	63	20	18	6	2	1	2	20	3	58	0	0	4	2	.667	0	19-22	16	2.51	2.08
2008	Col	NL	76	0	0	20	79.2	346	93	41	40	7	6	1	2	23	4	50	1	0	3	4	.429	0	4-13	19	4.55	4.52
2009	Col	NL	35	0	0	16	33.2	146	44	22	22	3	2	1	1	7	0	24	0	0	1	3	.250	0	1-3	7	5.24	5.88
2010	Col	NL	56	0	0	27	62.1	274	66	33	32	7	2	3	2	22	5	47	1	0	3	5	.375	0	10-14	2	4.25	4.62
2012	ChC	NL	48	0	0	11	46.2	205	50	27	26	7	1	0	5	16	3	28	1	0	0	2	.000	0	0-3	6	4.99	5.01
Postseason			9	0	0	8	10.1	37	6	1	1	0	0	0	1	0	0	7	0	0	1	0	1.000	0	5-6	0	0.90	0.87
6 ML YEARS			328	0	0	123	332.2	1413	352	156	151	33	13	6	14	96	16	234	5	0	12	18	.400	0	34-57	57	4.10	4.09

Carlos Corporan

Bats: B Throws: R Pos: C-24; PH-3   CORE-poor-run   Ht: 6'2" Wt: 220 Born: 1/7/1984 Age: 29

Year	Team	Lg	G	AB	H	2B	3B	HR	(Hm	Rd)	TB	R	RBI	RC	TBB	IBB	SO	HBP	SH	SF	SB	CS	SB%	GDP	Avg	OBP	Slg
2012	OKCity*	AAA	68	206	59	15	0	6	(-	-)	92	35	31	33	15	4	46	6	0	2	2	0	1.00	0	.286	.349	.447
2009	Mil	NL	1	1	1	0	0	0	(0	0)	1	1	0	1	0	0	0	0	0	0	0	0	-	0	1.000	1.000	1.000
2011	Hou	NL	52	154	29	8	1	0	(0	0)	39	9	11	11	10	4	49	4	3	2	0	0	-	5	.188	.253	.253
2012	Hou	NL	27	78	21	2	0	4	(3	1)	35	5	13	7	4	0	19	1	1	1	0	1	.00	2	.269	.310	.449
3 ML YEARS			80	233	51	10	1	4	(3	1)	75	15	24	19	14	4	68	5	4	3	0	1	.00	7	.219	.275	.322

Kevin Correia

Pitches: R Bats: R Pos: SP-28; RP-4   kore-AY-ah   Ht: 6'3" Wt: 200 Born: 8/24/1980 Age: 32

Year	Team	Lg	G	GS	CG	GF	IP	BFP	H	R	ER	HR	SH	SF	HB	TBB	IBB	SO	WP	Bk	W	L	Pct	Sh	Sv-Op	Hld	ERC	ERA
2003	SF	NL	10	7	0	1	39.1	173	41	16	16	6	1	1	4	18	1	28	2	0	3	1	.750	0	0-0	0	5.46	3.66
2004	SF	NL	12	1	0	5	19.0	92	25	20	17	3	3	3	1	10	0	14	0	0	0	1	.000	0	0-0	0	7.12	8.05
2005	SF	NL	16	11	0	1	58.1	264	61	31	30	12	5	1	4	31	2	44	2	0	2	5	.286	0	0-0	0	5.94	4.63
2006	SF	NL	48	0	0	9	69.2	295	64	27	27	5	1	4	3	22	0	57	0	0	2	0	1.000	0	0-1	10	3.25	3.49
2007	SF	NL	59	8	0	9	101.2	437	94	39	39	9	4	3	2	40	7	80	1	1	4	7	.364	0	0-3	12	3.48	3.45
2008	SF	NL	25	19	0	2	110.0	514	141	80	74	15	3	5	4	47	3	66	5	0	3	8	.273	0	0-0	0	6.19	6.05
2009	SD	NL	33	33	1	0	198.0	830	194	92	86	17	9	3	4	64	6	142	5	1	12	11	.522	1	0-0	0	3.64	3.91
2010	SD	NL	28	26	0	0	145.0	641	152	89	87	20	6	5	5	64	6	115	3	0	10	10	.500	0	0-0	0	4.87	5.40
2011	Pit	NL	27	26	1	1	154.0	660	175	90	82	24	7	2	2	39	0	77	3	1	12	11	.522	0	0-0	0	4.74	4.79
2012	Pit	NL	32	28	0	0	171.0	728	176	89	80	20	14	7	3	46	2	89	2	0	12	11	.522	0	0-0	0	3.86	4.21
10 ML YEARS			290	159	2	28	1066.0	4634	1123	573	538	131	53	34	32	381	27	712	23	3	60	65	.480	1	0-4	22	4.45	4.54

Mike Costanzo

Bats: L Throws: R Pos: PH-14; 1B-2; DH-1   Ht: 6'3" Wt: 215 Born: 9/9/1983 Age: 29

Year	Team	Lg	G	AB	H	2B	3B	HR	(Hm	Rd)	TB	R	RBI	RC	TBB	IBB	SO	HBP	SH	SF	SB	CS	SB%	GDP	Avg	OBP	Slg
2005	Batvia	A-	73	281	77	17	3	11	(-	-)	133	47	50	48	35	0	89	3	0	4	0	1	.00	3	.274	.356	.473
2006	Clrwtr	A+	135	504	130	33	1	14	(-	-)	207	72	81	74	74	4	133	11	2	2	3	2	.60	8	.258	.364	.411
2007	Rdng	AA	137	508	137	29	1	27	(-	-)	249	92	86	95	75	8	157	7	0	5	2	0	1.00	6	.270	.368	.490
2008	Norfolk	AAA	129	483	126	28	2	11	(-	-)	191	56	63	66	52	4	159	1	0	2	2	2	.50	7	.261	.333	.395
2009	Norfolk	AAA	22	68	14	4	2	0	(-	-)	22	8	8	8	13	1	21	1	0	1	0	0	-	2	.206	.337	.324
2009	Bowie	AA	60	204	41	12	1	3	(-	-)	64	25	29	19	27	3	58	0	0	2	0	2	.00	3	.201	.292	.314
2010	Carlina	AA	88	307	83	21	2	11	(-	-)	141	47	50	52	33	3	84	6	1	4	7	0	1.00	3	.270	.349	.459
2010	Lsvlle	AAA	6	12	2	1	0	0	(-	-)	3	2	1	1	3	0	5	0	0	0	0	0	-	0	.167	.333	.250
2011	Carlina	AA	73	255	69	18	5	8	(-	-)	121	43	36	43	33	1	68	0	0	3	2	3	.40	4	.271	.351	.475
2011	Lsvlle	AAA	47	153	33	6	0	5	(-	-)	54	15	26	15	14	0	59	1	0	5	1	1	.50	2	.216	.277	.353
2012	Penscla	AA	11	30	10	2	0	3	(-	-)	21	8	13	9	10	0	11	0	0	0	0	1	.00	0	.333	.500	.700
2012	Lsvlle	AAA	96	313	82	18	1	9	(-	-)	129	41	38	47	43	4	79	2	0	0	0	4	.00	7	.262	.355	.412
2012	Cin	NL	17	18	1	0	0	0	(0	0)	1	0	2	0	1	0	10	0	0	2	0	0	-	0	.056	.095	.056

Scott Cousins

Bats: L Throws: L Pos: PH-21; CF-18; RF-12; LF-6; PR-2   Ht: 6'1" Wt: 195 Born: 1/22/1985 Age: 28

Year	Team	Lg	G	AB	H	2B	3B	HR	(Hm	Rd)	TB	R	RBI	RC	TBB	IBB	SO	HBP	SH	SF	SB	CS	SB%	GDP	Avg	OBP	Slg
2012	NewOr*	AAA	61	233	69	13	2	7	(-	-)	107	36	36	41	24	2	58	2	1	2	14	3	.82	4	.296	.364	.459
2010	Fla	NL	27	37	11	2	2	0	(0	0)	17	2	2	4	1	0	13	0	0	0	0	0	-	0	.297	.316	.459
2011	Fla	NL	48	52	7	1	0	1	(1	0)	11	5	4	2	6	0	21	0	0	0	1	1	.50	0	.135	.224	.212
2012	Mia	NL	53	86	14	4	1	1	(0	1)	23	7	3	1	4	2	24	0	2	0	1	1	.50	2	.163	.200	.267
3 ML YEARS			128	175	32	7	3	2	(1	1)	51	14	9	7	11	2	58	0	2	0	2	2	.50	2	.183	.231	.291

Collin Cowgill

Bats: R **Throws:** L **Pos:** LF-16; CF-15; RF-8; PR-3; PH-2   **Ht:** 5'9" **Wt:** 185 **Born:** 5/22/1986 **Age:** 27

Year	Team	Lg	G	AB	H	2B	3B	HR	(Hm	Rd)	TB	R	RBI	RC	TBB	IBB	SO	HBP	SH	SF	SB	CS	SB%	GDP	Avg	OBP	Slg
2008	Yakima	A-	20	79	24	3	1	11	(-	-)	62	21	28	24	12	0	17	3	1	0	5	0	1.00	2	.304	.415	.785
2008	Sbend	A	50	201	50	13	3	1	(-	-)	72	31	17	27	25	0	61	5	0	0	1	0	1.00	4	.249	.346	.358
2009	Visalia	A+	61	220	61	9	5	6	(-	-)	98	39	36	39	29	3	49	7	0	4	11	4	.73	6	.277	.373	.445
2010	Mobile	AA	131	502	143	34	4	16	(-	-)	233	89	83	90	57	1	73	8	0	10	25	9	.74	23	.285	.360	.464
2011	Reno	AAA	98	395	140	24	8	13	(-	-)	219	95	70	96	51	0	63	2	7	1	30	3	.91	9	.354	.430	.554
2012	Scrmto	AAA	61	260	66	17	1	4	(-	-)	97	33	37	32	20	1	50	3	0	2	8	2	.80	9	.254	.312	.373
2012	Stcktn	A+	2	8	1	0	0	0	(-	-)	1	0	0	0	0	0	2	0	0	0	0	0	-	0	.125	.125	.125
2011	Ari	NL	37	92	22	3	0	1	(1	0)	28	8	9	8	8	1	28	0	0	0	4	2	.67	0	.239	.300	.304
2012	Oak	AL	38	104	28	2	0	1	(1	0)	33	10	9	14	11	0	27	0	0	1	3	4	.43	3	.269	.336	.317
	Postseason		2	1	1	0	0	0	(0	0)	1	0	2	1	0	0	0	0	0	0	0	0	-	0	1.000	1.000	1.000
	2 ML YEARS		75	196	50	5	0	2	(2	0)	61	18	18	22	19	1	55	0	0	1	7	6	.54	3	.255	.319	.311

Zack Cozart

Bats: R **Throws:** R **Pos:** SS-138; PH-2   COE-zart   **Ht:** 6'0" **Wt:** 195 **Born:** 8/12/1985 **Age:** 27

Year	Team	Lg	G	AB	H	2B	3B	HR	(Hm	Rd)	TB	R	RBI	RC	TBB	IBB	SO	HBP	SH	SF	SB	CS	SB%	GDP	Avg	OBP	Slg
2007	Dayton	A	53	184	44	7	2	2	(-	-)	61	28	18	18	11	0	36	2	3	1	3	1	.75	3	.239	.288	.332
2008	Dayton	A	109	418	117	20	6	14	(-	-)	191	57	49	64	24	0	77	10	6	6	3	3	.50	6	.280	.330	.457
2009	Carlina	AA	131	463	121	29	2	10	(-	-)	184	72	59	73	63	2	88	10	2	4	10	2	.83	8	.261	.359	.397
2010	Lsvlle	AAA	136	553	141	30	4	17	(-	-)	230	91	67	78	40	0	107	6	6	5	30	4	.88	15	.255	.310	.416
2011	Lsvlle	AAA	77	323	100	26	2	7	(-	-)	151	57	32	55	23	2	51	2	0	2	9	2	.82	4	.310	.357	.467
2011	Cin	NL	11	37	12	0	0	2	(2	0)	18	6	3	3	0	0	6	0	1	0	0	0	-	2	.324	.324	.486
2012	Cin	NL	138	561	138	33	4	15	(6	9)	224	72	35	51	31	0	113	3	2	3	4	0	1.00	11	.246	.288	.399
	2 ML YEARS		149	598	150	33	4	17	(8	9)	242	78	38	54	31	0	119	3	3	3	4	0	1.00	13	.251	.290	.405

Allen Craig

Bats: R **Throws:** R **Pos:** 1B-91; RF-23; LF-8; PH-6; DH-1   **Ht:** 6'2" **Wt:** 210 **Born:** 7/18/1984 **Age:** 28

Year	Team	Lg	G	AB	H	2B	3B	HR	(Hm	Rd)	TB	R	RBI	RC	TBB	IBB	SO	HBP	SH	SF	SB	CS	SB%	GDP	Avg	OBP	Slg
2012	PlmBh*	A+	3	11	4	0	0	1	(-	-)	7	1	1	2	1	0	2	0	0	0	0	0	-	0	.364	.417	.636
2012	Memp*	AAA	4	17	6	0	0	2	(-	-)	12	3	7	3	0	0	2	0	0	0	0	0	-	1	.353	.353	.706
2010	StL	NL	44	114	28	7	0	4	(3	1)	47	12	18	14	9	1	26	0	0	1	0	1	.00	1	.246	.298	.412
2011	StL	NL	75	200	63	15	0	11	(3	8)	111	33	40	37	15	0	40	1	1	2	5	0	1.00	7	.315	.362	.555
2012	StL	NL	119	469	144	35	0	22	(11	11)	245	76	92	89	37	1	89	1	0	7	2	1	.67	15	.307	.354	.522
	Postseason		15	37	9	0	1	4	(3	1)	23	9	8	8	8	0	13	1	1	0	0	2	.00	1	.243	.391	.622
	3 ML YEARS		238	783	235	57	0	37	(17	20)	403	121	150	140	61	2	155	2	1	10	7	2	.78	23	.300	.348	.515

Jesse Crain

Pitches: R **Bats:** R **Pos:** RP-51   **Ht:** 6'1" **Wt:** 215 **Born:** 7/5/1981 **Age:** 31

			HOW MUCH HE PITCHED						WHAT HE GAVE UP													THE RESULTS						
Year	Team	Lg	G	GS	CG	GF	IP	BFP	H	R	ER	HR	SH	SF	HB	TBB	IBB	SO	WP	Bk	W	L	Pct	Sh	Sv-Op Hld		ERC	ERA
2012	Charltt	AAA	2	2	0	0	2.0	7	0	0	0	0	0	0	1	0	0	3	0	0	0	0	-	0	0- -	-	0.27	0.00
2004	Min	AL	22	0	0	3	27.0	109	17	6	6	2	1	0	1	12	1	14	1	0	3	0	1.000	0	0-1	5	2.25	2.00
2005	Min	AL	75	0	0	17	79.2	326	61	28	24	6	9	3	5	29	7	25	2	0	12	5	.706	0	1-4	11	2.66	2.71
2006	Min	AL	68	0	0	24	76.2	325	79	31	30	6	1	2	2	18	2	60	1	0	4	5	.444	0	1-4	10	3.48	3.52
2007	Min	AL	18	0	0	5	16.1	71	19	16	10	4	0	1	1	4	0	10	0	1	1	2	.333	0	0-0	6	5.73	5.51
2008	Min	AL	66	0	0	14	62.2	268	62	29	25	6	0	2	1	24	3	50	2	0	5	4	.556	0	0-3	17	3.93	3.59
2009	Min	AL	56	0	0	15	51.2	230	48	28	27	3	3	3	5	27	3	43	1	1	7	4	.636	0	0-0	4	4.12	4.70
2010	Min	AL	71	0	0	16	68.0	278	53	27	23	5	3	0	1	27	4	62	3	0	1	1	.500	0	1-4	21	2.71	3.04
2011	CWS	AL	67	0	0	11	65.1	268	50	20	19	7	1	3	0	31	5	70	0	1	8	3	.727	0	1-7	24	3.08	2.62
2012	CWS	AL	51	0	0	6	48.0	194	29	14	13	5	0	0	4	23	1	60	4	0	2	3	.400	0	0-4	10	2.38	2.44
	Postseason		4	0	0	0	1.2	14	7	5	3	2	0	0	1	1	0	1	0	0	0	1	.000	0	0-0	0	40.37	16.20
	9 ML YEARS		494	0	0	111	495.1	2069	418	199	177	44	18	14	17	195	26	394	14	3	43	27	.614	0	4-27	105	3.19	3.22

Brandon Crawford

Bats: L **Throws:** R **Pos:** SS-139; PH-3; PR-2   **Ht:** 6'2" **Wt:** 215 **Born:** 1/21/1987 **Age:** 26

Year	Team	Lg	G	AB	H	2B	3B	HR	(Hm	Rd)	TB	R	RBI	RC	TBB	IBB	SO	HBP	SH	SF	SB	CS	SB%	GDP	Avg	OBP	Slg
2008	Giants	R	4	14	6	1	1	0	(-	-)	9	3	3	2	0	0	3	0	0	0	0	1	.00	1	.429	.429	.643
2008	SlmKzr	A-	1	2	0	0	0	0	(-	-)	0	0	0	0	0	0	0	0	0	0	0	0	-	0	.000	.000	.000
2009	SnJos	A+	25	105	39	2	2	6	(-	-)	63	21	17	25	10	0	32	4	0	0	2	4	.33	1	.371	.445	.600
2009	Conn	AA	108	392	101	29	2	4	(-	-)	142	38	31	42	20	0	100	1	8	2	12	7	.63	8	.258	.294	.362
2010	Rchmd	AA	79	291	70	12	3	7	(-	-)	109	43	22	41	39	0	77	6	1	5	4	1	.80	8	.241	.337	.375
2010	SnJos	A+	5	18	3	1	0	0	(-	-)	4	4	1	0	2	0	5	0	0	0	0	0	-	0	.167	.250	.222
2011	SnJos	A+	14	59	19	5	1	3	(-	-)	35	14	15	14	9	0	13	0	0	1	2	0	1.00	1	.322	.412	.593
2011	Fresno	AAA	29	107	25	5	1	1	(-	-)	35	13	9	10	9	1	20	0	1	0	5	2	.71	2	.234	.291	.327
2011	SF	NL	66	196	40	5	2	3	(0	3)	58	22	21	20	23	1	31	0	1	0	1	3	.25	4	.204	.288	.296
2012	SF	NL	143	435	108	26	3	4	(1	3)	152	44	45	40	33	6	95	3	2	3	1	4	.20	4	.248	.304	.349
	2 ML YEARS		209	631	148	31	5	7	(1	6)	210	66	66	60	56	7	126	3	3	3	2	7	.22	8	.235	.299	.333

Carl Crawford

Bats: L **Throws:** L **Pos:** LF-30; DH-1; PH-1   **Ht:** 6'2" **Wt:** 215 **Born:** 8/5/1981 **Age:** 31

										BATTING											BASERUNNING				AVERAGES		
Year	Team	Lg	G	AB	H	2B	3B	HR	(Hm	Rd)	TB	R	RBI	RC	TBB	IBB	SO	HBP	SH	SF	SB	CS	SB%	GDP	Avg	OBP	Slg
2012	RedSx*	R	5	14	3	1	0	0	(-	-)	4	2	0	1	5	1	4	0	0	0	0	1	.00	0	.214	.421	.286
2012	Portlnd*	AA	3	10	4	0	1	0	(-	-)	6	2	1	3	2	0	1	0	0	0	1	0	1.00	1	.400	.500	.600
2012	Pwtckt*	AAA	3	12	4	0	0	0	(-	-)	4	2	1	1	1	0	1	0	0	0	1	0	1.00	0	.333	.385	.333
2002	TB	AL	63	259	67	11	6	2	(1	1)	96	23	30	34	9	0	41	3	6	1	9	5	.64	0	.259	.290	.371
2003	TB	AL	151	630	177	18	9	5	(5	0)	228	80	54	80	26	4	102	1	1	3	55	10	.85	5	.281	.309	.362
2004	TB	AL	152	626	185	26	**19**	11	(6	5)	282	104	55	96	35	2	81	1	4	6	**59**	15	.80	2	.296	.331	.450
2005	TB	AL	156	644	194	33	15	15	(5	10)	302	101	81	102	27	1	84	5	5	6	46	8	.85	11	.301	.331	.469
2006	TB	AL	151	600	183	20	**16**	18	(7	11)	289	89	77	113	37	3	85	4	9	2	**58**	9	.87	8	.305	.348	.482
2007	TB	AL	143	584	184	37	9	11	(6	5)	272	93	80	97	32	5	112	5	1	2	**50**	10	.83	11	.315	.355	.466
2008	TB	AL	109	443	121	12	10	8	(3	5)	177	69	57	57	30	1	60	2	0	5	25	7	.78	10	.273	.319	.400
2009	TB	AL	156	606	185	28	8	15	(9	6)	274	96	68	91	51	1	99	8	2	5	60	16	.79	7	.305	.364	.452
2010	TB	AL	154	600	184	30	**13**	19	(11	8)	297	110	90	120	46	3	104	3	3	5	47	10	.82	2	.307	.356	.495
2011	Bos	AL	130	506	129	29	7	11	(4	7)	205	65	56	54	23	1	104	3	2	4	18	6	.75	7	.255	.289	.405
2012	Bos	AL	31	117	33	10	2	3	(2	1)	56	23	19	17	3	0	22	2	1	2	5	0	1.00	1	.282	.306	.479
	Postseason		21	83	21	3	1	3	(1	2)	35	10	9	11	3	0	14	1	0	0	8	0	1.00	1	.253	.287	.422
	11 ML YEARS		1396	5615	1642	254	114	118	(59	59)	2478	853	667	861	319	21	894	37	34	41	432	96	.82	64	.292	.332	.441

Evan Crawford

Pitches: L **Bats:** R **Pos:** RP-10   **Ht:** 6'2" **Wt:** 190 **Born:** 9/2/1986 **Age:** 26

			HOW MUCH HE PITCHED						WHAT HE GAVE UP										THE RESULTS						
Year	Team	Lg	G	GS	CG	GF	IP	BFP	H	R	ER	HR	SH	SF	HB	TBB	IBB	SO	WP	Bk	W	L	Pct	Sh	Sv-Op	Hld	ERC	ERA
2008	Auburn	A-	13	5	0	0	29.2	131	21	13	10	0	0	2	4	16	0	23	4	0	0	2	.000	0	0--	-	2.73	3.03
2009	Auburn	A-	14	14	1	0	57.2	260	60	35	26	1	1	2	3	31	1	38	3	0	1	5	.167	0	0--	-	4.40	4.06
2010	Lnsng	A	16	7	0	4	49.1	213	51	24	22	2	1	4	3	20	0	39	4	1	3	2	.600	0	0--	-	4.18	4.01
2010	Dnedin	A+	23	0	0	13	35.1	151	31	11	8	0	3	1	2	14	1	33	3	0	1	2	.333	0	3--	-	2.85	2.04
2011	NHam	AA	45	0	0	16	51.0	220	50	23	19	3	4	2	1	21	1	62	1	0	3	5	.375	0	2--	-	3.77	3.35
2012	NHam	AA	3	0	0	1	4.0	17	3	1	0	0	0	0	0	2	0	5	0	0	0	0	-	0	0--	-	2.40	0.00
2012	LsVgs	AAA	26	0	0	4	27.2	131	38	22	21	2	1	0	2	12	0	20	5	0	1	4	.200	0	0--	-	6.56	6.83
2012	Tor	AL	10	0	0	3	8.0	36	10	6	6	3	1	0	1	4	1	5	0	1	0	0	-	0	0-0	1	9.16	6.75

Coco Crisp

Bats: B **Throws:** R **Pos:** CF-97; LF-16; PH-6; DH-3; PR-3   **Ht:** 5'10" **Wt:** 185 **Born:** 11/1/1979 **Age:** 33

										BATTING											BASERUNNING				AVERAGES		
Year	Team	Lg	G	AB	H	2B	3B	HR	(Hm	Rd)	TB	R	RBI	RC	TBB	IBB	SO	HBP	SH	SF	SB	CS	SB%	GDP	Avg	OBP	Slg
2002	Cle	AL	32	127	33	9	2	1	(1	0)	49	16	9	19	11	0	19	0	3	2	4	1	.80	0	.260	.314	.386
2003	Cle	AL	99	414	110	15	6	3	(3	0)	146	55	27	48	23	1	51	0	7	3	15	9	.63	4	.266	.302	.353
2004	Cle	AL	139	491	146	24	2	15	(8	7)	219	78	71	72	36	4	69	0	9	2	20	13	.61	8	.297	.344	.446
2005	Cle	AL	145	594	178	42	4	16	(4	12)	276	86	69	92	44	1	81	0	**13**	5	15	6	.71	7	.300	.345	.465
2006	Bos	AL	105	413	109	22	2	8	(4	4)	159	58	36	51	31	1	67	1	7	0	22	4	.85	5	.264	.317	.385
2007	Bos	AL	145	526	141	28	7	6	(1	5)	201	85	60	68	50	1	84	1	9	5	28	6	.82	12	.268	.330	.382
2008	Bos	AL	118	361	102	18	3	7	(1	6)	147	55	41	49	35	0	59	1	8	4	20	7	.74	6	.283	.344	.407
2009	KC	AL	49	180	41	8	5	3	(0	3)	68	30	14	25	29	1	23	1	4	1	13	2	.87	4	.228	.336	.378
2010	Oak	AL	75	290	81	14	4	8	(6	2)	127	51	38	49	30	0	49	0	3	5	32	3	**.91**	6	.279	.342	.438
2011	Oak	AL	136	531	140	27	5	8	(4	4)	201	69	54	69	41	2	65	1	4	6	**49**	9	.84	11	.264	.314	.379
2012	Oak	AL	120	455	118	25	7	11	(6	5)	190	68	46	71	45	0	64	0	6	2	39	4	.91	9	.259	.325	.418
	Postseason		20	57	16	3	0	0	(0	0)	19	7	3	6	6	0	12	0	0	0	3	0	1.00	3	.281	.349	.333
	11 ML YEARS		1163	4382	1199	232	47	86	(38	48)	1783	651	465	613	375	11	631	5	73	35	257	64	.80	72	.274	.329	.407

Casey Crosby

Pitches: L **Bats:** R **Pos:** SP-3   **Ht:** 6'5" **Wt:** 225 **Born:** 9/17/1988 **Age:** 24

			HOW MUCH HE PITCHED						WHAT HE GAVE UP										THE RESULTS						
Year	Team	Lg	G	GS	CG	GF	IP	BFP	H	R	ER	HR	SH	SF	HB	TBB	IBB	SO	WP	Bk	W	L	Pct	Sh	Sv-Op	Hld	ERC	ERA
2008	Tigers	R	3	3	0	0	4.2	22	4	1	0	0	0	0	0	3	0	2	1	0	0	0	-	0	0--	-	3.21	0.00
2009	WMich	A	24	24	0	0	104.2	419	70	36	28	3	2	6	3	48	0	117	7	0	10	4	.714	0	0--	-	2.27	2.41
2010	Tigers	R	3	3	0	0	12.1	60	21	15	12	1	0	0	0	4	0	10	3	0	0	1	.000	0	0--	-	8.00	8.76
2011	Erie	AA	25	25	0	0	131.2	570	122	68	60	11	3	2	5	77	0	121	7	0	9	7	.563	0	0--	-	4.55	4.10
2012	Toledo	AAA	22	22	2	0	125.2	539	112	63	56	12	2	1	0	65	3	112	11	0	7	9	.438	0	0--	-	3.89	4.01
2012	Det	AL	3	3	0	0	12.1	59	15	13	13	2	0	0	0	11	0	9	1	0	1	1	.500	0	0-0	0	8.38	9.49

Aaron Crow

Pitches: R **Bats:** R **Pos:** RP-73   **Ht:** 6'3" **Wt:** 190 **Born:** 11/11/1986 **Age:** 26

			HOW MUCH HE PITCHED						WHAT HE GAVE UP										THE RESULTS						
Year	Team	Lg	G	GS	CG	GF	IP	BFP	H	R	ER	HR	SH	SF	HB	TBB	IBB	SO	WP	Bk	W	L	Pct	Sh	Sv-Op	Hld	ERC	ERA
2008	FtWth	IND	1	0	0	0	1.0	3	1	0	0	0	0	0	0	0	0	0	0	0	0	0	-	0	0--	-	2.79	0.00
2009	FtWth	IND	3	3	0	0	17.0	64	11	2	2	0	2	0	1	5	0	17	1	0	3	0	1.000	0	0--	-	1.65	1.06
2010	NWArk	AA	22	22	0	0	119.1	539	130	86	75	13	4	4	6	59	1	90	8	1	7	7	.500	0	0--	-	5.25	5.66
2010	Wilmg	A+	7	7	0	0	44.0	185	51	32	29	6	2	0	1	6	0	53	6	0	2	3	.400	0	0--	-	4.28	5.93
2011	KC	AL	57	0	0	19	62.0	266	55	20	19	8	3	0	0	31	2	65	9	1	4	4	.500	0	0-7	6	4.00	2.76
2012	KC	AL	73	0	0	20	64.2	260	54	27	25	4	1	2	1	22	2	65	4	0	3	1	.750	0	2-8	19	2.81	3.48
	2 ML YEARS		130	0	0	39	126.2	526	109	47	44	12	4	2	1	53	4	130	13	1	7	5	.583	0	2-15	27	3.38	3.13

Juan Cruz

Pitches: R Bats: R Pos: RP-43   **Ht: 6'2" Wt: 170 Born: 10/15/1978 Age: 34**

				HOW MUCH HE PITCHED							WHAT HE GAVE UP										THE RESULTS							
Year	Team	Lg	G	GS	CG	GF	IP	BFP	H	R	ER	HR	SH	SF	HB	TBB	IBB	SO	WP	Bk	W	L	Pct	Sh	Sv-Op	Hld	ERC	ERA
2012	Altna*	AA	2	2	0	0	1.1	9	5	2	2	0	0	0	0	0	0	2	0	0	0	0	-	0	0- -	-	20.38	13.50
2001	ChC	NL	8	8	0	0	44.2	185	40	16	16	4	2	0	2	17	1	39	0	0	3	1	.750	0	0-0	0	3.59	3.22
2002	ChC	NL	45	9	0	14	97.1	431	84	56	43	11	7	8	8	59	4	81	1	0	3	11	.214	0	1-4	3	4.49	3.98
2003	ChC	NL	25	6	0	3	61.0	284	66	44	41	7	7	2	7	28	0	65	4	0	2	7	.222	0	0-1	1	5.23	6.05
2004	Atl	NL	50	0	0	22	72.0	300	59	24	22	7	4	1	2	30	1	70	1	0	6	2	.750	0	0-0	2	3.25	2.75
2005	Oak	AL	28	0	0	14	32.2	159	38	33	27	5	0	4	2	22	4	34	3	0	0	3	.000	0	0-0	0	6.87	7.44
2006	Ari	NL	31	15	0	5	94.2	413	80	45	44	7	5	2	11	47	2	88	2	0	5	6	.455	0	0-0	0	3.82	4.18
2007	Ari	NL	53	0	0	15	61.0	262	45	28	21	7	2	2	5	32	3	87	1	2	6	1	.857	0	0-0	4	3.43	3.10
2008	Ari	NL	57	0	0	10	51.2	215	34	17	15	5	2	2	3	31	0	71	1	0	4	0	1.000	0	0-2	8	3.25	2.61
2009	KC	AL	46	0	0	18	50.1	219	46	34	32	6	1	1	1	29	1	38	6	0	3	4	.429	0	2-6	7	4.55	5.72
2010	KC	AL	5	0	0	1	5.1	28	9	2	2	1	0	1	0	4	0	7	0	0	0	0	-	0	0-1	0	9.07	3.38
2011	TB	AL	56	0	0	9	48.2	200	36	21	21	5	0	1	0	28	2	46	3	0	5	0	1.000	0	0-1	6	3.40	3.88
2012	Pit	NL	43	0	0	11	35.2	162	39	12	11	3	2	3	3	19	0	33	1	0	1	1	.500	0	3-4	14	5.45	2.78
	Postseason		10	0	0	2	11.0	52	8	5	4	0	1	0	1	10	1	17	1	0	0	0	-	0	0-0	0	3.79	3.27
	12 ML YEARS		447	38	0	122	655.0	2858	576	332	295	67	33	24	46	346	18	659	23	2	38	36	.514	0	6-19	45	4.17	4.05

Luis Cruz

Bats: R Throws: R Pos: 3B-51; SS-24; PH-3; 2B-2   **Ht: 6'2" Wt: 220 Born: 2/10/1984 Age: 29**

									BATTING												BASERUNNING				AVERAGES		
Year	Team	Lg	G	AB	H	2B	3B	HR	(Hm	Rd)	TB	R	RBI	RC	TBB	IBB	SO	HBP	SH	SF	SB	CS	SB%	GDP	Avg	OBP	Slg
2012	Albq*	AAA	74	289	92	31	3	8	(-	-)	153	46	46	51	13	1	34	1	0	2	1	2	.33	8	.318	.348	.529
2008	Pit	NL	22	67	15	3	0	0	(0	0)	18	6	3	4	3	0	2	2	2	0	1	1	.50	3	.224	.278	.269
2009	Pit	NL	27	70	15	1	0	0	(0	0)	16	5	2	3	6	1	7	1	0	1	0	0	-	1	.214	.282	.229
2010	Mil	NL	7	17	4	0	1	0	(0	0)	6	2	1	2	0	0	2	0	0	0	0	0	-	1	.235	.235	.353
2012	LAD	NL	78	283	84	20	0	6	(2	4)	122	26	40	39	9	1	34	2	1	1	2	1	.67	7	.297	.322	.431
	4 ML YEARS		134	437	118	24	1	6	(2	4)	162	39	46	48	18	2	45	5	3	2	3	2	.60	12	.270	.305	.371

Nelson Cruz

Bats: R Throws: R Pos: RF-151; DH-7; LF-6; PH-4   **Ht: 6'2" Wt: 240 Born: 7/1/1980 Age: 32**

									BATTING												BASERUNNING				AVERAGES		
Year	Team	Lg	G	AB	H	2B	3B	HR	(Hm	Rd)	TB	R	RBI	RC	TBB	IBB	SO	HBP	SH	SF	SB	CS	SB%	GDP	Avg	OBP	Slg
2005	Mil	NL	8	5	1	1	0	0	(0	0)	2	1	0	1	2	0	0	0	0	0	0	0	-	0	.200	.429	.400
2006	Tex	AL	41	130	29	3	0	6	(3	3)	50	15	22	18	7	0	32	0	0	1	1	0	1.00	6	.223	.261	.385
2007	Tex	AL	96	307	72	15	2	9	(4	5)	118	35	34	32	21	1	87	2	1	1	2	4	.33	5	.235	.287	.384
2008	Tex	AL	31	115	38	9	1	7	(4	3)	70	19	26	30	17	2	28	1	0	0	3	1	.75	1	.330	.421	.609
2009	Tex	AL	128	462	120	21	1	33	(18	15)	242	75	76	72	49	6	118	2	0	2	20	4	.83	9	.260	.332	.524
2010	Tex	AL	108	399	127	31	3	22	(13	9)	230	60	78	77	38	5	81	1	1	6	17	4	.81	12	.318	.374	.576
2011	Tex	AL	124	475	125	28	1	29	(19	10)	242	64	87	79	33	1	116	2	0	3	9	5	.64	8	.263	.312	.509
2012	Tex	AL	159	585	152	45	0	24	(18	6)	269	86	90	80	48	2	140	5	0	4	8	4	.67	7	.260	.319	.460
	Postseason		33	122	33	9	0	14	(9	5)	84	26	27	27	10	2	31	1	0	0	1	1	.50	3	.270	.331	.689
	8 ML YEARS		695	2478	664	153	8	130	(79	51)	1223	355	413	389	215	17	602	13	2	17	60	22	.73	43	.268	.328	.494

Rhiner Cruz

Pitches: R Bats: R Pos: RP-52   RYE-ner   **Ht: 6'2" Wt: 205 Born: 11/1/1986 Age: 26**

				HOW MUCH HE PITCHED							WHAT HE GAVE UP										THE RESULTS							
Year	Team	Lg	G	GS	CG	GF	IP	BFP	H	R	ER	HR	SH	SF	HB	TBB	IBB	SO	WP	Bk	W	L	Pct	Sh	Sv-Op	Hld	ERC	ERA
2004	Tigers	R	16	0	0	9	32.0	149	37	20	17	3	1	4	1	19	0	26	3	0	0	1	.000	0	0- -	-	5.88	4.78
2005	Tigers	R	14	0	0	8	28.0	136	35	15	14	5	0	1	5	12	0	23	4	0	1	0	1.000	0	1- -	-	6.92	4.50
2007	Mets	R	4	0	0	1	6.0	25	1	0	0	0	0	0	0	5	0	4	0	0	2	0	1.000	0	0- -	-	1.86	0.00
2007	Kngspt	R	11	0	0	8	12.2	54	7	1	1	0	2	0	0	14	0	13	0	0	1	1	.500	0	4- -	-	3.77	0.71
2008	Bklyn	A-	6	0	0	2	9.2	46	9	5	4	1	1	0	2	6	1	13	2	0	0	0	-	0	1- -	-	5.09	3.72
2008	Savann	A	15	0	0	7	30.1	133	27	20	17	4	2	0	2	14	0	33	2	0	2	2	.500	0	1- -	-	4.13	5.04
2009	Savann	A	50	0	0	37	61.0	253	42	14	13	2	1	2	8	31	0	55	8	0	3	3	.500	0	22- -	-	2.92	1.92
2010	StLuci	A+	51	0	0	23	75.1	341	62	34	29	6	5	4	12	53	3	66	9	0	5	5	.000	0	6- -	-	4.72	3.46
2011	StLuci	A+	8	0	0	5	13.0	55	9	4	4	1	1	1	2	6	0	18	3	0	2	1	.667	0	6- -	-	3.07	2.77
2011	Bnghtn	AA	36	0	0	21	58.2	260	43	27	27	4	1	1	5	39	1	51	7	0	3	2	.600	0	7- -	-	3.64	4.14
2012	OKCity	AAA	2	0	0	1	1.2	7	1	2	1	0	0	0	1	0	3	0	0	0	0	0	-	0	0- -	-	4.62	5.40
2012	Hou	NL	52	0	0	26	55.0	253	65	38	37	8	1	2	2	29	0	46	3	0	1	1	.500	0	0-1	0	6.24	6.05

Tony Cruz

Bats: R Throws: R Pos: C-47; PH-12; 1B-2   **Ht: 5'11" Wt: 205 Born: 8/18/1986 Age: 26**

									BATTING												BASERUNNING				AVERAGES		
Year	Team	Lg	G	AB	H	2B	3B	HR	(Hm	Rd)	TB	R	RBI	RC	TBB	IBB	SO	HBP	SH	SF	SB	CS	SB%	GDP	Avg	OBP	Slg
2007	Cards	R	7	32	12	5	0	0	(-	-)	17	8	4	6	1	0	7	0	0	1	1	0	1.00	0	.375	.382	.531
2007	JhsCty	R+	6	25	7	2	0	2	(-	-)	15	2	2	5	2	1	2	0	0	0	1	0	1.00	0	.280	.333	.600
2007	Batvia	A-	4	16	6	1	0	0	(-	-)	7	2	4	2	0	0	5	1	0	0	0	0	-	0	.375	.412	.438
2007	QuadC	A	49	195	55	10	1	5	(-	-)	82	26	34	29	17	0	25	1	0	3	3	1	.75	10	.282	.338	.421
2008	PlmBh	A+	89	351	98	22	3	8	(-	-)	150	41	58	49	19	0	50	2	1	5	3	0	1.00	17	.279	.316	.427
2009	Sprgfld	AA	111	405	89	25	2	10	(-	-)	148	44	48	43	34	2	85	1	2	3	1	0	1.00	16	.220	.280	.365
2010	PlmBh	A+	46	181	51	16	1	1	(-	-)	72	21	25	26	19	0	33	0	1	2	0	2	.00	5	.282	.348	.398
2010	Sprgfld	AA	40	149	43	10	0	6	(-	-)	71	26	20	26	17	3	30	1	1	1	0	0	-	5	.289	.363	.477
2010	Memp	AAA	4	14	3	0	0	1	(-	-)	6	1	0	1	0	0	0	0	0	0	0	0	-	1	.214	.267	.429

Year	Team	Lg	G	AB	H	2B	3B	HR	(Hm	Rd)	TB	R	RBI	RC	TBB	IBB	SO	HBP	SH	SF	SB	CS	SB%	GDP	Avg	OBP	Slg
2011	Memp	AAA	45	149	39	5	1	4	(-	-)	58	13	25	18	11	0	31	1	2	1	0	1	.00	7	.262	.315	.389
2011	StL	NL	38	65	17	5	0	0	(0	0)	22	8	6	7	6	1	13	1	0	0	0	1	.00	1	.262	.333	.338
2012	StL	NL	51	126	32	9	1	1	(0	1)	46	11	11	9	3	0	19	0	0	2	0	1	.00	4	.254	.267	.365
	2 ML YEARS		89	191	49	14	1	1	(0	1)	68	19	17	16	9	1	32	1	0	2	0	2	.00	5	.257	.291	.356

Michael Cuddyer

Bats: R **Throws:** R **Pos:** RF-74; 1B-26; PH-5   cuh-DYE-err   **Ht:** 6'2" **Wt:** 220 **Born:** 3/27/1979 **Age:** 34

Year	Team	Lg	G	AB	H	2B	3B	HR	(Hm	Rd)	TB	R	RBI	RC	TBB	IBB	SO	HBP	SH	SF	SB	CS	SB%	GDP	Avg	OBP	Slg
2012	ColSpr*	AAA	2	9	6	1	0	1	(-	-)	10	4	3	4	0	0	1	0	0	0	0	0	-	0	.667	.667	1.111
2001	Min	AL	8	18	4	2	0	0	(0	0)	6	1	1	2	2	0	6	0	0	0	1	0	1.00	1	.222	.300	.333
2002	Min	AL	41	112	29	7	0	4	(2	2)	48	12	13	14	8	0	30	1	1	1	2	0	1.00	3	.259	.311	.429
2003	Min	AL	35	102	25	1	3	4	(1	3)	44	14	8	10	12	0	19	0	0	0	1	1	.50	6	.245	.325	.431
2004	Min	AL	115	339	89	22	1	12	(8	4)	149	49	45	49	37	2	74	3	2	1	5	5	.50	8	.263	.339	.440
2005	Min	AL	126	422	111	25	3	12	(8	4)	178	55	42	43	41	5	93	3	1	3	3	4	.43	19	.263	.330	.422
2006	Min	AL	150	557	158	41	5	24	(15	9)	281	102	109	101	62	5	130	10	0	6	6	0	1.00	11	.284	.362	.504
2007	Min	AL	144	547	151	28	5	16	(8	8)	237	87	81	82	64	1	107	7	0	5	5	0	1.00	19	.276	.356	.433
2008	Min	AL	71	249	62	13	4	3	(1	2)	92	30	36	37	25	4	40	5	0	0	5	1	.83	7	.249	.330	.369
2009	Min	AL	153	588	162	34	7	32	(18	14)	306	93	94	89	54	3	118	6	0	2	6	1	.86	22	.276	.342	.520
2010	Min	AL	157	609	165	37	5	14	(7	7)	254	93	81	77	58	7	93	4	0	4	7	3	.70	26	.271	.336	.417
2011	Min	AL	139	529	150	29	2	20	(10	10)	243	70	70	75	48	3	95	4	0	3	11	1	.92	18	.284	.346	.459
2012	Col	NL	101	358	93	30	2	16	(9	7)	175	53	58	46	32	1	78	0	0	4	8	3	.73	12	.260	.317	.489
	Postseason		22	74	25	2	1	2	(2	0)	35	5	8	4	4	1	18	0	0	0	0	2	.00	1	.338	.372	.473
	12 ML YEARS		1240	4430	1199	269	37	157	(87	70)	2013	659	638	627	443	31	883	43	4	29	60	19	.76	152	.271	.341	.454

Johnny Cueto

Pitches: R **Bats:** R **Pos:** SP-33   KWAY-toe   **Ht:** 5'10" **Wt:** 215 **Born:** 2/15/1986 **Age:** 27

Year	Team	Lg	G	GS	CG	GF	IP	BFP	H	R	ER	HR	SH	SF	HB	TBB	IBB	SO	WP	Bk	W	L	Pct	Sh	Sv-Op	Hld	ERC	ERA
2008	Cin	NL	31	31	0	0	174.0	769	178	101	93	29	9	5	14	68	1	158	6	1	9	14	.391	0	0-0	0	4.95	4.81
2009	Cin	NL	30	30	0	0	171.1	740	172	90	84	24	5	3	14	61	0	132	4	0	11	11	.500	0	0-0	0	4.57	4.41
2010	Cin	NL	31	31	1	0	185.2	780	181	79	75	19	9	3	9	56	5	138	5	2	12	7	.632	1	0-0	0	3.75	3.64
2011	Cin	NL	24	24	3	0	156.0	631	123	51	40	8	10	4	10	47	0	104	5	1	9	5	.643	1	0-0	0	2.55	2.31
2012	Cin	NL	33	33	2	0	217.0	888	205	73	67	15	6	6	12	49	5	170	1	3	19	9	.679	0	0-0	0	3.13	2.78
	Postseason		1	1	0	0	5.0	22	5	2	1	1	1	0	0	1	0	2	0	0	0	1	.000	0	0-0	0	3.66	1.80
	5 ML YEARS		149	149	6	0	904.0	3808	859	394	359	95	39	21	59	281	11	702	21	7	60	46	.566	2	0-0	0	3.75	3.57

Charlie Culberson

Bats: R **Throws:** R **Pos:** 2B-6; PR-1   **Ht:** 6'1" **Wt:** 200 **Born:** 4/10/1989 **Age:** 24

Year	Team	Lg	G	AB	H	2B	3B	HR	(Hm	Rd)	TB	R	RBI	RC	TBB	IBB	SO	HBP	SH	SF	SB	CS	SB%	GDP	Avg	OBP	Slg
2007	Giants	R	46	161	46	8	5	1	(-	-)	67	32	16	30	19	1	38	5	0	2	19	1	.95	1	.286	.374	.416
2008	Augsta	A	81	282	66	11	2	3	(-	-)	90	31	27	26	18	0	57	6	3	4	6	6	.50	4	.234	.290	.319
2009	Augsta	A	132	509	125	19	3	2	(-	-)	156	71	36	51	33	1	110	10	4	2	15	4	.79	7	.246	.303	.306
2010	SnJos	A+	128	503	146	28	4	16	(-	-)	230	80	71	82	33	2	99	8	1	6	25	7	.78	15	.290	.340	.457
2011	Rchmd	AA	137	553	143	34	2	10	(-	-)	211	69	56	64	22	3	129	6	4	2	14	4	.78	6	.259	.293	.382
2012	Fresno	AAA	91	351	83	14	6	10	(-	-)	139	53	53	41	20	0	76	4	2	3	8	2	.80	10	.236	.283	.396
2012	ColSpr	AAA	30	125	42	11	1	2	(-	-)	61	17	12	20	1	0	18	1	0	1	6	2	.75	5	.336	.344	.488
2012	SF	NL	6	22	3	0	0	0	(0	0)	3	0	1	0	0	0	7	0	1	0	0	0	-	0	.136	.136	.136

Aaron Cunningham

Bats: R **Throws:** R **Pos:** LF-52; RF-13; CF-11; PR-3; DH-1; PH-1   **Ht:** 5'11" **Wt:** 195 **Born:** 4/24/1986 **Age:** 27

Year	Team	Lg	G	AB	H	2B	3B	HR	(Hm	Rd)	TB	R	RBI	RC	TBB	IBB	SO	HBP	SH	SF	SB	CS	SB%	GDP	Avg	OBP	Slg
2012	Clmbs*	AAA	22	74	15	4	0	2	(-	-)	25	6	5	7	8	0	21	0	2	0	0	0	-	1	.203	.280	.338
2008	Oak	AL	22	80	20	7	1	1	(1	0)	32	7	14	12	6	1	24	1	0	0	2	0	1.00	6	.250	.310	.400
2009	Oak	AL	23	53	8	2	0	1	(0	1)	13	6	6	3	3	0	16	1	0	0	0	0	-	3	.151	.211	.245
2010	SD	NL	53	132	38	12	1	1	(1	0)	55	17	15	16	7	1	28	3	2	3	1	3	.25	4	.288	.331	.417
2011	SD	NL	52	90	16	6	1	3	(1	2)	33	12	9	6	9	0	17	1	0	1	1	0	1.00	2	.178	.257	.367
2012	Cle	AL	72	97	17	4	0	1	(0	1)	24	5	7	4	9	1	25	0	3	0	0	3	.00	0	.175	.245	.247
	5 ML YEARS		222	452	99	31	3	7	(3	4)	157	47	51	41	34	3	110	6	5	4	4	6	.40	9	.219	.280	.347

Johnny Damon

Bats: L **Throws:** L **Pos:** LF-56; PH-6; DH-5   **Ht:** 6'2" **Wt:** 205 **Born:** 11/5/1973 **Age:** 39

Year	Team	Lg	G	AB	H	2B	3B	HR	(Hm	Rd)	TB	R	RBI	RC	TBB	IBB	SO	HBP	SH	SF	SB	CS	SB%	GDP	Avg	OBP	Slg
1995	KC	AL	47	188	53	11	5	3	(3	3)	83	32	23	29	12	0	22	1	2	0	7	0	1.00	2	.282	.324	.441
1996	KC	AL	145	517	140	22	5	6	(3	3)	190	61	50	64	31	3	64	3	10	5	25	5	.83	4	.271	.313	.368
1997	KC	AL	146	472	130	12	8	8	(3	5)	182	70	48	63	42	2	70	3	6	1	16	10	.62	3	.275	.338	.386
1998	KC	AL	161	642	178	30	10	18	(11	7)	282	104	66	98	58	4	84	4	3	3	26	12	.68	4	.277	.339	.439
1999	KC	AL	145	583	179	39	9	14	(5	9)	278	101	77	108	67	5	50	3	3	4	36	6	.86	13	.307	.379	.477
2000	KC	AL	159	655	214	42	10	16	(10	6)	324	136	88	129	65	4	60	1	8	12	46	9	.84	7	.327	.382	.495
2001	Oak	AL	155	644	165	34	4	9	(2	7)	234	108	49	79	61	1	70	5	5	4	27	12	.69	7	.256	.324	.363
2002	Bos	AL	154	623	178	34	11	14	(5	9)	276	118	63	101	65	6	70	6	3	5	31	6	.84	4	.286	.356	.443
2003	Bos	AL	145	608	166	32	6	12	(5	7)	246	103	67	92	68	4	74	2	6	6	30	6	.83	5	.273	.345	.405

(Batting — continued)

Year	Team	Lg	G	AB	H	2B	3B	HR	(Hm	Rd)	TB	R	RBI	RC	TBB	IBB	SO	HBP	SH	SF	SB	CS	SB%	GDP	Avg	OBP	Slg
2004	Bos	AL	150	621	189	35	6	20	(9	11)	296	123	94	115	76	1	71	2	0	3	19	8	.70	8	.304	.380	.477
2005	Bos	AL	148	624	197	35	6	10	(3	7)	274	117	75	105	53	3	69	2	0	9	18	1	.95	5	.316	.366	.439
2006	NYY	AL	149	593	169	35	5	24	(13	11)	286	115	80	99	67	1	85	4	2	5	25	10	.71	4	.285	.359	.482
2007	NYY	AL	141	533	144	27	2	12	(5	7)	211	93	63	84	66	1	79	2	1	3	27	3	.90	4	.270	.351	.396
2008	NYY	AL	143	555	168	27	5	17	(7	10)	256	95	71	109	64	0	82	1	2	1	29	8	.78	6	.303	.375	.461
2009	NYY	AL	143	550	155	36	3	24	(17	7)	269	107	82	97	71	1	98	2	2	1	12	0	1.00	5	.282	.365	.489
2010	Det	AL	145	539	146	36	5	8	(7	1)	216	81	51	73	69	2	90	2	2	1	11	1	.92	5	.271	.355	.401
2011	TB	AL	150	582	152	29	7	16	(6	10)	243	79	73	81	51	1	92	7	2	5	19	6	.76	4	.261	.326	.418
2012	Cle	AL	64	207	46	6	2	4	(1	3)	68	25	19	19	17	0	27	0	0	0	4	0	1.00	0	.222	.281	.329
	Postseason		59	261	72	12	2	10	(3	7)	118	39	33	38	17	0	40	1	0	0	13	1	.93	5	.276	.323	.452
	18 ML YEARS		2490	9736	2769	522	109	235	(113	122)	4214	1668	1139	1545	1003	38	1257	50	57	71	408	103	.80	94	.284	.352	.433

John Danks

Pitches: L **Bats:** L **Pos:** SP-9   **Ht:** 6'1" **Wt:** 215 **Born:** 4/15/1985 **Age:** 28

Year	Team	Lg	G	GS	CG	GF	IP	BFP	H	R	ER	HR	SH	SF	HB	TBB	IBB	SO	WP	Bk	W	L	Pct	Sh	Sv-Op	Hld	ERC	ERA
2012	Charltt*	AAA	1	1	0	0	4.0	17	4	3	1	0	0	0	1	0	1	0	0	0	0	0	-	0	0--	-	2.77	2.25
2007	CWS	AL	26	26	0	0	139.0	622	160	92	85	28	7	4	4	54	4	109	3	0	6	13	.316	0	0-0	0	5.73	5.50
2008	CWS	AL	33	33	0	0	195.0	804	182	74	72	15	2	2	4	57	1	159	7	0	12	9	.571	0	0-0	0	3.26	3.32
2009	CWS	AL	32	32	1	0	200.1	839	184	89	84	28	5	6	5	73	1	149	1	0	13	11	.542	0	0-0	0	3.89	3.77
2010	CWS	AL	32	32	1	0	213.0	878	189	93	88	18	5	0	4	70	2	162	2	1	15	11	.577	1	0-0	0	3.18	3.72
2011	CWS	AL	27	27	2	0	170.1	728	182	89	82	19	4	6	7	46	5	135	6	0	8	12	.400	1	0-0	0	4.16	4.33
2012	CWS	AL	9	9	0	0	53.2	238	57	35	34	7	3	2	1	23	0	30	5	0	3	4	.429	0	0-0	0	4.82	5.70
	Postseason		1	1	0	0	6.2	30	7	3	3	1	0	0	0	3	0	7	0	0	1	0	1.000	0	0-0	0	4.81	4.05
	6 ML YEARS		159	159	4	0	971.1	4109	954	472	445	115	26	20	25	323	13	744	24	1	57	60	.487	2	0-0	0	3.94	4.12

Jordan Danks

Bats: L **Throws:** R **Pos:** LF-21; PR-17; CF-14; RF-7; DH-3; PH-1   **Ht:** 6'4" **Wt:** 210 **Born:** 8/7/1986 **Age:** 26

Year	Team	Lg	G	AB	H	2B	3B	HR	(Hm	Rd)	TB	R	RBI	RC	TBB	IBB	SO	HBP	SH	SF	SB	CS	SB%	GDP	Avg	OBP	Slg
2008	Knapol	A	10	40	13	4	1	2	(-	-)	25	10	7	9	4	0	14	1	0	0	1	0	1.00	1	.325	.400	.625
2009	WinSa	A+	30	118	38	11	2	3	(-	-)	62	25	21	26	18	0	32	0	1	1	5	1	.83	4	.322	.409	.525
2009	Brham	AA	73	284	69	12	1	6	(-	-)	101	50	20	37	37	1	73	4	4	1	7	3	.70	2	.243	.337	.356
2010	Charltt	AAA	119	445	109	27	3	8	(-	-)	166	62	42	55	41	1	151	4	9	3	15	6	.71	6	.245	.312	.373
2011	Charltt	AAA	133	463	119	24	6	14	(-	-)	197	65	65	73	57	1	155	5	9	1	18	4	.82	6	.257	.344	.425
2012	Charltt	AAA	64	218	69	17	1	8	(-	-)	112	37	30	49	44	1	66	0	0	2	6	3	.67	0	.317	.428	.514
2012	CWS	AL	50	67	15	1	0	1	(1	0)	19	12	4	3	6	0	16	0	0	2	3	1	.75	1	.224	.280	.284

Chase d'Arnaud

Bats: R **Throws:** R **Pos:** PR-6; 2B-2; SS-1   dar-NO   **Ht:** 6'1" **Wt:** 205 **Born:** 1/21/1987 **Age:** 26

Year	Team	Lg	G	AB	H	2B	3B	HR	(Hm	Rd)	TB	R	RBI	RC	TBB	IBB	SO	HBP	SH	SF	SB	CS	SB%	GDP	Avg	OBP	Slg
2008	StCol	A-	43	168	48	10	5	1	(-	-)	71	26	21	23	11	0	30	2	0	2	14	2	.88	4	.286	.333	.423
2009	WV	A	62	213	62	14	3	3	(-	-)	91	32	31	36	30	1	31	8	1	3	17	3	.85	2	.291	.394	.427
2009	Lynbrg	A+	54	210	62	19	4	4	(-	-)	101	45	26	39	30	0	41	9	2	2	14	5	.74	0	.295	.402	.481
2010	Altna	AA	132	530	131	33	9	6	(-	-)	200	91	48	75	56	0	102	12	5	4	33	7	.83	5	.247	.331	.377
2011	Indy	AAA	74	288	76	12	6	4	(-	-)	112	43	37	41	23	0	53	5	4	1	20	4	.83	2	.264	.328	.389
2011	Bradtn	A+	4	12	4	1	0	1	(-	-)	8	3	3	1	1	0	0	0	0	0	2	0	1.00	0	.333	.385	.667
2012	Indy	AAA	98	381	96	24	4	6	(-	-)	146	63	38	54	37	0	93	5	3	1	34	5	.87	3	.252	.325	.383
2011	Pit	NL	48	143	31	6	2	0	(0	0)	41	17	6	8	4	0	36	1	2	1	12	2	.86	3	.217	.242	.287
2012	Pit	NL	8	6	0	0	0	0	(0	0)	0	2	1	0	0	0	2	0	0	0	1	0	1.00	0	.000	.000	.000
	2 ML YEARS		56	149	31	6	2	0	(0	0)	41	19	7	8	4	0	38	1	2	1	13	2	.87	3	.208	.232	.275

James Darnell

Bats: R **Throws:** R **Pos:** LF-4; PH-2; 3B-1   **Ht:** 6'2" **Wt:** 195 **Born:** 1/19/1987 **Age:** 26

Year	Team	Lg	G	AB	H	2B	3B	HR	(Hm	Rd)	TB	R	RBI	RC	TBB	IBB	SO	HBP	SH	SF	SB	CS	SB%	GDP	Avg	OBP	Slg
2008	Eugene	A-	16	67	25	6	1	2	(-	-)	39	9	15	17	11	1	12	0	0	0	1	1	.50	3	.373	.462	.582
2009	FtWyn	A	66	222	73	17	2	7	(-	-)	115	40	38	55	57	0	51	2	1	1	5	5	.50	5	.329	.468	.518
2009	Lk Els	A+	60	235	69	18	2	13	(-	-)	130	40	43	49	30	0	38	2	1	1	3	1	.75	2	.294	.377	.553
2010	SnAnt	AA	101	373	99	21	1	10	(-	-)	152	46	50	57	44	0	64	5	1	3	2	0	1.00	11	.265	.348	.408
2010	FtWyn	A	7	25	9	4	0	1	(-	-)	16	5	8	7	5	0	4	2	0	0	0	0	-	0	.360	.500	.640
2011	SnAnt	AA	76	288	96	25	1	17	(-	-)	174	62	62	74	52	4	48	2	0	4	2	1	.67	10	.333	.434	.604
2011	Tucsn	AAA	35	134	35	4	0	6	(-	-)	57	20	17	21	16	0	30	2	1	2	0	0	-	3	.261	.344	.425
2012	Tucsn	AAA	31	116	31	6	0	7	(-	-)	58	22	21	22	16	0	25	3	0	2	1	1	.50	1	.267	.365	.500
2011	SD	NL	18	45	10	2	0	1	(0	0)	15	7	2	4	5	0	7	0	1	0	1	0	1.00	6	.222	.294	.333
2012	SD	NL	7	17	4	1	0	1	(0	1)	8	1	1	0	2	0	2	0	0	0	0	0	-	0	.235	.316	.471
	2 ML YEARS		25	62	14	3	0	2	(0	2)	23	3	8	4	7	0	9	0	1	0	1	0	1.00	9	.226	.300	.371

Yu Darvish

Pitches: R Bats: R Pos: SP-29   YOO DARR-vish   Ht: 6'5" Wt: 215 Born: 8/16/1986 Age: 26

Year	Team	Lg	G	GS	CG	GF	IP	BFP	H	R	ER	HR	SH	SF	HB	TBB	IBB	SO	WP	Bk	W	L	Pct	Sh	Sv-Op Hld	ERC	ERA
2005	HNHF	Jap	14	14	2	-	94.1	428	97	37	37	7	-	-	3	48	1	52	2	0	5	5	.500	1	0- - -	4.50	3.53
2006	HNHF	Jap	25	24	3	-	149.2	641	128	55	48	12	-	-	6	64	0	115	5	1	12	5	.706	2	0- - -	3.37	2.89
2007	HNHF	Jap	26	26	12	-	207.2	790	123	48	42	9	-	-	13	49	1	210	4	0	15	5	.750	3	0- - -	1.47	1.82
2008	HNHF	Jap	25	24	10	-	200.2	764	136	44	42	11	-	-	9	44	0	208	4	1	16	4	.800	2	0- - -	1.75	1.88
2009	HNHF	Jap	23	23	8	-	182.0	701	118	36	35	9	-	-	6	45	0	167	5	0	15	5	.750	2	0- - -	1.63	1.73
2010	HNHF	Jap	26	25	10	-	202.0	805	158	48	40	5	-	-	7	47	0	222	6	0	12	8	.600	2	0- - -	2.01	1.78
2011	HNHF	Jap	28	28	10	-	232.0	885	156	42	37	5	-	-	6	36	0	276	10	1	18	6	.750	6	0- - -	1.37	1.44
2012	Tex	AL	29	29	0	0	191.1	816	156	89	83	14	2	7	10	89	1	221	8	0	16	9	.640	0	0-0 0	3.31	3.90

Chris Davis

Bats: L Throws: R Pos: DH-60; 1B-38; RF-30; LF-11; PH-1   Ht: 6'3" Wt: 232 Born: 3/17/1986 Age: 27

Year	Team	Lg	G	AB	H	2B	3B	HR	(Hm	Rd)	TB	R	RBI	RC	TBB	IBB	SO	HBP	SH	SF	SB	CS	SB%	GDP	Avg	OBP	Slg
2008	Tex	AL	80	295	84	23	2	17	(8	9)	162	51	55	44	20	1	88	1	0	1	1	2	.33	5	.285	.331	.549
2009	Tex	AL	113	391	93	15	1	21	(11	10)	173	48	59	50	24	2	150	2	0	2	0	0	-	6	.238	.284	.442
2010	Tex	AL	45	120	23	9	0	1	(0	1)	35	7	4	5	15	3	40	0	0	1	3	0	1.00	3	.192	.279	.292
2011	2 Tms	AL	59	199	53	12	0	5	(2	3)	80	25	19	23	11	1	63	0	0	0	1	0	1.00	4	.266	.305	.402
2012	Bal	AL	139	515	139	20	0	33	(22	11)	258	75	85	85	37	6	169	7	0	3	2	3	.40	8	.270	.326	.501
11	Tex	AL	28	76	19	3	0	3	(1	2)	31	9	6	7	5	0	24	0	0	0	0	0	-	2	.250	.296	.408
11	Bal	AL	31	123	34	9	0	2	(1	1)	49	16	13	16	6	1	39	0	0	0	1	0	1.00	2	.276	.310	.398
5 ML YEARS			436	1520	392	79	3	77	(43	34)	708	206	222	207	107	13	510	10	0	7	7	5	.58	26	.258	.310	.466

Ike Davis

Bats: L Throws: L Pos: 1B-148; PH-15   Ht: 6'4" Wt: 231 Born: 3/22/1987 Age: 26

Year	Team	Lg	G	AB	H	2B	3B	HR	(Hm	Rd)	TB	R	RBI	RC	TBB	IBB	SO	HBP	SH	SF	SB	CS	SB%	GDP	Avg	OBP	Slg
2010	NYM	NL	147	523	138	33	1	19	(8	11)	230	73	71	75	72	6	138	1	0	5	3	2	.60	13	.264	.351	.440
2011	NYM	NL	36	129	39	8	1	7	(5	2)	70	20	25	22	17	3	31	1	0	2	0	0	-	5	.302	.383	.543
2012	NYM	NL	156	519	118	26	0	32	(11	21)	240	66	90	68	61	3	141	1	0	3	0	2	.00	10	.227	.308	.462
3 ML YEARS			339	1171	295	67	2	58	(24	34)	540	159	186	165	150	12	310	3	0	10	3	4	.43	28	.252	.336	.461

Rajai Davis

Bats: R Throws: R Pos: LF-114; RF-24; PR-8; CF-6; PH-6; DH-5   RAHJ-ay   Ht: 5'9" Wt: 195 Born: 10/19/1980 Age: 32

Year	Team	Lg	G	AB	H	2B	3B	HR	(Hm	Rd)	TB	R	RBI	RC	TBB	IBB	SO	HBP	SH	SF	SB	CS	SB%	GDP	Avg	OBP	Slg
2006	Pit	NL	20	14	2	1	0	0	(0	0)	3	1	0	0	2	0	3	0	1	0	1	3	.25	0	.143	.250	.214
2007	2 Tms	NL	75	190	53	11	2	1	(0	1)	71	32	9	26	21	1	28	4	3	1	22	6	.79	1	.279	.361	.374
2008	2 Tms		113	214	52	5	4	3	(0	3)	74	30	19	24	8	0	40	1	2	1	29	6	.83	1	.243	.272	.346
2009	Oak	AL	125	390	119	27	5	3	(1	2)	165	65	48	63	29	0	70	7	2	4	41	12	.77	12	.305	.360	.423
2010	Oak	AL	143	525	149	28	5	5	(5	0)	198	66	52	62	26	0	78	4	1	5	50	11	.82	10	.284	.320	.377
2011	Tor	AL	95	320	76	21	6	1	(1	0)	112	44	29	32	15	0	63	1	1	1	34	11	.76	4	.238	.273	.350
2012	Tor	AL	142	447	115	24	3	8	(5	3)	169	64	43	59	29	3	102	6	1	4	46	13	.78	8	.257	.309	.378
07	Pit	NL	24	48	13	2	1	0	(0	0)	17	6	2	6	7	0	3	0	1	1	5	2	.71	1	.271	.357	.354
07	SF	NL	51	142	40	9	1	1	(0	1)	54	26	7	20	14	1	25	4	2	0	17	4	.81	0	.282	.363	.380
08	SF	NL	12	18	1	0	0	0	(0	0)	1	2	0	0	1	0	6	0	0	0	4	0	1.00	0	.056	.105	.056
08	Oak	AL	101	196	51	5	4	3	(0	3)	73	28	19	24	7	0	34	1	2	1	25	6	.81	1	.260	.288	.372
7 ML YEARS			713	2100	566	117	23	21	(12	9)	792	302	200	266	130	4	384	23	11	16	223	62	.78	36	.270	.317	.377

Wade Davis

Pitches: R Bats: R Pos: RP-54   Ht: 6'5" Wt: 225 Born: 9/7/1985 Age: 27

Year	Team	Lg	G	GS	CG	GF	IP	BFP	H	R	ER	HR	SH	SF	HB	TBB	IBB	SO	WP	Bk	W	L	Pct	Sh	Sv-Op Hld	ERC	ERA
2009	TB	AL	6	6	1	0	36.1	150	33	19	15	2	0	0	0	13	1	36	1	0	2	2	.500	1	0-0 0	3.12	3.72
2010	TB	AL	29	29	0	0	168.0	722	165	77	76	24	3	6	5	62	2	113	4	0	12	10	.545	0	0-0 0	4.25	4.07
2011	TB	AL	29	29	1	0	184.0	795	190	96	91	23	5	7	8	63	1	105	6	0	11	10	.524	0	0-0 0	4.38	4.45
2012	TB	AL	54	0	0	15	70.1	284	48	20	19	5	0	1	0	29	2	87	2	0	3	0	1.000	0	0-1 6	2.25	2.43
Postseason			3	1	0	2	7.1	33	8	2	2	1	0	0	0	4	0	8	0	0	1	0	1.000	0	0-0 0	5.52	2.45
4 ML YEARS			118	64	2	15	458.2	1951	436	212	201	54	8	14	13	167	6	341	13	0	28	22	.560	1	0-1 6	3.88	3.94

Alejandro De Aza

Bats: L Throws: L Pos: CF-125; LF-11; PH-2; PR-2; DH-1   day-AH-zah   Ht: 6'0" Wt: 190 Born: 4/11/1984 Age: 29

Year	Team	Lg	G	AB	H	2B	3B	HR	(Hm	Rd)	TB	R	RBI	RC	TBB	IBB	SO	HBP	SH	SF	SB	CS	SB%	GDP	Avg	OBP	Slg
2012	Charltt*	AAA	5	20	5	1	0	1	(-	-)	9	3	2	2	1	0	3	0	0	0	0	0	-	0	.250	.286	.450
2007	Fla	NL	45	144	33	8	2	0	(0	0)	45	14	8	11	6	1	37	1	5	2	2	0	1.00	2	.229	.261	.313
2009	Fla	NL	22	20	5	1	0	0	(0	0)	6	6	3	4	5	0	5	0	1	0	0	0	-	0	.250	.385	.300
2010	CWS	AL	19	30	9	3	0	0	(0	0)	12	7	2	4	1	0	4	0	1	0	2	1	.67	0	.300	.323	.400
2011	CWS	AL	54	152	50	11	3	4	(2	2)	79	29	23	34	17	1	34	1	1	0	12	5	.71	2	.329	.400	.520
2012	CWS	AL	131	524	147	29	6	9	(2	7)	215	81	50	79	47	3	109	9	4	1	26	12	.68	1	.281	.349	.410
5 ML YEARS			271	870	244	52	11	13	(4	9)	357	137	86	132	76	5	189	11	12	4	42	18	.70	5	.280	.344	.410

Justin De Fratus

Pitches: R Bats: B Pos: RP-13 duh-FRAY-tiss Ht: 6'4" Wt: 220 Born: 10/21/1987 Age: 25

				HOW MUCH HE PITCHED				WHAT HE GAVE UP													THE RESULTS							
Year	Team	Lg	G	GS	CG	GF	IP	BFP	H	R	ER	HR	SH	SF	HB	TBB	IBB	SO	WP	Bk	W	L	Pct	Sh	Sv-Op	Hld	ERC	ERA
2007	Phillies	R	10	8	0	0	46.0	194	51	25	22	1	1	1	2	3	0	34	1	0	2	3	.400	0	0--	-	2.95	4.30
2008	Wmspt	A-	14	14	1	0	83.1	367	87	39	34	1	4	1	2	25	0	74	5	0	6	5	.545	0	0--	-	3.29	3.67
2009	Lakwd	A	36	12	0	5	110.0	454	108	44	39	3	5	4	10	16	1	101	4	0	5	6	.455	0	3--	-	2.87	3.19
2010	Clrwtr	A+	29	0	0	28	40.1	159	31	9	8	1	1	1	2	11	0	43	3	0	2	0	1.000	0	15--	-	2.18	1.79
2010	Rdng	AA	20	0	0	17	24.2	94	17	6	6	2	1	1	0	5	1	28	0	0	1	0	1.000	0	6--	-	1.67	2.19
2011	Rdng	AA	23	0	0	21	34.1	148	28	11	8	1	4	2	3	14	2	43	2	0	4	0	1.000	0	8--	-	2.80	2.10
2011	LV	AAA	28	0	0	18	41.0	170	35	19	17	3	3	1	3	11	1	56	5	0	2	3	.400	0	7--	-	2.84	3.73
2012	Clrwtr	A+	2	1	0	0	2.0	7	2	0	0	0	0	0	0	0	0	1	0	0	0	0	-	0	0--	-	2.31	0.00
2012	Phillies	R	2	1	0	0	2.0	7	2	0	0	0	0	0	0	0	0	1	0	0	0	0	-	0	0--	-	2.31	0.00
2012	LV	AAA	17	0	0	8	21.2	81	15	6	6	2	3	1	0	3	0	22	2	0	0	1	.000	0	3--	-	1.61	2.49
2011	Phi	NL	5	0	0	2	4.0	17	1	2	1	0	1	0	1	3	1	3	1	0	1	0	1.000	0	0-0	-	1.39	2.25
2012	Phi	NL	13	0	0	2	10.2	44	7	5	4	0	0	0	0	5	1	8	1	0	0	0	-	0	0-0	5	1.75	3.38
	2 ML YEARS		18	0	0	4	14.2	61	8	7	5	0	1	0	1	8	2	11	2	0	1	0	1.000	0	0-0	5	1.65	3.07

Ivan De Jesus

Bats: R Throws: R Pos: PH-17; 2B-12; 3B-6; DH-2; SS-1; PR-1 ee-VAHN dey-HEY-soos Ht: 5'11" Wt: 200 Born: 5/1/1987 Age: 26

									BATTING														BASERUNNING				AVERAGES		
Year	Team	Lg	G	AB	H	2B	3B	HR	(Hm	Rd)	TB	R	RBI	RC	TBB	IBB	SO	HBP	SH	SF		SB	CS	SB%	GDP		Avg	OBP	Slg
2005	Ddgrs	R	33	121	41	5	0	0	(-	-)	46	18	11	19	10	0	22	0	1	0		8	2	.80	2		.339	.389	.380
2005	Ogden	R+	20	72	15	1	0	0	(-	-)	16	4	3	4	6	0	18	3	0	0		3	3	.50	1		.208	.296	.222
2006	Clmbs	A	126	483	134	17	2	1	(-	-)	158	65	44	66	63	0	85	4	6	7		16	5	.76	13		.277	.361	.327
2007	InldEm	A+	121	428	123	22	3	4	(-	-)	163	69	52	66	57	1	64	3	9	5		11	6	.65	20		.287	.371	.381
2008	Jaxnvl	AA	128	463	150	22	2	7	(-	-)	197	91	58	93	76	3	81	5	9	7		18	2	.90	18		.324	.419	.425
2009	Ddgrs	R	4	10	2	1	0	0	(-	-)	3	1	3	1	1	0	6	1	0	1		0	0	-	0		.200	.308	.300
2010	Albq	AAA	130	533	158	33	2	7	(-	-)	216	89	70	76	32	0	81	2	7	6		6	1	.86	14		.296	.335	.405
2011	Albq	AAA	100	387	120	19	2	8	(-	-)	167	61	59	68	45	0	68	6	3	2		4	1	.80	19		.310	.389	.432
2012	Albq	AAA	60	224	66	12	3	3	(-	-)	93	32	33	31	14	0	53	1	0	4		1	1	.50	5		.295	.333	.415
2012	Pwtckt	AAA	7	26	10	1	0	0	(-	-)	11	5	0	4	2	0	3	0	0	1		1	0	1.00	0		.385	.429	.423
2011	LAD	NL	17	32	6	0	0	0	(0	0)	6	2	1	1	2	0	11	0	1	0		0	0	-	1		.188	.235	.188
2012	2 Tms		31	41	9	3	0	0	(0	0)	12	5	4	4	3	0	13	0	0	1		1	1	.50	1		.220	.267	.293
12	LAD	NL	23	33	9	3	0	0	(0	0)	12	5	4	4	3	0	7	0	0	1		1	1	.50	1		.273	.324	.364
12	Bos	AL	8	8	0	0	0	0	(0	0)	0	0	0	0	0	0	6	0	0	0		0	0	-	0		.000	.000	.000
	2 ML YEARS		48	73	15	3	0	0	(0	0)	18	7	5	5	5	0	24	0	1	1		1	1	.50	2		.205	.253	.247

Dane de la Rosa

Pitches: R Bats: R Pos: RP-5 Ht: 6'7" Wt: 245 Born: 2/1/1983 Age: 30

				HOW MUCH HE PITCHED				WHAT HE GAVE UP													THE RESULTS							
Year	Team	Lg	G	GS	CG	GF	IP	BFP	H	R	ER	HR	SH	SF	HB	TBB	IBB	SO	WP	Bk	W	L	Pct	Sh	Sv-Op	Hld	ERC	ERA
2003	Yanks	R	5	1	0	2	9.0	37	5	3	3	0	0	0	0	6	0	12	3	1	0	0	-	0	0--	-	2.10	3.00
2004	Yanks	R	14	1	0	5	34.1	149	25	13	11	1	0	1	5	12	0	32	2	0	2	0	1.000	0	1--	-	2.39	2.88
2004	StIsInd	A-	1	0	0	1	1.2	8	1	2	0	0	0	0	0	2	0	1	0	0	0	0	-	0	0--	-	3.97	0.00
2007	Helena	R+	1	0	0	0	2.0	8	1	0	0	0	0	0	0	1	0	3	2	0	0	0	-	0	0--	-	1.41	0.00
2010	Charltt	A+	2	0	0	0	3.0	13	4	1	1	0	0	0	0	1	0	5	2	0	0	0	-	0	0--	-	3.56	3.00
2010	Mont	AA	47	0	0	16	73.0	301	66	20	16	3	6	3	1	26	5	75	8	0	9	3	.750	0	4--	-	3.00	1.97
2011	Drham	AAA	52	0	0	20	70.1	296	63	26	25	8	5	3	4	26	1	84	3	0	6	5	.545	0	6--	-	3.71	3.20
2012	Drham	AAA	54	0	0	36	67.2	277	36	22	21	2	1	2	4	42	1	87	5	0	0	4	.000	0	20--	-	2.21	2.79
2011	TB	AL	7	0	0	2	7.1	34	10	8	8	1	0	0	0	3	0	8	1	0	0	0	-	0	0-0	0	6.62	9.82
2012	TB	AL	5	0	0	5	5.0	22	7	7	7	2	0	0	0	2	0	5	0	0	0	0	-	0	0-0	0	9.62	12.60
	2 ML YEARS		12	0	0	7	12.1	56	17	15	15	3	0	0	0	5	0	13	1	0	0	0	-	0	0-0	0	7.79	10.95

Jorge de la Rosa

Pitches: L Bats: L Pos: SP-3 Ht: 6'1" Wt: 220 Born: 4/5/1981 Age: 32

				HOW MUCH HE PITCHED				WHAT HE GAVE UP													THE RESULTS							
Year	Team	Lg	G	GS	CG	GF	IP	BFP	H	R	ER	HR	SH	SF	HB	TBB	IBB	SO	WP	Bk	W	L	Pct	Sh	Sv-Op	Hld	ERC	ERA
2012	Mdest*	A+	2	2	0	0	5.2	27	7	4	3	0	0	0	0	3	0	7	0	0	0	0	-	0	0--	-	5.03	4.76
2012	Tulsa*	AA	2	2	0	0	5.0	25	8	5	5	0	1	0	0	3	0	5	1	0	0	0	-	0	0--	-	7.85	9.00
2012	ColSpr*	AAA	2	2	0	0	6.2	33	9	8	7	3	0	0	1	3	0	5	0	0	0	1	.000	0	0--	-	9.88	9.45
2012	GdJnct*	R+	1	1	0	0	3.0	12	3	0	0	0	0	0	0	0	0	5	0	0	0	0	-	0	0--	-	1.95	0.00
2004	Mil	NL	5	5	0	0	22.2	113	29	20	16	1	1	3	1	14	0	5	3	0	0	3	.000	0	0-0	0	6.12	6.35
2005	Mil	NL	38	0	0	13	42.1	208	48	23	21	1	2	2	1	38	4	42	6	0	2	2	.500	0	0-2	5	6.04	4.46
2006	2 Tms		28	13	0	4	79.0	367	81	59	57	14	2	4	2	54	1	67	6	1	5	6	.455	0	0-0	1	6.05	6.49
2007	KC	AL	26	23	0	1	130.0	589	160	88	84	20	2	4	3	53	6	82	4	1	8	12	.400	0	0-0	0	5.93	5.82
2008	Col	NL	28	23	0	0	130.0	571	128	77	71	13	6	7	7	42	3	128	14	1	10	8	.556	0	0-0	0	4.50	4.92
2009	Col	NL	33	32	0	0	185.0	799	172	95	90	20	11	6	9	83	3	193	12	1	16	9	.640	0	0-0	0	4.11	4.38
2010	Col	NL	20	20	0	0	121.2	512	105	62	57	15	3	3	5	55	4	113	9	1	8	7	.533	0	0-0	0	3.86	4.22
2011	Col	NL	10	10	1	0	59.0	245	48	25	23	4	4	1	2	22	0	52	6	1	5	2	.714	0	0-0	0	2.88	3.51
2012	Col	NL	3	3	0	0	10.2	53	17	14	11	5	1	0	0	2	0	6	2	0	0	2	.000	0	0-0	0	9.22	9.28
06	Mil	NL	18	3	0	4	30.1	146	32	30	29	4	1	3	1	22	1	31	4	0	2	2	.500	0	0-0	1	5.90	8.60
06	KC	AL	10	10	0	0	48.2	221	49	29	28	10	1	1	1	32	0	36	2	1	3	4	.429	0	0-0	0	6.14	5.18
	9 ML YEARS		191	129	1	18	780.1	3457	788	463	430	93	32	30	29	383	21	688	62	6	54	51	.514	0	0-2	6	4.75	4.96

Rubby de la Rosa

Pitches: R Bats: R Pos: RP-1   ROO-bee   Ht: 5'11" Wt: 205 Born: 3/4/1989 Age: 24

Year	Team	Lg	G	GS	CG	GF	IP	BFP	H	R	ER	HR	SH	SF	HB	TBB	IBB	SO	WP	Bk	W	L	Pct	Sh	Sv-Op	Hld	ERC	ERA
2009	Ddgrs	R	5	2	0	0	16.1	77	17	12	11	0	0	0	2	11	0	22	5	1	0	1	.000	0	0- -	-	5.08	6.06
2010	Gt Lks	A	14	5	0	8	59.1	242	49	23	21	3	0	0	5	17	0	55	7	0	4	1	.800	0	6- -	-	2.75	3.19
2010	Chatt	AA	8	8	0	0	51.0	202	38	12	8	1	3	0	1	21	0	39	2	1	3	1	.750	0	0- -	-	2.44	1.41
2011	Chatt	AA	8	8	0	0	40.0	174	30	19	12	1	1	1	2	19	0	52	1	0	2	2	.500	0	0- -	-	2.59	2.70
2012	RCuca	A+	3	2	0	0	9.0	32	4	0	0	0	0	0	0	3	0	9	0	0	1	0	1.000	0	0- -	-	1.01	0.00
2012	Ddgrs	R	1	1	0	0	3.0	10	1	0	0	0	0	0	0	0	0	3	0	0	0	0	-	0	0- -	-	0.25	0.00
2012	Chatt	AA	2	0	0	0	1.0	7	3	3	3	0	0	0	0	1	0	0	0	0	0	0	-	0	0- -	-	19.55	27.00
2011	LAD	NL	13	10	0	2	60.2	254	54	26	25	6	2	0	0	31	3	60	3	0	4	5	.444	0	0-1	1	3.94	3.71
2012	LAD	NL	1	0	0	0	0.2	4	0	2	2	0	0	0	0	2	0	0	0	0	0	0	-	0	0-0	0	7.00	27.00
	2 ML YEARS		14	10	0	2	61.1	258	54	28	27	6	2	0	0	33	3	60	3	0	4	5	.444	0	0-1	1	3.98	3.96

Fautino De Los Santos

Pitches: R Bats: R Pos: RP-6   faw-TEE-no   Ht: 6'2" Wt: 225 Born: 2/15/1986 Age: 27

Year	Team	Lg	G	GS	CG	GF	IP	BFP	H	R	ER	HR	SH	SF	HB	TBB	IBB	SO	WP	Bk	W	L	Pct	Sh	Sv-Op	Hld	ERC	ERA
2007	Knapol	A	21	15	0	1	97.2	384	49	33	26	5	2	6	8	36	1	121	18	3	9	4	.692	0	0- -	-	1.52	2.40
2007	WinSa	A+	5	5	0	0	24.2	99	20	12	10	3	0	0	1	7	0	32	1	0	1	1	.500	0	0- -	-	2.96	3.65
2008	Stcktn	A+	5	5	0	0	23.0	109	29	17	15	3	2	1	1	11	0	26	5	1	2	2	.500	0	0- -	-	6.28	5.87
2009	As	R	7	7	0	0	11.2	48	12	6	5	0	0	0	1	4	0	16	4	1	0	1	.000	0	0- -	-	3.87	3.86
2010	Stcktn	A+	12	0	0	7	15.2	61	13	4	4	0	0	0	0	3	0	22	0	0	1	0	1.000	0	1- -	-	1.88	2.30
2010	Mdland	AA	25	0	0	10	31.2	144	31	26	23	1	2	0	2	16	1	51	5	0	1	5	.167	0	0- -	-	3.95	6.54
2011	Mdland	AA	8	0	0	6	9.1	40	8	3	3	1	0	0	0	4	1	15	0	0	0	0	-	0	3- -	-	3.22	2.89
2011	Scrmto	AAA	15	0	0	1	19.2	86	18	4	4	0	0	1	0	12	0	21	3	0	0	0	-	0	0- -	-	3.72	1.83
2012	Scrmto	AAA	28	0	0	8	36.0	174	49	30	29	2	2	1	2	16	2	43	5	1	1	3	.250	0	0- -	-	6.04	7.25
2012	Nashv	AAA	11	0	0	3	13.2	61	17	3	3	0	2	0	1	4	2	17	0	0	1	0	1.000	0	0- -	-	4.35	1.98
2011	Oak	AL	34	0	0	8	33.1	143	27	19	16	4	2	1	0	17	1	43	9	0	3	2	.600	0	0-2	3	3.50	4.32
2012	Oak	AL	6	0	0	2	3.0	20	7	2	1	0	0	0	0	3	0	3	1	0	0	0	-	0	0-0	0	13.69	3.00
	2 ML YEARS		40	0	0	10	36.1	163	34	21	17	4	2	1	0	20	1	46	10	0	3	2	.600	0	0-2	3	4.23	4.21

Samuel Deduno

Pitches: R Bats: R Pos: SP-15   deh-DUE-noh   Ht: 6'3" Wt: 190 Born: 7/2/1983 Age: 29

Year	Team	Lg	G	GS	CG	GF	IP	BFP	H	R	ER	HR	SH	SF	HB	TBB	IBB	SO	WP	Bk	W	L	Pct	Sh	Sv-Op	Hld	ERC	ERA
2012	Roch*	AAA	9	9	0	0	42.0	174	27	13	10	2	1	1	4	22	0	46	2	0	1	2	.333	0	0- -	-	2.68	2.14
2010	Col	NL	4	0	0	3	2.2	12	3	1	1	0	0	0	1	0	0	3	0	0	0	0	-	0	0-0	1	6.59	3.38
2011	SD	NL	2	0	0	0	3.0	17	5	1	1	0	0	0	0	3	1	4	1	0	0	0	-	0	0-0	0	8.91	3.00
2012	Min	AL	15	15	0	0	79.0	347	69	40	39	10	1	2	5	53	0	57	5	0	6	5	.545	0	0-0	0	5.03	4.44
	3 ML YEARS		21	15	0	3	84.2	376	77	42	41	11	1	2	5	57	1	64	6	0	6	5	.545	0	0-0	1	5.22	4.36

David DeJesus

Bats: L Throws: L Pos: RF-100; CF-50; PH-12; LF-3   da-HAY-soos   Ht: 5'11" Wt: 190 Born: 12/20/1979 Age: 33

Year	Team	Lg	G	AB	H	2B	3B	HR	(Hm	Rd)	TB	R	RBI	RC	TBB	IBB	SO	HBP	SH	SF	SB	CS	SB%	GDP	Avg	OBP	Slg
2003	KC	AL	12	7	2	0	1	0	(0	0)	4	0	0	2	1	0	2	1	1	0	0	0	-	0	.286	.444	.571
2004	KC	AL	96	363	104	15	3	7	(2	5)	146	58	39	53	33	0	53	9	8	0	8	11	.42	6	.287	.360	.402
2005	KC	AL	122	461	135	31	6	9	(6	3)	205	69	56	77	42	1	76	9	5	6	5	5	.50	6	.293	.359	.445
2006	KC	AL	119	491	145	36	7	8	(4	4)	219	83	56	76	43	4	70	12	2	4	6	3	.67	10	.295	.364	.446
2007	KC	AL	157	605	157	29	9	7	(3	4)	225	101	58	87	64	7	83	23	7	4	10	4	.71	10	.260	.351	.372
2008	KC	AL	135	518	159	25	7	12	(6	6)	234	70	73	93	46	3	71	5	4	4	11	8	.58	10	.307	.366	.452
2009	KC	AL	144	558	157	28	9	13	(4	9)	242	74	71	83	51	0	87	8	5	5	4	9	.31	10	.281	.347	.434
2010	KC	AL	91	352	112	23	3	5	(2	3)	156	46	37	50	34	2	47	4	3	1	3	3	.50	10	.318	.384	.443
2011	Oak	AL	131	442	106	20	5	10	(4	6)	166	60	46	49	45	1	86	11	4	4	4	3	.57	14	.240	.323	.376
2012	ChC	NL	148	506	133	28	8	9	(4	5)	204	76	50	73	61	1	89	9	2	4	7	8	.47	9	.263	.350	.403
	10 ML YEARS		1155	4303	1210	235	58	80	(35	45)	1801	637	486	643	420	19	664	91	41	32	58	54	.52	85	.281	.355	.419

Enerio Del Rosario

Pitches: R Bats: R Pos: RP-19   en-AIR-ee-oh   Ht: 6'2" Wt: 190 Born: 10/16/1985 Age: 27

Year	Team	Lg	G	GS	CG	GF	IP	BFP	H	R	ER	HR	SH	SF	HB	TBB	IBB	SO	WP	Bk	W	L	Pct	Sh	Sv-Op	Hld	ERC	ERA
2012	OKCity*	AAA	36	0	0	9	41.1	187	43	25	23	5	2	1	2	20	2	18	3	0	4	1	.800	0	1- -	0	4.85	5.01
2010	2 Tms	NL	11	0	0	3	10.0	51	17	7	5	0	3	1	4	4	0	4	0	0	1	1	.500	0	0-2	0	7.90	4.50
2011	Hou	NL	54	0	0	13	53.0	250	59	30	27	3	3	1	3	31	3	31	2	1	0	3	.000	0	0-2	2	5.16	4.58
2012	Hou	NL	19	0	0	3	19.0	97	34	21	19	1	0	2	2	7	0	11	0	0	0	0	-	0	0-0	1	8.99	9.00
10	Cin	NL	9	0	0	2	8.2	42	13	4	2	0	3	1	0	4	0	3	0	0	1	1	.500	0	0-2	0	6.48	2.08
10	Hou	NL	2	0	0	1	1.1	9	4	3	3	0	0	0	1	0	0	1	0	0	0	0	-	0	0-0	0	18.29	20.25
	3 ML YEARS		84	0	0	19	82.0	398	110	58	51	4	6	4	6	42	3	46	2	1	1	4	.200	0	0-4	3	6.32	5.60

Steve Delabar

Pitches: R **Bats:** R **Pos:** RP-61 — DELL-uh-bar — **Ht:** 6'5" **Wt:** 220 **Born:** 7/17/1983 **Age:** 29

Year	Team	Lg	G	GS	CG	GF	IP	BFP	H	R	ER	HR	SH	SF	HB	TBB	IBB	SO	WP	Bk	W	L	Pct	Sh	Sv-Op	Hld	ERC	ERA
2004	Padres	R	14	6	0	1	45.1	200	51	32	22	1	3	2	6	21	0	39	2	1	3	4	.429	0	0--	-	5.21	4.37
2004	Eugene	A-	3	3	0	0	17.0	69	13	7	5	1	0	1	1	3	0	11	0	0	1	1	.500	0	0--	-	1.94	2.65
2005	Eugene	A-	16	16	0	0	75.2	340	84	45	40	7	2	4	15	18	0	59	4	0	4	6	.400	0	0--	-	4.74	4.76
2006	FtWyn	A	27	27	1	0	145.0	613	129	66	55	8	1	6	7	65	0	118	12	1	8	9	.471	0	0--	-	3.59	3.41
2007	Lk Els	A+	20	0	0	5	29.0	131	26	21	18	5	0	3	2	16	1	33	3	1	2	6	.250	0	0--	-	4.73	5.59
2007	FtWyn	A	21	12	0	1	68.0	318	63	49	45	8	0	5	13	46	0	48	6	0	2	5	.286	0	0--	-	5.68	5.96
2008	FtWyn	A	11	0	0	4	13.2	59	17	8	8	0	0	0	1	5	1	12	0	0	2	1	.667	0	0--	-	5.03	5.27
2011	Hi Dsrt	A+	7	0	0	4	12.1	59	12	6	6	0	0	0	2	8	0	20	3	0	1	1	.500	0	3--	-	4.61	4.38
2011	Jacksn	AA	23	0	0	17	30.2	139	23	10	7	0	2	0	1	26	3	30	0	0	1	3	.250	0	12--	-	3.57	2.05
2011	Tacom	AAA	10	0	0	7	13.0	58	11	1	1	0	1	0	2	6	1	18	2	0	1	1	.500	0	0--	-	3.12	0.69
2012	Tacom	AAA	9	0	0	3	12.0	60	11	10	5	0	0	1	1	12	0	12	1	1	0	1	.000	0	1--	-	5.31	3.75
2011	Sea	AL	6	0	0	4	7.0	28	5	2	2	1	0	0	1	4	1	7	0	0	1	1	.500	0	0-0	0	4.15	2.57
2012	2 Tms	AL	61	0	0	12	66.0	274	46	29	28	12	3	2	5	26	1	92	6	0	4	3	.571	0	0-2	12	3.18	3.82
12	Sea	AL	34	0	0	11	36.2	148	23	17	17	9	2	0	5	11	1	46	3	0	2	1	.667	0	0-2	3	3.07	4.17
12	Tor	AL	27	0	0	1	29.1	126	23	12	11	3	1	2	0	15	0	46	3	0	2	2	.500	0	0-0	9	3.27	3.38
	2 ML YEARS		67	0	0	16	73.0	302	51	31	30	13	3	2	6	30	2	99	6	0	5	4	.556	0	0-2	12	3.27	3.70

Randall Delgado

Pitches: R **Bats:** R **Pos:** SP-17; RP-1 — **Ht:** 6'3" **Wt:** 200 **Born:** 2/9/1990 **Age:** 23

Year	Team	Lg	G	GS	CG	GF	IP	BFP	H	R	ER	HR	SH	SF	HB	TBB	IBB	SO	WP	Bk	W	L	Pct	Sh	Sv-Op	Hld	ERC	ERA
2008	Danvle	R	14	14	0	0	69.0	292	63	32	24	5	2	2	5	30	1	81	9	2	3	8	.273	0	0--	-	3.89	3.13
2009	Rome	A	25	25	1	0	124.0	542	123	70	60	9	2	4	6	49	0	141	7	2	5	10	.333	0	0--	-	3.97	4.35
2010	MrtlBh	A+	20	20	0	0	117.1	469	89	46	36	7	6	1	7	32	1	120	6	0	4	7	.364	0	0--	-	2.32	2.76
2010	Missi	AA	8	8	0	0	43.2	190	36	26	23	2	3	3	2	20	0	42	2	0	3	5	.375	0	0--	-	3.05	4.74
2011	Missi	AA	21	21	2	0	117.1	508	116	58	50	11	5	3	4	46	1	110	5	3	5	5	.500	0	0--	-	4.05	3.84
2011	Gwnntt	AAA	4	4	0	0	21.2	92	19	10	10	4	0	1	0	11	0	25	2	1	2	2	.500	0	0--	-	4.47	4.15
2012	Gwnntt	AAA	8	8	1	0	44.1	195	47	20	20	6	0	2	1	21	0	51	3	0	4	3	.571	0	0--	-	5.15	4.06
2011	Atl	NL	7	7	0	0	35.0	147	29	12	11	5	0	0	1	14	1	18	2	0	1	1	.500	0	0-0	0	3.48	2.83
2012	Atl	NL	18	17	0	0	92.2	401	89	48	45	8	5	3	4	42	4	76	5	1	4	9	.308	0	0-0	0	4.10	4.37
	2 ML YEARS		25	24	0	0	127.2	548	118	60	56	13	5	3	5	56	5	94	7	1	5	10	.333	0	0-0	0	3.93	3.95

Sam Demel

Pitches: R **Bats:** R **Pos:** RP-1 — DEMM-ell — **Ht:** 6'0" **Wt:** 205 **Born:** 10/23/1985 **Age:** 27

Year	Team	Lg	G	GS	CG	GF	IP	BFP	H	R	ER	HR	SH	SF	HB	TBB	IBB	SO	WP	Bk	W	L	Pct	Sh	Sv-Op	Hld	ERC	ERA
2012	Reno*	AAA	56	0	0	11	66.1	278	60	34	30	11	2	0	1	22	3	75	4	0	1	4	.200	0	1--	-	3.70	4.07
2010	Ari	NL	37	0	0	10	37.0	165	42	27	22	5	0	1	1	12	2	33	5	0	2	1	.667	0	2-2	4	4.73	5.35
2011	Ari	NL	34	0	0	7	25.2	117	31	13	12	4	0	0	2	13	1	15	0	0	2	2	.500	0	0-1	6	6.64	4.21
2012	Ari	NL	1	0	0	1	1.0	6	2	1	1	0	1	0	0	1	1	0	0	0	0	1	.000	0	0-0	0	9.49	9.00
	3 ML YEARS		72	0	0	18	63.2	288	75	41	35	9	1	1	3	26	4	48	5	0	4	4	.500	0	2-3	10	5.55	4.95

Ryan Dempster

Pitches: R **Bats:** R **Pos:** SP-28 — **Ht:** 6'2" **Wt:** 215 **Born:** 5/3/1977 **Age:** 36

Year	Team	Lg	G	GS	CG	GF	IP	BFP	H	R	ER	HR	SH	SF	HB	TBB	IBB	SO	WP	Bk	W	L	Pct	Sh	Sv-Op	Hld	ERC	ERA
1998	Fla	NL	14	11	0	1	54.2	272	72	47	43	6	5	6	9	38	1	35	5	0	1	5	.167	0	0-1	0	8.14	7.08
1999	Fla	NL	25	25	0	0	147.0	666	146	77	77	21	3	6	6	93	1	126	8	0	7	8	.467	0	0-0	0	5.49	4.71
2000	Fla	NL	33	33	2	0	226.1	974	210	102	92	30	4	5	5	97	7	209	4	0	14	10	.583	1	0-0	0	4.04	3.66
2001	Fla	NL	34	34	2	0	211.1	954	218	123	116	21	15	7	10	112	5	171	5	0	15	12	.556	1	0-0	0	4.91	4.94
2002	2 Tms	NL	33	33	4	0	209.0	915	228	127	125	28	9	6	10	98	2	153	2	0	10	13	.435	0	0-0	0	5.35	5.38
2003	Cin	NL	22	20	0	1	115.2	545	134	89	84	14	9	4	5	70	4	84	3	0	3	7	.300	0	0-0	0	6.11	6.54
2004	ChC	NL	23	0	0	8	20.2	93	16	9	9	1	1	0	2	13	0	18	1	0	1	1	.500	0	0-2	3	3.61	3.92
2005	ChC	NL	63	6	0	53	92.0	401	83	35	32	4	5	0	4	49	7	89	4	0	5	3	.625	0	33-35	0	3.69	3.13
2006	ChC	NL	74	0	0	64	75.0	342	77	47	40	5	5	4	3	36	3	67	6	0	1	9	.100	0	24-33	2	4.26	4.80
2007	ChC	NL	66	0	0	58	66.2	282	59	36	35	8	3	2	1	30	4	55	2	1	2	7	.222	0	28-31	0	3.77	4.73
2008	ChC	NL	33	33	1	0	206.2	856	174	75	68	14	4	3	7	76	1	187	5	0	17	6	.739	0	0-0	0	3.03	2.96
2009	ChC	NL	31	31	1	0	200.0	842	196	94	81	22	10	8	6	65	4	172	11	0	11	9	.550	1	0-0	0	3.87	3.65
2010	ChC	NL	34	34	1	0	215.1	918	198	110	92	25	9	2	10	86	4	208	6	0	15	12	.556	0	0-0	0	3.91	3.85
2011	ChC	NL	34	34	0	0	202.1	881	211	111	108	23	12	3	5	82	2	191	7	0	10	14	.417	0	0-0	0	4.55	4.80
2012	2 Tms	NL	28	28	0	0	173.0	717	155	71	65	19	5	4	2	52	0	153	2	1	12	8	.600	0	0-0	0	3.23	3.38
02	Fla	NL	18	18	3	0	120.1	521	126	66	64	12	7	3	7	55	1	87	0	0	5	8	.385	0	0-0	0	4.95	4.79
02	Cin	NL	15	15	1	0	88.2	394	102	61	61	16	2	3	3	38	1	66	2	0	5	5	.500	0	0-0	0	5.90	6.19
12	ChC	NL	16	16	0	0	104.0	417	81	28	26	9	2	1	1	27	0	83	0	1	5	5	.500	0	0-0	0	2.34	2.25
12	Tex	AL	12	12	0	0	69.0	300	74	43	39	10	3	3	1	25	0	70	2	0	7	3	.700	0	0-0	0	4.73	5.09
	Postseason		2	1	0	1	5.2	27	4	4	4	1	0	0	0	7	0	4	0	0	1	0	.000	0	0-0	0	6.45	6.35
	15 ML YEARS		547	322	11	185	2215.2	9658	2177	1153	1067	241	99	60	85	992	46	1918	71	2	124	124	.500	3	87-102	5	4.36	4.33

Chris Denorfia

Bats: R **Throws:** R **Pos:** RF-79; LF-53; PH-33; CF-9; PR-1   denn-ORE-fee-ah   **Ht:** 6'0" **Wt:** 195 **Born:** 7/15/1980 **Age:** 32

Year	Team	Lg	G	AB	H	2B	3B	HR	(Hm	Rd)	TB	R	RBI	RC	TBB	IBB	SO	HBP	SH	SF	SB	CS	SB%	GDP	Avg	OBP	Slg
2005	Cin	NL	18	38	10	3	0	1	(1	0)	16	8	2	3	6	0	9	0	0	0	1	0	1.00	1	.263	.364	.421
2006	Cin	NL	49	106	30	6	0	1	(0	1)	39	14	7	13	11	1	21	1	2	0	1	1	.50	1	.283	.356	.368
2008	Oak	AL	29	62	18	3	0	1	(0	1)	24	10	9	9	6	0	16	1	2	0	2	0	1.00	3	.290	.362	.387
2009	Oak	AL	4	2	0	0	0	0	(0	0)	0	1	1	0	0	0	0	0	0	0	0	0	-	0	.000	.000	.000
2010	SD	NL	99	284	77	15	2	9	(3	6)	123	41	36	37	27	3	51	2	1	3	8	4	.67	5	.271	.335	.433
2011	SD	NL	111	307	85	13	2	5	(1	4)	117	38	19	34	28	1	49	1	2	2	11	6	.65	10	.277	.337	.381
2012	SD	NL	130	348	102	19	6	8	(3	5)	157	56	36	49	27	0	52	2	2	3	13	5	.72	9	.293	.345	.451
7 ML YEARS			440	1147	322	59	10	25	(8	17)	476	168	110	145	105	5	198	7	9	8	36	16	.69	29	.281	.343	.415

Mark DeRosa

Bats: R **Throws:** R **Pos:** PH-24; 3B-11; LF-9; RF-7; 1B-3; 2B-1; SS-1; PR-1   **Ht:** 6'1" **Wt:** 215 **Born:** 2/26/1975 **Age:** 38

Year	Team	Lg	G	AB	H	2B	3B	HR	(Hm	Rd)	TB	R	RBI	RC	TBB	IBB	SO	HBP	SH	SF	SB	CS	SB%	GDP	Avg	OBP	Slg
2012 Ptomc*		A+	4	11	1	0	0	0	(-	-)	1	1	2	0	4	0	3	0	0	0	0	0	-	0	.091	.333	.091
1998	Atl	NL	5	3	1	0	0	0	(0	0)	1	2	0	0	0	0	1	0	0	0	0	0	-	0	.333	.333	.333
1999	Atl	NL	7	8	0	0	0	0	(0	0)	0	0	0	0	0	0	2	0	0	0	0	0	-	0	.000	.000	.000
2000	Atl	NL	22	13	4	1	0	0	(0	0)	5	9	3	2	2	0	1	0	0	0	0	0	-	0	.308	.400	.385
2001	Atl	NL	66	164	47	8	0	3	(3	0)	64	27	20	22	12	6	19	5	1	2	2	1	.67	3	.287	.350	.390
2002	Atl	NL	72	212	63	9	2	5	(3	2)	91	24	23	27	12	3	24	3	2	3	2	3	.40	5	.297	.339	.429
2003	Atl	NL	103	266	70	14	0	6	(3	3)	102	40	22	28	16	0	49	5	0	1	1	0	1.00	6	.263	.316	.383
2004	Atl	NL	118	309	74	16	0	3	(0	3)	99	33	31	24	23	3	53	3	4	6	1	3	.25	6	.239	.293	.320
2005	Tex	AL	66	148	36	5	0	8	(1	7)	65	26	20	20	16	0	35	2	0	0	1	0	1.00	5	.243	.325	.439
2006	Tex	AL	136	520	154	40	2	13	(5	8)	237	78	74	78	44	1	102	6	0	2	4	4	.50	13	.296	.357	.456
2007	ChC	NL	149	502	147	28	3	10	(5	5)	211	64	72	76	58	2	93	7	3	4	1	2	.33	17	.293	.371	.420
2008	ChC	NL	149	505	144	30	3	21	(11	10)	243	103	87	95	69	0	106	9	2	8	6	0	1.00	9	.285	.376	.481
2009	2 Tms		139	515	129	23	1	23	(11	12)	223	78	78	68	47	1	121	7	2	5	3	2	.60	11	.250	.319	.433
2010	SF	NL	26	93	18	3	0	1	(0	1)	24	9	10	6	9	0	16	2	0	0	0	2	.00	6	.194	.279	.258
2011	SF	NL	47	86	24	2	0	0	(0	0)	26	9	12	10	8	0	18	2	0	1	1	1	.50	4	.279	.351	.302
2012	Was	NL	48	85	16	5	0	0	(0	0)	21	13	6	5	14	0	18	0	1	1	1	0	1.00	5	.188	.300	.247
09	Cle	AL	71	278	75	13	0	13	(8	5)	127	47	50	45	29	1	63	3	1	3	1	1	.50	6	.270	.342	.457
09	StL	NL	68	237	54	10	1	10	(3	7)	96	31	28	23	18	0	58	4	1	2	2	1	.67	5	.228	.291	.405
Postseason			22	53	19	6	1	1	(1	0)	30	8	10	7	4	0	8	1	0	0	0	0	-	2	.358	.414	.566
15 ML YEARS			1153	3429	927	184	11	93	(48	45)	1412	515	458	461	330	16	658	51	15	33	23	18	.56	88	.270	.340	.412

Daniel Descalso

Bats: L **Throws:** R **Pos:** 2B-96; SS-26; PH-23; 3B-22; 1B-5; PR-3   dess-CAL-so   **Ht:** 5'10" **Wt:** 190 **Born:** 10/19/1986 **Age:** 26

Year	Team	Lg	G	AB	H	2B	3B	HR	(Hm	Rd)	TB	R	RBI	RC	TBB	IBB	SO	HBP	SH	SF	SB	CS	SB%	GDP	Avg	OBP	Slg
2010	StL	NL	11	34	9	2	0	0	(0	0)	11	6	4	5	2	0	6	1	0	0	1	0	1.00	0	.265	.324	.324
2011	StL	NL	148	326	86	20	3	1	(1	0)	115	35	28	40	33	9	65	3	10	3	2	2	.50	3	.264	.334	.353
2012	StL	NL	143	374	85	10	7	4	(0	4)	121	41	26	29	37	3	83	5	7	3	6	3	.67	5	.227	.303	.324
Postseason			13	9	3	0	0	0	(0	0)	3	3	0	1	0	0	2	0	2	0	0	0	-	0	.333	.333	.333
3 ML YEARS			302	734	180	32	10	5	(1	4)	247	82	58	74	72	12	154	9	17	6	9	5	.64	8	.245	.318	.337

Ian Desmond

Bats: R **Throws:** R **Pos:** SS-128; PH-3; PR-1   **Ht:** 6'2" **Wt:** 205 **Born:** 9/20/1985 **Age:** 27

Year	Team	Lg	G	AB	H	2B	3B	HR	(Hm	Rd)	TB	R	RBI	RC	TBB	IBB	SO	HBP	SH	SF	SB	CS	SB%	GDP	Avg	OBP	Slg
2009	Was	NL	21	82	23	7	2	4	(2	2)	46	9	12	10	5	0	14	0	1	1	1	0	1.00	2	.280	.318	.561
2010	Was	NL	154	525	141	27	4	10	(8	2)	206	59	65	58	28	3	109	5	9	7	17	5	.77	9	.269	.308	.392
2011	Was	NL	154	584	148	27	5	8	(7	1)	209	65	49	65	35	2	139	4	11	5	25	10	.71	9	.253	.298	.358
2012	Was	NL	130	513	150	33	2	25	(16	9)	262	72	73	73	30	1	113	3	0	1	21	6	.78	17	.292	.335	.511
4 ML YEARS			459	1704	462	94	13	47	(33	14)	723	205	199	206	98	6	375	12	21	14	64	21	.75	37	.271	.313	.424

Ross Detwiler

Pitches: L **Bats:** R **Pos:** SP-27; RP-6   DETT-why-lerr   **Ht:** 6'5" **Wt:** 190 **Born:** 3/6/1986 **Age:** 27

			HOW MUCH HE PITCHED					WHAT HE GAVE UP												THE RESULTS						
Year	Team	Lg	G	GS	CG	GF	IP	BFP	H	R	ER	HR	SH	SF	HB	TBB	IBB	SO	WP	Bk	W	L	Pct	Sh	Sv-Op	Hld	ERC	ERA
2007	Was	NL	1	0	0	1	1.0	4	0	0	0	0	0	0	0	0	0	1	0	0	0	0	-	0	0-0	0	0.00	0.00
2009	Was	NL	15	14	1	0	75.2	341	87	43	42	3	4	1	2	33	3	43	4	0	1	6	.143	0	0-0	0	4.65	5.00
2010	Was	NL	8	5	0	1	29.2	135	34	22	14	5	2	0	1	14	1	17	1	0	1	3	.250	0	0-0	0	5.83	4.25
2011	Was	NL	15	10	0	0	66.0	277	63	26	22	7	7	3	0	20	2	41	2	0	4	5	.444	0	0-0	1	3.64	3.00
2012	Was	NL	33	27	0	1	164.1	686	149	75	62	15	8	3	5	52	0	105	4	1	10	8	.556	0	0-0	1	3.30	3.40
5 ML YEARS			72	56	1	3	336.2	1443	333	166	140	30	21	7	11	119	6	207	11	1	16	22	.421	0	0-0	2	3.85	3.74

Joey Devine

Pitches: R **Bats:** R **Pos:** P **Ht:** 6'0" **Wt:** 235 **Born:** 9/19/1983 **Age:** 29

Year	Team	Lg				HOW MUCH HE PITCHED					WHAT HE GAVE UP									THE RESULTS					
			G	GS	CG	GF	IP	BFP	H	R	ER	HR	SH	SF	HB	TBB	IBB	SO	WP	Bk	W	L	Pct	Sh	Sv-Op	Hld	ERC	ERA
2005	Atl	NL	5	0	0	1	5.0	26	6	7	7	2	0	0	0	5	1	3	0	0	0	1	.000	0	0-0	1	9.97	12.60
2006	Atl	NL	10	0	0	1	6.1	36	8	7	7	1	0	0	1	9	1	10	4	1	0	0	-	0	0-1	0	11.11	9.95
2007	Atl	NL	10	0	0	5	8.1	39	7	1	1	0	1	1	0	8	2	7	1	0	1	0	1.000	0	0-0	0	4.08	1.08
2008	Oak	AL	42	0	0	10	45.2	170	23	7	3	0	1	1	0	15	2	49	0	0	6	1	.857	0	1-2	11	1.09	0.59
2011	Oak	AL	26	0	0	3	23.0	100	18	9	9	0	1	2	2	11	0	20	0	0	1	1	.500	0	0-1	7	2.76	3.52
	Postseason		3	0	0	1	1.2	10	3	2	2	1	0	0	1	1	1	3	0	0	0	1	.000	0	0-0	0	16.60	10.80
	5 ML YEARS		93	0	0	20	88.1	371	62	31	27	3	3	4	3	48	6	89	5	1	8	3	.727	0	1-4	19	2.60	2.75

Cole DeVries

Pitches: R **Bats:** R **Pos:** SP-16; RP-1 **Ht:** 6'2" **Wt:** 180 **Born:** 2/12/1985 **Age:** 28

Year	Team	Lg				HOW MUCH HE PITCHED					WHAT HE GAVE UP									THE RESULTS					
			G	GS	CG	GF	IP	BFP	H	R	ER	HR	SH	SF	HB	TBB	IBB	SO	WP	Bk	W	L	Pct	Sh	Sv-Op	Hld	ERC	ERA
2007	Beloit	A	27	25	0	0	148.0	637	161	73	56	17	1	2	4	36	0	108	6	0	9	5	.643	0	0- -	-	4.12	3.41
2008	FtMyrs	A+	24	23	1	0	135.1	572	138	51	44	8	3	4	4	38	0	105	0	0	10	9	.526	0	0- -	-	3.57	2.93
2009	NwBrit	AA	26	26	1	0	137.2	613	162	88	74	16	1	4	6	46	2	90	7	0	7	14	.333	0	0- -	-	5.10	4.84
2010	Roch	AAA	39	2	0	16	68.1	314	87	53	44	10	2	2	3	25	0	63	6	0	1	5	.167	0	1- -	-	6.06	5.80
2010	Roch	AAA	9	3	0	3	23.1	109	25	17	15	2	1	0	0	14	1	24	3	1	0	3	.000	0	0- -	-	4.97	5.79
2011	NwBrit	AA	15	0	0	12	27.2	105	17	9	7	3	0	0	0	5	0	33	1	0	0	0	-	0	9- -	-	1.49	2.28
2011	Roch	AAA	30	2	0	10	62.1	270	74	30	27	4	2	2	0	18	2	42	0	0	4	2	.667	0	0- -	-	4.43	3.90
2012	Roch	AAA	12	12	0	0	70.0	290	75	37	34	7	2	2	1	10	0	50	1	1	3	5	.375	0	0- -	-	3.52	4.37
2012	Min	AL	17	16	0	1	87.2	375	88	48	40	16	4	0	4	18	0	58	1	0	5	5	.500	0	0-0	0	3.95	4.11

Blake DeWitt

Bats: L **Throws:** R **Pos:** PH-13; 2B-4; LF-1 **Ht:** 5'11" **Wt:** 195 **Born:** 8/20/1985 **Age:** 27

Year	Team	Lg						BATTING													BASERUNNING				AVERAGES		
			G	AB	H	2B	3B	HR	(Hm	Rd)	TB	R	RBI	RC	TBB	IBB	SO	HBP	SH	SF	SB	CS	SB%	GDP	Avg	OBP	Slg
2012	Iowa*	AAA	30	102	13	3	0	0	(-	-)	16	5	5	3	14	0	23	2	0	0	0	0	-	0	.127	.246	.157
2008	LAD	NL	117	368	97	13	2	9	(5	4)	141	45	52	51	45	9	68	3	0	5	3	0	1.00	6	.264	.344	.383
2009	LAD	NL	31	49	10	3	0	2	(1	1)	19	4	4	1	3	0	7	0	0	1	0	0	-	2	.204	.245	.388
2010	2 Tms	NL	135	440	115	24	5	5	(4	1)	164	47	52	62	47	8	86	4	2	3	3	2	.60	5	.261	.336	.373
2011	ChC	NL	121	230	61	11	4	5	(2	3)	95	21	26	25	12	1	31	1	0	0	1	0	1.00	6	.265	.305	.413
2012	ChC	NL	18	29	4	1	0	0	(0	0)	5	1	1	0	0	0	2	0	0	1	0	0	-	1	.138	.133	.172
10	LAD	NL	82	256	69	15	4	1	(1	0)	95	29	30	36	30	4	49	3	2	1	2	2	.50	4	.270	.352	.371
10	ChC	NL	53	184	46	9	1	4	(3	1)	69	18	22	26	17	4	37	1	0	2	1	0	1.00	1	.250	.314	.375
	Postseason		8	24	4	2	1	0	(0	0)	8	2	6	0	1	0	6	0	0	1	0	0	-	3	.167	.192	.333
	5 ML YEARS		422	1116	287	52	11	21	(12	9)	424	118	135	139	107	18	194	8	2	10	7	2	.78	20	.257	.324	.380

Scott Diamond

Pitches: L **Bats:** L **Pos:** SP-27 **Ht:** 6'3" **Wt:** 220 **Born:** 7/30/1986 **Age:** 26

Year	Team	Lg				HOW MUCH HE PITCHED					WHAT HE GAVE UP									THE RESULTS					
			G	GS	CG	GF	IP	BFP	H	R	ER	HR	SH	SF	HB	TBB	IBB	SO	WP	Bk	W	L	Pct	Sh	Sv-Op	Hld	ERC	ERA
2008	Rome	A	9	9	0	0	52.2	210	47	20	18	2	0	2	1	11	0	38	1	0	3	1	.750	0	0- -	-	2.52	3.08
2008	MrtlBh	A+	17	15	1	0	100.0	425	95	42	31	6	4	2	4	28	0	85	6	0	12	2	.857	1	0- -	-	3.17	2.79
2009	Missi	AA	23	23	0	0	131.0	583	152	68	51	5	6	5	2	53	0	111	4	0	5	10	.333	0	0- -	-	4.63	3.50
2010	Missi	AA	17	17	0	0	102.1	442	113	45	40	4	4	4	2	40	1	89	5	0	4	6	.400	0	0- -	-	4.34	3.52
2010	Gwnntt	AAA	10	10	1	0	56.1	226	53	25	21	2	3	3	1	15	0	33	4	0	4	1	.800	1	0- -	-	3.00	3.36
2011	Roch	AAA	23	23	2	0	123.0	553	158	85	76	11	2	6	1	36	2	90	4	1	4	14	.222	0	0- -	-	5.19	5.56
2012	Roch	AAA	6	6	0	0	34.2	141	35	12	10	1	3	0	1	7	1	26	0	0	4	1	.800	0	0- -	-	3.04	2.60
2011	Min	AL	7	7	0	0	39.0	181	51	25	22	3	2	1	0	17	3	19	3	0	1	5	.167	0	0-0	0	5.69	5.08
2012	Min	AL	27	27	1	0	173.0	714	184	76	68	17	3	5	4	31	2	90	10	0	12	9	.571	1	0-0	0	3.68	3.54
	2 ML YEARS		34	34	1	0	212.0	895	235	101	90	20	5	6	4	48	5	109	13	0	13	14	.481	1	0-0	0	4.04	3.82

Juan Diaz

Bats: B **Throws:** R **Pos:** SS-5 **Ht:** 6'4" **Wt:** 200 **Born:** 12/12/1988 **Age:** 24

Year	Team	Lg						BATTING													BASERUNNING				AVERAGES		
			G	AB	H	2B	3B	HR	(Hm	Rd)	TB	R	RBI	RC	TBB	IBB	SO	HBP	SH	SF	SB	CS	SB%	GDP	Avg	OBP	Slg
2007	Hi Dsrt	A+	6	20	3	0	1	0	(-	-)	5	1	2	0	2	0	8	0	0	0	0	0	-	1	.150	.227	.250
2007	Wisc	A	75	259	59	12	0	1	(-	-)	74	22	18	19	19	0	53	3	6	0	2	10	.17	7	.228	.288	.286
2008	Wisc	A	122	451	105	16	4	3	(-	-)	138	38	45	38	28	1	86	1	9	8	6	5	.55	8	.233	.275	.306
2009	Hi Dsrt	A+	84	325	101	22	5	4	(-	-)	145	55	29	52	23	0	65	0	3	0	5	2	.71	3	.311	.356	.446
2009	Ms	R	1	3	3	0	0	1	(-	-)	6	3	1	3	1	0	0	0	0	0	0	0	-	0	1.000	1.000	2.000
2010	Hi Dsrt	A+	70	254	75	8	3	7	(-	-)	110	36	41	39	19	0	45	1	1	1	8	2	.80	3	.295	.345	.433
2010	Knstn	A+	61	218	59	7	1	1	(-	-)	71	17	19	23	15	0	51	0	5	0	2	2	.50	2	.271	.318	.326
2011	Akron	AA	133	522	133	24	4	9	(-	-)	192	64	60	63	40	2	116	3	1	3	9	2	.82	15	.255	.310	.368
2012	Akron	AA	96	371	96	24	2	11	(-	-)	157	51	52	49	25	1	95	3	4	2	1	3	.25	8	.259	.309	.423
2012	Clmbs	AAA	19	72	22	5	0	2	(-	-)	33	12	11	11	4	0	18	0	0	0	0	0	-	3	.306	.342	.458
2012	Cle	AL	5	15	4	0	0	0	(0	0)	4	4	0	0	1	0	5	1	0	0	0	0	-	3	.267	.353	.267

Matt Diaz

Bats: R **Throws:** R **Pos:** PH-27; LF-19; RF-6; DH-2   DYE-azz   **Ht:** 6'0" **Wt:** 215 **Born:** 3/3/1978 **Age:** 35

								BATTING												BASERUNNING				AVERAGES		
Year	Team	Lg	G	AB	H	2B	3B	HR	(Hm	Rd)	TB	R	RBI	RC	TBB	IBB	SO	HBP	SH	SF	SB	CS	SB%	GDP	Avg	OBP	Slg
2003	TB	AL	4	9	1	0	0	0	(0	0)	1	2	0	0	1	0	3	0	0	0	0	0	-	0	.111	.200	.111
2004	TB	AL	10	21	4	1	1	1	(1	0)	10	3	3	2	1	0	6	2	0	0	0	0	-	0	.190	.292	.476
2005	KC	AL	34	89	25	4	2	1	(0	1)	36	7	9	11	4	0	15	2	1	1	0	1	.00	3	.281	.323	.404
2006	Atl	NL	124	297	97	15	4	7	(3	4)	141	37	32	40	11	3	49	9	1	4	5	5	.50	9	.327	.364	.475
2007	Atl	NL	135	358	121	21	0	12	(5	7)	178	44	45	53	16	3	63	4	1	5	4	0	1.00	8	.338	.368	.497
2008	Atl	NL	43	135	33	2	0	2	(2	0)	41	9	14	10	3	0	32	1	0	1	4	2	.67	4	.244	.264	.304
2009	Atl	NL	125	371	116	18	4	13	(4	9)	181	56	58	67	35	2	90	13	5	1	12	5	.71	14	.313	.390	.488
2010	Atl	NL	84	224	56	17	2	7	(5	2)	98	27	31	30	13	3	44	4	2	1	3	1	.75	6	.250	.302	.438
2011	2 Tms		116	251	66	13	1	0	(0	0)	81	16	20	20	12	0	52	3	0	2	5	2	.71	11	.263	.302	.323
2012	Atl	NL	51	108	24	6	0	2	(1	1)	36	10	13	8	9	1	21	0	0	1	0	0	-	4	.222	.280	.333
11	Pit	NL	100	216	56	12	1	0	(0	0)	70	14	19	19	11	0	44	3	0	1	4	2	.67	8	.259	.303	.324
11	Atl	NL	16	35	10	1	0	0	(0	0)	11	2	1	1	1	0	8	0	0	1	1	0	1.00	3	.286	.297	.314
	Postseason		4	10	1	0	0	0	(0	0)	1	0	0	0	0	0	2	0	0	0	0	0	-	0	.100	.100	.100
	10 ML YEARS		726	1863	543	97	14	45	(21	24)	803	211	225	241	105	12	375	38	10	16	33	16	.67	59	.291	.339	.431

Chris Dickerson

Bats: L **Throws:** L **Pos:** LF-18; PR-6; RF-5; PH-3; CF-2   **Ht:** 6'4" **Wt:** 230 **Born:** 4/10/1982 **Age:** 31

								BATTING												BASERUNNING				AVERAGES		
Year	Team	Lg	G	AB	H	2B	3B	HR	(Hm	Rd)	TB	R	RBI	RC	TBB	IBB	SO	HBP	SH	SF	SB	CS	SB%	GDP	Avg	OBP	Slg
2012	S-WB*	AAA	69	266	84	24	4	7	(-	-)	137	57	25	61	49	0	73	1	0	5	17	3	.85	4	.316	.417	.515
2008	Cin	NL	31	102	31	9	2	6	(4	2)	62	20	15	22	17	0	35	2	1	0	5	3	.63	0	.304	.413	.608
2009	Cin	NL	97	255	70	13	3	2	(0	2)	95	31	15	34	39	1	66	1	2	2	11	3	.79	3	.275	.370	.373
2010	2 Tms		45	97	20	2	2	0	(0	0)	26	11	5	6	6	0	34	0	2	1	4	0	1.00	1	.206	.250	.268
2011	NYY	AL	60	50	13	2	0	1	(0	1)	18	9	7	6	2	0	17	1	1	1	4	0	1.00	1	.260	.296	.360
2012	NYY	AL	25	14	4	0	0	2	(1	1)	10	5	5	4	3	0	5	0	0	0	3	0	1.00	1	.286	.412	.714
10	Cin	NL	20	44	9	1	1	0	(0	0)	12	9	0	3	1	0	19	0	0	0	3	0	1.00	1	.205	.222	.273
10	Mil	NL	25	53	11	1	1	0	(0	0)	14	2	5	3	5	0	15	0	2	1	1	0	1.00	0	.208	.271	.264
	Postseason		1	1	0	0	0	0	(0	0)	0	1	0	0	0	0	0	0	0	0	0	0	-	0	.000	.000	.000
	5 ML YEARS		258	518	138	26	7	11	(5	6)	211	76	47	72	67	1	157	4	6	4	27	6	.82	6	.266	.352	.407

R.A. Dickey

Pitches: R **Bats:** R **Pos:** SP-33; RP-1   **Ht:** 6'2" **Wt:** 216 **Born:** 10/29/1974 **Age:** 38

			HOW MUCH HE PITCHED					WHAT HE GAVE UP										THE RESULTS						
Year	Team	Lg	G	GS	CG	GF	IP	BFP	H	R	ER	HR	SH	SF	HB	TBB	IBB	SO	WP	Bk	W	L	Pct	Sh	Sv-Op	Hld	ERC	ERA
2001	Tex	AL	4	0	0	1	12.0	53	13	9	9	3	0	0	0	7	1	4	1	0	1	0	1.000	0	0-0	0	6.57	6.75
2003	Tex	AL	38	13	1	6	116.2	513	135	68	66	16	4	3	5	38	5	94	5	2	9	8	.529	1	1-1	3	5.09	5.09
2004	Tex	AL	25	15	0	2	104.1	480	136	77	65	17	3	3	4	33	1	57	5	1	6	7	.462	0	1-1	0	6.08	5.61
2005	Tex	AL	9	4	0	2	29.2	134	29	23	22	4	0	1	2	17	0	15	2	0	1	2	.333	0	0-0	0	5.18	6.67
2006	Tex	AL	1	1	0	0	3.1	18	8	7	7	6	0	0	0	1	0	1	0	0	0	1	.000	0	0-0	0	32.05	18.90
2008	Sea	AL	32	14	0	9	112.1	500	124	65	65	15	4	6	2	51	4	58	11	1	5	8	.385	0	0-0	0	5.19	5.21
2009	Min	AL	35	1	0	13	64.1	293	74	34	33	8	2	2	4	30	1	42	4	0	1	1	.500	0	0-0	1	5.66	4.62
2010	NYM	NL	27	26	2	0	174.1	713	165	62	55	13	7	3	4	42	3	104	11	0	11	9	.550	1	0-0	1	3.11	2.84
2011	NYM	NL	33	32	1	0	208.2	876	202	85	76	18	**16**	7	9	54	2	134	9	1	8	13	.381	0	0-0	1	3.40	3.28
2012	NYM	NL	34	**33**	5	1	233.2	927	192	78	71	24	9	7	9	54	2	**230**	4	1	20	6	.769	3	0-0	1	2.70	2.73
	10 ML YEARS		238	139	9	34	1059.1	4507	1078	508	469	124	45	32	39	327	19	739	52	6	61	56	.521	5	2-2	6	4.07	3.98

Brandon Dickson

Pitches: R **Bats:** R **Pos:** RP-4   **Ht:** 6'5" **Wt:** 190 **Born:** 11/3/1984 **Age:** 28

			HOW MUCH HE PITCHED					WHAT HE GAVE UP										THE RESULTS						
Year	Team	Lg	G	GS	CG	GF	IP	BFP	H	R	ER	HR	SH	SF	HB	TBB	IBB	SO	WP	Bk	W	L	Pct	Sh	Sv-Op	Hld	ERC	ERA
2006	JhsCty	R+	9	0	0	4	11.1	56	16	11	8	1	0	0	6	1	0	15	0	0	1	0	1.000	0	1--	-	6.65	6.35
2007	QuadC	A	31	23	0	4	144.0	626	148	74	56	9	2	2	12	41	1	84	11	0	11	7	.611	0	1--	-	3.78	3.50
2008	PlmBh	A+	23	17	1	1	115.1	488	119	49	45	7	3	3	2	37	0	66	5	0	7	8	.467	0	1--	-	3.78	3.51
2008	Sprgfld	AA	6	6	0	0	29.1	141	42	23	22	3	0	2	2	16	0	21	0	0	3	2	.600	0	0--	-	7.84	6.75
2009	Sprgfld	AA	28	20	1	2	147.2	637	160	75	62	12	6	3	7	50	3	112	9	0	8	10	.444	1	0--	-	4.39	3.78
2010	Memp	AAA	28	27	0	1	167.0	721	180	77	60	11	5	3	9	53	1	137	7	0	11	8	.579	0	0--	-	4.18	3.23
2011	Memp	AAA	26	25	1	0	157.1	656	169	75	69	22	5	4	4	32	1	124	5	1	8	9	.471	0	0--	-	4.13	3.95
2012	Memp	AAA	23	23	0	4	141.1	594	151	67	57	17	5	1	3	27	2	104	0	0	5	11	.313	0	0--	-	3.82	3.63
2011	StL	NL	4	1	0	0	8.1	34	9	3	3	2	0	0	0	3	0	7	0	0	0	0	-	0	0-0	0	5.77	3.24
2012	StL	NL	4	0	0	2	6.1	32	10	7	5	2	0	0	0	2	0	6	0	0	0	0	-	0	0-0	0	8.59	7.11
	2 ML YEARS		8	1	0	2	14.2	66	19	10	8	4	0	0	0	5	0	13	0	0	0	0	-	0	0-0	0	6.98	4.91

Jake Diekman

Pitches: L **Bats:** L **Pos:** RP-32   DEEK-man   **Ht:** 6'4" **Wt:** 200 **Born:** 1/21/1987 **Age:** 26

			HOW MUCH HE PITCHED					WHAT HE GAVE UP										THE RESULTS						
Year	Team	Lg	G	GS	CG	GF	IP	BFP	H	R	ER	HR	SH	SF	HB	TBB	IBB	SO	WP	Bk	W	L	Pct	Sh	Sv-Op	Hld	ERC	ERA
2007	Phillies	R	10	7	0	1	37.0	155	29	12	12	2	0	0	3	13	0	35	0	0	1	3	.250	0	0--	-	2.71	2.92
2007	Wmspt	A-	3	3	0	0	16.0	63	10	4	4	0	0	1	1	8	0	11	1	0	2	1	.667	0	0--	-	2.19	2.25
2008	Lakwd	A	19	19	0	0	96.1	443	120	72	58	4	1	3	5	47	0	53	12	3	5	3	.375	0	0--	-	5.71	5.42
2008	Wmspt	A-	8	8	1	0	45.0	196	41	24	22	4	2	1	1	25	0	43	2	0	1	4	.200	0	0--	-	4.23	4.40
2009	Lakwd	A	32	2	0	11	55.2	252	59	32	25	3	1	1	0	28	0	52	4	3	2	0	1.000	0	2--	-	4.40	4.04
2010	Lakwd	A	21	0	0	5	23.2	110	16	11	5	0	0	0	5	15	0	30	3	0	2	0	1.000	0	0--	-	3.06	1.90

Year Team	Lg	G	GS	CG	GF	IP	BFP	H	R	ER	HR	SH	SF	HB	TBB	IBB	SO	WP	Bk	W	L	Pct	Sh	Sv-Op	Hld	ERC	ERA
2010 Clrwtr	A+	24	0	0	7	32.0	144	22	20	13	2	1	1	6	23	0	26	2	0	0	2	.000	0	0--	-	3.99	3.66
2011 Rdng	AA	53	0	0	19	65.0	288	47	29	22	3	1	2	5	44	2	83	7	0	0	1	.000	0	3--	-	3.42	3.05
2012 LV	AAA	25	0	0	14	26.2	114	19	5	5	0	1	1	2	13	1	37	0	0	1	1	.500	0	7--	-	2.37	1.69
2012 Phi	NL	32	0	0	7	27.1	131	25	17	12	1	1	0	3	20	3	35	1	0	1	1	.500	0	0-1	4	4.45	3.95

Tim Dillard

Pitches: R **Bats:** R **Pos:** RP-34   **Ht:** 6'4" **Wt:** 219 **Born:** 7/19/1983 **Age:** 29

Year Team	Lg	G	GS	CG	GF	IP	BFP	H	R	ER	HR	SH	SF	HB	TBB	IBB	SO	WP	Bk	W	L	Pct	Sh	Sv-Op	Hld	ERC	ERA
2012 Nashv*	AAA	14	0	0	3	14.1	78	28	16	15	4	0	1	2	8	0	9	0	0	1	1	.500	0	0--	-	13.71	9.42
2012 Hntsvl*	AA	3	0	0	1	5.0	22	5	3	3	0	0	0	1	1	0	8	0	0	0	0	-	0	0--	-	3.28	5.40
2008 Mil	NL	13	0	0	5	14.1	65	17	12	7	2	0	1	0	6	2	5	1	0	0	0	-	0	0-0	1	5.24	4.40
2009 Mil	NL	2	0	0	0	4.1	23	7	6	6	1	0	1	0	5	1	1	0	0	0	1	.000	0	0-1	0	12.99	12.46
2011 Mil	NL	24	0	0	11	28.2	117	26	13	13	3	2	1	2	4	0	27	2	0	1	1	.500	0	0-0	1	2.85	4.08
2012 Mil	NL	34	0	0	15	37.0	166	45	21	18	3	2	0	1	14	2	29	0	0	0	2	.000	0	0-0	1	5.14	4.38
4 ML YEARS		73	0	0	31	84.1	371	95	52	44	9	4	3	3	29	5	62	3	0	1	4	.200	0	0-1	3	4.67	4.70

Andy Dirks

Bats: L **Throws:** L **Pos:** LF-59; RF-24; DH-10; PH-8; CF-1   **Ht:** 6'0" **Wt:** 195 **Born:** 1/24/1986 **Age:** 27

Year Team	Lg	G	AB	H	2B	3B	HR	(Hm	Rd)	TB	R	RBI	RC	TBB	IBB	SO	HBP	SH	SF	SB	CS	SB%	GDP	Avg	OBP	Slg
2008 WMich	A	3	10	1	0	0	0	(-	-)	1	0	2	0	1	0	2	0	0	0	0	0	-	0	.100	.182	.100
2008 Tigers	R	10	34	14	3	2	0	(-	-)	21	10	7	9	3	1	6	0	0	1	2	0	1.00	0	.412	.447	.618
2009 Lkland	A+	27	103	34	5	0	0	(-	-)	39	11	18	18	13	0	11	1	0	0	10	2	.83	2	.330	.410	.379
2009 Erie	AA	98	361	92	14	1	6	(-	-)	126	46	44	44	36	2	61	3	2	6	11	5	.69	2	.255	.323	.349
2010 Erie	AA	98	388	108	20	2	11	(-	-)	165	64	46	61	35	2	59	5	1	5	19	4	.83	8	.278	.342	.425
2010 Toledo	AAA	22	88	33	10	1	4	(-	-)	57	14	17	21	3	0	12	1	0	1	3	0	1.00	1	.375	.398	.648
2011 Toledo	AAA	41	157	51	8	1	7	(-	-)	82	30	24	31	12	0	28	0	1	2	12	2	.86	1	.325	.368	.522
2012 Toledo	AAA	10	37	8	1	0	2	(-	-)	15	4	5	4	4	0	8	0	0	2	2	0	1.00	2	.216	.293	.405
2011 Det	AL	78	219	55	13	0	7	(6	1)	89	34	28	27	11	1	36	3	2	0	5	2	.71	3	.251	.296	.406
2012 Det	AL	88	314	101	18	5	8	(3	5)	153	56	35	50	23	2	53	2	3	2	1	1	.50	4	.322	.370	.487
Postseason		2	5	1	0	0	0	(0	0)	1	1	0	0	0	0	1	0	0	0	1	0	1.00	0	.200	.200	.200
2 ML YEARS		166	533	156	31	5	15	(9	6)	242	90	63	77	34	3	89	5	5	2	6	3	.67	7	.293	.340	.454

Greg Dobbs

Bats: L **Throws:** R **Pos:** PH-47; 3B-36; LF-21; 1B-18; RF-16; DH-1   **Ht:** 6'1" **Wt:** 210 **Born:** 7/2/1978 **Age:** 34

Year Team	Lg	G	AB	H	2B	3B	HR	(Hm	Rd)	TB	R	RBI	RC	TBB	IBB	SO	HBP	SH	SF	SB	CS	SB%	GDP	Avg	OBP	Slg
2004 Sea	AL	18	53	12	1	0	1	(1	0)	16	4	9	5	1	0	14	1	0	1	0	0	-	0	.226	.250	.302
2005 Sea	AL	59	142	35	7	1	1	(0 | 1)	47	8	20	16	9	3	25	1	0	1	2	1	0	1.00	4	.246	.288	.331
2006 Sea	AL	23	27	10	3	1	0	(0	0)	15	4	3	5	0	0	4	1	0	0	0	1	.00	4	.370	.393	.556
2007 Phi	NL	142	324	88	20	4	10	(5	5)	146	45	55	42	29	4	67	1	0	4	3	0	1.00	7	.272	.330	.451
2008 Phi	NL	128	226	68	14	1	9	(3	6)	111	30	40	38	11	1	40	1	0	2	3	1	.75	4	.301	.333	.491
2009 Phi	NL	97	154	38	6	0	5	(3	2)	59	15	20	15	11	1	29	1	0	3	1	0	1.00	2	.247	.296	.383
2010 Phi	NL	88	163	32	7	0	5	(2	3)	54	13	15	14	12	1	39	0	1	1	1	1	.50	2	.196	.251	.331
2011 Fla	NL	134	411	113	23	4	8	(2	6)	160	38	49	40	22	3	83	1	2	3	0	0	-	12	.275	.311	.389
2012 Mia	NL	120	319	91	13	2	5	(3	2)	123	26	39	38	14	5	53	2	0	7	4	2	.67	8	.285	.313	.386
Postseason		16	21	7	1	0	0	(0	0)	8	2	0	2	3	2	6	0	0	0	0	0	-	0	.333	.417	.381
9 ML YEARS		809	1819	487	94	9	44	(19	25)	731	183	250	213	109	18	354	8	4	22	13	5	.72	39	.268	.308	.402

Rafael Dolis

Pitches: R **Bats:** R **Pos:** RP-34   DOE-leese   **Ht:** 6'4" **Wt:** 215 **Born:** 1/10/1988 **Age:** 25

Year Team	Lg	G	GS	CG	GF	IP	BFP	H	R	ER	HR	SH	SF	HB	TBB	IBB	SO	WP	Bk	W	L	Pct	Sh	Sv-Op	Hld	ERC	ERA
2006 Cubs	R	13	3	0	1	25.0	125	30	27	23	1	1	1	4	16	0	33	4	0	0	2	.000	0	0--	-	6.23	8.28
2007 Peoria	A	6	6	0	0	30.0	121	23	7	6	1	1	1	0	16	0	24	3	0	3	1	.750	0	0--	-	3.03	1.80
2009 Dytona	A+	27	25	0	0	99.2	420	78	46	42	4	4	3	7	53	0	75	8	1	3	9	.250	0	0--	-	3.31	3.79
2010 Dytona	A+	14	13	0	1	71.0	299	63	31	23	3	4	3	2	30	0	48	3	1	4	5	.444	0	0--	-	3.29	2.92
2010 Tenn	AA	12	12	0	0	55.1	251	65	32	25	3	1	2	1	27	0	45	7	0	5	4	.556	0	0--	-	5.20	4.07
2011 Tenn	AA	51	4	0	36	72.2	313	61	36	26	2	5	1	3	35	1	48	6	0	8	5	.615	0	17--	-	3.11	3.22
2012 Iowa	AAA	13	0	0	11	14.1	61	15	4	4	1	1	0	0	6	0	14	1	1	1	0	1.000	0	3--	-	4.32	2.51
2012 Cubs	R	5	0	0	0	5.2	26	7	5	4	0	0	0	0	2	0	5	2	0	1	1	.500	0	0--	-	4.35	6.35
2012 Tenn	AA	2	0	0	0	2.0	9	2	0	0	0	0	0	1	0	0	2	0	0	0	0	-	0	0--	-	3.63	0.00
2011 ChC	NL	1	0	0	0	1.1	4	0	0	0	0	0	0	0	1	0	1	0	0	0	0	-	0	0-0	0	0.71	0.00
2012 ChC	NL	34	0	0	15	38.0	173	40	29	27	5	2	1	3	23	1	24	1	0	2	4	.333	0	4-6	3	5.85	6.39
2 ML YEARS		35	0	0	15	39.1	177	40	29	27	5	2	1	3	24	1	25	1	0	2	4	.333	0	4-6	3	5.63	6.18

Matt Dominguez

Bats: R **Throws:** R **Pos:** 3B-31   **Ht:** 6'1" **Wt:** 215 **Born:** 8/28/1989 **Age:** 23

Year Team	Lg	G	AB	H	2B	3B	HR	(Hm	Rd)	TB	R	RBI	RC	TBB	IBB	SO	HBP	SH	SF	SB	CS	SB%	GDP	Avg	OBP	Slg
2007 Mrlns	R	5	20	2	0	0	0	(-	-)	2	0	2	0	1	0	2	0	0	1	0	0	-	0	.100	.136	.100
2007 Jmstwn	A-	10	37	7	2	0	1	(-	-)	12	3	4	2	1	0	12	0	0	0	0	0	-	0	.189	.211	.324
2008 Grnsbr	A	88	345	102	16	0	18	(-	-)	172	59	70	61	28	0	68	5	0	3	0	1	.00	13	.296	.354	.499
2009 Jupiter	A+	103	381	100	25	1	11	(-	-)	160	49	53	56	38	2	68	5	0	5	1	0	1.00	9	.262	.333	.420

Year	Team	Lg	G	AB	H	2B	3B	HR	(Hm	Rd)	TB	R	RBI	RC	TBB	IBB	SO	HBP	SH	SF	SB	CS	SB%	GDP	Avg	OBP	Slg
									BATTING												**BASERUNNING**				**AVERAGES**		
2009	Jaxnvl	AA	31	97	18	7	0	2	(-	-)	31	10	9	10	14	0	24	1	1	1	0	0	-	3	.186	.292	.320
2010	Jaxnvl	AA	138	504	127	34	2	14	(-	-)	207	61	81	73	56	3	96	9	1	7	0	2	.00	13	.252	.333	.411
2011	Jupiter	A+	4	18	3	0	0	0	(-	-)	3	0	2	0	1	0	3	1	0	0	0	0	-	0	.167	.250	.167
2011	Jaxnvl	AA	4	15	2	0	0	0	(-	-)	2	1	1	0	3	0	2	1	0	0	0	0	-	0	.133	.316	.133
2011	NewOr	AAA	87	325	84	18	1	12	(-	-)	140	47	55	45	24	0	50	3	0	4	1	1	.00	11	.258	.312	.431
2012	NewOr	AAA	78	286	67	14	0	7	(-	-)	102	27	46	31	23	2	31	1	2	3	0	1	.00	6	.234	.291	.357
2012	OKCity	AAA	45	161	48	10	0	2	(-	-)	64	21	23	23	11	0	21	2	1	2	0	0	-	4	.298	.347	.398
2011	Fla	NL	17	45	11	4	0	0	(0	0)	15	2	2	3	2	0	8	1	0	0	0	0	-	2	.244	.292	.333
2012	Hou	NL	31	109	31	2	2	5	(2	3)	52	14	16	13	4	1	17	0	0	0	0	0	-	4	.284	.310	.477
2 ML YEARS			48	154	42	6	2	5	(2	3)	67	16	18	16	6	1	25	1	0	0	0	0	-	6	.273	.304	.435

Jason Donald

Bats: R **Throws:** R **Pos:** 3B-12; SS-10; 2B-8; PR-7; LF-5; DH-4; CF-3; PH-2   **Ht:** 6'1" **Wt:** 195 **Born:** 9/4/1984 **Age:** 28

Year	Team	Lg	G	AB	H	2B	3B	HR	(Hm	Rd)	TB	R	RBI	RC	TBB	IBB	SO	HBP	SH	SF	SB	CS	SB%	GDP	Avg	OBP	Slg
2012	Clmbs*	AAA	65	256	71	19	3	6	(-	-)	114	46	31	42	30	1	58	6	3	1	5	5	.50	6	.277	.365	.445
2010	Cle	AL	88	296	75	19	3	4	(2	2)	112	39	24	29	22	2	70	3	4	0	5	1	.83	3	.253	.312	.378
2011	Cle	AL	39	132	42	6	1	1	(0	1)	53	13	8	18	7	0	35	3	0	1	3	2	.60	2	.318	.364	.402
2012	Cle	AL	43	124	25	2	1	2	(2	0)	35	18	11	7	5	0	40	3	1	2	4	0	1.00	0	.202	.246	.282
3 ML YEARS			170	552	142	27	5	7	(4	3)	200	70	43	54	34	2	145	9	5	3	12	3	.80	5	.257	.309	.362

Josh Donaldson

Bats: R **Throws:** R **Pos:** 3B-71; C-3; 1B-1   **Ht:** 6'0" **Wt:** 220 **Born:** 12/8/1985 **Age:** 27

Year	Team	Lg	G	AB	H	2B	3B	HR	(Hm	Rd)	TB	R	RBI	RC	TBB	IBB	SO	HBP	SH	SF	SB	CS	SB%	GDP	Avg	OBP	Slg
2007	Cubs	R	4	11	2	2	0	0	(-	-)	4	1	0	4	2	0	4	0	0	0	0	1	.00	0	.182	.308	.364
2007	Boise	A-	49	162	56	11	2	9	(-	-)	98	37	35	45	37	1	34	2	0	1	6	2	.75	3	.346	.470	.605
2008	Peoria	A	63	235	51	13	0	6	(-	-)	82	27	23	23	17	1	41	2	0	0	7	1	.88	3	.217	.276	.349
2008	Stcktn	A+	47	188	62	13	2	9	(-	-)	106	37	39	40	17	0	29	2	0	0	2	2	.00	2	.330	.391	.564
2009	Mdland	AA	124	455	123	37	1	9	(-	-)	189	67	91	78	79	2	92	4	3	2	7	2	.78	17	.270	.379	.415
2010	Scrmto	AAA	86	294	70	14	1	18	(-	-)	140	52	67	50	45	2	79	2	0	7	3	1	.75	15	.238	.336	.476
2011	Scrmto	AAA	115	444	116	28	0	17	(-	-)	195	79	70	71	51	1	100	6	0	2	13	4	.76	9	.261	.344	.439
2012	Scrmto	AAA	51	209	70	12	2	13	(-	-)	125	38	44	48	23	1	34	1	0	1	5	2	.71	13	.335	.402	.598
2010	Oak	AL	14	32	5	1	0	1	(0	1)	9	1	4	3	2	0	12	0	0	0	0	0	-	0	.156	.206	.281
2012	Oak	AL	75	274	66	16	0	9	(3	6)	109	34	33	33	14	0	61	5	0	1	4	1	.80	6	.241	.289	.398
2 ML YEARS			89	306	71	17	0	10	(3	7)	118	35	37	36	16	0	73	5	0	1	4	1	.80	6	.232	.280	.386

Sean Doolittle

Pitches: L **Bats:** L **Pos:** RP-44   **Ht:** 6'3" **Wt:** 210 **Born:** 9/26/1986 **Age:** 26

Year	Team	Lg	G	GS	CG	GF	IP	BFP	H	R	ER	HR	SH	SF	HB	TBB	IBB	SO	WP	Bk	W	L	Pct	Sh	Sv-Op	Hld	ERC	ERA
							HOW MUCH HE PITCHED				**WHAT HE GAVE UP**													**THE RESULTS**				
2011	As	R	1	0	0	0	1.0	4	0	1	1	0	0	0	0	1	0	2	0	0	0	0	-	0	0--	-	0.95	9.00
2012	Stcktn	A+	6	0	0	0	10.1	39	5	2	1	0	0	0	2	2	0	21	0	0	0	0	-	0	0--	-	1.18	0.87
2012	Mdland	AA	8	0	0	4	11.0	41	2	2	1	0	0	0	1	4	0	19	0	0	0	0	-	0	1--	-	0.53	0.82
2012	Scrmto	AAA	2	0	0	1	3.2	13	1	0	0	0	0	0	0	1	0	8	0	0	0	0	-	0	0--	-	0.47	0.00
2012	Oak	AL	44	0	0	7	47.1	191	40	18	16	3	2	2	0	11	1	60	0	0	2	1	.667	0	1-2	18	2.36	3.04

Octavio Dotel

Pitches: R **Bats:** R **Pos:** RP-57   OCK-tay-vee-oh dough-TELL   **Ht:** 6'0" **Wt:** 230 **Born:** 11/25/1973 **Age:** 39

Year	Team	Lg	G	GS	CG	GF	IP	BFP	H	R	ER	HR	SH	SF	HB	TBB	IBB	SO	WP	Bk	W	L	Pct	Sh	Sv-Op	Hld	ERC	ERA
							HOW MUCH HE PITCHED				**WHAT HE GAVE UP**													**THE RESULTS**				
1999	NYM	NL	19	14	0	1	85.1	368	69	52	51	12	3	5	6	49	1	85	3	2	8	3	.727	0	0-0	0	4.30	5.38
2000	Hou	NL	50	16	0	25	125.0	563	127	80	75	26	7	8	7	61	3	142	6	0	3	7	.300	0	16-23	0	5.47	5.40
2001	Hou	NL	61	4	0	20	105.0	438	79	35	31	5	2	2	2	47	2	145	4	0	7	5	.583	0	2-4	14	2.62	2.66
2002	Hou	NL	83	0	0	22	97.1	376	58	21	20	7	3	7	4	27	2	118	2	0	6	4	.600	0	6-10	31	1.61	1.85
2003	Hou	NL	76	0	0	13	87.0	346	53	25	24	9	2	1	3	31	2	97	2	0	6	4	.600	0	4-6	33	2.02	2.48
2004	2 Tms		77	0	0	70	85.1	356	68	38	35	13	4	2	4	33	7	122	4	1	6	6	.500	0	36-45	0	3.31	3.69
2005	Oak	AL	15	0	0	13	15.1	65	10	6	6	2	0	0	0	11	2	16	1	0	1	2	.333	0	7-11	0	3.44	3.52
2006	NYY	AL	14	0	0	7	10.0	59	18	13	12	2	0	1	2	11	1	7	3	0	0	0	-	0	0-0	1	12.97	10.80
2007	2 Tms		33	0	0	25	30.2	138	29	16	14	4	1	0	4	12	4	41	2	0	2	1	.667	0	11-15	1	4.12	4.11
2008	CWS	AL	72	0	0	10	67.0	288	52	34	28	12	4	0	5	29	3	92	4	0	4	4	.500	0	1-5	21	3.64	3.76
2009	CWS	NL	62	0	0	12	62.1	268	54	26	23	7	3	3	6	36	1	75	4	0	3	3	.500	0	0-3	16	4.14	3.32
2010	3 Tms	NL	68	0	0	50	64.0	279	52	32	29	9	2	4	3	32	5	75	8	0	3	4	.429	0	22-28	4	3.69	4.08
2011	2 Tms		65	0	0	21	54.0	218	36	23	21	6	3	1	2	17	2	62	1	0	5	4	.556	0	3-3	9	2.15	3.50
2012	Det	AL	57	0	0	15	58.0	234	50	23	23	3	2	2	1	12	4	62	2	0	5	3	.625	0	1-4	11	2.29	3.57
04	Hou	NL	32	0	0	29	34.2	146	27	15	12	4	2	1	1	15	4	50	3	1	0	4	.000	0	14-17	0	3.01	3.12
04	Oak	AL	45	0	0	41	50.2	210	41	23	23	9	2	1	3	18	3	72	1	0	6	2	.750	0	22-28	0	3.52	4.09
07	KC	AL	24	0	0	22	23.0	108	24	11	10	3	1	0	4	11	4	29	2	0	2	1	.667	0	11-14	0	5.13	3.91
07	Atl	NL	9	0	0	3	7.2	30	5	5	4	1	0	0	0	1	0	12	0	0	0	0	-	0	0-1	1	1.51	4.70
10	Pit	NL	41	0	0	37	40.0	173	35	21	19	6	2	3	3	17	2	48	2	0	2	2	.500	0	21-26	0	3.83	4.28
10	LAD	NL	19	0	0	12	18.2	78	11	7	7	3	0	1	0	11	3	21	3	0	1	1	.500	0	1-2	3	2.72	3.38
10	Col	NL	8	0	0	1	5.1	28	6	4	3	0	0	0	0	4	0	6	3	0	0	1	.000	0	0-0	1	6.30	5.06
11	Tor	AL	36	0	0	11	29.1	122	20	13	12	5	1	0	2	12	2	30	0	0	2	1	.667	0	1-1	4	2.97	3.68
11	StL	NL	29	0	0	10	24.2	96	16	10	9	1	2	1	0	5	0	32	1	0	3	3	.500	0	2-2	5	1.38	3.28
Postseason			20	0	0	2	18.1	80	17	11	10	2	0	1	2	6	2	27	2	0	3	1	.750	0	0-0	4	3.62	4.91
14 ML YEARS			752	34	0	304	946.1	3996	755	424	392	117	36	36	41	408	39	1139	46	4	59	50	.541	0	109-157	141	3.33	3.73

Felix Doubront

Pitches: L **Bats**: L **Pos**: SP-29   due-BRAWNDT   **Ht**: 6'2" **Wt**: 165 **Born**: 10/23/1987 **Age**: 25

Year	Team	Lg	G	GS	CG	GF	IP	BFP	H	R	ER	HR	SH	SF	HB	TBB	IBB	SO	WP	Bk	W	L	Pct	Sh	Sv-Op	Hld	ERC	ERA
2010	Bos	AL	12	3	0	5	25.0	113	27	16	12	3	1	1	1	10	0	23	3	0	2	2	.500	0	2-3	1	4.72	4.32
2011	Bos	AL	11	0	0	1	10.1	47	12	7	7	1	0	1	0	8	0	6	0	0	0	0	-	0	1-1	0	6.97	6.10
2012	Bos	AL	29	29	0	0	161.0	709	162	95	87	24	1	6	5	71	0	167	5	0	11	10	.524	0	0-0	0	4.73	4.86
	3 ML YEARS		52	32	0	6	196.1	869	201	118	106	28	2	8	6	89	0	196	8	0	13	12	.520	0	3-4	1	4.84	4.86

Ryan Doumit

Bats: B **Throws**: R **Pos**: C-59; DH-48; LF-16; PH-8; RF-6; 1B-1   DOE-mitt   **Ht**: 6'1" **Wt**: 220 **Born**: 4/3/1981 **Age**: 32

Year	Team	Lg	G	AB	H	2B	3B	HR	(Hm	Rd)	TB	R	RBI	RC	TBB	IBB	SO	HBP	SH	SF	SB	CS	SB%	GDP	Avg	OBP	Slg
2005	Pit	NL	75	231	59	13	1	6	(4	2)	92	25	35	32	11	1	48	13	1	1	2	1	.67	5	.255	.324	.398
2006	Pit	NL	61	149	31	9	0	5	(3	3)	58	15	17	17	15	1	42	11	1	2	0	0	-	3	.208	.322	.389
2007	Pit	NL	83	252	69	19	2	9	(7	2)	119	33	32	34	22	2	59	4	0	1	1	2	.33	5	.274	.341	.472
2008	Pit	NL	116	431	137	34	0	15	(8	7)	216	71	69	79	23	4	55	6	0	5	2	2	.50	10	.318	.357	.501
2009	Pit	NL	75	280	70	16	0	10	(4	4)	116	31	38	26	20	6	49	1	0	3	4	0	1.00	5	.250	.299	.414
2010	Pit	NL	124	406	102	22	1	13	(7	6)	165	42	45	47	41	4	87	8	0	1	1	0	1.00	18	.251	.331	.406
2011	Pit	NL	77	218	66	12	1	8	(6	2)	104	17	30	36	16	0	35	1	1	0	0	1	.00	5	.303	.353	.477
2012	Min	AL	134	484	133	34	1	18	(8	10)	223	56	75	61	29	5	98	7	0	8	0	0	-	17	.275	.320	.461
	8 ML YEARS		745	2451	667	159	6	85	(49	36)	1093	290	341	332	177	23	473	51	3	21	10	6	.63	75	.272	.331	.446

Darin Downs

Pitches: L **Bats**: R **Pos**: RP-18   **Ht**: 6'3" **Wt**: 208 **Born**: 12/26/1984 **Age**: 28

Year	Team	Lg	G	GS	CG	GF	IP	BFP	H	R	ER	HR	SH	SF	HB	TBB	IBB	SO	WP	Bk	W	L	Pct	Sh	Sv-Op	Hld	ERC	ERA
2003	Cubs	R	13	11	0	0	38.1	172	48	30	28	2	0	1	3	17	0	32	5	0	0	2	.000	0	0--		5.91	6.57
2004	Boise	A-	14	13	0	0	60.0	254	55	36	33	5	7	6	2	35	0	61	2	0	5	3	.625	0	0--		4.57	4.95
2005	Boise	A-	14	13	0	0	61.2	263	61	30	24	5	2	0	4	22	0	63	6	0	5	4	.556	0	0--		4.02	3.50
2005	Peoria	A	2	2	0	0	6.1	36	12	14	13	1	0	0	1	4	0	3	1	0	0	2	.000	0	0--		11.95	18.47
2006	Boise	A-	9	2	0	1	24.1	107	25	15	13	0	1	0	3	7	0	24	1	0	4	2	.667	0	0--		3.50	4.81
2006	Cubs	R	2	1	0	0	3.1	15	5	4	4	1	0	0	0	1	0	2	0	0	1	1	.500	0	0--		8.71	10.80
2007	Dytona	A+	34	2	0	14	61.1	263	61	39	28	10	4	2	1	17	2	65	5	0	3	7	.300	0	2--		3.91	4.11
2008	Dytona	A+	17	0	0	2	28.0	130	29	11	9	2	4	1	1	13	0	25	7	0	2	0	1.000	0	0--		4.21	2.89
2008	Tenn	AA	22	0	0	2	23.1	118	32	19	17	1	0	1	2	16	0	17	1	0	0	2	.000	0	0--		7.33	6.56
2008	VeroB	A+	10	1	0	3	21.0	96	24	15	14	1	0	0	0	9	0	24	2	0	0	3	.000	0	0--		4.49	6.00
2009	Charltt	A+	20	19	1	0	121.2	494	117	35	27	11	4	1	4	23	0	111	4	0	12	4	.750	0	0--		3.16	2.00
2009	Mont	AA	2	2	0	0	11.1	49	13	6	6	1	1	0	0	4	1	9	0	0	2	0	.000	0	0--		4.58	4.76
2010	Mont	AA	18	3	0	4	48.0	194	40	16	9	2	3	2	1	15	2	57	1	1	6	2	.750	0	0--		2.55	1.69
2010	Drham	AAA	23	1	0	7	40.1	181	44	21	20	4	0	1	4	17	2	45	5	0	6	2	.750	0	0--		5.01	4.46
2011	Jaxnvl	AAA	22	13	0	3	76.1	332	87	44	41	7	3	2	3	23	0	48	3	0	2	5	.286	0	0--		4.61	4.83
2011	NewOr	AAA	10	5	0	1	35.2	147	34	17	17	1	1	2	0	8	0	39	2	0	3	2	.600	0	0--		2.68	4.29
2012	Toledo	AAA	25	0	0	8	29.1	118	25	8	7	0	2	1	0	8	0	33	3	0	0	2	.000	0	0--		2.22	2.15
2012	Det	AL	18	0	0	5	20.2	86	18	8	8	1	0	0	1	9	2	20	1	0	2	1	.667	0	0-0	1	3.27	3.48

Matt Downs

Bats: R **Throws**: R **Pos**: PH-43; 1B-25; 3B-18; RF-11; 2B-3; LF-2; SS-1   **Ht**: 6'1" **Wt**: 190 **Born**: 3/19/1984 **Age**: 29

Year	Team	Lg	G	AB	H	2B	3B	HR	(Hm	Rd)	TB	R	RBI	RC	TBB	IBB	SO	HBP	SH	SF	SB	CS	SB%	GDP	Avg	OBP	Slg
2012	OKCity*	AAA	24	90	24	2	0	3	(-	-)	35	14	15	12	8	0	20	3	0	1	3	2	.60	2	.267	.343	.389
2009	SF	NL	17	53	9	2	0	1	(0	1)	14	6	2	1	6	1	13	0	0	1	1	0	1.00	1	.170	.250	.264
2010	2 Tms	NL	40	97	21	7	0	1	(1	0)	31	8	7	9	9	0	20	2	0	1	0	0	-	1	.216	.294	.320
2011	Hou	NL	106	199	55	18	0	10	(5	5)	103	29	41	37	17	0	47	5	0	1	0	0	-	3	.276	.347	.518
2012	Hou	NL	91	178	36	4	1	8	(3	5)	66	15	16	11	8	1	38	4	1	0	2	4	.33	5	.202	.253	.371
10	SF	NL	29	78	19	7	0	1	(1	0)	29	6	7	7	8	0	18	1	0	1	0	0	-	1	.244	.318	.372
10	Hou	NL	11	19	2	0	0	0	(0	0)	2	2	0	0	1	0	2	1	0	0	0	0	-	0	.105	.190	.105
	4 ML YEARS		254	527	121	31	1	20	(9	11)	214	58	66	58	40	2	118	11	1	3	3	4	.43	11	.230	.296	.406

Scott Downs

Pitches: L **Bats**: L **Pos**: RP-57   **Ht**: 6'2" **Wt**: 215 **Born**: 3/17/1976 **Age**: 37

Year	Team	Lg	G	GS	CG	GF	IP	BFP	H	R	ER	HR	SH	SF	HB	TBB	IBB	SO	WP	Bk	W	L	Pct	Sh	Sv-Op	Hld	ERC	ERA
2000	2 Tms	NL	19	19	0	0	97.0	442	122	62	57	13	2	4	5	40	1	63	1	0	4	3	.571	0	0-0	0	6.19	5.29
2003	Mon	NL	1	1	0	0	3.0	17	5	5	5	2	0	0	0	3	2	4	0	1	0	0	1.000	0	0-0	0	15.01	15.00
2004	Mon	NL	12	12	1	0	63.0	284	79	47	36	9	2	1	3	23	2	38	2	0	3	6	.333	1	0-0	0	5.97	5.14
2005	Tor	AL	26	13	0	0	94.0	407	93	49	45	12	0	1	5	34	0	75	3	0	4	3	.571	0	0-0	0	4.25	4.31
2006	Tor	AL	59	5	0	13	77.0	327	73	38	35	9	1	1	2	30	6	61	7	0	6	2	.750	0	1-4	6	3.87	4.09
2007	Tor	AL	81	0	0	13	58.0	239	47	15	14	3	1	2	1	24	3	57	2	1	4	2	.667	0	1-4	24	2.81	2.17
2008	Tor	AL	66	0	0	14	70.2	290	54	15	14	3	5	0	4	27	7	57	3	0	3	0	.000	0	5-9	24	2.47	1.78
2009	Tor	AL	48	0	0	24	46.2	200	46	18	16	4	0	2	2	13	1	43	1	0	1	3	.250	0	9-13	10	3.50	3.09
2010	Tor	AL	67	0	0	14	61.1	247	49	18	18	3	0	4	4	14	3	48	1	0	5	5	.500	0	0-2	26	2.14	2.64
2011	LAA	AL	60	0	0	11	53.2	218	39	11	8	3	5	2	0	15	3	35	2	0	6	3	.667	0	1-4	26	1.83	1.34
2012	LAA	AL	57	0	0	11	45.2	194	43	17	16	3	2	0	1	17	2	32	1	0	1	1	.500	0	9-12	25	3.33	3.15
00	ChC	NL	18	18	0	0	94.0	429	117	59	54	13	2	4	5	37	1	63	1	0	4	3	.571	0	0-0	0	6.07	5.17
00	Mon	NL	1	1	0	0	3.0	16	5	3	3	0	0	0	0	3	0	0	0	0	0	0	-	0	0-0	0	10.34	9.00
	11 ML YEARS		496	50	1	99	670.0	2859	648	296	264	64	16	15	26	240	30	513	23	2	34	32	.515	1	26-48	141	3.79	3.55

Brian Dozier

Bats: R **Throws:** R **Pos:** SS-83; PH-1; PR-1 DOUGH-zher **Ht:** 5'11" **Wt:** 190 **Born:** 5/15/1987 **Age:** 26

Year	Team	Lg	G	AB	H	2B	3B	HR	(Hm	Rd)	TB	R	RBI	RC	TBB	IBB	SO	HBP	SH	SF	SB	CS	SB%	GDP	Avg	OBP	Slg
2009	Twins	R	5	14	4	0	0	0	(-	-)	4	1	0	1	2	0	1	0	0	0	0	0	-	0	.286	.375	.286
2009	Elizab	R+	54	222	77	17	0	0	(-	-)	94	38	14	41	23	0	26	3	1	3	3	0	1.00	4	.347	.410	.423
2010	Beloit	A	39	151	42	7	1	0	(-	-)	51	24	17	20	16	0	16	0	0	3	6	1	.86	3	.278	.341	.338
2010	FtMyrs	A+	93	350	96	11	1	5	(-	-)	124	44	42	49	44	2	41	1	9	6	10	4	.71	9	.274	.352	.354
2011	FtMyrs	A+	49	180	58	11	5	2	(-	-)	85	32	22	39	27	2	20	6	3	2	13	4	.76	5	.322	.423	.472
2011	NwBrit	AA	78	311	99	22	7	7	(-	-)	156	60	34	59	28	0	46	5	7	0	11	7	.61	8	.318	.384	.502
2012	Roch	AAA	48	181	42	11	1	2	(-	-)	61	15	17	18	14	1	34	1	1	3	3	2	.60	5	.232	.286	.337
2012	Min	AL	84	316	74	11	1	6	(4	2)	105	33	33	24	16	0	58	1	4	3	9	2	.82	10	.234	.271	.332

Kyle Drabek

Pitches: R **Bats:** R **Pos:** SP-13 DRAY-beck **Ht:** 6'1" **Wt:** 230 **Born:** 12/8/1987 **Age:** 25

Year	Team	Lg	G	GS	CG	GF	IP	BFP	H	R	ER	HR	SH	SF	HB	TBB	IBB	SO	WP	Bk	W	L	Pct	Sh	Sv-Op	Hld	ERC	ERA
2010	Tor	AL	3	3	0	0	17.0	69	18	9	9	2	1	2	0	5	0	12	2	0	0	3	.000	0	0-0	0	4.34	4.76
2011	Tor	AL	18	14	0	2	78.2	365	87	54	53	10	3	5	1	55	0	51	11	0	4	5	.444	0	0-0	0	6.30	6.06
2012	Tor	AL	13	13	0	0	71.1	317	67	41	37	10	0	1	1	47	0	47	7	0	4	7	.364	0	0-0	0	5.21	4.67
	3 ML YEARS		34	30	0	2	167.0	751	172	104	99	22	4	8	2	107	0	110	20	0	8	15	.348	0	0-0	0	5.63	5.34

Stephen Drew

Bats: L **Throws:** R **Pos:** SS-75; PH-4 **Ht:** 6'0" **Wt:** 190 **Born:** 3/16/1983 **Age:** 30

Year	Team	Lg	G	AB	H	2B	3B	HR	(Hm	Rd)	TB	R	RBI	RC	TBB	IBB	SO	HBP	SH	SF	SB	CS	SB%	GDP	Avg	OBP	Slg
2012	Reno*	AAA	9	36	9	1	1	2	(-	-)	18	6	5	6	4	0	6	0	0	0	0	0	-	0	.250	.325	.500
2012	Mobile*	AA	2	5	1	0	0	0	(-	-)	1	0	0	1	4	0	1	0	0	0	0	0	-	0	.200	.556	.200
2006	Ari	NL	59	209	66	13	7	5	(2	3)	108	27	23	31	14	4	50	0	2	1	2	0	1.00	1	.316	.357	.517
2007	Ari	NL	150	543	129	28	4	12	(6	6)	201	60	60	71	60	5	100	3	5	8	9	0	1.00	4	.238	.313	.370
2008	Ari	NL	152	611	178	44	11	21	(9	12)	307	91	67	97	41	6	109	1	3	7	3	3	.50	5	.291	.333	.502
2009	Ari	NL	135	533	139	29	12	12	(4	8)	228	71	65	76	49	7	87	1	5	7	5	1	.83	5	.261	.320	.428
2010	Ari	NL	151	565	157	33	12	15	(5	10)	259	83	61	84	62	2	108	3	2	1	10	5	.67	8	.278	.352	.458
2011	Ari	NL	86	321	81	21	5	5	(3	2)	127	44	45	41	30	0	74	1	1	1	4	4	.50	3	.252	.317	.396
2012	2 Tms		79	287	64	13	1	7	(4	3)	100	38	28	30	37	2	76	0	0	3	1	2	.33	2	.223	.309	.348
12	Ari	NL	40	135	26	8	1	2	(0	2)	42	17	12	12	19	1	35	0	0	1	0	1	.00	1	.193	.290	.311
12	Oak	AL	39	152	38	5	0	5	(4	1)	58	21	16	18	18	1	41	0	0	2	1	1	.50	1	.250	.326	.382
	Postseason		7	31	12	1	1	2	(1	1)	21	6	4	5	1	0	7	0	0	0	1	0	1.00	1	.387	.406	.677
	7 ML YEARS		812	3069	814	181	52	77	(34	43)	1330	414	349	430	293	26	604	9	18	28	34	15	.69	28	.265	.328	.433

Lucas Duda

Bats: L **Throws:** R **Pos:** RF-81; LF-24; PH-11; 1B-6; DH-5 DOO-duh **Ht:** 6'4" **Wt:** 254 **Born:** 2/3/1986 **Age:** 27

Year	Team	Lg	G	AB	H	2B	3B	HR	(Hm	Rd)	TB	R	RBI	RC	TBB	IBB	SO	HBP	SH	SF	SB	CS	SB%	GDP	Avg	OBP	Slg
2012	Buffalo*	AAA	25	96	25	4	0	3	(-	-)	38	12	8	13	10	1	21	0	0	1	0	0	-	2	.260	.327	.396
2010	NYM	NL	29	84	17	6	0	4	(3	1)	35	11	13	5	6	0	22	1	0	1	0	0	-	2	.202	.261	.417
2011	NYM	NL	100	301	88	21	3	10	(2	8)	145	38	50	44	33	3	57	7	1	5	1	0	1.00	5	.292	.370	.482
2012	NYM	NL	121	401	96	15	0	15	(9	6)	156	43	57	58	51	0	120	4	0	3	1	0	1.00	5	.239	.329	.389
	3 ML YEARS		250	786	201	42	3	29	(14	15)	336	92	120	107	90	3	199	12	1	9	2	0	1.00	12	.256	.338	.427

Brian Duensing

Pitches: L **Bats:** L **Pos:** RP-44; SP-11 DUNN-sing **Ht:** 6'0" **Wt:** 205 **Born:** 2/22/1983 **Age:** 30

Year	Team	Lg	G	GS	CG	GF	IP	BFP	H	R	ER	HR	SH	SF	HB	TBB	IBB	SO	WP	Bk	W	L	Pct	Sh	Sv-Op	Hld	ERC	ERA
2009	Min	AL	24	9	0	3	84.0	359	84	37	34	7	3	2	3	31	1	53	1	0	5	2	.714	0	0-0	1	4.00	3.64
2010	Min	AL	53	13	1	11	130.2	535	122	42	38	11	4	0	3	35	5	78	1	0	10	3	.769	1	0-0	9	3.18	2.62
2011	Min	AL	32	28	1	0	161.2	711	193	102	94	21	7	6	1	52	3	115	3	0	9	14	.391	1	0-0	0	5.12	5.23
2012	Min	AL	55	11	0	8	109.0	472	126	71	62	10	2	3	2	27	3	69	5	0	4	12	.250	0	0-1	7	4.31	5.12
	Postseason		2	2	0	0	8.0	39	14	10	10	2	0	0	0	2	0	4	1	0	0	2	.000	0	0-0	0	9.43	11.25
	4 ML YEARS		164	61	2	22	485.1	2077	525	252	228	49	16	11	9	145	12	315	10	0	28	31	.475	2	0-1	17	4.20	4.23

Danny Duffy

Pitches: L **Bats:** L **Pos:** SP-6 **Ht:** 6'3" **Wt:** 200 **Born:** 12/21/1988 **Age:** 24

Year	Team	Lg	G	GS	CG	GF	IP	BFP	H	R	ER	HR	SH	SF	HB	TBB	IBB	SO	WP	Bk	W	L	Pct	Sh	Sv-Op	Hld	ERC	ERA
2007	Royals	R	11	9	0	0	37.1	157	24	14	6	0	1	1	3	17	0	63	5	0	2	3	.400	0	0--	-	2.01	1.45
2008	Burlgtn	A	17	17	0	0	81.2	325	56	26	20	4	3	3	4	25	0	102	10	0	8	4	.667	0	0--	-	1.99	2.20
2009	Wilmg	A+	24	24	1	0	126.2	516	108	49	42	6	2	2	1	41	0	125	8	1	9	3	.750	0	0--	-	2.72	2.98
2010	Royals	R	2	2	0	0	2.2	10	2	1	1	0	0	0	0	1	0	4	0	1	0	0	-	0	0--	-	2.27	3.38
2010	Idaho	R+	2	2	0	0	6.0	23	4	1	1	0	0	0	1	0	0	6	1	0	0	1	.000	0	0--	-	1.23	1.50
2010	Wilmg	A+	3	3	0	0	14.0	56	8	6	4	2	1	0	1	7	0	18	1	0	0	0	-	0	0--	-	2.80	2.57
2010	NWArk	AA	7	7	1	0	39.2	160	38	17	13	3	1	0	0	9	0	41	4	0	5	2	.714	1	0--	-	3.09	2.95
2011	Omha	AAA	8	8	0	0	42.0	171	37	17	16	5	1	1	3	10	0	48	1	0	3	1	.750	0	0--	-	3.25	3.43
2011	KC	AL	20	20	0	0	105.1	474	119	66	66	15	2	2	5	51	1	87	4	1	4	8	.333	0	0-0	0	5.76	5.64
2012	KC	AL	6	6	0	0	27.2	121	26	13	12	2	0	0	0	18	1	28	0	1	2	2	.500	0	0-0	0	4.58	3.90
	2 ML YEARS		26	26	0	0	133.0	595	145	79	78	17	2	2	5	69	2	115	4	2	6	10	.375	0	0-0	0	5.51	5.28

Zach Duke

Pitches: L Bats: L Pos: RP-8 Ht: 6'1" Wt: 205 Born: 4/19/1983 Age: 30

Year Team	Lg	G	GS	CG	GF	IP	BFP	H	R	ER	HR	SH	SF	HB	TBB	IBB	SO	WP	Bk	W	L	Pct	Sh	Sv-Op Hld	ERC	ERA
		HOW MUCH HE PITCHED						WHAT HE GAVE UP												THE RESULTS						
2012 Syrcse*	AAA	26	26	2	0	164.1	692	178	69	64	16	5	2	1	39	0	91	1	0	15	5	.750	1	0- -	-	3.93	3.51
2005 Pit	NL	14	14	0	0	84.2	341	79	20	17	3	3	1	2	23	2	58	1	0	8	2	.800	1	0-0	0	2.96	1.81
2006 Pit	NL	34	34	2	0	215.1	935	255	116	107	17	13	4	7	68	6	117	8	1	10	15	.400	1	0-0	0	4.82	4.47
2007 Pit	NL	20	19	0	0	107.1	482	161	74	66	14	2	4	3	25	2	41	0	1	3	8	.273	0	0-0	0	6.96	5.53
2008 Pit	NL	31	31	1	0	185.0	829	230	111	99	19	14	4	7	47	1	87	2	2	5	14	.263	1	0-0	0	4.99	4.82
2009 Pit	NL	32	32	3	0	213.0	891	231	101	96	23	18	10	3	49	0	106	2	1	11	16	.407	1	0-0	0	4.05	4.06
2010 Pit	NL	29	29	0	0	159.0	730	212	115	101	25	9	6	4	51	2	96	4	3	8	15	.348	0	0-0	0	6.22	5.72
2011 Ari	NL	21	9	0	5	76.2	338	101	42	42	6	3	3	1	19	0	32	1	0	3	4	.429	0	1-1	0	5.27	4.93
2012 Was	NL	8	0	0	3	13.2	56	11	2	2	0	0	0	0	4	0	10	0	0	1	0	1.000	0	0-0	0	2.00	1.32
8 ML YEARS		189	168	6	8	1054.2	4602	1280	581	530	107	62	32	27	286	13	547	18	8	49	74	.398	3	1-1	0	4.93	4.52

Shelley Duncan

Bats: R Throws: R Pos: LF-57; DH-17; PH-7; RF-2; PR-2; 1B-1 Ht: 6'5" Wt: 225 Born: 9/29/1979 Age: 33

Year Team	Lg	G	AB	H	2B	3B	HR	(Hm	Rd)	TB	R	RBI	RC	TBB	IBB	SO	HBP	SH	SF	SB	CS	SB%	GDP	Avg	OBP	Slg
				BATTING																BASERUNNING				AVERAGES		
2007 NYY	AL	34	74	19	1	0	7	(6	1)	41	16	17	14	8	0	20	0	1	0	0	0	-	2	.257	.329	.554
2008 NYY	AL	23	57	10	3	0	1	(1	0)	16	7	6	4	7	0	13	0	0	1	0	0	-	1	.175	.262	.281
2009 NYY	AL	11	15	3	0	0	0	(0	0)	3	1	1	1	0	0	5	0	0	0	0	0	-	1	.200	.200	.200
2010 Cle	AL	85	229	53	10	0	11	(9	2)	96	29	36	30	26	2	76	3	0	1	1	0	1.00	4	.231	.317	.419
2011 Cle	AL	76	223	58	17	0	11	(4	7)	108	29	47	38	19	1	56	3	0	2	0	1	.00	7	.260	.324	.484
2012 Cle	AL	81	232	47	10	0	11	(4	7)	90	29	31	22	28	1	59	1	0	3	1	2	.33	9	.203	.288	.388
Postseason		3	4	2	0	0	0	(0	0)	2	1	0	1	0	0	1	0	0	0	0	0	-	0	.500	.500	.500
6 ML YEARS		310	830	190	41	0	41	(24	17)	354	111	138	109	88	4	229	7	1	7	2	3	.40	24	.229	.306	.427

Adam Dunn

Bats: L Throws: R Pos: DH-93; 1B-52; LF-5; PH-2 Ht: 6'6" Wt: 285 Born: 11/9/1979 Age: 33

Year Team	Lg	G	AB	H	2B	3B	HR	(Hm	Rd)	TB	R	RBI	RC	TBB	IBB	SO	HBP	SH	SF	SB	CS	SB%	GDP	Avg	OBP	Slg
				BATTING																BASERUNNING				AVERAGES		
2001 Cin	NL	66	244	64	18	1	19	(8	11)	141	54	43	51	38	2	74	4	0	0	4	2	.67	4	.262	.371	.578
2002 Cin	NL	158	535	133	28	2	26	(13	13)	243	84	71	96	128	13	170	9	1	3	19	9	.68	8	.249	.400	.454
2003 Cin	NL	116	381	82	12	1	27	(16	11)	177	70	57	61	74	8	126	10	0	4	8	2	.80	4	.215	.354	.465
2004 Cin	NL	161	568	151	34	0	46	(25	21)	323	105	102	108	108	11	195	5	0	0	6	1	.86	8	.266	.388	.569
2005 Cin	NL	160	543	134	35	2	40	(26	14)	293	107	101	112	114	14	168	12	0	2	4	2	.67	6	.247	.387	.540
2006 Cin	NL	160	561	131	24	0	40	(22	18)	275	99	92	96	112	12	194	6	1	3	7	0	1.00	8	.234	.365	.490
2007 Cin	NL	152	522	138	27	2	40	(19	21)	289	101	106	103	101	8	165	5	0	4	9	2	.82	12	.264	.386	.554
2008 2 Tms	NL	158	517	122	23	0	40	(21	19)	265	79	100	101	122	13	164	7	0	5	2	1	.67	7	.236	.386	.513
2009 Was	NL	159	546	146	29	0	38	(19	19)	289	81	105	109	116	16	177	4	0	2	0	1	.00	8	.267	.398	.529
2010 Was	NL	158	558	145	36	2	38	(20	18)	299	85	103	88	77	10	199	9	0	4	0	1	.00	10	.260	.356	.536
2011 CWS	AL	122	415	66	16	0	11	(8	3)	115	36	42	34	75	0	177	4	0	2	0	1	.00	10	.159	.292	.277
2012 CWS	AL	151	539	110	19	0	41	(18	23)	252	87	96	85	105	3	222	1	0	4	2	1	.67	8	.204	.333	.468
08 Cin	NL	114	373	87	14	0	32	(16	16)	197	58	74	74	80	6	120	6	0	5	1	1	.50	4	.233	.373	.528
08 Ari	NL	44	144	35	9	0	8	(5	3)	68	21	26	27	42	7	44	1	0	0	1	0	1.00	3	.243	.417	.472
12 ML YEARS		1721	5929	1422	301	10	406	(215	191)	2961	988	1018	1044	1170	110	2031	76	2	33	61	23	.73	93	.240	.370	.499

Mike Dunn

Pitches: L Bats: L Pos: RP-60 Ht: 6'0" Wt: 220 Born: 5/23/1985 Age: 28

Year Team	Lg	G	GS	CG	GF	IP	BFP	H	R	ER	HR	SH	SF	HB	TBB	IBB	SO	WP	Bk	W	L	Pct	Sh	Sv-Op Hld	ERC	ERA
		HOW MUCH HE PITCHED						WHAT HE GAVE UP												THE RESULTS						
2012 NewOr*	AAA	12	0	0	1	17.2	78	19	11	9	0	2	0	0	7	0	24	0	0	1	1	.500	0	0- -	-	3.71	4.58
2009 NYY	AL	4	0	0	3	4.0	20	3	3	3	1	0	0	0	5	0	5	1	0	0	0	-	0	0-0	0	7.17	6.75
2010 Atl	NL	25	0	0	5	19.0	88	15	4	4	1	0	0	0	17	2	27	2	0	2	0	1.000	0	0-0	1	4.19	1.89
2011 Fla	NL	72	0	0	11	63.0	267	51	28	24	9	4	2	2	31	2	68	3	0	5	6	.455	0	0-4	15	3.77	3.43
2012 Mia	NL	60	0	0	8	44.0	208	49	31	24	3	2	4	0	29	8	47	2	0	0	3	.000	0	1-6	18	5.10	4.91
Postseason		3	0	0	0	1.1	6	2	0	0	0	0	0	0	0	0	2	0	0	0	0	-	0	0-1	0	4.47	0.00
4 ML YEARS		161	0	0	27	130.0	583	118	66	55	14	6	6	2	82	12	147	8	0	7	9	.438	0	1-10	34	4.39	3.81

Chad Durbin

Pitches: R Bats: R Pos: RP-76 DURR-binn Ht: 6'2" Wt: 220 Born: 12/3/1977 Age: 35

Year Team	Lg	G	GS	CG	GF	IP	BFP	H	R	ER	HR	SH	SF	HB	TBB	IBB	SO	WP	Bk	W	L	Pct	Sh	Sv-Op Hld	ERC	ERA
		HOW MUCH HE PITCHED						WHAT HE GAVE UP												THE RESULTS						
1999 KC	AL	1	0	0	0	2.1	9	1	0	0	0	0	0	0	1	0	3	1	0	0	0	-	0	0-0	0	1.08	0.00
2000 KC	AL	16	16	0	0	72.1	349	91	71	66	14	1	3	0	43	1	37	7	0	2	5	.286	0	0-0	0	7.05	8.21
2001 KC	AL	29	29	2	0	179.0	777	201	109	98	26	2	7	11	58	0	95	6	0	9	16	.360	0	0-0	0	5.15	4.93
2002 KC	AL	2	2	0	0	8.1	43	13	11	11	3	0	0	1	4	0	5	0	0	0	1	.000	0	0-0	0	10.58	11.88
2003 Cle	AL	3	1	0	0	8.2	45	18	12	7	2	0	0	0	3	0	8	2	0	0	1	.000	0	0-0	0	12.37	7.27
2004 2 Tms	AL	24	8	1	5	60.2	291	72	50	47	11	2	2	5	35	3	48	5	0	6	7	.462	0	0-0	1	6.75	6.97
2006 Det	AL	3	0	0	1	6.0	24	6	1	1	0	1	0	0	0	0	3	0	0	0	0	-	0	0-0	0	2.87	1.50
2007 Det	AL	36	19	0	7	127.2	561	133	71	67	21	1	7	8	49	4	66	2	0	8	7	.533	0	1-2	3	4.92	4.72
2008 Phi	NL	71	0	0	12	87.2	365	81	33	28	5	4	2	4	35	7	63	3	0	5	4	.556	0	1-7	17	3.51	2.87
2009 Phi	NL	59	0	0	15	69.2	314	56	38	34	8	3	3	7	47	2	62	0	0	2	2	.500	0	2-3	8	4.47	4.39
2010 Phi	NL	64	0	0	9	68.2	291	63	29	29	7	1	2	5	27	2	63	0	0	4	1	.800	0	0-1	15	3.90	3.80
2011 Cle	AL	56	0	0	11	68.1	318	86	45	42	12	1	7	3	26	3	59	6	0	2	2	.500	0	0-1	3	6.11	5.53
2012 Atl	NL	76	0	0	19	61.0	257	52	25	21	9	2	2	0	28	3	49	1	0	4	1	.800	0	1-3	15	3.76	3.10

Year	Team	Lg	G	GS	CG	GF	IP	BFP	H	R	ER	HR	SH	SF	HB	TBB	IBB	SO	WP	Bk	W	L	Pct	Sh	Sv-Op	Hld	ERC	ERA
04	Cle	AL	17	8	1	5	51.1	239	63	40	38	10	0	2	4	24	3	38	3	0	5	6	.455	0	0-0	1	6.70	6.66
04	Ari	NL	7	0	0	0	9.1	52	9	10	9	1	2	0	1	11	0	10	2	0	1	1	.500	0	0-0	1	6.92	8.68
	Postseason		15	0	0	2	10.0	51	12	8	7	1	1	0	2	8	0	7	0	0	2	0	1.000	0	0-1	3	7.77	6.30
	13 ML YEARS		440	75	3	79	820.1	3644	873	495	451	119	17	35	44	356	25	561	35	0	42	47	.472	0	5-17	62	5.10	4.95

Jarrod Dyson

Bats: L **Throws:** R **Pos:** CF-88; PR-13; DH-6; PH-3   juh-ROD   **Ht:** 5'9" **Wt:** 165 **Born:** 8/15/1984 **Age:** 28

Year	Team	Lg	G	AB	H	2B	3B	HR	(Hm	Rd)	TB	R	RBI	RC	TBB	IBB	SO	HBP	SH	SF	SB	CS	SB%	GDP	Avg	OBP	Slg
2012	Omha*	AAA	15	63	21	3	3	0	(-	-)	30	12	5	12	4	0	5	0	4	0	7	1	.88	3	.333	.373	.476
2010	KC	AL	18	57	12	4	2	1	(1	0)	23	11	5	9	4	0	16	0	2	0	9	1	.90	2	.211	.286	.404
2011	KC	AL	26	44	9	1	0	0	(0	0)	10	8	3	7	7	0	14	0	1	1	11	1	.92	0	.205	.308	.227
2012	KC	AL	102	292	76	8	5	0	(0	0)	94	52	9	36	30	1	56	1	4	3	30	5	.86	5	.260	.328	.322
	3 ML YEARS		146	393	97	13	7	1	(1	0)	127	71	17	52	43	1	86	1	7	4	50	7	.88	7	.247	.320	.323

Sam Dyson

Pitches: R **Bats:** R **Pos:** RP-2   **Ht:** 6'2" **Wt:** 205 **Born:** 5/7/1988 **Age:** 25

Year	Team	Lg	G	GS	CG	GF	IP	BFP	H	R	ER	HR	SH	SF	HB	TBB	IBB	SO	WP	Bk	W	L	Pct	Sh	Sv-Op	Hld	ERC	ERA
2012	Dnedin	A+	6	6	0	0	28.2	124	35	16	13	1	0	1	5	0	16	1	0	2	0	.-	0	0--	-	4.10	4.08
2012	NHam	AA	33	0	0	20	45.1	188	38	20	12	2	4	2	4	15	0	22	3	0	2	2	.500	0	9--	-	2.93	2.38
2012	Tor	AL	2	0	0	0	0.2	8	4	3	3	0	0	0	0	2	0	1	0	0	0	0	-	0	0-0	0	56.02	40.50

Adam Eaton

Bats: L **Throws:** L **Pos:** CF-21; LF-1; PH-1   **Ht:** 5'8" **Wt:** 184 **Born:** 12/6/1988 **Age:** 24

Year	Team	Lg	G	AB	H	2B	3B	HR	(Hm	Rd)	TB	R	RBI	RC	TBB	IBB	SO	HBP	SH	SF	SB	CS	SB%	GDP	Avg	OBP	Slg
2010	Msoula	R+	68	226	87	14	4	7	(-	-)	130	48	37	65	35	4	44	19	0	2	20	8	.71	1	.385	.500	.575
2011	Visalia	A+	65	244	81	15	3	6	(-	-)	120	54	39	59	42	0	41	14	0	1	24	8	.75	2	.332	.455	.492
2011	Mobile	AA	56	212	64	7	4	4	(-	-)	91	31	28	40	30	1	35	9	3	1	10	6	.63	0	.302	.409	.429
2012	Mobile	AA	11	40	12	1	0	0	(-	-)	13	11	3	8	6	0	8	5	0	0	6	1	.86	0	.300	.451	.325
2012	Reno	AAA	119	488	186	46	5	7	(-	-)	263	119	45	120	53	3	68	15	5	1	38	10	.79	9	.381	.456	.539
2012	Ari	NL	22	85	22	3	2	2	(1	1)	35	19	5	13	14	0	15	3	1	0	2	3	.40	0	.259	.382	.412

Josh Edgin

Pitches: L **Bats:** L **Pos:** RP-34   EDGE-inn   **Ht:** 6'1" **Wt:** 225 **Born:** 12/17/1986 **Age:** 26

Year	Team	Lg	G	GS	CG	GF	IP	BFP	H	R	ER	HR	SH	SF	HB	TBB	IBB	SO	WP	Bk	W	L	Pct	Sh	Sv-Op	Hld	ERC	ERA
2010	Kngspt	R	18	0	0	8	31.2	139	28	15	10	2	2	0	4	12	0	41	1	1	0	1	.000	0	3--	-	3.50	2.84
2010	Savann	A	2	0	0	0	3.0	11	3	0	0	0	0	0	0	0	0	5	0	0	0	0	-	0	0--	-	2.18	0.00
2011	Savann	A	24	0	0	19	31.0	118	14	4	3	0	3	1	0	10	1	41	3	0	1	0	1.000	0	16--	-	0.92	0.87
2011	StLuci	A+	25	0	0	17	35.0	146	30	10	8	2	1	2	1	13	1	35	1	0	2	1	.667	0	11--	-	2.98	2.06
2012	Bnghtn	AA	6	0	0	6	6.1	26	5	1	1	1	0	0	0	2	0	5	0	0	0	0	-	0	2--	-	2.94	1.42
2012	Buffalo	AAA	35	0	0	6	37.0	164	34	19	16	0	3	1	1	18	0	40	0	0	3	2	.600	0	1--	-	3.26	3.89
2012	NYM	NL	34	0	0	6	25.2	107	19	14	13	5	2	0	2	10	0	30	0	0	1	2	.333	0	0-2	5	3.52	4.56

Steve Edlefsen

Pitches: R **Bats:** R **Pos:** RP-14   ED-leff-sen   **Ht:** 6'2" **Wt:** 195 **Born:** 6/27/1985 **Age:** 28

Year	Team	Lg	G	GS	CG	GF	IP	BFP	H	R	ER	HR	SH	SF	HB	TBB	IBB	SO	WP	Bk	W	L	Pct	Sh	Sv-Op	Hld	ERC	ERA
2007	Salem	A+	18	0	0	6	33.1	127	14	8	6	0	0	0	3	16	1	26	2	0	2	0	1.000	0	2--	-	1.35	1.62
2008	SnJos	A+	40	0	0	10	77.2	330	71	34	29	5	0	1	7	38	1	77	7	0	8	5	.615	0	0--	-	4.17	3.36
2009	Conn	AA	6	0	0	2	11.1	50	10	4	4	1	0	0	2	8	1	8	2	0	2	0	1.000	0	0--	-	5.36	3.18
2009	SnJos	A+	21	0	0	16	28.0	114	15	4	3	1	0	0	0	13	1	40	1	0	1	1	.500	0	7--	-	1.53	0.96
2009	Fresno	AAA	22	0	0	8	30.0	129	23	9	8	2	0	0	3	16	2	24	2	1	5	0	1.000	0	2--	-	3.36	2.40
2010	Fresno	AAA	49	0	0	13	64.1	273	55	22	17	6	5	1	3	34	1	50	3	0	7	2	.778	0	6--	-	3.98	2.38
2011	Fresno	AAA	32	0	0	6	41.1	183	50	28	26	2	2	0	2	19	0	29	3	0	2	4	.333	0	1--	-	5.56	5.66
2011	Giants	R	4	0	0	0	3.1	20	4	4	1	0	0	0	0	4	1	6	1	0	0	0	-	0	0--	-	6.08	2.70
2012	Fresno	AAA	35	0	0	6	38.0	167	33	19	16	3	0	1	3	18	0	29	1	0	1	3	.250	0	0--	-	3.72	3.79
2011	SF	NL	13	0	0	2	11.1	60	17	12	12	1	0	0	0	10	0	6	0	0	0	0	-	0	0-0	1	10.57	9.53
2012	SF	NL	14	0	0	6	15.1	69	20	8	8	1	0	0	0	6	0	9	0	0	0	1	.000	0	0-0	0	5.66	4.70
	2 ML YEARS		27	0	0	8	26.2	129	37	20	20	3	0	0	1	16	0	15	0	0	0	1	.000	0	0-0	1	7.66	6.75

Jack Egbert

Pitches: R **Bats:** L **Pos:** RP-1   **Ht:** 6'3" **Wt:** 220 **Born:** 5/12/1983 **Age:** 30

Year	Team	Lg	G	GS	CG	GF	IP	BFP	H	R	ER	HR	SH	SF	HB	TBB	IBB	SO	WP	Bk	W	L	Pct	Sh	Sv-Op	Hld	ERC	ERA
2004	Gr Falls	R+	17	9	0	0	58.2	253	51	25	22	2	4	1	5	33	0	52	4	0	4	1	.800	0	0--	-	3.93	3.38
2005	Salem	A	30	24	4	1	147.0	610	127	66	51	5	4	2	16	48	0	107	10	0	10	5	.667	3	0--	-	3.08	3.12
2006	WinSa	A+	25	25	0	0	140.2	588	131	57	46	2	3	2	5	46	1	120	2	0	9	8	.529	2	0--	-	2.99	2.94
2006	Brham	AA	4	4	0	0	21.0	88	17	4	2	0	1	0	0	8	0	24	1	0	2	0	.000	0	0--	-	2.30	0.86
2007	Brham	AA	28	28	0	0	161.2	654	138	63	55	3	3	1	10	44	0	165	6	0	12	8	.600	0	0--	-	2.57	3.06
2008	Brham	AA	1	1	0	0	4.0	17	5	1	1	0	0	0	0	4	0	4	0	0	0	0	-	0	0--	-	4.32	2.25

Year Team	Lg	G	GS	CG	GF	IP	BFP	H	R	ER	HR	SH	SF	HB	TBB	IBB	SO	WP	Bk	W	L	Pct	Sh	Sv-Op	Hld	ERC	ERA
2008 Charltt	AAA	24	22	1	0	129.2	565	133	80	67	15	5	6	8	41	2	117	3	0	4	12	.250	1	0--	-	4.17	4.65
2009 Charltt	AAA	30	18	0	2	108.2	497	132	73	61	13	3	3	7	33	1	79	3	0	6	11	.353	0	1--	-	5.20	5.05
2011 StLuci	A+	5	5	0	0	22.2	102	33	15	11	0	1	1	1	4	0	12	0	0	0	2	.000	0	0--	-	5.31	4.37
2011 Buffalo	AAA	7	4	0	1	22.0	96	23	11	11	2	0	1	0	10	0	11	1	0	0	3	.000	0	0--	-	4.53	4.50
2011 Bnghtn	AA	7	0	0	6	24.0	94	17	6	5	2	0	0	1	6	1	17	1	1	1	1	.500	0	5--	-	2.05	1.88
2012 Buffalo	AAA	27	1	0	7	40.0	175	47	30	24	4	2	1	2	9	2	27	1	1	3	4	.429	0	0--	-	4.46	5.40
2009 CWS	AL	2	0	0	1	2.2	18	8	8	8	1	0	1	0	2	1	0	0	0	0	0	-	0	0-0		21.82	27.00
2012 NYM	NL	1	0	0	1	0.2	2	0	0	0	0	0	0	0	0	0	0	0	0	0	0	-	0	0-0		0.00	0.00
2 ML YEARS		3	0	0	2	3.1	20	8	8	8	1	0	1	0	2	1	0	0	0	0	0	-	0	0-0		15.56	21.60

Mike Ekstrom

Pitches: R **Bats:** R **Pos:** RP-15   ECK-strumm   **Ht:** 6'0" **Wt:** 190 **Born:** 8/30/1983 **Age:** 29

Year Team	Lg	G	GS	CG	GF	IP	BFP	H	R	ER	HR	SH	SF	HB	TBB	IBB	SO	WP	Bk	W	L	Pct	Sh	Sv-Op	Hld	ERC	ERA
2012 ColSpr*	AAA	43	0	0	12	57.0	236	47	17	16	0	4	1	3	18	2	57	1	0	3	1	.750	0	1--	-	2.31	2.53
2008 SD	NL	8	0	0	1	9.2	47	14	8	8	2	0	0	0	7	1	6	0	0	0	2	.000	0	0-0		9.38	7.45
2009 SD	NL	12	0	0	5	18.1	83	21	14	13	3	0	2	1	8	0	19	2	0	0	0	-	0	0-0		5.80	6.38
2010 TB	AL	15	0	0	6	16.1	68	12	6	6	0	0	1	2	9	1	10	1	0	0	1	.000	0	0-0		2.98	3.31
2011 TB	AL	1	0	0	1	1.0	4	1	0	0	0	0	0	0	0	0	1	0	0	0	0	-	0	0-0		1.95	0.00
2012 Col	NL	15	0	0	5	15.2	72	21	11	11	1	3	3	0	2	0	9	0	0	0	0	-	0	0-0		4.40	6.32
5 ML YEARS		51	0	0	22	61.0	274	69	39	38	6	3	6	3	26	2	45	3	0	0	3	.000	0	0-0		5.08	5.61

Scott Elbert

Pitches: L **Bats:** L **Pos:** RP-43   **Ht:** 6'2" **Wt:** 225 **Born:** 8/13/1985 **Age:** 27

Year Team	Lg	G	GS	CG	GF	IP	BFP	H	R	ER	HR	SH	SF	HB	TBB	IBB	SO	WP	Bk	W	L	Pct	Sh	Sv-Op	Hld	ERC	ERA
2012 Chatt*	AA	3	0	0	0	2.0	6	0	0	0	0	0	0	0	0	0	6	0	0	0	0	-	0	0--	-	0.00	0.00
2008 LAD	NL	10	0	0	1	6.0	31	9	8	8	2	0	0	1	4	0	4	0	0	0	1	.000	0	0-0	2	11.46	12.00
2009 LAD	NL	19	0	0	3	19.2	83	19	11	11	4	1	0	0	7	0	21	1	0	2	0	1.000	0	0-0	3	4.45	5.03
2010 LAD	NL	1	0	0	0	0.2	6	1	1	1	0	0	0	0	3	0	0	0	0	0	0	-	0	0-0	0	24.61	13.50
2011 LAD	NL	47	0	0	11	33.1	139	27	9	9	1	0	1	1	14	4	34	2	0	0	1	.000	0	2-2	7	2.60	2.43
2012 LAD	NL	43	0	0	12	32.2	133	27	8	8	3	0	2	1	13	1	29	3	0	1	1	.500	0	0-0	9	3.24	2.20
Postseason		1	0	0	0	0.1	3	0	0	0	0	0	0	0	2	0	0	1	0	0	0	-	0	0-0	0	19.60	0.00
5 ML YEARS		120	0	0	27	92.1	392	83	37	37	10	1	3	3	41	5	92	6	0	3	3	.500	0	2-2	21	3.83	3.61

Brad Eldred

Bats: R **Throws:** R **Pos:** DH-5; PR-1   **Ht:** 6'7" **Wt:** 270 **Born:** 7/12/1980 **Age:** 32

Year Team	Lg	G	AB	H	2B	3B	HR	(Hm	Rd)	TB	R	RBI	RC	TBB	IBB	SO	HBP	SH	SF	SB	CS	SB%	GDP	Avg	OBP	Slg
2012 Hshma*	Jap	60	208	55	10	0	11	(-	-)	98	20	34	32	18	1	64	2	0	2	0	0	-	2	.264	.326	.471
2012 Toledo*	AAA	63	236	72	18	1	24	(-	-)	164	49	65	59	24	2	73	3	0	2	5	0	1.00	5	.305	.374	.695
2005 Pit	NL	55	190	42	9	0	12	(4	8)	87	23	27	14	13	0	77	3	0	2	1	1	.50	5	.221	.279	.458
2007 Pit	NL	19	46	5	1	0	2	(1	1)	12	3	3	0	1	1	16	0	0	0	0	0	-	1	.109	.128	.261
2010 Col	NL	11	24	6	1	0	1	(1	0)	10	4	3	3	2	0	10	1	0	0	0	0	-	0	.250	.333	.417
2012 Det	AL	5	16	3	1	1	0	(0	0)	6	1	1	1	1	0	6	0	0	0	0	0	-	0	.188	.235	.375
4 ML YEARS		90	276	56	12	1	15	(6	9)	115	31	34	18	17	1	109	4	0	2	1	1	.50	6	.203	.258	.417

A.J. Ellis

Bats: R **Throws:** R **Pos:** C-131; PH-3   **Ht:** 6'3" **Wt:** 215 **Born:** 4/9/1981 **Age:** 32

Year Team	Lg	G	AB	H	2B	3B	HR	(Hm	Rd)	TB	R	RBI	RC	TBB	IBB	SO	HBP	SH	SF	SB	CS	SB%	GDP	Avg	OBP	Slg
2008 LAD	NL	4	3	0	0	0	0	(0	0)	0	1	0	0	2	0	0	0	0	0	0	0	-	0	.000	.000	.000
2009 LAD	NL	8	10	1	0	0	0	(0	0)	1	0	1	0	0	0	1	0	0	0	0	0	-	0	.100	.100	.100
2010 LAD	NL	44	108	30	5	0	0	(0	0)	35	6	16	16	14	1	18	1	4	1	0	0	-	5	.278	.363	.324
2011 LAD	NL	31	85	23	1	1	2	(0	2)	32	8	11	11	14	0	16	3	1	0	0	1	.00	2	.271	.392	.376
2012 LAD	NL	133	423	114	20	1	13	(6	7)	175	44	52	61	65	11	107	7	6	4	0	0	-	17	.270	.373	.414
5 ML YEARS		220	629	168	26	2	15	(6	9)	243	59	80	88	93	12	144	11	11	5	0	1	.00	24	.267	.369	.386

Mark Ellis

Bats: R **Throws:** R **Pos:** 2B-110; PH-2; PR-1   **Ht:** 5'10" **Wt:** 190 **Born:** 6/6/1977 **Age:** 36

Year Team	Lg	G	AB	H	2B	3B	HR	(Hm	Rd)	TB	R	RBI	RC	TBB	IBB	SO	HBP	SH	SF	SB	CS	SB%	GDP	Avg	OBP	Slg
2012 RCuca*	A+	4	14	4	0	0	0	(-	-)	4	3	3	1	2	0	3	0	0	0	0	0	-	0	.286	.375	.286
2002 Oak	AL	98	345	94	16	4	6	(6	0)	136	58	35	55	44	1	54	4	8	3	4	2	.67	3	.272	.359	.394
2003 Oak	AL	154	553	137	31	5	9	(7	2)	205	78	52	69	48	4	94	7	9	5	6	2	.75	7	.248	.313	.371
2005 Oak	AL	122	434	137	21	5	13	(5	8)	207	76	52	78	44	1	51	4	4	0	1	3	.25	10	.316	.384	.477
2006 Oak	AL	124	441	110	25	1	11	(7	4)	170	64	52	53	40	1	76	8	4	7	4	0	1.00	13	.249	.319	.385
2007 Oak	AL	150	583	161	33	3	19	(10	9)	257	84	76	76	44	1	94	10	2	3	9	4	.69	10	.276	.336	.441
2008 Oak	AL	117	442	103	20	3	12	(7	5)	165	55	41	54	33	2	65	5	5	2	14	2	.88	11	.233	.321	.373
2009 Oak	AL	105	377	99	23	0	10	(4	6)	152	52	61	54	23	1	54	2	3	4	10	3	.77	10	.263	.305	.403
2010 Oak	AL	124	436	127	24	0	5	(0	5)	166	45	49	66	40	4	56	8	3	5	7	6	.54	7	.291	.358	.381
2011 2 Tms		132	480	119	24	1	7	(6	1)	166	55	41	40	22	0	75	6	9	2	14	5	.74	8	.248	.288	.346
2012 LAD	NL	110	415	107	21	1	7	(6	1)	151	62	31	44	40	0	70	7	2	0	5	0	1.00	5	.258	.333	.364

Year	Team	Lg	G	AB	H	2B	3B	HR	(Hm	Rd)	TB	R	RBI	RC	TBB	IBB	SO	HBP	SH	SF	SB	CS	SB%	GDP	Avg	OBP	Slg
															BATTING						**BASERUNNING**				**AVERAGES**		
11	Oak	AL	62	217	47	11	1	1	(1	0)	63	21	16	10	8	0	32	3	4	1	7	2	.78	3	.217	.253	.290
11	Col	NL	70	263	72	13	0	6	(5	1)	103	34	25	30	14	0	43	3	5	1	7	3	.70	5	.274	.317	.392
	Postseason		12	43	11	2	0	1	(1	0)	16	3	4	6	5	0	11	1	0	0	0	0	-	0	.256	.347	.372
	10 ML YEARS		1236	4506	1194	238	23	99	(58	41)	1775	629	490	589	398	15	689	61	49	32	74	27	.73	84	.265	.331	.394

Jacoby Ellsbury

Bats: L **Throws:** L **Pos:** CF-73; DH-1   **Ht:** 6'1" **Wt:** 195 **Born:** 9/11/1983 **Age:** 29

Year	Team	Lg	G	AB	H	2B	3B	HR	(Hm	Rd)	TB	R	RBI	RC	TBB	IBB	SO	HBP	SH	SF	SB	CS	SB%	GDP	Avg	OBP	Slg
															BATTING						**BASERUNNING**				**AVERAGES**		
2012	RedSx*	R	4	10	2	1	0	1	(-	-)	6	3	3	2	4	0	3	0	0	0	0	0	-	0	.200	.429	.600
2012	PortInd*	AA	2	9	2	1	0	0	(-	-)	3	1	0	0	0	0	1	0	0	0	0	0	-	0	.222	.222	.333
2012	Pwtckt*	AAA	2	8	1	0	0	0	(-	-)	1	1	0	0	0	0	1	0	0	0	0	0	-	1	.125	.125	.125
2007	Bos	AL	33	116	41	7	1	3	(3	0)	59	20	18	26	8	0	15	1	0	2	9	0	1.00	2	.353	.394	.509
2008	Bos	AL	145	554	155	22	7	9	(4	5)	218	98	47	71	41	2	80	7	4	3	50	11	.82	10	.280	.336	.394
2009	Bos	AL	153	624	188	27	10	8	(4	4)	259	94	60	97	49	3	74	6	6	6	70	12	.85	13	.301	.355	.415
2010	Bos	AL	18	78	15	4	0	0	(0	0)	19	10	5	4	4	0	9	1	0	0	7	1	.88	0	.192	.241	.244
2011	Bos	AL	158	660	212	46	5	32	(15	17)	364	119	105	134	52	1	98	9	3	5	39	15	.72	8	.321	.376	.552
2012	Bos	AL	74	303	82	18	0	4	(3	1)	112	43	26	37	19	0	43	0	0	1	14	3	.82	5	.271	.313	.370
	Postseason		22	69	18	7	1	0	(0	0)	27	12	11	11	6	1	10	0	0	1	5	1	.83	2	.261	.316	.391
	6 ML YEARS		581	2335	693	124	23	56	(29	27)	1031	384	261	369	173	6	319	24	13	17	189	42	.82	38	.297	.349	.442

Jake Elmore

Bats: R **Throws:** R **Pos:** SS-17; PH-11; 2B-5   **Ht:** 5'10" **Wt:** 180 **Born:** 6/15/1987 **Age:** 26

Year	Team	Lg	G	AB	H	2B	3B	HR	(Hm	Rd)	TB	R	RBI	RC	TBB	IBB	SO	HBP	SH	SF	SB	CS	SB%	GDP	Avg	OBP	Slg
															BATTING						**BASERUNNING**				**AVERAGES**		
2008	MsnVjo*	R+	53	179	53	15	3	3	(-	-)	83	38	22	33	26	1	36	4	3	4	9	8	.53	2	.296	.390	.464
2009	Sbend	A	118	387	100	21	3	3	(-	-)	136	62	38	56	61	0	55	5	2	2	13	7	.65	11	.258	.365	.351
2010	Mobile	AA	124	388	107	17	2	2	(-	-)	134	64	31	57	58	1	57	4	7	5	25	13	.66	19	.276	.371	.345
2011	Mobile	AA	121	381	103	19	1	3	(-	-)	133	58	41	54	54	1	65	7	5	11	15	11	.58	9	.270	.362	.349
2012	Reno	AAA	108	419	144	30	9	1	(-	-)	195	95	73	95	74	1	54	5	7	6	32	8	.80	12	.344	.442	.465
2012	Ari	NL	30	68	13	4	0	0	(0	0)	17	1	7	3	5	0	6	0	0	0	0	0	-	1	.191	.247	.250

John Ely

Pitches: R **Bats:** R **Pos:** RP-2   **Ht:** 6'2" **Wt:** 200 **Born:** 5/13/1986 **Age:** 27

Year	Team	Lg	G	GS	CG	GF	IP	BFP	H	R	ER	HR	SH	SF	HB	TBB	IBB	SO	WP	Bk	W	L	Pct	Sh	Sv-Op Hld	ERC	ERA
					HOW MUCH HE PITCHED						**WHAT HE GAVE UP**											**THE RESULTS**					
2012	Albq*	AAA	27	27	1	0	168.2	682	150	68	60	18	7	5	4	36	0	165	9	0	14	7	.667	1	0- - -	2.92	3.20
2010	LAD	NL	18	18	0	0	100.0	430	105	63	61	12	4	4	2	40	2	76	4	0	4	10	.286	0	0-0 0	4.64	5.49
2011	LAD	NL	5	1	0	1	12.2	56	12	6	6	2	0	0	1	7	1	13	0	0	1	1	.000	0	0-0 0	4.66	4.26
2012	LAD	NL	2	0	0	1	2.2	19	6	6	6	0	1	0	1	4	2	3	0	0	0	2	.000	0	0-0 0	15.82	20.25
	3 ML YEARS		25	19	0	2	115.1	505	123	75	73	14	5	4	3	51	5	92	4	0	4	13	.235	0	0-0 0	4.88	5.70

Edwin Encarnacion

Bats: R **Throws:** R **Pos:** DH-82; 1B-68; LF-3; 3B-1   **Ht:** 6'2" **Wt:** 230 **Born:** 1/7/1983 **Age:** 30

Year	Team	Lg	G	AB	H	2B	3B	HR	(Hm	Rd)	TB	R	RBI	RC	TBB	IBB	SO	HBP	SH	SF	SB	CS	SB%	GDP	Avg	OBP	Slg
															BATTING						**BASERUNNING**				**AVERAGES**		
2005	Cin	NL	69	211	49	16	0	9	(3	6)	92	25	31	24	20	2	60	3	0	0	3	0	1.00	8	.232	.308	.436
2006	Cin	NL	117	406	112	33	1	15	(7	8)	192	60	72	66	41	3	78	13	0	3	6	3	.67	9	.276	.359	.473
2007	Cin	NL	139	502	145	25	1	16	(10	6)	220	66	76	86	39	4	86	14	0	1	8	1	.89	5	.289	.356	.438
2008	Cin	NL	146	506	127	29	1	26	(15	11)	236	75	68	72	61	1	102	10	0	5	1	0	1.00	13	.251	.340	.466
2009	2 Tms		85	293	66	11	2	13	(5	8)	120	35	39	37	37	0	67	5	0	3	2	1	.67	5	.225	.320	.410
2010	Tor	AL	96	332	81	16	0	21	(7	14)	160	47	51	41	29	1	60	2	0	4	1	0	1.00	9	.244	.305	.482
2011	Tor	AL	134	481	131	36	0	17	(14	3)	218	70	55	67	43	2	77	3	0	3	8	2	.80	17	.272	.334	.453
2012	Tor	AL	151	542	152	24	0	42	(23	19)	302	93	110	124	84	12	94	11	0	7	13	3	.81	6	.280	.384	.557
09	Cin	NL	43	139	29	6	1	5	(3	2)	52	10	16	19	24	0	38	2	0	0	1	1	.50	3	.209	.333	.374
09	Tor	AL	42	154	37	5	1	8	(2	6)	68	25	23	18	13	0	29	3	0	3	1	0	1.00	2	.240	.306	.442
	8 ML YEARS		937	3273	863	190	5	159	(84	75)	1540	471	502	517	354	25	624	61	0	26	42	10	.81	72	.264	.344	.471

Barry Enright

Pitches: R **Bats:** R **Pos:** RP-3   **Ht:** 6'3" **Wt:** 220 **Born:** 3/30/1986 **Age:** 27

Year	Team	Lg	G	GS	CG	GF	IP	BFP	H	R	ER	HR	SH	SF	HB	TBB	IBB	SO	WP	Bk	W	L	Pct	Sh	Sv-Op Hld	ERC	ERA
					HOW MUCH HE PITCHED						**WHAT HE GAVE UP**											**THE RESULTS**					
2012	Reno*	AAA	21	21	1	0	110.1	484	118	74	72	19	6	8	2	51	2	72	3	0	8	6	.571	0	0- - -	5.40	5.87
2012	Salt Lk*	AAA	8	8	1	0	52.2	212	42	19	16	3	0	2	2	19	0	30	1	0	5	1	.833	1	0- - -	2.79	2.73
2010	Ari	NL	17	17	0	0	99.0	410	97	43	43	20	8	1	1	29	0	49	0	0	6	7	.462	0	0-0 0	4.34	3.91
2011	Ari	NL	7	7	0	0	37.2	175	50	31	31	11	3	2	1	15	1	21	2	0	1	4	.200	0	0-0 0	7.65	7.41
2012	LAA	AL	3	0	0	2	3.2	20	7	6	6	1	0	0	1	1	0	0	0	0	0	0	-	0	0-0 0	10.06	14.73
	3 ML YEARS		27	24	0	2	140.1	605	154	80	80	32	11	3	2	45	1	70	2	0	7	11	.389	0	0-0 0	5.32	5.13

Nathan Eovaldi

Pitches: R **Bats:** R **Pos:** SP-22   eh-VOLL-dee   **Ht:** 6'2" **Wt:** 215 **Born:** 2/13/1990 **Age:** 23

Year	Team	Lg	G	GS	CG	GF	IP	BFP	H	R	ER	HR	SH	SF	HB	TBB	IBB	SO	WP	Bk	W	L	Pct	Sh	Sv-Op	Hld	ERC	ERA
2008	Ddgrs	R	6	0	0	4	8.0	33	6	1	1	0	1	0	0	3	0	9	2	0	0	1	.000	0	1- -	-	2.01	1.13
2008	Ogden	R+	1	0	0	0	2.2	8	1	0	0	0	0	0	0	0	0	2	0	0	0	0	-	0	0- -	-	0.35	0.00
2009	Gt Lks	A	26	16	0	4	96.1	417	95	48	35	2	1	10	6	41	0	71	5	1	3	5	.375	0	1- -	-	3.81	3.27
2010	InldEm	A+	16	14	2	0	85.0	369	99	46	42	3	3	1	4	33	0	58	6	0	3	5	.375	2	0- -	-	4.85	4.45
2010	Ddgrs	R	3	3	0	0	8.1	34	6	4	4	0	1	0	1	4	0	10	1	0	0	1	.000	0	0- -	-	2.76	4.32
2010	Ogden	R+	1	1	0	0	5.0	19	3	2	1	0	0	0	1	0	0	4	1	0	1	0	1.000	0	0- -	-	1.11	1.80
2011	Chatt	AA	20	19	0	0	103.0	427	76	41	30	3	1	4	2	46	2	99	6	0	6	5	.545	0	0- -	-	2.43	2.62
2012	Chatt	AA	9	8	0	0	35.0	141	30	12	12	2	2	1	2	13	0	30	0	1	2	2	.500	0	0- -	-	3.28	3.09
2011	LAD	NL	10	6	0	1	34.2	146	28	14	14	2	2	0	2	20	0	23	0	0	1	2	.333	0	0-0	1	3.75	3.63
2012	2 Tms	NL	22	22	0	0	119.1	526	133	59	57	10	1	6	3	47	3	78	1	0	4	13	.235	0	0-0	0	4.67	4.30
12	LAD	NL	10	10	0	0	56.1	241	63	27	26	5	0	3	0	20	2	34	1	0	1	6	.143	0	0-0	0	4.54	4.15
12	Mia	NL	12	12	0	0	63.0	285	70	32	31	5	1	3	3	27	1	44	0	0	3	7	.300	0	0-0	0	4.79	4.43
2 ML YEARS			32	28	0	1	154.0	672	161	73	71	12	3	6	5	67	3	101	1	0	5	15	.250	0	0-0	1	4.46	4.15

Cody Eppley

Pitches: R **Bats:** R **Pos:** RP-59   **Ht:** 6'5" **Wt:** 205 **Born:** 10/8/1985 **Age:** 27

Year	Team	Lg	G	GS	CG	GF	IP	BFP	H	R	ER	HR	SH	SF	HB	TBB	IBB	SO	WP	Bk	W	L	Pct	Sh	Sv-Op	Hld	ERC	ERA
2008	Rngrs	R	19	0	0	15	25.2	104	19	12	6	1	0	0	0	5	0	34	5	0	2	2	.500	0	7- -	-	1.61	2.10
2008	Clinton	A	2	0	0	2	2.0	9	2	2	2	0	0	0	1	0	0	3	1	0	0	0	-	0	0- -	-	3.63	9.00
2009	Hkry	A	37	0	0	21	67.2	278	65	31	22	4	1	2	3	6	0	76	5	0	1	3	.250	0	6- -	-	2.53	2.93
2010	Bkrsfld	A+	14	0	0	7	18.0	65	9	0	0	0	0	0	1	1	0	24	4	0	2	0	1.000	0	6- -	-	0.71	0.00
2010	Frisco	AA	19	0	0	16	22.2	88	12	3	3	0	1	0	0	9	1	27	0	0	1	1	.500	0	9- -	-	1.27	1.19
2010	OKCity	AAA	18	0	0	10	28.2	128	32	13	13	3	0	0	0	13	0	31	0	0	2	1	.667	0	1- -	-	5.00	4.08
2011	RdRck	AAA	43	0	0	29	55.1	250	51	27	24	3	0	1	1	34	4	55	7	0	4	2	.667	0	10- -	-	4.01	3.90
2012	S-WB	AAA	7	0	0	2	9.1	31	3	0	0	0	0	0	0	1	0	13	0	0	0	0	-	0	2- -	-	0.36	0.00
2011	Tex	AL	10	0	0	1	9.0	43	11	8	8	3	1	0	1	5	1	6	1	0	1	1	.500	0	0-1	2	8.30	8.00
2012	NYY	AL	59	0	0	14	46.0	194	46	19	17	3	4	0	0	17	2	32	2	0	1	2	.333	0	0-0	9	3.70	3.33
2 ML YEARS			69	0	0	15	55.0	237	57	27	25	6	5	0	1	22	3	38	3	0	2	3	.400	0	0-1	11	4.38	4.09

Edgmer Escalona

Pitches: R **Bats:** R **Pos:** RP-22   EGG-merr   **Ht:** 6'4" **Wt:** 235 **Born:** 10/6/1986 **Age:** 26

Year	Team	Lg	G	GS	CG	GF	IP	BFP	H	R	ER	HR	SH	SF	HB	TBB	IBB	SO	WP	Bk	W	L	Pct	Sh	Sv-Op	Hld	ERC	ERA
2012	ColSpr*	AAA	32	0	0	14	40.0	172	37	18	13	2	0	0	1	17	0	40	3	1	3	3	.500	0	5- -	-	3.49	2.93
2010	Col	NL	5	0	0	2	6.0	26	4	1	1	0	0	1	0	4	2	2	1	0	0	0	-	0	0-0	0	2.02	1.50
2011	Col	NL	14	0	0	5	25.2	99	17	5	5	3	1	0	0	7	2	14	0	0	0	0	-	0	0-0	0	1.92	1.75
2012	Col	NL	22	0	0	6	22.1	97	23	16	15	5	1	1	1	7	1	21	2	0	0	1	.000	0	0-0	2	4.83	6.04
3 ML YEARS			41	0	0	13	54.0	222	44	22	21	8	2	2	1	18	5	37	3	0	0	1	.000	0	0-0	2	3.06	3.50

Sergio Escalona

Pitches: L **Bats:** L **Pos:** P   **Ht:** 6'0" **Wt:** 215 **Born:** 8/3/1984 **Age:** 28

Year	Team	Lg	G	GS	CG	GF	IP	BFP	H	R	ER	HR	SH	SF	HB	TBB	IBB	SO	WP	Bk	W	L	Pct	Sh	Sv-Op	Hld	ERC	ERA
2007	Clrwtr	A+	1	1	0	0	4.0	21	8	1	1	0	1	0	0	2	0	4	0	0	0	0	-	0	0- -	-	10.21	2.25
2007	Wmspt	A-	7	7	0	0	27.1	128	32	26	23	2	0	1	2	19	0	26	2	0	2	2	.500	0	0- -	-	6.58	7.57
2007	Lakwd	A	7	7	0	0	39.0	177	51	25	18	4	2	4	1	11	0	32	1	0	1	4	.200	0	0- -	-	5.47	4.15
2008	Lakwd	A	28	0	0	8	44.2	181	36	18	17	1	1	1	0	18	1	60	5	0	5	1	.833	0	2- -	-	2.58	3.43
2008	Rdng	AA	15	0	0	5	24.1	112	27	12	6	3	1	0	1	14	0	29	0	0	1	1	.500	0	1- -	-	5.80	2.22
2009	Rdng	AA	32	0	0	22	40.2	168	31	12	8	1	2	0	3	14	1	38	3	0	2	1	.667	0	12- -	-	2.35	1.77
2009	LV	AAA	15	1	0	9	19.2	89	21	15	13	4	0	1	1	8	1	15	3	1	0	2	.000	0	2- -	-	5.26	5.95
2010	Rdng	AA	50	0	0	25	54.1	229	46	25	23	6	2	2	0	22	0	53	0	0	4	8	.333	0	10- -	-	3.29	3.81
2011	OKCity	AAA	14	0	0	10	17.0	70	13	6	6	1	2	1	1	5	0	18	2	0	1	0	1.000	0	3- -	-	2.36	3.18
2009	Phi	NL	14	0	0	4	13.2	60	12	7	7	0	0	2	3	5	1	10	1	0	1	0	1.000	0	0-0	2	3.24	4.61
2011	Hou	NL	49	0	0	5	27.2	115	24	10	9	3	2	0	2	11	1	25	2	0	2	1	.667	0	0-1	6	3.72	2.93
2 ML YEARS			63	0	0	9	41.1	175	36	17	16	3	2	2	5	16	2	35	3	0	3	1	.750	0	0-1	8	3.57	3.48

Alcides Escobar

Bats: R **Throws:** R **Pos:** SS-155   al-SEE-dess   **Ht:** 6'1" **Wt:** 190 **Born:** 12/16/1986 **Age:** 26

Year	Team	Lg	G	AB	H	2B	3B	HR	(Hm	Rd)	TB	R	RBI	RC	TBB	IBB	SO	HBP	SH	SF	SB	CS	SB%	GDP	Avg	OBP	Slg
2008	Mil	NL	9	4	2	0	0	0	(0	0)	2	2	0	0	0	0	1	0	0	0	0	0	-	0	.500	.500	.500
2009	Mil	NL	38	125	38	3	1	1	(0	1)	46	20	11	16	4	0	18	2	2	1	4	2	.67	0	.304	.333	.368
2010	Mil	NL	145	506	119	14	10	4	(3	1)	165	57	41	51	36	7	70	3	4	3	10	4	.71	8	.235	.288	.326
2011	KC	AL	158	548	139	21	8	4	(0	4)	188	69	46	46	25	1	73	4	18	3	26	9	.74	10	.254	.290	.343
2012	KC	AL	155	605	177	30	7	5	(5	0)	236	68	52	72	27	2	100	8	8	0	35	5	.88	14	.293	.331	.390
5 ML YEARS			505	1788	475	68	26	14	(8	6)	637	216	150	185	92	10	262	17	32	7	75	20	.79	32	.266	.307	.356

Eduardo Escobar

Bats: B **Throws:** R **Pos:** 3B-25; 2B-14; SS-10; PR-6; PH-4; LF-1; DH-1   **Ht:** 5'10" **Wt:** 165 **Born:** 1/5/1989 **Age:** 24

Year	Team	Lg	G	AB	H	2B	3B	HR	(Hm	Rd)	TB	R	RBI	RC	TBB	IBB	SO	HBP	SH	SF	SB	CS	SB%	GDP	Avg	OBP	Slg
2008	Gr Falls	R+	6	24	10	2	1	1	(-	-)	17	6	4	7	2	0	3	1	0	1	1	1	.50	0	.417	.464	.708
2008	Knapol	A	60	243	65	6	1	0	(-	-)	73	37	22	22	13	0	65	0	8	2	4	3	.57	1	.267	.302	.300
2009	Knapol	A	128	464	119	10	7	3	(-	-)	152	64	41	49	29	1	91	1	17	3	20	6	.77	9	.256	.300	.328
2010	WinSa	A+	87	368	105	18	8	3	(-	-)	148	57	39	50	23	3	76	2	11	4	8	5	.62	9	.285	.327	.402
2010	Brham	AA	49	202	53	8	3	3	(-	-)	76	22	22	23	9	0	35	0	5	0	3	0	1.00	5	.262	.294	.376
2011	Charltt	AAA	137	489	130	23	4	4	(-	-)	173	55	49	54	27	0	104	1	15	4	13	8	.62	6	.266	.303	.354
2012	Roch	AAA	35	138	30	3	3	1	(-	-)	42	19	9	11	8	0	26	0	4	1	3	1	.75	1	.217	.259	.304
2011	CWS	AL	9	7	2	0	0	0	(0	0)	2	0	0	1	0	0	1	0	0	0	0	0	-	0	.286	.286	.286
2012	2 Tms	AL	50	131	28	4	1	0	(0	0)	34	18	9	12	11	0	31	1	2	1	3	0	1.00	0	.214	.278	.260
12	CWS	AL	36	87	18	4	1	0	(0	0)	24	14	3	7	9	0	23	0	1	0	2	0	1.00	0	.207	.281	.276
12	Min	AL	14	44	10	0	0	0	(0	0)	10	4	6	5	2	0	8	1	1	1	1	0	1.00	0	.227	.271	.227
2 ML YEARS			59	138	30	4	1	0	(0	0)	36	18	9	13	11	0	32	1	2	1	3	0	1.00	0	.217	.278	.261

Yunel Escobar

Bats: R **Throws:** R **Pos:** SS-143; PH-3; DH-2   you-NELL   **Ht:** 6'2" **Wt:** 210 **Born:** 11/2/1982 **Age:** 30

Year	Team	Lg	G	AB	H	2B	3B	HR	(Hm	Rd)	TB	R	RBI	RC	TBB	IBB	SO	HBP	SH	SF	SB	CS	SB%	GDP	Avg	OBP	Slg
2007	Atl	NL	94	319	104	25	0	5	(3	2)	144	54	28	52	27	1	44	5	2	2	5	3	.63	6	.326	.385	.451
2008	Atl	NL	136	514	148	24	2	10	(5	5)	206	71	60	70	59	4	62	5	7	2	2	5	.29	24	.288	.366	.401
2009	Atl	NL	141	528	158	26	2	14	(7	7)	230	89	76	90	57	3	62	10	7	2	5	4	.56	21	.299	.377	.436
2010	2 Tms		135	497	127	19	0	4	(2	2)	158	60	35	53	56	1	57	5	9	0	6	2	.75	18	.256	.337	.318
2011	Tor	AL	133	513	149	24	3	11	(8	3)	212	77	48	84	61	1	70	6	5	5	3	3	.50	14	.290	.369	.413
2012	Tor	AL	145	558	141	22	1	9	(6	3)	192	58	51	51	35	1	70	4	7	4	5	1	.83	21	.253	.300	.344
10	Atl	NL	75	261	62	12	0	0	(0	0)	74	28	19	25	37	1	31	1	2	0	5	1	.83	9	.238	.334	.284
10	Tor	AL	60	236	65	7	0	4	(2	2)	84	32	16	28	19	0	26	4	7	0	1	1	.50	9	.275	.340	.356
6 ML YEARS			784	2929	827	140	8	53	(31	22)	1142	409	298	400	295	11	365	35	37	15	26	18	.59	104	.282	.353	.390

Danny Espinosa

Bats: B **Throws:** R **Pos:** 2B-126; SS-36; PH-6   **Ht:** 6'0" **Wt:** 195 **Born:** 4/25/1987 **Age:** 26

Year	Team	Lg	G	AB	H	2B	3B	HR	(Hm	Rd)	TB	R	RBI	RC	TBB	IBB	SO	HBP	SH	SF	SB	CS	SB%	GDP	Avg	OBP	Slg
2010	Was	NL	28	103	22	4	1	6	(4	2)	46	16	15	15	9	1	30	0	0	0	0	2	.00	4	.214	.277	.447
2011	Was	NL	158	573	135	29	5	21	(11	10)	237	72	66	83	57	4	166	19	5	4	17	6	.74	6	.236	.323	.414
2012	Was	NL	160	594	147	37	2	17	(7	10)	239	82	56	69	46	4	189	13	3	2	20	6	.77	11	.247	.315	.402
3 ML YEARS			346	1270	304	70	8	44	(22	22)	522	170	137	167	112	9	385	32	8	6	37	14	.73	17	.239	.315	.411

Marco Estrada

Pitches: R **Bats:** R **Pos:** SP-23; RP-6   **Ht:** 5'11" **Wt:** 200 **Born:** 7/5/1983 **Age:** 29

Year	Team	Lg	G	GS	CG	GF	IP	BFP	H	R	ER	HR	SH	SF	HB	TBB	IBB	SO	WP	Bk	W	L	Pct	Sh	Sv-Op	Hld	ERC	ERA
2012	Nashv*	AAA	2	2	0	0	8.0	35	7	1	1	0	1	0	0	5	0	5	0	1	0	0	-	0	0--	-	3.54	1.13
2008	Was	NL	11	0	0	3	12.2	63	17	13	11	4	0	0	2	5	1	10	0	1	0	0	-	0	0-1	3	8.13	7.82
2009	Was	NL	4	1	0	1	7.1	33	6	6	5	1	1	0	0	4	0	9	1	0	0	1	.000	0	0-0	1	3.67	6.14
2010	Mil	NL	7	1	0	0	11.1	58	14	13	12	3	1	0	1	6	0	13	2	0	0	0	-	0	0-0	7	7.17	9.53
2011	Mil	NL	43	7	0	12	92.2	381	83	45	42	11	7	1	2	29	2	88	4	2	4	8	.333	0	0-3	4	3.39	4.08
2012	Mil	NL	29	23	0	0	138.1	562	129	62	56	18	7	3	0	29	0	143	4	1	5	7	.417	0	0-0	1	3.18	3.64
Postseason			4	0	0	2	6.0	27	7	4	4	0	0	0	0	2	0	9	1	0	0	0	-	0	0-0	1	3.91	6.00
5 ML YEARS			94	32	0	16	262.1	1097	249	139	126	37	16	4	5	73	3	263	11	3	9	16	.360	0	0-4	8	3.64	4.32

Andre Ethier

Bats: L **Throws:** L **Pos:** RF-146; DH-2; PH-2; CF-1   EE-thee-er   **Ht:** 6'2" **Wt:** 205 **Born:** 4/10/1982 **Age:** 31

Year	Team	Lg	G	AB	H	2B	3B	HR	(Hm	Rd)	TB	R	RBI	RC	TBB	IBB	SO	HBP	SH	SF	SB	CS	SB%	GDP	Avg	OBP	Slg
2012	RCuca*	A+	2	4	0	0	0	0	(-	-)	0	0	1	0	1	0	1	0	0	0	0	0	-	1	.000	.200	.000
2006	LAD	NL	126	396	122	20	7	11	(9	2)	189	50	55	62	34	2	77	5	0	6	5	5	.50	11	.308	.365	.477
2007	LAD	NL	153	447	127	32	2	13	(8	5)	202	50	64	65	46	12	68	4	0	8	0	4	.00	10	.284	.350	.452
2008	LAD	NL	141	525	160	38	5	20	(10	10)	268	90	77	99	59	0	88	4	1	7	6	3	.67	6	.305	.375	.510
2009	LAD	NL	160	596	162	42	3	31	(22	9)	303	92	106	94	72	10	116	13	0	4	6	4	.60	19	.272	.361	.508
2010	LAD	NL	139	517	151	33	1	23	(14	9)	255	71	82	89	59	11	102	3	0	6	2	1	.67	11	.292	.364	.493
2011	LAD	NL	135	487	142	30	1	11	(8	3)	205	67	62	73	58	9	103	3	0	3	0	1	.00	8	.292	.368	.421
2012	LAD	NL	149	556	158	36	1	20	(14	6)	256	79	89	89	50	6	124	9	0	3	2	2	.50	13	.284	.351	.460
Postseason			18	64	17	4	1	3	(1	2)	32	13	6	8	8	0	16	1	0	0	0	1	.00	1	.266	.356	.500
7 ML YEARS			1003	3524	1022	231	19	129	(85	44)	1678	499	535	571	378	50	678	41	1	37	21	20	.51	78	.290	.362	.476

Dana Eveland

Pitches: L **Bats:** L **Pos:** RP-12; SP-2   EVE-land   **Ht:** 6'1" **Wt:** 235 **Born:** 10/29/1983 **Age:** 29

Year	Team	Lg	G	GS	CG	GF	IP	BFP	H	R	ER	HR	SH	SF	HB	TBB	IBB	SO	WP	Bk	W	L	Pct	Sh	Sv-Op	Hld	ERC	ERA
2012	Norfolk*	AAA	14	14	0	0	84.0	363	82	32	26	4	4	3	5	28	0	55	4	0	5	5	.500	0	0--	-	3.51	2.79
2005	Mil	NL	27	0	0	3	31.2	146	40	21	21	2	0	1	1	18	3	23	1	0	1	1	.500	0	1-2	7	6.16	5.97
2006	Mil	NL	9	5	0	1	27.2	141	39	25	25	4	1	1	5	16	2	32	2	0	0	3	.000	0	0-1	0	8.30	8.13
2007	Ari	NL	5	1	0	0	5.0	28	8	8	8	0	0	1	0	5	0	3	1	0	1	0	1.000	0	0-0	0	9.25	14.40

Year	Team	Lg	G	GS	CG	GF	IP	BFP	H	R	ER	HR	SH	SF	HB	TBB	IBB	SO	WP	Bk	W	L	Pct	Sh	Sv-Op	Hld	ERC	ERA
2008	Oak	AL	29	29	1	0	168.0	737	172	82	81	10	2	5	12	77	2	118	6	1	9	9	.500	0	0-0	0	4.47	4.34
2009	Oak	AL	13	9	0	2	44.0	221	70	39	35	4	1	2	10	26	1	22	2	0	2	4	.333	0	0-0	0	8.50	7.16
2010	2 Tms		12	10	0	1	54.1	262	72	44	41	4	0	4	4	32	2	24	4	0	3	5	.375	0	0-0	0	6.90	6.79
2011	LAD	NL	5	5	0	0	29.2	118	28	10	10	1	1	0	2	6	0	16	0	0	3	2	.600	0	0-0	0	2.98	3.03
2012	Bal		14	2	0	6	32.1	145	32	18	17	3	0	2	5	13	3	18	0	0	0	1	.000	0	0-0	0	4.38	4.73
10	Tor	AL	9	9	0	0	44.2	213	57	35	32	4	0	2	2	27	1	21	3	0	3	4	.429	0	0-0	0	6.69	6.45
10	Pit	NL	3	1	0	1	9.2	49	15	9	9	0	0	2	2	5	1	3	1	0	0	1	.000	0	0-0	0	7.85	8.38
	8 ML YEARS		114	61	1	13	392.2	1798	461	247	238	28	5	16	29	193	13	256	16	1	19	25	.432	0	1-3	7	5.54	5.46

Luis Exposito

Bats: R **Throws:** R **Pos:** C-9   ecks-puh-ZEE-toh   **Ht:** 6'3" **Wt:** 210 **Born:** 1/20/1987 **Age:** 26

										BATTING										BASERUNNING				AVERAGES		
Year	Team	Lg	G	AB	H	2B	3B	HR	(Hm | Rd)	TB	R	RBI	RC	TBB	IBB	SO	HBP	SH	SF	SB	CS	SB%	GDP	Avg	OBP	Slg
2006	Lowell	A-	57	208	52	13	0	1	(- | -)	68	18	23	21	13	0	44	3	2	2	1	1	.50	10	.250	.301	.327
2007	Grnville	A	9	30	7	0	0	0	(- | -)	7	3	2	1	2	0	5	0	0	0	0	0	-	0	.233	.281	.233
2008	Grnville	A	49	191	54	8	1	11	(- | -)	97	34	31	31	12	0	42	1	0	0	1	1	.50	7	.283	.328	.508
2008	Lancst	A+	55	226	68	13	2	10	(- | -)	115	31	37	37	9	0	47	2	0	2	0	1	.00	7	.301	.331	.509
2009	Salem	A+	76	288	78	24	1	6	(- | -)	122	28	45	42	23	1	49	4	0	4	3	1	.75	11	.271	.329	.424
2009	Portlnd	AA	23	92	31	5	0	3	(- | -)	45	14	12	15	4	0	27	1	0	0	1	2	.33	1	.337	.371	.489
2010	Portlnd	AA	125	473	123	39	1	11	(- | -)	197	65	94	71	55	1	92	6	0	8	1	2	.33	22	.260	.339	.416
2011	Pwtckt	AAA	89	330	80	17	0	8	(- | -)	121	33	36	36	26	0	79	1	0	2	0	2	.00	15	.242	.298	.367
2012	Pwtckt	AAA	3	10	2	2	0	0	(- | -)	4	1	1	1	1	0	2	0	0	0	0	0	-	0	.200	.273	.400
2012	Norfolk	AAA	55	205	55	11	1	6	(- | -)	86	26	23	28	18	0	35	0	0	1	0	2	.00	15	.268	.326	.420
2012	Orioles	R	5	17	4	0	0	0	(- | -)	4	1	1	0	0	0	0	0	0	0	0	0	-	3	.235	.235	.235
2012	Bal	AL	9	18	1	0	0	0	(0 | 0)	1	2	0	0	3	0	5	0	0	0	0	0	-	0	.056	.190	.056

Irving Falu

Bats: B **Throws:** R **Pos:** 2B-14; 3B-5; SS-5; PR-1   fuh-LOO   **Ht:** 5'10" **Wt:** 180 **Born:** 6/6/1983 **Age:** 30

										BATTING										BASERUNNING				AVERAGES		
Year	Team	Lg	G	AB	H	2B	3B	HR	(Hm | Rd)	TB	R	RBI	RC	TBB	IBB	SO	HBP	SH	SF	SB	CS	SB%	GDP	Avg	OBP	Slg
2003	Royals	R	36	139	36	6	2	1	(- | -)	49	26	11	21	24	0	22	5	4	0	8	6	.57	1	.259	.387	.353
2004	Royals	R	54	223	61	8	3	1	(- | -)	78	33	15	32	26	1	19	6	2	2	23	10	.70	2	.274	.362	.350
2004	Omha	AAA	3	6	3	0	0	0	(- | -)	3	1	0	1	0	0	1	0	0	0	0	0	-	0	.500	.500	.500
2005	Burlgtn	A	119	445	113	20	5	1	(- | -)	146	71	28	58	61	0	39	3	9	7	34	15	.69	8	.254	.343	.328
2005	Wichta	AA	6	17	4	1	0	0	(- | -)	5	1	2	1	1	0	0	0	0	0	0	0	-	1	.235	.278	.294
2006	Hi Dsrt	A+	126	531	159	23	7	3	(- | -)	205	87	49	77	40	1	46	3	10	1	31	11	.74	14	.299	.351	.386
2007	Wichta	AA	131	476	115	12	6	1	(- | -)	142	46	28	43	35	0	44	1	11	2	15	9	.63	13	.242	.294	.298
2008	NWArk	AA	101	362	109	11	2	5	(- | -)	139	57	42	53	38	0	31	0	4	1	11	9	.55	7	.301	.367	.384
2009	Omha	AAA	122	465	125	19	5	2	(- | -)	160	64	40	61	52	1	35	2	8	5	12	5	.71	9	.269	.342	.344
2010	Omha	AAA	119	503	137	14	6	1	(- | -)	166	75	46	59	42	2	39	0	5	2	15	4	.79	12	.272	.327	.330
2011	Omha	AAA	111	385	116	10	9	2	(- | -)	150	50	47	57	35	3	47	1	12	4	21	11	.66	11	.301	.358	.390
2012	Omha	AAA	88	365	120	22	3	7	(- | -)	169	69	50	66	28	1	41	0	11	2	21	6	.78	11	.329	.375	.463
2012	KC	AL	24	85	29	6	1	0	(0 | 0)	37	14	7	12	4	0	9	0	2	0	0	2	.00	2	.341	.371	.435

Jeurys Familia

Pitches: R **Bats:** R **Pos:** RP-7; SP-1   JAY-your-ees fuh-MEAL-yuh   **Ht:** 6'4" **Wt:** 230 **Born:** 10/10/1989 **Age:** 23

						HOW MUCH HE PITCHED					WHAT HE GAVE UP									THE RESULTS						
Year	Team	Lg	G	GS	CG	GF	IP	BFP	H	R	ER	HR	SH	SF	HB	TBB	IBB	SO	WP	Bk	W	L	Pct	Sh	Sv-Op	Hld	ERC	ERA
2008	Mets	R	11	11	0	0	51.2	216	46	20	16	2	2	0	3	13	0	38	4	2	2	2	.500	0	0- -	-	2.70	2.79
2009	Savann	A	24	23	0	1	134.0	558	109	46	40	3	2	5	12	46	0	109	17	5	10	6	.625	0	0- -	-	2.69	2.69
2010	StLuci	A+	24	24	0	0	121.0	556	117	87	75	7	7	5	15	74	0	137	25	3	6	9	.400	0	0- -	-	4.89	5.58
2011	StLuci	A+	6	6	0	0	36.1	135	21	7	6	1	2	1	1	8	0	36	1	0	1	1	.500	0	0- -	-	1.28	1.49
2011	Bnghtn	AA	17	17	0	0	87.2	388	85	43	35	10	3	0	8	35	0	96	10	0	4	4	.500	0	0- -	-	4.30	3.59
2012	Buffalo	AAA	28	28	1	0	137.0	625	145	84	80	8	4	1	4	73	0	128	13	2	9	9	.500	0	0- -	-	4.68	4.73
2012	NYM	NL	8	1	0	4	12.1	52	10	8	8	0	0	0	0	9	0	10	0	0	0	0	-	0	0-0	0	3.76	5.84

Kyle Farnsworth

Pitches: R **Bats:** R **Pos:** RP-34   **Ht:** 6'4" **Wt:** 230 **Born:** 4/14/1976 **Age:** 37

						HOW MUCH HE PITCHED					WHAT HE GAVE UP									THE RESULTS						
Year	Team	Lg	G	GS	CG	GF	IP	BFP	H	R	ER	HR	SH	SF	HB	TBB	IBB	SO	WP	Bk	W	L	Pct	Sh	Sv-Op	Hld	ERC	ERA
2012	Charltt*	A+	4	4	0	0	4.0	14	3	1	1	0	0	0	0	0	0	2	1	0	0	0	-	0	0- -	-	1.21	2.25
2012	Drham*	AAA	2	1	0	0	2.0	8	2	0	0	0	0	0	0	0	0	4	0	0	0	0	-	0	0- -	-	1.95	0.00
1999	ChC	NL	27	21	1	1	130.0	579	140	80	73	28	6	2	3	52	1	70	7	1	5	9	.357	1	0-0	0	5.39	5.05
2000	ChC	NL	46	5	0	8	77.0	371	90	58	55	14	4	4	4	50	8	74	3	0	2	9	.182	0	1-6	6	6.72	6.43
2001	ChC	NL	76	0	0	24	82.0	339	65	26	25	8	2	2	1	29	2	107	2	2	4	6	.400	0	2-3	24	2.76	2.74
2002	ChC	NL	45	0	0	17	46.2	213	53	47	38	9	2	5	1	24	7	46	1	0	4	6	.400	0	1-7	6	5.89	7.33
2003	ChC	NL	77	0	0	13	76.1	312	53	31	28	6	4	1	0	36	1	92	6	0	3	2	.600	0	0-3	19	2.58	3.30
2004	ChC	NL	72	0	0	25	66.2	298	67	39	35	10	5	0	2	33	1	78	1	0	4	5	.444	0	0-4	18	4.71	4.73
2005	2 Tms		72	0	0	34	70.0	277	44	18	17	5	2	1	3	27	0	87	3	1	1	1	.500	0	16-18	19	2.12	2.19
2006	NYY	AL	72	0	0	24	66.0	289	62	34	32	8	3	2	1	28	3	75	5	1	3	6	.333	0	6-10	19	3.88	4.36
2007	NYY	AL	64	0	0	11	60.0	266	60	35	32	9	1	2	2	27	2	48	4	2	2	1	.667	0	0-3	15	4.67	4.80
2008	2 Tms		61	0	0	11	60.1	261	70	32	30	15	3	1	1	22	4	61	1	1	2	3	.400	0	1-4	14	6.11	4.48
2009	KC	AL	41	0	0	18	37.1	168	43	22	19	3	1	2	1	14	2	42	2	1	1	5	.167	0	0-2	5	4.65	4.58
2010	2 Tms		60	0	0	15	64.2	267	55	25	24	4	3	2	4	19	1	61	3	0	3	2	.600	0	0-3	9	2.84	3.34
2011	TB	AL	63	0	0	51	57.2	231	45	15	14	5	1	2	2	12	1	51	1	0	5	1	.833	0	25-31	0	2.19	2.18
2012	TB	AL	34	0	0	15	27.0	120	22	13	12	1	2	1	1	14	2	25	0	0	1	6	.143	0	0-0	7	2.96	4.00
05	Det	AL	46	0	0	16	42.2	174	29	12	11	1	1	1	1	20	0	55	2	0	1	1	.500	0	6-8	15	2.26	2.32

Year	Team	Lg	G	GS	CG	GF	IP	BFP	H	R	ER	HR	SH	SF	HB	TBB	IBB	SO	WP	Bk	W	L	Pct	Sh	Sv-Op	Hld	ERC	ERA
05	Atl	NL	26	0	0	18	27.1	103	15	6	6	4	1	0	2	7	0	32	1	1	0	0	—	0	10-10	4	1.86	1.98
08	NYY	AL	45	0	0	6	44.1	185	43	18	18	11	3	1	1	17	3	43	1	1	1	2	.333	0	1-1	11	5.02	3.65
08	Det	AL	16	0	0	5	16.0	76	27	14	12	4	0	0	0	5	1	18	0	0	1	1	.500	0	0-3	3	9.43	6.75
10	KC	AL	37	0	0	9	44.2	185	40	13	12	2	1	1	4	12	0	36	2	0	3	0	1.000	0	0-2	7	3.01	2.42
10	Atl	NL	23	0	0	6	20.0	82	15	12	12	2	2	1	0	7	1	25	1	0	0	2	.000	0	0-1	2	2.46	5.40
	Postseason		15	0	0	5	16.0	66	12	9	9	2	1	1	1	6	2	17	0	0	1	0	1.000	0	0-0	2	2.86	5.06
	14 ML YEARS		810	26	1	260	921.2	3991	869	475	434	125	39	27	27	387	35	917	42	9	40	62	.392	1	52-94	161	4.11	4.24

Eric Farris

Bats: R **Throws:** R **Pos:** PH-8; PR-3; 2B-2; LF-1 **Ht:** 5'9" **Wt:** 180 **Born:** 3/3/1986 **Age:** 27

									BATTING													BASERUNNING				AVERAGES		
Year	Team	Lg	G	AB	H	2B	3B	HR	(Hm	Rd)	TB	R	RBI	RC	TBB	IBB	SO	HBP	SH	SF	SB	CS	SB%	GDP	Avg	OBP	Slg
2007	Helena	R+	63	239	78	16	2	1	(-	-)	101	34	34	41	16	0	22	2	9	3	21	5	.81	3	.326	.369	.423
2008	WV	A	103	454	133	21	4	3	(-	-)	171	73	54	61	24	0	50	5	4	5	32	10	.76	11	.293	.332	.377
2009	BrvdCt	A+	124	473	141	18	1	7	(-	-)	182	68	49	76	29	1	46	3	26	3	70	6	.92	10	.298	.341	.385
2010	Nashv	AAA	60	230	63	9	1	2	(-	-)	80	28	15	27	9	0	25	4	5	1	14	2	.88	8	.274	.311	.348
2010	Brewrs	R	10	32	8	5	0	1	(-	-)	16	5	9	4	1	0	3	0	0	2	1	0	1.00	0	.250	.257	.500
2011	Nashv	AAA	134	538	146	26	5	6	(-	-)	200	70	55	68	32	0	70	6	14	4	21	7	.75	17	.271	.317	.372
2012	Nashv	AAA	131	483	138	21	1	7	(-	-)	182	63	31	64	27	0	56	6	8	4	35	13	.73	9	.286	.329	.377
2011	Mil	NL	1	1	0	0	0	0	(0	0)	0	0	0	0	0	0	0	0	0	0	0	0	-	0	.000	.000	.000
2012	Mil	NL	13	8	1	0	0	0	(0	0)	1	1	0	0	1	0	2	0	0	0	1	0	1.00	0	.125	.222	.125
	2 ML YEARS		14	9	1	0	0	0	(0	0)	1	1	0	0	1	0	2	0	0	0	1	0	1.00	0	.111	.200	.111

Tim Federowicz

Bats: R **Throws:** R **Pos:** C-2; PH-1 fed-ur-OWE-vitch **Ht:** 5'10" **Wt:** 215 **Born:** 8/5/1987 **Age:** 25

									BATTING													BASERUNNING				AVERAGES		
Year	Team	Lg	G	AB	H	2B	3B	HR	(Hm	Rd)	TB	R	RBI	RC	TBB	IBB	SO	HBP	SH	SF	SB	CS	SB%	GDP	Avg	OBP	Slg
2008	Lowell	A-	36	127	31	6	0	1	(-	-)	40	14	15	16	19	0	24	0	0	2	10	3	.77	2	.244	.338	.315
2009	Grnville	A	55	226	78	19	0	10	(-	-)	127	34	34	48	15	1	42	4	0	2	1	0	1.00	2	.345	.393	.562
2009	Salem	A+	51	187	48	13	0	4	(-	-)	73	18	24	20	5	0	22	1	1	3	1	0	1.00	8	.257	.276	.390
2010	Salem	A+	109	407	103	34	1	4	(-	-)	151	47	61	51	43	1	86	2	0	5	1	1	.50	17	.253	.324	.371
2011	Portlnd	AA	90	339	94	20	0	8	(-	-)	138	46	52	50	32	1	63	3	0	8	1	0	1.00	14	.277	.338	.407
2011	Albq	AAA	25	83	27	7	0	6	(-	-)	52	17	17	22	15	0	20	2	0	2	0	0	-	4	.325	.431	.627
2012	Albq	AAA	115	412	121	34	1	11	(-	-)	190	71	76	73	52	1	91	3	1	7	0	1	.00	15	.294	.371	.461
2011	LAD	NL	7	13	2	0	0	0	(0	0)	2	0	1	1	2	0	4	1	0	0	0	0	-	0	.154	.313	.154
2012	LAD	NL	3	3	1	0	0	0	(0	0)	1	0	0	1	1	0	2	0	0	0	0	0	-	0	.333	.500	.333
	2 ML YEARS		10	16	3	0	0	0	(0	0)	3	0	1	2	3	0	6	1	0	0	0	0	-	0	.188	.350	.188

Scott Feldman

Pitches: R **Bats:** L **Pos:** SP-21; RP-8 **Ht:** 6'6" **Wt:** 230 **Born:** 2/7/1983 **Age:** 30

							HOW MUCH HE PITCHED			WHAT HE GAVE UP												THE RESULTS						
Year	Team	Lg	G	GS	CG	GF	IP	BFP	H	R	ER	HR	SH	SF	HB	TBB	IBB	SO	WP	Bk	W	L	Pct	Sh	Sv-Op	Hld	ERC	ERA
2005	Tex	AL	8	0	0	3	9.1	37	9	1	1	0	0	0	0	2	1	4	0	0	0	1	.000	0	0-0	1	2.48	0.96
2006	Tex	AL	36	0	0	5	41.1	175	42	19	18	4	2	1	4	10	0	30	0	0	0	2	.000	0	0-1	7	3.94	3.92
2007	Tex	AL	29	0	0	10	39.0	192	44	26	25	3	0	2	3	32	5	19	2	2	1	2	.333	0	0-0	0	6.40	5.77
2008	Tex	AL	28	25	0	2	151.1	651	161	103	89	22	1	9	10	56	2	74	4	2	6	8	.429	0	0-0	0	5.03	5.29
2009	Tex	AL	34	31	0	0	189.2	791	178	87	86	18	1	3	9	65	0	113	5	2	17	8	.680	0	0-0	0	3.74	4.08
2010	Tex	AL	29	22	0	2	141.1	641	181	98	86	18	5	8	5	45	2	75	11	0	7	11	.389	0	0-0	0	5.71	5.48
2011	Tex	AL	11	2	0	5	32.0	129	25	14	14	3	0	1	2	10	0	22	2	0	2	1	.667	0	0-0	0	2.83	3.94
2012	Tex	AL	29	21	0	5	123.2	536	139	79	70	14	0	5	1	32	2	96	2	1	6	11	.353	0	0-0	0	4.27	5.09
	Postseason		9	0	0	1	13.2	56	8	5	5	0	2	0	2	6	2	11	0	0	1	0	1.000	0	0-1	0	1.75	3.29
	8 ML YEARS		204	101	0	32	727.2	3152	779	427	389	82	9	29	34	252	12	433	26	7	39	44	.470	0	0-1	8	4.55	4.81

Pedro Feliciano

Pitches: L **Bats:** L **Pos:** P **Ht:** 5'10" **Wt:** 195 **Born:** 8/25/1976 **Age:** 36

							HOW MUCH HE PITCHED			WHAT HE GAVE UP												THE RESULTS						
Year	Team	Lg	G	GS	CG	GF	IP	BFP	H	R	ER	HR	SH	SF	HB	TBB	IBB	SO	WP	Bk	W	L	Pct	Sh	Sv-Op	Hld	ERC	ERA
2012	Yanks*	R	4	4	0	0	4.0	15	2	0	0	0	0	0	0	1	0	5	0	0	0	0	-	0	0--	-	0.94	0.00
2012	Tampa*	A+	1	0	0	0	1.0	7	4	2	2	0	0	0	0	0	0	1	0	0	0	0	-	0	0--	-	22.42	18.00
2012	Trntn*	AA	2	0	0	0	1.1	6	0	0	0	0	0	0	0	2	0	2	1	0	0	0	-	0	0--	-	1.96	0.00
2012	StIsInd*	A-	3	1	0	0	3.0	13	3	1	1	1	0	0	0	0	0	2	0	0	0	0	-	0	0--	-	3.45	3.00
2002	NYM	NL	6	0	0	3	6.0	26	9	5	5	0	0	0	0	1	0	4	0	0	0	0	-	0	0-0	0	5.56	7.50
2003	NYM	NL	23	0	0	8	48.1	218	52	21	18	6	1	0	3	21	3	43	3	1	0	0	-	0	0-0	4	4.77	3.35
2004	NYM	NL	22	0	0	3	18.1	82	14	12	11	2	1	1	1	12	0	14	1	0	1	1	.500	0	0-0	2	3.93	5.40
2006	NYM	NL	64	0	0	10	60.1	256	56	15	14	4	4	3	3	20	1	54	1	0	7	2	.778	0	0-3	10	3.34	2.09
2007	NYM	NL	78	0	0	12	64.0	275	47	26	22	3	2	2	5	31	4	61	1	1	2	2	.500	0	2-3	18	2.74	3.09
2008	NYM	NL	86	0	0	14	53.1	237	57	24	24	7	2	3	6	26	8	50	2	0	3	4	.429	0	2-4	21	5.11	4.05
2009	NYM	NL	88	0	0	11	59.1	242	51	25	20	7	2	1	0	18	4	59	2	0	6	4	.600	0	0-2	24	2.98	3.03
2010	NYM	NL	92	0	0	16	62.2	280	66	24	23	1	4	2	6	30	6	56	1	0	3	6	.333	0	0-1	23	4.30	3.30
	Postseason		6	0	0	0	4.2	18	2	1	1	1	0	0	0	2	0	3	1	0	1	0	1.000	0	0-0	1	1.92	1.93
	8 ML YEARS		459	0	0	77	372.1	1616	352	152	137	29	13	11	21	159	26	341	11	3	22	19	.537	0	4-13	98	3.82	3.31

Neftali Feliz

Pitches: R Bats: R Pos: SP-7; RP-1 | neff-TAH-lee | **Ht: 6'3" Wt: 215 Born: 5/2/1988 Age: 25**

Year	Team	Lg	G	GS	CG	GF	IP	BFP	H	R	ER	HR	SH	SF	HB	TBB	IBB	SO	WP	Bk	W	L	Pct	Sh	Sv-Op	Hld	ERC	ERA
2012	Frisco*	AA	1	1	0	0	2.0	9	1	1	0	0	0	0	0	2	0	4	0	0	0	1	.000	0	0- -	-	2.80	0.00
2012	RdRck*	AAA	2	2	0	0	4.2	23	4	4	1	0	0	0	1	3	0	4	2	1	0	1	.000	0	0- -	-	3.94	1.93
2009	Tex	AL	20	0	0	3	31.0	117	13	6	6	2	1	0	3	8	0	39	0	0	1	0	1.000	0	2-3	9	1.14	1.74
2010	Tex	AL	70	0	0	59	69.1	269	43	21	21	5	1	0	5	18	1	71	5	0	4	3	.571	0	40-43	3	1.75	2.73
2011	Tex	AL	64	0	0	56	62.1	252	42	22	19	4	3	2	0	30	1	54	2	1	2	3	.400	0	32-38	0	2.45	2.74
2012	Tex	AL	8	7	1	0	42.2	175	28	15	15	5	0	0	2	23	0	37	0	0	3	1	.750	0	0-0	0	3.11	3.16
	Postseason		18	0	0	15	18.2	76	8	4	4	1	1	0	1	13	1	23	1	0	0	0	-	0	7-8	0	2.04	1.93
4 ML YEARS			162	7	1	118	205.1	813	126	64	61	16	5	2	10	79	2	201	7	1	10	7	.588	0	74-84	12	2.09	2.67

Chuckie Fick

Pitches: R Bats: R Pos: RP-20 | **Ht: 6'5" Wt: 185 Born: 11/20/1985 Age: 27**

Year	Team	Lg	G	GS	CG	GF	IP	BFP	H	R	ER	HR	SH	SF	HB	TBB	IBB	SO	WP	Bk	W	L	Pct	Sh	Sv-Op	Hld	ERC	ERA
2007	JhsCty	R	8	0	0	4	14.0	57	9	3	2	0	0	0	0	6	0	12	4	0	1	0	1.000	0	2- -	-	1.71	1.29
2007	QuadC	A	9	0	0	0	25.0	108	27	10	6	1	1	1	2	5	0	13	5	0	1	0	1.000	0	0- -	-	3.58	2.16
2008	QuadC	A	20	13	0	3	93.2	388	97	50	33	6	2	1	2	15	2	67	2	0	6	5	.545	0	0- -	-	3.15	3.17
2009	QuadC	A	4	3	0	1	17.0	74	21	9	8	1	0	0	0	4	0	13	1	0	0	2	.000	0	0- -	-	4.47	4.24
2009	PlmBh	A+	20	7	0	2	56.2	239	67	33	31	6	1	2	2	8	1	26	1	0	3	3	.500	0	0- -	-	4.28	4.92
2009	Sprgfld	AA	10	3	0	5	24.0	100	19	5	4	1	2	0	2	10	1	12	2	0	1	2	.333	0	1- -	-	2.91	1.50
2010	Sprgfld	AA	11	3	0	2	27.0	104	19	8	6	0	3	0	0	6	0	32	0	0	2	0	1.000	0	0- -	-	1.48	2.00
2010	Memp	AAA	21	3	0	3	49.0	207	51	26	26	7	2	0	4	18	1	31	2	0	3	1	.750	0	0- -	-	5.00	4.78
2011	Memp	AAA	54	0	0	12	70.1	293	44	25	18	2	5	1	6	37	7	61	1	0	5	3	.625	0	1- -	-	2.26	2.30
2012	Memp	AAA	42	0	0	20	42.1	183	49	23	22	6	0	0	1	13	1	20	1	1	1	1	.500	0	2- -	-	5.05	4.68
2012	OKCity	AAA	5	0	0	2	3.2	16	3	4	4	0	0	0	1	2	1	3	0	0	1	1	.500	0	1- -	-	3.56	9.82
2012	2 Tms	NL	20	0	0	3	24.2	116	27	14	12	4	3	2	2	18	4	17	4	1	0	1	.000	0	0-0	0	6.67	4.38
12	StL	NL	2	0	0	1	1.2	9	3	1	1	0	1	0	0	1	0	0	0	0	0	0	-	0	0-0	0	8.83	5.40
12	Hou	NL	18	0	0	2	23.0	107	24	13	11	4	2	2	2	17	4	17	4	1	0	1	.000	0	0-0	0	6.51	4.30

Tommy Field

Bats: R Throws: R Pos: 2B-1; PR-1 | **Ht: 5'9" Wt: 175 Born: 2/22/1987 Age: 26**

Year	Team	Lg	G	AB	H	2B	3B	HR	(Hm	Rd)	TB	R	RBI	RC	TBB	IBB	SO	HBP	SH	SF	SB	CS	SB%	GDP	Avg	OBP	Slg
2008	TriCity	A-	56	182	45	8	2	5	(-	-)	72	34	32	33	42	0	34	6	1	1	10	6	.63	3	.247	.403	.396
2009	Ashvll	A	89	304	78	17	0	2	(-	-)	101	42	32	37	26	2	58	11	5	2	8	3	.73	3	.257	.335	.332
2010	Mdest	A+	124	440	125	21	7	15	(-	-)	205	84	72	88	66	2	114	21	9	7	16	5	.76	5	.284	.397	.466
2011	Tulsa	AA	134	472	128	22	3	17	(-	-)	207	77	61	78	53	1	108	12	3	4	9	4	.69	7	.271	.357	.439
2012	ColSpr	AAA	121	435	106	31	6	8	(-	-)	173	74	49	58	41	0	76	5	8	4	4	0	1.00	14	.244	.313	.398
2011	Col	NL	16	48	13	0	0	0	(0	0)	13	4	3	4	3	0	14	0	0	0	0	0	-	1	.271	.314	.271
2012	Col	NL	2	2	0	0	0	0	(0	0)	0	0	0	0	1	0	1	0	0	0	0	0	-	0	.000	.333	.000
2 ML YEARS			18	50	13	0	0	0	(0	0)	13	4	3	4	4	0	15	0	0	0	0	0	-	1	.260	.315	.260

Prince Fielder

Bats: L Throws: R Pos: 1B-159; DH-3 | **Ht: 5'11" Wt: 275 Born: 5/9/1984 Age: 29**

Year	Team	Lg	G	AB	H	2B	3B	HR	(Hm	Rd)	TB	R	RBI	RC	TBB	IBB	SO	HBP	SH	SF	SB	CS	SB%	GDP	Avg	OBP	Slg
2005	Mil	NL	39	59	17	4	0	2	(2	0)	27	2	10	10	2	0	17	0	0	1	0	0	-	0	.288	.306	.458
2006	Mil	NL	157	569	154	35	1	28	(11	17)	275	82	81	84	59	5	125	12	0	8	7	2	.78	17	.271	.347	.483
2007	Mil	NL	158	573	165	35	2	50	(27	23)	354	109	119	125	90	21	121	14	0	4	2	2	.50	9	.288	.395	.618
2008	Mil	NL	159	588	162	30	2	34	(18	16)	298	86	102	105	84	19	134	12	0	10	3	2	.60	12	.276	.372	.507
2009	Mil	NL	162	591	177	35	3	46	(23	23)	356	103	141	134	110	21	138	9	0	9	2	3	.40	14	.299	.412	.602
2010	Mil	NL	161	578	151	25	0	32	(18	14)	272	94	83	94	114	17	138	21	0	1	1	0	1.00	12	.261	.401	.471
2011	Mil	NL	162	569	170	36	1	38	(24	14)	322	95	120	120	107	32	106	10	0	6	1	1	.50	19	.299	.415	.566
2012	Det	AL	162	581	182	33	1	30	(18	12)	307	83	108	116	85	18	84	17	0	7	1	0	1.00	16	.313	.412	.528
	Postseason		15	52	10	4	0	4	(4	0)	26	7	8	6	8	4	14	2	0	1	0	0	-	2	.192	.317	.500
8 ML YEARS			1160	4108	1178	233	10	260	(141	119)	2211	654	764	788	651	133	863	95	0	46	17	10	.63	100	.287	.393	.538

Casey Fien

Pitches: R Bats: R Pos: RP-35 | FEEN | **Ht: 6'2" Wt: 205 Born: 10/21/1983 Age: 29**

Year	Team	Lg	G	GS	CG	GF	IP	BFP	H	R	ER	HR	SH	SF	HB	TBB	IBB	SO	WP	Bk	W	L	Pct	Sh	Sv-Op	Hld	ERC	ERA
2012	Roch*	AAA	33	0	0	20	46.0	189	39	23	22	5	2	1	0	14	3	42	1	0	2	5	.286	0	9- -	-	2.84	4.30
2009	Det	AL	9	0	0	5	11.1	53	13	11	10	2	0	2	0	6	0	9	0	0	1	0	1.000	0	0-0	0	5.92	7.94
2010	Det	AL	2	0	0	2	2.2	12	4	3	3	2	1	0	0	0	0	0	0	0	0	0	-	0	0-0	0	9.96	10.13
2012	Min	AL	35	0	0	7	35.0	141	25	9	8	3	1	2	1	9	4	32	0	0	2	1	.667	0	0-0	6	1.90	2.06
3 ML YEARS			46	0	0	14	49.0	206	42	23	21	7	2	4	1	15	4	41	0	0	2	2	.500	0	0-0	6	3.10	3.86

Mike Fiers

Pitches: R Bats: R Pos: SP-22; RP-1 **FIRES** Ht: 6'3" Wt: 195 Born: 6/15/1985 **Age: 28**

			HOW MUCH HE PITCHED						WHAT HE GAVE UP											THE RESULTS						
Year	Team	Lg	G	GS	CG	GF	IP	BFP	H	R	ER	HR	SH	SF	HB	TBB	IBB	SO	WP	Bk	W	L	Pct	Sh	Sv-Op	Hld	ERC	ERA
2009	Helena	R+	13	0	0	12	21.0	77	10	3	3	2	2	0	1	1	0	35	2	0	1	0	1.000	0	8--	-	0.86	1.29
2009	Wisc	A	3	0	0	3	6.0	24	4	0	0	0	0	0	1	2	0	8	0	0	0	0	-	0	1--	-	2.13	0.00
2009	BrvdCt	A+	6	0	0	5	13.2	51	10	3	3	2	0	0	0	2	0	16	0	0	1	0	1.000	0	2--	-	2.10	1.98
2010	BrvdCt	A+	17	15	0	1	93.1	378	78	37	36	6	1	2	11	23	0	94	5	0	4	8	.333	0	0--	-	2.89	3.47
2010	Hntsvl	AA	10	4	0	4	31.2	133	27	13	13	3	0	0	3	9	0	36	1	0	1	1	.500	0	1--	-	3.12	3.69
2011	Hntsvl	AA	22	8	0	10	61.1	241	42	21	18	7	2	1	2	14	0	63	1	2	5	3	.625	0	5--	-	2.02	2.64
2011	Nashv	AAA	12	10	1	1	64.2	263	41	18	8	4	3	0	3	22	0	69	1	0	8	0	1.000	1	0--	-	1.87	1.11
2012	Nashv	AAA	10	10	1	0	55.0	229	49	28	27	6	3	3	3	18	0	49	5	1	1	3	.250	1	0--	-	3.50	4.42
2011	Mil	NL	2	0	0	2	2.0	10	2	0	0	0	0	0	0	3	0	2	0	0	0	0	-	0	0-0	0	8.25	0.00
2012	Mil	NL	23	22	0	1	127.2	539	125	56	53	12	4	4	2	36	0	135	4	0	9	10	.474	0	0-0	0	3.50	3.74
	2 ML YEARS		25	22	0	3	129.2	549	127	56	53	12	4	4	2	39	0	137	4	0	9	10	.474	0	0-0	0	3.56	3.68

Stephen Fife

Pitches: R Bats: R Pos: SP-5 Ht: 6'3" Wt: 220 Born: 10/4/1986 **Age: 26**

			HOW MUCH HE PITCHED						WHAT HE GAVE UP											THE RESULTS						
Year	Team	Lg	G	GS	CG	GF	IP	BFP	H	R	ER	HR	SH	SF	HB	TBB	IBB	SO	WP	Bk	W	L	Pct	Sh	Sv-Op	Hld	ERC	ERA
2008	Lowell	A-	14	0	0	4	38.2	159	28	14	10	1	1	0	4	11	0	41	7	0	1	1	.500	0	2--	-	2.09	2.33
2009	Grnville	A	8	8	0	0	36.2	146	32	13	11	1	1	1	0	4	0	35	3	0	0	3	.000	0	0--	-	1.89	2.70
2009	Salem	A+	10	10	0	0	50.2	220	58	28	25	7	2	1	2	10	0	51	1	0	3	2	.600	0	0--	-	4.45	4.44
2010	Portlnd	AA	26	26	0	0	136.1	592	144	84	72	11	4	7	5	46	0	82	6	4	8	6	.571	0	0--	-	4.14	4.75
2011	Portlnd	AA	19	18	0	0	103.1	447	107	47	42	7	1	4	6	37	0	70	4	0	11	4	.733	0	0--	-	4.14	3.66
2011	Chatt	AA	6	6	0	0	33.2	152	36	18	15	2	2	1	1	15	0	25	0	0	3	0	1.000	0	0--	-	4.38	4.01
2012	Albq	AAA	25	24	0	0	135.1	607	157	85	70	13	7	3	10	44	1	93	10	1	11	7	.611	0	0--	-	4.91	4.66
2012	LAD	NL	5	5	0	0	26.2	115	25	8	8	2	3	0	2	12	0	20	4	0	0	2	.000	0	0-0	0	4.09	2.70

Chone Figgins

Bats: B Throws: R Pos: LF-38; 3B-10; PR-10; CF-9; PH-4; DH-3; RF-1 **SHAWN** Ht: 5'8" Wt: 180 Born: 1/22/1978 **Age: 35**

			BATTING																		BASERUNNING				AVERAGES		
Year	Team	Lg	G	AB	H	2B	3B	HR	(Hm	Rd)	TB	R	RBI	RC	TBB	IBB	SO	HBP	SH	SF	SB	CS	SB%	GDP	Avg	OBP	Slg
2002	LAA	AL	15	12	2	1	0	0	(0	0)	3	6	1	0	0	0	5	0	0	0	2	1	.67	1	.167	.167	.250
2003	LAA	AL	71	240	71	9	4	0	(0	0)	88	34	27	39	20	0	38	0	6	4	13	7	.65	1	.296	.345	.367
2004	LAA	AL	148	577	171	22	17	5	(3	2)	242	83	60	93	49	0	94	0	10	2	34	13	.72	6	.296	.350	.419
2005	LAA	AL	158	642	186	25	10	8	(2	6)	255	113	57	94	64	1	101	0	9	5	62	17	.78	9	.290	.352	.397
2006	LAA	AL	155	604	161	23	8	9	(2	7)	227	93	62	84	65	1	100	2	5	7	52	16	.76	6	.267	.336	.376
2007	LAA	AL	115	442	146	24	6	3	(1	2)	191	81	58	88	51	0	81	0	2	8	41	12	.77	7	.330	.393	.432
2008	LAA	AL	116	453	125	14	1	1	(0	1)	144	72	22	59	62	3	80	3	2	0	34	13	.72	7	.276	.367	.318
2009	LAA	AL	158	615	183	30	7	5	(2	3)	242	114	54	110	101	1	114	1	8	4	42	17	.71	8	.298	.395	.393
2010	Sea	AL	161	602	156	21	1	1	(0	1)	184	62	35	66	74	0	114	3	17	6	42	15	.74	20	.259	.340	.306
2011	Sea	AL	81	288	54	11	1	1	(0	1)	70	24	15	10	21	1	42	0	1	0	11	6	.65	6	.188	.241	.243
2012	Sea	AL	66	166	30	5	2	2	(1	1)	45	18	11	11	19	0	48	0	7	2	4	1	.80	3	.181	.262	.271
	Postseason		35	122	21	5	2	0	(0	0)	30	13	6	6	6	0	35	2	5	0	4	1	.80	1	.172	.223	.246
	11 ML YEARS		1244	4641	1285	185	58	35	(11	24)	1691	700	402	654	526	6	817	9	68	40	337	118	.74	74	.277	.349	.364

Pedro Figueroa

Pitches: L Bats: L Pos: RP-19 Ht: 6'0" Wt: 215 Born: 11/23/1985 **Age: 27**

			HOW MUCH HE PITCHED						WHAT HE GAVE UP											THE RESULTS						
Year	Team	Lg	G	GS	CG	GF	IP	BFP	H	R	ER	HR	SH	SF	HB	TBB	IBB	SO	WP	Bk	W	L	Pct	Sh	Sv-Op	Hld	ERC	ERA
2006	As	R	13	8	0	4	43.0	204	59	39	29	4	2	3	4	11	0	27	2	0	1	6	.143	0	0--	-	5.82	6.07
2007	Vancvr	A-	17	7	0	3	44.0	202	41	26	21	2	4	0	4	31	1	35	4	2	2	2	.500	0	1--	-	4.81	4.30
2008	Vancvr	A-	15	15	0	0	68.2	299	62	37	30	3	2	2	3	32	0	77	3	4	2	5	.286	0	0--	-	3.53	3.93
2009	Kane	A	16	16	0	0	86.1	370	89	37	31	6	2	0	4	31	0	78	6	2	10	2	.833	0	0--	-	4.11	3.23
2009	Stcktn	A+	11	11	0	0	65.2	285	62	27	26	3	2	0	1	35	1	67	4	0	3	4	.429	0	0--	-	3.97	3.56
2010	Mdland	AA	13	13	0	0	71.1	319	83	45	42	6	1	2	2	29	1	57	4	5	1	6	.143	0	0--	-	5.04	5.30
2011	As	R	2	2	0	0	2.0	10	3	1	1	0	0	0	0	0	0	0	0	0	0	0	-	0	0--	-	3.96	4.50
2012	Scrmto	AAA	32	0	0	7	44.2	187	35	17	13	1	1	0	3	18	0	40	0	0	0	2	.000	0	1--	-	2.66	2.62
2012	Oak	AL	19	0	0	6	21.2	89	16	9	8	2	0	0	0	15	1	14	2	0	0	0	-	0	0-0	0	3.87	3.32

Doug Fister

Pitches: R Bats: L Pos: SP-26 Ht: 6'8" Wt: 210 Born: 2/4/1984 **Age: 29**

			HOW MUCH HE PITCHED						WHAT HE GAVE UP											THE RESULTS						
Year	Team	Lg	G	GS	CG	GF	IP	BFP	H	R	ER	HR	SH	SF	HB	TBB	IBB	SO	WP	Bk	W	L	Pct	Sh	Sv-Op	Hld	ERC	ERA
2012	Toledo*	AAA	1	1	0	0	4.0	15	2	0	0	0	0	0	0	1	0	5	0	0	0	0	-	0	0--	-	0.94	0.00
2009	Sea	AL	11	10	0	0	61.0	256	63	29	28	11	0	0	2	15	0	36	1	0	3	4	.429	0	0-0	0	4.36	4.13
2010	Sea	AL	28	28	0	0	171.0	720	187	85	78	13	2	4	6	32	2	93	8	3	6	14	.300	0	0-0	0	3.73	4.11
2011	2 Tms	AL	32	31	3	0	216.1	875	193	76	68	11	4	9	12	37	2	146	3	1	11	13	.458	0	0-0	0	2.53	2.83
2012	Det	AL	26	26	2	0	161.2	673	156	73	62	15	3	0	7	37	1	137	1	0	10	10	.500	1	0-0	0	3.33	3.45
	11	Sea	AL	21	21	3	0	146.0	602	139	57	54	7	3	7	9	32	2	89	3	1	3	12	.200	0	0-0	0	3.02	3.33
	11	Det	AL	11	10	0	0	70.1	273	54	19	14	4	1	2	3	5	0	57	0	0	8	1	.889	0	0-0	0	1.63	1.79
	Postseason		3	2	0	0	17.0	72	19	9	9	1	1	0	1	4	0	13	0	1	2	1	.667	0	0-0	0	4.11	4.76
	4 ML YEARS		97	95	5	1	610.0	2524	599	263	236	50	9	13	27	121	5	412	13	4	30	41	.423	1	0-0	0	3.24	3.48

Ryan Flaherty

Bats: L **Throws:** R **Pos:** 2B-28; 3B-17; RF-17; PH-10; LF-7; PR-6; 1B-3; SS-1; DH-1   **Ht:** 6'3" **Wt:** 210 **Born:** 7/27/1986 **Age:** 26

									BATTING											BASERUNNING				AVERAGES		
Year	Team	Lg	G	AB	H	2B	3B	HR	(Hm | Rd)	TB	R	RBI	RC	TBB	IBB	SO	HBP	SH	SF	SB	CS	SB%	GDP	Avg	OBP	Slg
2008	Boise	A-	56	219	65	19	2	8	(- | -)	112	39	26	41	24	1	51	1	1	0	4	2	.67	2	.297	.369	.511
2009	Peoria	A	131	485	134	24	5	20	(- | -)	228	81	81	80	50	0	98	2	2	4	7	6	.54	9	.276	.344	.470
2010	Tenn	AA	23	71	13	2	0	1	(- | -)	18	10	9	6	10	2	12	1	0	2	1	0	1.00	0	.183	.286	.254
2010	Dytona	A+	108	420	120	34	3	9	(- | -)	187	65	63	68	41	2	74	4	1	9	6	3	.67	10	.286	.348	.445
2011	Tenn	AA	83	302	92	20	2	14	(- | -)	158	52	66	59	40	2	55	0	0	2	4	6	.40	12	.305	.384	.523
2011	Iowa	AAA	49	173	41	11	1	5	(- | -)	69	22	22	19	10	0	44	0	2	1	1	0	1.00	8	.237	.277	.399
2012	Norfolk	AAA	9	38	11	1	1	2	(- | -)	20	5	3	6	2	0	9	1	0	0	0	0	-	1	.289	.341	.526
2012	Bal	AL	77	153	33	2	1	6	(3 | 3)	55	15	19	15	6	0	43	3	3	1	1	0	1.00	3	.216	.258	.359

Jesus Flores

Bats: R **Throws:** R **Pos:** C-80; PH-3   **Ht:** 6'1" **Wt:** 210 **Born:** 10/26/1984 **Age:** 28

									BATTING											BASERUNNING				AVERAGES		
Year	Team	Lg	G	AB	H	2B	3B	HR	(Hm | Rd)	TB	R	RBI	RC	TBB	IBB	SO	HBP	SH	SF	SB	CS	SB%	GDP	Avg	OBP	Slg
2007	Was	NL	79	180	44	9	0	4	(1 | 3)	65	21	25	19	14	0	48	3	0	0	0	1	.00	5	.244	.310	.361
2008	Was	NL	90	301	77	18	1	8	(2 | 6)	121	23	59	45	15	1	78	4	0	4	0	1	.00	7	.256	.296	.402
2009	Was	NL	29	93	28	3	2	4	(0 | 4)	47	13	15	14	11	1	26	0	1	1	0	0	-	1	.301	.371	.505
2011	Was	NL	30	86	18	6	0	1	(1 | 0)	27	5	2	3	5	2	27	0	0	0	0	0	-	1	.209	.253	.314
2012	Was	NL	83	277	59	12	1	6	(5 | 1)	91	22	26	17	13	3	59	1	2	3	1	2	.33	7	.213	.248	.329
	5 ML YEARS		311	937	226	48	4	23	(9 | 14)	351	84	127	98	58	7	238	8	3	8	1	4	.20	21	.241	.289	.375

Pedro Florimon

Bats: B **Throws:** R **Pos:** SS-43   FLOOR-ih-moan   **Ht:** 6'2" **Wt:** 180 **Born:** 12/10/1986 **Age:** 26

									BATTING											BASERUNNING				AVERAGES		
Year	Team	Lg	G	AB	H	2B	3B	HR	(Hm | Rd)	TB	R	RBI	RC	TBB	IBB	SO	HBP	SH	SF	SB	CS	SB%	GDP	Avg	OBP	Slg
2006	Bluefld	R+	33	120	40	6	1	1	(- | -)	51	23	8	25	28	0	29	0	1	1	7	6	.54	0	.333	.456	.425
2006	Abrdn	A-	26	105	26	4	1	0	(- | -)	32	13	5	11	13	1	26	1	0	0	0	0	-	2	.248	.336	.305
2007	Dlmrva	A	111	371	73	14	1	4	(- | -)	101	50	34	26	28	0	107	3	13	3	16	6	.73	8	.197	.257	.272
2008	Dlmrva	A	81	269	60	18	1	0	(- | -)	80	28	19	27	27	0	97	3	3	3	13	2	.87	3	.223	.298	.297
2009	Frdrck	A+	115	430	115	32	5	9	(- | -)	184	76	68	66	42	1	107	5	4	5	26	9	.74	10	.267	.336	.428
2009	Bowie	AA	7	22	2	0	0	0	(- | -)	2	0	1	0	1	0	9	0	1	0	0	0	-	1	.091	.130	.091
2010	Bowie	AA	37	120	22	3	0	1	(- | -)	28	16	12	7	11	0	31	0	2	1	4	1	.80	3	.183	.250	.233
2010	Abrdn	A-	5	19	3	0	0	0	(- | -)	3	1	0	0	1	0	6	0	0	0	0	1	.00	0	.158	.200	.158
2010	Frdrck	A+	62	222	64	10	4	4	(- | -)	94	32	33	35	20	1	52	7	0	3	8	5	.62	4	.288	.361	.423
2011	Bowie	AA	133	454	121	27	4	8	(- | -)	180	53	60	64	51	5	114	5	6	4	15	12	.56	5	.267	.344	.396
2012	NwBrit	AA	30	113	32	4	0	2	(- | -)	42	11	8	16	11	0	28	0	3	0	8	1	.89	3	.283	.347	.372
2012	Roch	AAA	83	311	78	16	2	3	(- | -)	107	38	27	33	23	1	89	3	7	1	6	7	.46	8	.251	.308	.344
2011	Bal	AL	4	8	1	1	0	0	(0 | 0)	2	1	2	1	1	0	6	0	1	0	0	0	-	0	.125	.222	.250
2012	Min	AL	43	137	30	5	2	1	(1 | 0)	42	16	10	8	10	0	30	0	3	0	3	1	.75	3	.219	.272	.307
	2 ML YEARS		47	145	31	6	2	1	(1 | 0)	44	17	12	9	11	0	36	0	4	0	3	1	.75	3	.214	.269	.303

Tyler Flowers

Bats: R **Throws:** R **Pos:** C-49; 1B-2; PH-2; DH-1   **Ht:** 6'4" **Wt:** 245 **Born:** 1/24/1986 **Age:** 27

									BATTING											BASERUNNING				AVERAGES		
Year	Team	Lg	G	AB	H	2B	3B	HR	(Hm | Rd)	TB	R	RBI	RC	TBB	IBB	SO	HBP	SH	SF	SB	CS	SB%	GDP	Avg	OBP	Slg
2009	CWS	AL	10	16	3	1	0	0	(0 | 0)	4	3	0	2	3	0	8	1	0	0	0	0	-	1	.188	.350	.250
2010	CWS	AL	8	11	1	0	0	0	(0 | 0)	1	2	0	1	4	0	5	0	0	0	0	0	-	0	.091	.333	.091
2011	CWS	AL	38	110	23	5	1	5	(3 | 2)	45	13	16	13	14	0	38	1	0	2	0	1	.00	1	.209	.310	.409
2012	CWS	AL	52	136	29	6	0	7	(5 | 2)	56	19	13	13	12	0	56	4	1	0	2	1	.67	2	.213	.296	.412
	4 ML YEARS		108	273	56	12	1	12	(8 | 4)	106	37	29	29	33	0	107	8	1	2	2	2	.50	5	.205	.307	.388

Gavin Floyd

Pitches: R **Bats:** R **Pos:** SP-29   **Ht:** 6'6" **Wt:** 235 **Born:** 1/27/1983 **Age:** 30

			HOW MUCH HE PITCHED					WHAT HE GAVE UP												THE RESULTS						
Year	Team	Lg	G	GS	CG	GF	IP	BFP	H	R	ER	HR	SH	SF	HB	TBB	IBB	SO	WP	Bk	W	L	Pct	Sh	Sv-Op Hld	ERC	ERA
2004	Phi	NL	6	4	0	0	28.1	126	25	11	11	1	1	0	5	16	0	24	1	1	2	0	1.000	0	0-0 0	4.33	3.49
2005	Phi	NL	7	4	0	0	26.0	127	30	31	29	5	1	1	3	16	2	17	2	0	1	2	.333	0	0-0 0	6.82	10.04
2006	Phi	NL	11	11	1	0	54.1	264	70	48	44	14	2	5	3	32	3	34	2	0	4	3	.571	1	0-0 0	8.02	7.29
2007	CWS	AL	16	10	0	4	70.0	314	85	45	41	17	3	2	6	19	0	49	1	0	1	5	.167	0	0-0 0	6.22	5.27
2008	CWS	AL	33	33	1	0	206.1	878	190	107	88	30	7	5	9	70	6	145	9	0	17	8	.680	0	0-0 0	3.80	3.84
2009	CWS	AL	30	30	1	0	193.0	797	178	93	87	21	2	3	2	59	4	163	8	0	11	11	.500	2	0-0 0	3.38	4.06
2010	CWS	AL	31	31	1	0	187.1	798	199	92	85	14	3	4	6	58	4	151	9	1	10	13	.435	0	0-0 0	4.03	4.08
2011	CWS	AL	31	31	1	1	193.2	798	180	97	94	22	4	8	11	45	2	151	12	1	12	13	.480	0	0-0 0	3.36	4.37
2012	CWS	AL	29	29	0	0	168.0	724	166	84	80	22	3	3	14	63	2	144	8	0	12	11	.522	0	0-0 0	4.50	4.29
	Postseason		1	1	0	0	3.0	16	5	4	4	2	0	0	0	2	0	4	0	0	0	1	.000	0	0-0 0	14.65	12.00
	9 ML YEARS		194	182	5	5	1127.0	4826	1123	608	559	146	26	31	59	378	23	878	52	3	70	66	.515	1	0-0 0	4.20	4.46

Wilmer Font

Pitches: R **Bats:** R **Pos:** RP-3   FAHNT   **Ht:** 6'4" **Wt:** 210 **Born:** 5/24/1990 **Age:** 23

Year	Team	Lg	G	GS	CG	GF	IP	BFP	H	R	ER	HR	SH	SF	HB	TBB	IBB	SO	WP	Bk	W	L	Pct	Sh	Sv-Op	Hld	ERC	ERA
2007	Rngrs	R	14	10	0	0	45.2	206	41	33	23	2	1	3	6	24	0	61	3	3	2	3	.400	0	0- -	-	4.02	4.53
2008	Rngrs	R	3	0	0	0	4.1	18	1	5	5	1	0	0	3	1	0	6	0	0	1	0	1.000	0	0- -	-	2.79	10.38
2009	Hkry	A	29	24	0	0	108.1	481	93	51	42	4	5	5	9	59	1	105	16	2	8	3	.727	0	0- -	-	3.64	3.49
2010	Hkry	A	7	7	0	0	29.2	136	35	18	17	3	2	1	1	13	0	33	5	0	4	1	.800	0	0- -	-	5.37	5.16
2010	Bkrsfld	A+	9	9	0	0	49.0	212	38	26	21	5	1	2	2	32	0	52	1	0	1	2	.333	0	0- -	-	4.04	3.86
2012	MrtlBh	A+	23	19	0	2	83.1	337	58	41	39	10	4	0	3	37	0	109	8	1	2	5	.286	0	0- -	-	2.95	4.21
2012	Frisco	AA	10	0	0	3	15.0	62	9	5	5	1	1	0	1	7	1	29	1	0	2	0	1.000	0	1- -	-	2.14	3.00
2012	Tex	AL	3	0	0	0	2.0	10	0	2	2	0	0	0	0	4	0	1	1	0	0	0	-	0	0-0	0	3.47	9.00

Mike Fontenot

Bats: L **Throws:** R **Pos:** PH-19; 2B-17; 3B-12; PR-5; DH-1   FONT-uh-no   **Ht:** 5'8" **Wt:** 165 **Born:** 6/9/1980 **Age:** 33

Year	Team	Lg	G	AB	H	2B	3B	HR	(Hm	Rd)	TB	R	RBI	RC	TBB	IBB	SO	HBP	SH	SF	SB	CS	SB%	GDP	Avg	OBP	Slg
2012	LV*	AAA	16	52	16	6	0	1	(-	-)	25	5	7	9	5	0	11	0	1	0	0	0	-	1	.308	.368	.481
2005	ChC	NL	7	2	0	0	0	0	(0	0)	0	4	0	1	2	0	0	1	0	0	0	0	-	0	.000	.600	.000
2007	ChC	NL	86	234	65	12	4	3	(2	1)	94	32	29	26	22	0	43	0	1	3	5	4	.56	5	.278	.336	.402
2008	ChC	NL	119	243	74	22	1	9	(4	5)	125	42	40	49	34	2	51	3	3	1	2	0	1.00	1	.305	.395	.514
2009	ChC	NL	135	377	89	22	2	9	(3	6)	142	38	43	37	35	4	83	2	0	5	4	1	.80	7	.236	.301	.377
2010	2 Tms	NL	103	240	68	13	3	1	(0	1)	90	24	25	32	15	0	41	3	1	2	1	4	.20	3	.283	.331	.375
2011	SF	NL	85	220	50	15	3	4	(1	3)	83	22	21	22	25	3	48	1	2	4	5	1	.83	3	.227	.304	.377
2012	Phi	NL	47	97	28	2	0	1	(0	1)	33	13	5	10	7	2	23	1	0	0	0	1	.00	2	.289	.343	.340
10	ChC	NL	75	169	48	11	3	1	(0	1)	68	14	20	25	10	0	28	3	1	2	1	2	.33	3	.284	.332	.402
10	SF	NL	28	71	20	2	0	0	(0	0)	22	10	5	7	5	0	13	0	0	0	0	2	.00	0	.282	.329	.310
	Postseason		13	22	5	0	1	0	(0	0)	7	1	0	1	1	0	5	0	0	0	1	0	1.00	0	.227	.261	.318
	7 ML YEARS		582	1413	374	86	13	27	(10	17)	567	175	163	177	140	11	289	11	7	15	17	11	.61	21	.265	.332	.401

Lew Ford

Bats: R **Throws:** R **Pos:** LF-13; DH-8; RF-6; PH-3; PR-1   LOO   **Ht:** 6'0" **Wt:** 200 **Born:** 8/12/1976 **Age:** 36

Year	Team	Lg	G	AB	H	2B	3B	HR	(Hm	Rd)	TB	R	RBI	RC	TBB	IBB	SO	HBP	SH	SF	SB	CS	SB%	GDP	Avg	OBP	Slg
2012	Lng Isl*	IND	19	75	25	6	2	4	(-	-)	47	16	14	18	6	0	21	2	0	0	4	0	1.00	2	.333	.398	.627
2012	Norfolk*	AAA	62	242	80	14	3	11	(-	-)	133	35	40	51	23	2	43	1	0	1	8	2	.80	8	.331	.390	.550
2003	Min	AL	34	73	24	7	1	3	(2	1)	42	16	15	16	8	0	9	1	1	0	2	0	1.00	1	.329	.402	.575
2004	Min	AL	154	569	170	31	4	15	(6	9)	254	89	72	101	67	3	75	13	2	7	20	2	.91	15	.299	.381	.446
2005	Min	AL	147	522	138	30	4	7	(6	1)	197	70	53	70	45	2	85	16	2	5	13	6	.68	9	.264	.338	.377
2006	Min	AL	104	234	53	6	1	4	(2	2)	73	40	18	22	16	0	43	4	1	0	9	1	.90	5	.226	.287	.312
2007	Min	AL	55	116	27	6	0	3	(1	2)	42	13	14	13	11	0	24	3	0	1	3	1	.75	4	.233	.315	.362
2012	Bal	AL	25	71	13	3	0	3	(3	0)	25	7	4	3	7	0	13	0	1	0	1	0	1.00	3	.183	.256	.352
	Postseason		5	12	3	1	0	0	(0	0)	4	1	2	2	0	0	3	2	0	0	1	1	.50	0	.250	.357	.333
	6 ML YEARS		519	1585	425	83	10	35	(20	15)	633	235	176	225	154	5	249	37	7	12	48	10	.83	37	.268	.345	.399

Logan Forsythe

Bats: R **Throws:** R **Pos:** 2B-81; PH-8; SS-5; 3B-4; DH-2; PR-2   **Ht:** 6'1" **Wt:** 205 **Born:** 1/14/1987 **Age:** 26

Year	Team	Lg	G	AB	H	2B	3B	HR	(Hm	Rd)	TB	R	RBI	RC	TBB	IBB	SO	HBP	SH	SF	SB	CS	SB%	GDP	Avg	OBP	Slg
2008	Eugene	A-	3	9	3	1	0	0	(-	-)	4	2	0	1	1	0	3	1	0	0	0	0	-	0	.333	.455	.444
2008	Padres	R	9	26	6	0	0	0	(-	-)	6	2	0	3	5	0	8	4	0	0	0	0	-	0	.231	.429	.231
2009	Lk Els	A+	66	236	76	13	3	8	(-	-)	119	46	30	60	61	3	48	7	0	1	6	2	.75	9	.322	.472	.504
2009	SnAnt	AA	66	244	68	9	3	3	(-	-)	92	37	31	40	41	0	63	2	1	2	5	0	1.00	5	.279	.384	.377
2010	SnAnt	AA	107	392	99	22	1	3	(-	-)	132	66	38	59	75	2	95	4	0	1	17	5	.77	2	.253	.377	.337
2011	Tucsn	AAA	46	178	58	12	0	8	(-	-)	94	41	34	42	33	0	50	6	0	1	8	4	.67	0	.326	.445	.528
2012	Tucsn	AAA	16	58	15	2	3	1	(-	-)	26	12	9	12	13	1	18	3	0	0	3	0	1.00	1	.259	.419	.448
2011	SD	NL	62	150	32	9	1	0	(0	0)	43	12	12	15	12	3	33	3	2	2	3	1	.75	3	.213	.281	.287
2012	SD	NL	91	315	86	13	3	6	(5	1)	123	45	26	37	28	0	57	6	0	1	8	2	.80	6	.273	.343	.390
	2 ML YEARS		153	465	118	22	4	6	(5	1)	166	57	38	52	40	3	90	9	2	3	11	3	.79	9	.254	.323	.357

Dexter Fowler

Bats: B **Throws:** R **Pos:** CF-131; PH-14; PR-1   **Ht:** 6'4" **Wt:** 190 **Born:** 3/22/1986 **Age:** 27

Year	Team	Lg	G	AB	H	2B	3B	HR	(Hm	Rd)	TB	R	RBI	RC	TBB	IBB	SO	HBP	SH	SF	SB	CS	SB%	GDP	Avg	OBP	Slg
2008	Col	NL	13	26	4	0	0	0	(0	0)	4	3	0	0	0	0	5	1	0	0	0	1	.00	0	.154	.185	.154
2009	Col	NL	135	433	115	29	10	4	(2	2)	176	73	34	68	67	1	116	1	14	3	27	10	.73	4	.266	.363	.406
2010	Col	NL	132	439	114	20	14	6	(5	1)	180	73	36	68	57	0	104	2	7	0	13	8	.62	5	.260	.347	.410
2011	Col	NL	125	481	128	35	15	5	(3	2)	208	84	45	79	68	3	130	6	7	1	12	9	.57	6	.266	.363	.432
2012	Col	NL	143	454	136	18	11	13	(10	3)	215	72	53	81	68	1	128	0	6	2	12	5	.71	5	.300	.389	.474
	Postseason		4	14	3	0	0	0	(0	0)	3	1	2	1	1	0	3	0	1	0	0	0	-	0	.214	.235	.214
	5 ML YEARS		548	1833	497	102	50	28	(20	8)	783	305	168	296	260	5	483	10	34	6	64	33	.66	20	.271	.364	.427

Jeff Francis

Pitches: L **Bats:** L **Pos:** SP-24 **Ht:** 6'5" **Wt:** 220 **Born:** 1/8/1981 **Age:** 32

			HOW MUCH HE PITCHED						WHAT HE GAVE UP												THE RESULTS						
Year Team	Lg	G	GS	CG	GF	IP	BFP	H	R	ER	HR	SH	SF	HB	TBB	IBB	SO	WP	Bk	W	L	Pct	Sh	Sv-Op	Hld	ERC	ERA
2012 Lsvlle*	AAA	12	12	1	0	77.1	319	84	33	32	6	4	2	1	18	0	65	4	0	3	6	.333	1	0- -	-	3.92	3.72
2004 Col	NL	7	7	0	0	36.2	164	42	22	21	8	2	1	1	13	1	32	2	0	3	2	.600	0	0-0	0	5.62	5.15
2005 Col	NL	33	33	0	0	183.2	828	228	119	116	26	6	10	8	70	5	128	2	0	14	12	.538	0	0-0	0	5.94	5.68
2006 Col	NL	32	32	1	0	199.0	843	187	101	92	18	7	7	13	69	15	117	0	0	13	11	.542	1	0-0	0	3.63	4.16
2007 Col	NL	34	34	1	0	215.1	922	234	103	101	25	7	4	5	63	7	165	1	1	17	9	.654	1	0-0	0	4.37	4.22
2008 Col	NL	24	24	0	0	143.2	636	164	84	80	21	6	4	3	49	4	94	0	0	4	10	.286	0	0-0	0	5.00	5.01
2010 Col	NL	20	19	0	0	104.1	441	119	61	58	11	6	4	2	23	3	67	1	0	4	6	.400	0	0-0	0	4.29	5.00
2011 KC	AL	31	31	1	0	183.0	803	224	102	98	19	7	8	5	39	5	91	5	1	6	16	.273	0	0-0	0	4.67	4.82
2012 Col	NL	24	24	0	0	113.0	502	145	71	70	15	10	3	8	22	5	76	2	0	6	7	.462	0	0-0	0	5.34	5.58
Postseason		3	3	0	0	16.2	75	21	9	9	3	0	0	2	6	2	15	0	0	2	1	.667	0	0-0	0	6.57	4.86
8 ML YEARS		205	204	3	0	1178.2	5139	1343	663	636	143	51	41	47	348	45	770	13	2	67	73	.479	2	0-0	0	4.72	4.86

Ben Francisco

Bats: R **Throws:** R **Pos:** RF-29; LF-24; PH-23; DH-16; PR-3 **Ht:** 6'1" **Wt:** 185 **Born:** 10/23/1981 **Age:** 31

								BATTING												BASERUNNING				AVERAGES		
Year Team	Lg	G	AB	H	2B	3B	HR	(Hm	Rd)	TB	R	RBI	RC	TBB	IBB	SO	HBP	SH	SF	SB	CS	SB%	GDP	Avg	OBP	Slg
2012 Dnedin*	A+	2	6	0	0	0	0	(-	-)	0	0	0	0	1	0	1	0	0	0	0	0	-	0	.000	.143	.000
2012 NHam*	AA	9	36	8	3	0	0	(-	-)	11	2	2	3	3	0	4	0	0	0	0	0	-	2	.222	.282	.306
2007 Cle	AL	25	62	17	5	0	3	(2	1)	31	10	12	6	3	0	19	0	0	1	0	2	.00	2	.274	.303	.500
2008 Cle	AL	121	447	119	32	0	15	(7	8)	196	65	54	57	40	0	86	6	2	4	4	3	.57	10	.266	.332	.438
2009 2 Tms		126	405	104	30	1	15	(6	9)	181	58	46	56	38	0	83	9	4	3	14	7	.67	12	.257	.332	.447
2010 Phi	NL	88	179	48	13	0	6	(1	5)	79	24	28	26	14	1	35	2	1	1	8	0	1.00	6	.268	.327	.441
2011 Phi	NL	100	250	61	10	1	6	(4	2)	91	24	34	32	33	1	42	5	2	3	4	4	.50	5	.244	.340	.364
2012 3 Tms		82	192	46	14	1	4	(2	2)	74	14	15	17	13	0	49	0	0	2	0	1	.00	1	.240	.285	.385
09 Cle	AL	89	308	77	21	1	10	(4	6)	130	48	33	43	33	0	59	8	4	2	13	3	.81	11	.250	.336	.422
09 Phi	NL	37	97	27	9	0	5	(2	3)	51	10	13	13	5	0	24	1	0	1	1	4	.20	1	.278	.317	.526
12 Tor	AL	27	50	12	5	1	0	(0	0)	19	5	2	4	4	0	10	0	0	0	0	1	.00	0	.240	.296	.380
12 Hou	AL	31	85	21	4	0	2	(2	0)	31	5	5	8	5	0	23	0	0	0	0	0	-	0	.247	.289	.365
12 TB	AL	24	57	13	5	0	2	(0	2)	24	4	8	5	4	0	16	0	0	2	0	0	-	1	.228	.270	.421
Postseason		17	19	2	0	0	1	(0	1)	5	2	3	2	1	0	5	1	0	0	0	0	-	1	.105	.190	.263
6 ML YEARS		542	1535	395	104	3	49	(22	27)	652	195	189	194	141	2	314	22	9	14	30	17	.64	36	.257	.326	.425

Frank Francisco

Pitches: R **Bats:** R **Pos:** RP-48 **Ht:** 6'2" **Wt:** 250 **Born:** 9/11/1979 **Age:** 33

				HOW MUCH HE PITCHED						WHAT HE GAVE UP											THE RESULTS						
Year Team	Lg	G	GS	CG	GF	IP	BFP	H	R	ER	HR	SH	SF	HB	TBB	IBB	SO	WP	Bk	W	L	Pct	Sh	Sv-Op	Hld	ERC	ERA
2012 Bnghtn*	AA	5	0	0	1	4.2	21	6	2	2	0	0	0	0	1	0	4	0	0	0	0	-	0	1- -	-	4.11	3.86
2004 Tex	AL	45	0	0	7	51.1	216	36	19	19	4	2	1	3	28	2	60	4	1	5	1	.833	0	0-3	10	3.04	3.33
2006 Tex	AL	8	0	0	2	7.1	32	8	4	4	2	0	0	0	2	0	6	1	0	1	0	1.000	0	0-0	2	5.17	4.91
2007 Tex	AL	59	0	0	16	59.1	268	57	33	30	3	6	1	2	38	4	49	8	0	1	1	.500	0	0-0	21	4.44	4.55
2008 Tex	AL	58	0	0	18	63.1	264	47	24	22	7	0	3	0	26	2	83	5	0	3	5	.375	0	5-11	12	2.70	3.13
2009 Tex	AL	51	0	0	42	49.1	203	40	21	21	6	0	0	1	15	1	57	3	0	2	3	.400	0	25-29	4	2.85	3.83
2010 Tex	AL	56	0	0	20	52.2	221	49	23	22	5	3	1	1	18	2	60	2	1	6	4	.600	0	2-6	15	3.46	3.76
2011 Tor	AL	54	0	0	38	50.2	218	49	21	20	7	1	0	0	18	2	53	2	0	1	4	.200	0	17-21	2	3.85	3.55
2012 NYM	NL	48	0	0	38	42.1	197	47	27	26	5	0	1	0	21	1	47	2	1	1	3	.250	0	23-26	1	5.01	5.53
8 ML YEARS		379	0	0	181	376.1	1619	333	172	164	39	12	7	7	166	14	415	27	3	19	22	.463	0	72-96	67	3.60	3.92

Juan Francisco

Bats: L **Throws:** R **Pos:** 3B-49; PH-48; PR-2 **Ht:** 6'2" **Wt:** 245 **Born:** 6/24/1987 **Age:** 26

								BATTING												BASERUNNING				AVERAGES		
Year Team	Lg	G	AB	H	2B	3B	HR	(Hm	Rd)	TB	R	RBI	RC	TBB	IBB	SO	HBP	SH	SF	SB	CS	SB%	GDP	Avg	OBP	Slg
2009 Cin	NL	14	21	9	1	0	1	(1	0)	13	4	7	6	3	0	7	1	0	0	0	0	-	0	.429	.520	.619
2010 Cin	NL	36	55	15	3	0	1	(1	0)	21	3	7	3	4	0	20	0	0	0	0	1	.00	2	.273	.322	.382
2011 Cin	NL	31	93	24	7	1	3	(1	2)	42	10	15	12	4	1	24	0	0	0	1	0	1.00	1	.258	.289	.452
2012 Atl	NL	93	192	45	11	0	9	(4	5)	83	17	32	20	11	2	70	1	0	1	1	1	.50	5	.234	.278	.432
Postseason		1	1	0	0	0	0	(0	0)	0	0	0	0	0	0	0	0	0	0	0	0	-	0	.000	.000	.000
4 ML YEARS		174	361	93	22	1	14	(7	7)	159	34	61	41	22	3	121	2	0	1	2	2	.50	8	.258	.303	.440

Jeff Francoeur

Bats: R **Throws:** R **Pos:** RF-145; CF-3; DH-1; PH-1; PR-1 frann-COOR **Ht:** 6'4" **Wt:** 210 **Born:** 1/8/1984 **Age:** 29

								BATTING												BASERUNNING				AVERAGES		
Year Team	Lg	G	AB	H	2B	3B	HR	(Hm	Rd)	TB	R	RBI	RC	TBB	IBB	SO	HBP	SH	SF	SB	CS	SB%	GDP	Avg	OBP	Slg
2005 Atl	NL	70	257	77	20	1	14	(11	3)	141	41	45	50	11	3	58	4	0	2	3	2	.60	4	.300	.336	.549
2006 Atl	NL	162	651	169	24	6	29	(19	10)	292	83	103	91	23	6	132	9	0	3	1	6	.14	15	.260	.293	.449
2007 Atl	NL	162	642	188	40	0	19	(7	12)	285	84	105	97	42	5	129	5	0	7	5	2	.71	14	.293	.338	.444
2008 Atl	NL	155	599	143	33	4	11	(5	6)	215	70	71	49	39	5	111	10	0	4	1	0	1.00	18	.239	.294	.359
2009 2 Tms	NL	157	593	166	32	4	15	(7	8)	251	72	76	59	23	5	92	6	1	9	6	4	.60	13	.280	.309	.423
2010 2 Tms		139	454	113	18	2	13	(5	8)	174	52	65	46	30	8	81	8	0	11	8	3	.73	9	.249	.300	.383
2011 KC	AL	153	601	171	47	4	20	(10	10)	286	77	87	83	37	3	123	8	0	10	22	10	.69	17	.285	.329	.476
2012 KC	AL	148	561	132	26	3	16	(7	9)	212	58	49	50	34	9	119	7	0	1	4	7	.36	14	.235	.287	.378
09 Atl	NL	82	304	76	12	2	5	(3	2)	107	32	35	25	12	2	46	3	1	4	5	1	.83	10	.250	.282	.352
09 NYM	NL	75	289	90	20	2	10	(4	6)	144	40	41	34	11	3	46	3	0	5	1	3	.25	3	.311	.338	.498

Year	Team	Lg	G	AB	H	2B	3B	HR	(Hm	Rd)	TB	R	RBI	RC	TBB	IBB	SO	HBP	SH	SF	SB	CS	SB%	GDP	Avg	OBP	Slg
10	NYM	NL	124	401	95	16	2	11	(5	6)	148	43	54	39	29	8	76	7	0	10	8	2	.80	7	.237	.293	.369
10	Tex	AL	15	53	18	2	0	2	(0	2)	26	9	11	7	1	0	5	1	0	1	0	1	.00	2	.340	.357	.491
	Postseason		13	41	7	2	1	0			11	3	2	3	3	1	7	1	1	0	0	0	-	2	.171	.244	.268
	8 ML YEARS		1146	4358	1159	240	23	137	(71	66)	1856	537	601	525	239	44	845	57	1	47	49	35	.58	104	.266	.310	.426

Kevin Frandsen

Bats: R **Throws:** R **Pos:** 3B-52; PH-5   **Ht:** 6'0" **Wt:** 185 **Born:** 5/24/1982 **Age:** 31

Year	Team	Lg	G	AB	H	2B	3B	HR	(Hm	Rd)	TB	R	RBI	RC	TBB	IBB	SO	HBP	SH	SF	SB	CS	SB%	GDP	Avg	OBP	Slg
2012	LV*	AAA	99	391	118	34	0	1	(-	-)	155	38	33	52	14	2	31	8	2	3	2	4	.33	14	.302	.337	.396
2006	SF	NL	41	93	20	4	0	2	(0	2)	30	12	7	7	3	0	14	6	0	0	0	1	.00	3	.215	.284	.323
2007	SF	NL	109	264	71	12	1	5	(1	4)	100	26	31	29	21	3	24	5	3	3	4	3	.57	17	.269	.331	.379
2008	SF	NL	1	1	0	0	0	0	(0	0)	0	0	0	0	0	0	0	0	0	0	0	0	-	0	.000	.000	.000
2009	SF	NL	23	50	7	2	0	0	(0	0)	9	3	1	0	3	0	4	1	0	0	0	0	-	2	.140	.204	.180
2010	LAA	AL	54	160	40	11	0	0	(0	0)	51	24	14	16	9	0	10	1	3	0	2	0	1.00	5	.250	.294	.319
2012	Phi	NL	55	195	66	10	3	2	(1	1)	88	24	14	30	9	2	18	5	1	0	0	1	.00	4	.338	.383	.451
	6 ML YEARS		283	763	204	39	4	9	(2	7)	278	89	67	82	45	5	70	18	7	3	6	5	.55	31	.267	.322	.364

Jason Frasor

Pitches: R **Bats:** R **Pos:** RP-50   FRAY-zer   **Ht:** 5'9" **Wt:** 180 **Born:** 8/9/1977 **Age:** 35

			HOW MUCH HE PITCHED						WHAT HE GAVE UP										THE RESULTS						
Year	Team	Lg	G	GS	CG	GF	IP	BFP	H	R	ER	HR	SH	SF	HB	TBB	IBB	SO	WP	Bk	W	L	Pct	Sh	Sv-Op	Hld	ERC	ERA
2012	Dnedin*	A+	2	0	0	0	2.0	6	0	0	0	0	0	0	0	0	0	4	0	0	0	0	-	0	0--	-	0.00	0.00
2004	Tor	AL	63	0	0	37	68.1	299	64	31	31	4	3	3	2	36	3	54	4	2	4	6	.400	0	17-19	8	3.97	4.08
2005	Tor	AL	67	0	0	12	74.2	305	67	31	27	8	2	1	3	28	2	62	1	0	3	5	.375	0	1-3	15	3.72	3.25
2006	Tor	AL	51	0	0	12	50.0	215	47	24	24	8	0	3	2	17	1	51	3	0	3	2	.600	0	0-1	12	3.98	4.32
2007	Tor	AL	51	0	0	18	57.0	242	47	29	29	3	1	2	2	23	1	59	2	1	1	5	.167	0	3-6	4	2.88	4.58
2008	Tor	AL	49	0	0	21	47.1	208	36	23	22	4	0	2	1	32	4	42	6	0	1	2	.333	0	0-1	4	3.62	4.18
2009	Tor	AL	61	0	0	36	57.2	227	43	17	16	4	1	2	2	16	3	56	2	0	7	3	.700	0	11-14	4	2.22	2.50
2010	Tor	AL	69	0	0	18	63.2	279	61	30	26	4	1	0	4	27	6	65	5	0	3	4	.429	0	4-8	14	3.72	3.68
2011	2 Tms	AL	64	0	0	10	60.0	261	58	25	24	7	2	4	3	26	3	57	3	0	3	3	.500	0	0-2	15	4.26	3.60
2012	Tor	AL	50	0	0	9	43.2	191	42	20	20	6	1	2	2	22	1	53	5	1	1	1	.500	0	0-3	12	4.74	4.12
11	Tor	AL	44	0	0	6	42.1	178	38	15	14	4	2	3	2	15	1	37	2	0	2	1	.667	0	0-2	10	3.46	2.98
11	CWS	AL	20	0	0	4	17.2	83	20	10	10	3	0	1	1	11	2	20	1	0	1	2	.333	0	0-0	4	6.37	5.09
	9 ML YEARS		525	0	0	173	522.1	2227	465	230	219	48	11	19	21	227	24	499	31	4	26	31	.456	0	36-57	87	3.64	3.77

Todd Frazier

Bats: R **Throws:** R **Pos:** 3B-73; 1B-39; PH-13; LF-7; RF-1; DH-1   **Ht:** 6'3" **Wt:** 215 **Born:** 2/12/1986 **Age:** 27

Year	Team	Lg	G	AB	H	2B	3B	HR	(Hm	Rd)	TB	R	RBI	RC	TBB	IBB	SO	HBP	SH	SF	SB	CS	SB%	GDP	Avg	OBP	Slg
2007	Billings	R+	41	160	51	6	5	5	(-	-)	82	29	25	33	18	0	22	7	0	1	3	3	.50	2	.319	.409	.513
2007	Dayton	A	6	22	7	3	0	2	(-	-)	16	4	5	5	2	0	4	0	0	0	0	0	-	0	.318	.375	.727
2008	Dayton	A	30	112	36	10	0	7	(-	-)	67	25	20	25	15	0	28	0	0	0	4	2	.67	2	.321	.402	.598
2008	Srsota	A+	100	366	103	20	3	12	(-	-)	165	62	54	61	41	3	84	4	0	3	8	4	.67	9	.281	.357	.451
2009	Carlina	AA	119	451	131	40	2	14	(-	-)	217	59	67	76	42	1	67	2	0	5	7	8	.47	9	.290	.350	.481
2009	Lsvlle	AAA	16	63	19	5	0	2	(-	-)	30	9	9	11	6	0	12	0	0	0	2	0	1.00	2	.302	.362	.476
2010	Lsvlle	AAA	130	480	124	32	4	17	(-	-)	215	71	66	75	45	6	127	10	1	2	14	4	.78	11	.258	.333	.448
2011	Lsvlle	AAA	90	315	82	18	1	15	(-	-)	147	47	46	53	34	3	82	6	0	4	17	4	.81	7	.260	.340	.467
2012	Lsvlle	AAA	10	39	9	2	0	1	(-	-)	14	4	7	4	2	0	11	0	0	0	3	0	1.00	1	.231	.268	.359
2011	Cin	NL	41	112	26	5	0	6	(2	4)	49	17	15	13	7	0	27	2	0	1	1	0	1.00	2	.232	.289	.438
2012	Cin	NL	128	422	115	26	6	19	(10	9)	210	55	67	59	36	1	103	3	0	4	3	2	.60	9	.273	.331	.498
	2 ML YEARS		169	534	141	31	6	25	(12	13)	259	72	82	72	43	1	130	5	0	4	4	2	.67	11	.264	.323	.485

Freddie Freeman

Bats: L **Throws:** R **Pos:** 1B-146; PH-2   **Ht:** 6'5" **Wt:** 225 **Born:** 9/12/1989 **Age:** 23

Year	Team	Lg	G	AB	H	2B	3B	HR	(Hm	Rd)	TB	R	RBI	RC	TBB	IBB	SO	HBP	SH	SF	SB	CS	SB%	GDP	Avg	OBP	Slg
2010	Atl	NL	20	24	4	1	0	1	(0	1)	8	3	1	0	0	0	8	0	0	0	0	0	-	1	.167	.167	.333
2011	Atl	NL	157	571	161	32	0	21	(9	12)	256	67	76	79	53	3	142	6	0	5	4	4	.50	15	.282	.346	.448
2012	Atl	NL	147	540	140	33	2	23	(12	11)	246	91	94	82	64	4	129	7	0	9	2	0	1.00	10	.259	.340	.456
	3 ML YEARS		324	1135	305	66	2	45	(21	24)	510	161	171	161	117	7	279	13	0	14	6	4	.60	26	.269	.340	.449

Sam Freeman

Pitches: L **Bats:** R **Pos:** RP-24   **Ht:** 5'11" **Wt:** 170 **Born:** 6/24/1987 **Age:** 26

			HOW MUCH HE PITCHED						WHAT HE GAVE UP										THE RESULTS						
Year	Team	Lg	G	GS	CG	GF	IP	BFP	H	R	ER	HR	SH	SF	HB	TBB	IBB	SO	WP	Bk	W	L	Pct	Sh	Sv-Op	Hld	ERC	ERA
2008	JhsCty	R	20	0	0	10	24.1	108	23	15	10	2	0	3	1	12	1	34	4	0	4	1	.800	0	2--	-	4.04	3.70
2008	PlmBh	A+	1	0	0	0	2.0	7	0	0	0	0	0	0	0	1	0	4	0	0	0	0	-	0	0--	-	0.27	0.00
2009	PlmBh	A+	26	0	0	13	33.0	133	18	7	6	0	2	3	0	13	0	30	2	0	2	1	.667	0	1--	-	1.31	1.64
2009	Sprgfld	AA	15	0	0	4	23.0	97	19	9	9	6	3	0	1	14	3	17	2	0	1	0	.000	0	1--	-	5.28	3.52
2011	PlmBh	A+	7	0	0	2	9.0	37	8	5	4	0	0	2	0	4	0	7	0	0	0	0	-	0	0--	-	3.06	4.00
2011	Sprgfld	AA	52	0	0	25	59.1	255	53	28	20	5	3	1	2	28	0	52	3	1	2	2	.500	0	3--	-	3.80	3.03
2012	Sprgfld	AA	15	0	0	6	17.1	69	12	5	3	1	1	0	1	4	1	12	2	0	1	3	.250	0	1--	-	1.75	1.56
2012	Memp	AAA	27	0	0	6	30.1	123	25	7	7	3	0	1	0	12	2	27	2	0	2	2	.500	0	0--	-	3.09	2.08
2012	StL	NL	24	0	0	7	20.0	86	17	13	12	2	1	0	1	10	0	18	0	0	0	2	.000	0	0-0	2	3.84	5.40

David Freese

Bats: R Throws: R Pos: 3B-134; PH-11   FREEZE   Ht: 6'2" Wt: 220 Born: 4/28/1983 Age: 30

Year	Team	Lg	G	AB	H	2B	3B	HR	(Hm	Rd)	TB	R	RBI	RC	TBB	IBB	SO	HBP	SH	SF	SB	CS	SB%	GDP	Avg	OBP	Slg
2009	StL	NL	17	31	10	2	0	1	(0	1)	15	3	7	4	2	0	7	0	0				-	1	.323	.353	.484
2010	StL	NL	70	240	71	12	1	4	(3	1)	97	28	36	36	21	0	59	4	4	1	1	1	.50	7	.296	.361	.404
2011	StL	NL	97	333	99	16	1	10	(6	4)	147	41	55	50	24	0	75	4	0	2	1	0	1.00	18	.297	.350	.441
2012	StL	NL	144	501	147	25	1	20	(8	12)	234	70	79	79	57	2	122	7	0	2	3	3	.50	19	.293	.372	.467
	Postseason		18	63	25	8	1	5	(2	3)	50	12	21	22	7	1	14	1	0	0	0	0	-	3	.397	.465	.794
	4 ML YEARS		328	1105	327	55	3	35	(17	18)	493	142	177	169	104	2	263	15	4	6	5	4	.56	45	.296	.363	.446

Christian Friedrich

Pitches: L Bats: R Pos: SP-16   FREE-drick   Ht: 6'4" Wt: 215 Born: 7/8/1987 Age: 25

Year	Team	Lg	G	GS	CG	GF	IP	BFP	H	R	ER	HR	SH	SF	HB	TBB	IBB	SO	WP	Bk	W	L	Pct	Sh	Sv-Op	Hld	ERC	ERA
2008	TriCity	A-	8	8	0	0	36.0	147	31	16	13	2	2	0	1	8	0	50	7	0	2	1	.667	0	0- -	-	2.47	3.25
2008	Ashvll	A	3	3	0	0	12.0	59	14	10	10	2	0	0	0	7	0	15	3	0	0	1	.000	0	0- -	-	5.97	7.50
2009	Ashvll	A	8	8	0	0	45.1	181	35	14	11	2	1	1	1	15	0	66	5	0	3	3	.500	0	0- -	-	2.40	2.18
2009	Mdest	A+	14	14	0	0	74.1	312	59	25	21	3	3	2	5	28	0	93	12	0	3	2	.600	0	0- -	-	2.71	2.54
2010	Tulsa	AA	18	18	0	0	87.1	389	100	54	49	10	5	5	3	35	0	78	1	0	3	6	.333	0	0- -	-	5.19	5.05
2011	Tulsa	AA	25	25	0	0	133.1	600	156	88	74	20	6	3	3	43	0	103	17	1	6	10	.375	0	0- -	-	5.10	5.00
2012	ColSpr	AAA	5	5	1	0	30.0	118	23	12	10	1	3	2	1	4	0	27	0	0	2	1	.667	0	0- -	-	1.65	3.00
2012	Col	NL	16	16	0	0	84.2	377	102	61	58	14	6	2	2	30	0	74	8	0	5	8	.385	0	0-0	-	5.71	6.17

Ernesto Frieri

Pitches: R Bats: R Pos: RP-67   free-AIR-ee   Ht: 6'2" Wt: 200 Born: 7/19/1985 Age: 27

Year	Team	Lg	G	GS	CG	GF	IP	BFP	H	R	ER	HR	SH	SF	HB	TBB	IBB	SO	WP	Bk	W	L	Pct	Sh	Sv-Op	Hld	ERC	ERA
2009	SD	NL	2	0	0	2	2.0	7	0	0	0	0	0	0	0	1	0	2	0	0	0	0	-	0	0-0	0	0.27	0.00
2010	SD	NL	33	0	0	12	31.2	128	18	7	6	2	0	0	0	17	3	41	2	0	1	1	.500	0	0-0	7	1.99	1.71
2011	SD	NL	59	0	0	19	63.0	276	51	21	19	3	1	1	9	34	5	76	1	1	1	2	.333	0	0-0	4	3.60	2.71
2012	2 Tms		67	0	0	51	66.0	269	35	20	17	9	1	1	7	30	0	98	1	0	5	2	.714	0	23-26	7	2.43	2.32
12	SD	NL	11	0	0	5	11.2	50	9	5	3	2	0	0	2	4	0	18	0	0	1	0	1.000	0	0-0	1	3.67	2.31
12	LAA	AL	56	0	0	46	54.1	219	26	15	14	7	1	1	5	26	0	80	1	0	4	2	.667	0	23-26	6	2.18	2.32
	4 ML YEARS		161	0	0	84	162.2	680	104	48	42	14	2	2	16	82	8	217	4	1	7	5	.583	0	23-26	18	2.74	2.32

Eric Fryer

Bats: R Throws: R Pos: PH-5; LF-1; RF-1; PR-1   Ht: 6'2" Wt: 215 Born: 8/26/1985 Age: 27

Year	Team	Lg	G	AB	H	2B	3B	HR	(Hm	Rd)	TB	R	RBI	RC	TBB	IBB	SO	HBP	SH	SF	SB	CS	SB%	GDP	Avg	OBP	Slg
2007	Helena	R+	43	139	29	7	0	3	(-	-)	45	25	19	14	14	0	28	2	1	1	4	3	.57	5	.209	.288	.324
2008	WV	A	104	385	129	26	5	10	(-	-)	195	76	63	81	43	1	74	6	0	3	15	3	.83	3	.335	.407	.506
2009	Tampa	A+	59	224	56	11	2	2	(-	-)	77	34	24	27	27	0	43	2	0	2	11	5	.69	11	.250	.333	.344
2009	Lynbrg	A+	47	157	38	11	0	3	(-	-)	58	22	14	23	22	1	25	7	1	0	0	0	-	6	.242	.360	.369
2010	Bradtn	A+	83	287	86	16	5	8	(-	-)	136	53	48	55	37	0	64	8	2	3	10	1	.91	6	.300	.391	.474
2010	Pirates	R	3	7	1	0	0	0	(-	-)	1	1	0	1	5	0	0	0	0	0	1	0	1.00	3	.143	.500	.143
2011	Altna	AA	37	113	39	4	2	5	(-	-)	62	24	16	26	16	0	21	1	3	1	1	0	1.00	2	.345	.427	.549
2011	Indy	AAA	38	118	24	5	1	2	(-	-)	37	16	11	14	21	0	30	2	2	0	3	0	1.00	2	.203	.333	.314
2012	Indy	AAA	65	162	33	7	0	0	(-	-)	40	14	10	10	10	0	38	2	1	1	1	0	1.00	5	.204	.257	.247
2011	Pit	NL	10	26	7	0	0	0	(0	0)	7	5	0	2	3	1	7	0	0	0	1	1	.50	0	.269	.345	.269
2012	Pit	NL	6	4	1	0	0	0	(0	0)	1	0	0	1	1	0	1	0	0	0	0	0	-	0	.250	.400	.250
	2 ML YEARS		16	30	8	0	0	0	(0	0)	8	5	0	3	4	1	8	0	0	0	1	1	.50	0	.267	.353	.267

Brian Fuentes

Pitches: L Bats: L Pos: RP-32   foo-WHEN-tayz   Ht: 6'4" Wt: 230 Born: 8/9/1975 Age: 37

Year	Team	Lg	G	GS	CG	GF	IP	BFP	H	R	ER	HR	SH	SF	HB	TBB	IBB	SO	WP	Bk	W	L	Pct	Sh	Sv-Op	Hld	ERC	ERA
2012	Cards*	R	2	2	0	0	2.0	6	1	0	0	0	0	0	0	0	0	1	0	0	0	0	-	0	0- -	-	0.63	0.00
2012	Sprgfld*	AA	1	0	0	0	1.0	3	0	0	0	0	0	0	0	0	0	2	0	0	0	0	-	0	0- -	-	0.00	0.00
2001	Sea	AL	10	0	0	3	11.2	47	6	6	6	2	0	1	3	8	0	10	1	0	1	1	.500	0	0-1	1	4.39	4.63
2002	Col	NL	31	0	0	9	26.2	118	25	14	14	4	0	2	3	13	0	38	1	0	2	0	1.000	0	0-0	0	4.91	4.73
2003	Col	NL	75	0	0	23	75.1	320	64	24	23	7	0	3	6	34	2	82	2	1	3	3	.500	0	4-6	19	3.71	2.75
2004	Col	NL	47	0	0	12	44.2	201	46	30	28	5	7	0	4	19	6	48	3	0	2	4	.333	0	0-1	13	4.50	5.64
2005	Col	NL	78	0	0	55	74.1	321	59	25	24	6	5	1	10	34	4	91	8	0	2	5	.286	0	31-34	5	3.44	2.91
2006	Col	NL	66	0	0	58	65.1	274	50	25	24	8	2	1	6	26	4	73	6	0	3	4	.429	0	30-36	0	3.19	3.44
2007	Col	NL	64	0	0	38	61.1	255	46	26	21	6	1	1	7	23	0	56	2	0	3	5	.375	0	20-27	8	3.06	3.08
2008	Col	NL	67	0	0	62	62.2	256	47	22	19	3	3	1	1	22	1	82	1	0	1	5	.167	0	30-34	0	2.27	2.73
2009	LAA	AL	65	0	0	57	55.0	242	53	24	24	6	2	2	5	24	2	46	1	0	1	5	.167	0	**48-55**	0	4.37	3.93
2010	2 Tms	AL	48	0	0	35	48.0	196	31	17	15	5	2	2	1	20	1	47	3	1	4	1	.800	0	24-28	3	2.41	2.81
2011	Oak	AL	67	0	0	29	58.1	250	52	30	24	6	4	3	4	20	5	42	2	0	2	8	.200	0	12-15	9	3.35	3.70
2012	2 Tms		32	0	0	14	30.0	142	36	24	24	6	1	2	1	15	0	24	2	0	2	2	.500	0	5-8	3	6.45	7.20
10	LAA	AL	39	0	0	33	38.1	161	28	17	15	5	2	1	1	18	1	39	2	1	4	1	.800	0	23-27	0	3.11	3.52
10	Min	AL	9	0	0	2	9.2	35	3	0	0	0	0	1	0	2	0	8	1	0	0	0	-	0	1-1	3	0.60	0.00
12	Oak	AL	26	0	0	12	25.0	116	30	19	19	5	1	1	1	10	0	18	2	0	2	2	.500	0	5-8	2	6.04	6.84
12	StL	NL	6	0	0	2	5.0	26	6	5	5	1	0	1	0	5	0	6	0	0	0	0	-	0	0-0	1	8.54	9.00
	Postseason		17	0	0	4	17.0	76	16	8	8	3	0	0	1	9	2	16	1	0	1	0	1.000	0	3-4	1	4.82	4.24
	12 ML YEARS		650	0	0	381	613.1	2622	515	267	247	64	27	18	52	258	25	639	32	2	26	43	.377	0	204-245	68	3.55	3.62

116

Kosuke Fukudome

KOE-skay foo-koo-DOE-may

Bats: L **Throws:** R **Pos:** PH-11; LF-10; RF-4; DH-2; CF-1; PR-1   **Ht:** 6'0" **Wt:** 200 **Born:** 4/26/1977 **Age:** 36

								BATTING											BASERUNNING				AVERAGES		
Year	Team	Lg	G	AB	H	2B	3B	HR	(Hm | Rd)	TB	R	RBI	RC	TBB	IBB	SO	HBP	SH	SF	SB	CS	SB%	GDP	Avg	OBP	Slg
2012	Charltt*	AAA	4	13	2	0	0	0	(- | -)	2	0	0	0	3	0	4	0	0	0	0	0	-	0	.154	.313	.154
2012	S-WB*	AAA	39	127	35	5	1	2	(- | -)	48	17	16	25	37	3	25	1	0	1	1	1	.50	2	.276	.440	.378
2008	ChC	NL	150	501	129	25	3	10	(6 | 4)	190	79	58	77	81	9	104	1	2	5	12	4	.75	7	.257	.359	.379
2009	ChC	NL	146	499	129	38	5	11	(4 | 7)	210	79	54	76	93	3	112	3	3	5	6	10	.38	15	.259	.375	.421
2010	ChC	NL	130	358	94	20	2	13	(4 | 9)	157	45	44	59	64	1	67	0	3	4	7	8	.47	5	.263	.371	.439
2011	2 Tms		146	530	139	27	3	8	(8 | 0)	196	59	35	65	61	4	110	4	6	2	4	6	.40	8	.262	.342	.370
2012	CWS	AL	24	41	7	1	0	0	(0 | 0)	8	2	4	2	8	0	9	0	0	2	0	1	.00	0	.171	.294	.195
11	ChC	NL	87	293	80	15	2	3	(3 | 0)	108	33	13	46	46	1	57	1	5	0	2	2	.50	2	.273	.374	.369
11	Cle	AL	59	237	59	12	1	5	(5 | 0)	88	26	22	19	15	3	53	3	1	2	2	4	.33	6	.249	.300	.371
	Postseason		3	10	1	0	0	0	(0 | 0)	1	0	0	0	0	0	4	0	0	0	0	0	-	0	.100	.100	.100
	5 ML YEARS		596	1929	498	111	13	42	(22 | 20)	761	264	195	279	307	17	402	8	14	18	29	29	.50	35	.258	.359	.395

Sam Fuld

Bats: L **Throws:** L **Pos:** RF-15; LF-14; PH-9; CF-6; DH-6; PR-5   **Ht:** 5'10" **Wt:** 175 **Born:** 11/20/1981 **Age:** 31

								BATTING											BASERUNNING				AVERAGES		
Year	Team	Lg	G	AB	H	2B	3B	HR	(Hm | Rd)	TB	R	RBI	RC	TBB	IBB	SO	HBP	SH	SF	SB	CS	SB%	GDP	Avg	OBP	Slg
2012	Charltt*	AAA	5	13	2	0	0	0	(- | -)	2	0	0	0	2	0	3	0	0	0	0	1	.00	0	.154	.267	.154
2012	Drham*	AAA	5	18	3	1	0	0	(- | -)	4	0	0	0	3	0	3	0	0	0	0	1	.00	1	.167	.286	.222
2007	ChC	NL	14	6	0	0	0	0	(0 | 0)	0	3	0	0	3	0	3	0	0	0	0	0	-	0	.000	.333	.000
2009	ChC	NL	65	97	29	6	1	1	(1 | 0)	40	17	2	15	17	1	10	1	0	0	2	1	.67	1	.299	.409	.412
2010	ChC	NL	19	28	4	1	0	0	(0 | 0)	5	3	3	1	3	0	5	0	0	0	0	0	-	2	.143	.226	.179
2011	TB	AL	105	308	74	18	5	3	(2 | 1)	111	41	27	37	32	0	49	1	4	1	20	8	.71	3	.240	.313	.360
2012	TB	AL	44	98	25	3	2	0	(0 | 0)	32	14	5	13	8	0	14	1	0	0	7	2	.78	0	.255	.318	.327
	Postseason		3	3	0	0	0	0	(0 | 0)	0	0	0	0	0	0	1	0	0	0	0	0	-	0	.000	.000	.000
	5 ML YEARS		247	537	132	28	8	4	(3 | 1)	188	78	37	66	63	1	81	3	4	1	29	11	.73	6	.246	.328	.350

Charlie Furbush

FUR-bush

Pitches: L **Bats:** L **Pos:** RP-48   **Ht:** 6'5" **Wt:** 215 **Born:** 4/11/1986 **Age:** 27

			HOW MUCH HE PITCHED							WHAT HE GAVE UP											THE RESULTS						
Year	Team	Lg	G	GS	CG	GF	IP	BFP	H	R	ER	HR	SH	SF	HB	TBB	IBB	SO	WP	Bk	W	L	Pct	Sh	Sv-Op	Hld	ERC	ERA
2007	Tigers	R	4	3	0	1	16.0	62	11	5	5	2	0	0	0	3	0	23	1	0	2	0	1.000	0	0- -	-	1.83	2.81
2007	WMich	A	8	7	0	0	45.2	185	40	14	11	2	1	2	2	11	0	46	3	0	4	1	.800	0	0- -	-	2.65	2.17
2009	Lkland	A+	24	23	0	0	111.1	474	111	59	49	10	1	3	6	32	1	93	5	0	6	7	.462	0	0- -	-	3.74	3.96
2010	Lkland	A+	13	13	0	0	77.0	317	68	35	29	7	3	1	2	14	1	109	4	1	4	5	.444	0	0- -	-	2.58	3.39
2010	Erie	AA	5	5	0	0	33.1	138	31	12	12	5	1	1	1	10	1	37	0	0	1	0	1.000	0	0- -	-	3.75	3.24
2010	Toledo	AAA	9	9	0	0	48.2	212	59	37	34	9	3	3	0	16	0	37	2	1	3	4	.429	0	0- -	-	5.78	6.29
2011	Toledo	AAA	10	9	2	0	54.0	212	35	21	19	7	1	0	1	16	0	61	4	0	5	3	.625	1	0- -	-	2.13	3.17
2012	Tacom	AAA	7	0	0	0	10.0	40	7	4	4	1	0	0	0	3	0	13	0	0	1	0	1.000	0	0- -	-	2.13	3.60
2011	2 Tms	AL	28	12	0	1	85.1	372	97	59	52	16	2	4	6	30	2	67	2	1	4	10	.286	0	0-0	1	5.72	5.48
2012	Sea	AL	48	0	0	8	46.1	182	28	15	14	3	2	1	2	16	4	53	5	0	5	2	.714	0	0-0	6	1.72	2.72
11	Det	AL	17	2	0	1	32.1	139	36	18	13	5	2	1	3	14	1	26	0	1	1	3	.250	0	0-0	1	5.96	3.62
11	Sea	AL	11	10	0	0	53.0	233	61	41	39	11	0	3	3	16	1	41	2	0	3	7	.300	0	0-0	0	5.57	6.62
	2 ML YEARS		76	12	0	9	131.2	554	125	74	66	19	4	5	8	46	6	120	7	1	9	12	.429	0	0-0	7	4.14	4.51

Rafael Furcal

furr-CALL

Bats: B **Throws:** R **Pos:** SS-120; PH-3; PR-1   **Ht:** 5'8" **Wt:** 190 **Born:** 10/24/1977 **Age:** 35

								BATTING											BASERUNNING				AVERAGES		
Year	Team	Lg	G	AB	H	2B	3B	HR	(Hm | Rd)	TB	R	RBI	RC	TBB	IBB	SO	HBP	SH	SF	SB	CS	SB%	GDP	Avg	OBP	Slg
2000	Atl	NL	131	455	134	20	4	4	(1 | 3)	174	87	37	78	73	0	80	3	9	2	40	14	.74	2	.295	.394	.382
2001	Atl	NL	79	324	89	19	0	4	(3 | 1)	120	39	30	41	24	1	56	1	4	6	22	6	.79	5	.275	.321	.370
2002	Atl	NL	154	636	175	31	8	8	(4 | 4)	246	95	47	80	43	0	114	3	9	2	27	15	.64	8	.275	.323	.387
2003	Atl	NL	156	664	194	35	10	15	(4 | 11)	294	130	61	107	60	2	76	3	3	4	25	2	.93	1	.292	.352	.443
2004	Atl	NL	143	563	157	24	5	14	(5 | 9)	233	103	59	82	58	4	71	1	5	5	29	6	.83	9	.279	.344	.414
2005	Atl	NL	154	616	175	31	11	12	(9 | 3)	264	100	58	98	62	3	78	1	5	5	46	10	.82	11	.284	.348	.429
2006	LAD	NL	159	654	196	32	9	15	(12 | 3)	291	113	63	110	73	3	98	1	5	3	37	13	.74	7	.300	.369	.445
2007	LAD	NL	138	581	157	23	4	6	(4 | 2)	206	87	47	65	55	3	68	1	2	3	25	6	.81	11	.270	.333	.355
2008	LAD	NL	36	143	51	12	2	5	(3 | 2)	82	34	16	33	20	0	17	1	0	0	8	3	.73	3	.357	.439	.573
2009	LAD	NL	150	613	165	28	5	9	(5 | 4)	230	92	47	73	61	2	89	1	3	2	12	6	.67	11	.269	.335	.375
2010	LAD	NL	97	383	115	23	7	8	(5 | 3)	176	66	43	66	40	5	60	1	2	2	22	4	.85	5	.300	.366	.460
2011	2 Tms	NL	87	333	77	15	0	8	(5 | 3)	116	44	28	31	28	0	39	4	3	1	9	5	.64	3	.231	.298	.348
2012	StL	NL	121	477	126	18	3	5	(2 | 3)	165	69	49	57	44	1	57	1	5	4	12	4	.75	7	.264	.325	.346
11	LAD	NL	37	137	27	4	0	1	(1 | 0)	34	15	12	12	11	0	21	3	1	0	5	3	.63	0	.197	.272	.248
11	StL	NL	50	196	50	11	0	7	(4 | 3)	82	29	16	19	17	0	18	1	2	1	4	2	.67	3	.255	.316	.418
	Postseason		59	247	56	5	5	4	(3 | 1)	83	33	16	25	27	1	34	2	7	2	13	2	.87	2	.227	.306	.336
	13 ML YEARS		1605	6442	1811	311	68	113	(62 | 51)	2597	1059	585	921	641	24	903	22	55	39	314	94	.77	83	.281	.346	.403

Armando Galarraga

Pitches: R **Bats:** R **Pos:** SP-5 **Ht:** 6'3" **Wt:** 230 **Born:** 1/15/1982 **Age:** 31

Year	Team	Lg	G	GS	CG	GF	IP	BFP	H	R	ER	HR	SH	SF	HB	TBB	IBB	SO	WP	Bk	W	L	Pct	Sh	Sv-Op	Hld	ERC	ERA
2012	Lxngtn*	A	1	1	0	0	4.0	18	4	1	1	0	0	0	0	2	0	0	1	0	0	0	-	0	0- -	-	3.63	2.25
2012	OKCity*	AAA	9	9	0	0	43.2	188	37	20	20	7	1	1	4	18	1	31	3	0	3	2	.600	0	0- -	-	3.98	4.12
2007	Tex	AL	3	1	0	2	8.2	40	8	6	6	2	0	1	0	7	0	6	0	0	0	0	-	0	0-0	0	6.35	6.23
2008	Det	AL	30	28	0	0	178.2	746	152	83	74	28	2	4	6	61	2	126	6	0	13	7	.650	0	0-1	0	3.50	3.73
2009	Det	AL	29	25	0	1	143.2	642	158	93	90	24	1	11	6	67	1	95	1	0	6	10	.375	0	0-0	0	5.65	5.64
2010	Det	AL	25	24	2	0	144.1	617	143	75	72	21	1	7	4	51	1	74	4	3	4	9	.308	1	0-0	0	4.27	4.49
2011	Ari	NL	8	8	0	0	42.2	198	47	36	28	13	3	5	1	22	2	28	1	1	3	4	.429	0	0-0	0	6.60	5.91
2012	Hou	NL	5	5	0	0	24.0	120	28	20	18	6	1	1	2	18	1	17	1	1	0	4	.000	0	0-0	0	7.93	6.75
6 ML YEARS			100	91	2	3	542.0	2363	536	313	288	94	8	29	19	226	7	346	13	5	26	34	.433	1	0-1	0	4.72	4.78

Yovani Gallardo

Pitches: R **Bats:** R **Pos:** SP-33 guy-YARR-doe **Ht:** 6'2" **Wt:** 210 **Born:** 2/27/1986 **Age:** 27

Year	Team	Lg	G	GS	CG	GF	IP	BFP	H	R	ER	HR	SH	SF	HB	TBB	IBB	SO	WP	Bk	W	L	Pct	Sh	Sv-Op	Hld	ERC	ERA
2007	Mil	NL	20	17	0	1	110.1	466	103	48	45	8	4	3	2	37	2	101	3	0	9	5	.643	0	0-0	0	3.30	3.67
2008	Mil	NL	4	4	0	0	24.0	97	22	5	5	3	2	1	0	8	0	20	0	0	-	0	0-0	0	3.66	1.88
2009	Mil	NL	30	30	1	0	185.2	793	150	78	77	21	5	3	5	94	5	204	9	0	13	12	.520	0	0-0	0	3.57	3.73
2010	Mil	NL	31	31	2	0	185.0	803	178	89	79	12	11	4	3	75	5	200	7	1	14	7	.667	2	0-0	0	3.61	3.84
2011	Mil	NL	33	33	1	0	207.1	865	193	92	81	27	10	7	1	59	1	207	12	0	17	10	.630	1	0-0	0	3.43	3.52
2012	Mil	NL	33	33	0	0	204.0	860	185	86	83	26	11	6	0	81	3	204	5	0	16	9	.640	0	0-0	0	3.72	3.66
Postseason			5	4	0	0	26.0	109	22	9	6	2	1	0	0	13	3	20	4	0	1	2	.333	0	0-0	0	3.34	2.08
6 ML YEARS			151	148	4	1	916.1	3884	831	398	370	97	43	24	11	354	16	936	36	1	69	43	.616	3	0-0	0	3.56	3.63

Freddy Galvis

Bats: B **Throws:** R **Pos:** 2B-55; SS-5; PH-4 GAL-viss **Ht:** 5'10" **Wt:** 170 **Born:** 11/14/1989 **Age:** 23

Year	Team	Lg	G	AB	H	2B	3B	HR	(Hm	Rd)	TB	R	RBI	RC	TBB	IBB	SO	HBP	SH	SF	SB	CS	SB%	GDP	Avg	OBP	Slg
2007	Wmspt	A-	38	143	29	5	1	0	(-	-)	36	20	7	9	10	0	20	0	3	0	9	4	.69	1	.203	.255	.252
2008	Lakwd	A	127	458	109	12	1	3	(-	-)	132	59	42	43	39	0	58	4	16	6	14	7	.67	11	.238	.300	.288
2009	Clrwtr	A+	63	251	62	8	2	1	(-	-)	77	29	15	22	10	0	43	2	8	1	6	3	.67	4	.247	.280	.307
2009	Phillies	R	7	29	8	1	0	0	(-	-)	9	6	0	2	1	0	4	0	0	0	1	1	.50	3	.276	.300	.310
2009	Rdng	AA	16	61	12	0	0	1	(-	-)	15	6	5	2	2	0	7	0	0	0	0	1	.00	0	.197	.222	.246
2010	Rdng	AA	138	501	117	16	4	5	(-	-)	156	58	48	45	30	2	89	1	8	4	15	4	.79	8	.234	.276	.311
2011	Rdng	AA	104	422	115	22	4	8	(-	-)	169	63	35	56	28	0	68	6	7	1	19	11	.63	3	.273	.326	.400
2011	LV	AAA	33	121	36	6	1	0	(-	-)	44	15	8	13	3	1	18	0	2	0	4	2	.67	2	.298	.315	.364
2012	Phi	NL	58	190	43	15	1	3	(3	0)	69	14	24	14	7	0	29	0	3	0	0	0	-	6	.226	.254	.363

Mat Gamel

Bats: L **Throws:** R **Pos:** 1B-20; 3B-1; PH-1 GAMM-ell **Ht:** 6'0" **Wt:** 223 **Born:** 7/26/1985 **Age:** 27

Year	Team	Lg	G	AB	H	2B	3B	HR	(Hm	Rd)	TB	R	RBI	RC	TBB	IBB	SO	HBP	SH	SF	SB	CS	SB%	GDP	Avg	OBP	Slg
2008	Mil	NL	2	2	1	1	0	0	(0	0)	2	0	0	1	0	0	1	0	0	0	0	0	-	0	.500	.500	1.000
2009	Mil	NL	61	128	31	6	1	5	(4	1)	54	11	20	20	18	2	54	1	0	1	1	0	1.00	1	.242	.338	.422
2010	Mil	NL	12	15	3	1	0	0	(0	0)	4	1	1	1	1	0	8	1	0	0	0	0	-	0	.200	.294	.267
2011	Mil	NL	10	26	3	1	0	0	(0	0)	4	1	2	2	1	0	4	0	0	0	0	0	-	1	.115	.148	.154
2012	Mil	NL	21	69	17	2	1	1	(1	0)	24	10	6	8	4	0	15	1	0	1	3	0	1.00	0	.246	.293	.348
5 ML YEARS			106	240	55	11	2	6	(5	1)	88	23	29	32	24	2	82	3	0	2	4	0	1.00	3	.229	.305	.367

Avisail Garcia

Bats: R **Throws:** R **Pos:** RF-18; PH-4; PR-3; LF-2; CF-2 ah-vee-sigh-EEL **Ht:** 6'4" **Wt:** 240 **Born:** 6/12/1991 **Age:** 22

Year	Team	Lg	G	AB	H	2B	3B	HR	(Hm	Rd)	TB	R	RBI	RC	TBB	IBB	SO	HBP	SH	SF	SB	CS	SB%	GDP	Avg	OBP	Slg
2009	Lkland	A+	3	8	2	0	0	0	(-	-)	2	1	0	0	0	0	2	0	0	0	0	0	-	0	.250	.250	.250
2009	WMich	A	81	299	79	11	2	1	(-	-)	97	36	31	27	8	0	70	4	0	4	8	7	.53	13	.264	.289	.324
2010	WMich	A	125	494	139	17	4	4	(-	-)	176	58	63	59	20	1	113	5	0	5	20	4	.83	14	.281	.313	.356
2011	Lkland	A+	129	488	129	16	6	11	(-	-)	190	53	56	58	18	1	132	6	0	3	14	5	.74	17	.264	.297	.389
2012	Lkland	A+	67	266	77	8	5	8	(-	-)	119	47	36	40	11	1	57	5	0	5	14	4	.78	8	.289	.324	.447
2012	Erie	AA	55	215	67	9	3	6	(-	-)	100	31	22	34	7	0	38	4	0	0	9	4	.69	9	.312	.345	.465
2012	Det	AL	23	47	15	0	0	0	(0	0)	15	7	3	5	3	1	10	1	0	0	0	2	.00	1	.319	.373	.319

Christian Garcia

Pitches: R **Bats:** R **Pos:** RP-13 **Ht:** 6'5" **Wt:** 215 **Born:** 8/24/1985 **Age:** 27

Year	Team	Lg	G	GS	CG	GF	IP	BFP	H	R	ER	HR	SH	SF	HB	TBB	IBB	SO	WP	Bk	W	L	Pct	Sh	Sv-Op	Hld	ERC	ERA
2004	Yanks	R	13	6	0	0	38.0	159	26	13	12	1	0	2	2	17	0	47	3	0	3	4	.429	0	0- -	-	2.26	2.84
2005	CtnSC	A	21	20	0	0	106.0	476	102	57	46	3	1	2	10	53	0	103	8	3	5	6	.455	0	0- -	-	4.05	3.91
2005	Yanks	R	2	1	0	0	6.0	25	4	4	3	0	0	0	0	5	0	7	0	0	0	0	-	0	0- -	-	3.36	4.50
2006	Yanks	R	5	3	0	1	11.1	56	15	13	12	1	0	0	4	4	0	15	5	3	1	0	1.000	0	0- -	-	7.16	9.53
2006	CtnSC	A	7	7	0	0	41.2	166	37	19	16	2	0	1	1	12	0	45	3	0	2	3	.400	0	0- -	-	2.92	3.46
2008	Tampa	A+	10	10	0	0	49.2	210	45	20	16	2	0	2	4	17	0	60	8	0	4	2	.667	0	0- -	-	3.25	2.90
2008	Yanks	R	3	3	0	0	7.1	46	19	12	12	3	0	1	4	2	0	9	0	0	0	2	.000	0	0- -	-	20.72	14.73
2008	Trntn	AA	1	0	0	0	5.1	25	4	2	2	0	0	0	0	6	0	5	0	0	0	0	-	0	0- -	-	4.72	3.38

118

Year	Team	Lg	G	GS	CG	GF	IP	BFP	H	R	ER	HR	SH	SF	HB	TBB	IBB	SO	WP	Bk	W	L	Pct	Sh	Sv-Op	Hld	ERC	ERA
			HOW MUCH HE PITCHED						WHAT HE GAVE UP												THE RESULTS							
2009	Trntn	AA	5	5	0	0	25.1	106	15	3	2	1	1	0	1	17	0	24	1	2	2	0	1.000	0	0- -	-	2.68	0.71
2010	Trntn	AA	1	1	0	0	5.2	20	2	0	0	0	0	0	1	1	0	3	0	0	1	0	1.000	0	0- -	-	0.80	0.00
2011	Auburn	A-	10	0	0	2	18.1	76	17	6	6	1	0	0	3	2	0	28	3	0	3	1	.750	0	1- -	-	2.88	2.95
2011	Syrcse	AAA	1	0	0	0	2.0	7	0	0	0	0	0	0	0	1	0	2	0	0	0	0	-	0	0- -	-	0.27	0.00
2012	Hrsbrg	AA	18	0	0	12	20.0	80	13	6	3	0	0	2	0	6	0	28	2	0	1	0	1.000	0	7- -	-	1.43	1.35
2012	Syrcse	AAA	27	0	0	23	32.1	127	18	4	2	0	0	1	0	11	0	38	3	0	1	1	.500	0	14- -	-	1.25	0.56
2012	Was	NL	13	0	0	2	12.2	48	8	3	3	2	1	0	2	2	0	15	1	0	0	0	-	0	0-0	4	2.29	2.13

Freddy Garcia

Pitches: R **Bats:** R **Pos:** SP-17; RP-13   **Ht:** 6'4" **Wt:** 255 **Born:** 6/6/1976 **Age:** 37

Year	Team	Lg	G	GS	CG	GF	IP	BFP	H	R	ER	HR	SH	SF	HB	TBB	IBB	SO	WP	Bk	W	L	Pct	Sh	Sv-Op	Hld	ERC	ERA
			HOW MUCH HE PITCHED						WHAT HE GAVE UP												THE RESULTS							
1999	Sea	AL	33	33	2	0	201.1	888	205	96	91	18	3	6	10	90	4	170	12	3	17	8	.680	1	0-0	0	4.46	4.07
2000	Sea	AL	21	20	0	0	124.1	538	112	62	54	16	6	1	2	64	4	79	4	2	9	5	.643	0	0-0	0	4.20	3.91
2001	Sea	AL	34	34	4	0	238.2	971	199	88	81	16	8	5	5	69	6	163	3	1	18	6	.750	3	0-0	0	2.61	3.05
2002	Sea	AL	34	34	1	0	223.2	955	227	110	109	30	4	8	6	63	3	181	7	1	16	10	.615	0	0-0	0	3.98	4.39
2003	Sea	AL	33	33	1	0	201.1	862	196	109	101	31	2	8	11	71	2	144	11	0	12	14	.462	0	0-0	0	4.33	4.51
2004	2 Tms	AL	31	31	1	0	210.0	878	192	92	89	22	8	3	7	64	3	184	8	0	13	11	.542	0	0-0	0	3.37	3.81
2005	CWS	AL	33	33	2	0	228.0	943	225	102	98	26	5	5	3	60	2	146	20	1	14	8	.636	0	0-0	0	3.65	3.87
2006	CWS	AL	33	33	1	0	216.1	917	228	116	109	32	1	6	7	48	3	135	4	0	17	9	.654	0	0-0	0	4.09	4.53
2007	Phi	NL	11	11	0	0	58.0	264	74	39	38	12	4	3	5	19	3	50	5	0	1	5	.167	0	0-0	0	6.57	5.90
2008	Det	AL	3	3	0	0	15.0	61	11	8	7	3	0	0	1	6	0	12	0	0	1	1	.500	0	0-0	0	3.61	4.20
2009	CWS	AL	9	9	0	0	56.0	229	56	27	27	4	0	1	0	12	0	37	2	0	3	4	.429	0	0-0	0	3.21	4.34
2010	CWS	AL	28	28	0	0	157.0	671	171	85	81	23	5	4	3	45	5	89	4	0	12	6	.667	0	0-0	0	4.52	4.64
2011	NYY	AL	26	25	0	1	146.2	626	152	63	59	16	4	7	3	45	5	96	4	0	12	8	.600	0	0-0	0	4.01	3.62
2012	NYY	AL	30	17	0	10	107.1	461	112	64	62	18	4	4	3	35	2	89	10	1	7	6	.538	0	0-0	0	4.60	5.20
04	Sea		15	15	1	0	107.0	446	96	39	38	8	4	1	2	32	1	82	5	0	4	7	.364	0	0-0	0	3.00	3.20
04	CWS		16	16	0	0	103.0	432	96	53	51	14	4	2	5	32	2	102	3	0	9	4	.692	0	0-0	0	3.77	4.46
	Postseason		10	10	1	0	60.1	253	57	24	22	6	2	0	2	22	1	51	1	0	6	3	.667	0	0-0	0	3.80	3.28
	14 ML YEARS		359	344	12	11	2183.2	9264	2160	1061	1006	267	54	61	66	691	42	1575	94	9	152	101	.601	4	0-0	0	3.94	4.15

Jaime Garcia

Pitches: L **Bats:** L **Pos:** SP-20   HY-may   **Ht:** 6'2" **Wt:** 215 **Born:** 7/8/1986 **Age:** 26

Year	Team	Lg	G	GS	CG	GF	IP	BFP	H	R	ER	HR	SH	SF	HB	TBB	IBB	SO	WP	Bk	W	L	Pct	Sh	Sv-Op	Hld	ERC	ERA
			HOW MUCH HE PITCHED						WHAT HE GAVE UP												THE RESULTS							
2012	Cards*	R	1	1	0	0	2.1	10	4	0	0	0	0	0	0	0	0	1	0	0	0	0	-	0	0- -	-	6.33	0.00
2012	Sprgfld*	AA	2	2	0	0	10.1	39	8	6	6	2	0	0	0	0	0	11	0	0	1	0	1.000	0	0- -	-	1.91	5.23
2012	Memp*	AAA	1	1	0	0	5.0	21	4	2	2	1	0	0	0	3	0	8	1	0	0	1	.000	0	0- -	-	4.59	3.60
2008	StL	NL	10	1	0	4	16.0	69	14	10	10	4	0	0	1	8	0	8	3	0	1	1	.500	0	0-0	3	5.15	5.63
2010	StL	NL	28	28	1	0	163.1	695	151	64	49	9	3	3	3	64	4	132	4	1	13	8	.619	1	0-0	0	3.34	2.70
2011	StL	NL	32	32	2	0	194.2	826	207	100	77	15	10	5	2	50	2	156	12	1	13	7	.650	2	0-0	0	3.73	3.56
2012	StL	NL	20	20	0	0	121.2	515	136	58	53	7	8	7	0	30	1	98	12	1	7	7	.500	0	0-0	0	3.86	3.92
	Postseason		5	5	0	0	25.2	109	27	12	12	3	1	0	1	8	2	21	1	0	0	2	.000	0	0-0	0	4.24	4.21
	4 ML YEARS		90	81	3	4	495.2	2105	508	232	189	35	21	15	6	152	7	394	31	3	34	23	.596	3	0-0	3	3.68	3.43

Brett Gardner

Bats: L **Throws:** L **Pos:** LF-15; PR-3; PH-2   **Ht:** 5'10" **Wt:** 183 **Born:** 8/24/1983 **Age:** 29

Year	Team	Lg	G	AB	H	2B	3B	HR	(Hm	Rd)	TB	R	RBI	RC	TBB	IBB	SO	HBP	SH	SF	SB	CS	SB%	GDP	Avg	OBP	Slg
			BATTING																		BASERUNNING				AVERAGES		
2012	S-WB*	AAA	2	5	3	0	1	0	(-	-)	5	1	0	2	2	0	1	0	0	0	0	0	-	0	.600	.714	1.000
2012	CtnSC*	A	1	3	1	0	0	0	(-	-)	1	1	0	0	0	0	1	0	0	0	1	0	1.00	0	.333	.333	.333
2008	NYY	AL	42	127	29	5	2	0	(0	0)	38	18	16	17	8	0	30	2	3	1	13	1	.93	0	.228	.283	.299
2009	NYY	AL	108	248	67	6	6	3	(1	2)	94	48	23	38	26	0	40	3	6	1	26	5	.84	3	.270	.345	.379
2010	NYY	AL	150	477	132	20	7	5	(5	0)	181	97	47	77	79	1	101	5	3	5	47	9	.84	6	.277	.383	.379
2011	NYY	AL	159	510	132	19	8	7	(4	3)	188	87	36	77	60	1	93	8	8	2	49	13	.79	5	.259	.345	.369
2012	NYY	AL	16	31	10	2	0	0	(0	0)	12	7	3	7	5	0	7	0	1	0	2	2	.50	0	.323	.417	.387
	Postseason		28	57	14	1	0	0	(0	0)	15	8	7	5	4	0	16	0	0	2	3	2	.60	0	.246	.290	.263
	5 ML YEARS		475	1393	370	52	23	15	(10	5)	513	257	125	216	178	2	271	18	23	7	137	30	.82	14	.266	.355	.368

Matt Garza

Pitches: R **Bats:** R **Pos:** SP-18   **Ht:** 6'4" **Wt:** 215 **Born:** 11/26/1983 **Age:** 29

Year	Team	Lg	G	GS	CG	GF	IP	BFP	H	R	ER	HR	SH	SF	HB	TBB	IBB	SO	WP	Bk	W	L	Pct	Sh	Sv-Op	Hld	ERC	ERA
			HOW MUCH HE PITCHED						WHAT HE GAVE UP												THE RESULTS							
2006	Min	AL	10	9	0	0	50.0	232	62	33	32	6	0	3	0	23	0	38	1	0	3	6	.333	0	0-0	0	5.82	5.76
2007	Min	AL	16	15	0	1	83.0	367	96	44	34	8	1	4	4	32	4	67	4	0	5	7	.417	0	0-0	0	5.08	3.69
2008	TB	AL	30	30	3	0	184.2	772	170	83	76	19	3	9	6	59	2	128	3	2	11	9	.550	2	0-0	0	3.47	3.70
2009	TB	AL	32	32	0	0	203.0	861	177	93	89	25	2	8	11	79	0	189	3	0	8	12	.400	0	0-0	0	3.69	3.95
2010	TB	AL	33	32	3	1	204.2	855	193	94	89	28	1	6	7	63	2	150	12	2	15	10	.600	1	1-1	0	3.80	3.91
2011	ChC	NL	31	31	2	0	198.0	839	186	90	73	14	11	2	3	63	5	197	6	0	10	10	.500	0	0-0	0	3.21	3.32
2012	ChC	NL	18	18	0	0	103.2	424	90	48	45	15	5	1	4	32	0	96	1	0	5	7	.417	0	0-0	0	3.50	3.91
	Postseason		5	5	0	0	31.0	131	26	13	12	5	0	1	1	14	0	29	2	0	2	1	.667	0	0-0	0	3.95	3.48
	7 ML YEARS		170	167	8	2	1027.0	4350	974	485	438	115	23	33	35	351	13	865	30	4	57	61	.483	3	1-1	0	3.76	3.84

Chad Gaudin

Pitches: R Bats: R Pos: RP-46 goe-DANN **Ht: 5'10" Wt: 185 Born: 3/24/1983 Age: 30**

Year	Team	Lg	G	GS	CG	GF	IP	BFP	H	R	ER	HR	SH	SF	HB	TBB	IBB	SO	WP	Bk	W	L	Pct	Sh	Sv-Op	Hld	ERC	ERA
2003	TB	AL	15	3	0	5	40.0	173	37	18	16	4	0	2	1	16	0	23	1	0	2	0	1.000	0	0-0	0	3.70	3.60
2004	TB	AL	26	4	0	5	42.2	201	59	27	23	4	2	4	4	16	4	30	0	0	1	2	.333	0	0-1	5	6.46	4.85
2005	Tor	AL	5	3	0	0	13.0	74	31	19	19	6	0	1	1	6	0	12	0	0	1	3	.250	0	0-0	0	18.35	13.15
2006	Oak	AL	55	0	0	13	64.0	276	51	24	22	3	0	3	1	42	2	36	2	2	4	2	.667	0	2-3	11	3.62	3.09
2007	Oak	AL	34	34	1	0	199.1	886	205	108	98	21	3	6	8	100	8	154	3	1	11	13	.458	0	0-0	0	4.80	4.42
2008	2 Tms		50	6	0	14	90.0	382	92	50	44	11	2	2	3	27	3	71	2	2	9	5	.643	0	0-1	4	4.06	4.40
2009	2 Tms		31	25	0	4	147.1	664	146	85	76	14	7	8	8	76	4	139	7	1	6	10	.375	0	0-0	0	4.56	4.64
2010	2 Tms	AL	42	0	0	23	65.1	295	73	45	41	16	4	2	8	25	0	53	3	0	1	4	.200	0	0-1	1	6.33	5.65
2011	Was	NL	10	0	0	1	8.1	45	12	10	6	1	1	0	0	8	0	10	0	0	1	1	.500	0	0-0	2	9.20	6.48
2012	Mia	NL	46	0	0	11	69.1	302	72	39	35	6	8	2	3	26	5	57	3	1	4	2	.667	0	0-0	1	4.15	4.54
08	Oak	AL	26	6	0	9	62.2	263	63	29	25	6	2	1	3	17	1	44	2	1	5	3	.625	0	0-0	2	3.78	3.59
08	ChC	NL	24	0	0	5	27.1	119	29	21	19	5	0	1	0	10	2	27	0	1	4	2	.667	0	0-1	2	4.74	6.26
09	SD	NL	20	19	0	0	105.1	476	105	69	60	7	7	6	5	56	3	105	4	1	4	10	.286	0	0-0	0	4.41	5.13
09	NYY	AL	11	6	0	4	42.0	188	41	16	16	7	0	2	3	20	1	34	3	0	2	0	1.000	0	0-0	0	4.93	3.43
10	Oak	AL	12	0	0	6	17.1	86	27	18	17	5	2	1	3	5	0	20	0	0	0	2	.000	0	0-0	1	9.34	8.83
10	NYY	AL	30	0	0	17	48.0	209	46	27	24	11	2	1	5	20	0	33	3	0	1	2	.333	0	0-1	0	5.32	4.50
	Postseason		4	0	0	1	4.1	18	2	0	0	0	1	0	0	3	1	1	0	0	0	0	-	0	0-0	1	1.45	0.00
10 ML YEARS			314	75	1	76	739.1	3298	778	425	380	86	27	30	37	342	26	585	21	7	40	42	.488	0	2-6	24	4.89	4.63

Cory Gearrin

Pitches: R Bats: R Pos: RP-22 GARE-inn **Ht: 6'3" Wt: 200 Born: 4/14/1986 Age: 27**

Year	Team	Lg	G	GS	CG	GF	IP	BFP	H	R	ER	HR	SH	SF	HB	TBB	IBB	SO	WP	Bk	W	L	Pct	Sh	Sv-Op	Hld	ERC	ERA
2007	Danvle	R+	18	0	0	10	26.1	122	21	14	13	1	1	1	6	16	3	37	7	0	1	1	.500	0	0--	-	3.84	4.44
2008	Rome	A	19	0	0	15	22.1	105	19	11	7	1	2	1	0	15	0	36	4	0	3	2	.600	0	1--	-	3.62	2.82
2008	MrtlBh	A+	17	0	0	9	23.2	115	19	14	14	2	1	1	4	21	2	36	2	0	3	1	.750	0	0--	-	5.11	5.32
2009	MrtlBh	A+	27	0	0	24	29.1	115	22	6	6	2	0	0	1	3	0	32	0	0	0	2	.000	0	17--	-	1.65	1.84
2009	Missi	AA	20	0	0	10	25.1	102	19	9	8	2	2	0	3	8	1	20	1	0	1	2	.333	0	2--	-	2.75	2.84
2010	Gwnntt	AAA	52	0	0	15	80.1	339	72	32	30	6	2	3	9	32	1	66	12	0	3	5	.375	0	2--	-	3.83	3.36
2011	Gwnntt	AAA	35	0	0	17	50.0	211	42	11	10	0	1	1	3	20	1	60	4	0	4	1	.800	0	4--	-	2.72	1.80
2012	Gwnntt	AAA	39	0	0	29	54.2	227	43	21	14	0	3	2	2	22	1	66	3	0	3	3	.500	0	9--	-	2.40	2.30
2011	Atl	NL	18	0	0	4	18.1	85	17	16	16	0	0	1	2	12	4	25	1	0	1	1	.500	0	0-1	3	3.84	7.85
2012	Atl	NL	22	0	0	7	20.0	80	17	4	4	1	0	0	2	5	0	20	2	0	0	1	.000	0	0-1	4	2.86	1.80
2 ML YEARS			40	0	0	11	38.1	165	34	20	20	1	0	1	4	17	4	45	3	0	1	2	.333	0	0-2	7	3.35	4.70

Dillon Gee

Pitches: R Bats: R Pos: SP-17 JEE **Ht: 6'1" Wt: 205 Born: 4/28/1986 Age: 27**

Year	Team	Lg	G	GS	CG	GF	IP	BFP	H	R	ER	HR	SH	SF	HB	TBB	IBB	SO	WP	Bk	W	L	Pct	Sh	Sv-Op	Hld	ERC	ERA
2010	NYM	NL	5	5	0	0	33.0	136	25	10	8	2	3	0	0	15	2	17	0	0	2	2	.500	0	0-0	0	2.66	2.18
2011	NYM	NL	30	27	1	1	160.2	706	150	85	79	18	10	5	14	71	4	114	6	1	13	6	.684	0	0-0	0	4.23	4.43
2012	NYM	NL	17	17	0	0	109.2	463	108	56	50	12	2	3	6	29	0	97	0	1	6	7	.462	0	0-0	0	3.74	4.10
3 ML YEARS			52	49	1	1	303.1	1305	283	151	137	32	15	8	20	115	6	228	6	2	21	15	.583	0	0-0	0	3.87	4.06

Steve Geltz

Pitches: R Bats: R Pos: RP-2 **Ht: 5'10" Wt: 170 Born: 11/1/1987 Age: 25**

Year	Team	Lg	G	GS	CG	GF	IP	BFP	H	R	ER	HR	SH	SF	HB	TBB	IBB	SO	WP	Bk	W	L	Pct	Sh	Sv-Op	Hld	ERC	ERA
2008	Orem	R+	16	0	0	6	26.1	119	31	19	18	4	2	1	2	9	1	36	2	1	1	0	1.000	0	0--	-	5.47	6.15
2008	Angels	R	3	0	0	1	2.1	10	3	1	1	0	0	0	0	0	0	7	0	0	1	0	1.000	0	0--	-	3.32	3.86
2009	RCuca	A+	34	0	0	6	64.2	272	52	29	27	7	3	4	2	32	1	73	3	0	7	1	.875	0	0--	-	3.56	3.76
2010	RCuca	A+	22	0	0	9	34.0	134	20	14	13	4	1	0	3	10	0	51	1	1	3	1	.750	0	2--	-	2.01	3.44
2010	Ark	AA	16	0	0	7	18.2	79	9	5	5	0	0	0	1	16	1	36	2	0	1	0	1.000	0	0--	-	2.46	2.41
2011	Salt Lk	AAA	2	0	0	1	1.2	11	4	4	4	0	0	0	0	2	0	1	0	0	0	0	-	0	0--	-	15.90	21.60
2011	Ark	AA	32	0	0	18	46.2	181	31	16	16	5	1	2	1	14	3	67	1	0	3	3	.500	0	6--	-	2.07	3.09
2012	Ark	AA	21	0	0	13	25.1	95	13	1	1	0	0	0	1	6	2	37	1	0	3	0	1.000	0	6--	-	0.97	0.36
2012	Salt Lk	AAA	25	0	0	11	33.2	141	29	19	19	4	0	2	2	14	0	33	2	0	1	0	1.000	0	5--	-	3.80	5.08
2012	LAA	AL	2	0	0	2	2.0	11	2	1	1	0	0	1	0	3	0	1	0	0	0	0	-	0	0-0	0	7.45	4.50

Craig Gentry

Bats: R Throws: R Pos: CF-114; PH-16; PR-8; RF-3; DH-2 **Ht: 6'2" Wt: 190 Born: 11/29/1983 Age: 29**

Year	Team	Lg	G	AB	H	2B	3B	HR	(Hm	Rd)	TB	R	RBI	RC	TBB	IBB	SO	HBP	SH	SF	SB	CS	SB%	GDP	Avg	OBP	Slg
2009	Tex	AL	11	17	2	1	0	0	(0	0)	3	4	1	1	2	0	5	0	0	0	0	0	-	0	.118	.211	.176
2010	Tex	AL	20	33	7	0	0	0	(0	0)	7	4	3	1	1	0	11	0	0	1	1	0	1.00	1	.212	.229	.212
2011	Tex	AL	64	133	36	5	1	1	(1	0)	46	26	13	21	10	1	27	6	3	1	18	0	1.00	2	.271	.347	.346
2012	Tex	AL	122	240	73	12	3	1	(0	1)	94	31	26	33	14	1	41	10	5	0	13	7	.65	4	.304	.367	.392
	Postseason		13	15	5	0	0	0	(0	0)	5	2	1	3	1	0	4	1	1	0	2	1	.67	0	.333	.412	.333
4 ML YEARS			217	423	118	18	4	2	(1	1)	150	65	43	56	27	2	84	16	8	2	32	7	.82	7	.279	.344	.355

Justin Germano

Pitches: R Bats: R Pos: SP-12; RP-2   jerr-MAHN-oh   Ht: 6'2" Wt: 210 Born: 8/6/1982 Age: 30

				HOW	MUCH	HE	PITCHED				WHAT	HE	GAVE	UP									THE	RESULTS					
Year Team	Lg	G	GS	CG	GF	IP	BFP	H	R	ER	HR	SH	SF	HB	TBB	IBB	SO	WP	Bk	W	L	Pct	Sh	Sv-Op	Hld	ERC	ERA
2012 Pwtckt*	AAA	17	16	1	1	105.0	409	82	33	28	15	1	1	5	13	0	72	1	0	9	4	.692	0	0- -	-	2.34	2.40
2004 SD	NL	7	5	0	0	21.1	109	31	24	21	2	3	1	0	14	0	16	0	0	1	2	.333	0	0-0	0	7.69	8.86
2006 Cin	NL	2	1	0	0	6.2	31	8	4	4	1	0	0	1	3	1	4	0	0	0	1	.000	0	0-0	0	6.26	5.40
2007 SD	NL	26	23	0	3	133.1	566	133	72	66	14	4	0	8	40	3	78	1	0	7	10	.412	0	0-0	0	3.93	4.46
2008 SD	NL	12	6	0	4	43.2	194	54	31	29	8	2	1	1	13	2	17	4	0	0	3	.000	0	0-0	0	5.69	5.98
2010 Cle	AL	23	1	0	4	35.1	146	27	15	13	6	1	0	6	8	1	29	0	0	0	3	.000	0	0-1	2	3.17	3.31
2011 Cle	AL	9	0	0	5	12.2	60	15	8	8	1	1	0	2	5	0	5	0	0	0	1	.000	0	0-0	0	5.46	5.68
2012 2 Tms		14	12	0	1	69.2	320	86	52	48	7	5	3	7	21	2	52	5	0	2	10	.167	0	0-0	0	5.32	6.20
12 Bos	AL	1	0	0	1	5.2	24	5	0	0	0	0	0	0	2	0	7	1	0	0	0	-	0	0-0	0	2.55	0.00
12 ChC	NL	13	12	0	0	64.0	296	81	52	48	7	5	3	7	19	2	45	4	0	2	10	.167	0	0-0	0	5.59	6.75
7 ML YEARS		93	48	0	17	322.2	1426	354	206	189	39	16	5	25	104	9	205	10	0	10	30	.250	0	0-1	2	4.71	5.27

Chris Getz

Bats: L Throws: R Pos: 2B-61; PR-5; DH-1   GETS   Ht: 5'11" Wt: 185 Born: 8/30/1983 Age: 29

						BATTING												BASERUNNING				AVERAGES		
Year Team	Lg	G	AB	H	2B	3B	HR	(Hm | Rd)	TB	R	RBI	RC	TBB	IBB	SO	HBP	SH	SF	SB	CS	SB%	GDP	Avg	OBP	Slg
2012 Omha*	AAA	11	43	12	2	1	0	(- | -)	16	7	8	5	4	0	4	0	0	0	1	0	1.00	3	.279	.340	.372
2008 CWS	AL	10	7	2	0	0	0	(0 | 0)	2	2	1	1	0	0	1	0	0	0	1	1	.50	1	.286	.286	.286
2009 CWS	AL	107	375	98	18	4	2	(1 | 1)	130	49	31	47	30	1	54	6	1	3	25	2	.93	4	.261	.324	.347
2010 KC	AL	72	224	53	9	0	0	(0 | 0)	62	23	18	21	19	1	28	2	3	0	15	2	.88	3	.237	.302	.277
2011 KC	AL	118	380	97	6	3	0	(0 | 0)	109	50	26	43	30	4	45	3	14	2	21	7	.75	5	.255	.313	.287
2012 KC	AL	64	189	52	10	3	0	(0 | 0)	68	22	17	23	11	0	17	0	8	2	9	3	.75	3	.275	.312	.360
5 ML YEARS		371	1175	302	43	10	2	(1 | 1)	371	146	93	135	90	2	145	11	26	7	71	15	.83	15	.257	.314	.316

Jason Giambi

Bats: L Throws: R Pos: PH-41; 1B-13; DH-6   jee-AHM-bee   Ht: 6'3" Wt: 250 Born: 1/8/1971 Age: 42

						BATTING												BASERUNNING				AVERAGES		
Year Team	Lg	G	AB	H	2B	3B	HR	(Hm | Rd)	TB	R	RBI	RC	TBB	IBB	SO	HBP	SH	SF	SB	CS	SB%	GDP	Avg	OBP	Slg
2012 Tulsa*	AA	3	7	3	0	0	0	(- | -)	3	1	1	1	1	0	2	0	0	0	0	0	-	4	.429	.500	.429
2012 ColSpr*	AAA	2	6	2	1	0	0	(- | -)	3	0	0	0	0	0	2	0	0	0	0	0	-	1	.333	.333	.500
1995 Oak	AL	54	176	45	7	0	6	(3 | 3)	70	27	25	27	28	0	31	3	1	2	2	1	.67	4	.256	.364	.398
1996 Oak	AL	140	536	156	40	1	20	(6 | 14)	258	84	79	88	51	3	95	5	1	5	0	1	.00	15	.291	.355	.481
1997 Oak	AL	142	519	152	41	2	20	(14 | 6)	257	66	81	91	55	3	89	6	0	8	0	1	.00	11	.293	.362	.495
1998 Oak	AL	153	562	166	28	0	27	(12 | 15)	275	92	110	103	81	7	102	5	0	9	2	2	.50	16	.295	.384	.489
1999 Oak	AL	158	575	181	36	1	33	(17 | 16)	318	115	123	132	105	6	106	7	0	8	1	1	.50	11	.315	.422	.553
2000 Oak	AL	152	510	170	29	1	43	(23 | 20)	330	108	137	152	137	6	96	9	0	8	2	0	1.00	9	.333	.476	.647
2001 Oak	AL	154	520	178	47	2	38	(27 | 11)	343	109	120	153	129	24	83	13	0	7	2	0	1.00	17	.342	.477	.660
2002 NYY	AL	155	560	176	34	1	41	(19 | 22)	335	120	122	139	109	4	112	15	0	5	2	2	.50	18	.314	.435	.598
2003 NYY	AL	156	535	134	25	0	41	(12 | 29)	282	97	107	120	129	9	140	21	0	5	2	1	.67	9	.250	.412	.527
2004 NYY	AL	80	264	55	9	0	12	(5 | 7)	100	33	40	42	47	1	62	8	0	3	0	1	.00	5	.208	.342	.379
2005 NYY	AL	139	417	113	14	0	32	(16 | 16)	223	74	87	102	108	5	109	19	0	1	0	0	-	7	.271	.440	.535
2006 NYY	AL	139	446	113	25	0	37	(20 | 17)	249	92	113	106	110	12	106	16	0	7	2	0	1.00	10	.253	.413	.558
2007 NYY	AL	83	254	60	8	0	14	(6 | 8)	110	31	39	41	40	2	66	8	0	1	1	0	1.00	1	.236	.356	.433
2008 NYY	AL	145	458	113	19	1	32	(16 | 16)	230	68	96	79	76	5	111	22	0	9	2	1	.67	6	.247	.373	.502
2009 2 Tms		102	293	59	14	0	13	(7 | 6)	112	43	51	44	57	1	80	7	0	2	0	0	-	6	.201	.343	.382
2010 Col	NL	87	176	43	9	0	6	(4 | 2)	70	17	35	35	35	5	47	6	0	5	2	0	1.00	15	.244	.378	.398
2011 Col	NL	64	131	34	6	0	13	(6 | 7)	79	20	32	26	17	0	45	3	0	1	0	0	-	5	.260	.355	.603
2012 Col	NL	60	89	20	4	0	1	(1 | 0)	27	7	8	14	20	2	24	2	0	2	0	0	-	4	.225	.372	.303
09 Oak	AL	83	269	52	13	0	11	(7 | 4)	98	39	40	36	50	1	72	7	0	2	0	0	-	6	.193	.332	.364
09 Col	NL	19	24	7	1	0	2	(0 | 2)	14	4	11	8	7	0	8	0	0	0	0	0	-	0	.292	.452	.583
Postseason		45	138	40	6	0	7	(5 | 2)	67	19	19	25	30	2	30	4	0	2	2	0	1.00	3	.290	.425	.486
18 ML YEARS		2163	7021	1968	395	9	429	(214 | 215)	3668	1203	1405	1494	1334	95	1504	175	2	90	20	11	.65	155	.280	.403	.522

Johnny Giavotella

Bats: R Throws: R Pos: 2B-45; PH-6; DH-4   gee-uh-vo-TELL-uh   Ht: 5'8" Wt: 185 Born: 7/10/1987 Age: 25

						BATTING												BASERUNNING				AVERAGES		
Year Team	Lg	G	AB	H	2B	3B	HR	(Hm | Rd)	TB	R	RBI	RC	TBB	IBB	SO	HBP	SH	SF	SB	CS	SB%	GDP	Avg	OBP	Slg
2008 Burlgtn	A	68	278	83	18	2	4	(- | -)	117	50	26	42	25	0	34	1	3	3	10	7	.59	10	.299	.355	.421
2009 Wilmg	A+	133	476	123	24	8	6	(- | -)	181	84	52	71	66	0	54	4	11	4	26	9	.74	7	.258	.351	.380
2010 NWArk	AA	134	522	168	35	5	9	(- | -)	240	92	65	97	61	4	67	4	7	3	13	7	.65	17	.322	.395	.460
2011 Omha	AAA	110	453	153	34	2	9	(- | -)	218	67	72	85	40	1	57	2	3	5	9	5	.64	8	.338	.390	.481
2012 Omha	AAA	89	362	117	20	2	10	(- | -)	171	67	71	72	46	2	40	6	0	4	7	1	.88	12	.323	.404	.472
2011 KC	AL	46	178	44	9	4	2	(2 | 0)	67	20	21	15	6	0	32	1	0	2	5	2	.71	4	.247	.273	.376
2012 KC	AL	53	181	43	7	1	1	(1 | 0)	55	21	15	14	8	0	35	0	0	0	3	0	1.00	4	.238	.270	.304
2 ML YEARS		99	359	87	16	5	3	(3 | 0)	122	41	36	29	14	0	67	1	0	2	8	2	.80	8	.242	.271	.340

Conor Gillaspie

Bats: L Throws: R Pos: 3B-5; PH-1   gah-LESS-pee   Ht: 6'1" Wt: 195 Born: 7/18/1987 Age: 25

						BATTING												BASERUNNING				AVERAGES		
Year Team	Lg	G	AB	H	2B	3B	HR	(Hm | Rd)	TB	R	RBI	RC	TBB	IBB	SO	HBP	SH	SF	SB	CS	SB%	GDP	Avg	OBP	Slg
2012 Fresno*	AAA	108	413	116	18	3	14	(- | -)	182	60	49	65	41	3	54	2	4	5	0	0	-	8	.281	.345	.441

Year	Team	Lg	G	AB	H	2B	3B	HR	(Hm	Rd)	TB	R	RBI	RC	TBB	IBB	SO	HBP	SH	SF	SB	CS	SB%	GDP	Avg	OBP	Slg
									BATTING												**BASERUNNING**				**AVERAGES**		
2008	SF	NL	8	5	1	0	0	0	(0	0)	1	1	0	1	2	0	0	0	0	0	0	0	-	0	.200	.429	.200
2011	SF	NL	15	19	5	0	0	1	(1	0)	8	2	2	4	2	0	1	0	0	0	0	0	-	0	.263	.333	.421
2012	SF	NL	6	20	3	1	0	0	(0	0)	4	2	2	0	0	0	2	0	0	0	0	0	-	0	.150	.150	.200
3 ML YEARS			29	44	9	1	0	1	(1	0)	13	5	4	5	4	0	3	0	0	0	0	0	-	0	.205	.271	.295

Chris Gimenez

Bats: R **Throws:** R **Pos:** C-39; PH-3; 1B-1; 3B-1; LF-1; DH-1; PR-1   JIMM-inn-ezz   **Ht:** 6'2" **Wt:** 220 **Born:** 12/27/1982 **Age:** 30

Year	Team	Lg	G	AB	H	2B	3B	HR	(Hm	Rd)	TB	R	RBI	RC	TBB	IBB	SO	HBP	SH	SF	SB	CS	SB%	GDP	Avg	OBP	Slg
									BATTING												**BASERUNNING**				**AVERAGES**		
2012	Drham*	AAA	71	261	81	15	0	10	(-	-)	126	39	49	49	32	3	57	4	0	4	0	3	.00	7	.310	.389	.483
2009	Cle	AL	45	111	16	2	0	3	(0	3)	27	12	7	3	17	0	36	0	1	1	1	1	.50	3	.144	.256	.243
2010	Cle	AL	28	58	11	5	0	1	(1	0)	19	6	8	5	8	0	22	0	1	0	0	0	-	1	.190	.288	.328
2011	Sea	AL	24	59	12	1	0	1	(0	1)	16	6	6	5	10	0	13	0	0	1	0	1	.00	1	.203	.314	.271
2012	TB	AL	42	100	26	4	0	1	(0	1)	33	10	9	10	8	0	24	0	1	0	0	0	-	4	.260	.315	.330
4 ML YEARS			139	328	65	12	0	6	(1	5)	95	34	30	23	43	0	95	0	3	2	1	2	.33	9	.198	.290	.290

Hector Gimenez

Bats: B **Throws:** R **Pos:** C-3; PH-2; LF-1; RF-1; DH-1   hee-MEN-ezz   **Ht:** 5'10" **Wt:** 225 **Born:** 9/28/1982 **Age:** 30

Year	Team	Lg	G	AB	H	2B	3B	HR	(Hm	Rd)	TB	R	RBI	RC	TBB	IBB	SO	HBP	SH	SF	SB	CS	SB%	GDP	Avg	OBP	Slg
									BATTING												**BASERUNNING**				**AVERAGES**		
2012	Charltt*	AAA	99	375	97	22	2	14	(-	-)	165	50	57	55	37	0	89	0	4	2	2	1	.67	6	.259	.324	.440
2006	Hou	NL	2	2	0	0	0	0	(0	0)	0	0	0	0	0	0	1	0	0	0	0	0	-	0	.000	.000	.000
2011	LAD	NL	4	7	1	0	0	0	(0	0)	1	0	0	0	0	0	3	0	0	0	0	0	-	0	.143	.143	.143
2012	CWS	AL	5	11	5	0	0	0	(0	0)	5	1	1	3	0	0	3	0	0	0	0	0	-	0	.455	.455	.455
3 ML YEARS			11	20	6	0	0	0	(0	0)	6	1	1	3	0	0	7	0	0	0	0	0	-	0	.300	.300	.300

Graham Godfrey

Pitches: R **Bats:** R **Pos:** SP-4; RP-1   **Ht:** 6'3" **Wt:** 215 **Born:** 8/9/1984 **Age:** 28

Year	Team	Lg	G	GS	CG	GF	IP	BFP	H	R	ER	HR	SH	SF	HB	TBB	IBB	SO	WP	Bk	W	L	Pct	Sh	Sv-Op	Hld	ERC	ERA
							HOW MUCH HE PITCHED				**WHAT HE GAVE UP**											**THE RESULTS**						
2007	Lansng	A	21	21	0	0	110.2	481	132	63	49	8	2	3	3	36	1	74	5	0	6	7	.462	0	0- -	-	4.88	3.98
2008	Stcktn	A+	29	24	0	1	134.0	597	157	90	76	14	6	4	14	37	2	119	2	0	5	8	.385	0	0- -	-	4.99	5.10
2008	Scrmto	AAA	2	0	0	0	6.2	26	6	3	3	1	1	0	0	2	0	4	0	0	0	0	-	0	0- -	-	3.70	4.05
2009	Mdland	AA	28	28	1	0	159.1	686	153	70	62	8	4	7	7	51	0	110	5	0	11	8	.579	0	0- -	-	3.31	3.50
2010	Scrmto	AAA	24	16	0	4	106.1	479	108	76	66	9	5	7	8	53	3	87	4	0	4	7	.364	0	0- -	-	4.67	5.59
2010	Mdland	AA	5	4	0	0	18.2	84	22	9	8	0	1	0	1	9	1	16	1	0	1	0	1.000	0	0- -	-	4.88	3.86
2011	Mdland	AA	1	1	0	0	4.0	17	3	2	0	0	0	1	0	1	0	6	0	0	0	0	-	0	0- -	-	1.55	0.00
2011	Scrmto	AAA	19	18	0	0	107.1	446	92	38	32	6	1	2	7	30	0	89	1	0	14	3	.824	0	0- -	-	2.79	2.68
2012	Scrmto	AAA	20	17	0	3	104.0	424	98	39	38	8	4	4	9	26	0	60	2	0	9	2	.818	0	1- -	-	3.47	3.29
2011	Oak	AL	5	4	0	0	25.0	112	32	14	11	3	1	0	1	5	0	13	0	0	1	2	.333	0	0-0	-	5.11	3.96
2012	Oak	AL	5	4	0	1	21.0	98	26	18	15	4	0	3	3	10	0	10	0	0	0	4	.000	0	0-0	-	7.30	6.43
2 ML YEARS			10	8	0	1	46.0	210	58	32	26	7	1	3	4	15	0	23	0	0	1	6	.143	0	0-0	-	6.08	5.09

Paul Goldschmidt

Bats: R **Throws:** R **Pos:** 1B-139; PH-8   **Ht:** 6'3" **Wt:** 245 **Born:** 9/10/1987 **Age:** 25

Year	Team	Lg	G	AB	H	2B	3B	HR	(Hm	Rd)	TB	R	RBI	RC	TBB	IBB	SO	HBP	SH	SF	SB	CS	SB%	GDP	Avg	OBP	Slg
									BATTING												**BASERUNNING**				**AVERAGES**		
2009	Msoula	R+	74	287	96	27	3	18	(-	-)	183	51	62	71	36	0	74	3	0	5	4	3	.57	6	.334	.408	.638
2010	Visalia	A+	138	525	165	42	3	35	(-	-)	318	102	108	120	57	0	161	8	0	9	5	1	.83	9	.314	.384	.606
2011	Mobile	AA	103	366	112	21	3	30	(-	-)	229	84	94	99	82	12	92	5	0	4	8	3	.73	5	.306	.435	.626
2011	Ari	NL	48	156	39	9	1	8	(2	6)	74	28	26	26	20	0	53	0	0	1	4	0	1.00	4	.250	.333	.474
2012	Ari	NL	145	514	147	43	1	20	(10	10)	252	82	82	86	60	4	130	4	0	9	18	3	.86	9	.286	.359	.490
Postseason			4	16	7	0	0	2	(1	1)	13	4	6	5	2	0	5	1	0	0	1	0	1.00	0	.438	.526	.813
2 ML YEARS			193	670	186	52	2	28	(12	16)	326	110	108	112	80	4	183	4	0	10	22	3	.88	13	.278	.353	.487

Brandon Gomes

Pitches: R **Bats:** R **Pos:** RP-15   GOHMS   **Ht:** 5'11" **Wt:** 185 **Born:** 7/15/1984 **Age:** 28

Year	Team	Lg	G	GS	CG	GF	IP	BFP	H	R	ER	HR	SH	SF	HB	TBB	IBB	SO	WP	Bk	W	L	Pct	Sh	Sv-Op	Hld	ERC	ERA
							HOW MUCH HE PITCHED				**WHAT HE GAVE UP**											**THE RESULTS**						
2007	Eugene	A-	4	0	0	2	6.1	20	1	0	0	0	0	0	0	1	0	6	0	0	1	0	1.000	0	0- -	-	0.18	0.00
2007	FtWyn	A	14	11	0	2	59.2	261	65	41	31	3	2	0	6	11	0	44	6	2	1	4	.200	0	0- -	-	3.68	4.68
2008	FtWyn	A	29	2	0	3	56.2	242	63	24	22	5	1	5	3	19	1	45	1	0	4	2	.667	0	0- -	-	4.70	3.49
2008	Lk Els	A+	22	0	0	7	28.0	120	27	13	9	3	0	1	1	6	0	36	0	0	2	1	.667	0	0- -	-	3.21	2.89
2009	SnAnt	AA	65	0	0	22	72.0	294	54	27	21	4	1	1	2	28	2	100	5	0	4	1	.800	0	3- -	-	2.50	2.63
2010	SnAnt	AA	51	0	0	9	72.1	291	52	19	15	2	1	1	1	25	1	93	8	0	7	2	.778	0	1- -	-	2.01	1.87
2011	Drham	AAA	20	0	0	12	25.1	101	17	4	3	1	1	1	1	7	0	40	3	0	1	0	1.000	0	7- -	-	1.72	1.07
2012	Drham	AAA	40	0	0	20	55.1	222	44	19	19	5	2	1	3	14	1	73	5	0	5	4	.556	0	9- -	-	2.58	3.09
2011	TB	AL	40	0	0	17	37.0	160	34	15	12	3	1	3	1	16	0	32	1	0	2	1	.667	0	0-0	5	3.69	2.92
2012	TB	AL	15	0	0	4	17.2	83	16	12	10	2	0	1	2	12	3	15	1	0	2	2	.500	0	0-0	0	4.76	5.09
Postseason			3	0	0	2	2.1	10	1	2	2	1	0	0	0	2	0	3	0	0	0	0	-	0	0-0	0	4.86	7.71
2 ML YEARS			55	0	0	21	54.2	243	50	27	22	5	1	4	3	28	3	47	2	0	4	3	.571	0	0-0	5	4.04	3.62

Jonny Gomes

Bats: R **Throws:** R **Pos:** DH-52; LF-39; PH-18; RF-3; PR-1 GOHMS **Ht:** 6'1" **Wt:** 225 **Born:** 11/22/1980 **Age:** 32

Year	Team	Lg	G	AB	H	2B	3B	HR	(Hm	Rd)	TB	R	RBI	RC	TBB	IBB	SO	HBP	SH	SF	SB	CS	SB%	GDP	Avg	OBP	Slg
2003	TB	AL	8	15	2	1	0	0	(0	0)	3	1	0	0	0	0	6	1	0	0	0	0	-	0	.133	.188	.200
2004	TB	AL	5	14	1	0	0	0	(0	0)	1	0	1	0	1	0	6	0	0	0	0	0	-	0	.071	.133	.071
2005	TB	AL	101	348	98	13	6	21	(11	10)	186	61	54	62	39	1	113	14	1	5	9	5	.64	6	.282	.372	.534
2006	TB	AL	117	385	83	21	1	20	(7	13)	166	53	59	53	61	2	116	6	0	9	1	5	.17	10	.216	.325	.431
2007	TB	AL	107	348	85	20	2	17	(10	7)	160	48	49	47	35	1	126	7	0	4	12	4	.75	1	.244	.322	.460
2008	TB	AL	77	154	28	5	1	8	(2	6)	59	23	21	18	15	1	46	7	0	1	8	1	.89	1	.182	.282	.383
2009	Cin	NL	98	281	75	17	0	20	(11	9)	152	39	51	46	26	2	85	5	0	2	3	1	.75	8	.267	.338	.541
2010	Cin	NL	148	511	136	24	3	18	(11	7)	220	77	86	83	39	3	123	12	0	9	5	3	.63	4	.266	.327	.431
2011	2 Tms	NL	120	311	65	12	1	14	(8	6)	121	41	43	36	48	1	105	8	0	5	7	3	.70	2	.209	.325	.389
2012	Oak	AL	99	279	73	10	0	18	(7	11)	137	46	47	54	44	2	104	8	1	1	3	1	.75	2	.262	.377	.491
	11 Cin	NL	77	218	46	8	0	11	(7	4)	87	30	31	28	38	1	74	5	0	4	5	3	.63	1	.211	.336	.399
	11 Was	NL	43	93	19	4	1	3	(1	2)	34	11	12	8	10	0	31	3	0	1	2	0	1.00	1	.204	.299	.366
	Postseason		2	6	0	0	0	0	(0	0)	0	0	0	0	0	0	3	0	0	0	0	0	-	0	.000	.000	.000
	10 ML YEARS		880	2646	646	123	14	136	(67	69)	1205	389	411	399	308	13	830	68	2	36	48	23	.68	34	.244	.334	.455

Yan Gomes

Bats: R **Throws:** R **Pos:** 1B-20; C-9; 3B-8; PH-8; LF-4; DH-2 YAHN GOHMS **Ht:** 6'2" **Wt:** 215 **Born:** 7/19/1987 **Age:** 25

Year	Team	Lg	G	AB	H	2B	3B	HR	(Hm	Rd)	TB	R	RBI	RC	TBB	IBB	SO	HBP	SH	SF	SB	CS	SB%	GDP	Avg	OBP	Slg
2009	B Jays	R	4	14	5	0	0	0	(-	-)	5	1	2	2	3	0	2	0	0	0	0	0	-	0	.357	.471	.357
2009	Auburn	A-	60	223	66	23	2	2	(-	-)	99	22	44	36	22	1	37	2	0	1	0	2	.00	9	.296	.363	.444
2010	Dnedin	A+	68	233	64	21	1	9	(-	-)	114	37	40	35	9	0	64	4	0	1	0	0	-	6	.275	.312	.489
2010	Lansng	A	7	26	6	2	0	0	(-	-)	8	2	8	2	3	0	11	0	0	2	0	0	-	1	.231	.290	.308
2011	NHam	AA	79	276	69	18	1	13	(-	-)	128	34	51	42	25	1	75	4	0	4	0	0	-	7	.250	.317	.464
2011	LsVgs	AAA	4	14	3	1	0	0	(-	-)	4	1	1	1	1	0	4	0	0	0	0	0	-	1	.214	.267	.286
2012	LsVgs	AAA	79	305	100	29	1	13	(-	-)	170	44	58	63	25	0	72	2	0	2	4	0	1.00	4	.328	.380	.557
2012	Tor	AL	43	98	20	4	0	4	(3	1)	36	9	13	11	6	0	32	3	1	3	0	0	-	3	.204	.264	.367

Carlos Gomez

Bats: R **Throws:** R **Pos:** CF-128; PH-22; PR-5 **Ht:** 6'4" **Wt:** 210 **Born:** 12/4/1985 **Age:** 27

Year	Team	Lg	G	AB	H	2B	3B	HR	(Hm	Rd)	TB	R	RBI	RC	TBB	IBB	SO	HBP	SH	SF	SB	CS	SB%	GDP	Avg	OBP	Slg
2012	Wisc*	A	4	13	2	0	0	1	(-	-)	5	2	3	1	1	0	4	0	0	0	0	0	-	0	.154	.214	.385
2007	NYM	NL	58	125	29	3	0	2	(1	1)	38	14	12	11	8	2	27	3	0	3	12	3	.80	0	.232	.288	.304
2008	Min	AL	153	577	149	24	7	7	(3	4)	208	79	59	66	25	0	142	7	3	2	33	11	.75	7	.258	.296	.360
2009	Min	AL	137	315	72	15	5	3	(1	2)	106	51	28	33	22	0	72	4	7	1	14	7	.67	1	.229	.287	.337
2010	Mil	NL	97	291	72	11	3	5	(3	2)	104	38	24	28	17	1	72	4	6	0	18	3	.86	10	.247	.298	.357
2011	Mil	NL	94	231	52	11	3	8	(4	4)	93	37	24	25	15	0	64	2	8	2	16	2	.89	2	.225	.276	.403
2012	Mil	NL	137	415	108	19	4	19	(11	8)	192	72	51	59	20	1	98	8	6	3	37	6	.86	6	.260	.305	.463
	Postseason		9	18	5	0	0	1	(0	1)	8	4	2	2	1	0	4	2	2	0	2	1	.67	0	.278	.381	.444
	6 ML YEARS		676	1954	482	83	22	44	(23	21)	741	291	198	222	107	4	475	28	30	11	130	32	.80	26	.247	.294	.379

Jeanmar Gomez

Pitches: R **Bats:** R **Pos:** SP-17; RP-3 JENN-marr **Ht:** 6'3" **Wt:** 200 **Born:** 2/10/1988 **Age:** 25

			HOW MUCH HE PITCHED					WHAT HE GAVE UP										THE RESULTS						
Year	Team	Lg	G	GS	CG	GF	IP	BFP	H	R	ER	HR	SH	SF	HB	TBB	IBB	SO	WP	Bk	W	L	Pct	Sh	Sv-Op	Hld	ERC	ERA
2012	Clmbs*	AAA	11	11	1	0	69.1	294	75	39	34	6	1	0	1	17	0	54	2	0	6	5	.545	1	0- -	-	3.90	4.41
2010	Cle	AL	11	11	0	0	57.2	265	73	36	30	7	0	3	2	22	3	34	1	0	4	5	.444	0	0-0	0	5.75	4.68
2011	Cle	AL	11	10	0	0	58.1	259	73	31	29	6	0	2	1	15	1	31	2	0	5	3	.625	0	0-0	0	4.99	4.47
2012	Cle	AL	20	17	0	1	90.2	395	95	66	60	15	2	7	4	34	5	47	2	0	5	8	.385	0	0-0	0	4.83	5.96
	3 ML YEARS		42	38	0	1	206.2	919	241	133	119	28	2	12	7	71	9	112	5	0	14	16	.467	0	0-0	0	5.13	5.18

Mauro Gomez

Bats: R **Throws:** R **Pos:** 1B-16; PH-12; 3B-9; DH-6 MORE-oh **Ht:** 6'2" **Wt:** 230 **Born:** 9/7/1984 **Age:** 28

Year	Team	Lg	G	AB	H	2B	3B	HR	(Hm	Rd)	TB	R	RBI	RC	TBB	IBB	SO	HBP	SH	SF	SB	CS	SB%	GDP	Avg	OBP	Slg
2004	Rngrs	R	34	126	31	9	2	1	(-	-)	47	12	16	13	10	0	33	0	2	0	0	2	.00	1	.246	.301	.373
2005	Rngrs	R	4	13	5	2	0	1	(-	-)	10	5	4	4	3	0	2	0	0	0	0	0	-	0	.385	.471	.769
2006	Bkrsfld	A+	59	213	55	14	2	4	(-	-)	85	23	25	24	6	0	71	1	0	2	1	0	1.00	4	.258	.279	.399
2006	Bkrsfld	A+	11	44	18	3	0	3	(-	-)	30	9	14	12	5	1	5	1	0	0	1	1	.50	0	.409	.480	.682
2007	Clinton	A	132	497	130	28	4	21	(-	-)	221	72	74	71	23	1	115	18	0	3	2	3	.40	18	.262	.316	.445
2008	Bkrsfld	A+	80	316	77	13	0	8	(-	-)	114	30	41	32	14	1	93	3	1	2	0	0	-	9	.244	.281	.361
2009	Bkrsfld	A+	124	501	143	35	3	28	(-	-)	268	75	94	89	31	1	141	7	0	4	1	0	1.00	10	.285	.333	.535
2010	Missi	AA	133	495	138	42	2	16	(-	-)	232	67	80	83	46	3	122	10	0	8	1	2	.33	12	.279	.347	.469
2011	Gwnntt	AAA	135	506	154	34	2	24	(-	-)	264	76	94	94	38	6	131	4	1	6	6	2	.75	15	.304	.356	.522
2012	Pwtckt	AAA	100	387	120	34	1	24	(-	-)	228	65	74	82	35	3	88	3	0	1	1	0	1.00	10	.310	.371	.589
2012	Bos	AL	37	102	28	5	2	2	(2	0)	43	14	17	17	8	0	26	0	0	0	0	0	-	4	.275	.324	.422

Adrian Gonzalez

Bats: L **Throws:** L **Pos:** 1B-151; RF-18; DH-1; PH-1 — **Ht:** 6'2" **Wt:** 225 **Born:** 5/8/1982 **Age:** 31

Year Team	Lg	G	AB	H	2B	3B	HR	(Hm	Rd)	TB	R	RBI	RC	TBB	IBB	SO	HBP	SH	SF	SB	CS	SB%	GDP	Avg	OBP	Slg
2004 Tex	AL	16	42	10	3	0	1	(1	0)	16	7	7	7	2	0	6	0	0	0	0	0	-	0	.238	.273	.381
2005 Tex	AL	43	150	34	7	1	6	(3	3)	61	17	17	13	10	2	37	0	0	2	0	0	-	3	.227	.272	.407
2006 SD	NL	156	570	173	38	1	24	(10	14)	285	83	82	82	52	9	113	3	1	5	0	1	.00	24	.304	.362	.500
2007 SD	NL	161	646	182	46	3	30	(10	20)	324	101	100	108	65	9	140	3	0	6	0	0	-	6	.282	.347	.502
2008 SD	NL	162	616	172	32	1	36	(14	22)	314	103	119	107	74	18	142	7	0	3	0	0	-	24	.279	.361	.510
2009 SD	NL	160	552	153	27	2	40	(12	28)	304	90	99	109	119	22	109	5	1	4	1	1	.50	23	.277	.407	.551
2010 SD	NL	160	591	176	33	0	31	(11	20)	302	87	101	122	93	35	114	2	2	4	0	0	-	15	.298	.393	.511
2011 Bos	AL	159	630	213	45	3	27	(10	17)	345	108	117	121	74	20	119	6	0	5	1	0	1.00	28	.338	.410	.548
2012 2 Tms		159	629	188	47	1	18	(9	9)	291	75	108	113	42	5	110	5	0	8	2	0	1.00	15	.299	.344	.463
12 Bos	AL	123	484	145	37	0	15	(8	7)	227	63	86	89	31	4	81	5	0	7	0	0	-	9	.300	.343	.469
12 LAD	NL	36	145	43	10	1	3	(1	2)	64	12	22	24	11	1	29	0	0	1	2	0	1.00	1	.297	.344	.441
Postseason		4	14	5	0	0	0	(0	0)	5	2	0	1	3	0	3	0	0	0	0	0	-	0	.357	.471	.357
9 ML YEARS		1176	4426	1301	278	12	213	(80	133)	2242	671	750	782	531	120	890	31	4	37	4	2	.67	133	.294	.371	.507

Alberto Gonzalez

Bats: R **Throws:** R **Pos:** SS-9; 3B-8; 2B-5; PR-3; PH-2; DH-1 — **Ht:** 5'10" **Wt:** 195 **Born:** 4/18/1983 **Age:** 30

Year Team	Lg	G	AB	H	2B	3B	HR	(Hm	Rd)	TB	R	RBI	RC	TBB	IBB	SO	HBP	SH	SF	SB	CS	SB%	GDP	Avg	OBP	Slg
2012 RdRck*	AAA	14	51	16	2	0	2	(-	-)	24	5	6	7	0	0	11	1	1	0	0	0	-	2	.314	.327	.471
2007 NYY	AL	12	14	1	0	0	0	(0	0)	1	3	1	0	1	0	1	0	0	0	0	0	.00	1	.071	.133	.071
2008 2 Tms		45	101	26	8	0	1	(0	1)	37	13	10	11	8	0	14	1	2	0	0	1	.00	6	.257	.318	.366
2009 Was	NL	105	291	77	16	3	1	(1	0)	102	31	33	30	14	1	27	3	2	6	1	1	.50	8	.265	.299	.351
2010 Was	NL	115	186	46	8	1	0	(0	0)	56	19	5	9	7	0	30	1	3	1	0	0	-	8	.247	.277	.301
2011 SD	NL	102	247	53	10	2	1	(1	0)	70	18	32	20	13	3	37	2	1	4	1	2	.33	5	.215	.256	.283
2012 Tex	AL	24	54	13	2	1	0	(0	0)	17	7	4	3	0	0	9	0	1	0	0	0	-	2	.241	.241	.315
08 NYY	AL	28	52	9	2	0	0	(0	0)	11	4	1	0	4	0	8	0	2	0	0	0	-	4	.173	.232	.212
08 Was	AL	17	49	17	6	0	1	(0	1)	26	9	9	11	4	0	6	1	0	0	0	1	.00	2	.347	.407	.531
6 ML YEARS		403	893	216	44	7	3	(2	1)	283	91	85	73	43	4	118	7	9	11	2	5	.29	28	.242	.279	.317

Alex Gonzalez

Bats: R **Throws:** R **Pos:** SS-24 — **Ht:** 6'1" **Wt:** 208 **Born:** 2/15/1977 **Age:** 36

Year Team	Lg	G	AB	H	2B	3B	HR	(Hm	Rd)	TB	R	RBI	RC	TBB	IBB	SO	HBP	SH	SF	SB	CS	SB%	GDP	Avg	OBP	Slg
1998 Fla	NL	25	86	13	2	0	3	(1	2)	24	11	7	5	9	0	30	1	2	0	0	0	-	0	.151	.240	.279
1999 Fla	NL	136	560	155	28	8	14	(7	7)	241	81	59	69	15	0	113	12	1	3	3	5	.38	13	.277	.308	.430
2000 Fla	NL	109	385	77	17	4	7	(5	2)	123	35	42	26	13	0	77	2	5	2	7	1	.88	7	.200	.229	.319
2001 Fla	NL	145	515	129	36	1	9	(5	4)	194	57	48	56	30	6	107	10	3	3	2	2	.50	13	.250	.303	.377
2002 Fla	NL	42	151	34	7	1	2	(1	1)	49	15	18	14	12	1	32	4	3	2	3	1	.75	2	.225	.296	.325
2003 Fla	NL	150	528	135	33	6	18	(7	11)	234	52	77	67	33	13	106	13	3	5	0	4	.00	8	.256	.313	.443
2004 Fla	NL	159	561	130	30	3	23	(13	10)	235	67	79	58	27	9	126	4	3	4	3	1	.75	17	.232	.270	.419
2005 Fla	NL	130	435	115	30	0	5	(2	3)	160	45	45	47	31	10	81	5	4	3	5	3	.63	11	.264	.319	.368
2006 Bos	AL	111	388	99	24	2	9	(4	5)	154	48	50	40	22	1	67	5	7	7	1	0	1.00	6	.255	.299	.397
2007 Cin	NL	110	393	107	27	1	16	(8	8)	184	55	55	51	24	1	75	8	2	3	0	1	.00	13	.272	.325	.468
2009 2 Tms		112	391	93	22	0	8	(7	1)	139	42	41	40	20	4	65	4	10	4	2	1	.67	7	.238	.279	.355
2010 2 Tms		157	595	149	42	3	23	(11	12)	266	74	88	75	31	2	118	7	3	4	1	2	.33	16	.250	.294	.447
2011 Atl	NL	149	564	136	27	1	15	(7	8)	210	59	56	50	22	1	126	1	4	2	2	0	1.00	19	.241	.270	.372
2012 Mil	NL	24	81	21	4	0	4	(1	3)	37	8	15	12	6	0	15	2	0	0	1	1	.50	1	.259	.326	.457
09 Cin	NL	68	243	51	12	0	3	(2	1)	72	16	26	25	15	4	36	2	6	4	0	1	.00	3	.210	.258	.296
09 Bos	AL	44	148	42	10	0	5	(5	0)	67	26	15	15	5	0	29	2	4	0	2	0	1.00	4	.284	.316	.453
10 Tor	AL	85	328	85	25	1	17	(8	9)	163	47	50	47	17	0	65	1	0	2	1	0	1.00	9	.259	.296	.497
10 Atl	NL	72	267	64	17	2	6	(3	3)	103	27	38	28	14	2	53	6	3	2	0	2	.00	7	.240	.291	.386
Postseason		24	83	14	5	0	1	(1	0)	22	8	8	3	2	0	22	0	1	0	0	1	.00	2	.169	.188	.265
14 ML YEARS		1559	5633	1393	329	30	156	(79	77)	2250	649	680	610	295	48	1138	78	50	42	30	22	.58	135	.247	.292	.399

Carlos Gonzalez

Bats: L **Throws:** L **Pos:** LF-131; PH-4 — **Ht:** 6'1" **Wt:** 220 **Born:** 10/17/1985 **Age:** 27

Year Team	Lg	G	AB	H	2B	3B	HR	(Hm	Rd)	TB	R	RBI	RC	TBB	IBB	SO	HBP	SH	SF	SB	CS	SB%	GDP	Avg	OBP	Slg
2008 Oak	AL	85	302	73	22	1	4	(3	1)	109	31	26	30	13	1	81	0	1	0	4	1	.80	7	.242	.273	.361
2009 Col	NL	89	278	79	14	7	13	(7	6)	146	53	29	42	28	3	70	3	5	3	16	4	.80	3	.284	.353	.525
2010 Col	NL	145	587	197	34	9	34	(26	8)	351	111	117	118	40	8	135	2	0	7	26	8	.76	9	.336	.376	.598
2011 Col	NL	127	481	142	27	3	26	(16	10)	253	92	92	95	48	8	105	7	0	6	20	5	.80	11	.295	.363	.526
2012 Col	NL	135	518	157	31	5	22	(13	9)	264	89	85	88	56	11	115	2	0	3	20	5	.80	11	.303	.371	.510
Postseason		4	17	10	2	0	1	(1	0)	15	5	1	5	2	0	1	0	0	0	2	1	.67	0	.588	.632	.882
5 ML YEARS		581	2166	648	128	25	99	(65	34)	1123	376	349	373	185	31	506	14	6	19	86	23	.79	41	.299	.355	.518

Edgar Gonzalez

Pitches: R **Bats:** R **Pos:** SP-6 — **Ht:** 6'2" **Wt:** 210 **Born:** 2/23/1983 **Age:** 30

Year Team	Lg	G	GS	CG	GF	IP	BFP	H	R	ER	HR	SH	SF	HB	TBB	IBB	SO	WP	Bk	W	L	Pct	Sh	Sv-Op	Hld	ERC	ERA
2012 ColSpr*	AAA	15	7	0	0	46.2	210	54	32	28	5	1	2	5	11	0	40	3	0	3	3	.500	0	0--	-	4.68	5.40
2012 OKCity*	AAA	2	2	0	0	13.0	48	6	2	1	0	1	0	1	2	0	8	1	0	1	0	1.000	0	0--	-	0.82	0.69
2003 Ari	NL	9	2	0	1	18.1	85	28	10	10	3	1	1	0	7	2	14	2	0	2	1	.667	0	0-1	0	7.81	4.91
2004 Ari	NL	10	10	0	0	46.1	228	72	49	48	15	5	1	5	18	4	31	3	1	0	9	.000	0	0-0	0	9.78	9.32

(continued)

Year	Team	Lg	G	GS	CG	GF	IP	BFP	H	R	ER	HR	SH	SF	HB	TBB	IBB	SO	WP	Bk	W	L	Pct	Sh	Sv-Op	Hld	ERC	ERA
2005	Ari	NL	1	0	0	0	0.1	5	2	4	4	1	0	0	0	2	0	1	1	0	0	0	-	0	0-0	0	124.7	108.0
2006	Ari	NL	11	5	0	1	42.2	182	45	20	20	7	4	1	3	9	0	28	2	0	3	4	.429	0	0-0	1	4.33	4.22
2007	Ari	NL	32	12	0	5	102.0	437	110	61	57	18	2	3	4	28	4	62	5	1	8	4	.667	0	0-0	0	4.67	5.03
2008	Ari	NL	17	6	0	3	48.0	221	58	34	32	8	4	1	3	21	2	32	4	0	1	3	.250	0	0-0	0	6.16	6.00
2009	Oak	AL	26	6	0	10	65.1	299	76	41	40	4	2	3	6	28	4	39	4	0	0	4	.000	0	0-0	0	5.09	5.51
2011	Col	NL	1	0	0	1	2.0	11	5	2	2	0	0	0	0	1	0	1	0	0	0	0	-	0	0-0	0	14.52	9.00
2012	Hou	NL	6	6	0	0	25.0	105	23	14	14	3	1	0	0	8	0	18	1	0	3	1	.750	0	0-0	0	3.43	5.04
	9 ML YEARS		113	47	0	21	350.0	1573	419	235	227	59	19	10	21	122	16	226	22	2	17	26	.395	0	0-1	1	5.72	5.84

Gio Gonzalez

Pitches: L **Bats:** R **Pos:** SP-32   JEE-oh   **Ht:** 6'0" **Wt:** 200 **Born:** 9/19/1985 **Age:** 27

			HOW MUCH HE PITCHED						WHAT HE GAVE UP												THE RESULTS						
Year	Team	Lg	G	GS	CG	GF	IP	BFP	H	R	ER	HR	SH	SF	HB	TBB	IBB	SO	WP	Bk	W	L	Pct	Sh	Sv-Op	Hld	ERC	ERA
2008	Oak	AL	10	7	0	3	34.0	163	32	34	29	9	2	1	3	25	1	34	1	0	1	4	.200	0	0-0	0	6.54	7.68
2009	Oak	AL	20	17	0	0	98.2	455	113	68	63	14	2	3	1	56	2	109	2	0	6	7	.462	0	0-0	0	5.96	5.75
2010	Oak	AL	33	33	1	0	200.2	851	171	75	72	15	5	2	4	92	1	171	4	1	15	9	.625	0	0-0	0	3.39	3.23
2011	Oak	AL	32	32	0	0	202.0	864	175	81	70	17	3	2	8	**91**	1	197	6	1	16	12	.571	0	0-0	0	3.56	3.12
2012	Was	NL	32	32	2	0	199.1	822	149	69	64	9	9	7	5	76	3	207	10	1	**21**	8	.724	1	0-0	0	2.37	2.89
	5 ML YEARS		127	121	3	3	734.2	3155	640	327	298	64	21	15	21	340	8	718	23	3	59	40	.596	1	0-0	0	3.59	3.65

Marwin Gonzalez

Bats: B **Throws:** R **Pos:** SS-47; PH-18; 3B-14; 2B-6; PR-3   MARR-win   **Ht:** 6'1" **Wt:** 195 **Born:** 3/14/1989 **Age:** 24

			BATTING																	BASERUNNING				AVERAGES		
Year	Team	Lg	G	AB	H	2B	3B	HR	(Hm | Rd)	TB	R	RBI	RC	TBB	IBB	SO	HBP	SH	SF	SB	CS	SB%	GDP	Avg	OBP	Slg
2006	Cubs	R	24	86	17	4	1	0	(- | -)	23	9	11	5	8	0	19	0	0	0	2	2	.00	1	.198	.266	.267
2007	Cubs	R	17	59	17	3	3	1	(- | -)	29	12	10	11	9	0	10	1	0	0	1	2	.33	2	.288	.391	.492
2008	Peoria	A	33	116	26	7	0	0	(- | -)	33	6	9	7	3	0	15	0	1	2	1	1	.50	4	.224	.240	.284
2008	Boise	A-	65	244	68	15	3	0	(- | -)	89	29	43	29	13	0	36	2	6	2	15	7	.68	9	.279	.318	.365
2009	Dytona	A+	120	424	102	15	4	2	(- | -)	131	43	34	37	26	0	77	2	8	1	9	8	.53	11	.241	.287	.309
2010	Dytona	A+	23	85	23	3	0	0	(- | -)	26	7	5	10	7	0	13	1	2	1	7	1	.88	1	.271	.330	.306
2010	Tenn	AA	86	305	75	11	3	4	(- | -)	104	24	41	30	17	3	41	1	3	4	6	4	.60	7	.246	.284	.341
2011	Tenn	AA	64	216	65	18	1	2	(- | -)	91	29	20	33	17	2	27	3	2	1	4	2	.67	5	.301	.359	.421
2011	Iowa	AAA	60	197	54	12	1	2	(- | -)	74	24	19	26	16	2	21	1	8	4	3	1	.75	2	.274	.326	.376
2012	OKCity	AAA	13	39	13	4	0	1	(- | -)	20	2	10	7	3	1	7	1	0	0	0	0	-	1	.333	.395	.513
2012	Hou	NL	80	205	48	13	0	2	(1 | 1)	67	21	12	12	13	0	29	0	1	0	3	3	.50	9	.234	.280	.327

Michael Gonzalez

Pitches: L **Bats:** R **Pos:** RP-47   **Ht:** 6'2" **Wt:** 215 **Born:** 5/23/1978 **Age:** 35

			HOW MUCH HE PITCHED						WHAT HE GAVE UP												THE RESULTS						
Year	Team	Lg	G	GS	CG	GF	IP	BFP	H	R	ER	HR	SH	SF	HB	TBB	IBB	SO	WP	Bk	W	L	Pct	Sh	Sv-Op	Hld	ERC	ERA
2012	Syrcse*	AAA	1	0	0	0	1.1	4	0	0	0	0	0	0	0	0	0	2	0	0	0	0	-	0	0--	-	0.00	0.00
2003	Pit	NL	16	0	0	2	8.1	38	7	7	7	4	1	1	0	6	0	6	1	0	0	1	1.000	0	0-0	3	7.18	7.56
2004	Pit	NL	47	0	0	12	43.1	169	32	7	6	2	3	0	1	6	0	55	4	0	3	1	.750	0	1-4	13	1.60	1.25
2005	Pit	NL	51	0	0	15	50.0	212	35	15	15	2	0	2	1	31	2	58	3	0	1	3	.250	0	3-3	15	2.90	2.70
2006	Pit	NL	54	0	0	47	54.0	234	42	13	13	1	3	1	2	31	2	64	0	0	3	4	.429	0	24-24	3	3.00	2.17
2007	Atl	NL	18	0	0	5	17.0	70	15	3	3	0	0	1	0	8	0	13	0	0	2	0	1.000	0	2-2	5	3.13	1.59
2008	Atl	NL	36	0	0	29	33.2	142	26	21	16	6	1	2	1	14	3	44	0	0	0	0	.000	0	14-16	3	3.33	4.28
2009	Atl	NL	80	0	0	29	74.1	315	56	28	20	7	6	1	7	33	8	90	5	0	5	4	.556	0	10-17	17	3.04	2.42
2010	Bal	AL	29	0	0	7	24.2	106	18	11	11	1	3	1	0	14	4	31	3	0	1	3	.250	0	1-3	10	2.54	4.01
2011	2 Tms	AL	56	0	0	15	53.1	230	51	30	26	7	0	3	2	21	1	51	5	0	2	2	.500	0	1-2	8	4.13	4.39
2012	Was	NL	47	0	0	13	35.2	151	31	14	12	2	3	1	0	16	0	39	2	1	0	0	-	0	0-2	7	3.25	3.03
11	Bal	AL	49	0	0	14	46.1	202	46	26	22	7	0	2	2	18	1	46	4	0	2	2	.500	0	1-2	6	4.46	4.27
11	Tex	AL	7	0	0	1	7.0	28	5	4	4	0	0	1	0	3	0	5	1	0	0	0	-	0	0-0	2	2.11	5.14
	Postseason		8	0	0	1	4.1	17	3	2	2	1	0	1	0	1	0	4	0	0	0	0	-	0	0-0	1	2.55	4.15
	10 ML YEARS		434	0	0	174	394.1	1667	313	149	129	32	20	13	14	180	20	451	23	1	17	21	.447	0	56-73	81	3.09	2.94

Miguel Gonzalez

Pitches: R **Bats:** R **Pos:** SP-15; RP-3   **Ht:** 6'1" **Wt:** 170 **Born:** 5/27/1984 **Age:** 29

			HOW MUCH HE PITCHED						WHAT HE GAVE UP												THE RESULTS						
Year	Team	Lg	G	GS	CG	GF	IP	BFP	H	R	ER	HR	SH	SF	HB	TBB	IBB	SO	WP	Bk	W	L	Pct	Sh	Sv-Op	Hld	ERC	ERA
2005	RCuca	A+	2	0	0	0	4.2	15	0	0	0	0	0	0	0	2	0	3	0	0	0	0	-	0	0--	-	0.22	0.00
2005	CRpds	A	28	0	0	21	44.0	193	47	30	23	4	3	1	4	8	0	42	6	0	2	5	.286	0	8--	-	3.75	4.70
2005	Angels	R	3	0	0	1	4.0	12	0	0	0	0	0	0	0	0	0	7	0	0	1	0	1.000	0	0--	-	0.00	0.00
2006	RCuca	A+	14	0	0	3	26.1	102	17	5	5	2	0	0	1	2	0	24	0	0	1	0	1.000	0	1--	-	1.28	1.71
2006	Ark	AA	31	0	0	19	53.1	209	41	23	23	8	0	0	0	17	0	38	0	0	2	0	.000	0	4--	-	2.95	3.88
2007	Ark	AA	30	19	1	6	130.2	553	128	53	49	13	4	2	12	42	1	81	3	2	8	4	.667	1	1--	-	4.07	3.38
2010	Salem	A+	17	16	0	1	73.1	318	82	42	37	5	2	4	8	18	0	47	8	0	6	4	.600	0	0--	-	4.37	4.54
2011	Salem	A+	2	2	0	0	5.0	23	5	1	1	0	0	1	2	2	0	4	0	0	0	1	.000	0	0--	-	4.20	1.80
2011	Portlnd	AA	15	6	0	2	46.2	222	55	41	32	4	0	4	7	19	0	45	3	1	0	5	.000	0	0--	-	5.47	6.17
2011	Pwtckt	AAA	1	1	0	0	5.0	18	2	1	1	0	0	0	0	1	0	4	0	0	0	1	.000	0	0--	-	1.76	1.80
2012	Norfolk	AAA	14	6	0	1	44.2	165	22	12	8	1	1	0	0	10	0	53	1	0	3	2	.600	0	1--	-	0.96	1.61
2012	Bal	AL	18	15	0	0	105.1	434	92	38	38	13	1	2	5	35	2	77	3	2	9	4	.692	0	0-0	0	3.49	3.25

Alex Gordon

Bats: L **Throws:** R **Pos:** LF-160; PH-1　　　　　　　　　　**Ht:** 6'1" **Wt:** 220 **Born:** 2/10/1984 **Age:** 29

Year	Team	Lg	G	AB	H	2B	3B	HR	(Hm	Rd)	TB	R	RBI	RC	TBB	IBB	SO	HBP	SH	SF	SB	CS	SB%	GDP	Avg	OBP	Slg
2007	KC	AL	151	543	134	36	4	15	(8	7)	223	60	60	69	41	4	137	13	1	2	14	4	.78	12	.247	.314	.411
2008	KC	AL	134	493	128	35	1	16	(9	7)	213	72	59	71	66	5	120	6	1	5	9	2	.82	8	.260	.351	.432
2009	KC	AL	49	164	38	6	0	6	(2	4)	62	28	22	16	21	0	43	2	1	1	5	0	1.00	5	.232	.324	.378
2010	KC	AL	74	242	52	10	0	8	(5	3)	86	34	20	23	34	1	62	2	2	1	1	5	.17	9	.215	.315	.355
2011	KC	AL	151	611	185	45	4	23	(12	11)	307	101	87	103	67	2	139	7	0	3	17	8	.68	9	.303	.376	.502
2012	KC	AL	161	642	189	51	5	14	(6	8)	292	93	72	94	73	3	140	3	0	3	10	5	.67	14	.294	.368	.455
6 ML YEARS			720	2695	726	183	14	82	(42	40)	1183	388	320	376	302	15	641	33	5	15	56	24	.70	57	.269	.348	.439

Dee Gordon

Bats: L **Throws:** R **Pos:** SS-79; PR-7; PH-2　　　　　　　　　　**Ht:** 5'11" **Wt:** 160 **Born:** 4/22/1988 **Age:** 25

Year	Team	Lg	G	AB	H	2B	3B	HR	(Hm	Rd)	TB	R	RBI	RC	TBB	IBB	SO	HBP	SH	SF	SB	CS	SB%	GDP	Avg	OBP	Slg
2008	Ogden	R+	60	251	83	13	3	2	(-	-)	108	45	27	42	16	0	29	2	2	3	18	5	.78	3	.331	.371	.430
2009	Gt Lks	A	131	538	162	17	12	3	(-	-)	212	96	35	85	43	4	90	10	7	3	73	25	.74	7	.301	.362	.394
2010	Chatt	AA	133	555	154	17	10	2	(-	-)	197	86	39	72	40	1	89	7	9	3	53	20	.73	3	.277	.332	.355
2011	Albq	AAA	70	288	96	10	6	0	(-	-)	118	51	24	49	18	1	40	2	2	3	30	4	.88	1	.333	.373	.410
2011	RCuca	A+	3	11	3	0	0	0	(-	-)	3	4	0	1	1	0	1	0	0	0	2	1	.67	1	.273	.333	.273
2012	Albq	AAA	8	30	8	0	1	0	(-	-)	10	3	1	3	2	0	3	0	0	0	2	1	.67	0	.267	.313	.333
2011	LAD	NL	56	224	68	9	2	0	(0	0)	81	34	11	25	7	0	27	0	2	0	24	7	.77	1	.304	.325	.362
2012	LAD	NL	87	303	69	9	2	1	(0	1)	85	38	17	22	20	0	62	3	2	2	32	10	.76	5	.228	.280	.281
2 ML YEARS			143	527	137	18	4	1	(0	1)	166	72	28	47	27	0	89	3	4	2	56	17	.77	6	.260	.299	.315

Tom Gorzelanny

Pitches: L **Bats:** B **Pos:** RP-44; SP-1　　　　　gore-zah-LAWN-ee　　　　　**Ht:** 6'2" **Wt:** 205 **Born:** 7/12/1982 **Age:** 30

			HOW MUCH HE PITCHED						WHAT HE GAVE UP										THE RESULTS						
Year	Team	Lg	G	GS	CG	GF	IP	BFP	H	R	ER	HR	SH	SF	HB	TBB	IBB	SO	WP	Bk	W	L	Pct	Sh	Sv-Op Hld	ERC	ERA
2005	Pit	NL	3	1	0	0	6.0	32	10	8	8	1	1	0	0	3	0	3	0	0	0	1	.000	0	0-0 0	8.76	12.00
2006	Pit	NL	11	11	0	0	61.2	267	50	29	26	3	7	4	4	31	2	40	3	0	2	5	.286	0	0-0 0	3.23	3.79
2007	Pit	NL	32	32	1	0	201.2	874	214	90	87	18	3	9	11	68	3	135	5	1	14	10	.583	1	0-0 0	4.31	3.88
2008	Pit	NL	21	21	0	0	105.1	490	120	79	78	20	3	6	1	70	0	67	5	1	6	9	.400	0	0-0 0	6.86	6.66
2009	2 Tms	NL	22	7	0	2	47.0	204	45	30	29	6	3	3	1	17	0	47	1	0	7	3	.700	0	0-1 2	3.88	5.55
2010	ChC	NL	29	23	0	3	136.1	604	136	70	62	11	4	6	2	68	4	119	0	0	7	9	.438	0	1-1 1	4.30	4.09
2011	Was	NL	30	15	0	1	105.0	447	102	50	47	15	8	4	6	33	5	95	5	1	4	6	.400	0	0-1 4	4.03	4.03
2012	Was	NL	45	1	0	11	72.0	306	65	27	23	7	3	2	2	30	1	62	4	0	4	2	.667	0	1-1 9	3.68	2.88
09	Pit	NL	9	0	0	2	8.2	36	6	5	5	0	1	0	0	4	0	7	0	0	3	1	.750	0	0-1 1	2.02	5.19
09	ChC	NL	13	7	0	0	38.1	168	39	25	24	6	2	3	1	13	0	40	1	0	4	2	.667	0	0-0 1	4.33	5.63
8 ML YEARS			193	111	1	17	735.0	3224	742	383	360	81	32	34	27	320	15	568	23	3	44	45	.494	1	2-4 16	4.46	4.41

Anthony Gose

Bats: L **Throws:** L **Pos:** RF-24; CF-22; LF-15; PR-4; PH-3　　　GOASE　　　　　**Ht:** 6'1" **Wt:** 190 **Born:** 8/10/1990 **Age:** 22

Year	Team	Lg	G	AB	H	2B	3B	HR	(Hm	Rd)	TB	R	RBI	RC	TBB	IBB	SO	HBP	SH	SF	SB	CS	SB%	GDP	Avg	OBP	Slg
2008	Phillies	R	11	39	10	2	1	0	(-	-)	14	4	3	4	1	0	12	1	0	0	3	1	.75	0	.256	.293	.359
2009	Lakwd	A	131	510	132	24	9	2	(-	-)	180	72	52	68	35	2	110	15	9	3	76	20	.79	9	.259	.323	.353
2010	Clrwtr	A+	103	418	110	17	11	4	(-	-)	161	67	21	50	32	4	103	6	5	0	36	27	.57	6	.263	.325	.385
2010	Dnedin	A+	27	94	24	3	2	3	(-	-)	40	21	6	15	13	0	29	3	2	1	9	5	.64	0	.255	.360	.426
2011	NHam	AA	137	509	129	20	7	16	(-	-)	211	87	59	85	62	0	154	13	2	1	70	15	.82	3	.253	.349	.415
2012	LsVgs	AAA	102	420	120	21	10	5	(-	-)	176	87	43	69	49	1	101	5	4	1	34	12	.74	3	.286	.366	.419
2012	Tor	AL	56	166	37	7	3	1	(0	1)	53	25	11	21	17	0	59	2	4	0	15	3	.83	1	.223	.303	.319

Tyler Graham

Bats: R **Throws:** R **Pos:** PR-6; PH-2; CF-1; RF-1　　　　　　　　　　**Ht:** 6'0" **Wt:** 185 **Born:** 1/25/1984 **Age:** 29

Year	Team	Lg	G	AB	H	2B	3B	HR	(Hm	Rd)	TB	R	RBI	RC	TBB	IBB	SO	HBP	SH	SF	SB	CS	SB%	GDP	Avg	OBP	Slg
2006	SlmKzr	A-	50	125	30	3	0	0	(-	-)	33	23	9	13	11	0	38	6	7	2	14	4	.78	0	.240	.326	.264
2007	Augsta	A	66	231	67	8	4	2	(-	-)	89	45	30	35	20	0	51	3	2	2	29	8	.78	6	.290	.352	.385
2008	SnJos	A+	84	303	80	10	2	2	(-	-)	100	51	29	38	21	0	54	7	9	2	47	14	.77	5	.264	.324	.330
2009	Conn	AA	11	23	5	0	0	0	(-	-)	5	3	1	0	1	0	3	0	0	0	3	2	.60	0	.217	.250	.217
2009	Fresno	AAA	17	54	11	1	0	1	(-	-)	15	9	4	4	2	0	12	1	1	0	4	0	1.00	2	.204	.246	.278
2009	SnJos	A+	73	287	78	6	1	9	(-	-)	113	53	40	42	24	0	62	4	3	2	28	8	.78	4	.272	.334	.394
2010	Rchmd	AA	2	8	1	0	0	0	(-	-)	1	0	0	0	0	0	0	0	0	0	1	0	1.00	0	.125	.125	.125
2010	Fresno	AAA	109	341	117	23	2	2	(-	-)	150	60	34	63	24	1	54	6	5	3	35	11	.76	8	.343	.393	.440
2011	Fresno	AAA	127	414	113	18	3	1	(-	-)	140	82	31	58	31	0	80	11	8	4	60	12	.83	15	.273	.337	.338
2012	Fresno	AAA	5	19	5	1	0	0	(-	-)	6	3	0	2	1	0	1	0	0	0	1	0	1.00	1	.263	.300	.316
2012	DBcks	R	8	22	6	2	1	0	(-	-)	10	3	5	3	9	0	4	0	0	0	3	0	1.00	0	.273	.484	.455
2012	Reno	AAA	26	61	7	0	2	1	(-	-)	14	7	6	3	8	0	12	2	1	0	1	1	.50	4	.115	.239	.230
2012	Ari	NL	10	2	0	0	0	0	(0	0)	0	1	0	0	0	0	2	0	0	0	1	0	1.00	0	.000	.000	.000

Yasmani Grandal

Bats: B **Throws:** R **Pos:** C-55; PH-7 yaz-MON-ee gran-DAHL **Ht:** 6'2" **Wt:** 210 **Born:** 11/8/1988 **Age:** 24

Year	Team	Lg	G	AB	H	2B	3B	HR	(Hm	Rd)	TB	R	RBI	RC	TBB	IBB	SO	HBP	SH	SF	SB	CS	SB%	GDP	Avg	OBP	Slg
2010	Reds	R	8	28	8	1	0	0	(-	-)	9	4	1	3	4	0	4	1	0	0	0	1	.00	0	.286	.394	.321
2011	Bkrsfld	A+	56	206	61	14	0	10	(-	-)	105	47	40	45	41	0	57	1	0	3	0	0	-	6	.296	.410	.510
2011	Carlina	AA	45	156	47	15	0	4	(-	-)	74	20	26	26	13	1	39	2	0	1	0	1	.00	0	.301	.360	.474
2011	Lsvlle	AAA	4	12	6	2	0	0	(-	-)	8	2	2	5	5	0	1	1	0	0	0	0	-	0	.500	.667	.667
2012	Tucsn	AAA	56	194	65	18	0	6	(-	-)	101	40	35	46	37	4	35	2	0	2	0	0	-	7	.335	.443	.521
2012	Lk Els	A+	2	7	0	0	0	0	(-	-)	0	0	0	0	1	0	3	0	0	0	0	0	-	0	.000	.125	.000
2012	SD	NL	60	192	57	7	1	8	(3	5)	90	28	36	37	31	1	39	1	0	2	0	0	-	8	.297	.394	.469

Curtis Granderson

Bats: L **Throws:** R **Pos:** CF-157; PH-5; DH-1 **Ht:** 6'1" **Wt:** 195 **Born:** 3/16/1981 **Age:** 32

Year	Team	Lg	G	AB	H	2B	3B	HR	(Hm	Rd)	TB	R	RBI	RC	TBB	IBB	SO	HBP	SH	SF	SB	CS	SB%	GDP	Avg	OBP	Slg
2004	Det	AL	9	25	6	1	1	0	(0	0)	9	2	0	2	3	0	8	0	0	0	0	0	-	1	.240	.321	.360
2005	Det	AL	47	162	44	6	3	8	(5	3)	80	18	20	26	10	0	43	0	2	0	1	1	.50	2	.272	.314	.494
2006	Det	AL	159	596	155	31	9	19	(7	12)	261	90	68	89	66	0	174	4	7	6	8	5	.62	4	.260	.335	.438
2007	Det	AL	158	612	185	38	23	23	(10	13)	338	122	74	106	52	3	141	5	5	2	26	1	.96	3	.302	.361	.552
2008	Det	AL	141	553	155	26	13	22	(11	11)	273	112	66	100	71	1	111	3	1	1	12	4	.75	7	.280	.365	.494
2009	Det	AL	160	631	157	23	8	30	(10	20)	286	91	71	92	72	4	141	2	3	2	20	6	.77	1	.249	.327	.453
2010	NYY	AL	136	466	115	17	7	24	(14	10)	218	76	67	71	53	3	116	2	4	3	12	2	.86	3	.247	.324	.468
2011	NYY	AL	156	583	153	26	10	41	(21	20)	322	136	119	113	85	0	169	12	4	7	25	10	.71	12	.262	.364	.552
2012	NYY	AL	160	596	138	18	4	43	(26	17)	293	102	106	92	75	4	195	5	1	7	10	3	.77	5	.232	.319	.492
	Postseason		27	101	27	6	3	5	(3	2)	54	15	16	21	17	0	22	1	1	1	3	1	.75	2	.267	.375	.535
	9 ML YEARS		1126	4224	1108	186	78	210	(104	106)	2080	749	591	691	487	15	1098	33	27	28	114	32	.78	38	.262	.341	.492

Jeff Gray

Pitches: R **Bats:** R **Pos:** RP-49 **Ht:** 6'2" **Wt:** 210 **Born:** 11/19/1981 **Age:** 31

			HOW MUCH HE PITCHED					WHAT HE GAVE UP										THE RESULTS						
Year	Team	Lg	G	GS	CG	GF	IP	BFP	H	R	ER	HR	SH	SF	HB	TBB	IBB	SO	WP	Bk	W	L	Pct	Sh	Sv-Op	Hld	ERC	ERA
2008	Oak	AL	5	0	0	2	4.2	24	8	4	4	1	0	0	1	1	0	4	0	0	0	0	-	0	0-0	0	9.48	7.71
2009	Oak	AL	24	0	0	11	26.1	116	30	12	11	3	2	0	2	4	1	19	0	0	0	1	.000	0	0-0	1	4.07	3.76
2010	ChC	NL	7	0	0	0	9.1	45	12	9	7	1	1	0	1	5	0	4	1	0	1	0	1.000	0	0-0	0	6.85	6.75
2011	2 Tms	AL	30	0	0	11	48.1	215	52	23	23	4	1	3	1	21	2	23	2	0	1	1	.000	0	1-4	2	4.51	4.28
2012	Min	AL	49	0	0	11	52.0	236	58	34	33	9	0	1	4	22	0	26	5	1	6	1	.857	0	0-0	1	5.68	5.71
11	CWS	AL	6	0	0	5	13.1	57	13	4	4	1	0	1	1	4	0	7	1	0	0	0	-	0	0-0	0	3.65	2.70
11	Sea	AL	24	0	0	6	35.0	158	39	19	19	3	1	2	0	17	2	16	1	0	1	1	.000	0	1-4	2	4.84	4.89
5 ML YEARS			115	0	0	35	140.2	636	160	82	78	18	4	4	9	53	3	76	8	1	7	3	.700	0	1-4	4	5.15	4.99

Nick Green

Bats: R **Throws:** R **Pos:** 3B-3; 2B-2; SS-1; PH-1 **Ht:** 5'11" **Wt:** 185 **Born:** 9/10/1978 **Age:** 34

Year	Team	Lg	G	AB	H	2B	3B	HR	(Hm	Rd)	TB	R	RBI	RC	TBB	IBB	SO	HBP	SH	SF	SB	CS	SB%	GDP	Avg	OBP	Slg
2012	NewOr*	AAA	63	212	73	16	1	12	(-	-)	127	44	47	48	15	2	36	5	1	2	2	2	.50	5	.344	.397	.599
2004	Atl	NL	95	264	72	15	3	3	(3	0)	102	40	26	36	12	1	63	4	8	2	1	2	.33	0	.273	.312	.386
2005	TB	AL	111	318	76	15	2	5	(2	3)	110	53	29	38	33	0	86	11	10	3	3	1	.75	5	.239	.329	.346
2006	2 Tms	AL	63	114	21	5	0	2	(1	1)	32	12	4	10	11	0	40	1	1	0	1	4	.20	2	.184	.262	.281
2007	Sea	AL	6	7	0	0	0	0	(0	0)	0	0	0	0	0	0	3	0	0	0	0	0	-	0	.000	.000	.000
2009	Bos	AL	104	276	65	18	0	6	(4	2)	101	35	35	28	20	1	69	8	2	3	1	4	.20	10	.236	.303	.366
2010	2 Tms		14	21	3	0	0	0	(0	0)	3	2	2	1	1	0	5	1	0	0	0	0	-	0	.143	.217	.143
2012	Mia	NL	7	23	4	3	0	0	(0	0)	7	1	1	1	0	0	6	1	0	0	0	0	-	0	.174	.208	.304
06	TB	AL	17	39	3	0	0	0	(0	0)	3	4	0	0	6	0	11	0	0	0	0	3	.00	2	.077	.200	.077
06	NYY	AL	46	75	18	5	0	2	(1	1)	29	8	4	10	5	0	29	1	1	0	1	1	.50	0	.240	.296	.387
10	LAD	NL	5	8	1	0	0	0	(0	0)	1	0	1	0	0	0	2	1	0	0	0	0	-	0	.125	.222	.125
10	Tor	AL	9	13	2	0	0	0	(0	0)	2	2	1	1	1	0	3	0	0	0	0	0	-	0	.154	.214	.154
	Postseason		2	0	0	0	0	0	(0	0)	0	0	0	0	0	0	0	0	0	0	0	0	-	0	-	-	-
	7 ML YEARS		400	1023	241	56	5	16	(10	6)	355	143	97	114	77	2	272	26	21	8	6	11	.35	17	.236	.303	.347

Taylor Green

Bats: L **Throws:** R **Pos:** PH-28; 1B-18; 3B-13; 2B-4; DH-1; PR-1 **Ht:** 5'11" **Wt:** 197 **Born:** 11/2/1986 **Age:** 26

Year	Team	Lg	G	AB	H	2B	3B	HR	(Hm	Rd)	TB	R	RBI	RC	TBB	IBB	SO	HBP	SH	SF	SB	CS	SB%	GDP	Avg	OBP	Slg
2006	Helena	R+	62	221	51	12	1	1	(-	-)	68	36	23	25	29	0	35	4	4	2	0	1	.00	4	.231	.328	.308
2007	WV	A-	111	397	130	29	2	14	(-	-)	205	68	86	82	51	1	65	5	2	5	0	5	.00	6	.327	.406	.516
2008	BrvdCt	A+	114	418	121	19	0	15	(-	-)	185	46	73	75	61	7	59	4	3	4	4	2	.67	9	.289	.382	.443
2009	Wisc	A	6	20	8	1	0	1	(-	-)	12	6	6	4	4	0	4	2	0	0	0	0	-	0	.400	.538	.600
2009	Hntsvl	AA	87	306	79	15	0	5	(-	-)	109	34	43	39	33	1	37	2	0	4	0	1	.00	4	.258	.330	.356
2010	Hntsvl	AA	113	393	102	29	1	13	(-	-)	172	51	81	61	45	6	67	4	1	9	0	2	.00	10	.260	.336	.438
2011	Hntsvl	AA	3	11	4	1	0	0	(-	-)	5	2	3	2	0	0	3	1	0	1	0	0	-	0	.364	.385	.455
2011	Nashv	AAA	120	420	141	36	1	22	(-	-)	245	74	88	99	55	2	72	4	3	5	1	0	1.00	11	.336	.413	.583
2012	Nashv	AAA	77	282	77	17	0	7	(-	-)	115	29	40	28	22	5	57	3	0	1	1	3	.25	9	.273	.345	.408
2011	Mil	NL	20	37	10	3	0	0	(0	0)	13	2	1	3	0	0	6	0	0	0	0	0	-	1	.270	.270	.351
2012	Mil	NL	58	103	19	7	0	3	(2	1)	35	8	14	9	10	0	24	2	0	0	0	0	-	3	.184	.265	.340
	Postseason		3	2	0	0	0	0	(0	0)	0	0	0	0	0	0	0	0	0	0	0	0	-	0	.000	.000	.000
	2 ML YEARS		78	140	29	10	0	3	(2	1)	48	10	15	12	10	0	30	2	0	2	0	0	-	4	.207	.266	.343

Adam Greenberg

Bats: L Throws: L Pos: PH-1   Ht: 5'9" Wt: 180 Born: 2/21/1981 Age: 32

Year	Team	Lg	G	AB	H	2B	3B	HR	(Hm	Rd)	TB	R	RBI	RC	TBB	IBB	SO	HBP	SH	SF	SB	CS	SB%	GDP	Avg	OBP	Slg
2002	Lansng	A	35	116	26	7	2	1	(-	-)	40	20	11	15	15	2	22	4	4	1	2	1	.67	0	.224	.331	.345
2002	Dytona	A+	21	73	28	5	3	1	(-	-)	42	20	9	22	14	1	18	3	0	0	15	2	.88	0	.384	.500	.575
2003	Dytona	A+	72	271	81	11	5	3	(-	-)	111	42	27	47	38	0	46	2	2	2	26	9	.74	1	.299	.387	.410
2004	Dytona	A+	91	323	94	10	12	3	(-	-)	137	52	28	56	42	2	65	7	3	3	16	8	.67	4	.291	.381	.424
2004	WTenn	AA	32	112	31	7	2	3	(-	-)	51	22	10	20	14	1	30	3	2	2	3	0	1.00	1	.277	.366	.455
2004	Iowa	AAA	1	4	0	0	0	0	(-	-)	0	0	0	0	1	0	0	0	0	0	0	0	-	0	.000	.200	.000
2005	WTenn	AA	95	305	82	12	9	4	(-	-)	124	51	33	55	56	2	68	4	14	3	15	4	.79	1	.269	.386	.407
2006	WTenn	AA	32	84	15	2	0	0	(-	-)	17	9	1	4	9	2	27	1	4	0	3	2	.60	0	.179	.266	.202
2006	Iowa	AAA	11	17	2	0	0	0	(-	-)	2	1	0	0	0	0	5	0	0	0	0	1	.00	0	.118	.118	.118
2006	Jaxnvl	AA	75	219	50	9	3	1	(-	-)	68	36	17	33	51	1	70	7	6	2	9	3	.75	2	.228	.387	.311
2007	Wichita	AA	132	467	124	30	11	8	(-	-)	200	73	43	82	74	2	107	7	13	1	23	8	.74	1	.266	.373	.428
2008	Bdgprt	IND	13	45	13	2	2	0	(-	-)	19	11	5	10	10	0	9	4	3	1	2	1	.67	0	.289	.450	.422
2008	Ark	AA	70	262	71	8	3	2	(-	-)	91	47	15	36	32	0	55	5	4	0	16	7	.70	1	.271	.361	.347
2009	Bdgprt	IND	130	508	126	19	8	3	(-	-)	170	89	42	69	61	0	124	6	12	2	53	10	.84	2	.248	.334	.335
2010	Bdgprt	IND	105	384	99	9	6	4	(-	-)	132	67	39	64	75	0	98	6	11	4	44	11	.80	2	.258	.384	.344
2011	Bdgprt	IND	106	379	98	8	12	10	(-	-)	160	82	44	72	73	2	98	13	11	3	27	8	.77	1	.259	.393	.422
2005	ChC	NL	1	0	0	0	0	0	(0	0)	0	0	0	0	0	0	0	1	0	0	0	0	-	0	-	1.000	-
2012	Mia	NL	1	1	0	0	0	0	(0	0)	0	0	0	0	0	0	1	0	0	0	0	0	-	0	.000	.000	.000
	2 ML YEARS		2	1	0	0	0	0	(0	0)	0	0	0	0	0	0	1	1	0	0	0	0	-	0	.000	.500	.000

Tyler Greene

Bats: R Throws: R Pos: 2B-59; SS-43; PH-20; PR-11; RF-2; LF-1   Ht: 6'2" Wt: 190 Born: 8/17/1983 Age: 29

Year	Team	Lg	G	AB	H	2B	3B	HR	(Hm	Rd)	TB	R	RBI	RC	TBB	IBB	SO	HBP	SH	SF	SB	CS	SB%	GDP	Avg	OBP	Slg
2009	StL	NL	48	108	24	5	0	2	(1	1)	35	9	7	6	4	0	32	3	1	0	3	0	1.00	2	.222	.270	.324
2010	StL	NL	44	104	23	3	1	2	(2	0)	34	14	10	10	13	4	24	4	0	1	2	0	1.00	1	.221	.328	.327
2011	StL	NL	58	104	22	5	0	1	(0	1)	30	22	11	12	13	2	31	4	0	0	11	0	1.00	3	.212	.322	.288
2012	2 Tms	NL	116	305	70	15	2	11	(6	5)	122	34	30	27	19	1	95	1	2	3	12	4	.75	7	.230	.274	.400
12	StL	NL	77	179	39	9	2	4	(2	2)	64	16	19	16	13	1	56	1	2	2	9	2	.82	4	.218	.272	.358
12	Hou	NL	39	126	31	6	0	7	(4	3)	58	18	11	11	6	0	39	0	0	1	3	2	.60	3	.246	.278	.460
	4 ML YEARS		266	621	139	28	3	16	(9	7)	221	79	58	55	49	7	182	12	3	4	28	4	.88	13	.224	.292	.356

Luke Gregerson

Pitches: R Bats: L Pos: RP-77   Ht: 6'3" Wt: 200 Born: 5/14/1984 Age: 29

Year	Team	Lg	G	GS	CG	GF	IP	BFP	H	R	ER	HR	SH	SF	HB	TBB	IBB	SO	WP	Bk	W	L	Pct	Sh	Sv-Op	Hld	ERC	ERA
2009	SD	NL	72	0	0	7	75.0	318	62	29	27	3	3	1	3	31	9	93	4	0	2	4	.333	0	1-7	27	2.72	3.24
2010	SD	NL	80	0	0	9	78.1	297	47	30	28	8	1	1	1	18	2	89	0	0	4	7	.364	0	2-7	40	1.56	3.22
2011	SD	NL	61	0	0	11	55.2	241	57	23	17	2	5	1	2	19	3	34	2	0	3	3	.500	0	0-4	16	3.55	2.75
2012	SD	NL	77	0	0	15	71.2	294	57	19	19	7	5	0	3	21	3	72	3	0	2	0	1.000	0	9-13	24	2.64	2.39
	4 ML YEARS		290	0	0	42	280.2	1150	223	101	91	20	14	3	9	89	17	288	9	0	11	14	.440	0	12-31	107	2.51	2.92

Kevin Gregg

Pitches: R Bats: R Pos: RP-40   Ht: 6'6" Wt: 245 Born: 6/20/1978 Age: 35

Year	Team	Lg	G	GS	CG	GF	IP	BFP	H	R	ER	HR	SH	SF	HB	TBB	IBB	SO	WP	Bk	W	L	Pct	Sh	Sv-Op	Hld	ERC	ERA
2003	LAA	AL	5	3	0	0	24.2	97	18	9	9	3	0	0	1	8	0	14	0	0	2	0	1.000	0	0-0	0	2.74	3.28
2004	LAA	AL	55	0	0	23	87.2	377	86	43	41	6	4	5	3	28	3	84	13	1	5	2	.714	0	1-2	3	3.47	4.21
2005	LAA	AL	33	2	0	9	64.1	290	70	37	36	8	1	1	3	29	2	52	5	0	1	2	.333	0	0-1	1	5.08	5.04
2006	LAA	AL	32	3	0	12	78.1	341	88	41	36	10	0	3	2	21	0	71	6	0	3	4	.429	0	0-0	0	4.51	4.14
2007	Fla	NL	74	0	0	55	84.0	355	63	34	33	7	3	0	6	40	1	87	6	0	0	5	.000	0	32-36	6	3.15	3.54
2008	Fla	NL	72	0	0	59	68.2	296	51	30	26	3	3	1	4	37	4	58	7	0	7	8	.467	0	29-38	4	2.90	3.41
2009	ChC	NL	72	0	0	51	68.2	298	60	38	36	13	0	3	3	30	2	71	7	0	5	6	.455	0	23-30	1	4.19	4.72
2010	Tor	AL	63	0	0	56	59.0	254	52	24	23	4	1	3	1	30	1	58	3	0	2	6	.250	0	37-43	3	3.66	3.51
2011	Bal	AL	63	0	0	48	59.2	275	58	35	29	7	4	1	2	40	4	53	2	0	0	3	.000	0	22-29	0	5.10	4.37
2012	Bal	AL	40	0	0	13	43.2	200	50	26	24	6	0	1	3	24	2	37	0	0	3	2	.600	0	0-0	0	6.15	4.95
	Postseason		2	0	0	0	4.0	18	4	0	0	0	0	0	0	2	0	3	1	0	0	-	-	0	0-0	0	3.63	0.00
	10 ML YEARS		509	8	0	326	638.2	2783	596	317	293	67	16	18	28	287	19	585	49	1	28	38	.424	0	144-179	18	4.03	4.13

Didi Gregorius

Bats: L Throws: R Pos: SS-6; PR-2; PH-1   dee-dee greh-GORE-ee-us   Ht: 6'1" Wt: 185 Born: 2/18/1990 Age: 23

Year	Team	Lg	G	AB	H	2B	3B	HR	(Hm	Rd)	TB	R	RBI	RC	TBB	IBB	SO	HBP	SH	SF	SB	CS	SB%	GDP	Avg	OBP	Slg
2008	Reds	R	31	97	15	0	0	0	(-	-)	15	6	9	3	10	0	10	1	1	0	2	1	.67	3	.155	.241	.155
2009	Srsota	A+	22	71	18	4	0	0	(-	-)	22	8	2	6	1	0	9	1	1	0	0	0	-	0	.254	.274	.310
2009	Billings	R+	50	204	64	10	1	1	(-	-)	79	28	16	29	12	1	27	5	2	2	8	6	.57	6	.314	.363	.387
2010	Dayton	A	120	501	137	16	11	5	(-	-)	190	65	41	65	33	1	62	7	6	1	16	7	.70	3	.273	.327	.379
2010	Lynbrg	A+	7	25	6	0	0	0	(-	-)	6	4	0	2	2	0	6	1	1	0	0	0	-	0	.240	.321	.240
2011	Bkrsfld	A+	46	188	57	12	1	5	(-	-)	86	30	28	27	10	1	25	0	2	3	8	8	.50	2	.303	.333	.457
2011	Carlina	AA	38	148	40	6	3	2	(-	-)	58	18	16	18	9	0	25	0	3	0	3	2	.60	1	.270	.312	.392
2012	Penscla	AA	81	316	88	11	8	1	(-	-)	118	45	31	42	29	0	49	4	7	3	3	4	.43	4	.278	.344	.373
2012	Lsvlle	AAA	48	185	45	10	3	6	(-	-)	79	25	23	22	12	2	31	0	4	1	0	2	.00	1	.243	.288	.427
2012	Cin	NL	8	20	6	0	0	0	(0	0)	6	1	2	2	0	0	5	0	1	0	0	0	-	0	.300	.300	.300

Zack Greinke

Pitches: R **Bats:** R **Pos:** SP-34 GRAIN-key   **Ht:** 6'2" **Wt:** 200 **Born:** 10/21/1983 **Age:** 29

Year	Team	Lg	G	GS	CG	GF	IP	BFP	H	R	ER	HR	SH	SF	HB	TBB	IBB	SO	WP	Bk	W	L	Pct	Sh	Sv-Op	Hld	ERC	ERA
2004	KC	AL	24	24	0	0	145.0	599	143	64	64	26	3	2	8	26	3	100	1	1	8	11	.421	0	0-0	0	3.85	3.97
2005	KC	AL	33	33	2	0	183.0	829	233	125	118	23	4	4	13	53	0	114	4	2	5	17	.227	0	0-0	0	5.71	5.80
2006	KC	AL	3	0	0	1	6.1	28	7	3	3	1	0	0	0	3	2	5	0	0	1	0	1.000	0	0-0	0	4.93	4.26
2007	KC	AL	52	14	0	7	122.0	507	122	52	50	12	3	4	3	36	5	106	3	1	7	7	.500	0	1-1	12	3.77	3.69
2008	KC	AL	32	32	1	0	202.1	851	202	87	78	21	2	4	4	56	1	183	8	1	13	10	.565	0	0-0	0	3.68	3.47
2009	KC	AL	33	33	6	0	229.1	915	195	64	55	11	8	3	4	51	0	242	5	0	16	8	.667	3	0-0	0	**2.39**	2.16
2010	KC	AL	33	33	3	0	220.0	919	219	114	102	18	6	7	7	55	1	181	4	0	10	14	.417	0	0-0	0	3.48	4.17
2011	Mil	NL	28	28	0	0	171.2	715	161	82	73	19	6	1	4	45	0	201	10	0	16	6	.727	0	0-0	0	3.35	3.83
2012	2 Tms		34	34	0	0	212.1	868	200	84	82	18	7	2	2	54	0	200	8	0	15	5	.750	0	0-0	0	3.17	3.48
12	Mil	NL	21	21	0	0	123.0	504	120	49	47	7	3	0	0	28	0	122	4	0	9	3	.750	0	0-0	0	3.02	3.44
12	LAA	AL	13	13	0	0	89.1	364	80	35	35	11	4	2	2	26	0	78	4	0	6	2	.750	0	0-0	0	3.38	3.53
	Postseason		3	3	0	0	16.2	80	23	15	12	4	1	0	1	4	0	13	0	0	1	1	.500	0	0-0	0	6.67	6.48
	9 ML YEARS		272	231	12	8	1492.0	6231	1482	675	625	149	39	27	45	379	12	1332	43	5	91	78	.538	3	1-1	12	3.59	3.77

A.J. Griffin

Pitches: R **Bats:** R **Pos:** SP-15   **Ht:** 6'5" **Wt:** 230 **Born:** 1/28/1988 **Age:** 25

Year	Team	Lg	G	GS	CG	GF	IP	BFP	H	R	ER	HR	SH	SF	HB	TBB	IBB	SO	WP	Bk	W	L	Pct	Sh	Sv-Op	Hld	ERC	ERA
2010	As	R	4	0	0	1	5.0	16	1	0	0	0	0	0	0	0	0	6	0	0	0	0		0	0--	-	0.09	0.00
2010	Vancvr	A-	20	0	0	18	21.1	86	14	9	7	0	0	0	3	7	1	27	2	0	1	1	.500	0	15--	-	1.87	2.95
2011	Burlgtn	A	8	8	0	0	52.0	202	36	10	9	2	1	1	2	5	0	46	0	0	4	0	1.000	0	0--	-	1.35	1.56
2011	Stcktn	A+	12	12	0	0	70.2	283	64	31	28	8	4	3	2	14	0	82	3	1	5	3	.625	0	0--	-	3.04	3.57
2011	Scrmto	AAA	1	1	0	0	6.0	24	6	3	2	1	0	0	0	2	0	8	0	0	1	0	1.000	0	0--	-	4.57	3.00
2011	Mdland	AA	6	6	0	0	32.0	146	39	24	23	6	0	0	2	11	0	20	0	0	2	3	.400	0	0--	-	6.00	6.47
2012	Mdland	AA	7	7	0	0	43.1	164	31	12	12	4	1	1	1	7	0	44	1	0	3	1	.750	0	0--	-	1.85	2.49
2012	Scrmto	AAA	10	10	2	0	58.2	238	48	27	20	3	0	2	4	11	1	47	2	0	4	2	.667	0	0--	-	2.23	3.07
2012	Oak	AL	15	15	0	0	82.1	336	74	29	28	10	0	2	1	19	0	64	0	0	7	1	.875	0	0-0	0	3.06	3.06

Jason Grilli

Pitches: R **Bats:** R **Pos:** RP-64   GRILL-ee   **Ht:** 6'5" **Wt:** 225 **Born:** 11/11/1976 **Age:** 36

Year	Team	Lg	G	GS	CG	GF	IP	BFP	H	R	ER	HR	SH	SF	HB	TBB	IBB	SO	WP	Bk	W	L	Pct	Sh	Sv-Op	Hld	ERC	ERA
2000	Fla	NL	1	1	0	0	6.2	35	11	4	4	0	2	0	2	2	0	3	0	0	1	0	1.000	0	0-0	0	7.84	5.40
2001	Fla	NL	6	5	0	1	26.2	115	30	18	18	6	1	0	2	11	0	17	0	0	2	2	.500	0	0-0	0	6.44	6.08
2004	CWS	AL	8	8	1	0	45.0	203	52	38	37	11	2	1	3	20	0	26	2	0	2	3	.400	0	0-0	0	6.67	7.40
2005	Det	AL	3	2	0	0	16.0	63	14	6	6	1	1	1	0	6	0	5	0	0	1	1	.500	0	0-0	0	3.27	3.38
2006	Det	AL	51	0	0	18	62.0	270	61	31	29	6	2	4	5	25	3	31	5	0	2	3	.400	0	0-0	9	4.23	4.21
2007	Det	AL	57	0	0	13	79.2	352	81	46	42	5	1	5	5	32	1	62	5	0	5	5	.625	0	0-2	11	4.09	4.74
2008	2 Tms		60	0	0	16	75.0	323	67	27	25	2	1	3	2	38	7	69	4	0	3	3	.500	0	1-2	4	3.34	3.00
2009	2 Tms		52	0	0	11	45.2	212	50	27	27	4	2	1	1	27	2	49	2	0	2	3	.400	0	1-1	7	5.25	5.32
2011	Pit	NL	28	0	0	4	32.2	140	24	10	9	2	1	0	4	15	5	37	3	0	2	1	.667	0	1-1	9	2.79	2.48
2012	Pit	NL	64	0	0	11	58.2	244	45	20	19	7	2	1	2	22	4	90	0	0	1	6	.143	0	2-5	32	2.85	2.91
08	Det	AL	9	0	0	4	13.2	59	12	5	5	1	0	0	1	7	1	10	1	0	0	1	.000	0	0-1	0	3.85	3.29
08	Col		51	0	0	12	61.1	264	55	22	20	1	1	3	1	31	6	59	3	0	3	2	.600	0	1-1	4	3.23	2.93
09	Col	NL	22	0	0	6	19.1	99	29	13	13	2	1	1	0	13	2	22	2	0	0	1	.000	0	1-1	3	8.02	6.05
09	Tex	AL	30	0	0	5	26.1	113	21	14	14	2	1	0	1	14	0	27	0	0	2	2	.500	0	0-0	4	3.44	4.78
	Postseason		5	0	0	0	3.0	14	1	0	0	0	0	0	0	4	1	1	0	0	0	0		0	0-0	1	2.44	0.00
	10 ML YEARS		330	16	1	74	448.0	1957	435	227	216	44	15	16	26	198	22	389	21	0	21	25	.457	0	5-11	72	4.22	4.34

Justin Grimm

Pitches: R **Bats:** R **Pos:** RP-3; SP-2   **Ht:** 6'3" **Wt:** 195 **Born:** 8/16/1988 **Age:** 24

Year	Team	Lg	G	GS	CG	GF	IP	BFP	H	R	ER	HR	SH	SF	HB	TBB	IBB	SO	WP	Bk	W	L	Pct	Sh	Sv-Op	Hld	ERC	ERA
2011	Hkry	A	9	9	0	0	50.1	209	45	23	19	5	2	4	3	18	0	54	4	1	2	1	.667	0	0--	-	3.63	3.40
2011	MrtlBh	A+	16	16	0	0	90.1	386	84	40	34	2	6	4	6	30	0	73	4	0	5	2	.714	0	0--	-	3.12	3.39
2012	Frisco	AA	16	14	0	0	83.2	324	70	21	16	3	1	0	1	14	0	73	2	0	9	3	.750	0	0--	-	2.09	1.72
2012	RdRck	AAA	9	8	0	0	51.0	218	53	27	26	2	2	2	4	16	0	30	4	0	3	3	.400	0	0--	-	3.89	4.59
2012	Tex	AL	5	2	0	3	14.0	65	22	14	14	1	0	2	0	3	0	13	3	0	1	1	.500	0	0-0	0	6.54	9.00

Javy Guerra

Pitches: R **Bats:** R **Pos:** RP-45   GEHR-uh   **Ht:** 6'1" **Wt:** 200 **Born:** 10/31/1985 **Age:** 27

Year	Team	Lg	G	GS	CG	GF	IP	BFP	H	R	ER	HR	SH	SF	HB	TBB	IBB	SO	WP	Bk	W	L	Pct	Sh	Sv-Op	Hld	ERC	ERA
2004	Ddgrs	R	11	9	0	0	40.0	168	31	18	15	3	1	0	3	19	0	36	9	0	4	1	.800	0	0--	-	3.29	3.38
2005	Clmbs	A-	11	11	0	0	52.2	242	51	35	29	3	0	3	10	23	0	40	2	1	2	5	.286	0	0--	-	4.35	4.96
2006	Ogden	R+	7	7	0	0	28.0	140	37	18	15	1	3	1	4	20	0	22	6	0	1	3	.250	0	0--	-	7.45	4.82
2007	InldEm	A+	27	24	0	1	117.2	572	139	98	82	10	2	6	14	80	0	121	16	0	6	9	.400	0	1--	-	6.68	6.27
2008	InldEm	AA	31	3	0	10	66.1	317	68	34	30	0	3	6	4	44	0	63	5	0	5	4	.556	0	2--	-	4.55	4.07
2009	Gt Lks	A	28	0	0	23	41.0	162	23	7	7	1	2	1	1	15	3	55	8	0	3	1	.750	0	16--	-	1.40	1.54
2009	Chatt	AA	23	0	0	8	28.1	129	32	15	13	2	2	1	0	16	0	29	2	0	3	1	.750	0	0--	-	5.30	4.13
2010	Chatt	AA	28	0	0	10	27.0	125	24	12	7	1	2	0	1	22	2	27	5	0	2	0	1.000	0	5--	-	4.58	2.33
2010	Ddgrs	R	2	0	0	0	2.0	9	2	1	1	1	0	1	0	3	0	3	0	0	1	0	1.000	0	0--	-	7.30	4.50
2011	Chatt	AA	14	0	0	9	17.0	61	8	2	2	1	0	0	1	5	0	15	3	0	1	0	1.000	0	3--	-	1.20	1.06
2012	RCuca	A+	2	2	0	0	2.0	8	1	1	1	0	0	0	0	0	0	1	0	0	0	0		0	0--	-	0.47	4.50

	HOW MUCH HE PITCHED				WHAT HE GAVE UP						THE RESULTS				
Year Team Lg	G GS CG GF	IP	BFP	H R ER HR SH SF HB	TBB IBB	SO	WP Bk	W L	Pct	Sh	Sv-Op Hld	ERC	ERA
2012 Albq AAA	3 0 0 0	4.1	21	7 4 4 0 1 0 0	1 0	3	0 0	0 0	-	0	0-- -	6.07	8.31
2011 LAD NL	47 0 0 38	46.2	195	37 12 12 2 3 1 3	18 1	38	2 0	2 2	.500	0	21-23 0	2.73	2.31
2012 LAD NL	45 0 0 17	45.0	196	44 13 13 1 4 2 1	23 5	37	1 0	2 3	.400	0	8-13 4	3.76	2.60
2 ML YEARS	92 0 0 55	91.2	391	81 25 25 3 7 3 4	41 6	75	3 0	4 5	.444	0	29-36 4	3.23	2.45

Matt Guerrier

Pitches: R Bats: R Pos: RP-16   gurr-REAR   Ht: 6'3" Wt: 195 Born: 8/2/1978 Age: 34

	HOW MUCH HE PITCHED				WHAT HE GAVE UP						THE RESULTS				
Year Team Lg	G GS CG GF	IP	BFP	H R ER HR SH SF HB	TBB IBB	SO	WP Bk	W L	Pct	Sh	Sv-Op Hld	ERC	ERA
2012 RCuca* A+	5 3 0 0	5.0	18	3 2 2 0 1 0 0	0 0	5	1 0	0 0	-	0	0-- -	0.75	3.60
2004 Min AL	9 2 0 5	19.0	84	22 13 12 5 2 0 1	6 0	11	0 0	0 1	.000	0	0-0 0	6.10	5.68
2005 Min AL	43 0 0 14	71.2	306	71 29 27 6 4 1 3	24 5	46	3 0	0 0	-	0	0-0 1	3.71	3.39
2006 Min AL	39 1 0 13	69.2	300	78 29 26 9 3 4 0	21 0	37	6 0	1 0	1.000	0	1-1 2	4.59	3.36
2007 Min AL	73 0 0 16	88.0	351	71 23 23 9 0 3 5	21 1	68	6 0	2 4	.333	0	1-4 14	2.70	2.35
2008 Min AL	76 0 0 15	76.1	344	84 47 44 12 1 1 0	37 9	59	2 0	6 9	.400	0	1-5 20	5.20	5.19
2009 Min AL	79 0 0 15	76.1	304	58 23 20 10 3 1 4	16 2	47	6 0	5 1	.833	0	1-4 33	2.44	2.36
2010 Min AL	74 0 0 13	71.0	286	56 28 25 7 2 3 3	22 1	42	2 0	5 7	.417	0	1-7 23	2.78	3.17
2011 LAD NL	70 0 0 12	66.1	282	59 31 30 4 3 1 0	25 5	50	2 0	4 3	.571	0	1-4 13	2.95	4.07
2012 LAD NL	16 0 0 2	14.0	56	8 6 6 3 1 1 1	7 1	9	0 0	0 2	.000	0	0-1 3	3.15	3.86
Postseason	5 0 0 1	4.2	16	1 0 0 0 0 1 0	1 0	4	0 0	0 0	-	0	0-0 1	0.30	0.00
9 ML YEARS	479 3 0 105	552.1	2313	507 229 213 65 19 15 17	179 24	369	27 0	23 30	.434	0	6-26 109	3.51	3.47

Jeremy Guthrie

Pitches: R Bats: R Pos: SP-29; RP-4   Ht: 6'1" Wt: 205 Born: 4/8/1979 Age: 34

	HOW MUCH HE PITCHED				WHAT HE GAVE UP						THE RESULTS				
Year Team Lg	G GS CG GF	IP	BFP	H R ER HR SH SF HB	TBB IBB	SO	WP Bk	W L	Pct	Sh	Sv-Op Hld	ERC	ERA
2012 Mdest* A+	1 1 0 0	4.0	16	3 0 0 0 0 0 0	1 0	4	0 0	0 0	-	0	0-- -	1.65	0.00
2004 Cle AL	6 0 0 2	11.2	49	9 6 6 1 0 0 1	6 0	7	1 0	0 0	-	0	0-0 0	3.58	4.63
2005 Cle AL	1 0 0 1	6.0	29	9 4 4 2 1 1 0	2 0	3	0 0	0 0	-	0	0-0 0	8.58	6.00
2006 Cle AL	9 1 0 1	19.1	93	24 15 15 2 0 0 2	5 0	14	3 0	0 0	-	0	0-0 0	7.78	6.98
2007 Bal AL	32 26 0 3	175.1	723	165 78 72 23 4 6 4	47 2	123	8 1	7 5	.583	0	0-1 0	3.55	3.70
2008 Bal AL	30 30 1 0	190.2	796	176 82 77 24 2 2 7	58 2	120	3 0	10 12	.455	0	0-0 0	3.59	3.63
2009 Bal AL	33 33 1 0	200.0	874	224 120 112 35 1 8 9	60 1	110	1 1	10 17	.370	0	0-0 0	5.08	5.04
2010 Bal AL	32 32 0 0	209.1	872	193 93 89 25 3 9 16	50 1	119	1 1	11 14	.440	0	0-0 0	3.44	3.83
2011 Bal AL	34 32 2 1	208.0	889	213 113 100 26 5 10 9	66 5	130	0 0	9 17	.346	0	0-0 0	4.21	4.33
2012 2 Tms	33 29 0 0	181.2	788	206 109 96 30 8 6 9	50 2	101	2 2	8 12	.400	0	0-1 0	5.03	4.76
12 Col NL	19 15 0 0	90.2	422	122 72 64 21 5 3 7	31 2	45	1 1	3 9	.250	0	0-1 0	7.26	6.35
12 KC AL	14 14 0 0	91.0	366	84 37 32 9 3 3 2	19 0	56	1 1	5 3	.625	0	0-0 0	3.06	3.16
9 ML YEARS	210 183 4 8	1202.0	5113	1219 620 571 168 24 42 57	354 14	727	19 5	55 77	.417	0	0-2 0	4.20	4.28

Franklin Gutierrez

Bats: R Throws: R Pos: CF-38; PH-2; DH-1   Ht: 6'2" Wt: 190 Born: 2/21/1983 Age: 30

	BATTING																BASERUNNING				AVERAGES		
Year Team Lg	G	AB	H	2B	3B	HR	(Hm Rd)	TB	R	RBI	RC	TBB IBB	SO	HBP SH SF	SB	CS	SB%	GDP	Avg	OBP	Slg
2012 Tacom* AAA	17	62	16	5	0	2	(- -)	27	11	8	9	8 1	13	0 0 2	0	1	.00	1	.258	.333	.435
2005 Cle AL	7	1	0	0	0	0	(0 0)	0	2	0	0	1 0	0	0 0 0	0	0	-	0	.000	.500	.000
2006 Cle AL	43	136	37	9	0	1	(1 0)	49	21	8	12	3 0	28	0 2 0	0	0	-	4	.272	.288	.360
2007 Cle AL	100	271	72	13	2	13	(10 3)	128	41	36	36	21 1	77	1 5 3	8	3	.73	7	.266	.318	.472
2008 Cle AL	134	399	99	26	2	8	(6 2)	153	54	41	37	27 1	87	8 4 2	9	3	.75	10	.248	.307	.383
2009 Sea AL	153	565	160	24	1	18	(7 11)	240	85	70	80	46 3	122	3 13 2	16	5	.76	14	.283	.339	.425
2010 Sea AL	152	568	139	25	3	12	(6 6)	206	61	64	61	50 5	137	1 2 8	25	3	.89	10	.245	.303	.363
2011 Sea AL	92	322	72	13	0	1	(0 1)	88	26	19	25	16 1	56	1 3 2	13	2	.87	6	.224	.261	.273
2012 Sea AL	40	150	39	10	1	4	(2 2)	63	18	17	19	9 0	31	2 1 1	3	1	.75	5	.260	.309	.420
Postseason	10	29	6	0	0	1	(0 1)	9	5	4	3	5 0	11	0 0 0	0	0	-	1	.207	.324	.310
8 ML YEARS	721	2412	618	120	9	57	(32 25)	927	308	255	270	173 11	538	16 30 18	74	17	.81	56	.256	.308	.384

Brandon Guyer

Bats: R Throws: R Pos: LF-3   GYE-er   Ht: 6'2" Wt: 210 Born: 1/28/1986 Age: 27

	BATTING																BASERUNNING				AVERAGES		
Year Team Lg	G	AB	H	2B	3B	HR	(Hm Rd)	TB	R	RBI	RC	TBB IBB	SO	HBP SH SF	SB	CS	SB%	GDP	Avg	OBP	Slg
2007 Cubs R	17	72	16	4	1	1	(- -)	25	10	5	8	5 0	16	4 0 0	6	2	.75	0	.222	.309	.347
2007 Boise A-	19	71	19	1	0	0	(- -)	20	9	14	9	6 0	9	3 7 1	5	0	1.00	0	.268	.346	.282
2008 Peoria A	88	327	88	27	3	14	(- -)	163	55	38	56	19 0	63	13 1 3	22	7	.76	8	.269	.331	.498
2009 Tenn AA	57	189	36	12	2	1	(- -)	55	22	14	12	10 1	33	2 2 2	7	5	.58	3	.190	.236	.291
2009 Dytona A+	73	265	92	16	3	2	(- -)	120	40	32	55	24 1	34	8 0 8	23	2	.92	3	.347	.407	.453
2010 Tenn AA	102	369	127	39	6	13	(- -)	217	76	58	87	27 1	51	7 5 2	30	3	.91	6	.344	.398	.588
2011 Drham AAA	107	388	121	29	5	14	(- -)	202	78	61	78	35 1	79	12 6 2	16	6	.73	8	.312	.384	.521
2012 Drham AAA	22	85	25	3	1	3	(- -)	39	9	13	15	7 0	15	3 1 1	2	0	1.00	2	.294	.365	.459
2011 TB AL	15	41	8	1	0	2	(1 1)	15	7	3	7	1 0	9	0 1 0	0	0	-	1	.195	.214	.366
2012 TB AL	3	7	1	0	0	1	(0 1)	4	2	1	0	0 0	1	0 0 0	0	0	-	0	.143	.143	.571
2 ML YEARS	18	48	9	1	0	3	(1 2)	19	9	4	2	1 0	10	0 1 0	0	0	-	1	.188	.204	.396

Jesus Guzman

Bats: R Throws: R Pos: LF-52; PH-50; 1B-19; RF-7; 2B-4; DH-1 Ht: 6'1" Wt: 215 Born: 6/14/1984 Age: 29

									BATTING											BASERUNNING				AVERAGES		
Year	Team	Lg	G	AB	H	2B	3B	HR	(Hm Rd)	TB	R	RBI	RC	TBB	IBB	SO	HBP	SH	SF	SB	CS	SB%	GDP	Avg	OBP	Slg
2009	SF	NL	12	20	5	0	0	0	(0 0)	5	0	0	0	0	0	3	0	0	0	0	0	-	2	.250	.250	.250
2011	SD	NL	76	247	77	22	2	5	(4 1)	118	33	44	49	22	2	43	1	0	1	9	2	.82	6	.312	.369	.478
2012	SD	NL	120	287	71	18	2	9	(4 5)	120	32	48	40	29	3	71	2	1	2	3	3	.50	2	.247	.319	.418
3 ML YEARS			208	554	153	40	4	14	(8 6)	243	65	92	89	51	5	117	3	1	3	12	5	.71	10	.276	.339	.439

Tony Gwynn

Bats: L Throws: R Pos: CF-53; LF-38; PH-20; PR-4; RF-3 Ht: 5'11" Wt: 193 Born: 10/4/1982 Age: 30

									BATTING											BASERUNNING				AVERAGES		
Year	Team	Lg	G	AB	H	2B	3B	HR	(Hm Rd)	TB	R	RBI	RC	TBB	IBB	SO	HBP	SH	SF	SB	CS	SB%	GDP	Avg	OBP	Slg
2012	Albq*	AAA	19	68	23	4	1	0	(- -)	29	12	7	13	8	1	12	1	2	0	4	1	.80	1	.338	.416	.426
2006	Mil	NL	32	77	20	2	1	0	(0 0)	24	5	4	5	2	0	15	0	0	1	3	1	.75	2	.260	.275	.312
2007	Mil	NL	69	123	32	3	2	0	(0 0)	39	13	10	16	12	1	24	0	0	0	8	1	.89	0	.260	.326	.317
2008	Mil	NL	29	42	8	1	0	0	(0 0)	9	5	1	2	4	0	7	1	1	1	3	1	.75	1	.190	.271	.214
2009	SD	NL	119	393	106	11	6	2	(1 1)	135	59	21	48	48	2	65	2	5	3	11	7	.61	2	.270	.350	.344
2010	SD	NL	117	289	59	9	3	3	(2 1)	83	30	20	31	41	4	50	1	7	1	17	4	.81	3	.204	.304	.287
2011	LAD	NL	136	312	80	12	6	2	(0 2)	110	37	22	35	23	1	61	1	2	2	22	6	.79	2	.256	.308	.353
2012	LAD	NL	103	259	60	8	4	0	(0 0)	76	29	17	22	16	2	52	2	2	0	13	6	.68	6	.232	.276	.293
Postseason			3	3	1	0	0	0	(0 0)	1	0	0	0	0	0	1	0	0	0	0	0	-	0	.333	.333	.333
7 ML YEARS			605	1495	365	46	22	7	(3 4)	476	178	95	159	146	10	274	5	17	8	77	26	.75	16	.244	.312	.318

Eric Hacker

Pitches: R Bats: B Pos: RP-3; SP-1 Ht: 6'1" Wt: 230 Born: 3/26/1983 Age: 30

			HOW MUCH HE PITCHED						WHAT HE GAVE UP												THE RESULTS						
Year	Team	Lg	G	GS	CG	GF	IP	BFP	H	R	ER	HR	SH	SF	HB	TBB	IBB	SO	WP	Bk	W	L	Pct	Sh	Sv-Op	Hld	ERC	ERA
2012	Fresno*	AAA	26	25	0	0	150.1	623	149	70	67	12	3	6	7	43	1	103	3	1	12	6	.667	0	0--	-	3.71	4.01
2009	Pit	NL	3	0	0	2	3.0	14	4	2	2	0	0	0	0	2	0	1	0	0	0	0	-	0	0-0	0	6.62	6.00
2011	Min	AL	2	0	0	0	5.1	22	4	1	0	0	0	1	0	4	0	2	0	0	0	0	-	0	0-0	0	3.56	0.00
2012	SF	NL	4	1	0	2	9.2	45	14	6	6	2	0	1	2	2	1	8	0	0	0	1	.000	0	0-0	0	7.05	5.59
3 ML YEARS			9	1	0	4	18.0	81	22	9	8	2	0	1	1	8	1	11	0	0	0	1	.000	0	0-0	0	5.93	4.00

Travis Hafner

Bats: L Throws: R Pos: DH-61; PH-5 HAFF-nerr Ht: 6'3" Wt: 240 Born: 6/3/1977 Age: 36

									BATTING											BASERUNNING				AVERAGES		
Year	Team	Lg	G	AB	H	2B	3B	HR	(Hm Rd)	TB	R	RBI	RC	TBB	IBB	SO	HBP	SH	SF	SB	CS	SB%	GDP	Avg	OBP	Slg
2012	Clmbs*	AAA	3	10	1	0	0	0	(- -)	1	0	1	0	0	0	2	1	0	1	0	0	-	0	.100	.167	.100
2002	Tex	AL	23	62	15	4	1	1	(0 1)	24	6	6	7	8	1	15	0	0	0	0	1	.00	0	.242	.329	.387
2003	Cle	AL	91	291	74	19	3	14	(7 7)	141	35	40	42	22	2	81	10	0	1	2	1	.67	7	.254	.327	.485
2004	Cle	AL	140	482	150	41	3	28	(7 21)	281	96	109	103	68	7	111	17	0	6	3	2	.60	11	.311	.410	.583
2005	Cle	AL	137	486	148	42	0	33	(14 19)	289	94	108	115	79	7	123	9	0	4	0	0	-	9	.305	.408	.595
2006	Cle	AL	129	454	140	31	1	42	(21 21)	299	100	117	118	100	16	111	7	0	2	0	0	-	10	.308	**.439**	**.659**
2007	Cle	AL	152	545	145	25	2	24	(12 12)	246	80	100	94	102	17	115	7	0	5	1	1	.50	15	.266	.385	.451
2008	Cle	AL	57	198	39	10	0	5	(2 3)	64	21	24	21	27	6	55	5	0	3	1	1	.50	4	.197	.305	.323
2009	Cle	AL	94	338	92	19	0	16	(9 7)	159	46	49	49	41	6	67	3	0	1	0	0	-	7	.272	.355	.470
2010	Cle	AL	118	396	110	29	0	13	(10 3)	178	46	50	57	51	10	94	12	0	3	2	1	.67	2	.278	.374	.449
2011	Cle	AL	94	325	91	16	0	13	(9 4)	146	41	57	61	36	5	78	6	0	1	0	0	-	7	.280	.361	.449
2012	Cle	AL	66	219	50	6	2	12	(8 4)	96	23	34	22	32	2	47	9	0	3	0	0	-	9	.228	.346	.438
Postseason			11	43	8	1	0	2	(1 1)	15	6	4	3	7	1	15	0	0	0	0	0	-	1	.186	.300	.349
11 ML YEARS			1101	3796	1054	242	12	201	(99 102)	1923	588	694	689	566	79	897	85	0	29	9	7	.56	81	.278	.381	.507

Nick Hagadone

Pitches: L Bats: L Pos: RP-27 HAGG-uh-donn Ht: 6'5" Wt: 230 Born: 1/1/1986 Age: 27

			HOW MUCH HE PITCHED						WHAT HE GAVE UP												THE RESULTS						
Year	Team	Lg	G	GS	CG	GF	IP	BFP	H	R	ER	HR	SH	SF	HB	TBB	IBB	SO	WP	Bk	W	L	Pct	Sh	Sv-Op	Hld	ERC	ERA
2007	Lowell	A-	10	10	0	0	24.1	94	14	5	5	1	0	0	0	8	0	33	1	0	0	1	.000	0	0--	-	1.46	1.85
2008	Grnville	A	3	3	0	0	10.0	43	5	3	0	0	0	0	0	6	0	12	2	0	0	1	.500	0	0--	-	1.54	0.00
2009	Grnville	A	10	10	0	0	25.0	105	13	8	7	0	0	0	4	14	0	32	1	0	0	2	.000	0	0--	-	2.05	2.52
2009	Lk Cty	A	5	5	0	0	14.2	55	8	4	4	0	0	0	1	5	0	21	3	0	0	1	.000	0	0--	-	1.44	2.45
2009	Knstn	A+	2	2	0	0	5.1	25	5	3	3	0	0	0	0	5	0	6	1	0	0	0	-	0	0--	-	5.10	5.06
2010	Knstn	A+	10	10	0	0	37.2	167	28	11	10	2	2	0	0	29	0	45	2	0	1	3	.250	0	0--	-	3.71	2.39
2010	Akron	AA	19	7	0	3	48.0	218	44	27	24	5	1	0	1	34	0	44	7	0	2	2	.500	0	1--	-	4.94	4.50
2011	Akron	AA	12	0	0	1	22.2	88	14	4	4	0	1	0	0	7	0	24	1	0	2	1	.667	0	0--	-	1.39	1.59
2011	Clmbs	AAA	34	0	0	14	48.1	204	42	27	18	5	3	0	0	15	2	53	1	2	4	3	.571	0	4--	-	2.90	3.35
2012	Clmbs	AAA	5	0	0	0	7.1	25	4	0	0	0	0	0	0	1	0	7	0	0	0	0	-	0	0--	-	0.93	0.00
2011	Cle	AL	9	0	0	3	11.0	42	4	6	5	0	0	1	1	6	0	11	2	0	1	0	1.000	0	0-0	0	1.35	4.09
2012	Cle	AL	27	0	0	10	25.1	116	26	18	18	4	0	2	1	15	0	26	2	0	1	0	1.000	0	1-2	2	5.37	6.39
2 ML YEARS			36	0	0	13	36.1	158	30	24	23	4	0	3	1	21	0	37	4	0	2	0	1.000	0	1-2	2	3.97	5.70

Matt Hague

Bats: R **Throws:** R **Pos:** 1B-16; PH-14; DH-4 HAIG **Ht:** 6'3" **Wt:** 225 **Born:** 8/20/1985 **Age:** 27

Year	Team	Lg	G	AB	H	2B	3B	HR	(Hm	Rd)	TB	R	RBI	RC	TBB	IBB	SO	HBP	SH	SF	SB	CS	SB%	GDP	Avg	OBP	Slg
2008	StCol	A-	7	27	9	3	0	0	(-	-)	12	6	3	4	3	0	5	0	0	0	0	0	-	0	.333	.400	.444
2008	Hkry	A	57	215	69	14	0	6	(-	-)	101	25	29	40	20	0	28	4	0	3	1	0	1.00	10	.321	.384	.470
2009	Lynbrg	A+	122	454	133	30	0	8	(-	-)	187	52	50	70	40	1	67	8	0	6	3	2	.60	14	.293	.356	.412
2010	Altna	AA	135	509	150	29	0	15	(-	-)	224	90	86	87	61	5	62	7	0	4	3	6	.33	11	.295	.375	.440
2011	Indy	AAA	141	534	165	37	3	12	(-	-)	244	70	75	93	47	4	69	8	0	4	4	3	.57	12	.309	.372	.457
2012	Indy	AAA	91	367	104	13	0	4	(-	-)	129	41	54	45	26	1	50	2	1	3	3	1	.75	11	.283	.332	.351
2012	Pit	NL	30	70	16	2	0	0	(0	0)	18	5	7	4	3	0	14	1	0	0	1	0	1.00	1	.229	.270	.257

Jerry Hairston

Bats: R **Throws:** R **Pos:** 3B-32; 2B-30; LF-18; PH-10; SS-2; 1B-1; DH-1 **Ht:** 5'10" **Wt:** 195 **Born:** 5/29/1976 **Age:** 37

Year	Team	Lg	G	AB	H	2B	3B	HR	(Hm	Rd)	TB	R	RBI	RC	TBB	IBB	SO	HBP	SH	SF	SB	CS	SB%	GDP	Avg	OBP	Slg
2012	Albq*	AAA	2	6	0	0	0	0	(-	-)	0	0	0	0	0	0	0	0	0	0	0	0	-	0	.000	.000	.000
1998	Bal	AL	6	7	0	0	0	0	(0	0)	0	2	0	0	0	0	1	0	0	0	0	0	-	0	.000	.000	.000
1999	Bal	AL	50	175	47	12	1	4	(1	3)	73	26	17	24	11	0	24	3	4	0	9	4	.69	2	.269	.323	.417
2000	Bal	AL	49	180	46	5	0	5	(2	3)	66	27	19	22	21	0	22	6	5	0	8	5	.62	8	.256	.353	.367
2001	Bal	AL	159	532	124	25	5	8	(5	3)	183	63	47	57	44	0	73	13	9	4	29	11	.73	12	.233	.305	.344
2002	Bal	AL	122	426	114	25	3	5	(2	3)	160	55	32	55	34	0	55	7	8	4	21	6	.78	5	.268	.329	.376
2003	Bal	AL	58	218	59	12	2	2	(1	1)	81	25	21	32	23	0	25	6	10	2	14	5	.74	8	.271	.353	.372
2004	Bal	AL	86	287	87	19	1	2	(0	2)	114	43	24	45	29	1	29	8	6	4	13	8	.62	3	.303	.378	.397
2005	ChC	NL	114	380	99	25	4	4	(3	1)	140	51	30	46	31	0	46	12	7	0	8	9	.47	5	.261	.336	.368
2006	2 Tms		101	170	35	6	1	0	(0	0)	43	25	10	9	13	2	34	2	7	0	5	2	.71	5	.206	.270	.253
2007	Tex	AL	73	159	30	7	0	3	(1	2)	46	22	16	12	11	0	24	3	4	5	1	0	.83	5	.189	.249	.289
2008	Cin	NL	80	261	85	20	2	6	(3	3)	127	47	36	52	23	0	36	3	8	2	15	3	.83	0	.326	.384	.487
2009	2 Tms		131	383	96	23	1	10	(8	2)	151	62	39	42	32	0	54	6	8	4	7	4	.64	3	.251	.315	.394
2010	SD	NL	119	430	105	13	2	10	(7	3)	152	53	50	47	31	2	54	5	4	6	9	6	.60	5	.244	.299	.353
2011	2 Tms		120	337	91	21	1	5	(2	3)	129	43	31	41	33	1	46	5	1	0	3	2	.60	7	.270	.344	.383
2012	LAD	NL	78	238	65	13	1	4	(1	3)	92	19	26	31	23	2	27	3	1	2	1	2	.33	7	.273	.342	.387
06	ChC	NL	38	82	17	3	0	0	(0	0)	20	8	4	5	4	2	14	1	5	0	3	0	1.00	1	.207	.253	.244
06	Tex	AL	63	88	18	3	1	0	(0	0)	23	17	6	4	9	0	20	1	2	0	2	2	.50	4	.205	.286	.261
09	Cin	NL	86	307	78	18	1	8	(6	2)	122	47	27	30	21	0	46	3	6	3	7	3	.70	2	.254	.305	.397
09	NYY	AL	45	76	18	5	0	2	(2	0)	29	15	12	12	11	0	8	3	2	1	0	1	.00	1	.237	.352	.382
11	Was	NL	75	213	57	11	1	4	(2	2)	82	25	24	28	22	1	30	2	1	0	2	2	.50	3	.268	.342	.385
11	Mil	NL	45	124	34	10	0	1	(0	1)	47	18	7	13	11	0	16	3	0	0	1	0	1.00	4	.274	.348	.379
	Postseason		17	47	17	6	0	0	(0	0)	23	9	4	7	4	0	6	0	1	2	0	0	-	4	.362	.396	.489
	15 ML YEARS		1346	4183	1083	226	22	68	(36	32)	1557	563	398	515	359	8	550	82	85	32	147	68	.68	75	.259	.327	.372

Scott Hairston

Bats: R **Throws:** R **Pos:** LF-59; RF-48; PH-38; CF-14; PR-1 **Ht:** 6'0" **Wt:** 205 **Born:** 5/25/1980 **Age:** 33

Year	Team	Lg	G	AB	H	2B	3B	HR	(Hm	Rd)	TB	R	RBI	RC	TBB	IBB	SO	HBP	SH	SF	SB	CS	SB%	GDP	Avg	OBP	Slg
2004	Ari	NL	101	339	84	15	6	13	(6	7)	150	39	29	32	21	0	88	1	2	1	3	3	.50	4	.248	.293	.442
2005	Ari	NL	15	20	2	1	0	0	(0	0)	3	0	0	0	0	0	6	0	0	0	0	0	-	1	.100	.100	.150
2006	Ari	NL	9	15	6	2	0	0	(0	0)	8	2	2	2	1	0	5	0	0	0	0	0	-	0	.400	.438	.533
2007	2 Tms	NL	107	263	64	18	2	11	(6	5)	119	37	36	36	26	0	55	1	3	1	2	0	1.00	4	.243	.313	.452
2008	SD	NL	112	326	81	18	3	17	(9	8)	156	42	31	43	28	2	84	3	3	2	3	1	.75	2	.248	.312	.479
2009	2 Tms	NL	116	430	114	27	2	17	(9	8)	196	50	64	60	25	0	83	3	1	5	11	3	.79	9	.265	.307	.456
2010	SD	NL	104	295	62	10	0	10	(5	5)	102	34	36	28	31	1	69	6	0	4	6	1	.86	3	.210	.295	.346
2011	NYM	NL	79	132	31	8	1	7	(2	5)	62	20	24	16	11	2	34	2	0	0	1	1	.50	2	.235	.303	.470
2012	NYM	NL	134	377	99	25	3	20	(11	9)	190	52	57	53	19	0	83	1	1	1	8	2	.80	10	.263	.299	.504
07	Ari	NL	76	176	39	13	1	3	(1	2)	63	21	16	19	19	0	37	1	3	0	2	0	1.00	4	.222	.301	.358
07	SD	NL	31	87	25	5	1	8	(5	3)	56	16	20	17	7	0	18	0	0	1	0	0	-	0	.287	.337	.644
09	SD	NL	56	197	59	14	0	10	(5	5)	105	26	29	35	17	0	45	1	1	0	8	1	.89	4	.299	.358	.533
09	Oak	AL	60	233	55	13	1	7	(4	3)	91	24	35	25	8	0	38	2	0	5	3	2	.60	5	.236	.262	.391
	9 ML YEARS		777	2197	543	124	17	95	(48	47)	986	276	279	270	162	5	507	17	9	14	34	11	.76	36	.247	.302	.449

Bill Hall

Bats: R **Throws:** R **Pos:** DH-3; PH-2; PR-2; LF-1; RF-1 **Ht:** 6'0" **Wt:** 210 **Born:** 12/28/1979 **Age:** 33

Year	Team	Lg	G	AB	H	2B	3B	HR	(Hm	Rd)	TB	R	RBI	RC	TBB	IBB	SO	HBP	SH	SF	SB	CS	SB%	GDP	Avg	OBP	Slg
2012	Norfolk*	AAA	90	342	84	18	0	15	(-	-)	147	38	45	44	26	0	141	1	0	1	2	1	.67	9	.246	.300	.430
2002	Mil	NL	19	36	7	1	1	1	(0	1)	13	3	5	3	3	0	13	0	0	0	1	0	1.00	1	.194	.256	.361
2003	Mil	NL	52	142	37	9	2	5	(2	3)	65	23	20	18	7	0	28	1	4	1	1	2	.33	5	.261	.298	.458
2004	Mil	NL	126	390	93	20	3	9	(5	4)	146	43	53	41	20	1	119	1	2	2	12	6	.67	4	.238	.276	.374
2005	Mil	NL	146	501	146	39	6	17	(12	5)	248	69	62	73	39	2	103	1	2	3	18	6	.75	11	.291	.342	.495
2006	Mil	NL	148	537	145	39	4	35	(18	17)	297	101	85	87	63	6	162	1	3	4	8	9	.47	12	.270	.345	.553
2007	Mil	NL	136	452	115	35	0	14	(10	4)	192	59	63	59	40	1	128	3	1	7	4	5	.44	9	.254	.315	.425
2008	Mil	NL	128	404	91	22	1	15	(10	5)	160	50	55	43	37	2	124	3	1	3	5	6	.45	4	.225	.293	.396
2009	2 Tms		110	334	67	20	1	8	(4	4)	113	32	36	23	27	0	120	0	0	1	2	2	.50	11	.201	.258	.338
2010	Bos	AL	120	344	85	16	1	18	(8	10)	157	44	46	51	34	0	104	1	2	1	9	1	.90	4	.247	.316	.456
2011	2 Tms		62	185	39	9	2	2	(2	0)	58	24	14	11	11	1	63	2	0	1	3	2	.60	3	.211	.261	.314
2012	Bal	AL	7	9	2	0	0	1	(1	0)	5	2	1	2	5	1	7	0	0	0	0	0	-	0	.222	.500	.556
09	Mil	NL	76	214	43	12	0	6	(3	3)	73	22	24	15	19	0	72	0	0	1	1	0	1.00	10	.201	.265	.341
09	Sea	AL	34	120	24	8	1	2	(1	1)	40	10	12	8	8	0	48	0	0	3	1	2	.33	1	.200	.244	.333

							BATTING												BASERUNNING				AVERAGES		
Year	Team	Lg	G	AB	H	2B	3B	HR	(Hm | Rd)	TB	R	RBI	RC	TBB	IBB	SO	HBP	SH	SF	SB	CS	SB%	GDP	Avg	OBP	Slg
11	Hou	NL	46	147	33	7	2	2	(2 | 0)	50	18	13	11	8	1	55	2	0	1	1	1	.50	1	.224	.272	.340
11	SF	NL	16	38	6	2	0	0	(0 | 0)	8	6	1	0	3	0	8	0	0	0	2	1	.67	2	.158	.220	.211
	Postseason		3	8	2	0	0	0	(0 | 0)	2	1	0	1	1	0	3	0	0	0	0	0	-	0	.250	.333	.250
11 ML YEARS			1054	3334	827	210	21	125	(72 | 53)	1454	450	440	411	286	14	971	13	15	26	62	40	.61	64	.248	.308	.436

Roy Halladay

Pitches: R **Bats:** R **Pos:** SP-25   HAL-ah-day   **Ht:** 6'6" **Wt:** 230 **Born:** 5/14/1977 **Age:** 36

			HOW MUCH HE PITCHED						WHAT HE GAVE UP										THE RESULTS						
Year	Team	Lg	G	GS	CG	GF	IP	BFP	H	R	ER	HR	SH	SF	HB	TBB	IBB	SO	WP	Bk	W	L	Pct	Sh	Sv-Op	Hld	ERC	ERA
2012	Clrwtr*	A+	1	1	0	0	3.0	13	3	1	0	0	0	0	0	0	0	4	0	0	0	0	-	0	0- -	-	1.76	0.00
1998	Tor	AL	2	2	1	0	14.0	53	9	4	3	2	0	0	0	2	0	13	0	0	1	0	1.000	0	0-0	0	1.61	1.93
1999	Tor	AL	36	18	1	2	149.1	668	156	76	65	19	3	4	4	79	1	82	6	0	8	7	.533	1	1-1	2	5.19	3.92
2000	Tor	AL	19	13	0	4	67.2	349	107	87	80	14	2	3	2	42	0	44	6	1	4	7	.364	0	0-0	0	9.70	10.64
2001	Tor	AL	17	16	1	0	105.1	432	97	41	37	3	3	1	1	25	0	96	4	1	5	3	.625	1	0-0	0	2.61	3.16
2002	Tor	AL	34	34	2	0	239.1	993	223	93	78	10	9	2	7	62	6	168	4	1	19	7	.731	1	0-0	0	2.85	2.93
2003	Tor	AL	36	36	9	0	266.0	1071	253	111	96	26	3	2	9	32	1	204	6	1	22	7	.759	2	0-0	0	2.86	3.25
2004	Tor	AL	21	21	1	0	133.0	561	140	66	62	13	4	3	1	39	1	95	2	2	8	8	.500	1	0-0	0	4.00	4.20
2005	Tor	AL	19	19	5	0	141.2	553	118	39	38	11	2	1	7	18	2	108	2	1	12	4	.750	2	0-0	0	2.26	2.41
2006	Tor	AL	32	32	4	0	220.0	876	208	82	78	19	3	5	5	34	5	132	3	0	16	5	.762	0	0-0	0	2.87	3.19
2007	Tor	AL	31	31	7	0	225.1	927	232	101	93	15	2	7	3	48	3	139	4	0	16	7	.696	1	0-0	0	3.37	3.71
2008	Tor	AL	34	33	9	0	246.0	987	220	88	76	18	5	4	12	39	3	206	4	0	20	11	.645	2	0-0	1	2.62	2.78
2009	Tor	AL	32	32	9	0	239.0	963	234	82	74	22	1	9	5	35	0	208	2	0	17	10	.630	4	0-0	0	3.06	2.79
2010	Phi	NL	33	33	9	0	250.2	993	231	74	68	24	9	5	6	30	1	219	5	1	21	10	.677	4	0-0	0	2.69	2.44
2011	Phi	NL	32	32	8	0	233.2	933	208	65	61	10	15	7	4	35	4	220	2	1	19	6	.760	1	0-0	0	2.26	2.35
2012	Phi	NL	25	25	0	0	156.1	646	155	78	78	18	5	6	5	36	0	132	2	0	11	8	.579	0	0-0	0	3.63	4.49
	Postseason		5	5	1	0	38.0	143	23	10	10	3	1	0	0	5	1	35	1	0	3	2	.600	1	0-0	0	1.23	2.37
15 ML YEARS			403	377	66	6	2687.1	11005	2591	1087	987	224	66	59	71	556	27	2066	52	9	199	100	.666	20	1-1	3	3.14	3.31

Cole Hamels

Pitches: L **Bats:** L **Pos:** SP-31   **Ht:** 6'3" **Wt:** 200 **Born:** 12/27/1983 **Age:** 29

			HOW MUCH HE PITCHED						WHAT HE GAVE UP										THE RESULTS						
Year	Team	Lg	G	GS	CG	GF	IP	BFP	H	R	ER	HR	SH	SF	HB	TBB	IBB	SO	WP	Bk	W	L	Pct	Sh	Sv-Op	Hld	ERC	ERA
2006	Phi	NL	23	23	0	0	132.1	558	117	66	60	19	6	8	3	48	4	145	5	0	9	8	.529	0	0-0	0	3.61	4.08
2007	Phi	NL	28	28	2	0	183.1	743	163	72	69	25	5	6	3	43	4	177	6	0	15	5	.750	0	0-0	0	3.12	3.39
2008	Phi	NL	33	33	2	0	227.1	914	193	89	78	28	6	2	1	53	7	196	0	0	14	10	.583	2	0-0	0	2.76	3.09
2009	Phi	NL	32	32	2	0	193.2	814	206	95	93	24	7	5	5	43	4	168	1	0	10	11	.476	2	0-0	0	3.98	4.32
2010	Phi	NL	33	33	1	0	208.2	856	185	74	71	26	7	0	8	61	5	211	3	0	12	11	.522	0	0-0	0	3.36	3.06
2011	Phi	NL	32	31	3	0	216.0	850	169	68	67	19	9	3	5	44	2	194	3	3	14	9	.609	0	0-0	0	2.23	2.79
2012	Phi	NL	31	31	2	0	215.1	867	190	80	73	24	6	3	3	52	3	216	3	2	17	6	.739	2	0-0	0	2.98	3.05
	Postseason		13	13	1	0	81.2	326	65	29	28	9	3	2	2	21	1	77	0	0	7	4	.636	1	0-0	0	2.62	3.09
7 ML YEARS			212	211	12	0	1376.2	5602	1223	544	511	165	46	27	28	344	29	1307	20	5	91	60	.603	6	0-0	0	3.09	3.34

Josh Hamilton

Bats: L **Throws:** L **Pos:** CF-95; LF-84; DH-10; RF-2; PH-1   **Ht:** 6'4" **Wt:** 240 **Born:** 5/21/1981 **Age:** 32

							BATTING												BASERUNNING				AVERAGES		
Year	Team	Lg	G	AB	H	2B	3B	HR	(Hm	Rd)	TB	R	RBI	RC	TBB	IBB	SO	HBP	SH	SF	SB	CS	SB%	GDP	Avg	OBP	Slg
2007	Cin	NL	90	298	87	17	2	19	(11	8)	165	52	47	58	33	4	65	4	0	2	3	3	.50	6	.292	.368	.554
2008	Tex	AL	156	624	190	35	5	32	(19	13)	331	98	130	119	64	9	126	7	0	9	9	1	.90	8	.304	.371	.530
2009	Tex	AL	89	336	90	19	2	10	(6	4)	143	43	54	51	24	2	79	1	0	4	8	3	.73	5	.268	.315	.426
2010	Tex	AL	133	518	186	40	3	32	(22	10)	328	95	100	121	43	5	95	5	1	4	8	1	.89	11	.359	.411	.633
2011	Tex	AL	121	487	145	31	5	25	(14	11)	261	80	94	78	39	13	93	2	0	10	8	1	.89	8	.298	.346	.536
2012	Tex	AL	148	562	160	31	2	43	(22	21)	324	103	128	108	60	13	162	5	0	9	7	4	.64	9	.285	.354	.577
	Postseason		33	128	30	8	0	6	(2	4)	56	18	22	17	14	7	21	0	0	3	4	1	.80	3	.234	.303	.438
6 ML YEARS			737	2825	858	173	19	161	(94	67)	1552	471	553	535	263	46	620	24	1	38	43	13	.77	47	.304	.363	.549

Jason Hammel

Pitches: R **Bats:** R **Pos:** SP-20   **Ht:** 6'6" **Wt:** 225 **Born:** 9/2/1982 **Age:** 30

			HOW MUCH HE PITCHED						WHAT HE GAVE UP										THE RESULTS						
Year	Team	Lg	G	GS	CG	GF	IP	BFP	H	R	ER	HR	SH	SF	HB	TBB	IBB	SO	WP	Bk	W	L	Pct	Sh	Sv-Op	Hld	ERC	ERA
2012	Frdrck*	A+	1	1	0	0	5.0	20	3	0	0	0	0	0	0	1	0	7	0	0	1	0	1.000	0	0- -	-	1.06	0.00
2006	TB	AL	9	9	0	0	44.0	208	61	38	38	7	0	3	1	21	0	32	3	2	0	6	.000	0	0-0	0	7.40	7.77
2007	TB	AL	24	14	0	2	85.0	384	100	58	58	12	2	0	2	40	1	64	3	0	3	5	.375	0	0-0	0	5.86	6.14
2008	TB	AL	40	5	0	21	78.1	346	83	45	40	11	2	2	2	35	4	44	7	0	4	4	.500	0	2-2	1	4.94	4.60
2009	Col	NL	34	30	1	0	176.2	771	203	94	85	17	10	9	9	42	6	133	4	0	10	8	.556	0	0-0	0	4.37	4.33
2010	Col	NL	30	30	0	0	177.2	770	201	97	95	18	11	6	6	47	1	141	13	2	10	9	.526	0	0-0	0	4.41	4.81
2011	Col	NL	32	27	0	2	170.1	739	175	100	90	21	11	6	6	68	3	94	8	1	7	13	.350	0	1-1	0	4.54	4.76
2012	Bal	AL	20	20	1	0	118.0	493	104	48	45	9	3	1	2	42	2	113	3	0	8	6	.571	1	0-0	0	3.14	3.43
	Postseason		1	1	0	0	3.2	17	4	4	4	1	0	0	0	3	0	5	0	0	0	0	-	0	0-0	0	8.12	9.82
7 ML YEARS			189	135	2	25	850.0	3711	927	480	451	95	39	27	28	295	17	621	41	5	42	51	.452	1	3-3	1	4.57	4.78

Justin Hampson

Pitches: L Bats: L Pos: RP-13　　　　　　　　　　**Ht: 6'1" Wt: 206 Born: 5/24/1980 Age: 33**

Year Team	Lg	G	GS	CG	GF	IP	BFP	H	R	ER	HR	SH	SF	HB	TBB	IBB	SO	WP	Bk	W	L	Pct	Sh	Sv-Op	Hld	ERC	ERA
2012 Buffalo*	AAA	51	0	0	12	65.2	277	63	20	17	5	3	1	0	22	2	59	4	1	4	3	.571	0	4- -	-	3.38	2.33
2006 Col	NL	5	1	0	0	12.0	60	19	10	10	3	0	0	1	5	0	9	1	0	1	0	1.000	0	0-1	0	9.41	7.50
2007 SD	NL	39	0	0	12	53.1	219	48	17	16	1	1	1	3	16	4	34	0	0	2	3	.400	0	0-0	4	2.77	2.70
2008 SD	NL	35	0	0	8	30.2	126	31	11	10	1	1	4	0	10	2	19	0	0	2	1	.667	0	0-0	0	3.41	2.93
2012 NYM	NL	13	0	0	1	10.0	37	6	4	2	0	1	0	0	5	0	4	0	0	0	0	-	0	0-0	1	1.98	1.80
4 ML YEARS		92	1	0	21	106.0	442	104	42	38	5	3	5	4	36	6	66	1	0	5	4	.556	0	0-1	5	3.52	3.23

Brad Hand

Pitches: L Bats: L Pos: SP-1　　　　　　　　　　**Ht: 6'3" Wt: 220 Born: 3/20/1990 Age: 23**

Year Team	Lg	G	GS	CG	GF	IP	BFP	H	R	ER	HR	SH	SF	HB	TBB	IBB	SO	WP	Bk	W	L	Pct	Sh	Sv-Op	Hld	ERC	ERA
2008 Mrlns	R	9	7	0	0	32.2	132	25	16	9	0	1	0	2	11	0	34	4	0	2	0	1.000	0	0- -	-	2.23	2.48
2008 Jmstwn	A-	3	3	0	0	15.0	64	11	6	5	0	0	0	1	10	0	12	2	0	1	2	.333	0	0- -	-	3.24	3.00
2009 Grnsbr	A	26	26	0	0	127.2	571	130	83	69	12	2	4	7	66	2	122	22	2	7	13	.350	0	0- -	-	4.81	4.86
2010 Jupiter	A+	26	26	2	0	140.2	609	153	68	52	10	1	3	5	49	2	134	3	3	8	8	.500	2	0- -	-	4.32	3.33
2010 Jaxnvl	AA	1	1	0	0	6.0	24	3	2	2	0	0	0	0	3	0	4	0	0	1	0	1.000	0	0- -	-	1.41	3.00
2011 Jaxnvl	AA	19	18	0	1	108.2	447	90	42	41	11	5	2	1	50	0	71	0	2	11	4	.733	0	0- -	-	3.51	3.40
2011 Jupiter	A+	1	1	0	0	5.0	24	5	5	4	1	0	1	0	5	0	4	0	0	0	1	.000	0	0- -	-	7.56	7.20
2012 NewOr	AAA	27	27	0	0	148.1	626	129	72	66	15	5	5	0	75	4	141	7	1	11	7	.611	0	0- -	-	3.80	4.00
2011 Fla	NL	12	12	0	0	60.0	263	53	32	28	10	4	3	1	35	1	38	0	1	1	8	.111	0	0-0	0	4.68	4.20
2012 Mia	NL	1	1	0	0	3.2	23	6	7	7	1	0	0	0	6	1	3	0	0	0	1	.000	0	0-0	0	14.74	17.18
2 ML YEARS		13	13	0	0	63.2	286	59	39	35	11	4	3	1	41	2	41	0	1	1	9	.100	0	0-0	0	5.19	4.95

Ryan Hanigan

Bats: R Throws: R Pos: C-110; PH-2　　　HANN-eh-gann　　　**Ht: 6'0" Wt: 210 Born: 8/16/1980 Age: 32**

Year Team	Lg	G	AB	H	2B	3B	HR	(Hm	Rd)	TB	R	RBI	RC	TBB	IBB	SO	HBP	SH	SF	SB	CS	SB%	GDP	Avg	OBP	Slg
2007 Cin	NL	5	10	3	1	0	0	(0	0)	4	3	2	2	1	1	2	0	0	0	0	0	-	0	.300	.364	.400
2008 Cin	NL	31	85	23	2	0	2	(1	1)	31	9	9	12	10	1	9	3	0	0	0	0	-	2	.271	.367	.365
2009 Cin	NL	90	251	66	6	1	3	(3	0)	83	22	11	25	37	7	31	2	2	1	0	0	-	9	.263	.361	.331
2010 Cin	NL	70	203	61	11	0	5	(2	3)	87	25	40	41	33	4	21	4	1	2	0	0	-	6	.300	.405	.429
2011 Cin	NL	91	266	71	6	0	6	(4	2)	95	27	31	38	35	3	32	2	1	0	0	0	-	3	.267	.356	.357
2012 Cin	NL	112	317	87	14	0	2	(0	2)	107	25	24	40	44	13	37	3	4	3	0	0	-	6	.274	.365	.338
Postseason		2	4	0	0	0	0	(0	0)	0	0	0	0	0	0	0	0	0	0	0	0	-	0	.000	.000	.000
6 ML YEARS		399	1132	311	40	1	18	(10	8)	407	111	117	158	160	29	132	14	8	6	0	0	-	26	.275	.370	.360

Jack Hannahan

Bats: L Throws: R Pos: 3B-96; SS-7; PH-4; 1B-2; PR-2　　　　　　　　　　**Ht: 6'2" Wt: 210 Born: 3/4/1980 Age: 33**

Year Team	Lg	G	AB	H	2B	3B	HR	(Hm	Rd)	TB	R	RBI	RC	TBB	IBB	SO	HBP	SH	SF	SB	CS	SB%	GDP	Avg	OBP	Slg
2012 Clmbs*	AAA	1	4	0	0	0	0	(-	-)	0	0	0	0	0	0	2	0	0	0	0	0	-	0	.000	.000	.000
2012 Lk Cty*	A	2	8	1	0	0	0	(-	-)	1	0	1	0	0	0	4	0	0	0	0	0	-	0	.125	.125	.125
2006 Det	AL	3	9	0	0	0	0	(0	0)	0	0	0	0	1	0	1	0	0	0	0	0	-	0	.000	.100	.000
2007 Oak	AL	41	144	40	12	0	3	(1	2)	61	16	24	23	21	0	39	1	1	2	1	0	1.00	6	.278	.369	.424
2008 Oak	AL	143	436	95	27	0	4	(4	5)	149	48	47	38	55	4	131	2	3	5	2	0	1.00	5	.218	.305	.342
2009 2 Tms	AL	103	267	57	14	2	4	(2	2)	87	27	19	20	30	0	71	2	1	1	1	1	.50	4	.213	.297	.326
2011 Cle	AL	110	320	80	16	2	8	(7	1)	124	38	40	47	38	0	80	2	4	2	2	1	.67	7	.250	.331	.388
2012 Cle	AL	105	287	70	16	4	0	(3	1)	98	23	29	31	27	0	63	2	1	1	0	2	.00	9	.244	.312	.341
09 Oak	AL	52	119	23	6	2	1	(1	0)	36	12	8	7	13	0	36	1	1	0	0	0	-	2	.193	.278	.303
09 Sea	AL	51	148	34	8	0	3	(1	2)	51	15	11	13	17	0	35	1	0	1	1	1	.50	2	.230	.311	.345
6 ML YEARS		505	1463	342	85	4	28	(17	11)	519	152	159	159	172	4	385	9	10	11	6	4	.60	31	.234	.316	.355

Joel Hanrahan

Pitches: R Bats: R Pos: RP-63　　　　　　　　　　**Ht: 6'4" Wt: 250 Born: 10/6/1981 Age: 31**

Year Team	Lg	G	GS	CG	GF	IP	BFP	H	R	ER	HR	SH	SF	HB	TBB	IBB	SO	WP	Bk	W	L	Pct	Sh	Sv-Op	Hld	ERC	ERA
2007 Was	NL	12	11	0	0	51.0	247	59	35	34	9	2	1	0	38	0	43	3	0	5	3	.625	0	0-0	0	7.01	6.00
2008 Was	NL	69	0	0	34	84.1	364	73	40	37	9	2	6	1	42	7	93	6	0	6	3	.667	0	9-13	3	3.65	3.95
2009 2 Tms	NL	67	0	0	30	64.0	289	73	40	34	3	0	1	3	34	1	72	11	1	4	1	.200	0	5-10	9	5.12	4.78
2010 Pit	NL	72	0	0	27	69.2	294	58	28	28	6	0	1	4	26	0	100	5	0	4	1	.800	0	6-10	18	3.16	3.62
2011 Pit	NL	70	0	0	59	68.2	274	56	17	14	1	1	2	1	16	2	61	6	0	1	4	.200	0	40-44	0	2.00	1.83
2012 Pit	NL	63	0	0	57	59.2	254	40	18	18	8	3	0	1	36	0	67	6	0	5	2	.714	0	36-40	0	3.32	2.72
09 Was	NL	34	0	0	23	32.2	163	50	28	28	3	0	1	2	14	0	35	6	1	1	3	.250	0	5-10	2	7.49	7.71
09 Pit	NL	33	0	0	7	31.1	134	23	12	6	0	0	0	1	20	1	37	5	0	0	1	.000	0	0-0	7	2.92	1.72
6 ML YEARS		353	11	0	207	397.1	1730	359	178	165	36	8	11	10	192	10	436	37	1	22	17	.564	0	96-117	30	3.82	3.74

Tommy Hanson

Pitches: R **Bats:** R **Pos:** SP-31   **Ht:** 6'6" **Wt:** 220 **Born:** 8/28/1986 **Age:** 26

			HOW MUCH HE PITCHED						WHAT HE GAVE UP										THE RESULTS						
Year	Team	Lg	G	GS	CG	GF	IP	BFP	H	R	ER	HR	SH	SF	HB	TBB	IBB	SO	WP	Bk	W	L	Pct	Sh	Sv-Op Hld	ERC	ERA
2012	Gwnntt*	AAA	1	1	0	0	5.0	19	3	0	0	0	0	0	0	2	0	5	0	0	1	0	1.000	0	0- - -	1.59	0.00
2009	Atl	NL	21	21	0	0	127.2	522	105	42	41	10	4	1	5	46	1	116	2	0	11	4	.733	0	0-0 0	3.02	2.89
2010	Atl	NL	34	34	1	0	202.2	845	182	86	75	14	9	5	14	56	3	173	3	0	10	11	.476	0	0-0 0	3.08	3.33
2011	Atl	NL	22	22	0	0	130.0	540	106	55	52	17	4	3	3	46	3	142	5	0	11	7	.611	0	0-0 0	3.13	3.60
2012	Atl	NL	31	31	0	0	174.2	761	183	95	87	27	8	2	5	71	5	161	6	0	13	10	.565	0	0-0 0	4.88	4.48
	Postseason		1	1	0	0	4.0	17	5	4	4	1	0	0	0	1	0	5	0	0	0	0	-	0	0-0 0	6.26	9.00
	4 ML YEARS		108	108	1	0	635.0	2668	576	278	255	68	25	11	27	219	12	592	16	0	45	32	.584	0	0-0 0	3.55	3.61

J.A. Happ

Pitches: L **Bats:** L **Pos:** SP-24; RP-4   JAY   **Ht:** 6'6" **Wt:** 195 **Born:** 10/19/1982 **Age:** 30

			HOW MUCH HE PITCHED						WHAT HE GAVE UP										THE RESULTS						
Year	Team	Lg	G	GS	CG	GF	IP	BFP	H	R	ER	HR	SH	SF	HB	TBB	IBB	SO	WP	Bk	W	L	Pct	Sh	Sv-Op Hld	ERC	ERA
2007	Phi	NL	1	1	0	0	4.0	21	7	5	5	3	0	0	0	2	0	5	0	0	0	1	.000	0	0-0 0	15.13	11.25
2008	Phi	NL	8	4	0	1	31.2	138	28	13	13	3	2	1	1	14	1	26	1	0	1	0	1.000	0	0-0 1	3.55	3.69
2009	Phi	NL	35	23	3	4	166.0	685	149	55	54	20	7	6	5	56	2	119	2	0	12	4	.750	2	0-0 1	3.57	2.93
2010	2 Tms	NL	16	16	1	0	87.1	374	73	37	33	8	5	4	1	47	1	70	4	0	6	4	.600	1	0-0 0	3.69	3.40
2011	Hou	NL	28	28	0	0	156.1	698	157	103	93	21	12	8	2	83	5	134	3	2	6	15	.286	0	0-0 0	4.86	5.35
2012	2 Tms	NL	28	24	0	3	144.2	627	147	79	77	19	9	4	2	56	1	144	7	0	10	11	.476	0	0-0 1	4.37	4.79
10	Phi	NL	3	3	0	0	15.1	70	13	4	3	1	1	1	0	12	0	9	1	0	1	0	1.000	0	0-0 0	4.40	1.76
10	Hou	NL	13	13	1	0	72.0	304	60	33	30	7	4	3	1	35	1	61	3	0	5	4	.556	1	0-0 0	3.53	3.75
12	Hou	NL	18	18	0	0	104.1	457	112	58	56	17	7	2	1	39	0	98	5	0	7	9	.438	0	0-0 0	4.86	4.83
12	Tor	AL	10	6	0	3	40.1	170	35	21	21	2	2	2	1	17	1	46	2	0	3	2	.600	0	0-0 1	3.16	4.69
	Postseason		8	1	0	0	9.1	46	12	5	5	1	0	0	0	8	0	10	0	0	0	0	-	0	0-0 0	7.96	4.82
	6 ML YEARS		116	96	4	8	590.0	2543	561	292	275	74	35	23	11	258	10	498	17	2	35	35	.500	3	0-0 2	4.18	4.19

Aaron Harang

Pitches: R **Bats:** R **Pos:** SP-31   huh-RANG   **Ht:** 6'7" **Wt:** 260 **Born:** 5/9/1978 **Age:** 35

			HOW MUCH HE PITCHED						WHAT HE GAVE UP										THE RESULTS						
Year	Team	Lg	G	GS	CG	GF	IP	BFP	H	R	ER	HR	SH	SF	HB	TBB	IBB	SO	WP	Bk	W	L	Pct	Sh	Sv-Op Hld	ERC	ERA
2002	Oak	AL	16	15	0	0	78.1	354	78	44	42	7	3	4	3	45	2	64	1	0	5	4	.556	0	0-0 0	4.76	4.83
2003	2 Tms		16	15	0	1	76.1	327	89	47	45	11	5	1	1	19	0	42	3	1	5	6	.455	0	0-0 0	4.84	5.31
2004	Cin	NL	28	28	1	0	161.0	711	177	90	87	26	13	6	5	53	5	125	7	0	10	9	.526	0	0-0 0	4.81	4.86
2005	Cin	NL	32	32	1	0	211.2	887	217	93	90	22	11	5	8	51	3	163	6	0	11	13	.458	0	0-0 0	3.77	3.83
2006	Cin	NL	36	35	6	0	234.1	993	242	109	98	28	21	8	8	56	8	216	6	1	16	11	.593	2	0-0 0	3.82	3.76
2007	Cin	NL	34	34	2	0	231.2	948	213	100	96	28	4	5	8	52	3	218	12	1	16	6	.727	1	0-0 0	3.22	3.73
2008	Cin	NL	30	29	1	0	184.1	793	205	104	98	35	11	7	2	50	5	153	2	0	6	17	.261	1	0-0 0	4.83	4.78
2009	Cin	NL	26	26	2	0	162.1	703	186	82	76	24	6	2	4	43	6	142	6	0	6	14	.300	1	0-0 0	4.76	4.21
2010	Cin	NL	22	20	0	1	111.2	504	139	71	66	16	4	3	4	38	0	82	9	0	6	7	.462	0	0-0 0	5.75	5.32
2011	SD	NL	28	28	0	1	170.2	719	175	73	69	20	5	2	3	58	4	124	3	0	14	7	.667	0	0-0 0	4.22	3.64
2012	LAD	NL	31	31	0	0	179.2	786	167	85	72	14	9	10	4	85	10	131	4	0	10	10	.500	0	0-0 0	3.76	3.61
03	Oak	AL	7	6	0	1	30.1	136	41	19	18	5	2	1	0	9	0	16	0	1	1	3	.250	0	0-0 0	6.32	5.34
03	Cin	NL	9	9	0	0	46.0	191	48	28	27	6	3	0	1	10	0	26	3	0	4	3	.571	0	0-0 0	3.94	5.28
	11 ML YEARS		299	293	13	2	1802.0	7725	1888	898	839	231	92	53	50	550	46	1460	59	3	105	104	.502	6	0-0 0	4.24	4.19

J.J. Hardy

Bats: R **Throws:** R **Pos:** SS-158   **Ht:** 6'1" **Wt:** 190 **Born:** 8/19/1982 **Age:** 30

			BATTING																	BASERUNNING				AVERAGES		
Year	Team	Lg	G	AB	H	2B	3B	HR	(Hm	Rd)	TB	R	RBI	RC	TBB	IBB	SO	HBP	SH	SF	SB	CS	SB%	GDP	Avg	OBP	Slg
2005	Mil	NL	124	372	92	22	1	9	(6	3)	143	46	50	49	44	7	48	1	8	2	0	0	-	10	.247	.327	.384
2006	Mil	NL	35	128	31	5	0	5	(4	1)	51	13	14	13	10	0	23	0	0	1	1	1	.50	4	.242	.295	.398
2007	Mil	NL	151	592	164	30	1	26	(15	11)	274	89	80	84	40	1	73	1	4	1	2	3	.40	13	.277	.323	.463
2008	Mil	NL	146	569	161	31	4	24	(14	10)	272	78	74	78	52	3	98	1	5	2	2	1	.67	18	.283	.343	.478
2009	Mil	NL	115	414	95	16	2	11	(6	5)	148	53	47	32	43	0	85	2	1	5	0	1	.00	14	.229	.302	.357
2010	Min	AL	101	340	91	19	3	6	(1	5)	134	44	38	41	28	1	54	0	3	4	1	1	.50	8	.268	.320	.394
2011	Bal	AL	129	527	142	27	0	30	(15	15)	259	76	80	78	31	3	92	2	2	5	0	0	-	10	.269	.310	.491
2012	Bal	AL	158	663	158	30	2	22	(15	7)	258	85	68	71	38	4	106	3	7	2	0	0	-	21	.238	.282	.389
	Postseason		7	24	7	2	0	0	(0	0)	9	2	2	3	2	0	2	0	0	0	0	0	-	0	.292	.346	.375
	8 ML YEARS		959	3605	934	180	13	133	(76	57)	1539	484	451	446	286	19	579	10	30	22	6	7	.46	98	.259	.314	.427

Dan Haren

Pitches: R **Bats:** R **Pos:** SP-30   **Ht:** 6'5" **Wt:** 215 **Born:** 9/17/1980 **Age:** 32

			HOW MUCH HE PITCHED						WHAT HE GAVE UP										THE RESULTS						
Year	Team	Lg	G	GS	CG	GF	IP	BFP	H	R	ER	HR	SH	SF	HB	TBB	IBB	SO	WP	Bk	W	L	Pct	Sh	Sv-Op Hld	ERC	ERA
2012	InldEm*	A+	1	1	0	0	5.0	20	7	2	2	0	0	0	0	0	0	2	0	0	0	0	-	0	0- - -	4.37	3.60
2003	StL	NL	14	14	0	0	72.2	320	84	44	41	9	4	2	5	22	0	43	3	0	3	7	.300	0	0-0 0	5.07	5.08
2004	StL	NL	14	5	0	2	46.0	195	45	23	23	4	4	2	2	17	2	32	1	0	3	3	.500	0	0-0 0	3.91	4.50
2005	Oak	AL	34	34	3	0	217.0	897	212	101	90	26	3	5	6	53	5	163	6	0	14	12	.538	0	0-0 0	3.58	3.73
2006	Oak	AL	34	34	2	0	223.0	930	224	109	102	31	3	3	10	45	6	176	10	0	14	13	.519	0	0-0 0	3.72	4.12
2007	Oak	AL	34	34	0	0	222.2	935	214	91	76	24	2	8	3	55	1	192	10	0	15	9	.625	0	0-0 0	3.32	3.07
2008	Ari	NL	33	33	1	0	216.0	881	204	86	80	19	7	3	6	40	4	206	11	0	16	8	.667	1	0-0 0	2.96	3.33
2009	Ari	NL	33	33	3	0	229.1	909	192	83	80	27	8	3	4	38	2	223	13	0	14	10	.583	1	0-0 0	2.50	3.14
2010	2 Tms		35	35	2	0	235.0	994	245	110	102	31	6	10	5	54	6	216	12	2	12	12	.500	2	0-0 0	3.88	3.91
2011	LAA	AL	35	34	4	0	238.1	953	211	91	84	20	12	5	5	33	1	192	6	0	16	10	.615	3	0-0 0	2.45	3.17
2012	LAA	AL	30	30	1	0	176.2	747	190	95	85	28	7	8	3	38	3	142	5	1	12	13	.480	1	0-0 0	4.20	4.33

	HOW MUCH HE PITCHED						WHAT HE GAVE UP												THE RESULTS							
Year Team Lg	G	GS	CG	GF	IP	BFP	H	R	ER	HR	SH	SF	HB	TBB	IBB	SO	WP	Bk	W	L	Pct	Sh	Sv-Op	Hld	ERC	ERA
10 Ari NL	21	21	1	0	141.0	607	161	79	72	23	6	4	3	29	4	141	8	1	7	8	.467	0	0-0	0	4.55	4.60
10 LAA AL	14	14	1	0	94.0	387	84	31	30	8	0	6	2	25	2	75	4	1	5	4	.556	0	0-0	0	2.94	2.87
Postseason	7	2	0	0	19.1	86	24	7	7	3	1	0	0	7	0	16	2	0	2	0	1.000	0	0-0	0	5.83	3.26
10 ML YEARS	296	286	16	3	1876.2	7761	1821	833	763	219	56	49	49	395	30	1585	77	3	119	97	.551	6	0-0	0	3.36	3.66

Bryce Harper

Bats: L **Throws:** R **Pos:** CF-92; RF-65; LF-7; PH-2; PR-1   **Ht:** 6'3" **Wt:** 215 **Born:** 10/16/1992 **Age:** 20

	BATTING																	BASERUNNING				AVERAGES		
Year Team Lg	G	AB	H	2B	3B	HR	(Hm	Rd)	TB	R	RBI	RC	TBB	IBB	SO	HBP	SH	SF	SB	CS	SB%	GDP	Avg	OBP	Slg
2011 Hgrstn A	72	258	82	17	1	14	(-	-)	143	49	46	62	44	7	61	3	0	5	19	5	.79	5	.318	.423	.554
2011 Hrsbrg AA	37	129	33	7	1	3	(-	-)	51	14	12	18	15	0	26	0	1	2	7	2	.78	4	.256	.329	.395
2012 Syrcse AAA	21	74	18	4	1	1	(-	-)	27	8	3	9	9	0	14	0	1	0	1	1	.50	0	.243	.325	.365
2012 Was NL	139	533	144	26	9	22	(10	12)	254	98	59	82	56	0	120	2	3	3	18	6	.75	8	.270	.340	.477

Lucas Harrell

Pitches: R **Bats:** B **Pos:** SP-32   HAH-rell   **Ht:** 6'2" **Wt:** 210 **Born:** 6/3/1985 **Age:** 28

	HOW MUCH HE PITCHED						WHAT HE GAVE UP												THE RESULTS							
Year Team Lg	G	GS	CG	GF	IP	BFP	H	R	ER	HR	SH	SF	HB	TBB	IBB	SO	WP	Bk	W	L	Pct	Sh	Sv-Op	Hld	ERC	ERA
2010 CWS AL	8	3	0	3	24.0	119	34	18	13	2	1	0	0	17	1	15	1	0	1	0	1.000	0	0-0	0	7.77	4.88
2011 2 Tms	9	2	0	2	18.0	86	23	12	9	0	1	1	1	8	0	15	1	1	0	2	.000	0	0-0	0	5.16	4.50
2012 Hou NL	32	32	1	0	193.2	827	185	90	81	13	8	10	1	78	5	140	10	3	11	11	.500	1	0-0	0	3.59	3.76
11 CWS AL	3	0	0	2	5.0	26	11	4	4	0	0	0	0	1	0	5	0	0	0	0	-	0	0-0	0	10.11	7.20
11 Hou NL	6	2	0	0	13.0	60	12	8	5	0	1	1	1	7	0	10	1	1	0	2	.000	0	0-0	0	3.57	3.46
3 ML YEARS	49	37	1	5	235.2	1032	242	120	103	15	10	11	2	103	6	170	12	4	12	13	.480	1	0-0	0	4.09	3.93

Will Harris

Pitches: R **Bats:** R **Pos:** RP-20   **Ht:** 6'4" **Wt:** 225 **Born:** 8/28/1984 **Age:** 28

	HOW MUCH HE PITCHED						WHAT HE GAVE UP												THE RESULTS							
Year Team Lg	G	GS	CG	GF	IP	BFP	H	R	ER	HR	SH	SF	HB	TBB	IBB	SO	WP	Bk	W	L	Pct	Sh	Sv-Op	Hld	ERC	ERA
2006 TriCity A-	22	0	0	16	31.0	119	20	6	4	0	1	0	0	9	0	42	3	0	2	3	.400	0	6--	-	1.45	1.16
2007 Ashvll A	38	0	0	20	47.2	194	38	10	7	2	1	0	1	13	0	68	6	0	1	2	.333	0	1--	-	2.23	1.32
2008 Mdest A+	49	0	0	20	61.2	254	51	20	19	4	0	2	1	20	2	70	1	1	3	5	.375	0	3--	-	2.64	2.77
2009 TriCity A-	1	0	0	0	1.0	4	1	0	0	0	0	0	0	0	0	2	0	0	0	0	-	0	0--	-	1.95	0.00
2011 Mdest A+	33	0	0	15	47.0	202	45	29	29	4	4	0	0	21	1	55	4	0	3	2	.600	0	1--	-	3.90	5.55
2012 Tulsa AA	31	0	0	6	34.1	140	26	12	10	2	0	1	0	12	0	46	1	0	2	1	.667	0	1--	-	2.45	2.62
2012 ColSpr AAA	13	0	0	5	17.2	63	9	2	2	0	0	0	1	1	0	20	1	0	2	0	1.000	0	0--	-	0.64	1.02
2012 Col NL	20	0	0	10	17.2	89	27	18	16	3	2	1	1	6	1	19	4	0	1	1	.500	0	0-0	3	7.39	8.15

Willie Harris

Bats: L **Throws:** R **Pos:** PH-16; 2B-7; 3B-1; LF-1; DH-1   **Ht:** 5'9" **Wt:** 195 **Born:** 6/22/1978 **Age:** 35

	BATTING																	BASERUNNING				AVERAGES		
Year Team Lg	G	AB	H	2B	3B	HR	(Hm	Rd)	TB	R	RBI	RC	TBB	IBB	SO	HBP	SH	SF	SB	CS	SB%	GDP	Avg	OBP	Slg
2012 Lsvlle* AAA	74	250	56	13	0	3	(-	-)	78	22	20	24	23	3	52	3	1	2	4	3	.57	3	.224	.295	.312
2001 Bal AL	9	24	3	1	0	0	(0	0)	4	3	0	0	0	0	7	0	1	0	0	0	-	0	.125	.125	.167
2002 CWS AL	49	163	38	4	0	2	(2	0)	48	14	12	15	9	0	21	0	3	2	8	0	1.00	3	.233	.270	.294
2003 CWS AL	79	137	28	3	1	0	(0	0)	33	19	5	11	10	0	28	0	3	0	12	2	.86	1	.204	.259	.241
2004 CWS AL	129	409	107	15	2	2	(2	0)	132	68	27	53	51	0	79	1	7	3	19	7	.73	4	.262	.343	.323
2005 CWS AL	56	121	31	2	1	1	(1	0)	38	17	8	15	13	0	25	1	4	0	10	3	.77	1	.256	.333	.314
2006 Bos AL	47	45	7	2	0	0	(0	0)	9	17	1	1	4	0	11	2	0	1	6	3	.67	0	.156	.250	.200
2007 Atl NL	117	344	93	20	8	2	(1	1)	135	56	32	47	40	0	71	3	1	3	17	11	.61	3	.270	.349	.392
2008 Was NL	140	367	92	14	4	13	(4	9)	153	58	43	50	50	2	66	3	3	1	13	3	.81	8	.251	.344	.417
2009 Was NL	137	323	76	18	6	7	(6	1)	127	47	27	47	57	1	62	0	1	4	11	4	.73	4	.235	.364	.393
2010 Was NL	132	224	41	6	2	10	(7	3)	81	25	32	25	33	0	60	2	1	2	5	2	.71	3	.183	.291	.362
2011 NYM NL	126	240	59	11	0	2	(0	2)	76	36	23	26	36	3	62	4	1	2	4	4	.56	6	.246	.351	.317
2012 Cin NL	25	44	5	4	0	0	(0	0)	9	5	2	0	3	0	8	0	1	0	1	1	.50	0	.114	.170	.205
Postseason	3	2	2	0	0	0	(0	0)	2	1	1	2	0	0	0	0	0	0	1	0	1.00	0	1.000	1.000	1.000
12 ML YEARS	1046	2441	580	100	24	39	(23	16)	845	365	212	290	306	6	500	25	28	15	107	40	.73	33	.238	.327	.346

Josh Harrison

Bats: R **Throws:** R **Pos:** PH-33; 2B-28; SS-25; 3B-14; RF-12; PR-5; LF-1; DH-1   **Ht:** 5'8" **Wt:** 190 **Born:** 7/8/1987 **Age:** 25

	BATTING																	BASERUNNING				AVERAGES		
Year Team Lg	G	AB	H	2B	3B	HR	(Hm	Rd)	TB	R	RBI	RC	TBB	IBB	SO	HBP	SH	SF	SB	CS	SB%	GDP	Avg	OBP	Slg
2008 Boise A-	33	114	40	11	2	1	(-	-)	58	27	25	28	23	1	12	3	1	3	12	6	.67	1	.351	.462	.509
2008 Peoria A	31	122	32	4	1	1	(-	-)	41	15	4	12	3	0	11	1	0	0	6	2	.75	1	.262	.286	.336
2009 Peoria A	79	303	102	17	7	4	(-	-)	145	51	33	54	16	2	25	5	9	2	16	9	.64	5	.337	.377	.479
2009 Dytona A+	18	70	20	3	1	1	(-	-)	28	10	9	11	6	0	7	1	1	0	10	1	.91	1	.286	.351	.400
2009 Lynbrg A+	34	141	38	8	1	1	(-	-)	51	15	13	15	1	0	19	4	6	3	4	1	.80	1	.270	.289	.362
2010 Altna AA	135	520	156	33	3	4	(-	-)	207	74	74	77	32	2	52	9	14	10	19	7	.73	15	.300	.345	.398
2011 Indy AAA	62	226	70	15	2	5	(-	-)	104	35	23	39	15	0	28	6	5	2	13	5	.72	2	.310	.365	.460
2011 Pit NL	65	195	53	13	2	1	(1	0)	73	21	16	19	3	0	24	0	5	1	4	1	.80	6	.272	.281	.374
2012 Pit NL	104	249	58	9	5	3	(1	2)	86	34	16	22	10	0	37	7	7	3	7	3	.70	3	.233	.279	.345
2 ML YEARS	169	444	111	22	7	4	(2	2)	159	55	32	41	13	0	61	7	12	4	11	4	.73	9	.250	.280	.358

Matt Harrison

Pitches: L Bats: L Pos: SP-32 Ht: 6'4" Wt: 240 Born: 9/16/1985 Age: 27

							HOW MUCH HE PITCHED				WHAT HE GAVE UP											THE RESULTS							
Year	Team	Lg	G	GS	CG	GF	IP	BFP	H	R	ER	HR	SH	SF	HB	TBB	IBB	SO	WP	Bk	W	L	Pct	Sh	Sv-Op	Hld	ERC	ERA
2008	Tex	AL	15	15	1	0	83.2	372	100	57	51	12	1	5	2	31	2	42	2	2	9	3	.750	1	0-0	0	5.53	5.49
2009	Tex	AL	11	11	2	0	63.1	283	81	43	43	9	1	1	2	23	0	34	0	0	4	5	.444	0	0-0	0	6.17	6.11
2010	Tex	AL	37	6	0	9	78.1	356	80	45	41	10	2	8	2	39	3	46	4	0	3	2	.600	0	2-3	3	4.71	4.71
2011	Tex	AL	31	30	0	0	185.2	772	180	79	70	13	8	5	1	57	1	126	6	1	14	9	.609	0	0-0	0	3.40	3.39
2012	Tex	AL	32	32	4	0	213.1	876	210	82	78	22	1	2	1	59	0	133	2	0	18	11	.621	2	0-0	0	3.63	3.29
	Postseason		5	4	0	0	18.1	83	20	13	11	2	0	0	0	9	1	16	1	0	1	2	.333	0	0-0	0	4.88	5.40
	5 ML YEARS		126	94	7	9	624.1	2659	651	306	283	66	13	21	8	209	6	381	14	3	48	30	.615	4	2-3	3	4.18	4.08

Corey Hart

Bats: R Throws: R Pos: 1B-103; RF-53; PH-3 Ht: 6'6" Wt: 237 Born: 3/24/1982 Age: 31

									BATTING													BASERUNNING				AVERAGES		
Year	Team	Lg	G	AB	H	2B	3B	HR	(Hm	Rd)	TB	R	RBI	RC	TBB	IBB	SO	HBP	SH	SF	SB	CS	SB%	GDP	Avg	OBP	Slg
2004	Mil	NL	1	1	0	0	0	0	(0	0)	0	0	0	0	0	0	1	0	0	0	0	0	-	0	.000	.000	.000
2005	Mil	NL	21	57	11	2	1	2	(2	0)	21	9	7	4	6	0	11	0	0	0	2	0	1.00	6	.193	.270	.368
2006	Mil	NL	87	237	67	13	2	9	(6	3)	111	32	33	30	17	1	58	0	0	2	5	8	.38	7	.283	.328	.468
2007	Mil	NL	140	505	149	33	9	24	(15	9)	272	86	81	94	36	3	99	13	5	7	23	7	.77	6	.295	.353	.539
2008	Mil	NL	157	612	164	45	6	20	(7	13)	281	76	91	81	27	2	109	5	4	9	23	7	.77	17	.268	.300	.459
2009	Mil	NL	115	419	109	24	3	12	(9	3)	175	64	48	51	43	0	92	6	1	3	11	6	.65	9	.260	.335	.418
2010	Mil	NL	145	558	158	34	4	31	(16	15)	293	91	102	83	45	2	140	6	0	5	7	6	.54	14	.283	.340	.525
2011	Mil	NL	130	492	140	25	4	26	(17	9)	251	80	63	79	51	1	114	4	3	1	7	6	.54	12	.285	.356	.510
2012	Mil	NL	149	562	152	35	4	30	(22	8)	285	91	83	87	44	5	151	11	2	3	5	0	1.00	13	.270	.334	.507
	Postseason		14	54	13	0	0	2	(1	1)	19	6	5	4	3	0	11	1	1	1	0	0	-	1	.241	.288	.352
	9 ML YEARS		945	3443	950	211	33	154	(94	60)	1689	529	508	509	269	14	775	45	15	30	83	40	.67	84	.276	.334	.491

Matt Harvey

Pitches: R Bats: R Pos: SP-10 Ht: 6'4" Wt: 225 Born: 3/27/1989 Age: 24

							HOW MUCH HE PITCHED				WHAT HE GAVE UP											THE RESULTS							
Year	Team	Lg	G	GS	CG	GF	IP	BFP	H	R	ER	HR	SH	SF	HB	TBB	IBB	SO	WP	Bk	W	L	Pct	Sh	Sv-Op	Hld	ERC	ERA
2011	StLuci	A+	14	14	0	0	76.0	308	67	24	20	5	1	0	2	24	0	92	1	0	8	2	.800	0	0--	-	3.07	2.37
2011	Bnghtn	AA	12	12	0	0	59.2	259	59	32	31	4	3	2	3	23	0	64	5	0	5	3	.625	0	0--	-	3.91	4.68
2012	Buffalo	AAA	20	20	0	0	110.0	473	97	46	45	9	2	1	6	48	1	112	9	0	7	5	.583	0	0--	-	3.62	3.68
2012	NYM	NL	10	10	0	0	59.1	245	42	19	18	5	3	3	3	26	0	70	3	0	3	5	.375	0	0-0	0	2.75	2.73

Chris Hatcher

Pitches: R Bats: B Pos: RP-11 Ht: 6'2" Wt: 200 Born: 1/12/1985 Age: 28

							HOW MUCH HE PITCHED				WHAT HE GAVE UP											THE RESULTS							
Year	Team	Lg	G	GS	CG	GF	IP	BFP	H	R	ER	HR	SH	SF	HB	TBB	IBB	SO	WP	Bk	W	L	Pct	Sh	Sv-Op	Hld	ERC	ERA
2009	Jaxnvl	AA	1	0	0	1	0.1	1	0	0	0	0	0	0	0	0	0	0	0	0	0	0	-	0	0--	-	0.00	0.00
2010	Jaxnvl	AA	1	0	0	1	1.0	3	0	0	0	0	0	0	0	0	0	1	0	0	1	0	1.000	0	0--	-	0.00	0.00
2011	Jaxnvl	AA	42	0	0	12	47.1	189	32	11	10	2	1	2	0	19	0	57	9	1	2	2	.500	0	6--	-	2.07	1.90
2012	NewOr	AAA	37	0	0	22	47.0	188	33	6	4	1	1	2	2	15	1	45	3	0	1	0	1.000	0	11--	-	1.90	0.77
2011	Fla	NL	11	0	0	4	10.1	48	14	8	8	2	0	3	0	4	1	8	2	0	0	0	-	0	0-0	0	6.69	6.97
2012	Mia	NL	11	0	0	7	14.2	66	17	9	7	3	0	0	1	6	0	10	1	0	0	0	-	0	0-0	0	6.19	4.30
	2 ML YEARS		22	0	0	11	25.0	114	31	17	15	5	0	3	1	10	1	18	3	0	0	0	-	0	0-0	0	6.40	5.40

LaTroy Hawkins

Pitches: R Bats: R Pos: RP-48 Ht: 6'5" Wt: 220 Born: 12/21/1972 Age: 40

							HOW MUCH HE PITCHED				WHAT HE GAVE UP											THE RESULTS							
Year	Team	Lg	G	GS	CG	GF	IP	BFP	H	R	ER	HR	SH	SF	HB	TBB	IBB	SO	WP	Bk	W	L	Pct	Sh	Sv-Op	Hld	ERC	ERA
2012	InldEm*	A+	1	0	0	0	1.0	5	2	1	1	1	0	0	0	0	0	2	0	0	0	0	-	0	0--	-	16.28	9.00
2012	Salt Lk*	AAA	2	1	0	0	2.0	8	1	0	0	0	0	0	0	1	0	1	0	0	0	0	-	0	0--	-	1.41	0.00
1995	Min	AL	6	6	1	0	27.0	131	39	29	26	3	0	3	1	12	0	9	1	1	2	3	.400	0	0-0	0	7.14	8.67
1996	Min	AL	7	6	0	1	26.1	124	42	24	24	8	1	1	0	9	0	24	1	1	1	1	.500	0	0-0	0	9.49	8.20
1997	Min	AL	20	20	0	0	103.1	478	134	71	67	19	2	2	4	47	0	58	6	3	6	12	.333	0	0-0	0	7.01	5.84
1998	Min	AL	33	33	0	0	190.1	840	227	126	111	27	4	10	5	61	1	105	10	2	7	14	.333	0	0-0	0	5.31	5.25
1999	Min	AL	33	33	1	0	174.1	803	238	136	129	34	1	5	1	60	2	103	9	0	10	14	.417	0	0-0	0	6.55	6.66
2000	Min	AL	66	0	0	38	87.2	370	85	34	33	7	4	1	1	32	1	59	6	0	2	5	.286	0	14-14	7	3.70	3.39
2001	Min	AL	62	0	0	51	51.1	248	59	34	34	3	1	4	1	39	3	36	7	0	1	5	.167	0	28-37	1	6.02	5.96
2002	Min	AL	65	0	0	15	80.1	310	63	23	19	5	2	3	0	15	1	63	5	0	6	0	1.000	0	0-3	13	1.99	2.13
2003	Min	AL	74	0	0	12	77.1	310	69	20	16	4	4	1	1	15	1	75	0	0	9	3	.750	0	2-8	28	2.48	1.86
2004	ChC	NL	77	0	0	50	82.0	333	72	27	24	10	6	2	2	14	5	69	2	0	5	4	.556	0	25-34	4	2.66	2.63
2005	2 Tms	NL	66	0	0	21	56.1	247	58	27	24	7	3	1	0	24	3	43	1	0	2	8	.200	0	6-15	15	4.41	3.83
2006	Bal	AL	60	0	0	12	60.1	261	73	30	30	4	1	2	0	15	3	27	2	0	3	2	.600	0	0-4	16	4.37	4.48
2007	Col	NL	62	0	0	10	55.1	225	52	21	21	6	2	1	0	16	1	29	2	0	2	5	.286	0	0-5	18	3.43	3.42
2008	2 Tms	NL	57	0	0	15	62.0	252	53	29	27	3	1	3	0	22	4	48	3	0	3	1	.750	0	1-2	13	2.75	3.92
2009	Hou	NL	65	0	0	34	63.1	259	60	16	15	7	2	2	2	16	2	45	0	0	1	4	.200	0	11-15	19	3.42	2.13
2010	Mil	NL	18	0	0	5	16.0	74	21	15	15	2	0	1	0	6	1	18	1	0	0	2	.000	0	0-2	6	6.55	8.44
2011	Mil	NL	52	0	0	16	48.1	204	50	15	13	1	1	4	0	13	0	21	2	0	3	1	.750	0	0-0	20	2.91	2.42
2012	LAA	AL	48	0	0	7	42.0	178	45	20	17	5	3	1	0	13	1	23	0	0	2	3	.400	0	1-4	6	4.27	3.64
	05	ChC	NL	21	0	0	12	19.0	80	18	9	7	4	1	0	0	7	0	13	0	0	1	4	.200	0	4-8	0	4.44	3.32
	05	SF	NL	45	0	0	9	37.1	167	40	18	17	3	2	1	0	17	3	30	1	0	1	4	.200	0	2-7	15	4.36	4.10

Year Team Lg	G GS CG GF	IP	BFP	H R ER HR SH SF HB	TBB IBB	SO	WP Bk	W L Pct Sh Sv-Op Hld	ERC	ERA
08 NYY AL	33 0 0 11	41.0	173	42 26 26 3 1 2 0	17 3	23	2 0	1 1 .500 0 0-1 1	4.09	5.71
08 Hou NL	24 0 0 4	21.0	79	11 3 1 0 0 1 0	5 1	25	1 0	2 0 1.000 0 1-1 12	0.95	0.43
Postseason	19 0 0 4	15.2	65	13 7 6 0 3 1 0	6 1	17	0 0	1 0 1.000 0 0-0 4	2.35	3.45
18 ML YEARS	871 98 2 281	1303.2	5647	1440 697 645 150 39 43 20	426 30	862	65 7	65 88 .425 0 88-143 166	4.53	4.45

Blake Hawksworth

Pitches: R Bats: R Pos: P   Ht: 6'3" Wt: 195 Born: 3/1/1983 Age: 30

Year Team Lg	G GS CG GF	IP	BFP	H R ER HR SH SF HB	TBB IBB	SO	WP Bk	W L Pct Sh Sv-Op Hld	ERC	ERA
2012 RCuca* A+	2 2 0 0	2.0	8	1 1 1 0 0 0 0	0 0	2	0 0	0 0 - 0 0- - -	0.47	4.50
2009 StL NL	30 0 0 10	40.0	160	29 10 9 2 4 1 1	15 3	20	0 0	4 0 1.000 0 0-0 2	2.26	2.03
2010 StL NL	45 8 0 9	90.1	409	113 56 50 15 4 4 2	35 0	61	1 3	4 8 .333 0 0-0 4	6.15	4.98
2011 LAD NL	49 0 0 12	53.0	219	45 29 24 6 2 0 0	17 3	43	5 0	2 5 .286 0 0-1 7	2.94	4.08
Postseason	1 0 0 0	1.0	4	1 0 0 0 0 0 0	1 0	1	0 0	0 0 - 0 0-0 0	6.99	0.00
3 ML YEARS	124 8 0 31	183.1	788	187 95 83 23 10 5 3	67 6	124	6 3	10 13 .435 0 0-1 13	4.26	4.07

Brett Hayes

Bats: R Throws: R Pos: C-33; PR-4; PH-3   Ht: 6'0" Wt: 200 Born: 2/13/1984 Age: 29

Year Team Lg	G	AB	H	2B 3B HR	(Hm Rd)	TB	R	RBI	RC	TBB IBB	SO	HBP SH SF	SB CS SB% GDP	Avg	OBP	Slg
2012 NewOr* AAA	16	59	21	4 0 3	(- -)	34	9	8	12	3 0	13	1 0 0	0 0 - 0	.356	.397	.576
2009 Fla NL	14	11	3	1 0 1	(0 1)	7	5	2	1	0 0	4	1 0 0	0 0 - 1	.273	.333	.636
2010 Fla NL	26	77	16	6 1 2	(1 1)	30	6	6	7	6 1	26	0 0 0	0 0 - 1	.208	.265	.390
2011 Fla NL	64	130	30	9 0 5	(3 2)	54	19	16	13	11 2	39	0 3 0	0 0 - 2	.231	.291	.415
2012 Mia NL	39	114	23	6 0 0	(0 0)	29	7	3	2	4 3	49	0 0 0	1 0 1.00 1	.202	.229	.254
4 ML YEARS	143	332	72	22 1 8	(4 4)	120	37	27	23	21 6	118	1 3 0	1 0 1.00 5	.217	.266	.361

Chase Headley

Bats: B Throws: R Pos: 3B-159; PH-2; 1B-1   HEDD-lee   Ht: 6'2" Wt: 200 Born: 5/9/1984 Age: 29

Year Team Lg	G	AB	H	2B 3B HR	(Hm Rd)	TB	R	RBI	RC	TBB IBB	SO	HBP SH SF	SB CS SB% GDP	Avg	OBP	Slg
2007 SD NL	8	18	4	1 0 0	(0 0)	5	1	0	1	2 0	4	1 0 0	0 0 - 2	.222	.333	.278
2008 SD NL	91	331	89	19 2 9	(4 5)	139	34	38	42	30 1	104	5 0 2	4 1 .80 5	.269	.337	.420
2009 SD NL	156	543	142	31 2 12	(7 5)	213	62	64	68	62 3	133	5 0 2	10 2 .83 19	.262	.342	.392
2010 SD NL	161	610	161	29 3 11	(3 8)	229	77	58	70	56 3	139	3 1 4	17 5 .77 11	.264	.327	.375
2011 SD NL	113	381	110	28 1 4	(1 3)	152	43	44	61	52 8	92	2 1 3	13 2 .87 6	.289	.374	.399
2012 SD NL	161	604	173	31 2 31	(13 18)	301	95	115	112	86 2	157	4 0 5	17 6 .74 7	.286	.376	.498
6 ML YEARS	690	2487	679	139 10 67	(28 39)	1039	312	319	354	288 17	629	20 2 16	61 16 .79 50	.273	.351	.418

Deunte Heath

Pitches: R Bats: R Pos: RP-3   dee-UN-tay   Ht: 6'4" Wt: 215 Born: 8/8/1985 Age: 27

Year Team Lg	G GS CG GF	IP	BFP	H R ER HR SH SF HB	TBB IBB	SO	WP Bk	W L Pct Sh Sv-Op Hld	ERC	ERA
2007 Rome A	16 9 0 5	71.0	289	59 19 16 1 3 1 3	19 0	47	3 0	2 3 .400 0 0- - -	2.31	2.03
2007 MrtlBh A+	11 11 0 0	55.2	260	64 45 36 8 2 0 2	31 0	47	5 1	2 4 .333 0 0- - -	6.05	5.82
2008 MrtlBh A+	14 14 1 0	84.0	362	78 40 29 5 3 0 2	41 0	53	1 1	9 2 .818 0 0- - -	3.86	3.11
2008 Missi AA	13 11 0 1	66.1	307	76 50 41 5 2 0 5	32 0	46	7 1	4 5 .444 0 0- - -	5.32	5.56
2009 Missi AA	25 12 0 4	80.0	355	80 43 37 4 3 1 5	38 0	70	5 4	2 5 .286 0 1- - -	4.24	4.16
2009 Gwnntt AAA	7 2 0 1	18.2	95	27 21 20 2 0 0 0	12 0	18	2 0	0 1 .000 0 0- - -	7.71	9.64
2010 Brham AA	39 0 0 13	57.2	250	49 22 20 4 2 0 4	32 2	84	2 3	2 4 .333 0 2- - -	3.87	3.12
2011 Charltt AAA	30 16 0 1	102.2	465	98 62 51 12 1 4 4	62 0	117	8 1	4 7 .364 0 1- - -	4.87	4.47
2012 Charltt AAA	36 4 0 11	67.0	272	47 13 11 4 0 1 4	20 0	74	2 0	4 3 .571 0 3- - -	2.09	1.48
2012 CWS AL	3 0 0 2	2.0	7	1 1 1 1 0 0 0	1 0	1	0 0	0 0 - 0 0-0 0	4.74	4.50

Adeiny Hechavarria

Bats: R Throws: R Pos: 3B-18; SS-17; 2B-8; PH-1   a-DAY-nee hetch-a-VA-ree-a   Ht: 5'11" Wt: 180 Born: 4/15/1989 Age: 24

Year Team Lg	G	AB	H	2B 3B HR	(Hm Rd)	TB	R	RBI	RC	TBB IBB	SO	HBP SH SF	SB CS SB% GDP	Avg	OBP	Slg
2010 Dnedin A+	41	161	31	7 3 1	(- -)	47	21	7	10	5 0	25	0 1 0	7 0 1.00 4	.193	.217	.292
2010 NHam AA	61	253	69	11 1 3	(- -)	91	36	34	29	12 0	40	2 1 5	6 3 .67 9	.273	.305	.360
2011 NHam AA	111	464	109	22 6 6	(- -)	161	58	46	44	25 2	78	3 4 6	19 13 .59 9	.235	.275	.347
2011 LsVgs AAA	25	108	42	6 2 2	(- -)	58	16	11	23	8 0	21	0 0 0	1 2 .33 3	.389	.431	.537
2012 LsVgs AAA	102	443	138	20 6 6	(- -)	188	78	63	71	38 0	86	1 3 5	8 2 .80 14	.312	.363	.424
2012 Tor AL	41	126	32	8 0 2	(1 1)	46	10	15	15	4 0	32	1 5 1	0 0 - 2	.254	.280	.365

Jeremy Hefner

Pitches: R Bats: R Pos: SP-13; RP-13   HEFF-ner   Ht: 6'4" Wt: 215 Born: 3/11/1986 Age: 27

Year Team Lg	G GS CG GF	IP	BFP	H R ER HR SH SF HB	TBB IBB	SO	WP Bk	W L Pct Sh Sv-Op Hld	ERC	ERA
2007 Eugene A-	17 11 0 2	62.1	255	51 33 27 3 2 0 2	20 0	74	8 0	2 5 .286 0 0- - -	2.61	3.90
2008 FtWyn A	29 24 0 1	140.1	568	117 53 52 12 5 6 3	41 1	144	7 0	10 5 .667 0 0- - -	2.79	3.33
2008 Lk Els A+	1 1 0 0	5.0	21	3 2 2 0 1 0 0	2 0	6	0 0	0 0 - 0 0- - -	1.44	3.60
2009 Lk Els A+	27 27 0 0	150.2	635	165 81 69 13 3 1 11	38 0	142	9 0	14 9 .609 0 0- - -	4.34	4.12

	HOW MUCH HE PITCHED						WHAT HE GAVE UP												THE RESULTS							
Year Team	Lg	G	GS	CG	GF	IP	BFP	H	R	ER	HR	SH	SF	HB	TBB	IBB	SO	WP	Bk	W	L	Pct	Sh	Sv-Op	Hld	ERC	ERA
2009 Portlnd	AAA	1	1	0	0	5.1	24	7	2	2	0	0	0	0	2	0	5	0	0	0	0	-	0	0--	-	5.10	3.38
2010 SnAnt	AA	28	28	2	0	167.2	687	156	63	55	11	10	7	5	51	3	115	7	0	11	8	.579	0	0--	-	3.26	2.95
2011 Tucsn	AAA	28	28	0	0	157.1	704	178	101	87	21	6	4	3	61	1	120	7	0	9	7	.563	0	0--	-	5.05	4.98
2012 Buffalo	AAA	10	9	0	1	61.2	243	55	25	19	4	2	1	0	10	1	37	1	0	5	2	.714	0	0--	-	2.42	2.77
2012 NYM	NL	26	13	0	5	93.2	408	110	55	53	9	4	1	2	18	1	62	7	0	4	7	.364	0	0-0	0	4.20	5.09

Chris Heisey

Bats: R **Throws:** R **Pos:** LF-63; CF-36; PH-22; RF-13   HY-zee   **Ht:** 6'0" **Wt:** 220 **Born:** 12/14/1984 **Age:** 28

	BATTING																	BASERUNNING				AVERAGES		
Year Team	Lg	G	AB	H	2B	3B	HR	(Hm | Rd)	TB	R	RBI	RC	TBB	IBB	SO	HBP	SH	SF	SB	CS	SB%	GDP	Avg	OBP	Slg
2010 Cin	NL	97	201	51	10	1	8	(2 | 6)	87	33	21	22	16	1	57	6	1	2	1	2	.33	3	.254	.324	.433
2011 Cin	NL	120	279	71	9	1	18	(11 | 7)	136	44	50	40	19	3	78	5	1	4	6	1	.86	1	.254	.309	.487
2012 Cin	NL	120	347	92	16	5	7	(4 | 3)	139	44	31	42	18	0	81	7	3	0	6	3	.67	8	.265	.315	.401
Postseason		1	2	0	0	0	0	(0 | 0)	0	0	0	0	0	0	1	0	0	0	0	0	-	0	.000	.000	.000
3 ML YEARS		337	827	214	35	7	33	(17 | 16)	362	121	102	104	53	4	216	18	5	6	13	6	.68	12	.259	.315	.438

Jeremy Hellickson

Pitches: R **Bats:** R **Pos:** SP-31   **Ht:** 6'1" **Wt:** 190 **Born:** 4/8/1987 **Age:** 26

	HOW MUCH HE PITCHED						WHAT HE GAVE UP												THE RESULTS							
Year Team	Lg	G	GS	CG	GF	IP	BFP	H	R	ER	HR	SH	SF	HB	TBB	IBB	SO	WP	Bk	W	L	Pct	Sh	Sv-Op	Hld	ERC	ERA
2010 TB	AL	10	4	0	0	36.1	149	32	14	14	5	0	1	2	8	2	33	2	0	4	0	1.000	0	0-1	0	3.10	3.47
2011 TB	AL	29	29	2	0	189.0	774	146	64	62	21	1	2	4	72	8	117	8	1	13	10	.565	1	0-0	0	2.89	2.95
2012 TB	AL	31	31	0	0	177.0	741	163	68	61	25	4	3	4	59	3	124	5	0	10	11	.476	0	0-0	0	3.73	3.10
Postseason		1	1	0	0	4.0	16	4	3	3	0	0	0	0	1	0	1	0	0	0	1	.000	0	0-0	0	8.13	6.75
3 ML YEARS		70	64	2	0	402.1	1664	341	146	137	51	5	6	10	139	13	274	15	1	27	21	.563	1	0-1	0	3.27	3.06

Todd Helton

Bats: L **Throws:** L **Pos:** 1B-67; PH-4   **Ht:** 6'2" **Wt:** 220 **Born:** 8/20/1973 **Age:** 39

	BATTING																	BASERUNNING				AVERAGES		
Year Team	Lg	G	AB	H	2B	3B	HR	(Hm	Rd)	TB	R	RBI	RC	TBB	IBB	SO	HBP	SH	SF	SB	CS	SB%	GDP	Avg	OBP	Slg
2012 GdJnct*	R+	2	5	3	0	0	0	(-	-)	3	0	2	1	1	0	0	0	0	0	0	0	-	1	.600	.667	.600
1997 Col	NL	35	93	26	2	1	5	(3	2)	45	13	11	15	8	0	11	0	0	0	0	1	.00	1	.280	.337	.484
1998 Col	NL	152	530	167	37	1	25	(13	12)	281	78	97	101	53	5	54	6	1	5	3	3	.50	15	.315	.380	.530
1999 Col	NL	159	578	185	39	5	35	(23	12)	339	114	113	124	68	6	77	6	0	4	7	6	.54	14	.320	.395	.587
2000 Col	NL	160	580	216	59	2	42	(27	15)	405	138	147	169	103	22	61	4	0	10	5	3	.63	12	.372	.463	.698
2001 Col	NL	159	587	197	54	2	49	(27	22)	402	132	146	157	98	15	104	5	1	5	7	5	.58	14	.336	.432	.685
2002 Col	NL	156	553	182	39	4	30	(18	12)	319	107	109	127	99	21	91	5	0	10	5	1	.83	10	.329	.429	.577
2003 Col	NL	160	583	209	49	5	33	(23	10)	367	135	117	160	111	21	72	2	0	7	0	4	.00	19	.358	.458	.630
2004 Col	NL	154	547	190	49	2	32	(21	11)	339	115	96	143	127	19	72	3	0	6	3	0	1.00	12	.347	.469	.620
2005 Col	NL	144	509	163	45	2	20	(13	7)	272	92	79	114	106	22	80	9	1	1	3	0	1.00	14	.320	.445	.534
2006 Col	NL	145	546	165	40	5	15	(8	7)	260	94	81	118	91	15	64	6	0	6	3	2	.60	10	.302	.404	.476
2007 Col	NL	154	557	178	42	2	17	(9	8)	275	86	91	115	116	16	74	2	0	7	0	1	.00	15	.320	.434	.494
2008 Col	NL	83	299	79	16	0	7	(5	2)	116	39	29	45	61	8	50	1	0	0	0	0	-	9	.264	.391	.388
2009 Col	NL	151	544	177	38	3	15	(10	5)	266	79	86	108	89	5	73	2	0	10	0	1	.00	15	.325	.416	.489
2010 Col	NL	118	398	102	18	1	8	(4	4)	146	48	37	51	67	3	90	2	0	6	0	0	-	10	.256	.362	.367
2011 Col	NL	124	421	127	27	4	14	(8	6)	196	59	69	68	59	5	71	3	0	8	0	1	.00	6	.302	.385	.466
2012 Col	NL	69	240	57	16	1	7	(4	3)	96	31	37	36	39	1	44	1	0	3	1	1	.50	6	.238	.343	.400
Postseason		15	57	12	2	1	0	(0	0)	16	11	4	2	8	0	11	0	0	0	0	0	-	1	.211	.303	.281
16 ML YEARS		2123	7565	2420	570	36	354	(216	138)	4124	1360	1345	1651	1295	184	1088	57	3	88	37	29	.56	182	.320	.419	.545

Jim Henderson

Pitches: R **Bats:** L **Pos:** RP-36   **Ht:** 6'5" **Wt:** 190 **Born:** 10/21/1982 **Age:** 30

	HOW MUCH HE PITCHED						WHAT HE GAVE UP												THE RESULTS							
Year Team	Lg	G	GS	CG	GF	IP	BFP	H	R	ER	HR	SH	SF	HB	TBB	IBB	SO	WP	Bk	W	L	Pct	Sh	Sv-Op	Hld	ERC	ERA
2003 Expos	R	4	0	0	1	8.0	33	6	3	2	0	0	0	1	1	0	3	1	0	0	0	-	0	1--	-	1.60	2.25
2003 Vrmnt	A-	15	0	0	4	24.2	126	32	28	19	1	3	0	3	15	0	13	2	0	1	1	.500	0	0--	-	6.43	6.93
2004 Vrmnt	A-	14	13	0	0	76.1	313	60	34	22	2	6	8	2	27	1	39	0	0	2	6	.250	0	0--	-	2.38	2.59
2005 Savann	A	26	26	1	0	149.2	657	166	99	91	20	3	5	7	50	0	76	3	0	9	11	.450	1	0--	-	4.87	5.47
2006 Ptomc	A+	25	1	0	12	52.0	229	44	31	26	4	0	3	6	22	0	56	5	0	2	2	.500	0	1--	-	3.50	4.50
2006 Savann	A	3	0	0	1	5.1	22	6	2	2	1	1	0	1	0	0	6	0	0	1	0	1.000	0	0--	-	4.65	3.38
2007 Tenn	AA	42	0	0	22	58.0	242	50	15	12	7	4	0	4	25	2	49	2	0	4	3	.571	0	10--	-	3.90	1.86
2007 Iowa	AAA	8	0	0	1	13.0	59	16	8	8	2	0	0	0	6	0	6	0	0	3	0	1.000	0	0--	-	6.18	5.54
2008 Tenn	AA	5	0	0	4	6.1	24	5	1	0	0	0	0	0	1	0	4	1	0	0	1	.000	0	1--	-	1.64	0.00
2008 Iowa	AAA	3	0	0	1	3.0	17	2	5	5	1	0	0	1	5	0	4	0	0	0	0	-	0	0--	-	10.79	15.00
2009 Wisc	A	26	0	0	25	25.1	102	19	4	3	0	1	0	1	8	0	26	0	0	0	0	-	0	17--	-	2.00	1.07
2009 BrvdCt	A+	15	0	0	8	29.1	117	16	11	9	2	1	1	1	14	1	20	1	0	3	0	1.000	0	4--	-	1.93	2.76
2009 Hntsvl	AA	5	0	0	3	7.0	35	8	3	2	0	1	1	0	4	0	5	2	0	1	0	1.000	0	0--	-	4.37	2.57
2010 Hntsvl	AA	45	0	0	17	61.0	267	49	44	37	8	2	3	3	35	3	61	2	0	4	5	.444	0	7--	-	3.95	5.46
2011 Nashv	AAA	20	0	0	8	30.1	137	23	20	20	4	3	2	1	23	1	30	0	0	3	1	.750	0	0--	-	4.36	5.93
2011 Hntsvl	AA	22	0	0	11	30.2	124	22	9	9	4	2	0	3	8	0	39	2	0	4	1	.800	0	5--	-	2.60	2.64
2012 Nashv	AAA	35	0	0	29	48.0	195	36	10	9	2	2	1	2	22	2	56	0	0	4	3	.571	0	15--	-	2.75	1.69
2012 Mil	NL	36	0	0	6	30.2	131	26	12	12	1	1	3	1	13	0	45	1	0	1	3	.250	0	3-7	14	2.96	3.52

Liam Hendriks

Pitches: R Bats: R Pos: SP-16   Ht: 6'1" Wt: 205 Born: 2/10/1989 Age: 24

Year	Team	Lg	G	GS	CG	GF	IP	BFP	H	R	ER	HR	SH	SF	HB	TBB	IBB	SO	WP	Bk	W	L	Pct	Sh	Sv-Op	Hld	ERC	ERA
2007	Twins	R	10	10	0	0	44.0	182	41	14	10	2	0	0	1	11	0	52	0	0	4	2	.667	0	0- -	-	2.86	2.05
2009	Elizab	R	3	3	0	0	17.0	71	19	8	7	0	0	0	0	1	0	13	0	0	2	0	1.000	0	0- -	-	2.69	3.71
2009	Beloit	A	11	11	0	0	66.2	284	73	34	26	3	3	1	2	15	0	62	5	1	3	5	.375	0	0- -	-	3.65	3.51
2010	Beloit	A	6	6	0	0	34.0	123	16	6	5	0	1	1	1	4	0	39	2	0	2	1	.667	0	0- -	-	0.70	1.32
2010	FtMyrs	A+	13	12	1	0	74.2	292	63	20	16	2	2	1	1	8	0	66	3	0	6	3	.667	0	0- -	-	1.83	1.93
2011	NwBrit	AA	16	15	2	0	90.0	365	85	30	27	5	0	1	3	18	1	81	0	0	8	2	.800	0	0- -	-	2.88	2.70
2011	Roch	AAA	9	9	0	0	49.1	199	52	26	25	0	2	4	2	3	0	30	1	1	4	4	.500	0	0- -	-	2.62	4.56
2012	Roch	AAA	16	16	1	0	106.1	412	76	28	26	5	4	0	1	28	0	82	3	0	9	3	.750	1	0- -	-	1.88	2.20
2011	Min	AL	4	4	0	0	23.1	100	29	16	16	3	0	1	0	6	0	16	1	0	0	2	.000	0	0-0	0	5.26	6.17
2012	Min	AL	16	16	1	0	85.1	381	106	61	53	17	3	1	4	26	3	50	4	0	1	8	.111	0	0-0	0	6.03	5.59
	2 ML YEARS		20	20	1	0	108.2	481	135	77	69	20	3	2	4	32	3	66	5	0	1	10	.091	0	0-0	0	5.86	5.71

Clay Hensley

Pitches: R Bats: R Pos: RP-60   Ht: 5'11" Wt: 190 Born: 8/31/1979 Age: 33

Year	Team	Lg	G	GS	CG	GF	IP	BFP	H	R	ER	HR	SH	SF	HB	TBB	IBB	SO	WP	Bk	W	L	Pct	Sh	Sv-Op	Hld	ERC	ERA
2005	SD	NL	24	1	0	5	47.2	189	33	12	9	0	1	2	0	17	2	28	2	0	1	1	.500	0	0-0	2	1.70	1.70
2006	SD	NL	37	29	1	2	187.0	787	174	82	77	15	10	3	3	76	7	122	3	0	11	12	.478	1	0-1	1	3.64	3.71
2007	SD	NL	13	9	0	1	50.0	238	62	40	38	5	2	1	1	32	2	30	4	1	2	3	.400	0	0-0	0	6.54	6.84
2008	SD	NL	32	1	0	8	39.0	173	36	27	23	2	1	3	1	25	3	26	1	0	1	2	.333	0	0-1	3	4.23	5.31
2010	Fla	NL	68	0	0	23	75.0	307	54	20	18	3	3	1	4	29	4	77	2	0	3	4	.429	0	7-10	22	2.29	2.16
2011	Fla	NL	37	9	0	7	67.2	297	62	41	39	9	2	1	4	30	1	46	0	0	6	7	.462	0	0-2	8	4.16	5.19
2012	SF	NL	60	0	0	14	50.2	234	50	30	26	5	4	3	3	30	2	42	1	0	4	5	.444	0	3-4	8	4.82	4.62
	Postseason		5	0	0	1	7.1	32	6	2	2	0	1	0	0	4	0	1	0	0	0	0	-	0	0-0	0	2.87	2.45
	7 ML YEARS		271	49	1	60	517.0	2225	471	252	230	39	23	14	16	239	21	371	13	1	28	34	.452	1	10-18	44	3.71	4.00

Jeremy Hermida

Bats: L Throws: R Pos: PH-8; RF-6; LF-1   her-MEE-dah   Ht: 6'3" Wt: 222 Born: 1/30/1984 Age: 29

Year	Team	Lg	G	AB	H	2B	3B	HR	(Hm	Rd)	TB	R	RBI	RC	TBB	IBB	SO	HBP	SH	SF	SB	CS	SB%	GDP	Avg	OBP	Slg
2012	Tucsn*	AAA	44	151	38	7	0	3	(-	-)	54	21	22	18	15	0	43	1	0	3	1	0	1.00	5	.252	.318	.358
2005	Fla	NL	23	41	12	2	0	4	(4	0)	26	9	11	10	6	1	12	0	0	0	2	0	1.00	1	.293	.383	.634
2006	Fla	NL	99	307	77	19	1	5	(3	2)	113	37	28	38	33	3	70	5	2	1	4	1	.80	6	.251	.332	.368
2007	Fla	NL	123	429	127	32	1	18	(8	10)	215	54	63	69	47	2	105	4	1	3	3	4	.43	10	.296	.369	.501
2008	Fla	NL	142	502	125	22	3	17	(4	13)	204	74	61	65	48	5	138	7	1	1	6	1	.86	12	.249	.323	.406
2009	Fla	NL	129	429	111	14	2	13	(4	9)	168	48	47	57	56	4	101	4	0	2	5	2	.71	6	.259	.348	.392
2010	2 Tms	AL	73	222	48	12	0	6	(4	2)	78	19	29	20	16	0	58	0	0	1	1	0	1.00	6	.216	.268	.351
2011	2 Tms	NL	30	58	11	2	1	2	(2	0)	21	5	9	8	7	0	26	1	0	0	0	0	-	0	.190	.288	.362
2012	SD	NL	13	24	6	1	1	0	(0	0)	9	2	2	2	3	1	7	0	0	0	1	0	1.00	3	.250	.333	.375
10	Bos	AL	52	158	32	8	0	5	(4	1)	55	14	27	17	12	0	45	0	0	1	1	0	1.00	1	.203	.257	.348
10	Oak	AL	21	64	16	4	0	1	(0	1)	23	5	2	3	4	0	13	0	0	0	0	0	-	5	.250	.294	.359
11	Cin	NL	10	18	2	0	0	1	(1	0)	5	2	3	1	0	0	7	0	0	0	0	0	-	0	.111	.111	.278
11	SD	NL	20	40	9	2	1	1	(1	0)	16	3	6	7	7	0	19	1	0	0	0	0	-	0	.225	.354	.400
	8 ML YEARS		632	2012	517	104	9	65	(29	36)	834	248	250	269	216	16	517	21	4	8	22	8	.73	41	.257	.334	.415

David Hernandez

Pitches: R Bats: R Pos: RP-72   Ht: 6'2" Wt: 230 Born: 5/13/1985 Age: 28

Year	Team	Lg	G	GS	CG	GF	IP	BFP	H	R	ER	HR	SH	SF	HB	TBB	IBB	SO	WP	Bk	W	L	Pct	Sh	Sv-Op	Hld	ERC	ERA
2009	Bal	AL	20	19	0	0	101.1	462	118	62	61	27	2	3	1	46	0	68	3	0	4	10	.286	0	0-0	0	6.55	5.42
2010	Bal	AL	41	8	0	16	79.1	348	72	40	38	9	1	3	4	42	4	72	9	0	8	8	.500	0	2-6	2	4.28	4.31
2011	Ari	NL	74	0	0	28	69.1	291	49	27	26	4	3	2	2	30	1	77	7	1	5	3	.625	0	11-14	23	2.40	3.38
2012	Ari	NL	72	0	0	21	68.1	278	48	21	19	4	0	1	3	22	1	98	4	1	2	3	.400	0	4-10	25	2.10	2.50
	Postseason		4	0	0	1	5.0	17	2	2	2	1	0	0	0	0	0	5	0	0	0	0	-	0	0-0	0	0.74	3.60
	4 ML YEARS		207	27	0	65	318.1	1379	287	150	144	44	6	9	10	140	6	315	23	2	19	24	.442	0	17-30	50	4.00	4.07

Felix Hernandez

Pitches: R Bats: R Pos: SP-33   Ht: 6'3" Wt: 230 Born: 4/8/1986 Age: 27

Year	Team	Lg	G	GS	CG	GF	IP	BFP	H	R	ER	HR	SH	SF	HB	TBB	IBB	SO	WP	Bk	W	L	Pct	Sh	Sv-Op	Hld	ERC	ERA
2005	Sea	AL	12	12	0	0	84.1	328	61	26	25	5	1	2	2	23	0	77	3	0	4	4	.500	0	0-0	0	2.08	2.67
2006	Sea	AL	31	31	2	0	191.0	816	195	105	96	23	2	3	6	60	2	176	11	0	12	14	.462	1	0-0	0	4.11	4.52
2007	Sea	AL	30	30	1	0	190.1	808	209	88	83	20	6	1	3	53	4	165	7	1	14	7	.667	0	0-0	0	4.27	3.92
2008	Sea	AL	31	31	2	0	200.2	857	198	85	77	17	4	6	8	80	7	175	8	1	9	11	.450	0	0-0	0	4.05	3.45
2009	Sea	AL	34	34	2	0	238.2	977	200	81	66	15	6	11	8	71	0	217	17	1	19	5	.792	1	0-0	0	2.72	2.49
2010	Sea	AL	34	34	6	0	249.2	1001	194	80	63	17	6	3	8	70	1	232	14	1	13	12	.520	1	0-0	0	2.39	2.27
2011	Sea	AL	33	33	5	0	233.2	964	218	99	90	19	3	7	7	67	0	222	12	1	14	14	.500	1	0-0	0	3.31	3.47
2012	Sea	AL	33	33	5	0	232.0	939	209	84	79	14	2	2	12	56	0	223	13	2	13	9	.591	5	0-0	0	2.94	3.06
	8 ML YEARS		238	238	23	0	1620.1	6690	1484	648	579	130	30	35	54	480	14	1487	85	7	98	76	.563	9	0-0	0	3.24	3.22

Gorkys Hernandez

Bats: R **Throws:** R **Pos:** CF-37; PH-15; LF-14; RF-6; PR-4   GORE-keys   **Ht:** 6'0" **Wt:** 190 **Born:** 9/7/1987 **Age:** 25

Year	Team	Lg	G	AB	H	2B	3B	HR	(Hm	Rd)	TB	R	RBI	RC	TBB	IBB	SO	HBP	SH	SF	SB	CS	SB%	GDP	Avg	OBP	Slg
2006	Tigers	R	50	205	67	9	2	5	(-	-)	95	41	23	36	10	1	27	0	1	1	20	4	.83	1	.327	.356	.463
2007	WMich	A	124	481	141	25	5	4	(-	-)	188	84	50	74	36	1	69	5	4	7	54	11	.83	2	.293	.344	.391
2008	MrtlBh	A+	100	406	107	23	6	5	(-	-)	157	75	42	103	48	1	79	6	4	3	20	4	.83	10	.264	.348	.387
2009	Missi	AA	52	212	66	11	2	0	(-	-)	81	33	19	28	15	0	54	0	1	0	10	8	.56	5	.311	.357	.382
2009	Altna	AA	86	344	90	14	2	3	(-	-)	117	45	31	37	24	0	76	2	2	2	10	8	.56	7	.262	.312	.340
2010	Altna	AA	92	368	98	11	4	2	(-	-)	123	45	26	46	33	0	95	5	6	2	17	3	.85	10	.266	.333	.334
2011	Indy	AAA	126	424	120	25	9	1	(-	-)	166	48	40	61	35	0	91	8	7	1	21	9	.70	5	.283	.348	.392
2012	Indy	AAA	67	237	61	11	2	2	(-	-)	82	43	25	32	34	0	64	2	6	2	13	7	.65	0	.257	.353	.346
2012	2 Tms	NL	70	156	30	2	3	3	(2	1)	47	18	13	15	13	0	42	3	1	0	7	2	.78	2	.192	.267	.301
12	Pit	NL	25	24	2	0	0	0	(0	0)	2	2	2	0	1	0	5	1	0	0	2	0	1.00	1	.083	.154	.083
12	Mia	NL	45	132	28	2	3	3	(2	1)	45	16	11	15	12	0	37	2	1	0	5	2	.71	1	.212	.288	.341

Livan Hernandez

Pitches: R **Bats:** R **Pos:** RP-44   lee-VAHN   **Ht:** 6'2" **Wt:** 245 **Born:** 2/20/1975 **Age:** 38

Year	Team	Lg	G	GS	CG	GF	IP	BFP	H	R	ER	HR	SH	SF	HB	TBB	IBB	SO	WP	Bk	W	L	Pct	Sh	Sv-Op	Hld	ERC	ERA
1996	Fla	NL	1	0	0	0	3.0	13	3	0	0	0	0	0	0	2	0	2	0	0	0	0	-	0	0-0	0	4.60	0.00
1997	Fla	NL	17	17	0	0	96.1	405	81	39	34	5	4	7	3	38	1	72	0	0	9	3	.750	0	0-0	0	2.96	3.18
1998	Fla	NL	33	33	9	0	234.1	1040	265	133	123	37	8	5	6	104	8	162	4	3	10	12	.455	0	0-0	0	5.58	4.72
1999	2 Tms	NL	30	30	2	0	199.2	886	227	110	103	23	7	6	2	76	5	144	2	2	8	12	.400	0	0-0	0	4.88	4.64
2000	SF	NL	33	33	5	0	240.0	1030	254	114	100	22	12	9	4	73	3	165	3	0	17	11	.607	2	0-0	0	4.01	3.75
2001	SF	NL	34	34	2	0	226.2	1008	266	143	132	24	12	12	3	85	7	138	7	0	13	15	.464	0	0-0	0	5.03	5.24
2002	SF	NL	33	33	5	0	216.0	921	233	113	105	19	14	8	4	71	5	134	1	1	12	16	.429	3	0-0	0	4.26	4.38
2003	Mon	NL	33	33	8	0	233.1	967	225	92	83	27	6	4	10	57	3	178	6	1	15	10	.600	0	0-0	0	3.55	3.20
2004	Mon	NL	35	35	9	0	255.0	1053	234	105	102	26	11	4	10	83	9	186	1	0	11	15	.423	2	0-0	0	3.52	3.60
2005	Was	NL	35	35	2	0	246.1	1065	268	116	109	25	15	9	13	84	14	147	3	2	15	10	.600	0	0-0	0	4.54	3.98
2006	2 Tms	NL	34	34	0	0	216.0	959	246	125	116	29	16	8	4	78	6	128	1	0	13	13	.500	0	0-0	0	4.97	4.83
2007	Ari	NL	33	33	1	0	204.1	913	247	116	112	34	17	8	6	79	1	90	3	2	11	11	.500	0	0-0	0	5.94	4.93
2008	2 Tms		31	31	2	0	180.0	811	257	129	121	25	5	9	2	43	4	67	3	1	13	11	.542	0	0-0	0	6.35	6.05
2009	2 Tms		31	31	2	0	183.2	806	220	112	111	19	13	10	1	67	5	102	1	0	9	12	.429	0	0-0	0	5.17	5.44
2010	Was	NL	33	33	2	0	211.2	896	216	93	86	16	17	10	4	64	5	114	1	1	10	12	.455	1	0-0	0	3.69	3.66
2011	Was	NL	29	29	1	0	175.1	751	199	98	87	16	10	6	5	46	6	99	3	0	8	13	.381	1	0-0	0	4.34	4.47
2012	2 Tms	NL	44	0	0	17	67.1	292	84	48	48	15	7	3	1	16	4	48	2	0	4	1	.800	0	1-2	5	5.81	6.42
99	Fla	NL	20	20	2	0	136.0	612	161	78	72	17	3	4	2	55	3	97	2	1	5	9	.357	0	0-0	0	5.37	4.76
99	SF	NL	10	10	0	0	63.2	274	66	32	31	6	4	2	0	21	2	47	0	1	3	3	.500	0	0-0	0	3.88	4.38
06	Was	NL	24	24	0	0	146.2	661	176	94	87	22	10	7	2	52	4	89	0	0	9	8	.529	0	0-0	0	5.38	5.34
06	Ari	NL	10	10	0	0	69.1	298	70	31	29	7	6	1	2	26	2	39	1	0	4	5	.444	0	0-0	0	4.13	3.76
08	Min	AL	23	23	2	0	139.2	627	199	93	85	18	4	9	1	29	3	54	2	1	10	8	.556	0	0-0	0	6.06	5.48
08	Col	NL	8	8	0	0	40.1	184	58	36	36	7	1	0	1	14	1	13	1	0	3	3	.500	0	0-0	0	7.38	8.03
09	NYM	NL	23	23	1	0	135.0	593	164	83	82	16	8	8	1	51	3	75	1	0	7	8	.467	0	0-0	0	5.50	5.47
09	Was	NL	8	8	1	0	48.2	213	56	29	29	3	5	2	0	16	2	27	0	0	2	4	.333	0	0-0	0	4.30	5.36
12	Atl	NL	18	0	0	8	31.0	136	40	17	17	5	5	2	0	8	4	19	0	0	1	1	.500	0	1-1	3	5.50	4.94
12	Mil	NL	26	0	0	9	36.1	156	44	31	31	10	2	1	1	8	0	29	2	0	3	0	1.000	0	0-1	2	6.06	7.68
	Postseason		12	10	1	0	68.0	305	67	32	30	6	5	2	4	36	3	47	1	0	7	3	.700	0	0-0	0	4.56	3.97
	17 ML YEARS		519	474	50	17	3189.0	13816	3525	1686	1572	362	174	118	78	1066	86	1976	41	13	178	177	.501	9	1-2	2	4.60	4.44

Luis Hernandez

Bats: B **Throws:** R **Pos:** 3B-1; SS-1   **Ht:** 5'10" **Wt:** 190 **Born:** 6/26/1984 **Age:** 29

Year	Team	Lg	G	AB	H	2B	3B	HR	(Hm	Rd)	TB	R	RBI	RC	TBB	IBB	SO	HBP	SH	SF	SB	CS	SB%	GDP	Avg	OBP	Slg
2012	RdRck*	AAA	129	519	136	23	6	8	(-	-)	195	64	70	63	30	2	80	5	8	10	9	3	.75	15	.262	.303	.376
2007	Bal	AL	30	69	20	2	0	1	(1	0)	25	5	7	6	1	0	10	0	1	0	2	2	.50	1	.290	.300	.362
2008	Bal	AL	36	79	19	1	0	0	(0	0)	20	9	3	6	7	0	11	0	3	2	2	0	1.00	2	.241	.295	.253
2009	KC	AL	37	73	15	1	0	0	(0	0)	16	4	4	4	4	0	18	1	3	0	1	0	1.00	1	.205	.256	.219
2010	NYM	NL	17	44	11	1	0	2	(1	1)	18	4	6	6	2	0	7	1	0	0	1	0	1.00	1	.250	.298	.409
2012	Tex	AL	2	2	0	0	0	0	(0	0)	0	0	0	0	0	0	0	0	0	0	0	0	-	0	.000	.000	.000
	5 ML YEARS		122	267	65	5	0	3	(2	1)	79	22	20	22	14	0	46	2	7	2	6	2	.75	6	.243	.284	.296

Pedro Hernandez

Pitches: L **Bats:** L **Pos:** SP-1   **Ht:** 5'10" **Wt:** 200 **Born:** 4/12/1989 **Age:** 24

Year	Team	Lg	G	GS	CG	GF	IP	BFP	H	R	ER	HR	SH	SF	HB	TBB	IBB	SO	WP	Bk	W	L	Pct	Sh	Sv-Op	Hld	ERC	ERA
2009	Eugene	A-	6	4	0	0	16.1	85	31	21	18	4	1	1	2	4	0	15	3	2	0	2	.000	0	0--	-	10.89	9.92
2009	Padres	R	7	5	0	0	33.1	134	33	15	14	2	0	2	1	4	0	31	1	2	4	0	1.000	0	0--	-	2.85	3.78
2010	FtWyn	A	29	13	0	3	100.1	445	122	62	45	6	2	5	7	17	0	79	2	1	4	3	.571	0	0--	-	4.28	4.04
2011	Lk Els	A+	15	6	0	2	56.2	226	52	19	17	3	1	1	0	6	2	44	0	0	5	0	1.000	0	0--	-	2.20	2.70
2011	Tucsn	AAA	4	4	0	0	18.0	85	28	17	12	3	1	1	0	6	0	7	0	0	2	1	.667	0	0--	-	7.83	6.00
2011	SnAnt	AA	9	8	0	0	41.1	171	39	17	16	4	1	1	0	10	0	43	0	0	3	2	.600	0	0--	-	3.12	3.48
2012	Brham	AA	12	12	0	0	68.2	284	68	21	21	6	2	2	0	18	0	37	0	1	7	2	.778	0	0--	-	3.44	2.75
2012	Charltt	AAA	3	2	0	1	17.0	71	18	8	7	1	2	2	0	3	0	17	0	0	1	0	1.000	0	0--	-	3.23	3.71
2012	Roch	AAA	4	4	0	0	17.1	75	25	10	10	1	0	1	0	1	0	11	1	0	0	2	.000	0	0--	-	5.01	5.19
2012	CWS	AL	1	1	0	0	4.0	25	12	8	8	3	0	0	0	4	0	2	0	0	0	1	.000	0	0-0	0	24.35	18.00

Ramon Hernandez

Bats: R **Throws:** R **Pos:** C-46; PH-6; 1B-2   **Ht:** 6'0" **Wt:** 220 **Born:** 5/20/1976 **Age:** 37

Year	Team	Lg	G	AB	H	2B	3B	HR	(Hm	Rd)	TB	R	RBI	RC	TBB	IBB	SO	HBP	SH	SF	SB	CS	SB%	GDP	Avg	OBP	Slg
2012	ColSpr*	AAA	4	12	2	0	0	1	(-	-)	5	2	4	1	1	0	1	1	0	0	0	0	-	1	.167	.286	.417
1999	Oak	AL	40	136	38	7	0	3	(1	2)	54	13	21	20	18	0	11	1	1	2	1	0	1.00	5	.279	.363	.397
2000	Oak	AL	143	419	101	19	0	14	(7	7)	162	52	62	49	38	1	64	7	10	5	1	0	1.00	14	.241	.311	.387
2001	Oak	AL	136	453	115	25	0	15	(5	10)	185	55	60	58	37	3	68	6	9	4	1	1	.50	10	.254	.316	.408
2002	Oak	AL	136	403	94	20	0	7	(3	4)	135	51	42	41	43	1	64	5	3	3	0	0	-	11	.233	.313	.335
2003	Oak	AL	140	483	132	24	1	21	(9	12)	221	70	78	66	33	2	79	12	2	6	0	0	-	14	.273	.331	.458
2004	SD	NL	111	384	106	23	0	18	(10	8)	183	45	63	50	35	0	45	5	4	4	1	0	1.00	16	.276	.341	.477
2005	SD	NL	99	369	107	19	2	12	(5	7)	166	36	58	44	18	0	40	1	1	3	1	0	1.00	14	.290	.322	.450
2006	Bal	AL	144	501	138	29	2	23	(17	6)	240	66	91	82	43	2	79	11	0	5	1	0	1.00	13	.275	.343	.479
2007	Bal	AL	106	364	94	18	0	9	(4	5)	139	40	62	56	36	1	59	6	0	3	1	3	.25	9	.258	.333	.382
2008	Bal	AL	133	463	119	22	1	15	(10	5)	188	49	65	59	32	3	62	5	1	6	0	0	-	9	.257	.308	.406
2009	Cin	NL	81	287	74	13	1	5	(2	3)	104	25	37	42	33	2	34	3	4	4	1	0	1.00	7	.258	.336	.362
2010	Cin	NL	97	313	93	18	1	7	(3	4)	134	30	48	49	29	1	49	5	3	2	0	0	-	8	.297	.364	.428
2011	Cin	NL	91	298	84	13	0	12	(6	6)	133	28	36	36	23	6	41	5	0	2	0	0	-	11	.282	.341	.446
2012	Col	NL	52	184	40	10	0	5	(4	1)	65	16	28	16	6	1	32	2	2	2	0	1	.00	4	.217	.247	.353
	Postseason		25	76	16	3	0	1	(1	0)	22	6	6	7	5	0	13	3	2	0	0	0	-	2	.211	.286	.289
	14 ML YEARS		1509	5057	1335	260	8	166	(86	80)	2109	576	751	671	424	23	727	74	40	51	8	5	.62	145	.264	.327	.417

Roberto Hernandez

Pitches: R **Bats:** R **Pos:** SP-3   **Ht:** 6'4" **Wt:** 230 **Born:** 8/30/1980 **Age:** 32

Year	Team	Lg	G	GS	CG	GF	IP	BFP	H	R	ER	HR	SH	SF	HB	TBB	IBB	SO	WP	Bk	W	L	Pct	Sh	Sv-Op	Hld	ERC	ERA
2012	Lk Cty*	A	2	2	0	0	12.1	49	12	7	5	5	0	0	0	1	0	13	0	0	1	1	.500	0	0- -	-	4.51	3.65
2012	Clmbs*	AAA	2	2	0	0	12.0	51	13	6	6	0	0	0	0	3	0	7	1	0	1	0	1.000	0	0- -	-	3.25	4.50
2006	Cle	AL	38	7	0	12	74.2	340	88	46	45	9	2	4	7	31	3	58	3	1	1	10	.091	0	0-3	10	5.69	5.42
2007	Cle	AL	32	32	2	0	215.0	879	199	78	73	16	2	4	11	61	2	137	5	1	19	8	.704	1	0-0	0	3.32	3.06
2008	Cle	AL	22	22	1	0	120.2	549	126	80	73	7	1	4	9	70	0	58	8	1	8	7	.533	1	0-0	0	5.07	5.44
2009	Cle	AL	24	24	0	0	125.1	596	151	97	88	16	4	2	8	70	0	79	5	1	5	12	.294	0	0-0	0	6.38	6.32
2010	Cle	AL	33	33	4	0	210.1	880	203	98	88	17	0	9	9	72	0	124	3	0	13	14	.481	1	0-0	0	3.77	3.77
2011	Cle	AL	32	32	0	0	188.2	833	205	125	110	22	9	7	14	60	3	109	3	1	7	15	.318	0	0-0	0	4.59	5.25
2012	Cle	AL	3	3	0	0	14.1	62	17	15	12	4	0	2	1	3	0	2	1	0	0	3	.000	0	0-0	0	6.03	7.53
	Postseason		3	3	0	0	15.0	66	13	12	12	2	0	0	0	11	0	12	0	0	0	1	.000	0	0-0	0	5.02	7.20
	7 ML YEARS		184	153	7	12	949.0	4139	989	539	489	91	20	33	59	367	8	567	28	5	53	69	.434	3	0-3	10	4.50	4.64

David Herndon

Pitches: R **Bats:** R **Pos:** RP-5   **Ht:** 6'5" **Wt:** 230 **Born:** 9/4/1985 **Age:** 27

Year	Team	Lg	G	GS	CG	GF	IP	BFP	H	R	ER	HR	SH	SF	HB	TBB	IBB	SO	WP	Bk	W	L	Pct	Sh	Sv-Op	Hld	ERC	ERA
2010	Phi	NL	47	0	0	14	52.1	232	67	27	25	2	2	2	2	17	4	29	1	0	1	3	.250	0	0-1	5	5.06	4.30
2011	Phi	NL	45	0	0	22	57.0	243	54	26	21	9	7	1	2	24	7	39	3	0	1	4	.200	0	1-2	4	4.27	3.32
2012	Phi	NL	5	0	0	2	7.2	33	10	4	4	1	2	0	0	1	0	8	0	0	0	1	.000	0	0-0	0	4.99	4.70
	3 ML YEARS		97	0	0	38	117.0	508	131	57	50	12	11	3	4	42	11	76	4	0	2	8	.200	0	1-3	5	4.67	3.85

Elian Herrera

EH-lee-ahn

Bats: B **Throws:** R **Pos:** LF-22; 3B-20; PH-14; 2B-13; CF-9; RF-7; SS-2; PR-2   **Ht:** 5'10" **Wt:** 188 **Born:** 2/1/1985 **Age:** 28

Year	Team	Lg	G	AB	H	2B	3B	HR	(Hm	Rd)	TB	R	RBI	RC	TBB	IBB	SO	HBP	SH	SF	SB	CS	SB%	GDP	Avg	OBP	Slg
2006	Ddgrs	R	36	110	36	4	0	1	(-	-)	43	19	17	20	19	0	17	1	5	2	2	3	.40	1	.327	.424	.391
2007	InldEm	A+	11	30	6	2	0	0	(-	-)	8	3	4	1	2	0	12	0	2	1	1	2	.33	0	.200	.242	.267
2007	Gt Lks	A	9	36	6	2	0	0	(-	-)	8	3	3	2	1	0	10	3	0	0	3	1	.75	0	.167	.250	.222
2007	Ogden	R+	50	181	51	10	3	1	(-	-)	70	28	27	28	25	0	39	4	1	1	3	3	.50	0	.282	.379	.387
2008	Ogden	R+	33	124	37	12	1	5	(-	-)	66	28	27	26	16	0	32	2	1	1	5	0	1.00	0	.298	.385	.532
2009	Gt Lks	A	4	6	1	0	0	0	(-	-)	1	0	0	0	0	0	3	0	0	0	0	0	-	0	.167	.167	.167
2009	Gt Lks	A	13	40	10	0	0	0	(-	-)	10	6	2	2	1	0	9	0	0	1	1	2	.33	1	.250	.262	.250
2009	InldEm	A+	99	389	113	18	5	4	(-	-)	153	64	35	62	35	0	95	3	2	2	42	5	.89	6	.290	.352	.393
2010	Chatt	AA	97	299	77	11	4	2	(-	-)	102	44	38	44	47	1	71	4	12	3	31	10	.76	6	.258	.363	.341
2010	Albq	AAA	25	48	11	0	1	0	(-	-)	13	8	8	5	10	0	9	0	0	0	1	1	.50	2	.229	.356	.271
2011	Chatt	AA	116	378	105	17	6	3	(-	-)	143	69	35	60	58	0	103	1	6	6	32	11	.74	7	.278	.370	.378
2012	Albq	AAA	64	273	93	20	10	3	(-	-)	142	50	40	52	17	2	47	2	3	2	11	7	.61	3	.341	.381	.520
2012	LAD	NL	67	187	47	10	1	1	(0	1)	62	26	17	20	23	0	50	2	2	0	4	2	.67	5	.251	.340	.332

Jonathan Herrera

Bats: B **Throws:** R **Pos:** SS-42; 2B-19; PH-17; 3B-13; PR-1   **Ht:** 5'9" **Wt:** 180 **Born:** 11/3/1984 **Age:** 28

Year	Team	Lg	G	AB	H	2B	3B	HR	(Hm	Rd)	TB	R	RBI	RC	TBB	IBB	SO	HBP	SH	SF	SB	CS	SB%	GDP	Avg	OBP	Slg
2012	Tulsa*	AA	5	17	3	0	0	1	(-	-)	6	2	1	1	0	0	0	0	2	0	0	0	-	1	.176	.176	.353
2012	ColSpr*	AAA	4	12	2	1	0	0	(-	-)	3	1	1	0	0	0	1	0	0	0	0	0	-	0	.167	.167	.250
2008	Col	NL	28	61	14	1	1	0	(0	0)	17	5	3	6	4	0	10	0	1	0	1	1	.50	0	.230	.277	.279
2010	Col	NL	76	222	63	6	2	1	(0	1)	76	34	21	29	25	1	36	0	7	3	2	2	.50	2	.284	.352	.342
2011	Col	NL	104	281	68	5	1	3	(2	1)	84	28	14	24	28	0	40	1	10	0	4	4	.50	7	.242	.313	.299
2012	Col	NL	86	225	59	9	1	3	(3	0)	79	29	12	22	16	3	39	2	7	0	4	1	.80	5	.262	.317	.351
	4 ML YEARS		294	789	204	21	5	7	(5	2)	256	96	50	81	73	4	125	3	25	3	11	8	.58	14	.259	.323	.324

Kelvin Herrera

Pitches: R Bats: R Pos: RP-76   Ht: 5'9" Wt: 190 Born: 12/31/1989 Age: 23

Year	Team	Lg	G	GS	CG	GF	IP	BFP	H	R	ER	HR	SH	SF	HB	TBB	IBB	SO	WP	Bk	W	L	Pct	Sh	Sv-Op	Hld	ERC	ERA
2008	Burlgtn	R	11	8	0	0	50.2	198	48	17	8	0	1	0	3	5	0	45	2	1	2	2	.500	0	0- -	-	2.36	1.42
2008	Burlgtn	A	3	1	0	1	12.2	53	13	4	3	0	0	1	1	2	0	7	1	0	2	0	1.000	0	0- -	-	2.91	2.13
2009	Burlgtn	A	1	1	0	0	5.0	17	3	0	0	0	0	0	0	0	0	1	0	0	1	0	1.000	0	0- -	-	0.80	0.00
2010	Burlgtn	A	8	8	0	0	41.1	173	38	20	20	2	2	2	4	15	0	40	1	0	2	3	.400	0	0- -	-	3.60	4.35
2011	Wilmg	A+	8	0	0	6	14.2	53	8	1	1	1	0	0	0	2	0	12	0	0	2	1	.667	0	1- -	-	1.09	0.61
2011	NWArk	AA	23	0	0	17	36.0	138	22	9	7	4	3	3	1	6	2	40	0	1	4	0	1.000	0	7- -	-	1.46	1.75
2011	Omha	AAA	14	0	0	10	17.0	70	12	5	4	1	0	0	0	7	0	18	0	0	1	0	1.000	0	6- -	-	2.28	2.12
2011	KC	AL	2	0	0	0	2.0	9	2	3	3	1	1	0	1	0	0	0	0	0	0	0	.000	0	0-0	1	7.30	13.50
2012	KC	AL	76	0	0	10	84.1	344	79	24	22	4	5	0	2	21	6	77	3	1	4	3	.571	0	3-4	19	2.84	2.35
	2 ML YEARS		78	0	0	10	86.1	353	81	27	25	5	6	0	3	21	6	77	3	1	4	4	.500	0	3-4	20	2.94	2.61

Chris Herrmann

Bats: L Throws: R Pos: C-3; LF-2; DH-1; PH-1   HERR-men   Ht: 6'0" Wt: 198 Born: 11/24/1987 Age: 25

Year	Team	Lg	G	AB	H	2B	3B	HR	(Hm	Rd)	TB	R	RBI	RC	TBB	IBB	SO	HBP	SH	SF	SB	CS	SB%	GDP	Avg	OBP	Slg
2009	Elizab	R+	59	236	70	14	1	7	(-	-)	107	45	30	44	33	1	40	5	1	2	2	2	.50	4	.297	.391	.453
2010	FtMyrs	A+	107	356	78	17	3	2	(-	-)	107	34	30	36	41	0	74	7	2	2	3	2	.60	7	.219	.310	.301
2011	FtMyrs	A+	24	87	27	5	1	1	(-	-)	37	14	16	16	15	1	6	0	2	2	1	0	1.00	4	.310	.404	.425
2011	NwBrit	AA	97	337	87	14	5	7	(-	-)	132	53	46	56	64	3	68	2	3	0	9	3	.75	4	.258	.380	.392
2012	NwBrit	AA	127	490	135	25	1	10	(-	-)	192	91	61	72	58	2	89	1	1	6	2	1	.67	14	.276	.350	.392
2012	Min	AL	7	18	1	0	0	0	(0	0)	1	0	1	0	1	0	5	0	0	0	0	0	-	0	.056	.105	.056

Frank Herrmann

Pitches: R Bats: L Pos: RP-15   Ht: 6'4" Wt: 220 Born: 5/30/1984 Age: 29

Year	Team	Lg	G	GS	CG	GF	IP	BFP	H	R	ER	HR	SH	SF	HB	TBB	IBB	SO	WP	Bk	W	L	Pct	Sh	Sv-Op	Hld	ERC	ERA
2012	Clmbs*	AAA	42	0	0	18	52.2	226	58	31	28	8	1	3	1	15	1	58	4	0	2	2	.500	0	8- -	-	4.63	4.78
2010	Cle	AL	40	0	0	8	44.2	189	48	22	20	6	1	2	2	9	0	24	2	0	0	1	.000	0	1-2	7	4.12	4.03
2011	Cle	AL	40	0	0	17	56.1	253	71	35	32	7	2	0	0	16	1	34	1	0	4	0	1.000	0	0-0	0	5.20	5.11
2012	Cle	AL	15	0	0	7	19.1	71	12	5	5	1	0	0	0	4	0	14	0	0	0	0	-	0	0-0	0	1.42	2.33
	3 ML YEARS		95	0	0	32	120.1	513	131	62	57	14	3	2	2	29	1	72	3	0	4	1	.800	0	1-2	7	4.10	4.26

John Hester

Bats: R Throws: R Pos: C-38; PH-1; PR-1   Ht: 6'4" Wt: 230 Born: 9/14/1983 Age: 29

Year	Team	Lg	G	AB	H	2B	3B	HR	(Hm	Rd)	TB	R	RBI	RC	TBB	IBB	SO	HBP	SH	SF	SB	CS	SB%	GDP	Avg	OBP	Slg
2012	Norfolk*	AAA	10	34	9	4	0	1	(-	-)	16	7	1	5	3	0	8	1	0	0	0	0	-	1	.265	.342	.471
2012	Salt Lk*	AAA	26	92	20	4	2	3	(-	-)	37	13	13	10	9	0	32	0	2	2	0	1	.00	1	.217	.282	.402
2009	Ari	NL	15	28	7	2	0	1	(1	0)	12	4	4	5	2	0	7	0	0	0	0	0	-	0	.250	.300	.429
2010	Ari	NL	38	95	20	7	0	2	(1	1)	33	9	7	9	11	1	32	0	0	0	1	0	1.00	2	.211	.292	.347
2012	LAA	AL	39	85	18	1	0	3	(1	2)	28	14	4	4	8	0	25	1	1	0	0	0	-	1	.212	.287	.329
	3 ML YEARS		92	208	45	10	0	6	(3	3)	73	27	15	18	21	1	64	1	1	0	1	0	1.00	3	.216	.291	.351

Jason Heyward

Bats: L Throws: L Pos: RF-154; PH-3; CF-2   Ht: 6'5" Wt: 240 Born: 8/9/1989 Age: 23

Year	Team	Lg	G	AB	H	2B	3B	HR	(Hm	Rd)	TB	R	RBI	RC	TBB	IBB	SO	HBP	SH	SF	SB	CS	SB%	GDP	Avg	OBP	Slg
2010	Atl	NL	142	520	144	29	5	18	(9	9)	237	83	72	96	91	2	128	10	0	4	11	6	.65	13	.277	.393	.456
2011	Atl	NL	128	396	90	18	2	14	(5	9)	154	50	42	49	51	4	93	4	0	3	9	2	.82	7	.227	.319	.389
2012	Atl	NL	158	587	158	30	6	27	(9	18)	281	93	82	87	58	1	152	2	0	3	21	8	.72	5	.269	.335	.479
	Postseason		4	16	2	0	0	0	(0	0)	2	0	0	0	1	0	8	0	0	0	0	0	-	1	.125	.176	.125
	3 ML YEARS		428	1503	392	77	13	59	(23	36)	672	226	196	232	200	7	373	16	0	8	41	16	.72	25	.261	.352	.447

Brandon Hicks

Bats: R Throws: R Pos: SS-19; PH-3; 1B-1; 2B-1; PR-1   Ht: 6'2" Wt: 200 Born: 9/14/1985 Age: 27

Year	Team	Lg	G	AB	H	2B	3B	HR	(Hm	Rd)	TB	R	RBI	RC	TBB	IBB	SO	HBP	SH	SF	SB	CS	SB%	GDP	Avg	OBP	Slg
2012	Scrmto*	AAA	90	328	80	26	3	18	(-	-)	166	61	61	59	47	0	115	7	0	1	5	4	.56	14	.244	.350	.506
2010	Atl	NL	16	5	0	0	0	0	(0	0)	0	7	0	0	1	0	2	0	0	0	0	0	-	0	.000	.167	.000
2011	Atl	NL	17	21	1	0	0	0	(0	0)	1	1	1	0	1	0	9	0	0	0	0	0	-	0	.048	.091	.048
2012	Oak	AL	22	64	11	5	0	3	(2	1)	25	8	7	5	6	0	31	0	0	0	1	0	1.00	1	.172	.243	.391
	3 ML YEARS		55	90	12	5	0	3	(2	1)	26	16	8	5	8	0	42	0	0	0	1	0	1.00	1	.133	.204	.289

Aaron Hill

Bats: R Throws: R Pos: 2B-153; PH-3   Ht: 5'11" Wt: 205 Born: 3/21/1982 Age: 31

Year	Team	Lg	G	AB	H	2B	3B	HR	(Hm	Rd)	TB	R	RBI	RC	TBB	IBB	SO	HBP	SH	SF	SB	CS	SB%	GDP	Avg	OBP	Slg
2005	Tor	AL	105	361	99	25	3	3	(3	0)	139	49	40	50	34	0	41	5	3	4	2	1	.67	5	.274	.342	.385
2006	Tor	AL	155	546	159	28	3	6	(4	2)	211	70	50	68	42	5	66	9	4	5	3	2	.71	15	.291	.349	.386
2007	Tor	AL	160	608	177	47	2	17	(8	9)	279	87	78	88	41	1	102	0	3	5	4	3	.57	21	.291	.333	.459
2008	Tor	AL	55	205	54	14	0	2	(1	1)	74	19	20	24	16	0	31	3	4	1	4	2	.67	4	.263	.324	.361

Year	Team	Lg	G	AB	H	2B	3B	HR	(Hm	Rd)	TB	R	RBI	RC	TBB	IBB	SO	HBP	SH	SF	SB	CS	SB%	GDP	Avg	OBP	Slg
																				BATTING						**BASERUNNING**	**AVERAGES**
2009	Tor	AL	158	682	195	37	0	36	(21	15)	340	103	108	110	42	1	98	5	1	4	6	2	.75	17	.286	.330	.499
2010	Tor	AL	138	528	108	22	0	26	(15	11)	208	70	68	57	41	2	85	8	1	2	2	2	.50	8	.205	.271	.394
2011	2 Tms		137	520	128	27	3	8	(4	4)	185	61	61	61	35	1	72	7	2	7	21	7	.75	10	.246	.299	.356
2012	Ari	NL	156	609	184	44	6	26	(14	12)	318	93	85	101	52	7	86	4	1	2	14	5	.74	15	.302	.360	.522
11	Tor	AL	104	396	89	15	1	6	(3	3)	124	38	45	38	23	1	53	4	0	6	16	3	.84	8	.225	.270	.313
11	Ari	NL	33	124	39	12	2	2	(1	1)	61	23	16	23	12	0	19	3	2	1	5	4	.56	2	.315	.386	.492
	Postseason		5	18	5	0	0	1	(1	0)	8	3	1	2	5	0	3	0	0	0	0	0	-	1	.278	.435	.444
	8 ML YEARS		1064	4059	1104	244	17	124	(70	54)	1754	552	510	559	303	17	581	41	19	30	58	24	.71	95	.272	.327	.432

Koyie Hill

Bats: B **Throws:** R **Pos:** C-11
COY
Ht: 6'1" **Wt:** 210 **Born:** 3/9/1979 **Age:** 34

Year	Team	Lg	G	AB	H	2B	3B	HR	(Hm	Rd)	TB	R	RBI	RC	TBB	IBB	SO	HBP	SH	SF	SB	CS	SB%	GDP	Avg	OBP	Slg
																				BATTING						**BASERUNNING**	**AVERAGES**
2012	Pnscla*	AA	14	41	8	3	0	1	(-	-)	14	5	5	3	3	0	10	0	0	0	0	0	-	1	.195	.250	.341
2012	Syrcse*	AAA	31	104	17	1	0	2	(-	-)	24	14	9	5	9	2	26	0	2	1	1	0	1.00	1	.163	.226	.231
2012	RdRck*	AAA	15	55	13	1	0	1	(-	-)	17	4	3	5	4	0	16	1	0	0	0	0	-	2	.236	.300	.309
2003	LAD	NL	3	3	1	1	0	0	(0	0)	2	0	0	0	0	0	2	0	0	0	0	0	-	0	.333	.333	.667
2004	Ari	NL	13	36	9	1	0	1	(1	0)	13	3	6	5	2	1	6	0	0	0	1	0	1.00	1	.250	.289	.361
2005	Ari	NL	34	78	17	5	0	0	(0	0)	22	6	6	6	11	0	27	0	1	2	0	1	.00	4	.218	.308	.282
2007	ChC	NL	36	93	15	4	0	2	(1	1)	25	7	12	3	8	0	18	1	1	2	0	0	-	4	.161	.231	.269
2008	ChC	NL	10	21	2	1	0	0	(0	0)	3	0	1	0	0	0	12	0	1	0	0	0	-	0	.095	.095	.143
2009	ChC	NL	83	253	60	12	2	2	(1	1)	82	26	24	23	27	6	78	1	2	1	0	0	-	9	.237	.312	.324
2010	ChC	NL	77	215	46	13	1	1	(1	0)	64	18	17	17	12	3	61	0	3	1	1	0	1.00	5	.214	.254	.298
2011	ChC	NL	46	134	26	3	1	2	(1	1)	37	15	9	2	14	3	40	0	4	1	1	0	1.00	3	.194	.268	.276
2012	ChC	NL	11	39	7	1	0	0	(0	0)	8	3	1	1	0	0	7	0	0	0	0	0	-	0	.179	.179	.205
	9 ML YEARS		313	872	183	41	4	8	(5	3)	256	78	76	57	74	13	251	2	11	7	3	1	.75	22	.210	.271	.294

Rich Hill

Pitches: L **Bats:** L **Pos:** RP-25
Ht: 6'5" **Wt:** 220 **Born:** 3/11/1980 **Age:** 33

Year	Team	Lg	G	GS	CG	GF	IP	BFP	H	R	ER	HR	SH	SF	HB	TBB	IBB	SO	WP	Bk	W	L	Pct	Sh	Sv-Op	Hld	ERC	ERA
			HOW MUCH HE PITCHED						**WHAT HE GAVE UP**												**THE RESULTS**							
2012	Grnville*	A	2	2	0	0	2.0	8	2	1	1	0	0	0	0	0	0	5	0	0	0	0	-	0	0--	0	1.95	4.50
2012	Salem*	A+	3	3	0	0	4.0	15	1	0	0	0	0	0	1	1	0	8	0	0	0	0	-	0	0--	0	0.75	0.00
2012	Pwtckt*	AAA	8	0	0	1	8.0	29	3	1	1	1	0	0	0	2	0	10	0	0	1	0	1.000	0	0--	0	1.01	1.13
2012	RedSx*	R	2	1	0	0	1.1	6	0	2	2	0	0	0	1	2	0	3	0	0	0	1	.000	0	0--	0	1.96	13.50
2012	Portlnd*	AA	1	0	0	0	1.0	4	1	0	0	0	0	0	0	0	0	1	0	0	0	0	-	0	0--	0	1.95	0.00
2005	ChC	NL	10	4	0	1	23.2	115	25	24	24	3	1	0	1	17	1	21	0	0	0	2	.000	0	0-0	0	5.81	9.13
2006	ChC	NL	17	16	2	1	99.1	417	83	51	46	16	8	3	2	39	1	90	3	0	6	7	.462	1	0-0	0	3.59	4.17
2007	ChC	NL	32	32	0	0	195.0	812	170	89	85	27	9	4	12	63	3	183	1	1	11	8	.579	0	0-0	0	3.56	3.92
2008	ChC	NL	5	5	0	0	19.2	89	13	9	9	2	0	2	1	18	0	15	1	0	1	0	1.000	0	0-0	0	4.38	4.12
2009	Bal	AL	14	13	0	0	57.2	275	68	53	50	7	2	2	1	40	2	46	1	1	3	3	.500	0	0-0	0	6.55	7.80
2010	Bos	AL	6	0	0	0	4.0	18	5	0	0	0	0	0	0	1	0	3	0	0	0	0	1.000	0	0-0	1	4.05	0.00
2011	Bos	AL	9	0	0	3	8.0	30	3	0	0	0	0	0	1	3	0	12	1	0	0	0	-	0	0-0	3	1.10	0.00
2012	Bos	AL	25	0	0	3	19.2	83	17	4	4	0	0	0	0	11	1	21	0	0	1	0	1.000	0	0-0	6	3.24	1.83
	Postseason		1	1	0	0	3.0	18	6	3	3	1	0	0	1	2	0	3	0	0	0	1	.000	0	0-0	0	15.68	9.00
	8 ML YEARS		118	70	2	8	427.0	1839	384	230	218	55	20	11	18	192	8	391	7	2	23	20	.535	1	0-0	10	4.04	4.59

Shawn Hill

Pitches: R **Bats:** R **Pos:** RP-1
Ht: 6'2" **Wt:** 225 **Born:** 4/28/1981 **Age:** 32

Year	Team	Lg	G	GS	CG	GF	IP	BFP	H	R	ER	HR	SH	SF	HB	TBB	IBB	SO	WP	Bk	W	L	Pct	Sh	Sv-Op	Hld	ERC	ERA
			HOW MUCH HE PITCHED						**WHAT HE GAVE UP**												**THE RESULTS**							
2012	York*	IND	7	5	0	0	29.2	124	26	11	8	0	-	-	1	9	0	21	0	0	2	0	1.000	0	0--	0	2.49	2.43
2012	LsVgs*	AAA	15	15	0	0	89.2	400	115	49	45	10	0	2	7	22	0	52	2	0	9	2	.818	0	0--	0	5.55	4.52
2004	Mon	NL	3	3	0	0	9.0	51	17	16	16	1	0	2	1	7	0	10	0	0	1	2	.333	0	0-0	0	12.14	16.00
2006	Was	NL	6	6	0	0	36.2	163	43	20	19	2	2	1	3	12	2	16	1	0	1	3	.250	0	0-0	0	4.70	4.66
2007	Was	NL	16	16	0	0	97.1	399	86	42	37	9	2	1	5	25	2	65	2	0	4	5	.444	0	0-0	0	3.03	3.42
2008	Was	NL	12	12	0	0	63.1	296	88	47	41	5	3	3	1	23	2	39	2	1	1	5	.167	0	0-0	0	6.04	5.83
2009	SD	NL	3	3	0	0	12.0	56	15	7	7	1	2	1	1	3	0	7	0	0	1	1	.500	0	0-0	0	4.90	5.25
2010	Tor	AL	4	4	0	0	20.2	91	24	8	6	1	0	1	1	4	0	14	1	0	1	2	.333	0	0-0	0	3.89	2.61
2012	Tor	AL	1	0	0	0	3.0	11	0	0	0	0	0	0	0	2	0	0	0	0	1	0	1.000	0	0-0	0	0.46	0.00
	7 ML YEARS		45	44	0	0	242.0	1067	273	140	126	19	9	9	12	76	6	151	6	1	10	18	.357	0	0-0	0	4.44	4.69

Steven Hill

Bats: R **Throws:** R **Pos:** PH-8; 1B-1
Ht: 5'11" **Wt:** 200 **Born:** 3/14/1985 **Age:** 28

Year	Team	Lg	G	AB	H	2B	3B	HR	(Hm	Rd)	TB	R	RBI	RC	TBB	IBB	SO	HBP	SH	SF	SB	CS	SB%	GDP	Avg	OBP	Slg
																				BATTING						**BASERUNNING**	**AVERAGES**
2007	Batvia	A-	10	39	17	5	1	1	(-	-)	27	4	11	12	5	0	5	1	0	0	0	0	-	0	.436	.511	.692
2007	QuadC	A	62	261	79	15	0	11	(-	-)	127	38	44	41	9	0	58	2	0	1	1	1	.50	4	.303	.330	.487
2008	PlmBh	A+	46	172	49	11	2	9	(-	-)	91	28	34	31	15	0	42	0	0	2	0	0	-	5	.285	.339	.529
2008	Sprgfld	AA	26	99	30	3	1	5	(-	-)	50	13	9	16	3	0	31	1	0	0	0	0	-	1	.303	.330	.505
2008	Cards	R	4	16	5	1	0	3	(-	-)	15	4	5	4	0	0	7	0	0	0	0	0	-	1	.313	.313	.938
2009	Sprgfld	AA	120	464	131	26	2	19	(-	-)	218	62	64	73	36	6	106	2	0	6	1	2	.33	11	.282	.333	.470
2010	Sprgfld	AA	93	361	101	27	1	22	(-	-)	196	60	86	69	38	3	90	4	0	3	1	0	1.00	6	.280	.352	.543
2010	Memp	AAA	9	34	6	1	0	2	(-	-)	13	2	6	3	3	0	10	1	0	0	0	0	-	3	.176	.263	.382
2011	Sprgfld	AA	31	131	37	5	0	11	(-	-)	75	22	26	25	10	1	35	0	0	3	1	0	1.00	1	.282	.326	.573
2011	Memp	AAA	6	17	5	0	0	3	(-	-)	14	3	6	4	2	0	5	0	0	0	0	0	-	2	.294	.368	.824

Year Team	Lg	G	AB	H	2B	3B	HR	(Hm	Rd)	TB	R	RBI	RC	TBB	IBB	SO	HBP	SH	SF	SB	CS	SB%	GDP	Avg	OBP	Slg
2012 Memp	AAA	87	301	80	16	0	17	(-	-)	147	52	52	48	25	1	74	3	0	2	0	1	.00	5	.266	.326	.488
2010 StL	NL	1	3	1	0	0	1	(1	0)	4	1	1	0	0	0	1	0	0	0	0	0	-	0	.333	.333	1.333
2012 StL	NL	9	10	2	1	0	0	(0	0)	3	1	0	0	0	0	3	0	0	0	0	0	-	0	.200	.200	.300
2 ML YEARS		10	13	3	1	0	1	(1	0)	7	2	1	0	0	0	4	0	0	0	0	0	-	0	.231	.231	.538

Alex Hinshaw

Pitches: L Bats: L Pos: RP-33   Ht: 6'2" Wt: 175 Born: 10/31/1982 Age: 30

Year Team	Lg	G	GS	CG	GF	IP	BFP	H	R	ER	HR	SH	SF	HB	TBB	IBB	SO	WP	Bk	W	L	Pct	Sh	Sv-Op Hld	ERC	ERA
2012 Tucsn*	AAA	14	0	0	2	19.1	82	14	8	8	0	1	1	2	10	0	18	1	0	0	0	-	0	0- - -	2.74	3.72
2008 SF	NL	48	0	0	12	39.2	179	31	16	15	5	4	2	3	29	4	47	5	0	2	1	.667	0	0-0 4	4.43	3.40
2009 SF	NL	9	0	0	3	6.0	33	10	8	8	2	0	0	0	7	0	2	1	0	0	0	-	0	0-0 0	14.88	12.00
2012 2 Tms	NL	33	0	0	7	28.1	135	27	19	19	8	1	0	2	21	2	36	1	0	1	1	.500	0	0-1 1	6.67	6.04
12 SD	NL	31	0	0	7	28.0	129	23	14	14	5	1	0	2	20	2	36	1	0	1	1	.500	0	0-1 1	4.95	4.50
12 ChC	NL	2	0	0	0	0.1	6	4	5	5	3	0	0	0	1	0	0	0	0	0	0	-	0	0-0 0	277.5	135.0
3 ML YEARS		90	0	0	22	74.0	347	68	43	42	15	5	2	5	57	6	85	7	0	3	2	.600	0	0-1 5	6.00	5.11

Eric Hinske

Bats: L Throws: R Pos: PH-65; 1B-15; LF-6; RF-4; DH-4   Ht: 6'2" Wt: 235 Born: 8/5/1977 Age: 35

Year Team	Lg	G	AB	H	2B	3B	HR	(Hm	Rd)	TB	R	RBI	RC	TBB	IBB	SO	HBP	SH	SF	SB	CS	SB%	GDP	Avg	OBP	Slg
2002 Tor	AL	151	566	158	38	2	24	(15	9)	272	99	84	103	77	5	138	2	0	5	13	1	.93	12	.279	.365	.481
2003 Tor	AL	124	449	109	45	3	12	(4	8)	196	74	63	66	59	1	104	1	0	5	12	2	.86	11	.243	.329	.437
2004 Tor	AL	155	570	140	23	3	15	(6	9)	214	66	69	60	54	2	109	4	0	6	12	8	.60	14	.246	.312	.375
2005 Tor	AL	147	477	125	31	4	15	(7	8)	205	79	68	71	46	4	121	8	0	6	8	4	.67	8	.262	.333	.430
2006 2 Tms	AL	109	277	75	17	2	13	(7	6)	135	43	34	39	35	2	79	0	0	0	2	2	.50	8	.271	.353	.487
2007 Bos	AL	84	186	38	12	3	6	(4	2)	74	25	21	22	28	2	54	3	0	1	3	0	1.00	7	.204	.317	.398
2008 TB	AL	133	381	94	21	1	20	(8	12)	177	59	60	53	47	4	88	3	0	1	10	3	.77	13	.247	.333	.465
2009 2 Tms	NL	93	190	46	12	0	8	(2	6)	82	31	25	27	27	1	52	5	0	2	1	0	1.00	2	.242	.348	.432
2010 Atl	NL	131	281	72	21	1	11	(7	4)	128	38	51	40	33	5	75	3	0	3	0	0	-	4	.256	.338	.456
2011 Atl	NL	117	236	55	10	0	10	(3	7)	95	24	28	26	26	1	71	1	0	1	0	1	.00	5	.233	.311	.403
2012 Atl	NL	91	132	26	7	1	2	(0	2)	41	9	13	9	14	2	41	0	0	1	0	0	-	5	.197	.272	.311
06 Tor	AL	78	197	52	9	2	12	(6	6)	101	35	29	29	27	2	49	0	0	0	1	1	.50	6	.264	.353	.513
06 Bos	AL	31	80	23	8	0	1	(1	0)	34	8	5	10	8	0	30	0	0	0	1	1	.50	2	.288	.352	.425
09 Pit	NL	54	106	27	9	0	1	(0	1)	39	18	11	16	17	0	27	3	0	0	0	0	-	0	.255	.373	.368
09 NYY	AL	39	84	19	3	0	7	(2	5)	43	13	14	11	10	1	25	2	0	2	1	0	1.00	2	.226	.316	.512
Postseason		10	7	2	0	0	2	(1	1)	8	4	3	2	2	0	4	0	0	0	0	0	-	0	.286	.444	1.143
11 ML YEARS		1335	3745	938	237	18	136	(63	73)	1619	547	516	516	446	29	932	30	0	31	61	21	.74	89	.250	.333	.432

Luke Hochevar

Pitches: R Bats: R Pos: SP-32   HOE-chay-vur   Ht: 6'5" Wt: 220 Born: 9/15/1983 Age: 29

Year Team	Lg	G	GS	CG	GF	IP	BFP	H	R	ER	HR	SH	SF	HB	TBB	IBB	SO	WP	Bk	W	L	Pct	Sh	Sv-Op Hld	ERC	ERA
2007 KC	AL	4	1	0	1	12.2	54	11	4	3	1	1	0	3	4	0	5	1	0	0	1	.000	0	0-0 0	3.86	2.13
2008 KC	AL	22	22	0	0	129.0	566	143	84	79	12	1	2	5	47	1	72	7	0	6	12	.333	0	0-0 0	4.67	5.51
2009 KC	AL	25	25	0	0	143.0	631	167	109	104	23	2	0	8	46	0	106	9	0	7	13	.350	1	0-0 0	5.46	6.55
2010 KC	AL	18	17	1	0	103.0	450	110	61	55	9	2	2	4	37	1	76	2	1	6	6	.500	0	0-0 0	4.34	4.81
2011 KC	AL	31	31	0	0	198.0	835	192	110	103	23	2	2	7	62	4	128	7	2	11	11	.500	0	0-0 0	3.80	4.68
2012 KC	AL	32	32	0	0	185.1	800	202	127	118	27	4	3	13	61	3	144	8	0	8	16	.333	1	0-0 0	4.99	5.73
6 ML YEARS		132	128	5	1	771.0	3336	825	495	462	95	12	9	40	257	9	531	34	3	38	59	.392	2	0-0 0	4.60	5.39

L.J. Hoes

Bats: R Throws: R Pos: LF-1; PH-1; PR-1   HOSE   Ht: 6'0" Wt: 190 Born: 3/5/1990 Age: 23

Year Team	Lg	G	AB	H	2B	3B	HR	(Hm	Rd)	TB	R	RBI	RC	TBB	IBB	SO	HBP	SH	SF	SB	CS	SB%	GDP	Avg	OBP	Slg
2008 Orioles	R	48	159	49	4	3	1	(-	-)	62	36	18	30	30	0	22	0	1	1	10	0	1.00	8	.308	.416	.390
2009 Dlmrva	A	119	431	112	19	0	2	(-	-)	137	42	47	44	23	1	80	3	4	4	20	5	.80	10	.260	.299	.318
2010 Frdrck	A+	97	353	98	19	2	3	(-	-)	130	52	44	53	53	1	70	3	2	2	10	8	.56	17	.278	.375	.368
2010 Abrdn	A-	8	28	13	5	1	1	(-	-)	23	8	5	10	2	0	1	2	0	0	1	1	.50	1	.464	.531	.821
2010 Bowie	AA	3	9	2	0	0	0	(-	-)	2	1	1	0	0	0	1	0	0	0	0	0	-	1	.222	.222	.222
2011 Frdrck	A+	41	158	38	7	0	3	(-	-)	54	23	17	16	10	0	25	3	1	1	4	2	.67	7	.241	.297	.342
2011 Bowie	AA	95	344	105	17	1	6	(-	-)	142	47	54	57	43	0	56	0	3	3	16	7	.70	15	.305	.379	.413
2012 Bowie	AA	51	196	52	9	3	2	(-	-)	73	25	15	30	31	1	33	1	1	0	12	5	.71	9	.265	.368	.372
2012 Norfolk	AAA	82	317	95	14	4	3	(-	-)	126	54	38	49	34	0	43	4	1	1	8	7	.53	11	.300	.374	.397
2012 Bal	AL	2	1	0	0	0	0	(0	0)	0	0	0	0	0	0	0	0	0	0	0	0	-	0	.000	.000	.000

Bryan Holaday

Bats: R Throws: R Pos: C-6; PR-1   HAHL-ih-daye   Ht: 6'0" Wt: 205 Born: 11/19/1987 Age: 25

Year Team	Lg	G	AB	H	2B	3B	HR	(Hm	Rd)	TB	R	RBI	RC	TBB	IBB	SO	HBP	SH	SF	SB	CS	SB%	GDP	Avg	OBP	Slg
2010 Lkland	A+	44	159	35	8	0	3	(-	-)	52	14	12	19	21	2	43	7	1	0	0	0	-	2	.220	.337	.327
2011 Erie	AA	95	330	80	18	0	7	(-	-)	119	35	42	39	27	1	76	4	6	4	6	1	.86	7	.242	.304	.361
2012 Toledo	AAA	75	250	60	12	1	2	(-	-)	80	18	25	24	22	0	43	5	3	2	2	0	1.00	7	.240	.312	.320
2012 Det	AL	6	12	3	1	0	0	(0	0)	4	3	0	1	0	0	2	0	1	0	0	0	-	0	.250	.250	.333

Derek Holland

Pitches: L Bats: B Pos: SP-27; RP-2   Ht: 6'2" Wt: 195 Born: 10/9/1986 Age: 26

Year	Team	Lg	G	GS	CG	GF	IP	BFP	H	R	ER	HR	SH	SF	HB	TBB	IBB	SO	WP	Bk	W	L	Pct	Sh	Sv-Op Hld	ERC	ERA
2012	RdRck*	AAA	2	2	0	0	9.0	37	11	6	6	4	1	0	0	2	0	5	0	0	0	2	.000	0	0- - -	7.58	6.00
2009	Tex	AL	33	21	1	0	138.1	611	160	98	94	26	2	3	4	47	0	107	3	3	8	13	.381	1	0-1 2	5.52	6.12
2010	Tex	AL	14	10	0	2	57.1	253	55	30	26	6	0	2	4	24	0	54	0	1	3	4	.429	0	0-0 1	4.17	4.08
2011	Tex	AL	32	32	4	0	198.0	843	201	97	87	22	1	3	6	67	1	162	2	1	16	5	.762	4	0-0 0	4.15	3.95
2012	Tex	AL	29	27	0	1	175.1	730	162	100	91	32	5	4	3	52	0	145	1	0	12	7	.632	0	0-0 0	3.86	4.67
	Postseason		12	4	0	2	35.1	147	31	17	15	7	0	0	1	15	0	23	1	0	3	0	1.000	0	0-0 0	4.38	3.82
	4 ML YEARS		108	90	5	3	569.0	2437	578	325	298	86	8	12	17	190	1	468	6	5	39	29	.574	5	0-1 3	4.39	4.71

Greg Holland

Pitches: R Bats: R Pos: RP-67   Ht: 5'10" Wt: 195 Born: 11/20/1985 Age: 27

Year	Team	Lg	G	GS	CG	GF	IP	BFP	H	R	ER	HR	SH	SF	HB	TBB	IBB	SO	WP	Bk	W	L	Pct	Sh	Sv-Op Hld	ERC	ERA
2012	NWArk*	AA	2	2	0	0	2.0	7	1	1	0	0	0	0	0	0	0	3	1	0	0	1	.000	0	0- - -	0.54	0.00
2010	KC	AL	15	0	0	10	18.2	87	23	15	14	3	1	0	0	8	0	23	2	0	1	0	1.000	0	0-0 0	5.88	6.75
2011	KC	AL	46	0	0	15	60.0	233	37	13	12	3	1	1	1	19	3	74	7	0	5	1	.833	0	4-6 18	1.60	1.80
2012	KC	AL	67	0	0	36	67.0	289	58	22	22	2	4	3	0	34	7	91	3	1	7	4	.636	0	16-20 9	3.07	2.96
	3 ML YEARS		128	0	0	61	145.2	609	118	50	48	8	6	4	1	61	10	188	12	1	12	6	.667	0	20-26 27	2.74	2.97

Matt Holliday

Bats: R Throws: R Pos: LF-152; PH-3; DH-2   Ht: 6'4" Wt: 235 Born: 1/15/1980 Age: 33

Year	Team	Lg	G	AB	H	2B	3B	HR	(Hm	Rd)	TB	R	RBI	RC	TBB	IBB	SO	HBP	SH	SF	SB	CS	SB%	GDP	Avg	OBP	Slg
2004	Col	NL	121	400	116	31	3	14	(10	4)	195	65	57	61	31	0	86	6	1	1	3	3	.50	9	.290	.349	.488
2005	Col	NL	125	479	147	24	7	19	(12	7)	242	68	87	88	36	1	79	7	0	4	14	3	.82	11	.307	.361	.505
2006	Col	NL	155	602	196	45	5	34	(22	12)	353	119	114	112	47	3	110	15	0	3	10	5	.67	22	.326	.387	.586
2007	Col	NL	158	636	216	50	6	36	(25	11)	386	120	137	134	63	7	126	10	0	4	11	4	.73	23	.340	.405	.607
2008	Col	NL	139	539	173	38	2	25	(15	10)	290	107	88	104	74	6	104	8	0	2	28	2	.93	9	.321	.409	.538
2009	2 Tms		156	581	182	39	3	24	(16	8)	299	94	109	112	72	8	101	10	0	7	14	7	.67	13	.313	.394	.515
2010	StL	NL	158	596	186	45	1	28	(13	15)	317	95	103	107	69	10	93	8	0	2	9	5	.64	13	.312	.390	.532
2011	StL	NL	124	446	132	36	0	22	(12	10)	234	83	75	81	60	4	93	8	0	2	2	1	.67	21	.296	.388	.525
2012	StL	NL	157	599	177	36	2	27	(13	14)	298	95	102	99	75	3	132	9	0	5	4	4	.50	16	.295	.379	.497
09	Oak	AL	93	346	99	23	1	11	(7	4)	157	52	54	62	46	3	58	6	0	2	12	3	.80	8	.286	.378	.454
09	StL	NL	63	235	83	16	2	13	(9	4)	142	42	55	50	26	5	43	4	0	5	2	4	.33	5	.353	.419	.604
	Postseason		30	108	30	3	0	7	(4	3)	54	20	16	13	11	0	28	3	0	0	0	1	.00	4	.278	.361	.500
	9 ML YEARS		1293	4878	1525	344	29	229	(138	91)	2614	846	872	898	527	42	924	81	1	30	95	34	.74	137	.313	.387	.536

Brock Holt

Bats: L Throws: R Pos: 2B-14; PH-10   Ht: 5'10" Wt: 170 Born: 6/11/1988 Age: 25

Year	Team	Lg	G	AB	H	2B	3B	HR	(Hm	Rd)	TB	R	RBI	RC	TBB	IBB	SO	HBP	SH	SF	SB	CS	SB%	GDP	Avg	OBP	Slg
2009	StCol	A-	66	254	76	14	3	6	(-	-)	114	45	33	44	26	0	31	1	0	4	9	0	1.00	2	.299	.363	.449
2010	Bradtn	A+	47	194	68	12	1	1	(-	-)	85	31	27	35	19	3	30	2	1	2	6	6	.50	3	.351	.410	.438
2011	Altna	AA	132	511	147	30	9	1	(-	-)	198	62	40	75	50	1	85	7	6	5	18	10	.64	8	.288	.356	.387
2012	Altna	AA	102	382	123	24	6	2	(-	-)	165	52	43	65	40	0	51	4	3	3	11	11	.50	8	.322	.389	.432
2012	Indy	AAA	24	95	41	7	0	1	(-	-)	51	13	7	23	9	1	9	0	1	1	5	2	.71	2	.432	.476	.537
2012	Pit	NL	24	65	19	2	1	0	(0	0)	23	6	3	10	4	0	14	0	2	1	0	0	-	1	.292	.329	.354

J.J. Hoover

Pitches: R Bats: R Pos: RP-28   Ht: 6'3" Wt: 230 Born: 8/13/1987 Age: 25

Year	Team	Lg	G	GS	CG	GF	IP	BFP	H	R	ER	HR	SH	SF	HB	TBB	IBB	SO	WP	Bk	W	L	Pct	Sh	Sv-Op Hld	ERC	ERA
2008	Danvle	R	2	0	0	0	4.2	18	4	0	0	0	0	0	0	1	0	6	0	0	1	0	1.000	0	0- - -	2.13	0.00
2009	Rome	A	25	18	0	3	134.1	559	135	58	50	9	1	4	7	25	0	148	3	0	7	6	.538	0	1- - -	3.26	3.35
2009	MrtlBh	A+	1	1	0	0	3.0	17	3	3	3	1	0	0	0	5	1	2	1	0	0	0	-	0	0- - -	10.78	9.00
2010	MrtlBh	A+	24	24	0	0	132.2	564	126	56	48	7	3	5	6	35	1	118	6	0	11	6	.647	0	0- - -	3.06	3.26
2010	Missi	AA	4	4	0	0	20.2	90	15	8	8	1	1	0	0	15	1	34	0	0	3	1	.750	0	0- - -	3.36	3.48
2011	Missi	AA	31	12	0	5	87.0	352	65	30	24	5	3	1	4	28	0	86	4	1	2	5	.286	0	1- - -	2.37	2.48
2011	Gwnntt	AAA	12	2	0	3	18.2	82	12	8	7	0	0	0	0	12	0	31	0	0	1	1	.500	0	1- - -	2.28	3.38
2012	Lsvlle	AAA	30	0	0	21	37.0	138	15	9	5	1	0	1	1	12	0	55	3	0	4	0	1.000	0	13- - -	0.98	1.22
2012	Cin	NL	28	0	0	6	30.2	123	17	7	7	2	2	2	0	13	1	31	0	0	1	0	1.000	0	1-2 5	1.64	2.05

Jeremy Horst

Pitches: L Bats: L Pos: RP-32   Ht: 6'3" Wt: 217 Born: 10/1/1985 Age: 27

HOARST

Year	Team	Lg	G	GS	CG	GF	IP	BFP	H	R	ER	HR	SH	SF	HB	TBB	IBB	SO	WP	Bk	W	L	Pct	Sh	Sv-Op Hld	ERC	ERA
2007	Reds	R	2	0	0	0	2.0	12	3	4	1	0	0	0	0	2	0	4	1	0	0	0	-	0	0- - -	7.82	4.50
2007	Billings	R+	16	0	0	4	39.2	168	34	15	14	2	0	0	1	22	0	51	3	2	3	2	.600	0	2- - -	3.73	3.18
2008	Dayton	A	36	10	0	9	102.0	410	74	30	27	3	3	4	3	33	1	110	2	1	8	2	.800	0	4- - -	2.03	2.38
2009	Srsota	A+	23	23	1	0	133.0	569	136	61	48	15	4	7	9	41	0	101	2	1	6	13	.316	0	0- - -	4.23	3.25
2009	Carlina	AA	5	5	0	0	29.0	123	35	20	20	7	0	0	0	10	0	21	2	0	1	4	.200	0	0- - -	6.46	6.21
2010	Lynbrg	A+	11	0	0	4	14.2	67	17	8	7	1	1	1	1	4	1	17	1	0	0	2	.000	0	0- - -	4.21	4.30
2010	Carlina	AA	27	0	0	8	43.0	173	35	13	10	1	2	1	0	9	2	46	2	0	3	2	.600	0	0- - -	1.86	2.09

Year	Team	Lg	G	GS	CG	GF	IP	BFP	H	R	ER	HR	SH	SF	HB	TBB	IBB	SO	WP	Bk	W	L	Pct	Sh	Sv-Op	Hld	ERC	ERA
2010	Lsvlle	AAA	6	2	0	0	14.1	64	17	5	4	0	3	0	1	5	0	12	0	0	1	0	1.000	0	0--	-	4.48	2.51
2011	Lsvlle	AAA	36	0	0	9	51.1	210	41	18	16	2	4	3	2	14	0	42	1	0	1	4	.200	0	0--	-	2.28	2.81
2012	LV	AAA	26	0	0	12	38.1	173	43	11	9	3	1	0	2	18	1	32	0	0	2	1	.667	0	2--	-	5.08	2.11
2011	Cin	NL	12	0	0	4	15.1	69	18	6	5	2	0	1	0	6	1	9	0	1	0	0	-	0	0-0	0	5.11	2.93
2012	Phi	NL	32	0	0	9	31.1	125	21	8	4	1	1	0	1	14	1	40	1	0	2	0	1.000	0	0-0	6	2.23	1.15
2 ML YEARS			44	0	0	13	46.2	194	39	14	9	3	1	1	1	20	2	49	1	1	2	0	1.000	0	0-0	6	3.11	1.74

Eric Hosmer

Bats: L **Throws:** L **Pos:** 1B-148; RF-3; PH-1; PR-1   HOZZ-mer   **Ht:** 6'4" **Wt:** 230 **Born:** 10/24/1989 **Age:** 23

Year	Team	Lg	G	AB	H	2B	3B	HR	(Hm	Rd)	TB	R	RBI	RC	TBB	IBB	SO	HBP	SH	SF	SB	CS	SB%	GDP	Avg	OBP	Slg
2008	Idaho	R+	3	11	4	2	0	0	(-	-)	6	2	2	3	3	0	2	1	0	0	0	0	-	0	.364	.533	.545
2009	Burlgtn	A	79	280	71	17	2	5	(-	-)	107	31	49	41	44	3	68	0	0	3	3	2	.60	10	.254	.352	.382
2009	Wilmg	A+	27	97	20	2	2	1	(-	-)	29	9	10	8	9	0	22	1	0	0	0	0	-	1	.206	.280	.299
2010	Wilmg	A+	87	325	115	29	6	7	(-	-)	177	48	51	77	44	6	39	2	0	4	11	1	.92	12	.354	.429	.545
2010	NWArk	AA	50	195	61	14	3	13	(-	-)	120	39	35	42	15	2	27	1	0	0	3	1	.75	11	.313	.365	.615
2011	Omha	AAA	26	98	43	5	0	3	(-	-)	57	21	15	29	19	0	16	0	0	1	3	0	1.00	1	.439	.525	.582
2011	KC	AL	128	523	153	27	3	19	(3	16)	243	66	78	71	34	7	82	1	0	5	11	5	.69	13	.293	.334	.465
2012	KC	AL	152	535	124	22	2	14	(8	6)	192	65	60	61	56	4	95	2	0	5	16	1	.94	10	.232	.304	.359
2 ML YEARS			280	1058	277	49	5	33	(11	22)	435	131	138	132	90	11	177	3	0	10	27	6	.82	23	.262	.319	.411

Tommy Hottovy

Pitches: L **Bats:** L **Pos:** RP-9   HAWT-uh-vee   **Ht:** 6'1" **Wt:** 195 **Born:** 7/9/1981 **Age:** 31

Year	Team	Lg	G	GS	CG	GF	IP	BFP	H	R	ER	HR	SH	SF	HB	TBB	IBB	SO	WP	Bk	W	L	Pct	Sh	Sv-Op	Hld	ERC	ERA
2004	Lowell	A-	14	14	0	0	30.1	121	24	5	3	0	0	0	3	4	0	39	2	0	0	1	.000	0	0--	-	1.78	0.89
2005	Wilmg	A+	25	23	0	0	104.0	467	116	74	63	18	6	5	7	37	2	82	8	0	3	12	.200	0	0--	-	5.28	5.45
2006	Wilmg	A+	21	21	2	0	122.0	506	109	49	38	3	2	5	5	35	0	91	6	0	8	6	.571	0	0--	-	2.73	2.80
2006	Portlnd	AA	7	7	0	0	41.0	166	28	20	19	1	0	1	3	15	2	31	2	0	2	4	.333	0	0--	-	2.04	4.17
2007	Portlnd	AA	24	23	0	0	120.1	540	144	78	75	17	6	9	3	49	0	69	6	1	4	10	.286	0	0--	-	5.72	5.61
2008	Portlnd	AA	2	2	0	0	9.0	39	9	7	5	2	0	0	1	2	0	4	0	0	1	0	1.000	0	0--	-	4.55	5.00
2009	Lowell	A-	5	0	0	0	8.0	31	4	2	2	1	1	0	0	3	0	12	0	0	1	0	1.000	0	0--	-	1.64	2.25
2009	Portlnd	AA	16	0	0	5	26.0	115	26	12	10	2	2	2	2	10	0	29	3	0	0	2	.000	0	0--	-	4.09	3.46
2010	Portlnd	AA	15	0	0	6	39.2	182	49	25	23	6	0	0	0	20	1	34	5	1	3	2	.600	0	0--	-	6.32	5.22
2010	Pwtckt	AAA	26	0	0	6	35.2	169	37	19	18	5	0	2	4	23	2	22	5	0	1	0	1.000	0	0--	-	5.89	4.54
2011	Portlnd	AA	8	0	0	2	18.2	70	12	4	4	0	1	0	0	4	0	18	0	0	0	0	-	0	1--	-	1.29	1.93
2011	Pwtckt	AAA	24	0	0	3	36.0	138	23	13	11	8	1	0	1	9	0	29	0	0	2	0	1.000	0	1--	-	2.48	2.75
2012	Omha	AAA	41	0	0	22	50.0	210	42	18	14	6	0	1	1	16	0	61	0	0	2	2	.500	0	7--	-	3.31	2.52
2011	Bos	AL	8	0	0	1	4.0	19	4	3	3	0	0	0	1	3	0	2	0	0	0	0	-	0	0-0	2	5.79	6.75
2012	KC	AL	9	0	0	4	9.1	42	11	3	3	2	0	0	1	5	0	6	0	0	0	0	-	0	0-0	1	7.45	2.89
2 ML YEARS			17	0	0	5	13.1	61	15	6	6	2	0	0	2	8	0	8	0	0	0	0	-	0	0-0	3	6.98	4.05

Ryan Howard

Bats: L **Throws:** L **Pos:** 1B-67; PH-5   **Ht:** 6'4" **Wt:** 242 **Born:** 11/19/1979 **Age:** 33

Year	Team	Lg	G	AB	H	2B	3B	HR	(Hm	Rd)	TB	R	RBI	RC	TBB	IBB	SO	HBP	SH	SF	SB	CS	SB%	GDP	Avg	OBP	Slg
2012	Lakwd*	A	3	8	5	1	0	0	(-	-)	6	2	4	3	3	0	2	0	0	1	0	0	-	-	.625	.667	.750
2012	LV*	AAA	4	12	5	1	0	1	(-	-)	9	1	6	3	2	0	1	0	0	0	0	0	-	1	.417	.500	.750
2004	Phi	NL	19	39	11	5	0	2	(1	1)	22	5	5	7	2	0	13	1	0	0	0	0	-	2	.282	.333	.564
2005	Phi	NL	88	312	90	17	2	22	(11	11)	177	52	63	50	33	8	100	1	0	2	0	1	.00	6	.288	.356	.567
2006	Phi	NL	159	581	182	25	1	58	(29	29)	383	104	149	138	108	37	181	9	0	6	0	0	-	7	.313	.425	.659
2007	Phi	NL	144	529	142	26	0	47	(23	24)	309	94	136	119	107	35	199	5	0	7	1	0	1.00	13	.268	.392	.584
2008	Phi	NL	162	610	153	26	4	48	(26	22)	331	105	146	117	81	17	199	3	0	6	1	1	.50	11	.251	.339	.543
2009	Phi	NL	160	616	172	37	4	45	(18	27)	352	105	141	117	75	8	186	6	0	6	8	1	.89	11	.279	.360	.571
2010	Phi	NL	143	550	152	23	5	31	(16	15)	278	87	108	94	59	11	157	8	0	3	1	1	.50	14	.276	.353	.505
2011	Phi	NL	152	557	141	30	1	33	(17	16)	272	81	116	91	75	16	172	7	0	5	1	0	1.00	10	.253	.346	.488
2012	Phi	NL	71	260	57	11	0	14	(10	4)	110	28	56	35	25	7	99	4	0	3	0	0	-	8	.219	.295	.423
Postseason			46	170	44	13	1	8	(6	2)	83	22	33	28	26	7	67	1	0	2	1	1	.50	1	.259	.357	.488
9 ML YEARS			1098	4054	1100	200	17	300	(151	149)	2234	661	920	768	565	139	1306	44	0	38	12	4	.75	82	.271	.364	.551

J.P. Howell

Pitches: L **Bats:** L **Pos:** RP-55   **Ht:** 6'0" **Wt:** 190 **Born:** 4/25/1983 **Age:** 30

Year	Team	Lg	G	GS	CG	GF	IP	BFP	H	R	ER	HR	SH	SF	HB	TBB	IBB	SO	WP	Bk	W	L	Pct	Sh	Sv-Op	Hld	ERC	ERA
2005	KC	AL	15	15	0	0	72.2	328	73	55	50	9	3	3	6	39	0	54	7	0	3	5	.375	0	0-0	0	5.18	6.19
2006	TB	AL	8	8	0	0	42.1	187	52	25	24	4	0	2	3	14	0	33	1	0	1	3	.250	0	0-0	0	5.51	5.10
2007	TB	AL	10	10	0	0	51.0	244	69	45	43	8	2	1	3	21	0	49	3	0	1	6	.143	0	0-0	0	6.84	7.59
2008	TB	AL	64	0	0	9	89.1	370	62	29	22	6	6	1	4	39	1	92	5	0	6	1	.857	0	3-5	14	2.51	2.22
2009	TB	AL	69	0	0	41	66.2	278	47	22	21	7	2	1	3	33	3	79	3	1	7	5	.583	0	17-25	4	2.99	2.84
2011	TB	AL	46	0	0	9	30.2	138	30	24	21	5	1	1	2	18	1	26	2	2	2	3	.400	0	1-2	10	5.43	6.16
2012	TB	AL	55	0	0	10	50.1	203	39	17	17	7	2	0	4	22	2	42	1	0	1	0	1.000	0	0-0	3	3.68	3.04
Postseason			13	0	0	1	12.0	51	10	4	4	0	0	1	2	4	1	17	1	0	0	3	.000	0	0-0	4	2.73	3.00
7 ML YEARS			267	33	0	65	403.0	1748	372	217	198	46	16	9	25	186	7	375	22	3	21	23	.477	0	21-32	31	4.22	4.42

Daniel Hudson

Pitches: R **Bats:** R **Pos:** SP-9   **Ht:** 6'3" **Wt:** 225 **Born:** 3/9/1987 **Age:** 26

			HOW MUCH HE PITCHED					WHAT HE GAVE UP												THE RESULTS							
Year	Team	Lg	G	GS	CG	GF	IP	BFP	H	R	ER	HR	SH	SF	HB	TBB	IBB	SO	WP	Bk	W	L	Pct	Sh	Sv-Op	Hld	ERC	ERA
2012	Reno*	AAA	1	1	0	0	5.0	20	5	2	2	0	1	0	0	1	0	2	1	0	1	0	1.000	0	0--	-	2.76	3.60
2009	CWS	AL	6	2	0	1	18.2	82	16	9	7	3	0	1	1	9	0	14	1	0	1	1	.500	0	0-0	0	4.15	3.38
2010	2 Tms		14	14	0	0	95.1	372	68	26	26	8	2	2	4	27	1	84	5	0	8	2	.800	0	0-0	0	2.26	2.45
2011	Ari	NL	33	33	3	0	222.0	921	217	98	86	17	6	6	8	50	1	169	4	1	16	12	.571	0	0-0	0	3.26	3.49
2012	Ari	NL	9	9	0	0	45.1	202	62	37	37	9	2	1	0	12	0	37	2	0	3	2	.600	0	0-0	0	6.56	7.35
10	CWS	AL	3	3	0	0	15.2	71	17	11	11	1	1	1	0	11	0	14	2	0	1	1	.500	0	0-0	0	5.69	6.32
10	Ari	NL	11	11	0	0	79.2	301	51	15	15	7	1	1	4	16	1	70	3	0	7	1	.875	0	0-0	0	1.70	1.69
	Postseason		1	1	0	0	5.1	24	9	5	5	1	0	0	0	0	0	6	0	0	1	0	1.000	0	0-0	0	7.35	8.44
	4 ML YEARS		62	58	3	1	381.1	1577	363	170	156	37	10	10	13	98	2	304	12	1	28	17	.622	0	0-0	0	3.39	3.68

Orlando Hudson

Bats: B **Throws:** R **Pos:** 2B-44; 3B-29; PH-10; DH-4; PR-4   **Ht:** 6'0" **Wt:** 190 **Born:** 12/12/1977 **Age:** 35

									BATTING													BASERUNNING				AVERAGES		
Year	Team	Lg	G	AB	H	2B	3B	HR	(Hm	Rd)	TB	R	RBI	RC	TBB	IBB	SO	HBP	SH	SF		SB	CS	SB%	GDP	Avg	OBP	Slg
2012	Charltt*	AAA	5	15	5	1	0	0	(-	-)	6	1	1	2	1	0	1	0	0	0		2	0	1.00	0	.333	.375	.400
2002	Tor	AL	54	192	53	10	5	4	(2	2)	85	20	23	30	11	0	27	2	0	2		0	1	.00	6	.276	.319	.443
2003	Tor	AL	142	474	127	21	6	9	(5	4)	187	54	57	64	39	1	87	5	0	3		5	4	.56	13	.268	.328	.395
2004	Tor	AL	135	489	132	32	7	12	(5	7)	214	73	58	71	51	0	98	4	3	4		7	3	.70	12	.270	.341	.438
2005	Tor	AL	131	461	125	25	5	10	(4	6)	190	62	63	59	30	1	65	3	0	7		7	1	.88	10	.271	.315	.412
2006	Ari	NL	157	579	166	34	9	15	(7	8)	263	87	67	89	61	5	78	2	4	4		9	6	.60	17	.287	.354	.454
2007	Ari	NL	139	517	152	28	9	10	(7	3)	228	69	63	82	70	1	87	2	5	7		10	2	.83	21	.294	.376	.441
2008	Ari	NL	107	407	124	29	3	8	(6	2)	183	54	41	66	40	2	62	2	3	3		4	1	.80	18	.305	.367	.450
2009	LAD	NL	149	551	156	35	6	9	(4	5)	230	74	62	78	62	4	99	4	9	5		8	1	.89	16	.283	.357	.417
2010	Min	AL	126	497	133	24	5	6	(3	3)	185	80	37	56	50	0	87	4	5	3		10	3	.77	14	.268	.338	.372
2011	SD	NL	119	398	98	15	3	7	(4	3)	140	54	43	52	49	6	84	2	1	4		19	3	.86	5	.246	.329	.352
2012	2 Tms		86	260	53	3	8	3	(3	0)	81	21	28	23	20	1	51	0	3	0		6	3	.67	6	.204	.261	.312
12	SD	NL	35	123	26	0	5	1	(1	0)	39	11	11	9	8	0	27	0	0	0		3	2	.60	3	.211	.260	.317
12	CWS	AL	51	137	27	3	3	2	(2	0)	42	10	17	14	12	1	24	0	3	0		3	1	.75	3	.197	.262	.307
	Postseason		11	16	5	0	0	2	(1	1)	11	3	3	2	0	0	3	0	1	0		0	0	-	2	.313	.313	.688
	11 ML YEARS		1345	4825	1319	256	66	93	(50	43)	1986	648	542	670	483	21	825	30	33	42		85	28	.75	138	.273	.341	.412

Tim Hudson

Pitches: R **Bats:** R **Pos:** SP-28   **Ht:** 6'1" **Wt:** 175 **Born:** 7/14/1975 **Age:** 37

							HOW MUCH HE PITCHED		WHAT HE GAVE UP												THE RESULTS							
Year	Team	Lg	G	GS	CG	GF	IP	BFP	H	R	ER	HR	SH	SF	HB	TBB	IBB	SO	WP	Bk	W	L	Pct	Sh	Sv-Op	Hld	ERC	ERA
2012	Rome*	A	2	2	0	0	7.0	33	13	7	6	0	0	1	2	1	0	1	1	0	0	2	.000	0	0--	-	8.58	7.71
2012	Gwnntt*	AAA	2	2	0	0	10.2	47	8	2	1	0	0	0	0	5	0	8	0	0	2	0	1.000	0	0--	-	2.18	0.84
1999	Oak	AL	21	21	1	0	136.1	580	121	56	49	8	1	2	4	62	2	132	6	0	11	2	.846	0	0-0	0	3.50	3.23
2000	Oak	AL	32	32	2	0	202.1	847	169	100	93	24	5	7	7	82	5	169	7	0	20	6	.769	2	0-0	0	3.43	4.14
2001	Oak	AL	35	35	3	0	235.0	980	216	100	88	20	12	8	6	71	5	181	9	1	18	9	.667	0	0-0	0	3.22	3.37
2002	Oak	AL	34	34	4	0	238.1	983	237	87	79	19	6	5	8	62	9	152	7	1	15	9	.625	2	0-0	0	3.51	2.98
2003	Oak	AL	34	34	2	0	240.0	967	197	84	72	15	11	2	10	61	9	162	6	0	16	7	.696	2	0-0	0	2.47	2.70
2004	Oak	AL	27	27	3	0	188.2	793	194	82	74	8	7	4	12	44	3	103	4	1	12	6	.667	2	0-0	0	3.44	3.53
2005	Atl	NL	29	29	2	0	192.0	817	194	79	75	20	9	1	9	65	5	115	4	0	14	9	.609	0	0-0	0	4.12	3.52
2006	Atl	NL	35	35	2	0	218.1	959	235	129	118	25	8	3	9	79	10	141	7	0	13	12	.520	1	0-0	0	4.54	4.86
2007	Atl	NL	34	34	1	0	224.1	925	221	87	83	10	11	6	8	53	8	132	5	2	16	10	.615	1	0-0	0	3.12	3.33
2008	Atl	NL	23	22	1	0	142.0	573	125	53	50	11	5	4	2	40	5	85	3	1	11	7	.611	1	0-0	0	2.90	3.17
2009	Atl	NL	7	7	0	0	42.1	180	49	17	17	4	1	0	0	13	0	30	0	0	2	1	.667	0	0-0	0	4.70	3.61
2010	Atl	NL	34	34	1	0	228.2	920	189	74	72	20	9	2	9	74	8	139	5	0	17	9	.654	0	0-0	0	2.95	2.83
2011	Atl	NL	33	33	1	0	215.0	884	189	86	77	14	6	7	15	56	6	158	10	0	16	10	.615	1	0-0	0	2.91	3.22
2012	Atl	NL	28	28	1	0	179.0	749	168	77	72	12	10	4	9	48	2	102	3	0	16	7	.696	1	0-0	0	3.18	3.62
	Postseason		10	9	1	0	54.2	236	54	28	21	5	4	2	2	20	1	37	1	0	1	3	.250	0	0-0	0	3.91	3.46
	14 ML YEARS		406	405	25	0	2682.1	11157	2504	1111	1019	210	101	55	108	810	77	1801	76	6	197	104	.654	13	0-0	0	3.33	3.42

Aubrey Huff

Bats: L **Throws:** R **Pos:** PH-32; 1B-15; LF-5; 2B-1   **Ht:** 6'4" **Wt:** 225 **Born:** 12/20/1976 **Age:** 36

									BATTING													BASERUNNING				AVERAGES		
Year	Team	Lg	G	AB	H	2B	3B	HR	(Hm	Rd)	TB	R	RBI	RC	TBB	IBB	SO	HBP	SH	SF		SB	CS	SB%	GDP	Avg	OBP	Slg
2012	SnJos*	A+	5	16	4	1	0	1	(-	-)	8	3	3	3	3	0	4	0	0	0		0	0	-	1	.250	.368	.500
2012	Fresno*	AAA	4	13	2	0	0	0	(-	-)	2	1	1	0	1	0	1	0	0	0		0	0	-	0	.154	.214	.154
2000	TB	AL	39	122	35	7	0	4	(3	1)	54	12	14	15	5	1	18	1	0	1		0	0	-	6	.287	.318	.443
2001	TB	AL	111	411	102	25	1	8	(5	3)	153	42	45	37	23	2	72	0	0	0		1	3	.25	18	.248	.288	.372
2002	TB	AL	113	454	142	25	0	23	(17	6)	236	67	59	66	37	7	55	1	0	2		4	1	.80	17	.313	.364	.520
2003	TB	AL	162	636	198	47	3	34	(15	19)	353	91	107	112	53	17	80	8	0	9		2	3	.40	19	.311	.367	.555
2004	TB	AL	157	600	178	27	2	29	(16	13)	296	92	104	96	56	6	74	6	0	5		5	1	.83	9	.297	.360	.493
2005	TB	AL	154	575	150	26	2	22	(9	13)	246	70	92	77	49	13	88	5	0	7		8	7	.53	12	.261	.321	.428
2006	2 Tms		131	454	121	25	2	21	(9	12)	213	57	66	55	50	6	64	7	0	6		0	0	-	11	.267	.344	.469
2007	Bal	AL	151	550	154	34	5	15	(8	7)	243	68	72	79	48	2	87	1	0	4		1	1	.50	13	.280	.337	.442
2008	Bal	AL	154	598	182	48	2	32	(18	14)	330	96	108	111	53	7	89	3	0	7		4	0	1.00	9	.304	.360	.552
2009	2 Tms		150	536	129	30	1	15	(11	4)	206	59	85	67	51	7	87	5	0	5		0	6	.00	15	.241	.310	.384
2010	SF	NL	157	569	165	35	5	26	(12	14)	288	100	86	108	83	5	91	9	0	7		7	0	1.00	11	.290	.385	.506
2011	SF	NL	150	521	128	27	1	12	(3	9)	193	45	59	54	47	6	90	2	0	9		5	3	.63	11	.246	.306	.370
2012	SF	NL	52	78	15	4	0	1	(1	0)	22	7	7	6	16	1	12	0	0	3		0	0	-	3	.192	.326	.282
06	TB	AL	63	230	65	15	1	8	(4	4)	106	26	28	28	24	3	25	0	0	2		0	0	-	4	.283	.348	.461
06	Hou	NL	68	224	56	10	1	13	(5	8)	107	31	38	27	26	3	39	7	0	4		0	0	-	7	.250	.341	.478

BATTING																				BASERUNNING				AVERAGES		
Year Team	Lg	G	AB	H	2B	3B	HR	(Hm Rd)	TB	R	RBI	RC	TBB	IBB	SO	HBP	SH	SF		SB	CS	SB%	GDP		Avg	OBP	Slg
09 Bal	AL	110	430	109	24	1	13	(10 3)	174	51	72	58	41	7	74	4	0	5		0	6	.00	12		.253	.321	.405
09 Det	AL	40	106	20	6	0	2	(1 1)	32	8	13	9	10	0	13	1	0	-		0	0	-	3		.189	.265	.302
Postseason		15	56	15	2	0	1	(0 1)	20	7	8	7	5	1	10	1	1	0		0	2	.00	0		.268	.339	.357
13 ML YEARS		1681	6104	1699	360	24	242	(127 115)	2833	806	904	883	571	80	907	48	0	63		37	25	.60	160		.278	.342	.464

David Huff

Pitches: L Bats: B Pos: SP-4; RP-2

Ht: 6'2" Wt: 215 Born: 8/22/1984 Age: 28

HOW MUCH HE PITCHED							WHAT HE GAVE UP											THE RESULTS							
Year Team	Lg	G	GS	CG	GF	IP	BFP	H	R	ER	HR	SH	SF	HB	TBB	IBB	SO	WP	Bk	W	L	Pct	Sh	Sv-Op Hld	ERC	ERA
2012 Akron*	AA	1	1	0	0	4.0	13	1	0	0	0	0	0	0	1	0	3	0	0	0	0	-		0-- -	0.44	0.00
2012 Clmbs*	AAA	24	22	2	0	134.0	579	155	78	74	27	4	1	2	34	0	79	7	0	7	6	.538	1	0-- -	5.18	4.97
2009 Cle	AL	23	23	0	0	128.1	574	159	82	80	16	2	2	1	41	1	65	1	0	11	8	.579	0	0-0 0	5.33	5.61
2010 Cle	AL	15	15	1	0	79.2	369	101	61	55	14	3	3	3	34	1	37	2	0	2	11	.154	0	0-0 0	6.50	6.21
2011 Cle	AL	11	10	0	1	50.2	227	55	35	23	6	0	3	0	17	1	36	4	0	2	6	.250	0	0-0 0	4.23	4.09
2012 Cle	AL	6	4	0	1	26.2	114	30	14	10	5	0	1	1	5	0	19	0	0	3	1	.750	0	0-0 0	4.67	3.38
4 ML YEARS		55	52	1	1	285.1	1284	345	192	168	41	5	9	5	97	3	157	7	0	18	26	.409	0	0-0 0	5.38	5.30

Jared Hughes

Pitches: R Bats: R Pos: RP-66

Ht: 6'7" Wt: 245 Born: 7/4/1985 Age: 27

HOW MUCH HE PITCHED							WHAT HE GAVE UP											THE RESULTS							
Year Team	Lg	G	GS	CG	GF	IP	BFP	H	R	ER	HR	SH	SF	HB	TBB	IBB	SO	WP	Bk	W	L	Pct	Sh	Sv-Op Hld	ERC	ERA
2006 Wmspt	A-	5	5	0	0	23.0	88	14	7	7	2	0	0	3	7	0	11	3	0	1	2	.333	0	0-- -	2.23	2.74
2006 Hkry	A	10	10	0	0	48.1	226	46	38	31	6	3	2	6	31	0	25	8	0	5	4	.556	0	0-- -	5.37	5.77
2007 Hkry	A	27	27	0	0	145.1	659	162	94	75	11	10	8	10	54	2	109	27	0	8	9	.471	0	0-- -	4.59	4.64
2008 Lynbrg	A+	21	21	0	0	105.2	466	108	73	54	7	1	5	8	50	0	54	17	0	3	9	.250	0	0-- -	4.60	4.60
2008 Altna	AA	6	6	0	0	31.0	146	35	19	17	4	1	2	1	16	1	18	1	0	2	2	.500	0	0-- -	5.42	4.94
2009 Altna	AA	17	7	0	4	46.1	209	55	31	20	1	3	0	4	16	0	36	7	0	1	6	.143	0	3-- -	4.67	3.88
2009 Pirates	R	3	3	0	0	6.0	21	3	1	1	0	0	0	1	1	0	5	0	0	0	0	-	0	0-- -	1.20	1.50
2010 Altna	AA	30	23	0	2	150.2	656	166	93	74	15	4	8	11	41	0	120	15	0	12	8	.600	0	0-- -	4.43	4.42
2011 Altna	AA	13	11	0	0	61.2	270	62	31	28	2	4	1	8	18	0	33	3	0	3	4	.429	0	0-- -	3.66	4.09
2011 Indy	AAA	35	0	0	8	42.2	177	35	10	10	1	3	2	3	18	4	45	3	0	3	1	.750	0	0-- -	2.85	2.11
2012 Indy	AAA	2	0	0	1	2.0	8	1	0	0	0	0	0	0	1	0	3	0	0	0	0	-	0	0-- -	1.41	0.00
2011 Pit	NL	12	0	0	1	11.0	46	9	5	5	1	1	0	0	4	0	10	0	0	0	1	.000	0	0-0 0	2.85	4.09
2012 Pit	NL	66	0	0	20	75.2	316	65	30	24	7	1	0	5	22	4	50	5	0	2	2	.500	0	2-4 11	2.99	2.85
2 ML YEARS		78	0	0	21	86.2	362	74	35	29	8	2	0	5	26	4	60	5	0	2	3	.400	0	2-4 13	2.97	3.01

Luke Hughes

Bats: R Throws: R Pos: 3B-5; 2B-3; 1B-1; PH-1

Ht: 5'11" Wt: 205 Born: 8/2/1984 Age: 28

BATTING																				BASERUNNING				AVERAGES		
Year Team	Lg	G	AB	H	2B	3B	HR	(Hm Rd)	TB	R	RBI	RC	TBB	IBB	SO	HBP	SH	SF		SB	CS	SB%	GDP		Avg	OBP	Slg
2012 Scrmto*	AAA	35	102	24	6	0	2	(- -)	36	16	13	12	14	0	28	2	0	3		1	2	.33	2		.235	.331	.353
2012 Mdland*	AA	7	28	5	0	0	1	(- -)	8	1	2	2	3	0	9	0	0	0		1	0	1.00	0		.179	.258	.286
2012 LsVgs*	AAA	28	105	33	9	3	3	(- -)	57	20	13	22	13	0	32	1	1	1		1	0	1.00	5		.314	.392	.543
2010 Min	AL	2	7	2	0	0	1	(0 1)	5	1	1	0	0	0	3	0	0	0		1	0	1.00	0		.286	.286	.714
2011 Min	AL	96	287	64	12	0	7	(4 3)	97	31	30	29	24	0	79	3	2	1		3	2	.60	2		.223	.289	.338
2012 2 Tms	AL	8	23	3	0	0	0	(0 0)	3	0	2	1	0	0	10	0	0	1		1	0	1.00	0		.130	.125	.130
12 Min	AL	4	10	2	0	0	0	(0 0)	2	0	2	1	0	0	4	0	0	1		1	0	1.00	0		.200	.182	.200
12 Oak	AL	4	13	1	0	0	0	(0 0)	1	0	0	0	0	0	6	0	0	0		0	0	-	0		.077	.077	.077
3 ML YEARS		106	317	69	12	0	8	(4 4)	105	32	33	30	24	0	92	3	2	2		4	3	.57	2		.218	.277	.331

Phil Hughes

Pitches: R Bats: R Pos: SP-32

Ht: 6'5" Wt: 240 Born: 6/24/1986 Age: 27

HOW MUCH HE PITCHED							WHAT HE GAVE UP											THE RESULTS							
Year Team	Lg	G	GS	CG	GF	IP	BFP	H	R	ER	HR	SH	SF	HB	TBB	IBB	SO	WP	Bk	W	L	Pct	Sh	Sv-Op Hld	ERC	ERA
2007 NYY	AL	13	13	0	0	72.2	306	64	39	36	8	2	1	2	29	0	58	4	0	5	3	.625	0	0-0 0	3.61	4.46
2008 NYY	AL	8	8	0	0	34.0	157	43	26	25	3	1	3	1	15	0	23	0	0	0	4	.000	0	0-0 0	5.84	6.62
2009 NYY	AL	51	7	0	6	86.0	351	68	31	29	8	0	4	5	28	1	96	4	2	8	3	.727	0	3-6 18	2.86	3.03
2010 NYY	AL	31	29	0	0	176.1	730	162	83	82	25	2	5	0	58	1	146	9	1	18	8	.692	0	0-0 0	3.65	4.19
2011 NYY	AL	17	14	1	1	74.2	334	84	48	48	9	3	3	4	27	2	47	3	0	5	5	.500	1	0-0 0	4.92	5.79
2012 NYY	AL	32	32	1	0	191.1	815	196	101	90	35	1	4	6	46	0	165	3	0	16	13	.552	0	0-0 0	4.21	4.23
Postseason		16	3	0	2	30.0	134	34	18	18	3	1	0	0	12	3	29	3	0	2	3	.400	0	0-1 2	4.62	5.40
6 ML YEARS		152	103	2	7	635.0	2693	617	328	310	88	9	20	18	203	4	535	25	3	52	36	.591	1	3-6 18	3.96	4.39

Philip Humber

Pitches: R Bats: R Pos: SP-16; RP-10

UMM-burr

Ht: 6'3" Wt: 210 Born: 12/21/1982 Age: 30

HOW MUCH HE PITCHED							WHAT HE GAVE UP											THE RESULTS							
Year Team	Lg	G	GS	CG	GF	IP	BFP	H	R	ER	HR	SH	SF	HB	TBB	IBB	SO	WP	Bk	W	L	Pct	Sh	Sv-Op Hld	ERC	ERA
2012 Charltt*	AAA	2	2	0	0	6.1	30	8	4	4	1	0	0	0	4	0	4	0	0	0	1	.000	0	0-- -	7.18	5.68
2012 Brham*	AA	1	1	0	0	6.0	20	2	1	1	0	1	1	0	0	0	5	0	0	1	0	1.000	0	0-- -	0.25	1.50
2006 NYM	NL	2	0	0	0	2.0	7	0	0	0	0	0	0	0	1	0	2	0	0	0	0	-	0	0-0 0	0.27	0.00
2007 NYM	NL	3	1	0	2	7.0	32	9	6	6	1	0	0	0	2	0	2	0	0	0	0	-	0	0-0 0	5.46	7.71
2008 Min	AL	5	0	0	2	11.2	50	11	6	6	4	0	0	1	5	0	6	0	0	0	0	-	0	0-0 0	6.11	4.63
2009 Min	AL	8	0	0	3	9.0	50	17	8	8	1	0	0	0	9	2	9	1	0	0	0	-	0	0-0 0	12.62	8.00

Year Team	Lg	HOW MUCH HE PITCHED						WHAT HE GAVE UP													THE RESULTS							
		G	GS	CG	GF	IP	BFP	H	R	ER	HR	SH	SF	HB	TBB	IBB	SO	WP	Bk	W	L	Pct	Sh	Sv-Op	Hld	ERC	ERA
2010 KC	AL	8	1	0	1	21.2	94	22	10	10	1	0	1	1	7	2	16	2	0	2	1	.667	0	0-0	1	3.47	4.15
2011 CWS	AL	28	26	0	0	163.0	676	151	71	64	14	2	5	6	41	2	116	9	1	9	9	.500	0	0-0	0	3.13	3.75
2012 CWS	AL	26	16	1	6	102.0	462	113	74	73	23	1	4	4	44	1	85	9	0	5	5	.500	1	0-0	0	5.86	6.44
7 ML YEARS		80	44	1	15	316.1	1371	323	175	171	44	3	10	12	109	7	236	21	1	16	15	.516	1	0-0	1	4.34	4.87

Nick Hundley

Bats: R **Throws:** R **Pos:** C-56; PH-2 **Ht:** 6'1" **Wt:** 205 **Born:** 9/8/1983 **Age:** 29

Year Team	Lg	BATTING																		BASERUNNING				AVERAGES		
		G	AB	H	2B	3B	HR	(Hm	Rd)	TB	R	RBI	RC	TBB	IBB	SO	HBP	SH	SF	SB	CS	SB%	GDP	Avg	OBP	Slg
2012 Tucsn*	AAA	13	42	8	1	1	0	(-	-)	11	4	7	2	4	0	9	0	0	1	0	1	.00	2	.190	.255	.262
2008 SD	NL	60	198	47	7	1	5	(4	1)	71	21	24	17	11	0	52	2	0	5	0	0	-	1	.237	.278	.359
2009 SD	NL	78	256	61	15	2	8	(4	4)	104	23	30	33	28	1	76	1	1	3	5	1	.83	2	.238	.313	.406
2010 SD	NL	85	273	68	18	2	8	(7	1)	114	33	43	37	25	0	66	1	2	6	0	5	.00	8	.249	.308	.418
2011 SD	NL	82	281	81	16	5	9	(6	3)	134	34	29	40	22	3	74	4	0	1	1	1	.50	3	.288	.347	.477
2012 SD	NL	58	204	32	7	1	3	(1	2)	50	14	22	6	15	2	56	2	1	3	0	3	.00	4	.157	.219	.245
5 ML YEARS		363	1212	289	63	11	33	(22	11)	473	125	148	133	101	6	324	10	4	18	6	10	.38	18	.238	.298	.390

Tommy Hunter

Pitches: R **Bats:** R **Pos:** SP-20; RP-13 **Ht:** 6'3" **Wt:** 250 **Born:** 7/3/1986 **Age:** 26

Year Team	Lg	HOW MUCH HE PITCHED						WHAT HE GAVE UP													THE RESULTS							
		G	GS	CG	GF	IP	BFP	H	R	ER	HR	SH	SF	HB	TBB	IBB	SO	WP	Bk	W	L	Pct	Sh	Sv-Op	Hld	ERC	ERA
2012 Norfolk*	AAA	3	3	1	0	19.1	80	20	10	10	2	0	0	0	5	0	14	0	0	2	1	.667	0	0- -	-	3.81	4.66
2012 Bowie*	AA	2	1	1	1	10.0	34	3	0	0	0	0	0	0	1	0	6	0	0	1	0	1.000	1	1- -	-	0.31	0.00
2008 Tex	AL	3	3	0	0	11.0	63	23	20	20	4	0	0	1	3	0	9	0	0	0	2	.000	0	0-0	0	12.66	16.36
2009 Tex	AL	19	19	1	0	112.0	475	113	55	51	13	2	1	2	33	2	64	6	1	9	6	.600	0	0-0	0	3.86	4.10
2010 Tex	AL	23	22	1	0	128.0	536	126	55	53	21	3	2	3	33	0	68	1	0	13	4	.765	0	0-0	0	3.95	3.73
2011 2 Tms	AL	20	11	0	2	84.2	367	100	50	44	12	2	2	4	15	1	45	0	0	4	4	.500	0	0-1	1	4.65	4.68
2012 Bal	AL	33	20	0	5	133.2	573	161	85	81	32	3	6	4	27	2	77	0	1	7	8	.467	0	0-1	0	5.63	5.45
11 Tex	A+	8	0	0	2	15.1	62	12	6	5	1	1	1	0	5	0	10	0	0	1	1	.500	0	0-1	0	2.44	2.93
11 Bal	A+	12	11	0	0	69.1	305	88	44	39	11	1	1	4	10	1	35	0	0	3	3	.500	0	0-0	1	5.19	5.06
Postseason		3	3	0	0	11.1	52	16	8	7	2	0	0	1	1	0	13	0	1	0	2	.000	0	0-0	0	6.00	5.56
5 ML YEARS		98	75	2	7	469.1	2014	523	265	249	82	10	11	14	111	5	263	7	2	33	24	.579	0	0-2	1	4.69	4.77

Torii Hunter

Bats: R **Throws:** R **Pos:** RF-134; DH-6; PH-1; PR-1 **Ht:** 6'2" **Wt:** 225 **Born:** 7/18/1975 **Age:** 37

Year Team	Lg	BATTING																		BASERUNNING				AVERAGES		
		G	AB	H	2B	3B	HR	(Hm	Rd)	TB	R	RBI	RC	TBB	IBB	SO	HBP	SH	SF	SB	CS	SB%	GDP	Avg	OBP	Slg
1997 Min	AL	1	0	0	0	0	0	(0	0)	0	0	0	0	0	0	0	0	0	0	0	0	-	0	-	-	-
1998 Min	AL	6	17	4	1	0	0	(0	0)	5	0	2	1	2	0	6	0	0	0	0	1	.00	1	.235	.316	.294
1999 Min	AL	135	384	98	17	2	9	(2	7)	146	52	35	44	26	1	72	6	1	5	10	6	.63	9	.255	.309	.380
2000 Min	AL	99	336	94	14	7	5	(4	1)	137	44	44	39	18	2	68	2	0	2	4	3	.57	13	.280	.318	.408
2001 Min	AL	148	564	147	32	5	27	(13	14)	270	82	92	79	29	0	125	8	1	1	9	6	.60	12	.261	.306	.479
2002 Min	AL	148	561	162	37	4	29	(13	16)	294	89	94	85	35	3	118	5	0	3	23	8	.74	17	.289	.334	.524
2003 Min	AL	154	581	145	31	4	26	(12	14)	262	83	102	76	50	7	106	5	0	6	6	7	.46	15	.250	.312	.451
2004 Min	AL	138	520	141	37	0	23	(9	14)	247	79	81	69	40	4	101	7	0	2	21	7	.75	23	.271	.330	.475
2005 Min	AL	98	372	100	24	1	14	(6	8)	168	63	56	53	34	3	65	6	0	4	23	7	.77	8	.269	.337	.452
2006 Min	AL	147	557	155	21	2	31	(15	16)	273	86	98	81	45	2	108	5	0	4	12	6	.67	19	.278	.336	.490
2007 Min	AL	160	600	172	45	1	28	(11	17)	303	94	107	99	40	10	101	5	0	5	18	9	.67	17	.287	.334	.505
2008 LAA	AL	146	551	153	37	2	21	(10	11)	257	85	78	80	50	6	108	6	0	1	19	5	.79	15	.278	.344	.466
2009 LAA	AL	119	451	135	26	1	22	(15	7)	229	74	90	84	47	4	92	3	0	5	18	4	.82	9	.299	.366	.508
2010 LAA	AL	152	573	161	36	0	23	(8	15)	266	76	90	93	61	6	106	7	0	5	9	12	.43	22	.281	.354	.464
2011 LAA	AL	156	580	152	24	2	23	(15	8)	249	80	82	79	62	2	125	4	0	3	5	7	.42	24	.262	.336	.429
2012 LAA	AL	140	534	167	24	1	16	(7	9)	241	81	92	89	38	1	133	8	1	3	9	1	.90	15	.313	.365	.451
Postseason		34	131	40	10	1	4	(1	3)	64	19	18	18	13	2	19	1	2	1	3	1	.75	4	.305	.370	.489
16 ML YEARS		1947	7181	1986	406	32	297	(140	157)	3347	1068	1143	1051	577	51	1434	77	3	49	186	89	.68	219	.277	.335	.466

Drew Hutchison

Pitches: R **Bats:** L **Pos:** SP-11 **Ht:** 6'2" **Wt:** 195 **Born:** 8/22/1990 **Age:** 22

Year Team	Lg	HOW MUCH HE PITCHED						WHAT HE GAVE UP													THE RESULTS							
		G	GS	CG	GF	IP	BFP	H	R	ER	HR	SH	SF	HB	TBB	IBB	SO	WP	Bk	W	L	Pct	Sh	Sv-Op	Hld	ERC	ERA
2010 Auburn	A-	10	10	0	0	45.0	185	34	18	15	1	0	0	4	12	0	44	3	0	1	1	.500	0	0- -	-	2.11	3.00
2010 Lnsng	A	5	5	0	0	23.2	99	17	7	4	1	0	1	2	7	0	19	0	1	1	2	.333	0	0- -	-	2.08	1.52
2011 Lnsng	A	14	14	0	0	72.0	303	68	29	21	1	2	2	3	19	0	84	2	0	6	2	.750	0	0- -	-	2.81	2.63
2011 Dnedin	A+	11	10	0	0	62.1	239	42	20	19	3	2	3	4	14	1	66	1	0	5	3	.625	0	0- -	-	1.75	2.74
2011 NHam	AA	3	3	0	0	15.0	56	10	2	2	0	0	0	0	2	0	21	3	0	3	0	1.000	0	0- -	-	1.51	1.20
2012 NHam	AA	3	3	0	0	16.2	64	16	4	4	1	0	0	0	3	0	12	0	0	2	1	.667	0	0- -	-	2.97	2.16
2012 Tor	AL	11	11	0	0	58.2	257	59	31	30	8	1	1	5	20	0	49	1	0	5	3	.625	0	0-0	0	4.43	4.60

Chris Iannetta

Bats: R Throws: R Pos: C-78; PH-2   eye-ah-NETT-ah   Ht: 6'0" Wt: 230 Born: 4/8/1983 Age: 30

Year	Team	Lg	G	AB	H	2B	3B	HR	(Hm	Rd)	TB	R	RBI	RC	TBB	IBB	SO	HBP	SH	SF	SB	CS	SB%	GDP	Avg	OBP	Slg
2012	Salt Lk*	AAA	6	22	6	2	0	0	(-	-)	8	3	2	3	3	0	7	0	0	0	0	0	-	1	.273	.360	.364
2006	Col	NL	21	77	20	4	0	2	(0	2)	30	12	10	9	13	2	17	1	1	1	0	1	.00	1	.260	.370	.390
2007	Col	NL	67	197	43	8	3	4	(1	3)	69	22	27	27	29	3	58	5	1	2	0	0	-	3	.218	.330	.350
2008	Col	NL	104	333	88	22	2	18	(11	7)	168	50	65	65	56	0	92	14	2	2	0	0	-	6	.264	.390	.505
2009	Col	NL	93	289	66	15	2	16	(8	8)	133	41	52	47	43	3	75	11	1	6	0	1	.00	4	.228	.344	.460
2010	Col	NL	61	188	37	6	1	9	(7	2)	72	20	27	21	30	2	48	4	0	1	1	0	1.00	4	.197	.318	.383
2011	Col	NL	112	345	82	17	1	14	(10	4)	143	51	55	62	70	5	89	5	2	4	6	3	.67	10	.238	.370	.414
2012	LAA	AL	79	221	53	6	1	9	(3	6)	88	27	26	27	29	0	60	2	0	1	1	3	.25	4	.240	.332	.398
7 ML YEARS			537	1650	389	78	10	72	(40	32)	703	223	262	258	270	15	439	42	7	17	8	8	.50	32	.236	.354	.426

Raul Ibanez

Bats: L Throws: R Pos: LF-80; PH-30; DH-27; RF-13   ee-BAHN-yezz   Ht: 6'2" Wt: 220 Born: 6/2/1972 Age: 41

Year	Team	Lg	G	AB	H	2B	3B	HR	(Hm	Rd)	TB	R	RBI	RC	TBB	IBB	SO	HBP	SH	SF	SB	CS	SB%	GDP	Avg	OBP	Slg
1996	Sea	AL	4	5	0	0	0	0	(0	0)	0	0	0	0	0	0	1	1	0	0	0	0	-	0	.000	.167	.000
1997	Sea	AL	11	26	4	0	1	1	(1	0)	9	3	4	1	0	0	6	0	0	0	0	0	-	0	.154	.154	.346
1998	Sea	AL	37	98	25	7	1	2	(1	1)	40	12	12	10	5	0	22	0	0	0	0	0	-	4	.255	.291	.408
1999	Sea	AL	87	209	54	7	0	9	(3	6)	88	23	27	28	17	1	32	0	0	1	5	1	.83	4	.258	.313	.421
2000	Sea	AL	92	140	32	8	0	2	(2	0)	46	21	15	15	14	1	25	1	0	1	2	0	1.00	1	.229	.301	.329
2001	KC	AL	104	279	78	11	5	13	(5	8)	138	44	54	46	32	2	51	0	0	1	0	2	.00	6	.280	.353	.495
2002	KC	AL	137	497	146	37	6	24	(14	10)	267	70	103	89	40	5	76	2	1	4	5	3	.63	11	.294	.346	.537
2003	KC	AL	157	608	179	33	5	18	(8	10)	276	95	90	91	49	5	81	3	1	10	8	4	.67	10	.294	.345	.454
2004	Sea	AL	123	481	146	31	1	16	(9	7)	227	67	62	67	36	5	72	3	0	4	1	2	.33	10	.304	.353	.472
2005	Sea	AL	162	614	172	32	2	20	(9	11)	268	92	89	99	71	6	99	2	0	3	9	4	.69	12	.280	.355	.436
2006	Sea	AL	159	626	181	33	5	33	(17	16)	323	103	123	114	65	15	115	1	0	7	2	4	.33	13	.289	.353	.516
2007	Sea	AL	149	573	167	35	5	21	(7	14)	275	80	105	101	53	4	97	3	0	7	0	0	-	14	.291	.351	.480
2008	Sea	AL	162	635	186	43	3	23	(14	9)	304	85	110	110	64	11	110	3	0	5	2	4	.33	13	.293	.358	.479
2009	Phi	NL	134	500	136	32	3	34	(13	21)	276	93	93	80	56	8	119	4	0	5	4	0	1.00	16	.272	.347	.552
2010	Phi	NL	155	561	154	37	5	16	(9	7)	249	75	83	86	68	11	108	0	0	7	4	3	.57	15	.275	.349	.444
2011	Phi	NL	144	535	131	31	1	20	(15	5)	224	65	84	64	33	3	106	2	0	5	2	0	1.00	13	.245	.289	.419
2012	NYY	AL	130	384	92	19	3	19	(14	5)	174	50	62	50	35	5	67	4	0	2	3	0	1.00	14	.240	.308	.453
Postseason			36	117	27	8	0	3	(2	1)	44	12	17	14	8	1	32	0	0	0	0	0	-	2	.231	.280	.376
17 ML YEARS			1947	6771	1883	396	46	271	(141	130)	3184	978	1116	1048	638	82	1187	29	2	62	47	27	.64	156	.278	.340	.470

Ryota Igarashi

Pitches: R Bats: R Pos: RP-4   ree-OH-tah ig-ah-RAH-she   Ht: 5'11" Wt: 200 Born: 5/28/1979 Age: 34

Year	Team	Lg	G	GS	CG	GF	IP	BFP	H	R	ER	HR	SF	SH	HB	TBB	IBB	SO	WP	Bk	W	L	Pct	Sh	Sv-Op	Hld	ERC	ERA
2012	LsVgs*	AAA	19	0	0	5	21.0	76	10	3	3	0	1	0	0	3	0	28	2	0	1	1	.500	0	4--	-	0.71	1.29
2012	S-WB*	AAA	30	0	0	25	36.2	160	30	11	10	1	2	0	1	18	1	55	8	0	4	3	.571	0	10--	-	2.90	2.45
2010	NYM	NL	34	0	0	11	30.1	135	29	24	24	4	0	3	0	18	1	25	3	0	1	1	.500	0	0-0	2	4.78	7.12
2011	NYM	NL	45	0	0	9	38.2	190	43	20	20	2	2	0	4	28	2	42	3	0	4	1	.800	0	0-1	5	5.85	4.66
2012	2 Tms	AL	4	0	0	1	4.0	26	9	8	8	0	0	0	0	5	0	5	0	0	0	0	-	0	0-0	0	15.01	18.00
12	Tor	AL	2	0	0	0	1.0	10	5	4	4	0	0	0	0	2	0	2	0	0	0	0	-	0	0-0	0	41.68	36.00
12	NYY	AL	2	0	0	1	3.0	16	4	4	4	0	0	0	0	3	0	3	0	0	0	0	-	0	0-0	0	7.51	12.00
3 ML YEARS			83	0	0	21	73.0	351	81	52	52	6	2	3	4	51	3	72	6	0	5	2	.714	0	0-1	4	5.85	6.41

Jose Iglesias

Bats: R Throws: R Pos: SS-24; DH-1; PR-1   EE-glay-see-us   Ht: 5'11" Wt: 185 Born: 1/5/1990 Age: 23

Year	Team	Lg	G	AB	H	2B	3B	HR	(Hm	Rd)	TB	R	RBI	RC	TBB	IBB	SO	HBP	SH	SF	SB	CS	SB%	GDP	Avg	OBP	Slg
2010	Portlnd	AA	57	221	63	10	3	0	(-	-)	79	29	13	26	8	1	49	3	1	3	5	2	.71	6	.285	.315	.357
2010	Lowell	A-	13	40	14	2	2	0	(-	-)	20	8	7	9	7	0	8	1	0	2	2	1	.67	0	.350	.458	.500
2011	Pwtckt	AAA	101	357	84	9	0	1	(-	-)	96	35	31	29	21	0	58	4	5	0	12	4	.75	18	.235	.285	.269
2012	Pwtckt	AAA	88	353	94	9	1	1	(-	-)	108	46	23	38	27	0	46	2	9	5	12	3	.80	9	.266	.318	.306
2012	Lowell	A-	2	8	3	1	0	0	(-	-)	4	1	0	1	1	0	1	0	0	0	1	0	1.00	0	.375	.444	.500
2011	Bos	AL	10	6	2	0	0	0	(0	0)	2	3	0	0	0	0	2	0	0	0	0	0	-	0	.333	.333	.333
2012	Bos	AL	25	68	8	2	0	1	(0	1)	13	5	2	0	4	0	16	3	2	0	1	0	1.00	2	.118	.200	.191
2 ML YEARS			35	74	10	2	0	1	(0	1)	15	8	2	0	4	0	18	3	2	0	1	0	1.00	2	.135	.210	.203

Omar Infante

Bats: R Throws: R Pos: 2B-144; 3B-6; PH-4   in-FAHN-tay   Ht: 6'0" Wt: 197 Born: 12/26/1981 Age: 31

Year	Team	Lg	G	AB	H	2B	3B	HR	(Hm	Rd)	TB	R	RBI	RC	TBB	IBB	SO	HBP	SH	SF	SB	CS	SB%	GDP	Avg	OBP	Slg
2002	Det	AL	18	72	24	3	0	1	(0	1)	30	4	6	12	3	0	10	0	0	0	1	1	.00	0	.333	.360	.417
2003	Det	AL	69	221	49	6	1	0	(0	0)	57	24	8	16	18	0	37	0	3	2	6	3	.67	1	.222	.278	.258
2004	Det	AL	142	503	133	27	9	16	(7	9)	226	69	55	69	40	3	112	1	7	5	13	7	.65	4	.264	.317	.449
2005	Det	AL	121	406	90	28	2	9	(3	6)	149	36	43	38	16	0	73	2	8	2	8	0	1.00	5	.222	.254	.367
2006	Det	AL	78	224	62	11	4	4	(0	4)	93	35	25	26	14	0	45	3	2	2	3	2	.60	5	.277	.325	.415
2007	Det	AL	66	166	45	6	1	2	(1	1)	59	24	17	21	9	0	29	0	2	1	4	1	.80	4	.271	.307	.355
2008	Atl	NL	96	317	93	24	3	3	(1	2)	132	45	40	45	22	2	44	2	2	5	0	1	.00	4	.293	.338	.416
2009	Atl	NL	70	203	62	9	1	2	(1	1)	79	24	27	29	19	0	28	1	2	4	2	0	1.00	3	.305	.361	.389
2010	Atl	NL	134	471	151	15	3	8	(1	7)	196	65	47	70	29	1	62	0	4	2	7	6	.54	14	.321	.359	.416
2011	Fla	NL	148	579	160	24	8	7	(2	5)	221	55	49	66	34	1	67	2	**17**	8	4	2	.67	12	.276	.315	.382

Year Team	Lg	G	AB	H	2B	3B	HR	(Hm	Rd)	TB	R	RBI	RC	TBB	IBB	SO	HBP	SH	SF	SB	CS	SB%	GDP	Avg	OBP	Slg
2012 2 Tms		149	554	152	30	7	12	(5	7)	232	69	53	58	21	0	65	1	8	4	17	3	.85	9	.274	.300	.419
12 Mia	NL	85	328	94	23	2	8	(2	6)	145	42	33	36	12	0	42	1	4	2	10	1	.91	7	.287	.312	.442
12 Det	AL	64	226	58	7	5	4	(3	1)	87	27	20	22	9	0	23	0	4	2	7	2	.78	2	.257	.283	.385
Postseason		6	21	5	1	0	0	(0	0)	6	1	0	2	2	0	6	0	0	0	1	0	1.00	0	.238	.304	.286
11 ML YEARS		1091	3716	1021	183	39	64	(20	44)	1474	450	370	452	225	7	572	12	55	35	64	26	.71	63	.275	.315	.397

Brandon Inge

Bats: R Throws: R Pos: 3B-76; 2B-6; PH-2; DH-1   Ht: 5'11" Wt: 190 Born: 5/19/1977 Age: 36

Year Team	Lg	G	AB	H	2B	3B	HR	(Hm	Rd)	TB	R	RBI	RC	TBB	IBB	SO	HBP	SH	SF	SB	CS	SB%	GDP	Avg	OBP	Slg
2012 Toledo*	AAA	3	9	1	0	0	0	(-	-)	1	1	0	0	3	0	1	1	0	0	0	0	-	0	.111	.385	.111
2012 Scrmto*	AAA	8	27	10	4	0	2	(-	-)	20	6	9	8	5	0	9	0	0	0	0	0	-	0	.370	.469	.741
2001 Det	AL	79	189	34	11	0	0	(0	0)	45	13	15	6	9	0	41	0	2	2	1	4	.20	2	.180	.215	.238
2002 Det	AL	95	321	65	15	3	7	(3	4)	107	27	24	24	24	0	101	4	1	1	1	3	.25	7	.202	.266	.333
2003 Det	AL	104	330	67	15	3	8	(4	4)	112	32	30	23	24	0	79	5	4	3	4	4	.50	8	.203	.265	.339
2004 Det	AL	131	408	117	15	7	13	(9	4)	185	43	64	63	32	0	72	4	8	6	5	4	.56	4	.287	.340	.453
2005 Det	AL	160	616	161	31	9	16	(10	6)	258	75	72	82	63	1	140	3	6	6	7	6	.54	14	.261	.330	.419
2006 Det	AL	159	542	137	29	2	27	(12	15)	251	83	83	79	43	2	128	7	4	5	7	4	.64	12	.253	.313	.463
2007 Det	AL	151	508	120	25	2	14	(9	5)	191	64	71	65	47	5	150	11	7	4	9	2	.82	8	.236	.312	.376
2008 Det	AL	113	347	71	16	4	11	(8	3)	128	41	51	44	43	2	94	8	5	4	4	3	.57	4	.205	.303	.369
2009 Det	AL	161	562	129	16	1	27	(14	13)	228	71	84	70	54	1	170	17	1	3	2	5	.29	12	.230	.314	.406
2010 Det	AL	144	514	127	28	5	13	(4	9)	204	47	70	64	54	4	134	5	0	7	4	3	.57	12	.247	.321	.397
2011 Det	AL	102	269	53	10	2	3	(3	0)	76	29	23	12	24	0	74	2	5	3	1	1	.50	9	.197	.265	.283
2012 2 Tms		83	303	66	14	0	12	(8	4)	116	33	54	41	24	1	91	1	0	3	0	1	.00	8	.218	.275	.383
12 Det	AL	9	20	2	1	0	1	(0	1)	6	2	2	1	0	0	6	0	0	0	0	0	-	0	.100	.100	.300
12 Oak	AL	74	283	64	13	0	11	(8	3)	110	31	52	40	24	1	85	1	0	3	0	1	.00	8	.226	.286	.389
Postseason		23	66	19	4	0	2	(1	1)	29	10	5	7	7	2	18	1	2	1	0	0	-	1	.288	.360	.439
12 ML YEARS		1482	4909	1147	225	38	151	(84	67)	1901	558	641	573	441	16	1274	67	43	47	45	40	.53	100	.234	.303	.387

Travis Ishikawa

Bats: L Throws: L Pos: PH-55; 1B-43; RF-3   ee-shee-KAU-wuh   Ht: 6'3" Wt: 224 Born: 9/24/1983 Age: 29

Year Team	Lg	G	AB	H	2B	3B	HR	(Hm	Rd)	TB	R	RBI	RC	TBB	IBB	SO	HBP	SH	SF	SB	CS	SB%	GDP	Avg	OBP	Slg
2012 Nashv*	AAA	6	18	4	3	0	0	(-	-)	7	1	5	2	3	0	2	0	0	0	0	0	-	1	.222	.333	.389
2006 SF	NL	12	24	7	3	1	0	(0	0)	12	1	4	4	1	0	6	0	0	0	0	0	-	1	.292	.320	.500
2008 SF	NL	33	95	26	6	0	3	(1	2)	41	12	15	17	9	1	27	0	0	0	1	0	1.00	1	.274	.337	.432
2009 SF	NL	120	326	85	10	2	9	(7	2)	126	49	39	44	30	3	89	4	1	2	2	2	.50	7	.261	.329	.387
2010 SF	NL	116	158	42	11	0	3	(0	3)	62	18	22	19	13	2	29	0	1	1	0	0	-	3	.266	.320	.392
2012 Mil	NL	94	152	39	12	1	4	(2	2)	65	19	30	24	13	3	42	4	4	1	0	0	-	4	.257	.329	.428
Postseason		10	10	2	1	0	0	(0	0)	3	2	1	1	2	0	4	1	0	0	0	0	-	1	.200	.385	.300
5 ML YEARS		375	755	199	42	4	19	(10	9)	306	99	110	108	66	9	193	8	6	4	3	2	.60	16	.264	.328	.405

Jason Isringhausen

Pitches: R Bats: R Pos: RP-50   IZZ-ring-how-zen   Ht: 6'3" Wt: 235 Born: 9/7/1972 Age: 40

Year Team	Lg	G	GS	CG	GF	IP	BFP	H	R	ER	HR	SH	SF	HB	TBB	IBB	SO	WP	Bk	W	L	Pct	Sh	Sv-Op	Hld	ERC	ERA
1995 NYM	NL	14	14	1	0	93.0	385	88	29	29	6	3	5	2	31	2	55	4	1	9	2	.818	0	0-0	0	3.40	2.81
1996 NYM	NL	27	27	2	0	171.2	766	190	103	91	13	7	9	8	73	5	114	14	0	6	14	.300	1	0-0	0	4.75	4.77
1997 NYM	NL	6	6	0	0	29.2	145	40	27	25	3	1	2	1	22	0	25	3	0	2	2	.500	0	0-0	0	7.99	7.58
1999 2 Tms		33	5	0	20	64.2	286	64	35	34	9	0	1	3	34	4	51	4	0	1	4	.200	0	9-9	0	4.94	4.73
2000 Oak	AL	66	0	0	57	69.0	304	67	34	29	6	2	1	3	32	5	57	5	1	6	4	.600	0	33-40	0	4.09	3.78
2001 Oak	AL	65	0	0	54	71.1	293	54	24	21	5	3	1	0	23	5	74	2	0	4	3	.571	0	34-43	0	2.18	2.65
2002 StL	NL	60	0	0	51	65.1	257	46	22	18	0	4	3	1	18	1	68	0	0	3	2	.600	0	32-37	0	1.61	2.48
2003 StL	NL	40	0	0	31	62.0	174	31	14	11	2	1	0	0	18	1	41	6	0	0	1	.000	0	22-25	1	2.40	2.36
2004 StL	NL	74	0	0	66	75.1	308	55	27	24	5	6	1	2	23	4	71	1	0	4	2	.667	0	47-54	0	2.09	2.87
2005 StL	NL	63	0	0	52	59.0	245	43	14	14	4	3	1	1	27	5	51	2	0	1	2	.333	0	39-43	0	2.56	2.14
2006 StL	NL	59	0	0	51	58.1	257	47	25	23	10	1	3	3	38	3	52	3	0	4	8	.333	0	33-43	0	4.63	3.55
2007 StL	NL	63	0	0	54	65.1	267	42	21	18	4	1	1	2	28	3	54	3	0	4	0	1.000	0	32-34	0	2.11	2.48
2008 StL	NL	42	0	0	27	42.2	200	48	28	27	5	0	1	5	22	0	36	1	0	1	5	.167	0	12-19	5	5.84	5.70
2009 TB	AL	9	0	0	4	8.0	37	7	2	2	0	0	0	2	5	0	6	1	0	0	1	.000	0	0-1	0	3.64	2.25
2011 NYM	NL	53	0	0	15	46.2	200	36	23	21	6	2	2	1	24	2	44	1	0	3	3	.500	0	7-11	19	3.43	4.05
2012 LAA	AL	50	0	0	17	45.2	198	44	22	21	7	1	3	0	19	3	31	3	0	3	2	.600	0	0-5	4	4.16	4.14
99 NYM	NL	13	5	0	2	39.1	179	43	29	28	7	0	1	2	22	2	31	2	0	1	3	.250	0	1-1	0	6.07	6.41
99 Oak	AL	20	0	0	18	25.1	107	21	6	6	2	0	0	1	12	2	20	2	0	0	1	.000	0	8-8	0	3.33	2.13
Postseason		23	0	0	22	26.2	110	17	8	7	2	2	1	1	12	4	23	0	0	1	1	.500	0	11-12	2	2.10	2.36
16 ML YEARS		724	52	3	499	1007.2	4322	901	450	408	85	35	32	34	437	43	830	53	2	51	55	.481	1	300-364	27	3.56	3.64

Hisashi Iwakuma

Pitches: R Bats: R Pos: SP-16; RP-14   Ht: 6'3" Wt: 190 Born: 4/12/1981 Age: 32

Year Team	Lg	G	GS	CG	GF	IP	BFP	H	R	ER	HR	SH	SF	HB	TBB	IBB	SO	WP	Bk	W	L	Pct	Sh	Sv-Op	Hld	ERC	ERA
2001 Kintets	Jap	9	8	1	-	43.2	190	46	28	22	3	-	-	3	13	-	25	1	0	4	2	.667	1	0--	-	3.99	4.53
2002 Kintets	Jap	23	23	2	-	141.1	598	132	62	58	10	-	-	8	42	-	131	4	1	8	7	.533	0	0--	-	3.31	3.69
2003 Kintets	Jap	27	27	11	-	195.2	834	201	85	75	19	-	-	8	46	-	149	2	0	15	10	.600	0	0--	-	3.55	3.45
2004 Kintets	Jap	21	21	7	-	158.2	655	149	57	53	13	-	-	8	30	-	123	0	0	15	2	.882	1	0--	-	2.99	3.01
2005 Tohoku	Jap	27	27	9	-	182.1	805	218	113	101	19	-	-	6	40	-	124	7	0	9	15	.375	0	0--	-	4.55	4.99
2006 Tohoku	Jap	6	6	2	-	38.2	171	43	18	16	4	-	-	1	12	-	16	0	0	1	2	.333	0	0--	-	4.40	3.72

Year	Team	Lg	G	GS	CG	GF	IP	BFP	H	R	ER	HR	SH	SF	HB	TBB	IBB	SO	WP	Bk	W	L	Pct	Sh	Sv-Op	Hld	ERC	ERA
			HOW MUCH HE PITCHED						**WHAT HE GAVE UP**												**THE RESULTS**							
2007	Tohoku	Jap	16	16	0	-	90.0	388	95	47	34	6	-	-	2	23	-	84	0	0	5	5	.500	0	0- -	-	3.61	3.40
2008	Tohoku	Jap	28	28	5	-	201.2	802	161	48	42	3	-	-	4	36	-	159	4	0	21	4	.840	2	0- -	-	1.78	1.87
2009	Tohoku	Jap	24	24	5	-	169.0	729	179	62	61	15	-	-	6	43	-	121	3	0	13	6	.684	0	0- -	-	3.84	3.25
2010	Tohoku	Jap	28	28	4	-	201.0	823	184	68	63	11	-	-	12	36	-	153	1	1	10	9	.526	1	0- -	-	2.71	2.82
2011	Tohoku	Jap	17	17	2	-	119.0	482	106	34	32	6	-	-	5	19	-	90	1	0	6	7	.462	1	0- -	-	2.43	2.42
2012	Sea	AL	30	16	0	6	125.1	519	117	49	44	17	1	1	3	43	3	101	5	0	9	5	.643	0	2-2	0	3.87	3.16

Cesar Izturis

Bats: B Throws: R Pos: SS-46; PH-15; 3B-4; PR-3; 2B-2; 1B-1   izz-TOUR-iss   Ht: 5'9" Wt: 180 Born: 2/10/1980 Age: 33

Year	Team	Lg	G	AB	H	2B	3B	HR	(Hm	Rd)	TB	R	RBI	RC	TBB	IBB	SO	HBP	SH	SF	SB	CS	SB%	GDP	Avg	OBP	Slg
														BATTING								**BASERUNNING**			**AVERAGES**		
2012	Nashv*	AAA	4	12	1	0	0	0	(-	-)	1	1	0	0	0	0	1	0	1	0	0	0	-	0	.083	.083	.083
2001	Tor	AL	46	134	36	6	2	2	(1	1)	52	19	9	16	2	0	15	0	4	0	8	1	.89	6	.269	.279	.388
2002	LAD	NL	135	439	102	24	2	1	(0	1)	133	43	31	26	14	1	39	0	10	5	7	7	.50	12	.232	.253	.303
2003	LAD	NL	158	558	140	21	6	1	(0	1)	176	47	40	42	25	8	70	0	7	3	10	5	.67	8	.251	.282	.315
2004	LAD	NL	159	670	193	32	9	4	(1	3)	255	90	62	95	43	2	70	0	12	3	25	9	.74	6	.288	.330	.381
2005	LAD	NL	106	444	114	19	2	2	(1	1)	143	48	31	37	25	1	51	4	4	1	8	8	.50	11	.257	.302	.322
2006	2 Tms	NL	54	192	47	9	1	1	(1	0)	61	14	18	14	12	3	14	2	1	1	1	4	.20	4	.245	.295	.318
2007	2 Tms	NL	110	314	81	14	2	0	(0	0)	99	31	16	27	19	2	19	1	3	0	3	3	.50	7	.258	.302	.315
2008	StL	NL	135	414	109	10	3	1	(0	1)	128	50	24	39	29	1	26	6	3	2	24	6	.80	6	.263	.319	.309
2009	Bal	AL	114	387	99	14	4	2	(1	1)	127	34	30	37	18	0	38	3	4	0	12	4	.75	11	.256	.294	.328
2010	Bal	AL	150	473	109	13	1	1	(0	1)	127	42	28	32	25	1	53	6	7	2	11	5	.69	11	.230	.277	.268
2011	Bal	AL	18	30	6	0	0	0	(0	0)	6	4	1	2	2	0	10	0	1	0	0	0	-	0	.200	.250	.200
2012	2 Tms	NL	62	166	40	7	2	2	(2	0)	57	13	11	12	3	0	13	0	4	0	1	1	.50	7	.241	.254	.343
06	LAD	NL	32	119	30	7	1	1	(1	0)	42	10	12	10	7	3	6	2	0	1	1	3	.25	1	.252	.302	.353
06	ChC	NL	22	73	17	2	0	0	(0	0)	19	4	6	4	5	0	8	0	1	0	0	1	.00	3	.233	.282	.260
07	ChC	NL	65	191	47	11	0	0	(0	0)	58	15	8	13	13	2	16	1	2	0	3	0	1.00	6	.246	.298	.304
07	Pit	NL	45	123	34	3	2	0	(0	0)	41	16	8	14	6	0	3	0	1	0	0	3	.00	1	.276	.310	.333
12	Mil	NL	57	162	38	6	2	2	(2	0)	54	9	11	11	3	0	13	0	4	0	1	1	.50	7	.235	.248	.333
12	Was	NL	5	4	2	1	0	0	(0	0)	3	4	0	1	0	0	0	0	0	0	0	0	-	0	.500	.500	.750
	Postseason		4	17	3	1	0	0	(0	0)	4	1	0	0	1	0	2	0	0	0	0	0	-	0	.176	.222	.235
	12 ML YEARS		1247	4221	1076	169	34	17	(7	10)	1364	435	301	379	217	19	418	22	60	17	110	53	.67	83	.255	.294	.323

Maicer Izturis

Bats: B Throws: R Pos: 3B-30; 2B-29; SS-26; PH-26   MY-sare izz-TOUR-iss   Ht: 5'8" Wt: 170 Born: 9/12/1980 Age: 32

Year	Team	Lg	G	AB	H	2B	3B	HR	(Hm	Rd)	TB	R	RBI	RC	TBB	IBB	SO	HBP	SH	SF	SB	CS	SB%	GDP	Avg	OBP	Slg
														BATTING								**BASERUNNING**			**AVERAGES**		
2004	Mon	NL	32	107	22	5	2	1	(1	0)	34	10	4	8	10	1	20	2	2	0	4	0	1.00	1	.206	.286	.318
2005	LAA	AL	77	191	47	8	4	1	(0	1)	66	18	15	25	17	2	21	0	1	1	9	3	.75	5	.246	.306	.346
2006	LAA	AL	104	352	103	21	3	5	(1	4)	145	64	44	56	38	1	35	3	5	1	14	6	.70	7	.293	.365	.412
2007	LAA	AL	102	336	97	17	2	6	(4	2)	136	47	51	65	33	2	39	0	1	4	7	1	.88	6	.289	.349	.405
2008	LAA	AL	79	290	78	14	2	3	(1	2)	105	44	37	39	26	0	27	1	2	2	11	2	.85	9	.269	.329	.362
2009	LAA	AL	114	387	116	22	3	8	(3	5)	168	74	65	66	35	2	41	5	3	7	13	5	.72	7	.300	.359	.434
2010	LAA	AL	61	212	53	13	1	3	(0	3)	77	27	27	30	21	0	27	2	1	2	7	3	.70	1	.250	.321	.363
2011	LAA	AL	122	449	124	35	0	5	(1	4)	174	51	38	53	33	3	65	8	0	4	9	6	.60	6	.276	.334	.388
2012	LAA	AL	100	289	74	11	0	2	(0	2)	91	35	20	28	25	0	38	2	3	0	17	2	.89	10	.256	.320	.315
	Postseason		10	29	6	3	0	0	(0	0)	9	3	2	2	1	1	5	0	0	1	3	0	1.00	0	.207	.226	.310
	9 ML YEARS		791	2613	714	146	17	34	(11	23)	996	370	301	370	238	11	313	23	18	21	91	28	.76	50	.273	.337	.381

Austin Jackson

Bats: R Throws: R Pos: CF-137; PH-1; PR-1   Ht: 6'1" Wt: 185 Born: 2/1/1987 Age: 26

Year	Team	Lg	G	AB	H	2B	3B	HR	(Hm	Rd)	TB	R	RBI	RC	TBB	IBB	SO	HBP	SH	SF	SB	CS	SB%	GDP	Avg	OBP	Slg
														BATTING								**BASERUNNING**			**AVERAGES**		
2012	Toledo*	AAA	2	8	1	0	0	0	(-	-)	1	0	0	0	2	0	0	0	0	0	0	1	.00	0	.125	.222	.125
2010	Det	AL	151	618	181	34	10	4	(0	4)	247	103	41	84	47	4	170	4	3	3	27	6	.82	5	.293	.345	.400
2011	Det	AL	153	591	147	22	11	10	(5	5)	221	90	45	67	56	3	181	4	14	3	22	5	.81	11	.249	.317	.374
2012	Det	AL	137	543	163	29	10	16	(6	10)	260	103	66	90	67	0	134	2	2	3	12	9	.57	9	.300	.377	.479
	Postseason		11	41	8	2	0	1	(0	1)	13	6	4	5	7	0	19	1	1	0	1	1	.50	0	.195	.327	.317
	3 ML YEARS		441	1752	491	85	31	30	(11	19)	728	296	152	241	170	7	485	10	19	9	61	20	.75	25	.280	.346	.416

Brett Jackson

Bats: L Throws: R Pos: CF-39; PH-5; PR-1   Ht: 6'2" Wt: 210 Born: 8/2/1988 Age: 24

Year	Team	Lg	G	AB	H	2B	3B	HR	(Hm	Rd)	TB	R	RBI	RC	TBB	IBB	SO	HBP	SH	SF	SB	CS	SB%	GDP	Avg	OBP	Slg
														BATTING								**BASERUNNING**			**AVERAGES**		
2009	Cubs	R	3	11	5	0	1	0	(-	-)	7	6	4	3	3	0	4	0	0	1	0	0	-	0	.455	.533	.636
2009	Boise	A-	24	88	29	1	1	1	(-	-)	35	14	15	17	17	2	20	1	0	0	2	1	.67	1	.330	.443	.398
2009	Peoria	A	20	112	33	5	1	7	(-	-)	61	30	17	24	11	1	32	5	0	1	11	1	.92	0	.295	.383	.545
2010	Dytona	A+	67	263	83	19	8	6	(-	-)	136	56	38	57	43	2	63	5	0	1	12	7	.63	0	.316	.420	.517
2010	Tenn	AA	61	228	63	13	6	6	(-	-)	106	47	28	42	30	1	63	4	3	3	18	4	.82	2	.276	.366	.465
2011	Tenn	AA	67	246	63	10	3	10	(-	-)	109	45	32	44	45	1	74	2	2	2	15	6	.71	1	.256	.373	.443
2011	Iowa	AAA	48	185	55	13	2	10	(-	-)	102	39	26	40	28	3	64	0	1	1	6	1	.86	0	.297	.388	.551
2012	Iowa	AAA	106	407	104	22	12	15	(-	-)	195	66	47	71	47	1	158	6	2	5	27	5	.84	5	.256	.338	.479
2012	ChC	NL	44	120	21	6	1	4	(3	1)	41	14	9	11	22	0	59	0	0	0	0	3	.00	1	.175	.303	.342

Edwin Jackson

Pitches: R **Bats:** R **Pos:** SP-31 **Ht:** 6'3" **Wt:** 210 **Born:** 9/9/1983 **Age:** 29

Year Team	Lg	G	GS	CG	GF	IP	BFP	H	R	ER	HR	SH	SF	HB	TBB	IBB	SO	WP	Bk	W	L	Pct	Sh	Sv-Op	Hld	ERC	ERA
2003 LAD	NL	4	3	0	0	22.0	91	17	6	6	2	1	1	1	11	1	19	3	0	2	1	.667	0	0-0	0	3.36	2.45
2004 LAD	NL	8	5	0	1	24.2	113	31	20	20	7	1	0	0	11	1	16	0	0	2	1	.667	0	0-0	0	7.21	7.30
2005 LAD	NL	7	6	0	0	28.2	134	31	22	20	2	0	2	1	17	0	13	2	1	2	2	.500	0	0-0	0	5.13	6.28
2006 TB	AL	23	1	0	7	36.1	174	42	27	22	2	2	2	1	25	0	27	3	1	0	0	-	0	0-0	0	5.86	5.45
2007 TB	AL	32	31	1	0	161.0	755	195	116	103	19	5	6	4	88	3	128	7	1	5	15	.250	1	0-0	0	6.11	5.76
2008 TB	AL	32	31	0	0	183.1	792	199	91	90	23	3	3	2	77	1	108	7	1	14	11	.560	0	0-1	0	4.99	4.42
2009 Det	AL	33	33	1	0	214.0	890	200	93	86	27	4	2	5	70	3	161	6	0	13	9	.591	0	0-0	0	3.72	3.62
2010 2 Tms		32	32	1	0	209.1	902	214	111	104	21	6	4	6	78	4	181	20	0	10	12	.455	1	0-0	0	4.20	4.47
2011 2 Tms		32	31	1	1	199.2	861	225	92	84	16	15	6	2	62	4	148	9	2	12	9	.571	1	0-0	0	4.34	3.79
2012 Was	NL	31	31	1	0	189.2	790	173	90	85	23	9	8	2	58	5	168	3	0	10	11	.476	0	0-0	0	3.36	4.03
10 Ari	AL	21	21	1	0	134.1	587	141	80	77	13	6	2	5	60	2	104	13	0	6	10	.375	1	0-0	0	4.72	5.16
10 CWS	AL	11	11	0	0	75.0	315	73	31	27	8	0	2	1	18	2	77	7	0	4	2	.667	0	0-0	0	3.32	3.24
11 CWS	AL	19	19	1	0	121.2	522	134	55	53	8	6	4	0	39	2	97	7	1	7	7	.500	1	0-0	0	4.10	3.92
11 StL	NL	13	12	0	1	78.0	339	91	37	31	8	9	2	2	23	2	51	2	1	5	2	.714	0	0-0	0	4.73	3.58
Postseason		7	4	0	2	22.0	96	21	12	12	5	1	0	0	12	1	17	0	0	1	1	.500	0	0-0	0	5.32	4.91
10 ML YEARS		234	204	5	9	1268.2	5502	1327	668	620	142	46	34	24	497	22	969	60	6	70	71	.496	3	0-1	0	4.46	4.40

Ryan Jackson

Bats: R **Throws:** R **Pos:** 2B-8; PH-7; PR-2; SS-1 **Ht:** 6'3" **Wt:** 180 **Born:** 5/10/1988 **Age:** 25

Year Team	Lg	G	AB	H	2B	3B	HR	(Hm	Rd)	TB	R	RBI	RC	TBB	IBB	SO	HBP	SH	SF	SB	CS	SB%	GDP	Avg	OBP	Slg
2009 Batvia	A-	67	245	53	4	1	0	(-	-)	59	29	14	19	29	1	37	0	7	2	4	3	.57	6	.216	.297	.241
2010 QuadC	A	84	302	82	13	2	2	(-	-)	105	47	27	42	48	0	63	0	0	5	6	7	.46	8	.272	.366	.348
2010 PlmBh	A+	41	148	43	10	1	1	(-	-)	58	14	8	20	11	0	21	1	6	1	3	2	.60	2	.291	.342	.392
2011 Sprgfld	AA	135	533	148	34	3	11	(-	-)	221	65	73	78	44	2	91	4	12	6	2	0	1.00	17	.278	.334	.415
2012 Memp	AAA	117	445	121	23	1	10	(-	-)	176	60	47	62	43	2	75	0	12	3	2	0	1.00	18	.272	.334	.396
2012 StL	NL	13	17	2	0	0	0	(0	0)	2	2	0	0	1	0	3	0	0	0	0	0	-	1	.118	.167	.118

Mike Jacobs

Bats: L **Throws:** R **Pos:** PH-10; 1B-4 **Ht:** 6'3" **Wt:** 215 **Born:** 10/30/1980 **Age:** 32

Year Team	Lg	G	AB	H	2B	3B	HR	(Hm	Rd)	TB	R	RBI	RC	TBB	IBB	SO	HBP	SH	SF	SB	CS	SB%	GDP	Avg	OBP	Slg
2012 Reno*	AAA	101	333	93	15	0	18	(-	-)	162	59	60	59	44	4	83	0	0	1	2	2	.50	9	.279	.362	.486
2005 NYM	NL	30	100	31	7	0	11	(6	5)	71	19	23	21	10	0	22	1	0	1	0	0	-	5	.310	.375	.710
2006 Fla	NL	136	469	123	37	1	20	(12	8)	222	54	77	66	45	2	105	1	0	5	3	0	1.00	16	.262	.325	.473
2007 Fla	NL	114	426	113	27	2	17	(10	7)	195	57	54	51	31	3	101	2	0	1	1	2	.33	12	.265	.317	.458
2008 Fla	NL	141	477	118	27	2	32	(14	18)	245	67	93	69	36	10	119	1	0	5	1	0	1.00	9	.247	.299	.514
2009 KC	AL	128	434	99	16	1	19	(8	11)	174	46	61	50	41	2	132	2	0	1	0	0	-	9	.228	.297	.401
2010 NYM	NL	7	24	5	1	0	1	(1	0)	9	1	2	3	3	0	7	0	1	0	0	0	-	0	.208	.296	.375
2012 Ari	NL	13	19	4	1	0	0	(0	0)	5	4	2	3	4	1	6	0	0	0	0	0	-	0	.211	.348	.263
7 ML YEARS		569	1949	493	116	6	100	(51	49)	921	248	312	263	170	18	492	7	1	13	5	2	.71	49	.253	.313	.473

Paul Janish

Bats: R **Throws:** R **Pos:** SS-55 YONN-ish **Ht:** 6'2" **Wt:** 200 **Born:** 10/12/1982 **Age:** 30

Year Team	Lg	G	AB	H	2B	3B	HR	(Hm	Rd)	TB	R	RBI	RC	TBB	IBB	SO	HBP	SH	SF	SB	CS	SB%	GDP	Avg	OBP	Slg
2012 Lsvlle*	AAA	49	169	40	12	1	4	(-	-)	66	27	11	23	20	0	26	4	1	0	0	1	.00	5	.237	.332	.391
2008 Cin	NL	38	80	15	2	0	1	(1	0)	20	5	6	5	7	0	18	2	0	0	0	0	-	2	.188	.270	.250
2009 Cin	NL	90	256	54	21	0	1	(1	0)	78	36	16	18	26	1	40	5	5	0	2	0	1.00	4	.211	.296	.305
2010 Cin	NL	82	200	52	10	0	5	(0	5)	77	23	25	31	22	2	30	2	3	1	1	3	.25	4	.260	.338	.385
2011 Cin	NL	114	336	72	14	1	0	(0	0)	88	27	23	21	18	1	46	4	3	5	3	2	.60	7	.214	.259	.262
2012 Atl	NL	55	167	31	6	1	0	(0	0)	39	18	9	13	17	0	30	2	0	0	0	1	1.00	1	.186	.269	.234
Postseason		1	1	0	0	0	0	(0	0)	0	0	0	0	0	0	0	0	1	0	0	0	-	0	.000	.000	.000
5 ML YEARS		379	1039	224	53	2	7	(2	5)	302	109	79	88	90	4	164	15	11	6	7	5	.58	22	.216	.286	.291

Kenley Jansen

Pitches: R **Bats:** B **Pos:** RP-65 KEN-lee JANN-sen **Ht:** 6'5" **Wt:** 260 **Born:** 9/30/1987 **Age:** 25

Year Team	Lg	G	GS	CG	GF	IP	BFP	H	R	ER	HR	SH	SF	HB	TBB	IBB	SO	WP	Bk	W	L	Pct	Sh	Sv-Op	Hld	ERC	ERA
2010 LAD	NL	25	0	0	8	27.0	109	12	2	2	0	1	0	1	15	1	41	1	0	1	0	1.000	0	4-4	4	1.40	0.67
2011 LAD	NL	51	0	0	13	53.2	218	30	17	17	3	0	1	2	26	0	96	0	2	2	1	.667	0	5-6	9	1.96	2.85
2012 LAD	NL	65	0	0	40	65.0	252	33	18	17	6	0	1	3	22	1	99	3	0	5	3	.625	0	25-32	8	1.55	2.35
3 ML YEARS		141	0	0	61	145.2	579	75	37	36	9	1	2	6	63	2	236	4	2	8	4	.667	0	34-42	21	1.65	2.22

Casey Janssen

Pitches: R **Bats:** R **Pos:** RP-62 JANN-sen **Ht:** 6'3" **Wt:** 225 **Born:** 9/17/1981 **Age:** 31

Year Team	Lg	G	GS	CG	GF	IP	BFP	H	R	ER	HR	SH	SF	HB	TBB	IBB	SO	WP	Bk	W	L	Pct	Sh	Sv-Op	Hld	ERC	ERA
2006 Tor	AL	19	14	0	0	94.0	407	103	58	54	12	2	2	7	21	3	44	3	2	6	10	.375	0	0-0	0	4.32	5.07
2007 Tor	AL	70	0	0	21	72.2	297	67	22	19	4	0	3	3	20	2	39	4	0	2	3	.400	0	6-11	24	3.06	2.35
2009 Tor	AL	21	5	0	5	40.0	192	59	29	26	5	1	2	4	14	1	24	1	0	2	4	.333	0	1-1	7	7.04	5.85

Year	Team	Lg	G	GS	CG	GF	IP	BFP	H	R	ER	HR	SH	SF	HB	TBB	IBB	SO	WP	Bk	W	L	Pct	Sh	Sv-Op	Hld	ERC	ERA
			HOW MUCH HE PITCHED						**WHAT HE GAVE UP**												**THE RESULTS**							
2010	Tor	AL	56	0	0	16	68.2	298	74	29	28	8	0	1	4	21	1	63	3	0	5	2	.714	0	0-0	2	4.48	3.67
2011	Tor	AL	55	0	0	11	55.2	223	47	14	14	2	1	0	2	14	1	53	2	0	6	0	1.000	0	2-4	7	2.44	2.26
2012	Tor	AL	62	0	0	47	63.2	242	44	18	18	7	1	1	3	11	1	67	2	1	1	1	.500	0	22-25	1	1.93	2.54
6 ML YEARS			283	22	0	101	394.2	1659	394	170	158	38	5	9	21	101	9	290	15	3	22	20	.524	0	31-41	36	3.67	3.60

John Jaso

Bats: L **Throws:** R **Pos:** DH-46; C-43; PH-25   JAY-soe   **Ht:** 6'2" **Wt:** 205 **Born:** 9/19/1983 **Age:** 29

Year	Team	Lg	G	AB	H	2B	3B	HR	(Hm	Rd)	TB	R	RBI	RC	TBB	IBB	SO	HBP	SH	SF	SB	CS	SB%	GDP	Avg	OBP	Slg
			BATTING																		**BASERUNNING**				**AVERAGES**		
2008	TB	AL	5	10	2	0	0	0	(0	0)	2	2	0	0	0	0	2	0	0	0	0	0	-	1	.200	.200	.200
2010	TB	AL	109	339	89	18	3	5	(1	4)	128	57	44	57	59	1	39	2	1	3	4	0	1.00	8	.263	.372	.378
2011	TB	AL	89	246	55	15	1	5	(3	2)	87	26	27	20	25	0	36	1	1	0	1	2	.33	9	.224	.298	.354
2012	Sea	AL	108	294	81	19	2	10	(6	4)	134	41	50	68	56	1	51	5	1	5	5	0	1.00	6	.276	.394	.456
Postseason			5	14	3	0	0	0	(0	0)	3	0	1	1	1	0	3	0	0	0	0	0	-	0	.214	.267	.214
4 ML YEARS			311	889	227	52	6	20	(10	10)	351	126	121	145	140	2	128	8	3	8	10	2	.83	24	.255	.359	.395

Jon Jay

Bats: L **Throws:** L **Pos:** CF-116; PR-3; PH-1   **Ht:** 5'11" **Wt:** 200 **Born:** 3/15/1985 **Age:** 28

Year	Team	Lg	G	AB	H	2B	3B	HR	(Hm	Rd)	TB	R	RBI	RC	TBB	IBB	SO	HBP	SH	SF	SB	CS	SB%	GDP	Avg	OBP	Slg
			BATTING																		**BASERUNNING**				**AVERAGES**		
2012	Memp*	AAA	2	7	3	0	1	0	(-	-)	8	3	3	3	1	0	0	0	0	0	0	0	-	0	.429	.500	1.143
2010	StL	NL	105	287	86	19	2	4	(2	2)	121	47	27	40	24	0	50	3	8	1	2	4	.33	5	.300	.359	.422
2011	StL	NL	159	455	135	24	2	10	(5	5)	193	56	37	56	28	1	81	7	4	4	6	7	.46	11	.297	.344	.424
2012	StL	NL	117	443	135	22	4	4	(3	1)	177	70	40	65	34	3	71	15	9	1	19	7	.73	9	.305	.373	.400
Postseason			18	55	10	2	0	0			12	8	3	4	6	1	6	0	2	0	1	1	.50	2	.182	.262	.218
3 ML YEARS			381	1185	356	65	8	18	(10	8)	491	173	104	161	86	4	202	25	26	6	27	18	.60	25	.300	.359	.414

Jeremy Jeffress

Pitches: R **Bats:** R **Pos:** RP-13   JEFF-ress   **Ht:** 6'0" **Wt:** 195 **Born:** 9/21/1987 **Age:** 25

Year	Team	Lg	G	GS	CG	GF	IP	BFP	H	R	ER	HR	SH	SF	HB	TBB	IBB	SO	WP	Bk	W	L	Pct	Sh	Sv-Op	Hld	ERC	ERA
			HOW MUCH HE PITCHED						**WHAT HE GAVE UP**												**THE RESULTS**							
2012	Omha*	AAA	37	0	0	12	58.0	241	52	34	32	4	2	3	0	25	2	61	4	0	5	4	.556	0	2--	-	3.44	4.97
2012	NWArk*	AA	1	0	0	1	1.1	5	0	0	0	0	0	0	0	1	0	3	0	0	0	0	-	0	1--	-	0.57	0.00
2010	Mil	NL	10	0	0	5	10.0	42	8	4	3	0	0	1	0	6	1	8	1	0	1	0	1.000	0	0-0	0	2.96	2.70
2011	KC	AL	14	0	0	6	15.1	67	12	8	8	1	2	0	0	11	0	13	1	0	1	1	.500	0	1-2	0	3.87	4.70
2012	KC	AL	13	0	0	6	13.1	73	19	14	10	0	0	0	0	13	0	13	1	0	0	0	-	0	0-0	0	7.87	6.75
3 ML YEARS			37	0	0	17	38.2	182	39	26	21	1	2	1	0	30	1	34	3	0	2	1	.667	0	1-2	0	4.93	4.89

Chad Jenkins

Pitches: R **Bats:** R **Pos:** RP-10; SP-3   **Ht:** 6'4" **Wt:** 230 **Born:** 12/22/1987 **Age:** 25

Year	Team	Lg	G	GS	CG	GF	IP	BFP	H	R	ER	HR	SH	SF	HB	TBB	IBB	SO	WP	Bk	W	L	Pct	Sh	Sv-Op	Hld	ERC	ERA
			HOW MUCH HE PITCHED						**WHAT HE GAVE UP**												**THE RESULTS**							
2010	Lnsng	A	13	13	1	0	79.1	332	87	35	32	5	2	2	1	13	0	64	3	0	5	4	.556	0	0--	-	3.49	3.63
2010	Dnedin	A+	13	13	0	0	62.1	280	73	37	30	6	1	1	0	18	1	42	1	0	2	6	.250	0	0--	-	4.40	4.33
2011	Dnedin	A+	11	11	0	0	67.1	284	71	33	23	3	1	3	0	14	1	44	2	0	4	5	.444	0	0--	-	3.20	3.07
2011	NHam	AA	16	16	1	0	100.1	410	93	48	46	8	0	5	2	27	0	74	9	0	5	7	.417	0	0--	-	3.17	4.13
2012	NHam	AA	20	20	0	0	114.1	507	145	67	63	17	0	3	5	31	0	57	5	0	5	9	.357	0	0--	-	5.73	4.96
2012	Tor	AL	13	3	0	6	32.0	136	32	16	16	5	1	0	1	11	1	16	0	0	1	3	.250	0	0-0	0	4.36	4.50

Dan Jennings

Pitches: L **Bats:** L **Pos:** RP-22   **Ht:** 6'3" **Wt:** 215 **Born:** 4/17/1987 **Age:** 26

Year	Team	Lg	G	GS	CG	GF	IP	BFP	H	R	ER	HR	SH	SF	HB	TBB	IBB	SO	WP	Bk	W	L	Pct	Sh	Sv-Op	Hld	ERC	ERA
			HOW MUCH HE PITCHED						**WHAT HE GAVE UP**												**THE RESULTS**							
2008	Jmstwn	A-	13	13	0	0	58.2	267	79	31	23	2	1	1	1	18	0	62	4	0	1	4	.200	0	0--	-	5.28	3.53
2009	Grnsbr	A	34	0	0	12	49.1	206	42	21	15	1	5	3	0	21	3	54	8	0	1	2	.333	0	0--	-	2.76	2.74
2009	Jupiter	A+	8	0	0	6	11.2	42	5	0	0	0	0	0	0	4	0	13	1	0	0	0	-	0	6--	-	0.97	0.00
2009	Jaxnvl	AA	3	0	0	1	1.2	8	2	0	0	0	0	0	0	1	0	2	0	0	0	0	-	0	0--	-	5.10	0.00
2010	Jaxnvl	AA	37	0	0	4	52.2	223	49	18	15	0	4	2	0	26	1	44	9	0	4	2	.667	0	0--	-	3.39	2.56
2011	Jaxnvl	AA	21	0	0	7	25.2	112	26	11	9	1	2	1	0	11	0	29	0	0	4	1	.800	0	2--	-	3.80	3.16
2011	NewOr	AAA	24	0	0	8	30.2	137	34	24	24	3	3	4	0	17	2	27	1	0	1	3	.250	0	2--	-	5.31	7.04
2012	NewOr	AAA	42	0	0	10	51.2	212	48	19	18	2	5	1	0	16	0	48	6	0	1	3	.250	0	2--	-	2.99	3.14
2012	Mia	NL	22	0	0	4	19.0	86	18	5	4	2	0	0	2	11	1	8	0	0	1	0	1.000	0	0-0	2	4.85	1.89

Desmond Jennings

Bats: R **Throws:** R **Pos:** LF-111; CF-21; PH-5; RF-1   **Ht:** 6'2" **Wt:** 200 **Born:** 10/30/1986 **Age:** 26

Year	Team	Lg	G	AB	H	2B	3B	HR	(Hm	Rd)	TB	R	RBI	RC	TBB	IBB	SO	HBP	SH	SF	SB	CS	SB%	GDP	Avg	OBP	Slg
			BATTING																		**BASERUNNING**				**AVERAGES**		
2012	Charltt*	A+	1	3	1	1	0	0	(-	-)	2	1	0	0	0	0	0	0	0	0	0	0	-	0	.333	.333	.667
2012	Drham*	AAA	3	12	2	0	0	0	(-	-)	2	1	0	0	0	0	1	0	0	0	0	0	-	0	.167	.167	.167
2010	TB	AL	17	21	4	1	1	0	(0	0)	7	5	2	2	2	0	4	1	0	0	2	2	.50	0	.190	.292	.333

				BATTING																BASERUNNING				AVERAGES		
Year	Team	Lg	G	AB	H	2B	3B	HR	(Hm	Rd)	TB	R	RBI	RC	TBB	IBB	SO	HBP	SH	SF	SB	CS	SB%	GDP	Avg	OBP	Slg
2011	TB	AL	63	247	64	9	4	10	(3	7)	111	44	25	45	31	1	59	6	3	0	20	6	.77	1	.259	.356	.449
2012	TB	AL	132	505	124	19	7	13	(9	4)	196	85	47	62	46	1	120	5	6	1	31	2	.94	7	.246	.314	.388
	Postseason		6	17	5	1	0	2	(2	0)	12	4	2	3	3	0	2	0	0	0	0	0	-	0	.294	.400	.706
3 ML YEARS			212	773	192	29	12	23	(12	11)	314	134	74	109	79	2	183	12	9	1	53	10	.84	8	.248	.327	.406

Kevin Jepsen

Pitches: R **Bats:** R **Pos:** RP-49   **Ht:** 6'3" **Wt:** 230 **Born:** 7/26/1984 **Age:** 28

			HOW MUCH HE PITCHED						WHAT HE GAVE UP										THE RESULTS						
Year	Team	Lg	G	GS	CG	GF	IP	BFP	H	R	ER	HR	SH	SF	HB	TBB	IBB	SO	WP	Bk	W	L	Pct	Sh	Sv-Op Hld	ERC	ERA
2012	Salt Lk*	AAA	23	0	0	11	25.0	98	18	9	9	1	0	0	0	9	0	35	3	0	2	2	.500	0	2- -	2.18	3.24
2008	LAA	AL	9	0	0	0	8.1	36	8	5	4	0	0	0	0	4	0	7	1	0	0	1	.000	0	0-0 3	3.46	4.32
2009	LAA	AL	54	0	0	13	54.2	237	63	33	30	2	0	2	0	19	2	48	6	0	6	4	.600	0	1-2 17	4.27	4.94
2010	LAA	AL	68	0	0	4	59.0	253	54	26	26	2	4	2	2	29	5	61	8	0	2	4	.333	0	0-4 27	3.53	3.97
2011	LAA	AL	16	0	0	5	13.0	68	21	11	11	2	1	1	1	9	4	6	5	0	1	2	.333	0	0-1 2	9.45	7.62
2012	LAA	AL	49	0	0	11	44.2	178	39	17	15	3	3	1	2	12	1	38	1	0	3	2	.600	0	2-4 18	2.93	3.02
	Postseason		5	0	0	0	5.0	24	8	2	2	1	0	0	0	2	0	3	0	0	1	0	1.000	0	0-0 1	8.81	3.60
5 ML YEARS			196	0	0	33	179.2	772	185	92	86	9	8	6	5	73	12	160	21	0	12	13	.480	0	3-11 67	3.97	4.31

Derek Jeter

Bats: R **Throws:** R **Pos:** SS-135; DH-25   **Ht:** 6'3" **Wt:** 195 **Born:** 6/26/1974 **Age:** 39

				BATTING																BASERUNNING				AVERAGES		
Year	Team	Lg	G	AB	H	2B	3B	HR	(Hm	Rd)	TB	R	RBI	RC	TBB	IBB	SO	HBP	SH	SF	SB	CS	SB%	GDP	Avg	OBP	Slg
1995	NYY	AL	15	48	12	4	1	0	(0	0)	18	5	7	5	3	0	11	0	0	0	0	0	-	0	.250	.294	.375
1996	NYY	AL	157	582	183	25	6	10	(3	7)	250	104	78	92	48	1	102	9	6	9	14	7	.67	13	.314	.370	.430
1997	NYY	AL	159	654	190	31	7	10	(5	5)	265	116	70	99	74	0	125	10	8	2	23	12	.66	14	.291	.370	.405
1998	NYY	AL	149	626	203	25	8	19	(9	10)	301	127	84	115	57	1	119	5	3	3	30	6	.83	13	.324	.384	.481
1999	NYY	AL	158	627	219	37	9	24	(15	9)	346	134	102	146	91	5	116	12	3	6	19	8	.70	12	.349	.438	.552
2000	NYY	AL	148	593	201	31	4	15	(8	7)	285	119	73	118	68	4	99	12	3	3	22	4	.85	14	.339	.416	.481
2001	NYY	AL	150	614	191	35	3	21	(13	8)	295	110	74	112	56	3	99	10	5	1	27	3	.90	13	.311	.377	.480
2002	NYY	AL	157	644	191	26	0	18	(8	10)	271	124	75	108	73	2	114	7	3	3	32	3	.91	14	.297	.373	.421
2003	NYY	AL	119	482	156	25	3	10	(7	3)	217	87	52	86	43	2	88	13	3	1	11	5	.69	10	.324	.393	.450
2004	NYY	AL	154	643	188	44	1	23	(11	12)	303	111	78	100	46	1	99	14	16	3	23	4	.85	19	.292	.352	.471
2005	NYY	AL	159	654	202	25	5	19	(12	7)	294	122	70	105	77	3	117	11	7	3	14	5	.74	15	.309	.389	.450
2006	NYY	AL	154	623	214	39	3	14	(8	6)	301	118	97	132	69	4	102	12	7	4	34	5	.87	13	.343	.417	.483
2007	NYY	AL	156	639	206	39	4	12	(4	8)	289	102	73	112	56	3	100	14	3	2	15	8	.65	21	.322	.388	.452
2008	NYY	AL	150	596	179	25	3	11	(3	8)	243	88	69	88	52	0	85	9	7	4	11	5	.69	24	.300	.363	.408
2009	NYY	AL	153	634	212	27	1	18	(13	5)	295	107	66	109	72	4	90	5	4	1	30	5	.86	18	.334	.406	.465
2010	NYY	AL	157	663	179	30	3	10	(7	3)	245	111	67	86	63	4	106	9	1	3	18	5	.78	22	.270	.340	.370
2011	NYY	AL	131	546	162	24	4	6	(4	2)	212	84	61	75	46	0	81	6	4	5	16	6	.73	10	.297	.355	.388
2012	NYY	AL	159	683	216	32	0	15	(6	9)	293	99	58	98	45	1	90	5	6	1	9	4	.69	24	.316	.362	.429
	Postseason		152	623	191	31	4	20	(12	8)	290	107	59	95	64	3	125	5	8	4	18	5	.78	14	.307	.374	.465
18 ML YEARS			2585	10551	3304	524	65	255	(136	119)	4723	1868	1254	1786	1039	38	1743	163	89	53	348	95	.79	269	.313	.382	.448

Luis Jimenez

Bats: L **Throws:** L **Pos:** DH-4; PH-3   **Ht:** 6'4" **Wt:** 280 **Born:** 5/7/1982 **Age:** 31

				BATTING																BASERUNNING				AVERAGES		
Year	Team	Lg	G	AB	H	2B	3B	HR	(Hm	Rd)	TB	R	RBI	RC	TBB	IBB	SO	HBP	SH	SF	SB	CS	SB%	GDP	Avg	OBP	Slg
2001	As	R	24	70	15	1	1	0	(-	-)	18	8	12	6	8	0	23	0	0	4	2	0	1.00	0	.214	.280	.257
2002	Bluefld	R+	51	176	66	13	1	8	(-	-)	105	40	42	49	33	1	33	1	0	1	9	1	.90	7	.375	.474	.597
2003	Abrdn	A-	53	168	41	9	0	1	(-	-)	53	17	21	20	26	0	40	1	2	0	7	4	.64	2	.244	.349	.315
2004	Clmbs	A	110	392	113	24	1	20	(-	-)	199	62	75	75	51	2	104	3	1	3	6	2	.75	7	.288	.372	.508
2005	NwBrit	AA	114	423	118	29	1	16	(-	-)	197	61	68	70	44	2	101	2	0	0	3	2	.60	11	.279	.350	.466
2006	Portlnd	AA	115	395	109	22	2	17	(-	-)	186	74	70	73	58	5	90	5	0	6	9	2	.82	12	.276	.371	.471
2007	Pwtckt	AAA	25	81	12	2	0	1	(-	-)	17	4	7	3	9	1	21	0	0	1	1	0	1.00	3	.148	.231	.210
2007	Bowie	AA	89	320	105	18	0	22	(-	-)	189	57	80	73	41	6	71	0	0	5	1	1	.50	5	.328	.399	.591
2008	Hrsbrg	AA	77	246	64	8	0	14	(-	-)	114	35	42	42	35	6	44	0	0	1	3	0	1.00	11	.260	.351	.463
2008	Clmbs	AAA	33	91	30	4	0	1	(-	-)	37	9	10	15	12	3	22	0	0	1	0	0	-	5	.330	.404	.407
2011	Jacksn	AA	30	101	32	3	1	4	(-	-)	49	17	18	21	18	2	17	0	0	1	2	0	1.00	3	.317	.417	.485
2011	Tacom	AAA	74	284	81	13	1	12	(-	-)	132	51	57	51	39	2	55	1	0	3	2	1	.67	4	.285	.370	.465
2012	Tacom	AAA	125	471	146	32	2	20	(-	-)	242	64	81	96	64	2	97	1	0	0	3	0	1.00	14	.310	.394	.514
2012	Sea	AL	7	17	1	0	0	0	(0	0)	1	0	0	0	0	0	6	0	0	0	0	0	-	0	.059	.111	.059

Ubaldo Jimenez

Pitches: R **Bats:** R **Pos:** SP-31   ooh-BALL-doh   **Ht:** 6'5" **Wt:** 210 **Born:** 1/22/1984 **Age:** 29

			HOW MUCH HE PITCHED						WHAT HE GAVE UP										THE RESULTS						
Year	Team	Lg	G	GS	CG	GF	IP	BFP	H	R	ER	HR	SH	SF	HB	TBB	IBB	SO	WP	Bk	W	L	Pct	Sh	Sv-Op Hld	ERC	ERA
2006	Col	NL	2	1	0	0	7.2	30	5	4	3	1	0	0	0	3	0	3	0	0	0	0	-	0	0-0 0	2.48	3.52
2007	Col	NL	15	15	0	0	82.0	354	70	46	39	10	3	1	6	37	4	68	3	0	4	4	.500	0	0-0 0	3.80	4.28
2008	Col	NL	34	34	1	0	198.2	868	182	97	88	11	7	4	10	103	4	172	16	0	12	12	.500	0	0-0 0	3.92	3.99
2009	Col	NL	33	33	1	0	218.0	914	183	87	84	13	15	6	10	85	6	198	8	0	15	12	.556	0	0-0 0	3.03	3.47
2010	Col	NL	33	33	4	0	221.2	894	164	73	71	10	7	1	9	92	7	214	16	1	19	8	.704	2	0-0 0	2.57	2.88
2011	2 Tms		32	32	2	0	188.1	822	186	111	98	17	2	2	9	78	5	180	8	0	10	13	.435	1	0-0 0	4.13	4.68
2012	Cle	AL	31	31	0	0	176.2	805	190	116	106	25	2	3	8	95	3	143	16	1	9	17	.346	0	0-0 0	5.55	5.40
11 Col		NL	21	21	2	0	123.0	532	118	68	61	10	2	2	7	51	5	118	6	0	6	9	.400	1	0-0 0	3.94	4.46
11 Cle		AL	11	11	0	0	65.1	290	68	43	37	7	0	0	2	27	0	62	2	0	4	4	.500	0	0-0 0	4.48	5.10
	Postseason		5	5	0	0	28.0	123	26	11	11	3	0	1	1	16	2	24	1	0	0	2	.000	0	0-0 0	4.47	3.54
7 ML YEARS			180	179	8	0	1093.0	4687	980	534	489	87	36	17	52	493	29	978	67	5	69	66	.511	3	0-0 0	3.72	4.03

Chris Johnson

Bats: R **Throws:** R **Pos:** 3B-127; PH-7; 1B-6; RF-1   **Ht:** 6'3" **Wt:** 220 **Born:** 10/1/1984 **Age:** 28

								BATTING													BASERUNNING				AVERAGES		
Year	Team	Lg	G	AB	H	2B	3B	HR	(Hm	Rd)	TB	R	RBI	RC	TBB	IBB	SO	HBP	SH	SF	SB	CS	SB%	GDP	Avg	OBP	Slg
2009	Hou	NL	11	22	2	0	0	0	(0	0)	2	1	1	0	1	0	6	0	0	0	0	0	-	0	.091	.130	.091
2010	Hou	NL	94	341	105	22	2	11	(6	5)	164	40	52	55	15	2	91	2	0	4	3	0	1.00	8	.308	.337	.481
2011	Hou	NL	107	378	95	21	3	7	(2	5)	143	32	42	42	16	3	97	7	0	4	2	2	.50	2	.251	.291	.378
2012	2 Tms	NL	136	488	137	28	5	15	(8	7)	220	48	76	75	31	2	132	4	1	4	5	1	.83	18	.281	.326	.451
12	Hou	NL	92	341	95	21	3	8	(8	0)	146	36	41	47	23	1	92	3	0	1	4	1	.80	12	.279	.329	.428
12	Ari	NL	44	147	42	7	2	7	(0	7)	74	12	35	28	8	1	40	1	1	3	1	0	1.00	6	.286	.321	.503
	4 ML YEARS		348	1229	339	71	10	33	(16	17)	529	121	171	172	63	7	326	13	1	12	10	3	.77	28	.276	.315	.430

Dan Johnson

Bats: L **Throws:** R **Pos:** PH-9; DH-5; 1B-3   **Ht:** 6'2" **Wt:** 210 **Born:** 8/10/1979 **Age:** 33

								BATTING													BASERUNNING				AVERAGES		
Year	Team	Lg	G	AB	H	2B	3B	HR	(Hm	Rd)	TB	R	RBI	RC	TBB	IBB	SO	HBP	SH	SF	SB	CS	SB%	GDP	Avg	OBP	Slg
2012	Charltt*	AAA	137	476	127	21	1	28	(-	-)	234	77	85	98	94	9	94	7	0	10	1	0	1.00	8	.267	.388	.492
2005	Oak	AL	109	375	103	21	0	15	(2	13)	169	54	58	56	50	1	52	1	0	8	0	1	.00	1	.275	.355	.451
2006	Oak	AL	91	286	67	13	1	9	(4	5)	109	30	37	33	40	2	45	0	0	5	0	0	-	6	.234	.323	.381
2007	Oak	AL	117	416	98	20	1	18	(9	9)	174	53	62	58	72	4	77	3	0	4	0	0	-	12	.236	.349	.418
2008	2 Tms	AL	11	26	5	0	0	2	(1	1)	11	3	4	3	3	0	7	0	0	0	0	0	-	0	.192	.276	.423
2010	TB	AL	40	111	22	3	0	7	(4	3)	46	15	23	20	25	0	27	1	0	3	1	0	1.00	1	.198	.343	.414
2011	TB	AL	31	84	10	1	0	2	(1	1)	17	7	4	0	6	0	18	1	0	0	0	0	-	3	.119	.187	.202
2012	CWS	AL	14	22	8	1	0	3	(0	3)	18	8	6	9	9	1	3	0	0	0	0	0	-	0	.364	.548	.818
08	Oak	AL	1	1	0	0	0	0	(0	0)	0	0	0	0	0	0	0	0	0	0	0	0	-	0	.000	.000	.000
08	TB	AL	10	25	5	0	0	2	(1	1)	11	3	4	3	3	0	7	0	0	0	0	0	-	0	.200	.286	.440
	Postseason		5	9	2	1	0	0	(0	0)	3	1	0	1	3	0	4	0	0	0	0	0	-	1	.222	.417	.333
	7 ML YEARS		413	1320	313	59	2	56	(21	35)	544	170	194	179	205	8	229	6	0	20	1	1	.50	33	.237	.338	.412

Elliot Johnson

Bats: B **Throws:** R **Pos:** SS-100; 2B-13; PH-10; 3B-6; PR-6; LF-3; DH-2   **Ht:** 6'1" **Wt:** 190 **Born:** 3/9/1984 **Age:** 29

								BATTING													BASERUNNING				AVERAGES		
Year	Team	Lg	G	AB	H	2B	3B	HR	(Hm	Rd)	TB	R	RBI	RC	TBB	IBB	SO	HBP	SH	SF	SB	CS	SB%	GDP	Avg	OBP	Slg
2008	TB	AL	7	19	3	0	0	0	(0	0)	3	0	0	0	0	0	7	0	0	0	0	1	.00	0	.158	.158	.158
2011	TB	AL	70	160	31	7	2	4	(2	2)	54	20	17	10	14	0	53	0	6	1	6	7	.46	3	.194	.257	.338
2012	TB	AL	123	297	72	10	2	6	(1	5)	104	32	33	39	24	0	84	3	5	2	18	6	.75	3	.242	.304	.350
	Postseason		1	0	0	0	0	0	(0	0)	0	0	0	0	0	0	0	0	0	0	0	0	-	0	-	-	-
	3 ML YEARS		200	476	106	17	4	10	(3	7)	161	52	50	49	38	0	144	3	11	3	24	14	.63	6	.223	.283	.338

Jim Johnson

Pitches: R **Bats:** R **Pos:** RP-71   **Ht:** 6'6" **Wt:** 240 **Born:** 6/27/1983 **Age:** 30

			HOW MUCH HE PITCHED						WHAT HE GAVE UP											THE RESULTS						
Year	Team	Lg	G	GS	CG	GF	IP	BFP	H	R	ER	HR	SH	SF	HB	TBB	IBB	SO	WP	Bk	W	L	Pct	Sh	Sv-Op	Hld	ERC	ERA
2006	Bal	AL	1	1	0	0	3.0	21	9	8	8	1	0	1	0	3	0	0	0	0	0	1	.000	0	0-0	0	26.81	24.00
2007	Bal	AL	1	0	0	1	2.0	11	3	2	2	0	0	1	0	2	0	1	0	0	0	0	-	0	0-0	0	8.58	9.00
2008	Bal	AL	54	0	0	18	68.2	281	54	18	17	0	2	1	3	28	3	38	1	0	2	4	.333	0	1-1	19	2.45	2.23
2009	Bal	AL	64	0	0	29	70.0	300	73	32	32	8	2	3	3	23	3	49	2	1	4	6	.400	0	10-16	14	4.28	4.11
2010	Bal	AL	26	0	0	6	26.1	117	32	11	10	2	3	0	1	5	1	22	4	0	1	1	.500	0	1-6	11	4.26	3.42
2011	Bal	AL	69	0	0	20	91.0	366	80	30	27	5	4	2	2	21	3	58	2	1	6	5	.545	0	9-14	18	2.58	2.67
2012	Bal	AL	71	0	0	63	68.2	269	55	21	19	3	1	0	3	15	1	41	1	0	2	1	.667	0	51-54	0	2.22	2.49
	7 ML YEARS		286	1	0	137	329.2	1365	306	122	115	19	12	7	13	97	11	209	10	3	15	18	.455	0	72-91	62	3.13	3.14

Josh Johnson

Pitches: R **Bats:** L **Pos:** SP-31   **Ht:** 6'7" **Wt:** 250 **Born:** 1/31/1984 **Age:** 29

			HOW MUCH HE PITCHED						WHAT HE GAVE UP											THE RESULTS						
Year	Team	Lg	G	GS	CG	GF	IP	BFP	H	R	ER	HR	SH	SF	HB	TBB	IBB	SO	WP	Bk	W	L	Pct	Sh	Sv-Op	Hld	ERC	ERA
2005	Fla	NL	4	1	0	0	12.1	55	11	5	5	0	1	0	1	10	0	10	0	0	0	0	-	0	0-0	0	4.82	3.65
2006	Fla	NL	31	24	0	1	157.0	659	136	63	54	14	10	4	4	68	6	133	3	1	12	7	.632	0	0-1	0	3.48	3.10
2007	Fla	NL	4	4	0	0	15.2	82	26	17	13	1	2	1	0	12	3	14	1	0	0	3	.000	0	0-0	0	9.16	7.47
2008	Fla	NL	14	14	1	0	87.1	365	91	36	35	7	5	1	1	27	1	77	4	0	7	1	.875	0	0-0	0	3.94	3.61
2009	Fla	NL	33	33	2	0	209.0	855	184	77	75	14	11	4	6	58	6	191	10	0	15	5	.750	0	0-0	0	2.84	3.23
2010	Fla	NL	28	28	1	0	183.2	744	155	51	47	7	5	8	5	48	2	186	4	0	11	6	.647	0	0-0	0	2.44	2.30
2011	Fla	NL	9	9	0	0	60.1	234	39	13	11	2	1	1	1	20	2	56	2	1	3	1	.750	0	0-0	0	1.70	1.64
2012	Mia	NL	31	31	0	0	191.1	798	180	84	81	14	8	8	4	65	7	165	5	0	8	14	.364	0	0-0	0	3.40	3.81
	8 ML YEARS		154	144	4	1	916.2	3792	822	346	321	59	44	23	22	308	27	832	29	2	56	37	.602	0	0-1	0	3.11	3.15

Kelly Johnson

Bats: L **Throws:** R **Pos:** 2B-136; PH-5; DH-3   **Ht:** 6'1" **Wt:** 200 **Born:** 2/22/1982 **Age:** 31

								BATTING													BASERUNNING				AVERAGES		
Year	Team	Lg	G	AB	H	2B	3B	HR	(Hm	Rd)	TB	R	RBI	RC	TBB	IBB	SO	HBP	SH	SF	SB	CS	SB%	GDP	Avg	OBP	Slg
2005	Atl	NL	87	290	70	12	3	9	(2	7)	115	46	40	41	40	1	75	1	2	1	2	1	.67	11	.241	.334	.397
2007	Atl	NL	147	521	144	26	10	16	(5	11)	238	91	68	87	79	3	117	4	2	2	9	5	.64	8	.276	.375	.457
2008	Atl	NL	150	547	157	39	6	12	(5	7)	244	86	69	87	52	2	113	2	9	4	11	6	.65	3	.287	.349	.446
2009	Atl	NL	106	303	68	20	3	8	(4	4)	118	47	29	31	32	1	54	3	6	2	7	2	.78	4	.224	.303	.389
2010	Ari	NL	154	585	166	36	5	26	(16	10)	290	93	71	92	79	1	148	2	3	2	13	7	.65	12	.284	.370	.496
2011	2 Tms	NL	147	545	121	27	7	21	(10	11)	225	75	58	70	60	2	163	4	4	0	16	6	.73	3	.222	.304	.413

Year	Team	Lg	G	AB	H	2B	3B	HR	(Hm	Rd)	TB	R	RBI	RC	TBB	IBB	SO	HBP	SH	SF	SB	CS	SB%	GDP	Avg	OBP	Slg
2012	Tor	AL	142	507	114	19	2	16	(10	6)	185	61	55	63	62	4	159	5	2	4	14	2	.88	8	.225	.313	.365
11	Ari	NL	114	430	90	23	5	18	(10	8)	177	59	49	53	44	2	132	3	4	0	13	3	.81	3	.209	.287	.412
11	Tor	AL	33	115	31	4	2	3	(0	3)	48	16	9	17	16	0	31	1	0	0	3	3	.50	0	.270	.364	.417
	Postseason		4	2	0	0	0	0	(0	0)	0	0	0	0	1	0	0	0	0	0	0	0	-	0	.000	.333	.000
	7 ML YEARS		933	3298	840	179	36	108	(52	56)	1415	499	390	471	404	14	829	21	28	15	72	29	.71	49	.255	.338	.429

Nick Johnson

Bats: L Throws: L Pos: DH-20; PH-14; 1B-5   **Ht: 6'3" Wt: 235 Born: 9/19/1978 Age: 34**

Year	Team	Lg	G	AB	H	2B	3B	HR	(Hm	Rd)	TB	R	RBI	RC	TBB	IBB	SO	HBP	SH	SF	SB	CS	SB%	GDP	Avg	OBP	Slg
2001	NYY	AL	23	67	13	2	0	2	(1	1)	21	6	8	6	7	0	15	4	0	0	0	0	-	3	.194	.308	.313
2002	NYY	AL	129	378	92	15	0	15	(7	8)	152	56	58	59	48	5	98	12	3	0	1	3	.25	11	.243	.347	.402
2003	NYY	AL	96	324	92	19	0	14	(8	6)	153	60	47	65	70	4	57	8	3	1	5	2	.71	9	.284	.422	.472
2004	Mon	NL	73	251	63	16	0	7	(4	3)	100	35	33	36	40	2	58	3	0	1	6	3	.67	5	.251	.359	.398
2005	Was	NL	131	453	131	35	3	15	(7	8)	217	66	74	83	80	8	87	12	0	2	3	8	.27	15	.289	.408	.479
2006	Was	NL	147	500	145	46	0	23	(10	13)	260	100	77	104	110	15	99	13	2	3	10	3	.77	12	.290	.428	.520
2008	Was	NL	38	109	24	8	0	5	(2	3)	47	15	20	21	33	4	25	4	0	1	0	0	-	2	.220	.415	.431
2009	2 Tms	NL	133	457	133	24	2	8	(2	6)	185	71	62	85	99	4	84	12	1	5	2	4	.33	15	.291	.426	.405
2010	NYY	AL	24	72	12	4	0	2	(2	0)	22	12	8	12	24	0	23	2	0	0	1	0	1.00	4	.167	.388	.306
2012	Bal	AL	38	87	18	4	0	4	(4	0)	34	9	11	10	11	0	26	4	0	0	2	0	1.00	4	.207	.324	.391
09	Was	NL	98	353	104	16	2	6	(2	4)	142	47	44	60	63	3	66	6	0	2	2	2	.50	11	.295	.408	.402
09	Fla	NL	35	104	29	8	0	2	(0	2)	43	24	18	25	36	1	18	6	1	3	0	2	.00	4	.279	.477	.413
	Postseason		20	67	14	3	0	1	(1	0)	20	10	6	6	8	1	14	1	0	0	0	0	-	2	.209	.303	.299
	10 ML YEARS		832	2698	723	173	5	95	(47	48)	1191	430	398	481	522	42	572	74	9	13	29	24	.55	78	.268	.399	.441

Reed Johnson

Bats: R Throws: R Pos: PH-46; LF-37; CF-32; RF-29; PR-1   **Ht: 5'10" Wt: 180 Born: 12/8/1976 Age: 36**

Year	Team	Lg	G	AB	H	2B	3B	HR	(Hm	Rd)	TB	R	RBI	RC	TBB	IBB	SO	HBP	SH	SF	SB	CS	SB%	GDP	Avg	OBP	Slg
2003	Tor	AL	114	412	121	21	2	10	(6	4)	176	79	52	64	20	1	67	20	1	4	5	3	.63	10	.294	.353	.427
2004	Tor	AL	141	537	145	25	2	10	(8	2)	204	68	61	65	28	2	98	12	3	2	6	3	.67	17	.270	.320	.380
2005	Tor	AL	142	398	107	21	6	8	(4	4)	164	55	58	57	22	1	82	16	2	1	5	6	.45	8	.269	.332	.412
2006	Tor	AL	134	461	147	34	2	12	(4	8)	221	86	49	76	33	4	81	21	1	1	8	2	.80	9	.319	.390	.479
2007	Tor	AL	79	275	65	13	2	2	(1	1)	88	31	14	24	16	0	56	11	5	0	4	2	.67	7	.236	.305	.320
2008	ChC	NL	109	333	101	21	0	6	(3	3)	140	52	50	57	19	1	68	12	5	5	5	6	.45	3	.303	.358	.420
2009	ChC	NL	65	165	42	10	2	4	(3	1)	68	23	22	19	13	0	27	6	1	1	2	1	.67	5	.255	.330	.412
2010	LAD	NL	102	202	53	11	2	2	(0	2)	74	24	15	18	5	0	50	4	2	2	2	2	.50	7	.262	.291	.366
2011	ChC	NL	111	246	76	22	1	5	(4	1)	115	33	28	35	5	1	63	11	2	2	2	1	.67	4	.309	.348	.467
2012	2 Tms	NL	119	269	78	14	3	3	(0	3)	107	30	20	37	13	1	61	6	0	0	2	2	.50	4	.290	.337	.398
12	ChC	NL	76	169	51	9	3	3	(0	3)	75	23	16	26	10	1	43	4	0	0	2	1	.67	3	.302	.355	.444
12	Atl	NL	43	100	27	5	0	0	(0	0)	32	7	4	11	3	0	18	2	0	0	0	1	.00	1	.270	.305	.320
	10 ML YEARS		1116	3298	935	192	22	62	(34	28)	1357	481	369	452	174	11	653	119	22	18	41	28	.59	70	.284	.340	.411

Rob Johnson

Bats: R Throws: R Pos: C-17; PH-1   **Ht: 6'1" Wt: 220 Born: 7/22/1982 Age: 30**

Year	Team	Lg	G	AB	H	2B	3B	HR	(Hm	Rd)	TB	R	RBI	RC	TBB	IBB	SO	HBP	SH	SF	SB	CS	SB%	GDP	Avg	OBP	Slg
2012	Buffalo*	AAA	45	164	34	7	1	4	(-	-)	55	20	15	14	9	0	26	2	0	3	3	2	.60	5	.207	.253	.335
2007	Sea	AL	6	3	1	0	0	0	(0	0)	1	1	0	0	0	0	0	0	0	0	1	0	1.00	0	.333	.333	.333
2008	Sea	AL	14	31	4	0	0	1	(1	0)	7	2	2	0	0	0	6	0	1	0	0	0	-	1	.129	.129	.226
2009	Sea	AL	80	258	55	19	2	2	(2	0)	84	21	27	22	26	1	60	2	3	1	1	1	.50	11	.213	.289	.326
2010	Sea	AL	61	178	34	10	0	2	(0	2)	50	24	13	12	25	2	46	2	1	3	1	1	.50	5	.191	.293	.281
2011	SD	NL	67	179	34	6	1	3	(1	2)	51	9	16	12	14	1	58	3	2	1	3	0	1.00	3	.190	.259	.285
2012	NYM	NL	17	52	13	2	0	0	(0	0)	15	3	4	2	4	2	10	0	1	1	0	0	-	2	.250	.298	.288
	6 ML YEARS		245	701	141	37	3	8	(4	4)	208	60	62	48	69	6	180	7	8	6	6	2	.75	22	.201	.277	.297

Steve Johnson

Pitches: R Bats: R Pos: RP-8; SP-4   **Ht: 6'1" Wt: 220 Born: 8/31/1987 Age: 25**

Year	Team	Lg		HOW MUCH HE PITCHED								WHAT HE GAVE UP								THE RESULTS							
			G	GS	CG	GF	IP	BFP	H	R	ER	HR	SH	SF	HB	TBB	IBB	SO	WP	Bk	W	L	Pct	Sh	Sv-Op	Hld	ERC	ERA
2005	Ddgrs	R	6	3	0	0	11.1	59	18	12	12	1	1	0	4	4	0	14	1	1	0	2	.000	0	0--	-	8.90	9.53
2006	Jaxnvl	AA	2	0	0	0	4.2	18	2	0	0	0	0	0	1	2	0	3	0	0	0	0	.000	0	0--	-	1.57	0.00
2006	Ogden	R+	14	14	0	0	78.2	337	79	37	34	4	3	3	10	25	1	86	6	0	5	5	.500	0	0--	-	3.97	3.89
2007	Gt Lks	A	18	16	0	0	81.2	369	90	57	44	2	2	4	4	40	0	65	4	1	3	6	.333	0	0--	-	4.64	4.85
2008	Gt Lks	A	13	13	0	0	73.0	297	59	21	19	4	3	1	3	25	0	57	2	1	9	2	.818	0	0--	-	2.74	2.34
2008	InldEm	A+	11	11	0	0	52.0	238	68	47	41	9	0	2	1	21	0	55	0	0	3	6	.333	0	0--	-	6.66	7.10
2009	InldEm	A+	18	16	0	1	96.2	414	94	50	41	14	3	2	4	42	0	102	2	0	8	4	.667	0	0--	-	4.74	3.82
2009	Chatt	AA	2	2	0	0	10.2	45	8	5	2	1	1	1	1	3	0	15	0	0	1	1	.500	0	0--	-	2.50	1.69
2010	Bowie	AA	7	7	0	0	38.0	156	24	13	12	3	0	2	3	17	0	37	2	0	3	2	.600	0	0--	-	2.47	2.84
2010	Bowie	AA	28	28	0	0	145.0	652	144	87	83	24	4	2	11	78	1	128	13	0	7	8	.467	0	0--	-	5.40	5.15
2011	Bowie	AA	10	10	0	0	58.1	226	40	14	14	7	1	1	2	15	0	59	0	0	5	1	.833	0	0--	-	2.21	2.16
2011	Norfolk	AAA	17	17	0	0	87.1	404	101	56	54	7	4	4	4	47	0	63	5	0	2	7	.222	0	0--	-	5.58	5.56
2012	Norfolk	AAA	19	14	1	0	91.1	372	66	38	29	7	3	5	6	31	0	86	3	0	4	8	.333	0	0--	-	2.48	2.86
2012	Bal	AL	12	4	0	3	38.1	151	23	9	9	4	1	0	0	18	1	46	1	0	4	0	1.000	0	0-0	0	2.31	2.11

Adam Jones

Bats: R **Throws:** R **Pos:** CF-162; DH-1   **Ht:** 6'3" **Wt:** 225 **Born:** 8/1/1985 **Age:** 27

Year	Team	Lg	G	AB	H	2B	3B	HR	(Hm	Rd)	TB	R	RBI	RC	TBB	IBB	SO	HBP	SH	SF	SB	CS	SB%	GDP	Avg	OBP	Slg
2006	Sea	AL	32	74	16	4	0	1	(0	1)	23	6	8	4	2	0	22	0	0	0	3	1	.75	3	.216	.237	.311
2007	Sea	AL	41	65	16	2	1	2	(1	1)	26	16	4	5	4	0	21	1	1	0	2	1	.67	0	.246	.300	.400
2008	Bal	AL	132	477	129	21	7	9	(4	5)	191	61	57	56	23	0	108	7	2	5	10	3	.77	12	.270	.311	.400
2009	Bal	AL	119	473	131	22	3	19	(11	8)	216	83	70	71	36	3	93	7	0	3	10	4	.71	13	.277	.335	.457
2010	Bal	AL	149	581	165	25	5	19	(9	10)	257	76	69	72	23	1	119	13	2	2	7	7	.50	17	.284	.325	.442
2011	Bal	AL	151	567	159	26	2	25	(19	6)	264	68	83	77	29	2	113	9	1	12	12	4	.75	16	.280	.319	.466
2012	Bal	AL	162	648	186	39	3	32	(15	17)	327	103	82	101	34	0	126	13	0	2	16	7	.70	15	.287	.334	.505
7 ML YEARS			786	2885	802	139	21	107	(59	48)	1304	413	373	386	151	6	602	50	6	24	60	27	.69	76	.278	.323	.452

Andruw Jones

Bats: R **Throws:** R **Pos:** LF-47; PH-25; RF-23; DH-17; PR-2   ANN-drew   **Ht:** 6'1" **Wt:** 225 **Born:** 4/23/1977 **Age:** 36

Year	Team	Lg	G	AB	H	2B	3B	HR	(Hm	Rd)	TB	R	RBI	RC	TBB	IBB	SO	HBP	SH	SF	SB	CS	SB%	GDP	Avg	OBP	Slg
1996	Atl	NL	31	106	23	7	1	5	(3	2)	47	11	13	13	7	0	29	0	0	0	3	0	1.00	1	.217	.265	.443
1997	Atl	NL	153	399	92	18	1	18	(5	13)	166	60	70	54	56	2	107	4	5	3	20	11	.65	11	.231	.329	.416
1998	Atl	NL	159	582	158	33	8	31	(16	15)	300	89	90	97	40	8	129	4	1	4	27	4	.87	10	.271	.321	.515
1999	Atl	NL	162	592	163	35	5	26	(10	16)	286	97	84	103	76	11	103	9	0	2	24	12	.67	12	.275	.365	.483
2000	Atl	NL	161	656	199	36	6	36	(15	21)	355	122	104	127	59	0	100	9	0	5	21	6	.78	12	.303	.366	.541
2001	Atl	NL	161	625	157	25	2	34	(16	18)	288	104	104	90	56	3	142	3	0	9	11	4	.73	10	.251	.312	.461
2002	Atl	NL	154	560	148	34	0	35	(18	17)	287	91	94	94	83	4	135	10	0	6	8	3	.73	14	.264	.366	.513
2003	Atl	NL	156	595	165	28	2	36	(16	20)	305	101	116	92	53	2	125	5	0	6	4	3	.57	18	.277	.338	.513
2004	Atl	NL	154	570	149	34	4	29	(13	16)	278	85	91	75	71	9	147	3	0	2	6	6	.50	24	.261	.345	.488
2005	Atl	NL	160	586	154	24	3	51	(21	30)	337	95	128	91	64	13	112	15	0	7	5	3	.63	19	.263	.347	.575
2006	Atl	NL	156	565	148	29	0	41	(19	22)	300	107	129	108	82	9	127	13	0	9	4	1	.80	13	.262	.363	.531
2007	Atl	NL	154	572	127	27	2	26	(16	10)	236	83	94	71	70	4	138	8	0	9	5	2	.71	16	.222	.311	.413
2008	LAD	NL	75	209	33	8	1	3	(0	3)	52	21	14	6	27	0	76	1	0	1	0	1	.00	5	.158	.256	.249
2009	Tex	AL	82	281	60	18	0	17	(9	8)	129	43	43	42	45	3	72	2	0	3	5	1	.83	7	.214	.323	.459
2010	CWS	AL	107	278	64	12	1	19	(12	7)	135	41	48	45	45	0	73	3	0	2	9	2	.82	15	.230	.341	.486
2011	NYY	AL	77	190	47	8	0	13	(7	6)	94	27	33	36	29	0	62	3	0	0	0	0	-	3	.247	.356	.495
2012	NYY	AL	94	233	46	7	0	14	(6	8)	95	27	34	26	28	1	71	5	0	3	0	0	-	2	.197	.294	.408
Postseason			76	238	65	8	0	10	(5	5)	103	43	34	34	34	2	50	2	1	4	5	5	.50	5	.273	.363	.433
17 ML YEARS			2196	7599	1933	383	36	434	(202	232)	3690	1204	1289	1170	891	69	1748	97	6	71	152	59	.72	192	.254	.337	.486

Chipper Jones

Bats: B **Throws:** R **Pos:** 3B-103; PH-10; DH-1   **Ht:** 6'4" **Wt:** 210 **Born:** 4/24/1972 **Age:** 41

Year	Team	Lg	G	AB	H	2B	3B	HR	(Hm	Rd)	TB	R	RBI	RC	TBB	IBB	SO	HBP	SH	SF	SB	CS	SB%	GDP	Avg	OBP	Slg
2012 Rome*	A		2	4	1	0	0	0	(-	-)	1	0	1	0	2	0	1	0	0	0	0	0	-	0	.250	.500	.250
1993	Atl	NL	8	3	2	1	0	0	(0	0)	3	2	0	2	1	0	1	0	0	0	0	0	-	0	.667	.750	1.000
1995	Atl	NL	140	524	139	22	3	23	(15	8)	236	87	86	84	73	1	99	0	1	4	8	4	.67	10	.265	.353	.450
1996	Atl	NL	157	598	185	32	5	30	(18	12)	317	114	110	123	87	0	88	0	1	7	14	1	.93	14	.309	.393	.530
1997	Atl	NL	157	597	176	41	3	21	(7	14)	286	100	111	104	76	8	88	0	0	8	20	5	.80	19	.295	.371	.479
1998	Atl	NL	160	601	188	29	5	34	(17	17)	329	123	107	129	96	1	93	1	1	8	16	6	.73	17	.313	.404	.547
1999	Atl	NL	157	567	181	41	1	45	(20	25)	359	116	110	150	126	18	94	2	0	6	25	3	.89	20	.319	.441	.633
2000	Atl	NL	156	579	180	38	1	36	(18	18)	328	118	111	128	95	10	64	2	0	10	14	7	.67	14	.311	.404	.566
2001	Atl	NL	159	572	189	33	5	38	(19	19)	346	113	102	136	98	20	82	2	0	5	9	10	.47	13	.330	.427	.605
2002	Atl	NL	158	548	179	35	1	26	(19	7)	294	90	100	119	107	23	89	2	0	5	8	2	.80	18	.327	.435	.536
2003	Atl	NL	153	555	169	33	2	27	(16	11)	287	103	106	110	94	13	83	1	0	6	2	2	.50	10	.305	.402	.517
2004	Atl	NL	137	472	117	20	1	30	(19	11)	229	69	96	82	84	8	96	4	0	7	2	0	1.00	14	.248	.362	.485
2005	Atl	NL	109	358	106	30	0	21	(9	12)	199	66	72	78	72	5	56	0	0	2	5	1	.83	9	.296	.412	.556
2006	Atl	NL	110	411	133	28	3	26	(12	14)	245	87	86	94	61	4	73	1	0	4	6	1	.86	12	.324	.409	.596
2007	Atl	NL	134	513	173	42	4	29	(14	15)	310	108	102	110	82	10	75	0	0	5	5	1	.83	21	.337	.425	.604
2008	Atl	NL	128	439	160	24	1	22	(12	10)	252	82	75	98	90	16	61	1	0	4	4	0	1.00	13	.364	.470	.574
2009	Atl	NL	143	488	129	23	2	18	(10	8)	210	80	71	85	101	18	89	1	0	6	4	1	.80	14	.264	.388	.430
2010	Atl	NL	95	317	84	21	0	10	(9	1)	135	47	46	53	61	6	47	0	0	5	5	0	1.00	9	.265	.381	.426
2011	Atl	NL	126	455	125	33	1	18	(12	6)	214	56	70	72	51	10	80	0	0	6	2	2	.50	10	.275	.344	.470
2012	Atl	NL	112	387	111	23	0	14	(10	4)	176	58	62	63	57	6	51	1	0	3	1	0	1.00	15	.287	.377	.455
Postseason			92	333	96	18	0	13	(7	6)	153	58	47	60	72	11	60	1	1	5	8	3	.73	10	.288	.411	.459
19 ML YEARS			2499	8984	2726	549	38	468	(259	209)	4755	1619	1623	1820	1512	177	1409	18	3	97	150	46	.77	253	.303	.401	.529

Garrett Jones

Bats: L **Throws:** L **Pos:** 1B-72; RF-66; PH-16; DH-4   **Ht:** 6'4" **Wt:** 230 **Born:** 6/21/1981 **Age:** 32

Year	Team	Lg	G	AB	H	2B	3B	HR	(Hm	Rd)	TB	R	RBI	RC	TBB	IBB	SO	HBP	SH	SF	SB	CS	SB%	GDP	Avg	OBP	Slg
2007	Min	AL	31	77	16	2	1	2	(1	1)	26	7	5	3	6	0	20	0	0	1	1	1	.50	2	.208	.262	.338
2009	Pit	NL	82	314	92	21	1	21	(13	8)	178	45	44	47	40	8	76	1	0	3	10	2	.83	6	.293	.372	.567
2010	Pit	NL	158	592	146	34	1	21	(11	10)	245	64	86	69	53	2	123	1	0	8	7	3	.70	18	.247	.306	.414
2011	Pit	NL	148	423	103	30	1	16	(8	8)	183	51	58	57	48	2	104	2	0	4	6	3	.67	7	.243	.321	.433
2012	Pit	NL	145	475	130	28	3	27	(13	14)	245	68	86	84	33	2	103	0	0	7	2	0	1.00	3	.274	.317	.516
5 ML YEARS			564	1881	487	115	7	87	(46	41)	877	235	279	260	180	14	426	4	0	23	26	9	.74	36	.259	.321	.466

159

Nate Jones

Pitches: R Bats: R Pos: RP-65   **Ht: 6'5" Wt: 185 Born: 1/28/1986 Age: 27**

			HOW MUCH HE PITCHED							WHAT HE GAVE UP										THE RESULTS						
Year	Team	Lg	G	GS	CG	GF	IP	BFP	H	R	ER	HR	SH	SF	HB	TBB	IBB	SO	WP	Bk	W	L	Pct	Sh	Sv-Op Hld	ERC	ERA
2007	Bristol	R	13	10	0	0	47.1	212	44	33	27	4	1	2	4	29	0	42	11	0	0	4	.000	0	0- - -	4.79	5.13
2008	Knapol	A	18	10	1	2	56.2	263	63	45	43	8	1	2	1	35	0	71	7	0	1	7	.125	0	0- - -	6.02	6.83
2008	Bristol	R	4	1	0	1	6.2	31	6	4	1	0	0	1	1	2	0	12	3	1	1	0	1.000	0	0- - -	2.73	1.35
2008	WinSa	A+	2	0	0	1	2.2	11	1	1	1	0	0	0	0	2	0	1	1	0	0	-	-	0	0- - -	1.54	3.38
2009	Knapol	A	13	0	0	5	18.2	72	8	5	5	0	0	0	1	9	0	25	1	0	2	0	1.000	0	1- - -	1.31	2.41
2009	WinSa	A+	32	0	0	16	49.1	201	44	20	20	4	4	3	1	13	0	43	4	0	2	1	.667	0	1- - -	2.95	3.65
2010	WinSa	A+	28	28	1	0	152.1	671	176	77	69	10	2	7	12	56	0	109	7	1	11	6	.647	0	0- - -	5.01	4.08
2011	Brham	AA	42	0	0	26	63.1	272	58	27	23	3	0	4	2	27	1	67	8	0	2	3	.400	0	12- - -	3.43	3.27
2012	CWS	AL	65	0	0	11	71.2	301	67	19	19	4	2	4	1	32	3	65	5	0	8	1	1.000	0	0-3 7	3.67	2.39

Matt Joyce

Bats: L Throws: R Pos: RF-89; LF-33; PH-13; DH-4   **Ht: 6'2" Wt: 205 Born: 8/3/1984 Age: 28**

						BATTING														BASERUNNING				AVERAGES		
Year	Team	Lg	G	AB	H	2B	3B	HR	(Hm	Rd)	TB	R	RBI	RC	TBB	IBB	SO	HBP	SH	SF	SB	CS	SB%	GDP	Avg	OBP	Slg
2012	Drham*	AAA	1	2	0	0	0	0	(-	-)	0	0	0	0	1	0	0	0	0	0	0	1	.00	0	.000	.333	.000
2012	Charltt*	A+	2	8	2	1	0	0	(-	-)	3	2	2	1	1	0	1	0	0	0	0	0	-	0	.250	.333	.375
2008		AL	92	242	61	16	3	12	(6	6)	119	40	33	36	31	0	65	2	0	2	0	2	.00	3	.252	.339	.492
2009	TB	AL	11	32	6	1	0	3	(2	1)	16	3	7	5	3	0	7	1	0	1	1	0	1.00	0	.188	.270	.500
2010	TB	AL	77	216	52	15	3	10	(4	6)	103	30	40	41	40	2	55	2	0	3	2	2	.50	2	.241	.360	.477
2011	TB	AL	141	462	128	32	2	19	(11	8)	221	69	75	77	49	9	106	4	0	7	13	1	.93	7	.277	.347	.478
2012	TB	AL	124	399	96	18	3	17	(4	13)	171	55	59	59	55	4	102	6	1	1	4	3	.57	10	.241	.341	.429
	Postseason		8	24	5	1	0	1	(0	1)	9	1	4	3	1	0	9	0	0	0	1	0	1.00	0	.208	.240	.375
	5 ML YEARS		445	1351	343	82	11	61	(27	34)	630	197	214	218	178	15	335	15	1	14	20	8	.71	22	.254	.344	.466

Jair Jurrjens

Pitches: R Bats: R Pos: SP-10; RP-1   jye-AIR JURR-jens   **Ht: 6'1" Wt: 200 Born: 1/29/1986 Age: 27**

					HOW MUCH HE PITCHED						WHAT HE GAVE UP										THE RESULTS					
Year	Team	Lg	G	GS	CG	GF	IP	BFP	H	R	ER	HR	SH	SF	HB	TBB	IBB	SO	WP	Bk	W	L	Pct	Sh	Sv-Op Hld	ERC	ERA
2012	Gwnntt*	AAA	14	14	1	0	72.1	310	79	47	40	10	2	1	1	16	0	39	1	0	4	6	.400	0	0- - -	4.15	4.98
2007	Det	AL	7	7	0	0	30.2	122	24	16	16	4	0	1	0	11	0	13	2	0	3	1	.750	0	0-0 0	3.19	4.70
2008	Atl	NL	31	31	0	0	188.1	813	188	87	77	11	12	5	4	70	9	139	3	0	13	10	.565	0	0-0 0	3.65	3.68
2009	Atl	NL	34	34	0	0	215.0	884	186	71	62	15	16	4	3	75	1	152	3	2	14	10	.583	0	0-0 0	3.03	2.60
2010	Atl	NL	20	20	0	0	116.1	500	120	63	60	13	7	4	2	42	5	86	2	0	7	6	.538	0	0-0 0	4.20	4.64
2011	Atl	NL	23	23	2	0	152.0	627	142	52	50	14	6	3	4	44	5	90	4	2	13	6	.684	1	0-0 0	3.33	2.96
2012	Atl	NL	11	10	0	1	48.1	227	72	40	37	8	2	0	1	18	0	19	1	0	3	4	.429	0	0-0 0	7.70	6.89
	6 ML YEARS		126	125	2	1	750.2	3173	732	329	302	65	43	17	15	260	20	499	15	4	53	37	.589	1	0-0 0	3.70	3.62

Kila Ka'aihue

Bats: L Throws: R Pos: 1B-22; DH-12; PH-6   KEY-luh kuh-eye-HOO-ah   **Ht: 6'4" Wt: 235 Born: 3/29/1984 Age: 29**

						BATTING														BASERUNNING				AVERAGES		
Year	Team	Lg	G	AB	H	2B	3B	HR	(Hm	Rd)	TB	R	RBI	RC	TBB	IBB	SO	HBP	SH	SF	SB	CS	SB%	GDP	Avg	OBP	Slg
2012	Scrmto*	AAA	66	254	65	16	0	15	(-	-)	126	44	52	48	44	2	60	3	0	4	1	1	.50	6	.256	.367	.496
2008	KC	AL	12	21	6	0	0	1	(1	0)	9	4	1	3	3	0	2	0	0	0	0	0	-	0	.286	.375	.429
2010	KC	AL	52	180	39	6	1	8	(5	3)	71	22	25	15	24	2	39	0	1	1	0	1	.00	5	.217	.307	.394
2011	KC	AL	23	82	16	4	0	2	(1	1)	26	6	6	5	12	0	26	0	1	1	0	0	-	3	.195	.295	.317
2012	Oak	AL	39	128	30	9	0	4	(3	1)	51	13	14	13	10	0	28	1	0	0	1	0	1.00	6	.234	.295	.398
	4 ML YEARS		126	411	91	19	1	15	(10	5)	157	45	46	36	49	2	95	1	2	2	1	1	.50	14	.221	.305	.382

Ryan Kalish

Bats: L Throws: L Pos: CF-20; RF-9; LF-3; PH-3; PR-2; DH-1   KAY-lish   **Ht: 6'0" Wt: 215 Born: 3/28/1988 Age: 25**

						BATTING														BASERUNNING				AVERAGES		
Year	Team	Lg	G	AB	H	2B	3B	HR	(Hm	Rd)	TB	R	RBI	RC	TBB	IBB	SO	HBP	SH	SF	SB	CS	SB%	GDP	Avg	OBP	Slg
2006	RedSx	R	6	20	6	2	0	1	(-	-)	11	6	2	3	1	0	2	0	0	0	0	0	-	1	.300	.333	.550
2006	Lowell	A-	11	35	7	0	1	0	(-	-)	9	8	4	3	2	0	14	2	0	1	2	0	1.00	0	.200	.275	.257
2007	Lowell	A-	23	87	32	4	1	3	(-	-)	47	27	13	24	16	1	12	1	0	1	18	3	.86	0	.368	.471	.540
2008	Grnville	A	96	360	101	16	1	3	(-	-)	128	51	32	56	53	1	76	4	0	3	18	4	.82	9	.281	.376	.356
2008	Lancst	A+	18	73	17	6	0	2	(-	-)	29	6	14	9	8	0	23	0	0	1	1	0	1.00	2	.233	.305	.397
2009	Salem	A+	32	115	35	5	2	5	(-	-)	59	21	21	27	26	1	20	1	0	1	7	3	.70	2	.304	.434	.513
2009	PortInd	AA	103	391	106	19	4	13	(-	-)	172	63	56	62	42	0	87	1	0	3	14	3	.82	9	.271	.341	.440
2010	PortInd	AA	41	150	44	9	1	8	(-	-)	79	35	29	35	28	2	21	2	0	3	13	1	.93	1	.293	.404	.527
2010	Pwtckt	AAA	37	143	42	9	1	5	(-	-)	68	22	18	26	14	0	32	1	0	2	12	2	.86	3	.294	.356	.476
2011	Pwtckt	AAA	22	86	18	6	0	0	(-	-)	24	9	9	6	8	0	20	0	0	2	4	3	.57	0	.209	.271	.279
2011	Lowell	A-	2	6	3	0	0	0	(-	-)	3	2	1	1	1	0	3	0	0	0	1	0	1.00	0	.500	.571	.500
2012	Salem	A+	3	12	4	0	0	1	(-	-)	7	3	1	2	0	0	3	0	0	0	1	1	.50	0	.333	.333	.583
2012	PortInd	AA	3	9	2	1	0	0	(-	-)	3	0	1	0	4	0	3	0	0	0	0	0	-	0	.222	.462	.333
2012	Pwtckt	AAA	27	111	29	5	0	4	(-	-)	46	18	14	16	13	0	30	0	1	0	7	2	.78	3	.261	.336	.414
2010	Bos	AL	53	163	41	11	1	4	(2	2)	66	26	24	23	12	0	38	1	2	1	10	1	.91	5	.252	.305	.405
2012	Bos	AL	36	96	22	3	0	0	(0	0)	25	12	5	3	6	0	26	0	0	1	3	2	.60	4	.229	.272	.260
	2 ML YEARS		89	259	63	14	1	4	(2	2)	91	38	29	26	18	0	64	1	2	2	13	3	.81	9	.243	.293	.351

Jeff Karstens

Pitches: R Bats: R Pos: SP-15; RP-4 Ht: 6'3" Wt: 185 Born: 9/24/1982 Age: 30

				HOW MUCH HE PITCHED					WHAT HE GAVE UP													THE RESULTS							
Year	Team	Lg	G	GS	CG	GF	IP	BFP	H	R	ER	HR	SH	SF	HB	TBB	IBB	SO	WP	Bk	W	L	Pct	Sh	Sv-Op	Hld	ERC	ERA
2012	Altna*	AA	2	2	0	0	10.0	37	8	1	1	0	0	0	0	1	0	6	0	0	1	0	1.000	0	0--	-	1.56	0.90
2012	Indy*	AAA	3	3	0	0	13.2	56	11	13	7	1	1	0	1	3	0	13	1	0	0	2	.000	0	0--	-	2.43	4.61
2006	NYY	AL	8	6	0	2	42.2	179	40	20	18	6	0	2	1	11	2	16	3	1	2	1	.667	0	0-0	0	3.42	3.80
2007	NYY	AL	7	3	0	2	14.2	80	27	21	18	4	2	1	0	9	0	5	2	0	1	4	.200	0	0-0	0	11.86	11.05
2008	Pit	NL	9	9	1	0	51.1	220	56	32	23	7	2	4	0	13	0	23	1	0	2	6	.250	1	0-0	0	4.22	4.03
2009	Pit	NL	39	13	0	8	108.0	471	115	66	65	12	6	6	2	45	5	52	1	0	4	6	.400	0	0-0	1	4.64	5.42
2010	Pit	NL	26	19	0	1	122.2	525	146	72	67	21	2	9	1	27	5	72	0	1	3	10	.231	0	0-0	0	4.97	4.92
2011	Pit	NL	30	26	1	1	162.1	668	163	69	61	22	6	5	4	33	6	96	4	1	9	9	.500	1	0-0	0	3.64	3.38
2012	Pit	NL	19	15	0	0	90.2	372	89	41	40	8	7	1	1	15	0	66	3	1	5	4	.556	0	0-0	1	3.02	3.97
7 ML YEARS			138	91	2	14	592.1	2515	636	321	292	80	25	28	9	153	18	330	14	4	26	40	.394	2	0-0	2	4.20	4.44

Munenori Kawasaki

moo-neh-NO-ree kah-wah-SAH-kee

Bats: L Throws: R Pos: SS-38; PR-19; 2B-10; PH-4; DH-2; 3B-1 Ht: 5'10" Wt: 165 Born: 6/3/1981 Age: 32

									BATTING													BASERUNNING				AVERAGES		
Year	Team	Lg	G	AB	H	2B	3B	HR	(Hm	Rd)	TB	R	RBI	RC	TBB	IBB	SO	HBP	SH	SF		SB	CS	SB%	GDP		Avg	OBP	Slg
2001	Fk Dai	Jap	1	4	0	0	0	0	(-	-)	0	1	1	0	1	-	0	0	0	0		0	0	-	-		.000	.200	.000
2002	Fk Dai	Jap	36	112	26	4	5	0	(-	-)	40	13	8	10	4	-	21	0	6	0		3	2	.60	-		.232	.259	.357
2003	Fk Dai	Jap	133	493	145	17	9	2	(-	-)	186	78	51	69	41	-	74	4	28	2		30	16	.65	-		.294	.352	.377
2004	Fk Dai	Jap	133	564	171	19	18	4	(-	-)	238	87	45	92	48	-	63	3	15	3		42	13	.76	-		.303	.359	.422
2005	Fk Dai	Jap	102	399	108	12	3	4	(-	-)	138	53	36	49	26	-	52	8	22	3		21	10	.68	-		.271	.326	.346
2006	Fk Dai	Jap	115	449	140	21	7	3	(-	-)	184	69	27	71	32	-	54	5	27	0		24	9	.73	-		.312	.364	.410
2007	Fk Dai	Jap	95	383	126	12	7	4	(-	-)	164	57	43	65	29	-	46	4	10	1		23	8	.74	-		.329	.381	.428
2008	Fk Dai	Jap	99	424	136	16	6	1	(-	-)	167	55	34	61	16	-	40	6	6	5		19	9	.68	-		.321	.350	.394
2009	Fk Dai	Jap	143	540	140	26	8	4	(-	-)	194	73	34	70	47	-	90	7	43	3		44	17	.72	-		.259	.325	.359
2010	Fk Dai	Jap	144	602	190	27	5	4	(-	-)	239	74	50	93	43	-	86	7	10	0		30	11	.73	-		.316	.368	.397
2011	Fk Dai	Jap	144	603	161	19	7	1	(-	-)	197	71	37	66	36	-	84	3	9	4		31	10	.76	-		.267	.310	.327
2012	Sea	AL	61	104	20	1	0	0	(0	0)	21	13	7	7	8	0	18	1	2	0		2	2	.50	2		.192	.257	.202

Austin Kearns

Bats: R Throws: R Pos: PH-52; LF-22; RF-12; 1B-2; DH-2 Ht: 6'3" Wt: 240 Born: 5/20/1980 Age: 33

									BATTING													BASERUNNING				AVERAGES		
Year	Team	Lg	G	AB	H	2B	3B	HR	(Hm	Rd)	TB	R	RBI	RC	TBB	IBB	SO	HBP	SH	SF		SB	CS	SB%	GDP		Avg	OBP	Slg
2012	Jupiter*	A+	3	6	1	0	0	0	(-	-)	1	1	1	0	1	0	0	1	0	0		0	0	-	-		.167	.375	.167
2002	Cin	NL	107	372	117	24	3	13	(7	6)	186	66	56	70	54	3	81	6	0	3		6	3	.67	11		.315	.407	.500
2003	Cin	NL	82	292	77	11	0	15	(8	7)	133	39	58	52	41	1	68	5	0	0		5	2	.71	7		.264	.364	.455
2004	Cin	NL	64	217	50	10	2	9	(3	6)	91	28	32	26	28	0	71	1	0	0		2	1	.67	8		.230	.321	.419
2005	Cin	NL	112	387	93	26	1	18	(9	9)	175	62	67	55	48	2	107	4	0	5		0	0	-	8		.240	.333	.452
2006	2 Tms	NL	150	537	142	33	2	24	(12	12)	251	86	86	81	76	4	135	10	1	5		9	4	.69	18		.264	.363	.467
2007	Was	NL	161	587	156	35	1	16	(8	8)	241	84	74	87	71	5	106	12	0	4		2	2	.50	13		.266	.355	.411
2008	Was	NL	86	313	68	10	0	7	(1	6)	99	40	32	28	35	0	63	8	0	1		2	2	.50	11		.217	.311	.316
2009	Was	NL	80	174	34	6	2	3	(1	2)	53	20	17	17	32	1	51	5	0	0		1	1	.50	12		.195	.336	.305
2010	2 Tms	AL	120	403	106	21	1	10	(5	5)	159	55	49	51	46	2	116	10	0	2		4	1	.80	16		.263	.351	.395
2011	Cle	AL	57	150	30	5	1	2	(1	1)	43	18	7	11	18	0	48	4	2	0		0	4	.00	2		.200	.302	.287
2012	Mia	NL	87	147	36	6	0	4	(2	2)	54	21	16	21	22	1	44	6	0	0		2	1	.67	8		.245	.366	.367
06	Cin	NL	87	325	89	21	1	16	(8	8)	160	53	50	46	35	2	85	5	0	3		7	1	.88	14		.274	.351	.492
06	Was	NL	63	212	53	12	1	8	(4	4)	91	33	36	35	41	2	50	5	1	2		2	3	.40	4		.250	.381	.429
10	Cle	AL	84	301	82	18	1	8	(4	4)	126	42	42	43	34	2	78	5	0	2		4	1	.80	12		.272	.354	.419
10	NYY	AL	36	102	24	3	0	2	(1	1)	33	13	7	8	12	0	38	5	0	0		0	0	-	4		.235	.345	.324
11 ML YEARS			1106	3579	909	187	13	121	(57	64)	1485	519	494	499	471	19	890	75	3	20		33	21	.61	114		.254	.351	.415

Shawn Kelley

Pitches: R Bats: R Pos: RP-47 Ht: 6'2" Wt: 220 Born: 4/26/1984 Age: 29

				HOW MUCH HE PITCHED					WHAT HE GAVE UP													THE RESULTS							
Year	Team	Lg	G	GS	CG	GF	IP	BFP	H	R	ER	HR	SH	SF	HB	TBB	IBB	SO	WP	Bk	W	L	Pct	Sh	Sv-Op	Hld	ERC	ERA
2012	Tacom*	AAA	14	0	0	9	20.0	71	9	2	2	0	1	1	0	4	0	25	1	0	2	0	1.000	0	6--	-	0.76	0.90
2009	Sea	AL	41	0	0	12	46.0	191	45	23	23	9	2	2	3	9	1	41	2	1	5	4	.556	0	0-4	9	4.02	4.50
2010	Sea	AL	22	0	0	7	25.0	112	26	11	11	5	0	0	1	12	2	26	0	0	3	1	.750	0	0-0	3	5.38	3.96
2011	Sea	AL	10	0	0	2	12.2	47	7	0	0	0	0	0	0	3	1	10	0	0	0	0	-	0	0-0	1	1.01	0.00
2012	Sea	AL	47	0	0	10	44.1	190	43	20	16	5	4	3	0	15	6	45	2	1	2	4	.333	0	0-2	6	3.49	3.25
4 ML YEARS			120	0	0	31	128.0	540	121	54	50	19	6	5	4	39	10	122	4	2	10	9	.526	0	0-6	19	3.71	3.52

Casey Kelly

Pitches: R Bats: R Pos: SP-6 Ht: 6'3" Wt: 195 Born: 10/4/1989 Age: 23

				HOW MUCH HE PITCHED					WHAT HE GAVE UP													THE RESULTS							
Year	Team	Lg	G	GS	CG	GF	IP	BFP	H	R	ER	HR	SH	SF	HB	TBB	IBB	SO	WP	Bk	W	L	Pct	Sh	Sv-Op	Hld	ERC	ERA
2009	Grnville	A	9	9	0	0	48.1	183	32	9	6	0	0	0	0	9	0	39	3	0	6	1	.857	0	0--	-	1.28	1.12
2009	Salem	A+	8	8	0	0	46.2	178	33	21	16	4	2	0	1	7	0	35	2	0	1	4	.200	0	0--	-	1.71	3.09
2010	Portlnd	AA	21	21	0	0	95.0	428	118	60	56	10	3	3	2	35	0	81	7	1	3	5	.375	0	0--	-	5.51	5.31
2011	SnAnt	AA	27	27	0	0	142.1	615	153	74	63	8	6	5	8	46	0	105	7	2	11	6	.647	0	0--	-	4.14	3.98

Year	Team	Lg	G	GS	CG	GF	IP	BFP	H	R	ER	HR	SH	SF	HB	TBB	IBB	SO	WP	Bk	W	L	Pct	Sh	Sv-Op	Hld	ERC	ERA
							HOW MUCH HE PITCHED					**WHAT HE GAVE UP**											**THE RESULTS**					
2012	Tucsn	AAA	2	2	0	0	12.0	48	12	3	3	0	1	0	1	0	0	14	0	0	0	0	-	0	0--	-	2.28	2.25
2012	Padres	R	3	3	0	0	9.0	41	10	8	4	0	0	0	1	0	0	7	2	0	0	1	.000	0	0--	-	2.59	4.00
2012	SnAnt	AA	3	3	0	0	16.2	64	11	8	7	1	0	2	1	3	0	18	1	0	0	1	.000	0	0--	-	1.61	3.78
2012	SD	NL	6	6	0	0	29.0	136	39	23	20	5	3	0	2	10	1	26	0	0	2	3	.400	0	0-0	0	6.65	6.21

Don Kelly

Bats: L **Throws:** R **Pos:** RF-35; LF-18; 1B-8; CF-8; PR-6; PH-4; 3B-3; DH-3; 2B-1   **Ht:** 6'4" **Wt:** 190 **Born:** 2/15/1980 **Age:** 33

Year	Team	Lg	G	AB	H	2B	3B	HR	(Hm	Rd)	TB	R	RBI	RC	TBB	IBB	SO	HBP	SH	SF	SB	CS	SB%	GDP	Avg	OBP	Slg
2012	Toledo*	AAA	20	73	17	2	0	1	(-	-)	22	8	12	8	12	0	17	0	0	0	4	1	.80	1	.233	.341	.301
2007	Pit	AL	25	27	4	0	0	0	(0	0)	4	2	0	1	3	0	3	2	0	0	0	0	-	1	.148	.281	.148
2009	Det	AL	31	56	14	3	1	0	(0	0)	19	8	3	7	4	0	10	1	1	0	1	0	1.00	0	.250	.311	.339
2010	Det	AL	119	238	58	4	0	9	(4	5)	89	30	27	26	8	0	42	2	1	2	3	0	1.00	1	.244	.272	.374
2011	Det	AL	113	257	63	8	3	7	(1	6)	98	35	28	27	14	0	32	3	6	1	2	1	.67	8	.245	.291	.381
2012	Det	AL	75	113	21	2	1	1	(1	0)	28	14	7	6	14	0	22	0	0	0	2	0	1.00	0	.186	.276	.248
	Postseason		9	20	6	1	0	1	(0	1)	10	3	2	1	0	0	4	0	0	0	0	0	-	0	.300	.300	.500
	5 ML YEARS		363	691	160	17	5	17	(6	11)	238	89	65	67	43	0	109	8	8	3	8	1	.89	12	.232	.283	.344

Joe Kelly

Pitches: R **Bats:** R **Pos:** SP-16; RP-8   **Ht:** 6'1" **Wt:** 185 **Born:** 6/9/1988 **Age:** 25

Year	Team	Lg	G	GS	CG	GF	IP	BFP	H	R	ER	HR	SH	SF	HB	TBB	IBB	SO	WP	Bk	W	L	Pct	Sh	Sv-Op	Hld	ERC	ERA
2009	Batvia	A-	16	2	0	6	30.1	138	33	23	16	0	2	1	3	11	0	30	3	0	2	3	.400	0	1--	-	3.96	4.75
2010	QuadC	A	26	18	0	3	103.1	444	103	66	53	3	2	2	7	45	0	92	12	2	6	8	.429	0	1--	-	4.05	4.62
2011	PlmBh	A+	12	11	0	0	72.2	305	56	26	21	1	2	1	8	34	0	62	5	0	5	2	.714	0	0--	-	2.96	2.60
2011	Sprgfld	AA	11	11	0	0	59.1	264	70	40	33	7	3	2	5	25	2	51	2	1	6	4	.600	0	0--	-	5.82	5.01
2012	Memp	AAA	12	12	0	0	72.1	299	75	29	23	2	1	3	4	21	1	45	2	0	2	5	.286	0	0--	-	3.69	2.86
2012	StL	NL	24	16	0	4	107.0	457	112	50	42	10	4	1	3	36	2	75	4	0	5	7	.417	0	0-0	0	4.17	3.53

Matt Kemp

Bats: R **Throws:** R **Pos:** CF-105; PH-1   **Ht:** 6'4" **Wt:** 225 **Born:** 9/23/1984 **Age:** 28

Year	Team	Lg	G	AB	H	2B	3B	HR	(Hm	Rd)	TB	R	RBI	RC	TBB	IBB	SO	HBP	SH	SF	SB	CS	SB%	GDP	Avg	OBP	Slg
2012	Albq*	AAA	4	16	8	2	0	2	(-	-)	16	6	6	6	0	0	2	0	0	0	0	0	-	0	.500	.500	1.000
2012	RCuca*	A+	4	14	6	1	0	0	(-	-)	7	2	4	3	2	1	4	0	0	0	0	0	-	0	.429	.500	.500
2006	LAD	NL	52	154	39	7	1	7	(4	3)	69	30	23	20	9	1	53	0	0	3	6	0	1.00	1	.253	.289	.448
2007	LAD	NL	98	292	100	12	5	10	(9	1)	152	47	42	49	16	0	66	0	0	1	10	5	.67	6	.342	.373	.521
2008	LAD	NL	155	606	176	38	5	18	(14	4)	278	93	76	86	46	6	153	1	1	3	35	11	.76	11	.290	.340	.459
2009	LAD	NL	159	606	180	25	7	26	(13	13)	297	97	101	100	52	6	139	3	0	6	34	8	.81	14	.297	.352	.490
2010	LAD	NL	162	602	150	25	6	28	(15	13)	271	82	89	74	53	4	170	4	0	9	19	15	.56	14	.249	.310	.450
2011	LAD	NL	161	602	195	33	4	**39**	(19	20)	**353**	**115**	**126**	129	74	24	159	6	0	7	40	11	.78	16	.324	.399	.586
2012	LAD	NL	106	403	122	22	2	23	(13	10)	217	74	69	75	40	8	103	3	0	3	9	4	.69	10	.303	.367	.538
	Postseason		16	62	14	3	0	2	(1	1)	23	5	5	1	5	0	25	0	0	0	0	2	.00	2	.226	.284	.371
	7 ML YEARS		893	3265	962	162	30	151	(87	64)	1637	538	526	533	290	49	843	17	1	34	153	54	.74	72	.295	.352	.501

Howie Kendrick

Bats: R **Throws:** R **Pos:** 2B-143; PH-3; 1B-2; LF-2; DH-1; PR-1   **Ht:** 5'10" **Wt:** 205 **Born:** 7/12/1983 **Age:** 29

Year	Team	Lg	G	AB	H	2B	3B	HR	(Hm	Rd)	TB	R	RBI	RC	TBB	IBB	SO	HBP	SH	SF	SB	CS	SB%	GDP	Avg	OBP	Slg
2006	LAA	AL	72	267	76	21	1	4	(2	2)	111	25	30	32	9	2	44	4	0	3	6	0	1.00	5	.285	.314	.416
2007	LAA	AL	88	338	109	24	2	5	(3	2)	152	55	39	41	9	2	61	4	1	1	5	4	.56	15	.322	.347	.450
2008	LAA	AL	92	340	104	26	2	3	(1	2)	143	43	37	50	12	3	58	4	1	4	11	4	.73	8	.306	.333	.421
2009	LAA	AL	105	374	109	21	3	10	(5	5)	166	61	61	58	20	1	71	4	2	0	11	4	.73	8	.291	.334	.444
2010	LAA	AL	158	616	172	41	4	10	(4	6)	251	67	75	81	28	2	94	5	4	5	14	4	.78	16	.279	.313	.407
2011	LAA	AL	140	537	153	30	6	18	(5	13)	249	86	63	69	33	3	119	10	3	0	14	6	.70	18	.285	.338	.464
2012	LAA	AL	147	550	158	32	3	8	(4	4)	220	57	67	65	29	1	115	4	6	5	14	6	.70	26	.287	.325	.400
	Postseason		13	46	9	0	1	1	(1	0)	14	4	2	3	1	0	11	0	2	1	3	0	1.00	1	.196	.208	.304
	7 ML YEARS		802	3022	881	195	21	58	(24	34)	1292	394	372	396	140	14	562	35	17	18	75	28	.73	96	.292	.328	.428

Kyle Kendrick

Pitches: R **Bats:** R **Pos:** SP-25; RP-12   **Ht:** 6'3" **Wt:** 210 **Born:** 8/26/1984 **Age:** 28

Year	Team	Lg	G	GS	CG	GF	IP	BFP	H	R	ER	HR	SH	SF	HB	TBB	IBB	SO	WP	Bk	W	L	Pct	Sh	Sv-Op	Hld	ERC	ERA
2007	Phi	NL	20	20	0	0	121.0	499	129	53	52	16	4	2	7	25	3	49	0	0	10	4	.714	0	0-0	0	4.23	3.87
2008	Phi	NL	31	30	0	1	155.2	722	194	103	95	23	8	4	**14**	57	2	68	4	1	11	9	.550	0	0-0	0	6.05	5.49
2009	Phi	NL	9	2	0	2	26.1	112	27	11	10	1	1	2	1	9	0	15	0	1	3	1	.750	0	0-0	0	3.75	3.42
2010	Phi	NL	33	31	1	1	180.2	771	199	103	95	26	9	6	3	49	4	84	1	2	11	10	.524	0	0-0	0	4.51	4.73
2011	Phi	NL	34	15	0	5	114.2	478	110	50	41	14	6	3	7	30	5	59	1	1	8	6	.571	0	0-1	0	3.66	3.22
2012	Phi	NL	37	25	1	2	159.1	674	154	76	69	20	8	4	7	49	4	116	1	0	11	12	.478	1	0-1	2	3.84	3.90
	Postseason		1	1	0	0	3.2	18	5	5	5	2	0	0	0	2	1	2	0	0	1	0	1.000	0	0-0	0	9.97	12.27
	6 ML YEARS		164	123	2	11	757.2	3256	813	396	362	100	36	21	39	219	18	391	7	5	54	42	.563	1	0-2	2	4.47	4.30

Adam Kennedy

Bats: L **Throws:** R **Pos:** 3B-39; PH-33; 2B-16; 1B-3; PR-2; LF-1   **Ht:** 6'1" **Wt:** 195 **Born:** 1/10/1976 **Age:** 37

									BATTING													BASERUNNING				AVERAGES		
Year	Team	Lg	G	AB	H	2B	3B	HR	(Hm	Rd)	TB	R	RBI	RC	TBB	IBB	SO	HBP	SH	SF	SB	CS	SB%	GDP	Avg	OBP	Slg
2012	RCuca*	A+	5	16	4	0	1	0	(-	-)	6	4	1	1	1	0	4	0	0	0	0	0	-	1	.250	.294	.375
2012	Albq*	AAA	1	4	2	0	0	0	(-	-)	2	0	0	0	0	0	0	0	0	0	0	0	-	0	.500	.500	.500
1999	StL	NL	33	102	26	10	1	1	(1	0)	41	12	16	12	3	0	8	2	1	2	0	1	.00	1	.255	.284	.402
2000	LAA	AL	156	598	159	33	11	9	(7	2)	241	82	72	72	28	5	73	3	8	4	22	8	.73	10	.266	.300	.403
2001	LAA	AL	137	478	129	25	3	6	(4	2)	178	48	40	57	27	3	71	11	7	9	12	7	.63	7	.270	.318	.372
2002	LAA	AL	144	474	148	32	6	7	(6	1)	213	65	52	70	19	1	80	7	5	4	17	4	.81	5	.312	.345	.449
2003	LAA	AL	143	449	121	17	1	13	(8	5)	179	71	49	61	45	4	73	9	2	5	22	9	.71	7	.269	.344	.399
2004	LAA	AL	144	468	130	20	5	10	(5	5)	190	70	48	60	41	7	92	13	9	2	15	5	.75	10	.278	.351	.406
2005	LAA	AL	129	416	125	23	0	2	(1	1)	154	49	37	62	29	1	64	7	5	3	19	4	.83	5	.300	.354	.370
2006	LAA	AL	139	451	123	26	6	4	(3	1)	173	50	55	62	39	5	72	5	3	5	16	10	.62	15	.273	.334	.384
2007	StL	NL	87	279	61	9	1	3	(0	3)	81	27	18	19	22	6	33	3	1	1	6	2	.75	9	.219	.282	.290
2008	StL	NL	115	339	95	17	4	2	(1	1)	126	42	36	39	21	4	43	1	0	4	7	1	.88	13	.280	.321	.372
2009	Oak	AL	129	529	153	29	1	11	(4	7)	217	65	63	88	45	2	86	4	5	3	20	6	.77	8	.289	.348	.410
2010	Was	NL	135	342	85	16	1	3	(0	3)	112	43	31	37	37	1	44	5	1	4	14	2	.88	10	.249	.327	.327
2011	Sea	AL	114	380	89	23	1	7	(5	2)	135	36	38	35	22	3	67	1	4	2	8	2	.80	3	.234	.277	.355
2012	LAD	NL	86	168	44	8	1	2	(0	2)	60	22	16	19	23	1	33	1	1	1	1	1	.50	5	.262	.345	.357
	Postseason		25	78	24	3	1	4	(4	0)	41	13	13	11	1	0	15	1	3	2	2	2	.33	1	.308	.317	.526
	14 ML YEARS		1691	5473	1488	288	42	80	(45	35)	2100	682	571	693	401	43	839	72	55	53	179	62	.74	108	.272	.327	.384

Ian Kennedy

Pitches: R **Bats:** R **Pos:** SP-33   **Ht:** 6'0" **Wt:** 190 **Born:** 12/19/1984 **Age:** 28

				HOW MUCH HE PITCHED					WHAT HE GAVE UP											THE RESULTS						
Year	Team	Lg	G	GS	CG	GF	IP	BFP	H	R	ER	HR	SH	SF	HB	TBB	IBB	SO	WP	Bk	W	L	Pct	Sh	Sv-Op Hld	ERC	ERA
2007	NYY	AL	3	3	0	0	19.0	77	13	6	4	1	0	0	0	9	0	15	0	0	1	0	1.000	0	0-0 0	2.42	1.89
2008	NYY	AL	10	9	0	1	39.2	194	50	37	36	5	1	4	1	26	0	27	3	0	0	4	.000	0	0-0 0	6.93	8.17
2009	NYY	AL	1	0	0	0	1.0	6	0	0	0	0	0	0	1	2	0	1	0	0	0	0	-	0	0-0 1	7.00	0.00
2010	Ari	NL	32	32	0	0	194.0	810	163	87	82	26	11	5	10	70	2	168	16	0	9	10	.474	0	0-0 0	3.47	3.80
2011	Ari	NL	33	33	1	0	222.0	900	186	73	71	19	9	9	9	55	0	198	11	1	21	4	.840	1	0-0 0	2.71	2.88
2012	Ari	NL	33	33	1	0	208.1	899	216	101	93	28	13	5	14	55	4	187	5	4	15	12	.556	0	0-0 0	4.18	4.02
	Postseason		2	2	0	0	12.2	57	13	6	6	1	0	2	3	3	0	8	1	0	0	1	.000	0	0-0 0	4.25	4.26
	6 ML YEARS		112	110	2	1	684.0	2886	628	304	286	79	34	23	35	217	6	596	35	5	46	30	.605	1	0-0 1	3.58	3.76

Jeff Keppinger

Bats: R **Throws:** R **Pos:** 3B-50; 1B-27; 2B-27; DH-20; PH-9; PR-1   **Ht:** 6'0" **Wt:** 185 **Born:** 4/21/1980 **Age:** 33

									BATTING													BASERUNNING				AVERAGES		
Year	Team	Lg	G	AB	H	2B	3B	HR	(Hm	Rd)	TB	R	RBI	RC	TBB	IBB	SO	HBP	SH	SF	SB	CS	SB%	GDP	Avg	OBP	Slg
2012	Drham*	AAA	6	21	6	1	0	0	(-	-)	7	4	1	3	4	0	2	0	0	0	0	0	-	0	.286	.400	.333
2004	NYM	NL	33	116	33	2	0	3	(3	0)	44	9	9	12	6	0	7	0	0	1	2	1	.67	6	.284	.317	.379
2006	KC	NL	22	60	16	2	0	2	(0	2)	24	11	8	8	5	1	6	0	2	0	0	0	-	2	.267	.323	.400
2007	Cin	NL	67	241	80	16	2	5	(2	3)	115	39	32	42	24	0	12	4	6	1	2	1	.67	11	.332	.400	.477
2008	Cin	NL	121	459	122	24	2	3	(3	0)	159	45	43	52	30	3	24	2	6	5	3	1	.75	14	.266	.310	.346
2009	Hou	NL	107	305	78	13	3	7	(1	6)	118	35	29	28	27	3	33	3	7	2	0	2	.00	13	.256	.320	.387
2010	Hou	NL	137	514	148	34	1	6	(4	2)	202	62	59	72	51	1	36	1	5	4	4	1	.80	15	.288	.351	.393
2011	2 Tms	NL	99	379	105	20	0	6	(4	2)	143	39	35	38	12	0	24	2	2	4	0	1	.00	11	.277	.300	.377
2012	TB	AL	115	385	125	15	1	9	(5	4)	169	46	40	59	24	0	31	4	1	4	1	0	1.00	14	.325	.367	.439
11	Hou	NL	43	163	50	9	0	4	(3	1)	71	22	20	18	4	0	7	0	0	2	0	1	.00	5	.307	.320	.436
11	SF	NL	56	216	55	11	0	2	(1	1)	72	17	15	20	8	0	17	2	2	2	0	0	-	6	.255	.285	.333
	8 ML YEARS		701	2459	707	126	9	41	(22	19)	974	286	255	311	179	8	173	16	29	21	12	7	.63	86	.288	.337	.396

Clayton Kershaw

Pitches: L **Bats:** L **Pos:** SP-33   **Ht:** 6'3" **Wt:** 220 **Born:** 3/19/1988 **Age:** 25

				HOW MUCH HE PITCHED					WHAT HE GAVE UP											THE RESULTS						
Year	Team	Lg	G	GS	CG	GF	IP	BFP	H	R	ER	HR	SH	SF	HB	TBB	IBB	SO	WP	Bk	W	L	Pct	Sh	Sv-Op Hld	ERC	ERA
2008	LAD	NL	22	21	0	0	107.2	470	109	51	51	11	3	3	1	52	3	100	7	0	5	5	.500	0	0-0 1	4.53	4.26
2009	LAD	NL	31	30	0	1	171.0	701	119	55	53	7	11	2	1	91	4	185	11	2	8	8	.500	0	0-0 0	2.60	2.79
2010	LAD	NL	32	32	0	0	204.1	848	160	73	66	13	8	4	7	81	9	212	5	2	13	10	.565	1	0-0 0	2.72	2.91
2011	LAD	NL	33	33	5	0	233.1	912	174	66	59	15	11	2	3	54	2	248	5	1	21	5	.808	2	0-0 0	2.00	2.28
2012	LAD	NL	33	33	2	0	227.2	901	170	70	64	16	18	4	5	63	5	229	6	2	14	9	.609	2	0-0 0	2.20	2.53
	Postseason		5	2	0	0	15.1	68	15	10	10	3	3	0	1	9	1	11	4	0	0	1	.000	0	0-0 1	5.72	5.87
	5 ML YEARS		151	149	8	1	944.0	3832	732	315	293	62	51	15	17	341	23	974	34	7	61	37	.622	5	0-0 1	2.58	2.79

Dallas Keuchel

KYE-kull

Pitches: L **Bats:** L **Pos:** SP-16   **Ht:** 6'3" **Wt:** 210 **Born:** 1/1/1988 **Age:** 25

				HOW MUCH HE PITCHED					WHAT HE GAVE UP											THE RESULTS						
Year	Team	Lg	G	GS	CG	GF	IP	BFP	H	R	ER	HR	SH	SF	HB	TBB	IBB	SO	WP	Bk	W	L	Pct	Sh	Sv-Op Hld	ERC	ERA
2009	TriCity	A-	11	10	0	0	56.2	231	52	18	17	2	3	0	2	9	0	44	2	0	2	3	.400	0	0-- -	2.43	2.70
2010	Lancst	A+	19	18	3	0	120.2	505	129	58	45	10	5	1	2	25	1	97	3	0	5	8	.385	0	0-- -	3.66	3.36
2010	CpChr	AA	9	9	0	0	53.2	224	59	32	28	2	2	3	1	11	2	36	0	0	2	6	.250	0	0-- -	3.50	4.70
2011	CpChr	AA	20	20	1	0	127.2	513	116	49	45	9	6	1	4	27	0	76	6	0	9	6	.600	1	0-- -	2.85	3.17
2011	OKCity	AAA	7	7	0	0	36.0	165	52	30	30	5	2	4	0	12	1	15	0	1	1	1	.500	0	0-- -	6.85	7.50
2012	OKCity	AAA	16	16	2	0	92.1	375	92	46	40	5	3	3	0	20	3	50	1	1	6	4	.600	1	0-- -	3.06	3.90
2012	Hou	NL	16	16	1	0	85.1	377	93	56	50	14	9	3	1	39	1	38	2	0	3	8	.273	0	0-- -	5.39	5.27

Cole Kimball

Pitches: R Bats: R Pos: P   Ht: 6'4" Wt: 250 Born: 8/1/1985 Age: 27

			HOW MUCH HE PITCHED					WHAT HE GAVE UP										THE RESULTS						
Year	Team	Lg	G	GS	CG	GF	IP	BFP	H	R	ER	HR	SH	SF	HB	TBB	IBB	SO	WP	Bk	W	L	Pct	Sh	Sv-Op Hld	ERC	ERA
2006	Vrmnt	A-	16	5	0	3	34.0	169	43	26	22	3	0	2	3	24	0	28	6	0	1	4	.200	0	0- - -	7.17	5.82
2007	Vrmnt	A-	14	13	0	1	64.1	282	52	35	30	4	2	3	4	40	1	72	13	0	3	6	.333	0	1- - -	3.82	4.20
2008	Hgrstn	A	28	27	1	0	128.1	564	103	75	72	5	3	6	17	83	0	122	16	1	6	8	.429	1	0- - -	4.07	5.05
2009	Ptomc	A+	39	0	0	23	46.2	219	49	37	33	4	3	4	2	28	2	52	11	1	4	5	.444	0	9- - -	5.02	6.36
2010	Ptomc	A+	19	0	0	17	24.2	97	17	5	5	0	3	3	2	8	1	27	1	0	3	0	1.000	0	6- - -	1.88	1.82
2010	Hrsbrg	AA	38	0	0	24	54.0	235	33	21	14	4	2	4	5	31	2	74	14	3	5	1	.833	0	12- - -	2.65	2.33
2011	Syrcse	AAA	12	0	0	11	13.2	57	8	0	0	0	0	0	0	8	1	14	1	0	1	0	1.000	0	5- - -	1.82	0.00
2012	Nats	R	1	1	0	0	1.0	4	1	0	0	0	0	0	0	0	0	1	1	0	0	0	-	0	0- - -	1.95	0.00
2012	Hgrstn	A	1	1	0	0	1.0	4	1	0	0	0	0	0	0	0	0	2	0	0	0	0	-	0	0- - -	1.95	0.00
2012	Ptomc	A+	3	2	0	0	3.1	19	6	7	4	3	0	0	1	0	0	2	0	0	0	1	.000	0	0- - -	13.95	10.80
2012	Hrsbrg	AA	1	0	0	0	0.1	3	1	0	0	0	0	0	0	1	0	0	0	0	0	0	-	0	0- - -	29.63	0.00
2011	Was	NL	12	0	0	4	14.0	59	8	3	3	0	0	1	1	11	0	11	2	0	1	0	1.000	0	0-1 0	2.85	1.93

Craig Kimbrel

Pitches: R Bats: R Pos: RP-63   Ht: 5'11" Wt: 205 Born: 5/28/1988 Age: 25

KIM-brull

			HOW MUCH HE PITCHED					WHAT HE GAVE UP										THE RESULTS						
Year	Team	Lg	G	GS	CG	GF	IP	BFP	H	R	ER	HR	SH	SF	HB	TBB	IBB	SO	WP	Bk	W	L	Pct	Sh	Sv-Op Hld	ERC	ERA
2010	Atl	NL	21	0	0	7	20.2	88	9	2	1	0	0	0	0	16	1	40	4	0	4	0	1.000	0	1-1 2	1.72	0.44
2011	Atl	NL	79	0	0	64	77.0	306	48	19	18	3	1	2	1	32	1	127	4	0	4	3	.571	0	46-54	1.88	2.10
2012	Atl	NL	63	0	0	56	62.2	231	27	7	7	3	0	0	2	14	0	116	5	0	3	1	.750	0	42-45	1.01	1.01
	Postseason		4	0	0	2	4.1	13	1	2	1	0	0	0	0	1	0	7	0	0	0	1	.000	0	0-0 1	0.40	2.08
	3 ML YEARS		163	0	0	127	160.1	625	84	28	26	6	1	2	3	62	2	283	13	0	11	4	.733	0	89-100 2	1.44	1.46

Josh Kinney

Pitches: R Bats: R Pos: RP-35   Ht: 6'1" Wt: 214 Born: 3/31/1979 Age: 34

			HOW MUCH HE PITCHED					WHAT HE GAVE UP										THE RESULTS						
Year	Team	Lg	G	GS	CG	GF	IP	BFP	H	R	ER	HR	SH	SF	HB	TBB	IBB	SO	WP	Bk	W	L	Pct	Sh	Sv-Op Hld	ERC	ERA
2012	Tacom*	AAA	27	0	0	13	36.2	154	37	13	11	0	0	2	3	11	1	38	2	0	1	0	1.000	0	3- - -	3.39	2.70
2006	StL	NL	21	0	0	4	25.0	99	17	9	9	3	0	0	1	8	0	22	0	0	0	0	-	0	0-0 2	2.40	3.24
2008	StL	NL	7	0	0	1	7.0	25	3	0	0	0	0	0	0	1	0	8	0	0	0	0	-	0	0-0 0	0.60	0.00
2009	StL	NL	17	0	0	3	15.1	81	23	15	15	2	1	0	2	11	1	8	0	0	1	0	1.000	0	0-1 2	9.17	8.80
2011	CWS	AL	13	0	0	8	17.2	81	23	13	13	1	0	0	2	7	1	20	1	0	0	0	-	0	0-0 6	6.00	6.62
2012	Sea	AL	35	0	0	8	32.0	136	24	14	14	3	1	2	3	15	3	36	2	0	0	3	.000	0	1-2 9	3.13	3.94
	Postseason		7	0	0	1	6.1	25	3	0	0	0	0	0	1	4	0	6	0	0	1	0	1.000	0	0-0 3	2.24	0.00
	5 ML YEARS		93	0	0	24	97.0	422	90	51	51	9	2	2	8	42	5	94	3	0	1	3	.250	0	1-3 13	3.99	4.73

Ian Kinsler

Bats: R Throws: R Pos: 2B-144; DH-13; 3B-1   Ht: 6'0" Wt: 200 Born: 6/22/1982 Age: 31

			BATTING																	BASERUNNING				AVERAGES		
Year	Team	Lg	G	AB	H	2B	3B	HR	(Hm	Rd)	TB	R	RBI	RC	TBB	IBB	SO	HBP	SH	SF	SB	CS	SB%	GDP	Avg	OBP	Slg
2006	Tex	AL	120	423	121	27	1	14	(10	4)	192	65	55	65	40	1	64	3	1	7	11	4	.73	12	.286	.347	.454
2007	Tex	AL	130	483	127	22	2	20	(12	8)	213	96	61	79	62	2	83	9	8	4	23	2	.92	14	.263	.355	.441
2008	Tex	AL	121	518	165	41	4	18	(4	14)	268	102	71	106	45	1	67	6	7	7	26	2	.93	12	.319	.375	.517
2009	Tex	AL	144	566	143	32	4	31	(20	11)	276	101	86	99	59	0	77	6	3	6	31	5	.86	9	.253	.327	.488
2010	Tex	AL	103	391	112	20	1	9	(4	5)	161	73	45	59	56	2	57	7	2	4	15	5	.75	11	.286	.382	.412
2011	Tex	AL	155	620	158	34	4	32	(16	16)	296	121	77	100	89	2	71	8	4	2	30	4	.88	17	.255	.355	.477
2012	Tex	AL	157	655	168	42	5	19	(14	5)	277	105	72	83	60	0	90	10	1	5	21	9	.70	14	.256	.326	.423
	Postseason		33	119	36	7	1	4	(1	3)	57	17	20	24	22	1	16	1	1	1	6	5	.55	2	.303	.413	.479
	7 ML YEARS		930	3656	994	218	21	143	(80	63)	1683	663	467	591	411	8	509	49	26	35	157	31	.84	89	.272	.350	.460

Brandon Kintzler

Pitches: R Bats: R Pos: RP-14   Ht: 5'10" Wt: 187 Born: 8/1/1984 Age: 28

			HOW MUCH HE PITCHED					WHAT HE GAVE UP										THE RESULTS						
Year	Team	Lg	G	GS	CG	GF	IP	BFP	H	R	ER	HR	SH	SF	HB	TBB	IBB	SO	WP	Bk	W	L	Pct	Sh	Sv-Op Hld	ERC	ERA
2012	BrvdCt*	A+	6	0	0	2	6.0	27	7	2	2	0	0	0	0	3	0	9	1	0	0	1	.000	0	0- - -	4.72	3.00
2012	Hntsvl*	AA	31	0	0	21	35.2	146	35	15	13	1	1	1	2	12	3	20	3	0	0	2	.000	0	9- - -	3.48	3.28
2012	Nashv*	AAA	8	0	0	3	11.2	43	8	2	2	0	1	0	0	2	2	11	1	0	0	1	.000	0	1- - -	1.20	1.54
2010	Mil	NL	7	0	0	2	7.1	33	10	6	6	2	1	0	0	4	1	9	1	0	0	1	.000	0	0-0 -	8.67	7.36
2011	Mil	NL	9	0	0	3	14.2	61	14	9	6	3	0	2	0	3	0	15	0	1	1	1	.500	0	0-0 3	3.65	3.68
2012	Mil	NL	14	0	0	1	16.2	72	18	7	7	1	0	0	0	7	1	14	1	0	3	0	1.000	0	0-0 2	4.30	3.78
	3 ML YEARS		30	0	0	6	38.2	166	42	22	19	6	1	2	0	14	2	38	2	1	4	2	.667	0	0-0 2	4.80	4.42

Jason Kipnis

Bats: L Throws: R Pos: 2B-146; DH-4; PH-3   Ht: 5'11" Wt: 185 Born: 4/3/1987 Age: 26

KIP-niss

			BATTING																	BASERUNNING				AVERAGES		
Year	Team	Lg	G	AB	H	2B	3B	HR	(Hm	Rd)	TB	R	RBI	RC	TBB	IBB	SO	HBP	SH	SF	SB	CS	SB%	GDP	Avg	OBP	Slg
2009	MhVlly	A-	29	111	34	8	3	1	(-	-)	51	19	19	20	15	1	18	1	0	2	3	3	.50	1	.306	.388	.459
2010	Knstn	A+	54	203	61	12	3	6	(-	-)	97	33	31	38	24	1	46	6	2	2	2	3	.40	5	.300	.387	.478
2010	Akron	AA	79	315	98	20	5	10	(-	-)	158	63	43	62	31	1	61	7	2	0	7	1	.88	15	.311	.385	.502

			BATTING																				BASERUNNING				AVERAGES		
Year	Team	Lg	G	AB	H	2B	3B	HR	(Hm	Rd)	TB	R	RBI	RC	TBB	IBB	SO	HBP	SH	SF	SB	CS	SB%	GDP	Avg	OBP	Slg
2011	Clmbs	AAA	92	343	96	16	9	12	(-	-)	166	65	55	64	44	1	72	3	5	5	12	1	.92	5	.280	.362	.484
2011	Cle	AL	36	136	37	9	1	7	(3	4)	69	24	19	22	11	0	34	2	0	1	5	0	1.00		.272	.333	.507
2012	Cle	AL	152	591	152	22	4	14	(5	9)	224	86	76	88	67	2	109	5	3	6	31	7	.82	12	.257	.335	.379
	2 ML YEARS		188	727	189	31	5	21	(8	13)	293	110	95	110	78	2	143	7	3	7	36	7	.84	12	.260	.335	.403

Michael Kirkman

Pitches: L **Bats:** L **Pos:** RP-28 **Ht:** 6'4" **Wt:** 195 **Born:** 9/18/1986 **Age:** 26

			HOW MUCH HE PITCHED					WHAT HE GAVE UP											THE RESULTS							
Year	Team	Lg	G	GS	CG	GF	IP	BFP	H	R	ER	HR	SH	SF	HB	TBB	IBB	SO	WP	Bk	W	L	Pct	Sh	Sv-Op	Hld	ERC	ERA
2012	RdRck*	AAA	15	8	0	2	48.0	211	47	29	28	5	1	2	0	31	0	48	4	0	5	1	.833	0	0- -	-	5.13	5.25
2010	Tex	AL	14	0	0	2	16.1	68	9	3	3	0	0	2	0	10	1	16	0	0			-	0	0-1	2	1.76	1.65
2011	Tex	AL	15	0	0	7	27.1	122	26	22	20	5	1	2	3	12	2	21	2	0	1	1	.500	0	0-0	1	4.81	6.59
2012	Tex	AL	28	0	0	9	35.1	151	24	16	15	5	0	1	1	17	1	38	2	0	1	2	.333	0	0-2	1	2.88	3.82
	Postseason		3	0	0	2	2.2	13	4	1	1	0	1	0	0	2	0	2	0	0	0	0	-	0	0-0	0	8.14	3.38
	3 ML YEARS		57	0	0	18	79.0	341	59	41	38	10	1	5	4	39	4	75	4	0	2	3	.400	0	0-3	4	3.26	4.33

Corey Kluber

Pitches: R **Bats:** R **Pos:** SP-12 CLUE-burr **Ht:** 6'4" **Wt:** 215 **Born:** 4/10/1986 **Age:** 27

			HOW MUCH HE PITCHED					WHAT HE GAVE UP											THE RESULTS							
Year	Team	Lg	G	GS	CG	GF	IP	BFP	H	R	ER	HR	SH	SF	HB	TBB	IBB	SO	WP	Bk	W	L	Pct	Sh	Sv-Op	Hld	ERC	ERA
2007	Eugene	A-	10	7	0	0	33.1	143	28	16	13	1	2	2	2	15	0	33	0	0	1	1	.500	0	0- -	-	3.11	3.51
2008	Lk Els	A+	19	16	0	0	85.1	377	93	62	57	9	5	4	2	34	1	75	5	0	2	5	.286	0	0- -	-	4.69	6.01
2008	FtWyn	A	10	10	0	0	56.0	234	49	25	20	8	0	1	6	13	0	72	4	0	4	3	.571	0	0- -	-	3.41	3.21
2009	Lk Els	A+	19	19	0	0	109.0	469	110	65	55	9	5	1	6	36	0	124	8	0	7	9	.438	0	0- -	-	3.95	4.54
2009	SnAnt	AA	9	9	0	0	45.0	210	45	25	23	5	2	3	2	34	0	35	1	1	2	4	.333	0	0- -	-	5.81	4.60
2010	SnAnt	AA	22	21	0	0	122.2	525	121	59	47	7	5	4	9	40	0	136	5	0	6	6	.500	0	0- -	-	3.71	3.45
2010	Akron	AA	5	5	0	0	26.1	124	38	12	11	0	1	1	2	10	0	21	1	0	2	2	.500	0	0- -	-	6.22	3.76
2010	Clmbs	AAA	2	2	0	0	11.0	47	10	4	4	1	0	0	2	6	0	8	0	0	1	1	.500	0	0- -	-	5.11	3.27
2011	Clmbs	AAA	27	27	0	0	150.2	667	153	101	93	19	6	2	8	70	0	143	12	0	7	11	.389	0	0- -	-	4.84	5.56
2012	Clmbs	AAA	21	21	1	0	125.1	545	121	62	50	9	6	3	5	49	3	128	6	0	11	7	.611	0	0- -	-	3.72	3.59
2011	Cle	AL	3	0	0	2	4.1	25	6	4	4	0	0	0	2	3	0	5	1	0	0	0	-	0	0-0	0	8.12	8.31
2012	Cle	AL	12	12	0	0	63.0	281	76	44	36	9	1	0	4	18	0	54	2	0	2	5	.286	0	0-0	0	5.38	5.14
	2 ML YEARS		15	12	0	2	67.1	306	82	48	40	9	1	0	6	21	0	59	3	0	2	5	.286	0	0-0	0	5.57	5.35

Tom Koehler

Pitches: R **Bats:** R **Pos:** RP-7; SP-1 COLE-err **Ht:** 6'2" **Wt:** 225 **Born:** 6/29/1986 **Age:** 27

			HOW MUCH HE PITCHED					WHAT HE GAVE UP											THE RESULTS							
Year	Team	Lg	G	GS	CG	GF	IP	BFP	H	R	ER	HR	SH	SF	HB	TBB	IBB	SO	WP	Bk	W	L	Pct	Sh	Sv-Op	Hld	ERC	ERA
2008	Jmstwn	A-	15	13	0	0	66.0	297	66	33	27	0	2	3	10	29	0	58	3	0	5	5	.500	0	0- -	-	4.05	3.68
2009	Grnsbr	A	18	18	0	0	98.1	423	88	37	35	9	2	1	11	39	0	82	6	1	5	5	.500	0	0- -	-	3.87	3.20
2009	Jupiter	A+	6	6	0	0	34.2	141	35	15	13	0	0	1	2	9	0	25	3	0	4	1	.800	0	0- -	-	3.27	3.38
2010	Jaxnvl	AA	28	28	0	0	158.2	650	140	57	46	11	10	5	8	46	1	145	4	0	16	2	.889	0	0- -	-	3.04	2.61
2011	NewOr	AAA	28	28	0	0	150.1	664	144	90	83	18	5	7	5	79	1	116	4	1	12	7	.632	0	0- -	-	4.61	4.97
2012	NewOr	AAA	29	27	0	0	151.0	658	154	80	70	15	8	8	6	61	3	138	2	2	12	11	.522	0	0- -	-	4.33	4.17
2012	Mia	NL	8	1	0	0	13.1	56	15	8	8	4	0	0	0	2	1	13	0	0	0	1	.000	0	0-0	0	4.99	5.40

Michael Kohn

Pitches: R **Bats:** R **Pos:** OF KAHN **Ht:** 6'0" **Wt:** 200 **Born:** 6/26/1986 **Age:** 27

			HOW MUCH HE PITCHED					WHAT HE GAVE UP											THE RESULTS							
Year	Team	Lg	G	GS	CG	GF	IP	BFP	H	R	ER	HR	SH	SF	HB	TBB	IBB	SO	WP	Bk	W	L	Pct	Sh	Sv-Op	Hld	ERC	ERA
2008	Orem	R+	16	0	0	4	23.1	93	11	5	5	1	0	0	0	11	0	44	3	0	2	0	1.000	0	0- -	-	1.43	1.93
2009	CRpds	A	28	0	0	11	37.0	140	20	9	9	1	0	1	2	12	0	60	1	1	4	1	.800	0	6- -	-	1.45	2.19
2009	RCuca	A+	22	0	0	14	28.2	108	13	3	3	0	1	1	0	14	0	43	2	0	2	0	1.000	0	3- -	-	1.32	0.94
2010	Ark	AA	15	0	0	13	18.1	72	12	5	5	0	1	0	1	8	1	25	2	0	2	2	.500	0	3- -	-	2.00	2.45
2010	Salt Lk	AAA	26	0	0	23	27.2	115	16	7	6	3	3	0	1	17	2	32	0	0	3	2	.600	0	8- -	-	2.73	1.95
2011	Salt Lk	AAA	46	0	0	34	48.1	212	47	27	22	5	1	2	3	20	0	64	0	0	1	3	.250	0	12- -	-	4.21	4.10
2010	LAA	AL	24	0	0	8	21.1	95	17	5	5	0	4	0	0	16	1	20	0	0	2	0	1.000	0	1-1	1	3.45	2.11
2011	LAA	AL	14	0	0	7	12.1	60	14	10	10	6	0	1	1	9	0	9	1	0	0	1	.000	0	1-2	1	9.92	7.30
	2 ML YEARS		38	0	0	15	33.2	155	31	15	15	6	4	0	1	25	1	29	1	0	2	1	.667	0	2-3	2	5.66	4.01

Erik Komatsu

Bats: L **Throws:** L **Pos:** PH-11; RF-10; CF-5; PR-4; DH-3; LF-2 koh-MOTT-sue **Ht:** 5'10" **Wt:** 175 **Born:** 10/1/1987 **Age:** 25

			BATTING																				BASERUNNING				AVERAGES		
Year	Team	Lg	G	AB	H	2B	3B	HR	(Hm	Rd)	TB	R	RBI	RC	TBB	IBB	SO	HBP	SH	SF	SB	CS	SB%	GDP	Avg	OBP	Slg
2008	Helena	R+	68	277	89	19	4	11	(-	-)	149	61	47	58	30	1	42	5	1	3	8	4	.67	3	.321	.394	.538
2009	Wisc	A	21	66	16	2	0	1	(-	-)	21	6	5	7	8	0	14	3	1	2	0	2	.00	1	.242	.342	.318
2009	Brewrs	R	5	13	4	0	0	0	(-	-)	4	1	3	1	2	0	2	0	0	0	0	0	-	0	.308	.353	.308
2010	BrvdCt	A+	130	486	157	31	6	5	(-	-)	215	90	63	96	68	3	61	9	5	4	28	9	.76	8	.323	.413	.442
2011	Hntsvl	AA	93	320	94	19	1	6	(-	-)	133	48	40	57	53	2	44	2	0	4	13	6	.68	5	.294	.393	.416
2011	Hrsbrg	AA	31	128	30	5	0	1	(-	-)	38	12	8	12	11	0	22	1	1	1	8	3	.73	1	.234	.298	.297
2012	Syrcse	AAA	31	104	28	4	0	3	(-	-)	41	16	14	14	13	0	13	2	2	2	2	5	.29	1	.269	.355	.394
2012	2 Tms		30	51	11	0	0	0	(0	0)	11	5	1	3	6	0	5	0	0	1	0	0	-	2	.216	.293	.216
12	StL	NL	15	19	4	0	0	0	(0	0)	4	3	0	1	2	0	2	0	0	0	0	0	-	0	.211	.286	.211
12	Min	AL	15	32	7	0	0	0	(0	0)	7	2	1	2	4	0	3	0	0	1	0	0	-	2	.219	.297	.219

Paul Konerko

Bats: R **Throws:** R **Pos:** 1B-105; DH-38; PH-1 — kun-ER-ko — **Ht:** 6'2" **Wt:** 220 **Born:** 3/5/1976 **Age:** 37

							BATTING														BASERUNNING				AVERAGES		
Year	Team	Lg	G	AB	H	2B	3B	HR	(Hm	Rd)	TB	R	RBI	RC	TBB	IBB	SO	HBP	SH	SF	SB	CS	SB%	GDP	Avg	OBP	Slg
1997	LAD	NL	6	7	1	0	0	0	(0	0)	1	0	0	0	1	0	2	0	0	0	0	0	-	1	.143	.250	.143
1998	2 Tms	NL	75	217	47	4	0	7	(2	5)	72	21	29	17	16	0	40	3	0	3	0	1	.00	10	.217	.276	.332
1999	CWS	AL	142	513	151	31	4	24	(16	8)	262	71	81	86	45	0	68	2	1	3	1	0	1.00	19	.294	.352	.511
2000	CWS	AL	143	524	156	31	1	21	(10	11)	252	84	97	86	47	0	72	10	0	5	1	0	1.00	22	.298	.363	.481
2001	CWS	AL	156	582	164	35	0	32	(19	13)	295	92	99	99	54	6	89	9	0	5	1	0	1.00	17	.282	.349	.507
2002	CWS	AL	151	570	173	30	0	27	(13	14)	284	81	104	96	44	2	72	9	0	7	0	0	-	17	.304	.359	.498
2003	CWS	AL	137	444	104	19	0	18	(9	9)	177	49	65	42	43	7	50	4	0	4	0	0	-	28	.234	.305	.399
2004	CWS	AL	155	563	156	22	0	41	(29	12)	301	84	117	106	69	5	107	6	0	5	1	0	1.00	23	.277	.359	.535
2005	CWS	AL	158	575	163	24	0	40	(23	17)	307	98	100	106	81	10	109	5	0	3	0	0	-	9	.283	.375	.534
2006	CWS	AL	152	566	177	30	0	35	(21	14)	312	97	113	110	60	3	104	8	0	9	1	0	1.00	25	.313	.381	.551
2007	CWS	AL	151	549	142	34	0	31	(17	14)	269	71	90	88	78	9	102	3	0	6	0	1	.00	21	.259	.351	.490
2008	CWS	AL	122	438	105	19	1	22	(15	7)	192	59	62	60	65	4	80	7	0	4	2	0	1.00	17	.240	.344	.438
2009	CWS	AL	152	546	151	30	1	28	(18	10)	267	75	88	91	58	4	89	10	0	7	1	0	1.00	15	.277	.353	.489
2010	CWS	AL	149	548	171	30	1	39	(26	13)	320	89	111	118	72	7	110	5	0	6	0	1	.00	9	.312	.393	.584
2011	CWS	AL	149	543	163	25	0	31	(19	12)	281	69	105	100	77	17	89	8	0	11	1	1	.50	14	.300	.388	.517
2012	CWS	AL	144	533	159	22	0	26	(14	12)	259	66	75	86	56	4	83	7	0	2	0	0	-	16	.298	.371	.486
98	LAD	NL	49	144	31	1	0	4	(2	2)	44	14	16	10	10	0	30	2	0	2	0	1	.00	5	.215	.272	.306
98	Cin	NL	26	73	16	3	0	3	(0	3)	28	7	13	7	6	0	10	1	0	1	0	0	-	5	.219	.284	.384
	Postseason		19	74	18	2	0	7	(3	4)	41	10	17	12	5	2	10	1	0	0	0	0	-	4	.243	.300	.554
	16 ML YEARS		2142	7718	2183	386	8	422	(251	171)	3851	1106	1336	1291	866	78	1266	96	1	80	9	4	.69	263	.283	.359	.499

George Kontos

Pitches: R **Bats:** R **Pos:** RP-44 — CON-toes — **Ht:** 6'3" **Wt:** 225 **Born:** 6/12/1985 **Age:** 28

			HOW MUCH HE PITCHED						WHAT HE GAVE UP										THE RESULTS						
Year	Team	Lg	G	GS	CG	GF	IP	BFP	H	R	ER	HR	SH	SF	HB	TBB	IBB	SO	WP	Bk	W	L	Pct	Sh	Sv-Op Hld	ERC	ERA
2006	StIsInd	A-	14	14	0	0	78.1	313	64	25	23	3	4	6	2	19	0	82	3	0	7	3	.700	0	0- - -	2.27	2.64
2007	Tampa	A+	19	17	0	0	94.0	397	95	51	42	15	1	1	0	30	0	101	6	0	4	6	.400	0	0- - -	4.25	4.02
2008	Trntn	AA	27	27	0	0	151.2	635	134	76	62	14	4	8	4	57	1	152	2	0	6	11	.353	0	0- - -	3.40	3.68
2009	Trntn	AA	4	4	0	0	20.1	95	19	7	6	0	0	2	2	9	0	24	5	0	1	1	.500	0	0- - -	3.27	2.66
2009	S-WB	AAA	9	9	1	0	51.0	218	44	24	19	6	2	1	2	21	0	39	2	0	3	4	.429	0	0- - -	3.60	3.35
2010	Tampa	A+	5	2	0	2	10.1	40	7	3	3	0	0	1	0	3	0	8	0	0	0	1	.000	0	0- - -	1.55	2.61
2010	Trntn	AA	17	0	0	3	32.0	130	30	13	12	2	0	1	0	11	0	28	0	0	0	2	.000	0	0- - -	3.39	3.38
2010	S-WB	AAA	2	0	0	2	2.2	14	5	3	3	1	0	0	0	1	0	2	0	0	0	1	.000	0	0- - -	11.86	10.13
2011	S-WB	AAA	40	4	0	11	89.1	359	72	27	26	12	4	1	2	26	1	91	3	0	4	4	.500	0	2- - -	2.94	2.62
2012	Fresno	AAA	23	0	0	8	31.2	127	24	9	6	1	3	1	1	7	0	26	2	0	2	0	1.000	0	1- - -	1.86	1.71
2011	NYY	AL	7	0	0	4	6.0	24	4	2	2	1	0	0	0	3	0	6	0	0	0	0	-	0	0-0 0	3.20	3.00
2012	SF	NL	44	0	0	9	43.2	177	34	15	12	3	0	2	0	12	0	44	1	0	2	1	.667	0	0-1 5	2.23	2.47
	2 ML YEARS		51	0	0	13	49.2	201	38	17	14	4	0	2	0	15	0	50	1	0	2	1	.667	0	0-1 5	2.34	2.54

Bobby Korecky

Pitches: R **Bats:** R **Pos:** RP-1 — **Ht:** 5'11" **Wt:** 185 **Born:** 9/16/1979 **Age:** 33

			HOW MUCH HE PITCHED						WHAT HE GAVE UP										THE RESULTS						
Year	Team	Lg	G	GS	CG	GF	IP	BFP	H	R	ER	HR	SH	SF	HB	TBB	IBB	SO	WP	Bk	W	L	Pct	Sh	Sv-Op Hld	ERC	ERA
2012	LsVgs*	AAA	46	2	0	15	86.1	366	89	40	33	10	1	6	6	19	0	47	3	0	3	4	.429	0	0- - -	3.92	3.44
2008	Min	AL	16	0	0	9	17.2	74	19	9	9	2	0	0	0	8	0	6	0	0	2	0	1.000	0	0-0 1	5.13	4.58
2009	Ari	AL	5	0	0	0	6.0	32	11	9	9	0	1	1	0	4	0	3	3	0	0	0	-	0	0-0 1	9.65	13.50
2012	Tor	AL	1	0	0	1	1.0	5	1	2	2	1	0	0	0	1	0	0	0	0	0	0	-	0	0-0 0	14.27	18.00
	3 ML YEARS		22	0	0	10	24.2	111	31	20	20	3	1	1	0	13	0	9	3	0	2	0	1.000	0	0-0 1	6.56	7.30

Casey Kotchman

Bats: L **Throws:** L **Pos:** 1B-137; PH-10 — **Ht:** 6'3" **Wt:** 220 **Born:** 2/22/1983 **Age:** 30

							BATTING														BASERUNNING				AVERAGES		
Year	Team	Lg	G	AB	H	2B	3B	HR	(Hm	Rd)	TB	R	RBI	RC	TBB	IBB	SO	HBP	SH	SF	SB	CS	SB%	GDP	Avg	OBP	Slg
2004	LAA	AL	38	116	26	6	0	0	(0	0)	32	7	15	14	7	3	11	4	0	1	3	0	1.00	3	.224	.289	.276
2005	LAA	AL	47	126	35	5	0	7	(5	2)	61	16	22	21	15	0	18	0	1	1	1	1	.50	3	.278	.352	.484
2006	LAA	AL	29	79	12	2	0	1	(0	1)	17	6	6	1	7	0	13	0	2	0	0	1	.00	2	.152	.221	.215
2007	LAA	AL	137	443	131	37	3	11	(5	6)	207	64	68	74	53	1	43	4	3	5	2	4	.33	17	.296	.372	.467
2008	2 Tms	AL	143	525	143	28	1	14	(3	11)	215	65	74	70	36	5	39	9	0	3	2	1	.67	18	.272	.328	.410
2009	2 Tms	AL	126	385	103	23	0	7	(1	6)	147	37	48	49	39	6	42	4	0	3	1	0	1.00	11	.268	.339	.382
2010	Sea	AL	125	414	90	20	1	9	(5	4)	139	37	51	40	35	6	57	3	0	5	0	0	-	15	.217	.280	.336
2011	TB	AL	146	500	153	24	2	10	(3	7)	211	44	48	74	48	5	66	12	0	3	2	2	.50	13	.306	.378	.422
2012	Cle	AL	142	463	106	12	0	12	(6	6)	154	46	55	44	26	1	49	7	3	1	3	0	1.00	15	.229	.280	.333
08	LAA	AL	100	373	107	24	0	12	(2	10)	167	47	54	53	18	3	23	5	0	2	2	1	.67	14	.287	.327	.448
08	Atl	NL	43	152	36	4	1	2	(1	1)	48	18	20	17	18	2	16	4	0	1	0	0	-	4	.237	.331	.316
09	Atl	NL	87	298	84	20	0	6	(1	5)	122	28	41	43	32	6	28	3	0	3	0	0	-	7	.282	.354	.409
09	Bos	AL	39	87	19	3	0	1	(0	1)	25	9	7	6	7	0	14	1	0	0	1	0	1.00	4	.218	.284	.287
	Postseason		15	32	6	2	0	0	(0	0)	8	2	3	4	3	0	3	0	0	0	0	0	-	0	.188	.257	.250
	9 ML YEARS		933	3051	799	157	7	71	(32	39)	1183	322	387	387	266	27	338	43	9	22	14	9	.61	97	.262	.328	.388

Mark Kotsay

Bats: L Throws: L Pos: PH-52; LF-19; RF-9; 1B-5   Ht: 6'0" Wt: 210 Born: 12/2/1975 Age: 37

Year Team	Lg	G	AB	H	2B	3B	HR	(Hm	Rd)	TB	R	RBI	RC	TBB	IBB	SO	HBP	SH	SF	SB	CS	SB%	GDP	Avg	OBP	Slg
2012 Lk Els*	A+	1	4	0	0	0	0	(-	-)	0	0	0	0	0	0	0	0	0	0	0	0	-	0	.000	.000	.000
1997 Fla	NL	14	52	10	1	1	0	(0	0)	13	5	4	3	4	0	7	0	1	0	3	0	1.00	1	.192	.250	.250
1998 Fla	NL	154	578	161	25	7	11	(5	6)	233	72	68	70	34	2	61	1	7	3	10	5	.67	17	.279	.318	.403
1999 Fla	NL	148	495	134	23	9	8	(5	3)	199	57	50	58	29	5	50	0	2	9	7	6	.54	11	.271	.306	.402
2000 Fla	NL	152	530	158	31	5	12	(5	7)	235	87	57	78	42	2	46	0	2	4	19	9	.68	17	.298	.347	.443
2001 SD	NL	119	406	118	29	1	10	(3	7)	179	67	58	65	48	1	58	2	1	3	13	5	.72	11	.291	.366	.441
2002 SD	NL	153	578	169	27	7	17	(11	6)	261	82	61	92	59	0	89	3	2	4	11	9	.55	10	.292	.359	.452
2003 SD	NL	128	482	128	28	4	7	(1	6)	185	64	38	59	56	3	82	1	1	1	6	3	.67	8	.266	.343	.384
2004 Oak	AL	148	606	190	37	3	15	(9	6)	278	78	63	94	55	5	70	2	5	5	8	5	.62	6	.314	.370	.459
2005 Oak	AL	139	582	163	35	1	15	(4	11)	245	75	82	86	40	3	51	1	2	4	5	5	.50	13	.280	.325	.421
2006 Oak	AL	129	502	138	29	3	7	(1	6)	194	57	59	63	44	1	55	2	4	6	6	3	.67	18	.275	.332	.386
2007 Oak	AL	56	206	44	14	0	1	(0	1)	61	20	20	19	19	3	20	0	0	1	1	1	.50	4	.214	.279	.296
2008 2 Tms		110	402	111	25	4	6	(4	2)	162	45	49	49	32	3	45	0	1	1	2	4	.33	14	.276	.329	.403
2009 2 Tms		67	187	52	9	0	4	(4	0)	73	16	23	22	15	3	21	0	1	3	3	2	.60	6	.278	.327	.390
2010 CWS	AL	107	327	78	17	2	8	(4	4)	123	30	31	33	32	3	36	0	0	0	1	3	.25	9	.239	.306	.376
2011 Mil	NL	104	233	63	13	1	3	(1	2)	87	18	31	31	21	3	27	0	0	1	3	0	1.00	6	.270	.329	.373
2012 SD	NL	82	143	37	8	0	2	(1	1)	51	9	14	14	11	1	14	1	0	1	0	2	.00	2	.259	.314	.357
08 Atl	NL	88	318	92	17	3	6	(4	2)	133	39	37	37	25	2	34	0	1	1	2	3	.40	13	.289	.340	.418
08 Bos	AL	22	84	19	8	1	0	(0	0)	29	6	12	12	7	1	11	0	0	0	0	1	.00	1	.226	.286	.345
09 Bos	AL	27	74	19	2	0	1	(1	0)	24	4	5	6	4	1	12	0	0	1	2	1	.67	1	.257	.291	.324
09 CWS	AL	40	113	33	7	0	3	(3	0)	49	12	18	16	11	2	9	0	1	2	1	1	.50	5	.292	.344	.434
Postseason		26	82	17	5	0	2	(0	2)	28	9	3	3	5	1	12	0	0	0	0	0	-	4	.207	.253	.341
16 ML YEARS		1810	6309	1754	351	48	126	(58	68)	2579	782	708	836	541	38	732	13	29	46	98	62	.61	151	.278	.334	.409

George Kottaras

Bats: L Throws: R Pos: C-54; PH-30; 1B-6; DH-1   kah-TARR-iss   Ht: 6'0" Wt: 200 Born: 5/10/1983 Age: 30

Year Team	Lg	G	AB	H	2B	3B	HR	(Hm	Rd)	TB	R	RBI	RC	TBB	IBB	SO	HBP	SH	SF	SB	CS	SB%	GDP	Avg	OBP	Slg
2008 Bos	AL	3	5	1	1	0	0	(0	0)	2	1	0	0	0	0	2	0	0	0	0	0	-	0	.200	.200	.400
2009 Bos	AL	45	93	22	11	0	1	(1	0)	36	15	10	10	11	0	25	0	0	3	0	0	-	1	.237	.308	.387
2010 Mil	NL	67	212	43	12	1	9	(5	4)	84	24	26	22	33	1	44	0	1	4	2	0	1.00	5	.203	.305	.396
2011 Mil	NL	49	111	28	6	1	5	(1	4)	51	15	17	15	10	0	26	0	1	1	0	1	.00	2	.252	.311	.459
2012 2 Tms		85	171	36	6	1	9	(4	5)	71	20	31	30	37	1	48	0	1	0	0	0	-	4	.211	.351	.415
12 Mil	NL	58	86	18	4	0	3	(1	2)	31	10	12	15	29	1	24	0	1	0	0	0	-	2	.209	.409	.360
12 Oak	AL	27	85	18	2	1	6	(3	3)	40	10	19	15	8	0	24	0	0	0	0	0	-	2	.212	.280	.471
Postseason		3	8	0	0	0	0	(0	0)	0	0	0	2	1	0	2	0	0	0	0	0	-	0	.000	.111	.000
5 ML YEARS		249	592	130	36	3	24	(11	13)	244	75	84	77	91	2	145	0	3	8	2	1	.67	12	.220	.320	.412

Pete Kozma

Bats: R Throws: R Pos: SS-25; 2B-1; PH-1   KAHZ-muh   Ht: 6'0" Wt: 170 Born: 4/11/1988 Age: 25

Year Team	Lg	G	AB	H	2B	3B	HR	(Hm	Rd)	TB	R	RBI	RC	TBB	IBB	SO	HBP	SH	SF	SB	CS	SB%	GDP	Avg	OBP	Slg
2007 JhsCty	R+	30	106	28	8	0	2	(-	-)	42	16	9	15	12	0	21	2	0	0	3	2	.60	1	.264	.350	.396
2007 Cards	R	4	13	2	0	0	0	(-	-)	2	4	0	0	2	0	2	0	0	0	0	0	-	0	.154	.267	.154
2007 Batvia	A-	8	27	4	0	1	0	(-	-)	6	1	2	0	1	0	7	0	0	0	1	1	.50	0	.148	.179	.222
2008 QuadC	A	99	377	107	20	4	5	(-	-)	150	58	40	59	45	0	69	5	1	6	12	5	.71	7	.284	.363	.398
2008 PlmBh	A+	24	77	10	4	0	0	(-	-)	14	4	10	2	10	0	27	1	3	3	1	0	1.00	0	.130	.231	.182
2009 PlmBh	A+	18	73	23	5	0	0	(-	-)	28	8	8	11	8	0	16	1	0	2	1	0	1.00	0	.315	.381	.384
2009 Sprgfld	AA	113	407	88	15	3	6	(-	-)	127	52	37	39	42	0	88	1	4	5	4	2	.67	6	.216	.288	.312
2010 Sprgfld	AA	132	503	122	28	2	13	(-	-)	193	69	72	67	56	2	111	1	7	3	13	2	.87	9	.243	.318	.384
2011 Memp	AAA	112	398	85	17	2	3	(-	-)	115	48	47	33	36	3	91	3	5	6	2	2	.50	7	.214	.280	.289
2012 Memp	AAA	131	448	104	16	3	11	(-	-)	159	61	63	49	41	1	74	0	4	7	7	4	.64	6	.232	.292	.355
2011 StL	NL	16	17	3	1	0	0	(0	0)	4	2	1	2	4	0	4	0	1	0	0	0	-	0	.176	.333	.235
2012 StL	NL	26	72	24	5	3	2	(0	2)	41	11	14	13	7	1	19	0	1	2	2	0	1.00	4	.333	.383	.569
2 ML YEARS		42	89	27	6	3	2	(0	2)	45	13	15	15	11	1	23	0	2	2	2	0	1.00	4	.303	.373	.506

Erik Kratz

Bats: R Throws: R Pos: C-41; PH-10; PR-1   Ht: 6'4" Wt: 255 Born: 6/15/1980 Age: 33

Year Team	Lg	G	AB	H	2B	3B	HR	(Hm	Rd)	TB	R	RBI	RC	TBB	IBB	SO	HBP	SH	SF	SB	CS	SB%	GDP	Avg	OBP	Slg
2012 LV*	AAA	37	124	33	10	0	8	(-	-)	67	17	30	22	10	2	20	3	0	4	0	0	-	6	.266	.326	.540
2010 Pit	NL	9	34	4	0	0	0	(0	0)	4	2	1	0	2	0	9	0	0	0	0	0	-	0	.118	.167	.118
2011 Phi	NL	2	6	2	1	0	0	(0	0)	3	0	0	1	0	0	1	0	0	0	0	0	-	0	.333	.333	.500
2012 Phi	NL	50	141	35	9	0	9	(6	3)	71	14	26	20	11	2	34	2	0	3	0	0	-	2	.248	.306	.504
3 ML YEARS		61	181	41	10	0	9	(6	3)	78	16	27	21	13	2	44	2	0	3	0	0	-	2	.227	.281	.431

Jason Kubel

Bats: L Throws: R Pos: LF-124; PH-10; DH-6; RF-2   KOO-bull   Ht: 6'0" Wt: 220 Born: 5/25/1982 Age: 31

Year Team	Lg	G	AB	H	2B	3B	HR	(Hm	Rd)	TB	R	RBI	RC	TBB	IBB	SO	HBP	SH	SF	SB	CS	SB%	GDP	Avg	OBP	Slg
2004 Min	AL	23	60	18	2	0	2	(0	2)	26	10	7	13	6	0	9	0	0	1	1	1	.50	0	.300	.358	.433
2006 Min	AL	73	220	53	8	0	8	(3	5)	85	23	26	20	12	0	45	0	2	1	2	0	1.00	13	.241	.279	.386
2007 Min	AL	128	418	114	31	2	13	(6	7)	188	49	65	64	41	2	79	1	1	5	5	0	1.00	9	.273	.335	.450
2008 Min	AL	141	463	126	22	5	20	(9	11)	218	74	78	66	47	2	91	0	0	7	0	1	.00	12	.272	.335	.471

Year	Team	Lg	G	AB	H	2B	3B	HR	(Hm	Rd)	TB	R	RBI	RC	TBB	IBB	SO	HBP	SH	SF	SB	CS	SB%	GDP	Avg	OBP	Slg
																									BATTING → **BASERUNNING** → **AVERAGES**		
2009	Min	AL	146	514	154	35	2	28	(15	13)	277	73	103	101	56	9	106	3	0	5	1	1	.50	13	.300	.369	.539
2010	Min	AL	143	518	129	23	3	21	(8	13)	221	68	92	65	56	5	116	3	0	5	1	1	1.00	16	.249	.323	.427
2011	Min	AL	99	366	100	21	1	12	(4	8)	159	37	58	59	32	2	86	1	0	2	1	1	.50	8	.273	.332	.434
2012	Ari	NL	141	506	128	30	4	30	(18	12)	256	75	90	71	57	7	151	2	0	6	1	1	.50	11	.253	.327	.506
Postseason			8	29	2	1	0	0	(0	0)	3	0	0	0	3	0	13	0	0	0	0	0	-	0	.069	.156	.103
8 ML YEARS			894	3065	822	172	17	134	(63	71)	1430	409	519	453	307	27	683	10	3	32	11	6	.65	82	.268	.334	.467

Hiroki Kuroda

Pitches: R Bats: R Pos: SP-33   hih-ROE-kee kuh-ROE-duh   Ht: 6'1" Wt: 205 Born: 2/10/1975 Age: 38

			HOW MUCH HE PITCHED					WHAT HE GAVE UP												THE RESULTS							
Year	Team	Lg	G	GS	CG	GF	IP	BFP	H	R	ER	HR	SH	SF	HB	TBB	IBB	SO	WP	Bk	W	L	Pct	Sh	Sv-Op	Hld	ERC	ERA
2008	LAD	NL	31	31	2	0	183.1	776	181	85	76	13	5	5	7	42	8	116	5	0	9	10	.474	0	0-0	0	3.18	3.73
2009	LAD	NL	21	20	0	0	117.1	485	110	59	49	12	7	1	1	24	1	87	5	0	8	7	.533	0	0-0	0	2.98	3.76
2010	LAD	NL	31	31	0	0	196.1	810	180	87	74	15	9	7	5	48	13	159	12	0	11	13	.458	0	0-0	0	2.87	3.39
2011	LAD	NL	32	32	0	0	202.0	838	196	77	69	24	6	5	5	49	6	161	12	1	13	16	.448	0	0-0	0	3.49	3.07
2012	NYY	AL	33	33	3	0	219.2	891	205	86	81	25	7	3	6	51	2	167	13	0	16	11	.593	2	0-0	0	3.35	3.32
Postseason			3	3	0	0	13.2	60	17	8	8	1	1	0	0	3	1	8	0	0	2	1	.667	0	0-0	0	4.39	5.27
5 ML YEARS			148	147	5	0	918.2	3800	872	394	349	89	36	21	26	214	30	690	47	1	57	57	.500	4	0-0	0	3.19	3.42

John Lackey

Pitches: R Bats: R Pos: P   Ht: 6'6" Wt: 245 Born: 10/23/1978 Age: 34

			HOW MUCH HE PITCHED					WHAT HE GAVE UP												THE RESULTS							
Year	Team	Lg	G	GS	CG	GF	IP	BFP	H	R	ER	HR	SH	SF	HB	TBB	IBB	SO	WP	Bk	W	L	Pct	Sh	Sv-Op	Hld	ERC	ERA
2002	LAA	AL	18	18	1	0	108.1	465	113	52	44	10	4	4	4	33	0	69	7	2	9	4	.692	0	0-0	0	4.03	3.66
2003	LAA	AL	33	33	2	0	204.0	885	223	117	105	31	2	6	10	66	4	151	11	1	10	16	.385	2	0-0	0	4.88	4.63
2004	LAA	AL	33	32	1	0	198.1	855	215	108	103	22	9	4	8	60	4	144	11	1	14	13	.519	1	0-0	0	4.39	4.67
2005	LAA	AL	33	33	1	0	209.0	892	208	85	80	13	1	2	11	71	3	199	18	0	14	5	.737	0	0-0	0	3.76	3.44
2006	LAA	AL	33	33	3	0	217.2	922	203	98	86	14	8	6	9	72	4	190	16	0	13	11	.542	2	0-0	0	3.31	3.56
2007	LAA	AL	33	33	2	0	224.0	929	219	87	75	18	1	1	12	52	2	179	9	1	19	9	.679	2	0-0	0	3.40	3.01
2008	LAA	AL	24	24	3	0	163.1	675	161	71	68	26	5	1	10	40	1	130	5	0	12	5	.706	0	0-0	0	4.10	3.75
2009	LAA	AL	27	27	1	0	176.1	748	177	84	75	17	9	10	9	47	1	139	6	0	11	8	.579	1	0-0	0	3.73	3.83
2010	Bos	AL	33	33	0	0	215.0	930	233	114	105	18	4	5	9	72	2	156	3	0	14	11	.560	0	0-0	0	4.37	4.40
2011	Bos	AL	28	28	0	0	160.0	743	203	119	114	20	2	6	19	56	1	108	11	0	12	12	.500	0	0-0	0	6.11	6.41
Postseason			14	12	0	0	78.0	328	75	29	27	4	2	3	1	29	4	53	4	0	3	4	.429	0	0-0	0	3.43	3.12
10 ML YEARS			295	294	14	0	1876.0	8044	1955	935	855	189	41	45	101	569	22	1465	97	5	128	94	.577	8	0-0	0	4.15	4.10

Aaron Laffey

Pitches: L Bats: L Pos: SP-16; RP-6   LAFF-ee   Ht: 6'0" Wt: 200 Born: 4/15/1985 Age: 28

			HOW MUCH HE PITCHED					WHAT HE GAVE UP												THE RESULTS							
Year	Team	Lg	G	GS	CG	GF	IP	BFP	H	R	ER	HR	SH	SF	HB	TBB	IBB	SO	WP	Bk	W	L	Pct	Sh	Sv-Op	Hld	ERC	ERA
2012	LsVgs*	AAA	11	11	1	0	63.2	284	77	41	32	6	1	2	3	20	0	38	3	0	3	5	.375	0	0--	-	5.09	4.52
2007	Cle	AL	9	9	0	0	49.1	207	54	26	25	2	1	2	4	12	0	25	2	1	4	2	.667	0	0-0	0	4.02	4.56
2008	Cle	AL	16	16	0	0	93.2	409	103	52	44	10	2	0	9	31	1	43	5	1	5	7	.417	0	0-0	0	4.86	4.23
2009	Cle	AL	25	19	0	3	121.2	539	140	69	60	9	0	4	2	57	1	59	1	1	7	9	.438	0	1-1	0	5.20	4.44
2010	Cle	AL	29	5	0	1	55.2	253	62	30	28	1	0	3	2	28	1	28	1	0	2	3	.400	0	0-0	5	4.61	4.53
2011	2 Tms	AL	47	0	0	7	53.1	247	67	24	23	7	2	2	3	21	3	30	2	1	3	2	.600	0	0-1	5	5.89	3.88
2012	Tor	AL	22	16	0	1	100.2	429	100	56	51	17	2	0	5	37	1	48	2	0	4	6	.400	0	0-0	0	4.65	4.56
11	Sea	AL	36	0	0	7	42.2	197	54	20	19	7	2	1	1	16	3	24	2	1	1	1	.500	0	0-1	5	5.92	4.01
11	NYY	AL	11	0	0	0	10.2	50	13	4	4	0	0	1	2	5	0	6	0	0	2	1	.667	0	0-0	0	5.66	3.38
Postseason			1	0	0	0	4.2	16	1	0	0	0	0	0	0	1	0	3	0	0	0	0	-	0	0-0	0	0.30	0.00
6 ML YEARS			148	65	0	12	474.1	2084	526	257	231	46	7	11	25	186	7	233	13	4	25	29	.463	0	1-2	10	4.90	4.38

Bryan LaHair

Bats: L Throws: R Pos: 1B-58; PH-41; RF-34; LF-2   luh-HARE   Ht: 6'5" Wt: 240 Born: 11/5/1982 Age: 30

			BATTING																	BASERUNNING				AVERAGES		
Year	Team	Lg	G	AB	H	2B	3B	HR	(Hm	Rd)	TB	R	RBI	RC	TBB	IBB	SO	HBP	SH	SF	SB	CS	SB%	GDP	Avg	OBP	Slg
2008	Sea	AL	45	136	34	4	0	3	(0	3)	47	15	10	14	13	1	40	0	1	0	0	1	1.00	4	.250	.315	.346
2011	ChC	NL	20	59	17	5	1	2	(2	0)	30	9	6	9	9	0	18	0	0	1	0	0	-	4	.288	.377	.508
2012	ChC	NL	130	340	88	17	0	16	(5	11)	153	42	40	40	39	3	124	0	0	0	4	2	.67	8	.259	.334	.450
3 ML YEARS			195	535	139	26	1	21	(7	14)	230	66	56	63	61	4	182	0	1	2	4	3	.57	13	.260	.334	.430

Brandon Laird

Bats: R Throws: R Pos: 3B-8; PH-6; 1B-4   Ht: 6'1" Wt: 215 Born: 9/11/1987 Age: 25

			BATTING																	BASERUNNING				AVERAGES		
Year	Team	Lg	G	AB	H	2B	3B	HR	(Hm	Rd)	TB	R	RBI	RC	TBB	IBB	SO	HBP	SH	SF	SB	CS	SB%	GDP	Avg	OBP	Slg
2007	Yanks	R	45	168	57	14	1	8	(-	-)	97	27	29	34	6	0	26	2	1	1	0	0	-	4	.339	.367	.577
2008	CtnSC	A	122	454	124	31	1	23	(-	-)	226	71	86	78	40	0	86	5	0	7	1	0	1.00	15	.273	.334	.498
2009	Tampa	A+	124	451	120	20	4	13	(-	-)	187	53	75	64	39	3	75	6	0	5	1	1	.50	19	.266	.329	.415
2010	Trntn	AA	107	409	119	22	2	23	(-	-)	214	73	90	76	38	3	84	4	0	3	2	2	.50	14	.291	.345	.523
2010	S-WB	AAA	31	122	30	6	0	2	(-	-)	42	13	12	11	4	0	27	0	0	1	0	0	-	6	.246	.268	.344
2011	S-WB	AAA	123	462	120	27	0	16	(-	-)	195	69	69	57	17	1	84	4	0	6	0	0	-	14	.260	.288	.422
2012	S-WB	AAA	130	503	128	31	2	15	(-	-)	208	54	77	67	34	1	103	7	0	6	1	0	1.00	15	.254	.307	.414
2011	NYY	AL	11	21	4	0	0	0	(0	0)	4	3	1	2	3	0	4	0	1	0	0	0	-	1	.190	.292	.190
2012	Hou	NL	17	35	9	1	0	1	(0	1)	13	2	4	5	2	0	8	0	0	0	0	0	-	1	.257	.297	.371
2 ML YEARS			28	56	13	1	0	1	(0	1)	17	5	5	7	5	0	12	0	1	0	0	0	-	2	.232	.295	.304

Gerald Laird

Bats: R **Throws:** R **Pos:** C-56; PR-4; DH-2; PH-2   **Ht:** 6'1" **Wt:** 225 **Born:** 11/13/1979 **Age:** 33

Year	Team	Lg	G	AB	H	2B	3B	HR	(Hm	Rd)	TB	R	RBI	RC	TBB	IBB	SO	HBP	SH	SF	SB	CS	SB%	GDP	Avg	OBP	Slg
2003	Tex	AL	19	44	12	2	1	1	(0	1)	19	9	4	5	5	0	11	1	0	0	0	0	-	2	.273	.360	.432
2004	Tex	AL	49	147	33	6	0	1	(1	0)	42	20	16	11	12	0	35	2	4	3	0	1	.00	5	.224	.287	.286
2005	Tex	AL	13	40	9	2	0	1	(0	1)	14	7	4	4	2	0	7	0	0	0	0	0	-	1	.225	.262	.350
2006	Tex	AL	78	243	72	20	1	7	(3	4)	115	46	22	24	12	0	54	2	1	7	3	1	.75	7	.296	.332	.473
2007	Tex	AL	120	407	91	18	3	9	(6	3)	142	48	47	45	30	1	103	2	5	4	6	2	.75	3	.224	.278	.349
2008	Tex	AL	95	344	95	24	0	6	(3	3)	137	54	41	46	23	2	63	6	4	4	2	4	.33	5	.276	.329	.398
2009	Det	AL	135	413	93	23	2	4	(1	3)	132	49	33	41	40	0	68	10	10	4	5	0	1.00	11	.225	.306	.320
2010	Det	AL	89	270	56	11	0	5	(2	3)	82	22	25	22	18	0	57	3	6	2	3	1	.75	7	.207	.263	.304
2011	StL	NL	37	95	22	7	1	1	(1	0)	34	11	12	10	9	3	19	1	2	1	1	1	.50	3	.232	.302	.358
2012	Det	AL	63	174	49	8	1	2	(0	2)	65	24	11	19	14	0	21	1	1	1	0	0	-	4	.282	.337	.374
	Postseason		4	1	0	0	0	0	(0	0)	0	0	0	0	0	0	1	0	0	0	0	0	-	0	.000	.000	.000
	10 ML YEARS		698	2177	532	121	9	37	(17	20)	782	290	215	227	165	6	438	28	33	21	20	10	.67	48	.244	.303	.359

Blake Lalli

Bats: L **Throws:** R **Pos:** C-4; 1B-2; PH-1   LAHL-ee   **Ht:** 6'1" **Wt:** 205 **Born:** 5/12/1983 **Age:** 30

Year	Team	Lg	G	AB	H	2B	3B	HR	(Hm	Rd)	TB	R	RBI	RC	TBB	IBB	SO	HBP	SH	SF	SB	CS	SB%	GDP	Avg	OBP	Slg
2006	Boise	A-	3	7	0	0	0	0	(-	-)	0	0	0	0	1	0	1	0	0	0	0	0	-	0	.000	.125	.000
2006	Peoria	A	22	68	13	3	0	0	(-	-)	16	3	4	3	3	0	11	2	0	0	1	1	.50	3	.191	.247	.235
2007	Peoria	A	77	268	79	13	0	4	(-	-)	104	29	33	37	18	1	43	3	2	1	3	1	.75	5	.295	.345	.388
2008	Peoria	A	12	46	13	4	0	1	(-	-)	20	5	7	6	2	0	9	0	0	1	0	0	-	0	.283	.306	.435
2008	Dytona	A+	76	283	97	29	0	7	(-	-)	147	30	49	56	19	2	34	3	1	3	0	0	-	8	.343	.386	.519
2008	Tenn	AA	23	69	20	5	0	3	(-	-)	34	9	14	11	4	0	17	0	0	0	0	0	-	1	.290	.329	.493
2009	Tenn	AA	118	373	117	25	0	5	(-	-)	157	49	51	60	32	6	50	4	1	2	0	2	.00	12	.314	.372	.421
2010	Tenn	AA	130	453	141	23	0	4	(-	-)	176	63	52	76	68	9	53	2	0	1	0	2	.00	10	.311	.403	.389
2011	Tenn	AA	108	349	100	22	1	9	(-	-)	151	40	52	57	39	3	59	2	0	3	1	0	1.00	14	.287	.359	.433
2012	Iowa	AAA	93	301	78	20	0	7	(-	-)	119	33	40	36	17	1	54	0	0	6	0	1	.00	7	.259	.293	.395
2012	Scrmto	AAA	4	15	3	0	0	1	(-	-)	6	1	1	1	1	0	1	0	0	0	0	1	.00	1	.200	.250	.400
2012	ChC	NL	6	15	2	0	0	0	(0	0)	2	1	2	1	1	0	3	0	0	0	0	0	-	0	.133	.188	.133

Ryan Langerhans

Bats: L **Throws:** L **Pos:** LF-2   LANG-err-hans   **Ht:** 6'3" **Wt:** 220 **Born:** 2/20/1980 **Age:** 33

Year	Team	Lg	G	AB	H	2B	3B	HR	(Hm	Rd)	TB	R	RBI	RC	TBB	IBB	SO	HBP	SH	SF	SB	CS	SB%	GDP	Avg	OBP	Slg
2012	Salt Lk*	AAA	96	336	84	21	6	11	(-	-)	150	59	54	58	63	2	113	1	0	1	6	6	.50	2	.250	.369	.446
2002	Atl	NL	1	1	0	0	0	0	(0	0)	0	0	0	0	0	0	0	0	0	0	0	0	-	0	.000	.000	.000
2003	Atl	NL	16	15	4	0	0	0	(0	0)	4	2	0	1	0	0	6	0	0	0	0	0	-	1	.267	.267	.267
2005	Atl	NL	128	326	87	22	3	8	(3	5)	139	48	42	53	37	3	75	5	2	3	0	2	.00	4	.267	.348	.426
2006	Atl	NL	131	315	76	16	3	7	(3	4)	119	46	28	45	50	8	91	3	0	1	1	2	.33	9	.241	.350	.378
2007	3 Tms		125	210	35	7	2	6	(1	5)	64	27	23	22	29	2	81	2	1	2	3	1	.75	4	.167	.272	.305
2008	Was	NL	73	111	26	5	2	3	(1	2)	44	17	12	18	25	1	31	1	2	0	2	0	1.00	1	.234	.380	.396
2009	Sea	AL	38	101	22	6	1	3	(2	1)	39	12	10	11	14	1	28	1	3	3	0	1	.00	1	.218	.311	.386
2010	Sea	AL	60	107	21	2	1	3	(1	2)	34	16	4	11	24	1	51	0	1	0	4	1	.80	0	.196	.344	.318
2011	Sea	AL	19	52	9	1	0	3	(2	1)	18	6	6	5	11	0	22	0	1	0	1	0	1.00	0	.173	.317	.346
2012	LAA	AL	2	1	0	0	0	0	(0	0)	0	0	0	0	0	0	1	0	1	0	0	0	-	0	.000	.000	.000
07	Atl	NL	20	44	3	1	0	0	(0	0)	4	3	1	0	6	1	16	1	0	1	0	1	.00	3	.068	.192	.091
07	Oak	AL	2	4	0	0	0	0	(0	0)	0	0	0	0	1	0	2	0	0	0	0	0	-	0	.000	.200	.000
07	Was	NL	103	162	32	6	2	6	(1	5)	60	24	22	22	22	1	63	1	1	1	3	0	1.00	1	.198	.296	.370
	Postseason		4	12	4	1	0	0	(0	0)	5	1	0	2	3	1	3	1	0	0	1	0	1.00	0	.333	.500	.417
	10 ML YEARS		593	1239	280	58	12	33	(13	20)	461	174	125	166	190	16	386	12	11	9	10	8	.56	17	.226	.332	.372

John Lannan

Pitches: L **Bats:** L **Pos:** SP-6   **Ht:** 6'4" **Wt:** 235 **Born:** 9/27/1984 **Age:** 28

Year	Team	Lg	G	GS	CG	GF	IP	BFP	H	R	ER	HR	SH	SF	HB	TBB	IBB	SO	WP	Bk	W	L	Pct	Sh	Sv-Op	Hld	ERC	ERA
2012	Syrcse*	AAA	24	24	3	0	148.2	640	164	77	71	16	7	2	1	50	2	86	6	0	9	11	.450	2	0- -	-	4.52	4.30
2007	Was	NL	6	6	0	0	34.2	153	36	17	16	3	2	0	2	17	1	10	1	0	2	2	.500	0	0-0	0	4.82	4.15
2008	Was	NL	31	31	0	0	182.0	779	172	89	79	23	13	5	7	72	1	117	6	2	9	15	.375	0	0-0	0	4.09	3.91
2009	Was	NL	33	33	2	0	206.1	875	210	100	89	22	12	1	6	68	5	89	3	0	9	13	.409	1	0-0	0	4.07	3.88
2010	Was	NL	25	25	0	0	143.1	643	175	82	74	14	5	5	4	49	3	71	1	0	8	8	.500	0	0-0	0	5.18	4.65
2011	Was	NL	33	33	0	0	184.2	808	194	90	76	15	10	1	7	76	3	106	4	0	10	13	.435	0	0-0	0	4.42	3.70
2012	Was	NL	6	6	0	0	32.2	144	33	15	15	0	4	0	4	14	1	17	1	0	4	1	.800	0	0-0	0	3.97	4.13
	6 ML YEARS		134	134	2	0	783.2	3402	820	393	349	77	46	12	30	296	14	410	16	2	42	52	.447	1	0-0	0	4.39	4.01

Matt LaPorta

Bats: R **Throws:** R **Pos:** 1B-11; DH-9; PH-6   lah-POR-tah   **Ht:** 6'2" **Wt:** 215 **Born:** 1/8/1985 **Age:** 28

Year	Team	Lg	G	AB	H	2B	3B	HR	(Hm	Rd)	TB	R	RBI	RC	TBB	IBB	SO	HBP	SH	SF	SB	CS	SB%	GDP	Avg	OBP	Slg
2012	Clmbs*	AAA	101	375	99	19	1	19	(-	-)	177	56	62	64	44	2	81	9	0	6	0	3	.00	12	.264	.350	.472
2009	Cle	AL	52	181	46	13	0	7	(2	5)	80	29	21	22	12	0	37	3	0	2	2	0	1.00	6	.254	.308	.442
2010	Cle	AL	110	376	83	15	1	12	(9	3)	136	41	41	41	46	1	82	1	0	2	0	0	-	12	.221	.306	.362
2011	Cle	AL	107	352	87	23	1	11	(6	5)	145	34	53	46	23	1	87	5	0	5	1	0	1.00	7	.247	.299	.412
2012	Cle	AL	22	58	14	2	0	1	(0	1)	19	2	5	4	1	0	17	1	0	0	0	0	-	1	.241	.267	.328
	4 ML YEARS		291	967	230	53	2	31	(17	14)	380	106	120	113	82	2	223	10	0	9	3	1	1.00	21	.238	.301	.393

Adam LaRoche

Bats: L Throws: L Pos: 1B-153; PH-3   Ht: 6'3" Wt: 210 Born: 11/6/1979 Age: 33

Year	Team	Lg	G	AB	H	2B	3B	HR	(Hm	Rd)	TB	R	RBI	RC	TBB	IBB	SO	HBP	SH	SF	SB	CS	SB%	GDP	Avg	OBP	Slg
2004	Atl	NL	110	324	90	27	1	13	(7	6)	158	45	45	43	27	1	78	1	2	2	0	0	-	10	.278	.333	.488
2005	Atl	NL	141	451	117	28	0	20	(11	9)	205	53	78	63	39	7	87	4	2	6	0	2	.00	15	.259	.320	.455
2006	Atl	NL	149	492	140	38	1	32	(11	21)	276	89	90	83	55	5	128	2	1	7	0	2	.00	9	.285	.354	.561
2007	Pit	NL	152	563	152	42	0	21	(10	11)	258	71	88	84	62	5	131	3	0	4	1	1	.50	18	.272	.345	.458
2008	Pit	NL	136	492	133	32	3	25	(14	11)	246	66	85	76	54	7	122	2	0	6	1	1	.50	9	.270	.341	.500
2009	3 Tms		150	555	154	38	2	25	(15	10)	271	78	83	84	69	12	142	0	0	5	2	2	.50	11	.277	.355	.488
2010	Ari	NL	151	560	146	37	2	25	(13	12)	262	75	100	84	48	4	172	3	0	4	0	1	.00	8	.261	.320	.468
2011	Was	NL	43	151	26	4	0	3	(1	2)	39	15	15	11	25	0	37	0	0	1	1	0	1.00	2	.172	.288	.258
2012	Was	NL	154	571	155	35	1	33	(17	16)	291	76	100	92	67	7	138	0	0	9	1	1	.50	10	.271	.343	.510
09	Pit	NL	87	324	80	25	1	12	(7	5)	143	46	40	38	41	6	81	0	0	3	2	2	.50	9	.247	.329	.441
09	Bos	AL	6	19	5	2	0	1	(1	0)	10	2	3	3	0	0	2	0	0	0	0	0	-	1	.263	.263	.526
09	Atl	AL	57	212	69	11	1	12	(7	5)	118	30	40	43	28	6	59	0	0	2	0	0	-	1	.325	.401	.557
	Postseason		8	25	8	2	0	2	(0	2)	16	3	10	6	5	1	6	0	1	0	0	0	-	1	.320	.433	.640
	9 ML YEARS		1186	4159	1114	281	10	197	(99	98)	2006	568	684	620	446	48	1035	15	5	44	6	10	.38	92	.268	.338	.482

Mat Latos

Pitches: R Bats: R Pos: SP-33   LAY-tos   Ht: 6'6" Wt: 235 Born: 12/9/1987 Age: 25

Year	Team	Lg	G	GS	CG	GF	IP	BFP	H	R	ER	HR	SH	SF	HB	TBB	IBB	SO	WP	Bk	W	L	Pct	Sh	Sv-Op	Hld	ERC	ERA
2009	SD	NL	10	10	0	0	50.2	212	43	29	26	7	3	1	0	23	1	39	0	2	4	5	.444	0	0-0	0	3.72	4.62
2010	SD	NL	31	31	1	0	184.2	748	150	63	60	16	4	1	2	50	3	189	5	1	14	10	.583	1	0-0	0	2.52	2.92
2011	SD	NL	31	31	0	0	194.1	799	168	82	75	16	8	7	1	62	3	185	5	0	9	14	.391	0	0-0	0	2.93	3.47
2012	Cin	NL	33	33	2	0	209.1	858	179	87	81	25	9	3	4	64	9	185	3	1	14	4	.778	0	0-0	0	3.08	3.48
	4 ML YEARS		105	105	3	0	639.0	2617	540	261	242	64	24	12	7	199	16	598	13	4	41	33	.554	1	0-0	0	2.92	3.41

Ryan Lavarnway

Bats: R Throws: R Pos: C-28; DH-17; PH-3   luh-VARN-way   Ht: 6'4" Wt: 225 Born: 8/7/1987 Age: 25

Year	Team	Lg	G	AB	H	2B	3B	HR	(Hm	Rd)	TB	R	RBI	RC	TBB	IBB	SO	HBP	SH	SF	SB	CS	SB%	GDP	Avg	OBP	Slg
2008	Lowell	A-	22	71	15	5	0	2	(-	-)	26	10	9	8	8	0	18	3	0	0	0	0	-	1	.211	.317	.366
2009	Grnville	A	106	404	115	36	2	21	(-	-)	218	60	87	81	50	2	113	6	0	6	1	2	.33	7	.285	.367	.540
2010	Salem	A+	82	304	88	18	0	14	(-	-)	148	66	63	61	44	1	62	9	0	3	1	0	1.00	6	.289	.392	.487
2010	Portlnd	AA	44	158	45	9	0	8	(-	-)	78	25	39	32	26	2	42	4	0	2	0	0	-	2	.285	.395	.494
2011	Portlnd	AA	55	208	59	5	0	14	(-	-)	106	35	38	39	25	0	47	2	0	4	0	0	-	11	.284	.360	.510
2011	Pwtckt	AAA	61	227	67	18	0	18	(-	-)	139	40	55	53	32	2	60	4	0	1	1	1	.50	10	.295	.390	.612
2012	Pwtckt	AAA	83	319	94	22	0	8	(-	-)	140	52	43	55	40	6	62	4	0	4	1	0	1.00	8	.295	.376	.439
2011	Bos	AL	17	39	9	2	0	2	(0	2)	17	5	8	4	4	0	10	0	0	0	0	0	-	1	.231	.302	.436
2012	Bos	AL	46	153	24	8	0	2	(0	2)	38	11	12	4	11	0	41	0	0	2	0	0	-	4	.157	.211	.248
	2 ML YEARS		63	192	33	10	0	4	(0	4)	55	16	20	8	15	0	51	0	0	2	0	0	-	5	.172	.230	.286

Brett Lawrie

Bats: R Throws: R Pos: 3B-123; SS-1; DH-1   LORI   Ht: 6'0" Wt: 215 Born: 1/18/1990 Age: 23

Year	Team	Lg	G	AB	H	2B	3B	HR	(Hm	Rd)	TB	R	RBI	RC	TBB	IBB	SO	HBP	SH	SF	SB	CS	SB%	GDP	Avg	OBP	Slg
2009	Wisc	A	105	372	102	18	5	13	(-	-)	169	48	65	61	41	1	70	4	0	6	19	11	.63	6	.274	.348	.454
2009	Hntsvl	AA	13	52	14	0	1	0	(-	-)	16	6	0	3	0	0	14	1	0	0	0	2	.00	0	.269	.283	.308
2010	Hntsvl	AA	135	554	158	36	16	8	(-	-)	250	90	63	89	47	3	118	5	2	1	30	13	.70	6	.285	.346	.451
2011	LsVgs	AAA	69	292	103	24	6	18	(-	-)	193	64	61	76	26	0	53	6	4	1	13	2	.87	3	.353	.415	.661
2011	Dnedin	A+	4	8	1	0	0	0	(-	-)	1	0	1	0	0	0	1	3	0	0	0	0	-	0	.125	.364	.125
2012	B Jays	R	1	1	0	0	0	0	(-	-)	0	0	0	0	0	0	0	0	0	0	0	0	-	0	.000	.000	.000
2012	Dnedin	A+	1	3	0	0	0	0	(-	-)	0	0	0	0	0	0	1	0	0	0	0	0	-	0	.000	.000	.000
2011	Tor	AL	43	150	44	8	4	9	(5	4)	87	26	25	33	16	1	31	3	2	0	7	1	.88	0	.293	.373	.580
2012	Tor	AL	125	494	135	26	3	11	(7	4)	200	73	48	65	33	0	86	5	2	2	13	8	.62	9	.273	.324	.405
	2 ML YEARS		168	644	179	34	7	20	(12	8)	287	99	73	98	49	1	117	8	4	2	20	9	.69	9	.278	.336	.446

Tom Layne

Pitches: L Bats: L Pos: RP-26   Ht: 6'3" Wt: 185 Born: 11/2/1984 Age: 28

Year	Team	Lg	G	GS	CG	GF	IP	BFP	H	R	ER	HR	SH	SF	HB	TBB	IBB	SO	WP	Bk	W	L	Pct	Sh	Sv-Op	Hld	ERC	ERA
2007	Msoula	R+	16	16	0	0	79.2	348	94	49	41	9	0	5	2	23	0	66	7	1	4	8	.333	0	0- -	-	4.89	4.63
2008	Sbend	A	35	13	0	5	115.0	491	107	48	44	3	5	4	6	43	1	71	3	1	6	5	.545	0	0- -	-	3.26	3.44
2009	Visalia	A+	29	4	0	9	66.0	278	63	27	21	1	1	1	3	25	0	43	7	0	4	2	.667	0	0- -	-	3.39	2.86
2009	Mobile	AA	6	6	0	0	31.0	140	27	21	17	0	0	0	3	19	0	24	2	0	0	3	.000	0	0- -	-	3.76	4.94
2010	Mobile	AA	26	26	3	0	149.1	641	146	75	62	9	8	2	6	57	0	91	10	1	12	7	.632	1	0- -	-	3.77	3.74
2011	Reno	AAA	32	15	0	7	121.2	558	148	95	84	14	5	2	6	57	0	56	6	0	10	7	.588	0	0- -	-	6.01	6.21
2011	Mobile	AA	3	3	0	0	17.2	71	16	5	5	1	0	4	0	6	0	14	4	0	2	0	1.000	0	0- -	-	3.44	2.55
2012	Reno	AAA	5	4	0	0	20.0	100	30	24	23	4	0	0	2	9	0	14	1	0	0	2	.000	0	0- -	-	8.56	10.35
2012	Tucsn	AAA	5	5	0	0	22.0	110	28	20	19	4	2	0	3	15	0	19	0	0	0	3	.000	0	0- -	-	8.19	7.77
2012	SnAnt	AA	32	2	0	3	35.2	149	31	15	13	2	1	0	0	16	3	36	1	0	0	5	.000	0	1- -	-	3.16	3.28
2012	SD	NL	26	0	0	5	16.2	68	9	6	6	0	1	0	3	3	0	25	0	0	2	0	1.000	0	2-3	7	1.20	3.24

Brandon League

Pitches: R Bats: R Pos: RP-74   Ht: 6'2" Wt: 210 Born: 3/16/1983 Age: 30

Year	Team	Lg	G	GS	CG	GF	IP	BFP	H	R	ER	HR	SH	SF	HB	TBB	IBB	SO	WP	Bk	W	L	Pct	Sh	Sv-Op	Hld	ERC	ERA
2004	Tor	AL	3	0	0	0	4.2	18	3	0	0	0	0	0	0	1	0	2	0	0	1	0	1.000	0	0-0	1	1.26	0.00
2005	Tor	AL	20	0	0	4	35.2	162	42	27	26	8	0	1	2	20	1	17	5	0	1	0	1.000	0	0-0	1	7.24	6.56
2006	Tor	AL	33	0	0	8	42.2	173	34	17	12	3	2	0	3	9	2	29	0	0	1	2	.333	0	1-4	12	2.30	2.53
2007	Tor	AL	14	0	0	2	11.2	58	19	8	8	1	0	1	0	7	0	7	3	0	0	0	-	0	0-0	0	8.98	6.17
2008	Tor	AL	31	0	0	8	33.0	141	28	9	8	2	1	0	3	15	2	23	2	0	1	2	.333	0	1-1	5	3.45	2.18
2009	Tor	AL	67	0	0	18	74.2	313	72	40	38	8	5	0	7	21	2	76	9	0	3	6	.333	0	0-3	9	3.85	4.58
2010	Sea	AL	70	0	0	30	79.0	326	67	38	30	7	4	1	2	27	6	56	7	0	9	7	.563	0	6-12	13	2.96	3.42
2011	Sea	AL	65	0	0	60	61.1	250	56	25	19	3	4	0	2	10	2	45	4	0	1	5	.167	0	37-42	2	2.45	2.79
2012	2 Tms		74	0	0	39	72.0	301	65	27	25	1	3	0	1	33	7	54	4	0	2	6	.250	0	15-21	8	3.15	3.13
12	Sea	AL	46	0	0	24	44.2	193	48	20	18	1	3	0	0	19	3	27	3	0	0	5	.000	0	9-15	6	3.99	3.63
12	LAD	NL	28	0	0	15	27.1	108	17	7	7	0	0	0	1	14	4	27	1	0	2	1	.667	0	6-6	2	1.89	2.30
	9 ML YEARS		377	0	0	169	414.2	1742	386	191	166	33	19	3	20	143	22	309	34	0	19	28	.404	0	60-84	49	3.48	3.60

Mike Leake

Pitches: R Bats: R Pos: SP-30   LEEK   Ht: 6'0" Wt: 180 Born: 11/12/1987 Age: 25

Year	Team	Lg	G	GS	CG	GF	IP	BFP	H	R	ER	HR	SH	SF	HB	TBB	IBB	SO	WP	Bk	W	L	Pct	Sh	Sv-Op	Hld	ERC	ERA
2010	Cin	NL	24	22	0	0	138.1	604	158	77	65	19	7	3	3	49	2	91	2	0	8	4	.667	0	0-0	0	5.12	4.23
2011	Cin	NL	29	26	0	2	167.2	693	159	74	72	23	3	6	8	38	3	118	2	1	12	9	.571	0	0-0	0	3.53	3.86
2012	Cin	NL	30	30	2	0	179.0	757	201	97	91	26	6	7	3	41	3	116	3	0	8	9	.471	0	0-0	0	4.50	4.58
	3 ML YEARS		83	78	2	2	485.0	2054	518	248	228	68	16	16	14	128	8	325	7	1	28	22	.560	0	0-0	0	4.33	4.23

Wade LeBlanc

Pitches: L Bats: L Pos: RP-16; SP-9   lah-BLAHNK   Ht: 6'2" Wt: 215 Born: 8/7/1984 Age: 28

Year	Team	Lg	G	GS	CG	GF	IP	BFP	H	R	ER	HR	SH	SF	HB	TBB	IBB	SO	WP	Bk	W	L	Pct	Sh	Sv-Op	Hld	ERC	ERA
2012	NewOr*	AAA	16	16	0	0	98.2	403	91	43	41	10	4	4	1	20	1	91	5	0	5	5	.500	0	0- -	-	2.92	3.74
2008	SD	NL	5	4	0	0	21.1	104	29	19	19	7	1	0	0	15	2	14	0	0	1	3	.250	0	0-0	0	9.57	8.02
2009	SD	NL	9	9	0	0	46.1	194	35	19	19	6	3	1	4	19	1	30	0	0	3	1	.750	0	0-0	0	3.28	3.69
2010	SD	NL	26	25	0	0	146.0	625	157	69	69	24	7	2	2	51	5	110	2	0	8	12	.400	0	0-0	0	4.84	4.25
2011	SD	NL	14	14	0	0	79.2	339	84	42	41	7	3	3	1	28	1	51	1	1	5	6	.455	0	0-0	0	4.21	4.63
2012	Mia	NL	25	9	0	1	68.2	284	71	30	28	7	5	1	1	19	1	43	1	0	2	5	.286	0	0-0	1	3.94	3.67
	5 ML YEARS		79	61	0	1	362.0	1546	376	179	176	51	19	7	8	132	10	248	4	1	19	27	.413	0	0-0	1	4.56	4.38

Sam LeCure

Pitches: R Bats: R Pos: RP-48   leh-CURE   Ht: 6'1" Wt: 210 Born: 5/4/1984 Age: 29

Year	Team	Lg	G	GS	CG	GF	IP	BFP	H	R	ER	HR	SH	SF	HB	TBB	IBB	SO	WP	Bk	W	L	Pct	Sh	Sv-Op	Hld	ERC	ERA
2010	Cin	NL	15	6	0	4	48.0	217	50	24	24	6	1	2	5	25	3	37	1	0	2	5	.286	0	0-0	0	5.36	4.50
2011	Cin	NL	43	4	0	7	77.2	307	57	33	32	10	4	0	4	21	3	73	0	0	2	1	.667	0	0-0	5	2.55	3.71
2012	Cin	NL	48	0	0	12	57.1	237	46	22	20	3	4	1	1	23	2	61	2	0	3	3	.500	0	0-1	7	2.73	3.14
	3 ML YEARS		106	10	0	23	183.0	761	153	79	76	19	9	3	10	69	8	171	3	0	7	9	.438	0	0-1	12	3.29	3.74

Carlos Lee

Bats: R Throws: R Pos: 1B-145; DH-1; PH-1   Ht: 6'2" Wt: 270 Born: 6/20/1976 Age: 37

Year	Team	Lg	G	AB	H	2B	3B	HR	(Hm	Rd)	TB	R	RBI	RC	TBB	IBB	SO	HBP	SH	SF	SB	CS	SB%	GDP	Avg	OBP	Slg
2012	CpChr*	AA	3	10	5	0	0	1	(-	-)	8	1	2	3	0	0	2	0	0	0	0	0	-	0	.500	.500	.800
1999	CWS	AL	127	492	144	32	2	16	(10	6)	228	66	84	68	13	0	72	4	1	7	4	2	.67	11	.293	.312	.463
2000	CWS	AL	152	572	172	29	2	24	(12	12)	277	107	92	91	38	1	94	3	1	5	13	4	.76	17	.301	.345	.484
2001	CWS	AL	150	558	150	33	3	24	(12	12)	261	75	84	81	38	2	85	6	1	2	17	7	.71	15	.269	.321	.468
2002	CWS	AL	140	492	130	26	2	26	(14	12)	238	82	80	86	75	4	73	2	0	7	1	4	.20	5	.264	.359	.484
2003	CWS	AL	158	623	181	35	1	31	(18	13)	311	100	113	105	37	2	91	4	0	7	18	4	.82	20	.291	.331	.499
2004	CWS	AL	153	591	180	37	3	31	(17	14)	310	103	99	112	54	3	86	7	0	6	11	5	.69	10	.305	.366	.525
2005	Mil	NL	162	618	164	41	0	32	(15	17)	301	85	114	98	57	7	87	2	0	11	13	4	.76	8	.265	.324	.487
2006	2 Tms		161	624	187	37	1	37	(15	22)	337	102	116	113	58	6	65	2	0	11	19	2	.90	22	.300	.355	.540
2007	Hou	NL	162	627	190	43	1	32	(17	15)	331	93	119	104	53	10	63	4	0	13	10	5	.67	27	.303	.354	.528
2008	Hou	NL	115	436	137	27	0	28	(11	17)	248	61	100	85	37	7	49	3	0	5	4	1	.80	8	.314	.368	.569
2009	Hou	NL	160	610	183	35	1	26	(16	10)	298	65	102	85	41	5	51	3	0	8	5	3	.63	21	.300	.343	.489
2010	Hou	NL	157	605	149	29	1	24	(16	8)	252	67	89	75	37	1	59	3	0	4	3	3	.50	20	.246	.291	.417
2011	Hou	NL	155	585	161	38	4	18	(9	9)	261	66	94	83	59	8	60	3	0	6	4	3	.57	9	.275	.342	.446
2012	2 Tms		147	550	145	27	1	9	(6	3)	201	53	77	74	58	4	49	1	0	6	3	0	1.00	13	.264	.332	.365
06	Mil	NL	102	388	111	18	0	28	(10	18)	213	60	81	75	38	4	39	2	0	7	12	2	.86	13	.286	.347	.549
06	Tex	AL	59	236	76	19	1	9	(5	4)	124	42	35	38	20	2	26	0	0	4	7	0	1.00	9	.322	.369	.525
12	Hou	NL	66	258	74	15	1	5	(5	0)	106	24	29	33	19	2	17	0	0	0	0	0	-	7	.287	.334	.411
12	Mia	NL	81	292	71	12	0	4	(1	3)	95	29	48	41	39	2	32	1	0	6	3	0	1.00	6	.243	.328	.325
	Postseason		3	11	1	1	0	0	(0	0)	2	0	1	0	0	0	2	0	0	1	0	0	-	0	.091	.083	.182
	14 ML YEARS		2099	7983	2273	469	19	358	(188	170)	3854	1125	1363	1260	655	60	984	47	3	98	125	47	.73	206	.285	.339	.483

Cliff Lee

Pitches: L Bats: L Pos: SP-30   Ht: 6'3" Wt: 205 Born: 8/30/1978 Age: 34

			HOW MUCH HE PITCHED						WHAT HE GAVE UP											THE RESULTS							
Year	Team	Lg	G	GS	CG	GF	IP	BFP	H	R	ER	HR	SH	SF	HB	TBB	IBB	SO	WP	Bk	W	L	Pct	Sh	Sv-Op	Hld	ERC	ERA
2002	Cle	AL	2	2	0	0	10.1	44	6	2	2	0	1	0	0	8	1	6	0	1	0	1	.000	0	0-0	0	2.38	1.74
2003	Cle	AL	9	9	0	0	52.1	210	41	28	21	7	1	1	2	20	1	44	3	0	3	3	.500	0	0-0	0	3.29	3.61
2004	Cle	AL	33	33	0	0	179.0	802	188	113	108	30	2	6	11	81	1	161	6	0	14	8	.636	0	0-0	0	5.31	5.43
2005	Cle	AL	32	32	1	0	202.0	838	194	91	85	22	5	7	0	52	1	143	4	0	18	5	.783	0	0-0	0	3.35	3.79
2006	Cle	AL	33	33	1	0	200.2	882	224	114	98	29	3	6	8	58	3	129	3	0	14	11	.560	0	0-0	0	4.69	4.40
2007	Cle	AL	20	16	1	1	97.1	443	112	73	68	17	3	2	7	36	1	66	5	0	5	8	.385	0	0-0	0	5.59	6.29
2008	Cle	AL	31	31	4	0	223.1	891	214	68	63	12	2	3	5	34	1	170	4	0	22	3	.880	2	0-0	0	2.75	2.54
2009	2 Tms		34	34	6	0	231.2	969	245	88	83	17	11	9	5	43	1	181	7	0	14	13	.519	2	0-0	0	3.45	3.22
2010	2 Tms	AL	28	28	7	0	212.1	843	195	84	75	16	4	6	1	18	2	185	3	1	12	9	.571	1	0-0	0	2.31	3.18
2011	Phi	NL	32	32	6	0	232.2	920	197	66	62	18	6	4	6	42	0	238	0	0	17	8	.680	6	0-0	0	2.44	2.40
2012	Phi	NL	30	30	0	0	211.0	847	207	79	74	26	3	4	0	28	0	207	4	0	6	9	.400	0	0-0	0	3.11	3.16
09	Cle	AL	22	22	3	0	152.0	641	165	53	53	10	6	5	3	33	1	107	6	0	7	9	.438	1	0-0	0	3.68	3.14
09	Phi	NL	12	12	3	0	79.2	328	80	35	30	7	5	4	2	10	0	74	1	0	7	4	.636	1	0-0	0	3.03	3.39
10	Sea	AL	13	13	5	0	103.2	408	92	31	27	5	0	3	0	6	0	89	2	1	8	3	.727	1	0-0	0	1.91	2.34
10	Tex	AL	15	15	2	0	108.2	435	103	53	48	11	4	3	1	12	2	96	1	0	4	6	.400	0	0-0	0	2.71	3.98
	Postseason		11	11	3	0	82.0	320	66	27	23	2	1	0	1	10	0	89	2	0	7	3	.700	0	0-0	0	1.68	2.52
	11 ML YEARS		284	280	26	1	1852.2	7689	1823	806	739	194	41	48	45	420	12	1530	39	2	125	78	.616	11	0-0	0	3.44	3.59

DJ LeMahieu

Bats: R Throws: R Pos: 2B-67; 3B-9; PH-5; SS-2; PR-2; 1B-1   la-MAY-hugh   Ht: 6'4" Wt: 205 Born: 7/13/1988 Age: 24

						BATTING															BASERUNNING				AVERAGES		
Year	Team	Lg	G	AB	H	2B	3B	HR	(Hm	Rd)	TB	R	RBI	RC	TBB	IBB	SO	HBP	SH	SF	SB	CS	SB%	GDP	Avg	OBP	Slg
2009	Cubs	R	3	12	5	0	1	0	(-	-)	7	2	4	3	1	0	3	0	0	1	1	0	1.00	0	.417	.429	.583
2009	Peoria	A	38	152	48	4	2	0	(-	-)	56	19	30	21	12	1	22	2	1	1	2	2	.50	11	.316	.371	.368
2010	Dytona	A+	135	554	174	24	5	2	(-	-)	214	63	73	75	29	0	61	1	10	6	15	7	.68	18	.314	.346	.386
2011	Tenn	AA	50	187	67	15	2	2	(-	-)	92	32	27	35	11	0	22	0	0	4	4	3	.57	4	.358	.386	.492
2011	Iowa	AAA	58	227	65	7	1	3	(-	-)	83	23	23	28	14	0	27	2	0	4	5	5	.50	10	.286	.328	.366
2012	ColSpr	AAA	61	255	80	14	2	1	(-	-)	101	33	31	39	23	0	29	0	0	2	13	6	.68	4	.314	.368	.396
2011	ChC	NL	37	60	15	2	0	0	(0	0)	17	3	4	3	1	0	12	0	1	0	0	0	-	2	.250	.262	.283
2012	Col	NL	81	229	68	12	4	2	(1	1)	94	26	22	28	13	4	42	0	3	2	1	2	.33	8	.297	.332	.410
	2 ML YEARS		118	289	83	14	4	2	(1	1)	111	29	26	31	14	4	54	0	4	2	1	2	.33	10	.287	.318	.384

Sandy Leon

Bats: B Throws: R Pos: C-12; PH-1   lee-OWN   Ht: 5'11" Wt: 220 Born: 3/13/1989 Age: 24

						BATTING															BASERUNNING				AVERAGES		
Year	Team	Lg	G	AB	H	2B	3B	HR	(Hm	Rd)	TB	R	RBI	RC	TBB	IBB	SO	HBP	SH	SF	SB	CS	SB%	GDP	Avg	OBP	Slg
2007	Nats	R	31	94	19	0	0	0	(-	-)	19	10	11	7	17	1	15	0	4	0	0	0	-	2	.202	.324	.202
2008	Nats	R	26	74	14	1	1	0	(-	-)	17	12	11	5	9	0	18	2	1	0	1	2	.33	0	.189	.294	.230
2009	Hgrstn	A	23	78	17	3	0	0	(-	-)	20	7	6	5	5	0	21	0	0	0	0	0	-	0	.218	.265	.256
2009	Vrmnt	A-	50	166	41	10	1	2	(-	-)	59	16	18	22	24	0	29	2	1	2	1	1	.50	0	.247	.345	.355
2010	Hgrstn	A	98	325	81	10	6	2	(-	-)	109	48	36	41	50	0	79	0	5	5	3	5	.38	12	.249	.345	.335
2011	Ptomc	A+	109	370	93	21	1	6	(-	-)	134	36	43	43	33	2	69	1	9	3	1	3	.25	5	.251	.312	.362
2012	Hrsbrg	AA	40	135	42	12	0	1	(-	-)	57	15	19	21	9	0	16	2	1	2	1	0	1.00	3	.311	.358	.422
2012	Auburn	A-	5	15	5	2	0	0	(-	-)	7	3	3	3	3	0	2	0	0	0	0	0	-	0	.333	.444	.467
2012	Syrcse	AAA	19	52	18	5	0	2	(-	-)	29	8	4	13	12	1	12	0	0	0	0	0	-	0	.346	.469	.558
2012	Was	NL	12	30	8	2	0	0	(0	0)	10	2	2	2	4	0	11	2	0	0	0	0	-	1	.267	.389	.333

Chris Leroux

Pitches: R Bats: L Pos: RP-10   leh-RUE   Ht: 6'6" Wt: 230 Born: 4/14/1984 Age: 29

					HOW MUCH HE PITCHED						WHAT HE GAVE UP										THE RESULTS							
Year	Team	Lg	G	GS	CG	GF	IP	BFP	H	R	ER	HR	SH	SF	HB	TBB	IBB	SO	WP	Bk	W	L	Pct	Sh	Sv-Op	Hld	ERC	ERA
2012	Bradtn*	A+	1	1	0	0	3.0	11	2	1	1	0	0	0	0	1	0	2	0	0	0	1	.000	0	0--	-	1.73	3.00
2012	Indy*	AAA	21	7	0	4	63.2	259	52	22	22	6	1	2	8	14	1	56	10	0	4	0	1.000	0	0--	-	2.85	3.11
2009	Fla	NL	5	0	0	3	6.2	35	11	8	8	0	0	0	0	4	0	2	0	0	0	0	-	0	0-0	0	7.84	10.80
2010	2 Tms	NL	23	0	0	7	22.2	105	28	18	17	1	0	3	0	14	2	22	1	0	0	1	.000	0	0-2	3	5.86	6.75
2011	Pit	NL	23	0	0	5	25.0	110	26	9	8	0	1	0	1	7	2	24	2	0	1	1	.500	0	0-1	2	3.05	2.88
2012	Pit	NL	10	0	0	3	11.1	48	11	9	7	1	1	0	1	2	0	12	1	0	0	0	-	0	0-0	0	3.24	5.56
10	Fla	NL	17	0	0	5	18.0	84	24	15	14	1	0	3	0	11	2	18	0	0	0	0	-	0	0-1	3	6.58	7.00
10	Pit	NL	6	0	0	2	4.2	21	4	3	3	0	0	0	0	3	0	4	1	0	0	1	.000	0	0-1	0	3.39	5.79
	4 ML YEARS		61	0	0	18	65.2	298	76	44	40	2	2	3	2	27	4	60	4	0	1	2	.333	0	0-3	5	4.45	5.48

Steven Lerud

Bats: L Throws: R Pos: C-3   leh-ROOD   Ht: 6'1" Wt: 215 Born: 10/13/1984 Age: 28

						BATTING															BASERUNNING				AVERAGES		
Year	Team	Lg	G	AB	H	2B	3B	HR	(Hm	Rd)	TB	R	RBI	RC	TBB	IBB	SO	HBP	SH	SF	SB	CS	SB%	GDP	Avg	OBP	Slg
2004	Pirates	R	48	175	43	12	1	5	(-	-)	72	22	20	22	11	0	38	3	0	3	0	1	.00	3	.246	.297	.411
2004	Wmspt	A-	8	29	7	0	0	0	(-	-)	7	2	2	2	4	0	6	1	0	0	0	1	.00	1	.241	.353	.241
2005	Hkry	A	25	80	7	2	2	2	(-	-)	19	6	13	0	4	0	27	2	0	1	0	1	.00	1	.088	.149	.238
2005	Pirates	R	18	60	16	3	1	2	(-	-)	27	13	15	10	7	0	13	3	0	4	0	0	-	1	.267	.351	.450
2005	Wmspt	A-	10	32	4	0	0	1	(-	-)	7	3	2	0	2	0	14	0	0	0	0	0	-	1	.125	.176	.219
2006	Hkry	A	117	393	94	28	0	12	(-	-)	158	45	57	54	40	0	146	13	0	0	4	3	.57	9	.239	.330	.402
2007	Lynbrg	A+	84	287	58	17	1	4	(-	-)	89	27	31	28	31	1	63	9	0	1	3	2	.60	11	.202	.299	.310
2008	Lynbrg	A+	67	234	60	14	0	8	(-	-)	98	36	40	36	26	1	65	8	0	5	1	1	.50	4	.256	.344	.419
2008	Altna	AA	47	146	34	7	0	4	(-	-)	53	17	18	14	14	1	42	1	1	1	1	0	1.00	3	.233	.302	.363

172

Year	Team	Lg	G	AB	H	2B	3B	HR	(Hm	Rd)	TB	R	RBI	RC	TBB	IBB	SO	HBP	SH	SF	SB	CS	SB%	GDP	Avg	OBP	Slg
																									BATTING	BASERUNNING	AVERAGES
2009	Altna	AA	95	304	73	17	0	4	(-	-)	102	31	26	39	38	2	53	10	6	5	2	1	.67	6	.240	.339	.336
2010	Norfolk	AAA	9	21	2	1	0	0	(-	-)	3	2	2	1	7	0	6	0	0	0	0	0	-	0	.095	.321	.143
2010	Bowie	AA	49	153	31	7	1	6	(-	-)	58	18	14	19	18	1	47	7	1	0	0	0	-	2	.203	.315	.379
2011	Bowie	AA	73	228	44	8	1	5	(-	-)	69	25	30	19	20	1	86	5	5	4	0	1	.00	2	.193	.268	.303
2012	Rdng	AA	36	102	24	7	0	0	(-	-)	31	7	7	12	13	1	35	5	0	0	0	1	.00	1	.235	.350	.304
2012	Phi	NL	3	10	2	0	0	0	(0	0)	2	1	0	1	0	0	2	0	0	0	0	0	-	1	.200	.200	.200

Jon Lester

Pitches: L **Bats:** L **Pos:** SP-33 **Ht:** 6'4" **Wt:** 240 **Born:** 1/7/1984 **Age:** 29

Year	Team	Lg	G	GS	CG	GF	IP	BFP	H	R	ER	HR	SH	SF	HB	TBB	IBB	SO	WP	Bk	W	L	Pct	Sh	Sv-Op	Hld	ERC	ERA
			HOW MUCH HE PITCHED						WHAT HE GAVE UP												THE RESULTS							
2006	Bos	AL	15	15	0	0	81.1	367	91	43	43	7	2	8	5	43	1	60	5	0	7	2	.778	0	0-0	0	5.52	4.76
2007	Bos	AL	12	11	0	0	63.0	275	61	33	32	10	1	5	1	31	0	50	1	0	4	0	1.000	0	0-0	0	4.78	4.57
2008	Bos	AL	33	33	2	0	210.1	874	202	78	75	14	6	3	10	66	1	152	3	1	16	6	.727	2	0-0	0	3.55	3.21
2009	Bos	AL	32	32	2	0	203.1	843	186	80	77	20	4	6	3	64	0	225	6	0	15	8	.652	0	0-0	0	3.35	3.41
2010	Bos	AL	32	32	2	0	208.0	861	167	81	75	14	4	6	10	83	0	225	6	0	19	9	.679	0	0-0	0	3.00	3.25
2011	Bos	AL	31	31	0	0	191.2	799	166	77	74	20	2	2	11	75	0	182	4	0	15	9	.625	0	0-0	0	3.62	3.47
2012	Bos	AL	33	33	3	0	205.1	876	216	117	110	25	5	7	4	68	2	166	6	0	9	14	.391	0	0-0	0	4.36	4.82
	Postseason		8	6	0	2	42.0	175	34	14	12	5	2	0	0	13	0	39	0	0	2	3	.400	0	0-0	0	2.75	2.57
7 ML YEARS			188	187	9	0	1163.0	4895	1089	509	486	110	22	37	44	430	4	1060	31	1	85	48	.639	2	0-0	0	3.76	3.76

Colby Lewis

Pitches: R **Bats:** R **Pos:** SP-16 **Ht:** 6'4" **Wt:** 230 **Born:** 8/2/1979 **Age:** 33

Year	Team	Lg	G	GS	CG	GF	IP	BFP	H	R	ER	HR	SH	SF	HB	TBB	IBB	SO	WP	Bk	W	L	Pct	Sh	Sv-Op	Hld	ERC	ERA
			HOW MUCH HE PITCHED						WHAT HE GAVE UP												THE RESULTS							
2002	Tex	AL	15	4	0	4	34.1	168	42	26	24	4	2	0	2	26	2	28	3	1	1	3	.250	0	0-2	1	7.22	6.29
2003	Tex	AL	26	26	0	0	127.0	594	163	104	103	23	2	2	5	70	1	88	5	0	10	9	.526	0	0-0	0	7.38	7.30
2004	Tex	AL	3	3	0	0	15.1	71	13	7	7	1	0	0	1	13	0	11	0	0	1	1	.500	0	0-0	0	4.98	4.11
2006	Det	AL	2	0	0	1	3.0	18	8	1	1	1	0	0	0	1	0	5	0	0	0	0	-	0	0-0	0	17.35	3.00
2007	Oak	AL	26	1	0	8	37.2	170	44	28	27	7	1	2	3	14	3	23	1	1	0	2	.000	0	0-1	3	5.79	6.45
2010	Tex	AL	32	32	1	0	201.0	844	174	90	83	21	4	4	6	65	0	196	9	0	12	13	.480	0	0-0	0	3.15	3.72
2011	Tex	AL	32	32	2	0	200.1	839	187	103	98	35	4	5	6	56	1	169	4	0	14	10	.583	1	0-0	0	3.82	4.40
2012	Tex	AL	16	16	2	0	105.0	427	99	48	40	16	1	2	6	14	0	93	2	0	6	6	.500	0	0-0	0	3.28	3.43
	Postseason		8	8	0	0	50.0	204	32	15	13	7	0	0	2	22	0	44	3	0	4	1	.800	0	0-0	0	2.72	2.34
8 ML YEARS			152	114	5	13	723.2	3131	730	407	383	108	14	15	29	259	7	613	24	2	44	44	.500	1	0-3	4	4.44	4.76

Fred Lewis

Bats: L **Throws:** R **Pos:** PH-11; LF-4; RF-4; CF-1; PR-1 **Ht:** 6'2" **Wt:** 205 **Born:** 12/9/1980 **Age:** 32

Year	Team	Lg	G	AB	H	2B	3B	HR	(Hm	Rd)	TB	R	RBI	RC	TBB	IBB	SO	HBP	SH	SF	SB	CS	SB%	GDP	Avg	OBP	Slg
											BATTING										BASERUNNING				AVERAGES		
2012	Buffalo*	AAA	108	419	123	26	7	13	(-	-)	202	80	45	79	57	2	113	1	0	0	25	8	.76	8	.294	.379	.482
2006	SF	NL	13	11	5	1	0	0	(0	0)	6	5	2	4	0	0	3	0	0	0	0	0	-	0	.455	.455	.545
2007	SF	NL	58	157	45	6	2	3	(0	3)	64	34	19	27	19	0	32	3	1	0	5	1	.83	4	.287	.374	.408
2008	SF	NL	133	468	132	25	11	9	(4	5)	206	81	40	67	51	3	124	0	0	2	21	7	.75	5	.282	.351	.440
2009	SF	NL	122	295	76	21	3	4	(2	2)	115	49	20	37	36	3	84	5	0	0	8	4	.67	4	.258	.348	.390
2010	Tor	AL	110	428	112	31	5	8	(4	4)	177	70	36	56	38	1	104	9	1	4	17	6	.74	9	.262	.332	.414
2011	Cin	NL	81	183	42	7	0	3	(2	1)	58	20	19	17	22	2	38	3	1	1	2	5	.29	1	.230	.321	.317
2012	NYM	NL	18	20	3	0	0	0	(0	0)	3	2	0	1	4	1	5	1	0	0	0	0	-	0	.150	.320	.150
7 ML YEARS			535	1562	415	91	21	27	(12	15)	629	261	136	209	170	10	390	21	3	7	53	23	.70	23	.266	.344	.403

Alex Liddi

Bats: R **Throws:** R **Pos:** 3B-23; LF-7; 1B-5; PH-4   LID-ee   **Ht:** 6'4" **Wt:** 230 **Born:** 8/14/1988 **Age:** 24

Year	Team	Lg	G	AB	H	2B	3B	HR	(Hm	Rd)	TB	R	RBI	RC	TBB	IBB	SO	HBP	SH	SF	SB	CS	SB%	GDP	Avg	OBP	Slg
											BATTING										BASERUNNING				AVERAGES		
2006	Ms	R	47	182	57	13	6	3	(-	-)	91	31	25	33	12	0	48	1	0	2	9	2	.82	2	.313	.355	.500
2006	Wisc	A	11	38	7	1	0	0	(-	-)	8	4	2	0	1	0	8	0	0	1	0	1	.00	2	.184	.200	.211
2007	Wisc	A	113	400	96	28	3	8	(-	-)	154	41	52	49	36	1	123	5	4	5	5	4	.56	4	.240	.308	.385
2008	Wisc	A	125	447	109	26	4	6	(-	-)	161	65	53	54	42	3	115	4	1	2	17	5	.77	9	.244	.313	.360
2009	Hi Dsrt	A+	129	493	170	44	5	23	(-	-)	293	97	104	116	53	5	122	8	3	8	10	6	.63	11	.345	.411	.594
2010	WTenn	AA	134	502	141	37	8	15	(-	-)	239	78	92	84	50	4	145	7	4	2	5	7	.42	17	.281	.353	.476
2011	Tacom	AAA	138	559	145	32	3	30	(-	-)	273	121	104	95	61	0	170	5	2	10	5	1	.83	14	.259	.332	.488
2012	Tacom	AAA	76	296	80	18	2	11	(-	-)	135	39	30	44	24	1	75	1	0	2	9	6	.60	9	.270	.325	.456
2011	Sea	AL	15	40	9	3	0	3	(0	3)	21	7	6	8	3	0	17	1	0	0	1	0	1.00	1	.225	.295	.525
2012	Sea	AL	38	116	26	4	1	3	(1	2)	41	8	10	14	9	0	49	0	0	1	2	1	.67	0	.224	.278	.353
2 ML YEARS			53	156	35	7	1	6	(1	5)	62	15	16	22	12	0	66	1	0	1	3	1	.75	1	.224	.282	.397

Brad Lidge

Pitches: R **Bats:** R **Pos:** RP-11 **Ht:** 6'5" **Wt:** 210 **Born:** 12/23/1976 **Age:** 36

Year	Team	Lg	G	GS	CG	GF	IP	BFP	H	R	ER	HR	SH	SF	HB	TBB	IBB	SO	WP	Bk	W	L	Pct	Sh	Sv-Op	Hld	ERC	ERA
			HOW MUCH HE PITCHED						WHAT HE GAVE UP												THE RESULTS							
2012	Ptomc*	A+	2	1	0	0	1.1	7	2	1	1	0	0	0	0	1	0	3	0	0	0	1	.000	0	0--	-	7.52	6.75
2002	Hou	NL	6	1	0	2	8.2	48	12	6	6	0	1	0	2	9	1	12	0	0	1	0	1.000	0	0-0	0	8.90	6.23
2003	Hou	NL	78	0	0	9	85.0	349	60	36	34	6	2	3	5	42	7	97	4	1	6	3	.667	0	1-6	28	2.82	3.60
2004	Hou	NL	80	0	0	44	94.2	369	57	21	20	8	3	2	6	30	5	157	3	1	6	5	.545	0	29-33	17	1.85	1.90
2005	Hou	NL	70	0	0	65	70.2	291	58	21	18	5	4	1	3	23	1	103	8	0	4	4	.500	0	42-46	0	2.79	2.29

Year Team	Lg	G GS CG GF	IP	BFP	H	R	ER	HR	SH	SF	HB	TBB	IBB	SO	WP	Bk	W	L	Pct	Sh	Sv-Op	Hld	ERC	ERA
2006 Hou	NL	78 0 0 52	75.0	340	69	47	44	10	6	2	6	36	4	104	11	0	1	5	.167	0	32-38	6	4.25	5.28
2007 Hou	NL	66 0 0 34	67.0	287	54	29	25	9	5	1	4	30	4	88	6	0	5	3	.625	0	19-27	7	3.52	3.36
2008 Phi	NL	72 0 0 61	69.1	292	50	17	15	2	2	1	1	35	4	92	5	0	2	0	1.000	0	41-41	0	2.45	1.95
2009 Phi	NL	67 0 0 55	58.2	283	72	51	47	11	4	1	5	34	3	61	4	0	0	8	.000	0	31-42	1	7.11	7.21
2010 Phi	NL	50 0 0 38	45.2	193	32	16	15	5	3	0	1	24	4	52	3	1	1	1	.500	0	27-32	0	2.92	2.96
2011 Phi	NL	25 0 0 4	19.1	86	16	3	3	0	1	0	1	13	3	23	2	0	0	2	.000	0	1-1	8	3.34	1.40
2012 Was	NL	11 0 0 4	9.1	51	12	10	10	1	1	0	0	11	5	10	0	0	0	1	.000	0	2-4	0	7.79	9.64
Postseason		39 0 0 32	45.1	185	32	11	11	2	2	0	3	19	2	62	3	0	2	4	.333	0	18-20	0	2.44	2.18
11 ML YEARS		603 1 0 368	603.1	2589	492	257	237	57	32	11	34	287	41	799	46	3	26	32	.448	0	225-270	67	3.40	3.54

Brent Lillibridge

Bats: R **Throws:** R **Pos:** 1B-23; SS-21; LF-20; 3B-18; PR-18; PH-13; CF-11; 2B-6; RF-4; DH-2   **Ht:** 5'11" **Wt:** 185 **Born:** 9/18/1983 **Age:** 29

Year Team	Lg	G	AB	H	2B	3B	HR	(Hm	Rd)	TB	R	RBI	RC	TBB	IBB	SO	HBP	SH	SF	SB	CS	SB%	GDP	Avg	OBP	Slg
2008 Atl	NL	29	80	16	6	1	1	(0	1)	27	9	8	6	3	0	23	1	1	0	2	0	1.00	0	.200	.238	.338
2009 CWS	AL	46	95	15	2	0	0	(0	0)	17	9	3	5	14	0	26	1	2	0	6	3	.67	2	.158	.273	.179
2010 CWS	AL	64	98	22	5	2	2	(1	1)	37	19	16	11	3	0	36	0	0	0	5	3	.63	2	.224	.248	.378
2011 CWS	AL	97	186	48	5	1	13	(8	5)	94	38	29	30	17	1	62	7	4	2	10	6	.63	2	.258	.340	.505
2012 3 Tms	AL	102	190	37	6	0	3	(1	2)	52	25	10	9	11	0	71	4	1	3	14	2	.87	2	.195	.250	.274
12 CWS	AL	49	63	11	1	0	0	(0	0)	12	10	2	1	4	0	26	1	1	1	7	2	.78	0	.175	.232	.190
12 Bos	AL	10	16	2	0	0	0	(0	0)	2	0	0	0	0	0	5	0	0	0	1	0	-	0	.125	.125	.125
12 Cle	AL	43	111	24	5	0	3	(1	2)	38	15	8	8	7	0	40	3	0	2	6	0	1.00	2	.216	.276	.342
5 ML YEARS		338	649	138	24	4	19	(10	9)	227	100	66	61	48	1	218	13	8	5	36	14	.72	8	.213	.278	.350

Ted Lilly

Pitches: L **Bats:** L **Pos:** SP-8   **Ht:** 6'0" **Wt:** 190 **Born:** 1/4/1976 **Age:** 37

Year Team	Lg	G GS CG GF	IP	BFP	H	R	ER	HR	SH	SF	HB	TBB	IBB	SO	WP	Bk	W	L	Pct	Sh	Sv-Op	Hld	ERC	ERA
2012 RCuca*	A+	4 4 0 0	11.0	44	10	8	7	3	0	0	2	2	0	7	0	0	0	1	.000	0	0- -	-	3.82	5.73
1999 Mon	NL	9 3 0 1	23.2	110	30	20	20	7	0	1	3	9	0	28	1	0	0	1	.000	0	0-0	0	7.76	7.61
2000 NYY	AL	7 0 0 1	8.0	39	8	6	5	1	0	0	0	5	0	11	1	0	0	0	-	0	0-0	0	4.76	5.63
2001 NYY	AL	26 21 0 2	120.2	537	126	81	72	20	2	5	7	51	1	112	9	2	5	6	.455	0	0-0	0	5.10	5.37
2002 2 Tms	AL	22 16 2 1	100.0	413	80	43	41	15	0	3	6	31	3	77	6	1	5	7	.417	1	0-0	0	3.14	3.69
2003 Oak	AL	32 31 0 0	178.1	773	179	92	86	24	3	4	5	58	3	147	5	4	12	10	.545	0	0-0	0	4.06	4.34
2004 Tor	AL	32 32 2 0	197.1	845	171	92	89	26	3	3	6	89	2	168	6	4	12	10	.545	1	0-0	0	3.84	4.06
2005 Tor	AL	25 25 0 0	126.1	566	135	79	78	23	3	5	3	58	1	96	2	2	10	11	.476	0	0-0	0	5.38	5.56
2006 Tor	AL	32 32 0 0	181.2	797	179	98	87	28	4	2	4	81	6	160	7	4	15	13	.536	0	0-0	0	4.57	4.31
2007 ChC	NL	34 34 0 0	207.0	847	181	91	88	28	11	9	3	55	2	174	7	0	15	8	.652	0	0-0	0	3.14	3.83
2008 ChC	NL	34 **34** 0 0	204.2	861	187	96	93	32	5	3	7	64	2	184	4	4	17	9	.654	0	0-0	0	3.73	4.09
2009 ChC	NL	27 27 0 0	177.0	706	151	66	61	22	9	3	2	36	2	151	3	3	12	9	.571	0	0-0	0	2.74	3.10
2010 2 Tms	NL	30 30 1 0	193.2	785	165	83	78	32	14	2	5	44	4	166	2	2	10	12	.455	1	0-0	0	3.08	3.62
2011 LAD	NL	33 33 0 0	192.2	800	172	88	85	28	12	5	9	51	8	158	2	2	12	14	.462	0	0-0	0	3.36	3.97
2012 LAD	NL	8 8 0 0	48.2	202	36	23	17	3	2	2	2	19	1	31	3	0	5	1	.833	0	0-0	0	2.51	3.14
02 NYY	AL	16 11 2 1	76.2	314	57	31	29	10	0	3	5	24	3	59	6	0	3	6	.333	1	0-0	0	2.74	3.40
02 Oak	AL	6 5 0 0	23.1	99	23	12	12	5	0	0	1	7	0	18	0	1	2	1	.667	0	0-0	0	4.56	4.63
10 ChC	NL	18 18 0 0	117.0	480	104	53	48	19	8	1	2	29	3	89	2	2	3	8	.273	0	0-0	0	3.30	3.69
10 LAD	NL	12 12 1 0	76.2	305	61	30	30	13	6	1	3	15	1	77	0	0	7	4	.636	1	0-0	0	2.77	3.52
Postseason		5 2 0 0	16.1	76	19	13	12	2	1	0	1	7	0	14	1	0	0	2	.000	0	0-1	0	5.43	6.61
14 ML YEARS		351 326 5 5	1959.2	8281	1800	958	900	289	68	47	62	651	35	1663	58	29	130	111	.539	3	0-0	0	3.76	4.13

Che-Hsuan Lin

Bats: R **Throws:** R **Pos:** RF-6; CF-3; PR-2   CHAY-shwan   **Ht:** 6'0" **Wt:** 180 **Born:** 9/21/1988 **Age:** 24

Year Team	Lg	G	AB	H	2B	3B	HR	(Hm	Rd)	TB	R	RBI	RC	TBB	IBB	SO	HBP	SH	SF	SB	CS	SB%	GDP	Avg	OBP	Slg
2007 RedSx	R	43	175	46	10	6	4	(-	-)	80	33	22	29	17	0	42	3	0	5	14	3	.82	4	.263	.330	.457
2007 Lowell	A-	11	43	7	2	0	0	(-	-)	9	7	3	2	5	0	10	1	1	0	3	2	.60	1	.163	.265	.209
2008 Grnville	A	91	362	90	13	6	5	(-	-)	130	60	37	52	43	1	62	9	0	1	33	7	.83	3	.249	.342	.359
2009 Salem	A+	131	479	127	23	2	7	(-	-)	175	75	54	70	66	2	75	5	4	8	26	11	.70	14	.265	.355	.365
2010 PortInd	AA	119	458	126	17	4	2	(-	-)	157	88	34	70	72	0	63	11	1	1	26	12	.68	10	.275	.386	.343
2011 PortInd	AA	34	138	37	5	2	0	(-	-)	46	23	11	20	20	0	14	3	0	0	12	3	.80	3	.268	.373	.333
2011 Pwtckt	AAA	85	328	77	11	1	2	(-	-)	96	49	25	36	38	1	51	7	3	2	16	4	.80	6	.235	.325	.293
2012 Pwtckt	AAA	113	396	98	11	5	2	(-	-)	125	42	30	45	42	0	65	3	2	2	15	4	.79	7	.247	.323	.316
2012 Bos	AL	9	12	3	0	0	0	(0	0)	3	1	0	0	0	0	5	0	0	0	0	0	-	0	.250	.250	.250

Tim Lincecum

Pitches: R **Bats:** L **Pos:** SP-33   **Ht:** 5'11" **Wt:** 175 **Born:** 6/15/1984 **Age:** 29

Year Team	Lg	G GS CG GF	IP	BFP	H	R	ER	HR	SH	SF	HB	TBB	IBB	SO	WP	Bk	W	L	Pct	Sh	Sv-Op	Hld	ERC	ERA
2007 SF	NL	24 24 0 0	146.1	618	122	70	65	12	5	7	2	65	5	150	10	0	7	5	.583	0	0-0	0	3.21	4.00
2008 SF	NL	34 33 2 0	227.0	928	182	72	66	11	11	3	6	84	1	**265**	17	2	18	5	**.783**	1	0-0	0	**2.69**	2.62
2009 SF	NL	32 32 **4** 0	225.1	905	168	69	62	10	12	5	6	68	2	**261**	11	0	15	7	.682	**2**	0-0	0	**2.14**	2.48
2010 SF	NL	33 33 1 0	212.1	897	194	84	81	18	9	5	5	76	7	**231**	9	0	16	10	.615	1	0-0	0	3.37	3.43
2011 SF	NL	33 33 1 0	217.0	900	176	74	66	15	13	1	6	86	5	220	9	0	13	14	.481	1	0-0	0	2.92	2.74
2012 SF	NL	33 **33** 0 0	186.0	825	183	111	107	23	11	6	4	90	3	190	17	2	10	**15**	.400	0	0-0	0	4.50	5.18
Postseason		6 5 1 0	37.0	145	25	11	10	3	1	1	1	9	0	43	0	0	4	1	.800	1	0-0	1	1.84	2.43
6 ML YEARS		189 188 8 0	1214.0	5073	1025	480	447	89	61	27	29	469	23	1317	73	4	79	56	.585	5	0-0	0	3.06	3.31

Brad Lincoln

Pitches: R Bats: L Pos: RP-47; SP-5 Ht: 6'0" Wt: 210 Born: 5/25/1985 Age: 28

Year	Team	Lg	G	GS	CG	GF	IP	BFP	H	R	ER	HR	SH	SF	HB	TBB	IBB	SO	WP	Bk	W	L	Pct	Sh	Sv-Op	Hld	ERC	ERA
2012	Indy*	AAA	2	2	0	0	12.0	46	10	3	3	0	0	0	2	0	0	9	0	0	1	0	1.000	0	0--	-	1.84	2.25
2010	Pit	NL	11	9	0	0	52.2	240	66	42	39	9	3	4	5	15	0	25	1	0	1	4	.200	0	0-0	0	5.99	6.66
2011	Pit	NL	12	8	0	0	47.2	211	54	27	25	4	2	2	2	16	4	29	0	0	2	3	.400	0	0-0	4	4.46	4.72
2012	2 Tms		52	5	0	10	88.0	362	80	37	36	14	4	1	1	24	2	88	1	0	5	2	.714	0	1-2	9	3.49	3.68
12	Pit	NL	28	5	0	6	59.1	239	51	19	18	8	2	0	1	14	1	60	0	0	4	2	.667	0	1-2	5	2.97	2.73
12	Tor	AL	24	0	0	4	28.2	123	29	18	18	6	2	1	0	10	1	28	1	0	1	0	1.000	0	0-0	4	4.63	5.65
3 ML YEARS			75	22	0	10	188.1	813	200	106	100	27	9	7	8	55	6	142	2	0	8	9	.471	0	1-2	9	4.41	4.78

Adam Lind

Bats: L Throws: L Pos: 1B-61; DH-31; PH-8 Ht: 6'2" Wt: 210 Born: 7/17/1983 Age: 29

Year	Team	Lg	G	AB	H	2B	3B	HR	(Hm	Rd)	TB	R	RBI	RC	TBB	IBB	SO	HBP	SH	SF	SB	CS	SB%	GDP	Avg	OBP	Slg
2012	LsVgs*	AAA	32	125	49	10	0	8	(-	-)	83	24	29	34	15	0	26	0	0	3	1	0	1.00	0	.392	.448	.664
2012	NHam*	AA	3	11	6	0	0	1	(-	-)	9	2	1	4	2	1	4	0	0	0	0	0	-	0	.545	.615	.818
2006	Tor	AL	18	60	22	8	0	2	(0	2)	36	8	8	13	5	0	12	0	0	0	0	0	-	0	.367	.415	.600
2007	Tor	AL	89	290	69	14	0	11	(10	1)	116	34	46	38	16	0	65	1	2	2	1	2	.33	7	.238	.278	.400
2008	Tor	AL	88	326	92	16	4	9	(2	7)	143	48	40	39	16	3	59	2	1	4	2	0	1.00	8	.282	.316	.439
2009	Tor	AL	151	587	179	46	0	35	(14	21)	330	93	114	114	58	7	110	5	0	4	1	1	.50	15	.305	.370	.562
2010	Tor	AL	150	569	135	32	3	23	(15	8)	242	57	72	65	38	3	144	3	0	3	0	0	-	10	.237	.287	.425
2011	Tor	AL	125	499	125	16	0	26	(12	14)	219	56	87	67	32	4	107	3	0	8	1	1	.50	12	.251	.295	.439
2012	Tor	AL	93	321	82	14	2	11	(6	5)	133	28	45	47	29	1	61	0	0	3	0	0	-	10	.255	.314	.414
7 ML YEARS			714	2652	704	146	9	117	(59	58)	1219	324	412	383	194	18	558	14	3	24	5	4	.56	62	.265	.316	.460

Josh Lindblom

Pitches: R Bats: R Pos: RP-74 LIN-bloom Ht: 6'4" Wt: 239 Born: 6/15/1987 Age: 26

Year	Team	Lg	G	GS	CG	GF	IP	BFP	H	R	ER	HR	SH	SF	HB	TBB	IBB	SO	WP	Bk	W	L	Pct	Sh	Sv-Op	Hld	ERC	ERA
2008	Gt Lks	A	8	8	0	0	29.0	107	14	6	6	2	0	0	1	4	0	33	0	0	0	0	-	0	0--	-	0.96	1.86
2008	Jaxnvl	AA	1	1	0	0	5.0	20	5	2	2	0	0	0	0	1	0	4	1	0	0	0	-	0	0--	-	2.76	3.60
2009	Chatt	AA	14	11	0	1	57.1	243	55	35	30	4	1	3	5	14	2	46	3	0	3	5	.375	0	0--	-	3.30	4.71
2009	Albq	AAA	20	3	0	3	39.0	163	34	11	11	3	4	0	3	12	0	36	1	0	3	0	1.000	0	1--	-	3.17	2.54
2010	Albq	AAA	40	10	0	3	95.0	463	143	79	69	12	1	1	7	32	3	84	6	1	3	2	.600	0	0--	-	7.23	6.54
2011	Chatt	AA	34	0	0	27	42.1	167	30	10	10	3	2	1	4	14	3	54	2	0	1	3	.250	0	17--	-	2.45	2.13
2011	LAD	NL	27	0	0	8	29.2	116	21	9	9	0	2	3	2	10	3	28	3	0	1	0	1.000	0	0-1	3	1.90	2.73
2012	2 Tms	NL	74	0	0	18	71.0	304	61	31	28	13	2	0	4	35	2	70	2	0	3	5	.375	0	1-4	22	4.47	3.55
12	LAD	NL	48	0	0	12	47.2	197	42	16	16	9	2	0	3	18	0	43	1	0	2	2	.500	0	0-2	15	4.31	3.02
12	Phi	NL	26	0	0	6	23.1	107	19	15	12	4	0	0	1	17	2	27	1	0	1	3	.250	0	1-2	7	4.77	4.63
2 ML YEARS			101	0	0	26	100.2	420	82	40	37	13	4	3	6	45	5	98	5	0	4	5	.444	0	1-5	25	3.66	3.31

Matt Lindstrom

Pitches: R Bats: R Pos: RP-46 Ht: 6'3" Wt: 220 Born: 2/11/1980 Age: 33

Year	Team	Lg	G	GS	CG	GF	IP	BFP	H	R	ER	HR	SH	SF	HB	TBB	IBB	SO	WP	Bk	W	L	Pct	Sh	Sv-Op	Hld	ERC	ERA
2012	Orioles*	R	2	2	0	0	2.0	8	2	1	1	0	0	0	0	0	0	2	0	0	0	0	-	0	0--	-	1.95	4.50
2012	Bowie*	AA	2	1	0	0	2.1	12	4	3	1	0	0	0	0	1	0	1	0	0	0	0	-	0	0--	-	7.52	3.86
2007	Fla	NL	71	0	0	11	67.0	284	66	27	23	2	3	1	3	21	4	62	5	0	3	4	.429	0	0-2	19	3.26	3.09
2008	Fla	NL	66	0	0	27	57.1	245	57	21	20	1	6	1	1	26	4	43	4	0	3	3	.500	0	5-6	14	3.69	3.14
2009	Fla	NL	54	0	0	32	47.1	219	54	35	31	5	1	0	2	24	2	39	0	1	2	1	.667	0	15-17	8	5.41	5.89
2010	Hou	NL	58	0	0	41	53.1	244	68	26	26	5	2	0	0	20	1	43	8	0	2	5	.286	0	23-29	4	5.45	4.39
2011	Col	NL	63	0	0	16	54.0	226	52	21	18	3	3	3	2	14	4	36	2	0	2	2	.500	0	2-5	15	3.06	3.00
2012	2 Tms	NL	46	0	0	4	47.0	200	45	17	14	2	0	1	5	14	2	40	1	1	1	0	1.000	0	0-1	5	3.40	2.68
12	Bal	AL	34	0	0	3	36.1	155	35	14	11	2	0	1	4	12	2	30	1	1	1	0	1.000	0	0-1	2	3.66	2.72
12	Ari	NL	12	0	0	1	10.2	45	10	3	3	0	0	0	1	2	0	10	0	0	0	0	-	0	0-0	3	2.57	2.53
6 ML YEARS			358	0	0	133	326.0	1418	342	147	132	18	15	6	13	119	17	263	20	2	13	15	.464	0	45-60	65	3.97	3.64

Francisco Liriano

Pitches: L Bats: L Pos: SP-28; RP-6 Ht: 6'2" Wt: 215 Born: 10/26/1983 Age: 29

Year	Team	Lg	G	GS	CG	GF	IP	BFP	H	R	ER	HR	SH	SF	HB	TBB	IBB	SO	WP	Bk	W	L	Pct	Sh	Sv-Op	Hld	ERC	ERA
2005	Min	AL	6	4	0	2	23.2	93	19	15	15	4	0	0	4	7	0	33	0	0	1	2	.333	0	0-0	0	3.15	5.70
2006	Min	AL	28	16	0	2	121.0	473	89	31	29	9	4	2	1	32	0	144	9	1	12	3	.800	0	1-1	1	2.12	2.16
2008	Min	AL	14	14	0	0	76.0	329	74	40	33	7	2	3	1	32	1	67	3	0	6	4	.600	0	0-0	0	3.97	3.91
2009	Min	AL	29	24	0	0	136.2	609	147	93	88	21	5	6	6	65	0	122	5	1	5	13	.278	0	0-0	0	5.46	5.80
2010	Min	AL	31	31	0	0	191.2	806	184	77	77	9	6	2	10	58	0	201	10	1	14	10	.583	0	0-0	0	3.34	3.62
2011	Min	AL	26	24	1	0	134.1	591	125	81	76	14	6	6	7	75	1	112	9	0	9	10	.474	1	0-0	1	4.58	5.09
2012	2 Tms	AL	34	28	0	0	156.2	693	143	97	93	19	4	8	7	87	5	167	11	1	6	12	.333	0	0-0	1	4.47	5.34
12	Min	AL	22	17	0	2	100.0	440	89	63	59	12	2	7	4	55	4	109	6	1	3	10	.231	0	0-0	1	4.27	5.31
12	CWS	AL	12	11	0	0	56.2	253	54	34	34	7	2	1	3	32	1	58	5	0	3	2	.600	0	0-0	0	4.83	5.40
Postseason			2	1	0	0	7.2	34	7	6	5	1	0	0	0	4	0	8	1	0	0	0	-	0	0-0	0	4.19	5.87
7 ML YEARS			168	141	1	8	840.0	3594	781	434	411	83	21	27	32	356	7	846	47	4	53	54	.495	1	1-1	2	3.93	4.40

Jesse Litsch

Pitches: R Bats: R Pos: P   Ht: 6'1" Wt: 235 Born: 3/9/1985 Age: 28

			HOW MUCH HE PITCHED							WHAT HE GAVE UP										THE RESULTS							
Year	Team	Lg	G	GS	CG	GF	IP	BFP	H	R	ER	HR	SH	SF	HB	TBB	IBB	SO	WP	Bk	W	L	Pct	Sh	Sv-Op	Hld	ERC	ERA
2007	Tor	AL	20	20	0	0	111.0	478	116	56	47	14	3	3	7	36	2	50	2	0	7	9	.438	0	0-0	0	4.48	3.81
2008	Tor	AL	29	28	2	0	176.0	735	178	79	70	20	1	4	8	39	2	99	4	0	13	9	.591	2	0-0	0	3.71	3.58
2009	Tor	AL	2	2	0	0	9.0	42	14	9	9	4	0	0	1	1	0	8	0	0	0	1	.000	0	0-0	0	9.55	9.00
2010	Tor	AL	9	9	0	0	46.2	202	53	30	30	7	0	0	2	15	0	16	1	0	1	5	.167	0	0-0	0	5.18	5.79
2011	Tor	AL	28	8	0	4	75.0	317	69	40	37	10	2	2	3	28	2	66	3	0	6	3	.667	0	1-2	3	3.90	4.44
5 ML YEARS			88	67	2	4	417.2	1774	430	214	193	55	6	9	21	119	6	239	10	0	27	27	.500	2	1-2	3	4.22	4.16

Jose Lobaton

Bats: B Throws: R Pos: C-66; PH-8; DH-1; PR-1   LOE-bah-tone   Ht: 6'0" Wt: 210 Born: 10/21/1984 Age: 28

			BATTING																		BASERUNNING				AVERAGES		
Year	Team	Lg	G	AB	H	2B	3B	HR	(Hm	Rd)	TB	R	RBI	RC	TBB	IBB	SO	HBP	SH	SF	SB	CS	SB%	GDP	Avg	OBP	Slg
2012	Charltt*	A+	2	5	0	0	0	0	(-	-)	0	0	0	0	1	0	1	0	0	0	0	0	-	0	.000	.167	.000
2012	Mont*	AA	4	13	2	1	0	0	(-	-)	3	1	1	1	3	0	3	0	0	0	0	0	-	0	.154	.313	.231
2012	Drham*	AAA	4	15	1	1	0	0	(-	-)	2	0	0	0	0	0	5	0	0	0	0	0	-	0	.067	.067	.133
2009	SD	NL	7	17	3	0	0	0	(0	0)	3	0	0	0	0	0	5	0	0	0	0	0	-	1	.176	.176	.176
2011	TB	AL	15	34	4	1	0	0	(0	0)	5	2	0	0	4	0	8	1	0	0	0	0	-	2	.118	.231	.147
2012	TB	AL	69	167	37	10	0	2	(1	1)	53	16	20	19	24	1	46	2	2	2	0	1	.00	6	.222	.323	.317
3 ML YEARS			91	218	44	11	0	2	(1	1)	61	18	20	19	28	1	59	3	2	2	0	1	.00	9	.202	.299	.280

Jeff Locke

Pitches: L Bats: L Pos: SP-6; RP-2   Ht: 6'1" Wt: 180 Born: 11/20/1987 Age: 25

			HOW MUCH HE PITCHED							WHAT HE GAVE UP										THE RESULTS							
Year	Team	Lg	G	GS	CG	GF	IP	BFP	H	R	ER	SH	SF	HB	TBB	IBB	SO	WP	Bk	W	L	Sv-Op	Hld	ERC	ERA
2006	Braves	R	10	5	0	1	32.0	135	38	18	15	4	0	1	1	5	0	38	1	1	4	3	.571	0	0- -	-	4.53	4.22
2007	Danvle	R+	13	11	0	1	61.0	237	48	23	18	2	0	1	3	8	0	74	7	0	7	1	.875	0	1- -	-	1.81	2.66
2008	Rome	A	25	24	1	1	139.2	610	150	75	63	4	3	1	1	38	0	113	8	1	5	12	.294	0	0- -	-	3.61	4.06
2009	MrtlBh	A+	10	10	0	0	45.2	208	47	31	28	1	2	2	5	26	0	43	6	0	1	4	.200	0	0- -	-	4.78	5.52
2009	Lynbrg	A+	17	17	0	0	81.2	348	98	44	37	4	6	2	1	18	0	56	2	0	4	4	.500	0	0- -	-	4.25	4.08
2010	Bradtn	A+	17	17	0	0	86.1	353	82	42	34	6	0	1	7	14	0	83	0	0	9	3	.750	0	0- -	-	3.03	3.54
2010	Altna	AA	10	10	0	0	57.2	243	57	24	23	5	2	2	4	12	0	56	3	1	3	2	.600	0	0- -	-	3.42	3.59
2011	Altna	AA	23	22	0	0	125.0	535	118	68	56	9	5	5	8	46	0	114	10	1	7	8	.467	0	0- -	-	3.70	4.03
2011	Indy	AAA	5	5	0	0	28.1	114	25	8	7	1	1	0	0	9	1	25	0	0	1	2	.333	0	0- -	-	2.74	2.22
2012	Indy	AAA	24	24	0	0	141.2	585	126	42	39	9	10	3	7	43	1	131	2	0	10	5	.667	0	0- -	-	3.07	2.48
2011	Pit	NL	4	4	0	0	16.2	78	21	12	12	3	1	1	1	10	0	5	0	0	0	3	.000	0	0-0	0	7.62	6.48
2012	Pit	NL	8	6	0	1	34.1	148	36	21	21	6	1	0	1	11	0	34	0	0	1	3	.250	0	0-0	0	4.68	5.50
2 ML YEARS			12	10	0	1	51.0	226	57	33	33	9	2	1	2	21	0	39	0	0	1	6	.143	0	0-0	0	5.60	5.82

Kameron Loe

Pitches: R Bats: R Pos: RP-70   Ht: 6'8" Wt: 245 Born: 9/10/1981 Age: 31

			HOW MUCH HE PITCHED							WHAT HE GAVE UP										THE RESULTS							
Year	Team	Lg	G	GS	CG	GF	IP	BFP	H	R	ER	HR	SH	SF	HB	TBB	IBB	SO	WP	Bk	W	L	Pct	Sh	Sv-Op	Hld	ERC	ERA
2004	Tex	AL	2	1	0	0	6.2	29	6	5	4	0	0	0	1	6	0	3	0	0	0	0	-	0	0-0	0	5.87	5.40
2005	Tex	AL	48	8	0	13	92.0	392	89	43	35	7	5	1	2	31	6	45	2	0	9	6	.600	0	1-4	4	3.45	3.42
2006	Tex	AL	15	15	1	0	78.1	358	105	54	51	10	1	3	1	22	0	34	3	0	3	6	.333	1	0-0	0	5.79	5.86
2007	Tex	AL	28	23	0	0	136.0	615	162	96	81	13	1	5	4	56	6	78	6	0	6	11	.353	0	0-0	0	5.24	5.36
2008	Tex	AL	14	0	0	4	30.2	134	36	18	11	3	0	1	0	8	1	20	0	0	1	0	1.000	0	0-1	2	4.40	3.23
2010	Mil	NL	53	0	0	9	58.1	240	54	23	18	6	1	2	2	15	1	46	4	0	3	5	.375	0	0-2	22	3.27	2.78
2011	Mil	NL	72	0	0	19	72.0	291	65	30	28	4	2	0	2	16	2	61	5	0	4	7	.364	0	1-8	16	2.70	3.50
2012	Mil	NL	70	0	0	20	68.1	303	78	41	35	9	5	0	3	20	3	55	4	0	6	5	.545	0	2-7	7	4.72	4.61
Postseason			5	0	0	0	4.1	26	13	7	4	0	0	1	0	1	0	3	0	0	0	0	-	0	0-0	0	16.31	8.31
8 ML YEARS			302	47	1	65	542.1	2362	595	310	263	52	15	12	15	174	19	342	24	0	32	40	.444	1	4-22	51	4.32	4.36

Boone Logan

Pitches: L Bats: R Pos: RP-80   Ht: 6'5" Wt: 215 Born: 8/13/1984 Age: 28

			HOW MUCH HE PITCHED							WHAT HE GAVE UP										THE RESULTS							
Year	Team	Lg	G	GS	CG	GF	IP	BFP	H	R	ER	HR	SH	SF	HB	TBB	IBB	SO	WP	Bk	W	L	Pct	Sh	Sv-Op	Hld	ERC	ERA
2006	CWS	AL	21	0	0	4	17.1	93	21	18	16	2	1	1	3	15	2	15	1	0	0	0	-	0	1-2	2	7.56	8.31
2007	CWS	AL	68	0	0	13	50.2	226	59	30	28	7	2	6	0	20	3	35	2	0	2	1	.667	0	0-2	11	5.18	4.97
2008	CWS	AL	55	0	0	12	42.1	197	57	31	28	7	2	0	1	14	3	42	1	0	2	3	.400	0	0-1	3	6.24	5.95
2009	Atl	NL	20	0	0	4	17.1	82	21	12	10	1	0	0	1	9	3	10	0	0	1	1	.500	0	0-0	1	5.29	5.19
2010	NYY	AL	51	0	0	8	40.0	169	34	13	13	3	0	1	1	20	3	38	1	0	2	0	1.000	0	0-0	13	3.50	2.93
2011	NYY	AL	64	0	0	6	41.2	185	43	20	16	4	2	1	4	13	3	46	1	0	5	3	.625	0	0-2	10	4.04	3.46
2012	NYY	AL	80	0	0	8	55.1	239	48	23	23	6	1	3	2	28	6	68	3	0	7	2	.778	0	1-4	23	3.78	3.74
Postseason			8	0	0	1	4.0	17	4	2	2	1	0	0	0	1	0	7	0	1	0	0	-	0	0-0	2	4.38	4.50
7 ML YEARS			359	0	0	58	264.2	1191	283	147	134	30	8	12	12	119	23	254	9	0	19	10	.655	0	2-11	63	4.76	4.56

Kyle Lohse

Pitches: R **Bats:** R **Pos:** SP-33 — LOESH — **Ht:** 6'2" **Wt:** 210 **Born:** 10/4/1978 **Age:** 34

				HOW MUCH HE PITCHED				WHAT HE GAVE UP											THE RESULTS							
Year	Team	Lg	G	GS	CG	GF	IP	BFP	H	R	ER	HR	SH	SF	HB	TBB	IBB	SO	WP	Bk	W	L	Pct	Sh	Sv-Op	Hld	ERC	ERA
2001	Min	AL	19	16	0	2	90.1	402	102	60	57	16	1	5	8	29	0	64	5	0	4	7	.364	0	0-0	0	5.43	5.68
2002	Min	AL	32	31	1	0	180.2	783	181	92	85	26	3	3	9	70	2	124	8	0	13	8	.619	1	0-1	0	4.55	4.23
2003	Min	AL	33	33	2	0	201.0	850	211	107	103	28	8	5	5	45	1	130	10	1	14	11	.560	1	0-0	0	4.00	4.61
2004	Min	AL	35	34	1	1	194.0	883	240	118	115	28	5	7	7	76	5	111	6	0	9	13	.409	1	0-0	0	5.89	5.34
2005	Min	AL	31	30	0	1	178.2	769	211	85	83	22	3	7	9	44	5	86	4	1	9	13	.409	0	0-0	0	4.91	4.18
2006	2 Tms		34	19	0	6	126.2	566	150	83	82	15	8	5	6	44	4	97	3	1	5	10	.333	0	0-0	0	5.21	5.83
2007	2 Tms	NL	34	32	2	0	192.2	829	207	109	99	22	14	4	12	57	3	122	3	0	9	12	.429	1	0-0	0	4.45	4.62
2008	StL	NL	33	33	0	0	200.0	839	211	88	84	18	6	4	3	49	3	119	5	0	15	6	.714	0	0-0	0	3.77	3.78
2009	StL	NL	23	22	1	0	117.2	512	125	69	62	16	3	5	3	36	2	77	3	1	6	10	.375	1	0-0	0	4.33	4.74
2010	StL	NL	18	18	0	0	92.0	431	129	75	67	9	5	4	3	35	2	54	1	0	4	8	.333	0	0-0	0	6.50	6.55
2011	StL	NL	30	30	1	0	188.1	775	178	80	71	16	8	6	3	42	1	111	1	0	14	8	.636	1	0-0	0	3.05	3.39
2012	StL	NL	33	**33**	0	0	211.0	864	192	74	67	19	11	7	4	38	1	143	1	0	16	3	**.842**	0	0-0	0	2.72	2.86
06	Min	AL	22	8	0	5	63.2	295	80	50	50	8	1	3	6	25	2	46	1	1	2	5	.286	0	0-0	0	6.10	7.07
06	Cin		12	11	0	1	63.0	271	70	33	32	7	7	2	0	19	2	51	2	0	3	5	.375	0	0-0	0	4.36	4.57
07	Cin	NL	21	21	2	0	131.2	561	143	76	67	16	8	4	6	33	1	80	3	0	6	12	.333	1	0-0	0	4.32	4.58
07	Phi	NL	13	11	0	0	61.0	268	64	33	32	6	6	0	6	24	2	42	0	0	3	0	1.000	0	0-0	0	4.71	4.72
	Postseason		9	4	0	3	26.0	112	28	17	16	6	0	0	1	5	0	25	1	0	0	4	.000	0	0-0	0	4.62	5.54
	12 ML YEARS		355	331	8	10	1973.0	8503	2137	1050	975	235	75	62	72	565	29	1238	50	4	118	109	.520	6	0-1	0	4.35	4.45

Steve Lombardozzi

Bats: B **Throws:** R **Pos:** 2B-51; LF-41; PH-30; 3B-13; SS-1; PR-1 — lahm-bar-DOZE-ee — **Ht:** 6'0" **Wt:** 195 **Born:** 9/20/1988 **Age:** 24

									BATTING											BASERUNNING				AVERAGES		
Year	Team	Lg	G	AB	H	2B	3B	HR	(Hm	Rd)	TB	R	RBI	RC	TBB	IBB	SO	HBP	SH	SF	SB	CS	SB%	GDP	Avg	OBP	Slg
2008	Nats	R	48	152	43	4	1	0	(-	-)	49	23	24	22	21	0	32	2	6	3	4	1	.80	1	.283	.371	.322
2009	Hgrstn	A	128	496	147	26	7	3	(-	-)	196	90	58	80	62	0	80	5	6	7	16	7	.70	3	.296	.375	.395
2010	Ptomc	A+	110	440	129	30	9	1	(-	-)	180	71	38	72	49	1	60	6	10	2	20	10	.67	11	.293	.370	.409
2010	Hrsbrg	AA	27	105	31	5	2	5	(-	-)	55	19	12	20	12	0	15	1	0	0	4	2	.67	2	.295	.373	.524
2011	Hrsbrg	AA	65	262	81	12	7	4	(-	-)	119	40	23	46	18	0	38	6	4	1	16	3	.84	3	.309	.366	.454
2011	Syrcse	AAA	69	294	91	13	2	4	(-	-)	120	46	29	45	21	2	40	1	6	3	14	5	.74	4	.310	.354	.408
2011	Was	NL	13	31	6	1	0	0	(0	0)	7	3	1	2	1	0	4	0	0	0	0	0	-	0	.194	.219	.226
2012	Was	NL	126	384	105	16	3	3	(2	1)	136	40	27	46	19	1	46	6	6	1	5	3	.63	1	.273	.317	.354
	2 ML YEARS		139	415	111	17	3	3	(2	1)	143	43	28	48	20	1	50	6	6	1	5	3	.63	1	.267	.310	.345

James Loney

Bats: L **Throws:** L **Pos:** 1B-133; PH-22; PR-1 — **Ht:** 6'3" **Wt:** 220 **Born:** 5/7/1984 **Age:** 29

									BATTING											BASERUNNING				AVERAGES		
Year	Team	Lg	G	AB	H	2B	3B	HR	(Hm	Rd)	TB	R	RBI	RC	TBB	IBB	SO	HBP	SH	SF	SB	CS	SB%	GDP	Avg	OBP	Slg
2006	LAD	NL	48	102	29	6	5	4	(1	3)	57	20	18	17	8	1	10	1	0	0	1	0	1.00	8	.284	.342	.559
2007	LAD	NL	96	344	114	18	4	15	(5	10)	185	41	67	71	28	5	48	1	0	2	0	1	.00	6	.331	.381	.538
2008	LAD	NL	161	595	172	35	6	13	(5	8)	258	66	90	79	45	6	85	3	1	7	7	4	.64	25	.289	.338	.434
2009	LAD	NL	158	576	162	25	2	13	(1	12)	230	73	90	84	70	10	68	0	1	4	7	3	.70	16	.281	.357	.399
2010	LAD	NL	161	588	157	41	2	10	(6	4)	232	67	88	81	52	9	95	4	0	4	10	5	.67	14	.267	.329	.395
2011	LAD	NL	158	531	153	30	1	12	(7	5)	221	56	65	71	42	7	67	1	3	5	4	0	1.00	8	.288	.339	.416
2012	2 Tms		144	434	108	20	0	6	(0	6)	146	37	41	34	28	7	51	0	1	2	0	3	.00	21	.249	.293	.336
12	LAD	NL	114	334	85	18	0	4	(0	4)	115	32	33	28	23	7	39	0	1	1	0	3	.00	16	.254	.302	.344
12	Bos	AL	30	100	23	2	0	2	(0	2)	31	5	8	6	5	0	12	0	0	1	0	0	-	5	.230	.264	.310
	Postseason		17	63	22	3	0	3	(1	2)	34	5	14	13	7	1	10	0	0	0	0	0	-	2	.349	.414	.540
	7 ML YEARS		926	3170	895	175	20	73	(25	48)	1329	360	459	437	273	45	424	10	6	24	29	16	.64	98	.282	.339	.419

Evan Longoria

Bats: R **Throws:** R **Pos:** 3B-50; DH-25 — **Ht:** 6'2" **Wt:** 210 **Born:** 10/7/1985 **Age:** 27

									BATTING											BASERUNNING				AVERAGES		
Year	Team	Lg	G	AB	H	2B	3B	HR	(Hm	Rd)	TB	R	RBI	RC	TBB	IBB	SO	HBP	SH	SF	SB	CS	SB%	GDP	Avg	OBP	Slg
2012	Drham*	AAA	10	30	6	0	0	0	(-	-)	6	0	3	3	7	0	9	1	0	1	0	0	-	0	.200	.359	.200
2008	TB	AL	122	448	122	31	2	27	(18	9)	238	67	85	72	46	4	122	6	0	8	7	0	1.00	8	.272	.343	.531
2009	TB	AL	157	584	164	44	0	33	(16	17)	307	100	113	102	72	11	140	8	0	7	9	0	1.00	27	.281	.364	.526
2010	TB	AL	151	574	169	46	5	22	(10	12)	291	96	104	99	72	12	124	5	0	10	15	5	.75	15	.294	.372	.507
2011	TB	AL	133	483	118	26	1	31	(14	17)	239	78	99	91	80	6	93	6	0	5	3	2	.60	11	.244	.355	.495
2012	TB	AL	74	273	79	14	0	17	(8	9)	144	39	55	55	33	6	61	3	0	3	2	3	.40	14	.289	.369	.527
	Postseason		25	98	19	5	0	8	(3	5)	48	14	18	11	8	0	32	0	0	0	1	0	1.00	3	.194	.255	.490
	5 ML YEARS		637	2362	652	161	8	130	(66	64)	1219	380	456	419	303	39	540	28	0	33	36	10	.78	75	.276	.361	.516

Javier Lopez

Pitches: L **Bats:** L **Pos:** RP-70 — **Ht:** 6'4" **Wt:** 220 **Born:** 7/11/1977 **Age:** 35

				HOW MUCH HE PITCHED				WHAT HE GAVE UP											THE RESULTS							
Year	Team	Lg	G	GS	CG	GF	IP	BFP	H	R	ER	HR	SH	SF	HB	TBB	IBB	SO	WP	Bk	W	L	Pct	Sh	Sv-Op	Hld	ERC	ERA
2003	Col	NL	75	0	0	11	58.1	242	58	25	24	5	1	0	4	12	2	40	1	3	4	1	.800	0	1-2	15	3.44	3.70
2004	Col	NL	64	0	0	10	40.2	187	45	34	34	1	1	0	3	26	4	20	3	0	1	2	.333	0	0-1	12	5.28	7.52
2005	2 Tms	NL	32	0	0	6	16.1	87	26	20	20	2	1	0	1	11	3	12	0	0	1	1	.500	0	2-4	6	8.82	11.02
2006	Bos	AL	27	0	0	8	16.2	69	13	10	5	1	0	1	2	10	1	11	0	0	1	0	1.000	0	1-1	6	3.96	2.70
2007	Bos	AL	61	0	0	11	40.2	174	36	16	14	2	1	1	4	18	2	26	1	0	2	1	.667	0	0-2	13	3.59	3.10
2008	Bos	AL	70	0	0	10	59.1	247	53	18	16	4	1	1	2	27	0	38	1	0	2	0	1.000	0	0-1	16	3.73	2.43
2009	Bos	AL	14	0	0	5	11.2	64	20	13	12	1	1	1	2	9	0	5	1	0	0	2	.000	0	0-0	0	11.00	9.26
2010	2 Tms	NL	77	0	0	18	57.2	235	50	17	15	2	4	2	2	20	3	38	3	0	4	2	.667	0	0-0	11	2.85	2.34

177

			HOW MUCH HE PITCHED						WHAT HE GAVE UP												THE RESULTS							
Year	Team	Lg	G	GS	CG	GF	IP	BFP	H	R	ER	HR	SH	SF	HB	TBB	IBB	SO	WP	Bk	W	L	Pct	Sh	Sv-Op	Hld	ERC	ERA
2011	SF	NL	70	0	0	17	53.0	222	42	16	16	0	3	0	3	26	6	40	1	0	5	2	.714	0	1-3	20	2.69	2.72
2012	SF	NL	70	0	0	19	36.0	153	37	13	10	1	1	1	0	14	3	28	2	0	3	0	1.000	0	7-9	18	3.60	2.50
05	Col	NL	3	0	0	1	2.0	13	7	5	5	0	0	0	0	0	0	1	0	0	0	0	-	0	0-1	0	18.39	22.50
05	Ari	NL	29	0	0	5	14.1	74	19	15	15	2	1	0	1	11	3	11	0	0	1	1	.500	0	2-3	6	7.63	9.42
10	Pit	NL	50	0	0	14	38.2	166	39	14	12	2	1	2	2	18	3	22	3	0	2	2	.500	0	0-0	6	4.24	2.79
10	SF	NL	27	0	0	4	19.0	69	11	3	3	0	0	0	0	2	0	16	0	0	2	0	1.000	0	0-0	5	0.90	1.42
	Postseason		17	0	0	1	10.2	46	12	6	6	0	1	1	0	3	1	7	1	0	1	1	.500	0	0-0	6	3.44	5.06
10 ML YEARS			560	0	0	115	390.1	1680	380	182	166	19	11	7	23	173	24	258	13	3	23	11	.676	0	12-23	111	3.92	3.83

Jose Lopez

Bats: R **Throws:** R **Pos:** 3B-50; 1B-14; DH-13; PH-8; PR-6; 2B-4; RF-1   **Ht:** 6'0" **Wt:** 205 **Born:** 11/24/1983 **Age:** 29

							BATTING												BASERUNNING				AVERAGES		
Year	Team	Lg	G	AB	H	2B	3B	HR	(Hm | Rd)	TB	R	RBI	RC	TBB	IBB	SO	HBP	SH	SF	SB	CS	SB%	GDP	Avg	OBP	Slg
2012	Clmbs*	AAA	6	23	12	4	0	0	(- | -)	16	1	4	7	1	0	2	0	0	0	0	0	-	1	.522	.542	.696
2012	Charltt*	AAA	13	49	15	5	0	1	(- | -)	23	7	10	8	6	0	8	0	0	0	0	0	-	1	.306	.382	.469
2004	Sea	AL	57	207	48	13	0	5	(4 | 1)	76	28	22	20	8	0	31	1	1	1	0	1	.00	1	.232	.263	.367
2005	Sea	AL	54	190	47	19	0	2	(1 | 1)	72	18	25	24	6	0	25	4	1	2	4	2	.67	5	.247	.282	.379
2006	Sea	AL	151	603	170	28	8	10	(4 | 6)	244	78	79	84	26	1	80	9	12	5	5	2	.71	17	.282	.319	.405
2007	Sea	AL	149	524	132	17	2	11	(5 | 6)	186	58	62	52	20	0	64	5	9	3	2	3	.40	16	.252	.284	.355
2008	Sea	AL	159	644	191	41	1	17	(13 | 4)	285	80	89	83	27	5	67	1	6	9	6	3	.67	14	.297	.322	.443
2009	Sea	AL	153	613	167	42	0	25	(8 | 17)	284	69	96	71	24	5	69	6	3	7	3	3	.50	25	.272	.303	.463
2010	Sea	AL	150	593	142	29	0	10	(3 | 7)	201	49	58	42	23	1	66	3	0	3	3	2	.60	20	.239	.270	.339
2011	2 Tms	NL	82	231	50	12	0	8	(4 | 4)	86	23	21	17	7	1	28	2	1	1	2	0	1.00	6	.216	.245	.372
2012	2 Tms	NL	81	236	58	14	0	4	(2 | 2)	84	18	28	20	9	0	41	0	0	3	0	1	.00	9	.246	.270	.356
11	Col	NL	38	125	26	4	0	2	(1 | 1)	36	10	8	7	3	0	15	1	0	0	2	0	1.00	2	.208	.233	.288
11	Fla	NL	44	106	24	8	0	6	(3 | 3)	50	13	13	10	4	1	13	1	1	1	0	0	-	4	.226	.259	.472
12	Cle	AL	66	213	53	13	0	4	(2 | 2)	78	16	28	20	8	0	35	0	0	3	0	1	.00	8	.249	.272	.366
12	CWS	AL	15	23	5	1	0	0	(0 | 0)	6	2	0	0	1	0	6	0	0	0	0	0	-	1	.217	.250	.261
9 ML YEARS			1036	3841	1005	215	11	92	(44 | 48)	1518	421	480	413	150	13	471	31	33	34	25	17	.60	113	.262	.292	.395

Rodrigo Lopez

Pitches: R **Bats:** R **Pos:** RP-4   **Ht:** 6'1" **Wt:** 185 **Born:** 12/14/1975 **Age:** 37

			HOW MUCH HE PITCHED						WHAT HE GAVE UP												THE RESULTS							
Year	Team	Lg	G	GS	CG	GF	IP	BFP	H	R	ER	HR	SH	SF	HB	TBB	IBB	SO	WP	Bk	W	L	Pct	Sh	Sv-Op	Hld	ERC	ERA
2012	Iowa*	AAA	18	15	0	0	73.1	322	84	47	43	8	5	5	1	26	0	55	0	0	2	5	.286	0	0- -	-	4.88	5.28
2000	SD	NL	6	6	0	0	24.2	120	40	24	24	5	0	1	0	13	0	17	0	0	0	3	.000	0	0-0	0	9.78	8.76
2002	Bal	AL	33	28	1	0	196.2	809	172	83	78	23	2	4	5	62	4	136	2	1	15	9	.625	0	0-0	0	3.27	3.57
2003	Bal	AL	26	26	3	0	147.0	663	188	101	95	24	3	7	10	43	6	103	2	1	7	10	.412	1	0-0	0	6.00	5.82
2004	Bal	AL	37	23	1	3	170.2	714	164	71	68	21	5	2	2	54	2	121	4	1	14	9	.609	1	0-1	4	3.74	3.59
2005	Bal	AL	35	35	0	0	209.1	918	232	126	114	28	3	5	7	63	1	118	5	1	15	12	.556	0	0-0	0	4.62	4.90
2006	Bal	AL	36	29	0	2	189.0	874	234	129	124	32	5	5	4	59	2	136	6	1	9	18	.333	0	0-0	0	5.68	5.90
2007	Col	NL	14	14	0	0	79.1	333	83	43	39	11	3	5	0	21	6	43	0	0	5	4	.556	0	0-0	0	3.97	4.42
2009	Phi	NL	7	5	0	0	30.0	137	42	24	19	3	0	2	0	11	1	19	0	0	3	1	.750	0	0-0	0	6.39	5.70
2010	Ari	NL	33	33	0	0	200.0	874	227	126	111	37	14	7	3	56	1	116	2	0	7	16	.304	0	0-0	0	4.98	5.00
2011	ChC	NL	26	16	0	3	97.2	430	116	56	48	18	6	2	5	29	3	54	0	0	6	6	.500	0	0-0	0	5.58	4.42
2012	ChC	NL	4	0	0	2	6.1	34	8	6	4	0	2	1	1	5	0	2	0	0	0	1	.000	0	0-0	0	6.63	5.68
11 ML YEARS			257	215	5	10	1350.2	5879	1506	789	724	202	43	41	37	416	26	865	21	5	81	89	.476	2	0-1	4	4.80	4.82

Wilton Lopez

Pitches: R **Bats:** R **Pos:** RP-64   **Ht:** 6'0" **Wt:** 205 **Born:** 7/19/1983 **Age:** 29

			HOW MUCH HE PITCHED						WHAT HE GAVE UP												THE RESULTS							
Year	Team	Lg	G	GS	CG	GF	IP	BFP	H	R	ER	HR	SH	SF	HB	TBB	IBB	SO	WP	Bk	W	L	Pct	Sh	Sv-Op	Hld	ERC	ERA
2012	OKCity*	AAA	2	0	0	0	2.0	11	4	4	3	2	0	0	0	0	0	1	0	0	0	0	-	0	0- -	-	14.75	13.50
2009	Hou	NL	8	2	0	0	19.1	97	32	21	18	4	3	2	1	8	0	9	1	0	0	2	.000	0	0- -	-	9.39	8.38
2010	Hou	NL	68	0	0	14	67.0	262	66	23	22	4	2	2	0	5	1	50	2	2	5	2	.714	0	1-3	14	2.56	2.96
2011	Hou	NL	73	0	0	13	71.0	298	72	26	22	6	4	0	3	18	3	56	1	1	2	6	.250	0	0-6	14	3.60	2.79
2012	Hou	NL	64	0	0	28	66.1	260	61	18	16	4	4	2	2	8	2	54	1	0	6	3	.667	0	10-13	9	2.49	2.17
4 ML YEARS			213	2	0	55	223.2	917	231	88	78	18	13	6	6	39	6	169	5	3	13	13	.500	0	11-23	37	3.36	3.14

David Lough

Bats: L **Throws:** L **Pos:** CF-12; RF-5; PH-4; LF-1   LOW   **Ht:** 5'11" **Wt:** 185 **Born:** 1/20/1986 **Age:** 27

							BATTING												BASERUNNING				AVERAGES		
Year	Team	Lg	G	AB	H	2B	3B	HR	(Hm | Rd)	TB	R	RBI	RC	TBB	IBB	SO	HBP	SH	SF	SB	CS	SB%	GDP	Avg	OBP	Slg
2007	Burlgtn	A	24	86	29	6	0	2	(- | -)	41	15	12	16	4	0	13	2	0	0	6	1	.86	1	.337	.380	.477
2008	Burlgtn	A	126	488	131	21	11	16	(- | -)	222	76	62	73	35	2	70	10	8	2	12	11	.52	10	.268	.329	.455
2009	Wilmg	A+	65	222	71	15	2	5	(- | -)	105	28	30	39	12	0	34	7	7	2	6	4	.60	4	.320	.370	.473
2009	NWArk	AA	61	236	78	13	2	9	(- | -)	122	41	31	45	12	0	30	3	2	0	13	4	.76	2	.331	.371	.517
2010	Omha	AAA	120	460	129	15	12	11	(- | -)	201	65	58	74	40	2	72	8	19	4	14	5	.74	7	.280	.346	.437
2011	Omha	AAA	114	456	145	26	11	9	(- | -)	220	87	65	82	36	3	49	4	12	8	14	8	.64	10	.318	.367	.482
2012	Omha	AAA	130	491	135	19	11	10	(- | -)	206	69	69	71	25	5	65	8	14	6	26	4	.87	12	.275	.317	.420
2012	KC	AL	20	59	14	2	1	0	(0 | 0)	18	9	2	5	4	0	9	1	0	1	1	0	1.00	2	.237	.292	.305

Aaron Loup

Pitches: L Bats: L Pos: RP-33 　　LOOP 　　Ht: 5'11" Wt: 205 Born: 12/19/1987 Age: 25

			HOW MUCH HE PITCHED						WHAT HE GAVE UP										THE RESULTS							
Year	Team	Lg	G	GS	CG	GF	IP	BFP	H	R	ER	HR	SH	SF	HB	TBB	IBB	SO	WP	Bk	W	L	Pct	Sh	Sv-Op	Hld	ERC	ERA
2009	B Jays	R	13	0	0	8	16.1	71	17	9	7	0	0	2	3	3	0	19	1	0	2	1	.667	0	3--	-	3.43	3.86
2010	Lnsng	A	35	0	0	9	73.1	309	79	37	37	4	3	0	5	22	1	73	3	0	3	2	.600	0	2--	-	4.18	4.54
2011	Dnedin	A+	48	0	0	16	65.2	286	67	38	34	6	3	1	6	27	2	56	6	1	4	3	.571	0	5--	-	4.56	4.66
2012	NHam	AA	37	0	0	16	45.1	198	46	19	14	4	3	1	5	14	1	43	3	1	0	3	.000	0	3--	-	4.08	2.78
2012	Tor	AL	33	0	0	3	30.2	117	26	10	9	0	2	1	0	2	0	21	1	1	0	2	.000	0	0-1	6	1.59	2.64

Shane Loux

Pitches: R Bats: R Pos: RP-19 　　LUKES 　　Ht: 6'2" Wt: 225 Born: 8/31/1979 Age: 33

			HOW MUCH HE PITCHED						WHAT HE GAVE UP										THE RESULTS							
Year	Team	Lg	G	GS	CG	GF	IP	BFP	H	R	ER	HR	SH	SF	HB	TBB	IBB	SO	WP	Bk	W	L	Pct	Sh	Sv-Op	Hld	ERC	ERA
2012	Fresno*	AAA	23	0	0	5	32.0	120	23	6	5	0	3	1	1	5	0	22	1	0	4	1	.800	0	0--	-	1.48	1.41
2012	Giants*	R	1	1	0	0	1.0	3	0	0	0	0	0	0	0	0	0	1	0	0	0	0	-	0	0--	-	0.00	0.00
2002	Det	AL	3	3	0	0	14.0	64	19	16	14	4	0	0	1	3	0	7	1	0	0	3	.000	0	0-0	0	7.12	9.00
2003	Det	AL	11	4	0	1	30.1	140	37	24	24	4	1	1	4	12	1	8	1	0	1	1	.500	0	0-0	0	6.12	7.12
2008	LAA	AL	7	0	0	5	16.0	66	16	6	5	1	1	0	2	2	0	4	0	0	0	0	-	0	0-0	0	3.28	2.81
2009	LAA	AL	18	6	0	7	58.1	271	84	42	38	4	0	3	4	19	0	19	3	0	2	3	.400	0	0-0	0	6.54	5.86
2012	SF	NL	19	0	0	6	25.1	112	32	15	14	3	0	0	0	9	1	9	1	0	1	0	1.000	0	0-0	1	5.62	4.97
	5 ML YEARS		58	13	0	19	144.0	653	188	103	95	16	2	4	11	45	2	47	6	0	4	7	.364	0	0-0	1	5.96	5.94

Derek Lowe

Pitches: R Bats: R Pos: SP-21; RP-17 　　Ht: 6'6" Wt: 230 Born: 6/1/1973 Age: 40

			HOW MUCH HE PITCHED						WHAT HE GAVE UP										THE RESULTS							
Year	Team	Lg	G	GS	CG	GF	IP	BFP	H	R	ER	HR	SH	SF	HB	TBB	IBB	SO	WP	Bk	W	L	Pct	Sh	Sv-Op	Hld	ERC	ERA
1997	2 Tms	AL	20	9	0	1	69.0	298	74	49	47	11	4	2	4	23	3	52	2	0	2	6	.250	0	0-2	1	4.88	6.13
1998	Bos	AL	63	10	0	8	123.0	527	126	65	55	5	4	5	4	42	5	77	8	0	3	9	.250	0	4-9	12	3.64	4.02
1999	Bos	AL	74	0	0	32	109.1	436	84	35	32	7	1	2	4	25	1	80	1	0	6	3	.667	0	15-20	22	2.14	2.63
2000	Bos	AL	74	0	0	64	91.1	379	90	27	26	6	4	1	2	22	5	79	2	1	4	4	.500	0	42-47	0	3.17	2.56
2001	Bos	AL	67	3	0	50	91.2	404	103	39	36	7	5	1	5	29	9	82	4	0	5	10	.333	0	24-30	4	4.31	3.53
2002	Bos	AL	32	32	1	0	219.2	854	166	65	63	12	5	2	12	48	0	127	5	0	21	8	.724	1	0-0	0	2.13	2.58
2003	Bos	AL	33	33	1	0	203.1	886	216	113	101	17	3	5	11	72	4	110	3	0	17	7	.708	0	0-0	0	4.32	4.47
2004	Bos	AL	33	33	0	0	182.2	839	224	138	110	15	8	4	8	71	2	105	3	0	14	12	.538	0	0-0	0	5.31	5.42
2005	LAD	NL	35	35	2	0	222.0	934	223	113	89	28	12	5	5	55	1	146	3	2	12	15	.444	2	0-0	0	3.75	3.61
2006	LAD	NL	35	34	1	1	218.0	913	221	97	88	14	7	2	5	55	2	123	3	2	16	8	.667	0	0-0	0	3.42	3.63
2007	LAD	NL	33	32	3	0	199.1	831	194	100	86	20	6	2	1	59	2	147	3	1	12	14	.462	0	0-0	1	3.55	3.88
2008	LAD	NL	34	34	1	0	211.0	851	194	84	76	14	8	7	1	45	7	147	2	0	14	11	.560	0	0-0	0	2.72	3.24
2009	Atl	NL	34	34	0	0	194.2	855	232	109	101	16	11	6	4	63	7	111	4	2	15	10	.600	0	0-0	0	4.80	4.67
2010	Atl	NL	33	33	0	0	193.2	824	204	88	86	18	10	2	4	61	10	136	4	2	16	12	.571	0	0-0	0	4.03	4.00
2011	Atl	NL	34	34	0	0	187.0	830	212	110	105	14	9	5	3	70	4	137	1	2	9	17	.346	0	0-0	0	4.56	5.05
2012	2 Tms	AL	38	21	1	10	142.2	640	180	88	81	10	3	5	3	51	5	55	7	1	9	11	.450	0	1-1	1	5.27	5.11
97	Sea	AL	12	9	0	1	53.0	234	59	43	41	11	2	1	2	20	2	39	2	0	2	4	.333	0	0-0	0	5.55	6.96
97	Bos	AL	8	0	0	0	16.0	64	15	6	6	0	2	1	2	3	1	13	0	0	0	2	.000	0	0-2	1	2.78	3.38
12	Cle	AL	21	21	1	0	119.0	542	156	79	73	8	3	5	3	45	3	41	5	1	8	10	.444	0	0-0	0	5.67	5.52
12	NYY	AL	17	0	0	10	23.2	98	24	9	8	2	0	0	0	6	2	14	2	0	1	1	.500	0	1-1	1	3.39	3.04
	Postseason		23	12	0	3	95.1	399	78	42	34	10	6	4	1	32	6	69	1	0	5	7	.417	0	1-2	1	2.90	3.21
	16 ML YEARS		672	377	10	166	2658.1	11301	2743	1320	1182	214	100	56	76	791	67	1714	55	13	175	157	.527	4	86-109	41	3.80	4.00

Mark Lowe

Pitches: R Bats: L Pos: RP-36 　　Ht: 6'3" Wt: 210 Born: 6/7/1983 Age: 30

			HOW MUCH HE PITCHED						WHAT HE GAVE UP										THE RESULTS							
Year	Team	Lg	G	GS	CG	GF	IP	BFP	H	R	ER	HR	SH	SF	HB	TBB	IBB	SO	WP	Bk	W	L	Pct	Sh	Sv-Op	Hld	ERC	ERA
2012	Frisco*	AA	3	0	0	0	4.0	18	4	4	4	2	0	0	0	2	0	6	0	0	0	1	.000	0	0--	-	7.30	9.00
2012	RdRck*	AAA	2	0	0	1	2.0	6	0	0	0	0	0	0	0	0	0	4	0	0	0	0	-	0	0--	-	0.00	0.00
2006	Sea	AL	15	0	0	3	18.2	75	12	4	4	1	1	0	2	9	1	20	1	0	1	0	1.000	0	0-0	6	2.61	1.93
2007	Sea	AL	4	0	0	1	2.2	13	2	2	2	1	0	0	0	3	0	3	0	0	0	0	-	0	0-0	2	7.69	6.75
2008	Sea	AL	57	0	0	19	63.2	303	78	44	38	6	3	3	4	34	0	55	2	0	1	5	.167	0	1-5	6	6.10	5.37
2009	Sea	AL	75	0	0	18	80.0	339	71	39	29	7	0	4	0	29	1	69	4	0	2	7	.222	0	3-13	26	3.16	3.26
2010	2 Tms	AL	14	0	0	5	13.1	61	18	9	8	2	0	1	0	6	1	12	1	0	1	3	.250	0	0-0	0	6.82	5.40
2011	Tex	AL	52	0	0	10	45.0	196	46	26	19	6	1	1	0	19	4	42	3	0	2	3	.400	0	1-3	11	4.38	3.80
2012	Tex	AL	36	0	0	12	39.1	162	35	15	15	5	0	3	0	13	0	28	4	2	0	2	.000	0	0-0	1	3.41	3.43
10	Sea	AL	11	0	0	4	10.1	45	11	5	4	1	0	0	0	5	1	7	1	0	1	3	.250	0	0-0	0	4.70	3.48
10	Tex	AL	3	0	0	1	3.0	16	7	4	4	1	0	0	0	1	0	5	0	0	0	0	-	0	0-0	0	15.67	12.00
	Postseason		4	0	0	1	1.2	13	7	7	7	1	0	0	0	1	0	1	0	0	0	1	.000	0	0-0	0	35.40	37.80
	7 ML YEARS		253	0	0	68	262.2	1149	262	139	115	28	5	12	6	113	7	229	15	2	7	20	.259	0	5-21	51	4.25	3.94

Jed Lowrie

Bats: B Throws: R Pos: SS-93; PH-6 　　LAU-ree 　　Ht: 6'0" Wt: 180 Born: 4/17/1984 Age: 29

			BATTING																			BASERUNNING			AVERAGES		
Year	Team	Lg	G	AB	H	2B	3B	HR	(Hm	Rd)	TB	R	RBI	RC	TBB	IBB	SO	HBP	SH	SF		SB	CS	SB%	GDP	Avg	OBP	Slg
2012	OKCity*	AAA	2	6	3	0	0	0	(-	-)	3	1	3	1	0	1	0	0	0	1		0	0	-	0	.500	.500	.500
2008	Bos	AL	81	260	67	25	3	2	(0	2)	104	34	46	35	35	0	68	1	2	8		1	0	1.00	8	.258	.339	.400
2009	Bos	AL	32	68	10	2	0	2	(1	1)	18	5	11	5	6	0	20	0	0	2		0	0	-	0	.147	.211	.265
2010	Bos	AL	55	171	49	14	0	9	(3	6)	90	31	24	32	25	0	25	1	0	0		1	1	.50	2	.287	.381	.526

Year Team	Lg	G	AB	H	2B	3B	HR	(Hm	Rd)	TB	R	RBI	RC	TBB	IBB	SO	HBP	SH	SF	SB	CS	SB%	GDP	Avg	OBP	Slg
2011 Bos	AL	88	309	78	14	4	6	(3	3)	118	40	36	33	23	2	60	2	1	6	1	1	.50	6	.252	.303	.382
2012 Hou	NL	97	340	83	18	0	16	(9	7)	149	43	42	45	43	0	65	2	0	2	2	0	1.00	3	.244	.331	.438
Postseason		12	31	6	1	0	0	(0	0)	7	4	2	2	5	0	8	1	0	1	0	0	-	0	.194	.316	.226
5 ML YEARS		353	1148	287	73	7	35	(16	19)	479	153	159	150	132	2	238	6	3	18	5	2	.71	19	.250	.326	.417

Jonathan Lucroy

Bats: R **Throws:** R **Pos:** C-88; PH-13   LOO-croy   **Ht:** 6'0" **Wt:** 195 **Born:** 6/13/1986 **Age:** 27

Year Team	Lg	G	AB	H	2B	3B	HR	(Hm	Rd)	TB	R	RBI	RC	TBB	IBB	SO	HBP	SH	SF	SB	CS	SB%	GDP	Avg	OBP	Slg
2012 Wisc*	A	4	12	4	1	0	0	(-	-)	5	0	2	2	1	0	0	0	0	0	1	0	1.00	2	.333	.385	.417
2012 Nashv*	AAA	2	7	3	0	0	0	(-	-)	3	4	1	1	0	0	1	1	0	0	1	0	1.00	0	.429	.500	.429
2010 Mil	NL	75	277	70	9	0	4	(4	0)	91	24	26	23	18	1	44	1	0	1	4	2	.67	9	.253	.300	.329
2011 Mil	NL	136	430	114	16	1	12	(8	4)	168	45	59	50	29	0	99	2	4	3	2	1	.67	7	.265	.313	.391
2012 Mil	NL	96	316	101	17	4	12	(7	5)	162	46	58	61	22	1	44	4	1	3	4	1	.80	12	.320	.368	.513
Postseason		10	32	8	1	0	1	(1	0)	12	3	5	4	0	0	8	0	0	0	0	0	-	0	.250	.250	.375
3 ML YEARS		307	1023	285	42	5	28	(19	9)	421	115	143	134	69	2	187	7	5	7	10	4	.71	28	.279	.326	.412

Ryan Ludwick

Bats: R **Throws:** L **Pos:** LF-108; PH-15; DH-2   **Ht:** 6'3" **Wt:** 215 **Born:** 7/13/1978 **Age:** 34

Year Team	Lg	G	AB	H	2B	3B	HR	(Hm	Rd)	TB	R	RBI	RC	TBB	IBB	SO	HBP	SH	SF	SB	CS	SB%	GDP	Avg	OBP	Slg
2002 Tex	AL	23	81	19	6	0	1	(1	0)	28	10	9	6	7	0	24	0	0	0	2	1	.67	4	.235	.295	.346
2003 2 Tms	AL	47	162	40	8	1	7	(2	5)	71	17	26	28	12	1	48	0	1	0	2	0	1.00	1	.247	.299	.438
2004 Cle	AL	15	50	11	2	0	2	(0	2)	19	3	4	4	2	0	14	2	0	0	0	0	-	0	.220	.278	.380
2005 Cle	AL	19	41	9	0	0	4	(3	1)	21	8	5	3	7	0	13	0	0	0	0	1	.00	1	.220	.333	.512
2007 StL	NL	120	303	81	22	0	14	(7	7)	145	42	52	45	26	1	72	7	3	0	4	4	.50	1	.267	.339	.479
2008 StL	NL	152	538	161	40	3	37	(18	19)	318	104	113	100	62	3	146	8	1	8	4	4	.50	9	.299	.375	.591
2009 StL	NL	139	486	129	20	1	22	(4	18)	217	63	97	82	41	3	106	7	1	4	4	2	.67	6	.265	.329	.447
2010 2 Tms	NL	136	490	123	27	2	17	(8	9)	205	63	69	76	48	0	121	8	0	5	0	4	.00	13	.251	.325	.418
2011 2 Tms	NL	139	490	116	23	0	13	(6	7)	178	56	75	59	51	4	124	4	2	6	1	1	.50	9	.237	.310	.363
2012 Cin	NL	125	422	116	28	1	26	(16	10)	224	53	80	70	42	3	97	5	1	2	0	1	.00	9	.275	.346	.531
03 Tex	AL	8	26	4	1	0	0	(0	0)	5	3	0	1	4	0	9	0	0	0	0	0	-	0	.154	.267	.192
03 Cle	AL	39	136	36	7	1	7	(2	5)	66	14	26	27	8	1	39	0	1	0	2	0	1.00	1	.265	.306	.485
10 StL	NL	77	281	79	20	2	11	(4	7)	136	44	43	55	24	0	64	4	0	3	0	3	.00	4	.281	.343	.484
10 SD	NL	59	209	44	7	0	6	(4	2)	69	19	26	21	24	0	57	4	0	2	0	1	.00	9	.211	.301	.330
11 SD	NL	101	378	90	18	0	11	(5	6)	141	42	64	44	32	1	87	4	1	5	1	1	.50	8	.238	.301	.373
11 Pit	NL	38	112	26	5	0	2	(1	1)	37	14	11	15	19	3	37	0	1	1	0	0	-	1	.232	.341	.330
Postseason		3	12	4	0	0	0	(0	0)	4	1	1	1	1	0	0	0	0	0	0	0	-	0	.333	.385	.333
10 ML YEARS		915	3063	805	176	8	143	(65	78)	1426	419	530	473	298	15	765	41	9	25	17	18	.49	53	.263	.334	.466

Cory Luebke

Pitches: L **Bats:** R **Pos:** SP-5   LUBE-kee   **Ht:** 6'4" **Wt:** 205 **Born:** 3/4/1985 **Age:** 28

	HOW MUCH HE PITCHED						WHAT HE GAVE UP											THE RESULTS						
Year Team	Lg	G	GS	CG	GF	IP	BFP	H	R	ER	HR	SH	SF	HB	TBB	IBB	SO	WP	Bk	W	L	Pct	Sh	Sv-Op Hld	ERC	ERA
2010 SD	NL	4	3	0	1	17.2	76	17	8	8	3	0	0	1	6	0	18	0	0	1	1	.500	0	0-0	-3	4.30	4.08
2011 SD	NL	46	17	0	3	139.2	555	105	54	51	12	3	4	2	44	3	154	5	2	6	10	.375	0	0-0	-3	2.43	3.29
2012 SD	NL	5	5	0	0	31.0	130	28	10	9	1	2	0	0	8	0	23	0	0	3	1	.750	0	0-0	-3	2.51	2.61
3 ML YEARS		55	25	0	4	188.1	761	150	72	68	16	5	4	3	58	3	195	5	2	10	12	.455	0	0-0	-3	2.61	3.25

Josh Lueke

Pitches: R **Bats:** R **Pos:** RP-3   LOO-kee   **Ht:** 6'5" **Wt:** 235 **Born:** 12/5/1984 **Age:** 28

	HOW MUCH HE PITCHED						WHAT HE GAVE UP											THE RESULTS						
Year Team	Lg	G	GS	CG	GF	IP	BFP	H	R	ER	HR	SH	SF	HB	TBB	IBB	SO	WP	Bk	W	L	Pct	Sh	Sv-Op Hld	ERC	ERA
2007 Spkane	A-	2	0	0	0	2.2	11	2	0	0	0	0	0	1	0	0	6	0	0	0	0	-	0	0- -	-	2.01	0.00
2007 Clinton	A	20	0	0	4	35.0	145	29	19	13	4	3	0	3	10	0	31	3	0	0	3	.000	0	6- -	-	3.12	3.34
2008 Clinton	A	8	0	0	5	10.1	44	10	3	3	0	0	0	1	2	0	12	1	0	1	1	.500	0	2- -	-	2.75	2.61
2008 Bkrsfld	A+	35	0	0	22	59.0	266	65	39	33	6	1	4	4	16	0	72	3	0	2	6	.250	0	1- -	-	4.24	5.03
2009 Bkrsfld	A+	4	0	0	2	7.2	29	5	2	1	0	0	0	0	1	0	11	1	0	1	0	1.000	0	1- -	-	1.12	1.17
2010 Hkry	A	17	0	0	17	19.2	80	12	4	1	0	0	1	2	5	1	36	3	1	2	1	.667	0	10- -	-	1.37	0.46
2010 Frisco	AA	15	0	0	5	18.2	77	18	9	8	2	1	0	0	5	0	26	2	0	1	1	.500	0	2- -	-	3.44	3.86
2010 WTenn	AA	6	0	0	6	7.1	27	4	0	0	0	0	0	0	0	0	14	0	0	1	0	1.000	0	3- -	-	0.61	0.00
2010 Tacom	AAA	12	0	0	10	17.1	71	14	5	4	0	1	0	0	5	0	18	1	0	1	0	1.000	0	2- -	-	2.00	2.08
2011 Tacom	AAA	30	0	0	26	42.1	176	34	17	13	1	1	1	5	12	1	35	1	0	2	4	.333	0	11- -	-	2.48	2.76
2012 Drham	AAA	42	0	0	17	67.2	297	85	45	42	6	0	1	0	17	0	71	4	2	2	6	.250	0	2- -	-	4.88	5.59
2011 Sea	AL	25	0	0	8	32.2	142	34	22	22	2	2	1	0	13	1	29	5	0	1	1	.500	0	0-0	2	3.96	6.06
2012 TB	AL	3	0	0	2	3.1	21	9	7	7	0	0	2	0	3	0	2	0	0	0	0	-	0	0-0	0	17.54	18.90
2 ML YEARS		28	0	0	10	36.0	163	43	29	29	2	2	3	0	16	1	31	5	0	1	1	.500	0	0-0	2	4.99	7.25

Lucas Luetge

Pitches: L **Bats:** L **Pos:** RP-63 — LOOT-key — **Ht:** 6'4" **Wt:** 205 **Born:** 3/24/1987 **Age:** 26

Year	Team	Lg	G	GS	CG	GF	IP	BFP	H	R	ER	HR	SH	SF	HB	TBB	IBB	SO	WP	Bk	W	L	Pct	Sh	Sv-Op	Hld	ERC	ERA
2008	Helena	R+	5	1	0	1	14.0	54	5	2	0	0	0	0	1	5	0	13	4	0	4	0	1.000	0	0- -	-	0.88	0.00
2008	WV	A	8	6	0	0	36.1	150	35	16	15	2	0	1	0	10	0	33	4	1	2	1	.667	0	0- -	-	3.12	3.72
2009	BrvdCt	A+	27	7	0	4	92.1	405	93	55	46	6	4	4	9	38	0	75	5	0	6	7	.462	0	2- -	-	4.32	4.48
2010	BrvdCt	A+	16	1	0	2	35.1	145	36	10	9	1	1	1	1	10	1	21	6	0	1	1	.500	0	0- -	-	3.42	2.29
2010	Hntsvl	AA	23	2	0	3	44.0	203	52	25	17	4	1	1	2	17	1	47	6	0	3	2	.600	0	0- -	-	5.02	3.48
2011	Hntsvl	AA	46	1	0	6	69.0	286	63	29	24	3	4	3	1	23	4	69	6	0	1	3	.250	0	3- -	-	2.97	3.13
2012	Sea	AL	63	0	0	16	40.2	178	37	20	18	3	1	3	1	24	6	38	5	0	2	2	.500	0	2-3	12	4.01	3.98

Hector Luna

Bats: R **Throws:** R **Pos:** PH-15; 1B-10; LF-2; 3B-1 — LUE-na — **Ht:** 6'1" **Wt:** 190 **Born:** 2/1/1980 **Age:** 33

Year	Team	Lg	G	AB	H	2B	3B	HR	(Hm	Rd)	TB	R	RBI	RC	TBB	IBB	SO	HBP	SH	SF	SB	CS	SB%	GDP	Avg	OBP	Slg
2012	LV*	AAA	62	220	62	12	2	7	(-	-)	99	33	28	34	15	0	40	2	0	3	2	0	1.00	10	.282	.329	.450
2012	Indy*	AAA	4	16	8	1	0	1	(-	-)	12	5	5	5	1	0	1	0	0	0	0	0	-	0	.500	.529	.750
2004	StL	NL	83	173	43	7	2	3	(1	2)	63	25	22	20	13	0	37	2	1	3	6	3	.67	2	.249	.304	.364
2005	StL	NL	64	137	39	10	2	1	(0	1)	56	26	18	19	9	0	25	4	2	1	10	2	.83	4	.285	.344	.409
2006	2 Tms		113	350	100	21	2	6	(1	5)	143	41	38	46	27	1	60	1	0	1	5	4	.56	7	.286	.338	.409
2007	Tor	AL	22	42	7	0	0	1	(1	0)	10	5	4	1	2	0	10	1	0	1	2	0	1.00	6	.167	.217	.238
2008	Tor	AL	2	1	1	0	0	0	(0	0)	1	0	0	0	0	0	0	0	0	0	0	1	.00	0	1.000	1.000	1.000
2010	Fla	NL	27	29	4	1	0	2	(2	0)	11	2	4	0	0	0	13	0	0	1	0	1	.00	0	.138	.133	.379
2012	Phi	NL	28	62	14	2	0	2	(0	2)	22	5	10	7	4	0	14	0	0	0	0	0	-	1	.226	.273	.355
06	StL	NL	76	223	65	14	1	4	(1	3)	93	27	21	32	21	1	34	1	0	0	5	3	.63	3	.291	.355	.417
06	Cle		37	127	35	7	1	2	(0	2)	50	14	17	14	6	0	26	0	0	1	0	1	.00	4	.276	.306	.394
	Postseason		5	9	0	0	0	0	(0	0)	0	0	0	0	0	0	5	0	0	0	0	0	-	0	.000	.000	.000
7 ML YEARS			339	794	208	41	6	15	(5	10)	306	104	96	93	55	1	159	8	3	7	23	11	.68	14	.262	.314	.385

Zach Lutz

Bats: R **Throws:** R **Pos:** PH-6; 1B-1 — **Ht:** 6'1" **Wt:** 220 **Born:** 6/3/1986 **Age:** 27

Year	Team	Lg	G	AB	H	2B	3B	HR	(Hm	Rd)	TB	R	RBI	RC	TBB	IBB	SO	HBP	SH	SF	SB	CS	SB%	GDP	Avg	OBP	Slg
2007	Bklyn	A-	1	2	0	0	0	0	(-	-)	0	0	0	0	0	0	0	0	0	0	0	0	-	0	.000	.000	.000
2008	Bklyn	A-	24	72	24	4	0	3	(-	-)	37	9	12	15	14	0	12	0	0	0	0	2	.00	2	.333	.442	.514
2009	StLuci	A+	99	356	101	19	2	11	(-	-)	157	46	62	63	50	1	72	7	0	2	1	1	.50	10	.284	.381	.441
2009	Bnghtn	AA	8	29	6	1	0	0	(-	-)	7	0	2	2	5	0	7	0	0	0	0	0	-	1	.207	.324	.241
2010	Bnghtn	AA	61	225	65	14	0	17	(-	-)	130	42	42	49	33	0	63	4	1	0	0	2	.00	9	.289	.389	.578
2010	Mets	R	5	19	6	1	0	1	(-	-)	10	2	4	3	1	0	4	0	0	0	0	0	-	0	.316	.350	.526
2010	StLuci	A+	1	4	0	0	0	0	(-	-)	0	0	0	0	0	0	2	0	0	0	0	0	-	1	.000	.000	.000
2010	Buffalo	AAA	5	20	6	4	0	1	(-	-)	13	3	9	4	2	0	3	0	0	0	0	0	-	0	.300	.364	.650
2011	Buffalo	AAA	61	220	65	12	0	11	(-	-)	110	38	31	42	27	0	70	3	0	0	0	0	-	2	.295	.380	.500
2011	StLuci	A+	2	8	0	0	0	0	(-	-)	0	0	1	0	1	0	2	0	0	0	0	0	-	1	.000	.111	.000
2012	Buffalo	AAA	72	244	73	16	1	10	(-	-)	121	34	35	51	42	1	75	5	1	2	0	0	-	7	.299	.410	.496
2012	StLuci	A+	6	20	5	2	0	1	(-	-)	10	2	8	4	4	0	5	0	0	2	0	0	-	1	.250	.346	.500
2012	NYM	NL	7	11	1	0	0	0	(0	0)	1	1	0	0	0	0	5	0	0	0	0	0	-	0	.091	.091	.091

Jordan Lyles

Pitches: R **Bats:** R **Pos:** SP-25 — **Ht:** 6'4" **Wt:** 210 **Born:** 10/19/1990 **Age:** 22

Year	Team	Lg	G	GS	CG	GF	IP	BFP	H	R	ER	HR	SH	SF	HB	TBB	IBB	SO	WP	Bk	W	L	Pct	Sh	Sv-Op	Hld	ERC	ERA
2008	Grnville	R	13	13	0	0	49.2	208	44	26	22	4	0	2	3	10	0	64	1	0	3	3	.500	0	0- -	-	2.73	3.99
2008	TriCity	A-	2	2	0	0	5.2	31	7	5	4	2	0	0	0	7	0	4	1	0	0	0	-	0	0- -	1	11.36	6.35
2009	Lxngtn	A	26	26	0	0	144.2	601	134	56	52	5	1	5	14	38	1	167	6	0	7	11	.389	0	0- -	-	3.11	3.24
2010	CpChr	AA	21	20	1	0	127.0	541	133	54	44	10	1	4	6	35	2	115	3	1	7	9	.438	0	0- -	-	3.84	3.12
2010	RdRck	AAA	6	6	1	0	31.2	153	48	21	19	2	1	1	2	11	0	22	0	0	3	3	.000	0	0- -	-	6.89	5.40
2011	OKCity	AAA	12	10	0	0	62.1	257	64	25	25	4	2	2	5	17	2	42	0	0	3	3	.500	0	0- -	-	3.91	3.61
2012	OKCity	AAA	7	7	0	0	40.2	168	41	16	16	2	1	1	6	8	0	33	1	0	5	0	1.000	0	0- -	-	3.68	3.54
2011	Hou	NL	20	15	0	2	94.0	415	107	56	54	14	7	1	5	26	1	67	0	0	2	8	.200	0	0-0	-	4.87	5.36
2012	Hou	NL	25	25	1	0	141.1	628	159	97	80	20	6	4	5	42	4	99	2	0	5	12	.294	1	0-0	-	4.67	5.09
2 ML YEARS			45	40	1	2	235.1	1043	266	158	136	34	13	5	10	68	5	166	2	0	7	20	.259	1	0-0	0	4.75	5.20

Lance Lynn

Pitches: R **Bats:** R **Pos:** SP-29; RP-6 — **Ht:** 6'5" **Wt:** 250 **Born:** 5/12/1987 **Age:** 26

Year	Team	Lg	G	GS	CG	GF	IP	BFP	H	R	ER	HR	SH	SF	HB	TBB	IBB	SO	WP	Bk	W	L	Pct	Sh	Sv-Op	Hld	ERC	ERA
2008	Batvia	A-	6	4	0	1	18.2	73	12	5	2	0	1	0	1	4	0	22	1	0	1	0	1.000	0	0- -	-	1.36	0.96
2008	QuadC	A	2	2	0	0	8.0	34	8	2	2	0	0	0	1	2	0	7	0	0	0	1	.000	0	0- -	-	5.08	2.25
2009	PlmBh	A+	5	2	0	0	15.2	64	16	4	4	0	1	2	0	3	0	17	0	0	0	0	-	0	0- -	-	2.77	2.30
2009	Sprgfld	AA	22	22	0	0	126.1	532	117	51	41	5	5	5	4	51	0	98	5	0	11	4	.733	0	0- -	-	3.44	2.92
2009	Memp	AAA	1	1	0	0	6.2	28	5	2	2	0	0	0	0	3	0	9	1	0	0	0	-	0	0- -	-	2.24	2.70
2010	Memp	AAA	29	29	0	0	164.0	709	164	96	87	21	4	3	8	62	0	141	2	2	13	10	.565	0	0- -	-	4.40	4.77
2011	Memp	AAA	12	12	0	0	75.0	317	79	33	32	2	4	3	2	25	0	64	2	0	7	3	.700	0	0- -	-	3.78	3.84
2011	StL	NL	18	2	0	2	34.2	136	25	12	12	3	1	0	1	11	1	40	1	0	1	1	.500	0	1-2	3	2.37	3.12
2012	StL	NL	35	29	0	2	176.0	744	168	76	74	16	4	3	10	64	3	180	3	0	18	7	.720	0	0-0	1	3.87	3.78
	Postseason		10	0	0	1	11.0	44	10	4	4	2	0	2	0	5	2	5	0	0	2	0	1.000	0	0-0	1	4.39	3.27
2 ML YEARS			53	31	0	4	210.2	880	193	88	86	19	5	3	11	75	4	220	4	0	19	8	.704	0	1-2	4	3.61	3.67

Brandon Lyon

Pitches: R **Bats:** R **Pos:** RP-67 **Ht:** 6'1" **Wt:** 195 **Born:** 8/10/1979 **Age:** 33

Year	Team	Lg	G	GS	CG	GF	IP	BFP	H	R	ER	HR	SH	SF	HB	TBB	IBB	SO	WP	Bk	W	L	Pct	Sh	Sv-Op	Hld	ERC	ERA
2001	Tor	AL	11	11	0	0	63.0	261	63	31	30	6	2	6	1	15	0	35	0	1	5	4	.556	0	0-0	0	3.50	4.29
2002	Tor	AL	15	10	0	0	62.0	279	78	47	45	14	3	2	2	19	2	30	2	0	1	4	.200	0	0-1	0	6.24	6.53
2003	Bos	AL	49	0	0	31	59.0	273	73	33	27	6	1	4	2	19	5	50	0	0	4	6	.400	0	9-12	2	4.96	4.12
2005	Ari	NL	32	0	0	22	29.1	144	44	25	21	6	2	1	2	10	2	17	1	1	0	2	.000	0	14-15	1	7.72	6.44
2006	Ari	NL	68	0	0	22	69.1	293	68	32	30	7	3	4	0	22	7	46	1	0	2	4	.333	0	0-7	23	3.49	3.89
2007	Ari	NL	73	0	0	20	74.0	307	70	25	22	2	3	2	1	22	2	40	3	1	6	4	.600	0	2-5	35	2.93	2.68
2008	Ari	NL	61	0	0	50	59.1	265	75	34	31	7	2	1	0	13	1	44	1	0	3	5	.375	0	26-31	3	4.86	4.70
2009	Det	AL	65	0	0	27	78.2	314	56	25	25	7	5	3	2	31	9	57	3	0	6	5	.545	0	3-6	15	2.46	2.86
2010	Hou	NL	79	0	0	28	78.0	333	68	28	27	2	4	0	3	31	12	54	3	0	6	6	.500	0	20-22	19	2.73	3.12
2011	Hou	NL	15	0	0	13	13.1	71	27	17	17	4	0	0	0	5	1	6	1	0	3	3	.500	0	4-8	0	12.27	11.48
2012	2 Tms		67	0	0	21	61.0	258	56	21	21	5	1	1	3	20	3	63	6	0	4	2	.667	0	1-3	12	3.32	3.10
12	Hou	NL	37	0	0	11	36.0	154	37	13	13	3	0	0	2	11	2	35	5	0	0	2	.000	0	0-2	5	3.89	3.25
12	Tor	AL	30	0	0	10	25.0	104	19	8	8	2	1	1	1	9	1	28	1	0	4	0	1.000	0	1-1	7	2.57	2.88
	Postseason		5	0	0	1	6.0	20	1	0	0	0	0	0	0	1	0	5	0	0	0	0	-	0	0-0	2	0.19	0.00
	11 ML YEARS		535	21	0	234	647.0	2798	678	318	296	66	26	24	16	207	44	442	21	3	40	45	.471	0	79-110	110	4.00	4.12

Mike MacDougal

Pitches: R **Bats:** B **Pos:** RP-7 **Ht:** 6'4" **Wt:** 180 **Born:** 3/5/1977 **Age:** 36

Year	Team	Lg	G	GS	CG	GF	IP	BFP	H	R	ER	HR	SH	SF	HB	TBB	IBB	SO	WP	Bk	W	L	Pct	Sh	Sv-Op	Hld	ERC	ERA
2012	Iowa*	AAA	19	0	0	5	18.1	98	31	18	16	3	0	1	1	16	2	11	3	0	1	2	.333	0	1- -	-	11.55	7.85
2012	Syrcse*	AAA	12	0	0	8	10.2	46	9	5	5	1	0	0	0	8	1	14	1	0	1	1	.500	0	2- -	-	4.56	4.22
2001	KC	AL	3	3	0	0	15.1	67	18	10	8	2	0	0	1	4	0	7	3	0	1	1	.500	0	0-0	0	5.04	4.70
2002	KC	AL	6	0	0	1	9.0	38	5	5	5	0	0	0	0	7	1	10	1	0	0	1	.000	0	0-0	0	2.26	5.00
2003	KC	AL	68	0	0	61	64.0	285	64	36	29	4	3	2	8	32	0	57	6	0	3	5	.375	0	27-35	1	4.76	4.08
2004	KC	AL	13	0	0	8	11.1	61	16	8	7	2	0	0	1	9	0	14	2	0	1	1	.500	0	1-3	0	9.04	5.56
2005	KC	AL	68	0	0	53	70.1	298	69	32	26	6	1	1	3	24	2	72	6	1	5	6	.455	0	21-25	0	3.80	3.33
2006	2 Tms	AL	29	0	0	7	29.0	110	21	5	5	1	1	0	1	6	0	21	1	0	1	1	.500	0	1-2	11	1.80	1.55
2007	CWS	AL	54	0	0	8	42.1	208	50	37	32	3	0	1	2	33	3	39	8	0	2	5	.286	0	0-3	19	6.49	6.80
2008	CWS	AL	16	0	0	8	17.0	78	16	4	4	0	0	0	2	12	2	12	4	1	0	0	-	0	0-0	4	4.45	2.12
2009	2 Tms		57	0	0	41	54.1	246	52	31	26	3	2	3	3	38	3	34	10	0	1	1	.500	0	20-21	0	4.87	4.31
2010	StL	NL	17	0	0	7	18.2	92	23	15	15	1	1	0	1	12	2	14	1	0	1	1	.500	0	0-1	0	5.91	7.23
2011	LAD	NL	69	0	0	14	57.0	247	54	16	13	3	3	2	3	29	3	41	3	0	3	1	.750	0	1-2	14	4.05	2.05
2012	LAD	NL	7	0	0	1	5.2	32	9	5	5	0	0	0	0	6	0	4	0	0	0	0	-	0	0-0	2	9.43	7.94
06	KC	AL	4	0	0	3	4.0	13	2	0	0	0	0	0	0	0	0	2	0	0	0	0	-	0	1-1	0	0.58	0.00
06	CWS	AL	25	0	0	4	25.0	97	19	5	5	1	1	0	1	6	0	19	1	0	1	1	.500	0	0-1	11	2.10	1.80
09	CWS	AL	5	0	0	1	4.1	25	7	6	6	0	0	0	0	7	0	3	3	0	0	0	-	0	0-0	0	13.09	12.46
09	Was	NL	52	0	0	40	50.0	221	45	25	20	3	2	3	3	31	3	31	7	0	1	1	.500	0	20-21	0	4.26	3.60
	12 ML YEARS		407	3	0	209	394.0	1762	397	204	175	25	11	9	25	212	16	325	45	2	18	23	.439	0	71-92	47	4.60	4.00

Manny Machado

Bats: R **Throws:** R **Pos:** 3B-51 **Ht:** 6'3" **Wt:** 185 **Born:** 7/6/1992 **Age:** 20

Year	Team	Lg	G	AB	H	2B	3B	HR	(Hm	Rd)	TB	R	RBI	RC	TBB	IBB	SO	HBP	SH	SF	SB	CS	SB%	GDP	Avg	OBP	Slg
2010	Orioles	R	2	7	1	0	0	1	(-	-)	4	1	2	0	0	0	1	0	0	0	0	0	-	0	.143	.143	.571
2010	Abrdn	A-	7	29	10	1	1	0	(-	-)	13	2	3	5	3	0	2	0	0	0	0	0	-	0	.345	.406	.448
2011	Dlmrva	A	38	145	40	8	2	6	(-	-)	70	24	24	27	23	4	25	1	0	1	3	1	.75	8	.276	.376	.483
2011	Frdrck	A+	63	237	58	12	3	5	(-	-)	91	24	26	28	22	0	48	0	0	1	8	5	.62	6	.245	.308	.384
2012	Bowie	AA	109	402	107	26	5	11	(-	-)	176	60	59	66	48	0	70	6	1	2	13	4	.76	15	.266	.352	.438
2012	Bal	AL	51	191	50	8	3	7	(7	0)	85	24	26	29	9	0	38	0	1	1	2	0	1.00	6	.262	.294	.445

Jean Machi

Pitches: R **Bats:** R **Pos:** RP-8
GENE ma-SHEE **Ht:** 6'0" **Wt:** 260 **Born:** 2/1/1982 **Age:** 31

Year	Team	Lg	G	GS	CG	GF	IP	BFP	H	R	ER	HR	SH	SF	HB	TBB	IBB	SO	WP	Bk	W	L	Pct	Sh	Sv-Op	Hld	ERC	ERA
2002	Phillies	R	10	2	0	4	27.0	105	11	4	3	0	2	1	1	16	0	22	2	0	2	0	1.000	0	1- -	-	1.45	1.00
2003	Batvia	A-	8	8	0	0	32.0	139	30	21	17	1	1	2	7	13	0	19	2	0	2	4	.333	0	0- -	-	4.21	4.78
2005	Visalia	A+	31	14	0	9	97.0	456	113	76	65	8	0	5	10	58	0	106	16	1	3	11	.214	0	3- -	-	6.21	6.03
2005	Mont	AA	1	0	0	0	0.2	7	4	4	4	1	0	0	0	1	0	0	0	0	0	0	-	0	0- -	-	71.48	54.00
2006	Mont	AA	49	0	0	32	71.2	309	68	25	21	2	0	1	4	37	1	68	6	0	6	1	.857	0	16- -	-	4.01	2.64
2007	NHam	AA	48	0	0	15	81.2	333	68	35	32	8	1	2	3	24	3	56	5	2	2	4	.333	0	2- -	-	2.86	3.53
2008	NHam	AA	21	9	0	3	69.2	316	74	37	36	3	2	2	3	40	2	51	1	0	2	6	.250	0	1- -	-	4.84	4.65
2009	Altna	AA	28	0	0	22	34.2	142	28	12	8	2	4	1	0	13	2	25	5	0	2	3	.400	0	6- -	-	2.61	2.08
2009	Indy	AAA	13	0	0	11	17.0	62	8	4	4	1	0	2	0	6	0	12	0	0	1	1	.500	0	6- -	-	1.32	2.12
2010	Indy	AAA	58	0	0	53	59.2	260	51	29	26	6	2	3	2	32	2	58	5	0	5	5	.500	0	23- -	-	3.86	3.92
2011	Fresno	AAA	3	0	0	0	4.0	17	5	4	4	0	0	0	0	0	0	6	0	0	1	1	.500	0	0- -	-	3.14	9.00
2012	Fresno	AAA	53	0	0	34	56.2	257	67	29	25	7	3	1	3	17	1	44	0	0	2	1	.667	0	15- -	-	4.96	3.97
2012	SF	NL	8	0	0	5	6.2	28	7	5	5	2	0	0	0	1	0	4	0	0	0	0	-	0	0-0	0	4.56	6.75

Ryan Madson

Pitches: R Bats: L Pos: P   Ht: 6'6" Wt: 200 Born: 8/28/1980 Age: 32

Year Team	Lg	G	GS	CG	GF	IP	BFP	H	R	ER	HR	SH	SF	HB	TBB	IBB	SO	WP	Bk	W	L	Pct	Sh	Sv-Op	Hld	ERC	ERA
2003 Phi	NL	1	0	0	0	2.0	6	0	0	0	0	0	0	0	0	0	0	0	0	0	0	-	0	0-0	0	0.00	0.00
2004 Phi	NL	52	1	0	14	77.0	312	68	23	20	6	1	1	5	19	4	55	7	0	9	3	.750	0	1-2	7	2.95	2.34
2005 Phi	NL	78	0	0	10	87.0	365	84	44	40	11	5	5	6	25	6	79	6	1	6	5	.545	0	0-7	32	3.83	4.14
2006 Phi	NL	50	17	0	8	134.1	620	176	92	85	20	9	3	10	50	4	99	12	0	11	9	.550	0	2-4	6	6.50	5.69
2007 Phi	NL	38	0	0	9	56.0	237	48	19	19	5	2	2	2	23	4	43	2	2	2	2	.500	0	1-2	7	3.28	3.05
2008 Phi	NL	76	0	0	14	82.2	340	79	29	28	6	3	2	1	23	4	67	2	1	4	2	.667	0	1-3	17	3.20	3.05
2009 Phi	NL	79	0	0	28	77.1	320	73	29	28	7	3	1	3	22	3	78	1	0	5	5	.500	0	10-16	26	3.39	3.26
2010 Phi	NL	55	0	0	21	53.0	217	42	16	15	4	2	0	4	13	3	64	2	0	6	2	.750	0	5-10	15	2.42	2.55
2011 Phi	NL	62	0	0	46	60.2	246	54	16	16	2	6	1	1	16	8	62	0	0	4	2	.667	0	32-34	3	2.45	2.37
Postseason		33	0	0	11	35.0	145	33	9	9	2	2	2	1	10	2	43	2	0	2	1	.667	0	2-6	7	3.09	2.31
9 ML YEARS		491	18	0	150	630.0	2663	624	268	251	61	31	15	32	191	36	547	32	4	47	30	.610	0	52-78	113	3.76	3.59

Paul Maholm

Pitches: L Bats: L Pos: SP-31; RP-1   mah-HALL-uhm   Ht: 6'2" Wt: 220 Born: 6/25/1982 Age: 31

Year Team	Lg	G	GS	CG	GF	IP	BFP	H	R	ER	HR	SH	SF	HB	TBB	IBB	SO	WP	Bk	W	L	Pct	Sh	Sv-Op	Hld	ERC	ERA
2005 Pit	NL	6	6	0	0	41.1	168	31	10	10	2	0	0	3	17	0	26	0	0	3	1	.750	0	0-0	0	2.79	2.18
2006 Pit	NL	30	30	0	0	176.0	788	202	98	93	19	7	4	12	81	6	117	3	1	8	10	.444	0	0-0	0	5.58	4.76
2007 Pit	NL	29	29	2	0	177.2	765	204	110	99	22	13	6	6	49	3	105	5	0	10	15	.400	1	0-0	0	4.77	5.02
2008 Pit	NL	31	31	1	0	206.1	853	201	89	85	21	8	8	9	63	2	139	2	1	9	9	.500	0	0-0	0	3.84	3.71
2009 Pit	NL	31	31	0	0	194.2	836	221	102	96	14	7	1	6	60	4	119	11	1	8	9	.471	0	0-0	0	4.45	4.44
2010 Pit	NL	32	32	1	0	185.1	840	228	119	105	15	10	6	9	62	2	102	2	0	9	15	.375	1	0-0	0	5.14	5.10
2011 Pit	NL	26	26	1	0	162.1	687	160	72	66	11	8	10	8	50	6	97	3	0	6	14	.300	1	0-0	0	3.57	3.66
2012 2 Tms	NL	32	31	1	0	189.0	786	178	80	77	20	7	4	11	53	3	140	5	0	13	11	.542	1	0-0	0	3.57	3.67
12 ChC	NL	21	20	0	0	120.1	503	115	51	50	12	5	4	10	34	2	81	4	0	9	6	.600	0	0-0	0	3.73	3.74
12 Atl	NL	11	11	1	0	68.2	283	63	29	27	8	2	0	1	19	1	59	1	0	4	5	.444	1	0-0	0	3.31	3.54
8 ML YEARS		217	216	6	0	1332.2	5723	1425	680	631	124	60	39	64	435	26	845	31	3	66	84	.440	4	0-0	0	4.34	4.26

Joe Mahoney

Bats: L Throws: L Pos: 1B-2   Ht: 6'6" Wt: 240 Born: 2/1/1987 Age: 26

Year Team	Lg	G	AB	H	2B	3B	HR	(Hm	Rd)	TB	R	RBI	RC	TBB	IBB	SO	HBP	SH	SF	SB	CS	SB%	GDP	Avg	OBP	Slg
2007 Abrdn	A-	65	242	65	10	2	9	(-	-)	106	31	44	36	19	2	57	4	0	2	1	1	.50	5	.269	.330	.438
2008 Dlmrva	A	95	352	78	22	1	7	(-	-)	123	37	61	35	24	1	96	4	1	6	2	0	1.00	7	.222	.275	.349
2009 Dlmrva	A	108	395	110	16	7	7	(-	-)	161	61	53	60	30	2	93	3	0	4	29	1	.97	7	.278	.331	.408
2009 Frdrck	A+	7	30	8	4	0	1	(-	-)	15	2	5	3	0	0	10	0	0	1	0	1	.00	0	.267	.258	.500
2010 Frdrck	A+	72	271	81	18	0	9	(-	-)	126	37	49	45	22	5	56	4	0	2	5	3	.63	4	.299	.358	.465
2010 Bowie	AA	52	191	61	12	2	9	(-	-)	104	30	29	39	17	2	39	1	0	0	9	1	.90	2	.319	.378	.545
2011 Bowie	AA	85	315	91	24	5	11	(-	-)	158	43	67	56	25	1	84	6	0	9	7	2	.78	2	.289	.344	.502
2011 Frdrck	A+	3	8	4	2	0	0	(-	-)	6	0	2	3	4	0	1	0	0	0	0	0	-	0	.500	.667	.750
2012 Norfolk	AAA	132	491	130	29	1	10	(-	-)	191	54	56	63	34	6	95	6	0	4	4	2	.67	8	.265	.318	.389
2012 Bal	AL	2	4	0	0	0	0	(0	0)	0	0	0	0	0	0	0	0	0	0	0	0	-	0	.000	.000	.000

Mitch Maier

Bats: L Throws: R Pos: CF-16; PH-7; RF-6; DH-5; PR-5   MY-err   Ht: 6'3" Wt: 210 Born: 6/30/1982 Age: 31

Year Team	Lg	G	AB	H	2B	3B	HR	(Hm	Rd)	TB	R	RBI	RC	TBB	IBB	SO	HBP	SH	SF	SB	CS	SB%	GDP	Avg	OBP	Slg
2012 Omha*	AAA	38	132	38	4	1	4	(-	-)	56	25	17	23	21	1	31	1	0	2	2	1	.67	2	.288	.385	.424
2006 KC	AL	5	13	2	0	0	0	(0	0)	2	3	0	0	2	0	4	0	0	0	0	0	-	1	.154	.267	.154
2008 KC	AL	34	91	26	1	1	0	(0	0)	29	9	9	7	2	0	18	2	2	0	0	2	.00	3	.286	.316	.319
2009 KC	AL	127	341	83	15	3	3	(1	2)	113	42	31	42	43	2	76	4	7	2	9	2	.82	6	.243	.333	.331
2010 KC	AL	117	373	98	15	6	5	(1	4)	140	41	39	49	41	2	68	0	4	3	3	2	.60	3	.263	.333	.375
2011 KC	AL	45	95	22	4	3	0	(0	0)	32	19	7	11	16	0	32	1	0	1	1	0	1.00	1	.232	.345	.337
2012 KC	AL	32	64	11	1	1	2	(0	2)	20	8	7	5	8	0	24	0	1	1	2	0	1.00	0	.172	.260	.313
6 ML YEARS		360	977	242	36	14	10	(2	8)	336	122	93	114	112	4	222	7	14	7	15	6	.71	14	.248	.327	.344

Scott Maine

Pitches: L Bats: L Pos: RP-30   Ht: 6'3" Wt: 215 Born: 2/2/1985 Age: 28

Year Team	Lg	G	GS	CG	GF	IP	BFP	H	R	ER	HR	SH	SF	HB	TBB	IBB	SO	WP	Bk	W	L	Pct	Sh	Sv-Op	Hld	ERC	ERA
2012 Iowa*	AAA	28	0	0	20	34.1	141	21	12	11	1	0	0	3	13	1	29	1	0	4	2	.667	0	5- -	-	1.80	2.88
2012 Clmbs*	AAA	2	0	0	0	2.0	7	2	0	0	0	0	0	0	0	0	0	0	0	0	0	-	0	0- -	-	2.31	0.00
2010 ChC	NL	13	0	0	4	13.0	54	9	4	3	1	0	1	0	5	1	11	0	0	0	0	-	0	0-0	2	2.08	2.08
2011 ChC	NL	7	0	0	3	7.0	37	11	8	8	4	0	0	0	5	0	5	0	0	0	0	-	0	0-0	1	13.26	10.29
2012 2 Tms		30	0	0	9	26.2	127	30	18	18	3	1	4	5	15	0	32	3	0	2	3	.400	0	0-1	1	6.35	6.08
12 ChC	NL	21	0	0	5	20.2	94	17	11	11	2	1	3	4	12	0	26	2	0	1	1	.500	0	0-1	1	4.46	4.79
12 Cle	AL	9	0	0	4	6.0	33	13	7	7	1	0	1	1	3	0	6	1	0	1	2	.333	0	0-0	0	14.28	10.50
3 ML YEARS		50	0	0	16	46.2	218	50	30	29	8	1	5	5	25	1	48	3	0	2	3	.400	0	0-1	4	5.93	5.59

Carlos Maldonado

Bats: R Throws: R Pos: C-4; PR-1   Ht: 6'2" Wt: 290 Born: 1/3/1979 Age: 34

Year	Team	Lg	G	AB	H	2B	3B	HR	(Hm	Rd)	TB	R	RBI	RC	TBB	IBB	SO	HBP	SH	SF	SB	CS	SB%	GDP	Avg	OBP	Slg
2012	Syrcse*	AAA	51	157	33	7	0	6	(-	-)	58	20	11	20	27	0	42	0	3	0	0	0	-	7	.210	.326	.369
2012	Ptomc*	A+	3	9	1	0	0	0	(-	-)	1	0	0	0	2	0	4	0	0	0	0	0	-	0	.111	.273	.111
2006	Pit	NL	8	19	2	0	0	0	(0	0)	2	0	0	0	1	1	10	0	0	0	1	0	1.00	0	.105	.150	.105
2007	Pit	NL	13	24	5	1	0	2	(0	2)	12	2	4	2	5	2	8	0	0	1	0	0	-	2	.208	.333	.500
2010	Was	NL	4	11	3	0	0	1	(0	1)	6	1	3	3	1	0	2	0	0	0	0	0	-	0	.273	.333	.545
2012	Was	NL	4	9	0	0	0	0	(0	0)	0	0	1	0	2	0	4	0	1	0	0	0	-	0	.000	.182	.000
	4 ML YEARS		29	63	10	1	0	3	(0	3)	20	3	8	5	9	3	24	0	1	1	1	0	1.00	2	.159	.260	.317

Martin Maldonado

Bats: R Throws: R Pos: C-69; PH-15; 1B-4   Ht: 6'1" Wt: 224 Born: 8/16/1986 Age: 26

Year	Team	Lg	G	AB	H	2B	3B	HR	(Hm	Rd)	TB	R	RBI	RC	TBB	IBB	SO	HBP	SH	SF	SB	CS	SB%	GDP	Avg	OBP	Slg
2004	Angels	R	25	60	13	1	0	0	(-	-)	14	5	4	3	3	0	13	2	0	0	2	1	.67	4	.217	.277	.233
2005	Angels	R	27	86	22	2	0	0	(-	-)	24	6	10	6	2	0	9	1	1	1	0	0	-	3	.256	.278	.279
2005	Orem	R+	9	32	8	0	0	1	(-	-)	11	4	2	3	2	0	6	0	0	0	0	0	-	1	.250	.294	.344
2006	Angels	R	21	63	14	1	1	0	(-	-)	17	9	6	5	7	0	12	3	3	0	0	0	-	3	.222	.329	.270
2007	WV	A-	66	208	46	8	0	2	(-	-)	60	20	22	21	14	0	36	13	6	1	2	0	1.00	6	.221	.309	.288
2008	BrvdCt	A+	34	94	25	8	0	0	(-	-)	33	8	9	13	8	0	17	5	2	1	3	1	.75	4	.266	.352	.351
2008	Hntsvl	AA	31	98	19	2	0	2	(-	-)	27	4	8	5	4	0	24	0	4	0	0	0	-	5	.194	.225	.276
2009	BrvdCt	A+	81	251	50	9	0	2	(-	-)	65	25	21	22	30	0	51	7	9	2	2	1	.67	6	.199	.300	.259
2009	Nashv	AAA	7	18	6	1	0	0	(-	-)	7	1	3	2	1	0	2	0	0	1	0	0	-	0	.333	.350	.389
2009	Wisc	A	7	19	2	0	0	0	(-	-)	2	1	2	0	2	0	7	0	0	1	1	0	1.00	1	.105	.182	.105
2010	BrvdCt	A+	10	33	4	0	0	0	(-	-)	4	1	3	0	1	0	8	2	0	1	1	0	1.00	0	.121	.189	.121
2010	Hntsvl	AA	34	103	26	6	0	2	(-	-)	38	9	12	14	9	0	24	7	2	2	1	2	.33	5	.252	.347	.369
2010	Nashv	AAA	52	174	44	9	0	7	(-	-)	74	19	26	24	14	2	45	2	7	4	0	1	.00	6	.253	.309	.425
2011	Nashv	AAA	39	134	43	5	0	8	(-	-)	72	23	25	29	16	0	21	5	4	1	0	0	-	6	.321	.410	.537
2011	Hntsvl	AA	64	208	55	13	0	3	(-	-)	77	24	34	29	19	0	56	9	3	2	2	1	.67	6	.264	.349	.370
2012	Nashv	AAA	35	121	24	6	0	4	(-	-)	42	10	13	11	9	0	37	4	1	3	0	2	.00	3	.198	.270	.347
2011	Mil	NL	3	1	0	0	0	0	(0	0)	0	0	0	0	0	0	1	0	0	0	0	0	-	0	.000	.000	.000
2012	Mil	NL	78	233	62	9	0	8	(6	2)	95	22	30	28	17	0	56	2	4	0	1	1	.50	5	.266	.321	.408
	2 ML YEARS		81	234	62	9	0	8	(6	2)	95	22	30	28	17	0	57	2	4	0	1	1	.50	5	.265	.320	.406

Matt Maloney

Pitches: L Bats: L Pos: RP-9   Ht: 6'4" Wt: 210 Born: 1/16/1984 Age: 29

	HOW MUCH HE PITCHED						WHAT HE GAVE UP											THE RESULTS						
Year	Team	Lg	G	GS	CG	GF	IP	BFP	H	R	ER	HR	SH	SF	HB	TBB	IBB	SO	WP	Bk	W	L	Pct	Sh	Sv-Op	Hld	ERC	ERA
2012	Roch*	AAA	8	6	0	1	24.0	128	46	33	26	5	2	1	3	7	1	16	2	1	0	4	.000	0	0- -	-	10.70	9.75
2009	Cin	NL	7	7	0	0	40.2	170	43	22	22	9	2	4	3	8	1	28	0	0	2	4	.333	0	0-0	0	4.76	4.87
2010	Cin	NL	7	2	0	0	20.2	86	20	7	7	2	2	0	1	5	1	13	0	0	2	2	.500	0	0-0	0	3.39	3.05
2011	Cin	NL	8	2	0	1	18.2	96	36	21	19	7	1	2	1	4	0	13	0	0	0	3	.000	0	0-0	0	11.82	9.16
2012	Min	AL	9	0	0	2	11.0	52	17	10	10	2	0	1	1	1	0	5	0	0	1	0	1.000	0	0-0	0	6.91	8.18
	4 ML YEARS		31	11	0	3	91.0	404	116	60	58	20	5	7	6	18	2	59	0	0	5	9	.357	0	0-0	0	5.98	5.74

Jeff Manship

Pitches: R Bats: R Pos: RP-12   Ht: 6'2" Wt: 212 Born: 1/16/1985 Age: 28

	HOW MUCH HE PITCHED						WHAT HE GAVE UP											THE RESULTS						
Year	Team	Lg	G	GS	CG	GF	IP	BFP	H	R	ER	HR	SH	SF	HB	TBB	IBB	SO	WP	Bk	W	L	Pct	Sh	Sv-Op	Hld	ERC	ERA
2012	Roch*	AAA	22	11	0	2	80.1	337	79	27	26	5	0	1	1	35	0	52	1	0	6	3	.667	0	0- -	-	4.05	2.91
2009	Min	AL	11	5	0	1	31.2	146	39	21	20	4	1	3	1	15	0	21	2	0	1	1	.500	0	0-0	0	6.11	5.68
2010	Min	AL	13	1	0	1	29.0	124	34	20	17	3	1	1	0	6	0	21	0	0	2	1	.667	0	0-0	0	4.31	5.28
2011	Min	AL	5	0	0	1	3.1	19	5	3	3	0	0	2	0	4	1	2	0	0	0	0	-	0	0-0	0	8.73	8.10
2012	Min	AL	12	0	0	2	21.2	98	29	19	19	4	1	0	1	7	1	12	0	0	0	0	-	0	0-0	1	6.67	7.89
	4 ML YEARS		41	6	0	5	85.2	387	107	63	59	11	3	6	2	32	2	56	2	0	3	2	.600	0	0-0	1	5.73	6.20

Shaun Marcum

Pitches: R Bats: R Pos: SP-21   Ht: 6'0" Wt: 195 Born: 12/14/1981 Age: 31

	HOW MUCH HE PITCHED						WHAT HE GAVE UP											THE RESULTS						
Year	Team	Lg	G	GS	CG	GF	IP	BFP	H	R	ER	HR	SH	SF	HB	TBB	IBB	SO	WP	Bk	W	L	Pct	Sh	Sv-Op	Hld	ERC	ERA
2012	Wisc*	A	3	3	0	0	12.2	50	9	5	4	1	0	0	0	3	0	10	0	0	1	0	1.000	0	0- -	-	1.86	2.84
2005	Tor	AL	5	0	0	3	8.0	32	6	0	0	0	0	0	0	4	0	4	0	0	0	0	-	0	0-0	0	2.58	0.00
2006	Tor	AL	21	14	0	3	78.1	357	87	44	44	14	1	2	4	38	3	65	1	0	3	4	.429	0	0-0	0	5.80	5.06
2007	Tor	AL	38	25	0	6	159.0	660	149	76	73	27	3	3	5	49	1	122	1	0	12	6	.667	0	1-2	1	4.00	4.13
2008	Tor	AL	25	25	0	0	151.1	630	126	60	57	21	1	3	8	50	2	123	3	0	9	7	.563	0	0-0	0	3.32	3.39
2010	Tor	AL	31	31	1	0	195.1	800	181	84	79	24	1	3	6	43	3	165	3	0	13	8	.619	0	0-0	0	3.24	3.64
2011	Mil	NL	33	33	0	0	200.2	823	175	84	79	22	6	6	0	57	3	158	6	0	13	7	.650	0	0-0	0	2.97	3.54
2012	Mil	NL	21	21	0	0	124.0	527	116	57	51	16	6	2	4	41	2	109	3	2	7	4	.636	0	0-0	0	3.71	3.70
	Postseason		3	3	0	0	9.2	49	17	16	16	3	1	0	0	5	1	5	0	0	0	3	.000	0	0-0	0	11.38	14.90
	7 ML YEARS		174	149	1	12	916.2	3829	840	405	383	124	18	19	27	282	14	746	17	2	57	36	.613	0	1-2	1	3.58	3.76

Jhan Marinez

Pitches: R **Bats:** R **Pos:** RP-2

YAN mah-REE-nyez

Ht: 6'1" **Wt:** 200 **Born:** 8/12/1988 **Age:** 24

			HOW MUCH HE PITCHED					WHAT HE GAVE UP												THE RESULTS						
Year	Team	Lg	G	GS	CG	GF	IP	BFP	H	R	ER	HR	SH	SF	HB	TBB	IBB	SO	WP	Bk	W	L	Pct	Sh	Sv-Op	Hld	ERC	ERA
2007	Mrlns	R	3	0	0	0	3.1	19	5	5	4	0	0	0	1	4	0	4	1	0	0	0	-	0	0- -	-	11.36	10.80
2008	Mrlns	R	12	1	0	2	17.2	87	21	14	12	0	0	0	2	14	0	18	1	1	1	1	.500	0	0- -	-	6.46	6.11
2009	Jupiter	A+	29	0	0	10	43.0	179	28	17	15	4	1	3	4	20	0	42	3	0	1	1	.500	0	1- -	-	2.75	3.14
2010	Jupiter	A+	21	1	0	14	25.1	99	12	4	4	1	3	0	1	14	1	44	6	0	0	1	.000	0	4- -	-	1.73	1.42
2010	Jaxnvl	AA	15	0	0	11	16.2	63	9	5	4	1	0	1	0	7	0	20	2	0	1	0	1.000	0	6- -	-	1.69	2.16
2011	Jaxnvl	AA	56	0	0	20	58.0	259	47	26	23	7	4	1	1	42	0	74	13	2	3	8	.273	0	3- -	-	4.49	3.57
2012	Charltt	AAA	40	0	0	17	63.0	256	39	24	20	5	2	0	4	30	0	65	8	0	4	2	.667	0	4- -	-	2.49	2.86
2010	Fla	NL	4	0	0	2	2.2	14	3	3	2	1	0	0	0	3	0	3	0	0	1	1	.500	0	0-2	0	10.25	6.75
2012	CWS	AL	2	0	0	1	2.2	11	2	0	0	0	1	0	0	2	1	1	0	0	0	0	-	0	0-0	0	2.87	0.00
	2 ML YEARS		6	0	0	3	5.1	25	5	3	2	1	1	0	0	5	1	4	0	0	1	1	.500	0	0-2	0	6.37	3.38

Nick Markakis

Bats: L **Throws:** L **Pos:** RF-102; DH-2

mar-KAY-kiss

Ht: 6'1" **Wt:** 190 **Born:** 11/17/1983 **Age:** 29

			BATTING																		BASERUNNING				AVERAGES		
Year	Team	Lg	G	AB	H	2B	3B	HR	(Hm	Rd)	TB	R	RBI	RC	TBB	IBB	SO	HBP	SH	SF	SB	CS	SB%	GDP	Avg	OBP	Slg
2012	Bowie*	AA	3	10	3	1	0	2	(-	-)	10	4	4	3	2	0	2	0	0	0	0	0	-	0	.300	.417	1.000
2006	Bal	AL	147	491	143	25	2	16	(9	7)	220	72	62	67	43	3	72	3	3	2	2	0	1.00	15	.291	.351	.448
2007	Bal	AL	161	637	191	43	3	23	(15	8)	309	97	112	103	61	5	112	5	1	6	18	6	.75	22	.300	.362	.485
2008	Bal	AL	157	595	182	48	1	20	(11	9)	292	106	87	113	99	7	113	2	0	1	10	7	.59	10	.306	.406	.491
2009	Bal	AL	161	642	188	45	2	18	(8	10)	291	94	101	97	56	0	98	3	0	10	6	2	.75	12	.293	.347	.453
2010	Bal	AL	160	629	187	45	3	12	(8	4)	274	79	60	99	73	9	93	2	0	5	7	2	.78	18	.297	.370	.436
2011	Bal	AL	160	641	182	31	1	15	(8	7)	260	72	73	90	62	6	75	7	0	6	12	3	.80	16	.284	.351	.406
2012	Bal	AL	104	420	125	28	3	13	(9	4)	198	59	54	69	42	3	51	4	0	5	1	1	.50	11	.298	.363	.471
	7 ML YEARS		1050	4055	1198	265	15	117	(68	49)	1844	579	549	638	436	33	614	26	4	35	56	21	.73	104	.295	.365	.455

Carlos Marmol

Pitches: R **Bats:** R **Pos:** RP-61

mar-MOLE

Ht: 6'2" **Wt:** 215 **Born:** 10/14/1982 **Age:** 30

			HOW MUCH HE PITCHED					WHAT HE GAVE UP													THE RESULTS						
Year	Team	Lg	G	GS	CG	GF	IP	BFP	H	R	ER	HR	SH	SF	HB	TBB	IBB	SO	WP	Bk	W	L	Pct	Sh	Sv-Op	Hld	ERC	ERA
2012	Iowa*	AAA	2	0	0	0	2.0	9	1	0	0	0	0	0	0	2	0	4	2	0	0	0	-	0	0-0	-	2.80	0.00
2006	ChC	NL	19	13	0	1	77.0	356	71	54	52	14	6	2	5	59	2	59	3	1	5	7	.417	0	0-0	0	6.01	6.08
2007	ChC	NL	59	0	0	6	69.1	285	41	11	11	3	1	2	4	35	3	96	5	1	5	1	.833	0	1-2	16	2.11	1.43
2008	ChC	NL	82	0	0	22	87.1	348	40	30	26	10	2	3	6	41	3	114	6	1	2	4	.333	0	7-9	30	1.86	2.68
2009	ChC	NL	79	0	0	29	74.0	335	43	29	28	2	4	1	12	65	3	93	6	1	2	4	.333	0	15-19	27	3.55	3.41
2010	ChC	NL	77	0	0	70	77.2	332	40	23	22	1	0	0	8	52	4	138	2	2	2	3	.400	0	38-43	0	2.18	2.55
2011	ChC	NL	75	0	0	61	74.0	327	54	33	33	5	4	2	9	48	2	99	4	0	2	6	.250	0	34-44	2	3.71	4.01
2012	ChC	NL	61	0	0	47	55.1	247	40	24	21	4	0	0	2	45	0	72	2	0	3	3	.500	0	20-23	2	4.07	3.42
	Postseason		4	0	0	0	5.2	26	6	5	5	2	1	1	0	3	0	9	0	0	0	1	.000	0	0-0	0	6.73	7.94
	7 ML YEARS		452	13	0	236	514.2	2230	329	204	193	39	17	10	46	345	17	671	28	6	21	28	.429	0	115-140	77	3.24	3.38

Nick Maronde

Pitches: L **Bats:** B **Pos:** RP-12

ma-RON-day

Ht: 6'3" **Wt:** 205 **Born:** 9/5/1989 **Age:** 23

			HOW MUCH HE PITCHED					WHAT HE GAVE UP													THE RESULTS						
Year	Team	Lg	G	GS	CG	GF	IP	BFP	H	R	ER	HR	SH	SF	HB	TBB	IBB	SO	WP	Bk	W	L	Pct	Sh	Sv-Op	Hld	ERC	ERA
2011	Orem	R+	11	11	0	0	46.1	185	36	12	11	5	1	0	2	15	0	50	0	0	5	0	1.000	0	0- -	-	2.89	2.14
2012	InldEm	A+	10	10	0	0	59.1	228	40	13	12	4	0	0	0	14	0	60	1	0	3	1	.750	0	0- -	-	1.68	1.82
2012	Angels	R	3	3	0	0	8.0	32	3	4	1	0	0	1	1	2	0	9	0	0	0	1	.000	0	0- -	-	0.80	1.13
2012	Ark	AA	7	5	0	0	32.1	135	39	13	12	1	0	1	1	10	0	21	0	0	3	2	.600	0	0- -	-	3.72	3.34
2012	LAA	AL	12	0	0	1	6.0	27	6	1	1	0	0	1	0	3	0	7	0	0	0	0	-	0	0-0	3	3.63	1.50

Jason Marquis

Pitches: R **Bats:** L **Pos:** SP-22

marr-KEE

Ht: 6'1" **Wt:** 220 **Born:** 8/21/1978 **Age:** 34

			HOW MUCH HE PITCHED					WHAT HE GAVE UP													THE RESULTS						
Year	Team	Lg	G	GS	CG	GF	IP	BFP	H	R	ER	HR	SH	SF	HB	TBB	IBB	SO	WP	Bk	W	L	Pct	Sh	Sv-Op	Hld	ERC	ERA
2012	NwBrit*	AA	2	2	0	0	14.0	50	12	3	3	1	0	0	0	11	0	11	0	0	1	0	1.000	0	0- -	-	1.88	1.93
2012	SnAnt*	AA	1	1	0	0	7.0	26	5	1	1	0	0	0	0	2	0	5	2	0	1	0	1.000	0	0- -	-	1.76	1.29
2000	Atl	NL	15	0	0	7	23.1	103	23	16	13	4	1	1	1	12	1	17	1	0	1	0	1.000	0	0-1	1	5.13	5.01
2001	Atl	NL	38	16	0	9	129.1	556	113	62	50	14	6	5	4	59	4	98	1	2	5	6	.455	0	0-2	2	3.70	3.48
2002	Atl	NL	22	22	0	0	114.1	507	127	66	64	19	4	3	3	49	3	84	4	0	8	9	.471	0	0-0	0	5.43	5.04
2003	Atl	NL	21	2	0	10	40.2	182	43	27	25	3	0	3	2	18	2	19	2	0	0	0	-	0	1-1	0	4.45	5.53
2004	StL	NL	32	32	0	0	201.1	874	215	90	83	26	5	6	10	70	1	138	6	0	15	7	.682	0	0-0	0	4.69	3.71
2005	StL	NL	33	32	3	0	207.0	868	206	110	95	29	4	3	5	69	2	100	10	3	13	14	.481	1	0-0	0	4.23	4.13
2006	StL	NL	33	33	0	0	194.1	870	221	136	130	35	2	11	6	75	2	96	2	1	14	16	.467	0	0-0	0	5.79	6.02
2007	ChC	NL	34	33	1	0	191.2	846	190	111	98	22	13	1	13	76	6	109	3	0	12	9	.571	1	0-0	0	4.28	4.60
2008	ChC	NL	29	28	0	0	167.0	738	172	87	84	15	4	7	8	70	6	91	8	1	11	9	.550	0	0-0	0	4.35	4.53
2009	Col	NL	33	33	2	0	216.0	921	218	104	97	15	10	10	4	80	6	115	6	1	15	13	.536	1	0-0	0	3.86	4.04
2010	Was	NL	13	13	0	0	58.2	276	76	47	43	9	3	0	8	24	0	31	1	1	2	9	.182	0	0-0	0	6.93	6.60
2011	2 Tms	NL	23	23	1	0	132.0	587	154	74	65	11	9	5	5	43	1	76	1	0	8	6	.571	1	0-0	0	4.72	4.43
2012	2 Tms	NL	22	22	1	0	127.2	561	146	86	74	23	6	4	4	42	3	91	6	0	8	11	.421	1	0-0	0	5.31	5.22
	11	Was	NL	20	20	1	0	120.2	524	132	58	53	8	8	5	4	39	1	71	1	0	8	5	.615	1	0-0	0	4.19	3.95
	11	Ari	NL	3	3	0	0	11.1	63	22	16	12	3	1	0	1	4	0	5	0	0	0	1	.000	0	0-0	0	11.25	9.53

			HOW MUCH HE PITCHED						WHAT HE GAVE UP											THE RESULTS						
Year	Team	Lg	G	GS	CG	GF	IP	BFP	H	R	ER	HR	SH	SF	HB	TBB	IBB	SO	WP	Bk	W	L	Pct	Sh	Sv-Op Hld	ERC	ERA
12	Min	AL	7	7	0	0	34.0	160	52	33	32	9	1	2	3	14	0	12	1	0	2	4	.333	0	0-0 0	9.67	8.47
12	SD	NL	15	15	1	0	93.2	401	94	53	42	14	5	2	1	28	3	79	5	0	6	7	.462	1	0-0 0	3.97	4.04
	Postseason		11	3	0	6	23.2	115	25	17	12	6	4	1	0	18	1	14	0	0	2	2	.000	0	0-0 0	6.85	4.56
	13 ML YEARS		348	289	8	26	1803.1	7889	1904	1016	921	225	83	51	83	687	37	1065	51	9	112	109	.507	5	1-4 4	4.66	4.60

Sean Marshall

Pitches: L **Bats:** L **Pos:** RP-73   **Ht:** 6'7" **Wt:** 220 **Born:** 8/30/1982 **Age:** 30

			HOW MUCH HE PITCHED						WHAT HE GAVE UP											THE RESULTS						
Year	Team	Lg	G	GS	CG	GF	IP	BFP	H	R	ER	HR	SH	SF	HB	TBB	IBB	SO	WP	Bk	W	L	Pct	Sh	Sv-Op Hld	ERC	ERA
2006	ChC	NL	24	24	0	0	125.2	563	132	85	78	20	7	1	7	59	3	77	6	0	6	9	.400	0	0-0 0	5.27	5.59
2007	ChC	NL	21	19	0	0	103.1	446	107	52	45	13	7	2	1	35	3	67	4	0	7	8	.467	0	0-0 0	4.18	3.92
2008	ChC	NL	34	7	0	6	65.1	279	60	28	28	9	4	3	4	23	4	58	3	0	3	5	.375	0	1-2 3	3.82	3.86
2009	ChC	NL	55	9	1	10	85.1	373	91	43	41	10	7	1	1	32	4	68	2	0	3	7	.300	0	0-0 7	4.43	4.32
2010	ChC	NL	80	0	0	16	74.2	307	58	25	22	3	2	2	2	25	5	90	1	0	7	5	.583	0	1-3 22	2.26	2.65
2011	ChC	NL	78	0	0	18	75.2	307	66	21	19	1	6	0	2	17	4	79	0	1	6	6	.500	0	5-9 34	2.22	2.26
2012	Cin	NL	73	0	0	22	61.0	256	55	18	17	3	0	0	3	16	2	74	1	1	5	5	.500	0	9-13 22	2.78	2.51
	Postseason		2	0	0	0	3.1	13	2	1	1	1	0	0	0	1	0	5	0	0	0	0	-	0	0-0 0	2.70	2.70
	7 ML YEARS		365	59	1	72	591.0	2531	569	272	250	59	33	9	20	207	25	513	17	2	37	45	.451	0	16-27 88	3.72	3.81

Lou Marson

Bats: R **Throws:** R **Pos:** C-69; PR-2; DH-1   MARR-son   **Ht:** 6'1" **Wt:** 200 **Born:** 6/26/1986 **Age:** 27

			BATTING																			BASERUNNING				AVERAGES		
Year	Team	Lg	G	AB	H	2B	3B	HR	(Hm	Rd)	TB	R	RBI	RC	TBB	IBB	SO	HBP	SH	SF	SB	CS	SB%	GDP	Avg	OBP	Slg
2008	Phi	NL	1	4	2	0	0	1	(1	0)	5	2	2	2	0	0	2	0	0	0	0	0	-	0	.500	.500	1.250
2009	2 Tms		21	61	15	7	0	0	(0	0)	22	9	4	7	10	0	21	0	0	1	0	0	-	3	.246	.347	.361
2010	Cle	AL	87	262	51	15	0	3	(0	3)	75	29	22	17	26	0	55	3	2	1	8	1	.89	7	.195	.274	.286
2011	Cle	AL	79	243	56	9	2	1	(0	1)	72	26	19	19	24	0	68	1	2	2	4	2	.67	7	.230	.300	.296
2012	Cle	AL	70	195	44	8	2	0	(0	0)	56	27	13	18	36	1	44	1	2	1	4	2	.67	10	.226	.348	.287
09	Phi	NL	7	17	4	1	0	0	(0	0)	5	3	0	1	3	0	7	0	0	0	0	0	-	1	.235	.350	.294
09	Cle	AL	14	44	11	6	0	0	(0	0)	17	6	4	6	7	0	14	0	0	1	0	0	-	2	.250	.346	.386
	5 ML YEARS		258	765	168	39	4	5	(1	4)	230	93	60	63	96	1	190	5	6	5	16	5	.76	27	.220	.309	.301

Luis Marte

Pitches: R **Bats:** R **Pos:** RP-13   marr-TAY   **Ht:** 5'11" **Wt:** 199 **Born:** 8/26/1986 **Age:** 26

			HOW MUCH HE PITCHED						WHAT HE GAVE UP											THE RESULTS						
Year	Team	Lg	G	GS	CG	GF	IP	BFP	H	R	ER	HR	SH	SF	HB	TBB	IBB	SO	WP	Bk	W	L	Pct	Sh	Sv-Op Hld	ERC	ERA
2007	Tigers	R	2	2	1	0	12.0	45	8	1	1	0	0	0	1	1	0	12	1	0	2	0	1.000	0	0- -	1.26	0.75
2007	WMich	A	15	2	0	6	35.0	140	28	13	11	2	2	0	0	11	1	36	1	0	1	2	.333	0	3- -	2.43	2.83
2008	Lkland	A+	7	7	0	0	41.0	161	29	11	9	1	0	0	2	11	0	41	3	1	3	2	.600	0	0- -	1.85	1.98
2008	Erie	AA	10	10	0	0	57.0	247	57	35	32	8	1	3	1	26	0	32	5	0	4	4	.500	0	0- -	4.72	5.05
2008	Tigers	R	1	0	0	0	5.0	21	5	2	2	0	0	0	0	0	0	5	0	0	0	1	.000	0	0- -	1.83	3.60
2009	Erie	AA	19	17	0	1	105.1	445	106	57	47	18	3	3	2	28	1	84	4	0	5	8	.385	0	0- -	4.10	4.02
2010	Erie	AA	38	0	0	24	48.0	216	44	31	27	5	4	2	4	26	4	53	3	0	2	2	.500	0	7- -	4.32	5.06
2010	Toledo	AAA	1	0	0	1	1.0	5	1	1	0	0	0	0	0	1	0	0	0	0	0	0	-	0	0- -	5.48	0.00
2011	Erie	AA	23	1	0	13	53.0	204	29	10	10	3	1	1	1	18	0	68	3	1	3	0	1.000	0	3- -	1.51	1.70
2011	Toledo	AAA	2	0	0	1	3.1	18	3	2	2	0	0	0	0	4	1	2	0	0	1	0	1.000	0	0- -	6.15	5.40
2012	Lkland	A+	1	1	0	0	2.0	7	1	0	0	0	0	0	0	0	0	3	0	0	0	0	-	0	0- -	0.54	0.00
2012	Toledo	AAA	18	0	0	10	24.1	103	20	10	10	1	1	2	0	10	3	27	2	0	3	2	.600	0	2- -	2.53	3.70
2011	Det	AL	4	0	0	2	3.2	17	6	1	1	0	0	1	0	1	0	3	1	0	1	0	1.000	0	0-0 0	6.78	2.45
2012	Det	AL	13	0	0	4	22.1	93	19	7	7	4	0	0	1	9	0	19	1	0	1	0	1.000	0	0-0 0	4.04	2.82
	2 ML YEARS		17	0	0	6	26.0	110	25	8	8	4	0	1	1	10	0	22	2	0	2	0	1.000	0	0-0 0	4.41	2.77

Starling Marte

Bats: R **Throws:** R **Pos:** LF-43; CF-4; PH-3   marr-TAY   **Ht:** 6'0" **Wt:** 180 **Born:** 10/9/1988 **Age:** 24

			BATTING																			BASERUNNING				AVERAGES		
Year	Team	Lg	G	AB	H	2B	3B	HR	(Hm	Rd)	TB	R	RBI	RC	TBB	IBB	SO	HBP	SH	SF	SB	CS	SB%	GDP	Avg	OBP	Slg
2009	Pirates	R	2	7	0	0	0	0	(-	-)	0	1	0	0	0	0	1	0	0	0	0	0	-	0	.000	.000	.000
2009	WV	A	54	221	69	9	5	3	(-	-)	97	41	34	39	12	0	55	12	0	2	24	7	.77	9	.312	.377	.439
2009	Lynbrg	A+	1	2	2	0	0	0	(-	-)	2	0	1	1	0	0	0	0	0	0	0	0	-	0	1.000	1.000	1.000
2010	Bradtn	A+	60	222	70	16	5	0	(-	-)	96	41	33	39	12	0	59	15	2	2	22	8	.73	5	.315	.386	.432
2010	Pirates	R	8	26	9	3	0	2	(-	-)	18	6	5	6	1	0	6	1	0	0	4	1	.80	0	.346	.393	.692
2011	Altna	AA	129	536	178	38	8	12	(-	-)	268	91	50	97	22	3	100	11	1	2	24	12	.67	9	.332	.370	.500
2012	Indy	AAA	99	388	111	21	13	12	(-	-)	194	64	62	67	28	5	91	10	2	3	21	12	.64	3	.286	.347	.500
2012	StCol	A-	1	5	0	0	0	0	(-	-)	0	0	0	0	0	0	3	0	0	0	0	0	-	0	.000	.000	.000
2012	Pit	NL	47	167	43	3	6	5	(3	2)	73	18	17	21	8	0	50	3	2	2	12	5	.71	5	.257	.300	.437

Victor Marte

Pitches: R **Bats:** R **Pos:** RP-48   marr-TAY   **Ht:** 6'2" **Wt:** 255 **Born:** 11/8/1980 **Age:** 32

			HOW MUCH HE PITCHED						WHAT HE GAVE UP											THE RESULTS						
Year	Team	Lg	G	GS	CG	GF	IP	BFP	H	R	ER	HR	SH	SF	HB	TBB	IBB	SO	WP	Bk	W	L	Pct	Sh	Sv-Op Hld	ERC	ERA
2012	Memp*	AAA	12	0	0	10	12.0	50	9	4	4	0	1	0	0	7	3	10	1	0	0	2	.000	0	3- -	2.39	3.00
2009	KC	AL	8	0	0	4	12.0	58	13	12	11	2	0	0	0	12	1	7	1	0	0	0	-	0	0-0 0	7.71	8.25
2010	KC	AL	22	0	0	4	27.2	137	30	30	30	8	1	0	2	15	1	19	1	0	3	1	.750	0	0-0 1	8.71	9.76
2012	StL	NL	48	0	0	5	40.1	185	51	22	22	6	1	1	2	14	2	36	1	0	3	1	.600	0	0-2 9	5.86	4.91
	3 ML YEARS		78	0	0	13	80.0	380	102	64	63	16	2	1	4	41	4	62	3	0	6	2	.750	0	0-2 10	7.10	7.09

Leonys Martin

Bats: L **Throws:** R **Pos:** CF-14; PH-5; LF-4; PR-4; DH-1   lay-OH-niece mar-TEEN   **Ht:** 6'2" **Wt:** 190 **Born:** 3/6/1988 **Age:** 25

Year	Team	Lg	G	AB	H	2B	3B	HR	(Hm	Rd)	TB	R	RBI	RC	TBB	IBB	SO	HBP	SH	SF	SB	CS	SB%	GDP	Avg	OBP	Slg
2011	Frisco	AA	29	112	39	9	2	4	(-	-)	64	24	24	26	15	1	8	3	4	1	10	8	.56	3	.348	.435	.571
2011	Rngrs	R	4	15	4	0	2	0	(-	-)	8	2	1	2	1	0	6	0	0	0	0	1	1.00	0	.267	.313	.533
2011	RdRck	AAA	40	175	46	7	1	0	(-	-)	55	27	17	19	11	0	24	3	2	1	9	2	.82	4	.263	.316	.314
2012	RdRck	AAA	55	231	83	18	2	12	(-	-)	141	48	42	54	24	4	39	2	2	1	10	9	.53	2	.359	.422	.610
2011	Tex	AL	8	8	3	1	0	0	(0	0)	4	2	0	1	0	0	1	0	0	0	0	0	-	0	.375	.375	.500
2012	Tex	AL	24	46	8	5	2	0	(0	0)	17	6	6	4	4	0	12	0	1	1	3	0	1.00	2	.174	.235	.370
2 ML YEARS			32	54	11	6	2	0	(0	0)	21	8	6	5	4	0	13	0	1	1	3	0	1.00	2	.204	.254	.389

Russell Martin

Bats: R **Throws:** R **Pos:** C-128; PH-9; DH-4   **Ht:** 5'10" **Wt:** 205 **Born:** 2/15/1983 **Age:** 30

Year	Team	Lg	G	AB	H	2B	3B	HR	(Hm	Rd)	TB	R	RBI	RC	TBB	IBB	SO	HBP	SH	SF	SB	CS	SB%	GDP	Avg	OBP	Slg
2006	LAD	NL	121	415	117	26	4	10	(8	2)	181	65	65	58	45	8	57	4	1	3	10	5	.67	17	.282	.355	.436
2007	LAD	NL	151	540	158	32	3	19	(8	11)	253	87	87	84	67	1	89	7	0	6	21	9	.70	16	.293	.374	.469
2008	LAD	NL	155	553	155	25	0	13	(6	7)	219	87	69	89	90	8	83	5	0	2	18	6	.75	16	.280	.385	.396
2009	LAD	NL	143	505	126	19	0	7	(3	4)	166	63	53	62	69	9	80	11	2	1	11	6	.65	18	.250	.352	.329
2010	LAD	NL	97	331	82	13	0	5	(2	3)	110	45	26	40	48	7	61	4	1	3	6	2	.75	7	.248	.347	.332
2011	NYY	AL	125	417	99	17	0	18	(8	10)	170	57	65	56	50	1	81	5	1	3	8	2	.80	19	.237	.324	.408
2012	NYY	AL	133	422	89	18	0	21	(13	8)	170	50	53	53	53	0	95	8	2	0	6	1	.86	13	.211	.311	.403
Postseason			24	84	18	5	0	1	(0	1)	26	12	9	7	11	0	20	6	0	0	1	0	1.00	3	.214	.347	.310
7 ML YEARS			925	3183	826	150	7	93	(48	45)	1269	454	418	439	422	34	546	44	7	18	80	31	.72	106	.260	.352	.399

Cristhian Martinez

Pitches: R **Bats:** R **Pos:** RP-54   cris-tee-YAN   **Ht:** 6'1" **Wt:** 185 **Born:** 3/6/1982 **Age:** 31

Year	Team	Lg	G	GS	CG	GF	IP	BFP	H	R	ER	HR	SH	SF	HB	TBB	IBB	SO	WP	Bk	W	L	Pct	Sh	Sv-Op	Hld	ERC	ERA
2009	Fla	NL	15	0	0	4	26.1	112	27	16	15	2	1	0	0	8	1	18	1	0	1	1	.500	0	0-1	0	3.60	5.13
2010	Atl	NL	18	0	0	8	26.0	110	28	14	14	3	0	1	0	6	1	22	1	0	0	0	-	0	0-0	0	3.87	4.85
2011	Atl	NL	46	0	0	12	77.2	308	56	30	29	8	2	3	0	19	2	58	3	0	1	3	.250	0	0-0	3	2.18	3.36
2012	Atl	NL	54	0	0	26	73.2	313	80	33	32	6	3	2	0	19	4	65	2	1	5	4	.556	0	1-1	1	3.78	3.91
4 ML YEARS			133	0	0	50	203.2	843	191	93	90	19	6	3	3	52	8	163	7	1	7	8	.467	0	1-2	4	3.13	3.98

Fernando Martinez

Bats: L **Throws:** R **Pos:** LF-31; RF-6; PH-5   **Ht:** 6'1" **Wt:** 205 **Born:** 10/10/1988 **Age:** 24

Year	Team	Lg	G	AB	H	2B	3B	HR	(Hm	Rd)	TB	R	RBI	RC	TBB	IBB	SO	HBP	SH	SF	SB	CS	SB%	GDP	Avg	OBP	Slg
2012	OKCity	AAA	90	341	107	23	2	13	(-	-)	173	55	62	62	24	3	85	6	0	2	1	2	.33	13	.314	.367	.507
2009	NYM	NL	29	91	16	6	0	1	(0	1)	25	11	8	5	5	0	14	3	1	0	2	0	1.00	0	.176	.242	.275
2010	NYM	NL	7	18	3	0	0	0	(0	0)	3	1	2	1	1	0	5	2	0	1	0	1	.00	0	.167	.273	.167
2011	NYM	NL	11	22	5	2	0	1	(0	1)	10	3	2	1	1	0	7	0	0	0	0	0	-	0	.227	.261	.455
2012	Hou	NL	41	118	28	7	1	6	(2	4)	55	12	14	13	6	0	34	5	0	1	0	1	.00	1	.237	.300	.466
4 ML YEARS			88	249	52	15	1	8	(2	6)	93	27	26	20	13	0	60	10	1	2	2	2	.50	1	.209	.274	.373

J.D. Martinez

Bats: R **Throws:** R **Pos:** LF-100; PH-11; DH-5   **Ht:** 6'3" **Wt:** 205 **Born:** 8/21/1987 **Age:** 25

Year	Team	Lg	G	AB	H	2B	3B	HR	(Hm	Rd)	TB	R	RBI	RC	TBB	IBB	SO	HBP	SH	SF	SB	CS	SB%	GDP	Avg	OBP	Slg
2009	Grnville	R	19	77	31	9	1	5	(-	-)	57	17	23	22	5	1	14	1	0	0	0	0	-	1	.403	.446	.740
2009	TriCity	A-	53	187	61	15	2	7	(-	-)	101	25	33	38	15	2	30	3	0	3	1	0	1.00	9	.326	.380	.540
2010	Lxngtn	A	88	348	126	31	3	15	(-	-)	208	83	64	86	33	2	55	11	0	1	3	0	1.00	7	.362	.433	.598
2010	CpChr	AA	50	189	57	9	1	3	(-	-)	77	24	25	28	15	0	42	2	0	1	2	2	.50	9	.302	.357	.407
2011	CpChr	AA	88	317	107	25	1	13	(-	-)	173	50	72	72	42	2	55	4	0	7	1	0	1.00	6	.338	.414	.546
2012	OKCity	AAA	23	90	21	6	0	0	(-	-)	27	6	4	6	4	0	17	0	0	1	0	1	.00	3	.233	.263	.300
2011	Hou	NL	53	208	57	13	0	6	(3	3)	88	29	35	30	13	1	48	2	0	3	0	1	.00	4	.274	.319	.423
2012	Hou	NL	113	395	95	14	3	11	(5	6)	148	34	55	45	40	0	96	1	0	2	0	2	.00	18	.241	.311	.375
2 ML YEARS			166	603	152	27	3	17	(8	9)	236	63	90	75	53	1	144	3	0	5	0	3	.00	22	.252	.313	.391

Joe Martinez

Pitches: R **Bats:** L **Pos:** RP-1   **Ht:** 6'2" **Wt:** 190 **Born:** 2/26/1983 **Age:** 30

Year	Team	Lg	G	GS	CG	GF	IP	BFP	H	R	ER	HR	SH	SF	HB	TBB	IBB	SO	WP	Bk	W	L	Pct	Sh	Sv-Op	Hld	ERC	ERA
2012	Reno*	AAA	27	27	1	0	155.1	703	206	104	93	15	5	8	7	49	0	99	8	3	10	11	.476	0	0- -	-	5.88	5.39
2009	SF	NL	9	5	0	1	30.0	148	46	27	25	4	2	2	1	12	2	19	0	0	3	2	.600	0	0-0	0	7.49	7.50
2010	2 Tms	NL	9	1	0	0	19.2	94	26	11	9	1	0	1	2	9	2	9	1	1	0	0	1.000	0	0-0	0	6.02	4.12
2012	Ari	NL	1	0	0	1	1.0	5	2	1	1	0	0	0	0	0	0	1	0	0	0	0	-	0	0-0	0	7.48	9.00
10	SF	NL	4	1	0	0	11.0	53	15	6	6	1	0	1	1	6	2	3	0	0	0	1	.000	0	0-0	0	6.91	4.91
10	Pit	NL	5	0	0	0	8.2	41	11	5	3	0	0	0	1	3	0	6	1	1	0	0	-	0	0-0	0	4.96	3.12
3 ML YEARS			19	6	0	2	50.2	247	74	39	35	5	2	3	3	21	4	29	1	1	3	3	.500	0	0-0	0	6.92	6.22

Luis Martinez

Bats: R **Throws:** R **Pos:** C-10   **Ht:** 6'0" **Wt:** 210 **Born:** 4/3/1985 **Age:** 28

Year	Team	Lg	G	AB	H	2B	3B	HR	(Hm	Rd)	TB	R	RBI	RC	TBB	IBB	SO	HBP	SH	SF	SB	CS	SB%	GDP	Avg	OBP	Slg
2007	Eugene	A-	21	72	20	7	0	1	(-	-)	30	9	11	14	19	0	22	1	0	1	0	1	.00	2	.278	.430	.417
2007	FtWyn	A	24	78	18	3	0	1	(-	-)	24	12	6	7	8	0	23	0	1	1	0	0	-	2	.231	.299	.308
2008	FtWyn	A	94	305	68	12	1	3	(-	-)	91	30	19	35	51	0	66	2	6	0	3	1	.75	13	.223	.338	.298
2009	Lk Els	A+	83	280	84	20	0	4	(-	-)	116	39	41	48	34	0	58	7	0	0	2	1	.67	12	.300	.389	.414
2009	PortInd	AAA	11	35	6	0	0	0	(-	-)	6	3	0	1	4	1	7	0	0	0	0	0	-	3	.171	.256	.171
2010	SnAnt	AA	106	358	101	16	1	2	(-	-)	125	48	31	51	49	1	59	1	0	2	3	2	.60	8	.282	.368	.349
2011	Tucsn	AAA	58	198	64	17	1	1	(-	-)	86	24	27	33	17	1	46	2	0	2	2	0	1.00	9	.323	.379	.434
2012	RdRck	AAA	65	215	58	15	2	2	(-	-)	83	27	22	31	26	0	45	2	1	3	0	0	-	10	.270	.350	.386
2011	SD	NL	22	59	12	1	1	1	(1	0)	18	7	10	9	8	2	14	1	0	0	1	0	1.00	0	.203	.309	.305
2012	Tex	AL	10	18	2	0	0	0	(0	0)	2	1	0	0	0	0	4	1	0	0	0	0	-	0	.111	.158	.111
	2 ML YEARS		32	77	14	1	1	1	(1	0)	20	8	10	9	8	2	18	2	0	0	1	0	1.00	0	.182	.276	.260

Michael Martinez

Bats: B **Throws:** R **Pos:** 2B-16; 3B-10; SS-8; RF-4; CF-3; PH-3; PR-3; LF-2   **Ht:** 5'9" **Wt:** 175 **Born:** 9/16/1982 **Age:** 30

Year	Team	Lg	G	AB	H	2B	3B	HR	(Hm	Rd)	TB	R	RBI	RC	TBB	IBB	SO	HBP	SH	SF	SB	CS	SB%	GDP	Avg	OBP	Slg
2006	Savann	A	30	87	15	0	0	0	(-	-)	15	9	4	2	7	0	10	0	6	0	4	3	.57	2	.172	.234	.172
2006	Vrmnt	A-	45	159	51	5	2	1	(-	-)	63	26	19	22	9	0	28	2	8	1	6	8	.43	2	.321	.363	.396
2006	Ptomc	A+	7	23	5	2	0	0	(-	-)	7	1	2	2	1	0	1	1	0	0	1	0	1.00	1	.217	.280	.304
2007	Hgrstn	A	115	404	101	21	5	0	(-	-)	132	54	32	43	27	0	68	4	11	4	13	3	.81	9	.250	.301	.327
2008	Ptomc	A+	104	417	111	25	6	3	(-	-)	157	63	58	55	27	0	49	7	20	2	25	7	.78	7	.266	.320	.376
2009	Hrsbrg	AA	65	188	42	7	2	1	(-	-)	56	22	8	18	20	1	34	5	5	1	0	3	.00	5	.223	.313	.298
2009	Ptomc	A+	49	198	58	14	5	4	(-	-)	94	40	29	32	16	0	31	1	2	1	10	6	.63	3	.293	.347	.475
2010	Hrsbrg	AA	100	359	91	14	6	8	(-	-)	141	41	37	42	20	0	54	3	4	1	15	9	.63	4	.253	.298	.393
2010	Syrcse	AAA	33	126	41	7	0	3	(-	-)	57	16	19	20	3	1	20	3	2	1	8	3	.73	3	.325	.353	.452
2012	Clrwtr	A+	4	15	5	1	0	0	(-	-)	6	4	2	2	1	0	1	0	0	0	0	0	-	1	.333	.375	.400
2012	LV	AAA	32	107	29	4	2	2	(-	-)	43	12	15	15	10	2	12	1	1	3	3	1	.75	0	.271	.331	.402
2011	Phi	NL	88	209	41	5	2	3	(1	2)	59	25	24	20	18	0	35	0	5	2	3	0	1.00	2	.196	.258	.282
2012	Phi	NL	45	115	20	3	0	2	(1	1)	29	10	7	5	5	2	21	0	2	0	0	0	-	4	.174	.208	.252
	Postseason		2	0	0	0	0	0	(0	0)	0	1	0	0	0	0	0	0	0	0	0	0	-	0	-	-	-
	2 ML YEARS		133	324	61	8	2	5	(2	3)	88	35	31	25	23	2	56	0	7	2	3	0	1.00	6	.188	.241	.272

Victor Martinez

Bats: B **Throws:** R **Pos:** C   **Ht:** 6'2" **Wt:** 210 **Born:** 12/23/1978 **Age:** 34

Year	Team	Lg	G	AB	H	2B	3B	HR	(Hm	Rd)	TB	R	RBI	RC	TBB	IBB	SO	HBP	SH	SF	SB	CS	SB%	GDP	Avg	OBP	Slg
2002	Cle	AL	12	32	9	1	0	1	(1	0)	13	2	5	5	3	0	2	0	0	1	0	0	-	1	.281	.333	.406
2003	Cle	AL	49	159	46	4	0	1	(0	1)	53	15	16	17	13	0	21	1	0	1	1	1	.50	8	.289	.345	.333
2004	Cle	AL	141	520	147	38	1	23	(8	15)	256	77	108	90	60	11	69	5	0	6	0	1	.00	16	.283	.359	.492
2005	Cle	AL	147	547	167	33	0	20	(10	10)	260	73	80	90	63	9	78	5	0	7	0	1	.00	16	.305	.378	.475
2006	Cle	AL	153	572	181	37	0	16	(4	12)	266	82	93	96	71	8	78	3	0	6	0	-		27	.316	.391	.465
2007	Cle	AL	147	562	169	40	0	25	(12	13)	284	78	114	108	62	12	76	10	0	11	0	0	-	19	.301	.374	.505
2008	Cle	AL	73	266	74	17	0	2	(2	0)	97	30	35	36	24	4	32	1	0	3	0	0	-	12	.278	.337	.365
2009	2 Tms	AL	155	588	178	33	1	23	(7	16)	282	88	108	101	75	3	74	3	0	6	1	0	1.00	17	.303	.381	.480
2010	Bos	AL	127	493	149	32	1	20	(10	10)	243	64	79	74	40	5	52	0	0	5	1	0	1.00	17	.302	.351	.493
2011	Det	AL	145	540	178	40	0	12	(5	7)	254	76	103	103	46	6	51	2	0	7	1	0	1.00	20	.330	.380	.470
09	Cle	AL	99	377	107	21	1	15	(6	9)	175	56	67	64	51	3	51	2	0	5	0	0	-	11	.284	.368	.464
09	Bos	AL	56	211	71	12	0	8	(1	7)	107	32	41	37	24	0	23	1	0	1	1	0	1.00	6	.336	.405	.507
	Postseason		25	95	26	2	1	4	(3	1)	42	10	14	15	10	3	16	2	0	0	0	0	-	2	.274	.355	.442
	10 ML YEARS		1149	4279	1298	275	3	143	(59	84)	2008	585	741	720	457	58	533	30	0	53	4	3	.57	153	.303	.370	.469

Nick Masset

Pitches: R **Bats:** R **Pos:** P   MASS-it   **Ht:** 6'4" **Wt:** 235 **Born:** 5/17/1982 **Age:** 31

Year	Team	Lg	G	GS	CG	GF	IP	BFP	H	R	ER	HR	SH	SF	HB	TBB	IBB	SO	WP	Bk	W	L	Pct	Sh	Sv-Op	Hld	ERC	ERA
2012	Reds*	R	2	2	0	0	2.0		0	0	0	0	0	0	0	0	0	5	0	0	0	0	-	0	0- -	-	0.00	0.00
2012	Dayton*	A	1	1	0	0	1.0	4	1	0	0	0	0	0	0	0	0	1	0	0	0	0	-	0	0- -	-	1.95	0.00
2012	Lsvlle*	AAA	6	2	0	1	6.2	31	7	6	6	0	0	1	0	3	0	9	1	0	0	1	.000	0	0- -	-	4.26	8.10
2006	Tex	AL	8	0	0	7	8.2	36	9	4	4	0	0	2	2	2	0	4	0	0	0	0	-	0	0-0	0	4.05	4.15
2007	CWS	AL	27	1	0	4	39.1	193	52	33	31	2	1	3	2	26	5	21	4	0	2	3	.400	0	0-1	5	6.63	7.09
2008	2 Tms		42	1	0	12	62.0	271	71	32	27	7	3	1	2	26	4	43	3	1	2	0	1.000	0	1-3	5	5.27	3.92
2009	Cin	NL	74	0	0	15	76.0	292	54	22	20	6	1	1	0	24	0	70	6	0	5	1	.833	0	0-2	20	2.24	2.37
2010	Cin	NL	82	0	0	22	76.2	322	64	31	29	7	3	2	1	33	3	85	8	0	4	4	.500	0	2-5	20	3.23	3.40
2011	Cin	NL	75	0	0	21	70.1	313	76	30	29	5	2	1	1	31	6	62	2	4	3	6	.333	0	1-7	14	4.37	3.71
08	CWS	AL	32	1	0	11	44.2	203	55	26	23	4	3	1	2	21	4	32	2	1	1	0	1.000	0	1-1	1	5.78	4.63
08	Cin	NL	10	0	0	1	17.1	68	16	6	4	3	0	0	0	5	0	11	1	0	1	0	1.000	0	0-2	1	3.93	2.08
	Postseason		2	0	0	1	2.0	10	2	1	1	0	0	0	0	2	2	1	0	0	0	0	-	0	0-0	0	3.46	4.50
	6 ML YEARS		308	2	0	81	333.0	1427	326	152	140	27	10	10	8	142	18	285	23	5	16	14	.533	0	4-18	58	3.98	3.78

Justin Masterson

Pitches: R **Bats:** R **Pos:** SP-34 **Ht:** 6'6" **Wt:** 250 **Born:** 3/22/1985 **Age:** 28

			HOW MUCH HE PITCHED						WHAT HE GAVE UP											THE RESULTS							
Year	Team	Lg	G	GS	CG	GF	IP	BFP	H	R	ER	HR	SH	SF	HB	TBB	IBB	SO	WP	Bk	W	L	Pct	Sh	Sv-Op	Hld	ERC	ERA
2008	Bos	AL	36	9	0	6	88.1	365	68	31	31	10	1	1	8	40	3	68	1	0	6	5	.545	0	0-1	3	3.51	3.16
2009	2 Tms	AL	42	16	1	4	129.1	568	128	73	65	12	10	7	8	60	3	119	5	0	4	10	.286	0	0-1	6	4.45	4.52
2010	Cle	AL	34	29	1	0	180.0	802	197	107	94	14	5	4	11	73	4	140	12	0	6	13	.316	1	0-0	2	4.68	4.70
2011	Cle	AL	34	33	1	0	216.0	908	211	89	77	11	5	5	11	65	4	158	5	0	12	10	.545	0	0-0	0	3.43	3.21
2012	Cle	AL	34	34	1	0	206.1	906	212	122	113	18	6	11	13	88	1	159	14	0	11	15	.423	0	0-0	0	4.51	4.93
09	Bos		31	6	0	4	72.0	312	72	38	36	7	9	6	6	25	2	67	3	0	3	3	.500	0	0-1	6	4.13	4.50
09	Cle		11	10	1	0	57.1	256	56	35	29	5	1	1	2	35	1	52	2	0	1	7	.125	0	0-0	0	4.85	4.55
	Postseason		9	0	0	1	9.2	40	10	3	2	0	1	0	1	5	0	9	0	0	1	0	1.000	0	0-1	4	4.85	1.86
5 ML YEARS			180	121	4	10	820.0	3549	816	422	380	65	27	28	51	326	15	644	37	0	39	53	.424	1	0-2	11	4.14	4.17

Darin Mastroianni

mass-tree-AH-nee

Bats: R **Throws:** R **Pos:** RF-34; LF-25; PR-16; DH-5; PH-5; CF-4; 2B-1 **Ht:** 5'11" **Wt:** 190 **Born:** 8/26/1985 **Age:** 27

					BATTING															BASERUNNING				AVERAGES		
Year	Team	Lg	G	AB	H	2B	3B	HR	(Hm	Rd)	TB	R	RBI	RC	TBB	IBB	SO	HBP	SH	SF	SB	CS	SB%	GDP	Avg	OBP	Slg
2007	Auburn	A-	68	230	66	11	4	3	(-	-)	94	50	26	40	36	1	42	5	0	3	20	10	.67	4	.287	.391	.409
2008	Lnsng	A	95	325	74	10	4	3	(-	-)	101	51	25	38	31	0	77	4	8	1	30	1	.97	9	.228	.302	.311
2009	Dnedin	A+	61	231	75	11	2	0	(-	-)	90	55	26	46	37	0	38	4	2	0	32	7	.82	1	.325	.426	.390
2009	NHam	AA	70	247	67	10	2	1	(-	-)	84	39	25	39	39	0	45	1	4	1	38	8	.83	3	.271	.372	.340
2010	NHam	AA	132	525	158	25	7	4	(-	-)	209	101	46	94	77	0	96	3	7	5	46	10	.82	10	.301	.390	.398
2011	LsVgs	AAA	79	319	88	18	6	2	(-	-)	124	63	23	48	40	0	54	1	4	0	20	7	.74	6	.276	.358	.389
2011	NHam	AA	44	169	43	8	3	1	(-	-)	60	29	13	24	22	2	24	2	2	3	14	3	.82	1	.254	.342	.355
2012	NwBrit	AA	9	35	5	1	0	0	(-	-)	6	6	0	1	4	1	11	0	1	0	4	1	.80	0	.143	.231	.171
2012	Roch	AAA	20	78	27	2	2	0	(-	-)	33	10	11	14	5	0	14	1	1	0	10	1	.91	0	.346	.393	.423
2011	Tor	AL	1	2	0	0	0	0	(0	0)	0	0	0	0	0	0	1	0	1	0	0	0	-	0	.000	.000	.000
2012	Min	AL	77	163	41	3	2	3	(2	1)	57	22	17	24	18	0	45	1	3	1	21	3	.88	4	.252	.328	.350
2 ML YEARS			78	165	41	3	2	3	(2	1)	57	22	17	24	18	0	46	1	4	1	21	3	.88	4	.248	.324	.345

Marcos Mateo

Pitches: R **Bats:** R **Pos:** P **Ht:** 6'1" **Wt:** 220 **Born:** 4/18/1984 **Age:** 29

			HOW MUCH HE PITCHED						WHAT HE GAVE UP											THE RESULTS							
Year	Team	Lg	G	GS	CG	GF	IP	BFP	H	R	ER	HR	SH	SF	HB	TBB	IBB	SO	WP	Bk	W	L	Pct	Sh	Sv-Op	Hld	ERC	ERA
2005	Reds	R	13	4	0	6	44.0	192	54	26	21	2	3	1	3	10	0	23	7	0	2	3	.400	0	0--	-	4.61	4.30
2006	Billings	R+	18	0	0	1	45.0	191	43	17	16	2	1	3	3	20	0	30	5	0	5	1	.833	0	1--	-	3.99	3.20
2007	Dayton	A	41	0	0	22	72.0	300	68	29	28	2	7	4	3	24	3	63	8	0	2	4	.333	0	6--	-	3.17	3.50
2008	Peoria	A	8	0	0	6	15.0	54	4	3	2	1	0	0	0	7	0	20	1	0	1	0	1.000	0	1--	-	0.99	1.20
2008	Dytona	A+	25	16	0	3	88.1	380	87	42	35	6	2	3	7	29	0	65	10	2	4	3	.571	0	0--	-	3.79	3.57
2009	Dytona	A+	3	3	0	0	9.0	32	4	0	0	0	1	0	1	2	0	7	0	0	0	0	-	0	0--	-	1.01	0.00
2009	Tenn	AA	34	14	0	0	97.1	435	97	47	44	9	6	0	10	43	0	70	1	1	3	6	.333	0	0--	-	4.54	4.07
2010	Tenn	AA	17	1	0	9	20.2	92	23	8	5	2	0	0	0	3	0	29	0	0	0	0	-	0	4--	-	3.41	2.18
2010	Iowa	AAA	8	0	0	6	12.2	55	12	8	7	0	0	0	0	4	0	15	0	0	0	1	.000	0	0--	-	2.67	4.97
2010	Cubs	R	1	0	0	0	1.0	3	0	0	0	0	0	0	0	0	0	1	0	0	0	0	-	0	0--	-	0.00	0.00
2011	Iowa	AAA	16	0	0	11	18.1	85	20	14	14	3	0	2	2	10	2	18	2	0	1	3	.250	0	2--	-	5.96	6.87
2010	ChC	NL	21	0	0	5	21.2	93	20	15	14	6	0	2	1	9	1	26	1	0	0	1	.000	0	0-0	1	5.07	5.82
2011	ChC	NL	23	0	0	8	23.0	98	24	11	11	2	1	0	0	10	0	25	1	0	1	2	.333	0	0-0	2	4.50	4.30
2 ML YEARS			44	0	0	13	44.2	191	44	26	25	8	1	2	1	19	1	51	2	0	1	3	.250	0	0-0	3	4.80	5.04

Joe Mather

Bats: R **Throws:** R **Pos:** PH-33; CF-28; LF-25; 3B-18; RF-14; PR-4; 1B-2 **Ht:** 6'4" **Wt:** 215 **Born:** 7/23/1982 **Age:** 30

					BATTING															BASERUNNING				AVERAGES		
Year	Team	Lg	G	AB	H	2B	3B	HR	(Hm	Rd)	TB	R	RBI	RC	TBB	IBB	SO	HBP	SH	SF	SB	CS	SB%	GDP	Avg	OBP	Slg
2008	StL	NL	54	133	32	7	0	8	(2	6)	63	20	18	18	12	1	32	1	0	1	1	0	1.00	2	.241	.306	.474
2010	StL	NL	36	60	13	4	0	0	(0	0)	17	7	3	1	2	0	11	0	2	0	1	1	.50	2	.217	.242	.283
2011	Atl	NL	36	75	16	4	0	1	(0	1)	23	4	9	8	6	2	23	0	2	0	0	1	.00	1	.213	.272	.307
2012	ChC	NL	103	225	47	11	0	5	(4	1)	73	18	19	17	14	1	46	1	1	2	5	2	.71	4	.209	.256	.324
4 ML YEARS			229	493	108	26	0	14	(6	8)	176	49	49	44	34	4	112	2	5	3	7	4	.64	9	.219	.271	.357

Jeff Mathis

Bats: R **Throws:** R **Pos:** C-66; PH-5; DH-2; PR-2 **Ht:** 6'0" **Wt:** 200 **Born:** 3/31/1983 **Age:** 30

					BATTING															BASERUNNING				AVERAGES		
Year	Team	Lg	G	AB	H	2B	3B	HR	(Hm	Rd)	TB	R	RBI	RC	TBB	IBB	SO	HBP	SH	SF	SB	CS	SB%	GDP	Avg	OBP	Slg
2005	LAA	AL	5	3	1	0	0	0	(0	0)	1	1	0	0	0	0	1	0	0	0	0	0	-	0	.333	.333	.333
2006	LAA	AL	23	55	8	2	0	2	(1	1)	16	9	6	4	7	1	14	0	0	1	0	0	-	0	.145	.238	.291
2007	LAA	AL	59	171	36	12	0	4	(3	1)	60	24	23	15	15	0	49	2	3	4	0	1	.00	3	.211	.276	.351
2008	LAA	AL	94	283	55	8	0	9	(4	5)	90	35	42	33	30	4	90	3	8	4	2	2	.50	1	.194	.275	.318
2009	LAA	AL	84	237	50	8	0	5	(3	2)	73	26	28	24	22	0	73	4	8	1	2	3	.40	2	.211	.288	.308
2010	LAA	AL	68	205	40	6	1	3	(2	1)	57	19	18	10	6	0	59	1	3	3	3	0	1.00	3	.195	.219	.278
2011	LAA	AL	93	247	43	12	0	3	(1	2)	64	18	22	12	15	2	75	2	14	1	1	2	.33	1	.174	.225	.259
2012	Tor	AL	71	211	46	13	0	8	(5	3)	83	25	27	18	9	0	68	0	6	1	1	0	1.00	2	.218	.249	.393
	Postseason		10	20	9	5	0	0	(0	0)	14	2	2	3	0	0	5	0	1	0	0	0	-	0	.450	.450	.700
8 ML YEARS			497	1412	279	61	1	34	(19	15)	444	157	166	114	104	7	429	12	42	17	9	8	.53	14	.198	.256	.314

Hideki Matsui

Bats: L **Throws:** R **Pos:** DH-11; PH-11; LF-9; RF-6   **Ht:** 6'2" **Wt:** 210 **Born:** 6/12/1974 **Age:** 39

Year	Team	Lg	G	AB	H	2B	3B	HR	(Hm	Rd)	TB	R	RBI	RC	TBB	IBB	SO	HBP	SH	SF	SB	CS	SB%	GDP	Avg	OBP	Slg
2012	Drhm*	AAA	13	47	8	2	0	0	(-	-)	10	3	4	2	4	1	10	0	0	1	0	0	-	3	.170	.231	.213
2003	NYY	AL	**163**	623	179	42	1	16	(9	7)	271	82	106	96	63	5	86	3	0	6	2	2	.50	25	.287	.353	.435
2004	NYY	AL	**162**	584	174	34	2	31	(18	13)	305	109	108	117	88	2	103	3	0	5	3	0	1.00	11	.298	.390	.522
2005	NYY	AL	**162**	629	192	45	3	23	(15	8)	312	108	116	109	63	7	78	3	0	8	2	2	.50	16	.305	.367	.496
2006	NYY	AL	51	172	52	9	0	8	(1	7)	85	32	29	30	27	2	23	0	0	2	1	0	1.00	6	.302	.393	.494
2007	NYY	AL	143	547	156	28	4	25	(16	9)	267	100	103	91	73	2	73	3	0	10	4	2	.67	9	.285	.367	.488
2008	NYY	AL	93	337	99	17	0	9	(3	6)	143	43	45	56	38	6	47	3	0	0	0	0	-	10	.294	.370	.424
2009	NYY	AL	142	456	125	21	1	28	(13	15)	232	62	90	88	64	1	75	4	0	2	0	1	.00	4	.274	.367	.509
2010	LAA	AL	145	482	132	24	1	21	(10	11)	221	55	84	89	67	6	98	1	0	4	0	1	.00	10	.274	.361	.459
2011	Oak	AL	141	517	130	28	0	12	(4	8)	194	58	72	65	56	3	84	1	0	9	1	1	.50	10	.251	.321	.375
2012	TB	AL	34	95	14	1	0	2	(2	0)	21	7	7	3	8	1	22	0	0	0	0	0	-	5	.147	.214	.221
	Postseason		56	205	64	15	1	10	(5	5)	111	32	39	40	27	2	33	1	0	2	0	0	-	5	.312	.391	.541
	10 ML YEARS		1236	4442	1253	249	12	175	(91	84)	2051	656	760	744	547	35	689	21	0	46	13	9	.59	106	.282	.360	.462

Daisuke Matsuzaka

Pitches: R **Bats:** R **Pos:** SP-11   DICE-kay maht-soo-ZAH-kah   **Ht:** 6'0" **Wt:** 185 **Born:** 9/13/1980 **Age:** 32

			HOW MUCH HE PITCHED					WHAT HE GAVE UP										THE RESULTS							
Year	Team	Lg	G	GS	CG	GF	IP	BFP	H	R	ER	HR	SH	SF	HB	TBB	IBB	SO	WP	Bk	W	L	Pct	Sh	Sv-Op Hld	ERC	ERA
2012	Salem*	A+	1	1	0	0	4.0	18	6	3	3	2	0	0	0	0	0	3	0	0	0	1	.000	0	0- - -	8.13	6.75
2012	Portlnd*	AA	1	1	0	0	4.2	17	3	1	1	0	0	0	0	2	0	7	0	0	0	0	-	0	0- - -	1.98	1.93
2012	Pwtckt*	AAA	11	11	0	0	51.0	216	42	23	18	6	0	2	5	17	0	41	1	0	1	3	.250	0	0- - -	3.30	3.18
2007	Bos	AL	32	32	1	0	204.2	874	191	100	100	25	3	2	13	80	1	201	5	0	15	12	.556	0	0-0 0	4.10	4.40
2008	Bos	AL	29	29	0	0	167.2	716	128	58	54	12	3	4	7	94	1	154	5	0	18	3	.857	0	0-0 0	3.36	2.90
2009	Bos	AL	12	12	0	0	59.1	283	81	38	38	10	1	1	2	30	1	54	8	0	4	6	.400	0	0-0 0	7.45	5.76
2010	Bos	AL	25	25	0	0	153.2	664	137	84	80	13	3	8	8	74	1	133	4	0	9	6	.600	0	0-0 0	3.89	4.69
2011	Bos	AL	8	7	0	1	37.1	167	32	24	22	4	0	0	1	23	0	26	0	0	3	3	.500	0	0-0 0	4.21	5.30
2012	Bos	AL	11	11	0	0	45.2	215	58	43	42	11	0	3	3	20	0	41	3	0	1	7	.125	0	0-0 0	7.20	8.28
	Postseason		7	7	0	0	35.2	163	39	19	19	4	0	1	1	17	0	33	4	0	3	1	.750	0	0-0 0	5.04	4.79
	6 ML YEARS		117	116	1	1	668.1	2919	627	347	336	75	10	18	34	321	4	609	25	0	50	37	.575	0	0-0 0	4.33	4.52

Ryan Mattheus

Pitches: R **Bats:** R **Pos:** RP-66   MATH-uze   **Ht:** 6'3" **Wt:** 205 **Born:** 11/10/1983 **Age:** 29

			HOW MUCH HE PITCHED					WHAT HE GAVE UP										THE RESULTS							
Year	Team	Lg	G	GS	CG	GF	IP	BFP	H	R	ER	HR	SH	SF	HB	TBB	IBB	SO	WP	Bk	W	L	Pct	Sh	Sv-Op Hld	ERC	ERA
2004	Casper*	R+	7	7	0	0	27.1	125	27	16	15	2	2	1	5	14	0	16	7	0	3	3	.500	0	0- - -	4.98	4.94
2005	Ashvll	A	23	23	0	0	128.1	581	142	90	83	16	3	3	12	52	0	102	14	0	7	6	.538	0	0- - -	5.25	5.82
2006	Mdest	A+	28	28	1	0	156.0	718	198	103	90	5	2	8	11	65	0	131	6	1	7	12	.368	1	0- - -	5.51	5.19
2007	Tulsa	AA	26	26	1	0	158.2	704	182	100	98	13	12	5	14	55	2	102	5	0	9	11	.450	0	0- - -	4.95	5.56
2008	Tulsa	AA	58	0	0	40	57.2	244	50	27	21	5	10	2	1	27	2	56	6	0	2	5	.286	0	17- - -	3.56	3.28
2009	Mdest	A+	3	0	0	2	4.1	18	2	1	1	0	0	0	1	2	1	2	0	0	0	1	.000	0	0- - -	1.45	2.08
2009	Tulsa	AA	3	0	0	1	5.0	17	3	2	2	0	1	0	0	1	0	5	0	0	0	1	.000	0	0- - -	1.24	3.60
2009	ColSpr	AAA	13	0	0	6	16.2	75	19	8	8	3	1	0	0	8	2	20	0	0	1	1	.500	0	0- - -	5.64	4.32
2010	Nats	R	6	3	0	1	6.0	24	5	2	1	0	0	1	0	1	0	6	1	0	0	1	.000	0	0- - -	1.74	1.50
2010	Vrmnt	A-	4	1	0	1	5.1	22	3	1	0	0	0	0	0	2	0	5	0	0	1	0	1.000	0	0- - -	1.29	0.00
2011	Hrsbrg	AA	13	0	0	12	14.2	58	9	4	4	1	0	0	1	5	2	18	1	0	2	1	.667	0	4- - -	1.78	2.45
2011	Syrcse	AAA	9	0	0	7	10.0	35	3	0	0	0	0	0	0	3	0	10	0	0	0	0	-	0	2- - -	0.58	0.00
2012	Ptomc	A+	1	0	0	0	1.0	5	2	2	2	2	0	0	0	0	0	1	0	0	0	1	.000	0	0- - -	25.07	18.00
2012	Hrsbrg	AA	2	0	0	0	2.0	8	0	1	1	0	0	0	0	1	0	3	1	0	0	0	-	0	0- - -	0.24	4.50
2011	Was	NL	35	0	0	12	32.0	136	26	11	10	1	4	1	2	15	3	12	1	1	2	2	.500	0	0-0 8	2.94	2.81
2012	Was	NL	66	0	0	11	66.1	265	57	22	21	8	2	4	3	19	5	41	3	0	5	3	.625	0	0-0 18	3.19	2.85
	2 ML YEARS		101	0	0	23	98.1	401	83	33	31	9	6	5	5	34	8	53	4	1	7	5	.583	0	0-0 26	3.12	2.84

Kevin Mattison

Bats: L **Throws:** L **Pos:** PH-3; LF-1   **Ht:** 6'1" **Wt:** 195 **Born:** 9/20/1985 **Age:** 27

Year	Team	Lg	G	AB	H	2B	3B	HR	(Hm	Rd)	TB	R	RBI	RC	TBB	IBB	SO	HBP	SH	SF	SB	CS	SB%	GDP	Avg	OBP	Slg
2008	Jmstwn	A-	70	268	67	10	6	4	(-	-)	101	48	20	38	37	0	71	2	1	1	14	4	.78	0	.250	.344	.377
2009	Grnsbr	A	95	360	90	15	1	15	(-	-)	152	61	47	57	32	1	81	9	3	4	41	6	.87	6	.250	.323	.422
2010	Jupiter	A+	90	362	79	13	4	3	(-	-)	109	46	29	35	22	0	87	7	3	3	44	10	.81	4	.218	.274	.301
2010	NewOr	AAA	7	29	6	0	0	0	(-	-)	6	4	0	0	1	0	7	0	1	0	1	1	.50	0	.207	.233	.207
2010	Jaxnvl	AA	16	45	10	4	1	0	(-	-)	16	10	1	5	4	0	10	0	2	0	4	0	1.00	6	.222	.286	.356
2011	Jaxnvl	AA	130	503	131	17	16	8	(-	-)	204	87	49	79	58	2	127	17	8	5	37	16	.70	4	.260	.353	.406
2012	NewOr	AAA	121	482	116	23	6	13	(-	-)	190	80	41	62	44	2	145	6	3	3	26	12	.68	1	.241	.310	.394
2012	Mia	NL	3	5	0	0	0	0	(0	0)	0	0	0	0	0	0	2	0	0	0	0	0	-	0	.000	.000	.000

Brian Matusz

Pitches: L **Bats:** L **Pos:** RP-18; SP-16   MATT-uss   **Ht:** 6'4" **Wt:** 200 **Born:** 2/11/1987 **Age:** 26

			HOW MUCH HE PITCHED					WHAT HE GAVE UP										THE RESULTS							
Year	Team	Lg	G	GS	CG	GF	IP	BFP	H	R	ER	HR	SH	SF	HB	TBB	IBB	SO	WP	Bk	W	L	Pct	Sh	Sv-Op Hld	ERC	ERA
2012	Norfolk*	AAA	10	6	1	1	47.0	195	43	24	22	2	0	2	0	15	0	32	4	1	2	1	.667	1	1- - -	2.93	4.21
2009	Bal	AL	8	8	0	0	44.2	196	52	24	23	6	2	2	0	14	0	38	0	0	5	2	.714	0	0-0 0	4.91	4.63

			HOW MUCH HE PITCHED						WHAT HE GAVE UP											THE RESULTS							
Year	Team	Lg	G	GS	CG	GF	IP	BFP	H	R	ER	HR	SH	SF	HB	TBB	IBB	SO	WP	Bk	W	L	Pct	Sh	Sv-Op	Hld	ERC	ERA
2010	Bal	AL	32	32	0	0	175.2	760	173	88	84	19	6	6	7	63	3	143	1	0	10	12	.455	0	0-0	0	3.98	4.30
2011	Bal	AL	12	12	0	0	49.2	245	81	60	59	18	1	2	0	24	1	38	0	0	1	9	.100	0	0-0	0	10.88	10.69
2012	Bal	AL	34	16	0	2	98.0	441	112	61	53	15	2	3	0	41	4	81	0	0	6	10	.375	0	0-0	4	5.25	4.87
	4 ML YEARS		86	68	0	2	368.0	1642	418	233	219	58	11	13	7	142	8	300	1	0	22	33	.400	0	0-0	4	5.25	5.36

Joe Mauer

Bats: L **Throws:** R **Pos:** C-74; DH-42; 1B-30; PH-3   **Ht:** 6'5" **Wt:** 231 **Born:** 4/19/1983 **Age:** 30

								BATTING															BASERUNNING				AVERAGES		
Year	Team	Lg	G	AB	H	2B	3B	HR	(Hm	Rd)	TB	R	RBI	RC	TBB	IBB	SO	HBP	SH	SF		SB	CS	SB%	GDP		Avg	OBP	Slg
2004	Min	AL	35	107	33	8	1	6	(4	2)	61	18	17	21	11	0	14	1	0	3		1	0	1.00	1		.308	.369	.570
2005	Min	AL	131	489	144	26	2	9	(4	5)	201	61	55	78	61	12	64	1	0	3		13	1	.93	9		.294	.372	.411
2006	Min	AL	140	521	181	36	4	13	(3	10)	264	86	84	103	79	21	54	1	0	7		8	3	.73	24		.347	.429	.507
2007	Min	AL	109	406	119	27	3	7	(2	5)	173	62	60	69	57	10	51	3	2	3		7	1	.88	11		.293	.382	.426
2008	Min	AL	146	536	176	31	4	9	(7	2)	242	98	85	103	84	8	50	1	1	11		1	1	.50	21		.328	.413	.451
2009	Min	AL	138	523	191	30	1	28	(16	12)	307	94	96	123	76	14	63	2	0	5		4	1	.80	13		.365	.444	.587
2010	Min	AL	137	510	167	43	1	9	(1	8)	239	88	75	91	65	14	53	3	0	6		1	4	.20	19		.327	.402	.469
2011	Min	AL	82	296	85	15	0	3	(2	1)	109	38	30	39	32	7	38	3	0	2		0	0	-	9		.287	.360	.368
2012	Min	AL	147	545	174	31	4	10	(4	6)	243	81	85	108	90	10	88	2	1	3		8	4	.67	23		.319	.416	.446
	Postseason		9	35	10	1	0	0	(0	0)	11	1	1	2	4	0	7	0	0	0		0	0	-	0		.286	.359	.314
	9 ML YEARS		1065	3933	1270	247	20	94	(41	53)	1839	626	587	735	555	96	475	17	4	43		43	15	.74	130		.323	.405	.468

Justin Maxwell

Bats: R **Throws:** R **Pos:** CF-59; LF-38; PH-32; RF-20; PR-2   **Ht:** 6'5" **Wt:** 235 **Born:** 11/6/1983 **Age:** 29

								BATTING															BASERUNNING				AVERAGES		
Year	Team	Lg	G	AB	H	2B	3B	HR	(Hm	Rd)	TB	R	RBI	RC	TBB	IBB	SO	HBP	SH	SF		SB	CS	SB%	GDP		Avg	OBP	Slg
2012	OKCity*	AAA	3	10	2	1	0	0	(-	-)	3	1	0	0	0	0	3	0	0	0		0	0	-	0		.200	.200	.300
2012	CpChr*	AA	2	8	2	1	0	0	(-	-)	3	2	1	1	0	0	5	1	0	0		0	0	-	0		.250	.333	.375
2007	Was	NL	15	26	7	0	0	2	(0	2)	13	5	5	4	1	0	8	0	0	0		0	0	-	0		.269	.296	.500
2009	Was	NL	40	89	22	4	1	4	(1	3)	40	13	9	15	12	0	32	1	0	0		6	1	.86	1		.247	.343	.449
2010	Was	NL	67	104	15	6	0	3	(1	2)	30	16	12	11	25	2	43	0	0	2		5	1	.83	3		.144	.305	.288
2012	Hou	NL	124	315	72	13	3	18	(10	8)	145	46	53	52	32	0	114	3	0	2		9	4	.69	6		.229	.304	.460
	4 ML YEARS		246	534	116	23	4	27	(12	15)	228	80	79	82	70	2	197	4	0	4		20	6	.77	10		.217	.310	.427

John Mayberry

Bats: R **Throws:** R **Pos:** LF-70; CF-58; 1B-27; PH-23; PR-4; RF-3; DH-1   **Ht:** 6'6" **Wt:** 225 **Born:** 12/21/1983 **Age:** 29

								BATTING															BASERUNNING				AVERAGES		
Year	Team	Lg	G	AB	H	2B	3B	HR	(Hm	Rd)	TB	R	RBI	RC	TBB	IBB	SO	HBP	SH	SF		SB	CS	SB%	GDP		Avg	OBP	Slg
2009	Phi	NL	39	57	12	3	0	4	(1	3)	27	8	8	5	2	0	23	1	0	0		0	0	-	2		.211	.250	.474
2010	Phi	NL	11	12	4	0	0	2	(0	2)	10	4	6	4	1	0	4	0	0	0		0	1	.00	0		.333	.385	.833
2011	Phi	NL	104	267	73	17	1	15	(7	8)	137	37	49	44	26	2	55	2	0	1		8	3	.73	6		.273	.341	.513
2012	Phi	NL	149	441	108	24	0	14	(7	7)	174	53	46	47	34	2	111	2	0	2		1	0	1.00	17		.245	.301	.395
	Postseason		2	4	0	0	0	0	(0	0)	0	0	0	0	0	0	1	0	0	0		0	0	-	0		.000	.000	.000
	4 ML YEARS		303	777	197	44	1	35	(15	20)	348	102	109	100	63	4	193	5	0	3		9	4	.69	25		.254	.313	.448

Cameron Maybin

Bats: R **Throws:** R **Pos:** CF-145; PR-5; PH-1   **Ht:** 6'3" **Wt:** 210 **Born:** 4/4/1987 **Age:** 26

								BATTING															BASERUNNING				AVERAGES		
Year	Team	Lg	G	AB	H	2B	3B	HR	(Hm	Rd)	TB	R	RBI	RC	TBB	IBB	SO	HBP	SH	SF		SB	CS	SB%	GDP		Avg	OBP	Slg
2007	Det	AL	24	49	7	3	0	1	(0	1)	13	8	2	2	3	0	21	1	0	0		5	0	1.00	0		.143	.208	.265
2008	Fla	NL	8	32	16	2	0	0	(0	0)	18	9	2	8	3	0	8	0	1	0		4	0	1.00	0		.500	.543	.563
2009	Fla	NL	54	176	44	12	2	1	(1	3)	72	30	13	15	17	1	51	1	4	1		3	3	.25	2		.250	.318	.409
2010	Fla	NL	82	291	68	7	3	8	(5	3)	105	46	28	37	24	1	92	5	1	1		9	2	.82	4		.234	.302	.361
2011	SD	NL	137	516	136	24	8	9	(2	7)	203	82	40	69	44	2	125	2	4	2		40	8	.83	6		.264	.323	.393
2012	SD	NL	147	507	123	20	5	8	(3	5)	177	67	45	52	44	1	110	4	3	3		26	7	.79	12		.243	.306	.349
	6 ML YEARS		452	1571	394	68	18	30	(11	19)	588	242	130	183	135	5	407	13	13	7		85	20	.81	24		.251	.314	.374

Edwin Maysonet

Bats: R **Throws:** R **Pos:** SS-18; PH-8; 2B-3; PR-2; 3B-1   MACE-uh-nett   **Ht:** 6'1" **Wt:** 180 **Born:** 10/17/1981 **Age:** 31

								BATTING															BASERUNNING				AVERAGES		
Year	Team	Lg	G	AB	H	2B	3B	HR	(Hm	Rd)	TB	R	RBI	RC	TBB	IBB	SO	HBP	SH	SF		SB	CS	SB%	GDP		Avg	OBP	Slg
2012	Nashv*	AAA	69	231	48	13	2	3	(-	-)	74	20	19	20	16	0	43	4	5	3		2	1	.67	3		.208	.268	.320
2008	Hou	NL	7	7	1	0	0	0	(0	0)	1	0	0	0	0	0	2	0	0	0		0	0	-	0		.143	.143	.143
2009	Hou	NL	39	69	20	2	0	1	(0	1)	25	9	7	9	5	0	19	0	4	1		0	0	-	1		.290	.333	.362
2012	Mil	NL	30	60	15	1	1	1	(1	0)	21	7	4	5	3	0	9	1	2	0		1	0	1.00	1		.250	.297	.350
	3 ML YEARS		76	136	36	3	1	2	(1	1)	47	16	11	14	8	0	30	1	6	1		1	0	1.00	2		.265	.308	.346

Vin Mazzaro

Pitches: R **Bats:** R **Pos:** RP-12; SP-6 · muh-ZAIR-oh · **Ht:** 6'2" **Wt:** 220 **Born:** 9/27/1986 **Age:** 26

Year	Team	Lg	G	GS	CG	GF	IP	BFP	H	R	ER	HR	SH	SF	HB	TBB	IBB	SO	WP	Bk	W	L	Pct	Sh	Sv-Op Hld	ERC	ERA
2012	Omha*	AAA	22	8	0	12	67.0	276	69	28	27	4	1	4	3	20	0	62	6	0	2	2	.500	0	5-- -	3.91	3.63
2009	Oak	AL	17	17	0	0	91.1	423	120	61	54	12	1	3	4	39	3	59	5	0	4	9	.308	0	0-0 0	6.49	5.32
2010	Oak	AL	24	18	0	4	122.1	537	127	70	58	19	4	4	4	50	0	79	5	0	6	8	.429	0	0-0 0	4.86	4.27
2011	KC	AL	7	4	0	2	28.1	131	39	26	26	4	3	3	1	15	1	10	2	0	1	1	.500	0	0-0 0	7.67	8.26
2012	KC	AL	18	6	0	4	44.0	198	55	29	28	3	1	2	3	19	2	26	1	0	4	3	.571	0	0-0 0	5.80	5.73
	4 ML YEARS		66	45	0	10	286.0	1289	341	186	166	38	9	12	12	123	6	174	13	0	15	21	.417	0	0-0 0	5.78	5.22

Zach McAllister

Pitches: R **Bats:** R **Pos:** SP-22 · **Ht:** 6'6" **Wt:** 240 **Born:** 12/8/1987 **Age:** 25

Year	Team	Lg	G	GS	CG	GF	IP	BFP	H	R	ER	HR	SH	SF	HB	TBB	IBB	SO	WP	Bk	W	L	Pct	Sh	Sv-Op Hld	ERC	ERA
2006	Yanks	R	11	1	0	6	35.0	148	35	14	12	1	0	0	1	12	0	28	3	0	5	2	.714	0	0-- -	3.51	3.09
2007	StIslnd	A-	16	15	0	0	71.1	316	80	42	41	3	3	3	2	28	2	75	2	0	4	6	.400	0	0-- -	4.38	5.17
2008	CtnSC	A	10	10	0	0	62.1	253	59	28	17	3	1	1	2	8	0	53	3	0	6	3	.667	0	0-- -	2.54	2.45
2008	Tampa	A+	15	14	1	1	88.2	348	74	24	18	6	0	2	4	13	1	62	2	0	8	6	.571	1	1-- -	2.26	1.83
2009	Trntn	AA	22	22	0	0	121.0	493	98	39	30	4	3	3	7	33	0	96	0	1	7	5	.583	0	0-- -	2.39	2.23
2010	S-WB	AAA	24	24	1	0	132.2	591	166	82	78	20	3	7	6	38	0	88	7	0	8	10	.444	0	0-- -	5.68	5.29
2010	Clmbs	AAA	3	3	0	0	17.0	78	20	13	13	1	0	4	1	7	0	11	0	0	1	2	.333	0	0-- -	5.00	6.88
2011	Clmbs	AAA	25	25	3	0	154.2	644	155	61	57	11	6	7	6	31	0	128	1	0	12	3	.800	1	0-- -	3.27	3.32
2012	Clmbs	AAA	11	11	0	0	63.1	258	59	27	21	5	0	2	2	19	0	52	3	0	5	2	.714	0	0-- -	3.40	2.98
2011	Cle	AL	4	4	0	0	17.2	84	26	16	12	1	0	0	0	7	1	14	0	0	0	1	.000	0	0-0 0	6.41	6.11
2012	Cle	AL	22	22	0	0	125.1	543	133	78	59	19	2	5	1	38	0	110	0	2	6	8	.429	0	0-0 0	4.37	4.24
	2 ML YEARS		26	26	0	0	143.0	627	159	94	71	20	2	5	1	45	1	124	0	2	6	9	.400	0	0-0 0	4.62	4.47

Matt McBride

Bats: R **Throws:** R **Pos:** PH-13; RF-12; 1B-8 · **Ht:** 6'2" **Wt:** 215 **Born:** 5/23/1985 **Age:** 28

Year	Team	Lg	G	AB	H	2B	3B	HR	(Hm	Rd)	TB	R	RBI	RC	TBB	IBB	SO	HBP	SH	SF	SB	CS	SB%	GDP	Avg	OBP	Slg
2006	MhVlly	A-	52	184	50	12	0	4	(-	-)	74	24	31	28	16	2	22	9	0	2	5	2	.71	1	.272	.355	.402
2007	Lk Cty	A	105	421	119	35	2	8	(-	-)	182	66	66	67	38	1	54	8	0	7	1	0	1.00	13	.283	.348	.432
2007	Akron	AA	2	7	4	2	0	0	(-	-)	6	2	0	2	0	0	0	1	0	0	0	0	-	0	.571	.625	.857
2008	Indns	R	17	50	19	7	1	2	(-	-)	34	13	9	15	6	0	5	4	0	0	3	0	1.00	0	.380	.483	.680
2008	Knstn	A+	17	67	12	2	0	0	(-	-)	14	9	6	3	7	1	9	1	0	1	0	0	-	0	.179	.263	.209
2008	Lk Cty	A	11	39	12	4	0	1	(-	-)	19	6	7	7	5	1	5	0	0	0	0	0	-	1	.308	.386	.487
2009	Knstn	A+	31	126	51	15	0	6	(-	-)	84	24	36	34	11	0	15	1	0	0	0	0	-	2	.405	.453	.667
2009	Akron	AA	98	361	89	29	0	12	(-	-)	154	48	63	49	18	0	42	14	4	9	1	1	.50	4	.247	.301	.427
2010	Akron	AA	96	361	102	25	1	17	(-	-)	180	54	64	63	30	3	61	8	0	5	0	2	.00	6	.283	.347	.499
2010	Clmbs	AAA	32	120	32	6	0	4	(-	-)	50	17	11	15	5	0	17	0	2	1	0	0	-	4	.267	.294	.417
2011	Akron	AA	84	310	92	24	4	14	(-	-)	166	50	53	60	30	1	44	2	1	3	3	0	1.00	6	.297	.359	.535
2011	Clmbs	AAA	12	45	7	2	0	1	(-	-)	12	3	3	1	2	0	8	0	0	0	0	0	-	0	.156	.191	.267
2011	Tulsa		6	17	4	0	0	0	(-	-)	4	4	2	1	0	0	3	1	0	0	0	0	-	0	.235	.278	.235
2012	ColSpr	AAA	108	439	151	42	6	10	(-	-)	235	73	87	84	19	0	47	1	0	10	0	1	.00	4	.344	.365	.535
2012	Col	NL	31	78	16	2	0	2	(1	1)	24	8	11	7	1	0	17	1	0	1	0	0	-	4	.205	.222	.308

Brian McCann

Bats: L **Throws:** R **Pos:** C-114; PH-4; DH-3; PR-1 · **Ht:** 6'3" **Wt:** 230 **Born:** 2/20/1984 **Age:** 29

Year	Team	Lg	G	AB	H	2B	3B	HR	(Hm	Rd)	TB	R	RBI	RC	TBB	IBB	SO	HBP	SH	SF	SB	CS	SB%	GDP	Avg	OBP	Slg
2005	Atl	NL	59	180	50	7	0	5	(2	3)	72	20	23	25	18	5	26	1	4	1	1	1	.50	5	.278	.345	.400
2006	Atl	NL	130	442	147	34	0	24	(10	14)	253	61	93	94	41	8	54	3	0	6	2	0	1.00	12	.333	.388	.572
2007	Atl	NL	139	504	136	38	0	18	(6	12)	228	51	92	68	35	7	74	5	2	6	0	1	.00	19	.270	.320	.452
2008	Atl	NL	145	509	153	42	1	23	(10	13)	266	68	87	84	57	4	64	4	0	3	5	0	1.00	17	.301	.373	.523
2009	Atl	NL	138	488	137	35	1	21	(12	9)	237	63	94	83	49	3	83	5	3	6	4	1	.80	17	.281	.349	.486
2010	Atl	NL	143	479	129	25	0	21	(13	8)	217	63	77	76	74	10	98	9	0	4	5	2	.71	12	.269	.375	.453
2011	Atl	NL	128	466	126	19	0	24	(15	9)	217	51	71	76	57	14	89	2	0	2	3	2	.60	10	.270	.351	.466
2012	Atl	NL	121	439	101	14	0	20	(11	9)	175	44	67	45	44	7	76	1	0	3	3	0	1.00	15	.230	.300	.399
	Postseason		7	30	9	1	0	3	(2	1)	19	4	8	5	1	0	10	0	0	1	0	0	-	0	.300	.313	.633
	8 ML YEARS		1003	3507	979	214	2	156	(79	77)	1665	421	604	551	375	58	564	30	9	31	23	7	.77	107	.279	.351	.475

Brandon McCarthy

Pitches: R **Bats:** R **Pos:** SP-18 · **Ht:** 6'7" **Wt:** 200 **Born:** 7/7/1983 **Age:** 29

Year	Team	Lg	G	GS	CG	GF	IP	BFP	H	R	ER	HR	SH	SF	HB	TBB	IBB	SO	WP	Bk	W	L	Pct	Sh	Sv-Op Hld	ERC	ERA
2012	Scrmto*	AAA	2	2	0	0	9.2	39	9	6	6	1	0	0	0	3	0	11	0	0	0	1	.000	0	0-- -	3.50	5.59
2005	CWS	AL	12	10	0	0	67.0	277	62	30	30	13	1	1	2	17	0	48	1	1	3	2	.600	0	0-0 0	3.83	4.03
2006	CWS	AL	53	2	0	13	84.2	354	77	44	44	17	3	1	0	33	9	69	5	0	4	7	.364	0	0-1 11	4.10	4.68
2007	Tex	AL	23	22	0	0	101.2	459	111	62	55	9	3	5	3	48	0	59	4	1	5	10	.333	0	0-0 0	4.89	4.87
2008	Tex	AL	5	5	0	0	22.0	93	20	11	10	3	0	2	1	8	0	10	0	0	1	1	.500	0	0-0 0	3.87	4.09
2009	Tex	AL	17	17	1	0	97.1	420	96	55	50	13	0	5	3	36	0	65	0	0	7	4	.636	1	0-0 0	4.22	4.62
2011	Oak	AL	25	25	5	0	170.2	690	168	73	63	11	4	9	0	25	1	123	3	0	9	9	.500	1	0-0 0	2.80	3.32
2012	Oak	AL	18	18	0	0	111.0	469	115	44	40	10	5	4	6	24	2	73	0	0	8	6	.571	0	0-0 0	3.67	3.24
	7 ML YEARS		153	99	6	13	654.1	2762	649	319	292	76	16	27	15	191	12	447	13	2	37	39	.487	2	0-1 11	3.78	4.02

Kyle McClellan

Pitches: R Bats: R Pos: RP-16   Ht: 6'2" Wt: 215 Born: 6/12/1984 Age: 29

			HOW MUCH HE PITCHED						WHAT HE GAVE UP													THE RESULTS							
Year	Team	Lg	G	GS	CG	GF	IP	BFP	H	R	ER	HR	SH	SF	HB	TBB	IBB	SO	WP	Bk	W	L	Pct	Sh	Sv-Op	Hld	ERC	ERA
2008	StL	NL	68	0	0	17	75.2	327	79	37	34	7	2	1	4	26	2	59	6	0	2	7	.222	0	1-6	30	4.24	4.04
2009	StL	NL	66	0	0	14	66.2	288	56	27	25	4	5	2	2	34	2	51	4	0	4	4	.500	0	3-6	15	3.38	3.38
2010	StL	NL	68	0	0	18	75.1	307	58	20	19	9	4	1	3	23	3	60	2	0	1	4	.200	0	2-3	19	2.70	2.27
2011	StL	NL	43	17	0	5	141.2	607	143	71	66	21	6	2	6	43	3	76	6	0	12	7	.632	0	0-1	4	4.20	4.19
2012	StL	NL	16	0	0	6	18.2	83	16	11	11	2	0	0	2	9	0	11	1	0	1	0	1.000	0	0-0	1	3.98	5.30
	Postseason		2	0	0	0	1.0	8	3	1	1	0	1	0	1	1	0	0	0	0	0	0	-	0	0-0	0	24.59	9.00
	5 ML YEARS		261	17	0	50	378.0	1612	352	166	155	43	17	6	17	135	10	257	19	0	19	23	.452	0	6-16	69	3.74	3.69

Mike McClendon

Pitches: R Bats: R Pos: RP-9   Ht: 6'5" Wt: 225 Born: 4/3/1985 Age: 28

			HOW MUCH HE PITCHED						WHAT HE GAVE UP													THE RESULTS							
Year	Team	Lg	G	GS	CG	GF	IP	BFP	H	R	ER	HR	SH	SF	HB	TBB	IBB	SO	WP	Bk	W	L	Pct	Sh	Sv-Op	Hld	ERC	ERA
2012	Nashv*	AAA	33	0	0	7	43.0	184	40	24	20	2	4	2	3	18	2	27	2	0	4	3	.571	0	5--	-	3.62	4.19
2010	Mil	NL	17	0	0	3	21.0	84	15	7	7	2	0	0	7	0	0	21	1	0	2	0	1.000	0	0-1	3	2.31	3.00
2011	Mil	NL	9	0	0	7	13.2	59	15	5	4	1	0	0	1	3	0	10	2	0	3	0	1.000	0	0-0	0	3.99	2.63
2012	Mil	NL	9	0	0	3	14.0	69	20	11	10	1	3	0	3	5	0	4	1	0	0	0	-	0	0-0	0	7.07	6.43
	3 ML YEARS		35	0	0	13	48.2	212	50	23	21	4	3	0	4	15	0	35	4	0	5	0	1.000	0	0-1	3	4.03	3.88

Mike McCoy

Bats: R Throws: R Pos: PR-10; 2B-8; 3B-6; LF-4; CF-4; RF-3; DH-3; PH-3; SS-1   Ht: 5'9" Wt: 175 Born: 4/2/1981 Age: 32

			BATTING																	BASERUNNING				AVERAGES		
Year	Team	Lg	G	AB	H	2B	3B	HR	(Hm	Rd)	TB	R	RBI	RC	TBB	IBB	SO	HBP	SH	SF	SB	CS	SB%	GDP	Avg	OBP	Slg
2012	LsVgs*	AAA	85	278	73	14	1	3	(-	-)	98	46	31	45	58	0	51	1	7	5	21	10	.68	7	.263	.386	.353
2009	Col	NL	12	5	0	0	0	0	(0	0)	0	1	0	0	0	0	2	0	1	0	2	0	1.00	0	.000	.000	.000
2010	Tor	AL	46	82	16	4	0	0	(0	0)	20	9	3	5	8	0	20	0	0	0	5	1	.83	0	.195	.267	.244
2011	Tor	AL	80	197	39	8	0	2	(0	2)	53	26	10	17	25	1	41	1	5	0	12	2	.86	0	.198	.291	.269
2012	Tor	AL	32	52	9	1	0	1	(1	0)	13	10	7	2	4	0	6	0	0	0	2	1	.67	1	.173	.232	.250
	4 ML YEARS		170	336	64	13	0	3	(1	2)	86	46	20	24	37	1	69	1	6	0	21	4	.84	1	.190	.273	.256

Andrew McCutchen

Bats: R Throws: R Pos: CF-156; PH-1   Ht: 5'10" Wt: 185 Born: 10/10/1986 Age: 26

			BATTING																	BASERUNNING				AVERAGES		
Year	Team	Lg	G	AB	H	2B	3B	HR	(Hm	Rd)	TB	R	RBI	RC	TBB	IBB	SO	HBP	SH	SF	SB	CS	SB%	GDP	Avg	OBP	Slg
2009	Pit	NL	108	433	124	26	9	12	(8	4)	204	74	54	78	54	2	83	2	0	4	22	5	.81	3	.286	.365	.471
2010	Pit	NL	154	570	163	35	5	16	(8	8)	256	94	56	86	70	1	89	5	1	7	33	10	.77	6	.286	.365	.449
2011	Pit	NL	158	572	148	34	5	23	(10	13)	261	87	89	102	89	3	126	9	2	6	23	10	.70	7	.259	.364	.456
2012	Pit	NL	157	593	194	29	6	31	(15	16)	328	107	96	125	70	13	132	5	0	5	20	12	.63	9	.327	.400	.553
	4 ML YEARS		577	2168	629	124	25	82	(41	41)	1049	362	295	391	283	19	430	21	3	22	98	37	.73	25	.290	.374	.484

Daniel McCutchen

Pitches: R Bats: R Pos: RP-1   Ht: 6'2" Wt: 215 Born: 9/26/1982 Age: 30

			HOW MUCH HE PITCHED						WHAT HE GAVE UP													THE RESULTS							
Year	Team	Lg	G	GS	CG	GF	IP	BFP	H	R	ER	HR	SH	SF	HB	TBB	IBB	SO	WP	Bk	W	L	Pct	Sh	Sv-Op	Hld	ERC	ERA
2012	Indy*	AAA	36	1	0	9	63.1	258	54	25	21	3	4	2	3	14	3	55	2	1	7	2	.778	0	3--	-	2.39	2.98
2012	Bradtn*	A+	1	0	0	0	2.0	7	1	0	0	0	0	0	0	0	0	1	0	0	0	0	-	0	0--	-	0.54	0.00
2009	Pit	NL	6	6	0	0	36.1	155	38	17	17	6	3	0	1	11	2	19	0	0	1	2	.333	0	0-0	0	4.45	4.21
2010	Pit	NL	28	9	0	4	67.2	316	83	48	46	13	4	4	2	28	0	38	2	0	2	5	.286	0	0-0	0	6.16	6.12
2011	Pit	NL	73	0	0	15	84.2	364	87	38	35	7	4	3	4	33	5	47	7	0	5	3	.625	0	0-0	10	4.23	3.72
2012	Pit	NL	1	0	0	1	0.0	2	1	2	2	1	0	0	0	1	0	0	0	0	0	1	.000	0	0-0	0	-	-
	4 ML YEARS		108	15	0	20	188.2	837	209	105	100	27	11	7	7	73	7	104	9	0	8	11	.421	0	0-0	10	5.04	4.77

Darnell McDonald

Bats: R Throws: R Pos: LF-21; RF-12; CF-7; PH-7; PR-5; DH-3   Ht: 5'11" Wt: 205 Born: 11/17/1978 Age: 34

			BATTING																	BASERUNNING				AVERAGES		
Year	Team	Lg	G	AB	H	2B	3B	HR	(Hm	Rd)	TB	R	RBI	RC	TBB	IBB	SO	HBP	SH	SF	SB	CS	SB%	GDP	Avg	OBP	Slg
2012	Pwtckt*	AAA	6	21	4	3	0	0	(-	-)	7	2	2	1	0	0	6	1	0	1	0	0	-	0	.190	.217	.333
2012	S-WB*	AAA	31	108	21	1	0	3	(-	-)	31	18	7	9	15	1	29	1	0	0	1	2	.33	4	.194	.298	.287
2004	Bal	AL	17	32	5	1	0	0	(0	0)	6	3	1	2	2	0	6	0	0	0	1	0	1.00	0	.156	.206	.188
2007	Min	AL	4	10	1	0	0	0	(0	0)	1	0	0	0	1	0	3	0	0	0	0	0	-	0	.100	.182	.100
2009	Cin	NL	47	105	28	6	1	2	(2	0)	42	12	10	10	5	0	31	1	0	0	1	0	1.00	0	.267	.306	.400
2010	Bos	AL	117	319	86	18	3	9	(5	4)	137	40	34	46	30	1	85	2	12	0	9	1	.90	5	.270	.336	.429
2011	Bos	AL	79	157	37	6	1	6	(2	4)	63	26	24	19	14	0	33	2	0	2	2	3	.40	3	.236	.303	.401
2012	2 Tms	AL	42	88	18	7	0	2	(1	1)	31	17	9	8	12	0	19	0	2	1	1	1	.50	1	.205	.297	.352
12	Bos	AL	38	84	18	7	0	2	(1	1)	31	17	9	8	12	0	17	0	2	1	1	1	.50	1	.214	.309	.369
12	NYY	AL	4	4	0	0	0	0	(0	0)	0	0	0	0	0	0	2	0	0	0	0	0	-	0	.000	.000	.000
	6 ML YEARS		306	711	175	38	5	19	(10	9)	280	98	78	85	64	1	177	5	14	3	14	5	.74	13	.246	.312	.394

James McDonald

Pitches: R **Bats:** L **Pos:** SP-29; RP-1   **Ht:** 6'4" **Wt:** 205 **Born:** 10/19/1984 **Age:** 28

			HOW MUCH HE PITCHED							WHAT HE GAVE UP											THE RESULTS						
Year	Team	Lg	G	GS	CG	GF	IP	BFP	H	R	ER	HR	SH	SF	HB	TBB	IBB	SO	WP	Bk	W	L	Pct	Sh	Sv-Op	Hld	ERC	ERA
2008	LAD	NL	4	0	0	1	6.0	24	5	0	0	0	1	0	0	1	0	2	0	0	0	0	-	0	0-0	0	1.74	0.00
2009	LAD	NL	45	4	0	10	63.0	280	60	34	28	6	2	3	5	34	5	54	4	0	5	5	.500	0	0-0	5	4.53	4.00
2010	2 Tms	NL	15	12	0	0	71.2	306	70	32	32	4	5	3	0	29	5	68	5	0	4	6	.400	0	0-0	1	3.56	4.02
2011	Pit	NL	31	31	0	0	171.0	754	176	86	80	24	6	5	7	78	4	142	5	1	9	9	.500	0	0-0	0	4.92	4.21
2012	Pit	NL	30	29	1	0	171.0	713	147	85	80	21	5	4	4	69	6	151	3	0	12	8	.600	0	0-0	0	3.55	4.21
10	LAD	NL	4	1	0	0	7.2	38	11	7	7	1	0	1	0	5	1	7	0	0	0	1	.000	0	0-0	1	7.83	8.22
10	Pit	NL	11	11	0	0	64.0	268	59	25	25	3	5	2	0	24	4	61	5	0	4	5	.444	0	0-0	0	3.12	3.52
	Postseason		2	0	0	0	5.1	21	3	0	0	0	0	0	0	2	0	7	0	0	0	0	-	0	0-0	0	1.35	0.00
	5 ML YEARS		125	76	1	11	482.2	2077	458	237	220	55	19	15	16	211	20	417	17	1	30	28	.517	0	0-0	6	4.13	4.10

John McDonald

Bats: R **Throws:** R **Pos:** SS-54; PH-12; 3B-5; 2B-4   **Ht:** 5'9" **Wt:** 181 **Born:** 9/24/1974 **Age:** 38

			BATTING																			BASERUNNING				AVERAGES		
Year	Team	Lg	G	AB	H	2B	3B	HR	(Hm	Rd)	TB	R	RBI	RC	TBB	IBB	SO	HBP	SH	SF	SB	CS	SB%	GDP	Avg	OBP	Slg
2012	DBcks*	R	3	8	0	0	0	0	(-	-)	0	1	1	0	3	0	1	1	0	0	0	0	-	0	.000	.333	.000
1999	Cle	AL	18	21	7	0	0	0	(0	0)	7	2	0	1	0	0	3	0	0	0	0	1	.00	2	.333	.333	.333
2000	Cle	AL	9	9	4	0	0	0	(0	0)	4	0	0	2	0	0	1	0	0	0	0	0	-	0	.444	.444	.444
2001	Cle	AL	17	22	2	1	0	0	(0	0)	3	1	0	0	1	0	7	1	1	0	0	0	-	0	.091	.167	.136
2002	Cle	AL	93	264	66	11	3	1	(0	1)	86	35	12	24	10	0	50	5	7	2	3	0	1.00	4	.250	.288	.326
2003	Cle	AL	82	214	46	9	1	1	(0	1)	60	21	14	18	11	0	31	2	4	2	3	3	.50	4	.215	.258	.280
2004	Cle	AL	66	93	19	5	1	2	(0	2)	32	17	7	6	4	0	11	0	3	0	0	0	-	2	.204	.237	.344
2005	2 Tms	AL	68	166	46	6	1	0	(0	0)	54	18	16	19	11	0	24	2	3	2	6	1	.86	6	.277	.326	.325
2006	Tor	AL	104	260	58	7	3	3	(1	2)	80	35	23	20	16	0	41	2	6	2	7	2	.78	5	.223	.271	.308
2007	Tor	AL	123	327	82	20	2	1	(1	0)	109	32	31	35	11	0	48	2	12	1	7	2	.78	4	.251	.279	.333
2008	Tor	AL	84	186	39	8	0	1	(1	0)	50	21	18	11	10	0	25	2	7	2	3	1	.75	3	.210	.255	.269
2009	Tor	AL	73	151	39	7	0	4	(2	2)	58	18	13	16	1	0	18	2	1	1	0	2	.00	1	.258	.261	.384
2010	Tor	AL	63	152	38	9	2	6	(3	3)	69	27	23	20	6	0	26	0	2	3	2	1	.67	5	.250	.273	.454
2011	2 Tms	AL	84	227	52	10	1	2	(2	0)	70	21	22	23	12	0	27	1	3	2	2	4	.33	1	.229	.269	.308
2012	Ari	NL	70	197	49	9	0	6	(4	2)	76	16	22	21	12	5	33	1	2	0	0	1	.00	3	.249	.295	.386
05	Tor	AL	37	93	27	3	0	0	(0	0)	30	8	12	13	6	0	12	2	3	2	5	0	1.00	3	.290	.340	.323
05	Det	AL	31	73	19	3	1	0	(0	0)	24	10	4	6	5	0	12	0	0	0	1	1	.50	3	.260	.308	.329
11	Tor	AL	65	168	42	8	1	2	(2	0)	58	19	20	21	8	0	18	1	3	2	2	4	.33	1	.250	.285	.345
11	Ari	NL	19	59	10	2	0	0	(0	0)	12	2	2	2	4	0	9	0	0	0	0	0	-	0	.169	.222	.203
	Postseason		2	2	0	0	0	0	(0	0)	0	0	0	0	0	0	0	0	0	0	0	0	-	0	.000	.000	.000
	14 ML YEARS		954	2289	547	102	14	27	(14	13)	758	264	201	216	105	5	345	20	51	17	33	18	.65	43	.239	.276	.331

Jake McGee

Pitches: L **Bats:** L **Pos:** RP-69   **Ht:** 6'3" **Wt:** 230 **Born:** 8/6/1986 **Age:** 26

			HOW MUCH HE PITCHED							WHAT HE GAVE UP											THE RESULTS						
Year	Team	Lg	G	GS	CG	GF	IP	BFP	H	R	ER	HR	SH	SF	HB	TBB	IBB	SO	WP	Bk	W	L	Pct	Sh	Sv-Op	Hld	ERC	ERA
2010	TB	AL	8	0	0	3	5.0	20	2	1	1	0	0	0	0	3	0	6	0	0	0	0	-	0	0-0	1	1.32	1.80
2011	TB	AL	37	0	0	9	28.0	124	30	14	14	5	1	0	0	12	1	27	0	0	5	2	.714	0	0-0	4	5.09	4.50
2012	TB	AL	69	0	0	13	55.1	212	33	13	12	3	0	2	1	11	4	73	3	0	5	2	.714	0	0-2	19	1.26	1.95
	Postseason		1	0	0	0	0.1	2	0	0	0	0	1	0	0	0	0	0	0	0	0	0	-	0	0-0	0	7.00	0.00
	3 ML YEARS		114	0	0	25	88.1	356	65	28	27	8	1	2	1	26	5	106	3	0	10	4	.714	0	0-2	23	2.19	2.75

Casey McGehee

Bats: R **Throws:** R **Pos:** 1B-85; 3B-21; PH-17; DH-2; 2B-1   McGEE   **Ht:** 6'1" **Wt:** 220 **Born:** 10/12/1982 **Age:** 30

			BATTING																			BASERUNNING				AVERAGES		
Year	Team	Lg	G	AB	H	2B	3B	HR	(Hm	Rd)	TB	R	RBI	RC	TBB	IBB	SO	HBP	SH	SF	SB	CS	SB%	GDP	Avg	OBP	Slg
2012	CtnSC*	A	7	25	9	3	0	0	(-	-)	12	4	8	4	2	0	4	0	0	0	0	0	-	0	.360	.407	.480
2008	ChC	NL	9	24	4	1	0	0	(0	0)	5	1	5	0	0	0	8	0	0	1	0	0	-	1	.167	.160	.208
2009	Mil	NL	116	355	107	20	1	16	(6	10)	177	58	66	65	34	2	67	1	0	4	0	2	.00	13	.301	.360	.499
2010	Mil	NL	157	610	174	38	1	23	(13	10)	283	70	104	93	50	5	102	2	0	8	1	1	.50	18	.285	.337	.464
2011	Mil	NL	155	546	122	24	2	13	(8	5)	189	46	67	50	45	4	104	1	0	8	0	3	.00	19	.223	.280	.346
2012	2 Tms		114	318	69	16	1	9	(1	8)	114	36	41	30	29	0	70	2	0	3	1	1	.50	10	.217	.284	.358
12	Pit	NL	92	265	61	13	1	8	(1	7)	100	27	35	26	24	0	60	2	0	2	1	1	.50	7	.230	.297	.377
12	NYY	AL	22	53	8	3	0	1	(0	1)	14	9	6	4	5	0	10	0	0	1	0	0	-	3	.151	.220	.264
	Postseason		6	5	1	0	0	0	(0	0)	1	0	0	1	1	0	2	0	0	0	0	0	-	0	.200	.333	.200
	5 ML YEARS		551	1853	476	99	5	61	(28	33)	768	211	283	238	158	11	351	6	0	24	2	7	.22	61	.257	.314	.414

Dustin McGowan

Pitches: R **Bats:** R **Pos:** P   **Ht:** 6'3" **Wt:** 230 **Born:** 3/24/1982 **Age:** 31

			HOW MUCH HE PITCHED							WHAT HE GAVE UP											THE RESULTS						
Year	Team	Lg	G	GS	CG	GF	IP	BFP	H	R	ER	HR	SH	SF	HB	TBB	IBB	SO	WP	Bk	W	L	Pct	Sh	Sv-Op	Hld	ERC	ERA
2005	Tor	AL	13	7	0	2	45.1	205	49	34	32	7	0	4	7	17	0	34	7	0	1	3	.250	0	0-0	1	5.47	6.35
2006	Tor	AL	16	3	0	3	27.1	143	35	27	22	2	0	1	2	25	2	22	3	1	1	2	.333	0	0-1	1	7.72	7.24
2007	Tor	AL	27	27	2	0	169.2	705	146	80	77	14	0	6	2	61	3	144	13	0	12	10	.545	1	0-0	0	3.07	4.08
2008	Tor	AL	19	19	1	0	111.1	474	115	60	54	9	2	8	5	38	1	85	5	0	6	7	.462	0	0-0	0	4.13	4.37
2011	Tor	AL	5	4	0	0	21.0	96	20	15	15	4	0	1	1	13	0	20	3	0	0	2	.000	0	0-0	0	5.50	6.43
	5 ML YEARS		80	60	3	5	374.2	1623	365	216	200	36	2	20	17	154	6	305	31	1	20	24	.455	1	0-1	2	4.10	4.80

Collin McHugh

Pitches: R **Bats:** R **Pos:** SP-4; RP-4   **Ht:** 6'2" **Wt:** 195 **Born:** 6/19/1987 **Age:** 26

Year	Team	Lg	G	GS	CG	GF	IP	BFP	H	R	ER	HR	SH	SF	HB	TBB	IBB	SO	WP	Bk	W	L	Pct	Sh	Sv-Op	Hld	ERC	ERA
					HOW MUCH HE PITCHED						WHAT HE GAVE UP													THE RESULTS				
2008	Kngspt	R	12	8	0	2	41.0	186	47	25	19	5	1	3	1	16	0	41	1	1	0	0	-	0	1--	-	5.05	4.17
2009	Bklyn	A-	14	14	1	0	75.0	305	61	25	23	1	0	0	5	21	0	79	3	0	8	2	.800	1	0--	-	2.35	2.76
2010	Savann	A	28	20	0	6	132.1	575	139	65	49	7	2	4	12	38	0	129	5	2	7	8	.467	0	1--	-	3.92	3.33
2011	StLuci	A+	9	6	0	3	35.2	164	47	27	25	3	0	1	1	14	0	39	2	2	1	2	.333	0	1--	-	5.95	6.31
2011	Bnghtn	AA	18	16	1	2	93.1	394	78	32	30	2	3	2	8	32	3	100	7	0	8	2	.800	0	2--	-	2.70	2.89
2012	Bnghtn	AA	12	12	0	0	74.2	303	63	21	20	4	3	2	5	17	0	65	6	0	5	5	.500	0	0--	-	2.57	2.41
2012	Buffalo	AAA	13	13	0	0	73.2	312	60	32	28	8	0	3	2	29	0	70	2	0	2	4	.333	0	0--	-	3.14	3.42
2012	NYM	NL	8	4	0	1	21.1	99	27	21	18	5	2	1	2	8	2	17	0	0	0	4	.000	0	0-0	0	6.83	7.59

Michael McKenry

Bats: R **Throws:** R **Pos:** C-81; PH-16; PR-1   **Ht:** 5'10" **Wt:** 215 **Born:** 3/4/1985 **Age:** 28

Year	Team	Lg	G	AB	H	2B	3B	HR	(Hm	Rd)	TB	R	RBI	RC	TBB	IBB	SO	HBP	SH	SF	SB	CS	SB%	GDP	Avg	OBP	Slg
								BATTING															BASERUNNING			AVERAGES	
2010	Col	NL	6	8	0	0	0	0	(0	0)	0	0	0	0	1	0	5	0	0	0	0	0	-	0	.000	.111	.000
2011	Pit	NL	58	180	40	12	0	2	(1	1)	58	17	11	12	14	2	49	0	5	2	0	1	.00	3	.222	.276	.322
2012	Pit	NL	88	240	56	14	0	12	(3	9)	106	25	39	32	29	1	73	3	0	3	0	0	-	7	.233	.320	.442
	3 ML YEARS		152	428	96	26	0	14	(4	10)	164	42	50	44	44	3	127	3	5	5	0	1	.00	10	.224	.298	.383

Nate McLouth

Bats: L **Throws:** R **Pos:** LF-64; PH-19; CF-10; RF-3; PR-2   mc-CLOWTH   **Ht:** 5'11" **Wt:** 180 **Born:** 10/28/1981 **Age:** 31

Year	Team	Lg	G	AB	H	2B	3B	HR	(Hm	Rd)	TB	R	RBI	RC	TBB	IBB	SO	HBP	SH	SF	SB	CS	SB%	GDP	Avg	OBP	Slg
								BATTING															BASERUNNING			AVERAGES	
2012	Norfolk*	AAA	47	180	44	5	2	10	(-	-)	83	29	33	30	19	0	26	5	3	3	5	0	1.00	4	.244	.329	.461
2005	Pit	NL	41	109	28	6	0	5	(2	3)	49	20	12	9	3	0	20	5	2	1	2	0	1.00	3	.257	.305	.450
2006	Pit	NL	106	270	63	16	2	7	(3	4)	104	50	16	25	18	0	59	5	3	1	10	1	.91	7	.233	.293	.385
2007	Pit	NL	137	329	85	21	3	13	(5	8)	151	62	38	52	39	2	77	9	3	2	22	1	.96	5	.258	.351	.459
2008	Pit	NL	152	597	165	**46**	4	26	(15	11)	297	113	94	105	65	11	93	12	5	6	23	3	.88	5	.276	.356	.497
2009	2 Tms	NL	129	507	130	27	2	20	(9	11)	221	86	70	85	68	1	99	9	3	4	19	6	.76	8	.256	.352	.436
2010	Atl	NL	85	242	46	12	1	6	(5	1)	78	30	24	23	33	2	57	5	6	2	7	2	.78	3	.190	.298	.322
2011	Atl	NL	81	267	61	12	2	4	(4	0)	89	35	16	36	44	4	52	3	7	0	4	2	.67	4	.228	.344	.333
2012	2 Tms	NL	89	266	64	14	1	7	(4	3)	101	39	20	30	27	1	61	2	2	1	12	1	.92	2	.241	.314	.380
09	Pit	NL	45	168	43	7	1	9	(5	4)	79	27	34	33	21	0	29	4	0	2	7	0	1.00	2	.256	.349	.470
09	Atl	NL	84	339	87	20	1	11	(4	7)	142	59	36	52	47	1	70	5	3	2	12	6	.67	6	.257	.354	.419
12	Pit	NL	34	57	8	2	0	0	(0	0)	10	4	2	1	5	0	18	0	0	0	0	0	-	0	.140	.210	.175
12	Bal	AL	55	209	56	12	1	7	(4	3)	91	35	18	29	22	1	43	2	2	1	12	1	.92	2	.268	.342	.435
	Postseason		3	2	1	0	0	0	(0	0)	1	0	0	0	0	0	0	0	0	0	0	0	-	0	.500	.500	.500
	8 ML YEARS		820	2587	642	154	15	88	(47	41)	1090	435	290	365	297	21	518	50	31	17	99	16	.86	34	.248	.335	.421

Kyle McPherson

Pitches: R **Bats:** R **Pos:** RP-7; SP-3   **Ht:** 6'4" **Wt:** 220 **Born:** 11/11/1987 **Age:** 25

Year	Team	Lg	G	GS	CG	GF	IP	BFP	H	R	ER	HR	SH	SF	HB	TBB	IBB	SO	WP	Bk	W	L	Pct	Sh	Sv-Op	Hld	ERC	ERA
					HOW MUCH HE PITCHED						WHAT HE GAVE UP													THE RESULTS				
2007	Pirates	R	12	10	0	0	51.2	213	47	22	15	3	3	1	8	10	0	35	1	0	4	2	.667	0	0--	-	3.16	2.61
2007	StCol	A-	3	3	0	0	14.1	67	20	13	10	1	0	2	0	3	0	6	1	0	1	0	1.000	0	0--	-	5.14	6.28
2008	StCol	A-	15	7	0	3	55.2	224	52	29	27	10	1	0	1	5	0	41	2	0	1	3	.250	0	1--	-	3.03	4.37
2009	WV	A	13	8	0	3	51.0	210	53	32	28	3	1	2	4	6	0	32	0	0	5	2	.714	0	0--	-	3.26	4.94
2009	StCol	A-	13	13	0	0	75.1	302	70	27	25	5	1	5	3	11	0	57	0	0	3	4	.571	0	0--	-	2.70	2.99
2010	WV	A	26	21	0	4	117.2	488	96	58	47	14	1	2	9	31	0	124	3	0	9	9	.500	0	0--	-	2.93	3.59
2010	Bradtn	A+	2	0	0	1	4.0	15	2	0	0	0	0	0	0	0	0	7	1	0	0	0	-	0	0--	-	0.50	0.00
2011	Bradtn	A+	12	12	1	0	71.2	287	62	25	23	4	0	0	8	6	0	60	2	0	4	1	.800	0	0--	-	2.33	2.89
2011	Altna	AA	16	16	0	0	89.1	365	75	34	30	7	6	4	2	21	0	82	1	0	8	5	.615	0	0--	-	2.52	3.02
2012	Altna	AA	9	9	0	0	48.2	204	55	26	23	5	1	1	3	5	0	46	0	0	3	5	.375	0	0--	-	3.90	4.25
2012	Indy	AAA	3	3	0	0	18.1	69	11	3	2	1	1	0	0	4	0	17	1	0	1	0	1.000	0	0--	-	1.36	0.98
2012	Pit	NL	10	3	0	2	26.1	107	24	8	8	3	1	0	2	7	0	21	0	1	0	2	.000	0	0-0	0	3.57	2.73

Kris Medlen

Pitches: R **Bats:** B **Pos:** RP-38; SP-12   MEDD-linn   **Ht:** 5'10" **Wt:** 190 **Born:** 10/7/1985 **Age:** 27

Year	Team	Lg	G	GS	CG	GF	IP	BFP	H	R	ER	HR	SH	SF	HB	TBB	IBB	SO	WP	Bk	W	L	Pct	Sh	Sv-Op	Hld	ERC	ERA
					HOW MUCH HE PITCHED						WHAT HE GAVE UP													THE RESULTS				
2012	Gwnntt*	AAA	3	3	0	0	13.1	59	15	7	7	2	0	0	1	6	0	12	1	0	0	2	.000	0	0--	-	5.87	4.73
2009	Atl	NL	37	4	0	10	67.2	294	65	34	32	5	6	2	2	30	2	72	3	1	3	5	.375	0	0-2	1	3.90	4.26
2010	Atl	NL	31	14	0	5	107.2	438	108	48	44	13	7	3	3	21	0	83	1	1	6	2	.750	0	0-0	1	3.60	3.68
2011	Atl	NL	2	0	0	1	2.1	8	1	0	0	0	0	0	0	0	0	2	0	0	0	0	-	0	0-0	0	0.40	0.00
2012	Atl	NL	50	12	2	7	138.0	520	103	26	24	6	1	0	0	23	0	120	3	0	10	1	.909	1	1-2	7	1.69	1.57
	4 ML YEARS		120	30	2	23	315.2	1260	277	108	100	24	14	5	5	74	3	277	7	2	19	8	.704	1	1-4	9	2.75	2.85

Evan Meek

Pitches: R **Bats:** R **Pos:** RP-12   **Ht:** 6'0" **Wt:** 225 **Born:** 5/12/1983 **Age:** 30

Year	Team	Lg	G	GS	CG	GF	IP	BFP	H	R	ER	HR	SH	SF	HB	TBB	IBB	SO	WP	Bk	W	L	Pct	Sh	Sv-Op	Hld	ERC	ERA
2012	Indy*	AAA	36	0	0	12	46.0	198	33	16	14	3	3	1	4	26	3	41	3	0	3	2	.600	0	1- -	-	3.13	2.74
2008	Pit	NL	9	0	0	7	13.0	61	11	11	10	3	1	1	4	12	2	7	3	0	0	1	.000	0	0-0	0	6.46	6.92
2009	Pit	NL	41	0	0	14	47.0	195	34	18	18	2	2	1	0	29	2	42	5	0	1	1	.500	0	0-1	4	3.03	3.45
2010	Pit	NL	70	0	0	16	80.0	324	53	25	19	5	2	1	4	31	4	70	2	0	4	5	.556	0	4-10	15	2.15	2.14
2011	Pit	NL	24	0	0	6	20.2	100	27	11	8	1	1	0	0	12	0	17	2	0	1	1	.500	0	0-1	4	6.12	3.48
2012	Pit	NL	12	0	0	5	12.0	57	14	9	9	1	1	0	1	6	0	8	1	0	0	0	-	0	0-0	1	5.52	6.75
5 ML YEARS			156	0	0	48	172.2	737	139	74	64	12	7	3	6	90	8	144	13	0	7	7	.500	0	4-12	24	3.33	3.34

Jenrry Mejia

Pitches: R **Bats:** R **Pos:** SP-3; RP-2   HENN-ree mah-HEE-ah   **Ht:** 6'0" **Wt:** 205 **Born:** 10/11/1989 **Age:** 23

Year	Team	Lg	G	GS	CG	GF	IP	BFP	H	R	ER	HR	SH	SF	HB	TBB	IBB	SO	WP	Bk	W	L	Pct	Sh	Sv-Op	Hld	ERC	ERA
2008	Mets	R	3	3	1	0	15.0	58	9	1	1	0	0	0	0	3	0	15	0	0	2	0	1.000	1	0- -	-	1.09	0.60
2008	Bklyn	A-	11	11	0	0	56.2	228	42	22	22	4	2	1	1	23	0	52	3	0	3	2	.600	0	0- -	-	2.66	3.49
2009	StLuci	A+	9	9	0	0	50.1	209	41	18	11	0	2	0	2	16	0	44	2	1	4	1	.800	0	0- -	-	2.26	1.97
2009	Bnghtn	AA	10	10	0	0	44.1	202	44	28	22	2	5	1	4	23	1	47	2	0	5	0	.000	0	0- -	-	4.33	4.47
2010	Bnghtn	AA	6	6	1	0	27.1	111	19	5	4	0	2	0	0	14	0	26	1	0	2	0	1.000	1	0- -	-	2.28	1.32
2010	Mets	R	1	1	0	0	3.0	13	4	1	1	0	0	0	0	1	0	3	0	0	0	0	-	0	0- -	-	5.24	3.00
2010	StLuci	A+	1	1	0	0	4.0	13	1	0	0	0	0	0	0	0	0	7	1	0	0	0	-	0	0- -	-	0.14	0.00
2010	Buffalo	AAA	1	1	0	0	8.0	28	5	1	1	1	1	0	1	1	0	9	0	0	0	0	-	0	0- -	-	2.01	1.13
2011	Buffalo	AAA	5	5	0	0	28.1	113	16	10	9	1	1	1	2	14	0	21	0	0	1	2	.333	0	0- -	-	2.07	2.86
2012	StLuci	A+	2	2	0	0	11.0	41	7	3	3	1	0	1	0	2	0	8	0	0	1	0	1.000	0	0- -	-	1.53	2.45
2012	Bnghtn	AA	2	2	0	0	8.0	35	11	5	5	1	0	0	0	3	0	8	1	0	0	0	-	0	0- -	-	6.82	5.63
2012	Buffalo	AAA	26	10	0	3	73.2	313	75	38	29	4	0	3	1	24	1	39	6	0	3	4	.429	0	0- -	-	3.62	3.54
2010	NYM	NL	33	3	0	8	39.0	183	46	21	20	3	0	1	3	20	2	22	7	0	0	4	.000	0	0-1	2	5.57	4.62
2012	NYM	NL	5	3	0	1	16.0	74	20	10	10	2	1	0	0	9	0	8	1	0	1	2	.333	0	0-0	0	6.55	5.63
2 ML YEARS			38	6	0	9	55.0	257	66	31	30	5	1	1	3	29	2	30	8	0	1	6	.143	0	0-1	2	5.85	4.91

Mark Melancon

Pitches: R **Bats:** R **Pos:** RP-41   muh-LANN-sun   **Ht:** 6'2" **Wt:** 215 **Born:** 3/28/1985 **Age:** 28

Year	Team	Lg	G	GS	CG	GF	IP	BFP	H	R	ER	HR	SH	SF	HB	TBB	IBB	SO	WP	Bk	W	L	Pct	Sh	Sv-Op	Hld	ERC	ERA
2012	Pwtckt*	AAA	21	0	0	18	21.2	86	15	2	2	0	0	0	2	3	0	27	1	0	0	0	-	0	11- -	-	1.42	0.83
2009	NYY	AL	13	0	0	4	16.1	74	13	8	7	0	0	0	4	10	0	10	3	0	0	1	.000	0	0-1	0	3.94	3.86
2010	2 Tms		22	0	0	4	21.1	90	19	13	10	2	0	1	1	8	0	22	2	0	2	0	1.000	0	0-1	8	3.53	4.22
2011	Hou	NL	71	0	0	47	74.1	309	65	28	23	5	2	0	2	26	6	66	1	0	8	4	.667	0	20-25	3	2.98	2.78
2012	Bos	NL	41	0	0	17	45.0	194	45	31	31	8	1	2	3	12	1	41	2	0	0	2	.000	0	1-2	2	4.24	6.20
10 NYY		AL	2	0	0	2	4.0	19	7	5	4	1	0	1	0	0	0	3	0	0	0	0	-	0	0-0	0	7.95	9.00
10 Hou		NL	20	0	0	2	17.1	71	12	8	6	1	0	0	1	8	0	19	2	0	2	0	1.000	0	0-1	8	2.65	3.12
4 ML YEARS			147	0	0	72	157.0	667	142	80	71	15	3	3	10	56	7	139	8	0	10	7	.588	0	21-29	13	3.52	4.07

Luis Mendoza

Pitches: R **Bats:** R **Pos:** SP-25; RP-5   **Ht:** 6'3" **Wt:** 240 **Born:** 10/31/1983 **Age:** 29

Year	Team	Lg	G	GS	CG	GF	IP	BFP	H	R	ER	HR	SH	SF	HB	TBB	IBB	SO	WP	Bk	W	L	Pct	Sh	Sv-Op	Hld	ERC	ERA
2007	Tex	AL	6	3	0	2	16.0	64	13	4	4	1	0	2	2	4	0	7	0	0	1	0	1.000	0	0-0	0	2.83	2.25
2008	Tex	AL	25	11	0	6	63.1	316	97	74	61	7	0	2	6	25	4	35	5	0	3	8	.273	0	1-2	0	7.53	8.67
2009	Tex	AL	1	0	0	0	1.0	7	2	4	4	1	0	0	1	1	0	0	0	0	0	0	-	0	0-0	0	29.25	36.00
2010	KC	AL	4	0	0	1	4.0	25	10	10	10	4	0	0	0	3	0	1	0	0	0	1	.000	0	0-1	0	25.91	22.50
2011	KC	AL	2	2	0	0	14.2	60	11	3	2	0	0	1	2	5	0	7	0	0	2	0	1.000	0	0-0	0	2.42	1.23
2012	KC	AL	30	25	0	0	166.0	709	176	84	78	15	2	5	11	59	3	104	6	2	8	10	.444	0	0-0	0	4.53	4.23
6 ML YEARS			68	41	0	9	265.0	1181	309	179	159	28	2	10	22	97	7	154	11	2	14	19	.424	0	1-3	0	5.30	5.40

Jordy Mercer

Bats: R **Throws:** R **Pos:** SS-28; PH-8; 2B-7; PR-6; 3B-1   **Ht:** 6'3" **Wt:** 200 **Born:** 8/27/1986 **Age:** 26

Year	Team	Lg	G	AB	H	2B	3B	HR	(Hm	Rd)	TB	R	RBI	RC	TBB	IBB	SO	HBP	SH	SF	SB	CS	SB%	GDP	Avg	OBP	Slg
2008	StCol	A-	6	24	6	1	1	1	(-	-)	12	5	2	3	1	0	3	0	0	0	1	0	1.00	1	.250	.280	.500
2008	Hkry	A	50	192	48	7	0	4	(-	-)	67	21	18	20	12	0	44	2	1	1	4	3	.57	6	.250	.300	.349
2009	Lynbrg	A+	131	513	131	36	4	10	(-	-)	205	64	83	69	41	0	93	9	3	14	10	6	.63	11	.255	.314	.400
2010	Altna	AA	126	485	137	31	2	3	(-	-)	181	67	65	64	31	1	69	7	6	9	7	1	.88	10	.282	.329	.373
2011	Altna	AA	72	265	71	17	1	13	(-	-)	129	40	48	44	23	0	35	4	3	6	2	1	.67	3	.268	.329	.487
2011	Indy	AAA	60	226	54	13	1	6	(-	-)	87	39	21	27	13	0	43	8	3	0	3	3	.50	2	.239	.304	.385
2012	Indy	AAA	56	209	60	14	1	4	(-	-)	88	28	27	31	20	2	45	4	1	2	3	5	.38	3	.287	.357	.421
2012	Pit	NL	42	62	13	5	1	1	(1	0)	23	7	5	6	4	0	14	1	0	1	0	1	.00	0	.210	.265	.371

Melky Mesa

Bats: R Throws: R Pos: PH-2; CF-1; DH-1; PR-1   Ht: 6'1" Wt: 190 Born: 1/31/1987 Age: 26

								BATTING											BASERUNNING				AVERAGES		
Year	Team	Lg	G	AB	H	2B	3B	HR	(Hm | Rd)	TB	R	RBI	RC	TBB	IBB	SO	HBP	SH	SF	SB	CS	SB%	GDP	Avg	OBP	Slg
2006	Yanks	R	40	145	30	7	2	3	(- | -)	50	20	22	13	11	0	45	1	1	1	3	3	.50	0	.207	.266	.345
2007	Yanks	R	49	153	36	10	2	3	(- | -)	59	27	13	17	9	0	55	4	2	1	5	3	.63	2	.235	.293	.386
2008	StIslnd	A-	46	122	27	5	2	7	(- | -)	57	19	23	15	4	0	38	1	1	0	4	1	.80	1	.221	.252	.467
2009	CtnSC	A	133	497	112	24	7	20	(- | -)	210	76	74	69	51	3	168	11	0	5	18	6	.75	5	.225	.309	.423
2010	Tampa	A+	121	446	116	21	9	19	(- | -)	212	81	74	76	44	0	129	11	1	5	31	9	.78	5	.260	.338	.475
2011	Trntn	AA	105	386	97	24	4	9	(- | -)	156	58	46	52	36	1	129	9	1	1	18	13	.58	5	.251	.329	.404
2011	Tampa	A+	4	12	2	1	0	0	(- | -)	3	1	1	2	3	0	4	2	0	0	1	0	1.00	0	.167	.412	.250
2012	Trntn	AA	88	332	92	18	1	14	(- | -)	154	60	46	56	29	1	75	6	0	2	17	3	.85	7	.277	.344	.464
2012	S-WB	AAA	33	126	29	8	1	9	(- | -)	66	19	21	18	7	0	43	0	0	0	5	1	.83	0	.230	.271	.524
2012	NYY	AL	3	2	1	0	0	0	(0 | 0)	1	0	1	0	0	0	0	0	0	0	0	0	-	0	.500	.500	.500

Devin Mesoraco

Bats: R Throws: R Pos: C-53; PR-3   mezz-er-OCK-oh   Ht: 6'1" Wt: 225 Born: 6/19/1988 Age: 25

								BATTING											BASERUNNING				AVERAGES		
Year	Team	Lg	G	AB	H	2B	3B	HR	(Hm | Rd)	TB	R	RBI	RC	TBB	IBB	SO	HBP	SH	SF	SB	CS	SB%	GDP	Avg	OBP	Slg
2007	Reds	R	40	137	30	4	0	1	(- | -)	37	16	8	13	15	0	26	3	0	0	2	0	1.00	7	.219	.310	.270
2008	Dayton	A	83	306	80	13	1	9	(- | -)	122	29	42	40	20	0	64	4	0	4	2	3	.40	8	.261	.311	.399
2009	Srsota	A+	92	312	71	22	1	8	(- | -)	119	32	37	40	35	0	76	4	3	3	0	1	.00	11	.228	.311	.381
2010	Lynbrg	A+	43	158	53	11	2	10	(- | -)	98	24	31	39	19	1	29	3	0	1	2	2	.50	4	.335	.414	.620
2010	Carlina	AA	56	187	55	11	3	13	(- | -)	111	42	31	40	18	0	37	4	0	3	1	0	1.00	6	.294	.363	.594
2010	Lsvlle	AAA	14	52	12	3	0	3	(- | -)	24	5	13	7	6	0	14	0	0	0	0	1	.00	2	.231	.310	.462
2011	Lsvlle	AAA	120	436	126	36	2	15	(- | -)	211	60	71	80	52	6	83	7	0	4	1	1	.50	9	.289	.371	.484
2012	Lsvlle	AAA	5	18	3	1	0	0	(- | -)	4	0	0	0	1	0	2	0	0	0	0	0	-	0	.167	.211	.222
2011	Cin	NL	18	50	9	3	0	2	(2 | 0)	18	5	6	5	3	1	10	0	0	0	0	0	-	1	.180	.226	.360
2012	Cin	NL	54	165	35	8	0	5	(4 | 1)	58	17	14	10	17	4	33	1	0	1	1	1	.50	2	.212	.288	.352
	2 ML YEARS		72	215	44	11	0	7	(6 | 1)	76	22	20	15	20	5	43	1	0	1	1	1	.50	3	.205	.274	.353

Will Middlebrooks

Bats: R Throws: R Pos: 3B-72; PH-3; DH-1; PR-1   Ht: 6'4" Wt: 225 Born: 9/9/1988 Age: 24

								BATTING											BASERUNNING				AVERAGES		
Year	Team	Lg	G	AB	H	2B	3B	HR	(Hm | Rd)	TB	R	RBI	RC	TBB	IBB	SO	HBP	SH	SF	SB	CS	SB%	GDP	Avg	OBP	Slg
2008	Lowell	A-	59	209	53	17	2	1	(- | -)	77	21	21	25	12	1	73	2	1	2	10	0	1.00	9	.254	.298	.368
2009	Grnville	A	103	374	99	25	3	7	(- | -)	151	53	57	55	48	0	123	2	0	3	7	4	.64	7	.265	.349	.404
2010	Salem	A+	114	435	120	31	2	12	(- | -)	191	69	70	65	35	2	121	4	0	7	5	3	.63	6	.276	.331	.439
2011	Portlnd	AA	96	371	112	25	1	18	(- | -)	193	54	80	67	21	0	95	4	0	1	6	0	1.00	12	.302	.345	.520
2011	Lowell	A-	4	12	4	1	0	3	(- | -)	14	4	6	5	2	0	1	0	0	1	1	0	1.00	0	.333	.400	1.167
2011	Pwtckt	AAA	16	56	9	0	0	2	(- | -)	15	4	8	2	3	0	18	0	0	1	3	1	.75	0	.161	.200	.268
2012	Pwtckt	AAA	24	93	31	3	1	9	(- | -)	63	18	27	22	7	0	18	0	0	0	3	1	.75	1	.333	.380	.677
2012	Bos	AL	75	267	77	14	0	15	(9 | 6)	136	34	54	46	13	0	70	3	0	3	4	1	.80	8	.288	.325	.509

Jose Mijares

Pitches: L Bats: L Pos: RP-78   mee-HAHR-ess   Ht: 6'0" Wt: 230 Born: 10/29/1984 Age: 28

			HOW MUCH HE PITCHED						WHAT HE GAVE UP										THE RESULTS					
Year	Team	Lg	G	GS	CG	GF	IP	BFP	H	R	ER	HR	SH	SF	HB	TBB	IBB	SO	WP	Bk	W	L	Pct	Sh	Sv-Op Hld	ERC	ERA
2008	Min	AL	10	0	0	3	10.1	34	3	1	1	0	0	0	0	0	0	5	1	0	0	1	.000	0	0-0 2	0.19	0.87
2009	Min	AL	71	0	0	12	61.2	253	50	17	16	7	2	3	2	23	1	55	0	0	2	2	.500	0	0-1 27	3.18	2.34
2010	Min	AL	47	0	0	10	32.2	139	34	14	12	4	1	1	1	9	1	28	1	0	1	1	.500	0	0-0 9	4.04	3.31
2011	Min	AL	58	0	0	13	49.0	228	53	31	25	4	0	2	3	30	2	30	1	0	0	2	.000	0	0-2 10	5.42	4.59
2012	2 Tms		78	0	0	11	56.1	242	50	18	16	3	4	4	4	21	3	57	3	0	3	2	.600	0	0-1 18	3.18	2.56
	12 KC	AL	51	0	0	8	38.2	168	36	13	11	3	3	3	4	13	1	37	1	0	2	2	.500	0	0-1 11	3.59	2.56
	12 SF	NL	27	0	0	3	17.2	74	14	5	5	0	1	0	0	8	2	20	2	0	1	0	1.000	0	0-0 7	2.32	2.55
	Postseason		5	0	0	1	2.0	7	1	1	1	1	1	0	0	2	1	0	0	0	0	1	.000	0	0-0 0	7.39	4.50
	5 ML YEARS		264	0	0	49	210.0	896	190	81	70	18	7	9	10	83	7	175	6	0	6	8	.429	0	0-4 66	3.56	3.00

Miles Mikolas

Pitches: R Bats: R Pos: RP-25   MIKE-uh-liss   Ht: 6'5" Wt: 220 Born: 8/23/1988 Age: 24

			HOW MUCH HE PITCHED						WHAT HE GAVE UP										THE RESULTS					
Year	Team	Lg	G	GS	CG	GF	IP	BFP	H	R	ER	HR	SH	SF	HB	TBB	IBB	SO	WP	Bk	W	L	Pct	Sh	Sv-Op Hld	ERC	ERA
2009	Eugene	A-	15	11	0	0	53.0	250	77	47	35	1	3	1	5	9	0	39	3	0	1	8	.111	0	0-- -	5.39	5.94
2010	FtWyn	A	60	0	0	30	81.2	335	76	27	20	3	0	3	6	15	2	78	0	0	6	3	.667	0	13-- -	2.42	2.20
2011	Lk Els	A+	34	0	0	30	39.2	159	31	5	5	1	2	0	3	9	2	42	0	0	3	0	1.000	0	12-- -	2.06	1.13
2011	SnAnt	AA	28	0	0	20	32.1	130	29	6	6	0	3	0	0	6	0	27	1	0	1	0	1.000	0	9-- -	2.12	1.67
2012	SnAnt	AA	12	0	0	10	12.1	53	16	6	4	0	0	0	0	3	0	11	1	0	1	1	.500	0	4-- -	4.55	2.92
2012	Tucsn	AAA	17	0	0	6	19.2	87	20	8	7	1	1	1	0	8	0	17	1	0	2	1	.667	0	0-- -	3.75	3.20
2012	SD	NL	25	0	0	9	32.1	144	32	15	13	4	2	0	2	15	0	23	2	0	2	1	.667	0	0-1 1	4.65	3.62

Wade Miley

Pitches: L Bats: L Pos: SP-29; RP-3 — MY-lee — Ht: 6'0" Wt: 218 Born: 11/13/1986 Age: 26

Year	Team	Lg	HOW MUCH HE PITCHED						WHAT HE GAVE UP										THE RESULTS						
			G	GS	CG	GF	IP	BFP	H	R	ER	HR	SH	SF	HB	TBB	IBB	SO	WP	Bk	W	L	Pct	Sh	Sv-Op Hld	ERC	ERA
2008	Yakima	A-	7	0	0	0	11.0	49	11	6	6	0	0	0	0	5	0	11	0	0	1	1	.500	0	0- - -	3.47	4.91
2009	Sbend	A	21	21	0	0	113.2	480	127	60	52	8	1	4	4	29	0	91	7	0	5	9	.357	0	0- - -	4.19	4.12
2009	Visalia	A+	3	3	0	0	15.0	65	18	10	8	0	0	0	0	4	0	11	0	0	1	1	.500	0	0- - -	3.98	4.80
2010	Visalia	A+	14	14	0	0	80.1	345	81	36	29	1	2	0	1	37	0	50	10	0	4	5	.444	0	0- - -	3.85	3.25
2010	Mobile	AA	13	13	1	0	72.2	292	60	26	16	5	4	0	1	28	2	63	2	3	5	2	.714	0	0- - -	3.00	1.98
2011	Mobile	AA	14	14	0	0	75.1	322	74	49	40	6	1	2	3	28	0	46	3	2	4	2	.667	0	0- - -	3.91	4.78
2011	Reno	AAA	8	8	1	0	54.1	226	53	23	22	4	2	0	0	16	0	56	3	2	4	1	.800	0	0- - -	3.38	3.64
2011	Ari	NL	8	7	0	0	40.0	180	48	20	20	6	3	1	0	18	0	25	1	0	4	2	.667	0	0-0 0	5.90	4.50
2012	Ari	NL	32	29	0	0	194.2	807	193	79	72	14	8	3	2	37	0	144	6	1	16	11	.593	0	0-0 0	3.05	3.33
	2 ML YEARS		40	36	0	0	234.2	987	241	99	92	20	11	4	2	55	0	169	7	1	20	13	.606	0	0-0 0	3.49	3.53

Andrew Miller

Pitches: L Bats: L Pos: RP-53 — Ht: 6'7" Wt: 210 Born: 5/21/1985 Age: 28

Year	Team	Lg	HOW MUCH HE PITCHED						WHAT HE GAVE UP										THE RESULTS						
			G	GS	CG	GF	IP	BFP	H	R	ER	HR	SH	SF	HB	TBB	IBB	SO	WP	Bk	W	L	Pct	Sh	Sv-Op Hld	ERC	ERA
2012	Grnville*	A	2	1	0	0	2.0	8	2	0	0	0	0	0	1	0	0	3	0	0	0	0	-	0	0- - -	4.15	0.00
2012	Pwtckt*	AAA	10	0	0	1	11.0	53	4	7	7	1	0	0	1	14	0	23	1	0	0	0	-	0	1- - -	3.93	5.73
2006	Det	AL	8	0	0	3	10.1	51	8	9	7	0	0	0	2	10	0	6	1	0	0	1	.000	0	0-0 1	4.79	6.10
2007	Det	AL	13	13	0	0	64.0	309	73	43	40	8	3	1	7	39	0	56	4	1	5	5	.500	0	0-0 0	6.31	5.63
2008	Fla	NL	29	20	0	1	107.1	492	120	78	70	7	10	7	4	56	4	89	4	0	6	10	.375	0	0-0 2	5.04	5.87
2009	Fla	NL	20	14	0	1	80.0	366	85	52	43	7	6	4	2	43	1	59	10	0	3	5	.375	0	0-0 1	4.90	4.84
2010	Fla	NL	9	7	0	1	32.2	171	51	34	31	6	5	2	1	26	2	28	5	0	1	5	.167	0	0-0 0	10.20	8.54
2011	Bos	AL	17	12	0	2	65.0	310	77	43	40	8	6	5	3	41	0	50	2	1	6	3	.667	0	0-0 0	6.48	5.54
2012	Bos	AL	53	0	0	4	40.1	169	28	15	15	3	0	3	2	20	1	51	1	0	3	2	.600	0	0-0 13	2.76	3.35
	7 ML YEARS		149	66	0	12	399.2	1868	442	274	246	39	30	22	21	235	8	339	27	2	24	31	.436	0	0-0 17	5.56	5.54

Jim Miller

Pitches: R Bats: R Pos: RP-33 — Ht: 6'1" Wt: 200 Born: 4/28/1982 Age: 31

Year	Team	Lg	HOW MUCH HE PITCHED						WHAT HE GAVE UP										THE RESULTS						
			G	GS	CG	GF	IP	BFP	H	R	ER	HR	SH	SF	HB	TBB	IBB	SO	WP	Bk	W	L	Pct	Sh	Sv-Op Hld	ERC	ERA
2012	Scrmto*	AAA	16	0	0	9	19.1	78	15	6	6	0	1	1	0	4	1	21	0	0	0	3	.000	0	6- - -	1.57	2.79
2008	Bal	AL	8	0	0	5	7.2	39	9	3	1	0	1	1	1	5	2	8	1	0	0	2	.000	0	1-2 0	4.99	1.17
2011	Col	NL	6	0	0	4	7.0	29	3	2	2	0	0	2	0	4	0	5	0	0	0	0	-	0	0-0 0	1.30	2.57
2012	Oak	AL	33	0	0	18	48.2	211	39	15	14	6	0	1	3	27	2	44	1	0	2	1	.667	0	0-0 0	3.91	2.59
	3 ML YEARS		47	0	0	27	63.1	279	51	20	17	6	1	4	4	36	4	57	2	0	2	3	.400	0	1-2 0	3.69	2.42

Shelby Miller

Pitches: R Bats: R Pos: RP-5; SP-1 — Ht: 6'3" Wt: 195 Born: 10/10/1990 Age: 22

Year	Team	Lg	HOW MUCH HE PITCHED						WHAT HE GAVE UP										THE RESULTS						
			G	GS	CG	GF	IP	BFP	H	R	ER	HR	SH	SF	HB	TBB	IBB	SO	WP	Bk	W	L	Pct	Sh	Sv-Op Hld	ERC	ERA
2009	QuadC	A	2	2	0	0	3.0	16	5	3	2	0	0	0	0	2	0	2	0	0	0	0	-	0	0- - -	8.24	6.00
2010	QuadC	A	24	24	0	0	104.1	439	97	51	42	7	2	2	3	33	0	140	2	1	7	5	.583	0	0- - -	3.25	3.62
2011	PlmBh	A+	9	9	0	0	53.0	219	40	20	17	2	0	1	1	20	0	81	6	0	2	3	.400	0	0- - -	2.34	2.89
2011	Sprgfld	AA	16	16	0	0	86.2	355	72	28	26	2	3	0	4	33	0	89	3	2	9	3	.750	0	0- - -	2.82	2.70
2012	Memp	AAA	27	27	0	0	136.2	599	138	78	72	24	5	3	11	50	0	160	0	0	11	10	.524	0	0- - -	4.84	4.74
2012	StL	NL	6	1	0	1	13.2	54	9	2	2	0	0	0	1	4	0	16	0	0	1	0	1.000	0	0-0 1	1.65	1.32

Brad Mills

Pitches: L Bats: R Pos: SP-1 — Ht: 6'0" Wt: 185 Born: 3/5/1985 Age: 28

Year	Team	Lg	HOW MUCH HE PITCHED						WHAT HE GAVE UP										THE RESULTS						
			G	GS	CG	GF	IP	BFP	H	R	ER	HR	SH	SF	HB	TBB	IBB	SO	WP	Bk	W	L	Pct	Sh	Sv-Op Hld	ERC	ERA
2012	Salt Lk*	AAA	21	19	0	0	109.0	487	133	73	71	13	5	3	5	40	0	67	2	0	5	10	.333	0	0- - -	5.64	5.86
2009	Tor	AL	2	2	0	0	7.2	42	14	12	12	4	0	1	0	6	0	9	0	0	0	1	.000	0	0-0 0	15.52	14.09
2010	Tor	AL	7	3	0	0	22.1	98	20	14	14	2	0	1	1	13	1	18	1	0	1	0	1.000	0	0-0 1	4.26	5.64
2011	Tor	AL	5	4	0	0	18.1	91	23	20	20	4	0	0	2	12	1	18	1	0	1	2	.333	0	0-0 0	7.97	9.82
2012	LAA	AL	1	1	0	0	5.0	18	3	0	0	0	0	0	0	0	0	6	0	0	1	0	1.000	0	0-0 0	0.75	0.00
	4 ML YEARS		15	10	0	0	53.1	249	60	46	46	10	0	2	3	31	2	51	2	0	3	3	.500	0	0-0 1	6.41	7.76

Kevin Millwood

Pitches: R Bats: R Pos: SP-28 — Ht: 6'4" Wt: 230 Born: 12/24/1974 Age: 38

Year	Team	Lg	HOW MUCH HE PITCHED						WHAT HE GAVE UP										THE RESULTS						
			G	GS	CG	GF	IP	BFP	H	R	ER	HR	SH	SF	HB	TBB	IBB	SO	WP	Bk	W	L	Pct	Sh	Sv-Op Hld	ERC	ERA
1997	Atl	NL	12	8	0	2	51.1	227	55	26	23	1	3	5	2	21	1	42	1	0	5	3	.625	0	0-0 0	4.03	4.03
1998	Atl	NL	31	29	3	1	174.1	748	175	86	79	18	6	3	3	56	3	163	6	1	17	8	.680	1	0-0 1	3.81	4.08
1999	Atl	NL	33	33	2	0	228.0	906	168	80	68	24	9	3	4	59	2	205	5	0	18	7	.720	0	0-0 0	2.26	2.68
2000	Atl	NL	36	35	0	0	212.2	903	213	115	110	26	8	5	3	62	2	168	4	0	10	13	.435	0	0-0 0	3.83	4.66
2001	Atl	NL	21	21	0	0	121.0	515	121	66	58	20	7	2	1	40	6	84	5	1	7	7	.500	0	0-0 0	4.20	4.31
2002	Atl	NL	35	34	1	0	217.0	895	186	83	78	16	9	4	8	65	7	178	4	0	18	8	.692	1	0-0 0	2.85	3.24
2003	Phi	NL	35	35	5	0	222.0	930	210	103	99	19	12	5	4	68	6	169	2	0	14	12	.538	3	0-0 0	3.35	4.01
2004	Phi	NL	25	25	0	0	141.0	628	155	81	76	14	11	2	7	51	5	125	4	0	9	6	.600	0	0-0 0	4.57	4.85
2005	Cle	AL	30	30	1	0	192.0	799	182	72	61	20	6	4	4	52	0	146	2	0	9	11	.450	0	0-0 0	3.40	2.86
2006	Tex	AL	34	34	2	0	215.0	907	228	114	108	23	8	3	4	53	4	157	6	0	16	12	.571	0	0-0 0	3.92	4.52

Year	Team	Lg	G	GS	CG	GF	IP	BFP	H	R	ER	HR	SH	SF	HB	TBB	IBB	SO	WP	Bk	W	L	Pct	Sh	Sv-Op	Hld	ERC	ERA
2007	Tex	AL	31	31	0	0	172.2	788	213	111	99	19	1	4	8	67	2	123	4	0	10	14	.417	0	0-0	0	5.64	5.16
2008	Tex	AL	29	29	3	0	168.2	767	220	104	95	18	5	2	6	49	3	125	2	1	9	10	.474	0	0-0	0	5.54	5.07
2009	Tex	AL	31	31	3	0	198.2	850	195	88	81	26	4	5	11	71	0	123	8	0	13	10	.565	0	0-0	0	4.27	3.67
2010	Bal	AL	31	31	1	0	190.2	842	223	116	108	30	6	2	6	65	2	132	7	1	4	16	.200	0	0-0	0	5.39	5.10
2011	Col	NL	9	9	0	0	54.1	222	58	26	24	9	2	0	0	8	0	36	2	0	4	3	.571	0	0-0	0	3.93	3.98
2012	Sea	AL	28	28	1	0	161.0	689	168	86	76	13	6	4	3	56	3	107	5	0	6	12	.333	1	0-0	0	4.06	4.25
	Postseason		9	7	1	1	41.1	164	33	20	18	7	1	1	0	6	0	38	1	1	3	3	.500	0	1-1	0	2.41	3.92
	16 ML YEARS		451	443	22	3	2720.1	11616	2770	1357	1243	296	105	53	74	843	46	2083	67	4	169	152	.526	6	0-0	1	3.96	4.11

Tommy Milone

Pitches: L Bats: L Pos: SP-31   mah-LONE   **Ht: 6'0" Wt: 205 Born: 2/16/1987 Age: 26**

Year	Team	Lg	G	GS	CG	GF	IP	BFP	H	R	ER	HR	SH	SF	HB	TBB	IBB	SO	WP	Bk	W	L	Pct	Sh	Sv-Op	Hld	ERC	ERA
2008	Vrmnt	A-	8	3	0	0	21.2	91	27	12	11	4	0	0	0	3	0	22	0	0	1	3	.250	0	0--	-	5.14	4.57
2008	Hgrstn	A	7	7	0	0	37.1	150	36	16	12	0	3	1	0	6	0	27	0	0	3	0	.000	0	0--	-	2.38	2.89
2009	Ptomc	A+	27	25	0	0	151.1	611	144	57	49	9	5	4	5	36	2	106	8	1	12	5	.706	0	0--	-	3.13	2.91
2010	Hrsbrg	AA	27	27	2	0	158.0	650	161	57	50	10	3	3	4	23	0	155	7	2	12	5	.706	0	0--	-	3.05	2.85
2011	Syrcse	AAA	24	24	0	0	148.1	588	137	55	53	9	2	1	1	16	0	155	3	2	12	6	.667	0	0--	-	2.37	3.22
2011	Was	NL	5	5	0	0	26.0	110	28	11	11	2	3	2	2	4	2	15	0	0	1	0	1.000	0	0-0	0	3.55	3.81
2012	Oak	AL	31	31	1	0	190.0	791	207	90	79	24	3	3	4	36	2	137	2	0	13	10	.565	0	0-0	0	4.04	3.74
	2 ML YEARS		36	36	1	0	216.0	901	235	101	90	26	6	5	6	40	4	152	2	0	14	10	.583	0	0-0	0	3.98	3.75

Mike Minor

Pitches: L Bats: R Pos: SP-30   **Ht: 6'4" Wt: 205 Born: 12/26/1987 Age: 25**

Year	Team	Lg	G	GS	CG	GF	IP	BFP	H	R	ER	HR	SH	SF	HB	TBB	IBB	SO	WP	Bk	W	L	Pct	Sh	Sv-Op	Hld	ERC	ERA
2010	Atl	NL	9	8	0	0	40.2	185	53	28	27	6	1	3	1	11	0	43	0	0	3	2	.600	0	0-0	0	5.71	5.98
2011	Atl	NL	15	15	0	0	82.2	361	93	39	38	7	3	1	1	30	5	77	2	0	5	3	.625	0	0-0	0	4.51	4.14
2012	Atl	NL	30	30	0	0	179.1	728	151	88	82	26	8	8	5	56	7	145	3	0	11	10	.524	0	0-0	0	3.28	4.12
	3 ML YEARS		54	53	0	1	302.2	1274	297	155	147	39	12	12	7	97	12	265	5	0	19	15	.559	0	0-0	0	3.92	4.37

D.J. Mitchell

Pitches: R Bats: R Pos: RP-4   **Ht: 6'0" Wt: 160 Born: 5/13/1987 Age: 26**

Year	Team	Lg	G	GS	CG	GF	IP	BFP	H	R	ER	HR	SH	SF	HB	TBB	IBB	SO	WP	Bk	W	L	Pct	Sh	Sv-Op	Hld	ERC	ERA
2009	CtnSC	A	6	6	0	0	37.0	145	31	16	8	1	2	0	1	6	0	42	5	0	4	1	.800	0	0--	-	2.05	1.95
2009	Tampa	A+	19	18	1	0	103.1	431	93	41	33	1	2	4	8	38	2	83	10	1	8	6	.571	0	0--	-	3.12	2.87
2010	Trntn	AA	23	22	0	0	133.0	572	128	69	60	11	3	3	6	57	0	96	12	2	11	4	.733	0	0--	-	4.07	4.06
2010	S-WB	AAA	3	3	0	0	17.2	77	19	7	7	0	0	0	0	7	0	16	2	1	2	0	1.000	0	0--	-	3.76	3.57
2011	S-WB	AAA	28	24	3	1	161.1	683	155	60	57	10	3	3	6	63	1	112	16	0	13	9	.591	2	0--	-	3.84	3.18
2012	S-WB	AAA	15	14	0	1	85.2	365	85	49	48	8	2	2	6	29	0	72	3	1	6	4	.600	0	0--	-	4.07	5.04
2012	Tacom	AAA	8	8	0	0	48.2	205	41	19	16	4	0	1	1	19	0	33	4	0	3	2	.600	0	0--	-	3.11	2.96
2012	NYY	AL	4	0	0	3	4.2	24	7	2	2	1	0	0	0	3	0	2	1	0	0	0	-	0	0-0	0	9.04	3.86

Jose Molina

Bats: R Throws: R Pos: C-102; PH-1   **Ht: 6'2" Wt: 250 Born: 6/3/1975 Age: 38**

										BATTING														BASERUNNING				AVERAGES		
Year	Team	Lg	G	AB	H	2B	3B	HR	(Hm	Rd)	TB	R	RBI	RC	TBB	IBB	SO	HBP	SH	SF	SB	CS	SB%	GDP	Avg	OBP	Slg
1999	ChC	NL	10	19	5	1	0	0	(0	0)	6	3	1	2	2	1	4	0	0	0	0	0	-	0	.263	.333	.316
2001	LAA	AL	15	37	10	3	0	2	(0	2)	19	8	4	6	3	0	8	0	2	0	0	0	-	2	.270	.325	.514
2002	LAA	AL	29	70	19	3	0	0	(0	0)	22	5	5	4	5	0	15	0	4	0	2	0	.00	2	.271	.312	.314
2003	LAA	AL	53	114	21	4	0	0	(0	0)	25	12	6	5	1	0	26	3	4	1	0	0	-	1	.184	.210	.219
2004	LAA	AL	73	203	53	10	2	3	(1	2)	76	26	25	19	10	0	52	0	5	0	4	1	.80	6	.261	.296	.374
2005	LAA	AL	75	184	42	4	0	6	(2	4)	64	14	25	19	13	0	41	2	4	0	2	0	1.00	6	.228	.286	.348
2006	LAA	AL	78	225	54	17	0	4	(0	4)	83	18	22	21	9	0	49	2	7	2	1	0	1.00	6	.240	.273	.369
2007	2 Tms		69	191	49	13	0	1	(1	0)	65	18	19	20	5	0	43	0	5	1	2	1	.67	4	.257	.274	.340
2008	NYY	AL	100	268	58	17	0	3	(2	1)	84	32	18	18	12	0	52	6	8	3	0	0	-	6	.216	.263	.313
2009	NYY	AL	52	138	30	4	0	1	(0	1)	37	15	11	14	0	0	28	1	1	1	0	0	-	6	.217	.292	.268
2010	Tor	AL	57	167	41	4	0	6	(4	2)	63	13	12	12	9	1	36	5	2	0	1	0	1.00	6	.246	.304	.377
2011	Tor	AL	55	171	48	12	1	3	(1	2)	71	19	15	25	15	0	44	1	4	0	2	1	.67	2	.281	.342	.415
2012	TB	AL	102	251	56	9	0	8	(5	3)	89	27	32	23	20	0	60	2	1	1	3	1	.75	9	.223	.286	.355
07	LAA	AL	40	125	28	8	0	0	(0	0)	36	9	10	9	3	0	30	0	3	0	2	1	.67	3	.224	.242	.288
07	NYY	AL	29	66	21	5	0	1	(1	0)	29	9	9	11	2	0	13	0	2	1	0	0	-	1	.318	.333	.439
	Postseason		15	14	4	0	0	0	(0	0)	4	3	1	2	3	0	1	0	1	0	0	0	-	0	.286	.412	.286
	13 ML YEARS		768	2038	486	101	3	37	(16	21)	704	210	195	183	118	2	458	22	47	10	15	6	.71	59	.238	.286	.345

Yadier Molina

Bats: R Throws: R Pos: C-136; PH-4; 1B-3   YAH-dee-air   **Ht: 5'11" Wt: 225 Born: 7/13/1982 Age: 30**

										BATTING														BASERUNNING				AVERAGES		
Year	Team	Lg	G	AB	H	2B	3B	HR	(Hm	Rd)	TB	R	RBI	RC	TBB	IBB	SO	HBP	SH	SF	SB	CS	SB%	GDP	Avg	OBP	Slg
2004	StL	NL	51	135	36	6	0	2	(1	1)	48	12	15	15	13	3	20	0	2	1	0	1	.00	4	.267	.329	.356
2005	StL	NL	114	385	97	15	1	8	(6	2)	138	36	49	46	23	3	30	2	8	3	2	3	.40	10	.252	.295	.358
2006	StL	NL	129	417	90	26	0	6	(2	4)	134	29	49	35	26	2	41	8	8	2	1	2	.33	15	.216	.274	.321
2007	StL	NL	111	353	97	15	0	6	(4	2)	130	30	40	38	34	5	43	3	2	4	1	1	.50	18	.275	.340	.368
2008	StL	NL	124	444	135	18	0	7	(2	5)	174	37	56	57	32	4	29	1	3	5	0	2	.00	21	.304	.349	.392

		BATTING																				BASERUNNING				AVERAGES		
Year	Team	Lg	G	AB	H	2B	3B	HR	(Hm	Rd)	TB	R	RBI	RC	TBB	IBB	SO	HBP	SH	SF	SB	CS	SB%	GDP	Avg	OBP	Slg
2009	StL	NL	140	481	141	23	1	6	(5	1)	184	45	54	64	50	2	39	6	6	1	9	3	.75	27	.293	.366	.383
2010	StL	NL	136	465	122	19	0	6	(1	5)	159	34	62	55	42	6	51	7	2	5	4	1	.67	19	.262	.329	.342
2011	StL	NL	139	475	145	32	1	14	(5	9)	221	55	65	64	33	4	44	1	5	4	4	5	.44	21	.305	.349	.465
2012	StL	NL	138	505	159	28	0	22	(9	13)	253	65	76	91	45	4	55	5	3	5	12	3	.80	10	.315	.373	.501
	Postseason		50	175	54	13	0	2	(1	1)	73	14	23	21	13	4	21	0	0	1	1	1	.50	5	.309	.354	.417
	9 ML YEARS		1082	3660	1022	182	3	77	(35	42)	1441	343	466	465	298	33	352	33	39	30	37	24	.61	145	.279	.336	.394

Jesus Montero

Bats: R **Throws:** R **Pos:** DH-78; C-56; PH-3   **Ht:** 6'3" **Wt:** 235 **Born:** 11/28/1989 **Age:** 23

		BATTING																				BASERUNNING				AVERAGES		
Year	Team	Lg	G	AB	H	2B	3B	HR	(Hm	Rd)	TB	R	RBI	RC	TBB	IBB	SO	HBP	SH	SF	SB	CS	SB%	GDP	Avg	OBP	Slg
2007	Yanks	R	33	107	30	6	0	3	(-	-)	45	13	19	17	12	0	18	3	0	1	0	0	-	7	.280	.366	.421
2008	CtnSC	A	132	525	171	34	1	17	(-	-)	258	86	87	96	37	2	83	6	0	1	2	1	.67	16	.326	.376	.491
2009	Tampa	A+	48	180	64	15	1	8	(-	-)	105	26	37	40	14	1	26	2	1	1	0	0	-	3	.356	.406	.583
2009	Trntn	AA	44	167	53	10	0	9	(-	-)	90	19	33	32	14	1	21	0	0	0	0	0	-	10	.317	.370	.539
2010	S-WB	AAA	123	453	131	34	3	21	(-	-)	234	66	75	83	46	2	91	1	0	4	0	0	-	14	.289	.353	.517
2011	S-WB	AAA	109	420	121	19	1	18	(-	-)	196	52	66	69	36	6	98	4	0	3	0	0	-	16	.288	.348	.467
2011	NYY	AL	18	61	20	4	0	4	(3	1)	36	9	12	12	7	2	17	1	0	0	0	0	-	2	.328	.406	.590
2012	Sea	AL	135	515	134	20	0	15	(6	9)	199	46	62	52	29	4	99	2	0	7	0	2	.00	15	.260	.298	.386
	Postseason		1	2	2	0	0	0	(0	0)	2	1	1	2	0	0	0	0	0	0	0	0	-	0	1.000	1.000	1.000
	2 ML YEARS		153	576	154	24	0	19	(9	10)	235	55	74	64	36	6	116	3	0	7	0	2	.00	17	.267	.310	.408

Miguel Montero

Bats: L **Throws:** R **Pos:** C-139; PH-4   **Ht:** 5'11" **Wt:** 213 **Born:** 7/9/1983 **Age:** 29

		BATTING																				BASERUNNING				AVERAGES		
Year	Team	Lg	G	AB	H	2B	3B	HR	(Hm	Rd)	TB	R	RBI	RC	TBB	IBB	SO	HBP	SH	SF	SB	CS	SB%	GDP	Avg	OBP	Slg
2006	Ari	NL	6	16	4	1	0	0	(0	0)	5	0	3	2	1	0	3	0	0	0	0	0	-	0	.250	.294	.313
2007	Ari	NL	84	214	48	7	0	10	(7	3)	85	30	37	19	20	2	35	3	1	6	0	0	-	7	.224	.292	.397
2008	Ari	NL	70	184	47	16	1	5	(1	4)	80	24	18	21	19	3	49	2	1	1	0	0	-	1	.255	.330	.435
2009	Ari	NL	128	425	125	30	0	16	(5	11)	203	61	59	65	38	5	78	3	2	2	1	2	.33	6	.294	.355	.478
2010	Ari	NL	85	297	79	20	2	9	(0	9)	130	36	43	38	29	3	71	2	0	3	0	1	.00	10	.266	.332	.438
2011	Ari	NL	140	493	139	36	1	18	(8	10)	231	65	86	84	47	10	97	8	1	4	1	1	.50	14	.282	.351	.469
2012	Ari	NL	141	486	139	25	2	15	(4	11)	213	65	88	92	73	6	130	12	0	2	0	0	-	15	.286	.391	.438
	Postseason		9	27	8	2	0	0	(0	0)	10	4	2	3	3	1	6	0	0	0	0	0	-	0	.296	.367	.370
	7 ML YEARS		654	2115	581	135	6	73	(25	48)	947	281	334	321	227	29	463	30	5	18	2	4	.33	53	.275	.351	.448

Adam Moore

Bats: R **Throws:** R **Pos:** C-3; DH-1   **Ht:** 6'3" **Wt:** 220 **Born:** 5/8/1984 **Age:** 29

		BATTING																				BASERUNNING				AVERAGES		
Year	Team	Lg	G	AB	H	2B	3B	HR	(Hm	Rd)	TB	R	RBI	RC	TBB	IBB	SO	HBP	SH	SF	SB	CS	SB%	GDP	Avg	OBP	Slg
2012	Tacom*	AAA	24	86	18	5	0	3	(-	-)	32	10	11	8	5	0	14	0	1	2	0	0	-	3	.209	.247	.372
2012	Omha*	AAA	35	115	34	8	0	3	(-	-)	51	18	22	21	14	0	24	3	1	2	2	0	1.00	6	.296	.381	.443
2009	Sea	AL	6	23	5	1	0	1	(1	0)	9	4	2	2	0	0	7	1	0	0	1	0	1.00	1	.217	.250	.391
2010	Sea	AL	60	205	40	6	0	4	(1	3)	58	12	15	9	8	1	63	2	1	2	0	1	.00	3	.195	.230	.283
2011	Sea	AL	2	6	1	0	0	0	(0	0)	2	0	0	0	0	0	2	0	0	0	0	0	-	0	.167	.167	.333
2012	KC	AL	4	11	2	1	0	1	(1	0)	6	1	2	2	1	0	3	0	0	0	0	0	-	0	.182	.250	.545
	4 ML YEARS		72	245	48	9	0	6	(3	3)	75	17	19	13	9	1	75	3	1	2	1	1	.50	4	.196	.232	.306

Jeremy Moore

Bats: L **Throws:** R **Pos:** OF   **Ht:** 6'1" **Wt:** 195 **Born:** 6/29/1987 **Age:** 26

		BATTING																				BASERUNNING				AVERAGES		
Year	Team	Lg	G	AB	H	2B	3B	HR	(Hm	Rd)	TB	R	RBI	RC	TBB	IBB	SO	HBP	SH	SF	SB	CS	SB%	GDP	Avg	OBP	Slg
2005	Angels	R	34	110	25	3	1	0	(-	-)	30	15	11	9	11	0	46	1	2	0	12	6	.67	3	.227	.303	.273
2006	Angels	R	41	142	36	7	2	3	(-	-)	56	25	19	18	18	0	37	3	1	1	4	8	.33	4	.254	.348	.394
2007	Orem	R+	68	254	69	13	6	14	(-	-)	136	50	54	46	19	2	68	3	4	1	17	5	.77	5	.272	.329	.535
2008	CRpds	A	96	362	87	11	12	17	(-	-)	173	47	48	51	21	0	125	2	2	2	28	10	.74	1	.240	.284	.478
2009	RCuca	A+	124	470	131	20	12	11	(-	-)	208	61	58	68	34	2	144	4	4	4	17	13	.57	6	.279	.330	.443
2009	Ark	AA	7	21	7	0	1	2	(-	-)	15	5	10	5	3	0	7	1	0	1	1	1	.50	0	.333	.423	.714
2010	Ark	AA	128	456	138	14	10	13	(-	-)	211	72	61	77	39	2	122	3	5	5	24	10	.71	7	.303	.358	.463
2011	Salt Lk	AAA	113	426	127	24	18	15	(-	-)	232	76	66	76	21	0	114	3	4	6	21	10	.68	6	.298	.331	.545
2011	LAA	AL	8	8	1	0	0	0	(0	0)	1	3	0	0	0	0	2	0	0	0	0	0	-	0	.125	.125	.125

Matt Moore

Pitches: L **Bats:** L **Pos:** SP-31   **Ht:** 6'2" **Wt:** 205 **Born:** 6/18/1989 **Age:** 24

		HOW MUCH HE PITCHED						WHAT HE GAVE UP										THE RESULTS						
Year	Team	Lg	G	GS	CG	GF	IP	BFP	H	R	ER	HR	SH	SF	HB	TBB	IBB	SO	WP	Bk	W	L	Pct	Sh	Sv-Op Hld	ERC	ERA
2007	Princtn	R	8	3	0	0	20.1	93	12	6	6	1	0	2	2	16	0	29	2	0	0	0	-	0	0-- -	3.14	2.66
2008	Princtn	R	12	12	0	0	54.1	221	30	22	10	0	2	1	4	19	0	77	4	0	2	2	.500	0	0-- -	1.38	1.66
2009	BG	A	26	26	0	0	123.0	522	86	51	43	6	4	0	6	70	0	176	13	0	8	5	.615	0	0-- -	2.92	3.15
2010	Charltt	A+	26	26	0	0	144.2	598	109	62	54	7	6	4	8	61	0	208	10	2	6	11	.353	0	0-- -	2.73	3.36
2011	Mont	AA	18	18	1	0	102.1	400	68	31	25	8	2	1	5	28	0	131	3	1	8	3	.727	1	0-- -	1.97	2.20
2011	Drham	AAA	9	9	0	0	52.2	204	33	8	8	3	1	0	1	18	0	79	4	0	4	0	1.000	0	0-- -	1.83	1.37

Year	Team	Lg		HOW MUCH HE PITCHED						WHAT HE GAVE UP										THE RESULTS							
			G	GS	CG	GF	IP	BFP	H	R	ER	HR	SH	SF	HB	TBB	IBB	SO	WP	Bk	W	L	Pct	Sh	Sv-Op	Hld	ERC	ERA
2011	TB	AL	3	1	0	0	9.1	40	9	3	3	1	0	0	0	3	0	15	2	0	1	0	1.000	0	0-0	1	3.54	2.89
2012	TB	AL	31	31	0	0	177.1	759	158	85	75	18	3	4	7	81	5	175	8	1	11	11	.500	0	0-0	0	3.83	3.81
	Postseason		2	1	0	0	10.0	37	3	1	1	1	0	0	1	3	0	8	1	0	1	0	1.000	0	0-0	0	1.03	0.90
	2 ML YEARS		34	32	0	0	186.2	799	167	88	78	19	3	4	7	84	5	190	10	1	12	11	.522	0	0-0	1	3.82	3.76

Scott Moore

Bats: L **Throws:** R **Pos:** 3B-28; 1B-19; RF-15; PH-11; 2B-6; LF-2   **Ht:** 6'2" **Wt:** 195 **Born:** 11/17/1983 **Age:** 29

Year	Team	Lg						BATTING															BASERUNNING				AVERAGES		
			G	AB	H	2B	3B	HR	(Hm	Rd)	TB	R	RBI	RC	TBB	IBB	SO	HBP	SH	SF	SB	CS	SB%	GDP	Avg	OBP	Slg
2012	OKCity*	AAA	73	245	78	26	1	10	(-	-)	136	47	54	55	35	1	51	6	1	4	3	3	.50	6	.318	.410	.555
2006	ChC		16	38	10	2	0	2	(1	1)	18	6	5	5	2	0	10	1	1	0	0	0	-	1	.263	.317	.474
2007	2 Tms		19	52	12	2	0	1	(1	0)	17	2	11	6	1	0	17	0	0	2	1	1	.00	1	.231	.236	.327
2008	Bal	AL	4	8	1	0	0	1	(0	1)	4	1	1	1	1	0	3	0	0	0	0	0	-	0	.125	.222	.500
2010	Bal	AL	41	86	18	2	0	3	(2	1)	29	8	10	8	8	1	19	0	1	1	3	0	1.00	0	.209	.274	.337
2012	Hou	NL	72	201	52	11	0	9	(4	5)	90	23	26	28	16	2	56	7	1	3	0	1	.00	3	.259	.330	.448
07	ChC	NL	2	5	0	0	0	0	(0	0)	0	0	0	0	0	0	2	0	0	0	0	0	-	0	.000	.000	.000
07	Bal	AL	17	47	12	2	0	1	(1	0)	17	2	11	6	1	0	15	0	0	2	1	1	.00	1	.255	.260	.362
	5 ML YEARS		152	385	93	17	0	16	(8	8)	158	40	53	48	28	3	105	8	3	6	3	2	.60	5	.242	.302	.410

Tyler Moore

Bats: R **Throws:** R **Pos:** LF-40; PH-31; 1B-14; RF-2   **Ht:** 6'2" **Wt:** 215 **Born:** 1/30/1987 **Age:** 26

Year	Team	Lg						BATTING															BASERUNNING				AVERAGES		
			G	AB	H	2B	3B	HR	(Hm	Rd)	TB	R	RBI	RC	TBB	IBB	SO	HBP	SH	SF	SB	CS	SB%	GDP	Avg	OBP	Slg
2008	Vrmnt	A-	71	265	53	10	0	6	(-	-)	81	17	28	18	13	1	66	1	0	1	1	1	.50	5	.200	.239	.306
2009	Hgrstn	A	111	421	125	30	3	9	(-	-)	188	38	87	71	40	1	111	8	0	8	2	2	.50	6	.297	.363	.447
2010	Ptomc	A+	129	502	135	43	3	31	(-	-)	277	78	111	90	40	1	125	2	2	7	0	0	-	5	.269	.321	.552
2011	Hrsbrg	AA	137	519	140	35	4	31	(-	-)	276	70	90	88	30	2	139	6	0	6	2	0	1.00	6	.270	.314	.532
2012	Syrcse	AAA	29	101	31	6	1	9	(-	-)	66	15	26	24	12	0	26	0	0	2	1	0	1.00	2	.307	.374	.653
2012	Was	NL	75	156	41	9	0	10	(3	7)	80	20	29	26	14	0	46	1	0	0	3	0	1.00	3	.263	.327	.513

Franklin Morales

Pitches: L **Bats:** L **Pos:** RP-28; SP-9   **Ht:** 6'0" **Wt:** 210 **Born:** 1/24/1986 **Age:** 27

Year	Team	Lg		HOW MUCH HE PITCHED						WHAT HE GAVE UP												THE RESULTS							
			G	GS	CG	GF	IP	BFP	H	R	ER	HR	SH	SF	HB	TBB	IBB	SO	WP	Bk	W	L	Pct	Sh	Sv-Op	Hld	ERC	ERA
2007	Col	NL	8	8	0	0	39.1	163	34	15	15	2	4	2	2	14	1	26	0	0	3	2	.600	0	0-0	0	3.04	3.43
2008	Col	NL	5	5	0	0	25.1	120	28	18	18	2	2	2	1	17	2	9	1	3	1	2	.333	0	0-0	0	5.58	6.39
2009	Col	NL	40	2	0	14	40.0	179	38	22	20	4	3	0	1	23	4	41	2	0	3	2	.600	0	7-8	7	4.38	4.50
2010	Col	NL	35	0	0	15	28.2	140	28	22	20	5	1	2	3	24	2	27	3	2	0	4	.000	0	3-6	1	6.53	6.28
2011	2 Tms		50	0	0	13	46.1	193	40	21	19	6	2	1	2	19	1	42	2	1	1	2	.333	0	0-0	10	3.77	3.69
2012	Bos	AL	37	9	0	5	76.1	325	64	38	32	11	0	3	6	30	3	76	3	5	3	4	.429	0	1-1	8	3.68	3.77
11	Col	NL	14	0	0	4	14.0	59	10	6	6	2	1	1	0	8	1	11	1	0	0	1	.000	0	0-0	2	3.36	3.86
11	Bos	AL	36	0	0	9	32.1	134	30	15	13	4	1	0	2	11	0	31	1	1	1	1	.500	0	0-0	8	3.96	3.62
	Postseason		8	2	0	0	12.2	59	15	11	11	1	0	0	2	7	1	7	0	1	0	0	-	0	0-0	1	6.28	7.82
	6 ML YEARS		175	24	0	47	256.0	1120	232	136	124	30	12	10	15	127	13	221	11	11	11	16	.407	0	11-15	26	4.19	4.36

Kendrys Morales

Bats: B **Throws:** R **Pos:** DH-92; 1B-28; PH-14   KEN-dreez   **Ht:** 6'1" **Wt:** 225 **Born:** 6/20/1983 **Age:** 30

Year	Team	Lg						BATTING															BASERUNNING				AVERAGES		
			G	AB	H	2B	3B	HR	(Hm	Rd)	TB	R	RBI	RC	TBB	IBB	SO	HBP	SH	SF	SB	CS	SB%	GDP	Avg	OBP	Slg
2006	LAA	AL	57	197	46	10	1	5	(1	4)	73	21	22	19	17	1	28	0	0	1	1	1	.50	11	.234	.293	.371
2007	LAA	AL	43	119	35	10	4	0	(2	2)	57	12	15	15	6	2	21	1	0	0	0	1	.00	6	.294	.333	.479
2008	LAA	AL	27	61	13	2	0	3	(0	3)	24	7	8	3	4	0	7	1	0	0	0	1	.00	3	.213	.273	.393
2009	LAA	AL	152	566	173	43	2	34	(21	13)	322	86	108	105	46	10	117	2	0	8	3	7	.30	15	.306	.355	.569
2010	LAA	AL	51	193	56	5	0	11	(7	4)	94	29	39	34	12	3	31	5	0	1	0	0	.00	5	.290	.346	.487
2012	LAA	AL	134	484	132	26	1	22	(10	12)	226	61	73	68	31	1	116	4	0	3	0	1	.00	11	.273	.320	.467
	Postseason		16	47	9	1	0	2	(1	1)	16	3	7	3	2	0	8	1	0	1	0	0	-	1	.191	.235	.340
	6 ML YEARS		464	1620	455	96	4	79	(41	38)	796	216	265	244	116	17	320	13	0	13	4	12	.25	50	.281	.331	.491

Brent Morel

Bats: R **Throws:** R **Pos:** 3B-33; PR-4   more-ELL   **Ht:** 6'2" **Wt:** 220 **Born:** 4/21/1987 **Age:** 26

Year	Team	Lg						BATTING															BASERUNNING				AVERAGES		
			G	AB	H	2B	3B	HR	(Hm	Rd)	TB	R	RBI	RC	TBB	IBB	SO	HBP	SH	SF	SB	CS	SB%	GDP	Avg	OBP	Slg
2012	Charltt*	AAA	34	124	24	4	0	1	(-	-)	31	12	10	6	8	0	28	0	0	0	0	0	-	2	.194	.242	.250
2012	WinSa*	A+	7	22	5	4	0	0	(-	-)	9	2	2	2	2	0	4	0	0	0	0	0	-	2	.227	.292	.409
2010	CWS	AL	21	65	15	3	0	3	(3	0)	27	9	7	4	4	0	17	0	0	1	2	0	1.00	2	.231	.271	.415
2011	CWS	AL	126	413	101	18	1	10	(6	4)	151	44	41	36	22	0	57	3	5	1	5	4	.56	8	.245	.287	.366
2012	CWS	AL	35	113	20	2	0	0	(0	0)	22	14	5	4	7	0	39	0	5	0	4	1	.80	3	.177	.225	.195
	3 ML YEARS		182	591	136	23	1	13	(9	4)	200	67	53	44	33	0	113	3	10	2	11	5	.69	13	.230	.273	.338

Mitch Moreland

Bats: L **Throws:** L **Pos:** 1B-95; PH-19; DH-7; RF-3   **Ht:** 6'2" **Wt:** 230 **Born:** 9/6/1985 **Age:** 27

								BATTING													BASERUNNING				AVERAGES		
Year	Team	Lg	G	AB	H	2B	3B	HR	(Hm	Rd)	TB	R	RBI	RC	TBB	IBB	SO	HBP	SH	SF	SB	CS	SB%	GDP	Avg	OBP	Slg
2012	RdRck*	AAA	2	6	1	0	0	0	(-	-)	1	0	0	0	0	0	2	0	0	0	0	0	-	0	.167	.167	.167
2012	Frisco*	AA	3	13	4	2	0	0	(-	-)	6	4	1	2	0	0	2	1	0	0	0	0	-	0	.308	.357	.462
2010	Tex	AL	47	145	37	4	0	9	(3	6)	68	20	25	27	25	5	36	1	0	2	3	1	.75	3	.255	.364	.469
2011	Tex	AL	134	464	120	22	1	16	(7	9)	192	60	51	56	39	6	92	4	2	3	2	2	.50	9	.259	.320	.414
2012	Tex	AL	114	327	90	18	0	15	(10	5)	153	41	50	46	23	5	71	1	2	4	1	1	.50	8	.275	.321	.468
	Postseason		24	75	19	4	0	3	(3	0)	32	7	10	12	6	1	17	1	1	0	0	0	-	3	.253	.317	.427
	3 ML YEARS		295	936	247	44	1	40	(20	20)	413	121	126	129	87	16	199	6	4	9	6	4	.60	20	.264	.328	.441

Nyjer Morgan

Bats: L **Throws:** L **Pos:** CF-53; PH-39; RF-27; LF-19; PR-4; DH-1   NYE-jerr   **Ht:** 5'10" **Wt:** 184 **Born:** 7/2/1980 **Age:** 32

								BATTING													BASERUNNING				AVERAGES		
Year	Team	Lg	G	AB	H	2B	3B	HR	(Hm	Rd)	TB	R	RBI	RC	TBB	IBB	SO	HBP	SH	SF	SB	CS	SB%	GDP	Avg	OBP	Slg
2007	Pit	NL	28	107	32	3	4	1	(1	0)	46	15	7	18	9	0	19	1	1	0	7	3	.70	0	.299	.359	.430
2008	Pit	NL	58	160	47	13	0	0	(0	0)	60	26	7	18	10	0	32	3	1	1	9	5	.64	0	.294	.345	.375
2009	2 Tms	NL	120	469	144	15	7	3	(1	2)	182	74	39	69	40	2	74	9	10	5	42	17	.71	9	.307	.369	.388
2010	Was	NL	136	509	129	17	7	0	(0	0)	160	60	24	53	40	1	88	10	15	3	34	17	.67	2	.253	.319	.314
2011	Mil	NL	119	378	115	20	6	4	(0	4)	159	61	37	58	19	0	70	14	15	3	13	4	.76	1	.304	.357	.421
2012	Mil	NL	122	289	69	5	3	3	(3	0)	89	44	16	26	20	0	63	6	7	0	12	5	.71	4	.239	.302	.308
09	Pit	NL	71	278	77	6	5	2	(1	1)	99	39	27	37	29	2	49	5	5	4	18	10	.64	6	.277	.351	.356
09	Was	NL	49	191	67	9	2	1	(0	1)	83	35	12	32	11	0	25	4	5	1	24	7	.77	3	.351	.396	.435
	Postseason		10	28	5	2	0	0	(0	0)	7	2	3	2	2	0	11	2	0	0	0	0	-	1	.179	.281	.250
	6 ML YEARS		583	1912	536	73	27	11	(5	6)	696	280	130	242	138	3	346	43	49	12	117	51	.70	21	.280	.341	.364

Justin Morneau

Bats: L **Throws:** R **Pos:** 1B-99; DH-34; PH-1   MORE-no   **Ht:** 6'4" **Wt:** 222 **Born:** 5/15/1981 **Age:** 32

								BATTING													BASERUNNING				AVERAGES		
Year	Team	Lg	G	AB	H	2B	3B	HR	(Hm	Rd)	TB	R	RBI	RC	TBB	IBB	SO	HBP	SH	SF	SB	CS	SB%	GDP	Avg	OBP	Slg
2003	Min	AL	40	106	24	4	0	4	(1	3)	40	14	16	11	9	1	30	0	0	0	0	0	-	4	.226	.287	.377
2004	Min	AL	74	280	76	17	0	19	(9	10)	150	39	58	48	28	8	54	2	0	2	0	0	-	4	.271	.340	.536
2005	Min	AL	141	490	117	23	4	22	(9	13)	214	62	79	58	44	8	94	4	0	5	0	2	.00	12	.239	.304	.437
2006	Min	AL	157	592	190	37	1	34	(17	17)	331	97	130	118	53	9	93	5	0	11	3	3	.50	10	.321	.375	.559
2007	Min	AL	157	590	160	31	3	31	(15	16)	290	84	111	95	64	11	91	5	0	9	1	1	.50	17	.271	.343	.492
2008	Min	AL	163	623	187	47	4	23	(12	11)	311	97	129	122	76	16	85	3	0	10	0	1	.00	20	.300	.374	.499
2009	Min	AL	135	508	139	31	1	30	(14	16)	262	85	100	91	72	12	86	3	0	7	0	0	-	12	.274	.363	.516
2010	Min	AL	81	296	102	25	1	18	(4	14)	183	53	56	65	50	7	62	0	0	2	0	0	-	6	.345	.437	.618
2011	Min	AL	69	264	60	16	0	4	(0	4)	88	19	30	28	19	1	44	3	0	2	0	0	-	8	.227	.285	.333
2012	Min	AL	134	505	135	26	2	19	(7	12)	222	63	77	63	49	8	102	6	0	10	1	0	1.00	19	.267	.333	.440
	Postseason		7	29	9	3	0	2	(1	1)	18	4	4	3	0	0	3	0	0	0	0	0	-	0	.310	.310	.621
	10 ML YEARS		1151	4254	1190	257	16	204	(88	116)	2091	613	786	699	464	81	741	31	0	58	5	7	.42	112	.280	.351	.492

Bryan Morris

Pitches: R **Bats:** L **Pos:** RP-5   **Ht:** 6'3" **Wt:** 220 **Born:** 3/28/1987 **Age:** 26

			HOW MUCH HE PITCHED						WHAT HE GAVE UP										THE RESULTS							
Year	Team	Lg	G	GS	CG	GF	IP	BFP	H	R	ER	HR	SH	SF	HB	TBB	IBB	SO	WP	Bk	W	L	Pct	Sh	Sv-Op	Hld	ERC	ERA
2006	Ogden	R+	14	14	0	0	59.2	285	64	44	34	3	0	4	1	40	0	79	11	3	4	5	.444	0	0--	-	5.10	5.13
2008	Gt Lks	A	17	17	1	0	81.2	342	74	34	29	5	4	5	2	31	0	72	7	0	2	4	.333	1	0--	-	3.35	3.20
2008	Hkry	A	3	3	0	0	14.1	72	17	9	8	2	0	1	0	12	0	11	4	0	0	2	.000	0	0--	-	7.18	5.02
2009	Lynbrg	A+	15	15	0	0	72.2	334	87	58	45	2	4	1	0	34	0	32	10	0	4	9	.308	0	0--	-	4.87	5.57
2010	Bradtn	A+	8	8	0	0	44.2	180	37	8	3	0	1	2	2	7	0	40	2	1	3	0	1.000	0	0--	-	1.83	0.60
2010	Altna	AA	19	16	0	1	89.0	383	87	45	42	9	7	6	1	31	0	84	8	0	6	4	.600	0	0--	-	4.02	4.25
2011	Altna	AA	35	6	0	7	78.0	326	72	34	29	2	5	1	1	33	0	64	4	1	3	4	.429	0	3--	-	3.35	3.35
2012	Indy	AAA	46	0	0	14	81.0	335	76	32	24	8	0	1	0	17	0	79	9	1	2	2	.500	0	5--	-	2.95	2.67
2012	Pit	NL	5	0	0	2	5.0	20	2	2	1	0	0	1	0	2	0	6	1	0	0	0	-	0	0-0	-	1.32	1.80

Logan Morrison

Bats: L **Throws:** L **Pos:** LF-59; 1B-21; PH-14; DH-3   **Ht:** 6'3" **Wt:** 240 **Born:** 8/25/1987 **Age:** 25

								BATTING													BASERUNNING				AVERAGES		
Year	Team	Lg	G	AB	H	2B	3B	HR	(Hm	Rd)	TB	R	RBI	RC	TBB	IBB	SO	HBP	SH	SF	SB	CS	SB%	GDP	Avg	OBP	Slg
2010	Fla	NL	62	244	69	20	7	2	(1	1)	109	43	18	41	41	0	51	2	0	0	1	0	1.00	4	.283	.390	.447
2011	Fla	NL	123	462	114	25	4	23	(12	11)	216	54	72	55	54	3	99	5	0	4	2	1	.67	9	.247	.330	.468
2012	Mia	NL	93	296	68	15	1	11	(4	7)	118	30	36	27	31	2	58	4	0	3	1	0	1.00	9	.230	.308	.399
	3 ML YEARS		278	1002	251	60	12	36	(17	19)	443	127	126	123	126	5	208	11	0	7	3	2	.60	22	.250	.339	.442

Brandon Morrow

Pitches: R **Bats:** R **Pos:** SP-21   **Ht:** 6'3" **Wt:** 200 **Born:** 7/26/1984 **Age:** 28

			HOW MUCH HE PITCHED						WHAT HE GAVE UP										THE RESULTS							
Year	Team	Lg	G	GS	CG	GF	IP	BFP	H	R	ER	HR	SH	SF	HB	TBB	IBB	SO	WP	Bk	W	L	Pct	Sh	Sv-Op	Hld	ERC	ERA
2012	Dnedin*	A+	2	2	0	0	6.0	26	8	2	1	0	0	0	0	3	0	6	0	0	0	0	-	0	0--	-	6.18	1.50
2012	NHam*	AA	3	3	0	0	14.1	54	10	4	4	2	0	1	0	3	0	12	1	0	1	0	1.000	0	0--	-	2.12	2.51
2007	Sea	AL	60	0	0	18	63.1	289	56	29	29	3	4	4	1	50	5	66	4	0	3	4	.429	0	0-2	18	4.47	4.12
2008	Sea	AL	45	5	0	24	64.2	265	40	26	24	10	1	0	0	34	1	75	5	0	3	4	.429	0	10-12	3	2.84	3.34
2009	Sea	AL	26	10	0	9	69.2	313	66	38	34	10	1	2	0	44	1	63	3	0	2	4	.333	0	6-8	1	4.99	4.39

Year	Team	Lg	G	GS	CG	GF	IP	BFP	H	R	ER	HR	SH	SF	HB	TBB	IBB	SO	WP	Bk	W	L	Pct	Sh	Sv-Op	Hld	ERC	ERA
2010	Tor	AL	26	26	1	0	146.1	629	136	76	73	11	2	4	9	66	0	178	8	0	10	7	.588	0	0-0	0	3.99	4.49
2011	Tor	AL	30	30	0	0	179.1	777	162	103	94	21	4	9	12	69	1	203	12	1	11	11	.500	0	0-0	0	3.79	4.72
2012	Tor	AL	21	21	3	0	124.2	504	98	45	41	12	1	3	2	41	0	108	3	0	10	7	.588	3	0-0	0	2.73	2.96
6 ML YEARS			208	92	4	51	648.0	2777	558	317	295	67	13	22	24	304	8	693	35	1	39	37	.513	4	16-22	22	3.72	4.10

Michael Morse

Bats: R Throws: R Pos: LF-67; RF-36; DH-9; 1B-1 **Ht: 6'5" Wt: 245 Born: 3/22/1982 Age: 31**

						BATTING														BASERUNNING				AVERAGES		
Year	Team	Lg	G	AB	H	2B	3B	HR	(Hm	Rd)	TB	R	RBI	RC	TBB	IBB	SO	HBP	SH	SF	SB	CS	SB%	GDP	Avg	OBP	Slg
2012	Hrsbrg*	AA	3	8	3	2	0	1	(-	-)	8	1	4	3	1	1	3	0	0	0	0	0	-	0	.375	.444	1.000
2012	Hgrstn*	A	1	4	2	0	0	0	(-	-)	2	1	0	0	0	0	1	0	0	0	0	0	-	0	.500	.500	.500
2012	Ptomc*	A+	3	9	3	1	0	0	(-	-)	4	0	1	1	1	0	2	0	0	0	0	0	-	0	.333	.400	.444
2005	Sea	AL	72	230	64	10	1	3	(3	0)	85	27	23	28	18	0	50	8	0	2	3	1	.75	9	.278	.349	.370
2006	Sea	AL	21	43	16	5	0	0	(0	0)	21	5	11	9	3	0	7	0	0	2	1	0	1.00	2	.372	.396	.488
2007	Sea	AL	9	18	8	2	0	0	(0 | 0)	10	1	3	6	1	0	4	1	0	0	0	0	.444		0	.444	.500	.556
2008	Sea	AL	5	9	2	1	0	0	(0	0)	3	0	0	1	1	0	4	1	0	0	0	0	-	0	.222	.364	.333
2009	Was	NL	32	52	13	3	0	3	(3	0)	25	4	10	8	3	0	16	0	0	0	0	0	-	1	.250	.291	.481
2010	Was	NL	98	266	77	12	2	15	(6	9)	138	36	41	42	22	1	64	4	0	1	0	1	.00	6	.289	.352	.519
2011	Was	NL	146	522	158	36	0	31	(11	20)	287	73	95	96	36	5	126	13	0	4	2	3	.40	9	.303	.360	.550
2012	Was	NL	102	406	118	17	1	18	(7	11)	191	53	62	57	16	0	97	4	0	4	0	1	.00	14	.291	.321	.470
8 ML YEARS			485	1546	456	86	4	70	(30	40)	760	199	245	247	100	6	368	31	0	13	6	6	.50	41	.295	.347	.492

Clayton Mortensen

Pitches: R Bats: R Pos: RP-26 **Ht: 6'4" Wt: 185 Born: 4/10/1985 Age: 28**

			HOW MUCH HE PITCHED						WHAT HE GAVE UP												THE RESULTS							
Year	Team	Lg	G	GS	CG	GF	IP	BFP	H	R	ER	HR	SH	SF	HB	TBB	IBB	SO	WP	Bk	W	L	Pct	Sh	Sv-Op	Hld	ERC	ERA
2012	Pwtckt*	AAA	24	0	0	6	37.2	151	21	11	8	3	1	0	4	15	0	36	2	0	5	3	.625	0	2- -	0	2.06	1.91
2012	Portlnd*	AA	1	0	0	0	1.0	7	3	2	2	0	0	0	0	1	0	0	0	0	0	0	-	0	0- -	0	19.55	18.00
2009	2 Tms		7	6	0	1	30.2	149	42	34	26	6	1	4	3	13	0	13	1	0	2	4	.333	0	0-0	0	7.50	7.63
2010	Oak	AL	1	1	0	0	6.0	26	6	4	3	1	0	0	0	2	0	7	0	0	0	0	-	0	0-0	0	4.18	4.50
2011	Col	NL	16	6	0	6	58.1	244	55	30	25	9	4	0	2	24	2	30	3	0	2	4	.333	0	0-0	1	4.40	3.86
2012	Bos	AL	26	0	0	8	42.0	173	32	15	15	7	0	2	1	19	2	41	3	0	1	1	.500	0	0-0	1	3.49	3.21
09	StL	NL	1	0	0	0	3.0	16	5	6	2	1	1	1	1	1	0	2	0	0	0	0	-	0	0-0	0	11.45	6.00
09	Oak	AL	6	6	0	1	27.2	133	37	28	24	5	0	3	2	12	0	11	1	0	2	4	.333	0	0-0	0	7.10	7.81
4 ML YEARS			50	13	0	15	137.0	592	135	83	69	23	5	6	6	58	4	91	7	0	5	9	.357	0	0-0	1	4.75	4.53

Charlie Morton

Pitches: R Bats: R Pos: SP-9 **Ht: 6'5" Wt: 230 Born: 11/12/1983 Age: 29**

			HOW MUCH HE PITCHED						WHAT HE GAVE UP												THE RESULTS							
Year	Team	Lg	G	GS	CG	GF	IP	BFP	H	R	ER	HR	SH	SF	HB	TBB	IBB	SO	WP	Bk	W	L	Pct	Sh	Sv-Op	Hld	ERC	ERA
2012	Indy*	AAA	1	1	0	0	7.2	29	6	1	1	0	0	0	1	0	8	0	0	0	0	0	-	0	0- -	0	1.54	1.17
2008	Atl	NL	16	15	0	0	74.2	345	80	56	51	9	5	4	2	41	2	48	2	0	4	8	.333	0	0-0	0	5.21	6.15
2009	Pit	NL	18	18	1	0	97.0	416	102	49	49	7	1	1	5	40	0	62	4	0	5	9	.357	1	0-0	0	4.56	4.55
2010	Pit	NL	17	17	0	0	79.2	382	112	79	67	15	6	6	7	26	3	59	5	1	2	12	.143	0	0-0	0	7.10	7.57
2011	Pit	NL	29	29	2	0	171.2	769	186	82	73	6	12	6	13	77	5	110	9	1	10	10	.500	1	0-0	0	4.52	3.83
2012	Pit	NL	9	9	0	0	50.1	223	62	30	26	5	5	2	2	11	1	25	4	0	2	6	.250	0	0-0	0	4.74	4.65
5 ML YEARS			89	88	3	0	473.1	2135	542	296	266	42	29	19	29	195	11	304	24	2	23	45	.338	2	0-0	0	5.08	5.06

Guillermo Moscoso

Pitches: R Bats: R Pos: RP-20; SP-3 mahs-KOE-soe **Ht: 6'1" Wt: 200 Born: 11/14/1983 Age: 29**

			HOW MUCH HE PITCHED						WHAT HE GAVE UP												THE RESULTS							
Year	Team	Lg	G	GS	CG	GF	IP	BFP	H	R	ER	HR	SH	SF	HB	TBB	IBB	SO	WP	Bk	W	L	Pct	Sh	Sv-Op	Hld	ERC	ERA
2012	ColSpr*	AAA	18	18	0	0	98.1	434	127	68	67	14	1	7	0	26	0	85	4	0	8	6	.571	0	0- -	0	5.59	6.13
2009	Tex	AL	10	0	0	6	14.0	64	15	7	5	1	0	1	1	6	0	12	4	0	0	0	-	0	0-0	0	4.55	3.21
2010	Tex	AL	1	0	0	0	0.2	7	2	2	2	0	0	0	1	2	0	2	0	0	0	0	-	0	0-0	0	37.18	27.00
2011	Oak	AL	23	21	0	1	128.0	526	102	59	48	14	1	3	2	38	1	74	0	1	8	10	.444	0	0-0	0	2.67	3.38
2012	Col	NL	23	3	0	4	50.0	231	67	34	34	8	1	1	1	19	0	47	5	0	3	2	.600	0	0-1	1	6.60	6.12
4 ML YEARS			57	24	0	11	192.2	828	186	102	89	23	2	5	5	65	1	135	9	1	11	12	.478	0	0-1	1	3.81	4.16

Dustin Moseley

Pitches: R Bats: R Pos: SP-1 MOZE-lee **Ht: 6'4" Wt: 215 Born: 12/26/1981 Age: 31**

			HOW MUCH HE PITCHED						WHAT HE GAVE UP												THE RESULTS							
Year	Team	Lg	G	GS	CG	GF	IP	BFP	H	R	ER	HR	SH	SF	HB	TBB	IBB	SO	WP	Bk	W	L	Pct	Sh	Sv-Op	Hld	ERC	ERA
2006	LAA	AL	3	2	0	1	11.0	54	22	11	11	3	0	1	0	2	0	3	0	0	1	0	1.000	0	0-0	0	11.45	9.00
2007	LAA	AL	46	8	0	13	92.0	383	97	45	45	7	1	2	3	27	3	50	6	1	4	3	.571	0	0-0	4	4.00	4.40
2008	LAA	AL	12	10	0	1	50.1	237	70	38	38	6	1	3	2	20	0	37	3	1	2	4	.333	0	0-0	0	6.74	6.79
2009	LAA	AL	3	3	0	0	14.2	65	20	8	7	3	0	0	0	3	1	8	0	0	1	0	1.000	0	0-0	0	6.13	4.30
2010	NYY	AL	16	9	0	2	65.1	278	66	36	36	13	0	4	2	27	0	33	0	0	4	4	.500	0	0-0	0	5.17	4.96
2011	SD	NL	20	20	0	0	120.0	504	117	59	44	10	5	3	2	36	6	64	1	0	3	10	.231	0	0-0	0	3.43	3.30
2012	SD	NL	1	1	0	0	5.0	22	5	5	5	1	0	1	0	2	0	4	0	0	0	0	-	0	0-0	0	4.68	9.00
Postseason			2	0	0	1	3.0	10	1	0	0	0	0	0	0	0	0	5	0	0	1	0	1.000	0	0-0	0	0.25	0.00
7 ML YEARS			101	53	0	17	358.1	1543	397	202	186	43	7	14	9	117	10	199	10	2	15	21	.417	0	0-0	4	4.66	4.67

Brandon Moss

Bats: L **Throws:** R **Pos:** 1B-55; PH-15; RF-13; LF-11; DH-3 **Ht:** 6'0" **Wt:** 210 **Born:** 9/16/1983 **Age:** 29

Year	Team	Lg	G	AB	H	2B	3B	HR	(Hm	Rd)	TB	R	RBI	RC	TBB	IBB	SO	HBP	SH	SF	SB	CS	SB%	GDP	Avg	OBP	Slg
2012	Scrmto*	AAA	51	196	56	11	1	15	(-	-)	114	32	33	42	22	1	40	5	0	1	4	0	1.00	3	.286	.371	.582
2007	Bos	AL	15	25	7	2	1	0	(0	0)	11	6	1	3	4	0	6	0	0	0	0	0	-	1	.280	.379	.440
2008	2 Tms		79	236	58	15	3	8	(4	4)	103	19	34	30	21	1	70	1	0	5	1	2	.33	2	.246	.304	.436
2009	Pit	NL	133	385	91	20	4	7	(4	3)	140	47	41	37	34	3	84	4	0	1	1	5	.17	7	.236	.304	.364
2010	Pit	NL	17	26	4	1	0	0	(0	0)	5	2	2	2	1	0	6	0	0	0	0	0	-	1	.154	.185	.192
2011	Phi	NL	5	6	0	0	0	0	(0	0)	0	0	0	0	0	0	2	0	0	0	0	0	-	1	.000	.000	.000
2012	Oak	AL	84	265	77	18	0	21	(9	12)	158	48	52	50	26	2	90	3	0	2	1	1	.50	5	.291	.358	.596
08	Bos	AL	34	78	23	5	1	2	(1	1)	36	7	11	11	6	0	25	0	0	2	1	1	.50	0	.295	.337	.462
08	Pit	NL	45	158	35	10	2	6	(3	3)	67	12	23	19	15	1	45	1	0	3	0	1	.00	2	.222	.288	.424
6 ML YEARS			333	943	237	56	8	36	(17	19)	417	122	130	122	86	6	258	8	0	8	3	8	.27	17	.251	.317	.442

Guillermo Mota

Pitches: R **Bats:** R **Pos:** RP-26 **Ht:** 6'6" **Wt:** 240 **Born:** 7/25/1973 **Age:** 39

Year	Team	Lg	G	GS	CG	GF	IP	BFP	H	R	ER	HR	SH	SF	HB	TBB	IBB	SO	WP	Bk	W	L	Pct	Sh	Sv-Op	Hld	ERC	ERA
2012	Giants*	R	2	1	0	0	2.2	16	8	7	7	1	0	0	0	0	0	2	0	0	0	0	-	0	0--	-	18.64	23.63
2012	Fresno*	AAA	4	0	0	0	6.1	28	8	3	3	1	0	1	1	2	0	3	1	0	0	0	-	0	0--	-	6.73	4.26
1999	Mon	NL	51	0	0	18	55.1	243	54	24	18	5	3	3	2	25	3	27	1	1	2	4	.333	0	0-1	3	4.10	2.93
2000	Mon	NL	29	0	0	7	30.0	126	27	21	20	3	1	1	2	12	0	24	1	1	1	1	.500	0	0-0	5	3.86	6.00
2001	Mon	NL	53	0	0	20	49.2	212	51	30	29	9	3	2	1	18	1	31	1	0	1	3	.250	0	0-3	12	4.77	5.26
2002	LAD	NL	43	0	0	11	60.2	256	45	30	28	4	3	1	2	27	6	49	3	0	1	3	.250	0	0-1	4	2.57	4.15
2003	LAD	NL	76	0	0	18	105.0	410	78	23	23	7	3	1	1	26	4	99	0	0	6	3	.667	0	1-3	13	2.01	1.97
2004	2 Tms	NL	78	0	0	18	96.2	393	75	33	33	8	5	3	4	37	6	85	5	0	9	8	.529	0	4-8	30	2.82	3.07
2005	Fla	NL	56	0	0	24	67.0	293	65	38	35	5	1	3	1	32	7	60	4	0	2	2	.500	0	2-4	14	3.90	4.70
2006	2 Tms	NL	52	0	0	17	55.2	241	55	29	28	11	0	3	0	24	4	46	2	0	4	3	.571	0	0-0	9	4.71	4.53
2007	NYM	NL	52	0	0	10	59.1	261	63	39	38	8	2	0	2	18	2	47	2	0	2	2	.500	0	0-3	6	4.26	5.76
2008	Mil	NL	58	0	0	18	57.0	244	52	28	26	7	1	3	0	28	0	50	4	1	5	6	.455	0	1-4	11	4.14	4.11
2009	LAD	NL	61	0	0	27	65.1	273	53	25	25	6	3	4	5	24	8	39	3	0	3	4	.429	0	0-2	2	2.98	3.44
2010	SF	NL	56	0	0	17	54.0	228	49	29	26	4	0	4	0	22	5	38	5	0	1	3	.250	0	1-3	8	3.28	4.33
2011	SF	NL	52	0	0	11	80.1	333	71	34	34	10	3	2	2	30	4	77	1	1	2	2	.500	0	1-2	4	3.58	3.81
2012	SF	NL	26	0	0	4	20.2	91	24	13	12	3	0	1	2	8	0	24	0	0	0	1	.000	0	0-0	1	5.91	5.23
04	LAD	NL	52	0	0	11	63.0	259	51	15	15	4	4	2	2	27	5	52	5	0	8	4	.667	0	1-1	17	2.98	2.14
04	Fla	NL	26	0	0	7	33.2	134	24	18	18	4	1	1	2	10	1	33	0	0	1	4	.200	0	3-7	13	2.51	4.81
06	Cle	AL	34	0	0	13	37.2	173	45	27	26	9	0	3	0	19	3	27	2	0	1	3	.250	0	0-0	5	6.62	6.21
06	NYM	NL	18	0	0	4	18.0	68	10	2	2	2	0	0	0	5	1	19	0	0	3	0	1.000	0	0-0	4	1.51	1.00
	Postseason		11	0	0	5	12.1	50	13	6	6	1	0	0	0	4	0	7	0	0	1	0	1.000	0	0-2	3	4.20	4.38
14 ML YEARS			743	0	0	212	856.2	3604	762	396	375	90	28	31	24	331	50	696	32	4	39	45	.464	0	10-35	131	3.48	3.94

Jason Motte

Pitches: R **Bats:** R **Pos:** RP-67 MOTT **Ht:** 6'0" **Wt:** 200 **Born:** 6/22/1982 **Age:** 31

Year	Team	Lg	G	GS	CG	GF	IP	BFP	H	R	ER	HR	SH	SF	HB	TBB	IBB	SO	WP	Bk	W	L	Pct	Sh	Sv-Op	Hld	ERC	ERA
2008	StL	NL	12	0	0	4	11.0	40	5	2	1	0	1	0	0	3	0	16	0	0	0	0	-	0	1-1	4	0.89	0.82
2009	StL	NL	69	0	0	14	56.2	244	57	32	30	10	0	3	2	23	1	54	2	1	4	4	.500	0	0-3	15	4.86	4.76
2010	StL	NL	56	0	0	13	52.1	208	41	13	13	5	1	3	0	18	3	54	1	0	4	2	.667	0	2-3	12	2.68	2.24
2011	StL	NL	78	0	0	27	68.0	268	49	22	17	2	1	3	5	16	2	63	1	0	5	2	.714	0	9-13	18	1.87	2.25
2012	StL	NL	67	0	0	58	72.0	279	49	23	22	9	2	1	2	17	1	86	0	0	4	5	.444	0	42-49	0	2.08	2.75
	Postseason		13	0	0	10	13.1	46	5	4	3	1	0	0	0	1	0	8	0	0	0	1	.000	0	5-5	0	0.57	2.03
5 ML YEARS			282	0	0	116	260.0	1039	201	92	83	26	5	10	9	77	7	273	4	1	17	13	.567	0	54-69	49	2.62	2.87

Mike Moustakas

Bats: L **Throws:** R **Pos:** 3B-149 moo-STOCK-us **Ht:** 6'0" **Wt:** 215 **Born:** 9/11/1988 **Age:** 24

Year	Team	Lg	G	AB	H	2B	3B	HR	(Hm	Rd)	TB	R	RBI	RC	TBB	IBB	SO	HBP	SH	SF	SB	CS	SB%	GDP	Avg	OBP	Slg
2007	Idaho	R+	11	41	12	4	1	0	(-	-)	18	6	10	7	4	0	8	2	0	0	0	0	-	1	.293	.383	.439
2008	Burlgtn	A	126	496	135	25	3	22	(-	-)	232	77	71	80	43	4	86	7	0	3	8	4	.67	5	.272	.337	.468
2009	Wilmg	A+	129	492	123	32	2	16	(-	-)	207	66	86	63	32	5	90	2	1	3	10	6	.63	10	.250	.297	.421
2010	NWArk	AA	66	259	90	25	0	21	(-	-)	178	58	76	69	26	9	42	7	0	6	0	1	.00	7	.347	.413	.687
2010	Omha	AAA	52	225	66	16	0	15	(-	-)	127	36	48	40	8	1	25	0	0	3	2	0	1.00	8	.293	.314	.564
2011	Omha	AAA	55	223	64	15	1	10	(-	-)	111	38	44	39	19	0	44	3	2	3	1	1	.50	3	.287	.347	.498
2011	KC	AL	89	338	89	18	1	5	(3	2)	124	26	30	31	22	0	51	1	2	2	2	0	1.00	5	.263	.309	.367
2012	KC	AL	149	563	136	34	1	20	(10	10)	232	69	73	64	39	4	124	7	0	5	5	2	.71	4	.242	.296	.412
2 ML YEARS			238	901	225	52	2	25	(13	12)	356	95	103	95	61	4	175	8	2	7	7	2	.78	9	.250	.301	.395

Jamie Moyer

Pitches: L **Bats:** L **Pos:** SP-10 **Ht:** 6'0" **Wt:** 185 **Born:** 11/18/1962 **Age:** 50

Year	Team	Lg	G	GS	CG	GF	IP	BFP	H	R	ER	HR	SH	SF	HB	TBB	IBB	SO	WP	Bk	W	L	Pct	Sh	Sv-Op	Hld	ERC	ERA
2012	Norfolk*	AAA	3	3	0	0	16.0	62	11	4	3	1	0	0	1	0	0	16	0	0	1	1	.500	0	0--	-	1.25	1.69
2012	LsVgs*	AAA	2	2	0	0	11.0	55	17	10	10	3	2	0	0	3	0	9	0	0	1	1	.500	0	0--	-	7.77	8.18
1986	ChC	NL	16	16	1	0	87.1	395	107	52	49	10	3	3	3	42	1	45	3	3	7	4	.636	1	0-0	0	6.13	5.05
1987	ChC	NL	35	33	1	1	201.0	899	210	127	114	28	14	7	5	97	9	147	11	2	12	15	.444	0	0-0	0	4.96	5.10
1988	ChC	NL	34	30	3	1	202.0	855	212	84	78	20	14	4	4	55	7	121	4	0	9	15	.375	1	0-2	0	3.89	3.48
1989	Tex	AL	15	15	1	0	76.0	337	84	51	41	10	4	4	1	33	0	44	1	0	4	9	.308	1	0-0	0	5.20	4.86

Year	Team	Lg	G	GS	CG	GF	IP	BFP	H	R	ER	HR	SH	SF	HB	TBB	IBB	SO	WP	Bk	W	L	Pct	Sh	Sv-Op	Hld	ERC	ERA
							HOW MUCH HE PITCHED			**WHAT HE GAVE UP**														**THE RESULTS**				
1990	Tex	AL	33	10	1	6	102.1	447	115	59	53	6	1	7	4	39	4	58	1	0	2	6	.250	0	0-0	1	4.57	4.66
1991	StL	NL	8	7	0	1	31.1	142	38	21	20	5	4	2	1	16	0	20	2	1	0	5	.000	0	0-0	0	6.58	5.74
1993	Bal	AL	25	25	3	0	152.0	630	154	63	58	11	3	1	6	38	2	90	1	1	12	9	.571	1	0-0	0	3.58	3.43
1994	Bal	AL	23	23	0	0	149.0	631	158	81	79	23	5	2	2	38	3	87	1	0	5	7	.417	0	0-0	0	4.24	4.77
1995	Bal	AL	27	18	0	3	115.2	483	117	70	67	18	5	3	3	30	0	65	0	0	8	6	.571	0	0-0	0	4.11	5.21
1996	2 Tms	AL	34	21	0	1	160.2	703	177	86	71	23	7	6	2	46	5	79	3	1	13	3	.813	0	0-0	0	4.42	3.98
1997	Sea	AL	30	30	2	0	188.2	787	187	82	81	21	6	1	7	43	2	113	3	0	17	5	.773	0	0-0	0	3.56	3.86
1998	Sea	AL	34	34	4	0	234.1	974	234	99	92	23	4	3	10	42	2	158	3	1	15	9	.625	3	0-0	0	3.34	3.53
1999	Sea	AL	32	32	4	0	228.0	945	235	108	98	23	6	2	9	48	1	137	3	0	14	8	.636	0	0-0	0	3.71	3.87
2000	Sea	AL	26	26	0	0	154.0	678	173	103	94	22	3	3	3	53	2	98	4	1	13	10	.565	0	0-0	0	4.91	5.49
2001	Sea	AL	33	33	1	0	209.2	851	187	84	80	24	5	11	10	44	4	119	1	0	20	6	.769	0	0-0	0	3.03	3.43
2002	Sea	AL	34	34	4	0	230.2	931	198	89	85	28	5	7	9	50	4	147	3	0	13	8	.619	2	0-0	0	2.89	3.32
2003	Sea	AL	33	33	1	0	215.0	897	199	83	78	19	7	6	8	66	3	129	0	0	21	7	.750	0	0-0	0	3.37	3.27
2004	Sea	AL	34	33	1	1	202.0	888	217	127	117	**44**	9	6	11	63	3	125	1	0	7	13	.350	0	0-0	0	5.13	5.21
2005	Sea	AL	32	32	1	0	200.0	868	225	99	95	23	6	6	8	52	2	102	3	0	13	7	.650	0	0-0	0	4.46	4.28
2006	2 Tms		33	33	2	0	211.1	894	228	110	101	33	5	9	5	51	5	108	3	1	11	14	.440	1	0-0	0	4.36	4.30
2007	Phi	NL	33	33	1	0	199.1	867	222	118	111	30	11	5	5	66	3	133	2	0	14	12	.538	0	0-0	0	4.92	5.01
2008	Phi	NL	33	33	0	0	196.1	841	199	85	81	20	7	2	11	62	4	123	3	0	16	7	.696	0	0-0	0	4.03	3.71
2009	Phi	NL	30	25	0	1	162.0	699	177	91	89	27	8	4	10	43	1	94	1	1	12	10	.545	0	0-0	1	4.79	4.94
2010	Phi	NL	19	19	2	0	111.2	460	103	64	60	20	3	1	6	20	0	63	0	0	9	9	.500	1	0-0	0	3.47	4.84
2012	Col	NL	10	10	0	0	53.2	254	75	40	34	11	4	1	2	18	2	36	0	0	2	5	.286	0	0-0	0	7.01	5.70
96	Bos	AL	23	10	0	1	90.0	405	111	50	45	14	4	3	1	27	2	50	2	1	7	1	.875	0	0-0	0	5.37	4.50
96	Sea	AL	11	11	0	0	70.2	298	66	36	26	9	3	3	1	19	3	29	1	0	6	2	.750	0	0-0	0	3.31	3.31
06	Sea	AL	25	25	2	0	160.0	685	179	85	78	25	3	7	3	44	3	82	3	1	6	12	.333	1	0-0	0	4.74	4.39
06	Phi	NL	8	8	0	0	51.1	209	49	25	23	8	2	2	2	7	2	26	0	0	5	2	.714	0	0-0	0	3.24	4.03
	Postseason		8	8	0	0	41.1	168	37	19	19	3	2	2	2	10	0	29	1	0	3	3	.500	0			2.96	4.14
	25 ML YEARS		696	638	33	15	4074.0	17356	4231	2076	1926	522	146	106	146	1155	69	2441	57	12	269	209	.563	10	0-2	3	4.15	4.25

Peter Moylan

Pitches: R Bats: R Pos: RP-8　　　　　　　　　　**Ht:** 6'2" **Wt:** 225 **Born:** 12/2/1978 **Age:** 34

Year	Team	Lg	G	GS	CG	GF	IP	BFP	H	R	ER	HR	SH	SF	HB	TBB	IBB	SO	WP	Bk	W	L	Pct	Sh	Sv-Op	Hld	ERC	ERA
							HOW MUCH HE PITCHED			**WHAT HE GAVE UP**														**THE RESULTS**				
2012	Braves*	R	4	3	0	0	4.2	18	4	4	4	1	0	0	1	1	0	4	0	0	0	0	-	0	0--	0	4.60	7.71
2012	Rome*	A	4	0	0	0	4.0	19	5	4	4	0	0	0	1	2	0	3	0	0	0	1	.000	0	0--	0	6.32	9.00
2012	Missi*	AA	1	0	0	0	1.1	5	0	0	0	0	0	0	0	0	1	1	0	0	1	0	1.000	0	0--	0	0.00	0.00
2012	Gwnntt*	AAA	12	0	0	1	12.2	60	18	8	8	0	0	0	0	5	0	13	0	0	0	0	-	0		0	5.68	5.68
2006	Atl	NL	15	0	0	5	15.0	68	18	8	8	1	1	0	0	5	1	14	0	0	0	0	-	0	0-0	0	4.47	4.80
2007	Atl	NL	80	0	0	16	90.0	359	65	27	18	6	4	4	7	31	**12**	63	2	0	5	3	.625	0	1-2	8	2.36	1.80
2008	Atl	NL	7	0	0	2	5.2	25	5	1	1	0	0	1	0	1	0	5	0	0	0	1	.000	0	1-2	4	3.51	1.59
2009	Atl	NL	87	0	0	6	73.0	309	65	29	23	0	4	3	2	35	8	61	1	0	6	2	.750	0	0-5	25	3.06	2.84
2010	Atl	NL	85	0	0	7	63.2	271	53	24	21	5	5	2	2	37	6	52	3	0	6	2	.750	0	1-4	21	3.75	2.97
2011	Atl	NL	13	0	0	0	8.1	38	12	3	3	0	0	0	0	3	0	10	0	0	2	1	.667	0	0-0	2	5.87	3.24
2012	Atl	NL	8	0	0	3	5.0	21	3	3	1	1	1	0	0	2	0	2	1	0	1	0	1.000	0	1-1	1	2.40	1.80
	Postseason		4	0	0	1	6		1	0	0	0	0	0	0	0	0	1	0	0	0	0	-	0	0-1	0	1.26	0.00
	7 ML YEARS		295	0	0	41	260.2	1091	221	95	75	14	15	9	12	114	27	207	7	0	20	9	.690	0	4-14	61	3.14	2.59

Edward Mujica

Pitches: R Bats: R Pos: RP-70　　　　moo-HEE-kah　　　　**Ht:** 6'3" **Wt:** 225 **Born:** 5/10/1984 **Age:** 29

Year	Team	Lg	G	GS	CG	GF	IP	BFP	H	R	ER	HR	SH	SF	HB	TBB	IBB	SO	WP	Bk	W	L	Pct	Sh	Sv-Op	Hld	ERC	ERA
							HOW MUCH HE PITCHED			**WHAT HE GAVE UP**														**THE RESULTS**				
2012	Jupiter*	A+	2	2	0	0	3.0	9	0	0	0	0	0	0	0	0	0	2	0	0	0	0	-	0	0--	0	0.00	0.00
2006	Cle	AL	10	0	0	2	18.1	78	25	6	6	1	0	2	1	0	0	12	0	0	0	1	.000	0	0-0	0	4.50	2.95
2007	Cle	AL	10	0	0	5	13.0	60	19	12	12	3	0	1	0	2	0	7	0	0	0	0	-	0	0-0	0	6.63	8.31
2008	Cle	AL	33	0	0	13	38.2	168	46	29	29	5	0	4	1	10	3	27	1	0	3	2	.600	0	0-2	1	4.82	6.75
2009	SD	NL	67	4	0	15	93.2	393	101	47	41	14	1	3	0	19	4	76	3	1	3	5	.375	0	2-3	11	4.00	3.94
2010	SD	NL	59	0	0	24	69.2	268	59	29	28	14	1	0	0	6	0	72	1	0	2	1	.667	0	0-1	4	2.68	3.62
2011	Fla	NL	67	0	0	11	76.0	297	64	27	25	7	5	1	2	14	5	63	1	0	9	6	.600	0	0-3	17	2.46	2.96
2012	2 Tms	NL	70	0	0	16	65.1	258	56	24	22	7	1	1	1	12	3	47	1	0	0	3	.000	0	2-8	30	2.58	3.03
12	Mia	NL	41	0	0	14	39.0	161	36	21	19	6	0	1	1	9	2	26	0	0	0	3	.000	0	2-6	12	3.35	4.38
12	StL	NL	29	0	0	2	26.1	97	20	3	3	1	1	0	0	3	1	21	1	0	0	0	-	0	0-2	18	1.57	1.03
	7 ML YEARS		316	4	0	86	374.2	1522	370	174	163	51	8	12	5	63	15	304	7	1	17	18	.486	0	4-17	63	3.36	3.92

Daniel Murphy

Bats: L Throws: R Pos: 2B-138; PH-18; 1B-12　　　　**Ht:** 6'2" **Wt:** 205 **Born:** 4/1/1985 **Age:** 28

Year	Team	Lg	G	AB	H	2B	3B	HR	(Hm	Rd)	TB	R	RBI	RC	TBB	IBB	SO	HBP	SH	SF	SB	CS	SB%	GDP	Avg	OBP	Slg
						BATTING															**BASERUNNING**				**AVERAGES**		
2008	NYM	NL	49	131	41	9	3	2	(1	1)	62	24	17	26	18	1	28	1	0	1	0	2	.00	4	.313	.397	.473
2009	NYM	NL	155	508	135	38	4	12	(7	5)	217	60	63	60	38	4	69	0	4	6	4	2	.67	13	.266	.313	.427
2011	NYM	NL	109	391	125	28	2	6	(2	4)	175	49	49	57	24	2	42	3	3	2	5	5	.50	14	.320	.362	.448
2012	NYM	NL	156	571	166	40	3	6	(1	5)	230	62	65	78	36	5	82	1	0	4	10	2	.83	12	.291	.332	.403
	4 ML YEARS		469	1601	467	115	12	26	(11	15)	684	195	194	221	116	12	221	5	7	13	19	11	.63	43	.292	.339	.427

David Murphy

Bats: L **Throws:** L **Pos:** LF-120; RF-17; PH-16; DH-9; CF-2; PR-1   **Ht:** 6'4" **Wt:** 205 **Born:** 10/18/1981 **Age:** 31

											BATTING										BASERUNNING				AVERAGES		
Year	Team	Lg	G	AB	H	2B	3B	HR	(Hm	Rd)	TB	R	RBI	RC	TBB	IBB	SO	HBP	SH	SF	SB	CS	SB%	GDP	Avg	OBP	Slg
2006	Bos	AL	20	22	5	1	0	1	(0	1)	9	4	2	2	4	0	4	0	0	0	0	0	-	1	.227	.346	.409
2007	2 Tms	AL	46	105	36	12	2	2	(1	1)	58	17	14	23	7	0	20	0	0	0	0	0	-	1	.343	.384	.552
2008	Tex	AL	108	415	114	28	3	15	(8	7)	193	64	74	62	31	3	70	0	2	6	7	2	.78	7	.275	.321	.465
2009	Tex	AL	128	432	116	24	1	17	(8	9)	193	61	57	60	49	3	106	1	2	9	5	4	.69	5	.269	.338	.447
2010	Tex	AL	138	419	122	26	2	12	(7	5)	188	54	65	68	45	2	71	0	0	3	14	2	.88	6	.291	.358	.449
2011	Tex	AL	120	404	111	14	2	11	(8	3)	162	46	46	52	33	3	61	0	1	2	11	6	.65	11	.275	.328	.401
2012	Tex	AL	147	457	139	29	3	15	(7	8)	219	65	61	84	54	7	74	4	0	4	10	5	.67	7	.304	.380	.479
07	Bos	AL	3	2	1	0	1	0	(0	0)	3	1	0	1	0	0	1	0	0	0	0	0	-	0	.500	.500	1.500
07	Tex	AL	43	103	35	12	1	2	(1	1)	55	16	14	22	7	0	19	0	0	0	0	0	-	1	.340	.382	.534
Postseason			26	68	18	4	1	1	(1	0)	27	11	6	12	13	3	14	0	0	0	1	0	1.00	0	.265	.383	.397
7 ML YEARS			707	2254	643	134	13	73	(39	34)	1022	311	319	351	223	18	406	5	5	24	51	19	.73	38	.285	.348	.453

Donnie Murphy

Bats: R **Throws:** R **Pos:** 3B-22; PH-15; 2B-13; PR-5; SS-2   **Ht:** 5'10" **Wt:** 190 **Born:** 3/10/1983 **Age:** 30

											BATTING										BASERUNNING				AVERAGES		
Year	Team	Lg	G	AB	H	2B	3B	HR	(Hm	Rd)	TB	R	RBI	RC	TBB	IBB	SO	HBP	SH	SF	SB	CS	SB%	GDP	Avg	OBP	Slg
2012	NewOr*	AAA	33	106	32	6	0	13	(-	-)	77	21	25	29	14	0	28	4	0	1	1	0	1.00	2	.302	.400	.726
2012	Jupiter*	A+	4	17	6	1	1	1	(-	-)	12	4	6	3	0	0	3	0	0	1	0	0	-	0	.353	.333	.706
2004	KC	AL	7	27	5	3	0	0	(0	0)	8	1	3	2	0	0	7	0	0	0	1	0	1.00	1	.185	.185	.296
2005	KC	AL	32	77	12	5	0	1	(0	1)	20	4	8	1	9	0	23	0	1	1	0	1	.00	3	.156	.241	.260
2007	Oak	AL	42	118	26	8	0	6	(2	4)	52	21	21	16	10	0	35	2	1	1	1	0	1.00	3	.220	.290	.441
2008	Oak	AL	46	103	19	3	0	3	(2	1)	31	10	13	6	11	0	38	2	0	1	2	1	.67	1	.184	.274	.301
2010	Fla	NL	29	44	14	6	1	3	(2	1)	31	9	16	12	2	0	19	0	1	0	0	0	-	0	.318	.348	.705
2011	Fla	NL	36	92	17	4	1	2	(0	2)	29	10	9	5	4	1	21	3	0	1	0	0	-	0	.185	.240	.315
2012	Mia	NL	52	116	25	6	2	3	(2	1)	44	13	12	12	9	1	35	2	1	1	1	1	.50	4	.216	.281	.379
7 ML YEARS			244	577	118	35	4	18	(8	10)	215	68	82	54	45	2	178	9	4	5	5	3	.63	12	.205	.270	.373

Brett Myers

Pitches: R **Bats:** R **Pos:** RP-70   **Ht:** 6'4" **Wt:** 240 **Born:** 8/17/1980 **Age:** 32

			HOW MUCH HE PITCHED						WHAT HE GAVE UP											THE RESULTS						
Year	Team	Lg	G	GS	CG	GF	IP	BFP	H	R	ER	HR	SH	SF	HB	TBB	IBB	SO	WP	Bk	W	L	Pct	Sh	Sv-Op	Hld	ERC	ERA
2002	Phi	NL	12	12	1	0	72.0	307	73	38	34	11	6	2	6	29	1	34	2	1	4	5	.444	0	0-0	0	5.04	4.25
2003	Phi	NL	32	32	1	0	193.0	848	205	99	95	20	6	3	9	76	8	143	9	0	14	9	.609	1	0-0	0	4.56	4.43
2004	Phi	NL	32	31	1	1	176.0	778	196	113	108	31	9	3	6	62	4	116	5	0	11	11	.500	1	0-0	0	5.17	5.52
2005	Phi	NL	34	34	2	0	215.1	905	193	94	89	31	9	3	11	68	2	208	4	4	13	8	.619	0	0-0	0	3.64	3.72
2006	Phi	NL	31	31	1	0	198.0	833	194	93	86	29	7	4	3	63	3	189	3	0	12	7	.632	0	0-0	0	4.02	3.91
2007	Phi	NL	51	3	0	37	68.2	293	61	33	33	9	3	1	1	27	1	83	5	0	5	7	.417	0	21-24	3	3.63	4.33
2008	Phi	NL	30	30	2	0	190.0	817	197	103	96	29	4	3	6	65	6	163	2	0	10	13	.435	1	0-0	0	4.53	4.55
2009	Phi	NL	18	10	0	1	70.2	304	74	38	38	18	3	2	4	23	1	50	1	0	4	3	.571	0	0-0	3	5.41	4.84
2010	Hou	NL	33	33	2	0	223.2	936	212	88	78	20	9	4	3	66	3	180	2	0	14	8	.636	0	0-0	0	3.34	3.14
2011	Hou	NL	34	33	2	1	216.0	917	226	116	107	31	5	6	4	57	5	160	7	0	7	14	.333	0	0-0	0	4.13	4.46
2012	2 Tms		70	0	0	41	65.1	272	65	30	24	8	2	3	3	15	2	41	2	0	3	8	.273	0	19-21	8	3.69	3.31
12	Hou	NL	35	0	0	29	30.2	134	35	17	12	4	1	2	2	6	1	20	1	0	0	4	.000	0	19-21	0	4.41	3.52
12	CWS	AL	35	0	0	12	34.2	138	30	13	12	4	1	1	1	9	1	21	1	0	3	4	.429	0	0-0	8	3.08	3.12
Postseason			7	3	0	2	22.0	96	18	12	11	2	2	0	2	12	3	17	1	0	2	1	.667	0	0-0	0	3.69	4.50
11 ML YEARS			377	249	12	81	1688.2	7210	1696	845	788	237	63	34	56	551	36	1367	42	5	97	93	.511	3	40-45	14	4.19	4.20

Xavier Nady

Bats: R **Throws:** R **Pos:** LF-40; RF-15; PH-15; PR-1   **Ht:** 6'2" **Wt:** 215 **Born:** 11/14/1978 **Age:** 34

											BATTING										BASERUNNING				AVERAGES		
Year	Team	Lg	G	AB	H	2B	3B	HR	(Hm	Rd)	TB	R	RBI	RC	TBB	IBB	SO	HBP	SH	SF	SB	CS	SB%	GDP	Avg	OBP	Slg
2012	Ptomc*	A+	12	38	6	1	0	0	(-	-)	7	2	1	1	3	0	9	0	0	0	0	0	-	2	.158	.220	.184
2012	Fresno*	AAA	25	89	24	5	0	6	(-	-)	47	13	18	16	7	1	20	3	0	0	0	0	-	4	.270	.343	.528
2000	SD	NL	1	1	1	0	0	0	(0	0)	1	1	0	1	0	0	0	0	0	0	0	0	-	0	1.000	1.000	1.000
2003	SD	NL	110	371	99	17	1	9	(5	4)	145	50	39	39	24	0	74	6	2	1	6	2	.75	14	.267	.321	.391
2004	SD	NL	34	77	19	4	0	3	(1	2)	32	7	9	8	5	0	13	1	1	0	1	0	1.00	4	.247	.301	.416
2005	SD	NL	124	326	85	15	2	13	(5	8)	143	40	43	37	22	1	67	7	1	0	2	1	.67	5	.261	.321	.439
2006	2 Tms	NL	130	468	131	28	1	17	(10	7)	212	57	63	62	30	7	85	11	2	1	3	3	.50	12	.280	.337	.453
2007	Pit	NL	125	431	120	23	1	20	(7	13)	205	55	72	60	23	2	101	12	0	4	3	1	.75	16	.278	.330	.476
2008	2 Tms		148	555	169	37	1	25	(11	14)	283	76	97	93	39	2	103	9	0	4	2	1	.67	14	.305	.357	.510
2009	NYY	AL	7	28	8	4	0	0	(0	0)	12	4	2	2	1	0	6	0	0	0	0	0	-	2	.286	.310	.429
2010	ChC	NL	119	317	81	13	0	6	(2	4)	112	33	33	33	17	0	85	8	1	4	0	0	-	12	.256	.306	.353
2011	Ari	NL	82	206	51	11	0	4	(1	3)	74	26	35	22	10	1	46	3	0	4	2	0	1.00	4	.248	.287	.359
2012	2 Tms		59	152	28	6	1	4	(3	1)	48	12	13	5	13	2	37	1	0	0	1	0	1.00	6	.184	.253	.316
06	NYM	NL	75	265	70	15	1	14	(10	4)	129	37	40	35	19	4	51	6	1	1	2	1	.67	7	.264	.326	.487
06	Pit	NL	55	203	61	13	0	3	(0	3)	83	20	23	27	11	3	34	5	1	0	1	2	.33	5	.300	.352	.409
08	Pit	NL	89	327	108	26	1	13	(6	7)	175	50	57	59	25	1	55	5	0	3	1	0	1.00	9	.330	.383	.535
08	NYY	AL	59	228	61	11	0	12	(5	7)	108	26	40	34	14	1	48	4	0	1	1	1	.50	5	.268	.320	.474
12	Was	NL	40	102	16	3	0	3	(3	0)	28	6	6	0	7	2	24	0	0	0	1	0	1.00	3	.157	.211	.275
12	SF	NL	19	50	12	3	1	1	(0	1)	20	6	7	5	6	0	13	1	0	0	0	0	-	3	.240	.333	.400
Postseason			2	3	1	0	0	0	(0	0)	1	0	2	1	0	0	1	2	0	0	0	0	-	0	.333	.600	.333
11 ML YEARS			939	2932	792	158	7	101	(45	56)	1267	361	406	362	184	15	617	58	7	18	19	8	.70	91	.270	.324	.432

Mike Napoli

Bats: R **Throws:** R **Pos:** C-72; 1B-28; DH-9; PH-6 NAPP-uh-lee **Ht:** 6'0" **Wt:** 215 **Born:** 10/31/1981 **Age:** 31

Year	Team	Lg	G	AB	H	2B	3B	HR	(Hm	Rd)	TB	R	RBI	RC	TBB	IBB	SO	HBP	SH	SF	SB	CS	SB%	GDP	Avg	OBP	Slg
2006	LAA	AL	99	268	61	13	0	16	(10	6)	122	47	42	40	51	0	90	5	0	1	2	3	.40	2	.228	.360	.455
2007	LAA	AL	75	219	54	11	1	10	(5	5)	97	40	34	35	33	2	63	5	1	5	5	2	.71	5	.247	.351	.443
2008	LAA	AL	78	227	62	9	1	20	(10	10)	133	39	49	46	35	5	70	5	1	6	7	3	.70	3	.273	.374	.586
2009	LAA	AL	114	382	104	22	1	20	(10	10)	188	60	56	52	40	1	103	7	0	3	3	3	.50	6	.272	.350	.492
2010	LAA	AL	140	453	108	24	1	26	(13	13)	212	60	68	60	42	2	137	11	0	4	4	2	.67	15	.238	.316	.468
2011	Tex	AL	113	369	118	25	0	30	(13	17)	233	72	75	90	58	2	85	3	0	2	4	2	.67	10	.320	.414	.631
2012	Tex	AL	108	352	80	9	2	24	(11	13)	165	53	56	54	56	5	125	7	0	2	1	0	1.00	9	.227	.343	.469
	Postseason		31	89	25	2	0	5	(1	4)	42	15	19	20	12	2	23	3	0	2	1	0	1.00	1	.281	.377	.472
	7 ML YEARS		727	2270	587	113	6	146	(72	74)	1150	371	380	377	315	17	673	43	2	23	26	15	.63	50	.259	.356	.507

Chris Narveson

Pitches: L **Bats:** L **Pos:** SP-2 NARR-vih-son **Ht:** 6'3" **Wt:** 206 **Born:** 12/20/1981 **Age:** 31

			HOW MUCH HE PITCHED						WHAT HE GAVE UP										THE RESULTS						
Year	Team	Lg	G	GS	CG	GF	IP	BFP	H	R	ER	HR	SH	SF	HB	TBB	IBB	SO	WP	Bk	W	L	Pct	Sh	Sv-Op	Hld	ERC	ERA
2006	StL	NL	5	1	0	1	9.1	40	6	5	5	1	0	0	1	5	0	12	1	1	0	0	-	0	0-0	0	3.06	4.82
2009	Mil	NL	21	4	0	5	47.0	205	45	22	20	7	2	3	2	16	1	46	4	0	2	0	1.000	0	0-0	0	3.96	3.83
2010	Mil	NL	37	28	0	2	167.2	724	172	96	93	21	8	5	5	59	3	137	6	0	12	9	.571	0	0-1	3	4.30	4.99
2011	Mil	NL	30	28	0	0	161.2	699	160	82	80	17	6	4	1	65	1	126	4	1	11	8	.579	0	0-0	0	4.06	4.45
2012	Mil	NL	2	2	0	0	9.0	41	10	8	7	2	1	2	0	4	0	5	0	0	1	1	.500	0	0-0	0	5.69	7.00
	Postseason		6	0	0	2	7.1	33	7	9	9	5	0	1	0	2	1	13	0	0	0	0	-	0	0-0	0	6.33	11.05
	5 ML YEARS		95	63	0	8	394.2	1709	393	213	205	48	17	14	9	149	5	326	15	2	26	18	.591	0	0-1	3	4.16	4.67

Joe Nathan

Pitches: R **Bats:** R **Pos:** RP-66 **Ht:** 6'4" **Wt:** 225 **Born:** 11/22/1974 **Age:** 38

			HOW MUCH HE PITCHED						WHAT HE GAVE UP										THE RESULTS						
Year	Team	Lg	G	GS	CG	GF	IP	BFP	H	R	ER	HR	SH	SF	HB	TBB	IBB	SO	WP	Bk	W	L	Pct	Sh	Sv-Op	Hld	ERC	ERA
1999	SF	NL	19	14	0	2	90.1	395	84	45	42	17	2	0	1	46	0	54	2	0	7	4	.636	0	1-1	0	4.78	4.18
2000	SF	NL	20	15	0	0	93.1	426	89	63	54	12	5	5	4	63	4	61	5	0	5	2	.714	0	0-1	0	5.23	5.21
2002	SF	NL	4	0	0	3	3.2	12	1	0	0	0	0	0	0	0	0	2	0	0	0	0	-	0	0-0	0	0.17	0.00
2003	SF	NL	78	0	0	9	79.0	316	51	26	26	7	2	4	3	33	3	83	4	1	12	4	.750	0	0-3	20	2.34	2.96
2004	Min	AL	73	0	0	63	72.1	284	48	14	13	3	2	0	2	23	3	89	5	0	1	2	.333	0	44-47	0	1.78	1.62
2005	Min	AL	69	0	0	58	70.0	276	46	22	21	5	1	2	0	22	1	94	2	0	7	4	.636	0	43-48	0	1.83	2.70
2006	Min	AL	64	0	0	61	68.1	262	38	12	12	3	3	2	1	16	4	95	3	0	7	0	1.000	0	36-38	0	1.18	1.58
2007	Min	AL	68	0	0	60	71.2	282	54	15	15	4	2	2	1	19	2	77	3	0	4	2	.667	0	37-41	0	2.08	1.88
2008	Min	AL	68	0	0	57	67.2	261	43	13	13	5	1	0	2	18	4	74	2	0	1	2	.333	0	39-45	0	1.67	1.33
2009	Min	AL	70	0	0	62	68.2	271	42	16	16	7	1	0	2	22	1	89	4	0	2	2	.500	0	47-52	0	1.89	2.10
2011	Min	AL	48	0	0	33	44.2	191	38	26	24	7	1	2	3	14	2	43	3	0	2	1	.667	0	14-17	8	3.38	4.84
2012	Tex	AL	66	0	0	62	64.1	257	55	23	20	7	1	3	2	13	1	78	5	0	3	5	.375	0	37-40	0	2.73	2.80
	Postseason		8	0	0	3	8.0	43	12	7	7	2	0	0	0	7	3	10	1	0	0	2	.000	0	1-3	0	9.65	7.88
	12 ML YEARS		647	29	0	470	794.0	3233	589	275	253	77	21	20	21	289	25	839	38	1	51	28	.646	0	298-333	28	2.61	2.87

Daniel Nava

Bats: B **Throws:** L **Pos:** LF-76; PH-9; RF-4; DH-4; PR-2 NAH-vah **Ht:** 5'10" **Wt:** 200 **Born:** 2/22/1983 **Age:** 30

Year	Team	Lg	G	AB	H	2B	3B	HR	(Hm	Rd)	TB	R	RBI	RC	TBB	IBB	SO	HBP	SH	SF	SB	CS	SB%	GDP	Avg	OBP	Slg
2008	Lancst	A+	86	323	110	27	1	10	(-	-)	169	54	59	72	43	1	70	7	2	4	4	3	.57	8	.341	.424	.523
2009	Salem	A+	29	109	37	12	1	1	(-	-)	54	18	13	24	18	0	21	1	1	1	0	2	.00	5	.339	.434	.495
2009	Portlnd	AA	32	118	43	10	1	4	(-	-)	67	25	23	31	25	1	12	1	0	0	0	0	-	4	.364	.479	.568
2010	Pwtckt	AAA	77	284	82	16	1	10	(-	-)	130	41	48	50	28	0	64	11	0	2	4	2	.67	4	.289	.372	.458
2011	Pwtckt	AAA	121	441	118	27	2	10	(-	-)	179	69	48	73	70	4	88	6	1	4	10	3	.77	10	.268	.372	.406
2012	Pwtckt	AAA	29	99	31	7	1	4	(-	-)	52	20	18	22	16	0	15	4	0	1	1	1	.50	3	.313	.425	.525
2010	Bos	AL	60	161	39	14	1	1	(1	0)	58	23	26	26	19	1	46	8	0	0	1	1	.50	5	.242	.351	.360
2012	Bos	AL	88	267	65	21	0	6	(1	5)	104	38	33	33	37	1	63	9	2	2	3	0	1.00	5	.243	.352	.390
	2 ML YEARS		148	428	104	35	1	7	(2	5)	162	61	59	59	56	2	109	17	2	2	4	1	.80	10	.243	.352	.379

Dioner Navarro

Bats: B **Throws:** R **Pos:** C-21; PH-3 dee-AHN-err **Ht:** 5'9" **Wt:** 205 **Born:** 2/9/1984 **Age:** 29

Year	Team	Lg	G	AB	H	2B	3B	HR	(Hm	Rd)	TB	R	RBI	RC	TBB	IBB	SO	HBP	SH	SF	SB	CS	SB%	GDP	Avg	OBP	Slg
2012	Lsvlle*	AAA	62	207	66	12	0	5	(-	-)	93	24	32	37	23	2	24	2	2	6	0	0	-	6	.319	.382	.449
2004	NYY	AL	5	7	3	0	0	0	(0	0)	3	2	1	1	0	0	0	0	0	0	0	0	-	1	.429	.429	.429
2005	LAD	NL	50	176	48	9	0	3	(3	0)	66	21	14	18	20	1	21	2	1	0	0	0	-	3	.273	.354	.375
2006	2 Tms		81	268	68	9	0	6	(4	2)	95	28	28	27	31	6	51	1	1	1	2	1	.67	7	.254	.332	.354
2007	TB	AL	119	388	88	19	2	9	(5	4)	138	46	44	35	33	3	67	1	7	5	3	1	.75	11	.227	.286	.356
2008	TB	AL	120	427	126	27	0	7	(4	3)	174	43	54	59	34	1	49	3	3	3	0	4	.00	16	.295	.349	.407
2009	TB	AL	115	376	82	15	0	8	(4	4)	121	38	32	29	18	1	51	5	8	3	5	2	.71	14	.218	.261	.322
2010	TB	AL	48	124	24	5	0	1	(1	0)	32	11	7	4	12	0	20	1	5	0	1	0	.00	4	.194	.270	.258
2011	LAD	NL	64	176	34	6	1	5	(3	2)	57	13	17	14	20	4	35	1	3	2	0	0	-	3	.193	.276	.324
2012	Cin	NL	24	69	20	3	1	2	(0	2)	31	6	12	10	2	1	12	0	1	1	0	0	-	2	.290	.306	.449
	06	LAD	NL	25	75	21	2	0	2	(1 | 1)	29	5	8	8	11	4	18	0	0	0	1	0	1.00	1	.280	.372	.387
	06	TB	AL	56	193	47	7	0	4	(3 | 1)	66	23	20	19	20	2	33	1	1	1	1	1	.50	6	.244	.316	.342
	Postseason		16	58	17	4	0	0	(0	0)	21	4	5	6	4	0	11	0	0	0	1	0	.00	2	.293	.339	.362
	9 ML YEARS		626	2011	493	93	4	41	(24	17)	717	208	209	190	170	17	306	14	29	15	10	9	.53	59	.245	.306	.357

Yamaico Navarro

Bats: R Throws: R Pos: PH-15; LF-8; SS-3; 3B-2; RF-2; 2B-1   ya-MIKE-oh   Ht: 5'11" Wt: 215 Born: 10/31/1987 Age: 25

Year	Team	Lg	G	AB	H	2B	3B	HR	(Hm	Rd)	TB	R	RBI	RC	TBB	IBB	SO	HBP	SH	SF	SB	CS	SB%	GDP	Avg	OBP	Slg
2012	Indy*	AAA	66	222	62	14	3	9	(-	-)	109	41	35	41	32	2	41	0	0	3	9	4	.69	5	.279	.366	.491
2010	Bos	AL	20	42	6	0	0	0	(0	0)	6	4	5	1	2	1	17	0	0	2	0	0	-	0	.143	.174	.143
2011	2 Tms	AL	22	60	15	3	0	1	(0	1)	21	8	9	8	5	0	14	0	0	1	0	0	-	0	.250	.303	.350
2012	Pit	NL	29	50	8	0	0	1	(0	1)	11	4	4	1	5	0	13	0	0	1	0	2	.00	2	.160	.232	.220
11	Bos	AL	16	37	8	2	0	1	(0	1)	13	6	3	4	3	0	9	0	0	0	0	0	-	0	.216	.275	.351
11	KC	AL	6	23	7	1	0	0	(0	0)	8	2	6	4	2	0	5	0	0	1	0	0	-	0	.304	.346	.348
3 ML YEARS			71	152	29	3	0	2	(0	2)	38	16	18	10	12	1	44	0	0	4	0	2	.00	2	.191	.244	.250

Thomas Neal

Bats: R Throws: R Pos: LF-6; RF-2; PH-1   Ht: 6'2" Wt: 220 Born: 8/17/1987 Age: 25

Year	Team	Lg	G	AB	H	2B	3B	HR	(Hm	Rd)	TB	R	RBI	RC	TBB	IBB	SO	HBP	SH	SF	SB	CS	SB%	GDP	Avg	OBP	Slg
2006	SlmKzr	A-	50	176	44	6	2	4	(-	-)	66	26	20	18	7	0	44	3	0	1	1	3	.25	3	.250	.289	.375
2007	Giants	R	10	39	12	3	0	1	(-	-)	18	7	4	7	5	0	7	2	0	0	0	0	-	0	.308	.413	.462
2008	Augsta	A	117	428	118	25	1	15	(-	-)	190	69	81	71	48	1	103	12	1	8	3	4	.43	8	.276	.359	.444
2009	SnJos	A+	129	475	160	41	4	22	(-	-)	275	102	90	117	65	1	98	16	0	3	3	0	1.00	13	.337	.431	.579
2010	Rchmd	AA	136	525	154	40	1	12	(-	-)	232	69	69	86	46	3	94	11	0	3	11	5	.69	19	.293	.361	.442
2011	Fresno	AAA	60	220	65	13	3	2	(-	-)	90	35	25	31	13	0	50	6	0	0	7	6	.54	6	.295	.351	.409
2011	Clmbs	AAA	10	36	9	1	0	0	(-	-)	10	5	1	3	1	0	7	1	0	0	1	0	1.00	0	.250	.289	.278
2012	Akron	AA	117	405	127	24	1	12	(-	-)	189	77	51	77	46	1	71	14	3	2	12	8	.60	16	.314	.400	.467
2012	Cle	AL	9	23	5	1	0	0	(0	0)	6	2	2	1	0	0	6	1	0	0	0	0	-	1	.217	.250	.261

Kristopher Negron

Bats: R Throws: R Pos: PH-3; CF-1; PR-1   neh-GROAN   Ht: 6'0" Wt: 195 Born: 2/1/1986 Age: 27

Year	Team	Lg	G	AB	H	2B	3B	HR	(Hm	Rd)	TB	R	RBI	RC	TBB	IBB	SO	HBP	SH	SF	SB	CS	SB%	GDP	Avg	OBP	Slg
2006	RedSx	R	41	142	37	6	2	2	(-	-)	53	19	16	21	12	0	20	5	3	0	10	0	1.00	3	.261	.340	.373
2006	Lowell	A-	9	28	11	2	1	0	(-	-)	15	8	5	7	4	0	2	1	2	0	5	1	.83	1	.393	.485	.536
2007	Grnville	A	112	403	91	11	4	3	(-	-)	119	61	29	46	46	0	97	13	5	0	29	7	.81	10	.226	.325	.295
2007	Lancst	A+	3	11	2	0	0	0	(-	-)	2	3	0	1	0	0	2	2	0	0	2	0	1.00	1	.182	.308	.182
2008	Grnville	A	92	311	76	15	5	1	(-	-)	104	50	27	41	31	1	48	10	6	4	25	5	.83	9	.244	.329	.334
2008	Portlnd	AA	4	7	1	1	0	0	(-	-)	2	0	0	0	1	0	2	0	1	0	0	0	-	0	.143	.250	.286
2008	Lancst	A+	33	116	38	8	3	7	(-	-)	73	23	19	27	5	0	25	6	1	3	6	1	.86	2	.328	.377	.629
2009	Salem	A	111	409	108	17	4	3	(-	-)	142	69	34	54	39	1	83	8	6	2	20	3	.87	6	.264	.338	.347
2009	Srsota	A+	8	24	5	0	0	1	(-	-)	8	6	2	3	5	0	8	0	0	0	3	1	.75	0	.208	.345	.333
2009	Carlina	AA	15	54	13	2	0	2	(-	-)	21	11	5	9	8	0	7	4	1	0	4	1	.80	1	.241	.379	.389
2010	Carlina	AA	120	470	128	19	6	11	(-	-)	192	79	41	77	51	0	97	16	7	3	34	9	.79	5	.272	.361	.409
2010	Lsvlle	AAA	7	21	4	1	0	0	(-	-)	5	1	0	0	0	0	6	0	0	0	1	0	1.00	1	.190	.190	.238
2011	Lsvlle	AAA	123	417	90	16	4	9	(-	-)	141	54	45	41	22	0	102	10	11	5	11	1	.92	9	.216	.269	.338
2012	Lsvlle	AAA	74	284	62	14	2	6	(-	-)	98	34	20	31	22	0	77	6	5	2	17	3	.85	3	.218	.287	.345
2012	Cin	NL	4	4	1	0	0	0	(0	0)	1	2	0	1	1	0	2	0	0	0	0	0	-	0	.250	.400	.250

Chris Nelson

Bats: R Throws: R Pos: 3B-92; 2B-21; PH-11; PR-3; SS-1   Ht: 5'11" Wt: 205 Born: 9/3/1985 Age: 27

Year	Team	Lg	G	AB	H	2B	3B	HR	(Hm	Rd)	TB	R	RBI	RC	TBB	IBB	SO	HBP	SH	SF	SB	CS	SB%	GDP	Avg	OBP	Slg
2012	ColSpr*	AAA	13	51	15	4	1	0	(-	-)	21	12	8	6	2	0	12	1	0	0	1	1	.50	1	.294	.333	.412
2010	Col	NL	17	25	7	1	0	0	(0	0)	8	7	0	1	1	0	4	0	1	0	1	0	1.00	1	.280	.308	.320
2011	Col	NL	63	180	45	10	1	4	(3	1)	69	20	16	15	7	1	35	1	0	1	3	1	.75	5	.250	.280	.383
2012	Col	NL	111	345	104	21	3	9	(3	6)	158	45	53	56	27	4	84	1	2	2	2	1	.67	9	.301	.352	.458
3 ML YEARS			191	550	156	32	4	13	(6	7)	235	72	69	72	35	5	123	2	3	3	6	2	.75	15	.284	.327	.427

Pat Neshek

Pitches: R Bats: B Pos: RP-24   NEE-sheck   Ht: 6'3" Wt: 210 Born: 9/4/1980 Age: 32

Year	Team	Lg	G	GS	CG	GF	IP	BFP	H	R	ER	HR	SH	SF	HB	TBB	IBB	SO	WP	Bk	W	L	Pct	Sh	Sv-Op	Hld	ERC	ERA
2012	Norfolk*	AAA	35	0	0	23	44.0	178	42	13	13	1	2	0	1	7	1	49	2	0	3	2	.600	0	11--	-	2.50	2.66
2006	Min	AL	32	0	0	3	37.0	138	23	9	9	6	0	1	0	6	0	53	0	0	4	2	.667	0	0-2	10	1.68	2.19
2007	Min	AL	74	0	0	20	70.1	278	44	25	23	7	4	5	2	27	5	74	2	0	7	2	.778	0	0-3	15	2.12	2.94
2008	Min	AL	15	0	0	3	13.1	56	12	7	7	2	1	1	0	4	1	15	0	0	0	1	.000	0	0-2	6	3.29	4.73
2010	Min	AL	11	0	0	3	9.0	43	7	5	5	1	0	0	1	8	0	9	0	0	0	1	.000	0	0-1	1	5.13	5.00
2011	SD	NL	25	0	0	13	24.2	112	19	12	11	4	1	0	1	22	1	20	1	0	1	1	.500	0	0-0	0	5.37	4.01
2012	Oak	AL	24	0	0	5	19.2	77	10	3	3	3	0	2	1	6	1	16	1	0	2	1	.667	0	0-2	4	1.66	1.37
Postseason			2	0	0	1	1.0	4	1	1	1	0	0	0	0	0	1	0	0	0	0	1	.000	0	0-0	0	1.95	9.00
6 ML YEARS			181	0	0	47	174.0	704	115	61	58	23	6	9	5	73	8	187	4	0	14	8	.636	0	0-10	36	2.61	3.00

Juan Nicasio

Pitches: R Bats: R Pos: SP-11   nih-COSS-ee-oh   Ht: 6'3" Wt: 230 Born: 8/31/1986 Age: 26

Year	Team	Lg	G	GS	CG	GF	IP	BFP	H	R	ER	HR	SH	SF	HB	TBB	IBB	SO	WP	Bk	W	L	Pct	Sh	Sv-Op Hld	ERC	ERA
2007	Casper	R+	13	8	0	1	43.1	193	48	32	21	3	1	1	4	13	0	33	5	1	0	3	.000	0	0- -	4.37	4.36
2008	TriCity	A-	12	12	0	1	54.0	226	46	30	27	1	1	1	3	19	0	61	4	1	2	4	.333	0	0- -	2.76	4.50
2009	Ashvll	A	18	18	1	0	112.0	468	110	44	30	6	4	1	4	23	0	115	5	0	9	3	.750	1	0- -	3.03	2.41
2010	Mdest	A+	28	28	1	0	177.1	744	186	91	77	14	2	8	4	31	0	171	7	1	12	10	.545	0	0- -	3.38	3.91
2011	Tulsa	AA	9	9	1	0	56.2	219	48	15	14	3	3	0	0	10	1	63	3	2	5	1	.833	1	0- -	2.22	2.22
2011	Col	NL	13	13	0	0	71.2	299	73	35	33	8	1	0	1	18	3	58	1	0	4	4	.500	0	0-0	3.69	4.14
2012	Col	NL	11	11	0	0	58.0	257	72	37	34	7	3	1	1	22	1	54	4	0	2	3	.400	0	0-0	5.74	5.28
	2 ML YEARS		24	24	0	0	129.2	556	145	72	67	15	4	1	2	40	4	112	5	0	6	7	.462	0	0-0	4.57	4.65

Mike Nickeas

Bats: R Throws: R Pos: C-45; PH-3   NICK-ee-us   Ht: 6'0" Wt: 215 Born: 2/13/1983 Age: 30

Year	Team	Lg	G	AB	H	2B	3B	HR	(Hm	Rd)	TB	R	RBI	RC	TBB	IBB	SO	HBP	SH	SF	SB	CS	SB%	GDP	Avg	OBP	Slg
2012	Buffalo*	AAA	22	66	24	6	0	1	(-	-)	33	10	6	13	6	1	9	0	1	2	0	0	-	1	.364	.405	.500
2010	NYM	NL	5	10	2	0	0	0	(0	0)	2	0	0	0	0	0	5	0	0	0	0	0	-	1	.200	.200	.200
2011	NYM	NL	21	53	10	1	0	1	(1	0)	14	4	6	3	4	0	11	0	2	0	0	1	.00	1	.189	.246	.264
2012	NYM	NL	47	109	19	3	0	1	(1	0)	25	8	13	10	8	0	27	2	2	1	0	0	-	1	.174	.242	.229
	3 ML YEARS		73	172	31	4	0	2	(2	0)	41	12	19	13	12	0	43	2	4	1	0	1	.00	3	.180	.241	.238

Jeff Niemann

Pitches: R Bats: R Pos: SP-8   NEE-min   Ht: 6'9" Wt: 285 Born: 2/28/1983 Age: 30

Year	Team	Lg	G	GS	CG	GF	IP	BFP	H	R	ER	HR	SH	SF	HB	TBB	IBB	SO	WP	Bk	W	L	Pct	Sh	Sv-Op Hld	ERC	ERA
2012	Charltt*	A+	2	2	0	0	6.0	30	9	5	4	0	0	0	1	3	0	6	0	0	0	0	-	0	0- -	7.43	6.00
2012	Drham*	AAA	2	2	0	0	8.1	42	17	7	7	1	2	1	0	2	0	4	0	0	0	0	-	0	0- -	10.46	7.56
2008	TB	AL	5	2	0	2	16.0	76	18	12	9	3	2	0	1	8	0	14	0	0	2	2	.500	0	0-0	5.93	5.06
2009	TB	AL	31	30	2	1	180.2	769	185	84	79	17	2	4	9	59	1	125	6	0	13	6	.684	2	0-0	4.12	3.94
2010	TB	AL	30	29	1	0	174.1	733	159	86	85	25	5	2	7	61	6	131	4	0	12	8	.600	1	0-0	3.81	4.39
2011	TB	AL	23	23	1	0	135.1	572	131	65	61	18	2	4	5	37	1	105	7	0	11	7	.611	0	0-0	3.73	4.06
2012	TB	AL	8	8	0	0	38.0	156	30	17	13	2	0	1	2	12	0	34	2	0	2	3	.400	0	0-0	2.53	3.08
	Postseason		1	0	0	1	3.0	9	1	0	0	0	0	0	0	1	0	4	0	0	0	0	-	0	0-0	0.84	0.00
	5 ML YEARS		97	92	4	3	544.1	2306	523	264	247	65	11	11	24	177	8	409	19	0	40	26	.606	3	0-0	3.86	4.08

Jon Niese

Pitches: L Bats: L Pos: SP-30   NIECE   Ht: 6'4" Wt: 215 Born: 10/27/1986 Age: 26

Year	Team	Lg	G	GS	CG	GF	IP	BFP	H	R	ER	HR	SH	SF	HB	TBB	IBB	SO	WP	Bk	W	L	Pct	Sh	Sv-Op Hld	ERC	ERA
2008	NYM	NL	3	3	0	0	14.0	69	20	11	11	2	1	0	0	8	0	11	0	0	1	1	.500	0	0-0	7.71	7.07
2009	NYM	NL	5	5	0	0	25.2	110	27	12	12	1	2	1	0	9	0	18	1	0	1	1	.500	0	0-0	3.76	4.21
2010	NYM	NL	30	30	2	0	173.2	770	192	97	81	20	9	4	9	62	3	148	5	0	9	10	.474	1	0-0	4.77	4.20
2011	NYM	NL	27	26	0	0	157.1	694	178	88	77	14	16	2	5	44	4	138	3	0	11	11	.500	0	0-0	4.27	4.40
2012	NYM	NL	30	30	0	0	190.1	788	174	77	72	22	8	4	4	49	2	155	6	0	13	9	.591	0	0-0	3.21	3.40
	5 ML YEARS		95	94	2	0	561.0	2431	591	285	253	59	36	11	18	172	9	470	15	0	35	32	.522	1	0-0	4.11	4.06

Kirk Nieuwenhuis

Bats: L Throws: R Pos: CF-50; LF-23; RF-20; PH-15; PR-1   NEW-enn-hice   Ht: 6'3" Wt: 215 Born: 8/7/1987 Age: 25

Year	Team	Lg	G	AB	H	2B	3B	HR	(Hm	Rd)	TB	R	RBI	RC	TBB	IBB	SO	HBP	SH	SF	SB	CS	SB%	GDP	Avg	OBP	Slg
2008	Bklyn	A-	74	285	79	15	5	3	(-	-)	113	34	29	41	29	1	70	3	0	2	11	7	.61	4	.277	.348	.396
2009	StLuci	A+	123	482	132	35	5	16	(-	-)	225	91	71	84	53	0	118	10	1	1	16	4	.80	8	.274	.357	.467
2009	Bnghtn	AA	8	32	13	3	1	1	(-	-)	21	8	2	8	4	0	9	0	0	1	1	1	.50	1	.406	.472	.656
2010	Bnghtn	AA	94	394	114	35	2	16	(-	-)	201	81	60	60	30	0	93	1	3	5	13	7	.65	5	.289	.337	.510
2010	Buffalo	AAA	30	120	27	8	1	2	(-	-)	43	10	17	13	11	3	39	1	1	0	0	0	-	1	.225	.295	.358
2011	Buffalo	AAA	53	188	56	17	2	6	(-	-)	95	33	14	39	32	0	59	1	0	0	5	2	.71	2	.298	.403	.505
2012	Buffalo	AAA	5	11	2	1	0	0	(-	-)	3	0	3	1	2	0	4	0	0	0	1	0	1.00	0	.182	.308	.273
2012	NYM	NL	91	282	71	12	1	7	(5	2)	106	40	28	28	25	0	98	2	3	2	4	4	.50	2	.252	.315	.376

Wil Nieves

Bats: R Throws: R Pos: C-24; PH-11; 1B-2   Ht: 5'11" Wt: 190 Born: 9/25/1977 Age: 35

Year	Team	Lg	G	AB	H	2B	3B	HR	(Hm	Rd)	TB	R	RBI	RC	TBB	IBB	SO	HBP	SH	SF	SB	CS	SB%	GDP	Avg	OBP	Slg
2012	ColSpr*	AAA	34	111	34	4	0	3	(-	-)	47	15	16	16	6	2	20	0	4	2	1	1	.50	6	.306	.336	.423
2002	SD	NL	28	72	13	3	1	0	(0	0)	18	2	3	4	4	4	15	0	0	0	1	0	1.00	1	.181	.224	.250
2005	NYY	AL	3	4	0	0	0	0	(0	0)	0	0	0	0	0	0	1	0	0	0	0	0	-	0	.000	.000	.000
2006	NYY	AL	6	6	0	0	0	0	(0	0)	0	0	0	0	0	0	1	0	0	0	0	0	-	0	.000	.000	.000
2007	NYY	AL	26	61	10	4	0	0	(0	0)	14	6	8	4	2	0	9	0	3	0	0	0	-	3	.164	.190	.230
2008	Was	NL	68	176	46	9	1	1	(1	0)	60	15	20	20	13	1	29	0	5	2	0	1	.00	7	.261	.309	.341
2009	Was	NL	72	224	58	6	0	1	(0	1)	67	20	26	21	17	1	45	3	0	5	1	0	1.00	7	.259	.313	.299
2010	Was	NL	59	158	32	8	0	3	(1	2)	49	10	16	9	8	2	29	1	4	1	0	0	-	6	.203	.244	.310
2011	Mil	NL	20	50	7	2	0	0	(0	0)	9	2	0	4	3	1	12	0	1	0	0	0	-	3	.140	.189	.180

Year	Team	Lg	G	AB	H	2B	3B	HR	(Hm	Rd)	TB	R	RBI	RC	TBB	IBB	SO	HBP	SH	SF	SB	CS	SB%	GDP	Avg	OBP	Slg
2012	2 Tms	NL	32	83	25	3	0	2	(0	2)	34	7	8	9	4	2	17	0	1	1	0	1	.00	3	.301	.330	.410
12	Col	NL	16	47	14	2	0	1	(0	1)	19	3	5	6	3	1	9	0	0	1	0	0	-	3	.298	.333	.404
12	Ari	NL	16	36	11	1	0	1	(0	1)	15	4	3	3	1	1	8	0	1	0	0	1	.00	0	.306	.324	.417
	9 ML YEARS		314	834	191	35	2	7	(2	5)	251	62	81	67	51	11	158	4	14	9	2	2	.50	30	.229	.274	.301

Tsuyoshi Nishioka

Bats: B **Throws:** R **Pos:** 2B-3   soo-YO-shee nee-shee-OH-kah   **Ht:** 6'1" **Wt:** 176 **Born:** 7/27/1984 **Age:** 28

Year	Team	Lg	G	AB	H	2B	3B	HR	(Hm	Rd)	TB	R	RBI	RC	TBB	IBB	SO	HBP	SH	SF	SB	CS	SB%	GDP	Avg	OBP	Slg
2003	Chiba	Jap	7	9	3	2	0	0	(-	-)	5	3	1	2	2	-	1	0	0	0	0	0	-	0	.333	.455	.556
2004	Chiba	Jap	63	212	54	8	2	6	(-	-)	84	32	35	27	14	-	37	2	2	2	8	2	.80	2	.255	.304	.396
2005	Chiba	Jap	122	447	120	22	11	4	(-	-)	176	80	48	63	31	-	51	5	6	4	41	9	.82	6	.268	.320	.394
2006	Chiba	Jap	115	426	120	20	7	4	(-	-)	166	58	27	66	49	-	61	3	4	3	33	17	.66	6	.282	.358	.390
2007	Chiba	Jap	130	494	148	31	3	3	(-	-)	194	76	40	76	50	-	73	4	7	4	27	13	.68	3	.300	.366	.393
2008	Chiba	Jap	116	473	142	26	6	13	(-	-)	219	78	49	79	36	-	68	7	4	2	18	11	.62	3	.300	.357	.463
2009	Chiba	Jap	120	454	118	24	5	14	(-	-)	194	70	41	76	67	-	76	5	3	2	26	10	.72	6	.260	.360	.427
2010	Chiba	Jap	144	596	206	32	8	11	(-	-)	287	121	59	124	79	-	96	4	8	5	22	11	.67	8	.346	.423	.482
2011	FtMyrs	A+	4	12	4	1	0	0	(-	-)	5	4	1	2	2	0	2	1	0	0	1	0	1.00	0	.333	.467	.417
2011	Roch	AAA	3	12	4	1	0	0	(-	-)	5	0	1	2	2	0	1	0	0	0	0	0	-	1	.333	.429	.417
2012	Roch	AAA	101	392	101	18	1	2	(-	-)	127	42	34	41	32	2	53	1	5	1	7	7	.50	8	.258	.315	.324
2011	Min	AL	68	221	50	5	0	0	(0	0)	55	14	19	16	15	1	43	1	3	0	2	4	.33	1	.226	.278	.249
2012	Min	AL	3	12	0	0	0	0	(0	0)	0	0	1	0	1	0	1	0	0	1	0	0	-	0	.000	.071	.000
	2 ML YEARS		71	233	50	5	0	0	(0	0)	55	14	20	16	16	1	44	1	3	1	2	4	.33	1	.215	.267	.236

Jayson Nix

Bats: R **Throws:** R **Pos:** 3B-29; SS-18; 2B-13; LF-11; PH-6; DH-3; PR-3   **Ht:** 5'11" **Wt:** 195 **Born:** 8/26/1982 **Age:** 30

Year	Team	Lg	G	AB	H	2B	3B	HR	(Hm	Rd)	TB	R	RBI	RC	TBB	IBB	SO	HBP	SH	SF	SB	CS	SB%	GDP	Avg	OBP	Slg
2012	S-WB*	AAA	8	30	7	4	0	0	(-	-)	11	5	4	3	3	0	9	1	0	1	0	0	-	1	.233	.314	.367
2008	Col	NL	22	56	7	2	0	0	(0	0)	9	2	2	0	7	2	17	1	1	0	1	0	1.00	1	.125	.234	.161
2009	CWS	AL	94	255	57	11	0	12	(4	8)	104	36	32	31	28	1	64	4	1	2	10	2	.83	5	.224	.308	.408
2010	2 Tms	AL	102	331	74	15	0	14	(7	7)	131	32	34	35	20	2	87	7	3	2	1	2	.33	6	.224	.281	.396
2011	Tor	AL	46	136	23	5	1	4	(2	2)	42	15	16	12	12	1	42	2	0	1	4	1	.80	2	.169	.245	.309
2012	NYY	AL	74	177	43	13	0	4	(3	1)	68	24	18	23	14	0	53	2	9	0	6	3	.67	4	.243	.306	.384
10	CWS	AL	24	49	8	1	0	1	(0	1)	12	3	5	4	7	2	12	0	1	0	0	0	-	1	.163	.268	.245
10	Cle	AL	78	282	66	14	0	13	(7	6)	119	29	29	31	13	0	75	7	2	2	1	2	.33	5	.234	.283	.422
	5 ML YEARS		338	955	204	46	1	34	(16	18)	354	109	102	101	81	6	263	16	14	5	22	8	.73	18	.214	.285	.371

Laynce Nix

Bats: L **Throws:** L **Pos:** PH-36; LF-18; 1B-10; RF-10; CF-3   LANCE   **Ht:** 6'1" **Wt:** 220 **Born:** 10/30/1980 **Age:** 32

Year	Team	Lg	G	AB	H	2B	3B	HR	(Hm	Rd)	TB	R	RBI	RC	TBB	IBB	SO	HBP	SH	SF	SB	CS	SB%	GDP	Avg	OBP	Slg
2012	Clrwtr*	A+	6	16	4	2	0	1	(-	-)	9	1	4	3	4	0	2	0	0	0	0	0	-	1	.250	.400	.563
2012	LV*	AAA	2	8	2	0	0	0	(-	-)	2	1	0	0	1	0	3	0	0	0	0	0	-	0	.250	.333	.250
2003	Tex	AL	53	184	47	10	4	8	(7	1)	81	25	30	25	9	0	53	0	1	1	3	0	1.00	1	.255	.289	.440
2004	Tex	AL	115	371	92	20	4	14	(9	5)	162	58	46	44	23	4	113	2	1	3	1	1	.50	6	.248	.293	.437
2005	Tex	AL	63	229	55	12	3	6	(3	3)	91	28	32	26	9	3	45	0	0	2	2	0	1.00	3	.240	.267	.397
2006	2 Tms		19	67	11	2	0	1	(1	0)	16	3	10	3	0	0	28	2	0	1	0	0	-	1	.164	.186	.239
2007	Mil	NL	10	12	0	0	0	0	(0	0)	0	0	0	0	0	0	4	0	0	0	0	0	-	0	.000	.000	.000
2008	Mil	NL	10	12	1	0	0	0	(0	0)	1	1	0	0	1	0	3	0	0	0	0	0	-	0	.083	.154	.083
2009	Cin	NL	116	309	74	26	1	15	(5	10)	147	42	46	35	22	3	81	2	0	4	0	1	.00	5	.239	.291	.476
2010	Cin	NL	97	165	48	11	2	4	(1	3)	75	16	18	21	15	4	39	0	2	0	0	1	.00	5	.291	.350	.455
2011	Was	NL	124	324	81	15	1	16	(9	7)	146	38	44	37	23	2	82	1	0	3	2	2	.50	1	.250	.299	.451
2012	Phi	NL	70	114	28	10	0	3	(1	2)	47	13	16	16	12	0	42	0	0	0	0	0	-	1	.246	.315	.412
06	Tex	AL	9	32	3	1	0	0	(0	0)	4	1	4	0	0	0	17	1	0	1	0	0	-	1	.094	.118	.125
06	Mil	NL	10	35	8	1	0	1	(1	0)	12	2	6	3	0	0	11	1	0	0	0	0	-	0	.229	.250	.343
	Postseason		1	3	0	0	0	0	(0	0)	0	1	0	0	0	0	1	0	0	0	0	0	-	0	.000	.000	.000
	10 ML YEARS		677	1787	437	106	11	67	(36	31)	766	224	242	207	114	16	490	7	4	15	8	5	.62	23	.245	.290	.429

Hector Noesi

Pitches: R **Bats:** R **Pos:** SP-18; RP-4   NO-ess-ee   **Ht:** 6'3" **Wt:** 200 **Born:** 1/26/1987 **Age:** 26

			HOW MUCH HE PITCHED						WHAT HE GAVE UP											THE RESULTS						
Year	Team	Lg	G	GS	CG	GF	IP	BFP	H	R	ER	HR	SH	SF	HB	TBB	IBB	SO	WP	Bk	W	L	Pct	Sh	Sv-Op	Hld	ERC	ERA
2006	Yanks	R	5	0	0	2	7.0	27	5	1	1	0	0	0	1	0	11	0	0	0	0	-	1--	-	1	1.32	1.29
2007	CtnSC	A	5	5	0	0	20.0	91	25	10	10	2	1	1	0	8	0	11	2	0	1	1	.500	0	0--	-	5.53	4.50
2008	Yanks	R	9	2	0	1	24.2	98	23	11	10	2	2	1	1	3	1	24	1	0	2	1	.667	0	0--	-	2.68	3.65
2008	StlsInd	A-	5	5	0	0	24.0	99	20	12	8	5	2	0	1	7	0	31	3	1	1	1	.500	0	0--	-	3.58	3.00
2009	CtnSC	A+	17	11	0	0	75.2	297	62	24	20	3	2	0	0	11	0	78	0	1	3	4	.429	0	0--	-	1.86	2.38
2009	Tampa	A+	9	9	0	0	41.1	161	34	18	18	3	0	3	1	4	0	40	2	0	3	0	1.000	0	0--	-	1.98	3.92
2010	Tampa	A+	8	8	0	0	43.0	174	35	14	13	3	1	0	2	6	0	53	5	1	5	2	.714	0	0--	-	2.07	2.72
2010	Trntn	AA	17	16	2	1	98.2	395	90	37	34	7	1	3	2	18	1	86	5	0	8	4	.667	1	0--	-	2.70	3.10
2010	S-WB	AAA	3	3	1	0	18.2	81	23	10	10	1	0	2	1	4	0	14	1	0	1	1	.500	0	0--	-	4.60	4.82
2011	S-WB	AAA	6	5	0	0	24.2	111	28	11	9	0	0	0	2	9	0	17	2	1	1	1	.500	0	0--	-	4.24	3.28
2012	Tacom	AAA	11	11	0	0	64.1	295	80	46	41	7	3	4	2	22	0	55	5	0	2	6	.250	0	0--	-	5.35	5.74
2011	NYY	AL	30	2	0	14	56.1	247	63	29	28	6	1	2	2	22	4	45	4	0	2	2	.500	0	0-0	4	4.85	4.47
2012	Sea	AL	22	18	0	4	106.2	453	107	71	69	21	3	7	2	39	1	68	1	2	2	12	.143	0	0-0	0	4.77	5.82
	2 ML YEARS		52	20	0	18	163.0	700	170	100	97	27	4	9	4	61	5	113	5	2	4	14	.222	0	0-0	4	4.81	5.36

Ricky Nolasco

Pitches: R Bats: R Pos: SP-31   Ht: 6'2" Wt: 215 Born: 12/13/1982 Age: 30

			HOW MUCH HE PITCHED						WHAT HE GAVE UP												THE RESULTS						
Year	Team	Lg	G	GS	CG	GF	IP	BFP	H	R	ER	HR	SH	SF	HB	TBB	IBB	SO	WP	Bk	W	L	Pct	Sh	Sv-Op Hld	ERC	ERA
2006	Fla	NL	35	22	0	0	140.0	613	157	86	75	20	8	6	10	41	5	99	7	0	11	11	.500	0	0-0 2	4.89	4.82
2007	Fla	NL	5	4	0	0	21.1	99	26	16	13	3	3	5	1	9	2	11	1	0	1	2	.333	0	0-0 0	5.71	5.48
2008	Fla	NL	34	32	1	0	212.1	868	192	88	83	28	6	9	6	42	6	186	1	3	15	8	.652	1	0-0 0	3.03	3.52
2009	Fla	NL	31	31	2	0	185.0	785	188	111	104	23	8	5	2	44	7	195	2	0	13	9	.591	0	0-0 0	3.62	5.06
2010	Fla	NL	26	26	1	0	157.2	665	169	82	79	24	5	5	2	33	1	147	5	0	14	9	.609	0	0-0 0	4.11	4.51
2011	Fla	NL	33	33	2	0	206.0	891	**244**	117	107	20	11	5	3	44	8	148	6	0	10	12	.455	1	0-0 0	4.34	4.67
2012	Mia	NL	31	31	3	0	191.0	832	214	100	95	18	**19**	6	6	47	9	125	8	1	12	13	.480	2	0-0 0	4.14	4.48
	7 ML YEARS		195	179	9	0	1113.1	4753	1190	600	556	136	60	41	32	260	38	911	30	4	76	64	.543	4	0-0 2	3.99	4.49

Jordan Norberto

Pitches: L Bats: L Pos: RP-39   Ht: 6'0" Wt: 195 Born: 12/8/1986 Age: 26

			HOW MUCH HE PITCHED						WHAT HE GAVE UP												THE RESULTS						
Year	Team	Lg	G	GS	CG	GF	IP	BFP	H	R	ER	HR	SH	SF	HB	TBB	IBB	SO	WP	Bk	W	L	Pct	Sh	Sv-Op Hld	ERC	ERA
2012	Scrmto*	AAA	1	0	0	0	1.0	3	0	0	0	0	0	0	0	0	0	2	0	0	0	0	-	0	0-- -	0.00	0.00
2010	Ari	NL	33	0	0	5	20.0	94	16	13	13	3	1	0	0	22	1	15	2	0	0	2	.000	0	0-1 3	6.16	5.85
2011	Oak	AL	6	0	0	3	6.2	35	8	6	6	0	0	1	1	7	0	4	1	0	0	0	-	0	0-0 0	7.72	8.10
2012	Oak	AL	39	0	0	8	52.0	212	37	17	16	5	1	3	1	22	2	46	1	1	4	1	.800	0	1-3 4	2.64	2.77
	3 ML YEARS		78	0	0	16	78.2	341	61	36	35	8	2	4	2	51	3	65	4	1	4	3	.571	0	1-4 7	3.86	4.00

Bud Norris

Pitches: R Bats: R Pos: SP-29   Ht: 6'0" Wt: 230 Born: 3/2/1985 Age: 28

			HOW MUCH HE PITCHED						WHAT HE GAVE UP												THE RESULTS						
Year	Team	Lg	G	GS	CG	GF	IP	BFP	H	R	ER	HR	SH	SF	HB	TBB	IBB	SO	WP	Bk	W	L	Pct	Sh	Sv-Op Hld	ERC	ERA
2012	OKCity*	AAA	1	1	0	0	5.0	21	3	2	2	2	0	0	0	3	0	7	0	0	1	0	1.000	0	0-- -	4.54	3.60
2009	Hou	NL	11	10	0	0	55.2	249	59	29	28	9	1	3	3	25	1	54	3	0	6	3	.667	0	0-0 0	5.26	4.53
2010	Hou	NL	27	27	0	0	153.2	683	151	94	84	18	6	4	6	77	3	158	5	2	9	10	.474	0	0-0 0	4.61	4.92
2011	Hou	NL	31	31	0	0	186.0	795	177	93	78	24	9	4	5	70	7	176	3	2	6	11	.353	0	0-0 0	3.96	3.77
2012	Hou	NL	29	29	0	0	168.1	733	165	90	87	23	7	2	8	66	2	165	8	0	7	13	.350	0	0-0 0	4.34	4.65
	4 ML YEARS		98	97	0	0	563.2	2460	552	306	277	74	23	13	22	238	13	553	19	4	28	37	.431	0	0-0 0	4.37	4.42

Derek Norris

Bats: R Throws: R Pos: C-58; PH-4; DH-2   Ht: 6'0" Wt: 210 Born: 2/14/1989 Age: 24

			BATTING																	BASERUNNING				AVERAGES		
Year	Team	Lg	G	AB	H	2B	3B	HR	(Hm	Rd)	TB	R	RBI	RC	TBB	IBB	SO	HBP	SH	SF	SB	CS	SB%	GDP	Avg	OBP	Slg
2007	Nats	R	37	123	25	6	2	4	(-	-)	47	16	15	18	25	1	38	2	0	1	2	1	.67	1	.203	.344	.382
2008	Vrmnt	A-	70	227	63	12	0	10	(-	-)	105	42	38	51	63	4	56	8	0	4	11	9	.55	6	.278	.444	.463
2009	Hgrstn	A	126	437	125	30	0	23	(-	-)	224	78	84	97	90	9	116	8	0	5	6	3	.67	6	.286	.413	.513
2010	Ptomc	A+	94	298	70	19	0	12	(-	-)	125	67	49	61	89	2	94	8	0	4	6	3	.67	3	.235	.419	.419
2011	Hrsbrg	AA	104	334	70	17	1	20	(-	-)	149	75	46	61	77	1	117	7	3	2	13	4	.76	2	.210	.367	.446
2012	Scrmto	AAA	58	218	59	14	2	9	(-	-)	104	39	38	36	21	0	41	1	0	6	5	1	.83	7	.271	.329	.477
2012	Oak	AL	60	209	42	8	1	7	(3	4)	73	19	34	27	21	1	66	1	0	1	5	1	.83	6	.201	.276	.349

Ivan Nova

Pitches: R Bats: R Pos: SP-28   ee-VAHN   Ht: 6'4" Wt: 225 Born: 1/12/1987 Age: 26

			HOW MUCH HE PITCHED						WHAT HE GAVE UP												THE RESULTS						
Year	Team	Lg	G	GS	CG	GF	IP	BFP	H	R	ER	HR	SH	SF	HB	TBB	IBB	SO	WP	Bk	W	L	Pct	Sh	Sv-Op Hld	ERC	ERA
2010	NYY	AL	10	7	0	3	42.0	185	44	22	21	4	1	1	1	17	2	26	2	0	1	2	.333	0	0-1 0	4.31	4.50
2011	NYY	AL	28	27	0	1	165.1	704	163	74	68	13	2	6	6	57	3	98	11	0	16	4	.800	0	0-0 0	3.76	3.70
2012	NYY	AL	28	28	0	0	170.1	748	194	100	95	28	3	6	10	56	3	153	6	2	12	8	.600	0	0-0 0	5.32	5.02
	Postseason		2	1	0	0	8.1	34	7	4	4	2	0	0	0	4	0	8	0	0	1	1	.500	0	0-0 0	4.66	4.32
	3 ML YEARS		66	62	0	4	377.2	1637	401	196	184	45	6	13	17	130	8	277	19	2	29	14	.674	0	0-1 0	4.51	4.38

Eduardo Nunez

Bats: R Throws: R Pos: SS-16; 3B-9; PH-6; PR-6; DH-4; LF-3; 2B-1; RF-1   Ht: 6'0" Wt: 185 Born: 6/15/1987 Age: 26

			BATTING																	BASERUNNING				AVERAGES		
Year	Team	Lg	G	AB	H	2B	3B	HR	(Hm	Rd)	TB	R	RBI	RC	TBB	IBB	SO	HBP	SH	SF	SB	CS	SB%	GDP	Avg	OBP	Slg
2012	S-WB*	AAA	38	163	37	4	0	2	(-	-)	47	18	16	13	7	1	28	0	0	2	16	3	.84	9	.227	.256	.288
2012	Yanks*	R	4	10	2	0	0	1	(-	-)	5	1	1	1	0	0	0	0	0	0	0	0	-	0	.200	.200	.500
2012	Tampa*	A+	2	7	2	0	0	0	(-	-)	2	2	0	0	0	0	1	0	0	0	1	0	1.00	0	.286	.286	.286
2010	NYY	AL	30	50	14	1	0	1	(0	1)	18	12	7	8	3	0	2	0	0	0	5	0	1.00	4	.280	.321	.360
2011	NYY	AL	112	309	82	18	2	5	(2	3)	119	38	30	42	22	2	37	0	6	1	22	6	.79	6	.265	.313	.385
2012	NYY	AL	38	89	26	4	1	1	(1	0)	35	14	11	15	6	0	12	1	0	4	11	2	.85	1	.292	.330	.393
	Postseason		1	0	0	0	0	0	(0	0)	0	0	0	0	0	0	0	0	0	0	1	0	1.00	0	-	-	-
	3 ML YEARS		180	448	122	23	3	7	(3	4)	172	64	48	65	31	2	51	1	6	5	38	8	.83	11	.272	.318	.384

Darren O'Day

Pitches: R Bats: R Pos: RP-69   Ht: 6'4" Wt: 220 Born: 10/22/1982 Age: 30

Year	Team	Lg	G	GS	CG	GF	IP	BFP	H	R	ER	HR	SH	SF	HB	TBB	IBB	SO	WP	Bk	W	L	Pct	Sh	Sv-Op	Hld	ERC	ERA
2008	LAA	AL	30	0	0	17	43.1	194	49	24	22	2	2	1	4	14	6	29	1	0	0	1	.000	0	0-0	1	4.20	4.57
2009	2 Tms		68	0	0	15	58.2	233	41	14	12	3	1	3	5	18	1	56	1	0	2	1	.667	0	2-2	20	2.20	1.84
2010	Tex	AL	72	0	0	14	62.0	240	43	15	14	5	1	3	5	12	2	45	0	0	6	2	.750	0	0-2	22	1.93	2.03
2011	Tex	AL	16	0	0	7	16.2	74	17	10	10	7	1	1	2	5	0	18	0	0	0	1	.000	0	0-0	3	6.45	5.40
2012	Bal	AL	69	0	0	10	67.0	263	49	17	17	6	3	1	3	14	2	69	0	0	7	1	.875	0	0-2	15	2.06	2.28
09	NYM	NL	4	0	0	1	3.0	17	5	2	0	0	0	1	1	1	0	2	0	0	0	0	-	0	0-0	0	7.72	0.00
09	Tex		64	0	0	14	55.2	216	36	12	12	3	1	2	4	17	1	54	1	0	2	1	.667	0	2-2	20	1.95	1.94
	Postseason		11	0	0	1	4.2	23	6	4	4	2	0	0	1	1	0	8	0	0	0	1	.000	0	0-0	1	7.96	7.71
	5 ML YEARS		255	0	0	63	247.2	1004	199	80	75	23	8	9	19	63	11	217	2	0	15	6	.714	0	2-6	61	2.68	2.73

Jake Odorizzi

Pitches: R Bats: R Pos: SP-2   oh-duh-RIZZ-ee   Ht: 6'2" Wt: 185 Born: 3/27/1990 Age: 23

Year	Team	Lg	G	GS	CG	GF	IP	BFP	H	R	ER	HR	SH	SF	HB	TBB	IBB	SO	WP	Bk	W	L	Pct	Sh	Sv-Op	Hld	ERC	ERA
2008	Brewrs	R	11	4	0	0	20.2	93	18	10	8	2	0	1	1	9	0	19	0	1	1	2	.333	0	0--	-	3.45	3.48
2009	Helena	R+	12	10	0	0	47.0	203	55	27	23	3	2	4	2	9	0	43	5	0	1	4	.200	0	0--	-	4.10	4.40
2010	Wisc	A	23	20	0	1	120.2	505	99	52	46	7	2	4	9	40	0	135	5	0	7	3	.700	0	1--	-	2.83	3.43
2011	Wilmg	A+	15	15	0	0	78.1	317	68	30	25	4	3	1	2	22	0	103	6	0	5	4	.556	0	0--	-	2.75	2.87
2011	NWArk	AA	12	12	0	0	68.2	284	66	38	36	13	1	0	1	22	0	54	1	0	5	3	.625	0	0--	-	4.30	4.72
2012	NWArk	AA	7	7	0	0	38.0	152	27	15	14	2	0	1	0	10	0	47	4	0	4	2	.667	0	0--	-	1.78	3.32
2012	Omha	AAA	19	18	0	0	107.1	460	105	41	35	12	1	4	2	40	0	88	3	0	11	3	.786	0	0--	-	4.00	2.93
2012	KC	AL	2	2	0	0	7.1	34	8	4	4	1	0	0	0	4	0	4	0	0	0	1	.000	0	0-0	-	5.34	4.91

Eric O'Flaherty

Pitches: L Bats: L Pos: RP-64   Ht: 6'2" Wt: 220 Born: 2/5/1985 Age: 28

Year	Team	Lg	G	GS	CG	GF	IP	BFP	H	R	ER	HR	SH	SF	HB	TBB	IBB	SO	WP	Bk	W	L	Pct	Sh	Sv-Op	Hld	ERC	ERA
2006	Sea	AL	15	0	0	5	11.0	57	18	9	5	2	1	0	0	6	3	6	2	0	0	0	-	0	0-0	1	8.63	4.09
2007	Sea	AL	56	0	0	9	52.1	221	45	26	26	1	0	2	5	20	1	36	4	1	7	1	.875	0	0-1	4	3.04	4.47
2008	Sea	AL	7	0	0	1	6.2	42	16	15	15	1	0	1	2	4	2	4	0	0	0	1	.000	0	0-0	2	17.12	20.25
2009	Atl	NL	78	0	0	8	56.1	236	52	23	19	2	1	1	6	18	4	39	2	0	2	1	.667	0	0-2	15	3.26	3.04
2010	Atl	NL	56	0	0	7	44.0	181	37	14	12	2	1	0	1	18	2	36	3	0	3	2	.600	0	0-1	9	2.97	2.45
2011	Atl	NL	78	0	0	5	73.2	301	59	9	8	2	7	2	3	21	8	67	1	0	2	4	.333	0	0-4	32	2.13	0.98
2012	Atl	NL	64	0	0	7	57.1	230	47	14	11	3	3	1	2	19	2	46	1	0	3	0	1.000	0	0-3	28	2.71	1.73
	7 ML YEARS		354	0	0	42	301.1	1268	274	110	96	14	13	7	19	106	22	234	13	1	17	9	.654	0	0-11	91	3.18	2.87

Alexi Ogando

Pitches: R Bats: R Pos: RP-57; SP-1   oh-GONE-doh   Ht: 6'4" Wt: 195 Born: 10/5/1983 Age: 29

Year	Team	Lg	G	GS	CG	GF	IP	BFP	H	R	ER	HR	SH	SF	HB	TBB	IBB	SO	WP	Bk	W	L	Pct	Sh	Sv-Op	Hld	ERC	ERA
2012	RdRck*	AAA	2	1	0	0	3.0	10	1	0	0	0	0	0	0	0	0	6	0	0	0	0	-	0	0--	-	0.25	0.00
2010	Tex	AL	44	0	0	12	41.2	171	31	6	6	2	3	2	1	16	2	39	3	0	4	1	.800	0	0-2	7	2.34	1.30
2011	Tex	AL	31	29	1	2	169.0	693	149	73	66	16	2	3	7	43	0	126	5	0	13	8	.619	1	0-0	0	3.01	3.51
2012	Tex	AL	58	1	0	11	66.0	263	49	26	24	9	0	3	2	17	1	66	5	0	2	0	1.000	0	3-6	12	2.50	3.27
	Postseason		18	0	0	2	19.0	81	16	6	5	3	0	0	0	10	2	23	1	0	2	0	1.000	0	0-3	4	3.95	2.37
	3 ML YEARS		133	30	1	25	276.2	1127	229	105	96	27	5	8	10	76	3	231	13	0	19	9	.679	1	3-8	19	2.79	3.12

Ross Ohlendorf

Pitches: R Bats: R Pos: SP-9; RP-4   OH-lenn-dorf   Ht: 6'4" Wt: 240 Born: 8/8/1982 Age: 30

Year	Team	Lg	G	GS	CG	GF	IP	BFP	H	R	ER	HR	SH	SF	HB	TBB	IBB	SO	WP	Bk	W	L	Pct	Sh	Sv-Op	Hld	ERC	ERA
2012	Pwtckt*	AAA	10	10	0	0	52.2	233	57	28	27	5	2	2	8	15	0	37	4	0	4	3	.571	0	0--	-	4.65	4.61
2012	Tucsn*	AAA	3	0	0	2	17.0	71	19	8	8	2	0	1	1	3	0	17	1	0	1	1	.500	0	0--	-	4.30	4.24
2007	NYY	AL	6	0	0	3	6.1	26	5	2	2	1	0	0	0	2	0	9	0	0	0	0	-	0	0-0	1	2.94	2.84
2008	2 Tms		30	5	0	3	62.2	300	86	49	45	10	1	1	1	31	3	49	10	1	1	4	.200	0	0-0	4	7.16	6.46
2009	Pit	NL	29	29	0	0	176.2	725	165	80	77	25	11	8	7	53	1	109	2	1	11	10	.524	0	0-0	-	3.84	3.92
2010	Pit	NL	21	21	0	0	108.1	475	106	54	49	12	9	8	6	44	2	79	5	0	1	11	.083	0	0-0	-	4.20	4.07
2011	Pit	NL	9	9	0	0	38.2	194	60	38	35	9	5	3	6	15	2	27	2	0	1	3	.250	0	0-0	-	9.12	8.15
2012	SD	NL	13	9	0	2	48.2	233	62	44	42	7	4	0	1	24	0	39	2	1	4	4	.500	0	0-0	-	6.37	7.77
08	NYY	AL	25	0	0	3	40.0	187	50	31	29	7	0	0	1	19	3	36	6	0	1	1	.500	0	0-0	4	6.39	6.53
08	Pit	NL	5	5	0	0	22.2	113	36	18	16	3	1	1	0	12	0	13	4	1	0	3	.000	0	0-0	0	8.59	6.35
	Postseason		1	0	0	0	1.0	9	3	4	3	1	0	0	1	1	0	0	0	0	0	0	-	0	0-0	0	47.63	27.00
	6 ML YEARS		108	73	0	8	441.1	1953	484	267	250	64	30	20	21	169	8	312	21	3	18	32	.360	0	0-0	5	5.06	5.10

Will Ohman

Pitches: L Bats: L Pos: RP-32   OH-min   Ht: 6'2" Wt: 225 Born: 8/13/1977 Age: 35

Year	Team	Lg	G	GS	CG	GF	IP	BFP	H	R	ER	HR	SH	SF	HB	TBB	IBB	SO	WP	Bk	W	L	Pct	Sh	Sv-Op	Hld	ERC	ERA
2012	Lsvlle*	AAA	15	0	0	1	11.0	60	17	5	5	0	0	1	1	10	3	17	1	0	0	1	.000	0	0--	-	8.40	4.09
2000	ChC	NL	6	0	0	2	3.1	17	4	3	3	0	0	0	0	4	1	2	1	0	1	0	1.000	0	0-0	1	7.25	8.10
2001	ChC	NL	11	0	0	1	11.2	54	14	10	10	2	0	0	0	6	0	12	2	0	0	1	.000	0	0-0	1	6.26	7.71
2005	ChC	NL	69	0	0	13	43.1	187	32	14	14	6	1	0	3	24	3	45	6	1	2	2	.500	0	0-3	13	3.62	2.91

Year	Team	Lg	G	GS	CG	GF	IP	BFP	H	R	ER	HR	SH	SF	HB	TBB	IBB	SO	WP	Bk	W	L	Pct	Sh	Sv-Op	Hld	ERC	ERA
			HOW MUCH HE PITCHED						**WHAT HE GAVE UP**												**THE RESULTS**							
2006	ChC	NL	78	0	0	14	65.1	286	51	30	30	6	0	2	5	34	2	74	4	0	1	1	.500	0	0-0	9	3.44	4.13
2007	ChC	NL	56	0	0	11	36.1	168	42	20	20	3	2	0	1	16	4	33	2	0	2	4	.333	0	1-1	12	4.79	4.95
2008	Atl	NL	83	0	0	16	58.2	248	51	27	24	3	3	0	1	22	4	53	2	0	4	1	.800	0	1-4	23	2.87	3.68
2009	LAD	NL	21	0	0	5	12.1	54	12	8	8	4	0	0	0	8	1	7	0	0	1	0	1.000	0	1-2	4	6.76	5.84
2010	2 Tms		68	0	0	12	42.0	186	40	18	15	4	2	4	1	23	5	43	3	0	0	2	.000	0	0-1	18	4.24	3.21
2011	CWS	AL	59	0	0	15	53.1	232	53	26	25	8	2	1	4	17	5	54	1	0	1	3	.250	0	0-1	3	4.16	4.22
2012	CWS	AL	32	0	0	9	26.2	112	23	19	19	6	0	0	6	5	0	13	0	1	0	2	.000	0	0-2	1	4.21	6.41
10	Bal		51	0	0	9	30.0	135	30	12	11	3	2	3	1	18	4	29	2	0	0	0	-	0	0-1	15	4.80	3.30
10	Fla	NL	17	0	0	3	12.0	51	10	6	4	1	0	1	0	5	1	14	1	0	0	2	.000	0	0-0	3	2.94	3.00
10 ML YEARS			483	0	0	97	353.0	1544	322	175	168	42	10	7	21	159	25	336	21	2	12	16	.429	0	3-14	85	3.99	4.28

Darren Oliver

Pitches: L **Bats:** R **Pos:** RP-62   **Ht:** 6'2" **Wt:** 200 **Born:** 10/6/1970 **Age:** 42

Year	Team	Lg	G	GS	CG	GF	IP	BFP	H	R	ER	HR	SH	SF	HB	TBB	IBB	SO	WP	Bk	W	L	Pct	Sh	Sv-Op	Hld	ERC	ERA
			HOW MUCH HE PITCHED						**WHAT HE GAVE UP**												**THE RESULTS**							
1993	Tex	AL	2	0	0	0	3.1	14	2	1	1	1	0	0	0	1	1	4	0	0	0	0	-	0	0-0	0	2.15	2.70
1994	Tex	AL	43	0	0	10	50.0	226	40	24	19	4	6	0	6	35	4	50	2	2	4	0	1.000	0	2-3	9	4.29	3.42
1995	Tex	AL	17	7	0	2	49.0	222	47	25	23	3	5	1	1	32	1	39	4	0	4	2	.667	0	0-0	0	4.59	4.22
1996	Tex	AL	30	30	1	0	173.2	777	190	97	90	20	2	7	10	76	3	112	5	1	14	6	.700	1	0-0	0	5.10	4.66
1997	Tex	AL	32	32	3	0	201.1	887	213	111	94	29	2	5	11	82	3	104	7	0	13	12	.520	1	0-0	0	4.98	4.20
1998	2 Tms		29	29	2	0	160.1	749	204	115	102	18	8	8	10	66	2	87	7	4	10	11	.476	0	0-0	0	6.01	5.73
1999	StL	NL	30	30	2	0	196.1	842	197	96	93	16	11	4	11	74	4	119	6	2	9	9	.500	1	0-0	0	4.11	4.26
2000	Tex	AL	21	21	0	0	108.0	501	151	95	89	16	5	4	4	42	3	49	4	1	2	9	.182	0	0-0	0	7.04	7.42
2001	Tex	AL	28	28	1	0	154.0	696	189	109	103	23	1	5	6	65	0	104	8	2	11	11	.500	0	0-0	0	6.14	6.02
2002	Bos	AL	14	9	1	0	58.0	258	70	30	30	7	1	3	6	27	0	32	1	0	4	5	.444	1	0-0	0	6.49	4.66
2003	Col	NL	33	32	1	0	180.1	786	201	108	101	21	4	5	8	61	3	88	0	0	13	11	.542	0	0-0	0	4.80	5.04
2004	2 Tms		27	10	0	5	72.2	314	87	50	48	14	4	3	1	21	1	46	1	0	3	3	.500	0	0-0	0	5.59	5.94
2006	NYM	NL	45	0	0	10	81.0	333	70	33	31	13	2	4	3	21	2	60	1	0	4	1	.800	0	0-3	3	3.27	3.44
2007	LAA	AL	61	0	0	20	64.1	273	58	31	27	5	2	4	1	23	2	51	1	1	3	1	.750	0	0-0	8	3.19	3.78
2008	LAA	AL	54	0	0	9	72.0	291	67	24	23	5	4	3	4	16	2	48	3	0	7	1	.875	0	0-2	12	3.07	2.88
2009	LAA	AL	63	1	0	9	73.0	293	61	22	22	5	4	5	5	22	8	65	7	0	5	1	.833	0	0-1	20	2.81	2.71
2010	Tex	AL	64	0	0	7	61.2	244	53	20	17	4	5	3	2	15	4	65	0	0	1	2	.333	0	1-4	14	2.63	2.48
2011	Tex	AL	61	0	0	17	51.0	215	47	17	13	3	4	0	1	11	1	44	0	1	5	5	.500	0	2-6	16	2.64	2.29
2012	Tor	AL	62	0	0	11	56.2	221	43	13	13	3	1	0	4	15	0	52	3	0	3	4	.429	0	2-4	16	2.38	2.06
98	Tex	AL	19	19	2	0	103.1	493	140	84	75	11	3	6	10	43	1	58	6	1	6	7	.462	0	0-0	0	6.68	6.53
98	StL	NL	10	10	0	0	57.0	256	64	31	27	7	5	2	0	23	1	29	1	3	4	4	.500	0	0-0	0	4.85	4.26
04	Fla	NL	18	8	0	3	58.2	260	75	44	42	13	4	3	1	17	1	33	1	0	2	3	.400	0	0-0	0	6.30	6.44
04	Hou	NL	9	2	0	2	14.0	54	12	6	6	1	0	0	0	4	0	13	0	0	1	0	1.000	0	0-0	0	2.89	3.86
Postseason			30	1	0	4	41.2	165	34	20	20	3	4	0	1	12	2	31	1	0	2	2	.500	0	1-2	5	2.61	4.32
19 ML YEARS			716	229	11	100	1866.2	8142	1990	1021	939	210	71	64	94	705	44	1219	60	14	115	94	.550	4	7-20	98	4.66	4.53

Lester Oliveros

Pitches: R **Bats:** R **Pos:** RP-1   ahl-ih-VARE-us   **Ht:** 6'0" **Wt:** 226 **Born:** 5/28/1988 **Age:** 25

Year	Team	Lg	G	GS	CG	GF	IP	BFP	H	R	ER	HR	SH	SF	HB	TBB	IBB	SO	WP	Bk	W	L	Pct	Sh	Sv-Op	Hld	ERC	ERA
			HOW MUCH HE PITCHED						**WHAT HE GAVE UP**												**THE RESULTS**							
2008	Oneont	A-	15	0	0	9	20.2	83	15	4	4	1	1	0	0	6	1	34	0	0	1	2	.333	0	4--	-	1.86	1.74
2008	Lkland	A+	5	0	0	1	10.2	55	12	8	5	0	0	1	4	9	0	3	0	0	1	1	.500	0	0--	-	7.37	4.22
2009	Lkland	A+	34	0	0	14	54.0	235	53	27	25	5	1	1	4	16	1	58	2	1	4	2	.667	0	2--	-	3.69	4.17
2009	Toledo	AAA	1	0	0	0	2.0	9	2	0	0	0	0	0	0	1	0	3	0	0	0	0	-	0	0--	-	3.63	0.00
2010	Lkland	A+	20	0	0	13	19.0	76	13	5	4	0	0	1	2	6	0	24	2	0	0	1	.000	0	9--	-	1.93	1.89
2010	Erie	AA	24	0	0	20	25.1	117	20	14	14	3	2	0	2	21	4	36	0	1	1	2	.333	0	14--	-	4.70	4.97
2011	Erie	AA	10	0	0	6	17.0	63	11	1	1	0	1	0	1	4	1	28	1	0	2	0	1.000	0	0--	-	1.46	0.53
2011	Toledo	AAA	22	0	0	16	28.0	136	37	20	20	7	2	0	0	17	3	26	1	0	1	3	.250	0	5--	-	7.90	6.43
2011	Roch	AAA	2	0	0	0	3.0	11	2	1	1	1	0	0	0	0	0	4	0	0	1	0	1.000	0	0--	-	1.99	3.00
2012	NwBrit	AA	13	0	0	4	19.0	70	10	3	3	0	2	0	0	7	2	16	1	0	1	1	.500	0	2--	-	1.21	1.42
2012	Roch	AAA	19	0	0	9	29.1	117	24	10	10	2	2	2	0	8	2	35	0	0	1	2	.333	0	6--	-	2.38	3.07
2011	2 Tms	AL	19	0	0	6	21.1	91	21	11	11	0	0	2	0	11	2	13	1	0	0	0	-	0	0-0	1	3.67	4.64
2012	Min	AL	1	0	0	0	1.2	7	1	1	1	0	0	0	0	1	0	1	0	0	0	0	-	0	0-0	0	2.03	5.40
11	Det	AL	9	0	0	3	8.0	35	8	5	5	0	0	0	0	4	1	4	1	0	0	0	-	0	0-0	1	3.53	5.63
11	Min	AL	10	0	0	3	13.1	56	13	6	6	0	0	2	0	7	1	9	0	0	0	0	-	0	0-0	0	3.75	4.05
2 ML YEARS			20	0	0	6	23.0	98	22	12	12	0	0	2	0	12	2	14	1	0	0	0	-	0	0-0	1	3.54	4.70

Miguel Olivo

Bats: R **Throws:** R **Pos:** C-73; DH-12; PH-3; PR-1   oh-LEEV-oh   **Ht:** 6'0" **Wt:** 230 **Born:** 7/15/1978 **Age:** 34

Year	Team	Lg	G	AB	H	2B	3B	HR	(Hm	Rd)	TB	R	RBI	RC	TBB	IBB	SO	HBP	SH	SF	SB	CS	SB%	GDP	Avg	OBP	Slg
			BATTING																		**BASERUNNING**				**AVERAGES**		
2012	Tacom*	AAA	3	13	3	0	0	1	(-	-)	6	3	1	1	0	0	6	0	0	0	0	0	-	0	.231	.231	.462
2002	CWS	AL	6	19	4	1	0	1	(0	1)	8	2	5	4	2	0	5	0	0	0	0	0	-	1	.211	.286	.421
2003	CWS	AL	114	317	75	19	1	6	(4	2)	114	37	27	32	19	0	80	4	4	2	6	4	.60	3	.237	.287	.360
2004	2 Tms		96	301	70	15	4	13	(8	5)	132	46	40	33	20	2	84	3	4	1	7	6	.54	4	.233	.286	.439
2005	2 Tms		91	267	58	11	1	9	(5	4)	98	30	34	23	8	2	80	3	1	2	7	2	.78	7	.217	.246	.367
2006	Fla	NL	127	430	113	22	3	16	(7	9)	189	52	58	49	9	4	103	7	3	3	2	3	.40	9	.263	.287	.440
2007	Fla	NL	122	452	107	20	4	16	(11	5)	183	43	60	43	14	2	123	2	0	1	3	2	.60	13	.237	.262	.405
2008	KC	AL	84	306	78	22	0	12	(3	9)	136	29	41	35	7	2	82	3	0	1	7	0	1.00	6	.255	.278	.444
2009	KC	AL	114	390	97	15	5	23	(10	13)	191	51	65	47	19	0	126	5	1	1	5	2	.71	10	.249	.292	.490
2010	Col	NL	112	394	106	17	6	14	(4	10)	177	55	58	49	27	5	117	1	2	3	7	4	.64	6	.269	.315	.449
2011	Sea	AL	130	477	107	19	1	19	(10	9)	185	54	62	46	20	2	140	1	1	8	6	5	.55	7	.224	.253	.388
2012	Sea	AL	87	315	70	14	0	12	(5	7)	120	27	29	21	7	0	85	0	1	0	3	6	.33	8	.222	.239	.381

Year	Team	Lg	G	AB	H	2B	3B	HR	(Hm	Rd)	TB	R	RBI	RC	TBB	IBB	SO	HBP	SH	SF	SB	CS	SB%	GDP	Avg	OBP	Slg
																							BATTING									**BASERUNNING**				**AVERAGES**		
04	CWS	AL	46	141	38	7	2	7	(4	3)	70	21	26	21	10	1	29	0	4	1	5	4	.56	2	.270	.316	.496
04	Sea	AL	50	160	32	8	2	6	(4	2)	62	25	14	12	10	1	55	3	0	0	2	2	.50	2	.200	.260	.388
05	Sea	AL	54	152	23	4	0	5	(4	1)	42	14	18	6	4	0	49	0	0	1	1	1	.50	3	.151	.172	.276
05	SD	NL	37	115	35	7	1	4	(1	3)	56	16	16	17	4	2	31	3	1	1	6	1	.86	4	.304	.341	.487
	Postseason		1	1	0	0	0	0	(0	0)	0	0	0	0	0	0	0	0	0	0	0	0	-	1	.000	.000	.000
	11 ML YEARS		1083	3668	885	175	25	141	(73	68)	1533	426	479	380	152	19	1025	29	17	22	53	34	.61	74	.241	.275	.418

Ray Olmedo

Bats: B Throws: R Pos: 3B-10; PR-6; SS-5; 2B-2; DH-1; PH-1 ohl-MAY-doh **Ht: 5'11" Wt: 165 Born: 5/31/1981 Age: 32**

Year	Team	Lg	G	AB	H	2B	3B	HR	(Hm	Rd)	TB	R	RBI	RC	TBB	IBB	SO	HBP	SH	SF	SB	CS	SB%	GDP	Avg	OBP	Slg
2012	Charltt*	AAA	80	275	75	15	1	0	(-	-)	92	24	19	34	27	1	42	1	7	0	9	3	.75	9	.273	.340	.335
2003	Cin	NL	79	230	55	6	1	0	(0	0)	63	24	17	19	13	0	46	0	7	0	1	1	.50	4	.239	.280	.274
2004	Cin	NL	8	1	0	0	0	0	(0	0)	0	0	0	0	1	0	0	0	0	0	0	0	-	0	.000	.500	.000
2005	Cin	NL	54	77	17	4	1	1	(1	0)	26	10	4	6	6	0	22	1	3	1	4	0	1.00	1	.221	.282	.338
2006	Cin	NL	30	44	9	2	0	1	(0	1)	14	5	4	4	4	0	4	0	0	0	1	0	1.00	0	.205	.271	.318
2007	Tor	AL	27	51	11	4	0	0	(0	0)	15	6	1	2	2	0	9	0	1	0	0	0	-	1	.216	.245	.294
2012	CWS	AL	20	41	10	2	0	0	(0	0)	12	8	1	2	0	0	9	0	1	0	0	0	-	1	.244	.244	.293
	6 ML YEARS		218	444	102	18	2	2	(1	1)	130	53	27	33	26	0	90	1	12	1	6	1	.86	7	.230	.273	.293

Garrett Olson

Pitches: L Bats: R Pos: RP-1 **Ht: 6'1" Wt: 205 Born: 10/18/1983 Age: 29**

Year	Team	Lg	G	GS	CG	GF	IP	BFP	H	R	ER	HR	SH	SF	HB	TBB	IBB	SO	WP	Bk	W	L	Pct	Sh	Sv-Op	Hld	ERC	ERA
2012	Buffalo*	AAA	34	21	0	8	122.1	550	133	70	63	11	9	5	2	53	4	107	8	0	4	7	.364	0	0- -	-	4.57	4.63
2007	Bal	AL	7	7	0	0	32.1	162	42	28	28	4	0	3	2	28	1	28	1	1	1	3	.250	0	0-0	0	8.46	7.79
2008	Bal	AL	26	26	0	0	132.2	621	168	100	98	17	4	4	8	62	1	83	6	0	9	10	.474	0	0-0	0	6.40	6.65
2009	Sea	AL	31	11	0	5	80.1	347	79	52	50	19	1	2	4	34	0	47	2	0	3	5	.375	0	0-0	5	5.33	5.60
2010	Sea	AL	35	0	0	11	37.2	172	42	20	19	6	1	1	0	15	1	31	4	0	0	3	.000	0	1-1	4	4.94	4.54
2011	Pit	NL	4	0	0	1	4.1	21	2	1	1	0	1	1	0	3	1	4	1	0	1	1	.500	0	0-0	0	1.24	2.08
2012	NYM	NL	1	0	0	0	0.1	5	3	4	4	0	0	0	0	1	0	0	0	0	0	0	-	0	0-0	0	83.91	108.0
	6 ML YEARS		104	44	0	17	287.2	1328	336	205	200	46	7	11	14	143	4	193	14	1	14	22	.389	0	1-1	6	6.10	6.26

Mike Olt

Bats: R Throws: R Pos: 1B-8; 3B-5; RF-2; PH-1 OHLT **Ht: 6'2" Wt: 210 Born: 8/27/1988 Age: 24**

Year	Team	Lg	G	AB	H	2B	3B	HR	(Hm	Rd)	TB	R	RBI	RC	TBB	IBB	SO	HBP	SH	SF	SB	CS	SB%	GDP	Avg	OBP	Slg
2010	Spkane	A-	69	263	77	16	1	9	(-	-)	122	57	43	51	40	0	77	4	0	3	6	0	1.00	3	.293	.390	.464
2011	MrtlBh	A+	69	240	64	15	0	14	(-	-)	121	39	42	49	48	1	70	1	0	3	0	1	.00	7	.267	.387	.504
2011	Rngrs	R	4	14	3	0	0	1	(-	-)	6	2	4	1	1	0	5	0	0	0	0	0	-	0	.214	.267	.429
2012	Frisco	AA	95	354	102	17	1	28	(-	-)	205	65	82	82	61	5	101	4	0	1	4	0	1.00	13	.288	.398	.579
2012	Tex	AL	16	33	5	1	0	0	(0	0)	6	2	5	2	5	0	13	0	0	2	1	1	.50	1	.152	.250	.182

Brian Omogrosso

Pitches: R Bats: R Pos: RP-17 oh-muh-GRAH-so **Ht: 6'4" Wt: 230 Born: 4/24/1984 Age: 29**

Year	Team	Lg	G	GS	CG	GF	IP	BFP	H	R	ER	HR	SH	SF	HB	TBB	IBB	SO	WP	Bk	W	L	Pct	Sh	Sv-Op	Hld	ERC	ERA
2006	Brham	AA	22	0	0	7	36.2	150	27	14	13	2	3	1	4	13	2	23	6	0	1	2	.333	0	2- -	-	2.57	3.19
2007	WinSa	A+	40	14	1	13	120.1	524	94	60	50	7	5	2	14	57	1	108	15	0	8	8	.500	1	5- -	-	3.24	3.74
2008	Brham	AA	17	5	0	2	39.0	166	32	19	16	2	0	1	1	25	0	26	2	0	2	3	.400	0	1- -	-	3.89	3.69
2009	Brham	AA	13	13	0	0	73.0	320	67	40	34	4	0	1	6	40	0	64	4	1	7	2	.778	0	0- -	-	4.24	4.19
2009	Charltt	AAA	4	0	0	1	5.2	32	12	10	10	2	0	1	0	3	1	6	2	0	0	0	-	0	0- -	-	13.89	15.88
2010	Bristol	R	2	0	0	0	2.0	8	1	0	0	0	0	0	0	2	0	2	0	0	0	0	-	0	0- -	-	3.21	0.00
2010	Brham	AA	3	0	0	0	3.0	12	2	1	1	0	0	0	0	1	0	3	0	0	1	0	1.000	0	0- -	-	1.57	3.00
2011	Brham	AA	31	0	0	15	43.0	184	36	18	12	2	4	1	3	16	1	53	7	0	0	2	.000	0	2- -	-	2.89	2.51
2011	Charltt	AAA	11	1	0	0	22.1	97	24	11	10	1	2	2	0	8	0	19	0	0	1	1	.500	0	0- -	-	3.92	4.03
2012	Charltt	AAA	33	0	0	21	47.1	196	43	25	24	3	2	1	2	12	0	59	3	0	0	2	.000	0	9- -	-	2.93	4.56
2012	CWS	AL	17	0	0	1	21.0	90	20	6	6	3	0	0	0	9	0	18	0	0	0	0	-	0	0-1	1	4.23	2.57

Logan Ondrusek

Pitches: R Bats: R Pos: RP-63 ahn-DREW-seck **Ht: 6'8" Wt: 230 Born: 2/13/1985 Age: 28**

Year	Team	Lg	G	GS	CG	GF	IP	BFP	H	R	ER	HR	SH	SF	HB	TBB	IBB	SO	WP	Bk	W	L	Pct	Sh	Sv-Op	Hld	ERC	ERA
2012	Lsvlle*	AAA	3	0	0	1	4.0	24	8	4	4	1	1	0	0	4	0	5	0	0	0	1	.000	0	0- -	-	14.76	9.00
2010	Cin	NL	60	0	0	11	58.2	240	49	25	24	7	1	1	0	20	1	39	2	0	5	0	1.000	0	0-2	6	3.08	3.68
2011	Cin	NL	66	0	0	14	61.1	268	55	25	22	6	3	4	2	28	7	41	6	0	5	5	.500	0	0-3	14	3.58	3.23
2012	Cin	NL	63	0	0	20	54.2	243	51	23	21	8	1	1	3	31	4	39	5	0	5	2	.714	0	2-4	13	4.81	3.46
	Postseason		2	0	0	0	2.0	9	0	0	0	0	0	1	0	1	0	0	0	0	0	0	-	0	0-0	1	0.84	0.00
	3 ML YEARS		189	0	0	45	174.2	751	155	73	67	21	5	6	5	79	12	119	13	0	15	7	.682	0	2-9	33	3.78	3.45

Pete Orr

Bats: L **Throws:** R **Pos:** PH-19; 2B-13; 3B-4 **Ht:** 6'1" **Wt:** 195 **Born:** 6/8/1979 **Age:** 34

Year	Team	Lg	G	AB	H	2B	3B	HR	(Hm	Rd)	TB	R	RBI	RC	TBB	IBB	SO	HBP	SH	SF	SB	CS	SB%	GDP	Avg	OBP	Slg
2012	LV*	AAA	81	302	78	12	2	4	(-	-)	106	43	33	37	23	2	53	2	4	1	16	2	.89	4	.258	.314	.351
2005	Atl	NL	112	150	45	8	1	1	(0	1)	58	32	8	18	6	0	23	1	5	0	7	1	.88	2	.300	.331	.387
2006	Atl	NL	102	154	39	3	4	1	(1	0)	53	22	8	16	5	1	30	0	5	0	2	4	.33	1	.253	.277	.344
2007	Atl	NL	57	65	13	1	0	0	(0	0)	14	11	2	3	3	0	14	0	1	0	1	0	1.00	1	.200	.235	.215
2008	Was	NL	49	75	19	2	1	0	(0	0)	23	10	7	6	2	0	16	1	1	0	1	0	1.00	0	.253	.282	.307
2009	Was	NL	27	75	19	2	1	1	(0	1)	26	5	10	8	3	0	15	0	0	3	2	1	.67	0	.253	.272	.347
2011	Phi	NL	46	96	21	3	0	0	(0	0)	24	7	4	8	6	2	19	2	0	0	3	0	1.00	0	.219	.279	.250
2012	Phi	NL	35	54	17	5	1	0	(0	0)	24	6	7	9	1	0	18	0	2	0	3	1	.75	0	.315	.327	.444
	Postseason		3	2	0	0	0	0	(0	0)	0	0	0	0	0	0	0	0	0	0	0	0	-	0	.000	.000	.000
7 ML YEARS			428	669	173	24	8	3	(1	2)	222	93	46	68	26	3	135	4	14	3	19	7	.73	4	.259	.289	.332

Jose Ortega

Pitches: R **Bats:** R **Pos:** RP-2 **Ht:** 5'11" **Wt:** 187 **Born:** 10/12/1988 **Age:** 24

Year	Team	Lg	G	GS	CG	GF	IP	BFP	H	R	ER	HR	SH	SF	HB	TBB	IBB	SO	WP	Bk	W	L	Pct	Sh	Sv-Op	Hld	ERC	ERA
2009	Oneont	A-	25	0	0	13	34.0	152	28	19	15	2	1	0	1	23	2	32	3	0	2	2	.500	0	1--	-	3.83	3.97
2010	WMich	A	18	0	0	11	25.2	120	28	14	13	1	1	0	0	17	1	22	2	0	0	3	.000	0	1--	-	5.05	4.56
2010	Lkland	A+	10	0	0	6	19.0	74	14	2	2	0	0	0	1	7	1	20	1	0	2	1	.667	0	0--	-	2.19	0.95
2010	Erie	AA	15	1	0	4	23.2	100	22	8	8	2	0	1	1	7	1	19	1	0	1	0	1.000	0	0--	-	3.25	3.04
2011	Toledo	AAA	33	0	0	11	50.0	233	61	41	35	7	1	5	3	27	1	44	2	0	1	3	.250	0	0--	-	6.57	6.30
2012	Toledo	AAA	45	0	0	13	62.2	308	76	44	40	4	8	3	2	51	4	68	12	0	5	8	.385	0	1--	-	6.78	5.74
2012	Det	AL	2	0	0	0	2.2	13	3	1	1	1	0	0	0	1	0	4	0	0	0	0	-	0	0-1	0	6.04	3.38

Rafael Ortega

Bats: L **Throws:** R **Pos:** CF-1; PH-1 **Ht:** 5'11" **Wt:** 160 **Born:** 5/15/1991 **Age:** 22

Year	Team	Lg	G	AB	H	2B	3B	HR	(Hm	Rd)	TB	R	RBI	RC	TBB	IBB	SO	HBP	SH	SF	SB	CS	SB%	GDP	Avg	OBP	Slg
2010	Casper	R+	71	288	103	17	3	7	(-	-)	147	69	45	61	28	3	42	2	2	2	23	9	.72	2	.358	.416	.510
2011	Ashvll	A	113	479	141	26	8	9	(-	-)	210	77	66	70	28	1	90	5	3	6	32	19	.63	5	.294	.335	.438
2012	Mdest	A+	114	495	140	23	8	8	(-	-)	203	81	60	73	46	1	93	4	4	7	36	18	.67	8	.283	.344	.410
2012	Col	NL	2	4	2	0	0	0	(0	0)	2	0	0	2	1	0	2	1	0	0	1	0	1.00	0	.500	.667	.500

David Ortiz

Bats: L **Throws:** L **Pos:** DH-81; 1B-7; PH-2 **Ht:** 6'4" **Wt:** 250 **Born:** 11/18/1975 **Age:** 37

Year	Team	Lg	G	AB	H	2B	3B	HR	(Hm	Rd)	TB	R	RBI	RC	TBB	IBB	SO	HBP	SH	SF	SB	CS	SB%	GDP	Avg	OBP	Slg
1997	Min	AL	15	49	16	3	0	1	(0	1)	22	10	6	7	2	0	19	0	0	0	0	0	-	1	.327	.353	.449
1998	Min	AL	86	278	77	20	0	9	(2	7)	124	47	46	46	39	3	72	5	0	4	1	0	1.00	8	.277	.371	.446
1999	Min	AL	10	20	0	0	0	0	(0	0)	0	1	0	0	5	0	12	0	0	0	0	0	-	0	.000	.200	.000
2000	Min	AL	130	415	117	36	1	10	(7	3)	185	59	63	66	57	2	81	0	0	6	1	0	1.00	13	.282	.364	.446
2001	Min	AL	89	303	71	17	1	18	(6	12)	144	46	48	46	40	8	68	1	1	2	1	0	1.00	6	.234	.324	.475
2002	Min	AL	125	412	112	32	1	20	(5	15)	206	52	75	62	43	0	87	3	0	8	1	2	.33	8	.272	.339	.500
2003	Bos	AL	128	448	129	39	2	31	(17	14)	265	79	101	80	58	8	83	1	0	2	0	0	-	9	.288	.369	.592
2004	Bos	AL	150	582	175	47	3	41	(17	24)	351	94	139	127	75	8	133	4	0	8	0	0	-	12	.301	.380	.603
2005	Bos	AL	159	601	180	40	1	47	(20	27)	363	119	148	137	102	9	124	1	0	9	1	0	1.00	12	.300	.397	.604
2006	Bos	AL	151	558	160	29	2	54	(22	32)	355	115	137	129	119	23	117	4	0	5	1	0	1.00	12	.287	.413	.636
2007	Bos	AL	149	549	182	52	1	35	(16	19)	341	116	117	138	111	12	103	4	0	3	3	1	.75	16	.332	.445	.621
2008	Bos	AL	109	416	110	30	1	23	(12	11)	211	74	89	82	70	12	74	1	1	3	1	0	1.00	16	.264	.369	.507
2009	Bos	AL	150	541	129	35	1	28	(18	10)	250	77	99	79	74	5	134	5	0	7	0	2	.00	14	.238	.332	.462
2010	Bos	AL	145	518	140	36	1	32	(15	17)	274	86	102	94	82	14	145	2	0	4	0	1	.00	12	.270	.370	.529
2011	Bos	AL	146	525	162	40	1	29	(13	16)	291	84	96	97	78	12	83	1	0	1	1	1	.50	24	.309	.398	.554
2012	Bos	AL	90	324	103	26	0	23	(13	10)	198	65	60	75	56	13	51	0	0	3	0	1	.00	6	.318	.415	.611
	Postseason		66	244	69	18	2	12	(7	5)	127	39	47	51	41	7	64	2	0	2	0	1	.00	3	.283	.388	.520
16 ML YEARS			1832	6539	1863	482	16	401	(183	218)	3580	1124	1326	1265	1011	129	1386	32	2	65	11	8	.58	159	.285	.380	.547

Roy Oswalt

Pitches: R **Bats:** R **Pos:** SP-9; RP-8 OWES-walt **Ht:** 6'0" **Wt:** 190 **Born:** 8/29/1977 **Age:** 35

Year	Team	Lg	G	GS	CG	GF	IP	BFP	H	R	ER	HR	SH	SF	HB	TBB	IBB	SO	WP	Bk	W	L	Pct	Sh	Sv-Op	Hld	ERC	ERA
2012	RdRck*	AAA	3	3	0	0	12.0	52	15	7	7	1	0	0	0	3	0	10	0	0	1	1	.500	0	0--	-	4.86	5.25
2012	Frisco*	AA	1	1	0	0	3.1	17	5	3	3	0	0	0	0	1	0	3	1	0	0	0	-	0	0--	-	5.30	8.10
2001	Hou	NL	28	20	3	4	141.2	575	126	48	43	13	4	4	6	24	2	144	0	0	14	3	.824	1	0-0	0	2.68	2.73
2002	Hou	NL	35	34	0	0	233.0	956	215	86	78	17	12	7	5	62	4	208	3	0	19	9	.679	0	0-0	0	3.05	3.01
2003	Hou	NL	21	21	0	0	127.1	514	116	48	42	15	7	1	5	29	0	108	1	0	10	5	.667	0	0-0	0	3.26	2.97
2004	Hou	NL	36	35	2	0	237.0	983	233	100	92	17	11	4	11	62	5	206	5	1	20	10	.667	2	0-0	0	3.46	3.49
2005	Hou	NL	35	35	4	0	241.2	1002	243	85	79	18	12	7	8	48	3	184	5	1	20	12	.625	1	0-0	0	3.27	2.94
2006	Hou	NL	33	32	2	1	220.2	896	220	76	73	18	12	4	6	38	4	166	1	1	15	8	.652	0	0-0	0	3.19	2.98
2007	Hou	NL	33	32	1	0	212.0	910	221	80	75	14	6	4	7	60	6	154	1	1	14	7	.667	0	0-0	1	3.68	3.18
2008	Hou	NL	32	32	3	0	208.2	862	199	89	82	23	8	9	10	47	2	165	1	0	17	10	.630	2	0-0	0	3.40	3.54
2009	Hou	NL	30	30	3	0	181.1	757	183	83	83	19	12	5	8	42	4	138	4	0	8	6	.571	0	0-0	0	3.67	4.12
2010	2 Tms	NL	33	32	2	0	211.2	837	162	70	65	19	10	6	5	55	2	193	2	1	13	13	.500	2	0-0	0	2.37	2.76
2011	Phi	NL	23	23	0	0	139.0	594	153	60	57	10	7	3	5	33	2	93	3	0	9	10	.474	0	0-0	0	3.93	3.69
2012	Tex	AL	17	9	0	2	59.0	264	79	41	38	11	3	0	3	11	0	59	3	2	4	3	.571	0	0-0	0	6.05	5.80

Year Team	Lg	G	GS	CG	GF	IP	BFP	H	R	ER	HR	SH	SF	HB	TBB	IBB	SO	WP	Bk	W	L	Pct	Sh	Sv-Op	Hld	ERC	ERA
		HOW MUCH HE PITCHED						**WHAT HE GAVE UP**												**THE RESULTS**							
10 Hou	NL	20	20	1	0	129.0	521	109	52	49	13	4	5	2	34	2	120	2	1	6	12	.333	1	0-0	0	2.79	3.42
10 Phi	NL	13	12	1	0	82.2	316	53	18	16	6	6	1	3	21	0	73	0	0	7	1	.875	1	0-0	0	1.76	1.74
Postseason		13	11	0	2	72.1	314	73	32	30	9	4	4	6	24	0	56	1	0	5	2	.714	0	0-0	0	4.35	3.73
12 ML YEARS		356	335	20	7	2213.0	9150	2150	866	807	194	104	54	79	511	34	1818	29	7	163	96	.629	8	0-0	1	3.32	3.28

Dan Otero

Pitches: R Bats: R Pos: RP-12 oh-TEHR-oh **Ht:** 6'3" **Wt:** 215 **Born:** 2/19/1985 **Age:** 28

Year Team	Lg	G	GS	CG	GF	IP	BFP	H	R	ER	HR	SH	SF	HB	TBB	IBB	SO	WP	Bk	W	L	Pct	Sh	Sv-Op	Hld	ERC	ERA
2007 SlmKzr	A-	22	0	0	22	22.1	80	12	3	3	1	0	1	0	0	0	15	1	0	0	0	-	0	19--	-	0.72	1.21
2008 Augsta	A	25	0	0	23	27.0	109	22	2	1	0	1	1	0	4	1	26	3	0	0	0	-	0	18--	-	1.57	0.33
2008 SnJos	A+	27	0	0	23	27.0	124	34	14	11	1	3	1	2	3	0	23	0	0	1	1	.500	0	16--	-	3.97	3.67
2009 Conn	AA	39	0	0	32	39.0	163	40	6	5	0	2	1	2	10	4	31	2	0	0	3	.000	0	19--	-	3.06	1.15
2010 Giants	R	9	0	0	1	10.2	40	7	4	0	0	0	0	0	1	0	7	2	0	2	0	1.000	0	1--	-	1.06	0.00
2010 SnJos	A+	10	0	0	4	13.1	50	11	6	6	2	0	0	1	1	0	11	0	0	3	0	1.000	0	0--	-	2.31	4.05
2011 Rchmd	AA	23	0	0	8	38.0	153	34	8	6	0	4	0	2	4	1	40	2	0	2	1	.667	0	1--	-	1.96	1.42
2011 Fresno	AAA	33	0	0	23	36.0	154	38	15	13	4	2	1	0	7	0	36	1	0	2	3	.400	0	12--	-	3.54	3.25
2012 Fresno	AAA	48	0	0	14	62.0	258	70	26	20	4	5	3	3	8	1	45	1	0	5	5	.500	0	0--	-	3.70	2.90
2012 SF	NL	12	0	0	4	12.1	57	19	11	8	0	0	0	2	2	1	8	1	0	0	0	-	0	0-0	0	6.18	5.84

Adam Ottavino

Pitches: R Bats: B Pos: RP-53 ott-tah-VEE-no **Ht:** 6'5" **Wt:** 230 **Born:** 11/22/1985 **Age:** 27

Year Team	Lg	G	GS	CG	GF	IP	BFP	H	R	ER	HR	SH	SF	HB	TBB	IBB	SO	WP	Bk	W	L	Pct	Sh	Sv-Op	Hld	ERC	ERA
2006 StCol	A-	6	6	0	0	28.2	125	23	12	10	1	1	0	1	13	0	26	0	0	2	2	.500	0	0--	-	2.78	3.14
2006 QuadC	A	8	8	0	0	36.2	157	28	21	14	3	0	1	4	19	0	38	3	0	2	3	.400	0	0--	-	3.54	3.44
2007 PlmBh	A+	27	27	1	0	143.1	620	130	63	49	10	1	5	8	63	0	128	6	0	12	8	.600	0	0--	-	3.70	3.08
2008 Sprgfld	AA	24	24	1	0	115.1	530	133	75	67	16	5	6	10	52	0	96	6	0	3	7	.300	0	0--	-	5.82	5.23
2009 Memp	AAA	27	27	0	0	144.0	642	141	80	76	12	3	7	10	82	1	119	13	1	7	12	.368	0	0--	-	4.83	4.75
2010 Memp	AAA	9	9	0	0	47.2	196	43	23	21	5	1	0	3	12	0	43	3	0	5	3	.625	0	0--	-	3.28	3.97
2011 Memp	AAA	26	25	0	0	141.0	639	154	85	76	14	12	5	9	71	0	120	8	1	7	8	.467	0	0--	-	5.31	4.85
2012 ColSpr	AAA	13	0	0	3	19.2	89	22	8	7	2	0	0	0	7	0	25	1	0	0	0	-	0	0--	-	4.42	3.20
2010 StL	NL	5	3	0	0	22.1	110	37	21	21	5	1	0	0	9	1	12	1	0	0	2	.000	0	0-0	0	9.22	8.46
2012 Col	NL	53	0	0	6	79.0	339	76	42	40	9	3	1	1	34	7	81	8	0	5	1	.833	0	0-2	6	4.01	4.56
2 ML YEARS		58	3	0	6	101.1	449	113	63	61	14	4	1	1	43	8	93	9	0	5	3	.625	0	0-2	6	5.05	5.42

Josh Outman

Pitches: L Bats: L Pos: RP-20; SP-7 AWHT-min **Ht:** 6'1" **Wt:** 200 **Born:** 9/14/1984 **Age:** 28

Year Team	Lg	G	GS	CG	GF	IP	BFP	H	R	ER	HR	SH	SF	HB	TBB	IBB	SO	WP	Bk	W	L	Pct	Sh	Sv-Op	Hld	ERC	ERA
2012 Mdest*	A+	1	1	0	0	1.0	3	0	0	0	0	0	0	0	0	0	1	0	0	0	0	-	0	0--	-	0.00	0.00
2012 ColSpr*	AAA	2	0	0	0	2.0	7	1	1	0	1	0	0	0	0	0	1	1	0	0	0	-	0	0--	-	0.54	0.00
2012 Tulsa*	AA	14	11	0	0	69.1	291	64	32	28	4	2	2	3	30	0	71	9	0	2	5	.286	0	0--	-	3.76	3.63
2008 Oak	AL	6	4	0	0	25.2	116	34	14	13	1	0	2	2	8	1	19	1	0	1	2	.333	0	0-0	0	5.49	4.56
2009 Oak	AL	14	12	0	1	67.1	276	53	30	26	9	1	0	0	25	0	53	1	0	4	1	.800	0	0-0	0	3.04	3.48
2011 Oak	AL	13	9	0	2	58.1	254	62	27	24	4	4	3	0	23	0	35	3	0	3	5	.375	0	0-0	1	4.19	3.70
2012 Col	NL	27	7	0	3	40.2	185	47	37	37	7	2	1	0	20	0	40	5	0	1	3	.250	0	0-0	3	5.92	8.19
4 ML YEARS		60	32	0	6	192.0	831	196	108	100	21	7	6	2	76	1	147	10	0	9	11	.450	0	0-0	4	4.28	4.69

Lyle Overbay

Bats: L Throws: L Pos: PH-42; 1B-23; DH-1 **Ht:** 6'2" **Wt:** 235 **Born:** 1/28/1977 **Age:** 36

Year Team	Lg	G	AB	H	2B	3B	HR	(Hm	Rd)	TB	R	RBI	RC	TBB	IBB	SO	HBP	SH	SF	SB	CS	SB%	GDP	Avg	OBP	Slg
								BATTING												**BASERUNNING**				**AVERAGES**		
2012 Gwnntt*	AAA	7	22	6	3	0	0	(-	-)	9	3	3	4	6	0	6	0	0	0	0	0	-	0	.273	.429	.409
2001 Ari	NL	2	2	1	0	0	0	(0	0)	1	0	0	0	0	0	1	0	0	0	0	0	-	0	.500	.500	.500
2002 Ari	NL	10	10	1	0	0	0	(0	0)	1	0	1	0	0	0	5	0	0	0	0	0	-	0	.100	.100	.100
2003 Ari	NL	86	254	70	20	0	4	(2	2)	102	23	28	34	35	7	67	2	0	2	1	0	1.00	6	.276	.365	.402
2004 Mil	NL	159	579	174	53	1	16	(6	10)	277	83	87	94	81	9	128	2	0	6	2	1	.67	11	.301	.385	.478
2005 Mil	NL	158	537	148	34	1	19	(10	9)	241	80	72	84	78	8	98	2	1	4	1	0	1.00	17	.276	.367	.449
2006 Tor	AL	157	581	181	46	1	22	(17	5)	295	82	92	89	55	7	96	2	0	2	5	3	.63	19	.312	.372	.508
2007 Tor	AL	122	425	102	30	2	10	(6	4)	166	49	44	45	47	4	78	1	0	3	2	0	1.00	12	.240	.315	.391
2008 Tor	AL	158	544	147	32	2	15	(7	8)	228	74	69	73	74	3	116	3	1	5	1	2	.33	24	.270	.358	.419
2009 Tor	AL	132	423	112	35	1	16	(6	10)	197	57	64	64	74	6	95	0	0	3	0	0	-	8	.265	.372	.466
2010 Tor	AL	154	534	130	37	2	20	(13	7)	231	75	67	75	67	7	131	3	0	3	1	0	1.00	9	.243	.329	.433
2011 2 Tms	NL	121	394	92	21	1	9	(4	5)	142	43	47	41	42	2	88	2	1	1	2	1	.67	13	.234	.310	.360
2012 2 Tms	NL	65	116	30	10	0	2	(2	0)	46	12	10	11	13	2	34	0	0	1	0	0	-	4	.259	.331	.397
11 Pit	NL	103	352	80	17	1	8	(3	5)	123	40	37	33	36	1	77	1	1	1	1	1	.50	12	.227	.300	.349
11 Ari	NL	18	42	12	4	0	1	(1	0)	19	3	10	8	6	1	11	1	0	0	1	0	1.00	1	.286	.388	.452
12 Ari	NL	45	96	28	9	0	2	(2	0)	43	11	10	11	12	2	26	0	0	1	0	0	-	3	.292	.367	.448
12 Atl	NL	20	20	2	1	0	0	(0	0)	3	1	0	0	1	0	8	0	0	0	0	0	-	1	.100	.143	.150
Postseason		2	4	0	0	0	0	(0	0)	0	0	0	0	0	0	2	0	0	0	0	0	-	0	.000	.000	.000
12 ML YEARS		1324	4399	1188	318	11	133	(73	60)	1927	578	581	610	566	55	937	17	3	30	15	7	.68	125	.270	.353	.438

Juan Carlos Oviedo

Pitches: R Bats: R Pos: P Ht: 6'2" Wt: 190 Born: 8/14/1983 Age: 29

				HOW MUCH HE PITCHED				WHAT HE GAVE UP											THE RESULTS					
Year	Team	Lg	G	GS	CG	GF	IP	BFP	H	R	ER	HR	SH	SF	HB	TBB	IBB	SO	WP	Bk	W	L	Pct	Sh	Sv-Op Hld	ERC	ERA
2012	Jupiter*	A+	2	2	0	0	2.2	11	1	1	1	0	0	0	0	1	0	2	0	0	0	1	.000	0	0- -	0.77	3.38
2012	NewOr*	AAA	1	0	0	0	0.1	3	1	0	0	0	0	0	0	0	0	0	0	0	0	0	-	0	0- -	29.63	0.00
2005	KC	AL	41	0	0	10	53.2	246	73	45	45	9	1	2	3	18	2	32	1	0	3	2	.600	0	0-1 2	6.76	7.55
2006	KC	AL	7	0	0	5	13.1	58	15	7	7	2	0	1	2	5	0	7	0	0	0	0	-	0	0-0 0	5.98	4.73
2007	KC	AL	13	6	0	2	43.2	182	44	21	19	8	0	2	0	10	0	37	1	0	2	4	.333	0	0-0 1	3.98	3.92
2008	KC	AL	45	0	0	12	48.1	205	45	19	16	2	3	2	4	15	2	26	3	0	4	1	.800	0	0-3 7	3.20	2.98
2009	Fla	NL	75	0	0	41	68.2	293	59	33	31	13	4	2	6	27	5	60	1	1	4	6	.400	0	26-33 14	3.96	4.06
2010	Fla	NL	68	0	0	50	65.0	270	62	27	25	5	1	0	0	21	2	71	1	1	4	3	.571	0	30-38 5	3.36	3.46
2011	Fla	NL	68	0	0	51	64.1	268	57	30	29	8	1	2	1	21	2	55	1	0	1	4	.200	0	36-42 0	3.33	4.06
	7 ML YEARS		317	6	0	171	357.0	1522	355	182	172	47	10	11	14	117	13	288	8	2	18	20	.474	0	92-117 29	4.09	4.34

Micah Owings

Pitches: R Bats: R Pos: RP-6 MY-kuh Ht: 6'5" Wt: 220 Born: 9/28/1982 Age: 30

				HOW MUCH HE PITCHED				WHAT HE GAVE UP											THE RESULTS					
Year	Team	Lg	G	GS	CG	GF	IP	BFP	H	R	ER	HR	SH	SF	HB	TBB	IBB	SO	WP	Bk	W	L	Pct	Sh	Sv-Op Hld	ERC	ERA
2007	Ari	NL	29	27	2	0	152.2	651	146	81	73	20	7	3	14	50	2	106	5	0	8	8	.500	1	0-0 0	4.13	4.30
2008	2 Tms		22	18	0	2	104.2	466	104	73	69	14	2	4	12	41	0	87	4	0	6	9	.400	0	0-0 1	4.66	5.93
2009	Cin	NL	26	19	0	4	119.2	542	126	75	71	18	3	5	6	64	3	68	1	0	7	12	.368	0	1-1 0	5.48	5.34
2010	Cin	NL	22	0	0	9	33.1	153	28	20	20	3	2	1	3	25	0	35	1	1	3	2	.600	0	0-0 0	4.80	5.40
2011	Ari	NL	33	4	0	2	63.0	263	56	27	25	8	4	1	2	23	0	44	3	0	8	0	1.000	0	0-0 3	3.67	3.57
2012	SD	NL	6	0	0	3	9.2	41	8	4	3	1	0	0	1	5	0	7	0	0	2	0	.000	0	0-0 0	4.13	2.79
	Postseason		3	1	0	0	6.2	32	8	6	2	1	0	0	1	2	0	3	0	0	1	1	.500	0	0-0 0	5.50	2.70
	6 ML YEARS		138	68	2	20	483.0	2116	468	280	261	64	18	14	38	208	5	347	14	1	32	33	.492	1	1-1 4	4.56	4.86

Jordan Pacheco

Bats: R Throws: R Pos: 3B-82; 1B-43; PH-8; C-5; PR-1 puh-CHECK-oh Ht: 6'1" Wt: 200 Born: 1/30/1986 Age: 27

						BATTING													BASERUNNING				AVERAGES		
Year	Team	Lg	G	AB	H	2B	3B	HR	(Hm | Rd)	TB	R	RBI	RC	TBB	IBB	SO	HBP	SH	SF	SB	CS	SB%	GDP	Avg	OBP	Slg
2007	Casper	R+	55	192	56	10	2	3	(- | -)	79	27	29	32	21	0	36	7	3	1	3	1	.75	5	.292	.380	.411
2007	TriCity	A-	8	31	8	2	0	0	(- | -)	10	5	3	3	1	0	6	2	0	0	0	0	-	0	.258	.324	.323
2008	TriCity	A-	54	214	60	8	3	1	(- | -)	77	25	35	33	26	1	20	6	1	4	3	3	.50	8	.280	.368	.360
2009	Ashvll	A-	117	451	145	30	4	13	(- | -)	222	67	79	87	38	2	44	8	3	7	12	2	.86	7	.322	.379	.492
2010	Mdest	A+	104	390	125	27	3	5	(- | -)	173	59	70	75	54	2	36	8	1	7	5	6	.45	10	.321	.407	.444
2010	Tulsa	AA	21	78	26	5	0	1	(- | -)	34	11	19	14	6	0	6	4	0	3	1	1	.50	3	.333	.396	.436
2011	ColSpr	AAA	97	363	101	21	3	3	(- | -)	137	57	50	50	30	0	48	9	3	6	2	2	.50	15	.278	.343	.377
2012	ColSpr	AAA	17	67	29	4	0	3	(- | -)	42	10	10	18	3	0	5	3	1	0	1	0	1.00	1	.433	.479	.627
2011	Col	NL	21	84	24	1	0	2	(2 | 0)	31	5	14	12	3	0	9	1	0	0	0	0	-	2	.286	.318	.369
2012	Col	NL	132	475	147	32	3	5	(4 | 1)	200	51	54	64	22	2	61	3	1	4	7	2	.78	13	.309	.341	.421
	2 ML YEARS		153	559	171	33	3	7	(6 | 1)	231	56	68	76	25	2	70	4	1	4	7	2	.78	15	.306	.338	.413

Vicente Padilla

Pitches: R Bats: R Pos: RP-56 pah-DEE-ah Ht: 6'0" Wt: 230 Born: 9/27/1977 Age: 35

				HOW MUCH HE PITCHED				WHAT HE GAVE UP											THE RESULTS					
Year	Team	Lg	G	GS	CG	GF	IP	BFP	H	R	ER	HR	SH	SF	HB	TBB	IBB	SO	WP	Bk	W	L	Pct	Sh	Sv-Op Hld	ERC	ERA
1999	Ari	NL	5	0	0	2	2.2	19	7	5	5	1	1	0	0	3	0	0	0	0	0	1	.000	0	0-1 1	20.65	16.88
2000	2 Tms	NL	55	0	0	16	65.1	291	72	33	27	3	5	3	1	28	7	51	1	0	4	7	.364	0	2-7 15	4.22	3.72
2001	Phi	NL	23	0	0	5	34.0	144	36	18	16	1	0	0	0	12	0	29	1	0	3	1	.750	0	0-3 1	3.80	4.24
2002	Phi	NL	32	32	1	0	206.0	862	198	83	75	16	10	3	15	53	5	128	6	2	14	11	.560	1	0-0 0	3.42	3.28
2003	Phi	NL	32	32	1	0	208.2	876	196	94	84	22	11	7	16	62	4	133	3	2	14	12	.538	1	0-0 0	3.68	3.62
2004	Phi	NL	20	20	0	0	115.1	503	119	63	58	16	7	5	10	36	6	82	2	0	7	7	.500	0	0-0 0	4.42	4.53
2005	Phi	NL	27	27	0	0	147.0	654	146	79	77	22	7	3	8	74	9	103	1	0	9	12	.429	0	0-0 0	4.94	4.71
2006	Tex	AL	33	33	0	0	200.0	872	206	108	100	21	6	6	17	70	2	156	4	2	15	10	.600	0	0-0 0	4.41	4.50
2007	Tex	AL	23	23	0	0	120.1	553	146	88	77	16	3	2	9	50	1	71	2	0	6	10	.375	0	0-0 0	5.95	5.76
2008	Tex	AL	29	29	1	0	171.0	757	185	100	90	26	1	3	15	65	4	127	12	3	14	8	.636	1	0-0 0	5.20	4.74
2009	2 Tms		26	25	0	0	147.1	634	156	76	73	16	6	3	8	54	0	97	5	2	12	6	.667	0	0-0 0	4.65	4.46
2010	LAD	NL	16	16	1	0	95.0	389	79	46	43	14	5	3	7	24	4	84	0	1	6	5	.545	1	0-0 0	3.13	4.07
2011	LAD	NL	9	0	0	4	8.2	36	7	4	4	0	0	0	2	5	0	9	0	0	0	0	-	0	3-3 5	3.12	4.15
2012	Bos	AL	56	0	0	10	50.0	218	59	26	25	7	1	1	3	15	3	51	0	1	4	1	.800	0	1-5 23	5.25	4.50
	00 Ari	NL	27	0	0	12	35.0	143	32	10	9	0	1	0	1	10	2	30	0	0	2	1	.667	0	0-1 7	2.48	2.31
	00 Phi	NL	28	0	0	4	30.1	148	40	23	18	3	5	2	1	18	5	21	1	0	2	6	.250	0	2-6 8	6.52	5.34
	09 Tex	AL	18	18	0	0	108.0	475	120	61	59	12	3	2	8	42	0	59	4	2	8	6	.571	0	0-0 0	5.15	4.92
	09 LAD	NL	8	7	0	0	39.1	159	36	15	14	4	3	1	0	12	0	38	1	0	4	0	1.000	0	0-0 0	3.36	3.20
	Postseason		3	3	0	0	17.1	67	12	7	7	3	0	0	0	4	0	13	0	0	1	1	.500	0	0-0 0	2.29	3.63
	14 ML YEARS		386	237	4	37	1571.1	6808	1612	823	754	181	63	39	109	551	45	1121	37	12	108	91	.543	4	6-19 45	4.39	4.32

Angel Pagan

Bats: B Throws: R Pos: CF-151; PH-2; DH-1; PR-1 ANE-gell pah-GONN Ht: 6'2" Wt: 200 Born: 7/2/1981 Age: 31

						BATTING													BASERUNNING				AVERAGES		
Year	Team	Lg	G	AB	H	2B	3B	HR	(Hm | Rd)	TB	R	RBI	RC	TBB	IBB	SO	HBP	SH	SF	SB	CS	SB%	GDP	Avg	OBP	Slg
2006	ChC	NL	77	170	42	6	2	5	(4 | 1)	67	28	18	21	15	0	28	0	1	1	4	2	.67	3	.247	.306	.394
2007	ChC	NL	71	148	39	10	2	4	(3 | 1)	65	21	21	23	10	0	32	0	1	2	4	1	.80	0	.264	.306	.439
2008	NYM	NL	31	91	25	7	1	0	(0 | 0)	34	12	13	15	11	0	18	0	1	2	4	0	1.00	0	.275	.346	.374
2009	NYM	NL	88	343	105	22	11	6	(5 | 1)	167	54	32	53	26	2	56	0	5	3	14	7	.67	3	.306	.350	.487

								BATTING																BASERUNNING				AVERAGES		
Year	Team	Lg	G	AB	H	2B	3B	HR	(Hm	Rd)	TB	R	RBI	RC	TBB	IBB	SO	HBP	SH	SF					SB	CS	SB%	GDP	Avg	OBP	Slg
2010	NYM	NL	151	579	168	31	7	11	(6	5)	246	80	69	90	44	5	97	1	6	3					37	9	.80	9	.290	.340	.425
2011	NYM	NL	123	478	125	24	4	7	(4	3)	178	68	56	64	44	4	62	1	4	5					32	7	.82	4	.262	.322	.372
2012	SF	NL	154	605	174	38	15	8	(1	7)	266	95	56	91	48	5	97	0	2	4					29	7	.81	6	.288	.338	.440
7 ML YEARS			695	2414	678	138	42	41	(23	18)	1023	358	265	357	197	16	390	2	20	20					124	33	.79	25	.281	.333	.424

Matt Palmer

Pitches: R Bats: R Pos: RP-3   Ht: 6'2" Wt: 235 Born: 3/21/1979 Age: 34

				HOW MUCH HE PITCHED			WHAT HE GAVE UP										THE RESULTS								
Year	Team	Lg	G	GS	CG	GF	IP	BFP	H	R	ER	HR	SH	SF	HB	TBB	IBB	SO	WP	Bk	W	L	Pct	Sh	Sv-Op	Hld	ERC	ERA
2012	Tucsn*	AAA	21	20	0	0	98.2	455	120	69	62	3	6	5	8	42	0	64	9	0	6	9	.400	0	0- -	-	5.21	5.66
2008	SF	NL	3	3	0	0	12.2	67	17	13	12	1	1	0	2	13	1	3	0	0	0	2	.000	0	0-0	0	9.37	8.53
2009	LAA	AL	40	13	1	10	121.1	505	105	55	53	12	6	3	4	55	2	69	5	0	11	2	.846	0	0-0	0	3.74	3.93
2010	LAA	AL	14	1	0	3	33.2	157	38	20	17	1	1	0	1	20	1	17	2	0	1	2	.333	0	0-0	1	5.07	4.54
2011	LAA	AL	3	3	0	0	15.2	69	19	11	10	0	0	2	1	4	0	7	0	0	1	1	.500	0	0-0	0	4.24	5.74
2012	SD	NL	3	0	0	1	2.0	10	2	2	2	1	1	0	2	2	0	2	0	0	0	0	-	0	0-0	0	9.87	9.00
Postseason			2	0	0	2	2.2	14	5	4	4	1	0	0	0	1	0	2	0	0	0	0	-	0	0-0	0	11.86	13.50
5 ML YEARS			63	20	1	14	185.1	808	181	101	94	15	9	5	8	94	4	98	7	0	13	7	.650	0	0-0	1	4.44	4.56

Jonathan Papelbon

Pitches: R Bats: R Pos: RP-70   PAHP-ill-bonn   Ht: 6'4" Wt: 225 Born: 11/23/1980 Age: 32

				HOW MUCH HE PITCHED			WHAT HE GAVE UP										THE RESULTS								
Year	Team	Lg	G	GS	CG	GF	IP	BFP	H	R	ER	HR	SH	SF	HB	TBB	IBB	SO	WP	Bk	W	L	Pct	Sh	Sv-Op	Hld	ERC	ERA
2005	Bos	AL	17	3	0	4	34.0	148	33	11	10	4	1	0	3	17	2	34	1	0	3	1	.750	0	0-1	4	4.82	2.65
2006	Bos	AL	59	0	0	49	68.1	257	40	8	7	3	1	2	1	13	2	75	2	0	4	2	.667	0	35-41	1	1.22	0.92
2007	Bos	AL	59	0	0	53	58.1	224	30	12	12	5	0	0	4	15	0	84	0	0	1	3	.250	0	37-40	2	1.43	1.85
2008	Bos	AL	67	0	0	62	69.1	273	58	24	18	4	4	1	0	8	0	77	2	0	5	4	.556	0	41-46	0	1.92	2.34
2009	Bos	AL	66	0	0	59	68.0	285	54	15	14	5	1	2	4	24	1	76	0	0	1	1	.500	0	38-41	0	2.78	1.85
2010	Bos	AL	65	0	0	53	67.0	287	57	34	29	7	5	0	2	28	4	76	4	0	5	7	.417	0	37-45	0	3.32	3.90
2011	Bos	AL	63	0	0	54	64.1	255	50	22	21	3	0	1	3	10	1	87	1	0	4	1	.800	0	31-34	0	1.86	2.94
2012	Phi	NL	70	0	0	64	70.0	284	56	22	19	8	3	0	4	18	1	92	0	0	5	6	.455	0	38-42	0	2.75	2.44
Postseason			18	0	0	12	27.0	100	14	3	3	0	0	1	0	8	3	23	0	0	2	1	.667	0	7-9	0	1.01	1.00
8 ML YEARS			466	3	0	398	499.1	2013	378	148	130	39	15	6	21	133	11	601	10	0	28	25	.528	0	257-290	7	2.29	2.34

Jimmy Paredes

Bats: B Throws: R Pos: RF-15; 2B-5; PH-5; LF-1   pah-REY-dez   Ht: 6'3" Wt: 200 Born: 11/25/1988 Age: 24

								BATTING																BASERUNNING				AVERAGES		
Year	Team	Lg	G	AB	H	2B	3B	HR	(Hm	Rd)	TB	R	RBI	RC	TBB	IBB	SO	HBP	SH	SF					SB	CS	SB%	GDP	Avg	OBP	Slg
2008	Yanks	R	47	161	45	9	2	1	(-	-)	61	23	15	22	8	1	20	4	1	1					6	0	1.00	4	.280	.328	.379
2009	StIsInd	A-	54	205	62	8	4	2	(-	-)	84	36	17	30	10	1	30	2	1	3					23	9	.72	5	.302	.336	.410
2010	CtnSC	A	99	404	114	24	6	5	(-	-)	165	59	48	54	18	1	82	2	5	5					36	10	.78	3	.282	.312	.408
2010	Lxngtn	A	34	147	44	10	1	3	(-	-)	65	24	17	23	7	0	25	0	0	0					14	1	.93	1	.299	.331	.442
2011	CpChr	AA	93	385	104	22	4	10	(-	-)	164	69	41	50	15	0	84	2	4	1					29	12	.71	8	.270	.300	.426
2012	OKCity	AAA	124	507	161	28	7	13	(-	-)	242	92	59	86	22	1	101	3	2	2					37	10	.79	10	.318	.348	.477
2011	Hou	NL	46	168	48	8	2	2	(0	2)	66	16	18	23	9	0	47	0	1	1					5	4	.56	3	.286	.320	.393
2012	Hou	NL	24	74	14	1	1	0	(0	0)	17	7	3	3	6	0	21	0	0	2					2	1	.67	0	.189	.244	.230
2 ML YEARS			70	242	62	9	3	2	(0	2)	83	23	21	26	15	0	68	0	1	3					7	5	.58	3	.256	.296	.343

Blake Parker

Pitches: R Bats: R Pos: RP-7   Ht: 6'3" Wt: 225 Born: 6/19/1985 Age: 28

				HOW MUCH HE PITCHED			WHAT HE GAVE UP										THE RESULTS								
Year	Team	Lg	G	GS	CG	GF	IP	BFP	H	R	ER	HR	SH	SF	HB	TBB	IBB	SO	WP	Bk	W	L	Pct	Sh	Sv-Op	Hld	ERC	ERA
2007	Cubs	R	11	0	0	6	15.0	60	10	6	3	0	0	0	1	3	0	14	3	0	1	0	1.000	0	2- -	-	1.41	1.80
2007	Boise	A-	8	0	0	1	11.1	59	15	5	4	0	0	0	5	7	0	10	2	0	1	0	1.000	0	0- -	-	7.97	3.18
2008	Peoria	A	23	0	0	6	47.1	187	32	8	7	2	2	0	1	18	0	51	3	1	3	0	1.000	0	3- -	-	2.10	1.33
2008	Iowa	AAA	2	0	0	1	3.0	13	1	2	2	1	0	0	0	2	0	3	0	0	0	0	-	0	0- -	-	2.68	6.00
2008	Dytona	A+	20	0	0	15	21.1	89	17	8	8	0	1	0	1	10	1	21	0	0	1	2	.333	0	9- -	-	2.70	3.38
2009	Tenn	AA	10	0	0	8	12.1	50	8	2	2	0	1	0	0	8	0	19	1	0	0	0	-	0	3- -	-	2.57	1.46
2009	Iowa	AAA	45	0	0	38	51.0	218	36	20	17	3	4	0	3	27	1	58	3	1	2	3	.400	0	22- -	-	2.85	3.00
2010	Iowa	AAA	35	0	0	21	49.1	218	52	30	26	9	1	2	1	28	1	42	1	0	1	4	.200	0	2- -	-	5.93	4.74
2010	Tenn	AA	13	0	0	10	17.0	66	11	5	5	0	0	0	0	6	1	25	0	0	1	0	1.000	0	5- -	-	1.54	2.65
2011	Tenn	AA	16	0	0	12	24.0	105	20	14	11	1	1	2	1	13	2	20	1	0	1	2	.333	0	3- -	-	3.27	4.13
2011	Iowa	AAA	37	0	0	17	51.1	214	37	16	16	5	1	0	2	27	0	60	2	0	3	3	.500	0	4- -	-	3.21	2.81
2012	Iowa	AAA	21	0	0	15	23.2	92	16	9	9	3	0	2	0	6	0	22	0	0	1	1	.500	0	6- -	-	2.04	3.42
2012	ChC	NL	7	0	0	0	6.0	32	10	7	4	3	0	0	0	5	1	6	0	0	0	0	-	0	0-0	0	14.02	6.00

Jarrod Parker

Pitches: R Bats: R Pos: SP-29   Ht: 6'1" Wt: 195 Born: 11/24/1988 Age: 24

				HOW MUCH HE PITCHED			WHAT HE GAVE UP										THE RESULTS								
Year	Team	Lg	G	GS	CG	GF	IP	BFP	H	R	ER	HR	SH	SF	HB	TBB	IBB	SO	WP	Bk	W	L	Pct	Sh	Sv-Op	Hld	ERC	ERA
2008	Sbend	A	24	24	0	0	117.2	502	113	56	45	8	4	8	7	33	0	117	8	0	12	5	.706	0	0- -	-	3.36	3.44
2009	Visalia	A+	4	4	0	0	19.0	72	12	2	2	0	1	0	0	4	0	21	4	0	1	0	1.000	0	0- -	-	1.24	0.95
2009	Mobile	AA	16	16	0	0	78.1	345	82	35	33	2	1	1	7	34	0	74	9	0	4	6	.400	0	0- -	-	4.33	3.79
2011	Mobile	AA	26	26	0	0	130.2	550	112	61	55	7	5	5	11	55	0	112	8	3	11	8	.579	0	0- -	-	3.43	3.79
2012	Scrmto	AAA	4	4	0	0	20.2	87	22	6	5	2	1	0	0	6	0	21	0	0	1	0	1.000	0	0- -	-	4.04	2.18

	HOW MUCH HE PITCHED						WHAT HE GAVE UP										THE RESULTS							
Year Team Lg	G	GS	CG	GF	IP	BFP	H	R	ER	HR	SH	SF	HB	TBB	IBB	SO	WP	Bk	W	L	Pct	Sh	Sv-Op	Hld	ERC	ERA
2011 Ari NL	1	1	0	0	5.2	22	4	0	0	0	2	0	0	1	0	1	0	0	0	0	-	0	0-0	0	1.36	0.00
2012 Oak AL	29	29	0	0	181.1	751	166	71	70	11	7	8	3	63	3	140	10	0	13	8	.619	0	0-0	0	3.24	3.47
Postseason	1	0	0	0	0.1	4	2	1	1	0	1	0	0	1	0	0	0	0	0	0	-	0	0-0	0	56.02	27.00
2 ML YEARS	30	30	0	0	187.0	773	170	71	70	11	9	8	3	64	3	141	10	0	13	8	.619	0	0-0	0	3.17	3.37

Chris Parmelee

Bats: L **Throws:** L **Pos:** 1B-38; RF-18; PH-12; LF-1; DH-1   PAR-muh-lee   **Ht:** 6'1" **Wt:** 228 **Born:** 2/24/1988 **Age:** 25

	BATTING																		BASERUNNING				AVERAGES		
Year Team Lg	G	AB	H	2B	3B	HR	(Hm	Rd)	TB	R	RBI	RC	TBB	IBB	SO	HBP	SH	SF	SB	CS	SB%	GDP	Avg	OBP	Slg
2006 Twins R	45	154	43	7	4	8	(-	-)	82	29	32	30	23	1	47	0	0	2	3	3	.50	5	.279	.369	.532
2006 Beloit A	11	22	5	1	0	0	(-	-)	6	2	2	2	5	0	9	0	0	0	0	2	.00	0	.227	.370	.273
2007 Beloit A	128	447	107	23	5	15	(-	-)	185	56	70	60	46	1	137	4	0	4	8	4	.67	8	.239	.313	.414
2008 Beloit A	69	226	54	10	3	14	(-	-)	112	41	49	47	52	1	83	5	1	5	3	1	.75	2	.239	.385	.496
2009 FtMyrs A+	123	422	109	27	1	16	(-	-)	186	61	73	71	65	5	109	6	0	8	2	2	.50	4	.258	.359	.441
2010 NwBrit AA	111	411	113	25	2	6	(-	-)	160	51	44	58	43	2	70	2	0	7	3	2	.60	12	.275	.341	.389
2010 FtMyrs A+	22	80	27	2	1	2	(-	-)	37	9	17	16	13	0	11	0	0	1	0	1	.00	2	.338	.430	.463
2011 NwBrit AA	142	530	152	30	5	13	(-	-)	231	76	83	89	68	4	94	3	0	9	0	1	.00	6	.287	.366	.436
2012 Roch AAA	64	228	77	17	1	17	(-	-)	147	45	49	65	51	7	52	1	0	2	1	1	.50	2	.338	.457	.645
2011 Min AL	21	76	27	6	0	4	(2	2)	45	8	14	19	12	0	13	0	0	0	0	0	-	3	.355	.443	.592
2012 Min AL	64	192	44	10	2	5	(1	4)	73	18	20	18	13	1	52	4	0	1	0	0	-	4	.229	.290	.380
2 ML YEARS	85	268	71	16	2	9	(3	6)	118	26	34	37	25	1	65	4	0	1	0	0	-	7	.265	.336	.440

Bobby Parnell

Pitches: R **Bats:** R **Pos:** RP-74   **Ht:** 6'4" **Wt:** 200 **Born:** 9/8/1984 **Age:** 28

	HOW MUCH HE PITCHED						WHAT HE GAVE UP												THE RESULTS							
Year Team Lg	G	GS	CG	GF	IP	BFP	H	R	ER	HR	SH	SF	HB	TBB	IBB	SO	WP	Bk	W	L	Pct	Sh	Sv-Op	Hld	ERC	ERA
2008 NYM NL	6	0	0	3	5.0	19	3	3	3	0	0	0	0	2	0	3	1	0	0	0	-	0	0-0	0	1.59	5.40
2009 NYM NL	68	8	0	14	88.1	413	101	56	52	8	3	1	4	46	2	74	6	1	4	8	.333	0	1-5	16	5.37	5.30
2010 NYM NL	41	0	0	10	35.0	149	41	13	11	1	2	0	0	8	2	33	0	0	0	1	.000	0	0-2	9	3.80	2.83
2011 NYM NL	60	0	0	23	59.1	268	60	29	24	4	6	0	2	27	4	64	8	1	4	6	.400	0	6-12	11	4.01	3.64
2012 NYM NL	74	0	0	23	68.2	288	65	24	19	4	4	2	1	20	2	61	1	0	5	4	.556	0	7-12	18	3.08	2.49
5 ML YEARS	249	8	0	73	256.1	1137	270	125	109	17	15	3	7	103	10	235	16	2	13	19	.406	0	14-31	54	4.12	3.83

Gerardo Parra

Bats: L **Throws:** L **Pos:** CF-48; LF-47; PH-28; RF-17; PR-2   jer-AHR-doh PAH-ruh   **Ht:** 5'11" **Wt:** 200 **Born:** 5/6/1987 **Age:** 26

	BATTING																		BASERUNNING				AVERAGES		
Year Team Lg	G	AB	H	2B	3B	HR	(Hm	Rd)	TB	R	RBI	RC	TBB	IBB	SO	HBP	SH	SF	SB	CS	SB%	GDP	Avg	OBP	Slg
2009 Ari NL	120	455	132	21	8	5	(4	1)	184	59	60	58	25	1	89	1	4	6	5	7	.42	18	.290	.324	.404
2010 Ari NL	133	364	95	19	6	3	(1	2)	135	31	30	38	23	10	76	2	3	1	1	0	1.00	8	.261	.308	.371
2011 Ari NL	141	445	130	20	8	8	(3	5)	190	55	46	71	43	16	82	3	0	2	15	1	.94	8	.292	.357	.427
2012 Ari NL	133	385	105	21	2	7	(5	2)	151	58	36	50	33	4	77	4	6	2	15	9	.63	4	.273	.335	.392
Postseason	5	18	1	1	0	0	(0	0)	2	1	0	0	1	0	7	0	0	0	0	0	-	0	.056	.105	.111
4 ML YEARS	527	1649	462	81	24	23	(13	10)	660	203	172	217	124	31	324	10	13	11	36	17	.68	38	.280	.332	.400

Manny Parra

Pitches: L **Bats:** L **Pos:** RP-62   **Ht:** 6'3" **Wt:** 203 **Born:** 10/30/1982 **Age:** 30

	HOW MUCH HE PITCHED						WHAT HE GAVE UP												THE RESULTS							
Year Team Lg	G	GS	CG	GF	IP	BFP	H	R	ER	HR	SH	SF	HB	TBB	IBB	SO	WP	Bk	W	L	Pct	Sh	Sv-Op	Hld	ERC	ERA
2007 Mil NL	9	2	0	3	26.1	116	25	13	11	1	1	3	2	12	0	26	1	0	0	1	.000	0	0-0	1	3.83	3.76
2008 Mil NL	32	29	0	0	166.0	741	181	91	81	18	10	2	2	75	1	147	17	2	10	8	.556	0	0-0	0	4.89	4.39
2009 Mil NL	27	27	0	0	140.0	671	179	108	99	19	5	3	1	77	5	116	4	1	11	11	.500	0	0-0	0	6.51	6.36
2010 Mil NL	42	16	0	9	122.0	560	135	76	68	18	6	7	3	65	3	129	14	1	3	10	.231	0	0-0	0	5.53	5.02
2012 Mil NL	62	0	0	8	58.2	273	62	39	33	3	0	1	3	35	2	61	6	0	2	3	.400	0	0-2	9	4.88	5.06
Postseason	2	0	0	0	2.1	9	2	0	0	0	0	0	0	1	0	3	0	0	0	0	-	0	0-0	0	3.03	0.00
5 ML YEARS	172	74	0	20	513.0	2361	582	327	292	59	22	16	11	262	11	479	42	4	26	33	.441	0	0-2	10	5.42	5.12

Andy Parrino

Bats: B **Throws:** R **Pos:** SS-26; 2B-15; PH-14; 3B-2; PR-2; RF-1   **Ht:** 6'0" **Wt:** 180 **Born:** 10/31/1985 **Age:** 27

	BATTING																		BASERUNNING				AVERAGES		
Year Team Lg	G	AB	H	2B	3B	HR	(Hm	Rd)	TB	R	RBI	RC	TBB	IBB	SO	HBP	SH	SF	SB	CS	SB%	GDP	Avg	OBP	Slg
2007 Eugene A-	69	251	68	20	1	3	(-	-)	99	32	38	38	30	0	73	7	1	0	2	2	.50	7	.271	.365	.394
2008 FtWyn A	120	405	102	20	0	7	(-	-)	143	67	43	59	71	0	127	4	4	3	8	5	.62	7	.252	.366	.353
2009 Lk Els A+	95	311	73	16	1	2	(-	-)	97	52	29	39	51	1	85	4	1	4	8	2	.80	3	.235	.346	.312
2009 FtWyn A	5	18	9	2	0	0	(-	-)	11	3	3	5	3	0	3	0	0	0	0	0	-	0	.500	.571	.611
2010 SnAnt AA	125	410	101	28	4	11	(-	-)	170	70	49	67	68	8	115	8	4	2	4	2	.67	9	.246	.363	.415
2011 Tucsn AAA	48	153	50	13	1	3	(-	-)	74	26	24	30	16	0	25	5	0	4	2	1	.67	2	.327	.399	.484
2011 SnAnt AA	40	152	46	7	1	9	(-	-)	82	28	32	32	22	1	40	1	1	3	3	1	.75	1	.303	.388	.539
2012 Tucsn AAA	65	235	77	23	3	1	(-	-)	109	43	32	44	25	1	49	4	0	1	5	2	.71	3	.328	.400	.464
2011 SD NL	24	44	8	1	0	0	(0	0)	9	3	4	4	9	1	17	1	0	1	1	0	1.00	1	.182	.327	.205
2012 SD NL	55	116	24	5	0	1	(1	0)	32	9	6	9	17	7	35	2	2	1	1	0	1.00	2	.207	.316	.276
2 ML YEARS	79	160	32	6	0	1	(1	0)	41	12	10	13	26	8	52	3	2	2	2	0	1.00	3	.200	.319	.256

Tyler Pastornicky

Bats: R **Throws:** R **Pos:** SS-47; PH-28; PR-4; 2B-3   pas-tor-NICK-ee   **Ht:** 5'11" **Wt:** 190 **Born:** 12/13/1989 **Age:** 23

Year	Team	Lg	G	AB	H	2B	3B	HR	(Hm	Rd)	TB	R	RBI	RC	TBB	IBB	SO	HBP	SH	SF	SB	CS	SB%	GDP	Avg	OBP	Slg
2008	B Jays	R	50	160	42	6	3	1	(-	-)	57	32	17	25	21	0	21	2	0	3	27	5	.84	1	.263	.349	.356
2009	Lnsng	A	109	413	111	11	9	1	(-	-)	143	63	31	55	39	0	50	3	3	1	51	15	.77	10	.269	.336	.346
2009	Dnedin	A+	15	63	17	3	0	0	(-	-)	20	9	3	6	3	0	7	0	0	0	6	3	.67	1	.270	.303	.317
2010	Dnedin	A+	77	287	74	16	0	6	(-	-)	108	50	35	42	39	2	49	1	3	1	24	7	.77	5	.258	.348	.376
2010	Missi	AA	38	134	34	5	2	2	(-	-)	49	22	15	19	16	0	22	1	7	2	11	2	.85	4	.254	.333	.366
2011	Missi	AA	90	355	106	13	5	6	(-	-)	147	50	36	53	24	1	34	2	12	2	20	8	.71	4	.299	.345	.414
2011	Gwnntt	AAA	27	104	38	2	0	1	(-	-)	43	15	9	18	8	0	11	0	4	1	7	3	.70	3	.365	.407	.413
2012	Gwnntt	AAA	38	153	41	15	1	1	(-	-)	61	15	20	19	11	0	21	1	0	2	3	3	.50	1	.268	.317	.399
2012	Atl	NL	76	169	41	6	1	2	(1	1)	55	21	13	15	10	1	32	1	7	1	2	0	1.00	5	.243	.287	.325

Joe Paterson

Pitches: L **Bats:** R **Pos:** RP-6   **Ht:** 6'1" **Wt:** 210 **Born:** 5/19/1986 **Age:** 27

Year	Team	Lg	G	GS	CG	GF	IP	BFP	H	R	ER	HR	SH	SF	HB	TBB	IBB	SO	WP	Bk	W	L	Pct	Sh	Sv-Op	Hld	ERC	ERA
2007	Giants	R	4	0	0	2	5.0	16	1	1	0	0	0	0	0	0	0	8	0	0	1	0	1.000	0	0- -	-	0.09	0.00
2007	SlmKzr	A+	9	0	0	3	9.2	47	15	6	6	0	1	0	1	2	0	13	1	0	1	0	1.000	0	0- -	-	6.01	5.59
2008	Augsta	A	20	0	0	8	31.1	130	23	11	8	2	1	1	2	13	0	37	0	0	5	1	.833	0	1- -	-	2.71	2.30
2008	SnJos	A+	34	0	0	11	37.2	158	28	22	13	1	2	0	1	15	6	41	0	1	3	2	.600	0	7- -	-	2.06	3.11
2009	Conn	AA	55	0	0	26	69.0	274	47	18	15	3	5	3	3	24	3	69	1	3	5	6	.455	0	10- -	-	2.02	1.96
2010	Fresno	AAA	46	0	0	10	54.1	242	55	28	21	2	3	2	3	24	2	49	3	1	4	3	.571	0	2- -	-	3.95	3.48
2010	SnJos	A+	7	0	0	4	11.0	44	9	2	1	0	0	1	0	2	1	15	1	0	1	0	1.000	0	1- -	-	1.63	0.82
2012	Reno	AAA	48	0	0	16	43.1	189	41	20	20	7	4	0	4	16	2	40	0	0	2	2	.500	0	2- -	-	4.33	4.15
2011	Ari	NL	62	0	0	17	34.0	150	28	11	11	1	4	2	4	15	0	28	1	0	0	3	.000	0	1-1	10	3.12	2.91
2012	Ari	NL	6	0	0	0	2.2	26	15	11	11	2	0	0	0	3	0	0	0	0	0	0	-	0	0-0	1	53.93	37.13
	Postseason		1	0	0	0	0.1	1	0	0	0	0	0	0	0	0	0	1	0	0	0	0	-	0	0-0	0	0.00	0.00
	2 ML YEARS		68	0	0	17	36.2	176	43	22	22	3	4	2	4	18	0	28	1	0	0	3	.000	0	1-1	11	5.58	5.40

Troy Patton

Pitches: L **Bats:** B **Pos:** RP-54   **Ht:** 6'1" **Wt:** 179 **Born:** 9/3/1985 **Age:** 27

Year	Team	Lg	G	GS	CG	GF	IP	BFP	H	R	ER	HR	SH	SF	HB	TBB	IBB	SO	WP	Bk	W	L	Pct	Sh	Sv-Op	Hld	ERC	ERA
2007	Hou	NL	3	2	0	1	12.2	54	10	6	5	3	1	0	2	4	0	8	0	0	0	2	.000	0	0-0	0	4.04	3.55
2010	Bal	AL	1	0	0	0	0.2	4	1	0	0	0	0	0	0	1	0	1	0	0	0	0	-	0	0-0	0	10.76	0.00
2011	Bal	AL	20	0	0	4	30.0	119	25	10	10	2	1	1	0	5	1	22	0	0	2	1	.667	0	0-0	2	2.09	3.00
2012	Bal	AL	54	0	0	12	55.2	224	45	15	15	5	0	1	2	12	2	49	1	0	1	0	1.000	0	0-1	9	2.39	2.43
	4 ML YEARS		78	2	0	17	99.0	401	81	31	30	10	2	2	4	22	3	80	1	0	3	3	.500	0	0-1	11	2.54	2.73

Xavier Paul

Bats: L **Throws:** R **Pos:** PH-40; LF-17; RF-1   **Ht:** 5'9" **Wt:** 200 **Born:** 2/25/1985 **Age:** 28

Year	Team	Lg	G	AB	H	2B	3B	HR	(Hm	Rd)	TB	R	RBI	RC	TBB	IBB	SO	HBP	SH	SF	SB	CS	SB%	GDP	Avg	OBP	Slg
2012	Syrcse*	AAA	60	213	67	16	1	8	(-	-)	109	30	44	40	19	2	41	2	3	0	6	3	.67	3	.315	.376	.512
2012	Lsvlle*	AAA	6	25	12	2	0	1	(-	-)	17	4	4	7	1	0	5	0	0	0	3	0	1.00	0	.480	.500	.680
2009	LAD	NL	11	14	3	1	0	1	(0	1)	7	3	1	0	2	0	4	0	0	0	0	1	.00	1	.214	.313	.500
2010	LAD	NL	44	121	28	8	1	0	(0	0)	38	16	11	8	8	0	24	0	3	1	3	1	.75	3	.231	.277	.314
2011	2 Tms	NL	128	243	62	6	5	2	(1	1)	84	30	20	24	13	1	62	0	5	1	16	6	.73	2	.255	.292	.346
2012	Cin	NL	55	86	27	5	1	2	(1	1)	40	8	7	12	9	1	18	0	1	0	4	2	.67	2	.314	.379	.465
11	LAD	NL	7	11	3	0	0	0	(0	0)	3	0	0	1	0	0	5	0	0	0	0	0	-	0	.273	.273	.273
11	Pit	NL	121	232	59	6	5	2	(1	1)	81	30	20	23	13	1	57	0	5	1	16	6	.73	2	.254	.293	.349
	4 ML YEARS		238	464	120	20	7	5	(2	3)	169	57	39	44	32	2	108	0	9	2	23	10	.70	8	.259	.305	.364

David Pauley

Pitches: R **Bats:** R **Pos:** RP-10   **Ht:** 6'2" **Wt:** 215 **Born:** 6/17/1983 **Age:** 30

Year	Team	Lg	G	GS	CG	GF	IP	BFP	H	R	ER	HR	SH	SF	HB	TBB	IBB	SO	WP	Bk	W	L	Pct	Sh	Sv-Op	Hld	ERC	ERA
2012	Salt Lk*	AAA	9	5	0	1	30.2	124	27	8	6	4	0	0	0	7	0	21	0	0	2	0	1.000	0	0- -	-	2.97	1.76
2012	Tacom*	AAA	11	2	1	2	28.2	124	35	11	10	3	2	1	0	8	0	20	0	0	1	2	.333	0	0- -	-	4.98	3.14
2006	Bos	AL	3	3	0	0	16.0	82	31	14	14	1	0	0	2	6	1	10	0	0	2	.000	0	0-0	0	10.41	7.88
2008	Bos	AL	6	2	0	3	12.1	67	23	17	16	2	0	1	1	5	0	11	0	0	0	1	.000	0	0-0	0	10.16	11.68
2010	Sea	AL	19	15	0	2	90.2	390	89	44	41	13	2	3	4	30	2	51	4	0	4	9	.308	0	0-0	4	4.11	4.07
2011	2 Tms	AL	53	0	0	17	74.0	302	64	27	26	6	3	2	5	22	5	44	0	0	6	.455	0	0-2	8	3.05	3.16
2012	2 Tms	AL	10	0	0	6	16.2	82	27	13	12	2	1	1	2	5	1	6	0	0	0	1	.000	0	0-0	0	8.04	6.48
11	Sea	AL	39	0	0	13	54.1	213	38	13	13	2	2	1	4	16	4	34	0	0	5	4	.556	0	0-1	7	1.98	2.15
11	Det	AL	14	0	0	4	19.2	89	26	14	13	4	1	1	1	6	1	10	0	0	1	2	.000	0	0-1	1	6.60	5.95
12	LAA	AL	5	0	0	3	10.1	49	16	6	5	1	1	0	0	3	1	4	0	0	0	1	.000	0	0-0	0	6.68	4.35
12	Tor	AL	5	0	0	3	6.1	33	11	7	7	1	0	1	2	2	0	2	0	0	0	0	-	0	0-0	0	10.40	9.95
	5 ML YEARS		91	20	0	28	209.2	923	234	115	109	24	6	7	14	68	9	122	4	0	9	19	.321	0	0-2	8	4.74	4.68

Felipe Paulino

Pitches: R **Bats:** R **Pos:** SP-7   **Ht:** 6'2" **Wt:** 270 **Born:** 10/5/1983 **Age:** 29

				HOW MUCH HE PITCHED			WHAT HE GAVE UP										THE RESULTS							
Year	Team	Lg	G	GS	CG	GF	IP	BFP	H	R	ER	HR	SH	SF	HB	TBB	IBB	SO	WP	Bk	W	L	Pct	Sh	Sv-Op	Hld	ERC	ERA
2012	NWArk*	AA	3	3	0	0	13.1	56	12	6	6	3	0	0	0	4	0	14	0	0	1	0	1.000	0	0- --	-	3.87	4.05
2007	Hou	NL	5	3	0	0	19.0	85	22	15	15	5	2	0	0	7	1	11	1	0	2	1	.667	0	0-0	1	5.93	7.11
2009	Hou	NL	23	17	0	0	97.2	448	126	73	68	20	8	1	4	37	2	93	5	0	3	11	.214	0	0-1	0	6.70	6.27
2010	Hou	NL	19	14	0	0	91.2	411	95	63	52	4	6	3	3	46	4	83	6	1	1	9	.100	0	0-1	1	4.29	5.11
2011	2 Tms		39	20	0	8	139.1	599	146	74	69	13	5	7	8	55	2	133	7	1	4	10	.286	0	0-1	2	4.60	4.46
2012	KC	AL	7	7	0	0	37.2	156	31	8	7	3	1	1	0	15	0	39	1	0	3	1	.750	0	0-0	0	2.99	1.67
11	Col	NL	18	0	0	8	14.2	68	23	12	12	3	0	1	0	7	0	14	1	0	0	4	.000	0	0-1	2	9.44	7.36
11	KC	AL	21	20	0	0	124.2	531	123	62	57	10	5	6	8	48	2	119	6	1	4	6	.400	0	0-0	0	4.11	4.11
5 ML YEARS			93	61	0	8	385.1	1699	420	233	211	45	22	12	15	160	9	359	20	2	13	32	.289	0	0-3	4	4.94	4.93

Ronny Paulino

Bats: R **Throws:** R **Pos:** C-11; DH-8; PH-3   **Ht:** 6'3" **Wt:** 250 **Born:** 4/21/1981 **Age:** 32

									BATTING												BASERUNNING				AVERAGES		
Year	Team	Lg	G	AB	H	2B	3B	HR	(Hm	Rd)	TB	R	RBI	RC	TBB	IBB	SO	HBP	SH	SF	SB	CS	SB%	GDP	Avg	OBP	Slg
2012	Norfolk*	AAA	40	150	43	9	1	1	(-	-)	57	12	15	20	12	0	25	0	0	1	0	0	-	0	.287	.337	.380
2005	Pit	NL	2	4	2	0	0	0	(0	0)	2	1	0	1	1	0	0	0	0	0	0	0	-	0	.500	.600	.500
2006	Pit	NL	129	442	137	19	0	6	(2	4)	174	37	55	60	34	5	79	2	1	2	0	0	-	19	.310	.360	.394
2007	Pit	NL	133	457	120	25	0	11	(7	4)	178	56	55	49	33	0	79	2	0	2	2	2	.50	14	.263	.314	.389
2008	Pit	NL	40	118	25	5	0	2	(0	2)	36	8	18	14	11	1	24	0	0	1	0	0	-	4	.212	.277	.305
2009	Fla	NL	80	239	65	10	1	8	(4	4)	101	24	27	31	25	2	48	0	1	1	1	0	1.00	8	.272	.340	.423
2010	Fla	NL	91	316	82	18	0	4	(0	4)	112	31	37	32	25	4	51	0	0	3	1	0	1.00	11	.259	.311	.354
2011	NYM	NL	78	228	61	13	0	2	(1	1)	80	19	19	20	15	3	38	1	1	3	0	0	-	9	.268	.312	.351
2012	Bal	AL	20	63	16	3	0	0	(0	0)	19	5	5	3	1	0	9	0	0	0	0	0	-	6	.254	.266	.302
8 ML YEARS			573	1867	508	93	1	33	(14	19)	702	181	216	210	145	15	328	5	3	12	4	2	.67	69	.272	.324	.376

Carl Pavano

Pitches: R **Bats:** R **Pos:** SP-11   pah-VAH-no   **Ht:** 6'6" **Wt:** 264 **Born:** 1/8/1976 **Age:** 37

							HOW MUCH HE PITCHED			WHAT HE GAVE UP										THE RESULTS							
Year	Team	Lg	G	GS	CG	GF	IP	BFP	H	R	ER	HR	SH	SF	HB	TBB	IBB	SO	WP	Bk	W	L	Pct	Sh	Sv-Op	Hld	ERC	ERA
2012	FtMyrs*	A+	2	2	0	0	5.0	19	4	1	1	0	0	0	0	0	0	3	0	0	0	0	-	0	0- --	-	2.06	1.80
1998	Mon	NL	24	23	0	0	134.2	580	130	70	63	18	5	6	8	43	1	83	1	0	6	9	.400	0	0-0	0	3.97	4.21
1999	Mon	NL	19	18	1	0	104.0	457	117	66	65	8	5	2	4	35	1	70	1	3	6	8	.429	1	0-0	0	4.51	5.63
2000	Mon	NL	15	15	0	0	97.0	408	89	40	33	8	4	3	8	34	1	64	1	1	8	4	.667	0	0-0	0	3.67	3.06
2001	Mon	NL	8	8	0	0	42.2	199	59	33	30	7	2	1	2	16	1	36	0	1	1	6	.143	0	0-0	0	6.99	6.33
2002	2 Tms	NL	37	22	0	2	136.0	619	174	88	78	19	4	4	10	45	8	92	3	2	6	10	.375	0	0-0	3	5.98	5.16
2003	Fla	NL	33	32	2	1	201.0	846	204	99	96	19	9	10	7	49	10	133	3	2	12	13	.480	0	0-0	0	3.57	4.30
2004	Fla	NL	33	31	2	0	222.1	909	212	80	74	16	7	4	11	49	13	139	2	3	18	8	.692	2	0-0	0	3.10	3.00
2005	NYY	AL	17	17	1	0	100.0	442	129	66	53	17	4	3	8	18	1	56	2	1	4	6	.400	1	0-0	0	5.74	4.77
2007	NYY	AL	2	2	0	0	11.1	46	12	7	6	1	0	0	0	2	0	4	0	0	1	0	1.000	0	0-0	0	3.54	4.76
2008	NYY	AL	7	7	0	0	34.1	154	41	23	22	5	3	3	4	10	0	15	0	1	4	2	.667	0	0-0	0	5.60	5.77
2009	2 Tms	AL	33	33	0	0	199.1	854	235	119	113	26	2	7	6	39	1	147	5	0	14	12	.538	1	0-0	0	4.63	5.10
2010	Min	AL	32	32	7	0	221.0	906	227	95	92	24	5	5	6	37	2	117	4	0	17	11	.607	2	0-0	0	3.51	3.75
2011	Min	AL	33	33	3	0	222.0	955	262	123	106	23	7	9	8	40	0	102	4	2	9	13	.409	1	0-0	0	4.38	4.30
2012	Min	AL	11	11	0	0	63.0	268	80	46	42	9	1	1	2	8	2	33	0	0	2	5	.286	0	0-0	0	5.00	6.00
02	Mon	NL	15	14	0	0	74.1	350	98	55	52	14	2	2	7	31	5	51	2	1	3	8	.273	0	0-0	3	7.07	6.30
02	Fla	NL	22	8	0	2	61.2	269	76	33	26	5	2	2	3	14	3	41	1	1	3	2	.600	0	0-0	0	4.74	3.79
09	Cle	AL	21	21	0	0	125.2	534	150	80	75	19	1	6	3	23	0	88	4	0	9	8	.529	1	0-0	0	4.83	5.37
09	Min	AL	12	12	0	0	73.2	320	85	39	38	7	1	1	3	16	1	59	1	0	5	4	.556	0	0-0	0	4.29	4.64
Postseason			10	4	0	1	32.1	128	32	9	9	3	1	2	1	4	1	27	0	0	2	2	.500	0	0-0	0	3.09	2.51
14 ML YEARS			302	284	17	3	1788.2	7643	1971	955	873	200	58	58	84	425	41	1091	26	16	108	107	.502	8	0-0	3	4.26	4.39

Steve Pearce

Bats: R **Throws:** R **Pos:** LF-23; 1B-19; RF-19; PH-10; DH-2; PR-1   **Ht:** 5'11" **Wt:** 210 **Born:** 4/13/1983 **Age:** 30

									BATTING												BASERUNNING				AVERAGES		
Year	Team	Lg	G	AB	H	2B	3B	HR	(Hm	Rd)	TB	R	RBI	RC	TBB	IBB	SO	HBP	SH	SF	SB	CS	SB%	GDP	Avg	OBP	Slg
2012	S-WB*	AAA	53	192	61	15	0	11	(-	-)	109	37	30	45	29	4	33	5	0	1	3	1	.75	4	.318	.419	.568
2007	Pit	NL	23	68	20	5	1	0	(0	0)	27	13	6	9	5	0	12	0	0	0	2	1	.67	2	.294	.342	.397
2008	Pit	NL	37	109	27	7	0	4	(0	4)	46	6	15	13	5	0	22	3	0	2	2	0	1.00	1	.248	.294	.422
2009	Pit	NL	60	165	34	13	1	4	(3	1)	61	19	16	17	21	0	43	0	0	3	1	0	1.00	2	.206	.296	.370
2010	Pit	NL	15	29	8	2	1	0	(0	0)	12	4	5	7	0	0	6	0	0	2	0	0	-	0	.276	.395	.414
2011	Pit	NL	50	94	19	2	0	1	(1	0)	24	8	10	5	7	0	21	1	1	2	0	0	-	6	.202	.260	.255
2012	3 Tms		61	159	38	8	1	4	(2	2)	60	16	26	24	20	1	41	3	2	4	1	2	.33	4	.239	.328	.377
12	Bal	AL	28	71	18	4	0	3	(2	1)	31	8	14	12	8	0	17	0	2	2	0	1	.00	1	.254	.321	.437
12	Hou	NL	21	63	16	4	1	0	(0	0)	22	2	8	9	7	1	16	3	0	2	1	1	.50	3	.254	.347	.349
12	NYY	AL	12	25	4	0	0	1	(0	1)	7	6	4	3	5	0	8	0	0	0	0	0	-	0	.160	.300	.280
6 ML YEARS			246	624	146	37	4	13	(6	7)	230	66	78	73	65	1	145	7	3	10	6	3	.67	15	.234	.309	.369

Jake Peavy

Pitches: R **Bats:** R **Pos:** SP-32   **Ht:** 6'1" **Wt:** 195 **Born:** 5/31/1981 **Age:** 32

			HOW MUCH HE PITCHED						WHAT HE GAVE UP											THE RESULTS							
Year	Team	Lg	G	GS	CG	GF	IP	BFP	H	R	ER	HR	SH	SF	HB	TBB	IBB	SO	WP	Bk	W	L	Pct	Sh	Sv-Op	Hld	ERC	ERA
2002	SD	NL	17	17	0	0	97.2	430	106	54	49	11	5	2	3	33	4	90	4	1	6	7	.462	0	0-0	0	4.41	4.52
2003	SD	NL	32	32	0	0	194.2	827	173	94	89	33	7	5	6	82	3	156	2	0	12	11	.522	0	0-0	0	4.13	4.11
2004	SD	NL	27	27	0	0	166.1	694	146	49	42	13	5	6	11	53	4	173	1	1	15	6	.714	0	0-0	0	3.18	**2.27**
2005	SD	NL	30	30	3	0	203.0	812	162	70	65	18	4	5	7	50	3	**216**	3	1	13	7	.650	3	0-0	0	2.49	2.88
2006	SD	NL	32	32	2	0	202.1	846	187	93	92	23	5	1	6	62	11	215	4	0	11	14	.440	0	0-0	0	3.42	4.09
2007	SD	NL	34	34	0	0	223.1	898	169	67	63	13	5	7	6	68	5	**240**	4	0	**19**	6	.760	0	0-0	0	**2.27**	**2.54**
2008	SD	NL	27	27	1	0	173.2	709	146	57	55	17	7	1	5	59	1	166	6	0	10	11	.476	0	0-0	0	3.12	2.85
2009	2 Tms		16	16	1	0	101.2	410	80	41	39	8	3	2	1	34	0	110	2	2	9	6	.600	0	0-0	0	2.63	3.45
2010	CWS	AL	17	17	1	0	107.0	450	98	55	55	13	1	5	5	34	2	93	2	1	7	6	.538	1	0-0	0	3.59	4.63
2011	CWS	AL	19	18	1	0	111.2	470	117	61	61	10	1	5	3	24	4	95	4	0	7	7	.500	1	0-0	0	3.59	4.92
2012	CWS	AL	32	32	4	0	219.0	882	191	88	82	27	1	6	10	49	1	194	3	2	11	12	.478	1	0-0	0	3.07	3.37
09	SD	NL	13	13	1	0	81.2	335	69	38	36	7	2	2	1	28	0	92	2	1	6	6	.500	0	0-0	0	3.00	3.97
09	CWS	AL	3	3	0	0	20.0	75	11	3	3	1	1	0	0	6	0	18	0	1	3	0	1.000	0	0-0	0	1.38	1.35
Postseason			2	2	0	0	9.2	49	19	13	13	3	1	1	0	4	3	5	1	0	0	2	.000	0	0-0	0	12.16	12.10
11 ML YEARS			283	282	13	0	1800.1	7428	1575	729	692	186	44	45	63	548	38	1748	35	8	120	93	.563	6	0-0	0	3.17	3.46

Dustin Pedroia

Bats: R **Throws:** R **Pos:** 2B-139; DH-2   peh-DROY-uh   **Ht:** 5'8" **Wt:** 165 **Born:** 8/17/1983 **Age:** 29

						BATTING															BASERUNNING				AVERAGES		
Year	Team	Lg	G	AB	H	2B	3B	HR	(Hm	Rd)	TB	R	RBI	RC	TBB	IBB	SO	HBP	SH	SF	SB	CS	SB%	GDP	Avg	OBP	Slg
2006	Bos	AL	31	89	17	4	0	2	(1	1)	27	5	7	3	7	0	7	1	1	0	0	1	.00	1	.191	.258	.303
2007	Bos	AL	139	520	165	39	1	8	(5	3)	230	86	50	79	47	1	42	7	5	2	7	1	.88	8	.317	.380	.442
2008	Bos	AL	157	653	213	54	2	17	(7	10)	322	118	83	107	50	1	52	7	7	9	20	1	**.95**	17	.326	.376	.493
2009	Bos	AL	154	626	185	48	1	15	(10	5)	280	**115**	72	104	74	3	45	5	3	6	20	8	.71	19	.296	.371	.447
2010	Bos	AL	75	302	87	24	1	12	(4	8)	149	53	41	52	37	1	38	4	2	6	9	1	.90	7	.288	.367	.493
2011	Bos	AL	159	635	195	37	3	21	(13	8)	301	102	91	114	86	6	85	1	2	7	26	8	.76	12	.307	.387	.474
2012	Bos	AL	141	563	163	39	3	15	(9	6)	253	81	65	84	48	3	60	5	1	6	20	6	.77	9	.290	.347	.449
Postseason			28	115	29	9	0	5	(2	3)	53	22	18	18	14	0	12	2	1	0	2	1	.67	3	.252	.344	.461
7 ML YEARS			856	3388	1025	245	11	90	(49	41)	1562	560	409	543	349	15	329	30	21	36	102	26	.80	73	.303	.369	.461

Carlos Peguero

Bats: L **Throws:** L **Pos:** RF-11; DH-4; LF-2; PH-1; PR-1   peh-GEHR-oh   **Ht:** 6'5" **Wt:** 245 **Born:** 2/22/1987 **Age:** 26

						BATTING															BASERUNNING				AVERAGES		
Year	Team	Lg	G	AB	H	2B	3B	HR	(Hm	Rd)	TB	R	RBI	RC	TBB	IBB	SO	HBP	SH	SF	SB	CS	SB%	GDP	Avg	OBP	Slg
2006	Ms	R	34	134	42	10	7	7	(-	-)	87	27	30	31	13	0	49	2	0	1	3	2	.60	1	.313	.380	.649
2006	Everett	A-	25	93	19	4	1	2	(-	-)	31	7	9	5	2	1	34	0	0	0	0	2	.00	0	.204	.221	.333
2007	Wisc	A	79	297	78	21	6	9	(-	-)	138	35	50	43	16	0	97	7	0	1	4	3	.57	4	.263	.315	.465
2008	Hi Dsrt	A+	92	371	111	25	3	12	(-	-)	178	47	74	55	10	0	96	1	0	3	6	4	.60	5	.299	.317	.480
2009	Hi Dsrt	A+	126	491	133	21	14	31	(-	-)	275	92	98	91	42	2	172	7	1	3	3	4	.43	8	.271	.335	.560
2010	WTenn	AA	130	488	124	23	5	23	(-	-)	226	86	73	77	56	3	178	8	0	1	7	9	.44	8	.254	.340	.463
2011	Tacom	AAA	57	240	76	15	2	13	(-	-)	134	44	47	48	15	1	82	3	0	0	8	0	1.00	3	.317	.364	.558
2012	Tacom	AAA	76	281	80	12	1	21	(-	-)	157	47	54	57	29	3	103	9	0	3	2	2	.50	1	.285	.366	.559
2011	Sea	AL	46	143	28	3	2	6	(4	2)	53	14	19	12	8	2	54	3	0	1	0	1	.00	0	.196	.252	.371
2012	Sea	AL	17	56	10	2	1	2	(1	1)	20	2	7	5	1	0	28	0	0	0	0	0	-	0	.179	.193	.357
2 ML YEARS			63	199	38	5	3	8	(5	3)	73	16	26	17	9	2	82	3	0	1	0	1	.00	0	.191	.236	.367

Francisco Peguero

Bats: R **Throws:** R **Pos:** LF-8; PR-6; PH-4; RF-2   peh-GEHR-oh   **Ht:** 5'11" **Wt:** 195 **Born:** 6/1/1988 **Age:** 25

						BATTING															BASERUNNING				AVERAGES		
Year	Team	Lg	G	AB	H	2B	3B	HR	(Hm	Rd)	TB	R	RBI	RC	TBB	IBB	SO	HBP	SH	SF	SB	CS	SB%	GDP	Avg	OBP	Slg
2008	Augsta	A	50	180	47	2	4	2	(-	-)	63	23	15	22	12	0	43	1	0	1	15	1	.94	1	.261	.309	.350
2008	SlmKzr	A-	50	202	62	11	4	2	(-	-)	87	33	28	31	9	0	43	5	2	2	10	3	.77	4	.307	.349	.431
2009	Augsta	A	58	238	81	12	4	1	(-	-)	104	28	34	38	5	0	39	4	1	4	15	5	.75	6	.340	.359	.437
2009	SlmKzr	A-	17	71	28	3	1	0	(-	-)	33	14	12	15	3	0	9	1	0	1	7	0	1.00	4	.394	.421	.465
2010	SnJos	A+	122	510	168	19	16	10	(-	-)	249	78	77	87	18	3	88	6	2	2	40	22	.65	14	.329	.358	.488
2011	SnJos	A+	16	68	22	2	0	2	(-	-)	30	12	9	12	7	0	8	0	1	0	4	0	1.00	2	.324	.387	.441
2011	Rchmd	AA	71	285	88	12	6	5	(-	-)	127	34	37	41	5	0	45	1	0	5	8	1	.89	6	.309	.318	.446
2012	Fresno	AAA	105	449	122	20	10	5	(-	-)	177	46	68	54	15	1	82	3	4	5	1	0	1.00	20	.272	.297	.394
2012	SF	NL	17	16	3	0	0	0	(0	0)	3	6	0	1	0	0	7	0	0	0	3	0	1.00	0	.188	.188	.188

Mike Pelfrey

Pitches: R **Bats:** R **Pos:** SP-3   PELL-free   **Ht:** 6'7" **Wt:** 250 **Born:** 1/14/1984 **Age:** 29

						HOW MUCH HE PITCHED							WHAT HE GAVE UP											THE RESULTS						
Year	Team	Lg	G	GS	CG	GF	IP	BFP	H	R	ER	HR	SH	SF	HB	TBB	IBB	SO	WP	Bk	W	L	Pct	Sh	Sv-Op	Hld	ERC	ERA
2006	NYM	NL	4	4	0	0	21.1	99	25	14	13	1	1	1	3	12	0	13	2	0	2	1	.667	0	0-0	0	6.05	5.48
2007	NYM	NL	15	13	0	0	72.2	342	85	47	45	6	6	3	9	39	1	45	3	0	3	8	.273	0	0-0	0	5.99	5.57
2008	NYM	NL	32	32	2	0	200.2	851	209	86	83	12	11	5	13	64	0	110	2	0	13	11	.542	0	0-0	0	4.04	3.72
2009	NYM	NL	31	31	0	0	184.1	824	213	112	103	18	4	5	11	66	8	107	1	**6**	10	12	.455	0	0-0	0	4.83	5.03
2010	NYM	NL	34	33	0	1	204.0	870	213	88	83	12	**17**	4	6	68	5	113	1	1	15	9	.625	0	0-0	0	3.89	3.66
2011	NYM	NL	34	33	2	0	193.2	860	220	111	102	21	10	8	7	65	7	105	2	2	7	13	.350	0	0-0	0	4.70	4.74
2012	NYM	NL	3	3	0	0	19.2	85	24	5	5	0	1	0	0	4	0	13	1	0	0	0	-	0	0-0	0	3.82	2.29
7 ML YEARS			153	149	4	1	896.1	3931	989	463	434	70	54	26	45	318	22	506	12	9	50	54	.481	0	1-1	0	4.50	4.36

Brayan Pena

Bats: B **Throws:** R **Pos:** C-52; PH-8; DH-7; 1B-3 BRIAN **Ht:** 5'9" **Wt:** 230 **Born:** 1/7/1982 **Age:** 31

Year	Team	Lg	G	AB	H	2B	3B	HR	(Hm	Rd)	TB	R	RBI	RC	TBB	IBB	SO	HBP	SH	SF	SB	CS	SB%	GDP	Avg	OBP	Slg
2005	Atl	NL	18	39	7	2	0	0	(0	0)	9	2	4	0	1	1	7	0	0	0	0	0	-	1	.179	.200	.231
2006	Atl	NL	23	41	11	2	0	1	(0	1)	16	9	5	4	2	0	5	0	0	0	0	0	-	2	.268	.302	.390
2007	Atl	NL	16	33	7	0	0	1	(1	0)	10	2	3	0	0	0	3	0	0	0	0	1	.00	2	.212	.212	.303
2008	Atl	NL	14	14	4	1	0	0	(0	0)	5	3	0	0	1	0	2	0	0	0	0	0	-	0	.286	.333	.357
2009	KC	AL	64	165	45	10	0	6	(3	3)	73	17	18	18	12	2	18	0	4	2	0	0	-	5	.273	.318	.442
2010	KC	AL	60	158	40	10	0	1	(0	1)	53	11	19	16	12	0	27	1	1	2	2	0	1.00	8	.253	.306	.335
2011	KC	AL	72	222	55	11	0	3	(0	3)	75	17	24	23	12	0	24	2	0	4	0	0	-	6	.248	.288	.338
2012	KC	AL	68	212	50	10	1	2	(1	1)	68	16	25	19	9	0	24	0	1	4	0	1	.00	7	.236	.262	.321
8 ML YEARS			335	884	219	46	1	14	(5	9)	309	77	98	80	49	3	110	3	6	12	2	2	.50	31	.248	.286	.350

Carlos Pena

Bats: L **Throws:** L **Pos:** 1B-153; PH-12; DH-1 **Ht:** 6'2" **Wt:** 225 **Born:** 5/17/1978 **Age:** 35

Year	Team	Lg	G	AB	H	2B	3B	HR	(Hm	Rd)	TB	R	RBI	RC	TBB	IBB	SO	HBP	SH	SF	SB	CS	SB%	GDP	Avg	OBP	Slg
2001	Tex	AL	22	62	16	4	1	3	(2	1)	31	6	12	11	10	0	17	0	0	0	0	0	-	1	.258	.361	.500
2002	2 Tms	AL	115	397	96	17	4	19	(10	9)	178	43	52	56	41	0	111	3	0	2	2	2	.50	7	.242	.316	.448
2003	Det	AL	131	452	112	21	6	18	(8	10)	199	51	50	61	53	1	123	6	1	4	4	5	.44	6	.248	.332	.440
2004	Det	AL	142	481	116	22	4	27	(10	17)	227	89	82	73	70	2	146	3	2	5	7	1	.88	11	.241	.338	.472
2005	Det	AL	79	260	61	9	0	18	(14	4)	124	37	44	40	31	2	95	4	0	0	0	1	.00	3	.235	.325	.477
2006	Bos	AL	18	33	9	2	0	1	(1	0)	14	3	3	3	4	0	10	0	0	0	0	0	-	1	.273	.351	.424
2007	TB	AL	148	490	138	29	1	46	(23	23)	307	99	121	114	103	10	142	10	1	8	1	0	1.00	6	.282	.411	.627
2008	TB	AL	139	490	121	24	2	31	(14	17)	242	76	102	92	96	7	166	12	0	9	1	1	.50	6	.247	.377	.494
2009	TB	AL	135	471	107	25	2	39	(19	20)	253	91	100	88	87	11	163	9	0	3	3	3	.50	5	.227	.356	.537
2010	TB	AL	144	484	95	18	0	28	(18	10)	197	64	84	73	87	4	158	7	0	4	5	1	.83	2	.196	.325	.407
2011	ChC	NL	153	493	111	27	3	28	(12	16)	228	72	80	79	101	7	161	4	1	7	2	2	.50	6	.225	.357	.462
2012	TB	AL	160	497	98	17	2	19	(11	8)	176	72	61	60	87	2	182	13	0	3	2	3	.40	10	.197	.330	.354
02	Oak	AL	40	124	27	4	0	7	(5	2)	52	12	16	17	15	0	38	1	0	1	0	0	-	2	.218	.305	.419
02	Det	AL	75	273	69	13	4	12	(5	7)	126	31	36	39	26	0	73	2	0	1	2	2	.50	5	.253	.321	.462
Postseason			19	67	18	3	1	4	(0	4)	35	13	14	14	13	2	24	0	0	0	3	2	.60	1	.269	.388	.522
12 ML YEARS			1386	4610	1080	215	25	277	(142	135)	2176	703	791	750	770	46	1474	71	5	45	27	19	.59	65	.234	.350	.472

Ramiro Pena

Bats: B **Throws:** R **Pos:** PR-2; SS-1 **Ht:** 5'11" **Wt:** 185 **Born:** 7/18/1985 **Age:** 27

Year	Team	Lg	G	AB	H	2B	3B	HR	(Hm	Rd)	TB	R	RBI	RC	TBB	IBB	SO	HBP	SH	SF	SB	CS	SB%	GDP	Avg	OBP	Slg
2012	S-WB*	AAA	101	360	93	13	3	2	(-	-)	118	40	29	40	34	0	74	3	4	3	1	3	.25	4	.258	.325	.328
2009	NYY	AL	69	115	33	6	1	1	(1	0)	44	17	10	15	5	0	20	0	1	0	4	1	.80	2	.287	.317	.383
2010	NYY	AL	85	154	35	1	1	0	(0	0)	38	18	18	10	6	0	27	1	4	2	7	1	.88	4	.227	.258	.247
2011	NYY	AL	23	40	4	0	0	1	(1	0)	7	5	4	0	2	0	11	1	2	1	0	0	-	0	.100	.159	.175
2012	NYY	AL	3	4	1	0	0	0	(0	0)	1	0	0	0	0	0	0	0	0	0	0	0	-	0	.250	.250	.250
4 ML YEARS			180	313	73	7	2	2	(2	0)	90	40	32	25	13	0	58	2	7	3	11	2	.85	7	.233	.266	.288

Hunter Pence

Bats: R **Throws:** R **Pos:** RF-159; PH-2 **Ht:** 6'4" **Wt:** 220 **Born:** 4/13/1983 **Age:** 30

Year	Team	Lg	G	AB	H	2B	3B	HR	(Hm	Rd)	TB	R	RBI	RC	TBB	IBB	SO	HBP	SH	SF	SB	CS	SB%	GDP	Avg	OBP	Slg
2007	Hou	NL	108	456	147	30	9	17	(7	10)	246	57	69	77	26	0	95	1	0	1	11	5	.69	10	.322	.360	.539
2008	Hou	NL	157	595	160	34	4	25	(14	11)	277	78	83	82	40	2	124	4	0	3	11	10	.52	14	.269	.318	.466
2009	Hou	NL	159	585	165	26	5	25	(14	11)	276	76	72	80	58	1	109	1	0	3	14	11	.56	25	.282	.346	.472
2010	Hou	NL	156	614	173	29	3	25	(14	11)	283	93	91	89	41	2	105	0	0	3	18	9	.67	11	.282	.325	.461
2011	2 Tms	NL	154	606	190	38	5	22	(5	17)	304	84	97	102	56	3	124	1	0	5	8	2	.80	15	.314	.370	.502
2012	2 Tms	NL	160	617	156	26	4	24	(9	15)	262	87	104	81	56	2	145	7	1	7	5	2	.71	15	.253	.319	.425
11	Hou	NL	100	399	123	26	3	11	(4	7)	188	49	62	63	30	1	86	1	0	2	7	1	.88	7	.308	.356	.471
11	Phi	NL	54	207	67	12	2	11	(1	10)	116	35	35	39	26	2	38	0	0	3	1	1	.50	8	.324	.394	.560
12	Phi	NL	101	398	108	15	2	17	(7	10)	178	59	59	50	37	1	85	3	0	2	4	2	.67	14	.271	.336	.447
12	SF	NL	59	219	48	11	2	7	(2	5)	84	28	45	31	19	1	60	4	1	5	1	0	1.00	1	.219	.287	.384
Postseason			5	19	4	0	0	0	(0	0)	4	3	4	2	2	1	2	0	0	0	0	1	.00	0	.211	.286	.211
6 ML YEARS			894	3473	991	183	30	138	(63	75)	1648	475	516	511	277	10	702	14	1	22	67	39	.63	90	.285	.339	.475

Cliff Pennington

Bats: B **Throws:** R **Pos:** SS-93; 2B-32; PH-6 **Ht:** 5'10" **Wt:** 193 **Born:** 6/15/1984 **Age:** 29

Year	Team	Lg	G	AB	H	2B	3B	HR	(Hm	Rd)	TB	R	RBI	RC	TBB	IBB	SO	HBP	SH	SF	SB	CS	SB%	GDP	Avg	OBP	Slg
2012	Scrmto*	AAA	3	11	5	1	0	0	(-	-)	6	2	1	3	3	0	4	0	0	0	1	0	1.00	1	.455	.571	.545
2008	Oak	AL	36	99	24	5	0	0	(0	0)	29	14	9	12	13	0	18	2	2	1	4	1	.80	1	.242	.339	.293
2009	Oak	AL	60	208	58	11	3	4	(3	1)	87	27	21	29	19	0	46	1	1	0	7	5	.58	5	.279	.342	.418
2010	Oak	AL	156	508	127	26	8	6	(2	4)	187	64	46	66	50	0	96	3	12	3	29	5	.85	7	.250	.319	.368
2011	Oak	AL	148	515	136	26	2	8	(3	5)	190	57	58	73	42	1	104	1	8	4	14	9	.61	5	.264	.319	.369
2012	Oak	AL	125	418	90	18	2	6	(0	6)	130	50	28	37	35	0	90	2	5	2	15	6	.71	1	.215	.278	.311
5 ML YEARS			525	1748	435	86	15	24	(8	16)	623	212	162	217	159	1	354	9	28	10	69	26	.73	19	.249	.313	.356

Brad Penny

Pitches: R Bats: R Pos: RP-22   Ht: 6'4" Wt: 230 Born: 5/24/1978 Age: 35

Year	Team	Lg	G	GS	CG	GF	IP	BFP	H	R	ER	HR	SH	SF	HB	TBB	IBB	SO	WP	Bk	W	L	Pct	Sh	Sv-Op	Hld	ERC	ERA
2012	Sbank*	Jap	1	1	0	0	3.1	19	7	6	4	0	-	-	0	3	0	1	1	0	0	1	.000	0	0--	-	12.94	10.80
2012	Fresno*	AAA	8	0	0	0	9.1	41	10	8	5	1	0	0	0	3	0	3	1	0	1	0	1.000	0	0--	-	3.37	4.82
2012	Giants*	R	1	1	0	0	1.0	7	2	3	2	0	0	0	1	1	0	1	0	0	0	1	.000	0	0--	-	16.69	18.00
2012	SnJos*	A+	2	1	0	0	2.0	9	2	1	0	0	0	0	0	1	0	1	1	0	0	0	-	0	0--	-	3.63	0.00
2000	Fla	NL	23	22	0	0	119.2	529	120	70	64	13	6	2	5	60	4	80	4	1	8	7	.533	0	0-0	0	4.70	4.81
2001	Fla	NL	31	31	1	0	205.0	833	183	92	84	15	8	2	7	54	3	154	2	0	10	10	.500	1	0-0	0	2.96	3.69
2002	Fla	NL	24	24	1	0	129.1	574	148	76	67	18	6	4	1	50	7	93	4	0	8	7	.533	1	0-0	0	5.08	4.66
2003	Fla	NL	32	32	0	0	196.1	811	195	96	90	21	7	5	3	56	6	138	3	4	14	10	.583	0	0-0	0	3.73	4.13
2004	2 Tms	NL	24	24	0	0	143.0	590	130	55	50	12	3	3	3	45	6	111	5	0	9	10	.474	0	0-0	0	3.20	3.15
2005	LAD	NL	29	29	1	0	175.1	738	185	78	76	17	7	1	3	41	2	122	3	0	7	9	.438	0	0-0	0	3.77	3.90
2006	LAD	NL	34	33	0	0	189.0	813	206	94	91	19	8	3	9	54	4	148	6	0	16	9	.640	0	0-0	1	4.32	4.33
2007	LAD	NL	33	33	0	0	208.0	865	199	75	70	9	13	9	5	73	2	135	6	0	16	4	.800	0	0-0	0	3.41	3.03
2008	LAD	NL	19	17	0	1	94.2	426	112	68	66	13	10	2	3	42	0	51	1	1	6	9	.400	0	0-0	0	5.82	6.27
2009	2 Tms		30	30	1	0	173.1	751	191	102	94	22	0	7	5	51	0	109	6	0	11	9	.550	0	0-0	0	4.54	4.88
2010	StL	NL	9	9	0	0	55.2	232	63	25	20	4	2	3	3	9	1	35	1	0	3	4	.429	0	0-0	0	3.95	3.23
2011	Det	AL	31	31	0	0	181.2	803	222	117	107	24	5	6	4	62	1	74	9	0	11	11	.500	0	0-0	0	5.53	5.30
2012	SF	NL	22	0	0	8	28.0	133	42	22	19	4	1	0	1	9	2	10	2	0	1	0	1.000	0	0-0	2	7.13	6.11
04	Fla	NL	21	21	0	0	131.1	545	124	50	46	10	3	3	3	39	6	105	5	0	8	8	.500	0	0-0	0	3.26	3.15
04	LAD	NL	3	3	0	0	11.2	45	6	5	4	2	0	0	0	6	0	6	0	0	1	2	.333	0	0-0	0	2.51	3.09
09	Bos	AL	24	24	0	0	131.2	590	160	89	82	17	0	7	5	42	0	89	4	0	7	8	.467	0	0-0	0	5.35	5.61
09	SF	NL	6	6	1	0	41.2	161	31	13	12	5	0	0	0	9	0	20	2	0	4	1	.800	0	0-0	0	2.22	2.59
	Postseason		9	4	0	0	24.2	120	38	22	21	5	2	1	0	13	2	15	1	0	3	2	.600	0	0-1	0	8.87	7.66
	13 ML YEARS		341	315	4	9	1899.0	8098	1996	970	898	191	76	47	52	606	38	1260	52	6	119	100	.543	2	0-0	3	4.17	4.26

Jhonny Peralta

Bats: R Throws: R Pos: SS-149; DH-1; PH-1   pah-RALL-tah   Ht: 6'2" Wt: 215 Born: 5/28/1982 Age: 31

							BATTING													BASERUNNING				AVERAGES		
Year	Team	Lg	G	AB	H	2B	3B	HR	(Hm | Rd)	TB	R	RBI	RC	TBB	IBB	SO	HBP	SH	SF	SB	CS	SB%	GDP	Avg	OBP	Slg
2003	Cle	AL	77	242	55	10	1	4	(3 | 1)	79	24	21	24	20	0	65	4	2	2	1	3	.25	5	.227	.295	.326
2004	Cle	AL	8	25	6	1	0	0	(0 | 0)	7	2	2	2	3	0	6	0	0	0	0	1	.00	0	.240	.321	.280
2005	Cle	AL	141	504	147	35	4	24	(14 | 10)	262	82	78	87	58	3	128	3	1	4	0	2	.00	12	.292	.366	.520
2006	Cle	AL	149	569	146	28	3	13	(7 | 6)	219	84	68	66	56	0	152	1	3	3	0	1	.00	19	.257	.323	.385
2007	Cle	AL	152	574	155	27	1	21	(16 | 5)	247	87	72	85	61	2	146	4	1	7	4	4	.50	12	.270	.341	.430
2008	Cle	AL	154	605	167	42	4	23	(11 | 12)	286	104	89	84	48	2	126	4	2	5	3	1	.75	26	.276	.331	.473
2009	Cle	AL	151	582	148	35	1	11	(2 | 9)	218	57	83	63	51	0	134	4	2	6	0	2	.00	20	.254	.316	.375
2010	2 Tms	AL	148	551	137	30	2	15	(4 | 11)	216	60	81	71	53	2	103	1	0	10	1	0	1.00	11	.249	.311	.392
2011	Det	AL	146	525	157	25	3	21	(13 | 8)	251	68	86	77	40	2	95	2	0	9	0	2	.00	17	.299	.345	.478
2012	Det	AL	150	531	127	32	3	13	(6 | 7)	204	58	63	53	49	3	105	2	1	2	1	2	.33	22	.239	.305	.384
10	Cle	AL	91	334	82	23	2	7	(3 | 4)	130	37	43	41	32	1	69	1	0	6	1	0	1.00	7	.246	.308	.389
10	Det	AL	57	217	55	7	0	8	(1 | 7)	86	23	38	30	21	1	34	0	0	4	0	0	-	4	.253	.314	.396
	Postseason		22	83	23	8	0	4	(2 | 2)	43	8	13	13	7	0	19	1	1	1	1	0	1.00	3	.277	.337	.518
	10 ML YEARS		1276	4708	1245	265	22	145	(76 | 69)	1989	626	643	612	439	14	1060	25	12	48	10	18	.36	142	.264	.327	.422

Joel Peralta

Pitches: R Bats: R Pos: RP-77   joe-ELL pah-RALL-tah   Ht: 5'11" Wt: 205 Born: 3/23/1976 Age: 37

Year	Team	Lg	G	GS	CG	GF	IP	BFP	H	R	ER	HR	SH	SF	HB	TBB	IBB	SO	WP	Bk	W	L	Pct	Sh	Sv-Op	Hld	ERC	ERA
2005	LAA	AL	28	0	0	10	34.2	145	28	15	15	6	2	1	0	14	2	30	2	0	1	0	1.000	0	0-0	0	3.40	3.89
2006	KC	AL	64	0	0	21	73.2	304	74	37	36	10	1	3	2	17	2	57	5	0	1	3	.250	0	1-3	17	3.80	4.40
2007	KC	AL	62	0	0	18	87.2	366	93	39	37	9	2	4	2	19	5	66	2	0	1	3	.250	0	1-5	7	3.75	3.80
2008	KC	AL	40	0	0	12	52.2	224	56	37	35	15	1	3	2	14	0	38	1	0	1	2	.333	0	0-1	1	5.38	5.98
2009	Col	NL	27	0	0	6	24.2	113	27	17	17	3	0	1	3	12	2	22	0	0	0	3	.000	0	0-1	6	5.51	6.20
2010	Was	NL	39	0	0	10	49.0	189	30	12	11	5	2	1	1	9	4	49	0	0	1	0	1.000	0	0-2	9	1.43	2.02
2011	TB	AL	71	0	0	18	67.2	256	44	23	22	7	2	0	0	18	3	61	3	0	3	4	.429	0	6-8	19	1.84	2.93
2012	TB	AL	77	0	0	9	67.0	264	49	28	27	9	0	1	1	17	2	84	5	0	2	6	.250	0	2-5	37	2.36	3.63
	Postseason		3	0	0	2	2.1	10	1	0	0	0	0	0	0	2	0	0	0	0	0	0	-	0	0-0	0	2.03	0.00
	8 ML YEARS		408	0	0	104	457.0	1861	401	208	200	64	10	16	11	120	20	407	18	0	10	21	.323	0	10-25	96	3.19	3.94

Wily Peralta

Pitches: R Bats: R Pos: SP-5; RP-1   Ht: 6'2" Wt: 240 Born: 5/8/1989 Age: 24

Year	Team	Lg	G	GS	CG	GF	IP	BFP	H	R	ER	HR	SH	SF	HB	TBB	IBB	SO	WP	Bk	W	L	Pct	Sh	Sv-Op	Hld	ERC	ERA
2006	Brewrs	R	14	6	0	0	38.0	188	51	37	28	5	2	1	5	20	0	28	4	0	2	5	.286	0	0--	-	7.40	6.63
2008	Helena	R+	15	2	0	10	29.1	120	23	14	10	4	2	0	0	8	0	36	4	0	1	1	.500	0	2--	-	2.61	3.07
2008	WV	A	2	2	0	0	5.0	24	6	6	6	0	0	1	1	3	0	3	0	0	0	1	.000	0	0--	-	6.15	10.80
2009	Wisc	A	27	15	4	0	103.2	446	91	45	40	5	4	4	4	46	0	118	8	0	4	4	.500	0	1--	-	3.33	3.47
2010	BrvdCt	A+	19	17	0	0	105.0	454	102	50	45	5	3	2	6	40	0	75	3	1	6	3	.667	0	0--	-	3.68	3.86
2010	Hntsvl	AA	8	8	0	0	42.1	190	43	22	17	5	1	1	4	24	0	29	4	0	2	3	.400	0	0--	-	5.47	3.61
2011	Hntsvl	AA	21	21	1	0	119.2	496	106	57	46	9	3	5	4	48	0	117	8	0	9	7	.563	0	0--	-	3.50	3.46
2011	Nashv	AAA	5	5	0	0	31.0	122	21	7	7	0	0	1	1	11	0	40	1	0	2	0	1.000	0	0--	-	1.81	2.03
2012	Nashv	AAA	28	28	1	0	146.2	652	154	79	76	9	2	2	9	78	1	141	9	1	7	11	.389	0	0--	-	4.93	4.66
2012	Mil	NL	6	5	0	1	29.0	113	24	8	8	3	0	0	1	11	0	23	1	0	2	1	.667	0	0-0	0	2.61	2.48

Luis Perdomo

Pitches: R **Bats:** L **Pos:** RP-15   perr-DOH-moh   **Ht:** 6'0" **Wt:** 170 **Born:** 4/27/1984 **Age:** 29

				HOW MUCH HE PITCHED			WHAT HE GAVE UP												THE RESULTS						
Year	Team	Lg	G	GS	CG	GF	IP	BFP	H	R	ER	HR	SH	SF	HB	TBB	IBB	SO	WP	Bk	W	L	Pct	Sh	Sv-Op	Hld	ERC	ERA
2012	NwBrit*	AA	26	0	0	16	39.1	159	27	13	12	0	1	0	1	16	1	43	2	0	4	4	.500	0	2- -	-	1.92	2.75
2012	Roch*	AAA	19	0	0	12	33.1	134	27	9	9	4	1	3	0	6	0	25	1	0	4	1	.800	0	7- -	-	2.32	2.43
2009	SD	NL	35	0	0	10	60.0	268	57	36	32	11	1	1	0	34	3	55	8	0	1	0	1.000	0	0-1	0	4.94	4.80
2010	SD	NL	1	0	0	1	1.0	4	1	1	1	1	0	0	0	0	0	0	0	0	0	0	-	0	0-0	0	7.45	9.00
2012	Min	AL	15	0	0	9	17.0	78	15	8	6	0	0	1	2	12	1	8	1	0	0	0	-	0	0-0	0	4.17	3.18
3 ML YEARS			51	0	0	20	78.0	350	73	45	39	12	1	2	2	46	4	63	9	0	1	0	1.000	0	0-1	0	4.84	4.50

Chris Perez

Pitches: R **Bats:** R **Pos:** RP-61   **Ht:** 6'4" **Wt:** 230 **Born:** 7/1/1985 **Age:** 27

				HOW MUCH HE PITCHED			WHAT HE GAVE UP												THE RESULTS						
Year	Team	Lg	G	GS	CG	GF	IP	BFP	H	R	ER	HR	SH	SF	HB	TBB	IBB	SO	WP	Bk	W	L	Pct	Sh	Sv-Op	Hld	ERC	ERA
2008	StL	NL	41	0	0	23	41.2	177	34	18	16	5	1	3	1	22	0	42	2	0	3	3	.500	0	7-11	6	3.83	3.46
2009	2 Tms		61	0	0	16	57.0	239	41	28	27	8	0	2	6	27	0	68	8	0	1	2	.333	0	2-5	7	3.54	4.26
2010	Cle	AL	63	0	0	37	63.0	260	40	15	12	4	6	1	5	28	3	61	4	0	2	2	.500	0	23-27	9	2.30	1.71
2011	Cle	AL	64	0	0	57	59.2	248	46	24	22	5	4	1	3	26	4	39	1	0	4	7	.364	0	36-40	0	2.98	3.32
2012	Cle	AL	61	0	0	53	57.2	242	49	25	23	6	0	3	2	16	1	59	0	0	0	4	.000	0	39-43	0	2.85	3.59
09	StL	NL	29	0	0	8	23.2	106	17	12	11	3	0	1	3	15	0	30	4	0	1	1	.500	0	1-2	3	4.01	4.18
09	Cle	AL	32	0	0	8	33.1	133	24	16	16	5	0	1	3	12	0	38	4	0	0	1	.000	0	1-3	4	3.19	4.32
5 ML YEARS			290	0	0	186	279.0	1166	210	110	100	28	11	10	17	119	8	269	15	0	10	18	.357	0	107-126	22	3.03	3.23

Eury Perez

Bats: R **Throws:** R **Pos:** PR-8; CF-4; LF-3; PH-3   YERR-ee   **Ht:** 6'0" **Wt:** 180 **Born:** 5/30/1990 **Age:** 23

									BATTING													BASERUNNING				AVERAGES		
Year	Team	Lg	G	AB	H	2B	3B	HR	(Hm	Rd)	TB	R	RBI	RC	TBB	IBB	SO	HBP	SH	SF	SB	CS	SB%	GDP	Avg	OBP	Slg
2009	Nats	R	47	181	69	3	5	3	(-	-)	91	38	24	39	15	0	20	5	4	0	16	8	.67	3	.381	.443	.503
2010	Hgrstn	A	131	438	131	17	5	3	(-	-)	167	88	42	67	23	0	74	8	21	1	64	13	.83	11	.299	.345	.381
2011	Ptomc	A+	119	424	120	9	2	1	(-	-)	136	54	41	49	22	1	63	3	11	5	45	15	.75	4	.283	.319	.321
2012	Hrsbrg	AA	82	351	105	11	2	0	(-	-)	120	34	30	41	7	0	53	7	7	1	26	10	.72	0	.299	.325	.342
2012	Nats	R	5	22	9	1	0	0	(-	-)	10	4	2	5	1	0	0	0	0	0	5	0	1.00	1	.409	.435	.455
2012	Syrcse	AAA	40	159	53	7	1	0	(-	-)	62	21	10	25	8	0	26	2	4	0	20	5	.80	3	.333	.373	.390
2012	Was	NL	13	5	1	0	0	0	(0	0)	1	3	0	0	0	0	0	0	0	0	3	0	1.00	0	.200	.200	.200

Hernan Perez

Bats: R **Throws:** R **Pos:** 2B-1; PH-1; PR-1   HURR-nen   **Ht:** 6'1" **Wt:** 185 **Born:** 3/26/1991 **Age:** 22

									BATTING													BASERUNNING				AVERAGES		
Year	Team	Lg	G	AB	H	2B	3B	HR	(Hm	Rd)	TB	R	RBI	RC	TBB	IBB	SO	HBP	SH	SF	SB	CS	SB%	GDP	Avg	OBP	Slg
2009	Tigers	R	21	81	18	9	1	1	(-	-)	32	9	9	8	3	0	14	1	1	0	2	0	1.00	1	.222	.259	.395
2009	Lkland	A+	21	72	19	4	1	0	(-	-)	25	7	10	7	3	0	21	0	1	1	0	0	-	2	.264	.289	.347
2009	WMich	A	12	44	10	0	1	0	(-	-)	12	0	5	2	0	0	8	0	1	0	2	1	.67	1	.227	.227	.273
2010	WMich	A	124	473	111	15	0	5	(-	-)	141	45	50	39	25	0	98	2	2	5	5	1	.83	19	.235	.273	.298
2011	WMich	A	129	503	130	23	3	8	(-	-)	183	69	42	63	38	1	87	6	11	8	23	6	.79	9	.258	.314	.364
2012	Lkland	A+	124	441	115	11	4	5	(-	-)	149	50	44	50	24	0	70	2	6	6	27	4	.87	7	.261	.298	.338
2012	Det	AL	2	2	1	0	0	0	(0	0)	1	1	0	0	0	0	0	0	0	0	0	0	-	0	.500	.500	.500

Juan Perez

Pitches: L **Bats:** R **Pos:** RP-10   **Ht:** 6'0" **Wt:** 170 **Born:** 9/3/1978 **Age:** 34

				HOW MUCH HE PITCHED			WHAT HE GAVE UP												THE RESULTS						
Year	Team	Lg	G	GS	CG	GF	IP	BFP	H	R	ER	HR	SH	SF	HB	TBB	IBB	SO	WP	Bk	W	L	Pct	Sh	Sv-Op	Hld	ERC	ERA
2012	Nashv*	AAA	38	0	0	10	40.0	168	32	17	16	3	3	1	1	20	0	54	6	0	4	2	.667	0	0- -	-	3.33	3.60
2006	Pit	NL	7	0	0	0	3.1	17	5	3	3	1	0	1	2	1	0	3	0	0	0	1	.000	0	0-0	0	11.77	8.10
2007	Pit	NL	17	0	0	4	12.1	57	14	7	6	2	0	0	0	8	0	10	1	0	0	0	-	0	0-0	0	6.48	4.38
2011	Phi	NL	8	0	0	1	5.0	21	1	2	2	0	0	0	1	5	0	8	1	0	1	0	1.000	0	0-0	1	1.51	3.60
2012	Mil	NL	10	0	0	5	7.0	35	6	4	4	2	0	0	1	8	1	10	0	0	0	1	.000	0	0-0	0	8.29	5.14
4 ML YEARS			42	0	0	10	27.2	130	26	16	15	5	0	1	3	22	1	31	2	0	1	2	.333	0	0-0	1	6.42	4.88

Luis Perez

Pitches: L **Bats:** L **Pos:** RP-35   **Ht:** 6'0" **Wt:** 210 **Born:** 1/20/1985 **Age:** 28

				HOW MUCH HE PITCHED			WHAT HE GAVE UP												THE RESULTS						
Year	Team	Lg	G	GS	CG	GF	IP	BFP	H	R	ER	HR	SH	SF	HB	TBB	IBB	SO	WP	Bk	W	L	Pct	Sh	Sv-Op	Hld	ERC	ERA
2007	Auburn	A-	16	16	0	0	75.1	343	73	37	31	1	3	3	9	38	0	71	4	1	3	3	.500	0	0- -	-	4.05	3.70
2008	Lnsng	A	28	23	0	1	137.1	595	136	68	55	4	8	4	16	51	0	137	6	7	5	12	.294	0	0- -	-	3.89	3.60
2009	NHam	AA	28	27	2	0	162.1	693	145	78	64	11	3	3	13	67	2	112	6	0	9	11	.450	0	0- -	-	3.63	3.55
2010	NHam	AA	13	12	1	0	73.1	314	67	43	37	6	0	1	4	37	0	49	5	1	5	6	.455	0	0- -	-	4.19	4.54
2010	LsVgs	AAA	15	15	1	0	86.2	416	107	66	59	5	3	3	12	47	0	56	7	3	5	5	.500	0	0- -	-	6.27	6.13
2011	LsVgs	AAA	8	8	0	0	45.0	189	37	23	23	5	2	0	3	23	0	43	3	0	2	2	.500	0	0- -	-	3.98	4.60
2011	Tor	AL	37	4	0	7	65.0	294	74	40	37	9	1	3	5	27	1	54	4	0	3	3	.500	0	0-2	4	5.53	5.12
2012	Tor	AL	35	0	0	6	42.0	175	38	16	16	3	0	0	3	16	0	39	0	0	2	2	.500	0	0-0	4	3.66	3.43
2 ML YEARS			72	4	0	13	107.0	469	112	56	53	12	1	3	8	43	1	93	4	0	5	5	.500	0	0-2	8	4.77	4.46

Martin Perez

Pitches: L Bats: L Pos: SP-6; RP-6 · mar-TEEN · Ht: 6'0" Wt: 180 Born: 4/4/1991 Age: 22

			HOW MUCH HE PITCHED						WHAT HE GAVE UP												THE RESULTS						
Year	Team	Lg	G	GS	CG	GF	IP	BFP	H	R	ER	HR	SH	SF	HB	TBB	IBB	SO	WP	Bk	W	L	Pct	Sh	Sv-Op	Hld	ERC	ERA
2008	Spkane	A-	15	15	0	0	61.2	277	66	32	25	3	5	1	2	28	0	53	4	2	1	2	.333	0	0- -	-	4.39	3.65
2009	Hkry	A	22	14	0	3	93.2	391	82	35	24	3	5	4	1	33	0	105	5	5	5	5	.500	0	1- -	-	2.80	2.31
2009	Frisco	AA	5	5	0	0	21.0	95	29	16	13	2	0	1	0	5	0	14	1	0	1	3	.250	0	0- -	-	5.59	5.57
2010	Frisco	AA	24	23	0	0	99.2	461	117	73	66	12	4	3	0	50	1	101	6	2	5	8	.385	0	0- -	-	5.57	5.96
2011	Frisco	AA	17	16	1	0	88.1	368	80	35	31	6	3	2	1	36	0	83	4	2	4	2	.667	1	0- -	-	3.48	3.16
2011	RdRck	AAA	10	10	0	0	49.0	237	72	38	35	4	3	4	0	20	0	37	6	4	4	4	.500	0	0- -	-	6.67	6.43
2012	RdRck	AAA	22	21	2	0	127.0	544	122	70	60	10	6	5	4	56	0	69	3	0	7	6	.538	0	0- -	-	4.05	4.25
2012	Tex	AL	12	6	0	2	38.0	177	47	26	23	3	1	1	2	15	1	25	5	2	1	4	.200	0	0-0	0	5.33	5.45

Oliver Perez

Pitches: L Bats: L Pos: RP-33 · Ht: 6'3" Wt: 210 Born: 8/15/1981 Age: 31

			HOW MUCH HE PITCHED						WHAT HE GAVE UP												THE RESULTS						
Year	Team	Lg	G	GS	CG	GF	IP	BFP	H	R	ER	HR	SH	SF	HB	TBB	IBB	SO	WP	Bk	W	L	Pct	Sh	Sv-Op	Hld	ERC	ERA
2012	Tacom*	AAA	22	0	0	8	31.0	141	33	16	16	4	0	1	0	19	0	42	3	0	2	2	.500	0	1- -	-	5.57	4.65
2002	SD	NL	16	15	0	0	90.0	387	71	37	35	13	5	3	5	48	1	94	3	0	4	5	.444	0	0-0	0	3.93	3.50
2003	2 Tms	NL	24	24	0	0	126.2	579	129	80	77	22	5	2	4	77	3	141	7	1	4	10	.286	0	0-0	0	5.66	5.47
2004	Pit	NL	30	30	2	0	196.0	805	145	71	65	22	9	5	9	81	2	239	2	1	12	10	.545	1	0-0	0	2.99	2.98
2005	Pit	NL	20	20	0	0	103.0	471	102	68	67	23	5	4	6	70	1	97	3	0	7	5	.583	0	0-0	0	6.44	5.85
2006	2 Tms	NL	22	22	1	0	112.2	529	129	90	82	20	5	10	6	68	0	102	5	1	3	13	.188	1	0-0	0	6.62	6.55
2007	NYM	NL	29	29	0	0	177.0	765	153	90	70	22	4	7	7	79	1	174	6	0	15	10	.600	0	0-0	0	3.76	3.56
2008	NYM	NL	34	34	0	0	194.0	847	167	100	91	24	9	7	11	105	4	180	9	1	10	7	.588	0	0-0	0	4.21	4.22
2009	NYM	NL	14	14	0	0	66.0	324	69	51	50	12	5	4	4	58	2	62	2	0	3	4	.429	0	0-0	0	7.16	6.82
2010	NYM	NL	17	7	0	0	46.1	234	54	37	35	9	1	3	4	42	3	37	4	0	0	5	.000	0	0-0	0	8.27	6.80
2012	Sea	AL	33	0	0	6	29.2	123	27	7	7	1	1	1	0	10	2	24	2	0	1	3	.250	0	0-2	5	2.82	2.12
03	SD	NL	19	19	0	0	103.2	473	103	65	62	20	4	2	3	65	2	117	6	1	4	7	.364	0	0-0	0	5.74	5.38
03	Pit	NL	5	5	0	0	23.0	106	26	15	15	2	1	0	1	12	1	24	1	0	0	3	.000	0	0-0	0	5.29	5.87
06	Pit	NL	15	15	0	0	76.0	364	88	64	56	13	5	8	3	51	0	61	4	1	2	10	.167	0	0-0	0	6.85	6.63
06	NYM	NL	7	7	1	0	36.2	165	41	26	26	7	0	2	3	17	0	41	1	0	1	3	.250	1	0-0	0	6.16	6.38
	Postseason		2	2	0	0	11.2	50	13	6	6	3	2	0	1	3	1	7	0	0	1	0	1.000	0	0-0	0	5.61	4.63
	10 ML YEARS		239	195	3	10	1141.1	5064	1046	631	579	168	49	46	56	638	19	1150	43	4	59	72	.450	2	0-2	5	4.74	4.57

Rafael Perez

Pitches: L Bats: L Pos: RP-8 · Ht: 6'3" Wt: 195 Born: 5/15/1982 Age: 31

			HOW MUCH HE PITCHED						WHAT HE GAVE UP												THE RESULTS						
Year	Team	Lg	G	GS	CG	GF	IP	BFP	H	R	ER	HR	SH	SF	HB	TBB	IBB	SO	WP	Bk	W	L	Pct	Sh	Sv-Op	Hld	ERC	ERA
2012	Akron*	AA	3	1	0	0	4.0	13	2	0	0	0	0	0	0	0	0	0	0	0	0	0	-	0	0- -	-	0.58	0.00
2012	Clmbs*	AAA	2	0	0	0	2.0	7	1	0	0	0	0	0	0	1	0	1	0	0	0	0	-	0	0- -	-	1.62	0.00
2006	Cle	AL	18	0	0	5	12.1	56	10	6	6	2	1	0	0	6	1	15	4	1	0	0	-	0	0-1	1	3.37	4.38
2007	Cle	AL	44	0	0	11	60.2	236	41	15	12	5	1	1	0	15	2	62	4	0	1	2	.333	0	1-2	12	1.74	1.78
2008	Cle	AL	73	0	0	14	76.1	313	67	32	30	8	2	0	2	23	3	86	3	0	4	4	.500	0	2-7	25	3.14	3.54
2009	Cle	AL	54	0	0	12	48.0	230	66	41	39	5	4	2	2	25	6	32	1	2	4	3	.571	0	0-1	6	6.85	7.31
2010	Cle	AL	70	0	0	13	61.0	272	72	23	22	3	6	1	0	25	4	36	6	0	6	1	.857	0	0-4	13	4.68	3.25
2011	Cle	AL	71	0	0	7	63.0	257	59	27	21	2	3	2	0	19	0	33	3	1	5	2	.714	0	0-2	12	2.97	3.00
2012	Cle	AL	8	0	0	1	7.2	31	5	3	3	1	0	0	0	4	1	4	0	1	1	0	1.000	0	0-0	0	2.75	3.52
	Postseason		6	0	0	1	7.0	34	10	9	6	3	0	0	0	3	0	6	0	0	1	0	1.000	0	0-0	0	9.36	7.71
	7 ML YEARS		338	0	0	63	329.0	1395	320	147	133	26	17	6	4	117	17	268	21	5	21	12	.636	0	3-17	69	3.58	3.64

Salvador Perez

Bats: R Throws: R Pos: C-74; DH-1; PH-1 · Ht: 6'3" Wt: 245 Born: 5/10/1990 Age: 23

			BATTING																BASERUNNING				AVERAGES		
Year	Team	Lg	G	AB	H	2B	3B	HR	(Hm | Rd)	TB	R	RBI	RC	TBB	IBB	SO	HBP	SH	SF	SB	CS	SB%	GDP	Avg	OBP	Slg
2007	Royals	R	30	86	21	3	0	0	(- | -)	24	10	10	9	5	0	10	5	2	1	1	1	.50	1	.244	.320	.279
2008	Burlgtn	R+	13	40	13	0	1	0	(- | -)	15	4	10	7	5	0	5	1	2	1	0	0	-	0	.325	.404	.375
2008	Idaho	R+	12	43	17	3	1	1	(- | -)	25	7	6	9	2	0	5	0	0	1	0	1	.00	1	.395	.413	.581
2009	Burlgtn	A	36	127	24	6	0	0	(- | -)	30	10	7	5	6	0	15	1	2	1	0	0	-	3	.189	.230	.236
2009	Idaho	R+	59	233	72	14	3	2	(- | -)	98	35	38	37	19	0	25	1	1	5	0	1	.00	6	.309	.357	.421
2010	Wilmg	A+	99	365	106	21	1	7	(- | -)	150	35	53	50	18	1	38	3	1	9	1	1	.50	13	.290	.322	.411
2011	NWArk	AA	79	286	81	14	0	9	(- | -)	122	35	43	40	16	0	30	4	1	0	1	1	.00	12	.283	.329	.427
2011	Omha	AAA	12	48	16	5	0	1	(- | -)	24	5	10	8	0	0	6	1	0	0	0	0	-	1	.333	.347	.500
2012	Omha	AAA	12	50	17	2	0	0	(- | -)	19	11	7	7	2	0	5	0	1	0	0	0	-	2	.340	.365	.380
2011	KC	AL	39	148	49	8	2	3	(1 | 2)	70	20	21	26	7	0	20	1	0	2	0	0	-	5	.331	.361	.473
2012	KC	AL	76	289	87	16	0	11	(3 | 8)	136	38	39	36	12	3	27	1	0	3	0	0	-	14	.301	.328	.471
	2 ML YEARS		115	437	136	24	2	14	(4 | 10)	206	58	60	62	19	3	47	2	0	5	0	0	-	19	.311	.339	.471

Glen Perkins

Pitches: L Bats: L Pos: RP-70 · Ht: 6'0" Wt: 204 Born: 3/2/1983 Age: 30

			HOW MUCH HE PITCHED						WHAT HE GAVE UP												THE RESULTS						
Year	Team	Lg	G	GS	CG	GF	IP	BFP	H	R	ER	HR	SH	SF	HB	TBB	IBB	SO	WP	Bk	W	L	Pct	Sh	Sv-Op	Hld	ERC	ERA
2006	Min	AL	4	0	0	0	5.2	20	3	1	1	0	0	0	0	6	0	0	0	0	0	0	-	0	0-0	1	0.60	1.59
2007	Min	AL	19	0	0	3	28.2	115	23	10	10	2	1	1	2	12	0	20	2	0	0	0	-	0	0-0	3	3.32	3.14
2008	Min	AL	26	26	0	0	151.0	661	183	81	74	25	7	4	3	39	0	74	2	1	12	4	.750	0	0-0	0	5.30	4.41
2009	Min	AL	18	17	0	0	96.1	423	120	64	63	13	1	3	1	23	0	45	2	1	6	7	.462	0	0-0	0	5.14	5.89
2010	Min	AL	13	1	0	5	21.2	98	29	16	14	3	1	2	4	5	1	14	0	0	1	1	.500	0	0-0	0	6.56	5.82

Year Team Lg	G	GS	CG	GF	IP	BFP	H	R	ER	HR	SH	SF	HB	TBB	IBB	SO	WP	Bk	W	L	Pct	Sh	Sv-Op	Hld	ERC	ERA
2011 Min AL	65	0	0	17	61.2	253	55	19	17	2	5	1	1	21	5	65	3	0	4	4	.500	0	2-5	17	2.81	2.48
2012 Min AL	70	0	0	43	70.1	281	57	25	20	8	3	2	3	16	3	78	3	0	3	1	.750	0	16-20	11	2.63	2.56
Postseason	1	0	0	0	0.1	3	2	0	0	0	0	0	0	0	0	0	0	0	0	0	-	0	0-0	0	39.65	0.00
7 ML YEARS	215	44	0	70	435.1	1851	470	216	199	53	18	13	14	116	9	302	12	2	26	17	.605	0	18-25	32	4.28	4.11

Ryan Perry

Pitches: R Bats: R Pos: RP-7 **Ht: 6'4" Wt: 215 Born: 2/13/1987 Age: 26**

Year Team Lg	G	GS	CG	GF	IP	BFP	H	R	ER	HR	SH	SF	HB	TBB	IBB	SO	WP	Bk	W	L	Pct	Sh	Sv-Op	Hld	ERC	ERA
2012 Syrcse* AAA	11	0	0	7	12.0	53	16	6	6	0	0	0	1	7	1	14	6	0	1	1	.500	0	2- -		6.84	4.50
2012 Hrsbrg* AA	13	13	1	0	73.0	288	59	28	23	3	4	0	4	22	1	46	2	0	2	4	.333	0	0- -		2.61	2.84
2009 Det AL	53	0	0	12	61.2	273	56	30	26	7	3	3	1	38	5	60	6	1	0	1	.000	0	0-3	6	4.45	3.79
2010 Det AL	60	0	0	21	62.2	261	55	26	25	6	4	3	5	23	1	45	3	0	3	5	.375	0	2-5	19	3.61	3.59
2011 Det AL	36	0	0	6	37.0	168	39	25	22	1	1	3	2	21	3	24	3	1	2	0	1.000	0	0-1	4	4.58	5.35
2012 Was NL	7	0	0	4	8.0	35	12	9	9	2	0	0	0	2	0	3	0	0	1	0	1.000	0	0-0	0	8.17	10.13
Postseason	5	0	0	3	6.1	27	9	5	4	1	0	1	0	0	0	3	0	0	0	1	.000	0	0-0	0	5.36	5.68
4 ML YEARS	156	0	0	43	169.1	737	162	90	82	16	8	9	8	84	9	132	12	2	6	6	.500	0	2-9	29	4.32	4.36

Vinnie Pestano

Pitches: R Bats: R Pos: RP-70 peh-STAH-no **Ht: 6'0" Wt: 200 Born: 2/20/1985 Age: 28**

Year Team Lg	G	GS	CG	GF	IP	BFP	H	R	ER	HR	SH	SF	HB	TBB	IBB	SO	WP	Bk	W	L	Pct	Sh	Sv-Op	Hld	ERC	ERA
2010 Cle AL	5	0	0	5	5.0	23	4	2	2	0	0	0	0	5	0	8	0	0	0	0	-	0	1-1	0	4.56	3.60
2011 Cle AL	68	0	0	20	62.0	250	41	16	16	5	0	0	3	24	3	84	0	0	1	2	.333	0	2-6	23	2.26	2.32
2012 Cle AL	70	0	0	13	70.0	286	53	20	20	7	0	2	4	24	1	76	1	0	3	3	.500	0	2-5	36	2.77	2.57
3 ML YEARS	143	0	0	38	137.0	559	98	38	38	12	0	2	7	53	4	168	1	0	4	5	.444	0	5-12	59	2.60	2.50

Bryan Petersen

Bats: L Throws: R Pos: LF-51; CF-20; PH-15; RF-4; PR-4 **Ht: 6'0" Wt: 190 Born: 4/9/1986 Age: 27**

Year Team Lg	G	AB	H	2B	3B	HR	(Hm	Rd)	TB	R	RBI	RC	TBB	IBB	SO	HBP	SH	SF	SB	CS	SB%	GDP	Avg	OBP	Slg
2012 NewOr* AAA	64	243	78	8	2	3	(-	-)	99	45	28	38	20	0	43	5	0	3	8	7	.53	3	.321	.380	.407
2010 Fla NL	23	24	2	0	0	0	(0	0)	2	1	2	0	1	0	6	0	0	0	0	0	-	0	.083	.120	.083
2011 Fla NL	74	204	54	13	3	2	(2	0)	79	18	10	27	26	2	49	5	3	3	7	1	.88	4	.265	.357	.387
2012 Mia NL	84	241	47	9	3	0	(0	0)	62	29	17	19	25	0	58	1	5	1	8	2	.80	3	.195	.272	.257
3 ML YEARS	181	469	103	22	6	2	(2	0)	143	48	29	46	52	2	113	6	8	4	15	3	.83	7	.220	.303	.305

Yusmeiro Petit

Pitches: R Bats: R Pos: SP-1 USE-mere-oh pa-TEET **Ht: 6'1" Wt: 250 Born: 11/22/1984 Age: 28**

Year Team Lg	G	GS	CG	GF	IP	BFP	H	R	ER	HR	SH	SF	HB	TBB	IBB	SO	WP	Bk	W	L	Pct	Sh	Sv-Op	Hld	ERC	ERA
2012 Fresno* AAA	28	28	1	0	166.2	701	178	88	64	14	2	6	1	36	0	153	3	1	7	7	.500	0	0- -	-	3.64	3.46
2006 Fla NL	15	1	0	5	26.1	129	46	28	28	7	1	1	0	9	1	20	0	1	1	0	.500	0	0-0	0	10.07	9.57
2007 Ari NL	14	10	0	2	57.0	243	58	30	29	12	1	1	0	18	1	40	0	1	3	4	.429	0	0-0	0	4.56	4.58
2008 Ari NL	19	8	0	6	56.1	229	45	29	27	12	4	2	1	14	2	42	3	1	3	5	.375	0	0-0	0	3.08	4.31
2009 Ari NL	23	17	0	2	89.2	407	102	62	58	19	3	0	0	34	1	74	3	0	3	10	.231	0	0-0	0	5.44	5.82
2012 SF NL	1	1	0	0	4.2	22	7	2	2	0	1	0	0	4	0	1	1	0	0	0	-	0	0-0	0	9.14	3.86
5 ML YEARS	72	37	0	15	234.0	1030	258	151	144	50	10	4	1	79	5	177	7	2	10	20	.333	0	0-0	0	5.15	5.54

Andy Pettitte

Pitches: L Bats: L Pos: SP-12 PETT-it **Ht: 6'5" Wt: 225 Born: 6/15/1972 Age: 41**

Year Team Lg	G	GS	CG	GF	IP	BFP	H	R	ER	HR	SH	SF	HB	TBB	IBB	SO	WP	Bk	W	L	Pct	Sh	Sv-Op	Hld	ERC	ERA
2012 Tampa* A+	2	2	0	0	7.0	24	4	1	1	0	0	1	0	0	0	5	1	0	0	0	-	0	0- -	-	0.72	1.29
2012 Trntn* AA	1	1	0	0	5.0	24	7	4	3	0	0	0	0	1	0	3	0	0	0	1	.000	0	0- -	-	4.47	5.40
2012 S-WB* AAA	1	1	0	0	5.0	24	8	5	3	0	0	1	0	2	0	5	0	0	0	1	.000	0	0- -	-	6.98	5.40
1995 NYY AL	31	26	3	1	175.0	745	183	86	81	15	4	5	1	63	3	114	8	1	12	9	.571	0	0-0	0	4.13	4.17
1996 NYY AL	35	34	2	1	221.0	929	229	105	95	23	7	3	3	72	2	162	6	1	21	8	.724	0	0-0	0	4.14	3.87
1997 NYY AL	35	35	4	0	240.1	986	233	86	77	7	6	2	3	65	0	166	7	0	18	7	.720	1	0-0	0	3.05	2.88
1998 NYY AL	33	32	5	0	216.1	932	226	110	102	20	6	7	6	87	1	146	5	0	16	11	.593	0	0-0	0	4.46	4.24
1999 NYY AL	31	31	0	0	191.2	851	216	105	100	20	6	6	3	89	3	121	3	1	14	11	.560	0	0-0	0	5.22	4.70
2000 NYY AL	32	32	3	0	204.2	903	219	111	99	17	7	4	4	80	4	125	2	3	19	9	.679	1	0-0	0	4.32	4.35
2001 NYY AL	31	31	2	0	200.2	858	224	103	89	14	8	7	6	41	3	164	2	2	15	10	.600	0	0-0	0	3.82	3.99
2002 NYY AL	22	22	3	0	134.2	570	144	58	49	6	3	2	4	32	2	97	2	1	13	5	.722	1	0-0	0	3.55	3.27
2003 NYY AL	33	33	1	0	208.1	896	227	109	93	21	5	5	1	50	3	180	5	0	21	8	.724	1	0-0	0	3.89	4.02
2004 Hou NL	15	15	0	0	83.0	346	71	37	36	8	1	0	0	31	2	79	4	0	6	4	.600	0	0-0	0	3.12	3.90
2005 Hou NL	33	33	0	0	222.1	875	188	66	59	17	10	4	3	41	0	171	2	0	17	9	.654	0	0-0	0	2.40	2.39
2006 Hou NL	36	35	2	1	214.1	929	238	114	100	27	14	5	2	70	9	178	2	1	14	13	.519	0	0-0	0	4.58	4.20
2007 NYY AL	36	34	0	0	215.1	916	238	106	97	16	5	9	1	69	1	141	3	0	15	9	.625	0	0-0	1	4.27	4.05
2008 NYY AL	33	33	0	0	204.0	881	233	112	103	19	8	7	7	55	4	158	6	1	14	14	.500	0	0-0	0	4.45	4.54
2009 NYY AL	32	32	0	0	194.2	834	193	101	90	20	4	4	4	76	1	148	3	0	14	8	.636	0	0-0	0	4.11	4.16
2010 NYY AL	21	21	0	0	129.0	536	123	52	47	13	8	5	3	43	3	101	2	0	11	3	.786	0	0-0	0	3.62	3.28
2012 NYY AL	12	12	0	0	75.1	303	65	26	24	8	2	0	0	21	0	69	1	0	5	4	.556	0	0-0	0	2.96	2.87
Postseason	42	42	0	0	263.0	1098	271	116	112	31	12	9	3	72	3	173	4	1	19	10	.655	0	0-0	0	3.96	3.83
17 ML YEARS	501	491	25	3	3130.2	13290	3250	1487	1341	271	104	75	51	983	41	2320	63	11	245	142	.633	4	0-0	1	3.93	3.86

227

Cord Phelps

Bats: B Throws: R Pos: 2B-5; PH-5; DH-4; 3B-1; SS-1   Ht: 6'2" Wt: 200 Born: 1/23/1987 Age: 26

								BATTING													BASERUNNING				AVERAGES		
Year	Team	Lg	G	AB	H	2B	3B	HR	(Hm	Rd)	TB	R	RBI	RC	TBB	IBB	SO	HBP	SH	SF	SB	CS	SB%	GDP	Avg	OBP	Slg
2008	Indns	R	1	3	0	0	0	0	(-	-)	0	0	1	0	0	0	2	0	0	1	0	0	-	0	.000	.000	.000
2008	MhVlly	A-	35	141	44	10	2	0	(-	-)	64	24	21	24	15	0	22	0	0	1	4	3	.57	3	.312	.376	.454
2009	Knstn	A+	130	479	125	27	5	4	(-	-)	174	72	53	75	93	1	97	6	2	2	17	14	.55	18	.261	.386	.363
2010	Akron	AA	53	199	59	8	3	2	(-	-)	79	25	23	27	15	0	29	1	1	2	1	4	.20	10	.296	.346	.397
2010	Clmbs	AAA	66	243	77	20	4	6	(-	-)	123	41	31	47	24	1	39	4	1	1	3	2	.60	3	.317	.386	.506
2011	Clmbs	AAA	97	378	111	25	4	14	(-	-)	186	51	63	70	51	2	89	1	0	4	3	6	.33	10	.294	.376	.492
2012	Clmbs	AAA	135	503	139	34	3	16	(-	-)	227	82	62	88	71	3	94	4	1	3	9	4	.69	8	.276	.368	.451
2011	Cle	AL	35	71	11	2	1	1	(1	0)	18	10	6	3	8	0	17	0	1	0	1	0	1.00	2	.155	.241	.254
2012	Cle	AL	14	33	7	0	0	1	(0	1)	10	2	5	5	1	0	10	0	0	0	0	0	-	0	.212	.235	.303
	2 ML YEARS		49	104	18	2	1	2	(1	1)	28	12	11	8	9	0	27	0	1	0	1	0	1.00	2	.173	.239	.269

David Phelps

Pitches: R Bats: R Pos: RP-22; SP-11   Ht: 6'2" Wt: 200 Born: 10/9/1986 Age: 26

			HOW MUCH HE PITCHED					WHAT HE GAVE UP												THE RESULTS					
Year	Team	Lg	G	GS	CG	GF	IP	BFP	H	R	ER	HR	SH	SF	HB	TBB	IBB	SO	WP	Bk	W	L	Pct	Sh	Sv-Op	Hld	ERC	ERA
2008	StIsInd	A-	15	15	0	0	72.2	294	67	28	22	4	0	1	1	18	0	52	1	1	8	2	.800	0	0- -	-	2.89	2.72
2009	CtnSC	A	19	19	0	0	112.2	465	117	48	35	9	2	4	4	25	0	90	5	2	10	3	.769	0	0- -	-	3.68	2.80
2009	Tampa	A+	7	7	0	0	38.1	151	34	9	5	1	0	0	0	6	0	32	2	0	3	1	.750	0	0- -	-	2.16	1.17
2010	Trntn	AA	14	14	0	0	88.1	342	63	21	20	2	1	0	2	23	0	85	2	3	6	0	1.000	0	0- -	-	1.78	2.04
2010	S-WB	AAA	12	11	0	0	70.1	297	76	31	24	4	2	4	1	13	0	57	1	1	4	2	.667	0	0- -	-	3.41	3.07
2011	S-WB	AAA	18	18	1	0	107.1	449	115	42	38	11	4	1	4	26	0	90	0	0	6	6	.500	1	0- -	-	4.10	3.19
2011	Yanks	R	2	2	0	0	7.0	28	4	2	0	0	0	0	0	1	0	5	0	0	1	1	.500	0	0- -	-	0.87	0.00
2012	Tampa	A+	2	2	0	0	5.1	21	7	0	0	0	0	0	0	1	0	5	0	0	0	0	-	0	0- -	-	4.83	0.00
2012	Trntn	AA	1	1	0	0	6.2	22	1	0	0	0	0	0	0	1	0	11	0	0	1	0	1.000	0	0- -	-	0.15	0.00
2012	S-WB	AAA	1	1	0	0	6.2	27	4	0	0	0	0	0	0	3	0	7	0	0	1	0	1.000	0	0- -	-	1.61	0.00
2012	NYY	AL	33	11	0	5	99.2	414	81	38	37	14	4	3	6	38	2	96	2	2	4	4	.500	0	0-0	2	3.48	3.34

Brandon Phillips

Bats: R Throws: R Pos: 2B-146; PH-2   Ht: 6'0" Wt: 200 Born: 6/28/1981 Age: 32

								BATTING													BASERUNNING				AVERAGES		
Year	Team	Lg	G	AB	H	2B	3B	HR	(Hm	Rd)	TB	R	RBI	RC	TBB	IBB	SO	HBP	SH	SF	SB	CS	SB%	GDP	Avg	OBP	Slg
2002	Cle	AL	11	31	8	3	1	0	(0	0)	13	5	4	5	3	0	6	1	1	0	0	0	-	0	.258	.343	.419
2003	Cle	AL	112	370	77	18	1	6	(3	3)	115	36	33	22	14	0	77	3	5	1	4	5	.44	12	.208	.242	.311
2004	Cle	AL	6	22	4	2	0	0	(0	0)	6	1	1	0	2	0	5	0	0	0	0	2	.00	1	.182	.250	.273
2005	Cle	AL	6	9	0	0	0	0	(0	0)	0	1	0	0	0	0	4	0	0	0	0	0	-	0	.000	.000	.000
2006	Cin	NL	149	536	148	28	1	17	(9	8)	229	65	75	74	35	3	88	6	4	6	25	2	.93	19	.276	.324	.427
2007	Cin	NL	158	650	187	26	6	30	(17	13)	315	107	94	88	33	4	109	12	2	5	32	8	.80	26	.288	.331	.485
2008	Cin	NL	141	559	146	24	7	21	(13	8)	247	80	78	74	39	6	93	5	0	6	23	10	.70	13	.261	.312	.442
2009	Cin	NL	153	584	161	30	5	20	(10	10)	261	78	98	80	44	3	75	6	2	8	25	9	.74	21	.276	.329	.447
2010	Cin	NL	155	626	172	33	5	18	(10	8)	269	100	59	77	46	1	83	8	6	1	16	12	.57	14	.275	.332	.430
2011	Cin	NL	150	610	183	38	2	18	(14	4)	279	94	82	92	44	3	85	9	5	6	14	9	.61	15	.300	.353	.457
2012	Cin	NL	147	580	163	30	1	18	(15	3)	249	86	77	78	28	2	79	8	3	4	15	2	.88	19	.281	.321	.429
	Postseason		3	12	4	1	0	1	(0	1)	8	2	1	2	0	0	1	0	0	0	0	0	-	0	.333	.333	.667
	11 ML YEARS		1188	4577	1249	232	29	148	(91	57)	1983	653	601	590	288	22	704	58	28	37	154	59	.72	140	.273	.322	.433

Zach Phillips

Pitches: L Bats: L Pos: RP-6   Ht: 6'1" Wt: 190 Born: 9/21/1986 Age: 26

			HOW MUCH HE PITCHED					WHAT HE GAVE UP												THE RESULTS					
Year	Team	Lg	G	GS	CG	GF	IP	BFP	H	R	ER	HR	SH	SF	HB	TBB	IBB	SO	WP	Bk	W	L	Pct	Sh	Sv-Op	Hld	ERC	ERA
2005	Rngrs	R	14	11	0	0	50.1	216	52	26	22	3	0	0	3	13	0	73	2	0	1	3	.250	0	0- -	-	3.63	3.93
2005	Clinton	A	2	0	0	0	4.0	19	7	3	3	0	1	0	0	0	0	4	0	0	0	0	-	0	0- -	-	5.92	6.75
2006	Clinton	A	28	28	0	0	142.0	648	178	106	94	5	7	4	6	66	0	126	16	3	5	12	.294	0	0- -	-	5.59	5.96
2007	Clinton	A	27	27	0	0	151.2	618	139	56	49	6	3	3	5	43	0	157	8	1	11	7	.611	0	0- -	-	2.97	2.91
2008	Bkrsfld	A+	28	28	1	0	144.2	661	161	102	89	10	4	4	7	73	0	117	6	1	8	9	.471	0	0- -	-	5.09	5.54
2009	Bkrsfld	A+	16	3	0	3	44.0	168	19	7	6	1	1	1	0	11	0	46	4	0	2	3	.400	0	2- -	-	0.82	1.23
2009	Frisco	AA	20	0	0	4	33.2	152	27	11	6	1	3	1	1	19	0	29	1	0	0	0	-	0	2- -	-	3.06	1.60
2010	Frisco	AA	12	0	0	9	16.2	63	9	2	2	0	0	0	0	5	0	23	1	1	0	0	-	0	4- -	-	1.16	1.08
2010	OKCity	AAA	33	1	0	9	50.1	225	50	22	18	1	7	1	1	29	2	40	2	0	3	2	.600	0	1- -	-	4.14	3.22
2011	RdRck	AAA	33	0	0	14	44.2	204	50	26	22	3	4	1	1	21	2	38	3	0	1	3	.250	0	3- -	-	4.73	4.43
2011	Norfolk	AAA	14	0	0	8	13.2	57	12	5	4	0	0	1	0	7	1	7	1	0	1	1	.500	0	1- -	-	3.12	2.63
2012	Norfolk	AAA	42	0	0	23	54.0	236	56	22	19	1	3	1	2	22	4	45	2	0	2	2	.500	0	7- -	-	3.74	3.17
2011	Bal	AL	10	0	0	2	8.0	33	6	1	1	1	0	0	0	2	0	8	0	0	0	0	-	0	0-0	0	2.24	1.13
2012	Bal	AL	6	0	0	3	6.0	28	7	4	4	2	0	0	0	3	1	5	0	0	0	0	-	0	0-0	0	6.85	6.00
	2 ML YEARS		16	0	0	5	14.0	61	13	5	5	3	0	0	0	5	1	13	0	0	0	0	-	0	0-0	0	4.01	3.21

Denis Phipps

Bats: R Throws: R Pos: PH-3; PR-3; CF-1; RF-1   DENN-iss FIPPS   Ht: 6'3" Wt: 210 Born: 7/22/1985 Age: 27

								BATTING													BASERUNNING				AVERAGES		
Year	Team	Lg	G	AB	H	2B	3B	HR	(Hm	Rd)	TB	R	RBI	RC	TBB	IBB	SO	HBP	SH	SF	SB	CS	SB%	GDP	Avg	OBP	Slg
2006	Reds	R	43	164	46	10	1	3	(-	-)	67	21	22	21	8	0	31	3	0	1	6	6	.50	0	.280	.324	.409
2006	Billings	R+	17	54	17	3	0	1	(-	-)	23	7	10	9	5	0	19	0	2	1	6	0	1.00	1	.315	.367	.426
2007	Dayton	A	125	450	107	14	2	9	(-	-)	152	65	53	52	41	2	98	10	0	4	18	6	.75	7	.238	.313	.338
2008	Dayton	A	124	474	121	19	4	7	(-	-)	169	57	57	52	34	0	113	4	0	6	10	10	.50	8	.255	.307	.357
2009	Srsota	A+	134	493	118	32	5	10	(-	-)	190	51	55	57	31	0	108	5	5	6	18	8	.69	8	.239	.288	.385

Year	Team	Lg	G	AB	H	2B	3B	HR	(Hm	Rd)	TB	R	RBI	RC	TBB	IBB	SO	HBP	SH	SF	SB	CS	SB%	GDP	Avg	OBP	Slg
2009	Carlina	AA	3	4	0	0	0	0	(-	-)	0	0	0	0	0	0	1	0	0	0	0	0	-	0	.000	.000	.000
2010	Carlina	AA	104	372	85	22	3	4	(-	-)	125	44	35	37	32	2	86	4	1	2	8	9	.47	7	.228	.295	.336
2010	Lynbrg	A+	25	93	31	10	1	8	(-	-)	67	23	21	26	10	0	19	0	0	0	9	1	.90	2	.333	.398	.720
2011	Carlina	AA	82	305	100	22	5	7	(-	-)	153	53	38	58	27	0	83	2	0	4	10	6	.63	4	.328	.382	.502
2011	Lsvlle	AAA	40	158	60	12	2	5	(-	-)	91	30	26	37	13	0	41	1	0	1	4	1	.80	3	.380	.428	.576
2012	Lsvlle	AAA	92	357	79	19	0	15	(-	-)	143	48	45	43	33	0	103	4	2	2	4	2	.67	13	.221	.293	.401
2012	Reds	R	5	20	8	0	1	2	(-	-)	16	6	5	5	0	0	5	1	0	0	0	0	-	0	.400	.429	.800
2012	Cin	NL	8	10	3	1	0	1	(1	0)	7	4	2	2	1	0	4	0	0	0	0	0	-	0	.300	.364	.700

Juan Pierre

Bats: L Throws: L Pos: LF-107; PH-20; PR-6   **Ht: 5'11" Wt: 175 Born: 8/14/1977 Age: 35**

Year	Team	Lg	G	AB	H	2B	3B	HR	(Hm	Rd)	TB	R	RBI	RC	TBB	IBB	SO	HBP	SH	SF	SB	CS	SB%	GDP	Avg	OBP	Slg
2000	Col	NL	51	200	62	2	0	0	(0	0)	64	26	20	23	13	0	15	1	4	1	7	6	.54	2	.310	.353	.320
2001	Col	NL	156	617	202	26	11	2	(0	2)	256	108	55	101	41	1	29	10	14	1	46	17	.73	6	.327	.378	.415
2002	Col	NL	152	592	170	20	5	1	(0	1)	203	90	35	79	31	0	52	9	8	0	47	12	.80	7	.287	.332	.343
2003	Fla	NL	162	668	204	28	7	1	(1	0)	249	100	41	92	55	1	35	5	15	3	65	20	.76	9	.305	.361	.373
2004	Fla	NL	162	678	221	22	12	3	(1	2)	276	100	49	101	45	1	35	9	15	2	45	24	.65	9	.326	.374	.407
2005	Fla	NL	162	656	181	19	13	2	(1	1)	232	96	47	76	41	1	45	9	10	2	57	17	.77	10	.276	.326	.354
2006	ChC	NL	162	699	204	32	13	3	(1	2)	271	87	40	84	32	0	38	8	10	1	58	20	.74	6	.292	.330	.388
2007	LAD	NL	162	668	196	24	8	0	(0	0)	236	96	41	75	33	0	37	6	20	2	64	15	.81	10	.293	.331	.353
2008	LAD	NL	119	375	106	10	2	1	(0	1)	123	44	28	48	22	1	24	3	5	1	40	12	.77	3	.283	.327	.328
2009	LAD	NL	145	380	117	16	8	0	(0	0)	149	57	31	58	27	3	27	8	9	1	30	12	.71	7	.308	.365	.392
2010	CWS	AL	160	651	179	18	3	1	(0	1)	206	96	47	84	45	0	47	21	15	2	68	18	.79	8	.275	.341	.316
2011	CWS	AL	158	639	178	17	4	2	(2	0)	209	80	50	80	43	0	41	7	19	3	27	17	.61	7	.279	.329	.327
2012	Phi	NL	130	394	121	10	6	1	(0	1)	146	59	25	55	23	0	27	4	17	1	37	7	.84	4	.307	.351	.371
	Postseason		26	79	24	5	2	0	(0	0)	33	16	7	14	8	2	4	1	2	0	3	5	.38	0	.304	.375	.418
13 ML YEARS			1881	7217	2141	244	92	17	(7	10)	2620	1039	509	956	451	8	452	99	161	20	591	197	.75	88	.297	.346	.363

A.J. Pierzynski

Bats: L Throws: R Pos: C-126; PH-9; DH-5   perr-ZINN-ski   **Ht: 6'3" Wt: 235 Born: 12/30/1976 Age: 36**

Year	Team	Lg	G	AB	H	2B	3B	HR	(Hm	Rd)	TB	R	RBI	RC	TBB	IBB	SO	HBP	SH	SF	SB	CS	SB%	GDP	Avg	OBP	Slg
1998	Min	AL	7	10	3	0	0	0	(0	0)	3	1	1	2	1	0	2	1	0	1	0	0	-	0	.300	.385	.300
1999	Min	AL	9	22	6	2	0	0	(0	0)	8	3	3	3	1	0	4	1	0	0	0	0	-	0	.273	.333	.364
2000	Min	AL	33	88	27	5	1	2	(1	1)	40	12	11	14	5	0	14	2	0	1	1	0	1.00	1	.307	.354	.455
2001	Min	AL	114	381	110	33	2	7	(3	4)	168	51	55	50	16	4	57	4	1	3	1	7	.13	7	.289	.322	.441
2002	Min	AL	130	440	132	31	6	6	(2	4)	193	54	49	60	13	1	61	11	2	3	1	2	.33	14	.300	.334	.439
2003	Min	AL	137	487	152	35	3	11	(6	5)	226	63	74	80	24	12	55	15	2	5	3	1	.75	13	.312	.360	.464
2004	SF	NL	131	471	128	28	2	11	(3	8)	193	45	77	58	19	4	27	15	2	3	0	1	.00	27	.272	.319	.410
2005	CWS	AL	128	460	118	21	0	18	(12	6)	193	61	56	55	23	5	68	12	1	1	0	2	.00	13	.257	.308	.420
2006	CWS	AL	140	509	150	24	0	16	(9	7)	222	65	64	68	22	6	72	8	3	1	1	0	1.00	14	.295	.333	.436
2007	CWS	AL	136	472	124	24	0	14	(8	6)	190	54	50	49	25	5	66	8	1	3	1	1	.50	21	.263	.309	.403
2008	CWS	AL	134	534	150	31	1	13	(7	6)	222	66	60	64	19	5	71	8	3	6	1	0	1.00	14	.281	.312	.416
2009	CWS	AL	138	504	151	22	1	13	(8	5)	214	57	49	59	24	6	52	1	3	3	1	1	.50	18	.300	.331	.425
2010	CWS	AL	128	474	128	29	0	9	(7	2)	184	43	56	51	15	2	39	6	6	2	3	4	.43	17	.270	.300	.388
2011	CWS	AL	129	464	133	29	1	8	(5	3)	188	38	48	53	23	6	33	5	2	6	0	0	-	19	.287	.323	.405
2012	CWS	AL	135	479	133	18	4	27	(18	9)	240	68	77	79	28	5	78	8	1	4	0	0	-	8	.278	.326	.501
	Postseason		30	100	30	5	1	5	(3	2)	52	16	17	19	10	1	13	2	1	1	2	3	.40	2	.300	.372	.520
15 ML YEARS			1629	5795	1645	332	21	155	(89	66)	2484	681	730	745	258	61	699	105	27	42	13	19	.41	182	.284	.324	.429

Brett Pill

Bats: R Throws: R Pos: 1B-24; PH-19; LF-7; 3B-1   **Ht: 6'4" Wt: 225 Born: 9/9/1984 Age: 28**

Year	Team	Lg	G	AB	H	2B	3B	HR	(Hm	Rd)	TB	R	RBI	RC	TBB	IBB	SO	HBP	SH	SF	SB	CS	SB%	GDP	Avg	OBP	Slg
2006	SlmKzr	A-	60	223	49	16	0	5	(-	-)	80	37	35	25	22	1	39	3	0	2	3	2	.60	10	.220	.296	.359
2007	Augsta	A	137	536	144	47	1	10	(-	-)	223	72	91	75	38	2	81	7	1	7	4	2	.67	17	.269	.321	.416
2008	SnJos	A+	131	458	122	32	0	9	(-	-)	181	73	65	62	33	1	85	8	0	9	5	2	.71	13	.266	.321	.395
2009	Conn	AA	139	527	157	37	1	19	(-	-)	253	71	109	90	37	7	72	8	0	9	6	3	.67	13	.298	.348	.480
2010	Fresno	AAA	140	520	143	34	0	16	(-	-)	225	63	84	75	30	2	65	8	0	9	7	2	.78	21	.275	.319	.433
2011	Fresno	AAA	133	536	167	36	3	25	(-	-)	284	82	107	96	25	1	54	4	2	9	6	6	.50	16	.312	.341	.530
2012	Fresno	AAA	60	246	70	18	1	11	(-	-)	123	35	45	42	13	1	36	7	0	2	0	0	-	9	.285	.336	.500
2011	SF	NL	15	50	15	3	2	2	(0	2)	28	7	9	6	2	0	8	0	0	1	0	1	.00	2	.300	.321	.560
2012	SF	NL	48	105	22	3	0	4	(0	4)	37	10	11	7	6	1	19	2	1	0	1	0	1.00	5	.210	.265	.352
2 ML YEARS			63	155	37	6	2	6	(0	6)	65	17	20	13	8	1	27	2	1	1	1	1	.50	7	.239	.283	.419

Manny Pina

Bats: R Throws: R Pos: C-1; PH-1   PEEN-yah   **Ht: 6'0" Wt: 215 Born: 6/5/1987 Age: 26**

Year	Team	Lg	G	AB	H	2B	3B	HR	(Hm	Rd)	TB	R	RBI	RC	TBB	IBB	SO	HBP	SH	SF	SB	CS	SB%	GDP	Avg	OBP	Slg
2005	Rngrs	R	27	85	21	3	1	0	(-	-)	26	13	10	11	7	1	12	8	0	1	2	0	1.00	4	.247	.356	.306
2006	Rngrs	R	14	45	11	4	0	0	(-	-)	15	1	3	4	2	0	4	2	0	1	0	0	-	0	.244	.300	.333
2007	Clinton	A	86	281	64	13	0	1	(-	-)	80	20	23	23	15	0	28	6	0	4	0	0	-	4	.228	.278	.285
2008	Bkrsfld	A+	61	223	59	10	1	3	(-	-)	80	31	24	26	14	0	22	3	1	3	1	0	1.00	7	.265	.313	.359
2008	Frisco	AA	23	80	22	7	0	0	(-	-)	29	7	9	10	5	0	12	2	1	1	1	0	1.00	4	.275	.330	.363
2009	Frisco	AA	86	321	83	17	1	8	(-	-)	126	36	42	41	19	1	58	8	3	4	1	0	1.00	9	.259	.313	.393
2010	NWArk	AA	74	266	69	16	0	7	(-	-)	106	39	44	36	24	0	37	2	4	6	0	0	-	9	.259	.319	.398

	BATTING																			BASERUNNING				AVERAGES		
Year Team	Lg	G	AB	H	2B	3B	HR	(Hm	Rd)	TB	R	RBI	RC	TBB	IBB	SO	HBP	SH	SF	SB	CS	SB%	GDP	Avg	OBP	Slg
2010 Omha	AAA	17	55	12	2	0	2	(-	-)	20	5	5	5	3	0	7	1	0	1	0	0	-	4	.218	.267	.364
2011 Omha	AAA	68	210	50	13	0	5	(-	-)	78	34	25	32	34	0	37	8	6	1	0	0	-	6	.238	.364	.371
2011 NWArk	AA	3	8	2	1	0	0	(-	-)	3	0	3	1	2	0	3	0	0	0	0	0	-	0	.250	.400	.375
2012 Royals	R	6	13	6	2	0	0	(-	-)	8	3	5	5	6	0	2	1	0	1	0	0	-	1	.462	.619	.615
2012 NWArk	AA	43	131	34	3	0	5	(-	-)	52	9	20	23	24	0	24	5	0	2	0	0	-	1	.260	.389	.397
2011 KC	AL	4	14	3	2	0	0	(0	0)	5	2	0	1	1	0	2	0	0	0	0	0	-	1	.214	.267	.357
2012 KC	AL	1	2	0	0	0	0	(0	0)	0	0	0	0	0	0	0	0	0	0	0	0	-	0	.000	.000	.000
2 ML YEARS		5	16	3	2	0	0	(0	0)	5	2	0	1	1	0	2	0	0	0	0	0	-	1	.188	.235	.313

Michael Pineda

Pitches: R **Bats:** R **Pos:** P 　　　　pih-NAY-duh 　　　　**Ht:** 6'7" **Wt:** 265 **Born:** 1/18/1989 **Age:** 24

	HOW MUCH HE PITCHED						WHAT HE GAVE UP												THE RESULTS							
Year Team	Lg	G	GS	CG	GF	IP	BFP	H	R	ER	HR	SH	SF	HB	TBB	IBB	SO	WP	Bk	W	L	Pct	Sh	Sv-Op	Hld	ERC	ERA
2008 Wisc	A	26	21	1	0	138.1	551	109	38	30	7	3	4	5	35	0	128	6	3	8	6	.571	1	0--	-	2.28	1.95
2009 Hi Dsrt	A+	10	8	0	0	44.1	168	29	16	14	3	1	2	6	17	0	48	2	0	4	2	.667	0	0--	-	1.74	2.84
2009 Ms	R	2	2	0	0	3.0	10	2	0	0	0	0	0	0	0	0	4	0	0	0	0	-	0	0--	-	1.01	0.00
2010 WTenn	AA	13	13	0	0	77.0	316	67	23	19	1	1	0	4	17	1	78	2	0	8	1	.889	0	0--	-	2.32	2.22
2010 Tacom	AAA	12	12	0	0	62.1	260	54	33	33	7	2	0	3	17	0	76	0	0	3	3	.500	0	0--	-	3.28	4.76
2011 Sea	AL	28	28	0	0	171.0	696	133	76	71	18	4	3	5	55	1	173	9	0	9	10	.474	0	0-0	0	2.73	3.74

Trevor Plouffe

Bats: R **Throws:** R **Pos:** 3B-95; RF-15; 2B-4; 1B-3; LF-2; DH-2; PH-2; SS-1 　　PLOOF 　　**Ht:** 6'2" **Wt:** 203 **Born:** 6/15/1986 **Age:** 27

	BATTING																			BASERUNNING				AVERAGES		
Year Team	Lg	G	AB	H	2B	3B	HR	(Hm	Rd)	TB	R	RBI	RC	TBB	IBB	SO	HBP	SH	SF	SB	CS	SB%	GDP	Avg	OBP	Slg
2012 Roch*	AAA	2	8	0	0	0	0	(-	-)	0	0	0	0	1	0	2	0	0	0	0	0	-	0	.000	.111	.000
2010 Min	AL	22	41	6	1	0	2	(1	1)	13	7	6	2	0	0	14	0	2	1	0	0	-	0	.146	.143	.317
2011 Min	AL	81	286	68	18	1	8	(3	5)	112	47	31	31	25	0	71	4	2	3	3	3	.50	6	.238	.305	.392
2012 Min	AL	119	422	99	19	1	24	(15	9)	192	56	55	48	37	0	92	4	0	2	1	3	.25	9	.235	.301	.455
3 ML YEARS		222	749	173	38	2	34	(19	15)	317	110	92	81	62	0	177	8	4	6	4	6	.40	15	.231	.295	.423

Scott Podsednik

Bats: L **Throws:** L **Pos:** LF-31; CF-23; PH-6; RF-5; DH-3; PR-1 　　puh-SEDD-nik 　　**Ht:** 6'0" **Wt:** 185 **Born:** 3/18/1976 **Age:** 37

	BATTING																			BASERUNNING				AVERAGES		
Year Team	Lg	G	AB	H	2B	3B	HR	(Hm	Rd)	TB	R	RBI	RC	TBB	IBB	SO	HBP	SH	SF	SB	CS	SB%	GDP	Avg	OBP	Slg
2012 LV*	AAA	23	76	15	1	0	0	(-	-)	16	13	4	5	8	0	12	1	0	0	6	1	.86	4	.197	.282	.211
2012 Pwtckt*	AAA	25	89	25	2	1	1	(-	-)	32	10	11	11	8	0	13	0	2	3	4	2	.67	2	.281	.330	.360
2001 Sea	AL	5	6	1	0	1	0	(0	0)	3	1	3	0	0	0	1	0	0	0	0	0	-	1	.167	.167	.500
2002 Sea	AL	14	20	4	0	0	1	(0	1)	7	2	5	3	4	0	6	0	0	1	0	0	-	1	.200	.320	.350
2003 Mil	NL	154	558	175	29	8	9	(7	2)	247	100	58	101	56	2	91	4	8	2	43	10	.81	11	.314	.379	.443
2004 Mil	NL	154	640	156	27	7	12	(3	9)	233	85	39	76	58	2	105	7	6	1	70	13	.84	7	.244	.313	.364
2005 CWS	AL	129	507	147	28	1	0	(0	0)	177	80	25	64	47	0	75	3	6	5	59	23	.72	7	.290	.351	.349
2006 CWS	AL	139	524	137	27	6	3	(2	1)	185	86	45	65	54	1	96	2	8	4	40	19	.68	7	.261	.330	.353
2007 CWS	AL	62	214	52	13	4	2	(1	1)	79	30	11	17	13	0	36	4	4	0	12	5	.71	9	.243	.299	.369
2008 Col	NL	93	162	41	8	1	1	(0	1)	54	22	15	19	6	0	28	1	1	1	12	4	.75	3	.253	.322	.333
2009 CWS	AL	132	537	160	25	6	7	(3	4)	221	75	48	78	39	1	74	3	6	2	30	13	.70	8	.304	.353	.412
2010 2 Tms	AL	134	539	160	14	7	6	(1	5)	206	63	51	73	40	1	83	0	10	6	35	15	.70	10	.297	.342	.382
2012 Bos	AL	63	199	60	7	0	1	(0	1)	70	19	12	23	6	0	35	1	8	2	8	2	.80	3	.302	.322	.352
10 KC	AL	95	390	121	8	6	5	(1	4)	156	46	44	59	29	1	57	0	10	6	30	12	.71	5	.310	.353	.400
10 LAD	NL	39	149	39	6	1	1	(0	1)	50	17	7	14	11	0	26	0	0	0	5	3	.63	5	.262	.313	.336
Postseason		12	49	14	1	3	2	(2	0)	27	9	6	10	7	0	10	2	1	0	6	3	.67	1	.286	.397	.551
11 ML YEARS		1079	3906	1096	178	41	42	(17	25)	1482	563	312	519	333	7	630	25	57	24	309	104	.75	67	.281	.339	.379

Placido Polanco

Bats: R **Throws:** R **Pos:** 3B-80; PH-13 　　PLAH-si-doh puh-LAHN-ko 　　**Ht:** 5'10" **Wt:** 189 **Born:** 10/10/1975 **Age:** 37

	BATTING																			BASERUNNING				AVERAGES		
Year Team	Lg	G	AB	H	2B	3B	HR	(Hm	Rd)	TB	R	RBI	RC	TBB	IBB	SO	HBP	SH	SF	SB	CS	SB%	GDP	Avg	OBP	Slg
2012 Clrwtr*	A+	3	12	5	0	0	0	(-	-)	5	3	2	2	0	0	0	0	0	0	0	0	-	0	.417	.417	.417
1998 StL	NL	45	114	29	3	2	1	(1	0)	39	10	11	12	5	0	9	1	2	0	2	0	1.00	0	.254	.292	.342
1999 StL	NL	88	220	61	9	3	1	(0	1)	79	24	19	23	15	1	24	0	3	2	1	3	.25	7	.277	.321	.359
2000 StL	NL	118	323	102	12	3	5	(2	3)	135	50	39	44	16	0	26	1	7	3	4	4	.50	8	.316	.347	.418
2001 StL	NL	144	564	173	26	4	3	(1	2)	216	87	38	70	25	0	43	6	14	1	12	3	.80	22	.307	.342	.383
2002 2 Tms	NL	147	548	158	32	2	9	(8	1)	221	75	49	64	26	1	41	8	13	0	5	3	.63	15	.288	.330	.403
2003 Phi	NL	122	492	142	30	3	14	(7	7)	220	87	63	74	42	1	38	8	8	4	14	2	.88	16	.289	.352	.447
2004 Phi	NL	126	503	150	21	0	17	(10	7)	222	74	55	71	27	0	39	12	7	6	7	4	.64	13	.298	.345	.441
2005 2 Tms	NL	129	501	166	27	2	9	(6	3)	224	84	56	86	33	0	25	11	2	4	4	3	.57	12	.331	.383	.447
2006 Det	AL	110	461	136	18	1	4	(2	2)	168	58	52	65	17	0	27	7	8	2	1	2	.33	18	.295	.329	.364
2007 Det	AL	142	587	200	36	3	9	(7	2)	269	105	67	100	37	3	30	11	2	4	7	3	.70	9	.341	.388	.458
2008 Det	AL	141	580	178	34	3	8	(2	6)	242	90	58	81	26	2	43	6	4	4	7	1	.88	14	.307	.350	.417
2009 Det	AL	153	618	176	31	4	10	(5	5)	245	82	72	84	36	2	46	9	7	5	7	2	.78	15	.285	.331	.396
2010 Phi	NL	132	554	165	27	2	6	(4	2)	214	76	52	68	32	1	47	7	1	8	5	0	1.00	14	.298	.339	.386
2011 Phi	NL	122	469	130	14	0	5	(4	1)	159	46	50	56	42	0	44	3	1	8	3	0	1.00	15	.277	.335	.339
2012 Phi	NL	90	303	78	15	0	2	(5	0)	99	28	19	27	18	1	25	2	4	1	0	0	-	7	.257	.302	.327
02 StL	NL	94	342	97	19	1	5	(5	0)	133	47	27	38	12	1	27	4	9	0	3	1	.75	12	.284	.316	.389
02 Phi	NL	53	206	61	13	1	4	(3	1)	88	28	22	26	14	0	14	4	4	0	2	2	.50	3	.296	.353	.427

			BATTING																	BASERUNNING				AVERAGES		
Year	Team	Lg	G	AB	H	2B	3B	HR	(Hm	Rd)	TB	R	RBI	RC	TBB	IBB	SO	HBP	SH	SF	SB	CS	SB%	GDP	Avg	OBP	Slg
05	Phi	NL	43	158	50	7	0	3	(2	1)	66	26	20	26	12	0	9	3	0	0	0	0	-	3	.316	.376	.418
05	Det	AL	86	343	116	20	2	6	(4	2)	158	58	36	60	21	0	16	8	2	4	4	3	.57	9	.338	.386	.461
	Postseason		38	129	32	4	0	0	(0	0)	36	11	13	13	11	2	9	2	3	2	3	1	.75	6	.248	.313	.279
15 ML YEARS			1809	6837	2044	335	32	103	(61	42)	2752	976	700	925	406	12	507	92	83	52	79	30	.72	186	.299	.344	.403

A.J. Pollock

Bats: R Throws: R Pos: CF-14; PH-10; LF-7; RF-4   Ht: 6'1" Wt: 193 Born: 12/5/1987 Age: 25

			BATTING																	BASERUNNING				AVERAGES		
Year	Team	Lg	G	AB	H	2B	3B	HR	(Hm	Rd)	TB	R	RBI	RC	TBB	IBB	SO	HBP	SH	SF	SB	CS	SB%	GDP	Avg	OBP	Slg
2009	Sbend	A	63	255	69	12	3	3	(-	-)	96	36	22	32	16	0	36	3	1	2	10	4	.71	3	.271	.319	.376
2011	Mobile	AA	133	550	169	41	5	8	(-	-)	244	103	73	94	44	2	86	4	1	9	36	7	.84	11	.307	.357	.444
2012	Reno	AAA	106	428	136	25	3	3	(-	-)	176	65	52	68	32	0	52	5	2	4	21	8	.72	5	.318	.369	.411
2012	Ari	NL	31	81	20	4	1	2	(2	0)	32	8	8	9	9	1	11	0	1	2	1	2	.33	2	.247	.315	.395

Drew Pomeranz

Pitches: L Bats: R Pos: SP-22   POMM-er-anze   Ht: 6'5" Wt: 240 Born: 11/22/1988 Age: 24

			HOW MUCH HE PITCHED					WHAT HE GAVE UP										THE RESULTS							
Year	Team	Lg	G	GS	CG	GF	IP	BFP	H	R	ER	HR	SH	SF	HB	TBB	IBB	SO	WP	Bk	W	L	Pct	Sh	Sv-Op Hld	ERC	ERA
2011	Knstn	A+	15	15	0	0	77.0	313	56	22	16	2	2	1	1	32	0	95	6	0	3	2	.600	0	0-- -	2.30	1.87
2011	Akron	AA	3	3	0	0	14.0	57	10	4	4	1	0	1	0	6	0	17	0	0	1	0	.000	0	0-- -	2.50	2.57
2011	Tulsa	AA	2	2	0	0	10.0	32	2	0	0	0	0	0	0	0	0	7	0	0	1	0	1.000	0	0-- -	0.09	0.00
2012	Tulsa	AA	1	1	0	0	4.0	19	4	0	0	0	0	0	1	1	0	4	1	0	0	0	-	0	0-- -	3.41	0.00
2012	ColSpr	AAA	9	9	0	0	46.2	212	52	23	13	2	1	1	0	20	0	46	0	0	4	4	.500	0	0-- -	4.30	2.51
2011	Col	NL	4	4	0	0	18.1	77	19	11	11	0	1	0	1	5	0	13	1	0	2	1	.667	0	0-0 0	3.36	5.40
2012	Col	NL	22	22	0	0	96.2	434	97	57	53	14	8	4	4	46	2	83	8	1	2	9	.182	0	0-0 0	4.78	4.93
2 ML YEARS			26	26	0	0	115.0	511	116	68	64	14	9	4	5	51	2	96	9	1	4	10	.286	0	0-0 0	4.55	5.01

Stuart Pomeranz

Pitches: R Bats: R Pos: RP-3   POMM-er-anze   Ht: 6'7" Wt: 220 Born: 12/17/1984 Age: 28

			HOW MUCH HE PITCHED					WHAT HE GAVE UP										THE RESULTS							
Year	Team	Lg	G	GS	CG	GF	IP	BFP	H	R	ER	HR	SH	SF	HB	TBB	IBB	SO	WP	Bk	W	L	Pct	Sh	Sv-Op Hld	ERC	ERA
2003	JhsCty	R+	4	3	0	0	14.2	62	13	10	10	2	0	0	3	4	0	14	0	0	1	1	.500	0	0-- -	4.06	6.14
2004	Peoria	A	17	17	0	0	101.1	424	95	59	40	10	6	5	8	25	0	88	6	1	12	4	.750	0	0-- -	3.44	3.55
2005	PlmBh	A+	8	8	0	0	48.1	209	56	26	18	1	3	3	3	10	0	29	2	0	2	5	.286	0	0-- -	3.88	3.35
2005	Sprgfld	AA	18	18	0	0	98.2	449	110	65	58	12	2	6	5	40	0	66	7	0	5	6	.455	0	0-- -	5.03	5.29
2006	Sprgfld	AA	18	18	0	0	98.1	419	107	50	48	13	3	5	1	30	0	64	4	0	7	4	.636	0	0-- -	4.52	4.39
2007	Cards	R	3	3	0	0	4.2	19	4	3	3	1	1	1	0	1	0	4	0	0	0	0	-	0	0-- -	3.23	5.79
2007	PlmBh	A+	3	3	0	0	9.2	44	12	9	7	4	0	1	1	2	0	5	0	1	1	2	.333	0	0-- -	7.33	6.52
2010	Tulsa	AA	51	0	0	35	49.0	223	57	24	20	5	0	2	1	20	1	53	4	0	1	6	.143	0	18-- -	5.03	3.67
2011	Chatt	AA	2	0	0	0	1.1	11	3	5	4	0	0	0	0	3	0	2	1	0	0	0	-	0	0-- -	17.96	27.00
2012	Bowie	AA	5	0	0	1	13.1	48	7	2	0	0	0	0	0	1	0	20	0	0	0	0	-	0	1-- -	0.71	0.00
2012	Norfolk	AAA	5	0	0	4	10.0	33	2	0	0	0	0	0	0	2	0	15	1	0	0	0	-	0	2-- -	0.27	0.00
2012	Bal	AL	3	0	0	0	6.0	26	7	2	2	1	0	0	0	1	0	3	0	0	0	0	-	0	0-0 0	4.43	3.00

Rick Porcello

Pitches: R Bats: R Pos: SP-31   pore-SELL-oh   Ht: 6'5" Wt: 200 Born: 12/27/1988 Age: 24

			HOW MUCH HE PITCHED					WHAT HE GAVE UP										THE RESULTS							
Year	Team	Lg	G	GS	CG	GF	IP	BFP	H	R	ER	HR	SH	SF	HB	TBB	IBB	SO	WP	Bk	W	L	Pct	Sh	Sv-Op Hld	ERC	ERA
2009	Det	AL	31	31	0	0	170.2	720	176	81	75	23	4	2	3	52	0	89	6	1	14	9	.609	0	0-0 0	4.24	3.96
2010	Det	AL	27	27	0	0	162.2	700	188	96	89	18	1	2	7	38	2	84	11	3	10	12	.455	0	0-0 0	4.56	4.92
2011	Det	AL	31	31	0	0	182.0	784	210	103	96	18	5	5	8	46	1	104	12	0	14	9	.609	0	0-0 0	4.57	4.75
2012	Det	AL	31	31	0	0	176.1	783	226	101	90	16	2	3	6	44	3	107	6	0	10	12	.455	0	0-0 0	5.16	4.59
	Postseason		4	2	0	0	15.0	64	15	9	8	0	0	1	2	2	2	12	0	0	0	1	.000	0	0-0 0	2.62	4.80
4 ML YEARS			120	120	0	0	691.2	2987	800	381	350	75	12	12	24	180	6	384	35	4	48	42	.533	0	0-0 0	4.63	4.55

Buster Posey

Bats: R Throws: R Pos: C-114; 1B-29; PH-5; DH-3   Ht: 6'1" Wt: 220 Born: 3/27/1987 Age: 26

			BATTING																	BASERUNNING				AVERAGES		
Year	Team	Lg	G	AB	H	2B	3B	HR	(Hm	Rd)	TB	R	RBI	RC	TBB	IBB	SO	HBP	SH	SF	SB	CS	SB%	GDP	Avg	OBP	Slg
2009	SF	NL	7	17	2	0	0	0	(0	0)	2	1	0	0	0	0	4	0	0	0	0	0	-	0	.118	.118	.118
2010	SF	NL	108	406	124	23	2	18	(6	12)	205	58	67	70	30	5	55	4	0	3	0	2	.00	12	.305	.357	.505
2011	SF	NL	45	162	46	5	0	4	(1	3)	63	17	21	26	18	3	30	4	0	1	3	0	1.00	4	.284	.368	.389
2012	SF	NL	148	530	178	39	1	24	(7	17)	291	78	103	111	69	7	96	2	0	9	1	1	.50	19	.336	.408	.549
	Postseason		15	59	17	3	0	1	(0	1)	23	6	5	6	6	1	18	0	0	1	1	0	1.00	1	.288	.354	.390
4 ML YEARS			308	1115	350	67	3	46	(14	32)	561	154	191	207	117	15	185	10	0	13	4	3	.57	35	.314	.380	.503

Martin Prado

mar-TEEN PRAH-doe

Bats: R **Throws:** R **Pos:** LF-119; 3B-25; SS-13; 2B-10; 1B-4; PH-2   **Ht:** 6'1" **Wt:** 190 **Born:** 10/27/1983 **Age:** 29

Year	Team	Lg	G	AB	H	2B	3B	HR	(Hm	Rd)	TB	R	RBI	RC	TBB	IBB	SO	HBP	SH	SF	SB	CS	SB%	GDP	Avg	OBP	Slg
2006	Atl	NL	24	42	11	1	1	1	(1	0)	17	3	9	9	5	0	7	0	2	0	0	0	-	2	.262	.340	.405
2007	Atl	NL	28	59	17	3	0	0	(0	0)	20	5	2	6	3	0	6	0	0	0	0	0	-	0	.288	.323	.339
2008	Atl	NL	78	228	73	18	4	2	(1	1)	105	36	33	39	21	0	29	1	2	2	3	1	.75	3	.320	.377	.461
2009	Atl	NL	128	450	138	38	0	11	(4	7)	209	64	49	57	36	1	59	2	11	4	1	3	.25	17	.307	.358	.464
2010	Atl	NL	140	599	184	40	3	15	(4	11)	275	100	66	86	40	2	86	3	3	6	5	3	.63	13	.307	.350	.459
2011	Atl	NL	129	551	143	26	2	13	(9	4)	212	66	57	57	34	1	52	1	1	3	4	8	.33	16	.260	.302	.385
2012	Atl	NL	156	617	186	42	6	10	(6	4)	270	81	70	96	58	2	69	2	4	9	17	4	.81	19	.301	.359	.438
7 ML YEARS			683	2546	752	168	16	52	(25	27)	1108	355	286	350	197	6	308	9	23	24	30	19	.61	70	.295	.345	.435

Alex Presley

Bats: L **Throws:** L **Pos:** LF-81; PH-20; RF-8; CF-4; PR-1   **Ht:** 5'10" **Wt:** 185 **Born:** 7/25/1985 **Age:** 27

Year	Team	Lg	G	AB	H	2B	3B	HR	(Hm	Rd)	TB	R	RBI	RC	TBB	IBB	SO	HBP	SH	SF	SB	CS	SB%	GDP	Avg	OBP	Slg
2012	Indy*	AAA	40	153	47	3	4	5	(-	-)	73	24	22	30	24	2	26	0	1	1	7	2	.78	2	.307	.399	.477
2010	Pit	NL	19	23	6	1	0	0	(0	0)	7	2	0	1	1	0	8	0	1	0	1	1	.50	0	.261	.292	.304
2011	Pit	NL	52	215	64	12	6	4	(1	3)	100	27	20	35	13	1	40	1	1	1	9	3	.75	1	.298	.339	.465
2012	Pit	NL	104	346	82	14	7	10	(2	8)	140	46	25	31	18	0	72	2	4	0	9	7	.56	5	.237	.279	.405
3 ML YEARS			175	584	152	27	13	14	(3	11)	247	75	45	67	32	1	120	3	6	1	19	11	.63	6	.260	.302	.423

David Price

Pitches: L **Bats:** L **Pos:** SP-31   **Ht:** 6'6" **Wt:** 220 **Born:** 8/26/1985 **Age:** 27

	HOW MUCH HE PITCHED						WHAT HE GAVE UP										THE RESULTS						
Year	Team	Lg	G	GS	CG	GF	IP	BFP	H	R	ER	HR	SH	SF	HB	TBB	IBB	SO	WP	Bk	W	L	Pct	Sh	Sv-Op	Hld	ERC	ERA
2008	TB	AL	5	1	0	0	14.0	57	9	4	3	1	0	1	4	0	12	0	0	0	0	-	0	0-0	1	1.86	1.93
2009	TB	AL	23	23	0	0	128.1	557	119	72	63	17	3	2	4	54	0	102	2	0	10	7	.588	0	0-0	0	4.05	4.42
2010	TB	AL	32	31	2	0	208.2	861	170	71	63	15	4	3	5	79	1	188	5	3	19	6	.760	1	0-0	0	2.91	2.72
2011	TB	AL	34	34	0	0	224.1	918	192	93	87	22	4	7	9	63	5	218	2	0	12	13	.480	0	0-0	0	2.97	3.49
2012	TB	AL	31	31	2	0	211.0	836	173	63	60	16	2	3	5	59	2	205	8	1	20	5	.800	1	0-0	0	2.67	2.56
Postseason			8	3	0	5	25.0	106	26	13	11	4	0	0	0	5	0	25	1	0	1	3	.250	0	1-1	0	3.82	3.96
5 ML YEARS			125	120	4	0	786.1	3229	663	303	276	71	13	16	24	259	8	725	17	4	61	31	.663	2	0-0	1	3.02	3.16

Jason Pridie

PRY-dee

Bats: L **Throws:** R **Pos:** PH-7; CF-1; RF-1   **Ht:** 6'1" **Wt:** 203 **Born:** 10/9/1983 **Age:** 29

Year	Team	Lg	G	AB	H	2B	3B	HR	(Hm	Rd)	TB	R	RBI	RC	TBB	IBB	SO	HBP	SH	SF	SB	CS	SB%	GDP	Avg	OBP	Slg
2012	LV*	AAA	49	178	53	7	3	5	(-	-)	81	17	22	29	16	2	38	0	0	0	4	0	1.00	5	.298	.356	.455
2008	Min	AL	10	4	0	0	0	0	(0	0)	0	3	0	0	1	0	1	0	1	0	0	0	-	0	.000	.200	.000
2009	Min	AL	1	0	0	0	0	0	(0	0)	0	0	0	0	0	0	0	0	0	0	0	0	-	-	-	-	-
2011	NYM	NL	101	208	48	11	3	4	(3	1)	77	28	20	22	24	2	64	0	3	1	7	1	.88	2	.231	.309	.370
2012	Phi	NL	9	10	3	1	0	1	(1	0)	7	1	3	2	0	0	0	0	0	0	0	0	-	0	.300	.300	.700
4 ML YEARS			121	222	51	12	3	5	(4	1)	84	32	23	24	25	2	65	0	4	1	7	1	.88	2	.230	.306	.378

Jurickson Profar

JURR-ick-sun PRO-farr

Bats: B **Throws:** R **Pos:** 2B-5; SS-3; PH-1; PR-1   **Ht:** 6'0" **Wt:** 165 **Born:** 2/20/1993 **Age:** 20

Year	Team	Lg	G	AB	H	2B	3B	HR	(Hm	Rd)	TB	R	RBI	RC	TBB	IBB	SO	HBP	SH	SF	SB	CS	SB%	GDP	Avg	OBP	Slg
2010	Spkane	A-	63	252	63	19	0	4	(-	-)	94	42	23	33	28	0	46	0	6	2	8	3	.73	8	.250	.323	.373
2011	Hkry	A	115	430	123	37	8	12	(-	-)	212	86	65	87	65	2	63	11	6	4	23	9	.72	7	.286	.390	.493
2012	Frisco	AA	126	480	135	26	7	14	(-	-)	217	76	62	86	66	5	79	5	2	9	16	4	.80	11	.281	.368	.452
2012	Tex	AL	9	17	3	2	0	1	(0	1)	8	2	2	1	0	0	4	0	0	0	0	0	-	1	.176	.176	.471

Stephen Pryor

Pitches: R **Bats:** R **Pos:** RP-26   **Ht:** 6'4" **Wt:** 245 **Born:** 7/23/1989 **Age:** 23

	HOW MUCH HE PITCHED						WHAT HE GAVE UP										THE RESULTS						
Year	Team	Lg	G	GS	CG	GF	IP	BFP	H	R	ER	HR	SH	SF	HB	TBB	IBB	SO	WP	Bk	W	L	Pct	Sh	Sv-Op	Hld	ERC	ERA
2010	Everett	A-	11	0	0	7	18.1	68	7	1	1	0	2	0	0	7	0	26	1	0	0	0	-	0	4- -	-	0.89	0.49
2010	Clinton	A	12	0	0	4	17.0	76	17	12	7	0	1	0	1	6	0	29	3	1	0	2	.000	0	1- -	-	3.27	3.71
2011	Hi Dsrt	A+	22	0	0	9	27.0	134	28	24	23	2	0	0	2	26	0	34	5	0	1	0	1.000	0	4- -	-	6.66	7.67
2011	Jacksn	AA	17	0	0	13	22.2	84	9	4	3	0	1	2	1	7	0	27	1	0	2	1	.667	0	6- -	-	0.88	1.19
2012	Jacksn	AA	11	0	0	10	16.0	61	7	3	2	0	0	0	0	5	0	24	0	0	1	0	1.000	0	7- -	-	0.88	1.13
2012	Tacom	AAA	16	0	0	12	20.0	80	11	0	0	0	0	0	0	11	0	20	1	0	0	0	-	0	3- -	-	1.72	0.00
2012	Hi Dsrt	A+	2	1	0	0	2.2	10	0	2	2	0	0	0	0	3	0	3	0	0	0	0	-	0	0- -	-	1.28	6.75
2012	Sea	AL	26	0	0	8	23.0	104	22	13	10	5	2	0	0	13	2	27	3	0	3	1	.750	0	0-0	5	5.10	3.91

Albert Pujols

Bats: R **Throws:** R **Pos:** 1B-120; DH-34; 3B-3   **Ht:** 6'3" **Wt:** 230 **Born:** 1/16/1980 **Age:** 33

Year	Team	Lg	G	AB	H	2B	3B	HR	(Hm	Rd)	TB	R	RBI	RC	TBB	IBB	SO	HBP	SH	SF	SB	CS	SB%	GDP	Avg	OBP	Slg
2001	StL	NL	161	590	194	47	4	37	(18	19)	360	112	130	132	69	6	93	9	1	7	1	3	.25	21	.329	.403	.610
2002	StL	NL	157	590	185	40	2	34	(14	20)	331	118	127	121	72	13	69	9	0	4	2	4	.33	20	.314	.394	.561
2003	StL	NL	157	591	**212**	**51**	1	43	(21	**22)**	**394**	**137**	124	**160**	79	12	65	10	0	5	5	1	.83	13	**.359**	.439	.667
2004	StL	NL	154	592	196	51	2	46	(18	28)	389	133	123	143	84	12	52	7	0	9	5	5	.50	21	.331	.415	.657
2005	StL	NL	161	591	195	38	2	41	(23	18)	360	**129**	117	139	97	**27**	65	9	0	3	16	2	.89	19	.330	.430	.609
2006	StL	NL	143	535	177	33	1	49	(24	25)	359	119	137	146	92	28	50	4	0	3	7	2	.78	20	.331	**.431**	**.671**
2007	StL	NL	158	565	185	38	1	32	(12	20)	321	99	103	118	99	22	58	7	0	8	2	6	.25	**27**	.327	.429	.568
2008	StL	NL	148	524	187	44	0	37	(19	18)	**342**	100	116	**130**	104	**34**	54	5	0	8	7	3	.70	16	.357	.462	**.653**
2009	StL	NL	160	568	186	45	1	**47**	(22	25)	**374**	**124**	135	145	115	**44**	64	9	0	8	16	4	.80	23	.327	**.443**	**.658**
2010	StL	NL	159	587	183	39	1	**42**	(16	21)	350	115	118	131	103	38	76	4	0	6	14	4	.78	23	.312	.414	.596
2011	StL	NL	147	579	173	29	0	37	(16	21)	313	105	99	100	61	15	58	4	0	7	9	1	.90	**29**	.299	.366	.541
2012	LAA	AL	154	607	173	50	0	30	(14	16)	313	85	105	100	52	16	76	5	0	6	8	1	.89	19	.285	.343	.516
	Postseason		74	267	88	18	1	18	(7	11)	162	54	52	67	48	20	39	5	0	1	1	2	.33	6	.330	.439	.607
	12 ML YEARS		1859	6919	2246	505	15	475	(218	257)	4206	1376	1434	1565	1027	267	780	82	1	74	92	36	.72	251	.325	.414	.608

Nick Punto

Bats: B **Throws:** R **Pos:** 3B-31; 2B-26; PH-26; PR-7; SS-6; 1B-5; DH-2   POON-toh   **Ht:** 5'9" **Wt:** 190 **Born:** 11/8/1977 **Age:** 35

Year	Team	Lg	G	AB	H	2B	3B	HR	(Hm	Rd)	TB	R	RBI	RC	TBB	IBB	SO	HBP	SH	SF	SB	CS	SB%	GDP	Avg	OBP	Slg
2001	Phi	NL	4	5	2	0	0	0	(0	0)	2	0	0	1	0	0	0	0	0	0	0	0	-	0	.400	.400	.400
2002	Phi	NL	9	6	1	0	0	0	(0	0)	1	0	0	0	0	0	3	0	1	0	0	0	-	0	.167	.167	.167
2003	Phi	NL	64	92	20	2	0	1	(0	1)	25	14	4	7	7	1	22	0	0	0	2	1	.67	0	.217	.273	.272
2004	Min	AL	38	91	23	0	0	2	(2	0)	29	17	12	15	12	0	19	0	0	0	6	0	1.00	0	.253	.340	.319
2005	Min	AL	112	394	94	18	4	4	(3	1)	132	45	26	35	36	0	86	0	7	2	13	8	.62	9	.239	.301	.335
2006	Min	AL	135	459	133	21	7	1	(0	1)	171	73	45	59	47	0	68	1	10	7	17	5	.77	8	.290	.352	.373
2007	Min	AL	150	472	99	18	4	1	(0	1)	128	53	25	37	55	1	90	0	6	3	16	6	.73	7	.210	.291	.271
2008	Min	AL	99	338	96	19	4	2	(1	1)	129	43	28	42	32	1	57	0	5	2	15	6	.71	10	.284	.344	.382
2009	Min	AL	125	359	82	15	1	1	(0	1)	102	56	38	46	61	1	70	1	13	6	16	3	.84	7	.228	.337	.284
2010	Min	AL	88	252	60	11	1	1	(0	1)	76	24	20	25	28	2	50	1	4	3	6	2	.75	3	.238	.313	.302
2011	StL	NL	63	133	37	8	4	1	(0	1)	56	21	20	25	25	3	21	0	6	2	1	1	.50	3	.278	.388	.421
2012	2 Tms		87	160	35	7	0	1	(0	1)	45	20	10	15	25	0	42	0	4	2	6	0	1.00	5	.219	.321	.281
	12 Bos	AL	65	125	25	6	0	1	(0	1)	34	14	10	10	19	0	33	0	2	2	5	0	1.00	5	.200	.301	.272
	12 LAD	NL	22	35	10	1	0	0	(0	0)	11	6	0	5	6	0	9	0	2	0	1	0	1.00	0	.286	.390	.314
	Postseason		21	56	12	1	0	0	(0	0)	13	0	4	4	10	2	19	0	2	1	0	0	-	0	.214	.328	.232
	12 ML YEARS		974	2761	682	119	25	15	(6	9)	896	366	228	307	328	9	528	3	56	27	98	32	.75	54	.247	.325	.325

Luke Putkonen

Pitches: R **Bats:** R **Pos:** RP-12   putt-COE-nen   **Ht:** 6'6" **Wt:** 210 **Born:** 5/10/1986 **Age:** 27

			HOW MUCH HE PITCHED						WHAT HE GAVE UP										THE RESULTS						
Year	Team	Lg	G	GS	CG	GF	IP	BFP	H	R	ER	HR	SH	SF	HB	TBB	IBB	SO	WP	Bk	W	L	Pct	Sh	Sv-Op Hld	ERC	ERA
2007	Tigers	R	3	3	0	0	8.2	35	8	5	4	0	0	0	0	0	0	9	0	0	0	1	.000	0	0- - -	1.59	4.15
2008	Oneont	A-	6	6	0	0	24.2	98	24	10	10	1	0	0	1	8	0	17	0	0	2	1	.667	0	0- - -	3.65	3.65
2009	WMich	A	28	28	1	0	149.1	631	148	63	52	3	1	2	9	47	0	115	9	0	7	8	.467	1	0- - -	3.41	3.13
2010	Lkland	A+	27	26	1	0	152.2	617	144	55	54	8	3	3	6	44	1	87	6	1	9	7	.563	0	0- - -	3.29	3.18
2011	Erie	AA	11	11	0	0	52.1	247	68	50	44	8	4	2	2	22	0	23	2	0	1	7	.125	0	0- - -	6.42	7.57
2011	Lkland	A+	18	8	1	6	65.0	285	77	46	40	10	0	3	2	18	1	52	2	1	2	6	.250	0	0- - -	5.23	5.54
2012	Toledo	AAA	24	0	0	6	56.2	249	68	37	31	3	0	3	2	19	0	46	2	0	3	3	.500	0	0- - -	4.84	4.92
2012	Det	AL	12	0	0	6	16.0	72	19	7	7	0	1	0	0	8	1	10	2	0	0	2	.000	0	1-2 0	4.74	3.94

Zach Putnam

Pitches: R **Bats:** R **Pos:** RP-2   **Ht:** 6'1" **Wt:** 225 **Born:** 7/3/1987 **Age:** 25

			HOW MUCH HE PITCHED						WHAT HE GAVE UP										THE RESULTS						
Year	Team	Lg	G	GS	CG	GF	IP	BFP	H	R	ER	HR	SH	SF	HB	TBB	IBB	SO	WP	Bk	W	L	Pct	Sh	Sv-Op Hld	ERC	ERA
2008	MhVlly	A-	3	3	0	0	9.2	40	7	5	4	0	0	1	0	5	0	8	0	0	0	1	.000	0	0- - -	2.41	3.72
2009	Knstn	A+	5	5	0	0	24.0	96	22	12	11	1	1	1	0	5	0	23	0	0	2	0	1.000	0	0- - -	2.58	4.13
2009	Akron	AA	33	0	0	9	56.2	245	59	29	26	2	0	0	1	18	3	57	1	0	4	2	.667	0	0- - -	3.47	4.13
2010	Akron	AA	20	7	0	9	51.1	217	58	25	22	2	3	2	0	9	0	41	1	0	4	1	.800	0	3- - -	3.48	3.86
2010	Clmbs	AAA	17	0	0	5	24.1	99	20	10	9	2	1	1	0	7	0	24	1	0	0	1	.000	0	0- - -	2.58	3.33
2011	Clmbs	AAA	44	0	0	16	69.0	292	61	30	28	6	1	2	1	23	1	68	6	0	6	3	.667	0	9- - -	3.07	3.65
2012	ColSpr	AAA	49	0	0	33	60.2	276	73	35	28	5	1	2	1	27	3	49	5	0	3	4	.429	0	12- - -	5.29	4.15
2011	Cle	AL	8	0	0	3	7.1	34	10	5	5	1	0	0	2	0	0	9	1	0	1	1	.500	0	0-1 0	5.82	6.14
2012	Col	NL	2	0	0	0	2.0	9	3	0	0	0	1	0	0	1	0	0	0	0	0	0	-	0	0-0 0	7.26	0.00
	2 ML YEARS		10	0	0	3	9.1	43	13	5	5	1	1	0	2	1	0	9	1	0	1	1	.500	0	0-1 0	6.13	4.82

J.J. Putz

Pitches: R **Bats:** R **Pos:** RP-57   PUTS   **Ht:** 6'5" **Wt:** 250 **Born:** 2/22/1977 **Age:** 36

			HOW MUCH HE PITCHED						WHAT HE GAVE UP										THE RESULTS						
Year	Team	Lg	G	GS	CG	GF	IP	BFP	H	R	ER	HR	SH	SF	HB	TBB	IBB	SO	WP	Bk	W	L	Pct	Sh	Sv-Op Hld	ERC	ERA
2003	Sea	AL	3	0	0	0	3.2	18	4	2	2	0	0	0	0	3	0	3	0	0	0	0	-	0	0-0 0	5.31	4.91
2004	Sea	AL	54	0	0	30	63.0	275	66	35	33	10	3	2	5	24	4	47	1	0	0	3	.000	0	9-13 3	4.97	4.71
2005	Sea	AL	64	0	0	20	60.0	259	58	27	24	8	3	3	2	23	2	45	2	0	6	5	.545	0	1-4 21	4.11	3.60
2006	Sea	AL	72	0	0	57	78.1	303	59	20	20	4	1	2	2	13	1	104	1	0	4	1	.800	0	36-43 5	1.78	2.30
2007	Sea	AL	68	0	0	65	71.2	260	37	11	11	4	0	1	2	13	0	82	3	0	6	1	.857	0	40-42 0	1.21	1.38
2008	Sea	AL	47	0	0	35	46.1	211	46	20	20	4	0	1	2	28	2	56	2	0	6	5	.545	0	15-23 5	4.82	3.88

	HOW MUCH HE PITCHED						WHAT HE GAVE UP											THE RESULTS						
Year Team	Lg	G	GS	CG	GF	IP	BFP	H	R	ER	HR	SH	SF	HB	TBB	IBB	SO	WP	Bk	W	L	Pct	Sh	Sv-Op Hld	ERC	ERA
2009 NYM	NL	29	0	0	6	29.1	135	29	18	17	1	1	2	0	11	4	19	1	0	1	4	.200	0	2-4 10	4.16	5.22
2010 CWS	AL	60	0	0	16	54.0	219	41	18	17	4	1	1	1	15	2	65	4	0	7	5	.583	0	3-7 14	2.19	2.83
2011 Ari	NL	60	0	0	52	58.0	229	41	15	14	4	2	3	2	12	0	61	2	0	2	2	.500	0	45-49 0	1.80	2.17
2012 Ari	NL	57	0	0	52	54.1	218	45	18	17	4	2	1	2	11	1	65	3	0	1	5	.167	0	32-37 0	2.38	2.82
Postseason		3	0	0	3	2.1	11	3	1	1	0	0	0	0	1	0	0	0	0	0	1	.000	0	0-0 0	4.93	3.86
10 ML YEARS		514	0	0	333	518.2	2127	426	184	175	45	15	16	18	161	16	547	19	0	33	31	.516	0	183-222 53	2.78	3.04

Chad Qualls

Pitches: R Bats: R Pos: RP-60　　　　**Ht: 6'5" Wt: 220 Born: 8/17/1978 Age: 34**

	HOW MUCH HE PITCHED						WHAT HE GAVE UP											THE RESULTS						
Year Team	Lg	G	GS	CG	GF	IP	BFP	H	R	ER	HR	SH	SF	HB	TBB	IBB	SO	WP	Bk	W	L	Pct	Sh	Sv-Op Hld	ERC	ERA
2012 Indy*	AAA	1	1	0	0	1.0	3	0	0	0	0	0	0	0	0	0	3	0	0	0	0	-	0	0- -	0.00	0.00
2004 Hou	NL	25	0	0	4	33.0	141	34	13	13	3	0	1	4	8	1	24	0	0	4	0	1.000	0	1-2 9	4.02	3.55
2005 Hou	NL	77	0	0	19	79.2	329	73	33	29	7	4	3	6	23	2	60	1	0	6	4	.600	0	0-0 22	3.42	3.28
2006 Hou	NL	81	0	0	13	88.2	356	76	38	37	10	4	4	6	28	6	56	0	0	7	3	.700	0	0-6 23	3.36	3.76
2007 Hou	NL	79	0	0	16	82.2	345	84	29	28	10	6	2	3	25	5	78	2	0	6	5	.545	0	5-10 21	4.07	3.05
2008 Ari	NL	77	0	0	21	73.2	300	61	29	23	4	4	3	3	18	2	71	6	0	4	8	.333	0	9-17 22	2.40	2.81
2009 Ari	NL	51	0	0	44	52.0	217	53	23	21	5	1	0	2	7	2	45	2	0	2	2	.500	0	24-29 0	3.17	3.63
2010 2 Tms		70	0	0	29	59.0	281	85	56	48	7	4	4	2	21	4	49	4	0	3	4	.429	0	12-19 11	6.63	7.32
2011 SD	NL	77	0	0	20	74.1	306	73	30	29	7	7	1	0	20	5	43	4	0	6	8	.429	0	0-5 22	3.38	3.51
2012 3 Tms		60	0	0	15	52.1	231	63	34	31	7	2	2	0	14	4	27	3	0	2	1	.667	0	0-5 14	4.78	5.33
10 Ari	NL	43	0	0	28	38.0	190	61	41	35	5	4	2	1	15	4	34	3	0	1	4	.200	0	12-16 3	7.80	8.29
10 TB	AL	27	0	0	1	21.0	91	24	15	13	2	0	2	1	6	0	15	1	0	2	0	1.000	0	0-3 8	4.64	5.57
12 Phi	NL	35	0	0	6	31.1	140	39	18	16	7	1	0	0	9	3	19	2	0	1	1	.500	0	0-5 12	5.74	4.60
12 NYY	AL	8	0	0	4	7.1	33	10	5	5	0	0	1	0	3	1	2	1	0	1	0	1.000	0	0-0 0	5.38	6.14
12 Pit	NL	17	0	0	5	13.2	58	14	11	10	0	1	1	0	2	0	6	0	0	0	0	-	0	0-0 2	2.48	6.59
Postseason		17	0	0	0	22.2	94	24	13	13	3	1	0	0	7	3	17	0	0	1	1	.500	0	0-2 2	4.20	5.16
9 ML YEARS		597	0	0	181	595.1	2506	602	285	259	60	32	20	26	164	31	453	22	0	40	35	.533	0	51-93 144	3.78	3.92

Carlos Quentin

Bats: R Throws: R Pos: LF-69; PH-9; DH-5; RF-3　　　　**Ht: 6'2" Wt: 235 Born: 8/28/1982 Age: 30**

				BATTING																BASERUNNING				AVERAGES		
Year Team	Lg	G	AB	H	2B	3B	HR	(Hm Rd)	TB	R	RBI	RC	TBB	IBB	SO	HBP	SH	SF	SB	CS	SB%	GDP	Avg	OBP	Slg
2012 Tucsn*	AAA	5	14	4	0	0	1	(- -)	7	4	4	3	2	0	3	1	0	0	0	0	-	0	.286	.412	.500
2012 Lk Els*	A+	4	14	6	1	0	1	(- -)	10	3	5	4	0	0	2	1	0	0	0	0	-	0	.429	.467	.714
2006 Ari	NL	57	166	42	13	3	9	(3 6)	88	23	32	29	15	2	34	8	1	1	1	0	1.00	6	.253	.342	.530
2007 Ari	NL	81	229	49	16	0	5	(5 0)	80	29	31	27	18	1	54	11	1	4	2	2	.50	5	.214	.298	.349
2008 CWS	AL	130	480	138	26	1	36	(21 15)	274	96	100	104	66	0	80	20	0	3	7	3	.70	16	.288	.394	.571
2009 CWS	AL	99	351	83	14	0	21	(12 9)	160	47	56	47	31	2	52	15	0	2	3	0	1.00	14	.236	.323	.456
2010 CWS	AL	131	453	110	25	2	26	(19 7)	217	73	87	78	50	3	83	20	0	4	2	2	.50	16	.243	.342	.479
2011 CWS	AL	118	421	107	31	0	24	(7 17)	210	53	77	72	34	0	84	23	0	5	1	1	.50	7	.254	.340	.499
2012 SD	NL	86	284	74	21	0	16	(7 9)	143	44	46	45	36	2	41	17	0	3	0	1	.00	6	.261	.374	.504
7 ML YEARS		702	2384	603	146	6	137	(74 63)	1172	365	429	402	250	10	428	114	2	22	16	9	.64	67	.253	.349	.492

Jose Quintana

Pitches: L Bats: R Pos: SP-22; RP-3　　KIN-tahn-ah　　**Ht: 6'0" Wt: 215 Born: 1/24/1989 Age: 24**

	HOW MUCH HE PITCHED						WHAT HE GAVE UP											THE RESULTS						
Year Team	Lg	G	GS	CG	GF	IP	BFP	H	R	ER	HR	SH	SF	HB	TBB	IBB	SO	WP	Bk	W	L	Pct	Sh	Sv-Op Hld	ERC	ERA
2010 Yanks	R	15	0	0	10	23.1	97	14	11	6	0	0	0	3	8	0	32	1	0	3	1	.750	0	1- - -	1.63	2.31
2010 CtnSC	A	5	3	0	0	15.1	68	11	10	8	1	0	0	1	10	0	12	0	0	1	0	1.000	0	0- - -	3.41	4.70
2011 Tampa	A+	30	12	0	3	102.0	402	86	35	33	5	5	4	1	28	0	88	7	0	10	2	.833	0	1- - -	2.58	2.91
2012 Brham	AA	9	9	0	0	48.2	196	43	17	15	1	2	1	0	14	0	41	2	0	1	3	.250	0	0- - -	2.58	2.77
2012 CWS	AL	25	22	0	2	136.1	568	142	62	57	14	5	1	3	42	4	81	10	2	6	6	.500	0	0-0 0	4.13	3.76

Omar Quintanilla

Bats: L Throws: R Pos: 2B-34; SS-30; PH-7; PR-1　　keen-tah-NEE-yah　　**Ht: 5'9" Wt: 185 Born: 10/24/1981 Age: 31**

				BATTING																BASERUNNING				AVERAGES		
Year Team	Lg	G	AB	H	2B	3B	HR	(Hm Rd)	TB	R	RBI	RC	TBB	IBB	SO	HBP	SH	SF	SB	CS	SB%	GDP	Avg	OBP	Slg
2012 Buffalo*	AAA	48	156	44	11	2	6	(- -)	77	18	27	25	14	3	27	1	1	0	1	3	.25	5	.282	.345	.494
2005 Col	NL	39	128	28	1	1	0	(0 0)	31	16	7	9	9	0	15	0	6	0	2	1	.67	3	.219	.270	.242
2006 Col	NL	11	34	6	1	1	0	(0 0)	9	3	3	2	3	1	9	0	1	0	1	1	.50	1	.176	.243	.265
2007 Col	NL	27	70	16	4	0	0	(0 0)	20	6	5	6	5	0	15	0	0	0	0	0	-	3	.229	.280	.286
2008 Col	NL	81	210	50	17	0	2	(1 1)	73	28	15	18	15	3	46	0	8	1	0	0	-	3	.238	.288	.348
2009 Col	NL	58	58	10	2	0	0	(0 0)	12	7	2	4	8	0	27	0	3	0	0	0	-	0	.172	.273	.207
2011 Tex	AL	11	22	1	0	1	0	(0 0)	3	3	2	0	0	0	9	0	1	0	0	0	-	0	.045	.045	.136
2012 2 Tms		65	169	41	8	0	4	(3 1)	61	25	16	14	16	1	42	2	1	2	0	1	.00	3	.243	.312	.361
12 NYM	NL	29	70	18	5	0	1	(0 1)	26	13	4	6	8	1	17	2	0	0	0	-	2	.257	.350	.371
12 Bal	AL	36	99	23	3	0	3	(3 0)	35	12	12	8	8	0	25	0	1	2	0	1	.00	1	.232	.284	.354
7 ML YEARS		292	691	152	33	3	6	(4 2)	209	88	50	53	56	5	163	2	20	3	1	3	.50	13	.220	.279	.302

Humberto Quintero

Bats: R Throws: R Pos: C-43; PH-1   oom-BARE-toe keen-TARE-oh   Ht: 5'9" Wt: 215 Born: 8/2/1979 Age: 33

Year Team	Lg	G	AB	H	2B	3B	HR	(Hm	Rd)	TB	R	RBI	RC	TBB	IBB	SO	HBP	SH	SF	SB	CS	SB%	GDP	Avg	OBP	Slg
2012 NewOr*	AAA	5	15	2	0	0	0	(-	-)	2	1	3	0	2	1	3	0	0	0	0	0	-	2	.133	.235	.133
2012 Nashv*	AAA	25	95	25	8	0	1	(-	-)	36	9	12	10	1	0	21	2	1	1	0	0	-	3	.263	.283	.379
2003 SD	NL	12	23	5	0	0	0	(0	0)	5	1	2	2	1	1	6	0	0	0	0	0	-	0	.217	.250	.217
2004 SD	NL	23	72	18	3	0	2	(1	1)	27	7	10	6	5	0	16	0	0	1	0	2	.00	5	.250	.295	.375
2005 Hou	NL	18	54	10	1	0	1	(1	0)	14	6	8	2	1	1	10	0	2	0	0	0	-	3	.185	.200	.259
2006 Hou	NL	11	21	7	2	0	0	(0	0)	9	2	2	1	1	0	3	0	0	0	0	0	-	2	.333	.364	.429
2007 Hou	NL	29	53	12	2	0	0	(0	0)	14	2	1	3	2	1	13	2	0	0	0	0	-	2	.226	.281	.264
2008 Hou	NL	59	168	38	6	0	2	(1	1)	50	16	12	10	6	0	34	4	5	0	0	0	-	5	.226	.270	.298
2009 Hou	NL	60	157	37	8	1	4	(3	1)	59	11	14	13	7	1	41	4	0	0	0	0	-	8	.236	.286	.376
2010 Hou	NL	88	265	62	10	0	4	(2	2)	84	13	20	20	8	2	59	2	1	0	0	0	-	5	.234	.262	.317
2011 Hou	NL	79	262	63	12	1	2	(2	0)	83	22	25	14	6	2	53	1	1	2	1	0	1.00	10	.240	.258	.317
2012 KC	AL	43	138	32	12	0	1	(1	0)	47	7	19	10	4	0	28	1	0	1	0	1	.00	1	.232	.257	.341
10 ML YEARS		422	1213	284	56	2	16	(11	5)	392	87	113	81	41	8	263	14	9	4	1	3	.25	41	.234	.267	.323

Guillermo Quiroz

Bats: R Throws: R Pos: C-1; PH-1   key-ROSE   Ht: 6'1" Wt: 215 Born: 11/29/1981 Age: 31

Year Team	Lg	G	AB	H	2B	3B	HR	(Hm	Rd)	TB	R	RBI	RC	TBB	IBB	SO	HBP	SH	SF	SB	CS	SB%	GDP	Avg	OBP	Slg
2012 Tacom*	AAA	89	302	84	15	1	15	(-	-)	146	45	52	54	36	1	70	5	2	2	0	0	-	4	.278	.362	.483
2004 Tor	AL	17	52	11	2	0	0	(0	0)	13	2	6	4	2	0	8	2	0	1	1	0	1.00	1	.212	.263	.250
2005 Tor	AL	12	36	7	2	0	0	(0	0)	9	3	4	3	2	0	13	1	0	0	0	0	-	3	.194	.256	.250
2006 Sea	AL	1	2	0	0	0	0	(0	0)	0	0	0	0	0	0	2	0	0	0	0	0	-	0	.000	.000	.000
2007 Tex	AL	9	10	4	1	0	0	(0	0)	5	1	2	3	1	0	2	0	0	0	0	0	-	0	.400	.455	.500
2008 Bal	AL	56	134	25	5	0	2	(1	1)	36	12	14	10	12	0	34	1	1	0	0	0	-	3	.187	.259	.269
2009 Sea	AL	4	14	4	0	0	0	(0	0)	4	0	2	1	0	0	3	0	1	0	0	0	-	0	.286	.286	.286
2010 Sea	AL	2	7	2	1	0	0	(0	0)	3	1	0	0	0	0	1	0	0	0	0	0	-	0	.286	.286	.429
2012 Bos	AL	2	2	0	0	0	0	(0	0)	0	0	0	0	0	0	1	0	0	0	0	0	-	0	.000	.000	.000
8 ML YEARS		103	257	53	11	0	2	(1	1)	70	19	28	21	17	0	64	4	2	1	1	0	1.00	4	.206	.265	.272

Ryan Raburn

Bats: R Throws: R Pos: 2B-32; LF-30; RF-22; PH-5; DH-2   RAY-burn   Ht: 6'0" Wt: 185 Born: 4/17/1981 Age: 32

Year Team	Lg	G	AB	H	2B	3B	HR	(Hm	Rd)	TB	R	RBI	RC	TBB	IBB	SO	HBP	SH	SF	SB	CS	SB%	GDP	Avg	OBP	Slg
2012 Toledo*	AAA	15	60	15	2	0	4	(-	-)	29	8	12	9	5	0	15	1	0	0	1	0	1.00	7	.250	.318	.483
2004 Det	AL	12	29	4	1	0	0	(0	0)	5	4	1	1	2	0	15	0	0	0	1	0	1.00	0	.138	.194	.172
2007 Det	AL	49	138	42	12	2	4	(2	2)	70	28	27	21	8	1	33	0	1	1	3	0	1.00	7	.304	.340	.507
2008 Det	AL	92	182	43	10	1	4	(2	2)	67	26	20	20	16	1	49	0	1	0	3	1	.75	2	.236	.298	.368
2009 Det	AL	113	261	76	11	2	16	(9	7)	139	44	45	42	26	2	60	2	1	1	4	5	.44	6	.291	.359	.533
2010 Det	AL	113	371	104	25	1	15	(5	10)	176	54	62	54	27	0	92	8	1	3	2	2	.50	8	.280	.340	.474
2011 Det	AL	121	387	99	22	2	14	(7	7)	167	53	49	48	21	2	114	3	4	3	1	1	.50	4	.256	.297	.432
2012 Det	AL	66	205	35	14	0	1	(0	1)	52	14	12	8	13	0	53	2	1	1	1	1	.50	7	.171	.226	.254
Postseason		9	28	8	1	0	2	(1	1)	15	4	5	4	4	0	7	0	0	0	0	0	-	3	.286	.375	.536
7 ML YEARS		566	1573	403	95	8	54	(25	29)	676	223	216	194	113	6	416	15	9	9	16	9	.64	34	.256	.311	.430

Brooks Raley

Pitches: L Bats: L Pos: SP-5   RAIL-ee   Ht: 6'3" Wt: 185 Born: 6/29/1988 Age: 25

Year Team	Lg	G	GS	CG	GF	IP	BFP	H	R	ER	HR	SH	SF	HB	TBB	IBB	SO	WP	Bk	W	L	Pct	Sh	Sv-Op	Hld	ERC	ERA
2009 Cubs	R	3	3	0	0	4.1	18	2	4	2	1	0	0	0	2	0	3	1	0	0	1	.000	0	0- -	-	2.12	4.15
2009 Boise	A-	2	0	0	0	6.1	31	3	1	1	1	0	0	0	1	0	2	0	0	0	0	-	0	0- -	-	1.29	1.42
2010 Dytona	A+	27	27	0	0	136.1	584	151	62	53	9	3	2	4	43	0	97	5	2	8	6	.571	0	0- -	-	4.30	3.50
2011 Tenn	AA	26	25	0	0	136.1	619	170	86	64	16	14	4	3	45	0	80	7	0	8	10	.444	0	0- -	-	5.39	4.22
2012 Tenn	AA	8	8	0	0	48.2	199	47	19	19	2	2	0	4	12	0	29	1	0	2	2	.500	0	0- -	-	3.32	3.51
2012 Iowa	AAA	14	14	1	0	82.0	356	87	39	33	7	1	4	3	28	0	69	2	0	4	8	.333	1	0- -	-	4.23	3.62
2012 ChC	NL	5	5	0	0	24.1	116	33	23	22	7	1	0	0	11	0	16	0	0	1	2	.333	0	0-0	0	7.87	8.14

Alexei Ramirez

Bats: R Throws: R Pos: SS-158; PR-1   ah-lexx-AY   Ht: 6'2" Wt: 180 Born: 9/22/1981 Age: 31

Year Team	Lg	G	AB	H	2B	3B	HR	(Hm	Rd)	TB	R	RBI	RC	TBB	IBB	SO	HBP	SH	SF	SB	CS	SB%	GDP	Avg	OBP	Slg
2008 CWS	AL	136	480	139	22	2	21	(13	8)	228	65	77	78	18	3	61	3	4	4	13	9	.59	14	.290	.317	.475
2009 CWS	AL	148	542	150	14	1	15	(9	6)	211	71	68	74	49	3	66	1	6	8	14	5	.74	15	.277	.333	.389
2010 CWS	AL	156	585	165	29	2	18	(11	7)	252	83	70	72	27	2	82	2	7	5	13	8	.62	12	.282	.313	.431
2011 CWS	AL	158	614	165	31	2	15	(7	8)	245	81	70	74	51	1	84	6	8	5	7	5	.58	19	.269	.328	.399
2012 CWS	AL	158	593	157	24	4	9	(6	3)	216	59	73	70	16	2	77	4	4	4	20	7	.74	15	.265	.287	.364
Postseason		4	12	3	0	0	0	(0	0)	3	1	2	1	1	0	1	0	0	0	0	0	-	0	.250	.267	.250
5 ML YEARS		756	2814	776	120	11	78	(46	32)	1152	359	358	368	161	11	370	16	29	26	67	34	.66	75	.276	.316	.409

Aramis Ramirez

Bats: R Throws: R Pos: 3B-143; DH-3; PH-3   ah-RAH-miss   Ht: 6'1" Wt: 205 Born: 6/25/1978 Age: 35

Year	Team	Lg	G	AB	H	2B	3B	HR	(Hm	Rd)	TB	R	RBI	RC	TBB	IBB	SO	HBP	SH	SF	SB	CS	SB%	GDP	Avg	OBP	Slg
1998	Pit	NL	72	251	59	9	1	6	(3	3)	88	23	24	26	18	0	72	4	1	1	0	1	.00	3	.235	.296	.351
1999	Pit	NL	18	56	10	2	1	0	(0	0)	14	2	7	4	6	0	9	0	1	0	0	0	-	0	.179	.254	.250
2000	Pit	NL	73	254	65	15	2	6	(4	2)	102	19	35	28	10	0	36	5	1	4	0	0	-	9	.256	.293	.402
2001	Pit	NL	158	603	181	40	0	34	(16	18)	323	83	112	108	40	4	100	8	0	4	5	4	.56	9	.300	.350	.536
2002	Pit	NL	142	522	122	26	0	18	(7	11)	202	51	71	49	29	3	95	8	0	11	2	0	1.00	17	.234	.279	.387
2003	2 Tms	NL	159	607	165	32	2	27	(10	17)	282	75	106	88	42	3	99	10	0	11	2	2	.50	21	.272	.324	.465
2004	ChC	NL	145	547	174	32	1	36	(22	14)	316	99	103	100	49	6	62	3	0	7	0	2	.00	25	.318	.373	.578
2005	ChC	NL	123	463	140	30	0	31	(11	20)	263	72	92	79	35	4	60	6	0	2	1	0	1.00	15	.302	.358	.568
2006	ChC	NL	157	594	173	38	4	38	(14	24)	333	93	119	109	50	4	63	9	0	7	2	1	.67	15	.291	.352	.561
2007	ChC	NL	132	506	157	35	4	26	(17	9)	278	72	101	95	43	8	66	4	0	5	0	0	-	13	.310	.366	.549
2008	ChC	NL	149	554	160	44	1	27	(17	10)	287	97	111	108	74	7	94	11	0	6	2	2	.50	13	.289	.380	.518
2009	ChC	NL	82	306	97	14	1	15	(7	8)	158	46	65	66	28	3	43	8	0	0	2	1	.67	8	.317	.389	.516
2010	ChC	NL	124	465	112	21	1	25	(14	11)	210	61	83	64	34	3	90	3	0	5	0	0	-	10	.241	.294	.452
2011	ChC	NL	149	565	173	35	1	26	(14	12)	288	80	93	96	43	5	69	10	0	8	1	1	.50	12	.306	.361	.510
2012	Mil	NL	149	570	171	**50**	3	27	(15	12)	308	92	105	97	44	3	82	12	0	4	9	2	.82	14	.300	.360	.540
03	Pit	NL	96	375	105	25	1	12	(6	6)	168	44	67	49	25	3	68	7	0	8	1	1	.50	17	.280	.330	.448
03	ChC	NL	63	232	60	7	1	15	(4	11)	114	31	39	39	17	0	31	3	0	3	1	1	.50	4	.259	.314	.491
	Postseason		18	67	13	2	1	4	(1	3)	29	7	10	8	9	0	15	1	0	0	0	0	-	5	.194	.299	.433
	15 ML YEARS		1832	6863	1959	423	22	342	(171	171)	3452	965	1227	1117	545	53	1040	101	3	76	25	17	.60	184	.285	.343	.503

Elvin Ramirez

Pitches: R Bats: R Pos: RP-20   ELL-vinn   Ht: 6'3" Wt: 210 Born: 10/10/1987 Age: 25

			HOW MUCH HE PITCHED					WHAT HE GAVE UP										THE RESULTS						
Year	Team	Lg	G	GS	CG	GF	IP	BFP	H	R	ER	HR	SH	SF	HB	TBB	IBB	SO	WP	Bk	W	L	Pct	Sh	Sv-Op	Hld	ERC	ERA
2007	Kngspt	R	12	12	0	0	45.2	221	52	34	28	5	1	3	2	29	0	48	8	0	1	4	.200	0	0- -	-	5.93	5.52
2008	Savann	A	18	18	0	0	81.0	359	81	38	33	1	3	2	3	36	0	62	8	0	6	7	.462	0	0- -	-	3.70	3.67
2009	Savann	A	15	15	0	0	72.2	328	73	40	33	2	2	1	6	39	0	48	4	0	3	7	.300	0	0- -	-	4.41	4.09
2010	StLuci	A+	49	0	0	16	73.1	325	56	37	34	0	5	4	9	43	2	65	8	0	4	3	.571	0	0- -	-	3.13	4.17
2010	Bnghtn	AA	3	0	0	1	6.2	30	5	3	3	2	0	0	0	6	0	7	1	0	0	1	.000	0	0- -	-	6.29	4.05
2012	Bnghtn	AA	8	0	0	4	13.0	53	7	2	2	0	0	0	0	7	0	16	2	0	1	0	.000	0	1- -	-	1.61	1.38
2012	Buffalo	AAA	33	0	0	5	42.0	177	26	14	11	2	2	1	2	25	1	41	6	0	3	1	.750	0	1- -	-	2.55	2.36
2012	NYM	NL	20	0	0	7	21.1	102	24	13	13	1	0	1	0	20	1	22	1	0	0	1	.000	0	0-0	1	6.70	5.48

Erasmo Ramirez

Pitches: R Bats: R Pos: SP-8; RP-8   ehh-RAZ-mo   Ht: 5'11" Wt: 205 Born: 5/2/1990 Age: 23

			HOW MUCH HE PITCHED					WHAT HE GAVE UP										THE RESULTS						
Year	Team	Lg	G	GS	CG	GF	IP	BFP	H	R	ER	HR	SH	SF	HB	TBB	IBB	SO	WP	Bk	W	L	Pct	Sh	Sv-Op	Hld	ERC	ERA
2010	Clinton	A	26	23	1	1	151.2	611	142	63	50	13	3	1	13	21	0	117	2	0	10	4	.714	0	1- -	-	3.02	2.97
2011	Jacksn	AA	19	19	0	0	110.1	481	127	74	58	10	6	3	8	19	0	81	5	0	7	6	.538	0	0- -	-	4.18	4.73
2011	Tacom	AAA	7	7	0	0	42.1	184	51	27	24	4	0	1	2	13	0	35	0	0	3	2	.600	0	0- -	-	5.17	5.10
2012	Tacom	AAA	15	15	0	0	77.1	339	81	45	32	5	3	4	4	18	0	58	8	0	6	3	.667	0	0- -	-	3.51	3.72
2012	Sea	AL	16	8	0	2	59.0	238	47	26	22	6	1	5	3	12	1	48	0	0	1	3	.250	0	0-0	0	2.42	3.36

Hanley Ramirez

Bats: R Throws: R Pos: 3B-98; SS-57; DH-2; PR-1   Ht: 6'2" Wt: 229 Born: 12/23/1983 Age: 29

Year	Team	Lg	G	AB	H	2B	3B	HR	(Hm	Rd)	TB	R	RBI	RC	TBB	IBB	SO	HBP	SH	SF	SB	CS	SB%	GDP	Avg	OBP	Slg
2005	Bos	AL	2	2	0	0	0	0	(0	0)	0	0	0	0	0	0	2	0	0	0	0	0	-	0	.000	.000	.000
2006	Fla	NL	158	633	185	46	11	17	(9	8)	304	119	59	101	56	0	128	4	5	2	51	15	.77	7	.292	.353	.480
2007	Fla	NL	154	639	212	48	6	29	(15	14)	359	125	81	115	52	3	95	7	4	4	51	14	.78	10	.332	.386	.562
2008	Fla	NL	153	589	177	34	4	33	(17	16)	318	125	67	116	92	9	122	8	0	4	35	12	.74	5	.301	.400	.540
2009	Fla	NL	151	576	197	42	1	24	(17	7)	313	101	106	122	61	14	101	9	1	5	27	8	.77	9	**.342**	.410	.543
2010	Fla	NL	142	543	163	28	2	21	(12	9)	258	92	76	90	64	12	93	7	0	5	32	10	.76	14	.300	.378	.475
2011	Fla	NL	92	338	82	16	0	10	(5	5)	128	55	45	46	44	3	66	2	1	0	20	10	.67	6	.243	.333	.379
2012	2 Tms	NL	157	604	155	29	4	24	(11	13)	264	79	92	81	54	4	132	6	0	3	21	7	.75	17	.257	.322	.437
12	Mia	NL	93	353	87	18	2	14	(7	7)	151	49	48	42	37	1	72	3	0	2	14	4	.78	11	.246	.322	.428
12	LAD	NL	64	251	68	11	2	10	(4	6)	113	30	44	39	17	3	60	3	0	1	7	3	.70	6	.271	.324	.450
	8 ML YEARS		1009	3924	1171	243	28	158	(86	72)	1944	696	526	671	423	45	739	43	11	23	237	76	.76	68	.298	.371	.495

Ramon Ramirez

Pitches: R Bats: R Pos: RP-58   Ht: 5'11" Wt: 200 Born: 8/31/1981 Age: 31

			HOW MUCH HE PITCHED					WHAT HE GAVE UP										THE RESULTS						
Year	Team	Lg	G	GS	CG	GF	IP	BFP	H	R	ER	HR	SH	SF	HB	TBB	IBB	SO	WP	Bk	W	L	Pct	Sh	Sv-Op	Hld	ERC	ERA
2012	StLuci*	A+	2	1	0	0	2.0	11	5	3	3	0	0	0	0	0	0	0	0	0	0	0	-	0	0- -	-	10.86	13.50
2012	Buffalo*	AAA	1	0	0	0	0.2	7	4	3	3	0	0	1	0	1	0	0	0	0	0	1	.000	0	0- -	-	47.92	40.50
2006	Col	NL	61	0	0	14	67.2	285	58	28	26	5	2	3	1	27	3	61	2	0	4	3	.571	0	0-2	10	3.09	3.46
2007	Col	NL	22	0	0	5	17.1	78	21	16	16	2	2	2	1	6	2	15	2	0	2	2	.500	0	0-0	3	5.24	8.31
2008	KC	AL	71	0	0	15	71.2	295	57	23	21	2	4	3	0	31	6	70	6	1	3	2	.600	0	1-5	21	2.53	2.64
2009	Bos	AL	70	0	0	16	69.2	301	61	26	22	7	3	0	4	32	4	52	2	2	7	4	.636	0	0-4	12	3.73	2.84
2010	2 Tms	NL	69	0	0	23	69.1	284	52	24	23	7	2	4	0	27	3	46	5	2	1	3	.250	0	3-3	6	2.64	2.99
2011	SF	NL	66	0	0	22	68.2	282	54	24	20	3	2	1	3	26	5	66	6	1	3	3	.500	0	4-5	11	2.57	2.62
2012	NYM	NL	58	0	0	18	63.2	277	58	33	30	4	3	3	0	35	4	52	4	0	3	4	.429	0	1-3	1	3.80	4.24

Year Team	Lg	G	GS	CG	GF	IP	BFP	H	R	ER	HR	SH	SF	HB	TBB	IBB	SO	WP	Bk	W	L	Pct	Sh	Sv-Op	Hld	ERC	ERA
				HOW MUCH HE PITCHED							**WHAT HE GAVE UP**											**THE RESULTS**					
10 Bos	AL	44	0	0	17	42.1	178	39	21	21	6	2	4	0	16	2	31	4	1	0	3	.000	0	2-2	2	3.78	4.46
10 SF		25	0	0	6	27.0	106	13	3	2	1	0	0	0	11	1	15	1	1	0	1	1.000	0	1-1	4	1.28	0.67
Postseason		6	0	0	2	4.0	24	6	8	8	2	1	0	1	3	1	2	0	0	0	1	.000	0	0-0	0	11.88	18.00
7 ML YEARS		417	0	0	113	428.0	1802	361	174	158	30	18	16	9	184	27	362	27	6	23	21	.523	0	9-22	64	3.12	3.32

A.J. Ramos

Pitches: R **Bats:** R **Pos:** RP-11   **Ht:** 5'10" **Wt:** 210 **Born:** 9/20/1986 **Age:** 26

Year Team	Lg	G	GS	CG	GF	IP	BFP	H	R	ER	HR	SH	SF	HB	TBB	IBB	SO	WP	Bk	W	L	Pct	Sh	Sv-Op	Hld	ERC	ERA
				HOW MUCH HE PITCHED							**WHAT HE GAVE UP**											**THE RESULTS**					
2009 Jmstwn	A-	25	0	0	21	33.2	140	22	9	8	0	1	1	3	14	0	50	6	1	2	2	.500	0	9- --	-	1.98	2.14
2010 Grnsbr	A	49	0	0	45	58.1	245	40	26	24	3	1	5	5	32	3	78	7	1	3	7	.300	0	28- -	-	2.89	3.70
2011 Jupiter	A+	49	0	0	48	50.2	212	37	12	10	2	1	2	5	19	1	71	4	0	1	4	.200	0	25- -	-	2.46	1.78
2012 Jaxnvl	AA	55	0	0	46	68.2	261	36	14	11	3	1	0	0	21	0	89	2	1	3	3	.500	0	21- -	-	1.27	1.44
2012 Mia	NL	11	0	0	4	9.1	40	8	4	4	2	0	0	1	4	0	13	0	0	0	0	-	0	0-1	1	4.65	3.86

Cesar Ramos

Pitches: L **Bats:** L **Pos:** RP-16; SP-1   **Ht:** 6'2" **Wt:** 205 **Born:** 6/22/1984 **Age:** 29

Year Team	Lg	G	GS	CG	GF	IP	BFP	H	R	ER	HR	SH	SF	HB	TBB	IBB	SO	WP	Bk	W	L	Pct	Sh	Sv-Op	Hld	ERC	ERA
				HOW MUCH HE PITCHED							**WHAT HE GAVE UP**											**THE RESULTS**					
2012 Drham*	AAA	25	7	0	6	62.0	255	58	30	26	10	2	0	0	16	0	46	0	0	5	5	.500	0	1- -	-	3.58	3.77
2009 SD	NL	5	2	0	0	14.2	62	19	5	5	0	0	0	0	4	0	10	0	0	0	1	.000	0	0-0	4	4.78	3.07
2010 SD	NL	14	0	0	4	8.1	47	18	11	11	1	0	0	0	4	0	9	1	1	0	1	.000	0	0-0	1	11.97	11.88
2011 TB	AL	59	0	0	9	43.2	192	36	22	19	4	1	2	3	25	8	31	1	0	0	1	.000	0	0-2	3	3.64	3.92
2012 TB	AL	17	1	0	9	30.0	120	19	7	7	2	0	0	2	10	0	29	0	0	1	0	1.000	0	0-0	1	1.98	2.10
4 ML YEARS		95	3	0	22	96.2	421	92	45	42	7	1	2	5	43	8	79	2	1	1	3	.250	0	0-2	5	3.84	3.91

Wilson Ramos

Bats: R **Throws:** R **Pos:** C-24; PH-1   **Ht:** 6'0" **Wt:** 250 **Born:** 8/10/1987 **Age:** 25

Year Team	Lg	G	AB	H	2B	3B	HR	(Hm	Rd)	TB	R	RBI	RC	TBB	IBB	SO	HBP	SH	SF	SB	CS	SB%	GDP	Avg	OBP	Slg
						BATTING															**BASERUNNING**				**AVERAGES**	
2010 2 Tms		22	79	22	7	0	1	(1	0)	32	5	5	10	2	0	12	1	0	0	0	0	-	2	.278	.305	.405
2011 Was	NL	113	389	104	22	1	15	(8	7)	173	48	52	43	38	8	76	2	4	2	0	2	.00	19	.267	.334	.445
2012 Was	NL	25	83	22	2	0	3	(1	2)	33	11	10	12	12	2	19	0	0	1	0	0	-	1	.265	.354	.398
10 Min	AL	7	27	8	3	0	0	(0	0)	11	2	1	3	0	0	3	1	0	0	0	0	-	0	.296	.321	.407
10 Was	NL	15	52	14	4	0	1	(1	0)	21	3	4	7	2	0	9	0	0	0	0	0	-	1	.269	.296	.404
3 ML YEARS		160	551	148	31	1	19	(10	9)	238	64	67	65	52	10	107	3	4	3	0	2	.00	22	.269	.333	.432

Cody Ransom

Bats: R **Throws:** R **Pos:** SS-48; 3B-35; PH-17; 2B-6; 1B-1; DH-1; PR-1   **Ht:** 6'2" **Wt:** 203 **Born:** 2/17/1976 **Age:** 37

Year Team	Lg	G	AB	H	2B	3B	HR	(Hm	Rd)	TB	R	RBI	RC	TBB	IBB	SO	HBP	SH	SF	SB	CS	SB%	GDP	Avg	OBP	Slg
						BATTING															**BASERUNNING**				**AVERAGES**	
2012 Reno	AAA	10	34	10	2	0	2	(-	-)	18	5	9	7	6	0	14	0	0	0	0	0	-	0	.294	.400	.529
2001 SF	NL	9	7	0	0	0	0	(0	0)	0	1	0	0	0	0	5	0	0	0	0	0	-	0	.000	.000	.000
2002 SF	NL	7	3	2	0	0	0	(0	0)	2	2	1	1	1	1	1	0	0	0	0	0	-	0	.667	.750	.667
2003 SF	NL	20	27	6	1	0	1	(1	0)	10	7	1	1	1	0	11	0	0	0	0	0	-	0	.222	.250	.370
2004 SF	NL	78	68	17	6	0	1	(0	1)	26	13	11	9	6	0	20	1	3	0	2	2	.50	2	.250	.320	.382
2007 Hou	AL	19	35	8	2	0	1	(1	0)	13	9	3	6	9	1	9	2	0	0	0	0	-	0	.229	.413	.371
2008 NYY	AL	33	43	13	3	0	4	(1	3)	28	9	8	10	6	0	12	1	1	0	0	0	-	0	.302	.400	.651
2009 NYY	AL	31	79	15	9	1	0	(0	0)	26	11	10	5	7	0	25	0	0	0	2	0	1.00	3	.190	.256	.329
2010 Phi	NL	22	42	8	0	0	2	(2	0)	14	6	5	5	3	0	11	0	1	0	1	0	1.00	3	.190	.244	.333
2011 Ari	NL	12	33	5	2	0	1	(1	0)	10	3	4	2	3	0	7	1	0	0	1	0	1.00	3	.152	.243	.303
2012 2 Tms	NL	90	246	54	14	0	11	(6	5)	101	29	42	31	30	0	109	3	3	0	0	1	.00	6	.220	.312	.411
12 Ari	NL	26	78	21	7	0	5	(3	2)	43	11	16	12	7	0	30	3	0	0	0	0	-	1	.269	.352	.551
12 Mil	NL	64	168	33	7	0	6	(3	3)	58	18	26	19	23	0	79	0	3	0	0	1	.00	5	.196	.293	.345
10 ML YEARS		321	583	128	37	1	21	(12	9)	230	90	85	70	66	2	212	8	8	0	6	3	.67	15	.220	.307	.395

Clay Rapada

Pitches: L **Bats:** R **Pos:** RP-70   ruh-PAH-duh   **Ht:** 6'5" **Wt:** 200 **Born:** 3/9/1981 **Age:** 32

Year Team	Lg	G	GS	CG	GF	IP	BFP	H	R	ER	HR	SH	SF	HB	TBB	IBB	SO	WP	Bk	W	L	Pct	Sh	Sv-Op	Hld	ERC	ERA
				HOW MUCH HE PITCHED							**WHAT HE GAVE UP**											**THE RESULTS**					
2007 2 Tms		5	0	0	2	2.2	13	3	3	3	2	0	0	0	2	0	4	2	0	0	0	-	0	0-0	0	11.59	10.13
2008 Det	AL	25	0	0	3	21.1	94	19	11	10	0	1	0	1	14	1	15	1	0	3	0	1.000	0	0-0	2	3.87	4.22
2009 Det	AL	3	0	0	1	3.1	16	4	2	2	1	0	0	0	2	1	2	0	0	0	0	-	0	0-0	0	7.00	5.40
2010 Tex	AL	13	0	0	2	9.0	39	6	4	4	2	0	0	0	7	1	5	0	0	0	0	-	0	0-1	3	4.42	4.00
2011 Bal	AL	32	0	0	4	16.1	69	14	11	11	3	0	1	0	7	0	18	0	0	2	0	1.000	0	0-0	5	3.95	6.06
2012 NYY	AL	70	0	0	7	38.1	155	29	14	12	2	1	1	1	17	1	38	1	2	3	0	1.000	0	0-0	6	2.77	2.82
07 ChC	NL	1	0	0	0	0.1	1	0	0	0	0	0	0	0	0	0	0	0	0	0	0	-	0	0-0	0	0.00	0.00
07 Det	AL	4	0	0	2	2.1	12	3	3	3	2	0	0	0	2	0	4	2	0	0	0	-	0	0-0	0	14.48	11.57
Postseason		3	0	0	0	0.1	3	1	0	0	0	0	0	0	1	0	1	0	0	0	0	-	0	0-1	0	29.63	0.00
6 ML YEARS		148	0	0	19	91.0	386	75	45	42	10	2	2	2	49	4	82	4	2	8	0	1.000	0	0-1	16	3.78	4.15

Colby Rasmus

Bats: L **Throws:** L **Pos:** CF-145; PH-6; DH-4   **Ht:** 6'2" **Wt:** 200 **Born:** 8/11/1986 **Age:** 26

Year	Team	Lg	G	AB	H	2B	3B	HR	(Hm	Rd)	TB	R	RBI	RC	TBB	IBB	SO	HBP	SH	SF	SB	CS	SB%	GDP	Avg	OBP	Slg
2009	StL	NL	147	474	119	22	2	16	(7	9)	193	72	52	60	36	3	95	3	5	2	3	1	.75	5	.251	.307	.407
2010	StL	NL	144	464	128	28	3	23	(11	12)	231	85	66	76	63	9	148	1	2	4	12	8	.60	5	.276	.361	.498
2011	2 Tms		129	471	106	24	6	14	(4	10)	184	75	53	50	50	2	116	0	2	3	5	2	.71	10	.225	.298	.391
2012	Tor	AL	151	565	126	21	5	23	(8	15)	224	75	75	74	47	5	149	7	2	4	4	3	.57	7	.223	.289	.400
11	StL	NL	94	338	83	14	6	11	(4	7)	142	61	40	43	45	2	77	0	1	2	5	2	.71	8	.246	.332	.420
11	Tor	AL	35	133	23	10	0	3	(0	3)	42	14	13	7	5	0	39	0	1	1	0	0	-	2	.173	.201	.316
	Postseason		3	9	4	3	0	0	(0	0)	7	1	1	1	2	0	1	0	0	0	0	0	-	1	.444	.545	.778
	4 ML YEARS		571	1974	479	95	16	76	(30	46)	834	307	246	260	196	19	508	11	11	13	24	14	.63	27	.243	.313	.422

Jon Rauch

Pitches: R **Bats:** R **Pos:** RP-73   RAUSH   **Ht:** 6'11" **Wt:** 290 **Born:** 9/27/1978 **Age:** 34

Year	Team	Lg	G	GS	CG	GF	IP	BFP	H	R	ER	HR	SH	SF	HB	TBB	IBB	SO	WP	Bk	W	L	Pct	Sh	Sv-Op	Hld	ERC	ERA
2002	CWS	AL	8	6	0	1	28.2	130	28	26	21	7	0	1	2	14	2	19	1	1	2	1	.667	0	0-0	0	5.41	6.59
2004	2 Tms		11	4	0	1	32.0	131	30	10	10	1	2	1	0	11	2	22	2	0	4	1	.800	0	0-0	0	3.05	2.81
2005	Was	NL	15	1	0	4	30.0	124	24	12	12	3	1	1	1	11	2	23	2	0	2	4	.333	0	0-0	0	2.90	3.60
2006	Was	NL	85	0	0	19	91.1	383	78	37	34	13	1	6	2	36	6	86	4	1	4	5	.444	0	2-5	18	3.52	3.35
2007	Was	NL	88	0	0	26	87.1	354	75	37	35	7	2	5	0	21	4	71	2	0	8	4	.667	0	4-10	33	2.53	3.61
2008	2 Tms	NL	74	0	0	51	71.2	295	69	36	33	11	6	3	0	16	2	66	1	0	4	8	.333	0	18-24	6	3.48	4.14
2009	2 Tms	NL	75	0	0	15	70.0	299	70	30	28	6	3	4	2	23	1	49	6	0	7	3	.700	0	2-5	17	3.78	3.60
2010	Min	AL	59	0	0	41	57.2	245	61	20	20	3	1	1	1	14	0	46	1	0	3	1	.750	0	21-25	2	3.50	3.12
2011	Tor	AL	53	0	0	28	52.0	225	56	28	28	11	2	0	1	14	1	36	2	0	5	4	.556	0	11-16	4	4.75	4.85
2012	NYM	NL	73	0	0	22	57.2	233	45	28	23	7	1	4	1	12	2	42	1	0	3	7	.300	0	4-8	16	2.30	3.59
04	CWS	AL	2	2	0	0	8.2	43	16	6	6	0	1	1	0	4	0	4	1	0	1	1	.500	0	0-0	0	9.15	6.23
04	Mon	NL	9	2	0	1	23.1	88	14	4	4	1	1	0	0	7	2	18	1	0	3	0	1.000	0	0-0	0	1.44	1.54
08	Was	NL	48	0	0	41	48.1	192	42	18	16	5	3	1	0	7	1	44	0	0	4	2	.667	0	17-22	5	2.41	2.98
08	Ari	NL	26	0	0	10	23.1	103	27	18	17	6	3	2	0	9	1	22	1	0	0	6	.000	0	1-2	6	6.09	6.56
09	Ari	NL	58	0	0	13	54.1	235	57	27	25	5	1	2	1	17	0	35	6	0	2	2	.500	0	2-3	12	3.98	4.14
09	Min	AL	17	0	0	2	15.2	64	13	3	3	1	2	2	1	6	1	14	0	0	5	1	.833	0	0-2	5	3.09	1.72
	Postseason		5	0	0	1	3.0	12	1	1	1	0	0	0	0	2	0	1	0	0	0	0	-	0	0-0	0	1.26	3.00
	10 ML YEARS		541	11	0	208	578.1	2419	536	264	244	69	19	26	10	172	22	460	22	2	42	38	.525	0	62-93	96	3.40	3.80

Anthony Recker

Bats: R **Throws:** R **Pos:** C-17; PH-5; 1B-1; DH-1   **Ht:** 6'2" **Wt:** 240 **Born:** 8/29/1983 **Age:** 29

Year	Team	Lg	G	AB	H	2B	3B	HR	(Hm	Rd)	TB	R	RBI	RC	TBB	IBB	SO	HBP	SH	SF	SB	CS	SB%	GDP	Avg	OBP	Slg
2005	Vancvr	A-	43	150	35	8	0	5	(-	-)	58	16	18	19	16	0	40	2	1	0	0	0	-	5	.233	.315	.387
2006	Kane	A	109	407	117	24	3	14	(-	-)	189	52	57	68	42	2	115	3	0	1	5	5	.50	10	.287	.358	.464
2007	Stcktn	A+	56	207	66	17	2	13	(-	-)	126	39	47	50	27	0	48	5	0	5	2	0	1.00	5	.319	.402	.609
2007	Mdland	AA	58	201	41	12	0	4	(-	-)	65	16	20	17	17	0	63	1	0	0	0	1	.00	8	.204	.269	.323
2008	Mdland	AA	117	430	118	29	4	11	(-	-)	188	57	64	66	43	0	140	5	2	2	1	2	.33	11	.274	.346	.437
2009	Scrmto	AAA	78	272	71	11	2	12	(-	-)	122	30	45	42	28	0	80	2	3	1	2	0	1.00	4	.261	.333	.449
2009	Mdland	AA	16	57	17	4	0	3	(-	-)	30	11	9	11	8	0	22	0	0	0	0	0	-	1	.298	.385	.526
2010	Mdland	AA	11	38	8	1	0	1	(-	-)	12	8	5	7	0	12	2	0	0	1	0	1.00	0	.211	.362	.316
2010	Scrmto	AAA	80	250	72	18	2	10	(-	-)	124	36	42	42	22	1	62	0	0	4	0	1	.00	5	.288	.341	.496
2011	Scrmto	AAA	99	345	99	24	1	16	(-	-)	173	61	48	69	56	2	81	4	2	5	7	5	.58	6	.287	.388	.501
2012	Scrmto	AAA	52	200	53	7	0	9	(-	-)	87	29	29	32	28	0	56	1	0	0	3	1	.75	7	.265	.358	.435
2012	Iowa	AAA	3	7	2	1	0	0	(-	-)	3	1	0	1	2	0	2	0	0	0	0	0	-	0	.286	.444	.429
2012	Tenn	AA	4	15	3	1	0	1	(-	-)	7	1	4	1	0	0	7	0	0	0	0	0	-	0	.200	.200	.467
2011	Oak	AL	5	17	3	1	0	0	(0	0)	4	3	0	0	4	0	7	0	0	0	0	0	-	0	.176	.333	.235
2012	2 Tms		22	49	7	2	0	1	(0	1)	12	4	4	0	6	0	15	2	1	0	0	0	-	1	.143	.263	.245
12	Oak	AL	13	31	4	1	0	0	(0	0)	5	3	0	0	4	0	13	1	1	0	0	0	-	0	.129	.250	.161
12	ChC	NL	9	18	3	1	0	1	(0	1)	7	1	4	0	2	0	2	1	0	0	0	0	-	1	.167	.286	.389
	2 ML YEARS		27	66	10	3	0	1	(0	1)	16	7	4	0	10	0	22	2	1	0	0	0	-	1	.152	.282	.242

Josh Reddick

Bats: L **Throws:** R **Pos:** RF-136; CF-14; DH-12; PH-3   **Ht:** 6'2" **Wt:** 180 **Born:** 2/19/1987 **Age:** 26

Year	Team	Lg	G	AB	H	2B	3B	HR	(Hm	Rd)	TB	R	RBI	RC	TBB	IBB	SO	HBP	SH	SF	SB	CS	SB%	GDP	Avg	OBP	Slg
2009	Bos	AL	27	59	10	4	0	2	(0	2)	20	5	4	4	2	0	17	1	0	0	0	0	-	0	.169	.210	.339
2010	Bos	AL	29	62	12	3	1	1	(1	0)	20	5	5	1	1	0	15	0	0	0	1	0	1.00	1	.194	.206	.323
2011	Bos	AL	87	254	71	18	3	7	(2	5)	116	41	28	33	19	1	50	1	0	4	1	2	.33	1	.280	.327	.457
2012	Oak	AL	156	611	148	29	5	32	(18	14)	283	85	85	73	55	8	151	2	1	4	11	1	.92	15	.242	.305	.463
	4 ML YEARS		299	986	241	54	9	42	(21	21)	439	136	122	111	77	9	233	4	1	8	13	3	.81	17	.244	.300	.445

Todd Redmond

Pitches: R **Bats:** R **Pos:** SP-1   **Ht:** 6'3" **Wt:** 215 **Born:** 5/17/1985 **Age:** 28

Year	Team	Lg	G	GS	CG	GF	IP	BFP	H	R	ER	HR	SH	SF	HB	TBB	IBB	SO	WP	Bk	W	L	Pct	Sh	Sv-Op	Hld	ERC	ERA
2005	Wmspt	A-	15	14	0	0	72.2	295	62	22	16	2	1	0	6	21	0	63	2	0	1	2	.333	0	0- -	-	2.78	1.98
2006	Hkry	A	27	27	0	0	160.1	659	137	64	49	13	2	2	17	33	0	148	3	0	13	6	.684	0	0- -	-	2.83	2.75
2007	Lynbrg	A+	25	25	0	0	142.2	608	151	82	72	13	7	9	10	32	0	95	2	0	7	12	.368	0	0- -	-	3.92	4.54
2007	Altna	AA	3	3	0	0	17.1	70	15	6	6	2	0	0	1	3	0	12	1	0	1	1	.500	0	0- -	-	2.81	3.12
2008	Missi	AA	28	27	0	0	166.1	686	164	72	65	17	5	3	6	33	2	133	4	0	13	5	.722	0	0- -	-	3.37	3.52

Year	Team	Lg	G	GS	CG	GF	IP	BFP	H	R	ER	HR	SH	SF	HB	TBB	IBB	SO	WP	Bk	W	L	Pct	Sh	Sv-Op	Hld	ERC	ERA
2009	Gwnntt	AAA	27	24	0	0	145.0	635	152	85	71	21	6	9	7	47	1	106	1	0	9	6	.600	0	0--	-	4.49	4.41
2010	Gwnntt	AAA	28	28	1	0	162.2	679	156	86	77	21	3	6	1	44	0	142	1	0	9	10	.474	1	0--	-	3.55	4.26
2011	Gwnntt	AAA	28	27	2	1	169.2	693	152	58	55	18	3	4	8	47	0	142	1	1	10	8	.556	1	0--	-	3.31	2.92
2012	Gwnntt	AAA	18	18	1	0	105.2	446	107	50	42	11	4	2	2	28	5	96	1	0	6	6	.500	1	0--	-	3.64	3.58
2012	Lsvlle	AAA	8	7	0	0	43.0	178	43	21	18	7	1	0	1	11	0	40	0	0	2	5	.286	0	0--	-	4.09	3.77
2012	Cin	NL	1	1	0	0	3.1	22	7	4	4	1	0	0	0	5	0	2	0	0	0	1	.000	0	0-0	0	18.68	10.80

Addison Reed

Pitches: R Bats: L Pos: RP-62 Ht: 6'4" Wt: 220 Born: 12/27/1988 Age: 24

Year	Team	Lg	G	GS	CG	GF	IP	BFP	H	R	ER	HR	SH	SF	HB	TBB	IBB	SO	WP	Bk	W	L	Pct	Sh	Sv-Op	Hld	ERC	ERA
2010	Gr Falls	R+	13	2	0	3	30.0	115	17	7	6	1	1	1	2	6	0	44	1	0	1	0	1.000	0	1--	-	1.27	1.80
2011	Knapol	A	4	0	0	1	8.0	29	4	1	1	0	1	0	0	1	0	11	1	0	0	0	-	0	0--	-	0.73	1.13
2011	WinSa	A+	15	0	0	4	28.1	114	21	8	5	1	1	0	2	4	0	39	3	0	2	0	1.000	0	1--	-	1.65	1.59
2011	Brham	AA	13	0	0	7	20.2	77	10	2	2	0	0	0	1	6	0	33	0	0	0	1	.000	0	2--	-	1.09	0.87
2011	Charltt	AAA	11	0	0	3	21.1	73	8	3	3	2	0	0	1	3	0	28	2	0	0	0	-	0	2--	-	0.74	1.27
2011	CWS	AL	6	0	0	2	7.1	33	10	3	3	1	0	0	0	1	0	12	0	0	0	0	-	0	0-0	0	5.24	3.68
2012	CWS	AL	62	0	0	44	55.0	238	57	30	29	6	0	4	2	18	3	54	0	1	3	2	.600	0	29-33	4	4.09	4.75
	2 ML YEARS		68	0	0	46	62.1	271	67	33	32	7	0	4	2	19	3	66	0	1	3	2	.600	0	29-33	4	4.22	4.62

Nolan Reimold

Bats: R Throws: R Pos: LF-15; PH-2; DH-1 RYE-mold Ht: 6'4" Wt: 205 Born: 10/12/1983 Age: 29

Year	Team	Lg	G	AB	H	2B	3B	HR	(Hm	Rd)	TB	R	RBI	RC	TBB	IBB	SO	HBP	SH	SF	SB	CS	SB%	GDP	Avg	OBP	Slg
2009	Bal	AL	104	358	100	18	2	15	(8	7)	167	49	45	57	47	1	77	3	0	3	8	2	.80	8	.279	.365	.466
2010	Bal	AL	39	116	24	5	0	3	(0	3)	38	9	14	6	12	0	26	1	0	2	0	0	-	6	.207	.282	.328
2011	Bal	AL	87	267	66	10	3	13	(8	5)	121	40	45	48	28	1	57	6	0	4	7	2	.78	4	.247	.328	.453
2012	Bal	AL	16	67	21	6	0	5	(0	5)	42	10	10	15	2	0	14	0	0	0	1	0	1.00	3	.313	.333	.627
	4 ML YEARS		246	808	211	39	5	36	(16	20)	368	108	114	126	89	2	174	10	0	9	16	4	.80	21	.261	.338	.455

Jason Repko

Bats: R Throws: R Pos: CF-4; PR-1 Ht: 5'11" Wt: 200 Born: 12/27/1980 Age: 32

Year	Team	Lg	G	AB	H	2B	3B	HR	(Hm	Rd)	TB	R	RBI	RC	TBB	IBB	SO	HBP	SH	SF	SB	CS	SB%	GDP	Avg	OBP	Slg
2012	Pwtckt*	AAA	47	178	40	6	4	7	(-	-)	75	30	26	22	15	0	40	3	1	2	4	3	.57	2	.225	.293	.421
2012	Grnville*	A	7	22	6	0	1	1	(-	-)	11	5	2	5	6	0	10	1	0	0	1	0	1.00	0	.273	.448	.500
2005	LAD	NL	129	276	61	15	3	8	(4	4)	106	43	30	28	16	1	80	7	2	0	5	0	1.00	7	.221	.281	.384
2006	LAD	NL	69	130	33	5	1	3	(1	2)	49	21	16	21	15	1	24	3	2	0	10	4	.71	2	.254	.345	.377
2008	LAD	NL	22	18	3	1	0	0	(0	0)	4	0	0	0	2	0	9	0	0	0	1	0	1.00	0	.167	.250	.222
2009	LAD	NL	10	5	0	0	0	0	(0	0)	0	1	1	0	0	0	2	1	0	1	1	0	1.00	0	.000	.143	.000
2010	Min	AL	58	127	29	6	0	3	(0	3)	44	19	9	12	13	0	38	5	1	0	3	2	.60	2	.228	.324	.346
2011	Min	AL	67	133	30	2	0	2	(1	1)	38	21	11	14	6	0	38	2	3	0	7	2	.78	0	.226	.270	.286
2012	Bos	AL	5	11	1	0	0	0	(0	0)	1	0	0	0	0	0	4	0	0	0	0	0	-	0	.091	.091	.091
	Postseason		2	0	0	0	0	0	(0	0)	0	0	0	0	0	0	0	0	0	0	0	0	-	0	-	-	-
	7 ML YEARS		360	700	157	29	4	16	(6	10)	242	105	67	75	52	2	195	18	8	1	27	8	.77	11	.224	.294	.346

Chris Resop

Pitches: R Bats: R Pos: RP-61 REE-sawp Ht: 6'3" Wt: 225 Born: 11/4/1982 Age: 30

Year	Team	Lg	G	GS	CG	GF	IP	BFP	H	R	ER	HR	SH	SF	HB	TBB	IBB	SO	WP	Bk	W	L	Pct	Sh	Sv-Op	Hld	ERC	ERA
2005	Fla	NL	15	0	0	6	17.0	80	22	16	16	1	0	2	1	9	0	15	3	0	2	0	1.000	0	0-0	0	6.35	8.47
2006	Fla	NL	22	0	0	10	21.1	101	26	9	8	1	0	1	0	16	5	19	0	0	1	2	.333	0	0-1	2	6.30	3.38
2007	LAA	AL	4	0	0	3	4.1	17	4	2	2	1	2	1	0	1	0	2	0	0	0	0	-	0	0-0	0	4.00	4.15
2008	Atl	NL	16	0	0	9	18.1	82	16	12	12	2	2	1	2	10	2	13	0	0	0	1	.000	0	0-0	2	4.19	5.89
2010	2 Tms	NL	23	0	0	5	21.0	91	15	9	9	1	1	2	0	13	0	26	0	1	0	0	-	0	0-0	5	2.93	3.86
2011	Pit	NL	76	0	0	12	69.2	309	73	34	34	8	0	5	3	30	9	79	4	1	5	4	.556	0	1-6	15	4.52	4.39
2012	Pit	NL	61	0	0	13	73.2	330	81	35	32	6	5	6	2	24	6	46	2	0	1	4	.200	0	1-2	8	4.05	3.91
10	Atl	NL	1	0	0	0	2.0	14	5	5	5	0	0	0	0	3	0	2	0	0	0	0	-	0	0-0	0	18.12	22.50
10	Pit	NL	22	0	0	5	19.0	77	10	4	4	1	1	2	0	10	0	24	0	1	0	0	-	0	0-0	5	1.80	1.89
	7 ML YEARS		217	0	0	58	225.1	1010	237	117	113	20	10	17	8	103	22	191	9	2	9	11	.450	0	2-9	32	4.46	4.51

Ben Revere

Bats: L Throws: R Pos: RF-84; CF-39; LF-5; PH-3; PR-1 Ht: 5'9" Wt: 172 Born: 5/3/1988 Age: 25

Year	Team	Lg	G	AB	H	2B	3B	HR	(Hm	Rd)	TB	R	RBI	RC	TBB	IBB	SO	HBP	SH	SF	SB	CS	SB%	GDP	Avg	OBP	Slg
2012	Roch*	AAA	23	94	31	1	0	0	(-	-)	32	9	6	12	4	0	6	1	1	1	6	2	.75	2	.330	.360	.340
2010	Min	AL	13	14	5	0	0	0	(0	0)	5	1	2	0	2	0	5	0	0	0	0	1	.00	1	.179	.233	.179
2011	Min	AL	117	450	120	9	5	0	(0	0)	139	56	30	51	26	1	41	2	3	0	34	9	.79	7	.267	.310	.309
2012	Min	AL	124	511	150	13	6	0	(0	0)	175	70	32	62	29	0	54	3	6	4	40	9	.82	8	.294	.333	.342
	3 ML YEARS		254	989	275	22	11	0	(0	0)	319	127	64	113	57	1	100	5	9	4	74	19	.80	16	.278	.319	.323

Jose Reyes

Bats: B Throws: R Pos: SS-160   Ht: 6'1" Wt: 195 Born: 6/11/1983 Age: 30

							BATTING													BASERUNNING				AVERAGES		
Year	Team	Lg	G	AB	H	2B	3B	HR	(Hm	Rd)	TB	R	RBI	RC	TBB	IBB	SO	HBP	SH	SF	SB	CS	SB%	GDP	Avg	OBP	Slg
2003	NYM	NL	69	274	84	12	4	5	(1	4)	119	47	32	46	13	0	36	0	2	3	13	3	.81	1	.307	.334	.434
2004	NYM	NL	53	220	56	16	2	2	(1	1)	82	33	14	25	5	0	31	0	4	0	19	2	.90	1	.255	.271	.373
2005	NYM	NL	161	696	190	24	17	7	(2	5)	269	99	58	84	27	0	78	2	4	4	60	15	.80	7	.273	.300	.386
2006	NYM	NL	153	647	194	30	17	19	(9	10)	315	122	81	121	53	6	81	1	2	0	64	17	.79	6	.300	.354	.487
2007	NYM	NL	160	681	191	36	12	12	(7	5)	287	119	57	99	77	13	78	1	5	1	78	21	.79	6	.280	.354	.421
2008	NYM	NL	159	688	204	37	19	16	(9	7)	327	113	68	117	66	8	82	1	5	3	56	15	.79	9	.297	.358	.475
2009	NYM	NL	36	147	41	7	2	2	(1	1)	58	18	15	20	18	1	19	0	0	1	11	2	.85	2	.279	.355	.395
2010	NYM	NL	133	563	159	29	10	11	(8	3)	241	83	54	76	31	4	63	2	4	3	30	10	.75	8	.282	.321	.428
2011	NYM	NL	126	537	181	31	16	7	(4	3)	265	101	44	90	43	9	41	0	2	4	39	7	.85	5	.337	.384	.493
2012	Mia	NL	160	642	184	37	12	11	(4	7)	278	86	57	92	63	9	56	0	5	6	40	11	.78	10	.287	.347	.433
	Postseason		10	44	11	1	1	1	(1	0)	17	7	5	6	3	1	5	0	0	0	3	1	.75	0	.250	.298	.386
	10 ML YEARS		1210	5095	1484	259	111	92	(46	46)	2241	821	480	770	396	50	565	7	33	25	410	103	.80	55	.291	.342	.440

Mark Reynolds

Bats: R Throws: R Pos: 1B-108; 3B-15; DH-12; PH-3   Ht: 6'2" Wt: 220 Born: 8/3/1983 Age: 29

							BATTING													BASERUNNING				AVERAGES		
Year	Team	Lg	G	AB	H	2B	3B	HR	(Hm	Rd)	TB	R	RBI	RC	TBB	IBB	SO	HBP	SH	SF	SB	CS	SB%	GDP	Avg	OBP	Slg
2012	Bowie*	AA	2	7	1	0	0	0	(-	-)	1	0	0	0	2	0	4	0	0	0	0	0	-	0	.143	.333	.143
2007	Ari	NL	111	366	102	20	4	17	(7	10)	181	62	62	62	37	4	129	5	1	5	0	1	.00	5	.279	.349	.495
2008	Ari	NL	152	539	129	28	3	28	(13	15)	247	87	97	82	64	0	204	3	1	6	11	2	.85	10	.239	.320	.458
2009	Ari	NL	155	578	150	30	1	44	(19	25)	314	98	102	94	76	3	223	5	0	3	24	9	.73	8	.260	.349	.543
2010	Ari	NL	145	499	99	17	2	32	(21	11)	216	79	85	77	83	7	211	9	0	5	7	4	.64	8	.198	.320	.433
2011	Bal	AL	155	534	118	27	1	37	(17	20)	258	84	86	77	75	2	196	7	0	4	6	4	.60	11	.221	.323	.483
2012	Bal	AL	135	457	101	26	0	23	(11	12)	196	65	69	68	73	2	159	6	0	2	1	3	.25	19	.221	.335	.429
	Postseason		7	26	4	0	0	2	(1	1)	10	3	2	1	2	0	9	1	0	0	0	0	-	0	.154	.241	.385
	6 ML YEARS		853	2973	699	148	11	181	(88	93)	1412	475	501	460	408	18	1122	35	2	25	49	23	.68	61	.235	.332	.475

Matt Reynolds

Pitches: L Bats: L Pos: RP-71   Ht: 6'5" Wt: 240 Born: 10/2/1984 Age: 28

			HOW MUCH HE PITCHED					WHAT HE GAVE UP										THE RESULTS						
Year	Team	Lg	G	GS	CG	GF	IP	BFP	H	R	ER	HR	SH	SF	HB	TBB	IBB	SO	WP	Bk	W	L	Pct	Sh	Sv-Op	Hld	ERC	ERA
2010	Col	NL	21	0	0	2	18.0	70	10	4	4	2	1	1	2	5	0	17	1	0	1	0	1.000	0	0-0	2	1.87	2.00
2011	Col	NL	73	0	0	14	50.2	211	48	24	23	10	1	4	0	18	5	50	5	2	1	2	.333	0	0-2	18	4.18	4.09
2012	Col	NL	71	0	0	16	57.1	249	65	31	28	11	6	3	0	17	4	51	5	1	3	1	.750	0	0-0	2	4.96	4.40
	3 ML YEARS		165	0	0	27	126.0	530	123	59	55	23	8	8	2	40	9	118	11	3	5	3	.625	0	0-2	22	4.16	3.93

Will Rhymes

Bats: L Throws: R Pos: 2B-31; 3B-15; PH-6; PR-3   Ht: 5'9" Wt: 155 Born: 4/1/1983 Age: 30

							BATTING													BASERUNNING				AVERAGES		
Year	Team	Lg	G	AB	H	2B	3B	HR	(Hm	Rd)	TB	R	RBI	RC	TBB	IBB	SO	HBP	SH	SF	SB	CS	SB%	GDP	Avg	OBP	Slg
2012	Drham*	AAA	46	172	44	5	3	4	(-	-)	67	19	21	22	18	0	19	1	1	2	2	3	.40	3	.256	.326	.390
2010	Det	AL	54	191	58	12	3	1	(1	0)	79	30	19	27	14	0	16	0	7	1	0	3	.00	1	.304	.350	.414
2011	Det	AL	29	85	20	3	0	0	(0	0)	23	13	2	8	11	0	12	0	3	0	1	0	1.00	2	.235	.323	.271
2012	TB	AL	47	123	28	2	1	1	(0	1)	35	11	8	10	10	0	17	3	0	1	1	2	.33	1	.228	.299	.285
	3 ML YEARS		130	399	106	17	4	2	(1	1)	137	54	29	45	35	0	45	3	10	2	2	5	.29	4	.266	.328	.343

Clayton Richard

Pitches: L Bats: L Pos: SP-33   Ht: 6'5" Wt: 245 Born: 9/12/1983 Age: 29

			HOW MUCH HE PITCHED					WHAT HE GAVE UP										THE RESULTS						
Year	Team	Lg	G	GS	CG	GF	IP	BFP	H	R	ER	HR	SH	SF	HB	TBB	IBB	SO	WP	Bk	W	L	Pct	Sh	Sv-Op	Hld	ERC	ERA
2008	CWS	AL	13	8	0	3	47.2	215	61	37	32	5	0	1	0	13	2	29	1	1	2	5	.286	0	0-0	0	5.06	6.04
2009	2 Tms		38	26	1	3	153.0	663	154	81	75	17	8	5	3	71	0	114	7	3	9	5	.643	0	0-0	0	4.60	4.41
2010	SD	NL	33	33	1	0	201.2	861	206	89	84	16	6	2	4	78	6	153	4	2	14	9	.609	1	0-0	0	4.09	3.75
2011	SD	NL	18	18	0	0	99.2	427	104	52	43	8	4	1	2	38	2	53	3	1	5	9	.357	0	0-0	0	4.22	3.88
2012	SD	NL	33	33	1	0	218.2	910	228	110	97	31	3	6	6	42	4	107	4	2	14	14	.500	1	0-0	0	3.87	3.99
09	CWS	AL	26	14	1	3	89.0	387	94	50	46	10	3	4	3	37	0	66	5	2	4	5	.571	0	0-0	0	4.76	4.65
09	SD	NL	12	12	0	0	64.0	276	60	31	29	7	5	1	0	34	0	48	2	1	5	2	.714	0	0-0	0	4.38	4.08
	Postseason		2	0	0	0	6.1	25	5	1	1	0	0	0	0	3	0	6	0	0	0	0	-	0	0-0	0	2.74	1.42
	5 ML YEARS		135	118	3	6	720.2	3076	753	369	331	77	21	15	15	242	14	456	19	9	44	42	.512	2	0-0	0	4.22	4.13

Garrett Richards

Pitches: R Bats: R Pos: RP-21; SP-9   Ht: 6'3" Wt: 215 Born: 5/27/1988 Age: 25

			HOW MUCH HE PITCHED					WHAT HE GAVE UP										THE RESULTS						
Year	Team	Lg	G	GS	CG	GF	IP	BFP	H	R	ER	HR	SH	SF	HB	TBB	IBB	SO	WP	Bk	W	L	Pct	Sh	Sv-Op	Hld	ERC	ERA
2009	Orem	R+	8	8	0	0	35.1	141	37	6	6	0	2	0	2	4	0	30	4	0	3	1	.750	0	0--	-	2.91	1.53
2010	CRpds	A	19	19	2	0	108.1	443	92	46	41	6	3	1	3	34	0	108	1	1	8	4	.667	0	0--	-	2.78	3.41
2010	RCuca	A+	7	7	0	0	34.2	147	38	17	15	4	0	2	1	9	0	41	4	1	4	1	.800	0	0--	-	4.34	3.89
2011	Ark	AA	22	21	3	0	143.0	579	123	58	50	10	3	1	8	40	0	103	7	0	12	2	.857	0	0--	-	2.95	3.15
2012	Salt Lk	AAA	14	14	0	0	77.0	348	87	36	36	5	4	2	6	35	0	65	6	0	7	3	.700	0	0--	-	5.13	4.21
2011	LAA	AL	7	3	0	2	14.0	62	16	11	9	4	0	0	0	7	0	9	2	0	0	2	.000	0	0-0	0	6.97	5.79
2012	LAA	AL	30	9	0	4	71.0	318	77	46	37	7	2	4	3	34	1	47	2	0	4	3	.571	0	1-3	5	5.04	4.69
	2 ML YEARS		37	12	0	6	85.0	380	93	57	46	11	2	4	3	41	1	56	4	0	4	5	.444	0	1-3	5	5.35	4.87

Scott Richmond

Pitches: R **Bats:** R **Pos:** RP-3   **Ht:** 6'5" **Wt:** 220 **Born:** 8/30/1979 **Age:** 33

Year	Team	Lg	G	GS	CG	GF	IP	BFP	H	R	ER	HR	SH	SF	HB	TBB	IBB	SO	WP	Bk	W	L	Pct	Sh	Sv-Op	Hld	ERC	ERA
2012	LsVgs*	AAA	27	25	0	0	134.2	595	163	93	84	21	4	4	4	43	0	112	9	0	11	7	.611	0	0- -	-	5.57	5.61
2008	Tor	AL	5	5	1	0	27.0	113	32	12	12	2	0	1	2	2	0	20	0	0	1	3	.250	1	0-0	0	3.99	4.00
2009	Tor	AL	27	24	1	1	138.2	610	147	90	85	27	1	2	0	59	1	117	5	1	8	11	.421	0	0-0	0	5.20	5.52
2011	Tor	AL	1	0	0	1	0.1	1	0	0	0	0	0	0	0	0	0	0	0	0	0	0	-	0	0-0	0	0.00	0.00
2012	Tor	AL	3	0	0	2	3.0	15	5	2	2	1	0	1	0	0	0	2	1	0	0	0	-	0	0-1	0	7.47	6.00
4 ML YEARS			36	29	2	4	169.0	739	184	104	99	30	1	4	2	61	1	139	6	1	9	14	.391	1	0-1	0	5.02	5.27

Alex Rios

Bats: R **Throws:** R **Pos:** RF-156; PH-1   **Ht:** 6'5" **Wt:** 215 **Born:** 2/18/1981 **Age:** 32

Year	Team	Lg	G	AB	H	2B	3B	HR	(Hm	Rd)	TB	R	RBI	RC	TBB	IBB	SO	HBP	SH	SF	SB	CS	SB%	GDP	Avg	OBP	Slg
2004	Tor	AL	111	426	122	24	7	1	(0	1)	163	55	28	49	31	0	84	2	1	0	15	3	.83	14	.286	.338	.383
2005	Tor	AL	146	481	126	23	6	10	(5	5)	191	71	59	56	28	1	101	5	0	5	14	9	.61	14	.262	.306	.397
2006	Tor	AL	128	450	136	33	6	17	(12	5)	232	68	82	83	35	1	89	3	0	10	15	6	.71	10	.302	.349	.516
2007	Tor	AL	161	643	191	43	7	24	(13	11)	320	114	85	105	55	3	103	6	0	7	17	4	.81	9	.297	.354	.498
2008	Tor	AL	155	635	185	47	8	15	(9	6)	293	91	79	92	44	2	112	2	0	5	32	8	.80	20	.291	.337	.461
2009	2 Tms	AL	149	582	144	31	2	17	(15	2)	230	63	71	64	37	1	107	6	1	7	24	5	.83	21	.247	.296	.395
2010	CWS	AL	147	567	161	29	3	21	(10	11)	259	89	88	84	38	4	93	7	0	5	34	14	.71	21	.284	.334	.457
2011	CWS	AL	145	537	122	22	2	13	(7	6)	187	64	44	35	27	4	68	2	0	4	11	6	.65	20	.227	.265	.348
2012	CWS	AL	157	605	184	37	8	25	(16	9)	312	93	91	103	26	3	92	4	0	5	23	6	.79	18	.304	.334	.516
09	Tor	AL	108	436	115	25	2	14	(12	2)	186	52	62	60	31	1	78	6	0	6	19	3	.86	14	.264	.317	.427
09	CWS	AL	41	146	29	6	0	3	(3	0)	44	11	9	4	6	0	29	0	1	1	5	2	.71	7	.199	.229	.301
9 ML YEARS			1299	4926	1371	289	49	143	(87	56)	2187	708	627	671	321	19	849	37	2	48	185	61	.75	147	.278	.324	.444

Juan Rivera

Bats: R **Throws:** R **Pos:** 1B-54; LF-37; PH-28; RF-10; DH-1   **Ht:** 6'2" **Wt:** 220 **Born:** 7/3/1978 **Age:** 34

Year	Team	Lg	G	AB	H	2B	3B	HR	(Hm	Rd)	TB	R	RBI	RC	TBB	IBB	SO	HBP	SH	SF	SB	CS	SB%	GDP	Avg	OBP	Slg
2012	Albq*	AAA	2	5	2	0	0	1	(-	-)	5	2	3	2	1	0	2	1	0	0	0	0	-	0	.400	.571	1.000
2012	RCuca*	A+	2	7	1	0	0	1	(-	-)	4	1	2	0	0	0	1	0	0	0	0	0	-	0	.143	.143	.571
2001	NYY	AL	3	4	0	0	0	0	(0	0)	0	0	0	0	0	0	0	0	0	0	0	0	-	0	.000	.000	.000
2002	NYY	AL	28	83	22	5	0	1	(0	1)	30	9	6	8	6	0	10	0	1	1	1	1	.50	4	.265	.311	.361
2003	NYY	AL	57	173	46	14	0	7	(4	3)	81	22	26	23	10	1	27	0	1	1	0	0	-	6	.266	.304	.468
2004	Mon	NL	134	391	120	24	1	12	(6	6)	182	48	49	60	34	7	45	1	0	0	6	2	.75	11	.307	.364	.465
2005	LAA	AL	106	350	95	17	1	15	(8	7)	159	46	59	49	23	0	44	0	2	1	1	9	.10	15	.271	.316	.454
2006	LAA	AL	124	448	139	27	0	23	(12	11)	235	65	85	80	33	0	59	7	0	6	0	4	.00	14	.310	.362	.525
2007	LAA	AL	14	43	12	1	0	2	(1	1)	19	3	8	5	1	0	4	0	0	0	0	0	-	5	.279	.295	.442
2008	LAA	AL	89	256	63	13	0	12	(5	7)	112	31	45	28	16	0	33	0	0	8	1	1	.50	10	.246	.282	.438
2009	LAA	AL	138	529	152	24	1	25	(11	14)	253	72	88	82	36	1	57	2	0	5	0	1	.00	15	.287	.332	.478
2010	LAA	AL	124	416	105	20	0	15	(4	11)	170	53	52	50	33	4	58	4	0	2	2	2	.50	10	.252	.312	.409
2011	2 Tms	AL	132	466	120	23	1	11	(6	5)	178	46	74	58	43	1	76	3	0	9	5	3	.63	16	.258	.319	.382
2012	LAD	NL	109	312	76	14	0	9	(5	4)	117	30	47	32	18	1	35	3	0	6	1	3	.25	15	.244	.286	.375
11	Tor	AL	70	247	60	11	0	6	(3	3)	89	22	28	23	22	1	41	2	0	4	3	2	.60	11	.243	.305	.360
11	LAD	NL	62	219	60	12	1	5	(3	2)	89	24	46	35	21	0	35	1	0	5	2	1	.67	5	.274	.333	.406
Postseason			36	105	25	5	0	1	(1	0)	33	10	8	5	8	2	14	0	1	0	1	0	1.00	5	.238	.292	.314
12 ML YEARS			1058	3471	950	182	4	132	(62	70)	1536	425	539	475	253	15	448	20	4	39	17	26	.40	127	.274	.323	.443

Mariano Rivera

Pitches: R **Bats:** R **Pos:** RP-9   **Ht:** 6'2" **Wt:** 195 **Born:** 11/29/1969 **Age:** 43

Year	Team	Lg	G	GS	CG	GF	IP	BFP	H	R	ER	HR	SH	SF	HB	TBB	IBB	SO	WP	Bk	W	L	Pct	Sh	Sv-Op	Hld	ERC	ERA
1995	NYY	AL	19	10	0	2	67.0	301	71	43	41	11	0	2	2	30	0	51	0	1	5	3	.625	0	0-1	0	5.14	5.51
1996	NYY	AL	61	0	0	14	107.2	425	73	25	25	1	2	1	2	34	3	130	1	0	8	3	.727	0	5-8	27	1.65	2.09
1997	NYY	AL	66	0	0	56	71.2	301	65	17	15	5	3	4	0	20	6	68	2	0	6	4	.600	0	43-52	0	2.73	1.88
1998	NYY	AL	54	0	0	49	61.1	246	48	13	13	3	2	3	1	17	1	36	0	0	3	0	1.000	0	36-41	0	2.21	1.91
1999	NYY	AL	66	0	0	63	69.0	268	43	15	14	2	0	2 ·	3	18	3	52	2	1	4	3	.571	0	45-49	0	1.47	1.83
2000	NYY	AL	66	0	0	61	75.2	311	58	26	24	4	5	2	0	25	3	58	2	0	7	4	.636	0	36-41	0	2.20	2.85
2001	NYY	AL	71	0	0	66	80.2	310	61	24	21	5	4	1	1	12	2	83	1	0	4	6	.400	0	50-57	0	1.74	2.34
2002	NYY	AL	45	0	0	37	46.0	187	35	16	14	3	2	0	2	11	2	41	1	1	1	4	.200	0	28-32	2	2.08	2.74
2003	NYY	AL	64	0	0	57	70.2	277	61	15	13	3	1	2	4	10	1	63	0	0	5	2	.714	0	40-46	0	2.29	1.66
2004	NYY	AL	74	0	0	69	78.2	316	65	17	17	3	2	0	5	20	3	66	0	0	4	2	.667	0	53-57	0	2.45	1.94
2005	NYY	AL	71	0	0	67	78.1	306	50	18	12	2	0	1	4	18	0	80	0	0	7	4	.636	0	43-47	0	1.48	1.38
2006	NYY	AL	63	0	0	59	75.0	293	61	16	15	3	1	2	5	11	4	55	0	0	5	5	.500	0	34-37	0	2.03	1.80
2007	NYY	AL	67	0	0	59	71.1	295	68	25	25	4	1	1	6	12	2	74	1	0	3	4	.429	0	30-34	0	2.92	3.15
2008	NYY	AL	64	0	0	60	70.2	259	41	11	11	4	1	1	2	6	0	77	1	0	6	5	.545	0	39-40	0	1.09	1.40
2009	NYY	AL	66	0	0	55	66.1	257	48	14	13	7	0	0	1	12	1	72	1	0	3	3	.500	0	44-46	0	1.93	1.76
2010	NYY	AL	61	0	0	55	60.0	230	39	14	12	2	0	1	5	11	3	45	0	0	3	3	.500	0	33-38	0	1.50	1.80
2011	NYY	AL	64	0	0	54	61.1	233	47	13	13	3	2	2	2	8	2	60	1	0	1	2	.333	0	44-49	0	1.75	1.91
2012	NYY	AL	9	0	0	9	8.1	32	6	2	2	0	0	0	2	2	2	8	0	0	1	1	.500	0	5-6	0	1.36	2.16
Postseason			96	0	0	78	141.0	527	86	13	11	2	7	3	3	21	4	110	3	0	8	1	.889	0	42-47	4	1.12	0.70
18 ML YEARS			1051	10	0	892	1219.2	4847	940	324	300	65	26	25	45	277	38	1119	13	3	76	58	.567	0	608-681	29	2.07	2.21

Anthony Rizzo

Bats: L **Throws:** L **Pos:** 1B-85; PH-2   **Ht:** 6'3" **Wt:** 220 **Born:** 8/8/1989 **Age:** 23

Year	Team	Lg	G	AB	H	2B	3B	HR	(Hm	Rd)	TB	R	RBI	RC	TBB	IBB	SO	HBP	SH	SF	SB	CS	SB%	GDP	Avg	OBP	Slg
2007	RedSx	R	6	21	6	0	0	1	(-	-)	9	6	3	3	1	0	2	2	0	0	0	0	-	1	.286	.375	.429
2008	Grnville	A	21	83	31	6	0	0	(-	-)	37	9	11	14	3	0	15	1	0	0	0	0	-	2	.373	.402	.446
2009	Grnville	A	64	245	73	21	0	9	(-	-)	121	40	42	44	25	0	60	2	0	2	2	1	.67	1	.298	.365	.494
2009	Salem	A+	55	200	59	16	0	3	(-	-)	84	23	24	33	25	5	39	1	0	3	2	0	1.00	4	.295	.371	.420
2010	Salem	A+	29	117	29	12	0	5	(-	-)	56	26	20	20	16	2	32	0	0	2	3	0	1.00	4	.248	.333	.479
2010	Portlnd	AA	107	414	109	30	0	20	(-	-)	199	66	80	70	45	3	100	2	0	6	7	1	.88	6	.263	.334	.481
2011	Tucsn	AAA	93	356	118	34	1	26	(-	-)	232	64	101	89	43	5	89	6	0	8	7	6	.54	4	.331	.404	.652
2012	Iowa	AAA	70	257	88	18	2	23	(-	-)	179	48	62	66	23	2	52	4	0	0	2	2	.50	10	.342	.405	.696
2011	SD	NL	49	128	18	8	1	1	(1	0)	31	9	9	7	21	1	46	4	0	0	2	1	.67	2	.141	.281	.242
2012	ChC	NL	87	337	96	15	0	15	(7	8)	156	44	48	57	27	1	62	3	0	1	3	2	.60	7	.285	.342	.463
	2 ML YEARS		136	465	114	23	1	16	(8	8)	187	53	57	64	48	2	108	7	0	1	5	3	.63	9	.245	.324	.402

Brian Roberts

Bats: B **Throws:** R **Pos:** 2B-17   **Ht:** 5'9" **Wt:** 175 **Born:** 10/9/1977 **Age:** 35

Year	Team	Lg	G	AB	H	2B	3B	HR	(Hm	Rd)	TB	R	RBI	RC	TBB	IBB	SO	HBP	SH	SF	SB	CS	SB%	GDP	Avg	OBP	Slg
2012	Bowie*	AA	7	16	4	3	0	1	(-	-)	10	4	3	4	4	0	3	0	0	1	0	0	-	1	.250	.381	.625
2012	Dlmrva*	A	2	5	1	0	0	0	(-	-)	1	0	0	0	1	0	1	0	0	0	0	0	-	0	.200	.333	.200
2012	Norfolk*	AAA	5	21	5	2	0	0	(-	-)	7	2	1	2	2	0	4	0	0	0	0	0	-	0	.238	.304	.333
2012	Abrdn*	A-	1	4	0	0	0	0	(-	-)	0	1	0	0	1	0	2	0	0	0	0	0	-	0	.000	.200	.000
2001	Bal	AL	75	273	69	12	3	2	(0	2)	93	42	17	27	13	0	36	0	3	3	12	3	.80	3	.253	.284	.341
2002	Bal	AL	38	128	29	6	0	1	(1	0)	38	18	11	12	15	0	21	1	3	2	9	2	.82	3	.227	.308	.297
2003	Bal	AL	112	460	124	22	4	5	(3	2)	169	65	41	62	46	1	58	1	4	1	23	6	.79	9	.270	.337	.367
2004	Bal	AL	159	641	175	50	2	4	(0	4)	241	107	53	91	71	1	95	1	15	6	29	12	.71	3	.273	.344	.376
2005	Bal	AL	143	561	176	45	7	18	(9	9)	289	92	73	106	67	5	83	3	5	4	27	10	.73	6	.314	.387	.515
2006	Bal	AL	138	563	161	34	3	10	(6	4)	231	85	55	74	55	4	66	0	6	5	36	7	.84	16	.286	.347	.410
2007	Bal	AL	156	621	180	42	5	12	(6	6)	268	103	57	105	89	6	99	0	2	4	50	7	.88	8	.290	.377	.432
2008	Bal	AL	155	611	181	51	8	9	(6	3)	275	107	57	101	82	3	104	2	3	6	40	10	.80	8	.296	.378	.450
2009	Bal	AL	159	632	179	56	1	16	(4	12)	285	110	79	106	74	3	112	2	1	8	30	7	.81	7	.283	.356	.451
2010	Bal	AL	59	230	64	14	0	4	(2	2)	90	28	15	31	26	1	40	2	1	2	12	2	.86	2	.278	.354	.391
2011	Bal	AL	39	163	36	7	1	3	(1	2)	54	18	19	18	12	0	21	0	2	1	6	1	.86	4	.221	.273	.331
2012	Bal	AL	17	66	12	0	0	0	(0	0)	12	2	5	3	5	0	12	0	1	2	1	1	.50	0	.182	.233	.182
	12 ML YEARS		1250	4949	1386	339	34	84	(38	46)	2045	777	482	736	555	24	747	12	46	44	275	68	.80	69	.280	.351	.413

Ryan Roberts

Bats: R **Throws:** R **Pos:** 3B-78; 2B-54; PH-23; LF-1; DH-1   **Ht:** 5'11" **Wt:** 185 **Born:** 9/19/1980 **Age:** 32

Year	Team	Lg	G	AB	H	2B	3B	HR	(Hm	Rd)	TB	R	RBI	RC	TBB	IBB	SO	HBP	SH	SF	SB	CS	SB%	GDP	Avg	OBP	Slg
2006	Tor	AL	9	13	1	0	0	1	(0	1)	4	1	1	0	1	0	4	0	0	0	0	0	-	1	.077	.143	.308
2007	Tor	AL	8	13	1	0	0	0	(0	0)	1	2	0	0	2	0	7	1	0	0	0	0	-	0	.077	.250	.077
2008	Tex	AL	1	1	0	0	0	0	(0	0)	0	0	0	0	0	0	1	0	0	0	0	0	-	0	.000	.000	.000
2009	Ari	NL	110	305	85	17	2	7	(3	4)	127	41	25	41	40	1	55	3	2	1	7	3	.70	2	.279	.367	.416
2010	Ari	NL	36	66	13	4	0	2	(1	1)	23	8	9	7	3	1	17	0	1	1	0	0	-	0	.197	.229	.348
2011	Ari	NL	143	482	120	25	2	19	(9	10)	206	86	65	75	66	2	98	2	3	2	18	9	.67	6	.249	.341	.427
2012	2 Tms		143	439	103	19	0	12	(5	7)	158	51	52	46	40	1	92	1	3	6	10	6	.63	13	.235	.296	.360
12	Ari	NL	83	252	63	9	0	6	(4	2)	90	28	34	25	22	1	45	0	2	4	6	3	.67	10	.250	.306	.357
12	TB		60	187	40	10	0	6	(1	5)	68	23	18	21	18	0	47	1	1	2	4	3	.57	3	.214	.284	.364
	Postseason		5	20	7	1	0	2	(1	1)	14	2	6	2	0	0	4	0	0	0	0	1	.00	0	.350	.350	.700
	7 ML YEARS		450	1319	323	65	4	41	(18	23)	519	189	152	169	152	5	274	7	9	10	35	18	.66	22	.245	.324	.393

David Robertson

Pitches: R **Bats:** R **Pos:** RP-65   **Ht:** 5'11" **Wt:** 195 **Born:** 4/9/1985 **Age:** 28

Year	Team	Lg	G	GS	CG	GF	IP	BFP	H	R	ER	HR	SH	SF	HB	TBB	IBB	SO	WP	Bk	W	L	Pct	Sh	Sv-Op	Hld	ERC	ERA
2012	S-WB*	AAA	2	1	0	0	2.0	6	0	0	0	0	0	0	0	0	0	2	0	0	0	0	-	0	0- -	-	0.00	0.00
2008	NYY	AL	25	0	0	8	30.1	131	29	18	18	3	0	3	0	15	2	36	6	0	4	0	1.000	0	0-0	0	4.12	5.34
2009	NYY	AL	45	0	0	10	43.2	191	36	19	16	4	0	0	1	23	1	63	6	0	2	1	.667	0	1-1	5	3.51	3.30
2010	NYY	AL	64	0	0	10	61.1	273	59	26	26	5	5	3	3	33	6	71	7	2	4	5	.444	0	1-3	14	4.29	3.82
2011	NYY	AL	70	0	0	8	66.2	272	40	9	8	1	1	0	1	35	6	100	6	1	4	0	1.000	0	1-4	34	1.85	1.08
2012	NYY	AL	65	0	0	17	60.2	248	52	19	18	5	0	1	1	19	0	81	1	1	2	7	.222	0	2-5	30	2.95	2.67
	Postseason		13	0	0	3	10.2	51	12	6	6	1	1	0	1	5	3	10	1	0	2	0	1.000	0	0-0	2	4.66	5.06
	5 ML YEARS		269	0	0	63	262.2	1115	216	91	86	18	6	7	6	125	15	351	26	4	16	13	.552	0	5-13	83	3.17	2.95

Tyler Robertson

Pitches: L **Bats:** L **Pos:** RP-40   **Ht:** 6'5" **Wt:** 255 **Born:** 12/23/1987 **Age:** 25

Year	Team	Lg	G	GS	CG	GF	IP	BFP	H	R	ER	HR	SH	SF	HB	TBB	IBB	SO	WP	Bk	W	L	Pct	Sh	Sv-Op	Hld	ERC	ERA
2006	Twins	R	11	10	0	0	48.2	214	54	23	23	2	1	1	4	15	0	54	6	1	4	2	.667	0	0- -	-	4.22	4.25
2007	Beloit	A	18	16	2	2	102.1	421	87	33	26	3	1	0	2	33	1	123	11	1	9	5	.643	0	1- -	-	2.59	2.29
2008	FtMyrs	A+	15	15	1	0	82.2	353	78	36	25	3	1	3	2	31	0	73	6	0	5	3	.625	0	0- -	-	3.31	2.72
2009	FtMyrs	A+	26	26	0	0	143.1	606	139	64	53	7	8	4	7	51	0	103	7	0	8	8	.500	0	0- -	-	3.62	3.33
2010	NwBrit	AA	27	27	0	0	144.2	658	181	100	87	17	1	6	7	57	1	91	13	1	4	13	.235	0	0- -	-	5.90	5.41

Year	Team	Lg	G	GS	CG	GF	IP	BFP	H	R	ER	HR	SH	SF	HB	TBB	IBB	SO	WP	Bk	W	L	Pct	Sh	Sv-Op Hld	ERC	ERA
			HOW MUCH HE PITCHED						WHAT HE GAVE UP												THE RESULTS						
2010	Roch	AAA	1	1	0	0	5.0	25	6	3	3	0	0	0	1	2	0	6	0	0	0	1	.000		0- -	4.87	5.40
2011	NwBrit	AA	55	0	0	43	89.2	384	87	42	36	6	5	2	3	29	1	88	13	1	10	3	.769	0	16- -	3.46	3.61
2012	Roch	AAA	33	0	0	13	28.2	129	26	18	12	2	2	1	0	13	2	33	1	0	2	2	.500	0	2- -	3.24	3.77
2012	Min	AL	40	0	0	2	25.0	111	21	16	15	4	1	1	1	14	3	26	1	0	2	2	.500	0	0-1 5	4.10	5.40

Clint Robinson

Bats: L **Throws:** L **Pos:** PH-4   **Ht:** 6'5" **Wt:** 240 **Born:** 2/16/1985 **Age:** 28

Year	Team	Lg	G	AB	H	2B	3B	HR	(Hm	Rd)	TB	R	RBI	RC	TBB	IBB	SO	HBP	SH	SF	SB	CS	SB%	GDP	Avg	OBP	Slg
						BATTING															BASERUNNING				AVERAGES		
2007	Idaho	R+	67	253	85	18	1	15	(-	-)	150	39	66	56	19	3	42	4	0	2	2	0	1.00	6	.336	.388	.593
2008	Burlgtn	A	106	379	100	22	3	17	(-	-)	179	53	64	60	37	2	67	4	1	3	0	3	.00	5	.264	.333	.472
2009	Wilmg	A+	124	436	130	31	1	13	(-	-)	202	65	57	73	35	4	79	7	0	5	4	3	.57	11	.298	.356	.463
2010	NWArk	AA	129	477	160	41	5	29	(-	-)	298	90	98	117	58	4	86	6	2	5	4	3	.57	7	.335	.410	.625
2011	Omha	AAA	134	503	164	35	0	23	(-	-)	268	86	100	106	58	5	88	6	1	4	2	1	.67	18	.326	.399	.533
2012	Omha	AAA	131	487	142	37	1	13	(-	-)	220	70	67	91	79	4	65	3	0	1	1	0	1.00	17	.292	.393	.452
2012	KC	AL	4	4	0	0	0	0	(0	0)	0	0	0	0	0	0	2	0	0	0	0	0	-	0	.000	.000	.000

Shane Robinson

Bats: R **Throws:** R **Pos:** PH-56; CF-37; LF-15; RF-11; PR-3   **Ht:** 5'9" **Wt:** 160 **Born:** 10/30/1984 **Age:** 28

Year	Team	Lg	G	AB	H	2B	3B	HR	(Hm	Rd)	TB	R	RBI	RC	TBB	IBB	SO	HBP	SH	SF	SB	CS	SB%	GDP	Avg	OBP	Slg
						BATTING															BASERUNNING				AVERAGES		
2012	Memp*	AAA	18	70	21	4	2	0	(-	-)	29	15	3	12	8	0	15	2	0	0	5	0	1.00	2	.300	.388	.414
2009	StL	NL	11	25	6	1	0	0	(0	0)	7	1	1	1	0	0	2	0	0	1	1	0	1.00	1	.240	.231	.280
2011	StL	NL	9	7	0	0	0	0	(0	0)	0	0	0	0	1	0	2	0	0	0	0	0	-	1	.000	.125	.000
2012	StL	NL	102	166	42	8	0	3	(1	2)	59	20	16	15	14	2	32	0	0	1	1	0	1.00	5	.253	.309	.355
3 ML YEARS			122	198	48	9	0	3	(1	2)	66	21	17	16	15	2	36	0	0	2	2	0	1.00	7	.242	.293	.333

Trayvon Robinson

Bats: B **Throws:** R **Pos:** LF-46; PH-2   trey-VONN   **Ht:** 5'10" **Wt:** 200 **Born:** 9/1/1987 **Age:** 25

Year	Team	Lg	G	AB	H	2B	3B	HR	(Hm	Rd)	TB	R	RBI	RC	TBB	IBB	SO	HBP	SH	SF	SB	CS	SB%	GDP	Avg	OBP	Slg
						BATTING															BASERUNNING				AVERAGES		
2005	Ddgrs	R	40	115	34	7	2	3	(-	-)	54	19	15	19	8	0	25	3	0	0	6	4	.60	2	.296	.357	.470
2005	Ogden	R+	8	23	5	0	0	1	(-	-)	8	2	2	1	0	0	9	0	0	0	0	0	-	0	.217	.217	.348
2006	Ddgrs	R	39	134	34	7	2	2	(-	-)	51	24	20	19	16	0	48	2	2	1	5	1	.83	0	.254	.340	.381
2006	VeroB	A+	3	5	2	0	0	0	(-	-)	2	1	1	0	0	0	2	0	0	0	1	0	1.00	0	.400	.400	.400
2007	Gt Lks	A	110	396	100	9	4	2	(-	-)	123	50	31	41	32	0	119	4	10	1	22	9	.71	6	.253	.314	.311
2008	InldEm	A+	112	439	121	20	8	4	(-	-)	169	67	42	58	33	0	104	4	8	5	22	12	.65	5	.276	.328	.385
2009	InldEm	A+	117	470	144	28	9	15	(-	-)	235	82	54	90	50	4	125	4	1	4	43	18	.70	8	.306	.375	.500
2009	Chatt	AA	19	57	14	1	2	2	(-	-)	25	8	10	9	10	0	18	0	3	0	4	2	.67	3	.246	.358	.439
2010	Chatt	AA	120	434	129	23	5	9	(-	-)	189	80	57	83	73	2	125	5	8	3	38	15	.72	5	.297	.402	.435
2011	Albq	AAA	100	368	108	9	6	26	(-	-)	207	70	71	75	45	2	122	3	0	1	8	6	.57	4	.293	.375	.563
2011	Tacom	AAA	3	9	1	0	0	0	(-	-)	1	1	0	0	3	0	4	0	0	0	1	0	1.00	0	.111	.333	.111
2012	Tacom	AAA	83	340	90	18	2	9	(-	-)	139	50	41	50	34	2	85	1	3	3	19	5	.79	4	.265	.331	.409
2011	Sea	AL	44	143	30	12	0	2	(0	2)	48	12	14	14	8	0	61	0	3	1	1	0	1.00	1	.210	.250	.336
2012	Sea	AL	46	145	32	4	1	3	(1	2)	47	16	12	14	14	1	43	1	4	0	6	3	.67	2	.221	.294	.324
2 ML YEARS			90	288	62	16	1	5	(1	4)	95	28	26	24	22	1	104	1	7	1	7	3	.70	3	.215	.272	.330

Fernando Rodney

Pitches: R **Bats:** R **Pos:** RP-76   **Ht:** 5'11" **Wt:** 220 **Born:** 3/18/1977 **Age:** 36

Year	Team	Lg	G	GS	CG	GF	IP	BFP	H	R	ER	HR	SH	SF	HB	TBB	IBB	SO	WP	Bk	W	L	Pct	Sh	Sv-Op Hld	ERC	ERA
			HOW MUCH HE PITCHED						WHAT HE GAVE UP												THE RESULTS						
2002	Det	AL	20	0	0	10	18.0	89	25	15	12	2	2	1	0	10	2	10	0	1	1	3	.250	0	0-4	6.77	6.00
2003	Det	AL	27	0	0	11	29.2	143	35	20	20	2	3	3	1	17	1	33	0	0	1	3	.250	0	3-6 3	5.46	6.07
2005	Det	AL	39	0	0	26	44.0	185	39	14	14	5	2	0	2	17	3	42	2	0	2	3	.400	0	9-15 3	3.59	2.86
2006	Det	AL	63	0	0	30	71.2	304	51	36	28	6	2	0	8	34	4	65	3	0	7	4	.636	0	7-11 18	3.01	3.52
2007	Det	AL	48	0	0	12	50.2	223	46	27	24	5	4	2	3	21	0	54	4	0	2	6	.250	0	1-3 12	3.74	4.26
2008	Det	AL	38	0	0	25	40.1	188	34	22	22	3	1	2	3	30	5	49	3	0	0	6	.000	0	13-19 5	4.29	4.91
2009	Det	AL	73	0	0	65	75.2	330	70	38	37	8	4	2	2	41	4	61	5	0	2	5	.286	0	37-38 0	4.31	4.40
2010	LAA	AL	72	0	0	30	68.0	308	70	33	32	4	1	0	5	35	1	53	4	0	4	3	.571	0	14-21 21	4.63	4.24
2011	LAA	AL	39	0	0	15	32.0	150	26	18	16	1	3	0	3	28	0	26	2	0	3	5	.375	0	3-7 10	4.66	4.50
2012	TB	AL	76	0	0	65	74.2	282	43	9	5	2	4	2	3	15	1	76	4	0	2	2	.500	0	48-50	1.22	0.60
Postseason			7	0	0	0	7.2	33	6	4	2	0	2	0	0	5	1	9	0	0	0	0	-	0	0-1 2	2.94	2.35
10 ML YEARS			495	0	0	289	504.2	2202	439	232	210	38	26	12	30	248	21	469	27	1	24	40	.375	0	135-174 72	3.66	3.75

Alex Rodriguez

Bats: R **Throws:** R **Pos:** 3B-81; DH-38; PH-3   **Ht:** 6'3" **Wt:** 225 **Born:** 7/27/1975 **Age:** 37

Year	Team	Lg	G	AB	H	2B	3B	HR	(Hm	Rd)	TB	R	RBI	RC	TBB	IBB	SO	HBP	SH	SF	SB	CS	SB%	GDP	Avg	OBP	Slg
						BATTING															BASERUNNING				AVERAGES		
2012	Tampa*	A+	2	7	0	0	0	0	(-	-)	0	1	0	0	1	0	4	0	0	0	0	0	-	0	.000	.125	.000
1994	Sea	AL	17	54	11	0	0	0	(0	0)	11	4	2	3	3	0	20	0	1	1	3	0	1.00	0	.204	.241	.204
1995	Sea	AL	48	142	33	6	2	5	(1	4)	58	15	19	15	6	0	42	0	1	0	4	2	.67	0	.232	.264	.408
1996	Sea	AL	146	601	215	54	1	36	(18	18)	379	141	123	144	59	1	104	4	6	7	15	4	.79	15	.358	.414	.631
1997	Sea	AL	141	587	176	40	3	23	(16	7)	291	100	84	100	41	1	99	5	4	1	29	6	.83	14	.300	.350	.496
1998	Sea	AL	161	686	213	35	5	42	(18	24)	384	123	124	135	45	0	121	10	3	4	46	13	.78	12	.310	.360	.560
1999	Sea	AL	129	502	143	25	0	42	(20	22)	294	110	111	102	56	2	109	5	1	8	21	7	.75	12	.285	.357	.586

Year	Team	Lg	G	AB	H	2B	3B	HR	(Hm	Rd)	TB	R	RBI	RC	TBB	IBB	SO	HBP	SH	SF	SB	CS	SB%	GDP	Avg	OBP	Slg
									BATTING														**BASERUNNING**			**AVERAGES**	
2000	Sea	AL	148	554	175	34	2	41	(13	28)	336	134	132	138	100	5	121	7	0	11	15	4	.79	10	.316	.420	.606
2001	Tex	AL	162	632	201	34	1	52	(26	26)	393	133	135	148	75	6	131	16	0	9	18	3	.86	17	.318	.399	.622
2002	Tex	AL	162	624	187	27	2	57	(34	23)	389	125	142	152	87	12	122	10	0	4	9	4	.69	14	.300	.392	.623
2003	Tex	AL	161	607	181	30	6	47	(26	21)	364	124	118	131	87	10	126	15	0	6	17	3	.85	16	.298	.396	.600
2004	NYY	AL	155	601	172	24	2	36	(17	19)	308	112	106	112	80	6	131	10	0	7	28	4	.88	18	.286	.375	.512
2005	NYY	AL	162	605	194	29	1	48	(26	22)	369	124	130	137	91	8	139	16	0	3	21	6	.78	8	.321	.421	.610
2006	NYY	AL	154	572	166	26	1	35	(20	15)	299	113	121	112	90	8	139	8	0	4	15	4	.79	22	.290	.392	.523
2007	NYY	AL	158	583	183	31	0	54	(26	28)	376	143	156	159	95	11	120	21	0	9	24	4	.86	15	.314	.422	.645
2008	NYY	AL	138	510	154	33	0	35	(21	14)	292	104	103	97	65	9	117	14	0	5	18	3	.86	16	.302	.392	.573
2009	NYY	AL	124	444	127	17	1	30	(18	12)	236	78	100	89	80	7	97	8	0	3	14	2	.88	13	.286	.402	.532
2010	NYY	AL	137	522	141	29	2	30	(15	15)	264	74	125	93	59	1	98	3	0	11	4	3	.57	7	.270	.341	.506
2011	NYY	AL	99	373	103	21	0	16	(9	7)	172	67	62	61	47	1	80	5	0	3	4	1	.80	13	.276	.362	.461
2012	NYY	AL	122	463	126	17	1	18	(8	10)	199	74	57	66	51	3	116	10	0	5	13	1	.93	13	.272	.353	.430
Postseason			68	249	69	16	0	13	(5	8)	124	42	41	43	37	4	63	9	1	3	8	3	.73	5	.277	.386	.498
19 ML YEARS			2524	9662	2901	512	30	647	(332	315)	5414	1898	1950	1994	1217	91	2032	167	16	101	318	74	.81	235	.300	.384	.560

Aneury Rodriguez

Pitches: R **Bats:** R **Pos:** SP-1   uh-NURR-ee   **Ht:** 6'4" **Wt:** 250 **Born:** 12/13/1987 **Age:** 25

Year	Team	Lg	G	GS	CG	GF	IP	BFP	H	R	ER	HR	SH	SF	HB	TBB	IBB	SO	WP	Bk	W	L	Pct	Sh	Sv-Op	Hld	ERC	ERA
			HOW MUCH HE PITCHED						**WHAT HE GAVE UP**												**THE RESULTS**							
2005	Casper	R+	15	15	0	0	62.0	285	77	54	52	7	2	1	7	26	0	47	11	1	3	4	.429	0	0- -		6.25	7.55
2006	TriCity	A-	15	15	1	0	76.0	337	78	42	35	2	2	0	6	30	0	69	6	0	4	4	.500	0	0- -		3.93	4.14
2007	Ashvll	A	28	28	1	0	152.0	675	182	105	87	19	1	5	10	48	1	160	14	2	9	9	.500	1	0- -		5.37	5.15
2008	Mdest	A+	27	27	2	0	156.1	650	148	78	65	12	3	6	10	40	2	139	7	3	9	10	.474	2	0- -		3.32	3.74
2009	Mont	AA	27	27	1	0	142.0	606	122	78	71	17	4	4	12	59	0	111	6	0	9	11	.450	1	0- -		3.83	4.50
2010	Mont	AA	2	2	0	0	10.0	41	9	6	3	0	0	2	0	2	0	6	2	0	1	0	1.000	0	0- -		2.14	2.70
2010	Drham	AAA	27	17	0	7	113.2	490	104	52	48	10	1	4	2	49	2	94	7	0	6	5	.545	0	0- -		3.65	3.80
2012	OKCity	AAA	29	13	0	2	92.2	443	130	71	68	10	5	6	1	44	6	75	7	1	4	7	.364	0	0- -		6.79	6.60
2011	Hou	NL	43	8	0	16	85.1	369	83	57	50	13	3	3	2	32	3	64	3	0	1	6	.143	0	0-0	1	4.18	5.27
2012	Hou	NL	1	1	0	0	6.0	22	2	2	2	2	1	0	0	2	0	6	0	0	0	0	-	0	0-0	0	1.69	3.00
2 ML YEARS			44	9	0	16	91.1	391	85	59	52	15	4	3	2	34	3	70	3	0	1	6	.143	0	0-0	1	4.02	5.12

Eddy Rodriguez

Bats: R **Throws:** R **Pos:** C-2   **Ht:** 6'0" **Wt:** 205 **Born:** 12/1/1985 **Age:** 27

Year	Team	Lg	G	AB	H	2B	3B	HR	(Hm	Rd)	TB	R	RBI	RC	TBB	IBB	SO	HBP	SH	SF	SB	CS	SB%	GDP	Avg	OBP	Slg
									BATTING														**BASERUNNING**			**AVERAGES**	
2006	Reds	R	7	17	4	2	0	1	(-	-)	9	1	4	2	1	0	5	1	0	1	0	0	-	0	.235	.300	.529
2007	Dayton	A	83	280	66	15	0	6	(-	-)	99	32	33	28	16	0	61	4	0	2	1	1	.50	8	.236	.285	.354
2008	Srsota	A+	70	229	46	5	1	5	(-	-)	68	20	20	17	14	0	63	3	1	1	0	0	-	7	.201	.255	.297
2008	Chatt	AA	7	25	6	1	0	2	(-	-)	13	4	7	4	2	0	8	1	0	0	0	0	-	1	.240	.321	.520
2011	Tucsn	AAA	6	19	3	0	0	1	(-	-)	6	3	3	1	2	0	5	0	0	0	0	0	-	3	.158	.238	.316
2011	Lk Els	A+	46	158	43	10	0	8	(-	-)	77	23	21	25	12	0	41	2	2	1	0	0	-	3	.272	.329	.487
2011	SnAnt	AA	18	67	14	3	0	1	(-	-)	20	7	6	5	4	1	18	1	0	0	0	0	-	3	.209	.264	.299
2012	Lk Els	A+	87	328	73	13	0	13	(-	-)	125	37	36	34	19	0	100	3	0	3	2	1	.67	3	.223	.269	.381
2012	Tucsn	AAA	14	50	9	4	0	1	(-	-)	16	3	6	3	2	0	13	1	0	0	0	0	-	1	.180	.226	.320
2012	SD	NL	2	5	1	0	0	1	(0	1)	4	1	1	1	2	0	3	0	0	0	0	0	-	0	.200	.429	.800

Fernando Rodriguez

Pitches: R **Bats:** R **Pos:** RP-71   **Ht:** 6'3" **Wt:** 235 **Born:** 6/18/1984 **Age:** 29

Year	Team	Lg	G	GS	CG	GF	IP	BFP	H	R	ER	HR	SH	SF	HB	TBB	IBB	SO	WP	Bk	W	L	Pct	Sh	Sv-Op	Hld	ERC	ERA
			HOW MUCH HE PITCHED						**WHAT HE GAVE UP**												**THE RESULTS**							
2009	LAA	AL	1	0	0	0	0.2	6	1	3	2	1	0	0	0	2	0	1	1	0	0	0	-	0	0-0	0	31.03	27.00
2011	Hou	NL	47	0	0	11	52.1	231	51	24	23	6	5	0	3	30	5	57	2	0	2	3	.400	0	0-0	13	4.90	3.96
2012	Hou	NL	71	0	0	9	70.1	309	68	45	42	10	2	2	1	34	7	78	10	0	2	10	.167	0	0-4	13	4.39	5.37
3 ML YEARS			119	0	0	20	123.1	546	120	72	67	17	7	2	4	66	12	136	13	0	4	13	.235	0	0-4	19	4.72	4.89

Francisco Rodriguez

Pitches: R **Bats:** R **Pos:** RP-78   **Ht:** 6'0" **Wt:** 195 **Born:** 1/7/1982 **Age:** 31

Year	Team	Lg	G	GS	CG	GF	IP	BFP	H	R	ER	HR	SH	SF	HB	TBB	IBB	SO	WP	Bk	W	L	Pct	Sh	Sv-Op	Hld	ERC	ERA
			HOW MUCH HE PITCHED						**WHAT HE GAVE UP**												**THE RESULTS**							
2002	LAA	AL	5	0	0	4	5.2	21	3	0	0	0	0	0	1	2	1	13	0	0	0	0	-	0	0-0	0	1.52	0.00
2003	LAA	AL	59	0	0	23	86.0	334	50	30	29	12	2	4	2	35	5	95	7	0	8	3	.727	0	2-6	7	2.25	3.03
2004	LAA	AL	69	0	0	29	84.0	335	51	21	17	2	2	1	1	33	1	123	5	0	4	1	.800	0	12-19	27	1.64	1.82
2005	LAA	AL	66	0	0	58	67.1	279	45	20	20	7	1	1	0	32	3	91	8	0	2	5	.286	0	**45-50**	0	2.52	2.67
2006	LAA	AL	69	0	0	58	73.0	296	52	16	14	6	3	0	1	28	5	98	10	0	2	3	.400	0	**47-51**	0	2.35	1.73
2007	LAA	AL	64	0	0	56	67.1	285	50	22	21	3	1	4	1	34	0	90	7	1	5	2	.714	0	40-46	0	2.74	2.81
2008	LAA	AL	76	0	0	69	68.1	288	54	21	17	4	1	1	2	34	4	77	6	0	2	3	.400	0	**62-69**	0	3.06	2.24
2009	NYM	NL	70	0	0	68	68.0	295	51	34	28	7	4	1	1	38	6	73	1	0	3	6	.333	0	35-42	0	3.18	3.71
2010	NYM	NL	53	0	0	46	57.1	236	45	14	14	3	1	1	2	21	4	67	3	1	4	2	.667	0	25-30	0	2.53	2.20
2011	2 Tms	NL	73	0	0	36	71.2	307	67	22	21	4	2	1	2	26	4	79	4	0	6	2	.750	0	23-29	17	2.64	2.64
2012	Mil	NL	78	0	0	13	72.0	305	65	37	35	8	1	3	0	31	1	72	6	0	2	7	.222	0	3-10	32	3.73	4.38
11 NYM	NL		42	0	0	34	42.2	187	44	15	15	3	2	1	2	16	4	46	2	0	2	2	.500	0	23-26	0	3.49	3.16
11 Mil	NL		31	0	0	2	29.0	120	23	7	6	1	0	0	0	10	0	33	2	0	4	0	1.000	0	0-3	17	2.32	1.86
Postseason			26	0	0	8	36.2	158	32	15	12	5	1	3	1	18	2	49	5	0	5	4	.556	0	3-5	6	3.99	2.95
11 ML YEARS			682	0	0	458	720.2	2981	533	237	216	56	18	17	13	314	34	878	57	2	38	34	.528	0	294-352	83	2.67	2.70

Henry Rodriguez

Bats: B **Throws:** R **Pos:** PH-10; 2B-2   **Ht:** 5'10" **Wt:** 150 **Born:** 2/9/1990 **Age:** 23

									BATTING												BASERUNNING				AVERAGES		
Year	Team	Lg	G	AB	H	2B	3B	HR	(Hm	Rd)	TB	R	RBI	RC	TBB	IBB	SO	HBP	SH	SF	SB	CS	SB%	GDP	Avg	OBP	Slg
2009	Reds	R	41	150	49	10	1	1	(-	-)	64	23	19	24	6	0	17	1	0	1	9	0	1.00	5	.327	.354	.427
2010	Dayton	A	124	514	158	37	3	14	(-	-)	243	76	78	84	22	3	70	4	1	6	33	13	.72	13	.307	.337	.473
2010	Lynbrg	A+	6	24	6	0	0	0	(-	-)	6	2	4	1	0	0	4	0	0	0	0	0	-	1	.250	.250	.250
2011	Bkrsfld	A+	58	238	81	17	0	8	(-	-)	122	37	44	44	14	0	35	1	0	1	12	7	.63	4	.340	.378	.513
2011	Carlina	AA	69	278	84	19	1	5	(-	-)	120	39	37	48	25	1	43	4	4	1	18	3	.86	4	.302	.367	.432
2012	Penscla	AA	33	132	46	6	0	2	(-	-)	58	19	15	23	9	2	18	0	1	2	3	0	1.00	5	.348	.385	.439
2012	Reds	R	5	17	4	1	0	0	(-	-)	5	1	1	1	1	0	2	0	0	0	0	0	-	0	.235	.278	.294
2012	Lsvlle	AAA	51	213	52	10	0	3	(-	-)	71	23	20	18	6	0	35	0	1	1	5	4	.56	4	.244	.264	.333
2012	Cin	NL	12	14	3	1	0	0	(0	0)	4	0	2	1	2	0	2	0	0	0	0	0	-	1	.214	.313	.286

Henry Rodriguez

Pitches: R **Bats:** R **Pos:** RP-35   **Ht:** 6'1" **Wt:** 225 **Born:** 2/25/1987 **Age:** 26

			HOW MUCH HE PITCHED					WHAT HE GAVE UP										THE RESULTS						
Year	Team	Lg	G	GS	CG	GF	IP	BFP	H	R	ER	HR	SH	SF	HB	TBB	IBB	SO	WP	Bk	W	L	Pct	Sh	Sv-Op	Hld	ERC	ERA
2012	Syrcse*	AAA	4	0	0	4	4.0	16	0	0	0	0	0	0	0	4	0	3	0	0	0	0	-	0	2- -	-	0.95	0.00
2012	Hrsbrg*	AA	3	0	0	0	3.0	10	0	0	0	0	0	0	0	1	0	4	0	0	0	0	-	0	0- -	-	0.13	0.00
2009	Oak	AL	3	0	0	1	4.0	20	4	2	1	0	0	0	1	2	0	4	3	0	0	0	-	0	0-0	0	4.28	2.25
2010	Oak	AL	29	0	0	8	27.2	121	25	16	14	2	2	1	1	13	0	33	7	0	1	0	1.000	0	0-1	3	3.70	4.55
2011	Was	NL	59	0	0	21	65.2	295	54	30	26	1	1	1	2	45	1	70	14	1	3	3	.500	0	2-5	10	3.59	3.56
2012	Was	NL	35	0	0	20	29.1	131	19	20	19	4	2	1	1	22	0	31	10	1	1	3	.250	0	9-12	2	3.76	5.83
	4 ML YEARS		126	0	0	50	126.2	567	102	68	60	7	5	3	5	82	1	138	34	2	5	6	.455	0	11-18	15	3.68	4.26

Paco Rodriguez

Pitches: L **Bats:** L **Pos:** RP-11   **Ht:** 6'3" **Wt:** 215 **Born:** 4/16/1991 **Age:** 22

			HOW MUCH HE PITCHED					WHAT HE GAVE UP										THE RESULTS						
Year	Team	Lg	G	GS	CG	GF	IP	BFP	H	R	ER	HR	SH	SF	HB	TBB	IBB	SO	WP	Bk	W	L	Pct	Sh	Sv-Op	Hld	ERC	ERA
2012	Gt Lks	A	6	0	0	4	6.0	22	4	0	0	0	0	0	0	0	0	10	0	0	0	0	-	0	2- -	-	0.91	0.00
2012	Chatt	AA	16	0	0	5	13.2	55	7	2	2	0	1	0	1	6	1	22	0	0	1	0	1.000	0	3- -	-	1.41	1.32
2012	LAD	NL	11	0	0	2	6.2	26	3	1	1	0	0	0	0	4	1	6	0	0	0	1	.000	0	0-0	0	1.37	1.35

Sean Rodriguez

Bats: R **Throws:** R **Pos:** 3B-49; SS-47; 2B-37; PH-12; PR-5; DH-4   **Ht:** 6'0" **Wt:** 200 **Born:** 4/26/1985 **Age:** 28

									BATTING												BASERUNNING				AVERAGES		
Year	Team	Lg	G	AB	H	2B	3B	HR	(Hm	Rd)	TB	R	RBI	RC	TBB	IBB	SO	HBP	SH	SF	SB	CS	SB%	GDP	Avg	OBP	Slg
2012	Drham*	AAA	2	6	3	2	0	1	(-	-)	8	2	4	3	1	0	2	0	1	0	0	0	-	0	.500	.571	1.333
2008	LAA	AL	59	167	34	8	1	3	(2	1)	53	18	10	12	14	0	55	3	2	1	3	1	.75	3	.204	.276	.317
2009	LAA	AL	12	25	5	0	0	2	(0	2)	11	4	4	2	3	0	7	0	0	1	0	0	-	2	.200	.276	.440
2010	TB	AL	118	343	86	19	2	9	(5	4)	136	53	40	38	21	1	97	6	8	5	13	3	.81	10	.251	.308	.397
2011	TB	AL	131	373	83	20	3	8	(4	4)	133	45	36	41	38	2	87	18	5	2	11	7	.61	8	.223	.323	.357
2012	TB	AL	112	301	64	14	1	6	(3	3)	98	36	32	32	27	1	75	3	8	3	5	0	1.00	7	.213	.281	.326
	Postseason		8	22	4	1	0	0	(0	0)	5	5	1	1	2	0	5	0	0	0	0	0	-	0	.182	.250	.227
	5 ML YEARS		432	1209	272	61	7	28	(14	14)	431	156	122	125	103	4	321	32	20	8	32	11	.74	30	.225	.301	.356

Wandy Rodriguez

Pitches: L **Bats:** B **Pos:** SP-33; RP-1   WONN-dee   **Ht:** 5'10" **Wt:** 195 **Born:** 1/18/1979 **Age:** 34

			HOW MUCH HE PITCHED					WHAT HE GAVE UP										THE RESULTS						
Year	Team	Lg	G	GS	CG	GF	IP	BFP	H	R	ER	HR	SH	SF	HB	TBB	IBB	SO	WP	Bk	W	L	Pct	Sh	Sv-Op	Hld	ERC	ERA
2005	Hou	NL	25	22	0	0	128.2	560	135	82	79	19	3	3	8	53	2	80	3	3	10	10	.500	0	0-0	0	5.08	5.53
2006	Hou	NL	30	24	0	1	135.2	611	154	96	85	17	7	4	6	63	7	98	6	0	9	10	.474	0	0-0	0	5.45	5.64
2007	Hou	NL	31	31	1	0	182.2	782	179	102	93	22	6	4	5	62	2	158	3	0	9	13	.409	1	0-0	0	3.94	4.58
2008	Hou	NL	25	25	0	0	137.1	587	136	65	54	14	2	5	5	44	3	131	2	3	9	7	.563	0	0-0	0	3.82	3.54
2009	Hou	NL	33	33	1	0	205.2	849	192	77	69	21	8	4	6	63	5	193	2	1	14	12	.538	1	0-0	0	3.47	3.02
2010	Hou	NL	32	32	0	0	195.0	822	183	95	78	16	6	5	9	68	3	178	8	0	11	12	.478	0	0-0	0	3.60	3.60
2011	Hou	NL	30	30	0	0	191.0	808	182	81	74	25	7	3	5	69	7	166	5	0	11	11	.500	0	0-0	0	3.95	3.49
2012	2 Tms	NL	34	33	0	1	205.2	875	205	99	86	21	6	5	3	56	4	139	5	0	12	13	.480	0	0-0	0	3.55	3.76
12	Hou	NL	21	21	0	0	130.2	558	134	66	55	13	5	3	2	32	2	89	5	0	7	9	.438	0	0-0	0	3.57	3.79
12	Pit	NL	13	12	0	1	75.0	317	71	33	31	8	1	2	1	24	2	50	0	0	5	4	.556	0	0-0	0	3.50	3.72
	Postseason		3	0	0	1	4.2	22	5	2	2	2	1	0	0	5	1	4	0	0	0	1	.000	0	0-0	0	10.58	3.86
	8 ML YEARS		240	230	2	2	1381.2	5894	1366	697	618	155	45	33	46	478	33	1143	34	7	85	88	.491	2	0-0	0	3.99	4.03

Josh Roenicke

Pitches: R **Bats:** R **Pos:** RP-63   RENN-ick-kee   **Ht:** 6'3" **Wt:** 200 **Born:** 8/4/1982 **Age:** 30

			HOW MUCH HE PITCHED					WHAT HE GAVE UP										THE RESULTS						
Year	Team	Lg	G	GS	CG	GF	IP	BFP	H	R	ER	HR	SH	SF	HB	TBB	IBB	SO	WP	Bk	W	L	Pct	Sh	Sv-Op	Hld	ERC	ERA
2008	Cin	NL	5	0	0	0	3.0	18	6	3	3	0	0	0	1	2	0	6	0	0	0	0	-	0	0-0	0	12.01	9.00
2009	2 Tms	NL	24	0	0	5	31.0	138	32	19	18	2	0	1	1	16	1	33	2	0	0	0	-	0	0-0	1	4.55	5.23
2010	Tor	AL	16	0	0	3	19.0	91	18	15	12	1	0	0	2	13	0	18	1	0	1	0	1.000	0	0-0	2	4.76	5.68
2011	Col	NL	19	0	0	6	16.2	68	14	7	7	1	0	0	1	7	1	12	1	0	0	0	-	0	0-0	4	3.28	3.78
2012	Col	NL	63	0	0	14	88.2	383	85	40	32	9	6	4	2	43	3	54	8	0	4	2	.667	0	1-3	8	4.28	3.25
09	Cin	NL	11	0	0	2	13.1	54	13	4	4	0	0	0	0	4	0	14	1	0	0	0	-	0	0-0	0	3.00	2.70
09	Tor	AL	13	0	0	3	17.2	84	19	15	14	2	0	1	1	12	1	19	1	0	0	0	-	0	0-0	1	5.81	7.13
	5 ML YEARS		127	0	0	28	158.1	698	155	84	72	13	6	5	7	81	5	123	12	0	5	2	.714	0	1-3	15	4.41	4.09

Esmil Rogers

Pitches: R Bats: R Pos: RP-67   ESS-mill   Ht: 6'1" Wt: 190 Born: 8/14/1985 Age: 27

			HOW MUCH HE PITCHED						WHAT HE GAVE UP											THE RESULTS						
Year	Team	Lg	G	GS	CG	GF	IP	BFP	H	R	ER	HR	SH	SF	HB	TBB	IBB	SO	WP	Bk	W	L	Pct	Sh	Sv-Op	Hld	ERC	ERA
2009	Col	NL	1	1	0	0	4.0	16	3	2	2	0	0	1	0	2	0	3	0	0	0	0	-	0	0-0	0	2.58	4.50
2010	Col	NL	28	8	0	5	72.0	333	94	59	49	5	3	3	5	26	2	66	5	2	2	3	.400	0	0-1	1	5.70	6.13
2011	Col	NL	18	13	0	1	83.0	404	110	65	65	14	4	3	6	47	5	63	5	1	6	6	.500	0	0-0	0	7.49	7.05
2012	2 Tms		67	0	0	19	78.2	348	83	42	41	7	2	2	5	30	4	83	10	0	3	3	.500	0	0-2	8	4.37	4.69
12	Col	NL	23	0	0	6	25.2	131	36	23	23	2	0	0	2	18	2	29	5	0	0	2	.000	0	0-2	2	7.71	8.06
12	Cle	AL	44	0	0	13	53.0	217	47	19	18	5	2	2	3	12	2	54	5	0	3	1	.750	0	0-0	6	2.93	3.06
4 ML YEARS			114	22	0	25	237.2	1101	290	168	157	26	9	9	16	105	11	215	20	3	11	12	.478	0	0-3	9	5.79	5.95

Mark Rogers

Pitches: R Bats: R Pos: SP-7   Ht: 6'2" Wt: 226 Born: 1/30/1986 Age: 27

			HOW MUCH HE PITCHED						WHAT HE GAVE UP											THE RESULTS						
Year	Team	Lg	G	GS	CG	GF	IP	BFP	H	R	ER	HR	SH	SF	HB	TBB	IBB	SO	WP	Bk	W	L	Pct	Sh	Sv-Op	Hld	ERC	ERA
2004	Brewers	R	9	6	0	0	26.2	120	30	21	14	0	0	1	3	14	0	35	5	1	0	3	.000	0	0--	-	5.13	4.73
2005	WV	A	25	20	0	2	98.2	451	87	65	56	11	1	2	12	70	0	109	11	0	2	9	.182	0	1--	-	5.25	5.11
2006	BrvdCt	A+	16	16	0	0	71.0	329	68	46	40	6	2	2	3	53	0	96	12	0	1	2	.333	0	0--	-	5.27	5.07
2006	Brewrs	R	3	3	0	0	4.0	19	5	1	1	0	0	0	0	2	0	5	2	0	0	0	-	0	0--	-	5.00	2.25
2009	BrvdCt	A+	23	22	0	0	64.2	260	46	16	12	2	0	0	2	29	0	67	7	0	1	3	.250	0	0--	-	2.47	1.67
2010	Hntsvl	AA	24	24	0	0	111.2	490	86	60	46	3	3	3	6	69	0	111	12	1	6	8	.429	0	0--	-	3.29	3.71
2010	Nashv	AAA	1	1	0	0	4.1	19	3	1	1	0	0	0	0	3	0	3	0	0	0	0	-	0	0--	-	2.74	2.08
2011	Nashv	AAA	5	5	0	0	15.0	87	21	23	22	1	1	1	0	22	0	12	1	0	0	2	.000	0	0--	-	10.77	13.20
2011	BrvdCt	A+	5	5	0	0	16.1	92	22	20	17	4	0	2	2	15	0	17	2	0	0	3	.000	0	0--	-	9.69	9.37
2011	Brewrs	R	5	3	0	0	13.0	58	13	9	7	1	1	0	0	5	0	11	3	0	0	0	-	0	0--	-	3.69	4.85
2012	Nashv	AAA	18	18	0	0	95.1	415	92	52	50	13	2	2	5	49	0	74	5	1	6	6	.500	0	0--	-	4.91	4.72
2010	Mil	NL	4	2	0	1	10.0	36	2	2	2	0	1	1	1	3	0	11	0	0	0	0	-	0	0-0	0	0.50	1.80
2012	Mil	NL	7	7	0	0	39.0	165	36	17	17	5	1	1	1	14	0	41	1	0	3	1	.750	0	0-0	0	3.78	3.92
2 ML YEARS			11	9	0	1	49.0	201	38	19	19	5	2	2	2	17	0	52	1	0	3	1	.750	0	0-0	0	2.84	3.49

Scott Rolen

Bats: R Throws: R Pos: 3B-87; PH-6   Ht: 6'4" Wt: 245 Born: 4/4/1975 Age: 38

			BATTING																BASERUNNING				AVERAGES		
Year	Team	Lg	G	AB	H	2B	3B	HR	(Hm | Rd)	TB	R	RBI	RC	TBB	IBB	SO	HBP	SH	SF	SB	CS	SB%	GDP	Avg	OBP	Slg
2012	Lsvlle*	AAA	2	6	2	0	0	1	(- | -)	5	1	3	1	0	0	2	0	0	0	0	0	-	0	.333	.333	.833
1996	Phi	NL	37	130	33	7	0	4	(2 | 2)	52	10	18	16	13	0	27	1	0	2	0	2	.00	4	.254	.322	.400
1997	Phi	NL	156	561	159	35	3	21	(11 | 10)	263	93	92	103	76	4	138	13	0	7	16	6	.73	6	.283	.377	.469
1998	Phi	NL	160	601	174	45	4	31	(19 | 12)	320	120	110	124	93	6	141	11	0	6	14	7	.67	10	.290	.391	.532
1999	Phi	NL	112	421	113	28	1	26	(9 | 17)	221	74	77	83	67	2	114	3	0	6	12	2	.86	8	.268	.368	.525
2000	Phi	NL	128	483	144	32	6	26	(12 | 14)	266	88	89	97	51	9	99	5	0	2	8	1	.89	4	.298	.370	.551
2001	Phi	NL	151	554	160	39	1	25	(12 | 13)	276	96	107	108	74	6	127	13	0	12	16	5	.76	6	.289	.378	.498
2002	2 Tms	NL	155	580	154	29	8	31	(14 | 17)	292	89	110	98	72	4	102	12	0	3	8	4	.67	22	.266	.357	.503
2003	StL	NL	154	559	160	49	1	28	(12 | 16)	295	98	104	104	82	5	104	9	0	7	13	3	.81	19	.286	.382	.528
2004	StL	NL	142	500	157	32	4	34	(10 | 24)	299	109	124	124	72	5	92	13	1	7	4	3	.57	8	.314	.409	.598
2005	StL	NL	56	196	46	12	1	5	(2 | 3)	75	28	28	22	25	1	28	1	0	1	1	2	.33	3	.235	.323	.383
2006	StL	NL	142	521	154	48	1	22	(12 | 10)	270	94	95	89	56	7	69	9	0	8	7	4	.64	10	.296	.369	.518
2007	StL	NL	112	392	104	24	2	8	(4 | 4)	156	55	58	47	37	2	56	5	0	7	5	3	.63	13	.265	.331	.398
2008	Tor	AL	115	408	107	30	4	11	(6 | 5)	176	58	50	57	46	2	71	10	0	3	5	0	1.00	12	.262	.349	.431
2009	2 Tms	NL	128	475	145	36	1	11	(8 | 3)	216	76	67	82	45	1	62	7	0	8	5	4	.56	4	.305	.368	.455
2010	Cin	NL	133	471	134	34	3	20	(10 | 10)	234	66	83	73	50	3	82	8	0	8	1	2	.33	12	.285	.358	.497
2011	Cin	NL	65	252	61	20	2	5	(3 | 2)	100	31	36	26	10	0	36	4	0	3	1	0	1.00	4	.242	.279	.397
2012	Cin	NL	92	294	72	17	2	8	(6 | 2)	117	26	39	37	30	0	62	3	0	5	2	1	.67	5	.245	.318	.398
02	Phi	NL	100	375	97	21	4	17	(8 | 9)	177	52	66	60	52	2	68	8	0	3	5	2	.71	12	.259	.358	.472
02	StL	NL	55	205	57	8	4	14	(6 | 8)	115	37	44	38	20	2	34	4	0	0	3	2	.60	10	.278	.354	.561
09	Tor	AL	88	338	108	29	0	8	(6 | 2)	161	52	43	60	26	1	42	4	0	5	4	2	.67	2	.320	.370	.476
09	Cin	NL	40	137	37	7	1	3	(2 | 1)	55	24	24	22	19	0	20	3	0	3	1	2	.33	2	.270	.364	.401
Postseason			35	125	27	7	0	5	(3 | 2)	49	17	11	14	14	0	30	2	0	1	0	1	.00	5	.216	.303	.392
17 ML YEARS			2038	7398	2077	517	43	316	(152 | 164)	3628	1211	1287	1290	899	57	1410	127	1	93	118	49	.71	150	.281	.364	.490

Jimmy Rollins

Bats: B Throws: R Pos: SS-156; PH-3   Ht: 5'8" Wt: 180 Born: 11/27/1978 Age: 34

			BATTING																BASERUNNING				AVERAGES		
Year	Team	Lg	G	AB	H	2B	3B	HR	(Hm | Rd)	TB	R	RBI	RC	TBB	IBB	SO	HBP	SH	SF	SB	CS	SB%	GDP	Avg	OBP	Slg
2000	Phi	NL	14	53	17	1	1	0	(0 | 0)	20	5	5	8	2	0	7	0	0	0	3	0	1.00	0	.321	.345	.377
2001	Phi	NL	158	656	180	29	12	14	(8 | 6)	275	97	54	96	48	2	108	2	9	5	46	8	.85	5	.274	.323	.419
2002	Phi	NL	154	637	156	33	10	11	(3 | 8)	242	82	60	72	54	3	103	4	6	4	31	13	.70	14	.245	.306	.380
2003	Phi	NL	156	628	165	42	6	8	(5 | 3)	243	85	62	76	54	4	113	0	5	2	20	12	.63	9	.263	.320	.387
2004	Phi	NL	154	657	190	43	12	14	(6 | 8)	299	119	73	108	57	3	73	3	6	2	30	9	.77	4	.289	.348	.455
2005	Phi	NL	158	677	196	38	11	12	(5 | 7)	292	115	54	100	47	8	71	4	2	2	41	6	.87	5	.290	.338	.431
2006	Phi	NL	158	689	191	45	9	25	(15 | 10)	329	127	83	114	57	2	80	5	0	7	36	4	.90	12	.277	.334	.478
2007	Phi	NL	162	716	212	38	20	30	(18 | 12)	380	139	94	124	49	5	85	7	0	6	41	6	.87	11	.296	.344	.531
2008	Phi	NL	137	556	154	38	9	11	(5 | 6)	243	76	59	95	58	7	55	5	3	3	47	3	.94	11	.277	.349	.437
2009	Phi	NL	155	672	168	43	5	21	(10 | 11)	284	100	77	88	44	1	70	2	2	5	31	8	.79	7	.250	.296	.423
2010	Phi	NL	88	350	85	16	3	8	(4 | 4)	131	48	41	54	40	2	32	1	0	3	17	1	.94	4	.243	.320	.374
2011	Phi	NL	142	567	152	22	2	16	(7 | 9)	226	87	63	82	58	5	59	3	0	4	30	8	.79	6	.268	.338	.399
2012	Phi	NL	156	632	158	33	5	23	(11 | 12)	270	102	68	88	62	2	96	0	2	3	30	5	.86	9	.250	.316	.427
Postseason			46	188	47	12	1	3	(1 | 2)	70	27	15	16	16	0	34	2	1	1	11	4	.73	5	.250	.314	.372
13 ML YEARS			1792	7490	2024	421	105	193	(99 | 94)	3234	1182	793	1105	630	44	952	36	35	45	403	83	.83	104	.270	.328	.432

J.C. Romero

Pitches: L Bats: B Pos: RP-16   Ht: 5'11" Wt: 205 Born: 6/4/1976 Age: 37

Year Team	Lg	G	GS	CG	GF	IP	BFP	H	R	ER	HR	SH	SF	HB	TBB	IBB	SO	WP	Bk	W	L	Pct	Sh	Sv-Op	Hld	ERC	ERA
2012 Norfolk*	AAA	17	1	0	6	14.1	59	10	4	4	0	1	0	1	5	0	13	1	0	1	0	1.000	0	2- -	-	1.91	2.51
2012 Clmbs*	AAA	8	0	0	4	8.2	32	4	3	3	0	0	0	0	3	0	7	0	0	0	0	-	0	1- -	-	2.50	3.12
1999 Min	AL	5	0	0	3	9.2	39	13	4	4	0	0	0	0	0	0	4	0	0	0	0	-	0	0-0	0	3.95	3.72
2000 Min	AL	12	11	0	0	57.2	268	72	51	45	8	4	2	1	30	0	50	2	1	2	7	.222	0	0-0	0	6.48	7.02
2001 Min	AL	14	11	0	1	65.0	286	71	48	45	10	3	2	1	24	1	39	1	0	1	4	.200	0	0-0	0	4.89	6.23
2002 Min	AL	81	0	0	15	81.0	332	62	17	17	3	1	0	4	36	4	76	9	0	9	2	.818	0	1-5	33	2.74	1.89
2003 Min	AL	73	0	0	17	63.0	295	66	37	35	7	4	0	6	42	7	50	9	2	2	0	1.000	0	0-4	22	5.72	5.00
2004 Min	AL	74	0	0	12	74.1	319	61	32	29	4	3	1	5	38	6	69	5	0	7	4	.636	0	1-8	16	3.33	3.51
2005 Min	AL	68	0	0	11	57.0	264	50	26	22	6	5	1	6	39	8	48	1	1	4	3	.571	0	0-1	11	4.62	3.47
2006 LAA	AL	65	0	0	16	48.1	226	57	40	36	3	1	5	1	28	2	31	1	0	1	2	.333	0	0-1	7	5.54	6.70
2007 2 Tms		74	0	0	10	56.1	237	39	12	12	3	1	1	2	40	5	42	4	0	2	2	.500	0	1-2	24	3.35	1.92
2008 Phi	NL	81	0	0	14	59.0	255	41	18	18	5	4	0	5	38	5	52	2	1	4	4	.500	0	1-5	24	3.42	2.75
2009 Phi	NL	21	0	0	5	16.2	73	13	6	5	2	0	0	0	13	0	12	0	0	0	0	-	0	0-1	6	5.20	2.70
2010 Phi	NL	60	0	0	14	36.2	171	30	17	15	3	2	0	5	29	7	28	0	1	1	0	1.000	0	3-6	9	4.58	3.68
2011 2 Tms		36	0	0	6	24.2	116	28	14	11	1	2	0	1	15	2	19	0	0	1	0	1.000	0	0-0	3	5.19	4.01
2012 2 Tms		16	0	0	4	12.0	62	21	13	12	4	0	1	1	3	0	6	1	0	0	0	-	0	0-0	2	10.17	9.00
07 Bos	AL	23	0	0	5	20.0	94	24	7	7	2	0	1	0	15	3	11	0	0	1	0	1.000	0	1-1	2	6.61	3.15
07 Phi	NL	51	0	0	5	36.1	143	15	5	5	1	1	0	2	25	2	31	4	0	1	2	.333	0	0-1	22	1.86	1.24
11 Phi	NL	24	0	0	4	16.1	75	16	7	7	0	1	0	1	12	2	10	0	0	0	0	-	0	0-0	3	4.56	3.86
11 Col	NL	12	0	0	2	8.1	41	12	7	4	1	1	0	0	3	0	9	0	0	1	0	1.000	0	0-0	0	6.37	4.32
12 StL	NL	11	0	0	2	8.0	41	14	9	9	3	0	0	1	2	0	5	0	0	0	0	-	0	0-0	1	10.94	10.13
12 Bal	AL	5	0	0	2	4.0	21	7	4	3	1	0	1	0	1	0	1	1	0	0	0	-	0	0-0	1	8.72	6.75
Postseason		25	0	0	7	20.0	82	15	7	7	1	2	1	0	9	1	15	1	0	2	2	.500	0	0-0	6	2.56	3.15
14 ML YEARS		680	22	0	128	661.1	2943	624	335	306	59	30	13	40	375	47	526	35	6	34	28	.548	0	7-33	157	4.47	4.16

Ricky Romero

Pitches: L Bats: R Pos: SP-32   Ht: 6'0" Wt: 220 Born: 11/6/1984 Age: 28

Year Team	Lg	G	GS	CG	GF	IP	BFP	H	R	ER	HR	SH	SF	HB	TBB	IBB	SO	WP	Bk	W	L	Pct	Sh	Sv-Op	Hld	ERC	ERA
2009 Tor	AL	29	29	2	0	178.0	771	192	88	85	18	3	3	10	79	0	141	6	1	13	9	.591	0	0-0	0	5.12	4.30
2010 Tor	AL	32	32	3	0	210.0	882	189	98	87	15	9	3	8	82	3	174	18	1	14	9	.609	1	0-0	0	3.46	3.73
2011 Tor	AL	32	32	4	0	225.0	917	176	85	73	26	6	1	14	80	2	178	9	1	15	11	.577	2	0-0	0	3.11	2.92
2012 Tor	AL	32	32	1	0	181.0	829	198	122	116	21	7	4	10	105	1	124	8	0	9	14	.391	0	0-0	0	5.75	5.77
4 ML YEARS		125	125	8	0	794.0	3399	755	393	361	80	25	11	42	346	6	617	41	3	51	43	.543	3	0-0	0	4.21	4.09

Andrew Romine

Bats: L Throws: R Pos: SS-8; PR-3; 2B-1; 3B-1; DH-1; PH-1   ROW-mine   Ht: 6'1" Wt: 190 Born: 12/24/1985 Age: 27

Year Team	Lg	G	AB	H	2B	3B	HR	(Hm	Rd)	TB	R	RBI	RC	TBB	IBB	SO	HBP	SH	SF	SB	CS	SB%	GDP	Avg	OBP	Slg
2012 Salt Lk*	AAA	87	351	100	11	7	4	(-	-)	137	57	39	48	24	1	46	4	7	2	23	10	.70	2	.285	.336	.390
2010 LAA	AL	5	11	1	0	0	0	(0	0)	1	0	0	0	0	0	4	0	1	0	0	0	-	0	.091	.091	.091
2011 LAA	AL	10	16	2	0	0	0	(0	0)	2	2	0	0	1	0	6	0	1	0	1	0	1.00	0	.125	.176	.125
2012 LAA	AL	12	17	7	0	0	0	(0	0)	7	2	1	5	3	0	3	0	1	0	1	0	1.00	0	.412	.500	.412
3 ML YEARS		27	44	10	0	0	0	(0	0)	10	4	1	5	4	0	13	0	3	0	2	0	1.00	0	.227	.292	.227

Sergio Romo

Pitches: R Bats: R Pos: RP-69   Ht: 5'10" Wt: 185 Born: 3/4/1983 Age: 30

Year Team	Lg	G	GS	CG	GF	IP	BFP	H	R	ER	HR	SH	SF	HB	TBB	IBB	SO	WP	Bk	W	L	Pct	Sh	Sv-Op	Hld	ERC	ERA
2008 SF	NL	29	0	0	8	34.0	130	16	13	8	3	2	1	3	8	1	33	0	0	3	1	.750	0	0-0	5	1.27	2.12
2009 SF	NL	45	0	0	9	34.0	143	30	15	15	1	2	0	1	11	0	41	2	0	5	2	.714	0	2-2	10	4.89	3.97
2010 SF	NL	68	0	0	13	62.0	247	46	16	15	6	2	2	4	14	2	70	0	0	5	3	.625	0	0-4	21	2.26	2.18
2011 SF	NL	65	0	0	16	48.0	175	29	8	8	2	2	0	0	5	1	70	0	0	3	1	.750	0	1-2	23	1.08	1.50
2012 SF	NL	69	0	0	27	55.1	215	37	11	11	5	2	0	3	10	1	63	2	0	4	2	.667	0	14-15	23	1.72	1.79
Postseason		6	0	0	1	3.2	17	6	3	3	1	0	0	0	1	0	4	0	0	1	0	1.000	0	0-2	0	9.25	7.36
5 ML YEARS		276	0	0	73	233.1	910	158	63	57	17	10	3	11	48	5	277	4	0	20	9	.690	0	17-23	82	1.72	2.20

Adam Rosales

Bats: R Throws: R Pos: 2B-21; SS-11; 1B-7; 3B-3; PR-3; PH-1   Ht: 6'1" Wt: 195 Born: 5/20/1983 Age: 30

Year Team	Lg	G	AB	H	2B	3B	HR	(Hm	Rd)	TB	R	RBI	RC	TBB	IBB	SO	HBP	SH	SF	SB	CS	SB%	GDP	Avg	OBP	Slg
2012 Scrmto*	AAA	76	275	77	21	1	8	(-	-)	124	46	47	44	26	0	57	2	1	6	4	2	.67	6	.280	.340	.451
2008 Cin	NL	18	29	6	1	0	0	(0	0)	7	0	2	2	1	0	4	0	0	0	1	0	1.00	0	.207	.233	.241
2009 Cin	NL	87	230	49	10	1	4	(2	2)	73	23	19	22	26	0	46	5	2	3	1	2	.33	2	.213	.303	.317
2010 Oak	AL	80	255	69	8	2	7	(1	6)	102	31	31	31	19	0	65	1	2	2	2	2	.50	1	.271	.321	.400
2011 Oak	AL	24	61	6	0	0	2	(0	2)	12	5	8	0	4	0	13	1	0	2	0	0	-	4	.098	.162	.197
2012 Oak	AL	42	99	22	5	0	2	(1	1)	33	12	8	6	11	1	24	0	0	1	0	0	-	4	.222	.297	.333
5 ML YEARS		251	674	152	24	3	15	(4	11)	227	71	68	61	61	1	152	7	4	8	4	4	.50	11	.226	.293	.337

Sandy Rosario

Pitches: R Bats: R Pos: RP-4 — roh-SORRY-oh — Ht: 6'1" Wt: 210 Born: 8/22/1985 Age: 27

			HOW MUCH HE PITCHED						WHAT HE GAVE UP											THE RESULTS						
Year	Team	Lg	G	GS	CG	GF	IP	BFP	H	R	ER	HR	SH	SF	HB	TBB	IBB	SO	WP	Bk	W	L	Pct	Sh	Sv-Op Hld	ERC	ERA
2012	NewOr*	AAA	25	0	0	22	26.0	99	20	4	3	0	1	1	1	2	2	24	1	0	0	2	.000	0	16-- -	1.38	1.04
2012	Jupiter*	A+	4	2	0	1	3.2	16	3	3	3	1	0	0	0	2	0	1	1	0	0	0	-	0	0-- -	4.74	7.36
2012	Jaxnvl*	AA	2	0	0	1	2.0	10	3	1	1	1	0	0	0	1	0	4	0	0	0	0	-	0	1-- -	10.88	4.50
2010	Fla	NL	2	0	0	0	1.0	12	9	6	6	2	0	0	0	1	0	0	0	0	0	0	-	0	0-0 0	115.7	54.00
2011	Fla	NL	4	0	0	1	3.2	18	5	1	1	0	0	0	0	2	0	2	0	0	0	0	-	0	0-0 0	5.84	2.45
2012	Mia	NL	4	0	0	1	3.0	17	8	6	6	0	0	0	0	0	0	2	0	0	0	0	-	0	0-0 0	12.05	18.00
	3 ML YEARS		10	0	0	2	7.2	47	22	13	13	2	0	0	0	3	0	4	0	0	0	0	-	0	0-0 0	18.88	15.26

Wilin Rosario

Bats: R Throws: R Pos: C-105; PH-11; 3B-3; 1B-1; PR-1 — wih-LEAN roh-SORRY-oh — Ht: 5'11" Wt: 215 Born: 2/23/1989 Age: 24

			BATTING																		BASERUNNING				AVERAGES		
Year	Team	Lg	G	AB	H	2B	3B	HR	(Hm	Rd)	TB	R	RBI	RC	TBB	IBB	SO	HBP	SH	SF	SB	CS	SB%	GDP	Avg	OBP	Slg
2007	Casper	R+	34	115	24	4	0	2	(-	-)	34	11	9	9	11	0	38	1	0	0	2	2	.50	3	.209	.283	.296
2008	Casper	R+	66	263	83	15	3	12	(-	-)	140	48	49	52	24	0	57	1	0	3	4	3	.57	5	.316	.351	.532
2009	Mdest	A+	58	203	54	12	2	4	(-	-)	82	17	33	25	10	0	55	1	3	5	2	1	.67	4	.266	.297	.404
2010	Tulsa	AA	73	270	77	13	1	19	(-	-)	149	42	52	51	21	2	57	3	2	1	1	0	1.00	9	.285	.342	.552
2011	Tulsa	AA	102	405	101	15	3	21	(-	-)	185	52	48	53	19	0	91	1	0	1	1	2	.33	15	.249	.284	.457
2011	Col	NL	16	54	11	3	1	3	(1	2)	25	6	8	4	2	0	20	0	0	1	0	0	-	1	.204	.228	.463
2012	Col	NL	117	396	107	19	0	28	(18	10)	210	67	71	56	25	2	99	1	0	4	4	5	.44	10	.270	.312	.530
	2 ML YEARS		133	450	118	22	1	31	(19	12)	235	73	79	60	27	2	119	1	0	5	4	5	.44	11	.262	.302	.522

B.J. Rosenberg

Pitches: R Bats: R Pos: RP-21; SP-1 — Ht: 6'3" Wt: 220 Born: 9/17/1985 Age: 27

			HOW MUCH HE PITCHED						WHAT HE GAVE UP											THE RESULTS						
Year	Team	Lg	G	GS	CG	GF	IP	BFP	H	R	ER	HR	SH	SF	HB	TBB	IBB	SO	WP	Bk	W	L	Pct	Sh	Sv-Op Hld	ERC	ERA
2008	Wmspt	A-	21	0	0	20	36.0	145	26	9	4	2	2	1	0	15	0	52	3	1	3	1	.750	0	10-- -	2.43	1.00
2009	Lakwd	A	37	0	0	31	50.1	198	37	7	5	0	0	1	2	10	1	65	5	0	7	2	.778	0	19-- -	1.58	0.89
2009	Rdng	AA	10	0	0	6	10.2	43	10	3	3	0	0	0	1	4	0	8	0	0	0	1	.000	0	3-- -	3.55	2.53
2010	Rdng	AA	11	0	0	3	13.2	60	15	14	14	6	0	0	1	5	0	15	0	0	1	0	1.000	0	0-- -	7.45	9.22
2010	Clrwtr	A+	10	0	0	4	13.0	51	9	2	2	2	0	0	0	4	0	17	1	0	1	0	1.000	0	1-- -	2.47	1.38
2010	Phillies	R	1	0	0	0	1.0	4	1	0	0	0	0	0	0	0	0	1	0	0	0	0	-	0	0-- -	1.95	0.00
2011	Rdng	AA	39	14	0	9	109.1	474	114	56	52	11	8	3	8	38	1	103	1	0	5	7	.417	0	2-- -	4.43	4.28
2012	Rdng	AA	5	0	0	4	8.0	32	5	1	1	0	0	0	0	2	0	10	2	0	1	0	1.000	0	3-- -	1.69	1.13
2012	LV	AAA	20	6	0	4	54.0	221	49	14	12	4	1	0	3	16	0	63	2	0	4	2	.667	0	0-- -	3.29	2.00
2012	Phi	NL	22	1	0	3	25.0	106	18	17	17	4	2	0	2	14	0	24	0	0	1	2	.333	0	0-0 2	3.92	6.12

Trevor Rosenthal

Pitches: R Bats: R Pos: RP-19 — Ht: 6'2" Wt: 190 Born: 5/29/1990 Age: 23

			HOW MUCH HE PITCHED						WHAT HE GAVE UP											THE RESULTS						
Year	Team	Lg	G	GS	CG	GF	IP	BFP	H	R	ER	HR	SH	SF	HB	TBB	IBB	SO	WP	Bk	W	L	Pct	Sh	Sv-Op Hld	ERC	ERA
2009	Cards	R	14	0	0	2	24.0	111	25	17	13	0	1	1	4	10	0	26	3	1	4	1	.800	0	0-- -	4.15	4.88
2010	JhsCty	R	10	6	0	1	32.0	125	23	10	8	1	0	0	2	7	0	30	0	1	3	0	1.000	0	1-- -	1.83	2.25
2011	QuadC	A	22	22	1	0	120.1	509	111	62	55	7	4	3	13	39	0	133	7	0	7	7	.500	0	0-- -	3.52	4.11
2012	Sprgfld	AA	17	17	0	0	94.0	379	67	33	29	6	5	3	2	37	0	83	5	1	8	6	.571	0	0-- -	2.42	2.78
2012	Memp	AAA	3	3	0	0	15.0	61	11	7	7	1	1	0	2	5	0	21	1	0	0	0	-	0	0-- -	2.74	4.20
2012	StL	NL	19	0	0	7	22.2	89	14	7	7	2	1	0	1	7	0	25	1	0	0	2	.000	0	0-0 3	1.89	2.78

Cody Ross

Bats: R Throws: L Pos: RF-96; LF-22; DH-14; CF-7; PH-3 — Ht: 5'10" Wt: 195 Born: 12/23/1980 Age: 32

			BATTING																		BASERUNNING				AVERAGES		
Year	Team	Lg	G	AB	H	2B	3B	HR	(Hm	Rd)	TB	R	RBI	RC	TBB	IBB	SO	HBP	SH	SF	SB	CS	SB%	GDP	Avg	OBP	Slg
2012	Pwtckt*	AAA	2	7	1	0	0	0	(-	-)	1	1	0	0	1	0	0	1	0	0	0	0	-	0	.143	.333	.143
2003	Det	AL	6	19	4	1	0	1	(1	0)	8	1	5	4	1	0	3	1	1	0	0	0	-	0	.211	.286	.421
2005	LAD	NL	14	25	4	1	0	0	(0	0)	5	1	1	0	1	0	10	0	0	0	0	0	-	1	.160	.192	.200
2006	3 Tms	NL	101	269	61	12	2	13	(6	7)	116	34	46	36	22	0	65	4	1	2	1	1	.50	8	.227	.293	.431
2007	Fla	NL	66	173	58	19	0	12	(8	4)	113	35	39	42	20	3	38	3	0	1	2	0	1.00	2	.335	.411	.653
2008	Fla	NL	145	461	120	29	5	22	(7	15)	225	59	73	68	33	2	116	7	0	5	6	1	.86	5	.260	.316	.488
2009	Fla	NL	151	559	151	37	1	24	(13	11)	262	73	90	75	34	1	122	9	0	2	5	2	.71	18	.270	.321	.469
2010	2 Tms	NL	153	525	141	28	3	14	(5	9)	217	71	65	68	37	4	121	5	0	2	9	2	.82	9	.269	.322	.413
2011	SF	NL	121	405	97	25	0	14	(6	8)	164	54	52	53	49	4	96	4	0	3	5	2	.71	10	.240	.325	.405
2012	Bos	AL	130	476	127	34	1	22	(13	9)	229	70	81	76	42	3	129	3	1	6	2	3	.40	11	.267	.326	.481
06	LAD	NL	8	14	7	1	1	2	(0	2)	16	4	9	6	0	0	2	0	0	0	1	0	1.00	0	.500	.500	1.143
06	Cin	NL	2	5	1	0	0	0	(0	0)	1	0	0	1	0	0	2	0	0	0	0	0	-	0	.200	.200	.200
06	Fla	NL	91	250	53	11	1	11	(6	5)	99	30	37	29	22	0	61	4	1	2	0	1	.00	8	.212	.284	.396
10	Fla	NL	120	452	120	24	3	11	(5	6)	183	60	58	58	30	4	100	4	0	1	9	1	.90	7	.265	.316	.405
10	SF	NL	33	73	21	4	0	3	(0	3)	34	11	7	10	7	0	21	1	0	1	0	1	.00	2	.288	.354	.466
	Postseason		15	51	15	5	0	5	(0	5)	35	11	10	12	7	0	11	1	0	0	0	0	-	1	.294	.390	.686
	9 ML YEARS		887	2912	763	186	12	122	(59	63)	1339	398	452	422	239	17	700	36	3	21	30	11	.73	64	.262	.324	.460

David Ross

Bats: R Throws: R Pos: C-54; PH-9   Ht: 6'2" Wt: 205 Born: 3/19/1977 Age: 36

Year	Team	Lg	G	AB	H	2B	3B	HR	(Hm	Rd)	TB	R	RBI	RC	TBB	IBB	SO	HBP	SH	SF	SB	CS	SB%	GDP	Avg	OBP	Slg
2002	LAD	NL	8	10	2	1	0	1	(0	1)	6	2	2	2	2	0	4	1	0	0	0	0	-	0	.200	.385	.600
2003	LAD	NL	40	124	32	7	0	10	(5	5)	69	19	18	18	13	0	42	2	0	1	0	0	-	4	.258	.336	.556
2004	LAD	NL	70	165	28	3	1	5	(2	3)	48	13	15	11	15	1	62	5	0	5	0	0	-	3	.170	.253	.291
2005	2 Tms	NL	51	125	30	8	1	3	(2	1)	49	11	15	13	6	0	28	2	2	3	0	0	-	3	.240	.279	.392
2006	Cin	NL	90	247	63	15	1	21	(13	8)	143	37	52	43	37	7	75	3	4	5	0	0	-	4	.255	.353	.579
2007	Cin	NL	112	311	63	10	0	17	(12	5)	124	32	39	27	30	4	92	0	5	2	0	0	-	9	.203	.271	.399
2008	2 Tms	NL	60	142	32	9	0	3	(1	2)	50	18	13	19	32	4	39	1	6	1	0	1	.00	3	.225	.369	.352
2009	Atl	NL	54	128	35	9	0	7	(2	5)	65	18	20	20	21	0	39	1	1	0	0	0	-	1	.273	.380	.508
2010	Atl	NL	59	121	35	13	2	2	(2	0)	58	15	28	22	20	0	28	1	2	1	0	1	.00	5	.289	.392	.479
2011	Atl	NL	52	152	40	7	0	6	(2	4)	65	14	23	22	16	0	51	0	2	0	0	1	.00	4	.263	.333	.428
2012	Atl	NL	62	176	45	7	0	9	(4	5)	79	18	23	21	18	0	60	0	0	2	1	0	1.00	5	.256	.321	.449
05	Pit	NL	40	108	24	8	0	3	(2	1)	41	9	15	9	6	0	24	1	1	3	0	0	-	3	.222	.263	.380
05	SD	NL	11	17	6	0	1	0	(0	0)	8	2	0	4	0	0	4	1	1	0	0	0	-	0	.353	.389	.471
08	Cin	NL	52	134	31	9	0	3	(1	2)	49	17	13	19	32	4	36	1	5	1	0	1	.00	3	.231	.381	.366
08	Bos	AL	8	8	1	0	0	0	(0	0)	1	1	0	0	0	0	3	0	1	0	0	0	-	0	.125	.125	.125
	Postseason		5	3	0	0	0	0	(0	0)	0	0	0	0	1	0	0	0	0	0	0	0	-	0	.000	.250	.000
	11 ML YEARS		658	1701	405	89	5	84	(45	39)	756	197	248	218	210	16	520	16	22	20	1	3	.25	41	.238	.324	.444

Robbie Ross

Pitches: L Bats: L Pos: RP-58   Ht: 5'11" Wt: 185 Born: 6/24/1989 Age: 24

			HOW MUCH HE PITCHED					WHAT HE GAVE UP											THE RESULTS						
Year	Team	Lg	G	GS	CG	GF	IP	BFP	H	R	ER	HR	SH	SF	HB	TBB	IBB	SO	WP	Bk	W	L	Pct	Sh	Sv-Op Hld	ERC	ERA
2009	Spkane	A-	15	15	0	0	74.1	315	68	28	22	5	4	1	10	17	0	76	6	2	4	4	.500	0	0- - -	3.21	2.66
2010	Hkry	A	16	16	0	0	94.0	401	89	38	27	2	5	1	11	20	0	62	2	1	8	7	.533	0	0- - -	2.93	2.59
2010	Bkrsfld	A+	11	11	0	0	52.0	242	67	38	31	4	1	0	4	17	0	49	4	1	4	4	.500	0	0- - -	5.51	5.37
2011	MrtlBh	A+	21	20	1	0	123.1	491	102	37	31	1	6	2	6	28	0	98	5	0	9	4	.692	0	0- - -	2.18	2.26
2011	Frisco	AA	6	6	0	0	38.0	149	33	13	11	5	0	1	0	5	0	36	1	0	1	1	.500	0	0- - -	2.57	2.61
2012	Tex	AL	58	0	0	9	65.0	265	55	21	16	3	1	2	2	23	3	47	1	1	6	0	1.000	0	0-0 9	2.83	2.22

Tyson Ross

Pitches: R Bats: R Pos: SP-13; RP-5   Ht: 6'6" Wt: 230 Born: 4/22/1987 Age: 26

			HOW MUCH HE PITCHED					WHAT HE GAVE UP											THE RESULTS						
Year	Team	Lg	G	GS	CG	GF	IP	BFP	H	R	ER	HR	SH	SF	HB	TBB	IBB	SO	WP	Bk	W	L	Pct	Sh	Sv-Op Hld	ERC	ERA
2012	Scrmto*	AAA	15	13	1	0	78.1	330	69	33	26	4	2	2	3	29	0	64	4	0	6	2	.750	0	0- - -	3.12	2.99
2010	Oak	AL	26	2	0	9	39.1	169	39	24	24	4	1	4	0	20	0	32	5	0	1	4	.200	0	1-2 2	4.60	5.49
2011	Oak	AL	9	6	0	1	36.0	145	33	12	11	1	4	0	0	13	1	24	2	0	3	3	.500	0	0-0 0	3.09	2.75
2012	Oak	AL	18	13	0	3	73.1	342	96	56	53	7	3	3	5	37	3	46	2	1	2	11	.154	0	0-0 0	6.68	6.50
	3 ML YEARS		53	21	0	13	148.2	656	168	92	88	12	5	7	5	70	4	102	9	1	6	18	.250	0	1-2 2	5.20	5.33

Vinny Rottino

Bats: R Throws: R Pos: LF-18; 1B-7; PH-6; DH-3; PR-3; C-2; 3B-2; RF-2   row-TEEN-oh   Ht: 6'1" Wt: 215 Born: 4/7/1980 Age: 33

Year	Team	Lg	G	AB	H	2B	3B	HR	(Hm	Rd)	TB	R	RBI	RC	TBB	IBB	SO	HBP	SH	SF	SB	CS	SB%	GDP	Avg	OBP	Slg
2012	Buffalo*	AAA	36	140	43	10	1	4	(-	-)	67	22	25	24	12	0	20	1	0	2	5	3	.63	2	.307	.361	.479
2012	Clmbs*	AAA	60	234	68	18	1	5	(-	-)	103	38	41	38	22	5	33	3	0	6	9	3	.75	3	.291	.351	.440
2006	Mil	NL	9	14	3	1	0	0	(0	0)	4	1	1	1	1	0	2	0	0	0	1	0	1.00	0	.214	.267	.286
2007	Mil	NL	8	9	2	1	0	0	(0	0)	3	0	3	2	0	0	1	0	0	0	0	0	-	0	.222	.222	.333
2008	Mil	NL	1	1	0	0	0	0	(0	0)	0	0	0	0	0	0	0	0	0	0	0	0	-	0	.000	.000	.000
2011	Fla	NL	8	12	2	0	0	0	(0	0)	2	1	0	0	2	0	4	0	0	0	0	0	-	0	.167	.286	.167
2012	2 Tms		36	61	9	2	0	3	(2	1)	20	12	7	6	7	1	17	0	2	1	4	0	1.00	0	.148	.232	.328
12	NYM	NL	18	33	6	1	0	2	(2	0)	13	8	5	6	6	1	9	0	0	0	3	0	1.00	0	.182	.308	.394
12	Cle	AL	18	28	3	1	0	1	(0	1)	7	4	2	0	1	0	8	0	2	1	1	0	1.00	0	.107	.133	.250
	5 ML YEARS		62	97	16	4	0	3	(2	1)	29	14	11	9	10	1	24	0	2	1	5	0	1.00	0	.165	.241	.299

Darin Ruf

Bats: R Throws: R Pos: LF-6; 1B-3; PH-3   ROUGH   Ht: 6'3" Wt: 220 Born: 7/28/1986 Age: 26

Year	Team	Lg	G	AB	H	2B	3B	HR	(Hm	Rd)	TB	R	RBI	RC	TBB	IBB	SO	HBP	SH	SF	SB	CS	SB%	GDP	Avg	OBP	Slg
2009	Phillies	R	20	43	14	3	0	0	(-	-)	17	5	6	7	3	0	8	3	0	1	0	0	-	2	.326	.400	.395
2009	Wmspt	A-	37	133	40	17	0	3	(-	-)	66	17	24	25	14	1	22	3	0	1	1	1	.00	2	.301	.377	.496
2010	Lakwd	A	32	115	38	7	3	4	(-	-)	63	25	17	28	21	0	23	3	1	1	3	2	.60	1	.330	.443	.548
2010	Clrwtr	A+	97	368	102	34	2	5	(-	-)	155	45	50	53	26	0	87	8	0	4	2	2	.50	10	.277	.335	.421
2011	Clrwtr	A+	133	484	149	43	1	17	(-	-)	245	72	82	96	56	1	95	10	0	4	0	1	.00	15	.308	.388	.506
2012	Rdng	AA	139	489	155	32	1	38	(-	-)	303	93	104	122	65	0	102	18	0	11	2	0	1.00	17	.317	.408	.620
2012	Phi	NL	12	33	11	2	1	3	(1	2)	24	4	10	5	2	1	12	0	0	2	0	0	-	1	.333	.351	.727

Justin Ruggiano

Bats: R **Throws:** R **Pos:** CF-52; LF-31; RF-15; PH-10; PR-3   rouge-ee-AH-no   **Ht:** 6'2" **Wt:** 205 **Born:** 4/12/1982 **Age:** 31

Year Team	Lg	G	AB	H	2B	3B	HR	(Hm	Rd)	TB	R	RBI	RC	TBB	IBB	SO	HBP	SH	SF	SB	CS	SB%	GDP	Avg	OBP	Slg
2012 OKCity*	AAA	39	117	38	13	1	5	(-	-)	68	21	29	27	18	1	24	0	0	2	5	3	.63	1	.325	.409	.581
2007 TB	AL	7	14	3	0	0	0	(0	0)	3	2	3	1	1	0	5	0	0	0	0	0	-	0	.214	.267	.214
2008 TB	AL	45	76	15	4	0	2	(2	0)	25	9	7	4	4	0	27	1	0	0	2	0	1.00	2	.197	.247	.329
2011 TB	AL	46	105	26	4	0	4	(3	1)	42	11	13	16	4	0	26	0	1	1	1	1	.50	2	.248	.273	.400
2012 Mia	NL	91	288	90	23	1	13	(4	9)	154	38	36	46	29	0	84	0	1	1	14	8	.64	6	.313	.374	.535
4 ML YEARS		189	483	134	31	1	19	(9	10)	224	60	59	67	38	0	142	1	2	2	17	9	.65	10	.277	.330	.464

Carlos Ruiz

Bats: R **Throws:** R **Pos:** C-106; PH-15; PR-1   **Ht:** 5'10" **Wt:** 206 **Born:** 1/22/1979 **Age:** 34

Year Team	Lg	G	AB	H	2B	3B	HR	(Hm	Rd)	TB	R	RBI	RC	TBB	IBB	SO	HBP	SH	SF	SB	CS	SB%	GDP	Avg	OBP	Slg
2006 Phi	NL	27	69	18	1	1	3	(2	1)	30	5	10	10	5	2	8	1	2	1	0	0	-	3	.261	.316	.435
2007 Phi	NL	115	374	97	29	2	6	(4	2)	148	42	54	49	42	10	49	5	5	3	6	1	.86	17	.259	.340	.396
2008 Phi	NL	117	320	70	14	0	4	(2	2)	96	47	31	28	44	6	38	4	4	1	1	2	.33	14	.219	.320	.300
2009 Phi	NL	107	322	82	26	1	9	(5	4)	137	32	43	49	47	8	39	4	4	2	3	2	.60	8	.255	.355	.425
2010 Phi	NL	121	371	112	28	1	8	(3	5)	166	43	53	62	55	13	54	6	0	1	0	1	.00	8	.302	.400	.447
2011 Phi	NL	132	410	116	23	0	6	(1	5)	157	49	40	59	48	10	48	10	3	1	1	0	1.00	7	.283	.371	.383
2012 Phi	NL	114	372	121	32	0	16	(8	8)	201	56	68	75	29	6	50	16	0	4	4	0	1.00	6	.325	.394	.540
Postseason		46	142	36	8	1	4	(3	1)	58	19	15	24	24	3	16	5	1	0	3	0	1.00	2	.254	.380	.408
7 ML YEARS		733	2238	616	153	5	52	(25	27)	935	274	299	332	270	55	286	46	18	13	15	6	.71	63	.275	.363	.418

Dan Runzler

Pitches: L **Bats:** L **Pos:** RP-6   **Ht:** 6'4" **Wt:** 235 **Born:** 3/30/1985 **Age:** 28

Year Team	Lg	G	GS	CG	GF	IP	BFP	H	R	ER	HR	SH	SF	HB	TBB	IBB	SO	WP	Bk	W	L	Pct	Sh	Sv-Op	Hld	ERC	ERA
2012 SnJos*	A+	3	2	0	0	3.0	13	3	3	2	1	0	0	0	1	0	1	0	0	0	2	.000	0	0- -	-	5.31	6.00
2012 Fresno*	AAA	29	0	0	10	27.0	127	36	21	18	2	3	1	1	14	0	33	0	0	0	2	.000	0	1- -	-	6.60	6.00
2009 SF	NL	11	0	0	0	8.2	38	6	1	1	0	0	0	0	5	0	11	0	0	0	0	-	0	0-0	2	3.54	1.04
2010 SF	NL	41	0	0	7	32.2	144	29	12	11	1	4	0	1	20	3	37	2	0	3	0	1.000	0	0-0	5	3.74	3.03
2011 SF	NL	31	1	0	9	27.1	120	29	21	19	0	0	1	0	16	1	25	1	0	1	2	.333	0	0-0	3	4.48	6.26
2012 SF	NL	6	0	0	0	3.2	15	1	0	0	0	0	1	1	3	1	5	1	0	0	0	-	0	0-0	1	1.73	0.00
4 ML YEARS		89	1	0	16	72.1	317	65	34	31	2	4	2	3	44	5	78	4	0	4	2	.667	0	0-0	10	3.88	3.86

Chris Rusin

Pitches: L **Bats:** L **Pos:** SP-7   RUSS-inn   **Ht:** 6'2" **Wt:** 195 **Born:** 10/22/1986 **Age:** 26

Year Team	Lg	G	GS	CG	GF	IP	BFP	H	R	ER	HR	SH	SF	HB	TBB	IBB	SO	WP	Bk	W	L	Pct	Sh	Sv-Op	Hld	ERC	ERA
2009 Cubs	R	2	1	0	0	5.0	18	1	0	0	0	0	0	0	3	0	2	0	0	0	0	-	0	0- -	-	0.84	0.00
2009 Boise	A-	8	8	0	0	31.0	136	33	14	12	1	0	1	4	9	0	27	3	0	0	4	.000	0	0- -	-	4.01	3.48
2010 Dytona	A+	20	17	0	1	91.0	366	79	43	34	6	2	0	7	15	0	84	1	0	4	3	.571	0	0- -	-	2.58	3.36
2010 Tenn	AA	4	4	0	0	19.0	81	21	8	4	0	2	0	1	4	0	15	0	0	2	1	.667	0	0- -	-	3.43	1.89
2011 Tenn	AA	15	15	0	0	76.0	324	80	39	33	5	4	1	5	16	0	49	2	0	3	2	.600	0	0- -	-	3.62	3.91
2011 Iowa	AAA	11	9	0	0	62.2	259	70	29	28	8	5	0	1	14	0	46	0	1	5	2	.714	0	0- -	-	4.44	4.02
2012 Iowa	AAA	25	25	0	0	140.1	615	146	81	71	17	4	4	8	53	2	94	7	1	8	9	.471	0	0- -	-	4.57	4.55
2012 Tenn	AA	1	1	0	0	3.0	9	0	0	0	0	0	0	0	0	0	1	0	0	0	0	-	0	0- -	-	0.00	0.00
2012 ChC	NL	7	7	0	0	29.2	135	38	22	21	4	0	0	3	11	0	21	0	0	2	3	.400	0	0-0	0	6.46	6.37

James Russell

Pitches: L **Bats:** L **Pos:** RP-77   **Ht:** 6'4" **Wt:** 200 **Born:** 1/8/1986 **Age:** 27

Year Team	Lg	G	GS	CG	GF	IP	BFP	H	R	ER	HR	SH	SF	HB	TBB	IBB	SO	WP	Bk	W	L	Pct	Sh	Sv-Op	Hld	ERC	ERA
2010 ChC	NL	57	0	0	11	49.0	219	55	37	27	11	3	4	4	11	0	42	2	0	1	1	.500	0	0-2	6	5.12	4.96
2011 ChC	NL	64	5	0	10	67.2	292	76	37	31	12	4	6	2	14	4	43	1	0	1	6	.143	0	0-2	6	4.51	4.12
2012 ChC	NL	77	0	0	19	69.1	292	67	28	25	5	2	3	1	23	7	55	1	1	7	1	.875	0	2-5	13	3.35	3.25
3 ML YEARS		198	5	0	40	186.0	803	198	102	83	28	9	13	7	48	11	140	4	1	9	8	.529	0	2-9	25	4.23	4.02

Josh Rutledge

Bats: R **Throws:** R **Pos:** SS-57; PH-10; 2B-7   **Ht:** 6'1" **Wt:** 190 **Born:** 4/21/1989 **Age:** 24

Year Team	Lg	G	AB	H	2B	3B	HR	(Hm	Rd)	TB	R	RBI	RC	TBB	IBB	SO	HBP	SH	SF	SB	CS	SB%	GDP	Avg	OBP	Slg
2010 TriCity	A-	11	39	5	0	0	0	(-	-)	5	6	4	0	4	0	10	1	1	0	1	0	1.00	1	.128	.227	.128
2011 Mdest	A+	113	460	160	33	9	9	(-	-)	238	91	71	99	41	1	91	12	8	2	16	3	.84	5	.348	.414	.517
2012 Tulsa	AA	87	356	109	27	3	13	(-	-)	181	57	35	62	14	1	69	5	0	4	14	4	.78	6	.306	.338	.508
2012 Col	NL	73	277	76	20	5	8	(5	3)	130	37	37	37	9	0	54	4	0	1	7	0	1.00	8	.274	.306	.469

Brendan Ryan

Bats: R **Throws:** R **Pos:** SS-138; PH-2; PR-1   **Ht:** 6'2" **Wt:** 195 **Born:** 3/26/1982 **Age:** 31

Year	Team	Lg	G	AB	H	2B	3B	HR	(Hm	Rd)	TB	R	RBI	RC	TBB	IBB	SO	HBP	SH	SF	SB	CS	SB%	GDP	Avg	OBP	Slg
2007	StL	NL	67	180	52	9	0	4	(2	2)	73	30	12	21	15	0	19	1	3	0	7	0	1.00	3	.289	.347	.406
2008	StL	NL	80	197	48	9	0	0	(0	0)	57	30	10	12	16	0	31	2	3	0	7	2	.78	4	.244	.307	.289
2009	StL	NL	129	390	114	19	7	3	(1	2)	156	55	37	48	24	3	56	6	6	3	14	7	.67	9	.292	.340	.400
2010	StL	NL	139	439	98	19	3	2	(0	2)	129	50	36	37	33	5	60	2	9	3	11	4	.73	6	.223	.279	.294
2011	Sea	AL	123	436	108	19	3	3	(0	3)	142	51	39	46	34	0	87	10	9	5	13	3	.81	7	.248	.313	.326
2012	Sea	AL	141	407	79	19	3	3	(2	1)	113	42	31	35	44	0	98	5	8	6	11	5	.69	4	.194	.277	.278
	Postseason		3	12	1	1	0	0	(0	0)	2	0	0	0	0	0	2	0	0	0	0	0	-	0	.083	.083	.167
	6 ML YEARS		679	2049	499	94	16	15	(5	10)	670	258	165	199	166	8	351	26	38	17	63	21	.75	33	.244	.306	.327

Marc Rzepczynski

Pitches: L **Bats:** L **Pos:** RP-70   zepp-CHINN-ski   **Ht:** 6'1" **Wt:** 205 **Born:** 8/29/1985 **Age:** 27

Year	Team	Lg	G	GS	CG	GF	IP	BFP	H	R	ER	HR	SH	SF	HB	TBB	IBB	SO	WP	Bk	W	L	Pct	Sh	Sv-Op	Hld	ERC	ERA
2009	Tor	AL	11	11	0	0	61.1	261	51	27	25	7	2	1	1	30	0	60	4	1	2	4	.333	0	0-0	0	3.65	3.67
2010	Tor	AL	14	12	0	0	63.2	287	72	37	35	8	1	2	5	30	1	57	4	1	4	4	.500	0	0-0	2	5.71	4.95
2011	2 Tms		71	0	0	7	62.0	256	50	27	23	3	2	0	4	26	1	61	6	0	2	6	.250	0	0-4	18	3.04	3.34
2012	StL	NL	70	0	0	14	46.2	196	46	22	22	7	0	0	0	17	2	33	3	0	1	3	.250	0	0-5	18	4.21	4.24
11	Tor	AL	43	0	0	6	39.1	158	28	16	13	2	1	0	3	15	0	33	5	0	2	3	.400	0	0-3	10	2.52	2.97
11	StL	NL	28	0	0	1	22.2	98	22	11	10	1	1	0	1	11	1	28	1	0	0	3	.000	0	0-1	8	4.01	3.97
	Postseason		12	0	0	0	8.1	33	7	4	4	0	0	0	1	1	0	9	1	0	1	0	1.000	0	0-0	6	2.07	4.32
	4 ML YEARS		166	23	0	21	233.2	1000	219	113	105	25	5	3	10	103	4	211	17	2	9	17	.346	0	0-9	38	4.13	4.04

CC Sabathia

Pitches: L **Bats:** L **Pos:** SP-28   **Ht:** 6'7" **Wt:** 290 **Born:** 7/21/1980 **Age:** 32

Year	Team	Lg	G	GS	CG	GF	IP	BFP	H	R	ER	HR	SH	SF	HB	TBB	IBB	SO	WP	Bk	W	L	Pct	Sh	Sv-Op	Hld	ERC	ERA
2001	Cle	AL	33	33	0	0	180.1	763	149	93	88	19	3	5	7	95	1	171	7	3	17	5	.773	0	0-0	0	3.86	4.39
2002	Cle	AL	33	33	2	0	210.0	891	198	109	102	17	5	10	1	88	2	149	6	3	13	11	.542	0	0-0	0	3.74	4.37
2003	Cle	AL	30	30	2	0	197.2	832	190	85	79	19	10	4	6	66	3	141	4	2	13	9	.591	1	0-0	0	3.70	3.60
2004	Cle	AL	30	30	1	0	188.0	787	176	90	86	20	3	6	7	72	3	139	1	1	11	10	.524	1	0-0	0	3.91	4.12
2005	Cle	AL	31	31	1	0	196.2	823	185	92	88	19	5	3	7	62	1	161	7	0	15	10	.600	0	0-0	0	3.55	4.03
2006	Cle	AL	28	28	6	0	192.2	802	182	83	69	17	8	5	7	44	3	172	3	0	12	11	.522	2	0-0	0	3.13	3.22
2007	Cle	AL	34	34	4	0	241.0	975	238	94	86	20	6	6	8	37	1	209	1	0	19	7	.731	1	0-0	0	3.12	3.21
2008	2 Tms		35	35	10	0	253.0	1023	223	85	76	19	9	6	7	59	1	251	2	2	17	10	.630	5	0-0	0	2.78	2.70
2009	NYY	AL	34	34	2	0	230.0	938	197	96	86	18	4	9	9	67	7	197	5	0	19	8	.704	1	0-0	0	2.89	3.37
2010	NYY	AL	34	34	2	0	237.2	970	209	92	84	20	5	8	7	74	6	197	8	1	21	7	.750	0	0-0	0	3.11	3.18
2011	NYY	AL	33	33	3	0	237.1	985	230	87	79	17	8	7	7	61	4	230	2	1	19	8	.704	1	0-0	0	3.27	3.00
2012	NYY	AL	28	28	2	0	200.0	833	184	89	75	22	4	3	8	44	2	197	4	1	15	6	.714	0	0-0	0	3.10	3.38
08	Cle	AL	18	18	3	0	122.1	507	117	54	52	13	3	3	3	34	1	123	1	2	6	8	.429	2	0-0	0	3.52	3.83
08	Mil	NL	17	17	7	0	130.2	516	106	31	24	6	6	3	4	25	0	128	1	0	11	2	.846	3	0-0	0	2.13	1.65
	Postseason		16	15	0	0	86.0	386	93	48	46	12	4	0	5	46	8	82	4	1	7	4	.636	0	0-0	0	5.58	4.81
	12 ML YEARS		383	383	35	0	2564.1	10622	2361	1095	998	227	71	72	81	769	34	2214	50	14	191	102	.652	12	0-0	0	3.31	3.50

Takashi Saito

Pitches: R **Bats:** L **Pos:** RP-16   tuh-KAH-shee SYE-toe   **Ht:** 6'2" **Wt:** 200 **Born:** 2/14/1970 **Age:** 43

Year	Team	Lg	G	GS	CG	GF	IP	BFP	H	R	ER	HR	SH	SF	HB	TBB	IBB	SO	WP	Bk	W	L	Pct	Sh	Sv-Op	Hld	ERC	ERA
2012	Visalia*	A+	1	1	0	0	1.0	4	1	0	0	0	0	0	0	1	0	0	0	0	0	0	-	0	0--	-	6.99	0.00
2012	Reno*	AAA	4	0	0	0	2.2	16	7	3	3	1	0	0	0	1	0	2	0	0	0	1	.000	0	0--	-	17.70	10.13
2012	DBcks*	R	4	4	0	0	4.0	13	2	0	0	0	0	0	0	0	0	4	0	0	0	0	-	0	0--	-	0.58	0.00
2006	LAD	NL	72	0	0	48	78.1	303	48	19	18	3	3	4	2	23	3	107	0	0	6	2	.750	0	24-26	7	1.52	2.07
2007	LAD	NL	63	0	0	55	64.1	234	33	10	10	5	0	0	3	13	0	78	0	0	2	1	.667	0	39-43	1	1.28	1.40
2008	LAD	NL	45	0	0	35	47.0	197	40	14	13	1	0	2	2	16	3	60	1	0	4	4	.500	0	18-22	0	2.57	2.49
2009	Bos	AL	56	0	0	30	55.2	240	50	16	15	6	1	4	5	25	2	52	1	0	3	3	.500	0	2-4	3	4.08	2.43
2010	Atl	NL	56	0	0	14	54.0	221	41	20	17	4	2	0	0	17	2	69	2	0	2	3	.400	0	1-2	17	2.24	2.83
2011	Mil	NL	30	0	0	5	26.2	108	21	6	6	2	1	0	1	9	2	23	2	0	4	2	.667	0	0-2	10	2.62	2.03
2012	Ari	NL	16	0	0	2	12.0	60	17	14	9	4	1	0	1	5	1	11	1	0	0	2	.000	0	0-1	2	8.51	6.75
	Postseason		10	0	0	3	10.2	40	9	2	2	0	0	0	2	0	0	9	0	0	1	0	1.000	0	0-0	2	2.03	1.69
	7 ML YEARS		338	0	0	189	338.0	1363	250	99	88	25	8	10	14	108	13	400	9	0	21	15	.583	0	84-100	40	2.36	2.34

Fernando Salas

Pitches: R **Bats:** R **Pos:** RP-65   SAH-lahss   **Ht:** 6'2" **Wt:** 200 **Born:** 5/30/1985 **Age:** 28

Year	Team	Lg	G	GS	CG	GF	IP	BFP	H	R	ER	HR	SH	SF	HB	TBB	IBB	SO	WP	Bk	W	L	Pct	Sh	Sv-Op	Hld	ERC	ERA
2012	Memp*	AAA	4	0	0	4	4.0	17	6	4	4	2	0	0	0	0	0	5	0	0	1	0	1.000	0	1--	-	8.64	9.00
2010	StL	NL	27	0	0	11	30.2	133	28	13	12	4	1	1	0	15	2	29	2	0	1	0	1.000	0	0-0	1	4.03	3.52
2011	StL	NL	68	0	0	46	75.0	295	50	20	19	7	3	0	2	21	3	75	2	0	5	6	.455	0	24-30	6	1.94	2.28
2012	StL	NL	65	0	0	23	58.2	256	56	28	28	5	5	0	1	27	5	60	4	0	1	4	.200	0	0-3	7	3.85	4.30
	Postseason		11	0	0	1	13.1	58	12	7	5	0	0	0	0	4	1	12	1	1	0	0	-	0	0-0	4	2.25	3.38
	3 ML YEARS		160	0	0	80	164.1	684	134	61	59	16	9	1	3	63	10	164	8	0	6	10	.375	0	24-34	14	2.96	3.23

Chris Sale

Pitches: L **Bats:** L **Pos:** SP-29; RP-1 — SAIL — **Ht:** 6'6" **Wt:** 180 **Born:** 3/30/1989 **Age:** 24

			HOW MUCH HE PITCHED						WHAT HE GAVE UP										THE RESULTS						
Year	Team	Lg	G	GS	CG	GF	IP	BFP	H	R	ER	HR	SH	SF	HB	TBB	IBB	SO	WP	Bk	W	L	Pct	Sh	Sv-Op Hld	ERC	ERA
2010	CWS	AL	21	0	0	8	23.1	92	15	5	5	2	1	0	0	10	0	32	1	0	2	1	.667	0	4-4 2	2.30	1.93
2011	CWS	AL	58	0	0	17	71.0	288	52	22	22	6	3	0	2	27	3	79	2	0	2	2	.500	0	8-10 16	2.55	2.79
2012	CWS	AL	30	29	1	0	192.0	772	167	66	65	19	1	3	6	51	5	192	6	0	17	8	.680	0	0-1 0	3.00	3.05
	3 ML YEARS		109	29	1	25	286.1	1152	234	93	92	27	5	3	8	88	8	303	9	0	21	11	.656	0	12-15 18	2.83	2.89

Jarrod Saltalamacchia

Bats: B **Throws:** R **Pos:** C-104; PH-14; DH-12; 1B-1 — salt-ah-luh-MOCK-ee-ah — **Ht:** 6'4" **Wt:** 235 **Born:** 5/2/1985 **Age:** 28

			BATTING																		BASERUNNING				AVERAGES		
Year	Team	Lg	G	AB	H	2B	3B	HR	(Hm	Rd)	TB	R	RBI	RC	TBB	IBB	SO	HBP	SH	SF	SB	CS	SB%	GDP	Avg	OBP	Slg
2007	2 Tms		93	308	82	13	1	11	(6	5)	130	39	33	32	19	1	75	1	0	1	0	0	-	8	.266	.310	.422
2008	Tex	AL	61	198	50	13	0	3	(2	1)	72	27	26	29	31	1	74	0	0	1	0	2	.00	1	.253	.352	.364
2009	Tex	AL	84	283	66	12	0	9	(6	3)	105	34	34	30	22	1	97	1	3	1	0	2	.00	3	.233	.290	.371
2010	2 Tms		12	24	4	3	0	0	(0	0)	7	2	2	3	6	0	5	0	0	0	0	0	-	0	.167	.333	.292
2011	Bos	AL	103	358	84	23	3	16	(6	10)	161	52	56	43	24	1	119	3	0	1	1	0	1.00	7	.235	.288	.450
2012	Bos	AL	121	405	90	17	1	25	(12	13)	184	55	59	49	38	0	139	1	0	4	0	1	.00	5	.222	.288	.454
07	Atl	NL	47	141	40	6	0	4	(4	0)	58	11	12	13	10	1	28	1	0	1	0	0	-	4	.284	.333	.411
07	Tex	NL	46	167	42	7	1	7	(2	5)	72	28	21	19	9	0	47	0	0	0	0	0	-	4	.251	.290	.431
10	Tex	AL	2	5	1	0	0	0	(0	0)	1	0	1	1	0	0	1	0	0	0	0	0	-	0	.200	.200	.200
10	Bos	AL	10	19	3	3	0	0	(0	0)	6	2	1	2	6	0	4	0	0	0	0	0	-	0	.158	.360	.316
	6 ML YEARS		474	1576	376	81	5	64	(32	32)	659	209	210	186	140	4	509	6	3	8	1	5	.17	24	.239	.302	.418

Jeff Samardzija

Pitches: R **Bats:** R **Pos:** SP-28 — suh-MAHR-jah — **Ht:** 6'5" **Wt:** 225 **Born:** 1/23/1985 **Age:** 28

			HOW MUCH HE PITCHED						WHAT HE GAVE UP											THE RESULTS						
Year	Team	Lg	G	GS	CG	GF	IP	BFP	H	R	ER	HR	SH	SF	HB	TBB	IBB	SO	WP	Bk	W	L	Pct	Sh	Sv-Op Hld	ERC	ERA
2008	ChC	NL	26	0	0	6	27.2	124	24	12	7	0	1	1	1	15	2	25	2	0	1	0	1.000	0	1-4 3	3.08	2.28
2009	ChC	NL	20	2	0	7	34.2	161	46	29	29	7	4	1	1	15	1	21	2	0	1	3	.250	0	0-0 0	7.13	7.53
2010	ChC	NL	7	3	0	0	19.1	100	21	22	18	4	0	0	2	20	1	9	1	0	2	2	.500	0	0-0 0	8.45	8.38
2011	ChC	NL	75	0	0	18	88.0	380	64	35	29	5	3	2	5	50	3	87	8	0	8	4	.667	0	0-2 13	3.05	2.97
2012	ChC	NL	28	28	1	0	174.2	723	157	79	74	20	5	4	4	56	2	180	10	0	9	13	.409	0	0-0 0	3.41	3.81
	Postseason		1	0	0	0	1.0	4	2	1	1	0	0	0	0	0	0	0	0	0	0	0	-	0	0-0 0	9.49	9.00
	5 ML YEARS		156	33	1	31	344.1	1488	312	177	157	36	13	8	13	156	9	322	23	0	21	22	.488	0	1-6 16	3.88	4.10

Brian Sanches

Pitches: R **Bats:** R **Pos:** RP-6 — **Ht:** 6'1" **Wt:** 191 **Born:** 8/8/1978 **Age:** 34

			HOW MUCH HE PITCHED						WHAT HE GAVE UP											THE RESULTS						
Year	Team	Lg	G	GS	CG	GF	IP	BFP	H	R	ER	HR	SH	SF	HB	TBB	IBB	SO	WP	Bk	W	L	Pct	Sh	Sv-Op Hld	ERC	ERA
2012	LV*	AAA	25	1	0	8	39.2	164	41	15	11	2	2	1	4	8	0	31	1	0	3	2	.600	0	0- - -	3.29	2.50
2012	OKCity*	AAA	12	0	0	3	12.1	55	16	9	9	3	0	0	0	2	0	10	0	1	2	3	.400	0	0- - -	5.73	6.57
2006	Phi	NL	18	0	0	5	21.1	98	23	14	14	5	0	0	0	13	3	22	0	1	0	0	-	0	0-0 0	6.18	5.91
2007	Phi	NL	12	0	0	4	14.2	68	13	11	9	6	1	0	1	12	2	9	1	0	1	1	.500	0	0-0 1	7.73	5.52
2008	Was	NL	12	0	0	2	11.0	54	16	10	9	2	0	1	1	5	0	10	0	0	2	0	1.000	0	0-1 0	8.15	7.36
2009	Fla	NL	47	0	0	7	56.1	248	50	18	16	5	3	0	6	26	8	51	5	0	4	2	.667	0	0-3 9	3.75	2.56
2010	Fla	NL	61	0	0	14	63.2	254	43	20	16	7	1	3	1	27	0	54	5	0	2	2	.500	0	0-1 12	2.63	2.26
2011	Fla	NL	39	2	0	8	61.2	270	52	32	27	7	1	2	2	36	6	53	4	1	4	1	.800	0	0-0 0	3.97	3.94
2012	Phi	NL	6	0	0	3	6.1	34	12	7	7	4	0	0	0	3	1	5	0	0	1	0	.000	0	0-0 0	14.67	9.95
	7 ML YEARS		195	2	0	43	235.0	1026	209	112	98	36	6	6	11	122	20	204	15	2	13	7	.650	0	0-5 22	4.35	3.75

Anibal Sanchez

Pitches: R **Bats:** R **Pos:** SP-31 — ah-NEE-bahl — **Ht:** 6'0" **Wt:** 205 **Born:** 2/27/1984 **Age:** 29

			HOW MUCH HE PITCHED						WHAT HE GAVE UP											THE RESULTS						
Year	Team	Lg	G	GS	CG	GF	IP	BFP	H	R	ER	HR	SH	SF	HB	TBB	IBB	SO	WP	Bk	W	L	Pct	Sh	Sv-Op Hld	ERC	ERA
2006	Fla	NL	18	17	2	0	114.1	469	90	39	36	9	3	1	4	46	1	72	4	1	10	3	.769	1	0-0 0	2.96	2.83
2007	Fla	NL	6	6	0	0	30.0	151	43	17	16	3	2	2	2	19	1	14	3	0	2	1	.667	0	0-0 0	7.90	4.80
2008	Fla	NL	10	10	0	0	51.2	241	54	35	32	7	4	2	6	27	2	50	1	0	2	5	.286	0	0-0 0	5.40	5.57
2009	Fla	NL	16	16	0	0	86.0	383	84	39	37	10	2	2	1	46	5	71	0	1	4	8	.333	0	0-0 0	4.51	3.87
2010	Fla	NL	32	32	1	0	195.0	841	192	89	77	10	13	3	7	70	5	157	7	0	13	12	.520	1	0-0 0	3.56	3.55
2011	Fla	NL	32	32	3	0	196.1	830	187	85	80	20	12	1	5	64	8	202	4	5	8	9	.471	2	0-0 0	3.57	3.67
2012	2 Tms		31	31	1	0	195.2	820	200	95	84	20	5	7	5	48	3	167	7	1	9	13	.409	1	0-0 0	3.70	3.86
12	Mia	NL	19	19	0	0	121.0	504	119	59	53	12	4	5	2	33	2	110	4	1	5	7	.417	0	0-0 0	3.55	3.94
12	Det	AL	12	12	1	0	74.2	316	81	36	31	8	1	2	3	15	1	57	3	0	4	6	.400	1	0-0 0	3.95	3.74
	7 ML YEARS		145	144	7	0	869.0	3735	850	399	362	79	41	18	30	320	25	733	26	8	48	51	.485	5	0-0 0	3.85	3.75

Eduardo Sanchez

Pitches: R **Bats:** R **Pos:** RP-17 — **Ht:** 5'11" **Wt:** 170 **Born:** 2/16/1989 **Age:** 24

			HOW MUCH HE PITCHED						WHAT HE GAVE UP											THE RESULTS						
Year	Team	Lg	G	GS	CG	GF	IP	BFP	H	R	ER	HR	SH	SF	HB	TBB	IBB	SO	WP	Bk	W	L	Pct	Sh	Sv-Op Hld	ERC	ERA
2007	Cards	R	7	0	0	6	6.0	26	2	2	1	0	0	0	0	6	0	7	0	0	0	1	.000	0	3- - -	2.02	1.50
2007	JhsCty	R+	12	0	0	9	15.1	57	8	2	2	0	2	0	0	3	0	22	3	1	2	1	.667	0	5- - -	0.90	1.17
2008	QuadC	A	24	5	0	9	56.2	233	40	23	18	1	5	4	8	25	0	55	3	0	5	1	.833	0	1- - -	2.70	2.86
2009	PlmBh	A+	19	0	0	9	25.0	93	12	4	4	2	2	1	3	5	0	26	1	0	1	0	1.000	0	3- - -	1.32	1.44
2009	Sprgfld	AA	41	0	0	19	50.0	197	32	16	15	4	1	1	4	20	1	56	4	1	2	0	1.000	0	10- - -	2.46	2.70

			HOW MUCH HE PITCHED						WHAT HE GAVE UP													THE RESULTS							
Year	Team	Lg	G	GS	CG	GF	IP	BFP	H	R	ER	HR	SH	SF	HB	TBB	IBB	SO	WP	Bk	W	L	Pct	Sh	Sv-Op	Hld	ERC	ERA
2010	Sprgfld	AA	24	0	0	19	26.0	106	22	13	9	2	0	1	2	8	0	27	2	0	1	1	.500	0	11--	-	3.10	3.12
2010	Memp	AAA	26	0	0	10	27.0	110	19	7	5	2	1	0	2	12	1	31	8	0	0	0		0	3--	-	2.78	1.67
2011	Memp	AAA	2	0	0	1	3.0	9	0	0	0	0	0	0	0	0	0	3	0	0	1	0	1.000	0	0--	-	0.00	0.00
2011	Sprgfld	AA	3	0	0	0	4.1	20	3	3	2	0	1	0	2	2	0	3	2	0	0	0		0	0--	-	3.50	4.15
2012	Memp	AAA	30	0	0	23	27.2	135	27	19	18	3	0	1	6	21	1	26	2	0	2	3	.400	0	9--	-	6.21	5.86
2011	StL	NL	26	0	0	11	30.0	118	14	6	6	1	0	2	3	16	0	35	5	0	3	1	.750	0	5-7	7	1.85	1.80
2012	StL	NL	17	0	0	4	15.0	70	11	11	11	2	1	1	1	13	4	13	4	0	0	1	.000	0	0-0	4	4.32	6.60
	2 ML YEARS		43	0	0	15	45.0	188	25	17	17	3	1	3	4	29	4	48	9	0	3	2	.600	0	5-7	11	2.62	3.40

Freddy Sanchez

Bats: R Throws: R Pos: 2B   **Ht: 6'0" Wt: 200 Born: 12/21/1977 Age: 35**

			BATTING																		BASERUNNING				AVERAGES		
Year	Team	Lg	G	AB	H	2B	3B	HR	(Hm	Rd)	TB	R	RBI	RC	TBB	IBB	SO	HBP	SH	SF	SB	CS	SB%	GDP	Avg	OBP	Slg
2012	SnJos*	A+	3	10	4	0	0	0	(-	-)	4	1	3	1	0	0	1	0	0	0	0	0	-	2	.400	.400	.400
2002	Bos	AL	12	16	3	0	0	0	(0	0)	3	3	2	1	2	0	3	0	0	0	0	0	-	0	.188	.278	.188
2003	Bos	AL	20	34	8	2	0	0	(0	0)	10	6	2	1	0	0	8	0	0	0	0	0	-	0	.235	.235	.294
2004	Pit	NL	9	19	3	0	0	0	(0	0)	3	2	2	2	0	0	3	0	1	0	0	0	-	0	.158	.158	.158
2005	Pit	NL	132	453	132	26	4	5	(3	2)	181	54	35	57	27	1	36	5	4	3	2	2	.50	6	.291	.336	.400
2006	Pit	NL	157	582	200	53	2	6	(2	4)	275	85	85	101	31	6	52	7	3	9	3	2	.60	12	.344	.378	.473
2007	Pit	NL	147	602	183	42	4	11	(5	6)	266	77	81	94	32	2	76	8	2	9	0	1	.00	13	.304	.343	.442
2008	Pit	NL	145	569	154	26	2	9	(1	8)	211	75	52	61	21	1	63	4	8	6	0	1	.00	13	.271	.298	.371
2009	2 Tms	NL	111	457	134	29	3	7	(3	4)	190	56	41	59	22	4	76	2	4	4	5	1	.83	5	.293	.326	.416
2010	SF	NL	111	431	126	22	1	7	(1	6)	171	55	47	59	32	1	68	3	8	5	3	1	.75	9	.292	.342	.397
2011	SF	NL	60	239	69	15	1	3	(0	3)	95	21	24	30	13	3	35	3	5	1	0	1	.00	2	.289	.332	.397
09	Pit	NL	86	355	105	28	3	6	(3	3)	157	45	34	49	20	4	60	2	2	3	5	1	.83	5	.296	.334	.442
09	SF	NL	25	102	29	1	0	1	(0	1)	33	11	7	10	2	0	16	0	2	1	0	0	-	3	.284	.295	.324
	Postseason		15	63	16	4	0	0	(0	0)	20	5	3	5	1	0	8	1	2	0	0	0	-	2	.254	.277	.317
	10 ML YEARS		904	3402	1012	215	17	48	(15	33)	1405	434	371	465	180	18	420	32	35	37	13	9	.59	67	.297	.335	.413

Gaby Sanchez

Bats: R Throws: R Pos: 1B-95; PH-16; PR-1   GABB-ee   **Ht: 6'1" Wt: 230 Born: 9/2/1983 Age: 29**

			BATTING																		BASERUNNING				AVERAGES		
Year	Team	Lg	G	AB	H	2B	3B	HR	(Hm	Rd)	TB	R	RBI	RC	TBB	IBB	SO	HBP	SH	SF	SB	CS	SB%	GDP	Avg	OBP	Slg
2012	NewOr*	AAA	34	116	35	7	0	5	(-	-)	57	20	18	25	22	1	23	5	0	1	2	2	.50	6	.302	.431	.491
2008	Fla	NL	5	8	3	2	0	0	(2	0)	5	0	1	2	0	0	2	0	0	0	0	0	-	1	.375	.375	.625
2009	Fla	NL	21	21	5	0	0	2	(2	0)	11	2	3	3	2	0	3	0	0	0	0	0	-	1	.238	.304	.524
2010	Fla	NL	151	572	156	37	3	19	(7	12)	256	72	85	88	57	2	101	5	3	6	5	0	1.00	14	.273	.341	.448
2011	Fla	NL	159	572	152	35	0	19	(11	8)	244	72	78	77	74	4	97	6	2	7	3	1	.75	18	.266	.352	.427
2012	2 Tms	NL	105	299	65	16	0	7	(1	6)	102	30	30	21	25	2	56	1	0	1	1	0	1.00	13	.217	.279	.341
12	Mia	NL	55	183	37	10	0	3	(1	2)	56	12	17	10	12	1	36	0	0	1	1	0	1.00	7	.202	.250	.306
12	Pit	NL	50	116	28	6	0	4	(0	4)	46	18	13	11	13	1	20	1	0	0	0	0	-	6	.241	.323	.397
	5 ML YEARS		441	1472	381	90	3	47	(21	26)	618	176	197	191	158	8	259	12	5	14	9	1	.90	46	.259	.333	.420

Hector Sanchez

Bats: B Throws: R Pos: C-56; PH-19; DH-1   **Ht: 5'11" Wt: 225 Born: 11/17/1989 Age: 23**

			BATTING																		BASERUNNING				AVERAGES		
Year	Team	Lg	G	AB	H	2B	3B	HR	(Hm	Rd)	TB	R	RBI	RC	TBB	IBB	SO	HBP	SH	SF	SB	CS	SB%	GDP	Avg	OBP	Slg
2009	Giants	R	33	117	35	8	1	1	(-	-)	48	13	22	21	16	0	21	5	0	1	0	0	-	1	.299	.403	.410
2010	Augsta	A	89	310	85	20	1	5	(-	-)	122	29	31	41	28	2	50	1	2	0	0	2	.00	14	.274	.336	.394
2011	SnJos	A+	52	212	64	14	1	11	(-	-)	113	31	58	38	11	1	49	2	0	3	0	1	.00	6	.302	.338	.533
2011	Fresno	AAA	46	153	40	9	0	1	(-	-)	52	15	26	17	13	2	22	0	0	2	0	1	.00	6	.261	.315	.340
2012	Fresno	AAA	4	15	1	0	0	0	(-	-)	1	0	1	0	0	0	1	0	0	0	0	0	-	0	.067	.067	.067
2011	SF	NL	13	31	8	2	0	0	(0	0)	10	0	1	2	3	0	6	0	0	0	0	0	-	1	.258	.324	.323
2012	SF	NL	74	218	61	15	0	3	(1	2)	85	22	34	22	5	0	52	1	0	3	0	0	-	8	.280	.295	.390
	2 ML YEARS		87	249	69	17	0	3	(1	2)	95	22	35	24	8	0	58	1	0	3	0	0	-	9	.277	.299	.382

Jonathan Sanchez

Pitches: L Bats: L Pos: SP-15   **Ht: 6'0" Wt: 198 Born: 11/19/1982 Age: 30**

			HOW MUCH HE PITCHED						WHAT HE GAVE UP													THE RESULTS							
Year	Team	Lg	G	GS	CG	GF	IP	BFP	H	R	ER	HR	SH	SF	HB	TBB	IBB	SO	WP	Bk	W	L	Pct	Sh	Sv-Op	Hld	ERC	ERA
2012	Omha*	AAA	3	3	0	0	13.1	61	14	10	10	5	0	0	1	7	0	13	1	0	1	1	.500	0	0--	-	7.31	6.75
2006	SF	NL	27	4	0	4	40.0	185	39	26	22	2	0	4	2	23	0	33	2	0	3	1	.750	0	0-0	5	4.54	4.95
2007	SF	NL	33	4	0	8	52.0	238	57	34	34	8	2	2	5	28	1	62	4	0	1	5	.167	0	0-0	2	6.06	5.88
2008	SF	NL	29	29	0	0	158.0	695	154	90	88	14	8	7	5	75	1	157	7	0	9	12	.429	0	0-0	0	4.31	5.01
2009	SF	NL	32	29	1	2	163.1	710	135	82	77	19	3	1	6	88	5	177	11	0	8	12	.400	1	0-0	1	3.83	4.24
2010	SF	NL	34	33	0	0	193.1	812	142	74	66	21	7	4	9	96	4	205	15	1	13	9	.591	0	0-0	1	3.21	3.07
2011	SF	NL	19	19	0	0	101.1	444	80	54	48	9	4	6	2	66	2	102	5	0	4	7	.364	0	0-0	0	4.02	4.26
2012	2 Tms		15	15	0	0	64.2	327	82	60	58	11	2	6	5	53	2	45	6	1	1	9	.100	0	0-0	0	8.37	8.07
12	KC	AL	12	12	0	0	53.1	270	65	47	46	8	2	4	5	44	1	36	4	1	1	6	.143	0	0-0	0	7.92	7.76
12	Col	NL	3	3	0	0	11.1	57	17	13	12	3	0	2	0	9	1	9	2	0	0	3	.000	0	0-0	0	10.60	9.53
	Postseason		4	4	0	0	20.0	86	16	10	9	2	0	2	1	9	0	22	1	0	0	2	.000	0	0-0	0	3.30	4.05
	7 ML YEARS		189	133	1	14	772.2	3411	689	420	393	84	27	24	42	429	15	781	50	2	39	55	.415	1	0-0	9	4.31	4.58

Pablo Sandoval

Bats: B **Throws:** R **Pos:** 3B-102; 1B-3; PH-3; DH-2   **Ht:** 5'11" **Wt:** 240 **Born:** 8/11/1986 **Age:** 26

Year	Team	Lg	G	AB	H	2B	3B	HR	(Hm	Rd)	TB	R	RBI	RC	TBB	IBB	SO	HBP	SH	SF	SB	CS	SB%	GDP	Avg	OBP	Slg
2012	SnJos*	A+	6	22	6	2	0	1	(-	-)	11	1	1	3	1	0	5	0	0	0	0	0	-	1	.273	.304	.500
2012	Fresno*	AAA	3	11	3	1	0	2	(-	-)	10	3	2	3	1	0	0	0	0	0	0	0	-	0	.273	.333	.909
2008	SF	NL	41	145	50	10	1	3	(1	2)	71	24	24	24	4	1	14	1	0	4	0	0	-	6	.345	.357	.490
2009	SF	NL	153	572	189	44	5	25	(13	12)	318	79	90	113	52	13	83	4	0	5	5	5	.50	10	.330	.387	.556
2010	SF	NL	152	563	151	34	3	13	(9	4)	230	61	63	55	47	12	81	1	0	5	3	2	.60	26	.268	.323	.409
2011	SF	NL	117	426	134	26	3	23	(7	16)	235	55	70	72	32	9	63	0	1	7	2	4	.33	12	.315	.357	.552
2012	SF	NL	108	396	112	25	2	12	(7	5)	177	59	63	60	38	4	59	1	0	7	1	1	.50	13	.283	.342	.447
	Postseason		6	17	3	1	0	0	(0	0)	4	0	2	1	2	1	3	0	0	0	0	0	-	3	.176	.263	.235
	5 ML YEARS		571	2102	636	139	14	76	(37	39)	1031	278	310	324	173	39	300	7	1	28	11	12	.48	67	.303	.353	.490

Jerry Sands

Bats: R **Throws:** R **Pos:** LF-6; PH-2; 1B-1; RF-1   **Ht:** 6'4" **Wt:** 225 **Born:** 9/28/1987 **Age:** 25

Year	Team	Lg	G	AB	H	2B	3B	HR	(Hm	Rd)	TB	R	RBI	RC	TBB	IBB	SO	HBP	SH	SF	SB	CS	SB%	GDP	Avg	OBP	Slg
2008	Ddgrs	R	46	146	30	4	0	10	(-	-)	64	29	33	25	29	0	43	5	0	5	1	0	1.00	4	.205	.346	.438
2009	Gt Lks	A	32	104	27	7	2	5	(-	-)	53	22	19	20	15	0	32	2	1	1	1	0	1.00	2	.260	.361	.510
2009	Ogden*	R+	41	163	57	9	2	14	(-	-)	112	41	39	44	22	1	28	0	0	0	1	0	1.00	1	.350	.427	.687
2010	Gt Lks	A	69	243	81	16	3	18	(-	-)	157	48	46	66	40	6	61	3	0	1	14	2	.88	5	.333	.432	.646
2010	Chatt	AA	68	259	70	12	2	17	(-	-)	137	54	47	51	33	2	62	6	0	5	4	0	1.00	9	.270	.360	.529
2011	Albq	AAA	94	370	103	21	3	29	(-	-)	217	78	88	75	38	2	86	3	0	7	3	1	.75	11	.278	.344	.586
2012	Albq	AAA	119	452	134	17	4	26	(-	-)	237	84	107	91	59	1	106	0	1	8	1	0	1.00	11	.296	.375	.524
2011	LAD	NL	61	198	50	15	0	4	(2	2)	77	20	26	25	25	0	51	1	2	1	3	3	.50	5	.253	.338	.389
2012	LAD	NL	9	23	4	2	0	0	(0	0)	6	2	1	1	1	0	9	0	0	0	0	0	-	0	.174	.208	.261
	2 ML YEARS		70	221	54	17	0	4	(2	2)	83	22	27	26	26	0	60	1	2	1	3	3	.50	5	.244	.325	.376

Carlos Santana

Bats: B **Throws:** R **Pos:** C-100; DH-27; 1B-21; LF-1; PH-1   **Ht:** 5'11" **Wt:** 200 **Born:** 4/8/1986 **Age:** 27

Year	Team	Lg	G	AB	H	2B	3B	HR	(Hm	Rd)	TB	R	RBI	RC	TBB	IBB	SO	HBP	SH	SF	SB	CS	SB%	GDP	Avg	OBP	Slg
2012	Lk Cty*	A	1	4	1	0	0	1	(-	-)	4	1	2	1	0	0	0	0	0	0	0	0	-	0	.250	.250	1.000
2010	Cle	AL	46	150	39	13	0	6	(2	4)	70	23	22	25	37	2	29	1	0	4	3	0	1.00	3	.260	.401	.467
2011	Cle	AL	155	552	132	35	2	27	(14	13)	252	84	79	81	97	7	133	2	0	7	5	3	.63	15	.239	.351	.457
2012	Cle	AL	143	507	128	27	2	18	(7	11)	213	72	76	77	91	4	101	3	0	8	3	5	.38	21	.252	.365	.420
	3 ML YEARS		344	1209	299	75	4	51	(23	28)	535	179	177	183	225	13	263	6	0	19	11	8	.58	39	.247	.363	.443

Ervin Santana

Pitches: R **Bats:** R **Pos:** SP-30   **Ht:** 6'2" **Wt:** 185 **Born:** 12/12/1982 **Age:** 30

			HOW MUCH HE PITCHED					WHAT HE GAVE UP											THE RESULTS						
Year	Team	Lg	G	GS	CG	GF	IP	BFP	H	R	ER	HR	SH	SF	HB	TBB	IBB	SO	WP	Bk	W	L	Pct	Sh	Sv-Op	Hld	ERC	ERA
2005	LAA	AL	23	23	1	0	133.2	583	139	73	69	17	1	4	8	47	2	99	4	0	12	8	.600	1	0-0	0	4.51	4.65
2006	LAA	AL	33	33	0	0	204.0	846	181	106	97	21	4	10	11	70	2	141	10	2	16	8	.667	0	0-0	0	3.51	4.28
2007	LAA	AL	28	26	0	1	150.0	675	174	103	96	26	3	2	8	58	3	126	7	0	7	14	.333	0	0-0	0	5.69	5.76
2008	LAA	AL	32	32	2	0	219.0	897	198	89	85	23	3	5	8	47	2	214	5	1	16	7	.696	1	0-0	0	3.00	3.49
2009	LAA	AL	24	23	2	0	139.2	614	159	83	78	24	2	1	10	47	4	107	4	0	8	8	.500	2	0-0	1	5.47	5.03
2010	LAA	AL	33	33	4	0	222.2	954	221	104	97	27	8	8	12	73	2	169	11	1	17	10	.630	1	0-0	0	4.10	3.92
2011	LAA	AL	33	33	4	0	228.2	949	207	95	86	26	4	7	8	72	4	178	10	1	11	12	.478	1	0-0	0	3.45	3.38
2012	LAA	AL	30	30	1	0	178.0	764	165	109	102	39	2	2	9	61	2	133	4	0	9	13	.409	1	0-0	0	4.38	5.16
	Postseason		8	2	0	3	22.2	101	21	17	14	4	1	1	3	9	1	14	0	0	2	2	.500	0	0-0	0	4.55	5.56
	8 ML YEARS		236	233	14	1	1475.2	6282	1444	762	710	203	27	39	74	475	21	1167	55	5	96	80	.545	7	0-0	1	4.09	4.33

Johan Santana

Pitches: L **Bats:** L **Pos:** SP-21   YOE-hahn   **Ht:** 6'0" **Wt:** 210 **Born:** 3/13/1979 **Age:** 34

			HOW MUCH HE PITCHED					WHAT HE GAVE UP											THE RESULTS						
Year	Team	Lg	G	GS	CG	GF	IP	BFP	H	R	ER	HR	SH	SF	HB	TBB	IBB	SO	WP	Bk	W	L	Pct	Sh	Sv-Op	Hld	ERC	ERA
2012	Bklyn*	A-	1	1	0	0	3.0	11	1	0	0	0	0	0	0	1	0	3	0	0	0	0	-	0	0- -	-	0.69	0.00
2000	Min	AL	30	5	0	9	86.0	398	102	64	62	11	1	3	2	54	0	64	5	2	2	3	.400	0	0-0	0	6.59	6.49
2001	Min	AL	15	4	0	5	43.2	195	50	25	23	6	2	3	3	16	0	28	3	0	1	0	1.000	0	0-0	0	5.36	4.74
2002	Min	AL	27	14	0	2	108.1	452	84	41	36	7	3	3	1	49	0	137	15	2	8	6	.571	0	1-1	3	2.86	2.99
2003	Min	AL	45	18	0	7	158.1	644	127	56	54	17	2	4	3	47	1	169	6	2	12	3	.800	0	0-0	5	2.73	3.07
2004	Min	AL	34	34	1	0	228.0	881	156	70	66	24	3	3	9	54	0	265	7	0	20	6	.769	1	0-0	0	2.07	2.61
2005	Min	AL	33	33	3	0	231.2	910	180	77	74	22	6	2	1	45	1	238	8	0	16	7	.696	2	0-0	0	2.14	2.87
2006	Min	AL	34	34	1	0	233.2	923	186	79	72	24	6	4	4	47	0	245	4	1	19	6	.760	0	0-0	0	2.36	2.77
2007	Min	AL	33	33	1	0	219.0	878	183	88	81	33	4	4	4	52	0	235	7	1	15	13	.536	1	0-0	0	2.98	3.33
2008	NYM	NL	34	34	3	0	234.1	964	206	74	66	23	9	1	4	63	5	206	9	2	16	7	.696	2	0-0	0	2.93	2.53
2009	NYM	NL	25	25	0	0	166.2	701	156	67	58	20	8	3	3	46	3	146	1	0	13	9	.591	0	0-0	0	3.37	3.13
2010	NYM	NL	29	29	4	0	199.0	817	179	67	66	16	10	5	2	55	2	144	2	2	11	9	.550	2	0-0	0	2.96	2.98
2012	NYM	NL	21	21	2	0	117.0	499	117	65	63	17	4	3	0	39	1	111	1	0	6	9	.400	2	0-0	0	4.09	4.85
	Postseason		11	5	0	0	34.0	143	35	15	15	2	0	0	1	10	1	32	2	0	1	3	.250	0	0-0	1	3.66	3.97
	12 ML YEARS		360	284	15	23	2025.2	8262	1726	773	721	220	58	38	36	567	13	1988	68	12	139	78	.641	10	1-1	8	2.94	3.20

Hector Santiago

Pitches: L **Bats:** R **Pos:** RP-38; SP-4　　　　**Ht:** 6'0" **Wt:** 210 **Born:** 12/16/1987 **Age:** 25

Year	Team	Lg	G	GS	CG	GF	IP	BFP	H	R	ER	HR	SH	SF	HB	TBB	IBB	SO	WP	Bk	W	L	Pct	Sh	Sv-Op	Hld	ERC	ERA
2007	Bristol	R	17	0	0	4	32.2	129	19	7	6	1	4	0	1	16	0	38	1	0	1	1	.500	0	0- -	-	1.99	1.65
2008	Knapol	A	38	0	0	12	64.1	291	57	37	29	1	6	1	3	44	0	83	8	2	5	1	.833	0	1- -	-	4.06	4.06
2009	WinSa	A+	38	0	0	15	58.0	248	54	34	25	5	3	3	3	25	3	66	3	1	4	4	.500	0	1- -	-	3.88	3.88
2010	WinSa	A+	37	1	0	9	60.2	269	63	29	28	4	3	7	3	19	1	61	1	1	4	5	.444	0	2- -	-	3.75	4.15
2011	WinSa	A+	8	8	0	0	44.0	181	38	18	18	7	2	1	3	14	0	43	3	0	2	3	.400	0	0- -	-	3.73	3.68
2011	Brham	AA	15	15	0	0	83.1	350	71	34	33	4	3	2	4	39	1	74	6	3	7	5	.583	0	0- -	-	3.40	3.56
2012	Charltt	AAA	3	3	0	0	14.2	54	9	0	0	0	0	0	0	6	0	13	0	0	1	0	1.000	0	0- -	-	1.73	0.00
2011	CWS	AL	2	0	0	1	5.1	18	1	0	0	0	0	0	0	1	1	2	1	0			-	0	0-0	0	0.16	0.00
2012	CWS	AL	42	4	0	19	70.1	306	54	26	26	10	2	1	7	40	1	79	5	2	4	1	.800	0	4-6	4	4.11	3.33
	2 ML YEARS		44	4	0	20	75.2	324	55	26	26	10	2	1	7	41	2	81	6	2	4	1	.800	0	4-6	4	3.66	3.09

Ramon Santiago

Bats: B **Throws:** R **Pos:** 2B-71; SS-20; PH-9; 3B-6; PR-1　　　　**Ht:** 5'11" **Wt:** 175 **Born:** 8/31/1979 **Age:** 33

Year	Team	Lg	G	AB	H	2B	3B	HR	(Hm	Rd)	TB	R	RBI	RC	TBB	IBB	SO	HBP	SH	SF	SB	CS	SB%	GDP	Avg	OBP	Slg
2002	Det	AL	65	222	54	5	5	4	(3	1)	81	33	20	23	13	0	48	8	4	2	8	5	.62	2	.243	.306	.365
2003	Det	AL	141	444	100	18	1	2	(1	1)	126	41	29	38	33	0	66	10	18	2	10	4	.71	9	.225	.292	.284
2004	Sea	AL	19	39	7	1	0	0	(0	0)	8	8	2	1	3	0	3	1	2	0	0	0	-	1	.179	.256	.205
2005	Sea	AL	8	8	1	0	0	0	(0	0)	1	2	0	1	1	0	2	3	1	0	0	0	-	0	.125	.417	.125
2006	Det	AL	43	80	18	1	1	0	(0	0)	21	9	3	3	3	0	14	1	4	0	2	0	1.00	1	.225	.244	.263
2007	Det	AL	32	67	19	5	1	0	(0	0)	26	10	7	11	1	0	10	3	3	0	3	0	1.00	0	.284	.324	.388
2008	Det	AL	58	124	35	6	2	4	(4	0)	57	30	18	26	22	0	17	5	5	0	1	0	1.00	1	.282	.411	.460
2009	Det	AL	93	262	70	6	2	7	(4	3)	101	29	35	33	17	1	57	4	10	3	1	2	.33	3	.267	.318	.385
2010	Det	AL	112	320	84	9	1	3	(3	0)	104	38	22	37	30	0	56	7	8	2	2	2	.50	6	.263	.337	.325
2011	Det	AL	101	258	67	11	3	5	(3	2)	99	29	30	25	17	0	38	4	11	4	0	0	-	5	.260	.311	.384
2012	Det	AL	93	228	47	7	1	2	(1	1)	62	19	17	17	20	1	39	5	5	1	1	0	1.00	1	.206	.283	.272
	Postseason		16	50	12	2	0	0	(0	0)	14	1	2	3	1	0	9	0	3	0	0	0	-	3	.240	.255	.280
	11 ML YEARS		765	2052	502	69	17	27	(19	8)	686	248	183	215	158	2	350	51	71	14	28	13	.68	35	.245	.313	.334

Omir Santos

Bats: R **Throws:** R **Pos:** C-3　　　　OH-meer　　　　**Ht:** 6'0" **Wt:** 213 **Born:** 4/29/1981 **Age:** 32

Year	Team	Lg	G	AB	H	2B	3B	HR	(Hm	Rd)	TB	R	RBI	RC	TBB	IBB	SO	HBP	SH	SF	SB	CS	SB%	GDP	Avg	OBP	Slg
2012	Toledo*	AAA	23	84	26	7	1	0	(-	-)	35	7	9	11	2	0	17	0	0	3	0	1	.00	0	.310	.315	.417
2012	ColSpr*	AAA	38	119	37	9	0	2	(-	-)	52	12	21	16	2	0	17	0	1	1	0	0	-	5	.311	.320	.437
2008	Bal	AL	11	10	1	0	0	0	(0	0)	1	0	0	0	0	0	2	0	0	0	0	0	-	0	.100	.100	.100
2009	NYM	NL	96	281	73	14	1	7	(2	5)	110	28	40	29	15	1	44	2	2	6	0	0	-	9	.260	.296	.391
2011	Det	AL	11	22	5	0	0	0	(0	0)	5	1	0	0	0	0	4	0	0	0	0	0	-	0	.227	.227	.227
2012	Det	AL	3	8	1	0	0	0	(0	0)	1	0	1	0	0	0	1	0	1	1	0	0	-	2	.125	.111	.125
	Postseason		1	0	0	0	0	0	(0	0)	0	0	0	0	0	0	0	0	0	0	0	0	-	0	-	-	-
	4 ML YEARS		121	321	80	14	1	7	(2	5)	117	29	41	29	15	1	51	2	3	7	0	0	-	11	.249	.281	.364

Sergio Santos

Pitches: R **Bats:** R **Pos:** RP-6　　　　**Ht:** 6'3" **Wt:** 240 **Born:** 7/4/1983 **Age:** 29

Year	Team	Lg	G	GS	CG	GF	IP	BFP	H	R	ER	HR	SH	SF	HB	TBB	IBB	SO	WP	Bk	W	L	Pct	Sh	Sv-Op	Hld	ERC	ERA
2010	CWS	AL	56	0	0	13	51.2	235	53	18	17	2	2	1	3	26	3	56	8	0	2	2	.500	0	1-3	14	4.22	2.96
2011	CWS	AL	63	0	0	50	63.1	260	41	25	25	6	1	1	3	29	5	92	5	0	4	5	.444	0	30-36	2	2.46	3.55
2012	Tor	AL	6	0	0	4	5.0	24	6	5	5	1	0	1	0	4	0	4	1	0	0	1	.000	0	2-4	0	7.98	9.00
	3 ML YEARS		125	0	0	67	120.0	519	100	48	47	9	3	3	6	59	8	152	14	0	6	8	.429	0	33-43	16	3.39	3.53

Dave Sappelt

Bats: R **Throws:** R **Pos:** RF-20; PH-8; LF-4; PR-1　　　　sap-PELT　　　　**Ht:** 5'9" **Wt:** 195 **Born:** 1/2/1987 **Age:** 26

Year	Team	Lg	G	AB	H	2B	3B	HR	(Hm	Rd)	TB	R	RBI	RC	TBB	IBB	SO	HBP	SH	SF	SB	CS	SB%	GDP	Avg	OBP	Slg
2008	Billings	R+	62	254	76	19	5	7	(-	-)	126	47	35	44	21	0	45	1	2	1	6	3	.67	5	.299	.354	.496
2009	Dayton	A	74	301	81	14	7	3	(-	-)	118	44	25	40	23	1	46	2	2	3	26	11	.70	4	.269	.322	.392
2009	Srsota	A+	62	251	74	10	3	4	(-	-)	102	27	21	34	13	0	29	2	4	1	21	11	.66	2	.295	.333	.406
2010	Lynbrg	A+	19	71	20	5	0	0	(-	-)	25	7	4	8	5	0	15	1	0	0	6	4	.60	1	.282	.338	.352
2010	Carlina	AA	89	330	119	19	8	9	(-	-)	181	53	62	71	31	3	46	3	4	4	15	13	.54	5	.361	.416	.548
2010	Lsvlle	AAA	25	108	35	8	3	1	(-	-)	52	12	8	19	6	0	13	1	0	0	4	1	.80	0	.324	.365	.481
2011	Lsvlle	AAA	74	297	93	16	3	7	(-	-)	136	40	29	52	30	2	39	2	4	3	4	4	.50	3	.313	.377	.458
2012	Iowa	AAA	133	500	133	26	4	7	(-	-)	188	50	54	63	36	1	73	2	6	6	15	6	.71	13	.266	.314	.376
2011	Cin	NL	38	107	26	8	0	0	(0	0)	34	14	5	9	7	0	17	0	4	0	1	1	.50	1	.243	.289	.318
2012	ChC	NL	26	69	19	6	0	2	(0	2)	31	8	8	11	7	1	9	1	1	0	0	0	-	1	.275	.351	.449
	2 ML YEARS		64	176	45	14	0	2	(0	2)	65	22	13	20	14	1	26	1	5	0	1	1	.50	2	.256	.314	.369

Josh Satin

Bats: R **Throws:** R **Pos:** PH-1   SAT-inn   **Ht:** 6'2" **Wt:** 200 **Born:** 12/23/1984 **Age:** 28

Year	Team	Lg	G	AB	H	2B	3B	HR	(Hm	Rd)	TB	R	RBI	RC	TBB	IBB	SO	HBP	SH	SF	SB	CS	SB%	GDP	Avg	OBP	Slg
2008	Bklyn	A-	45	143	40	10	2	4	(-	-)	66	21	13	23	16	0	28	0	4	1	0	1	.00	4	.280	.350	.462
2008	Kngspt	R	3	12	7	2	0	1	(-	-)	12	3	2	5	1	0	2	0	0	0	0	0	-	0	.583	.615	1.000
2009	Savann	A	125	440	125	38	0	7	(-	-)	184	62	60	75	73	1	103	2	0	5	0	3	.00	6	.284	.385	.418
2009	StLuci	A+	7	22	8	2	0	1	(-	-)	13	6	5	6	5	0	7	0	0	1	0	0	-	0	.364	.464	.591
2010	StLuci	A+	58	209	66	15	0	5	(-	-)	96	27	35	39	30	0	50	3	1	2	1	5	.17	6	.316	.406	.459
2010	Bnghtn	AA	79	286	88	24	1	7	(-	-)	135	49	39	55	36	0	71	7	0	3	1	0	1.00	8	.308	.395	.472
2011	Bnghtn	AA	94	338	110	35	2	11	(-	-)	182	60	60	77	57	0	91	4	0	5	2	2	.50	6	.325	.423	.538
2011	Buffalo	AAA	38	145	46	8	0	1	(-	-)	57	17	16	22	14	0	33	1	0	0	1	2	.33	4	.317	.381	.393
2012	Buffalo	AAA	131	441	126	25	1	14	(-	-)	195	72	60	81	77	2	109	3	0	6	3	4	.43	18	.286	.391	.442
2011	NYM	NL	15	25	5	1	0	0	(0	0)	6	3	2	1	1	0	11	1	0	0	0	0	-	1	.200	.259	.240
2012	NYM	NL	1	1	0	0	0	0	(0	0)	0	0	0	0	0	0	1	0	0	0	0	0	-	0	.000	.000	.000
	2 ML YEARS		16	26	5	1	0	0	(0	0)	6	3	2	1	1	0	12	1	0	0	0	0	-	1	.192	.250	.231

Joe Saunders

Pitches: L **Bats:** L **Pos:** SP-28   **Ht:** 6'3" **Wt:** 210 **Born:** 6/16/1981 **Age:** 32

				HOW MUCH HE PITCHED					WHAT HE GAVE UP											THE RESULTS						
Year	Team	Lg	G	GS	CG	GF	IP	BFP	H	R	ER	HR	SH	SF	HB	TBB	IBB	SO	WP	Bk	W	L	Pct	Sh	Sv-Op	Hld	ERC	ERA
2012	DBcks*	R	1	1	0	0	4.1	22	3	5	3	0	0	0	0	5	0	7	0	0	0	1	.000	0	0- -	-	4.09	6.23
2005	LAA	AL	2	2	0	0	9.1	41	10	8	8	3	0	0	0	4	0	4	1	0	0	0	-	0	0-0	0	6.27	7.71
2006	LAA	AL	13	13	0	0	70.2	302	71	42	37	6	1	2	1	29	1	51	2	1	7	3	.700	0	0-0	0	4.13	4.71
2007	LAA	AL	18	18	0	0	107.1	473	129	56	53	11	0	5	1	34	1	69	3	0	8	5	.615	0	0-0	0	4.96	4.44
2008	LAA	AL	31	31	1	0	198.0	807	187	82	75	21	5	2	6	53	2	103	3	0	17	7	.708	0	0-0	0	3.49	3.41
2009	LAA	AL	31	31	1	0	186.0	805	202	102	95	29	6	4	6	64	2	101	5	1	16	7	.696	1	0-0	0	4.91	4.60
2010	2 Tms		33	33	3	0	203.1	880	232	120	101	25	6	8	5	64	1	114	6	0	9	17	.346	1	0-0	0	4.86	4.47
2011	Ari	NL	33	33	1	0	212.0	874	210	94	87	29	9	5	3	67	4	108	3	0	12	13	.480	0	0-0	0	4.10	3.69
2012	2 Tms		28	28	1	0	174.2	745	195	88	79	21	7	3	2	39	2	112	3	0	9	13	.409	1	0-0	0	4.19	4.07
10	LAA	AL	20	20	2	0	120.2	522	135	70	62	14	5	5	1	45	1	64	3	0	6	10	.375	1	0-0	0	4.88	4.62
10	Ari	NL	13	13	1	0	82.2	358	97	50	39	11	1	3	4	19	0	50	3	0	3	7	.300	0	0-0	0	4.84	4.25
12	Ari	NL	21	21	1	0	130.0	561	146	68	61	17	5	2	2	31	1	89	2	0	6	10	.375	1	0-0	0	4.36	4.22
12	Bal	AL	7	7	0	0	44.2	184	49	20	18	4	2	1	0	8	1	23	1	0	3	3	.500	0	0-0	0	3.71	3.63
	Postseason		4	4	0	0	18.0	86	23	12	12	1	1	0	1	12	0	8	0	0	0	1	.000	0	0-0	0	6.85	6.00
	8 ML YEARS		189	189	7	0	1161.1	4927	1236	592	535	145	34	29	24	354	13	662	26	2	78	65	.545	3	0-0	0	4.36	4.15

Michael Saunders

Bats: L **Throws:** R **Pos:** CF-113; LF-22; RF-5; PH-5; PR-1   **Ht:** 6'4" **Wt:** 215 **Born:** 11/19/1986 **Age:** 26

									BATTING												BASERUNNING				AVERAGES		
Year	Team	Lg	G	AB	H	2B	3B	HR	(Hm	Rd)	TB	R	RBI	RC	TBB	IBB	SO	HBP	SH	SF	SB	CS	SB%	GDP	Avg	OBP	Slg
2009	Sea	AL	46	122	27	3	0	6	(0	0)	34	13	4	8	6	0	40	0	1	0	4	1	.80	1	.221	.258	.279
2010	Sea	AL	100	289	61	11	2	10	(5	5)	106	29	33	31	35	0	84	0	2	1	6	3	.67	1	.211	.295	.367
2011	Sea	AL	58	161	24	5	0	2	(1	1)	35	16	8	2	12	1	56	0	5	1	6	2	.75	1	.149	.207	.217
2012	Sea	AL	139	507	125	31	3	19	(8	11)	219	71	57	67	43	0	132	1	1	1	21	4	.84	6	.247	.306	.432
	4 ML YEARS		343	1079	237	48	8	31	(14	17)	394	129	102	108	96	1	312	1	9	3	37	10	.79	9	.220	.283	.365

Joe Savery

Pitches: L **Bats:** L **Pos:** RP-19   SAVE-uh-ree   **Ht:** 6'3" **Wt:** 235 **Born:** 11/4/1985 **Age:** 27

				HOW MUCH HE PITCHED					WHAT HE GAVE UP											THE RESULTS						
Year	Team	Lg	G	GS	CG	GF	IP	BFP	H	R	ER	HR	SH	SF	HB	TBB	IBB	SO	WP	Bk	W	L	Pct	Sh	Sv-Op	Hld	ERC	ERA
2007	Wmspt	A-	7	7	0	0	26.1	116	22	9	8	0	0	0	0	13	0	22	1	0	2	3	.400	0	0- -	-	2.72	2.73
2008	Clrwtr	A+	27	24	0	0	150.1	667	171	84	69	10	1	3	6	60	1	122	6	0	9	10	.474	0	0- -	-	4.80	4.13
2009	Rdng	AA	21	20	1	0	112.1	488	111	55	55	13	7	4	1	53	1	77	6	0	12	4	.750	0	0- -	-	4.46	4.41
2009	LV	AAA	7	7	1	0	39.0	180	42	23	19	0	3	4	1	24	0	19	2	0	4	2	.667	0	0- -	-	4.67	4.38
2010	LV	AAA	28	19	0	3	127.1	578	154	78	66	13	3	12	4	51	1	67	1	1	1	12	.077	0	0- -	-	5.42	4.66
2011	Clrwtr	A+	1	0	0	0	2.0	8	2	0	0	0	0	0	0	0	0	1	0	0	0	0	-	0	0- -	-	1.95	0.00
2011	Rdng	AA	6	0	0	0	9.0	33	7	1	1	0	0	0	0	6	0	14	0	0	1	0	1.000	0	0- -	-	1.24	1.00
2011	LV	AAA	18	0	0	3	25.0	100	23	6	5	0	3	2	0	6	0	26	1	0	4	0	1.000	0	2- -	-	2.47	1.80
2012	LV	AAA	20	0	0	8	23.1	107	27	14	11	3	1	0	1	9	1	26	1	0	1	1	.500	0	2- -	-	5.11	4.24
2011	Phi	NL	4	0	0	1	2.2	9	1	0	0	1	0	0	0	0	0	2	0	0	0	0	-	0	0-0	1	0.31	0.00
2012	Phi	NL	19	0	0	8	25.0	108	26	17	15	4	2	2	1	8	1	16	0	1	1	2	.333	0	0-0	1	4.49	5.40
	2 ML YEARS		23	0	0	9	27.2	117	27	17	15	4	3	2	1	8	1	18	0	1	1	2	.333	0	0-0	2	3.89	4.88

Rob Scahill

Pitches: R **Bats:** L **Pos:** RP-6   SKAY-hill   **Ht:** 6'2" **Wt:** 220 **Born:** 2/15/1987 **Age:** 26

				HOW MUCH HE PITCHED					WHAT HE GAVE UP											THE RESULTS						
Year	Team	Lg	G	GS	CG	GF	IP	BFP	H	R	ER	HR	SH	SF	HB	TBB	IBB	SO	WP	Bk	W	L	Pct	Sh	Sv-Op	Hld	ERC	ERA
2009	TriCity	A-	15	15	0	0	63.0	267	58	30	22	2	1	8	7	20	0	58	7	0	1	4	.200	0	0- -	-	3.37	3.14
2010	Mdest	A+	27	27	1	0	156.0	689	173	91	82	9	1	9	10	59	0	140	13	0	10	7	.588	0	0- -	-	4.58	4.73
2011	Tulsa	AA	27	26	1	1	160.2	693	164	81	70	12	7	5	5	60	0	104	16	0	12	11	.522	0	0- -	-	4.05	3.92
2012	ColSpr	AAA	29	29	1	0	152.0	693	168	109	96	11	10	3	7	74	0	159	8	0	9	11	.450	0	0- -	-	4.97	5.68
2012	Col	NL	6	0	0	3	8.2	33	7	1	1	0	0	0	0	3	0	4	0	0	0	0	-	0	0-0	1	2.43	1.04

Jordan Schafer

Bats: L **Throws:** L **Pos:** CF-87; PH-14; PR-8   **Ht:** 6'1" **Wt:** 190 **Born:** 9/4/1986 **Age:** 26

Year	Team	Lg	G	AB	H	2B	3B	HR	(Hm	Rd)	TB	R	RBI	RC	TBB	IBB	SO	HBP	SH	SF	SB	CS	SB%	GDP	Avg	OBP	Slg
2012	Astros*	R	1	2	1	0	0	0	(-	-)	1	0	0	0	0	0	0	0	0	0	0	0	-	0	.500	.500	.500
2012	OKCity*	AAA	4	13	2	0	0	0	(-	-)	2	2	0	0	2	0	1	0	0	0	2	0	1.00	0	.154	.267	.154
2009	Atl	NL	50	167	34	8	0	2	(0	2)	48	18	8	11	27	3	63	0	0	1	2	1	.67	2	.204	.313	.287
2011	2 Tms	NL	82	302	73	10	3	2	(0	2)	95	46	13	34	28	0	70	2	4	1	22	4	.85	4	.242	.309	.315
2012	Hou	NL	106	313	66	10	2	4	(4	0)	92	40	23	32	36	3	106	3	6	1	27	9	.75	3	.211	.297	.294
11	Atl	NL	52	196	47	6	3	1	(0	1)	62	32	7	22	18	0	42	1	4	0	15	4	.79	3	.240	.307	.316
11	Hou	NL	30	106	26	4	0	1	(0	1)	33	14	6	12	10	0	28	1	0	1	7	0	1.00	1	.245	.314	.311
3 ML YEARS			238	782	173	28	5	8	(4	4)	235	104	44	77	91	6	239	5	10	3	51	14	.78	9	.221	.305	.301

Logan Schafer

Bats: L **Throws:** L **Pos:** PH-9; CF-5; LF-2; RF-2   **Ht:** 6'1" **Wt:** 180 **Born:** 9/8/1986 **Age:** 26

Year	Team	Lg	G	AB	H	2B	3B	HR	(Hm	Rd)	TB	R	RBI	RC	TBB	IBB	SO	HBP	SH	SF	SB	CS	SB%	GDP	Avg	OBP	Slg
2008	Helena	R+	8	25	6	0	1	2	(-	-)	14	4	8	5	5	0	4	0	0	1	1	0	1.00	1	.240	.355	.560
2008	WV	A	43	181	50	13	2	0	(-	-)	67	25	20	18	8	0	42	1	3	3	3	8	.27	1	.276	.306	.370
2009	BrvdCt	A+	113	457	143	31	6	6	(-	-)	204	76	58	77	38	1	53	5	1	4	16	8	.67	5	.313	.369	.446
2009	Hntsvl	AA	7	23	5	0	1	0	(-	-)	7	4	0	3	4	0	3	2	1	0	1	0	1.00	0	.217	.379	.304
2010	BrvdCt	A+	7	23	4	2	0	0	(-	-)	6	7	1	2	4	0	6	0	0	1	0	0	-	1	.174	.286	.261
2011	BrvdCt	A+	9	36	11	0	0	0	(-	-)	11	4	1	4	5	0	4	0	0	0	1	1	.50	0	.306	.390	.306
2011	Hntsvl	AA	51	190	57	9	4	0	(-	-)	74	32	19	28	17	0	25	3	2	0	10	5	.67	0	.300	.367	.389
2011	Nashv	AAA	40	169	56	13	2	5	(-	-)	88	31	23	35	17	0	18	4	2	2	5	3	.63	1	.331	.401	.521
2012	Nashv	AAA	124	464	129	23	9	11	(-	-)	203	72	40	70	29	0	72	10	7	3	16	7	.70	5	.278	.332	.438
2011	Mil	NL	8	3	1	0	0	0	(0	0)	1	1	0	0	1	0	1	0	1	0	0	0	-	0	.333	.500	.333
2012	Mil	NL	16	23	7	1	2	0	(0	0)	12	3	5	4	1	0	3	0	0	1	0	1	.00	0	.304	.320	.522
2 ML YEARS			24	26	8	1	2	0	(0	0)	13	4	5	4	2	0	4	0	1	1	0	1	.00	0	.308	.345	.500

Tanner Scheppers

Pitches: R **Bats:** R **Pos:** RP-39   **Ht:** 6'4" **Wt:** 220 **Born:** 1/17/1987 **Age:** 26

Year	Team	Lg	G	GS	CG	GF	IP	BFP	H	R	ER	HR	SH	SF	HB	TBB	IBB	SO	WP	Bk	W	L	Pct	Sh	Sv-Op Hld	ERC	ERA
2010	Frisco	AA	6	0	0	5	11.0	38	3	1	1	1	0	0	0	0	0	19	1	0	0	0	-	0	2- -	0.28	0.82
2010	OKCity	AAA	30	7	0	11	69.0	320	82	45	42	5	2	4	8	30	0	71	7	0	1	3	.250	0	4- -	5.56	5.48
2011	RdRck	AAA	11	1	0	6	20.2	94	23	10	10	0	1	1	2	12	0	20	2	0	2	0	1.000	0	2- -	5.19	4.35
2011	Frisco	AA	17	0	0	8	23.0	97	18	10	8	1	1	1	1	9	1	24	2	1	2	1	.667	0	0- -	2.56	3.13
2012	RdRck	AAA	27	0	0	26	31.0	127	30	12	12	2	2	1	3	4	0	31	2	0	1	2	.333	0	11- -	3.02	3.48
2012	Tex	AL	39	0	0	13	32.1	152	47	18	16	6	3	1	2	9	3	30	4	0	1	1	.500	0	1-1 4	7.05	4.45

Max Scherzer

Pitches: R **Bats:** R **Pos:** SP-32   SHERR-zer   **Ht:** 6'3" **Wt:** 220 **Born:** 7/27/1984 **Age:** 28

Year	Team	Lg	G	GS	CG	GF	IP	BFP	H	R	ER	HR	SH	SF	HB	TBB	IBB	SO	WP	Bk	W	L	Pct	Sh	Sv-Op Hld	ERC	ERA
2008	Ari	NL	16	7	0	2	56.0	237	48	24	19	5	4	2	5	21	1	66	2	0	0	4	.000	0	0-0 0	3.45	3.05
2009	Ari	NL	30	30	0	0	170.1	741	166	94	78	20	5	6	10	63	1	174	5	1	9	11	.450	0	0-0 0	4.12	4.12
2010	Det	AL	31	31	0	0	195.2	800	174	84	76	20	5	5	7	70	1	184	8	0	12	11	.522	0	0-0 0	3.56	3.50
2011	Det	AL	33	33	0	0	195.0	833	207	101	96	29	3	7	7	56	1	174	12	0	15	9	.625	0	0-0 0	4.48	4.43
2012	Det	AL	32	32	0	0	187.2	787	179	82	78	23	5	1	5	60	2	231	2	1	16	7	.696	0	0-0 0	3.77	3.74
Postseason			4	3	0	0	15.2	72	15	10	10	1	0	0	1	9	0	14	0	0	1	1	.500	0	0-0 1	4.39	5.74
5 ML YEARS			142	133	0	2	804.2	3398	774	385	347	97	22	21	34	270	6	829	29	2	52	42	.553	0	0-0 0	3.94	3.88

Nate Schierholtz

Bats: L **Throws:** R **Pos:** RF-80; PH-38; CF-7; DH-2; PR-1   SHEER-holtz   **Ht:** 6'1" **Wt:** 205 **Born:** 2/15/1984 **Age:** 29

Year	Team	Lg	G	AB	H	2B	3B	HR	(Hm	Rd)	TB	R	RBI	RC	TBB	IBB	SO	HBP	SH	SF	SB	CS	SB%	GDP	Avg	OBP	Slg
2012	LV*	AAA	4	17	2	0	0	0	(-	-)	2	1	1	0	0	0	3	0	0	0	0	0	-	0	.118	.118	.118
2007	SF	NL	39	112	34	5	3	0	(0	0)	45	9	10	14	2	0	19	1	0	2	3	1	.75	0	.304	.316	.402
2008	SF	NL	19	75	24	8	1	1	(1	0)	37	12	5	12	3	0	8	3	0	0	1	0	1.00	1	.320	.370	.493
2009	SF	NL	116	285	76	19	2	5	(1	4)	114	33	29	35	16	3	58	1	0	6	3	1	.75	5	.267	.302	.400
2010	SF	NL	137	227	55	13	3	3	(0	3)	83	34	17	26	20	5	38	3	1	1	4	5	.44	3	.242	.311	.366
2011	SF	NL	115	335	93	22	1	9	(4	5)	144	42	41	46	21	3	61	4	0	2	7	4	.64	5	.278	.326	.430
2012	2 Tms	NL	114	241	62	8	5	6	(0	6)	98	20	21	31	23	2	46	1	1	3	3	2	.60	1	.257	.321	.407
12	SF	NL	77	175	44	4	5	5	(0	5)	73	15	16	23	18	2	36	1	0	2	3	2	.60	1	.251	.321	.417
12	Phi	NL	37	66	18	4	0	1	(0	1)	25	5	5	8	5	0	10	0	1	1	0	0	-	0	.273	.319	.379
Postseason			11	12	2	0	0	0	(0	0)	2	2	1	1	1	0	5	0	0	0	0	0	-	0	.167	.231	.167
6 ML YEARS			540	1275	344	75	15	24	(6	18)	521	150	123	164	85	13	230	13	2	14	20	14	.59	15	.270	.319	.409

Daniel Schlereth

Pitches: L **Bats:** L **Pos:** RP-6   SHLARE-ith   **Ht:** 6'0" **Wt:** 198 **Born:** 5/9/1986 **Age:** 27

Year	Team	Lg	G	GS	CG	GF	IP	BFP	H	R	ER	HR	SH	SF	HB	TBB	IBB	SO	WP	Bk	W	L	Pct	Sh	Sv-Op	Hld	ERC	ERA
2012	Lkland*	A+	8	6	0	0	8.0	37	6	1	1	0	1	0	0	7	1	9	1	0	0	0	-	0	0--	-	3.42	1.13
2012	Toledo*	AAA	3	0	0	0	1.2	12	3	2	2	0	0	0	0	4	0	2	2	0	0	0	-	0	0--	-	17.05	10.80
2009	Ari	NL	21	0	0	4	18.1	86	15	13	12	1	2	0	1	15	1	22	4	0	1	4	.200	0	0-3	0	4.32	5.89
2010	Det	AL	18	0	0	6	18.2	87	20	7	6	2	1	1	1	10	3	19	1	0	2	0	1.000	0	1-2	1	4.89	2.89
2011	Det	AL	49	0	0	16	49.0	212	36	20	19	6	3	1	5	31	3	44	6	0	2	2	.500	0	0-1	7	4.02	3.49
2012	Det	AL	6	0	0	2	7.0	39	14	10	8	3	0	0	0	5	2	6	1	0	0	0	-	0	0-0	0	14.88	10.29
	Postseason		3	0	0	1	1.2	10	5	3	3	0	0	0	0	0	0	4	1	0	0	0	-	0	0-0	0	14.52	16.20
	4 ML YEARS		94	0	0	28	93.0	424	85	50	45	12	6	2	7	61	9	91	12	0	5	6	.455	0	1-6	8	4.93	4.35

Konrad Schmidt

Bats: R **Throws:** R **Pos:** C-2; PH-2   **Ht:** 5'10" **Wt:** 229 **Born:** 8/2/1984 **Age:** 28

					BATTING																	BASERUNNING				AVERAGES		
Year	Team	Lg	G	AB	H	2B	3B	HR	(Hm | Rd)	TB	R	RBI	RC	TBB	IBB	SO	HBP	SH	SF	SB	CS	SB%	GDP	Avg	OBP	Slg
2007	Yakima	A-	45	164	41	10	0	6	(- | -)	69	19	24	20	4	0	38	6	0	1	1	0	1.00	9	.250	.291	.421
2008	Sbend	A	62	216	56	10	0	2	(- | -)	72	21	18	25	20	1	41	4	1	3	3	3	.50	11	.259	.329	.333
2008	Visalia	A+	40	152	50	10	1	1	(- | -)	65	21	19	23	3	1	26	4	0	1	0	0	-	2	.329	.356	.428
2009	Visalia	A+	106	411	125	28	1	9	(- | -)	182	54	50	67	30	1	75	7	0	3	0	3	.00	14	.304	.359	.443
2009	Reno	AAA	5	16	7	2	0	0	(- | -)	9	1	4	3	0	0	1	0	0	0	0	0	-	0	.438	.438	.563
2010	Mobile	AA	107	394	124	30	3	11	(- | -)	193	48	65	73	32	10	63	8	0	6	7	3	.70	10	.315	.373	.490
2011	Reno	AAA	92	346	97	24	3	9	(- | -)	154	47	45	50	21	0	66	5	1	1	1	3	.25	10	.280	.330	.445
2012	Reno	AAA	93	332	92	24	0	7	(- | -)	137	43	47	49	25	2	69	8	4	5	2	0	1.00	10	.277	.338	.413
2010	Ari	NL	4	8	1	0	0	0	(0 | 0)	1	0	0	0	1	0	0	0	0	0	0	0	-	0	.125	.222	.125
2012	Ari	NL	4	7	0	0	0	0	(0 | 0)	0	1	2	0	1	0	2	0	0	0	0	0	-	0	.000	.125	.000
	2 ML YEARS		8	15	1	0	0	0	(0 | 0)	1	1	2	0	2	0	2	0	0	0	0	0	-	0	.067	.176	.067

Brian Schneider

Bats: L **Throws:** R **Pos:** C-29; PH-5   SHNY-derr   **Ht:** 6'1" **Wt:** 210 **Born:** 11/26/1976 **Age:** 36

					BATTING																	BASERUNNING				AVERAGES		
Year	Team	Lg	G	AB	H	2B	3B	HR	(Hm	Rd)	TB	R	RBI	RC	TBB	IBB	SO	HBP	SH	SF	SB	CS	SB%	GDP	Avg	OBP	Slg
2012	Clrwtr*	A+	6	22	4	2	0	0	(-	-)	6	2	2	1	1	0	6	0	0	1	0	0	-	1	.182	.217	.273
2000	Mon	NL	45	115	27	6	0	0	(0	0)	33	6	11	8	7	2	24	0	0	1	0	1	.00	1	.235	.276	.287
2001	Mon	NL	27	41	13	3	0	1	(1	0)	19	4	6	8	6	1	3	0	0	1	0	0	-	0	.317	.396	.463
2002	Mon	NL	73	207	57	19	2	5	(3	2)	95	21	29	29	21	8	41	0	2	2	1	2	.33	7	.275	.339	.459
2003	Mon	NL	108	335	77	26	1	9	(9	0)	132	34	46	36	37	8	75	2	1	2	0	2	.00	12	.230	.309	.394
2004	Mon	NL	135	436	112	20	3	12	(5	7)	174	40	49	52	42	10	63	3	5	2	0	1	.00	8	.257	.325	.399
2005	Was	NL	116	369	99	20	1	10	(5	5)	151	38	44	48	29	7	48	6	2	2	1	0	1.00	14	.268	.330	.409
2006	Was	NL	124	410	105	18	0	4	(3	1)	135	30	55	45	38	10	67	2	2	3	2	2	.50	14	.256	.320	.329
2007	Was	NL	129	408	96	21	1	6	(2	4)	137	33	54	41	56	7	56	2	4	7	0	0	-	15	.235	.326	.336
2008	NYM	NL	110	335	86	10	0	9	(4	5)	123	30	38	36	42	9	53	1	4	2	0	0	-	11	.257	.339	.367
2009	NYM	NL	59	170	37	11	0	3	(3	0)	57	11	24	16	18	1	21	1	2	3	0	0	-	5	.218	.292	.335
2010	Phi	NL	47	125	30	4	1	4	(2	2)	48	17	15	17	19	2	25	1	2	0	0	0	-	3	.240	.345	.384
2011	Phi	NL	41	125	22	4	0	2	(0	2)	32	11	9	7	11	1	35	1	1	1	0	0	-	3	.176	.246	.256
2012	Phi	NL	34	89	20	5	0	2	(1	1)	31	9	7	7	5	0	15	3	1	0	0	0	-	4	.225	.289	.348
	13 ML YEARS		1048	3165	781	167	9	67	(38	29)	1167	284	387	350	331	66	526	22	26	26	4	8	.33	93	.247	.320	.369

Skip Schumaker

Bats: L **Throws:** R **Pos:** 2B-61; PH-35; CF-15; RF-10; LF-1   SHOO-mock-er   **Ht:** 5'10" **Wt:** 195 **Born:** 2/3/1980 **Age:** 33

					BATTING																	BASERUNNING				AVERAGES		
Year	Team	Lg	G	AB	H	2B	3B	HR	(Hm	Rd)	TB	R	RBI	RC	TBB	IBB	SO	HBP	SH	SF	SB	CS	SB%	GDP	Avg	OBP	Slg
2012	Memp*	AAA	7	21	6	2	0	0	(-	-)	8	5	0	3	4	0	3	0	0	0	1	0	1.00	1	.286	.400	.381
2005	StL	NL	27	24	6	1	0	0	(0	0)	7	9	1	2	2	0	2	0	1	0	1	0	1.00	0	.250	.308	.292
2006	StL	NL	28	54	10	1	0	1	(0	1)	14	3	2	2	5	1	6	0	1	0	2	1	.67	1	.185	.254	.259
2007	StL	NL	88	177	59	12	2	2	(1	1)	81	19	19	30	8	0	20	0	1	2	1	1	.50	5	.333	.358	.458
2008	StL	NL	153	540	163	22	5	8	(4	4)	219	87	46	74	47	2	60	2	4	1	8	2	.80	19	.302	.359	.406
2009	StL	NL	153	532	161	34	1	4	(2	2)	209	85	35	74	52	2	69	0	1	1	2	2	.50	4	.303	.364	.393
2010	StL	NL	137	476	126	18	1	5	(1	4)	161	66	42	61	43	2	64	4	2	4	5	3	.63	7	.265	.328	.338
2011	StL	NL	117	367	104	19	0	2	(1	1)	129	34	38	43	27	3	50	2	1	3	2	0	.00	10	.283	.333	.351
2012	StL	NL	107	272	75	14	4	1	(1	0)	100	37	28	34	27	2	50	0	3	2	1	1	.50	6	.276	.339	.368
	Postseason		13	27	10	3	0	0	(0	0)	13	3	5	5	1	0	3	1	0	0	0	0	-	1	.370	.414	.481
	8 ML YEARS		810	2442	704	121	13	23	(10	13)	920	340	211	320	211	12	321	8	13	13	20	12	.63	52	.288	.345	.377

Michael Schwimer

Pitches: R **Bats:** R **Pos:** RP-35   SHWIMM-ur   **Ht:** 6'8" **Wt:** 240 **Born:** 2/19/1986 **Age:** 27

Year	Team	Lg	G	GS	CG	GF	IP	BFP	H	R	ER	HR	SH	SF	HB	TBB	IBB	SO	WP	Bk	W	L	Pct	Sh	Sv-Op	Hld	ERC	ERA
2008	Wmspt	A-	22	0	0	19	41.1	173	33	12	9	0	3	0	3	15	2	62	3	0	0	2	.000	0	8--	-	2.38	1.96
2009	Clrwtr	A+	48	0	0	36	60.0	239	44	21	19	2	1	1	2	19	0	82	2	1	2	1	.667	0	20--	-	2.12	2.85
2009	Rdng	AA	5	0	0	3	4.2	7	7	4	4	0	0	1	0	2	0	7	1	0	2	1	.667	0	0--	-	6.19	7.71
2010	Rdng	AA	32	0	0	27	40.0	170	34	16	16	5	3	0	2	14	1	58	1	1	5	3	.625	0	11--	-	3.32	3.60
2010	LV	AAA	16	0	0	7	20.0	85	16	6	3	1	2	0	1	7	1	18	1	0	2	2	.500	0	0--	-	2.52	1.35
2011	LV	AAA	47	0	0	29	68.0	277	51	15	14	4	2	1	1	22	1	86	4	0	9	1	.900	0	10--	-	2.24	1.85

Year	Team	Lg	G	GS	CG	GF	IP	BFP	H	R	ER	HR	SH	SF	HB	TBB	IBB	SO	WP	Bk	W	L	Pct	Sh	Sv-Op	Hld	ERC	ERA
2012	LV	AAA	15	0	0	10	18.1	79	17	11	8	2	2	0	1	5	0	19	0	0	2	1	.667	0	6--	-	3.33	3.93
2011	Phi	NL	12	0	0	5	14.1	64	15	8	8	2	2	0	1	7	1	16	0	0	1	1	.500	0	0-2	0	5.21	5.02
2012	Phi	NL	35	0	0	16	34.1	147	30	18	17	3	3	3	2	16	2	36	1	0	2	1	.667	0	0-1	1	3.70	4.46
2 ML YEARS			47	0	0	21	48.2	211	45	26	25	5	5	3	3	23	3	52	1	0	3	2	.600	0	0-3	1	4.13	4.62

Chris Schwinden

Pitches: R **Bats:** R **Pos:** SP-2; RP-1   SCHWINN-den   **Ht:** 6'3" **Wt:** 215 **Born:** 9/22/1986 **Age:** 26

			HOW MUCH HE PITCHED						WHAT HE GAVE UP												THE RESULTS							
Year	Team	Lg	G	GS	CG	GF	IP	BFP	H	R	ER	HR	SH	SF	HB	TBB	IBB	SO	WP	Bk	W	L	Pct	Sh	Sv-Op	Hld	ERC	ERA
2008	Bklyn	A-	14	8	0	2	62.2	245	53	21	14	3	1	2	2	12	1	70	2	0	4	1	.800	0	0--	-	2.34	2.01
2009	Savann	A	21	17	0	2	115.1	476	126	51	42	6	2	2	5	15	0	88	6	0	9	6	.600	0	0--	-	3.43	3.28
2009	StLuci	A+	2	2	0	0	11.1	48	12	5	5	0	0	0	2	3	0	4	1	0	0	1	.000	0	0--	-	4.00	3.97
2010	StLuci	A+	7	2	0	2	34.1	139	34	8	7	2	1	0	1	5	0	23	1	0	3	0	1.000	0	0--	-	2.93	1.83
2010	Bnghtn	AA	17	14	1	0	79.1	352	100	53	49	8	0	2	4	19	1	69	3	0	4	7	.364	1	0--	-	5.13	5.56
2011	Bnghtn	AA	2	0	0	0	3.0	10	2	0	0	0	0	0	0	0	0	5	0	0	0	0	-	0	0--	-	1.01	0.00
2011	Buffalo	AAA	26	26	0	0	145.2	615	138	71	64	14	4	1	10	48	2	134	6	0	8	8	.500	0	0--	-	3.77	3.95
2012	Buffalo	AAA	21	19	2	1	106.2	447	102	39	32	7	2	4	2	30	1	92	9	0	8	6	.571	0	0--	-	3.19	2.70
2012	LsVgs	AAA	1	1	0	0	3.0	18	8	8	7	1	0	0	0	1	0	2	1	0	1	0	1.000	0	0--	-	17.35	21.00
2012	Clmbs	AAA	3	3	0	0	15.1	68	16	11	10	4	0	0	0	6	0	5	2	0	1	2	.333	0	0--	-	5.33	5.87
2012	S-WB	AAA	1	1	0	0	4.0	21	8	4	3	0	0	0	0	1	0	2	1	0	0	1	.000	0	0--	-	8.60	6.75
2011	NYM	NL	4	4	0	0	21.0	95	23	13	11	1	2	2	1	6	2	17	1	0	0	2	.000	0	0-0	0	3.63	4.71
2012	NYM	NL	3	2	0	1	8.2	46	15	13	12	4	1	0	0	3	0	1	0	0	0	1	.000	0	0-0	0	10.90	12.46
2 ML YEARS			7	6	0	1	29.2	141	38	26	23	5	3	2	1	9	2	18	1	0	0	3	.000	0	0-0	0	5.55	6.98

Luke Scott

Bats: L **Throws:** R **Pos:** DH-82; PH-12; 1B-6   **Ht:** 6'0" **Wt:** 205 **Born:** 6/25/1978 **Age:** 35

			BATTING																	BASERUNNING				AVERAGES		
Year	Team	Lg	G	AB	H	2B	3B	HR	(Hm	Rd)	TB	R	RBI	RC	TBB	IBB	SO	HBP	SH	SF	SB	CS	SB%	GDP	Avg	OBP	Slg
2012	Drham*	AAA	2	8	3	0	0	2	(-	-)	9	3	4	3	0	0	1	1	0	1	0	0	-	0	.375	.400	1.125
2012	Charltt*	A+	8	26	8	1	0	2	(-	-)	15	6	6	6	6	2	7	0	0	2	0	0	-	2	.308	.438	.577
2005	Hou	NL	34	80	15	4	2	0	(0	0)	23	6	4	6	9	1	23	0	0	0	1	1	.50	1	.188	.270	.288
2006	Hou	NL	65	214	72	19	6	10	(8	2)	133	31	37	48	30	4	43	4	0	1	2	1	.67	2	.336	.426	.621
2007	Hou	NL	132	369	94	28	5	18	(8	10)	186	49	64	55	53	4	95	2	0	1	3	1	.75	8	.255	.351	.504
2008	Bal	AL	148	475	122	29	2	23	(11	12)	224	67	65	68	53	10	102	5	0	3	2	2	.50	7	.257	.336	.472
2009	Bal	AL	128	449	116	26	1	25	(18	7)	219	61	77	69	55	5	104	1	0	1	0	0	-	4	.258	.340	.488
2010	Bal	AL	131	447	127	29	1	27	(19	8)	239	70	72	71	59	4	98	4	0	7	2	0	1.00	9	.284	.368	.535
2011	Bal	AL	64	209	46	11	0	9	(5	4)	84	24	22	24	24	1	54	1	0	2	1	1	.50	2	.220	.301	.402
2012	TB	AL	96	314	72	22	1	14	(6	8)	138	35	55	40	21	3	80	5	0	4	5	0	1.00	9	.229	.285	.439
Postseason			2	2	0	0	0	0	(0	0)	0	1	0	1	0	1	0	0	0	0	0	0	-	0	.000	.333	.000
8 ML YEARS			798	2557	664	168	18	126	(75	51)	1246	343	396	381	304	32	599	22	0	19	16	6	.73	41	.260	.341	.487

Evan Scribner

Pitches: R **Bats:** R **Pos:** RP-30   SKRIBB-nurr   **Ht:** 6'3" **Wt:** 190 **Born:** 7/19/1985 **Age:** 27

			HOW MUCH HE PITCHED						WHAT HE GAVE UP												THE RESULTS							
Year	Team	Lg	G	GS	CG	GF	IP	BFP	H	R	ER	HR	SH	SF	HB	TBB	IBB	SO	WP	Bk	W	L	Pct	Sh	Sv-Op	Hld	ERC	ERA
2007	Msoula	R+	18	0	0	10	37.0	158	35	13	12	1	0	2	3	9	0	48	3	0	0	1	.000	0	2--	-	2.93	2.92
2007	Sbend	A	5	0	0	2	10.1	43	7	3	3	1	0	0	0	5	0	13	0	0	1	0	1.000	0	0--	-	2.61	2.61
2008	Sbend	A	23	0	0	22	34.1	136	23	7	6	0	1	0	3	8	2	52	1	0	3	2	.400	0	8--	-	1.51	1.57
2008	Visalia	A+	5	0	0	3	9.2	36	5	2	2	1	0	0	0	2	0	10	1	0	1	0	.000	0	1--	-	1.24	1.86
2008	Lk Els	A+	20	0	0	8	23.1	90	14	7	7	3	1	0	2	3	0	31	0	0	2	1	.667	0	1--	-	1.57	2.70
2009	SnAnt	AA	58	0	0	51	70.1	294	60	27	24	4	5	1	0	20	3	77	2	0	8	4	.667	0	21--	-	2.45	3.07
2010	SnAnt	AA	57	0	0	36	66.0	263	51	22	19	6	2	1	5	15	2	81	1	0	4	5	.444	0	16--	-	2.45	2.59
2011	Tucsn	AAA	28	0	0	20	28.2	123	27	15	15	2	2	3	0	12	1	27	1	0	2	3	.400	0	10--	-	3.54	4.71
2012	Scrmto	AAA	26	0	0	17	35.2	140	26	12	12	4	1	1	0	10	0	38	1	0	1	0	1.000	0	8--	-	2.32	3.03
2011	SD	NL	10	0	0	5	14.0	64	18	11	11	1	0	0	0	4	0	10	0	0	0	0	-	0	0-0	0	4.92	7.07
2012	Oak	AL	30	0	0	13	35.1	148	30	11	10	2	0	0	0	12	0	30	1	0	2	0	1.000	0	1-1	1	2.70	2.55
2 ML YEARS			40	0	0	18	49.1	212	48	22	21	3	0	0	0	16	0	40	1	0	2	0	1.000	0	1-1	1	3.29	3.83

Marco Scutaro

Bats: R **Throws:** R **Pos:** 2B-118; SS-27; 3B-15; PH-2   SKOO-tah-row   **Ht:** 5'10" **Wt:** 185 **Born:** 10/30/1975 **Age:** 37

			BATTING																	BASERUNNING				AVERAGES		
Year	Team	Lg	G	AB	H	2B	3B	HR	(Hm	Rd)	TB	R	RBI	RC	TBB	IBB	SO	HBP	SH	SF	SB	CS	SB%	GDP	Avg	OBP	Slg
2002	NYM	NL	27	36	8	0	1	1	(0	1)	13	2	6	2	0	0	11	0	1	1	0	1	.00	1	.222	.216	.361
2003	NYM	NL	48	75	16	4	0	2	(0	2)	26	10	6	10	13	2	14	1	1	1	2	0	1.00	1	.213	.333	.347
2004	Oak	AL	137	455	124	32	1	7	(6	1)	179	50	43	48	16	1	58	0	5	1	0	0	-	9	.273	.297	.393
2005	Oak	AL	118	381	94	22	3	9	(5	4)	149	48	37	45	36	1	48	0	4	4	5	2	.71	6	.247	.310	.391
2006	Oak	AL	117	365	97	21	6	5	(1	4)	145	52	41	41	50	0	66	0	3	5	5	1	.83	16	.266	.350	.397
2007	Oak	AL	104	338	88	13	0	7	(2	5)	122	49	41	42	35	1	40	2	2	2	2	1	.67	13	.260	.332	.361
2008	Tor	AL	145	517	138	23	1	7	(2	5)	184	76	60	72	57	0	65	5	6	7	7	2	.78	8	.267	.341	.356
2009	Tor	AL	144	574	162	35	1	12	(7	5)	235	100	60	97	90	0	75	4	5	7	14	5	.74	12	.282	.379	.409
2010	Bos	AL	150	632	174	38	0	11	(6	5)	245	92	56	81	53	1	71	3	4	3	5	4	.56	13	.275	.333	.388
2011	Bos	AL	113	395	118	26	1	7	(4	3)	167	59	54	56	38	1	36	1	7	4	4	2	.67	12	.299	.358	.423
2012	2 Tms	NL	156	620	190	32	4	7	(4	3)	251	87	74	86	40	0	49	4	10	9	9	4	.69	12	.306	.348	.405
12	Col	NL	95	377	102	16	3	4	(3	1)	136	47	30	40	27	0	35	4	4	3	7	3	.70	5	.271	.324	.361
12	SF	NL	61	243	88	16	1	3	(1	2)	115	40	44	46	13	0	14	0	6	6	2	1	.67	7	.362	.385	.473
Postseason			7	27	5	4	0	0	(0	0)	9	1	6	3	0	0	4	0	0	0	0	0	-	0	.185	.185	.333
11 ML YEARS			1259	4388	1209	246	18	75	(40	35)	1716	625	478	586	428	7	533	20	48	42	53	22	.71	103	.276	.340	.391

Kyle Seager

Bats: L **Throws:** R **Pos:** 3B-138; 2B-18; DH-2; PH-2 — SEE-gurr — **Ht:** 6'0" **Wt:** 195 **Born:** 11/3/1987 **Age:** 25

									BATTING											BASERUNNING				AVERAGES		
Year	Team	Lg	G	AB	H	2B	3B	HR	(Hm	Rd)	TB	R	RBI	RC	TBB	IBB	SO	HBP	SH	SF	SB	CS	SB%	GDP	Avg	OBP	Slg
2009	Ms	R	1	3	0	0	0	0	(-	-)	0	0	0	0	0	0	1	0	0	0	0	0	-	0	.000	.000	.000
2009	Clinton	A	41	153	42	8	0	1	(-	-)	53	17	22	21	22	1	20	0	0	3	4	2	.67	2	.275	.360	.346
2009	Hi Dsrt	A+	2	5	0	0	0	0	(-	-)	0	1	0	0	0	0	0	0	0	0	0	0	-	0	.000	.000	.000
2010	Hi Dsrt	A+	135	557	192	40	3	14	(-	-)	280	126	74	117	71	0	94	5	3	7	13	12	.52	5	.345	.419	.503
2011	Jacksn	AA	66	266	83	25	1	4	(-	-)	122	33	37	47	26	1	38	5	0	2	8	5	.62	5	.312	.381	.459
2011	Tacom	AAA	24	106	41	8	2	3	(-	-)	62	24	17	26	11	0	12	0	0	0	3	1	.75	6	.387	.444	.585
2011	Sea	AL	53	182	47	13	0	3	(0	3)	69	22	13	16	13	0	36	2	2	2	3	1	.75	4	.258	.312	.379
2012	Sea	AL	155	594	154	35	1	20	(5	15)	251	62	86	88	46	1	110	5	2	4	13	5	.72	9	.259	.316	.423
	2 ML YEARS		208	776	201	48	1	23	(5	18)	320	84	99	104	59	1	146	7	4	6	16	6	.73	13	.259	.315	.412

Chris Seddon

Pitches: L **Bats:** L **Pos:** RP-15; SP-2 — SEDD-un — **Ht:** 6'4" **Wt:** 220 **Born:** 10/13/1983 **Age:** 29

			HOW MUCH HE PITCHED						WHAT HE GAVE UP										THE RESULTS						
Year	Team	Lg	G	GS	CG	GF	IP	BFP	H	R	ER	HR	SH	SF	HB	TBB	IBB	SO	WP	Bk	W	L	Pct	Sh	Sv-Op	Hld	ERC	ERA
2012	Clmbs*	AAA	20	20	1	0	123.0	494	112	55	47	16	4	6	2	27	0	108	4	0	11	5	.688	0	0- -	-	3.21	3.44
2007	Fla	NL	7	4	0	1	17.1	91	29	19	17	2	1	1	1	5	0	10	0	0	0	2	.000	0	0-0	0	7.56	8.83
2010	Sea	AL	14	0	0	5	22.1	95	21	14	14	4	0	1	0	10	0	16	2	0	1	0	1.000	0	0-0	0	4.55	5.64
2012	Cle	AL	17	2	0	3	34.1	147	35	15	14	2	0	2	0	13	1	18	1	0	1	1	.500	0	0-0	1	3.78	3.67
	3 ML YEARS		38	6	0	9	74.0	333	85	48	45	8	1	4	1	28	1	44	3	0	2	3	.400	0	0-0	1	4.86	5.47

Jean Segura

Bats: R **Throws:** R **Pos:** SS-44; PH-1 — GENE seg-ER-uh — **Ht:** 5'10" **Wt:** 165 **Born:** 3/17/1990 **Age:** 23

									BATTING											BASERUNNING				AVERAGES		
Year	Team	Lg	G	AB	H	2B	3B	HR	(Hm	Rd)	TB	R	RBI	RC	TBB	IBB	SO	HBP	SH	SF	SB	CS	SB%	GDP	Avg	OBP	Slg
2008	Angels	R	11	36	9	0	0	0	(-	-)	9	13	4	4	6	0	5	1	0	0	1	0	1.00	1	.250	.372	.250
2009	Salt Lk	AAA	7	19	8	2	0	0	(-	-)	10	2	2	3	0	0	4	0	0	0	0	0	-	0	.421	.421	.526
2009	Orem	A-	36	162	56	10	4	3	(-	-)	83	33	21	33	11	1	11	2	1	1	11	3	.79	1	.346	.392	.512
2010	CRpds	A	130	515	161	24	12	10	(-	-)	239	89	79	95	45	3	72	2	11	8	50	10	.83	5	.313	.365	.464
2011	InldEm	A+	44	185	52	9	4	3	(-	-)	78	26	21	28	15	3	26	1	0	1	18	6	.75	4	.281	.337	.422
2011	Angels	R	8	30	11	4	0	1	(-	-)	18	5	5	6	0	0	3	0	0	0	0	0	-	0	.367	.367	.600
2012	Ark	AA	94	374	110	10	5	7	(-	-)	151	50	40	55	23	3	57	8	6	3	33	13	.72	6	.294	.346	.404
2012	Hntsvl	AA	8	30	13	3	0	0	(-	-)	16	7	4	8	4	0	4	1	1	1	2	0	1.00	0	.433	.500	.533
2012	2 Tms		45	151	39	4	3	0	(0	0)	49	19	14	16	13	3	23	0	1	1	7	1	.88	1	.258	.315	.325
12	LAA	AL	1	3	0	0	0	0	(0	0)	0	0	0	0	0	0	2	0	0	0	0	0	-	0	.000	.000	.000
12	Mil	NL	44	148	39	4	3	0	(0	0)	49	19	14	16	13	3	21	0	1	1	7	1	.88	1	.264	.321	.331

Justin Sellers

Bats: R **Throws:** R **Pos:** SS-9; 3B-7; 2B-3; PH-3 — **Ht:** 5'10" **Wt:** 155 **Born:** 2/1/1986 **Age:** 27

									BATTING											BASERUNNING				AVERAGES		
Year	Team	Lg	G	AB	H	2B	3B	HR	(Hm	Rd)	TB	R	RBI	RC	TBB	IBB	SO	HBP	SH	SF	SB	CS	SB%	GDP	Avg	OBP	Slg
2005	Vancvr	A-	47	175	48	8	1	0	(-	-)	58	31	13	25	19	0	24	8	4	1	8	3	.73	0	.274	.369	.331
2006	Kane	A	119	411	99	21	2	5	(-	-)	139	75	46	56	58	0	65	11	10	5	17	5	.77	7	.241	.346	.338
2007	Stcktn	A+	114	434	119	25	4	4	(-	-)	164	72	37	63	46	0	69	8	1	6	11	4	.73	11	.274	.350	.378
2007	Mdland	AA	14	45	7	1	0	0	(-	-)	8	2	3	1	3	0	10	1	2	0	2	0	1.00	1	.156	.224	.178
2008	Mdland	AA	124	442	112	15	8	6	(-	-)	161	72	46	58	48	0	77	7	9	5	10	6	.63	11	.253	.333	.364
2009	Chatt	AA	116	393	110	27	1	2	(-	-)	145	44	33	59	50	1	70	10	6	5	10	8	.56	12	.280	.371	.369
2010	InldEm	A+	24	96	25	7	0	0	(-	-)	32	15	12	11	9	0	16	1	1	2	2	0	1.00	1	.260	.324	.333
2010	Albq	AAA	90	288	82	17	1	14	(-	-)	143	51	56	55	40	0	49	3	7	6	5	3	.63	6	.285	.371	.497
2011	Albq	AAA	89	270	82	17	2	14	(-	-)	145	57	49	58	41	2	57	5	2	4	3	3	.50	6	.304	.400	.537
2012	Albq	AAA	2	7	2	1	0	0	(-	-)	3	1	1	0	0	0	2	0	0	1	0	0	-	0	.286	.250	.429
2012	RCuca	A+	3	7	2	1	1	0	(-	-)	5	1	0	1	1	0	1	0	0	0	1	0	1.00	0	.286	.375	.714
2011	LAD	NL	36	123	25	9	0	1	(1	0)	37	20	13	15	12	0	21	2	1	1	1	0	1.00	1	.203	.283	.301
2012	LAD	NL	19	44	9	3	1	1	(1	0)	17	6	2	2	5	1	14	0	1	0	0	0	-	0	.205	.286	.386
	2 ML YEARS		55	167	34	12	1	2	(2	0)	54	26	15	17	17	1	35	2	2	1	1	0	1.00	1	.204	.283	.323

Leyson Septimo

Pitches: L **Bats:** L **Pos:** RP-21 — LAY-sun SEP-tuh-moh — **Ht:** 6'1" **Wt:** 195 **Born:** 7/7/1985 **Age:** 27

			HOW MUCH HE PITCHED						WHAT HE GAVE UP										THE RESULTS						
Year	Team	Lg	G	GS	CG	GF	IP	BFP	H	R	ER	HR	SH	SF	HB	TBB	IBB	SO	WP	Bk	W	L	Pct	Sh	Sv-Op	Hld	ERC	ERA
2008	Visalia	A+	27	0	0	7	41.0	197	42	27	25	4	0	1	3	33	0	44	9	2	0	2	.000	0	1- -	-	6.12	5.49
2009	Visalia	A+	26	0	0	14	38.1	170	29	18	15	1	1	2	4	26	0	44	6	1	2	1	.667	0	6- -	-	3.65	3.52
2009	Mobile	AA	19	0	0	8	16.1	95	20	17	16	2	2	0	3	18	1	25	6	2	0	1	.000	0	3- -	-	7.58	7.85
2010	Mobile	AA	26	0	0	13	28.1	121	16	17	13	1	4	1	2	23	1	37	8	0	2	2	.500	0	4- -	-	3.07	4.13
2010	Reno	AAA	16	0	0	4	17.0	101	15	25	21	2	1	1	4	30	0	20	6	0	0	1	.000	0	0- -	-	9.89	11.12
2011	Mobile	AA	21	0	0	4	29.2	132	20	23	21	1	1	1	6	25	0	22	1	2	2	1	.667	0	0- -	-	4.38	6.37
2011	Brham	AA	22	0	0	10	26.1	121	23	16	12	1	0	2	3	16	0	38	1	0	2	1	.667	0	0- -	-	4.04	4.10
2012	Charltt	AAA	24	0	0	11	34.1	137	16	5	5	1	0	1	1	20	0	43	2	0	2	1	.667	0	1- -	-	1.71	1.31
2012	CWS	AL	21	0	0	5	14.1	58	8	8	8	3	0	0	1	6	1	14	2	0	0	2	.000	0	0-0	0	2.63	5.02

Bryan Shaw

Pitches: R Bats: B Pos: RP-64   Ht: 6'1" Wt: 210 Born: 11/8/1987 Age: 25

			HOW MUCH HE PITCHED						WHAT HE GAVE UP												THE RESULTS							
Year	Team	Lg	G	GS	CG	GF	IP	BFP	H	R	ER	HR	SH	SF	HB	TBB	IBB	SO	WP	Bk	W	L	Pct	Sh	Sv-Op	Hld	ERC	ERA
2008	Msoula	R+	10	0	0	5	17.1	87	24	19	13	2	0	0	4	7	0	17	4	0	0	1	.000	0	2--	-	7.35	6.75
2008	Sbend	A	11	0	0	4	22.1	90	18	12	10	0	0	0	1	6	0	16	1	0	0	1	.000	0	0--	-	2.13	4.03
2009	Visalia	A+	30	19	0	2	107.1	461	96	65	56	7	2	2	11	40	1	95	11	0	3	7	.300	0	0--	-	3.51	4.70
2010	Mobile	AA	33	13	0	9	101.1	447	102	57	48	4	7	3	10	43	3	75	11	0	4	9	.308	0	2--	-	4.11	4.26
2011	Mobile	AA	15	0	0	14	20.2	84	15	5	2	1	1	0	0	8	0	15	0	0	3	1	.750	0	7--	-	2.26	0.87
2011	Reno	AAA	16	0	0	12	17.2	70	14	9	9	4	1	0	2	4	0	15	2	0	1	0	1.000	0	9--	-	3.63	4.58
2012	Reno	AAA	8	0	0	4	8.0	31	6	2	2	0	0	0	0	2	0	10	1	0	0	0	.	-	0	2--	-	1.71	2.25
2011	Ari	NL	33	0	0	8	28.1	122	30	9	8	2	0	0	4	8	1	24	1	0	1	0	1.000	0	0-0	9	4.31	2.54
2012	Ari	NL	64	0	0	19	59.1	252	60	29	23	4	4	2	2	24	3	41	4	1	1	6	.143	0	2-4	10	4.08	3.49
	Postseason		4	0	0	1	4.0	13	0	0	0	0	0	1	0	1	0	3	0	0	0	0	-	0	0-0	1	0.07	0.00
	2 ML YEARS		97	0	0	27	87.2	374	90	38	31	6	4	2	6	32	4	65	5	1	2	6	.250	0	2-4	19	4.16	3.18

Ben Sheets

Pitches: R Bats: R Pos: SP-9   Ht: 6'1" Wt: 220 Born: 7/18/1978 Age: 34

			HOW MUCH HE PITCHED						WHAT HE GAVE UP												THE RESULTS							
Year	Team	Lg	G	GS	CG	GF	IP	BFP	H	R	ER	HR	SH	SF	HB	TBB	IBB	SO	WP	Bk	W	L	Pct	Sh	Sv-Op	Hld	ERC	ERA
2012	Missi*	AA	2	2	0	0	10.2	45	12	7	6	0	0	0	1	1	0	10	0	0	0	1	.000	0	0--	-	3.25	5.06
2001	Mil	NL	25	25	1	0	151.1	653	166	89	80	23	8	5	5	48	6	94	3	0	11	10	.524	1	0-0	0	4.78	4.76
2002	Mil	NL	34	34	1	0	216.2	934	237	105	100	21	10	0	10	70	10	170	9	0	11	16	.407	0	0-0	0	4.45	4.15
2003	Mil	NL	34	34	1	0	220.2	931	232	122	109	29	11	6	6	43	2	157	7	0	11	13	.458	0	0-0	0	3.83	4.45
2004	Mil	NL	34	34	5	0	237.0	937	201	85	71	25	6	4	4	32	1	264	8	1	12	14	.462	0	0-0	0	2.37	2.70
2005	Mil	NL	22	22	3	0	156.2	633	142	66	58	19	6	2	2	25	1	141	7	0	10	9	.526	0	0-0	0	2.81	3.33
2006	Mil	NL	17	17	0	0	106.0	430	105	47	45	9	6	5	2	11	1	116	3	0	6	7	.462	0	0-0	0	2.84	3.82
2007	Mil	NL	24	24	2	0	141.1	592	138	62	60	17	4	5	1	37	2	106	4	0	12	5	.706	0	0-0	0	3.53	3.82
2008	Mil	NL	31	31	5	0	198.1	812	181	74	68	17	6	7	1	47	2	158	8	0	13	9	.591	3	0-0	0	2.89	3.09
2010	Oak	AL	20	20	0	0	119.1	511	123	65	60	18	3	0	1	43	2	84	3	0	4	9	.308	0	0-0	0	4.45	4.53
2012	Atl	NL	9	9	0	0	49.1	207	52	21	19	6	4	0	1	13	1	35	1	0	4	4	.500	0	0-0	0	4.09	3.47
	10 ML YEARS		250	250	18	0	1596.2	6640	1577	736	670	184	64	37	32	369	28	1325	53	1	94	96	.495	4	0-0	0	3.50	3.78

George Sherrill

Pitches: L Bats: L Pos: RP-2   Ht: 6'0" Wt: 225 Born: 4/19/1977 Age: 36

			HOW MUCH HE PITCHED						WHAT HE GAVE UP												THE RESULTS							
Year	Team	Lg	G	GS	CG	GF	IP	BFP	H	R	ER	HR	SH	SF	HB	TBB	IBB	SO	WP	Bk	W	L	Pct	Sh	Sv-Op	Hld	ERC	ERA
2004	Sea	AL	21	0	0	4	23.2	104	24	12	10	3	0	1	1	9	1	16	4	1	2	1	.667	0	0-0	3	4.31	3.80
2005	Sea	AL	29	0	0	2	19.0	77	13	12	11	3	1	1	1	7	2	24	0	0	4	3	.571	0	0-0	9	2.70	5.21
2006	Sea	AL	72	0	0	6	40.0	174	30	19	19	4	2	0	2	27	4	42	0	0	2	4	.333	0	1-1	17	2.86	4.28
2007	Sea	AL	73	0	0	16	45.2	182	28	12	12	4	4	4	1	17	1	56	1	1	2	0	1.000	0	3-7	22	1.96	2.36
2008	Bal	AL	57	0	0	49	53.1	239	47	28	28	6	1	3	1	33	6	58	1	0	3	5	.375	0	31-37	1	4.18	4.73
2009	2 Tms		72	0	0	39	69.0	282	53	13	13	4	1	1	2	24	4	61	1	0	1	1	.500	0	21-26	11	2.41	1.70
2010	LAD	NL	65	0	0	12	36.1	180	46	28	27	4	5	2	1	24	4	25	1	0	2	2	.500	0	0-4	7	6.56	6.69
2011	Atl	NL	51	0	0	9	36.0	149	33	12	12	3	2	1	1	12	1	38	1	0	3	1	.750	0	0-1	7	3.37	3.00
2012	Sea	AL	2	0	0	1	1.1	10	6	4	4	2	0	0	0	1	0	0	1	0	0	0	-	0	0-0	0	56.84	27.00
09	Bal	AL	42	0	0	38	41.1	171	34	11	11	3	0	1	2	13	2	39	0	0	0	1	.000	0	20-23	0	2.72	2.40
09	LAD	NL	30	0	0	1	27.2	111	19	2	2	1	1	0	0	11	2	22	1	0	1	0	1.000	0	1-3	11	1.96	0.65
	Postseason		6	0	0	1	4.1	22	3	4	4	1	0	0	3	4	0	2	1	0	1	0	1.000	0	0-0	2	8.61	8.31
	9 ML YEARS		442	0	0	138	324.1	1397	280	140	136	29	18	15	8	154	23	320	9	2	19	17	.528	0	56-76	76	3.49	3.77

James Shields

Pitches: R Bats: R Pos: SP-33   Ht: 6'4" Wt: 215 Born: 12/20/1981 Age: 31

			HOW MUCH HE PITCHED						WHAT HE GAVE UP												THE RESULTS							
Year	Team	Lg	G	GS	CG	GF	IP	BFP	H	R	ER	HR	SH	SF	HB	TBB	IBB	SO	WP	Bk	W	L	Pct	Sh	Sv-Op	Hld	ERC	ERA
2006	TB	AL	21	21	1	0	124.2	540	141	69	67	18	4	3	5	38	5	104	9	0	6	8	.429	0	0-0	0	4.92	4.84
2007	TB	AL	31	31	1	0	215.0	874	202	98	92	28	4	5	10	36	0	184	9	0	12	8	.600	0	0-0	0	3.24	3.85
2008	TB	AL	33	33	3	0	215.0	877	208	94	85	24	6	0	12	40	0	160	6	0	14	8	.636	2	0-0	0	3.41	3.56
2009	TB	AL	33	33	0	0	219.2	930	239	113	101	29	6	3	1	52	1	167	3	1	11	12	.478	0	0-0	0	4.16	4.14
2010	TB	AL	34	33	0	0	203.1	899	246	128	117	34	5	2	5	51	2	187	13	2	13	15	.464	0	0-0	0	5.21	5.18
2011	TB	AL	33	33	11	0	249.1	975	195	83	78	26	5	3	5	65	1	225	4	0	16	12	.571	4	0-0	0	2.58	2.82
2012	TB	AL	33	33	3	0	227.2	944	208	103	89	25	3	2	11	58	2	223	7	1	15	10	.600	2	0-0	0	3.28	3.52
	Postseason		6	6	0	0	34.1	152	40	20	19	4	1	1	5	8	0	25	3	0	2	4	.333	0	0-0	0	5.08	4.98
	7 ML YEARS		218	217	19	0	1454.2	6039	1439	688	629	184	33	18	49	340	11	1250	51	4	87	73	.544	8	0-0	0	3.69	3.89

Kelly Shoppach

Bats: R Throws: R Pos: C-73; PH-7; DH-1   SHOP-ick   Ht: 6'0" Wt: 220 Born: 4/29/1980 Age: 33

			BATTING																			BASERUNNING				AVERAGES		
Year	Team	Lg	G	AB	H	2B	3B	HR	(Hm	Rd)	TB	R	RBI	RC	TBB	IBB	SO	HBP	SH	SF	SB	CS	SB%	GDP	Avg	OBP	Slg
2005	Bos	AL	9	15	0	0	0	0	(0	0)	0	1	0	0	0	0	7	1	0	0	0	0	-	0	.000	.063	.000
2006	Cle	AL	41	110	27	6	0	3	(2	1)	42	7	16	13	8	0	45	0	2	0	0	0	-	2	.245	.297	.382
2007	Cle	AL	59	161	42	13	0	7	(4	3)	76	26	30	24	11	0	56	1	3	1	0	0	-	2	.261	.310	.472
2008	Cle	AL	112	352	92	27	0	21	(9	12)	182	67	55	58	36	3	133	11	3	1	0	0	-	7	.261	.348	.517
2009	Cle	AL	89	271	58	14	0	12	(5	7)	108	33	40	32	33	0	98	18	2	3	0	0	-	8	.214	.335	.399
2010	TB	AL	63	158	31	8	0	5	(4	1)	54	17	17	18	20	0	71	6	2	1	0	0	-	2	.196	.308	.342
2011	TB	AL	87	221	39	3	0	11	(4	7)	75	23	22	15	19	0	79	9	3	1	0	0	-	3	.176	.268	.339
2012	2 Tms		76	219	51	14	2	8	(3	5)	93	23	27	31	16	3	89	8	2	0	1	0	1.00	2	.233	.309	.425

Year	Team	Lg	G	AB	H	2B	3B	HR	(Hm	Rd)	TB	R	RBI	RC	TBB	IBB	SO	HBP	SH	SF	SB	CS	SB%	GDP	Avg	OBP	Slg
12	Bos	AL	48	140	35	12	2	5	(3	2)	66	16	17	22	11	1	62	5	2	0	1	0	1.00	2	.250	.327	.471
12	NYM	NL	28	79	16	2	0	3	(0	3)	27	7	10	9	5	2	27	3	0	0	0	0	-	0	.203	.276	.342
	Postseason		9	25	7	2	0	2	(0	2)	15	4	6	6	2	0	9	2	0	0	0	0	-	1	.280	.379	.600
	8 ML YEARS		536	1507	340	85	2	67	(31	36)	630	197	207	191	143	6	578	54	17	7	1	0	1.00	28	.226	.314	.418

Moises Sierra

Bats: R **Throws:** R **Pos:** RF-39; PH-6; DH-5; PR-1   **Ht:** 6'0" **Wt:** 225 **Born:** 9/24/1988 **Age:** 24

Year	Team	Lg	G	AB	H	2B	3B	HR	(Hm	Rd)	TB	R	RBI	RC	TBB	IBB	SO	HBP	SH	SF	SB	CS	SB%	GDP	Avg	OBP	Slg
2007	B Jays	R	43	143	29	5	1	5	(-	-)	51	17	15	12	5	0	39	4	1	1	2	2	.50	1	.203	.248	.357
2008	Lnsng	A	130	451	111	16	5	9	(-	-)	164	50	39	48	26	0	114	8	1	3	12	11	.52	14	.246	.297	.364
2009	Dnedin	A+	110	405	116	24	2	5	(-	-)	159	56	56	62	34	3	66	15	1	4	10	2	.83	11	.286	.360	.393
2009	NHam	AA	8	34	12	1	0	1	(-	-)	16	1	6	5	1	0	8	0	0	1	0	1	.00	2	.353	.361	.471
2010	B Jays	R	10	34	9	2	0	1	(-	-)	14	4	3	5	4	0	8	0	0	0	0	0	-	2	.265	.342	.412
2010	Dnedin	A+	10	37	6	1	0	1	(-	-)	10	4	5	1	1	0	11	0	0	2	0	1	.00	0	.162	.175	.270
2011	NHam	AA	133	495	137	19	3	18	(-	-)	216	81	67	74	39	2	93	12	1	4	16	14	.53	12	.277	.342	.436
2012	LsVgs	AAA	100	377	109	16	1	17	(-	-)	178	62	63	64	39	2	86	4	0	2	7	6	.54	12	.289	.360	.472
2012	Tor	AL	49	147	33	4	0	6	(3	3)	55	14	15	10	8	0	44	2	0	0	1	0	1.00	3	.224	.274	.374

Andrelton Simmons

Bats: R **Throws:** R **Pos:** SS-49   ANN-drel-ton   **Ht:** 6'2" **Wt:** 170 **Born:** 9/4/1989 **Age:** 23

Year	Team	Lg	G	AB	H	2B	3B	HR	(Hm	Rd)	TB	R	RBI	RC	TBB	IBB	SO	HBP	SH	SF	SB	CS	SB%	GDP	Avg	OBP	Slg
2010	Danvle	R+	62	239	66	11	1	2	(-	-)	85	36	26	33	16	0	14	9	1	4	18	4	.82	3	.276	.340	.356
2011	Lynbrg	A+	131	517	161	35	6	1	(-	-)	211	69	52	75	29	2	43	6	12	6	26	18	.59	12	.311	.351	.408
2012	Missi	AA	44	174	51	9	2	3	(-	-)	73	29	21	30	20	1	20	3	4	2	10	2	.83	4	.293	.372	.420
2012	Atl	NL	49	166	48	8	2	3	(3	0)	69	17	19	23	12	1	21	1	0	3	1	0	1.00	5	.289	.335	.416

Alfredo Simon

Pitches: R **Bats:** R **Pos:** RP-36   si-MOHN   **Ht:** 6'6" **Wt:** 260 **Born:** 5/8/1981 **Age:** 32

			HOW MUCH HE PITCHED						WHAT HE GAVE UP											THE RESULTS						
Year	Team	Lg	G	GS	CG	GF	IP	BFP	H	R	ER	HR	SH	SF	HB	TBB	IBB	SO	WP	Bk	W	L	Pct	Sh	Sv-Op	Hld	ERC	ERA
2008	Bal	AL	4	1	0	0	13.0	59	16	10	9	4	0	1	2	2	0	8	2	0	0	0	-	0	0-0	0	6.45	6.23
2009	Bal	AL	2	2	0	0	6.1	28	8	7	7	5	0	0	0	2	0	3	0	0	0	1	.000	0	0-0	0	10.74	9.95
2010	Bal	AL	49	0	0	35	49.1	222	54	30	27	10	1	2	2	22	2	37	1	0	4	2	.667	0	17-21	1	5.66	4.93
2011	Bal	AL	23	16	0	1	115.2	499	128	69	63	15	1	4	4	40	6	83	2	2	4	9	.308	0	0-0	0	4.83	4.90
2012	Cin	NL	36	0	0	13	61.0	269	65	22	18	2	2	3	6	22	1	52	9	0	3	2	.600	0	1-1	1	4.16	2.66
	5 ML YEARS		114	19	0	49	245.1	1077	271	138	124	36	4	10	14	88	9	183	14	2	11	14	.440	0	18-22	2	5.06	4.55

Tony Sipp

Pitches: L **Bats:** L **Pos:** RP-63   **Ht:** 6'0" **Wt:** 190 **Born:** 7/12/1983 **Age:** 29

			HOW MUCH HE PITCHED						WHAT HE GAVE UP											THE RESULTS						
Year	Team	Lg	G	GS	CG	GF	IP	BFP	H	R	ER	HR	SH	SF	HB	TBB	IBB	SO	WP	Bk	W	L	Pct	Sh	Sv-Op	Hld	ERC	ERA
2009	Cle	AL	46	0	0	8	40.0	168	27	16	13	5	3	1	0	25	2	48	3	0	2	0	1.000	0	0-0	9	3.29	2.93
2010	Cle	AL	70	0	0	16	63.0	266	48	30	29	12	3	2	2	39	3	69	4	0	2	2	.500	0	1-3	15	4.42	4.14
2011	Cle	AL	69	0	0	17	62.1	251	45	22	21	10	1	2	0	24	3	57	1	0	6	3	.667	0	0-1	24	2.87	3.03
2012	Cle	AL	63	0	0	7	55.0	233	47	29	27	9	2	1	1	23	1	51	3	0	1	2	.333	0	1-2	12	3.80	4.42
	4 ML YEARS		248	0	0	48	220.1	918	167	97	90	36	9	6	3	111	9	225	12	1	11	7	.611	0	2-6	60	3.61	3.68

Grady Sizemore

Bats: L **Throws:** L **Pos:** OF   **Ht:** 6'2" **Wt:** 200 **Born:** 8/2/1982 **Age:** 30

Year	Team	Lg	G	AB	H	2B	3B	HR	(Hm	Rd)	TB	R	RBI	RC	TBB	IBB	SO	HBP	SH	SF	SB	CS	SB%	GDP	Avg	OBP	Slg
2004	Cle	AL	43	138	34	6	2	4	(2	2)	56	15	24	21	14	0	34	5	0	2	1	0	1.00	6	.246	.333	.406
2005	Cle	AL	158	640	185	37	11	22	(10	12)	310	111	81	101	52	1	132	7	5	2	22	10	.69	17	.289	.348	.484
2006	Cle	AL	162	655	190	53	11	28	(14	14)	349	134	76	121	78	8	153	13	1	4	22	6	.79	2	.290	.375	.533
2007	Cle	AL	162	628	174	34	5	24	(11	13)	290	118	78	123	101	9	155	17	0	2	33	10	.77	3	.277	.390	.462
2008	Cle	AL	157	634	170	39	5	33	(21	12)	318	101	90	121	98	14	130	11	0	2	38	5	.88	5	.268	.374	.502
2009	Cle	AL	106	436	108	20	6	18	(5	13)	194	73	64	68	60	1	92	4	2	1	13	8	.62	4	.248	.343	.445
2010	Cle	AL	33	128	27	6	2	0	(0	0)	37	15	13	11	9	0	35	2	0	1	4	2	.67	1	.211	.271	.289
2011	Cle	AL	71	268	60	21	1	10	(6	4)	113	34	32	28	18	1	85	6	0	3	2	0	.00	4	.224	.285	.422
	Postseason		11	43	12	2	1	2	(0	2)	22	9	3	5	8	3	9	1	0	1	2	1	.67	2	.279	.396	.512
	8 ML YEARS		892	3527	948	216	43	139	(69	70)	1667	601	458	594	430	34	816	65	8	17	134	43	.76	36	.269	.357	.473

Scott Sizemore

Bats: R **Throws:** R **Pos:** 2B   **Ht:** 6'0" **Wt:** 185 **Born:** 1/4/1985 **Age:** 28

Year	Team	Lg	G	AB	H	2B	3B	HR	(Hm	Rd)	TB	R	RBI	RC	TBB	IBB	SO	HBP	SH	SF	SB	CS	SB%	GDP	Avg	OBP	Slg
2006	Oneont	A-	70	294	96	15	4	3	(-	-)	128	49	37	52	32	2	47	2	3	2	7	5	.58	4	.327	.394	.435
2007	WMich	A	125	438	116	33	5	4	(-	-)	171	78	48	72	73	1	60	9	4	6	16	10	.62	11	.265	.376	.390
2008	Lkland	A+	53	203	58	11	1	4	(-	-)	83	32	20	34	24	1	44	3	1	3	14	3	.82	2	.286	.365	.409
2009	Erie	AA	59	228	70	17	4	9	(-	-)	122	39	33	49	35	0	46	2	3	1	7	3	.70	5	.307	.402	.535
2009	Toledo	AAA	71	292	90	22	1	8	(-	-)	138	49	33	55	49	0	49	4	5	0	14	1	.93	6	.308	.378	.473

Year	Team	Lg	G	AB	H	2B	3B	HR	(Hm	Rd)	TB	R	RBI	RC	TBB	IBB	SO	HBP	SH	SF	SB	CS	SB%	GDP	Avg	OBP	Slg
										BATTING													BASERUNNING			AVERAGES	
2010	Toledo	AAA	76	299	89	23	1	9	(-	-)	141	49	37	54	31	0	77	9	1	2	2	2	.50	3	.298	.378	.472
2011	Toledo	AAA	23	76	31	7	1	2	(-	-)	46	17	15	21	12	0	19	2	1	1	3	1	.75	1	.408	.495	.605
2011	Scrmto	AAA	9	30	8	2	0	1	(-	-)	13	11	3	7	12	0	4	0	0	1	2	1	.67	2	.267	.465	.433
2010	Det	AL	48	143	32	7	0	3	(1	2)	48	19	14	13	15	0	40	0	4	1	0	0	-	4	.224	.296	.336
2011	2 Tms	AL	110	368	90	22	1	11	(4	7)	147	50	56	60	53	0	112	2	5	1	5	3	.63	8	.245	.342	.399
11	Det	AL	17	63	14	1	0	0	(0	0)	15	8	4	8	10	0	19	0	1	0	1	1	.50	0	.222	.329	.238
11	Oak	AL	93	305	76	21	1	11	(4	7)	132	42	52	52	43	0	93	2	4	1	4	2	.67	8	.249	.345	.433
2 ML YEARS			158	511	122	29	1	14	(5	9)	195	69	70	73	68	0	152	2	9	2	5	3	.63	12	.239	.329	.382

Tyler Skaggs

Pitches: L **Bats:** L **Pos:** SP-6 **Ht:** 6'3" **Wt:** 197 **Born:** 7/13/1991 **Age:** 21

Year	Team	Lg	G	GS	CG	GF	IP	BFP	H	R	ER	HR	SH	SF	HB	TBB	IBB	SO	WP	Bk	W	L	Pct	Sh	Sv-Op	Hld	ERC	ERA
					HOW MUCH HE PITCHED							WHAT HE GAVE UP												THE RESULTS				
2009	Angels	R	3	2	0	0	6.0	24	4	0	0	0	0	0	1	1	0	7	0	1	0	0	-	0	0--	-	1.57	0.00
2009	Orem	R+	2	0	0	0	4.0	19	5	4	2	0	0	0	1	1	0	6	0	0	0	0	-	0	0--	-	3.81	4.50
2010	CRpds	A	19	14	0	3	82.1	341	78	35	33	6	7	0	4	21	1	82	1	1	8	4	.667	0	0--	-	3.24	3.61
2010	Sbend	A	4	4	0	0	16.0	62	13	3	3	1	0	0	0	4	0	20	1	0	1	1	.500	0	0--	-	2.40	1.69
2011	Visalia	A+	17	17	0	0	100.2	413	81	39	36	6	1	3	5	34	0	125	4	1	5	5	.500	0	0--	-	2.74	3.22
2011	Mobile	AA	10	10	0	0	57.2	228	45	20	16	4	1	2	1	15	0	73	2	0	4	1	.800	0	0--	-	2.39	2.50
2012	Mobile	AA	13	13	0	0	69.2	290	63	27	22	8	5	2	1	21	1	71	8	1	4	5	.444	0	0--	-	3.29	2.84
2012	Reno	AAA	9	9	0	0	52.2	213	49	22	17	4	1	1	1	16	0	45	2	2	4	2	.667	0	0--	-	3.36	2.91
2012	Ari	NL	6	6	0	0	29.1	133	30	20	19	6	1	0	2	13	0	21	1	0	1	3	.250	0	0-0	0	5.31	5.83

Doug Slaten

Pitches: L **Bats:** L **Pos:** RP-10 SLATE-enn **Ht:** 6'5" **Wt:** 215 **Born:** 2/4/1980 **Age:** 33

Year	Team	Lg	G	GS	CG	GF	IP	BFP	H	R	ER	HR	SH	SF	HB	TBB	IBB	SO	WP	Bk	W	L	Pct	Sh	Sv-Op	Hld	ERC	ERA
					HOW MUCH HE PITCHED							WHAT HE GAVE UP												THE RESULTS				
2012	Indy*	AAA	40	0	0	23	42.2	168	30	11	10	5	2	1	2	13	2	24	1	0	3	3	.500	0	10--	-	2.43	2.11
2006	Ari	NL	9	0	0	0	5.2	21	3	0	0	0	1	0	0	2	1	3	0	0	0	0	-	0	0-0	2	1.11	0.00
2007	Ari	NL	61	0	0	13	36.1	163	41	15	11	4	0	0	4	14	0	28	3	0	3	2	.600	0	0-1	7	4.74	2.72
2008	Ari	NL	45	0	0	13	32.1	147	33	20	17	4	1	1	4	14	1	20	0	0	0	3	.000	0	0-0	4	4.86	4.73
2009	Ari	NL	11	0	0	1	6.1	30	10	5	5	1	0	0	0	4	0	4	0	0	0	0	-	0	0-0	0	6.82	7.11
2010	Was	NL	49	0	0	13	40.2	174	34	18	14	2	0	0	4	19	2	36	2	0	4	1	.800	0	0-0	3	3.40	3.10
2011	Was	NL	31	0	0	11	16.1	84	26	10	8	3	1	0	1	9	3	13	0	0	0	2	.000	0	0-0	3	8.95	4.41
2012	Pit	NL	10	0	0	4	13.0	55	9	4	4	1	1	0	0	8	0	6	1	0	0	0	-	0	0-0	2	3.07	2.77
Postseason			3	0	0	1	1.1	7	1	0	0	0	0	0	0	2	1	1	1	0	0	0	-	0	0-0	0	4.29	0.00
7 ML YEARS			216	0	0	55	150.2	674	156	72	59	15	4	1	9	67	7	110	6	0	7	8	.467	0	0-1	22	4.57	3.52

Joe Smith

Pitches: R **Bats:** R **Pos:** RP-72 **Ht:** 6'2" **Wt:** 205 **Born:** 3/22/1984 **Age:** 29

Year	Team	Lg	G	GS	CG	GF	IP	BFP	H	R	ER	HR	SH	SF	HB	TBB	IBB	SO	WP	Bk	W	L	Pct	Sh	Sv-Op	Hld	ERC	ERA
					HOW MUCH HE PITCHED							WHAT HE GAVE UP												THE RESULTS				
2007	NYM	NL	54	0	0	14	44.1	205	48	18	17	3	2	0	7	21	4	45	2	0	3	2	.600	0	0-0	10	5.04	3.45
2008	NYM	NL	82	0	0	12	63.1	271	51	28	25	4	0	4	4	31	4	52	1	0	6	3	.667	0	0-3	18	3.23	3.55
2009	Cle	AL	37	0	0	5	34.0	142	30	16	13	4	1	1	0	13	0	30	2	0	0	0	-	0	0-1	5	3.49	3.44
2010	Cle	AL	53	0	0	7	40.0	170	30	18	17	4	1	0	1	24	2	32	0	1	2	2	.500	0	0-1	17	3.53	3.83
2011	Cle	AL	71	0	0	13	67.0	267	52	16	15	1	2	2	2	21	1	45	2	0	3	3	.500	0	0-3	16	2.19	2.01
2012	Cle	AL	72	0	0	12	67.0	278	53	27	22	4	1	1	2	25	4	53	1	1	7	4	.636	0	0-3	21	2.60	2.96
6 ML YEARS			369	0	0	63	315.2	1333	264	123	109	20	11	4	16	135	15	257	8	2	21	14	.600	0	0-11	92	3.17	3.11

Seth Smith

Bats: L **Throws:** L **Pos:** LF-57; DH-50; PH-21; RF-13 **Ht:** 6'3" **Wt:** 210 **Born:** 9/30/1982 **Age:** 30

Year	Team	Lg	G	AB	H	2B	3B	HR	(Hm	Rd)	TB	R	RBI	RC	TBB	IBB	SO	HBP	SH	SF	SB	CS	SB%	GDP	Avg	OBP	Slg
										BATTING													BASERUNNING			AVERAGES	
2012	Scrmto*	AAA	1	3	2	0	0	0	(-	-)	2	0	0	1	0	0	0	1	0	0	0	0	-	0	.667	.750	.667
2007	Col	NL	7	8	5	0	1	0	(0	0)	7	4	0	3	0	0	1	0	0	0	0	0	-	0	.625	.625	.875
2008	Col	NL	67	108	28	7	0	4	(2	2)	47	13	15	18	15	0	23	0	0	0	1	0	1.00	0	.259	.350	.435
2009	Col	NL	133	335	98	20	4	15	(8	7)	171	61	55	63	46	3	67	2	1	3	4	1	.80	5	.293	.378	.510
2010	Col	NL	133	358	88	19	5	17	(12	5)	168	55	52	51	35	1	67	2	0	3	2	1	.67	5	.246	.314	.469
2011	Col	NL	147	476	135	32	9	15	(9	6)	230	67	59	73	46	7	93	4	0	7	10	2	.83	9	.284	.347	.483
2012	Oak	AL	125	383	92	23	2	14	(6	8)	161	55	52	52	50	7	98	5	0	3	2	2	.50	4	.240	.333	.420
Postseason			9	11	4	1	0	0	(0	0)	5	2	2	3	1	1	2	0	0	0	0	0	-	0	.364	.417	.455
6 ML YEARS			612	1668	446	101	21	65	(37	28)	784	255	233	260	192	18	349	13	1	16	19	6	.76	23	.267	.345	.470

Will Smith

Pitches: L **Bats:** R **Pos:** SP-16 **Ht:** 6'5" **Wt:** 240 **Born:** 7/10/1989 **Age:** 23

Year	Team	Lg	G	GS	CG	GF	IP	BFP	H	R	ER	HR	SH	SF	HB	TBB	IBB	SO	WP	Bk	W	L	Pct	Sh	Sv-Op	Hld	ERC	ERA
					HOW MUCH HE PITCHED							WHAT HE GAVE UP												THE RESULTS				
2008	Orem	R+	16	14	0	0	73.0	298	73	28	25	6	1	0	2	6	0	76	2	1	8	2	.800	0	0--	-	2.81	3.08
2009	CRpds	A	20	19	0	0	115.0	473	109	61	48	11	2	7	2	24	0	95	3	0	10	5	.667	0	0--	-	3.08	3.76
2010	RCuca	A+	6	6	0	0	37.1	156	36	23	19	4	3	1	0	13	0	31	1	0	2	2	.500	0	0--	-	3.78	4.58
2010	Salt Lk	AAA	9	9	0	0	53.0	239	65	36	33	6	4	2	0	20	3	40	0	1	2	4	.333	0	0--	-	5.28	5.60
2010	Ark	AA	4	4	0	0	18.2	96	33	16	15	3	3	0	1	9	0	8	2	0	1	2	.333	0	0--	-	10.19	7.23

Year	Team	Lg	G	GS	CG	GF	IP	BFP	H	R	ER	HR	SH	SF	HB	TBB	IBB	SO	WP	Bk	W	L	Pct	Sh	Sv-Op	Hld	ERC	ERA
2010	Wilmg	A+	8	8	0	0	54.2	213	48	20	17	6	1	1	4	4	0	51	1	0	4	1	.800	0	0- -	-	2.35	2.80
2011	NWArk	AA	27	27	2	0	161.1	678	171	78	69	13	6	7	6	45	2	108	4	0	13	9	.591	1	0- -	-	4.01	3.85
2012	Omha	AAA	15	15	0	0	89.2	388	104	44	36	8	3	2	2	22	0	74	1	0	4	4	.500	0	0- -	-	4.38	3.61
2012	KC	AL	16	16	0	0	89.2	396	111	54	53	12	2	5	1	33	1	59	4	0	6	9	.400	0	0-0	0	5.75	5.32

Justin Smoak

Bats: B Throws: L Pos: 1B-131; DH-1 SMOKE **Ht: 6'4" Wt: 230 Born: 12/5/1986 Age: 26**

								BATTING													BASERUNNING				AVERAGES		
Year	Team	Lg	G	AB	H	2B	3B	HR	(Hm	Rd)	TB	R	RBI	RC	TBB	IBB	SO	HBP	SH	SF	SB	CS	SB%	GDP	Avg	OBP	Slg
2012	Tacom*	AAA	20	66	16	6	1	0	(-	-)	24	10	4	11	16	1	16	0	0	0	1	0	1.00	1	.242	.390	.364
2010	2 Tms	AL	100	348	76	14	0	13	(4	9)	129	40	48	42	46	4	91	0	0	3	1	0	1.00	3	.218	.307	.371
2011	Sea	AL	123	427	100	24	0	15	(10	5)	169	38	55	55	55	4	105	3	0	4	1	0	-	10	.234	.323	.396
2012	Sea	AL	132	483	105	14	0	19	(4	15)	176	49	51	50	49	2	111	1	0	2	1	0	1.00	12	.217	.290	.364
10	Tex	AL	70	235	49	10	0	8	(4	4)	83	29	34	30	38	4	57	0	0	2	1	0	1.00	6	.209	.316	.353
10	Sea	AL	30	113	27	4	0	5	(0	5)	46	11	14	12	8	0	34	0	0	1	0	0	-	3	.239	.287	.407
	3 ML YEARS		355	1258	281	52	0	47	(18	29)	474	127	154	147	150	10	307	4	0	9	2	0	1.00	31	.223	.306	.377

Drew Smyly

Pitches: L Bats: L Pos: SP-18; RP-5 SMILE-ee **Ht: 6'3" Wt: 190 Born: 6/13/1989 Age: 24**

			HOW MUCH HE PITCHED						WHAT HE GAVE UP										THE RESULTS								
Year	Team	Lg	G	GS	CG	GF	IP	BFP	H	R	ER	HR	SH	SF	HB	TBB	IBB	SO	WP	Bk	W	L	Pct	Sh	Sv-Op	Hld	ERC	ERA
2011	Lkland	A+	14	14	0	0	80.1	323	71	32	23	1	4	1	3	21	0	77	5	0	7	3	.700	0	0- -	-	2.58	2.58
2011	Erie	AA	8	7	0	0	45.2	178	31	10	6	1	2	1	1	15	0	53	2	0	4	3	.571	0	0- -	-	1.84	1.18
2012	Toledo	AAA	7	7	0	0	17.2	83	22	13	12	3	3	0	1	8	0	25	2	1	0	2	.000	0	0- -	-	6.47	6.11
2012	Det	AL	23	18	0	0	99.1	416	93	49	44	12	2	3	2	33	1	94	3	0	4	3	.571	0	0-0	1	3.68	3.99

Travis Snider

Bats: L Throws: L Pos: RF-33; PH-17; LF-15 **Ht: 6'0" Wt: 235 Born: 2/2/1988 Age: 25**

								BATTING													BASERUNNING				AVERAGES		
Year	Team	Lg	G	AB	H	2B	3B	HR	(Hm	Rd)	TB	R	RBI	RC	TBB	IBB	SO	HBP	SH	SF	SB	CS	SB%	GDP	Avg	OBP	Slg
2012	LsVgs*	AAA	56	209	70	16	0	13	(-	-)	125	49	57	50	34	2	42	0	0	3	2	4	.33	4	.335	.423	.598
2012	Dnedin*	A+	5	22	5	1	0	0	(-	-)	6	3	1	1	1	0	5	0	0	0	2	0	1.00	0	.227	.261	.273
2008	Tor	AL	24	73	22	6	0	2	(1	1)	34	9	13	13	5	0	23	0	0	2	0	0	-	0	.301	.338	.466
2009	Tor	AL	77	241	58	14	1	9	(5	4)	101	34	29	30	29	1	78	3	2	1	1	1	.50	5	.241	.328	.419
2010	Tor	AL	82	298	76	20	0	14	(9	5)	138	36	32	40	21	2	79	0	0	0	6	3	.67	3	.255	.304	.463
2011	Tor	AL	49	187	42	14	0	3	(2	1)	65	23	30	21	11	1	56	1	1	2	3	1	.75	5	.225	.269	.348
2012	2 Tms		60	164	41	7	1	4	(3	1)	62	23	17	21	17	0	48	1	0	3	2	0	1.00	2	.250	.319	.378
12	Tor	AL	10	36	9	2	0	3	(2	1)	20	6	8	7	3	0	14	0	0	1	0	0	-	0	.250	.300	.556
12	Pit	NL	50	128	32	5	1	1	(1	0)	42	17	9	14	14	0	34	1	0	2	2	0	1.00	2	.250	.324	.328
	5 ML YEARS		292	963	239	61	2	32	(20	12)	400	125	121	125	83	4	284	5	3	8	18	7	.72	15	.248	.309	.415

Brandon Snyder

Bats: R Throws: R Pos: PH-14; 1B-11; 3B-7; PR-6; LF-5; RF-5; DH-3; C-1 **Ht: 6'2" Wt: 215 Born: 11/23/1986 Age: 26**

								BATTING													BASERUNNING				AVERAGES		
Year	Team	Lg	G	AB	H	2B	3B	HR	(Hm	Rd)	TB	R	RBI	RC	TBB	IBB	SO	HBP	SH	SF	SB	CS	SB%	GDP	Avg	OBP	Slg
2012	RdRck*	AAA	23	87	22	7	0	2	(-	-)	35	12	9	10	4	0	30	0	1	0	0	0	-	1	.253	.286	.402
2010	Bal	AL	10	20	6	2	0	0	(0	0)	8	1	3	3	0	0	3	0	0	0	0	1	.00	0	.300	.300	.400
2011	Bal	AL	6	13	3	1	0	0	(0	0)	4	2	1	1	3	0	4	1	0	0	0	0	-	0	.231	.412	.308
2012	Tex	AL	40	65	18	2	0	3	(1	2)	29	11	9	7	3	0	26	0	1	0	0	0	-	1	.277	.309	.446
	3 ML YEARS		56	98	27	5	0	3	(1	2)	41	14	13	11	6	0	33	1	1	0	0	1	.00	1	.276	.324	.418

Chris Snyder

Bats: R Throws: R Pos: C-72; PH-5; 1B-1 **Ht: 6'4" Wt: 240 Born: 2/12/1981 Age: 32**

								BATTING													BASERUNNING				AVERAGES		
Year	Team	Lg	G	AB	H	2B	3B	HR	(Hm	Rd)	TB	R	RBI	RC	TBB	IBB	SO	HBP	SH	SF	SB	CS	SB%	GDP	Avg	OBP	Slg
2004	Ari	NL	29	96	23	6	0	5	(1	4)	44	10	15	11	13	1	25	0	0	1	0	0	-	0	.240	.327	.458
2005	Ari	NL	115	326	66	14	0	6	(2	4)	98	24	28	25	40	5	87	4	3	0	0	1	.00	8	.202	.297	.301
2006	Ari	NL	61	184	51	9	0	6	(4	2)	78	19	32	27	22	4	39	1	1	5	0	0	-	5	.277	.349	.424
2007	Ari	NL	110	326	82	20	0	13	(4	9)	141	37	47	48	40	3	67	7	3	4	0	1	.00	9	.252	.342	.433
2008	Ari	NL	115	334	79	22	1	16	(6	10)	151	47	64	53	56	5	101	4	5	5	0	0	-	7	.237	.348	.452
2009	Ari	NL	61	165	33	7	0	6	(3	3)	58	20	22	17	32	4	47	2	1	2	0	0	-	5	.200	.333	.352
2010	2 Tms	NL	105	319	66	9	0	15	(6	9)	120	34	48	38	52	10	94	2	1	2	0	0	-	11	.207	.320	.376
2011	Pit	NL	34	96	26	3	0	3	(0	3)	38	13	17	17	17	0	23	1	2	3	1	0	.00	2	.271	.376	.396
2012	Hou	NL	76	221	39	8	0	7	(3	4)	68	23	24	21	33	4	70	4	0	0	0	0	-	5	.176	.295	.308
10	Ari	NL	65	195	45	8	0	10	(5	5)	83	22	32	30	36	6	61	1	1	0	0	0	-	5	.231	.352	.426
10	Pit	NL	40	124	21	1	0	5	(1	4)	37	12	16	8	16	4	33	1	0	1	0	0	-	6	.169	.268	.298
	Postseason		6	19	5	2	0	1	(0	1)	10	3	3	2	2	0	6	0	0	0	0	0	-	3	.263	.333	.526
	9 ML YEARS		706	2067	465	98	1	77	(29	48)	796	227	297	257	305	36	553	25	16	22	0	3	.00	50	.225	.329	.385

Miguel Socolovich

Pitches: R **Bats:** R **Pos:** RP-12   sah-COE-lah-vitch   **Ht:** 6'1" **Wt:** 190 **Born:** 7/24/1986 **Age:** 26

Year	Team	Lg	G	GS	CG	GF	IP	BFP	H	R	ER	HR	SH	SF	HB	TBB	IBB	SO	WP	Bk	W	L	Pct	Sh	Sv-Op	Hld	ERC	ERA
2006	RedSx	R	14	2	0	2	25.1	104	20	12	9	1	0	1	0	11	0	18	3	2	4	0	1.000	0	2- -	-	2.72	3.20
2007	Grnville	A	11	0	0	2	21.2	105	30	20	16	4	1	1	0	10	0	21	2	0	2	2	.500	0	0- -	-	7.17	6.65
2007	Lowell	A-	14	13	0	0	68.1	285	55	31	27	7	0	1	4	34	0	51	5	0	5	4	.556	0	0- -	-	3.73	3.56
2008	Knapol	A	21	18	0	0	90.1	385	86	53	47	12	3	3	6	33	0	72	5	0	6	6	.500	0	0- -	-	4.20	4.68
2009	WinSa	A+	29	5	0	17	54.1	239	65	30	29	6	3	3	1	20	3	41	0	0	3	4	.429	0	7- -	-	5.24	4.80
2009	Brham	AA	4	0	0	1	4.1	16	2	0	0	0	0	0	0	0	0	0	0	0	1	0	1.000	0	0- -	-	0.43	0.00
2010	Brham	AA	33	0	0	14	52.1	223	34	28	20	2	1	1	2	27	3	47	1	1	4	5	.444	0	2- -	-	2.23	3.44
2010	Charltt	AAA	18	0	0	8	26.0	121	22	10	9	2	2	0	0	18	4	30	1	0	3	1	.750	0	0- -	-	3.71	3.12
2011	Charltt	AAA	29	2	0	7	48.0	214	46	24	21	2	2	0	0	25	1	63	5	0	3	2	.600	0	1- -	-	3.78	3.94
2011	Brham	AA	5	0	0	3	7.0	22	0	0	0	0	0	0	0	2	0	7	0	0	0	0	-	0	1- -	-	0.10	0.00
2012	Norfolk	AAA	28	0	0	12	52.0	203	33	13	11	4	0	2	3	14	0	52	1	0	4	0	1.000	0	2- -	-	1.83	1.90
2012	Iowa	AAA	3	0	0	0	3.1	13	3	3	2	1	0	0	0	0	0	5	0	0	0	0	-	0	0- -	-	3.05	5.40
2012	2 Tms		12	0	0	2	16.1	72	15	11	11	3	0	0	0	9	0	12	0	1	0	0	-	0	0-1	1	4.79	6.06
12	Bal	AL	6	0	0	1	10.1	47	11	8	8	2	0	0	0	6	0	6	0	1	0	0	-	0	0-1	0	5.91	6.97
12	ChC	NL	6	0	0	1	6.0	25	4	3	3	1	0	0	0	3	0	6	0	0	0	0	-	0	0-0	1	3.05	4.50

Eric Sogard

Bats: L **Throws:** R **Pos:** SS-15; 3B-14; 2B-6; PH-6; PR-2   SO-guard   **Ht:** 5'10" **Wt:** 190 **Born:** 5/22/1986 **Age:** 27

Year	Team	Lg	G	AB	H	2B	3B	HR	(Hm	Rd)	TB	R	RBI	RC	TBB	IBB	SO	HBP	SH	SF	SB	CS	SB%	GDP	Avg	OBP	Slg
2012	Scrmto*	AAA	37	157	52	5	2	5	(-	-)	76	29	22	33	23	0	17	0	0	0	11	3	.79	3	.331	.417	.484
2010	Oak	AL	4	7	3	0	0	0	(0	0)	3	0	0	1	2	0	1	0	0	0	0	1	.00	0	.429	.556	.429
2011	Oak	AL	27	70	14	3	0	2	(0	2)	23	7	4	3	4	0	13	0	0	0	0	0	-	2	.200	.243	.329
2012	Oak	AL	37	102	17	3	1	2	(0	2)	28	8	7	7	5	0	17	0	1	0	2	0	1.00	1	.167	.206	.275
	3 ML YEARS		68	179	34	6	1	4	(0	4)	54	15	11	11	11	0	31	0	1	0	2	1	.67	3	.190	.237	.302

Donovan Solano

Bats: R **Throws:** R **Pos:** 2B-58; PH-18; 3B-10; LF-10; SS-5   sol-ON-oh   **Ht:** 5'9" **Wt:** 190 **Born:** 12/17/1987 **Age:** 25

Year	Team	Lg	G	AB	H	2B	3B	HR	(Hm	Rd)	TB	R	RBI	RC	TBB	IBB	SO	HBP	SH	SF	SB	CS	SB%	GDP	Avg	OBP	Slg
2005	JhsCty	R+	45	145	38	4	0	0	(-	-)	42	27	11	15	14	0	22	3	1	1	3	2	.60	6	.262	.337	.290
2005	NewJrs	A-	22	77	19	5	0	0	(-	-)	24	7	11	9	7	0	12	4	1	0	1	0	1.00	3	.247	.341	.312
2006	StCol	A-	44	149	42	2	0	0	(-	-)	44	22	13	16	12	0	17	2	3	1	2	1	.67	4	.282	.341	.295
2007	QuadC	A	82	292	75	8	0	0	(-	-)	83	31	30	26	14	0	25	6	2	2	5	2	.71	12	.257	.303	.284
2007	PlmBh	A+	50	163	34	2	1	0	(-	-)	38	17	11	8	8	0	21	1	1	1	0	1	.00	6	.209	.249	.233
2008	PlmBh	A+	107	402	115	15	4	1	(-	-)	141	56	31	52	37	0	63	2	4	0	1	2	.33	9	.286	.349	.351
2008	Sprgfld	AA	26	106	28	5	0	1	(-	-)	36	11	11	12	5	0	22	4	4	1	2	1	.67	7	.264	.319	.340
2009	Sprgfld	AA	64	251	52	7	1	1	(-	-)	64	27	16	17	21	0	39	1	3	0	1	0	1.00	8	.207	.271	.255
2009	Memp	AAA	52	164	52	7	0	0	(-	-)	59	22	14	24	10	0	27	2	2	0	3	0	1.00	5	.317	.364	.360
2010	Memp	AAA	102	330	84	12	1	4	(-	-)	110	41	27	31	11	1	35	2	1	0	2	1	.67	9	.255	.283	.333
2011	Memp	AAA	81	229	65	21	1	1	(-	-)	91	22	23	33	19	0	35	1	5	4	2	0	1.00	9	.284	.336	.397
2011	Sprgfld	AA	27	101	23	7	0	2	(-	-)	36	5	10	9	3	0	16	0	0	0	0	0	-	3	.228	.250	.356
2012	NewOr	AAA	36	141	37	7	1	0	(-	-)	46	14	14	17	10	0	27	4	4	1	4	0	1.00	3	.262	.327	.326
2012	Mia	NL	93	285	84	11	3	2	(0	2)	107	29	28	35	21	1	58	2	3	5	7	0	1.00	5	.295	.342	.375

Jhonatan Solano

Bats: R **Throws:** R **Pos:** C-11; PH-1   sol-ON-oh   **Ht:** 5'9" **Wt:** 205 **Born:** 8/12/1985 **Age:** 27

Year	Team	Lg	G	AB	H	2B	3B	HR	(Hm	Rd)	TB	R	RBI	RC	TBB	IBB	SO	HBP	SH	SF	SB	CS	SB%	GDP	Avg	OBP	Slg
2006	Nats	R	37	129	33	3	0	0	(-	-)	36	16	11	11	6	0	15	3	4	2	3	1	.75	2	.256	.300	.279
2007	Hgrstn	A	83	298	74	15	0	3	(-	-)	98	39	38	37	42	1	53	4	3	1	0	3	.00	8	.248	.348	.329
2008	Hgrstn	A	16	55	12	2	0	1	(-	-)	17	6	5	5	6	0	6	1	2	1	1	1	.50	2	.218	.302	.309
2008	Ptomc	A+	68	225	58	11	0	4	(-	-)	81	35	24	27	16	0	30	4	2	3	2	1	.67	3	.258	.315	.360
2009	Hrsbrg	AA	26	93	26	6	0	1	(-	-)	35	7	11	10	2	0	16	0	0	0	0	0	-	5	.280	.295	.376
2009	Syrcse	AAA	63	183	37	11	0	1	(-	-)	51	17	17	12	9	0	24	1	2	4	2	1	.67	10	.202	.239	.279
2010	Hrsbrg	AA	90	317	80	15	0	6	(-	-)	113	28	42	35	21	1	29	3	1	3	1	1	.50	9	.252	.302	.356
2011	Syrcse	AAA	78	255	70	14	0	5	(-	-)	99	27	33	33	19	1	36	1	2	2	1	1	.50	11	.275	.325	.388
2012	Syrcse	AAA	13	52	13	2	0	0	(-	-)	15	8	2	4	3	0	6	1	0	1	0	0	-	1	.250	.298	.288
2012	Nats	R	2	3	1	0	0	0	(-	-)	2	1	1	0	0	0	0	0	0	0	0	0	-	0	.333	.250	.667
2012	Hrsbrg	AA	11	41	8	1	0	1	(-	-)	12	4	7	2	0	0	12	1	0	1	0	0	-	1	.195	.209	.293
2012	Was	NL	12	35	11	3	0	2	(1	1)	20	6	6	6	2	1	5	0	0	0	1	0	1.00	0	.314	.351	.571

Ali Solis

Bats: R **Throws:** R **Pos:** PH-4; C-2   ah-LEE so-LEASE   **Ht:** 6'0" **Wt:** 175 **Born:** 9/29/1987 **Age:** 25

Year	Team	Lg	G	AB	H	2B	3B	HR	(Hm	Rd)	TB	R	RBI	RC	TBB	IBB	SO	HBP	SH	SF	SB	CS	SB%	GDP	Avg	OBP	Slg
2006	Padres	R	17	56	14	5	0	0	(-	-)	19	7	6	6	7	0	10	0	0	0	0	0	-	1	.250	.333	.339
2007	Padres	R	27	79	20	4	0	0	(-	-)	24	11	14	10	11	0	21	3	1	1	0	0	-	1	.253	.362	.304
2007	Eugene	A-	1	5	1	0	0	1	(-	-)	4	1	2	0	0	0	1	0	0	0	0	0	-	0	.200	.200	.800
2008	FtWyn	A	35	113	18	6	0	2	(-	-)	30	10	16	7	14	0	40	0	2	1	0	0	-	2	.159	.250	.265
2008	Eugene	A-	8	31	10	2	0	1	(-	-)	15	6	1	6	4	0	7	2	0	0	0	0	-	0	.323	.432	.484
2009	Lk Els	A+	45	138	28	4	3	2	(-	-)	44	16	19	16	7	0	37	2	3	2	1	0	1.00	6	.203	.248	.319
2009	FtWyn	A	13	48	10	2	0	4	(-	-)	24	10	10	7	4	0	14	1	0	1	0	0	-	1	.208	.278	.500
2009	SnAnt	AA	10	27	4	0	0	0	(-	-)	4	4	3	0	1	0	10	0	0	0	0	0	-	0	.148	.179	.148

Year	Team	Lg	G	AB	H	2B	3B	HR	(Hm	Rd)	TB	R	RBI	RC	TBB	IBB	SO	HBP	SH	SF	SB	CS	SB%	GDP	Avg	OBP	Slg
									BATTING												BASERUNNING				AVERAGES		
2010	SnAnt	AA	11	18	2	0	0	0	(-	-)	2	0	1	0	0	0	5	1	0	0	0	0	-	1	.111	.158	.111
2010	Lk Els	A+	12	37	10	1	0	4	(-	-)	23	6	8	7	2	0	10	0	0	0	0	0	-	1	.270	.308	.622
2011	SnAnt	AA	73	255	67	14	1	6	(-	-)	101	30	26	31	12	2	65	5	1	1	0	0	-	9	.263	.308	.396
2011	Tucsn	AAA	11	38	8	2	0	0	(-	-)	10	3	3	1	1	0	14	0	0	0	0	0	-	2	.211	.231	.263
2012	SnAnt	AA	87	329	93	25	1	6	(-	-)	138	26	40	42	11	0	77	1	1	1	1	1	.50	11	.283	.307	.419
2012	SD	NL	5	4	0	0	0	0	(0	0)	0	0	0	0	0	0	2	0	0	0	0	0	-	0	.000	.000	.000

Joakim Soria

Pitches: R Bats: R Pos: P   WAH-keem SORE-ee-uh   Ht: 6'3" Wt: 200 Born: 5/18/1984 Age: 29

				HOW MUCH HE PITCHED						WHAT HE GAVE UP									THE RESULTS							
Year	Team	Lg	G	GS	CG	GF	IP	BFP	H	R	ER	HR	SH	SF	HB	TBB	IBB	SO	WP	Bk	W	L	Pct	Sh	Sv-Op	Hld	ERC	ERA
2007	KC	AL	62	0	0	38	69.0	270	46	20	19	3	1	3	1	19	3	75	2	0	2	3	.400	0	17-21	9	1.63	2.48
2008	KC	AL	63	0	0	57	67.1	260	39	13	12	5	2	2	6	19	1	66	1	1	2	3	.400	0	42-45	0	1.72	1.60
2009	KC	AL	47	0	0	41	53.0	222	44	14	13	5	1	2	2	16	1	69	3	0	3	2	.600	0	30-33	0	2.80	2.21
2010	KC	AL	66	0	0	56	65.2	270	53	13	13	4	3	4	2	16	1	71	3	1	1	2	.333	0	43-46	0	2.27	1.78
2011	KC	AL	60	0	0	47	60.1	256	60	29	27	7	3	2	2	17	0	60	1	0	5	5	.500	0	28-35	0	3.80	4.03
5 ML YEARS			298	0	0	239	315.1	1278	242	89	84	24	10	13	13	87	6	341	10	2	13	15	.464	0	160-180	9	2.35	2.40

Alfonso Soriano

Bats: R Throws: R Pos: LF-145; DH-6; PH-2   Ht: 6'1" Wt: 195 Born: 1/7/1976 Age: 37

										BATTING											BASERUNNING				AVERAGES		
Year	Team	Lg	G	AB	H	2B	3B	HR	(Hm	Rd)	TB	R	RBI	RC	TBB	IBB	SO	HBP	SH	SF	SB	CS	SB%	GDP	Avg	OBP	Slg
1999	NYY	AL	9	8	1	0	0	1	(1	0)	4	2	1	0	0	0	3	0	0	0	0	1	.00	0	.125	.125	.500
2000	NYY	AL	22	50	9	3	0	2	(0	2)	18	5	3	4	1	0	15	0	2	0	2	0	1.00	0	.180	.196	.360
2001	NYY	AL	158	574	154	34	3	18	(8	10)	248	77	73	77	29	0	125	3	3	5	43	14	.75	7	.268	.304	.432
2002	NYY	AL	156	696	209	51	2	39	(17	22)	381	128	102	121	23	1	157	14	1	7	41	13	.76	8	.300	.332	.547
2003	NYY	AL	156	682	198	36	5	38	(15	23)	358	114	91	110	38	7	130	12	0	2	35	8	.81	8	.290	.338	.525
2004	Tex	AL	145	608	170	32	4	28	(12	16)	294	77	91	90	33	4	121	10	0	7	18	5	.78	7	.280	.324	.484
2005	Tex	AL	156	637	171	43	2	36	(25	11)	326	102	104	93	33	3	125	7	0	5	30	2	.94	6	.268	.309	.512
2006	Was	NL	159	647	179	41	2	46	(24	22)	362	119	95	114	67	16	160	9	2	3	41	17	.71	3	.277	.351	.560
2007	ChC	NL	135	579	173	42	5	33	(13	20)	324	97	70	91	31	4	130	4	0	3	19	6	.76	9	.299	.337	.560
2008	ChC	NL	109	453	127	27	0	29	(17	12)	241	76	75	77	43	11	103	3	0	4	19	3	.86	9	.280	.344	.532
2009	ChC	NL	117	477	115	25	1	20	(7	13)	202	64	55	61	40	6	118	3	0	2	9	2	.82	7	.241	.303	.423
2010	ChC	NL	147	496	128	40	3	24	(11	13)	246	67	79	75	45	3	123	3	1	3	5	1	.83	12	.258	.322	.496
2011	ChC	NL	137	475	116	27	1	26	(12	14)	223	50	88	59	27	4	113	4	0	2	2	1	.67	15	.244	.289	.469
2012	ChC	NL	151	561	147	33	2	32	(15	17)	280	68	108	89	44	5	153	7	0	3	6	2	.75	18	.262	.322	.499
Postseason			44	174	37	3	0	4	(3	1)	52	14	18	14	9	0	53	3	0	0	10	3	.77	3	.213	.263	.299
14 ML YEARS			1757	6943	1897	434	30	372	(177	195)	3507	1046	1035	1061	454	64	1576	79	9	46	270	75	.78	109	.273	.323	.505

Rafael Soriano

Pitches: R Bats: R Pos: RP-69   Ht: 6'1" Wt: 230 Born: 12/19/1979 Age: 33

				HOW MUCH HE PITCHED						WHAT HE GAVE UP									THE RESULTS							
Year	Team	Lg	G	GS	CG	GF	IP	BFP	H	R	ER	HR	SH	SF	HB	TBB	IBB	SO	WP	Bk	W	L	Pct	Sh	Sv-Op	Hld	ERC	ERA
2002	Sea	AL	10	8	0	1	47.1	202	45	25	24	8	1	0	0	16	1	32	2	0	0	3	.000	0	1-1	0	3.93	4.56
2003	Sea	AL	40	0	0	12	53.0	201	30	9	9	2	0	1	3	12	1	68	0	0	3	0	1.000	0	1-2	5	1.32	1.53
2004	Sea	AL	6	0	0	0	3.1	23	9	6	5	0	0	0	0	3	0	3	0	0	0	3	.000	0	0-1	0	15.97	13.50
2005	Sea	AL	7	0	0	4	7.1	30	6	2	2	0	0	1	1	1	0	9	0	0	0	0	-	0	0-0	1	2.00	2.45
2006	Sea	AL	53	0	0	14	60.0	241	44	15	15	6	1	1	2	21	0	65	2	0	1	2	.333	0	2-6	18	2.64	2.25
2007	Atl	NL	71	0	0	28	72.0	276	47	26	24	12	0	0	2	15	2	70	0	0	3	3	.500	0	9-12	19	2.05	3.00
2008	Atl	NL	14	0	0	5	14.0	57	7	5	4	1	0	0	1	9	2	16	1	0	0	1	.000	0	3-4	0	2.27	2.57
2009	Atl	NL	77	0	0	52	75.2	307	53	25	25	6	4	2	1	27	4	102	0	0	1	6	.143	0	27-31	6	2.18	2.97
2010	TB	AL	64	0	0	56	62.1	237	36	14	12	4	0	1	1	14	2	57	0	0	3	2	.600	0	45-48	0	1.33	1.73
2011	NYY	AL	42	0	0	8	39.1	164	33	18	18	4	1	0	1	18	2	36	0	0	2	3	.400	0	2-5	23	3.51	4.12
2012	NYY	AL	69	0	0	54	67.2	279	55	17	17	6	0	1	1	24	4	69	3	0	2	1	.667	0	42-46	4	2.79	2.26
Postseason			6	0	0	3	7.2	27	5	4	4	3	0	0	0	0	0	5	0	0	0	1	.000	0	1-1	1	2.25	4.70
11 ML YEARS			453	8	0	234	502.0	2017	365	162	155	49	7	7	13	160	18	527	8	0	15	24	.385	0	132-156	76	2.38	2.78

Geovany Soto

Bats: R Throws: R Pos: C-96; PH-2; DH-1   Ht: 6'1" Wt: 220 Born: 1/20/1983 Age: 30

										BATTING											BASERUNNING				AVERAGES		
Year	Team	Lg	G	AB	H	2B	3B	HR	(Hm	Rd)	TB	R	RBI	RC	TBB	IBB	SO	HBP	SH	SF	SB	CS	SB%	GDP	Avg	OBP	Slg
2012	Iowa*	AAA	5	16	3	2	0	0	(-	-)	5	1	0	1	0	0	5	1	0	0	0	0	-	1	.188	.235	.313
2005	ChC	NL	1	1	0	0	0	0	(0	0)	0	0	0	0	0	0	0	0	0	0	0	0	-	0	.000	.000	.000
2006	ChC	NL	11	25	5	1	0	0	(0	0)	6	1	2	0	0	0	5	1	0	0	0	0	-	0	.200	.231	.240
2007	ChC	NL	18	54	21	6	0	3	(2	1)	36	12	8	13	5	0	14	0	0	1	0	0	-	1	.389	.433	.667
2008	ChC	NL	141	494	141	35	2	23	(11	12)	249	66	86	81	62	6	121	2	0	5	0	1	.00	11	.285	.364	.504
2009	ChC	NL	102	331	72	19	1	11	(6	5)	126	27	47	34	50	3	77	3	0	5	1	0	1.00	19	.218	.321	.381
2010	ChC	NL	105	322	90	19	0	17	(12	5)	160	47	53	59	62	4	83	0	0	3	0	1	.00	16	.280	.393	.497
2011	ChC	NL	125	421	96	26	0	17	(7	10)	173	46	54	43	45	3	124	6	0	0	0	0	-	12	.228	.310	.411
2012	2 Tms		99	324	64	12	1	11	(3	8)	111	45	39	30	30	1	76	3	2	2	1	0	1.00	12	.198	.270	.343
12	ChC	NL	52	176	35	6	1	6	(2	4)	61	26	14	15	19	1	35	2	0	0	0	0	-	6	.199	.284	.347
12	Tex	AL	47	148	29	6	0	5	(1	4)	50	19	25	15	11	0	41	1	2	2	1	0	1.00	6	.196	.253	.338
Postseason			5	17	3	1	0	1	(0	1)	7	1	2	1	3	0	4	0	0	0	0	0	-	0	.176	.300	.412
8 ML YEARS			602	1972	489	118	4	82	(41	41)	861	244	289	260	254	17	500	15	2	18	2	2	.50	60	.248	.336	.437

Denard Span

Bats: L Throws: L Pos: CF-125; PR-3; PH-2; DH-1   Ht: 6'0" Wt: 212 Born: 2/27/1984 Age: 29

Year	Team	Lg	G	AB	H	2B	3B	HR	(Hm	Rd)	TB	R	RBI	RC	TBB	IBB	SO	HBP	SH	SF	SB	CS	SB%	GDP	Avg	OBP	Slg
2008	Min	AL	93	347	102	16	7	6	(2	4)	150	70	47	68	50	3	60	4	8	2	18	7	.72	3	.294	.387	.432
2009	Min	AL	145	578	180	16	10	8	(5	3)	240	97	68	100	70	3	89	10	12	6	23	10	.70	7	.311	.392	.415
2010	Min	AL	153	629	166	24	10	3	(0	3)	219	85	58	85	60	0	74	4	10	2	26	4	.87	12	.264	.331	.348
2011	Min	AL	70	284	75	11	5	2	(1	1)	102	37	16	32	27	0	36	0	0	0	6	1	.86	3	.264	.328	.359
2012	Min	AL	128	516	146	38	4	4	(2	2)	204	71	41	69	47	0	62	0	4	1	17	6	.74	10	.283	.342	.395
	Postseason		6	28	10	1	0	0	(0	0)	11	1	1	2	0	0	2	0	0	0	1	0	1.00	1	.357	.357	.393
5 ML YEARS			589	2354	669	105	36	23	(10	13)	915	360	230	354	254	6	321	18	34	11	90	28	.76	35	.284	.357	.389

Nate Spears

Bats: L Throws: R Pos: PH-3; LF-2; 2B-1; 3B-1   Ht: 5'11" Wt: 175 Born: 5/3/1985 Age: 28

Year	Team	Lg	G	AB	H	2B	3B	HR	(Hm	Rd)	TB	R	RBI	RC	TBB	IBB	SO	HBP	SH	SF	SB	CS	SB%	GDP	Avg	OBP	Slg
2003	Orioles	R	56	180	52	7	5	1	(-	-)	72	38	19	37	40	0	32	5	4	2	18	5	.78	2	.289	.427	.400
2004	Dlmrva	A	97	371	102	12	11	5	(-	-)	151	50	38	57	47	0	63	3	7	3	7	6	.54	3	.275	.358	.407
2005	Frdrck	A+	112	445	131	30	6	6	(-	-)	191	63	41	68	36	1	82	2	14	1	8	4	.67	1	.294	.349	.429
2006	Dytona	A+	97	321	79	15	1	1	(-	-)	99	45	25	35	31	1	53	7	7	3	7	4	.64	4	.246	.323	.308
2007	Dytona	A+	78	249	65	13	3	1	(-	-)	87	36	26	34	28	0	44	6	15	2	4	1	.80	2	.261	.347	.349
2007	Tenn	AA	38	114	34	2	2	4	(-	-)	52	22	11	21	13	0	19	3	4	1	2	0	1.00	4	.298	.382	.456
2008	Tenn	AA	115	384	115	22	5	7	(-	-)	168	71	51	71	58	3	72	6	19	6	6	5	.55	3	.299	.394	.438
2008	Iowa	AAA	5	18	5	1	0	0	(-	-)	6	5	1	2	3	0	0	0	0	1	1	0	1.00	2	.278	.381	.333
2009	Iowa	AAA	128	368	93	20	4	2	(-	-)	127	48	37	43	35	1	43	2	4	2	6	5	.55	8	.253	.319	.345
2010	Portlnd	AA	136	514	140	30	4	20	(-	-)	238	104	82	99	84	2	93	11	1	10	13	1	.93	7	.272	.380	.463
2011	Pwtckt	AAA	96	315	78	19	2	8	(-	-)	125	49	45	51	49	2	69	6	3	5	13	1	.93	3	.248	.355	.397
2012	Pwtckt	AAA	108	346	83	16	4	10	(-	-)	137	46	38	47	43	1	86	3	3	0	3	2	.60	6	.240	.329	.396
2011	Bos	AL	3	4	0	0	0	0	(0	0)	0	0	0	0	0	0	1	0	0	0	0	0	-	0	.000	.000	.000
2012	Bos	AL	4	4	0	0	0	0	(0	0)	0	0	0	0	0	0	3	0	0	0	0	0	-	0	.000	.000	.000
2 ML YEARS			7	8	0	0	0	0	(0	0)	0	0	0	0	0	0	4	0	0	0	0	0	-	0	.000	.000	.000

Josh Spence

Pitches: L Bats: L Pos: RP-11   Ht: 6'1" Wt: 190 Born: 1/22/1988 Age: 25

Year	Team	Lg	G	GS	CG	GF	IP	BFP	H	R	ER	HR	SH	SF	HB	TBB	IBB	SO	WP	Bk	W	L	Pct	Sh	Sv-Op	Hld	ERC	ERA
2010	Padres	R	1	0	0	0	1.0	5	1	0	0	0	0	0	0	0	0	3	1	0	0	0	-	0	0- -		1.51	0.00
2010	Eugene	A-	2	2	0	0	6.0	21	4	1	1	1	0	0	0	1	0	8	0	0	0	0	-	0	0- -		2.11	1.50
2010	FtWyn	A	7	3	0	0	17.0	69	14	7	7	2	0	1	1	6	0	31	1	0	2	2	.500	0	0- -		3.38	3.71
2011	SnAnt	AA	35	0	0	7	47.1	176	29	9	9	4	3	0	1	11	1	42	0	1	3	1	.750	0	0- -		1.61	1.71
2012	Tucsn	AAA	31	4	0	7	49.1	218	48	27	23	4	1	3	1	20	0	36	2	0	4	2	.667	0	0- -		3.78	4.20
2011	SD	NL	40	0	0	8	29.2	123	14	9	9	2	1	1	2	19	5	31	0	0	0	2	.000	0	0-2	7	1.99	2.73
2012	SD	NL	11	0	0	3	10.1	48	13	5	5	1	0	0	0	5	1	10	0	0	0	1	.000	0	0-0	0	5.71	4.35
2 ML YEARS			51	0	0	11	40.0	171	27	14	14	3	1	1	2	24	6	41	0	0	0	3	.000	0	0-2	7	2.84	3.15

Craig Stammen

Pitches: R Bats: R Pos: RP-59   STAMM-enn   Ht: 6'4" Wt: 225 Born: 3/9/1984 Age: 29

Year	Team	Lg	G	GS	CG	GF	IP	BFP	H	R	ER	HR	SH	SF	HB	TBB	IBB	SO	WP	Bk	W	L	Pct	Sh	Sv-Op	Hld	ERC	ERA
2009	Was	NL	19	19	1	0	105.2	448	112	67	60	14	4	3	3	24	1	48	7	0	4	7	.364	0	0-0	0	4.03	5.11
2010	Was	NL	35	19	0	3	128.0	562	151	78	73	13	5	6	1	41	4	85	3	0	4	4	.500	0	0-0	1	4.79	5.13
2011	Was	NL	7	0	0	2	10.1	38	3	1	1	0	0	0	0	4	0	12	1	0	1	1	.500	0	0-0	1	0.67	0.87
2012	Was	NL	59	0	0	15	88.1	370	70	27	23	7	5	1	2	36	4	87	3	0	6	1	.857	0	1-2	10	2.84	2.34
4 ML YEARS			120	38	1	20	332.1	1418	336	173	157	34	14	10	6	105	9	232	14	0	15	13	.536	0	1-2	12	3.84	4.25

Giancarlo Stanton

Bats: R Throws: R Pos: RF-117; PH-5; DH-1   john-CAHR-loh   Ht: 6'5" Wt: 245 Born: 11/8/1989 Age: 23

Year	Team	Lg	G	AB	H	2B	3B	HR	(Hm	Rd)	TB	R	RBI	RC	TBB	IBB	SO	HBP	SH	SF	SB	CS	SB%	GDP	Avg	OBP	Slg
2012	Jupiter*	A+	4	16	5	1	0	2	(-	-)	12	2	5	3	0	0	1	0	0	0	0	0	-	0	.313	.313	.750
2010	Fla	NL	100	359	93	21	1	22	(7	15)	182	45	59	56	34	6	123	2	0	1	5	2	.71	7	.259	.326	.507
2011	Fla	NL	150	516	135	30	5	34	(16	18)	277	79	87	81	70	6	166	9	0	6	5	5	.50	11	.262	.356	.537
2012	Mia	NL	123	449	130	30	1	37	(16	21)	273	75	86	79	46	9	143	5	0	1	6	2	.75	5	.290	.361	.608
3 ML YEARS			373	1324	358	81	7	93	(39	54)	732	199	232	216	150	21	432	16	0	8	16	9	.64	23	.270	.350	.553

Tim Stauffer

Pitches: R Bats: R Pos: SP-1   STOFF-er   Ht: 6'1" Wt: 225 Born: 6/2/1982 Age: 31

Year	Team	Lg	G	GS	CG	GF	IP	BFP	H	R	ER	HR	SH	SF	HB	TBB	IBB	SO	WP	Bk	W	L	Pct	Sh	Sv-Op	Hld	ERC	ERA
2012	Lk Els*	A+	4	4	0	0	13.1	55	15	5	5	0	0	0	0	2	0	11	0	0	0	1	.000	0	0- -		3.17	3.38
2012	Tucsn*	AAA	2	2	0	0	8.0	31	10	3	3	1	0	0	0	1	0	2	0	0	0	1	.000	0	0- -		5.10	3.38
2012	Padres*	R	1	1	0	0	1.0	5	1	1	0	0	0	0	1	0	0	1	0	0	0	0	-	0	0- -		1.51	0.00
2005	SD	NL	15	14	0	0	81.0	355	92	50	48	10	2	0	2	29	0	49	0	0	3	6	.333	0	0-0	0	5.00	5.33
2006	SD	NL	1	1	0	0	6.0	21	3	2	1	0	0	0	0	1	0	2	0	0	1	0	1.000	0	0-0	0	0.84	1.50
2007	SD	NL	2	2	0	0	7.2	45	15	18	18	5	0	0	1	6	0	6	0	0	0	1	.000	0	0-0	0	18.32	21.13
2009	SD	NL	14	14	0	0	73.0	316	71	31	29	8	2	1	5	34	1	53	1	0	4	7	.364	0	0-0	0	4.60	3.58

Year	Team	Lg	G	GS	CG	GF	IP	BFP	H	R	ER	HR	SH	SF	HB	TBB	IBB	SO	WP	Bk	W	L	Pct	Sh	Sv-Op	Hld	ERC	ERA
2010	SD	NL	32	7	0	12	82.2	326	65	18	17	3	3	0	2	24	5	61	0	0	6	5	.545	0	0-0	0	2.23	1.85
2011	SD	NL	31	31	0	0	185.2	777	180	81	77	20	14	3	8	53	5	128	4	1	9	12	.429	0	0-0	0	3.67	3.73
2012	SD	NL	1	1	0	0	5.0	24	7	4	3	1	0	0	0	3	0	5	0	0	0	-	0	0-0	0	8.40	5.40
7 ML YEARS			96	70	0	12	441.0	1864	433	204	193	47	21	4	18	150	11	304	5	1	23	31	.426	0	0-0	0	3.96	3.94

Chris Stewart

Bats: R **Throws:** R **Pos:** C-54; PH-2   **Ht:** 6'4" **Wt:** 210 **Born:** 2/19/1982 **Age:** 31

Year	Team	Lg	G	AB	H	2B	3B	HR	(Hm	Rd)	TB	R	RBI	RC	TBB	IBB	SO	HBP	SH	SF	SB	CS	SB%	GDP	Avg	OBP	Slg
2006	CWS	AL	6	8	0	0	0	0	(0	0)	0	0	0	0	0	0	2	0	0	0	0	0	-	0	.000	.000	.000
2007	Tex	AL	17	37	9	2	0	0	(0	0)	11	4	3	3	3	0	6	0	3	0	0	0	-	2	.243	.300	.297
2008	NYY	AL	1	3	0	0	0	0	(0	0)	0	0	0	0	0	0	1	0	0	0	0	0	-	0	.000	.000	.000
2010	SD	NL	2	5	0	0	0	0	(0	0)	0	0	0	0	0	0	0	0	0	0	0	0	-	0	.000	.000	-
2011	SF	NL	67	162	33	8	0	3	(1	2)	50	20	10	10	16	4	18	2	3	0	0	0	-	2	.204	.283	.309
2012	NYY	AL	55	141	34	8	0	1	(1	0)	45	15	13	10	10	0	21	1	3	2	2	0	1.00	1	.241	.292	.319
6 ML YEARS			148	351	76	18	0	4	(2	2)	106	39	26	23	29	4	48	3	9	2	2	0	1.00	5	.217	.281	.302

Ian Stewart

Bats: L **Throws:** R **Pos:** 3B-52; PH-3; PR-1   **Ht:** 6'3" **Wt:** 215 **Born:** 4/5/1985 **Age:** 28

Year	Team	Lg	G	AB	H	2B	3B	HR	(Hm	Rd)	TB	R	RBI	RC	TBB	IBB	SO	HBP	SH	SF	SB	CS	SB%	GDP	Avg	OBP	Slg
2007	Col	NL	35	43	9	4	0	1	(1	0)	16	3	9	5	1	0	17	2	0	0	0	0	-	0	.209	.261	.372
2008	Col	NL	81	266	69	18	2	10	(5	5)	121	33	41	44	30	4	94	7	0	1	1	1	.50	3	.259	.349	.455
2009	Col	NL	147	425	97	19	3	25	(13	12)	197	74	70	59	56	3	138	5	0	5	7	4	.64	7	.228	.322	.464
2010	Col	NL	121	386	99	14	2	18	(6	12)	171	54	61	51	45	8	110	5	0	5	5	2	.71	8	.256	.338	.443
2011	Col	NL	48	122	19	6	1	0	(0	0)	27	14	6	4	14	2	37	0	0	0	3	2	.60	1	.156	.243	.221
2012	ChC	NL	55	179	36	5	2	5	(2	3)	60	16	17	16	21	4	46	2	0	0	0	3	.00	5	.201	.292	.335
Postseason			2	1	0	0	0	0	(0	0)	0	0	0	0	1	0	1	0	0	0	0	0	-	0	.000	.500	.000
6 ML YEARS			487	1421	329	66	10	59	(27	32)	592	194	204	179	167	21	442	21	0	11	16	12	.57	24	.232	.319	.417

Zach Stewart

Pitches: R **Bats:** R **Pos:** RP-17; SP-3   **Ht:** 6'2" **Wt:** 205 **Born:** 9/28/1986 **Age:** 26

Year	Team	Lg	G	GS	CG	GF	IP	BFP	H	R	ER	HR	SH	SF	HB	TBB	IBB	SO	WP	Bk	W	L	Pct	Sh	Sv-Op	Hld	ERC	ERA
2008	Dayton	A	11	0	0	10	16.1	61	10	2	1	0	0	0	1	3	0	13	0	0	1	2	.333	0	3- -	-	1.27	0.55
2008	Srsota	A+	13	0	0	11	16.2	75	16	5	3	0	1	1	1	11	2	23	0	0	0	2	.000	0	2- -	-	4.17	1.62
2009	Srsota	A+	7	7	1	0	42.1	177	47	17	10	1	1	1	1	8	0	32	1	0	1	1	.500	0	0- -	-	3.47	2.13
2009	Carlina	AA	7	7	0	0	37.0	145	29	7	6	1	1	0	1	10	0	31	1	0	3	0	1.000	0	0- -	-	2.19	1.46
2009	Lsvlle	AAA	9	0	0	4	12.1	55	11	2	1	0	0	0	0	8	0	16	1	0	0	0	-	0	0- -	-	3.67	0.73
2009	LsVgs	AAA	11	0	0	3	13.1	62	18	8	5	1	0	1	0	6	0	14	1	0	0	0	-	0	0- -	-	6.21	3.38
2010	NHam	AA	26	26	0	0	136.1	575	131	59	55	13	1	2	5	54	0	106	5	2	8	3	.727	0	0- -	-	4.05	3.63
2011	NHam	AA	16	16	1	0	94.1	403	106	49	44	6	2	2	1	27	0	75	3	1	5	5	.500	0	0- -	-	4.16	4.20
2011	Charltt	AAA	1	1	0	0	6.1	28	10	3	3	0	0	0	0	0	0	5	0	0	1	0	1.000	0	0- -	-	5.11	4.26
2012	Pwtckt	AAA	11	11	0	0	59.1	248	58	26	26	6	0	2	2	14	0	42	1	0	3	5	.375	0	0- -	-	3.44	3.94
2011	2 Tms	AL	13	11	1	1	67.1	297	90	44	44	11	2	2	2	18	2	45	2	1	2	6	.250	1	0-0	0	6.25	5.88
2012	2 Tms	AL	20	3	0	8	35.2	168	58	40	34	14	1	1	1	4	0	19	0	1	1	4	.200	0	0-0	0	9.07	8.58
11	Tor	AL	3	3	0	0	16.2	75	26	9	9	2	0	1	1	5	1	10	1	1	0	1	.000	0	0-0	0	7.90	4.86
11	CWS	AL	10	8	1	1	50.2	222	64	35	35	9	2	1	1	13	1	35	1	0	2	5	.286	1	0-0	0	5.73	6.22
12	CWS	AL	18	1	0	8	30.0	134	41	26	20	10	1	1	0	4	0	16	0	1	1	2	.333	0	0-0	0	6.74	6.00
12	Bos	AL	2	2	0	0	5.2	34	17	14	14	4	0	0	1	0	0	3	0	0	0	2	.000	0	0-0	0	24.09	22.24
2 ML YEARS			33	14	1	9	103.0	465	148	84	78	25	3	3	3	22	2	64	2	2	3	10	.231	1	0-0	0	7.22	6.82

Josh Stinson

Pitches: R **Bats:** R **Pos:** RP-5; SP-1   **Ht:** 6'4" **Wt:** 210 **Born:** 3/14/1988 **Age:** 25

Year	Team	Lg	G	GS	CG	GF	IP	BFP	H	R	ER	HR	SH	SF	HB	TBB	IBB	SO	WP	Bk	W	L	Pct	Sh	Sv-Op	Hld	ERC	ERA
2006	Mets	R	9	4	0	1	27.0	110	27	10	6	0	3	3	0	5	0	14	1	0	1	2	.333	0	0- -	-	2.64	2.00
2006	Hgrstn	A	3	3	0	0	13.1	53	11	2	2	0	1	0	2	4	0	5	0	0	0	1	.000	0	0- -	-	2.83	1.35
2007	Savann	A	26	21	0	2	109.1	491	131	77	59	13	1	4	8	33	0	52	14	0	3	11	.214	0	0- -	-	5.24	4.86
2008	Savann	A	21	6	0	10	71.2	319	78	36	28	7	1	2	5	32	0	46	5	0	3	6	.333	0	3- -	-	5.10	3.52
2008	StLuci	A+	7	2	0	2	14.2	68	17	12	10	0	1	2	2	5	1	14	3	0	0	2	.000	0	0- -	-	4.28	6.14
2009	Savann	A	25	1	0	7	42.1	175	45	17	17	1	3	0	4	10	0	49	3	0	2	2	.500	0	2- -	-	3.78	3.61
2009	StLuci	A+	25	0	0	19	36.1	151	22	12	8	0	1	0	0	19	1	35	5	1	3	1	.750	0	6- -	-	1.77	1.98
2010	Bnghtn	AA	32	14	0	7	110.1	481	108	57	52	7	5	6	4	50	0	68	10	0	9	3	.750	0	1- -	-	4.05	4.24
2010	Buffalo	AAA	4	4	1	0	28.0	112	22	10	8	5	0	0	0	8	0	21	0	0	2	2	.500	0	0- -	-	2.99	2.57
2011	Bnghtn	AA	27	2	0	15	47.1	205	46	22	21	1	3	4	3	16	2	39	3	0	4	3	.571	0	6- -	-	3.35	3.99
2011	Buffalo	AAA	13	13	0	0	61.2	286	77	54	51	7	4	1	1	33	1	32	4	0	3	7	.300	0	0- -	-	6.33	7.44
2012	Hntsvl	AA	29	24	1	1	145.1	666	167	70	51	7	9	2	11	71	0	91	12	0	11	9	.550	1	1- -	-	5.22	3.16
2011	NYM	NL	14	0	0	3	13.0	57	14	10	10	1	1	0	0	7	0	8	0	0	0	2	.000	0	1-2	4	5.05	6.92
2012	Mil	NL	6	1	0	2	9.1	38	7	1	1	1	0	0	0	5	0	3	0	0	0	0	-	0	0-0	0	3.42	0.96
2 ML YEARS			20	1	0	5	22.1	95	21	11	11	2	1	0	0	12	0	11	0	0	0	2	.000	0	1-2	4	4.35	4.43

Drew Storen

Pitches: R **Bats:** B **Pos:** RP-37

STORE-inn

Ht: 6'2" **Wt:** 190 **Born:** 8/11/1987 **Age:** 25

Year	Team	Lg	G	GS	CG	GF	IP	BFP	H	R	ER	HR	SH	SF	HB	TBB	IBB	SO	WP	Bk	W	L	Pct	Sh	Sv-Op	Hld	ERC	ERA
2012	Ptomc*	A+	5	1	0	1	6.0	24	4	3	2	1	1	1	0	1	0	8	1	0	1	0	1.000	0	0- -	-	1.77	3.00
2012	Hrsbrg*	AA	1	0	0	0	0.2	6	3	4	4	1	0	1	0	1	0	0	0	0	0	0	-	0	0- -	-	56.63	54.00
2010	Was	NL	54	0	0	22	55.1	232	48	24	22	3	6	2	3	22	3	52	3	0	4	4	.500	0	5-7	10	3.19	3.58
2011	Was	NL	73	0	0	52	75.1	303	57	24	23	8	1	1	2	20	4	74	2	0	6	3	.667	0	43-48	1	2.35	2.75
2012	Was	NL	37	0	0	17	30.1	116	22	8	8	0	0	2	1	8	0	24	1	0	3	1	.750	0	4-5	10	1.79	2.37
	3 ML YEARS		164	0	0	91	161.0	651	127	56	53	11	7	5	6	50	7	150	6	0	13	8	.619	0	52-60	23	2.52	2.96

Mickey Storey

Pitches: R **Bats:** R **Pos:** RP-26

Ht: 6'2" **Wt:** 185 **Born:** 3/16/1986 **Age:** 27

Year	Team	Lg	G	GS	CG	GF	IP	BFP	H	R	ER	HR	SH	SF	HB	TBB	IBB	SO	WP	Bk	W	L	Pct	Sh	Sv-Op	Hld	ERC	ERA
2008	As	R	14	0	0	4	22.0	89	17	8	8	2	0	1	1	6	0	23	1	0	2	2	.500	0	1- -	-	2.51	3.27
2009	Kane	A	13	0	0	10	17.1	60	5	1	1	0	0	0	2	1	0	23	0	0	0	0	-	0	9- -	-	0.38	0.52
2009	Stcktn	A+	22	0	0	19	23.2	97	19	10	6	2	1	0	1	6	0	35	1	0	1	1	.500	0	9- -	-	2.50	2.28
2009	Scrmto	AAA	2	0	0	1	3.0	9	0	0	0	0	0	0	0	0	0	4	0	0	0	0	-	0	0- -	-	0.00	0.00
2009	Mdland	AA	4	0	0	0	7.2	27	3	0	0	0	0	0	1	1	0	9	0	0	1	0	1.000	0	0- -	-	0.73	0.00
2010	Mdland	AA	43	1	0	23	71.0	294	58	31	26	5	2	6	3	22	2	63	5	1	5	4	.556	0	8- -	-	2.66	3.30
2010	Scrmto	AAA	11	0	0	6	13.0	60	15	10	8	3	0	1	0	5	0	14	1	1	1	1	.500	0	1- -	-	5.64	5.54
2011	Mdland	AA	27	0	0	12	38.0	165	41	17	17	3	1	2	3	13	2	31	3	1	3	3	.500	0	4- -	-	4.43	4.03
2011	OKCity	AAA	23	0	0	7	29.1	130	35	13	13	3	0	0	0	12	0	28	1	0	1	0	1.000	0	2- -	-	5.33	3.99
2012	OKCity	AAA	38	2	0	9	65.0	273	62	24	22	8	4	2	3	14	1	72	3	1	7	4	.636	0	2- -	-	3.36	3.05
2012	Hou	NL	26	0	0	3	30.1	127	27	14	13	2	2	0	1	10	0	34	0	0	0	1	.000	0	0-0	3	3.10	3.86

Dan Straily

Pitches: R **Bats:** R **Pos:** SP-7

Ht: 6'2" **Wt:** 215 **Born:** 12/1/1988 **Age:** 24

Year	Team	Lg	G	GS	CG	GF	IP	BFP	H	R	ER	HR	SH	SF	HB	TBB	IBB	SO	WP	Bk	W	L	Pct	Sh	Sv-Op	Hld	ERC	ERA
2009	Vancvr	A-	16	11	0	1	59.0	256	66	27	27	5	1	5	1	18	0	66	2	0	5	3	.625	0	0- -	-	4.68	4.12
2010	Kane	A	28	28	0	0	148.0	623	138	75	71	13	5	6	7	61	3	149	10	1	10	7	.588	0	0- -	-	3.91	4.32
2011	Stcktn	A+	28	26	0	0	160.2	683	160	78	69	10	6	8	14	40	1	154	5	0	11	9	.550	0	0- -	-	3.54	3.87
2012	Mdland	AA	14	14	0	0	85.1	347	69	36	32	6	3	4	5	23	1	108	6	0	3	4	.429	0	0- -	-	2.59	3.38
2012	Scrmto	AAA	11	11	0	0	66.2	255	40	15	15	3	2	0	1	19	0	82	3	0	6	3	.667	0	0- -	-	1.51	2.03
2012	Oak	AL	7	7	0	0	39.1	172	36	19	17	11	1	1	2	16	1	32	0	0	2	1	.667	0	0-0	0	4.94	3.89

Stephen Strasburg

Pitches: R **Bats:** R **Pos:** SP-28

STRAHS-berg

Ht: 6'4" **Wt:** 220 **Born:** 7/20/1988 **Age:** 24

Year	Team	Lg	G	GS	CG	GF	IP	BFP	H	R	ER	HR	SH	SF	HB	TBB	IBB	SO	WP	Bk	W	L	Pct	Sh	Sv-Op	Hld	ERC	ERA
2010	Was	NL	12	12	0	0	68.0	274	56	25	22	5	2	2	0	17	0	92	2	0	5	3	.625	0	0-0	0	2.41	2.91
2011	Was	NL	5	5	0	0	24.0	88	15	5	4	0	1	1	0	2	0	24	0	0	1	1	.500	0	0-0	0	0.97	1.50
2012	Was	NL	28	28	0	0	159.1	653	136	62	56	15	6	4	4	48	1	197	5	0	15	6	.714	0	0-0	0	2.97	3.16
	3 ML YEARS		45	45	0	0	251.1	1015	207	92	82	20	9	7	4	67	1	313	7	0	21	10	.677	0	0-0	0	2.57	2.94

Huston Street

Pitches: R **Bats:** R **Pos:** RP-40

Ht: 6'0" **Wt:** 190 **Born:** 8/2/1983 **Age:** 29

Year	Team	Lg	G	GS	CG	GF	IP	BFP	H	R	ER	HR	SH	SF	HB	TBB	IBB	SO	WP	Bk	W	L	Pct	Sh	Sv-Op	Hld	ERC	ERA
2012	Lk Els*	A+	2	2	0	0	2.0	8	1	2	2	1	0	0	0	1	0	1	0	0	0	0	-	0	0- -	-	4.08	9.00
2005	Oak	AL	67	0	0	47	78.1	306	53	17	15	3	3	2	2	26	4	72	1	0	5	1	.833	0	23-27	0	1.87	1.72
2006	Oak	AL	69	0	0	55	70.2	290	64	28	26	4	3	3	2	13	3	67	4	0	4	4	.500	0	37-48	1	2.49	3.31
2007	Oak	AL	48	0	0	35	50.0	199	35	20	16	5	2	1	0	12	3	63	0	0	5	2	.714	0	16-21	5	1.84	2.88
2008	Oak	AL	63	0	0	37	70.0	287	58	29	29	6	3	3	1	27	6	69	2	0	7	5	.583	0	18-25	6	2.98	3.73
2009	Col	NL	64	0	0	52	61.2	240	43	22	21	7	3	2	0	13	4	70	0	0	4	1	.800	0	35-37	2	1.83	3.06
2010	Col	NL	44	0	0	39	47.1	187	39	21	19	5	0	1	2	11	4	45	2	1	4	4	.500	0	20-25	0	2.66	3.61
2011	Col	NL	62	0	0	47	58.1	239	62	28	25	10	3	1	1	9	1	55	0	0	1	4	.200	0	29-33	4	4.03	3.86
2012	SD	NL	40	0	0	36	39.0	144	17	8	8	2	1	1	0	11	1	47	1	0	2	1	.667	0	23-24	0	0.99	1.85
	Postseason		8	0	0	7	9.0	43	14	9	9	2	1	1	0	4	0	5	0	0	0	3	.000	0	3-4	1	8.97	9.00
	8 ML YEARS		457	0	0	348	475.1	1892	371	173	159	42	18	14	8	122	26	488	10	1	32	22	.593	0	201-240	18	2.32	3.01

Pedro Strop

Pitches: R **Bats:** R **Pos:** RP-70

STROPE

Ht: 6'0" **Wt:** 215 **Born:** 6/13/1985 **Age:** 28

Year	Team	Lg	G	GS	CG	GF	IP	BFP	H	R	ER	HR	SH	SF	HB	TBB	IBB	SO	WP	Bk	W	L	Pct	Sh	Sv-Op	Hld	ERC	ERA
2009	Tex	AL	7	0	0	3	7.0	30	6	6	6	0	0	0	0	4	0	9	0	0	0	0	-	0	0-0	0	3.27	7.71
2010	Tex	AL	15	0	0	5	10.2	60	17	12	12	2	1	0	1	11	0	11	5	1	0	0	-	0	0-0	1	11.92	10.13
2011	2 Tms	AL	23	0	0	6	22.0	90	15	5	5	0	2	1	1	10	0	21	2	2	2	1	.667	0	0-2	4	2.15	2.05
2012	Bal	AL	70	0	0	17	66.1	283	52	18	18	2	1	1	4	37	2	58	5	0	5	2	.714	0	3-10	24	3.22	2.44
11	Tex	AL	11	0	0	4	9.2	44	7	4	4	0	1	1	1	7	0	9	2	2	0	1	.000	0	0-1	0	3.34	3.72
11	Bal	AL	12	0	0	2	12.1	46	8	1	1	0	1	0	0	3	0	12	0	0	2	0	1.000	0	0-1	4	1.39	0.73
	4 ML YEARS		115	0	0	31	106.0	463	90	41	41	4	4	2	6	62	2	99	12	3	7	3	.700	0	3-12	29	3.71	3.48

Drew Stubbs

Bats: R Throws: R Pos: CF-135; PR-2   Ht: 6'4" Wt: 205 Born: 10/4/1984 Age: 28

Year Team	Lg	G	AB	H	2B	3B	HR	(Hm	Rd)	TB	R	RBI	RC	TBB	IBB	SO	HBP	SH	SF	SB	CS	SB%	GDP	Avg	OBP	Slg
2012 Dayton*	A	3	10	1	0	0	0	(-	-)	1	0	1	0	2	0	0	0			0	0	-	0	.100	.182	.100
2009 Cin	NL	42	180	48	5	1	8	(7	1)	79	27	17	22	15	0	49	0	1	0	10	4	.71	1	.267	.323	.439
2010 Cin	NL	150	514	131	19	6	22	(13	9)	228	91	77	74	55	2	168	5	3	6	30	6	.83	6	.255	.329	.444
2011 Cin	NL	158	604	147	22	3	15	(9	6)	220	92	44	66	63	1	205	7	6	1	40	10	.80	2	.243	.321	.364
2012 Cin	NL	136	493	105	13	2	14	(6	8)	164	75	40	45	42	0	166	2	6	1	30	7	.81	2	.213	.277	.333
Postseason		3	9	1	0	0	0	(0	0)	1	0	0	0	2	0	4	0	0	0	0	0	-	0	.111	.273	.111
4 ML YEARS		486	1791	431	59	12	59	(35	24)	691	285	178	207	175	3	588	14	16	8	110	27	.80	11	.241	.312	.386

Eric Stults

Pitches: L Bats: L Pos: SP-15; RP-5   Ht: 6'0" Wt: 225 Born: 12/9/1979 Age: 33

Year Team	Lg	G	GS	CG	GF	IP	BFP	H	R	ER	HR	SH	SF	HB	TBB	IBB	SO	WP	Bk	W	L	Pct	Sh	Sv-Op	Hld	ERC	ERA
2012 Charltt*	AAA	5	5	0	0	28.2	115	25	7	7	0	1	1	0	10	0	26	1	0	1	1	.500	0	0- -	-	2.64	2.20
2012 Tucsn*	AAA	2	2	0	0	6.2	34	7	5	4	0	0	0	0	4	0	10	0	0	0	0	-	0	0- -	-	3.83	5.40
2006 LAD	NL	6	2	0	2	17.2	73	17	12	11	4	2	0	0	7	0	5	0	0	1	0	1.000	0	0-0	0	4.91	5.60
2007 LAD	NL	12	5	0	0	38.2	179	50	26	25	5	1	1	1	17	2	30	2	0	1	4	.200	0	0-0	1	6.25	5.82
2008 LAD	NL	7	7	1	0	38.2	167	38	18	15	6	2	0	1	13	2	30	0	0	2	3	.400	1	0-0	0	4.07	3.49
2009 LAD	NL	10	10	1	0	50.0	223	51	27	27	3	3	0	4	26	2	33	2	0	4	3	.571	1	0-0	0	4.67	4.86
2011 Col	NL	6	0	0	2	12.0	53	11	8	8	4	0	0	1	4	1	7	0	0	0	0	-	0	0-0	0	4.94	6.00
2012 2 Tms		20	15	0	2	99.0	413	92	38	32	7	9	5	2	27	0	55	1	1	8	3	.727	0	0-0	0	3.06	2.91
12 CWS	AL	2	1	0	1	6.2	30	6	2	2	0	0	0	1	4	0	4	0	0	0	0	-	0	0-0	0	4.14	2.70
12 SD	NL	18	14	0	1	92.1	383	86	36	30	7	9	5	1	23	0	51	1	1	8	3	.727	0	0-0	0	2.98	2.92
6 ML YEARS		61	39	2	6	256.0	1108	259	129	118	29	17	6	9	94	7	160	5	1	16	13	.552	2	0-0	1	4.19	4.15

Michael Stutes

Pitches: R Bats: R Pos: RP-6   STOOTS   Ht: 6'1" Wt: 185 Born: 9/4/1986 Age: 26

Year Team	Lg	G	GS	CG	GF	IP	BFP	H	R	ER	HR	SH	SF	HB	TBB	IBB	SO	WP	Bk	W	L	Pct	Sh	Sv-Op	Hld	ERC	ERA
2008 Wmspt	A-	6	6	0	0	27.0	105	16	5	4	2	0	0	1	11	0	31	1	0	2	1	.667	0	0- -	-	2.06	1.33
2008 Lakwd	A	7	7	0	0	42.2	164	20	8	7	1	0	0	2	18	0	53	4	1	5	1	.833	0	0- -	-	1.39	1.48
2009 Rdng	AA	27	27	0	0	145.2	632	147	78	69	15	6	5	8	58	0	109	6	1	8	8	.500	0	0- -	-	4.39	4.26
2010 Rdng	AA	25	0	0	12	35.2	159	28	15	15	2	1	1	7	21	0	37	2	1	3	0	1.000	0	2- -	-	4.05	3.79
2010 LV	AAA	28	0	0	5	40.2	170	29	15	14	5	1	0	1	23	1	42	3	1	4	1	.800	0	1- -	-	3.41	3.10
2011 LV	AAA	7	0	0	5	10.0	41	9	3	2	0	0	0	0	4	0	14	1	0	2	1	.667	0	1- -	-	2.95	1.80
2011 Phi	NL	57	0	0	11	62.0	259	49	25	25	7	2	2	2	28	2	58	0	0	6	2	.750	0	0-0	13	3.31	3.63
2012 Phi	NL	6	0	0	5	5.2	29	7	6	4	0	0	0	0	4	0	5	1	0	0	0	-	0	0-0	1	5.50	6.35
Postseason		1	0	0	0	0.1	5	3	3	3	0	0	0	0	1	0	1	0	0	0	0	-	0	0-0	0	83.91	81.00
2 ML YEARS		63	0	0	15	67.2	288	56	31	29	7	2	2	2	32	2	63	1	0	6	2	.750	0	0-0	14	3.50	3.86

Jeff Suppan

Pitches: R Bats: R Pos: SP-6   SOO-pahn   Ht: 6'2" Wt: 230 Born: 1/2/1975 Age: 38

Year Team	Lg	G	GS	CG	GF	IP	BFP	H	R	ER	HR	SH	SF	HB	TBB	IBB	SO	WP	Bk	W	L	Pct	Sh	Sv-Op	Hld	ERC	ERA
2012 Tucsn*	AAA	2	2	0	0	6.2	39	17	9	9	0	1	0	3	0	2	0	0	0	0	1	.000	0	0- -	-	13.75	12.15
1995 Bos	AL	8	3	0	1	22.2	100	29	15	15	4	1	1	0	5	1	19	0	0	1	2	.333	0	0-0	1	5.43	5.96
1996 Bos	AL	8	4	0	2	22.2	107	29	19	19	3	1	4	1	13	0	13	3	0	1	1	.500	0	0-0	0	7.03	7.54
1997 Bos	AL	23	22	0	1	112.1	503	140	75	71	12	0	4	4	36	1	67	5	0	7	3	.700	0	0-0	0	5.39	5.69
1998 2 Tms		17	14	1	2	78.2	345	91	56	50	13	3	2	1	22	1	51	2	0	1	7	.125	0	0-0	0	4.95	5.72
1999 KC	AL	32	32	4	0	208.2	887	222	113	105	28	7	5	3	62	4	103	5	1	10	12	.455	1	0-0	0	4.33	4.53
2000 KC	AL	35	33	3	0	217.0	948	240	121	119	36	5	6	7	84	3	128	7	1	10	9	.526	1	0-0	0	5.31	4.94
2001 KC	AL	34	34	1	0	218.1	946	227	120	106	26	5	6	12	74	3	120	6	0	10	14	.417	0	0-0	0	4.40	4.37
2002 KC	AL	33	33	3	0	208.0	912	229	134	123	32	4	11	7	68	3	109	10	1	9	16	.360	1	0-0	0	4.84	5.32
2003 2 Tms		32	31	3	0	204.0	873	217	98	95	23	11	6	8	51	5	110	7	0	13	11	.542	2	0-0	0	4.03	4.19
2004 StL	NL	31	31	0	0	188.0	811	192	98	87	25	8	5	8	65	1	110	4	1	16	9	.640	0	0-0	0	4.38	4.16
2005 StL	NL	32	32	0	0	194.1	834	206	93	77	24	11	5	7	63	1	114	6	1	16	10	.615	0	0-0	0	4.46	3.57
2006 StL	NL	32	32	0	0	190.0	837	207	100	87	21	9	3	8	69	6	104	8	0	12	7	.632	0	0-0	0	4.62	4.12
2007 Mil	NL	34	34	1	0	206.2	919	243	113	106	18	14	11	11	68	10	114	7	0	12	12	.500	0	0-0	0	4.84	4.62
2008 Mil	NL	31	31	0	0	177.2	780	207	110	98	30	10	4	4	67	7	90	3	1	10	10	.500	0	0-0	0	5.58	4.96
2009 Mil	NL	30	30	0	0	161.2	748	200	106	95	25	14	4	11	74	8	80	12	0	7	12	.368	0	0-0	0	6.39	5.29
2010 2 Tms		30	15	0	10	101.1	452	130	61	57	13	9	3	2	37	1	51	4	0	3	8	.273	0	0-0	0	6.02	5.06
2012 SD	NL	6	6	0	0	30.2	137	34	19	18	4	3	0	0	13	3	7	0	0	2	3	.400	0	0-0	0	4.81	5.28
98 Ari	NL	13	13	1	0	66.0	299	82	55	49	12	3	2	1	21	1	39	2	0	1	7	.125	0	0-0	0	5.73	6.68
98 KC	AL	4	1	0	2	12.2	46	9	1	1	1	0	0	0	1	0	12	0	0	0	0	-	0	0-0	0	1.51	0.71
03 Pit	NL	21	21	3	0	141.0	597	147	57	56	11	10	2	6	31	5	78	3	0	10	7	.588	2	0-0	0	3.55	3.57
03 Bos	AL	11	10	0	0	63.0	276	70	41	39	12	1	4	2	20	0	32	4	0	3	4	.429	0	0-0	0	5.15	5.57
10 Mil	NL	15	2	0	9	31.0	148	50	29	27	4	4	2	1	12	1	18	1	0	0	2	.000	0	0-0	0	8.38	7.84
10 StL	NL	15	13	0	1	70.1	304	80	32	30	9	5	1	1	25	0	33	3	0	3	6	.333	0	0-0	0	5.06	3.84
Postseason		10	10	0	0	57.0	241	46	24	23	9	1	2	3	24	4	36	1	0	3	4	.429	0	0-0	0	3.56	3.63
17 ML YEARS		448	417	16	16	2542.2	11139	2843	1451	1328	337	112	80	94	871	58	1390	89	6	140	146	.490	5	0-0	1	4.89	4.70

Eric Surkamp

Pitches: L **Bats:** L **Pos:** P **Ht:** 6'5" **Wt:** 215 **Born:** 7/16/1987 **Age:** 25

			HOW MUCH HE PITCHED				WHAT HE GAVE UP											THE RESULTS					
Year	Team	Lg	G	GS	CG	GF	IP	BFP	H	R	ER	HR	SH	SF	HB	TBB	IBB	SO	WP	Bk	W	L	Pct	Sh	Sv-Op Hld	ERC	ERA
2008	Giants	R	2	0	0	0	3.1	13	3	1	1	0	0	0	0	0	0	7	0	0	0	0	-	0	0- - -	1.57	2.70
2008	SlmKzr	A-	5	4	0	0	14.0	66	20	10	10	1	3	0	1	5	0	16	0	0	0	2	.000	0	0- - -	6.57	6.43
2009	Augsta	A	23	23	2	0	131.0	551	129	57	48	6	2	4	4	39	0	169	9	0	11	5	.688	0	0- - -	3.36	3.30
2010	SnJos	A+	17	17	1	0	101.1	398	79	39	35	4	4	2	6	22	0	108	5	0	4	2	.667	1	0- - -	2.21	3.11
2011	Rchmd	AA	23	22	1	0	142.1	572	110	37	32	5	6	0	5	44	0	165	5	1	10	4	.714	0	0- - -	2.30	2.02
2011	SnJos	A+	1	1	0	0	6.0	22	4	0	0	0	0	0	0	1	0	5	0	0	1	0	1.000	0	0- - -	1.29	0.00
2011	SF	NL	6	6	0	0	26.2	126	32	18	17	1	2	2	2	17	1	13	0	0	2	2	.500	0	0-0 0	6.03	5.74

Drew Sutton

Bats: B **Throws:** R **Pos:** LF-13; 3B-11; PH-10; 2B-8; RF-8; 1B-3 **Ht:** 6'3" **Wt:** 200 **Born:** 6/30/1983 **Age:** 30

						BATTING														BASERUNNING				AVERAGES		
Year	Team	Lg	G	AB	H	2B	3B	HR	(Hm	Rd)	TB	R	RBI	RC	TBB	IBB	SO	HBP	SH	SF	SB	CS	SB%	GDP	Avg	OBP	Slg
2012	Gwnntt*	AAA	38	137	37	10	2	0	(-	-)	51	19	15	20	20	0	24	4	1	2	2	3	.40	1	.270	.374	.372
2012	Indy*	AAA	12	21	1	1	0	0	(-	-)	2	2	1	0	4	0	7	1	0	0	1	0	1.00	0	.048	.231	.095
2009	Cin	NL	42	66	14	4	1	1	(1	0)	23	10	9	12	7	0	20	1	2	0	0	2	.00	1	.212	.297	.348
2010	2 Tms		13	39	10	1	0	2	(1	1)	17	5	8	7	3	0	13	0	0	0	0	0	-	1	.256	.310	.436
2011	Bos	AL	31	54	17	7	0	0	(0	0)	24	11	7	9	3	0	13	1	2	0	0	0	-	0	.315	.362	.444
2012	2 Tms		42	122	31	12	1	1	(1	0)	48	12	13	16	6	0	42	1	0	1	0	1	.00	1	.254	.292	.393
10	Cin	NL	2	3	2	0	0	1	(1	0)	5	1	4	3	0	0	1	0	0	0	0	0	-	0	.667	.667	1.667
10	Cle	AL	11	36	8	1	0	1	(0	1)	12	4	4	4	3	0	12	0	0	0	0	0	-	1	.222	.282	.333
12	TB	AL	18	48	13	4	0	0	(0	0)	17	2	6	7	2	0	16	1	0	0	0	0	-	0	.271	.314	.354
12	Pit	NL	24	74	18	8	1	1	(1	0)	31	10	7	9	4	0	26	0	0	1	0	1	.00	1	.243	.278	.419
	4 ML YEARS		128	281	72	24	2	4	(3	1)	112	38	37	44	19	0	88	3	4	1	0	3	.00	3	.256	.309	.399

Ichiro Suzuki

EE-chee-row soo-ZOO-kee

Bats: L **Throws:** R **Pos:** RF-132; LF-35; CF-7; PH-6; DH-3; PR-1 **Ht:** 5'11" **Wt:** 170 **Born:** 10/22/1973 **Age:** 39

						BATTING														BASERUNNING				AVERAGES		
Year	Team	Lg	G	AB	H	2B	3B	HR	(Hm	Rd)	TB	R	RBI	RC	TBB	IBB	SO	HBP	SH	SF	SB	CS	SB%	GDP	Avg	OBP	Slg
2001	Sea	AL	157	692	242	34	8	8	(5	3)	316	127	69	124	30	10	53	8	4	4	56	14	.80	3	.350	.381	.457
2002	Sea	AL	157	647	208	27	8	8	(4	4)	275	111	51	110	68	27	62	5	3	5	31	15	.67	3	.321	.388	.425
2003	Sea	AL	159	679	212	29	8	13	(8	5)	296	111	62	107	36	7	69	6	3	1	34	8	.81	3	.312	.352	.436
2004	Sea	AL	161	704	262	24	5	8	(4	4)	320	101	60	125	49	19	63	4	2	3	36	11	.77	6	.372	.414	.455
2005	Sea	AL	162	679	206	21	12	15	(8	7)	296	111	68	107	48	23	66	4	2	5	33	8	.80	5	.303	.350	.436
2006	Sea	AL	161	695	224	20	9	9	(6	3)	289	110	49	107	49	16	71	5	1	2	45	2	.96	2	.322	.370	.416
2007	Sea	AL	161	678	238	22	7	6	(3	3)	292	111	68	128	49	13	77	3	4	2	37	8	.82	7	.351	.396	.431
2008	Sea	AL	162	686	213	20	7	6	(3	3)	265	103	42	100	51	12	65	5	3	4	43	4	.91	8	.310	.361	.386
2009	Sea	AL	146	639	225	31	4	11	(6	5)	297	88	46	111	32	15	71	4	2	1	26	9	.74	1	.352	.386	.465
2010	Sea	AL	162	680	214	30	3	6	(1	5)	268	74	43	96	45	13	86	3	3	1	42	9	.82	3	.315	.359	.394
2011	Sea	AL	161	677	184	22	3	5	(4	1)	227	80	47	80	39	13	69	0	1	4	40	7	.85	11	.272	.310	.335
2012	2 Tms	AL	162	629	178	28	6	9	(6	3)	245	77	55	63	22	5	61	2	5	5	29	7	.81	12	.283	.307	.390
12	Sea	AL	95	402	105	15	5	4	(1	3)	142	49	28	33	17	4	40	0	0	4	15	2	.88	10	.261	.288	.353
12	NYY	AL	67	227	73	13	1	5	(5	0)	103	28	27	30	5	1	21	2	5	1	14	5	.74	2	.322	.340	.454
	Postseason		10	38	16	2	0	0	(0	0)	18	7	3	8	5	2	4	0	0	0	3	2	.60	0	.421	.488	.474
	12 ML YEARS		1911	8085	2606	308	80	104	(58	46)	3386	1204	660	1260	518	173	813	49	33	38	452	102	.82	69	.322	.365	.419

Kurt Suzuki

Bats: R **Throws:** R **Pos:** C-117; PH-2 **Ht:** 5'11" **Wt:** 195 **Born:** 10/4/1983 **Age:** 29

						BATTING														BASERUNNING				AVERAGES		
Year	Team	Lg	G	AB	H	2B	3B	HR	(Hm	Rd)	TB	R	RBI	RC	TBB	IBB	SO	HBP	SH	SF	SB	CS	SB%	GDP	Avg	OBP	Slg
2007	Oak	AL	68	213	53	13	0	7	(4	3)	87	27	39	33	24	0	39	3	3	5	0	0	-	4	.249	.327	.408
2008	Oak	AL	148	530	148	25	1	7	(2	5)	196	54	42	66	44	2	69	11	2	1	2	3	.40	20	.279	.346	.370
2009	Oak	AL	147	570	156	37	1	15	(8	7)	240	74	88	77	28	0	59	8	1	7	8	2	.80	14	.274	.313	.421
2010	Oak	AL	131	495	120	18	2	13	(8	5)	181	55	71	54	33	3	49	12	0	4	3	2	.60	22	.242	.303	.366
2011	Oak	AL	134	460	109	26	1	14	(8	6)	177	54	44	42	38	1	64	7	3	7	2	2	.50	14	.237	.301	.385
2012	2 Tms		118	408	96	20	0	6	(3	3)	134	36	43	39	20	3	73	5	4	5	2	0	1.00	5	.235	.276	.328
12	Oak	AL	75	262	57	15	0	1	(1	0)	75	19	18	16	9	0	53	3	2	1	1	0	1.00	3	.218	.250	.286
12	Was	NL	43	146	39	5	0	5	(2	3)	59	17	25	23	11	3	20	2	2	3	1	0	1.00	2	.267	.321	.404
	6 ML YEARS		746	2676	682	139	4	62	(36	26)	1015	300	327	311	187	9	353	46	13	29	17	9	.65	79	.255	.311	.379

Anthony Swarzak

Pitches: R **Bats:** R **Pos:** RP-39; SP-5 SWORE-zack **Ht:** 6'4" **Wt:** 209 **Born:** 9/10/1985 **Age:** 27

						HOW MUCH HE PITCHED			WHAT HE GAVE UP												THE RESULTS				
Year	Team	Lg	G	GS	CG	GF	IP	BFP	H	R	ER	HR	SH	SF	HB	TBB	IBB	SO	WP	Bk	W	L	Pct	Sh	Sv-Op Hld	ERC	ERA
2009	Min	AL	12	12	0	0	59.0	268	76	43	41	12	1	1	2	20	0	34	0	0	3	7	.300	0	0-0 0	6.50	6.25
2011	Min	AL	27	11	0	2	102.0	441	111	53	49	9	2	3	6	26	1	55	3	1	4	7	.364	0	0-0 0	4.11	4.32
2012	Min	AL	44	5	0	9	96.2	413	106	57	54	15	3	6	0	31	8	62	3	0	3	6	.333	0	0-1 1	4.63	5.03
	3 ML YEARS		83	28	0	11	257.2	1122	293	153	144	36	6	10	8	77	9	151	6	1	10	20	.333	0	0-1 1	4.83	5.03

Ryan Sweeney

Bats: L **Throws:** L **Pos:** RF-49; CF-19; PH-6   **Ht:** 6'4" **Wt:** 225 **Born:** 2/20/1985 **Age:** 28

Year	Team	Lg	G	AB	H	2B	3B	HR	(Hm	Rd)	TB	R	RBI	RC	TBB	IBB	SO	HBP	SH	SF	SB	CS	SB%	GDP	Avg	OBP	Slg
2012	PortInd*	AA	2	7	1	0	0	0	(-	-)	1	0	0	0	0	0	0	0	0	0	0	0	-	0	.143	.143	.143
2006	CWS	AL	18	35	8	0	0	0	(0	0)	8	1	5	1	0	0	7	0	0	0	0	0	-	1	.229	.229	.229
2007	CWS	AL	15	45	9	3	0	1	(1	0)	15	5	5	2	4	0	5	0	0	0	0	1	.00	2	.200	.265	.333
2008	Oak	AL	115	384	110	18	2	5	(1	4)	147	53	45	56	38	3	67	3	2	6	9	1	.90	9	.286	.350	.383
2009	Oak	AL	134	484	142	31	3	6	(2	4)	197	68	53	63	40	1	67	3	2	5	6	5	.55	14	.293	.348	.407
2010	Oak	AL	82	303	89	20	2	1	(1	0)	116	41	36	38	24	2	41	0	1	3	1	1	.50	14	.294	.342	.383
2011	Oak	AL	108	264	70	11	3	1	(1	0)	90	34	25	35	33	3	48	0	1	1	1	1	.50	7	.265	.346	.341
2012	Bos	AL	63	204	53	19	2	0	(0	0)	76	22	16	20	12	0	43	1	1	1	0	0	-	1	.260	.303	.373
	7 ML YEARS		535	1719	481	102	12	14	(6	8)	649	224	185	215	151	9	278	7	7	16	17	9	.65	48	.280	.338	.378

Nick Swisher

Bats: B **Throws:** L **Pos:** RF-109; 1B-41; DH-12; PH-2   **Ht:** 5'11" **Wt:** 200 **Born:** 11/25/1980 **Age:** 32

Year	Team	Lg	G	AB	H	2B	3B	HR	(Hm	Rd)	TB	R	RBI	RC	TBB	IBB	SO	HBP	SH	SF	SB	CS	SB%	GDP	Avg	OBP	Slg
2004	Oak	AL	20	60	15	4	0	2	(1	1)	25	11	8	8	8	0	11	2	0	1	0	0	-	2	.250	.352	.417
2005	Oak	AL	131	462	109	32	1	21	(11	10)	206	66	74	62	55	3	110	4	0	1	0	1	.00	9	.236	.322	.446
2006	Oak	AL	157	556	141	24	2	35	(17	18)	274	106	95	95	97	7	152	11	2	6	1	2	.33	13	.254	.372	.493
2007	Oak	AL	150	539	141	36	1	22	(8	14)	245	84	78	89	100	12	131	10	1	9	3	2	.60	13	.262	.381	.455
2008	CWS	AL	153	497	109	21	1	24	(19	5)	204	86	69	69	82	6	135	4	1	4	3	3	.50	14	.219	.332	.410
2009	NYY	AL	150	498	124	35	1	29	(8	21)	248	84	82	84	97	2	126	3	3	6	0	0	-	13	.249	.371	.498
2010	NYY	AL	150	566	163	33	3	29	(15	14)	289	91	89	100	58	0	139	6	3	2	1	2	.33	13	.288	.359	.511
2011	NYY	AL	150	526	137	30	0	23	(12	11)	236	81	85	90	95	6	125	5	1	8	2	2	.50	18	.260	.374	.449
2012	NYY	AL	148	537	146	36	0	24	(11	13)	254	75	93	98	77	2	141	4	1	5	2	3	.40	9	.272	.364	.473
	Postseason		38	124	21	7	0	4	(3	1)	40	16	6	9	21	0	36	1	1	0	0	0	-	2	.169	.295	.323
	9 ML YEARS		1209	4241	1085	251	9	209	(102	107)	1981	684	673	695	669	38	1070	49	12	42	12	15	.44	104	.256	.361	.467

Jose Tabata

Bats: R **Throws:** R **Pos:** RF-77; LF-32; PH-11   TAH-bah-tah   **Ht:** 5'11" **Wt:** 215 **Born:** 8/12/1988 **Age:** 24

Year	Team	Lg	G	AB	H	2B	3B	HR	(Hm	Rd)	TB	R	RBI	RC	TBB	IBB	SO	HBP	SH	SF	SB	CS	SB%	GDP	Avg	OBP	Slg
2012	Indy*	AAA	41	158	47	9	0	0	(-	-)	56	21	15	21	10	0	20	4	0	1	5	2	.71	4	.297	.353	.354
2010	Pit	NL	102	405	121	21	4	4	(3	1)	162	61	35	59	28	0	57	2	5	1	19	7	.73	7	.299	.346	.400
2011	Pit	NL	91	334	89	18	1	4	(3	1)	121	53	21	41	40	1	61	4	1	3	16	7	.70	8	.266	.349	.362
2012	Pit	NL	103	333	81	20	3	3	(1	2)	116	43	16	31	29	0	58	6	6	0	8	12	.40	7	.243	.315	.348
	3 ML YEARS		296	1072	291	59	8	11	(7	4)	399	157	72	131	97	1	176	12	12	4	43	26	.62	22	.271	.338	.372

Hisanori Takahashi

Pitches: L **Bats:** L **Pos:** RP-51   EES-ah-nore-ee tah-ka-HA-shee   **Ht:** 5'10" **Wt:** 175 **Born:** 4/2/1975 **Age:** 38

Year	Team	Lg	G	GS	CG	GF	IP	BFP	H	R	ER	HR	SH	SF	HB	TBB	IBB	SO	WP	Bk	W	L	Pct	Sh	Sv-Op	Hld	ERC	ERA
2012	Salt Lk*	AAA	1	0	0	0	1.0	3	0	0	0	0	0	0	0	0	0	0	0	0	0	0	-	0	0--	-	0.00	0.00
2010	NYM	NL	53	12	0	21	122.0	516	116	51	49	13	10	3	0	43	7	114	1	1	10	6	.625	0	8-8	3	3.57	3.61
2011	LAA	AL	61	0	0	18	68.0	281	58	30	26	7	3	3	0	25	8	52	1	0	4	3	.571	0	2-5	7	3.01	3.44
2012	2 Tms		51	0	0	11	50.1	212	49	32	31	8	2	1	0	14	1	52	0	0	0	3	.000	0	0-1	3	3.77	5.54
12	LAA	AL	42	0	0	9	42.0	173	39	24	23	6	1	1	0	10	1	41	0	0	0	3	.000	0	0-1	3	3.28	4.93
12	Pit	NL	9	0	0	2	8.1	39	10	8	8	2	1	0	0	4	0	11	0	0	0	0	-	0	0-0	0	6.53	8.64
	3 ML YEARS		165	12	0	50	240.1	1009	223	113	106	28	15	7	0	82	16	218	2	1	14	12	.538	0	10-14	13	3.45	3.97

Yoshinori Tateyama

Pitches: R **Bats:** R **Pos:** RP-14   YO-shin-nor-ee TAH-tay-yah-mah   **Ht:** 5'10" **Wt:** 165 **Born:** 12/26/1975 **Age:** 37

Year	Team	Lg	G	GS	CG	GF	IP	BFP	H	R	ER	HR	SH	SF	HB	TBB	IBB	SO	WP	Bk	W	L	Pct	Sh	Sv-Op	Hld	ERC	ERA
1999	HNHF	Jap	22	-	1	-	106.0	442	101	43	34	11	-	-	1	29	-	62	0	0	6	5	.545	1	0--	-	3.38	2.89
2000	HNHF	Jap	28	-	2	-	89.1	396	106	57	55	15	-	-	2	29	-	55	1	0	6	8	.429	0	0--	-	5.45	5.54
2001	HNHF	Jap	10	-	0	-	14.1	72	22	17	17	5	-	-	2	9	-	9	0	0	1	0	1.000	0	0--	-	11.80	10.67
2002	HNHF	Jap	45	-	0	-	59.0	231	40	16	15	7	-	-	4	13	-	41	1	0	3	2	.600	0	4--	-	2.12	2.29
2003	HNHF	Jap	32	-	0	-	37.1	138	24	9	9	5	-	-	0	4	-	31	2	0	2	1	.667	0	15--	-	1.51	2.17
2004	HNHF	Jap	41	-	0	-	46.1	190	39	17	12	4	-	-	2	7	-	39	1	0	1	3	.250	0	0--	-	2.30	2.33
2005	HNHF	Jap	45	-	0	-	51.1	211	50	22	21	10	-	-	2	8	-	35	1	0	4	6	.400	0	2--	-	3.72	3.68
2006	HNHF	Jap	46	-	0	-	47.0	193	42	18	16	6	-	-	2	10	-	30	1	1	3	3	.500	0	0--	-	3.10	3.06
2007	HNHF	Jap	7	-	1	-	41.0	167	33	20	19	7	-	-	2	9	-	31	0	0	2	4	.333	0	0--	-	3.26	4.17
2008	HNHF	Jap	58	-	0	-	67.1	276	61	23	23	3	-	-	4	12	-	53	1	0	1	2	.333	0	2--	-	2.59	3.07
2009	HNHF	Jap	46	-	0	-	47.2	209	53	24	20	3	-	-	1	15	-	43	1	0	5	7	.417	0	4--	-	4.15	3.78
2010	HNHF	Jap	58	-	0	-	55.0	218	43	11	11	3	-	-	2	11	-	59	0	0	1	2	.333	0	4--	-	2.07	1.80
2011	RdRck	AAA	14	0	0	6	21.0	86	17	5	5	1	0	0	3	4	0	26	2	0	1	0	1.000	0	1--	-	2.47	2.14
2012	RdRck	AAA	32	0	0	19	39.2	153	29	8	5	2	1	1	1	7	1	45	0	0	4	0	1.000	0	6--	-	1.70	1.13
2011	Tex	AL	39	0	0	8	44.0	181	37	23	22	8	0	0	2	11	4	43	1	0	2	0	1.000	0	1-1	4	3.16	4.50
2012	Tex	AL	14	0	0	5	17.0	76	18	19	17	4	0	0	0	6	1	18	0	0	1	0	1.000	0	0-0	0	4.90	9.00
	Postseason		1	0	0	1	0.2	3	1	0	0	0	0	0	0	0	0	0	0	0	0	0	-	0	0-0	0	4.47	0.00
	2 ML YEARS		53	0	0	13	61.0	257	55	42	39	12	0	0	2	17	5	61	1	0	3	0	1.000	0	1-1	4	3.63	5.75

Andrew Taylor

Pitches: L Bats: R Pos: RP-3   Ht: 6'2" Wt: 195 Born: 8/18/1986 Age: 26

		HOW MUCH HE PITCHED						WHAT HE GAVE UP										THE RESULTS						
Year	Team	Lg	G	GS	CG	GF	IP	BFP	H	R	ER	HR	SH	SF	HB	TBB	IBB	SO	WP	Bk	W	L	Pct	Sh	Sv-Op Hld	ERC	ERA
2008	Orem	R+	21	3	0	10	35.0	151	33	22	17	4	2	1	2	13	0	39	4	0	2	1	.667	0	5- -	-	3.94	4.37
2009	CRpds	A	40	0	0	23	51.1	199	29	7	7	0	4	1	0	19	0	83	1	0	3	0	1.000	0	8- -	-	1.36	1.23
2009	RCuca	A+	5	0	0	0	5.2	34	8	8	6	2	1	0	0	8	0	8	1	0	1	0	1.000	0	0- -	-	13.12	9.53
2010	RCuca	A+	20	0	0	6	35.0	144	24	9	8	1	1	0	0	14	0	39	3	0	4	1	.800	0	0- -	-	1.96	2.06
2010	Ark	AA	15	4	0	4	38.1	167	38	21	20	2	2	1	2	18	0	21	4	0	1	3	.250	0	0- -	-	4.21	4.70
2011	Ark	AA	29	19	0	7	112.0	529	125	86	64	13	8	6	9	71	0	73	4	0	2	11	.154	0	0- -	-	6.17	5.14
2012	Ark	AA	37	0	0	13	41.0	184	44	22	21	4	4	2	3	14	0	39	3	0	2	4	.333	0	2- -	-	4.42	4.61
2012	Salt Lk	AAA	16	0	0	1	18.0	83	16	7	7	3	0	0	2	11	0	17	1	0	1	0	1.000	0	0- -	-	5.11	3.50
2012	LAA	AL	3	0	0	2	2.1	14	3	3	3	0	0	0	0	4	0	0	1	0	0	0	-	0	0-0	0	10.22	11.57

Michael Taylor

Bats: R Throws: R Pos: RF-4; LF-2; PH-1   Ht: 6'5" Wt: 255 Born: 12/19/1985 Age: 27

									BATTING												BASERUNNING				AVERAGES		
Year	Team	Lg	G	AB	H	2B	3B	HR	(Hm	Rd)	TB	R	RBI	RC	TBB	IBB	SO	HBP	SH	SF	SB	CS	SB%	GDP	Avg	OBP	Slg
2007	Wmspt	A-	66	233	53	14	0	6	(-	-)	85	30	33	27	23	0	53	2	1	2	8	2	.80	10	.227	.300	.365
2008	Lakwd	A	67	249	90	12	3	10	(-	-)	138	40	50	60	31	1	43	6	0	2	10	3	.77	5	.361	.441	.554
2008	Clrwtr	A+	65	243	80	27	1	9	(-	-)	136	36	38	49	19	3	46	2	0	2	5	6	.45	10	.329	.380	.560
2009	Rdng	AA	86	318	106	22	4	15	(-	-)	181	59	65	74	35	7	51	7	0	3	18	4	.82	14	.333	.408	.569
2009	LV	AAA	30	110	31	6	1	5	(-	-)	54	15	19	20	13	0	19	2	0	3	3	1	.75	3	.282	.359	.491
2010	Scrmto	AAA	127	464	126	26	6	6	(-	-)	182	79	78	68	51	1	92	5	0	3	16	5	.76	22	.272	.348	.392
2011	Scrmto	AAA	93	349	95	16	0	16	(-	-)	159	51	64	60	46	1	80	3	0	2	14	5	.74	8	.272	.360	.456
2012	Scrmto	AAA	120	449	129	31	1	12	(-	-)	198	81	67	89	86	2	105	5	0	3	18	3	.86	8	.287	.405	.441
2011	Oak	AL	11	30	6	0	0	1	(1	0)	9	4	1	4	5	0	11	0	0	0	0	0	-	0	.200	.314	.300
2012	Oak	AL	6	21	3	1	0	0	(0	0)	4	2	0	0	0	0	10	0	0	0	0	0	-	1	.143	.143	.190
	2 ML YEARS		17	51	9	1	0	1	(1	0)	13	6	1	4	5	0	21	0	0	0	0	0	-	1	.176	.250	.255

Junichi Tazawa

Pitches: R Bats: R Pos: RP-37   joo-NEE-chee tuh-ZAH-wah   Ht: 5'11" Wt: 180 Born: 6/6/1986 Age: 27

			HOW MUCH HE PITCHED						WHAT HE GAVE UP											THE RESULTS						
Year	Team	Lg	G	GS	CG	GF	IP	BFP	H	R	ER	HR	SH	SF	HB	TBB	IBB	SO	WP	Bk	W	L	Pct	Sh	Sv-Op Hld	ERC	ERA
2012	Pwtckt*	AAA	25	0	0	8	42.1	179	34	18	12	2	0	1	0	17	0	56	3	1	3	2	.600	0	4- -	-	2.61	2.55
2009	Bos	AL	6	4	0	1	25.1	130	43	23	21	4	0	3	3	9	0	13	0	0	2	3	.400	0	0-0	0	9.14	7.46
2011	Bos	AL	3	0	0	2	3.0	13	3	2	2	1	0	0	0	1	0	4	0	0	0	0	-	0	0-0	0	5.31	6.00
2012	Bos	AL	37	0	0	13	44.0	172	37	7	7	1	1	1	2	5	0	45	0	0	1	1	.500	0	1-1	5	1.94	1.43
	3 ML YEARS		46	4	0	16	72.1	315	83	32	30	6	1	4	5	15	0	62	0	0	3	4	.429	0	1-1	5	4.26	3.73

Everett Teaford

Pitches: L Bats: L Pos: RP-13; SP-5   Ht: 6'0" Wt: 165 Born: 5/15/1984 Age: 29

			HOW MUCH HE PITCHED						WHAT HE GAVE UP											THE RESULTS						
Year	Team	Lg	G	GS	CG	GF	IP	BFP	H	R	ER	HR	SH	SF	HB	TBB	IBB	SO	WP	Bk	W	L	Pct	Sh	Sv-Op Hld	ERC	ERA
2006	Idaho	R+	15	12	0	1	63.0	262	54	29	26	3	1	0	4	20	1	51	5	2	5	1	.833	0	0- -	-	2.86	3.71
2007	Burlgtn	A	27	21	0	1	134.2	578	147	83	70	11	4	10	5	36	0	84	10	2	6	8	.429	0	0- -	-	4.09	4.68
2008	Wilmg	A+	28	23	0	2	144.1	605	135	70	61	15	5	2	3	46	1	116	7	2	8	6	.571	0	1- -	-	3.50	3.80
2009	Wilmg	A+	11	11	0	0	64.0	250	51	19	17	7	2	2	1	12	0	49	2	2	7	1	.875	0	0- -	-	2.37	2.39
2009	NWArk	AA	16	16	1	0	81.0	361	86	53	46	12	3	1	3	34	0	42	2	1	3	7	.300	0	0- -	-	4.97	5.11
2010	NWArk	AA	27	12	0	4	99.0	416	91	39	37	7	3	3	3	32	0	113	4	1	14	3	.824	0	0- -	-	3.25	3.36
2010	Omha	AAA	1	1	0	0	4.2	23	8	7	7	2	0	0	0	1	0	4	0	0	0	1	.000	0	0- -	-	10.29	13.50
2011	Omha	AAA	16	3	0	2	35.0	138	23	14	13	5	0	0	1	11	0	33	1	0	3	2	.600	0	0- -	-	2.35	3.34
2012	Omha	AAA	7	6	0	1	33.0	125	24	4	4	2	0	0	1	8	1	25	0	0	4	0	1.000	0	0- -	-	2.04	1.09
2011	KC	AL	26	3	0	7	44.0	175	36	17	16	8	1	3	1	14	0	28	2	0	2	1	.667	0	1-1	1	3.50	3.27
2012	KC	AL	18	5	0	3	61.1	263	68	34	34	11	0	1	2	21	0	35	2	1	1	4	.200	0	0-0	0	5.31	4.99
	2 ML YEARS		44	8	0	10	105.1	438	104	51	50	19	1	4	3	35	0	63	4	1	3	5	.375	0	1-1	1	4.53	4.27

Taylor Teagarden

Bats: R Throws: R Pos: C-21; PH-2; DH-1   Ht: 6'0" Wt: 215 Born: 12/21/1983 Age: 29

									BATTING												BASERUNNING				AVERAGES		
Year	Team	Lg	G	AB	H	2B	3B	HR	(Hm	Rd)	TB	R	RBI	RC	TBB	IBB	SO	HBP	SH	SF	SB	CS	SB%	GDP	Avg	OBP	Slg
2012	Orioles*	R	3	8	1	0	0	0	(-	-)	1	0	0	0	2	0	2	1	0	0	0	0	-	0	.125	.364	.125
2012	Bowie*	AA	3	7	2	1	0	0	(-	-)	3	1	0	1	3	0	3	0	0	0	0	0	-	0	.286	.500	.429
2012	Dlmrva*	A	3	9	3	2	0	0	(-	-)	5	0	3	2	2	0	5	0	0	1	0	0	-	0	.333	.417	.556
2008	Tex	AL	16	47	15	5	0	6	(3	3)	38	10	17	15	5	0	19	1	0	0	0	0	-	0	.319	.396	.809
2009	Tex	AL	60	198	43	10	0	6	(2	4)	74	26	24	16	14	0	76	1	3	2	0	0	-	6	.217	.270	.374
2010	Tex	AL	28	71	11	1	0	4	(1	3)	24	10	6	5	8	0	34	2	4	0	0	0	-	0	.155	.259	.338
2011	Tex	AL	14	34	8	2	0	0	(0	0)	10	3	2	2	2	0	13	0	0	0	0	0	-	0	.235	.278	.294
2012	Bal	AL	22	57	9	3	0	2	(2	0)	18	4	9	6	5	0	23	0	2	0	0	0	-	1	.158	.226	.316
	5 ML YEARS		140	407	86	24	0	18	(8	10)	164	53	58	44	34	0	165	4	9	2	0	0	-	7	.211	.277	.403

Julio Teheran

Pitches: R Bats: R Pos: SP-1; RP-1   tay-RONN   Ht: 6'2" Wt: 175 Born: 1/27/1991 Age: 22

			HOW MUCH HE PITCHED						WHAT HE GAVE UP											THE RESULTS						
Year	Team	Lg	G	GS	CG	GF	IP	BFP	H	R	ER	HR	SH	SF	HB	TBB	IBB	SO	WP	Bk	W	L	Pct	Sh	Sv-Op Hld	ERC	ERA
2008	Danvle	R+	6	6	0	0	15.0	66	18	12	11	2	0	1	2	4	0	17	0	0	1	2	.333	0	0- -	5.63	6.60
2009	Danvle	R+	7	7	0	0	43.2	173	36	17	13	2	2	0	7	7	0	39	1	0	2	1	.667	0	0- -	2.59	2.68
2009	Rome	A	7	7	0	0	37.2	163	42	20	20	2	0	1	5	11	0	28	4	0	1	3	.250	0	0- -	4.61	4.78
2010	Rome	A	7	7	0	0	39.1	154	23	8	5	1	1	1	5	10	0	45	1	0	2	2	.500	0	0- -	1.55	1.14
2010	MrtlBh	A+	10	10	0	0	63.1	260	56	22	21	6	2	0	5	13	1	76	3	1	4	4	.500	0	0- -	2.95	2.98
2010	Missi	AA	7	7	0	0	40.0	162	29	15	15	2	1	1	1	17	0	38	2	0	3	2	.600	0	0- -	2.53	3.38
2011	Gwnntt	AAA	25	24	0	0	144.2	590	123	46	41	5	1	6	5	48	2	122	3	1	15	3	.833	0	0- -	2.75	2.55
2012	Gwnntt	AAA	26	26	1	0	131.0	576	146	81	74	18	6	7	15	43	1	97	4	2	7	9	.438	0	0- -	5.25	5.08
2011	Atl	NL	5	3	0	0	19.2	87	21	11	11	4	2	1	0	8	0	10	1	0	1	1	.500	0	0-0	0	5.19	5.03
2012	Atl	NL	2	1	0	0	6.1	24	5	4	4	0	0	0	0	1	0	5	0	0	0	0	-	0	0-0	0	1.64	5.68
	2 ML YEARS		7	4	0	0	26.0	111	26	15	15	4	2	1	0	9	0	15	1	0	1	1	.500	0	0-0	0	4.23	5.19

Mark Teixeira

Bats: B Throws: R Pos: 1B-119; DH-4; PH-2   tuh-SHARE-uh   Ht: 6'3" Wt: 215 Born: 4/11/1980 Age: 33

						BATTING																BASERUNNING				AVERAGES		
Year	Team	Lg	G	AB	H	2B	3B	HR	(Hm	Rd)	TB	R	RBI	RC	TBB	IBB	SO	HBP	SH	SF		SB	CS	SB%	GDP	Avg	OBP	Slg
2003	Tex	AL	146	529	137	29	5	26	(19	7)	254	66	84	78	44	5	120	14	0	2		1	2	.33	14	.259	.331	.480
2004	Tex	AL	145	545	153	34	2	38	(18	20)	305	101	112	120	68	12	117	10	0	2		4	1	.80	6	.281	.370	.560
2005	Tex	AL	**162**	644	194	41	3	43	(30	13)	**370**	112	144	**148**	72	5	124	11	0	3		4	0	1.00	18	.301	.379	.575
2006	Tex	AL	**162**	628	177	45	1	33	(12	21)	323	99	110	114	89	12	128	4	0	6		2	0	1.00	17	.282	.371	.514
2007	2 Tms		132	494	151	33	2	30	(14	16)	278	86	105	104	72	13	112	7	0	2		0	0	-	7	.306	.400	.563
2008	2 Tms		157	574	177	41	0	33	(19	14)	317	102	121	119	97	13	93	7	0	7		2	0	1.00	17	.308	.410	.552
2009	NYY	AL	156	609	178	43	3	**39**	(24	15)	**344**	103	**122**	112	81	9	114	12	0	5		2	1	.67	13	.292	.383	.565
2010	NYY	AL	158	601	154	36	0	33	(19	14)	289	**113**	108	110	93	6	122	13	0	5		0	1	.00	15	.256	.365	.481
2011	NYY	AL	156	589	146	26	1	39	(22	17)	291	90	111	106	76	3	110	11	0	8		4	1	.80	12	.248	.341	.494
2012	NYY	AL	123	451	113	27	1	24	(12	12)	214	66	84	69	54	1	83	7	0	**12**		2	1	.67	11	.251	.332	.475
07	Tex	AL	78	286	85	24	1	13	(5	8)	150	48	49	58	45	10	66	3	0	1		0	0	-	5	.297	.397	.524
07	Atl	NL	54	208	66	9	1	17	(9	8)	128	38	56	58	27	3	46	4	0	1		0	0	-	2	.317	.404	.615
08	Atl	NL	103	381	108	27	0	20	(11	9)	195	63	78	69	65	9	70	3	0	2		0	0	-	13	.283	.390	.512
08	LAA	AL	54	193	69	14	0	13	(8	5)	122	39	43	50	32	4	23	4	0	5		2	0	1.00	4	.358	.449	.632
	Postseason		31	121	25	5	0	3	(2	1)	39	19	13	10	16	1	31	4	0	2		0	0	-	2	.207	.315	.322
	10 ML YEARS		1497	5664	1580	355	18	338	(189	149)	2985	938	1101	1092	746	79	1123	96	0	52		21	6	.78	130	.279	.369	.527

Ruben Tejada

Bats: R Throws: R Pos: SS-112; PH-2   Ht: 5'11" Wt: 185 Born: 10/27/1989 Age: 23

						BATTING																BASERUNNING				AVERAGES		
Year	Team	Lg	G	AB	H	2B	3B	HR	(Hm	Rd)	TB	R	RBI	RC	TBB	IBB	SO	HBP	SH	SF		SB	CS	SB%	GDP	Avg	OBP	Slg
2012	Buffalo*	AAA	6	20	4	1	0	0	(-	-)	5	3	2	1	1	0	3	0	0	0		0	0	-	1	.200	.238	.250
2012	StLuci*	A+	2	9	1	1	0	0	(-	-)	2	1	0	0	0	0	2	0	0	0		0	0	-	0	.111	.111	.222
2010	NYM	NL	78	216	46	12	0	1	(0	1)	61	28	15	16	22	3	38	8	6	3		2	2	.50	2	.213	.305	.282
2011	NYM	NL	96	328	93	15	1	0	(0	0)	110	31	36	41	35	3	50	6	4	3		5	1	.83	6	.284	.360	.335
2012	NYM	NL	114	464	134	26	0	1	(0	1)	163	53	25	49	27	0	73	5	3	2		4	4	.50	9	.289	.333	.351
	3 ML YEARS		288	1008	273	53	1	2	(0	2)	334	112	76	106	84	6	161	19	13	8		11	7	.61	17	.271	.336	.331

Blake Tekotte

Bats: L Throws: R Pos: PH-7; LF-2; CF-1; RF-1; PR-1   tee-COAT-ee   Ht: 5'11" Wt: 180 Born: 5/24/1987 Age: 26

						BATTING																BASERUNNING				AVERAGES		
Year	Team	Lg	G	AB	H	2B	3B	HR	(Hm	Rd)	TB	R	RBI	RC	TBB	IBB	SO	HBP	SH	SF		SB	CS	SB%	GDP	Avg	OBP	Slg
2008	Eugene	A-	47	193	55	15	0	6	(-	-)	88	43	29	35	27	0	45	4	1	3		7	4	.64	0	.285	.379	.456
2009	FtWyn	A	134	530	137	24	5	13	(-	-)	210	83	56	79	68	3	97	4	4	4		30	12	.71	6	.258	.345	.396
2010	Lk Els	A+	59	203	63	17	1	8	(-	-)	106	41	27	46	36	0	46	2	0	0		22	8	.73	2	.310	.419	.522
2010	SnAnt	AA	67	268	67	8	7	10	(-	-)	119	44	37	37	26	2	63	4	2	1		6	9	.40	1	.250	.324	.444
2011	SnAnt	AA	106	414	118	27	2	19	(-	-)	206	77	67	86	67	0	108	8	7	2		36	12	.75	1	.285	.393	.498
2012	Tucsn	AAA	89	321	78	20	2	9	(-	-)	129	38	26	36	18	0	92	1	6	1		9	8	.53	3	.243	.284	.402
2011	SD	NL	19	34	6	1	1	0	(0	0)	9	1	1	1	4	0	21	0	2	0		2	1	.67	0	.176	.263	.265
2012	SD	NL	11	15	2	0	0	0	(0	0)	2	0	0	0	0	0	4	0	0	0		1	0	1.00	0	.133	.133	.133
	2 ML YEARS		30	49	8	1	1	0	(0	0)	11	1	1	1	4	0	25	0	2	0		3	1	.75	0	.163	.226	.224

Eric Thames

Bats: L Throws: R Pos: LF-44; RF-35; PH-12; DH-2; PR-2   THAIMS   Ht: 6'0" Wt: 205 Born: 11/10/1986 Age: 26

						BATTING																BASERUNNING				AVERAGES		
Year	Team	Lg	G	AB	H	2B	3B	HR	(Hm	Rd)	TB	R	RBI	RC	TBB	IBB	SO	HBP	SH	SF		SB	CS	SB%	GDP	Avg	OBP	Slg
2009	Dnedin	A+	52	195	61	15	5	3	(-	-)	95	33	38	37	21	1	40	3	0	1		1	1	.50	0	.313	.386	.487
2009	B Jays	R	7	21	6	3	0	0	(-	-)	9	4	1	3	3	0	5	0	0	1		0	0	-	0	.286	.360	.429
2010	NHam	AA	130	496	143	25	6	27	(-	-)	261	95	104	98	50	2	121	18	2	7		9	5	.64	10	.288	.370	.526
2011	LsVgs	AAA	53	210	74	25	4	7	(-	-)	128	38	45	52	23	5	41	5	0	3		5	2	.71	4	.352	.423	.610
2012	LsVgs	AAA	54	197	65	15	3	6	(-	-)	104	31	32	36	26	1	42	3	0	5		1	1	.50	5	.330	.407	.528
2011	Tor	AL	95	362	95	24	5	12	(10	2)	165	58	37	42	23	0	88	5	1	3		2	1	.67	7	.262	.313	.456
2012	2 Tms	AL	86	271	63	12	3	9	(6	3)	108	27	25	25	15	0	87	1	1	2		1	1	.50	7	.232	.273	.399
12	Tor	AL	46	148	36	7	1	3	(1	2)	54	17	11	13	9	0	40	1	0	2		0	1	.00	7	.243	.288	.365
12	Sea	AL	40	123	27	5	2	6	(5	1)	54	10	14	12	6	0	47	0	1	0		1	0	1.00	0	.220	.256	.439
	2 ML YEARS		181	633	158	36	8	21	(16	5)	273	85	62	67	38	0	175	6	2	5		3	2	.60	14	.250	.296	.431

Joe Thatcher

Pitches: L **Bats:** L **Pos:** RP-55   **Ht:** 6'2" **Wt:** 230 **Born:** 10/4/1981 **Age:** 31

Year	Team	Lg	G	GS	CG	GF	IP	BFP	H	R	ER	HR	SH	SF	HB	TBB	IBB	SO	WP	Bk	W	L	Pct	Sh	Sv-Op	Hld	ERC	ERA
2012	Lk Els*	A+	1	1	0	0	1.0	3	0	0	0	0	0	0	0	0	0	1	0	0	0	0	-	0	0--	-	0.00	0.00
2007	SD	NL	22	0	0	5	21.0	85	13	6	3	1	0	0	1	6	2	16	0	0	2	2	.500	0	0-0	2	1.49	1.29
2008	SD	NL	25	0	0	7	25.2	128	42	25	24	4	2	3	0	13	2	17	0	0	0	4	.000	0	0-3	5	8.91	8.42
2009	SD	NL	52	0	0	7	45.0	188	37	14	14	2	1	2	4	18	7	55	2	1	1	0	1.000	0	0-1	9	2.87	2.80
2010	SD	NL	65	0	0	12	35.0	137	23	5	5	1	3	2	1	7	2	45	0	0	1	0	1.000	0	0-0	11	1.37	1.29
2011	SD	NL	18	0	0	5	10.0	44	8	5	5	1	0	0	0	7	1	9	0	0	0	0	-	0	0-0	2	3.96	4.50
2012	SD	NL	55	0	0	13	31.2	141	30	13	12	2	2	2	3	14	3	39	0	1	1	4	.200	0	1-1	14	3.82	3.41
	6 ML YEARS		237	0	0	49	168.1	723	153	68	63	11	8	9	9	65	17	181	2	2	5	10	.333	0	1-5	43	3.30	3.37

Dale Thayer

Pitches: R **Bats:** R **Pos:** RP-64   **Ht:** 6'0" **Wt:** 195 **Born:** 12/17/1980 **Age:** 32

Year	Team	Lg	G	GS	CG	GF	IP	BFP	H	R	ER	HR	SH	SF	HB	TBB	IBB	SO	WP	Bk	W	L	Pct	Sh	Sv-Op	Hld	ERC	ERA
2012	Tucsn*	AAA	7	0	0	1	8.1	29	2	0	0	0	0	0	0	2	0	5	0	0	0	0	-	0	0--	-	0.37	0.00
2009	TB	AL	11	0	0	3	13.2	59	18	9	7	3	0	0	0	1	0	8	1	0	0	0	-	0	1-1	0	5.38	4.61
2010	TB	AL	1	0	0	0	2.0	13	7	6	6	1	0	0	0	0	0	2	0	0	0	0	-	0	0-0	0	24.30	27.00
2011	NYM	NL	11	0	0	7	10.1	42	12	4	4	0	1	2	0	0	0	5	0	0	0	3	.000	0	0-0	0	2.78	3.48
2012	SD	NL	64	0	0	21	57.2	235	53	24	22	4	4	4	1	12	4	47	2	0	2	2	.500	0	7-10	22	2.68	3.43
	4 ML YEARS		87	0	0	31	83.2	349	90	43	39	8	5	6	1	13	4	62	3	0	2	5	.286	0	8-11	22	3.47	4.20

Ryan Theriot

Bats: R **Throws:** R **Pos:** 2B-91; PH-18; LF-2   TARE-ee-oh   **Ht:** 5'11" **Wt:** 185 **Born:** 12/7/1979 **Age:** 33

Year	Team	Lg	G	AB	H	2B	3B	HR	(Hm	Rd)	TB	R	RBI	RC	TBB	IBB	SO	HBP	SH	SF	SB	CS	SB%	GDP	Avg	OBP	Slg
2005	ChC	NL	9	13	2	1	0	0	(0	0)	3	3	0	0	1	0	2	0	0	0	0	0	-	0	.154	.214	.231
2006	ChC	NL	53	134	44	11	3	3	(3	0)	70	34	16	31	17	0	18	2	6	0	13	2	.87	5	.328	.412	.522
2007	ChC	NL	148	537	143	30	2	3	(3	0)	186	80	45	64	49	1	50	0	8	3	28	4	.88	12	.266	.326	.346
2008	ChC	NL	149	580	178	19	4	1	(1	0)	208	85	38	78	73	1	58	3	4	1	22	13	.63	19	.307	.387	.359
2009	ChC	NL	154	602	171	20	5	7	(5	2)	222	81	54	79	51	1	93	6	13	5	21	10	.68	13	.284	.343	.369
2010	2 Tms	NL	150	586	158	15	2	2	(1	1)	183	72	29	58	41	3	74	4	7	2	20	9	.69	13	.270	.321	.312
2011	StL	NL	132	442	120	26	1	1	(0	1)	151	46	47	46	29	0	41	4	6	2	4	6	.40	15	.271	.321	.342
2012	SF	NL	104	352	95	16	1	0	(0	0)	113	45	28	36	24	1	47	1	4	3	13	5	.72	12	.270	.316	.321
10	ChC	NL	96	388	110	10	2	1	(0	1)	127	45	21	43	19	3	46	2	2	1	16	6	.73	8	.284	.320	.327
10	LAD	NL	54	198	48	5	0	1	(1	0)	56	27	8	15	22	0	28	2	5	1	4	3	.57	5	.242	.323	.283
	Postseason		18	56	14	2	0	0	(0	0)	16	3	4	4	3	1	9	0	1	0	2	0	1.00	2	.250	.288	.286
	8 ML YEARS		899	3246	911	138	18	17	(13	4)	1136	446	257	392	285	7	383	20	48	16	121	49	.71	89	.281	.341	.350

Josh Thole

Bats: L **Throws:** R **Pos:** C-100; PH-12   TOE-lee   **Ht:** 6'1" **Wt:** 215 **Born:** 10/28/1986 **Age:** 26

Year	Team	Lg	G	AB	H	2B	3B	HR	(Hm	Rd)	TB	R	RBI	RC	TBB	IBB	SO	HBP	SH	SF	SB	CS	SB%	GDP	Avg	OBP	Slg
2012	Buffalo*	AAA	2	5	1	0	0	0	(-	-)	1	0	0	0	0	0	0	0	0	0	0	0	-	0	.200	.200	.200
2009	NYM	NL	17	53	17	2	1	0	(0	0)	21	2	9	9	4	0	5	0	0	2	1	0	1.00	1	.321	.356	.396
2010	NYM	NL	73	202	56	7	1	3	(2	1)	74	17	17	28	24	1	25	1	0	0	1	0	1.00	8	.277	.357	.366
2011	NYM	NL	114	340	91	17	0	3	(1	2)	117	22	40	39	38	6	47	4	1	3	0	2	.00	8	.268	.345	.344
2012	NYM	NL	104	321	75	15	0	1	(0	1)	93	24	21	24	27	6	50	1	4	1	0	0	-	12	.234	.294	.290
	4 ML YEARS		308	916	239	41	2	7	(3	4)	305	65	87	100	93	13	127	6	5	6	2	2	.50	29	.261	.331	.333

Clete Thomas

Bats: L **Throws:** R **Pos:** RF-10; LF-3; PH-2; PR-2; CF-1   **Ht:** 5'11" **Wt:** 195 **Born:** 11/14/1983 **Age:** 29

Year	Team	Lg	G	AB	H	2B	3B	HR	(Hm	Rd)	TB	R	RBI	RC	TBB	IBB	SO	HBP	SH	SF	SB	CS	SB%	GDP	Avg	OBP	Slg
2012	Roch*	AAA	109	393	91	22	5	12	(-	-)	159	47	47	47	47	1	109	1	3	2	15	4	.79	3	.232	.281	.405
2008	Det	AL	40	116	33	9	1	1	(1	0)	47	7	9	17	14	1	26	1	2	0	2	0	1.00	1	.284	.366	.405
2009	Det	AL	102	275	66	13	3	7	(4	3)	106	46	39	36	33	0	77	1	1	0	3	0	1.00	3	.240	.324	.385
2012	2 Tms	AL	15	28	4	1	0	1	(1	0)	8	3	4	4	0	0	16	1	0	0	0	0	-	0	.143	.172	.286
12	Det	AL	3	0	0	0	0	0	(0	0)	0	1	0	0	0	0	0	0	0	0	0	0	-	0	-	-	-
12	Min	AL	12	28	4	1	0	1	(1	0)	8	2	4	4	0	0	16	1	0	0	0	0	-	0	.143	.172	.286
	3 ML YEARS		157	419	103	23	4	9	(6	3)	161	56	52	57	47	1	119	3	3	0	5	0	1.00	4	.246	.326	.384

Justin Thomas

Pitches: L **Bats:** L **Pos:** RP-11   **Ht:** 6'3" **Wt:** 220 **Born:** 1/18/1984 **Age:** 29

Year	Team	Lg	G	GS	CG	GF	IP	BFP	H	R	ER	HR	SH	SF	HB	TBB	IBB	SO	WP	Bk	W	L	Pct	Sh	Sv-Op	Hld	ERC	ERA
2012	Pwtckt*	AAA	4	0	0	0	5.1	22	5	2	2	0	0	0	0	0	0	5	0	0	0	0	-	0	0--	-	1.61	3.38
2012	S-WB*	AAA	30	6	0	5	57.1	234	49	23	22	3	3	2	1	20	1	49	1	0	2	1	.667	0	1--	-	2.88	3.45
2008	Sea	AL	8	0	0	2	4.0	22	9	3	3	0	1	0	0	2	0	2	1	0	0	1	.000	0	0-1	1	12.01	6.75
2010	Pit	NL	12	0	0	6	13.0	62	21	9	9	3	0	1	0	5	1	5	0	0	0	1	.000	0	0-0	0	9.03	6.23
2012	2 Tms	AL	11	0	0	0	7.2	37	12	7	7	1	0	1	1	3	0	7	1	0	0	0	-	0	0-0	0	8.62	8.22
12	Bos	AL	7	0	0	0	4.2	25	10	4	4	0	0	1	1	2	0	4	1	0	0	0	-	0	0-0	0	12.33	7.71
12	NYY	AL	4	0	0	0	3.0	12	2	3	3	1	0	0	0	1	0	3	0	0	0	0	-	0	0-0	0	3.37	9.00
	3 ML YEARS		31	0	0	8	24.2	121	42	19	19	4	1	2	1	10	1	14	2	0	0	2	.000	0	0-1	1	9.39	6.93

Jim Thome

Bats: L Throws: R Pos: DH-36; PH-19; 1B-4   TOE-may   Ht: 6'4" Wt: 250 Born: 8/27/1970 Age: 42

											BATTING									BASERUNNING				AVERAGES		
Year	Team	Lg	G	AB	H	2B	3B	HR	(Hm	Rd)	TB	R	RBI	RC	TBB	IBB	SO	HBP	SH	SF	SB	CS	SB%	GDP	Avg	OBP	Slg
2012	Clrwtr*	A+	3	10	5	2	0	0	(-	-)	7	3	4	3	3	0	2	0	0	0	0	0	.500	5	.500	.615	.700
1991	Cle	AL	27	98	25	4	2	1	(0	1)	36	7	9	9	5	1	16	1	0	0	1	1	.50	4	.255	.298	.367
1992	Cle	AL	40	117	24	3	1	2	(1	1)	35	8	12	9	10	2	34	2	0	2	2	0	1.00	3	.205	.275	.299
1993	Cle	AL	47	154	41	11	0	7	(5	2)	73	28	22	30	29	1	36	4	0	5	2	1	.67	3	.266	.385	.474
1994	Cle	AL	98	321	86	20	1	20	(10	10)	168	58	52	56	46	5	84	0	1	1	3	3	.50	11	.268	.359	.523
1995	Cle	AL	137	452	142	29	3	25	(13	12)	252	92	73	109	97	3	113	5	0	3	4	3	.57	8	.314	.438	.558
1996	Cle	AL	151	505	157	28	5	38	(18	20)	309	122	116	132	123	8	141	6	0	2	2	2	.50	13	.311	.450	.612
1997	Cle	AL	147	496	142	25	0	40	(17	23)	287	104	102	120	120	9	146	3	0	8	1	1	.50	9	.286	.423	.579
1998	Cle	AL	123	440	129	34	2	30	(18	12)	257	89	85	104	89	8	141	4	0	4	1	0	1.00	7	.293	.413	.584
1999	Cle	AL	146	494	137	27	2	33	(19	14)	267	101	108	116	127	13	171	4	0	4	0	0	-	6	.277	.426	.540
2000	Cle	AL	158	557	150	33	1	37	(21	16)	296	106	106	119	118	4	171	4	0	5	1	0	1.00	8	.269	.398	.531
2001	Cle	AL	156	526	153	26	1	49	(30	19)	328	101	124	130	111	14	185	4	0	3	0	1	.00	9	.291	.416	.624
2002	Cle	AL	147	480	146	19	2	52	(30	22)	325	101	118	139	122	18	139	5	0	6	1	2	.33	5	.304	.445	.677
2003	Phi	NL	159	578	154	30	3	47	(28	19)	331	111	131	125	111	11	182	4	0	5	0	3	.00	5	.266	.385	.573
2004	Phi	NL	143	508	139	28	1	42	(19	23)	295	97	105	97	104	26	144	2	0	4	0	2	.00	10	.274	.396	.581
2005	Phi	NL	59	193	40	7	0	7	(6	1)	68	26	30	25	45	4	59	2	0	2	0	0	-	5	.207	.360	.352
2006	CWS	AL	143	490	141	26	0	42	(25	17)	293	108	109	120	107	12	147	6	0	7	0	0	-	8	.288	.416	.598
2007	CWS	AL	130	432	119	19	0	35	(21	14)	243	79	96	104	95	11	134	6	0	3	0	1	.00	10	.275	.410	.563
2008	CWS	AL	149	503	123	28	0	34	(19	15)	253	93	90	96	91	9	147	4	0	4	1	0	1.00	18	.245	.362	.503
2009	2 Tms		124	362	90	15	0	23	(14	9)	174	55	77	65	69	3	123	0	0	3	0	0	-	8	.249	.366	.481
2010	Min	AL	108	276	78	16	2	25	(15	10)	173	48	59	61	60	4	82	2	0	2	0	0	-	8	.283	.412	.627
2011	2 Tms	AL	93	277	71	16	0	15	(8	7)	132	32	50	54	46	4	92	0	0	1	0	0	-	6	.256	.361	.477
2012	2 Tms		58	163	41	7	0	8	(2	6)	72	17	25	23	22	3	61	1	0	0	0	0	-	6	.252	.344	.442
09	CWS	AL	107	345	86	15	0	23	(14	9)	170	55	74	65	69	3	116	0	0	3	0	0	-	8	.249	.372	.493
09	LAD	AL	17	17	4	0	0	0	(0	0)	4	0	3	0	0	0	7	0	0	0	0	0	-	0	.235	.235	.235
11	Min	AL	71	206	50	12	0	12	(6	6)	98	21	40	40	35	3	69	0	0	1	0	0	-	5	.243	.351	.476
11	Cle	AL	22	71	21	4	0	3	(2	1)	34	11	10	14	11	1	23	0	0	0	0	0	-	1	.296	.390	.479
12	Phi	NL	30	62	15	2	0	5	(1	4)	32	9	15	10	8	1	21	1	0	0	0	0	-	2	.242	.338	.516
12	Bal	AL	28	101	26	5	0	3	(1	2)	40	8	10	13	14	2	40	0	0	0	0	0	-	4	.257	.348	.396
	Postseason		67	217	47	2	1	17	(13	4)	102	35	37	31	29	1	68	4	1	0	0	0	-	3	.217	.320	.470
22	ML YEARS		2543	8422	2328	451	26	612	(339	273)	4667	1583	1699	1843	1747	173	2548	69	1	74	19	20	.49	166	.276	.402	.554

Rich Thompson

Pitches: R Bats: R Pos: RP-3   Ht: 6'1" Wt: 210 Born: 7/1/1984 Age: 28

			HOW MUCH HE PITCHED						WHAT HE GAVE UP											THE RESULTS						
Year	Team	Lg	G	GS	CG	GF	IP	BFP	H	R	ER	HR	SH	SF	HB	TBB	IBB	SO	WP	Bk	W	L	Pct	Sh	Sv-Op	Hld	ERC	ERA
2012	Scrmto*	AAA	46	0	0	15	62.0	251	46	24	23	7	3	2	0	23	2	58	5	0	4	2	.667	0	3--	-	2.64	3.34
2007	LAA	AL	7	0	0	2	6.2	32	10	8	8	4	0	0	0	3	0	9	2	0	0	0	-	0	0-0	0	11.85	10.80
2008	LAA	AL	2	0	0	1	2.0	12	4	5	5	0	0	0	0	2	0	1	1	0	0	0	-	0	0-0	0	12.01	22.50
2009	LAA	AL	13	0	0	2	19.1	92	27	11	11	6	1	1	1	7	0	21	5	0	0	0	-	0	0-0	0	8.17	5.12
2010	LAA	AL	13	0	0	7	19.2	75	12	4	3	2	1	0	0	4	0	15	4	0	2	0	1.000	0	0-0	1	1.50	1.37
2011	LAA	AL	44	0	0	16	54.0	228	46	18	18	5	1	2	0	20	0	56	1	1	1	3	.250	0	0-1	3	3.05	3.00
2012	2 Tms	AL	3	0	0	3	3.0	16	6	4	4	1	0	0	0	1	0	3	0	0	0	1	.000	0	0-0	0	12.18	12.00
12	LAA	AL	2	0	0	2	2.1	13	5	4	4	1	0	0	0	1	0	3	0	0	0	1	.000	0	0-0	0	14.73	15.43
12	Oak	AL	1	0	0	1	0.2	3	1	0	0	0	0	0	0	0	0	0	0	0	0	0	-	0	0-0	0	4.47	0.00
6	ML YEARS		82	0	0	31	104.2	455	105	50	49	18	3	3	1	37	0	105	13	1	3	4	.429	0	0-1	4	4.37	4.21

Rich Thompson

Bats: L Throws: R Pos: PR-12; LF-7; CF-5; DH-3; PH-2   Ht: 6'3" Wt: 185 Born: 4/23/1979 Age: 34

											BATTING									BASERUNNING				AVERAGES		
Year	Team	Lg	G	AB	H	2B	3B	HR	(Hm	Rd)	TB	R	RBI	RC	TBB	IBB	SO	HBP	SH	SF	SB	CS	SB%	GDP	Avg	OBP	Slg
2000	Queens	A-	68	252	66	9	5	1	(-	-)	88	42	27	42	45	1	57	6	5	0	28	8	.78	0	.262	.386	.349
2001	Dnedin	A+	112	454	141	14	6	1	(-	-)	170	90	60	74	44	1	72	9	3	4	39	11	.78	3	.311	.380	.374
2001	Syrcse	AAA	17	53	13	0	1	0	(-	-)	15	5	3	5	4	0	12	0	3	1	5	1	.83	1	.245	.293	.283
2002	Tenn	AA	135	554	155	13	4	2	(-	-)	182	109	44	79	50	0	86	20	7	0	45	13	.78	1	.280	.361	.329
2003	NwHav	AA	49	182	57	5	1	0	(-	-)	64	39	9	28	10	0	24	8	2	1	15	3	.83	2	.313	.352	.352
2003	Syrcse	AAA	28	112	33	2	1	0	(-	-)	37	13	7	17	9	0	10	5	3	0	11	1	.92	0	.295	.373	.330
2003	Nashv	AAA	35	109	28	3	2	0	(-	-)	35	17	11	15	9	0	21	4	1	1	22	3	.88	0	.257	.333	.321
2004	Nashv	AAA	112	411	118	7	13	5	(-	-)	166	73	36	63	26	1	62	13	10	1	40	15	.73	0	.287	.348	.404
2005	Indy	AAA	29	91	19	1	2	1	(-	-)	27	9	3	11	9	0	12	4	3	0	13	2	.87	1	.209	.308	.297
2005	Altna	AA	94	346	89	11	5	3	(-	-)	119	58	30	48	30	1	60	8	10	1	45	6	.88	3	.257	.330	.344
2006	Altna	AA	14	50	17	3	0	0	(-	-)	20	11	5	8	8	0	11	1	0	0	1	3	.25	0	.340	.441	.400
2006	Indy	AAA	80	232	65	12	6	2	(-	-)	95	43	22	41	31	4	39	12	11	1	16	8	.67	1	.280	.391	.409
2007	Tucsn	AAA	111	325	96	18	6	3	(-	-)	135	60	41	53	28	1	49	5	9	0	15	2	.88	4	.295	.360	.415
2008	Rdng	AA	3	10	3	0	1	0	(-	-)	5	1	1	1	0	0	2	0	0	0	1	0	-	1	.300	.273	.500
2008	LV	AAA	97	352	93	18	5	4	(-	-)	133	41	42	53	39	4	72	4	7	3	25	2	.93	4	.264	.342	.378
2009	LV	AAA	119	445	118	22	7	3	(-	-)	163	86	39	61	38	0	73	8	2	0	26	4	.87	8	.265	.334	.366
2010	LV	AAA	99	348	96	14	4	4	(-	-)	130	47	31	49	24	1	55	5	8	3	28	4	.88	7	.276	.329	.374
2010	Rdng	AA	33	128	38	4	3	1	(-	-)	51	23	14	21	9	0	20	4	4	1	13	0	1.00	3	.297	.359	.398
2011	LV	AAA	124	424	117	25	8	5	(-	-)	173	81	30	73	37	2	84	16	10	3	48	4	.92	9	.276	.354	.408
2012	LV	AAA	30	88	27	4	2	0	(-	-)	35	6	11	15	9	0	18	4	1	0	7	2	.78	1	.307	.396	.398
2012	Drham	AAA	63	251	78	13	5	2	(-	-)	107	41	19	43	20	1	35	3	8	0	22	5	.81	2	.311	.369	.426
2004	KC	AL	6	1	0	0	0	0	(0	0)	0	1	0	0	0	0	0	0	0	0	1	0	1.00	1	.000	.000	.000
2012	TB	AL	23	22	2	0	0	0	(0	0)	2	5	1	0	0	0	5	2	0	0	6	2	.75	1	.091	.167	.091
2	ML YEARS		29	23	2	0	0	0	(0	0)	2	6	1	0	0	0	5	2	0	0	7	2	.78	2	.087	.160	.087

Tyler Thornburg

Pitches: R **Bats:** R **Pos:** RP-5; SP-3   **Ht:** 6'0" **Wt:** 190 **Born:** 9/29/1988 **Age:** 24

		HOW MUCH HE PITCHED						WHAT HE GAVE UP											THE RESULTS						
Year	Team	Lg	G	GS	CG	GF	IP	BFP	H	R	ER	HR	SH	SF	HB	TBB	IBB	SO	WP	Bk	W	L	Pct	Sh	Sv-Op Hld	ERC	ERA
2010	Helena	R+	9	6	0	1	23.1	97	15	6	5	2	0	0	2	11	0	38	3	2	1	0	1.000	0	1-- -	2.66	1.93
2011	Wisc	A	12	12	2	0	68.2	274	49	14	12	3	3	1	4	25	0	76	5	3	7	0	1.000	1	0-- -	2.36	1.57
2011	BrvdCt	A+	12	12	0	0	68.0	282	45	30	27	5	3	0	4	33	0	84	4	0	3	6	.333	0	0-- -	2.64	3.57
2012	Hntsvl	AA	13	13	0	0	75.0	307	57	36	25	6	5	7	2	24	0	71	2	0	8	1	.889	0	0-- -	2.45	3.00
2012	Nashv	AAA	8	8	0	0	37.2	162	38	16	15	1	3	0	2	13	0	42	0	0	2	3	.400	0	0-- -	3.61	3.58
2012	Mil	NL	8	3	0	3	22.0	95	24	11	11	8	1	0	1	7	0	20	1	0	0	0	-	0	0-0 0	6.44	4.50

Matt Thornton

Pitches: L **Bats:** L **Pos:** RP-74   **Ht:** 6'6" **Wt:** 240 **Born:** 9/15/1976 **Age:** 36

		HOW MUCH HE PITCHED						WHAT HE GAVE UP											THE RESULTS						
Year	Team	Lg	G	GS	CG	GF	IP	BFP	H	R	ER	HR	SH	SF	HB	TBB	IBB	SO	WP	Bk	W	L	Pct	Sh	Sv-Op Hld	ERC	ERA
2004	Sea	AL	19	1	0	8	32.2	148	30	15	15	2	2	1	0	25	1	30	2	0	1	2	.333	0	0-0 0	4.75	4.13
2005	Sea	AL	55	0	0	15	57.0	262	54	33	33	13	1	1	0	42	2	57	7	0	0	4	.000	0	0-1 5	6.06	5.21
2006	CWS	AL	63	0	0	20	54.0	227	46	20	20	5	1	3	1	21	4	49	1	0	5	3	.625	0	2-5 18	3.12	3.33
2007	CWS	AL	68	0	0	13	56.1	249	59	31	30	4	0	2	2	26	6	55	3	0	4	4	.500	0	2-7 17	4.35	4.79
2008	CWS	AL	74	0	0	12	67.1	268	48	20	20	5	1	4	2	19	2	77	3	0	5	3	.625	0	1-6 20	2.07	2.67
2009	CWS	AL	70	0	0	17	72.1	291	58	22	22	5	2	1	1	20	2	87	4	0	6	3	.667	0	4-9 24	2.40	2.74
2010	CWS	AL	61	0	0	13	60.2	239	41	18	18	3	0	2	2	20	5	81	1	0	5	4	.556	0	8-10 21	1.89	2.67
2011	CWS	AL	62	0	0	20	59.2	262	60	34	22	3	3	3	0	21	5	63	2	0	2	5	.286	0	3-7 20	3.32	3.32
2012	CWS	AL	74	0	0	18	65.0	266	63	27	25	4	1	0	3	17	4	53	2	0	4	10	.286	0	3-7 26	3.29	3.46
	Postseason		3	0	0	1	3.1	14	2	0	0	0	0	0	0	2	1	2	0	0	0	0	-	0	0-0 1	1.62	0.00
9 ML YEARS			546	1	0	136	525.0	2212	459	220	205	44	11	14	11	211	31	552	25	0	32	38	.457	0	23-52 151	3.28	3.51

Chris Tillman

Pitches: R **Bats:** R **Pos:** SP-15   **Ht:** 6'5" **Wt:** 210 **Born:** 4/15/1988 **Age:** 25

		HOW MUCH HE PITCHED						WHAT HE GAVE UP											THE RESULTS						
Year	Team	Lg	G	GS	CG	GF	IP	BFP	H	R	ER	HR	SH	SF	HB	TBB	IBB	SO	WP	Bk	W	L	Pct	Sh	Sv-Op Hld	ERC	ERA
2012	Norfolk*	AAA	16	15	1	0	89.1	378	85	36	36	5	3	1	3	30	0	92	1	0	8	8	.500	0	0-- -	3.39	3.63
2012	Bowie*	AA	1	1	0	0	3.1	15	4	3	3	0	0	0	0	2	0	2	1	0	0	1	.000	0	0-- -	5.47	8.10
2009	Bal	AL	12	12	0	0	65.0	285	77	40	39	15	0	0	2	24	1	39	4	0	2	5	.286	0	0-0 -	6.28	5.40
2010	Bal	AL	11	11	0	0	53.2	236	51	37	35	9	1	3	1	31	1	31	2	0	2	5	.286	0	0-0 -	5.12	5.87
2011	Bal	AL	13	13	0	0	62.0	287	77	41	38	5	1	1	4	25	0	46	1	1	3	5	.375	0	0-0 -	5.58	5.52
2012	Bal	AL	15	15	0	0	86.0	347	66	38	28	12	1	2	1	24	0	66	5	0	9	3	.750	0	0-0 -	2.65	2.93
4 ML YEARS			51	51	0	0	266.2	1155	271	156	140	41	3	6	8	104	2	182	12	1	16	18	.471	0	0-0 -	4.64	4.73

Shawn Tolleson

Pitches: R **Bats:** R **Pos:** RP-40   TAHL-eh-son   **Ht:** 6'2" **Wt:** 220 **Born:** 1/19/1988 **Age:** 25

		HOW MUCH HE PITCHED						WHAT HE GAVE UP											THE RESULTS						
Year	Team	Lg	G	GS	CG	GF	IP	BFP	H	R	ER	HR	SH	SF	HB	TBB	IBB	SO	WP	Bk	W	L	Pct	Sh	Sv-Op Hld	ERC	ERA
2010	Ogden	R+	26	0	0	25	28.2	104	17	2	2	1	1	1	0	5	0	39	2	0	1	1	.500	0	17-- -	1.21	0.63
2011	Gt Lks	A	14	0	0	13	15.0	56	8	1	0	0	0	0	0	4	0	33	2	0	1	0	1.000	0	10-- -	1.08	0.00
2011	RCuca	A+	5	0	0	5	9.2	36	2	3	1	1	0	0	0	3	0	17	0	0	1	0	1.000	0	3-- -	0.62	0.93
2011	Chatt	AA	38	0	0	22	44.1	181	42	14	8	2	1	0	2	11	1	55	2	0	4	2	.667	0	12-- -	3.05	1.62
2012	Chatt	AA	11	0	0	9	13.0	49	8	2	2	2	0	0	0	4	0	19	0	0	0	0	-	0	5-- -	2.16	1.38
2012	Albq	AAA	8	0	0	2	9.1	37	8	5	5	1	0	0	0	1	0	15	3	0	0	1	.000	0	0-- -	2.24	4.82
2012	LAD	NL	40	0	0	12	37.2	160	30	19	18	4	2	1	1	20	1	39	0	0	3	1	.750	0	0-0 2	3.59	4.30

Steve Tolleson

Bats: R **Throws:** R **Pos:** 3B-12; LF-7; PH-5; 2B-4; SS-3; DH-3; PR-1   TAHL-eh-son   **Ht:** 5'11" **Wt:** 185 **Born:** 11/1/1983 **Age:** 29

			BATTING																			BASERUNNING				AVERAGES		
Year	Team	Lg	G	AB	H	2B	3B	HR	(Hm	Rd)	TB	R	RBI	RC	TBB	IBB	SO	HBP	SH	SF	SB	CS	SB%	GDP	Avg	OBP	Slg
2005	Elizab	R+	16	56	18	6	1	2	(-	-)	32	18	8	14	11	0	4	3	3	0	2	1	.67	2	.321	.457	.571
2005	Beloit	A	31	102	18	2	0	3	(-	-)	29	16	10	11	17	0	23	3	4	0	3	0	1.00	3	.176	.311	.284
2006	Beloit	A	47	171	49	8	2	2	(-	-)	67	23	16	26	27	0	34	2	4	0	7	9	.44	3	.287	.390	.392
2006	Twins	R	2	8	2	0	0	0	(-	-)	2	1	1	0	0	0	0	0	0	1	0	0	-	0	.250	.222	.250
2006	FtMyrs	A+	49	157	42	8	1	4	(-	-)	64	23	23	25	22	0	24	1	2	4	3	1	.75	4	.268	.353	.408
2007	FtMyrs	A+	132	487	139	24	4	5	(-	-)	186	75	35	81	79	1	97	3	1	1	27	10	.73	10	.285	.388	.382
2008	NwBrit	AA	93	343	102	28	1	9	(-	-)	159	54	50	62	44	1	74	3	4	3	12	6	.67	6	.297	.379	.464
2009	NwBrit	AA	38	151	39	10	2	2	(-	-)	59	21	13	22	16	0	20	4	1	1	6	2	.75	5	.258	.343	.391
2009	Roch	AAA	92	352	95	17	1	6	(-	-)	132	57	27	47	36	1	52	2	1	3	7	6	.54	7	.270	.338	.375
2010	Scrmto	AAA	80	292	97	17	3	9	(-	-)	147	52	43	64	37	0	50	4	4	2	8	2	.80	6	.332	.412	.503
2011	Scrmto	AAA	46	175	48	6	0	5	(-	-)	69	29	19	30	31	0	37	2	0	1	8	2	.80	11	.274	.388	.394
2011	Tucsn	AAA	77	312	86	21	2	4	(-	-)	123	48	36	46	29	0	56	3	1	3	16	3	.84	2	.276	.340	.394
2012	Norfolk	AAA	51	162	45	8	0	1	(-	-)	56	15	21	26	23	0	32	0	3	5	3	2	.60	5	.278	.358	.346
2010	Oak	AL	25	49	14	3	0	1	(1	0)	20	5	4	7	4	0	9	0	0	0	0	0	-	0	.286	.340	.408
2012	Bal	AL	29	71	13	3	0	2	(2	0)	22	4	6	7	4	0	17	0	1	0	1	0	1.00	1	.183	.227	.310
2 ML YEARS			54	120	27	6	0	3	(3	0)	42	9	10	14	8	0	26	0	1	0	1	0	1.00	2	.225	.273	.350

Josh Tomlin

Pitches: R Bats: R Pos: SP-16; RP-5   TOM-lynn   Ht: 6'1" Wt: 190 Born: 10/19/1984 Age: 28

			HOW MUCH HE PITCHED							WHAT HE GAVE UP											THE RESULTS						
Year	Team	Lg	G	GS	CG	GF	IP	BFP	H	R	ER	HR	SH	SF	HB	TBB	IBB	SO	WP	Bk	W	L	Pct	Sh	Sv-Op	Hld	ERC	ERA
2010	Cle	AL	12	12	1	0	73.0	301	72	38	37	10	3	3	3	19	3	43	1	0	6	4	.600	0	0-0	0	3.89	4.56
2011	Cle	AL	26	26	0	0	165.1	662	157	80	78	24	1	3	3	21	2	89	3	0	12	7	.632	0	0-0	0	3.11	4.25
2012	Cle	AL	21	16	0	0	103.1	452	126	74	73	18	2	3	3	25	3	56	4	0	5	8	.385	0	0-0	0	5.34	6.36
3 ML YEARS			59	54	1	0	341.2	1415	355	192	188	52	6	9	9	65	8	188	8	0	23	19	.548	0	0-0	0	3.92	4.95

Yorvit Torrealba

Bats: R Throws: R Pos: C-60; PH-4; 1B-1; PR-1   your-VEET tore-ree-AL-bah   Ht: 5'11" Wt: 200 Born: 7/19/1978 Age: 34

			BATTING																	BASERUNNING				AVERAGES		
Year	Team	Lg	G	AB	H	2B	3B	HR	(Hm	Rd)	TB	R	RBI	RC	TBB	IBB	SO	HBP	SH	SF	SB	CS	SB%	GDP	Avg	OBP	Slg
2012	NHam*	AA	4	12	5	0	0	0	(-	-)	5	1	1	3	3	0	1	0	0	0	1	0	1.00	0	.417	.533	.417
2001	SF	NL	3	4	2	0	1	0	(0	0)	4	0	2	2	0	0	0	0	0	0	0	0	-	0	.500	.500	1.000
2002	SF	NL	53	136	38	10	0	2	(0	2)	54	17	14	16	14	2	20	2	3	0	0	0	-	11	.279	.355	.397
2003	SF	NL	66	200	52	10	2	4	(3	1)	78	22	29	25	14	1	39	2	3	2	1	0	1.00	3	.260	.312	.390
2004	SF	NL	64	172	39	7	3	6	(3	3)	70	19	23	18	17	3	31	2	4	1	2	0	1.00	7	.227	.302	.407
2005	2 Tms		76	201	47	12	0	3	(2	1)	68	32	15	14	16	1	50	2	5	0	1	0	1.00	8	.234	.297	.338
2006	Col	NL	65	223	55	16	3	7	(3	4)	98	23	43	30	11	1	49	4	2	1	4	3	.57	7	.247	.293	.439
2007	Col	NL	113	396	101	22	1	8	(6	2)	149	47	47	34	34	1	73	6	6	1	1	.67		19	.255	.323	.376
2008	Col	NL	70	236	58	17	0	6	(5	1)	93	19	31	23	12	0	44	5	5	3	0	4	.00	10	.246	.293	.394
2009	Col	NL	64	213	62	11	1	2	(1	1)	81	27	31	37	21	5	42	1	3	4	1	1	.50	4	.291	.351	.380
2010	SD	NL	95	325	88	14	0	7	(4	3)	123	31	37	41	33	2	67	3	1	1	7	5	.58	12	.271	.343	.378
2011	Tex	AL	113	396	108	27	1	7	(7	0)	158	40	37	41	20	0	65	0	1	2	0	2	.00	11	.273	.306	.399
2012	3 Tms		64	194	44	8	0	4	(2	2)	64	19	14	17	17	0	40	2	3	2	1	1	.50	2	.227	.293	.330
05	SF	NL	34	93	21	8	0	1	(1	0)	32	18	7	7	9	1	25	1	2	0	1	0	1.00	3	.226	.301	.344
05	Sea	AL	42	108	26	4	0	2	(1	1)	36	14	8	7	7	0	25	1	3	0	0	0	-	5	.241	.293	.333
12	Tex	AL	49	161	38	8	0	3	(2	1)	55	16	12	15	14	0	31	2	3	2	1	1	.50	2	.236	.302	.342
12	Tor	AL	10	28	6	0	0	1	(0	1)	9	3	2	2	2	0	7	0	0	0	0	0	-	0	.214	.267	.321
12	Mil	NL	5	5	0	0	0	0	(0	0)	0	0	0	0	1	0	2	0	0	0	0	0	-	0	.000	.167	.000
	Postseason		24	73	21	5	0	2	(1	1)	32	7	13	12	5	1	16	0	3	1	0	0	-	2	.288	.329	.438
12 ML YEARS			846	2696	694	154	12	56	(36	20)	1040	296	323	298	209	16	520	29	36	17	19	17	.53	94	.257	.316	.386

Andres Torres

Bats: B Throws: R Pos: CF-124; PH-10; PR-5; DH-1   Ht: 5'10" Wt: 195 Born: 1/26/1978 Age: 35

			BATTING																	BASERUNNING				AVERAGES		
Year	Team	Lg	G	AB	H	2B	3B	HR	(Hm	Rd)	TB	R	RBI	RC	TBB	IBB	SO	HBP	SH	SF	SB	CS	SB%	GDP	Avg	OBP	Slg
2012	StLuci*	A+	3	12	4	1	0	0	(-	-)	5	3	1	2	0	0	0	0	0	0	2	0	1.00	0	.333	.333	.417
2012	Buffalo*	AAA	2	7	1	0	0	0	(-	-)	1	1	0	0	2	0	3	0	1	0	1	0	1.00	0	.143	.333	.143
2002	Det	AL	19	70	14	1	1	0	(0	0)	17	7	3	2	6	0	16	1	0	2	2	2	.50	2	.200	.266	.243
2003	Det	AL	59	168	37	4	3	1	(1	0)	50	23	9	9	10	0	35	0	6	1	5	5	.50	5	.220	.263	.298
2004	Det	AL	3	0	0	0	0	0	(0	0)	0	1	0	0	0	0	0	0	0	0	0	0	-	0	-	-	-
2005	Tex	AL	8	19	3	1	0	0	(0	0)	4	2	1	1	1	0	6	0	0	1	1	0	1.00	0	.158	.190	.211
2009	SF	NL	75	152	41	6	8	6	(4	2)	81	30	23	31	16	0	45	1	1	0	6	1	.86	0	.270	.343	.533
2010	SF	NL	139	507	136	43	8	16	(7	9)	243	84	63	87	56	2	128	2	5	0	26	7	.79	10	.268	.343	.479
2011	SF	NL	112	348	77	24	1	4	(1	3)	115	50	19	38	42	0	95	4	4	0	19	6	.76	3	.221	.312	.330
2012	NYM	NL	132	374	86	17	7	3	(1	2)	126	47	35	45	52	2	90	3	1	2	13	5	.72	9	.230	.327	.337
	Postseason		15	58	16	4	0	1	(0	1)	23	6	3	6	3	0	18	1	1	0	2	3	.40	0	.276	.323	.397
8 ML YEARS			547	1638	394	96	28	30	(14	16)	636	244	153	213	183	4	415	11	17	6	73	26	.74	29	.241	.320	.388

Carlos Torres

Pitches: R Bats: R Pos: RP-31   Ht: 6'1" Wt: 190 Born: 10/22/1982 Age: 30

			HOW MUCH HE PITCHED							WHAT HE GAVE UP											THE RESULTS						
Year	Team	Lg	G	GS	CG	GF	IP	BFP	H	R	ER	HR	SH	SF	HB	TBB	IBB	SO	WP	Bk	W	L	Pct	Sh	Sv-Op	Hld	ERC	ERA
2012	ColSpr*	AAA	14	13	0	0	61.0	261	62	30	27	6	1	0	1	25	0	59	6	0	5	4	.556	0	0--	-	4.34	3.98
2009	CWS	AL	8	5	0	2	28.1	130	30	20	19	5	3	3	2	17	2	22	0	0	1	2	.333	0	0-0	0	6.05	6.04
2010	CWS	AL	5	1	0	1	13.2	71	23	13	13	2	0	1	0	9	1	13	0	0	0	1	.000	0	0-0	0	9.84	8.56
2012	Col	NL	31	0	0	9	53.0	231	49	31	31	2	6	4	4	26	1	42	6	0	5	3	.625	0	0-0	1	3.85	5.26
3 ML YEARS			44	6	0	12	95.0	432	102	64	63	9	9	8	6	52	4	77	6	0	6	6	.500	0	0-0	1	5.27	5.97

Chad Tracy

Bats: L Throws: R Pos: PH-54; 1B-14; 3B-10   Ht: 6'1" Wt: 220 Born: 5/22/1980 Age: 33

			BATTING																	BASERUNNING				AVERAGES		
Year	Team	Lg	G	AB	H	2B	3B	HR	(Hm	Rd)	TB	R	RBI	RC	TBB	IBB	SO	HBP	SH	SF	SB	CS	SB%	GDP	Avg	OBP	Slg
2012	Ptomc*	A+	6	18	4	0	0	0	(-	-)	4	3	2	1	1	0	1	0	0	1	0	0	-	0	.222	.250	.222
2012	Syrcse*	AAA	6	19	9	0	0	1	(-	-)	12	2	3	5	1	0	2	0	0	0	0	0	-	2	.474	.500	.632
2004	Ari	NL	143	481	137	29	3	8	(6	2)	196	45	53	63	45	3	60	0	1	5	2	3	.40	11	.285	.343	.407
2005	Ari	NL	145	503	155	34	4	27	(9	18)	278	73	72	82	35	4	78	8	1	6	3	1	.75	10	.308	.359	.553
2006	Ari	NL	154	597	168	41	0	20	(14	6)	269	91	80	85	54	5	129	5	1	5	5	1	.83	11	.281	.343	.451
2007	Ari	NL	76	227	60	18	2	7	(3	4)	103	30	35	33	29	4	43	1	0	3	0	0	-	8	.264	.346	.454
2008	Ari	NL	88	273	73	16	0	8	(3	5)	113	25	39	32	16	2	49	1	0	2	0	0	-	5	.267	.308	.414
2009	Ari	NL	98	257	61	15	0	8	(7	1)	100	29	39	28	26	7	38	1	0	4	1	0	1.00	3	.237	.306	.389
2010	2 Tms	NL	69	146	36	8	0	1	(0	1)	47	11	15	14	11	0	36	2	0	0	0	0	-	2	.247	.306	.322
2012	Was	NL	73	93	25	7	0	3	(3	0)	41	7	14	14	10	3	15	1	0	1	0	0	-	1	.269	.343	.441
10	ChC	NL	28	44	11	2	0	0	(0	0)	13	6	5	6	5	0	15	0	0	0	0	0	-	0	.250	.327	.295
10	Fla	NL	41	102	25	6	0	1	(0	1)	34	5	10	8	6	0	21	2	0	0	0	0	-	2	.245	.297	.333
8 ML YEARS			846	2577	715	168	9	82	(45	37)	1147	311	347	351	226	28	448	19	3	27	11	5	.69	51	.277	.337	.445

Matt Treanor

Bats: R Throws: R Pos: C-35; PH-2   TRAY-ner   Ht: 6'0" Wt: 200 Born: 3/3/1976 Age: 37

Year	Team	Lg	G	AB	H	2B	3B	HR	(Hm	Rd)	TB	R	RBI	RC	TBB	IBB	SO	HBP	SH	SF	SB	CS	SB%	GDP	Avg	OBP	Slg
2004	Fla	NL	29	55	13	2	0	0	(0	0)	15	7	1	4	4	0	13	2	0	0	0	0	-	3	.236	.311	.273
2005	Fla	NL	58	134	27	8	0	0	(0	0)	35	10	13	13	16	1	28	3	1	0	0	0	-	5	.201	.301	.261
2006	Fla	NL	67	157	36	6	1	2	(0	2)	50	12	14	16	19	4	34	5	2	2	0	1	.00	4	.229	.328	.318
2007	Fla	NL	55	171	46	7	1	4	(2	2)	67	16	19	26	19	1	29	5	2	1	0	0	-	2	.269	.357	.392
2008	Fla	NL	65	206	49	7	0	2	(1	1)	62	18	23	25	18	1	53	3	5	2	1	0	1.00	4	.238	.306	.301
2009	Det	AL	4	13	0	0	0	0	(0	0)	0	0	0	0	1	0	4	0	0	0	0	0	-	3	.000	.071	.000
2010	Tex	AL	82	237	50	6	1	5	(4	1)	73	22	27	19	22	0	43	5	4	4	1	2	.33	4	.211	.287	.308
2011	2 Tms		72	196	42	6	0	3	(2	1)	57	24	22	25	34	0	53	4	5	3	2	2	.50	3	.214	.338	.291
2012	LAD	NL	36	103	18	3	1	2	(1	1)	29	11	10	6	14	2	29	2	1	2	1	1	.50	2	.175	.281	.282
11	KC	AL	65	186	42	6	0	3	(2	1)	57	24	21	25	33	0	49	4	5	2	2	2	.50	3	.226	.351	.306
11	Tex	AL	7	10	0	0	0	0	(0	0)	0	0	1	0	1	0	4	0	0	1	0	0	-	0	.000	.083	.000
	Postseason		4	10	2	0	0	1	(0	1)	5	3	2	2	2	0	2	2	0	0	0	0	-	0	.200	.429	.500
	9 ML YEARS		468	1272	281	45	4	18	(10	8)	388	120	129	134	147	9	286	29	20	14	5	6	.45	28	.221	.313	.305

Carlos Triunfel

Bats: R Throws: R Pos: SS-7; 2B-2; PH-2   TRUE-en-fell   Ht: 5'11" Wt: 200 Born: 2/27/1990 Age: 23

Year	Team	Lg	G	AB	H	2B	3B	HR	(Hm	Rd)	TB	R	RBI	RC	TBB	IBB	SO	HBP	SH	SF	SB	CS	SB%	GDP	Avg	OBP	Slg
2007	Wisc	A	43	152	47	8	2	0	(-	-)	59	18	14	18	5	1	23	3	3	1	4	8	.33	1	.309	.342	.388
2007	Ms	R	3	11	3	0	0	0	(-	-)	3	1	3	0	0	0	1	0	0	2	0	0	-	0	.273	.231	.273
2007	Hi Dsrt	A+	50	208	60	10	2	0	(-	-)	74	32	22	24	12	0	31	2	3	0	3	4	.43	6	.288	.333	.356
2008	Hi Dsrt	A+	108	436	125	20	4	8	(-	-)	177	75	49	64	30	0	52	5	3	5	30	9	.77	7	.287	.336	.406
2009	WTenn	AA	7	26	6	1	0	0	(-	-)	7	2	4	2	1	0	2	1	0	0	0	0	-	0	.231	.286	.269
2009	Ms	R	4	16	4	1	0	0	(-	-)	5	0	4	1	0	0	2	0	0	0	1	0	1.00	1	.250	.250	.313
2010	WTenn	AA	129	470	121	12	1	7	(-	-)	156	51	42	43	13	1	54	7	5	3	2	8	.20	18	.257	.286	.332
2011	Jacksn	AA	105	395	111	22	2	6	(-	-)	155	45	35	53	25	2	71	10	3	0	5	7	.42	2	.281	.340	.392
2011	Tacom	AAA	27	111	31	6	1	0	(-	-)	39	7	10	12	2	0	17	2	1	1	1	0	1.00	3	.279	.302	.351
2012	Tacom	AAA	131	496	129	31	2	10	(-	-)	194	74	63	62	23	0	89	13	7	4	3	2	.60	12	.260	.308	.391
2012	Sea	AL	10	22	5	2	0	0	(0	0)	7	2	3	3	1	0	4	0	1	0	0	0	-	0	.227	.261	.318

Mike Trout

Bats: R Throws: R Pos: CF-110; LF-67; RF-4; PR-1   Ht: 6'1" Wt: 210 Born: 8/7/1991 Age: 21

Year	Team	Lg	G	AB	H	2B	3B	HR	(Hm	Rd)	TB	R	RBI	RC	TBB	IBB	SO	HBP	SH	SF	SB	CS	SB%	GDP	Avg	OBP	Slg
2009	Angels	R	39	164	59	7	7	1	(-	-)	83	29	25	36	18	0	28	0	3	2	13	2	.87	2	.360	.418	.506
2009	CRpds	A	5	15	4	0	0	0	(-	-)	4	1	0	2	4	0	6	0	1	0	0	0	-	0	.267	.421	.267
2010	CRpds	A	81	312	113	19	7	6	(-	-)	164	76	39	79	46	2	52	7	2	1	45	9	.83	1	.362	.454	.526
2010	RCuca	A+	50	196	60	9	2	4	(-	-)	85	30	19	33	27	1	33	1	5	3	11	6	.65	2	.306	.388	.434
2011	Ark	AA	91	353	115	18	13	11	(-	-)	192	82	38	81	45	1	76	9	4	1	33	10	.77	2	.326	.414	.544
2012	Salt Lk	AAA	20	77	31	4	5	1	(-	-)	48	21	13	22	11	0	16	1	1	3	6	1	.86	1	.403	.467	.623
2011	LAA	AL	40	123	27	6	0	5	(1	4)	48	20	16	14	9	0	30	2	0	1	4	0	1.00	2	.220	.281	.390
2012	LAA	AL	139	559	182	27	8	30	(16	14)	315	129	83	127	67	4	139	6	0	7	49	5	.91	7	.326	.399	.564
	2 ML YEARS		179	682	209	33	8	35	(17	18)	363	149	99	141	76	4	169	8	0	8	53	5	.91	9	.306	.379	.532

Mark Trumbo

Bats: R Throws: R Pos: LF-66; RF-35; DH-23; 1B-21; 3B-8; PR-1   Ht: 6'4" Wt: 225 Born: 1/16/1986 Age: 27

Year	Team	Lg	G	AB	H	2B	3B	HR	(Hm	Rd)	TB	R	RBI	RC	TBB	IBB	SO	HBP	SH	SF	SB	CS	SB%	GDP	Avg	OBP	Slg
2010	LAA	AL	8	15	1	0	0	0	(0	0)	1	2	2	0	1	0	8	0	0	0	0	0	-	0	.067	.125	.067
2011	LAA	AL	149	539	137	31	1	29	(14	15)	257	65	87	69	25	6	120	5	0	4	9	4	.69	17	.254	.291	.477
2012	LAA	AL	144	544	146	19	3	32	(12	20)	267	66	95	80	36	3	153	4	0	2	4	5	.44	12	.268	.317	.491
	3 ML YEARS		301	1098	284	50	4	61	(26	35)	525	133	184	149	62	9	281	9	0	6	13	9	.59	29	.259	.302	.478

Troy Tulowitzki

Bats: R Throws: R Pos: SS-47   too-luh-WIT-skee   Ht: 6'3" Wt: 215 Born: 10/10/1984 Age: 28

Year	Team	Lg	G	AB	H	2B	3B	HR	(Hm	Rd)	TB	R	RBI	RC	TBB	IBB	SO	HBP	SH	SF	SB	CS	SB%	GDP	Avg	OBP	Slg
2012	ColSpr*	AAA	6	17	6	1	0	2	(-	-)	13	2	4	4	1	0	4	0	0	0	0	0	-	1	.353	.389	.765
2012	Tulsa*	AA	3	10	3	1	0	1	(-	-)	7	1	2	2	0	0	2	0	0	0	0	0	-	0	.300	.300	.700
2006	Col	NL	25	96	23	2	0	1	(0	1)	28	15	6	10	10	3	25	1	1	0	3	0	1.00	1	.240	.318	.292
2007	Col	NL	155	609	177	33	5	24	(15	9)	292	104	99	95	57	3	130	9	5	2	7	6	.54	14	.291	.359	.479
2008	Col	NL	101	377	99	24	2	8	(4	4)	151	48	46	42	38	5	56	2	2	1	1	6	.14	16	.263	.332	.401
2009	Col	NL	151	543	161	25	9	32	(17	15)	300	101	92	96	73	4	112	3	0	9	20	11	.65	20	.297	.377	.552
2010	Col	NL	122	470	148	32	3	27	(15	12)	267	89	95	88	48	4	78	5	1	5	11	2	.85	17	.315	.381	.568
2011	Col	NL	143	537	162	36	2	30	(17	13)	292	81	105	101	59	12	79	4	1	5	9	3	.75	16	.302	.372	.544
2012	Col	NL	47	181	52	8	2	8	(3	5)	88	33	27	27	19	1	19	2	0	1	2	2	.50	7	.287	.360	.486
	Postseason		15	57	12	5	0	1	(0	1)	20	3	6	3	4	0	17	1	0	1	0	1	.00	3	.211	.270	.351
	7 ML YEARS		744	2813	822	160	23	130	(71	59)	1418	471	470	459	304	32	499	26	10	24	53	30	.64	91	.292	.364	.504

Jacob Turner

Pitches: R **Bats:** R **Pos:** SP-10

Ht: 6'5" **Wt:** 210 **Born:** 5/21/1991 **Age:** 22

Year	Team	Lg	G	GS	CG	GF	IP	BFP	H	R	ER	HR	SH	SF	HB	TBB	IBB	SO	WP	Bk	W	L	Pct	Sh	Sv-Op	Hld	ERC	ERA
2010	WMich	A	11	10	0	1	54.0	228	53	26	22	4	0	2	1	9	0	51	1	0	2	3	.400	0	0--	-	2.87	3.67
2010	Lkland	A+	13	13	0	0	61.1	252	53	22	20	3	0	2	7	14	0	51	0	1	4	2	.667	0	0--	-	2.81	2.93
2011	Erie	AA	17	17	0	0	113.2	473	102	47	44	9	4	4	7	32	1	90	8	0	3	5	.375	0	0--	-	3.15	3.48
2011	Toledo	AAA	3	3	0	0	17.1	69	15	6	6	1	0	0	0	3	0	20	2	0	1	0	1.000	0	0--	-	2.27	3.12
2012	Lkland	A+	4	4	0	0	21.2	86	17	8	4	1	0	0	1	7	0	17	1	0	1	2	.333	0	0--	-	2.57	1.66
2012	Toledo	AAA	10	10	1	0	62.2	258	52	23	22	2	1	3	2	24	1	40	1	0	4	2	.667	1	0--	-	2.78	3.16
2012	NewOr	AAA	5	5	0	0	27.1	116	27	6	6	2	2	1	0	12	1	16	2	0	2	0	1.000	0	0--	-	4.00	1.98
2011	Det	AL	3	3	0	0	12.2	60	17	13	12	3	0	1	1	4	0	8	0	0	0	1	.000	0	0-0	-	7.03	8.53
2012	2 Tms	AL	10	10	0	0	55.0	231	50	32	27	9	1	2	0	16	3	36	5	0	2	5	.286	0	0-0	-	3.42	4.42
12	Det	AL	3	3	0	0	12.1	61	17	11	11	4	0	1	0	7	1	7	1	0	1	1	.500	0	0-0	-	8.66	8.03
12	Mia	NL	7	7	0	0	42.2	170	33	21	16	5	1	1	0	9	2	29	4	0	1	4	.200	0	0-0	-	2.20	3.38
	2 ML YEARS		13	13	0	0	67.2	291	67	45	39	12	1	3	1	20	3	44	5	0	2	6	.250	0	0-0	-	4.03	5.19

Justin Turner

Bats: R **Throws:** R **Pos:** PH-56; 2B-14; 1B-11; 3B-11; SS-10; PR-1

Ht: 6'0" **Wt:** 210 **Born:** 11/23/1984 **Age:** 28

Year	Team	Lg	G	AB	H	2B	3B	HR	(Hm	Rd)	TB	R	RBI	RC	TBB	IBB	SO	HBP	SH	SF	SB	CS	SB%	GDP	Avg	OBP	Slg
2012	Buffalo*	AAA	2	8	2	0	0	0	(-	-)	2	0	0	0	0	0	0	0	0	0	0	0	-	2	.250	.250	.250
2009	Bal	AL	12	18	3	0	0	0	(0	0)	3	2	3	1	4	0	3	0	0	0	0	0	-	1	.167	.318	.167
2010	2 Tms		9	17	1	1	0	0	(0	0)	2	1	0	0	1	0	3	0	0	0	0	0	-	0	.059	.111	.118
2011	NYM	NL	117	435	113	30	4	0	(3	1)	155	49	51	59	39	2	59	10	2	1	7	2	.78	9	.260	.334	.356
2012	NYM	NL	94	171	46	13	1	2	(2	0)	67	20	19	19	9	0	24	4	0	1	1	1	.50	9	.269	.319	.392
10	Bal	AL	5	9	0	0	0	0	(0	0)	0	0	0	0	0	0	3	0	0	0	0	0	-	0	.000	.000	.000
10	NYM	NL	4	8	1	1	0	0	(0	0)	2	1	0	0	1	0	0	0	0	0	0	0	-	0	.125	.222	.250
	4 ML YEARS		232	641	163	44	1	6	(5	1)	227	72	73	79	53	2	89	14	2	2	8	3	.73	19	.254	.324	.354

Koji Uehara

Pitches: R **Bats:** R **Pos:** RP-37

KOH-jee ooh-ih-HAR-uh

Ht: 6'1" **Wt:** 190 **Born:** 4/3/1975 **Age:** 38

Year	Team	Lg	G	GS	CG	GF	IP	BFP	H	R	ER	HR	SH	SF	HB	TBB	IBB	SO	WP	Bk	W	L	Pct	Sh	Sv-Op	Hld	ERC	ERA
2012	RdRck*	AAA	3	0	0	0	3.0	11	3	0	0	0	0	0	0	0	0	4	0	0	0	0	-	0	0--	-	2.18	0.00
2009	Bal	AL	12	12	0	0	66.2	279	71	33	30	7	1	3	0	12	1	48	0	0	2	4	.333	0	0-0	-	3.56	4.05
2010	Bal	AL	43	0	0	22	44.0	174	37	15	14	5	1	0	0	5	0	55	1	0	1	2	.333	0	13-15	6	2.22	2.86
2011	2 Tms	AL	65	0	0	22	65.0	243	38	17	17	11	1	1	0	9	1	85	0	0	2	3	.400	0	0-1	22	1.48	2.35
2012	Tex	AL	37	0	0	13	36.0	130	20	7	7	4	1	1	0	3	0	43	1	0	0	0	-	0	1-1	7	1.12	1.75
11	Bal	AL	43	0	0	19	47.0	174	25	9	9	6	1	1	0	8	1	62	0	0	1	1	.500	0	0-1	13	1.27	1.72
11	Tex	AL	22	0	0	3	18.0	69	13	8	8	5	0	0	0	1	0	23	0	0	1	2	.333	0	0-0	9	2.21	4.00
	Postseason		3	0	0	0	1.1	11	5	5	5	3	0	0	0	2	0	1	0	0	0	0	-	0	0-0	-	59.72	33.75
	4 ML YEARS		157	12	0	57	211.2	826	166	72	68	27	4	5	0	29	2	231	2	0	5	9	.357	0	14-17	35	2.12	2.89

Dan Uggla

Bats: R **Throws:** R **Pos:** 2B-152; PH-3

UGG-luh

Ht: 5'11" **Wt:** 205 **Born:** 3/11/1980 **Age:** 33

Year	Team	Lg	G	AB	H	2B	3B	HR	(Hm	Rd)	TB	R	RBI	RC	TBB	IBB	SO	HBP	SH	SF	SB	CS	SB%	GDP	Avg	OBP	Slg
2006	Fla	NL	154	611	172	26	7	27	(10	17)	293	105	90	97	48	1	123	9	7	8	6	6	.50	5	.282	.339	.480
2007	Fla	NL	159	632	155	49	3	31	(18	13)	303	113	88	81	68	0	167	13	4	11	2	1	.67	10	.245	.326	.479
2008	Fla	NL	146	531	138	37	1	32	(15	17)	273	97	92	93	77	6	171	8	0	3	5	5	.50	10	.260	.360	.514
2009	Fla	NL	158	564	137	27	1	31	(21	10)	259	84	90	81	92	4	150	7	1	4	2	1	.67	10	.243	.354	.459
2010	Fla	NL	159	589	169	31	0	33	(14	19)	299	100	105	101	78	2	149	2	0	5	4	1	.80	10	.287	.369	.508
2011	Atl	NL	161	600	140	22	1	36	(18	18)	272	88	82	78	62	2	156	7	0	3	1	3	.25	9	.233	.311	.453
2012	Atl	NL	154	523	115	29	0	19	(7	12)	201	86	78	83	94	5	168	10	0	3	4	3	.57	8	.220	.348	.384
	7 ML YEARS		1091	4050	1026	221	13	209	(103	106)	1900	673	625	614	519	20	1084	56	12	37	24	20	.55	62	.253	.343	.469

B.J. Upton

Bats: R **Throws:** R **Pos:** CF-142; DH-3; PH-2

Ht: 6'3" **Wt:** 185 **Born:** 8/21/1984 **Age:** 28

Year	Team	Lg	G	AB	H	2B	3B	HR	(Hm	Rd)	TB	R	RBI	RC	TBB	IBB	SO	HBP	SH	SF	SB	CS	SB%	GDP	Avg	OBP	Slg
2012	Chrltt*	A+	4	11	1	0	0	0	(-	-)	1	1	1	0	1	0	1	0	0	0	2	0	1.00	2	.091	.167	.091
2012	Mont*	AA	3	10	2	0	0	0	(-	-)	2	1	1	0	1	0	1	0	0	0	0	0	-	0	.200	.273	.200
2004	TB	AL	45	159	41	8	2	4	(2	2)	65	19	12	22	15	0	46	1	1	1	4	1	.80	1	.258	.324	.409
2006	TB	AL	50	175	43	5	0	1	(1	0)	51	20	10	17	13	0	40	1	0	0	11	3	.79	5	.246	.302	.291
2007	TB	AL	129	474	142	25	1	24	(13	11)	241	86	82	93	65	4	154	4	1	4	22	8	.73	14	.300	.386	.508
2008	TB	AL	145	531	145	37	2	9	(4	5)	213	85	67	87	97	4	134	2	3	7	44	16	.73	13	.273	.383	.401
2009	TB	AL	144	560	135	33	4	11	(7	4)	209	79	55	68	57	0	152	3	3	3	42	14	.75	7	.241	.313	.373
2010	TB	AL	154	536	127	38	4	18	(7	11)	227	89	62	74	67	1	164	2	1	4	42	9	.82	13	.237	.322	.424
2011	TB	AL	153	560	136	27	4	23	(9	14)	240	82	81	79	71	4	161	4	2	3	36	12	.75	16	.243	.331	.429
2012	TB	AL	146	573	141	29	3	28	(17	11)	260	79	78	71	45	0	169	1	4	8	31	6	.84	13	.246	.298	.454
	Postseason		25	101	27	6	1	7	(2	5)	56	19	18	17	9	1	29	0	0	1	9	2	.82	4	.267	.324	.554
	8 ML YEARS		966	3568	910	202	20	118	(60	58)	1506	539	447	511	430	13	1020	18	15	30	232	69	.77	78	.255	.336	.422

Justin Upton

Bats: R Throws: R Pos: RF-149; PR-1   Ht: 6'2" Wt: 205 Born: 8/25/1987 Age: 25

Year	Team	Lg	G	AB	H	2B	3B	HR	(Hm	Rd)	TB	R	RBI	RC	TBB	IBB	SO	HBP	SH	SF	SB	CS	SB%	GDP	Avg	OBP	Slg
2007	Ari	NL	43	140	31	8	3	2	(2	0)	51	17	11	13	11	4	37	1	0	0	2	0	1.00	3	.221	.283	.364
2008	Ari	NL	108	356	89	19	6	15	(12	3)	165	52	42	47	54	6	121	4	0	3	1	4	.20	3	.250	.353	.463
2009	Ari	NL	138	526	158	30	7	26	(14	12)	280	84	86	94	55	3	137	2	1	4	20	5	.80	10	.300	.366	.532
2010	Ari	NL	133	495	135	27	3	17	(8	9)	219	73	69	73	64	5	152	4	1	7	18	8	.69	20	.273	.356	.442
2011	Ari	NL	159	592	171	39	5	31	(20	11)	313	105	88	103	59	9	126	19	0	1	21	9	.70	8	.289	.369	.529
2012	Ari	NL	150	554	155	24	4	17	(11	6)	238	107	67	82	63	5	121	5	0	6	18	8	.69	7	.280	.355	.430
	Postseason		11	34	9	1	1	2	(0	2)	18	5	4	6	6	0	9	2	0	0	1	0	1.00	0	.265	.405	.529
	6 ML YEARS		731	2663	739	147	28	108	(67	41)	1266	438	363	412	306	32	694	35	2	24	80	34	.70	51	.278	.357	.475

Juan Uribe

Bats: R Throws: R Pos: 3B-46; PH-20; SS-1   yer-EE-bay   Ht: 6'0" Wt: 240 Born: 3/22/1979 Age: 34

Year	Team	Lg	G	AB	H	2B	3B	HR	(Hm	Rd)	TB	R	RBI	RC	TBB	IBB	SO	HBP	SH	SF	SB	CS	SB%	GDP	Avg	OBP	Slg
2012	RCuca*	A+	3	10	3	0	1	0	(-	-)	8	1	3	2	0	0	4	0	0	1	0	0	-	0	.300	.273	.800
2001	Col	NL	72	273	82	15	11	8	(3	5)	143	32	53	44	8	1	55	2	0	0	3	0	1.00	6	.300	.325	.524
2002	Col	NL	155	566	136	25	7	6	(4	2)	193	69	49	53	34	1	120	5	7	6	9	2	.82	17	.240	.286	.341
2003	Col	NL	87	316	80	19	3	10	(6	4)	135	45	33	45	17	0	60	3	6	1	7	2	.78	3	.253	.297	.427
2004	CWS	AL	134	502	142	31	6	23	(16	7)	254	82	74	81	32	1	96	3	11	5	9	11	.45	10	.283	.327	.506
2005	CWS	AL	146	481	121	23	3	16	(10	6)	198	58	71	59	34	0	77	4	11	10	4	6	.40	7	.252	.301	.412
2006	CWS	AL	132	463	109	28	2	21	(13	8)	204	53	71	52	13	1	82	3	9	7	1	1	.50	10	.235	.257	.441
2007	CWS	AL	150	513	120	18	2	20	(15	5)	202	55	68	52	34	2	112	4	7	5	1	9	.10	5	.234	.284	.394
2008	CWS	AL	110	324	80	22	1	7	(5	2)	125	38	40	43	22	0	64	1	5	1	1	3	.25	5	.247	.296	.386
2009	SF	NL	122	398	115	26	4	16	(9	7)	197	50	55	55	25	2	82	1	3	5	3	1	.75	7	.289	.329	.495
2010	SF	NL	148	521	129	24	2	24	(13	11)	229	64	85	68	45	6	92	4	0	5	1	2	.33	20	.248	.310	.440
2011	LAD	NL	77	270	55	12	0	4	(3	1)	79	21	28	13	17	2	60	6	0	2	2	0	1.00	12	.204	.264	.293
2012	LAD	NL	66	162	31	9	0	2	(1	1)	46	15	17	13	13	0	37	2	1	1	0	1	.00	6	.191	.258	.284
	Postseason		30	101	21	5	0	3	(2	1)	35	11	16	11	7	0	27	1	2	1	2	0	1.00	2	.208	.264	.347
	12 ML YEARS		1399	4789	1200	252	41	157	(98	59)	2005	582	644	578	294	16	937	38	60	48	41	38	.52	109	.251	.296	.419

Chase Utley

Bats: L Throws: R Pos: 2B-81; PH-2   UTT-lee   Ht: 6'1" Wt: 200 Born: 12/17/1978 Age: 34

Year	Team	Lg	G	AB	H	2B	3B	HR	(Hm	Rd)	TB	R	RBI	RC	TBB	IBB	SO	HBP	SH	SF	SB	CS	SB%	GDP	Avg	OBP	Slg
2012	Clrwtr*	A+	9	32	5	0	0	1	(-	-)	8	3	5	2	3	0	5	2	0	1	1	0	1.00	0	.156	.263	.250
2012	LV*	AAA	1	5	2	0	0	1	(-	-)	5	1	1	1	0	0	2	0	0	0	0	0	-	0	.400	.400	1.000
2003	Phi	NL	43	134	32	10	1	2	(1	1)	50	13	21	19	11	0	22	6	0	1	2	0	1.00	3	.239	.322	.373
2004	Phi	NL	94	267	71	11	2	13	(8	5)	125	36	57	37	15	1	40	2	1	2	4	1	.80	6	.266	.308	.468
2005	Phi	NL	147	543	158	39	6	28	(12	16)	293	93	105	102	69	5	109	9	0	7	16	3	.84	10	.291	.376	.540
2006	Phi	NL	160	658	203	40	4	32	(16	16)	347	131	102	122	63	1	132	14	0	4	15	4	.79	9	.309	.379	.527
2007	Phi	NL	132	530	176	48	5	22	(14	8)	300	104	103	111	50	1	89	25	1	7	9	1	.90	7	.332	.410	.566
2008	Phi	NL	159	607	177	41	4	33	(20	13)	325	113	104	113	64	14	104	27	1	8	14	2	.88	9	.292	.380	.535
2009	Phi	NL	156	571	161	28	4	31	(16	15)	290	112	93	115	88	10	110	24	0	1.00	23	0	1.00	5	.282	.397	.508
2010	Phi	NL	115	425	117	20	2	16	(10	6)	189	75	65	83	63	3	63	18	0	5	13	2	.87	4	.275	.387	.445
2011	Phi	NL	103	398	103	21	6	11	(8	3)	169	54	44	57	39	4	47	14	1	2	14	0	1.00	3	.259	.344	.425
2012	Phi	NL	83	301	77	15	2	11	(8	3)	129	48	45	49	43	7	43	12	0	6	11	1	.92	4	.256	.365	.429
	Postseason		46	164	43	7	1	10	(5	5)	82	38	25	34	34	3	38	5	0	1	10	2	.83	3	.262	.402	.500
	10 ML YEARS		1192	4434	1275	273	36	199	(113	86)	2217	779	739	808	505	39	759	151	4	46	121	14	.90	60	.288	.376	.500

Luis Valbuena

Bats: L Throws: R Pos: 3B-82; PH-12; 2B-5   val-BWAY-nah   Ht: 5'10" Wt: 195 Born: 11/30/1985 Age: 27

Year	Team	Lg	G	AB	H	2B	3B	HR	(Hm	Rd)	TB	R	RBI	RC	TBB	IBB	SO	HBP	SH	SF	SB	CS	SB%	GDP	Avg	OBP	Slg
2012	Iowa*	AAA	58	211	64	17	1	8	(2	6)	107	38	31	41	28	1	50	1	0	6	1	1	.50	3	.303	.378	.507
2008	Sea	AL	18	49	12	5	0	0	(0	0)	17	6	1	5	4	0	11	1	0	0	0	0	-	0	.245	.315	.347
2009	Cle	AL	103	368	92	25	3	10	(2	8)	153	52	31	35	26	0	83	0	2	2	2	3	.40	8	.250	.298	.416
2010	Cle	AL	91	275	53	12	0	2	(1	1)	71	22	24	21	28	1	61	3	2	2	1	2	.33	5	.193	.273	.258
2011	Cle	AL	17	43	9	0	0	1	(1	0)	12	4	1	2	1	0	9	0	0	0	1	0	1.00	0	.209	.227	.279
2012	ChC	NL	90	265	58	20	0	4	(2	2)	90	26	24	27	36	1	55	0	0	2	0	2	.00	6	.219	.310	.340
	5 ML YEARS		319	1000	224	62	3	17	(5	12)	343	110	85	90	95	2	219	4	4	6	4	7	.36	19	.224	.292	.343

Raul Valdes

Pitches: L Bats: L Pos: RP-26; SP-1   Ht: 5'11" Wt: 190 Born: 11/27/1977 Age: 35

			HOW MUCH HE PITCHED					WHAT HE GAVE UP										THE RESULTS						
Year	Team	Lg	G	GS	CG	GF	IP	BFP	H	R	ER	HR	SH	SF	HB	TBB	IBB	SO	WP	Bk	W	L	Pct	Sh	Sv-Op Hld	ERC	ERA
2012	LV*	AAA	16	0	0	6	30.0	114	26	12	9	3	1	0	0	2	0	41	1	0	1	2	.333	0	3- -	-	2.20	2.70
2010	NYM	NL	38	1	0	8	58.2	262	59	33	32	7	2	2	4	27	1	56	2	0	3	3	.500	0	1-3	1	4.70	4.91
2011	2 Tms		13	0	0	3	12.0	55	14	4	4	1	0	0	1	6	2	15	0	0	0	1	.000	0	0-0	1	5.42	3.00
2012	Phi	NL	27	1	0	7	31.0	113	18	10	10	3	1	0	0	5	1	35	0	0	3	2	.600	0	0-1	2	1.32	2.90
11	StL	NL	7	0	0	3	5.1	27	6	2	2	0	0	0	1	4	2	7	0	0	0	1	.000	0	0-0	0	5.20	3.38
11	NYY	AL	6	0	0	0	6.2	28	8	2	2	1	0	0	0	2	0	8	0	0	0	0	-	0	0-0	0	5.47	2.70
	3 ML YEARS		78	2	0	18	101.2	430	91	47	46	11	3	2	5	38	4	106	2	0	6	6	.500	0	1-4	3	3.59	4.07

Jordany Valdespin

jor-DAN-ee VAL-dah-spin

Bats: L **Throws:** R **Pos:** PH-48; LF-21; 2B-16; CF-11; RF-10; SS-4; DH-2; PR-2   **Ht:** 6'0" **Wt:** 190 **Born:** 12/23/1987 **Age:** 25

								BATTING												BASERUNNING				AVERAGES		
Year	Team	Lg	G	AB	H	2B	3B	HR	(Hm | Rd)	TB	R	RBI	RC	TBB	IBB	SO	HBP	SH	SF	SB	CS	SB%	GDP	Avg	OBP	Slg
2008	Mets	R	34	134	38	6	3	3	(- | -)	59	23	22	20	7	0	10	1	1	2	9	2	.82	3	.284	.319	.440
2009	Savann	A	39	152	49	9	3	3	(- | -)	73	30	18	27	11	0	32	0	0	1	7	2	.78	1	.322	.366	.480
2009	Mets	R	6	23	4	0	0	0	(- | -)	4	0	0	0	1	0	3	0	0	0	1	0	1.00	0	.174	.208	.174
2009	Bklyn	A-	18	68	19	3	1	1	(- | -)	27	10	5	9	5	0	16	1	2	0	4	3	.57	3	.279	.338	.397
2010	StLuci	A+	65	270	78	16	3	6	(- | -)	118	40	33	37	8	0	45	6	3	1	13	10	.57	1	.289	.323	.437
2010	Bnghtn	AA	28	112	26	8	0	0	(- | -)	34	8	8	7	2	0	23	0	2	1	4	2	.67	4	.232	.243	.304
2011	Bnghtn	AA	107	404	120	23	3	15	(- | -)	194	62	51	67	21	2	68	7	7	2	33	14	.70	5	.297	.341	.480
2011	Buffalo	AAA	27	107	30	8	0	2	(- | -)	44	7	9	12	4	0	25	0	1	1	4	4	.50	1	.280	.304	.411
2012	Buffalo	AAA	39	151	43	2	1	5	(- | -)	62	22	23	20	10	0	22	1	0	1	10	8	.56	3	.285	.331	.411
2012	NYM	NL	94	191	46	9	1	8	(5 | 3)	81	28	26	20	10	0	44	2	3	0	10	3	.77	2	.241	.286	.424

Jose Valdez

Pitches: R **Bats:** R **Pos:** RP-12   **Ht:** 6'4" **Wt:** 200 **Born:** 1/22/1983 **Age:** 30

			HOW MUCH HE PITCHED					WHAT HE GAVE UP												THE RESULTS							
Year	Team	Lg	G	GS	CG	GF	IP	BFP	H	R	ER	HR	SH	SF	HB	TBB	IBB	SO	WP	Bk	W	L	Pct	Sh	Sv-Op	Hld	ERC	ERA
2002	StIsInd	A-	4	4	0	0	20.0	88	19	14	12	0	2	0	1	9	0	21	2	0	1	3	.250	0	0- -	-	3.42	5.40
2002	Yanks	R	8	7	0	0	40.1	174	45	19	15	2	1	2	2	10	0	28	1	0	1	4	.200	0	0- -	-	3.96	3.35
2003	Btl Crk	A	22	22	0	0	133.2	568	132	67	54	14	3	5	8	42	1	76	8	4	11	7	.611	0	0- -	-	3.95	3.64
2003	Tampa	A+	3	3	0	0	15.2	61	11	7	7	2	1	1	0	4	0	9	1	0	1	1	.500	0	0- -	-	2.18	4.02
2004	Tampa	A+	23	20	0	1	111.2	482	116	69	53	7	6	4	7	38	1	76	10	2	7	7	.500	0	0- -	-	4.05	4.27
2006	Yanks	R	9	0	0	1	10.1	42	12	7	3	2	0	0	0	1	0	7	0	0	1	1	.500	0	1- -	-	4.52	2.61
2006	CtnSC	A	5	0	0	3	8.1	32	8	1	1	0	0	0	0	2	1	6	0	0	0	0	-	0	2- -	-	2.64	1.08
2007	Tampa	A+	37	0	0	20	59.2	251	54	21	19	4	1	4	0	21	3	60	6	1	3	4	.429	0	3- -	-	3.05	2.87
2008	Tampa	A+	27	0	0	16	36.0	141	30	13	11	4	2	0	0	9	3	32	1	1	6	2	.750	0	3- -	-	2.67	2.75
2008	Trntn	AA	17	0	0	13	24.1	96	17	7	6	4	0	1	1	7	0	23	1	0	1	0	1.000	0	4- -	-	2.64	2.22
2009	Trntn	AA	34	0	0	26	38.1	171	32	17	13	2	5	2	3	23	5	42	14	0	1	1	.500	0	10- -	-	3.61	3.05
2009	S-WB	AAA	9	0	0	3	19.1	86	23	9	9	2	1	0	0	10	1	18	2	0	2	1	.667	0	0- -	-	5.80	4.19
2010	Astros	R	4	0	0	0	4.0	13	2	0	0	0	0	0	0	0	0	4	0	0	0	0	-	0	0- -	-	0.58	0.00
2010	CpChr	AA	9	0	0	6	12.1	48	5	2	2	0	0	0	2	4	0	11	0	0	0	0	-	0	0- -	-	1.12	1.46
2011	OKCity	AAA	20	0	0	13	20.2	99	23	16	13	4	2	1	1	9	3	26	2	0	1	0	1.000	0	9- -	-	5.16	5.66
2011	Astros	R	4	0	0	0	4.0	17	3	3	2	0	0	0	0	1	0	7	1	0	0	1	.000	0	0- -	-	1.55	4.50
2012	OKCity	AAA	46	0	0	36	43.2	205	53	27	24	5	3	1	1	12	5	59	6	0	5	0	.000	0	21- -	-	4.48	4.95
2012	Astros	R	5	5	0	0	5.0	19	2	0	0	0	0	0	0	1	0	7	0	0	0	0	-	0	0- -	-	0.60	0.00
2011	Hou	NL	12	0	0	7	14.0	65	17	14	14	2	0	1	1	7	1	15	1	0	0	0	-	0	0-0	1	6.31	9.00
2012	Hou	NL	12	0	0	3	12.0	57	12	4	3	1	3	0	0	8	1	10	1	0	0	0	-	0	0-0	4	4.64	2.25
	2 ML YEARS		24	0	0	10	26.0	122	29	18	17	3	3	1	1	15	2	25	2	0	0	0	-	0	0-0	5	5.51	5.88

Wilson Valdez

Bats: R **Throws:** R **Pos:** SS-33; 2B-22; PH-15; 3B-14; CF-5; PR-2   **Ht:** 5'11" **Wt:** 170 **Born:** 5/20/1978 **Age:** 35

								BATTING												BASERUNNING				AVERAGES		
Year	Team	Lg	G	AB	H	2B	3B	HR	(Hm | Rd)	TB	R	RBI	RC	TBB	IBB	SO	HBP	SH	SF	SB	CS	SB%	GDP	Avg	OBP	Slg
2004	CWS	AL	19	43	10	1	0	1	(1 | 0)	14	8	4	2	2	0	5	0	1	0	1	2	.33	1	.233	.267	.326
2005	2 Tms		51	139	28	7	1	0	(0 | 0)	37	9	9	8	8	0	26	0	1	0	2	2	.50	2	.201	.245	.266
2007	LAD	NL	41	74	16	2	1	0	(0 | 0)	20	12	7	7	4	0	12	1	0	1	1	0	1.00	6	.216	.263	.270
2009	NYM	NL	41	86	22	3	2	0	(0 | 0)	29	11	7	6	8	0	10	1	0	0	0	1	.00	6	.256	.326	.337
2010	Phi	NL	111	333	86	16	3	4	(2 | 2)	120	37	35	34	21	7	43	2	7	0	7	0	1.00	20	.258	.306	.360
2011	Phi	NL	99	273	68	14	4	1	(1 | 0)	93	39	30	30	18	3	41	0	7	2	3	3	.50	13	.249	.294	.341
2012	Cin	NL	77	194	40	4	0	0	(0 | 0)	44	15	15	9	8	0	36	0	5	1	3	1	.75	4	.206	.236	.227
05	Sea	AL	42	126	25	5	1	0	(0 | 0)	32	9	8	6	6	0	25	0	1	0	2	2	.50	1	.198	.235	.254
05	SD	AL	9	13	3	2	0	0	(0 | 0)	5	0	1	2	2	0	1	0	0	0	0	0	-	1	.231	.333	.385
	Postseason		3	3	1	0	0	0	(0 | 0)	1	1	0	0	0	0	0	0	0	0	0	0	-	0	.333	.333	.333
	7 ML YEARS		439	1142	270	47	11	6	(4 | 2)	357	131	107	96	69	10	173	4	21	4	17	9	.65	46	.236	.281	.313

Danny Valencia

vuh-LENN-see-yah

Bats: R **Throws:** R **Pos:** 3B-44; PH-1; PR-1   **Ht:** 6'2" **Wt:** 220 **Born:** 9/19/1984 **Age:** 28

								BATTING												BASERUNNING				AVERAGES		
Year	Team	Lg	G	AB	H	2B	3B	HR	(Hm | Rd)	TB	R	RBI	RC	TBB	IBB	SO	HBP	SH	SF	SB	CS	SB%	GDP	Avg	OBP	Slg
2012	Roch*	AAA	69	268	67	17	1	7	(- | -)	107	30	37	31	15	0	40	0	0	1	1	2	.33	7	.250	.289	.399
2012	Pwtckt*	AAA	13	49	15	3	0	1	(- | -)	21	3	8	6	3	0	12	1	0	0	0	2	.00	1	.306	.358	.429
2010	Min	AL	85	299	93	18	1	7	(4 | 3)	134	30	40	50	20	0	46	0	0	3	2	0	1.00	11	.311	.351	.448
2011	Min	AL	154	564	139	28	2	15	(9 | 6)	216	63	72	57	40	2	102	0	0	4	2	6	.25	15	.246	.294	.383
2012	2 Tms	AL	44	154	29	6	1	3	(3 | 0)	46	14	21	7	3	0	38	0	0	6	1	0	.00	6	.188	.199	.299
12	Min	AL	34	126	25	6	1	2	(2 | 0)	39	13	17	7	3	0	32	0	0	3	1	0	.00	5	.198	.212	.310
12	Bos	AL	10	28	4	0	0	1	(1 | 0)	7	1	4	0	0	0	6	0	0	1	0	0	-	1	.143	.138	.250
	Postseason		3	9	2	1	0	0	(0 | 0)	3	1	2	1	1	0	3	0	0	0	0	0	-	0	.222	.273	.333
	3 ML YEARS		283	1017	261	52	4	25	(16 | 9)	396	107	133	114	63	2	186	0	0	11	4	7	.36	32	.257	.297	.389

Jose Valverde

Pitches: R **Bats:** R **Pos:** RP-71   val-VARE-day   **Ht:** 6'4" **Wt:** 254 **Born:** 3/24/1978 **Age:** 35

Year	Team	Lg	G	GS	CG	GF	IP	BFP	H	.	R	ER	HR	SH	SF	HB	TBB	IBB	SO	WP	Bk	W	L	Pct	Sh	Sv-Op	Hld	ERC	ERA
2003	Ari	NL	54	0	0	33	50.1	204	24	16	12	4	0	1	2	26	2	71	2	0	2	1	.667	0	10-11	8	1.77	2.15
2004	Ari	NL	29	0	0	20	29.2	131	23	17	14	7	3	2	1	17	4	38	4	0	1	2	.333	0	8-10	5	4.25	4.25
2005	Ari	NL	61	0	0	34	66.1	268	51	19	18	5	3	1	2	20	1	75	3	0	3	4	.429	0	15-17	7	2.43	2.44
2006	Ari	NL	44	0	0	35	49.1	223	50	32	32	6	1	3	2	22	3	69	2	0	2	3	.400	0	18-22	1	4.42	5.84
2007	Ari	NL	65	0	0	59	64.1	265	46	21	19	7	0	1	3	26	1	78	1	0	1	4	.200	0	47-54	0	2.77	2.66
2008	Hou	NL	74	0	0	71	72.0	303	62	28	27	10	0	2	2	23	6	83	3	2	6	3	.667	0	44-51	0	3.18	3.38
2009	Hou	NL	52	0	0	45	54.0	219	40	15	14	5	1	2	2	21	1	56	1	0	4	2	.667	0	25-29	1	2.76	2.33
2010	Det	AL	60	0	0	55	63.0	259	41	24	21	5	0	1	3	32	1	63	3	0	2	4	.333	0	26-29	0	2.67	3.00
2011	Det	AL	75	0	0	70	72.1	301	52	21	18	5	2	0	3	34	4	69	3	1	2	4	.333	0	49-49	0	2.71	2.24
2012	Det	AL	71	0	0	67	69.0	294	59	34	29	3	2	3	4	27	5	48	1	0	3	4	.429	0	35-40	0	2.95	3.78
	Postseason		10	0	0	7	12.0	56	9	7	7	2	0	1	1	10	2	14	0	0	0	2	.000	0	4-4	0	4.79	5.25
	10 ML YEARS		585	0	0	489	590.1	2467	448	227	204	57	12	16	24	248	28	650	23	3	26	31	.456	0	277-312	22	2.89	3.11

Scott Van Slyke

Bats: R **Throws:** R **Pos:** RF-12; LF-11; PH-6; 1B-5   **Ht:** 6'5" **Wt:** 250 **Born:** 7/24/1986 **Age:** 26

Year	Team	Lg	G	AB	H	2B	3B	HR	(Hm	Rd)	TB	R	RBI	RC	TBB	IBB	SO	HBP	SH	SF	SB	CS	SB%	GDP	Avg	OBP	Slg
2005	Ddgrs	R	24	85	24	4	1	2	(-	-)	36	15	15	12	4	0	19	3	1	2	4	3	.57	4	.282	.330	.424
2006	Ogden	R+	45	156	40	5	2	2	(-	-)	55	18	17	18	14	0	41	1	0	1	5	3	.63	7	.256	.320	.353
2007	Gt Lks	A	104	351	89	18	1	2	(-	-)	115	38	35	37	27	0	68	4	3	5	4	4	.50	5	.254	.310	.328
2008	Gt Lks	A	22	61	9	4	0	0	(-	-)	13	4	7	4	12	0	11	0	1	2	0	0	-	2	.148	.280	.213
2008	InldEm	A+	48	176	46	9	2	5	(-	-)	74	29	26	23	11	0	35	2	1	2	7	4	.64	3	.261	.309	.420
2009	InldEm	A+	132	496	146	42	4	23	(-	-)	265	75	100	98	61	0	128	3	0	3	10	7	.59	10	.294	.373	.534
2009	Albq	AAA	3	6	1	0	0	0	(-	-)	1	1	0	0	2	0	1	0	0	0	0	0	-	0	.167	.375	.167
2010	Chatt	AA	65	217	51	7	3	4	(-	-)	76	28	29	24	18	1	37	3	1	2	4	2	.67	5	.235	.300	.350
2010	InldEm	A+	48	189	58	12	2	9	(-	-)	101	34	35	37	17	1	39	2	0	1	3	1	.75	17	.307	.368	.534
2010	Albq	AAA	12	38	11	4	0	1	(-	-)	18	5	5	5	0	0	7	0	0	0	0	0	-	0	.289	.289	.474
2011	Chatt	AA	130	457	158	45	4	20	(-	-)	271	81	92	111	65	7	100	2	0	5	6	5	.55	5	.346	.425	.593
2012	Albq	AAA	95	358	117	34	1	18	(-	-)	207	68	67	82	46	1	64	3	0	4	5	3	.63	9	.327	.404	.578
2012	LAD	NL	27	54	9	2	0	2	(1	1)	17	4	7	4	2	0	14	0	1	0	1	0	1.00	2	.167	.196	.315

Rick VandenHurk

Pitches: R **Bats:** R **Pos:** RP-4   VANN-denn-herk   **Ht:** 6'5" **Wt:** 215 **Born:** 5/22/1985 **Age:** 28

Year	Team	Lg	G	GS	CG	GF	IP	BFP	H	R	ER	HR	SH	SF	HB	TBB	IBB	SO	WP	Bk	W	L	Pct	Sh	Sv-Op	Hld	ERC	ERA
2012	Bradtn*	A+	1	1	0	0	6.0	26	8	4	4	1	0	0	0	1	0	5	0	0	1	0	1.000	0	0- -	-	5.64	6.00
2012	Indy*	AAA	21	19	0	1	123.1	521	112	46	40	8	6	5	11	35	1	113	5	0	13	5	.722	0	0- -	-	3.20	2.92
2007	Fla	NL	18	17	0	0	81.2	379	94	63	62	15	5	3	3	48	5	82	4	4	4	6	.400	0	0-0	0	6.50	6.83
2008	Fla	NL	4	4	0	0	14.0	74	20	12	12	1	2	0	0	10	0	20	0	0	1	1	.500	0	0-0	0	8.20	7.71
2009	Fla	NL	11	11	0	0	58.2	256	57	29	28	11	3	2	4	21	3	49	2	0	3	2	.600	0	0-0	0	4.49	4.30
2010	2 Tms		9	1	0	2	17.2	76	16	14	10	2	0	1	2	8	0	18	0	0	0	1	.000	0	0-0	0	4.38	5.09
2011	Bal	AL	4	2	0	1	9.0	46	12	9	8	4	0	0	1	8	0	7	0	0	0	0	-	0	0-0	0	12.32	8.00
2012	Pit	NL	4	0	0	3	2.2	16	5	4	4	0	0	0	1	1	0	3	2	0	0	1	.000	0	0-0	0	9.34	13.50
	10 Fla	NL	2	0	0	0	1.1	9	3	4	1	0	0	0	0	1	0	1	0	0	0	0	-	0	0-0	0	11.17	6.75
	10 Bal	AL	7	1	0	2	16.1	67	13	10	9	2	0	1	2	7	0	17	0	0	0	1	.000	0	0-0	0	3.86	4.96
	6 ML YEARS		50	35	0	6	183.2	847	204	131	124	33	10	6	13	96	8	179	8	4	8	11	.421	0	0-0	0	6.05	6.08

Jason Vargas

Pitches: L **Bats:** L **Pos:** SP-33   **Ht:** 6'0" **Wt:** 215 **Born:** 2/2/1983 **Age:** 30

Year	Team	Lg	G	GS	CG	GF	IP	BFP	H	R	ER	HR	SH	SF	HB	TBB	IBB	SO	WP	Bk	W	L	Pct	Sh	Sv-Op	Hld	ERC	ERA
2005	Fla	NL	17	13	1	0	73.2	325	71	34	33	4	4	1	4	31	4	59	0	0	5	5	.500	0	0-0	0	3.68	4.03
2006	Fla	NL	12	5	0	3	43.0	213	50	39	35	9	4	4	4	30	3	25	2	0	1	2	.333	0	0-0	0	7.30	7.33
2007	NYM	NL	2	2	0	0	10.1	51	17	14	14	4	0	0	0	2	1	4	1	1	0	1	.000	0	0-0	0	8.95	12.19
2009	Sea	AL	23	14	0	4	91.2	385	98	53	50	16	3	6	3	24	1	54	1	0	3	6	.333	0	0-0	0	4.64	4.91
2010	Sea	AL	31	31	0	0	192.2	811	187	86	81	18	4	7	1	54	3	116	1	4	9	12	.429	0	0-0	0	3.37	3.78
2011	Sea	AL	32	32	4	0	201.0	857	205	105	95	22	3	4	4	59	4	131	3	1	10	13	.435	3	0-0	0	3.86	4.25
2012	Sea	AL	33	33	2	0	217.1	887	201	94	93	35	3	6	3	55	1	141	5	0	14	11	.560	2	0-0	0	3.57	3.85
	7 ML YEARS		150	130	7	7	829.2	3529	829	425	401	108	21	28	19	255	17	530	13	6	42	50	.457	3	0-0	0	3.96	4.35

Anthony Varvaro

Pitches: R **Bats:** R **Pos:** RP-12   var-VAR-oh   **Ht:** 6'0" **Wt:** 195 **Born:** 10/31/1984 **Age:** 28

Year	Team	Lg	G	GS	CG	GF	IP	BFP	H	R	ER	HR	SH	SF	HB	TBB	IBB	SO	WP	Bk	W	L	Pct	Sh	Sv-Op	Hld	ERC	ERA
2012	Gwnntt*	AAA	33	1	0	13	44.1	195	39	12	11	1	1	0	1	24	2	47	1	0	0	2	.000	0	6- -	-	3.36	2.23
2010	Sea	AL	4	0	0	2	4.0	24	6	5	5	2	0	0	0	6	0	5	1	0	0	1	.000	0	0-0	0	16.26	11.25
2011	Atl	NL	18	0	0	9	24.0	96	15	7	7	3	2	1	0	11	4	23	1	0	0	2	.000	0	0-1	5	2.28	2.63
2012	Atl	NL	12	0	0	5	16.2	76	16	11	10	2	1	0	2	9	1	21	3	0	1	1	.500	0	0-0	0	4.88	5.40
	3 ML YEARS		34	0	0	16	44.2	196	37	23	22	7	3	1	2	26	5	49	5	0	1	4	.200	0	0-1	1	4.20	4.43

Esmerling Vasquez

Pitches: R Bats: R Pos: SP-6   Ht: 6'1" Wt: 200 Born: 11/7/1983 Age: 29

Year	Team	Lg	G	GS	CG	GF	IP	BFP	H	R	ER	HR	SH	SF	HB	TBB	IBB	SO	WP	Bk	W	L	Pct	Sh	Sv-Op	Hld	ERC	ERA
2012	Roch*	AAA	31	8	1	6	100.1	403	74	33	31	8	1	3	7	39	1	98	5	1	9	6	.600	0	0- -	-	2.84	2.78
2009	Ari	NL	53	0	0	10	53.0	238	52	27	26	4	1	1	3	29	2	45	4	0	3	3	.500	0	0-4	4	4.51	4.42
2010	Ari	NL	57	0	0	16	53.2	240	46	32	31	6	0	1	6	38	3	55	3	1	1	6	.143	0	0-2	6	5.04	5.20
2011	Ari	NL	31	0	0	5	30.1	132	27	16	14	2	0	2	4	13	2	20	0	0	1	1	.500	0	0-2	6	3.74	4.15
2012	Min	AL	6	6	0	0	31.2	141	32	20	20	2	1	3	1	19	0	14	1	0	0	2	.000	0	0-0	0	4.87	5.68
	4 ML YEARS		147	6	0	31	168.2	751	157	95	91	14	2	7	14	99	7	134	8	1	5	12	.294	0	0-8	16	4.60	4.86

Donnie Veal

Pitches: L Bats: L Pos: RP-24   Ht: 6'4" Wt: 240 Born: 9/18/1984 Age: 28

Year	Team	Lg	G	GS	CG	GF	IP	BFP	H	R	ER	HR	SH	SF	HB	TBB	IBB	SO	WP	Bk	W	L	Pct	Sh	Sv-Op	Hld	ERC	ERA
2005	Cubs	R	4	3	0	0	10.2	45	8	6	6	2	0	0	1	5	0	14	2	0	1	0	1.000	0	0- -	-	3.95	5.06
2005	Boise	A-	7	6	0	0	19.0	117	18	11	8	2	1	1	0	15	0	34	4	3	1	2	.333	0	0- -	-	2.36	2.48
2006	Peoria	A	14	14	0	0	73.2	296	45	26	22	4	1	2	2	40	0	86	9	0	5	3	.625	0	0- -	-	2.44	2.69
2006	Dytona	A+	14	14	0	0	80.2	317	46	18	15	3	2	1	2	42	0	88	8	1	6	2	.750	0	0- -	-	2.08	1.67
2007	Tenn	AA	28	27	0	0	130.1	585	126	80	72	11	9	5	6	73	0	131	6	3	8	10	.444	0	0- -	-	4.57	4.97
2008	Tenn	AA	29	29	1	0	145.1	643	150	89	74	19	8	5	5	81	0	123	17	2	5	10	.333	0	0- -	-	5.40	4.58
2009	Indy	AAA	9	1	0	2	14.0	62	6	10	10	0	1	1	0	16	0	13	1	0	0	1	.000	0	0- -	-	3.01	6.43
2009	Altna	AAA	7	5	0	0	13.1	55	5	2	2	0	0	1	1	10	0	18	1	0	0	0	-	0	0- -	-	1.75	1.35
2010	Indy	AAA	9	9	0	0	49.2	214	42	26	24	3	1	3	6	23	0	41	1	1	3	2	.600	0	0- -	-	3.68	4.35
2011	Bradtn	A+	7	4	0	1	19.1	82	17	6	6	1	1	0	3	6	0	18	3	0	0	1	.000	0	0- -	-	3.35	2.79
2011	Altna	AA	4	0	0	2	4.2	24	9	4	4	3	1	0	0	0	0	3	0	0	0	1	.000	0	0- -	-	12.01	7.71
2011	Indy	AAA	7	0	0	2	6.1	31	5	4	4	0	0	0	1	7	1	7	0	0	0	0	-	0	0- -	-	5.10	5.68
2011	Pirates	R	1	1	0	0	1.2	9	1	1	1	0	0	0	1	2	0	3	0	0	0	0	-	0	0- -	-	6.15	5.40
2012	Charltt	AAA	35	0	0	15	52.0	220	40	17	12	0	2	0	5	23	0	61	4	1	7	3	.700	0	2- -	-	2.67	2.08
2009	Pirates	NL	19	0	0	10	16.1	87	18	13	13	2	0	1	2	20	0	16	2	0	1	0	1.000	0	0-0	1	8.89	7.16
2012	CWS	AL	24	0	0	5	13.0	49	5	2	2	0	0	0	0	4	0	19	0	0	0	0	-	0	1-1	4	0.75	1.38
	2 ML YEARS		43	0	0	15	29.1	136	23	15	15	2	0	1	2	24	0	35	2	0	1	0	1.000	0	1-1	5	4.43	4.60

Gil Velazquez

Bats: R Throws: R Pos: 3B-17; PH-2   veh-LAZZ-kezz   Ht: 6'2" Wt: 185 Born: 10/17/1979 Age: 33

Year	Team	Lg	G	AB	H	2B	3B	HR	(Hm	Rd)	TB	R	RBI	RC	TBB	IBB	SO	HBP	SH	SF	SB	CS	SB%	GDP	Avg	OBP	Slg
2012	NewOr*	AAA	110	398	124	15	1	4	(-	-)	153	52	42	63	49	3	50	4	8	2	6	8	.43	9	.312	.391	.384
2008	Bos	AL	3	8	1	0	0	0	(0	0)	1	0	1	1	0	0	0	0	0	0	0	0	-	0	.125	.125	.125
2009	Bos	AL	6	2	0	0	0	0	(0	0)	0	0	0	0	0	0	0	1	0	0	0	0	-	0	.000	.333	.000
2011	LAA	AL	4	6	3	0	0	0	(0	0)	3	0	1	1	0	0	0	0	0	1	0	0	-	0	.500	.429	.500
2012	Mia	NL	19	56	13	1	0	0	(0	0)	14	2	2	3	1	0	11	0	0	0	0	0	-	0	.232	.246	.250
	4 ML YEARS		32	72	17	1	0	0	(0	0)	18	2	4	5	1	0	11	1	0	1	0	0	-	0	.236	.253	.250

Will Venable

Bats: L Throws: L Pos: RF-114; PH-26; CF-21; LF-10; PR-1   VENN-uh-bull   Ht: 6'2" Wt: 200 Born: 10/29/1982 Age: 30

Year	Team	Lg	G	AB	H	2B	3B	HR	(Hm	Rd)	TB	R	RBI	RC	TBB	IBB	SO	HBP	SH	SF	SB	CS	SB%	GDP	Avg	OBP	Slg
2008	SD	NL	28	110	29	4	2	2	(0	2)	43	16	10	15	13	1	21	0	0	1	1	1	.50	1	.264	.339	.391
2009	SD	NL	95	293	75	14	2	12	(5	7)	129	38	38	34	25	2	89	4	2	0	6	1	.86	6	.256	.323	.440
2010	SD	NL	131	392	96	11	7	13	(6	7)	160	60	51	57	45	8	128	3	0	5	29	7	.81	3	.245	.324	.408
2011	SD	NL	121	370	91	14	7	9	(6	3)	146	49	44	52	31	4	92	5	1	4	26	3	.90	2	.246	.310	.395
2012	SD	NL	148	417	110	26	8	9	(2	7)	179	62	45	66	41	2	94	5	5	2	24	6	.80	2	.264	.335	.429
	5 ML YEARS		523	1582	401	69	26	45	(19	26)	657	225	188	224	155	17	424	17	8	12	86	18	.83	14	.253	.324	.415

Jonny Venters

Pitches: L Bats: L Pos: RP-66   Ht: 6'3" Wt: 195 Born: 3/20/1985 Age: 28

Year	Team	Lg	G	GS	CG	GF	IP	BFP	H	R	ER	HR	SH	SF	HB	TBB	IBB	SO	WP	Bk	W	L	Pct	Sh	Sv-Op	Hld	ERC	ERA
2012	Gwnntt*	AAA	1	1	0	0	1.0	3	0	0	0	0	0	0	0	0	0	0	0	0	0	0	-	0	0- -	-	0.00	0.00
2010	Atl	NL	79	0	0	17	83.0	350	61	30	18	1	2	1	8	39	2	93	4	0	4	4	.500	0	1-5	24	2.64	1.95
2011	Atl	NL	85	0	0	10	88.0	357	53	19	18	2	7	1	5	43	7	96	4	0	6	2	.750	0	5-9	35	1.96	1.84
2012	Atl	NL	66	0	0	12	58.2	262	61	23	21	6	3	0	5	28	3	69	9	0	5	4	.556	0	0-3	26	4.92	3.22
	Postseason		4	0	0	0	5.1	20	7	0	0	0	0	0	0	0	0	8	0	0	0	0	-	0	0-0	0	4.06	0.00
	3 ML YEARS		230	0	0	39	229.2	969	175	72	57	9	12	2	18	110	12	258	17	0	15	10	.600	0	6-17	79	2.90	2.23

Jose Veras

Pitches: R Bats: R Pos: RP-72   Ht: 6'6" Wt: 235 Born: 10/20/1980 Age: 32

Year	Team	Lg	G	GS	CG	GF	IP	BFP	H	R	ER	HR	SH	SF	HB	TBB	IBB	SO	WP	Bk	W	L	Pct	Sh	Sv-Op	Hld	ERC	ERA
2006	NYY	AL	12	0	0	4	11.0	43	8	5	5	2	0	0	0	5	0	6	1	1	0	0	-	0	1-1	1	3.55	4.09
2007	NYY	AL	9	0	0	3	9.1	41	6	6	6	0	0	0	0	7	1	7	1	0	0	0	-	0	2-2	1	2.52	5.79
2008	NYY	AL	60	0	0	15	57.2	253	52	23	23	7	2	1	3	29	6	63	4	0	5	3	.625	0	0-2	10	4.09	3.59
2009	2 Tms	AL	47	0	0	19	50.1	225	42	33	29	8	4	0	6	28	0	40	0	1	4	3	.571	0	0-0	6	4.60	5.19
2010	Fla	NL	48	0	0	11	48.0	201	32	20	20	5	1	0	1	29	0	54	2	0	3	3	.500	0	0-2	19	3.19	3.75
2011	Pit	NL	79	0	0	19	71.0	305	54	32	30	6	2	3	4	34	3	79	5	1	2	4	.333	0	1-8	27	3.06	3.80

Year	Team	Lg	G	GS	CG	GF	IP	BFP	H	R	ER	HR	SH	SF	HB	TBB	IBB	SO	WP	Bk	W	L	Pct	Sh	Sv-Op	Hld	ERC	ERA
2012	Mil	NL	72	0	0	17	67.0	300	61	29	27	5	1	2	2	40	1	79	1	0	5	4	.556	0	1-2	10	4.20	3.63
09	NYY	AL	25	0	0	10	25.2	118	23	17	17	5	2	0	4	14	0	18	0	0	3	1	.750	0	0-0	3	5.29	5.96
09	Cle	AL	22	0	0	9	24.2	107	19	16	12	3	2	0	2	14	0	22	0	1	1	2	.333	0	0-0	3	3.92	4.38
	Postseason		2	0	0	0	0.2	4	1	0	0	0	0	0	0	1	1	1	0	0	0	0	-	0	0-0	0	6.98	0.00
	7 ML YEARS		327	0	0	88	314.1	1368	255	148	140	33	10	6	16	172	11	328	14	3	19	17	.528	0	5-17	74	3.75	4.01

Ryan Verdugo

Pitches: L Bats: L Pos: SP-1   Ht: 6'0" Wt: 195 Born: 4/10/1987 Age: 26

Year	Team	Lg	G	GS	CG	GF	IP	BFP	H	R	ER	HR	SH	SF	HB	TBB	IBB	SO	WP	Bk	W	L	Pct	Sh	Sv-Op	Hld	ERC	ERA
2008	Giants	R	8	0	0	4	13.0	52	9	3	3	0	1	0	0	6	0	19	2	0	1	0	1.000	0	2--	-	2.12	2.08
2008	SlmKzr	A-	1	0	0	0	2.0	7	1	1	1	1	0	0	0	1	0	3	0	0	0	0	-	0	0--	-	4.74	4.50
2009	Giants	R	2	0	0	1	3.0	11	0	0	0	0	0	0	1	0	0	6	0	0	0	0	-	0	0--	-	0.11	0.00
2009	Augsta	A	21	0	0	5	32.1	132	19	6	5	0	0	0	1	19	2	45	4	0	4	0	1.000	0	0--	-	2.01	1.39
2010	Augsta	A	22	0	0	6	32.0	133	26	8	8	0	3	0	0	14	0	50	3	0	4	1	.800	0	1--	-	2.56	2.25
2010	SnJos	A+	22	1	0	6	30.2	120	15	5	5	3	0	0	0	19	1	44	3	0	4	1	1.000	0	0--	-	2.28	1.47
2011	Rchmd	AA	25	25	0	0	130.1	556	115	68	63	14	7	3	4	63	1	133	8	0	8	6	.571	0	0--	-	3.95	4.35
2012	Omha	AAA	27	24	0	2	136.2	581	114	60	57	19	4	4	4	67	0	118	5	0	12	4	.750	0	0--	-	3.92	3.75
2012	KC	AL	1	1	0	0	1.2	15	8	6	6	1	0	0	0	2	0	2	0	0	0	1	.000	0	0-0	0	44.44	32.40

Justin Verlander

Pitches: R Bats: R Pos: SP-33   Ht: 6'6" Wt: 225 Born: 2/20/1983 Age: 30

Year	Team	Lg	G	GS	CG	GF	IP	BFP	H	R	ER	HR	SH	SF	HB	TBB	IBB	SO	WP	Bk	W	L	Pct	Sh	Sv-Op	Hld	ERC	ERA
2005	Det	AL	2	2	0	0	11.1	54	15	9	9	1	0	0	1	5	0	7	1	0	0	2	.000	0	0-0	0	6.41	7.15
2006	Det	AL	30	30	1	0	186.0	776	187	78	75	21	2	4	6	60	1	124	5	1	17	9	.654	1	0-0	0	4.12	3.63
2007	Det	AL	32	32	1	0	201.2	866	181	88	82	20	3	1	19	67	3	183	17	2	18	6	.750	1	0-0	0	3.53	3.66
2008	Det	AL	33	33	1	0	201.0	880	195	119	108	18	4	6	14	87	8	163	6	3	11	17	.393	1	0-0	0	4.17	4.84
2009	Det	AL	35	35	3	0	240.0	982	219	99	92	20	6	4	6	63	5	269	8	4	19	9	.679	1	0-0	0	3.06	3.45
2010	Det	AL	33	33	4	0	224.1	925	190	89	84	14	6	8	6	71	0	219	11	2	18	9	.667	0	0-0	0	2.79	3.37
2011	Det	AL	34	34	4	0	251.0	969	174	73	67	24	2	3	3	57	0	250	7	2	24	5	.828	2	0-0	0	1.92	2.40
2012	Det	AL	33	33	6	0	238.1	956	192	81	70	19	4	3	5	60	2	239	2	1	17	8	.680	1	0-0	0	2.45	2.64
	Postseason		8	8	0	0	42.0	191	45	29	26	7	1	1	1	20	0	48	5	1	3	3	.500	0	0-0	0	5.30	5.57
	8 ML YEARS		232	232	20	0	1553.2	6408	1353	636	587	137	27	29	60	470	19	1454	57	15	124	65	.656	6	0-0	0	3.07	3.40

Dayan Viciedo

Bats: R Throws: R Pos: LF-131; DH-12; PH-5; PR-1   DYE-yahn vee-see-AY-doe   Ht: 5'11" Wt: 240 Born: 3/10/1989 Age: 24

Year	Team	Lg	G	AB	H	2B	3B	HR	(Hm	Rd)	TB	R	RBI	RC	TBB	IBB	SO	HBP	SH	SF	SB	CS	SB%	GDP	Avg	OBP	Slg
2010	CWS	AL	38	104	32	7	0	5	(4	1)	54	17	13	15	2	0	25	0	0	0	1	0	1.00	5	.308	.321	.519
2011	CWS	AL	29	102	26	3	0	1	(0	1)	32	11	6	12	9	0	23	2	0	0	1	0	1.00	4	.255	.327	.314
2012	CWS	AL	147	505	129	18	1	25	(13	12)	224	64	78	65	28	0	120	6	0	4	0	2	.00	19	.255	.300	.444
	3 ML YEARS		214	711	187	28	1	31	(17	14)	310	92	97	92	39	0	168	8	0	4	2	2	.50	28	.263	.307	.436

Shane Victorino

Bats: B Throws: R Pos: CF-109; LF-48; RF-1   Ht: 5'9" Wt: 190 Born: 11/30/1980 Age: 32

Year	Team	Lg	G	AB	H	2B	3B	HR	(Hm	Rd)	TB	R	RBI	RC	TBB	IBB	SO	HBP	SH	SF	SB	CS	SB%	GDP	Avg	OBP	Slg
2003	SD	NL	36	73	11	2	0	0	(0	0)	13	8	4	1	7	0	17	1	1	1	7	2	.78	5	.151	.232	.178
2005	Phi	NL	21	17	5	0	0	1	(1	1)	11	5	8	4	0	0	3	0	0	2	0	0	-	0	.294	.263	.647
2006	Phi	NL	153	415	119	19	8	6	(3	3)	172	70	46	58	24	0	54	14	8	1	4	3	.57	5	.287	.346	.414
2007	Phi	NL	131	456	128	23	3	12	(6	6)	193	78	46	65	37	1	62	10	5	2	37	4	.90	10	.281	.347	.423
2008	Phi	NL	146	570	167	30	8	14	(6	8)	255	102	58	86	45	2	69	7	5	0	36	11	.77	5	.293	.352	.447
2009	Phi	NL	156	620	181	39	13	10	(4	6)	276	102	62	99	60	1	71	6	4	4	25	8	.76	5	.292	.358	.445
2010	Phi	NL	147	587	152	26	10	18	(13	5)	252	84	69	89	53	5	79	7	0	1	34	6	.85	7	.259	.327	.429
2011	Phi	NL	132	519	145	27	16	17	(6	11)	255	95	61	86	55	1	63	6	6	0	19	3	.86	4	.279	.355	.491
2012	2 Tms	NL	154	595	152	29	7	11	(4	7)	228	72	55	76	53	1	80	6	9	3	39	6	.87	5	.255	.321	.383
12	Phi	NL	101	387	101	17	5	9	(6	6)	155	46	40	50	35	1	49	2	5	2	24	4	.86	4	.261	.324	.401
12	LAD	NL	53	208	51	12	2	2	(1	1)	73	26	15	26	18	0	31	4	4	1	15	2	.88	1	.245	.316	.351
	Postseason		46	175	47	9	2	6	(3	3)	78	25	30	29	15	4	15	4	3	1	8	1	.89	3	.269	.338	.446
	9 ML YEARS		1076	3852	1060	195	65	90	(43	47)	1655	616	409	564	334	11	498	57	38	14	201	43	.82	49	.275	.341	.430

Carlos Villanueva

Pitches: R Bats: R Pos: RP-22; SP-16   vee-ah-nue-AY-vah   Ht: 6'2" Wt: 235 Born: 11/28/1983 Age: 29

Year	Team	Lg	G	GS	CG	GF	IP	BFP	H	R	ER	HR	SH	SF	HB	TBB	IBB	SO	WP	Bk	W	L	Pct	Sh	Sv-Op	Hld	ERC	ERA
2006	Mil	NL	10	6	0	2	53.2	215	43	22	22	8	1	0	4	11	1	39	0	0	2	2	.500	0	0-0	0	2.85	3.69
2007	Mil	NL	59	6	0	8	114.1	489	101	52	50	16	4	1	3	53	3	99	3	0	8	5	.615	0	1-3	16	4.03	3.94
2008	Mil	NL	47	9	0	9	108.1	464	112	53	49	18	9	1	3	30	1	93	4	0	4	7	.364	0	1-1	11	4.29	4.07
2009	Mil	NL	64	6	0	23	96.0	422	102	58	57	13	4	0	2	35	8	83	4	0	4	10	.286	0	3-8	9	4.44	5.34
2010	Mil	NL	50	0	0	5	52.2	231	48	27	27	7	0	3	4	22	1	67	5	0	2	0	1.000	0	1-4	14	4.08	4.61
2011	Tor	AL	33	13	0	3	107.0	454	103	49	48	11	1	6	4	32	3	68	4	0	6	4	.600	0	0-1	0	3.57	4.04
2012	Tor	AL	38	16	0	9	125.1	521	113	59	58	23	2	4	3	46	4	122	6	1	7	7	.500	0	0-2	4	4.08	4.16
	Postseason		2	0	0	0	3.2	11	0	0	0	0	0	0	0	0	0	3	0	0	0	0	-	0	0-0	1	0.00	0.00
	7 ML YEARS		301	56	0	59	657.1	2796	622	320	311	96	21	15	23	229	21	571	26	1	33	35	.485	0	6-17	52	3.97	4.26

Brayan Villarreal

Pitches: R **Bats:** R **Pos:** RP-50

BRIAN VEE-yuh-ray-al

Ht: 6'0" **Wt:** 170 **Born:** 5/10/1987 **Age:** 26

Year	Team	Lg	G	GS	CG	GF	IP	BFP	H	R	ER	HR	SH	SF	HB	TBB	IBB	SO	WP	Bk	W	L	Pct	Sh	Sv-Op	Hld	ERC	ERA
2007	Tigers	R	1	1	0	0	4.1	20	4	4	3	0	0	0	0	3	0	5	0	0	0	0	-	0	0--	-	3.91	6.23
2008	Tigers	R	11	6	1	1	37.0	152	26	19	15	0	2	2	5	11	0	37	2	2	1	5	.167	0	0--	-	1.99	3.65
2008	WMich	A	1	1	0	0	3.1	18	7	7	6	1	0	0	1	1	0	0	0	0	0	1	.000	0	0--	-	14.81	16.20
2009	WMich	A	26	16	0	3	103.1	429	85	40	33	5	7	6	13	34	0	118	6	0	5	5	.500	0	2--	-	3.02	2.87
2010	Lkland	A+	16	16	1	0	85.2	350	73	37	33	8	3	4	6	23	0	90	2	0	7	4	.636	0	0--	-	3.03	3.47
2010	Erie	AA	8	8	0	0	43.2	184	37	21	18	6	2	2	4	16	0	46	4	0	0	4	.000	0	0--	-	3.73	3.71
2011	Toledo	AAA	17	10	0	3	66.0	290	65	40	37	6	0	1	11	29	0	40	6	0	3	5	.375	0	0--	-	4.85	5.05
2012	Toledo	AAA	8	0	2	2	14.0	51	5	2	2	1	3	0	1	7	0	22	1	1	0	0	-	0	1--	-	1.54	1.29
2011	Det	AL	16	0	0	4	16.0	76	21	12	12	3	1	0	0	10	2	14	1	0	1	1	.500	0	0-0	1	7.53	6.75
2012	Det	AL	50	0	0	15	54.2	226	38	20	16	3	1	6	1	28	3	66	9	2	3	5	.375	0	0-0	9	2.58	2.63
	2 ML YEARS		66	0	0	19	70.2	302	59	32	28	6	2	6	1	38	5	80	10	2	4	6	.400	0	0-0	10	3.56	3.57

Pedro Villarreal

Pitches: R **Bats:** R **Pos:** RP-1

VEE-uh-ree-al

Ht: 6'1" **Wt:** 225 **Born:** 12/9/1987 **Age:** 25

Year	Team	Lg	G	GS	CG	GF	IP	BFP	H	R	ER	HR	SH	SF	HB	TBB	IBB	SO	WP	Bk	W	L	Pct	Sh	Sv-Op	Hld	ERC	ERA
2008	Reds	R	2	0	0	0	2.1	18	6	5	2	0	0	0	1	2	0	3	1	0	0	0	-	0	0--	-	15.60	7.71
2009	Reds	R	5	5	0	0	18.1	71	15	6	3	1	0	1	2	6	0	9	0	0	1	2	.333	0	0--	-	3.21	1.47
2009	Srsota	A+	9	3	0	2	31.1	145	30	20	19	2	1	2	5	18	0	12	1	0	0	3	.000	0	0--	-	4.82	5.46
2010	Dayton	A	26	14	0	7	96.0	414	89	52	41	7	3	2	9	29	0	77	10	0	4	7	.364	0	2--	-	3.40	3.84
2010	Lynbrg	A+	6	5	0	0	19.2	91	26	17	15	3	1	0	1	8	0	16	0	0	0	3	.000	0	0--	-	6.73	6.86
2011	Bkrsfld	A+	10	10	0	0	58.0	242	68	31	28	9	0	1	2	8	0	41	2	1	4	3	.571	0	0--	-	4.62	4.34
2011	Carlina	AA	17	17	1	0	91.2	391	92	52	45	11	2	5	7	20	0	68	4	2	7	4	.636	0	0--	-	3.77	4.42
2012	Penscla	AA	6	6	0	0	35.1	138	31	16	14	2	1	1	1	6	0	26	2	0	1	2	.333	0	0--	-	2.49	3.57
2012	Lsvlle	AAA	20	20	0	0	113.1	499	129	70	58	9	6	5	3	32	0	81	3	1	3	12	.200	0	0--	-	4.29	4.61
2012	Cin	NL	1	0	0	1	1.0	3	0	0	0	0	0	0	0	0	0	1	0	0	0	0	-	0	0-0	0	0.00	0.00

Nick Vincent

Pitches: R **Bats:** R **Pos:** RP-27

Ht: 6'0" **Wt:** 175 **Born:** 7/12/1986 **Age:** 26

Year	Team	Lg	G	GS	CG	GF	IP	BFP	H	R	ER	HR	SH	SF	HB	TBB	IBB	SO	WP	Bk	W	L	Pct	Sh	Sv-Op	Hld	ERC	ERA
2008	Eugene	A-	16	8	0	7	43.1	187	42	32	26	6	2	1	2	20	0	38	3	0	3	3	.500	0	2--	-	4.69	5.40
2008	Portlnd	AAA	1	1	0	0	5.0	19	2	4	3	1	0	0	1	1	0	4	0	0	1	0	1.000	0	0--	-	1.65	5.40
2009	Lk Els	A+	59	0	0	24	64.1	270	66	27	22	3	3	0	1	18	1	74	0	0	4	2	.667	0	2--	-	3.45	3.08
2010	Lk Els	A+	48	1	0	5	81.2	333	60	24	17	7	4	2	5	23	0	76	1	1	4	0	1.000	0	0--	-	2.35	1.87
2011	SnAnt	AA	66	0	0	16	79.1	310	54	20	20	6	7	4	3	20	2	89	1	0	8	2	.800	0	3--	-	1.88	2.27
2012	Tucsn	AAA	23	0	0	7	21.2	102	27	14	14	2	2	1	2	11	0	19	1	0	1	1	.500	0	2--	-	6.33	5.82
2012	SnAnt	AA	9	0	0	0	9.2	34	4	2	2	0	0	0	1	0	0	15	0	0	1	0	1.000	0	0--	-	0.52	1.86
2012	SD	NL	27	0	0	3	26.1	105	19	5	5	2	1	0	1	7	0	28	1	0	2	0	1.000	0	0-1	5	2.13	1.71

Josh Vitters

Bats: R **Throws:** R **Pos:** 3B-29; PH-12

Ht: 6'2" **Wt:** 200 **Born:** 8/27/1989 **Age:** 23

Year	Team	Lg	G	AB	H	2B	3B	HR	(Hm	Rd)	TB	R	RBI	RC	TBB	IBB	SO	HBP	SH	SF	SB	CS	SB%	GDP	Avg	OBP	Slg
2007	Cubs	R	7	30	2	0	0	0	(-	-)	2	0	2	0	1	0	9	0	0	1	0	0	-	1	.067	.094	.067
2007	Boise	A-	7	21	4	0	0	0	(-	-)	4	2	1	0	2	0	5	0	0	0	1	1	.50	0	.190	.261	.190
2008	Peoria	A	4	14	3	3	0	0	(-	-)	6	1	1	1	0	0	5	0	0	1	0	0	-	1	.214	.214	.429
2008	Boise	A-	61	259	85	25	2	5	(-	-)	129	38	37	45	13	2	45	3	0	2	1	3	.25	5	.328	.365	.498
2009	Peoria	A	70	269	85	12	1	15	(-	-)	144	42	46	50	7	0	42	9	0	3	4	0	1.00	6	.316	.351	.535
2009	Dytona	A+	50	189	45	7	2	3	(-	-)	65	21	22	16	5	0	23	1	0	1	2	1	.67	2	.238	.260	.344
2010	Dytona	A+	28	110	32	8	0	3	(-	-)	49	16	13	17	8	0	22	2	0	0	4	1	.80	1	.291	.350	.445
2010	Tenn	AA	63	206	46	12	0	7	(-	-)	79	28	26	24	13	1	41	7	2	0	2	1	1.00	4	.223	.292	.383
2011	Tenn	AA	129	449	127	28	2	14	(-	-)	201	56	81	64	22	1	54	8	1	8	4	10	.29	16	.283	.322	.448
2012	Iowa	AAA	110	415	126	32	2	17	(-	-)	213	54	68	75	30	4	77	5	0	2	6	3	.67	8	.304	.356	.513
2012	ChC	NL	36	99	12	2	0	2	(0	2)	20	7	5	0	7	0	33	2	0	1	2	0	1.00	6	.121	.193	.202

Arodys Vizcaino

Pitches: R **Bats:** R **Pos:** P

uh-ROAD-eese

Ht: 6'0" **Wt:** 190 **Born:** 11/13/1990 **Age:** 22

Year	Team	Lg	G	GS	CG	GF	IP	BFP	H	R	ER	HR	SH	SF	HB	TBB	IBB	SO	WP	Bk	W	L	Pct	Sh	Sv-Op	Hld	ERC	ERA
2008	Yanks	R	12	6	0	2	44.0	186	38	22	18	5	0	1	1	13	0	48	6	1	3	2	.600	0	0--	-	3.01	3.68
2009	StsInd	A-	10	10	0	0	42.1	179	34	18	10	2	1	1	1	15	0	52	2	2	2	4	.333	0	0--	-	2.52	2.13
2010	Rome	A	14	14	0	0	71.2	292	63	25	19	1	2	3	3	9	0	68	6	2	9	4	.692	0	0--	-	2.01	2.39
2010	MrtlBh	A+	3	3	0	0	13.2	61	16	9	7	1	2	1	1	3	0	11	1	1	0	0	-	0	0--	-	4.31	4.61
2011	Lynbrg	A+	9	9	0	0	40.1	161	31	14	11	3	1	0	0	10	0	37	4	1	2	2	.500	0	0--	-	2.14	2.45
2011	Missi	AA	11	8	0	0	49.2	210	44	21	21	3	1	0	3	18	1	55	4	1	3	3	.500	0	0--	-	3.24	3.81
2011	Gwnntt	AAA	6	0	0	0	7.0	28	7	3	1	1	1	0	0	0	0	8	0	0	1	0	1.000	0	0--	-	2.74	1.29
2011	Atl	NL	17	0	0	2	17.1	77	16	9	9	1	0	0	1	9	1	17	5	0	1	1	.500	0	0-2	5	3.89	4.67

Omar Vizquel

vizz-KELL

Bats: B **Throws:** R **Pos:** 2B-24; 3B-18; PH-12; SS-10; 1B-2; LF-1; DH-1; PR-1   **Ht:** 5'9" **Wt:** 180 **Born:** 4/24/1967 **Age:** 46

Year	Team	Lg	G	AB	H	2B	3B	HR	(Hm	Rd)	TB	R	RBI	RC	TBB	IBB	SO	HBP	SH	SF	SB	CS	SB%	GDP	Avg	OBP	Slg
1989	Sea	AL	143	387	85	7	3	1	(1	0)	101	45	20	25	28	0	40	1	13	2	1	4	.20	6	.220	.273	.261
1990	Sea	AL	81	255	63	3	2	2	(0	2)	76	19	18	22	18	0	22	0	10	2	4	1	.80	7	.247	.295	.298
1991	Sea	AL	142	426	98	16	4	1	(1	0)	125	42	41	39	45	0	37	0	8	3	7	2	.78	8	.230	.302	.293
1992	Sea	AL	136	483	142	20	4	0	(0	0)	170	49	21	54	32	0	38	2	9	1	15	13	.54	14	.294	.340	.352
1993	Sea	AL	158	560	143	14	2	2	(1	1)	167	68	31	53	50	2	71	4	13	3	12	14	.46	7	.255	.319	.298
1994	Cle	AL	69	286	78	10	1	1	(0	1)	93	39	33	32	23	0	23	0	11	2	13	4	.76	4	.273	.325	.325
1995	Cle	AL	136	542	144	28	0	6	(3	3)	190	87	56	70	59	0	59	1	10	10	29	11	.73	4	.266	.333	.351
1996	Cle	AL	151	542	161	36	1	9	(2	7)	226	98	64	87	56	0	42	4	12	9	35	9	.80	10	.297	.362	.417
1997	Cle	AL	153	565	158	23	6	5	(3	2)	208	89	49	75	57	1	58	2	16	2	43	12	.78	16	.280	.347	.368
1998	Cle	AL	151	576	166	30	6	2	(0	2)	214	86	50	82	62	1	64	4	12	6	37	12	.76	10	.288	.358	.372
1999	Cle	AL	144	574	191	36	4	5	(3	2)	250	112	66	106	65	0	50	1	17	7	42	9	.82	8	.333	.397	.436
2000	Cle	AL	156	613	176	27	3	7	(1	6)	230	101	66	92	87	0	72	5	7	5	22	10	.69	13	.287	.377	.375
2001	Cle	AL	155	611	156	26	8	2	(2	0)	204	84	50	66	61	0	72	2	15	4	13	9	.59	14	.255	.323	.334
2002	Cle	AL	151	582	160	31	5	14	(9	5)	243	85	72	91	56	3	64	8	7	10	18	10	.64	7	.275	.341	.418
2003	Cle	AL	64	250	61	13	2	2	(2	0)	84	43	19	25	29	0	20	0	5	1	8	3	.73	11	.244	.321	.336
2004	Cle	AL	148	567	165	28	3	7	(2	5)	220	82	59	86	57	0	62	1	20	6	19	6	.76	12	.291	.353	.388
2005	SF	NL	152	568	154	28	4	3	(0	3)	199	66	45	76	56	0	58	5	20	2	24	10	.71	10	.271	.341	.350
2006	SF	NL	153	579	171	22	10	4	(2	2)	225	88	58	90	56	3	51	6	13	5	24	7	.77	13	.295	.361	.389
2007	SF	NL	145	513	126	18	3	4	(2	2)	162	54	51	53	44	6	48	1	14	3	14	6	.70	14	.246	.305	.316
2008	SF	NL	92	266	59	10	1	0	(0	0)	71	24	23	24	24	9	29	0	7	3	5	4	.56	4	.222	.283	.267
2009	Tex	AL	62	177	47	7	2	1	(0	1)	61	17	14	24	13	0	27	0	5	0	4	0	1.00	6	.266	.316	.345
2010	CWS	AL	108	344	95	11	1	2	(1	1)	114	36	30	41	34	0	45	2	7	4	11	7	.61	8	.276	.341	.331
2011	CWS	AL	58	167	42	7	1	0	(0	0)	51	18	8	11	9	0	18	0	4	2	1	2	.33	2	.251	.287	.305
2012	Tor	AL	60	153	36	5	1	0	(0	0)	43	13	7	9	7	0	17	0	1	2	3	2	.60	5	.235	.265	.281
	Postseason		57	228	57	7	4	0	(0	0)	72	28	20	27	25	0	36	2	7	2	23	3	.88	0	.250	.327	.316
	24 ML YEARS		2968	10586	2877	456	77	80	(35	45)	3727	1445	951	1333	1028	25	1087	49	256	94	404	167	.71	207	.272	.336	.352

Ryan Vogelsong

VOH-gull-song

Pitches: R **Bats:** R **Pos:** SP-31   **Ht:** 6'4" **Wt:** 215 **Born:** 7/22/1977 **Age:** 35

			HOW MUCH HE PITCHED						WHAT HE GAVE UP									THE RESULTS						
Year	Team	Lg	G	GS	CG	GF	IP	BFP	H	R	ER	HR	SH	SF	HB	TBB	IBB	SO	WP	Bk	W	L	Pct	Sh	Sv-Op	Hld	ERC	ERA
2012	Fresno*	AAA	2	2	0	0	10.0	41	9	2	2	0	0	0	0	4	0	12	0	0	1	0	1.000	0	0- -	-	2.95	1.80
2000	SF	NL	4	0	0	3	6.0	24	4	0	0	0	0	0	0	2	0	6	0	0	0	0	-	0	0-0	0	1.57	0.00
2001	2 Tms	NL	15	2	0	8	34.2	164	39	31	26	6	0	1	2	20	1	24	2	0	0	5	.000	0	0-0	0	6.20	6.75
2003	Pit	NL	6	5	0	0	22.0	108	30	19	16	1	3	1	2	9	3	15	1	0	2	2	.500	0	0-0	0	5.72	6.55
2004	Pit	NL	31	26	0	4	133.0	610	148	97	96	22	8	6	10	67	7	92	3	0	6	13	.316	0	0-0	0	5.89	6.50
2005	Pit	NL	44	0	0	19	81.1	369	82	43	40	5	1	4	8	40	1	52	7	0	2	2	.500	0	0-1	1	4.51	4.43
2006	Pit	NL	20	0	0	7	38.0	178	44	27	27	2	5	4	7	16	2	27	4	1	0	0	-	0	0-0	0	5.31	6.39
2011	SF	NL	30	28	1	1	179.2	752	164	62	54	15	10	3	5	61	6	139	1	1	13	7	.650	1	0-0	0	3.32	2.71
2012	SF	NL	31	31	0	0	189.2	788	171	76	71	17	7	4	8	62	7	158	3	0	14	9	.609	0	0-0	0	3.33	3.37
01	SF	NL	13	0	0	8	28.2	130	29	21	18	5	0	1	2	14	0	17	2	0	0	3	.000	0	0-0	0	5.55	5.65
01	Pit	NL	2	2	0	0	6.0	34	10	10	8	1	0	0	0	6	1	7	0	0	0	2	.000	0	0-0	0	11.03	12.00
	8 ML YEARS		181	92	1	42	684.1	2993	682	355	330	68	34	23	42	277	27	513	21	2	37	38	.493	1	0-1	1	4.24	4.34

Stephen Vogt

VOTE

Bats: L **Throws:** R **Pos:** PH-10; C-7; DH-5; LF-2; PR-1   **Ht:** 6'0" **Wt:** 215 **Born:** 11/1/1984 **Age:** 28

			BATTING																BASERUNNING				AVERAGES		
Year	Team	Lg	G	AB	H	2B	3B	HR	(Hm	Rd)	TB	R	RBI	RC	TBB	IBB	SO	HBP	SH	SF	SB	CS	SB%	GDP	Avg	OBP	Slg
2007	HudVal	A-	70	240	72	8	0	4	(-	-)	92	40	48	38	31	1	31	0	1	7	6	1	.86	3	.300	.371	.383
2008	Clmbs	A	113	392	114	22	3	6	(-	-)	160	57	54	63	47	0	48	3	2	4	6	1	.86	4	.291	.368	.408
2009	Charltt	A+	10	35	6	2	0	0	(-	-)	8	0	3	1	2	0	4	0	0	0	0	1	.00	2	.171	.216	.229
2010	Charltt	A+	106	368	127	31	3	8	(-	-)	188	56	47	75	31	4	46	6	3	6	3	1	.75	5	.345	.399	.511
2011	Mont	AA	97	386	116	21	6	13	(-	-)	188	52	85	66	30	3	51	1	0	10	4	2	.67	9	.301	.344	.487
2011	Drham	AAA	31	124	36	14	1	4	(-	-)	64	15	20	19	4	0	29	0	0	3	0	0	-	6	.290	.305	.516
2012	Drham	AAA	94	349	95	18	4	9	(-	-)	148	48	43	54	42	2	61	1	2	2	1	0	1.00	3	.272	.350	.424
2012	TB	AL	18	25	0	0	0	0	(0	0)	0	0	0	0	2	0	2	0	0	0	0	0	-	0	.000	.074	.000

Edinson Volquez

VOLE-kezz

Pitches: R **Bats:** R **Pos:** SP-32   **Ht:** 6'0" **Wt:** 225 **Born:** 7/3/1983 **Age:** 29

			HOW MUCH HE PITCHED						WHAT HE GAVE UP									THE RESULTS						
Year	Team	Lg	G	GS	CG	GF	IP	BFP	H	R	ER	HR	SH	SF	HB	TBB	IBB	SO	WP	Bk	W	L	Pct	Sh	Sv-Op	Hld	ERC	ERA
2005	Tex	AL	6	3	0	0	12.2	75	25	22	20	3	0	1	2	10	0	11	0	0	0	4	.000	0	0-0	0	14.15	14.21
2006	Tex	AL	8	8	0	0	33.1	164	52	28	27	7	0	1	1	17	0	15	0	0	1	6	.143	0	0-0	0	9.27	7.29
2007	Tex	AL	6	6	0	0	34.0	149	34	18	17	4	0	2	2	15	0	29	0	0	2	1	.667	0	0-0	0	4.63	4.50
2008	Cin	NL	33	32	0	1	196.0	838	167	82	70	14	6	5	14	93	5	206	10	1	17	6	.739	0	0-0	0	3.61	3.21
2009	Cin	NL	9	9	0	0	49.2	218	34	25	24	6	2	1	5	32	0	47	2	1	4	2	.667	0	0-0	0	3.77	4.35
2010	Cin	NL	12	12	0	0	62.2	275	59	30	30	6	3	1	3	35	0	67	5	0	4	3	.571	0	0-0	0	4.60	4.31
2011	Cin	NL	20	20	0	0	108.2	489	106	72	69	19	5	6	4	65	3	104	5	2	5	7	.417	0	0-0	0	5.42	5.71
2012	SD	NL	32	32	1	0	182.2	802	160	88	84	14	5	4	9	105	6	174	9	1	11	11	.500	1	0-0	0	4.14	4.14
	Postseason		1	1	0	0	1.2	11	4	4	4	0	0	0	0	2	0	0	0	0	0	1	.000	0	0-0	0	15.90	21.60
	8 ML YEARS		126	122	1	1	679.2	3010	637	365	341	73	21	21	40	372	14	653	31	5	44	40	.524	1	0-0	0	4.58	4.52

Chris Volstad

Pitches: R **Bats:** R **Pos:** SP-21 VOHL-stadd **Ht:** 6'8" **Wt:** 230 **Born:** 9/23/1986 **Age:** 26

			HOW MUCH HE PITCHED						WHAT HE GAVE UP										THE RESULTS						
Year	Team	Lg	G	GS	CG	GF	IP	BFP	H	R	ER	HR	SH	SF	HB	TBB	IBB	SO	WP	Bk	W	L	Pct	Sh	Sv-Op Hld	ERC	ERA
2012	Iowa*	AAA	12	12	0	0	71.1	315	86	48	41	7	0	1	4	19	0	52	0	2	3	5	.375	0	0- - -	4.94	5.17
2008	Fla	NL	15	14	0	0	84.1	365	76	30	27	3	6	1	5	36	4	52	0	0	6	4	.600	0	0-0	3.30	2.88
2009	Fla	NL	29	29	1	0	159.0	682	169	100	92	29	8	3	3	59	3	107	8	0	9	13	.409	1	0-0	5.05	5.21
2010	Fla	NL	30	30	2	0	175.0	758	187	94	89	17	8	7	6	60	5	102	8	1	12	9	.571	1	0-0	4.38	4.58
2011	Fla	NL	29	29	0	0	165.2	719	187	96	90	23	12	10	1	49	6	117	2	1	5	13	.278	0	0-0	4.63	4.89
2012	ChC	NL	21	21	0	0	111.1	507	137	81	78	16	5	8	1	43	4	61	2	1	3	12	.200	0	0-0	5.73	6.31
	5 ML YEARS		124	123	3	0	695.1	3031	756	401	376	88	39	29	20	247	22	439	20	3	35	51	.407	2	0-0	4.67	4.87

Joey Votto

Bats: L **Throws:** R **Pos:** 1B-109; PH-2 VAH-toe **Ht:** 6'3" **Wt:** 225 **Born:** 9/10/1983 **Age:** 29

			BATTING																		BASERUNNING				AVERAGES		
Year	Team	Lg	G	AB	H	2B	3B	HR	(Hm	Rd)	TB	R	RBI	RC	TBB	IBB	SO	HBP	SH	SF	SB	CS	SB%	GDP	Avg	OBP	Slg
2012	Dayton*	A	3	5	1	0	0	0	(-	-)	1	1	1	1	3	0	1	0	0	1	0	0	-	0	.200	.444	.200
2012	Lsvlle*	AAA	2	6	1	0	0	0	(-	-)	4	1	1	0	0	0	4	0	0	0	0	0	-	0	.167	.167	.667
2007	Cin	NL	24	84	27	7	0	4	(4	0)	46	11	17	17	5	1	15	0	0	0	1	0	1.00	0	.321	.360	.548
2008	Cin	NL	151	526	156	32	3	24	(14	10)	266	69	84	91	59	9	102	2	0	2	7	5	.58	7	.297	.368	.506
2009	Cin	NL	131	469	151	38	1	25	(14	11)	266	82	84	99	70	10	106	4	0	1	4	1	.80	8	.322	.414	.567
2010	Cin	NL	150	547	177	36	2	37	(18	19)	328	106	113	132	91	8	125	7	0	3	16	5	.76	11	.324	.424	.600
2011	Cin	NL	161	599	185	40	3	29	(13	16)	318	101	103	131	110	15	129	4	0	6	8	6	.57	20	.309	.416	.531
2012	Cin	NL	111	419	126	44	0	14	(10	4)	212	59	56	97	94	18	85	5	0	2	5	3	.63	8	.337	.474	.567
	Postseason		3	10	1	0	0	0	(0	0)	1	0	1	0	0	0	2	0	0	1	0	0	-	1	.100	.091	.100
	6 ML YEARS		728	2599	822	197	9	133	(73	60)	1436	428	457	567	429	61	562	22	0	14	41	20	.67	54	.316	.415	.553

Tsuyoshi Wada

Pitches: L **Bats:** L **Pos:** P soo-YO-shee WAH-dah **Ht:** 5'11" **Wt:** 180 **Born:** 2/21/1981 **Age:** 32

			HOW MUCH HE PITCHED						WHAT HE GAVE UP										THE RESULTS						
Year	Team	Lg	G	GS	CG	GF	IP	BFP	H	R	ER	HR	SH	SF	HB	TBB	IBB	SO	WP	Bk	W	L	Pct	Sh	Sv-Op Hld	ERC	ERA
2003	Fk Dai	Jap	26	-	8	-	189.0	781	165	77	71	26	-	-	1	61	-	195	1	0	14	5	.737	2	0- -	3.35	3.38
2004	Fk Dai	Jap	19	-	7	-	128.1	534	110	67	62	23	-	-	3	38	-	115	2	0	10	6	.625	0	0- -	3.45	4.35
2005	Sbank	Jap	25	-	4	-	181.2	741	154	69	66	17	-	-	2	57	-	167	4	0	12	8	.600	0	0- -	2.95	3.27
2006	Sbank	Jap	24	-	6	-	163.1	657	137	57	54	18	-	-	1	42	-	136	2	0	14	6	.700	3	0- -	2.78	2.98
2007	Sbank	Jap	26	26	2	0	182.0	757	168	65	57	15	-	5	42	-	169	6	1	12	10	.545	1	0- -	2.96	2.82
2008	Sbank	Jap	23	23	3	0	162.0	671	167	65	65	12	-	-	3	36	-	123	3	0	8	8	.500	0	0- -	3.49	3.61
2009	Sbank	Jap	15	13	1	-	84.1	337	72	39	38	13	-	-	1	24	-	87	1	0	4	5	.444	1	0- -	3.32	4.06
2010	Sbank	Jap	26	26	1	0	169.1	696	145	59	59	11	-	-	1	55	-	169	2	0	17	8	.680	0	0- -	2.82	3.14
2011	Sbank	Jap	26	-	4	0	184.2	726	145	33	31	7	-	-	4	40	-	168	5	0	16	5	.762	2	0- -	2.02	1.51
2012	Norfolk	AAA	1	1	0	0	2.2	18	6	6	6	1	0	0	0	4	0	1	0	0	0	1	.000	0	0- -	20.79	20.25

Cory Wade

Pitches: R **Bats:** R **Pos:** RP-39 **Ht:** 6'2" **Wt:** 185 **Born:** 5/28/1983 **Age:** 30

			HOW MUCH HE PITCHED						WHAT HE GAVE UP										THE RESULTS						
Year	Team	Lg	G	GS	CG	GF	IP	BFP	H	R	ER	HR	SH	SF	HB	TBB	IBB	SO	WP	Bk	W	L	Pct	Sh	Sv-Op Hld	ERC	ERA
2012	S-WB*	AAA	17	0	0	8	31.2	128	22	12	8	3	1	1	1	9	0	20	2	0	2	0	1.000	0	5- - -	2.10	2.27
2008	LAD	NL	55	0	0	21	71.1	275	51	22	18	7	2	1	4	15	3	51	2	0	2	1	.667	0	0-1 8	2.11	2.27
2009	LAD	NL	27	0	0	2	27.2	121	28	17	17	3	0	1	1	10	3	18	4	0	2	3	.400	0	0-6 7	3.96	5.53
2011	NYY	AL	40	0	0	8	39.2	157	33	10	9	5	0	0	0	8	0	30	1	0	6	1	.857	0	0-1 8	2.61	2.04
2012	NYY	AL	39	0	0	7	39.0	171	46	29	28	8	0	1	1	8	1	38	0	0	1	1	.500	0	0-2 8	5.04	6.46
	Postseason		8	0	0	1	9.1	37	8	3	3	1	1	0	0	1	0	6	1	0	0	1	.000	0	0-1 2	2.24	2.89
	4 ML YEARS		161	0	0	38	177.2	724	158	78	72	23	2	3	6	41	7	137	7	0	11	6	.647	0	0-10 31	3.10	3.65

Adam Wainwright

Pitches: R **Bats:** R **Pos:** SP-32 **Ht:** 6'7" **Wt:** 230 **Born:** 8/30/1981 **Age:** 31

			HOW MUCH HE PITCHED						WHAT HE GAVE UP										THE RESULTS						
Year	Team	Lg	G	GS	CG	GF	IP	BFP	H	R	ER	HR	SH	SF	HB	TBB	IBB	SO	WP	Bk	W	L	Pct	Sh	Sv-Op Hld	ERC	ERA
2005	StL	NL	2	0	0	1	2.0	9	2	3	3	1	0	0	1	1	0	0	0	0	0	0	-	0	0-0 0	7.30	13.50
2006	StL	NL	61	0	0	10	75.0	309	64	26	26	6	4	1	4	22	2	72	3	0	2	1	.667	0	3-5 17	2.92	3.12
2007	StL	NL	32	32	1	0	202.0	882	212	93	83	13	9	5	9	70	4	136	6	0	14	12	.538	0	0-0 0	4.01	3.70
2008	StL	NL	20	20	1	0	132.0	544	122	51	47	12	6	4	3	34	1	91	3	0	11	3	.786	0	0-0 0	3.14	3.20
2009	StL	NL	34	34	1	0	233.0	970	216	75	68	17	10	5	3	66	1	212	7	0	19	8	.704	0	0-0 0	3.08	2.63
2010	StL	NL	33	33	5	0	230.1	910	186	68	62	15	13	6	4	56	2	213	2	0	20	11	.645	2	0-0 0	2.36	2.42
2012	StL	NL	32	32	3	0	198.2	831	196	96	87	15	9	6	6	52	3	184	5	2	14	13	.519	2	0-0 0	3.41	3.94
	Postseason		10	1	0	9	17.2	67	10	1	1	1	0	0	1	3	0	22	1	0	1	0	1.000	0	4-5 0	1.27	0.51
	7 ML YEARS		214	151	11	11	1073.0	4455	998	412	376	79	51	27	29	301	13	908	26	2	80	48	.625	4	3-5 17	3.15	3.15

Jordan Walden

Pitches: R **Bats:** R **Pos:** RP-45 **Ht:** 6'5" **Wt:** 235 **Born:** 11/16/1987 **Age:** 25

			HOW MUCH HE PITCHED						WHAT HE GAVE UP										THE RESULTS						
Year	Team	Lg	G	GS	CG	GF	IP	BFP	H	R	ER	HR	SH	SF	HB	TBB	IBB	SO	WP	Bk	W	L	Pct	Sh	Sv-Op Hld	ERC	ERA
2012	Salt Lk*	AAA	3	0	0	0	2.2	12	3	4	2	0	0	1	1	0	0	3	0	0	0	1	.000	0	0- - -	3.84	6.75

288

Year	Team	Lg	G	GS	CG	GF	IP	BFP	H	R	ER	HR	SH	SF	HB	TBB	IBB	SO	WP	Bk	W	L	Pct	Sh	Sv-Op	Hld	ERC	ERA
2010	LAA	AL	16	0	0	5	15.1	65	13	4	4	1	0	0	0	7	0	23	1	1	0	1	.000	0	1-1	6	3.21	2.35
2011	LAA	AL	62	0	0	42	60.1	253	49	22	20	3	4	2	1	26	3	67	6	0	5	5	.500	0	32-42	2	2.82	2.98
2012	LAA	AL	45	0	0	20	39.0	172	35	15	15	3	0	1	0	18	1	48	7	0	3	2	.600	0	1-2	8	3.42	3.46
3 ML YEARS			123	0	0	67	114.2	490	97	41	39	7	4	3	1	51	4	138	14	1	8	8	.500	0	34-45	16	3.08	3.06

Kyle Waldrop

Pitches: R Bats: R Pos: RP-17 Ht: 6'6" Wt: 220 Born: 10/27/1985 Age: 27

Year	Team	Lg	G	GS	CG	GF	IP	BFP	H	R	ER	HR	SH	SF	HB	TBB	IBB	SO	WP	Bk	W	L	Pct	Sh	Sv-Op	Hld	ERC	ERA
2004	Twins	R	7	7	0	0	38.0	146	32	9	6	1	1	0	1	4	0	30	1	1	3	2	.600	0	0- -	-	1.90	1.42
2004	Elizab	R+	4	4	0	0	25.0	100	21	10	9	1	1	0	1	3	0	25	0	0	2	0	1.000	0	0- -	-	1.97	3.24
2005	Beloit	A	27	27	2	0	151.2	667	182	93	84	17	5	5	8	23	1	108	9	0	6	11	.353	1	0- -	-	4.40	4.98
2006	Beloit	A	18	18	1	0	110.0	460	110	54	47	8	3	1	14	17	0	62	8	0	6	3	.667	1	0- -	-	3.45	3.85
2006	FtMyrs	A+	8	7	1	0	45.1	201	48	27	18	4	2	1	0	17	1	25	2	0	3	2	.600	0	0- -	-	4.08	3.57
2007	FtMyrs	A+	16	16	0	0	92.2	383	90	42	35	3	2	2	9	24	0	57	5	1	7	5	.583	0	0- -	-	3.38	3.40
2007	NwBrit	AA	11	11	0	0	59.0	274	74	42	35	7	2	1	10	19	1	33	3	0	3	6	.333	0	0- -	-	6.06	5.34
2009	FtMyrs	A+	20	0	0	11	35.0	149	43	15	12	0	2	0	2	7	1	20	1	0	3	2	.600	0	3- -	-	4.15	3.09
2009	NwBrit	AA	31	0	0	8	55.2	237	51	14	9	2	3	2	7	18	4	30	4	0	2	3	.400	0	0- -	-	3.26	1.46
2010	Roch	AAA	59	0	0	20	87.2	369	89	38	25	5	0	2	7	20	4	60	4	1	5	3	.625	0	2- -	-	3.46	2.57
2011	Roch	AAA	56	0	0	22	79.0	328	84	39	34	7	1	1	4	18	4	44	4	0	5	5	.500	0	3- -	-	3.90	3.87
2012	FtMyrs	A+	4	0	0	1	4.0	15	2	0	0	0	0	0	0	1	0	5	0	0	0	0	-	0	0- -	-	0.94	0.00
2012	Roch	AAA	24	0	0	11	35.0	150	35	14	13	1	1	1	2	13	3	16	1	0	0	0	-	0	4- -	-	3.58	3.34
2011	Min	AL	7	0	0	1	11.0	50	10	7	7	1	1	0	0	6	2	5	1	0	1	0	1.000	0	0-0	0	3.59	5.73
2012	Min	AL	17	0	0	3	21.1	94	27	6	6	2	0	0	3	6	1	7	1	0	0	1	.000	0	0-1	2	5.83	2.53
2 ML YEARS			24	0	0	4	32.1	144	37	13	13	3	1	0	3	12	3	12	2	0	1	1	.500	0	0-1	2	5.01	3.62

Neil Walker

Bats: B Throws: R Pos: 2B-125; PH-4; DH-1 Ht: 6'3" Wt: 210 Born: 9/10/1985 Age: 27

Year	Team	Lg	G	AB	H	2B	3B	HR	(Hm	Rd)	TB	R	RBI	RC	TBB	IBB	SO	HBP	SH	SF	SB	CS	SB%	GDP	Avg	OBP	Slg
2009	Pit	NL	17	36	7	1	0	0	(0	0)	8	5	0	2	4	0	11	0	0	0	1	0	1.00	1	.194	.275	.222
2010	Pit	NL	110	426	126	29	3	12	(5	7)	197	57	66	66	34	1	83	3	2	4	2	3	.40	4	.296	.349	.462
2011	Pit	NL	159	596	163	36	4	12	(4	8)	243	76	83	77	54	5	112	4	0	8	9	6	.60	15	.273	.334	.408
2012	Pit	NL	129	472	132	27	0	14	(7	7)	201	62	69	72	47	1	104	2	1	8	7	5	.58	11	.280	.342	.426
4 ML YEARS			415	1530	428	93	7	38	(16	22)	649	200	218	217	139	7	310	9	3	20	19	14	.58	31	.280	.339	.424

Josh Wall

Pitches: R Bats: R Pos: RP-7 Ht: 6'6" Wt: 220 Born: 1/21/1987 Age: 26

Year	Team	Lg	G	GS	CG	GF	IP	BFP	H	R	ER	HR	SH	SF	HB	TBB	IBB	SO	WP	Bk	W	L	Pct	Sh	Sv-Op	Hld	ERC	ERA
2005	Ddgrs	R	5	4	0	0	14.0	62	13	8	6	2	1	0	0	8	0	5	1	1	1	3	.250	0	0- -	-	4.64	3.86
2006	Ogden	R+	14	14	0	0	66.0	307	80	56	43	5	4	3	4	33	1	41	12	0	3	5	.375	0	0- -	-	5.77	5.86
2007	Gt Lks	A	26	24	1	1	129.1	570	136	71	60	8	3	2	10	48	1	103	10	1	6	10	.375	0	1- -	-	4.26	4.18
2008	InldEm	A+	27	25	0	0	129.0	592	152	92	90	12	1	5	11	63	0	101	13	1	9	6	.600	0	0- -	-	5.85	6.28
2009	InldEm	A+	23	22	0	0	111.1	506	135	85	74	9	5	4	11	51	1	77	10	1	5	8	.385	0	0- -	-	5.95	5.98
2010	Gt Lks	A	26	26	1	0	153.0	670	144	80	72	11	1	6	14	68	0	151	20	0	9	7	.563	1	0- -	-	4.08	4.24
2011	Chatt	AA	51	0	0	22	68.2	299	71	34	30	6	3	0	3	27	1	57	4	0	4	5	.444	0	1- -	-	4.32	3.93
2012	Albq	AAA	55	0	0	48	53.2	231	50	30	27	7	1	1	2	20	0	52	4	0	2	1	.667	0	28- -	-	3.90	4.53
2012	LAD	NL	7	0	0	6	5.2	21	3	3	3	1	0	0	1	1	0	4	2	0	1	0	1.000	0	0-0	0	2.05	4.76

Brett Wallace

Bats: L Throws: R Pos: 1B-58; 3B-8; PH-4 Ht: 6'2" Wt: 260 Born: 8/26/1986 Age: 26

Year	Team	Lg	G	AB	H	2B	3B	HR	(Hm	Rd)	TB	R	RBI	RC	TBB	IBB	SO	HBP	SH	SF	SB	CS	SB%	GDP	Avg	OBP	Slg
2012	OKCity*	AAA	86	310	93	16	0	16	(-	-)	157	54	57	59	27	1	87	13	0	1	0	1	.00	7	.300	.379	.506
2010	Hou	NL	51	144	32	6	1	2	(1	1)	46	14	13	10	8	3	50	7	0	0	0	0	-	3	.222	.296	.319
2011	Hou	NL	115	336	87	22	0	5	(3	2)	124	37	29	31	36	4	91	3	1	2	1	1	.50	12	.259	.334	.369
2012	Hou	NL	66	229	58	10	1	9	(1	8)	97	24	24	27	18	1	73	6	0	1	0	0	-	2	.253	.323	.424
3 ML YEARS			232	709	177	38	2	16	(4	12)	267	75	66	68	62	8	214	16	1	3	1	1	.50	17	.250	.323	.377

P.J. Walters

Pitches: R Bats: R Pos: SP-12 Ht: 6'4" Wt: 215 Born: 3/12/1985 Age: 28

Year	Team	Lg	G	GS	CG	GF	IP	BFP	H	R	ER	HR	SH	SF	HB	TBB	IBB	SO	WP	Bk	W	L	Pct	Sh	Sv-Op	Hld	ERC	ERA
2012	Roch*	AAA	14	14	1	0	58.1	252	67	28	26	7	1	2	1	15	0	47	2	0	3	3	.500	0	0- -	-	4.57	4.01
2009	StL	NL	8	1	0	4	16.0	80	21	19	17	6	1	1	0	9	1	14	0	0	0	0	-	0	0-0	0	8.42	9.56
2010	StL	NL	7	3	0	3	30.0	129	32	20	20	5	1	2	0	10	0	22	0	0	2	0	1.000	0	0-0	0	4.67	6.00
2011	2 Tms		5	0	0	2	5.0	21	3	4	4	1	0	0	0	3	0	4	0	0	0	0	-	0	0-0	0	3.28	7.20
2012	Min	AL	12	12	1	0	61.2	271	71	41	39	12	1	1	3	22	1	42	1	0	2	5	.286	0	0-0	0	5.75	5.69
11	StL	NL	4	0	0	2	4.0	18	3	4	4	1	0	0	0	2	0	3	0	0	0	0	-	0	0-0	0	3.76	9.00
11	Tor	AL	1	0	0	0	1.0	3	0	0	0	0	0	0	0	1	0	1	0	0	0	0	-	0	0-0	0	1.26	0.00
4 ML YEARS			32	16	1	9	112.2	501	127	84	80	24	3	4	3	44	2	82	1	0	4	5	.444	0	0-0	0	5.70	6.39

Chien-Ming Wang

Pitches: R **Bats:** R **Pos:** SP-5; RP-5
CHENN-MING WONG
Ht: 6'4" **Wt:** 225 **Born:** 3/31/1980 **Age:** 33

Year	Team	Lg	G	GS	CG	GF	IP	BFP	H	R	ER	HR	SH	SF	HB	TBB	IBB	SO	WP	Bk	W	L	Pct	Sh	Sv-Op	Hld	ERC	ERA
2012	Ptomc*	A+	2	2	0	0	8.0	33	7	4	4	0	0	0	0	2	0	4	1	0	0	1	.000	0	0- -	-	2.18	4.50
2012	Hgrstn*	A	1	1	0	0	6.0	23	3	2	1	1	0	0	0	1	0	7	0	0	1	0	1.000	0	0- -	-	1.24	1.50
2012	Syrcse*	AAA	3	3	0	0	20.2	90	26	10	10	1	1	1	2	5	0	8	1	0	2	1	.000	0	0- -	-	5.09	4.35
2012	Hrsbrg*	AA	9	9	1	0	45.1	201	59	36	34	7	4	4	0	9	1	33	3	0	1	5	.167	0	0- -	-	5.32	6.75
2005	NYY	AL	18	17	0	0	116.1	486	113	58	52	9	3	4	6	32	3	47	3	0	8	5	.615	0	0-0	0	3.47	4.02
2006	NYY	AL	34	33	2	1	218.0	900	233	92	88	12	3	2	2	52	4	76	6	1	19	6	.760	1	1-1	0	3.62	3.63
2007	NYY	AL	30	30	1	0	199.1	823	199	84	82	9	2	3	8	59	1	104	9	1	19	7	.731	0	0-0	0	3.54	3.70
2008	NYY	AL	15	15	1	0	95.0	402	90	44	43	4	0	3	3	35	1	54	0	0	8	2	.800	0	0-0	0	3.39	4.07
2009	NYY	AL	12	9	0	2	42.0	206	66	46	45	7	3	1	2	19	1	29	3	0	1	6	.143	0	0-0	0	8.67	9.64
2011	Was	NL	11	11	0	0	62.1	264	67	35	28	8	2	2	1	13	0	25	2	0	4	3	.571	0	0-0	0	3.97	4.04
2012	Was	NL	10	5	0	0	32.1	158	50	24	24	5	4	3	3	15	0	15	5	0	2	3	.400	0	0-0	0	8.80	6.68
	Postseason		4	4	0	0	19.0	90	28	19	16	5	2	0	3	5	0	7	0	0	1	3	.250	0	0-0	0	8.53	7.58
	7 ML YEARS		130	120	4	3	765.1	3239	818	383	362	54	17	18	25	225	10	350	28	2	61	32	.656	1	1-1	0	4.02	4.26

Adam Warren

Pitches: R **Bats:** R **Pos:** SP-1
Ht: 6'2" **Wt:** 225 **Born:** 8/25/1987 **Age:** 25

Year	Team	Lg	G	GS	CG	GF	IP	BFP	H	R	ER	HR	SH	SF	HB	TBB	IBB	SO	WP	Bk	W	L	Pct	Sh	Sv-Op	Hld	ERC	ERA
2009	StsInd	A-	12	12	0	0	56.2	220	49	12	9	1	1	1	0	10	0	50	3	0	4	2	.667	0	0- -	-	2.11	1.43
2010	Tampa	A+	15	15	1	0	81.0	333	72	23	20	2	3	1	6	17	0	67	0	0	7	5	.583	1	0- -	-	2.55	2.22
2010	Trntn	AA	10	10	0	0	54.1	232	49	26	19	2	0	2	3	16	0	59	4	0	2	2	.667	0	0- -	-	2.85	3.15
2011	S-WB	AAA	27	27	1	0	152.1	650	145	68	61	13	4	3	8	53	0	111	4	0	6	8	.429	0	0- -	-	3.71	3.60
2012	S-WB	AAA	26	26	2	0	152.2	657	167	64	63	11	0	3	4	46	1	107	9	0	7	8	.467	1	0- -	-	4.13	3.71
2012	NYY	AL	1	1	0	0	2.1	17	8	6	6	2	0	0	0	2	0	1	0	0	0	0	-	0	0-0	0	33.34	23.14

Tony Watson

Pitches: L **Bats:** L **Pos:** RP-68
Ht: 6'4" **Wt:** 210 **Born:** 5/30/1985 **Age:** 28

Year	Team	Lg	G	GS	CG	GF	IP	BFP	H	R	ER	HR	SH	SF	HB	TBB	IBB	SO	WP	Bk	W	L	Pct	Sh	Sv-Op	Hld	ERC	ERA
2007	StCol	A-	10	10	0	0	53.2	214	47	17	15	4	1	1	1	7	0	40	1	0	6	1	.857	0	0- -	-	2.32	2.52
2007	Hkry	A	3	3	0	0	14.0	57	14	6	6	2	0	1	2	1	0	18	0	0	1	1	.500	0	0- -	-	3.70	3.86
2008	Lynbrg	A+	28	28	0	0	151.2	632	149	70	60	16	8	4	9	36	0	104	1	0	8	12	.400	1	0- -	-	3.64	3.56
2009	Altna	AA	5	5	0	0	15.1	78	22	18	14	2	1	0	2	11	0	14	0	0	3	0	.000	0	0- -	-	8.29	8.22
2010	Altna	AA	34	9	0	5	111.1	437	82	33	33	11	3	2	5	24	1	105	2	0	6	4	.600	0	2- -	-	2.19	2.67
2011	Indy	AAA	26	1	0	6	34.1	140	24	10	9	2	2	1	2	11	2	35	2	0	3	3	.500	0	0- -	-	2.06	2.36
2011	Pit	NL	43	0	0	6	41.0	174	34	18	18	6	2	1	1	20	4	37	0	0	2	2	.500	0	0-1	10	3.75	3.95
2012	Pit	NL	68	0	0	10	53.1	215	37	21	20	5	2	2	1	23	1	53	1	0	5	2	.714	0	0-2	16	2.62	3.38
	2 ML YEARS		111	0	0	16	94.1	389	71	39	38	11	4	3	2	43	5	90	1	0	7	4	.636	0	0-3	26	3.10	3.63

Jered Weaver

Pitches: R **Bats:** R **Pos:** SP-30
Ht: 6'7" **Wt:** 210 **Born:** 10/4/1982 **Age:** 30

Year	Team	Lg	G	GS	CG	GF	IP	BFP	H	R	ER	HR	SH	SF	HB	TBB	IBB	SO	WP	Bk	W	L	Pct	Sh	Sv-Op	Hld	ERC	ERA
2006	LAA	AL	19	19	0	0	123.0	490	94	36	35	15	2	3	3	33	1	105	2	0	11	2	.846	0	0-0	0	2.57	2.56
2007	LAA	AL	28	28	0	0	161.0	695	178	77	70	17	5	5	2	45	3	115	4	0	13	7	.650	0	0-0	0	4.24	3.91
2008	LAA	AL	30	30	0	0	176.2	745	173	88	85	20	1	4	6	54	4	152	3	0	11	10	.524	0	0-0	0	3.80	4.33
2009	LAA	AL	33	33	4	0	211.0	882	196	91	88	26	6	8	4	66	3	174	3	0	16	8	.667	2	0-0	0	3.56	3.75
2010	LAA	AL	34	34	0	0	224.1	905	187	83	75	23	2	5	0	54	0	233	7	1	13	12	.520	0	0-0	0	2.59	3.01
2011	LAA	AL	33	33	4	0	235.2	926	182	65	63	20	5	5	3	56	0	198	8	0	18	8	.692	2	0-0	0	2.27	2.41
2012	LAA	AL	30	30	0	0	188.2	739	147	63	59	20	0	4	4	45	0	142	2	0	20	5	.800	2	0-0	0	2.48	2.81
	Postseason		6	3	0	2	20.2	83	12	6	6	5	0	0	0	10	0	22	0	0	2	1	.667	0	0-0	1	3.04	2.61
	7 ML YEARS		207	207	11	0	1320.1	5382	1157	503	475	141	21	33	22	353	11	1119	29	1	102	52	.662	6	0-0	0	3.01	3.24

Ryan Webb

Pitches: R **Bats:** R **Pos:** RP-65
Ht: 6'5" **Wt:** 230 **Born:** 2/5/1986 **Age:** 27

Year	Team	Lg	G	GS	CG	GF	IP	BFP	H	R	ER	HR	SH	SF	HB	TBB	IBB	SO	WP	Bk	W	L	Pct	Sh	Sv-Op	Hld	ERC	ERA
2012	NewOr*	AAA	3	0	0	1	5.2	20	3	1	1	0	0	0	0	1	0	1	1	0	2	0	1.000	0	0- -	-	0.93	1.59
2009	SD	NL	28	0	0	9	25.2	117	27	14	11	3	2	1	1	11	1	19	4	0	2	1	.667	0	0-0	6	4.54	3.86
2010	SD	NL	54	0	0	15	59.0	253	64	21	19	1	1	1	1	19	5	44	2	1	3	1	.750	0	0-2	9	3.61	2.90
2011	Fla	NL	53	0	0	10	50.2	214	48	20	18	2	3	1	2	20	5	31	1	1	2	4	.333	0	0-4	8	3.39	3.20
2012	Mia	NL	65	0	0	21	60.1	270	72	30	27	2	0	2	4	20	8	44	0	0	4	3	.571	0	0-0	10	4.44	4.03
	4 ML YEARS		200	0	0	55	195.2	854	211	85	75	8	6	5	8	70	19	138	7	2	11	9	.550	0	0-6	33	3.93	3.45

Thad Weber

Pitches: R **Bats:** R **Pos:** RP-2
Ht: 6'2" **Wt:** 205 **Born:** 9/28/1984 **Age:** 28

Year	Team	Lg	G	GS	CG	GF	IP	BFP	H	R	ER	HR	SH	SF	HB	TBB	IBB	SO	WP	Bk	W	L	Pct	Sh	Sv-Op	Hld	ERC	ERA
2008	Tigers	R	2	1	0	0	4.0	13	1	0	0	0	0	0	0	0	0	9	0	0	0	0	-	0	0- -	-	0.14	0.00
2008	WMich	A	11	11	0	0	56.1	225	46	20	16	3	0	1	3	11	0	49	5	1	1	4	.200	0	0- -	-	2.28	2.56
2009	Lkland	A+	12	12	1	0	67.2	262	54	19	16	6	0	1	1	11	0	40	5	0	4	4	.500	0	0- -	-	2.18	2.13
2009	Erie	AA	13	13	1	0	75.1	311	78	38	34	7	1	2	4	18	1	44	2	0	7	3	.700	1	0- -	-	3.90	4.06

Year	Team	Lg	G	GS	CG	GF	IP	BFP	H	R	ER	HR	SH	SF	HB	TBB	IBB	SO	WP	Bk	W	L	Pct	Sh	Sv-Op	Hld	ERC	ERA
2010	Erie	AA	25	25	2	0	167.2	707	176	87	76	17	7	7	8	41	1	113	7	1	9	12	.429	0	0- -	-	3.97	4.08
2010	Toledo	AAA	3	3	0	0	22.0	78	14	4	4	2	0	0	0	3	0	17	2	0	2	1	.667	0	0- -	-	1.48	1.64
2011	Toledo	AAA	27	27	1	0	151.1	667	176	98	95	28	4	3	5	49	1	111	4	1	5	11	.313	0	0- -	-	5.48	5.65
2012	Toledo	AAA	22	21	1	0	128.2	536	123	62	60	16	2	6	6	31	0	97	5	1	7	11	.389	0	0- -	-	3.56	4.20
2012	Tucsn	AAA	3	3	0	0	18.1	78	22	9	9	1	3	0	1	3	0	14	0	0	1	0	1.000	0	0- -	-	4.23	4.42
2012	Det	AL	2	0	0	1	4.0	24	10	4	4	0	0	0	0	2	0	1	0	0	0	1	.000	0	0-0	0	13.27	9.00

Jemile Weeks

Bats: B Throws: R Pos: 2B-113; PH-4; PR-2; DH-1 jah-MYLE Ht: 5'9" Wt: 160 Born: 1/26/1987 Age: 26

Year	Team	Lg	G	AB	H	2B	3B	HR	(Hm	Rd)	TB	R	RBI	RC	TBB	IBB	SO	HBP	SH	SF	SB	CS	SB%	GDP	Avg	OBP	Slg
2008	Kane	A	19	74	22	3	1	1	(-	-)	30	11	8	14	13	0	12	3	0	0	6	2	.75	1	.297	.422	.405
2009	Stcktn	A+	50	201	60	9	2	7	(-	-)	94	29	31	38	26	0	40	3	1	1	5	1	.83	5	.299	.385	.468
2009	Mdland	AA	30	105	25	5	0	2	(-	-)	36	10	13	12	10	0	16	1	4	3	4	0	1.00	0	.238	.303	.343
2010	Mdland	AA	67	273	73	14	7	3	(-	-)	110	43	33	39	28	0	37	3	2	6	11	6	.65	5	.267	.335	.403
2010	As	R	10	36	11	2	1	0	(-	-)	15	9	1	7	7	0	4	1	0	0	5	1	.83	1	.306	.432	.417
2011	Scrmto	AAA	45	184	59	6	4	3	(-	-)	82	30	22	36	29	0	32	2	1	1	10	4	.71	6	.321	.417	.446
2012	Scrmto	AAA	10	45	15	4	0	0	(-	-)	19	5	10	8	6	0	8	0	0	0	1	0	1.00	3	.333	.412	.422
2011	Oak	AL	97	406	123	26	8	2	(1	1)	171	50	36	64	21	1	62	4	2	4	22	11	.67	3	.303	.340	.421
2012	Oak	AL	118	444	98	15	8	2	(1	1)	135	54	20	42	50	0	70	5	9	3	16	5	.76	5	.221	.305	.304
	2 ML YEARS		215	850	221	41	16	4	(2	2)	306	104	56	106	71	1	132	9	11	7	38	16	.70	8	.260	.321	.360

Rickie Weeks

Bats: R Throws: R Pos: 2B-152; PH-3; DH-2 Ht: 5'10" Wt: 220 Born: 9/13/1982 Age: 30

Year	Team	Lg	G	AB	H	2B	3B	HR	(Hm	Rd)	TB	R	RBI	RC	TBB	IBB	SO	HBP	SH	SF	SB	CS	SB%	GDP	Avg	OBP	Slg
2003	Mil	NL	7	12	2	1	0	0	(0	0)	3	1	0	0	1	0	6	1	0	0	0	0	.00	0	.167	.286	.250
2005	Mil	NL	96	360	86	13	2	13	(8	5)	142	56	42	49	40	2	96	11	2	1	15	2	.88	11	.239	.333	.394
2006	Mil	NL	95	359	100	15	3	8	(6	2)	145	73	34	53	30	1	92	19	2	3	19	5	.79	6	.279	.363	.404
2007	Mil	NL	118	409	96	21	6	16	(5	11)	177	87	36	65	78	5	116	14	3	2	25	2	.93	3	.235	.374	.433
2008	Mil	NL	129	475	111	22	7	14	(3	11)	189	89	46	67	66	0	115	14	1	4	19	5	.79	5	.234	.342	.398
2009	Mil	NL	37	147	40	5	2	9	(7	2)	76	28	24	27	12	0	39	3	0	0	2	2	.50	1	.272	.340	.517
2010	Mil	NL	160	651	175	32	4	29	(16	13)	302	112	83	110	76	0	184	25	0	1	11	4	.73	5	.269	.366	.464
2011	Mil	NL	118	453	122	26	2	20	(10	10)	212	77	49	68	50	3	107	8	1	3	9	2	.82	6	.269	.350	.468
2012	Mil	NL	157	588	135	29	4	21	(10	11)	235	85	63	77	74	2	169	13	0	2	16	3	.84	9	.230	.328	.400
	Postseason		14	45	6	1	1	2	(2	0)	15	5	4	2	2	0	8	2	0	0	0	0	-	3	.133	.204	.333
	9 ML YEARS		917	3454	867	164	30	130	(65	65)	1481	608	377	516	427	13	924	108	9	17	116	25	.82	46	.251	.350	.429

Kyle Weiland

Pitches: R Bats: L Pos: SP-3 WHY-lend Ht: 6'4" Wt: 195 Born: 9/12/1986 Age: 26

Year	Team	Lg	G	GS	CG	GF	IP	BFP	H	R	ER	HR	SH	SF	HB	TBB	IBB	SO	WP	Bk	W	L	Pct	Sh	Sv-Op	Hld	ERC	ERA
2008	Lowell	A-	15	10	0	1	60.0	238	36	17	10	1	2	1	8	10	0	68	1	1	3	3	.500	0	0- -	-	1.35	1.50
2009	Salem	A+	26	26	0	0	132.2	575	119	65	51	4	5	2	16	57	0	112	10	3	7	9	.438	0	0- -	-	3.60	3.46
2010	Portlnd	AA	25	25	0	0	128.1	543	112	70	63	13	3	1	16	49	0	120	7	2	9	7	.357	0	0- -	-	3.86	4.42
2011	Pwtckt	AAA	24	24	0	0	128.1	537	108	54	51	10	7	2	8	55	0	126	9	2	8	10	.444	0	0- -	-	3.47	3.58
2011	Bos	AL	7	5	0	2	24.2	118	29	22	21	5	0	1	4	12	0	13	0	0	0	3	.000	0	0-0	0	6.89	7.66
2012	Hou	NL	3	3	0	0	17.2	79	24	13	13	5	0	0	0	7	0	13	1	1	0	3	.000	0	0-0	0	8.02	6.62
	2 ML YEARS		10	8	0	2	42.1	197	53	35	34	10	0	1	4	19	0	26	1	1	0	6	.000	0	0-0	0	7.36	7.23

Casper Wells

Bats: R Throws: R Pos: LF-52; RF-25; CF-11; PH-7; PR-2; DH-1 Ht: 6'2" Wt: 220 Born: 11/23/1984 Age: 28

Year	Team	Lg	G	AB	H	2B	3B	HR	(Hm	Rd)	TB	R	RBI	RC	TBB	IBB	SO	HBP	SH	SF	SB	CS	SB%	GDP	Avg	OBP	Slg
2012	Tacom*	AAA	22	71	17	7	2	2	(-	-)	34	18	14	15	20	0	17	2	1	1	2	1	.67	0	.239	.415	.479
2010	Det	AL	36	93	30	6	1	4	(1	3)	50	14	17	16	6	0	19	0	0	0	0	1	.00	2	.323	.364	.538
2011	2 Tms	AL	95	215	51	11	0	11	(7	4)	95	30	27	30	18	2	71	7	1	0	3	2	.60	3	.237	.317	.442
2012	Sea	AL	93	285	65	12	3	10	(4	6)	113	42	36	39	26	0	80	4	1	0	3	0	1.00	3	.228	.302	.396
11	Det	AL	64	113	29	10	0	4	(1	3)	51	16	12	15	9	0	29	2	1	0	1	0	1.00	2	.257	.323	.451
11	Sea	AL	31	102	22	1	0	7	(6	1)	44	14	15	15	9	2	42	5	0	0	2	2	.50	1	.216	.310	.431
	3 ML YEARS		224	593	146	29	4	25	(12	13)	258	86	80	85	50	2	170	11	2	0	6	3	.67	8	.246	.317	.435

Kip Wells

Pitches: R Bats: R Pos: SP-7 Ht: 6'3" Wt: 205 Born: 4/21/1977 Age: 36

Year	Team	Lg	G	GS	CG	GF	IP	BFP	H	R	ER	HR	SH	SF	HB	TBB	IBB	SO	WP	Bk	W	L	Pct	Sh	Sv-Op	Hld	ERC	ERA
2012	Tucsn*	AAA	10	8	0	0	50.2	228	60	38	27	4	0	5	7	26	1	22	3	0	2	4	.333	0	0- -	-	5.63	4.80
1999	CWS	AL	7	7	0	0	35.2	153	33	17	16	2	0	2	3	15	0	29	1	2	4	1	.800	0	0-0	0	3.80	4.04
2000	CWS	AL	20	20	0	0	98.2	468	126	76	66	15	1	3	3	58	4	71	7	0	6	9	.400	0	0-0	0	7.07	6.02
2001	CWS	AL	40	20	0	3	133.1	603	145	80	71	14	8	6	12	61	5	99	14	0	10	11	.476	0	0-2	6	5.16	4.79
2002	Pit	NL	33	33	1	0	198.1	845	197	92	79	21	7	5	7	71	11	134	7	0	12	14	.462	1	0-0	0	4.00	3.58
2003	Pit	NL	31	31	1	0	197.1	835	171	77	72	24	15	2	7	76	7	147	7	0	10	9	.526	0	0-0	0	3.49	3.28
2004	Pit	NL	24	24	0	0	138.1	621	145	71	70	14	6	6	6	66	4	116	3	0	5	7	.417	0	0-0	0	4.77	4.55
2005	Pit	NL	33	33	1	0	182.0	828	186	116	103	23	9	10	12	99	8	132	8	0	8	18	.308	1	0-0	0	5.14	5.09
2006	2 Tms		9	9	0	0	44.1	208	61	33	32	3	1	1	4	21	1	20	5	0	2	5	.286	0	0-0	0	6.90	6.50

			HOW MUCH HE PITCHED						WHAT HE GAVE UP											THE RESULTS							
Year	Team	Lg	G	GS	CG	GF	IP	BFP	H	R	ER	HR	SH	SF	HB	TBB	IBB	SO	WP	Bk	W	L	Pct	Sh	Sv-Op	Hld	ERC	ERA
2007	StL	NL	34	26	0	4	162.2	750	186	116	103	19	8	7	9	78	9	122	8	1	7	17	.292	0	0-0	0	5.44	5.70
2008	2 Tms		25	2	0	8	37.2	176	39	29	26	4	3	0	2	30	2	31	3	0	1	3	.250	0		0	6.20	6.21
2009	2 Tms	NL	33	7	0	9	72.2	314	60	43	43	6	4	1	5	40	1	43	0	0	2	5	.286	0	2-2	5	3.84	5.33
2012	SD	NL	7	7	0	0	37.1	169	41	23	19	6	1	2	1	20	1	19	4	0	2	4	.333	0	0-0	0	5.78	4.58
06	Pit	NL	7	7	0	0	36.1	168	46	27	27	3	1	1	4	18	1	16	5	0	1	5	.167	0	0-0	0	6.51	6.69
06	Tex	AL	2	2	0	0	8.0	40	15	6	5	0	0	0	0	3	0	4	0	0	1	0	1.000	0	0-0	0	8.77	5.63
08	Col	NL	15	2	0	6	27.1	126	29	19	16	3	3	0	1	19	2	22	2	0	1	2	.333	0	0-0	0	5.82	5.27
08	KC	AL	10	0	0	2	10.1	50	10	10	10	1	0	0	1	11	0	9	1	0	0	1	.000	0		0	7.23	8.71
09	Was	NL	23	0	0	8	26.1	117	23	19	19	1	1	1	0	18	1	18	0	0	0	2	.000	0	2-2	5	3.95	6.49
09	Cin	NL	10	7	0	1	46.1	197	37	24	24	5	3	0	5	22	0	25	0	0	2	3	.400	0	0-0	0	3.77	4.66
12 ML YEARS			296	219	3	24	1338.1	5970	1390	773	700	151	62	45	71	635	53	963	67	3	69	103	.401	2	2-4	12	4.84	4.71

Randy Wells

Pitches: R **Bats:** R **Pos:** RP-8; SP-4   **Ht:** 6'5" **Wt:** 230 **Born:** 8/28/1982 **Age:** 30

			HOW MUCH HE PITCHED						WHAT HE GAVE UP											THE RESULTS							
Year	Team	Lg	G	GS	CG	GF	IP	BFP	H	R	ER	HR	SH	SF	HB	TBB	IBB	SO	WP	Bk	W	L	Pct	Sh	Sv-Op	Hld	ERC	ERA
2012	Iowa*	AAA	9	9	0	0	43.1	201	52	39	38	6	2	2	3	18	0	29	2	0	3	3	.500	0	0- -	-	5.81	7.89
2008	2 Tms		4	0	0	2	5.1	18	0	0	0	0	0	0	0	3	0	1	0	0	0	0		0	0-0	0	0.35	0.00
2009	ChC	NL	27	27	0	0	165.1	694	165	67	56	14	7	4	6	46	4	104	3	1	12	10	.545	0	0-0	0	3.62	3.05
2010	ChC	NL	32	32	0	0	194.1	843	209	97	92	19	8	0	6	63	5	144	2	0	8	14	.364	0	0-0	0	4.26	4.26
2011	ChC	NL	23	23	2	0	135.1	583	141	76	75	23	3	6	2	47	4	82	8	0	7	6	.538	1	0-0	0	4.62	4.99
2012	ChC	NL	12	4	0	2	28.2	143	35	18	17	1	4	1	2	24	1	14	1	0	1	2	.333	0	0-1	0	6.88	5.34
08	Tor	AL	1	0	0	1	1.0	4	0	0	0	0	0	0	0	1	0	0	0	0	0	0		0	0-0	0	0.95	0.00
08	ChC	NL	3	0	0	1	4.1	14	0	0	0	0	0	0	0	2	0	1	0	0	0	0		0	0-0	0	0.25	0.00
5 ML YEARS			98	86	2	4	529.0	2281	550	258	240	57	22	11	16	183	14	345	14	1	28	32	.467	1	0-1	0	4.23	4.08

Vernon Wells

Bats: R **Throws:** R **Pos:** LF-69; CF-6; PR-3; RF-2; DH-1; PH-1   **Ht:** 6'1" **Wt:** 230 **Born:** 12/8/1978 **Age:** 34

			BATTING																BASERUNNING				AVERAGES		
Year	Team	Lg	G	AB	H	2B	3B	HR	(Hm | Rd)	TB	R	RBI	RC	TBB	IBB	SO	HBP	SH	SF	SB	CS	SB%	GDP	Avg	OBP	Slg
2012	Salt Lk*	AAA	7	26	8	1	0	2	(- | -)	15	2	3	5	0	0	6	2	0	0	3	0	1.00	0	.308	.357	.577
1999	Tor	AL	24	88	23	5	0	1	(1 | 0)	31	8	8	7	4	0	18	0	0	0	1	1	.50	6	.261	.293	.352
2000	Tor	AL	3	2	0	0	0	0	(0 | 0)	0	0	0	0	0	0	0	0	0	0	0	0	-	0	.000	.000	.000
2001	Tor	AL	30	96	30	8	0	1	(1 | 0)	41	14	6	16	5	0	15	1	0	1	5	0	1.00	4	.313	.350	.427
2002	Tor	AL	159	608	167	34	4	23	(10 | 13)	278	87	100	88	27	0	85	3	2	8	9	4	.69	15	.275	.305	.457
2003	Tor	AL	161	678	215	49	5	33	(13 | 20)	373	118	117	124	42	2	80	7	0	8	4	1	.80	21	.317	.359	.550
2004	Tor	AL	134	536	146	34	2	23	(14 | 9)	253	82	67	72	51	2	83	2	0	1	9	2	.82	17	.272	.337	.472
2005	Tor	AL	156	620	167	30	3	28	(14 | 14)	287	78	97	96	47	3	86	3	0	8	8	3	.73	13	.269	.320	.463
2006	Tor	AL	154	611	185	40	5	32	(24 | 8)	331	91	106	107	54	0	90	3	0	9	17	4	.81	13	.303	.357	.542
2007	Tor	AL	149	584	143	36	4	16	(8 | 8)	235	85	80	74	49	4	89	3	0	6	10	4	.71	9	.245	.304	.402
2008	Tor	AL	108	427	128	21	2	20	(11 | 9)	212	63	78	68	29	5	46	3	0	7	4	2	.67	16	.300	.343	.496
2009	Tor	AL	158	630	164	37	3	15	(8 | 7)	252	84	66	65	48	2	86	1	0	5	17	4	.81	18	.260	.311	.400
2010	Tor	AL	157	590	161	44	3	31	(20 | 11)	304	79	88	92	50	5	84	3	0	3	6	4	.60	18	.273	.331	.515
2011	LAA	AL	131	505	110	15	4	25	(8 | 17)	208	60	66	52	20	0	86	1	0	3	9	4	.69	8	.218	.248	.412
2012	LAA	AL	77	243	56	9	0	11	(5 | 6)	98	36	29	17	16	0	35	1	0	2	3	1	.75	5	.230	.279	.403
14 ML YEARS			1601	6218	1695	363	34	259	(137 | 122)	2903	885	908	878	442	23	883	31	2	61	102	34	.75	159	.273	.321	.467

Andrew Werner

Pitches: L **Bats:** L **Pos:** SP-8   **Ht:** 6'2" **Wt:** 215 **Born:** 2/25/1987 **Age:** 26

			HOW MUCH HE PITCHED						WHAT HE GAVE UP											THE RESULTS							
Year	Team	Lg	G	GS	CG	GF	IP	BFP	H	R	ER	HR	SH	SF	HB	TBB	IBB	SO	WP	Bk	W	L	Pct	Sh	Sv-Op	Hld	ERC	ERA
2011	FtWyn	A	12	12	0	0	68.0	280	70	30	26	4	3	0	4	13	0	52	7	1	2	6	.250	0	0- -	-	3.24	3.44
2011	Lk Els	A+	13	13	0	0	68.1	288	72	26	23	1	1	0	3	13	1	55	2	0	5	2	.714	0	0- -	-	3.11	3.03
2012	SnAnt	AA	18	18	0	0	103.0	427	107	46	37	6	5	0	3	25	3	89	2	0	4	8	.333	0	0- -	-	3.53	3.23
2012	Tucsn	AAA	4	4	1	0	23.1	102	26	18	15	1	0	0	0	6	0	20	0	1	1	2	.333	1	0- -	-	3.66	5.79
2012	SD	NL	8	8	0	0	40.1	177	45	26	25	5	2	2	1	14	1	35	1	1	2	3	.400	0	0-0	0	4.76	5.58

Jayson Werth

Bats: R **Throws:** R **Pos:** RF-76; CF-11; PH-2   **Ht:** 6'5" **Wt:** 225 **Born:** 5/20/1979 **Age:** 34

			BATTING																BASERUNNING				AVERAGES		
Year	Team	Lg	G	AB	H	2B	3B	HR	(Hm | Rd)	TB	R	RBI	RC	TBB	IBB	SO	HBP	SH	SF	SB	CS	SB%	GDP	Avg	OBP	Slg
2012	Ptomc*	A+	2	6	3	1	0	0	(- | -)	4	2	1	2	2	0	1	0	0	0	0	0	-	0	.500	.625	.667
2012	Syrcse*	AAA	7	21	5	2	0	0	(- | -)	7	4	4	3	6	1	5	0	0	0	0	0	-	1	.238	.407	.333
2002	Tor	AL	15	46	12	2	1	0	(0 | 0)	16	4	6	5	6	0	11	0	0	1	1	0	1.00	4	.261	.340	.348
2003	Tor	AL	26	48	10	4	0	2	(0 | 2)	20	7	10	6	3	0	22	0	0	0	1	0	1.00	0	.208	.255	.417
2004	LAD	NL	89	290	76	11	3	16	(11 | 5)	141	56	47	47	30	0	85	4	1	1	4	1	.80	1	.262	.338	.486
2005	LAD	NL	102	337	79	22	3	7	(1 | 6)	126	46	43	44	48	2	114	6	1	3	11	2	.85	10	.234	.338	.374
2007	Phi	NL	94	255	76	11	3	8	(1 | 7)	117	43	49	57	44	1	73	2	2	1	7	1	.88	0	.298	.404	.459
2008	Phi	NL	134	418	114	16	3	24	(11 | 13)	208	73	67	74	57	1	119	4	0	3	20	1	.95	2	.273	.363	.498
2009	Phi	NL	159	571	153	26	1	36	(21 | 15)	289	98	99	107	91	8	156	8	0	6	20	3	.87	11	.268	.373	.506
2010	Phi	NL	156	554	164	46	2	27	(18 | 9)	295	106	85	91	82	6	147	7	0	9	13	3	.81	11	.296	.388	.532
2011	Was	NL	150	561	130	26	1	20	(10 | 10)	218	69	58	74	74	5	160	10	0	4	19	3	.86	10	.232	.330	.389
2012	Was	NL	81	300	90	21	3	5	(4 | 1)	132	42	31	48	42	2	57	1	0	1	8	2	.80	3	.300	.387	.440
Postseason			44	153	41	9	2	13	(9 | 4)	93	30	26	29	27	4	52	1	0	1	5	0	1.00	3	.268	.379	.608
10 ML YEARS			1006	3380	904	185	19	145	(77 | 68)	1562	544	495	553	477	25	944	42	4	29	104	16	.87	52	.267	.362	.462

Jake Westbrook

Pitches: R **Bats:** R **Pos:** SP-28   **Ht:** 6'3" **Wt:** 210 **Born:** 9/29/1977 **Age:** 35

			HOW MUCH HE PITCHED			WHAT HE GAVE UP											THE RESULTS							
Year	Team	Lg	G	GS	CG	GF	IP	BFP	H	R	ER	HR	SH	SF	HB	TBB	IBB	SO	WP	Bk	W	L	Pct	Sh	Sv-Op	Hld	ERC	ERA
2000	NYY	AL	3	2	0	1	6.2	38	15	10	10	1	0	2	0	4	1	1	0	0	0	2	.000	0	0-0	0	13.53	13.50
2001	Cle	AL	23	6	0	3	64.2	290	79	43	42	6	1	5	4	22	4	48	4	0	4	4	.500	0	0-0	5	5.25	5.85
2002	Cle	AL	11	4	0	1	41.2	185	50	30	27	6	2	1	1	12	1	20	1	0	1	3	.250	0	0-2	1	5.12	5.83
2003	Cle	AL	34	22	0	4	133.0	580	142	70	64	9	4	3	12	56	1	58	3	0	7	10	.412	0	0-0	1	4.78	4.33
2004	Cle	AL	33	30	5	2	215.2	895	208	95	81	19	6	6	5	61	3	116	4	1	14	9	.609	1	0-0	0	3.45	3.38
2005	Cle	AL	34	34	2	0	210.2	895	218	121	105	19	5	4	7	56	3	119	3	0	15	15	.500	0	0-0	0	3.78	4.49
2006	Cle	AL	32	32	3	0	211.1	904	247	106	98	15	5	4	4	55	4	109	5	0	15	10	.600	2	0-0	0	4.39	4.17
2007	Cle	AL	25	25	0	0	152.0	648	159	78	73	13	6	4	6	55	5	93	5	0	6	9	.400	0	0-0	0	4.28	4.32
2008	Cle	AL	5	5	1	0	34.2	139	33	13	12	5	0	2	1	7	0	19	1	0	1	2	.333	0	0-0	0	3.54	3.12
2010	2 Tms		33	33	1	0	202.2	860	203	99	95	20	5	3	8	68	4	128	8	0	10	11	.476	0	0-0	0	3.99	4.22
2011	StL	NL	33	33	0	0	183.1	809	208	103	95	16	11	5	2	73	8	104	3	0	12	9	.571	0	0-0	0	4.75	4.66
2012	StL	NL	28	28	1	0	174.2	751	191	85	77	12	8	5	8	52	0	106	5	0	13	11	.542	0	0-0	0	4.20	3.97
10	Cle	AL	21	21	1	0	127.2	543	133	68	66	15	3	3	6	44	4	73	6	0	6	7	.462	0	0-0	0	4.45	4.65
10	StL	NL	12	12	0	0	75.0	317	70	31	29	5	2	0	2	24	0	55	2	0	4	4	.500	0	0-0	0	3.25	3.48
	Postseason		5	3	0	2	19.2	82	27	11	11	2	0	1	0	5	1	8	0	0	2	2	.500	0	0-0	0	6.10	5.03
	12 ML YEARS		294	254	14	11	1631.0	6994	1753	853	779	141	53	44	58	521	34	921	40	1	98	95	.508	3	0-2	7	4.24	4.30

Dan Wheeler

Pitches: R **Bats:** R **Pos:** RP-13   **Ht:** 6'3" **Wt:** 220 **Born:** 12/10/1977 **Age:** 35

			HOW MUCH HE PITCHED			WHAT HE GAVE UP											THE RESULTS							
Year	Team	Lg	G	GS	CG	GF	IP	BFP	H	R	ER	HR	SH	SF	HB	TBB	IBB	SO	WP	Bk	W	L	Pct	Sh	Sv-Op	Hld	ERC	ERA
2012	Clmbs*	AAA	36	0	0	14	42.2	180	38	14	11	4	1	1	3	13	2	30	0	0	3	3	.500	0	5--	-	3.24	2.32
1999	TB	AL	6	6	0	0	30.2	136	35	20	20	7	1	0	0	13	1	32	1	0	0	4	.000	0	0-0	0	5.96	5.87
2000	TB	AL	11	2	0	6	23.0	111	29	14	14	2	1	1	2	11	2	17	2	0	1	1	.500	0	0-1	1	5.87	5.48
2001	TB	AL	13	0	0	3	17.2	87	30	17	17	3	0	2	0	5	0	12	1	1	1	0	1.000	0	0-0	0	8.38	8.66
2003	NYM	NL	35	0	0	10	51.0	215	49	23	21	6	0	3	1	17	4	35	1	0	1	3	.250	0	2-3	0	3.69	3.71
2004	2 Tms	NL	46	1	0	11	65.0	287	76	33	31	10	2	1	1	20	2	55	4	1	3	1	.750	0	0-0	5	5.05	4.29
2005	Hou	NL	71	0	0	20	73.1	288	53	18	18	7	5	1	3	19	3	69	0	0	2	3	.400	0	3-5	17	2.22	2.21
2006	Hou	NL	75	0	0	25	71.1	295	58	22	20	5	3	3	2	24	8	68	0	0	3	5	.375	0	9-12	24	2.57	2.52
2007	2 Tms		70	0	0	29	74.2	321	74	48	44	11	3	3	3	23	3	82	2	0	1	9	.100	0	11-18	18	4.04	5.30
2008	TB	AL	70	0	0	26	66.1	264	44	25	23	10	0	2	0	22	4	53	1	0	5	6	.455	0	13-18	26	2.28	3.12
2009	TB	AL	69	0	0	20	57.2	219	41	22	21	11	3	1	0	9	2	45	3	0	4	5	.444	0	2-6	16	2.17	3.28
2010	TB	AL	64	0	0	13	48.1	195	36	20	18	7	1	3	1	16	2	46	3	0	2	4	.333	0	3-6	9	2.77	3.35
2011	Bos	AL	47	0	0	22	49.1	201	47	24	24	7	1	1	0	8	1	39	0	0	2	2	.500	0	0-0	4	3.11	4.38
2012	Cle	AL	13	0	0	2	12.1	61	17	12	12	3	0	2	0	7	0	2	2	0	0	0	-	0	0-0	1	8.12	8.76
04	NYM	NL	32	1	0	7	50.2	232	65	29	27	9	2	1	0	17	2	46	4	1	3	1	.750	0	0-0	3	5.91	4.80
04	Hou	NL	14	0	0	4	14.1	55	11	4	4	1	0	0	1	3	0	9	0	0	0	0	-	0	0-0	2	2.35	2.51
07	Hou	NL	45	0	0	25	49.2	205	46	28	28	8	1	1	2	13	1	56	1	0	1	4	.200	0	11-15	6	3.69	5.07
07	TB	AL	25	0	0	4	25.0	116	28	20	16	3	2	2	1	10	2	26	1	0	0	5	.000	0	0-3	12	4.72	5.76
	Postseason		21	0	0	5	26.2	111	21	10	10	3	1	0	3	8	1	28	1	0	1	0	1.000	0	1-3	5	2.98	3.38
	13 ML YEARS		590	9	0	187	640.2	2680	589	298	283	89	20	23	13	194	32	555	20	2	25	43	.368	0	43-69	121	3.50	3.98

Ryan Wheeler

Bats: L **Throws:** R **Pos:** PH-25; 3B-23; 1B-4; PR-1   **Ht:** 6'3" **Wt:** 237 **Born:** 7/10/1988 **Age:** 24

			BATTING											BASERUNNING							AVERAGES		
Year	Team	Lg	G	AB	H	2B	3B	HR	(Hm | Rd)	TB	R	RBI	RC	TBB	IBB	SO	HBP	SH	SF	SB	CS	SB%	GDP	Avg	OBP	Slg
2009	Yakima	A-	64	234	85	20	3	5	(- | -)	126	44	36	58	37	3	28	7	0	2	7	4	.64	4	.363	.461	.538
2009	Sbend	A	8	29	10	1	1	1	(- | -)	16	4	5	7	5	0	4	2	0	0	0	1	.00	1	.345	.472	.552
2010	Visalia	A+	113	465	132	25	2	9	(- | -)	188	62	57	66	35	2	98	5	0	1	3	1	.75	15	.284	.340	.404
2010	Mobile	AA	19	67	17	3	0	3	(- | -)	29	8	10	9	5	0	16	1	0	0	0	0	-	1	.254	.315	.433
2011	Mobile	AA	131	480	141	30	2	16	(- | -)	223	69	89	80	45	7	102	4	0	2	3	3	.50	14	.294	.358	.465
2012	Reno	AAA	93	362	127	27	4	15	(- | -)	207	56	90	78	26	2	67	2	0	9	3	1	.75	9	.351	.388	.572
2012	Ari	NL	50	109	26	6	1	1	(0 | 1)	37	11	10	7	9	0	22	0	0	1	1	0	1.00	4	.239	.294	.339

Alex White

Pitches: R **Bats:** R **Pos:** SP-20; RP-3   **Ht:** 6'3" **Wt:** 215 **Born:** 8/29/1988 **Age:** 24

			HOW MUCH HE PITCHED			WHAT HE GAVE UP											THE RESULTS							
Year	Team	Lg	G	GS	CG	GF	IP	BFP	H	R	ER	HR	SH	SF	HB	TBB	IBB	SO	WP	Bk	W	L	Pct	Sh	Sv-Op	Hld	ERC	ERA
2010	Knstn	A+	8	8	0	0	44.0	183	32	18	14	4	5	1	0	19	0	41	1	0	2	3	.400	0	0--	-	2.64	2.86
2010	Akron	AA	18	17	0	0	106.2	439	91	45	27	8	4	4	2	27	0	76	5	0	8	7	.533	0	0--	-	2.61	2.28
2011	Clmbs	AAA	4	4	0	0	23.2	97	19	7	5	1	0	0	2	5	0	28	1	0	1	0	1.000	0	0--	-	2.25	1.90
2011	Tulsa	AA	4	4	0	0	16.1	60	10	3	3	1	0	0	1	1	0	10	0	0	1	1	.500	0	0--	-	1.22	1.65
2012	ColSpr	AAA	11	11	0	0	60.2	255	54	28	25	3	2	1	2	23	0	45	8	0	3	4	.429	0	0--	-	3.19	3.71
2011	2 Tms		10	10	0	0	51.1	237	62	42	40	15	2	3	4	25	3	37	5	0	3	4	.429	0	0-0	0	7.55	7.01
2012	Col	NL	23	20	0	0	98.0	459	114	66	60	13	5	2	5	51	9	64	6	0	2	9	.182	0	0-0	0	5.75	5.51
11	Cle	AL	3	3	0	0	15.0	66	14	7	6	3	1	1	0	9	2	13	0	0	1	0	1.000	0	0-0	0	5.06	3.60
11	Col	NL	7	7	0	0	36.1	171	48	35	34	12	1	2	4	16	1	24	5	0	2	4	.333	0	0-0	0	8.66	8.42
	2 ML YEARS		33	30	0	0	149.1	696	176	108	100	28	7	5	9	76	12	101	11	0	5	13	.278	0	0-0	0	6.35	6.03

Eli Whiteside

Bats: R **Throws:** R **Pos:** C-11; PR-2   **Ht:** 6'2" **Wt:** 220 **Born:** 10/22/1979 **Age:** 33

Year	Team	Lg	G	AB	H	2B	3B	HR	(Hm	Rd)	TB	R	RBI	RC	TBB	IBB	SO	HBP	SH	SF	SB	CS	SB%	GDP	Avg	OBP	Slg
2012	Fresno*	AAA	60	201	45	11	1	1	(-	-)	61	27	20	19	17	1	43	5	3	3	0	1	.00	4	.224	.296	.303
2005	Bal	AL	9	12	3	0	0	0	(0	0)	3	1	1	0	0	0	2	0	0	0	0	0	-	1	.250	.250	.250
2009	SF	NL	49	127	29	6	1	2	(1	1)	43	15	13	11	4	1	30	3	0	0	0	0	-	4	.228	.269	.339
2010	SF	NL	56	126	30	6	1	4	(3	1)	50	19	10	9	8	0	35	3	3	0	1	2	.33	4	.238	.299	.397
2011	SF	NL	82	213	42	8	2	4	(3	1)	66	14	17	11	18	3	59	2	1	2	2	1	.67	9	.197	.264	.310
2012	SF	NL	12	11	1	1	0	0	(0	0)	2	3	2	1	1	0	4	1	0	1	0	0	-	0	.091	.214	.182
	5 ML YEARS		208	489	105	21	4	10	(7	3)	164	52	43	32	31	4	130	9	4	3	3	3	.50	18	.215	.273	.335

Joe Wieland

Pitches: R **Bats:** R **Pos:** SP-5   WEE-lend   **Ht:** 6'3" **Wt:** 195 **Born:** 1/21/1990 **Age:** 23

Year	Team	Lg	G	GS	CG	GF	IP	BFP	H	R	ER	HR	SH	SF	HB	TBB	IBB	SO	WP	Bk	W	L	Pct	Sh	Sv-Op	Hld	ERC	ERA
2008	Rngrs	R	13	7	0	1	43.2	172	32	8	7	2	0	0	4	8	0	41	3	0	5	1	.833	0	0- -	-	1.94	1.44
2009	Hkry	A	19	18	0	0	83.0	381	102	67	49	7	5	6	5	24	4	73	6	0	4	6	.400	0	0- -	-	4.85	5.31
2010	Hkry	A	15	15	2	0	89.0	357	84	36	33	4	2	2	3	15	0	71	1	0	7	4	.636	1	0- -	-	2.72	3.34
2010	Bkrsfld	A+	11	10	0	0	59.0	258	67	36	34	6	4	5	2	10	0	62	4	1	4	3	.571	0	0- -	-	3.93	5.19
2011	MrtlBh	A+	14	13	1	0	85.2	333	78	23	20	7	2	0	2	4	0	96	7	0	6	3	.667	1	0- -	-	2.29	2.10
2011	Frisco	AA	7	7	1	0	44.0	175	35	9	6	2	1	1	0	11	0	36	1	0	4	0	1.000	1	0- -	-	2.14	1.23
2011	SnAnt	AA	5	5	0	0	26.0	108	23	10	8	0	2	2	2	6	0	18	1	0	3	1	.750	0	0- -	-	2.44	2.77
2012	Tucsn	AAA	2	2	0	0	7.2	34	10	3	3	0	0	0	0	2	0	11	0	0	1	0	1.000	0	0- -	-	4.53	3.52
2012	SD	NL	5	5	0	0	27.2	119	26	16	14	5	1	2	1	9	2	24	1	0	0	4	.000	0	0-0	0	3.94	4.55

Matt Wieters

Bats: B **Throws:** R **Pos:** C-134; DH-9; PH-3   WEE-ters   **Ht:** 6'5" **Wt:** 240 **Born:** 5/21/1986 **Age:** 27

Year	Team	Lg	G	AB	H	2B	3B	HR	(Hm	Rd)	TB	R	RBI	RC	TBB	IBB	SO	HBP	SH	SF	SB	CS	SB%	GDP	Avg	OBP	Slg
2009	Bal	AL	96	354	102	15	1	9	(5	4)	146	35	43	43	28	2	86	1	0	2	0	0	-	11	.288	.340	.412
2010	Bal	AL	130	446	111	22	1	11	(3	8)	168	37	55	47	47	7	94	2	0	7	0	1	.00	13	.249	.319	.377
2011	Bal	AL	139	500	131	28	0	22	(13	9)	225	72	68	76	48	3	84	2	0	1	1	0	1.00	16	.262	.328	.450
2012	Bal	AL	144	526	131	27	1	23	(11	12)	229	67	83	73	60	4	112	4	0	3	3	0	1.00	17	.249	.329	.435
	4 ML YEARS		509	1826	475	92	3	65	(32	33)	768	211	249	239	183	16	376	9	0	13	4	1	.80	57	.260	.328	.421

Ty Wigginton

Bats: R **Throws:** R **Pos:** 1B-71; PH-41; 3B-22; LF-7   **Ht:** 6'0" **Wt:** 230 **Born:** 10/11/1977 **Age:** 35

Year	Team	Lg	G	AB	H	2B	3B	HR	(Hm	Rd)	TB	R	RBI	RC	TBB	IBB	SO	HBP	SH	SF	SB	CS	SB%	GDP	Avg	OBP	Slg
2002	NYM	NL	46	116	35	8	0	6	(4	2)	61	18	18	15	8	0	19	2	0	1	2	1	.67	4	.302	.354	.526
2003	NYM	NL	156	573	146	36	6	11	(4	7)	227	73	71	76	46	2	124	9	1	4	12	2	.86	15	.255	.318	.396
2004	2 Tms	NL	144	494	129	30	2	17	(6	11)	214	63	66	59	45	6	82	2	1	3	7	1	.88	15	.261	.324	.433
2005	Pit	NL	57	155	40	9	1	7	(1	6)	72	20	25	22	14	0	30	1	1	0	0	1	.00	3	.258	.324	.465
2006	TB	AL	122	444	122	25	1	24	(18	6)	221	55	79	69	32	3	97	6	1	3	4	3	.57	11	.275	.330	.498
2007	2 Tms	NL	148	547	152	33	0	22	(15	7)	251	71	67	64	41	0	113	8	0	8	3	4	.43	16	.278	.333	.459
2008	Hou	NL	111	386	110	22	1	23	(15	8)	203	50	58	57	32	1	69	8	0	3	4	6	.40	9	.285	.350	.526
2009	Bal	AL	122	410	112	19	0	11	(9	2)	164	44	41	41	23	1	57	2	0	1	1	2	.33	16	.273	.314	.400
2010	Bal	AL	154	581	144	19	1	22	(12	10)	241	63	76	62	50	3	116	8	1	9	0	1	.00	23	.248	.312	.415
2011	Col	NL	130	401	97	21	2	15	(7	8)	167	52	47	38	38	4	84	5	1	1	8	1	.89	10	.242	.315	.416
2012	Phi	NL	125	315	74	11	0	11	(6	5)	118	40	43	32	37	2	81	2	0	6	1	0	1.00	5	.235	.314	.375
04	NYM	NL	86	312	89	23	2	12	(5	7)	152	46	42	38	23	4	48	1	1	2	6	1	.86	11	.285	.334	.487
04	Pit	NL	58	182	40	7	0	5	(1	4)	62	17	24	21	22	2	34	1	0	1	1	0	1.00	4	.220	.306	.341
07	TB	AL	98	378	104	21	0	16	(9	7)	173	47	49	42	28	0	73	5	0	6	1	4	.20	8	.275	.329	.458
07	Hou	NL	50	169	48	12	0	6	(6	0)	78	24	18	22	13	0	40	3	0	2	2	0	1.00	8	.284	.342	.462
	11 ML YEARS		1315	4422	1161	243	14	169	(96	73)	1939	549	591	535	366	22	872	53	6	39	42	22	.66	127	.263	.324	.438

Tom Wilhelmsen

Pitches: R **Bats:** R **Pos:** RP-73   will-HELM-senn   **Ht:** 6'6" **Wt:** 230 **Born:** 12/16/1983 **Age:** 29

Year	Team	Lg	G	GS	CG	GF	IP	BFP	H	R	ER	HR	SH	SF	HB	TBB	IBB	SO	WP	Bk	W	L	Pct	Sh	Sv-Op	Hld	ERC	ERA
2003	Beloit	A	15	15	1	0	88.0	361	78	35	27	6	0	0	4	27	0	63	2	0	5	5	.500	0	0- -	-	3.12	2.76
2003	Brewrs	R	2	2	0	0	4.0	22	5	2	2	0	0	0	1	4	0	4	0	0	1	0	1.000	0	0- -	-	8.02	4.50
2010	Ms	R	5	3	0	0	15.0	54	4	1	1	0	0	1	0	2	0	22	2	0	0	0	-	0	0- -	-	0.36	0.60
2010	Everett	A-	3	3	0	0	14.2	59	14	6	6	1	1	0	1	2	0	14	2	0	1	0	1.000	0	0- -	-	2.93	3.68
2010	Clinton	A	7	6	1	0	44.1	187	33	16	11	1	1	2	2	15	0	37	4	0	6	1	.857	0	0- -	-	2.09	2.23
2011	Jacksn	AA	14	12	0	1	60.2	273	66	45	37	8	2	4	7	26	0	46	6	1	4	5	.444	0	0- -	-	5.45	5.49
2011	Sea	AL	25	0	0	10	32.2	136	25	13	12	2	0	2	2	13	0	30	6	1	2	0	1.000	0	0-0	3	2.78	3.31
2012	Sea	AL	73	0	0	48	79.1	326	59	24	22	5	1	2	2	29	3	87	3	0	4	3	.571	0	29-34	7	2.38	2.50
	2 ML YEARS		98	0	0	58	112.0	462	84	37	34	7	1	4	4	42	3	117	9	1	6	3	.667	0	29-34	10	2.49	2.73

Adam Wilk

Pitches: L Bats: L Pos: SP-3   Ht: 6'2" Wt: 181 Born: 12/9/1987 Age: 25

Year	Team	Lg	G	GS	CG	GF	IP	BFP	H	R	ER	HR	SH	SF	HB	TBB	IBB	SO	WP	Bk	W	L	Pct	Sh	Sv-Op	Hld	ERC	ERA
2009	Oneont	A-	7	7	1	0	37.1	140	23	7	6	0	1	0	1	5	0	34	0	0	2	0	1.000	1	0--	-	1.09	1.45
2009	WMich	A	7	7	0	0	36.1	138	30	7	6	2	0	0	1	2	0	33	1	0	2	1	.667	0	0--	-	1.81	1.49
2010	Lkland	A+	24	24	1	0	143.2	588	139	58	48	8	3	6	4	19	0	100	5	0	9	5	.643	0	0--	-	2.68	3.01
2010	Erie	AA	3	3	0	0	23.2	84	10	3	3	1	0	0	1	5	0	14	0	0	2	0	1.000	0	0--	-	0.92	1.14
2011	Toledo	AAA	18	18	0	0	102.2	422	105	45	37	15	2	2	3	14	0	76	3	0	8	6	.571	0	0--	-	3.58	3.24
2012	Toledo	AAA	24	24	3	0	149.2	595	123	61	46	13	7	4	0	28	1	128	2	0	7	11	.389	0	0--	-	2.25	2.77
2011	Det	AL	5	0	0	1	13.1	57	14	10	8	3	0	0	0	3	0	10	0	0	0	0	-	0	0-0	0	5.40	
2012	Det	AL	3	3	0	0	11.0	55	21	11	10	4	0	1	0	3	0	7	0	0	0	3	.000	0	0-0	0	11.90	8.18
	2 ML YEARS		8	3	0	1	24.1	112	35	21	18	7	0	1	0	6	0	17	0	0	0	3	.000	0	0-0	0	7.50	6.66

Jerome Williams

Pitches: R Bats: R Pos: RP-17; SP-15   Ht: 6'3" Wt: 240 Born: 12/4/1981 Age: 31

Year	Team	Lg	G	GS	CG	GF	IP	BFP	H	R	ER	HR	SH	SF	HB	TBB	IBB	SO	WP	Bk	W	L	Pct	Sh	Sv-Op	Hld	ERC	ERA
2012	InldEm*	A+	2	2	0	0	11.0	46	11	4	4	1	0	0	1	1	0	9	0	0	1	0	1.000	0	0--	-	3.10	3.27
2012	Salt Lk*	AAA	2	2	0	0	8.0	36	13	9	7	1	0	0	0	0	0	8	0	0	1	0	1.000	0	0--	-	6.33	7.88
2003	SF	NL	21	21	2	0	131.0	545	116	54	48	10	6	3	7	49	3	88	2	1	7	5	.583	1	0-0	-	3.42	3.30
2004	SF	NL	22	22	0	0	129.1	559	123	69	61	14	4	9	17	44	1	80	2	1	10	7	.588	0	0-0	0	4.14	4.24
2005	2 Tms	NL	22	20	0	0	122.2	532	119	62	58	14	11	8	10	49	1	70	2	0	6	10	.375	0	0-0	1	4.34	4.26
2006	ChC	NL	5	2	0	1	12.1	61	15	12	10	2	0	3	1	11	1	5	0	0	0	2	.000	0	0-0	0	8.42	7.30
2007	Was	NL	6	6	0	0	30.0	140	34	26	24	6	1	1	0	18	0	15	2	1	0	5	.000	0	0-0	0	6.43	7.20
2011	LAA	AL	10	6	0	1	44.0	184	45	20	18	6	0	1	1	15	0	28	0	0	4	0	1.000	0	0-0	0	4.45	3.68
2012	LAA	AL	32	15	1	7	137.2	572	139	73	70	17	0	4	5	35	1	98	1	0	6	8	.429	1	1-1	0	3.91	4.58
05	SF	NL	4	3	0	0	16.2	73	21	12	12	2	1	0	1	4	1	11	0	0	0	2	.000	0	0-0	0	5.32	6.48
05	ChC	NL	18	17	0	0	106.0	459	98	50	46	12	10	8	9	45	0	59	2	0	6	8	.429	0	0-1	1	4.19	3.91
	Postseason		1	1	0	0	2.0	13	5	3	3	0	1	0	0	1	0	1	0	0	0	0	-	0	0-0	0	12.20	13.50
	7 ML YEARS		118	92	3	9	607.0	2593	591	316	289	69	22	29	41	221	7	384	9	3	33	37	.471	2	1-1	1	4.18	4.29

Josh Willingham

Bats: R Throws: R Pos: LF-119; DH-25; PH-2   Ht: 6'2" Wt: 228 Born: 2/17/1979 Age: 34

Year	Team	Lg	G	AB	H	2B	3B	HR	(Hm	Rd)	TB	R	RBI	RC	TBB	IBB	SO	HBP	SH	SF	SB	CS	SB%	GDP	Avg	OBP	Slg
2004	Fla	NL	12	25	5	0	0	1	(0	1)	8	2	1	1	4	0	8	0	0	0	0	0	-	1	.200	.310	.320
2005	Fla	NL	16	23	7	1	0	0	(0	0)	8	3	4	3	2	0	5	2	1	0	0	0	-	1	.304	.407	.348
2006	Fla	NL	142	502	139	28	2	26	(11	15)	249	62	74	74	54	2	109	11	0	6	2	0	1.00	13	.277	.356	.496
2007	Fla	NL	144	521	138	32	4	21	(10	11)	241	75	89	94	66	1	122	16	0	1	8	1	.89	11	.265	.364	.463
2008	Fla	NL	102	351	89	21	5	15	(6	9)	165	54	51	56	48	2	82	14	1	2	3	2	.60	7	.254	.364	.470
2009	Was	NL	133	427	111	29	0	24	(7	17)	212	70	61	61	72	4	104	12	0	2	4	3	.57	11	.260	.367	.496
2010	Was	NL	114	370	99	19	2	16	(11	5)	170	54	56	65	67	3	85	9	0	4	8	0	1.00	8	.268	.389	.459
2011	Oak	AL	136	488	120	26	0	29	(15	14)	233	69	98	86	56	3	150	11	0	8	4	1	.80	6	.246	.332	.477
2012	Min	AL	145	519	135	30	1	35	(21	14)	272	85	110	99	76	4	141	14	0	6	3	2	.60	15	.260	.366	.524
	9 ML YEARS		944	3226	843	186	14	167	(81	86)	1558	474	544	539	434	17	806	89	2	29	32	9	.78	73	.261	.362	.483

Bobby Wilson

Bats: R Throws: R Pos: C-72; 1B-4; DH-1; PH-1   Ht: 6'0" Wt: 220 Born: 4/8/1983 Age: 30

Year	Team	Lg	G	AB	H	2B	3B	HR	(Hm	Rd)	TB	R	RBI	RC	TBB	IBB	SO	HBP	SH	SF	SB	CS	SB%	GDP	Avg	OBP	Slg
2012	InldEm*	A+	1	2	0	0	0	0	(-	-)	0	0	0	0	0	0	0	0	0	0	0	0	-	1	.000	.000	.000
2012	Salt Lk*	AAA	2	7	2	0	0	0	(-	-)	2	0	0	0	0	0	1	0	0	0	0	0	-	0	.286	.286	.286
2008	LAA	AL	7	6	1	0	0	0	(0	0)	1	0	1	0	1	0	3	0	0	0	0	0	-	1	.167	.286	.167
2009	LAA	AL	12	5	1	1	0	0	(0	0)	2	0	0	0	0	0	1	0	1	0	0	0	-	1	.200	.200	.400
2010	LAA	AL	40	96	22	6	0	4	(3	1)	40	12	15	12	8	0	23	0	2	0	0	0	-	3	.229	.288	.417
2011	LAA	AL	57	111	21	8	0	1	(0	1)	32	5	8	7	10	1	16	0	4	2	0	2	.00	7	.189	.252	.288
2012	LAA	AL	75	171	36	5	0	3	(2	1)	50	19	13	13	15	0	33	1	13	1	0	0	-	7	.211	.277	.292
	5 ML YEARS		191	389	81	20	0	8	(5	3)	125	36	37	32	34	1	76	1	20	3	0	2	.00	13	.208	.272	.321

Brian Wilson

Pitches: R Bats: R Pos: RP-2   Ht: 6'2" Wt: 205 Born: 3/16/1982 Age: 31

Year	Team	Lg	G	GS	CG	GF	IP	BFP	H	R	ER	HR	SH	SF	HB	TBB	IBB	SO	WP	Bk	W	L	Pct	Sh	Sv-Op	Hld	ERC	ERA
2006	SF	NL	31	0	0	9	30.0	141	32	19	18	1	1	4	1	21	2	23	0	0	2	3	.400	0	1-2	4	5.11	5.40
2007	SF	NL	24	0	0	9	23.2	93	16	6	6	1	0	0	1	7	0	5	0	0	1	2	.333	0	6-7	9	1.87	2.28
2008	SF	NL	63	0	0	54	62.1	274	62	32	32	7	2	5	3	28	4	67	2	0	3	2	.600	0	41-47	5	4.41	4.62
2009	SF	NL	68	0	0	60	72.1	303	60	27	22	3	4	2	1	27	4	83	4	0	5	6	.455	0	38-45	1	2.61	2.74
2010	SF	NL	70	0	0	59	74.2	311	62	16	15	3	1	4	2	26	5	93	0	0	3	3	.500	0	**48-53**	0	2.51	1.81
2011	SF	NL	57	0	0	45	55.0	243	50	20	19	2	1	1	2	31	0	54	2	0	6	4	.600	0	36-41	0	3.87	3.11
2012	SF	NL	2	0	0	2	2.0	12	4	2	2	0	0	0	0	2	0	2	1	0	0	0	-	0	1-1	0	12.01	9.00
	Postseason		10	0	0	9	11.2	44	5	1	0	0	1	1	1	4	0	16	0	0	1	0	1.000	0	6-7	0	1.10	0.00
	7 ML YEARS		315	0	0	238	320.0	1377	286	122	114	17	9	12	9	142	15	340	9	0	20	20	.500	0	171-196	14	3.34	3.21

C.J. Wilson

Pitches: L **Bats:** L **Pos:** SP-34   **Ht:** 6'1" **Wt:** 210 **Born:** 11/18/1980 **Age:** 32

			HOW MUCH HE PITCHED						WHAT HE GAVE UP											THE RESULTS						
Year	Team	Lg	G	GS	CG	GF	IP	BFP	H	R	ER	HR	SH	SF	HB	TBB	IBB	SO	WP	Bk	W	L	Pct	Sh	Sv-Op	Hld	ERC	ERA
2005	Tex	AL	24	6	0	5	48.0	220	63	39	37	5	1	2	2	18	1	30	4	1	1	7	.125	0	1-1	4	6.03	6.94
2006	Tex	AL	44	0	0	12	44.1	191	39	23	20	7	1	0	5	18	1	43	0	0	2	4	.333	0	1-2	7	4.25	4.06
2007	Tex	AL	66	0	0	22	68.1	285	50	25	23	4	2	4	6	33	1	63	5	0	2	1	.667	0	12-14	15	3.01	3.03
2008	Tex	AL	50	0	0	41	46.1	214	49	35	31	8	1	1	2	27	2	41	3	0	2	2	.500	0	24-28	1	5.77	6.02
2009	Tex	AL	74	0	0	30	73.2	323	66	29	23	3	3	0	6	32	3	84	3	0	5	6	.455	0	14-18	19	3.40	2.81
2010	Tex	AL	33	33	3	0	204.0	850	161	83	76	10	1	3	10	93	0	170	7	1	15	8	.652	0	0-0	0	3.03	3.35
2011	Tex	AL	34	34	0	0	223.1	915	191	89	73	16	3	5	10	74	0	206	6	0	16	7	.696	1	0-0	0	3.07	2.94
2012	LAA	AL	34	34	0	0	202.1	865	181	102	86	19	4	6	6	91	2	173	4	1	13	10	.565	0	0-0	0	3.75	3.83
	Postseason		10	9	0	0	52.1	231	46	32	28	10	3	1	4	29	6	43	3	0	1	5	.167	0	0-0	0	4.79	4.82
	8 ML YEARS		359	107	6	110	910.1	3863	800	425	369	72	16	21	47	386	10	810	32	3	56	45	.554	1	52-63	46	3.56	3.65

Jack Wilson

Bats: R **Throws:** R **Pos:** SS-29; PH-12; PR-3; 2B-2   **Ht:** 6'0" **Wt:** 200 **Born:** 12/29/1977 **Age:** 35

					BATTING														BASERUNNING				AVERAGES		
Year	Team	Lg	G	AB	H	2B	3B	HR	(Hm | Rd)	TB	R	RBI	RC	TBB	IBB	SO	HBP	SH	SF	SB	CS	SB%	GDP	Avg	OBP	Slg
2012	Gwnntt*	AAA	19	64	12	4	0	0	(- | -)	16	7	6	3	4	0	9	1	1	2	1	2	.33	2	.188	.239	.250
2001	Pit	NL	108	390	87	17	1	3	(0 | 3)	115	44	25	27	16	2	70	1	17	1	1	3	.25	4	.223	.255	.295
2002	Pit	NL	147	527	133	22	4	4	(2 | 2)	175	77	47	60	37	2	74	4	17	1	5	2	.71	7	.252	.306	.332
2003	Pit	NL	150	558	143	21	3	9	(2 | 7)	197	58	62	62	36	3	74	4	11	6	5	5	.50	11	.256	.303	.353
2004	Pit	NL	157	652	201	41	12	11	(7 | 4)	299	82	59	84	26	0	71	3	7	5	8	4	.67	15	.308	.335	.459
2005	Pit	NL	158	587	151	24	7	8	(3 | 5)	213	60	52	60	31	6	58	6	11	4	7	3	.70	11	.257	.299	.363
2006	Pit	NL	142	543	148	27	1	8	(5 | 3)	201	70	35	58	33	0	65	4	9	5	4	3	.57	15	.273	.316	.370
2007	Pit	NL	135	477	141	29	2	12	(3 | 9)	210	67	56	70	38	9	46	6	7	7	2	5	.29	8	.296	.350	.440
2008	Pit	NL	87	305	83	18	1	1	(1 | 0)	106	24	22	32	13	0	27	5	6	1	2	2	.50	6	.272	.312	.348
2009	2 Tms		106	373	95	23	1	5	(2 | 3)	135	37	39	40	21	2	48	0	5	3	3	1	.75	6	.255	.292	.362
2010	Sea	AL	61	193	48	11	1	0	(0 | 0)	61	17	14	16	7	0	35	3	5	3	1	2	.33	2	.249	.282	.316
2011	2 Tms		79	214	52	9	0	0	(0 | 0)	61	25	11	19	10	0	39	0	6	2	5	2	.71	2	.243	.274	.285
2012	Atl	NL	40	71	12	1	1	0	(0 | 0)	15	4	4	0	2	1	12	0	3	1	0	-	-	1	.169	.189	.211
09	Pit	NL	75	266	71	18	1	4	(1 | 3)	103	26	31	31	15	2	31	0	3	2	2	1	.67	4	.267	.304	.387
09	Sea	AL	31	107	24	5	0	1	(1 | 0)	32	11	8	9	6	0	17	0	2	1	1	0	1.00	2	.224	.263	.299
11	Sea	AL	62	173	43	8	0	0	(0 | 0)	51	22	11	18	9	0	27	0	3	2	5	2	.71	2	.249	.283	.295
11	Atl	NL	17	41	9	1	0	0	(0 | 0)	10	3	0	1	1	0	12	0	3	0	0	-	-	0	.220	.238	.244
	12 ML YEARS		1370	4890	1294	243	34	61	(25 | 36)	1788	565	426	528	270	25	619	36	104	39	43	32	.57	88	.265	.306	.366

Justin Wilson

Pitches: L **Bats:** L **Pos:** RP-8   **Ht:** 6'2" **Wt:** 220 **Born:** 8/18/1987 **Age:** 25

			HOW MUCH HE PITCHED						WHAT HE GAVE UP											THE RESULTS						
Year	Team	Lg	G	GS	CG	GF	IP	BFP	H	R	ER	HR	SH	SF	HB	TBB	IBB	SO	WP	Bk	W	L	Pct	Sh	Sv-Op	Hld	ERC	ERA
2009	Lynbrg	A+	26	26	0	0	116.0	514	118	64	58	14	1	0	7	55	0	94	6	0	6	8	.429	0	0- -	-	4.89	4.50
2010	Altna	AA	27	26	0	0	142.2	600	109	59	49	4	8	7	7	71	0	134	6	1	11	8	.579	0	0- -	-	2.88	3.09
2011	Indy	AAA	30	21	0	5	124.1	557	121	68	57	12	7	3	4	67	1	94	4	0	10	8	.556	0	0- -	-	4.52	4.13
2012	Indy	AAA	29	25	1	0	135.2	564	91	60	57	12	4	6	7	66	1	138	6	0	9	6	.600	1	0- -	-	2.74	3.78
2012	Pit	NL	8	0	0	3	4.2	26	10	1	1	0	1	0	0	3	0	7	1	0	0	0	-	0	0-0	0	11.83	1.93

DeWayne Wise

Bats: L **Throws:** L **Pos:** LF-53; CF-38; RF-11; PH-11; PR-9   **Ht:** 6'0" **Wt:** 200 **Born:** 2/24/1978 **Age:** 35

					BATTING														BASERUNNING				AVERAGES		
Year	Team	Lg	G	AB	H	2B	3B	HR	(Hm	Rd)	TB	R	RBI	RC	TBB	IBB	SO	HBP	SH	SF	SB	CS	SB%	GDP	Avg	OBP	Slg
2012	S-WB*	AAA	21	76	25	7	0	4	(-	-)	44	17	10	17	9	0	16	0	0	0	2	0	1.00	3	.329	.400	.579
2012	Charltt*		7	31	5	1	1	0	(-	-)	8	3	3	1	1	0	8	0	0	1	1	0	1.00	1	.161	.182	.258
2000	Tor	AL	28	22	3	0	0	0	(0	0)	3	3	0	0	1	0	5	1	0	0	1	0	1.00	0	.136	.208	.136
2002	Tor	AL	42	112	20	4	1	3	(2	1)	35	14	13	8	4	0	15	0	0	0	5	0	1.00	0	.179	.207	.313
2004	Atl	NL	77	162	37	9	4	6	(3	3)	72	24	17	20	9	1	28	1	2	1	6	1	.86	1	.228	.272	.444
2006	Cin	NL	31	38	7	2	0	0	(0	0)	9	3	1	0	0	0	6	0	0	0	0	0	-	0	.184	.184	.237
2007	Cin	NL	5	5	1	0	1	0	(0	0)	3	1	1	1	1	1	1	0	0	0	0	0	-	0	.200	.333	.600
2008	CWS	AL	57	129	32	4	2	6	(2	4)	58	20	18	14	8	0	32	1	3	2	9	0	1.00	5	.248	.293	.450
2009	CWS	AL	84	142	32	8	3	2	(2	0)	52	17	11	10	3	0	27	4	4	0	4	5	.44	1	.225	.262	.366
2010	Tor	AL	52	112	28	3	2	3	(1	2)	44	20	14	17	4	0	29	1	1	0	4	0	1.00	1	.250	.282	.393
2011	2 Tms		69	99	20	2	1	2	(0	2)	30	10	7	5	3	0	36	1	0	1	6	2	.75	0	.202	.231	.303
2012	2 Tms	AL	101	224	58	10	2	8	(5	3)	96	31	30	29	11	0	52	1	0	3	19	4	.83	2	.259	.293	.429
11	Fla	NL	49	67	16	2	0	0	(0	0)	18	6	5	5	3	0	21	1	0	1	4	2	.67	0	.239	.278	.269
11	Tor	AL	20	32	4	0	1	2	(0	2)	12	4	2	0	0	0	15	0	0	0	2	0	1.00	0	.125	.125	.375
12	NYY	AL	56	61	16	3	1	3	(2	1)	30	11	8	10	2	0	12	0	0	0	7	0	1.00	1	.262	.286	.492
12	CWS	AL	45	163	42	7	1	5	(3	2)	66	20	22	19	9	0	40	1	0	3	12	4	.75	1	.258	.295	.405
	Postseason		8	12	3	2	0	1	(0	1)	8	3	5	3	1	0	4	0	0	0	1	0	1.00	0	.250	.308	.667
	10 ML YEARS		546	1045	238	42	16	30	(15	15)	402	143	112	104	44	2	231	10	12	7	54	12	.82	12	.228	.264	.385

Randy Wolf

Pitches: L **Bats:** L **Pos:** SP-26; RP-4
Ht: 6'0" **Wt:** 205 **Born:** 8/22/1976 **Age:** 36

Year	Team	Lg	G	GS	CG	GF	IP	BFP	H	R	ER	HR	SH	SF	HB	TBB	IBB	SO	WP	Bk	W	L	Pct	Sh	Sv-Op	Hld	ERC	ERA
1999	Phi	NL	22	21	0	0	121.2	552	126	78	75	20	5	1	5	67	0	116	4	0	6	9	.400	0	0-0	0	5.54	5.55
2000	Phi	NL	32	32	1	0	206.1	889	210	107	100	25	10	8	8	83	2	160	1	0	11	9	.550	0	0-0	0	4.54	4.36
2001	Phi	NL	28	25	4	1	163.0	684	150	74	67	15	11	7	10	51	4	152	1	0	10	11	.476	2	0-0	0	3.46	3.70
2002	Phi	NL	31	31	3	0	210.2	855	172	77	75	23	7	6	7	63	5	172	4	0	11	9	.550	2	0-0	0	2.88	3.20
2003	Phi	NL	33	33	2	0	200.0	850	176	101	94	27	8	4	6	78	4	177	6	0	16	10	.615	2	0-0	0	3.67	4.23
2004	Phi	NL	23	23	1	0	136.2	585	145	73	65	20	6	3	5	36	4	89	2	0	5	8	.385	1	0-0	0	4.29	4.28
2005	Phi	NL	13	13	0	0	80.0	346	87	40	39	14	4	1	6	26	2	61	1	0	6	4	.600	0	0-0	0	5.17	4.39
2006	Phi	NL	12	12	0	0	56.2	261	63	37	35	13	2	3	2	33	2	44	2	0	4	0	1.000	0	0-0	0	6.63	5.56
2007	LAD	NL	18	18	0	0	102.2	458	110	55	54	10	5	5	6	39	2	94	4	0	9	6	.600	0	0-0	0	4.52	4.73
2008	2 Tms	NL	33	33	1	0	190.1	823	191	100	91	21	10	4	12	71	4	162	3	0	12	12	.500	1	0-0	0	4.30	4.30
2009	LAD	NL	34	34	0	0	214.1	862	178	81	77	24	12	2	6	58	1	160	4	0	11	7	.611	0	0-0	0	2.89	3.23
2010	Mil	NL	34	34	1	0	215.2	936	213	107	100	29	9	6	9	87	6	142	2	0	13	12	.520	1	0-0	0	4.39	4.17
2011	Mil	NL	33	33	0	0	212.1	903	214	95	87	23	13	6	13	66	1	134	4	1	13	10	.565	0	0-0	0	4.10	3.69
2012	2 Tms	NL	30	26	0	1	157.2	699	196	103	99	23	10	4	7	52	1	104	2	2	5	10	.333	0	0-0	0	5.85	5.65
08	SD	NL	21	21	0	0	119.2	522	123	69	63	14	6	2	8	47	0	105	2	0	6	10	.375	0	0-0	0	4.63	4.74
08	Hou	NL	12	12	1	0	70.2	301	68	31	28	7	4	2	4	24	4	57	1	0	6	2	.750	1	0-0	0	3.77	3.57
12	Mil	NL	25	24	0	0	142.1	633	179	94	90	21	8	4	6	45	1	96	2	2	3	10	.231	0	0-0	0	5.86	5.69
12	Bal	AL	5	2	0	1	15.1	66	17	9	9	2	2	0	1	7	0	8	0	0	2	0	1.000	0	0-0	0	5.74	5.28
	Postseason		4	4	0	0	19.0	92	24	14	14	5	1	0	1	11	2	12	0	0	1	1	.500	0	0-0	0	7.71	6.63
14 ML YEARS			376	368	13	2	2268.0	9703	2231	1128	1058	287	112	60	102	810	38	1767	40	3	132	117	.530	9	0-0	0	4.17	4.20

Blake Wood

Pitches: R **Bats:** R **Pos:** P
Ht: 6'5" **Wt:** 240 **Born:** 8/8/1985 **Age:** 27

Year	Team	Lg	G	GS	CG	GF	IP	BFP	H	R	ER	HR	SH	SF	HB	TBB	IBB	SO	WP	Bk	W	L	Pct	Sh	Sv-Op	Hld	ERC	ERA
2006	Idaho	R+	12	12	0	0	52.0	224	50	28	26	1	2	3	10	15	0	46	2	0	3	1	.750	0	0--	-	3.63	4.50
2007	Royals	R	4	4	0	0	9.2	36	9	2	0	0	0	0	0	0	0	15	0	0	0	0	-	0	0--	-	1.78	0.00
2007	Burlgtn	A	7	7	0	0	35.2	152	32	12	12	3	1	0	3	14	0	26	0	0	2	1	.667	0	0--	-	3.72	3.03
2007	Wilmg	A+	2	2	0	0	9.2	41	9	5	5	1	0	0	3	3	0	11	0	0	0	1	.000	0	0--	-	4.84	4.66
2008	Wilmg	A+	10	10	0	0	57.1	212	32	17	17	3	1	3	2	15	0	63	6	0	3	2	.600	0	0--	-	1.43	2.67
2008	NWArk	AA	18	18	2	0	86.2	383	96	55	51	7	3	2	7	32	0	76	11	0	5	7	.417	2	0--	-	4.79	5.30
2009	NWArk	AA	17	13	1	3	78.2	338	92	52	51	8	6	1	5	27	1	49	7	0	2	8	.200	0	0--	-	5.30	5.83
2009	Royals	R	3	2	0	0	4.0	18	4	1	0	0	0	1	0	1	0	4	2	0	0	1	.000	0	0--	-	2.58	0.00
2010	Omha	AAA	12	0	0	10	16.2	67	12	5	4	0	1	1	0	7	0	12	1	0	2	1	.667	0	5--	-	2.09	2.16
2011	Omha	AAA	3	0	0	0	5.0	15	2	0	0	0	0	0	0	0	0	6	0	0	0	0	-	0	0--	-	0.40	0.00
2010	KC	AL	51	0	0	13	49.2	220	54	29	28	6	2	6	1	22	5	31	3	0	1	3	.250	0	0-4	15	4.83	5.07
2011	KC	AL	55	0	0	20	69.2	303	66	30	29	5	5	3	3	32	7	62	2	0	5	3	.625	0	1-3	5	3.82	3.75
2 ML YEARS			106	0	0	33	119.1	523	120	59	57	11	7	9	4	54	12	93	5	0	6	6	.500	0	1-7	20	4.23	4.30

Kerry Wood

Pitches: R **Bats:** R **Pos:** RP-10
Ht: 6'5" **Wt:** 210 **Born:** 6/16/1977 **Age:** 36

Year	Team	Lg	G	GS	CG	GF	IP	BFP	H	R	ER	HR	SH	SF	HB	TBB	IBB	SO	WP	Bk	W	L	Pct	Sh	Sv-Op	Hld	ERC	ERA
1998	ChC	NL	26	26	1	0	166.2	699	117	69	63	14	2	4	11	85	1	233	6	3	13	6	.684	1	0-0	0	3.03	3.40
2000	ChC	NL	23	23	1	0	137.0	603	112	77	73	17	7	5	9	87	0	132	5	1	8	7	.533	0	0-0	0	4.43	4.80
2001	ChC	NL	28	28	1	0	174.1	740	127	70	65	16	4	5	10	92	3	217	9	0	12	6	.667	1	0-0	0	3.22	3.36
2002	ChC	NL	33	33	4	0	213.2	895	169	92	87	22	13	5	16	97	5	217	8	1	12	11	.522	1	0-0	0	3.46	3.66
2003	ChC	NL	32	32	4	0	211.0	887	152	77	75	24	11	6	21	100	2	266	10	0	14	11	.560	2	0-0	0	3.31	3.20
2004	ChC	NL	22	22	0	0	140.1	595	127	62	58	16	6	6	11	51	0	144	7	0	8	9	.471	0	0-0	0	3.83	3.72
2005	ChC	NL	21	10	0	4	66.0	273	52	32	31	14	2	1	2	26	0	77	0	0	3	4	.429	0	0-0	4	3.75	4.23
2006	ChC	NL	4	4	0	0	19.2	86	19	13	9	5	0	2	1	8	0	13	1	0	1	2	.333	0	0-0	0	5.17	4.12
2007	ChC	NL	22	0	0	2	24.1	101	18	9	9	0	1	0	0	13	1	24	1	0	1	1	.500	0	0-0	0	2.49	3.33
2008	ChC	NL	65	0	0	56	66.1	276	54	24	24	3	2	2	7	18	4	84	1	0	5	4	.556	0	34-40	0	2.52	3.26
2009	Cle	AL	58	0	0	50	55.0	241	48	26	26	7	1	3	3	28	0	63	5	0	3	3	.500	0	20-26	0	4.16	4.25
2010	2 Tms	AL	47	0	0	19	46.0	201	35	17	16	4	2	0	3	29	4	49	5	1	3	4	.429	0	8-12	11	3.65	3.13
2011	ChC	NL	55	0	0	7	51.0	224	45	23	19	5	3	3	5	21	2	57	5	0	3	5	.375	0	1-7	21	3.69	3.35
2012	ChC	NL	10	0	0	0	8.2	42	8	8	8	1	0	1	0	11	0	6	1	0	0	2	.000	0	0-2	3	7.68	8.31
10	Cle	AL	23	0	0	18	20.0	93	21	15	14	3	0	0	2	11	2	18	2	1	1	4	.200	0	8-11	5	5.52	6.30
10	NYY	AL	24	0	0	1	26.0	108	14	2	2	1	2	0	1	18	2	31	3	0	2	0	1.000	0	0-1	10	2.36	0.69
	Postseason		15	5	0	2	44.2	190	35	18	17	3	1	1	0	23	3	45	2	0	2	2	.500	0	0-0	3	2.98	3.43
14 ML YEARS			446	178	11	138	1380.0	5863	1083	599	563	148	54	43	99	666	22	1582	64	6	86	75	.534	5	63-87	39	3.53	3.67

Travis Wood

Pitches: L **Bats:** R **Pos:** SP-26
Ht: 5'11" **Wt:** 175 **Born:** 2/6/1987 **Age:** 26

Year	Team	Lg	G	GS	CG	GF	IP	BFP	H	R	ER	HR	SH	SF	HB	TBB	IBB	SO	WP	Bk	W	L	Pct	Sh	Sv-Op	Hld	ERC	ERA
2012	Iowa*	AAA	7	7	0	0	41.1	176	48	22	21	5	0	1	1	11	0	39	1	1	3	3	.500	0	0--	-	4.83	4.57
2010	Cin	NL	17	17	0	0	102.2	419	85	45	40	9	3	3	4	26	1	86	0	1	5	4	.556	0	0-0	0	2.64	3.51
2011	Cin	NL	22	18	0	2	106.0	463	118	57	57	10	9	7	4	40	5	76	2	0	6	6	.500	0	0-0	0	4.73	4.84
2012	ChC	NL	26	26	0	0	156.0	649	133	80	74	25	9	4	8	54	3	119	2	1	6	13	.316	0	0-0	0	3.65	4.27
	Postseason		1	0	0	0	3.1	12	1	0	0	0	0	0	0	1	1	3	0	0	0	0	-	0	0-0	0	0.38	0.00
3 ML YEARS			65	61	0	2	364.2	1531	336	182	171	44	21	14	16	120	9	281	4	2	17	23	.425	0	0-0	0	3.65	4.22

Vance Worley

Pitches: R **Bats:** R **Pos:** SP-23   **Ht:** 6'2" **Wt:** 230 **Born:** 9/25/1987 **Age:** 25

Year	Team	Lg	G	GS	CG	GF	IP	BFP	H	R	ER	HR	SH	SF	HB	TBB	IBB	SO	WP	Bk	W	L	Pct	Sh	Sv-Op	Hld	ERC	ERA
2010	Phi	NL	5	2	0	2	13.0	51	8	2	2	1	2	0	0	4	0	12	1	0	1	1	.500	0	0-0	1	1.66	1.38
2011	Phi	NL	25	21	1	0	131.2	553	116	47	44	10	9	5	3	46	2	119	2	1	11	3	.786	0	0-0	2	3.12	3.01
2012	Phi	NL	23	23	0	0	133.0	590	154	69	62	12	11	3	6	47	4	107	1	0	6	9	.400	0	0-0	0	4.87	4.20
	Postseason		2	0	0	0	1.1	8	3	1	1	0	0	0	0	1	0	0	0	0	0	0	-	0	0-0	1	12.64	6.75
	3 ML YEARS		53	46	1	2	277.2	1194	278	118	108	23	22	8	9	97	6	238	4	1	18	13	.581	0	0-0	2	3.85	3.50

Danny Worth

Bats: R **Throws:** R **Pos:** 2B-31; PR-8; 3B-5; SS-3; PH-2; DH-1   **Ht:** 6'1" **Wt:** 185 **Born:** 9/30/1985 **Age:** 27

Year	Team	Lg	G	AB	H	2B	3B	HR	(Hm	Rd)	TB	R	RBI	RC	TBB	IBB	SO	HBP	SH	SF	SB	CS	SB%	GDP	Avg	OBP	Slg
2012	Toledo*	AAA	60	216	57	15	2	5	(-	-)	91	30	24	35	31	0	58	4	2	2	10	5	.67	4	.264	.364	.421
2010	Det	AL	39	106	27	5	0	2	(2	0)	38	10	8	11	6	0	13	0	3	0	1	2	.33	0	.255	.295	.358
2011	Det	AL	30	37	10	2	0	0	(0	0)	12	6	3	3	2	0	9	0	0	0	0	0	-	0	.270	.308	.324
2012	Det	AL	43	74	16	3	0	0	(0	0)	19	9	3	7	13	0	23	0	2	1	0	0	-	1	.216	.330	.257
	Postseason		1	0	0	0	0	0	(0	0)	0	0	0	0	0	0	0	0	0	0	0	0	-	0	-	-	-
	3 ML YEARS		112	217	53	10	0	2	(2	0)	69	25	14	21	21	0	45	0	5	1	1	2	.33	1	.244	.310	.318

David Wright

Bats: R **Throws:** R **Pos:** 3B-155; SS-1; PH-1   **Ht:** 6'0" **Wt:** 210 **Born:** 12/20/1982 **Age:** 30

Year	Team	Lg	G	AB	H	2B	3B	HR	(Hm	Rd)	TB	R	RBI	RC	TBB	IBB	SO	HBP	SH	SF	SB	CS	SB%	GDP	Avg	OBP	Slg
2004	NYM	NL	69	263	77	17	1	14	(8	6)	138	41	40	42	14	0	40	3	0	3	6	0	1.00	7	.293	.332	.525
2005	NYM	NL	160	575	176	42	1	27	(12	15)	301	99	102	105	72	2	113	7	0	3	17	7	.71	16	.306	.388	.523
2006	NYM	NL	154	582	181	40	5	26	(13	13)	309	96	116	119	66	13	113	5	0	8	20	5	.80	15	.311	.381	.531
2007	NYM	NL	160	604	196	42	1	30	(16	14)	330	113	107	127	94	6	115	6	0	7	34	5	.87	14	.325	.416	.546
2008	NYM	NL	160	626	189	42	2	33	(21	12)	334	115	124	116	94	5	118	4	0	11	15	5	.75	15	.302	.390	.534
2009	NYM	NL	144	535	164	39	3	10	(5	5)	239	88	72	86	74	8	140	3	0	6	27	9	.75	16	.307	.390	.447
2010	NYM	NL	157	587	166	36	3	29	(12	17)	295	87	103	97	69	9	161	2	0	12	19	11	.63	12	.283	.354	.503
2011	NYM	NL	102	389	99	23	1	14	(5	9)	166	60	61	58	52	4	97	3	0	3	13	2	.87	5	.254	.345	.427
2012	NYM	NL	156	581	178	41	2	21	(12	9)	286	91	93	105	81	16	112	3	0	5	15	10	.60	15	.306	.391	.492
	Postseason		10	37	8	3	0	1	(0	1)	14	3	6	5	5	1	8	0	0	0	0	0	-	0	.216	.310	.378
	9 ML YEARS		1262	4742	1426	322	19	204	(104	100)	2398	790	818	855	616	63	1009	36	0	58	166	54	.75	115	.301	.381	.506

Jamey Wright

Pitches: R **Bats:** R **Pos:** RP-66   **Ht:** 6'6" **Wt:** 235 **Born:** 12/24/1974 **Age:** 38

Year	Team	Lg	G	GS	CG	GF	IP	BFP	H	R	ER	HR	SH	SF	HB	TBB	IBB	SO	WP	Bk	W	L	Pct	Sh	Sv-Op	Hld	ERC	ERA
1996	Col	NL	16	15	0	0	91.1	406	105	60	50	8	4	2	7	41	1	45	1	2	4	4	.500	0	0-0	1	5.50	4.93
1997	Col	NL	26	26	1	0	149.2	698	198	113	104	19	8	3	11	71	3	59	6	2	8	12	.400	0	0-0	0	6.96	6.25
1998	Col	NL	34	34	1	0	206.1	919	235	143	130	24	8	6	11	95	3	86	6	3	9	14	.391	0	0-0	0	5.57	5.67
1999	Col	NL	16	16	0	0	94.1	423	110	52	51	10	3	4	4	54	3	49	3	0	4	3	.571	0	0-0	0	6.19	4.87
2000	Mil	NL	26	25	0	1	164.2	718	157	81	75	12	4	6	18	88	5	96	9	2	7	9	.438	0	0-0	0	4.67	4.10
2001	Mil	NL	33	33	1	0	194.2	868	201	115	106	26	7	5	20	98	10	129	6	1	11	12	.478	1	0-0	0	5.36	4.90
2002	2 Tms	NL	23	22	1	0	129.1	585	130	80	76	17	9	6	11	75	9	77	9	0	7	13	.350	1	0-0	0	5.35	5.29
2003	KC	AL	4	4	2	0	25.1	106	23	14	12	1	0	0	1	11	0	19	0	0	1	2	.333	1	0-0	0	3.53	4.26
2004	Col	NL	14	14	0	0	78.2	363	82	39	36	8	1	1	6	45	3	41	3	0	2	3	.400	0	0-0	0	5.26	4.12
2005	Col	NL	34	27	0	1	171.1	782	201	119	104	22	4	3	15	81	4	101	2	2	8	16	.333	0	0-0	0	6.02	5.46
2006	SF	NL	34	21	0	2	156.0	676	167	95	90	16	5	4	10	64	4	79	6	0	6	10	.375	0	0-0	0	4.89	5.19
2007	Tex	AL	20	9	0	3	77.0	330	72	35	31	6	3	2	5	41	2	39	4	0	4	5	.444	0	0-0	1	4.44	3.62
2008	Tex	AL	75	0	0	17	84.1	379	93	57	48	5	4	4	8	35	3	60	5	0	8	7	.533	0	0-6	17	4.74	5.12
2009	KC	AL	65	0	0	14	79.0	350	73	51	38	8	4	0	7	44	5	60	7	0	3	5	.375	0	0-3	12	4.56	4.33
2010	2 Tms	NL	46	0	0	17	56.1	249	55	33	27	3	3	3	3	25	1	28	4	1	1	3	.250	0	0-1	9	3.75	4.17
2011	Sea	AL	60	0	0	19	68.1	286	61	26	24	6	2	1	5	30	3	48	4	0	2	3	.400	0	1-5	16	3.89	3.16
2012	LAD	NL	66	0	0	22	67.2	306	72	35	28	2	3	2	4	30	7	54	2	0	5	3	.625	0	0-0	6	4.07	3.72
02	Mil	NL	19	19	1	0	114.1	515	115	72	68	15	9	6	11	63	8	69	8	0	5	13	.278	1	0-0	0	5.28	5.35
02	StL	NL	4	3	0	0	15.0	70	15	8	8	2	0	0	0	12	1	8	1	0	2	0	1.000	0	0-0	0	5.87	4.80
10	Cle	AL	18	0	0	9	21.1	98	25	18	13	1	1	1	2	9	0	9	1	0	1	2	.333	0	0-0	1	5.10	5.48
10	Sea	AL	28	0	0	8	37.0	151	30	15	14	2	2	2	1	16	1	19	3	1	0	1	.000	0	0-1	8	3.03	3.41
	17 ML YEARS		592	246	6	96	1896.1	8442	2035	1148	1030	193	71	52	146	928	66	1070	77	13	90	124	.421	3	1-15	63	5.22	4.89

Wesley Wright

Pitches: L **Bats:** R **Pos:** RP-77   **Ht:** 5'11" **Wt:** 180 **Born:** 1/28/1985 **Age:** 28

Year	Team	Lg	G	GS	CG	GF	IP	BFP	H	R	ER	HR	SH	SF	HB	TBB	IBB	SO	WP	Bk	W	L	Pct	Sh	Sv-Op	Hld	ERC	ERA
2008	Hou	NL	71	0	0	15	55.2	250	45	34	31	8	1	4	4	34	4	57	2	1	4	3	.571	0	1-1	13	4.21	5.01
2009	Hou	NL	49	0	0	5	44.2	204	53	27	27	9	1	0	2	25	3	47	2	0	3	4	.429	0	0-2	6	6.64	5.44
2010	Hou	NL	14	4	0	3	33.0	148	37	27	21	6	2	1	3	13	0	29	0	0	1	2	.333	0	0-0	0	5.78	5.73
2011	Hou	NL	21	0	0	5	12.0	44	6	2	2	1	0	0	0	5	0	11	1	0	0	0	-	0	0-1	3	1.68	1.50
2012	Hou	NL	77	0	0	13	52.1	223	45	20	19	4	1	0	6	17	0	54	1	0	2	2	.500	0	1-2	19	3.26	3.27
	5 ML YEARS		232	4	0	41	197.2	869	186	110	100	28	4	4	13	94	7	198	6	1	10	11	.476	0	2-6	41	4.54	4.55

Kevin Youkilis

Bats: R **Throws:** R **Pos:** 3B-111; 1B-26; PH-1   YOU-kih-liss   **Ht:** 6'1" **Wt:** 220 **Born:** 3/15/1979 **Age:** 34

								BATTING												BASERUNNING				AVERAGES		
Year	Team	Lg	G	AB	H	2B	3B	HR	(Hm Rd)	TB	R	RBI	RC	TBB	IBB	SO	HBP	SH	SF	SB	CS	SB%	GDP	Avg	OBP	Slg
2012	Pwtckt*	AAA	4	11	4	2	0	0	(- -)	6	1	1	2	3	0	4	0	0	0	0	1	.00	0	.364	.500	.545
2004	Bos	AL	72	208	54	11	0	7	(2 5)	86	38	35	36	33	0	45	4	0	3	0	1	.00	1	.260	.367	.413
2005	Bos	AL	44	79	22	7	0	1	(0 1)	32	11	9	13	14	0	19	2	0	0	0	1	.00	0	.278	.400	.405
2006	Bos	AL	147	569	159	42	2	13	(6 7)	244	100	72	104	91	0	120	9	0	11	5	2	.71	12	.279	.381	.429
2007	Bos	AL	145	528	152	35	2	16	(8 8)	239	85	83	101	77	0	105	15	0	5	4	2	.67	9	.288	.390	.453
2008	Bos	AL	145	538	168	43	4	29	(17 12)	306	91	115	120	62	7	108	12	0	9	3	5	.38	11	.312	.390	.569
2009	Bos	AL	136	491	150	36	1	27	(14 13)	269	99	94	114	77	6	125	16	0	4	7	2	.78	9	.305	.413	.548
2010	Bos	AL	102	362	111	26	5	19	(8 11)	204	77	62	77	58	3	67	10	0	5	4	1	.80	4	.307	.411	.564
2011	Bos	AL	120	431	111	32	2	17	(8 9)	198	68	80	81	68	3	100	14	0	4	3	0	1.00	14	.258	.373	.459
2012	2 Tms	AL	122	438	103	15	2	19	(12 7)	179	72	60	63	51	2	108	17	0	3	0	0	-	10	.235	.336	.409
12	Bos	AL	42	146	34	7	1	4	(2 2)	55	25	14	17	14	0	39	4	0	1	0	0	-	4	.233	.315	.377
12	CWS	AL	80	292	69	8	1	15	(10 5)	124	47	46	46	37	2	69	13	0	2	0	0	-	6	.236	.346	.425
	Postseason		29	111	34	9	1	6	(2 4)	63	22	17	20	13	0	18	0	0	1	0	0	-	4	.306	.376	.568
	9 ML YEARS		1033	3644	1030	247	18	148	(75 73)	1757	641	610	709	531	21	797	99	0	44	26	14	.65	70	.283	.384	.482

Chris Young

Pitches: R **Bats:** R **Pos:** SP-20   **Ht:** 6'10" **Wt:** 260 **Born:** 5/25/1979 **Age:** 34

			HOW MUCH HE PITCHED						WHAT HE GAVE UP											THE RESULTS							
Year	Team	Lg	G	GS	CG	GF	IP	BFP	H	R	ER	HR	SH	SF	HB	TBB	IBB	SO	WP	Bk	W	L	Pct	Sh	Sv-Op Hld	ERC	ERA
2012	StLuci*	A+	3	3	0	0	17.0	67	17	6	6	1	0	0	1	2	0	7	1	1	1	0	1.000	0	0- -	3.09	3.18
2012	Buffalo*	AAA	1	1	0	0	6.0	24	2	0	0	0	0	0	0	3	0	2	0	0	0	0	-	0	0- -	0.92	0.00
2004	Tex	AL	7	7	0	0	36.1	158	36	21	19	7	1	0	2	10	0	27	1	0	3	2	.600	0	0-0	4.26	4.71
2005	Tex	AL	31	31	0	0	164.2	700	162	84	78	19	2	4	7	45	2	137	3	0	12	7	.632	0	0-0	3.71	4.26
2006	SD	NL	31	31	0	0	179.1	735	134	72	69	28	8	3	6	69	4	164	6	1	11	5	.688	0	0-0	3.12	3.46
2007	SD	NL	30	30	0	0	173.0	705	118	66	60	10	3	6	7	72	0	167	7	4	9	8	.529	0	0-0	2.35	3.12
2008	SD	NL	18	18	1	0	102.1	434	84	46	45	13	4	1	1	48	4	93	3	1	7	6	.538	0	0-0	3.50	3.96
2009	SD	NL	14	14	0	0	76.0	336	70	47	44	12	4	5	2	40	3	50	1	0	4	6	.400	0	0-0	4.55	5.21
2010	SD	NL	4	4	0	0	20.0	82	10	2	2	1	1	0	0	11	0	15	1	0	2	0	1.000	0	0-0	1.72	0.90
2011	NYM	NL	4	4	0	0	24.0	95	12	5	5	3	1	0	1	11	0	22	0	0	1	0	1.000	0	0-0	2.04	1.88
2012	NYM	NL	20	20	0	0	115.0	493	119	58	53	16	9	4	2	36	5	80	3	0	4	9	.308	0	0-0	4.19	4.15
	Postseason		1	1	0	0	6.2	25	4	0	0	0	0	0	0	2	1	9	0	0	1	0	1.000	0	0-0	1.22	0.00
	9 ML YEARS		159	159	1	0	890.2	3738	745	401	375	109	33	23	28	342	18	755	25	6	53	43	.552	0	0-0	3.34	3.79

Chris Young

Bats: R **Throws:** R **Pos:** CF-87; PH-14; DH-2   **Ht:** 6'2" **Wt:** 192 **Born:** 9/5/1983 **Age:** 29

								BATTING												BASERUNNING				AVERAGES		
Year	Team	Lg	G	AB	H	2B	3B	HR	(Hm Rd)	TB	R	RBI	RC	TBB	IBB	SO	HBP	SH	SF	SB	CS	SB%	GDP	Avg	OBP	Slg
2012	Visalia*	A+	3	13	4	3	0	1	(- -)	10	3	7	3	0	0	4	0	0	0	0	0	-	0	.308	.308	.769
2012	Reno*	AAA	1	2	0	0	0	0	(- -)	0	0	1	0	0	0	1	0	0	0	0	0	-	0	.000	.000	.000
2006	Ari	NL	30	70	17	4	0	2	(1 1)	27	10	10	11	6	0	12	1	0	1	2	1	.67	0	.243	.308	.386
2007	Ari	NL	148	569	135	29	3	32	(14 18)	266	85	68	68	43	1	141	6	1	5	27	6	.82	5	.237	.295	.467
2008	Ari	NL	160	625	155	42	7	22	(9 13)	277	85	85	84	62	2	165	1	6	5	14	5	.74	10	.248	.315	.443
2009	Ari	NL	134	433	92	28	4	15	(7 8)	173	54	42	47	59	2	133	4	3	2	11	4	.73	3	.212	.311	.400
2010	Ari	NL	156	584	150	33	0	27	(20 7)	264	94	91	86	74	0	145	2	1	3	28	7	.80	10	.257	.341	.452
2011	Ari	NL	156	567	134	38	3	20	(14 6)	238	89	71	84	80	4	139	4	1	7	22	9	.71	3	.236	.331	.420
2012	Ari	NL	101	325	75	24	0	14	(5 9)	141	36	41	46	36	0	79	2	0	0	8	3	.73	4	.231	.311	.434
	Postseason		12	43	14	2	0	5	(3 2)	31	9	9	12	9	0	18	1	0	0	3	2	.60	0	.326	.453	.721
	7 ML YEARS		885	3173	758	198	17	132	(70 62)	1386	453	408	426	360	9	814	20	12	23	112	35	.76	35	.239	.318	.437

Delmon Young

Bats: R **Throws:** R **Pos:** DH-118; LF-31; PH-6   **Ht:** 6'3" **Wt:** 240 **Born:** 9/14/1985 **Age:** 27

								BATTING												BASERUNNING				AVERAGES		
Year	Team	Lg	G	AB	H	2B	3B	HR	(Hm Rd)	TB	R	RBI	RC	TBB	IBB	SO	HBP	SH	SF	SB	CS	SB%	GDP	Avg	OBP	Slg
2006	TB	AL	30	126	40	9	1	3	(1 2)	60	16	10	15	1	0	24	3	0	1	2	2	.50	0	.317	.336	.476
2007	TB	AL	162	645	186	38	0	13	(9 4)	263	65	93	90	26	2	127	3	0	7	10	3	.77	23	.288	.316	.408
2008	Min	AL	152	575	167	28	4	10	(7 3)	233	80	69	74	35	7	105	7	1	5	14	5	.74	19	.290	.336	.405
2009	Min	AL	108	395	112	16	2	12	(7 5)	168	50	60	46	12	1	92	4	0	5	2	5	.29	17	.284	.308	.425
2010	Min	AL	153	570	170	46	1	21	(6 15)	281	77	112	94	28	5	81	6	0	9	5	4	.56	16	.298	.333	.493
2011	2 Tms	AL	124	473	127	21	1	12	(8 4)	186	54	64	57	23	2	85	2	0	5	1	0	1.00	12	.268	.302	.393
2012	Det	AL	151	574	153	27	1	18	(9 9)	236	54	74	62	20	1	112	7	0	7	0	2	.00	20	.267	.296	.411
11	Min	AL	84	305	81	16	0	4	(1 3)	109	26	32	32	18	2	55	0	0	2	1	0	1.00	12	.266	.305	.357
11	Det	AL	40	168	46	5	1	8	(7 1)	77	28	32	25	5	0	30	2	0	3	0	0	-	7	.274	.298	.458
	Postseason		15	58	13	1	1	5	(3 2)	31	8	6	6	4	0	13	1	0	0	1	0	1.00	0	.224	.286	.534
	7 ML YEARS		880	3358	955	185	10	89	(47 42)	1427	396	482	438	145	18	626	32	1	39	34	21	.62	114	.284	.317	.425

Eric Young

Bats: B **Throws:** R **Pos:** PH-61; CF-15; RF-11; LF-8; PR-6; DH-1   **Ht:** 5'10" **Wt:** 180 **Born:** 5/25/1985 **Age:** 28

								BATTING												BASERUNNING				AVERAGES		
Year	Team	Lg	G	AB	H	2B	3B	HR	(Hm Rd)	TB	R	RBI	RC	TBB	IBB	SO	HBP	SH	SF	SB	CS	SB%	GDP	Avg	OBP	Slg
2009	Col	NL	30	57	14	1	0	1	(1 0)	18	7	1	2	4	0	12	0	0	0	4	4	.50	1	.246	.295	.316
2010	Col	NL	51	172	42	5	1	0	(0 0)	49	26	8	16	17	0	32	0	0	0	17	6	.74	2	.244	.312	.285

BATTING																				BASERUNNING				AVERAGES		
Year	Team	Lg	G	AB	H	2B	3B	HR	(Hm Rd)	TB	R	RBI	RC	TBB	IBB	SO	HBP	SH	SF	SB	CS	SB%	GDP	Avg	OBP	Slg
2011	Col	NL	77	198	49	4	3	0	(0 0)	59	34	10	27	26	0	38	3	1	1	27	4	.87	1	.247	.342	.298
2012	Col	NL	98	174	55	7	2	4	(2 2)	78	36	15	29	13	0	31	4	5	0	14	2	.88	1	.316	.377	.448
Postseason			2	1	0	0	0	0	(0 0)	0	0	0	0	0	0	0	0	0	0	0	0	-	0	.000	.000	.000
4 ML YEARS			256	601	160	17	6	5	(3 2)	204	103	34	74	60	0	113	7	6	1	62	16	.79	5	.266	.339	.339

Matt Young

Bats: L **Throws:** R **Pos:** LF-3; 2B-2; PH-2; RF-1   **Ht:** 5'9" **Wt:** 175 **Born:** 10/3/1982 **Age:** 30

BATTING																				BASERUNNING				AVERAGES		
Year	Team	Lg	G	AB	H	2B	3B	HR	(Hm Rd)	TB	R	RBI	RC	TBB	IBB	SO	HBP	SH	SF	SB	CS	SB%	GDP	Avg	OBP	Slg
2005	Rome	A	114	423	132	15	4	6	(- -)	173	85	52	75	66	0	65	7	7	2	10	11	.48	3	.312	.412	.409
2006	MrtlBh	A+	118	424	119	30	2	2	(- -)	159	65	52	71	71	1	55	8	9	6	21	10	.68	11	.281	.389	.375
2006	Missi	AA	13	50	11	1	0	0	(- -)	12	3	6	4	7	0	9	0	1	1	1	1	.50	1	.220	.310	.240
2007	MrtlBh	A+	65	243	68	7	3	1	(- -)	84	29	18	36	37	1	36	4	1	2	14	7	.67	5	.280	.381	.346
2007	Missi	AA	33	95	23	4	1	0	(- -)	29	6	15	8	10	1	18	0	1	2	0	3	.00	6	.242	.308	.305
2008	Missi	AA	135	491	142	16	11	3	(- -)	189	74	50	81	68	0	62	9	7	2	30	12	.71	9	.289	.384	.385
2009	Missi	AA	130	460	133	22	10	4	(- -)	187	81	33	91	94	8	59	12	3	2	42	16	.72	7	.289	.421	.407
2009	Gwnntt	AAA	7	26	5	1	0	1	(- -)	9	6	3	2	3	0	5	0	0	0	1	1	.50	1	.192	.276	.346
2010	Gwnntt	AAA	134	487	146	33	5	3	(- -)	198	88	35	85	57	3	53	7	2	2	39	7	.85	13	.300	.380	.407
2011	Gwnntt	AAA	99	366	100	16	4	1	(- -)	127	64	24	54	57	0	59	2	1	2	17	7	.71	15	.273	.372	.347
2012	Toledo	AAA	96	293	62	6	5	1	(- -)	81	44	24	39	68	4	68	3	3	2	16	4	.80	10	.212	.363	.276
2012	Memp	AAA	13	43	19	2	0	0	(- -)	21	7	5	9	3	0	12	0	0	0	2	0	1.00	0	.442	.478	.488
2011	Atl	NL	20	48	10	1	0	0	(0 0)	11	4	1	3	4	0	6	0	0	0	0	1	.00	0	.208	.269	.229
2012	Det	AL	5	10	1	1	0	0	(0 0)	2	2	1	0	0	0	9	1	0	0	0	0	-	0	.100	.182	.200
2 ML YEARS			25	58	11	2	0	0	(0 0)	13	6	2	3	4	0	15	1	0	0	0	1	.00	0	.190	.254	.224

Michael Young

Bats: R **Throws:** R **Pos:** DH-72; 1B-41; 3B-25; 2B-16; SS-4; PH-1   **Ht:** 6'1" **Wt:** 200 **Born:** 10/19/1976 **Age:** 36

BATTING																				BASERUNNING				AVERAGES		
Year	Team	Lg	G	AB	H	2B	3B	HR	(Hm Rd)	TB	R	RBI	RC	TBB	IBB	SO	HBP	SH	SF	SB	CS	SB%	GDP	Avg	OBP	Slg
2000	Tex	AL	2	2	0	0	0	0	(0 0)	0	0	0	0	0	0	1	0	0	0	0	0	-	0	.000	.000	.000
2001	Tex	AL	106	386	96	18	4	11	(7 4)	155	57	49	45	26	0	91	3	9	5	3	1	.75	9	.249	.298	.402
2002	Tex	AL	156	573	150	26	8	9	(3 6)	219	77	62	64	41	1	112	0	13	6	6	7	.46	14	.262	.308	.382
2003	Tex	AL	160	666	204	33	9	14	(9 5)	297	106	72	106	36	1	103	1	3	7	13	2	.87	14	.306	.339	.446
2004	Tex	AL	160	690	216	33	9	22	(9 13)	333	114	99	124	44	1	89	1	0	4	12	3	.80	11	.313	.353	.483
2005	Tex	AL	159	668	221	40	5	24	(12 12)	343	114	91	131	58	0	91	3	0	3	5	2	.71	20	.331	.385	.513
2006	Tex	AL	162	691	217	52	3	14	(8 6)	317	93	103	120	48	0	96	1	0	8	7	3	.70	27	.314	.356	.459
2007	Tex	AL	156	639	201	37	1	9	(8 1)	267	80	94	107	47	5	107	5	0	1	13	3	.81	21	.315	.366	.418
2008	Tex	AL	155	645	183	36	2	12	(8 4)	259	102	82	86	55	0	109	2	0	6	10	0	1.00	19	.284	.339	.402
2009	Tex	AL	135	541	174	36	2	22	(10 12)	280	76	68	87	47	2	90	1	0	4	8	3	.73	16	.322	.374	.518
2010	Tex	AL	157	656	186	36	3	21	(16 5)	291	99	91	85	50	4	115	1	0	11	4	2	.67	21	.284	.330	.444
2011	Tex	AL	159	631	213	41	6	11	(10 1)	299	88	106	118	47	7	78	2	0	9	6	2	.75	17	.338	.380	.474
2012	Tex	AL	156	611	169	27	3	8	(1 7)	226	79	67	67	33	3	70	1	0	6	2	2	.50	26	.277	.312	.370
Postseason			33	137	33	10	0	3	(2 1)	52	11	19	12	5	0	30	0	0	1	0	0	-	5	.241	.266	.380
13 ML YEARS			1823	7399	2230	415	55	177	(101 76)	3286	1085	984	1140	532	24	1152	21	25	70	89	30	.75	215	.301	.347	.444

Mike Zagurski

Pitches: L **Bats:** L **Pos:** RP-45   zah-GURR-skee   **Ht:** 6'0" **Wt:** 225 **Born:** 1/27/1983 **Age:** 30

HOW MUCH HE PITCHED									WHAT HE GAVE UP											THE RESULTS						
Year	Team	Lg	G	GS	CG	GF	IP	BFP	H	R	ER	HR	SH	SF	HB	TBB	IBB	SO	WP	Bk	W	L	Pct	Sh	Sv-Op	Hld	ERC	ERA
2012	Reno*	AAA	6	0	0	1	9.0	32	3	2	2	1	0	0	1	2	0	7	0	0	0	0	-	0	0- -	-	1.05	2.00
2007	Phi	NL	25	0	0	4	21.1	101	25	14	14	3	1	1	1	11	2	21	2	0	1	0	1.000	0	0-2	5	5.75	5.91
2010	Phi	NL	8	0	0	1	7.0	34	8	8	8	1	1	2	5	0	11	1	0	0	0	-	0	0-0	0	8.12	10.29
2011	Phi	NL	4	0	0	1	3.1	17	4	2	2	1	0	0	0	3	0	4	0	0	0	0	-	0	0-0	0	8.99	5.40
2012	Ari	NL	45	0	0	13	37.1	163	37	24	23	5	2	5	1	19	0	34	5	0	0	0	-	0	0-1	4	4.90	5.54
4 ML YEARS			82	0	0	21	69.0	315	74	48	47	10	4	7	4	38	2	70	8	0	1	0	1.000	0	0-3	9	5.66	6.13

Carlos Zambrano

Pitches: R **Bats:** B **Pos:** SP-20; RP-15   **Ht:** 6'4" **Wt:** 275 **Born:** 6/1/1981 **Age:** 32

HOW MUCH HE PITCHED									WHAT HE GAVE UP											THE RESULTS						
Year	Team	Lg	G	GS	CG	GF	IP	BFP	H	R	ER	HR	SH	SF	HB	TBB	IBB	SO	WP	Bk	W	L	Pct	Sh	Sv-Op	Hld	ERC	ERA
2001	ChC	NL	6	1	0	0	7.2	42	11	13	13	2	1	1	6	8	0	4	1	0	1	2	.333	0	0-1	0	11.86	15.26
2002	ChC	NL	32	16	0	3	108.1	477	94	53	44	9	9	1	4	63	2	93	6	0	4	8	.333	0	0-0	0	4.02	3.66
2003	ChC	NL	32	32	3	0	214.0	907	188	88	74	9	11	6	10	94	12	168	6	1	13	11	.542	1	0-0	0	3.28	3.11
2004	ChC	NL	31	31	1	0	209.2	887	174	73	64	14	10	3	20	81	4	188	6	2	16	8	.667	1	0-0	0	3.20	2.75
2005	ChC	NL	33	33	2	0	223.1	909	170	88	81	21	9	5	8	86	3	202	7	0	14	6	.700	2	0-0	0	2.86	3.26
2006	ChC	NL	33	33	0	0	214.0	917	162	91	80	20	11	4	9	115	4	210	9	1	16	7	.696	0	0-0	0	3.34	3.41
2007	ChC	NL	34	34	1	0	216.1	925	187	100	95	23	6	3	14	101	4	177	3	0	18	13	.581	0	0-0	0	3.88	3.95
2008	ChC	NL	30	30	1	0	188.2	796	172	85	82	18	5	0	6	72	1	130	4	0	14	6	.700	1	0-0	0	3.62	3.91
2009	ChC	NL	28	28	1	0	169.1	733	155	78	71	10	10	5	9	78	6	152	7	0	9	7	.563	1	0-0	0	3.70	3.77
2010	ChC	NL	36	20	0	2	129.2	571	119	55	48	7	9	3	6	69	0	117	7	1	11	6	.647	0	0-0	4	3.97	3.33
2011	ChC	NL	24	24	0	0	145.2	634	154	80	78	19	12	5	5	56	4	101	1	0	9	7	.563	0	0-0	0	4.69	4.82
2012	Mia	NL	35	20	1	5	132.1	591	123	75	66	9	7	4	9	75	1	95	1	0	7	10	.412	1	0-0	2	4.38	4.49
Postseason			5	5	0	0	29.0	132	35	19	14	6	1	1	2	8	0	27	1	0	0	2	.000	0	0-0	0	5.72	4.34
12 ML YEARS			354	302	10	11	1959.0	8389	1709	879	797	161	100	44	102	898	41	1637	58	5	132	91	.592	5	0-1	6	3.65	3.66

Brad Ziegler

Pitches: R Bats: R Pos: RP-77
ZIGG-lerr
Ht: 6'4" Wt: 210 Born: 10/10/1979 Age: 33

Year	Team	Lg	G	GS	CG	GF	IP	BFP	H	R	ER	HR	SH	SF	HB	TBB	IBB	SO	WP	Bk	W	L	Pct	Sh	Sv-Op Hld	ERC	ERA
2008	Oak	AL	47	0	0	21	59.2	229	47	8	7	2	4	3	1	22	3	30	0	0	3	0	1.000	0	11-13 9	2.60	1.06
2009	Oak	AL	69	0	0	23	73.1	313	82	27	25	2	1	3	1	28	4	54	0	0	2	4	.333	0	7-10 14	4.25	3.07
2010	Oak	AL	64	0	0	12	60.2	257	54	24	22	4	1	1	3	28	9	41	0	1	3	7	.300	0	0-4 18	3.48	3.26
2011	2 Tms		66	0	0	16	58.1	239	53	21	14	0	1	2	1	19	3	44	1	0	3	2	.600	0	1-2 10	2.68	2.16
2012	Ari	NL	77	0	0	15	68.2	263	54	21	19	2	2	2	1	21	2	42	1	0	6	1	.857	0	0-2 17	2.33	2.49
11	Oak	AL	43	0	0	12	37.2	160	38	14	10	0	1	1	1	13	3	29	1	0	3	2	.600	0	1-2 6	3.21	2.39
11	Oak	NL	23	0	0	4	20.2	79	15	7	4	0	0	1	0	6	0	15	0	0	0	0	-	0	0-0 4	1.77	1.74
Postseason			2	0	0	0	0.1	7	4	4	4	0	0	0	0	2	1	0	0	1	0	0	-	0	0-0 0	115.8	108.0
5 ML YEARS			323	0	0	87	320.2	1301	290	101	87	10	9	11	7	118	21	211	2	1	17	14	.548	0	19-31 68	3.08	2.44

Ryan Zimmerman

Bats: R Throws: R Pos: 3B-145; PH-1
Ht: 6'3" Wt: 230 Born: 9/28/1984 Age: 28

Year	Team	Lg	G	AB	H	2B	3B	HR	(Hm	Rd)	TB	R	RBI	RC	TBB	IBB	SO	HBP	SH	SF	SB	CS	SB%	GDP	Avg	OBP	Slg
2005	Was	NL	20	58	23	10	0	0	(0	0)	33	6	6	9	3	0	12	0	0	1	0	0	-	1	.397	.419	.569
2006	Was	NL	157	614	176	47	3	20	(10	10)	289	84	110	101	61	7	120	2	1	4	11	8	.58	15	.287	.351	.471
2007	Was	NL	162	653	174	43	5	24	(11	13)	299	99	91	83	61	3	125	3	0	5	4	1	.80	26	.266	.330	.458
2008	Was	NL	106	428	121	24	1	14	(7	7)	189	51	51	48	31	1	71	3	0	4	1	1	.50	12	.283	.333	.442
2009	Was	NL	157	610	178	37	3	33	(17	16)	320	110	106	96	72	9	119	2	0	9	2	0	1.00	22	.292	.364	.525
2010	Was	NL	142	525	161	32	0	25	(9	16)	268	85	85	97	69	6	98	4	0	5	4	1	.80	16	.307	.388	.510
2011	Was	NL	101	395	114	21	2	12	(7	5)	175	52	49	58	41	4	73	1	0	3	3	1	.75	14	.289	.355	.443
2012	Was	NL	145	578	163	36	1	25	(16	9)	276	93	95	84	57	8	116	2	0	4	5	2	.71	20	.282	.346	.478
8 ML YEARS			990	3861	1110	250	15	153	(77	76)	1849	580	593	576	395	38	734	17	1	35	30	14	.68	126	.287	.353	.479

Jordan Zimmermann

Pitches: R Bats: R Pos: SP-32
Ht: 6'2" Wt: 220 Born: 5/23/1986 Age: 27

Year	Team	Lg	G	GS	CG	GF	IP	BFP	H	R	ER	HR	SH	SF	HB	TBB	IBB	SO	WP	Bk	W	L	Pct	Sh	Sv-Op Hld	ERC	ERA
2009	Was	NL	16	16	0	0	91.1	391	95	51	47	10	5	3	4	29	0	92	0	0	3	5	.375	0	0-0 0	4.25	4.63
2010	Was	NL	7	7	0	0	31.0	135	31	20	17	8	1	1	2	10	1	27	0	0	1	2	.333	0	0-0 0	5.02	4.94
2011	Was	NL	26	26	1	0	161.1	662	154	62	57	12	8	2	7	31	2	124	3	1	8	11	.421	0	0-0 0	3.02	3.18
2012	Was	NL	32	32	0	0	195.2	805	186	69	64	18	8	4	8	43	2	153	3	0	12	8	.600	0	0-0 0	3.22	2.94
4 ML YEARS			81	81	1	0	479.1	1993	466	202	185	48	22	10	21	113	5	396	6	1	24	26	.480	0	0-0 0	3.45	3.47

Barry Zito

Pitches: L Bats: L Pos: SP-32
Ht: 6'2" Wt: 205 Born: 5/13/1978 Age: 35

Year	Team	Lg	G	GS	CG	GF	IP	BFP	H	R	ER	HR	SH	SF	HB	TBB	IBB	SO	WP	Bk	W	L	Pct	Sh	Sv-Op Hld	ERC	ERA
2000	Oak	AL	14	14	1	0	92.2	376	64	30	28	6	1	0	2	45	2	78	2	0	7	4	.636	1	0-0 0	2.63	2.72
2001	Oak	AL	35	35	3	0	214.1	902	184	92	83	18	5	4	13	80	0	205	6	1	17	8	.680	2	0-0 0	3.33	3.49
2002	Oak	AL	35	35	1	0	229.1	939	182	79	70	24	9	7	9	78	2	182	2	1	23	5	.821	0	0-0 0	2.92	2.75
2003	Oak	AL	35	35	0	0	231.2	957	186	98	85	19	7	7	6	88	3	146	0	1	14	12	.538	1	0-0 0	2.91	3.30
2004	Oak	AL	34	34	0	0	213.0	926	216	116	106	28	7	9	4	81	2	163	4	1	11	11	.500	0	0-0 0	4.45	4.48
2005	Oak	AL	35	35	0	0	228.1	953	185	106	98	26	8	7	13	89	0	171	4	0	14	13	.519	0	0-0 0	3.32	3.86
2006	Oak	AL	34	34	0	0	221.0	945	211	99	94	27	7	6	13	99	5	151	4	2	16	10	.615	0	0-0 0	4.47	3.83
2007	SF	NL	34	33	0	0	196.2	850	182	105	99	24	12	4	4	83	4	131	5	0	11	13	.458	0	0-0 0	3.91	4.53
2008	SF	NL	32	32	0	0	180.0	818	186	115	103	16	8	14	4	102	10	120	3	0	10	17	.370	0	0-0 0	4.81	5.15
2009	SF	NL	33	33	1	0	192.0	818	179	89	86	21	11	1	8	81	8	154	2	2	10	13	.435	0	0-0 0	4.00	4.03
2010	SF	NL	34	33	1	1	199.1	848	184	97	92	20	13	7	7	84	7	150	7	0	9	14	.391	1	0-0 0	3.85	4.15
2011	SF	NL	13	9	0	3	53.2	225	51	35	35	10	0	2	0	24	1	32	1	0	3	4	.429	0	0-0 0	4.71	5.87
2012	SF	NL	32	32	1	0	184.1	799	186	91	85	20	12	4	5	70	6	114	1	0	15	8	.652	1	0-0 0	4.15	4.15
Postseason			7	7	0	0	44.1	184	34	16	16	6	1	0	3	17	0	33	1	0	4	3	.571	0	0-0 0	3.24	3.25
13 ML YEARS			400	394	12	4	2436.1	10356	2196	1152	1064	259	100	72	93	1004	50	1797	45	7	160	132	.548	5	0-0 0	3.75	3.93

Ben Zobrist

Bats: B Throws: R Pos: RF-71; 2B-58; SS-47; DH-4
ZOH-brist
Ht: 6'3" Wt: 210 Born: 5/26/1981 Age: 32

Year	Team	Lg	G	AB	H	2B	3B	HR	(Hm	Rd)	TB	R	RBI	RC	TBB	IBB	SO	HBP	SH	SF	SB	CS	SB%	GDP	Avg	OBP	Slg
2006	TB	AL	52	183	41	6	2	2	(2	0)	57	10	18	13	10	1	26	0	2	3	2	3	.40	2	.224	.260	.311
2007	TB	AL	31	97	15	2	0	1	(0	1)	20	8	9	0	3	0	21	1	2	2	2	0	1.00	1	.155	.184	.206
2008	TB	AL	62	198	50	10	2	12	(4	8)	100	32	30	31	25	1	37	2	0	2	3	0	1.00	6	.253	.339	.505
2009	TB	AL	152	501	149	28	7	27	(18	9)	272	91	91	109	91	4	104	2	1	4	17	6	.74	7	.297	.405	.543
2010	TB	AL	151	541	129	28	2	10	(3	7)	191	77	75	84	92	1	107	3	7	12	24	3	.89	10	.238	.346	.353
2011	TB	AL	156	588	158	46	6	20	(9	11)	276	99	91	100	77	1	128	2	2	5	19	6	.76	9	.269	.353	.469
2012	TB	AL	157	560	151	39	7	20	(8	12)	264	88	74	102	97	7	103	3	2	6	14	9	.61	13	.270	.377	.471
Postseason			16	48	11	2	0	1	(1	0)	16	4	2	2	4	0	10	1	0	0	0	0	-	0	.229	.302	.333
7 ML YEARS			761	2668	693	159	26	92	(44	48)	1180	405	388	439	395	15	526	13	16	34	81	27	.75	46	.260	.354	.442

2012 Fielding Statistics

We made some subtle changes to the Fielding Statistics section this year corresponding to enhancements in our defensive statistics published in *The Fielding Bible—Volume III*. Among other improvements to the Defensive Runs Saved system, we introduced a new component, Good Fielding Play/Defensive Misplay Runs Saved, which measures the run impact of first baseman scoops of low throws, home run robberies, and catcher blocks of pitches in the dirt, among many other miscellaneous plays recorded by Baseball Info Solutions' video scouts.

The resulting system provides the most comprehensive and objective defensive analysis ever released.

Thanks to his sparkling range and a 141-game errorless streak, Darwin Barney saved the Cubs 28 runs more (28 Defensive Runs Saved) than an average second baseman this year, the highest total in baseball. This effort won him the Fielding Bible Award.

Some details about this section:

We split fielders between "Regulars" and "All Others". Based on a suggestion from a loyal reader, we changed the innings minimums for regulars this year to include more fielders at each position. The new thresholds are at least 750 innings at a given position or 600 innings as a catcher.

Plus/Minus (PM) and Defensive Runs Saved (Runs Saved for short) numbers are supplied for each player, as well as traditional stats such as putouts, assists, and errors. For lineup regulars we list players by position in order of best-to-worst Runs Saved. For each position we evaluate at least three separate aspects of defensive play at the position; we also report each Runs Saved components individually in the following pages. For catchers, we have grouped Bunt Runs Saved and Good Fielding Play/Defensive Misplay Runs Saved together into the "Other" category. A more detailed explanation of Runs Saved can be found in the glossary.

You can find pitcher fielding data in the "Pitchers Hitting, Fielding, and Holding Runners" section.

First Basemen - Regulars

Player	Tm	G	GS	Inn	PO	A	E	DP	Pct.	PM	+/-	Runs Saved GFP/ DME	Bunts/ GDP	Total
Teixeira,Mark	NYY	119	117	1032.0	986	69	1	91	.999	+17	12	3	2	17
Gonzalez,Adrian	TOT	151	139	1246.0	1264	137	3	134	.998	+15	11	3	2	16
Votto,Joey	Cin	109	109	969.0	850	116	6	69	.994	+9	6	5	-2	9
Pujols,Albert	LAA	120	118	1021.2	1013	97	7	95	.994	+8	6	2	0	8
LaRoche,Adam	Was	153	149	1323.1	1259	100	7	113	.995	+5	3	2	3	8
Loney,James	TOT	133	107	982.1	915	74	6	85	.994	+8	6	0	0	6
Belt,Brandon	SF	139	102	976.1	913	73	8	85	.992	+4	3	-1	3	5
Freeman,Freddie	Atl	146	145	1289.1	1294	74	12	122	.991	0	1	3	-1	3
Alonso,Yonder	SD	149	144	1276.1	1269	96	12	77	.991	-3	-2	2	2	2
Goldschmidt,Paul	Ari	139	136	1205.1	1234	65	7	106	.995	+1	1	2	-2	1
Pena,Carlos	TB	153	134	1237.0	1182	95	7	119	.995	+5	3	-2	-1	0
Morneau,Justin	Min	99	99	879.2	879	72	6	105	.994	+2	1	0	-1	0
Smoak,Justin	Sea	131	129	1155.2	1094	70	4	119	.997	-1	-1	2	-1	0
Kotchman,Casey	Cle	137	120	1087.0	1099	108	6	114	.995	-1	0	0	-1	-1
Reynolds,Mark	Bal	108	105	957.0	926	40	5	84	.995	-8	-6	4	0	-2
Davis,Ike	NYM	148	137	1222.1	1157	71	8	106	.994	-4	-3	1	-1	-3
Craig,Allen	StL	91	86	773.2	761	40	4	64	.995	-6	-5	1	1	-3
Fielder,Prince	Det	159	159	1392.2	1256	105	11	113	.992	-3	-2	-2	0	-4
Lee,Carlos	TOT	145	145	1250.2	1219	104	6	114	.995	-6	-4	-1	0	-5
Hart,Corey	Mil	103	97	849.1	733	64	4	67	.995	-7	-5	0	0	-5
Hosmer,Eric	KC	148	142	1277.0	1183	103	9	132	.993	-10	-7	1	1	-5
Konerko,Paul	CWS	105	105	886.0	818	60	1	96	.999	-14	-10	0	-1	-11

Second Basemen - Regulars

Player	Tm	G	GS	Inn	PO	A	E	DP	Pct.	Range	PM	+/-	Runs Saved GFP/ DME	GDP	Total
Barney,Darwin	ChC	155	146	1270.1	311	418	2	96	.997	5.16	+29	22	4	2	28
Cano,Robinson	NYY	154	150	1343.1	285	435	6	92	.992	4.82	+22	17	-2	0	15
Phillips,Brandon	Cin	146	144	1251.0	241	391	5	73	.992	4.55	+13	10	2	-1	11
Ackley,Dustin	Sea	142	142	1259.1	237	395	7	91	.989	4.52	+12	9	0	2	11
Pedroia,Dustin	Bos	139	139	1216.0	228	392	5	100	.992	4.59	+6	5	3	3	11
Ellis,Mark	LAD	110	100	910.1	211	274	3	59	.994	4.79	+11	8	2	0	10
Infante,Omar	TOT	144	141	1246.1	233	452	17	98	.976	4.95	+8	6	-2	2	6
Johnson,Kelly	Tor	136	133	1179.2	247	385	11	100	.983	4.82	+11	9	-3	-1	5
Andino,Robert	Bal	108	96	899.2	183	286	13	66	.973	4.69	+5	4	-1	2	5
Uggla,Dan	Atl	152	151	1348.1	258	471	12	103	.984	4.87	+4	3	1	0	4
Kipnis,Jason	Cle	146	145	1293.1	240	440	6	94	.991	4.73	+6	4	-2	1	3
Espinosa,Danny	Was	126	119	1069.2	193	329	6	67	.989	4.39	+4	3	0	0	3
Kinsler,Ian	Tex	144	144	1265.0	203	386	18	81	.970	4.19	+1	0	0	1	1
Kendrick,Howie	LAA	143	142	1242.0	238	407	14	81	.979	4.67	-4	-2	4	-1	1
Hill,Aaron	Ari	153	151	1336.2	264	487	6	94	.992	5.06	-2	-2	2	-2	-2
Walker,Neil	Pit	125	124	1068.2	234	361	9	76	.985	5.01	-4	-3	-1	0	-4
Scutaro,Marco	TOT	118	109	955.2	230	301	8	72	.985	5.00	-1	0	-3	-3	-6
Beckham,Gordon	CWS	149	148	1308.2	280	411	7	110	.990	4.75	-12	-9	1	2	-6
Murphy,Daniel	NYM	138	129	1127.2	228	325	15	69	.974	4.41	-10	-8	-2	-1	-11
Weeks,Jemile	Oak	113	112	1013.2	181	293	11	63	.977	4.21	-16	-12	-1	-1	-14
Altuve,Jose	Hou	147	142	1226.2	256	410	11	83	.984	4.89	-19	-14	-2	-2	-18
Weeks,Rickie	Mil	152	152	1344.1	236	374	16	78	.974	4.08	-34	-26	-3	-1	-30

Third Basemen - Regulars

Player	Tm	G	GS	Inn	PO	A	E	DP	Pct.	Range	PM	+/-	Runs Saved GFP/ DME	Bunts/ GDP	Total
Lawrie,Brett	Tor	123	123	1072.0	84	274	17	23	.955	3.01	+28	21	-1	0	20
Wright,David	NYM	155	155	1348.1	107	267	10	20	.974	2.50	+19	14	2	0	16
Moustakas,Mike	KC	149	147	1314.1	127	312	15	41	.967	3.01	+20	15	3	-4	14
Beltre,Adrian	Tex	129	129	1125.1	95	209	8	23	.974	2.43	+12	9	0	4	13
Callaspo,Alberto	LAA	131	122	1106.2	77	235	12	19	.963	2.54	+8	6	0	1	7
Ramirez,Aramis	Mil	143	143	1242.1	71	222	7	14	.977	2.12	+4	4	-1	1	4
Freese,David	StL	134	132	1153.2	77	259	18	29	.949	2.62	+1	1	0	1	2
Jones,Chipper	Atl	103	100	895.2	41	181	11	8	.953	2.23	-5	-4	3	1	0
Youkilis,Kevin	TOT	111	107	894.1	62	177	9	20	.964	2.41	-4	-3	1	1	-1
Zimmerman,Ryan	Was	145	144	1280.1	76	284	19	28	.950	2.53	-9	-7	2	4	-1
Headley,Chase	SD	159	159	1397.0	100	315	10	20	.976	2.67	+2	1	-2	-2	-3
Cabrera,Miguel	Det	154	154	1322.0	127	243	13	31	.966	2.52	-11	-8	2	2	-4
Sandoval,Pablo	SF	102	101	842.0	63	207	13	13	.954	2.89	+4	3	-4	-4	-5
Alvarez,Pedro	Pit	145	143	1273.0	73	264	27	23	.926	2.38	-2	-2	-1	-2	-5

Player	Tm	G	GS	Inn	PO	A	E	DP	Pct.	Range	PM	+/-	Runs Saved GFP/DME	Bunts/GDP	Total
Seager,Kyle	Sea	138	137	1208.2	99	226	13	20	.962	2.42	-6	-4	-1	-2	-7
Plouffe,Trevor	Min	95	93	804.2	64	180	17	14	.935	2.73	-12	-9	1	0	-8
Johnson,Chris	TOT	127	123	1069.1	73	223	19	15	.940	2.49	-12	-10	0	-1	-11
Ramirez,Hanley	TOT	98	97	860.1	69	137	9	20	.958	2.15	-17	-13	1	1	-11

Shortstops - Regulars

Player	Tm	G	GS	Inn	PO	A	E	DP	Pct.	Range	PM	+/-	Runs Saved GFP/DME	GDP	Total
Ryan,Brendan	Sea	138	134	1170.2	197	396	9	104	.985	4.56	+27	21	2	4	27
Hardy,J.J.	Bal	158	158	1439.0	244	529	6	113	.992	4.83	+19	14	4	0	18
Escobar,Yunel	Tor	143	140	1250.2	240	431	12	100	.982	4.83	+22	17	-2	-1	14
Aviles,Mike	Bos	128	123	1107.2	207	369	15	89	.975	4.68	+19	14	-2	2	14
Ramirez,Alexei	CWS	158	157	1392.0	227	434	12	93	.982	4.27	+17	12	0	2	14
Barmes,Clint	Pit	142	135	1159.0	147	399	16	72	.972	4.24	+14	11	1	1	13
Cozart,Zack	Cin	138	131	1163.2	204	349	14	68	.975	4.28	+16	12	0	0	12
Crawford,Brandon	SF	139	122	1101.0	196	394	18	74	.970	4.82	+13	10	1	1	12
Andrus,Elvis	Tex	153	150	1333.0	233	414	16	91	.976	4.37	+12	9	-2	1	8
Pennington,Cliff	Oak	93	90	805.0	150	272	9	58	.979	4.72	+5	4	0	1	5
Castro,Starlin	ChC	162	161	1402.2	266	465	27	97	.964	4.69	+12	9	-4	-2	3
Aybar,Erick	LAA	139	137	1189.2	232	359	15	86	.975	4.47	-2	-1	3	1	3
Tejada,Ruben	NYM	112	110	964.2	164	280	12	72	.974	4.14	-4	-3	3	0	0
Peralta,Jhonny	Det	149	145	1277.2	229	359	7	75	.988	4.14	0	0	-1	0	-1
Escobar,Alcides	KC	155	155	1379.2	242	408	19	97	.972	4.24	-3	-3	1	0	-2
Lowrie,Jed	Hou	93	90	773.1	102	284	8	48	.980	4.49	-1	-1	-2	0	-3
Cabrera,Everth	SD	111	104	915.1	140	315	16	34	.966	4.47	0	0	-1	-3	-4
Furcal,Rafael	StL	120	116	1034.1	173	349	15	68	.972	4.54	-5	-4	0	0	-4
Cabrera,Asdrubal	Cle	136	133	1161.1	224	408	19	99	.971	4.90	-7	-6	-1	2	-5
Desmond,Ian	Was	128	126	1139.1	171	306	15	65	.970	3.77	-9	-7	0	1	-6
Rollins,Jimmy	Phi	156	152	1364.0	204	377	13	74	.978	3.83	-14	-10	3	-1	-8
Reyes,Jose	Mia	160	160	1410.2	226	419	18	105	.973	4.12	-18	-14	-2	0	-16
Jeter,Derek	NYY	135	133	1186.1	172	324	10	67	.980	3.76	-26	-20	3	-1	-18

Left Fielders - Regulars

Player	Tm	G	GS	Inn	PO	A	E	DP	Pct.	Range	PM	+/-	Runs Saved GFP/DME	Throws	Total
Gordon,Alex	KC	160	159	1424.1	319	17	2	3	.994	2.12	+14	8	7	9	24
Prado,Martin	Atl	119	111	985.2	179	9	3	1	.984	1.72	+7	4	3	5	12
Jennings,Desmond	TB	111	105	932.1	174	4	0	0	1.000	1.72	+17	9	-1	1	9
Braun,Ryan	Mil	151	151	1318.0	276	6	6	1	.979	1.93	+16	9	-1	-1	7
Murphy,David	Tex	120	106	913.0	177	4	1	2	.995	1.78	+14	8	0	-1	7
Pierre,Juan	Phi	107	98	799.2	156	1	1	0	.994	1.77	+2	1	1	0	2
Viciedo,Dayan	CWS	131	129	1093.0	233	13	2	0	.992	2.03	0	0	0	2	2
Davis,Rajai	Tor	114	96	856.1	171	8	7	1	.962	1.88	-11	-6	2	5	1
Cabrera,Melky	SF	106	101	898.0	185	6	4	3	.979	1.91	-7	-4	1	2	-1
Martinez,J.D.	Hou	100	97	833.0	131	9	2	0	.986	1.51	-7	-4	1	1	-2
Soriano,Alfonso	ChC	145	143	1183.0	253	12	1	6	.996	2.02	-6	-3	-1	-1	-5
Ludwick,Ryan	Cin	108	107	929.1	191	0	1	0	.995	1.85	-9	-5	-1	1	-5
Holliday,Matt	StL	152	152	1312.2	226	6	3	1	.987	1.59	-10	-6	1	-1	-6
Kubel,Jason	Ari	124	123	1061.1	182	13	1	3	.995	1.65	-20	-11	3	2	-6
Willingham,Josh	Min	119	118	1027.2	237	6	4	2	.984	2.13	-9	-5	-3	-5	-13
Gonzalez,Carlos	Col	131	131	1127.2	207	7	4	0	.982	1.71	-13	-7	-4	-2	-13

Center Fielders - Regulars

Player	Tm	G	GS	Inn	PO	A	E	DP	Pct.	Range	PM	+/-	Runs Saved GFP/DME	Throws	Total
Bourn,Michael	Atl	153	151	1340.1	383	3	2	0	.995	2.59	+37	21	1	2	24
Trout,Mike	LAA	110	108	885.2	264	2	2	1	.993	2.70	+34	19	6	-2	23
Span,Denard	Min	125	122	1073.1	339	6	4	3	.989	2.89	+31	18	1	1	20
Maybin,Cameron	SD	145	136	1210.1	330	4	3	1	.991	2.48	+15	8	4	-3	9
Rasmus,Colby	Tor	145	138	1237.1	304	7	6	1	.981	2.26	+4	3	0	4	7
Jackson,Austin	Det	137	135	1184.0	339	5	1	1	.997	2.61	+8	4	2	-1	5
Torres,Andres	NYM	124	101	904.2	261	6	2	1	.993	2.66	+3	2	0	1	3
Gomez,Carlos	Mil	128	98	911.1	255	9	5	4	.981	2.61	+1	0	0	3	3
Jay,Jon	StL	116	108	993.1	291	1	0	0	1.000	2.65	+5	3	1	-2	2
Stubbs,Drew	Cin	135	123	1107.1	272	5	5	1	.982	2.25	0	0	0	2	2
Crisp,Coco	Oak	97	94	840.0	245	4	2	2	.992	2.67	-4	-2	3	-1	0

Player	Tm	G	GS	Inn	PO	A	E	DP	Pct.	Range	PM	+/-	GFP/DME	Throws	Total
Brantley,Michael	Cle	144	140	1237.0	336	5	1	3	.997	2.48	-7	-4	3	0	-1
Victorino,Shane	TOT	109	103	939.1	247	7	2	3	.992	2.43	-13	-7	1	3	-3
Upton,B.J.	TB	142	141	1254.2	290	10	3	4	.990	2.15	-4	-2	0	-2	-4
McCutchen,Andrew	Pit	156	156	1364.0	367	3	1	1	.997	2.44	-1	0	-2	-3	-5
De Aza,Alejandro	CWS	125	122	1078.2	314	4	3	1	.991	2.65	-3	-2	-2	-1	-5
Pagan,Angel	SF	151	148	1279.1	377	7	5	2	.987	2.70	-3	-1	-3	-2	-6
Fowler,Dexter	Col	131	116	1026.0	257	4	6	2	.978	2.29	-7	-4	-2	-4	-10
Granderson,Curtis	NYY	157	152	1364.1	346	3	0	0	1.000	2.30	-17	-10	1	-1	-10
Saunders,Michael	Sea	113	107	974.0	268	2	4	1	.985	2.49	-23	-13	0	0	-13
Kemp,Matt	LAD	105	105	911.0	208	7	1	1	.995	2.12	-32	-18	1	4	-13
Jones,Adam	Bal	162	161	1458.0	439	7	8	0	.982	2.75	-23	-13	-2	-1	-16

Right Fielders - Regulars

Player	Tm	G	GS	Inn	PO	A	E	DP	Pct.	Range	PM	+/-	GFP/DME	Throws	Total
Reddick,Josh	Oak	136	131	1179.2	275	14	5	3	.983	2.20	+22	13	3	6	22
Heyward,Jason	Atl	154	149	1337.2	331	11	5	4	.986	2.30	+40	23	0	-3	20
Hunter,Torii	LAA	134	128	1112.2	240	14	4	5	.984	2.05	+5	3	3	9	15
Suzuki,Ichiro	TOT	132	117	1072.1	239	4	1	0	.996	2.04	+15	9	2	0	11
Stanton,Giancarlo	Mia	117	116	1034.1	257	6	7	1	.974	2.29	+19	11	-3	2	10
Aoki,Norichika	Mil	107	99	896.0	194	7	2	2	.990	2.02	+12	7	1	0	8
Rios,Alex	CWS	156	156	1369.0	333	9	7	2	.980	2.25	+7	4	4	-1	7
Beltran,Carlos	StL	132	125	1126.2	210	10	2	0	.991	1.76	+4	2	2	3	7
Bautista,Jose	Tor	90	90	775.2	155	11	2	4	.988	1.93	-10	-6	3	6	3
Upton,Justin	Ari	149	148	1280.2	309	6	5	1	.984	2.21	+13	7	-2	-3	2
Ethier,Andre	LAD	146	142	1256.1	234	3	3	1	.988	1.70	+11	6	0	-4	2
Swisher,Nick	NYY	109	107	907.2	214	4	3	0	.986	2.16	+1	1	1	-2	0
Ross,Cody	Bos	96	90	766.2	164	7	1	2	.994	2.01	+1	0	0	0	0
DeJesus,David	ChC	100	86	767.0	168	5	2	1	.989	2.03	+8	5	-2	-4	-1
Bruce,Jay	Cin	154	149	1343.1	297	8	6	1	.981	2.04	-8	-5	0	1	-4
Markakis,Nick	Bal	102	102	926.0	187	3	2	0	.990	1.85	-13	-7	0	0	-7
Boesch,Brennan	Det	121	115	909.2	167	5	2	1	.989	1.70	-16	-9	2	-1	-8
Pence,Hunter	TOT	159	158	1408.1	271	11	7	0	.976	1.80	-17	-10	-2	3	-9
Choo,Shin-Soo	Cle	154	151	1331.2	293	7	2	1	.993	2.03	-20	-11	0	-1	-12
Cruz,Nelson	Tex	151	146	1286.0	286	4	4	2	.987	2.06	-20	-12	-2	2	-12
Francoeur,Jeff	KC	145	144	1283.1	242	19	4	3	.985	1.83	-34	-20	0	8	-12

Catchers - Regulars

Player	Tm	G	GS	Inn	PO	A	E	DP	PB	Pct.	SBA	CS	PCS	CS%	CERA	GFP/DME	SB	Other	Total
Molina,Yadier	StL	136	133	1161.1	962	88	3	12	6	.997	70	32	3	.46	3.60	1	8	7	16
Perez,Salvador	KC	74	74	653.2	522	53	4	4	3	.993	40	15	3	.38	4.35	1	7	1	9
Hanigan,Ryan	Cin	110	98	877.0	781	48	4	6	3	.995	60	26	6	.43	3.04	0	6	1	7
Avila,Alex	Det	113	107	937.2	897	57	6	7	10	.994	107	28	6	.26	3.61	2	2	2	6
Wieters,Matt	Bal	134	132	1188.2	994	52	10	7	5	.991	80	29	3	.36	3.79	-3	6	2	5
Lucroy,Jonathan	Mil	88	80	717.1	714	34	7	4	2	.991	86	16	3	.19	4.25	8	-2	-2	4
Thole,Josh	NYM	100	90	798.1	690	50	6	3	18	.992	70	13	4	.19	3.77	-1	-1	6	4
Ruiz,Carlos	Phi	106	95	856.1	856	73	6	8	5	.994	85	21	12	.25	4.12	5	1	-3	3
Arencibia,J.P.	Tor	94	91	800.0	622	57	4	1	9	.994	65	12	10	.18	4.76	5	-3	1	3
Flores,Jesus	Was	80	75	687.2	648	52	4	5	6	.994	58	7	2	.12	3.35	2	-1	1	2
Santana,Carlos	Cle	100	95	851.1	628	65	7	3	10	.990	93	23	2	.25	4.69	-1	3	0	2
Buck,John	Mia	105	103	915.0	715	57	7	4	7	.991	59	11	7	.19	3.88	1	-1	2	2
Ellis,A.J.	LAD	131	128	1151.0	1007	87	6	12	11	.995	102	28	8	.27	3.30	-1	2	1	2
Suzuki,Kurt	TOT	117	113	1014.0	815	61	5	7	6	.994	85	20	8	.24	3.51	2	4	-4	2
Olivo,Miguel	Sea	73	68	625.2	505	46	5	5	8	.991	66	19	2	.29	3.91	0	4	-4	0
Posey,Buster	SF	114	111	973.0	855	69	8	9	2	.991	118	31	7	.26	3.50	1	2	-3	0
Iannetta,Chris	LAA	78	71	623.0	495	35	2	3	8	.996	59	13	3	.22	3.90	2	-1	-1	0
Castro,Jason	Hou	79	73	646.2	525	40	6	6	8	.989	69	12	1	.17	4.34	-2	-1	3	0
McKenry,Michael	Pit	81	64	607.1	495	41	3	1	2	.994	71	10	3	.14	4.10	4	-2	-2	0
Montero,Miguel	Ari	139	136	1190.0	1008	78	9	8	5	.992	67	23	9	.34	3.87	-3	2	0	-1
Molina,Jose	TB	102	80	709.2	657	41	4	8	6	.994	54	15	4	.28	3.22	-4	4	-1	-1
McCann,Brian	Atl	114	113	994.2	845	51	2	4	6	.998	93	17	7	.18	3.35	-2	-1	2	-1
Rosario,Wilin	Col	105	100	878.0	694	78	13	5	21	.983	88	24	6	.27	5.01	-5	3	1	-1
Napoli,Mike	Tex	72	69	619.1	511	37	4	1	8	.993	50	8	3	.16	4.32	1	-2	-3	-4
Saltalamacchia,J	Bos	104	95	852.0	715	41	7	3	6	.991	95	15	3	.16	4.85	1	-3	-3	-5
Pierzynski,A.J.	CWS	126	121	1071.1	899	71	6	8	8	.994	95	19	8	.20	4.06	-8	2	1	-5
Mauer,Joe	Min	74	72	628.1	425	25	3	5	1	.993	61	5	4	.08	4.90	-1	-3	-2	-6
Martin,Russell	NYY	128	116	1045.0	923	62	6	3	9	.994	79	16	4	.20	4.05	-1	0	-5	-6

Player	Tm	G	GS	Inn	PO	A	E	DP	PB	Pct.	SBA	CS	PCS	CS%	CERA	GFP/ DME	SB	Other	Total
																Runs Saved			
Soto,Geovany	TOT	96	92	806.2	714	37	8	3	2	.989	78	13	8	.17	4.17	-4	-2	-2	-8
Barajas,Rod	Pit	99	98	826.0	700	41	6	4	7	.992	97	4	2	.04	3.77	-1	-10	-1	-12

All Other Fielders

Player	Tm	Pos	G	GS	Inn	PO	A	E	DP	Pct.	Rng	+/-	RS
Abreu, B	TOT	LF	52	48	364	66	2	1	1	.986	1.68	-12	-7
	TOT	RF	2	2	13	4	0	0	0	1.000	2.77	-1	0
Abreu, T	KC	2B	11	10	99	19	32	1	10	.981	4.64	+1	2
	KC	3B	6	4	34	3	10	0	2	1.000	3.44	-1	-2
	KC	SS	4	3	27	5	5	0	3	1.000	3.25	-1	-1
Ackley, D	Sea	1B	11	5	58	51	4	1	5	.982	-	-1	0
Adams, M	StL	1B	24	23	194	210	12	3	13	.987	-	+2	1
Allen, B	TOT	1B	3	2	20	25	2	0	1	1.000	-	+1	1
	TOT	LF	3	3	23	4	0	0	0	1.000	1.57	-2	-1
Amarista, A	TOT	2B	52	43	378	80	99	3	15	.984	4.26	-5	-4
	TOT	3B	1	0	0	0	0	0	0	-	.00	0	0
	TOT	SS	12	8	73	8	28	1	6	.973	4.44	0	0
	TOT	LF	27	7	87	21	1	0	1	1.000	2.27	+3	2
	TOT	CF	11	6	50	8	0	0	0	1.000	1.44	-3	-2
	TOT	RF	4	0	5	3	0	0	0	1.000	5.06	0	0
Anderson, B	StL	1B	1	1	9	5	1	1	1	.857	-	0	-1
Anderson, L	Bos	1B	2	0	3	4	0	0	0	1.000	-	0	0
	Bos	LF	4	1	9	1	0	0	0	1.000	1.00	0	0
Andino, R	Bal	3B	15	9	90	8	13	0	1	1.000	2.09	-1	-1
	Bal	SS	2	2	17	4	7	0	4	1.000	5.82	0	0
	Bal	LF	1	0	1	0	0	0	0	-	.00		0
	Bal	CF	1	0	4	0	0	0	0	-	.00	0	0
Ankiel, R	Was	CF	62	37	382	115	2	2	0	.983	2.76	-10	-7
Aoki, N	Mil	LF	13	7	76	14	0	0	0	1.000	1.66	-2	-1
	Mil	CF	19	13	120	22	1	1	0	.958	1.73	-4	-2
Arias, J	SF	2B	4	2	17	6	7	1	1	.929	6.75	-1	-1
	SF	3B	74	39	404	26	90	4	8	.967	2.58	+4	3
	SF	SS	50	38	328	41	98	4	16	.972	3.81	-10	-7
Avery, X	Bal	LF	27	23	216	49	1	2	0	.962	2.08	0	-2
	Bal	CF	1	0	1	0	0	0	0	-	.00	0	0
Aviles, M	Bos	2B	2	1	10	1	3	0	0	1.000	3.60	0	0
	Bos	3B	1	1	8	0	3	0	0	1.000	3.24	-1	-1
Baker, J	TOT	1B	20	20	156	143	7	2	11	.987	-	-6	-6
	TOT	2B	9	3	36	6	12	0	3	1.000	4.46	-1	-1
	TOT	3B	4	2	19	3	4	1	1	.875	3.32	-1	-1
	TOT	LF	5	3	30	4	0	0	0	1.000	1.20	0	0
	TOT	RF	26	20	155	30	0	0	0	1.000	1.74	0	0
Barajas, R	Pit	1B	1	0	1	1	0	0	0	1.000	-		0
Barmes, C	Pit	1B	1	0	2	0	0	0	0	-	-		0
Barnes, B	Hou	LF	1	0	2	0	0	0	0	-	.00		0
	Hou	CF	32	23	211	65	2	0	1	1.000	2.85	+5	5
	Hou	RF	5	1	54	0	1	0	0	1.000	.64	-2	0
Barney, D	ChC	SS	3	1	11	4	8	1	2	.923	9.82	+2	1
Bartlett, J	SD	SS	27	26	233	32	68	5	12	.952	3.85	-3	-3
Barton, D	Oak	1B	43	33	313	319	17	0	30	1.000	-	+5	2
Bautista, J	Tor	1B	4	0	7	8	2	0	1	1.000	-	0	0
	Tor	3B	1	0	4	0	0	0	0	-	.00	-1	0
Baxter, M	NYM	LF	18	10	99	17	1	1	1	.947	1.64	+1	-2
	NYM	CF	1	1	7	1	0	0	0	1.000	1.29	-1	0
	NYM	RF	45	33	300	63	2	0	1	1.000	1.95	0	2
Bay, J	NYM	LF	65	54	457	113	2	2	0	.983	2.26	-8	-3
Bell, J	Ari	3B	12	12	106	6	18	1	1	.960	2.04	+1	0
Belt, B	SF	LF	4	4	27	4	0	0	0	1.000	1.32	-1	-1
Beltran, C	StL	CF	9	7	47	11	0	0	0	1.000	2.09	-5	-3
Berkman, L	StL	1B	23	22	173	170	13	4	22	.979	-	-2	0
Bernadina, R	Was	LF	57	19	208	39	1	0	0	1.000	1.73	-3	-4
	Was	CF	37	27	263	70	1	0	0	1.000	2.43	+3	2
	Was	RF	7	3	32	8	1	0	1	1.000	2.51	0	1
Berry, Q	Det	LF	64	46	436	97	1	2	0	.980	2.02	-1	-1
	Det	CF	22	20	175	61	1	0	0	1.000	3.18	-5	-4
	Det	RF	5	4	32	9	0	0	0	1.000	2.53	0	0
Betancourt, Y	KC	2B	46	43	382	89	107	5	40	.975	4.61	-13	-10
	KC	3B	8	6	58	3	11	0	1	1.000	2.17	0	0
	KC	SS	1	1	9	1	3	1	1	.800	4.00	-2	-1
Betemit, W	Bal	1B	15	13	125	123	6	1	10	.992	-	+1	0
	Bal	3B	75	69	608	41	115	13	9	.923	2.31	-8	-6
	Bal	LF	5	5	47	8	0	1	0	.889	1.53	+3	0
Bianchi, J	Mil	2B	4	1	13	1	2	0	0	1.000	2.08	0	0
	Mil	3B	6	1	19	3	3	0	0	1.000	2.84	0	0
	Mil	SS	14	13	119	14	34	1	7	.980	3.63	+1	0
Bixler, B	Hou	2B	5	4	41	5	16	0	0	1.000	4.61	0	-1
	Hou	3B	4	1	15	1	0	0	1	1.000	3.45	-1	-1

Player	Tm	Pos	G	GS	Inn	PO	A	E	DP	Pct.	Rng	+/-	RS
	Hou	SS	6	4	43	8	11	0	4	1.000	3.95	-2	-2
	Hou	LF	3	2	18	4	0	0	0	1.000	2.00	0	1
	Hou	RF	9	7	59	11	0	0	0	1.000	1.68	+6	3
Blackmon, C	Col	LF	15	12	114	31	2	0	1	1.000	2.59	0	3
	Col	CF	1	1	8	0	0	0	0	-	.00	0	0
	Col	RF	17	11	107	23	2	0	1	1.000	2.10	+1	2
Blanco, G	SF	LF	53	25	278	44	2	0	0	1.000	1.49	+3	3
	SF	CF	30	14	168	51	0	1	0	.981	2.72	-1	-1
	SF	RF	54	50	431	86	1	1	0	.989	1.82	+11	5
Blanks, K	SD	1B	1	1	9	6	0	0	0	1.000	-	0	0
	SD	LF	1	0	0	0	0	0	0	-	.00		0
Bloomquist, W	Ari	2B	1	1	6	1	0	1	0	.500	1.50	0	-1
	Ari	3B	11	11	94	5	21	1	1	.963	2.48	+1	1
	Ari	SS	64	61	528	85	139	4	31	.982	3.82	-11	-11
	Ari	LF	1	0	5	0	0	0	0	-	.00	0	0
	Ari	RF	1	0	2	0	0	0	0	-	.00		0
Blum, G	Ari	3B	6	5	44	1	13	0	2	1.000	2.86	+2	1
Bogusevic, B	Hou	LF	1	0	2	0	0	0	0	-	.00	0	0
	Hou	CF	20	10	116	32	0	1	0	.970	2.48	+2	-1
	Hou	RF	104	73	689	155	5	4	3	.976	2.09	-1	3
Bonifacio, E	Mia	2B	15	14	122	19	40	3	7	.952	4.33	-1	-1
	Mia	CF	51	50	427	111	1	1	0	.991	2.36	+1	-2
Bourgeois, J	KC	LF	2	1	10	1	0	0	0	1.000	.90	0	0
	KC	CF	23	15	130	43	3	3	1	.939	3.17	-7	-5
Bourjos, P	LAA	CF	90	48	501	164	2	1	1	.994	2.98	+13	9
Brignac, R	TB	2B	1	0	1	0	1	0	0	1.000	9.00	0	0
	TB	3B	4	0	9	0	3	0	0	1.000	3.00	-1	-1
	TB	SS	11	5	54	13	20	1	11	.971	5.50	0	1
	TB	LF	1	0	0	0	0	0	0	-	.00		0
Brown, A	Col	LF	12	9	85	19	3	1	0	.957	2.31	-2	3
	Col	RF	24	19	148	36	0	1	0	.973	2.18	0	0
Brown, C	Was	LF	7	1	18	7	0	0	0	1.000	3.50	0	1
	Was	CF	2	1	12	5	0	0	0	1.000	3.65	+2	1
	Was	RF	2	0	7	2	0	0	0	1.000	2.57	+1	1
Brown, D	Phi	LF	29	13	141	31	3	0	0	1.000	2.16	-4	0
	Phi	RF	38	38	308	63	4	0	1	1.000	1.96	-10	-6
Buck, T	Hou	LF	11	8	71	14	1	0	0	1.000	1.88	+2	2
	Hou	RF	10	9	74	26	0	1	0	.963	3.15	+1	0
Burriss, E	SF	2B	37	30	269	42	65	2	13	.982	3.58	-4	-3
	SF	3B	6	2	28	1	6	1	0	.875	2.25	-2	-2
	SF	SS	6	2	21	6	6	1	1	.923	5.06	-2	-2
	SF	RF	1	0	1	0	0	0	0	-	.00		0
Burroughs, S	Min	1B	1	0	3	4	0	0	1	1.000	-	0	0
	Min	3B	3	3	22	3	5	0	1	1.000	3.27	0	0
Butler, B	KC	1B	20	20	165	147	15	3	18	.982	-	-3	-3
Byrd, M	TOT	CF	47	39	352	104	1	2	0	.981	2.68	+4	3
	TOT	RF	2	1	10	1	0	0	0	1.000	.90	0	0
Cabrera, E	SD	2B	6	5	36	6	11	0	0	1.000	4.21	-1	0
	SD	3B	1	0	2	0	2	0	0	1.000	9.00	0	0
Cabrera, M	SF	RF	11	11	81	13	1	0	0	1.000	1.54	-1	1
Cabrera, M	Det	1B	2	0	3	4	0	0	1	1.000	-	0	0
Cain, L	KC	LF	1	1	10	5	0	0	0	1.000	4.50	0	0
	KC	CF	50	45	403	117	3	4	1	.968	2.68	+14	6
	KC	RF	9	9	80	22	0	0	0	1.000	2.48	+3	2
Cairo, M	Cin	1B	24	16	158	156	14	1	7	.994	-	0	-1
	Cin	2B	8	4	49	15	22	1	7	.974	6.75	+3	1
	Cin	3B	13	10	77	8	12	3	1	.870	2.33	-4	-3
Calhoun, K	LAA	LF	4	2	19	4	0	0	0	1.000	1.89	0	0
	LAA	RF	14	1	33	9	0	0	0	1.000	2.45	+2	1
Campana, T	ChC	LF	11	5	51	9	0	0	0	1.000	1.59	+2	1
	ChC	CF	55	33	326	82	1	0	0	1.000	2.29	+2	1
	ChC	RF	4	0	4	0	0	0	0	-	.00	0	0
Canzler, R	Cle	1B	8	7	56	52	2	1	5	.982	-	0	0
	Cle	LF	11	11	88	20	1	0	0	1.000	2.15	-5	-2
Cardenas, A	ChC	2B	12	7	61	16	15	0	2	1.000	4.52	+2	0
	ChC	3B	1	1	8	1	1	2	0	.500	2.25	-1	-1
	ChC	LF	3	1	11	1	0	0	0	1.000	.82	0	0
Carp, M	Sea	1B	23	23	199	188	13	0	15	1.000	-	+1	1
	Sea	LF	24	21	169	41	1	2	0	.955	2.24	-1	-1
Carpenter, M	StL	1B	44	30	281	316	12	3	32	.991	-	-3	-2
	StL	2B	5	2	18	3	4	0	2	1.000	3.50	-1	-1
	StL	3B	33	22	217	13	44	3	3	.950	2.36	+3	1
	StL	LF	7	3	36	3	1	0	0	1.000	1.00	-1	-1
	StL	RF	15	10	72	16	0	3	0	.842	1.99	-2	-3

Player	Tm	Pos	G	GS	Inn	PO	A	E	DP	Pct.	Rng	+/-	RS
Carrera, E	Cle	LF	36	24	236	68	1	1	0	.986	2.62	+3	0
	Cle	CF	15	13	117	44	0	0	0	1.000	3.38	+3	1
	Cle	RF	1	0	0	0	0	0	0	-	.00	0	0
Carroll, B	Was	CF	3	0	4	0	0	0	0	-	.00	0	0
Carroll, J	Min	2B	66	64	566	115	194	6	46	.981	4.91	+7	9
	Min	3B	44	30	287	25	63	4	10	.957	2.76	+3	4
	Min	SS	37	36	310	53	120	2	29	.989	5.02	+2	1
Carson, M	Min	LF	15	8	75	15	2	0	1	1.000	2.02	+1	3
	Min	RF	9	8	67	10	1	0	0	1.000	1.47	+1	1
Carter, C	Oak	1B	55	51	469	433	14	6	29	.987	-	-4	-5
Casilla, A	Min	2B	96	83	744	178	263	9	81	.980	5.33	+14	15
	Min	3B	4	1	12	0	4	0	1	1.000	3.00	-1	0
Castellanos, A	LAD	LF	11	2	32	6	0	0	0	1.000	1.67	-3	-2
	LAD	RF	4	2	19	5	0	1	0	.833	2.37	0	0
Castillo, W	ChC	1B	1	0	0	0	0	0	0	-	-	0	0
Cedeno, R	NYM	2B	28	18	148	29	45	2	9	.974	4.48	-2	-2
	NYM	3B	3	2	21	1	1	0	0	1.000	.86	+1	0
	NYM	SS	27	22	191	18	52	2	10	.972	3.29	-1	-2
Cespedes, Y	Oak	LF	56	56	468	93	6	3	0	.971	1.90	-6	1
	Oak	CF	48	46	432	128	3	0	0	1.000	2.73	-1	-8
Chambers, A	StL	LF	10	1	32	9	1	0	0	1.000	2.81	+5	3
	StL	CF	10	6	60	14	0	0	0	1.000	2.09	+1	1
	StL	RF	8	1	22	9	0	0	0	1.000	3.57	+2	1
Chavez, E	Bal	LF	35	21	213	37	2	1	0	.975	1.65	-1	1
	Bal	CF	3	0	6	2	0	0	0	1.000	3.00	+1	1
	Bal	RF	21	13	146	36	0	1	0	.973	2.22	+2	0
Chavez, E	NYY	1B	10	6	61	49	5	1	2	.982	-	+1	1
	NYY	3B	64	50	446	36	86	5	5	.961	2.46	-1	-2
Chisenhall, L	Cle	3B	30	28	255	16	54	6	7	.921	2.47	-6	-4
Christian, J	SF	LF	10	4	37	13	0	1	0	.929	3.11	+2	0
	SF	CF	1	0	3	1	0	1	0	.500	3.00	0	0
	SF	RF	8	5	49	14	0	0	0	1.000	2.55	+3	2
Ciriaco, P	Bos	2B	16	11	104	13	29	0	1	1.000	3.63	+2	1
	Bos	3B	35	35	298	28	79	8	9	.930	3.23	-1	-1
	Bos	SS	12	11	95	15	35	1	9	.980	4.70	+2	2
	Bos	LF	2	1	10	1	0	0	0	1.000	.90	0	1
	Bos	CF	3	1	7	6	0	0	0	1.000	7.71	-3	-2
	Bos	RF	2	0	3	0	0	0	0	-	.00	0	0
Clement, J	Pit	1B	1	1	6	7	1	0	0	1.000	-	-1	-1
Clevenger, S	ChC	1B	9	3	35	31	3	0	3	1.000	-	+1	0
	ChC	3B	1	0	0	0	0	0	0	-	.00	0	0
Coghlan, C	Mia	LF	21	12	120	32	0	0	0	1.000	2.39	+1	0
	Mia	CF	13	10	91	20	0	0	0	1.000	1.98	-2	-2
	Mia	RF	2	1	10	2	0	0	0	1.000	1.74	-1	0
Colvin, T	Col	1B	31	18	167	167	7	2	11	.989	-	+4	1
	Col	LF	10	5	52	6	0	0	0	1.000	1.04	-1	-2
	Col	CF	38	32	274	84	2	3	0	.966	2.82	+11	7
	Col	RF	59	44	397	89	6	0	1	1.000	2.15	-1	-2
Conrad, B	TOT	1B	7	4	32	35	1	0	1	1.000	-	0	0
	TOT	2B	13	7	69	14	20	0	3	1.000	4.39	+3	2
	TOT	3B	16	10	96	7	18	2	1	.926	2.34	+1	0
	TOT	SS	1	0	1	0	0	0	0	-	.00		0
Constanza, J	Atl	LF	21	17	150	36	2	0	0	1.000	2.28	+8	7
	Atl	CF	5	3	32	5	0	0	0	1.000	1.41	0	0
Cooper, D	Tor	1B	29	26	225	217	25	1	22	.996	-	-5	-3
Costanzo, M	Cin	1B	2	1	7	9	0	1	0	.900	-	0	-1
Cousins, S	Mia	LF	6	0	11	2	0	0	0	1.000	1.59	+2	1
	Mia	CF	18	8	91	29	0	0	0	1.000	2.87	0	1
	Mia	RF	12	6	58	13	0	0	0	1.000	1.99	-2	-1
Cowgill, C	Oak	LF	16	11	100	27	0	0	0	1.000	2.42	-1	0
	Oak	CF	15	12	98	26	1	0	1	1.000	2.47	-5	-3
	Oak	RF	8	5	56	16	2	0	1	1.000	2.86	+5	6
Craig, A	StL	LF	8	5	47	10	1	0	0	1.000	2.11	-2	-1
	StL	RF	23	21	165	31	0	0	0	1.000	1.68	-3	-3
Crawford, C	Bos	LF	30	30	245	42	0	1	0	.977	1.54	+2	0
Crisp, C	Oak	LF	16	15	132	27	0	1	0	1.000	1.83	+4	1
Cruz, L	LAD	2B	2	2	17	5	9	0	2	1.000	7.41	+2	1
	LAD	3B	51	48	427	29	92	2	9	.984	2.55	+11	8
	LAD	SS	24	23	205	44	58	2	12	.981	4.47	0	0
Cruz, N	Tex	LF	6	2	21	2	0	0	0	1.000	.86	-2	-1
Cruz, T	StL	1B	2	0	2	1	1	0	2	1.000	-	0	0
Cuddyer, M	Col	1B	26	24	205	217	15	2	22	.991	-	+1	1
	Col	RF	74	68	593	122	6	3	3	.977	1.94	-17	-8
Culberson, C	SF	2B	6	5	48	9	11	0	1	1.000	3.72	-1	0

Player	Tm	Pos	G	GS	Inn	PO	A	E	DP	Pct.	Rng	+/-	RS
Cunningham, A	Cle	LF	52	7	168	37	2	0	0	1.000	2.09	-2	2
	Cle	CF	11	6	56	13	1	0	1	1.000	2.25	-2	0
	Cle	RF	13	8	75	15	1	0	0	1.000	1.92	-1	0
Damon, J	Cle	LF	56	52	396	99	1	2	0	.980	2.27	0	1
Danks, J	CWS	LF	21	6	76	16	0	0	0	1.000	1.88	0	0
	CWS	CF	14	8	84	20	0	0	0	1.000	2.13	+3	2
	CWS	RF	7	1	22	8	0	0	0	1.000	3.27	+1	1
d'Arnaud, C	Pit	2B	2	1	9	1	1	0	0	1.000	2.00	0	0
	Pit	SS	1	0	4	0	1	0	0	1.000	1.93	0	0
Darnell, J	SD	3B	1	1	8	1	1	1	0	.667	2.25	-1	-1
	SD	LF	4	3	27	2	0	1	0	1.000	.67	-1	-1
Davis, C	Bal	1B	38	38	343	342	28	4	37	.989	-	0	-4
	Bal	LF	11	11	86	23	0	1	0	.958	2.41	-1	-1
	Bal	RF	30	28	230	59	3	1	0	.984	2.43	-1	0
Davis, R	Tor	CF	6	5	34	5	0	0	0	1.000	1.32	+2	1
	Tor	RF	24	14	147	35	0	1	0	.972	2.14	+2	1
De Aza, A	CWS	LF	11	5	54	12	0	0	0	1.000	1.98	0	0
De Jesus, I	TOT	2B	12	4	45	7	10	1	3	.944	3.35	0	-1
	TOT	3B	6	1	14	1	2	1	0	.750	1.88	-1	0
	TOT	SS	1	0	2	1	1	0	1	1.000	9.00	0	1
DeJesus, D	ChC	LF	3	3	22	4	0	0	0	1.000	1.64	+2	1
	ChC	CF	50	36	336	90	3	0	0	1.000	2.49	-8	-4
Denorfia, C	SD	LF	53	13	187	38	1	0	0	1.000	1.87	+2	2
	SD	CF	9	4	40	8	0	0	0	1.000	1.80	+1	1
	SD	RF	79	60	507	94	3	1	0	.990	1.72	-3	1
DeRosa, M	Was	1B	3	0	4	4	0	0	1	1.000	-	0	0
	Was	2B	1	0	3	0	0	0	0	-	.00		0
	Was	3B	11	2	37	5	9	0	0	1.000	2.43	0	0
	Was	SS	1	1	9	3	5	1	1	.889	8.00	0	0
	Was	LF	9	7	62	8	0	0	0	1.000	1.15	-3	-2
	Was	RF	7	6	48	7	1	0	0	1.000	1.50	-5	-3
Descalso, D	StL	1B	5	0	18	20	3	0	1	1.000	-	+1	1
	StL	2B	96	66	626	137	225	5	47	.986	5.20	0	0
	StL	3B	22	8	91	8	17	2	0	.926	2.46	-1	-1
	StL	SS	26	20	184	24	69	8	17	.921	4.55	-8	-7
DeWitt, B	ChC	2B	4	4	30	12	8	0	2	1.000	5.87	0	-1
	ChC	LF	1	1	6	1	0	0	0	1.000	1.50	0	0
Diaz, J	Cle	SS	5	4	36	8	9	1	4	.944	4.25	-2	-3
Diaz, M	Atl	LF	19	17	141	35	2	0	2	1.000	2.36	-4	-3
	Atl	RF	6	5	41	15	0	0	0	1.000	3.27	+1	-1
Dickerson, C	NYY	LF	18	1	32	3	0	0	0	1.000	.84	-1	0
	NYY	CF	2	2	15	8	0	0	0	1.000	4.80	+1	1
	NYY	RF	5	1	12	0	0	0	0	-	.00	0	0
Dirks, A	Det	LF	59	56	463	91	1	1	0	.989	1.79	+10	3
	Det	CF	1	0	2	0	0	0	0	-	.00		0
	Det	RF	24	13	139	16	0	2	0	.889	1.03	+3	-1
Dobbs, G	Mia	1B	18	14	133	127	7	1	10	.993	-	0	-1
	Mia	3B	36	30	262	13	35	10	1	.828	1.65	-13	-10
	Mia	LF	21	11	105	19	0	0	0	1.000	1.62	-1	-3
	Mia	RF	16	15	122	24	0	0	0	1.000	1.77	-9	-5
Dominguez, M	Hou	3B	31	27	245	18	59	1	9	.987	2.82	-1	0
Donald, J	Cle	2B	8	8	61	7	16	2	5	.920	3.39	+1	1
	Cle	3B	12	11	99	5	17	4	1	.846	2.00	-3	-3
	Cle	SS	10	9	79	13	17	1	4	.968	3.42	+1	0
	Cle	LF	5	4	33	7	0	0	0	1.000	1.91	+2	1
	Cle	CF	3	1	14	5	0	0	0	1.000	3.21	+2	1
Donaldson, J	Oak	1B	1	0	3	3	1	0	0	1.000	-	0	0
	Oak	3B	71	71	633	53	152	12	14	.945	2.91	+6	4
Doumit, R	Min	1B	1	0	3	3	0	0	0	1.000	-	0	0
	Min	LF	16	16	135	36	0	3	0	.923	2.39	+1	-1
	Min	RF	6	6	49	6	0	0	0	1.000	1.10	-4	-2
Downs, M	Hou	1B	25	14	138	135	16	3	10	.981	-		-1
	Hou	2B	3	2	22	5	9	0	2	1.000	5.73	-3	-2
	Hou	3B	18	11	102	5	26	3	1	.912	2.73	-1	0
	Hou	SS	1	0	1	0	0	0	0	-	.00		0
	Hou	RF	11	8	56	7	1	0	0	1.000	1.27	-4	-1
Dozier, B	Min	SS	83	81	732	111	287	15	70	.964	4.89	-3	1
Drew, S	TOT	SS	75	75	658	84	190	8	42	.972	3.74	-8	-7
Duda, L	NYM	1B	6	4	32	20	4	1	1	.960	-	+1	2
	NYM	LF	24	23	175	36	2	0	0	1.000	1.95	-10	-2
	NYM	RF	81	77	670	128	3	4	0	.970	1.76	-21	-16
Duncan, S	Cle	1B	1	0	1	1	0	0	0	1.000	-		0
	Cle	LF	57	52	404	77	4	2	0	.976	1.80	-6	-3

Player	Tm	Pos	G	GS	Inn	PO	A	E	DP	Pct.	Rng	+/-	RS
	Cle	RF	2	0	6	1	0	0	0	1.000	1.50	-1	-1
Dunn, A	CWS	1B	52	51	452	387	34	2	31	.995	-	+2	-1
	CWS	LF	5	5	32	8	0	0	0	1.000	2.25	-5	-3
Dyson, J	KC	CF	88	79	699	231	8	6	4	.976	3.08	+8	5
Eaton, A	Ari	LF	1	1	0	0	0	0	0	-	.00		0
	Ari	CF	21	20	185	37	2	1	1	.975	1.89	+1	2
Ellsbury, J	Bos	CF	73	71	611	164	2	3	1	.982	2.44	+11	3
Elmore, J	Ari	2B	5	1	13	3	6	0	3	1.000	6.23	+1	0
	Ari	SS	17	14	129	22	50	2	9	.973	5.00	-3	-3
Encarnacion, E	Tor	1B	68	66	583	602	32	3	61	.995	-	-2	-1
	Tor	3B	1	1	8	2	0	1	0	.667	2.25	-1	-1
	Tor	LF	3	2	17	3	0	0	0	1.000	1.59	-3	-2
Escobar, E	TOT	2B	14	12	106	28	35	0	8	1.000	5.33	-1	1
	TOT	3B	25	15	152	4	32	1	3	.973	2.13	+5	3
	TOT	SS	10	6	59	10	26	1	5	.973	5.49	+1	1
	TOT	LF	1	0	7	2	0	0	0	1.000	2.57	-1	0
Espinosa, D	Was	SS	36	34	309	43	110	7	23	.956	4.46	+7	4
Ethier, A	LAD	CF	1	1	9	4	0	0	0	1.000	4.00	+1	1
Falu, I	KC	2B	14	11	110	19	37	1	9	.982	4.58	-3	-1
	KC	3B	5	5	45	4	13	2	1	.895	3.40	+2	2
	KC	SS	5	3	35	6	9	0	3	1.000	3.86	-2	-1
Farris, E	Mil	2B	2	0	2	1	0	0	0	1.000	4.50	0	0
	Mil	LF	1	0	2	0	0	0	0	-	.00		0
Field, T	Col	2B	1	0	4	1	0	0	0	1.000	1.93	0	0
Figgins, C	Sea	3B	10	6	67	6	17	0	1	1.000	3.06	+3	3
	Sea	LF	38	29	270	49	2	1	1	.981	1.70	-6	-4
	Sea	CF	9	8	68	20	0	0	0	1.000	2.65	-7	-4
	Sea	RF	1	1	9	3	0	0	0	1.000	3.00	-2	-1
Flaherty, R	Bal	1B	3	0	3	3	0	0	1	1.000	-	0	0
	Bal	2B	28	20	172	36	56	1	13	.989	4.80	+4	1
	Bal	3B	17	7	80	2	14	1	1	.941	1.80	-2	-1
	Bal	SS	1	0	1	0	0	0	0	-	.00	0	0
	Bal	LF	7	6	50	12	0	1	0	.923	2.13	0	0
	Bal	RF	17	9	88	15	0	0	0	1.000	1.53	+1	0
Florimon, P	Min	SS	43	42	367	69	125	7	26	.965	4.76	+11	7
Flowers, T	CWS	1B	2	1	11	10	1	0	2	1.000	-	-1	-1
Fontenot, M	Phi	2B	17	13	123	28	30	3	5	.951	4.22	+3	2
	Phi	3B	12	9	77	5	18	2	3	.920	2.69	0	-1
Ford, L	Bal	LF	13	9	72	16	2	0	0	1.000	2.25	0	1
	Bal	RF	6	3	33	11	0	0	0	1.000	3.00	+2	1
Forsythe, L	SD	2B	81	73	647	166	187	12	35	.967	4.91	-11	-11
	SD	3B	4	1	17	0	2	0	0	1.000	1.06	0	0
	SD	SS	5	2	21	4	7	0	1	1.000	4.57	+1	1
Francisco, B	TOT	LF	24	12	119	18	0	1	0	.947	1.36	0	-4
	TOT	RF	29	21	170	25	1	0	0	1.000	1.37	-3	-4
Francisco, J	Atl	3B	49	42	363	20	67	6	9	.935	2.16	+2	1
Francoeur, J	KC	CF	3	2	16	0	0	0	0	-	.00	-4	-2
Frandsen, K	Phi	3B	52	49	442	35	76	7	4	.941	2.26	+1	2
Frazier, T	Cin	1B	39	36	318	315	21	2	30	.994	-	-8	-6
	Cin	3B	73	66	589	45	105	5	4	.968	2.29	+8	3
	Cin	LF	7	6	49	12	0	0	0	1.000	2.19	+4	2
	Cin	RF	1	1	7	0	0	0	0	-	.00	0	0
Fryer, E	Pit	LF	1	0	1	0	0	0	0	-	.00	0	0
	Pit	RF	1	0	0	0	0	0	0	-	-	0	0
Fukudome, K	CWS	LF	10	7	59	17	0	0	0	1.000	2.59	+3	3
	CWS	CF	1	1	9	2	0	0	0	1.000	2.00	+1	0
	CWS	RF	4	3	29	3	0	0	0	1.000	.93	-4	-2
Fuld, S	TB	LF	14	9	94	19	1	0	0	1.000	1.91	+3	3
	TB	CF	6	3	33	11	0	0	0	1.000	3.00	-1	-1
	TB	RF	15	11	105	21	1	1	0	.957	1.89	+2	2
Galvis, F	Phi	2B	55	45	416	92	151	1	31	.996	5.26	+4	7
	Phi	SS	5	4	36	4	18	0	3	1.000	5.45	+2	2
Gamel, M	Mil	1B	20	20	157	134	8	3	15	.979	-	+1	0
	Mil	3B	1	0	2	0	0	0	0	-	.00	0	0
Garcia, A	Det	LF	2	1	11	4	1	0	1	1.000	4.09	+1	1
	Det	CF	2	0	6	1	0	0	0	1.000	1.50	0	0
	Det	RF	18	10	104	18	0	0	0	1.000	1.55	-1	-2
Gardner, B	NYY	LF	15	8	85	14	1	0	0	1.000	1.58	+1	1
Gentry, C	Tex	CF	114	66	648	189	7	0	2	1.000	2.72	+14	16
	Tex	RF	3	0	6	1	0	0	0	1.000	1.50	0	0
Getz, C	KC	2B	61	55	483	95	143	4	40	.983	4.43	-5	-2
Giambi, J	Col	1B	13	12	89	86	3	0	7	1.000	-	0	0
Giavotella, J	KC	2B	45	43	376	84	93	6	21	.967	4.23	-3	-4
Gillaspie, C	SF	3B	5	5	45	3	9	2	0	.857	2.40	-2	-3

Player	Tm	Pos	G	GS	Inn	PO	A	E	DP	Pct.	Rng	+/-	RS
Gimenez, C	TB	1B	1	0	2	2	0	0	1	1.000	-	0	0
	TB	3B	1	0	1	0	0	0	0	-	.00	0	0
	TB	LF	1	0	1	1	0	0	0	1.000	9.00	0	0
Gimenez, H	CWS	LF	1	0	1	0	0	0	0	-	.00	0	0
	CWS	RF	1	0	1	1	0	0	0	1.000	9.00	+1	0
Gomes, J	Oak	LF	39	25	258	56	1	2	0	.966	1.98	0	-2
	Oak	RF	3	3	23	9	0	0	0	1.000	3.52	-1	0
Gomes, Y	Tor	1B	20	13	119	106	7	1	7	.991	-	+1	0
	Tor	3B	8	6	54	7	12	0	2	1.000	3.17	+1	1
	Tor	LF	4	0	8	0	0	0	0	-	.00	0	0
Gomez, M	Bos	1B	16	13	125	112	14	1	13	.992	-	0	-1
	Bos	3B	5	4	49	7	7	4	0	.778	2.57	-2	-3
Gonzalez, A	TOT	RF	18	18	127	18	1	2	1	.905	1.35	-2	-2
Gonzalez, A	Tex	2B	5	2	29	4	7	0	2	1.000	3.41	0	0
	Tex	3B	8	5	56	4	11	0	2	1.000	2.41	+2	1
	Tex	SS	5	5	49	7	17	2	2	.923	4.41	+1	1
Gonzalez, A	Mil	SS	24	24	203	30	67	3	17	.970	4.30	-3	-2
Gonzalez, M	Hou	2B	6	4	31	5	15	0	1	1.000	5.81	0	0
	Hou	3B	14	6	52	2	16	0	0	1.000	3.08	+2	2
	Hou	SS	47	38	347	56	112	5	19	.971	4.35	0	0
Gordon, D	LAD	SS	79	73	651	127	186	18	38	.946	4.32	-14	-14
Gose, A	Tor	LF	15	13	110	22	2	0	2	1.000	1.96	0	2
	Tor	CF	22	15	146	46	0	0	0	1.000	2.83	+6	2
	Tor	RF	24	21	181	38	0	1	0	.974	1.88	-2	-1
Graham, T	Ari	LF	1	0	1	0	0	0	0	-	.00		0
	Ari	RF	1	0	1	0	0	0	0	-	.00		0
Green, N	Mia	2B	2	2	17	1	7	0	3	1.000	4.24	+1	1
	Mia	3B	3	3	27	2	6	2	1	.800	2.67	0	-1
	Mia	SS	1	1	9	2	3	0	1	1.000	5.00	0	0
Green, T	Mil	1B	18	14	116	110	10	0	10	1.000	-	-2	-1
	Mil	2B	4	1	14	0	6	0	0	1.000	3.86	+2	2
	Mil	3B	13	7	72	6	12	2	2	.900	2.24	+1	1
Greene, T	TOT	2B	59	43	379	72	138	4	29	.981	4.98	-11	-8
	TOT	SS	43	34	304	46	98	7	17	.954	4.25	-4	-3
	TOT	LF	1	0	1	0	0	0	0	-	.00		0
	TOT	RF	2	0	2	1	0	0	0	1.000	3.86	+2	1
Gregorius, D	Cin	SS	4	4	46	8	10	0	4	1.000	3.52	+1	1
Gutierrez, F	Sea	CF	38	38	322	98	1	1	0	.990	2.76	-5	-4
Guyer, B	TB	LF	3	2	14	2	0	1	0	.667	1.29	0	0
Guzman, J	SD	1B	19	14	123	116	12	0	8	1.000	-	+1	1
	SD	2B	4	0	7	0	1	0	0	1.000	1.23	+1	0
	SD	LF	52	43	363	73	4	2	1	.975	1.91	+2	0
	SD	RF	7	7	49	12	0	0	0	1.000	2.17	-1	-1
Gwynn, T	LAD	LF	38	13	163	44	2	0	0	1.000	2.54	+4	2
	LAD	CF	53	43	403	103	4	1	0	.991	2.39	-8	-0
	LAD	RF	3	1	12	2	0	0	0	1.000	1.50	0	0
Hague, M	Pit	1B	16	14	111	114	12	1	13	.992	-	+1	1
Hairston, J	LAD	1B	1	0	1	0	0	0	0	-	-		0
	LAD	2B	30	26	226	44	66	3	16	.973	4.37	-7	-6
	LAD	3B	32	23	206	15	56	4	2	.947	3.10	+2	2
	LAD	SS	2	0	4	1	1	1	0	.667	4.50	-1	-1
	LAD	LF	18	13	109	35	1	1	0	.973	2.97	+8	5
Hairston, S	NYM	LF	59	37	361	58	1	1	0	.983	1.47	+1	3
	NYM	CF	14	11	82	17	0	0	0	1.000	1.86	-3	-3
	NYM	RF	48	38	329	77	0	0	0	1.000	2.10	-4	-4
Hall, B	Bal	LF	1	1	8	1	0	0	0	1.000	1.13	0	0
	Bal	RF	1	1	8	0	0	0	0	-	.00	-2	-1
Hamilton, J	Tex	LF	84	52	481	96	3	3	0	.971	1.85	+4	2
	Tex	CF	95	84	687	177	2	4	2	.978	2.34	-13	-11
	Tex	RF	2	0	4	0	0	0	0	-	.00	0	0
Hannahan, J	Cle	1B	2	1	10	9	1	1	3	.909	-	0	-1
	Cle	3B	96	80	724	63	180	13	18	.949	3.02	+5	2
	Cle	SS	2	0	13	4	6	0	1	1.000	6.92	0	0
Harper, B	Was	LF	7	6	58	14	0	0	0	1.000	2.17	+3	2
	Was	CF	92	86	715	200	4	4	1	.981	2.57	+17	13
	Was	RF	65	41	414	97	4	3	2	.971	2.19	-6	-1
Harris, W	Cin	2B	7	5	44	8	18	1	4	.963	5.32	-1	-1
	Cin	3B	1	1	9	0	2	0	1	1.000	2.00	+1	1
	Cin	LF	1	1	9	1	0	0	0	1.000	1.00	0	0
Harrison, J	Pit	2B	28	18	180	34	52	1	5	.989	4.30	+2	1
	Pit	3B	54	39	374	5	16	1	1	.955	2.54	+2	1
	Pit	SS	25	18	158	26	40	4	6	.943	3.74	-3	-4
	Pit	LF	1	0	1	0	0	0	0	-	.00		0
	Pit	RF	12	10	84	16	1	0	0	1.000	1.81	-3	-3

Player	Tm	Pos	G	GS	Inn	PO	A	E	DP	Pct.	Rng	+/-	RS
Hart, C	Mil	RF	53	49	408	80	0	2	0	.976	1.76	+8	1
Headley, C	SD	1B	1	0	2	0	0	0	0	-	-		0
Hechavarria, A	Tor	2B	8	8	70	17	20	0	4	1.000	4.71	-1	-2
	Tor	3B	18	18	156	8	40	1	5	.980	2.77	-3	-1
	Tor	SS	17	13	114	14	32	2	12	.958	3.63	+2	2
Heisey, C	Cin	LF	63	36	355	83	3	3	0	.966	2.18	-1	-3
	Cin	CF	36	34	297	80	0	0	0	1.000	2.42	-7	-2
	Cin	RF	13	10	84	18	1	0	0	1.000	2.02	+1	0
Helton, T	Col	1B	67	64	558	566	57	2	53	.997	-		1
Hermida, J	SD	LF	1	0	2	0	0	0	0	-	.00	0	0
	SD	RF	6	4	37	11	0	0	0	1.000	2.63	+3	2
Hernandez, G	TOT	1B	14	2	48	17	0	0	0	1.000	3.17	+5	3
	TOT	CF	37	31	283	87	1	0	0	1.000	2.79	-9	-6
	TOT	RF	6	0	12	2	0	0	0	1.000	1.50	+2	1
Hernandez, L	Tex	3B	1	0	1	0	0	0	0	-	.00	0	0
	Tex	SS	1	1	7	1	2	0	0	1.000	3.86	0	0
Hernandez, R	Col	1B	2	0	2	1	0	0	0	1.000	-		0
Herrera, E	LAD	2B	13	9	79	21	23	1	7	.978	4.99	-1	-2
	LAD	3B	20	14	117	10	20	1	3	.968	2.29	-2	-2
	LAD	SS	2	0	3	1	0	0	0	1.000	3.00	0	0
	LAD	LF	22	9	104	25	0	1	0	.962	2.16	+3	-2
	LAD	CF	9	9	71	13	0	0	0	1.000	1.65	-3	-2
	LAD	RF	7	3	32	10	1	0	1	1.000	3.06	+2	1
Herrera, J	Col	2B	19	12	112	26	32	0	6	1.000	4.66	-1	0
	Col	3B	13	9	82	7	13	0	2	1.000	2.20	0	-1
	Col	SS	42	34	315	53	101	3	15	.981	4.40	-5	-5
Herrmann, C	Min	LF	2	1	9	1	0	0	0	1.000	1.00	0	0
Heyward, J	Atl	CF	2	2	18	4	0	0	0	1.000	2.00	-1	0
Hicks, B	Oak	1B	1	1	8	3	1	0	1	1.000	-	0	0
	Oak	2B	1	1	9	1	3	0	0	1.000	4.00	0	0
	Oak	SS	19	16	143	24	37	3	4	.953	3.84	0	-1
Hill, S	StL	1B	1	0	1	1	0	0	0	1.000	-	0	0
Hinske, E	Atl	1B	15	11	107	95	8	2	6	.981	-	+2	0
	Atl	LF	6	3	32	4	0	0	0	1.000	1.10	-3	-2
	Atl	RF	4	4	31	5	0	0	0	1.000	1.45	-1	0
Hoes, L	Bal	LF	1	0	1	0	0	0	0	-	.00	0	0
Holt, B	Pit	2B	14	14	123	22	38	4	3	.938	4.37	-1	-2
Hosmer, E	KC	RF	3	2	16	1	0	0	0	.667	1.13	-2	-1
Howard, R	Phi	1B	67	66	589	495	30	5	37	.991	-	-2	-6
Hudson, O	TOT	2B	44	41	365	87	112	2	27	.990	4.90	+7	5
	TOT	3B	29	25	233	17	51	4	6	.944	2.62	0	0
Huff, A	SF	1B	15	11	88	83	7	1	3	.989	-	+1	1
	SF	2B	1	0	1	0	0	0	0	1.000	13.50	0	0
	SF	LF	5	4	32	7	0	0	0	1.000	1.97	+1	0
Hughes, L	TOT	1B	1	1	8	10	0	0	0	1.000	-	0	0
	TOT	2B	3	2	18	5	7	1	0	.923	6.00	+1	0
	TOT	3B	5	4	35	3	6	3	1	.750	2.29	-2	-1
Ibanez, R	NYY	LF	80	65	545	118	2	0	0	1.000	1.98	+5	-1
	NYY	RF	13	11	106	13	0	0	0	1.000	1.10	-7	-4
Iglesias, J	Bos	SS	24	23	193	27	71	2	16	.980	4.55	+6	7
Infante, O	TOT	3B	6	2	27	0	1	1	0	.500	.33	-1	1
Inge, B	TOT	2B	6	5	43	11	17	1	3	.966	5.86	-2	-3
	TOT	3B	76	74	673	74	141	7	18	.968	2.88	+5	6
Ishikawa, T	Mil	1B	43	27	277	269	17	2	21	.993	-	+4	5
	Mil	RF	3	0	3	0	0	0	0	-	.00	0	0
Izturis, C	TOT	1B	1	0	1	2	0	0	0	1.000	-	0	0
	TOT	2B	2	0	3	0	0	0	0	-	.00	-1	-1
	TOT	3B	4	1	13	2	6	0	1	1.000	5.54	+1	1
	TOT	SS	46	39	357	42	112	3	16	.981	3.88	+1	0
Izturis, M	LAA	2B	29	20	190	26	68	0	14	1.000	4.44	+2	2
	LAA	3B	30	30	246	12	40	5	4	.912	1.90	-2	-1
	LAA	SS	26	20	191	29	56	5	8	.944	4.00	-10	-9
Jackson, B	ChC	CF	39	38	313	94	0	2	0	.979	2.70	+3	0
Jackson, R	StL	2B	8	3	29	2	11	1	1	.929	3.99	0	0
	StL	SS	1	0	0	0	0	0	0	-	.00		0
Jacobs, M	Ari	1B	4	3	28	26	3	1	4	.967	-	-2	-1
Janish, P	Atl	SS	55	49	450	63	166	2	34	.991	4.58	+4	4
Jennings, D	TB	CF	21	18	162	45	0	0	0	1.000	2.50	+1	0
	TB	RF	1	1	6	1	0	0	0	1.000	1.50	-1	0
Johnson, C	TOT	1B	6	4	35	42	3	0	2	1.000	-	+1	1
	TOT	RF	1	0	1	0	0	0	0	-	.00	0	0
Johnson, D	CWS	1B	3	1	14	12	1	0	2	1.000	-	0	-1
Johnson, E	TB	2B	13	8	71	20	25	1	5	.978	5.65	0	1
	TB	3B	6	3	41	5	12	2	0	.895	3.73	0	0
	TB	SS	100	68	675	102	204	11	50	.965	4.08	-4	-6
	TB	LF	3	0	9	2	0	0	0	1.000	2.00	-3	-2
Johnson, N	Bal	1B	5	5	43	51	3	1	7	.982	-	0	-1
Johnson, R	TOT	LF	37	16	168	32	0	1	0	.970	1.71	-1	-1
	TOT	CF	32	22	192	41	2	1	1	.977	2.02	-3	-2
	TOT	RF	29	16	145	29	1	0	0	1.000	1.85	0	0
Jones, A	NYY	LF	47	41	321	56	2	0	2	1.000	1.63	+7	2
	NYY	RF	23	14	131	25	1	1	0	.963	1.78	-1	-1
Jones, G	Pit	1B	72	65	529	500	48	5	46	.991	-	-5	-5
	Pit	RF	66	58	467	103	3	4	1	.964	2.04	+3	-3
Joyce, M	TB	LF	33	28	245	48	2	0	0	1.000	1.83	-4	3
	TB	RF	89	78	712	133	0	2	0	.985	1.68	+4	0
Ka'aihue, K	Oak	1B	22	21	179	160	12	0	24	.989	-	0	-2
Kalish, R	Bos	LF	3	1	10	3	0	1	0	.750	2.70	0	0
	Bos	CF	20	16	149	44	0	2	0	.957	2.65	-3	-4
	Bos	RF	9	8	71	15	0	1	0	.938	1.88	0	-1
Kawasaki, M	Sea	2B	10	4	39	6	13	0	3	1.000	4.31	0	-1
	Sea	3B	1	0	1	0	0	0	0	-	.00	0	0
	Sea	SS	38	25	246	50	65	0	13	1.000	4.21	-1	0
Kearns, A	Mia	1B	2	1	11	14	1	0	2	1.000	-	-1	0
	Mia	LF	22	17	142	54	0	1	0	.982	3.42	-2	-2
	Mia	RF	12	11	93	36	0	0	0	1.000	3.48	+4	2
Kelly, D	Det	1B	8	3	35	30	2	0	3	1.000	-	-1	-1
	Det	2B	1	0	1	0	0	0	0	-	.00		0
	Det	3B	3	2	19	1	3	0	0	1.000	1.89	0	0
	Det	LF	18	13	117	27	3	2	0	.938	2.30	0	2
	Det	CF	8	7	63	15	0	0	0	1.000	2.14	0	-1
	Det	RF	35	4	87	19	0	1	0	.950	1.97	-5	-3
Kendrick, H	LAA	1B	2	0	4	4	1	0	0	1.000	-	+1	1
	LAA	LF	2	0	3	2	0	1	0	.667	4.91	0	0
Kennedy, A	LAD	1B	3	0	6	3	1	0	0	1.000	-	0	0
	LAD	2B	16	15	118	35	33	3	3	.958	5.16	-4	-4
	LAD	3B	39	25	225	20	68	3	5	.967	3.52	+3	0
	LAD	LF	1	0	1	0	0	0	0	-	.00		0
Keppinger, J	TB	1B	27	21	168	157	7	1	13	.994	-	-1	-1
	TB	2B	27	23	164	32	52	0	12	1.000	4.61	-4	-3
	TB	3B	50	41	340	23	59	2	10	.976	2.17	+6	7
Kinsler, I	Tex	3B	1	0	2	0	0	0	0	-	.00		0
Komatsu, E	TOT	LF	2	1	12	1	0	1	0	.500	.75	-2	-1
	TOT	CF	5	2	31	9	0	0	0	1.000	2.61	-1	-1
	TOT	RF	10	7	64	16	1	0	0	1.000	2.38	+2	1
Kotsay, M	SD	1B	5	3	23	26	0	0	2	1.000	-	0	0
	SD	LF	19	19	127	27	1	1	1	.966	1.98	+1	2
	SD	RF	9	7	65	14	1	0	1	1.000	2.08	-4	-2
Kottaras, G	TOT	1B	6	0	9	10	0	0	2	1.000	-	0	0
Kozma, P	StL	1B	1	0	2	3	0	0	0	1.000	13.50	0	0
	StL	SS	25	22	197	22	60	3	10	.965	3.75	+2	2
Kubel, J	Ari	RF	2	1	14	3	1	0	0	1.000	2.45	0	1
LaHair, B	ChC	1B	58	53	474	445	18	3	44	.994	-	-6	-4
	ChC	LF	2	1	7	1	0	0	0	1.000	1.29	0	0
	ChC	RF	34	32	241	58	0	2	0	.967	2.17	-6	-6
Laird, B	Hou	1B	4	3	23	21	0	0	1	1.000	-	0	0
	Hou	3B	8	5	45	2	10	1	0	.923	2.38	+1	1
Lalli, B	ChC	1B	2	0	3	4	0	0	1	1.000	-	0	0
Langerhans, R	LAA	LF	2	0	1	0	0	0	0	-	.00	-2	-1
LaPorta, M	Cle	1B	11	8	69	56	6	0	5	1.000	-	0	-2
Lawrie, B	Tor	SS	1	0	4	1	0	0	0	1.000	2.25	0	0
LeMahieu, D	Col	1B	1	0	3	1	0	0	0	1.000	-	0	0
	Col	2B	67	60	509	105	204	2	33	.994	5.46	+11	8
	Col	3B	9	5	46	2	8	0	0	1.000	1.96	0	0
	Col	SS	2	0	2	0	0	0	0	-	.00	0	0
Lewis, F	NYM	LF	4	0	9	0	0	0	0	-	.00	-1	-1
	NYM	CF	1	0	3	0	0	0	0	-	.00	0	0
	NYM	RF	4	3	16	4	0	0	0	1.000	2.25	-1	-1
Liddi, A	Sea	1B	5	5	43	45	3	1	3	.980	-	0	0
	Sea	3B	23	19	179	8	33	3	4	.932	2.06	+1	0
	Sea	LF	7	6	46	9	0	1	0	.900	1.76	0	-1
Lillibridge, B	TOT	1B	23	3	52	40	4	0	3	1.000	-	+1	0
	TOT	2B	6	3	29	6	8	1	2	.933	4.25	0	0
	TOT	3B	18	15	118	11	21	1	4	.970	2.44	+2	1
	TOT	SS	15	14	143	14	33	6	5	.887	2.94	-5	-4
	TOT	LF	20	3	61	11	0	0	0	1.000	1.61	+1	0
	TOT	CF	11	7	65	15	0	0	0	1.000	2.08	0	0
	TOT	RF	4	1	13	5	0	0	0	1.000	3.46	+1	0

Player	Tm	Pos	G	GS	Inn	PO	A	E	DP	Pct.	Rng	+/-	RS
Lin, C	Bos	CF	3	2	18	4	0	0	0	1.000	2.00	-1	-1
	Bos	RF	6	1	22	2	0	0	0	1.000	.82	+1	0
Lind, A	Tor	1B	61	57	500	545	37	5	64	.991	-	+3	1
Lombardozzi, S	Was	2B	51	43	394	95	141	2	27	.992	5.39	-1	0
	Was	3B	13	10	94	3	19	2	2	.917	2.11	-1	-1
	Was	SS	1	1	9	0	2	0	0	1.000	2.00	-2	-1
	Was	LF	41	29	252	48	2	0	0	1.000	1.78	+1	1
Longoria, E	TB	3B	50	49	413	37	81	8	7	.937	2.57	+1	1
Lopez, J	TOT	1B	14	6	61	60	2	0	2	1.000	-	-2	-1
	TOT	2B	4	2	23	2	4	0	1	1.000	2.35	+2	1
	TOT	3B	50	38	340	18	65	3	9	.965	2.19	0	1
	TOT	RF	1	0	0	0	0	0	0	-	.00		
Lough, D	KC	LF	1	1	7	4	0	0	0	1.000	5.14	+2	1
	KC	CF	12	8	76	23	0	1	0	.958	2.70	-1	-1
	KC	RF	5	5	44	3	0	0	0	1.000	.61	-1	0
Luna, H	Phi	1B	10	8	79	72	6	0	7	1.000	-	+2	0
	Phi	3B	1	1	7	1	1	0	0	1.000	2.57	0	1
	Phi	LF	2	2	15	5	0	0	0	1.000	3.00	0	0
Lutz, Z	NYM	1B	1	1	8	10	1	1	0	.917	-	0	0
Machado, M	Bal	3B	51	51	468	44	102	5	4	.967	2.81	+8	7
Mahoney, J	Bal	1B	2	1	12	10	0	0	0	1.000	-	0	0
Maier, M	KC	CF	16	13	126	30	0	0	0	1.000	2.14	-5	-4
	KC	RF	6	2	28	8	0	0	0	1.000	2.57	-1	-2
Maldonado, M	Mil	1B	4	0	9	9	0	0	1	1.000	-	+1	1
Marte, S	Pit	LF	43	38	338	63	3	3	0	.957	1.76	+8	6
	Pit	CF	4	1	13	3	0	0	0	1.000	2.08	0	0
Martin, L	Tex	LF	4	1	14	7	0	0	0	1.000	4.50	+1	1
	Tex	CF	14	12	105	32	1	0	1	1.000	2.83	-2	-1
Martinez, F	Hou	LF	31	29	225	42	1	0	0	1.000	1.71	-6	-5
	Hou	RF	6	6	50	7	0	0	0	1.000	1.26	-1	-2
Martinez, M	Phi	2B	16	14	121	24	26	2	9	.962	3.72	-1	0
	Phi	3B	10	8	70	4	19	2	2	.920	2.94	+1	2
	Phi	SS	8	6	51	8	16	0	2	1.000	4.24	-1	1
	Phi	1B	2	0	4	0	0	0	0	-	.00		-1
	Phi	CF	3	2	17	4	0	0	0	1.000	2.08	+1	1
	Phi	RF	4	4	29	5	1	0	1	1.000	1.82	+1	2
Mastroianni, D	Min	2B	1	0	1	0	0	0	0	-	.00		
	Min	3B	25	10	111	23	0	1	0	.958	1.86	+1	1
	Min	CF	4	4	32	10	0	0	0	1.000	2.78	+1	1
	Min	RF	34	27	254	67	2	2	0	.972	2.44	+5	3
Mather, J	ChC	1B	2	0	5	3	1	0	0	1.000	-	0	0
	ChC	3B	18	16	132	2	18	3	3	.870	1.36	-3	-3
	ChC	LF	25	4	71	16	0	0	0	1.000	2.03	-2	-1
	ChC	CF	28	26	196	64	0	0	0	1.000	2.94	-10	-6
	ChC	RF	14	4	54	11	0	0	0	1.000	1.81	-3	-1
Matsui, H	TB	LF	9	7	57	6	0	0	0	1.000	.95	0	0
	TB	RF	6	6	39	8	0	0	0	1.000	1.83	-3	-3
Mattison, K	Mia	LF	1	0	2	0	0	0	0	-	.00	-1	-1
Mauer, J	Min	1B	30	30	260	265	17	2	22	.993	-	-4	-1
Maxwell, J	Hou	LF	38	17	151	41	0	0	0	1.000	2.10	-2	-2
	Hou	CF	59	47	403	121	4	0	0	1.000	2.79	+21	12
	Hou	RF	20	13	114	23	1	2	0	.923	1.89	-1	-2
Mayberry, J	Phi	1B	27	22	185	175	11	1	13	.995	-	+1	1
	Phi	LF	70	30	330	82	2	1	1	.988	2.29	0	0
	Phi	CF	58	52	474	124	2	1	0	.992	2.39	-2	-2
	Phi	RF	3	3	24	4	2	0	1	1.000	2.25	0	3
Maysonet, E	Mil	2B	3	3	26	3	10	1	2	.929	4.50	-1	-1
	Mil	3B	1	0	2	0	1	0	0	1.000	4.50	0	0
	Mil	SS	18	10	107	25	46	3	14	.959	5.97	+1	1
McBride, M	Col	1B	8	8	64	59	0	2	3	.967	-	-3	-2
	Col	RF	12	9	79	20	0	0	0	1.000	2.28	0	-1
McCoy, M	Tor	2B	8	3	29	6	12	0	2	1.000	5.52	0	0
	Tor	3B	6	4	38	2	12	0	1	1.000	3.32	+2	1
	Tor	SS	1	0	2	0	0	0	0	-	.00		0
	Tor	LF	4	1	12	2	0	0	0	1.000	1.46	0	0
	Tor	CF	4	4	26	5	0	0	0	1.000	1.73	+1	0
	Tor	RF	3	0	10	1	1	0	0	1.000	1.80	0	1
McDonald, D	TOT	LF	21	16	149	38	2	0	0	1.000	2.41	+3	2
	TOT	CF	7	5	34	8	0	0	0	1.000	2.12	-1	-2
	TOT	RF	12	3	43	12	0	2	0	.857	2.51	+1	2
McDonald, J	Ari	2B	4	3	26	6	10	0	2	1.000	5.54	+1	1
	Ari	3B	5	1	16	2	3	0	0	1.000	2.70	0	0
	Ari	SS	54	47	426	67	141	1	31	.995	4.39	+5	7
McGehee, C	TOT	1B	85	61	569	557	45	2	51	.997	-	0	2
	TOT	2B	1	0	1	0	0	0	0	-	.00		0
	TOT	3B	21	17	146	12	21	1	2	.971	2.03	+1	-3
McLouth, N	TOT	LF	64	55	515	96	1	1	0	.990	1.69	+2	-2
	TOT	CF	10	4	46	14	0	0	0	1.000	2.74	0	0
	TOT	RF	3	3	23	3	0	0	0	1.000	1.17	+3	2
Mercer, J	Pit	2B	7	4	41	4	19	0	4	1.000	5.05	+2	2
	Pit	3B	1	0	1	0	0	0	0	-	.00		0
	Pit	SS	28	9	104	16	39	1	4	.982	4.74	+1	1
Mesa, M	NYY	CF	1	0	0	0	0	0	0	-	.00		0
Middlebrooks, W	Bos	3B	72	69	606	32	134	9	13	.949	2.46	0	-3
Molina, Y	StL	1B	3	0	9	11	2	0	0	1.000	-	0	0
Moore, S	Hou	1B	19	15	136	136	9	1	10	.993	-	-2	0
	Hou	2B	6	3	36	11	17	0	3	1.000	7.00	+2	1
	Hou	3B	28	22	179	9	36	5	3	.900	2.26	-7	-5
	Hou	LF	2	1	9	2	0	0	0	1.000	2.00	0	0
	Hou	RF	15	12	80	20	0	0	0	1.000	2.23	-3	-2
Moore, T	Was	1B	14	7	69	70	6	0	7	1.000	-	0	1
	Was	LF	40	28	229	27	1	0	0	1.000	1.10	-10	-8
	Was	RF	2	0	6	2	0	0	0	1.000	3.00	-1	0
Morales, K	LAA	1B	28	28	241	199	13	1	18	.995	-	+1	-1
Morel, B	CWS	3B	33	31	281	25	51	3	2	.962	2.43	-1	0
Moreland, M	Tex	1B	95	82	739	691	57	3	68	.996	-	-1	0
	Tex	RF	3	0	4	3	0	0	0	1.000	6.75	0	0
Morgan, N	Mil	LF	19	4	52	15	1	0	0	1.000	2.77	+4	1
	Mil	CF	53	48	392	111	1	0	1	1.000	2.57	+10	7
	Mil	RF	27	14	143	28	0	0	0	1.000	1.76	0	1
Morrison, L	Mia	1B	21	16	155	148	26	1	18	.994	-	+5	4
	Mia	LF	59	59	479	89	4	4	2	.959	1.75	-5	-5
Morse, M	Was	1B	1	0	5	8	1	0	0	1.000	-	+1	0
	Was	LF	67	57	493	82	2	0	0	1.000	1.53	-3	-4
	Was	RF	36	35	280	64	1	1	0	.985	2.08	+3	0
Moss, B	Oak	1B	55	51	443	407	24	8	38	.982	-	-4	0
	Oak	LF	11	5	60	10	1	0	0	1.000	1.64	-1	0
	Oak	RF	13	10	98	25	1	1	0	.963	2.39	-3	-1
Murphy, D	NYM	1B	12	7	60	46	4	0	5	1.000	-	+1	0
Murphy, D	Tex	CF	2	0	2	0	0	0	0	-	.00	0	0
	Tex	RF	17	12	110	20	0	0	0	1.000	1.64	0	-1
Murphy, D	Mia	2B	13	8	80	16	25	0	3	1.000	4.57	+3	2
	Mia	3B	22	17	152	9	20	1	1	.967	1.71	-7	-4
	Mia	SS	2	1	12	3	4	0	2	1.000	5.25	0	0
Nady, X	TOT	LF	40	30	248	40	2	1	0	.977	1.52	-4	-1
	TOT	RF	15	9	71	12	0	0	0	1.000	1.51	+1	2
Napoli, M	Tex	1B	28	24	207	174	15	3	13	.984	-	-1	0
Nava, D	Bos	LF	76	66	611	107	5	2	0	.982	1.65	-5	3
	Bos	RF	4	2	20	4	0	0	0	1.000	1.77	+1	0
Navarro, Y	Pit	2B	1	1	9	2	3	0	1	1.000	5.00	0	0
	Pit	3B	2	2	18	0	5	0	0	1.000	2.50	+1	1
	Pit	SS	3	0	6	1	1	0	1	1.000	2.70	0	0
	Pit	LF	8	5	42	8	0	0	0	1.000	1.71	-2	1
	Pit	RF	2	2	15	3	1	0	1	1.000	2.40	0	1
Neal, T	Cle	LF	6	5	38	10	1	1	1	.917	2.61	+2	-1
	Cle	RF	2	2	16	1	0	0	0	1.000	.56	-2	-1
Negron, K	Cin	CF	1	0	4	0	0	0	0	-	.00	0	0
Nelson, C	Col	2B	21	18	155	39	54	1	13	.989	5.39	-5	-4
	Col	3B	92	68	647	45	118	12	14	.931	2.27	-22	-18
	Col	SS	1	0	2	1	0	0	0	1.000	4.50	-1	0
Nieuwenhuis, K	NYM	LF	23	20	170	33	0	0	0	1.000	1.74	+2	1
	NYM	CF	50	43	372	120	0	4	0	.968	2.90	-1	-1
	NYM	RF	20	6	70	21	0	0	0	1.000	2.67	-1	-2
Nieves, W	TOT	1B	2	0	4	1	0	0	0	1.000	-	0	0
Nishioka, T	Min	2B	3	3	26	6	11	2	6	.895	5.88	-2	-2
Nix, J	NYY	2B	13	11	93	16	24	0	4	1.000	3.87	+1	1
	NYY	3B	29	17	159	15	39	2	6	.964	3.05	+2	1
	NYY	SS	18	15	134	24	34	1	8	.983	3.90	-3	-2
	NYY	LF	11	9	76	11	0	1	0	.917	1.30	0	0
Nix, L	Phi	1B	10	10	72	68	6	2	8	.974	-	0	0
	Phi	LF	16	6	67	14	0	0	0	1.000	1.88	+2	1
	Phi	CF	3	3	23	5	0	1	0	.833	1.96	-2	-1
	Phi	RF	10	7	64	13	0	0	0	1.000	1.83	0	0
Nunez, E	NYY	2B	1	1	8	0	2	1	0	.667	2.25	0	0
	NYY	3B	15	5	51	6	12	2	1	.900	3.18	0	0
	NYY	SS	16	13	116	20	34	4	7	.931	4.19	-1	-1
	NYY	LF	3	3	25	6	0	0	0	1.000	2.88	0	0
	NYY	RF	1	0	0	0	0	0	0	-	.00	0	0

Player	Tm	Pos	G	GS	Inn	PO	A	E	DP	Pct.	Rng	+/-	RS
Olmedo, R	CWS	2B	2	2	16	4	6	0	2	1.000	5.63	+1	1
	CWS	3B	10	5	56	4	10	0	0	1.000	2.22	0	0
	CWS	SS	5	2	23	2	5	1	1	.875	2.74	-1	-1
Olt, M	Tex	1B	8	8	57	46	6	1	2	.981	-	0	0
	Tex	3B	5	2	24	0	8	1	0	.889	2.92	+1	1
	Tex	RF	2	1	8	3	0	1	0	.750	3.38	-1	0
Orr, P	Phi	2B	13	9	70	12	20	3	4	.914	4.09	0	-1
	Phi	3B	4	2	14	1	3	0	0	1.000	2.57	0	1
Ortega, R	Col	CF	1	1	8	3	0	0	0	1.000	3.38	0	0
Ortiz, D	Bos	1B	7	7	52	54	2	0	4	1.000	-	-1	-1
Overbay, L	TOT	1B	23	23	196	190	14	1	26	.995	-	+2	1
Pacheco, J	Col	1B	43	35	319	324	16	4	26	.988	-	0	0
	Col	3B	82	80	642	21	142	9	15	.948	2.29	-19	-13
Paredes, J	Hou	2B	5	4	35	5	13	3	2	.857	4.63	-1	-1
	Hou	LF	1	1	8	0	0	0	0	-	.00	0	0
	Hou	RF	15	13	111	23	1	2	0	.923	1.95	+4	0
Parmelee, C	Min	1B	38	31	272	296	25	2	43	.994	-	-5	-3
	Min	LF	1	1	9	4	0	0	0	1.000	4.00	-1	0
	Min	RF	18	16	132	26	1	0	0	1.000	1.84	0	-1
Parra, G	Ari	LF	47	33	316	59	2	2	0	.968	1.74	+3	2
	Ari	CF	48	44	398	98	3	2	0	.981	2.28	-1	1
	Ari	RF	17	13	127	32	3	0	1	1.000	2.47	+7	5
Parrino, A	SD	2B	15	8	78	18	20	0	5	1.000	4.38	-2	-1
	SD	3B	2	1	10	0	4	0	0	1.000	3.60	+1	1
	SD	SS	26	22	191	26	68	6	11	.940	4.43	0	1
	SD	RF	1	0	0	0	0	0	0	-	.00		0
Pastornicky, T	Atl	2B	3	2	13	3	5	0	1	1.000	5.54	+1	1
	Atl	SS	47	40	332	43	84	7	21	.948	3.44	-18	-16
Paul, X	Cin	LF	17	12	109	15	1	0	0	1.000	1.31	-2	-1
	Cin	RF	1	1	9	0	1	0	0	1.000	1.00	-2	-1
Pearce, S	TOT	1B	19	14	123	131	2	1	14	.993	-	0	-1
	TOT	LF	23	16	147	31	1	0	0	1.000	1.95	+1	2
	TOT	RF	19	14	123	17	1	0	0	1.000	1.31	+2	1
Peguero, C	Sea	LF	2	2	21	5	0	0	0	1.000	2.11	+1	0
	Sea	RF	11	10	90	23	0	0	0	1.000	2.29	-3	-2
Peguero, F	SF	LF	8	2	22	7	0	0	0	1.000	2.86	+4	2
	SF	RF	2	1	14	7	1	0	0	1.000	5.14	+4	4
Pena, B	KC	1B	3	0	8	8	0	0	0	1.000	-	0	0
Pena, R	NYY	SS	1	1	9	0	4	0	0	1.000	4.00	+1	0
Pennington, C	Oak	2B	32	26	247	67	85	2	12	.987	5.54	+8	7
Perez, E	Was	LF	3	0	3	0	0	0	0	-	.00	0	0
	Was	CF	4	0	8	1	0	0	0	1.000	1.13	0	0
Perez, H	Det	2B	1	0	2	1	0	0	0	1.000	4.50		0
Petersen, B	Mia	LF	51	39	367	76	2	1	1	.987	1.91	+3	0
	Mia	CF	20	15	139	34	2	0	0	1.000	2.33	-11	-5
	Mia	RF	4	3	22	5	0	0	0	1.000	2.01	+1	1
Phelps, C	Cle	2B	5	4	35	4	12	0	2	1.000	4.11	+1	1
	Cle	3B	1	0	1	0	0	0	0	-	.00	0	0
	Cle	SS	1	1	9	2	6	0	3	1.000	8.00	0	0
Phipps, D	Cin	CF	1	1	9	3	0	0	0	1.000	3.00	-2	-1
	Cin	RF	1	1	9	1	0	0	0	1.000	1.00	0	0
Pill, B	SF	1B	24	18	158	157	13	2	15	.988	-	+2	1
	SF	3B	1	0	1	0	0	0	0	-	.00	0	0
	SF	LF	7	7	44	9	0	0	0	1.000	1.72	0	0
Plouffe, T	Min	1B	3	1	12	14	0	0	2	1.000	-	0	0
	Min	2B	4	2	20	5	8	0	2	1.000	5.85	0	0
	Min	SS	1	0	1	0	1	1	0	.500	9.00	0	0
	Min	LF	2	2	17	1	1	0	0	1.000	1.06	-2	0
	Min	RF	15	13	115	24	1	1	0	.962	1.96	+1	0
Podsednik, S	Bos	LF	31	28	238	44	3	0	1	1.000	1.78	0	-2
	Bos	CF	23	18	166	35	0	1	0	.972	1.90	+3	2
	Bos	RF	5	4	32	9	0	0	0	1.000	2.53	+1	1
Polanco, P	Phi	3B	80	72	664	57	148	2	10	.990	2.78	-1	2
Pollock, A	Ari	LF	7	5	48	13	0	0	0	1.000	2.44	+3	2
	Ari	CF	14	14	124	42	0	0	0	1.000	3.05	0	0
	Ari	RF	4	0	8	3	0	0	0	1.000	3.38	0	0
Posey, B	SF	1B	29	29	216	204	6	2	13	.991	-	0	-1
Prado, M	Atl	1B	4	4	33	35	7	0	8	1.000	-	+1	1
	Atl	2B	10	8	73	8	20	0	4	1.000	3.45	+2	1
	Atl	3B	25	20	186	13	35	1	6	.980	2.32	+2	2
	Atl	SS	13	11	92	15	28	0	4	1.000	4.19	+6	3
Presley, A	Pit	LF	81	69	607	138	1	2	1	.986	2.06	+11	-1
	Pit	CF	4	2	20	4	0	1	0	.800	1.77	0	0
	Pit	RF	8	7	60	11	1	0	0	1.000	1.80	-4	-3
Pridie, J	Phi	CF	1	1	9	2	0	0	0	1.000	2.00	0	0
	Phi	RF	1	0	1	0	0	0	0	-	.00		0
Profar, J	Tex	2B	5	2	24	3	5	0	1	1.000	3.00	-1	-1
	Tex	SS	3	2	20	0	3	0	0	1.000	1.35	0	0
Pujols, A	LAA	3B	3	2	15	1	3	0	2	1.000	2.30	+2	1
Punto, N	TOT	1B	5	0	6	4	1	0	0	1.000	-	0	0
	TOT	2B	26	16	156	36	51	1	14	.989	5.01	+4	4
	TOT	3B	31	15	166	11	46	1	6	.983	3.08	+2	1
	TOT	SS	6	5	44	8	19	0	1	1.000	5.52	+3	2
Quentin, C	SD	LF	69	69	565	94	2	3	0	.970	1.53	-10	-10
	SD	RF	3	3	25	2	0	0	0	1.000	.72	0	0
Quintanilla, O	TOT	2B	34	27	245	39	77	4	13	.967	4.25	-1	-3
	TOT	SS	30	23	210	31	62	2	14	.979	3.99	+2	1
Raburn, R	Det	2B	32	31	226	36	63	3	13	.971	3.94	-6	-3
	Det	LF	30	15	154	29	2	1	0	.969	1.81	0	1
	Det	RF	22	8	92	15	0	0	0	1.000	1.46	0	1
Ramirez, H	TOT	SS	57	56	503	72	150	6	35	.974	3.97	-6	-7
Ransom, C	TOT	1B	1	0	1	1	0	0	0	1.000	-	0	0
	TOT	2B	6	2	25	7	14	0	4	1.000	7.46	+2	1
	TOT	3B	35	26	238	12	58	6	8	.921	2.65	-2	-3
	TOT	SS	48	37	325	51	98	2	24	.987	4.07	0	1
Recker, A	TOT	1B	1	1	9	7	0	0	2	1.000	-	0	0
Reddick, J	Oak	CF	14	10	99	35	1	1	0	.973	3.25	-3	-3
Reimold, N	Bal	LF	15	14	126	26	0	3	0	.897	1.86	-1	-1
Repko, J	Bos	CF	4	4	32	12	0	0	0	1.000	3.38	+3	2
Revere, B	Min	LF	5	5	44	15	0	0	0	1.000	3.07	+3	0
	Min	CF	39	34	309	87	2	0	1	1.000	2.59	-3	-3
	Min	RF	84	79	708	172	6	0	2	1.000	2.26	+18	11
Reynolds, M	Bal	1B	15	15	142	10	24	6	2	.850	2.15	-8	-7
Rhymes, W	TB	2B	31	22	214	40	83	5	27	.961	5.17	-3	-2
	TB	3B	15	13	85	3	21	3	1	.889	2.54	-1	-1
Rivera, J	LAD	1B	54	39	327	301	19	5	20	.985	-	-4	-2
	LAD	LF	37	30	249	43	3	0	0	1.000	1.66	0	0
	LAD	RF	5	5	51	9	0	0	0	1.000	1.58	+1	0
Rizzo, A	ChC	1B	85	85	730	685	46	4	76	.995	-	+3	4
Roberts, B	Bal	2B	17	17	149	30	48	1	9	.987	4.71	-8	-6
Roberts, R	TOT	2B	54	46	408	90	135	0	34	1.000	4.96	0	3
	TOT	3B	78	68	617	40	149	9	8	.955	2.75	+6	6
	TOT	LF	1	0	2	1	0	0	0	1.000	4.50	0	0
Robinson, S	StL	LF	15	1	30	9	0	0	0	1.000	2.70	+2	1
	StL	CF	37	27	250	60	3	2	1	.969	2.26	-3	0
	StL	RF	11	1	24	5	0	0	0	1.000	1.88	+1	1
Robinson, T	Sea	LF	46	39	367	100	0	2	0	.980	2.45	+10	2
Rodriguez, A	NYY	3B	81	81	709	57	119	8	13	.957	2.23	0	-2
Rodriguez, H	Cin	2B	2	1	9	5	5	0	2	1.000	9.31	-1	0
Rodriguez, S	TB	2B	37	17	178	40	63	0	15	1.000	5.21	+4	3
	TB	3B	49	27	285	23	70	11	8	.894	2.94	+4	1
	TB	SS	47	42	338	50	115	7	18	.959	4.39	+2	1
Rolen, S	Cin	3B	87	80	719	45	139	10	6	.948	2.30	+2	0
Romine, A	LAA	2B	1	0	1	0	0	0	0	-	.00	0	0
	LAA	3B	1	0	2	0	1	0	0	1.000	.00	-1	-1
	LAA	SS	8	4	43	9	20	1	6	.967	6.02	-1	-1
Rosales, A	Oak	1B	7	3	33	26	7	0	1	1.000	-	0	0
	Oak	2B	21	18	151	46	41	0	14	1.000	5.19	+4	5
	Oak	3B	3	1	16	2	4	0	0	1.000	3.38	+1	0
	Oak	SS	11	9	83	14	27	0	3	1.000	4.45	-1	-1
Rosario, W	Col	1B	1	1	8	8	0	1	1	.889	-	0	0
	Col	3B	4	0	4	0	1	1	0	.500	1.93	0	0
Ross, C	Bos	LF	22	19	166	21	2	0	0	1.000	1.24	-4	-1
	Bos	CF	7	3	39	13	0	0	0	1.000	3.00	-1	-1
Rottino, V	TOT	1B	7	5	40	36	2	0	6	1.000	-	+1	0
	TOT	3B	2	0	7	0	1	0	0	1.000	1.29	0	0
	TOT	LF	18	9	85	18	1	0	0	1.000	2.00	+1	1
	TOT	RF	2	1	12	2	0	0	0	1.000	1.50	-1	-1
Ruf, D	Phi	1B	3	3	26	16	0	0	0	1.000	-	0	0
	Phi	LF	6	6	46	5	0	0	0	1.000	.98	+1	0
Ruggiano, J	Mia	LF	31	16	150	28	3	0	0	1.000	1.86	-6	-4
	Mia	CF	52	48	412	135	4	3	0	.978	2.94	+13	6
	Mia	RF	15	10	99	17	0	0	0	1.000	1.54	-1	-1
Rutledge, J	Col	2B	7	7	64	15	18	0	4	1.000	4.59	+2	1
	Col	SS	57	56	483	83	157	11	33	.956	4.47	-11	-11
Saltalamacchia, J	Bos	1B	1	1	9	1	0	0	0	1.000	-	0	0
Sanchez, G	TOT	1B	95	77	697	695	71	3	58	.996	-	+12	6
Sandoval, P	SF	1B	3	2	12	10	1	0	1	1.000	-	+2	1

Player	Tm	Pos	G	GS	Inn	PO	A	E	DP	Pct.	Rng	+/-	RS
Sands, J	LAD	1B	1	1	8	9	1	0	1	1.000	-	0	0
	LAD	LF	6	4	34	6	0	0	0	1.000	1.59	+2	1
	LAD	RF	1	1	7	2	0	0	0	1.000	2.57	0	0
Santana, C	Cle	1B	21	20	162	160	13	2	21	.989	-	+1	1
	Cle	LF	1	0	4	2	0	0	0	1.000	4.50	0	0
Santiago, R	Det	2B	71	45	440	75	149	1	32	.996	4.58	-2	-1
	Det	3B	6	2	28	0	5	1	0	.833	1.57	+1	1
	Det	SS	20	15	139	13	34	4	4	.922	3.04	-4	-2
Sappelt, D	ChC	LF	4	0	7	0	0	0	0	-	.00	0	0
	ChC	RF	20	16	143	37	2	0	1	1.000	2.45	+4	2
Saunders, M	Sea	LF	22	22	183	41	1	0	0	1.000	2.06	0	1
	Sea	RF	5	4	31	6	0	0	0	1.000	1.74	+1	0
Schafer, J	Hou	CF	87	82	692	178	4	2	1	.989	2.36	-7	-6
Schafer, L	Mil	LF	2	0	5	3	0	0	0	1.000	4.76	+1	0
	Mil	CF	5	3	30	11	0	0	0	1.000	3.30	+2	1
	Mil	RF	2	0	3	3	0	0	0	1.000	9.00	+1	0
Schierholtz, N	TOT	LF	7	5	44	9	0	0	0	1.000	1.84	-1	-1
	TOT	RF	80	47	489	100	1	0	0	.990	1.84	+8	3
Schumaker, S	StL	2B	61	51	439	101	143	4	35	.984	4.99	-1	-1
	StL	LF	1	0	1	1	0	0	0	1.000	9.00	-1	0
	StL	CF	15	14	98	27	1	0	0	1.000	2.57	-3	0
	StL	RF	10	3	36	8	0	0	0	1.000	1.96	+1	0
Scott, L	TB	1B	6	6	41	28	2	0	3	1.000	-	+1	0
Scutaro, M	TOT	3B	15	15	131	14	36	2	3	.962	3.44	-2	-2
	TOT	SS	27	25	216	40	89	3	17	.977	5.38	-3	-2
Seager, K	Sea	2B	18	14	140	40	52	0	17	1.000	5.89	+4	3
Segura, J	TOT	SS	44	44	389	65	96	10	20	.942	3.72	-1	0
Sellers, J	LAD	2B	3	1	8	1	1	0	0	1.000	2.25	0	0
	LAD	3B	7	2	27	2	5	0	2	1.000	2.33	+1	1
	LAD	SS	9	9	73	17	22	1	4	.975	4.76	+1	1
Sierra, M	Tor	RF	39	35	316	67	3	0	0	1.000	1.99	-13	-7
Simmons, A	Atl	SS	49	49	426	67	158	3	31	.987	4.75	+20	19
Smith, S	Oak	LF	57	49	439	102	3	1	0	.991	2.15	-1	2
	Oak	RF	13	9	75	13	0	1	0	.929	1.55	+1	0
Snider, T	TOT	LF	15	12	115	26	0	1	0	.963	2.03	0	0
	TOT	RF	33	29	233	58	1	0	1	1.000	2.28	+6	3
Snyder, B	Tex	1B	11	8	75	67	6	0	5	1.000	-	+1	1
	Tex	3B	7	1	18	0	1	0	0	1.000	.50	0	0
	Tex	LF	5	1	13	3	0	0	0	1.000	2.08	-1	0
	Tex	RF	5	3	24	7	0	0	0	1.000	2.63	0	0
Snyder, C	Hou	1B	1	0	1	0	0	1	0	.000	-	0	0
Sogard, E	Oak	2B	6	5	49	10	17	0	4	1.000	4.93	+1	2
	Oak	3B	14	12	116	11	24	2	2	.946	2.72	+3	3
	Oak	SS	15	8	89	14	34	0	6	1.000	4.85	-1	-2
Solano, D	Mia	2B	58	56	488	88	166	2	28	.992	4.68	+4	1
	Mia	3B	10	8	74	5	13	2	2	.900	2.19	-1	-1
	Mia	SS	5	0	9	1	5	0	2	1.000	6.00	0	0
	Mia	LF	10	8	63	13	0	0	0	1.000	1.86	-3	-3
Spears, N	Bos	2B	1	0	1	0	1	0	0	1.000	9.00	0	0
	Bos	3B	1	0	5	1	1	0	0	1.000	3.60	-1	-1
	Bos	LF	2	0	4	0	0	0	0	-	.00	0	0
Stewart, I	ChC	3B	52	49	436	21	86	5	4	.955	2.21	+1	3
Sutton, D	TOT	1B	3	1	11	8	0	0	1	1.000	-	0	0
	TOT	2B	8	2	25	6	6	0	2	1.000	4.21	0	0
	TOT	3B	11	9	82	7	22	3	0	.906	3.17	-1	0
	TOT	LF	13	12	85	18	0	2	0	.900	1.91	+5	1
	TOT	RF	8	4	41	8	0	0	0	1.000	1.73	-7	-5
Suzuki, I	TOT	LF	35	26	236	50	0	0	0	1.000	1.91	0	-2
	TOT	CF	7	5	38	10	0	0	0	1.000	2.61	-3	0
Sweeney, R	Bos	CF	19	15	126	31	1	0	0	1.000	2.29	+1	1
	Bos	RF	49	35	341	80	2	2	2	.976	2.16	+5	4
Swisher, N	NYY	1B	41	27	259	255	18	3	23	.989	-	+4	5
Tabata, J	Pit	LF	32	30	240	59	2	0	0	1.000	2.28	+4	1
	Pit	RF	77	49	496	107	4	3	0	.974	2.01	+5	3
Taylor, M	Oak	LF	2	1	10	2	0	0	0	1.000	1.80	+1	0
	Oak	RF	4	4	37	12	0	0	0	1.000	2.92	+3	2
Tekotte, B	SD	LF	2	1	11	1	0	0	0	1.000	.82	-1	-1
	SD	CF	1	0	3	2	0	0	0	1.000	6.00	0	0
	SD	RF	1	1	7	0	0	0	0	-	.00	0	0
Thames, E	TOT	LF	44	39	341	75	0	1	0	.987	1.98	-4	-4
	TOT	RF	35	31	278	70	1	2	0	.973	2.30	-2	-3
Theriot, R	SF	2B	91	81	736	151	201	9	52	.975	4.30	-14	-12
	SF	LF	2	0	4	1	0	0	0	1.000	2.25	0	0
Thomas, C	TOT	LF	3	0	3	0	0	0	0	-	.00	0	0

Player	Tm	Pos	G	GS	Inn	PO	A	E	DP	Pct.	Rng	+/-	RS
	TOT	CF	1	0	6	4	0	0	0	1.000	6.00	+1	0
	TOT	RF	10	7	62	15	1	0	0	1.000	2.32	+2	2
Thome, J	TOT	1B	4	4	27	35	2	1	4	.974	-	0	1
Thompson, R	TB	LF	7	4	47	7	0	0	0	1.000	1.34	-1	-1
	TB	CF	5	0	10	1	0	0	0	1.000	.90	-2	-1
Tolleson, S	Bal	2B	4	2	19	7	6	0	2	1.000	6.16	0	0
	Bal	3B	12	11	94	2	27	4	0	.879	2.78	+2	1
	Bal	SS	3	0	3	1	1	0	1	1.000	6.00	0	0
	Bal	LF	7	6	50	11	0	0	0	1.000	1.98	+1	0
Torrealba, Y	TOT	1B	1	0	3	2	0	0	0	1.000	-	0	0
Tracy, C	Was	1B	14	6	66	64	4	1	6	.986	-	0	0
	Was	3B	10	6	55	3	13	0	0	1.000	2.62	+3	2
Triunfel, C	Sea	2B	2	2	17	1	8	0	1	1.000	4.76	0	0
	Sea	SS	7	3	40	11	15	1	5	.963	5.85	+2	1
Trout, M	LAA	LF	67	29	328	75	0	1	0	.987	2.06	+2	-1
	LAA	RF	4	1	12	1	1	1	0	.667	1.50	-2	-1
Trumbo, M	LAA	1B	21	16	159	145	5	0	8	1.000	-	-1	0
	LAA	3B	8	8	63	5	5	4	0	.714	1.43	-3	-2
	LAA	LF	66	66	497	102	4	0	0	1.000	1.92	+7	7
	LAA	RF	35	31	263	42	0	3	0	.933	1.43	-7	-6
Tulowitzki, T	Col	SS	47	47	404	76	140	8	31	.964	4.81	-8	-6
Turner, J	NYM	1B	11	8	71	53	2	1	6	.982	-	-1	0
	NYM	2B	14	10	91	29	26	1	7	.982	5.44	-1	-1
	NYM	3B	11	5	57	5	8	0	1	1.000	2.03	0	-1
	NYM	SS	10	8	66	9	20	0	5	1.000	3.93	-1	-1
Uribe, J	LAD	3B	46	41	357	21	84	4	7	.963	2.65	+6	4
	LAD	SS	1	1	9	2	2	1	1	.800	4.00	-1	0
Utley, C	Phi	2B	81	81	720	156	209	7	32	.981	4.56	+13	8
Valbuena, L	ChC	2B	2	1	16	2	4	0	1	1.000	3.24	-1	-1
	ChC	3B	82	72	638	45	137	7	18	.963	2.57	+6	5
Valdespin, J	NYM	2B	16	5	64	19	19	0	9	1.000	5.34	-2	-2
	NYM	SS	4	1	18	3	5	3	2	.727	3.86	-4	-3
	NYM	LF	21	15	134	24	0	0	0	1.000	1.61	-5	-4
	NYM	CF	11	6	64	21	0	0	0	1.000	2.92	-4	-2
	NYM	RF	10	5	47	15	1	0	0	1.000	3.06	+2	1
Valdez, W	Cin	2B	22	8	99	14	27	1	3	.976	3.73	-5	-5
	Cin	3B	14	5	57	5	13	2	1	.900	2.81	-1	-1
	Cin	SS	33	27	243	47	54	1	15	.990	3.74	-5	-4
	Cin	CF	5	4	35	6	0	0	0	1.000	1.54	+1	0
Valencia, D	TOT	3B	44	40	357	26	83	4	9	.965	2.75	-1	-1
Van Slyke, S	LAD	1B	5	5	34	23	4	0	2	1.000	-	-2	0
	LAD	LF	11	1	26	5	0	0	0	1.000	1.73	+1	0
	LAD	RF	12	7	65	17	1	0	1	1.000	2.47	+1	1
Velazquez, G	Mia	3B	17	15	134	16	31	2	3	.959	3.14	+1	2
Venable, W	SD	LF	10	7	63	10	0	1	0	.909	1.43	+3	0
	SD	CF	21	16	131	28	0	0	0	1.000	1.92	-1	0
	SD	RF	114	80	737	171	1	6	0	.966	2.10	+15	1
Victorino, S	TOT	LF	48	48	411	95	2	0	1	1.000	2.12	+13	7
	TOT	RF	1	0	1	0	0	0	0	-	.00	0	0
Vitters, J	ChC	3B	29	24	197	9	41	4	4	.926	2.28	-2	-3
Vizquel, O	Tor	1B	2	0	5	6	0	0	0	1.000	-	0	0
	Tor	2B	24	18	164	32	52	0	13	1.000	4.61	0	2
	Tor	3B	18	10	111	10	31	3	3	.932	3.30	+1	1
	Tor	SS	10	9	73	10	20	0	3	1.000	3.70	+3	1
	Tor	LF	1	0	0	0	0	0	0	-	.00	0	0
Vogt, S	TB	LF	2	0	3	1	0	0	0	1.000	3.00	0	0
Wallace, B	Hou	1B	58	54	466	455	39	7	41	.986	-	0	-5
	Hou	3B	8	5	49	2	8	2	3	.833	1.82	-3	-2
Wells, C	Sea	1B	52	42	390	82	3	0	1	1.000	1.96	-1	1
	Sea	CF	11	9	92	28	0	0	0	1.000	2.74	+2	1
	Sea	RF	25	23	212	41	5	0	1	1.000	1.95	-1	2
Wells, V	LAA	LF	69	59	539	128	0	1	0	.992	2.14	+9	5
	LAA	CF	6	6	46	9	0	0	0	1.000	1.76	-2	-2
	LAA	RF	2	0	4	0	0	0	0	-	.00	0	0
Werth, J	Was	CF	11	11	83	14	0	1	0	.933	1.51	-8	-5
	Was	RF	76	68	608	152	4	0	1	1.000	2.31	-10	-7
Wheeler, R	Ari	1B	4	2	20	21	1	0	1	1.000	-	+1	1
	Ari	3B	23	21	193	11	36	2	4	.959	2.19	0	-1
Wigginton, T	Phi	1B	71	49	471	421	38	4	34	.991	-	-3	-3
	Phi	3B	22	21	175	10	30	8	3	.833	2.05	-9	-7
	Phi	LF	7	7	48	13	0	0	0	1.000	2.44	-5	-3
Wilson, B	LAA	1B	4	0	7	10	2	0	1	1.000	-	0	0
Wilson, J	Atl	2B	2	1	9	1	5	1	1	.857	6.00	-1	-1
	Atl	SS	29	13	144	21	49	1	14	.986	4.38	+1	-1

Player	Tm	Pos	G	GS	Inn	PO	A	E	DP	Pct.	Rng	+/-	RS
Wise, D	TOT	LF	53	17	199	36	2	1	0	.974	1.72	+2	0
	TOT	CF	38	30	265	77	1	0	0	1.000	2.64	-2	-3
	TOT	RF	11	6	69	12	1	0	0	1.000	1.70	0	1
Worth, D	Det	2B	31	22	200	36	50	1	13	.989	3.87	-3	-3
	Det	3B	5	0	12	0	1	0	0	1.000	.75	0	0
	Det	SS	3	2	14	2	7	0	3	1.000	5.79	0	0
Wright, D	NYM	SS	1	0	6	0	2	0	0	1.000	3.00	0	0
Wright, W	Hou	RF	1	0	0	0	0	0	0	-	-	0	0
Youkilis, K	TOT	1B	26	14	125	117	9	0	20	1.000	-	0	1
Young, C	Ari	CF	87	84	725	201	4	2	1	.990	2.54	+13	7
Young, D	Det	LF	31	29	226	35	1	2	0	.947	1.43	-4	-3
Young, E	Col	LF	8	5	42	7	0	0	0	1.000	1.50	+1	0
	Col	CF	15	12	105	40	0	0	0	1.000	3.41	+12	6
	Col	RF	11	11	97	17	0	0	0	1.000	1.58	-3	-2
Young, M	Det	2B	2	0	4	1	1	0	1	1.000	4.50	0	0
	Det	LF	3	1	13	7	0	0	0	1.000	4.85	+1	1
	Det	RF	1	0	2	0	0	0	0	-	.00	0	-1
Young, M	Tex	1B	41	40	363	358	24	2	37	.995	-	-3	-2
	Tex	2B	16	14	124	24	31	2	8	.965	3.99	-4	-3
	Tex	3B	25	25	215	18	38	2	3	.966	2.34	-6	-6
	Tex	SS	4	4	33	6	6	0	0	1.000	3.27	-1	-1
Zobrist, B	TB	2B	58	46	408	73	107	6	27	.968	3.97	-4	-5
	TB	SS	47	47	392	46	139	4	27	.979	4.25	-4	0
	TB	RF	71	59	541	113	6	2	1	.983	1.98	+9	9

All Other Catchers

Player	Tm	G	GS	Inn	PO	A	E	DP	PB	Pct.	SBA	CS	PCS	CS%	CERA	GFP/DME	SB	Other	Total
																Runs Saved			
Anderson,Bryan	StL	2	1	8.0	9	0	0	0	0	1.000	0	0	0	-	4.50	0	0	0	0
Baker,John	SD	56	52	460.1	368	23	4	0	7	.990	54	5	4	.09	3.95	-1	-2	2	-1
Blanco,Henry	Ari	21	18	160.2	141	14	2	5	2	.987	6	3	0	.50	4.87	-1	1	0	0
Boscan,J.C.	Atl	6	2	29.0	37	1	1	0	0	.974	3	0	0	.00	3.72	0	0	0	0
Brantly,Rob	Mia	28	28	247.2	191	16	2	1	6	.990	21	3	1	.14	3.85	0	-2	0	-2
Butera,Drew	Min	41	32	298.2	242	15	1	2	4	.996	27	4	3	.15	4.04	0	0	2	2
Carlin,Luke	Cle	4	3	31.0	32	1	0	0	1	1.000	3	0	1	.00	6.68	0	0	0	0
Castillo,Welington	ChC	49	46	413.2	345	24	7	2	4	.981	40	7	4	.18	4.83	2	0	0	2
Cervelli,Francisco	NYY	3	0	5.0	8	0	0	0	0	1.000	0	0	0	-	0.00	0	0	0	0
Clevenger,Steve	ChC	51	49	412.2	319	18	4	0	4	.988	51	6	1	.12	4.47	0	-3	1	-2
Conger,Hank	LAA	7	6	55.0	48	4	1	0	0	.981	8	2	0	.25	4.75	0	0	0	0
Corporan,Carlos	Hou	24	22	185.2	164	23	2	3	2	.989	19	5	2	.26	4.85	2	0	0	2
Cruz,Tony	StL	47	28	293.1	255	23	2	3	3	.993	26	8	0	.31	4.14	1	-1	-2	-2
Donaldson,Josh	Oak	3	3	24.0	20	2	1	0	0	.957	4	0	2	.00	4.88	0	0	0	0
Doumit,Ryan	Min	59	56	492.2	290	22	2	3	2	.994	37	6	3	.16	5.08	-2	-1	-3	-6
Exposito,Luis	Bal	9	6	57.0	43	3	0	0	1	1.000	1	0	1	.00	5.37	0	0	0	0
Federowicz,Tim	LAD	2	1	10.0	13	0	0	0	0	1.000	0	0	1	-	0.90	0	0	0	0
Flowers,Tyler	CWS	49	40	360.2	324	29	2	5	1	.994	40	12	2	.30	4.04	1	4	0	5
Gimenez,Chris	TB	39	31	266.0	262	12	3	2	0	.989	25	5	0	.20	3.21	1	1	0	2
Gimenez,Hector	CWS	3	1	13.2	16	0	0	0	0	1.000	0	0	0	-	0.66	0	0	0	0
Gomes,Yan	Tor	9	5	49.1	35	0	0	0	0	1.000	0	0	0	-	5.29	-1	0	0	-1
Grandal,Yasmani	SD	55	52	461.1	386	38	5	2	8	.988	55	11	2	.20	4.00	7	0	-1	6
Hayes,Brett	Mia	33	31	278.0	221	21	5	1	1	.980	27	5	1	.19	5.08	1	0	-2	-1
Hernandez,Ramon	Col	46	45	400.0	336	17	2	4	1	.994	43	7	5	.16	5.45	-4	-1	-2	-7
Herrmann,Chris	Min	3	2	19.0	9	0	0	0	1	1.000	1	0	0	.00	3.79	0	0	0	0
Hester,John	LAA	38	27	253.2	195	9	0	2	1	1.000	33	3	2	.09	3.97	0	-3	-1	-4
Hill,Koyie	ChC	11	10	87.0	71	8	1	0	0	.988	8	2	0	.25	4.76	0	0	0	0
Holaday,Bryan	Det	6	3	37.0	25	2	0	1	0	1.000	3	0	1	.00	4.14	0	0	0	0
Hundley,Nick	SD	56	56	492.0	426	48	4	1	3	.992	73	19	6	.26	4.12	2	3	1	6
Jaso,John	Sea	43	39	343.1	263	15	0	1	5	1.000	33	6	1	.18	3.41	-3	0	2	-1
Johnson,Rob	NYM	17	15	134.2	130	6	0	0	2	1.000	10	1	0	.10	5.55	0	-1	0	-1
Kottaras,George	TOT	54	49	410.1	326	15	4	0	3	.988	40	2	6	.05	4.50	2	-4	-2	-4
Kratz,Erik	Phi	41	38	343.1	339	26	1	3	3	.997	30	12	3	.40	3.43	1	3	2	6
Laird,Gerald	Det	56	49	429.0	393	22	4	2	2	.990	49	7	3	.14	4.01	0	-3	-2	-5
Lalli,Blake	ChC	4	3	26.2	20	0	0	0	0	1.000	4	0	0	.00	4.05	0	-1	0	-1
Lavarnway,Ryan	Bos	28	25	219.0	183	11	2	0	0	.990	31	3	0	.10	5.84	-1	-2	-1	-4
Leon,Sandy	Was	12	9	83.1	73	5	1	1	3	.987	7	1	0	.14	3.13	0	0	0	0
Lerud,Steven	Phi	3	3	23.0	21	0	0	0	0	1.000	0	0	0	-	3.13	0	0	0	0
Lobaton,Jose	TB	66	50	467.0	448	28	4	3	0	.992	49	7	1	.14	3.24	-2	-1	-1	-4
Maldonado,Carlos	Was	4	3	28.0	24	0	0	0	0	1.000	2	0	0	.00	4.18	0	0	0	0
Maldonado,Martin	Mil	69	58	537.1	523	47	6	6	2	.990	44	12	3	.27	3.89	2	1	1	4
Marson,Lou	Cle	69	64	555.2	433	18	2	3	2	.996	77	10	1	.13	4.86	-4	-4	0	-8
Martinez,Luis	Tex	10	6	57.0	54	1	0	0	6	1.000	6	0	0	.00	2.84	0	-1	0	-1
Mathis,Jeff	Tor	66	59	532.2	433	37	2	5	6	.996	42	13	7	.31	4.39	2	3	0	5
Mesoraco,Devin	Cin	53	48	420.2	368	24	1	1	3	.997	48	9	1	.19	4.19	1	-3	-2	-4
Montero,Jesus	Sea	56	55	487.2	409	22	3	3	7	.993	63	9	2	.14	3.82	-2	-3	0	-5
Moore,Adam	KC	3	2	22.0	11	1	1	0	1	.923	4	0	0	.00	6.55	0	-1	0	-1
Navarro,Dioner	Cin	21	16	155.1	131	9	1	0	1	.993	6	1	0	.17	2.78	0	0	0	0
Nickeas,Mike	NYM	45	35	305.0	280	20	2	3	8	.993	23	5	1	.22	4.10	-2	-1	0	-3
Nieves,Wil	TOT	24	19	174.0	140	10	2	2	1	.987	18	1	2	.06	4.40	-1	-2	0	-3
Norris,Derek	Oak	58	53	496.2	438	19	5	0	4	.989	40	6	6	.15	3.10	-2	0	2	0
Pacheco,Jordan	Col	5	5	40.0	29	1	1	0	0	.968	5	0	0	.00	6.75	0	-1	0	-1
Paulino,Ronny	Bal	11	9	85.1	62	4	0	1	3	1.000	5	0	1	.00	3.38	0	-1	0	-1
Pena,Brayan	KC	52	46	417.2	344	18	4	4	5	.989	62	10	6	.16	4.22	3	-1	-1	1
Pina,Manny	KC	1	0	3.0	4	0	0	0	0	1.000	0	0	0	-	9.00	0	0	0	0
Quintero,Humberto	KC	43	40	355.0	310	28	5	5	2	.985	43	11	6	.26	4.11	3	1	1	5
Quiroz,Guillermo	Bos	1	0	2.0	1	1	0	0	1	1.000	0	0	0	-	4.50	0	0	0	0
Ramos,Wilson	Was	24	24	216.2	189	14	1	1	2	.995	22	3	1	.14	3.07	0	-1	0	-1
Recker,Anthony	TOT	17	12	111.2	84	8	1	3	2	.989	13	6	1	.46	3.06	1	1	-1	1
Rodriguez,Eddy	SD	2	2	17.0	20	1	0	0	0	1.000	3	0	0	.00	4.24	0	0	0	0
Ross,David	Atl	54	47	421.2	366	27	2	4	4	.995	33	14	1	.42	3.56	-3	4	-1	0
Rottino,Vinny	TOT	2	0	4.0	0	0	0	0	0	1.000	0	0	0	-	0.00	0	0	0	0
Sanchez,Hector	SF	56	48	441.0	350	26	7	4	3	.982	51	11	1	.22	4.00	-1	0	1	0
Santos,Omir	Det	3	3	27.0	21	0	2	0	2	.913	7	0	0	.00	5.00	0	-1	0	-1
Schmidt,Konrad	Ari	2	1	13.0	11	3	0	0	1	1.000	0	0	0	-	4.85	-1	0	0	-1
Schneider,Brian	Phi	29	26	228.2	197	21	0	2	1	1.000	24	7	1	.29	3.58	0	0	-1	-1
Shoppach,Kelly	TOT	73	64	566.0	454	29	10	3	8	.980	44	12	4	.27	3.99	-3	2	4	3
Snyder,Brandon	Tex	1	0	1.0	1	0	0	0	0	1.000	0	0	0	-	0.00	0	0	0	0
Snyder,Chris	Hou	72	67	591.0	498	39	3	5	3	.994	75	15	2	.20	4.72	-2	0	-1	-3
Solano,Jhonatan	Was	11	10	88.1	55	10	0	2	2	1.000	8	3	0	.38	3.26	1	0	-1	0
Solis,Ali	SD	2	0	4.0	0	0	1	0	0	.889	2	0	0	.00	0.00	0	0	0	0
Stewart,Chris	NYY	54	46	395.1	379	25	4	3	8	.990	34	7	1	.21	3.41	2	0	2	4
Teagarden,Taylor	Bal	21	15	152.0	110	7	0	0	1	1.000	8	2	0	.25	4.50	-1	-1	0	-2
Torrealba,Yorvit	TOT	60	53	470.0	432	21	2	2	4	.996	42	7	3	.17	4.04	-4	-2	-1	-7
Treanor,Matt	LAD	35	33	288.2	261	21	3	3	0	.989	21	3	3	.14	3.65	1	-2	0	-1
Vogt,Stephen	TB	7	1	17.0	19	2	0	0	0	1.000	1	1	0	1.00	0.53	0	0	0	0
Whiteside,Eli	SF	11	3	37.0	32	5	0	0	0	1.000	4	2	1	.50	4.62	-1	1	0	0
Wilson,Bobby	LAA	72	58	501.2	420	32	4	6	2	.991	60	15	3	.25	4.11	4	1	1	6

2012 Baserunning

Bill James

Mike Trout was on first base when a single was hit 45 times in his first season in the majors, and he made it to third base 28 times, which is 62%. Carlos Santana was on first base when a single was hit 34 times and motored over to third 4 times, which is 12%.

Trout was on a second when a single was hit 29 times. He scored on 20 of the 29 singles, which is 69%. Santana was on second when a single was hit 20 times. He scored 7 times, which is 35%.

Trout was on first when the batter hit a double 10 times, and he came around to score 7 times. That's 70%. Santana was on first when the batter hit a double 16 times, and he scored 3 times. That's 19%.

You might get the impression that Mike Trout was a better base runner than Carlos Santana, in which case you would be among the last people to get the memo on that. We have Trout as the best base runner in the major leagues in 2012 (+51) bases, and Santana as the worst (-45 bases). The difference between them as base runners is 20 runs, more or less. Trout's rating as a base runner is knocked backward a substantial distance by the fact that he made 9 unforced outs on the bases. He ran into an out 5 times and was doubled off 4 times; the total of 9 base running outs, was one of the highest in the majors. (His teammate, Albert Pujols, led the majors with 13 base running outs. The Angels, always aggressive on the bases, make a lot of outs on the bases but compensate by manufacturing some runs going first-to-third and things of that nature.) Anyway, my point was that if a player picks up five bases by being aggressive on the bases but runs into five outs, that's not a breakeven; that's a pretty significant net loss for the offense. You have to gain about three bases for each out before you break even on those, so Trout's nine outs on the bases offset 27 bases gained, which is not a negligible thing.

On the other hand, Carlos Santana made seven outs on the bases himself, so, comparing Santana to Trout. . .not that much difference on that scale, small advantage for Santana. It's the only one. Trout batted 87 times with a runner on first and less than two out, and grounded into 7 double plays. Santana batted 124 times with a runner on first and less than two out, and grounded into 21 double plays. Trout moved up 21 bases on Sacrifice Flies, Passed Balls, Wild Pitches, Balks and Defensive Indifference; Santana moved up only 9 bases on those events. Summarizing all of those differences, we have Trout +12 as a base runner, not counting his stolen base attempts, and Santana -38.   Trout also stole 49 bases in 54 attempts; Santana stole 3 bases in 8 attempts.   When we include base stealing, we have Trout +51 as a base runner, and Santana -45.

You would have known, without our data, that Mike Trout was a better base runner than Carlos Santana, but you cannot know, unless you actually study the data, how large the differences are, and you cannot know, unless you study the data, how many runs are gained and lost in this area.   You also cannot know, unless you study the data, how every player ranks in this area.   Who is a better at going first-to-third on a single: Carlos Pena or Jhonny Peralta? (Carlos Pena, by a mile.)

Without hard data, the impact of base running on the offense can be ignored, or it can be exaggerated.   We've tried to measure it so that it can neither be ignored nor exaggerated, but accurately evaluated.   We haven't yet measured everything involved in base running.   If one runner moves second-to-third on an infield out while another runner stays at second on a similar play, our system does not capture that.   If one runner makes a groundout a 4-3, advance, while another runners makes the same play a 4-6 forceout, our system does not pick up that difference.   We're still not capturing everything.   But we're working on the problem like busy little beavers, and we're making some progress.

In past seasons we have had two base running charts for you, one for individuals and one for teams. This year there is a third chart.   The third chart is career data.

In his career, the only major league player who has gone from first to third on a single 50% of the time is Chone Figgins.   Figgins—whose career began in the same year as our data in this area begins, 2002—has gone from first to third 148 times in 282 chances, or 52%. . .no one else is over 50%.

Prince Fielder is last on the list, at 10%.

Chase Utley is the only major league player who has scored from second on a single 75% of the time, 111 for 148.   (Utley is also second on the list, behind Figgins, in going first-to-third on a single.)

Brian McCann is last on that list, at 32%.

Jose Reyes has scored from first on a double 34 times in 52 chances over the years, or 65%.

Jim Thome is last on that list, at 15%.

Over the last eleven seasons, the ten best base runners in baseball have been 1) Ichiro (+372 bases), 2) Jimmy Rollins (+349), 3) Carl Crawford (+347), 4) Juan Pierre (+326), 5) Carlos Beltran (+308), 6-7) Johnny Damon and Jose Reyes (+280), 8) Chase Utley (+254), 9) Coco Crisp (+235), and 10) Shane Victorino (+233).   The worst base runner has been Paul Konerko, -183 bases.

Our job, as I see it, is to turn observation into knowledge.   These are among the things we know. Thanks for reading, and I hope you get something out of having the data.

2012 Baserunning

Player	1st to 3rd Moved	1st to 3rd Chances	2nd to Home Moved	2nd to Home Chances	1st to Home Moved	1st to Home Chances	Bases Taken	Out Adv	Doubled Off	BR Outs	GDP	GDP Opps	BR Gain	SB Gain	Net Gain
Abreu,Bobby	4	24	3	8	1	3	14	0	0	0	7	56	+6	+2	+8
Ackley,Dustin	12	49	11	17	4	5	26	1	3	4	3	97	+18	+7	+25
Alonso,Yonder	7	38	9	14	3	13	10	6	3	11	14	120	-34	+3	-31
Altuve,Jose	6	20	15	28	4	8	20	4	3	7	8	87	-5	+11	+6
Alvarez,Pedro	7	27	10	15	3	6	9	0	0	0	10	102	+8	+1	+9
Amarista,Alexi	1	7	9	14	2	2	12	2	0	2	2	48	+8	0	+8
Andino,Robert	5	16	3	10	3	3	12	1	3	4	13	93	-6	-5	-11
Andrus,Elvis	20	32	13	20	7	9	24	4	3	7	15	115	+11	+1	+12
Aoki,Norichika	5	21	10	18	2	4	12	4	1	5	6	64	-8	+14	+6
Arencibia,J.P.	2	11	8	12	1	3	6	1	1	2	4	55	0	+1	+1
Arias,Joaquin	7	15	3	8	1	2	13	1	0	1	12	76	+5	+3	+8
Avila,Alex	3	25	8	14	2	6	4	3	1	4	12	78	-19	+2	-17
Aviles,Mike	8	22	12	17	4	8	12	1	1	2	6	94	+11	+2	+13
Aybar,Erick	13	27	19	23	4	6	17	3	1	4	11	114	+15	+12	+27
Baker,Jeff	1	7	2	7	0	0	5	1	1	2	7	38	-8	+2	-6
Baker,John	1	8	0	4	5	5	3	0	0	0	4	36	+1	0	+1
Barajas,Rod	1	14	3	10	1	5	1	0	1	1	4	57	-9	0	-9
Barmes,Clint	3	13	6	9	0	4	9	1	0	1	9	87	+2	-4	-2
Barney,Darwin	7	33	11	16	9	11	20	0	0	0	11	97	+19	+4	+23
Barton,Daric	1	9	2	2	4	5	5	1	0	1	1	24	+4	+1	+5
Bautista,Jose	11	20	7	9	3	4	8	1	1	2	11	93	+7	+1	+8
Baxter,Mike	6	12	4	4	3	4	8	1	0	1	0	37	+13	-1	+12
Bay,Jason	3	9	2	2	3	4	2	0	0	0	3	47	+6	+3	+9
Beckham,Gordon	10	27	10	16	2	6	7	4	2	6	10	103	-11	-3	-14
Belt,Brandon	9	28	6	19	2	5	11	8	1	9	3	99	-16	+8	-8
Beltran,Carlos	6	26	5	13	5	9	12	0	1	1	9	127	+7	+1	+8
Beltre,Adrian	8	31	13	20	3	12	18	5	0	5	8	112	+1	+1	+2
Bernadina,Roger	6	17	5	11	4	7	6	2	0	2	2	41	+1	+9	+10
Berry,Quintin	7	20	11	15	5	6	11	2	2	4	4	69	+6	+21	+27
Betancourt,Yuniesky	2	7	2	6	0	2	4	1	1	2	10	55	-10	-2	-12
Betemit,Wilson	5	13	3	6	1	7	7	1	1	2	8	66	-3	-2	-5
Blanco,Gregor	10	25	5	12	5	6	12	3	2	5	0	61	+4	+14	+18
Bloomquist,Willie	5	14	9	13	2	6	9	0	0	0	5	41	+8	-13	-5
Boesch,Brennan	3	20	8	13	7	9	8	2	1	3	11	97	-4	0	-4
Bogusevic,Brian	12	25	4	10	3	5	8	0	1	1	6	67	+7	+7	+14
Bonifacio,Emilio	6	10	6	9	0	2	6	1	0	1	3	50	+6	+24	+30
Bourjos,Peter	5	12	9	10	1	1	9	0	0	0	2	43	+15	+1	+16
Bourn,Michael	10	32	8	12	7	9	30	0	2	2	2	84	+31	+16	+47
Brantley,Michael	10	38	9	18	4	7	12	1	2	3	7	118	+3	-6	-3
Braun,Ryan	8	28	12	23	8	13	14	3	1	4	12	123	-1	+16	+15
Brown,Domonic	2	15	0	5	1	3	9	2	1	3	6	53	-7	0	-7
Bruce,Jay	4	27	9	16	3	9	12	5	1	6	5	113	-7	+3	-4
Buck,John	1	10	3	11	0	0	1	0	2	2	8	66	-13	0	-13
Burriss,Emmanuel	1	4	2	3	3	3	4	0	0	0	6	36	+3	-1	+2
Butler,Billy	6	36	5	16	2	10	13	2	1	3	20	117	-19	0	-19
Cabrera,Asdrubal	13	31	14	20	2	5	21	4	0	4	18	126	+7	+1	+8
Cabrera,Everth	6	13	11	13	3	4	14	3	1	4	3	69	+10	+36	+46
Cabrera,Melky	9	30	10	14	6	11	25	2	0	2	8	103	+22	+3	+25
Cabrera,Miguel	14	46	14	23	6	8	21	8	0	8	28	146	-16	+2	-14
Cain,Lorenzo	3	11	3	4	2	5	2	3	1	4	4	37	-11	+10	-1
Callaspo,Alberto	6	25	14	16	3	5	13	2	0	2	6	89	+11	-2	+9
Campana,Tony	6	11	6	11	0	0	13	0	0	0	0	30	+17	+24	+41
Cano,Robinson	16	38	12	23	2	10	24	5	5	10	22	166	-14	-1	-15
Carp,Mike	6	14	2	5	0	3	5	0	0	0	7	38	+1	+1	+2
Carpenter,Matt	3	19	6	9	4	5	12	2	0	2	10	86	+3	-1	+2
Carrera,Ezequiel	2	9	4	6	2	3	1	0	0	0	3	30	+1	+6	+7
Carroll,Jamey	11	37	15	25	3	10	19	3	0	3	9	89	+6	-1	+5
Carter,Chris	2	12	5	9	1	4	8	0	0	0	4	46	+5	0	+5
Casilla,Alexi	3	11	11	12	1	4	11	0	0	0	6	48	+11	+19	+30
Castillo,Welington	1	5	2	3	0	3	5	1	0	1	4	30	-1	0	-1
Castro,Jason	5	13	7	10	0	0	8	1	0	1	8	67	+5	0	+5
Castro,Starlin	12	32	10	11	7	13	18	4	1	5	15	128	+5	-1	+4

2012 Baserunning

Player	1st to 3rd Moved	1st to 3rd Chances	2nd to Home Moved	2nd to Home Chances	1st to Home Moved	1st to Home Chances	Bases Taken	Out Adv	Doubled Off	BR Outs	GDP	GDP Opps	BR Gain	SB Gain	Net Gain
Cedeno,Ronny	1	7	0	2	2	3	2	1	0	1	10	41	-9	-2	-11
Cespedes,Yoenis	8	24	6	8	5	9	16	2	0	2	9	101	+12	+8	+20
Chavez,Endy	0	5	4	5	0	1	3	0	0	0	2	31	+3	-1	+2
Chavez,Eric	4	13	4	7	0	2	5	1	1	2	10	50	-8	0	-8
Choo,Shin-Soo	17	43	9	21	3	10	18	3	2	5	11	97	-3	+7	+4
Ciriaco,Pedro	7	19	6	7	2	3	11	0	0	0	2	46	+16	+10	+26
Clevenger,Steve	4	9	5	8	2	2	5	1	1	2	10	50	-4	-2	-6
Colvin,Tyler	10	26	12	19	2	4	8	2	0	2	6	70	+4	+1	+5
Cozart,Zack	7	24	10	16	3	5	23	1	0	1	11	68	+14	+4	+18
Craig,Allen	11	24	7	19	5	10	11	2	0	2	15	101	-2	0	-2
Crawford,Brandon	3	19	12	16	2	3	3	2	1	3	4	95	-2	-7	-9
Crisp,Coco	2	18	13	20	2	5	20	1	1	2	9	69	+7	+31	+38
Cruz,Luis	6	8	3	8	2	4	8	0	1	1	7	52	+4	0	+4
Cruz,Nelson	4	31	14	22	0	7	15	6	2	8	7	116	-14	0	-14
Cuddyer,Michael	6	13	10	13	3	5	5	3	0	3	12	78	-5	+2	-3
Damon,Johnny	5	11	3	4	2	3	0	2	0	2	0	44	+1	+4	+5
Davis,Chris	7	21	4	9	2	8	10	1	1	2	8	98	+2	-4	-2
Davis,Ike	4	22	8	16	0	2	11	1	2	3	10	106	-4	0	-4
Davis,Rajai	8	12	8	11	3	7	16	2	2	4	8	66	+6	+20	+26
De Aza,Alejandro	10	24	17	26	4	5	15	3	2	5	1	68	+9	+2	+11
DeJesus,David	14	33	14	21	2	7	19	3	1	4	9	59	+5	-9	-4
Denorfia,Chris	5	21	6	9	5	7	9	1	3	4	9	56	-7	+3	-4
Descalso,Daniel	9	18	10	13	3	4	9	1	0	1	5	77	+14	0	+14
Desmond,Ian	8	21	4	15	5	7	17	1	2	3	17	89	-4	+9	+5
Dirks,Andy	5	25	8	12	4	6	9	2	0	2	4	58	+3	-1	+2
Dobbs,Greg	1	14	7	10	1	3	4	1	1	2	8	58	-8	0	-8
Donaldson,Josh	8	17	5	9	1	3	5	1	0	1	6	46	+2	+2	+4
Doumit,Ryan	4	22	9	17	2	5	8	5	1	6	17	120	-21	0	-21
Downs,Matt	1	4	1	2	0	1	4	0	0	0	5	32	+1	-6	-5
Dozier,Brian	7	13	1	7	1	4	9	2	2	4	10	66	-8	+5	-3
Drew,Stephen	1	14	3	10	0	5	9	1	0	1	2	45	-1	-3	-4
Duda,Lucas	7	22	3	8	2	9	6	0	1	1	5	83	+1	+1	+2
Duncan,Shelley	4	10	2	4	1	5	4	0	2	2	9	53	-7	-3	-10
Dunn,Adam	6	32	12	21	2	10	11	1	1	2	8	138	+3	0	+3
Dyson,Jarrod	12	24	15	17	4	6	17	0	0	0	5	49	+26	+20	+46
Ellis,A.J.	7	27	6	16	0	2	9	1	0	1	17	99	-9	0	-9
Ellis,Mark	7	29	10	17	1	5	14	3	1	4	5	58	-2	+5	+3
Ellsbury,Jacoby	6	12	7	14	3	5	9	1	0	1	5	52	+7	+8	+15
Encarnacion,Edwin	15	33	11	17	1	8	16	4	2	6	6	124	+5	+7	+12
Escobar,Alcides	11	31	14	23	8	12	15	2	1	3	14	120	+6	+25	+31
Escobar,Eduardo	7	12	2	5	1	1	4	1	1	2	0	26	+3	+3	+6
Escobar,Yunel	10	33	10	16	0	4	18	3	2	5	21	109	-11	+3	-8
Espinosa,Danny	9	32	15	23	2	8	16	4	2	6	11	133	-3	+8	+5
Ethier,Andre	6	30	19	24	3	6	13	3	0	3	13	133	+4	-2	+2
Fielder,Prince	7	43	9	19	3	10	13	4	2	6	19	128	-24	+1	-23
Figgins,Chone	6	12	3	6	0	0	6	0	0	0	3	24	+6	+2	+8
Flores,Jesus	3	8	3	5	0	1	2	1	0	1	7	51	-3	-3	-6
Forsythe,Logan	8	22	8	11	4	5	12	1	1	2	6	55	+9	+4	+13
Fowler,Dexter	18	28	9	15	4	5	21	4	3	7	5	70	+11	+2	+13
Francisco,Ben	0	4	2	5	0	2	4	0	1	1	1	33	-1	-2	-3
Francisco,Juan	1	6	1	1	1	1	2	1	0	1	5	33	-3	-1	-4
Francoeur,Jeff	13	33	9	16	1	11	14	4	1	5	14	106	-8	-10	-18
Frandsen,Kevin	1	10	3	5	1	4	8	0	0	0	4	38	+4	-2	+2
Frazier,Todd	7	18	5	10	6	9	14	1	0	1	9	92	+12	-1	+11
Freeman,Freddie	5	24	16	18	1	10	20	4	0	4	10	125	+8	+2	+10
Freese,David	7	35	10	18	3	14	15	5	3	8	19	96	-28	-3	-31
Furcal,Rafael	15	33	16	21	3	8	10	3	2	5	7	62	0	+4	+4
Galvis,Freddy	3	12	6	10	0	1	1	0	0	0	6	38	-3	0	-3
Gentry,Craig	3	14	10	12	0	3	4	0	0	0	4	61	+5	-1	+4
Getz,Chris	7	11	3	4	0	1	6	1	0	1	3	34	+6	+3	+9
Giavotella,Johnny	5	15	5	8	1	1	6	1	0	1	4	31	+3	+3	+6
Goldschmidt,Paul	9	32	17	26	5	6	15	1	3	4	9	104	+5	+12	+17
Gomes,Jonny	3	11	8	9	1	4	8	0	2	2	2	64	+4	+1	+5
Gomez,Carlos	2	10	17	20	2	2	7	2	2	4	6	78	0	+25	+25

2012 Baserunning

Player	1st to 3rd Moved	1st to 3rd Chances	2nd to Home Moved	2nd to Home Chances	1st to Home Moved	1st to Home Chances	Bases Taken	Out Adv	Doubled Off	BR Outs	GDP	GDP Opps	BR Gain	SB Gain	Net Gain
Gonzalez,Adrian	5	34	7	19	4	14	14	4	1	5	10	125	-13	+2	-11
Gonzalez,Carlos	5	23	15	23	4	8	20	2	0	2	11	113	+12	+10	+22
Gonzalez,Marwin	0	12	4	13	0	1	4	2	0	2	9	43	-15	-3	-18
Gordon,Alex	6	36	17	29	6	10	18	0	3	3	14	120	0	0	0
Gordon,Dee	2	6	5	8	2	3	8	1	0	1	5	46	+4	+12	+16
Gose,Anthony	7	8	3	5	2	2	11	0	1	1	1	30	+15	+9	+24
Grandal,Yasmani	3	15	2	7	0	4	5	1	0	1	8	52	-7	0	-7
Granderson,Curtis	5	19	9	16	4	7	23	1	2	3	5	140	+21	+4	+25
Greene,Tyler	4	11	3	6	1	2	10	0	0	0	7	69	+9	+4	+13
Gutierrez,Franklin	3	8	3	4	1	2	4	2	0	3	5	31	-6	+1	-5
Guzman,Jesus	4	11	5	7	0	2	5	1	0	1	2	68	+6	-3	+3
Gwynn,Tony	3	14	6	9	3	6	8	3	0	3	6	46	-4	+1	-3
Hafner,Travis	1	13	1	2	1	4	2	1	0	1	9	48	-10	0	-10
Hairston,Jerry	2	10	4	7	0	2	6	0	0	0	7	36	-1	-3	-4
Hairston,Scott	2	17	12	17	2	4	4	3	0	3	10	70	-10	+4	-6
Hamilton,Josh	16	40	14	17	2	4	15	0	1	1	9	125	+22	-1	+21
Hanigan,Ryan	2	15	9	11	1	3	10	0	0	0	6	53	+7	0	+7
Hannahan,Jack	3	10	6	11	1	1	7	1	2	3	9	55	-7	-4	-11
Hardy,J.J.	11	29	10	16	4	12	16	0	0	0	21	134	+8	0	+8
Harper,Bryce	13	25	14	22	8	12	16	5	3	8	8	120	+3	+6	+9
Harrison,Josh	3	8	6	7	3	5	13	1	0	1	3	36	+13	+1	+14
Hart,Corey	8	23	12	21	4	6	13	2	1	3	13	95	0	+5	+5
Headley,Chase	11	38	15	25	3	7	19	3	2	6	7	126	+3	+5	+8
Heisey,Chris	4	16	11	15	2	5	11	1	0	1	8	66	+6	0	+6
Helton,Todd	4	16	6	8	0	5	7	2	1	3	6	51	-6	-1	-7
Hernandez,Gorkys	2	8	1	2	1	1	5	1	2	3	2	25	-4	+3	-1
Hernandez,Ramon	1	5	3	6	0	3	0	2	0	2	4	31	-10	-2	-12
Herrera,Elian	4	14	6	8	1	2	12	1	0	1	5	34	+8	0	+8
Herrera,Jonathan	7	13	1	5	1	4	6	0	0	0	5	45	+5	+2	+7
Heyward,Jason	15	32	18	22	6	9	18	1	2	3	5	145	+29	+5	+34
Hill,Aaron	9	30	9	13	4	7	25	2	1	3	15	112	+11	+4	+15
Holliday,Matt	11	46	18	26	2	12	19	1	1	2	16	170	+8	-4	+4
Hosmer,Eric	8	28	14	23	2	3	16	2	1	3	10	94	+5	+14	+19
Howard,Ryan	1	10	2	9	0	2	7	3	0	3	8	57	-11	0	-11
Hudson,Orlando	5	9	4	6	0	3	7	1	0	1	6	53	+4	0	+4
Hundley,Nick	3	7	3	6	0	2	5	1	0	1	4	44	+1	-6	-5
Hunter,Torii	13	33	14	15	9	14	16	5	1	6	15	100	+1	+7	+8
Iannetta,Chris	3	13	2	4	0	1	6	1	0	1	4	55	+2	-5	-3
Ibanez,Raul	4	16	5	7	1	4	5	1	0	1	14	98	-4	+3	-1
Infante,Omar	9	17	7	13	6	8	11	2	6	8	9	114	-7	+11	+4
Inge,Brandon	2	11	3	4	1	2	7	0	0	0	8	54	+3	-2	+1
Ishikawa,Travis	3	10	1	3	0	1	5	0	0	0	4	34	+3	0	+3
Izturis,Cesar	3	7	3	5	0	1	4	0	0	0	7	37	+1	-1	0
Izturis,Maicer	6	21	8	14	0	2	14	0	1	1	10	50	+3	+13	+16
Jackson,Austin	15	43	20	28	4	6	22	3	4	7	9	88	+5	-6	-1
Janish,Paul	1	3	1	5	1	2	4	1	0	1	1	26	0	+1	+1
Jaso,John	7	18	10	12	2	4	11	4	0	4	6	62	+2	+5	+7
Jay,Jon	11	30	9	12	4	8	20	1	1	3	9	90	+13	+5	+18
Jennings,Desmond	6	14	12	17	6	6	19	1	1	2	7	79	+18	+27	+45
Jeter,Derek	10	43	11	24	4	13	21	1	3	4	24	102	-16	+1	-15
Johnson,Chris	3	19	7	11	2	4	17	1	2	3	18	100	-4	+3	-1
Johnson,Elliot	3	13	6	8	3	4	10	4	0	4	3	66	+2	+6	+8
Johnson,Kelly	6	25	6	12	0	2	19	1	1	2	8	94	+9	+10	+19
Johnson,Reed	3	17	1	3	4	6	7	1	1	2	4	43	-2	-2	-4
Jones,Adam	14	34	9	13	7	11	18	3	2	5	15	124	+5	+2	+7
Jones,Andruw	4	8	1	4	0	0	7	0	1	1	2	57	+7	0	+7
Jones,Chipper	5	28	7	15	1	6	10	3	0	4	15	91	-17	+1	-16
Jones,Garrett	5	30	6	9	2	8	14	4	1	5	3	108	0	+2	+2
Joyce,Matt	3	12	12	17	7	7	15	1	2	3	10	82	+8	-2	+6
Kawasaki,Munenori	4	7	2	3	0	0	3	1	0	1	2	15	+1	-2	-1
Kearns,Austin	2	10	3	5	2	3	4	0	0	0	8	34	-2	0	-2
Kemp,Matt	14	31	14	20	5	7	5	5	3	8	10	93	-13	+1	-12
Kendrick,Howie	10	32	6	15	3	5	23	3	1	4	26	115	-8	+2	-6
Kennedy,Adam	2	13	3	5	0	0	6	0	0	0	5	43	+3	-1	+2

2012 Baserunning

Player	1st to 3rd Moved	Chances	2nd to Home Moved	Chances	1st to Home Moved	Chances	Bases Taken	Out Adv	Doubled Off	BR Outs	GDP	GDP Opps	BR Gain	SB Gain	Net Gain
Keppinger,Jeff	5	29	6	10	4	11	10	4	1	5	14	81	-17	+1	-16
Kinsler,Ian	15	32	20	31	4	10	24	1	3	4	14	94	+11	+3	+14
Kipnis,Jason	15	39	11	20	4	9	18	3	3	6	12	146	+3	+17	+20
Konerko,Paul	5	39	4	7	2	12	14	0	1	1	16	107	-7	0	-7
Kotchman,Casey	1	24	7	10	2	10	8	3	0	3	15	109	-14	+3	-11
Kottaras,George	1	9	1	2	2	6	4	0	2	2	4	46	-5	0	-5
Kubel,Jason	6	20	11	19	4	13	11	4	0	4	11	113	-4	-1	-5
LaHair,Bryan	4	13	3	5	0	6	10	1	2	3	8	67	-4	0	-4
Laird,Gerald	2	14	3	9	0	2	6	0	1	2	4	35	-7	0	-7
LaRoche,Adam	4	32	11	18	2	8	13	3	0	3	10	117	-3	-1	-4
Lawrie,Brett	14	27	11	14	4	6	14	5	0	5	9	79	+5	-3	+2
Lee,Carlos	11	33	10	15	1	4	14	5	0	5	13	95	-6	+3	-3
LeMahieu,DJ	4	8	3	6	1	1	6	0	1	1	8	35	-1	-3	-4
Lillibridge,Brent	4	14	3	4	2	2	4	0	1	1	2	45	+4	+9	+13
Lind,Adam	2	13	1	5	1	5	7	2	1	4	10	70	-14	0	-14
Lobaton,Jose	0	15	2	8	1	1	0	1	0	1	6	38	-13	-2	-15
Lombardozzi,Steve	5	18	8	13	2	6	7	2	1	3	1	45	-1	-1	-2
Loney,James	5	25	7	10	3	6	10	0	0	0	21	85	-5	-6	-11
Longoria,Evan	3	11	3	9	1	5	6	0	0	0	14	64	-7	-4	-11
Lopez,Jose	1	12	2	6	0	1	6	1	0	1	9	53	-6	-2	-8
Lowrie,Jed	6	15	5	6	2	6	13	2	1	3	3	59	+8	+2	+10
Lucroy,Jonathan	2	16	4	7	2	4	9	1	0	1	12	71	-3	+2	-1
Ludwick,Ryan	6	24	5	13	3	3	10	2	2	4	9	85	-7	-2	-9
Machado,Manny	1	4	5	5	0	0	5	1	1	2	6	42	-2	+2	0
Maldonado,Martin	2	9	1	5	1	1	6	3	0	3	5	47	-6	-1	-7
Markakis,Nick	6	27	12	16	2	9	11	3	2	5	11	71	-12	-1	-13
Marson,Lou	3	10	7	9	1	4	5	1	1	2	10	47	-7	0	-7
Marte,Starling	3	5	1	4	1	2	3	0	1	1	5	21	-3	+2	-1
Martin,Russell	3	21	8	13	3	5	7	1	2	3	13	90	-10	+4	-6
Martinez,J.D.	7	25	3	4	2	6	9	1	1	2	18	85	-9	-4	-13
Mastroianni,Darin	4	8	4	5	0	0	5	1	2	3	4	41	-2	+15	+13
Mather,Joe	4	10	5	7	0	0	3	2	0	2	4	45	-1	+1	0
Mathis,Jeff	1	6	6	9	1	2	2	0	1	1	2	32	0	+1	+1
Mauer,Joe	12	35	16	17	2	14	14	0	2	2	23	147	0	0	0
Maxwell,Justin	8	15	7	8	2	2	7	0	1	1	6	61	+10	+1	+11
Mayberry,John	4	23	7	15	7	10	13	5	2	7	17	89	-20	+1	-19
Maybin,Cameron	11	26	14	22	5	8	16	0	3	3	12	110	+9	+12	+21
McCann,Brian	5	29	6	11	1	6	5	3	0	3	15	103	-16	+3	-13
McCutchen,Andrew	22	46	20	21	5	8	20	1	1	2	9	124	+31	-4	+27
McDonald,John	1	4	1	6	0	0	4	1	0	1	3	34	-2	-2	-4
McGehee,Casey	6	16	7	14	0	2	7	1	0	1	10	57	-2	-1	-3
McKenry,Michael	3	9	7	8	0	1	5	2	1	3	7	64	-3	0	-3
McLouth,Nate	4	13	9	10	0	2	8	0	1	1	2	43	+8	+10	+18
Mesoraco,Devin	0	6	2	5	1	1	4	0	0	0	2	25	+2	-1	+1
Middlebrooks,Will	1	6	2	4	2	9	9	0	0	0	8	53	+2	+2	+4
Molina,Jose	2	8	0	4	0	2	4	0	1	1	9	46	-8	+1	-7
Molina,Yadier	4	29	4	7	3	8	17	7	2	9	10	109	-17	+6	-11
Montero,Jesus	3	22	4	11	1	4	12	2	4	6	15	96	-20	-4	-24
Montero,Miguel	5	35	3	12	9	19	15	7	2	9	15	118	-27	0	-27
Moore,Scott	2	8	2	4	1	3	11	0	0	0	3	34	+9	-2	+7
Moore,Tyler	0	9	1	4	1	1	3	1	0	1	3	26	-5	+3	-2
Morales,Kendrys	9	36	6	11	1	4	15	3	1	4	11	77	-5	-2	-7
Moreland,Mitch	1	11	4	10	1	8	10	2	0	2	8	73	-5	-1	-6
Morgan,Nyjer	2	21	5	7	3	5	8	1	2	3	4	53	-4	+2	-2
Morneau,Justin	3	27	3	12	0	10	10	2	2	4	19	126	-24	+1	-23
Morrison,Logan	0	16	2	6	2	3	10	2	0	2	9	56	-6	+1	-5
Morse,Michael	5	20	5	12	1	8	11	3	1	4	14	74	-15	-2	-17
Moss,Brandon	2	7	6	12	3	4	7	0	0	0	5	61	+7	-1	+6
Moustakas,Mike	6	31	9	19	0	6	23	2	2	4	4	115	+8	+1	+9
Murphy,Daniel	9	34	9	12	5	10	14	1	4	5	12	116	-3	+6	+3
Murphy,David	5	15	7	16	7	10	13	2	1	3	7	95	+4	0	+4
Napoli,Mike	2	21	5	13	0	4	7	1	1	2	9	90	-9	+1	-8
Nava,Daniel	2	11	10	14	3	6	10	0	0	0	5	47	+9	+3	+12
Nelson,Chris	9	30	5	10	1	1	7	1	0	1	9	54	-2	0	-2

2012 Baserunning

Player	1st to 3rd Moved	1st to 3rd Chances	2nd to Home Moved	2nd to Home Chances	1st to Home Moved	1st to Home Chances	Bases Taken	Out Adv	Doubled Off	BR Outs	GDP	GDP Opps	BR Gain	SB Gain	Net Gain
Nieuwenhuis,Kirk	6	16	4	6	4	5	8	0	0	0	2	44	+13	-4	+9
Nix,Jayson	6	11	4	7	1	2	5	1	0	1	4	40	+4	0	+4
Norris,Derek	4	7	4	7	0	0	9	0	0	0	6	35	+7	+3	+10
Olivo,Miguel	5	12	0	2	1	2	4	1	0	1	8	60	-2	-9	-11
Ortiz,David	1	17	8	15	2	9	5	5	3	8	6	80	-26	-2	-28
Pacheco,Jordan	14	28	8	15	1	8	13	2	0	2	13	80	+2	+3	+5
Pagan,Angel	13	38	16	24	4	10	36	3	2	5	6	112	+26	+15	+41
Parmelee,Chris	1	6	1	5	2	3	4	0	0	0	4	39	+1	0	+1
Parra,Gerardo	10	26	10	14	3	6	19	4	2	6	4	58	+5	-3	+2
Parrino,Andy	1	4	1	1	2	3	7	0	1	1	2	24	+5	+1	+6
Pastornicky,Tyler	2	6	4	7	1	2	5	0	0	0	5	41	+3	+2	+5
Pearce,Steve	2	10	4	5	0	0	8	1	0	1	4	34	+4	-3	+1
Pedroia,Dustin	7	26	17	26	5	12	23	4	1	5	9	97	+6	+8	+14
Pena,Brayan	3	15	4	7	0	3	7	3	0	3	7	36	-9	-2	-11
Pena,Carlos	13	39	7	14	3	11	15	6	2	8	10	110	-12	-4	-16
Pence,Hunter	11	45	12	21	9	14	26	1	2	3	15	144	+14	+1	+15
Pennington,Cliff	6	16	12	18	2	3	16	0	1	1	1	63	+20	+3	+23
Peralta,Jhonny	1	22	9	20	5	7	10	5	0	5	20	128	-21	-3	-24
Perez,Salvador	4	15	8	11	0	7	6	1	2	3	14	57	-15	0	-15
Petersen,Bryan	6	17	9	10	1	3	9	2	0	2	3	46	+7	+4	+11
Phillips,Brandon	13	30	9	16	5	9	18	1	0	1	19	105	+9	+11	+20
Pierre,Juan	10	25	11	18	4	7	14	2	2	4	4	66	+6	+23	+29
Pierzynski,A.J.	4	22	10	19	0	3	11	5	1	6	8	92	-13	0	-13
Plouffe,Trevor	5	20	10	13	1	3	13	3	1	4	9	89	0	-5	-5
Podsednik,Scott	3	13	3	6	3	5	5	2	2	4	3	32	-8	+4	-4
Polanco,Placido	3	17	7	11	1	9	6	0	0	0	7	56	-2	0	-2
Posey,Buster	5	36	9	15	3	15	24	1	1	2	19	126	-1	-1	-2
Prado,Martin	18	36	9	12	7	11	28	4	1	5	19	120	+14	+9	+23
Presley,Alex	5	10	4	7	0	1	14	0	0	0	5	43	+13	-5	+8
Pujols,Albert	14	32	13	17	1	8	11	12	0	13	19	134	-31	+6	-25
Punto,Nick	6	14	3	7	1	1	6	1	0	1	5	38	+2	+6	+8
Quentin,Carlos	5	18	6	7	1	1	5	1	1	2	6	58	-1	-2	-3
Quintanilla,Omar	4	11	2	3	3	5	3	1	0	1	3	29	+1	-2	-1
Raburn,Ryan	4	9	7	7	0	2	10	0	0	0	7	55	+11	-1	+10
Ramirez,Alexei	7	22	15	19	1	1	14	1	0	1	15	107	+9	+6	+15
Ramirez,Aramis	4	24	9	18	2	11	18	2	1	3	14	110	-5	+5	0
Ramirez,Hanley	13	24	14	16	5	7	10	6	1	7	17	138	-4	+7	+3
Ransom,Cody	4	10	4	5	0	2	9	0	1	1	6	63	+7	-2	+5
Rasmus,Colby	7	24	10	13	3	3	14	4	4	8	7	102	-5	-2	-7
Reddick,Josh	9	29	11	15	6	9	23	1	0	1	15	148	+22	+9	+31
Revere,Ben	9	39	17	20	3	6	23	3	1	4	8	86	+12	+22	+34
Reyes,Jose	14	41	18	24	2	3	26	6	0	6	10	103	+11	+18	+29
Reynolds,Mark	7	25	6	9	5	8	10	1	0	1	19	104	-2	-5	-7
Rios,Alex	10	26	11	20	2	6	17	2	3	5	18	128	-5	+11	+6
Rivera,Juan	4	19	2	6	3	4	9	2	1	3	15	71	-11	-5	-16
Rizzo,Anthony	5	14	5	11	4	7	7	4	1	5	7	74	-9	-1	-10
Roberts,Ryan	2	18	13	18	2	4	11	2	1	3	13	107	-3	-2	-5
Robinson,Shane	5	12	9	11	1	1	8	1	3	4	5	31	-2	+1	-1
Robinson,Trayvon	1	4	2	5	0	0	2	0	0	0	2	31	+1	0	+1
Rodriguez,Alex	5	27	8	14	0	5	21	2	1	3	13	112	+2	+11	+13
Rodriguez,Sean	7	20	7	9	2	3	10	1	1	2	7	58	+5	+5	+10
Rolen,Scott	7	18	3	7	1	3	12	3	1	4	5	65	0	0	0
Rollins,Jimmy	10	41	17	21	3	6	30	2	0	2	9	87	+24	+20	+44
Rosario,Wilin	8	27	15	17	2	6	12	2	2	4	10	67	-1	-6	-7
Ross,Cody	11	26	8	13	2	7	16	2	1	3	11	110	+8	-4	+4
Ross,David	2	5	4	5	0	4	2	0	1	1	5	34	-4	+1	-3
Ruggiano,Justin	2	13	6	10	1	2	3	4	0	4	6	60	-12	-2	-14
Ruiz,Carlos	8	26	10	14	4	7	8	2	0	3	6	60	0	+4	+4
Rutledge,Josh	4	15	3	7	4	5	5	1	0	1	8	60	-1	+7	+6
Ryan,Brendan	9	19	2	8	2	2	15	3	0	3	4	80	+10	+1	+11
Saltalamacchia,J	9	19	4	6	3	5	11	2	0	2	5	80	+11	-2	+9
Sanchez,Gaby	4	15	3	5	0	1	6	1	0	1	13	70	-5	-4	-4
Sanchez,Hector	0	7	3	8	2	2	8	0	1	1	8	51	-1	0	-1
Sandoval,Pablo	1	25	13	15	3	10	11	1	0	1	13	97	-1	-1	-2

2012 Baserunning

Player	1st to 3rd Moved	Chances	2nd to Home Moved	Chances	1st to Home Moved	Chances	Bases Taken	Out Adv	Doubled Off	BR Outs	GDP	GDP Opps	BR Gain	SB Gain	Net Gain
Santana,Carlos	4	34	7	20	3	16	9	6	1	7	21	124	-38	-7	-45
Santiago,Ramon	4	18	2	5	0	3	7	0	0	0	7	57	+1	+1	+2
Saunders,Michael	12	26	4	8	3	6	13	2	3	5	6	104	+4	+13	+17
Schafer,Jordan	4	13	6	11	1	4	10	2	2	4	3	47	-3	+9	+6
Schierholtz,Nate	2	9	1	4	2	2	5	1	3	4	1	43	-6	-1	-7
Schumaker,Skip	4	14	7	11	2	3	11	0	1	1	6	65	+8	-1	+5
Scott,Luke	2	14	1	6	1	1	8	0	0	0	9	60	0	+5	+5
Scutaro,Marco	13	36	9	15	3	7	25	2	2	4	12	111	+11	+1	+12
Seager,Kyle	5	20	4	13	6	11	11	1	2	3	9	112	-2	+3	+1
Segura,Jean	3	8	4	7	1	2	4	1	0	1	1	30	+3	+5	+8
Shoppach,Kelly	0	5	3	7	2	3	6	1	0	1	2	52	+3	+1	+4
Simmons,Andrelton	2	7	2	4	1	1	8	0	1	1	5	35	+3	+1	+4
Smith,Seth	6	19	8	10	4	5	10	2	0	2	4	67	+9	-2	+7
Smoak,Justin	3	25	4	13	1	7	6	3	0	3	12	100	-17	+1	-16
Snider,Travis	2	8	3	6	2	4	8	2	0	2	2	29	+1	+2	+3
Snyder,Chris	2	7	4	11	1	3	3	2	0	2	5	30	-9	0	-9
Solano,Donovan	6	18	5	8	3	5	8	0	0	0	5	58	+9	+7	+16
Soriano,Alfonso	6	19	10	15	1	8	11	2	0	2	18	110	-5	+2	-3
Soto,Geovany	4	15	5	8	3	6	10	1	1	2	12	62	-3	+1	-2
Span,Denard	11	28	19	32	3	6	13	3	2	5	10	73	-5	+5	0
Stanton,Giancarlo	5	21	9	18	4	7	17	2	0	2	5	91	+11	+2	+13
Stewart,Ian	2	5	2	3	1	3	4	0	1	1	5	32	-1	-6	-7
Stubbs,Drew	11	22	11	14	8	13	10	2	3	5	2	73	+7	+16	+23
Suzuki,Ichiro	11	33	15	23	2	8	17	3	0	3	12	124	+7	+15	+22
Suzuki,Kurt	2	12	8	15	0	3	4	0	0	0	5	73	+1	+2	+3
Sweeney,Ryan	2	10	5	8	4	5	4	0	1	1	1	35	+4	0	+4
Swisher,Nick	8	23	5	10	4	11	17	2	1	3	9	142	+10	-4	+6
Tabata,Jose	5	14	7	16	1	5	17	1	0	1	7	53	+8	-16	-8
Teixeira,Mark	4	25	7	14	3	6	11	3	3	6	11	131	-11	0	-11
Tejada,Ruben	8	23	11	17	6	11	14	3	1	4	9	69	0	-4	-4
Thames,Eric	4	11	3	5	1	1	2	1	1	2	7	43	-6	-1	-7
Theriot,Ryan	6	26	9	18	2	6	15	0	0	0	12	66	+4	+3	+7
Thole,Josh	4	21	5	8	0	3	5	1	0	1	12	62	-8	0	-8
Thome,Jim	0	7	0	2	0	0	3	2	0	2	6	35	-9	0	-9
Torrealba,Yorvit	2	13	4	8	1	3	5	1	0	1	2	42	0	-1	-1
Torres,Andres	7	23	19	21	2	6	15	2	3	5	9	66	+1	+3	+4
Trout,Mike	28	45	20	29	7	10	21	5	4	9	7	87	+12	+39	+51
Trumbo,Mark	9	26	2	10	4	9	17	1	1	2	12	103	+5	-6	-1
Tulowitzki,Troy	5	11	2	6	0	1	12	0	1	1	7	42	+5	-2	+3
Turner,Justin	2	11	5	8	1	3	2	3	0	3	9	37	-15	-1	-16
Uggla,Dan	13	32	11	14	10	17	17	1	0	1	8	107	+23	-2	+21
Upton,B.J.	9	19	8	13	1	2	29	4	1	5	13	111	+14	+19	+33
Upton,Justin	14	37	15	20	10	15	21	2	2	4	7	125	+21	+2	+23
Uribe,Juan	2	8	4	5	1	2	5	1	0	1	6	38	0	-2	-2
Utley,Chase	9	15	7	11	4	5	13	0	1	1	4	76	+19	+9	+28
Valbuena,Luis	4	11	5	9	0	3	5	4	0	4	6	50	-10	-4	-14
Valdespin,Jordany	2	6	2	6	0	1	5	0	0	0	2	41	+5	+4	+9
Valdez,Wilson	2	8	3	4	1	1	4	1	1	2	4	42	-2	+1	-1
Venable,Will	7	22	13	21	4	5	13	0	1	1	2	54	+14	+12	+26
Viciedo,Dayan	2	25	9	11	0	4	6	2	1	3	19	95	-19	-4	-23
Victorino,Shane	12	35	11	17	8	10	12	2	2	4	5	122	+10	+27	+37
Votto,Joey	11	31	9	19	2	7	14	4	4	8	8	102	-12	-1	-13
Walker,Neil	12	31	4	9	6	9	16	2	1	3	11	96	+7	-3	+4
Wallace,Brett	1	8	6	9	0	1	5	0	0	0	2	43	+5	0	+5
Weeks,Jemile	9	24	10	16	3	6	11	0	2	2	5	69	+7	+6	+13
Weeks,Rickie	8	30	11	23	4	9	22	1	4	5	9	108	+2	+10	+12
Wells,Casper	4	15	8	10	3	6	6	3	0	3	3	59	+1	+3	+4
Wells,Vernon	5	12	9	10	1	1	10	2	1	3	5	49	+5	+1	+6
Werth,Jayson	6	19	6	10	0	3	10	0	0	0	3	40	+8	+4	+12
Wieters,Matt	4	29	6	18	2	9	10	2	0	2	17	102	-16	+3	-13
Wigginton,Ty	2	17	8	13	3	8	3	1	2	3	5	60	-10	+1	-9
Willingham,Josh	13	32	7	14	4	14	15	1	1	2	15	136	+5	-1	+4
Wilson,Bobby	3	8	4	6	2	5	3	0	0	0	7	36	0	0	0
Wise,DeWayne	3	13	8	12	1	1	5	2	0	2	2	42	+1	+11	+12

2012 Baserunning

Player	1st to 3rd		2nd to Home		1st to Home		Bases Taken	Out Adv	Doubled Off	BR Outs	GDP	GDP Opps	BR Gain	SB Gain	Net Gain
	Moved	Chances	Moved	Chances	Moved	Chances									
Wright,David	7	30	14	17	7	10	13	2	1	5	15	141	-2	-5	-7
Youkilis,Kevin	5	27	6	12	3	9	9	3	0	3	10	99	-7	0	-7
Young,Chris (Ari)	4	15	4	4	4	4	7	1	0	1	4	76	+10	+2	+12
Young,Delmon	3	19	9	15	3	9	12	5	0	6	20	134	-18	-4	-22
Young,Eric	9	15	4	6	3	4	5	1	0	1	1	29	+9	+10	+19
Young,Michael	4	38	10	21	4	13	15	1	1	2	26	107	-21	-2	-23
Zimmerman,Ryan	11	27	13	20	4	9	22	4	0	4	20	143	+6	+1	+7
Zobrist,Ben	10	35	12	21	4	11	19	4	3	7	13	120	-8	-4	-12

Career Baserunning
Players with 1000 Career Games
(Data goes back to 2002)

Player	1st to 3rd Moved	1st to 3rd Chances	2nd to Home Moved	2nd to Home Chances	1st to Home Moved	1st to Home Chances	Bases Taken	Out Adv	Doubled Off	BR Outs	GDP	GDP Opps	BR Gain	SB Gain	Net Gain
Abreu,Bobby	101	349	158	255	51	107	193	30	9	40	117	1479	+80	+112	+192
Barajas,Rod	23	151	42	103	15	44	52	14	2	16	61	665	-46	-2	-48
Bay,Jason	81	279	87	169	43	102	129	14	9	23	78	1017	+47	+60	+107
Beltran,Carlos	126	343	130	203	53	97	192	14	12	27	102	1246	+152	+156	+308
Beltre,Adrian	93	302	110	186	39	90	160	33	3	36	169	1378	-1	+23	+22
Berkman,Lance	89	412	111	207	46	103	159	38	9	47	124	1263	-51	-4	-55
Betancourt,Yuniesky	70	201	74	132	17	31	95	24	16	41	101	740	-58	-30	-88
Blum,Geoff	30	141	48	77	31	51	45	11	4	15	67	617	-18	-12	-30
Byrd,Marlon	58	222	93	144	38	74	129	16	6	23	87	799	+40	+1	+41
Cabrera,Miguel	100	412	130	235	35	105	164	27	11	39	194	1315	-84	-3	-87
Cairo,Miguel	43	119	46	91	20	35	59	12	5	17	48	478	+1	+34	+35
Cano,Robinson	73	251	122	183	31	64	129	24	17	41	153	1111	-40	-23	-63
Carroll,Jamey	82	263	115	169	36	75	130	14	9	24	58	630	+65	+2	+67
Chavez,Eric	64	209	74	113	31	62	81	10	7	18	99	933	+20	+13	+33
Crawford,Carl	57	236	144	204	51	96	228	32	19	54	64	1124	+107	+240	+347
Crisp,Coco	74	216	113	165	45	76	157	16	8	24	72	774	+106	+129	+235
Cuddyer,Michael	110	261	94	154	38	71	128	38	9	49	151	998	-48	+21	-27
Damon,Johnny	129	388	159	245	69	137	227	31	15	47	54	1143	+153	+127	+280
DeJesus,David	125	317	101	158	34	65	157	24	13	37	85	744	+58	-50	+8
DeRosa,Mark	50	208	77	118	23	58	102	19	11	30	85	706	-24	-13	-37
Dunn,Adam	63	342	97	187	37	106	143	20	6	27	89	1368	+24	+15	+39
Ellis,Mark	83	264	114	196	48	85	147	17	6	24	84	937	+78	+20	+98
Ethier,Andre	49	248	100	135	29	60	86	15	7	23	78	834	+6	-19	-13
Fielder,Prince	30	292	51	128	24	80	110	22	9	31	101	914	-105	-3	-108
Figgins,Chone	148	282	127	189	45	72	200	33	27	60	74	894	+104	+101	+205
Francoeur,Jeff	77	214	80	130	29	74	117	27	14	43	105	928	-28	-21	-49
Furcal,Rafael	136	359	156	241	36	73	204	21	15	36	76	756	+113	+104	+217
Giambi,Jason	54	260	57	100	14	73	80	24	6	31	72	1016	-44	+1	-43
Gonzalez,Adrian	43	269	68	161	33	90	111	24	11	36	133	1025	-117	0	-117
Gonzalez,Alex	47	145	69	116	21	42	78	25	4	29	100	868	-30	-10	-40
Granderson,Curtis	72	234	90	154	45	75	131	10	15	25	38	833	+98	+50	+148
Hafner,Travis	54	260	69	122	35	83	95	27	7	35	81	887	-48	-5	-53
Hairston,Jerry	64	184	66	115	24	48	97	17	10	27	53	586	+16	+5	+21
Hall,Bill	48	136	63	92	34	55	93	17	7	26	64	718	+36	-18	+18
Harris,Willie	34	139	67	97	16	30	87	10	2	12	33	439	+54	+27	+81
Helton,Todd	88	398	136	210	51	147	176	40	9	49	126	1234	-35	-7	-42
Hernandez,Ramon	45	222	59	134	16	67	73	34	7	43	116	874	-156	-3	-159
Hill,Aaron	60	215	78	122	25	51	116	15	7	22	95	882	+31	+10	+41
Hinske,Eric	61	230	92	134	25	52	105	13	11	24	89	909	+29	+19	+48
Holliday,Matt	111	325	136	200	44	78	153	27	14	41	137	1142	+26	+27	+53
Howard,Ryan	32	232	64	140	28	92	92	24	8	32	82	955	-74	+4	-70
Hudson,Orlando	106	286	117	173	41	79	141	21	15	37	138	1037	+16	+29	+45
Huff,Aubrey	97	346	115	194	37	80	148	23	12	35	136	1174	-2	-8	-10
Hunter,Torii	139	293	122	192	42	82	185	46	15	62	184	1247	-19	+17	-2
Ibanez,Raul	88	347	118	220	53	92	154	23	11	35	141	1301	-1	-8	-9
Infante,Omar	63	183	74	124	24	49	87	15	14	30	63	723	+2	+12	+14
Inge,Brandon	57	241	71	135	24	48	116	12	15	29	98	984	-9	-28	-37
Izturis,Cesar	58	228	97	136	19	47	79	22	8	30	83	700	-36	-2	-38
Jeter,Derek	141	461	151	240	56	125	228	28	11	40	190	1309	+26	+103	+129
Johnson,Reed	57	210	81	124	35	65	115	19	4	24	70	571	+23	-15	+8
Jones,Andruw	67	255	80	130	42	90	112	21	7	28	136	1131	-16	+2	-14
Jones,Chipper	92	365	114	184	53	108	125	13	10	27	146	1331	0	+24	+24
Kearns,Austin	53	203	73	116	36	69	102	12	9	22	114	874	-4	-9	-13
Kennedy,Adam	75	265	104	159	22	58	145	26	16	42	90	858	-1	+53	+52
Konerko,Paul	58	382	78	181	15	92	120	23	10	33	194	1255	-183	0	-183
Kotsay,Mark	76	239	76	134	21	58	123	31	6	37	94	897	-13	-28	-41
LaRoche,Adam	41	217	60	124	18	58	96	21	7	28	92	912	-49	-14	-63
Lee,Carlos	97	337	105	214	39	107	135	45	11	56	163	1323	-123	+23	-100
Lopez,Jose	41	194	61	114	24	56	86	21	6	27	113	812	-64	-9	-73
Markakis,Nick	69	272	106	160	29	67	113	18	4	23	104	862	+6	+14	+20

327

Career Baserunning
Players with 1000 Career Games
(Data goes back to 2002)

Player	1st to 3rd Moved	1st to 3rd Chances	2nd to Home Moved	2nd to Home Chances	1st to Home Moved	1st to Home Chances	Bases Taken	Out Adv	Doubled Off	BR Outs	GDP	GDP Opps	BR Gain	SB Gain	Net Gain
Martinez,Victor	50	277	70	145	21	89	126	24	6	30	153	1052	-97	-2	-99
Matsui,Hideki	73	271	94	142	26	77	124	18	3	21	106	1096	+39	-5	+34
Mauer,Joe	85	271	106	153	37	84	152	12	8	22	130	945	+49	+13	+62
McCann,Brian	37	187	31	98	11	67	56	24	7	32	107	854	-139	+9	-130
Molina,Yadier	38	209	41	105	15	43	77	21	7	29	145	780	-142	-11	-153
Morneau,Justin	40	215	70	131	19	67	116	29	4	33	112	1011	-53	-9	-62
Olivo,Miguel	45	141	52	87	16	28	94	24	7	32	74	775	-3	-15	-18
Ortiz,David	54	339	74	188	25	107	143	36	14	51	129	1448	-123	-8	-131
Overbay,Lyle	57	261	60	127	30	81	110	19	8	27	125	924	-65	+1	-64
Pena,Carlos	99	289	64	123	29	83	143	24	9	33	64	1047	+64	-11	+53
Peralta,Jhonny	42	242	84	158	25	79	121	30	8	38	142	1053	-98	-26	-124
Phillips,Brandon	94	216	94	137	29	47	156	32	10	44	140	906	+7	+36	+43
Pierre,Juan	160	410	171	255	48	83	239	28	22	51	80	945	+136	+190	+326
Pierzynski,A.J.	53	272	76	167	17	60	131	41	4	46	174	1166	-144	-13	-157
Podsednik,Scott	64	193	95	148	32	52	139	14	16	30	66	544	+40	+101	+141
Polanco,Placido	106	378	146	224	45	108	186	22	9	33	148	1139	+32	+20	+52
Pujols,Albert	149	418	167	225	53	116	205	52	13	67	230	1705	-26	+25	-1
Ramirez,Aramis	60	295	82	181	27	101	129	33	10	43	163	1271	-130	-4	-134
Ramirez,Hanley	71	200	105	161	37	60	126	31	9	40	68	745	+24	+85	+109
Reyes,Jose	93	259	134	198	34	52	201	38	15	53	55	710	+76	+204	+280
Rios,Alex	66	220	118	175	35	65	129	14	13	27	147	1107	+13	+63	+76
Rivera,Juan	51	201	59	96	18	48	60	27	13	41	127	729	-140	-35	-175
Roberts,Brian	88	282	123	199	32	78	160	23	18	41	66	788	+33	+133	+166
Rodriguez,Alex	113	346	146	218	46	111	181	32	14	46	155	1494	+33	+97	+130
Rolen,Scott	93	277	106	161	39	85	148	33	8	42	112	1069	+19	0	+19
Rollins,Jimmy	126	380	178	254	45	89	238	28	8	36	99	983	+145	+204	+349
Schneider,Brian	27	126	45	94	12	26	52	10	2	12	92	629	-47	-10	-57
Scutaro,Marco	76	266	98	158	40	97	146	20	11	31	103	869	+15	+9	+24
Soriano,Alfonso	101	252	128	198	27	62	162	23	14	37	102	1131	+74	+105	+179
Suzuki,Ichiro	138	513	188	297	57	119	270	29	14	43	66	1149	+152	+220	+372
Swisher,Nick	87	270	73	131	34	76	122	20	16	36	104	1040	-1	-18	-19
Teixeira,Mark	73	325	114	187	41	104	157	36	8	44	130	1458	-8	+9	+1
Thome,Jim	49	296	83	158	13	88	103	27	6	33	85	1132	-61	-14	-75
Uggla,Dan	81	244	84	122	52	89	115	24	8	32	62	824	+55	-16	+39
Uribe,Juan	73	202	77	120	14	43	109	12	11	24	103	914	+24	-38	-14
Utley,Chase	119	243	111	148	47	76	140	18	10	28	60	1033	+161	+93	+254
Victorino,Shane	82	211	86	125	38	64	139	7	12	21	49	693	+118	+115	+233
Vizquel,Omar	71	226	93	151	26	73	124	28	8	37	86	861	-4	+17	+13
Wells,Vernon	105	277	117	171	52	88	158	28	10	39	153	1321	+49	+30	+79
Werth,Jayson	63	210	71	107	24	52	100	12	4	17	52	700	+60	+72	+132
Wigginton,Ty	39	216	74	137	26	60	88	29	10	39	127	943	-112	-2	-114
Wilson,Jack	72	195	92	151	38	65	129	18	15	35	84	919	+38	-16	+22
Wright,David	89	279	105	157	48	105	150	26	13	42	115	1133	+19	+58	+77
Youkilis,Kevin	73	256	87	147	41	94	138	21	10	31	70	901	+43	-2	+41
Young,Michael	94	405	154	245	71	130	182	17	11	28	206	1349	-10	+28	+18

2002-2012 MLB Averages

1st to 3rd	2nd to Home	1st to Home
28%	59%	45%

2012 Team Baserunning

Team	1st to 3rd Moved	Chances	2nd to Home Moved	Chances	1st to Home Moved	Chances	Bases Taken	Out Adv	Doubled Off	BR Outs	GDP	GDP Opps	BR Gain	SB Gain	Net Gain
Oakland Athletics	67	243	103	159	38	75	166	10	13	24	97	1045	+86	+58	+144
Atlanta Braves	83	272	96	145	41	90	162	22	7	30	109	1108	+63	+37	+100
Los Angeles Angels	126	336	128	186	37	73	179	37	12	50	138	1095	+24	+68	+92
San Francisco Giants	83	332	97	187	42	89	203	24	12	36	115	1226	+49	+40	+89
Philadelphia Phillies	80	304	107	183	47	92	148	20	13	34	115	1056	+6	+70	+76
San Diego Padres	78	272	110	175	40	78	149	22	19	44	100	1070	+7	+63	+70
Milwaukee Brewers	55	245	98	177	36	76	140	21	13	34	111	1066	-15	+80	+65
Cincinnati Reds	84	270	90	158	38	74	153	22	14	36	100	1044	+30	+33	+63
Boston Red Sox	79	265	109	187	46	106	168	30	11	41	104	1092	+23	+35	+58
Pittsburgh Pirates	83	258	94	151	26	65	154	15	8	23	98	1019	+74	-31	+43
Minnesota Twins	90	308	120	190	24	82	160	24	15	39	148	1172	-21	+61	+40
Colorado Rockies	117	313	106	177	30	70	151	25	10	35	132	1061	+17	+20	+37
Miami Marlins	72	267	93	160	28	51	132	30	12	42	114	1043	-32	+67	+35
Seattle Mariners	90	286	70	132	25	59	140	25	14	40	95	1033	+1	+34	+35
Tampa Bay Rays	71	263	90	157	41	77	165	29	13	42	133	1097	-12	+46	+34
Kansas City Royals	94	314	116	201	30	84	169	28	16	44	130	1052	-23	+56	+33
New York Yankees	78	280	97	178	25	72	170	20	20	40	136	1243	-7	+39	+32
Toronto Blue Jays	101	263	96	152	24	62	148	34	18	53	109	1043	-15	+41	+26
St Louis Cardinals	97	333	116	186	40	94	168	27	15	43	135	1239	+3	+17	+20
Houston Astros	70	239	82	153	23	52	146	19	13	32	114	994	+2	+13	+15
Chicago White Sox	79	281	108	176	21	65	146	26	14	40	113	1069	-14	+23	+9
Arizona D-Backs	78	285	107	179	47	88	156	28	12	40	108	1121	+17	-9	+8
Los Angeles Dodgers	79	312	113	189	33	63	150	26	8	34	139	1130	-10	+16	+6
Chicago Cubs	81	243	88	140	36	81	148	29	10	39	125	1022	-1	+4	+3
Washington Nationals	81	282	101	195	31	81	143	30	13	43	111	1083	-36	+35	-1
Texas Rangers	84	293	118	200	32	89	158	25	14	39	121	1105	-7	+3	-4
New York Mets	73	282	107	160	41	84	122	19	13	34	118	1099	-8	+3	-5
Cleveland Indians	89	323	92	170	29	85	124	27	14	41	142	1207	-70	+22	-48
Baltimore Orioles	77	260	84	143	30	81	127	23	12	35	152	1109	-49	0	-49
Detroit Tigers	74	332	116	198	47	86	153	35	14	51	156	1184	-80	+13	-67
MLB Totals	2493	8556	3052	5144	1028	2324	4598	752	392	1158	3618	32927			

Relief Pitching

This section documents the bullpen performance of each major league team and every major league reliever. For this season, we are only showing pitchers with at least 10 relief appearances for his team. We show each relief pitcher's role on his team last year along with his performance in twenty-some bullpen-specific performance categories. A modern bullpen consists of a Closer (CL), a Set Up Man or two set-up men (SU), some left-handers whose job is to get out left-handed hitters (LT), a Long Man (LM), and some auditioning relievers who pitch as they are needed and try to work their way into a better role, categorized as Utilty Relievers (UR). Of course, there's the occasional starting pitcher or position player called to pitch in relief. We call these Emergency Relievers (ER).

The data in this section is:

Usage: Games in Relief (Rel G), the number of times the pitcher entered the game before the seventh inning (Early Entry), pitching on consecutive days (Cons Days), long outings (LO), and Leverage Index (Lev Ind). We use the Leverage Index calculated by Tom Tango and published on FanGraphs.com. An average Leverage Index is 1.0. If a pitcher pitches frequently with the game on the line, his Leverage index will be high. If he pitches generally in the 6th inning of 7-2 ballgames, his leverage index will be very low.

Inherited Runners: The total (#), the number that scored (Scrd), and Percentage that scored (Pct).

Saves: A Save is considered "Easy" if the relief pitcher enters the game, pitches one inning or less, and the first batter he faces does not at least represent the tying run. A "Tough" Save is one in which the reliever enters with the tying run on base and a "Regular" Save is a Save Opportunity which is neither easy nor tough.

Relief Results: A Clean Outing (Clean) is any appearance in which a reliever does not allow a run to score and does not allow an inherited run to score. A BS Win is a Blown Save/Win. Sv-Opp is the number of saves and save opportunities. Holds are credited to any pitcher who enters the game with a Save Opportunity, records at least one out, does not surrender the lead, and passes the ball to another reliever. We also display a pitcher's Save/Hold Percentage, Opponent OPS, and ERA (as a reliever only).

Arizona Diamondbacks

Pitcher	Pos	T	Usage					Inherited Runners			Saves			Relief Results						
			Rel G	Early Entry	Cons Days	Long	Lev Ind	#	Scrd	Pct	Easy	Reg	Tough	Clean	BS Win	Sv-Opp	Holds	Sv/Hld Pct	Opp OPS	Rel ERA
Putz, J.J.	CL	R	57	0	14	2	1.7	3	0	.00	23 - 23	9 - 14	0 - 0	47	0	32 - 37	0	.86	.600	2.82
Hernandez, David	SU	R	72	0	19	3	1.4	10	2	.20	0 - 1	4 - 9	0 - 0	58	0	4 - 10	25	.83	.544	2.50
Zagurski, Mike	LT	L	45	10	12	4	0.5	31	12	.39	0 - 0	0 - 0	0 - 1	23	0	0 - 1	4	.80	.817	5.54
Breslow, Craig	LM	L	40	13	7	12	0.7	23	7	.30	0 - 0	0 - 0	0 - 0	27	0	0 - 0	4	1.00	.673	2.70
Bergesen, Brad	LM	R	19	9	1	6	0.6	4	2	.50	0 - 0	0 - 0	0 - 1	10	0	0 - 1	0	.00	.717	3.64
Collmenter, Josh	LM	R	17	7	0	11	0.6	6	4	.67	0 - 0	0 - 0	0 - 0	10	0	0 - 0	0		.619	1.32
Ziegler, Brad	UR	R	77	11	26	2	0.9	54	11	.20	0 - 0	0 - 2	0 - 0	54	1	0 - 2	17	.89	.578	2.49
Shaw, Bryan	UR	R	64	8	19	6	0.9	28	5	.18	0 - 1	1 - 1	1 - 2	46	0	2 - 4	10	.86	.747	3.49
Albers, Matt	UR	R	23	10	3	0	0.8	14	5	.36	0 - 0	0 - 1	0 - 1	17	0	0 - 2	2	.50	.622	2.57
Saito, Takashi	UR	R	16	0	0	0	0.6	6	2	.33	0 - 0	0 - 1	0 - 0	8	0	0 - 1	2	.67	1.088	6.75
Lindstrom, Matt	UR	R	12	0	2	0	0.7	3	0	.00	0 - 0	0 - 0	0 - 0	10	0	0 - 0	3	1.00	.598	2.53

Atlanta Braves

Pitcher	Pos	T	Usage					Inherited Runners			Saves			Relief Results						
			Rel G	Early Entry	Cons Days	Long	Lev Ind	#	Scrd	Pct	Easy	Reg	Tough	Clean	BS Win	Sv-Opp	Holds	Sv/Hld Pct	Opp OPS	Rel ERA
Kimbrel, Craig	CL	R	63	0	17	4	1.8	4	0	.00	26 - 26	15 - 18	1 - 1	56	0	42 - 45	0	.93	.358	1.01
Venters, Jonny	SU	L	66	6	16	5	1.2	25	9	.36	0 - 0	0 - 2	0 - 1	49	1	0 - 3	20	.87	.739	3.22
O'Flaherty, Eric	SU	L	64	2	19	3	1.7	22	1	.05	0 - 2	0 - 1	0 - 0	54	0	0 - 3	28	.90	.602	1.73
Avilan, Luis	LM	L	31	13	9	7	0.4	32	8	.25	0 - 0	0 - 0	0 - 0	22	0	0 - 0	5	1.00	.547	2.00
Hernandez, Livan	LM	R	18	7	2	9	0.8	10	6	.60	0 - 0	1 - 1	0 - 0	10	0	1 - 1	0	1.00	.862	4.94
Durbin, Chad	UR	R	76	15	19	4	0.8	44	11	.25	0 - 0	1 - 1	0 - 2	57	0	1 - 3	15	.89	.709	3.10
Martinez, Cristhian	UR	R	54	18	15	18	0.6	32	8	.25	0 - 0	1 - 1	0 - 0	31	0	1 - 1	1	1.00	.745	3.91
Medlen, Kris	UR	R	38	13	6	10	0.8	17	9	.53	0 - 0	1 - 1	0 - 1	26	0	1 - 2	7	.89	.598	2.48
Gearrin, Cory	UR	R	22	7	8	1	0.8	13	4	.31	0 - 0	0 - 0	0 - 1	15	0	0 - 1	4	.80	.642	1.80
Varvaro, Anthony	UR	R	12	4	2	7	0.7	5	3	.60	0 - 0	0 - 0	0 - 0	4	0	0 - 0	0		.766	5.40

Baltimore Orioles

Pitcher	Pos	T	Usage					Inherited Runners			Saves			Relief Results						
			Rel G	Early Entry	Cons Days	Long	Lev Ind	#	Scrd	Pct	Easy	Reg	Tough	Clean	BS Win	Sv-Opp	Holds	Sv/Hld Pct	Opp OPS	Rel ERA
Johnson, Jim	CL	R	71	0	20	4	2.1	8	6	.75	33 - 34	18 - 20	0 - 0	60	1	51 - 54	0	.94	.556	2.49
Strop, Pedro	SU	R	70	0	16	5	1.7	23	10	.43	1 - 3	2 - 5	0 - 2	52	1	3 - 10	24	.79	.613	2.44
Patton, Troy	LT	L	54	9	11	9	0.9	28	6	.21	0 - 0	0 - 1	0 - 0	39	0	0 - 1	9	.90	.598	2.43
Matusz, Brian	LT	L	18	1	5	0	1.0	14	0	.00	0 - 0	0 - 0	0 - 0	16	0	0 - 0	4	1.00	.352	1.35
Eveland, Dana	LT	L	12	4	0	6	0.4	4	2	.50	0 - 0	0 - 0	0 - 0	6	0	0 - 0	0		.667	3.57
Gregg, Kevin	LM	R	40	14	6	13	0.5	20	8	.40	0 - 0	0 - 0	0 - 0	26	0	0 - 0	0		.838	4.95
Lindstrom, Matt	LM	R	34	9	5	6	0.9	17	4	.24	0 - 0	0 - 1	0 - 0	24	0	0 - 1	2	.67	.655	2.72
O'Day, Darren	UR	R	69	9	14	7	1.1	43	6	.14	0 - 0	0 - 2	0 - 0	54	0	0 - 2	15	.88	.613	2.28
Ayala, Luis	UR	R	66	18	7	13	1.1	50	22	.44	1 - 1	0 - 0	0 - 2	42	0	1 - 3	11	.86	.717	2.64
Hunter, Tommy	UR	R	13	4	2	4	1.1	7	3	.43	0 - 0	0 - 0	0 - 1	8	1	0 - 1	0	.00	.839	3.71

Boston Red Sox

Pitcher	Pos	T	Usage					Inherited Runners			Saves			Relief Results						
			Rel G	Early Entry	Cons Days	Long	Lev Ind	#	Scrd	Pct	Easy	Reg	Tough	Clean	BS Win	Sv-Opp	Holds	Sv/Hld Pct	Opp OPS	Rel ERA
Aceves, Alfredo	CL	R	69	7	18	16	1.5	23	8	.35	14 - 16	10 - 13	1 - 4	41	1	25 - 33	0	.76	.748	5.36
Bailey, Andrew	CL	R	19	0	6	1	2.0	2	0	.00	2 - 4	3 - 4	1 - 1	14	0	6 - 9	1	.70	.862	7.04
Padilla, Vicente	SU	R	56	2	9	5	1.6	34	5	.15	0 - 1	0 - 2	1 - 2	39	0	1 - 5	23	.86	.845	4.50
Morales, Franklin	SU	L	28	5	2	7	1.0	14	1	.07	1 - 1	0 - 0	0 - 0	20	0	1 - 1	8	1.00	.614	3.23
Miller, Andrew	LT	L	53	14	12	2	1.0	46	7	.15	0 - 0	0 - 0	0 - 0	37	0	0 - 0	13	1.00	.588	3.35
Hill, Rich	LT	L	25	7	1	2	1.0	14	6	.43	0 - 0	0 - 0	0 - 0	18	0	0 - 0	6	1.00	.685	1.83
Breslow, Craig	LT	L	23	4	4	0	1.1	16	8	.50	0 - 0	0 - 0	0 - 1	15	0	0 - 1	5	.83	.579	2.70
Albers, Matt	LM	R	40	10	10	4	1.0	35	12	.34	0 - 0	0 - 1	0 - 3	24	2	0 - 4	7	.64	.653	2.29
Mortensen, Clayton	LM	R	26	13	1	11	0.6	23	9	.39	0 - 0	0 - 0	0 - 0	13	0	0 - 0	1	1.00	.691	3.21
Atchison, Scott	UR	R	42	14	10	9	0.7	32	11	.34	0 - 0	0 - 0	0 - 1	30	0	0 - 1	5	.83	.549	1.58
Melancon, Mark	UR	R	41	4	5	9	0.6	18	7	.39	1 - 2	0 - 0	0 - 0	27	0	1 - 2	2	.75	.754	6.20
Tazawa, Junichi	UR	R	37	9	10	5	0.6	26	10	.38	0 - 0	1 - 1	0 - 0	23	0	1 - 1	5	1.00	.558	1.43

Chicago Cubs

Pitcher	Pos	T	Usage					Inherited Runners			Saves			Relief Results						
			Rel G	Early Entry	Cons Days	Long	Lev Ind	#	Scrd	Pct	Easy	Reg	Tough	Clean	BS Win	Sv-Opp	Holds	Sv/Hld Pct	Opp OPS	Rel ERA
Marmol, Carlos	CL	R	61	0	14	6	1.3	5	3	.60	16 - 16	4 - 5	0 - 2	46	0	20 - 23	2	.88	.662	3.42
Camp, Shawn	SU	R	80	7	27	7	1.0	22	7	.32	1 - 2	1 - 4	0 - 0	53	1	2 - 6	18	.83	.719	3.59
Chapman, Jaye	SU	R	14	4	5	1	1.2	5	1	.20	0 - 0	0 - 0	0 - 0	11	0	0 - 0	5	1.00	.660	3.75
Russell, James	LT	L	77	6	24	8	1.0	29	9	.31	2 - 2	0 - 1	0 - 2	55	1	2 - 5	13	.83	.732	3.25
Maine, Scott	LT	L	21	9	2	5	0.6	15	5	.33	0 - 0	0 - 0	0 - 1	12	0	0 - 1	1	.50	.720	4.79
Bowden, Michael	LM	R	30	12	5	9	0.4	23	11	.48	0 - 0	0 - 1	0 - 0	19	0	0 - 1	2	.67	.682	2.95
Beliveau, Jeff	LM	L	22	9	7	5	0.3	13	6	.46	0 - 0	0 - 0	0 - 0	14	0	0 - 0	1	1.00	.956	4.58
Corpas, Manuel	UR	R	48	12	13	4	0.8	23	9	.39	0 - 0	0 - 2	0 - 1	30	0	0 - 3	6	.67	.818	5.01
Dolis, Rafael	UR	R	34	8	7	8	1.1	14	7	.50	1 - 1	3 - 4	0 - 1	16	0	4 - 6	3	.78	.858	6.39
Cabrera, Alberto	UR	R	25	6	6	4	0.6	10	3	.30	0 - 0	0 - 0	0 - 0	13	0	0 - 0	1	1.00	.678	5.40
Coleman, Casey	UR	R	16	7	2	4	0.4	5	3	.60	0 - 0	0 - 1	0 - 0	9	0	0 - 1	0	.00	.951	7.32
Castillo, Lendy	UR	R	13	8	1	6	0.2	4	2	.50	0 - 0	0 - 0	0 - 0	4	0	0 - 0	0		.925	7.88
Asencio, Jairo	UR	R	12	5	3	3	0.3	11	3	.27	0 - 0	0 - 0	0 - 0	7	0	0 - 0	0		.683	3.07
Wood, Kerry	UR	R	10	0	0	0	2.3	3	1	.33	0 - 0	0 - 1	0 - 1	5	0	0 - 2	3	.60	.886	8.31

Chicago White Sox

Pitcher	Pos	T	Usage					Inherited Runners			Saves			Relief Results						
			Rel G	Early Entry	Cons Days	Long	Lev Ind	#	Scrd	Pct	Easy	Reg	Tough	Clean	BS Win	Sv-Opp	Holds	Sv/Hld Pct	Opp OPS	Rel ERA
Reed, Addison	CL	R	62	0	14	2	2.0	18	7	.39	15 - 16	11 - 13	3 - 4	42	1	29 - 33	4	.89	.753	4.75
Thornton, Matt	SU	L	74	2	22	3	1.6	32	10	.31	0 - 0	2 - 3	1 - 4	48	1	3 - 7	26	.88	.685	3.46
Santiago, Hector	LT	L	38	7	3	13	0.8	19	2	.11	3 - 5	1 - 1	0 - 0	24	0	4 - 6	4	.80	.741	3.88
Ohman, Will	LT	L	32	11	8	2	0.5	17	5	.29	0 - 0	0 - 0	0 - 2	20	0	0 - 2	1	.33	.729	6.41
Veal, Donnie	LT	L	24	5	8	1	0.9	23	2	.09	0 - 0	1 - 1	0 - 0	20	0	1 - 1	4	1.00	.361	1.38
Septimo, Leyson	LT	L	21	6	2	0	0.7	20	6	.30	0 - 0	0 - 0	0 - 0	14	0	0 - 0	0		.592	5.02
Omogrosso, Brian	LM	R	17	9	2	8	0.5	13	4	.31	0 - 0	0 - 0	0 - 1	10	0	0 - 1	1	.50	.742	2.57
Jones, Nate	UR	R	65	24	17	14	1.0	54	24	.44	0 - 0	0 - 1	0 - 2	41	0	0 - 3	7	.70	.686	2.39
Crain, Jesse	UR	R	51	3	12	5	1.2	24	5	.21	0 - 0	0 - 0	0 - 4	38	1	0 - 4	10	.71	.561	2.44
Myers, Brett	UR	R	35	0	12	3	1.4	18	2	.11	0 - 0	0 - 0	0 - 0	26	0	0 - 0	8	1.00	.681	3.12
Stewart, Zach	UR	R	17	6	3	5	0.4	6	1	.17	0 - 0	0 - 0	0 - 0	9	0	0 - 0	0		.866	5.18
Humber, Philip	UR	R	10	4	1	3	0.3	5	1	.20	0 - 0	0 - 0	0 - 0	6	0	0 - 0	0		.915	8.36

Cincinnati Reds

Pitcher	Pos	T	Rel G	Early Entry	Cons Days	Long	Lev Ind	#	Scrd	Pct	Easy	Reg	Tough	Clean	BS Win	Sv- Opp	Holds	Sv/Hld Pct	Opp OPS	Rel ERA
			Usage					**Inherited Runners**			**Saves**			**Relief Results**						
Chapman, Aroldis	CL	L	68	0	20	10	1.8	15	3	.20	23 - 23	13 - 18	2 - 2	59	0	38 - 43	6	.90	.450	1.51
Marshall, Sean	SU	L	73	0	18	3	1.5	34	9	.26	6 - 7	2 - 3	1 - 3	53	0	9 - 13	22	.89	.597	2.51
Broxton, Jonathan	SU	R	25	0	6	0	1.6	3	0	.00	2 - 2	2 - 4	0 - 0	20	1	4 - 6	10	.88	.637	2.82
Bray, Bill	LT	L	14	3	1	1	0.9	11	3	.27	0 - 0	0 - 1	0 - 1	9	0	0 - 2	1	.33	.984	5.19
Simon, Alfredo	LM	R	36	18	2	21	0.7	16	4	.25	0 - 0	1 - 1	0 - 0	20	0	1 - 1	1	1.00	.747	2.66
Arredondo, Jose	UR	R	66	10	15	8	0.9	25	9	.36	0 - 0	0 - 0	1 - 2	44	0	1 - 2	12	.93	.704	2.95
Ondrusek, Logan	UR	R	63	3	10	7	1.4	42	4	.10	1 - 2	0 - 0	1 - 2	49	0	2 - 4	13	.88	.752	3.46
LeCure, Sam	UR	R	48	16	5	14	0.9	31	5	.16	0 - 0	0 - 0	0 - 1	30	0	0 - 1	7	.88	.627	3.14
Hoover, J.J.	UR	R	28	10	1	5	1.1	11	5	.45	0 - 0	1 - 2	0 - 0	21	0	1 - 2	1	.67	.512	2.05

Cleveland Indians

Pitcher	Pos	T	Rel G	Early Entry	Cons Days	Long	Lev Ind	#	Scrd	Pct	Easy	Reg	Tough	Clean	BS Win	Sv- Opp	Holds	Sv/Hld Pct	Opp OPS	Rel ERA
			Usage					**Inherited Runners**			**Saves**			**Relief Results**						
Perez, Chris	CL	R	61	0	14	6	1.9	6	1	.17	28 - 31	11 - 12	0 - 0	47	0	39 - 43	0	.91	.652	3.59
Smith, Joe	SU	R	72	10	17	8	1.2	47	10	.21	0 - 2	0 - 0	0 - 1	49	2	0 - 3	21	.88	.594	2.96
Pestano, Vinnie	SU	R	70	0	20	11	1.8	21	3	.14	0 - 0	1 - 3	1 - 2	55	0	2 - 5	36	.93	.631	2.57
Sipp, Tony	LT	L	63	12	21	5	0.7	28	8	.29	0 - 0	1 - 1	0 - 1	40	0	1 - 2	12	.93	.739	4.42
Hagadone, Nick	LT	L	27	4	3	4	0.7	14	4	.29	0 - 0	1 - 2	0 - 0	16	0	1 - 2	2	.75	.778	6.39
Barnes, Scott	LT	L	16	7	1	6	0.4	7	2	.29	0 - 0	0 - 0	0 - 0	12	0	0 - 0	1	1.00	.718	4.26
Rogers, Esmil	LM	R	44	11	6	13	0.7	28	8	.29	0 - 0	0 - 0	0 - 0	27	0	0 - 0	6	1.00	.657	3.06
Accardo, Jeremy	LM	R	26	7	4	10	0.2	7	1	.14	0 - 0	0 - 0	0 - 0	16	0	0 - 0	0		.820	4.58
Asencio, Jairo	LM	R	18	6	3	7	0.6	10	3	.30	0 - 0	0 - 0	0 - 0	11	0	0 - 0	0		.848	5.96
Seddon, Chris	LM	L	15	10	3	7	0.5	10	4	.40	0 - 0	0 - 0	0 - 0	8	0	0 - 0	1	1.00	.604	3.00
Allen, Cody	UR	R	27	3	3	9	0.5	10	3	.30	0 - 0	0 - 1	0 - 0	18	0	0 - 1	1	.50	.710	3.72
Herrmann, Frank	UR	R	15	6	2	3	0.2	10	1	.10	0 - 0	0 - 0	0 - 0	11	0	0 - 0	0		.539	2.33
Wheeler, Dan	UR	R	13	5	1	2	0.4	7	4	.57	0 - 0	0 - 0	0 - 0	4	0	0 - 0	1	1.00	.970	8.76

Colorado Rockies

Pitcher	Pos	T	Rel G	Early Entry	Cons Days	Long	Lev Ind	#	Scrd	Pct	Easy	Reg	Tough	Clean	BS Win	Sv- Opp	Holds	Sv/Hld Pct	Opp OPS	Rel ERA
			Usage					**Inherited Runners**			**Saves**			**Relief Results**						
Betancourt, Rafael	CL	R	60	0	9	2	2.0	10	6	.60	20 - 21	11 - 16	0 - 1	47	1	31 - 38	1	.82	.655	2.81
Belisle, Matt	SU	R	80	5	21	10	1.6	40	9	.23	0 - 0	2 - 6	1 - 4	53	0	3 - 10	26	.81	.722	3.71
Brothers, Rex	SU	L	75	7	20	9	1.3	33	7	.21	0 - 0	0 - 4	0 - 1	51	1	0 - 5	18	.78	.732	3.86
Reynolds, Matt	LT	L	71	21	19	8	0.6	51	15	.29	0 - 0	0 - 0	0 - 0	45	0	0 - 0	2	1.00	.853	4.40
Outman, Josh	LT	L	20	9	4	1	0.9	19	0	.00	0 - 0	0 - 0	0 - 0	14	0	0 - 0	3	1.00	.700	6.91
Roenicke, Josh	LM	R	63	35	10	25	0.7	28	11	.39	1 - 1	0 - 1	0 - 1	38	0	1 - 3	8	.82	.753	3.25
Ottavino, Adam	LM	R	53	31	8	27	0.9	17	5	.29	0 - 0	0 - 1	0 - 1	31	0	0 - 2	6	.75	.717	4.56
Torres, Carlos	LM	R	31	19	3	19	0.8	9	3	.33	0 - 0	0 - 0	0 - 0	16	0	0 - 0	1	1.00	.723	5.26
Moscoso, Guillermo	LM	R	20	14	1	12	0.7	6	3	.50	0 - 0	0 - 1	0 - 0	12	0	0 - 1	1	.50	.834	4.42
Rogers, Esmil	UR	R	23	8	4	10	0.8	15	7	.47	0 - 0	0 - 2	0 - 0	12	0	0 - 2	2	.50	.905	8.06
Escalona, Edgmer	UR	R	22	8	6	3	0.7	16	5	.31	0 - 0	0 - 0	0 - 0	12	0	0 - 0	2	1.00	.840	6.04
Harris, Will	UR	R	20	0	3	1	0.6	5	3	.60	0 - 0	0 - 0	0 - 0	11	0	0 - 0	3	1.00	.922	8.15
Ekstrom, Mike	UR	R	15	1	5	3	0.3	4	1	.25	0 - 0	0 - 0	0 - 0	8	0	0 - 0	0		.802	6.32

Detroit Tigers

Pitcher	Pos	T	Usage					Inherited Runners			Saves			Relief Results						
			Rel G	Early Entry	Cons Days	Long	Lev Ind	#	Scrd	Pct	Easy	Reg	Tough	Clean	BS Win	Sv- Opp	Holds	Sv/Hld Pct	Opp OPS	Rel ERA
Valverde, Jose	CL	R	71	0	31	7	1.7	4	2	.50	27 - 28	8 - 12	0 - 0	51	2	35 - 40	0	.88	.649	3.78
Benoit, Joaquin	SU	R	73	0	23	5	1.4	18	3	.17	2 - 2	0 - 4	0 - 0	51	1	2 - 6	30	.89	.720	3.68
Coke, Phil	SU	L	66	11	18	5	1.3	43	12	.28	1 - 1	0 - 0	0 - 2	39	0	1 - 3	20	.91	.854	4.00
Downs, Darin	LT	L	18	4	1	5	0.6	14	2	.14	0 - 0	0 - 0	0 - 0	12	0	0 - 0	1	1.00	.655	3.48
Below, Duane	LM	L	26	12	2	10	0.4	20	5	.25	0 - 0	0 - 0	0 - 0	15	0	0 - 0	0		.701	3.92
Dotel, Octavio	UR	R	57	5	14	6	1.0	22	4	.18	1 - 2	0 - 1	0 - 1	41	1	1 - 4	11	.80	.617	3.57
Villarreal, Brayan	UR	R	50	13	9	12	1.0	25	11	.44	0 - 0	0 - 0	0 - 0	30	0	0 - 0	9	1.00	.595	2.63
Marte, Luis	UR	R	13	9	0	6	0.7	10	3	.30	0 - 0	0 - 0	0 - 0	7	0	0 - 0	0		.721	2.82
Putkonen, Luke	UR	R	12	4	1	3	1.1	12	4	.33	0 - 0	1 - 2	0 - 0	5	0	1 - 2	0	.50	.777	3.94
Balester, Collin	UR	R	11	7	3	7	0.7	13	8	.62	0 - 0	0 - 0	0 - 0	0	0	0 - 0	0		.830	6.50

Houston Astros

Pitcher	Pos	T	Usage					Inherited Runners			Saves			Relief Results						
			Rel G	Early Entry	Cons Days	Long	Lev Ind	#	Scrd	Pct	Easy	Reg	Tough	Clean	BS Win	Sv- Opp	Holds	Sv/Hld Pct	Opp OPS	Rel ERA
Myers, Brett	CL	R	35	0	8	2	1.9	3	3	1.00	11 - 12	8 - 9	0 - 0	26	0	19 - 21	0	.90	.762	3.52
Lopez, Wilton	SU	R	64	4	17	4	1.6	28	9	.32	4 - 4	4 - 6	2 - 3	47	1	10 - 13	9	.86	.626	2.17
Wright, Wesley	LT	L	77	9	19	1	0.9	47	16	.34	0 - 0	1 - 1	0 - 1	55	0	1 - 2	19	.95	.638	3.27
Cedeno, Xavier	LT	L	44	13	14	1	0.7	45	14	.31	0 - 0	0 - 1	1 - 2	29	0	1 - 3	6	.78	.704	3.77
Abad, Fernando	LT	L	31	7	6	1	0.4	23	7	.30	0 - 0	0 - 0	0 - 0	19	0	0 - 0	3	1.00	.848	3.80
Carpenter, David	LM	R	30	6	7	6	1.0	15	6	.40	0 - 0	0 - 0	0 - 1	14	0	0 - 1	2	.67	.895	6.07
Storey, Mickey	LM	R	26	13	4	9	0.6	15	4	.27	0 - 0	0 - 0	0 - 0	14	0	0 - 0	3	1.00	.681	3.86
Del Rosario, Enerio	LM	R	19	6	6	7	0.2	14	3	.21	0 - 0	0 - 0	0 - 0	6	0	0 - 0	1	1.00	1.001	9.00
Fick, Chuckie	LM	R	18	10	3	7	0.5	14	6	.43	0 - 0	0 - 0	0 - 0	6	0	0 - 0	2	1.00	.910	4.30
Rodriguez, Fernando	UR	R	71	19	16	15	1.1	55	14	.25	0 - 0	0 - 1	0 - 3	34	0	0 - 4	13	.76	.761	5.37
Cruz, Rhiner	UR	R	52	11	10	11	0.3	26	12	.46	0 - 0	0 - 0	0 - 1	28	0	0 - 1	0	.00	.870	6.05
Lyon, Brandon	UR	R	37	5	10	8	0.8	10	1	.10	0 - 0	0 - 1	0 - 1	25	0	0 - 2	5	.71	.686	3.25
Ambriz, Hector	UR	R	18	5	4	3	1.1	10	4	.40	0 - 0	0 - 0	0 - 0	12	0	0 - 0	3	1.00	.613	4.19
Valdez, Jose	UR	R	12	3	2	3	0.6	5	1	.20	0 - 0	0 - 0	0 - 0	9	0	0 - 0	4	1.00	.718	2.25

Kansas City Royals

Pitcher	Pos	T	Usage					Inherited Runners			Saves			Relief Results						
			Rel G	Early Entry	Cons Days	Long	Lev Ind	#	Scrd	Pct	Easy	Reg	Tough	Clean	BS Win	Sv- Opp	Holds	Sv/Hld Pct	Opp OPS	Rel ERA
Holland, Greg	CL	R	67	1	20	9	1.8	27	11	.41	11 - 12	5 - 6	0 - 2	49	0	16 - 20	9	.86	.653	2.96
Broxton, Jonathan	CL	R	35	0	8	2	2.6	2	0	.00	13 - 14	10 - 13	0 - 0	27	1	23 - 27	0	.85	.697	2.27
Herrera, Kelvin	SU	R	76	20	12	12	1.3	43	12	.28	1 - 1	2 - 2	0 - 1	49	0	3 - 4	19	.96	.643	2.35
Crow, Aaron	SU	R	73	4	15	2	1.1	45	13	.29	1 - 2	1 - 2	0 - 4	51	1	2 - 8	19	.78	.601	3.48
Collins, Tim	LT	L	72	25	16	16	1.1	55	22	.40	0 - 2	0 - 1	0 - 1	46	1	0 - 4	11	.73	.692	3.36
Mijares, Jose	LT	L	51	8	17	2	1.0	37	15	.41	0 - 0	0 - 0	0 - 1	32	0	0 - 1	11	.92	.701	2.56
Bueno, Francisley	LT	L	18	3	4	1	1.0	14	0	.00	0 - 0	0 - 0	0 - 0	14	0	0 - 0	4	1.00	.568	1.56
Teaford, Everett	LM	L	13	10	0	11	0.5	11	3	.27	0 - 0	0 - 0	0 - 0	3	0	0 - 0	0		.742	4.17
Coleman, Louis	UR	R	42	10	4	15	0.5	29	7	.24	0 - 0	0 - 0	0 - 0	25	0	0 - 0	2	1.00	.762	3.71
Jeffress, Jeremy	UR	R	13	0	1	3	0.4	4	2	.50	0 - 0	0 - 0	0 - 0	7	0	0 - 0	0		.838	6.75
Mazzaro, Vin	UR	R	12	3	1	3	0.6	9	3	.33	0 - 0	0 - 0	0 - 0	8	0	0 - 0	0		.747	4.67
Adcock, Nathan	UR	R	10	7	1	5	0.8	9	4	.44	0 - 0	0 - 0	0 - 0	3	0	0 - 0	1	1.00	.744	1.32

Los Angeles Angels

Pitcher	Pos	T	Rel G	Early Entry	Cons Days	Long	Lev Ind	#	Scrd	Pct	Easy	Reg	Tough	Clean	BS Win	Sv- Opp	Holds	Sv/Hld Pct	Opp OPS	Rel ERA
Frieri, Ernesto	CL	R	56	0	13	8	1.6	13	2	.15	12 - 12	8 - 11	3 - 3	48	1	23 - 26	6	.91	.530	2.32
Downs, Scott	SU	L	57	1	14	0	1.3	25	7	.28	5 - 6	3 - 3	1 - 3	45	0	9 - 12	25	.92	.658	3.15
Jepsen, Kevin	SU	R	49	2	12	2	1.3	19	2	.11	0 - 0	1 - 2	1 - 2	39	0	2 - 4	18	.91	.647	3.02
Richards, Garrett	SU	R	21	4	6	1	1.2	11	5	.45	0 - 0	1 - 1	0 - 2	14	0	1 - 3	5	.75	.719	5.50
Maronde, Nick	LT	L	12	6	3	0	0.9	13	3	.23	0 - 0	0 - 0	0 - 0	9	0	0 - 0	3	1.00	.638	1.50
Takahashi, Hisanori	LM	L	42	15	12	10	0.6	24	9	.38	0 - 0	0 - 0	0 - 1	25	0	0 - 1	3	.75	.745	4.93
Carpenter, David	LM	R	28	11	6	9	0.6	22	8	.36	0 - 0	0 - 0	0 - 0	12	0	0 - 0	2	1.00	.781	4.76
Williams, Jerome	LM	R	17	10	1	9	0.3	15	5	.33	0 - 0	1 - 1	0 - 0	8	0	1 - 1	0	1.00	.723	4.08
Isringhausen, Jason	UR	R	50	4	10	3	0.6	12	9	.75	0 - 0	0 - 4	0 - 1	33	1	0 - 5	4	.44	.743	4.14
Hawkins, LaTroy	UR	R	48	14	11	4	0.9	29	9	.31	0 - 0	0 - 2	1 - 2	31	0	1 - 4	6	.70	.735	3.64
Walden, Jordan	UR	R	45	2	6	4	0.8	9	3	.33	1 - 1	0 - 1	0 - 0	32	0	1 - 2	8	.90	.674	3.46

Los Angeles Dodgers

Pitcher	Pos	T	Rel G	Early Entry	Cons Days	Long	Lev Ind	#	Scrd	Pct	Easy	Reg	Tough	Clean	BS Win	Sv- Opp	Holds	Sv/Hld Pct	Opp OPS	Rel ERA
Jansen, Kenley	CL	R	65	0	17	8	1.6	12	4	.33	14 - 15	11 - 15	0 - 2	50	4	25 - 32	8	.83	.504	2.35
Belisario, Ronald	SU	R	68	0	20	5	1.4	31	13	.42	0 - 1	1 - 2	0 - 2	48	2	1 - 5	23	.86	.558	2.54
Lindblom, Josh	SU	R	48	8	8	6	1.1	16	6	.38	0 - 0	0 - 0	0 - 2	35	0	0 - 2	15	.88	.754	3.02
Elbert, Scott	LT	L	43	10	11	0	0.9	42	10	.24	0 - 0	0 - 0	0 - 0	33	0	0 - 0	9	1.00	.642	2.20
Choate, Randy	LT	L	36	4	17	0	1.0	32	6	.19	0 - 0	0 - 0	0 - 0	29	0	0 - 0	5	1.00	.714	4.05
Rodriguez, Paco	LT	L	11	5	2	0	1.0	12	1	.08	0 - 0	0 - 0	0 - 0	9	0	0 - 0	0		.406	1.35
Wright, Jamey	UR	R	66	16	15	14	0.7	45	10	.22	0 - 0	0 - 0	0 - 0	42	0	0 - 0	6	1.00	.676	3.72
Guerra, Javy	UR	R	45	9	8	4	1.6	17	8	.47	3 - 3	5 - 9	0 - 1	31	0	8 - 13	4	.71	.685	2.60
Tolleson, Shawn	UR	R	40	15	6	8	0.6	31	6	.19	0 - 0	0 - 0	0 - 0	28	0	0 - 0	2	1.00	.698	4.30
League, Brandon	UR	R	28	1	7	4	1.3	6	0	.00	3 - 3	3 - 3	0 - 0	23	0	6 - 6	2	1.00	.511	2.30
Coffey, Todd	UR	R	23	2	3	0	0.4	6	2	.33	0 - 0	0 - 0	0 - 0	16	0	0 - 0	2	1.00	.718	4.66
Guerrier, Matt	UR	R	16	2	2	0	1.6	3	0	.00	0 - 1	0 - 0	0 - 0	11	0	0 - 1	3	.75	.682	3.86

Miami Marlins

Pitcher	Pos	T	Rel G	Early Entry	Cons Days	Long	Lev Ind	#	Scrd	Pct	Easy	Reg	Tough	Clean	BS Win	Sv- Opp	Holds	Sv/Hld Pct	Opp OPS	Rel ERA
Bell, Heath	CL	R	73	0	22	9	1.9	11	5	.45	12 - 14	7 - 13	0 - 0	52	0	19 - 27	13	.80	.780	5.09
Cishek, Steve	CL	R	68	0	20	8	1.8	25	6	.24	8 - 9	5 - 6	2 - 4	48	1	15 - 19	13	.88	.663	2.69
Dunn, Mike	SU	L	60	5	21	9	1.2	26	8	.31	1 - 2	0 - 1	0 - 3	40	0	1 - 6	18	.79	.806	4.91
Choate, Randy	SU	L	44	0	16	0	1.3	34	8	.24	0 - 0	0 - 0	0 - 1	30	0	1 - 1	15	1.00	.483	2.49
Mujica, Edward	SU	R	41	1	10	3	1.3	15	3	.20	1 - 3	1 - 3	0 - 0	30	0	2 - 6	12	.78	.692	4.38
LeBlanc, Wade	LT	L	16	8	3	4	0.5	5	0	.00	0 - 0	0 - 0	0 - 0	11	0	0 - 0	1	1.00	.702	2.53
Gaudin, Chad	LM	R	46	19	7	19	0.6	29	9	.31	0 - 0	0 - 0	0 - 0	22	0	0 - 0	1	1.00	.754	4.54
Jennings, Dan	LM	L	22	11	5	1	0.4	14	4	.29	0 - 0	0 - 0	0 - 0	18	0	0 - 0	2	1.00	.771	1.89
Webb, Ryan	UR	R	65	9	15	13	1.0	49	18	.37	0 - 0	0 - 0	0 - 0	36	0	0 - 0	10	1.00	.749	4.03
Zambrano, Carlos	UR	R	15	7	1	6	1.0	4	3	.75	0 - 0	0 - 0	0 - 0	8	0	0 - 0	2	1.00	.734	4.15
Ramos, A.J.	UR	R	11	0	3	1	0.8	5	0	.00	0 - 0	0 - 1	0 - 0	8	0	0 - 1	1	.50	.754	3.86
Hatcher, Chris	UR	R	11	3	2	6	0.1	5	3	.60	0 - 0	0 - 0	0 - 0	6	0	0 - 0	0		.889	4.30

Milwaukee Brewers

Pitcher	Pos	T	Rel G	Early Entry	Cons Days	Long	Lev Ind	#	Scrd	Pct	Easy	Reg	Tough	Clean	BS Win	Sv-Opp	Holds	Sv/Hld Pct	Opp OPS	Rel ERA
			Usage					Inherited Runners			Saves			Relief Results						
Axford, John	CL	R	75	2	27	12	1.9	23	6	.26	22 - 24	12 - 19	1 - 1	50	0	35 - 44	3	.81	.717	4.67
Rodriguez, Francisco	SU	R	78	0	28	7	1.7	7	0	.00	2 - 5	1 - 5	0 - 0	56	0	3 - 10	32	.83	.708	4.38
Henderson, Jim	SU	R	36	3	13	2	1.5	13	4	.31	1 - 2	2 - 5	0 - 0	25	0	3 - 7	14	.81	.609	3.52
Parra, Manny	LT	L	62	13	20	13	1.0	28	13	.46	0 - 0	0 - 2	0 - 0	33	0	0 - 2	9	.82	.738	5.06
Perez, Juan	LT	L	10	0	4	1	0.8	8	2	.25	0 - 0	0 - 0	0 - 0	5	0	0 - 0	0		.929	5.14
Hernandez, Livan	LM	R	26	12	3	9	0.5	11	1	.09	0 - 0	0 - 1	0 - 0	11	1	0 - 1	2	.67	.914	7.68
Veras, Jose	UR	R	72	10	17	12	1.0	26	4	.15	0 - 0	0 - 0	1 - 2	51	0	1 - 2	10	.92	.694	3.63
Loe, Kameron	UR	R	70	20	20	8	1.1	39	15	.38	1 - 2	0 - 1	1 - 4	42	1	2 - 7	7	.64	.786	4.61
Dillard, Tim	UR	R	34	5	9	8	0.5	15	3	.20	0 - 0	0 - 0	0 - 0	16	0	0 - 0	1	1.00	.816	4.38
Kintzler, Brandon	UR	R	14	7	4	2	1.0	1	0	.00	0 - 0	0 - 0	0 - 0	10	0	0 - 0	2	1.00	.732	3.78

Minnesota Twins

Pitcher	Pos	T	Rel G	Early Entry	Cons Days	Long	Lev Ind	#	Scrd	Pct	Easy	Reg	Tough	Clean	BS Win	Sv-Opp	Holds	Sv/Hld Pct	Opp OPS	Rel ERA
			Usage					Inherited Runners			Saves			Relief Results						
Perkins, Glen	CL	L	70	0	18	4	1.3	6	3	.50	9 - 11	7 - 9	0 - 0	55	0	16 - 20	11	.87	.631	2.56
Capps, Matt	CL	R	30	0	5	1	1.7	1	0	.00	6 - 6	8 - 9	0 - 0	21	0	14 - 15	0	.93	.672	3.68
Burton, Jared	SU	R	64	0	11	3	1.4	13	1	.08	2 - 3	3 - 6	0 - 0	53	0	5 - 9	18	.85	.549	2.18
Duensing, Brian	LT	L	44	15	5	10	1.1	32	5	.16	0 - 0	0 - 0	0 - 1	31	0	0 - 1	7	.88	.598	3.47
Robertson, Tyler	LT	L	40	5	14	0	1.0	38	9	.24	0 - 1	0 - 0	0 - 1	23	0	0 - 1	5	.83	.700	5.40
Swarzak, Anthony	LM	R	39	25	1	21	0.7	23	7	.30	0 - 0	0 - 0	0 - 1	16	0	0 - 1	1	.50	.726	4.05
Burnett, Alex	UR	R	67	19	10	12	0.8	52	18	.35	0 - 0	0 - 1	0 - 0	38	0	0 - 1	10	.91	.666	3.52
Gray, Jeff	UR	R	49	11	7	6	0.8	32	6	.19	0 - 0	0 - 0	0 - 0	28	0	0 - 0	1	1.00	.834	5.71
Fien, Casey	UR	R	35	7	7	7	1.1	25	11	.44	0 - 0	0 - 0	0 - 0	25	0	0 - 0	6	1.00	.578	2.06
Waldrop, Kyle	UR	R	17	6	1	3	0.6	11	6	.55	0 - 0	0 - 0	0 - 1	8	0	0 - 1	2	.67	.795	2.53
Perdomo, Luis	UR	R	15	1	3	3	0.1	5	3	.60	0 - 0	0 - 0	0 - 0	9	0	0 - 0	0		.705	3.18
Manship, Jeff	UR	R	12	8	0	6	0.4	5	3	.60	0 - 0	0 - 0	0 - 0	4	0	0 - 0	1	1.00	.898	7.89

New York Mets

Pitcher	Pos	T	Rel G	Early Entry	Cons Days	Long	Lev Ind	#	Scrd	Pct	Easy	Reg	Tough	Clean	BS Win	Sv-Opp	Holds	Sv/Hld Pct	Opp OPS	Rel ERA
			Usage					Inherited Runners			Saves			Relief Results						
Francisco, Frank	CL	R	48	0	11	3	1.5	9	5	.56	16 - 16	7 - 9	0 - 1	30	1	23 - 26	1	.89	.791	5.53
Parnell, Bobby	SU	R	74	3	20	9	1.5	28	9	.32	4 - 4	3 - 7	0 - 1	53	0	7 - 12	18	.83	.648	2.49
Rauch, Jon	SU	R	73	2	16	1	1.1	26	6	.23	3 - 3	0 - 2	1 - 3	54	1	4 - 8	16	.83	.617	3.59
Byrdak, Tim	SU	L	56	1	23	1	1.3	41	7	.17	0 - 0	0 - 2	0 - 0	42	0	0 - 2	17	.89	.576	4.40
Edgin, Josh	LT	L	34	4	12	2	1.0	23	7	.30	0 - 0	0 - 1	0 - 1	24	1	0 - 2	5	.71	.693	4.56
Carson, Robert	LT	L	17	4	4	2	0.5	6	1	.17	0 - 0	0 - 0	0 - 0	11	0	0 - 0	1	1.00	.779	4.73
Hampson, Justin	LT	L	13	5	2	1	0.5	8	1	.13	0 - 0	0 - 0	0 - 0	8	0	0 - 0	1	1.00	.564	1.80
Batista, Miguel	LM	R	25	7	4	6	0.5	18	7	.39	0 - 0	0 - 0	0 - 0	13	0	0 - 0	0		.779	4.56
Ramirez, Ramon	UR	R	58	16	7	12	0.8	25	9	.36	0 - 1	1 - 2	0 - 0	37	0	1 - 3	1	.50	.698	4.24
Acosta, Manny	UR	R	45	19	11	9	0.7	18	4	.22	1 - 1	0 - 0	0 - 1	28	0	1 - 2	4	.83	.748	6.46
Ramirez, Elvin	UR	R	20	4	3	6	0.8	7	2	.29	0 - 0	0 - 0	0 - 0	10	0	0 - 0	1	1.00	.876	5.48
Hefner, Jeremy	UR	R	13	6	0	6	0.3	6	6	1.00	0 - 0	0 - 0	0 - 0	6	0	0 - 0	0		.778	4.44

New York Yankees

Pitcher	Pos	T	Rel G	Early Entry	Cons Days	Long	Lev Ind	#	Scrd	Pct	Easy	Reg	Tough	Clean	BS Win	Sv- Opp	Holds	Sv/Hld Pct	Opp OPS	Rel ERA
Soriano, Rafael	CL	R	69	0	19	6	1.9	19	3	.16	26 - 27	13 - 16	3 - 3	53	0	42 - 46	4	.92	.639	2.26
Logan, Boone	SU	L	80	17	27	6	1.2	64	15	.23	0 - 0	1 - 1	0 - 3	57	0	1 - 4	23	.89	.718	3.74
Robertson, David	SU	R	65	0	20	5	1.5	22	7	.32	2 - 2	0 - 1	0 - 2	52	0	2 - 5	30	.91	.638	2.67
Rapada, Clay	LT	L	70	24	20	2	0.6	57	7	.12	0 - 0	0 - 0	0 - 0	53	0	0 - 0	6	1.00	.601	2.82
Phelps, David	LM	R	22	11	0	15	0.7	16	5	.31	0 - 0	0 - 0	0 - 0	12	0	0 - 0	2	1.00	.640	2.76
Eppley, Cody	UR	R	59	15	14	6	0.8	42	5	.12	0 - 0	0 - 0	0 - 0	38	0	0 - 0	9	1.00	.690	3.33
Wade, Cory	UR	R	39	5	7	6	0.9	22	4	.18	0 - 0	0 - 1	0 - 1	22	0	0 - 2	8	.80	.874	6.46
Chamberlain, Joba	UR	R	22	5	4	4	0.9	24	13	.54	0 - 0	0 - 0	0 - 0	8	0	0 - 0	4	1.00	.835	4.35
Lowe, Derek	UR	R	17	6	2	6	0.8	9	1	.11	0 - 0	1 - 1	0 - 0	9	0	1 - 1	1	1.00	.676	3.04
Garcia, Freddy	UR	R	13	1	0	6	0.8	3	1	.33	0 - 0	0 - 0	0 - 0	9	0	0 - 0	0		.565	2.42

Oakland Athletics

Pitcher	Pos	T	Rel G	Early Entry	Cons Days	Long	Lev Ind	#	Scrd	Pct	Easy	Reg	Tough	Clean	BS Win	Sv- Opp	Holds	Sv/Hld Pct	Opp OPS	Rel ERA
Balfour, Grant	CL	R	75	5	20	5	1.6	21	10	.48	18 - 18	6 - 7	0 - 1	59	0	24 - 26	15	.95	.495	2.53
Cook, Ryan	SU	R	71	2	18	5	1.7	25	8	.32	10 - 12	4 - 7	0 - 2	58	1	14 - 21	21	.83	.517	2.09
Doolittle, Sean	SU	L	44	4	11	7	1.4	22	3	.14	0 - 0	1 - 2	0 - 0	32	1	1 - 2	18	.95	.611	3.04
Blevins, Jerry	LT	L	63	17	12	11	1.0	45	12	.27	0 - 0	0 - 0	1 - 1	43	0	1 - 1	14	1.00	.637	2.48
Fuentes, Brian	LT	L	26	2	5	3	1.2	2	0	.00	0 - 0	2 - 3	0 - 0	16	0	5 - 8	2	.70	.871	6.84
Norberto, Jordan	LM	L	39	16	6	11	1.0	24	4	.17	0 - 1	0 - 1	1 - 1	26	0	1 - 3	4	.71	.614	2.77
Figueroa, Pedro	LM	L	19	10	2	3	0.4	12	2	.17	0 - 0	0 - 0	0 - 0	12	0	0 - 0	0		.659	3.32
Miller, Jim	UR	R	33	9	6	15	0.4	18	8	.44	0 - 0	0 - 0	0 - 0	16	0	0 - 0	0		.688	2.59
Scribner, Evan	UR	R	30	5	4	9	0.5	13	4	.31	0 - 0	1 - 1	0 - 0	23	0	1 - 1	1	1.00	.637	2.55
Neshek, Pat	UR	R	24	8	5	3	1.0	17	5	.29	0 - 0	0 - 2	0 - 0	20	0	0 - 2	4	.67	.530	1.37
Carignan, Andrew	UR	R	11	1	1	2	0.4	2	2	1.00	0 - 0	0 - 0	0 - 0	7	0	0 - 0	0		.722	4.66

Philadelphia Phillies

Pitcher	Pos	T	Rel G	Early Entry	Cons Days	Long	Lev Ind	#	Scrd	Pct	Easy	Reg	Tough	Clean	BS Win	Sv- Opp	Holds	Sv/Hld Pct	Opp OPS	Rel ERA
Papelbon, Jonathan	CL	R	70	0	19	7	1.7	8	4	.50	23 - 26	13 - 14	2 - 2	54	1	38 - 42	0	.90	.621	2.44
Bastardo, Antonio	SU	L	65	0	19	6	1.7	19	7	.37	1 - 2	0 - 1	0 - 2	46	0	1 - 5	26	.87	.662	4.33
Qualls, Chad	SU	R	35	3	10	2	1.3	15	9	.60	0 - 2	0 - 1	0 - 2	21	1	0 - 5	12	.71	.883	4.60
Lindblom, Josh	SU	R	26	5	3	3	1.2	10	5	.50	0 - 0	1 - 1	0 - 1	17	0	1 - 2	7	.89	.750	4.63
Aumont, Phillippe	SU	R	18	0	5	0	1.3	6	2	.33	2 - 2	0 - 0	0 - 1	14	0	2 - 3	5	.88	.544	3.68
Diekman, Jake	LT	L	32	2	3	6	0.9	25	6	.24	0 - 0	0 - 0	0 - 1	19	0	0 - 1	4	.80	.696	3.95
Horst, Jeremy	LT	L	32	7	8	5	0.6	13	3	.23	0 - 0	0 - 0	0 - 0	22	0	0 - 0	6	1.00	.566	1.15
Valdes, Raul	LT	L	26	11	6	4	0.7	19	2	.11	0 - 0	0 - 0	0 - 1	21	0	0 - 0	2	.67	.414	2.17
Savery, Joe	LM	L	19	8	2	6	0.7	9	2	.22	0 - 0	0 - 0	0 - 0	8	0	0 - 0	1	1.00	.804	5.40
Schwimer, Michael	UR	R	35	3	8	6	1.0	19	10	.53	0 - 0	0 - 0	0 - 1	23	0	0 - 1	1	.50	.724	4.46
Rosenberg, B.J.	UR	R	21	7	2	3	0.7	11	0	.00	0 - 0	0 - 0	0 - 0	14	0	0 - 0	2	1.00	.748	6.86
Contreras, Jose	UR	R	17	1	3	0	0.9	5	2	.40	0 - 0	0 - 0	0 - 0	12	0	0 - 0	4	1.00	.696	5.27
De Fratus, Justin	UR	R	13	1	3	1	0.7	4	0	.00	0 - 0	0 - 0	0 - 0	10	0	0 - 0	5	1.00	.478	3.38
Kendrick, Kyle	UR	R	12	2	2	5	1.4	7	0	.00	0 - 1	0 - 0	0 - 0	9	0	0 - 1	2	.67	.692	3.95

Pittsburgh Pirates

Pitcher	Pos	T	Usage				Inherited Runners			Saves			Relief Results						
			Rel G	Early Entry	Cons Days	Long	Lev Ind	#	Scrd	Pct	Easy	Reg	Tough	Clean	BS Win	Sv-Opp	Holds	Sv/Hld Pct	Opp OPS	Rel ERA
Hanrahan, Joel	CL	R	63	0	17	4	1.8	7	0	.00	23 - 23	13 - 17	0 - 0	51	2	36 - 40	0	.90	.648	2.72
Grilli, Jason	SU	R	64	0	12	3	1.7	6	0	.00	0 - 0	2 - 5	0 - 0	49	1	2 - 5	32	.92	.635	2.91
Cruz, Juan	SU	R	43	1	7	2	1.5	7	1	.14	1 - 1	2 - 3	0 - 0	32	0	3 - 4	14	.94	.789	2.78
Watson, Tony	LT	L	68	13	14	3	1.1	61	11	.18	0 - 0	0 - 1	0 - 1	48	1	0 - 2	16	.89	.623	3.38
Slaten, Doug	LT	L	10	6	1	4	0.3	6	2	.33	0 - 0	0 - 0	0 - 0	8	0	0 - 0	2	1.00	.597	2.77
Resop, Chris	LM	R	61	25	6	11	0.8	27	10	.37	0 - 0	1 - 1	0 - 1	36	0	1 - 2	8	.90	.722	3.91
Hughes, Jared	UR	R	66	17	12	13	0.9	38	10	.26	0 - 0	2 - 3	0 - 1	47	0	2 - 4	11	.87	.677	2.85
Lincoln, Brad	UR	R	23	7	1	8	0.9	11	0	.00	0 - 0	1 - 2	0 - 0	20	0	1 - 2	5	.86	.519	0.50
Qualls, Chad	UR	R	17	2	1	0	0.5	5	1	.20	0 - 0	0 - 0	0 - 0	12	0	0 - 0	2	1.00	.614	6.59
Meek, Evan	UR	R	12	2	2	1	0.5	5	4	.80	0 - 0	0 - 0	0 - 0	7	0	0 - 0	1	1.00	.763	6.75
Leroux, Chris	UR	R	10	4	1	4	0.5	6	1	.17	0 - 0	0 - 0	0 - 0	5	0	0 - 0	0		.639	5.56

San Diego Padres

Pitcher	Pos	T	Usage				Inherited Runners			Saves			Relief Results						
			Rel G	Early Entry	Cons Days	Long	Lev Ind	#	Scrd	Pct	Easy	Reg	Tough	Clean	BS Win	Sv-Opp	Holds	Sv/Hld Pct	Opp OPS	Rel ERA
Street, Huston	CL	R	40	0	11	1	1.5	13	4	.31	13 - 13	8 - 9	2 - 2	32	0	23 - 24	0	.96	.425	1.85
Gregerson, Luke	SU	R	77	1	24	5	1.5	25	5	.20	3 - 3	4 - 6	2 - 4	62	0	9 - 13	24	.89	.612	2.39
Thayer, Dale	SU	R	64	3	17	6	1.2	27	8	.30	4 - 5	3 - 4	0 - 1	47	0	7 - 10	22	.91	.627	3.43
Cashner, Andrew	SU	R	28	2	10	2	1.6	6	5	.83	0 - 0	0 - 2	0 - 2	18	0	0 - 4	6	.60	.676	3.67
Layne, Tom	SU	L	26	2	11	0	1.0	15	3	.20	1 - 1	0 - 0	1 - 2	21	0	2 - 3	7	.90	.421	3.24
Thatcher, Joe	LT	L	55	6	14	1	1.3	46	7	.15	1 - 1	0 - 0	0 - 0	40	0	1 - 1	14	1.00	.680	3.41
Spence, Josh	LT	L	11	4	1	1	0.5	7	1	.14	0 - 0	0 - 0	0 - 0	7	0	0 - 0	0		.770	4.35
Hinshaw, Alex	LM	R	31	11	5	3	0.4	20	2	.10	0 - 0	0 - 1	0 - 0	21	0	0 - 1	1	.50	.748	4.50
Mikolas, Miles	LM	R	25	11	3	7	0.4	19	6	.32	0 - 0	0 - 1	0 - 0	13	0	0 - 1	1	.50	.761	3.62
Boxberger, Brad	LM	R	24	10	3	11	0.6	22	9	.41	0 - 0	0 - 0	0 - 0	13	0	0 - 0	1	1.00	.734	2.60
Brach, Brad	UR	R	67	21	16	14	1.0	46	5	.11	0 - 0	0 - 0	0 - 1	46	0	0 - 1	15	.94	.674	3.78
Vincent, Nick	UR	R	27	12	5	3	0.7	33	12	.36	0 - 0	0 - 1	0 - 0	19	0	0 - 1	5	.83	.551	1.71
Burns, Cory	UR	R	17	4	4	4	0.5	5	2	.40	0 - 0	0 - 0	0 - 0	11	0	0 - 0	0		.859	5.50
Frieri, Ernesto	UR	R	11	3	1	4	0.5	2	0	.00	0 - 0	0 - 0	0 - 0	7	0	0 - 0	1	1.00	.664	2.31

San Francisco Giants

Pitcher	Pos	T	Usage				Inherited Runners			Saves			Relief Results						
			Rel G	Early Entry	Cons Days	Long	Lev Ind	#	Scrd	Pct	Easy	Reg	Tough	Clean	BS Win	Sv-Opp	Holds	Sv/Hld Pct	Opp OPS	Rel ERA
Casilla, Santiago	CL	R	73	0	25	4	1.8	41	9	.22	18 - 20	6 - 9	1 - 2	52	2	25 - 31	12	.86	.656	2.84
Lopez, Javier	SU	L	70	0	22	1	1.3	51	7	.14	0 - 0	5 - 5	1 - 3	54	0	7 - 9	18	.93	.700	2.50
Romo, Sergio	SU	R	69	0	21	1	1.5	43	9	.21	3 - 4	10 - 10	1 - 1	56	0	14 - 15	23	.97	.525	1.79
Affeldt, Jeremy	SU	L	67	7	16	5	1.0	39	12	.31	0 - 0	3 - 4	0 - 0	47	0	3 - 4	16	.95	.640	2.70
Mijares, Jose	LT	L	27	12	10	1	0.8	18	2	.11	0 - 0	0 - 0	0 - 0	23	0	0 - 0	7	1.00	.609	2.55
Loux, Shane	LM	R	19	9	2	6	0.2	6	3	.50	0 - 0	0 - 0	0 - 0	11	0	0 - 0	1	1.00	.879	4.97
Hensley, Clay	UR	R	60	5	15	8	1.0	28	5	.18	0 - 0	0 - 1	3 - 3	37	0	3 - 4	8	.92	.747	4.62
Kontos, George	UR	R	44	15	10	7	0.4	28	12	.43	0 - 0	0 - 0	0 - 1	30	0	0 - 1	5	.83	.591	2.47
Mota, Guillermo	UR	R	26	9	7	2	0.9	13	3	.23	0 - 0	0 - 0	0 - 1	19	0	0 - 1	10	.91	.911	5.23
Penny, Brad	UR	R	22	5	0	5	0.5	7	0	.00	0 - 0	0 - 0	0 - 0	12	0	0 - 0	2	1.00	.902	6.11
Edlefsen, Steve	UR	R	14	3	1	2	0.3	8	3	.38	0 - 0	0 - 0	0 - 0	8	0	0 - 0	0		.805	4.70
Otero, Dan	UR	R	12	4	3	3	0.3	10	0	.00	0 - 0	0 - 0	0 - 0	8	0	0 - 0	0		.894	5.84

Seattle Mariners

Pitcher	Pos	T	Usage					Inherited Runners			Saves			Relief Results						
			Rel G	Early Entry	Cons Days	Long	Lev Ind	#	Scrd	Pct	Easy	Reg	Tough	Clean	BS Win	Sv-Opp	Holds	Sv/Hld Pct	Opp OPS	Rel ERA
Wilhelmsen, Tom	CL	R	73	0	19	5	1.7	19	7	.37	18 - 18	9 - 12	2 - 4	52	0	29 - 34	7	.88	.578	2.50
League, Brandon	SU	R	46	3	12	4	1.7	10	3	.30	5 - 5	4 - 9	0 - 1	33	0	9 - 15	6	.71	.692	3.63
Kinney, Josh	SU	R	35	3	10	3	1.4	17	2	.12	0 - 0	0 - 1	1 - 1	23	0	1 - 2	9	.91	.668	3.94
Luetge, Lucas	LT	L	63	5	17	4	1.1	50	8	.16	1 - 1	1 - 1	0 - 1	47	1	2 - 3	12	.93	.693	3.98
Furbush, Charlie	LT	L	48	11	3	10	1.1	27	8	.30	0 - 0	0 - 0	0 - 0	31	0	0 - 0	6	1.00	.529	2.72
Perez, Oliver	LT	L	33	8	6	4	1.0	29	9	.31	0 - 0	0 - 0	0 - 2	22	1	0 - 2	5	.71	.628	2.12
Capps, Carter	LM	R	18	8	1	11	0.4	7	0	.00	0 - 0	0 - 0	0 - 0	11	0	0 - 0	2	1.00	.667	3.96
Iwakuma, Hisashi	LM	R	14	10	2	8	0.5	3	2	.67	1 - 1	1 - 1	0 - 0	4	0	2 - 2	0	1.00	.806	4.75
Kelley, Shawn	UR	R	47	10	10	8	1.0	26	10	.38	0 - 0	0 - 0	0 - 2	31	0	0 - 2	6	.75	.717	3.25
Delabar, Steve	UR	R	34	7	4	4	0.6	18	5	.28	0 - 1	0 - 1	0 - 0	23	0	0 - 2	3	.60	.683	4.17
Pryor, Stephen	UR	R	27	2	5	5	1.3	17	10	.59	0 - 0	0 - 0	0 - 0	16	0	0 - 0	5	1.00	.849	3.91

St Louis Cardinals

Pitcher	Pos	T	Usage					Inherited Runners			Saves			Relief Results						
			Rel G	Early Entry	Cons Days	Long	Lev Ind	#	Scrd	Pct	Easy	Reg	Tough	Clean	BS Win	Sv-Opp	Holds	Sv/Hld Pct	Opp OPS	Rel ERA
Motte, Jason	CL	R	67	0	17	6	1.7	20	3	.15	30 - 31	6 - 11	6 - 7	51	2	42 - 49	0	.86	.576	2.75
Boggs, Mitchell	SU	R	78	0	24	5	1.4	34	6	.18	0 - 0	0 - 2	0 - 1	62	0	0 - 3	34	.92	.570	2.21
Rzepczynski, Marc	SU	L	70	4	16	2	1.2	53	11	.21	0 - 1	0 - 3	0 - 1	51	1	0 - 5	18	.78	.729	4.24
Mujica, Edward	SU	R	29	3	12	0	1.3	11	3	.27	0 - 0	0 - 0	0 - 2	25	0	0 - 2	18	.90	.562	1.03
Freeman, Sam	LT	L	24	5	5	0	0.6	14	7	.50	0 - 0	0 - 0	0 - 0	13	0	0 - 0	2	1.00	.654	5.40
Browning, Barret	LT	L	22	5	7	3	0.9	5	3	.60	0 - 0	0 - 0	0 - 0	13	0	0 - 0	4	1.00	.702	5.12
Romero, J.C.	LT	L	11	3	2	1	0.4	6	2	.33	0 - 0	0 - 0	0 - 0	6	0	0 - 0	1	1.00	1.073	10.13
Salas, Fernando	UR	R	65	8	14	12	1.2	32	9	.28	0 - 1	0 - 1	0 - 1	43	0	0 - 3	7	.70	.720	4.30
Marte, Victor	UR	R	48	13	10	2	1.0	40	11	.28	0 - 0	0 - 0	0 - 2	23	1	0 - 2	9	.82	.855	4.91
Rosenthal, Trevor	UR	R	19	6	2	6	0.6	6	0	.00	0 - 0	0 - 0	0 - 0	15	0	0 - 0	3	1.00	.513	2.78
Sanchez, Eduardo	UR	R	17	2	4	2	0.9	8	4	.50	0 - 0	0 - 0	0 - 0	10	0	0 - 0	4	1.00	.714	6.60
McClellan, Kyle	UR	R	16	2	3	2	0.6	1	0	.00	0 - 0	0 - 0	0 - 0	9	0	0 - 0	1	1.00	.700	5.30

Tampa Bay Rays

Pitcher	Pos	T	Usage					Inherited Runners			Saves			Relief Results						
			Rel G	Early Entry	Cons Days	Long	Lev Ind	#	Scrd	Pct	Easy	Reg	Tough	Clean	BS Win	Sv-Opp	Holds	Sv/Hld Pct	Opp OPS	Rel ERA
Rodney, Fernando	CL	R	76	0	28	4	1.8	18	2	.11	34 - 34	11 - 13	3 - 3	67	0	48 - 50	0	.96	.417	0.60
Peralta, Joel	SU	R	77	1	27	4	1.2	26	9	.35	1 - 1	0 - 1	1 - 3	55	0	2 - 5	37	.93	.629	3.63
McGee, Jake	SU	L	69	17	19	5	1.3	54	14	.26	0 - 0	0 - 0	0 - 2	51	0	0 - 2	19	.90	.452	1.95
Howell, J.P.	LT	L	55	17	13	3	0.7	25	6	.24	0 - 0	0 - 0	0 - 0	42	0	0 - 0	3	1.00	.706	3.04
Ramos, Cesar	LT	L	16	6	1	7	0.3	5	0	.00	0 - 0	0 - 0	0 - 0	11	0	0 - 0	0		.507	2.30
Badenhop, Burke	UR	R	66	18	20	7	0.8	37	9	.24	0 - 0	0 - 0	0 - 0	46	0	0 - 0	5	1.00	.687	3.03
Davis, Wade	UR	R	54	13	6	20	0.8	20	5	.25	0 - 0	0 - 1	0 - 0	39	0	0 - 1	6	.86	.570	2.43
Farnsworth, Kyle	UR	R	34	6	4	2	1.2	5	2	.40	0 - 0	0 - 0	0 - 0	25	0	0 - 0	7	1.00	.588	4.00
Gomes, Brandon	UR	R	15	3	4	5	0.9	7	1	.14	0 - 0	0 - 0	0 - 0	7	0	0 - 0	0		.773	5.09

Texas Rangers

Pitcher	Pos	T	Rel G	Early Entry	Cons Days	Long	Lev Ind	#	Scrd	Pct	Easy	Reg	Tough	Clean	BS Win	Sv- Opp	Holds	Sv/Hld Pct	Opp OPS	Rel ERA
					Usage				Inherited Runners			Saves			Relief Results					
Nathan, Joe	CL	R	66	0	21	9	1.6	3	0	.00	22 - 24	15 - 16	0 - 0	53	0	37 - 40	0	.93	.631	2.80
Adams, Mike	SU	R	61	0	17	3	1.6	17	6	.35	1 - 1	0 - 0	0 - 1	45	0	1 - 2	27	.97	.718	3.27
Ogando, Alexi	SU	R	57	8	13	8	1.3	36	11	.31	3 - 3	0 - 2	0 - 1	38	0	3 - 6	12	.83	.638	3.43
Ross, Robbie	LT	L	58	20	15	13	0.9	45	10	.22	0 - 0	0 - 0	0 - 0	42	0	0 - 0	9	1.00	.624	2.22
Kirkman, Michael	LT	L	28	7	4	9	0.7	23	5	.22	0 - 0	0 - 1	0 - 1	17	0	0 - 2	1	.33	.611	3.82
Scheppers, Tanner	UR	R	39	7	7	2	0.7	26	10	.38	1 - 1	0 - 0	0 - 0	23	0	1 - 1	4	1.00	.908	4.45
Uehara, Koji	UR	R	37	2	9	0	0.6	17	5	.29	0 - 0	0 - 0	1 - 1	30	0	1 - 1	7	1.00	.466	1.75
Lowe, Mark	UR	R	36	8	3	5	0.3	8	5	.63	0 - 0	0 - 0	0 - 0	26	0	0 - 0	1	1.00	.707	3.43
Tateyama, Yoshinori	UR	R	14	7	2	4	0.3	9	3	.33	0 - 0	0 - 0	0 - 0	7	0	0 - 0	0		.816	9.00

Toronto Blue Jays

Pitcher	Pos	T	Rel G	Early Entry	Cons Days	Long	Lev Ind	#	Scrd	Pct	Easy	Reg	Tough	Clean	BS Win	Sv- Opp	Holds	Sv/Hld Pct	Opp OPS	Rel ERA
					Usage				Inherited Runners			Saves			Relief Results					
Janssen, Casey	CL	R	62	0	17	8	1.2	12	2	.17	12 - 12	10 - 13	0 - 0	48	0	22 - 25	1	.88	.564	2.54
Oliver, Darren	SU	L	62	2	11	4	1.3	13	5	.38	1 - 1	1 - 1	0 - 2	50	0	2 - 4	16	.90	.575	2.06
Frasor, Jason	SU	R	50	10	10	4	1.0	31	12	.39	0 - 0	0 - 1	0 - 2	36	0	0 - 3	12	.80	.799	4.12
Delabar, Steve	SU	R	27	6	3	7	1.4	11	2	.18	0 - 0	0 - 0	0 - 0	19	0	0 - 0	9	1.00	.693	3.38
Perez, Luis	LT	L	35	10	7	7	0.9	24	5	.21	0 - 0	0 - 0	0 - 0	25	0	0 - 0	4	1.00	.672	3.43
Loup, Aaron	LT	L	33	8	5	2	0.9	19	4	.21	0 - 0	0 - 0	0 - 1	25	0	0 - 1	6	.86	.547	2.64
Cecil, Brett	LT	L	12	5	3	3	0.6	6	0	.00	0 - 0	0 - 0	0 - 0	7	0	0 - 0	1	1.00	.773	5.73
Crawford, Evan	LT	L	10	1	1	2	0.6	3	0	.00	0 - 0	0 - 0	0 - 0	7	0	0 - 0	1	1.00	1.129	6.75
Cordero, Francisco	UR	R	41	0	10	4	1.5	8	1	.13	2 - 3	0 - 2	0 - 0	27	1	2 - 5	6	.73	.943	5.77
Lyon, Brandon	UR	R	30	6	6	2	1.1	15	4	.27	0 - 0	1 - 1	0 - 0	22	0	1 - 1	7	1.00	.619	2.88
Lincoln, Brad	UR	R	24	8	1	5	0.9	19	8	.42	0 - 0	0 - 0	0 - 0	15	0	0 - 0	4	1.00	.831	5.65
Villanueva, Carlos	UR	R	22	5	2	9	0.9	9	1	.11	0 - 0	0 - 0	0 - 0	17	0	0 - 0	2	1.00	.718	3.24
Beck, Chad	UR	R	15	6	3	2	0.5	15	8	.53	0 - 0	0 - 0	0 - 0	5	0	0 - 0	0		.891	6.32
Jenkins, Chad	UR	R	10	4	2	4	0.7	6	1	.17	0 - 0	0 - 0	0 - 0	5	0	0 - 0	0		.760	4.91

Washington Nationals

Pitcher	Pos	T	Rel G	Early Entry	Cons Days	Long	Lev Ind	#	Scrd	Pct	Easy	Reg	Tough	Clean	BS Win	Sv- Opp	Holds	Sv/Hld Pct	Opp OPS	Rel ERA
					Usage				Inherited Runners			Saves			Relief Results					
Clippard, Tyler	CL	R	74	0	21	7	1.8	9	2	.22	26 - 27	6 - 9	0 - 1	51	0	32 - 37	13	.90	.621	3.72
Burnett, Sean	SU	L	70	0	22	1	1.4	29	12	.41	0 - 0	0 - 2	2 - 2	53	0	2 - 5	31	.92	.673	2.38
Storen, Drew	SU	R	37	0	11	0	1.4	12	2	.17	3 - 3	0 - 1	1 - 1	32	1	4 - 5	10	.93	.496	2.37
Gonzalez, Michael	LT	L	47	4	12	2	0.9	33	7	.21	0 - 0	0 - 1	0 - 1	32	0	0 - 2	7	.78	.692	3.03
Stammen, Craig	LM	R	59	23	7	27	1.0	27	5	.19	1 - 1	0 - 0	0 - 0	38	0	1 - 2	10	.92	.636	2.34
Gorzelanny, Tom	LM	L	44	21	1	19	0.8	13	4	.31	0 - 0	1 - 1	0 - 0	27	0	1 - 1	9	1.00	.708	2.90
Mattheus, Ryan	UR	R	66	3	19	6	1.0	29	7	.24	0 - 0	0 - 0	0 - 0	45	0	0 - 0	18	1.00	.710	2.85
Rodriguez, Henry	UR	R	35	0	8	3	1.6	3	0	.00	6 - 7	3 - 5	0 - 0	22	0	9 - 12	2	.79	.640	5.83
Garcia, Christian	UR	R	13	5	3	0	0.7	6	0	.00	0 - 0	0 - 0	0 - 0	11	0	0 - 0	4	1.00	.627	2.13
Lidge, Brad	UR	R	11	0	2	3	2.5	1	1	1.00	0 - 2	2 - 2	0 - 0	6	0	2 - 4	0	.50	1.024	9.64

Pitchers Hitting, Fielding, & Holding Runners, and Hitters Pitching

Pitchers are notoriously poor hitters and this section displays the carnage. Many pitchers have batting averages well below their weight (and sometimes below their IQ), especially American League pitchers who only get the opportunity to hit through interleague play. 2012 and career hitting statistics for each pitcher are printed in this section.

Alex White, Mike Leake, and Madison Bumgarner each hit two home runs in 2012, which was the best of all pitchers. Bumgarner had six RBI, besting Leake's three and White's five. None of them, nor any other pitcher, could beat Yovani Gallardo's nine RBI.

This section also includes 2012 fielding statistics for pitchers and data on how well they held runners last season. A pitcher's Runs Saved (RS) is the sum of Plus/Minus Runs Saved to evaluate range, Stolen Base Runs Saved, which measures the ability to control the running game, and Good Fielding Play/Defensive Misplay Runs Saved, which account for the defensive plays and the mistakes made on the field that are not normally counted, but Bill James and Baseball Info Solutions do. Mark Buehrle of the Marlins led all pitchers with 12 Runs Saved.

The final piece of this section is Hitters Pitching. The Orioles' Chris Davis is your hitters pitching Triple Crown winner in 2012, recording a win, no earned runs, and two strikeouts(!) in two innings pitched. Career statistics are listed for all active position players who have pitched, as well as any 2011 pitching statistics that they may have accrued.

Pitchers Hitting, Fielding and Holding Runners

Pitcher	T	2012 Hitting						Career Hitting											2012 Fielding and Holding Runners											
		Avg	AB	H	HR	RBI	SH	Avg	AB	H	2B	3B	HR	RBI	BB	SO	SH	Inn	PO	A	E	DP	Pct	SBA	CS	PCS	PPO	CS%	RS
Aardsma,David, NYY	R	-	0	0	0	0	0	.000	3	0	0	0	0	0	0	1	1	1.0	0	0	0	0	-	0	0	0	0	-	0
Abad,Fernando, Hou	L	.143	7	1	0	0	0	.125	8	1	0	0	0	0	4	4	0	46.0	3	6	0	0	1.000	3	3	0	0	1.00	-1
Accardo,Jeremy, Cle-Oak	R	-	0	0	0	0	0	.143	7	1	0	0	0	0	0	1	0	37.1	2	7	0	2	1.000	6	1	0	0	.17	1
Aceves,Alfredo, Bos	R	-	0	0	0	0	0	.000	2	0	0	0	0	0	0	1	0	84.0	9	12	2	1	.913	7	1	0	1	.14	1
Acosta,Manny, NYM	R	-	0	0	0	0	0	.000	6	0	0	0	0	0	1	4	0	47.1	3	2	1	0	.833	5	1	0	0	.20	-1
Adams,Mike, Tex	R		0	0	0	0	0	.000	2	0	0	0	0	0	0	0	0	52.1	5	12	0	2	1.000	12	1	0	0	.08	2
Adcock,Nathan, KC	R	.000	1	0	0	0	0	.000	1	0	0	0	0	0	0	1	0	34.2	1	5	2	0	.750	6	3	0	0	.50	1
Affeldt,Jeremy, SF	L	.000	1	0	0	0	0	.200	15	3	0	0	0	2	2	4	0	63.1	5	13	1	1	.947	5	2	1	0	.40	-1
Albaladejo,J, Ari	R	-	0	0	0	0	0	-	0	0	0	0	0	0	0	0	0	3.0	0	0	0	0	-	0	0	0	0	-	0
Albers,Matt, Bos-Ari	R	-	0	0	0	0	0	.059	34	2	0	0	0	0	0	21	3	60.1	1	8	1	1	.900	8	2	0	0	.25	0
Alburquerque,Al, Det	R	-	0	0	0	0	0	-	0	0	0	0	0	0	0	0	0	13.1	0	2	0	0	1.000	2	1	0	0	.50	1
Allen,Cody, Cle	R	-	0	0	0	0	0	-	0	0	0	0	0	0	0	0	0	29.0	3	2	0	0	1.000	4	2	0	1	.50	0
Alvarez,Henderson, Tor	R	.000	1	0	0	0	0	.000	1	0	0	0	0	0	0	1	0	187.1	15	35	4	2	.926	2	0	0	0	.00	3
Ambriz,Hector, Hou	R	-	0	0	0	0	0	-	0	0	0	0	0	0	0	0	0	19.1	2	3	0	0	1.000	3	1	0	0	.33	1
Anderson,Brett, Oak	L	-	0	0	0	0	0	.000	4	0	0	0	0	0	0	2	0	35.0	1	0	1	0	1.000	2	1	1	0	.50	-3
Archer,Chris, TB	R	.000	3	0	0	0	0	.000	3	0	0	0	0	0	0	1	0	29.1	1	4	1	0	.833	3	2	1	0	.67	0
Arredondo,Jose, Cin	R	-	0	0	0	0	0	.500	2	1	0	0	0	0	0	1	0	61.0	7	9	1	1	.941	9	3	0	1	.33	0
Arrieta,Jake, Bal	R	.000	3	0	0	0	0	.100	10	1	0	0	0	1	2	4	1	114.2	4	18	3	2	.880	12	3	0	0	.25	-2
Arroyo,Bronson, Cin	R	.143	63	9	1	3	6	.130	517	67	16	0	6	29	14	228	62	202.0	16	31	0	1	1.000	12	5	1	1	.42	4
Asencio,Jairo, Cle-ChC	R	-	0	0	0	0	0	-	0	0	0	0	0	0	0	0	0	40.1	0	1	0	0	1.000	6	1	0	0	.17	1
Atchison,Scott, Bos	R	-	0	0	0	0	0	.000	2	0	0	0	0	0	0	1	0	51.1	8	10	0	0	1.000	2	0	0	0	.00	2
Aumont,Phillippe, Phi	R	-	0	0	0	0	0	-	0	0	0	0	0	0	0	0	0	14.2	0	3	0	0	1.000	2	1	0	0	.50	1
Avilan,Luis, Atl	L	.333	3	1	0	0	0	.333	3	1	0	0	0	0	0	0	0	36.0	1	2	1	1	.750	2	0	0	0	.00	-2
Axelrod,Dylan, CWS	R	-	0	0	0	0	0	-	0	0	0	0	0	0	0	0	0	51.0	2	6	0	0	1.000	8	2	0	0	.25	-1
Axford,John, Mil	R	.000	1	0	0	0	0	.000	1	0	0	0	0	0	0	1	0	69.1	2	4	1	0	.857	6	2	0	0	.33	-1
Ayala,Luis, Bal	R	-	0	0	0	0	0	.286	14	4	1	0	0	0	3	3	3	75.0	4	13	0	1	1.000	5	0	0	0	.00	2
Badenhop,Burke, TB	R	.000	1	0	0	0	0	.097	31	3	1	0	0	2	1	18	5	62.1	3	4	2	1	.778	1	0	0	0	.00	-1
Bailey,Andrew, Bos	R	-	0	0	0	0	0	-	0	0	0	0	0	0	0	0	0	15.1	1	0	1	0	1.000	2	1	0	0	.50	1
Bailey,Homer, Cin	R	.114	70	8	0	5	5	.164	201	33	5	0	0	13	4	82	22	208.0	14	26	3	0	.930	23	7	0	0	.30	4
Balester,Collin, Det	R	-	0	0	0	0	0	.148	27	4	0	0	0	1	2	10	11	18.0	1	0	0	0	1.000	3	0	0	0	.00	0
Balfour,Grant, Oak	R	.000	1	0	0	0	0	.000	2	0	0	0	0	0	0	2	0	74.2	6	7	0	0	1.000	6	3	0	0	.50	1
Bard,Daniel, Bos	R	.000	2	0	0	0	0	.000	2	0	0	0	0	0	0	1	0	59.1	4	8	3	1	1.000	12	3	1	0	.25	-1
Barnes,Scott, Cle	L	-	0	0	0	0	0	-	0	0	0	0	0	0	0	0	0	19.0	2	3	0	0	1.000	2	0	0	0	.00	0
Bass,Anthony, SD	R	.129	31	4	0	5	0	.111	36	4	0	1	0	5	0	16	1	97.0	9	12	0	0	1.000	18	3	0	2	.17	-1
Bastardo,Antonio, Phi	L	-	0	0	0	0	0	.000	6	0	0	0	0	0	0	3	1	52.0	2	0	1	1	.667	8	1	0	0	.13	-1
Batista,Miguel, NYM-Atl	R	.000	6	0	0	0	1	.090	311	28	5	0	2	9	11	173	28	52.2	0	7	1	0	.875	11	3	0	0	.27	0
Bauer,Trevor, Ari	R	.000	4	0	0	0	1	.000	4	0	0	0	0	0	0	0	0	16.1	1	3	2	1	.667	4	0	0	0	.00	-2
Beachy,Brandon, Atl	R	.185	27	5	0	4	2	.120	75	9	1	0	0	5	4	43	8	81.0	1	7	0	1	1.000	9	3	0	0	.33	0
Beato,Pedro, NYM-Bos	R	-	0	0	0	0	0	-	0	0	0	0	0	0	0	0	0	12.0	0	1	0	0	1.000	2	1	0	0	.50	0
Beavan,Blake, Sea	R	.000	2	0	0	0	1	.000	2	0	0	0	0	0	0	1	1	152.1	6	19	1	3	.962	19	4	0	0	.21	1
Beck,Chad, Tor	R	-	0	0	0	0	0	-	0	0	0	0	0	0	0	0	0	15.2	1	2	1	0	.750	3	1	1	0	.33	0
Beckett,Josh, Bos-LAD	R	.048	21	1	0	0	1	.136	242	33	9	0	3	16	10	93	27	170.1	13	19	1	2	.970	22	3	0	1	.14	-4
Bedard,Erik, Pit	L	.108	37	4	0	0	6	.158	57	9	1	0	1	2	21	7	125.2	5	9	0	2	1.000	6	0	0	0	.00	-1
Belisario,Ronald, LAD	R	-	0	0	0	0	0	.000	4	0	0	0	0	0	0	3	0	71.0	4	11	1	0	.947	5	1	0	0	.20	2
Belisle,Matt, Col	R	.000	3	0	0	0	0	.084	83	7	3	0	0	3	3	46	18	80.0	6	7	1	0	.929	1	0	0	0	.00	-3
Beliveau,Jeff, ChC	L	-	0	0	0	0	0	-	0	0	0	0	0	0	0	0	0	17.2	0	4	0	0	1.000	1	1	1	0	1.00	0
Bell,Heath, Mia	R	-	0	0	0	0	0	.000	6	0	0	0	0	0	0	2	1	63.2	1	14	0	2	1.000	6	2	0	0	.33	1
Below,Duane, Det	L	.000	1	0	0	0	0	.000	1	0	0	0	0	0	0	0	0	46.1	2	8	0	0	1.000	8	2	2	0	.25	0
Benoit,Joaquin, Det	R	-	0	0	0	0	0	.000	0	0	0	0	0	0	0	4	0	71.0	4	8	0	0	1.000	2	1	0	0	.50	3
Bergesen,Brad, Ari	R	.000	0	0	0	0	0	.222	9	2	0	0	0	0	0	0	0	29.2	1	4	1	0	.833	1	0	0	0	.00	0
Berken,Jason, Bal-ChC	R	.000	5	0	0	0	0	.000	6	0	0	0	0	0	0	2	0	19.2	1	5	0	0	1.000	0	0	0	0	-	0
Betancourt,Rafael, Col	R	-	0	0	0	0	0	.000	1	0	0	0	0	0	0	1	0	57.2	3	1	0	0	1.000	0	0	0	0	.00	-2
Billingsley,Chad, LAD	R	.190	42	8	0	2	5	.142	339	48	8	0	2	20	19	162	33	149.2	9	29	1	2	.974	15	5	0	0	.33	4
Blackburn,Nick, Min	R	.000	2	0	0	0	0	.083	12	1	0	0	0	0	0	3	0	98.2	10	14	0	2	1.000	6	1	1	0	.17	0
Blackley,Travis, SF-Oak	L	.000	2	0	0	0	0	.200	5	1	0	0	0	0	0	3	0	107.2	9	14	1	1	.958	6	4	4	3	.67	1
Blanton,Joe, Phi-LAD	R	.073	55	4	0	1	7	.107	206	22	0	0	0	6	8	89	31	191.0	14	25	4	3	.907	15	7	0	0	.47	-1
Blevins,Jerry, Oak	L	-	0	0	0	0	0	-	0	0	0	0	0	0	0	0	0	65.1	0	7	0	0	1.000	7	3	1	0	.43	2
Boggs,Mitchell, StL	R	-	0	0	0	0	0	.037	27	1	1	0	0	0	0	14	3	73.1	3	15	1	2	.947	6	0	0	0	.00	0
Bowden,M, Bos-ChC	R	.000	2	0	0	0	0	.000	2	0	0	0	0	0	0	2	0	39.2	0	4	0	0	1.000	6	0	0	0	.00	-1
Boxberger,Brad, SD	R	.000	1	0	0	0	0	.000	1	0	0	0	0	0	0	1	1	27.2	0	0	3	0	.000	6	1	1	0	.17	-1
Brach,Brad, SD	R	-	0	0	0	0	0	.000	0	0	0	0	0	0	0	0	0	66.2	2	6	2	1	.800	13	2	1	0	.15	-2
Bray,Bill, Cin	L	-	0	0	0	0	0	.000	1	0	0	0	0	0	0	1	0	8.2	1	2	0	0	1.000	3	1	0	0	.33	0
Breslow,Craig, Ari-Bos	L	.000	3	0	0	0	0	.000	4	0	0	0	0	0	0	2	0	63.1	1	6	0	0	1.000	5	3	1	0	.60	0
Britton,Zach, Bal	L	-	0	0	0	0	0	.625	8	5	1	0	2	0	1	0	60.1	1	10	1	0	.917	3	2	0	0	.67	0
Brothers,Rex, Col	L	.000	2	0	0	0	0	.000	3	0	0	0	0	0	0	1	0	67.2	1	5	0	1	1.000	9	4	0	0	.44	0
Browning,Barret, StL	L	.000	1	0	0	0	0	.000	1	0	0	0	0	0	0	0	0	19.1	0	7	0	0	1.000	1	0	0	0	.00	0
Broxton,J, KC-Cin	R	-	0	0	0	0	0	.000	5	0	0	0	0	0	0	2	1	58.0	4	7	0	0	1.000	7	2	1	0	.29	1
Brummett,Tyson, Phi	R	-	0	0	0	0	0	-	0	0	0	0	0	0	0	0	0	0.2	0	0	0	0	-	0	0	0	0	-	0

Pitchers Hitting, Fielding and Holding Runners

Pitcher	T	2012 Hitting						Career Hitting										2012 Fielding and Holding Runners											
		Avg	AB	H	HR	RBI	SH	Avg	AB	H	2B	3B	HR	RBI	BB	SO	SH	Inn	PO	A	E	DP	Pct	SBA	CS	PCS	PPO	CS%	RS
Bruney,Brian, CWS	R	-	0	0	0	0	0	.000	1	0	0	0	0	0	0	0	0	1.0	0	0	0	0	-	0	0	0	0	-	0
Buchholz,Clay, Bos	R	.000	2	0	0	0	1	.333	3	1	0	0	0	0	0	0	0	189.1	29	14	3	2	.935	11	2	0	1	.18	0
Buehrle,Mark, Mia	L	.045	67	3	0	1	4	.070	114	8	2	0	1	3	1	54	12	202.1	13	47	0	5	1.000	8	3	3	2	.38	12
Bueno,Francisley, KC	L	-	0	0	0	0	0	-	0	0	0	0	0	0	0	0	0	17.1	1	3	0	1	1.000	0	0	0	0	-	1
Bumgarner,Madison, SF	L	.162	68	11	2	6	6	.149	168	25	6	0	2	12	8	55	20	208.1	7	36	2	0	.956	37	10	5	0	.27	1
Bundy,Dylan, Bal	R	-	0	0	0	0	0	-	0	0	0	0	0	0	0	0	0	1.2	0	0	0	0	-	0	0	0	0	-	0
Burnett,A.J., Pit	R	.063	63	4	0	2	5	.117	332	39	6	3	3	11	15	165	42	202.1	21	36	1	1	.983	40	2	2	2	.05	-3
Burnett,Alex, Min	R	-	0	0	0	0	0	-	0	0	0	0	0	0	0	0	0	71.2	4	10	0	1	1.000	9	0	0	0	.00	-3
Burnett,Sean, Was	L	-	0	0	0	0	0	.069	29	2	1	0	0	0	4	9	2	56.2	7	10	0	2	1.000	6	0	0	0	.00	0
Burns,Cory, SD	R	.000	1	0	0	0	0	.000	1	0	0	0	0	0	0	1	0	18.0	2	2	1	0	.800	2	0	0	0	.00	0
Burton,Jared, Min	R	-	0	0	0	0	0	.000	2	0	0	0	0	0	0	2	0	62.0	2	11	1	0	.929	6	0	0	0	.00	1
Byrdak,Tim, NYM	L	-	0	0	0	0	0	.154	13	2	1	0	0	0	0	4	0	30.2	1	5	0	1	1.000	3	2	1	0	.67	1
Cabrera,Alberto, ChC	R	-	0	0	0	0	0	-	0	0	0	0	0	0	0	0	0	21.2	2	1	1	0	.750	5	1	0	0	.20	0
Cabrera,Edwar, Col	L	.000	1	0	0	0	0	.000	1	0	0	0	0	0	0	0	0	5.2	0	0	0	0	-	2	0	0	0	.00	0
Cahill,Trevor, Ari	R	.119	67	8	0	4	5	.117	77	9	0	0	0	4	1	27	7	200.0	16	31	5	0	.904	19	7	0	0	.37	0
Cain,Matt, SF	R	.176	74	13	1	6	8	.127	457	58	10	1	6	24	17	227	57	219.1	10	24	2	1	.944	27	9	0	0	.33	1
Camp,Shawn, ChC	R	-	0	0	0	0	0	1.000	1	1	0	0	0	0	0	0	1	77.2	4	10	2	0	.875	11	4	2	1	.36	1
Capps,Carter, Sea	R	-	0	0	0	0	0	-	0	0	0	0	0	0	0	0	0	25.0	1	3	0	1	1.000	9	1	1	0	.11	-1
Capps,Matt, Min	R	-	0	0	0	0	0	.200	5	1	0	0	0	0	0	3	0	29.1	1	1	0	1	1.000	3	0	0	0	.00	-2
Capuano,Chris, LAD	L	.093	54	5	0	3	13	.130	346	45	10	0	1	20	8	168	34	198.1	5	27	1	1	.970	9	3	2	2	.33	4
Carignan,Andrew, Oak	R	-	0	0	0	0	0	-	0	0	0	0	0	0	0	0	0	9.2	0	0	0	0	-	0	0	0	0	-	-1
Carpenter,Andrew, Tor	R	-	2	0	0	0	0	.000	4	0	0	0	0	0	0	1	0	9.0	0	1	0	0	1.000	1	0	0	0	.00	0
Carpenter,Chris, StL	R	.167	6	1	0	0	0	.118	439	52	8	0	2	21	12	144	47	17.0	0	2	0	0	1.000	1	0	0	0	.00	-1
Carpenter,Chris, Bos	R	-	0	0	0	0	0	-	0	0	0	0	0	0	0	0	0	6.0	0	1	0	0	1.000	3	0	0	0	.00	0
Carpenter,David, Hou-Tor	R	.500	2	1	0	0	0	.500	2	1	0	0	0	0	0	0	0	32.1	2	2	0	0	1.000	3	0	0	0	.00	0
Carpenter,David, LAA	R	-	0	0	0	0	0	-	0	0	0	0	0	0	0	0	0	39.2	2	5	0	2	1.000	9	2	0	0	.22	-1
Carrasco,D.J., NYM	R	-	0	0	0	0	0	.000	15	0	0	0	0	0	0	5	2	3.2	1	1	0	0	1.000	0	0	0	0	-	0
Carreno,Joel, Tor	R	.000	1	0	0	0	0	.000	1	0	0	0	0	0	0	0	0	22.0	1	1	1	0	.667	5	2	0	0	.40	0
Carson,Robert, NYM	L	-	0	0	0	0	0	-	0	0	0	0	0	0	0	0	0	13.1	0	1	0	0	1.000	1	0	0	0	.00	-1
Cashner,Andrew, SD	R	.143	7	1	0	0	0	.100	10	1	0	0	0	0	1	5	2	46.1	5	8	0	0	1.000	14	2	0	0	.14	-3
Casilla,Santiago, SF	R	.333	3	1	0	1	0	.333	3	1	0	0	0	0	1	1	0	63.1	1	7	2	1	.800	6	1	1	0	.17	-1
Cassevah,Bobby, LAA	R	-	0	0	0	0	0	-	0	0	0	0	0	0	0	0	0	5.0	0	1	1	0	.500	0	0	0	0	-	0
Castillo,Lendy, ChC	R	-	0	0	0	0	0	-	0	0	0	0	0	0	0	0	0	16.0	1	1	0	0	1.000	0	0	0	0	.00	-2
Cecil,Brett, Tor	L	.000	2	0	0	0	0	.000	6	0	0	0	0	0	0	6	0	61.1	0	7	1	1	.875	5	2	1	0	.40	0
Cedeno,Xavier, Hou	L	.000	1	0	0	0	0	.000	1	0	0	0	0	0	0	1	0	31.0	4	2	0	0	1.000	3	0	0	0	.00	-2
Chacin,Jhoulys, Col	R	.292	24	7	0	3	1	.160	125	20	3	0	0	8	3	24	10	69.0	7	11	3	1	.857	4	2	1	1	.50	2
Chamberlain,Joba, NYY	R	-	0	0	0	0	0	.000	5	0	0	0	0	0	1	1	2	20.2	0	2	0	0	1.000	4	0	0	0	.00	-1
Chapman,Aroldis, Cin	L	-	0	0	0	0	0	-	0	0	0	0	0	0	0	0	0	71.2	2	3	1	0	.833	6	1	0	0	.17	1
Chapman,Jaye, ChC	R	-	0	0	0	0	0	-	0	0	0	0	0	0	0	0	0	12.0	0	2	0	0	1.000	6	3	1	0	.50	0
Chatwood,Tyler, Col	R	.250	16	4	0	1	6	.316	19	6	1	0	0	1	1	3	8	64.2	5	13	1	2	.947	12	4	0	0	.33	0
Chavez,Jesse, Tor-Oak	R	-	2	0	0	0	0	.000	4	0	0	0	0	0	0	4	1	24.2	0	2	1	0	.667	0	0	0	0	-	-1
Chen,Bruce, KC	L	.200	5	1	0	0	0	.146	123	18	1	0	0	3	3	57	19	191.2	7	28	1	0	.972	26	8	4	0	.31	0
Chen,Wei-Yin, Bal	L	.000	3	0	0	0	1	.000	3	0	0	0	0	0	0	2	1	192.2	7	31	1	2	.974	14	3	2	0	.21	3
Choate,Randy, Mia-LAD	L	-	0	0	0	0	0	.000	5	0	0	0	0	0	0	3	0	38.2	6	6	0	1	1.000	2	0	0	0	.00	1
Chulk,Vinnie, Mil	R	-	0	0	0	0	0	.250	4	1	0	0	0	0	0	0	0	9.0	1	0	0	0	1.000	1	0	0	0	.00	0
Cingrani,Tony, Cin	L	.000	1	0	0	0	0	.000	1	0	0	0	0	0	0	1	0	5.0	1	0	1	0	.500	0	0	0	0	-	-1
Cishek,Steve, Mia	R	.000	1	0	0	0	0	.000	1	0	0	0	0	0	0	1	0	63.2	9	5	1	0	.933	3	0	0	0	.00	-1
Cleto,Maikel, StL	R	.000	1	0	0	0	0	.000	2	0	0	0	0	0	0	2	0	9.0	1	0	0	0	1.000	1	1	0	0	1.00	0
Clippard,Tyler, Was	R	-	0	0	0	0	0	.214	14	3	1	0	0	0	0	6	3	72.2	3	8	2	0	.846	8	0	0	0	.00	0
Cloyd,Tyler, Phi	R	.091	11	1	0	0	0	.091	11	1	0	0	0	0	3	3	0	33.0	2	6	0	2	1.000	0	0	0	0	-	1
Cobb,Alex, TB	R	-	0	0	0	0	0	-	0	0	0	0	0	0	0	0	0	136.1	18	27	1	3	.978	21	2	1	0	.10	5
Coello,Robert, Tor	R	-	0	0	0	0	0	-	0	0	0	0	0	0	0	0	0	6.1	0	0	0	0	-	0	0	0	0	-	0
Coffey,Todd, LAD	R	-	0	0	0	0	0	.000	7	0	0	0	0	0	0	5	3	19.1	0	6	0	1	1.000	2	1	0	0	.50	2
Coke,Phil, Det	L	-	0	0	0	0	0	.000	3	0	0	0	0	0	0	3	0	54.0	4	7	0	1	1.000	7	2	1	0	.29	-1
Coleman,Casey, ChC	R	.333	3	1	0	0	0	.146	48	7	2	1	0	2	1	18	6	24.1	3	2	0	0	1.000	1	0	0	0	.00	-1
Coleman,Louis, KC	R	-	0	0	0	0	0	.000	1	0	0	0	0	0	0	1	0	51.0	0	3	0	0	1.000	2	2	0	0	1.00	2
Collins,Tim, KC	L	.000	1	0	0	0	0	.000	1	0	0	0	0	0	0	1	0	69.2	3	9	0	0	1.000	9	0	0	0	.00	-1
Collmenter,Josh, Ari	R	.063	16	1	0	2	6	.125	56	7	0	0	0	3	3	21	10	90.1	5	11	0	1	1.000	7	4	0	0	.57	2
Colon,Bartolo, Oak	R	.000	4	0	0	0	0	.111	90	10	0	0	0	5	0	53	6	152.1	6	18	4	2	.857	1	0	0	0	.00	0
Colon,Roman, KC	R	.000	1	0	0	0	0	.000	8	0	0	0	0	0	0	5	1	8.0	1	2	0	0	1.000	0	0	0	0	-	0
Contreras,Jose, Phi	R	-	0	0	0	0	0	.000	29	0	0	0	0	0	3	18	1	13.2	1	2	0	0	1.000	4	1	0	0	.25	0
Cook,Aaron, Bos	R	-	0	0	0	0	0	.152	382	58	7	1	0	19	21	130	67	94.0	15	16	5	1	.861	4	2	0	2	.50	1
Cook,Ryan, Oak	R	-	0	0	0	0	0	-	0	0	0	0	0	0	0	0	0	73.1	7	6	0	2	1.000	6	2	0	0	.33	1
Corbin,Patrick, Ari	L	.111	36	4	0	4	6	.111	36	4	0	1	0	4	1	17	6	107.0	3	17	0	2	1.000	7	2	2	0	.29	4
Cordero,F, Tor-Hou	R	-	0	0	0	0	0	.000	3	0	0	0	0	0	0	1	0	39.1	2	5	0	0	1.000	7	0	0	0	.00	-3
Corpas,Manuel, ChC	R	.000	1	0	0	0	0	.000	7	0	0	0	0	0	2	4	0	46.2	4	3	0	1	1.000	5	2	0	0	.40	0
Correia,Kevin, Pit	R	.106	47	5	0	0	8	.116	276	32	5	0	0	12	11	116	41	171.0	23	23	1	1	.979	11	4	1	0	.36	0
Crain,Jesse, CWS	R	-	0	0	0	0	0	.000	1	0	0	0	0	0	0	1	0	48.0	0	4	1	0	.800	8	2	0	2	.25	0
Crawford,Evan, Tor	L	-	0	0	0	0	0	-	0	0	0	0	0	0	0	0	0	8.0	0	1	0	0	1.000	2	1	0	0	.50	0
Crosby,Casey, Det	L	-	0	0	0	0	0	-	0	0	0	0	0	0	0	0	0	12.1	1	1	0	1	1.000	2	0	0	0	.00	0

Pitchers Hitting, Fielding and Holding Runners

Pitcher	T	2012 Hitting						Career Hitting										2012 Fielding and Holding Runners											
		Avg	AB	H	HR	RBI	SH	Avg	AB	H	2B	3B	HR	RBI	BB	SO	SH	Inn	PO	A	E	DP	Pct	SBA	CS	PCS	PPO	CS%	RS
Crow,Aaron, KC	R	-	0	0	0	0	0	-	0	0	0	0	0	0	0	0	0	64.2	4	5	0	0	1.000	4	2	0	0	.50	-1
Cruz,Juan, Pit	R	-	0	0	0	0	0	.114	70	8	1	1	0	2	4	28	7	35.2	1	4	0	0	1.000	2	1	0	1	.50	1
Cruz,Rhiner, Hou	R	.000	1	0	0	0	0	.000	1	0	0	0	0	0	0	1	0	55.0	6	6	1	0	.923	6	1	0	0	.17	0
Cueto,Johnny, Cin	R	.090	67	6	0	2	17	.089	259	23	1	0	0	6	8	89	50	217.0	19	44	5	0	.926	10	9	4	6	.90	8
Danks,John, CWS	L	.000	3	0	0	0	0	.053	19	1	0	0	0	0	1	6	1	53.2	3	13	3	0	.842	2	1	0	0	.50	3
Darvish,Yu, Tex	R	.333	3	1	0	0	0	.333	3	1	0	0	0	0	0	1	0	191.1	19	14	0	1	1.000	27	4	0	0	.15	-2
Davis,Wade, TB	R	.500	2	1	0	0	0	.400	5	2	0	0	0	0	2	2	0	70.1	6	4	1	0	.909	6	2	0	0	.33	1
De Fratus,Justin, Phi	R	-	0	0	0	0	0	-	0	0	0	0	0	0	0	0	0	10.2	0	2	1	0	.667	2	0	0	0	.00	0
de la Rosa,Dane, TB	R	-	0	0	0	0	0	-	0	0	0	0	0	0	0	0	0	5.0	0	0	0	0	-	1	1	0	0	1.00	-1
de la Rosa,Jorge, Col	R	.400	5	2	0	1	0	.150	180	27	4	0	0	17	1	81	15	10.2	0	0	0	0	-	1	0	0	0	.00	0
de la Rosa,Rubby, LAD	R	-	0	0	0	0	0	.214	14	3	0	0	0	1	1	1	1	0.2	0	0	0	0	-	1	0	0	0	.00	0
De Los Santos,F, Oak	R	-	0	0	0	0	0	-	0	0	0	0	0	0	0	0	0	3.0	0	0	0	0	-	0	0	0	0	-	0
Deduno,Samuel, Min	R	-	0	0	0	0	0	-	0	0	0	0	0	0	0	0	0	79.0	11	13	2	5	.923	9	1	0	2	.11	-1
Del Rosario,Enerio, Hou	R	-	0	0	0	0	0	-	0	0	0	0	0	0	0	0	0	19.0	3	2	2	0	.714	6	0	0	0	.00	-1
Delabar,Steve, Sea-Tor	R	-	0	0	0	0	0	-	0	0	0	0	0	0	0	0	0	66.0	5	3	0	0	1.000	4	2	0	0	.50	1
Delgado,Randall, Atl	R	.240	25	6	0	1	3	.171	35	6	0	0	0	1	0	15	4	92.2	6	16	0	0	1.000	5	4	1	0	.80	1
Demel,Sam, Ari	R	-	0	0	0	0	0	-	0	0	0	0	0	0	0	0	0	1.0	1	0	0	0	1.000	0	0	0	0	-	0
Dempster,Ryan, ChC-Tex	R	.094	32	3	0	1	1	.099	588	58	9	2	0	17	13	221	85	173.0	10	26	1	0	.973	26	4	1	1	.15	3
Detwiler,Ross, Was	L	.044	45	2	0	1	3	.056	90	5	0	0	0	3	1	40	6	164.1	12	18	1	2	.968	5	2	0	1	.40	1
DeVries,Cole, Min	R	-	0	0	0	0	0	-	0	0	0	0	0	0	0	0	0	87.2	5	7	1	0	.923	3	1	0	0	.33	0
Diamond,Scott, Min	L	.143	7	1	0	0	1	.143	7	1	0	0	0	0	0	4	1	173.0	10	21	0	1	1.000	19	4	3	0	.21	1
Dickey,R.A., NYM	R	.153	72	11	0	3	10	.182	187	34	2	0	0	10	4	33	26	233.2	12	44	4	6	.933	7	3	1	4	.43	6
Dickson,Brandon, StL	R	.500	2	1	0	0	0	.600	5	3	0	0	0	0	0	2	0	6.1	0	1	0	0	1.000	0	0	0	0	-	0
Diekman,Jake, Phi	L	-	0	0	0	0	0	-	0	0	0	0	0	0	0	0	0	27.1	1	3	2	0	.667	6	1	1	0	.17	-1
Dillard,Tim, Mil	R	-	0	0	0	0	0	.500	2	1	0	0	0	0	0	1	0	37.0	3	4	0	0	1.000	1	1	0	0	1.00	0
Dolis,Rafael, ChC	R	-	0	0	0	0	0	-	0	0	0	0	0	0	0	0	0	38.0	0	4	1	0	.800	0	0	0	0	-	-1
Doolittle,Sean, Oak	L	-	0	0	0	0	0	-	0	0	0	0	0	0	0	0	0	47.1	0	4	2	0	.667	6	1	1	0	.17	-1
Dotel,Octavio, Det	R	-	0	0	0	0	0	.065	77	5	0	0	0	1	5	44	9	58.0	1	4	1	0	.833	13	3	0	0	.23	-1
Doubront,Felix, Bos	L	.000	1	0	0	0	1	.000	1	0	0	0	0	0	0	0	1	161.0	7	17	1	2	.960	22	3	1	0	.14	-3
Downs,Darin, Det	L	-	0	0	0	0	0	-	0	0	0	0	0	0	0	0	0	20.2	1	3	0	1	1.000	4	1	1	0	.25	1
Downs,Scott, LAA	L	-	0	0	0	0	0	.067	45	3	0	0	0	1	3	17	10	45.2	6	9	1	1	.938	2	0	0	0	.00	1
Drabek,Kyle, Tor	R	.000	2	0	0	0	0	.000	2	0	0	0	0	0	0	1	0	71.1	3	8	3	1	.786	3	3	0	0	1.00	1
Duensing,Brian, Min	L	.000	1	0	0	0	0	.000	6	0	0	0	0	0	0	4	0	109.0	5	13	0	1	1.000	6	1	0	0	.17	-3
Duffy,Danny, KC	L	-	0	0	0	0	0	.000	3	0	0	0	0	0	0	2	0	27.2	0	2	0	0	1.000	3	1	1	1	.33	1
Duke,Zach, Was	L	.000	1	0	0	0	0	.175	314	55	7	0	2	23	12	116	42	13.2	0	4	0	0	1.000	3	0	0	0	.00	0
Dunn,Mike, Mia	L	.000	1	0	0	0	0	.000	4	0	0	0	0	0	0	1	0	44.0	3	4	1	0	.875	2	0	0	0	.00	0
Durbin,Chad, Atl	R	-	0	0	0	0	0	.083	24	2	0	0	0	1	0	8	1	61.0	1	8	1	0	.900	6	2	0	1	.33	2
Dyson,Sam, Tor	R	-	0	0	0	0	0	-	0	0	0	0	0	0	0	0	0	0.2	0	0	0	0	-	1	0	0	0	.00	0
Edgin,Josh, NYM	L	-	0	0	0	0	0	-	0	0	0	0	0	0	0	0	0	25.2	0	2	1	0	.667	1	0	0	0	.00	0
Edlefsen,Steve, SF	R	.000	1	0	0	0	0	.000	2	0	0	0	0	0	0	1	0	15.1	1	1	1	0	.667	1	1	0	0	1.00	-1
Egbert,Jack, NYM	R	-	0	0	0	0	0	-	0	0	0	0	0	0	0	0	0	-	0	0	0	0	-	0	0	0	0	-	0
Ekstrom,Mike, Col	R	-	0	0	0	0	0	.000	2	0	0	0	0	0	0	1	1	15.2	2	3	0	1	1.000	2	0	0	0	.00	0
Elbert,Scott, LAD	L	-	0	0	0	0	0	.167	6	1	1	0	0	1	0	2	0	32.2	1	3	0	1	1.000	4	1	0	0	.25	-2
Ely,John, LAD	R	-	0	0	0	0	0	.067	30	2	0	0	0	1	2	15	4	2.2	0	0	0	0	-	0	0	0	0	-	0
Enright,Barry, LAA	R	-	0	0	0	0	0	.222	45	10	1	0	1	8	2	11	4	3.2	0	0	0	0	-	0	0	0	0	-	-1
Eovaldi,Nathan, LAD-Mia	R	.094	32	3	0	0	3	.093	43	4	0	0	0	0	2	29	3	119.1	7	16	0	1	1.000	6	2	0	1	.33	1
Eppley,Cody, NYY	R	-	0	0	0	0	0	-	0	0	0	0	0	0	0	0	0	46.0	1	11	0	1	1.000	3	0	0	0	.00	2
Escalona,Edgmer, Col	R	-	0	0	0	0	1	.000	3	0	0	0	0	0	0	3	1	22.1	0	2	0	0	1.000	4	0	0	0	.00	-1
Estrada,Marco, Mil	R	.100	40	4	0	3	3	.132	53	7	3	0	0	3	3	26	10	138.1	4	16	0	1	1.000	20	5	0	2	.25	-1
Eveland,Dana, Bal	L	-	0	0	0	0	0	.045	22	1	0	0	0	0	2	13	5	32.1	6	2	0	0	1.000	2	0	0	0	.00	0
Familia,Jeurys, NYM	R	.000	1	0	0	0	0	.000	1	0	0	0	0	0	0	1	0	12.1	0	3	0	0	1.000	3	2	0	0	.67	0
Farnsworth,Kyle, TB	R	-	0	0	0	0	0	.074	54	4	1	0	0	3	2	18	8	27.0	1	4	0	0	1.000	0	0	0	0	.00	0
Feldman,Scott, Tex	R	.250	4	1	0	1	1	.167	18	3	1	0	0	1	0	7	4	123.2	6	14	0	0	1.000	23	3	0	0	.13	-4
Feliz,Neftali, Tex	R	.000	2	0	0	0	0	.000	2	0	0	0	0	0	0	1	0	42.2	0	4	0	0	1.000	3	0	0	0	.00	0
Fick,Chuckie, StL-Hou	R	-	0	0	0	0	0	-	0	0	0	0	0	0	0	0	0	24.2	2	6	0	1	1.000	1	1	0	0	1.00	1
Fien,Casey, Min	R	-	0	0	0	0	0	-	0	0	0	0	0	0	0	0	0	35.0	1	2	0	0	1.000	3	0	0	0	.00	0
Fiers,Mike, Mil	R	.094	32	3	0	2	6	.094	32	3	0	0	0	2	0	17	6	127.2	8	14	5	1	.815	13	3	0	0	.23	3
Fife,Stephen, LAD	R	.286	7	2	0	0	1	.286	7	2	1	0	0	0	0	2	1	26.2	3	4	0	0	1.000	1	0	0	0	.00	1
Figueroa,Pedro, Oak	L	-	0	0	0	0	0	-	0	0	0	0	0	0	0	0	0	21.2	1	0	0	0	1.000	2	0	0	0	.00	-1
Fister,Doug, Det	R	.000	2	0	0	0	0	.200	10	2	1	0	0	1	0	4	1	161.2	10	24	2	3	.944	6	4	2	0	.67	2
Floyd,Gavin, CWS	R	.000	1	0	0	0	0	.056	54	3	0	0	0	2	2	29	4	168.0	10	26	1	2	.973	12	4	0	1	.33	3
Font,Wilmer, Tex	R	-	0	0	0	0	0	-	0	0	0	0	0	0	0	0	0	2.0	0	0	0	0	-	0	0	0	0	-	0
Francis,Jeff, Col	L	.065	31	2	0	0	6	.118	287	34	6	0	0	15	23	97	51	113.0	5	23	0	1	1.000	13	3	1	1	.23	4
Francisco,Frank, NYM	R	-	0	0	0	0	0	-	0	0	0	0	0	0	0	0	0	42.1	0	4	0	0	1.000	6	0	0	0	.00	-2
Frasor,Jason, Tor	R	-	0	0	0	0	0	-	0	0	0	0	0	0	0	0	0	43.2	5	2	1	0	.875	8	2	0	0	.25	0
Freeman,Sam, StL	L	-	0	0	0	0	0	-	0	0	0	0	0	0	0	0	0	20.0	0	3	1	0	.750	1	1	0	0	.00	0
Friedrich,Christian, Col	L	.080	25	2	0	0	1	.080	25	2	0	0	0	3	15	1	84.2	3	8	3	0	.786	1	1	1	0	1.00	-2
Frieri,Ernesto, SD-LAA	R	-	0	0	0	0	0	.000	1	0	0	0	0	0	0	1	0	66.0	1	4	0	1	1.000	5	1	0	0	.20	0
Fuentes,Brian, Oak-StL	L	-	0	0	0	0	0	.000	1	0	0	0	0	0	0	1	0	30.0	1	2	0	0	1.000	3	1	0	0	.33	0
Furbush,Charlie, Sea	L	-	0	0	0	0	0	-	0	0	0	0	0	0	0	0	0	46.1	1	6	1	0	.875	13	3	2	0	.23	-1

Pitchers Hitting, Fielding and Holding Runners

Pitcher	T	2012 Hitting						Career Hitting										2012 Fielding and Holding Runners											
		Avg	AB	H	HR	RBI	SH	Avg	AB	H	2B	3B	HR	RBI	BB	SO	SH	Inn	PO	A	E	DP	Pct	SBA	CS	PCS	PPO	CS%	RS
Galarraga,Armando, Hou	R	.000	8	0	0	0	0	.000	31	0	0	0	0	1	3	16	2	24.0	1	0	0	0	1.000	5	0	0	0	.00	-1
Gallardo,Yovani, Mil	R	.164	67	11	1	9	8	.207	305	63	17	0	10	37	11	100	23	204.0	13	27	1	3	.976	12	3	0	1	.25	3
Garcia,Christian, Was	R	-	0	0	0	0	0	-	0	0	0	0	0	0	0	0	0	12.2	0	1	0	0	1.000	0	0	0	0	-	0
Garcia,Freddy, NYY	R	.000	1	0	0	0	0	.174	69	12	2	0	0	4	2	21	17	107.1	8	7	0	0	1.000	18	3	0	0	.17	-4
Garcia,Jaime, StL	L	.250	40	10	1	3	4	.166	157	26	2	1	2	11	7	47	13	121.2	3	22	1	0	.962	9	5	1	0	.56	0
Garza,Matt, ChC	R	.067	30	2	0	0	4	.076	105	8	1	0	0	1	2	74	12	103.2	4	12	3	0	.842	5	3	2	0	.60	-5
Gaudin,Chad, Mia	R	.000	8	0	0	0	0	.025	40	1	0	0	0	0	2	20	3	69.1	7	14	0	0	1.000	4	2	1	0	.50	1
Gearrin,Cory, Atl	R	-	0	0	0	0	0	-	0	0	0	0	0	0	0	0	0	20.0	1	3	0	0	1.000	1	0	0	0	.00	1
Gee,Dillon, NYM	R	.148	27	4	0	1	5	.129	85	11	3	0	0	6	4	37	13	109.2	9	16	2	3	.926	10	3	0	0	.30	1
Geltz,Steve, LAA	R	-	0	0	0	0	0	-	0	0	0	0	0	0	0	0	0	2.0	0	0	0	0	-	0	0	0	0	-	0
Germano,J, Bos-ChC	R	.059	17	1	0	0	6	.149	67	10	2	0	0	3	4	31	17	69.2	5	14	0	2	1.000	6	1	0	0	.17	0
Godfrey,Graham, Oak	R	-	0	0	0	0	0	.000	2	0	0	0	0	0	0	1	0	21.0	1	3	0	1	1.000	3	2	0	0	.67	-1
Gomes,Brandon, TB	R	.000	1	0	0	1	0	.000	1	0	0	0	0	1	1	1	0	17.2	2	1	1	0	.750	3	0	0	0	.00	0
Gomez,Jeanmar, Cle	R	.250	4	1	0	0	0	.250	4	1	0	0	0	0	0	1	0	90.2	8	10	0	2	1.000	7	2	0	1	.29	1
Gonzalez,Edgar, Hou	R	.111	9	1	0	1	1	.167	72	12	1	0	0	3	2	18	8	25.0	1	1	1	0	.667	4	0	0	0	.00	-1
Gonzalez,Gio, Was	L	.094	64	6	1	4	9	.085	71	6	1	0	1	4	1	29	11	199.1	10	22	2	1	.941	13	1	0	0	.08	-1
Gonzalez,Michael, Was	L	-	0	0	0	0	0	.333	3	1	1	0	0	2	0	0	0	35.2	1	2	0	1	1.000	4	0	0	0	.00	-3
Gonzalez,Miguel, Bal	R	-	0	0	0	0	0	-	0	0	0	0	0	0	0	0	0	105.1	3	7	0	1	1.000	5	3	0	0	.60	-1
Gorzelanny,Tom, Was	L	.333	6	2	0	1	0	.095	199	19	0	0	0	13	9	92	23	72.0	8	12	1	2	.952	6	1	0	0	.17	3
Gray,Jeff, Min	R	-	0	0	0	0	0	-	0	0	0	0	0	0	0	0	0	52.0	3	5	0	0	1.000	6	1	0	0	.17	0
Gregerson,Luke, SD	R	.000	1	0	0	0	0	.000	2	0	0	0	0	0	0	1	1	71.2	3	20	1	1	.958	6	1	0	0	.17	1
Gregg,Kevin, Bal	R	-	0	0	0	0	0	.000	6	0	0	0	0	0	0	5	0	43.2	4	5	0	1	1.000	3	1	0	0	.33	1
Greinke,Zack, Mil-LAA	R	.212	33	7	1	2	4	.170	106	18	5	0	3	4	3	23	13	212.1	22	31	0	3	1.000	16	7	1	4	.44	6
Griffin,A.J., Oak	R	-	0	0	0	0	0	-	0	0	0	0	0	0	0	0	0	82.1	4	7	0	0	1.000	4	3	1	0	.75	1
Grilli,Jason, Pit	R	-	0	0	0	0	0	.200	15	3	0	0	1	3	0	3	0	58.2	5	4	0	0	1.000	3	0	0	0	.00	-1
Grimm,Justin, Tex	R	-	0	0	0	0	0	-	0	0	0	0	0	0	0	0	0	14.0	1	4	0	0	1.000	4	2	0	0	.50	0
Guerra,Javy, LAD	R	-	0	0	0	0	0	-	0	0	0	0	0	0	0	0	0	45.0	1	0	0	0	1.000	1	0	0	0	.00	1
Guerrier,Matt, LAD	R	-	0	0	0	0	0	.000	2	0	0	0	0	1	1	1	0	14.0	1	3	0	0	1.000	4	1	0	0	.25	1
Guthrie,Jeremy, Col-KC	R	.080	25	2	0	1	4	.085	47	4	2	0	1	1	1	24	4	181.2	13	15	4	1	.875	12	4	0	2	.33	1
Hacker,Eric, SF	R	.000	3	0	0	0	0	.000	3	0	0	0	0	0	0	1	0	9.2	0	2	0	0	1.000	3	1	0	0	.33	0
Hagadone,Nick, Cle	L	-	0	0	0	0	0	-	0	0	0	0	0	0	0	0	0	25.1	1	0	1	0	1.000	5	1	1	0	.20	-1
Halladay,Roy, Phi	R	.170	53	9	0	2	4	.132	257	34	2	0	0	11	3	120	25	156.1	8	20	2	2	.933	19	6	3	0	.32	-1
Hamels,Cole, Phi	L	.217	69	15	1	5	8	.169	450	76	11	1	1	23	16	188	38	215.1	10	25	4	0	.897	34	11	5	0	.32	-2
Hammel,Jason, Bal	R	.000	4	0	0	0	3	.123	163	20	4	0	1	7	4	72	25	118.0	4	23	1	1	.964	10	4	1	0	.40	4
Hampson,Justin, NYM	L	.000	1	0	0	0	0	.000	9	0	0	0	0	0	1	3	1	10.0	1	0	0	0	1.000	3	1	1	0	.33	-1
Hand,Brad, Mia	L	.000	1	0	0	0	0	.111	18	2	0	0	0	1	0	7	3	3.2	0	0	0	0	-	2	0	0	0	.00	-1
Hanrahan,Joel, Pit	R	-	0	0	0	0	0	.235	17	4	2	1	0	3	0	5	4	59.2	2	6	0	0	1.000	9	0	0	0	.00	-1
Hanson,Tommy, Atl	R	.020	49	1	0	0	10	.059	187	11	0	0	0	5	5	92	32	174.2	2	15	5	1	.773	42	11	1	1	.26	-6
Happ,J.A., Hou-Tor	L	.094	32	3	0	1	5	.092	152	14	2	0	1	6	8	62	24	144.2	8	21	0	1	1.000	11	1	0	0	.09	-2
Harang,Aaron, LAD	R	.071	56	4	0	2	7	.091	550	50	7	0	1	20	3	241	51	179.2	10	31	2	1	.953	12	4	0	0	.33	0
Haren,Dan, LAA	R	.000	4	0	0	0	0	.223	264	59	21	0	2	27	8	68	22	176.2	11	19	3	3	.909	11	2	0	1	.18	1
Harrell,Lucas, Hou	R	.153	59	9	0	1	3	.145	62	9	0	0	0	1	1	35	3	193.2	12	39	0	2	1.000	23	5	0	0	.22	2
Harris,Will, Col	R	-	0	0	0	0	0	-	0	0	0	0	0	0	0	0	0	17.2	1	3	0	0	1.000	0	0	0	0	-	0
Harrison,Matt, Tex	L	.000	5	0	0	0	2	.000	16	0	0	0	0	0	1	11	2	213.1	13	25	1	3	.974	4	3	3	0	.75	3
Harvey,Matt, NYM	R	.333	18	6	0	3	3	.333	18	6	2	0	0	3	0	7	3	59.1	1	13	0	0	1.000	0	0	0	0	-	2
Hatcher,Chris, Mia	R	.000	1	0	0	0	0	.000	7	0	0	0	0	0	2	6	0	14.2	1	1	0	0	1.000	0	0	0	0	-	0
Hawkins,LaTroy, LAA	R	-	0	0	0	0	0	.000	6	0	0	0	0	0	0	5	1	42.0	3	4	1	1	.875	14	1	0	2	.07	-3
Heath,Deunte, CWS	R	-	0	0	0	0	0	-	0	0	0	0	0	0	0	0	0	2.0	0	0	0	0	-	0	0	0	0	-	0
Hefner,Jeremy, NYM	R	.100	20	2	1	1	6	.100	20	2	0	0	1	1	0	11	6	93.0	7	11	0	1	1.000	6	1	0	0	.17	-1
Hellickson,Jeremy, TB	R	.000	1	0	0	0	0	.000	3	0	0	0	0	0	0	2	1	177.0	17	21	2	2	.950	10	3	0	1	.30	2
Henderson,Jim, Mil	R	-	0	0	0	0	0	-	0	0	0	0	0	0	0	0	0	30.2	0	3	0	0	1.000	5	0	0	0	.00	0
Hendriks,Liam, Min	R	.000	2	0	0	0	0	.000	2	0	0	0	0	0	0	1	0	85.1	5	7	0	1	1.000	9	2	0	0	.22	-2
Hensley,Clay, SF	R	.000	1	0	0	0	0	.092	87	8	0	0	0	4	4	46	10	50.2	4	5	1	2	.900	9	0	0	0	.00	-3
Hernandez,David, Ari	R	1.000	1	1	0	0	0	.250	4	1	0	0	0	0	0	1	0	68.1	0	1	1	0	.500	2	0	0	0	.00	-1
Hernandez,Felix, Sea	R	.333	3	1	0	2	0	.148	27	4	1	0	1	7	1	13	4	232.0	11	24	2	3	.946	24	7	1	1	.29	0
Hernandez,Livan, Atl-Mil	R	.000	4	0	0	0	0	.221	973	215	38	2	10	85	10	130	123	67.1	4	11	0	1	1.000	2	1	0	0	.50	0
Hernandez,Pedro, CWS	L	-	0	0	0	0	0	-	0	0	0	0	0	0	0	0	0	4.0	0	0	0	0	-	0	0	0	0	-	-1
Hernandez,Roberto, Cle	R	-	0	0	0	0	0	.000	14	0	0	0	0	0	0	8	2	14.1	1	1	0	0	1.000	2	1	0	0	.50	0
Herndon,David, Phi	R	.000	1	0	0	0	0	.000	7	0	0	0	0	0	0	6	0	7.2	1	2	0	0	1.000	2	1	0	0	.50	-1
Herrera,Kelvin, KC	R	-	0	0	0	0	0	-	0	0	0	0	0	0	0	0	0	84.1	8	9	0	1	1.000	16	4	0	0	.25	-1
Herrmann,Frank, Cle	R	-	0	0	0	0	0	.000	1	0	0	0	0	0	0	0	0	19.1	1	1	0	0	1.000	2	1	0	0	.50	0
Hill,Rich, Bos	L	-	0	0	0	0	0	.123	114	14	3	0	0	6	2	51	6	19.2	4	4	0	1	1.000	6	1	1	0	.17	1
Hill,Shawn, Tor	R	-	0	0	0	0	0	.067	45	3	0	0	0	6	19	15	3.0	0	0	1	0	.000	0	0	0	0	-	0
Hinshaw,Alex, SD-ChC	L	.000	1	0	0	0	0	.000	1	0	0	0	0	0	1	1	0	28.1	0	3	0	0	1.000	2	0	0	0	.00	0
Hochevar,Luke, KC	R	.200	5	1	0	0	0	.063	16	1	0	0	0	0	0	10	1	185.1	7	18	0	1	1.000	22	7	1	0	.32	3
Holland,Derek, Tex	L	.000	2	0	0	0	0	.000	7	0	0	0	0	0	3	1	0	175.1	9	28	2	1	.949	12	3	3	2	.25	2
Holland,Greg, KC	R	-	0	0	0	0	0	-	0	0	0	0	0	0	0	0	0	67.0	2	3	0	1	1.000	4	2	0	0	.50	-2
Hoover,J.J., Cin	R	-	0	0	0	0	0	-	0	0	0	0	0	0	0	0	0	30.2	0	1	0	0	1.000	1	0	0	0	.00	-1
Horst,Jeremy, Phi	L	-	0	0	0	0	0	1.000	1	1	0	0	0	1	0	0	0	31.1	3	4	0	1	1.000	4	3	2	0	.75	0
Hottovy,Tommy, KC	L	-	0	0	0	0	0	-	0	0	0	0	0	0	0	0	0	9.1	1	1	0	0	-	0	0	0	0	-	0

Pitchers Hitting, Fielding and Holding Runners

Pitcher	T	2012 Hitting Avg	AB	H	HR	RBI	SH	Career Hitting Avg	AB	H	2B	3B	HR	RBI	BB	SO	SH	2012 Fielding and Holding Runners Inn	PO	A	E	DP	Pct	SBA	CS	PCS	PPO	CS%	RS
Howell,J.P., TB	L	-	0	0	0	0	0	.200	10	2	0	0	0	1	0	4	0	50.1	2	8	0	0	1.000	7	4	1	1	.57	1
Hudson,Daniel, Ari	R	-	0	0	0	1	0	.229	105	24	5	0	1	21	5	34	14	45.1	0	5	0	1	1.000	4	1	0	0	.25	-1
Hudson,Tim, Atl	R	.218	55	12	0	6	7	.171	484	83	16	1	2	37	19	145	52	179.0	13	20	1	0	.971	7	5	0	1	.71	-1
Huff,David, Cle	L	-	0	0	0	0	0	.000	4	0	0	0	0	0	0	2	2	26.2	0	2	0	1	1.000	3	2	1	0	.67	1
Hughes,Jared, Pit	R	.000	1	0	0	0	0	.000	1	0	0	0	0	0	0	1	0	75.2	8	15	1	2	.958	17	0	0	0	.00	-1
Hughes,Phil, NYY	R	.000	2	0	0	0	0	.000	3	0	0	0	0	0	0	1	1	191.1	7	14	1	0	.955	7	3	0	0	.43	-1
Humber,Philip, CWS	R	.200	5	1	0	1	0	.091	11	1	0	0	0	1	0	4	2	102.0	8	5	0	0	1.000	16	1	0	0	.06	-5
Hunter,Tommy, Bal	R	.000	2	0	0	0	0	.000	3	0	0	0	0	0	0	2	0	133.2	8	29	0	4	1.000	5	4	0	0	.80	4
Hutchison,Drew, Tor	R	.000	2	0	0	0	0	.000	2	0	0	0	0	0	0	0	0	58.2	2	7	0	0	1.000	6	1	0	0	.17	1
Igarashi,Ryota, Tor-NYY	R	-	0	0	0	0	0	-	0	0	0	0	0	0	0	0	0	4.0	1	1	0	0	1.000	0	0	0	0	-	1
Isringhausen,Jason, LAA	R	-	0	0	0	0	0	.202	104	21	4	1	2	16	5	36	8	45.2	3	5	1	0	.889	8	1	1	1	.13	-1
Iwakuma,Hisashi, Sea	R	-	0	0	0	0	0	-	0	0	0	0	0	0	0	0	0	125.1	7	10	1	1	.944	17	7	0	0	.41	0
Jackson,Edwin, Was	R	.228	57	13	0	0	5	.200	155	31	0	0	1	7	9	62	13	189.2	17	20	3	1	.925	12	5	2	0	.42	0
Jansen,Kenley, LAD	R	-	0	0	0	0	0	1.000	1	1	0	0	0	0	1	0	0	65.0	1	5	1	0	.857	5	0	0	0	.00	0
Janssen,Casey, Tor	R	-	0	0	0	0	0	.000	3	0	0	0	0	0	0	2	1	63.2	7	6	0	0	1.000	5	2	0	0	.40	1
Jeffress,Jeremy, KC	R	-	0	0	0	0	0	-	0	0	0	0	0	0	0	0	0	13.1	2	3	0	0	1.000	2	0	0	0	.00	1
Jenkins,Chad, Tor	R	-	0	0	0	0	0	-	0	0	0	0	0	0	0	0	0	32.0	5	3	1	0	.889	2	0	0	0	.00	0
Jennings,Dan, Mia	L	.000	1	0	0	0	0	.000	1	0	0	0	0	0	0	0	0	19.0	2	2	0	1	1.000	1	0	0	0	.00	0
Jepsen,Kevin, LAA	R	-	0	0	0	0	0	-	0	0	0	0	0	0	0	0	0	44.2	2	3	1	0	.833	5	1	0	0	.20	-1
Jimenez,Ubaldo, Cle	R	.000	5	0	0	0	0	.115	270	31	0	0	0	9	16	91	32	176.2	12	16	1	3	.966	37	5	0	0	.14	-3
Johnson,Jim, Bal	R	-	0	0	0	0	0	-	0	0	0	0	0	0	0	0	0	68.2	6	12	0	1	1.000	5	2	0	0	.40	0
Johnson,Josh, Mia	R	.094	53	5	0	2	5	.125	271	34	5	0	3	25	13	145	32	191.1	25	33	1	3	.983	30	3	1	1	.10	-4
Johnson,Steve, Bal	R	-	0	0	0	0	0	-	0	0	0	0	0	0	0	0	0	38.1	0	2	0	0	1.000	4	4	0	0	1.00	1
Jones,Nate, CWS	R	-	0	0	0	0	0	-	0	0	0	0	0	0	0	0	0	71.2	6	6	1	0	.923	4	1	0	0	.25	0
Jurrjens,Jair, Atl	R	.077	13	1	0	0	3	.113	222	25	3	1	0	7	18	75	28	48.1	2	13	0	1	1.000	13	4	1	0	.31	0
Karstens,Jeff, Pit	R	.107	28	3	0	2	1	.090	145	13	1	0	0	4	8	79	15	90.2	4	8	1	0	.923	8	0	0	1	.00	-3
Kelley,Shawn, Sea	R	-	0	0	0	0	0	-	0	0	0	0	0	0	0	0	0	44.1	2	8	0	0	1.000	3	1	0	0	.33	1
Kelly,Casey, SD	R	.200	10	2	0	0	2	.200	10	2	0	0	0	0	0	4	2	29.0	2	6	0	1	1.000	3	2	0	0	.67	-1
Kelly,Joe, StL	R	.152	33	5	0	2	2	.152	33	5	2	0	0	2	0	13	2	107.0	11	19	2	3	.938	13	5	0	2	.38	2
Kendrick,Kyle, Phi	R	.139	36	5	0	0	6	.135	208	28	5	0	4	13	90	29	159.1	11	22	1	1	.971	11	3	0	0	.27	2
Kennedy,Ian, Ari	R	.078	51	4	0	6	10	.139	166	23	4	1	0	12	22	77	24	208.1	9	22	4	1	.886	7	3	0	0	.43	0
Kershaw,Clayton, LAD	L	.207	58	12	0	2	14	.146	261	38	1	0	0	9	9	78	60	227.2	9	42	0	1	1.000	20	12	9	2	.60	6
Keuchel,Dallas, Hou	L	.100	20	2	0	1	5	.100	20	2	0	0	0	1	1	10	5	85.1	8	19	2	2	.931	11	2	1	0	.18	0
Kimbrel,Craig, Atl	R	-	0	0	0	0	0	-	0	0	0	0	0	0	0	0	0	62.2	0	5	0	0	1.000	9	1	0	0	.11	-1
Kinney,Josh, Sea	R	-	0	0	0	0	0	.000	1	0	0	0	0	0	0	1	0	32.0	2	6	0	0	1.000	4	0	0	0	.00	1
Kintzler,Brandon, Mil	R	-	0	0	0	0	0	.000	1	0	0	0	0	0	0	1	0	16.2	2	4	0	0	1.000	1	1	1	1	1.00	2
Kirkman,Michael, Tex	L	-	0	0	0	0	0	-	0	0	0	0	0	0	0	0	0	35.1	3	1	0	0	1.000	1	0	0	0	.00	0
Kluber,Corey, Cle	R	-	0	0	0	0	0	-	0	0	0	0	0	0	0	0	0	63.0	9	5	0	1	1.000	18	3	0	0	.17	-2
Koehler,Tom, Mia	R	.000	1	0	0	0	0	.000	1	0	0	0	0	0	0	1	0	13.1	0	1	0	0	1.000	0	0	0	0	-	0
Kontos,George, SF	R	.000	1	0	0	0	0	.000	1	0	0	0	0	0	0	0	0	43.2	4	4	1	0	.889	5	2	0	0	.40	0
Korecky,Bobby, Tor	R	-	0	0	0	0	0	1.000	1	1	0	0	0	0	0	0	0	1.0	0	1	0	0	1.000	0	0	0	0	-	0
Kuroda,Hiroki, NYY	R	.000	2	0	0	0	0	.105	200	21	1	0	0	3	13	69	32	219.2	11	31	0	3	1.000	25	8	0	1	.32	2
Laffey,Aaron, Tor	L	.000	1	0	0	0	0	.250	4	1	0	0	0	0	0	0	0	100.2	5	22	0	2	1.000	6	2	1	0	.33	4
Lannan,John, Was	L	.111	9	1	0	0	1	.097	226	22	4	0	1	10	14	100	19	33.2	0	9	0	1	1.000	4	1	1	0	.25	0
Latos,Mat, Cin	R	.185	65	12	1	4	10	.119	194	23	4	0	3	8	4	98	26	209.1	18	22	0	0	1.000	20	3	1	0	.15	0
Layne,Tom, SD	L	-	0	0	0	0	0	-	0	0	0	0	0	0	0	0	0	16.2	1	2	0	0	.500	1	0	0	0	.00	-1
League,B, Sea-LAD	R	-	0	0	0	0	0	-	0	0	0	0	0	0	0	0	0	72.0	4	7	1	1	.917	14	3	0	0	.21	-3
Leake,Mike, Cin	R	.295	61	18	2	3	7	.274	164	45	6	0	2	8	7	58	23	179.0	25	30	2	3	.965	14	6	0	1	.43	6
LeBlanc,Wade, Mia	L	.083	12	1	0	0	3	.263	99	26	1	0	0	2	3	23	14	68.2	3	13	0	1	1.000	7	5	2	0	.71	3
LeCure,Sam, Cin	R	.000	1	0	0	0	0	.095	21	2	2	0	0	1	8	2	57.1	7	9	0	2	1.000	5	3	0	0	.60	2
Lee,Cliff, Phi	L	.156	64	10	0	4	6	.164	207	34	6	0	2	12	3	76	13	211.0	6	22	3	3	.903	7	3	0	0	.43	-2
Leroux,Chris, Pit	R	.000	1	0	0	0	0	.000	1	0	0	0	0	0	0	0	0	11.1	0	2	0	0	1.000	2	0	0	0	.00	-1
Lester,Jon, Bos	L	.000	5	0	0	0	1	.000	25	0	0	0	0	1	1	15	4	205.1	14	21	2	3	.946	16	3	0	0	.19	0
Lewis,Colby, Tex	R	.500	4	2	0	2	0	.250	20	5	1	0	0	4	0	7	1	105.0	4	7	2	0	.846	11	3	0	0	.27	-1
Lidge,Brad, Was	R	-	0	0	0	0	0	.286	7	2	1	0	0	2	0	4	0	9.1	0	1	0	0	1.000	3	0	0	0	.00	0
Lilly,Ted, LAD	L	.067	15	1	0	0	4	.102	342	35	6	1	0	17	8	144	37	48.2	0	4	0	0	1.000	9	2	0	0	.22	-1
Lincecum,Tim, SF	R	.089	45	4	0	3	10	.116	352	41	3	1	0	17	25	174	56	186.0	15	22	0	1	1.000	27	2	0	1	.07	-2
Lincoln,Brad, Pit-Tor	R	.200	10	2	0	0	0	.243	37	9	1	0	0	4	1	14	4	88.0	8	14	0	1	1.000	11	2	0	0	.18	-1
Lindblom,Josh, LAD-Phi	R	-	0	0	0	0	0	.000	1	0	0	0	0	0	0	1	0	71.0	3	8	1	1	.917	9	5	0	1	.56	0
Lindstrom,Matt, Bal-Ari	R	-	0	0	0	0	0	.000	1	0	0	0	0	0	0	1	0	47.0	3	4	0	1	1.000	8	0	0	0	.00	-3
Liriano,F, Min-CWS	L	.000	3	0	0	0	0	.118	17	2	0	0	0	2	2	9	2	156.2	6	23	0	2	1.000	18	2	2	1	.11	2
Locke,Jeff, Pit	L	.091	11	1	0	0	0	.063	16	1	0	0	0	0	0	11	0	34.1	2	2	0	1	1.000	6	2	1	0	.33	-3
Loe,Kameron, Mil	R	-	0	0	0	0	1	.200	5	1	0	0	0	0	1	3	1	68.1	5	15	2	0	.909	9	2	1	0	.22	0
Logan,Boone, NYY	L	-	0	0	0	0	0	-	0	0	0	0	0	0	0	0	1	55.1	2	8	0	0	1.000	4	1	0	0	.25	-1
Lohse,Kyle, StL	R	.094	64	6	0	3	12	.153	354	54	8	0	0	22	6	101	51	211.0	17	26	0	2	1.000	10	4	0	1	.40	1
Lopez,Javier, SF	L	-	0	0	0	0	0	.091	11	1	0	0	0	1	0	5	1	36.0	5	8	0	0	1.000	1	0	0	0	.00	1
Lopez,Rodrigo, ChC	R	-	0	0	0	0	0	.062	145	9	0	0	0	1	3	75	9	6.1	1	0	0	0	1.000	1	1	0	0	1.00	0
Lopez,Wilton, Hou	R	-	0	0	0	0	0	.000	5	0	0	0	0	0	0	2	0	66.1	10	12	1	1	.957	1	0	0	1	.00	2
Loup,Aaron, Tor	L	.000	1	0	0	0	0	.000	1	0	0	0	0	0	0	0	0	30.2	2	7	0	0	1.000	6	3	3	0	.50	1
Loux,Shane, SF	R	.000	0	0	0	0	0	.000	1	0	0	0	0	0	0	0	0	25.1	3	2	1	0	.833	2	2	0	0	1.00	1

Pitchers Hitting, Fielding and Holding Runners

Pitcher	T	2012 Hitting						Career Hitting										2012 Fielding and Holding Runners											
		Avg	AB	H	HR	RBI	SH	Avg	AB	H	2B	3B	HR	RBI	BB	SO	SH	Inn	PO	A	E	DP	Pct	SBA	CS	PCS	PPO	CS%	RS
Lowe,Derek, Cle-NYY	R	.500	4	2	0	0	0	.149	436	65	13	0	1	25	29	129	67	142.2	11	14	1	0	.962	9	2	0	0	.22	-8
Lowe,Mark, Tex	R	-	0	0	0	0	0	.000	1	0	0	0	0	0	0	1	0	39.1	2	2	0	1	1.000	1	1	0	0	1.00	-1
Luebke,Cory, SD	L	.000	11	0	0	0	1	.143	49	7	0	0	0	0	2	27	2	31.0	2	7	1	0	.900	5	2	1	0	.40	1
Lueke,Josh, TB	R	-	0	0	0	0	0	-	0	0	0	0	0	0	0	0	0	3.1	0	0	0	0	-	0	0	0	0	-	0
Luetge,Lucas, Sea	L	-	0	0	0	0	0	-	0	0	0	0	0	0	0	0	0	40.2	1	1	0	1	1.000	4	0	0	0	.00	0
Lyles,Jordan, Hou	R	.158	38	6	1	4	7	.143	63	9	1	0	1	4	3	27	9	141.1	7	19	1	2	.963	14	4	0	0	.29	-2
Lynn,Lance, StL	R	.060	50	3	0	1	10	.056	54	3	0	0	1	3	3	37	10	176.0	5	16	1	1	.955	18	9	1	1	.50	1
Lyon,Brandon, Hou-Tor	R	-	0	0	0	0	0	1.000	1	1	1	0	0	1	1	0	0	61.0	3	5	0	0	1.000	17	2	0	0	.12	-1
MacDougal,Mike, LAD	R	-	0	0	0	0	0	-	0	0	0	0	0	0	0	0	0	5.2	0	0	0	0	-	1	0	0	0	.00	0
Machi,Jean, SF	R	-	0	0	0	0	0	-	0	0	0	0	0	0	0	0	0	6.2	0	2	0	1	1.000	0	0	0	0	-	0
Maholm,Paul, ChC-Atl	L	.063	63	4	1	3	3	.108	417	45	2	0	2	16	21	221	26	189.0	5	26	2	1	.939	12	6	3	1	.50	1
Maine,Scott, ChC-Cle	L	.000	2	0	0	0	0	.000	2	0	0	0	0	0	0	1	0	26.2	0	1	0	0	1.000	3	0	0	0	.00	1
Maloney,Matt, Min	L	-	0	0	0	0	0	.211	19	4	0	0	0	1	6	4	11.0	0	3	0	1	1.000	2	0	0	0	.00	0
Manship,Jeff, Min	R	-	0	0	0	0	0	.000	1	0	0	0	0	0	0	1	0	21.2	1	3	0	1	1.000	1	0	0	0	.00	-1
Marcum,Shaun, Mil	R	.105	38	4	0	1	3	.131	107	14	4	0	1	8	9	39	16	124.0	11	16	1	0	.964	16	3	0	0	.19	-1
Marinez,Jhan, CWS	R	-	0	0	0	0	0	-	0	0	0	0	0	0	0	0	0	2.2	0	1	0	0	1.000	0	0	0	0	-	0
Marmol,Carlos, ChC	R	-	0	0	0	0	0	.200	30	6	1	0	1	1	0	11	3	55.1	5	5	1	4	.909	6	0	0	0	.00	0
Maronde,Nick, LAA	L	-	0	0	0	0	0	-	0	0	0	0	0	0	0	0	0	6.0	0	1	0	0	1.000	0	0	0	0	-	0
Marquis,Jason, Min-SD	R	.281	32	9	0	1	3	.202	605	122	33	2	5	54	13	151	40	127.2	7	23	2	0	.938	24	7	0	0	.29	-1
Marshall,Sean, Cin	L	-	0	0	0	0	0	.158	101	16	1	0	1	5	2	48	8	61.0	4	11	0	1	1.000	3	2	1	0	.67	2
Marte,Luis, Det	R	.000	1	0	0	0	0	.000	1	0	0	0	0	0	0	0	0	22.1	1	3	0	0	1.000	0	0	0	0	-	1
Marte,Victor, StL	R	-	0	0	0	0	0	-	0	0	0	0	0	0	0	0	0	40.1	2	5	0	0	1.000	5	1	0	0	.20	1
Martinez,Cristhian, Atl	R	.000	3	0	0	0	0	.133	15	2	1	0	0	2	0	5	2	73.2	8	7	0	1	1.000	4	0	0	0	.00	-1
Martinez,Joe, Ari	R	-	0	0	0	0	0	.182	11	2	1	0	0	0	0	2	1	1.0	0	0	0	0	-	0	0	0	0	-	0
Masterson,Justin, Cle	R	.000	2	0	0	0	0	.118	17	2	0	0	0	0	0	8	1	206.1	24	34	1	2	.983	32	7	0	0	.22	1
Matsuzaka,Daisuke, Bos	R	.000	2	0	0	0	0	.143	14	2	0	0	1	0	5	1	45.2	6	2	0	1	1.000	11	0	0	1	.00	-1
Mattheus,Ryan, Was	R	.000	1	0	0	0	0	.000	1	0	0	0	0	0	0	1	0	66.1	7	7	0	0	1.000	3	1	0	0	.33	0
Matusz,Brian, Bal	L	.250	4	1	0	0	0	.125	8	1	0	0	0	0	0	2	0	98.0	2	10	0	1	1.000	5	3	1	0	.60	-3
Mazzaro,Vin, KC	R	.500	4	2	0	1	1	.200	10	2	0	0	0	1	0	6	5	44.0	3	6	0	0	1.000	14	2	1	0	.14	-2
McAllister,Zach, Cle	R	-	0	0	0	0	0	-	0	0	0	0	0	0	0	0	0	125.1	4	5	1	0	.900	19	1	0	0	.05	-6
McCarthy,Brandon, Oak	R	-	0	0	0	0	0	.000	9	0	0	0	0	0	0	4	0	111.0	7	14	0	1	1.000	16	3	0	0	.19	-2
McClellan,Kyle, StL	R	.000	1	0	0	0	0	.130	46	6	1	0	0	4	1	18	6	18.2	1	0	0	0	1.000	1	0	0	0	.00	0
McClendon,Mike, Mil	R	.000	2	0	0	0	0	.250	4	1	0	0	0	0	0	1	0	14.0	0	5	0	0	1.000	4	0	0	0	.00	0
McCutchen,Daniel, Pit	R	-	0	0	0	0	0	.067	30	2	0	0	0	1	1	8	3	0.0	0	0	0	0	-	1	0	0	0	.00	0
McDonald,James, Pit	R	.143	49	7	0	1	6	.097	134	13	2	0	4	12	70	13	171.0	14	15	1	1	.967	16	4	0	0	.25	1
McGee,Jake, TB	L	-	0	0	0	0	0	-	0	0	0	0	0	0	0	0	0	55.1	2	7	0	1	1.000	0	0	0	0	-	1
McHugh,Collin, NYM	R	.000	4	0	0	0	0	.000	4	0	0	0	0	0	0	2	0	21.1	0	3	0	0	1.000	4	2	0	0	.50	0
McPherson,Kyle, Pit	R	.000	5	0	0	0	0	.000	5	0	0	0	0	0	1	3	0	26.1	3	1	0	0	1.000	6	2	0	0	.33	0
Medlen,Kris, Atl	R	.121	33	4	0	2	2	.123	73	9	2	0	4	7	36	4	138.0	12	26	1	1	.974	7	2	1	2	.29	3
Meek,Evan, Pit	R	-	0	0	0	0	0	1.000	1	1	0	0	0	0	0	0	1	12.0	3	1	0	0	1.000	1	0	0	0	.00	0
Mejia,Jenrry, NYM	R	.000	3	0	0	1	2	.167	6	1	0	0	0	1	0	3	2	16.0	0	2	1	0	.667	2	0	0	0	.00	-4
Melancon,Mark, Bos	R	-	0	0	0	0	0	-	0	0	0	0	0	0	1	0	0	45.0	5	8	0	0	1.000	1	1	0	0	1.00	1
Mendoza,Luis, KC	R	.000	2	0	0	0	0	.000	3	0	0	0	0	0	0	3	1	166.0	19	25	1	1	.978	14	7	1	2	.50	4
Mijares,Jose, KC-SF	L	.000	1	0	0	0	0	.000	1	0	0	0	0	0	0	1	0	56.1	1	6	2	0	.778	7	1	1	1	.14	0
Mikolas,Miles, SD	R	.000	3	0	0	0	0	.000	3	0	0	0	0	0	0	1	0	32.1	0	7	1	0	.875	1	0	0	0	.00	1
Miley,Wade, Ari	L	.169	65	11	0	2	8	.154	78	12	2	0	0	3	4	22	9	194.2	2	28	1	1	.968	9	6	4	0	.67	5
Miller,Andrew, Bos	L	-	0	0	0	0	0	.056	72	4	0	0	0	3	0	36	4	40.1	1	2	1	0	.750	0	0	0	0	-	-1
Miller,Jim, Oak	R	-	0	0	0	0	0	-	0	0	0	0	0	0	0	0	0	48.2	5	4	0	1	1.000	10	0	0	0	.00	-2
Miller,Shelby, StL	R	.667	3	2	0	0	0	.667	3	2	1	0	0	0	0	0	0	13.2	1	2	0	0	1.000	5	0	0	0	.00	0
Mills,Brad, LAA	L	-	0	0	0	0	0	.000	1	0	0	0	0	0	0	0	0	5.0	0	0	0	0	-	0	0	0	0	-	0
Millwood,Kevin, Sea	R	.000	5	0	0	0	0	.121	472	57	15	0	4	27	21	219	55	161.0	11	17	0	2	1.000	21	3	0	0	.14	-4
Milone,Tommy, Oak	L	.200	5	1	0	0	0	.182	11	2	0	0	1	5	0	2	4	190.0	5	18	1	1	.958	18	10	6	0	.56	3
Minor,Mike, Atl	L	.073	55	4	0	0	4	.076	92	7	3	0	0	0	6	48	6	179.1	2	22	0	1	1.000	12	2	2	0	.17	0
Mitchell,D.J., NYY	R	-	0	0	0	0	0	-	0	0	0	0	0	0	0	0	0	4.2	0	1	1	0	.500	0	0	0	0	-	0
Moore,Matt, TB	L	.000	4	0	0	1	1	.000	4	0	0	0	0	1	0	2	1	177.1	6	20	2	3	.929	23	4	2	0	.17	-2
Morales,Franklin, Bos	L	.500	2	1	0	0	0	.267	30	8	0	0	2	1	10	2	76.1	5	6	1	0	.917	10	2	2	2	.20	0
Morris,Bryan, Pit	R	-	0	0	0	0	0	-	0	0	0	0	0	0	0	0	0	5.0	1	1	0	0	1.000	0	0	0	0	.00	0
Morrow,Brandon, Tor	R	-	0	0	0	0	0	.000	12	0	0	0	0	0	0	4	0	124.2	4	8	1	0	.923	5	1	0	0	.20	-1
Mortensen,Clayton, Bos	R	.000	1	0	0	0	0	.000	15	0	0	0	0	1	1	10	0	42.0	5	8	0	0	1.000	6	2	0	0	.33	2
Morton,Charlie, Pit	R	.000	13	0	0	0	2	.073	137	10	4	0	0	3	1	79	20	50.1	3	6	3	0	.750	4	0	0	0	.00	-2
Moscoso,Guillermo, Col	R	.182	11	2	0	1	1	.154	32	3	1	0	1	0	7	2	50.0	3	9	0	2	1.000	8	1	1	2	.13	0
Moseley,Dustin, SD	R	.000	1	0	0	0	0	.133	30	4	0	0	0	1	11	6	5.0	0	0	0	0	-	2	0	0	0	.00	0
Mota,Guillermo, SF	R	-	0	0	0	0	0	.188	48	9	2	0	2	7	0	21	2	20.2	2	3	0	0	1.000	4	2	0	1	.50	1
Motte,Jason, StL	R	-	0	0	0	0	0	.000	4	0	0	0	0	0	0	4	0	72.0	5	2	0	0	1.000	5	2	0	0	.40	2
Moyer,Jamie, Col	L	.154	13	2	0	2	3	.128	400	51	5	0	0	15	35	152	64	53.2	3	11	0	0	1.000	9	2	1	0	.22	0
Moylan,Peter, Atl	R	-	0	0	0	0	0	.000	7	0	0	0	0	0	1	6	0	5.0	0	0	0	0	-	1	0	0	0	.00	0
Mujica,Edward, Mia-StL	R	-	0	0	0	0	0	.222	9	2	0	0	0	0	0	2	2	65.1	6	12	1	1	.947	2	1	0	0	.50	2
Myers,Brett, Hou-CWS	R	-	0	0	0	0	0	.134	471	63	11	0	0	12	25	161	60	65.1	12	6	0	2	1.000	3	2	0	0	.67	-1
Narveson,Chris, Mil	L	.000	3	0	0	0	0	.227	110	25	3	0	0	12	5	42	15	9.0	0	1	0	0	1.000	1	0	0	0	.00	0
Nathan,Joe, Tex	R	-	0	0	0	0	0	.159	63	10	3	0	2	4	3	17	10	64.1	3	4	1	0	.875	4	1	0	0	.25	0

349

Pitchers Hitting, Fielding and Holding Runners

Pitcher	T	2012 Hitting						Career Hitting										2012 Fielding and Holding Runners											
		Avg	AB	H	HR	RBI	SH	Avg	AB	H	2B	3B	HR	RBI	BB	SO	SH	Inn	PO	A	E	DP	Pct	SBA	CS	PCS	PPO	CS%	RS
Neshek,Pat, Oak	R	-	0	0	0	0	0	-	0	0	0	0	0	0	0	0	0	19.2	0	1	0	0	1.000	2	0	0	0	.00	0
Nicasio,Juan, Col	R	.111	18	2	0	1	1	.125	40	5	2	0	0	1	2	29	2	58.0	5	6	0	0	1.000	8	5	1	1	.63	1
Niemann,Jeff, TB	R	-	0	0	0	0	0	.077	13	1	0	0	0	0	0	9	1	38.0	2	6	0	2	1.000	9	1	0	0	.11	1
Niese,Jon, NYM	L	.218	55	12	0	2	7	.158	171	27	2	1	0	6	18	86	20	190.1	5	26	2	2	.939	10	2	2	0	.20	3
Noesi,Hector, Sea	R	.500	4	2	0	0	0	.500	4	2	0	0	0	0	0	2	0	106.2	9	5	1	0	.933	11	5	1	0	.45	0
Nolasco,Ricky, Mia	R	.161	56	9	0	8	10	.141	319	45	10	0	1	25	15	147	54	191.0	22	21	1	3	.977	18	4	0	0	.22	-5
Norberto,Jordan, Oak	L	-	0	0	0	0	0	-	0	0	0	0	0	0	0	0	0	52.0	1	6	1	0	.875	5	2	2	0	.40	0
Norris,Bud, Hou	R	.100	50	5	0	3	8	.135	163	22	5	0	0	10	4	57	30	168.1	16	17	2	2	.943	23	10	1	1	.43	2
Nova,Ivan, NYY	R	.143	7	1	0	0	2	.091	11	1	0	0	0	0	0	10	3	170.1	9	9	1	2	.947	10	3	0	0	.30	-3
O'Day,Darren, Bal	R	-	0	0	0	0	0	-	0	0	0	0	0	0	0	0	0	67.0	3	6	0	0	1.000	6	2	1	0	.33	0
Odorizzi,Jake, KC	R	-	0	0	0	0	0	-	0	0	0	0	0	0	0	0	0	7.1	2	1	0	0	1.000	2	0	0	0	.00	0
O'Flaherty,Eric, Atl	L	-	0	0	0	0	0	.000	2	0	0	0	0	0	0	2	0	57.1	1	6	0	0	1.000	3	2	1	0	.67	0
Ogando,Alexi, Tex	R	.500	2	1	0	0	0	.600	5	3	0	0	0	0	0	2	0	66.0	3	7	0	0	1.000	5	0	0	0	.00	-1
Ohlendorf,Ross, SD	R	.063	16	1	0	0	1	.082	122	10	0	0	1	4	3	56	8	48.2	3	6	1	0	.900	10	0	0	1	.00	-2
Ohman,Will, CWS	L	-	0	0	0	0	0	.400	5	2	0	0	0	1	1	2	1	26.2	0	1	0	1	1.000	0	0	0	0	-	0
Oliver,Darren, Tor	L	-	0	0	0	0	0	.221	217	48	11	0	1	20	8	74	15	56.2	1	3	0	0	1.000	12	4	2	0	.33	-2
Oliveros,Lester, Min	R	-	0	0	0	0	0	-	0	0	0	0	0	0	0	0	0	1.2	0	0	0	0	-	0	0	0	0	-	0
Olson,Garrett, NYM	L	-	0	0	0	0	0	.167	6	1	0	0	0	1	0	2	2	0.1	0	0	0	0	-	0	0	0	0	-	0
Omogrosso,Brian, CWS	R	-	0	0	0	0	0	-	0	0	0	0	0	0	0	0	0	21.0	0	0	0	0	-	3	1	0	0	.33	-1
Ondrusek,Logan, Cin	R	-	0	0	0	0	0	.000	4	0	0	0	0	0	0	4	0	54.2	4	5	0	1	1.000	1	0	0	0	.00	-2
Ortega,Jose, Det	R	-	0	0	0	0	0	-	0	0	0	0	0	0	0	0	0	2.2	0	0	0	0	-	0	0	0	0	-	0
Oswalt,Roy, Tex	R	-	0	0	0	0	0	.152	651	99	7	0	1	36	27	179	105	59.0	2	4	0	1	1.000	4	2	1	0	.50	-1
Otero,Dan, SF	R	.000	1	0	0	0	0	.000	1	0	0	0	0	0	0	1	0	12.1	0	3	0	1	1.000	2	1	0	0	.50	0
Ottavino,Adam, Col	R	.111	9	1	0	0	3	.067	15	1	0	0	0	1	1	12	3	79.0	5	10	0	0	1.000	17	1	0	0	.06	-3
Outman,Josh, Col	L	.083	12	1	0	1	0	.053	19	1	0	0	0	1	1	10	0	40.2	1	5	0	0	1.000	4	1	0	0	.25	0
Owings,Micah, SD	R	.000	2	0	0	0	0	.283	205	58	14	2	9	35	8	72	3	9.2	0	3	0	0	1.000	1	1	0	0	1.00	1
Padilla,Vicente, Bos	R	.000	1	0	0	0	0	.108	251	27	4	1	0	17	16	130	30	50.0	4	3	1	0	.875	5	1	0	0	.20	-2
Palmer,Matt, SD	R	-	0	0	0	0	0	.200	10	2	0	0	0	0	1	5	1	2.0	0	1	0	1	1.000	0	0	0	0	-	0
Papelbon,Jonathan, Phi	R	-	0	0	0	0	0	-	0	0	0	0	0	0	0	0	0	70.0	1	9	0	0	1.000	11	3	1	0	.27	-1
Parker,Blake, ChC	R	-	0	0	0	0	0	-	0	0	0	0	0	0	0	0	0	6.0	0	0	1	0	.000	1	0	0	0	.00	-1
Parker,Jarrod, Oak	R	.000	6	0	0	0	1	.125	8	1	1	0	0	0	0	5	1	181.1	9	15	3	2	.889	27	6	2	1	.22	-2
Parnell,Bobby, NYM	R	-	0	0	0	0	1	.111	9	1	0	0	0	0	0	3	5	68.2	7	18	0	2	1.000	1	0	0	0	.00	4
Parra,Manny, Mil	L	.000	1	0	0	0	0	.183	142	26	11	1	0	13	6	58	10	58.2	4	6	0	0	1.000	15	3	2	0	.20	-4
Paterson,Joe, Ari	L	-	0	0	0	0	0	-	0	0	0	0	0	0	0	0	0	2.2	0	0	0	0	-	0	0	0	0	-	-2
Patton,Troy, Bal	L	-	0	0	0	0	0	.333	3	1	0	0	0	0	0	1	0	55.2	3	1	1	1	.800	1	0	0	0	.00	-1
Pauley,David, LAA-Tor	R	-	0	0	0	0	0	-	0	0	0	0	0	0	0	0	0	16.2	0	1	0	0	1.000	1	0	0	0	.00	0
Paulino,Felipe, KC	R	-	0	0	0	0	0	.143	56	8	1	0	0	1	1	29	9	37.2	3	6	0	0	1.000	4	2	1	1	.50	0
Pavano,Carl, Min	R	.000	2	0	0	0	0	.141	311	44	8	2	2	14	4	123	36	63.0	5	5	0	0	1.000	8	1	0	0	.13	-1
Peavy,Jake, CWS	R	.000	5	0	0	1	0	.177	418	74	14	1	2	27	19	122	45	219.0	14	22	1	3	.973	17	8	0	1	.47	4
Pelfrey,Mike, NYM	R	.167	6	1	0	0	1	.098	264	26	5	0	0	13	13	70	24	19.2	3	4	1	0	.875	3	1	0	0	.33	0
Penny,Brad, SF	R	.000	1	0	0	0	0	.155	523	81	16	2	3	34	3	170	41	28.0	3	4	0	2	1.000	4	1	0	0	.25	-1
Peralta,Joel, TB	R	-	0	0	0	0	0	.250	4	1	1	0	0	2	0	2	0	67.0	6	2	0	1	1.000	4	1	0	0	.25	0
Peralta,Wily, Mil	R	.091	11	1	0	0	0	.091	11	1	1	0	0	0	0	5	0	29.0	4	4	1	0	.889	4	3	0	0	.75	1
Perdomo,Luis, Min	R	-	0	0	0	0	0	.000	6	0	0	0	0	0	0	5	0	17.0	6	3	0	1	1.000	2	0	0	0	.00	0
Perez,Chris, Cle	R	-	0	0	0	0	0	.000	1	0	0	0	0	0	0	1	0	57.2	7	2	0	1	1.000	3	0	0	0	.00	0
Perez,Juan, Mil	L	.000	1	0	0	0	0	.000	1	0	0	0	0	0	0	1	0	7.0	0	0	0	0	-	1	0	0	0	.00	-1
Perez,Luis, Tor	L	-	0	0	0	0	0	-	0	0	0	0	0	0	0	0	0	42.0	1	3	1	0	.800	2	1	1	0	.50	0
Perez,Martin, Tex	L	-	0	0	0	0	0	-	0	0	0	0	0	0	0	0	0	38.0	2	1	0	1	1.000	2	1	1	0	.50	-1
Perez,Oliver, Sea	L	-	0	0	0	0	0	.158	341	54	1	0	0	15	14	116	39	29.2	2	5	0	0	1.000	0	0	0	0	.00	0
Perez,Rafael, Cle	L	-	0	0	0	0	0	.000	1	0	0	0	0	0	0	1	0	7.2	2	0	0	0	1.000	1	0	0	0	.00	0
Perkins,Glen, Min	L	-	0	0	0	0	0	.000	4	0	0	0	0	0	0	4	3	70.1	2	13	1	0	.938	5	3	2	0	.60	0
Perry,Ryan, Was	R	-	0	0	0	0	0	-	0	0	0	0	0	0	0	0	0	8.0	0	1	0	0	1.000	3	1	0	0	.33	0
Pestano,Vinnie, Cle	R	-	0	0	0	0	0	-	0	0	0	0	0	0	0	0	0	70.0	3	7	0	1	1.000	6	2	0	0	.33	2
Petit,Yusmeiro, SF	R	.000	1	0	0	0	0	.048	62	3	0	0	0	1	1	26	4	4.2	0	2	0	0	1.000	3	2	0	1	.67	2
Pettitte,Andy, NYY	L	.250	4	1	0	0	1	.139	194	27	6	0	1	13	6	65	34	75.1	1	12	0	0	1.000	9	5	3	0	.56	-2
Phelps,David, NYY	R	-	0	0	0	0	0	-	0	0	0	0	0	0	0	0	0	99.2	4	10	3	0	.824	4	1	0	3	.25	0
Phillips,Zach, Bal	L	-	0	0	0	0	0	-	0	0	0	0	0	0	0	0	0	1.0	0	1	0	0	1.000	0	0	0	0	-	0
Pomeranz,Drew, Col	L	.231	26	6	1	1	4	.226	31	7	2	0	1	1	1	18	6	96.2	6	14	1	0	.952	12	2	1	0	.17	-3
Pomeranz,Stuart, Bal	R	-	0	0	0	0	0	-	0	0	0	0	0	0	0	0	0	6.0	0	0	0	0	-	0	0	0	0	-	0
Porcello,Rick, Det	R	.000	2	0	0	0	1	.214	14	3	0	0	0	2	0	6	2	176.1	12	30	5	0	.894	23	5	0	1	.22	0
Price,David, TB	L	.000	4	0	0	0	0	.111	18	2	0	0	0	2	9	0	211.0	6	28	3	4	.919	21	10	1	0	.48	5		
Pryor,Stephen, Sea	R	-	0	0	0	0	0	-	0	0	0	0	0	0	0	0	0	23.0	2	2	0	0	1.000	2	0	0	0	.00	0
Putkonen,Luke, Det	R	-	0	0	0	0	0	-	0	0	0	0	0	0	0	0	0	16.0	2	2	0	0	1.000	2	1	0	0	.50	-1
Putnam,Zach, Col	R	-	0	0	0	0	0	-	0	0	0	0	0	0	0	0	0	2.0	0	0	0	0	-	0	0	0	0	-	0
Putz,J.J., Ari	R	-	0	0	0	0	0	-	0	0	0	0	0	0	0	0	0	54.1	1	6	0	0	1.000	0	0	0	0	-	1
Qualls,Chad, Phi-NYY-Pit	R	-	0	0	0	0	0	.000	6	0	0	0	0	0	0	5	0	52.1	7	9	2	0	.889	13	1	0	0	.08	-1
Quintana,Jose, CWS	L	.000	3	0	0	0	1	.000	3	0	0	0	0	0	1	3	1	136.1	7	21	1	2	.966	11	4	2	0	.36	1
Raley,Brooks, ChC	L	.200	10	2	0	0	0	.200	10	2	0	0	0	0	0	1	0	24.1	1	3	0	0	1.000	3	1	0	0	.33	0
Ramirez,Elvin, NYM	R	.000	1	0	0	0	0	.000	1	0	0	0	0	0	0	1	0	21.0	0	2	0	0	1.000	2	1	0	0	.50	-1
Ramirez,Erasmo, Sea	R	.000	3	0	0	0	0	.000	3	0	0	0	0	0	0	1	0	59.0	3	9	0	0	1.000	4	0	0	0	.00	1

Pitchers Hitting, Fielding and Holding Runners

Pitcher	T	2012 Hitting Avg	AB	H	HR	RBI	SH	Career Hitting Avg	AB	H	2B	3B	HR	RBI	BB	SO	SH	2012 Fielding and Holding Runners Inn	PO	A	E	DP	Pct	SBA	CS	PCS	PPO	CS%	RS
Ramirez,Ramon, NYM	R	-	0	0	0	0	0	.333	6	2	0	0	0	0	0	3	1	63.2	3	6	0	0	1.000	12	2	0	0	.17	-3
Ramos,A.J., Mia	R	-	0	0	0	0	0	-	0	0	0	0	0	0	0	0	0	9.1	0	1	0	0	1.000	1	1	0	0	1.00	0
Ramos,Cesar, TB	L	.000	1	0	0	0	0	.000	5	0	0	0	0	0	0	3	0	30.0	5	4	0	1	1.000	3	0	0	0	.00	0
Rapada,Clay, NYY	L	-	0	0	0	0	0	-	0	0	0	0	0	0	0	0	0	38.1	0	8	3	1	.727	1	0	0	1	.00	-1
Rauch,Jon, NYM	R	-	0	0	0	0	0	.095	21	2	0	0	1	3	0	15	2	57.2	2	7	0	0	1.000	5	0	0	0	.00	0
Redmond,Todd, Cin	R	.000	1	0	0	0	0	.000	1	0	0	0	0	0	0	1	0	3.1	0	1	1	0	.500	2	0	0	0	.00	0
Reed,Addison, CWS	R	-	0	0	0	0	0	-	0	0	0	0	0	0	0	0	0	55.0	5	4	0	2	1.000	8	1	0	0	.13	-1
Resop,Chris, Pit	R	.000	3	0	0	0	1	.000	4	0	0	0	0	0	1	3	1	73.2	7	10	3	0	.850	7	1	0	0	.14	0
Reynolds,Matt, Col	L	.000	3	0	0	0	1	.000	5	0	0	0	0	0	1	3	1	57.1	5	11	2	1	.889	5	3	2	0	.60	1
Richard,Clayton, SD	L	.087	69	6	1	7	8	.110	181	20	6	0	1	16	3	83	22	218.2	17	42	6	1	.908	12	4	3	1	.33	3
Richards,Garrett, LAA	R	.000	2	0	0	0	0	.000	2	0	0	0	0	0	0	1	0	71.0	1	5	1	0	.857	10	2	0	0	.20	-2
Richmond,Scott, Tor	R	-	0	0	0	0	0	.000	6	0	0	0	0	0	0	5	0	3.0	0	0	1	0	.000	0	0	0	0	-	-1
Rivera,Mariano, NYY	R	-	0	0	0	0	0	.000	3	0	0	0	0	0	1	1	1	8.1	1	2	0	0	1.000	0	0	0	0	-	1
Robertson,David, NYY	R	-	0	0	0	0	0	-	0	0	0	0	0	0	0	0	0	60.2	4	1	0	0	1.000	9	1	0	0	.11	-2
Robertson,Tyler, Min	L	-	0	0	0	0	0	-	0	0	0	0	0	0	0	0	0	25.0	1	5	1	0	.857	5	2	1	0	.40	0
Rodney,Fernando, TB	R	-	0	0	0	0	0	.000	1	0	0	0	0	0	0	0	0	74.2	13	13	0	1	1.000	3	1	0	0	.33	1
Rodriguez,Aneury, Hou	R	1.000	1	1	0	0	0	.100	10	1	0	0	0	0	0	5	2	6.0	0	0	0	0	-	1	0	0	0	.00	0
Rodriguez,F, Hou	R	.000	3	0	0	0	0	.000	4	0	0	0	0	0	0	3	0	70.1	3	5	2	0	.800	21	1	0	0	.05	-5
Rodriguez,Francisco, Mil	R	-	0	0	0	0	0	.500	2	1	0	0	0	0	0	1	0	72.0	3	2	0	0	1.000	12	0	0	1	.00	-3
Rodriguez,Henry, Was	R	-	0	0	0	0	0	.000	2	0	0	0	0	0	2	0	0	29.1	0	3	1	0	.750	9	2	0	0	.22	-2
Rodriguez,Paco, LAD	L	-	0	0	0	0	0	-	0	0	0	0	0	0	0	0	0	6.2	3	0	0	0	1.000	1	0	0	0	.00	-1
Rodriguez,W, Hou-Pit	L	.066	61	4	0	2	8	.133	415	55	10	0	0	20	10	120	51	205.2	7	24	3	1	.912	20	4	2	0	.20	-6
Roenicke,Josh, Col	R	.083	12	1	0	0	0	.083	12	1	0	0	0	0	0	6	0	88.2	3	20	1	0	.958	5	2	0	2	.40	2
Rogers,Esmil, Col-Cle	R	.333	3	1	0	0	0	.224	49	11	3	0	0	1	0	20	7	78.2	9	8	1	1	.944	2	1	0	0	.50	-2
Rogers,Mark, Mil	R	.214	14	3	0	0	2	.250	16	4	2	0	0	0	0	6	2	39.0	4	6	0	1	1.000	3	0	0	0	.00	1
Romero,J.C., StL-Bal	L	-	0	0	0	0	0	.250	4	1	1	0	0	0	0	1	0	12.0	2	4	1	0	.857	2	0	0	0	.00	0
Romero,Ricky, Tor	L	.200	5	1	0	0	0	.095	21	2	0	0	2	0	11	0	181.0	5	34	2	2	.951	23	10	8	0	.43	6
Romo,Sergio, SF	R	-	0	0	0	0	0	.000	4	0	0	0	0	0	0	3	0	55.1	1	5	0	0	1.000	9	1	0	0	.11	0
Rosario,Sandy, Mia	R	-	0	0	0	0	0	-	0	0	0	0	0	0	0	0	0	3.0	0	0	0	0	-	1	0	0	0	.00	-1
Rosenberg,B.J., Phi	R	.333	3	1	0	1	1	.333	3	1	0	0	0	1	0	1	1	25.0	3	2	0	0	1.000	1	0	0	1	.00	0
Rosenthal,Trevor, StL	R	-	0	0	0	0	0	-	0	0	0	0	0	0	0	0	0	22.2	1	1	0	0	1.000	2	1	0	0	.50	2
Ross,Robbie, Tex	L	.000	2	0	0	0	0	.000	2	0	0	0	0	0	0	1	0	65.0	4	12	0	3	1.000	2	1	0	0	.50	0
Ross,Tyson, Oak	R	.000	2	0	0	0	0	.000	3	0	0	0	0	0	2	0	73.1	8	16	0	1	1.000	13	3	1	0	.23	-1
Runzler,Dan, SF	L	-	0	0	0	0	0	.000	1	0	0	0	0	0	1	1	0	3.2	0	0	0	0	-	1	0	0	0	.00	0
Rusin,Chris, ChC	L	.167	12	2	0	0	0	.167	12	2	0	1	0	0	0	5	0	29.2	1	6	0	0	1.000	3	1	1	0	.33	-1
Russell,James, ChC	L	.000	1	0	0	0	0	.077	13	1	0	0	0	0	0	5	0	69.1	9	2	1	0	.917	9	2	1	0	.22	-1
Rzepczynski,Marc, StL	L	-	0	0	0	0	0	-	0	0	0	0	0	0	0	0	0	46.2	2	10	0	1	1.000	4	2	0	0	.50	2
Sabathia,CC, NYY	L	.000	5	0	0	0	0	.238	105	25	3	0	3	14	1	28	3	200.0	1	27	0	0	1.000	12	2	1	0	.17	2
Saito,Takashi, Ari	R	-	0	0	0	0	0	.000	2	0	0	0	0	0	0	2	0	12.0	1	0	0	0	1.000	1	0	0	0	.00	0
Salas,Fernando, StL	R	.000	1	0	0	0	0	.000	2	0	0	0	0	0	0	1	0	58.2	3	9	0	0	1.000	6	3	0	0	.50	-1
Sale,Chris, CWS	L	.000	2	0	0	0	1	.000	2	0	0	0	0	0	0	2	1	192.0	8	25	1	0	.971	24	10	6	0	.42	-1
Samardzija,Jeff, ChC	R	.100	50	5	0	3	7	.109	64	7	0	0	1	5	5	23	9	174.2	13	25	2	1	.950	20	5	0	0	.25	1
Sanches,Brian, Phi	R	.000	1	0	0	0	0	.091	11	1	0	0	0	1	0	3	1	6.1	0	0	0	0	-	0	0	0	0	-	0
Sanchez,Anibal, Mia-Det	R	.100	30	3	0	0	4	.091	232	21	0	1	0	6	15	105	29	195.2	16	26	2	4	.955	27	4	0	1	.15	-1
Sanchez,Eduardo, StL	R	-	0	0	0	0	0	.000	2	0	0	0	0	0	0	1	0	15.0	1	0	0	0	1.000	0	0	0	0	-	-1
Sanchez,J, KC-Col	L	.000	5	0	0	0	0	.118	195	23	6	1	0	9	7	99	22	64.2	2	8	4	0	.714	15	4	4	0	.27	-3
Santana,Ervin, LAA	R	.000	4	0	0	0	1	.143	21	3	1	0	0	2	0	13	1	178.0	17	16	1	1	.971	18	2	0	1	.11	-2
Santana,Johan, NYM	L	.086	35	3	0	0	5	.161	248	40	12	1	1	9	9	78	22	117.0	7	16	0	2	1.000	10	3	2	0	.30	1
Santiago,Hector, CWS	L	-	0	0	0	0	0	-	0	0	0	0	0	0	0	0	0	70.1	4	8	0	1	1.000	11	1	0	0	.09	0
Santos,Sergio, Tor	R	-	0	0	0	0	0	-	0	0	0	0	0	0	0	0	0	5.0	0	2	0	0	1.000	2	0	0	0	.00	0
Saunders,Joe, Ari-Bal	L	.086	35	3	0	1	7	.138	123	17	1	0	0	6	6	32	14	174.2	12	23	1	2	.972	10	6	2	0	.60	4
Savery,Joe, Phi	L	.000	2	0	0	0	0	.000	2	0	0	0	0	0	0	1	0	25.0	1	7	1	0	.889	3	3	2	1	1.00	1
Scahill,Rob, Col	R	.000	1	0	0	0	1	.000	1	0	0	0	0	0	1	0	1	8.2	0	1	0	0	1.000	1	1	0	0	1.00	0
Scheppers,Tanner, Tex	R	-	0	0	0	0	0	-	0	0	0	0	0	0	0	0	0	32.1	2	5	0	2	1.000	6	0	0	0	.00	-1
Scherzer,Max, Det	R	.000	2	0	0	0	2	.162	74	12	2	0	0	3	4	22	8	187.2	8	13	1	0	.955	24	9	1	2	.38	-3
Schlereth,Daniel, Det	L	-	0	0	0	0	0	-	0	0	0	0	0	0	0	0	0	7.0	0	0	0	0	-	0	0	0	0	-	0
Schwimer,Michael, Phi	R	-	0	0	0	0	0	.000	1	0	0	0	0	0	0	1	0	34.1	1	4	0	0	1.000	6	5	0	0	.83	1
Schwinden,Chris, NYM	R	.250	4	1	0	1	0	.200	10	2	0	0	0	1	1	3	0	8.2	2	2	1	0	.800	2	0	0	0	.00	-1
Scribner,Evan, Oak	R	-	0	0	0	0	0	-	0	0	0	0	0	0	0	0	0	35.1	0	2	0	0	1.000	2	0	0	0	.00	0
Seddon,Chris, Cle	L	-	0	0	0	0	0	.000	3	0	0	0	0	0	0	2	0	34.1	2	1	1	0	.750	3	0	0	0	.00	-2
Septimo,Leyson, CWS	L	-	0	0	0	0	0	-	0	0	0	0	0	0	0	0	0	14.1	0	1	1	0	.500	4	0	0	1	.00	0
Shaw,Bryan, Ari	R	-	0	0	0	0	0	-	0	0	0	0	0	0	0	0	0	59.1	2	9	1	1	.917	6	3	0	1	.50	1
Sheets,Ben, Atl	R	.000	13	0	0	0	3	.076	449	34	3	0	0	12	19	212	45	49.1	5	6	0	0	1.000	4	0	0	1	.00	-1
Sherrill,George, Sea	L	-	0	0	0	0	0	-	0	0	0	0	0	0	0	0	0	1.1	0	0	0	0	-	0	0	0	0	-	0
Shields,James, TB	R	.200	5	1	0	1	0	.189	37	7	0	0	0	3	2	11	1	227.2	16	21	5	0	.881	16	2	0	3	.13	-3
Simon,Alfredo, Cin	R	.000	4	0	0	0	0	.000	4	0	0	0	0	0	0	2	0	61.0	6	6	1	0	.923	9	3	0	0	.33	0
Sipp,Tony, Cle	L	-	0	0	0	0	0	-	0	0	0	0	0	0	0	0	0	55.0	5	8	0	0	1.000	5	2	1	0	.40	1
Skaggs,Tyler, Ari	L	.000	7	0	0	0	2	.000	7	0	0	0	0	0	0	4	2	29.1	0	8	0	0	1.000	1	1	0	0	1.00	2
Slaten,Doug, Pit	L	-	0	0	0	0	0	-	0	0	0	0	0	0	0	0	0	13.0	0	1	0	0	1.000	1	0	0	0	.00	0
Smith,Joe, Cle	R	-	0	0	0	0	0	.000	2	0	0	0	0	0	0	2	0	67.0	1	15	1	1	.941	4	2	1	0	.50	2

Pitchers Hitting, Fielding and Holding Runners

Pitcher	T	2012 Hitting Avg	AB	H	HR	RBI	SH	Career Hitting Avg	AB	H	2B	3B	HR	RBI	BB	SO	SH	2012 Fielding and Holding Runners Inn	PO	A	E	DP	Pct	SBA	CS	PCS	PPO	CS%	RS
Smith,Will, KC	L	-	0	0	0	0	0	-	0	0	0	0	0	0	0	0	0	89.2	2	8	0	1	1.000	11	3	1	0	.27	-3
Smyly,Drew, Det	L	.000	1	0	0	0	0	.000	1	0	0	0	0	0	0	0	0	99.1	3	12	3	1	.833	14	6	2	0	.43	2
Socolovich,M, Bal-ChC	R	-	0	0	0	0	0	-	0	0	0	0	0	0	0	0	0	16.1	0	3	0	0	1.000	3	0	0	0	.00	0
Soriano,Rafael, NYY	R	-	0	0	0	0	0	.000	4	0	0	0	0	0	0	1	0	67.2	1	4	1	0	.833	4	1	0	0	.25	-2
Spence,Josh, SD	L	-	0	0	0	0	0	-	0	0	0	0	0	0	0	0	0	10.1	1	5	0	0	1.000	2	1	1	0	.50	0
Stammen,Craig, Was	R	.000	6	0	0	0	2	.208	77	16	6	0	0	10	3	29	9	88.1	5	8	1	0	.929	13	1	0	0	.08	-1
Stauffer,Tim, SD	R	.000	1	0	0	1	1	.160	125	20	3	0	0	12	4	57	16	5.0	1	1	0	0	1.000	2	1	0	0	.50	0
Stewart,Zach, CWS-Bos	R	-	0	0	0	0	0	.000	2	0	0	0	0	0	0	2	0	35.2	2	2	1	0	.800	5	1	0	0	.20	-1
Stinson,Josh, Mil	R	.000	1	0	0	0	0	.000	1	0	0	0	0	0	1	1	0	9.1	0	0	0	0	-	1	0	0	0	.00	0
Storen,Drew, Was	R	-	0	0	0	0	0	.500	2	1	0	0	0	0	0	1	0	30.1	1	2	0	0	1.000	6	0	0	0	.00	-1
Storey,Mickey, Hou	R	-	0	0	0	0	0	-	0	0	0	0	0	0	0	0	0	30.1	1	2	1	0	.750	2	0	0	0	.00	1
Straily,Dan, Oak	R	-	0	0	0	0	0	-	0	0	0	0	0	0	0	0	0	39.1	1	1	0	0	1.000	4	1	0	0	.25	0
Strasburg,Stephen, Was	R	.277	47	13	1	7	2	.192	73	14	4	0	1	8	3	23	6	159.1	15	13	0	0	1.000	16	2	1	0	.13	-2
Street,Huston, SD	R	-	0	0	0	0	0	.000	2	0	0	0	0	0	0	1	0	39.0	4	7	0	0	1.000	1	0	1	0	.00	1
Strop,Pedro, Bal	R	-	0	0	0	0	0	-	0	0	0	0	0	0	0	0	0	66.1	6	12	0	1	1.000	2	1	0	0	.50	0
Stults,Eric, CWS-SD	L	.250	28	7	0	3	6	.234	77	18	5	0	0	7	5	30	9	99.0	3	16	0	1	1.000	11	3	1	0	.27	2
Stutes,Michael, Phi	R	-	0	0	0	0	0	-	0	0	0	0	0	0	0	0	0	5.2	0	0	0	0	-	5	0	0	0	.00	-1
Suppan,Jeff, SD	R	.100	10	1	0	0	3	.173	439	76	7	0	1	24	24	101	70	30.2	5	7	0	1	1.000	2	0	0	0	.00	1
Swarzak,Anthony, Min	R	.000	2	0	0	0	0	.000	4	0	0	0	0	0	0	3	0	96.2	6	9	0	1	1.000	2	1	0	0	.50	1
Takahashi,H LAA-Pit	L	-	0	0	0	0	0	.063	16	1	0	0	0	0	0	3	4	50.1	4	4	0	0	1.000	3	2	1	0	.67	0
Tateyama,Yoshinori, Tex	R	-	0	0	0	0	0	-	0	0	0	0	0	0	0	0	0	17.0	2	0	0	0	1.000	1	0	0	0	.00	0
Taylor,Andrew, LAA	L	-	0	0	0	0	0	-	0	0	0	0	0	0	0	0	0	2.1	0	0	0	0	-	0	0	0	0	-	0
Tazawa,Junichi, Bos	R	-	0	0	0	0	0	-	0	0	0	0	0	0	0	0	1	44.0	2	4	0	1	1.000	5	1	0	0	.20	1
Teaford,Everett, KC	L	-	0	0	0	0	0	-	0	0	0	0	0	0	0	0	0	61.1	1	8	0	2	1.000	4	2	1	0	.50	-1
Teheran,Julio, Atl	R	.000	1	0	0	0	0	.000	5	0	0	0	0	0	1	1	1	6.1	1	1	0	0	1.000	0	0	1	0	-	0
Thatcher,Joe, SD	L	-	0	0	0	0	0	.000	1	0	0	0	0	0	0	1	0	31.2	0	3	0	0	1.000	4	2	2	0	.50	-1
Thayer,Dale, SD	R	-	0	0	0	0	0	.000	1	0	0	0	0	0	0	0	0	57.2	1	3	0	0	1.000	13	1	0	0	.08	-4
Thomas,Justin, Bos-NYY	L	-	0	0	0	0	0	.000	1	0	0	0	0	0	0	1	0	7.2	0	0	0	0	-	2	1	0	0	.50	0
Thompson,R, LAA-Oak	R	-	0	0	0	0	0	-	0	0	0	0	0	0	0	0	0	3.0	0	0	0	0	-	2	0	0	0	.00	0
Thornburg,Tyler, Mil	R	.200	5	1	0	0	0	.200	5	1	1	0	0	0	0	2	0	22.0	1	5	0	1	1.000	1	1	0	0	1.00	1
Thornton,Matt, CWS	L	-	0	0	0	0	0	.000	1	0	0	0	0	0	0	1	0	65.0	2	14	0	2	1.000	6	2	2	0	.33	3
Tillman,Chris, Bal	R	-	0	0	0	0	0	.000	1	0	0	0	0	0	0	0	0	86.0	2	7	1	0	.900	6	2	0	0	.33	-1
Tolleson,Shawn, LAD	R	-	0	0	0	0	0	-	0	0	0	0	0	0	0	0	0	37.2	1	3	0	0	1.000	1	0	0	1	.00	0
Tomlin,Josh, Cle	R	.400	5	2	0	0	0	.571	7	4	0	0	0	1	0	3	0	103.1	14	8	0	1	1.000	5	2	0	0	.40	1
Torres,Carlos, Col	R	.222	9	2	0	1	3	.167	12	2	0	0	0	1	1	7	3	53.0	1	9	1	0	.909	6	1	0	1	.17	-1
Turner,Jacob, Det-Mia	R	.000	14	0	0	0	2	.000	14	0	0	0	0	0	0	8	2	55.0	2	9	0	0	1.000	4	4	0	0	.50	2
Uehara,Koji, Tex	R	-	0	0	0	0	0	.000	2	0	0	0	0	0	1	1	0	36.0	4	1	1	0	.833	1	0	0	0	.00	0
Valdes,Raul, Phi	L	-	0	0	0	0	0	.400	10	4	1	0	0	1	0	3	4	31.0	1	1	0	0	1.000	1	1	0	0	1.00	0
Valdez,Jose, Hou	R	-	0	0	0	0	0	-	0	0	0	0	0	0	0	0	0	12.0	0	1	0	0	1.000	0	0	0	0	-	-1
Valverde,Jose, Det	R	-	0	0	0	0	0	.500	2	1	1	0	0	0	0	1	0	69.0	4	0	1	0	.800	13	1	0	0	.08	-5
VandenHurk,Rick, Pit	R	-	0	0	0	0	0	.021	47	1	0	0	0	0	1	31	6	2.2	0	0	0	0	-	0	0	0	0	-	0
Vargas,Jason, Sea	L	.400	5	2	0	1	0	.262	61	16	3	0	4	3	16	2	217.1	7	28	2	0	.946	16	6	0	0	.38	4		
Varvaro,Anthony, Atl	R	-	0	0	0	0	0	-	0	0	0	0	0	0	0	0	0	16.2	0	1	0	0	1.000	0	0	0	0	-	-1
Vasquez,Esmerling, Min	R	-	0	0	0	0	0	.000	2	0	0	0	0	0	0	1	0	31.2	0	6	0	0	1.000	4	2	0	0	.50	1
Veal,Donnie, CWS	L	-	0	0	0	0	0	-	0	0	0	0	0	0	0	0	1	13.0	0	1	1	0	.500	0	0	0	0	-	0
Venters,Jonny, Atl	L	-	0	0	0	0	0	.000	1	0	0	0	0	0	0	0	0	58.2	1	9	2	0	.833	5	0	0	0	.00	-3
Veras,Jose, Mil	R	-	0	0	0	0	0	-	0	0	0	0	0	0	1	0	0	67.0	2	6	0	0	1.000	12	2	0	0	.17	0
Verdugo,Ryan, KC	L	-	0	0	0	0	0	-	0	0	0	0	0	0	0	0	0	0.0	0	0	0	0	-	0	0	0	0	-	0
Verlander,Justin, Det	R	.000	4	0	0	0	4	.000	24	0	0	0	0	0	0	14	9	238.1	25	24	4	3	.925	20	4	0	1	.20	5
Villanueva,Carlos, Tor	R	.500	2	1	0	0	0	.091	66	6	0	0	3	3	31	10	125.1	7	11	0	0	1.000	11	5	0	0	.45	0
Villarreal,Brayan, Det	R	-	0	0	0	0	0	-	0	0	0	0	0	0	0	0	0	54.2	1	4	2	1	.714	13	2	0	0	.15	-2
Villarreal,Pedro, Cin	R	-	0	0	0	0	0	-	0	0	0	0	0	0	0	0	0	1.0	0	0	0	0	-	0	0	0	0	-	0
Vincent,Nick, SD	R	.000	1	0	0	0	0	.000	1	0	0	0	0	0	0	1	0	26.1	1	3	0	0	1.000	2	1	0	0	.50	0
Vogelsong,Ryan, SF	R	.093	54	5	0	0	8	.169	166	28	6	0	0	5	9	70	25	189.2	6	20	0	3	1.000	19	9	1	0	.47	2
Volquez,Edinson, SD	R	.071	56	4	0	1	5	.091	176	16	1	0	0	2	3	88	26	182.2	9	18	0	1	1.000	32	10	1	0	.31	-5
Volstad,Chris, ChC	R	.179	28	5	0	0	6	.139	201	28	6	0	0	7	2	94	28	111.1	4	21	1	2	.962	21	2	1	1	.10	-1
Wade,Cory, NYY	R	-	0	0	0	0	0	.000	2	0	0	0	0	0	0	1	0	39.0	2	3	1	0	.833	9	0	0	0	.00	-1
Wainwright,Adam, StL	R	.121	66	8	1	4	3	.204	367	75	18	1	6	27	16	119	25	198.2	15	19	1	2	.971	5	3	0	0	.60	-1
Walden,Jordan, LAA	R	-	0	0	0	0	0	-	0	0	0	0	0	0	0	0	0	39.0	1	3	0	0	1.000	7	2	0	0	.29	0
Waldrop,Kyle, Min	R	-	0	0	0	0	0	-	0	0	0	0	0	0	0	0	0	21.1	3	7	0	2	1.000	2	0	0	0	.00	0
Wall,Josh, LAD	R	-	0	0	0	0	0	-	0	0	0	0	0	0	0	0	0	5.2	0	1	0	0	1.000	1	0	1	0	1.00	0
Walters,P.J., Min	R	-	0	0	0	0	0	.000	10	0	0	0	0	0	1	6	3	61.2	5	7	1	1	.923	7	1	0	0	.14	1
Wang,Chien-Ming, Was	R	.167	6	1	0	0	0	.051	39	2	1	0	0	1	2	21	1	32.1	2	8	0	2	1.000	7	3	0	0	.43	2
Warren,Adam, NYY	R	-	0	0	0	0	0	-	0	0	0	0	0	0	0	0	0	2.1	0	0	0	0	-	1	0	0	0	.00	-1
Watson,Tony, Pit	L	.000	1	0	0	0	0	.000	2	0	0	0	0	0	0	2	0	53.1	1	8	2	0	.818	11	1	1	0	.10	1
Weaver,Jered, LAA	R	.500	2	1	0	0	0	.143	28	4	0	0	0	1	2	9	0	188.2	12	14	0	3	1.000	17	8	1	1	.47	2
Webb,Ryan, Mia	R	.000	1	0	0	0	0	.000	2	0	0	0	0	0	0	2	0	60.1	5	1	1	0	.857	14	3	1	0	.21	-6
Weber,Thad, Det	R	-	0	0	0	0	0	-	0	0	0	0	0	0	0	0	0	4.0	0	1	0	0	1.000	1	0	0	0	.00	-1
Weiland,Kyle, Hou	R	.000	5	0	0	0	1	.000	5	0	0	0	0	0	0	1	1	17.2	1	0	2	0	.333	2	2	0	0	1.00	-1
Wells,Kip, SD	R	.083	12	1	0	0	1	.190	331	63	10	1	4	17	4	143	34	37.1	2	2	1	0	.800	5	3	0	0	.60	-2

Pitchers Hitting, Fielding and Holding Runners

Pitcher	T	2012 Hitting						Career Hitting										2012 Fielding and Holding Runners											
		Avg	AB	H	HR	RBI	SH	Avg	AB	H	2B	3B	HR	RBI	BB	SO	SH	Inn	PO	A	E	DP	Pct	SBA	CS	PCS	PPO	CS%	RS
Wells,Randy, ChC	R	.250	4	1	0	0	0	.171	146	25	5	0	0	6	5	37	27	28.2	2	7	0	0	1.000	5	2	0	0	.40	1
Werner,Andrew, SD	L	.083	12	1	0	0	2	.083	12	1	0	0	0	0	0	4	2	40.1	0	3	1	1	.750	8	1	1	0	.13	-4
Westbrook,Jake, StL	R	.122	49	6	0	0	5	.119	135	16	5	0	1	10	9	67	19	174.2	12	43	5	1	.917	9	6	1	2	.67	11
Wheeler,Dan, Cle	R	-	0	0	0	0	0	.143	7	1	0	0	0	0	0	1	1	12.1	1	0	0	0	1.000	0	0	0	0	-	-1
White,Alex, Col	R	.179	28	5	2	5	4	.146	41	6	2	0	2	5	0	18	5	98.0	8	20	2	0	.933	17	4	0	0	.24	-1
Wieland,Joe, SD	R	.250	8	2	0	2	0	.250	8	2	1	0	0	2	0	2	0	27.2	2	2	0	0	1.000	0	0	0	0	-	0
Wilhelmsen,Tom, Sea	R	-	0	0	0	0	0	-	0	0	0	0	0	0	0	0	0	79.1	4	8	2	0	.857	13	1	0	0	.08	-4
Wilk,Adam, Det	L	-	0	0	0	0	0	.000	1	0	0	0	0	0	0	1	0	11.0	0	2	0	0	1.000	2	1	1	0	.50	0
Williams,Jerome, LAA	R	.250	4	1	0	0	0	.117	120	14	3	0	0	1	1	54	19	137.2	12	17	0	2	1.000	17	3	0	2	.18	1
Wilson,Brian, SF	R	-	0	0	0	0	0	.000	9	0	0	0	0	0	0	2	1	2.0	0	0	0	0	-	0	0	0	0	-	0
Wilson,C.J., LAA	L	.000	5	0	0	0	0	.077	13	1	0	1	0	0	1	2	2	202.1	7	33	2	0	.952	34	12	5	0	.35	3
Wilson,Justin, Pit	L	-	0	0	0	0	0	-	0	0	0	0	0	0	0	0	0	4.2	0	1	0	0	1.000	2	0	0	0	.00	0
Wolf,Randy, Mil-Bal	L	.150	40	6	0	4	5	.185	687	127	33	0	5	58	32	230	79	157.2	6	38	0	4	1.000	15	6	4	0	.40	7
Wood,Kerry, ChC	R	.000	1	0	0	0	0	.171	346	59	6	0	7	32	11	114	46	8.2	1	1	0	0	1.000	3	0	0	1	.00	0
Wood,Travis, ChC	L	.189	53	10	1	4	2	.158	120	19	5	1	3	10	0	49	12	156.0	10	22	2	1	.941	7	1	0	0	.14	2
Worley,Vance, Phi	R	.081	37	3	0	2	7	.153	85	13	2	0	0	7	1	30	9	133.0	4	22	1	2	.963	11	6	0	0	.55	-1
Wright,Jamey, LAD	R	.000	2	0	0	0	0	.146	438	64	15	1	1	17	12	176	51	67.2	9	10	5	1	.792	11	1	1	1	.09	-4
Wright,Wesley, Hou	L	.000	2	0	0	0	1	.067	15	1	0	0	0	0	0	7	1	52.1	5	10	1	1	.938	4	1	1	0	.25	1
Young,Chris, NYM	R	.129	31	4	0	2	4	.144	201	29	6	1	1	14	10	81	27	115.0	6	8	1	0	.933	22	3	0	1	.14	-5
Zagurski,Mike, Ari	L	-	0	0	0	0	0	-	0	0	0	0	0	0	0	0	0	37.1	0	6	0	0	1.000	3	3	2	0	1.00	0
Zambrano,Carlos, Mia	R	.176	34	6	1	2	2	.238	693	165	26	3	24	71	10	240	37	132.1	12	18	2	2	.938	1	1	1	0	1.00	2
Ziegler,Brad, Ari	R	.250	4	1	0	0	0	.250	4	1	0	0	0	0	0	2	0	68.2	3	21	1	2	.960	1	0	0	0	.00	4
Zimmermann,J, Was	R	.193	57	11	1	4	5	.190	137	26	3	0	1	9	7	38	22	195.2	12	28	2	2	.952	12	2	0	0	.17	3
Zito,Barry, SF	L	.075	53	4	0	2	10	.097	310	30	0	0	0	9	18	91	47	184.1	2	26	1	1	.966	16	7	1	0	.44	1

Hitters Pitching

Player	2012 Pitching											Career Pitching										
	G	W	L	Sv	IP	H	R	ER	BB	SO	ERA	G	W	L	Sv	IP	H	R	ER	BB	SO	ERA
Ankiel,Rick, Was	0	0	0	0	0.0	0	0	0	0	0	-	51	13	10	1	242.0	198	119	105	130	269	3.90
Bogusevic,Brian, Hou	1	0	0	0	1.0	3	2	2	0	0	18.00	1	0	0	0	1.0	3	2	2	0	0	18.00
Burroughs,Sean, Min	0	0	0	0	0.0	0	0	0	0	0	-	1	0	0	0	1.0	4	3	3	0	0	27.00
Butera,Drew, Min	1	0	0	0	1.0	0	0	0	1	1	0.00	1	0	0	0	1.0	0	0	0	1	1	0.00
Cuddyer,Michael, Col	0	0	0	0	0.0	0	0	0	0	0	-	1	0	0	0	1.0	2	0	0	1	0	0.00
Davis,Chris, Bal	1	1	0	0	2.0	2	0	0	1	2	0.00	1	1	0	0	2.0	2	0	0	1	2	0.00
Gentry,Craig, Tex	1	0	0	0	1.0	3	2	2	1	0	18.00	1	0	0	0	1.0	3	2	2	1	0	18.00
Green,Nick, Mia	0	0	0	0	0.0	0	0	0	0	0	-	1	0	0	0	2.0	0	0	0	3	0	0.00
Hall,Bill, Bal	0	0	0	0	0.0	0	0	0	0	0	-	1	0	0	0	1.0	0	0	0	0	0	0.00
Janish,Paul, Atl	0	0	0	0	0.0	0	0	0	0	0	-	2	0	0	0	2.0	9	11	11	2	3	49.50
Johnson,Rob, NYM	1	0	0	0	1.0	0	0	0	0	1	0.00	1	0	0	0	1.0	0	0	0	0	1	0.00
Kelly,Don, Det	0	0	0	0	0.0	0	0	0	0	0	-	1	0	0	0	0.1	0	0	0	0	0	0.00
Maier,Mitch, KC	1	0	0	0	1.0	1	0	0	0	0	0.00	2	0	0	0	2.0	2	0	0	0	0	0.00
Mather,Joe, ChC	1	0	0	0	0.1	0	0	0	0	0	0.00	2	0	1	0	2.1	3	2	2	3	0	7.71
Mathis,Jeff, Tor	2	0	0	0	2.0	4	2	2	1	0	9.00	2	0	0	0	2.0	4	2	2	1	0	9.00
McCoy,Mike, Tor	0	0	0	0	0.0	0	0	0	0	0	-	1	0	0	0	1.0	0	0	0	0	0	0.00
McDonald,Darnell, Bos-NYY	1	0	1	0	1.0	2	3	3	2	0	27.00	2	0	1	0	2.0	3	5	5	4	0	22.50
Petersen,Bryan, Mia	0	0	0	0	0.0	0	0	0	0	0	-	1	0	0	0	1.0	0	0	0	1	0	0.00
Ross,Cody, Bos	0	0	0	0	0.0	0	0	0	0	0	-	1	0	0	0	1.0	1	0	0	0	0	0.00
Schumaker,Skip, StL	0	0	0	0	0.0	0	0	0	0	0	-	1	0	0	0	1.0	1	2	2	1	2	18.00
Swisher,Nick, NYY	0	0	0	0	0.0	0	0	0	0	0	-	1	0	0	0	1.0	1	0	0	1	1	0.00
Valdez,Wilson, Cin	0	0	0	0	0.0	0	0	0	0	0	-	1	1	0	0	1.0	0	0	0	0	0	0.00
Wise,DeWayne, NYY-CWS	2	0	0	0	1.2	1	0	0	1	0	0.00	2	0	0	0	1.2	1	0	0	1	0	0.00

2012 Pitch Repertoire

How many curveballs did Stephen Strasburg throw this year? The answer is 19% of all of his pitches. How fast was Aroldis Chapman's fastball? It was really fast: 97.7 miles per hour on average. What pitches did Josh Tomlin use this season? Fastballs, cutters, curves, and change-ups. Does anyone still throw screwballs? Yes, in fact, Hector Santiago is still practicing that ancient craft. He threw a screwball 6% of the time in 2012.

This section contains that information, which is a pretty nice view into our advanced pitch charting data for the 2012 season. Within, you can find every pitcher from this season, including the Blue Jays' catcher Jeff Mathis and the rest of the hitters forced onto the mound in 2012, his average fastball velocity and the breakdown of his pitch usage throughout the season.

Player	Fastball Velocity	Fastball	Cutter	Curve	Slider	Change	Splitter	Other
Aardsma,David	91.5	54%	-	-	4%	-	42%	
Abad,Fernando	90.1	54%	-	34%	-	12%	-	
Accardo,Jeremy	91.1	63%	7%	-	-	-	30%	
Aceves,Alfredo	94.0	48%	12%	25%	-	10%	5%	
Acosta,Manny	94.0	43%	-	-	34%	23%	-	
Adams,Mike	91.3	40%	45%	12%	-	3%	-	
Adcock,Nathan	91.3	69%	-	9%	14%	7%	-	
Affeldt,Jeremy	91.4	59%	-	28%	-	-	13%	
Albaladejo,Jonathan	89.7	63%	-	17%	-	20%	-	
Albers,Matt	93.7	72%	-	13%	15%	<1%	-	
Alburquerque,Al	94.5	38%	-	-	62%	-	-	
Allen,Cody	94.8	76%	<1%	24%	-	-	-	
Alvarez,Henderson	93.3	69%	4%	-	11%	16%	-	
Ambriz,Hector	93.7	54%	-	8%	38%	-	-	
Anderson,Brett	91.5	50%	-	11%	33%	6%	-	
Archer,Chris	93.9	64%	-	1%	27%	8%	-	
Arredondo,Jose	90.9	34%	-	-	11%	-	55%	
Arrieta,Jake	93.4	60%	-	16%	16%	8%	-	
Arroyo,Bronson	87.2	38%	7%	19%	23%	13%	-	
Asencio,Jairo	92.1	41%	-	-	20%	39%	-	
Atchison,Scott	90.5	32%	52%	15%	-	<1%	-	
Aumont,Phillippe	95.7	72%	-	23%	-	-	6%	
Avilan,Luis	92.5	68%	-	19%	-	14%	-	
Axelrod,Dylan	88.5	42%	-	9%	38%	11%	-	
Axford,John	96.2	73%	-	18%	9%	-	-	
Ayala,Luis	90.8	55%	17%	2%	13%	14%	-	
Badenhop,Burke	89.5	74%	-	-	17%	9%	-	
Bailey,Andrew	94.3	58%	31%	12%	-	-	-	
Bailey,Homer	92.5	62%	-	10%	19%	-	9%	
Balester,Collin	92.9	68%	-	27%	-	4%	-	
Balfour,Grant	92.8	69%	-	8%	23%	<1%	-	
Bard,Daniel	93.1	63%	-	-	27%	10%	-	
Barnes,Scott	91.8	47%	-	-	40%	13%	-	
Bass,Anthony	91.9	52%	12%	-	20%	15%	-	
Bastardo,Antonio	91.8	63%	-	-	37%	<1%	-	
Batista,Miguel	91.7	60%	33%	1%	-	6%	-	
Bauer,Trevor	92.2	52%	-	22%	<1%	16%	10%	
Beachy,Brandon	91.0	63%	-	9%	18%	9%	-	
Beato,Pedro	92.2	53%	7%	20%	-	20%	-	
Beavan,Blake	90.9	64%	-	10%	23%	4%	-	
Beck,Chad	93.7	63%	-	-	25%	-	11%	
Beckett,Josh	91.4	48%	21%	18%	-	13%	-	
Bedard,Erik	89.4	53%	10%	28%	-	10%	-	
Belisario,Ronald	94.0	88%	-	-	9%	-	2%	
Belisle,Matt	90.7	60%	-	12%	27%	<1%	-	
Beliveau,Jeff	90.5	60%	13%	14%	-	14%	-	
Bell,Heath	93.6	68%	-	28%	-	5%	-	
Below,Duane	89.8	55%	22%	10%	-	14%	-	
Benoit,Joaquin	93.7	51%	-	<1%	16%	33%	-	
Bergesen,Brad	91.2	63%	-	-	34%	3%	-	
Berken,Jason	90.4	68%	-	<1%	21%	11%	-	
Betancourt,Rafael	91.4	75%	-	18%	-	6%	-	
Billingsley,Chad	91.5	61%	9%	17%	8%	5%	-	
Blackburn,Nick	90.4	61%	11%	14%	-	14%	-	

Player	Fastball Velocity	Fastball	Cutter	Curve	Slider	Change	Splitter	Other
Blackley,Travis	90.5	52%	-	17%	18%	13%	-	
Blanton,Joe	90.4	47%	13%	10%	11%	18%	-	
Blevins,Jerry	89.8	49%	25%	12%	-	14%	-	
Boggs,Mitchell	95.8	66%	-	-	24%	10%	-	
Bogusevic,Brian	87.8	96%	-	-	-	4%	-	
Bowden,Michael	91.3	58%	-	-	23%	-	19%	
Boxberger,Brad	91.6	63%	-	-	4%	33%	-	
Brach,Brad	91.9	66%	-	-	24%	-	10%	
Bray,Bill	88.9	65%	-	-	33%	2%	-	
Breslow,Craig	90.9	54%	34%	2%	-	10%	-	
Britton,Zach	92.0	68%	-	-	22%	9%	-	
Brothers,Rex	95.3	69%	-	-	28%	3%	-	
Browning,Barret	86.9	59%	-	-	34%	7%	-	
Broxton,Jonathan	94.7	66%	5%	3%	27%	-	-	
Brummett,Tyson	90.8	36%	-	-	45%	18%	-	
Bruney,Brian	94.5	59%	-	-	36%	5%	-	
Buchholz,Clay	92.2	44%	21%	17%	-	14%	5%	
Buehrle,Mark	85.0	37%	10%	11%	15%	27%	-	
Bueno,Francisley	91.1	79%	-	7%	7%	8%	-	
Bumgarner,Madison	91.1	43%	-	10%	39%	8%	-	
Bundy,Dylan	93.7	66%	14%	3%	-	17%	-	
Burnett,A.J.	92.3	60%	-	34%	-	6%	-	
Burnett,Alex	92.7	63%	-	17%	20%	<1%	-	
Burnett,Sean	89.8	76%	-	-	16%	8%	-	
Burns,Cory	89.2	32%	-	-	5%	63%	-	
Burton,Jared	92.9	46%	-	-	16%	39%	-	
Butera,Drew	89.7	76%	-	-	-	24%	-	
Byrdak,Tim	88.5	39%	-	-	56%	5%	-	
Cabrera,Alberto	93.3	62%	-	-	32%	6%	-	
Cabrera,Edwar	90.4	61%	-	12%	-	27%	-	
Cahill,Trevor	89.4	63%	-	7%	11%	19%	-	
Cain,Matt	91.2	51%	-	14%	20%	16%	-	
Camp,Shawn	87.6	44%	-	-	46%	11%	-	
Capps,Carter	98.3	79%	-	17%	-	4%	-	
Capps,Matt	92.4	70%	-	-	16%	14%	-	
Capuano,Chris	88.0	57%	4%	9%	4%	26%	-	
Carignan,Andrew	94.4	86%	-	-	14%	-	-	
Carpenter,Andrew	89.9	53%	-	-	26%	-	21%	
Carpenter,Chris (Stl)	90.5	56%	-	14%	25%	5%	-	
Carpenter,Chris (Bos)	94.1	66%	-	-	31%	3%	-	
Carpenter,David (LAA)	89.0	72%	-	-	21%	7%	-	
Carpenter,David (Tor)	94.4	63%	-	-	36%	1%	-	
Carrasco,D.J.	89.4	47%	28%	8%	10%	7%	-	
Carreno,Joel	91.2	53%	-	-	41%	6%	-	
Carson,Robert	94.7	72%	-	<1%	26%	1%	-	
Cashner,Andrew	97.7	64%	-	-	14%	22%	-	
Casilla,Santiago	93.9	70%	-	15%	15%	-	-	
Cassevah,Bobby	91.4	64%	-	-	27%	-	8%	
Castillo,Lendy	92.3	66%	-	-	32%	2%	-	
Cecil,Brett	89.1	44%	<1%	24%	16%	16%	-	
Cedeno,Xavier	89.1	45%	8%	43%	-	3%	-	
Chacin,Jhoulys	90.3	60%	-	6%	20%	14%	-	
Chamberlain,Joba	94.7	48%	-	12%	38%	3%	-	
Chapman,Aroldis	97.7	88%	-	-	12%	-	-	
Chapman,Jaye	90.0	34%	-	-	26%	40%	-	
Chatwood,Tyler	93.8	72%	-	11%	12%	5%	-	
Chavez,Jesse	92.8	50%	25%	12%	5%	8%	-	

Player	Fastball Velocity	Fastball	Cutter	Curve	Slider	Change	Splitter	Other
Chen,Bruce	86.3	42%	-	13%	30%	15%	-	
Chen,Wei-Yin	91.0	65%	-	6%	15%	14%	-	
Choate,Randy	86.6	67%	-	-	33%	-	-	
Chulk,Vinnie	91.1	57%	-	39%	-	4%	-	
Cingrani,Tony	92.0	91%	-	-	5%	4%	-	
Cishek,Steve	92.2	60%	-	-	34%	5%	-	
Cleto,Maikel	96.8	65%	-	-	34%	1%	-	
Clippard,Tyler	92.8	52%	10%	2%	-	36%	-	
Cloyd,Tyler	86.2	51%	30%	11%	-	8%	-	
Cobb,Alex	90.3	47%	-	19%	-	34%	-	
Coello,Robert	92.3	82%	-	-	9%	<1%	8%	
Coffey,Todd	93.1	65%	-	-	32%	-	3%	
Coke,Phil	93.1	51%	-	-	37%	12%	-	
Coleman,Casey	90.8	59%	-	18%	14%	9%	-	
Coleman,Louis	90.3	57%	-	-	40%	4%	-	
Collins,Tim	93.2	55%	-	28%	-	18%	-	
Collmenter,Josh	87.5	71%	-	5%	-	24%	-	
Colon,Bartolo	90.2	89%	-	-	7%	4%	-	
Colon,Roman	94.5	57%	-	-	34%	-	9%	
Contreras,Jose	92.0	50%	-	-	33%	-	16%	
Cook,Aaron	89.8	75%	15%	7%	3%	<1%		
Cook,Ryan	95.1	69%	-	-	28%	3%	-	
Corbin,Patrick	90.9	69%	-	-	16%	15%	-	
Cordero,Francisco	92.3	43%	-	6%	27%	24%	-	
Corpas,Manuel	89.2	39%	-	-	61%	-	-	
Correia,Kevin	90.3	48%	21%	12%	8%	11%	-	
Crain,Jesse	93.7	50%	-	6%	37%	7%	-	
Crawford,Evan	90.3	57%	-	22%	21%	-	-	
Crosby,Casey	90.0	54%	7%	22%	-	17%	-	
Crow,Aaron	94.5	56%	-	2%	42%	<1%	-	
Cruz,Juan	93.6	41%	30%	-	18%	10%	-	
Cruz,Rhiner	95.0	65%	-	-	28%	7%	-	
Cueto,Johnny	92.7	54%	5%	<1%	21%	18%	-	
Danks,John	90.1	49%	26%	6%	-	19%	-	
Darvish,Yu	92.8	47%	17%	14%	14%	<1%	6%	
Davis,Chris	86.2	87%	-	-	-	13%	-	
Davis,Wade	93.5	66%	-	21%	11%	3%	-	
De Fratus,Justin	93.3	65%	-	-	26%	9%	-	
de la Rosa,Dane	92.1	76%	-	22%	-	2%	-	
de la Rosa,Jorge	90.5	53%	-	<1%	10%	36%	-	
de la Rosa,Rubby	94.3	75%	-	-	5%	20%	-	
De Los Santos,Fautino	94.4	81%	-	-	16%	3%	-	
Deduno,Samuel	90.7	53%	-	25%	8%	13%	-	
Del Rosario,Enerio	88.1	78%	-	-	21%	1%	-	
Delabar,Steve	94.6	61%	-	-	4%	-	35%	
Delgado,Randall	92.0	66%	-	13%	<1%	20%	-	
Demel,Sam	92.8	44%	-	-	56%	-	-	
Dempster,Ryan	89.7	45%	11%	-	30%	-	14%	
Detwiler,Ross	92.7	80%	-	13%	-	7%	-	
DeVries,Cole	89.7	56%	-	16%	19%	9%	-	
Diamond,Scott	89.4	60%	-	29%	-	11%	-	
Dickey,R.A.	83.4	14%	-	-	-	<1%	-	Knuckleball 85%
Dickson,Brandon	89.4	60%	-	-	34%	7%	-	
Diekman,Jake	95.0	68%	-	-	27%	5%	-	
Dillard,Tim	86.8	60%	-	-	37%	3%	-	
Dolis,Rafael	95.1	84%	-	-	15%	<1%	-	
Doolittle,Sean	93.6	87%	-	9%	-	4%	-	

Player	Fastball Velocity	Fastball	Cutter	Curve	Slider	Change	Splitter	Other
Dotel,Octavio	92.4	80%	-	8%	12%	-	-	
Doubront,Felix	92.7	63%	6%	16%	-	15%	-	
Downs,Darin	90.6	49%	-	13%	33%	5%	-	
Downs,Scott	88.7	82%	-	18%	-	-	-	
Drabek,Kyle	92.6	62%	15%	12%	-	11%	-	
Duensing,Brian	91.7	58%	-	9%	24%	10%	-	
Duffy,Danny	95.3	68%	-	18%	3%	11%	-	
Duke,Zach	89.0	61%	-	13%	8%	17%	-	
Dunn,Mike	94.4	61%	-	10%	29%	<1%	-	
Durbin,Chad	90.4	48%	38%	8%	-	7%	-	
Dyson,Sam	92.0	88%	-	4%	-	8%	-	
Edgin,Josh	93.3	69%	-	-	28%	3%	-	
Edlefsen,Steve	90.8	69%	-	-	21%	10%	-	
Egbert,Jack	87.5	57%	-	-	14%	29%	-	
Ekstrom,Mike	92.3	61%	-	-	37%	2%	-	
Elbert,Scott	92.2	59%	-	-	39%	2%	-	
Ely,John	90.2	60%	7%	1%	-	31%	-	
Enright,Barry	90.3	56%	-	11%	25%	8%	-	
Eovaldi,Nathan	94.1	64%	-	9%	21%	6%	-	
Eppley,Cody	87.8	82%	-	-	15%	3%	-	
Escalona,Edgmer	94.2	60%	-	-	35%	5%	-	
Estrada,Marco	90.2	60%	<1%	22%	-	18%	-	
Eveland,Dana	89.2	52%	8%	2%	29%	10%	-	
Familia,Jeurys	95.6	80%	-	-	15%	5%	-	
Farnsworth,Kyle	93.2	56%	12%	-	32%	-	-	
Feldman,Scott	91.7	34%	32%	23%	-	-	11%	
Feliz,Neftali	94.7	65%	-	5%	16%	14%	-	
Fick,Chuckie	89.7	63%	-	-	28%	9%	-	
Fien,Casey	92.8	54%	27%	-	19%	-	-	
Fiers,Mike	88.1	54%	14%	21%	-	10%	-	
Fife,Stephen	89.1	54%	-	23%	18%	5%	-	
Figueroa,Pedro	95.0	77%	-	-	14%	10%	-	
Fister,Doug	88.9	53%	-	20%	14%	13%	-	
Floyd,Gavin	91.5	45%	30%	19%	-	6%	-	
Font,Wilmer	94.9	77%	-	-	13%	9%	-	
Francis,Jeff	85.3	50%	7%	20%	-	23%	-	
Francisco,Frank	93.9	65%	-	4%	2%	-	28%	
Frasor,Jason	93.0	75%	-	-	14%	-	11%	
Freeman,Sam	93.4	72%	-	-	18%	10%	-	
Friedrich,Christian	91.8	62%	-	13%	13%	11%	-	
Frieri,Ernesto	94.2	86%	-	7%	7%	<1%	-	
Fuentes,Brian	90.4	76%	-	-	7%	17%	-	
Furbush,Charlie	91.3	55%	-	9%	35%	1%	-	
Galarraga,Armando	88.6	50%	-	-	34%	16%	-	
Gallardo,Yovani	91.8	57%	-	18%	23%	2%	-	
Garcia,Christian	95.2	70%	-	11%	-	19%	-	
Garcia,Freddy	87.5	31%	-	10%	37%	8%	13%	
Garcia,Jaime	88.7	57%	17%	8%	-	18%	-	
Garza,Matt	93.6	59%	-	10%	26%	5%	-	
Gaudin,Chad	92.4	61%	-	-	27%	12%	-	
Gearrin,Cory	90.7	65%	-	-	24%	11%	-	
Gee,Dillon	90.2	51%	1%	12%	13%	23%	-	
Geltz,Steve	92.5	83%	-	-	7%	10%	-	
Gentry,Craig	82.8	100%	-	-	-	-	-	
Germano,Justin	86.1	52%	-	31%	7%	10%	-	
Godfrey,Graham	88.5	68%	-	13%	10%	10%	-	
Gomes,Brandon	90.1	42%	-	-	35%	-	22%	

Player	Fastball Velocity	Pitch Repertoire						
		Fastball	Cutter	Curve	Slider	Change	Splitter	Other
Gomez,Jeanmar	90.1	58%	10%	<1%	17%	15%	-	
Gonzalez,Edgar	89.5	52%	4%	10%	19%	15%	-	
Gonzalez,Gio	93.1	71%	-	21%	-	8%	-	
Gonzalez,Michael	91.5	56%	-	-	36%	8%	-	
Gonzalez,Miguel	91.4	62%	-	9%	17%	-	12%	
Gorzelanny,Tom	90.9	56%	6%	-	22%	16%	-	
Gray,Jeff	92.9	54%	-	-	41%	-	5%	
Gregerson,Luke	89.2	29%	-	-	69%	2%	-	
Gregg,Kevin	91.4	51%	27%	-	16%	-	6%	
Greinke,Zack	92.4	53%	11%	17%	13%	7%	-	
Griffin,A.J.	89.8	57%	-	17%	13%	13%	-	
Grilli,Jason	93.6	72%	-	-	28%	-	-	
Grimm,Justin	92.4	61%	-	33%	-	6%	-	
Guerra,Javy	93.5	65%	-	11%	22%	2%	-	
Guerrier,Matt	90.4	36%	-	22%	38%	4%	-	
Guthrie,Jeremy	92.8	62%	-	10%	18%	10%	-	
Hacker,Eric	87.4	50%	-	24%	26%	-	-	
Hagadone,Nick	94.3	81%	-	-	19%	-	-	
Halladay,Roy	90.6	19%	42%	24%	-	-	15%	
Hamels,Cole	91.2	47%	18%	9%	-	26%	-	
Hammel,Jason	93.6	60%	-	10%	22%	7%	-	
Hampson,Justin	85.7	32%	-	20%	44%	4%	-	
Hand,Brad	90.0	68%	-	21%	-	11%	-	
Hanrahan,Joel	95.9	75%	-	-	25%	-	-	
Hanson,Tommy	89.7	55%	-	14%	30%	2%	-	
Happ,J.A.	90.5	65%	-	11%	14%	10%	-	
Harang,Aaron	89.7	60%	5%	8%	22%	5%	-	
Haren,Dan	88.5	40%	36%	6%	-	-	18%	
Harrell,Lucas	92.5	71%	12%	9%	-	8%	-	
Harris,Will	91.0	80%	-	19%	-	<1%	-	
Harrison,Matt	92.1	64%	-	15%	8%	13%	-	
Harvey,Matt	94.7	65%	-	10%	13%	12%	-	
Hatcher,Chris	93.4	68%	-	-	21%	11%	-	
Hawkins,LaTroy	92.3	70%	-	9%	19%	2%	-	
Heath,Deunte	93.5	83%	-	4%	9%	4%	-	
Hefner,Jeremy	90.2	55%	-	15%	17%	14%	-	
Hellickson,Jeremy	91.4	52%	7%	12%	-	28%	-	
Henderson,Jim	95.0	66%	-	-	34%	-	-	
Hendriks,Liam	90.0	65%	-	13%	14%	8%	-	
Hensley,Clay	85.5	65%	-	20%	6%	8%	-	
Hernandez,David	94.7	63%	-	34%	-	3%	-	
Hernandez,Felix	92.1	56%	-	13%	13%	18%	-	
Hernandez,Livan	84.0	50%	-	19%	26%	6%	-	
Hernandez,Pedro	89.8	53%	25%	2%	-	20%	-	
Hernandez,Roberto	91.4	66%	-	-	13%	21%	-	
Herndon,David	91.3	67%	-	-	23%	10%	-	
Herrera,Kelvin	98.5	65%	-	7%	<1%	29%	-	
Herrmann,Frank	94.6	73%	-	5%	22%	-	-	
Hill,Rich	92.0	43%	3%	54%	-	-	-	
Hill,Shawn	87.8	88%	-	-	5%	8%	-	
Hinshaw,Alex	91.7	53%	-	10%	37%	<1%	-	
Hochevar,Luke	92.6	53%	10%	21%	10%	5%	-	
Holland,Derek	93.0	69%	-	15%	11%	6%	-	
Holland,Greg	96.1	56%	-	<1%	40%	-	3%	
Hoover,J.J.	92.8	73%	-	20%	2%	6%	-	
Horst,Jeremy	90.6	58%	-	-	25%	17%	-	
Hottovy,Tommy	88.1	60%	-	36%	-	3%	-	

Player	Fastball Velocity	Pitch Repertoire						
		Fastball	Cutter	Curve	Slider	Change	Splitter	Other
Howell,J.P.	86.0	44%	-	40%	-	16%	-	
Hudson,Daniel	92.8	62%	5%	-	13%	20%	-	
Hudson,Tim	89.0	58%	2%	11%	21%	1%	8%	
Huff,David	90.8	63%	5%	10%	-	21%	-	
Hughes,Jared	92.4	87%	-	-	10%	3%	-	
Hughes,Phil	92.1	65%	2%	18%	4%	10%	-	
Humber,Philip	90.5	53%	-	17%	22%	8%	-	
Hunter,Tommy	92.0	60%	20%	14%	-	6%	-	
Hutchison,Drew	91.4	76%	-	-	15%	9%	-	
Igarashi,Ryota	94.7	55%	-	5%	4%	-	36%	
Isringhausen,Jason	90.0	50%	29%	21%	-	<1%	-	
Iwakuma,Hisashi	90.3	51%	-	7%	20%	-	23%	
Jackson,Edwin	93.5	54%	5%	5%	28%	8%	-	
Jansen,Kenley	91.9	94%	-	-	6%	-	-	
Janssen,Casey	91.7	51%	29%	15%	5%	<1%	-	
Jeffress,Jeremy	94.7	77%	-	21%	2%	-	-	
Jenkins,Chad	90.9	70%	-	<1%	19%	10%	-	
Jennings,Dan	90.3	64%	-	-	34%	2%	-	
Jepsen,Kevin	96.6	73%	14%	13%	-	-	-	
Jimenez,Ubaldo	92.5	57%	-	9%	16%	13%	5%	
Johnson,Jim	94.3	75%	-	12%	-	13%	-	
Johnson,Josh	92.8	55%	-	16%	24%	5%	-	
Johnson,Rob	85.0	70%	10%	20%	-	-	-	
Johnson,Steve	89.0	66%	-	14%	6%	14%	-	
Jones,Nate	97.6	67%	-	<1%	24%	8%	-	
Jurrjens,Jair	88.6	55%	-	-	14%	30%	-	
Karstens,Jeff	89.3	54%	<1%	21%	12%	12%	-	
Kelley,Shawn	92.4	51%	-	-	48%	1%	-	
Kelly,Casey	91.2	65%	-	27%	-	8%	-	
Kelly,Joe	94.4	69%	-	4%	14%	13%	-	
Kendrick,Kyle	89.9	49%	22%	3%	-	26%	-	
Kennedy,Ian	89.7	66%	8%	8%	<1%	17%	-	
Kershaw,Clayton	93.2	62%	-	11%	23%	4%	-	
Keuchel,Dallas	88.0	58%	12%	15%	-	15%	-	
Kimbrel,Craig	96.8	68%	-	32%	-	-	-	
Kinney,Josh	90.9	35%	-	14%	51%	-	-	
Kintzler,Brandon	92.7	62%	-	-	29%	10%	-	
Kirkman,Michael	94.3	65%	-	-	29%	-	6%	
Kluber,Corey	92.6	44%	26%	14%	-	17%	-	
Koehler,Tom	93.7	57%	9%	30%	-	4%	-	
Kontos,George	90.9	44%	-	-	52%	4%	-	
Korecky,Bobby	86.9	67%	-	19%	-	14%	-	
Kuroda,Hiroki	91.8	50%	-	6%	30%	-	14%	
Laffey,Aaron	86.3	54%	31%	3%	2%	9%	-	
Lannan,John	89.4	65%	-	9%	8%	18%	-	
Latos,Mat	92.6	59%	-	13%	25%	4%	-	
Layne,Tom	89.5	46%	28%	23%	-	4%	-	
League,Brandon	95.2	67%	-	-	6%	-	27%	
Leake,Mike	89.6	46%	24%	9%	10%	10%	-	
LeBlanc,Wade	87.0	43%	27%	8%	-	22%	-	
LeCure,Sam	89.6	59%	-	17%	18%	6%	-	
Lee,Cliff	91.7	54%	20%	9%	<1%	16%	-	
Leroux,Chris	91.2	42%	-	-	57%	<1%	-	
Lester,Jon	92.6	52%	22%	14%	-	12%	-	
Lewis,Colby	87.9	55%	-	14%	22%	9%	-	
Lidge,Brad	90.2	40%	-	-	60%	-	-	
Lilly,Ted	87.6	50%	-	14%	14%	22%	-	

Player	Fastball Velocity	Fastball	Cutter	Curve	Slider	Change	Splitter	Other
Lincecum,Tim	90.4	52%	-	11%	17%	20%	-	
Lincoln,Brad	93.4	63%	-	32%	-	-	5%	
Lindblom,Josh	92.2	65%	-	7%	25%	4%	-	
Lindstrom,Matt	94.8	65%	-	-	33%	-	2%	
Liriano,Francisco	93.0	50%	-	-	33%	17%	-	
Locke,Jeff	90.8	64%	-	20%	-	16%	-	
Loe,Kameron	89.5	73%	-	26%	<1%	<1%	-	
Logan,Boone	93.5	46%	-	-	52%	2%	-	
Lohse,Kyle	89.5	53%	-	4%	23%	19%	-	
Lopez,Javier	86.8	60%	26%	-	6%	8%	-	
Lopez,Rodrigo	87.5	59%	-	-	24%	17%	-	
Lopez,Wilton	92.4	77%	-	-	5%	18%	-	
Loup,Aaron	92.1	77%	-	-	20%	3%	-	
Loux,Shane	91.2	75%	-	10%	9%	5%	-	
Lowe,Derek	87.9	65%	8%	-	15%	11%	-	
Lowe,Mark	93.9	61%	-	-	37%	2%	-	
Luebke,Cory	91.2	62%	-	7%	15%	16%	-	
Lueke,Josh	92.8	71%	-	17%	-	-	13%	
Luetge,Lucas	89.3	44%	-	7%	49%	<1%	-	
Lyles,Jordan	91.8	61%	15%	19%	-	5%	-	
Lynn,Lance	92.8	70%	-	18%	5%	7%	-	
Lyon,Brandon	90.2	35%	37%	26%	-	3%	-	
MacDougal,Mike	93.1	76%	4%	-	20%	-	-	
Machi,Jean	93.0	50%	-	-	12%	-	39%	
Maholm,Paul	87.4	41%	-	14%	30%	14%	-	
Maier,Mitch	74.4	100%	-	-	-	-	-	
Maine,Scott	91.5	62%	6%	23%	2%	7%	-	
Maloney,Matt	87.6	56%	-	-	24%	20%	-	
Manship,Jeff	91.0	54%	-	5%	29%	12%	-	
Marcum,Shaun	86.5	31%	21%	15%	14%	20%	-	
Marinez,Jhan	94.7	66%	-	-	34%	-	-	
Marmol,Carlos	94.0	51%	-	-	49%	-	-	
Maronde,Nick	92.5	76%	-	-	22%	2%	-	
Marquis,Jason	88.6	55%	5%	-	26%	14%	-	
Marshall,Sean	90.8	32%	12%	38%	17%	-	-	
Marte,Luis	91.6	49%	10%	-	26%	15%	-	
Marte,Victor	93.6	54%	-	-	34%	-	12%	
Martinez,Cristhian	89.2	45%	-	-	24%	31%	-	
Martinez,Joe	90.2	81%	-	13%	-	6%	-	
Masterson,Justin	91.9	81%	-	-	19%	-	-	
Mather,Joe	80.0	50%	-	50%	-	-	-	
Mathis,Jeff	84.0	86%	-	-	-	14%	-	
Matsuzaka,Daisuke	90.9	46%	23%	<1%	21%	8%	2%	
Mattheus,Ryan	93.4	80%	-	-	12%	-	8%	
Matusz,Brian	91.1	58%	-	8%	21%	13%	-	
Mazzaro,Vin	92.5	62%	-	<1%	31%	7%	-	
McAllister,Zach	92.1	70%	-	15%	7%	8%	-	
McCarthy,Brandon	90.7	39%	40%	19%	-	2%	-	
McClellan,Kyle	90.0	53%	22%	18%	-	8%	-	
McClendon,Mike	88.2	62%	-	-	31%	7%	-	
McCutchen,Daniel	91.3	50%	-	8%	-	-	42%	
McDonald,Darnell	83.1	100%	-	-	-	-	-	
McDonald,James	91.8	62%	-	18%	17%	3%	-	
McGee,Jake	95.7	87%	-	-	6%	7%	-	
McHugh,Collin	90.0	58%	-	26%	13%	3%	-	
McPherson,Kyle	93.0	66%	-	26%	-	8%	-	
Medlen,Kris	90.0	61%	-	18%	1%	20%	-	

362

Player	Fastball Velocity	Fastball	Cutter	Curve	Slider	Change	Splitter	Other
Meek,Evan	92.8	54%	23%	18%	5%	-	-	
Mejia,Jenrry	93.9	72%	-	20%	2%	6%	-	
Melancon,Mark	93.3	44%	26%	25%	-	5%	-	
Mendoza,Luis	92.3	68%	-	23%	-	10%	-	
Mijares,Jose	91.2	68%	-	-	26%	7%	-	
Mikolas,Miles	93.0	62%	-	35%	-	3%	-	
Miley,Wade	90.9	72%	-	1%	14%	12%	-	
Miller,Andrew	94.9	58%	-	-	39%	2%	-	
Miller,Jim	92.9	68%	-	9%	23%	-	-	
Miller,Shelby	92.9	69%	-	19%	-	11%	-	
Mills,Brad	84.7	52%	6%	13%	-	30%	-	
Millwood,Kevin	90.2	50%	20%	6%	19%	5%	-	
Milone,Tommy	87.7	48%	16%	11%	-	26%	-	
Minor,Mike	90.3	59%	-	12%	14%	15%	-	
Mitchell,D.J.	89.4	68%	-	18%	-	14%	-	
Moore,Matt	94.4	66%	-	17%	-	17%	-	
Morales,Franklin	94.4	62%	-	19%	2%	17%	-	
Morris,Bryan	94.0	48%	41%	-	11%	-	-	
Morrow,Brandon	93.0	61%	<1%	5%	21%	12%	-	
Mortensen,Clayton	88.6	35%	-	-	40%	26%	-	
Morton,Charlie	89.9	53%	-	24%	14%	8%	-	
Moscoso,Guillermo	91.3	62%	-	14%	11%	13%	-	
Moseley,Dustin	87.3	53%	13%	16%	-	18%	-	
Mota,Guillermo	91.8	58%	-	-	20%	23%	-	
Motte,Jason	96.8	72%	26%	-	-	2%	-	
Moyer,Jamie	78.6	33%	28%	9%	-	30%	-	
Moylan,Peter	88.8	86%	-	-	13%	2%	-	
Mujica,Edward	91.9	45%	-	-	9%	-	45%	
Myers,Brett	91.6	48%	-	28%	19%	5%	-	
Narveson,Chris	86.6	53%	-	17%	5%	25%	-	
Nathan,Joe	94.0	59%	-	15%	25%	<1%	-	
Neshek,Pat	89.3	10%	-	-	83%	6%	-	
Nicasio,Juan	93.5	68%	-	-	25%	7%	-	
Niemann,Jeff	90.1	58%	4%	18%	10%	-	11%	
Niese,Jon	90.4	49%	28%	19%	-	4%	-	
Noesi,Hector	92.5	60%	-	6%	19%	15%	-	
Nolasco,Ricky	90.0	45%	-	17%	24%	-	15%	
Norberto,Jordan	92.6	67%	-	-	19%	14%	-	
Norris,Bud	91.8	57%	-	-	37%	7%	-	
Nova,Ivan	93.0	54%	-	29%	14%	3%	-	
O'Day,Darren	85.1	55%	-	-	45%	-	-	
Odorizzi,Jake	90.5	71%	-	14%	3%	12%	-	
O'Flaherty,Eric	91.1	73%	-	-	24%	3%	-	
Ogando,Alexi	97.0	64%	-	-	35%	1%	-	
Ohlendorf,Ross	90.8	54%	1%	-	31%	14%	-	
Ohman,Will	88.8	59%	-	3%	37%	1%	-	
Oliver,Darren	88.3	60%	15%	-	24%	1%	-	
Oliveros,Lester	93.3	66%	-	-	25%	9%	-	
Olson,Garrett	90.2	85%	-	10%	-	5%	-	
Omogrosso,Brian	93.8	58%	-	18%	16%	8%	-	
Ondrusek,Logan	93.5	46%	24%	25%	-	-	6%	
Ortega,Jose	96.9	87%	-	-	13%	-	-	
Oswalt,Roy	91.5	58%	-	18%	7%	18%	-	
Otero,Dan	89.9	70%	-	2%	23%	4%	-	
Ottavino,Adam	94.1	52%	-	-	46%	2%	-	
Outman,Josh	93.5	57%	-	4%	23%	16%	-	
Owings,Micah	87.2	11%	71%	-	17%	1%	-	

Player	Fastball Velocity	Fastball	Cutter	Curve	Slider	Change	Splitter	Other
Padilla,Vicente	93.1	77%	-	9%	6%	9%	-	
Palmer,Matt	89.8	29%	46%	22%	-	2%	-	
Papelbon,Jonathan	93.8	71%	-	-	8%	-	20%	
Parker,Blake	91.9	54%	-	-	40%	6%	-	
Parker,Jarrod	92.4	63%	-	2%	13%	22%	-	
Parnell,Bobby	95.7	74%	-	26%	-	-	-	
Parra,Manny	92.6	56%	-	19%	<1%	11%	14%	
Paterson,Joe	83.2	56%	-	-	35%	9%	-	
Patton,Troy	89.9	50%	-	5%	34%	11%	-	
Pauley,David	88.1	61%	-	12%	16%	11%	-	
Paulino,Felipe	95.1	58%	-	7%	27%	8%	-	
Pavano,Carl	86.8	59%	-	-	13%	22%	5%	
Peavy,Jake	90.8	51%	11%	12%	15%	11%	-	
Pelfrey,Mike	93.5	63%	7%	10%	9%	-	12%	
Penny,Brad	92.3	60%	-	18%	15%	<1%	6%	
Peralta,Joel	90.3	44%	-	24%	-	-	32%	
Peralta,Wily	95.5	70%	-	2%	22%	6%	-	
Perdomo,Luis	91.8	58%	-	-	34%	8%	-	
Perez,Chris	94.0	70%	-	-	30%	-	-	
Perez,Juan	93.0	47%	-	-	53%	-	-	
Perez,Luis	93.3	61%	-	-	19%	20%	-	
Perez,Martin	92.0	61%	-	12%	8%	19%	-	
Perez,Oliver	93.7	65%	-	-	35%	-	-	
Perez,Rafael	87.7	12%	-	-	61%	28%	-	
Perkins,Glen	94.9	64%	-	-	36%	<1%	-	
Perry,Ryan	93.5	56%	10%	-	24%	10%	-	
Pestano,Vinnie	91.8	77%	-	-	23%	-	-	
Petit,Yusmeiro	88.2	60%	-	13%	21%	7%	-	
Pettitte,Andy	87.8	54%	25%	12%	-	8%	-	
Phelps,David	90.8	57%	17%	19%	-	7%	-	
Phillips,Zach	89.1	55%	-	10%	22%	13%	-	
Pomeranz,Drew	91.2	79%	-	14%	-	7%	-	
Pomeranz,Stuart	94.1	74%	-	26%	-	-	-	
Porcello,Rick	92.0	67%	-	4%	15%	14%	-	
Price,David	95.5	61%	16%	11%	-	12%	-	
Pryor,Stephen	96.3	73%	25%	2%	-	<1%	-	
Putkonen,Luke	94.6	65%	-	20%	-	-	15%	
Putnam,Zach	90.8	60%	-	-	3%	-	37%	
Putz,J.J.	92.9	70%	6%	-	-	-	23%	
Qualls,Chad	93.1	68%	-	-	30%	-	2%	
Quintana,Jose	90.4	54%	26%	15%	-	5%	-	
Raley,Brooks	88.2	50%	29%	12%	-	9%	-	
Ramirez,Elvin	93.6	78%	-	1%	7%	14%	-	
Ramirez,Erasmo	92.8	59%	-	6%	13%	22%	-	
Ramirez,Ramon (NYM)	91.1	44%	-	-	22%	34%	-	
Ramos,A.J.	93.9	48%	11%	14%	14%	13%	-	
Ramos,Cesar	91.6	69%	-	14%	7%	10%	-	
Rapada,Clay	85.4	52%	-	-	47%	1%	-	
Rauch,Jon	90.8	54%	-	5%	36%	5%	-	
Redmond,Todd	89.4	74%	-	-	21%	5%	-	
Reed,Addison	94.6	75%	-	-	14%	11%	-	
Resop,Chris	92.7	71%	5%	20%	-	4%	-	
Reynolds,Matt	89.0	53%	-	-	29%	<1%	18%	
Richard,Clayton	90.7	62%	10%	-	10%	18%	-	
Richards,Garrett	95.0	67%	-	3%	24%	5%	-	
Richmond,Scott	91.3	61%	-	39%	-	-	-	
Rivera,Mariano	90.5	7%	93%	-	-	-	-	

Player	Fastball Velocity	Pitch Repertoire						
		Fastball	Cutter	Curve	Slider	Change	Splitter	Other
Robertson,David	92.2	81%	-	18%	-	1%	-	
Robertson,Tyler	88.8	45%	-	-	53%	2%	-	
Rodney,Fernando	96.1	63%	-	-	<1%	37%	-	
Rodriguez,Aneury	91.3	63%	-	-	31%	6%	-	
Rodriguez,Fernando	93.9	66%	<1%	28%	-	6%	-	
Rodriguez,Francisco (Mil)	91.8	61%	-	19%	-	20%	-	
Rodriguez,Henry	97.7	76%	-	-	18%	6%	-	
Rodriguez,Paco	90.2	42%	37%	-	18%	4%	-	
Rodriguez,Wandy	89.3	59%	-	31%	-	10%	-	
Roenicke,Josh	92.3	62%	29%	9%	-	<1%	-	
Rogers,Esmil	95.8	64%	-	20%	16%	<1%	-	
Rogers,Mark	93.6	63%	-	11%	24%	2%	-	
Romero,J.C.	89.5	65%	-	-	19%	16%	-	
Romero,Ricky	91.2	45%	22%	14%	<1%	19%	-	
Romo,Sergio	87.7	34%	-	-	62%	5%	-	
Rosario,Sandy	94.2	65%	-	-	18%	17%	-	
Rosenberg,B.J.	95.3	70%	-	-	19%	11%	-	
Rosenthal,Trevor	97.6	80%	6%	12%	-	2%	-	
Ross,Robbie	91.8	82%	-	-	18%	-	-	
Ross,Tyson	92.5	67%	-	-	26%	7%	-	
Runzler,Dan	95.0	76%	-	13%	11%	-	-	
Rusin,Chris	88.1	48%	32%	8%	-	13%	-	
Russell,James	89.1	33%	9%	6%	39%	13%	-	
Rzepczynski,Marc	92.0	72%	-	-	23%	4%	-	
Sabathia,CC	92.3	54%	-	7%	26%	13%	-	
Saito,Takashi	90.5	70%	-	11%	19%	-	<1%	
Salas,Fernando	91.8	54%	-	-	21%	25%	-	
Sale,Chris	91.6	60%	-	-	26%	14%	-	
Samardzija,Jeff	95.0	54%	9%	2%	16%	-	19%	
Sanches,Brian	88.1	49%	-	5%	24%	-	23%	
Sanchez,Anibal	91.8	48%	-	10%	23%	20%	-	
Sanchez,Eduardo	95.0	70%	-	29%	-	<1%	-	
Sanchez,Jonathan	89.0	61%	-	-	15%	24%	-	
Santana,Ervin	91.7	57%	-	-	35%	7%	-	
Santana,Johan	88.4	58%	-	-	20%	22%	-	
Santiago,Hector	93.2	65%	8%	-	8%	13%	-	Screwball 6%
Santos,Sergio	94.8	60%	-	-	27%	13%	-	
Saunders,Joe	88.9	71%	-	15%	-	15%	-	
Savery,Joe	91.1	63%	-	-	35%	2%	-	
Scahill,Rob	94.9	76%	-	11%	12%	2%	-	
Scheppers,Tanner	96.2	68%	-	28%	-	3%	-	
Scherzer,Max	94.2	61%	-	-	20%	20%	-	
Schlereth,Daniel	90.5	45%	-	55%	-	-	-	
Schwimer,Michael	92.6	48%	-	-	45%	-	6%	
Schwinden,Chris	89.0	60%	19%	13%	-	7%	-	
Scribner,Evan	90.2	62%	4%	33%	-	1%	-	
Seddon,Chris	90.2	58%	-	5%	19%	18%	-	
Septimo,Leyson	92.6	62%	-	-	37%	2%	-	
Shaw,Bryan	90.3	2%	81%	1%	13%	2%	-	
Sheets,Ben	90.2	52%	-	28%	12%	7%	-	
Sherrill,George	85.9	77%	-	-	23%	-	-	
Shields,James	92.3	34%	19%	18%	-	29%	-	
Simon,Alfredo	94.4	53%	-	23%	13%	-	11%	
Sipp,Tony	90.7	64%	-	-	30%	6%	-	
Skaggs,Tyler	89.4	70%	-	17%	-	12%	-	
Slaten,Doug	87.9	69%	-	-	17%	13%	-	
Smith,Joe	89.5	70%	-	-	30%	-	-	

Player	Fastball Velocity	Fastball	Cutter	Curve	Slider	Change	Splitter	Other
Smith,Will	90.5	60%	-	22%	6%	13%	-	
Smyly,Drew	91.6	54%	12%	-	29%	6%	-	
Socolovich,Miguel	92.5	57%	-	-	21%	22%	-	
Soriano,Rafael	92.2	60%	-	-	40%	-	-	
Spence,Josh	83.9	45%	-	-	38%	17%	-	
Stammen,Craig	91.6	57%	-	11%	31%	<1%	-	
Stauffer,Tim	90.9	42%	32%	14%	-	12%	-	
Stewart,Zach	89.6	59%	-	3%	20%	19%	-	
Stinson,Josh	92.7	72%	-	4%	20%	3%	-	
Storen,Drew	94.6	71%	-	-	25%	4%	-	
Storey,Mickey	89.8	37%	-	22%	35%	5%	-	
Straily,Dan	91.3	58%	-	4%	25%	13%	-	
Strasburg,Stephen	95.7	65%	-	19%	-	16%	-	
Street,Huston	89.0	43%	-	-	39%	18%	-	
Strop,Pedro	96.9	69%	-	-	28%	-		4%
Stults,Eric	87.4	47%	-	10%	18%	24%	-	
Stutes,Michael	92.3	64%	-	9%	28%	-	-	
Suppan,Jeff	85.9	44%	-	11%	29%	17%	-	
Swarzak,Anthony	92.2	66%	-	7%	21%	6%	-	
Takahashi,Hisanori	88.7	54%	<1%	6%	19%	20%	-	
Tateyama,Yoshinori	87.0	55%	<1%	-	28%	16%	-	
Taylor,Andrew	87.8	40%	-	-	60%	-	-	
Tazawa,Junichi	93.7	56%	-	8%	4%	-	32%	
Teaford,Everett	90.4	41%	26%	23%	-	10%	-	
Teheran,Julio	92.1	67%	-	24%	-	9%	-	
Thatcher,Joe	86.1	73%	-	-	27%	-	-	
Thayer,Dale	93.9	71%	-	-	26%	4%	-	
Thomas,Justin	90.4	54%	-	-	20%	26%	-	
Thompson,Rich	89.0	13%	70%	18%	-	-	-	
Thornburg,Tyler	92.5	64%	-	26%	-	10%	-	
Thornton,Matt	95.0	76%	4%	-	20%	-	-	
Tillman,Chris	92.4	61%	8%	17%	-	14%	-	
Tolleson,Shawn	92.6	62%	-	-	38%	-	-	
Tomlin,Josh	89.5	39%	33%	14%	-	13%	-	
Torres,Carlos	91.4	45%	35%	19%	-	1%	-	
Turner,Jacob	91.2	57%	-	18%	16%	9%	-	
Uehara,Koji	88.9	52%	4%	-	-	-	44%	
Valdes,Raul	87.9	62%	-	-	33%	6%	-	
Valdez,Jose	93.8	44%	-	-	-	-	56%	
Valverde,Jose	93.4	82%	-	-	-	-	18%	
VandenHurk,Rick	93.7	74%	-	8%	18%	-	-	
Vargas,Jason	88.0	57%	9%	7%	-	27%	-	
Varvaro,Anthony	93.2	66%	-	28%	-	6%	-	
Vasquez,Esmerling	90.8	48%	-	10%	14%	28%	-	
Veal,Donnie	92.4	43%	-	54%	-	2%	-	
Venters,Jonny	93.7	70%	-	-	23%	7%	-	
Veras,Jose	93.8	54%	-	41%	-	-	5%	
Verdugo,Ryan	89.0	64%	-	2%	22%	13%	-	
Verlander,Justin	94.3	56%	-	15%	12%	17%	-	
Villanueva,Carlos	89.0	44%	-	12%	20%	24%	-	
Villarreal,Brayan	97.1	83%	-	-	17%	-	-	
Villarreal,Pedro	92.6	58%	-	-	33%	8%	-	
Vincent,Nick	89.7	40%	58%	-	-	2%	-	
Vogelsong,Ryan	90.8	57%	12%	18%	-	13%	-	
Volquez,Edinson	93.6	50%	-	25%	-	26%	-	
Volstad,Chris	91.2	60%	-	7%	24%	9%	-	
Wade,Cory	88.2	51%	4%	24%	6%	15%	-	

Player	Fastball Velocity	Pitch Repertoire						
		Fastball	Cutter	Curve	Slider	Change	Splitter	Other
Wainwright,Adam	90.1	42%	14%	25%	13%	6%	-	
Walden,Jordan	96.3	79%	-	-	18%	3%	-	
Waldrop,Kyle	89.0	80%	-	15%	-	5%	-	
Wall,Josh	93.5	53%	-	-	45%	1%	-	
Walters,P.J.	88.6	50%	12%	23%	-	14%	-	
Wang,Chien-Ming	91.0	77%	-	9%	9%	5%	-	
Warren,Adam	91.7	56%	-	18%	17%	9%	-	
Watson,Tony	93.6	68%	-	-	26%	7%	-	
Weaver,Jered	87.8	62%	-	11%	13%	14%	-	
Webb,Ryan	94.3	63%	-	-	29%	7%	-	
Weber,Thad	89.8	68%	-	26%	-	6%	-	
Weiland,Kyle	90.9	54%	29%	10%	-	7%	-	
Wells,Kip	89.8	49%	5%	17%	17%	13%	-	
Wells,Randy	89.2	54%	6%	-	23%	18%	-	
Werner,Andrew	87.9	50%	-	7%	13%	30%	-	
Westbrook,Jake	90.6	62%	17%	-	8%	6%	7%	
Wheeler,Dan	88.4	52%	32%	6%	-	11%	-	
White,Alex	91.2	68%	-	-	20%	-	12%	
Wieland,Joe	89.7	57%	-	21%	10%	11%	-	
Wilhelmsen,Tom	96.3	66%	-	29%	-	5%	-	
Wilk,Adam	87.2	52%	14%	8%	-	26%	-	
Williams,Jerome	91.7	51%	28%	10%	-	10%	-	
Wilson,Brian	93.4	23%	68%	-	9%	-	-	
Wilson,C.J.	91.7	51%	16%	14%	9%	9%	-	
Wilson,Justin	93.9	74%	-	3%	23%	-	-	
Wise,DeWayne	76.4	95%	-	-	-	5%	-	
Wolf,Randy	88.4	52%	-	20%	18%	10%	-	
Wood,Kerry	94.1	47%	42%	12%	-	-	-	
Wood,Travis	89.4	48%	30%	3%	9%	11%	-	
Worley,Vance	89.8	64%	20%	7%	4%	6%	-	
Wright,Jamey	91.4	48%	22%	25%	5%	-	-	
Wright,Wesley	90.7	58%	-	12%	30%	<1%	-	
Young,Chris	84.6	74%	-	1%	22%	3%	-	
Zagurski,Mike	91.8	74%	4%	-	21%	2%	-	
Zambrano,Carlos	90.0	46%	19%	2%	11%	-	21%	
Ziegler,Brad	86.1	84%	-	-	10%	7%	-	
Zimmermann,Jordan	93.9	62%	-	12%	24%	2%	-	
Zito,Barry	83.9	37%	-	20%	33%	11%	-	

Pitcher Analysis

Bill James

The eight pages of data which follow this article present a simple summary of the performance of each major league pitcher in 2012, giving for each pitcher:

a) the number of pitches that he threw,

b) the number of batters that he faced,

c-d) the number of strikeouts and walks resulting,

e-f-g) the number of ground balls, line drives, and fly balls hit off of the pitcher,

h) the number of times the pitcher was behind the batter 1-0 (one ball, no strikes),

i) the number of times the pitcher was ahead of the batter 0-1,

j) the number of times the pitcher ran a full count,

k) the number of times the pitcher had two strikes on a batter, and

l) the number of times the pitcher had a 3-ball count on a batter.

Just to hit some highlights. . .Justin Verlander led the major leagues in the number of pitches thrown (3,768), the number of batters faced (956) and the number of strikeouts (239). Edinson Volquez and Ricky Romero walked the most hitters (105 each).

Clayton Richard of the Padres got the most ground balls (400), although other pitchers got more ground balls as a percentage of batters faced. Who would be the leader would depend on what standard we use for qualification. If the standard is 162 innings, the leader would be Henderson Alvarez; if 100 innings, Derek Lowe; if 50 innings, Brad Ziegler.

The pitcher who gave up the most line drives was Kyle Lohse, 156 line drives—an interesting fact, in that Lohse was able to go 16-3 despite giving up a lot of hard contact. Giving up line drives is generally not a good thing.

This is kind of off-topic, but I'll break off topic to avoid misleading people. Pitchers who give up line drives, in general, are ineffective; in fact, the percentage of line drives surrendered is one of the MOST definitive things that marks an effective or ineffective pitcher. If you sort all major league pitchers by the percentage of line drives surrendered in 2012 (LD/BFP), you will find that the top 20% (most line drives) had an aggregate ERA of 4.50, the next 20% had an

ERA of 4.26, the middle group had an ERA of 3.99, the fourth group an ERA of 3.59, and the group that allowed the fewest line drives had an aggregate ERA of 3.42. There are very few "sorts" you can do which will so effectively distinguish levels of effectiveness.

Successful pitching is, to a large extent, simply a matter of avoiding giving up line drives. The entire reason that strikeout pitchers tend to be effective pitchers is that the strikeouts reduce the number of line drives the pitcher surrenders. Kyle Lohse gave up line drives to 18.7% of the hitters he faced—a high percentage, but not terribly high. But to lead the majors in a category like line drives surrendered, you have to throw innings, and to throw innings, you have to get outs. Whoever led the majors in line drives surrendered, then, would have to be an effective pitcher, because he would have to throw innings. So the pitchers who give up the most line drives are pitchers who pitch a lot of innings without walking anybody.

Back to business. The pitcher who surrendered the most fly balls in 2012 was Phil Hughes (282), followed by Bruce Chen (278) and Jake Peavy (278). The pitcher who was behind the most hitters 1-0 was Ricky Romero (386), followed by the Cleveland Indian combination of Ubaldo and Masterson, 383 each.

Working *ahead* of the most hitters 0-1 was. . .who would you guess? It's actually *not* Verlander; Verlander is fourth on the list. It's Cliff Lee. Lee was 0-1 on 505 hitters, followed by Clayton Kershaw, Kyle Lohse, Verlander and R. A. Dickey. The five pitchers who worked 0-1 the most often had a combined won-lost record in 2012 of 73-35—despite Cliff Lee's odd season.

Lee was #1 not only in the number of 0-1 counts, but in the percentage of 0-1 counts vs. 1-0 counts. . .#1 among starters. Lee was ahead of the hitter after one pitch 68% of the time (not counting balls in play on the first pitch), a figure exceeded by relievers Jason Motte and Craig Kimbrel, 42 Saves apiece.

Yovani Gallardo had not only the most full counts on batters, 161, but *by far* the most full counts; six other pitchers had 130 or more, but the other five were between 130 and 135. Gallardo is an outlier on that scale.

Verlander had the most two-strike counts on batters, 522, followed by Clayton Kershaw. Kershaw and Verlander both got strikeouts from 46% of their two-strike situations. The norm is 40%, but a lot of relievers have numbers that are way up there. Kimbrel got strikeouts in 69% of his two-strike situations, and Aroldis Chapman 64%. Starters never have strikeout percentages (from two-strike situations) anywhere near that high. The highest percentages for starters were for two Washington guys, Strasburg (52%) and Gio Gonzalez (50.49%).

On the other hand, Blake Beavan of Seattle was able to get strikeouts in only 23% of his two-strike situations. Have you seen Blake Beavan, by the way? The man is a beast. He's the only pitcher I've ever seen who can stand in the center of the pitcher's mound and have two shoulders in foul territory, one on each side. I'll tell you, there ain't *nobody* charging the mound on that guy. I get the feeling he's not that far away from being a dominant pitcher, but he's going to have to come up with some kind of a strikeout pitch.

Anyway, Yovani Gallardo had the most three-ball counts, 219, followed by C. J. Wilson, 205. Pitchers typically issue a walk on about 42% of three-ball counts, but the data is interesting. Jake Peavy, for example, took 169 hitters to 3-ball counts, but walked only 49 of them—suggesting that he attacks the zone when he gets to 3 balls, or perhaps that he eliminates the cutter with three balls on the hitter and uses the straight fastball. Yu Darvish took fewer hitters to three balls (168), but walked 89 of them. Big difference.

Let's talk a little bit about what we learn in a general way from having this data.

a) Pitchers are pitching ahead (0-1) more often than they are pitching behind (1-0). 80% of pitchers have more 0-1 counts than 1-0 counts. The imbalance is modest, however; the norm is 54% (that is, 54% of 0-1 and 1-0 counts on hitters are 0-1.)

b) There are few if any successful pitchers who work consistently behind the hitters. The two most successful pitchers of 2012 who worked behind the hitters more often than ahead of the hitters were Jarrod Parker of the A's and Edinson Volquez of San Diego. Parker had a pretty decent year despite working behind 51% of the hitters. Jerry Blevins and Pedro Strop had good years out of the bullpen, working behind the hitters. But of the pitchers who started out 1-0 more often than 0-1, almost half had ERAs over 5.00.

c) Is there such a thing as throwing *too many* strikes?

Not within this data, no. This profile doesn't capture everything. I've heard about the pitcher who throws too many strikes all my life, but this data doesn't show evidence of such a creature. If we sort the data into five sectors, those pitchers who started out 0-1 the highest percentage of the time had a 3.58 ERA and a .550 Winning Percentage. Those who started out 1-0 most often had a 4.62 ERA and a .428 Winning Percentage. There is no evidence in the data of a diminishing return to starting out ahead more often.

d) Does throwing a strike on the first pitch reduce the number of pitches per batter?

Not meaningfully, no. The pitchers who throw strikes on the first pitch most often threw 3.80 pitches per batter. The second group threw 3.81, the third group 3.82, the fourth group 3.88, the bottom group 3.85.

There is a very meaningful reduction in pitches thrown *per inning* when the pitcher throws a first-pitch strike. The pitchers who throw the most first-pitch strikes average 15.78 pitches per inning; those who throw the fewest average

17.03.   But that advantage comes from getting more **outs** per batter faced, thus shortening the innings, rather than from reducing the number of pitches per batter.

e) Perhaps the most surprising finding in the data is that there is very, very little variation in the number of 3-2 counts between different types of pitchers. When I sorted the pitchers by the percentage of first-pitch strikes, those who threw the most first-pitch strikes—the Cliff Lee group—had 3-2 counts on 12% of the hitters they faced. Those who threw the fewest first-pitch strikes had 3-2 counts on 13% of the hitters they faced.   Jason Motte had the one of the highest first-pitch strike percentage in the major leagues; Christian Friedrich had one of the lowest—but Motte faced more 3-2 counts than Friedrich did.

There were a very few pitchers—most notably Yovani Gallardo—who had individual outlier data on the percentage of 3-2 counts,   Gallardo faced a 3-2 count on 19% of the hitters he faced; Aaron Cook went 3-2 on only 7%. That's a meaningful difference.

But when you sort pitchers in any other way—by ERA, for example, or strikeout to walk ratio, or even by the percentage of balls put in play—you find that the scale for groups runs only, at most, from 11% to 14%, and usually only from 12% to 13%. There just isn't much difference between most pitchers as to the number of 3-2 counts that they face.

f) Working ahead of the hitters, however, clearly *does* help to control the running game.   Those pitchers who worked ahead of the hitters most often allowed an average of .53 stolen bases per nine innings. This number increases steadily as we move down the scale, and those who work behind the hitters most often allow an average of .87 stolen bases per nine innings. There is little or no difference in the stolen base *percentage* between the groups, but the number of stolen bases allowed increases substantially when pitchers work behind the hitters.

g) As has been shown by other studies, ground ball pitchers are generally not effective pitchers. Measuring ground ball rates by Ground Balls per Batter Faced, the **most** effective pitchers are those who throw the fewest ground balls, and the least effective are those who throw the most ground balls. Of course, you do get different results if you measure ground ball tendencies only by balls put in play.

I wanted to present this data, in part, because it is an essential first step toward understanding the game on a deeper level.   Suppose that you wanted to create a simulation of baseball which operated pitch by pitch. To do that, you have to know what percentage of pitches thrown by each pitcher are strikes, what percentage are balls, etc.   You have to know the things that are presented in this chart.

Maybe twenty years ago, I tried to create a pitch-by-pitch simulation of the game, but failed because I couldn't make the strike percentages and the ballin-play percentages work out right—and I could only guess at the symbiotic relationship between throwing strikes and getting good results in other categories. I realized then that this data was essential to understanding the game on a deeper level—more data than this, but at least this is a down payment.

Pitcher Analysis
Pitchers with 50+ Batters Faced in 2012

| Pitcher | Pitches | BF | K | BB | GB | LD | FB | Counts | | | | |
								1-0	0-1	Full	2 Strike	3 Ball
Fernando Abad	818	208	38	19	63	31	52	81	108	29	111	37
Jeremy Accardo	624	162	29	16	53	27	36	70	74	19	80	31
Alfredo Aceves	1419	361	75	31	90	54	99	139	179	42	205	61
Manny Acosta	818	216	46	25	54	36	48	78	113	33	103	50
Mike Adams	865	228	45	17	74	33	51	83	121	32	125	44
Nathan Adcock	521	148	22	13	54	19	36	68	56	15	54	35
Jeremy Affeldt	1004	267	57	23	106	36	35	103	130	32	135	46
Matt Albers	895	241	44	22	94	32	44	91	111	30	112	52
Al Alburquerque	228	53	18	8	17	3	7	24	26	8	38	13
Cody Allen	539	126	27	15	32	20	31	60	56	23	71	30
Henderson Alvarez	2865	807	79	54	375	123	160	332	369	82	329	131
Hector Ambriz	324	83	22	11	21	7	15	37	38	11	42	19
Brett Anderson	527	137	25	7	61	24	17	53	74	11	66	20
Chris Archer	490	122	36	13	31	13	27	46	67	16	63	28
Jose Arredondo	1090	263	62	34	74	33	56	116	130	42	145	70
Jake Arrieta	1956	496	109	35	149	81	110	214	232	67	246	112
Bronson Arroyo	2958	835	129	35	271	138	245	267	442	78	387	111
Jairo Asencio	679	175	29	19	51	30	44	85	72	28	86	43
Scott Atchison	699	200	36	9	84	26	42	77	97	16	85	29
Phillippe Aumont	248	65	14	9	29	1	9	32	25	10	32	17
Luis Avilan	548	142	33	10	45	19	31	64	64	17	67	29
Dylan Axelrod	948	231	40	21	74	31	60	95	114	41	130	55
John Axford	1405	310	93	39	81	42	52	143	146	67	194	98
Luis Ayala	1206	320	51	14	121	48	78	127	156	37	146	51
Burke Badenhop	918	262	42	12	108	46	50	89	143	22	117	33
Andrew Bailey	310	74	14	8	17	12	23	33	33	16	41	21
Homer Bailey	3334	874	168	52	287	126	226	301	476	106	436	145
Collin Balester	298	83	12	11	18	9	29	39	33	10	32	20
Grant Balfour	1263	289	72	28	67	44	76	114	161	53	184	75
Daniel Bard	1045	277	38	43	80	40	63	120	132	31	118	73
Scott Barnes	337	82	16	7	20	13	22	38	39	12	45	17
Anthony Bass	1524	411	80	39	137	57	90	176	189	51	187	82
Antonio Bastardo	948	224	81	26	31	25	56	94	110	39	136	60
Miguel Batista	970	244	36	33	78	38	53	129	98	30	108	63
Trevor Bauer	323	77	17	13	20	11	13	28	40	15	38	23
Brandon Beachy	1331	319	68	29	90	39	89	125	169	41	181	64
Pedro Beato	212	51	12	5	16	6	10	25	25	9	32	11
Blake Beavan	2303	638	67	24	193	115	220	220	344	64	287	97
Chad Beck	262	72	9	5	29	12	17	32	31	7	30	12
Josh Beckett	2630	730	132	52	225	110	194	283	356	72	341	111
Erik Bedard	2134	557	118	56	159	86	122	212	282	77	293	119
Ronald Belisario	1075	286	69	29	118	38	27	111	146	31	143	53
Matt Belisle	1281	348	69	18	127	60	64	121	194	24	186	38
Jeff Beliveau	361	86	17	12	24	6	25	37	45	10	52	17
Heath Bell	1185	286	59	29	90	45	57	117	146	49	159	69
Duane Below	692	189	29	8	57	40	52	79	90	17	95	25
Joaquin Benoit	1209	288	84	22	63	36	77	120	149	36	178	59
Brad Bergesen	412	121	18	7	40	24	28	41	64	8	49	14
Jason Berken	333	95	11	7	36	15	24	37	46	5	32	13
Rafael Betancourt	916	236	57	12	59	30	75	102	106	19	131	31
Chad Billingsley	2381	634	128	45	203	96	148	250	310	75	305	114
Nick Blackburn	1628	456	42	26	173	73	137	195	211	46	170	67
Travis Blackley	1661	444	71	32	158	58	115	182	209	58	207	89
Joe Blanton	2927	806	166	34	263	138	189	309	401	79	391	108
Jerry Blevins	1021	261	54	25	65	30	74	125	110	33	127	57
Mitchell Boggs	1077	296	58	21	107	39	57	105	150	34	126	56
Michael Bowden	649	165	32	17	44	17	51	53	94	22	86	33
Brad Boxberger	567	120	33	18	27	9	31	65	54	18	83	35
Brad Brach	1169	280	75	33	59	34	75	124	137	40	152	66
Craig Breslow	1067	261	61	22	77	33	61	109	123	38	134	58
Zach Britton	1069	270	53	32	110	29	42	133	119	38	133	65
Rex Brothers	1160	295	83	37	80	39	51	144	122	29	156	66
Barret Browning	300	84	11	7	31	13	18	36	37	9	39	14
Jonathan Broxton	937	238	45	17	91	37	41	101	114	30	124	49
Clay Buchholz	2900	802	129	64	278	114	192	298	393	86	360	140
Mark Buehrle	3061	828	125	40	260	141	229	323	407	97	367	151

Pitcher Analysis
Pitchers with 50+ Batters Faced in 2012

Pitcher	Pitches	BF	K	BB	GB	LD	FB	Counts				
								1-0	0-1	Full	2 Strike	3 Ball
Francisley Bueno	214	69	7	2	33	9	16	26	33	5	20	8
Madison Bumgarner	3269	849	191	49	282	111	196	318	431	116	435	157
A.J. Burnett	3042	851	180	62	333	110	142	331	396	102	406	149
Alex Burnett	1141	309	36	26	125	44	71	119	157	30	150	53
Sean Burnett	948	239	57	12	93	32	37	96	121	29	127	42
Cory Burns	335	92	18	10	35	13	13	37	46	8	42	15
Jared Burton	939	245	55	16	81	28	58	87	125	22	133	43
Tim Byrdak	525	125	34	18	23	16	29	59	60	21	72	33
Alberto Cabrera	390	99	27	18	22	10	20	45	45	12	51	26
Trevor Cahill	3172	839	156	74	350	92	130	312	427	108	394	168
Matt Cain	3345	876	193	51	223	125	249	327	449	104	447	138
Shawn Camp	1188	327	54	21	118	48	83	131	158	31	153	56
Carter Capps	472	109	28	11	28	19	22	49	52	19	70	25
Matt Capps	446	120	18	4	41	19	38	47	64	7	54	14
Chris Capuano	2976	817	162	54	232	118	225	271	445	85	397	134
Chris Carpenter (Stl)	259	72	12	3	21	11	22	20	40	7	32	10
David Carpenter (Tor)	627	163	31	16	46	25	39	62	80	20	86	31
David Carpenter (LAA)	637	172	28	17	57	27	41	85	66	22	70	41
Joel Carreno	386	97	16	14	24	12	28	47	41	19	46	31
Robert Carson	230	57	5	4	15	10	20	26	28	7	28	11
Andrew Cashner	792	196	52	19	64	27	29	89	89	36	110	49
Santiago Casilla	1001	272	55	22	105	29	57	129	117	24	118	43
Lendy Castillo	342	88	13	12	21	18	19	35	43	15	44	23
Brett Cecil	1021	270	51	23	68	40	76	128	118	33	130	49
Xavier Cedeno	558	138	36	14	42	13	29	69	57	19	78	29
Jhoulys Chacin	1160	314	45	32	89	56	86	130	146	36	142	68
Joba Chamberlain	361	95	22	6	29	15	20	44	47	8	49	17
Aroldis Chapman	1203	276	122	23	47	25	54	128	129	47	192	65
Jaye Chapman	205	50	12	10	13	6	8	25	23	6	23	16
Tyler Chatwood	1166	294	41	33	120	45	48	136	135	42	130	73
Jesse Chavez	474	123	30	11	28	22	27	46	60	16	69	22
Bruce Chen	3193	827	140	47	203	139	278	296	430	83	440	118
Wei-Yin Chen	3137	818	154	57	218	122	247	327	408	89	424	140
Randy Choate	649	168	38	18	64	20	19	81	73	21	82	37
Steve Cishek	1102	275	68	29	87	27	52	118	127	39	146	60
Tyler Clippard	1290	307	84	29	54	25	103	115	155	45	179	61
Tyler Cloyd	528	138	30	7	31	18	47	41	79	14	68	23
Alex Cobb	2169	569	106	40	238	81	86	215	292	73	283	102
Todd Coffey	325	83	18	9	33	10	11	38	37	12	39	16
Phil Coke	932	245	51	18	82	35	51	106	116	21	125	39
Casey Coleman	460	119	16	12	37	21	31	56	53	14	47	27
Louis Coleman	950	217	65	26	24	27	69	92	104	40	142	54
Tim Collins	1229	295	93	34	65	26	68	137	126	54	179	72
Josh Collmenter	1500	375	80	22	98	51	113	153	190	44	200	66
Bartolo Colon	2141	636	91	23	234	92	186	207	334	43	280	73
Jose Contreras	214	56	15	3	19	8	10	28	23	8	29	13
Aaron Cook	1353	411	20	21	214	67	84	157	195	27	141	54
Ryan Cook	1137	288	80	27	81	27	65	145	126	32	161	58
Patrick Corbin	1597	454	86	25	153	78	104	189	204	42	192	67
Francisco Cordero	750	192	31	18	53	32	49	93	79	28	86	43
Manuel Corpas	707	205	28	16	68	29	57	75	87	15	81	34
Kevin Correia	2565	728	89	46	292	112	166	279	326	83	304	120
Jesse Crain	851	194	60	23	40	21	47	87	92	37	117	53
Casey Crosby	241	59	9	11	20	9	10	23	31	12	32	18
Aaron Crow	965	260	65	22	90	32	48	121	115	28	130	48
Juan Cruz	671	162	33	19	39	32	34	76	77	31	87	42
Rhiner Cruz	980	253	46	29	68	43	63	99	129	43	116	67
Johnny Cueto	3449	888	170	49	314	139	189	327	460	114	443	163
John Danks	834	238	30	23	73	39	65	104	97	21	99	41
Yu Darvish	3166	816	221	89	225	108	154	340	399	106	441	168
Wade Davis	1236	284	87	29	64	36	66	122	144	50	189	65
Jorge de la Rosa	204	53	6	2	15	6	23	20	30	3	27	6
Samuel Deduno	1335	347	57	53	134	49	47	158	155	44	157	82
Enerio Del Rosario	361	97	11	7	31	21	25	48	38	10	43	18
Steve Delabar	1142	274	92	26	63	23	61	118	136	43	160	63
Randall Delgado	1616	401	76	42	135	59	75	160	204	67	197	104
Ryan Dempster	2748	717	153	52	217	104	178	281	359	85	375	123
Ross Detwiler	2541	686	105	52	257	83	166	271	334	79	316	129
Cole DeVries	1471	375	58	18	90	69	131	152	184	52	182	76

Pitcher Analysis
Pitchers with 50+ Batters Faced in 2012

Pitcher	Pitches	BF	K	BB	GB	LD	FB	Counts				
								1-0	0-1	Full	2 Strike	3 Ball
Scott Diamond	2520	714	90	31	311	122	149	274	360	59	304	91
R.A. Dickey	3359	927	230	54	287	123	212	350	478	73	484	113
Jake Diekman	535	131	35	20	36	17	16	59	62	19	74	38
Tim Dillard	605	166	29	14	65	23	32	67	75	19	75	31
Rafael Dolis	654	173	24	23	55	38	28	92	66	20	70	47
Sean Doolittle	787	191	60	11	40	17	57	64	104	20	117	27
Octavio Dotel	915	234	62	12	62	30	63	86	118	24	137	38
Felix Doubront	2868	709	167	71	200	107	151	295	354	106	405	157
Darin Downs	352	86	20	9	22	16	17	39	39	14	45	23
Scott Downs	712	194	32	17	87	26	31	75	96	21	84	35
Kyle Drabek	1305	317	47	47	119	39	62	159	136	52	139	96
Brian Duensing	1706	472	69	27	175	74	121	187	225	51	204	79
Danny Duffy	527	121	28	18	26	16	122	33	149	58	54	21	66	38
Zach Duke	217	56	10	4	16	11	13	26	22	9	30	15
Mike Dunn	897	208	47	29	43	36	49	95	98	38	123	57
Chad Durbin	996	257	49	28	84	28	64	101	124	40	117	64
Josh Edgin	426	107	30	10	24	9	29	52	45	12	56	21
Steve Edlefsen	253	69	9	6	35	11	8	36	28	11	28	14
Mike Ekstrom	259	72	9	2	26	14	17	29	31	8	29	10
Scott Elbert	551	133	29	13	30	21	36	60	60	23	78	32
Nathan Eovaldi	2066	526	78	47	179	91	123	222	249	62	250	110
Cody Eppley	743	194	32	17	85	29	27	79	88	27	96	41
Edgmer Escalona	379	97	21	7	24	14	29	45	45	6	45	13
Marco Estrada	2246	562	143	29	130	77	172	216	289	71	329	98
Dana Eveland	511	145	18	13	52	19	37	65	58	19	59	29
Jeurys Familia	208	52	10	9	16	6	11	30	20	6	21	16
Kyle Farnsworth	439	120	25	14	43	10	25	42	61	19	63	25
Scott Feldman	2106	536	96	32	171	105	129	208	274	72	264	106
Neftali Feliz	737	175	37	23	42	17	54	82	80	29	94	49
Chuckie Fick	439	116	17	18	34	19	22	53	53	12	49	27
Casey Fien	594	141	32	9	24	24	49	61	64	23	82	33
Mike Fiers	2152	539	135	36	116	100	139	214	272	65	306	95
Stephen Fife	421	115	20	12	31	18	27	45	56	12	53	22
Pedro Figueroa	342	89	14	15	24	10	25	45	35	12	42	23
Doug Fister	2517	673	137	37	247	108	129	252	346	73	335	110
Gavin Floyd	2758	724	144	63	234	90	172	290	342	99	361	142
Jeff Francis	1858	502	76	22	190	71	117	216	240	47	207	80
Frank Francisco	798	197	47	21	42	36	50	94	86	31	107	47
Jason Frasor	822	191	53	22	43	26	43	65	114	33	122	42
Sam Freeman	346	86	18	10	25	8	21	38	42	9	42	20
Christian Friedrich	1394	377	74	30	111	61	91	181	149	42	170	70
Ernesto Frieri	1199	269	98	30	35	28	70	119	134	43	184	59
Brian Fuentes	526	142	24	15	36	24	36	70	65	14	65	25
Charlie Furbush	745	182	53	16	44	23	39	75	86	24	108	40
Armando Galarraga	433	120	17	18	34	15	32	55	43	16	49	28
Yovani Gallardo	3479	860	204	81	265	116	175	375	389	161	448	219
Freddy Garcia	1767	461	89	35	132	82	114	188	223	61	220	85
Jaime Garcia	1757	515	98	30	201	76	97	190	247	50	232	77
Matt Garza	1699	424	96	32	131	54	92	160	223	57	239	82
Chad Gaudin	1154	302	57	26	84	50	72	122	141	36	156	61
Cory Gearrin	279	80	20	5	29	12	12	29	38	10	39	12
Dillon Gee	1752	463	97	29	160	64	94	186	239	47	238	71
Justin Germano	1154	320	52	21	106	51	75	122	158	29	147	48
Graham Godfrey	365	98	10	10	21	20	32	49	42	12	37	22
Brandon Gomes	328	83	15	12	19	12	21	32	42	8	41	19
Jeanmar Gomez	1460	395	47	34	148	57	101	173	181	51	158	80
Edgar Gonzalez	426	105	18	8	36	14	28	41	55	19	54	27
Gio Gonzalez	3198	822	207	76	249	113	155	337	387	132	410	183
Michael Gonzalez	618	151	39	16	37	21	35	76	56	29	82	45
Miguel Gonzalez	1686	434	77	35	109	70	133	148	240	45	241	69
Tom Gorzelanny	1156	306	62	30	87	42	74	152	120	37	148	66
Jeff Gray	845	236	26	22	74	43	65	89	122	22	105	34
Luke Gregerson	1101	294	72	21	96	34	61	118	142	25	163	43
Kevin Gregg	811	200	37	24	65	25	46	77	108	35	104	51
Zack Greinke	3383	868	200	54	297	131	176	354	433	130	428	177
A.J. Griffin	1421	336	64	19	94	59	98	129	185	45	194	68
Jason Grilli	998	244	90	22	39	31	57	103	115	33	152	47
Justin Grimm	249	65	13	3	21	14	13	26	32	8	31	12
Javy Guerra	749	196	37	23	62	28	38	96	80	27	85	44

Pitcher Analysis
Pitchers with 50+ Batters Faced in 2012

Pitcher	Pitches	BF	K	BB	GB	LD	FB	Counts 1-0	0-1	Full	2 Strike	3 Ball
Matt Guerrier	218	56	9	7	15	4	18	27	22	4	28	9
Jeremy Guthrie	2922	788	101	50	251	142	222	320	384	82	339	140
Nick Hagadone	463	116	26	15	25	16	32	47	56	17	59	27
Roy Halladay	2388	646	132	36	208	107	150	224	348	68	338	90
Cole Hamels	3316	867	216	52	250	124	202	322	443	102	463	140
Jason Hammel	1932	493	113	42	176	62	93	215	225	71	256	106
Joel Hanrahan	1012	254	67	36	55	23	64	102	130	35	139	58
Tommy Hanson	2916	761	161	71	202	105	200	286	374	116	371	173
J.A. Happ	2538	627	144	56	180	70	159	229	337	104	341	140
Aaron Harang	3096	786	131	85	211	112	224	341	358	120	371	182
Dan Haren	2849	747	142	38	218	114	218	268	402	91	357	121
Lucas Harrell	3188	827	140	78	341	121	134	343	402	103	383	163
Will Harris	333	89	19	6	22	14	24	41	35	9	46	15
Matt Harrison	3247	876	133	59	331	136	209	335	430	104	398	156
Matt Harvey	978	245	70	26	53	34	52	96	121	32	140	50
Chris Hatcher	292	66	10	6	18	11	20	31	32	12	39	19
LaTroy Hawkins	705	178	23	13	79	24	36	91	75	25	78	36
Jeremy Hefner	1508	408	62	18	138	62	115	146	210	43	185	61
Jeremy Hellickson	2994	741	124	59	227	114	202	295	380	113	390	155
Jim Henderson	532	131	45	13	30	16	25	45	74	15	81	27
Liam Hendriks	1463	381	50	26	121	71	103	174	166	48	173	74
Clay Hensley	898	234	42	30	77	21	54	96	109	38	119	54
David Hernandez	1083	278	98	22	48	34	71	97	153	39	173	51
Felix Hernandez	3420	939	223	56	311	143	182	350	459	110	457	148
Livan Hernandez	1111	292	48	16	87	47	84	131	133	44	131	65
Roberto Hernandez	231	62	2	3	28	10	17	26	28	8	25	12
Kelvin Herrera	1291	344	77	21	131	47	58	143	171	31	179	54
Frank Herrmann	295	71	14	4	21	9	23	32	34	15	42	20
Rich Hill	347	83	21	11	22	12	17	31	46	9	53	18
Alex Hinshaw	546	135	36	21	30	15	30	72	57	11	72	32
Luke Hochevar	3007	800	144	61	247	124	200	325	391	100	376	157
Derek Holland	2756	730	145	52	226	88	210	295	348	97	343	143
Greg Holland	1156	289	91	34	72	29	58	144	125	37	162	66
J.J. Hoover	521	123	31	13	18	15	43	50	64	27	72	35
Jeremy Horst	494	125	40	14	30	11	27	47	67	16	72	25
J.P. Howell	822	203	42	22	64	26	41	85	103	36	116	52
Daniel Hudson	801	202	37	12	56	40	54	90	92	29	104	39
Tim Hudson	2623	749	102	48	319	111	145	285	350	74	320	109
David Huff	432	114	19	5	33	15	39	38	68	14	55	22
Jared Hughes	1162	316	50	22	140	41	54	145	122	39	130	62
Phil Hughes	3219	815	165	46	192	118	282	280	457	113	445	145
Philip Humber	1767	462	85	44	113	72	139	165	257	70	232	102
Tommy Hunter	2079	573	77	27	207	91	158	230	268	50	259	75
Drew Hutchison	987	257	49	20	79	45	53	119	115	34	125	54
Jason Isringhausen	776	198	31	19	65	30	51	96	87	22	93	42
Hisashi Iwakuma	1916	519	101	43	191	75	100	210	249	53	257	81
Edwin Jackson	2968	790	168	58	259	92	196	299	391	86	379	143
Kenley Jansen	1052	252	99	22	42	24	62	99	146	31	168	43
Casey Janssen	948	242	67	11	68	34	58	91	126	29	138	41
Jeremy Jeffress	287	73	13	13	22	12	12	34	29	10	34	23
Chad Jenkins	454	136	16	11	46	15	35	53	60	10	52	18
Dan Jennings	337	86	8	11	29	13	23	45	36	14	33	27
Kevin Jepsen	709	178	38	12	43	28	51	86	74	28	88	38
Ubaldo Jimenez	3123	805	143	95	212	129	211	383	351	118	376	202
Jim Johnson	1022	269	41	15	129	34	44	115	121	35	114	54
Josh Johnson	3145	798	165	65	254	130	166	337	380	130	401	182
Steve Johnson	671	151	46	18	20	21	44	62	82	29	100	37
Nate Jones	1168	301	65	32	91	45	64	136	134	40	150	64
Jair Jurrjens	830	227	19	18	72	41	73	80	118	28	104	37
Jeff Karstens	1313	372	66	15	103	74	103	129	197	25	172	38
Shawn Kelley	750	190	45	15	36	25	64	76	95	22	102	39
Casey Kelly	505	136	26	10	53	16	26	65	58	15	65	24
Joe Kelly	1695	457	75	36	171	69	91	184	215	58	199	92
Kyle Kendrick	2511	674	116	49	229	87	176	247	344	78	325	120
Ian Kennedy	3380	899	187	55	230	127	260	310	457	97	449	140
Clayton Kershaw	3469	901	229	63	272	111	197	319	491	117	493	167
Dallas Keuchel	1388	377	38	39	150	50	88	168	161	54	149	83
Craig Kimbrel	936	231	116	14	48	19	31	68	147	23	170	32
Josh Kinney	526	136	36	15	35	12	32	49	71	14	77	25

Pitcher Analysis
Pitchers with 50+ Batters Faced in 2012

Pitcher	Pitches	BF	K	BB	GB	LD	FB	Counts				
								1-0	0-1	Full	2 Strike	3 Ball
Brandon Kintzler	298	72	14	7	26	14	11	22	42	12	42	16
Michael Kirkman	629	151	38	17	35	20	40	67	69	24	79	39
Corey Kluber	1083	281	54	18	91	45	67	121	135	37	137	56
Tom Koehler	209	56	13	2	10	11	20	22	24	6	29	9
George Kontos	647	177	44	12	61	18	40	71	88	18	93	25
Hiroki Kuroda	3330	891	167	51	342	119	193	367	427	96	409	139
Aaron Laffey	1558	429	48	37	166	63	104	200	175	43	160	77
John Lannan	509	144	17	14	58	22	22	66	61	15	52	30
Mat Latos	3271	858	185	64	268	108	212	324	460	87	441	138
Tom Layne	280	68	25	3	18	8	10	30	34	11	40	13
Brandon League	1107	301	54	33	105	56	48	146	123	35	128	64
Mike Leake	2714	757	116	41	287	144	156	283	359	90	323	126
Wade LeBlanc	1078	284	43	19	73	42	97	102	152	33	138	48
Sam LeCure	950	237	61	23	70	31	46	80	134	41	140	53
Cliff Lee	3099	847	207	28	268	108	220	242	505	80	459	112
Jon Lester	3424	876	166	68	307	137	180	366	429	117	422	178
Colby Lewis	1627	427	93	14	103	66	143	131	254	44	228	62
Brad Lidge	208	51	10	11	15	4	10	19	29	8	22	18
Ted Lilly	707	202	31	19	60	30	55	64	109	20	91	36
Tim Lincecum	3299	825	190	90	239	124	158	369	385	135	421	195
Brad Lincoln	1323	362	88	24	98	53	94	147	159	34	184	56
Josh Lindblom	1237	304	70	35	68	39	83	132	133	50	163	67
Matt Lindstrom	774	200	40	14	71	31	38	81	94	28	103	42
Francisco Liriano	2715	693	167	87	185	90	147	321	316	94	342	174
Jeff Locke	563	148	34	11	49	15	36	56	74	21	78	28
Kameron Loe	1076	303	55	20	125	43	50	119	150	27	137	44
Boone Logan	953	239	68	28	53	31	54	91	129	35	138	54
Kyle Lohse	3127	864	143	38	265	156	233	272	489	82	413	123
Javier Lopez	568	153	28	14	65	21	23	60	80	14	73	30
Wilton Lopez	931	260	54	8	104	45	40	88	133	22	131	29
Aaron Loup	434	117	21	2	51	16	25	50	63	13	53	20
Shane Loux	409	112	9	9	46	23	24	44	53	15	41	23
Derek Lowe	2338	640	55	51	311	104	110	276	287	72	234	131
Mark Lowe	637	162	28	13	41	27	53	60	81	30	83	41
Cory Luebke	512	130	23	8	46	18	32	47	67	18	68	22
Lucas Luetge	711	178	38	24	53	27	33	70	90	33	91	47
Jordan Lyles	2364	628	99	42	253	80	136	243	309	83	300	119
Lance Lynn	3002	744	180	64	210	115	154	291	395	107	407	162
Brandon Lyon	979	258	63	20	63	31	74	105	125	37	124	55
Paul Maholm	2971	786	140	53	291	121	156	286	414	112	380	151
Scott Maine	527	127	32	15	20	24	30	66	56	23	72	36
Matt Maloney	147	52	5	1	19	10	16	19	21	3	14	4
Jeff Manship	387	98	12	7	39	16	22	40	49	15	47	21
Shaun Marcum	2069	527	109	41	129	84	151	198	285	80	278	108
Carlos Marmol	1110	247	72	45	52	25	51	129	106	56	156	83
Jason Marquis	2046	561	91	42	218	86	111	263	245	61	232	111
Sean Marshall	1007	256	74	16	90	32	38	108	124	27	145	38
Luis Marte	344	93	19	9	19	10	34	34	49	8	48	13
Victor Marte	637	185	36	14	61	31	37	79	76	17	78	30
Cristhian Martinez	1179	313	65	19	104	50	71	116	168	31	160	45
Justin Masterson	3426	906	159	88	352	122	158	383	411	111	424	178
Daisuke Matsuzaka	846	215	41	20	59	27	63	98	91	31	109	45
Ryan Mattheus	1012	265	41	19	98	42	57	108	127	32	125	57
Brian Matusz	1702	441	81	41	126	61	123	175	220	50	236	81
Vin Mazzaro	712	198	26	19	67	40	39	88	85	19	78	34
Zach McAllister	2119	543	110	38	158	75	157	213	277	62	287	93
Brandon McCarthy	1652	469	73	24	143	86	124	155	260	45	202	63
Kyle McClellan	280	83	11	9	27	11	23	33	37	9	38	13
Mike McClendon	230	69	4	5	27	12	15	27	34	6	26	14
James McDonald	2802	713	151	69	185	101	186	321	322	83	359	151
Jake McGee	920	212	73	11	55	24	46	80	109	27	144	35
Collin McHugh	396	99	17	8	23	19	27	39	48	12	52	20
Kyle McPherson	441	107	21	7	35	10	31	41	57	11	55	20
Kris Medlen	1885	520	120	23	199	69	105	179	281	44	279	57
Evan Meek	195	57	8	6	14	15	12	26	24	4	22	10
Jenrry Mejia	299	74	8	9	37	6	12	34	35	9	39	16
Mark Melancon	739	194	41	12	68	32	36	72	100	23	100	34
Luis Mendoza	2532	709	104	59	273	109	142	296	314	74	267	130
Jose Mijares	970	242	57	21	54	41	61	101	125	23	138	44

Pitcher Analysis
Pitchers with 50+ Batters Faced in 2012

Pitcher	Pitches	BF	K	BB	GB	LD	FB	Counts 1-0	0-1	Full	2 Strike	3 Ball
Miles Mikolas	518	144	23	15	54	20	28	64	57	17	64	26
Wade Miley	3002	807	144	37	262	139	204	325	395	74	390	111
Andrew Miller	687	169	51	20	41	22	32	76	80	33	94	45
Jim Miller	853	211	44	27	48	28	60	90	102	37	117	51
Shelby Miller	196	54	16	4	14	5	14	23	28	5	29	9
Kevin Millwood	2596	689	107	56	228	111	171	283	334	101	326	142
Tommy Milone	3033	791	137	36	230	149	225	250	449	80	411	109
Mike Minor	2863	728	145	56	180	106	222	301	357	97	365	153
Matt Moore	3023	759	175	81	183	96	210	304	383	106	412	171
Franklin Morales	1342	325	76	30	84	41	87	142	164	57	175	74
Brandon Morrow	1970	504	108	41	143	66	139	203	252	68	266	105
Clayton Mortensen	700	173	41	19	51	19	42	79	83	20	91	38
Charlie Morton	795	223	25	11	100	37	40	86	111	25	96	34
Guillermo Moscoso	911	231	47	19	56	41	65	93	118	35	119	47
Guillermo Mota	383	91	24	8	20	16	20	38	43	19	51	28
Jason Motte	1125	279	86	17	70	34	68	80	171	35	171	48
Jamie Moyer	919	254	36	18	81	36	73	106	113	30	97	48
Edward Mujica	887	258	47	12	97	31	64	78	136	23	113	30
Brett Myers	986	272	41	15	108	47	56	108	130	29	138	40
Joe Nathan	1073	257	78	13	74	35	54	89	155	35	167	45
Pat Neshek	332	77	16	6	19	9	26	28	45	11	53	16
Juan Nicasio	1023	257	54	22	69	43	62	103	128	49	139	65
Jeff Niemann	646	156	34	12	55	20	32	68	75	30	84	39
Jon Niese	3029	788	155	49	274	119	174	294	422	91	414	130
Hector Noesi	1707	453	68	39	125	60	153	162	238	58	228	82
Ricky Nolasco	2972	832	125	47	291	135	198	311	406	74	370	116
Jordan Norberto	884	212	46	22	64	17	59	96	92	45	117	66
Bud Norris	2819	733	165	66	189	102	191	310	345	103	372	144
Ivan Nova	2691	748	153	56	236	117	169	309	358	69	327	119
Darren O'Day	1007	263	69	14	58	40	73	91	145	28	141	39
Eric O'Flaherty	845	230	46	19	105	26	28	92	111	30	102	40
Alexi Ogando	1044	263	66	17	66	37	73	108	132	33	152	46
Ross Ohlendorf	905	233	39	24	45	37	74	91	111	33	114	49
Will Ohman	397	112	13	5	43	15	30	46	51	13	49	19
Darren Oliver	875	221	52	15	65	32	50	71	129	26	119	39
Brian Omogrosso	380	90	18	9	22	15	26	39	41	17	56	21
Logan Ondrusek	925	243	39	31	72	25	69	105	113	28	120	52
Roy Oswalt	1001	264	59	11	84	44	59	97	137	25	154	33
Dan Otero	186	57	8	2	30	10	5	20	32	0	20	3
Adam Ottavino	1349	339	81	34	104	57	56	140	167	44	193	68
Josh Outman	751	185	40	20	57	24	40	78	92	32	101	49
Vicente Padilla	850	218	51	15	64	28	53	89	110	21	115	41
Jonathan Papelbon	1148	284	92	18	68	30	66	109	143	38	172	52
Jarrod Parker	2830	751	140	63	237	137	161	337	323	89	362	147
Bobby Parnell	1125	288	61	20	123	34	43	119	141	46	148	63
Manny Parra	1046	273	61	35	84	41	46	128	117	36	133	65
Troy Patton	832	224	49	12	80	30	49	74	126	18	125	28
David Pauley	307	82	6	5	22	21	25	41	32	11	36	18
Felipe Paulino	637	156	39	15	45	19	37	76	72	17	83	32
Carl Pavano	915	268	33	8	91	46	84	106	122	20	112	29
Jake Peavy	3486	882	194	49	228	118	278	322	468	133	492	169
Mike Pelfrey	305	85	13	4	35	18	13	31	45	8	35	13
Brad Penny	444	133	10	9	56	28	27	56	48	18	47	23
Joel Peralta	1082	264	84	17	48	29	83	105	139	39	165	51
Wily Peralta	454	113	23	11	42	16	18	45	57	19	55	32
Luis Perdomo	303	78	8	12	28	14	14	43	30	12	31	21
Chris Perez	972	242	59	16	67	32	66	97	119	23	141	39
Luis Perez	670	175	39	16	55	21	39	78	74	22	98	33
Martin Perez	662	177	25	15	65	28	40	72	84	23	77	42
Oliver Perez	461	123	24	10	29	20	38	45	62	12	65	20
Glen Perkins	1059	281	78	16	76	34	69	103	149	23	161	37
Vinnie Pestano	1206	286	76	24	74	30	77	111	157	45	170	62
Andy Pettitte	1131	303	69	21	117	31	60	104	167	43	146	52
David Phelps	1678	414	96	38	115	50	103	159	221	63	218	91
Drew Pomeranz	1702	434	83	46	128	58	103	192	205	55	213	92
Rick Porcello	2828	783	107	44	328	149	139	291	390	72	332	121
David Price	3332	836	205	59	299	112	152	311	444	103	471	144
Stephen Pryor	439	104	27	13	23	11	28	44	49	14	59	25
Luke Putkonen	301	72	10	8	27	11	15	34	31	12	37	19

Pitcher Analysis
Pitchers with 50+ Batters Faced in 2012

Pitcher	Pitches	BF	K	BB	GB	LD	FB	Counts 1-0	0-1	Full	2 Strike	3 Ball
J.J. Putz	817	218	65	11	63	29	46	90	104	21	117	33
Chad Qualls	844	231	27	14	103	35	48	96	100	34	106	45
Jose Quintana	2168	568	81	42	202	93	133	224	287	72	256	104
Brooks Raley	415	116	16	11	33	20	34	53	49	13	42	24
Elvin Ramirez	430	102	22	20	24	15	21	42	46	22	58	36
Erasmo Ramirez	885	238	48	12	69	41	61	85	125	22	123	37
Ramon Ramirez (NYM)	1079	277	52	35	85	25	72	141	112	39	129	66
Cesar Ramos	429	120	29	10	43	16	20	44	58	9	56	20
Clay Rapada	612	155	38	17	44	22	30	53	89	22	82	31
Jon Rauch	929	233	42	12	64	32	79	98	112	33	123	45
Addison Reed	921	238	54	18	54	40	70	82	127	20	134	35
Chris Resop	1162	330	46	24	125	38	85	121	160	29	145	49
Matt Reynolds	978	249	51	17	74	43	55	98	125	29	129	43
Clayton Richard	3166	910	107	42	400	137	207	338	467	75	371	122
Garrett Richards	1192	318	47	34	105	50	76	142	143	35	132	69
David Robertson	974	248	81	19	66	29	52	88	140	30	146	43
Tyler Robertson	441	111	26	14	35	11	20	48	55	15	58	24
Fernando Rodney	1105	282	76	15	106	32	45	111	143	36	164	49
Fernando Rodriguez	1264	309	78	34	68	35	89	126	152	54	168	76
Francisco Rodriguez (Mil)	1221	305	72	31	83	51	65	120	154	52	167	73
Henry Rodriguez (Wsh)	556	131	31	22	28	14	33	61	62	28	73	40
Wandy Rodriguez	3204	875	139	56	316	135	208	299	456	89	386	147
Josh Roenicke	1444	383	54	43	138	60	77	145	193	57	167	89
Esmil Rogers	1460	348	83	30	108	52	68	143	178	51	190	80
Mark Rogers	669	165	41	14	42	23	41	64	85	30	93	40
J.C. Romero	207	62	6	3	23	12	17	28	27	5	25	7
Ricky Romero	3084	829	124	105	308	116	152	386	352	110	360	187
Sergio Romo	806	215	63	10	66	29	41	70	126	17	119	27
B.J. Rosenberg	410	106	24	14	25	15	24	32	57	18	54	23
Trevor Rosenthal	368	89	25	7	29	7	18	37	41	13	47	19
Robbie Ross	1070	265	47	23	118	34	37	111	132	42	141	62
Tyson Ross	1288	342	46	37	123	58	67	154	149	47	148	75
Chris Rusin	507	135	21	11	44	24	29	64	61	13	62	25
James Russell	1184	292	55	23	77	44	85	113	153	44	157	65
Marc Rzepczynski	736	196	33	17	86	32	28	106	71	28	82	44
CC Sabathia	3028	833	197	44	276	121	176	305	432	82	407	116
Takashi Saito	238	60	11	5	17	6	18	21	34	7	32	12
Fernando Salas	1042	256	60	27	62	39	61	86	145	34	148	55
Chris Sale	3019	772	192	51	230	118	164	337	371	95	416	136
Jeff Samardzija	2767	723	180	56	210	105	156	286	357	76	378	122
Anibal Sanchez	3057	820	167	48	270	125	187	280	434	105	423	136
Eduardo Sanchez	275	70	13	13	16	7	17	34	31	6	35	16
Jonathan Sanchez	1339	327	45	53	87	41	91	162	136	52	155	102
Ervin Santana	2859	764	133	61	239	108	206	294	372	103	350	155
Johan Santana	1940	499	111	39	112	81	145	207	242	70	259	106
Hector Santiago	1362	306	79	40	68	36	74	133	160	68	194	90
Joe Saunders	2709	745	112	39	249	123	206	324	332	96	312	136
Joe Savery	404	108	16	8	35	18	27	51	46	10	48	18
Tanner Scheppers	562	152	30	9	46	22	40	71	64	20	72	28
Max Scherzer	3278	787	231	60	175	106	199	306	410	114	482	158
Michael Schwimer	608	147	36	16	27	20	43	55	80	25	88	30
Evan Scribner	598	148	30	12	40	26	40	59	77	22	89	29
Chris Seddon	527	147	18	13	48	29	39	62	67	16	64	26
Leyson Septimo	198	58	14	6	17	4	16	23	23	5	25	12
Bryan Shaw	947	252	41	24	102	38	41	108	112	34	116	50
Ben Sheets	768	207	35	13	62	41	49	87	96	21	94	36
James Shields	3617	944	223	58	336	120	186	367	469	111	487	153
Alfredo Simon	1009	269	52	22	100	39	46	99	138	30	132	47
Tony Sipp	955	233	51	23	50	38	64	111	101	32	129	55
Tyler Skaggs	522	133	21	13	32	17	45	64	58	16	62	28
Doug Slaten	196	55	6	8	20	8	12	25	21	7	19	13
Joe Smith	1086	278	53	25	112	33	48	119	131	32	144	50
Will Smith	1411	396	59	33	126	69	105	172	174	38	164	68
Drew Smyly	1748	416	94	33	112	53	116	174	212	68	234	93
Miguel Socolovich	282	72	12	9	20	8	22	31	34	15	32	21
Rafael Soriano	1107	279	69	24	66	45	73	123	132	30	148	56
Craig Stammen	1386	370	87	36	108	48	84	151	181	44	183	69
Zach Stewart	619	168	19	4	72	24	46	71	75	20	70	26
Drew Storen	395	116	24	8	44	15	23	48	49	12	52	18

Pitcher Analysis
Pitchers with 50+ Batters Faced in 2012

Pitcher	Pitches	BF	K	BB	GB	LD	FB	Counts 1-0	0-1	Full	2 Strike	3 Ball
Mickey Storey	509	127	34	10	30	10	40	53	65	14	76	19
Dan Straily	673	172	32	16	36	18	66	84	77	16	83	29
Stephen Strasburg	2607	653	197	48	175	90	131	247	336	96	377	136
Huston Street	581	144	47	11	35	17	32	54	72	17	89	24
Pedro Strop	1105	283	58	37	117	29	36	132	121	42	147	70
Eric Stults	1521	413	55	27	129	82	108	159	208	40	179	64
Jeff Suppan	505	137	7	13	64	20	30	68	48	22	55	33
Anthony Swarzak	1459	413	62	31	137	67	112	166	191	42	174	72
Hisanori Takahashi	835	212	52	14	53	24	66	95	97	31	110	46
Yoshinori Tateyama	296	76	18	6	18	10	24	26	37	11	41	15
Junichi Tazawa	656	172	45	5	58	29	32	56	97	17	97	21
Everett Teaford	1040	263	35	21	89	41	73	107	135	32	130	51
Joe Thatcher	534	141	39	14	35	15	31	52	77	15	75	24
Dale Thayer	954	235	47	12	70	35	65	97	124	33	129	43
Tyler Thornburg	381	95	20	7	28	13	25	45	42	14	54	18
Matt Thornton	1020	266	53	17	102	38	48	107	135	27	139	41
Chris Tillman	1438	347	66	24	87	53	112	157	168	51	187	73
Shawn Tolleson	658	160	39	20	37	21	39	53	82	26	92	39
Josh Tomlin	1610	452	56	25	151	77	135	161	226	45	196	66
Carlos Torres	898	231	42	26	67	42	44	98	114	26	108	50
Jacob Turner	897	231	36	16	80	34	63	99	114	23	108	42
Koji Uehara	513	130	43	3	27	14	42	43	79	7	82	9
Raul Valdes	472	113	35	5	17	19	36	38	64	20	68	22
Jose Valdez	226	57	10	8	18	4	14	24	26	4	26	14
Jose Valverde	1139	294	48	27	71	46	92	126	142	31	141	56
Jason Vargas	3354	887	141	55	272	131	274	354	444	112	424	163
Anthony Varvaro	322	76	21	9	18	7	18	31	38	9	45	17
Esmerling Vasquez	547	141	14	19	33	21	51	54	71	24	61	40
Jonny Venters	962	262	69	28	98	33	25	107	118	30	124	56
Jose Veras	1301	300	79	40	78	44	56	142	151	62	174	91
Justin Verlander	3768	956	239	60	271	142	228	370	482	126	522	171
Carlos Villanueva	2014	521	122	46	126	66	151	217	257	66	259	104
Brayan Villarreal	943	226	66	28	39	26	63	95	104	28	135	50
Nick Vincent	448	105	28	7	25	16	26	47	48	17	61	25
Ryan Vogelsong	3056	788	158	62	238	101	208	308	395	103	410	155
Edinson Volquez	3221	802	174	105	253	106	141	381	371	126	425	202
Chris Volstad	1891	507	61	43	191	88	109	214	230	70	217	108
Cory Wade	676	171	38	8	50	25	48	50	95	25	94	32
Adam Wainwright	3091	831	184	52	292	132	151	297	428	98	428	133
Jordan Walden	730	172	48	18	42	26	38	69	90	36	105	47
Kyle Waldrop	346	94	7	6	55	13	10	42	42	8	40	16
P.J. Walters	1019	271	42	22	82	53	67	119	126	34	118	53
Chien-Ming Wang	565	158	15	15	64	22	35	73	74	10	64	24
Tony Watson	866	215	53	23	54	24	56	78	111	23	117	41
Jered Weaver	2859	739	142	45	196	115	233	285	383	105	363	145
Ryan Webb	1019	270	44	20	104	54	43	101	137	27	127	49
Kyle Weiland	303	79	13	7	22	14	20	42	29	13	36	17
Kip Wells	638	169	19	20	61	23	44	89	63	22	75	40
Randy Wells	547	143	14	24	39	30	28	59	65	26	62	43
Andrew Werner	666	177	35	14	66	19	40	61	95	21	85	34
Jake Westbrook	2678	751	106	52	332	119	120	292	355	91	324	127
Dan Wheeler	253	61	2	7	23	7	22	29	27	16	27	22
Alex White	1794	459	64	51	179	71	81	218	199	54	194	106
Joe Wieland	467	119	24	9	34	17	32	49	58	20	62	27
Tom Wilhelmsen	1220	326	87	29	100	34	73	139	156	44	174	62
Adam Wilk	194	55	7	3	14	8	19	21	24	7	23	10
Jerome Williams	2035	572	98	35	232	79	122	230	274	57	257	92
C.J. Wilson	3442	865	173	91	296	117	176	372	419	133	444	205
Randy Wolf	2710	699	104	52	223	119	178	281	346	107	331	155
Travis Wood	2499	649	119	54	154	98	197	272	298	94	315	133
Vance Worley	2192	590	107	47	190	100	123	232	285	69	271	114
Jamey Wright	1116	306	54	30	142	44	25	138	132	32	138	58
Wesley Wright	833	223	54	17	79	31	34	79	123	23	110	37
Chris Young	1847	493	80	36	80	70	209	184	251	62	256	90
Mike Zagurski	639	163	34	19	44	27	35	67	74	25	91	38
Carlos Zambrano	2294	591	95	75	196	90	113	266	256	94	287	143
Brad Ziegler	930	263	42	21	148	33	15	93	138	25	113	40
Jordan Zimmermann	3089	805	153	43	253	135	195	245	475	95	432	127
Barry Zito	3068	799	114	70	236	117	231	362	363	101	377	158

Pinch Hitting

Bill James

I will confess to you that until I was assigned to write this article, I had never heard of Jordany Valdespin. When I saw that Valdespin had hit five pinch hit homers in 2012 I thought that was probably a misprint. Willie Mays hit five pinch hit home runs in his career, and, while it is true that Willie was often in the starting lineup, he did pinch hit 129 times. I always said that Willie Mays was no Jordany Valdespin.

In the past we have printed complete pinch hitting records for every player who had one pinch hit opportunity during the season. This led to very long charts in which 80% of the numbers were zero, and this year we decided that it was not meant that trees should die for such a purpose. It is inherently improbable, to begin with, that a player becomes a better or worse hitter than he otherwise is because he is pinch hitting, and, if a player goes 1-for-4 as a pinch hitter, what do we learn from that? We decided this year to limit the pinch hitting charts to players who actually were used with some consistency in the pinch hitting role.

Valdespin's first major league hit was a three-run pinch-hit homer, and later on, he hit another one. This made Jordany one of four major league players to drive in 10 runs as a pinch hitter—Valdespin, Matt Carpenter, Jesus Guzman and Chad Tracy. Guzman led in that category, with 12 RBI; he's a San Diego Padre who appears to have lost the competition for the first base job to Yonder Alonso, although frankly it is hard to see why. Travis Buck hit .538 as a pinch hitter (7-for-13), while Austin Kearns had ten walks and a .481 on base percentage as a pinch hitter—and he pinch hit in one-third of his team's games.

Matt Stairs, the best pinch hitter of the last generation, has moved on to the broadcast booth, taking his 23 career pinch hit bombs with him. Greg Dobbs is now the only active player with 10 home runs as a substitute batter; he also leads active players in pinch hitting at bats (327), hits (85), doubles (19) and RBI (68). The only active players who have a .300 average in 100 or more plate appearances as a PH are Jamey Carroll (.350), Seth Smith (.318), Tony Gwynn Jr. (.305) and Nate Schierholtz (.305).

Pinch Hitting
Pinch Hitters with 10+ PAs or 10+ Total Bases in 2012

Batter	B	AB	H	2B	3B	HR	RBI	TBB	IBB	SO	GDP	Avg	OBP	Slg	OPS
Bobby Abreu	L	35	9	0	0	1	4	8	2	11	0	.257	.395	.343	.738
Alexi Amarista	L	24	5	2	0	0	1	2	0	4	0	.208	.269	.292	.561
Rick Ankiel	L	11	2	0	1	0	2	1	0	5	1	.182	.250	.364	.614
Norichika Aoki	L	22	9	0	0	0	3	1	0	6	0	.409	.435	.409	.844
Joaquin Arias	R	13	2	1	0	0	1	1	0	3	0	.154	.214	.231	.445
Jeff Baker	R	24	4	1	0	2	7	3	1	9	0	.167	.259	.458	.718
Mike Baxter	L	24	11	6	0	0	8	8	3	4	0	.458	.559	.708	1.267
Brandon Belt	L	13	4	1	2	0	4	1	0	5	0	.308	.357	.692	1.049
Carlos Beltran	B	13	5	2	0	0	5	2	1	2	0	.385	.467	.538	1.005
Lance Berkman	B	6	1	0	0	1	1	4	1	3	0	.167	.500	.667	1.167
Roger Bernadina	L	33	8	2	0	0	1	5	0	8	0	.242	.359	.303	.662
Jeff Bianchi	R	12	2	1	0	0	1	1	0	4	0	.167	.231	.250	.481
Brian Bixler	R	10	0	0	0	0	0	0	0	5	0	.000	.000	.000	.000
Charlie Blackmon	L	10	2	1	0	0	1	1	0	2	0	.200	.273	.300	.573
Gregor Blanco	L	14	4	2	0	0	4	3	0	4	0	.286	.368	.429	.797
Geoff Blum	B	11	2	0	0	0	0	1	0	4	0	.182	.250	.182	.432
Brian Bogusevic	L	33	8	1	0	1	5	3	0	10	1	.242	.306	.364	.669
Andrew Brown	R	11	1	0	0	0	0	1	0	5	0	.091	.167	.091	.258
Corey Brown	L	11	3	1	0	0	1	0	0	3	0	.273	.273	.364	.636
Travis Buck	L	13	7	3	1	0	2	1	0	1	0	.538	.571	.923	1.495
Emmanuel Burriss	B	9	1	0	0	0	0	0	0	4	0	.111	.111	.111	.222
Miguel Cairo	R	24	6	2	1	0	3	0	0	2	1	.250	.250	.417	.667
Alberto Callaspo	B	9	4	0	0	1	6	1	0	2	0	.444	.500	.778	1.278
Tony Campana	L	21	6	0	0	0	1	1	0	6	0	.286	.318	.286	.604
Adrian Cardenas	L	30	4	2	0	0	1	2	1	8	0	.133	.188	.200	.388
Mike Carp	L	10	0	0	0	0	0	1	0	5	1	.000	.091	.000	.091
Matt Carpenter	L	31	8	5	0	0	11	2	0	15	2	.258	.278	.419	.697
Jason Castro	L	8	2	1	0	0	1	2	1	3	1	.250	.400	.375	.775
Ronny Cedeno	R	20	6	1	0	2	3	3	0	5	1	.300	.391	.650	1.041
Adron Chambers	L	13	2	0	0	0	0	0	0	9	0	.154	.154	.154	.308
Eric Chavez	L	34	4	0	0	1	1	2	0	13	0	.118	.167	.206	.373
Justin Christian	R	14	2	0	0	0	0	1	0	2	0	.143	.200	.143	.343
Jeff Clement	L	20	3	1	0	0	1	2	0	6	2	.150	.227	.200	.427
Steve Clevenger	L	14	5	1	0	0	1	1	0	1	0	.357	.400	.429	.829
Tyler Colvin	L	22	5	0	1	2	6	1	0	11	0	.227	.261	.591	.852
Brooks Conrad	B	22	2	1	0	0	1	1	0	11	1	.091	.130	.136	.267
Mike Costanzo	L	13	0	0	0	0	1	0	0	8	0	.000	.000	.000	.000
Scott Cousins	L	20	2	0	0	1	1	1	0	6	0	.100	.143	.250	.393
Tony Cruz	R	11	2	0	0	0	1	0	0	3	1	.182	.167	.182	.348
Ike Davis	L	15	5	1	0	0	5	0	0	5	0	.333	.333	.400	.733
Ivan De Jesus	R	14	3	0	0	0	2	2	0	2	1	.214	.294	.214	.508
David DeJesus	L	10	3	0	0	1	6	1	0	1	0	.300	.417	.600	1.017
Chris Denorfia	R	29	8	3	0	0	5	3	0	8	3	.276	.333	.379	.713
Mark DeRosa	R	18	7	2	0	0	5	5	0	4	0	.389	.522	.500	1.022
Daniel Descalso	L	21	2	0	0	0	1	0	0	7	0	.095	.095	.095	.190
Blake DeWitt	L	12	1	1	0	0	1	0	0	1	1	.083	.077	.167	.244
Matt Diaz	R	26	5	0	0	0	1	1	0	12	0	.192	.222	.192	.415
Greg Dobbs	L	41	11	1	0	1	8	2	1	7	1	.268	.289	.366	.655
Matt Downs	R	37	4	1	0	0	1	6	1	14	1	.108	.233	.135	.368
Lucas Duda	L	8	1	0	0	0	1	2	0	2	0	.125	.364	.125	.489
Jake Elmore	R	9	1	0	0	0	1	2	0	1	0	.111	.273	.111	.384
Ryan Flaherty	L	10	2	0	0	0	0	0	0	3	0	.200	.200	.200	.400
Mike Fontenot	L	18	5	0	0	0	1	1	0	5	0	.278	.316	.278	.594
Dexter Fowler	B	11	3	0	0	2	2	3	0	7	0	.273	.429	.818	1.247
Ben Francisco	R	22	4	1	1	0	2	1	0	11	0	.182	.217	.318	.536
Juan Francisco	L	41	5	0	0	1	5	4	0	20	2	.122	.217	.195	.413
Todd Frazier	R	12	6	2	2	0	3	1	0	1	0	.500	.538	1.000	1.538
David Freese	R	7	0	0	0	0	0	4	1	3	1	.000	.364	.000	.364
Kosuke Fukudome	L	10	2	0	0	0	0	1	0	3	0	.200	.273	.200	.473
Craig Gentry	R	13	2	1	0	0	1	1	0	0	0	.154	.313	.231	.543
Jason Giambi	L	32	7	0	0	3	3	8	1	11	1	.219	.390	.313	.703
Jonny Gomes	R	12	2	0	0	1	3	4	1	6	0	.167	.389	.417	.806
Carlos Gomez	R	20	6	2	0	1	1	1	0	5	0	.300	.333	.550	.883
Mauro Gomez	R	11	2	0	0	0	5	0	0	2	1	.182	.182	.182	.364
Marwin Gonzalez	B	17	4	0	0	1	1	1	0	4	1	.235	.278	.412	.690
Taylor Green	L	21	3	0	0	2	6	5	0	8	0	.143	.308	.429	.736

Pinch Hitting
Pinch Hitters with 10+ PAs or 10+ Total Bases in 2012

												Pinch Hitting			
Batter	B	AB	H	2B	3B	HR	RBI	TBB	IBB	SO	GDP	Avg	OBP	Slg	OPS
Tyler Greene	R	17	1	0	0	0	0	2	0	9	1	.059	.158	.059	.217
Jesus Guzman	R	43	11	3	0	2	12	6	1	12	0	.256	.340	.465	.805
Tony Gwynn	L	20	8	1	1	0	5	0	0	4	0	.400	.400	.550	.950
Matt Hague	R	14	4	0	0	0	2	0	0	1	0	.286	.286	.286	.571
Scott Hairston	R	33	7	1	0	3	5	5	0	9	2	.212	.316	.515	.831
Willie Harris	L	14	3	2	0	0	0	1	0	4	0	.214	.267	.357	.624
Josh Harrison	R	29	4	0	0	0	3	1	0	4	1	.138	.161	.138	.299
Chris Heisey	R	19	6	3	0	0	4	3	0	5	0	.316	.409	.474	.883
Gorkys Hernandez	R	13	3	0	0	0	2	2	0	4	1	.231	.333	.231	.564
Elian Herrera	B	10	4	0	0	0	0	3	0	2	0	.400	.538	.400	.938
Jonathan Herrera	B	15	1	0	0	0	0	2	0	3	0	.067	.176	.067	.243
Eric Hinske	L	57	8	2	0	1	4	5	0	17	3	.140	.210	.228	.438
Brock Holt	L	6	1	0	0	0	0	3	0	3	0	.167	.444	.167	.611
Orlando Hudson	B	8	3	0	0	1	4	2	0	3	0	.375	.500	.750	1.250
Aubrey Huff	L	26	7	1	0	0	1	6	0	3	0	.269	.406	.308	.714
Raul Ibanez	L	25	8	2	0	2	7	3	1	3	2	.320	.379	.640	1.019
Travis Ishikawa	L	50	13	2	1	0	8	3	1	12	0	.260	.315	.340	.655
Cesar Izturis	B	13	3	0	0	0	0	0	0	1	0	.231	.231	.231	.462
Maicer Izturis	B	22	2	0	0	0	2	2	0	5	1	.091	.167	.091	.258
Mike Jacobs	L	9	1	0	0	0	1	1	0	1	0	.111	.200	.111	.311
John Jaso	L	18	6	1	0	0	4	3	0	3	0	.333	.409	.389	.798
Elliot Johnson	B	8	0	0	0	0	0	2	0	7	0	.000	.200	.000	.200
Nick Johnson	L	13	2	0	0	0	0	1	0	3	3	.154	.214	.154	.368
Reed Johnson	R	43	18	2	0	1	5	3	0	13	0	.419	.457	.535	.991
Andruw Jones	R	22	4	0	0	2	3	1	1	9	0	.182	.280	.455	.735
Chipper Jones	B	8	3	1	0	1	3	2	0	0	1	.375	.500	.875	1.375
Garrett Jones	L	13	3	0	0	0	2	2	1	2	0	.231	.333	.231	.564
Matt Joyce	L	10	2	2	0	0	1	3	1	5	0	.200	.385	.400	.785
Austin Kearns	R	40	13	1	0	1	5	10	0	14	2	.325	.481	.425	.906
Adam Kennedy	L	28	8	1	0	0	1	2	1	4	1	.286	.355	.321	.676
Erik Komatsu	L	9	2	0	0	0	0	2	0	3	0	.222	.364	.222	.586
Casey Kotchman	L	9	2	0	0	0	1	1	1	0	1	.222	.300	.222	.522
Mark Kotsay	L	48	13	4	0	2	9	3	0	6	1	.271	.314	.479	.793
George Kottaras	L	23	6	3	0	1	5	5	0	11	2	.261	.393	.522	.915
Erik Kratz	R	10	2	0	0	2	3	0	0	2	0	.200	.200	.800	1.000
Jason Kubel	L	8	1	0	0	0	0	2	0	3	1	.125	.300	.125	.425
Bryan LaHair	L	36	10	3	0	1	6	2	0	16	1	.278	.316	.444	.760
Fred Lewis	L	10	0	0	0	0	0	1	1	4	0	.000	.091	.000	.091
Brent Lillibridge	R	13	2	1	0	1	2	0	0	8	0	.154	.154	.462	.615
Steve Lombardozzi	B	26	8	2	0	0	0	1	0	6	0	.308	.379	.385	.764
James Loney	L	20	4	0	0	0	2	1	1	2	0	.200	.238	.200	.438
Jonathan Lucroy	R	11	4	1	1	0	6	2	0	2	0	.364	.462	.636	1.098
Ryan Ludwick	R	15	4	2	0	1	3	0	0	6	0	.267	.267	.600	.867
Hector Luna	R	12	1	0	0	1	4	2	0	3	1	.083	.214	.333	.548
Martin Maldonado	R	14	1	0	0	0	1	1	0	9	0	.071	.133	.071	.205
J.D. Martinez	R	10	3	0	0	0	1	1	0	5	0	.300	.364	.300	.664
Joe Mather	R	31	5	1	0	1	2	0	0	10	1	.161	.182	.290	.472
Hideki Matsui	L	10	1	1	0	0	0	1	1	3	0	.100	.182	.200	.382
Justin Maxwell	R	28	7	2	0	3	8	3	0	12	0	.250	.313	.643	.955
John Mayberry	R	23	7	1	0	0	1	0	0	7	0	.304	.304	.348	.652
Matt McBride	R	13	4	0	0	0	2	0	0	3	0	.308	.308	.308	.615
John McDonald	R	12	4	0	0	1	1	0	0	1	0	.333	.333	.583	.917
Casey McGehee	R	15	7	2	0	0	4	2	0	2	1	.467	.529	.600	1.129
Michael McKenry	R	15	3	0	0	0	1	1	0	5	1	.200	.250	.200	.450
Nate McLouth	L	14	0	0	0	0	0	4	0	5	0	.000	.222	.000	.222
Scott Moore	L	5	3	0	0	0	0	5	1	2	0	.600	.818	.600	1.418
Tyler Moore	R	29	6	2	0	2	7	1	0	12	1	.207	.258	.483	.741
Kendrys Morales	B	13	3	1	0	1	6	0	0	3	0	.231	.214	.538	.753
Mitch Moreland	L	18	4	1	0	1	3	1	0	5	1	.222	.263	.444	.708
Nyjer Morgan	L	36	7	1	1	0	3	1	0	8	1	.194	.237	.278	.515
Logan Morrison	L	13	5	0	0	2	4	1	0	2	0	.385	.429	.846	1.275
Brandon Moss	L	10	5	0	0	1	4	4	0	2	0	.500	.600	.800	1.400
Daniel Murphy	L	16	4	1	1	0	1	2	1	3	0	.250	.333	.438	.771
David Murphy	L	11	3	0	0	1	4	4	1	3	0	.273	.438	.545	.983
Donnie Murphy	R	14	2	0	0	1	2	1	0	5	0	.143	.200	.357	.557
Xavier Nady	R	13	6	1	0	2	3	2	1	2	0	.462	.533	1.000	1.533
Yamaico Navarro	R	12	0	0	0	0	0	3	0	7	0	.000	.200	.000	.200
Chris Nelson	R	8	2	0	0	1	1	3	0	2	1	.250	.455	.625	1.080
Kirk Nieuwenhuis	L	11	4	1	0	0	2	3	0	4	0	.364	.500	.455	.955

Pinch Hitting
Pinch Hitters with 10+ PAs or 10+ Total Bases in 2012

Batter	B	AB	H	2B	3B	HR	RBI	TBB	IBB	SO	GDP	Avg	OBP	Slg	OPS
Wil Nieves	R	11	4	0	0	0	0	0	0	2	0	.364	.364	.364	.727
Laynce Nix	L	26	4	2	0	0	3	1	0	12	1	.154	.185	.231	.416
Pete Orr	L	15	5	1	0	0	0	1	0	9	0	.333	.375	.400	.775
Lyle Overbay	L	36	7	1	0	0	2	1	0	15	1	.194	.216	.222	.438
Chris Parmelee	L	11	2	0	1	0	2	0	0	4	0	.182	.250	.364	.614
Gerardo Parra	L	26	5	2	0	1	3	0	0	7	0	.192	.222	.385	.607
Andy Parrino	B	13	3	0	0	0	1	1	0	8	1	.231	.286	.231	.516
Tyler Pastornicky	R	20	4	0	0	1	1	4	1	7	1	.200	.333	.350	.683
Xavier Paul	L	36	12	3	1	1	2	3	1	5	2	.333	.385	.556	.940
Steve Pearce	R	10	3	1	0	0	1	0	0	2	1	.300	.300	.400	.700
Carlos Pena	L	10	2	0	0	1	2	1	0	3	0	.200	.333	.500	.833
Bryan Petersen	L	9	1	0	0	0	0	6	0	3	1	.111	.467	.111	.578
Juan Pierre	L	16	3	0	0	0	0	2	0	2	0	.188	.316	.188	.503
Brett Pill	R	15	2	0	0	1	3	2	1	3	0	.133	.278	.333	.611
Placido Polanco	R	10	2	0	0	0	0	2	0	1	1	.200	.333	.200	.533
A.J. Pollock	R	10	3	0	0	0	1	0	0	1	0	.300	.300	.300	.600
Alex Presley	L	17	2	0	0	1	2	2	0	5	1	.118	.250	.294	.544
Nick Punto	B	17	3	2	0	0	0	6	0	6	0	.176	.391	.294	.685
Cody Ransom	R	15	4	2	0	0	3	0	0	6	0	.267	.267	.400	.667
Juan Rivera	R	23	6	0	0	0	4	2	1	5	2	.261	.346	.261	.607
Ryan Roberts	R	22	6	1	0	0	2	1	0	1	0	.273	.304	.318	.623
Shane Robinson	R	50	11	3	0	0	3	6	0	10	1	.220	.304	.280	.584
Henry Rodriguez (Cin)	B	9	2	0	0	0	0	1	0	2	1	.222	.300	.222	.522
Sean Rodriguez	R	6	1	0	0	0	0	3	0	2	0	.167	.500	.167	.667
Wilin Rosario	R	11	3	0	0	1	2	0	0	2	0	.273	.273	.545	.818
Justin Ruggiano	R	9	3	1	0	1	1	0	0	5	0	.333	.333	.778	1.111
Carlos Ruiz	R	14	4	0	0	1	3	0	0	1	1	.286	.267	.500	.767
Josh Rutledge	R	10	6	1	1	1	5	0	0	1	0	.600	.600	1.200	1.800
Jarrod Saltalamacchia	B	13	3	0	0	1	4	1	0	6	0	.231	.286	.462	.747
Gaby Sanchez	R	12	2	1	0	1	3	3	0	3	2	.167	.375	.500	.875
Hector Sanchez	B	19	5	2	0	0	4	0	0	7	1	.263	.263	.368	.632
Jordan Schafer	L	12	3	1	0	0	0	2	0	3	0	.250	.357	.333	.690
Nate Schierholtz	L	34	9	0	1	0	3	3	0	7	0	.265	.316	.324	.639
Skip Schumaker	L	26	5	2	0	0	3	5	1	6	0	.192	.323	.269	.592
Luke Scott	L	12	5	2	0	1	4	0	0	1	1	.417	.417	.833	1.250
Seth Smith	L	20	4	1	0	0	5	1	0	8	0	.200	.238	.250	.488
Travis Snider	L	16	4	1	0	0	0	1	0	6	1	.250	.294	.313	.607
Brandon Snyder	R	12	2	0	0	1	1	2	0	6	0	.167	.286	.417	.702
Donovan Solano	R	15	6	0	1	0	2	2	0	3	0	.400	.471	.533	1.004
Drew Sutton	B	8	1	1	0	0	1	1	0	4	0	.125	.300	.250	.550
Jose Tabata	R	8	1	0	0	0	1	3	0	3	0	.125	.364	.125	.489
Eric Thames	L	11	1	0	0	0	1	0	0	5	0	.091	.091	.091	.182
Ryan Theriot	R	18	5	2	0	0	1	0	0	3	2	.278	.278	.389	.667
Josh Thole	L	11	2	0	0	0	0	1	0	3	0	.182	.250	.182	.432
Jim Thome	L	18	2	1	0	1	1	1	1	12	0	.111	.158	.333	.491
Andres Torres	B	9	1	1	0	0	0	1	0	3	1	.111	.200	.222	.422
Chad Tracy	L	46	12	3	0	1	11	5	3	9	0	.261	.340	.391	.731
Justin Turner	R	48	12	3	0	0	6	5	0	7	4	.250	.327	.313	.640
Juan Uribe	R	15	3	0	0	0	1	3	0	5	1	.200	.350	.200	.550
Luis Valbuena	L	12	4	1	0	0	1	0	0	2	0	.333	.333	.417	.750
Jordany Valdespin	L	42	9	1	0	5	10	4	0	13	0	.214	.298	.595	.893
Wilson Valdez	R	12	1	0	0	0	1	0	0	4	0	.083	.083	.083	.167
Will Venable	L	23	2	0	0	0	2	3	0	7	0	.087	.192	.087	.279
Josh Vitters	R	10	1	1	0	0	2	2	0	4	1	.100	.250	.200	.450
Omar Vizquel	B	12	3	0	0	0	0	0	0	0	2	.250	.250	.250	.500
Stephen Vogt	L	8	0	0	0	0	0	2	0	1	0	.000	.200	.000	.200
Ryan Wheeler	R	23	5	1	0	0	1	1	0	6	1	.217	.250	.261	.511
Ty Wigginton	R	33	5	1	0	0	3	6	1	10	0	.152	.293	.182	.475
Jack Wilson	R	9	1	0	1	0	0	1	0	3	0	.111	.200	.333	.533
DeWayne Wise	L	11	2	1	0	0	1	0	0	2	0	.182	.182	.273	.455
Chris Young (Ari)	R	10	4	0	0	1	3	3	0	3	0	.400	.538	.700	1.238
Eric Young	B	53	13	1	0	1	4	5	0	13	0	.245	.333	.321	.654

Career Pinch Hitting

Active Pinch Hitters with 100+ PAs in their careers

Batter	B	AB	H	2B	3B	HR	RBI	TBB	IBB	SO	GDP	Avg	OBP	Slg	OPS
Bobby Abreu	L	87	18	0	1	1	11	19	5	30	0	.207	.349	.264	.613
Jeff Baker	R	163	30	6	1	5	19	15	2	61	6	.184	.256	.325	.581
Wilson Betemit	B	152	36	9	0	5	20	26	0	59	3	.237	.346	.395	.741
Geoff Blum	B	254	62	12	1	1	35	35	6	53	6	.244	.339	.311	.650
Sean Burroughs	L	99	25	5	0	1	8	7	0	20	4	.253	.302	.333	.635
Miguel Cairo	R	276	74	14	3	2	43	21	3	40	6	.268	.321	.362	.684
Jamey Carroll	R	117	41	4	0	1	14	17	0	23	4	.350	.430	.410	.840
Endy Chavez	L	119	31	6	3	1	13	7	1	13	3	.261	.302	.387	.688
Brooks Conrad	B	160	29	9	0	7	26	15	1	64	2	.181	.251	.369	.620
Mark DeRosa	R	141	39	6	0	2	19	18	0	26	0	.277	.364	.362	.726
Blake DeWitt	L	110	24	5	1	3	17	6	0	20	6	.218	.269	.364	.633
Matt Diaz	R	225	57	8	2	1	23	9	0	55	8	.253	.289	.320	.609
Greg Dobbs	L	327	85	19	2	10	68	27	4	69	7	.260	.313	.422	.735
Ryan Doumit	B	95	27	4	0	3	20	8	2	27	5	.284	.349	.421	.770
Matt Downs	R	94	21	6	0	3	18	14	1	30	1	.223	.333	.383	.716
Mike Fontenot	L	155	35	12	0	2	21	16	1	41	1	.226	.299	.342	.641
Ben Francisco	R	117	28	10	1	1	18	15	0	35	3	.239	.328	.368	.696
Jason Giambi	L	159	38	3	0	8	32	29	5	60	2	.239	.363	.409	.771
Jonny Gomes	R	113	16	5	0	3	17	15	1	50	1	.142	.261	.265	.527
Tony Gwynn	L	131	40	7	3	0	12	13	1	26	2	.305	.372	.405	.777
Scott Hairston	R	174	32	5	0	9	20	23	1	64	4	.184	.283	.368	.651
Bill Hall	R	120	23	5	0	6	19	9	1	47	0	.192	.246	.383	.629
Willie Harris	L	220	47	8	0	4	21	28	0	51	3	.214	.311	.305	.616
Eric Hinske	L	262	57	11	1	8	36	36	1	75	6	.218	.317	.359	.676
Raul Ibanez	L	133	25	6	0	4	21	15	2	26	5	.188	.267	.323	.590
Travis Ishikawa	L	119	33	8	1	1	14	9	1	26	1	.277	.333	.387	.720
Reed Johnson	R	175	50	10	0	4	22	9	1	44	3	.286	.339	.411	.750
Andruw Jones	R	88	17	3	0	5	17	15	1	29	1	.193	.324	.398	.722
Austin Kearns	R	99	27	3	1	3	18	21	0	36	3	.273	.419	.414	.833
Adam Kennedy	L	140	33	7	0	1	14	9	2	29	5	.236	.286	.307	.593
Mark Kotsay	L	181	54	10	0	5	30	13	2	32	4	.298	.345	.436	.782
Ryan Langerhans	L	93	22	4	1	4	8	13	0	35	1	.237	.330	.430	.760
Fred Lewis	L	107	27	7	1	1	16	13	2	38	0	.252	.344	.364	.709
Ryan Ludwick	R	95	25	7	0	5	15	10	2	26	1	.263	.340	.495	.834
Nate McLouth	L	111	21	4	1	1	10	9	0	29	0	.189	.260	.270	.530
Xavier Nady	R	117	30	4	0	6	18	17	1	29	6	.256	.367	.444	.811
Laynce Nix	L	160	29	7	0	2	14	18	4	52	4	.181	.263	.263	.525
Pete Orr	L	195	53	6	2	2	15	8	0	47	1	.272	.298	.354	.651
David Ortiz	L	84	15	3	1	4	17	20	1	22	2	.179	.333	.381	.714
Lyle Overbay	L	93	19	5	0	2	16	9	2	33	3	.204	.269	.323	.592
Xavier Paul	L	95	19	6	1	2	4	4	1	30	4	.200	.232	.347	.580
Juan Pierre	L	106	31	1	2	0	4	12	1	8	0	.292	.375	.340	.715
A.J. Pierzynski	L	99	22	4	0	3	17	12	5	16	6	.222	.307	.354	.661
Scott Podsednik	L	97	20	1	2	1	10	12	0	20	2	.206	.306	.289	.595
Placido Polanco	R	89	22	3	0	1	16	8	0	9	3	.247	.306	.315	.621
Juan Rivera	R	95	21	6	0	1	15	8	3	19	8	.221	.302	.316	.618
Nate Schierholtz	L	131	40	7	1	2	18	10	0	28	1	.305	.347	.420	.767
Skip Schumaker	L	136	34	7	0	1	13	8	1	24	2	.250	.299	.324	.623
Luke Scott	L	92	24	10	0	3	14	8	1	24	2	.261	.320	.467	.787
Seth Smith	L	157	50	12	5	5	39	26	2	42	2	.318	.409	.554	.963
Jim Thome	L	138	30	10	0	5	15	22	2	64	2	.217	.331	.399	.730
Chad Tracy	L	156	39	12	0	6	35	20	3	37	2	.250	.339	.442	.781
Ty Wigginton	R	103	24	3	0	3	24	16	3	26	2	.233	.347	.350	.696
Eric Young	B	93	23	2	1	1	4	15	0	17	2	.247	.364	.323	.686

Manufactured Runs, Productive Outs, & Unproductive Outs

Bill James

There are two questions that sound the same but have very different consequences:

    1) What is a Manufactured Run?, and

    2) What exactly is a Manufactured Run?

The term "Manufactured Run" in baseball has been generally used in the last three or four decades to mean a run that is created not by hitting, but by moving runners and taking advantage of opportunities. A walk, a stolen base, take third on a ground out and come home on a bunt; that's a manufactured run.

The problem comes when you have to ask what is not a manufactured run. Where do you draw the line between a manufactured run and one that is not? Single, single, runner takes third on a ground out and scores on a sac fly, is that a manufactured run or not?

It is by our definition. Our job is to decide what <u>exactly</u> is a manufactured run, meaning to decide what looks like a manufactured run maybe, but isn't. Our definition is

    1) A run that is driven in by an extra-base hit is NEVER a manufactured run, with a few exceptions,

    2) A run that scores without a hit is always a manufactured run, and

    3) Otherwise, it's a manufactured run if two of the four bases result from the batter/runner doing something other than playing station-to-station baseball.

The exception to the rule that a run driven in by an extra base hit is not a Manufactured Run is that it may still be a Manufactured Run if there were *two* deliberate actions taken to advance the runner, such as bunts, stolen bases, and the use of a pinch runner. If a team has a single, puts in a pinch runner and the pinch runner steals second, then scores on a double, then that is a manufactured run, because the team has done two things in the effort to manufacture the run—put in the pinch runner, and stolen the base. Deliberate efforts to manufacture a run carry a little more weight than things like moving up on a ground out or scoring on a fly ball. But a run that scores on a home run is never counted as a manufactured run, ever.

It turns out that by this definition major league teams manufacture about one run per game, on average.   The Los Angeles Angels led the majors in Manufactured Runs in 2012, as they often do, with 196.   196 is a very good figure, but two years ago the Texas Rangers manufactured 230.   A more striking figure than the 196 runs manufactured by the Angels is that Cincinnati Reds opponents manufactured only 96 runs all year, whereas their American League cousins, the Indians, allowed opponents to manufacture 205.   That's certainly a tribute to the Reds' defensive play, that they were so successful at preventing the opposition from manufacturing runs.

Related to Manufactured Runs are Productive Outs. . .Productive Outs lead to Manufactured Runs.   About Productive Outs, let me quote General George S. Patton: I want you to remember that no bastard ever won a war by dying for his country.   He won it by making the other poor, dumb bastard die for *his* country.

There's a corollary there: nobody ever won a pennant by making productive outs.   He won the pennant by making the *other* team make productive outs.   I'm sure that's not an absolute truth, but. . .the Angels were the best team in the majors in 2012 at manufacturing a run.   The Oakland A's were the worst team at manufacturing a run.   Draw your own conclusions.

A "productive out" is any out that moves a runner.   The productive out is defined from the standpoint of the team, not from the standpoint of the individual. If a pitcher throws a wild pitch while the batter is at the plate, that becomes a productive out (if the batter makes an out), because the baserunner has moved up while the batter was hitting.   If the team gains a base while the batter is at bat but the runner makes an out which is not the third out, that's a productive out—period. You can agree with that definition or not, but I think that's the way to do it.   If a player gets himself out on the first pitch, there's no opportunity for the pitcher to throw a wild pitch.   If a wild pitch occurs, then, the batter **has** contributed to that, in general, by forcing the pitcher to make pitches.   Taking pitches can be productive for the offense.   I don't think it would be right to screen that out.

Martin Prado led the majors in productive outs in 2012, with 48.   An average major league team makes about 250 productive outs in a season, so 48 is about one-fifth of a team total.   About 6% of all outs are productive outs.   For Prado, it was over 10%.

Many of the guys who are near the top of the list of productive outs are the guys you would expect to be there. . .middle infielders who bunt and such like. Elvis Andrus, Marco Scutaro, Jason Kipnis.   But many of the people who are near the top of the "productive outs" leader board are people that you would never expect to see there, like Josh Hamilton, Miguel Cabrera and Freddie Freeman.

An <u>un</u>productive out is any out which

a) occurs with runners on base,

b) is not the third out, and

c) does not advance the runners.

The Oakland A's, the worst team in the majors at Manufacturing a Run, were also at the bottom of the list in Productive Outs (195), and had the most Unproductive Outs (726) in all of baseball to boot.

We have re-designed these charts this year. One chart has a heading "Manufactured Runs", which should actually be "Player contributions to Manufactured Runs". Ian Kinsler contributed to 38 Manufactured Runs either as a batter or a baserunner, the most of any major league player. It was the second consecutive season that Kinsler had led the majors in that department; he contributed to 45 Manufactured Runs in 2011.

It's a legitimate skill, and I'm glad we measure it. I don't want to overstate its importance. As the A's remind us, you can win without it.

Manufactured Runs, Productive Outs, & Unproductive Outs Produced by Team

Team	Manufactured Runs	Productive Outs	Unproductive Outs
Arizona Diamondbacks	134	251	711
Atlanta Braves	164	305	683
Baltimore Orioles	135	234	679
Boston Red Sox	149	264	671
Chicago White Sox	142	233	648
Chicago Cubs	159	263	658
Cincinnati Reds	133	244	673
Cleveland Indians	154	280	691
Colorado Rockies	160	302	634
Detroit Tigers	136	241	705
Houston Astros	132	245	661
Kansas City Royals	176	266	663
Los Angeles Dodgers	155	299	668
Los Angeles Angels	196	296	655
Miami Marlins	151	303	670
Milwaukee Brewers	168	262	702
Minnesota Twins	177	293	674
New York Yankees	150	260	702
New York Mets	139	285	668
Oakland Athletics	118	195	726
Philadelphia Phillies	140	264	669
Pittsburgh Pirates	150	249	628
San Diego Padres	156	273	677
San Francisco Giants	176	339	703
Seattle Mariners	133	213	647
St Louis Cardinals	159	321	712
Tampa Bay Rays	144	225	696
Texas Rangers	169	293	631
Toronto Blue Jays	177	238	665
Washington Nationals	149	248	674

Manufactured Runs, Productive Outs, & Unproductive Outs Allowed by Team

Team	Manufactured Runs	Productive Outs	Unproductive Outs
Arizona Diamondbacks	144	276	695
Atlanta Braves	128	260	602
Baltimore Orioles	137	231	720
Boston Red Sox	187	288	643
Chicago White Sox	123	197	673
Chicago Cubs	151	262	692
Cincinnati Reds	96	235	625
Cleveland Indians	205	309	665
Colorado Rockies	191	353	702
Detroit Tigers	148	255	665
Houston Astros	196	285	705
Kansas City Royals	166	237	722
Los Angeles Dodgers	154	294	648
Los Angeles Angels	145	243	648
Miami Marlins	179	314	667
Milwaukee Brewers	151	270	698
Minnesota Twins	189	272	685
New York Yankees	119	243	679
New York Mets	133	257	732
Oakland Athletics	153	226	672
Philadelphia Phillies	128	244	659
Pittsburgh Pirates	161	303	652
San Diego Padres	167	279	659
San Francisco Giants	142	271	689
Seattle Mariners	140	260	688
St Louis Cardinals	157	310	651
Tampa Bay Rays	140	214	637
Texas Rangers	156	224	676
Toronto Blue Jays	131	272	694
Washington Nationals	164	300	701

Players with the most Manufactured Runs, Productive Outs, & Unproductive Outs

Manufactured Runs	
Kinsler, Ian, Tex	38
Bourn, Michael, Atl	37
Trout, Mike, LAA	36
Andrus, Elvis, Tex	34
Rollins, Jimmy, Phi	33
Reyes, Jose, Mia	33
Pagan, Angel, SF	30
Harper, Bryce, Was	29
Aoki, Norichika, Mil	29
De Aza, Alejandro, CWS	28
Revere, Ben, Min	28
DeJesus, David, ChC	27
Ackley, Dustin, Sea	27
Heyward, Jason, Atl	26
Jackson, Austin, Det	26
Altuve, Jose, Hou	26
Aybar, Erick, LAA	25
Choo, Shin-Soo, Cle	25
Escobar, Alcides, KC	25
McCutchen, Andrew, Pit	25
Castro, Starlin, ChC	24
Upton, B.J., TB	24
Barney, Darwin, ChC	24
Suzuki, Ichiro, Sea-NYY	24
Gomez, Carlos, Mil	24
Davis, Rajai, Tor	23
Brantley, Michael, Cle	23
Escobar, Yunel, Tor	23
Furcal, Rafael, StL	23
Kipnis, Jason, Cle	22
Kendrick, Howie, LAA	22
Span, Denard, Min	22
Rios, Alex, CWS	22
Jones, Adam, Bal	22
Moustakas, Mike, KC	21
Freeman, Freddie, Atl	21
Callaspo, Alberto, LAA	21
Stubbs, Drew, Cin	21
Pierre, Juan, Phi	21
Dyson, Jarrod, KC	21
Beltre, Adrian, Tex	21
Scutaro, Marco, Col-SF	21
Maybin, Cameron, SD	21
Ramirez, Hanley, Mia-LAD	21
Jeter, Derek, NYY	21
Jennings, Desmond, TB	21
Gordon, Alex, KC	21
Pedroia, Dustin, Bos	20
Parra, Gerardo, Ari	20
Hunter, Torii, LAA	20
Cabrera, Asdrubal, Cle	20
Encarnacion, Edwin, Tor	20
Fowler, Dexter, Col	20
Blanco, Gregor, SF	20

Productive Outs	
Prado, Martin, Atl	48
Andrus, Elvis, Tex	47
Scutaro, Marco, Col-SF	42
Hamilton, Josh, Tex	42
Kipnis, Jason, Cle	41
Reyes, Jose, Mia	39
Victorino, Shane, Phi-LAD	38
Gonzalez, Carlos, Col	38
Holliday, Matt, StL	36
Freeman, Freddie, Atl	36
Cabrera, Miguel, Det	35
Ramirez, Hanley, Mia-LAD	35
Hardy, J.J., Bal	35
LaRoche, Adam, Was	34
Kotchman, Casey, Cle	34
Suzuki, Ichiro, Sea-NYY	34
Brantley, Michael, Cle	33
Pujols, Albert, LAA	33
Pence, Hunter, Phi-SF	33
Zimmerman, Ryan, Was	32
Beltran, Carlos, StL	32
Revere, Ben, Min	32
Morneau, Justin, Min	32
Teixeira, Mark, NYY	31
Barney, Darwin, ChC	31
Callaspo, Alberto, LAA	31
Mauer, Joe, Min	31
Heyward, Jason, Atl	31
Cabrera, Melky, SF	31
Escobar, Yunel, Tor	31
Hosmer, Eric, KC	31
Hunter, Torii, LAA	31
Cano, Robinson, NYY	30
Infante, Omar, Mia-Det	30
Butler, Billy, KC	29
Gonzalez, Adrian, Bos-LAD	29
Murphy, Daniel, NYM	29
Carroll, Jamey, Min	29
Pedroia, Dustin, Bos	29
Upton, Justin, Ari	28
Sandoval, Pablo, SF	28
Reddick, Josh, Oak	28
Headley, Chase, SD	28
Young, Michael, Tex	28
Pierzynski, A.J., CWS	28
Castro, Starlin, ChC	28
McCann, Brian, Atl	28
Gordon, Alex, KC	27
Jones, Garrett, Pit	27
Jeter, Derek, NYY	27
Beltre, Adrian, Tex	27
Beckham, Gordon, CWS	27
Wright, David, NYM	27
McCutchen, Andrew, Pit	27
Aybar, Erick, LAA	27
Rasmus, Colby, Tor	27
Ramirez, Alexei, CWS	27

Unproductive Outs	
Reddick, Josh, Oak	106
Granderson, Curtis, NYY	98
Pence, Hunter, Phi-SF	98
Weeks, Rickie, Mil	90
Dunn, Adam, CWS	89
Holliday, Matt, StL	89
Young, Delmon, Det	89
Swisher, Nick, NYY	89
Espinosa, Danny, Was	89
Hardy, J.J., Bal	88
Ramirez, Hanley, Mia-LAD	87
Heyward, Jason, Atl	85
Gordon, Alex, KC	85
Zimmerman, Ryan, Was	84
Headley, Chase, SD	83
Pujols, Albert, LAA	82
Cabrera, Miguel, Det	81
Hamilton, Josh, Tex	81
Moustakas, Mike, KC	81
Cabrera, Asdrubal, Cle	80
Upton, Justin, Ari	80
Pena, Carlos, TB	80
Upton, B.J., TB	79
Wright, David, NYM	79
Infante, Omar, Mia-Det	79
Freeman, Freddie, Atl	79
Braun, Ryan, Mil	78
Uggla, Dan, Atl	78
Castro, Starlin, ChC	77
Peralta, Jhonny, Det	77
McCutchen, Andrew, Pit	77
Ethier, Andre, LAD	77
Victorino, Shane, Phi-LAD	77
Francoeur, Jeff, KC	76
Jones, Adam, Bal	76
Reynolds, Mark, Bal	75
Doumit, Ryan, Min	75
Harper, Bryce, Was	75
Seager, Kyle, Sea	74
Maybin, Cameron, SD	74
Hill, Aaron, Ari	74
Plouffe, Trevor, Min	74
Rodriguez, Alex, NYY	73
Johnson, Kelly, Tor	73
Kipnis, Jason, Cle	73
Rasmus, Colby, Tor	73
Escobar, Alcides, KC	73
Aybar, Erick, LAA	72
Pagan, Angel, SF	72
Hunter, Torii, LAA	72
Cano, Robinson, NYY	72
Zobrist, Ben, TB	72
Kubel, Jason, Ari	72

The Manager's Record

The purpose of this section is to document and quantify, as much as we can, the objective differences between managers.   Is a manager quick to go to his bullpen, or slow?   Is he willing to bring back a reliever he used yesterday, or not so much?   Does he like to have runners in motion, or not?

The tools we have to evaluate managers are divided into several categories:

Lineups: Number of Different Lineups Used (LUp), the percentage of players who had the platoon advantage at the start of the game (PL%).

Substitution: Pinch Hitters Used (PH), Pinch Runners Used (PR), Defensive Substitutes Used (DS).

Pitchers Usage: Quick Hooks (Quick), Slow Hooks (Slow), Long Outings by Starting Pitchers (LO), Relievers Used on Consecutive Days (RCD), Long Saves (LS), Relievers Used (Rel).

For Quick Hooks, we calculate a "Damage Score" for each pitcher and each game, which is his pitches thrown, plus 10 times his runs allowed.   The bottom 25% of the games in each league are Quick Hooks.   If the manager takes his pitcher out after 92 pitches and 1 run allowed (102), that will be a quick hook. The top 25% are Slow Hooks.   If a pitcher throws 114 pitches and gives up 4 runs (154), that will be a Slow Hook.   If a pitcher throws more than 110 pitches in a start, that's a Long Outing.   Yes, this *is* redundant of Slow Hooks; thanks for noticing.

Tactics: Stolen Base Attempts (SBA), Sacrifice Bunts Attempts (SacA), Runners Moving with the Pitch (RM), Pitchouts ordered (PO).

Intentional Walks: Intentional Walks issued (#), Intentional Walks resulting in a Good Outcome (Good), Intentional Walks resulting Not in a Good Outcome (NG), Intentional Walks Blowing up on the Manager (Bomb).

A good result is 1) The next hitter grounds into a double play, or
2) The team in the field gets out of the inning without additional runs scoring. A "Bomb" means that *Multiple* runs score in the inning after the intentional walk. If the hitter after the IBB grounds into a double play, then we count that intentional walk as a success, even if multiple runs score after the IBB.

Results: Wins (W), Losses (L) and Winning Percentage (Pct.).

Manny Acta

Year	Team	Lg	G	LUp	PL%	PH	PR	DS	Quick	Slow	LO	RCD	LS	Rel	SBA	SacA	RM	PO	#	Good	NG	Bomb	W	L	Pct
2007	Nationals	NL	162	101	.65	295	32	78	53	28	5	183	1	588	92	86	70	28	44	28	16	8	73	89	.451
2008	Nationals	NL	161	133	.62	293	31	39	38	46	6	119	4	517	124	95	63	24	44	27	17	8	59	102	.366
2009	Nationals	NL	87	66	.62	145	11	20	14	25	1	91	1	282	54	43	62	5	26	13	13	6	26	61	.299
2010	Indians	AL	162	142	.63	79	20	39	44	49	18	81	6	470	124	41	142	20	36	17	19	10	69	93	.426
2011	Indians	AL	162	134	.71	76	44	43	47	49	20	107	0	483	131	40	144	29	34	20	14	10	80	82	.494
2012	Indians	AL	156	116	.76	68	20	72	38	54	14	94	1	464	149	21	135	23	27	12	15	9	65	91	.417
162-Game Average				126	.67	174	29	53	43	46	12	123	2	510	123	59	112	23	38	21	17	9	68	94	.420

Sandy Alomar, Jr.

Year	Team	Lg	G	LUp	PL%	PH	PR	DS	Quick	Slow	LO	RCD	LS	Rel	SBA	SacA	RM	PO	#	Good	NG	Bomb	W	L	Pct
2012	Indians	AL	6	6	.61	12	2	1	1	1	0	9	0	30	5	3	3	0	0	0	0	0	3	3	.500
162-Game Average				162	.61	324	54	27	27	27	0	243	0	810	135	81	81	0	0	0	0	0	81	81	.500

Dusty Baker

Year	Team	Lg	G	LUp	PL%	PH	PR	DS	Quick	Slow	LO	RCD	LS	Rel	SBA	SacA	RM	PO	#	Good	NG	Bomb	W	L	Pct
1994	Giants	NL	115	76	.53	177	16	9	29	25	2	86	12	288	154	88		78	40	24	16	8	55	60	.478
1995	Giants	NL	144	96	.41	230	36	13	32	50	8	90	8	381	184	101		77	51	32	19	14	67	77	.465
1996	Giants	NL	162	129	.51	250	17	15	24	58	15	94	8	425	166	103		96	60	37	23	15	68	94	.420
1997	Giants	NL	162	114	.71	212	17	22	46	25	17	132	4	481	170	85		93	57	36	21	12	90	72	.556
1998	Giants	NL	163	130	.62	224	20	12	43	38	8	113	5	433	153	111		41	68	42	26	9	89	74	.546
1999	Giants	NL	162	120	.62	233	16	16	30	51	27	111		450	165	113		40	41	25	16	10	86	76	.531
2000	Giants	NL	162	82	.56	233	26	22	38	50	25	91	3	384	118	86		37	26	17	9	2	97	65	.599
2001	Giants	NL	162	122	.48	261	22	19	40	48	10	114	4	439	99	95		45	49	33	16	6	90	72	.556
2002	Giants	NL	162	118	.43	223	32	38	29	56	53	106	8	417	95	89	42	41	44	28	16	10	95	66	.590
2003	Cubs	NL	162	114	.49	272	25	43	24	58	65	111	3	420	104	93	31	24	36	23	13	4	88	74	.543
2004	Cubs	NL	162	113	.44	254	16	19	37	41	42	129	8	460	94	108	71	62	33	22	11	7	89	73	.549
2005	Cubs	NL	162	121	.59	240	21	29	40	46	36	103	2	457	104	88	107	70	48	27	21	7	79	83	.488
2006	Cubs	NL	162	133	.58	271	9	26	45	39	22	165	2	542	170	108	139	46	44	28	16	11	66	96	.407
2008	Reds	NL	162	119	.58	285	28	27	26	63	39	124	2	507	132	100	101	37	40	28	12	4	74	88	.457
2009	Reds	NL	162	130	.45	252	15	35	30	62	35	115	1	478	136	120	118	23	36	29	7	6	78	84	.481
2010	Reds	NL	162	120	.46	258	19	49	36	41	22	140	0	502	136	91	157	13	32	22	10	9	91	71	.562
2011	Reds	NL	162	142	.42	240	29	42	34	51	20	115	0	501	147	102	226	33	47	26	21	5	79	83	.488
2012	Reds	NL	162	121	.43	201	19	39	33	39	30	78	4	425	114	108	148	19	33	22	11	3	97	65	.599
162-Game Average				119	.52	245	22	27	35	48	27	115	4	454	139	102	114	50	45	28	16	8	84	78	.519

Bud Black

Year	Team	Lg	G	LUp	PL%	PH	PR	DS	Quick	Slow	LO	RCD	LS	Rel	SBA	SacA	RM	PO	#	Good	NG	Bomb	W	L	Pct
2007	Padres	NL	162	115	.62	279	18	13	63	28	13	122	0	485	79	85	73	56	48	28	20	11	89	74	.546
2008	Padres	NL	162	113	.63	286	25	20	55	36	17	109	0	491	53	75	78	31	61	30	31	17	63	99	.389
2009	Padres	NL	162	137	.64	264	8	34	50	37	8	118	5	527	111	99	84	55	58	42	16	6	75	87	.463
2010	Padres	NL	162	135	.61	285	16	45	55	33	10	132	7	499	174	99	135	31	51	35	16	8	90	72	.556
2011	Padres	NL	162	140	.58	288	20	43	40	36	10	110	2	490	214	69	184	41	56	31	25	13	71	91	.438
2012	Padres	NL	162	132	.74	280	26	35	45	49	11	126	5	529	201	89	162	21	48	34	14	7	76	86	.469
162-Game Average				129	.64	280	19	32	51	36	11	119	3	503	139	86	119	39	54	33	20	10	77	85	.475

Bruce Bochy

Year	Team	Lg	G	LUp	PL%	PH	PR	DS	Quick	Slow	LO	RCD	LS	Rel	SBA	SacA	RM	PO	#	Good	NG	Bomb	W	L	Pct
1995	Padres	NL	144	96	.59	262	30	23	44	41	17	38	3	337	170	68		38	37	19	18	11	70	74	.486
1996	Padres	NL	162	114	.52	289	29	15	51	33	10	67	12	411	164	73		65	47	29	18	12	91	71	.562
1997	Padres	NL	162	111	.60	291	26	9	45	45	3	81	11	426	200	84		58	37	20	17	11	76	86	.469
1998	Padres	NL	162	110	.65	280	62	14	44	45	9	81	12	369	116	84		27	45	31	14	10	98	64	.605
1999	Padres	NL	162	137	.60	298	51	21	44	36	4	68	5	403	241	60		29	48	29	19	13	74	88	.457
2000	Padres	NL	162	134	.52	285	44	14	41	47	14	105	5	443	184	52		27	50	21	29	11	76	86	.469
2001	Padres	NL	162	116	.60	255	54	27	32	47	6	85	10	422	173	43		23	54	31	23	13	79	83	.488
2002	Padres	NL	162	123	.66	259	44	56	39	40	17	106	4	459	115	63	74	14	61	38	23	14	66	96	.407
2003	Padres	NL	162	134	.58	339	20	29	34	43	16	100	3	473	115	63	41	6	52	33	19	12	64	98	.395
2004	Padres	NL	162	96	.54	261	28	47	47	32	15	76	3	437	77	75	96	14	39	24	15	14	87	75	.537
2005	Padres	NL	162	128	.58	285	31	49	46	36	23	87	1	456	143	89	111	16	45	33	12	8	82	80	.506
2006	Padres	NL	162	111	.60	264	64	28	43	42	24	111	2	475	154	77	110	21	63	43	20	10	88	74	.543
2007	Giants	NL	162	128	.72	264	50	45	26	50	36	132	2	496	152	86	119	10	41	29	12	3	71	91	.438
2008	Giants	NL	162	134	.68	276	32	39	24	59	42	97	6	478	154	77	155	5	59	40	19	8	72	90	.444
2009	Giants	NL	162	134	.65	231	21	52	42	40	32	84	8	457	106	93	118	5	49	32	17	10	88	74	.543

Year	Team	Lg	G	LUp	PL%	PH	PR	DS	Quick	Slow	LO	RCD	LS	Rel	SBA	SacA	RM	PO	# Good	NG	Bomb	W	L	Pct
2010	Giants	NL	162	126	.55	224	45	70	29	37	40	118	12	477	87	102	144	12	58	41	17	8	92	70	.568
2011	Giants	NL	162	138	.62	245	49	42	38	38	44	108	3	480	136	79	175	11	46	36	10	6	86	76	.531
2012	Giants	NL	162	112	.75	220	32	55	22	50	31	136	9	526	157	87	176	15	42	30	12	5	94	68	.580
162-Game Average				122	.61	270	40	38	39	43	21	94	6	449	148	76	120	22	49	31	18	10	81	81	.500

Daren Brown

Year	Team	Lg	G	LUp	PL%	PH	PR	DS	Quick	Slow	LO	RCD	LS	Rel	SBA	SacA	RM	PO	# Good	NG	Bomb	W	L	Pct
2010	Mariners	AL	50	39	.60	9	12	2	15	8	6	14	2	104	52	19	71	9	8	5	3	2	19	31	.380
162-Game Average				126	.60	29	39	6	49	26	19	45	6	337	168	62	230	29	26	16	10	6	62	100	.383

Dave Clark

Year	Team	Lg	G	LUp	PL%	PH	PR	DS	Quick	Slow	LO	RCD	LS	Rel	SBA	SacA	RM	PO	# Good	NG	Bomb	W	L	Pct
2009	Astros	NL	13	9	.63	28	1	4	3	5	0	15	0	48	7	5	8	0	3	1	2	1	4	9	.308
162-Game Average				112	.63	349	12	50	37	62	0	187	0	598	87	62	100	0	37	12	25	12	50	112	.309

Terry Collins

Year	Team	Lg	G	LUp	PL%	PH	PR	DS	Quick	Slow	LO	RCD	LS	Rel	SBA	SacA	RM	PO	# Good	NG	Bomb	W	L	Pct
1994	Astros	NL	115	74	.54	185	20	13	6	6	0	37	4	268	168	90		37	28	17	11	5	66	49	.574
1995	Astros	NL	144	106	.49	302	38	11	15	7	8	100	8	394	236	97		44	39	27	12	8	76	68	.528
1996	Astros	NL	162	111	.41	257	30	38	13	12	9	70	10	371	243	94		35	42	30	12	6	82	80	.506
1997	Angels	AL	162	117	.70	86	34	22	10	16	15	67	8	400	198	55		60	25	13	12	4	84	78	.519
1998	Angels	AL	162	119	.57	100	64	33	15	11	28	86	11	415	138	69		38	16	6	10	4	85	77	.525
1999	Angels	AL	133	113	.56	93	26	16	10	16	10	68	2	315	93	39		7	10	1	9	3	51	82	.383
2011	Mets	NL	162	121	.68	312	18	28	32	44	23	126	5	514	165	88	151	9	48	35	13	9	77	85	.475
2012	Mets	NL	162	141	.69	329	16	38	39	36	19	113	0	505	117	75	149	8	29	18	11	3	74	88	.457
162-Game Average				122	.58	224	33	27	19	20	15	90	6	429	183	82	150	32	32	20	12	6	80	82	.494

Cecil Cooper

Year	Team	Lg	G	LUp	PL%	PH	PR	DS	Quick	Slow	LO	RCD	LS	Rel	SBA	SacA	RM	PO	# Good	NG	Bomb	W	L	Pct
2007	Astros	NL	31	26	.42	63	8	23	10	5	2	11	0	88	19	16	20	4	14	8	6	4	15	16	.484
2008	Astros	NL	161	115	.58	252	16	47	60	35	14	108	2	488	166	81	112	5	53	35	18	11	86	75	.534
2009	Astros	NL	149	94	.54	238	26	36	48	34	14	116	6	449	150	86	77	8	53	30	23	12	70	79	.470
162-Game Average				112	.55	263	24	50	56	35	14	112	4	487	159	87	99	8	57	35	22	13	81	81	.500

Don Cooper

Year	Team	Lg	G	LUp	PL%	PH	PR	DS	Quick	Slow	LO	RCD	LS	Rel	SBA	SacA	RM	PO	# Good	NG	Bomb	W	L	Pct
2011	White Sox	AL	2	2	.39	0	1	0	1	0	0	2	1	6	1	1	1	0	1	0	1	1	1	1	.500
162-Game Average				162	.39	0	81	0	81	0	0	162	81	486	81	81	81	0	81	0	81	81	81	81	.500

Bobby Cox

Year	Team	Lg	G	LUp	PL%	PH	PR	DS	Quick	Slow	LO	RCD	LS	Rel	SBA	SacA	RM	PO	# Good	NG	Bomb	W	L	Pct
1994	Braves	NL	114	64	.60	163	30	25	22	31	5	60	5	244	79	83		44	52	33	19	9	68	46	.596
1995	Braves	NL	144	59	.56	224	48	40	41	34	13	80	6	339	116	77		41	46	31	15	4	90	54	.625
1996	Braves	NL	162	89	.62	254	32	27	48	43	19	110	9	408	126	90		34	64	38	26	14	96	66	.593
1997	Braves	NL	162	87	.64	276	58	29	40	37	23	90	4	374	166	112		13	56	42	14	10	101	61	.623
1998	Braves	NL	162	80	.64	245	28	25	44	33	14	70	1	354	141	97		40	37	22	15	8	106	56	.654
1999	Braves	NL	162	76	.58	272	51	34	44	39	13	99	4	394	214	89		54	55	35	20	11	103	59	.636
2000	Braves	NL	162	103	.59	252	72	11	52	41	6	81	13	376	204	109		59	52	35	17	5	95	67	.586
2001	Braves	NL	162	113	.57	278	50	23	49	40	4	93	8	412	131	84		90	77	49	28	13	88	74	.543
2002	Braves	NL	161	105	.48	282	33	44	60	30	20	113	9	469	115	89	47	51	63	41	22	12	101	59	.631
2003	Braves	NL	162	69	.52	262	49	45	40	45	23	113	10	489	90	85	23	49	69	51	18	11	101	61	.623
2004	Braves	NL	162	105	.70	243	57	28	50	34	25	128	16	483	118	105	87	25	50	30	20	14	96	66	.593
2005	Braves	NL	162	110	.69	247	54	35	46	27	20	125	7	484	124	104	93	11	52	34	18	14	90	72	.556
2006	Braves	NL	162	85	.58	299	24	35	44	38	24	144	3	522	87	99	58	24	69	48	21	12	79	83	.488
2007	Braves	NL	162	86	.68	290	33	21	60	24	10	143	1	528	94	77	68	28	89	58	31	16	84	78	.519
2008	Braves	NL	162	117	.67	294	31	17	59	34	6	134	6	545	85	90	77	23	80	45	35	20	72	90	.444
2009	Braves	NL	162	112	.62	252	37	32	48	34	19	142	1	488	84	125	47	21	59	35	24	14	86	76	.531
2010	Braves	NL	162	109	.65	263	51	50	49	31	9	140	1	490	92	89	121	48	64	36	28	14	91	71	.562
162-Game Average				95	.61	265	45	31	48	36	15	112	6	446	125	97	69	40	62	40	22	12	93	69	.574

Tony DeFrancesco

Year	Team	Lg	G	LUp	PL%	PH	PR	DS	Quick	Slow	LO	RCD	LS	Rel	SBA	SacA	RM	PO	#	Good	NG	Bomb	W	L	Pct
2012	Astros	NL	41	41	.64	82	10	12	21	7	2	24	5	150	34	16	45	14	15	9	6	4	16	25	.390
162-Game Average				162	.64	324	40	47	83	28	8	95	20	593	134	63	178	55	59	36	24	16	63	99	.389

John Farrell

Year	Team	Lg	G	LUp	PL%	PH	PR	DS	Quick	Slow	LO	RCD	LS	Rel	SBA	SacA	RM	PO	#	Good	NG	Bomb	W	L	Pct
2011	Blue Jays	AL	162	131	.43	64	48	22	40	41	26	62	3	474	28	40	181	22	28	17	11	5	81	81	.500
2012	Blue Jays	AL	162	131	.50	94	30	16	49	44	7	84	3	495	164	46	211	15	20	11	9	7	73	89	.451
162-Game Average				131	.47	79	39	19	45	43	17	73	3	485	174	43	196	19	24	14	10	6	77	85	.475

Terry Francona

Year	Team	Lg	G	LUp	PL%	PH	PR	DS	Quick	Slow	LO	RCD	LS	Rel	SBA	SacA	RM	PO	#	Good	NG	Bomb	W	L	Pct
1997	Phillies	NL	162	98	.66	288	19	28	28	54	22	102	9	409	148	91		30	42	23	19	9	68	94	.420
1998	Phillies	NL	162	84	.53	256	20	19	34	57	20	88	7	385	142	85		16	27	10	17	8	75	87	.463
1999	Phillies	NL	162	85	.51	239	13	31	29	41	16	111	7	441	160	81		27	24	14	10	6	77	85	.475
2000	Phillies	NL	162	108	.53	278	17	14	38	43	25	102	5	414	132	89		16	32	22	10	7	65	97	.401
2004	Red Sox	AL	162	141	.65	116	65	58	41	48	32	105	8	437	98	18	91	28	28	22	6	4	98	64	.605
2005	Red Sox	AL	162	104	.67	110	46	37	25	55	30	99	3	442	57	21	79	11	28	18	10	5	95	67	.586
2006	Red Sox	AL	162	116	.59	93	54	49	36	44	13	94	9	454	74	33	98	16	25	11	14	7	86	76	.531
2007	Red Sox	AL	162	109	.60	84	34	23	41	35	32	89	4	451	120	45	90	14	20	14	6	4	96	66	.593
2008	Red Sox	AL	162	131	.59	62	40	40	50	30	20	90	11	466	155	40	87	8	17	10	7	4	95	67	.586
2009	Red Sox	AL	162	113	.58	85	47	28	36	50	30	68	6	463	165	29	68	9	24	15	9	6	95	67	.586
2010	Red Sox	AL	162	143	.62	125	48	34	32	63	49	84	3	443	85	36	125	26	30	17	13	4	89	73	.549
2011	Red Sox	AL	162	123	.67	89	44	11	52	46	27	89	4	444	144	29	163	34	11	6	5	2	90	72	.556
162-Game Average				113	.60	152	37	31	37	47	26	93	6	437	123	50	100	20	26	15	11	6	86	76	.531

Ron Gardenhire

Year	Team	Lg	G	LUp	PL%	PH	PR	DS	Quick	Slow	LO	RCD	LS	Rel	SBA	SacA	RM	PO	#	Good	NG	Bomb	W	L	Pct
2002	Twins	AL	161	111	.69	141	36	42	54	25	10	84	1	435	141	48	44	11	24	16	8	4	94	67	.584
2003	Twins	AL	162	126	.63	144	50	26	49	33	13	85	2	399	138	59	37	14	35	16	19	6	90	72	.556
2004	Twins	AL	162	131	.59	129	45	29	56	21	20	106	4	435	162	66	121	18	27	15	12	7	92	70	.568
2005	Twins	AL	162	135	.58	104	45	26	50	21	5	87	1	396	146	59	138	16	38	28	10	3	83	79	.512
2006	Twins	AL	162	97	.62	93	36	21	60	31	3	82	5	421	143	48	130	11	25	14	11	4	96	66	.593
2007	Twins	AL	162	139	.63	104	42	25	45	30	8	99	4	438	142	45	148	11	33	14	19	9	79	83	.488
2008	Twins	AL	162	103	.64	109	26	12	47	29	5	115	3	485	144	73	143	17	38	25	13	8	88	75	.540
2009	Twins	AL	163	129	.63	83	54	34	43	25	12	115	3	480	117	62	100	21	20	9	11	6	87	76	.534
2010	Twins	AL	162	112	.62	86	55	30	57	28	5	106	4	465	96	47	140	14	19	12	7	4	94	68	.580
2011	Twins	AL	162	150	.58	93	48	21	34	44	17	82	1	457	131	44	170	5	37	21	16	9	63	99	.389
2012	Twins	AL	162	121	.62	64	45	24	42	31	4	82	1	499	172	49	207	10	43	27	16	6	66	96	.407
162-Game Average				123	.62	104	44	26	49	29	9	95	2	446	139	55	125	13	31	18	13	6	85	77	.525

Cito Gaston

Year	Team	Lg	G	LUp	PL%	PH	PR	DS	Quick	Slow	LO	RCD	LS	Rel	SBA	SacA	RM	PO	#	Good	NG	Bomb	W	L	Pct
1994	Blue Jays	AL	115	59	.55	41	16	21	7	14	2	23	5	221	105	44		48	23	15	8	6	55	60	.478
1995	Blue Jays	AL	144	82	.65	85	24	7	15	27	40	29	10	265	91	47		57	42	24	18	10	56	88	.389
1996	Blue Jays	AL	162	87	.70	126	23	11	12	27	23	41	4	303	154	63		34	37	23	14	9	74	88	.457
1997	Blue Jays	AL	157	90	.59	71	19	6	13	22	36	74	6	322	177	50		30	29	20	9	2	72	85	.459
2008	Blue Jays	AL	88	65	.59	36	18	30	18	19	25	40	0	216	37	41	37	11	16	8	8	6	51	37	.580
2009	Blue Jays	AL	162	105	.49	48	36	18	36	47	25	83	3	445	96	32	64	25	26	15	11	6	75	87	.463
2010	Blue Jays	AL	162	103	.45	40	40	13	51	33	12	77	4	455	78	22	88	23	35	19	16	6	85	77	.525
162-Game Average				97	.57	73	29	17	25	31	27	60	5	364	121	49	74	37	34	20	14	7	77	85	.475

Bob Geren

Year	Team	Lg	G	LUp	PL%	PH	PR	DS	Quick	Slow	LO	RCD	LS	Rel	SBA	SacA	RM	PO	#	Good	NG	Bomb	W	L	Pct
2007	Athletics	AL	162	140	.57	64	31	24	39	43	14	112	9	446	72	31	91	22	60	38	22	10	76	86	.469
2008	Athletics	AL	161	133	.59	91	57	37	49	32	5	87	8	441	109	44	62	18	45	25	20	10	75	86	.466
2009	Athletics	AL	162	129	.59	77	27	40	54	40	5	108	11	488	181	37	71	5	30	15	15	7	75	87	.463
2010	Athletics	AL	162	126	.63	108	28	26	57	30	19	81	8	423	194	58	138	11	29	16	13	3	81	81	.500
2011	Athletics	AL	63	47	.62	42	9	3	25	11	7	50	2	177	57	18	54	9	15	7	8	4	27	36	.429
162-Game Average				131	.60	87	35	30	51	36	11	100	9	451	140	43	95	15	41	23	18	8	76	86	.469

Kirk Gibson

Year	Team	Lg	G	LINEUPS		SUBSTITUTION			PITCHER USAGE						TACTICS				INTENTIONAL BB				RESULTS		
				LUp	PL%	PH	PR	DS	Quick	Slow	LO	RCD	LS	Rel	SBA	SacA	RM	PO	#	Good	NG	Bomb	W	L	Pct
2010	Diamondbacks	NL	83	57	.64	154	7	11	25	21	8	43	1	247	69	28	62	19	19	13	6	2	34	49	.410
2011	Diamondbacks	NL	162	118	.57	253	9	13	33	51	15	116	2	463	188	74	143	12	16	10	6	3	94	68	.580
2012	Diamondbacks	NL	162	140	.56	231	11	9	35	50	16	104	4	461	144	77	120	8	18	11	7	1	81	81	.500
	162-Game Average			125	.58	254	11	13	37	49	16	105	3	466	160	71	129	16	21	14	8	2	83	79	.512

Joe Girardi

Year	Team	Lg	G	LINEUPS		SUBSTITUTION			PITCHER USAGE						TACTICS				INTENTIONAL BB				RESULTS		
				LUp	PL%	PH	PR	DS	Quick	Slow	LO	RCD	LS	Rel	SBA	SacA	RM	PO	#	Good	NG	Bomb	W	L	Pct
2006	Marlins	NL	162	117	.50	250	44	**66**	46	40	28	76	3	438	168	97	108	42	58	37	21	7	78	84	.481
2008	Yankees	AL	162	114	.63	97	37	42	**60**	37	12	88	10	475	157	38	**173**	**36**	37	22	15	8	89	73	.549
2009	Yankees	AL	162	106	**.73**	97	**61**	42	36	45	27	88	**13**	461	139	44	83	33	28	14	14	9	**103**	59	.636
2010	Yankees	AL	162	114	**.72**	117	44	31	43	39	33	76	3	430	133	47	152	20	37	26	11	6	95	67	.586
2011	Yankees	AL	162	94	.69	72	41	53	51	36	21	88	2	465	193	50	151	26	43	30	13	4	**97**	65	.599
2012	Yankees	AL	162	107	.70	149	33	48	37	53	21	115	7	485	120	47	145	10	32	17	15	6	**95**	67	.586
	162-Game Average			109	.66	130	43	47	46	42	24	89	6	459	152	54	135	28	39	24	15	7	93	69	.574

Fredi Gonzalez

Year	Team	Lg	G	LINEUPS		SUBSTITUTION			PITCHER USAGE						TACTICS				INTENTIONAL BB				RESULTS		
				LUp	PL%	PH	PR	DS	Quick	Slow	LO	RCD	LS	Rel	SBA	SacA	RM	PO	#	Good	NG	Bomb	W	L	Pct
2007	Marlins	NL	162	96	.50	284	29	34	33	**56**	20	138	5	560	139	91	79	22	60	36	24	**16**	71	91	.438
2008	Marlins	NL	161	106	.51	255	38	49	38	39	8	120	3	511	104	61	75	17	66	42	24	14	84	77	.522
2009	Marlins	NL	162	97	.58	281	28	49	48	26	12	116	0	**530**	110	86	88	20	60	38	22	15	87	75	.537
2010	Marlins	NL	70	31	.41	104	12	16	14	13	11	35	1	193	56	33	64	10	18	11	7	5	34	36	.486
2011	Braves	NL	162	120	.60	260	27	29	53	36	21	**144**	0	510	121	95	139	19	**73**	**49**	24	13	89	73	.549
2012	Braves	NL	162	110	.61	268	18	27	50	34	9	115	4	460	133	67	116	20	40	28	12	11	94	68	.580
	162-Game Average			103	.55	268	28	38	43	38	15	123	2	509	122	80	103	20	58	38	21	14	85	77	.525

Ozzie Guillen

Year	Team	Lg	G	LINEUPS		SUBSTITUTION			PITCHER USAGE						TACTICS				INTENTIONAL BB				RESULTS		
				LUp	PL%	PH	PR	DS	Quick	Slow	LO	RCD	LS	Rel	SBA	SacA	RM	PO	#	Good	NG	Bomb	W	L	Pct
2004	White Sox	AL	162	134	.58	**132**	35	15	28	**65**	**48**	86	8	399	129	**84**	97	17	36	15	**21**	8	83	79	.512
2005	White Sox	AL	162	112	.51	100	32	21	31	**56**	**35**	114	5	412	204	**68**	148	15	**42**	27	15	6	**99**	63	.611
2006	White Sox	AL	162	87	.60	**135**	42	38	28	**68**	**35**	83	7	398	141	61	85	27	**59**	**39**	20	9	90	72	.556
2007	White Sox	AL	162	124	.56	100	26	23	26	53	**33**	131	2	463	123	54	92	13	50	24	**26**	**15**	72	90	.444
2008	White Sox	AL	163	100	.52	75	49	37	42	48	14	100	3	463	101	44	98	8	42	29	13	6	89	74	.546
2009	White Sox	AL	162	124	.52	105	48	19	50	37	16	70	4	415	162	45	114	15	41	23	**18**	**10**	79	83	.488
2010	White Sox	AL	162	115	.51	85	46	36	41	51	24	61	**8**	407	**234**	60	220	25	41	26	15	10	88	74	.543
2011	White Sox	AL	160	111	.52	73	47	28	34	45	28	63	**8**	404	133	65	172	40	**49**	**35**	14	7	78	82	.488
2012	Marlins	NL	162	116	.60	234	23	29	24	39	27	126	2	483	190	89	137	**23**	61	**38**	23	13	69	93	.426
	162-Game Average			114	.55	116	39	27	34	51	29	93	5	427	158	63	129	20	47	28	18	9	83	79	.512

Trey Hillman

Year	Team	Lg	G	LINEUPS		SUBSTITUTION			PITCHER USAGE						TACTICS				INTENTIONAL BB				RESULTS		
				LUp	PL%	PH	PR	DS	Quick	Slow	LO	RCD	LS	Rel	SBA	SacA	RM	PO	#	Good	NG	Bomb	W	L	Pct
2008	Royals	AL	162	134	.55	71	44	34	35	48	19	78	2	439	117	50	96	15	15	9	6	3	75	87	.463
2009	Royals	AL	162	141	.63	90	34	38	41	**54**	34	72	7	426	117	51	110	27	28	13	15	**10**	65	97	.401
2010	Royals	AL	35	24	.57	12	12	1	9	13	4	21	2	109	38	25	41	8	3	2	1	1	12	23	.343
	162-Game Average			135	.59	78	41	33	38	52	26	77	5	440	123	57	111	23	21	11	10	6	69	93	.426

A.J. Hinch

Year	Team	Lg	G	LINEUPS		SUBSTITUTION			PITCHER USAGE						TACTICS				INTENTIONAL BB				RESULTS		
				LUp	PL%	PH	PR	DS	Quick	Slow	LO	RCD	LS	Rel	SBA	SacA	RM	PO	#	Good	NG	Bomb	W	L	Pct
2009	Diamondbacks	NL	133	115	.63	222	10	13	24	50	24	61	5	392	113	64	41	5	24	12	12	6	58	75	.436
2010	Diamondbacks	NL	79	56	.53	120	7	4	12	40	21	39	1	207	58	19	51	7	19	9	10	9	31	48	.392
	162-Game Average			131	.59	261	13	13	28	69	34	76	5	458	131	63	70	9	33	16	17	11	68	94	.420

Clint Hurdle

Year	Team	Lg	G	LINEUPS		SUBSTITUTION			PITCHER USAGE						TACTICS				INTENTIONAL BB				RESULTS		
				LUp	PL%	PH	PR	DS	Quick	Slow	LO	RCD	LS	Rel	SBA	SacA	RM	PO	#	Good	NG	Bomb	W	L	Pct
2002	Rockies	NL	140	100	.52	274	28	41	33	45	17	104	3	437	139	46	50	13	38	22	16	11	67	73	.479
2003	Rockies	NL	162	108	.47	317	17	32	35	40	5	87	4	500	100	82	26	16	51	31	20	13	74	88	.457
2004	Rockies	NL	162	131	.57	289	18	35	36	**63**	20	74	1	473	77	**128**	67	12	**84**	**54**	**30**	12	68	94	.420
2005	Rockies	NL	162	135	.60	273	21	40	42	**60**	17	89	2	459	97	114	119	22	54	28	26	**15**	67	**95**	.414

Year	Team	Lg	G	LUp	PL%	PH	PR	DS	Quick	Slow	LO	RCD	LS	Rel	SBA	SacA	RM	PO	# Good	NG	Bomb	W	L	Pct
2006	Rockies	NL	162	111	.49	259	17	22	34	**52**	17	107	2	499	135	**156**	114	28	81	45	**36**	**23**	76	86	.469
2007	Rockies	NL	163	96	.51	283	32	29	45	37	13	112	1	529	131	**112**	109	26	61	30	**31**	14	**90**	73	.552
2008	Rockies	NL	162	131	.49	253	20	31	40	43	16	85	2	485	**178**	**111**	116	**43**	49	31	18	6	74	88	.457
2009	Rockies	NL	46	42	.60	73	8	10	11	14	3	31	0	135	45	26	34	3	11	8	3	1	18	28	.391
2011	Pirates	NL	162	134	.60	278	26	63	**58**	27	1	134	3	**549**	160	101	173	20	65	39	**26**	13	72	90	.444
2012	Pirates	NL	162	133	.55	270	26	**60**	50	33	3	74	2	483	125	82	120	17	30	18	12	3	79	83	.488
	162-Game Average			122	.54	281	23	40	42	45	12	98	2	497	130	105	101	22	57	33	24	12	75	87	.463

Brandon Hyde

Year	Team	Lg	G	LUp	PL%	PH	PR	DS	Quick	Slow	LO	RCD	LS	Rel	SBA	SacA	RM	PO	# Good	NG	Bomb	W	L	Pct
2011	Marlins	NL	1	1	.44	0	0	0	0	0	1	1	0	3	0	0	1	0	1	1	0	0	0	1	.000
	162-Game Average			162	.44	0	0	0	0	0	162	162	0	486	0	0	162	0	162	162	0	0	0	162	.000

Davey Johnson

Year	Team	Lg	G	LUp	PL%	PH	PR	DS	Quick	Slow	LO	RCD	LS	Rel	SBA	SacA	RM	PO	# Good	NG	Bomb	W	L	Pct
1994	Reds	NL	115	79	.54	195	22	12	32	28	2	56	12	261	170	86	0	41	23	15	8	1	66	48	.579
1995	Reds	NL	144	105	.55	257	18	31	56	18	1	60	16	329	258	88	0	10	32	16	16	10	85	59	.590
1996	Orioles	AL	163	99	.68	85	33	38	48	43	13	67	9	378	117	62	0	6	35	13	22	11	88	74	.543
1997	Orioles	AL	162	109	.56	104	36	43	65	23	5	84	11	400	89	75	0	10	31	16	15	9	98	64	.605
1999	Dodgers	NL	162	109	.53	236	22	9	36	40	8	67	4	399	235	126	0	19	26	17	9	7	77	85	.475
2000	Dodgers	NL	162	89	.59	252	26	11	20	15	10		6	371	137	80	51	11	14	8	6	2	86	76	.531
2011	Nationals	NL	83	59	.45	143	20	23	40	13	1	51	1	271	58	51	85	6	19	10	9	6	40	43	.482
2012	Nationals	NL	162	93	.60	252	30	42	57	30	10	105	1	482	140	67	158	2	32	21	11	7	**98**	64	.605
	162-Game Average			99	.33	226	30	17	47	35	17	63	16	347	177	88	194	19	34	19	15	8	93	69	.574

Tony LaRussa

Year	Team	Lg	G	LUp	PL%	PH	PR	DS	Quick	Slow	LO	RCD	LS	Rel	SBA	SacA	RM	PO	# Good	NG	Bomb	W	L	Pct
1994	Athletics	AL	114	97	.62	89	28	14	43	21	5	60	4	308	130	31		32	30	20	10	4	51	63	.447
1995	Athletics	AL	144	120	.54	113	38	24	33	38	19	46	7	358	158	42		42	26	18	8	4	67	77	.465
1996	Cardinals	NL	162	120	.52	246	25	13	32	48	24	90	8	413	207	117		41	43	28	15	7	88	74	.543
1997	Cardinals	NL	162	146	.54	307	17	18	34	42	16	81	2	399	224	77		79	34	26	8	2	73	89	.451
1998	Cardinals	NL	162	146	.52	259	7	18	62	31	13	82	14	429	174	85		34	38	25	13	8	83	79	.512
1999	Cardinals	NL	161	138	.47	264	32	28	50	41	13	96	14	454	182	103		30	38	20	18	11	75	86	.466
2000	Cardinals	NL	162	137	.53	240	35	25	40	31	11	63	18	386	138	107		34	28	21	7	6	95	67	.586
2001	Cardinals	NL	162	117	.47	256	26	13	46	36	7	140	7	485	126	102		25	36	21	15	4	93	69	.574
2002	Cardinals	NL	162	117	.52	**340**	27	41	58	33	23	110	6	472	128	106	75	13	39	25	14	8	97	65	.599
2003	Cardinals	NL	162	126	.50	**352**	28	51	38	49	36	113	9	460	114	**108**	**56**	9	36	28	8	2	85	77	.525
2004	Cardinals	NL	162	119	.53	275	25	**69**	30	48	31	120	**16**	469	148	88	**158**	9	24	17	7	4	**105**	57	.648
2005	Cardinals	NL	162	138	.55	270	25	48	40	38	22	88	4	436	119	92	**153**	9	27	16	11	7	**100**	62	.617
2006	Cardinals	NL	161	131	.56	272	11	53	50	34	21	95	6	469	91	86	123	13	35	21	14	3	83	78	.516
2007	Cardinals	NL	162	**150**	.60	**317**	19	37	46	44	8	102	5	516	89	85	120	23	25	10	15	11	78	84	.481
2008	Cardinals	NL	162	**153**	.64	275	26	57	52	40	16	101	**11**	506	105	87	114	18	21	13	8	1	86	76	.531
2009	Cardinals	NL	162	131	.52	**289**	12	51	55	38	17	102	8	481	106	93	91	17	23	15	8	1	91	71	.562
2010	Cardinals	NL	162	**147**	.55	**292**	16	28	52	40	16	80	5	455	120	87	151	22	32	17	15	8	86	76	.531
2011	Cardinals	NL	162	127	.57	262	36	**86**	47	44	20	94	**8**	468	96	101	179	17	44	23	21	**14**	90	72	.556
	162-Game Average			134	.54	268	25	38	46	40	18	95	9	453	140	91	122	27	33	21	12	6	87	75	.537

Jim Leyland

Year	Team	Lg	G	LUp	PL%	PH	PR	DS	Quick	Slow	LO	RCD	LS	Rel	SBA	SacA	RM	PO	# Good	NG	Bomb	W	L	Pct
1994	Pirates	NL	114	94	.56	170	16	13	12	9	1	48	4	285	78	48		38	52	29	23	15	53	61	.465
1995	Pirates	NL	144	124	.56	282	8	4	13	12	11	71	4	391	139	69		51	50	30	20	10	58	86	.403
1996	Pirates	NL	162	117	.53	299	18	14	27	8	11	60	11	422	175	101		46	50	23	27	13	73	89	.451
1997	Marlins	NL	162	105	.59	258	36	31	21	12	18	65	2	404	173	91		38	41	25	16	9	92	70	.568
1998	Marlins	NL	162	96	.59	277	13	15	18	24	31	73	4	420	172	91		31	61	36	25	11	54	108	.333
1999	Rockies	NL	162	124	.56	294	11	12	11	29	21	72	5	421	113	88		11	46	24	22	14	72	90	.444
2006	Tigers	AL	162	120	.53	81	34	38	52	32	16	52	3	390	100	57	128	9	35	23	12	9	95	67	.586
2007	Tigers	AL	162	108	.53	77	31	49	46	43	14	70	5	443	133	35	123	20	44	24	17	13	88	74	.543
2008	Tigers	AL	162	131	.51	66	25	**50**	29	47	20	72	7	440	94	40	114	10	**63**	37	**26**	13	74	88	.457
2009	Tigers	AL	163	126	.55	125	52	**50**	47	47	**38**	86	3	439	105	60	132	19	42	26	16	6	86	77	.528
2010	Tigers	AL	162	129	.58	130	11	**47**	36	54	45	70	6	416	99	54	174	**31**	29	14	15	9	81	81	.500
2011	Tigers	AL	162	127	.63	86	42	**87**	43	39	39	84	1	421	69	62	172	7	34	17	**17**	**10**	95	67	.586
2012	Tigers	AL	162	121	.58	76	33	62	38	41	**37**	103	0	420	82	46	151	14	35	21	14	7	88	74	.543
	162-Game Average			121	.56	176	26	37	31	32	24	73	5	422	122	67	142	26	46	26	20	11	80	82	.494

Ken Macha

Year	Team	Lg	G	LUp	PL%	PH	PR	DS	Quick	Slow	LO	RCD	LS	Rel	SBA	SacA	RM	PO	#	Good	NG	Bomb	W	L	Pct
2003	Athletics	AL	162	111	.57	140	29	23	44	38	30	72	12	364	62	31	28	9	42	25	17	10	96	66	.593
2004	Athletics	AL	162	119	.60	123	13	14	37	47	39	94	5	414	69	30	63	2	49	31	18	9	91	71	.562
2005	Athletics	AL	162	127	.62	83	17	11	43	36	30	79	13	410	53	29	53	13	42	27	15	6	88	74	.543
2006	Athletics	AL	162	121	.58	62	33	23	39	47	28	104	8	444	81	29	70	22	47	26	21	11	93	69	.574
2009	Brewers	NL	162	111	.48	267	7	32	35	51	19	120	1	512	105	70	90	12	60	35	25	17	80	82	.494
2010	Brewers	NL	162	95	.47	226	14	22	42	55	27	102	9	495	107	52	138	5	42	27	15	11	77	85	.475
	162-Game Average			114	.55	150	19	21	40	46	29	95	8	440	80	40	74	11	47	29	19	11	88	74	.543

Joe Maddon

Year	Team	Lg	G	LUp	PL%	PH	PR	DS	Quick	Slow	LO	RCD	LS	Rel	SBA	SacA	RM	PO	#	Good	NG	Bomb	W	L	Pct
1996	Angels	AL	22	19	.64	21	5	0	7	6	6	10	3	48	11	20		6	4	3	1	1	8	14	.364
1998	Angels	AL	8	4	.57	2	4	0	1	5	3	5	3	12	2	7		0	1	0	1	0	6	2	.750
1999	Angels	AL	29	19	.58	29	4	1	6	0	4	20	0	85	23	12		7	3	1	2	1	19	10	.655
2006	Devil Rays	AL	162	145	.54	81	26	51	41	39	16	79	10	444	186	51	132	48	39	19	20	13	61	101	.377
2007	Devil Rays	AL	162	122	.53	80	19	16	31	56	19	113	1	483	179	40	118	50	31	18	13	4	66	96	.407
2008	Rays	AL	162	115	.69	133	16	39	48	37	14	112	7	448	192	31	113	26	29	15	14	8	97	65	.599
2009	Rays	AL	162	123	.66	140	21	18	28	51	23	139	3	510	255	29	99	15	22	10	12	7	84	78	.519
2010	Rays	AL	162	129	.67	174	31	18	41	34	26	135	2	491	219	45	166	12	34	28	6	3	96	66	.593
2011	Rays	AL	162	130	.67	137	16	31	34	36	47	112	6	438	217	42	187	4	38	23	15	6	91	71	.562
2012	Rays	AL	162	151	.62	156	37	52	43	38	33	123	3	472	178	40	181	7	35	25	10	6	90	72	.556
	162-Game Average			130	.62	129	24	31	38	41	26	115	5	466	199	43	142	24	32	19	13	7	84	78	.519

Charlie Manuel

Year	Team	Lg	G	LUp	PL%	PH	PR	DS	Quick	Slow	LO	RCD	LS	Rel	SBA	SacA	RM	PO	#	Good	NG	Bomb	W	L	Pct
2000	Indians	AL	162	102	.64	73	40	26	21	12	20	104	7	462	147	59		30	45	28	17	9	90	72	.556
2001	Indians	AL	162	114	.61	105	30	49	28	17	10	120	3	484	120	67		43	44	30	14	11	91	71	.562
2002	Indians	AL	86	67	.61	57	10	19	14	17	25	47	0	222	57	21	34	3	21	12	9	4	39	47	.453
2005	Phillies	NL	162	80	.64	265	36	19	42	28	13	119	6	442	143	86	76	11	51	35	16	9	88	74	.543
2006	Phillies	NL	162	81	.65	301	42	49	28	43	22	126	2	500	117	79	74	16	63	35	28	12	85	77	.525
2007	Phillies	NL	162	87	.64	264	56	75	40	40	19	128	6	498	157	84	90	30	62	41	21	16	89	73	.549
2008	Phillies	NL	162	77	.65	291	62	60	33	42	24	124	1	468	161	88	92	34	64	46	18	11	92	70	.568
2009	Phillies	NL	162	68	.67	283	20	16	32	55	32	107	3	459	147	74	65	3	31	19	12	3	93	69	.574
2010	Phillies	NL	162	94	.64	276	17	19	37	50	39	114	1	451	129	64	120	3	42	27	15	6	97	65	.599
2011	Phillies	NL	162	105	.69	264	26	22	49	39	48	74	1	394	120	80	141	5	41	31	10	5	102	60	.630
2012	Phillies	NL	162	131	.68	281	22	48	35	56	30	93	5	440	139	91	125	6	33	21	12	5	81	81	.500
	162-Game Average			96	.65	234	34	38	34	38	27	110	3	458	136	75	96	17	47	31	16	9	90	72	.556

Jerry Manuel

Year	Team	Lg	G	LUp	PL%	PH	PR	DS	Quick	Slow	LO	RCD	LS	Rel	SBA	SacA	RM	PO	#	Good	NG	Bomb	W	L	Pct
1998	White Sox	AL	162	110	.56	65	19	31	43	35	6	72	14	405	173	54		26	20	14	6	4	80	82	.494
1999	White Sox	AL	161	109	.58	79	35	39	35	42	9	78	8	409	160	69		22	31	20	11	7	75	86	.466
2000	White Sox	AL	162	84	.53	84	35	20	41	31	8	91	18	466	161	75		32	27	16	11	10	95	67	.586
2001	White Sox	AL	162	115	.53	104	34	50	45	39	5	93	16	466	182	95		41	38	24	14	9	83	79	.512
2002	White Sox	AL	162	104	.55	86	10	39	50	44	17	86	10	423	106	73	38	18	31	17	14	11	81	81	.500
2003	White Sox	AL	162	105	.55	146	40	71	39	36	27	74	10	361	106	66	39	20	30	18	12	7	86	76	.531
2008	Mets	NL	93	58	.76	167	7	31	12	30	23	95	2	324	89	54	81	6	37	18	19	6	55	38	.591
2009	Mets	NL	162	117	.72	289	11	37	34	51	22	137	2	511	166	112	104	3	60	38	22	14	70	92	.432
2010	Mets	NL	162	124	.67	290	19	25	39	47	32	145	9	491	174	100	169	8	55	42	13	6	79	83	.488
	162-Game Average			108	.60	153	25	40	39	41	17	102	10	443	154	81	94	21	38	24	14	9	82	80	.506

Mike Matheny

Year	Team	Lg	G	LUp	PL%	PH	PR	DS	Quick	Slow	LO	RCD	LS	Rel	SBA	SacA	RM	PO	#	Good	NG	Bomb	W	L	Pct
2012	Cardinals	NL	162	122	.62	286	37	33	53	37	8	118	5	506	128	95	144	16	28	13	15	7	88	74	.543
	162-Game Average			122	.62	286	37	33	53	37	8	118	5	506	128	95	144	16	28	13	15	7	88	74	.543

Don Mattingly

Year	Team	Lg	G	LUp	PL%	PH	PR	DS	Quick	Slow	LO	RCD	LS	Rel	SBA	SacA	RM	PO	#	Good	NG	Bomb	W	L	Pct
2011	Dodgers	NL	161	140	.57	233	29	44	45	40	30	86	1	461	166	93	181	13	48	27	21	12	82	79	.509
2012	Dodgers	NL	162	127	.59	247	22	43	51	39	20	118	2	506	148	105	153	8	62	38	24	15	86	76	.531
	162-Game Average			134	.58	241	26	44	48	40	25	102	2	485	157	99	168	11	55	33	23	14	84	78	.519

Jack McKeon

Year	Team	Lg	G	LUp	PL%	PH	PR	DS	Quick	Slow	LO	RCD	LS	Rel	SBA	SacA	RM	PO	#	Good	NG	Bomb	W	L	Pct
1997	Reds	NL	63	50	.46	102	18	7	23	11	5	44	3	154	79	42		18	16	6	10	7	33	30	.524
1998	Reds	NL	162	132	.55	288	30	25	49	25	10	107	20	366	137	98		7	42	29	13	8	77	85	.475
1999	Reds	NL	163	95	.50	251	30	38	58	23	9	93	28	381	218	88		14	46	30	16	5	96	67	.589
2000	Reds	NL	163	117	.51	270	31	41	52	27	10	96	24	387	138	82		24	53	36	17	10	85	77	.525
2003	Marlins	NL	124	57	.43	171	26	21	32	35	33	63	6	280	150	92	41	17	28	16	12	10	75	49	.605
2004	Marlins	NL	162	90	.48	224	27	34	42	37	20	95	12	404	139	104	96	19	61	40	21	13	83	79	.512
2005	Marlins	NL	162	82	.43	246	24	36	44	35	36	103	7	449	134	106	106	16	57	37	20	10	83	79	.512
2011	Marlins	NL	90	65	.53	146	22	16	29	15	13	63	0	278	87	74	67	10	43	25	18	10	40	50	.444
162-Game Average				102	.49	253	31	32	49	31	20	99	15	402	161	102	93	19	52	33	19	11	85	77	.525

John McLaren

Year	Team	Lg	G	LUp	PL%	PH	PR	DS	Quick	Slow	LO	RCD	LS	Rel	SBA	SacA	RM	PO	#	Good	NG	Bomb	W	L	Pct
2007	Mariners	AL	84	52	.48	55	40	18	17	23	19	49	6	247	56	20	76	18	19	10	9	5	43	41	.512
2008	Mariners	AL	72	48	.50	31	16	4	17	24	9	45	1	197	65	17	63	11	12	6	6	5	25	47	.347
2011	Nationals	NL	3	3	.56	2	0	1	1	0	2	3	0	12	6	2	8	1	2	1	1	0	2	1	.667
162-Game Average				105	.49	90	57	23	36	48	31	99	7	465	129	40	150	31	34	17	16	10	71	91	.438

Bob Melvin

Year	Team	Lg	G	LUp	PL%	PH	PR	DS	Quick	Slow	LO	RCD	LS	Rel	SBA	SacA	RM	PO	#	Good	NG	Bomb	W	L	Pct
2003	Mariners	AL	162	111	.62	81	62	33	27	46	43	56	6	366	145	44	37	5	24	14	10	4	93	69	.574
2004	Mariners	AL	162	151	.59	109	66	26	26	63	43	82	5	414	152	56	123	24	32	18	14	8	63	99	.389
2005	Diamondbacks	NL	162	120	.68	310	26	38	26	56	36	123	11	458	93	93	101	30	43	27	16	9	77	85	.475
2006	Diamondbacks	NL	162	114	.72	278	11	35	37	42	15	86	0	461	106	83	61	30	44	28	16	8	76	86	.469
2007	Diamondbacks	NL	162	146	.57	243	11	61	35	42	31	96	2	469	133	74	70	25	38	30	8	4	90	72	.556
2008	Diamondbacks	NL	162	134	.57	263	27	30	41	39	16	102	0	444	81	87	79	28	41	27	14	9	82	80	.506
2009	Diamondbacks	NL	29	29	.62	47	6	8	7	4	3	17	0	91	29	17	13	3	3	1	2	2	12	17	.414
2011	Athletics	AL	99	87	.71	33	13	17	24	23	18	59	2	283	103	34	87	23	9	5	4	3	47	52	.475
2012	Athletics	AL	162	132	.71	111	17	18	63	29	5	93	2	462	154	41	116	30	34	21	13	6	94	68	.580
162-Game Average				131	.64	189	31	34	37	44	27	92	4	443	128	68	88	25	34	22	12	7	81	81	.500

Brad Mills

Year	Team	Lg	G	LUp	PL%	PH	PR	DS	Quick	Slow	LO	RCD	LS	Rel	SBA	SacA	RM	PO	#	Good	NG	Bomb	W	L	Pct
2010	Astros	NL	162	128	.50	280	17	51	29	52	41	121	1	507	136	90	122	8	39	30	9	5	76	86	.469
2011	Astros	NL	162	121	.49	284	31	31	25	65	38	125	2	503	115	95	135	11	59	38	21	9	56	106	.346
2012	Astros	NL	121	103	.60	181	22	22	20	49	12	102	0	391	117	54	115	10	25	12	13	6	39	82	.322
162-Game Average				128	.53	271	25	38	27	60	33	127	1	510	147	87	135	11	45	29	16	7	62	100	.383

Lou Piniella

Year	Team	Lg	G	LUp	PL%	PH	PR	DS	Quick	Slow	LO	RCD	LS	Rel	SBA	SacA	RM	PO	#	Good	NG	Bomb	W	L	Pct
1994	Mariners	AL	112	98	.49	113	24	6	30	35	4	54	9	252	69	54		37	39	21	18	9	49	63	.438
1995	Mariners	AL	145	98	.56	137	41	22	37	39	30	58	20	324	151	66		40	37	18	19	12	79	66	.545
1996	Mariners	AL	161	99	.55	190	28	14	56	21	15	91	14	403	129	65		40	52	31	21	13	85	76	.528
1997	Mariners	AL	162	84	.57	147	35	27	38	47	25	79	11	392	129	61		32	36	18	18	10	90	72	.556
1998	Mariners	AL	161	111	.53	99	38	43	38	54	32	81	4	368	154	58		20	23	8	15	7	76	85	.472
1999	Mariners	AL	162	130	.46	122	38	30	31	40	21	51	10	346	175	49		31	39	15	24	8	79	83	.488
2000	Mariners	AL	162	130	.50	109	43	52	51	37	1	64	11	383	178	73		22	37	20	17	8	91	71	.562
2001	Mariners	AL	162	115	.64	121	44	64	55	33	5	62	9	392	216	62		33	28	19	9	3	116	46	.716
2002	Mariners	AL	162	129	.64	95	129	50	49	39	34	52	7	343	195	61	43	25	34	15	19	11	93	69	.574
2003	Devil Rays	AL	162	124	.60	188	43	26	38	41	29	59	5	372	184	53	52	23	37	21	16	10	63	99	.389
2004	Devil Rays	AL	161	137	.63	97	25	36	51	34	23	57	15	401	174	45	104	16	35	16	19	9	70	91	.435
2005	Devil Rays	AL	162	135	.54	127	18	52	38	54	32	67	10	401	200	53	128	16	41	19	22	13	67	95	.414
2007	Cubs	NL	162	125	.51	263	52	51	35	38	33	98	3	478	119	60	89	17	46	28	18	4	85	77	.525
2008	Cubs	NL	161	112	.47	286	22	31	42	37	27	111	9	478	121	93	98	15	45	28	17	9	97	64	.602
2009	Cubs	NL	161	131	.57	277	14	55	47	40	20	127	3	480	90	81	92	23	46	21	25	13	83	78	.516
2010	Cubs	NL	125	101	.53	192	10	37	31	41	32	93	6	371	68	65	103	16	33	17	16	9	51	74	.408
162-Game Average				121	.55	167	39	39	44	41	24	79	9	403	153	65	91	26	40	21	19	10	83	79	.512

Mike Quade

Year	Team	Lg	G	LUp	PL%	PH	PR	DS	Quick	Slow	LO	RCD	LS	Rel	SBA	SacA	RM	PO	#	Good	NG	Bomb	W	L	Pct
				LINEUPS		**SUBSTITUTION**			**PITCHER USAGE**						**TACTICS**				**INTENTIONAL BB**				**RESULTS**		
2010	Cubs	NL	37	32	.52	44	1	15	10	11	6	20	3	111	18	14	16	4	9	8	1	0	24	13	.649
2011	Cubs	NL	162	125	.50	259	30	66	30	56	35	125	4	495	92	78	113	23	45	32	13	9	71	91	.438
162-Game Average				128	.50	247	25	66	33	55	33	118	6	493	90	75	105	22	44	33	11	7	77	85	.475

Jim Riggleman

Year	Team	Lg	G	LUp	PL%	PH	PR	DS	Quick	Slow	LO	RCD	LS	Rel	SBA	SacA	RM	PO	#	Good	NG	Bomb	W	L	Pct
1994	Padres	NL	117	93	.63	184	28	19	11	5	3	53	10	273	116	80		52	62	34	28	11	47	70	.402
1995	Cubs	NL	144	92	.56	196	9	30	15	8	13	119	12	414	142	90		53	68	45	23	12	73	71	.507
1996	Cubs	NL	162	87	.54	326	34	21	17	11	7	114	11	439	158	79		65	55	33	22	10	76	86	.469
1997	Cubs	NL	162	127	.50	280	40	44	13	5	2	113	9	441	176	103		74	51	38	13	6	68	94	.420
1998	Cubs	NL	163	104	.60	273	26	35	16	14	20	133	6	449	109	89		26	48	22	26	15	90	73	.552
1999	Cubs	NL	162	122	.61	312	25	30	16	19	8	105	4	441	104	94		20	48	21	27	15	67	95	.414
2008	Mariners	AL	90	70	.60	75	30	22	21	25	19	50	4	272	57	27	88	10	25	17	8	3	36	54	.400
2009	Nationals	NL	75	60	.51	115	15	33	24	16	4	63	6	250	59	44	36	8	33	17	16	8	33	42	.440
2010	Nationals	NL	162	131	.58	271	33	67	50	32	9	101	5	494	151	101	158	13	57	37	20	10	69	93	.426
2011	Nationals	NL	75	61	.58	105	22	23	24	15	2	54	5	220	80	47	89	3	22	16	6	3	38	37	.507
162-Game Average				117	.57	264	32	40	26	19	11	112	9	456	142	93	150	40	58	35	23	11	74	88	.457

Edwin Rodriguez

Year	Team	Lg	G	LUp	PL%	PH	PR	DS	Quick	Slow	LO	RCD	LS	Rel	SBA	SacA	RM	PO	#	Good	NG	Bomb	W	L	Pct
2010	Marlins	NL	92	60	.42	152	12	20	22	23	13	72	1	288	62	37	69	9	24	17	7	3	46	46	.500
2011	Marlins	NL	71	50	.51	114	10	10	14	17	14	49	0	227	49	47	62	5	28	19	9	4	32	39	.451
162-Game Average				109	.46	264	22	30	36	40	27	120	1	512	110	83	130	14	52	36	16	7	78	84	.481

Ron Roenicke

Year	Team	Lg	G	LUp	PL%	PH	PR	DS	Quick	Slow	LO	RCD	LS	Rel	SBA	SacA	RM	PO	#	Good	NG	Bomb	W	L	Pct
2011	Brewers	NL	162	105	.45	260	31	36	36	43	31	92	1	434	125	**104**	141	14	16	9	7	4	96	66	.593
2012	Brewers	NL	162	110	.45	322	20	25	36	50	23	**149**	1	512	197	91	152	8	20	12	8	2	83	79	.512
162-Game Average				108	.45	291	26	31	36	47	27	121	1	473	161	98	147	11	18	11	8	3	90	72	.556

John Russell

Year	Team	Lg	G	LUp	PL%	PH	PR	DS	Quick	Slow	LO	RCD	LS	Rel	SBA	SacA	RM	PO	#	Good	NG	Bomb	W	L	Pct
2008	Pirates	NL	162	128	.51	290	17	13	29	47	15	111	0	497	76	92	54	19	31	21	10	4	67	95	.414
2009	Pirates	NL	161	121	.60	251	3	5	44	45	12	89	0	456	122	78	97	15	37	20	17	10	62	**99**	.385
2010	Pirates	NL	162	119	.60	275	13	10	48	44	8	122	0	**517**	123	81	124	32	40	26	14	4	57	**105**	.352
162-Game Average				123	.57	273	11	9	40	45	12	108	0	491	107	84	92	22	36	22	14	6	62	100	.383

Juan Samuel

Year	Team	Lg	G	LUp	PL%	PH	PR	DS	Quick	Slow	LO	RCD	LS	Rel	SBA	SacA	RM	PO	#	Good	NG	Bomb	W	L	Pct
2010	Orioles	AL	51	39	.63	27	14	3	11	17	6	33	0	157	40	18	39	2	18	12	6	5	17	34	.333
162-Game Average				124	.63	86	44	10	35	54	19	105	0	499	127	57	124	6	57	38	19	16	54	108	.333

Mike Scioscia

Year	Team	Lg	G	LUp	PL%	PH	PR	DS	Quick	Slow	LO	RCD	LS	Rel	SBA	SacA	RM	PO	#	Good	NG	Bomb	W	L	Pct
2000	Angels	AL	162	75	.62	110	41	4	56	42	6	95	9	441	145	63		40	44	28	16	7	82	80	.506
2001	Angels	AL	162	130	.62	118	30	8	29	41	5	81	9	384	168	66		50	47	22	25	12	75	87	.463
2002	Angels	AL	162	102	.64	**162**	57	26	36	33	34	88	8	400	168	62	52	30	24	15	9	5	99	63	.611
2003	Angels	AL	162	130	.64	134	54	40	50	48	11	60	4	375	**190**	64	79	25	38	26	12	3	77	85	.475
2004	Angels	AL	162	126	.57	94	32	44	37	40	22	61	11	343	**189**	70	**229**	33	27	18	9	3	92	70	.568
2005	Angels	AL	162	124	.65	92	37	37	47	37	24	88	9	379	**218**	58	**160**	43	24	15	9	4	95	67	.586
2006	Angels	AL	162	114	.63	103	45	38	38	49	21	99	9	380	**205**	37	**166**	22	27	18	9	6	89	73	.549
2007	Angels	AL	162	127	.66	103	26	19	39	40	14	94	4	396	**194**	41	**166**	44	22	12	10	5	94	68	.580
2008	Angels	AL	162	125	.63	74	30	36	37	48	**21**	87	1	383	177	39	151	31	32	22	10	6	**100**	62	.617
2009	Angels	AL	162	123	.69	80	26	37	47	47	33	91	1	434	**211**	55	**137**	**40**	35	22	13	6	97	65	.599
2010	Angels	AL	162	133	.59	96	31	23	41	52	48	76	0	410	156	58	**223**	28	33	17	16	8	80	82	.494

Year	Team	Lg	G	LUp	PL%	PH	PR	DS	Quick	Slow	LO	RCD	LS	Rel	SBA	SacA	RM	PO	#	Good	NG	Bomb	W	L	Pct
				LINEUPS		SUBSTITUTION			PITCHER USAGE						TACTICS				INTENTIONAL BB				RESULTS		
2011	Angels	AL	162	129	.64	88	14	24	31	37	55	57	1	386	187	69	212	46	34	25	9	5	86	76	.531
2012	Angels	AL	162	121	.55	73	33	47	37	47	31	96	8	444	167	61	236	33	20	11	9	7	89	73	.549
162-Game Average				120	.62	102	35	29	40	43	25	83	6	397	183	57	165	36	31	19	12	6	89	73	.549

Buck Showalter

Year	Team	Lg	G	LUp	PL%	PH	PR	DS	Quick	Slow	LO	RCD	LS	Rel	SBA	SacA	RM	PO	#	Good	NG	Bomb	W	L	Pct
				LINEUPS		SUBSTITUTION			PITCHER USAGE						TACTICS				INTENTIONAL BB				RESULTS		
1994	Yankees	AL	113	79	.59	95	31	3	24	30	0	38	7	241	95	34		22	24	13	11	4	70	43	.619
1995	Yankees	AL	145	107	.68	124	30	20	29	42	37	57	6	302	80	27		29	21	14	7	1	79	65	.549
1998	Diamondbacks	NL	162	124	.62	252	17	15	34	40	7	43	6	368	111	68		13	32	16	16	9	65	97	.401
1999	Diamondbacks	NL	162	97	.63	220	20	17	37	48	25	74	3	382	176	75		15	48	29	19	8	100	62	.617
2000	Diamondbacks	NL	162	99	.60	250	32	11	46	26	18	74	12	390	141	89		10	53	28	25	16	85	77	.525
2003	Rangers	AL	162	133	.61	88	51	41	35	33	12	93	7	494	90	35	80	12	45	24	21	14	71	91	.438
2004	Rangers	AL	162	120	.64	86	15	24	53	30	12	82	10	468	105	30	88	5	29	19	10	3	89	73	.549
2005	Rangers	AL	162	98	.59	57	22	11	42	39	17	79	8	454	82	11	103	5	31	10	21	16	79	83	.488
2006	Rangers	AL	162	95	.57	39	34	22	41	27	10	85	4	489	77	30	72	8	18	11	7	5	80	82	.494
2010	Orioles	AL	57	42	.74	20	11	13	23	9	10	24	1	144	38	13	31	1	10	9	1	1	34	23	.596
2011	Orioles	AL	162	117	.53	60	39	27	43	40	14	61	2	478	106	32	133	6	42	31	11	5	69	93	.426
2012	Orioles	AL	162	120	.62	78	28	31	37	42	10	88	0	492	87	46	145	6	36	25	11	5	93	69	.574
162-Game Average				113	.61	125	30	21	41	37	16	73	6	430	109	45	103	12	36	21	15	8	84	78	.519

Dale Sveum

Year	Team	Lg	G	LUp	PL%	PH	PR	DS	Quick	Slow	LO	RCD	LS	Rel	SBA	SacA	RM	PO	#	Good	NG	Bomb	W	L	Pct
				LINEUPS		SUBSTITUTION			PITCHER USAGE						TACTICS				INTENTIONAL BB				RESULTS		
2008	Brewers	NL	12	3	.48	32	2	1	7	2	1	12	0	46	5	13	6	1	2	1	1	0	7	5	.583
2012	Cubs	NL	162	101	.60	277	23	44	46	48	8	117	1	493	139	61	153	13	36	24	12	8	61	101	.377
162-Game Average				97	.59	288	23	42	49	47	8	120	1	502	134	69	148	13	35	23	12	7	63	99	.389

Joe Torre

Year	Team	Lg	G	LUp	PL%	PH	PR	DS	Quick	Slow	LO	RCD	LS	Rel	SBA	SacA	RM	PO	#	Good	NG	Bomb	W	L	Pct
				LINEUPS		SUBSTITUTION			PITCHER USAGE						TACTICS				INTENTIONAL BB				RESULTS		
1994	Cardinals	NL	115	79	.68	192	9	0	36	29	6	106	4	330	122	57		33	28	18	10	6	53	61	.465
1995	Cardinals	NL	47	36	.51	99	6	4	17	11	1	41	2	146	42	26		14	16	10	6	2	20	27	.426
1996	Yankees	AL	162	131	.57	92	62	55	59	23	22	97	10	411	142	53		19	35	17	18	14	92	70	.568
1997	Yankees	AL	162	118	.61	75	70	23	35	41	19	84	14	368	157	54		14	41	23	18	10	96	66	.593
1998	Yankees	AL	162	96	.62	94	36	28	43	38	27	71	17	334	216	44		9	25	17	8	4	114	48	.704
1999	Yankees	AL	162	95	.63	114	63	10	29	51	26	80	12	359	161	31		12	27	17	10	8	98	64	.605
2000	Yankees	AL	161	112	.63	86	49	27	43	53	27	92	16	382	147	22		8	23	9	14	7	87	74	.540
2001	Yankees	AL	161	94	.56	76	33	14	37	45	10	77	17	362	214	41		21	29	20	9	6	95	65	.594
2002	Yankees	AL	161	108	.58	89	53	31	39	49	44	86	13	334	138	35	46	18	44	33	11	4	103	58	.640
2003	Yankees	AL	163	104	.65	118	48	18	26	51	52	75	10	367	131	39	69	33	36	21	15	8	101	61	.623
2004	Yankees	AL	162	116	.65	86	35	46	48	35	29	129	10	436	117	50	126	36	32	16	16	9	101	61	.623
2005	Yankees	AL	162	117	.64	94	65	47	44	45	28	92	7	418	111	40	123	50	25	11	14	9	95	67	.586
2006	Yankees	AL	162	120	.66	108	50	59	50	30	9	109	7	489	174	48	118	50	41	22	19	4	97	65	.599
2007	Yankees	AL	162	102	.68	99	34	22	51	29	10	113	13	522	163	51	152	41	33	17	16	7	94	68	.580
2008	Dodgers	NL	162	124	.53	277	43	66	61	30	17	94	8	461	169	75	133	38	58	46	12	5	84	78	.519
2009	Dodgers	NL	162	113	.59	263	22	22	62	23	18	125	8	526	164	107	163	17	68	45	23	12	95	67	.586
2010	Dodgers	NL	162	127	.55	255	18	47	42	37	30	92	5	475	142	108	192	8	75	53	22	11	80	82	.494
162-Game Average				112	.61	139	44	33	45	39	23	98	11	421	157	55	125	26	40	25	15	8	94	68	.580

Jim Tracy

Year	Team	Lg	G	LUp	PL%	PH	PR	DS	Quick	Slow	LO	RCD	LS	Rel	SBA	SacA	RM	PO	#	Good	NG	Bomb	W	L	Pct
				LINEUPS		SUBSTITUTION			PITCHER USAGE						TACTICS				INTENTIONAL BB				RESULTS		
2001	Dodgers	NL	162	111	.50	264	34	20	46	42	8	84	4	409	131	81		10	37	19	18	9	86	76	.531
2002	Dodgers	NL	162	102	.52	317	39	37	49	36	21	118	9	423	133	81	46	18	45	31	14	5	92	70	.568
2003	Dodgers	NL	162	103	.64	269	22	64	52	29	22	148	11	438	116	97	32	10	35	23	12	8	85	77	.525
2004	Dodgers	NL	162	94	.70	295	25	19	49	34	16	128	16	459	143	81	93	7	47	32	15	8	93	69	.574
2005	Dodgers	NL	162	129	.66	303	31	37	44	40	20	126	2	459	93	76	97	17	34	21	13	6	71	91	.438
2006	Pirates	NL	162	121	.43	264	22	22	37	43	12	156	3	505	91	80	75	12	62	39	23	15	67	95	.414
2007	Pirates	NL	162	124	.49	240	12	26	33	40	13	113	0	495	98	80	90	12	55	30	25	11	68	94	.420
2009	Rockies	NL	116	87	.63	186	25	28	28	27	27	83	3	349	116	73	82	9	40	28	12	7	74	42	.638
2010	Rockies	NL	162	135	.65	257	30	41	38	40	34	128	0	513	141	64	135	11	54	34	20	10	83	79	.512
2011	Rockies	NL	162	134	.62	252	21	30	35	47	21	129	1	517	160	94	231	18	47	27	20	11	73	89	.451
2012	Rockies	NL	162	140	.55	264	33	33	74	33	6	111	2	575	140	88	165	18	61	36	25	12	64	98	.395
162-Game Average				119	.58	272	27	33	45	38	19	124	5	480	127	84	108	13	48	30	18	10	80	82	.494

Dave Trembley

Year	Team	Lg	G	LUp	PL%	PH	PR	DS	Quick	Slow	LO	RCD	LS	Rel	SBA	SacA	RM	PO	#	Good	NG	Bomb	W	L	Pct
2007	Orioles	AL	93	71	.60	63	29	16	21	25	16	47	3	279	124	32	83	32	29	15	14	8	40	53	.430
2008	Orioles	AL	161	119	.58	117	36	25	41	44	11	87	4	492	118	38	143	11	44	18	**26**	12	68	**93**	.422
2009	Orioles	AL	162	132	.68	99	26	21	43	39	11	66	4	484	113	20	86	6	**45**	**28**	17	9	64	98	.395
2010	Orioles	AL	54	50	.62	24	14	7	6	16	10	33	1	153	32	10	24	2	17	7	10	5	15	39	.278
162-Game Average				128	.62	104	36	24	38	43	17	80	4	485	133	34	116	18	47	23	23	12	64	98	.395

Bobby Valentine

Year	Team	Lg	G	LUp	PL%	PH	PR	DS	Quick	Slow	LO	RCD	LS	Rel	SBA	SacA	RM	PO	#	Good	NG	Bomb	W	L	Pct
1996	Mets	NL	31	28	.67	88	7	3	7	4	1	11	1	75	20	27	0	2	14	8	6	2	12	19	.387
1997	Mets	NL	162	131	.65	313	39	23	52	30	8	70	11	376	171	102	0	27	43	28	15	6	88	74	.543
1998	Mets	NL	162	124	.64	305	42	34	45	36	23	80	7	399	108	157	0	50	59	42	17	10	88	74	.543
1999	Mets	NL	163	76	.57	323	43	26	56	24	14	108	8	439	211	109	0	43	53	35	18	9	97	66	.595
2000	Mets	NL	162	118	.34	299	38	32	37	37	18	90	7	411	112	118	0	0	42	27	15	7	94	68	.580
2001	Mets	NL	161	143	.43	298	33	34	38	40	7	83	6	397	114	88	0	0	60	30	30	16	82	80	.506
2002	Mets	NL	162	122	.62	323	**48**	32	15	42	29	87	2	451	129	98	**81**	41	75	49	26	13	75	86	.466
2012	Red Sox	AL	162	143	.61	107	30	25	34	52	21	91	6	489	128	44	148	18	33	22	11	5	69	93	.426
162-Game Average				125	.61	243	45	14	38	46	31	79	14	369	158	90	115	25	45	27	18	10	82	80	.506

Robin Ventura

Year	Team	Lg	G	LUp	PL%	PH	PR	DS	Quick	Slow	LO	RCD	LS	Rel	SBA	SacA	RM	PO	#	Good	NG	Bomb	W	L	Pct
2012	White Sox	AL	162	75	.48	72	**64**	23	39	44	34	104	4	466	152	42	174	13	29	17	12	7	85	77	.525
162-Game Average				75	.48	72	64	23	39	44	34	104	4	466	152	42	174	13	29	17	12	7	85	77	.525

Don Wakamatsu

Year	Team	Lg	G	LUp	PL%	PH	PR	DS	Quick	Slow	LO	RCD	LS	Rel	SBA	SacA	RM	PO	#	Good	NG	Bomb	W	L	Pct
2009	Mariners	AL	162	138	.51	58	31	18	50	27	18	76	1	410	122	61	91	4	13	3	10	6	85	77	.525
2010	Mariners	AL	112	93	.61	49	21	12	37	21	20	39	2	254	129	40	124	12	25	11	14	8	42	70	.375
162-Game Average				137	.55	63	31	18	51	28	22	68	2	393	148	60	127	12	22	8	14	8	75	87	.463

Ron Washington

Year	Team	Lg	G	LUp	PL%	PH	PR	DS	Quick	Slow	LO	RCD	LS	Rel	SBA	SacA	RM	PO	#	Good	NG	Bomb	W	L	Pct
2007	Rangers	AL	162	139	.60	89	30	**53**	47	46	4	78	9	467	113	**76**	67	13	38	19	19	11	75	87	.463
2008	Rangers	AL	162	129	.64	118	16	14	31	**53**	11	85	3	458	106	53	74	20	44	19	25	**20**	79	83	.488
2009	Rangers	AL	162	123	.55	48	11	11	39	47	28	80	9	436	185	44	80	5	14	9	5	3	87	75	.537
2010	Rangers	AL	162	112	.52	86	39	31	46	42	35	110	4	481	171	**68**	160	10	24	15	9	0	90	72	.556
2011	Rangers	AL	162	106	.48	66	18	23	43	39	40	76	2	417	188	52	182	3	21	12	9	6	96	66	.593
2012	Rangers	AL	162	79	.47	94	25	37	30	48	33	91	0	428	135	46	155	22	15	10	5	5	93	69	.574
162-Game Average				115	.55	84	23	28	39	46	25	87	5	448	150	57	120	12	26	14	12	8	87	75	.537

Eric Wedge

Year	Team	Lg	G	LUp	PL%	PH	PR	DS	Quick	Slow	LO	RCD	LS	Rel	SBA	SacA	RM	PO	#	Good	NG	Bomb	W	L	Pct
2003	Indians	AL	162	**145**	.67	117	43	27	47	34	18	89	5	428	147	67	54	12	37	22	15	8	68	94	.420
2004	Indians	AL	162	114	**.72**	91	34	20	44	38	22	121	0	**479**	149	57	129	28	47	26	**21**	**18**	80	82	.494
2005	Indians	AL	162	111	.66	88	18	16	45	45	15	90	3	409	98	53	79	9	20	11	9	7	93	69	.574
2006	Indians	AL	162	111	.59	98	13	13	31	52	27	48	1	377	78	40	83	15	35	21	14	11	78	84	.481
2007	Indians	AL	162	117	.60	116	41	25	34	38	20	79	2	395	113	40	108	6	42	24	18	9	**96**	66	.593
2008	Indians	AL	162	**136**	.54	112	31	18	40	35	17	78	4	399	106	56	98	5	28	6	22	11	81	81	.500
2009	Indians	AL	162	**148**	.59	63	28	11	32	41	21	67	3	445	115	52	74	8	31	14	17	9	65	97	.401
2011	Mariners	AL	162	**152**	.68	52	30	22	39	45	30	50	1	351	165	43	161	7	27	20	7	6	67	95	.414
2012	Mariners	AL	162	141	.69	87	36	21	44	35	14	89	5	451	139	45	116	8	39	20	**19**	7	75	87	.463
162-Game Average				131	.64	92	30	19	40	40	20	79	3	415	123	50	100	12	34	18	16	10	78	84	.481

Ned Yost

Year	Team	Lg	G	LUp	PL%	PH	PR	DS	Quick	Slow	LO	RCD	LS	Rel	SBA	SacA	RM	PO	#	Good	NG	Bomb	W	L	Pct
2003	Brewers	NL	162	97	.44	304	22	39	23	**59**	18	90	6	460	138	85	40	23	43	28	15	9	68	94	.420
2004	Brewers	NL	161	131	.60	283	25	20	39	41	27	63	2	423	**178**	79	108	8	27	16	11	8	67	94	.416
2005	Brewers	NL	162	99	.46	259	18	35	26	41	**42**	71	2	395	113	89	97	50	52	23	**29**	10	81	81	.500

				LINEUPS		SUBSTITUTION			PITCHER USAGE						TACTICS				INTENTIONAL BB				RESULTS		
Year	Team	Lg	G	LUp	PL%	PH	PR	DS	Quick	Slow	LO	RCD	LS	Rel	SBA	SacA	RM	PO	#	Good	NG	Bomb	W	L	Pct
2006	Brewers	NL	162	106	.48	238	12	14	33	44	18	77	4	427	108	80	82	16	34	14	20	12	75	87	.463
2007	Brewers	NL	162	109	.60	259	11	41	37	42	18	117	7	492	128	74	94	19	37	28	9	9	83	79	.512
2008	Brewers	NL	150	93	.48	217	5	16	37	39	23	69	5	399	141	61	105	31	30	17	13	7	83	67	.553
2010	Royals	AL	127	80	.57	56	25	6	22	39	20	65	0	332	127	40	128	18	25	16	9	5	55	72	.433
2011	Royals	AL	162	87	.58	36	28	16	42	42	21	56	7	420	211	65	203	19	42	27	15	5	71	91	.438
2012	Royals	AL	162	118	.57	60	34	15	48	37	10	108	1	**500**	170	37	149	25	**44**	**29**	15	**11**	72	90	.444
	162-Game Average			106	.53	197	21	23	35	44	23	82	4	442	151	70	116	24	38	23	16	9	75	87	.463

Categories of this record are Games Managed (G), Number of Different Lineups Used (LUp), the percentage of players who had the platoon advantage at the start of the game (PL%), Pinch Hitters Used (PH), Pinch Runners Used (PR), Defensive Substitutes Used (DS), Quick Hooks (Quick), Slow Hooks (Slow), Long Outings by Starting Pitchers (LO), Relievers Used on Consecutive Days (RCD), Long Saves (LS), Relievers Used (Rel), Stolen Base Attempts (SBA), Sacrifice Bunt Attempts (SacA), Runners Moving with the Pitch (RM), Pitchouts ordered (PO), Intentional Walks issued (#), Intentional Walks resulting in a Good Outcome (Good), Intentional Walks resulting Not in a Good Outcome (NG), Intentional Walks Blowing Up on the Manager (Bomb), Wins (W), Losses (L), and Winning Percentage (Pct).

2012 American League Managers

Manager	G	LINEUPS LUp	PL%	SUBSTITUTION PH	PR	DS	PITCHER USAGE Quick	Slow	LO	RCD	LS	Rel	TACTICS SBA	SacA	RM	PO	INTENTIONAL BB #	Good	NG	Bomb	RESULTS W	L	Pct
Bobby Valentine, Bos	162	143	.61	107	30	25	34	52	21	91	6	489	128	44	148	18	33	22	11	5	69	93	.426
Jim Leyland, Det	162	121	.58	76	33	62	38	41	**37**	103	0	420	82	46	151	14	35	21	14	7	88	74	.543
Joe Maddon, TB	162	**151**	.62	**156**	37	52	43	38	33	**123**	3	472	**178**	40	181	7	35	25	10	6	90	72	.556
Joe Girardi, NYY	162	107	.70	149	33	48	37	53	21	115	7	485	120	47	145	10	32	17	15	6	**95**	67	.586
Ron Washington, Tex	162	79	.47	94	25	37	30	48	33	91	0	428	135	46	155	22	15	10	5	5	93	69	.574
Manny Acta, Cle	156	116	**.76**	68	20	**72**	38	**54**	14	94	1	464	149	21	135	23	27	12	15	9	65	91	.417
John Farrell, Tor	162	131	.50	94	30	16	49	44	7	84	3	495	164	46	211	15	20	11	9	7	73	89	.451
Robin Ventura, CWS	162	75	.48	72	**64**	23	39	44	34	104	4	466	152	42	174	13	29	17	12	7	85	77	.525
Mike Scioscia, LAA	162	121	.55	73	33	47	37	47	31	96	8	444	167	**61**	**236**	**33**	20	11	9	7	89	73	.549
Eric Wedge, Sea	162	141	.69	87	36	21	44	35	14	89	5	451	139	45	116	8	39	20	**19**	7	75	87	.463
Ron Gardenhire, Min	162	121	.62	64	45	24	42	31	4	82	1	499	172	49	207	10	43	27	16	6	66	**96**	.407
Bob Melvin, Oak	162	132	.71	111	17	18	**63**	29	5	93	2	462	154	41	116	30	34	21	13	6	94	68	.580
Buck Showalter, Bal	162	120	.62	78	28	31	37	42	10	88	0	492	87	46	145	6	36	25	11	5	93	69	.574
Ned Yost, KC	162	118	.57	60	34	15	48	37	10	108	1	**500**	170	37	149	25	**44**	29	15	**11**	72	90	.444
162-Game Average		120	.61	92	33	35	41	43	20	97	3	470	143	44	162	17	32	19	7	6	82	80	.506

Manager	G	LINEUPS LUp	PL%	SUBSTITUTION PH	PR	DS	PITCHER USAGE Quick	Slow	LO	RCD	LS	Rel	TACTICS SBA	SacA	RM	PO	INTENTIONAL BB #	Good	NG	Bomb	RESULTS W	L	Pct
Sandy Alomar, Jr., Cle	6	6	.61	12	2	1	1	1	0	9	0	30	5	3	3	0	0	0	0	0	3	3	.500

2012 National League Managers

Manager	G	LINEUPS LUp	PL%	SUBSTITUTION PH	PR	DS	PITCHER USAGE Quick	Slow	LO	RCD	LS	Rel	TACTICS SBA	SacA	RM	PO	INTENTIONAL BB #	Good	NG	Bomb	RESULTS W	L	Pct
Charlie Manuel, Phi	162	131	.68	281	22	48	35	**56**	30	93	5	440	139	91	125	6	33	21	12	5	81	81	.500
Ozzie Guillen, Mia	162	116	.60	234	23	29	24	39	27	126	2	483	190	89	137	23	61	**38**	23	13	69	93	.426
Fredi Gonzalez, Atl	162	110	.61	268	18	27	50	34	9	115	4	460	133	67	116	20	40	28	12	11	94	68	.580
Bud Black, SD	162	132	.74	280	26	35	45	49	11	126	5	529	**201**	89	162	21	48	34	14	7	76	86	.469
Dale Sveum, ChC	162	101	.60	277	23	44	46	48	8	117	1	493	139	61	153	13	36	24	12	8	61	**101**	.377
Kirk Gibson, Ari	162	140	.56	231	11	9	35	50	16	104	4	461	144	77	120	8	18	11	7	1	81	81	.500
Terry Collins, NYM	162	**141**	.69	**329**	16	38	39	36	19	113	0	505	117	75	149	8	29	18	11	3	74	88	.457
Don Mattingly, LAD	162	127	.59	247	22	43	51	39	20	118	2	506	148	105	153	8	**62**	**38**	24	**15**	86	76	.531
Ron Roenicke, Mil	162	110	.45	322	20	25	36	50	23	**149**	1	512	197	91	152	8	20	12	8	2	83	79	.512
Davey Johnson, Was	162	93	.60	252	30	42	57	30	10	105	1	482	140	67	158	2	32	21	11	7	**98**	64	.605
Mike Matheny, StL	162	122	.62	286	**37**	33	53	37	8	118	5	506	128	95	144	16	28	13	15	7	88	74	.543
Dusty Baker, Cin	162	121	.43	201	19	39	33	39	30	78	4	425	114	**108**	148	19	33	22	11	3	97	65	.599
Clint Hurdle, Pit	162	133	.55	270	26	**60**	33		3	74	2	483	125	82	120	17	30	18	12	3	79	83	.488
Jim Tracy, Col	162	140	.55	264	33	33	**74**	33	6	111	2	**575**	140	88	165	18	61	36	**25**	12	64	98	.395
Bruce Bochy, SF	162	112	**.75**	220	32	55	22	50	**31**	136	9	526	157	87	**176**	15	42	30	12	5	94	68	.580
162-Game Average		123	.60	263	24	37	42	43	17	114	3	494	148	84	146	13	38	24	7	7	80	82	.494

Manager	G	LINEUPS LUp	PL%	SUBSTITUTION PH	PR	DS	PITCHER USAGE Quick	Slow	LO	RCD	LS	Rel	TACTICS SBA	SacA	RM	PO	INTENTIONAL BB #	Good	NG	Bomb	RESULTS W	L	Pct
Brad Mills, Hou	121	103	.60	181	22	22	20	49	12	102	0	391	117	54	115	10	25	12	13	6	39	82	.322
Tony DeFrancesco, Hou	41	41	.64	82	10	12	21	7	2	24	5	150	34	16	45	14	15	9	6	4	16	25	.390

2012 Ballparks and Park Indices

Bill James

The fact that baseball parks have a significant impact on the statistics of those who play in them has been known in a general way at least since 1880, and efforts to document this effect date back a hundred years or more. In 1914 Gavvy Cravath led the National League in home runs, with 19, hitting all 19 home runs in his "home" park, none on the road. This fact was known and published at that time.

However, a general understanding of park effects has not really permeated the public to this day. Among all of the things that sabermetrics has developed knowledge about, the area of park effects stands out for its failure to dissolve into the public's understanding. When Felix Abraham (Garcia) Hernandez won the Cy Young Award in 2010 despite a won-lost record of 13-12, this was widely reported (and denounced) as a triumph for the sabermetric viewpoint, that a pitcher could be recognized as the best in the league even though his won-lost record was not impressive. But what was rarely commented on and little understood in that debate was that Hernandez was pitching in an extreme pitcher-friendly environment, and that this was actually making him look better than he was. While I am very happy that Hernandez won the Cy Young Award that year, because Felix is a great pitcher every year and deserves to win an Award sometime, it is not all that clear to me that Hernandez in 2010 was actually better than CC Sabathia, who finished third in the voting. Hernandez finished 13-12 with a 2.27 ERA; Sabathia finished 21-7 with a 3.18 ERA. The voters got the fact that Hernandez' won-lost record was knocked backward by his lack of offensive support, but missed the fact that Sabathia's ERA was at a serious disadvantage because of the park that he was playing in.

Park effects get overlooked, I think, because it is difficult to adjust for them on a constantly-updated basis during the season. Analysts "build in" park adjustments after the season—too late to have impact on the voting.

Our park effects this year have a new category, which is "FO" or "Foul Outs" in the park. In Fenway Park, where the seats crowd in around the infield, there were 88 Foul Outs last season (by the two teams combined), whereas in Red Sox road games there were 119 Foul Outs. In Tampa Bay's Tropicana Field, where tribes of alligators have periodically taken up residence in foul territory, there were 133 Foul Outs, as opposed to 99 in Tampa Bay Road games. That's a park index, for that area of performance, of 136.   If a park increases runs scored by 10%, that's a park run index of 110.   If a park reduces the number of triples hit there by 55% (as Dodger Stadium in fact does), that creates a park triples effect of 45.

But the new data shows that the impact of foul outs on the runs scored in the park is nowhere near as large as I would have guessed that it was, nor as large as I have speculated that it is.   If you compare Fenway Park to Tropicana Field (or Oakland), the difference is less than 50 Foul Outs per season for the two teams combined.   Per batting order position, that's three foul outs.   So this fact, by itself, would appear to have relatively little impact on the batting averages of the players who play in those two parks, or on the ERAs of the pitchers.

We have added something else to these charts this year, which is dimensions.   Nationals Park in Washington: 336 feet to left, 403 to center, 335 to right.   Obvious.   Don't know why it took us so long to put that in the book.

We measure the effects of each park over the last year, and over a three-year period.   The single-season data gives imperfect estimates of the effects of the park, because the sample is too small, and the multi-year data gives imperfect estimates because some park in the league changes something every year, so that the sampling procedure is compromised.   It's one of those things. . .there is no right way to do it; we just do the best we can.

New park this year in Miami; the Marlins I think were also ordered by a court to stop claiming that they represented the entire state of Florida.   Unless you spend time in Florida you actually can't believe how big the state is. This is true: if you're driving west out of Florida, then once you hit the central time zone you're still 160 miles from the end of the state.

Finally, the 2012 season opened with a two-game series between the Mariners and the Athletics in Japan. Oakland was the official home team in those contests, but for the purposes of Park Indices, both teams were considered "Away."   Far, far away.

Park Index Charts begin on the next page.

Arizona Diamondbacks - Chase Field
LF: 330   CF: 407   RF:334

	2012 Season							2010-2012						
	Home Games			Away Games				Home Games			Away Games			
	D'Backs	Opp	Total	D'Backs	Opp	Total	Index	D'Backs	Opp	Total	D'Backs	Opp	Total	Index
G	81	81	162	81	81	162		243	243	486	243	243	486	
Avg	.264	.269	.267	.255	.252	.253	105	.262	.265	.263	.244	.262	.253	104
AB	2660	2847	5507	2802	2644	5446	101	8029	8530	16559	8327	8000	16327	101
R	391	376	767	343	312	655	117	1175	1129	2304	1003	1057	2060	112
H	701	767	1468	715	665	1380	106	2106	2257	4363	2033	2092	4125	106
2B	157	171	328	150	129	279	116	473	468	941	428	408	836	111
3B	24	16	40	9	25	34	116	72	54	126	32	51	83	150
HR	84	90	174	81	65	146	118	275	273	548	242	251	493	110
BB	260	207	467	279	210	489	94	845	640	1485	814	767	1581	93
SO	628	618	1246	638	582	1220	101	1967	1730	3697	2077	1598	3675	99
Foul Outs	48	59	107	52	44	96	110	157	208	365	173	166	339	106
E	44	40	84	46	46	92	91	137	109	246	145	126	271	91
E-Infield	22	21	43	21	18	39	110	61	47	108	61	54	115	94
LHB-Avg	.263	.275	.270	.238	.252	.245	110	.265	.266	.265	.249	.256	.252	105
LHB-HR	31	32	63	29	20	49	122	99	108	207	108	91	199	102
RHB-Avg	.264	.265	.264	.266	.251	.259	102	.261	.264	.262	.241	.265	.253	104
RHB-HR	53	58	111	52	45	97	116	176	165	341	134	160	294	115

Atlanta Braves - Turner Field
LF: 335   CF: 401   RF:330

	2012 Season							2010-2012						
	Home Games			Away Games				Home Games			Away Games			
	Braves	Opp	Total	Braves	Opp	Total	Index	Braves	Opp	Total	Braves	Opp	Total	Index
G	81	81	162	81	81	162		243	243	486	243	243	486	
Avg	.249	.244	.247	.245	.241	.243	101	.258	.237	.247	.241	.249	.245	101
AB	2628	2777	5405	2797	2621	5418	100	8016	8335	16351	8400	8000	16400	100
R	351	311	662	349	289	638	104	1067	889	1956	1012	945	1957	100
H	655	678	1333	686	632	1318	101	2072	1973	4045	2025	1995	4020	101
2B	139	141	280	124	110	234	120	414	377	791	405	364	769	103
3B	18	8	26	12	13	25	104	43	29	72	28	57	85	85
HR	70	67	137	79	78	157	87	234	182	416	227	214	441	95
BB	306	219	525	261	245	506	104	878	720	1598	827	770	1597	100
SO	643	648	1291	646	584	1230	105	1800	2046	3846	1889	1759	3648	106
Foul Outs	55	56	111	58	36	94	118	165	146	311	184	130	314	99
E	49	55	104	37	40	77	135	158	164	322	137	133	270	119
E-Infield	18	22	40	18	15	33	121	67	75	142	60	61	121	117
LHB-Avg	.258	.245	.252	.248	.237	.243	103	.263	.243	.254	.248	.253	.250	101
LHB-HR	45	32	77	55	27	82	97	136	80	216	133	83	216	102
RHB-Avg	.240	.243	.242	.242	.245	.243	99	.254	.232	.242	.234	.246	.241	101
RHB-HR	25	35	60	24	51	75	78	98	102	200	94	131	225	88

Baltimore Orioles - Oriole Park at Camden Yards
LF: 337   CF: 406   RF:320

	2012 Season							2010-2012						
	Home Games			Away Games				Home Games			Away Games			
	Orioles	Opp	Total	Orioles	Opp	Total	Index	Orioles	Opp	Total	Orioles	Opp	Total	Index
G	81	81	162	81	81	162		243	243	486	243	243	486	
Avg	.258	.264	.261	.237	.241	.239	109	.261	.269	.265	.248	.264	.256	103
AB	2726	2907	5633	2834	2769	5603	101	8222	8748	16970	8477	8184	16661	102
R	387	378	765	325	327	652	117	1069	1214	2283	964	1136	2100	109
H	704	766	1470	671	667	1338	110	2143	2351	4494	2106	2158	4264	105
2B	143	136	279	127	135	262	106	427	461	888	380	462	842	104
3B	5	8	13	11	8	19	68	18	34	52	32	41	73	70
HR	127	99	226	87	85	172	131	305	313	618	233	267	500	121
BB	242	245	487	238	236	474	102	685	780	1465	671	756	1427	101
SO	622	614	1236	693	563	1256	98	1666	1681	3347	1825	1547	3372	97
Foul Outs	63	45	108	70	72	142	76	195	167	362	203	189	392	91
E	49	56	105	57	35	92	114	144	138	282	177	139	316	89
E-Infield	25	27	52	19	11	30	173	77	62	139	79	48	127	109
LHB-Avg	.264	.251	.257	.245	.240	.243	106	.267	.269	.268	.249	.261	.255	105
LHB-HR	61	40	101	40	40	80	129	124	140	264	85	117	202	129
RHB-Avg	.253	.274	.264	.230	.242	.236	112	.256	.269	.262	.248	.266	.257	102
RHB-HR	66	59	125	47	45	92	133	181	173	354	148	150	298	116

Boston Red Sox - Fenway Park
LF: 310   CF: 420   RF:302

| | 2012 Season | | | | | | | 2010-2012 | | | | | | |
| | Home Games | | | Away Games | | | | Home Games | | | Away Games | | | |
	Red Sox	Opp	Total	Red Sox	Opp	Total	Index	Red Sox	Opp	Total	Red Sox	Opp	Total	Index
G	81	81	162	81	81	162		243	243	486	243	243	486	
Avg	.279	.271	.275	.242	.253	.247	111	.283	.263	.273	.256	.245	.251	109
AB	2828	2882	5710	2776	2639	5415	105	8421	8589	17010	8539	8008	16547	103
R	419	423	842	315	383	698	121	1298	1226	2524	1129	1061	2190	115
H	788	782	1570	671	667	1338	117	2385	2256	4641	2185	1961	4146	112
2B	211	167	378	128	125	253	142	599	507	1106	450	379	829	130
3B	9	16	25	7	11	18	132	38	35	73	35	40	75	95
HR	88	97	185	77	93	170	103	277	245	522	302	253	555	91
BB	229	258	487	199	271	470	98	806	822	1628	787	827	1614	98
SO	592	599	1191	605	577	1182	96	1690	1822	3512	1755	1774	3529	97
Foul Outs	46	42	88	48	71	119	70	147	157	304	172	208	380	78
E	48	50	98	53	38	91	108	170	152	322	134	122	256	126
E-Infield	19	20	39	18	13	31	126	68	66	134	51	56	107	125
LHB-Avg	.293	.272	.282	.249	.255	.252	112	.284	.260	.272	.257	.252	.254	107
LHB-HR	38	36	74	38	47	85	82	133	89	222	160	121	281	77
RHB-Avg	.267	.271	.269	.236	.251	.243	111	.282	.265	.273	.255	.239	.247	111
RHB-HR	50	61	111	39	46	85	125	144	156	300	142	132	274	106

Chicago Cubs - Wrigley Field
LF: 355   CF: 400   RF:353

| | 2012 Season | | | | | | | 2010-2012 | | | | | | |
| | Home Games | | | Away Games | | | | Home Games | | | Away Games | | | |
	Cubs	Opp	Total	Cubs	Opp	Total	Index	Cubs	Opp	Total	Cubs	Opp	Total	Index
G	81	81	162	81	81	162		243	243	486	243	243	486	
Avg	.245	.248	.246	.235	.271	.252	98	.256	.257	.256	.246	.261	.253	101
AB	2647	2770	5417	2764	2631	5395	100	8079	8463	16542	8393	7962	16355	101
R	332	362	694	281	397	678	102	1008	1150	2158	944	1132	2076	104
H	648	687	1335	649	712	1361	98	2066	2171	4237	2068	2076	4144	102
2B	141	138	279	124	135	259	107	432	403	835	416	422	838	99
3B	22	18	40	14	29	43	93	59	51	110	40	57	97	112
HR	65	88	153	72	87	159	96	212	256	468	222	235	457	101
BB	247	295	542	200	278	478	113	706	897	1603	645	861	1506	105
SO	588	596	1184	647	532	1179	100	1754	1930	3684	1919	1690	3609	101
Foul Outs	37	37	74	40	39	79	93	124	134	258	155	152	307	83
E	62	57	119	43	53	96	124	197	174	371	168	147	315	118
E-Infield	30	26	56	21	24	45	124	86	83	169	71	65	136	124
LHB-Avg	.241	.229	.235	.233	.275	.252	93	.242	.252	.248	.228	.263	.247	100
LHB-HR	24	31	55	31	36	67	80	65	83	148	77	91	168	91
RHB-Avg	.247	.260	.254	.236	.268	.252	101	.262	.259	.261	.255	.259	.257	101
RHB-HR	41	57	98	41	51	92	107	147	173	320	145	144	289	107

Chicago White Sox - U.S. Cellular Field
LF: 330   CF: 400   RF: 335

| | 2012 Season | | | | | | | 2010-2012 | | | | | | |
| | Home Games | | | Away Games | | | | Home Games | | | Away Games | | | |
	White Sox	Opp	Total	White Sox	Opp	Total	Index	White Sox	Opp	Total	White Sox	Opp	Total	Index
G	81	81	162	81	81	162		243	243	486	243	243	486	
Avg	.268	.254	.261	.243	.245	.244	107	.264	.257	.261	.253	.259	.256	102
AB	2719	2801	5520	2799	2669	5468	101	8069	8467	16536	8435	8197	16632	99
R	417	379	796	331	297	628	127	1134	1113	2247	1020	973	1993	113
H	730	711	1441	679	654	1333	108	2132	2176	4308	2131	2123	4254	101
2B	124	131	255	104	121	225	112	370	417	787	373	385	758	104
3B	15	8	23	14	12	26	88	34	26	60	32	45	77	78
HR	120	108	228	91	78	169	134	317	267	584	225	202	427	138
BB	252	275	527	209	228	437	119	770	778	1548	633	654	1287	121
SO	580	644	1224	623	602	1225	99	1524	1919	3443	1590	1696	3286	105
Foul Outs	68	58	126	60	61	121	103	209	190	399	186	153	339	118
E	33	56	89	37	44	81	110	124	141	265	128	154	282	94
E-Infield	11	20	31	15	15	30	103	44	55	99	51	63	114	87
LHB-Avg	.249	.261	.256	.246	.252	.249	103	.256	.263	.260	.255	.261	.258	101
LHB-HR	44	47	91	44	33	77	116	78	107	185	62	94	156	119
RHB-Avg	.280	.248	.265	.241	.240	.240	110	.269	.252	.261	.252	.257	.254	103
RHB-HR	76	61	137	47	45	92	149	239	160	399	163	108	271	149

Cincinnati Reds - Great American Ballpark
LF: 328   CF: 404   RF:325

| | 2012 Season | | | | | | | 2010-2012 | | | | | | |
| | Home Games | | | Away Games | | | | Home Games | | | Away Games | | | |
	Reds	Opp	Total	Reds	Opp	Total	Index	Reds	Opp	Total	Reds	Opp	Total	Index
G	81	81	162	81	81	162		243	243	486	243	243	486	
Avg	.256	.250	.253	.247	.244	.245	103	.265	.252	.258	.255	.252	.253	102
AB	2648	2798	5446	2829	2694	5523	99	8078	8453	16531	8590	8110	16700	99
R	352	310	662	317	278	595	111	1139	1019	2158	1055	974	2029	106
H	679	699	1378	698	657	1355	102	2141	2132	4273	2189	2042	4231	101
2B	133	123	256	163	139	302	86	393	388	781	460	429	889	89
3B	17	18	35	13	17	30	118	42	36	78	37	44	81	97
HR	103	96	199	69	56	125	161	310	282	592	233	213	446	134
BB	257	205	462	224	222	446	105	764	738	1502	774	752	1526	99
SO	638	636	1274	628	612	1240	104	1821	1820	3641	1913	1670	3583	103
Foul Outs	56	53	109	55	52	107	103	171	181	352	176	152	328	108
E	37	41	78	52	63	115	68	110	149	259	142	174	316	82
E-Infield	17	15	32	17	32	49	65	59	60	119	46	76	122	98
LHB-Avg	.285	.256	.265	.272	.243	.252	105	.276	.257	.264	.290	.251	.266	99
LHB-HR	32	43	75	18	23	41	183	106	121	227	88	97	185	121
RHB-Avg	.248	.244	.247	.240	.245	.242	102	.261	.248	.256	.243	.252	.247	103
RHB-HR	71	53	124	51	33	84	151	204	161	365	145	116	261	143

Cleveland Indians - Progressive Field
LF: 325   CF: 405   RF:325

| | 2012 Season | | | | | | | 2010-2012 | | | | | | |
| | Home Games | | | Away Games | | | | Home Games | | | Away Games | | | |
	Indians	Opp	Total	Indians	Opp	Total	Index	Indians	Opp	Total	Indians	Opp	Total	Index
G	81	81	162	81	81	162		243	243	486	243	243	486	
Avg	.249	.257	.253	.252	.281	.266	95	.250	.258	.254	.250	.276	.263	97
AB	2749	2916	5665	2776	2687	5463	104	8105	8614	16719	8416	8111	16527	101
R	323	393	716	344	452	796	90	997	1116	2113	1020	1241	2261	93
H	685	748	1433	700	755	1455	98	2027	2222	4249	2100	2240	4340	98
2B	141	156	297	125	161	286	100	419	493	912	427	454	881	102
3B	9	5	14	15	28	43	31	35	27	62	35	66	101	61
HR	64	85	149	72	89	161	89	217	224	441	201	250	451	97
BB	271	266	537	284	277	561	92	808	753	1561	786	825	1611	96
SO	539	595	1134	548	491	1039	105	1744	1613	3357	1796	1464	3260	102
Foul Outs	56	55	111	58	53	111	96	163	162	325	195	156	351	92
E	52	57	109	44	39	83	131	161	151	312	155	109	264	118
E-Infield	19	26	45	17	19	36	125	70	65	135	70	45	115	117
LHB-Avg	.254	.272	.262	.261	.269	.264	99	.258	.271	.264	.254	.281	.266	99
LHB-HR	49	52	101	49	47	96	102	148	134	282	125	106	231	120
RHB-Avg	.235	.241	.239	.232	.294	.270	89	.237	.245	.242	.242	.272	.259	94
RHB-HR	15	33	48	23	42	65	71	69	90	159	76	144	220	72

Colorado Rockies - Coors Field
LF: 347   CF: 415   RF:350

| | 2012 Season | | | | | | | 2010-2012 | | | | | | |
| | Home Games | | | Away Games | | | | Home Games | | | Away Games | | | |
	Rockies	Opp	Total	Rockies	Opp	Total	Index	Rockies	Opp	Total	Rockies	Opp	Total	Index
G	81	81	162	81	81	162		243	243	486	243	243	486	
Avg	.306	.306	.306	.241	.273	.257	119	.293	.284	.288	.236	.257	.247	117
AB	2827	2972	5799	2750	2667	5417	107	8358	8703	17061	8293	7946	16239	105
R	486	523	1009	272	367	639	158	1404	1329	2733	859	1052	1911	143
H	864	909	1773	662	728	1390	128	2446	2469	4915	1961	2044	4005	123
2B	174	171	345	132	150	282	114	474	498	972	376	404	780	119
3B	38	29	67	14	20	34	184	100	68	168	46	62	108	148
HR	100	118	218	66	80	146	139	302	298	600	200	215	415	138
BB	259	269	528	191	297	488	101	862	742	1604	728	871	1599	95
SO	546	574	1120	667	570	1237	85	1685	1752	3437	2003	1744	3747	87
Foul Outs	30	42	72	48	63	111	61	123	148	271	183	151	334	77
E	64	70	134	58	54	112	120	159	174	333	162	146	308	108
E-Infield	16	26	42	24	21	45	93	56	63	119	64	67	131	91
LHB-Avg	.319	.287	.302	.235	.274	.255	119	.303	.284	.294	.243	.256	.249	118
LHB-HR	42	45	87	22	23	45	183	148	122	270	88	82	170	155
RHB-Avg	.298	.318	.308	.244	.272	.258	119	.285	.283	.284	.232	.258	.245	116
RHB-HR	58	73	131	44	57	101	120	154	176	330	112	133	245	126

Detroit Tigers - Comerica Park
LF: 345   CF: 420   RF:330

	2012 Season							2010-2012						
	Home Games			Away Games				Home Games			Away Games			
	Tigers	Opp	Total	Tigers	Opp	Total	Index	Tigers	Opp	Total	Tigers	Opp	Total	Index
G	81	81	162	81	81	162		243	243	486	243	243	486	
Avg	.278	.252	.265	.258	.261	.260	102	.283	.255	.269	.260	.262	.261	103
AB	2696	2821	5517	2780	2675	5455	101	8168	8469	16637	8514	8010	16524	101
R	393	329	722	333	341	674	107	1217	1016	2233	1047	1108	2155	104
H	749	711	1460	718	698	1416	103	2308	2160	4468	2214	2100	4314	104
2B	136	128	264	143	143	286	91	438	377	815	446	396	842	96
3B	27	19	46	12	18	30	152	67	61	128	38	48	86	148
HR	92	67	159	71	84	155	101	256	202	458	228	240	468	97
BB	253	216	469	258	222	480	97	773	687	1460	805	780	1585	91
SO	488	684	1172	615	634	1249	93	1506	1749	3255	1887	1740	3627	89
Foul Outs	67	62	129	41	61	102	125	209	218	427	158	192	350	121
E	54	43	97	45	43	88	110	178	153	331	133	140	273	121
E-Infield	20	12	32	12	17	29	110	70	49	119	46	61	107	111
LHB-Avg	.276	.259	.267	.260	.267	.263	101	.280	.256	.267	.259	.257	.258	103
LHB-HR	39	31	70	24	39	63	112	101	96	197	74	123	197	98
RHB-Avg	.279	.245	.263	.257	.255	.256	103	.284	.254	.270	.261	.267	.263	103
RHB-HR	53	36	89	47	45	92	94	155	106	261	154	117	271	96

Houston Astros - Minute Maid Park
LF: 315   CF: 435   RF:326

	2012 Season							2010-2012						
	Home Games			Away Games				Home Games			Away Games			
	Astros	Opp	Total	Astros	Opp	Total	Index	Astros	Opp	Total	Astros	Opp	Total	Index
G	81	81	162	81	81	162		243	243	486	243	243	486	
Avg	.239	.255	.247	.233	.285	.259	96	.250	.254	.252	.244	.278	.261	97
AB	2657	2849	5506	2750	2690	5440	101	8095	8505	16600	8362	8117	16479	101
R	311	355	666	272	439	711	94	933	1093	2026	876	1226	2102	96
H	636	726	1362	640	767	1407	97	2025	2162	4187	2041	2254	4295	97
2B	114	137	251	124	139	263	94	399	442	841	400	417	817	102
3B	18	14	32	10	25	35	90	50	46	96	31	61	92	104
HR	79	79	158	67	94	161	97	188	251	439	161	250	411	106
BB	262	251	513	201	289	490	103	677	811	1488	602	837	1439	103
SO	687	628	1315	678	542	1220	106	1756	1916	3672	1798	1655	3453	106
Foul Outs	60	49	109	66	59	125	86	166	146	312	188	156	344	90
E	63	65	128	55	48	103	124	169	175	344	168	143	311	111
E-Infield	33	18	51	19	24	43	119	77	68	145	73	62	135	107
LHB-Avg	.227	.246	.237	.236	.287	.261	91	.247	.261	.255	.239	.267	.254	100
LHB-HR	28	26	54	32	40	72	80	47	97	144	48	89	137	104
RHB-Avg	.248	.260	.254	.231	.284	.257	99	.252	.250	.251	.246	.284	.264	95
RHB-HR	51	53	104	35	54	89	109	141	154	295	113	161	274	107

Kansas City Royals - Kauffman Stadium
LF: 330   CF: 410   RF:330

	2012 Season							2010-2012						
	Home Games			Away Games				Home Games			Away Games			
	Royals	Opp	Total	Royals	Opp	Total	Index	Royals	Opp	Total	Royals	Opp	Total	Index
G	81	81	162	81	81	162		243	243	486	243	243	486	
Avg	.278	.265	.271	.252	.276	.264	103	.278	.268	.273	.264	.274	.269	101
AB	2767	2859	5626	2869	2708	5577	101	8302	8645	16947	8610	8117	16727	101
R	341	382	723	335	364	699	103	1072	1157	2229	1010	1196	2206	101
H	768	757	1525	724	747	1471	104	2312	2316	4628	2274	2228	4502	103
2B	156	135	291	139	145	284	102	445	464	909	454	438	892	101
3B	20	24	44	17	18	35	125	72	60	132	37	48	85	153
HR	62	87	149	69	76	145	102	175	237	412	206	265	471	86
BB	202	268	470	202	274	476	98	666	811	1477	651	839	1490	98
SO	450	593	1043	582	584	1166	89	1358	1663	3021	1585	1629	3214	93
Foul Outs	63	68	131	61	74	135	96	174	186	360	192	221	413	86
E	49	43	92	64	45	109	84	161	151	312	168	148	316	99
E-Infield	18	19	37	27	14	41	90	66	66	132	64	55	119	111
LHB-Avg	.273	.264	.268	.240	.277	.257	104	.280	.268	.274	.260	.277	.268	102
LHB-HR	25	34	59	27	24	51	112	71	94	165	100	100	200	81
RHB-Avg	.282	.266	.273	.263	.275	.269	102	.277	.268	.273	.268	.273	.270	101
RHB-HR	37	53	90	42	52	94	97	104	143	247	106	165	271	90

Los Angeles Angels - Angel Stadium of Anaheim
LF: 330   CF: 400   RF:330

| | 2012 Season | | | | | | | 2010-2012 | | | | | | |
| | Home Games | | | Away Games | | | | Home Games | | | Away Games | | | |
	Angels	Opp	Total	Angels	Opp	Total	Index	Angels	Opp	Total	Angels	Opp	Total	Index
G	81	81	162	81	81	162		243	243	486	243	243	486	
Avg	.272	.234	.253	.276	.259	.268	94	.256	.240	.248	.261	.263	.262	95
AB	2646	2732	5378	2890	2702	5592	96	8002	8396	16398	8535	8119	16654	98
R	348	309	657	419	390	809	81	972	918	1890	1143	1116	2259	84
H	720	638	1358	798	701	1499	91	2046	2015	4061	2229	2134	4363	93
2B	141	108	249	132	142	274	94	402	379	781	436	471	907	87
3B	13	10	23	9	12	21	114	33	27	60	42	46	88	69
HR	82	79	161	105	107	212	79	213	216	429	284	260	544	80
BB	193	212	405	256	271	527	80	644	719	1363	713	805	1518	91
SO	503	632	1135	610	525	1135	104	1539	1802	3341	1730	1543	3273	104
Foul Outs	57	46	103	57	63	120	89	157	144	301	196	193	389	79
E	49	52	101	49	61	110	92	153	161	314	151	178	329	95
E-Infield	25	16	41	17	27	44	93	66	51	117	62	76	138	85
LHB-Avg	.277	.214	.236	.246	.257	.253	93	.259	.234	.243	.259	.264	.262	93
LHB-HR	13	36	49	17	49	66	76	52	91	143	71	114	185	78
RHB-Avg	.270	.251	.262	.287	.261	.277	95	.254	.246	.251	.262	.262	.262	96
RHB-HR	69	43	112	88	58	146	81	161	125	286	213	146	359	81

Los Angeles Dodgers - Dodger Stadium
LF: 330   CF: 395   RF:330

| | 2012 Season | | | | | | | 2010-2012 | | | | | | |
| | Home Games | | | Away Games | | | | Home Games | | | Away Games | | | |
	Dodgers	Opp	Total	Dodgers	Opp	Total	Index	Dodgers	Opp	Total	Dodgers	Opp	Total	Index
G	81	81	162	81	81	162		243	243	486	242	242	484	
Avg	.259	.227	.243	.245	.248	.247	99	.256	.233	.244	.251	.249	.250	98
AB	2653	2715	5368	2785	2657	5442	99	7956	8213	16169	8344	7926	16270	99
R	305	268	573	332	329	661	87	927	915	1842	1021	986	2007	91
H	687	617	1304	682	660	1342	97	2036	1916	3952	2096	1971	4067	97
2B	118	116	234	151	133	284	84	364	366	730	412	388	800	92
3B	8	10	18	15	22	37	49	33	20	53	47	71	118	45
HR	59	67	126	57	55	112	114	173	201	374	180	187	367	103
BB	246	257	503	235	282	517	99	771	787	1558	741	798	1539	102
SO	577	673	1250	579	603	1182	107	1641	1990	3631	1786	1825	3611	101
Foul Outs	42	49	91	55	62	117	79	146	184	330	157	184	341	97
E	52	42	94	46	55	101	93	137	139	276	144	173	317	87
E-Infield	23	22	45	19	24	43	105	52	55	107	64	73	137	78
LHB-Avg	.264	.241	.254	.230	.258	.244	104	.263	.234	.249	.251	.258	.254	98
LHB-HR	16	28	44	18	21	39	115	60	76	136	55	75	130	105
RHB-Avg	.255	.219	.235	.255	.242	.249	95	.250	.233	.241	.252	.243	.247	98
RHB-HR	43	39	82	39	34	73	114	113	125	238	125	112	237	101

Miami Marlins - Marlins Park
LF: 340   CF: 416   RF:335

| | 2012 Season | | | | | | | 2009-2011 | | | | | | |
| | Home Games | | | Away Games | | | | Home Games | | | Away Games | | | |
	Marlins	Opp	Total	Marlins	Opp	Total	Index	Marlins	Opp	Total	Marlins	Opp	Total	Index
G	81	81	162	81	81	162		237	237	474	249	249	498	
Avg	.249	.259	.254	.239	.268	.253	100	.256	.255	.256	.256	.259	.257	99
AB	2641	2807	5448	2796	2697	5493	99	7967	8347	16314	8644	8241	16885	102
R	305	363	668	304	361	665	100	1035	1115	2150	1081	1070	2151	105
H	658	726	1384	669	722	1391	99	2043	2130	4173	2211	2131	4342	101
2B	129	128	257	132	142	274	95	406	443	849	458	396	854	103
3B	23	21	44	16	19	35	127	50	50	100	42	73	115	90
HR	55	58	113	82	75	157	73	222	208	430	238	235	473	94
BB	255	241	496	229	254	483	104	859	868	1727	765	782	1547	116
SO	594	575	1169	634	538	1172	101	1929	1984	3913	1916	1650	3566	114
Foul Outs	66	48	114	64	51	115	100	147	210	357	171	173	344	107
E	57	45	102	46	54	100	102	175	148	323	147	169	316	107
E-Infield	28	16	44	17	24	41	107	63	53	116	58	64	122	100
LHB-Avg	.231	.266	.251	.245	.263	.255	98	.251	.258	.255	.261	.253	.256	100
LHB-HR	11	24	35	19	33	52	69	45	99	144	49	103	152	92
RHB-Avg	.259	.253	.256	.236	.272	.252	102	.259	.253	.256	.254	.263	.258	99
RHB-HR	44	34	78	63	42	105	74	177	109	286	189	132	321	96

416

Milwaukee Brewers - Miller Park
LF: 344 CF: 400 RF:345

| | 2012 Season | | | | | | | 2010-2012 | | | | | | |
| | Home Games | | | Away Games | | | | Home Games | | | Away Games | | | |
	Brewers	Opp	Total	Brewers	Opp	Total	Index	Brewers	Opp	Total	Brewers	Opp	Total	Index
G	81	81	162	81	81	162		243	243	486	243	243	486	
Avg	.266	.252	.259	.253	.269	.261	99	.267	.254	.261	.255	.262	.258	101
AB	2717	2872	5589	2840	2722	5562	100	8102	8574	16676	8508	8075	16583	101
R	437	376	813	339	357	696	117	1191	1094	2285	1056	1081	2137	107
H	723	725	1448	719	733	1452	100	2166	2180	4346	2169	2113	4282	101
2B	154	139	293	146	151	297	98	439	445	884	430	437	867	101
3B	24	16	40	15	15	30	133	56	38	94	47	44	91	103
HR	119	111	230	83	58	141	162	321	276	597	248	213	461	129
BB	253	257	510	213	268	481	106	793	769	1562	700	778	1478	105
SO	616	772	1388	624	630	1254	110	1727	2113	3840	1812	1804	3616	106
Foul Outs	66	57	123	44	38	82	149	175	155	330	169	140	309	106
E	45	66	111	54	58	112	99	154	165	319	157	166	323	99
E-Infield	18	27	45	20	23	43	105	70	66	136	65	70	135	101
LHB-Avg	.270	.253	.259	.230	.271	.256	101	.258	.252	.255	.252	.264	.259	98
LHB-HR	16	51	67	11	23	34	189	72	120	192	63	81	144	130
RHB-Avg	.265	.252	.259	.261	.268	.264	98	.271	.256	.264	.256	.260	.258	102
RHB-HR	103	60	163	72	35	107	155	249	156	405	185	132	317	128

Minnesota Twins - Target Field
LF: 339 CF: 411 RF:328

| | 2012 Season | | | | | | | 2010-2012 | | | | | | |
| | Home Games | | | Away Games | | | | Home Games | | | Away Games | | | |
	Twins	Opp	Total	Twins	Opp	Total	Index	Twins	Opp	Total	Twins	Opp	Total	Index
G	81	81	162	81	81	162		243	243	486	243	243	486	
Avg	.274	.267	.270	.247	.281	.264	103	.269	.268	.269	.252	.279	.265	101
AB	2735	2864	5599	2827	2746	5573	100	8101	8580	16681	8516	8204	16720	100
R	366	417	783	335	415	750	104	1055	1131	2186	1046	1176	2222	98
H	750	764	1514	698	772	1470	103	2183	2303	4486	2143	2290	4433	101
2B	137	139	276	133	146	279	98	432	436	868	415	447	862	101
3B	20	20	40	10	11	21	190	57	57	114	39	52	91	126
HR	69	98	167	62	100	162	103	167	242	409	209	272	481	85
BB	273	231	504	232	234	466	108	784	655	1439	720	673	1393	104
SO	497	501	998	572	442	1014	98	1436	1530	2966	1648	1401	3049	98
Foul Outs	42	55	97	49	69	118	82	155	167	322	172	191	363	89
E	46	45	91	61	65	126	72	150	145	295	154	177	331	89
E-Infield	20	15	35	26	26	52	67	59	58	117	50	74	124	94
LHB-Avg	.287	.251	.271	.256	.285	.269	101	.280	.256	.269	.260	.278	.268	100
LHB-HR	20	41	61	34	38	72	86	67	90	157	111	104	215	74
RHB-Avg	.258	.278	.269	.235	.278	.259	104	.258	.277	.269	.242	.280	.262	103
RHB-HR	49	57	106	28	62	90	116	100	152	252	98	168	266	94

New York Mets - Citi Field 2012
LF: 335 CF: 408 RF:330

| | 2012 Season | | | | | | | 2009-2011 | | | | | | |
| | Home Games | | | Away Games | | | | Home Games | | | Away Games | | | |
	Mets	Opp	Total	Mets	Opp	Total	Index	Mets	Opp	Total	Mets	Opp	Total	Index
G	81	81	162	81	81	162		243	243	486	243	243	486	
Avg	.242	.241	.242	.256	.261	.258	93	.264	.249	.256	.258	.277	.268	96
AB	2637	2762	5399	2813	2687	5500	98	8066	8438	16504	8452	8185	16637	99
R	287	347	634	363	362	725	87	1005	999	2004	1040	1152	2192	91
H	638	666	1304	719	702	1421	92	2129	2102	4231	2181	2270	4451	95
2B	117	124	241	169	138	307	80	429	422	851	441	473	914	94
3B	10	12	22	11	24	35	64	79	42	121	49	49	98	124
HR	67	88	155	72	73	145	109	162	186	348	169	254	423	83
BB	250	237	487	253	251	504	98	809	846	1655	790	829	1619	103
SO	624	642	1266	626	598	1224	105	1507	1713	3220	1601	1550	3151	103
Foul Outs	40	75	115	58	68	126	93	170	212	382	185	159	344	112
E	37	43	80	64	43	107	75	155	147	302	145	170	315	96
E-Infield	12	20	32	28	24	52	62	69	60	129	61	74	135	96
LHB-Avg	.244	.251	.247	.243	.275	.257	96	.271	.247	.260	.266	.266	.266	98
LHB-HR	33	41	74	43	30	73	102	71	81	152	71	104	175	90
RHB-Avg	.240	.234	.236	.269	.251	.260	91	.257	.251	.253	.249	.285	.269	94
RHB-HR	34	47	81	29	43	72	116	91	105	196	98	150	248	78

New York Yankees - Yankee Stadium
LF: 318   CF: 408   RF:314

| | 2012 Season | | | | | | | 2010-2012 | | | | | | |
| | Home Games | | | Away Games | | | | Home Games | | | Away Games | | | |
	Yankees	Opp	Total	Yankees	Opp	Total	Index	Yankees	Opp	Total	Yankees	Opp	Total	Index
G	81	81	162	81	81	162		243	243	486	243	243	486	
Avg	.266	.239	.252	.264	.266	.265	95	.273	.247	.260	.257	.258	.258	101
AB	2668	2790	5458	2856	2752	5608	97	8091	8393	16484	8518	8121	16639	99
R	406	327	733	398	341	739	99	1350	1031	2381	1180	987	2167	110
H	709	668	1377	753	733	1486	93	2208	2075	4283	2191	2098	4289	100
2B	122	151	273	158	152	310	90	400	419	819	422	422	844	98
3B	3	8	11	10	16	26	43	31	25	56	47	37	84	67
HR	138	94	232	107	96	203	117	375	289	664	293	232	525	128
BB	277	223	500	288	208	496	104	927	734	1661	927	744	1671	100
SO	572	672	1244	604	646	1250	102	1666	1879	3545	1784	1815	3599	99
Foul Outs	46	63	109	63	59	122	92	155	177	332	185	188	373	90
E	39	38	77	35	50	85	91	123	142	265	122	132	254	104
E-Infield	13	18	31	23	24	47	66	47	64	111	57	57	114	97
LHB-Avg	.276	.234	.256	.264	.249	.257	100	.275	.249	.262	.258	.254	.256	103
LHB-HR	91	48	139	63	35	98	146	246	151	397	167	93	260	153
RHB-Avg	.255	.244	.249	.263	.282	.273	91	.271	.246	.257	.257	.262	.260	99
RHB-HR	47	46	93	44	61	105	91	129	138	267	126	139	265	102

Oakland Athletics - O.co Coliseum
LF: 330   CF: 400   RF:330

| | 2012 Season | | | | | | | 2010-2012 | | | | | | |
| | Home Games | | | Away Games | | | | Home Games | | | Away Games | | | |
	Athletics	Opp	Total	Athletics	Opp	Total	Index	Athletics	Opp	Total	Athletics	Opp	Total	Index
G	79	79	158	83	83	166		241	241	482	245	245	490	
Avg	.236	.232	.234	.240	.259	.249	94	.249	.231	.240	.244	.263	.253	95
AB	2634	2758	5392	2893	2782	5675	100	7914	8227	16141	8513	8204	16717	98
R	337	278	615	376	336	712	91	1026	863	1889	995	1056	2051	94
H	622	640	1262	693	720	1413	94	1968	1899	3867	2073	2156	4229	93
2B	115	122	237	152	142	294	85	399	337	736	424	404	828	92
3B	15	9	24	17	5	22	115	51	27	78	40	30	70	115
HR	89	64	153	106	83	189	85	185	186	371	233	250	483	80
BB	287	220	507	263	242	505	106	830	723	1553	756	770	1526	105
SO	642	558	1200	745	578	1323	95	1655	1732	3387	1887	1634	3521	100
Foul Outs	110	97	207	60	84	144	151	278	273	551	211	209	420	136
E	53	42	95	58	45	103	97	173	152	325	161	154	315	105
E-Infield	26	11	37	24	20	44	88	67	51	118	64	67	131	92
LHB-Avg	.234	.243	.239	.243	.258	.250	96	.248	.239	.244	.250	.266	.257	95
LHB-HR	46	36	82	54	39	93	91	77	75	152	109	116	225	69
RHB-Avg	.238	.223	.230	.236	.259	.248	93	.249	.225	.236	.238	.260	.250	95
RHB-HR	43	28	71	52	44	96	79	108	111	219	124	134	258	88

Philadelphia Phillies - Citizens Bank Park
LF: 329   CF: 401   RF:329

| | 2012 Season | | | | | | | 2010-2012 | | | | | | |
| | Home Games | | | Away Games | | | | Home Games | | | Away Games | | | |
	Phillies	Opp	Total	Phillies	Opp	Total	Index	Phillies	Opp	Total	Phillies	Opp	Total	Index
G	81	81	162	81	81	162		246	246	492	240	240	480	
Avg	.253	.248	.250	.257	.255	.256	98	.258	.241	.249	.254	.256	.255	98
AB	2677	2787	5464	2867	2737	5604	98	8251	8518	16769	8453	8033	16486	99
R	324	347	671	360	333	693	97	1101	919	2020	1068	930	1998	99
H	676	690	1366	738	697	1435	95	2126	2050	4176	2148	2059	4207	97
2B	131	141	272	140	135	275	101	413	412	825	406	399	805	101
3B	14	8	22	14	17	31	73	54	25	79	46	51	97	80
HR	82	93	175	76	85	161	111	253	238	491	224	228	452	107
BB	230	218	448	224	191	415	111	796	620	1416	757	609	1366	102
SO	516	729	1245	578	656	1234	103	1529	2053	3582	1653	1814	3467	102
Foul Outs	50	62	112	57	65	122	94	173	203	376	180	173	353	105
E	50	47	97	51	49	100	97	133	141	274	125	152	277	97
E-Infield	31	20	51	24	18	42	121	69	58	127	56	72	128	97
LHB-Avg	.243	.248	.245	.257	.271	.263	93	.252	.246	.249	.246	.263	.253	99
LHB-HR	38	35	73	33	29	62	120	154	94	248	111	87	198	122
RHB-Avg	.262	.247	.254	.257	.244	.250	101	.264	.237	.249	.262	.252	.257	97
RHB-HR	44	58	102	43	56	99	107	99	144	243	113	141	254	95

Pittsburgh Pirates - PNC Park
LF: 325   CF: 399   RF:320

| | 2012 Season | | | | | | | 2010-2012 | | | | | | |
| | Home Games | | | Away Games | | | | Home Games | | | Away Games | | | |
	Pirates	Opp	Total	Pirates	Opp	Total	Index	Pirates	Opp	Total	Pirates	Opp	Total	Index
G	81	81	162	81	81	162		243	243	486	243	243	486	
Avg	.235	.234	.234	.250	.263	.257	91	.245	.257	.251	.241	.277	.259	97
AB	2588	2718	5306	2824	2737	5561	95	7844	8398	16242	8375	8214	16589	98
R	297	277	574	354	397	751	76	917	1040	1957	931	1212	2143	91
H	607	636	1243	706	721	1427	87	1922	2161	4083	2019	2276	4295	95
2B	128	122	250	113	128	241	109	410	453	863	384	432	816	108
3B	19	9	28	18	21	39	75	49	38	87	50	49	99	90
HR	67	58	125	103	95	198	66	180	190	370	223	282	505	75
BB	207	207	414	237	283	520	83	656	735	1391	740	828	1568	91
SO	620	575	1195	734	617	1351	93	1718	1601	3319	2151	1648	3799	89
Foul Outs	53	37	90	60	50	110	86	127	140	267	162	144	306	89
E	60	64	124	52	45	97	128	187	162	349	164	139	303	115
E-Infield	27	33	60	20	21	41	146	83	87	170	68	66	134	127
LHB-Avg	.248	.219	.233	.248	.241	.245	95	.243	.258	.250	.239	.279	.258	97
LHB-HR	35	26	61	47	34	81	82	96	78	174	113	110	223	83
RHB-Avg	.226	.245	.235	.251	.280	.265	89	.246	.257	.252	.242	.276	.260	97
RHB-HR	32	32	64	56	61	117	56	84	112	196	110	172	282	69

San Diego Padres - PETCO Park
LF: 322   CF: 396   RF:334

| | 2012 Season | | | | | | | 2010-2012 | | | | | | |
| | Home Games | | | Away Games | | | | Home Games | | | Away Games | | | |
	Padres	Opp	Total	Padres	Opp	Total	Index	Padres	Opp	Total	Padres	Opp	Total	Index
G	81	81	162	81	81	162		243	243	486	243	243	486	
Avg	.244	.240	.242	.249	.257	.253	96	.236	.232	.234	.251	.257	.253	92
AB	2651	2799	5450	2771	2665	5436	100	7897	8307	16204	8376	8011	16387	99
R	309	318	627	342	392	734	85	886	867	1753	1023	1035	2058	85
H	648	672	1320	691	684	1375	96	1862	1930	3792	2099	2055	4154	91
2B	134	129	263	138	134	272	96	346	374	720	409	396	805	90
3B	25	19	44	18	17	35	125	62	51	113	47	39	86	133
HR	47	62	109	74	100	174	62	152	182	334	192	244	436	77
BB	268	272	540	271	267	538	100	822	791	1613	756	786	1542	106
SO	616	649	1265	622	556	1178	107	1877	1935	3812	1864	1704	3568	108
Foul Outs	40	55	95	56	57	113	84	150	169	319	178	162	340	95
E	66	53	119	55	58	113	105	148	147	295	139	169	308	96
E-Infield	19	21	40	21	26	47	85	52	56	108	55	76	131	82
LHB-Avg	.248	.219	.235	.267	.250	.260	90	.237	.232	.234	.262	.254	.258	91
LHB-HR	16	15	31	37	35	72	44	53	48	101	90	89	179	57
RHB-Avg	.241	.254	.248	.231	.261	.247	100	.235	.233	.234	.243	.258	.250	93
RHB-HR	31	47	78	37	65	102	75	99	134	233	102	155	257	92

San Francisco Giants - AT&T Park
LF: 339   CF: 399   RF:309

| | 2012 Season | | | | | | | 2010-2012 | | | | | | |
| | Home Games | | | Away Games | | | | Home Games | | | Away Games | | | |
	Giants	Opp	Total	Giants	Opp	Total	Index	Giants	Opp	Total	Giants	Opp	Total	Index
G	81	81	162	81	81	162		243	243	486	243	243	486	
Avg	.267	.234	.250	.271	.262	.267	94	.257	.228	.242	.255	.250	.252	96
AB	2665	2753	5418	2893	2740	5633	96	7996	8243	16239	8536	8094	16630	98
R	308	272	580	410	377	787	74	891	797	1688	1094	1013	2107	80
H	711	643	1354	784	718	1502	90	2055	1879	3934	2178	2021	4199	94
2B	141	134	275	146	162	308	93	428	386	814	425	428	853	98
3B	29	13	42	28	24	52	84	60	41	101	51	65	116	89
HR	31	53	84	72	89	161	54	148	156	304	238	216	454	69
BB	246	245	491	237	244	481	106	699	800	1499	719	826	1545	99
SO	511	623	1134	586	614	1200	98	1572	2014	3586	1746	1870	3616	102
Foul Outs	54	59	113	55	47	102	115	158	176	334	213	183	396	86
E	48	47	95	67	55	122	78	140	148	288	152	160	312	92
E-Infield	24	18	42	32	20	52	81	66	51	117	71	56	127	92
LHB-Avg	.271	.214	.247	.255	.270	.261	94	.259	.216	.239	.255	.250	.253	95
LHB-HR	15	19	34	26	29	55	65	64	51	115	108	80	188	63
RHB-Avg	.262	.246	.253	.287	.256	.271	93	.256	.235	.244	.255	.250	.252	97
RHB-HR	16	34	50	46	60	106	49	84	105	189	130	136	266	72

Seattle Mariners - Safeco Field
LF: 331   CF: 405   RF:327

| | 2012 Season | | | | | | 2010-2012 | | | | | |
| | Home Games | | | Away Games | | | Home Games | | | Away Games | | |
	Mariners	Opp	Total	Mariners	Opp	Total	Index	Mariners	Opp	Total	Mariners	Opp	Total	Index
G	81	81	162	81	81	162		246	246	492	240	240	480	
Avg	.220	.229	.225	.247	.266	.256	88	.226	.236	.231	.242	.267	.254	91
AB	2598	2741	5339	2896	2743	5639	95	7943	8409	16352	8381	8036	16417	97
R	257	260	517	362	391	753	69	761	889	1650	927	1135	2062	78
H	571	629	1200	714	730	1444	83	1792	1986	3778	2030	2144	4174	88
2B	106	96	202	135	150	285	75	324	356	680	397	436	833	82
3B	8	11	19	19	17	36	56	27	26	53	38	48	86	62
HR	56	60	116	93	106	199	62	148	206	354	211	262	473	75
BB	248	210	458	218	239	457	106	730	651	1381	630	686	1316	105
SO	598	616	1214	661	550	1211	106	1902	1715	3617	1821	1512	3333	109
Foul Outs	89	81	170	74	56	130	138	234	236	470	208	185	393	120
E	35	43	78	37	53	90	87	124	133	257	166	161	327	77
E-Infield	14	25	39	14	22	36	108	56	59	115	76	71	147	76
LHB-Avg	.220	.227	.223	.252	.276	.262	85	.226	.239	.232	.249	.269	.258	90
LHB-HR	35	27	62	60	39	99	68	93	85	178	122	92	214	85
RHB-Avg	.220	.232	.227	.237	.258	.249	91	.225	.234	.230	.233	.265	.251	92
RHB-HR	21	33	54	33	67	100	55	55	121	176	89	170	259	67

St Louis Cardinals - Busch Stadium
LF: 336   CF: 400   RF:335

| | 2012 Season | | | | | | 2010-2012 | | | | | |
| | Home Games | | | Away Games | | | Home Games | | | Away Games | | |
	Cardinals	Opp	Total	Cardinals	Opp	Total	Index	Cardinals	Opp	Total	Cardinals	Opp	Total	Index
G	81	81	162	81	81	162		243	243	486	243	243	486	
Avg	.285	.248	.266	.258	.262	.260	102	.275	.245	.260	.264	.270	.267	97
AB	2793	2866	5659	2829	2705	5534	102	8125	8447	16572	8571	8238	16809	99
R	404	297	701	361	351	712	98	1140	914	2054	1123	1067	2190	94
H	795	712	1507	731	708	1439	105	2236	2066	4302	2259	2227	4486	96
2B	165	134	299	125	138	263	111	447	388	835	436	445	881	96
3B	21	10	31	16	22	38	80	41	35	76	36	60	96	80
HR	76	64	140	83	70	153	89	210	182	392	261	221	482	82
BB	255	217	472	278	219	497	93	834	664	1498	782	697	1479	103
SO	570	646	1216	622	572	1194	100	1478	1772	3250	1719	1638	3357	98
Foul Outs	56	45	101	38	44	82	120	161	146	307	151	130	281	111
E	51	42	93	56	55	111	84	163	139	302	159	156	315	96
E-Infield	29	17	46	24	25	49	94	84	56	140	76	66	142	99
LHB-Avg	.282	.265	.273	.254	.258	.256	107	.269	.255	.261	.266	.266	.266	98
LHB-HR	24	32	56	20	30	50	110	65	83	148	75	83	158	98
RHB-Avg	.287	.236	.261	.261	.265	.263	99	.279	.238	.258	.262	.273	.268	97
RHB-HR	52	32	84	63	40	103	79	145	99	244	186	138	324	75

Tampa Bay Rays - Tropicana Field Surface: FieldTurf
LF: 315   CF: 404   RF:322

| | 2012 Season | | | | | | 2010-2012 | | | | | |
| | Home Games | | | Away Games | | | Home Games | | | Away Games | | |
	Rays	Opp	Total	Rays	Opp	Total	Index	Rays	Opp	Total	Rays	Opp	Total	Index
G	81	81	162	81	81	162		243	243	486	243	243	486	
Avg	.231	.218	.224	.248	.238	.243	92	.236	.225	.231	.250	.246	.248	93
AB	2614	2763	5377	2784	2650	5434	99	7853	8302	16155	8420	8022	16442	98
R	329	265	594	368	312	680	87	990	843	1833	1216	997	2213	83
H	603	603	1206	690	630	1320	91	1857	1869	3726	2103	1974	4077	91
2B	115	110	225	135	109	244	93	366	368	734	452	397	849	88
3B	15	12	27	15	6	21	130	50	46	96	54	36	90	109
HR	82	55	137	93	84	177	78	241	216	457	266	259	525	89
BB	298	223	521	273	246	519	101	914	698	1612	900	753	1653	99
SO	623	760	1383	700	623	1323	106	1795	1992	3787	2013	1723	3736	103
Foul Outs	72	61	133	53	46	99	136	211	262	473	171	176	347	139
E	53	40	93	61	43	104	89	123	125	248	149	180	329	75
E-Infield	23	21	44	28	24	52	85	47	57	104	62	80	142	73
LHB-Avg	.209	.218	.214	.234	.249	.241	89	.233	.222	.227	.247	.253	.250	91
LHB-HR	32	25	57	43	38	81	63	115	96	211	121	117	238	86
RHB-Avg	.250	.218	.234	.258	.230	.244	96	.240	.228	.234	.252	.241	.246	95
RHB-HR	50	30	80	50	46	96	93	126	120	246	145	142	287	91

Texas Rangers - Rangers Ballpark in Arlington
LF: 332   CF: 400   RF:325

	2012 Season							2010-2012						
	Home Games			Away Games				Home Games			Away Games			
	Rangers	Opp	Total	Rangers	Opp	Total	Index	Rangers	Opp	Total	Rangers	Opp	Total	Index
G	81	81	162	81	81	162		243	243	486	243	243	486	
Avg	.285	.259	.272	.261	.240	.251	108	.290	.254	.272	.265	.238	.252	108
AB	2772	2863	5635	2818	2655	5473	103	8342	8543	16885	8542	7936	16478	102
R	447	374	821	361	333	694	118	1375	1111	2486	1075	960	2035	122
H	790	742	1532	736	636	1372	112	2417	2172	4589	2264	1888	4152	111
2B	164	145	309	139	128	267	112	468	427	895	413	374	787	111
3B	16	19	35	16	18	34	100	52	38	90	37	38	75	117
HR	108	94	202	92	81	173	113	327	277	604	245	230	475	124
BB	240	222	462	238	224	462	97	746	719	1465	718	739	1457	98
SO	520	685	1205	583	601	1184	99	1407	1849	3256	1612	1797	3409	93
Foul Outs	42	54	96	61	76	137	68	137	188	325	171	210	381	83
E	38	73	111	47	41	88	126	166	210	376	138	153	291	129
E-Infield	16	32	48	24	21	45	107	80	101	181	59	61	120	151
LHB-Avg	.307	.257	.275	.258	.233	.242	114	.294	.257	.273	.270	.235	.251	109
LHB-HR	39	42	81	35	30	65	123	111	121	232	87	83	170	133
RHB-Avg	.277	.261	.270	.262	.245	.255	106	.288	.252	.271	.263	.240	.253	107
RHB-HR	69	52	121	57	51	108	108	216	156	372	158	147	305	119

Toronto Blue Jays - Rogers Centre Surface: FieldTurf
LF: 328   CF: 400   RF:328

	2012 Season							2010-2012						
	Home Games			Away Games				Home Games			Away Games			
	Blue Jays	Opp	Total	Blue Jays	Opp	Total	Index	Blue Jays	Opp	Total	Blue Jays	Opp	Total	Index
G	81	81	162	81	81	162		240	240	480	246	246	492	
Avg	.249	.259	.254	.242	.263	.252	101	.253	.261	.257	.243	.254	.248	103
AB	2647	2814	5461	2840	2703	5543	99	7998	8468	16466	8543	8148	16691	101
R	368	385	753	348	399	747	101	1142	1151	2293	1072	1122	2194	107
H	659	728	1387	687	711	1398	99	2020	2208	4228	2074	2071	4145	105
2B	127	174	301	120	160	280	109	425	505	930	426	446	872	108
3B	14	7	21	8	8	16	133	44	45	89	33	34	67	135
HR	102	102	204	96	102	198	105	351	278	629	290	255	545	117
BB	244	256	500	229	318	547	93	735	769	1504	734	884	1618	94
SO	605	587	1192	646	555	1201	101	1718	1813	3531	1881	1682	3563	100
Foul Outs	74	52	126	66	58	124	103	249	183	432	235	163	398	110
E	47	58	105	54	50	104	101	142	155	297	161	147	308	99
E-Infield	18	21	39	20	19	39	100	53	66	119	53	63	116	105
LHB-Avg	.244	.254	.249	.230	.254	.243	103	.243	.255	.250	.239	.253	.247	101
LHB-HR	28	42	70	33	50	83	84	101	103	204	88	104	192	105
RHB-Avg	.252	.263	.257	.249	.270	.258	99	.258	.265	.261	.245	.255	.249	105
RHB-HR	74	60	134	63	52	115	120	250	175	425	202	151	353	124

Washington Nationals - Nationals Park
LF: 336   CF: 403   RF:335

	2012 Season							2010-2012						
	Home Games			Away Games				Home Games			Away Games			
	Nationals	Opp	Total	Nationals	Opp	Total	Index	Nationals	Opp	Total	Nationals	Opp	Total	Index
G	81	81	162	81	81	162		242	242	484	243	243	486	
Avg	.267	.240	.253	.256	.233	.245	103	.260	.247	.253	.244	.253	.248	103
AB	2784	2838	5622	2831	2636	5467	103	8081	8444	16525	8393	8044	16437	101
R	367	303	670	364	291	655	102	1005	966	1971	1005	1013	2018	98
H	743	681	1424	725	615	1340	106	2098	2131	4229	2044	2037	4081	104
2B	138	159	297	163	134	297	97	403	421	824	405	405	810	101
3B	11	20	31	14	12	26	116	36	42	78	42	48	90	86
HR	101	64	165	93	65	158	102	258	205	463	239	204	443	104
BB	242	232	474	237	265	502	92	724	648	1372	728	838	1566	87
SO	597	674	1271	728	651	1379	90	1770	1756	3526	2098	1686	3784	93
Foul Outs	75	51	126	54	53	107	115	180	176	356	151	177	328	108
E	50	53	103	44	54	98	105	160	142	302	165	160	325	93
E-Infield	18	23	41	19	21	40	103	62	58	120	76	67	143	84
LHB-Avg	.270	.248	.259	.256	.228	.243	106	.251	.256	.254	.235	.249	.242	105
LHB-HR	40	28	68	46	28	74	92	105	75	180	100	90	190	96
RHB-Avg	.265	.235	.250	.256	.237	.247	101	.266	.250	.258	.250	.256	.253	102
RHB-HR	61	36	97	47	37	84	110	153	130	283	139	114	253	110

2012 American League Ballpark Index Rankings

Home Park	Avg	AB	R	H	2B	3B	HR	BB	SO	FO	E	E-Inf	LHB Avg	LHB HR	RHB Avg	RHB HR
White Sox (U.S. Cellular Field)	107	101	127	108	112	88	134	119	99	103	110	103	103	116	110	149
Red Sox (Fenway Park)	111	105	121	117	142	132	103	98	96	70	108	126	112	82	111	125
Rangers (Rangers Ballpark in Arlington)	108	103	118	112	112	100	113	97	99	68	126	107	114	123	106	108
Orioles (Oriole Park at Camden Yards)	109	101	117	110	106	68	131	102	98	76	114	173	106	129	112	133
Tigers (Comerica Park)	102	101	107	103	91	152	101	97	93	125	110	110	101	112	103	94
Twins (Target Field)	103	100	104	103	98	190	103	108	98	82	72	67	101	86	104	116
Royals (Kauffman Stadium)	103	101	103	104	102	125	102	98	89	96	84	90	104	112	102	97
Blue Jays (Rogers Centre)	101	99	101	99	109	133	105	93	101	103	101	100	103	84	99	120
Yankees (Yankee Stadium)	95	97	99	93	90	43	117	104	102	92	91	66	100	146	91	91
Athletics (O.co Coliseum)	94	100	91	94	85	115	85	106	95	151	97	88	96	91	93	79
Indians (Progressive Field)	95	104	90	98	100	31	89	92	105	96	131	125	99	102	89	71
Rays (Tropicana Field)	92	99	87	91	93	130	78	101	106	136	89	85	89	63	96	93
Angels (Angel Stadium of Anaheim)	94	96	81	91	94	114	79	80	104	89	92	93	93	76	95	81
Mariners (Safeco Field)	88	95	69	83	75	56	62	106	106	138	87	108	85	68	91	55

2012 National League Ballpark Index Rankings

Home Park	Avg	AB	R	H	2B	3B	HR	BB	SO	FO	E	E-Inf	LHB Avg	LHB HR	RHB Avg	RHB HR
Rockies (Coors Field)	119	107	158	128	114	184	139	101	85	61	120	93	119	183	119	120
Diamondbacks (Chase Field)	105	101	117	106	116	116	118	94	101	110	91	110	110	122	102	116
Brewers (Miller Park)	99	100	117	100	98	133	162	106	110	149	99	105	101	189	98	155
Reds (Great American Ballpark)	103	99	111	102	86	118	161	105	104	103	68	65	105	183	102	151
Braves (Turner Field)	101	100	104	101	120	104	87	104	105	118	135	121	103	97	99	78
Cubs (Wrigley Field)	98	100	102	98	107	93	96	113	100	93	124	124	93	80	101	107
Nationals (Nationals Park)	103	103	102	106	97	116	102	92	90	115	105	103	106	92	101	110
Marlins (Marlins Park)	100	99	100	99	95	127	73	104	101	100	102	107	98	69	102	74
Cardinals (Busch Stadium)	102	102	98	105	111	80	89	93	100	120	84	94	107	110	99	79
Phillies (Citizens Bank Park)	98	98	97	95	101	73	111	111	103	94	97	121	93	120	101	107
Astros (Minute Maid Park)	96	101	94	97	94	90	97	103	106	86	124	119	91	80	99	109
Mets (Citi Field 2012)	93	98	87	92	80	64	109	98	105	93	75	62	96	102	91	116
Dodgers (Dodger Stadium)	99	99	87	97	84	49	114	99	107	79	93	105	104	115	95	114
Padres (PETCO Park)	96	100	85	96	96	125	62	100	107	84	105	85	90	44	100	75
Pirates (PNC Park)	91	95	76	87	109	75	66	83	93	86	128	146	95	82	89	56
Giants (AT&T Park)	94	96	74	90	93	84	54	106	98	115	78	81	94	65	93	49

2012 AL Home Runs

Home Park	Index
White Sox	134
Orioles	131
Yankees	117
Rangers	113
Blue Jays	105
Red Sox	103
Twins	103
Royals	102
Tigers	101
Indians	89
Athletics	85
Angels	79
Rays	78
Mariners	62

2012 AL LHB Home Runs

Home Park	Index
Yankees	146
Orioles	129
Rangers	123
White Sox	116
Royals	112
Tigers	112
Indians	102
Athletics	91
Twins	86
Blue Jays	84
Red Sox	82
Angels	76
Mariners	68
Rays	63

2012 AL RHB Home Runs

Home Park	Index
White Sox	149
Orioles	133
Red Sox	125
Blue Jays	120
Twins	116
Rangers	108
Royals	97
Tigers	94
Rays	93
Yankees	91
Angels	81
Athletics	79
Indians	71
Mariners	55

2012 NL Home Runs

Home Park	Index
Brewers	162
Reds	161
Rockies	139
Diamondbacks	118
Dodgers	114
Phillies	111
Mets	109
Nationals	102
Astros	97
Cubs	96
Cardinals	89
Braves	87
Marlins	73
Pirates	66
Padres	62
Giants	54

2012 NL LHB Home Runs

Home Park	Index
Brewers	189
Reds	183
Rockies	183
Diamondbacks	122
Phillies	120
Dodgers	115
Cardinals	110
Mets	102
Braves	97
Nationals	92
Pirates	82
Cubs	80
Astros	80
Marlins	69
Giants	65
Padres	44

2012 NL RHB Home Runs

Home Park	Index
Brewers	155
Reds	151
Rockies	120
Diamondbacks	116
Mets	116
Dodgers	114
Nationals	110
Astros	109
Cubs	107
Phillies	107
Cardinals	79
Braves	78
Padres	75
Marlins	74
Pirates	56
Giants	49

2012 AL Avg	
Home Park	Index
Red Sox	111
Orioles	109
Rangers	108
White Sox	107
Royals	103
Twins	103
Tigers	102
Blue Jays	101
Yankees	95
Indians	95
Angels	94
Athletics	94
Rays	92
Mariners	88

2012 AL LHB Avg	
Home Park	Index
Rangers	114
Red Sox	112
Orioles	106
Royals	104
Blue Jays	103
White Sox	103
Tigers	101
Twins	101
Yankees	100
Indians	99
Athletics	96
Angels	93
Rays	89
Mariners	85

2012 AL RHB Avg	
Home Park	Index
Orioles	112
Red Sox	111
White Sox	110
Rangers	106
Twins	104
Tigers	103
Royals	102
Blue Jays	99
Rays	96
Angels	95
Athletics	93
Yankees	91
Mariners	91
Indians	89

2012 NL Avg	
Home Park	Index
Rockies	119
Diamondbacks	105
Nationals	103
Reds	103
Cardinals	102
Braves	101
Marlins	100
Brewers	99
Dodgers	99
Cubs	98
Phillies	98
Padres	96
Astros	96
Giants	94
Mets	93
Pirates	91

2012 NL LHB Avg	
Home Park	Index
Rockies	119
Diamondbacks	110
Cardinals	107
Nationals	106
Reds	105
Dodgers	104
Braves	103
Brewers	101
Marlins	98
Mets	96
Pirates	95
Giants	94
Cubs	93
Phillies	93
Astros	91
Padres	90

2012 NL RHB Avg	
Home Park	Index
Rockies	119
Diamondbacks	102
Reds	102
Marlins	102
Phillies	101
Nationals	101
Cubs	101
Padres	100
Braves	99
Cardinals	99
Astros	99
Brewers	98
Dodgers	95
Giants	93
Mets	91
Pirates	89

2012 AL Doubles	
Home Park	Index
Red Sox	142
Rangers	112
White Sox	112
Blue Jays	109
Orioles	106
Royals	102
Indians	100
Twins	98
Angels	94
Rays	93
Tigers	91
Yankees	90
Athletics	85
Mariners	75

2012 AL Triples	
Home Park	Index
Twins	190
Tigers	152
Blue Jays	133
Red Sox	132
Rays	130
Royals	125
Athletics	115
Angels	114
Rangers	100
White Sox	88
Orioles	68
Mariners	56
Yankees	43
Indians	31

2012 AL Errors	
Home Park	Index
Indians	131
Rangers	126
Orioles	114
Tigers	110
White Sox	110
Red Sox	108
Blue Jays	101
Athletics	97
Angels	92
Yankees	91
Rays	89
Mariners	87
Royals	84
Twins	72

2012 NL Doubles	
Home Park	Index
Braves	120
Diamondbacks	116
Rockies	114
Cardinals	111
Pirates	109
Cubs	107
Phillies	101
Brewers	98
Nationals	97
Padres	96
Marlins	95
Astros	94
Giants	93
Reds	86
Dodgers	84
Mets	80

2012 NL Triples	
Home Park	Index
Rockies	184
Brewers	133
Marlins	127
Padres	125
Reds	118
Diamondbacks	116
Nationals	116
Braves	104
Cubs	93
Astros	90
Giants	84
Cardinals	80
Pirates	75
Phillies	73
Mets	64
Dodgers	49

2012 NL Errors	
Home Park	Index
Braves	135
Pirates	128
Astros	124
Cubs	124
Rockies	120
Padres	105
Nationals	105
Marlins	102
Brewers	99
Phillies	97
Dodgers	93
Diamondbacks	91
Cardinals	84
Giants	78
Mets	75
Reds	68

2010-2012 American League Ballpark Index Rankings

Home Park	Avg	AB	R	H	2B	3B	HR	BB	SO	FO	E	E-Inf	LHB Avg	LHB HR	RHB Avg	RHB HR
Rangers (Rangers Ballpark in Arlington)	108	102	122	111	111	117	124	98	93	83	129	151	109	133	107	119
Red Sox (Fenway Park)	109	103	115	112	130	95	91	98	97	78	126	125	107	77	111	106
White Sox (U.S. Cellular Field)	102	99	113	101	104	78	138	121	105	118	94	87	101	119	103	149
Yankees (Yankee Stadium)	101	99	110	100	98	67	128	100	99	90	104	97	103	153	99	102
Orioles (Oriole Park at Camden Yards)	103	102	109	105	104	70	121	101	97	91	89	109	105	129	102	116
Blue Jays (Rogers Centre)	103	101	107	105	108	135	117	94	100	110	99	105	101	105	105	124
Tigers (Comerica Park)	103	101	104	104	96	148	97	91	89	121	121	111	103	98	103	96
Royals (Kauffman Stadium)	101	101	101	103	101	153	86	98	93	86	99	111	102	81	101	90
Twins (Target Field)	101	100	98	101	101	126	85	104	98	89	89	94	100	74	103	94
Athletics (O.co Coliseum)	95	98	94	93	92	115	80	105	100	136	105	92	95	69	95	88
Indians (Progressive Field)	97	101	93	98	102	61	97	96	102	92	118	117	99	120	94	72
Angels (Angel Stadium of Anaheim)	95	98	84	93	87	69	80	91	104	79	95	85	93	78	96	81
Rays (Tropicana Field)	93	98	83	91	88	109	89	99	103	139	75	73	91	86	95	91
Mariners (Safeco Field)	91	97	78	88	82	62	75	105	109	120	77	76	90	85	92	67

2010-2012 National League Ballpark Index Rankings

Home Park	Avg	AB	R	H	2B	3B	HR	BB	SO	FO	E	E-Inf	LHB Avg	LHB HR	RHB Avg	RHB HR
Rockies (Coors Field)	117	105	143	123	119	148	138	95	87	77	108	91	118	155	116	126
Diamondbacks (Chase Field)	104	101	112	106	111	150	110	93	99	106	91	94	105	102	104	115
Brewers (Miller Park)	101	101	107	101	101	103	129	105	106	106	99	101	98	130	102	128
Reds (Great American Ballpark)	102	99	106	101	89	97	134	99	103	108	82	98	99	121	103	143
Cubs (Wrigley Field)	101	101	104	102	99	112	101	105	101	83	118	124	100	91	101	107
Marlins (Marlins Park)*	100	99	100	99	95	127	73	104	101	100	102	107	98	69	102	74
Braves (Turner Field)	101	100	100	101	103	85	95	100	106	99	119	117	101	102	101	88
Phillies (Citizens Bank Park)	98	99	99	97	101	80	107	102	102	105	97	97	99	122	97	95
Nationals (Nationals Park)	103	101	98	104	101	86	104	87	93	108	93	84	105	96	102	110
Astros (Minute Maid Park)	97	101	96	97	102	104	106	103	106	90	111	107	100	104	95	107
Cardinals (Busch Stadium)	97	99	94	96	96	80	82	103	98	111	96	99	98	98	97	75
Dodgers (Dodger Stadium)	98	99	91	97	92	45	103	102	101	97	87	78	98	105	98	101
Pirates (PNC Park)	97	98	91	95	108	90	75	91	89	89	115	127	97	83	97	69
Mets (Citi Field 2012)*	93	98	87	92	80	64	109	98	105	93	75	62	96	102	91	116
Padres (PETCO Park)	92	99	85	91	90	133	77	106	108	95	96	82	91	57	93	92
Giants (AT&T Park)	96	98	80	94	98	89	69	99	102	86	92	92	95	63	97	72

2010-2012 AL Home Runs		2010-2012 AL LHB Home Runs		2010-2012 AL RHB Home Runs	
Home Park	Index	Home Park	Index	Home Park	Index
White Sox	138	Yankees	153	White Sox	149
Yankees	128	Rangers	133	Blue Jays	124
Rangers	124	Orioles	129	Rangers	119
Orioles	121	Indians	120	Orioles	116
Blue Jays	117	White Sox	119	Red Sox	106
Tigers	97	Blue Jays	105	Yankees	102
Indians	97	Tigers	98	Tigers	96
Red Sox	91	Rays	86	Twins	94
Rays	89	Mariners	85	Rays	91
Royals	86	Royals	81	Royals	90
Twins	85	Angels	78	Athletics	88
Angels	80	Red Sox	77	Angels	81
Athletics	80	Twins	74	Indians	72
Mariners	75	Athletics	69	Mariners	67

2010-2012 NL Home Runs		2010-2012 NL LHB Home Runs		2010-2012 NL RHB Home Runs	
Home Park	Index	Home Park	Index	Home Park	Index
Rockies	138	Rockies	155	Reds	143
Reds	134	Brewers	130	Brewers	128
Brewers	129	Phillies	122	Rockies	126
Diamondbacks	110	Reds	121	Mets*	116
Mets*	109	Dodgers	105	Diamondbacks	115
Phillies	107	Astros	104	Nationals	110
Astros	106	Mets*	102	Astros	107
Nationals	104	Diamondbacks	102	Cubs	107
Dodgers	103	Braves	102	Dodgers	101
Cubs	101	Cardinals	98	Phillies	95
Braves	95	Nationals	96	Padres	92
Cardinals	82	Cubs	91	Braves	88
Padres	77	Pirates	83	Cardinals	75
Pirates	75	Marlins*	69	Marlins*	74
Marlins*	73	Giants	63	Giants	72
Giants	69	Padres	57	Pirates	69

* Park Data is for 2012 only

2010-2012 AL Avg	
Home Park	Index
Red Sox	109
Rangers	108
Orioles	103
Blue Jays	103
Tigers	103
White Sox	102
Royals	101
Twins	101
Yankees	101
Indians	97
Athletics	95
Angels	95
Rays	93
Mariners	91

2010-2012 AL LHB Avg	
Home Park	Index
Rangers	109
Red Sox	107
Orioles	105
Tigers	103
Yankees	103
Royals	102
Blue Jays	101
White Sox	101
Twins	100
Indians	99
Athletics	95
Angels	93
Rays	91
Mariners	90

2010-2012 AL RHB Avg	
Home Park	Index
Red Sox	111
Rangers	107
Blue Jays	105
White Sox	103
Tigers	103
Twins	103
Orioles	102
Royals	101
Yankees	99
Angels	96
Rays	95
Athletics	95
Indians	94
Mariners	92

2010-2012 NL Avg	
Home Park	Index
Rockies	117
Diamondbacks	104
Nationals	103
Reds	102
Cubs	101
Brewers	101
Braves	101
Marlins*	100
Dodgers	98
Phillies	98
Cardinals	97
Pirates	97
Astros	97
Giants	96
Mets*	93
Padres	92

2010-2012 NL LHB Avg	
Home Park	Index
Rockies	118
Diamondbacks	105
Nationals	105
Braves	101
Astros	100
Cubs	100
Reds	99
Phillies	99
Brewers	98
Cardinals	98
Marlins*	98
Dodgers	98
Pirates	97
Mets*	96
Giants	95
Padres	91

2010-2012 NL RHB Avg	
Home Park	Index
Rockies	116
Diamondbacks	104
Reds	103
Brewers	102
Nationals	102
Marlins*	102
Cubs	101
Braves	101
Dodgers	98
Pirates	97
Giants	97
Phillies	97
Cardinals	97
Astros	95
Padres	93
Mets*	91

2010-2012 AL Doubles	
Home Park	Index
Red Sox	130
Rangers	111
Blue Jays	108
White Sox	104
Orioles	104
Indians	102
Twins	101
Royals	101
Yankees	98
Tigers	96
Athletics	92
Rays	88
Angels	87
Mariners	82

2010-2012 AL Triples	
Home Park	Index
Royals	153
Tigers	148
Blue Jays	135
Twins	126
Rangers	117
Athletics	115
Rays	109
Red Sox	95
White Sox	78
Orioles	70
Angels	69
Yankees	67
Mariners	62
Indians	61

2010-2012 AL Errors	
Home Park	Index
Rangers	129
Red Sox	126
Tigers	121
Indians	118
Athletics	105
Yankees	104
Blue Jays	99
Royals	99
Angels	95
White Sox	94
Orioles	89
Twins	89
Mariners	77
Rays	75

2010-2012 NL Doubles	
Home Park	Index
Rockies	119
Diamondbacks	111
Pirates	108
Braves	103
Astros	102
Brewers	101
Nationals	101
Phillies	101
Cubs	99
Giants	98
Cardinals	96
Marlins*	95
Dodgers	92
Padres	90
Reds	89
Mets*	80

2010-2012 NL Triples	
Home Park	Index
Diamondbacks	150
Rockies	148
Padres	133
Marlins*	127
Cubs	112
Astros	104
Brewers	103
Reds	97
Pirates	90
Giants	89
Nationals	86
Braves	85
Cardinals	80
Phillies	80
Mets*	64
Dodgers	45

2010-2012 NL Errors	
Home Park	Index
Braves	119
Cubs	118
Pirates	115
Astros	111
Rockies	108
Marlins*	102
Brewers	99
Phillies	97
Cardinals	96
Padres	96
Nationals	93
Giants	92
Diamondbacks	91
Dodgers	87
Reds	82
Mets*	75

* Data is for 2012 only

2012 Lefty/Righty Statistics

We used to fill this section with a complete record of lefty/right splits for pitchers and hitters. The section wound up cluttered with too many meaningless zeroes and insignificant sample sizes. Frankly, it detracted from the section as a whole. With this year's Handbook, we've focused on the players with more substantial samples, specifically those with at least 20 plate appearances (for hitters) or 20 batters faced (for pitchers).

On the following pages, you will find the batting average, on-base percentage, and slugging percentage along with a count of at-bats, hits, doubles, triples, home runs, RBI, walks, and strikeouts for hitters against pitchers of each type. For example, Ichiro, Adam Jones, Josh Hamilton, and Miguel Cabrera didn't seem to care which arm the pitcher threw with this year.

For pitchers, these stats reflect the results of opposing batters. For example, Yankees lefty Clay Rapada is the classic (LOOGY) Left-handed One Out GuY, brought in almost exclusively to face left-handed hitters in tight spots. He did his job well, limiting lefties to a .186 average. When he stayed in to face a righty in 2012, however, the opposition hit over .300. On the other hand, we have Pat Neshek who might have the funkiest motion in baseball. Neshek, a righty, is used primarily against opposing middle-of-the order righties, holding them to a ridiculous .094 average.

Batters vs. Left-Handed and Right-Handed Pitchers

Batter	vs	Avg	AB	H	2B	3B	HR	RBI	BB	SO	OBP	Slg
Abreu,Bobby	L	.267	45	12	2	0	1	5	5	15	.340	.378
Bats Left	R	.236	174	41	9	1	2	19	32	41	.353	.333
Abreu,Tony	L	.207	29	6	1	0	0	4	0	5	.207	.241
Bats Both	R	.293	41	12	1	1	1	11	2	8	.333	.439
Ackley,Dustin	L	.246	211	52	5	1	6	20	20	44	.310	.365
Bats Left	R	.215	396	85	17	1	6	30	39	80	.285	.308
Adams,Matt	L	.150	20	3	2	0	0	0	1	6	.190	.250
Bats Left	R	.273	66	18	4	0	2	13	4	18	.314	.424
Alonso,Yonder	L	.261	153	40	13	0	1	16	14	28	.327	.366
Bats Left	R	.278	396	110	26	0	8	46	48	73	.356	.404
Altuve,Jose	L	.359	156	56	15	1	2	5	10	17	.405	.506
Bats Right	R	.264	420	111	19	3	5	32	30	57	.317	.360
Alvarez,Pedro	L	.207	140	29	6	0	6	23	11	58	.270	.379
Bats Left	R	.257	385	99	19	1	24	62	46	122	.334	.499
Amarista,Alexi	L	.266	64	17	3	3	0	2	3	14	.299	.406
Bats Left	R	.232	211	49	12	2	5	30	14	28	.278	.379
Andino,Robert	L	.216	125	27	6	0	2	10	13	29	.295	.312
Bats Right	R	.208	259	54	7	1	5	18	24	71	.277	.301
Andrus,Elvis	L	.265	170	45	10	3	0	15	16	23	.328	.359
Bats Right	R	.294	459	135	21	6	3	47	41	73	.356	.386
Ankiel,Rick	L	.174	23	4	2	0	0	1	0	10	.174	.261
Bats Left	R	.237	135	32	8	2	5	14	12	49	.299	.437
Aoki,Norichika	L	.270	185	50	14	1	2	12	9	17	.322	.389
Bats Left	R	.299	335	100	23	3	8	38	34	38	.372	.457
Arencibia,J.P.	L	.244	90	22	5	0	6	17	4	28	.274	.500
Bats Right	R	.230	257	59	11	0	12	39	14	80	.275	.412
Arias,Joaquin	L	.303	152	46	5	3	3	15	7	19	.333	.434
Bats Right	R	.240	167	40	8	2	2	19	6	25	.278	.347
Avery,Xavier	L	.125	16	2	1	0	0	0	5	6	.333	.188
Bats Left	R	.244	78	19	5	1	1	6	6	17	.298	.372
Avila,Alex	L	.176	85	15	2	0	1	9	16	30	.304	.235
Bats Left	R	.262	282	74	19	2	8	39	45	74	.367	.429
Aviles,Mike	L	.286	147	42	6	0	5	15	9	19	.325	.429
Bats Right	R	.236	365	86	22	0	8	45	14	58	.264	.362
Aybar,Erick	L	.336	137	46	14	2	2	14	7	11	.368	.511
Bats Both	R	.274	380	104	17	3	6	31	15	50	.308	.382
Baker,Jeff	L	.240	129	31	10	0	3	17	7	34	.277	.388
Bats Right	R	.237	59	14	2	1	1	8	4	14	.281	.356
Baker,John	L	.229	35	8	1	0	0	3	5	10	.325	.257
Bats Left	R	.241	158	38	7	0	0	11	15	31	.306	.285
Barajas,Rod	L	.167	72	12	1	0	1	5	9	16	.250	.222
Bats Right	R	.217	249	54	10	0	10	26	20	53	.292	.378
Barmes,Clint	L	.274	95	26	6	0	1	7	13	18	.373	.368
Bats Right	R	.217	360	78	10	1	7	38	7	88	.243	.308
Barnes,Brandon	L	.234	47	11	3	0	0	4	2	17	.280	.298
Bats Right	R	.176	51	9	0	0	1	3	3	12	.222	.235
Barney,Darwin	L	.257	144	37	7	1	1	5	8	15	.296	.340
Bats Right	R	.252	404	102	19	3	6	39	25	43	.300	.359
Bartlett,Jason	L	.160	25	4	1	0	0	2	3	7	.241	.200
Bats Right	R	.121	58	7	4	0	0	2	9	20	.239	.190
Barton,Daric	L	.188	32	6	2	0	0	4	4	9	.297	.250
Bats Left	R	.210	81	17	5	0	1	2	18	23	.354	.309
Bautista,Jose	L	.200	85	17	3	0	5	14	12	13	.306	.412
Bats Right	R	.255	247	63	11	0	22	51	47	50	.375	.567
Baxter,Mike	L	.053	19	1	1	0	0	0	3	8	.182	.105
Bats Left	R	.288	160	46	13	2	3	17	22	37	.386	.450
Bay,Jason	L	.172	93	16	0	0	4	15	12	23	.264	.301
Bats Right	R	.158	101	16	2	0	4	5	7	35	.211	.297
Beckham,Gordon	L	.227	119	27	7	0	3	12	19	18	.333	.361
Bats Right	R	.236	406	96	17	0	13	48	21	71	.284	.374
Bell,Josh	L	.083	12	1	0	0	0	0	1	7	.154	.083
Bats Both	R	.200	40	8	2	0	1	4	3	7	.256	.325
Belt,Brandon	L	.242	128	31	8	2	5	17	12	35	.315	.453
Bats Left	R	.290	283	82	19	4	2	39	42	71	.380	.406
Beltran,Carlos	L	.276	145	40	9	1	9	29	12	36	.329	.538
Bats Both	R	.266	402	107	17	0	23	68	53	88	.352	.480
Beltre,Adrian	L	.269	156	42	6	0	6	19	10	28	.314	.423
Bats Right	R	.339	448	152	27	2	30	83	26	54	.375	.609
Berkman,Lance	L	.176	17	3	1	0	1	2	2	5	.300	.412
Bats Both	R	.281	64	18	6	1	1	5	12	14	.403	.453
Bernadina,Roger	L	.417	24	10	1	0	0	0	2	8	.481	.458
Bats Left	R	.276	203	56	10	0	5	25	26	45	.359	.399
Berry,Quintin	L	.214	56	12	2	3	0	3	2	23	.237	.357
Bats Left	R	.268	235	63	8	3	2	26	23	57	.351	.353
Betancourt,Yuniesky	L	.247	85	21	7	1	1	10	2	11	.264	.388
Bats Right	R	.215	130	28	7	0	6	26	7	14	.250	.408
Betemit,Wilson	L	.140	86	12	1	0	1	10	9	27	.219	.186
Bats Both	R	.302	255	77	18	0	11	30	22	76	.357	.502
Bianchi,Jeff	L	.091	22	2	0	0	1	3	1	6	.130	.227
Bats Right	R	.234	47	11	2	0	2	6	3	7	.275	.404
Bixler,Brian	L	.262	42	11	3	0	1	3	4	14	.326	.405
Bats Right	R	.130	46	6	3	0	1	4	3	22	.184	.261
Blackmon,Charlie	L	.348	23	8	3	0	0	1	0	3	.375	.478
Bats Left	R	.267	90	24	5	0	2	8	4	14	.313	.389
Blanco,Gregor	L	.248	133	33	4	1	3	11	17	33	.333	.361
Bats Left	R	.242	260	63	10	4	2	23	34	71	.332	.335
Blanco,Henry	L	.162	37	6	2	0	0	3	2	9	.205	.216
Bats Right	R	.222	27	6	1	0	1	4	1	9	.250	.370
Bloomquist,Willie	L	.317	104	33	8	3	0	10	5	16	.345	.452
Bats Right	R	.295	220	65	13	2	0	13	7	39	.316	.373
Blum,Geoff	L	.000	3	0	0	0	0	0	0	1	.000	.000
Bats Both	R	.160	25	4	0	0	0	1	2	6	.214	.160
Boesch,Brennan	L	.230	126	29	5	1	2	14	9	38	.292	.333
Bats Left	R	.244	344	84	17	1	10	40	17	66	.284	.387
Bogusevic,Brian	L	.156	64	10	1	0	1	4	4	22	.217	.219
Bats Left	R	.213	291	62	8	2	6	24	37	74	.313	.316
Bonifacio,Emilio	L	.210	81	17	0	0	1	4	5	24	.256	.247
Bats Both	R	.282	163	46	3	4	0	7	20	28	.364	.350
Bourgeois,Jason	L	.265	49	13	2	1	0	5	4	2	.321	.347
Bats Right	R	.231	13	3	0	0	0	0	0	2	.231	.231
Bourjos,Peter	L	.232	69	16	4	0	1	10	4	15	.273	.333
Bats Right	R	.212	99	21	3	0	2	9	11	29	.304	.303
Bourn,Michael	L	.273	227	62	7	6	2	21	23	61	.345	.383
Bats Left	R	.275	397	109	19	4	7	36	47	94	.350	.395
Brantley,Michael	L	.265	181	48	12	2	0	18	18	26	.327	.354
Bats Left	R	.299	371	111	25	2	6	42	35	30	.359	.426
Brantly,Rob	L	.200	20	4	1	0	0	0	2	5	.273	.250
Bats Left	R	.313	80	25	7	0	3	8	11	11	.396	.513
Braun,Ryan	L	.363	146	53	7	1	17	41	20	26	.435	.774
Bats Right	R	.305	452	138	29	2	24	71	43	102	.377	.538
Brignac,Reid	L	.200	5	1	0	0	0	1	0	3	.200	.200
Bats Left	R	.063	16	1	0	0	0	0	1	2	.118	.063
Brown,Andrew	L	.275	40	11	2	0	1	3	7	12	.375	.400
Bats Right	R	.208	72	15	5	0	4	8	5	22	.256	.444
Brown,Corey	L	.250	4	1	0	0	1	1	0	2	.250	1.000
Bats Left	R	.190	21	4	2	0	0	2	1	7	.227	.286
Brown,Domonic	L	.196	51	10	4	0	1	7	7	8	.288	.333
Bats Left	R	.250	136	34	7	2	4	19	14	26	.327	.419
Bruce,Jay	L	.225	169	38	3	1	11	32	18	56	.304	.450
Bats Left	R	.263	391	103	32	4	23	67	44	99	.337	.542
Buck,John	L	.162	105	17	4	1	2	9	18	35	.288	.276
Bats Right	R	.206	238	49	11	0	10	32	31	68	.301	.378
Buck,Travis	L	.286	7	2	0	0	0	0	0	3	.286	.286
Bats Left	R	.209	67	14	5	1	0	6	6	15	.284	.313
Burriss,Emmanuel	L	.094	32	3	1	0	0	0	3	9	.171	.125
Bats Both	R	.250	104	26	0	0	0	7	7	16	.301	.250
Butera,Drew	L	.118	34	4	1	0	0	1	3	8	.189	.147
Bats Right	R	.234	77	18	5	0	1	4	6	18	.306	.338
Butler,Billy	L	.331	160	53	8	1	12	29	25	26	.417	.619
Bats Right	R	.306	454	139	24	0	17	78	29	85	.356	.471
Byrd,Marlon	L	.327	49	16	1	0	1	4	1	9	.353	.408
Bats Right	R	.149	94	14	1	0	0	5	4	22	.188	.160
Cabrera,Asdrubal	L	.286	182	52	11	1	5	24	17	30	.356	.440
Bats Both	R	.263	373	98	24	0	11	44	35	69	.329	.416
Cabrera,Everth	L	.195	113	22	4	0	1	11	11	36	.266	.257
Bats Both	R	.267	285	76	15	3	1	13	32	74	.347	.351
Cabrera,Melky	L	.395	129	51	7	2	8	27	13	18	.444	.667
Bats Both	R	.327	330	108	18	8	3	33	23	45	.368	.458
Cabrera,Miguel	L	.314	159	50	13	0	4	17	35	28	.441	.472
Bats Right	R	.335	463	155	27	0	40	122	31	70	.375	.652
Cain,Lorenzo	L	.306	72	22	2	1	3	12	7	17	.358	.486
Bats Right	R	.247	150	37	7	1	4	19	8	39	.294	.387
Cairo,Miguel	L	.239	46	11	3	1	0	2	0	3	.234	.348
Bats Right	R	.163	104	17	4	1	1	11	4	17	.202	.250
Calhoun,Kole	L	.000	5	0	0	0	0	0	0	3	.000	.000
Bats Left	R	.222	18	4	1	0	0	1	2	3	.300	.278
Callaspo,Alberto	L	.306	134	41	7	0	5	19	12	12	.363	.470
Bats Both	R	.229	323	74	13	0	5	34	44	47	.318	.316
Campana,Tony	L	.229	35	8	0	0	0	0	5	8	.325	.229
Bats Left	R	.273	139	38	6	0	0	5	6	35	.303	.317
Cano,Robinson	L	.239	243	58	6	0	6	26	20	47	.309	.337
Bats Left	R	.359	384	138	42	1	27	68	41	49	.423	.685

Batters vs. Left-Handed and Right-Handed Pitchers

Batter	vs	Avg	AB	H	2B	3B	HR	RBI	BB	SO	OBP	Slg
Canzler,Russ	L	.393	28	11	2	0	2	4	1	7	.414	.679
Bats Right	R	.215	65	14	1	0	1	7	3	15	.250	.277
Cardenas,Adrian	L	.250	4	1	1	0	0	0	1	2	.400	.500
Bats Left	R	.179	56	10	5	0	0	2	6	11	.258	.268
Carp,Mike	L	.310	42	13	3	0	0	3	1	13	.341	.381
Bats Left	R	.180	122	22	3	0	5	17	20	33	.303	.328
Carpenter,Matt	L	.265	98	26	4	1	5	16	3	24	.305	.480
Bats Left	R	.308	198	61	18	4	1	30	31	39	.391	.455
Carrera,Ezequiel	L	.333	45	15	2	1	0	6	3	9	.388	.422
Bats Left	R	.245	102	25	4	2	2	5	5	26	.278	.382
Carroll,Jamey	L	.338	136	46	8	1	1	13	16	14	.405	.434
Bats Right	R	.240	334	80	10	0	0	27	36	51	.318	.269
Carson,Matt	L	.238	21	5	1	0	0	1	2	2	.304	.286
Bats Right	R	.222	45	10	0	0	0	3	0	19	.217	.222
Carter,Chris	L	.241	83	20	6	0	5	17	24	26	.404	.494
Bats Right	R	.237	135	32	6	0	11	22	15	57	.311	.526
Casilla,Alexi	L	.296	71	21	5	0	0	8	5	9	.338	.366
Bats Both	R	.224	228	51	12	2	1	22	11	43	.264	.307
Castellanos,Alex	L	.000	13	0	0	0	0	0	0	6	.000	.000
Bats Right	R	.400	10	4	0	1	1	3	0	2	.417	.900
Castillo,Welington	L	.476	42	20	5	0	1	9	4	8	.532	.667
Bats Right	R	.195	128	25	6	0	4	13	13	43	.273	.336
Castro,Jason	L	.148	54	8	2	0	0	3	2	21	.175	.185
Bats Left	R	.286	203	58	13	2	6	26	29	40	.373	.458
Castro,Starlin	L	.293	150	44	8	2	2	13	16	23	.361	.413
Bats Right	R	.280	496	139	21	10	12	65	20	77	.310	.435
Cedeno,Ronny	L	.277	94	26	9	1	1	10	8	20	.333	.426
Bats Right	R	.236	72	17	2	0	3	12	9	15	.329	.389
Cespedes,Yoenis	L	.298	151	45	6	2	7	25	11	24	.350	.503
Bats Right	R	.289	336	97	19	3	16	57	32	78	.358	.506
Chambers,Adron	L	.077	13	1	0	0	0	0	1	4	.143	.077
Bats Left	R	.268	41	11	0	2	0	4	4	14	.348	.366
Chavez,Endy	L	.185	27	5	0	0	0	0	0	1	.185	.185
Bats Left	R	.206	131	27	6	0	2	12	6	23	.246	.298
Chavez,Eric	L	.152	33	5	0	0	0	3	4	13	.231	.152
Bats Left	R	.298	245	73	12	0	16	34	26	46	.365	.543
Chisenhall,Lonnie	L	.184	38	7	2	0	0	1	0	9	.205	.237
Bats Left	R	.298	104	31	4	1	5	15	8	18	.348	.500
Choo,Shin-Soo	L	.199	206	41	12	0	2	13	28	60	.318	.286
Bats Left	R	.327	392	128	31	2	14	54	45	90	.403	.523
Christian,Justin	L	.121	33	4	1	0	0	1	3	0	.194	.152
Bats Right	R	.130	23	3	0	0	0	1	2	3	.200	.130
Ciriaco,Pedro	L	.304	79	24	3	1	2	4	2	13	.321	.443
Bats Right	R	.289	180	52	12	1	0	15	6	34	.312	.367
Clement,Jeff	L	-	0	0	0	0	0	0	0	0	-	-
Bats Left	R	.136	22	3	1	0	0	1	2	7	.208	.182
Clevenger,Steve	L	.069	29	2	0	0	0	1	0	7	.069	.069
Bats Left	R	.224	170	38	12	0	1	15	16	32	.290	.312
Coghlan,Chris	L	.050	20	1	0	0	0	0	2	4	.136	.050
Bats Left	R	.164	73	12	1	0	1	10	7	8	.232	.219
Colvin,Tyler	L	.270	100	27	7	4	1	12	3	31	.302	.450
Bats Left	R	.297	320	95	20	6	17	60	18	86	.334	.556
Conrad,Brooks	L	.178	45	8	3	0	3	12	2	18	.208	.444
Bats Both	R	.094	53	5	2	0	1	3	4	25	.158	.189
Constanza,Jose	L	.182	11	2	0	0	0	0	0	3	.182	.182
Bats Left	R	.262	65	17	2	0	0	4	8	18	.342	.292
Cooper,David	L	.294	34	10	3	0	0	0	0	6	.294	.382
Bats Left	R	.302	106	32	8	0	4	11	4	16	.333	.491
Corporan,Carlos	L	.222	18	4	0	0	0	4	0	2	.211	.222
Bats Both	R	.283	60	17	2	0	4	9	4	17	.338	.517
Cousins,Scott	L	.000	14	0	0	0	0	0	0	6	.000	.000
Bats Left	R	.194	72	14	4	1	1	3	4	18	.237	.319
Cowgill,Collin	L	.318	44	14	2	0	1	3	7	11	.412	.432
Bats Right	R	.233	60	14	0	0	0	6	4	16	.277	.233
Cozart,Zack	L	.265	132	35	8	1	3	11	5	28	.290	.409
Bats Right	R	.240	429	103	25	3	12	24	26	85	.287	.396
Craig,Allen	L	.354	127	45	11	0	8	22	5	19	.381	.630
Bats Right	R	.289	342	99	24	0	14	70	32	70	.345	.482
Crawford,Brandon	L	.254	114	29	5	0	1	15	8	33	.306	.325
Bats Left	R	.246	321	79	21	3	3	30	25	62	.303	.358
Crawford,Carl	L	.282	39	11	2	1	2	7	1	9	.317	.538
Bats Left	R	.282	78	22	8	1	1	12	2	13	.301	.449
Crisp,Coco	L	.248	157	39	10	1	3	11	12	30	.300	.382
Bats Both	R	.265	298	79	15	6	8	35	33	34	.337	.436
Cruz,Luis	L	.302	86	26	5	0	3	11	2	5	.326	.465
Bats Right	R	.294	197	58	15	0	3	29	7	29	.320	.416

Batter	vs	Avg	AB	H	2B	3B	HR	RBI	BB	SO	OBP	Slg
Cruz,Nelson	L	.309	139	43	16	0	6	16	19	26	.390	.554
Bats Right	R	.244	446	109	29	0	18	74	29	114	.296	.430
Cruz,Tony	L	.195	41	8	2	0	0	3	0	8	.195	.244
Bats Right	R	.282	85	24	7	1	1	8	3	11	.300	.424
Cuddyer,Michael	L	.258	97	25	5	1	8	18	14	13	.351	.577
Bats Right	R	.261	261	68	25	1	8	40	18	65	.304	.456
Culberson,Charlie	L	.250	12	3	0	0	0	0	0	5	.250	.250
Bats Right	R	.000	10	0	0	0	0	1	0	2	.000	.000
Cunningham,Aaron	L	.179	39	7	2	0	1	3	7	9	.304	.308
Bats Right	R	.172	58	10	2	0	0	4	2	16	.200	.207
Damon,Johnny	L	.205	44	9	2	0	1	3	2	9	.239	.318
Bats Left	R	.227	163	37	4	2	3	16	15	18	.292	.331
Danks,Jordan	L	.179	28	5	0	0	0	0	1	9	.207	.179
Bats Left	R	.256	39	10	1	0	1	4	5	7	.326	.359
Davis,Chris	L	.265	113	30	5	0	7	15	4	33	.297	.496
Bats Left	R	.271	402	109	15	0	26	70	33	136	.333	.502
Davis,Ike	L	.174	167	29	3	0	8	19	11	50	.225	.335
Bats Left	R	.253	352	89	23	0	24	71	50	91	.345	.523
Davis,Rajai	L	.285	151	43	9	1	4	14	12	35	.345	.437
Bats Right	R	.243	296	72	15	2	4	29	17	67	.290	.348
De Aza,Alejandro	L	.248	129	32	8	2	1	8	13	28	.336	.364
Bats Left	R	.291	395	115	21	4	8	42	34	81	.354	.425
De Jesus,Ivan	L	.143	21	3	0	0	0	1	2	5	.217	.143
Bats Right	R	.300	20	6	3	0	0	3	1	8	.318	.450
DeJesus,David	L	.149	94	14	0	0	0	6	13	21	.289	.149
Bats Left	R	.289	412	119	28	8	9	44	48	68	.365	.461
Denorfia,Chris	L	.337	178	60	11	3	4	22	15	16	.390	.500
Bats Right	R	.247	170	42	8	3	4	14	12	36	.297	.400
DeRosa,Mark	L	.225	40	9	4	0	0	2	6	9	.326	.325
Bats Right	R	.156	45	7	1	0	0	4	8	9	.278	.178
Descalso,Daniel	L	.309	94	29	6	1	1	9	9	16	.387	.426
Bats Left	R	.200	280	56	4	6	3	17	28	67	.275	.289
Desmond,Ian	L	.303	119	36	9	1	7	18	5	25	.331	.571
Bats Right	R	.289	394	114	24	1	18	55	25	88	.336	.492
DeWitt,Blake	L	-	0	0	0	0	0	0	0	0	-	-
Bats Left	R	.138	29	4	1	0	0	1	0	2	.133	.172
Diaz,Matt	L	.269	78	21	5	0	2	10	7	10	.329	.410
Bats Right	R	.100	30	3	1	0	0	3	2	11	.152	.133
Dirks,Andy	L	.274	73	20	0	0	3	4	8	8	.354	.397
Bats Left	R	.336	241	81	18	5	5	31	15	45	.375	.515
Dobbs,Greg	L	.279	43	12	2	0	0	3	1	9	.295	.326
Bats Left	R	.286	276	79	11	2	5	36	13	44	.315	.395
Dominguez,Matt	L	.250	24	6	0	0	1	3	1	1	.280	.375
Bats Right	R	.294	85	25	2	2	4	13	3	16	.318	.506
Donald,Jason	L	.175	57	10	1	0	2	5	2	18	.213	.298
Bats Right	R	.224	67	15	1	1	0	6	3	22	.274	.269
Donaldson,Josh	L	.229	83	19	4	0	4	10	4	15	.281	.422
Bats Right	R	.246	191	47	12	0	5	23	10	46	.293	.387
Doumit,Ryan	L	.247	154	38	9	0	5	22	6	29	.287	.403
Bats Both	R	.288	330	95	25	1	13	53	23	69	.335	.488
Downs,Matt	L	.184	98	18	3	0	6	10	5	24	.231	.398
Bats Right	R	.225	80	18	1	1	2	6	3	14	.279	.338
Dozier,Brian	L	.256	78	20	5	1	4	10	2	14	.275	.500
Bats Right	R	.227	238	54	6	0	2	23	14	44	.270	.277
Drew,Stephen	L	.198	86	17	3	0	2	8	8	27	.260	.302
Bats Left	R	.234	201	47	10	1	5	20	29	49	.329	.368
Duda,Lucas	L	.239	134	32	4	0	4	11	11	51	.304	.358
Bats Left	R	.240	267	64	11	0	11	46	40	69	.341	.404
Duncan,Shelley	L	.212	113	24	6	0	5	17	13	30	.297	.398
Bats Right	R	.193	119	23	4	0	6	14	15	29	.279	.378
Dunn,Adam	L	.191	183	35	5	0	15	35	29	86	.302	.464
Bats Left	R	.211	356	75	14	0	26	61	76	136	.348	.469
Dyson,Jarrod	L	.206	63	13	1	0	0	2	8	16	.288	.222
Bats Left	R	.275	229	63	7	5	0	7	22	40	.340	.349
Eaton,Adam	L	.313	32	10	2	0	1	3	4	1	.421	.469
Bats Left	R	.226	53	12	1	2	1	2	10	14	.359	.377
Ellis,A.J.	L	.224	107	24	6	1	2	7	17	24	.346	.355
Bats Right	R	.285	316	90	14	0	11	45	48	83	.382	.434
Ellis,Mark	L	.321	134	43	6	0	6	15	10	19	.377	.500
Bats Right	R	.228	281	64	15	1	1	16	30	51	.313	.299
Ellsbury,Jacoby	L	.292	106	31	4	0	0	5	4	17	.318	.330
Bats Left	R	.259	197	51	14	0	4	21	15	26	.310	.391
Elmore,Jake	L	.158	19	3	1	0	0	1	2	1	.238	.211
Bats Right	R	.204	49	10	3	0	0	6	3	5	.250	.265
Encarnacion,Edwin	L	.301	136	41	8	0	14	31	27	31	.417	.669
Bats Right	R	.273	406	111	16	0	28	79	57	63	.372	.520

Batters vs. Left-Handed and Right-Handed Pitchers

Batter	vs	Avg	AB	H	2B	3B	HR	RBI	BB	SO	OBP	Slg
Escobar,Alcides	L	.277	173	48	8	0	1	11	15	24	.335	.341
Bats Right	R	.299	432	129	22	7	4	41	12	76	.330	.410
Escobar,Eduardo	L	.351	37	13	2	1	0	6	2	3	.385	.459
Bats Both	R	.160	94	15	2	0	0	3	9	28	.238	.181
Escobar,Yunel	L	.258	151	39	2	1	2	16	14	17	.319	.325
Bats Right	R	.251	407	102	20	0	7	35	21	53	.292	.351
Espinosa,Danny	L	.281	167	47	16	0	3	15	13	47	.344	.431
Bats Both	R	.234	427	100	21	2	14	41	33	142	.303	.391
Ethier,Andre	L	.222	221	49	10	1	4	29	11	63	.276	.330
Bats Left	R	.325	335	109	26	0	16	60	39	61	.398	.546
Falu,Irving	L	.385	26	10	1	0	0	4	1	1	.407	.423
Bats Both	R	.322	59	19	5	1	0	3	3	8	.355	.441
Fielder,Prince	L	.289	218	63	14	1	6	46	22	39	.363	.445
Bats Left	R	.328	363	119	19	0	24	62	63	45	.439	.579
Figgins,Chone	L	.183	60	11	3	0	0	1	7	19	.269	.233
Bats Both	R	.179	106	19	2	2	2	10	12	29	.258	.292
Flaherty,Ryan	L	.250	12	3	0	1	0	2	0	3	.250	.417
Bats Left	R	.213	141	30	2	0	6	17	6	40	.258	.355
Flores,Jesus	L	.189	90	17	4	1	4	10	7	17	.247	.389
Bats Right	R	.225	187	42	8	0	2	16	6	42	.249	.299
Florimon,Pedro	L	.255	47	12	1	1	0	3	3	8	.300	.319
Bats Both	R	.200	90	18	4	1	1	7	7	22	.258	.300
Flowers,Tyler	L	.269	52	14	2	0	5	9	3	20	.309	.596
Bats Right	R	.179	84	15	4	0	2	4	9	36	.289	.298
Fontenot,Mike	L	.067	15	1	0	0	0	0	1	8	.176	.067
Bats Left	R	.329	82	27	2	0	1	5	6	15	.375	.390
Ford,Lew	L	.224	49	11	2	0	3	4	6	9	.309	.449
Bats Right	R	.091	22	2	1	0	0	0	1	4	.130	.136
Forsythe,Logan	L	.384	99	38	5	1	3	8	13	12	.465	.545
Bats Right	R	.222	216	48	8	2	3	18	15	45	.284	.319
Fowler,Dexter	L	.315	143	45	8	2	3	14	19	32	.395	.462
Bats Both	R	.293	311	91	10	9	10	39	49	96	.387	.479
Francisco,Ben	L	.213	94	20	3	1	3	8	7	25	.265	.362
Bats Right	R	.265	98	26	11	0	1	7	6	24	.305	.408
Francisco,Juan	L	.189	37	7	2	0	0	3	1	13	.225	.243
Bats Left	R	.245	155	38	9	0	9	29	10	57	.291	.477
Francoeur,Jeff	L	.225	160	36	9	1	5	13	18	35	.307	.388
Bats Right	R	.239	401	96	17	2	11	36	16	84	.278	.374
Frandsen,Kevin	L	.400	65	26	6	2	0	2	2	5	.426	.554
Bats Right	R	.308	130	40	4	1	2	12	7	13	.362	.400
Frazier,Todd	L	.298	124	37	8	1	6	22	7	29	.333	.524
Bats Right	R	.262	298	78	18	5	13	45	29	74	.330	.487
Freeman,Freddie	L	.237	228	54	16	0	7	34	22	67	.315	.399
Bats Left	R	.276	312	86	17	2	16	60	42	62	.358	.497
Freese,David	L	.320	122	39	4	1	5	24	15	28	.394	.492
Bats Right	R	.285	379	108	21	0	15	55	42	94	.365	.459
Fukudome,Kosuke	L	.250	4	1	0	0	0	1	1	0	.333	.250
Bats Left	R	.162	37	6	1	0	0	3	7	9	.289	.189
Fuld,Sam	L	.250	36	9	1	1	0	1	1	6	.289	.333
Bats Left	R	.258	62	16	2	1	0	4	7	8	.333	.323
Furcal,Rafael	L	.284	155	44	7	1	3	20	13	20	.337	.400
Bats Both	R	.255	322	82	11	2	2	29	31	37	.319	.320
Galvis,Freddy	L	.267	60	16	4	0	2	8	3	8	.302	.433
Bats Both	R	.208	130	27	11	1	1	16	4	21	.231	.331
Gamel,Mat	L	.286	14	4	0	0	0	1	1	3	.375	.286
Bats Left	R	.236	55	13	2	1	1	5	3	12	.271	.364
Garcia,Avisail	L	.333	30	10	0	0	0	0	3	6	.412	.333
Bats Right	R	.294	17	5	0	0	0	3	0	4	.294	.294
Gardner,Brett	L	.857	7	6	2	0	0	3	2	1	.889	1.143
Bats Left	R	.167	24	4	0	0	0	0	3	6	.259	.167
Gentry,Craig	L	.343	99	34	6	0	1	12	8	13	.425	.434
Bats Right	R	.277	141	39	6	3	0	14	6	28	.325	.362
Getz,Chris	L	.229	48	11	3	0	0	5	2	9	.255	.292
Bats Left	R	.291	141	41	7	3	0	12	9	8	.331	.383
Giambi,Jason	L	.296	27	8	2	0	1	3	3	6	.367	.481
Bats Left	R	.194	62	12	2	0	0	5	17	18	.373	.226
Giavotella,Johnny	L	.203	69	14	4	1	0	7	5	15	.257	.290
Bats Right	R	.259	112	29	3	0	1	8	3	20	.278	.313
Gillaspie,Conor	L	.000	5	0	0	0	0	1	0	0	.000	.000
Bats Left	R	.200	15	3	1	0	0	1	0	2	.200	.267
Gimenez,Chris	L	.357	56	20	4	0	0	6	5	14	.410	.429
Bats Right	R	.136	44	6	0	0	1	3	3	10	.191	.205
Goldschmidt,Paul	L	.343	172	59	20	1	10	34	26	34	.423	.645
Bats Right	R	.257	342	88	23	0	10	48	34	96	.326	.412
Gomes,Jonny	L	.299	164	49	10	0	11	26	27	58	.413	.561
Bats Right	R	.209	115	24	0	0	7	21	17	46	.324	.391

Batter	vs	Avg	AB	H	2B	3B	HR	RBI	BB	SO	OBP	Slg
Gomes,Yan	L	.217	46	10	2	0	3	6	1	13	.245	.457
Bats Right	R	.192	52	10	2	0	1	7	5	19	.279	.288
Gomez,Carlos	L	.261	153	40	9	3	6	17	8	36	.301	.477
Bats Right	R	.260	262	68	10	1	13	34	12	62	.307	.454
Gomez,Mauro	L	.229	48	11	2	0	0	5	4	13	.288	.271
Bats Right	R	.315	54	17	3	2	2	12	4	13	.356	.556
Gonzalez,Adrian	L	.322	230	74	19	1	6	46	10	39	.355	.491
Bats Left	R	.286	399	114	28	0	12	62	32	71	.337	.446
Gonzalez,Alberto	L	.227	22	5	1	0	0	1	0	6	.227	.273
Bats Right	R	.250	32	8	1	1	0	3	0	3	.250	.344
Gonzalez,Alex	L	.211	19	4	1	0	1	5	1	6	.250	.421
Bats Right	R	.274	62	17	3	0	3	10	5	9	.348	.468
Gonzalez,Carlos	L	.266	192	51	10	1	6	27	14	40	.321	.422
Bats Left	R	.325	326	106	21	4	16	58	42	75	.400	.561
Gonzalez,Marwin	L	.113	53	6	2	0	0	1	2	9	.145	.151
Bats Both	R	.276	152	42	11	0	2	11	11	20	.325	.388
Gordon,Alex	L	.248	230	57	14	1	3	23	19	52	.311	.357
Bats Left	R	.320	412	132	37	4	11	49	54	88	.398	.510
Gordon,Dee	L	.172	99	17	1	0	0	4	7	20	.234	.182
Bats Left	R	.255	204	52	8	2	1	13	13	42	.303	.328
Gose,Anthony	L	.290	31	9	2	1	0	3	0	11	.290	.419
Bats Left	R	.207	135	28	5	2	1	8	17	48	.305	.296
Grandal,Yasmani	L	.308	52	16	4	0	4	12	5	13	.356	.615
Bats Both	R	.293	140	41	3	1	4	24	26	26	.407	.414
Granderson,Curtis	L	.218	216	47	6	2	14	35	26	79	.304	.458
Bats Left	R	.239	380	91	12	2	29	71	49	116	.328	.511
Green,Nick	L	.182	11	2	1	0	0	0	0	2	.182	.273
Bats Right	R	.167	12	2	2	0	0	1	0	4	.231	.333
Green,Taylor	L	.200	5	1	0	0	0	1	3	0	.556	.200
Bats Left	R	.184	98	18	7	0	3	13	7	24	.241	.347
Greene,Tyler	L	.280	118	33	6	1	6	14	7	34	.318	.500
Bats Right	R	.198	187	37	9	1	5	16	12	61	.246	.337
Gregorius,Didi	L	.500	2	1	0	0	0	0	0	1	.500	.500
Bats Left	R	.278	18	5	0	0	0	2	0	4	.278	.278
Gutierrez,Franklin	L	.400	65	26	7	1	4	13	5	14	.437	.723
Bats Right	R	.153	85	13	3	0	0	4	4	17	.209	.188
Guzman,Jesus	L	.303	122	37	7	2	6	22	20	23	.401	.541
Bats Right	R	.206	165	34	11	0	3	26	9	48	.253	.327
Gwynn,Tony	L	.209	86	18	1	1	0	5	7	21	.269	.244
Bats Left	R	.243	173	42	7	3	0	12	9	31	.280	.318
Hafner,Travis	L	.197	61	12	1	1	4	10	8	17	.306	.443
Bats Left	R	.241	158	38	5	1	8	24	24	30	.361	.437
Hague,Matt	L	.304	23	7	0	0	0	3	1	4	.333	.304
Bats Right	R	.191	47	9	2	0	0	4	2	10	.240	.234
Hairston,Jerry	L	.293	92	27	5	1	2	11	10	12	.365	.435
Bats Right	R	.260	146	38	8	0	2	15	13	15	.327	.356
Hairston,Scott	L	.286	189	54	17	0	11	30	8	34	.317	.550
Bats Right	R	.239	188	45	8	3	9	27	11	49	.281	.457
Hamilton,Josh	L	.291	175	51	10	0	10	41	11	54	.333	.520
Bats Left	R	.282	387	109	21	2	33	87	49	108	.363	.602
Hanigan,Ryan	L	.329	70	23	1	0	1	8	17	6	.455	.386
Bats Right	R	.259	247	64	13	0	1	16	27	31	.337	.324
Hannahan,Jack	L	.167	72	12	1	0	1	7	8	20	.259	.222
Bats Left	R	.270	215	58	15	0	3	22	19	43	.331	.381
Hardy,J.J.	L	.277	166	46	7	2	5	19	14	28	.333	.434
Bats Right	R	.225	497	112	23	0	17	49	24	78	.264	.374
Harper,Bryce	L	.240	183	44	6	4	6	23	15	51	.300	.415
Bats Left	R	.286	350	100	20	5	16	36	41	69	.360	.509
Harris,Willie	L	-	0	0	0	0	0	0	0	0	-	-
Bats Left	R	.114	44	5	4	0	0	2	3	8	.170	.205
Harrison,Josh	L	.198	86	17	3	2	2	8	3	12	.231	.349
Bats Right	R	.252	163	41	6	3	1	8	7	25	.303	.344
Hart,Corey	L	.290	131	38	15	1	5	13	9	33	.359	.534
Bats Right	R	.265	431	114	20	3	25	70	35	118	.326	.499
Hayes,Brett	L	.156	32	5	2	0	0	1	2	17	.206	.219
Bats Right	R	.220	82	18	4	0	0	2	2	32	.238	.268
Headley,Chase	L	.265	185	49	7	0	11	46	16	38	.320	.481
Bats Both	R	.296	419	124	24	2	20	69	70	119	.400	.506
Hechavarria,Adeiny	L	.234	47	11	2	0	1	4	1	10	.250	.340
Bats Right	R	.266	79	21	6	0	1	11	3	22	.298	.380
Heisey,Chris	L	.274	84	23	4	2	4	12	4	15	.315	.512
Bats Right	R	.262	263	69	12	3	3	19	14	66	.314	.365
Helton,Todd	L	.184	87	16	6	0	2	12	9	22	.268	.322
Bats Left	R	.268	153	41	10	1	5	25	30	22	.382	.444
Hermida,Jeremy	L	.500	2	1	1	0	0	0	0	0	.500	1.000
Bats Left	R	.227	22	5	0	1	0	2	3	7	.320	.318

Batters vs. Left-Handed and Right-Handed Pitchers

Batter	vs	Avg	AB	H	2B	3B	HR	RBI	BB	SO	OBP	Slg
Hernandez,Gorkys	L	.159	63	10	1	0	1	3	6	20	.232	.222
Bats Right	R	.215	93	20	1	3	2	10	7	22	.291	.355
Hernandez,Ramon	L	.152	46	7	2	0	0	4	0	5	.152	.196
Bats Right	R	.239	138	33	8	0	5	24	6	27	.277	.406
Herrera,Elian	L	.265	68	18	7	0	1	7	8	12	.342	.412
Bats Both	R	.244	119	29	3	1	0	10	15	38	.338	.286
Herrera,Jonathan	L	.231	52	12	1	0	2	6	3	6	.273	.365
Bats Both	R	.272	173	47	8	1	1	6	13	33	.330	.347
Hester,John	L	.216	37	8	0	0	1	1	5	10	.310	.297
Bats Right	R	.208	48	10	1	0	2	3	3	15	.269	.354
Heyward,Jason	L	.224	237	53	10	0	7	28	19	71	.280	.354
Bats Left	R	.300	350	105	20	6	20	54	39	81	.372	.563
Hicks,Brandon	L	.159	44	7	2	0	3	3	5	21	.245	.409
Bats Right	R	.200	20	4	3	0	0	4	1	10	.238	.350
Hill,Aaron	L	.271	188	51	16	0	8	27	24	27	.355	.484
Bats Right	R	.316	421	133	28	6	18	58	28	59	.362	.539
Hill,Koyie	L	.150	20	3	1	0	0	1	0	4	.150	.200
Bats Both	R	.211	19	4	0	0	0	0	0	3	.211	.211
Hinske,Eric	L	.118	17	2	2	0	0	1	1	9	.167	.235
Bats Left	R	.209	115	24	5	1	2	12	13	32	.287	.322
Holliday,Matt	L	.316	155	49	13	0	11	31	23	43	.408	.613
Bats Right	R	.288	444	128	23	2	16	71	52	89	.369	.457
Holt,Brock	L	.267	15	4	0	0	0	2	0	3	.250	.267
Bats Left	R	.300	50	15	2	1	0	1	4	11	.352	.380
Hosmer,Eric	L	.220	182	40	5	1	3	14	15	39	.284	.308
Bats Left	R	.238	353	84	17	1	11	46	41	56	.315	.385
Howard,Ryan	L	.173	98	17	2	0	6	18	5	45	.226	.378
Bats Left	R	.247	162	40	9	0	8	38	20	54	.333	.451
Hudson,Orlando	L	.218	78	17	0	0	0	5	7	14	.282	.218
Bats Both	R	.198	182	36	3	8	3	23	13	37	.251	.352
Huff,Aubrey	L	.111	9	1	1	0	0	0	1	1	.200	.222
Bats Left	R	.203	69	14	3	0	1	7	15	11	.341	.290
Hundley,Nick	L	.098	82	8	2	0	1	4	5	23	.148	.159
Bats Right	R	.197	122	24	5	1	2	18	10	33	.265	.303
Hunter,Torii	L	.340	144	49	6	0	4	14	15	32	.403	.465
Bats Right	R	.303	390	118	18	1	12	78	23	101	.351	.446
Iannetta,Chris	L	.208	48	10	1	0	1	3	10	14	.345	.292
Bats Right	R	.249	173	43	5	1	8	23	19	46	.328	.428
Ibanez,Raul	L	.197	61	12	1	1	0	5	2	13	.246	.246
Bats Left	R	.248	323	80	18	2	19	57	33	54	.319	.492
Iglesias,Jose	L	.172	29	5	1	0	1	1	2	7	.226	.310
Bats Right	R	.077	39	3	1	0	0	1	2	9	.182	.103
Infante,Omar	L	.317	161	51	8	2	8	24	4	16	.331	.540
Bats Right	R	.257	393	101	22	5	4	29	17	49	.287	.369
Inge,Brandon	L	.209	115	24	6	0	6	22	10	35	.276	.417
Bats Right	R	.223	188	42	8	0	6	32	14	56	.275	.362
Ishikawa,Travis	L	.286	28	8	3	0	1	11	0	8	.276	.500
Bats Left	R	.250	124	31	9	1	3	19	13	34	.340	.411
Izturis,Cesar	L	.188	48	9	0	0	0	2	1	4	.204	.188
Bats Both	R	.263	118	31	7	2	2	9	2	9	.275	.407
Izturis,Maicer	L	.231	78	18	1	0	0	4	2	10	.259	.244
Bats Both	R	.265	211	56	10	0	2	16	23	28	.340	.341
Jackson,Austin	L	.289	159	46	11	2	5	20	24	40	.378	.478
Bats Right	R	.305	384	117	18	8	11	46	43	94	.377	.479
Jackson,Brett	L	.167	18	3	2	0	0	2	1	8	.211	.278
Bats Left	R	.176	102	18	4	1	4	7	21	51	.317	.353
Janish,Paul	L	.194	62	12	2	0	0	2	8	7	.286	.226
Bats Right	R	.181	105	19	4	1	0	7	9	23	.259	.238
Jaso,John	L	.119	42	5	1	0	0	3	6	9	.250	.143
Bats Left	R	.302	252	76	18	2	10	47	50	42	.419	.508
Jay,Jon	L	.281	128	36	7	0	0	11	14	18	.361	.336
Bats Left	R	.314	315	99	15	4	4	29	20	53	.378	.425
Jennings,Desmond	L	.246	126	31	5	4	2	10	18	30	.338	.397
Bats Right	R	.245	379	93	14	3	11	37	28	90	.306	.385
Jeter,Derek	L	.364	214	78	14	0	8	27	13	23	.399	.542
Bats Right	R	.294	469	138	18	0	7	31	32	67	.346	.377
Johnson,Chris	L	.245	139	34	4	1	4	18	9	42	.298	.374
Bats Right	R	.295	349	103	24	4	11	58	22	90	.338	.481
Johnson,Dan	L	.400	5	2	0	0	2	4	1	0	.500	1.600
Bats Left	R	.353	17	6	1	0	1	2	8	3	.560	.588
Johnson,Elliot	L	.175	97	17	5	0	3	10	11	29	.266	.320
Bats Both	R	.275	200	55	5	2	3	23	13	55	.323	.365
Johnson,Kelly	L	.201	139	28	3	0	4	14	18	42	.297	.309
Bats Left	R	.234	368	86	16	2	12	41	44	117	.319	.386
Johnson,Nick	L	.250	12	3	1	0	1	5	1	3	.438	.583
Bats Left	R	.200	75	15	3	0	3	6	10	23	.302	.360

Batter	vs	Avg	AB	H	2B	3B	HR	RBI	BB	SO	OBP	Slg
Johnson,Reed	L	.311	151	47	10	2	2	10	8	25	.354	.444
Bats Right	R	.263	118	31	4	1	1	10	5	36	.315	.339
Johnson,Rob	L	.227	22	5	1	0	0	2	1	6	.250	.273
Bats Right	R	.267	30	8	1	0	0	2	3	4	.333	.300
Jones,Adam	L	.292	161	47	8	0	7	16	8	36	.327	.472
Bats Right	R	.285	487	139	31	3	25	66	26	90	.337	.515
Jones,Andruw	L	.202	168	34	5	0	10	24	20	44	.294	.411
Bats Right	R	.185	65	12	2	0	4	10	8	27	.293	.400
Jones,Chipper	L	.298	171	51	13	0	4	23	21	18	.376	.444
Bats Both	R	.278	216	60	10	0	10	39	36	33	.378	.463
Jones,Garrett	L	.189	74	14	2	0	2	10	5	13	.235	.297
Bats Left	R	.289	401	116	26	3	25	76	28	90	.332	.556
Joyce,Matt	L	.209	91	19	2	0	3	15	10	33	.301	.330
Bats Left	R	.250	308	77	16	3	14	44	45	69	.352	.458
Ka'aihue,Kila	L	.297	37	11	3	0	1	4	2	10	.333	.459
Bats Left	R	.209	91	19	6	0	3	10	8	18	.280	.374
Kalish,Ryan	L	.333	15	5	1	0	0	1	1	5	.375	.400
Bats Left	R	.210	81	17	2	0	0	4	5	21	.253	.235
Kawasaki,Munenori	L	.105	19	2	0	0	0	0	1	7	.150	.105
Bats Left	R	.212	85	18	1	0	0	7	7	11	.280	.224
Kearns,Austin	L	.196	97	19	4	0	2	9	13	27	.304	.299
Bats Right	R	.340	50	17	2	0	2	7	9	17	.476	.500
Kelly,Don	L	.083	12	1	0	0	0	2	2	5	.214	.083
Bats Left	R	.198	101	20	2	1	1	5	12	17	.283	.267
Kemp,Matt	L	.363	124	45	6	0	11	31	14	28	.428	.677
Bats Right	R	.276	279	77	16	2	12	38	26	75	.341	.477
Kendrick,Howie	L	.309	165	51	13	2	2	15	10	33	.349	.448
Bats Right	R	.278	385	107	19	1	6	52	19	82	.315	.379
Kennedy,Adam	L	.233	30	7	1	0	0	2	1	5	.258	.267
Bats Left	R	.268	138	37	7	1	2	14	22	28	.361	.377
Keppinger,Jeff	L	.376	117	44	5	0	4	14	6	6	.402	.521
Bats Right	R	.302	268	81	10	1	5	26	18	25	.352	.403
Kinsler,Ian	L	.350	160	56	10	0	8	20	19	18	.425	.563
Bats Right	R	.226	495	112	32	5	11	52	41	72	.293	.378
Kipnis,Jason	L	.215	209	45	4	2	2	24	24	39	.298	.282
Bats Left	R	.280	382	107	18	2	12	52	43	70	.355	.432
Komatsu,Erik	L	.400	5	2	0	0	0	0	1	0	.500	.400
Bats Left	R	.196	46	9	0	0	0	1	5	5	.269	.196
Konerko,Paul	L	.271	129	35	8	0	6	19	20	21	.373	.473
Bats Right	R	.307	404	124	14	0	20	56	36	62	.371	.490
Kotchman,Casey	L	.221	113	25	3	0	2	11	4	11	.273	.301
Bats Left	R	.231	350	81	9	0	10	44	22	38	.282	.343
Kotsay,Mark	L	.250	12	3	0	0	0	0	1	3	.357	.250
Bats Left	R	.260	131	34	8	0	2	14	10	11	.310	.366
Kottaras,George	L	.231	26	6	0	1	0	4	9	6	.429	.308
Bats Left	R	.207	145	30	6	0	9	27	28	42	.335	.434
Kozma,Pete	L	.333	18	6	1	2	0	5	2	3	.400	.611
Bats Right	R	.333	54	18	4	1	2	9	5	16	.377	.556
Kratz,Erik	L	.256	43	11	4	0	3	8	4	8	.319	.558
Bats Right	R	.245	98	24	5	0	6	18	7	26	.300	.480
Kubel,Jason	L	.234	184	43	12	3	7	35	15	60	.291	.446
Bats Left	R	.264	322	85	18	1	23	55	42	91	.348	.540
LaHair,Bryan	L	.063	48	3	0	0	1	1	6	27	.167	.125
Bats Left	R	.291	292	85	17	0	15	39	33	97	.362	.503
Laird,Brandon	L	.211	19	4	0	0	0	2	1	2	.250	.211
Bats Right	R	.313	16	5	1	0	1	2	1	6	.353	.563
Laird,Gerald	L	.204	98	20	6	1	2	9	10	12	.275	.347
Bats Right	R	.382	76	29	2	0	0	2	4	9	.420	.408
LaPorta,Matt	L	.286	35	10	1	0	1	3	0	9	.306	.400
Bats Right	R	.174	23	4	1	0	0	2	1	8	.208	.217
LaRoche,Adam	L	.268	168	45	7	0	11	28	15	51	.319	.506
Bats Left	R	.273	403	110	28	1	22	72	52	87	.353	.511
Lavarnway,Ryan	L	.180	50	9	2	0	1	5	3	12	.226	.280
Bats Right	R	.146	103	15	6	0	1	7	8	29	.204	.233
Lawrie,Brett	L	.319	135	43	9	0	3	11	8	24	.361	.452
Bats Right	R	.256	359	92	17	3	8	37	25	62	.310	.387
Lee,Carlos	L	.206	141	29	7	0	2	24	11	8	.261	.298
Bats Right	R	.284	409	116	20	1	7	53	47	41	.355	.389
LeMahieu,DJ	L	.233	60	14	4	3	0	4	4	9	.281	.400
Bats Right	R	.320	169	54	8	1	2	18	9	33	.350	.414
Leon,Sandy	L	.500	8	4	2	0	0	2	1	1	.556	.750
Bats Both	R	.182	22	4	0	0	0	0	3	10	.333	.182
Lewis,Fred	L	.000	1	0	0	0	0	0	0	1	.000	.000
Bats Left	R	.158	19	3	0	0	0	0	4	4	.333	.158
Liddi,Alex	L	.197	61	12	1	0	1	4	5	29	.258	.262
Bats Right	R	.255	55	14	3	1	2	6	4	20	.300	.455

Batters vs. Left-Handed and Right-Handed Pitchers

Batter	vs	Avg	AB	H	2B	3B	HR	RBI	BB	SO	OBP	Slg
Lillibridge,Brent	L	.184	87	16	3	0	3	6	5	24	.234	.322
Bats Right	R	.204	103	21	3	0	0	4	6	47	.263	.233
Lind,Adam	L	.202	89	18	1	1	2	11	6	17	.250	.303
Bats Left	R	.276	232	64	13	1	9	34	23	44	.339	.457
Lobaton,Jose	L	.310	58	18	5	0	0	4	4	12	.355	.397
Bats Both	R	.174	109	19	5	0	2	16	20	34	.308	.275
Lombardozzi,Steve	L	.231	91	21	3	0	0	6	4	13	.268	.264
Bats Both	R	.287	293	84	13	3	3	21	15	33	.332	.382
Loney,James	L	.217	92	20	4	0	0	10	4	16	.247	.261
Bats Left	R	.257	342	88	16	0	6	31	24	35	.305	.357
Longoria,Evan	L	.318	66	21	5	0	6	17	9	13	.397	.667
Bats Right	R	.280	207	58	9	0	11	38	24	48	.359	.483
Lopez,Jose	L	.277	94	26	7	0	2	11	3	11	.293	.415
Bats Right	R	.225	142	32	7	0	2	17	6	30	.255	.317
Lough,David	L	.167	6	1	0	0	0	0	0	1	.286	.167
Bats Left	R	.245	53	13	2	1	0	2	4	8	.293	.321
Lowrie,Jed	L	.184	87	16	4	0	3	13	12	16	.290	.333
Bats Both	R	.265	253	67	14	0	13	29	31	49	.345	.474
Lucroy,Jonathan	L	.400	80	32	7	2	5	22	8	12	.444	.725
Bats Right	R	.292	236	69	10	2	7	36	14	32	.341	.441
Ludwick,Ryan	L	.263	118	31	7	0	10	25	16	21	.360	.576
Bats Right	R	.280	304	85	21	1	16	55	26	76	.340	.513
Luna,Hector	L	.148	27	4	0	0	0	3	1	5	.179	.148
Bats Right	R	.286	35	10	2	0	2	7	3	9	.342	.514
Machado,Manny	L	.280	50	14	0	2	2	5	3	11	.321	.480
Bats Right	R	.255	141	36	8	1	5	21	6	27	.284	.433
Maier,Mitch	L	.176	17	3	0	0	2	3	0	7	.176	.529
Bats Left	R	.170	47	8	1	1	0	4	8	17	.286	.234
Maldonado,Martin	L	.250	56	14	1	0	0	3	8	18	.344	.268
Bats Right	R	.271	177	48	8	0	8	27	9	38	.314	.452
Markakis,Nick	L	.313	128	40	8	1	5	24	9	15	.369	.508
Bats Left	R	.291	292	85	20	2	8	30	33	36	.361	.455
Marson,Lou	L	.221	86	19	6	1	0	6	14	18	.327	.314
Bats Right	R	.229	109	25	2	1	0	7	22	26	.364	.266
Marte,Starling	L	.318	44	14	1	3	3	8	4	16	.360	.682
Bats Right	R	.236	123	29	2	3	2	9	4	34	.277	.350
Martin,Leonys	L	.125	8	1	0	1	0	2	0	2	.125	.375
Bats Left	R	.184	38	7	5	1	0	4	4	10	.256	.368
Martin,Russell	L	.226	124	28	7	0	10	21	23	28	.356	.524
Bats Right	R	.205	298	61	11	0	11	32	30	67	.290	.352
Martinez,Fernando	L	.077	13	1	0	0	0	0	0	5	.077	.077
Bats Left	R	.257	105	27	7	1	6	14	6	29	.325	.514
Martinez,J.D.	L	.255	106	27	3	0	3	11	11	25	.322	.368
Bats Right	R	.235	289	68	11	3	8	44	29	71	.306	.377
Martinez,Michael	L	.241	54	13	1	0	1	3	0	7	.241	.315
Bats Both	R	.115	61	7	2	0	1	4	5	14	.182	.197
Mastroianni,Darin	L	.288	66	19	0	0	1	8	9	17	.377	.333
Bats Right	R	.227	97	22	3	2	2	9	9	28	.292	.361
Mather,Joe	L	.202	114	23	5	0	2	8	10	21	.264	.298
Bats Right	R	.216	111	24	6	0	3	11	4	25	.248	.351
Mathis,Jeff	L	.219	64	14	3	0	3	5	3	18	.254	.406
Bats Right	R	.218	147	32	10	0	5	22	6	50	.247	.388
Matsui,Hideki	L	.222	36	8	0	0	1	3	3	7	.282	.306
Bats Left	R	.102	59	6	1	0	1	4	5	15	.172	.169
Mauer,Joe	L	.287	188	54	9	1	1	22	32	40	.392	.362
Bats Left	R	.336	357	120	22	3	9	63	58	48	.428	.490
Maxwell,Justin	L	.272	103	28	5	2	5	18	19	30	.387	.505
Bats Right	R	.208	212	44	8	1	13	35	13	84	.259	.439
Mayberry,John	L	.271	166	45	13	0	8	19	10	32	.317	.494
Bats Right	R	.229	275	63	11	0	6	27	24	79	.291	.335
Maybin,Cameron	L	.240	150	36	9	1	2	11	7	28	.277	.353
Bats Right	R	.244	357	87	11	4	6	34	37	82	.318	.347
Maysonet,Edwin	L	.118	17	2	0	0	0	0	2	2	.211	.118
Bats Right	R	.302	43	13	1	1	1	4	1	7	.333	.442
McBride,Matt	L	.194	31	6	0	0	1	5	0	5	.219	.290
Bats Right	R	.213	47	10	2	0	1	6	1	12	.224	.319
McCann,Brian	L	.236	157	37	6	0	7	29	7	30	.265	.408
Bats Left	R	.227	282	64	8	0	13	38	37	46	.318	.394
McCoy,Mike	L	.150	20	3	1	0	1	3	4	1	.292	.350
Bats Right	R	.188	32	6	0	0	0	4	0	5	.188	.188
McCutchen,Andrew	L	.392	130	51	9	2	8	30	17	19	.464	.677
Bats Right	R	.309	463	143	20	4	23	66	53	113	.381	.518
McDonald,Darnell	L	.196	46	9	3	0	1	6	7	11	.302	.326
Bats Right	R	.214	42	9	4	0	1	3	5	8	.292	.381
McDonald,John	L	.318	66	21	5	0	3	5	5	7	.366	.530
Bats Right	R	.214	131	28	4	0	3	17	7	26	.259	.313

Batter	vs	Avg	AB	H	2B	3B	HR	RBI	BB	SO	OBP	Slg
McGehee,Casey	L	.231	117	27	5	1	5	16	16	27	.326	.419
Bats Right	R	.209	201	42	11	0	4	25	13	43	.258	.323
McKenry,Michael	L	.241	54	13	4	0	3	12	8	15	.333	.481
Bats Right	R	.231	186	43	10	0	9	27	21	58	.316	.430
McLouth,Nate	L	.197	66	13	3	0	1	2	7	17	.293	.288
Bats Left	R	.255	200	51	11	1	6	18	20	44	.321	.410
Mercer,Jordy	L	.100	10	1	1	0	0	1	1	1	.167	.200
Bats Right	R	.231	52	12	4	1	1	4	3	13	.286	.404
Mesoraco,Devin	L	.308	39	12	3	0	1	3	2	5	.341	.462
Bats Right	R	.183	126	23	5	0	4	11	15	28	.273	.317
Middlebrooks,Will	L	.300	90	27	5	0	6	20	8	23	.350	.556
Bats Right	R	.282	177	50	9	0	9	34	5	47	.312	.486
Molina,Jose	L	.170	47	8	1	0	0	3	7	12	.278	.191
Bats Right	R	.235	204	48	8	0	8	29	13	48	.288	.392
Molina,Yadier	L	.342	111	38	12	0	6	16	13	16	.408	.613
Bats Right	R	.307	394	121	16	0	16	60	32	39	.363	.470
Montero,Jesus	L	.322	177	57	7	0	6	22	12	28	.366	.463
Bats Right	R	.228	338	77	13	0	9	40	17	71	.262	.346
Montero,Miguel	L	.259	162	42	9	0	6	34	15	40	.341	.426
Bats Left	R	.299	324	97	16	2	9	54	58	90	.414	.444
Moore,Scott	L	.182	11	2	0	0	0	1	0	3	.250	.182
Bats Left	R	.263	190	50	11	0	9	25	16	53	.335	.463
Moore,Tyler	L	.247	93	23	6	0	5	11	7	26	.307	.473
Bats Right	R	.286	63	18	3	0	5	18	7	20	.357	.571
Morales,Kendrys	L	.229	70	16	2	0	5	15	5	15	.289	.471
Bats Both	R	.280	414	116	24	1	17	58	26	101	.325	.466
Morel,Brent	L	.200	25	5	0	0	0	1	3	5	.286	.200
Bats Right	R	.170	88	15	2	0	0	4	4	34	.207	.193
Moreland,Mitch	L	.239	46	11	1	0	3	9	2	14	.280	.457
Bats Left	R	.281	281	79	17	0	12	41	21	57	.328	.470
Morgan,Nyjer	L	.263	19	5	0	0	0	2	1	4	.333	.263
Bats Left	R	.237	270	64	5	3	3	14	19	59	.299	.311
Morneau,Justin	L	.232	198	46	7	0	2	21	10	45	.271	.298
Bats Left	R	.290	307	89	19	2	17	56	39	57	.371	.531
Morrison,Logan	L	.213	80	17	3	0	4	13	4	19	.259	.400
Bats Left	R	.236	216	51	12	1	7	23	27	39	.325	.398
Morse,Michael	L	.290	107	31	5	0	4	17	3	24	.306	.449
Bats Right	R	.291	299	87	12	1	14	45	13	73	.326	.478
Moss,Brandon	L	.293	58	17	2	0	2	8	4	15	.339	.431
Bats Left	R	.290	207	60	16	0	19	44	22	75	.363	.643
Moustakas,Mike	L	.254	169	43	12	1	4	14	10	41	.296	.408
Bats Left	R	.236	394	93	22	0	16	59	29	83	.297	.414
Murphy,Daniel	L	.283	187	53	13	0	1	25	7	37	.311	.369
Bats Left	R	.294	384	113	27	3	5	40	29	45	.341	.419
Murphy,David	L	.347	75	26	5	1	0	6	5	16	.405	.440
Bats Left	R	.296	382	113	24	2	15	55	49	58	.375	.487
Murphy,Donnie	L	.128	47	6	2	0	1	2	4	14	.196	.234
Bats Right	R	.275	69	19	4	2	2	10	5	21	.338	.478
Nady,Xavier	L	.213	75	16	5	1	2	6	7	17	.289	.387
Bats Right	R	.156	77	12	1	0	2	7	6	20	.217	.247
Napoli,Mike	L	.179	112	20	2	0	8	19	17	40	.295	.411
Bats Right	R	.250	240	60	7	2	16	37	39	85	.365	.496
Nava,Daniel	L	.185	81	15	3	0	3	10	11	22	.280	.333
Bats Both	R	.269	186	50	18	0	3	23	26	41	.383	.414
Navarro,Dioner	L	.200	20	4	1	0	2	3	0	3	.200	.550
Bats Both	R	.327	49	16	2	1	0	9	2	9	.346	.408
Navarro,Yamaico	L	.222	27	6	0	0	1	3	3	5	.290	.333
Bats Right	R	.087	23	2	0	0	0	1	2	8	.160	.087
Neal,Thomas	L	.154	13	2	0	0	0	1	0	3	.214	.154
Bats Right	R	.300	10	3	1	0	0	1	0	3	.300	.400
Nelson,Chris	L	.307	101	31	8	1	1	11	7	21	.352	.436
Bats Right	R	.299	244	73	13	2	8	42	20	63	.352	.467
Nickeas,Mike	L	.217	60	13	2	0	0	6	6	14	.284	.250
Bats Right	R	.122	49	6	1	0	1	7	2	13	.189	.204
Nieuwenhuis,Kirk	L	.180	61	11	0	0	1	2	8	26	.286	.230
Bats Left	R	.271	221	60	12	1	6	26	17	72	.324	.416
Nieves,Wil	L	.318	22	7	0	0	2	5	1	4	.348	.591
Bats Right	R	.295	61	18	3	0	0	3	3	13	.323	.344
Nix,Jayson	L	.255	98	25	9	0	2	10	9	28	.318	.408
Bats Right	R	.228	79	18	4	0	2	8	5	25	.291	.354
Nix,Laynce	L	.222	9	2	1	0	1	2	1	5	.300	.667
Bats Left	R	.248	105	26	9	0	2	14	11	37	.316	.390
Norris,Derek	L	.209	86	18	4	1	2	15	6	25	.269	.349
Bats Right	R	.195	123	24	4	0	5	19	15	41	.281	.350
Nunez,Eduardo	L	.360	50	18	3	1	0	6	4	4	.400	.460
Bats Right	R	.205	39	8	1	0	1	5	2	8	.244	.308

Batters vs. Left-Handed and Right-Handed Pitchers

Batter	vs	Avg	AB	H	2B	3B	HR	RBI	BB	SO	OBP	Slg
Olivo,Miguel	L	.221	140	31	6	0	7	16	4	40	.243	.414
Bats Right	R	.223	175	39	8	0	5	13	3	45	.236	.354
Olmedo,Ray	L	.143	14	2	0	0	0	0	0	4	.143	.143
Bats Both	R	.296	27	8	2	0	0	1	0	5	.296	.370
Olt,Mike	L	.176	17	3	0	0	0	4	1	8	.211	.176
Bats Right	R	.125	16	2	1	0	0	1	4	5	.286	.188
Orr,Pete	L	.000	2	0	0	0	0	0	0	1	.000	.000
Bats Left	R	.327	52	17	5	1	0	7	1	17	.340	.462
Ortiz,David	L	.320	125	40	9	0	9	22	12	24	.377	.608
Bats Left	R	.317	199	63	17	0	14	38	44	27	.437	.613
Overbay,Lyle	L	.214	14	3	1	0	0	0	1	7	.267	.286
Bats Left	R	.265	102	27	9	0	2	10	12	27	.339	.412
Pacheco,Jordan	L	.351	131	46	5	1	1	16	10	12	.394	.427
Bats Right	R	.294	344	101	27	2	4	38	12	49	.320	.419
Pagan,Angel	L	.271	210	57	14	3	4	14	13	33	.313	.424
Bats Both	R	.296	395	117	24	12	4	42	35	64	.351	.448
Paredes,Jimmy	L	.063	16	1	0	0	0	1	2	6	.158	.063
Bats Both	R	.224	58	13	1	1	0	2	4	15	.270	.276
Parmelee,Chris	L	.245	53	13	4	1	0	5	3	16	.322	.358
Bats Left	R	.223	139	31	6	1	5	15	10	36	.278	.388
Parra,Gerardo	L	.256	86	22	2	0	2	11	2	20	.283	.349
Bats Left	R	.278	299	83	19	2	5	25	31	57	.349	.405
Parrino,Andy	L	.214	42	9	2	0	0	2	7	12	.333	.262
Bats Both	R	.203	74	15	3	0	1	4	10	23	.306	.284
Pastornicky,Tyler	L	.196	56	11	2	0	1	6	4	12	.250	.286
Bats Right	R	.265	113	30	4	1	1	7	6	20	.306	.345
Paul,Xavier	L	.000	3	0	0	0	0	0	1	2	.250	.000
Bats Left	R	.325	83	27	5	1	2	7	8	16	.385	.482
Paulino,Ronny	L	.207	29	6	2	0	0	1	1	3	.233	.276
Bats Right	R	.294	34	10	1	0	0	4	0	6	.294	.324
Pearce,Steve	L	.240	75	18	2	0	4	15	10	17	.333	.427
Bats Right	R	.238	84	20	6	1	0	11	10	24	.323	.333
Pedroia,Dustin	L	.305	164	50	13	1	4	20	19	14	.378	.470
Bats Right	R	.283	399	113	26	2	11	45	29	46	.334	.441
Peguero,Carlos	L	.000	14	0	0	0	0	0	0	10	.000	.000
Bats Left	R	.238	42	10	2	1	2	7	1	18	.256	.476
Pena,Brayan	L	.265	68	18	4	0	1	12	2	10	.278	.368
Bats Both	R	.222	144	32	6	1	1	13	7	14	.255	.299
Pena,Carlos	L	.176	153	27	3	0	7	24	21	72	.302	.333
Bats Left	R	.206	344	71	14	2	12	37	66	110	.342	.363
Pence,Hunter	L	.235	162	38	5	2	8	29	11	36	.289	.438
Bats Right	R	.259	455	118	21	2	16	75	45	109	.329	.420
Pennington,Cliff	L	.168	107	18	3	1	0	6	5	30	.205	.215
Bats Both	R	.232	311	72	15	1	6	22	30	60	.301	.344
Peralta,Jhonny	L	.214	154	33	8	0	6	21	21	34	.309	.383
Bats Right	R	.249	377	94	24	3	7	42	28	71	.303	.385
Perez,Salvador	L	.358	81	29	8	0	5	18	4	5	.379	.642
Bats Right	R	.279	208	58	8	0	6	21	8	22	.307	.404
Petersen,Bryan	L	.137	51	7	0	1	0	3	8	20	.254	.176
Bats Left	R	.211	190	40	9	2	0	14	17	38	.278	.279
Phelps,Cord	L	.400	10	4	0	0	1	3	0	3	.400	.700
Bats Both	R	.130	23	3	0	0	0	2	1	7	.167	.130
Phillips,Brandon	L	.269	160	43	13	0	4	22	9	19	.316	.425
Bats Right	R	.286	420	120	17	1	14	55	19	60	.323	.431
Pierre,Juan	L	.190	63	12	0	0	0	2	1	6	.227	.190
Bats Left	R	.329	331	109	10	6	1	23	22	21	.374	.405
Pierzynski,A.J.	L	.248	113	28	7	0	3	14	3	19	.283	.389
Bats Left	R	.287	366	105	11	4	24	63	25	59	.338	.536
Pill,Brett	L	.200	75	15	3	0	2	7	5	11	.268	.320
Bats Right	R	.233	30	7	0	0	2	4	1	8	.258	.433
Plouffe,Trevor	L	.242	124	30	5	0	12	22	16	22	.338	.573
Bats Right	R	.232	298	69	14	1	12	33	21	70	.285	.406
Podsednik,Scott	L	.395	38	15	0	0	0	5	0	5	.375	.395
Bats Left	R	.280	161	45	7	0	1	7	6	30	.310	.342
Polanco,Placido	L	.226	93	21	7	0	1	6	7	11	.277	.333
Bats Right	R	.271	210	57	8	0	1	13	11	14	.314	.324
Pollock,A.J.	L	.269	52	14	3	1	2	6	5	6	.328	.481
Bats Right	R	.207	29	6	1	0	0	2	4	5	.294	.241
Posey,Buster	L	.433	164	71	18	1	13	47	14	21	.470	.793
Bats Right	R	.292	366	107	21	0	11	56	55	75	.382	.440
Prado,Martin	L	.323	217	70	22	3	2	20	23	20	.384	.479
Bats Right	R	.290	400	116	20	3	8	50	35	49	.345	.415
Presley,Alex	L	.262	61	16	3	1	1	5	3	13	.297	.393
Bats Left	R	.232	285	66	11	6	9	20	15	59	.275	.407
Pujols,Albert	L	.290	155	45	15	0	10	32	11	15	.345	.581
Bats Right	R	.283	452	128	35	0	20	73	41	61	.343	.493

Batter	vs	Avg	AB	H	2B	3B	HR	RBI	BB	SO	OBP	Slg
Punto,Nick	L	.280	25	7	1	0	0	0	5	5	.400	.320
Bats Both	R	.207	135	28	6	0	1	10	20	37	.306	.274
Quentin,Carlos	L	.329	82	27	12	0	3	7	11	7	.433	.585
Bats Right	R	.233	202	47	9	0	13	39	25	34	.350	.470
Quintanilla,Omar	L	.261	46	12	1	0	0	1	3	13	.306	.283
Bats Left	R	.236	123	29	7	0	4	15	13	29	.314	.390
Quintero,Humberto	L	.152	33	5	4	0	0	5	2	9	.200	.273
Bats Right	R	.257	105	27	8	0	1	14	2	19	.275	.362
Raburn,Ryan	L	.165	91	15	8	0	0	2	7	18	.224	.253
Bats Right	R	.175	114	20	6	0	1	10	6	35	.228	.254
Ramirez,Alexei	L	.290	131	38	6	1	3	17	3	16	.304	.420
Bats Right	R	.258	462	119	18	3	6	56	13	61	.282	.348
Ramirez,Aramis	L	.338	139	47	16	0	10	30	6	21	.380	.669
Bats Right	R	.288	431	124	34	3	17	75	38	61	.354	.499
Ramirez,Hanley	L	.263	175	46	11	1	7	23	18	36	.337	.457
Bats Right	R	.254	429	109	18	3	17	69	36	96	.316	.429
Ramos,Wilson	L	.300	10	3	0	0	0	0	3	3	.462	.300
Bats Right	R	.260	73	19	2	0	3	10	9	16	.337	.411
Ransom,Cody	L	.264	87	23	8	0	6	29	10	35	.340	.563
Bats Right	R	.195	159	31	6	0	5	13	20	74	.297	.327
Rasmus,Colby	L	.182	154	28	4	2	3	12	12	44	.262	.292
Bats Left	R	.238	411	98	17	3	20	63	35	105	.299	.440
Recker,Anthony	L	.063	16	1	0	0	1	1	2	7	.167	.250
Bats Right	R	.182	33	6	2	0	0	3	4	8	.308	.242
Reddick,Josh	L	.237	224	53	13	2	12	34	11	56	.277	.473
Bats Left	R	.245	387	95	16	3	20	51	44	95	.320	.457
Reimold,Nolan	L	.313	16	5	0	0	2	4	2	5	.389	.688
Bats Right	R	.314	51	16	6	0	3	6	0	9	.314	.608
Revere,Ben	L	.314	169	53	4	0	0	13	6	16	.339	.337
Bats Left	R	.284	342	97	9	6	0	19	23	38	.330	.345
Reyes,Jose	L	.277	188	52	10	3	3	11	19	17	.343	.410
Bats Both	R	.291	454	132	27	9	8	46	44	39	.349	.443
Reynolds,Mark	L	.227	119	27	8	0	3	14	21	40	.352	.370
Bats Right	R	.219	338	74	18	0	20	55	52	119	.328	.450
Rhymes,Will	L	.000	20	0	0	0	0	0	2	9	.130	.000
Bats Left	R	.272	103	28	2	1	1	8	8	8	.333	.340
Rios,Alex	L	.293	147	43	11	1	7	21	8	22	.333	.524
Bats Right	R	.308	458	141	26	7	18	70	18	70	.335	.513
Rivera,Juan	L	.260	127	33	4	0	6	20	9	12	.312	.433
Bats Right	R	.232	185	43	10	0	3	27	9	23	.269	.335
Rizzo,Anthony	L	.208	101	21	3	0	4	17	5	21	.243	.356
Bats Left	R	.318	236	75	12	0	11	31	22	41	.383	.508
Roberts,Brian	L	.250	12	3	0	0	0	0	2	1	.357	.250
Bats Both	R	.167	54	9	0	0	0	5	3	11	.203	.167
Roberts,Ryan	L	.231	156	36	9	0	4	12	12	35	.282	.365
Bats Right	R	.237	283	67	10	0	8	40	28	57	.304	.357
Robinson,Shane	L	.256	82	21	5	0	1	10	11	15	.340	.354
Bats Right	R	.250	84	21	3	0	2	6	3	17	.276	.357
Robinson,Trayvon	L	.192	52	10	3	0	0	4	4	8	.250	.250
Bats Both	R	.237	93	22	1	1	3	8	10	35	.317	.366
Rodriguez,Alex	L	.308	146	45	4	1	8	24	24	33	.410	.514
Bats Right	R	.256	317	81	13	0	10	33	27	83	.326	.391
Rodriguez,Sean	L	.228	101	23	6	0	0	10	20	18	.368	.287
Bats Right	R	.205	200	41	8	1	6	22	7	57	.230	.345
Rolen,Scott	L	.234	77	18	4	0	1	5	9	13	.322	.325
Bats Right	R	.249	217	54	13	2	7	34	21	49	.317	.424
Rollins,Jimmy	L	.218	202	44	10	2	3	11	18	29	.281	.332
Bats Both	R	.265	430	114	23	3	20	57	44	67	.332	.472
Rosales,Adam	L	.219	64	14	2	0	1	3	4	19	.261	.297
Bats Right	R	.229	35	8	3	0	1	5	7	5	.357	.400
Rosario,Wilin	L	.348	112	39	4	0	14	29	6	21	.381	.759
Bats Right	R	.239	284	68	15	0	14	42	19	78	.286	.440
Ross,Cody	L	.295	132	39	7	1	12	35	16	25	.373	.636
Bats Right	R	.256	344	88	27	0	10	46	26	104	.308	.422
Ross,David	L	.241	79	19	1	0	4	8	8	27	.307	.405
Bats Right	R	.268	97	26	6	0	5	15	10	33	.333	.485
Rottino,Vinny	L	.154	39	6	1	0	2	6	6	7	.261	.333
Bats Right	R	.136	22	3	1	0	1	1	1	10	.174	.318
Ruf,Darin	L	.375	16	6	1	1	2	8	1	6	.389	.938
Bats Right	R	.294	17	5	1	0	1	2	1	6	.316	.529
Ruggiano,Justin	L	.330	91	30	12	1	7	15	14	20	.415	.714
Bats Right	R	.305	197	60	11	0	6	21	15	64	.354	.452
Ruiz,Carlos	L	.320	103	33	5	0	5	18	11	11	.392	.515
Bats Right	R	.327	269	88	27	0	11	50	18	39	.395	.550
Rutledge,Josh	L	.247	81	20	7	3	3	12	3	24	.279	.519
Bats Right	R	.286	196	56	13	2	5	25	6	30	.317	.449

Batters vs. Left-Handed and Right-Handed Pitchers

Batter	vs	Avg	AB	H	2B	3B	HR	RBI	BB	SO	OBP	Slg
Ryan,Brendan	L	.234	158	37	10	2	1	13	14	29	.295	.342
Bats Right	R	.169	249	42	9	1	2	18	30	69	.266	.237
Saltalamacchia,J	L	.170	53	9	3	0	1	6	3	22	.211	.283
Bats Both	R	.230	352	81	14	1	24	53	35	117	.299	.480
Sanchez,Gaby	L	.240	96	23	6	0	3	13	13	18	.333	.396
Bats Right	R	.207	203	42	10	0	4	17	12	38	.251	.315
Sanchez,Hector	L	.304	79	24	7	0	1	15	0	15	.296	.430
Bats Both	R	.266	139	37	8	0	2	19	5	37	.295	.367
Sandoval,Pablo	L	.299	127	38	6	1	2	16	8	18	.336	.409
Bats Both	R	.275	269	74	19	1	10	47	30	41	.344	.465
Sands,Jerry	L	.158	19	3	1	0	0	0	0	7	.158	.211
Bats Right	R	.250	4	1	1	0	0	1	1	2	.400	.500
Sàntana,Carlos	L	.272	169	46	7	0	6	31	34	26	.388	.420
Bats Both	R	.243	338	82	20	2	12	45	57	75	.352	.420
Santiago,Ramon	L	.140	57	8	4	0	1	3	4	12	.219	.263
Bats Both	R	.228	171	39	3	1	1	14	16	27	.305	.275
Sappelt,Dave	L	.440	25	11	4	0	1	2	3	2	.517	.720
Bats Right	R	.182	44	8	2	0	1	6	4	7	.250	.295
Saunders,Michael	L	.261	180	47	11	1	8	18	12	44	.307	.467
Bats Left	R	.239	327	78	20	2	11	39	31	88	.306	.413
Schafer,Jordan	L	.100	50	5	0	0	1	3	6	24	.196	.160
Bats Left	R	.232	263	61	10	2	3	20	30	82	.316	.319
Schafer,Logan	L	.000	3	0	0	0	0	0	1	0	.250	.000
Bats Left	R	.350	20	7	1	2	0	5	0	3	.333	.600
Schierholtz,Nate	L	.175	63	11	2	1	0	4	3	17	.206	.238
Bats Left	R	.287	178	51	6	4	6	17	20	29	.360	.466
Schneider,Brian	L	.176	17	3	1	0	0	0	2	3	.333	.235
Bats Left	R	.236	72	17	4	0	2	7	3	12	.276	.375
Schumaker,Skip	L	.158	38	6	0	2	0	3	4	10	.233	.263
Bats Left	R	.295	234	69	14	2	1	25	23	40	.357	.385
Scott,Luke	L	.149	87	13	4	0	2	10	4	26	.211	.264
Bats Left	R	.260	227	59	18	1	12	45	17	54	.313	.507
Scutaro,Marco	L	.301	193	58	10	0	2	17	11	16	.335	.383
Bats Right	R	.309	427	132	22	4	5	57	29	33	.353	.415
Seager,Kyle	L	.237	215	51	7	1	7	35	12	44	.281	.377
Bats Left	R	.272	379	103	28	0	13	51	34	66	.335	.449
Segura,Jean	L	.081	37	3	0	0	0	1	6	9	.209	.081
Bats Right	R	.316	114	36	4	3	0	13	7	14	.352	.404
Sellers,Justin	L	.174	23	4	2	0	0	0	4	6	.296	.261
Bats Right	R	.238	21	5	1	1	1	2	1	8	.273	.524
Shoppach,Kelly	L	.239	113	27	9	1	3	13	8	44	.301	.416
Bats Right	R	.226	106	24	5	1	5	14	8	45	.317	.434
Sierra,Moises	L	.286	56	16	2	0	3	7	4	12	.333	.482
Bats Right	R	.187	91	17	2	0	3	8	4	32	.237	.308
Simmons,Andrelton	L	.305	59	18	3	0	2	7	4	5	.338	.458
Bats Right	R	.280	107	30	5	2	1	12	8	16	.333	.393
Smith,Seth	L	.157	70	11	2	0	2	8	8	20	.250	.271
Bats Left	R	.259	313	81	21	2	12	44	42	78	.352	.454
Smoak,Justin	L	.235	170	40	7	0	7	17	17	28	.303	.400
Bats Both	R	.208	313	65	7	0	12	34	32	83	.282	.345
Snider,Travis	L	.364	33	12	3	0	3	8	1	9	.382	.727
Bats Left	R	.221	131	29	4	1	1	9	16	39	.305	.290
Snyder,Brandon	L	.318	44	14	2	0	3	8	2	17	.348	.568
Bats Right	R	.190	21	4	0	0	0	1	1	9	.227	.190
Snyder,Chris	L	.169	77	13	4	0	4	14	13	21	.297	.377
Bats Right	R	.181	144	26	4	0	3	10	20	49	.293	.271
Sogard,Eric	L	.200	20	4	1	0	0	1	0	6	.200	.250
Bats Left	R	.159	82	13	2	1	2	6	5	11	.207	.280
Solano,Donovan	L	.291	103	30	5	1	0	8	5	25	.324	.359
Bats Right	R	.297	182	54	6	2	2	20	16	33	.351	.385
Solano,Jhonatan	L	.444	9	4	1	0	1	3	1	0	.500	.889
Bats Right	R	.269	26	7	2	0	1	3	1	5	.296	.462
Soriano,Alfonso	L	.260	131	34	6	0	8	25	15	40	.342	.489
Bats Right	R	.263	430	113	27	2	24	83	29	113	.315	.502
Soto,Geovany	L	.239	88	21	3	0	3	11	8	25	.302	.375
Bats Right	R	.182	236	43	9	1	8	28	22	51	.259	.331
Span,Denard	L	.301	156	47	8	1	0	17	18	20	.374	.365
Bats Left	R	.275	360	99	30	3	4	24	29	42	.328	.408
Stanton,Giancarlo	L	.302	116	35	11	0	10	24	12	36	.369	.655
Bats Right	R	.285	333	95	19	1	27	62	34	107	.358	.592
Stewart,Chris	L	.214	56	12	3	0	1	10	3	10	.258	.321
Bats Right	R	.259	85	22	5	0	0	3	7	11	.315	.318
Stewart,Ian	L	.179	39	7	1	0	0	2	0	15	.200	.205
Bats Left	R	.207	140	29	4	2	5	15	21	31	.315	.371
Stubbs,Drew	L	.283	138	39	2	1	7	17	8	46	.324	.464
Bats Right	R	.186	355	66	11	1	7	23	34	120	.259	.282

Batter	vs	Avg	AB	H	2B	3B	HR	RBI	BB	SO	OBP	Slg
Sutton,Drew	L	.275	40	11	3	0	1	6	3	14	.341	.425
Bats Both	R	.244	82	20	9	1	0	7	3	28	.267	.378
Suzuki,Ichiro	L	.284	229	65	9	1	2	17	3	16	.291	.358
Bats Left	R	.283	400	113	19	5	7	38	19	45	.316	.408
Suzuki,Kurt	L	.242	95	23	8	0	1	9	4	19	.270	.358
Bats Right	R	.233	313	73	12	0	5	34	16	54	.278	.319
Sweeney,Ryan	L	.100	20	2	1	0	0	0	2	7	.182	.150
Bats Left	R	.277	184	51	18	2	0	16	10	36	.316	.397
Swisher,Nick	L	.270	185	50	7	0	5	22	32	33	.380	.389
Bats Both	R	.273	352	96	29	0	19	71	45	108	.356	.517
Tabata,Jose	L	.241	79	19	6	1	1	5	8	9	.326	.380
Bats Right	R	.244	254	62	14	2	2	11	21	49	.312	.339
Taylor,Michael	L	.083	12	1	0	0	0	0	0	6	.083	.083
Bats Right	R	.222	9	2	1	0	0	0	0	4	.222	.333
Teagarden,Taylor	L	.154	26	4	1	0	1	3	0	12	.154	.308
Bats Right	R	.161	31	5	2	0	1	6	5	11	.278	.323
Teixeira,Mark	L	.269	175	47	16	0	10	29	17	27	.333	.531
Bats Both	R	.239	276	66	11	1	14	55	37	56	.331	.438
Tejada,Ruben	L	.320	153	49	11	0	0	3	10	26	.367	.392
Bats Right	R	.273	311	85	15	0	1	22	17	47	.316	.331
Thames,Eric	L	.212	52	11	2	1	1	2	5	16	.281	.346
Bats Left	R	.237	219	52	10	2	8	23	10	71	.272	.411
Theriot,Ryan	L	.272	125	34	7	1	0	6	8	15	.319	.344
Bats Right	R	.269	227	61	9	0	0	22	16	32	.314	.308
Thole,Josh	L	.211	76	16	4	0	1	7	4	20	.259	.303
Bats Left	R	.241	245	59	11	0	0	14	23	30	.305	.286
Thomas,Clete	L	.167	6	1	1	0	0	1	0	4	.286	.333
Bats Left	R	.136	22	3	0	0	1	3	0	12	.136	.273
Thome,Jim	L	.179	28	5	0	0	3	5	2	10	.233	.500
Bats Left	R	.267	135	36	7	0	5	20	20	51	.365	.430
Thompson,Rich	L	.154	13	2	0	0	0	1	0	3	.214	.154
Bats Left	R	.000	9	0	0	0	0	0	0	2	.100	.000
Tolleson,Steve	L	.192	52	10	2	0	2	6	4	10	.250	.346
Bats Right	R	.158	19	3	1	0	0	0	0	7	.158	.211
Torrealba,Yorvit	L	.203	79	16	6	0	0	5	9	14	.289	.278
Bats Right	R	.243	115	28	2	0	4	9	8	26	.296	.365
Torres,Andres	L	.286	147	42	10	2	0	9	22	31	.382	.381
Bats Both	R	.194	227	44	7	5	3	26	30	59	.291	.308
Tracy,Chad	L	.333	9	3	0	0	1	4	0	2	.333	.667
Bats Left	R	.262	84	22	7	0	2	10	10	13	.344	.417
Treanor,Matt	L	.218	55	12	2	1	2	5	6	14	.302	.400
Bats Right	R	.125	48	6	1	0	0	5	8	15	.259	.146
Triunfel,Carlos	L	.300	10	3	2	0	0	1	0	2	.300	.500
Bats Right	R	.167	12	2	0	0	0	2	1	2	.231	.167
Trout,Mike	L	.267	146	39	8	2	7	17	24	35	.368	.493
Bats Right	R	.346	413	143	19	6	23	66	43	104	.410	.588
Trumbo,Mark	L	.266	158	42	5	0	11	29	8	46	.301	.506
Bats Right	R	.269	386	104	14	3	21	66	28	107	.324	.484
Tulowitzki,Troy	L	.173	52	9	1	1	3	7	7	5	.267	.404
Bats Right	R	.333	129	43	7	1	5	20	12	14	.399	.519
Turner,Justin	L	.241	83	20	5	1	1	9	4	7	.289	.361
Bats Right	R	.295	88	26	8	0	1	10	5	17	.347	.420
Uggla,Dan	L	.220	168	37	7	0	8	24	39	56	.371	.405
Bats Right	R	.220	355	78	22	0	11	54	55	112	.336	.375
Upton,B.J.	L	.238	151	36	9	1	8	22	21	53	.322	.470
Bats Right	R	.249	422	105	20	2	20	56	24	116	.289	.448
Upton,Justin	L	.275	160	44	3	3	6	17	28	27	.386	.444
Bats Right	R	.282	394	111	21	1	11	50	35	94	.342	.424
Uribe,Juan	L	.143	63	9	4	0	0	4	3	9	.179	.206
Bats Right	R	.222	99	22	5	0	2	13	10	28	.306	.333
Utley,Chase	L	.215	121	26	3	1	4	10	16	17	.324	.355
Bats Left	R	.283	180	51	12	1	7	35	27	26	.391	.478
Valbuena,Luis	L	.196	56	11	4	0	1	9	9	15	.303	.321
Bats Left	R	.225	209	47	16	0	3	19	27	40	.312	.344
Valdespin,Jordany	L	.226	31	7	3	0	0	6	1	7	.250	.323
Bats Left	R	.244	160	39	6	1	8	20	9	37	.292	.444
Valdez,Wilson	L	.308	52	16	1	0	0	5	3	8	.345	.327
Bats Right	R	.169	142	24	3	0	0	10	5	28	.196	.190
Valencia,Danny	L	.226	53	12	0	1	2	12	0	9	.214	.377
Bats Right	R	.168	101	17	6	0	1	9	3	29	.190	.257
Van Slyke,Scott	L	.154	26	4	0	0	2	5	0	5	.154	.385
Bats Right	R	.179	28	5	2	0	0	2	2	9	.233	.250
Velazquez,Gil	L	.263	19	5	0	0	0	1	1	3	.300	.263
Bats Right	R	.216	37	8	1	0	0	1	0	8	.216	.243
Venable,Will	L	.231	65	15	4	1	1	7	7	18	.315	.369
Bats Left	R	.270	352	95	22	7	8	38	34	76	.339	.440

Batters vs. Left-Handed and Right-Handed Pitchers

Batter	vs	Avg	AB	H	2B	3B	HR	RBI	BB	SO	OBP	Slg
Viciedo,Dayan	L	.350	123	43	9	0	9	23	9	17	.391	.642
Bats Right	R	.225	382	86	9	1	16	55	19	103	.271	.380
Victorino,Shane	L	.323	164	53	10	2	6	15	16	26	.388	.518
Bats Both	R	.230	431	99	19	5	5	40	37	54	.295	.332
Vitters,Josh	L	.111	45	5	1	0	1	2	2	13	.146	.200
Bats Right	R	.130	54	7	1	0	1	3	5	20	.230	.204
Vizquel,Omar	L	.217	46	10	2	0	0	2	2	7	.250	.261
Bats Both	R	.243	107	26	3	1	0	5	5	10	.272	.290
Vogt,Stephen	L	.000	2	0	0	0	0	0	0	0	.000	.000
Bats Left	R	.000	23	0	0	0	0	0	2	2	.080	.000
Votto,Joey	L	.288	118	34	10	0	4	15	23	34	.413	.475
Bats Left	R	.359	256	92	34	0	10	41	71	51	.500	.609
Walker,Neil	L	.246	118	29	5	0	0	15	13	19	.314	.288
Bats Both	R	.291	354	103	22	0	14	54	34	85	.352	.472
Wallace,Brett	L	.273	55	15	2	0	2	6	1	13	.293	.418
Bats Left	R	.247	174	43	8	1	7	18	17	60	.332	.425
Weeks,Jemile	L	.232	151	35	5	5	1	6	19	25	.318	.351
Bats Both	R	.215	293	63	10	3	1	14	31	45	.298	.280
Weeks,Rickie	L	.248	133	33	5	0	3	9	28	41	.387	.353
Bats Right	R	.224	455	102	24	4	18	54	46	128	.309	.413
Wells,Casper	L	.267	131	35	7	3	7	20	19	38	.364	.527
Bats Right	R	.195	154	30	5	0	3	16	7	42	.244	.286
Wells,Vernon	L	.227	75	17	5	0	2	8	7	12	.298	.373
Bats Right	R	.232	168	39	4	0	9	21	9	23	.270	.417
Werth,Jayson	L	.395	76	30	6	2	1	6	11	7	.471	.566
Bats Right	R	.268	224	60	15	1	4	25	31	50	.358	.397
Wheeler,Ryan	L	.067	15	1	0	0	0	0	0	5	.067	.067
Bats Left	R	.266	94	25	6	1	1	10	9	17	.327	.383
Wieters,Matt	L	.323	133	43	7	1	5	21	17	33	.404	.504
Bats Both	R	.224	393	88	20	0	18	62	43	79	.303	.412
Wigginton,Ty	L	.234	124	29	4	0	6	15	24	32	.360	.411
Bats Right	R	.236	191	45	7	0	5	28	13	49	.281	.351
Willingham,Josh	L	.231	156	36	5	1	15	37	30	40	.356	.564
Bats Right	R	.273	363	99	25	0	20	73	46	101	.370	.507
Wilson,Bobby	L	.220	50	11	2	0	2	5	9	13	.339	.380
Bats Right	R	.207	121	25	3	0	1	8	6	20	.248	.256
Wilson,Jack	L	.194	31	6	1	1	0	2	1	3	.219	.290
Bats Right	R	.150	40	6	0	0	0	2	1	9	.167	.150
Wise,DeWayne	L	.188	64	12	2	1	2	10	3	18	.221	.344
Bats Left	R	.288	160	46	8	1	6	20	8	34	.322	.463
Worth,Danny	L	.297	37	11	0	0	0	2	7	11	.400	.297
Bats Right	R	.135	37	5	3	0	0	1	6	12	.256	.216
Wright,David	L	.320	178	57	10	1	6	27	34	21	.428	.489
Bats Right	R	.300	403	121	31	1	15	66	47	91	.374	.494
Youkilis,Kevin	L	.275	120	33	2	0	8	19	22	24	.386	.492
Bats Right	R	.220	318	70	13	2	11	41	29	84	.316	.377
Young,Chris	L	.267	120	32	9	0	5	12	13	23	.343	.467
Bats Right	R	.210	205	43	15	0	9	29	23	56	.293	.415
Young,Delmon	L	.308	182	56	12	1	7	26	4	33	.333	.500
Bats Right	R	.247	392	97	15	0	11	48	16	79	.279	.370
Young,Eric	L	.383	47	18	2	1	1	4	4	7	.442	.532
Bats Both	R	.291	127	37	5	1	3	11	9	24	.353	.417
Young,Michael	L	.333	156	52	7	2	1	23	10	13	.371	.423
Bats Right	R	.257	455	117	20	1	7	44	23	57	.291	.352
Zimmerman,Ryan	L	.307	153	47	11	0	5	26	19	27	.384	.477
Bats Right	R	.273	425	116	25	1	20	69	38	89	.333	.478
Zobrist,Ben	L	.308	169	52	15	2	4	28	24	36	.388	.491
Bats Both	R	.253	391	99	24	5	16	46	73	67	.372	.463
AL	L	.255	-	-	-	-	-	-	-	-	.321	.407
	R	.256	-	-	-	-	-	-	-	-	.319	.413
NL	L	.252	-	-	-	-	-	-	-	-	.314	.400
	R	.255	-	-	-	-	-	-	-	-	.320	.400
MLB	L	.253	-	-	-	-	-	-	-	-	.317	.404
	R	.255	-	-	-	-	-	-	-	-	.320	.406

Pitchers vs. Left-Handed and Right-Handed Batters

Pitcher	vs	Avg	AB	H	2B	3B	HR	RBI	BB	SO	OBP	Slg
Abad,Fernando	L	.277	65	18	3	1	2	17	5	14	.333	.446
Throws Left	R	.331	118	39	11	1	4	15	14	24	.410	.542
Accardo,Jeremy	L	.217	60	13	4	0	1	10	10	11	.319	.333
Throws Right	R	.358	81	29	10	1	2	11	6	18	.393	.580
Aceves,Alfredo	L	.269	160	43	12	0	6	28	20	39	.358	.456
Throws Right	R	.239	155	37	6	1	5	25	11	36	.290	.387
Acosta,Manny	L	.253	79	20	2	0	3	16	11	18	.348	.392
Throws Right	R	.264	106	28	2	0	4	16	14	28	.358	.396
Adams,Mike	L	.290	107	31	7	0	2	11	11	23	.372	.411
Throws Right	R	.248	101	25	5	0	2	9	6	22	.290	.356
Adcock,Nathan	L	.237	59	14	3	0	1	6	9	7	.348	.339
Throws Right	R	.319	72	23	4	0	3	9	4	15	.346	.500
Affeldt,Jeremy	L	.236	106	25	5	1	0	9	11	30	.319	.302
Throws Left	R	.244	131	32	8	1	1	15	12	27	.313	.344
Albers,Matt	L	.207	82	17	1	0	4	14	16	16	.337	.366
Throws Right	R	.220	132	29	1	0	5	19	6	28	.259	.341
Alburquerque,Al	L	.136	22	3	0	0	0	0	2	10	.208	.136
Throws Right	R	.130	23	3	1	0	0	1	6	8	.310	.174
Allen,Cody	L	.240	50	12	3	0	2	5	9	10	.356	.420
Throws Right	R	.288	59	17	1	0	0	8	6	17	.348	.305
Alvarez,Henderson	L	.312	404	126	29	2	16	55	39	39	.372	.512
Throws Right	R	.265	340	90	14	1	13	42	15	40	.298	.426
Ambriz,Hector	L	.174	23	4	1	0	0	1	2	8	.269	.217
Throws Right	R	.222	45	10	4	0	0	9	9	14	.364	.311
Anderson,Brett	L	.219	32	7	1	0	0	0	2	3	.265	.250
Throws Left	R	.227	97	22	5	0	1	6	5	22	.272	.309
Archer,Chris	L	.300	40	12	1	0	2	10	9	15	.440	.475
Throws Right	R	.164	67	11	1	0	1	5	4	21	.211	.224
Arredondo,Jose	L	.165	103	17	4	1	2	13	20	31	.299	.282
Throws Right	R	.277	119	33	7	0	5	17	14	31	.351	.462
Arrieta,Jake	L	.291	244	71	14	1	12	45	19	60	.342	.504
Throws Right	R	.249	205	51	9	0	4	26	16	49	.313	.351
Arroyo,Bronson	L	.287	407	117	23	0	17	45	23	51	.325	.469
Throws Right	R	.245	375	92	19	0	9	36	12	78	.274	.368
Asencio,Jairo	L	.264	72	19	3	3	1	17	8	15	.338	.431
Throws Right	R	.241	83	20	5	1	4	12	11	14	.337	.470
Atchison,Scott	L	.188	85	16	4	0	0	8	7	17	.250	.235
Throws Right	R	.252	103	26	3	0	2	10	2	19	.262	.340
Aumont,Phillippe	L	.167	12	2	0	0	0	1	4	4	.412	.167
Throws Right	R	.195	41	8	2	0	0	4	5	10	.283	.244
Avilan,Luis	L	.180	50	9	1	0	1	3	5	18	.268	.260
Throws Left	R	.231	78	18	4	0	0	11	5	15	.277	.282
Axelrod,Dylan	L	.277	94	26	6	0	5	15	11	14	.361	.500
Throws Right	R	.273	110	30	7	0	3	13	10	26	.341	.418
Axford,John	L	.225	138	31	5	2	2	18	22	46	.337	.333
Throws Right	R	.234	128	30	1	1	8	22	17	47	.322	.445
Ayala,Luis	L	.284	134	38	8	0	4	22	9	17	.326	.433
Throws Right	R	.262	164	43	11	0	3	19	5	34	.299	.384
Badenhop,Burke	L	.300	80	24	5	2	2	11	7	6	.356	.488
Throws Right	R	.239	163	39	6	0	4	18	5	36	.260	.350
Bailey,Andrew	L	.364	33	12	1	1	2	6	5	6	.447	.636
Throws Right	R	.273	33	9	1	0	0	4	3	8	.333	.303
Bailey,Homer	L	.245	363	89	13	5	8	26	28	85	.307	.375
Throws Right	R	.265	441	117	16	4	18	59	24	83	.305	.442
Balester,Collin	L	.250	24	6	2	0	1	8	8	3	.424	.458
Throws Right	R	.186	43	8	2	0	4	11	3	9	.280	.512
Balfour,Grant	L	.157	134	21	5	1	1	11	16	40	.245	.231
Throws Right	R	.163	123	20	5	0	3	16	12	32	.239	.276
Bard,Daniel	L	.260	123	32	7	0	4	15	24	14	.388	.415
Throws Right	R	.286	98	28	5	0	5	19	19	24	.423	.490
Barnes,Scott	L	.200	30	6	1	1	0	5	4	8	.314	.300
Throws Left	R	.262	42	11	5	0	1	5	3	8	.340	.452
Bass,Anthony	L	.251	179	45	14	2	4	24	21	42	.330	.419
Throws Right	R	.234	188	44	9	1	6	29	18	38	.301	.388
Bastardo,Antonio	L	.169	83	14	1	1	3	15	9	34	.255	.313
Throws Left	R	.236	110	26	5	0	4	12	17	47	.341	.391
Batista,Miguel	L	.317	101	32	6	0	3	16	15	17	.402	.465
Throws Right	R	.250	104	26	6	0	3	14	18	19	.363	.394
Bauer,Trevor	L	.281	32	9	4	0	1	8	4	7	.351	.500
Throws Right	R	.172	29	5	2	0	1	3	9	10	.385	.345
Beachy,Brandon	L	.148	122	18	5	0	0	4	17	30	.257	.189
Throws Right	R	.189	164	31	2	0	6	15	12	38	.242	.311
Beato,Pedro	L	.294	17	5	0	0	0	1	1	2	.333	.294
Throws Right	R	.214	28	6	1	0	1	5	4	10	.333	.357
Beavan,Blake	L	.304	299	91	21	3	11	33	14	35	.339	.505
Throws Right	R	.258	299	77	18	1	12	38	10	32	.296	.445

Pitcher	vs	Avg	AB	H	2B	3B	HR	RBI	BB	SO	OBP	Slg
Beck,Chad	L	.310	29	9	2	1	2	9	4	4	.394	.655
Throws Right	R	.324	37	12	4	0	0	8	1	5	.333	.432
Beckett,Josh	L	.280	354	99	18	4	13	51	34	73	.338	.463
Throws Right	R	.245	306	75	14	1	8	33	18	59	.296	.376
Bedard,Erik	L	.218	87	19	1	1	2	7	10	26	.306	.322
Throws Left	R	.272	404	110	27	2	12	60	46	92	.348	.438
Belisario,Ronald	L	.250	104	26	8	1	1	15	15	18	.350	.375
Throws Right	R	.142	148	21	4	0	2	14	14	51	.230	.209
Belisle,Matt	L	.313	134	42	8	1	1	14	14	29	.378	.410
Throws Right	R	.259	189	49	10	1	4	24	4	40	.286	.386
Beliveau,Jeff	L	.360	25	9	1	0	3	7	4	5	.467	.760
Throws Left	R	.255	47	12	3	0	2	8	8	12	.364	.447
Bell,Heath	L	.239	109	26	6	0	1	11	20	25	.357	.321
Throws Right	R	.317	139	44	12	1	4	26	9	34	.357	.504
Below,Duane	L	.304	79	24	1	1	2	9	0	12	.309	.418
Throws Left	R	.260	96	25	2	0	4	17	8	17	.311	.406
Benoit,Joaquin	L	.237	139	33	5	0	7	17	12	47	.296	.424
Throws Right	R	.217	120	26	2	2	7	16	10	37	.278	.442
Bergesen,Brad	L	.326	46	15	6	0	0	3	2	8	.354	.457
Throws Right	R	.222	63	14	1	1	2	9	5	10	.286	.365
Berken,Jason	L	.286	35	10	2	0	3	8	3	5	.333	.600
Throws Right	R	.380	50	19	4	2	2	11	4	6	.436	.660
Betancourt,Rafael	L	.304	102	31	8	0	1	5	7	22	.349	.412
Throws Right	R	.186	118	22	4	0	5	17	5	35	.216	.347
Billingsley,Chad	L	.260	304	79	20	7	6	36	24	70	.313	.431
Throws Right	R	.255	271	69	17	2	5	26	21	58	.318	.387
Blackburn,Nick	L	.376	186	70	11	1	9	33	20	19	.435	.591
Throws Right	R	.311	235	73	19	1	14	46	6	23	.322	.579
Blackley,Travis	L	.241	116	28	3	2	2	13	4	20	.276	.353
Throws Left	R	.244	287	70	17	3	8	37	28	51	.311	.408
Blanton,Joe	L	.293	379	111	21	4	12	42	23	78	.334	.464
Throws Right	R	.254	378	96	16	2	17	51	11	88	.277	.442
Blevins,Jerry	L	.182	110	20	4	0	4	15	7	30	.248	.327
Throws Left	R	.219	114	25	7	0	3	9	18	24	.333	.360
Boggs,Mitchell	L	.241	108	26	4	0	2	8	13	25	.322	.333
Throws Right	R	.191	157	30	2	0	3	16	8	33	.249	.261
Bowden,Michael	L	.212	52	11	1	0	2	6	9	13	.323	.346
Throws Right	R	.233	90	21	6	0	3	17	8	19	.300	.400
Boxberger,Brad	L	.239	46	11	2	1	2	6	8	14	.364	.457
Throws Right	R	.208	53	11	3	0	1	12	10	19	.338	.321
Brach,Brad	L	.239	92	22	3	0	3	12	15	29	.349	.370
Throws Right	R	.188	149	28	3	0	8	20	18	46	.276	.369
Bray,Bill	L	.000	11	0	0	0	0	3	9	4	.409	.000
Throws Left	R	.375	16	6	2	0	2	4	5	3	.524	.875
Breslow,Craig	L	.222	108	24	6	1	2	18	3	32	.246	.352
Throws Left	R	.228	123	28	4	1	3	15	19	29	.333	.350
Britton,Zach	L	.235	81	19	2	1	3	11	10	24	.319	.395
Throws Left	R	.273	154	42	10	1	3	17	22	29	.369	.409
Brothers,Rex	L	.206	102	21	5	0	1	11	14	41	.303	.284
Throws Left	R	.282	149	42	8	3	4	16	23	42	.376	.456
Browning,Barret	L	.194	36	7	0	0	2	6	5	7	.286	.361
Throws Left	R	.297	37	11	5	0	0	4	2	4	.325	.432
Broxton,Jonathan	L	.219	96	21	6	0	1	6	13	24	.315	.313
Throws Right	R	.294	119	35	4	2	1	11	4	21	.328	.387
Buchholz,Clay	L	.266	380	101	22	1	12	45	37	68	.337	.424
Throws Right	R	.260	331	86	15	1	13	39	27	61	.322	.429
Buehrle,Mark	L	.217	180	39	4	1	7	20	16	34	.279	.367
Throws Left	R	.271	583	158	33	1	19	65	24	91	.302	.429
Bueno,Francisley	L	.263	38	10	2	0	0	1	1	2	.300	.316
Throws Left	R	.222	27	6	1	0	0	2	1	5	.241	.259
Bumgarner,Madison	L	.208	168	35	5	2	4	17	9	47	.247	.333
Throws Left	R	.241	614	148	31	5	19	62	40	144	.294	.401
Burnett,A.J.	L	.248	391	97	14	2	11	36	34	89	.316	.379
Throws Right	R	.245	376	92	16	0	7	39	28	91	.298	.343
Burnett,Alex	L	.215	93	20	0	0	1	9	16	19	.336	.247
Throws Right	R	.279	183	51	5	3	3	30	10	17	.320	.388
Burnett,Sean	L	.211	90	19	4	0	1	12	1	28	.245	.289
Throws Left	R	.298	131	39	7	0	3	13	11	29	.347	.420
Burns,Cory	L	.325	40	13	3	1	1	3	3	8	.372	.525
Throws Right	R	.317	41	13	3	0	0	5	7	10	.429	.390
Burton,Jared	L	.235	85	20	6	0	3	7	10	21	.337	.412
Throws Right	R	.154	136	21	1	1	2	10	6	34	.200	.221
Byrdak,Tim	L	.154	65	10	0	1	2	10	9	29	.260	.277
Throws Left	R	.229	35	8	1	0	0	3	9	5	.386	.257
Cabrera,Alberto	L	.133	30	4	2	1	0	0	5	9	.257	.267
Throws Right	R	.250	48	12	2	0	1	10	13	18	.413	.354

Pitchers vs. Left-Handed and Right-Handed Batters

Pitcher	vs	Avg	AB	H	2B	3B	HR	RBI	BB	SO	OBP	Slg
Cabrera,Edwar	L	.333	9	3	1	0	0	1	1	3	.400	.444
Throws Left	R	.353	17	6	0	0	3	6	6	2	.522	.882
Cahill,Trevor	L	.253	411	104	22	4	6	38	39	80	.326	.370
Throws Right	R	.246	325	80	16	1	10	42	35	76	.324	.394
Cain,Matt	L	.257	382	98	22	1	9	31	34	94	.321	.390
Throws Right	R	.191	414	79	19	2	12	35	17	99	.229	.333
Camp,Shawn	L	.263	114	30	3	4	2	11	11	20	.328	.412
Throws Right	R	.259	189	49	10	2	5	24	10	34	.294	.413
Capps,Carter	L	.318	44	14	1	1	0	1	7	11	.412	.386
Throws Right	R	.212	52	11	4	0	0	5	4	17	.263	.288
Capps,Matt	L	.175	57	10	1	0	1	4	2	11	.203	.246
Throws Right	R	.305	59	18	3	0	4	8	2	7	.328	.559
Capuano,Chris	L	.231	156	36	4	0	3	12	13	39	.288	.314
Throws Left	R	.260	585	152	29	4	22	59	41	123	.309	.436
Carignan,Andrew	L	.273	11	3	0	0	0	1	4	2	.467	.273
Throws Right	R	.227	22	5	2	0	0	4	6	6	.393	.318
Carpenter,Andrew	L	.214	14	3	1	0	2	2	4	3	.389	.714
Throws Right	R	.200	20	4	0	0	2	2	2	6	.273	.500
Carpenter,Chris (Stl)	L	.385	26	10	2	1	0	3	3	4	.467	.538
Throws Right	R	.150	40	6	2	0	2	4	0	8	.171	.350
Carpenter,Chris (Bos)	L	.600	10	6	2	0	1	4	6	2	.750	1.100
Throws Right	R	.083	12	1	0	0	0	1	4	0	.313	.083
Carpenter,D (Tor)	L	.446	56	25	4	1	1	14	8	8	.516	.607
Throws Right	R	.299	87	26	1	1	4	14	8	23	.371	.471
Carpenter,D (LAA)	L	.308	65	20	2	0	1	8	10	6	.400	.385
Throws Right	R	.253	87	22	4	0	5	15	7	22	.305	.471
Carreno,Joel	L	.231	39	9	1	0	2	5	11	7	.400	.410
Throws Right	R	.295	44	13	5	0	5	9	3	9	.340	.750
Carson,Robert	L	.286	28	8	3	0	1	4	3	5	.375	.500
Throws Left	R	.227	22	5	0	0	1	2	1	0	.292	.364
Cashner,Andrew	L	.197	76	15	2	0	1	8	7	26	.262	.263
Throws Right	R	.281	96	27	4	0	4	17	12	26	.367	.448
Casilla,Santiago	L	.265	98	26	6	0	2	9	11	18	.339	.388
Throws Right	R	.197	147	29	4	0	6	19	11	37	.261	.347
Cassevah,Bobby	L	.333	9	3	1	0	1	5	5	2	.500	.778
Throws Right	R	.200	10	2	0	0	1	3	1	0	.333	.500
Castillo,Lendy	L	.423	26	11	1	0	2	7	2	3	.448	.692
Throws Right	R	.295	44	13	2	0	0	8	10	10	.456	.341
Cecil,Brett	L	.214	56	12	3	0	1	4	3	15	.281	.321
Throws Left	R	.319	182	58	10	1	10	31	20	36	.384	.549
Cedeno,Xavier	L	.213	61	13	0	0	2	8	7	27	.304	.311
Throws Left	R	.298	57	17	5	0	1	12	7	9	.358	.439
Chacin,Jhoulys	L	.293	147	43	6	2	8	21	23	20	.386	.524
Throws Right	R	.282	131	37	7	0	2	12	9	25	.338	.382
Chamberlain,Joba	L	.226	31	7	1	0	0	4	5	10	.351	.258
Throws Right	R	.345	55	19	5	0	3	16	1	12	.362	.600
Chapman,Aroldis	L	.108	74	8	2	0	0	1	6	43	.195	.135
Throws Left	R	.155	174	27	5	1	4	14	17	79	.237	.264
Chapman,Jaye	L	.125	16	2	1	0	0	1	7	7	.391	.188
Throws Right	R	.250	24	6	1	1	0	2	3	5	.333	.375
Chatwood,Tyler	L	.311	132	41	6	2	4	22	23	22	.413	.477
Throws Right	R	.268	123	33	4	2	5	18	10	19	.319	.455
Chavez,Jesse	L	.375	40	15	1	0	4	12	4	15	.444	.700
Throws Right	R	.279	68	19	6	1	3	21	7	15	.359	.529
Chen,Bruce	L	.314	191	60	13	1	6	21	15	39	.365	.487
Throws Left	R	.271	573	155	32	5	27	81	32	101	.315	.485
Chen,Wei-Yin	L	.232	203	47	10	1	7	24	15	52	.288	.394
Throws Left	R	.257	540	139	24	3	22	63	42	102	.311	.435
Choate,Randy	L	.158	101	16	3	0	1	11	9	30	.243	.218
Throws Left	R	.325	40	13	1	0	0	2	9	8	.471	.350
Chulk,Vinnie	L	.368	19	7	1	1	0	5	2	4	.429	.526
Throws Right	R	.400	25	10	4	0	0	5	2	6	.444	.560
Cingrani,Tony	L	.200	10	2	0	0	0	1	2	5	.333	.200
Throws Left	R	.200	10	2	0	0	1	1	0	4	.200	.500
Cishek,Steve	L	.279	111	31	8	1	1	10	16	38	.391	.396
Throws Right	R	.185	124	23	2	2	2	12	13	30	.266	.282
Cleto,Maikel	L	.280	25	7	0	1	3	6	0	12	.280	.720
Throws Right	R	.462	13	6	1	0	1	1	2	3	.563	.769
Clippard,Tyler	L	.170	135	23	5	2	1	15	16	40	.260	.259
Throws Right	R	.239	134	32	6	0	6	16	13	44	.307	.418
Cloyd,Tyler	L	.314	51	16	2	0	4	6	5	7	.397	.588
Throws Right	R	.224	76	17	3	0	4	12	2	23	.244	.421
Cobb,Alex	L	.256	285	73	16	1	8	32	29	65	.331	.404
Throws Right	R	.252	226	57	10	0	3	26	11	41	.297	.336
Coello,Robert	L	.364	11	4	3	0	0	1	3	4	.500	.636
Throws Right	R	.353	17	6	0	1	2	4	1	7	.421	.824

Pitcher	vs	Avg	AB	H	2B	3B	HR	RBI	BB	SO	OBP	Slg
Coffey,Todd	L	.167	24	4	0	1	0	1	5	3	.333	.250
Throws Right	R	.277	47	13	3	1	1	8	4	15	.340	.447
Coke,Phil	L	.263	118	31	5	1	2	13	8	30	.313	.373
Throws Left	R	.396	101	40	8	2	3	18	10	21	.446	.604
Coleman,Casey	L	.435	46	20	4	0	3	10	11	7	.544	.717
Throws Right	R	.283	60	17	2	0	2	13	1	9	.295	.417
Coleman,Louis	L	.235	68	16	3	1	5	11	6	17	.297	.529
Throws Right	R	.210	119	25	7	0	5	14	20	48	.329	.395
Collins,Tim	L	.239	117	28	7	2	4	22	16	38	.333	.436
Throws Left	R	.196	138	27	5	1	4	19	18	55	.293	.333
Collmenter,Josh	L	.313	176	55	11	0	5	20	9	27	.346	.460
Throws Right	R	.215	172	37	7	1	8	18	13	53	.270	.407
Colon,Bartolo	L	.274	325	89	16	2	14	34	21	55	.317	.465
Throws Right	R	.257	280	72	8	1	3	23	2	36	.262	.325
Colon,Roman	L	.385	13	5	3	0	0	2	1	1	.429	.615
Throws Right	R	.333	21	7	2	0	0	5	2	2	.391	.429
Contreras,Jose	L	.200	15	3	1	0	1	4	2	4	.333	.467
Throws Right	R	.278	36	10	3	0	0	5	1	11	.289	.361
Cook,Aaron	L	.340	209	71	18	2	7	31	14	9	.382	.545
Throws Right	R	.261	176	46	8	0	8	26	7	11	.288	.443
Cook,Ryan	L	.171	117	20	4	1	3	10	15	35	.269	.299
Throws Right	R	.162	136	22	4	1	1	10	12	45	.245	.228
Corbin,Patrick	L	.325	80	26	5	1	0	8	6	23	.368	.413
Throws Left	R	.269	338	91	18	4	14	42	19	63	.312	.470
Cordero,Francisco	L	.380	79	30	5	0	2	15	11	14	.462	.519
Throws Right	R	.348	89	31	6	0	7	19	7	17	.402	.652
Corpas,Manuel	L	.328	58	19	5	2	2	10	7	9	.435	.586
Throws Right	R	.248	125	31	6	0	5	19	9	19	.304	.416
Correia,Kevin	L	.248	306	76	16	1	11	40	34	44	.320	.415
Throws Right	R	.284	352	100	13	4	9	44	12	45	.311	.420
Crain,Jesse	L	.232	69	16	3	0	3	8	8	23	.312	.406
Throws Right	R	.129	101	13	2	0	2	7	15	37	.248	.208
Crawford,Evan	L	.118	17	2	1	0	1	1	0	3	.118	.353
Throws Left	R	.615	13	8	1	0	2	3	4	2	.722	1.154
Crosby,Casey	L	.250	16	4	1	0	1	4	4	4	.400	.500
Throws Left	R	.344	32	11	3	1	1	8	7	5	.462	.594
Crow,Aaron	L	.188	85	16	2	0	2	6	10	20	.274	.282
Throws Right	R	.255	149	38	1	1	2	22	12	45	.311	.315
Cruz,Juan	L	.254	59	15	4	0	1	6	13	13	.400	.373
Throws Right	R	.316	76	24	3	0	2	5	6	20	.365	.434
Cruz,Rhiner	L	.315	89	28	7	1	5	17	11	19	.390	.584
Throws Right	R	.285	130	37	7	1	3	18	18	27	.375	.423
Cueto,Johnny	L	.279	437	122	18	3	7	36	26	90	.326	.382
Throws Right	R	.220	378	83	18	3	8	28	23	80	.274	.347
Danks,John	L	.307	88	27	4	1	3	14	6	10	.354	.477
Throws Left	R	.248	121	30	9	0	4	17	17	20	.338	.421
Darvish,Yu	L	.231	403	93	26	4	5	47	54	120	.322	.352
Throws Right	R	.207	305	63	13	0	9	34	35	101	.302	.338
Davis,Wade	L	.161	112	18	3	0	0	5	18	37	.277	.188
Throws Right	R	.211	142	30	8	1	5	17	11	50	.266	.387
De Fratus,Justin	L	.250	16	4	1	0	0	1	2	2	.333	.313
Throws Right	R	.130	23	3	0	0	0	2	3	6	.231	.130
de la Rosa,Dane	L	.375	8	3	1	0	0	3	0	1	.375	.500
Throws Right	R	.333	12	4	1	0	2	4	2	4	.429	.917
de la Rosa,Jorge	L	.125	8	1	0	0	0	0	0	3	.125	.125
Throws Left	R	.381	42	16	3	0	5	9	2	3	.409	.810
De Los Santos,F	L	.250	4	1	0	0	0	0	1	2	.400	.250
Throws Right	R	.462	13	6	1	0	0	1	2	1	.533	.538
Deduno,Samuel	L	.256	164	42	5	1	2	10	34	41	.388	.335
Throws Right	R	.221	122	27	4	1	8	25	19	16	.338	.467
Del Rosario,Enerio	L	.425	40	17	3	1	1	10	1	4	.432	.625
Throws Right	R	.370	46	17	6	0	0	9	6	7	.453	.500
Delabar,Steve	L	.171	105	18	8	0	2	10	11	35	.246	.305
Throws Right	R	.211	133	28	6	0	10	21	15	57	.314	.481
Delgado,Randall	L	.263	171	45	7	0	5	19	23	35	.352	.392
Throws Right	R	.250	176	44	14	0	3	19	19	41	.330	.381
Dempster,Ryan	L	.218	339	74	13	2	8	27	29	93	.278	.339
Throws Right	R	.257	315	81	18	2	11	37	23	60	.310	.432
Detwiler,Ross	L	.170	147	25	4	0	3	11	12	32	.255	.259
Throws Left	R	.263	471	124	31	2	12	55	40	73	.320	.414
DeVries,Cole	L	.236	161	38	6	0	6	17	13	32	.305	.385
Throws Right	R	.266	188	50	11	0	10	26	5	26	.289	.484
Diamond,Scott	L	.291	182	53	10	3	6	24	6	29	.314	.478
Throws Left	R	.268	489	131	29	2	11	49	25	61	.306	.403
Dickey,R.A.	L	.237	380	90	13	3	11	29	36	108	.308	.374
Throws Right	R	.218	468	102	22	1	13	41	18	122	.252	.353

Pitchers vs. Left-Handed and Right-Handed Batters

Pitcher	vs	Avg	AB	H	2B	3B	HR	RBI	BB	SO	OBP	Slg
Dickson,Brandon	L	.455	11	5	1	1	1	3	1	2	.500	1.000
Throws Right	R	.263	19	5	0	0	1	4	1	4	.300	.421
Diekman,Jake	L	.200	45	9	2	0	0	6	8	18	.345	.244
Throws Left	R	.258	62	16	5	0	1	10	12	17	.387	.387
Dillard,Tim	L	.340	53	18	5	0	2	9	5	8	.397	.547
Throws Right	R	.281	96	27	6	1	1	12	9	21	.349	.396
Dolis,Rafael	L	.141	64	9	5	0	1	3	10	11	.257	.266
Throws Right	R	.388	80	31	6	1	4	26	13	13	.485	.638
Doolittle,Sean	L	.286	63	18	9	0	1	8	3	18	.318	.476
Throws Left	R	.195	113	22	2	0	2	7	8	42	.244	.265
Dotel,Octavio	L	.288	80	23	6	2	0	7	8	19	.360	.413
Throws Right	R	.197	137	27	4	1	3	14	4	43	.217	.307
Doubront,Felix	L	.259	174	45	10	2	5	23	16	41	.335	.425
Throws Left	R	.259	451	117	24	1	19	65	55	126	.337	.443
Downs,Darin	L	.171	35	6	0	0	0	3	3	10	.237	.171
Throws Left	R	.293	41	12	4	0	1	4	6	10	.396	.463
Downs,Scott	L	.190	84	16	4	0	0	8	7	20	.250	.238
Throws Left	R	.297	91	27	5	0	3	13	10	12	.363	.451
Drabek,Kyle	L	.199	141	28	9	0	3	10	26	22	.325	.326
Throws Right	R	.307	127	39	14	0	7	23	21	25	.405	.583
Duensing,Brian	L	.250	164	41	8	1	4	29	9	28	.294	.384
Throws Left	R	.310	274	85	18	2	6	29	18	41	.352	.456
Duffy,Danny	L	.192	26	5	2	0	0	0	1	10	.222	.269
Throws Left	R	.273	77	21	8	0	2	11	17	18	.404	.455
Duke,Zach	L	.267	15	4	1	0	0	0	1	4	.313	.333
Throws Left	R	.189	37	7	1	1	0	2	3	6	.250	.270
Dunn,Mike	L	.293	92	27	7	0	2	16	9	28	.350	.435
Throws Left	R	.272	81	22	9	0	1	15	20	19	.408	.420
Durbin,Chad	L	.274	84	23	3	0	4	15	6	22	.322	.452
Throws Right	R	.206	141	29	5	1	5	17	22	27	.309	.362
Edgin,Josh	L	.164	55	9	1	0	3	11	4	18	.246	.345
Throws Left	R	.263	38	10	2	0	2	4	6	12	.364	.474
Edlefsen,Steve	L	.316	19	6	1	0	0	2	2	3	.381	.368
Throws Right	R	.318	44	14	3	0	1	7	4	6	.375	.455
Ekstrom,Mike	L	.524	21	11	1	1	1	5	0	2	.500	.810
Throws Right	R	.233	43	10	3	0	0	7	2	7	.255	.302
Elbert,Scott	L	.271	70	19	2	0	2	7	7	11	.342	.386
Throws Left	R	.170	47	8	1	0	1	8	6	18	.259	.255
Enright,Barry	L	.273	11	3	1	0	0	1	1	0	.333	.364
Throws Right	R	.500	8	4	0	0	1	5	0	0	.500	.875
Eovaldi,Nathan	L	.318	274	87	16	3	6	42	32	41	.381	.464
Throws Right	R	.236	195	46	11	1	4	14	15	37	.300	.364
Eppley,Cody	L	.352	54	19	5	0	0	3	9	10	.444	.444
Throws Right	R	.227	119	27	2	0	3	8	8	22	.276	.319
Escalona,Edgmer	L	.242	33	8	2	1	3	8	2	10	.278	.636
Throws Right	R	.278	54	15	1	1	2	10	5	11	.350	.444
Estrada,Marco	L	.247	243	60	14	2	8	27	22	63	.308	.420
Throws Right	R	.246	280	69	16	1	10	33	7	80	.263	.418
Eveland,Dana	L	.239	46	11	2	0	1	8	6	8	.351	.348
Throws Left	R	.266	79	21	4	0	2	8	7	10	.341	.392
Familia,Jeurys	L	.316	19	6	0	0	0	2	4	3	.435	.316
Throws Right	R	.167	24	4	0	1	0	2	5	7	.310	.250
Farnsworth,Kyle	L	.225	40	9	2	0	1	6	9	11	.373	.350
Throws Right	R	.210	62	13	1	0	0	1	5	14	.269	.226
Feldman,Scott	L	.276	268	74	10	3	8	44	21	45	.327	.425
Throws Right	R	.283	230	65	10	2	6	30	11	51	.314	.422
Feliz,Neftali	L	.173	81	14	1	1	3	10	13	18	.295	.321
Throws Right	R	.203	69	14	2	0	2	5	10	19	.313	.319
Fick,Chuckie	L	.419	31	13	4	1	1	3	11	0	.581	.710
Throws Right	R	.233	60	14	1	0	3	10	7	17	.314	.400
Fien,Casey	L	.173	52	9	1	0	1	7	5	11	.241	.250
Throws Right	R	.211	76	16	3	2	2	11	4	21	.256	.382
Fiers,Mike	L	.265	245	65	14	0	5	28	15	64	.307	.384
Throws Right	R	.242	248	60	15	1	7	25	21	71	.303	.395
Fife,Stephen	L	.224	49	11	2	0	1	4	8	13	.333	.327
Throws Right	R	.286	49	14	1	0	1	3	4	7	.364	.367
Figueroa,Pedro	L	.179	28	5	0	0	0	1	2	8	.233	.179
Throws Left	R	.239	46	11	1	0	2	6	13	6	.407	.391
Fister,Doug	L	.270	371	100	24	5	9	35	13	81	.300	.434
Throws Right	R	.220	255	56	6	0	6	27	24	56	.297	.314
Floyd,Gavin	L	.291	327	95	16	1	16	42	41	74	.379	.492
Throws Right	R	.226	314	71	14	2	6	32	22	70	.292	.341
Francis,Jeff	L	.270	100	27	3	2	2	6	0	19	.277	.400
Throws Left	R	.329	359	118	26	1	13	58	22	57	.376	.515
Francisco,Frank	L	.273	88	24	3	3	3	13	13	23	.363	.477
Throws Right	R	.264	87	23	7	0	2	13	8	24	.326	.414

Pitcher	vs	Avg	AB	H	2B	3B	HR	RBI	BB	SO	OBP	Slg
Frasor,Jason	L	.273	66	18	6	0	3	13	15	18	.415	.500
Throws Right	R	.245	98	24	6	1	3	18	7	35	.296	.418
Freeman,Sam	L	.290	31	9	0	0	1	8	7	8	.421	.387
Throws Left	R	.186	43	8	1	0	1	6	3	10	.255	.279
Friedrich,Christian	L	.288	73	21	4	0	3	10	7	19	.350	.466
Throws Left	R	.307	264	81	18	1	11	41	23	55	.364	.508
Frieri,Ernesto	L	.095	105	10	0	1	2	5	14	62	.202	.171
Throws Right	R	.200	125	25	2	0	7	12	16	36	.322	.384
Fuentes,Brian	L	.250	40	10	2	1	1	5	4	8	.326	.425
Throws Left	R	.313	83	26	5	0	5	18	11	16	.389	.554
Furbush,Charlie	L	.147	75	11	3	0	0	6	6	29	.217	.187
Throws Left	R	.198	86	17	4	0	3	8	10	24	.289	.349
Galarraga,Armando	L	.244	45	11	3	1	2	7	13	8	.414	.489
Throws Right	R	.321	53	17	4	0	4	10	5	9	.393	.623
Gallardo,Yovani	L	.256	371	95	20	2	12	41	48	102	.341	.418
Throws Right	R	.230	391	90	10	1	14	38	33	102	.286	.368
Garcia,Christian	L	.267	15	4	2	0	1	2	1	3	.313	.600
Throws Right	R	.143	28	4	0	0	1	1	1	12	.226	.250
Garcia,Freddy	L	.282	220	62	15	0	9	31	23	41	.349	.473
Throws Right	R	.256	195	50	8	0	9	26	12	48	.303	.436
Garcia,Jaime	L	.260	96	25	4	0	2	9	4	27	.284	.365
Throws Left	R	.297	374	111	22	3	5	42	26	71	.338	.412
Garza,Matt	L	.247	190	47	5	1	10	26	14	53	.302	.442
Throws Right	R	.224	192	43	6	1	5	20	18	43	.299	.344
Gaudin,Chad	L	.322	121	39	6	2	3	24	16	17	.396	.479
Throws Right	R	.232	142	33	8	0	3	19	10	40	.297	.352
Gearrin,Cory	L	.345	29	10	2	1	1	4	3	4	.406	.586
Throws Right	R	.159	44	7	1	0	0	4	2	16	.229	.182
Gee,Dillon	L	.287	230	66	10	1	7	29	16	49	.340	.430
Throws Right	R	.219	192	42	7	0	5	22	13	48	.276	.333
Germano,Justin	L	.274	106	29	3	2	1	5	8	21	.345	.368
Throws Right	R	.320	178	57	10	0	6	34	13	31	.372	.478
Godfrey,Graham	L	.333	51	17	4	0	2	10	7	6	.426	.529
Throws Right	R	.290	31	9	1	0	2	8	3	4	.351	.516
Gomes,Brandon	L	.333	27	9	2	1	1	2	6	2	.455	.593
Throws Right	R	.171	41	7	2	0	1	7	6	13	.300	.293
Gomez,Jeanmar	L	.258	155	40	9	0	9	32	18	19	.331	.490
Throws Right	R	.285	193	55	15	0	6	25	16	28	.344	.456
Gonzalez,Edgar	L	.279	43	12	2	2	2	5	5	9	.354	.558
Throws Right	R	.208	53	11	3	0	1	9	3	9	.250	.321
Gonzalez,Gio	L	.231	156	36	8	1	3	18	17	53	.307	.353
Throws Left	R	.199	569	113	27	2	6	43	59	154	.276	.285
Gonzalez,Michael	L	.179	67	12	3	0	1	6	7	23	.257	.269
Throws Left	R	.297	64	19	7	1	1	12	9	16	.378	.484
Gonzalez,Miguel	L	.250	200	50	8	1	5	20	21	52	.326	.375
Throws Right	R	.220	191	42	11	0	8	19	14	25	.282	.403
Gorzelanny,Tom	L	.237	118	28	8	1	3	10	8	26	.289	.398
Throws Left	R	.245	151	37	9	1	4	17	22	36	.343	.397
Gray,Jeff	L	.317	82	26	5	2	6	19	9	9	.394	.646
Throws Right	R	.252	127	32	6	0	3	17	13	17	.331	.370
Gregerson,Luke	L	.214	98	21	2	0	3	6	16	30	.336	.327
Throws Right	R	.216	167	36	8	0	4	10	5	42	.243	.335
Gregg,Kevin	L	.286	77	22	6	1	3	13	15	19	.404	.506
Throws Right	R	.295	95	28	2	0	3	19	9	18	.368	.411
Greinke,Zack	L	.249	409	102	18	2	11	39	32	106	.307	.384
Throws Right	R	.249	394	98	14	2	7	39	22	94	.287	.348
Griffin,A.J.	L	.245	163	40	2	0	5	15	7	37	.279	.350
Throws Right	R	.225	151	34	4	0	5	14	12	27	.280	.351
Grilli,Jason	L	.168	101	17	0	1	1	5	14	50	.267	.218
Throws Right	R	.241	116	28	8	0	6	12	8	40	.302	.466
Grimm,Justin	L	.406	32	13	3	0	1	5	1	4	.412	.594
Throws Right	R	.321	28	9	5	0	0	6	2	9	.355	.500
Guerra,Javy	L	.314	70	22	4	0	0	9	12	15	.410	.371
Throws Right	R	.229	96	22	2	1	1	12	11	22	.312	.302
Guerrier,Matt	L	.316	19	6	1	0	2	4	4	2	.435	.684
Throws Right	R	.074	27	2	0	0	1	2	3	7	.188	.185
Guthrie,Jeremy	L	.303	366	111	23	1	18	53	23	56	.348	.519
Throws Right	R	.272	349	95	24	0	12	45	27	45	.331	.444
Hacker,Eric	L	.368	19	7	0	0	1	2	2	4	.429	.526
Throws Right	R	.304	23	7	3	0	1	4	0	4	.333	.565
Hagadone,Nick	L	.200	45	9	2	0	1	2	6	14	.294	.311
Throws Left	R	.315	54	17	2	0	3	17	9	12	.400	.519
Halladay,Roy	L	.273	322	88	15	1	10	43	23	65	.319	.419
Throws Right	R	.246	272	67	12	2	8	32	13	67	.290	.393
Hamels,Cole	L	.242	215	52	5	1	4	19	17	62	.299	.330
Throws Left	R	.235	587	138	27	3	20	56	35	154	.279	.394

Pitchers vs. Left-Handed and Right-Handed Batters

Pitcher	vs	Avg	AB	H	2B	3B	HR	RBI	BB	SO	OBP	Slg
Hammel,Jason	L	.203	231	47	12	0	4	19	23	62	.278	.307
Throws Right	R	.266	214	57	6	0	5	19	19	51	.328	.364
Hampson,Justin	L	.150	20	3	0	0	0	2	2	3	.227	.150
Throws Left	R	.273	11	3	0	1	0	0	3	1	.429	.455
Hand,Brad	L	.500	4	2	0	0	1	3	1	1	.600	1.250
Throws Left	R	.308	13	4	2	0	0	2	5	2	.500	.462
Hanrahan,Joel	L	.135	104	14	2	0	4	8	16	42	.256	.269
Throws Right	R	.236	110	26	5	1	4	10	20	25	.354	.409
Hanson,Tommy	L	.295	352	104	25	1	18	51	37	75	.363	.526
Throws Right	R	.245	323	79	20	1	9	32	34	86	.323	.396
Happ,J.A.	L	.259	147	38	10	0	5	23	8	37	.301	.429
Throws Left	R	.267	409	109	29	5	14	49	48	107	.342	.465
Harang,Aaron	L	.260	334	87	20	3	7	30	54	60	.360	.401
Throws Right	R	.233	344	80	22	1	7	42	31	71	.299	.363
Haren,Dan	L	.234	363	85	25	2	16	41	24	88	.285	.446
Throws Right	R	.320	328	105	17	0	12	43	14	54	.343	.482
Harrell,Lucas	L	.248	323	80	15	2	7	30	48	74	.341	.372
Throws Right	R	.258	407	105	12	5	6	47	30	66	.306	.356
Harris,Will	L	.265	34	9	1	0	1	5	3	8	.342	.382
Throws Right	R	.400	45	18	5	0	2	15	3	11	.429	.644
Harrison,Matt	L	.209	211	44	6	2	5	11	10	37	.244	.327
Throws Left	R	.276	602	166	34	5	17	61	49	96	.330	.434
Harvey,Matt	L	.212	118	25	6	1	4	14	10	45	.280	.381
Throws Right	R	.185	92	17	6	0	1	3	16	25	.309	.283
Hatcher,Chris	L	.357	28	10	1	0	3	8	3	2	.419	.714
Throws Right	R	.226	31	7	4	0	0	3	3	8	.314	.355
Hawkins,LaTroy	L	.214	84	18	2	0	2	9	6	16	.267	.310
Throws Right	R	.351	77	27	3	0	3	17	7	7	.400	.506
Hefner,Jeremy	L	.302	199	60	18	2	6	29	7	29	.325	.503
Throws Right	R	.272	184	50	10	1	3	24	11	33	.318	.386
Hellickson,Jeremy	L	.241	374	90	18	1	13	40	34	64	.305	.398
Throws Right	R	.247	295	73	11	0	12	20	25	60	.311	.407
Henderson,Jim	L	.294	51	15	1	1	0	9	9	23	.381	.353
Throws Right	R	.177	62	11	2	0	1	6	4	22	.239	.258
Hendriks,Liam	L	.257	179	46	8	1	8	25	16	29	.321	.447
Throws Right	R	.357	168	60	11	3	9	33	10	21	.401	.619
Hensley,Clay	L	.241	83	20	1	0	3	13	12	19	.347	.361
Throws Right	R	.270	111	30	7	1	2	10	18	23	.371	.405
Hernandez,David	L	.240	121	29	7	0	3	11	12	47	.311	.372
Throws Right	R	.145	131	19	2	1	1	8	10	51	.217	.198
Hernandez,Felix	L	.248	512	127	18	2	9	37	33	125	.299	.344
Throws Right	R	.231	355	82	12	2	5	37	23	98	.290	.318
Hernandez,Livan	L	.323	130	42	8	0	8	23	7	18	.357	.569
Throws Right	R	.311	135	42	3	1	7	25	9	30	.352	.504
Hernandez,Pedro	L	.667	9	6	1	0	1	2	0	1	.667	1.111
Throws Left	R	.400	15	6	0	0	2	6	1	1	.438	.800
Hernandez,Roberto	L	.364	33	12	2	1	2	6	3	1	.405	.667
Throws Right	R	.217	23	5	2	0	2	5	0	1	.240	.565
Herndon,David	L	.429	14	6	2	0	1	1	0	4	.429	.786
Throws Right	R	.250	16	4	1	0	0	3	1	4	.294	.313
Herrera,Kelvin	L	.275	120	33	4	2	2	12	14	25	.351	.392
Throws Right	R	.235	196	46	7	1	2	12	7	52	.268	.311
Herrmann,Frank	L	.138	29	4	1	0	1	4	2	7	.194	.276
Throws Right	R	.211	38	8	5	0	0	1	2	7	.250	.342
Hill,Rich	L	.205	39	8	1	2	0	5	8	8	.340	.333
Throws Left	R	.273	33	9	3	0	0	4	3	13	.333	.364
Hinshaw,Alex	L	.191	47	9	3	0	1	6	10	15	.345	.319
Throws Left	R	.281	64	18	1	0	7	15	11	21	.395	.625
Hochevar,Luke	L	.298	386	115	28	5	14	58	40	82	.372	.505
Throws Right	R	.261	333	87	16	1	13	48	21	62	.317	.432
Holland,Derek	L	.243	144	35	5	1	2	11	14	29	.323	.333
Throws Left	R	.243	522	127	24	4	30	80	38	116	.293	.477
Holland,Greg	L	.194	108	21	8	1	0	13	15	38	.290	.287
Throws Right	R	.264	140	37	4	2	2	18	19	53	.348	.364
Hoover,J.J.	L	.120	50	6	2	0	1	4	6	16	.207	.220
Throws Right	R	.196	56	11	1	1	1	8	7	15	.286	.304
Horst,Jeremy	L	.170	47	8	1	0	0	4	4	17	.250	.191
Throws Left	R	.210	62	13	5	0	1	3	10	23	.319	.339
Hottovy,Tommy	L	.250	20	5	1	0	0	2	3	4	.375	.300
Throws Left	R	.375	16	6	3	0	2	6	2	2	.444	.938
Howell,J.P.	L	.200	85	17	3	0	2	8	13	20	.306	.306
Throws Left	R	.244	90	22	4	0	5	12	9	22	.340	.456
Hudson,Daniel	L	.340	103	35	8	0	7	22	6	13	.373	.621
Throws Right	R	.321	84	27	4	0	2	10	6	24	.367	.440
Hudson,Tim	L	.235	370	87	16	3	9	42	30	49	.301	.368
Throws Right	R	.263	308	81	13	3	3	31	18	53	.309	.354

Pitcher	vs	Avg	AB	H	2B	3B	HR	RBI	BB	SO	OBP	Slg
Huff,David	L	.333	36	12	1	1	2	6	1	8	.359	.583
Throws Left	R	.254	71	18	3	0	3	8	4	11	.293	.423
Hughes,Jared	L	.248	133	33	11	2	3	18	10	13	.306	.429
Throws Right	R	.206	155	32	6	2	4	19	12	37	.281	.348
Hughes,Phil	L	.211	388	82	13	2	11	25	29	81	.270	.340
Throws Right	R	.308	370	114	29	1	24	70	17	84	.342	.586
Humber,Philip	L	.302	232	70	12	0	12	39	28	49	.384	.509
Throws Right	R	.243	177	43	5	2	11	28	16	36	.303	.480
Hunter,Tommy	L	.294	282	83	9	1	16	36	19	36	.337	.504
Throws Right	R	.311	251	78	9	2	16	40	8	41	.337	.554
Hutchison,Drew	L	.254	122	31	7	1	4	12	11	26	.324	.426
Throws Right	R	.259	108	28	7	0	4	17	9	23	.333	.435
Isringhausen,Jason	L	.241	79	19	2	0	4	15	14	19	.344	.418
Throws Right	R	.260	96	25	7	0	3	13	5	12	.297	.427
Iwakuma,Hisashi	L	.246	224	55	12	0	7	21	25	44	.323	.393
Throws Right	R	.251	247	62	10	0	10	25	18	57	.307	.413
Jackson,Edwin	L	.249	370	92	18	5	16	47	31	82	.304	.454
Throws Right	R	.236	343	81	24	3	7	39	27	86	.293	.385
Jansen,Kenley	L	.147	116	17	3	1	4	9	11	47	.225	.293
Throws Right	R	.145	110	16	4	1	2	10	11	52	.236	.255
Janssen,Casey	L	.172	116	20	2	0	2	5	7	30	.226	.241
Throws Right	R	.218	110	24	2	2	5	13	4	37	.256	.409
Jeffress,Jeremy	L	.192	26	5	1	0	0	5	7	4	.364	.231
Throws Right	R	.412	34	14	2	1	0	5	6	9	.500	.529
Jenkins,Chad	L	.283	60	17	3	0	3	10	6	9	.348	.483
Throws Right	R	.238	63	15	2	0	2	6	5	7	.304	.365
Jennings,Dan	L	.282	39	11	2	0	1	5	5	7	.378	.410
Throws Left	R	.206	34	7	2	1	1	4	6	1	.341	.412
Jepsen,Kevin	L	.286	77	22	2	1	1	7	8	22	.368	.377
Throws Right	R	.205	83	17	3	0	2	6	4	16	.239	.313
Jimenez,Ubaldo	L	.273	355	97	18	5	15	44	55	75	.375	.479
Throws Right	R	.272	342	93	18	2	10	59	40	68	.354	.424
Johnson,Jim	L	.225	138	31	5	0	2	18	10	17	.277	.304
Throws Right	R	.214	112	24	2	0	1	6	5	24	.267	.259
Johnson,Josh	L	.263	411	108	20	3	5	41	39	97	.328	.363
Throws Right	R	.238	302	72	9	1	9	35	26	68	.297	.364
Johnson,Steve	L	.169	65	11	2	0	2	4	9	24	.270	.292
Throws Right	R	.179	67	12	1	0	2	4	9	22	.276	.284
Jones,Nate	L	.170	94	16	3	0	2	10	12	25	.262	.266
Throws Right	R	.304	168	51	8	1	2	30	20	40	.375	.399
Jurrjens,Jair	L	.345	113	39	10	0	4	17	11	11	.403	.540
Throws Right	R	.355	93	33	6	0	4	17	7	8	.406	.548
Karstens,Jeff	L	.243	148	36	8	0	4	19	6	27	.277	.378
Throws Right	R	.265	200	53	9	1	4	21	9	39	.295	.380
Kelley,Shawn	L	.265	49	13	2	0	1	5	9	13	.379	.367
Throws Right	R	.252	119	30	6	1	4	20	6	32	.281	.420
Kelly,Casey	L	.318	66	21	3	0	3	9	7	13	.392	.500
Throws Right	R	.327	55	18	5	0	2	9	3	13	.373	.527
Kelly,Joe	L	.318	176	56	15	2	6	21	20	22	.389	.528
Throws Right	R	.236	237	56	5	1	4	22	16	53	.290	.316
Kendrick,Kyle	L	.238	298	71	15	2	8	26	31	57	.318	.383
Throws Right	R	.269	308	83	19	0	12	42	18	59	.312	.448
Kennedy,Ian	L	.265	423	112	22	6	17	62	34	109	.324	.466
Throws Right	R	.267	389	104	28	3	11	32	21	78	.319	.440
Kershaw,Clayton	L	.181	149	27	6	0	4	10	18	60	.268	.302
Throws Left	R	.216	661	143	32	3	12	50	45	169	.270	.328
Keuchel,Dallas	L	.250	72	18	3	0	3	13	8	8	.333	.417
Throws Left	R	.296	253	75	12	0	11	34	31	30	.369	.474
Kimbrel,Craig	L	.116	112	13	0	0	1	3	9	61	.189	.143
Throws Right	R	.136	103	14	1	0	2	3	5	55	.183	.204
Kinney,Josh	L	.205	39	8	4	0	0	3	7	11	.333	.308
Throws Right	R	.211	76	16	4	0	3	8	8	25	.299	.382
Kintzler,Brandon	L	.290	31	9	2	0	0	4	5	5	.389	.355
Throws Right	R	.265	34	9	2	0	1	2	2	9	.306	.412
Kirkman,Michael	L	.216	51	11	3	0	2	6	7	18	.317	.392
Throws Left	R	.160	81	13	2	0	3	13	10	20	.253	.296
Kluber,Corey	L	.301	146	44	9	2	5	21	13	35	.366	.493
Throws Right	R	.286	112	32	9	0	4	18	5	19	.328	.473
Koehler,Tom	L	.250	20	5	2	0	1	2	2	6	.318	.500
Throws Right	R	.294	34	10	3	0	3	8	0	7	.294	.647
Kontos,George	L	.167	54	9	0	0	1	3	6	16	.246	.222
Throws Right	R	.229	109	25	7	2	2	20	6	28	.267	.385
Kuroda,Hiroki	L	.253	474	120	31	2	15	50	36	87	.312	.422
Throws Right	R	.244	348	85	19	0	10	32	15	80	.279	.385
Laffey,Aaron	L	.239	117	28	4	0	6	18	8	17	.305	.427
Throws Left	R	.269	268	72	14	1	11	32	29	31	.344	.451

Pitchers vs. Left-Handed and Right-Handed Batters

Pitcher	vs	Avg	AB	H	2B	3B	HR	RBI	BB	SO	OBP	Slg
Lannan,John	L	.281	32	9	1	0	0	2	4	8	.378	.313
Throws Left	R	.267	90	24	6	2	0	7	10	9	.359	.378
Latos,Mat	L	.252	393	99	24	4	14	46	33	87	.313	.440
Throws Right	R	.208	384	80	17	0	11	34	31	98	.269	.339
Layne,Tom	L	.083	36	3	1	0	0	2	1	15	.175	.111
Throws Left	R	.240	25	6	0	1	0	2	2	10	.296	.320
League,Brandon	L	.292	120	35	6	0	1	11	19	21	.388	.367
Throws Right	R	.208	144	30	2	1	0	11	14	33	.283	.236
Leake,Mike	L	.297	384	114	24	2	13	49	23	63	.335	.471
Throws Right	R	.275	316	87	22	3	13	41	18	53	.315	.487
LeBlanc,Wade	L	.280	75	21	2	0	6	10	4	10	.316	.547
Throws Left	R	.273	183	50	8	1	1	16	15	33	.330	.344
LeCure,Sam	L	.208	96	20	5	1	1	11	12	29	.300	.313
Throws Right	R	.232	112	26	4	1	2	10	11	32	.301	.339
Lee,Cliff	L	.263	175	46	8	0	2	9	5	40	.283	.343
Throws Left	R	.253	637	161	35	3	24	65	23	167	.277	.430
Leroux,Chris	L	.143	14	2	0	0	0	1	1	5	.200	.143
Throws Right	R	.300	30	9	1	0	1	5	1	7	.344	.433
Lester,Jon	L	.259	212	55	9	1	8	27	14	49	.313	.425
Throws Left	R	.278	580	161	40	4	17	81	54	117	.337	.448
Lewis,Colby	L	.252	230	58	11	2	12	28	11	47	.297	.474
Throws Right	R	.236	174	41	10	2	4	17	3	46	.256	.385
Lidge,Brad	L	.545	11	6	3	1	1	5	8	2	.737	1.273
Throws Right	R	.214	28	6	2	0	0	3	3	8	.290	.286
Lilly,Ted	L	.209	43	9	1	1	1	7	2	6	.277	.349
Throws Left	R	.201	134	27	3	1	2	15	17	25	.288	.284
Lincecum,Tim	L	.232	362	84	20	4	10	38	51	102	.330	.392
Throws Right	R	.282	351	99	22	1	13	57	39	88	.352	.462
Lincoln,Brad	L	.212	151	32	7	1	4	16	11	44	.270	.351
Throws Right	R	.265	181	48	11	1	10	29	13	44	.313	.503
Lindblom,Josh	L	.261	115	30	6	0	7	13	17	30	.370	.496
Throws Right	R	.209	148	31	5	0	6	25	18	40	.299	.365
Lindstrom,Matt	L	.284	74	21	3	0	1	10	6	17	.372	.365
Throws Right	R	.226	106	24	2	1	1	9	8	23	.281	.292
Liriano,Francisco	L	.221	140	31	5	1	1	14	15	41	.310	.293
Throws Left	R	.251	447	112	20	3	18	69	72	126	.354	.430
Locke,Jeff	L	.297	37	11	1	0	2	7	3	11	.350	.486
Throws Left	R	.255	98	25	2	0	4	12	8	23	.318	.398
Loe,Kameron	L	.307	114	35	9	0	3	14	12	18	.378	.465
Throws Right	R	.267	161	43	9	0	6	28	8	37	.310	.435
Logan,Boone	L	.231	121	28	8	0	3	20	10	42	.293	.372
Throws Left	R	.238	84	20	6	0	3	8	18	26	.371	.417
Lohse,Kyle	L	.253	379	96	18	1	9	31	17	64	.287	.377
Throws Right	R	.226	425	96	23	2	10	32	21	79	.263	.360
Lopez,Javier	L	.191	89	17	5	1	1	11	6	22	.240	.303
Throws Left	R	.417	48	20	3	0	0	5	8	6	.500	.479
Lopez,Rodrigo	L	.300	10	3	0	2	0	3	2	1	.417	.700
Throws Right	R	.333	15	5	1	0	0	2	3	1	.450	.400
Lopez,Wilton	L	.231	91	21	1	0	1	8	5	16	.265	.275
Throws Right	R	.261	153	40	9	1	3	14	3	38	.285	.392
Loup,Aaron	L	.207	58	12	2	0	0	4	1	11	.220	.241
Throws Left	R	.259	54	14	4	1	0	4	1	10	.268	.370
Loux,Shane	L	.302	43	13	2	1	2	5	2	3	.333	.535
Throws Right	R	.322	59	19	7	0	1	11	7	6	.394	.492
Lowe,Derek	L	.345	255	88	23	1	7	39	30	19	.412	.525
Throws Right	R	.285	323	92	13	0	3	40	21	36	.330	.353
Lowe,Mark	L	.239	71	17	4	1	4	10	2	14	.257	.493
Throws Right	R	.240	75	18	4	0	1	9	11	14	.330	.333
Luebke,Cory	L	.259	27	7	1	1	0	6	2	10	.310	.370
Throws Left	R	.226	93	21	4	1	1	4	6	13	.273	.323
Lueke,Josh	L	.667	9	6	2	1	0	4	1	0	.636	1.111
Throws Right	R	.429	7	3	0	0	0	3	2	2	.500	.429
Luetge,Lucas	L	.193	83	16	1	0	1	10	12	26	.289	.241
Throws Left	R	.318	66	21	2	1	2	11	12	12	.425	.470
Lyles,Jordan	L	.300	247	74	12	3	12	38	28	39	.368	.518
Throws Right	R	.263	323	85	14	0	8	46	14	60	.302	.381
Lynn,Lance	L	.272	309	84	14	5	11	39	53	69	.384	.456
Throws Right	R	.237	354	84	22	2	5	33	11	111	.271	.353
Lyon,Brandon	L	.213	75	16	5	0	1	5	12	24	.337	.320
Throws Right	R	.253	158	40	6	0	4	18	8	39	.292	.367
MacDougal,Mike	L	.182	11	2	1	0	0	1	2	3	.308	.273
Throws Right	R	.467	15	7	1	0	0	3	4	1	.579	.533
Machi,Jean	L	.143	14	2	0	0	0	0	0	1	.143	.143
Throws Right	R	.385	13	5	1	0	2	6	1	3	.429	.923
Maholm,Paul	L	.265	162	43	8	1	3	14	9	39	.320	.383
Throws Left	R	.246	549	135	29	5	17	58	44	101	.308	.410

Pitcher	vs	Avg	AB	H	2B	3B	HR	RBI	BB	SO	OBP	Slg
Maine,Scott	L	.188	32	6	0	0	0	5	8	11	.378	.188
Throws Left	R	.343	70	24	6	0	3	20	7	21	.407	.557
Maloney,Matt	L	.389	18	7	4	1	0	4	1	1	.450	.722
Throws Left	R	.323	31	10	4	0	2	9	0	4	.313	.645
Manship,Jeff	L	.238	42	10	2	0	2	6	5	5	.333	.429
Throws Right	R	.404	47	19	3	0	2	12	2	7	.429	.596
Marcum,Shaun	L	.263	236	62	18	0	9	27	27	55	.338	.453
Throws Right	R	.227	238	54	7	3	7	27	14	54	.278	.370
Marmol,Carlos	L	.221	104	23	5	0	3	14	19	36	.347	.356
Throws Right	R	.177	96	17	5	0	1	8	26	36	.358	.260
Maronde,Nick	L	.385	13	5	1	0	0	1	2	4	.438	.462
Throws Left	R	.100	10	1	0	0	0	2	1	3	.182	.100
Marquis,Jason	L	.302	242	73	15	3	14	44	31	35	.381	.562
Throws Right	R	.278	263	73	13	1	9	33	11	56	.310	.437
Marshall,Sean	L	.173	98	17	3	0	0	3	4	34	.206	.204
Throws Left	R	.273	139	38	4	1	3	19	12	40	.344	.381
Marte,Luis	L	.281	32	9	2	0	2	6	6	3	.395	.531
Throws Right	R	.196	51	10	1	0	2	3	3	16	.255	.333
Marte,Victor	L	.318	66	21	5	0	1	9	8	16	.392	.439
Throws Right	R	.297	101	30	8	0	5	18	6	20	.345	.525
Martinez,Cristhian	L	.241	141	34	7	2	0	13	14	31	.310	.319
Throws Right	R	.311	148	46	14	0	6	26	5	34	.329	.527
Masterson,Justin	L	.296	456	135	27	2	13	85	56	72	.376	.450
Throws Right	R	.232	332	77	9	0	5	29	32	87	.308	.304
Matsuzaka,Daisuke	L	.333	96	32	5	1	8	28	12	23	.400	.656
Throws Right	R	.280	93	26	6	1	3	11	8	18	.352	.462
Mattheus,Ryan	L	.241	87	21	5	0	5	9	9	15	.313	.471
Throws Right	R	.240	150	36	9	1	3	17	10	26	.293	.373
Matusz,Brian	L	.175	114	20	5	0	3	11	8	40	.230	.298
Throws Left	R	.327	281	92	21	1	12	40	33	41	.394	.537
Mazzaro,Vin	L	.329	70	23	4	0	2	15	13	11	.437	.471
Throws Right	R	.311	103	32	2	0	1	6	6	15	.355	.359
McAllister,Zach	L	.243	276	67	20	0	10	37	23	57	.300	.424
Throws Right	R	.299	221	66	13	0	9	32	15	53	.340	.480
McCarthy,Brandon	L	.288	222	64	13	0	6	21	15	33	.342	.428
Throws Right	R	.245	208	51	11	0	4	19	9	40	.281	.356
McClellan,Kyle	L	.200	30	6	1	0	2	8	6	7	.333	.433
Throws Right	R	.238	42	10	4	0	0	2	3	4	.319	.333
McClendon,Mike	L	.357	28	10	2	0	1	8	5	1	.471	.536
Throws Right	R	.333	30	10	3	0	0	8	0	3	.375	.433
McDonald,James	L	.207	323	67	16	3	9	32	38	75	.294	.359
Throws Right	R	.260	308	80	19	2	12	45	31	76	.328	.451
McGee,Jake	L	.259	85	22	2	1	2	17	3	29	.289	.376
Throws Left	R	.098	112	11	1	0	1	5	8	44	.157	.134
McHugh,Collin	L	.361	36	13	3	3	2	12	4	8	.415	.778
Throws Right	R	.280	50	14	2	2	3	12	4	9	.357	.580
McPherson,Kyle	L	.225	40	9	0	0	2	3	2	7	.262	.375
Throws Right	R	.263	57	15	3	0	1	2	5	14	.344	.368
Medlen,Kris	L	.208	250	52	9	2	1	13	13	63	.247	.272
Throws Right	R	.207	246	51	8	0	5	17	10	57	.238	.301
Meek,Evan	L	.429	21	9	1	0	0	7	3	0	.500	.476
Throws Right	R	.179	28	5	1	0	1	6	3	8	.281	.321
Mejia,Jenrry	L	.267	30	8	3	1	0	3	6	3	.389	.433
Throws Right	R	.353	34	12	1	0	2	5	3	5	.405	.559
Melancon,Mark	L	.291	79	23	3	0	5	20	7	17	.356	.519
Throws Right	R	.227	97	22	6	0	3	14	5	24	.274	.381
Mendoza,Luis	L	.292	332	97	18	3	6	36	38	45	.371	.419
Throws Right	R	.263	300	79	11	2	9	36	21	59	.321	.403
Mijares,Jose	L	.211	123	26	8	1	1	11	7	35	.269	.317
Throws Left	R	.276	87	24	4	1	2	15	14	22	.375	.414
Mikolas,Miles	L	.231	52	12	2	1	1	8	4	11	.298	.365
Throws Right	R	.274	73	20	4	0	3	12	11	12	.376	.452
Miley,Wade	L	.200	160	32	8	3	1	11	7	28	.238	.306
Throws Left	R	.270	597	161	38	6	13	62	30	116	.304	.419
Miller,Andrew	L	.149	87	13	0	0	1	11	10	33	.245	.184
Throws Left	R	.263	57	15	5	0	2	5	10	18	.373	.456
Miller,Jim	L	.136	81	11	2	0	3	8	9	20	.237	.272
Throws Right	R	.283	99	28	6	0	3	12	18	24	.398	.434
Miller,Shelby	L	.167	18	3	0	0	0	1	4	8	.318	.167
Throws Right	R	.194	31	6	1	0	0	1	0	8	.219	.226
Millwood,Kevin	L	.255	298	76	14	1	6	45	37	60	.339	.369
Throws Right	R	.286	322	92	15	4	7	40	19	47	.326	.422
Milone,Tommy	L	.263	194	51	3	1	9	27	15	43	.321	.428
Throws Left	R	.283	551	156	30	1	15	56	21	94	.311	.423
Minor,Mike	L	.239	159	38	8	0	7	19	14	40	.303	.421
Throws Left	R	.230	492	113	22	3	19	54	42	105	.292	.402

Pitchers vs. Left-Handed and Right-Handed Batters

Pitcher	vs	Avg	AB	H	2B	3B	HR	RBI	BB	SO	OBP	Slg
Mitchell,D.J.	L	.364	11	4	0	0	0	2	0	0	.364	.364
Throws Right	R	.300	10	3	1	0	1	1	3	2	.462	.700
Moore,Matt	L	.243	152	37	6	0	3	18	20	30	.343	.342
Throws Left	R	.237	511	121	32	1	15	57	61	145	.321	.391
Morales,Franklin	L	.184	98	18	1	0	1	7	7	26	.265	.224
Throws Left	R	.245	188	46	8	1	10	22	23	50	.330	.457
Morris,Bryan	L	.000	6	0	0	0	0	1	1	2	.125	.000
Throws Right	R	.200	10	2	0	0	0	2	1	4	.333	.200
Morrow,Brandon	L	.188	250	47	14	0	5	18	23	62	.257	.304
Throws Right	R	.246	207	51	14	0	7	25	18	46	.308	.415
Mortensen,Clayton	L	.179	67	12	2	0	3	5	13	20	.317	.343
Throws Right	R	.238	84	20	4	0	4	15	6	21	.286	.429
Morton,Charlie	L	.301	103	31	6	2	0	11	6	12	.342	.398
Throws Right	R	.310	100	31	6	1	5	17	5	13	.346	.540
Moscoso,Guillermo	L	.304	92	28	2	1	4	15	15	21	.398	.478
Throws Right	R	.333	117	39	8	1	4	19	4	26	.361	.521
Moseley,Dustin	L	.231	13	3	2	0	0	2	1	3	.286	.385
Throws Right	R	.333	6	2	0	0	1	3	1	1	.375	.833
Mota,Guillermo	L	.375	24	9	2	1	0	1	3	8	.444	.542
Throws Right	R	.268	56	15	6	0	3	10	5	16	.344	.536
Motte,Jason	L	.122	123	15	2	0	2	7	10	43	.194	.187
Throws Right	R	.254	134	34	7	0	7	19	7	43	.294	.463
Moyer,Jamie	L	.333	78	26	6	0	5	9	2	20	.350	.603
Throws Left	R	.325	151	49	11	0	6	27	16	16	.394	.517
Moylan,Peter	L	.500	2	1	0	0	0	0	1	0	.667	.500
Throws Right	R	.125	16	2	0	0	1	2	1	2	.176	.313
Mujica,Edward	L	.243	115	28	4	1	4	12	4	28	.269	.400
Throws Right	R	.219	128	28	6	1	3	13	8	19	.268	.352
Myers,Brett	L	.283	106	30	4	1	4	20	8	10	.333	.453
Throws Right	R	.245	143	35	6	1	4	15	7	31	.288	.385
Narveson,Chris	L	.286	14	4	1	0	1	2	0	1	.267	.571
Throws Left	R	.300	20	6	2	0	1	6	4	4	.400	.550
Nathan,Joe	L	.232	142	33	5	0	4	11	6	46	.265	.352
Throws Right	R	.229	96	22	4	0	3	10	7	32	.286	.365
Neshek,Pat	L	.333	15	5	0	0	2	3	1	1	.375	.733
Throws Right	R	.094	53	5	2	0	1	4	5	15	.180	.189
Nicasio,Juan	L	.299	107	32	3	3	6	18	8	28	.350	.551
Throws Right	R	.325	123	40	8	1	1	17	14	26	.394	.431
Niemann,Jeff	L	.280	82	23	5	1	1	11	5	19	.330	.402
Throws Right	R	.119	59	7	1	0	1	2	7	15	.221	.186
Niese,Jon	L	.243	144	35	7	0	4	12	7	36	.290	.375
Throws Left	R	.240	579	139	22	0	18	59	42	119	.291	.371
Noesi,Hector	L	.278	216	60	13	2	12	34	23	38	.342	.523
Throws Right	R	.253	186	47	9	2	9	34	16	30	.314	.468
Nolasco,Ricky	L	.299	385	115	17	4	11	51	35	60	.360	.449
Throws Right	R	.270	366	99	15	5	7	43	12	65	.299	.396
Norberto,Jordan	L	.225	71	16	4	0	2	6	9	20	.313	.366
Throws Left	R	.184	114	21	5	0	3	13	13	26	.266	.307
Norris,Bud	L	.263	319	84	20	1	10	37	46	75	.358	.426
Throws Right	R	.245	331	81	17	1	13	42	20	90	.300	.420
Nova,Ivan	L	.272	327	89	25	2	16	42	34	79	.341	.508
Throws Right	R	.303	346	105	27	5	12	50	22	74	.357	.514
O'Day,Darren	L	.207	87	18	5	1	4	9	3	20	.239	.425
Throws Right	R	.200	155	31	11	1	2	11	11	49	.262	.323
Odorizzi,Jake	L	.280	25	7	1	1	1	4	4	3	.379	.520
Throws Right	R	.200	5	1	0	0	0	0	0	1	.200	.200
O'Flaherty,Eric	L	.113	71	8	0	0	0	0	6	20	.192	.113
Throws Left	R	.291	134	39	6	0	3	15	13	26	.356	.403
Ogando,Alexi	L	.234	107	25	4	1	3	13	5	31	.263	.374
Throws Right	R	.179	134	24	4	0	6	18	12	35	.255	.343
Ohlendorf,Ross	L	.286	98	28	8	2	2	12	16	21	.391	.469
Throws Right	R	.321	106	34	8	0	5	22	8	18	.368	.538
Ohman,Will	L	.186	59	11	1	0	2	5	3	8	.250	.305
Throws Left	R	.286	42	12	1	0	4	10	2	5	.375	.595
Oliver,Darren	L	.234	94	22	3	0	2	5	9	23	.314	.330
Throws Left	R	.196	107	21	4	0	1	8	6	29	.252	.262
Omogrosso,Brian	L	.281	32	9	1	0	1	3	5	5	.378	.406
Throws Right	R	.224	49	11	4	0	2	5	4	13	.283	.429
Ondrusek,Logan	L	.190	84	16	4	0	2	4	17	20	.333	.310
Throws Right	R	.285	123	35	4	0	6	18	14	19	.364	.463
Oswalt,Roy	L	.306	111	34	9	3	4	12	7	22	.358	.550
Throws Right	R	.331	136	45	8	0	7	21	4	37	.355	.544
Otero,Dan	L	.389	18	7	2	0	0	3	1	1	.450	.500
Throws Right	R	.343	35	12	3	1	0	6	1	7	.378	.486
Ottavino,Adam	L	.286	119	34	7	0	1	16	17	25	.375	.370
Throws Right	R	.232	181	42	4	1	8	25	17	56	.300	.398

Pitcher	vs	Avg	AB	H	2B	3B	HR	RBI	BB	SO	OBP	Slg
Outman,Josh	L	.197	61	12	2	0	3	6	4	26	.246	.377
Throws Left	R	.347	101	35	9	1	4	22	16	14	.432	.574
Owings,Micah	L	.286	14	4	2	0	0	1	0	5	.333	.429
Throws Right	R	.190	21	4	0	0	1	6	5	2	.346	.333
Padilla,Vicente	L	.280	93	26	6	1	4	15	8	21	.346	.495
Throws Right	R	.314	105	33	7	1	3	9	7	30	.363	.486
Papelbon,Jonathan	L	.208	125	26	3	1	4	15	12	41	.283	.344
Throws Right	R	.224	134	30	4	0	4	9	6	51	.273	.343
Parker,Blake	L	.143	7	1	0	0	1	2	5	2	.500	.571
Throws Right	R	.450	20	9	0	0	2	2	0	4	.450	.750
Parker,Jarrod	L	.247	348	86	18	2	7	34	35	72	.314	.371
Throws Right	R	.248	322	80	19	0	4	30	28	68	.309	.345
Parnell,Bobby	L	.235	119	28	5	1	2	13	8	37	.281	.345
Throws Right	R	.261	142	37	6	0	2	17	12	24	.321	.345
Parra,Manny	L	.229	109	25	6	0	1	11	12	33	.323	.312
Throws Left	R	.296	125	37	10	0	2	26	23	28	.403	.424
Paterson,Joe	L	.500	10	5	3	0	0	4	2	0	.583	.800
Throws Left	R	.769	13	10	1	0	2	7	1	0	.786	1.308
Patton,Troy	L	.212	113	24	6	0	1	10	6	31	.262	.292
Throws Left	R	.219	96	21	4	0	4	8	6	18	.265	.385
Pauley,David	L	.357	28	10	2	0	1	8	2	2	.406	.536
Throws Right	R	.378	45	17	2	0	1	6	3	4	.429	.489
Paulino,Felipe	L	.190	84	16	5	0	2	3	10	25	.274	.321
Throws Right	R	.273	55	15	3	2	1	4	5	14	.333	.455
Pavano,Carl	L	.319	138	44	9	1	6	26	5	18	.345	.529
Throws Right	R	.305	118	36	12	0	3	17	3	15	.328	.483
Peavy,Jake	L	.252	468	118	26	1	16	43	26	101	.299	.415
Throws Right	R	.210	348	73	10	3	11	38	23	93	.263	.351
Pelfrey,Mike	L	.298	47	14	1	0	0	4	4	6	.353	.319
Throws Right	R	.303	33	10	1	1	0	1	0	7	.303	.394
Penny,Brad	L	.392	51	20	4	0	3	9	5	5	.446	.647
Throws Right	R	.310	71	22	4	0	1	10	4	5	.355	.408
Peralta,Joel	L	.173	127	22	5	1	4	16	9	50	.234	.323
Throws Right	R	.229	118	27	9	0	5	18	8	34	.276	.432
Peralta,Wily	L	.265	49	13	2	0	0	3	5	12	.333	.306
Throws Right	R	.220	50	11	2	0	0	1	6	11	.304	.260
Perdomo,Luis	L	.156	32	5	5	0	0	4	6	4	.300	.313
Throws Right	R	.323	31	10	1	0	0	3	6	4	.447	.355
Perez,Chris	L	.181	116	21	4	1	2	8	11	34	.254	.284
Throws Right	R	.267	105	28	4	3	4	17	5	25	.304	.476
Perez,Juan	L	.154	13	2	1	0	0	2	4	5	.389	.231
Throws Left	R	.308	13	4	0	0	2	4	4	5	.471	.769
Perez,Luis	L	.194	62	12	3	0	1	10	6	23	.296	.290
Throws Left	R	.277	94	26	4	0	2	8	10	16	.346	.383
Perez,Martin	L	.240	50	12	2	0	0	4	4	14	.316	.280
Throws Left	R	.324	108	35	8	3	3	13	11	11	.387	.537
Perez,Oliver	L	.281	57	16	4	0	0	9	4	14	.328	.351
Throws Left	R	.204	54	11	2	0	1	3	6	10	.279	.296
Perez,Rafael	L	.231	13	3	2	0	1	4	3	1	.375	.615
Throws Left	R	.143	14	2	0	0	0	1	1	3	.200	.143
Perkins,Glen	L	.192	99	19	3	0	1	4	6	34	.236	.253
Throws Left	R	.241	158	38	6	1	7	19	10	44	.297	.424
Perry,Ryan	L	.333	18	6	1	1	0	3	2	2	.400	.500
Throws Right	R	.400	15	6	1	0	2	4	0	1	.400	.867
Pestano,Vinnie	L	.241	137	33	13	0	4	13	16	29	.329	.423
Throws Right	R	.168	119	20	2	0	3	9	8	47	.227	.261
Petit,Yusmeiro	L	.385	13	5	0	0	0	1	3	1	.500	.385
Throws Right	R	.500	4	2	0	0	0	0	1	0	.600	.500
Pettitte,Andy	L	.202	84	17	1	0	2	6	3	27	.230	.286
Throws Left	R	.245	196	48	5	1	6	17	18	42	.308	.372
Phelps,David	L	.227	163	37	8	1	9	21	23	44	.332	.454
Throws Right	R	.220	200	44	4	0	5	19	15	52	.282	.315
Phillips,Zach	L	.417	12	5	1	0	2	5	1	2	.462	1.000
Throws Left	R	.154	13	2	1	0	0	1	2	3	.267	.231
Pomeranz,Drew	L	.169	83	14	1	0	1	8	8	30	.247	.217
Throws Left	R	.287	289	83	16	2	13	44	38	53	.372	.491
Pomeranz,Stuart	L	.250	8	2	0	0	0	0	1	0	.333	.250
Throws Right	R	.294	17	5	0	0	1	2	0	3	.294	.471
Porcello,Rick	L	.325	378	123	32	1	11	53	33	54	.381	.503
Throws Right	R	.294	350	103	21	1	5	43	11	53	.322	.403
Price,David	L	.205	176	36	3	0	3	13	8	45	.247	.273
Throws Left	R	.232	591	137	20	0	13	44	51	160	.295	.332
Pryor,Stephen	L	.243	37	9	1	0	2	5	4	6	.317	.432
Throws Right	R	.260	50	13	4	1	3	16	9	21	.361	.560
Putkonen,Luke	L	.333	33	11	3	1	0	3	4	2	.405	.485
Throws Right	R	.267	30	8	1	0	0	6	4	8	.353	.300

Pitchers vs. Left-Handed and Right-Handed Batters

Pitcher	vs	Avg	AB	H	2B	3B	HR	RBI	BB	SO	OBP	Slg
Putz,J.J.	L	.219	105	23	6	0	2	7	6	33	.259	.333
Throws Right	R	.227	97	22	4	0	2	9	5	32	.279	.330
Qualls,Chad	L	.337	89	30	9	0	5	17	7	7	.381	.607
Throws Right	R	.268	123	33	7	0	2	17	7	20	.305	.374
Quintana,Jose	L	.252	151	38	7	1	5	12	7	30	.289	.411
Throws Left	R	.284	366	104	21	2	9	47	35	51	.349	.426
Raley,Brooks	L	.214	14	3	0	0	1	2	2	3	.313	.429
Throws Left	R	.333	90	30	3	0	6	20	9	13	.394	.567
Ramirez,Elvin	L	.250	44	11	3	0	1	6	7	14	.353	.386
Throws Right	R	.351	37	13	4	1	0	8	13	8	.510	.514
Ramirez,Erasmo	L	.207	111	23	4	0	4	9	9	29	.260	.351
Throws Right	R	.226	106	24	4	2	2	13	3	19	.263	.358
Ramirez,R (NYM)	L	.273	110	30	8	2	1	13	19	27	.380	.409
Throws Right	R	.224	125	28	0	1	3	23	16	25	.306	.312
Ramos,A.J.	L	.118	17	2	0	0	0	1	4	7	.318	.118
Throws Right	R	.333	18	6	1	0	2	3	0	6	.333	.722
Ramos,Cesar	L	.222	54	12	0	0	0	3	3	13	.288	.222
Throws Left	R	.130	54	7	0	0	2	4	7	16	.230	.241
Rapada,Clay	L	.186	102	19	1	0	2	9	11	33	.263	.255
Throws Left	R	.303	33	10	4	0	0	4	6	5	.425	.424
Rauch,Jon	L	.262	84	22	5	1	3	10	7	11	.312	.452
Throws Right	R	.176	131	23	6	0	4	16	5	31	.209	.313
Redmond,Todd	L	.364	11	4	0	0	1	2	5	2	.563	.636
Throws Right	R	.500	6	3	1	0	0	1	0	0	.500	.667
Reed,Addison	L	.293	99	29	7	0	2	15	8	21	.349	.424
Throws Right	R	.243	115	28	8	1	4	16	10	33	.302	.435
Resop,Chris	L	.237	114	27	5	0	4	15	12	19	.308	.386
Throws Right	R	.302	179	54	9	1	2	22	12	27	.344	.397
Reynolds,Matt	L	.269	104	28	9	1	2	14	10	27	.325	.433
Throws Left	R	.311	119	37	6	0	9	24	7	24	.349	.588
Richard,Clayton	L	.241	199	48	6	1	2	17	6	34	.280	.312
Throws Left	R	.275	654	180	38	2	29	82	36	73	.312	.472
Richards,Garrett	L	.321	137	44	11	1	3	22	24	25	.418	.482
Throws Right	R	.239	138	33	8	0	4	18	10	22	.298	.384
Rivera,Mariano	L	.154	13	2	0	1	0	2	1	4	.214	.308
Throws Right	R	.235	17	4	1	0	0	0	1	4	.278	.294
Robertson,David	L	.208	120	25	4	2	1	13	11	40	.275	.300
Throws Right	R	.252	107	27	4	0	4	11	8	41	.308	.402
Robertson,Tyler	L	.190	63	12	2	0	2	11	6	22	.268	.317
Throws Left	R	.290	31	9	0	0	2	6	8	4	.436	.484
Rodney,Fernando	L	.166	145	24	1	0	2	8	10	37	.222	.214
Throws Right	R	.168	113	19	1	0	0	1	5	39	.217	.177
Rodriguez,Aneury	L	.000	8	0	0	0	0	0	1	1	.111	.000
Throws Right	R	.182	11	2	0	0	2	2	1	5	.250	.727
Rodriguez,Fernando	L	.226	93	21	3	1	3	12	14	27	.327	.376
Throws Right	R	.266	177	47	8	2	7	35	20	51	.340	.452
Rodriguez,F (Mil)	L	.224	147	33	6	2	8	19	9	43	.268	.456
Throws Right	R	.260	123	32	7	0	0	14	22	29	.367	.317
Rodriguez,Henry	L	.208	48	10	1	0	2	6	11	11	.356	.354
Throws Right	R	.158	57	9	1	0	2	7	11	20	.300	.281
Rodriguez,Paco	L	.143	14	2	0	0	0	0	1	4	.200	.143
Throws Left	R	.125	8	1	0	0	0	1	3	2	.364	.125
Rodriguez,Wandy	L	.255	161	41	11	0	3	17	12	33	.310	.379
Throws Left	R	.255	644	164	30	3	18	76	44	106	.302	.394
Roenicke,Josh	L	.231	130	30	5	1	2	18	17	17	.315	.331
Throws Right	R	.278	198	55	9	3	7	26	26	37	.364	.460
Rogers,Esmil	L	.248	149	37	7	1	1	15	21	38	.347	.329
Throws Right	R	.288	160	46	9	2	6	30	9	45	.335	.481
Rogers,Mark	L	.253	79	20	4	0	4	7	10	19	.333	.456
Throws Right	R	.232	69	16	6	0	1	10	4	22	.284	.362
Romero,J.C.	L	.385	26	10	0	0	2	9	1	4	.414	.615
Throws Left	R	.355	31	11	3	0	2	6	2	2	.394	.645
Romero,Ricky	L	.310	229	71	17	0	9	38	28	40	.397	.502
Throws Left	R	.268	474	127	31	0	12	60	77	84	.373	.409
Romo,Sergio	L	.167	54	9	1	0	1	2	4	6	.250	.241
Throws Right	R	.192	146	28	5	0	4	15	6	57	.229	.308
Rosenberg,B.J.	L	.188	32	6	3	0	0	4	12	11	.422	.281
Throws Right	R	.214	56	12	2	0	4	9	2	13	.254	.464
Rosenthal,Trevor	L	.143	35	5	0	0	1	2	1	10	.167	.229
Throws Right	R	.200	45	9	1	0	1	1	6	15	.308	.289
Ross,Robbie	L	.225	102	23	5	1	1	9	10	24	.289	.324
Throws Left	R	.237	135	32	5	0	2	14	13	23	.313	.319
Ross,Tyson	L	.356	149	53	12	0	4	23	25	22	.458	.517
Throws Right	R	.297	145	43	7	0	3	23	12	24	.352	.407
Rusin,Chris	L	.273	33	9	1	1	0	6	1	5	.314	.364
Throws Left	R	.330	88	29	5	1	4	12	10	16	.410	.545

Pitcher	vs	Avg	AB	H	2B	3B	HR	RBI	BB	SO	OBP	Slg
Russell,James	L	.262	103	27	5	1	3	11	6	21	.309	.417
Throws Left	R	.250	160	40	17	2	2	18	17	34	.317	.419
Rzepczynski,Marc	L	.255	94	24	4	0	2	13	9	21	.320	.362
Throws Left	R	.259	85	22	2	0	5	15	8	12	.323	.459
Sabathia,CC	L	.227	194	44	10	3	6	22	7	72	.265	.402
Throws Left	R	.241	580	140	29	0	16	61	37	125	.291	.374
Saito,Takashi	L	.261	23	6	3	0	2	7	1	6	.320	.652
Throws Right	R	.367	30	11	5	0	2	7	4	5	.441	.733
Salas,Fernando	L	.270	89	24	6	0	0	10	10	24	.343	.337
Throws Right	R	.239	134	32	7	1	5	18	17	36	.329	.418
Sale,Chris	L	.233	193	45	12	1	2	16	7	56	.265	.337
Throws Left	R	.236	518	122	25	0	17	43	44	136	.300	.382
Samardzija,Jeff	L	.241	328	79	20	5	12	45	37	83	.317	.442
Throws Right	R	.239	326	78	10	1	8	29	19	97	.287	.350
Sanches,Brian	L	.375	16	6	2	0	2	4	3	2	.474	.875
Throws Right	R	.400	15	6	0	0	2	7	0	3	.400	.800
Sanchez,Anibal	L	.243	404	98	10	4	8	45	29	94	.299	.347
Throws Right	R	.291	351	102	24	2	12	30	19	73	.324	.473
Sanchez,Eduardo	L	.226	31	7	1	0	1	5	6	7	.342	.355
Throws Right	R	.174	23	4	1	0	1	5	7	6	.387	.348
Sanchez,Jonathan	L	.258	66	17	3	2	2	9	14	15	.402	.455
Throws Left	R	.333	195	65	13	5	9	48	39	30	.440	.590
Santana,Ervin	L	.262	370	97	21	3	23	63	44	79	.345	.522
Throws Right	R	.213	320	68	12	0	16	38	17	54	.264	.400
Santana,Johan	L	.281	114	32	7	0	5	25	7	26	.322	.474
Throws Left	R	.251	339	85	20	1	12	36	32	85	.313	.422
Santiago,Hector	L	.211	109	23	0	0	1	4	20	32	.353	.239
Throws Left	R	.211	147	31	5	0	9	17	20	47	.316	.429
Santos,Sergio	L	.182	11	2	0	0	1	3	2	1	.286	.455
Throws Right	R	.500	8	4	2	0	0	1	2	3	.600	.750
Saunders,Joe	L	.199	166	33	5	0	0	10	4	38	.222	.229
Throws Left	R	.307	528	162	33	3	21	68	35	74	.349	.500
Savery,Joe	L	.243	37	9	2	0	1	6	0	7	.250	.378
Throws Left	R	.293	58	17	5	0	3	8	8	9	.379	.534
Scahill,Rob	L	.111	9	1	0	0	0	0	2	1	.273	.111
Throws Right	R	.286	21	6	2	0	0	1	1	3	.318	.381
Scheppers,Tanner	L	.302	53	16	2	0	4	9	6	13	.383	.566
Throws Right	R	.369	84	31	4	0	2	12	3	17	.393	.488
Scherzer,Max	L	.292	387	113	24	5	11	40	46	109	.366	.465
Throws Right	R	.201	329	66	9	1	12	33	14	122	.244	.343
Schlereth,Daniel	L	.231	13	3	0	1	1	3	0	3	.231	.615
Throws Left	R	.524	21	11	4	0	2	8	5	3	.615	1.000
Schwimer,Michael	L	.262	42	11	3	0	1	10	4	15	.340	.405
Throws Right	R	.235	81	19	2	2	2	16	12	21	.330	.383
Schwinden,Chris	L	.429	21	9	1	1	1	7	2	1	.478	.714
Throws Right	R	.286	21	6	1	1	3	7	1	0	.318	.857
Scribner,Evan	L	.278	54	15	4	0	2	8	8	14	.371	.463
Throws Right	R	.183	82	15	8	0	0	3	4	16	.221	.280
Seddon,Chris	L	.229	48	11	0	0	0	5	4	7	.283	.229
Throws Left	R	.286	84	24	3	2	2	12	9	11	.351	.440
Septimo,Leyson	L	.161	31	5	0	0	3	10	5	8	.278	.452
Throws Left	R	.150	20	3	0	0	0	0	1	6	.227	.150
Shaw,Bryan	L	.333	111	37	6	1	2	16	12	15	.403	.459
Throws Right	R	.211	109	23	6	1	2	12	12	26	.290	.339
Sheets,Ben	L	.265	117	31	9	1	2	9	5	18	.301	.410
Throws Right	R	.292	72	21	4	0	4	10	8	17	.363	.514
Shields,James	L	.232	466	108	22	4	19	60	33	113	.288	.418
Throws Right	R	.248	403	100	14	3	6	29	25	110	.303	.342
Simon,Alfredo	L	.267	116	31	9	3	0	17	14	25	.348	.397
Throws Right	R	.283	120	34	6	1	2	7	8	27	.348	.400
Sipp,Tony	L	.209	110	23	4	1	5	18	7	25	.263	.400
Throws Left	R	.250	96	24	7	1	4	12	16	26	.354	.469
Skaggs,Tyler	L	.167	18	3	0	0	0	0	0	2	.167	.167
Throws Left	R	.273	99	27	4	0	6	19	13	19	.368	.495
Slaten,Doug	L	.077	13	1	0	0	0	0	1	3	.143	.077
Throws Left	R	.242	33	8	1	0	1	6	7	3	.375	.364
Smith,Joe	L	.218	101	22	5	0	1	7	9	24	.288	.297
Throws Right	R	.209	148	31	6	0	3	18	16	29	.289	.311
Smith,Will	L	.356	101	36	8	0	2	17	9	19	.402	.495
Throws Left	R	.295	254	75	11	3	10	33	24	40	.355	.480
Smyly,Drew	L	.224	116	26	5	1	4	16	9	39	.283	.388
Throws Left	R	.258	260	67	15	4	8	31	24	55	.321	.438
Socolovich,Miguel	L	.243	37	9	1	0	2	8	5	6	.333	.432
Throws Right	R	.231	26	6	0	1	1	2	4	6	.333	.423
Soriano,Rafael	L	.221	136	30	7	1	5	11	18	37	.316	.397
Throws Right	R	.214	117	25	5	1	1	6	6	32	.250	.299

Pitchers vs. Left-Handed and Right-Handed Batters

Pitcher	vs	Avg	AB	H	2B	3B	HR	RBI	BB	SO	OBP	Slg
Spence,Josh	L	.158	19	3	0	0	0	1	1	5	.200	.158
Throws Left	R	.417	24	10	1	0	1	3	4	5	.500	.583
Stammen,Craig	L	.198	121	24	8	1	2	10	13	29	.274	.331
Throws Right	R	.224	205	46	10	0	5	17	23	58	.309	.346
Stauffer,Tim	L	.286	14	4	0	0	1	2	1	4	.333	.500
Throws Right	R	.429	7	3	0	0	0	1	2	1	.556	.429
Stewart,Zach	L	.352	71	25	6	0	5	18	0	4	.352	.648
Throws Right	R	.367	90	33	3	0	9	22	4	15	.396	.700
Stinson,Josh	L	.222	18	4	2	0	0	0	4	1	.364	.333
Throws Right	R	.200	15	3	0	0	1	2	1	2	.250	.400
Storen,Drew	L	.289	38	11	2	0	0	4	1	8	.293	.342
Throws Right	R	.164	67	11	0	0	0	2	7	16	.253	.164
Storey,Mickey	L	.167	36	6	2	0	0	3	3	6	.231	.222
Throws Right	R	.269	78	21	6	1	2	12	7	28	.337	.449
Straily,Dan	L	.271	59	16	1	0	7	10	13	11	.403	.644
Throws Right	R	.215	93	20	4	0	4	8	3	21	.253	.387
Strasburg,Stephen	L	.271	310	84	14	2	6	28	27	88	.326	.387
Throws Right	R	.185	281	52	11	1	9	31	21	109	.251	.327
Street,Huston	L	.127	63	8	2	0	0	2	8	29	.225	.159
Throws Right	R	.132	68	9	3	1	2	9	3	18	.167	.294
Strop,Pedro	L	.252	115	29	6	0	0	17	20	29	.370	.304
Throws Right	R	.184	125	23	4	0	2	7	17	29	.292	.264
Stults,Eric	L	.161	93	15	3	0	3	12	2	21	.192	.290
Throws Left	R	.278	277	77	12	4	4	25	25	34	.334	.394
Stutes,Michael	L	.167	12	2	0	1	0	2	3	4	.333	.333
Throws Right	R	.385	13	5	2	0	0	4	1	1	.429	.538
Suppan,Jeff	L	.340	47	16	5	1	3	11	3	2	.380	.681
Throws Right	R	.243	74	18	3	1	1	7	10	5	.333	.351
Swarzak,Anthony	L	.254	169	43	13	0	7	28	17	32	.316	.456
Throws Right	R	.309	204	63	9	0	8	30	14	30	.350	.471
Takahashi,Hisanori	L	.234	107	25	7	2	4	16	5	31	.268	.449
Throws Left	R	.273	88	24	8	0	4	17	9	21	.337	.500
Tateyama,Yoshinori	L	.300	30	9	3	0	4	12	5	7	.400	.800
Throws Right	R	.225	40	9	2	0	0	7	1	11	.244	.275
Tazawa,Junichi	L	.234	64	15	2	0	0	6	1	15	.254	.266
Throws Right	R	.222	99	22	5	1	1	9	4	30	.260	.323
Teaford,Everett	L	.300	90	27	2	1	3	10	9	10	.364	.444
Throws Left	R	.275	149	41	7	0	8	19	12	25	.335	.483
Teheran,Julio	L	.125	8	1	0	0	0	0	0	2	.125	.125
Throws Right	R	.267	15	4	0	0	0	1	1	3	.313	.267
Thatcher,Joe	L	.175	63	11	0	0	2	9	6	31	.239	.270
Throws Left	R	.333	57	19	3	1	0	5	8	8	.441	.421
Thayer,Dale	L	.253	91	23	2	0	2	9	8	24	.313	.341
Throws Right	R	.244	123	30	4	1	2	18	4	23	.265	.341
Thomas,Justin	L	.235	17	4	1	0	0	3	1	5	.300	.294
Throws Left	R	.533	15	8	2	0	1	7	2	2	.588	.867
Thornburg,Tyler	L	.268	41	11	1	0	2	3	3	12	.318	.439
Throws Right	R	.289	45	13	1	0	6	8	4	8	.360	.711
Thornton,Matt	L	.256	121	31	6	1	1	10	7	35	.313	.347
Throws Left	R	.258	124	32	8	0	3	16	10	18	.313	.395
Tillman,Chris	L	.216	199	43	12	0	5	18	9	44	.249	.352
Throws Right	R	.192	120	23	6	0	7	12	15	22	.285	.417
Tolleson,Shawn	L	.316	57	18	5	0	3	11	10	16	.426	.561
Throws Right	R	.152	79	12	4	0	1	10	10	23	.244	.241
Tomlin,Josh	L	.303	218	66	13	4	14	48	17	24	.353	.592
Throws Right	R	.299	201	60	10	3	4	23	8	32	.330	.438
Torres,Carlos	L	.225	80	18	2	1	1	10	15	18	.347	.313
Throws Right	R	.279	111	31	8	2	1	17	11	24	.354	.414
Turner,Jacob	L	.189	95	18	3	0	2	5	10	17	.264	.284
Throws Right	R	.274	117	32	5	3	7	23	6	19	.306	.547
Uehara,Koji	L	.188	69	13	2	0	3	10	1	21	.197	.348
Throws Right	R	.125	56	7	2	0	1	2	2	22	.155	.214
Valdes,Raul	L	.149	47	7	0	0	2	4	1	19	.167	.277
Throws Left	R	.183	60	11	1	0	1	4	4	16	.234	.250
Valdez,Jose	L	.222	18	4	0	0	1	2	2	6	.300	.389
Throws Right	R	.286	28	8	1	0	0	3	6	4	.412	.321
Valverde,Jose	L	.257	144	37	8	3	3	23	19	21	.337	.417
Throws Right	R	.193	114	22	6	0	0	9	8	27	.270	.246
Vargas,Jason	L	.239	201	48	10	0	8	26	17	30	.297	.408
Throws Left	R	.247	619	153	25	2	27	60	38	111	.292	.425
Varvaro,Anthony	L	.273	33	9	1	0	2	5	5	8	.385	.485
Throws Right	R	.226	31	7	1	1	0	3	4	13	.333	.323
Vasquez,Esmerling	L	.361	61	22	3	0	2	9	9	8	.431	.508
Throws Right	R	.179	56	10	3	0	0	7	10	6	.309	.232
Veal,Donnie	L	.094	32	3	2	0	0	1	2	14	.147	.156
Throws Left	R	.154	13	2	1	0	0	1	2	5	.267	.231

Pitcher	vs	Avg	AB	H	2B	3B	HR	RBI	BB	SO	OBP	Slg
Venters,Jonny	L	.250	80	20	2	0	1	5	8	30	.341	.313
Throws Left	R	.281	146	41	4	0	5	19	20	39	.375	.411
Veras,Jose	L	.260	123	32	5	1	2	14	19	43	.359	.366
Throws Right	R	.220	132	29	4	1	3	13	21	36	.331	.333
Verlander,Justin	L	.213	497	106	28	2	11	38	35	140	.264	.344
Throws Right	R	.222	387	86	12	0	8	33	25	99	.278	.315
Villanueva,Carlos	L	.239	226	54	9	1	15	35	30	57	.330	.487
Throws Right	R	.246	240	59	15	0	8	21	16	65	.295	.408
Villarreal,Brayan	L	.190	63	12	3	1	1	10	19	18	.360	.317
Throws Right	R	.206	126	26	4	0	2	9	9	48	.261	.286
Vincent,Nick	L	.139	36	5	1	0	1	6	4	7	.225	.250
Throws Right	R	.233	60	14	2	0	1	9	3	21	.281	.317
Vogelsong,Ryan	L	.254	351	89	19	3	9	31	35	85	.321	.402
Throws Right	R	.230	356	82	19	1	8	38	27	73	.297	.357
Volquez,Edinson	L	.230	304	70	22	3	4	40	48	75	.338	.362
Throws Right	R	.240	375	90	14	1	10	37	57	99	.348	.363
Volstad,Chris	L	.283	187	53	11	3	7	30	18	20	.345	.487
Throws Right	R	.322	261	84	10	2	9	48	25	41	.378	.479
Wade,Cory	L	.278	72	20	6	1	2	10	2	15	.297	.472
Throws Right	R	.292	89	26	11	0	6	17	6	23	.340	.618
Wainwright,Adam	L	.261	348	91	11	6	8	46	34	86	.327	.397
Throws Right	R	.256	410	105	29	2	7	37	18	98	.293	.388
Walden,Jordan	L	.171	76	13	7	0	2	8	10	31	.264	.342
Throws Right	R	.286	77	22	3	1	1	7	8	17	.353	.390
Waldrop,Kyle	L	.237	38	9	0	0	0	3	4	3	.326	.237
Throws Right	R	.383	47	18	2	0	2	9	2	4	.431	.553
Wall,Josh	L	.000	7	0	0	0	0	0	0	1	.125	.000
Throws Right	R	.250	12	3	1	0	1	3	1	3	.308	.583
Walters,P.J.	L	.318	129	41	2	1	5	14	17	21	.395	.465
Throws Right	R	.261	115	30	4	1	7	21	5	21	.309	.496
Wang,Chien-Ming	L	.413	63	26	6	1	4	15	8	3	.479	.730
Throws Right	R	.343	70	24	5	0	1	12	7	12	.407	.457
Watson,Tony	L	.183	93	17	5	0	2	9	9	21	.252	.301
Throws Left	R	.213	94	20	4	1	3	16	14	32	.318	.372
Weaver,Jered	L	.199	392	78	11	0	8	20	28	81	.252	.288
Throws Right	R	.235	294	69	13	1	12	35	17	61	.282	.408
Webb,Ryan	L	.314	102	32	10	1	0	16	11	16	.377	.431
Throws Right	R	.282	142	40	6	0	2	22	9	28	.340	.366
Weber,Thad	L	.500	8	4	2	0	0	1	1	0	.556	.750
Throws Right	R	.429	14	6	1	0	0	2	1	1	.467	.500
Weiland,Kyle	L	.343	35	12	1	0	2	5	4	6	.410	.543
Throws Right	R	.324	37	12	3	0	3	7	3	7	.375	.649
Wells,Kip	L	.279	61	17	2	2	1	6	8	9	.352	.426
Throws Right	R	.286	84	24	2	0	5	14	12	10	.381	.488
Wells,Randy	L	.353	51	18	9	0	1	8	16	8	.515	.588
Throws Right	R	.279	61	17	3	1	0	10	8	6	.366	.361
Werner,Andrew	L	.205	44	9	5	0	0	6	6	14	.314	.318
Throws Left	R	.316	114	36	5	2	5	20	8	21	.355	.526
Westbrook,Jake	L	.297	317	94	15	3	7	38	25	45	.351	.429
Throws Right	R	.269	361	97	17	0	5	32	27	61	.326	.357
Wheeler,Dan	L	.520	25	13	2	0	3	12	3	0	.571	.960
Throws Right	R	.148	27	4	2	0	0	2	4	2	.242	.222
White,Alex	L	.285	214	61	14	6	4	36	28	27	.370	.463
Throws Right	R	.291	182	53	11	0	9	24	23	37	.380	.500
Wieland,Joe	L	.250	52	13	3	2	1	5	5	13	.305	.442
Throws Right	R	.241	54	13	3	0	4	11	4	11	.305	.519
Wilhelmsen,Tom	L	.223	148	33	6	1	3	13	16	36	.299	.338
Throws Right	R	.181	144	26	4	1	2	16	13	51	.255	.264
Wilk,Adam	L	.417	12	5	0	0	0	2	1	1	.462	.417
Throws Left	R	.410	39	16	0	0	4	8	2	6	.429	.718
Williams,Jerome	L	.263	270	71	11	3	9	37	22	48	.321	.426
Throws Right	R	.264	258	68	14	3	8	35	13	50	.304	.434
Wilson,C.J.	L	.217	180	39	4	1	3	23	17	54	.290	.300
Throws Left	R	.246	578	142	26	2	16	63	74	119	.333	.381
Wilson,Justin	L	.364	11	4	3	0	0	6	1	4	.417	.636
Throws Left	R	.545	11	6	0	0	0	1	2	3	.615	.545
Wolf,Randy	L	.267	135	36	7	1	6	26	15	30	.342	.467
Throws Left	R	.326	491	160	35	5	17	67	37	74	.378	.521
Wood,Kerry	L	.214	14	3	0	0	1	2	3	2	.333	.429
Throws Right	R	.313	16	5	0	1	0	5	8	4	.542	.438
Wood,Travis	L	.195	118	23	5	1	4	9	7	31	.258	.356
Throws Left	R	.241	456	110	34	2	21	65	47	88	.316	.463
Worley,Vance	L	.312	260	81	16	4	5	35	30	62	.386	.462
Throws Right	R	.280	261	73	19	0	7	28	17	45	.331	.433
Wright,Jamey	L	.252	115	29	3	0	0	9	21	28	.365	.278
Throws Right	R	.283	152	43	6	0	2	28	9	26	.337	.362

Pitchers vs. Left-Handed and Right-Handed Batters

Pitcher	vs	Avg	AB	H	2B	3B	HR	RBI	BB	SO	OBP	Slg
Wright,Wesley	L	.198	121	24	1	1	2	13	9	39	.265	.273
Throws Left	R	.269	78	21	2	2	2	13	8	15	.367	.423
Young,Chris	L	.278	212	59	11	3	9	31	26	33	.357	.486
Throws Right	R	.261	230	60	19	0	7	23	10	47	.292	.435
Zagurski,Mike	L	.298	57	17	1	2	1	13	7	16	.364	.439
Throws Left	R	.253	79	20	6	0	4	18	12	18	.347	.481
Zambrano,Carlos	L	.244	254	62	8	3	3	33	48	42	.365	.335
Throws Right	R	.257	237	61	10	1	6	38	27	53	.347	.384
Ziegler,Brad	L	.268	71	19	3	1	1	8	12	9	.369	.380
Throws Right	R	.211	166	35	3	0	1	17	9	33	.254	.247
Zimmermann,Jordan	L	.234	380	89	23	0	7	25	30	82	.300	.350
Throws Right	R	.268	362	97	19	3	11	37	13	71	.295	.428
Zito,Barry	L	.209	177	37	8	1	2	8	7	36	.259	.299
Throws Left	R	.281	530	149	35	5	18	69	63	78	.355	.468
AL	L	.254	-	-	-	-	-	-	-	-	.323	.409
	R	.256	-	-	-	-	-	-	-	-	.315	.409
NL	L	.254	-	-	-	-	-	-	-	-	.325	.398
	R	.255	-	-	-	-	-	-	-	-	.315	.405
MLB	L	.254	-	-	-	-	-	-	-	-	.324	.403
	R	.255	-	-	-	-	-	-	-	-	.315	.407

2012 Leaderboards

This section contains all the leader boards you traditionally see, but way more of those that you never see. For example, Miguel Cabrera, who led the American League in RBIs, also led all of baseball with 46 RBIs that either tied the game or gave his team the lead.

Some of the leader boards derive from the complex pitch data collected by Baseball Info Solutions. For example, the two best pitchers in baseball at throwing pitches in the strike-zone in 2012 were Cliff Lee of the Phillies and the Mets' knuckleballer R.A. Dickey, with 51.9% and 49.3% of their pitches thrown in the strikezone, respectively.

Bill James provides his own leader boards including Runs Created, Tough Losses and Power/Speed Numbers. This year, he has updated his speed score formula. The fastest players in 2012 were, in order, Michael Bourn, Shane Victorino, Angel Pagan, Jose Reyes, and Drew Stubbs.

In short, if there's any kind of leader board that we thought would be interesting, we put it here.

Some details:

Our home run distance leader boards are fueled by Hit Tracker data. Please check out www.hittrackeronline.com and thank you ESPN Stats & Information Group.

In the past we measured hitter performance against various pitch types by result only. The problem with that approach was that if a hitter regularly looked silly on non-result-pitch curveballs, but mashed just a few along the way, he could look like a great curveball hitter, even though nothing was further from the truth. Bill James designed a formula to rate hitters not only on the result pitches, but on every pitch the batter faced. The hitters you'll now see in these leader boards are a much better representation of the guys who mastered each pitch type this past year.

Here are some definitions to help clarify parts of the leader boards that may not be familiar to all readers:

BPS stands for "Batting Average plus Slugging Percentage." We feel that BPS makes more sense than OPS for some leader boards that involve pitches.

OutZ is "Pitches Outside the Strike Zone."

Holds Adjusted Save Percentage is calculated by dividing holds plus saves by holds plus save opportunities.

2012 American League Batting Leaders

Batting Average (minimum 502 PA)		On Base Percentage (minimum 502 PA)		Slugging Average (minimum 502 PA)		Home Runs	
Cabrera,Miguel, Det	.330	Mauer,Joe, Min	.416	Cabrera,Miguel, Det	.606	Cabrera,Miguel, Det	44
Trout,Mike, LAA	.326	Fielder,Prince, Det	.412	Hamilton,Josh, Tex	.577	Granderson,Curtis, NYY	43
Beltre,Adrian, Tex	.321	Trout,Mike, LAA	.399	Trout,Mike, LAA	.564	Hamilton,Josh, Tex	43
Mauer,Joe, Min	.319	Cabrera,Miguel, Det	.393	Beltre,Adrian, Tex	.561	Encarnacion,Edwin, Tor	42
Jeter,Derek, NYY	.316	Encarnacion,Edwin, Tor	.384	Encarnacion,Edwin, Tor	.557	Dunn,Adam, CWS	41
Fielder,Prince, Det	.313	Murphy,David, Tex	.380	Cano,Robinson, NYY	.550	Beltre,Adrian, Tex	36
Hunter,Torii, LAA	.313	Cano,Robinson, NYY	.379	Fielder,Prince, Det	.528	Willingham,Josh, Min	35
Butler,Billy, KC	.313	Jackson,Austin, Det	.377	Willingham,Josh, Min	.524	Cano,Robinson, NYY	33
Cano,Robinson, NYY	.313	Zobrist,Ben, TB	.377	Rios,Alex, CWS	.516	Davis,Chris, Bal	33
Murphy,David, Tex	.304	Choo,Shin-Soo, Cle	.373	Pujols,Albert, LAA	.516	3 tied with	32

Games		Plate Appearances		At Bats		Hits	
Fielder,Prince, Det	162	Jeter,Derek, NYY	740	Jeter,Derek, NYY	683	Jeter,Derek, NYY	216
Jones,Adam, Bal	162	Kinsler,Ian, Tex	731	Hardy,J.J., Bal	663	Cabrera,Miguel, Det	205
Suzuki,Ichiro, Sea-NYY	162	Gordon,Alex, KC	721	Kinsler,Ian, Tex	655	Cano,Robinson, NYY	196
Butler,Billy, KC	161	Hardy,J.J., Bal	713	Jones,Adam, Bal	648	Beltre,Adrian, Tex	194
Cabrera,Miguel, Det	161	Andrus,Elvis, Tex	711	Gordon,Alex, KC	642	Butler,Billy, KC	192
Cano,Robinson, NYY	161	Cabrera,Miguel, Det	697	Andrus,Elvis, Tex	629	Gordon,Alex, KC	189
Gordon,Alex, KC	161	Cano,Robinson, NYY	697	Suzuki,Ichiro, Sea-NYY	629	Jones,Adam, Bal	186
Granderson,Curtis, NYY	160	Jones,Adam, Bal	697	Cano,Robinson, NYY	627	Rios,Alex, CWS	184
Pena,Carlos, TB	160	Fielder,Prince, Det	690	Cabrera,Miguel, Det	622	Fielder,Prince, Det	182
2 tied with	159	Choo,Shin-Soo, Cle	686	Butler,Billy, KC	614	Trout,Mike, LAA	182

Singles		Doubles		Triples		Total Bases	
Jeter,Derek, NYY	169	Gordon,Alex, KC	51	Jackson,Austin, Det	10	Cabrera,Miguel, Det	377
Andrus,Elvis, Tex	137	Pujols,Albert, LAA	50	Andrus,Elvis, Tex	9	Cano,Robinson, NYY	345
Escobar,Alcides, KC	135	Cano,Robinson, NYY	48	Rios,Alex, CWS	8	Beltre,Adrian, Tex	339
Suzuki,Ichiro, Sea-NYY	135	Cruz,Nelson, Tex	45	Trout,Mike, LAA	8	Jones,Adam, Bal	327
Revere,Ben, Min	131	Choo,Shin-Soo, Cle	43	Weeks,Jemile, Oak	8	Hamilton,Josh, Tex	324
Young,Michael, Tex	131	Kinsler,Ian, Tex	42	Crisp,Coco, Oak	7	Trout,Mike, LAA	315
Butler,Billy, KC	130	Cabrera,Miguel, Det	40	Escobar,Alcides, KC	7	Butler,Billy, KC	313
Mauer,Joe, Min	129	Jones,Adam, Bal	39	Jennings,Desmond, TB	7	Pujols,Albert, LAA	313
Hunter,Torii, LAA	126	Pedroia,Dustin, Bos	39	Zobrist,Ben, TB	7	Rios,Alex, CWS	312
Beltre,Adrian, Tex	123	Zobrist,Ben, TB	39	4 tied with	6	Fielder,Prince, Det	307

Runs Scored		RBI		Walks		Strikeouts	
Trout,Mike, LAA	129	Cabrera,Miguel, Det	139	Dunn,Adam, CWS	105	Dunn,Adam, CWS	222
Cabrera,Miguel, Det	109	Hamilton,Josh, Tex	128	Zobrist,Ben, TB	97	Granderson,Curtis, NYY	195
Cano,Robinson, NYY	105	Encarnacion,Edwin, Tor	110	Santana,Carlos, Cle	91	Pena,Carlos, TB	182
Kinsler,Ian, Tex	105	Willingham,Josh, Min	110	Mauer,Joe, Min	90	Davis,Chris, Bal	169
Hamilton,Josh, Tex	103	Fielder,Prince, Det	108	Pena,Carlos, TB	87	Upton,B.J., TB	169
Jackson,Austin, Det	103	Butler,Billy, KC	107	Fielder,Prince, Det	85	Hamilton,Josh, Tex	162
Jones,Adam, Bal	103	Granderson,Curtis, NYY	106	Encarnacion,Edwin, Tor	84	Johnson,Kelly, Tor	159
Granderson,Curtis, NYY	102	Pujols,Albert, LAA	105	Swisher,Nick, NYY	77	Reynolds,Mark, Bal	159
Jeter,Derek, NYY	99	Beltre,Adrian, Tex	102	Willingham,Josh, Min	76	Trumbo,Mark, LAA	153
Beltre,Adrian, Tex	95	Dunn,Adam, CWS	96	Granderson,Curtis, NYY	75	Reddick,Josh, Oak	151

2012 American League Batting Leaders

Intentional Walks

Fielder,Prince, Det	18
Cabrera,Miguel, Det	17
Pujols,Albert, LAA	16
Hamilton,Josh, Tex	13
Ortiz,David, Bos	13
Brantley,Michael, Cle	12
Encarnacion,Edwin, Tor	12
Cano,Robinson, NYY	10
Mauer,Joe, Min	10
2 tied with	9

BA Bases Loaded
(minimum 10 PA)

Seager,Kyle, Sea	.667
Ackley,Dustin, Sea	.538
Scott,Luke, TB	.500
Zobrist,Ben, TB	.500
Andrus,Elvis, Tex	.462
Gonzalez,Adrian, Bos	.455
Jennings,Desmond, TB	.429
Hosmer,Eric, KC	.417
Jackson,Austin, Det	.417
Granderson,Curtis, NYY	.400

Sacrifice Hits

Andrus,Elvis, Tex	17
Wilson,Bobby, LAA	13
Nix,Jayson, NYY	9
Weeks,Jemile, Oak	9
Beckham,Gordon, CWS	8
Escobar,Alcides, KC	8
Getz,Chris, KC	8
Podsednik,Scott, Bos	8
Rodriguez,Sean, TB	8
Ryan,Brendan, Sea	8

Sacrifice Flies

Teixeira,Mark, NYY	12
Morneau,Justin, Min	10
Beltre,Adrian, Tex	9
Hamilton,Josh, Tex	9
Doumit,Ryan, Min	8
Santana,Carlos, Cle	8
Upton,B.J., TB	8
7 tied with	7

BA Close & Late
(minimum 50 PA)

Teixeira,Mark, NYY	.390
Hunter,Torii, LAA	.350
Butler,Billy, KC	.340
Dirks,Andy, Det	.340
Cabrera,Miguel, Det	.337
Thames,Eric, Tor-Sea	.333
Carroll,Jamey, Min	.325
Escobar,Alcides, KC	.324
Cespedes,Yoenis, Oak	.324
Brantley,Michael, Cle	.318

Batting Average w/ RISP
(minimum 100 PA)

Gonzalez,Adrian, Bos	.398
Jaso,John, Sea	.378
Mauer,Joe, Min	.372
Cabrera,Miguel, Det	.356
Andrus,Elvis, Tex	.350
Rios,Alex, CWS	.348
Murphy,David, Tex	.347
Cespedes,Yoenis, Oak	.345
Hunter,Torii, LAA	.344
Fielder,Prince, Det	.338

SLG vs. LHP
(minimum 125 PA)

Encarnacion,Edwin, Tor	.669
Viciedo,Dayan, CWS	.642
Ross,Cody, Bos	.636
Butler,Billy, KC	.619
Ortiz,David, Bos	.608
Pujols,Albert, LAA	.581
Plouffe,Trevor, Min	.573
Willingham,Josh, Min	.564
Kinsler,Ian, Tex	.563
Gomes,Jonny, Oak	.561

SLG vs. RHP
(minimum 377 PA)

Cano,Robinson, NYY	.685
Cabrera,Miguel, Det	.652
Beltre,Adrian, Tex	.609
Hamilton,Josh, Tex	.602
Trout,Mike, LAA	.588
Fielder,Prince, Det	.579
Pierzynski,A.J., CWS	.536
Choo,Shin-Soo, Cle	.523
Encarnacion,Edwin, Tor	.520
Swisher,Nick, NYY	.517

Leadoff Hitters OBP
(minimum 150 PA)

Trout,Mike, LAA	.399
Markakis,Nick, Bal	.390
Choo,Shin-Soo, Cle	.389
Gordon,Alex, KC	.379
Jackson,Austin, Det	.378
Jeter,Derek, NYY	.364
De Aza,Alejandro, CWS	.349
Crisp,Coco, Oak	.348
Span,Denard, Min	.339
Lawrie,Brett, Tor	.327

Cleanup Hitters SLG
(minimum 150 PA)

Cano,Robinson, NYY	.624
Encarnacion,Edwin, Tor	.590
Beltre,Adrian, Tex	.569
Butler,Billy, KC	.543
Fielder,Prince, Det	.528
Willingham,Josh, Min	.526
Jones,Adam, Bal	.517
Gonzalez,Adrian, Bos	.496
Konerko,Paul, CWS	.482
Longoria,Evan, TB	.480

BA vs. LHP
(minimum 125 PA)

Keppinger,Jeff, TB	.376
Jeter,Derek, NYY	.364
Kinsler,Ian, Tex	.350
Viciedo,Dayan, CWS	.350
Hunter,Torii, LAA	.340
Carroll,Jamey, Min	.338
Aybar,Erick, LAA	.336
Young,Michael, Tex	.333
Butler,Billy, KC	.331
Wieters,Matt, Bal	.323

BA vs. RHP
(minimum 377 PA)

Cano,Robinson, NYY	.359
Trout,Mike, LAA	.346
Beltre,Adrian, Tex	.339
Mauer,Joe, Min	.336
Cabrera,Miguel, Det	.335
Fielder,Prince, Det	.328
Choo,Shin-Soo, Cle	.327
Gordon,Alex, KC	.320
Rios,Alex, CWS	.308
Konerko,Paul, CWS	.307

Home BA
(minimum 251 PA)

Beltre,Adrian, Tex	.346
Mauer,Joe, Min	.342
Fielder,Prince, Det	.337
Murphy,David, Tex	.335
Cabrera,Miguel, Det	.332
Span,Denard, Min	.332
Konerko,Paul, CWS	.325
Rios,Alex, CWS	.324
Butler,Billy, KC	.322
Cespedes,Yoenis, Oak	.319

Away BA
(minimum 251 PA)

Jeter,Derek, NYY	.347
Trout,Mike, LAA	.332
Cabrera,Miguel, Det	.327
Cano,Robinson, NYY	.321
Kendrick,Howie, LAA	.319
Hunter,Torii, LAA	.314
Brantley,Michael, Cle	.310
Butler,Billy, KC	.303
Jackson,Austin, Det	.297
Zobrist,Ben, TB	.297

OBP vs. LHP
(minimum 125 PA)

Cabrera,Miguel, Det	.441
Kinsler,Ian, Tex	.425
Butler,Billy, KC	.417
Encarnacion,Edwin, Tor	.417
Gomes,Jonny, Oak	.413
Rodriguez,Alex, NYY	.410
Carroll,Jamey, Min	.405
Wieters,Matt, Bal	.404
Hunter,Torii, LAA	.403
Keppinger,Jeff, TB	.402

OBP vs. RHP
(minimum 377 PA)

Fielder,Prince, Det	.439
Mauer,Joe, Min	.428
Cano,Robinson, NYY	.423
Trout,Mike, LAA	.410
Choo,Shin-Soo, Cle	.403
Gordon,Alex, KC	.398
Jackson,Austin, Det	.377
Beltre,Adrian, Tex	.375
Murphy,David, Tex	.375
Cabrera,Miguel, Det	.375

2012 American League Batting Leaders

Stolen Bases

Trout,Mike, LAA	49
Davis,Rajai, Tor	46
Revere,Ben, Min	40
Crisp,Coco, Oak	39
Escobar,Alcides, KC	35
Jennings,Desmond, TB	31
Kipnis,Jason, Cle	31
Upton,B.J., TB	31
Dyson,Jarrod, KC	30
Suzuki,Ichiro, Sea-NYY	29

Caught Stealing

Davis,Rajai, Tor	13
De Aza,Alejandro, CWS	12
Andrus,Elvis, Tex	10
Brantley,Michael, Cle	9
Jackson,Austin, Det	9
Kinsler,Ian, Tex	9
Revere,Ben, Min	9
Zobrist,Ben, TB	9
Lawrie,Brett, Tor	8
7 tied with	7

Highest SB Success Pct
(minimum 20 SBA)

Berry,Quintin, Det	100.0
Casilla,Alexi, Min	95.5
Jennings,Desmond, TB	93.9
Trout,Mike, LAA	90.7
Crisp,Coco, Oak	90.7
Escobar,Alcides, KC	87.5
Mastroianni,Darin, Min	87.5
Dyson,Jarrod, KC	85.7
Saunders,Michael, Sea	84.0
Upton,B.J., TB	83.8

Lowest SB Success Pct
(minimum 20 SBA)

Brantley,Michael, Cle	57.1
Jackson,Austin, Det	57.1
Zobrist,Ben, TB	60.9
Lawrie,Brett, Tor	61.9
Gentry,Craig, Tex	65.0
Andrus,Elvis, Tex	67.7
De Aza,Alejandro, CWS	68.4
Jones,Adam, Bal	69.6
3 tied with	70.0

Steals of Third

Davis,Rajai, Tor	17
Crisp,Coco, Oak	14
Mastroianni,Darin, Min	8
Escobar,Alcides, KC	7
Revere,Ben, Min	7
Cespedes,Yoenis, Oak	6
Suzuki,Ichiro, Sea-NYY	6
Trout,Mike, LAA	6
7 tied with	5

Grounded Into DP

Cabrera,Miguel, Det	28
Kendrick,Howie, LAA	26
Young,Michael, Tex	26
Jeter,Derek, NYY	24
Mauer,Joe, Min	23
Cano,Robinson, NYY	22
Escobar,Yunel, Tor	21
Hardy,J.J., Bal	21
Santana,Carlos, Cle	21
3 tied with	20

Grounded Into DP Pct
(minimum 50 GIDP Ops)

De Aza,Alejandro, CWS	1.47
Pennington,Cliff, Oak	1.59
Ackley,Dustin, Sea	3.09
Gomes,Jonny, Oak	3.13
Moustakas,Mike, KC	3.48
Jones,Andruw, NYY	3.51
Granderson,Curtis, NYY	3.57
Johnson,Elliot, TB	4.55
Encarnacion,Edwin, Tor	4.84
Ryan,Brendan, Sea	5.00

Hit By Pitch

Fielder,Prince, Det	17
Youkilis,Kevin, Bos-CWS	17
Choo,Shin-Soo, Cle	14
Willingham,Josh, Min	14
Jones,Adam, Bal	13
Pena,Carlos, TB	13
Encarnacion,Edwin, Tor	11
Gentry,Craig, Tex	10
Kinsler,Ian, Tex	10
Rodriguez,Alex, NYY	10

Pitches Seen

Granderson,Curtis, NYY	2921
Kinsler,Ian, Tex	2902
Gordon,Alex, KC	2894
Dunn,Adam, CWS	2876
Choo,Shin-Soo, Cle	2811
Hardy,J.J., Bal	2799
Andrus,Elvis, Tex	2778
Mauer,Joe, Min	2767
Jeter,Derek, NYY	2740
Zobrist,Ben, TB	2724

At Bats Per Home Run
(minimum 502 PA)

Encarnacion,Edwin, Tor	12.9
Hamilton,Josh, Tex	13.1
Dunn,Adam, CWS	13.1
Granderson,Curtis, NYY	13.9
Cabrera,Miguel, Det	14.1
Willingham,Josh, Min	14.8
Davis,Chris, Bal	15.6
Beltre,Adrian, Tex	16.8
Trumbo,Mark, LAA	17.0
Pierzynski,A.J., CWS	17.7

Highest GB/FB Ratio
(minimum 502 PA)

Revere,Ben, Min	4.61
Jeter,Derek, NYY	3.94
Carroll,Jamey, Min	2.81
Kendrick,Howie, LAA	2.81
Andrus,Elvis, Tex	2.72
Mauer,Joe, Min	2.35
Escobar,Alcides, KC	2.25
Escobar,Yunel, Tor	2.25
Span,Denard, Min	2.24
Young,Michael, Tex	2.22

Lowest GB/FB Ratio
(minimum 502 PA)

Reddick,Josh, Oak	0.59
Encarnacion,Edwin, Tor	0.67
Moustakas,Mike, KC	0.68
Granderson,Curtis, NYY	0.75
Dunn,Adam, CWS	0.78
Seager,Kyle, Sea	0.85
Ross,Cody, Bos	0.85
Pena,Carlos, TB	0.87
Reynolds,Mark, Bal	0.87
Willingham,Josh, Min	0.88

Pitches Per Plate App
(minimum 502 PA)

Dunn,Adam, CWS	4.43
Youkilis,Kevin, Bos-CWS	4.36
Mauer,Joe, Min	4.32
Santana,Carlos, Cle	4.27
Granderson,Curtis, NYY	4.27
Reynolds,Mark, Bal	4.27
Swisher,Nick, NYY	4.26
Willingham,Josh, Min	4.21
Encarnacion,Edwin, Tor	4.19
Jackson,Austin, Det	4.15

Pct Pitches Taken
(minimum 1500 Pitches)

Mauer,Joe, Min	65.2
Zobrist,Ben, TB	63.1
Youkilis,Kevin, Bos-CWS	63.1
Bautista,Jose, Tor	62.5
Carroll,Jamey, Min	62.0
Santana,Carlos, Cle	61.2
Andrus,Elvis, Tex	61.1
Avila,Alex, Det	60.8
Span,Denard, Min	60.7
Weeks,Jemile, Oak	60.7

Best BPS on OutZ
(minimum 502 PA)

Fielder,Prince, Det	.677
Cabrera,Miguel, Det	.670
Beltre,Adrian, Tex	.640
Mauer,Joe, Min	.632
Cespedes,Yoenis, Oak	.623
Cano,Robinson, NYY	.615
Butler,Billy, KC	.613
Pedroia,Dustin, Bos	.606
Murphy,David, Tex	.601
Morneau,Justin, Min	.590

Worst BPS on OutZ
(minimum 502 PA)

Youkilis,Kevin, Bos-CWS	.234
Dunn,Adam, CWS	.295
Pena,Carlos, TB	.319
De Aza,Alejandro, CWS	.321
Boesch,Brennan, Det	.325
Smoak,Justin, Sea	.326
Johnson,Kelly, Tor	.329
Reynolds,Mark, Bal	.336
Willingham,Josh, Min	.336
Trumbo,Mark, LAA	.346

2012 American League Batting Leaders

Best OPS vs Fastballs
(minimum 251 PA)

Cabrera,Miguel, Det	1.008
Butler,Billy, KC	.991
Encarnacion,Edwin, Tor	.972
Granderson,Curtis, NYY	.936
Hamilton,Josh, Tex	.930
Fielder,Prince, Det	.917
Morales,Kendrys, LAA	.915
Joyce,Matt, TB	.911
Jones,Adam, Bal	.910
Konerko,Paul, CWS	.910

Best OPS vs Curveballs
(minimum 50 PA)

Fielder,Prince, Det	1.272
Encarnacion,Edwin, Tor	1.202
Reynolds,Mark, Bal	1.181
Beltre,Adrian, Tex	1.130
Jackson,Austin, Det	1.100
Trumbo,Mark, LAA	.962
Kinsler,Ian, Tex	.940
Hamilton,Josh, Tex	.906
Morales,Kendrys, LAA	.905
Murphy,David, Tex	.886

Best OPS vs Changeups
(minimum 50 PA)

Trout,Mike, LAA	1.301
Cano,Robinson, NYY	1.244
Trumbo,Mark, LAA	1.224
Morneau,Justin, Min	1.176
Encarnacion,Edwin, Tor	1.103
Reddick,Josh, Oak	1.092
Rios,Alex, CWS	1.090
Viciedo,Dayan, CWS	1.090
Moreland,Mitch, Tex	1.086
Cabrera,Miguel, Det	1.018

Best OPS vs Sliders
(minimum 32 PA)

Moss,Brandon, Oak	1.293
Cain,Lorenzo, KC	1.163
Markakis,Nick, Bal	1.132
Bautista,Jose, Tor	1.088
Trout,Mike, LAA	1.068
Lind,Adam, Tor	1.059
Gonzalez,Adrian, Bos	1.042
Callaspo,Alberto, LAA	1.022
Dirks,Andy, Det	1.007
Pierzynski,A.J., CWS	1.006

OPS
(minimum 502 PA)

Cabrera,Miguel, Det	.999
Trout,Mike, LAA	.963
Encarnacion,Edwin, Tor	.941
Fielder,Prince, Det	.940
Hamilton,Josh, Tex	.930
Cano,Robinson, NYY	.929
Beltre,Adrian, Tex	.921
Willingham,Josh, Min	.890
Butler,Billy, KC	.882
2 tied with	.861

OPS First Half
(minimum 260 PA)

Hamilton,Josh, Tex	1.016
Ortiz,David, Bos	1.013
Trumbo,Mark, LAA	.965
Trout,Mike, LAA	.959
Cano,Robinson, NYY	.953
Jackson,Austin, Det	.953
Encarnacion,Edwin, Tor	.947
Cabrera,Miguel, Det	.938
Konerko,Paul, CWS	.932
Willingham,Josh, Min	.913

OPS Second Half
(minimum 201 PA)

Cabrera,Miguel, Det	1.074
Fielder,Prince, Det	1.006
Trout,Mike, LAA	.966
Beltre,Adrian, Tex	.965
Moss,Brandon, Oak	.951
Pujols,Albert, LAA	.935
Encarnacion,Edwin, Tor	.932
Butler,Billy, KC	.917
Cespedes,Yoenis, Oak	.909
Cano,Robinson, NYY	.902

OPS by Catchers
(minimum 251 PA)

Mauer,Joe, Min	.952
Napoli,Mike, Tex	.850
Pierzynski,A.J., CWS	.841
Perez,Salvador, KC	.795
Wieters,Matt, Bal	.784
Saltalamacchia,J, Bos	.755
Santana,Carlos, Cle	.737
Iannetta,Chris, LAA	.736
Avila,Alex, Det	.736
Martin,Russell, NYY	.726

OPS by First Basemen
(minimum 251 PA)

Encarnacion,Edwin, Tor	.966
Fielder,Prince, Det	.945
Pujols,Albert, LAA	.895
Konerko,Paul, CWS	.887
Gonzalez,Adrian, Bos	.844
Teixeira,Mark, NYY	.811
Morneau,Justin, Min	.792
Reynolds,Mark, Bal	.779
Moreland,Mitch, Tex	.760
Pena,Carlos, TB	.685

OPS by Second Basemen
(minimum 251 PA)

Cano,Robinson, NYY	.925
Pedroia,Dustin, Bos	.792
Kinsler,Ian, Tex	.747
Kendrick,Howie, LAA	.729
Kipnis,Jason, Cle	.728
Carroll,Jamey, Min	.693
Johnson,Kelly, Tor	.673
Beckham,Gordon, CWS	.668
Ackley,Dustin, Sea	.634
Weeks,Jemile, Oak	.615

OPS by Third Basemen
(minimum 251 PA)

Cabrera,Miguel, Det	1.003
Beltre,Adrian, Tex	.908
Middlebrooks,Will, Bos	.828
Plouffe,Trevor, Min	.795
Betemit,Wilson, Bal	.775
Rodriguez,Alex, NYY	.764
Seager,Kyle, Sea	.742
Lawrie,Brett, Tor	.734
Youkilis,Kevin, Bos-CWS	.713
Moustakas,Mike, KC	.708

OPS by Shortstops
(minimum 251 PA)

Cabrera,Asdrubal, Cle	.765
Jeter,Derek, NYY	.760
Aybar,Erick, LAA	.739
Andrus,Elvis, Tex	.727
Escobar,Alcides, KC	.721
Peralta,Jhonny, Det	.689
Johnson,Elliot, TB	.675
Hardy,J.J., Bal	.671
Aviles,Mike, Bos	.664
Ramirez,Alexei, CWS	.651

OPS by Left Fielders
(minimum 251 PA)

Willingham,Josh, Min	.909
Murphy,David, Tex	.861
Gordon,Alex, KC	.824
Nava,Daniel, Bos	.789
Viciedo,Dayan, CWS	.742
Jennings,Desmond, TB	.720
Ibanez,Raul, NYY	.716
Trumbo,Mark, LAA	.688
Davis,Rajai, Tor	.657

OPS by Center Fielders
(minimum 251 PA)

Hamilton,Josh, Tex	.979
Trout,Mike, LAA	.946
Jackson,Austin, Det	.858
Jones,Adam, Bal	.839
Granderson,Curtis, NYY	.810
Crisp,Coco, Oak	.779
Upton,B.J., TB	.761
De Aza,Alejandro, CWS	.759
Brantley,Michael, Cle	.757
Saunders,Michael, Sea	.745

OPS by Right Fielders
(minimum 251 PA)

Zobrist,Ben, TB	.911
Bautista,Jose, Tor	.883
Ross,Cody, Bos	.847
Rios,Alex, CWS	.847
Markakis,Nick, Bal	.841
Hunter,Torii, LAA	.814
Choo,Shin-Soo, Cle	.810
Swisher,Nick, NYY	.806
Cruz,Nelson, Tex	.761
Reddick,Josh, Oak	.760

OPS by Designated Hitters
(minimum 125 PA)

Ortiz,David, Bos	1.025
Encarnacion,Edwin, Tor	.923
Butler,Billy, KC	.873
Doumit,Ryan, Min	.858
Rodriguez,Alex, NYY	.837
Gomes,Jonny, Oak	.824
Jaso,John, Sea	.820
Davis,Chris, Bal	.818
Dunn,Adam, CWS	.772
Morales,Kendrys, LAA	.770

2012 American League Batting Leaders

OPS Batting Left vs. LHP		OPS Batting Left vs. RHP		OPS Batting Right vs. LHP		OPS Batting Right vs. RHP	
(minimum 125 PA)		(minimum 377 PA)		(minimum 125 PA)		(minimum 377 PA)	
Ortiz,David, Bos	.985	Cano,Robinson, NYY	1.108	Encarnacion,Edwin, Tor	1.086	Cabrera,Miguel, Det	1.027
Markakis,Nick, Bal	.877	Fielder,Prince, Det	1.017	Butler,Billy, KC	1.042	Trout,Mike, LAA	.999
Hamilton,Josh, Tex	.853	Hamilton,Josh, Tex	.965	Viciedo,Dayan, CWS	1.033	Beltre,Adrian, Tex	.985
Gonzalez,Adrian, Bos	.824	Choo,Shin-Soo, Cle	.926	Ross,Cody, Bos	1.010	Encarnacion,Edwin, Tor	.892
Fielder,Prince, Det	.808	Mauer,Joe, Min	.918	Kinsler,Ian, Tex	.988	Willingham,Josh, Min	.877
Saunders,Michael, Sea	.774	Gordon,Alex, KC	.908	Gomes,Jonny, Oak	.974	Cespedes,Yoenis, Oak	.864
Dunn,Adam, CWS	.767	Pierzynski,A.J., CWS	.874	Cruz,Nelson, Tex	.944	Konerko,Paul, CWS	.861
Granderson,Curtis, NYY	.762	Swisher,Nick, NYY	.873	Jeter,Derek, NYY	.941	Jackson,Austin, Det	.856
Mauer,Joe, Min	.754	Murphy,David, Tex	.862	Pujols,Albert, LAA	.926	Jones,Adam, Bal	.852
Reddick,Josh, Oak	.751	Granderson,Curtis, NYY	.839	Rodriguez,Alex, NYY	.924	Rios,Alex, CWS	.848

OPS vs. LHP		OPS vs. RHP		RC Per 27 Outs vs. LHP		RC Per 27 Outs vs. RHP	
(minimum 125 PA)		(minimum 377 PA)		(minimum 125 PA)		(minimum 377 PA)	
Encarnacion,Edwin, Tor	1.086	Cano,Robinson, NYY	1.108	Encarnacion,Edwin, Tor	10.2	Trout,Mike, LAA	9.9
Butler,Billy, KC	1.036	Cabrera,Miguel, Det	1.027	Gomes,Jonny, Oak	9.0	Cano,Robinson, NYY	9.0
Viciedo,Dayan, CWS	1.033	Fielder,Prince, Det	1.017	Ross,Cody, Bos	8.5	Mauer,Joe, Min	8.1
Ross,Cody, Bos	1.010	Trout,Mike, LAA	.999	Ortiz,David, Bos	8.0	Cabrera,Miguel, Det	8.0
Kinsler,Ian, Tex	.988	Beltre,Adrian, Tex	.985	Wieters,Matt, Bal	7.6	Beltre,Adrian, Tex	7.9
Ortiz,David, Bos	.985	Hamilton,Josh, Tex	.965	Viciedo,Dayan, CWS	7.6	Fielder,Prince, Det	7.7
Gomes,Jonny, Oak	.974	Choo,Shin-Soo, Cle	.926	Kinsler,Ian, Tex	7.6	Encarnacion,Edwin, Tor	7.4
Cruz,Nelson, Tex	.944	Mauer,Joe, Min	.918	Rodriguez,Alex, NYY	7.5	Hamilton,Josh, Tex	7.2
Jeter,Derek, NYY	.941	Gordon,Alex, KC	.908	Zobrist,Ben, TB	7.5	Choo,Shin-Soo, Cle	7.1
Pujols,Albert, LAA	.926	Encarnacion,Edwin, Tor	.892	Butler,Billy, KC	7.4	Swisher,Nick, NYY	7.1

Highest RBI %		Lowest RBI %		Highest Strikeout per PA		Lowest Strikeout per PA	
(minimum 502 PA)		(minimum 502 PA)		(minimum 502 PA)		(minimum 502 PA)	
Hamilton,Josh, Tex	47.69	Weeks,Jemile, Oak	14.91	Dunn,Adam, CWS	.342	Brantley,Michael, Cle	.092
Encarnacion,Edwin, Tor	47.13	Revere,Ben, Min	21.16	Pena,Carlos, TB	.303	Suzuki,Ichiro, Sea-NYY	.092
Cabrera,Miguel, Det	43.88	Francoeur,Jeff, KC	24.79	Davis,Chris, Bal	.301	Pedroia,Dustin, Bos	.096
Trout,Mike, LAA	43.07	Carroll,Jamey, Min	25.45	Reynolds,Mark, Bal	.296	Revere,Ben, Min	.098
Cespedes,Yoenis, Oak	41.88	Aybar,Erick, LAA	25.64	Granderson,Curtis, NYY	.285	Young,Michael, Tex	.108
Fielder,Prince, Det	41.35	Smoak,Justin, Sea	26.09	Johnson,Kelly, Tor	.274	Span,Denard, Min	.109
Willingham,Josh, Min	40.56	Escobar,Alcides, KC	26.36	Upton,B.J., TB	.267	Aybar,Erick, LAA	.110
Butler,Billy, KC	40.53	Escobar,Yunel, Tor	26.72	Trumbo,Mark, LAA	.261	Callaspo,Alberto, LAA	.113
Pujols,Albert, LAA	39.91	Span,Denard, Min	26.73	Hamilton,Josh, Tex	.255	Pujols,Albert, LAA	.113
Beltre,Adrian, Tex	39.86	Jennings,Desmond, TB	27.29	Ross,Cody, Bos	.244	Escobar,Yunel, Tor	.115

Home Runs At Home		Home Runs Away		Longest Avg Home Run		Shortest Avg Home Run	
				(min 10 over the wall)		(min 10 over the wall)	
Cabrera,Miguel, Det	28	Dunn,Adam, CWS	23	Cruz,Nelson, Tex	419	Callaspo,Alberto, LAA	376
Granderson,Curtis, NYY	26	Hamilton,Josh, Tex	21	Hamilton,Josh, Tex	416	Perez,Salvador, KC	376
Encarnacion,Edwin, Tor	23	Trumbo,Mark, LAA	20	Trumbo,Mark, LAA	415	Martin,Russell, NYY	377
Cano,Robinson, NYY	22	Encarnacion,Edwin, Tor	19	Encarnacion,Edwin, Tor	413	Crisp,Coco, Oak	379
Davis,Chris, Bal	22	Butler,Billy, KC	18	Dunn,Adam, CWS	413	Beckham,Gordon, CWS	380
Hamilton,Josh, Tex	22	Granderson,Curtis, NYY	17	Rodriguez,Alex, NYY	413	Betemit,Wilson, Bal	381
Willingham,Josh, Min	21	Jones,Adam, Bal	17	Hunter,Torii, LAA	411	Granderson,Curtis, NYY	383
Beltre,Adrian, Tex	20	4 tied with	16	Moreland,Mitch, Tex	410	Hardy,J.J., Bal	383
5 tied with	18			Trout,Mike, LAA	410	Markakis,Nick, Bal	385
				Moss,Brandon, Oak	409	Wells,Casper, Sea	385

2012 American League Batting Leaders

Under Age 26: AB Per HR
(minimum 502 PA)

Trout,Mike, LAA	18.6
Reddick,Josh, Oak	19.1
Viciedo,Dayan, CWS	20.2
Smoak,Justin, Sea	25.4
Saunders,Michael, Sea	26.7
Moustakas,Mike, KC	28.2
Seager,Kyle, Sea	29.7
Jackson,Austin, Det	33.9
Montero,Jesus, Sea	34.3
Hosmer,Eric, KC	38.2

Under Age 26: OPS
(minimum 502 PA)

Trout,Mike, LAA	.963
Jackson,Austin, Det	.856
Reddick,Josh, Oak	.768
Brantley,Michael, Cle	.750
Viciedo,Dayan, CWS	.744
Saunders,Michael, Sea	.738
Seager,Kyle, Sea	.738
Lawrie,Brett, Tor	.729
Andrus,Elvis, Tex	.727
Escobar,Alcides, KC	.721

Under Age 26: RC/27 Outs
(minimum 502 PA)

Trout,Mike, LAA	8.6
Jackson,Austin, Det	6.0
Seager,Kyle, Sea	5.1
Kipnis,Jason, Cle	5.1
Andrus,Elvis, Tex	5.0
Brantley,Michael, Cle	4.9
Lawrie,Brett, Tor	4.6
Saunders,Michael, Sea	4.6
Viciedo,Dayan, CWS	4.3
Revere,Ben, Min	4.3

Longest Home Run

Encarnacion,E, Tor, 9/1	488
Cruz,Nelson, Tex, 6/3	484
Hafner,Travis, Cle, 4/15	481
Cruz,Nelson, Tex, 8/1	470
Hamilton,Josh, Tex, 4/17	469
Encarnacion,E, Tor, 7/14	467
Cabrera,Miguel, Det, 6/2	466
Saltalamacchia,J, Bos, 5/20	466
Cruz,Nelson, Tex, 7/30	464
Moustakas,Mike, KC, 6/24	464

Swing and Miss %
(minimum 1500 Pitches Seen)

Hamilton,Josh, Tex	36.0
Pena,Carlos, TB	34.5
Reynolds,Mark, Bal	32.9
Dunn,Adam, CWS	31.7
Upton,B.J., TB	31.0
Saltalamacchia,J, Bos	30.9
Napoli,Mike, Tex	30.7
Trumbo,Mark, LAA	30.2
Johnson,Kelly, Tor	30.0
Davis,Chris, Bal	29.9

Highest First Swing %
(minimum 502 PA)

Hamilton,Josh, Tex	47.0
Upton,B.J., TB	43.5
Young,Delmon, Det	41.9
Davis,Chris, Bal	39.3
Jones,Adam, Bal	36.2
Morneau,Justin, Min	35.5
Cabrera,Asdrubal, Cle	34.7
Aybar,Erick, LAA	33.6
Jeter,Derek, NYY	33.4
Montero,Jesus, Sea	32.9

Lowest First Swing %
(minimum 502 PA)

Youkilis,Kevin, Bos-CWS	7.3
Mauer,Joe, Min	7.7
Trout,Mike, LAA	7.7
Hardy,J.J., Bal	8.1
Pedroia,Dustin, Bos	8.1
Revere,Ben, Min	8.8
Carroll,Jamey, Min	10.9
Teixeira,Mark, NYY	13.0
Weeks,Jemile, Oak	13.8
Ackley,Dustin, Sea	14.2

Home RC Per 27 Outs
(minimum 251 PA)

Encarnacion,Edwin, Tor	9.2
Fielder,Prince, Det	8.9
Cabrera,Miguel, Det	8.7
Cespedes,Yoenis, Oak	8.7
Willingham,Josh, Min	8.6
Murphy,David, Tex	8.2
Beltre,Adrian, Tex	8.0
Trout,Mike, LAA	7.8
Pierzynski,A.J., CWS	7.5
Mauer,Joe, Min	7.2

Road RC Per 27 Outs
(minimum 251 PA)

Trout,Mike, LAA	9.2
Encarnacion,Edwin, Tor	7.2
Mauer,Joe, Min	7.2
Zobrist,Ben, TB	7.1
Swisher,Nick, NYY	6.8
Butler,Billy, KC	6.7
Seager,Kyle, Sea	6.6
Hamilton,Josh, Tex	6.6
Cano,Robinson, NYY	6.4
Hunter,Torii, LAA	6.2

Lead Changing RBI

Cabrera,Miguel, Det	46
Beltre,Adrian, Tex	36
Jones,Adam, Bal	36
Willingham,Josh, Min	36
Fielder,Prince, Det	35
Butler,Billy, KC	34
Hamilton,Josh, Tex	34
Granderson,Curtis, NYY	32
Pujols,Albert, LAA	32
2 tied with	31

2012 National League Batting Leaders

Batting Average (minimum 502 PA)		On Base Percentage (minimum 502 PA)		Slugging Average (minimum 502 PA)		Home Runs	
Cabrera,Melky, SF	.346	Votto,Joey, Cin	.474	Stanton,Giancarlo, Mia	.608	Braun,Ryan, Mil	41
Posey,Buster, SF	.336	Posey,Buster, SF	.408	Braun,Ryan, Mil	.595	Stanton,Giancarlo, Mia	37
McCutchen,Andrew, Pit	.327	McCutchen,Andrew, Pit	.400	McCutchen,Andrew, Pit	.553	Bruce,Jay, Cin	34
Braun,Ryan, Mil	.319	Braun,Ryan, Mil	.391	Posey,Buster, SF	.549	LaRoche,Adam, Was	33
Molina,Yadier, StL	.315	Wright,David, NYM	.391	Ramirez,Aramis, Mil	.540	Beltran,Carlos, StL	32
Pacheco,Jordan, Col	.309	Montero,Miguel, Ari	.391	Craig,Allen, StL	.522	Davis,Ike, NYM	32
Craig,Allen, StL	.307	Fowler,Dexter, Col	.389	Hill,Aaron, Ari	.522	Soriano,Alfonso, ChC	32
Scutaro,Marco, Col-SF	.306	Holliday,Matt, StL	.379	Jones,Garrett, Pit	.516	Headley,Chase, SD	31
Wright,David, NYM	.306	Headley,Chase, SD	.376	Bruce,Jay, Cin	.514	McCutchen,Andrew, Pit	31
Jay,Jon, StL	.305	Jay,Jon, StL	.373	Desmond,Ian, Was	.511	3 tied with	30

Games		Plate Appearances		At Bats		Hits	
Castro,Starlin, ChC	162	Reyes,Jose, Mia	716	Castro,Starlin, ChC	646	McCutchen,Andrew, Pit	194
Headley,Chase, SD	161	Bourn,Michael, Atl	703	Reyes,Jose, Mia	642	Braun,Ryan, Mil	191
Espinosa,Danny, Was	160	Headley,Chase, SD	699	Rollins,Jimmy, Phi	632	Scutaro,Marco, Col-SF	190
Pence,Hunter, Phi-SF	160	Rollins,Jimmy, Phi	699	Bourn,Michael, Atl	624	Prado,Martin, Atl	186
Reyes,Jose, Mia	160	Castro,Starlin, ChC	691	Scutaro,Marco, Col-SF	620	Hill,Aaron, Ari	184
Heyward,Jason, Atl	158	Prado,Martin, Atl	690	Pence,Hunter, Phi-SF	617	Reyes,Jose, Mia	184
Holliday,Matt, StL	157	Holliday,Matt, StL	688	Prado,Martin, Atl	617	Castro,Starlin, ChC	183
McCutchen,Andrew, Pit	157	Pence,Hunter, Phi-SF	688	Hill,Aaron, Ari	609	Posey,Buster, SF	178
Ramirez,Hanley, Mia-LAD	157	Scutaro,Marco, Col-SF	683	Pagan,Angel, SF	605	Wright,David, NYM	178
Weeks,Rickie, Mil	157	2 tied with	677	2 tied with	604	Holliday,Matt, StL	177

Singles		Doubles		Triples		Total Bases	
Scutaro,Marco, Col-SF	147	Ramirez,Aramis, Mil	50	Pagan,Angel, SF	15	Braun,Ryan, Mil	356
Castro,Starlin, ChC	128	Hill,Aaron, Ari	44	Castro,Starlin, ChC	12	McCutchen,Andrew, Pit	328
McCutchen,Andrew, Pit	128	Votto,Joey, Cin	44	Reyes,Jose, Mia	12	Hill,Aaron, Ari	318
Prado,Martin, Atl	128	Goldschmidt,Paul, Ari	43	Fowler,Dexter, Col	11	Ramirez,Aramis, Mil	308
Bourn,Michael, Atl	126	Prado,Martin, Atl	42	Bourn,Michael, Atl	10	Headley,Chase, SD	301
Reyes,Jose, Mia	124	Wright,David, NYM	41	Cabrera,Melky, SF	10	Holliday,Matt, StL	298
Altuve,Jose, Hou	122	Murphy,Daniel, NYM	40	Colvin,Tyler, Col	10	LaRoche,Adam, Was	291
Murphy,Daniel, NYM	117	Alonso,Yonder, SD	39	Harper,Bryce, Was	9	Posey,Buster, SF	291
3 tied with	114	Posey,Buster, SF	39	DeJesus,David, ChC	8	Bruce,Jay, Cin	288
		Pagan,Angel, SF	38	Venable,Will, SD	8	Wright,David, NYM	286

Runs Scored		RBI		Walks		Strikeouts	
Braun,Ryan, Mil	108	Headley,Chase, SD	115	Uggla,Dan, Atl	94	Espinosa,Danny, Was	189
McCutchen,Andrew, Pit	107	Braun,Ryan, Mil	112	Votto,Joey, Cin	94	Alvarez,Pedro, Pit	180
Upton,Justin, Ari	107	Soriano,Alfonso, ChC	108	Headley,Chase, SD	86	Weeks,Rickie, Mil	169
Rollins,Jimmy, Phi	102	Ramirez,Aramis, Mil	105	Wright,David, NYM	81	Uggla,Dan, Atl	168
Harper,Bryce, Was	98	Pence,Hunter, Phi-SF	104	Holliday,Matt, StL	75	Stubbs,Drew, Cin	166
Bourn,Michael, Atl	96	Posey,Buster, SF	103	Weeks,Rickie, Mil	74	Headley,Chase, SD	157
Headley,Chase, SD	95	Holliday,Matt, StL	102	Montero,Miguel, Ari	73	Bourn,Michael, Atl	155
Holliday,Matt, StL	95	LaRoche,Adam, Was	100	Bourn,Michael, Atl	70	Bruce,Jay, Cin	155
Pagan,Angel, SF	95	Bruce,Jay, Cin	99	McCutchen,Andrew, Pit	70	Soriano,Alfonso, ChC	153
3 tied with	93	Beltran,Carlos, StL	97	Posey,Buster, SF	69	Heyward,Jason, Atl	152

2012 National League Batting Leaders

Intentional Walks		BA Bases Loaded		Sacrifice Hits		Sacrifice Flies	
		(minimum 10 PA)					
Votto,Joey, Cin	18	Lombardozzi,Steve, Was	.600	Cueto,Johnny, Cin	17	Freeman,Freddie, Atl	9
Wright,David, NYM	16	Hart,Corey, Mil	.545	Pierre,Juan, Phi	17	Goldschmidt,Paul, Ari	9
Beltran,Carlos, StL	15	Morse,Michael, Was	.545	Kershaw,Clayton, LAD	14	LaRoche,Adam, Was	9
Braun,Ryan, Mil	15	Holliday,Matt, StL	.500	Capuano,Chris, LAD	13	Posey,Buster, SF	9
Hanigan,Ryan, Cin	13	Stanton,Giancarlo, Mia	.500	Lohse,Kyle, StL	12	Prado,Martin, Atl	9
McCutchen,Andrew, Pit	13	Uggla,Dan, Atl	.471	9 tied with	10	Scutaro,Marco, Col-SF	9
Bruce,Jay, Cin	11	Lucroy,Jonathan, Mil	.455			Walker,Neil, Pit	8
Ellis,A.J., LAD	11	Ramirez,Hanley, Mia-LAD	.455			7 tied with	7
Gonzalez,Carlos, Col	11	Barmes,Clint, Pit	.438				
3 tied with	9	Montero,Miguel, Ari	.417				

BA Close & Late		Batting Average w/ RISP		SLG vs. LHP		SLG vs. RHP	
(minimum 50 PA)		(minimum 100 PA)		(minimum 125 PA)		(minimum 377 PA)	
Cabrera,Melky, SF	.394	Craig,Allen, StL	.400	Posey,Buster, SF	.793	Heyward,Jason, Atl	.563
Reyes,Jose, Mia	.386	Lucroy,Jonathan, Mil	.389	Braun,Ryan, Mil	.774	Jones,Garrett, Pit	.556
McCutchen,Andrew, Pit	.370	Votto,Joey, Cin	.370	Kemp,Matt, LAD	.677	Ethier,Andre, LAD	.546
Amarista,Alexi, SD	.358	Ruiz,Carlos, Phi	.368	McCutchen,Andrew, Pit	.677	Bruce,Jay, Cin	.542
Cruz,Luis, LAD	.351	Nelson,Chris, Col	.363	Ramirez,Aramis, Mil	.669	Hill,Aaron, Ari	.539
Phillips,Brandon, Cin	.349	Venable,Will, SD	.353	Cabrera,Melky, SF	.667	Braun,Ryan, Mil	.538
Nelson,Chris, Col	.345	Montero,Miguel, Ari	.345	Stanton,Giancarlo, Mia	.655	Davis,Ike, NYM	.523
Pierre,Juan, Phi	.328	Posey,Buster, SF	.340	Goldschmidt,Paul, Ari	.645	McCutchen,Andrew, Pit	.518
Votto,Joey, Cin	.322	Colvin,Tyler, Col	.336	Craig,Allen, StL	.630	LaRoche,Adam, Was	.511
Torres,Andres, NYM	.321	Johnson,Chris, Hou-Ari	.336	Holliday,Matt, StL	.613	Harper,Bryce, Was	.509

Leadoff Hitters OBP		Cleanup Hitters SLG		BA vs. LHP		BA vs. RHP	
(minimum 150 PA)		(minimum 150 PA)		(minimum 125 PA)		(minimum 377 PA)	
Werth,Jayson, Was	.388	Davis,Ike, NYM	.602	Posey,Buster, SF	.433	Ethier,Andre, LAD	.325
Fowler,Dexter, Col	.384	Stanton,Giancarlo, Mia	.554	Cabrera,Melky, SF	.395	Hill,Aaron, Ari	.316
Parra,Gerardo, Ari	.374	Posey,Buster, SF	.551	McCutchen,Andrew, Pit	.392	Scutaro,Marco, Col-SF	.309
Jay,Jon, StL	.362	Kubel,Jason, Ari	.541	Braun,Ryan, Mil	.363	McCutchen,Andrew, Pit	.309
DeJesus,David, ChC	.358	Ramirez,Aramis, Mil	.540	Kemp,Matt, LAD	.363	Molina,Yadier, StL	.307
Denorfia,Chris, SD	.354	Cuddyer,Michael, Col	.531	Altuve,Jose, Hou	.359	Braun,Ryan, Mil	.305
Aoki,Norichika, Mil	.353	Jones,Garrett, Pit	.526	Craig,Allen, StL	.354	Wright,David, NYM	.300
Bourn,Michael, Atl	.346	Tulowitzki,Troy, Col	.512	Pacheco,Jordan, Col	.351	Heyward,Jason, Atl	.300
Furcal,Rafael, StL	.341	Quentin,Carlos, SD	.507	Goldschmidt,Paul, Ari	.343	Montero,Miguel, Ari	.299
Blanco,Gregor, SF	.340	Hairston,Scott, NYM	.506	Molina,Yadier, StL	.342	Aoki,Norichika, Mil	.299

Home BA		Away BA		OBP vs. LHP		OBP vs. RHP	
(minimum 251 PA)		(minimum 251 PA)		(minimum 125 PA)		(minimum 377 PA)	
Jay,Jon, StL	.384	Cabrera,Melky, SF	.367	Posey,Buster, SF	.470	Montero,Miguel, Ari	.414
Gonzalez,Carlos, Col	.368	Posey,Buster, SF	.330	McCutchen,Andrew, Pit	.464	Headley,Chase, SD	.400
Pacheco,Jordan, Col	.345	McCutchen,Andrew, Pit	.326	Cabrera,Melky, SF	.444	Ethier,Andre, LAD	.398
Posey,Buster, SF	.343	Braun,Ryan, Mil	.325	Braun,Ryan, Mil	.435	Posey,Buster, SF	.382
Fowler,Dexter, Col	.332	Wright,David, NYM	.318	Wright,David, NYM	.428	Ellis,A.J., LAD	.382
Ethier,Andre, LAD	.331	Goldschmidt,Paul, Ari	.315	Kemp,Matt, LAD	.428	McCutchen,Andrew, Pit	.381
Molina,Yadier, StL	.331	Walker,Neil, Pit	.305	Goldschmidt,Paul, Ari	.423	Braun,Ryan, Mil	.377
McCutchen,Andrew, Pit	.329	Jones,Garrett, Pit	.303	Votto,Joey, Cin	.413	Wright,David, NYM	.374
Scutaro,Marco, Col-SF	.324	Headley,Chase, SD	.300	Molina,Yadier, StL	.408	Aoki,Norichika, Mil	.372
Craig,Allen, StL	.324	Molina,Yadier, StL	.300	Holliday,Matt, StL	.408	Heyward,Jason, Atl	.372

2012 National League Batting Leaders

Stolen Bases		Caught Stealing		Highest SB Success Pct (minimum 20 SBA)		Lowest SB Success Pct (minimum 20 SBA)	
Cabrera,Everth, SD	44	Bourn,Michael, Atl	13	Cabrera,Everth, SD	91.7	Tabata,Jose, Pit	40.0
Bourn,Michael, Atl	42	Castro,Starlin, ChC	13	Bonifacio,Emilio, Mia	90.9	Wright,David, NYM	60.0
Reyes,Jose, Mia	40	McCutchen,Andrew, Pit	12	Campana,Tony, ChC	90.9	McCutchen,Andrew, Pit	62.5
Victorino,Shane, Phi-LAD	39	Tabata,Jose, Pit	12	Victorino,Shane, Phi-LAD	86.7	Parra,Gerardo, Ari	62.5
Gomez,Carlos, Mil	37	Altuve,Jose, Hou	11	Gomez,Carlos, Mil	86.0	Ruggiano,Justin, Mia	63.6
Pierre,Juan, Phi	37	Reyes,Jose, Mia	11	Goldschmidt,Paul, Ari	85.7	Castro,Starlin, ChC	65.8
Altuve,Jose, Hou	33	Bloomquist,Willie, Ari	10	Rollins,Jimmy, Phi	85.7	Upton,Justin, Ari	69.2
Gordon,Dee, LAD	32	Gordon,Dee, LAD	10	Pierre,Juan, Phi	84.1	Heyward,Jason, Atl	72.4
6 tied with	30	Wright,David, NYM	10	Blanco,Gregor, SF	81.3	Jay,Jon, StL	73.1
		2 tied with	9	2 tied with	81.1	Headley,Chase, SD	73.9

Steals of Third		Grounded Into DP		Grounded Into DP Pct (minimum 50 GIDP Ops)		Hit By Pitch	
Rollins,Jimmy, Phi	12	Zimmerman,Ryan, Was	20	Blanco,Gregor, SF	0.00	Quentin,Carlos, SD	17
Cabrera,Everth, SD	11	Freese,David, StL	19	Bourn,Michael, Atl	2.38	Ruiz,Carlos, Phi	16
Campana,Tony, ChC	11	Phillips,Brandon, Cin	19	Stubbs,Drew, Cin	2.74	Jay,Jon, StL	15
Reyes,Jose, Mia	11	Posey,Buster, SF	19	Jones,Garrett, Pit	2.78	Aoki,Norichika, Mil	13
Pierre,Juan, Phi	10	Prado,Martin, Atl	19	Guzman,Jesus, SD	2.94	Espinosa,Danny, Was	13
Aoki,Norichika, Mil	9	Johnson,Chris, Hou-Ari	18	Belt,Brandon, SF	3.03	Weeks,Rickie, Mil	13
Bourn,Michael, Atl	9	Martinez,J.D., Hou	18	Heyward,Jason, Atl	3.45	Montero,Miguel, Ari	12
Braun,Ryan, Mil	7	Soriano,Alfonso, ChC	18	Venable,Will, SD	3.70	Ramirez,Aramis, Mil	12
6 tied with	6	4 tied with	17	Victorino,Shane, Phi-LAD	4.10	Utley,Chase, Phi	12
				Crawford,Brandon, SF	4.21	2 tied with	11

Pitches Seen		At Bats Per Home Run (minimum 502 PA)		Highest GB/FB Ratio (minimum 502 PA)		Lowest GB/FB Ratio (minimum 502 PA)	
Bourn,Michael, Atl	2917	Braun,Ryan, Mil	14.6	Jay,Jon, StL	3.06	Uggla,Dan, Atl	0.72
Headley,Chase, SD	2835	Davis,Ike, NYM	16.2	Bourn,Michael, Atl	2.19	Kubel,Jason, Ari	0.76
Weeks,Rickie, Mil	2761	Bruce,Jay, Cin	16.5	Murphy,Daniel, NYM	2.03	LaRoche,Adam, Was	0.76
Prado,Martin, Atl	2712	Kubel,Jason, Ari	16.9	Aoki,Norichika, Mil	2.00	Hill,Aaron, Ari	0.77
Ramirez,Hanley, Mia-LAD	2691	Beltran,Carlos, StL	17.1	Furcal,Rafael, StL	1.99	Bruce,Jay, Cin	0.80
Holliday,Matt, StL	2677	LaRoche,Adam, Was	17.3	Freese,David, StL	1.98	Soriano,Alfonso, ChC	0.82
Pence,Hunter, Phi-SF	2638	Alvarez,Pedro, Pit	17.5	Maybin,Cameron, SD	1.95	Ramirez,Aramis, Mil	0.91
Uggla,Dan, Atl	2633	Soriano,Alfonso, ChC	17.5	Altuve,Jose, Hou	1.94	Rollins,Jimmy, Phi	0.95
Heyward,Jason, Atl	2624	Jones,Garrett, Pit	17.6	Gonzalez,Carlos, Col	1.66	Jones,Garrett, Pit	0.96
LaRoche,Adam, Was	2616	Hart,Corey, Mil	18.7	Prado,Martin, Atl	1.65	Davis,Ike, NYM	0.97

Pitches Per Plate App (minimum 502 PA)		Pct Pitches Taken (minimum 1500 Pitches)		Best BPS on OutZ (minimum 502 PA)		Worst BPS on OutZ (minimum 502 PA)	
Ellis,A.J., LAD	4.44	Votto,Joey, Cin	63.5	Braun,Ryan, Mil	.737	Weeks,Rickie, Mil	.200
Posey,Buster, SF	4.26	Ellis,A.J., LAD	63.3	Molina,Yadier, StL	.709	Stubbs,Drew, Cin	.289
Kubel,Jason, Ari	4.25	Prado,Martin, Atl	62.5	Reyes,Jose, Mia	.685	Barney,Darwin, ChC	.295
Uggla,Dan, Atl	4.18	Duda,Lucas, NYM	61.0	Posey,Buster, SF	.653	Bruce,Jay, Cin	.318
Bourn,Michael, Atl	4.15	Weeks,Rickie, Mil	60.1	Pacheco,Jordan, Col	.643	Freeman,Freddie, Atl	.319
Weeks,Rickie, Mil	4.08	Rollins,Jimmy, Phi	59.9	Prado,Martin, Atl	.632	Davis,Ike, NYM	.343
DeJesus,David, ChC	4.07	Torres,Andres, NYM	59.8	McCutchen,Andrew, Pit	.621	Alonso,Yonder, SD	.349
Headley,Chase, SD	4.06	Werth,Jayson, Was	59.8	Zimmerman,Ryan, Was	.618	Maybin,Cameron, SD	.355
Davis,Ike, NYM	4.05	DeJesus,David, ChC	59.6	Hill,Aaron, Ari	.577	Uggla,Dan, Atl	.356
LaRoche,Adam, Was	4.04	Ellis,Mark, LAD	59.6	Ramirez,Aramis, Mil	.571	Alvarez,Pedro, Pit	.372

2012 National League Batting Leaders

Best OPS vs Fastballs	
(minimum 251 PA)	
McCutchen,Andrew, Pit	1.034
Kemp,Matt, LAD	1.018
Posey,Buster, SF	1.001
Braun,Ryan, Mil	1.000
Jones,Garrett, Pit	.992
Soriano,Alfonso, ChC	.982
Molina,Yadier, StL	.973
Ramirez,Aramis, Mil	.960
Colvin,Tyler, Col	.959
Headley,Chase, SD	.947

Best OPS vs Curveballs	
(minimum 50 PA)	
Holliday,Matt, StL	1.330
Braun,Ryan, Mil	1.178
Alonso,Yonder, SD	.973
Frazier,Todd, Cin	.950
Craig,Allen, StL	.948
Weeks,Rickie, Mil	.909
Hart,Corey, Mil	.906
Ramirez,Aramis, Mil	.892
Walker,Neil, Pit	.889
Cabrera,Melky, SF	.883

Best OPS vs Changeups	
(minimum 50 PA)	
Posey,Buster, SF	1.460
Votto,Joey, Cin	1.131
Bruce,Jay, Cin	1.127
Hart,Corey, Mil	1.061
Wright,David, NYM	1.018
Headley,Chase, SD	.979
Goldschmidt,Paul, Ari	.974
Pagan,Angel, SF	.944
Cabrera,Melky, SF	.943
2 tied with	.909

Best OPS vs Sliders	
(minimum 32 PA)	
Bernadina,Roger, Was	1.098
Ruiz,Carlos, Phi	1.091
Cuddyer,Michael, Col	1.029
Hill,Aaron, Ari	1.023
Ethier,Andre, LAD	1.018
Rolen,Scott, Cin	.954
Ruggiano,Justin, Mia	.954
Maldonado,Martin, Mil	.951
LaRoche,Adam, Was	.942
Amarista,Alexi, SD	.935

OPS	
(minimum 502 PA)	
Braun,Ryan, Mil	.987
Posey,Buster, SF	.957
McCutchen,Andrew, Pit	.953
Ramirez,Aramis, Mil	.901
Wright,David, NYM	.883
Hill,Aaron, Ari	.882
Gonzalez,Carlos, Col	.881
Holliday,Matt, StL	.877
Craig,Allen, StL	.876
Headley,Chase, SD	.875

OPS First Half	
(minimum 260 PA)	
Votto,Joey, Cin	1.087
McCutchen,Andrew, Pit	1.039
Wright,David, NYM	1.004
Ruiz,Carlos, Phi	.995
Braun,Ryan, Mil	.990
Gonzalez,Carlos, Col	.967
Fowler,Dexter, Col	.937
Beltran,Carlos, StL	.924
Goldschmidt,Paul, Ari	.920
Stanton,Giancarlo, Mia	.919

OPS Second Half	
(minimum 201 PA)	
Posey,Buster, SF	1.102
Ramirez,Aramis, Mil	.990
Braun,Ryan, Mil	.983
Headley,Chase, SD	.978
Ludwick,Ryan, Cin	.959
Zimmerman,Ryan, Was	.945
Hill,Aaron, Ari	.906
Molina,Yadier, StL	.894
Davis,Ike, NYM	.888
Rosario,Wilin, Col	.881

OPS by Catchers	
(minimum 251 PA)	
Ruiz,Carlos, Phi	.941
Posey,Buster, SF	.937
Molina,Yadier, StL	.874
Lucroy,Jonathan, Mil	.873
Rosario,Wilin, Col	.841
Montero,Miguel, Ari	.829
Ellis,A.J., LAD	.785
McKenry,Michael, Pit	.782
Castro,Jason, Hou	.734
McCann,Brian, Atl	.718

OPS by First Basemen	
(minimum 251 PA)	
Votto,Joey, Cin	1.036
Goldschmidt,Paul, Ari	.861
Craig,Allen, StL	.861
LaRoche,Adam, Was	.851
Hart,Corey, Mil	.831
Jones,Garrett, Pit	.810
Rizzo,Anthony, ChC	.810
Freeman,Freddie, Atl	.799
Belt,Brandon, SF	.774
Davis,Ike, NYM	.772

OPS by Second Basemen	
(minimum 251 PA)	
Hill,Aaron, Ari	.880
Utley,Chase, Phi	.792
Walker,Neil, Pit	.770
Phillips,Brandon, Cin	.750
Infante,Omar, Mia	.749
Altuve,Jose, Hou	.739
Uggla,Dan, Atl	.735
Weeks,Rickie, Mil	.730
Scutaro,Marco, Col-SF	.728
Forsythe,Logan, SD	.725

OPS by Third Basemen	
(minimum 251 PA)	
Ramirez,Aramis, Mil	.906
Wright,David, NYM	.889
Headley,Chase, SD	.876
Freese,David, StL	.846
Jones,Chipper, Atl	.826
Zimmerman,Ryan, Was	.822
Frazier,Todd, Cin	.819
Nelson,Chris, Col	.806
Sandoval,Pablo, SF	.798
Johnson,Chris, Hou-Ari	.793

OPS by Shortstops	
(minimum 251 PA)	
Desmond,Ian, Was	.845
Reyes,Jose, Mia	.780
Lowrie,Jed, Hou	.764
Castro,Starlin, ChC	.753
Bloomquist,Willie, Ari	.746
Rollins,Jimmy, Phi	.746
Cozart,Zack, Cin	.689
Tejada,Ruben, NYM	.687
Furcal,Rafael, StL	.674
Crawford,Brandon, SF	.646

OPS by Left Fielders	
(minimum 251 PA)	
Braun,Ryan, Mil	.989
Cabrera,Melky, SF	.909
Gonzalez,Carlos, Col	.888
Quentin,Carlos, SD	.885
Holliday,Matt, StL	.872
Ludwick,Ryan, Cin	.863
Kubel,Jason, Ari	.849
Prado,Martin, Atl	.839
Soriano,Alfonso, ChC	.800
Pierre,Juan, Phi	.731

OPS by Center Fielders	
(minimum 251 PA)	
McCutchen,Andrew, Pit	.955
Kemp,Matt, LAD	.908
Fowler,Dexter, Col	.853
Harper,Bryce, Was	.851
Pagan,Angel, SF	.779
Jay,Jon, StL	.774
Gomez,Carlos, Mil	.762
Bourn,Michael, Atl	.740
Young,Chris, Ari	.737
Victorino,Shane, Phi-LAD	.707

OPS by Right Fielders	
(minimum 251 PA)	
Stanton,Giancarlo, Mia	.983
Bruce,Jay, Cin	.839
Beltran,Carlos, StL	.837
Heyward,Jason, Atl	.823
Venable,Will, SD	.823
Ethier,Andre, LAD	.818
Cuddyer,Michael, Col	.808
Denorfia,Chris, SD	.806
Aoki,Norichika, Mil	.789
Upton,Justin, Ari	.785

OPS by Pitchers	
(minimum 50 PA)	
Leake,Mike, Cin	.763
Strasburg,Stephen, Was	.759
Hamels,Cole, Phi	.560
Zimmermann,Jordan, Was	.527
Hudson,Tim, Atl	.523
Niese,Jon, NYM	.513
Wood,Travis, ChC	.500
Jackson,Edwin, Was	.495
Latos,Mat, Cin	.475
Kershaw,Clayton, LAD	.454

2012 National League Batting Leaders

OPS Batting Left vs. LHP
(minimum 125 PA)

Votto,Joey, Cin	.887
LaRoche,Adam, Was	.825
Belt,Brandon, SF	.768
Montero,Miguel, Ari	.767
Bruce,Jay, Cin	.754
Gonzalez,Carlos, Col	.742
Kubel,Jason, Ari	.736
Bourn,Michael, Atl	.728
Harper,Bryce, Was	.715
Freeman,Freddie, Atl	.714

OPS Batting Left vs. RHP
(minimum 377 PA)

Ethier,Andre, LAD	.945
Heyward,Jason, Atl	.934
Headley,Chase, SD	.918
Jones,Garrett, Pit	.888
Bruce,Jay, Cin	.879
Harper,Bryce, Was	.869
Davis,Ike, NYM	.868
LaRoche,Adam, Was	.864
Montero,Miguel, Ari	.859
Alvarez,Pedro, Pit	.833

OPS Batting Right vs. LHP
(minimum 125 PA)

Posey,Buster, SF	1.262
Braun,Ryan, Mil	1.208
McCutchen,Andrew, Pit	1.140
Cabrera,Melky, SF	1.111
Kemp,Matt, LAD	1.105
Goldschmidt,Paul, Ari	1.068
Ramirez,Aramis, Mil	1.049
Stanton,Giancarlo, Mia	1.024
Holliday,Matt, StL	1.021
Molina,Yadier, StL	1.021

OPS Batting Right vs. RHP
(minimum 377 PA)

Braun,Ryan, Mil	.915
Hill,Aaron, Ari	.901
McCutchen,Andrew, Pit	.900
Wright,David, NYM	.867
Ramirez,Aramis, Mil	.853
Molina,Yadier, StL	.833
Desmond,Ian, Was	.828
Craig,Allen, StL	.827
Holliday,Matt, StL	.827
Hart,Corey, Mil	.825

OPS vs. LHP
(minimum 125 PA)

Posey,Buster, SF	1.262
Braun,Ryan, Mil	1.208
McCutchen,Andrew, Pit	1.140
Cabrera,Melky, SF	1.111
Kemp,Matt, LAD	1.105
Goldschmidt,Paul, Ari	1.068
Ramirez,Aramis, Mil	1.049
Stanton,Giancarlo, Mia	1.024
Holliday,Matt, StL	1.021
Molina,Yadier, StL	1.021

OPS vs. RHP
(minimum 377 PA)

Ethier,Andre, LAD	.945
Heyward,Jason, Atl	.934
Braun,Ryan, Mil	.915
Headley,Chase, SD	.906
Hill,Aaron, Ari	.901
McCutchen,Andrew, Pit	.900
Jones,Garrett, Pit	.888
Bruce,Jay, Cin	.879
Harper,Bryce, Was	.869
Davis,Ike, NYM	.868

RC Per 27 Outs vs. LHP
(minimum 125 PA)

Posey,Buster, SF	13.9
McCutchen,Andrew, Pit	13.8
Kemp,Matt, LAD	10.4
Cabrera,Melky, SF	10.4
Braun,Ryan, Mil	10.2
Molina,Yadier, StL	9.4
Goldschmidt,Paul, Ari	9.3
Stanton,Giancarlo, Mia	8.6
Craig,Allen, StL	7.8
Ramirez,Aramis, Mil	7.7

RC Per 27 Outs vs. RHP
(minimum 377 PA)

Ethier,Andre, LAD	8.2
Montero,Miguel, Ari	7.5
Headley,Chase, SD	7.1
Jones,Garrett, Pit	7.0
Braun,Ryan, Mil	7.0
Heyward,Jason, Atl	6.9
Craig,Allen, StL	6.6
McCutchen,Andrew, Pit	6.4
Wright,David, NYM	6.3
DeJesus,David, ChC	6.2

Highest RBI %
(minimum 502 PA)

Jones,Garrett, Pit	44.08
Braun,Ryan, Mil	43.73
Craig,Allen, StL	42.46
McCutchen,Andrew, Pit	42.33
Posey,Buster, SF	41.28
Headley,Chase, SD	41.25
Soriano,Alfonso, ChC	41.14
Ramirez,Aramis, Mil	40.90
Montero,Miguel, Ari	40.09
Beltran,Carlos, StL	39.32

Lowest RBI %
(minimum 502 PA)

Cozart,Zack, Cin	20.95
Altuve,Jose, Hou	24.98
Maybin,Cameron, SD	25.06
Barney,Darwin, ChC	25.51
Espinosa,Danny, Was	25.65
Stubbs,Drew, Cin	27.12
Alonso,Yonder, SD	27.80
Reyes,Jose, Mia	28.76
Weeks,Rickie, Mil	28.87
Furcal,Rafael, StL	29.29

Highest Strikeout per PA
(minimum 502 PA)

Alvarez,Pedro, Pit	.307
Stubbs,Drew, Cin	.305
Espinosa,Danny, Was	.287
Uggla,Dan, Atl	.267
Kubel,Jason, Ari	.264
Johnson,Chris, Hou-Ari	.250
Weeks,Rickie, Mil	.250
Soriano,Alfonso, ChC	.249
Bruce,Jay, Cin	.245
Hart,Corey, Mil	.243

Lowest Strikeout per PA
(minimum 502 PA)

Scutaro,Marco, Col-SF	.072
Reyes,Jose, Mia	.078
Lee,Carlos, Hou-Mia	.080
Aoki,Norichika, Mil	.094
Molina,Yadier, StL	.098
Barney,Darwin, ChC	.099
Prado,Martin, Atl	.100
Furcal,Rafael, StL	.107
Altuve,Jose, Hou	.117
Victorino,Shane, Phi-LAD	.120

Home Runs At Home

Braun,Ryan, Mil	24
Hart,Corey, Mil	22
Bruce,Jay, Cin	21
Beltran,Carlos, StL	20
Kubel,Jason, Ari	18
Rosario,Wilin, Col	18
LaRoche,Adam, Was	17
4 tied with	16

Home Runs Away

Davis,Ike, NYM	21
Stanton,Giancarlo, Mia	21
Alvarez,Pedro, Pit	18
Headley,Chase, SD	18
Heyward,Jason, Atl	18
Braun,Ryan, Mil	17
Posey,Buster, SF	17
Soriano,Alfonso, ChC	17
LaRoche,Adam, Was	16
McCutchen,Andrew, Pit	16

Longest Avg Home Run
(min 10 over the wall)

Upton,Justin, Ari	415
Ruggiano,Justin, Mia	414
Gonzalez,Carlos, Col	414
Stanton,Giancarlo, Mia	413
Harper,Bryce, Was	413
Rosario,Wilin, Col	413
Weeks,Rickie, Mil	412
Holliday,Matt, StL	411
Freeman,Freddie, Atl	411
Montero,Miguel, Ari	411

Shortest Avg Home Run
(min 10 over the wall)

Lowrie,Jed, Hou	374
Rollins,Jimmy, Phi	374
Mayberry,John, Phi	378
Victorino,Shane, Phi-LAD	383
Cozart,Zack, Cin	384
Greene,Tyler, StL-Hou	385
Hill,Aaron, Ari	386
Barajas,Rod, Pit	387
3 tied with	388

2012 National League Batting Leaders

Under Age 26: AB Per HR
(minimum 502 PA)

Davis,Ike, NYM	16.2
Bruce,Jay, Cin	16.5
Alvarez,Pedro, Pit	17.5
McCutchen,Andrew, Pit	19.1
Heyward,Jason, Atl	21.7
Posey,Buster, SF	22.1
Freeman,Freddie, Atl	23.5
Harper,Bryce, Was	24.2
Goldschmidt,Paul, Ari	25.7
Upton,Justin, Ari	32.6

Under Age 26: OPS
(minimum 502 PA)

Posey,Buster, SF	.957
McCutchen,Andrew, Pit	.953
Goldschmidt,Paul, Ari	.850
Bruce,Jay, Cin	.841
Harper,Bryce, Was	.817
Heyward,Jason, Atl	.814
Freeman,Freddie, Atl	.796
Upton,Justin, Ari	.785
Alvarez,Pedro, Pit	.784
Davis,Ike, NYM	.771

Under Age 26: RC/27 Outs
(minimum 502 PA)

McCutchen,Andrew, Pit	7.9
Posey,Buster, SF	7.8
Goldschmidt,Paul, Ari	5.9
Harper,Bryce, Was	5.4
Bruce,Jay, Cin	5.2
Freeman,Freddie, Atl	5.2
Heyward,Jason, Atl	5.2
Upton,Justin, Ari	5.2
Alvarez,Pedro, Pit	5.0
Castro,Starlin, ChC	4.9

Longest Home Run

Stanton,Giancarlo, Mia, 8/17	494
Maybin,Cameron, SD, 7/2	485
Maxwell,Justin, Hou, 5/28	471
Ludwick,Ryan, Cin, 6/27	469
Morse,Michael, Was, 7/20	465
Stanton,Giancarlo, Mia, 8/18	465
Beltran,Carlos, StL, 5/8	464
Freese,David, StL, 7/31	464
3 tied with	462

Swing and Miss %
(minimum 1500 Pitches Seen)

Stanton,Giancarlo, Mia	32.8
Espinosa,Danny, Was	31.4
Uggla,Dan, Atl	31.4
Alvarez,Pedro, Pit	30.5
Rosario,Wilin, Col	30.0
Soriano,Alfonso, ChC	29.2
Hart,Corey, Mil	29.1
Colvin,Tyler, Col	28.9
LaHair,Bryan, ChC	28.8
Buck,John, Mia	28.3

Highest First Swing %
(minimum 502 PA)

Desmond,Ian, Was	44.8
Freeman,Freddie, Atl	44.2
Molina,Yadier, StL	42.4
Alvarez,Pedro, Pit	39.4
Espinosa,Danny, Was	39.1
Alonso,Yonder, SD	38.3
Harper,Bryce, Was	38.1
Ramirez,Aramis, Mil	36.9
Maybin,Cameron, SD	34.9
2 tied with	34.0

Lowest First Swing %
(minimum 502 PA)

Prado,Martin, Atl	6.9
Ellis,A.J., LAD	9.5
Zimmerman,Ryan, Was	13.2
Scutaro,Marco, Col-SF	13.3
Rollins,Jimmy, Phi	14.1
Kubel,Jason, Ari	14.5
Jay,Jon, StL	15.1
DeJesus,David, ChC	16.5
Victorino,Shane, Phi-LAD	16.9
Aoki,Norichika, Mil	17.2

Home RC Per 27 Outs
(minimum 251 PA)

Gonzalez,Carlos, Col	8.6
McCutchen,Andrew, Pit	8.6
Fowler,Dexter, Col	8.5
Ramirez,Aramis, Mil	8.2
Braun,Ryan, Mil	7.9
Molina,Yadier, StL	7.5
Jay,Jon, StL	7.5
Upton,Justin, Ari	7.4
Posey,Buster, SF	7.2
Craig,Allen, StL	7.1

Road RC Per 27 Outs
(minimum 251 PA)

Cabrera,Melky, SF	9.4
Posey,Buster, SF	8.2
Headley,Chase, SD	8.0
Braun,Ryan, Mil	7.4
McCutchen,Andrew, Pit	7.2
Venable,Will, SD	6.9
Wright,David, NYM	6.7
Goldschmidt,Paul, Ari	6.6
Jones,Garrett, Pit	6.6
Montero,Miguel, Ari	6.5

Lead Changing RBI

Ramirez,Aramis, Mil	41
Beltran,Carlos, StL	38
Headley,Chase, SD	38
Posey,Buster, SF	38
Wright,David, NYM	37
Jones,Garrett, Pit	36
Braun,Ryan, Mil	35
Pence,Hunter, Phi-SF	35
Soriano,Alfonso, ChC	34
3 tied with	33

2012 American League Pitching Leaders

Earned Run Average
(minimum 162 IP)

Price,David, TB	2.56
Verlander,Justin, Det	2.64
Weaver,Jered, LAA	2.81
Sale,Chris, CWS	3.05
Hernandez,Felix, Sea	3.07
Hellickson,Jeremy, TB	3.10
Harrison,Matt, Tex	3.29
Kuroda,Hiroki, NYY	3.32
Peavy,Jake, CWS	3.37
Sabathia,CC, NYY	3.38

Winning Percentage
(minimum 15 Decisions)

Price,David, TB	.800
Weaver,Jered, LAA	.800
Sabathia,CC, NYY	.714
Scherzer,Max, Det	.696
Sale,Chris, CWS	.680
Verlander,Justin, Det	.680
Darvish,Yu, Tex	.640
Holland,Derek, Tex	.632
Harrison,Matt, Tex	.621
Parker,Jarrod, Oak	.619

Opponent Batting Average
(minimum 162 IP)

Weaver,Jered, LAA	.214
Verlander,Justin, Det	.217
Darvish,Yu, Tex	.220
Price,David, TB	.226
Peavy,Jake, CWS	.234
Sale,Chris, CWS	.235
Sabathia,CC, NYY	.238
Moore,Matt, TB	.238
Wilson,C.J., LAA	.239
Santana,Ervin, LAA	.239

Baserunners Per 9 IP
(minimum 162 IP)

Weaver,Jered, LAA	9.35
Verlander,Justin, Det	9.71
Price,David, TB	10.11
Peavy,Jake, CWS	10.27
Sale,Chris, CWS	10.50
Sabathia,CC, NYY	10.62
Vargas,Jason, Sea	10.73
Hernandez,Felix, Sea	10.75
Kuroda,Hiroki, NYY	10.82
Shields,James, TB	10.95

Games

Logan,Boone, NYY	80
Peralta,Joel, TB	77
Herrera,Kelvin, KC	76
Rodney,Fernando, TB	76
Balfour,Grant, Oak	75
Thornton,Matt, CWS	74
Benoit,Joaquin, Det	73
Crow,Aaron, KC	73
Wilhelmsen,Tom, Sea	73
2 tied with	72

Games Started

Chen,Bruce, KC	34
Masterson,Justin, Cle	34
Wilson,C.J., LAA	34
Hernandez,Felix, Sea	33
Kuroda,Hiroki, NYY	33
Lester,Jon, Bos	33
Shields,James, TB	33
Vargas,Jason, Sea	33
Verlander,Justin, Det	33
7 tied with	32

Complete Games

Verlander,Justin, Det	6
Hernandez,Felix, Sea	5
Harrison,Matt, Tex	4
Peavy,Jake, CWS	4
Kuroda,Hiroki, NYY	3
Lester,Jon, Bos	3
Morrow,Brandon, Tor	3
Shields,James, TB	3
Weaver,Jered, LAA	3
8 tied with	2

Shutouts

Hernandez,Felix, Sea	5
Morrow,Brandon, Tor	3
Harrison,Matt, Tex	2
Kuroda,Hiroki, NYY	2
Shields,James, TB	2
Weaver,Jered, LAA	2
18 tied with	1

Wins

Price,David, TB	20
Weaver,Jered, LAA	20
Harrison,Matt, Tex	18
Sale,Chris, CWS	17
Verlander,Justin, Det	17
Darvish,Yu, Tex	16
Hughes,Phil, NYY	16
Kuroda,Hiroki, NYY	16
Scherzer,Max, Det	16
2 tied with	15

Losses

Jimenez,Ubaldo, Cle	17
Hochevar,Luke, KC	16
Masterson,Justin, Cle	15
Alvarez,Henderson, Tor	14
Chen,Bruce, KC	14
Lester,Jon, Bos	14
Romero,Ricky, Tor	14
Haren,Dan, LAA	13
Hughes,Phil, NYY	13
Santana,Ervin, LAA	13

No Decisions

Hernandez,Felix, Sea	11
Smyly,Drew, Det	11
Wilson,C.J., LAA	11
Buchholz,Clay, Bos	10
Hellickson,Jeremy, TB	10
Lester,Jon, Bos	10
Liriano,Francisco, Min-CWS	10
Millwood,Kevin, Sea	10
Quintana,Jose, CWS	10
9 tied with	9

Wild Pitches

Jimenez,Ubaldo, Cle	16
Masterson,Justin, Cle	14
Hernandez,Felix, Sea	13
Kuroda,Hiroki, NYY	13
Liriano,Francisco, Min-CWS	11
Diamond,Scott, Min	10
Garcia,Freddy, NYY	10
Parker,Jarrod, Oak	10
Quintana,Jose, CWS	10
2 tied with	9

Strikeouts

Verlander,Justin, Det	239
Scherzer,Max, Det	231
Hernandez,Felix, Sea	223
Shields,James, TB	223
Darvish,Yu, Tex	221
Price,David, TB	205
Sabathia,CC, NYY	197
Peavy,Jake, CWS	194
Sale,Chris, CWS	192
Moore,Matt, TB	175

Walks Allowed

Romero,Ricky, Tor	105
Jimenez,Ubaldo, Cle	95
Wilson,C.J., LAA	91
Darvish,Yu, Tex	89
Masterson,Justin, Cle	88
Liriano,Francisco, Min-CWS	87
Moore,Matt, TB	81
Doubront,Felix, Bos	71
Lester,Jon, Bos	68
Buchholz,Clay, Bos	64

Intentional Walks Allowed

Collins,Tim, KC	8
Swarzak,Anthony, Min	8
Holland,Greg, KC	7
Herrera,Kelvin, KC	6
Kelley,Shawn, Sea	6
Logan,Boone, NYY	6
Luetge,Lucas, Sea	6
9 tied with	5

Hit Batters

Floyd,Gavin, CWS	14
Hochevar,Luke, KC	13
Masterson,Justin, Cle	13
Buchholz,Clay, Bos	12
Hernandez,Felix, Sea	12
Mendoza,Luis, KC	11
Shields,James, TB	11
5 tied with	10

2012 American League Pitching Leaders

Runs Allowed		Hits Allowed		Doubles Allowed		Home Runs Allowed	
Hochevar,Luke, KC	127	Porcello,Rick, Det	226	Porcello,Rick, Det	53	Santana,Ervin, LAA	39
Masterson,Justin, Cle	122	Alvarez,Henderson, Tor	216	Nova,Ivan, NYY	52	Hughes,Phil, NYY	35
Romero,Ricky, Tor	122	Lester,Jon, Bos	216	Kuroda,Hiroki, NYY	50	Vargas,Jason, Sea	35
Lester,Jon, Bos	117	Chen,Bruce, KC	215	Lester,Jon, Bos	49	Chen,Bruce, KC	33
Jimenez,Ubaldo, Cle	116	Masterson,Justin, Cle	212	Romero,Ricky, Tor	48	Holland,Derek, Tex	32
Chen,Bruce, KC	114	Harrison,Matt, Tex	210	Chen,Bruce, KC	45	Hunter,Tommy, Bal	32
Alvarez,Henderson, Tor	110	Hernandez,Felix, Sea	209	Hochevar,Luke, KC	44	Alvarez,Henderson, Tor	29
Santana,Ervin, LAA	109	Shields,James, TB	208	Alvarez,Henderson, Tor	43	Chen,Wei-Yin, Bal	29
Buchholz,Clay, Bos	104	Milone,Tommy, Oak	207	Haren,Dan, LAA	42	Haren,Dan, LAA	28
Shields,James, TB	103	Kuroda,Hiroki, NYY	205	Hughes,Phil, NYY	42	Nova,Ivan, NYY	28

Run Support Per Nine IP (minimum 162 IP)		% Pitches In Strike Zone (minimum 162 IP)		Pitches Per Start (minimum 30 GS)		Pitches Per Batter (minimum 162 IP)	
Diamond,Scott, Min	6.97	Moore,Matt, TB	47.1	Verlander,Justin, Det	114.2	Diamond,Scott, Min	3.53
Weaver,Jered, LAA	6.54	Harrison,Matt, Tex	46.9	Shields,James, TB	109.6	Alvarez,Henderson, Tor	3.55
Sabathia,CC, NYY	6.12	Hughes,Phil, NYY	46.5	Peavy,Jake, CWS	108.9	Mendoza,Luis, KC	3.57
Wilson,C.J., LAA	5.96	Alvarez,Henderson, Tor	46.2	Price,David, TB	107.5	Nova,Ivan, NYY	3.60
Holland,Derek, Tex	5.95	Chen,Wei-Yin, Bal	46.1	Lester,Jon, Bos	103.8	Porcello,Rick, Det	3.61
Scherzer,Max, Det	5.71	Sale,Chris, CWS	45.9	Hernandez,Felix, Sea	103.6	Buchholz,Clay, Bos	3.62
Moore,Matt, TB	5.53	Holland,Derek, Tex	45.7	Scherzer,Max, Det	102.4	Sabathia,CC, NYY	3.64
Sale,Chris, CWS	5.48	Wilson,C.J., LAA	45.7	Vargas,Jason, Sea	101.6	Hernandez,Felix, Sea	3.64
Buchholz,Clay, Bos	5.42	Hochevar,Luke, KC	45.0	Harrison,Matt, Tex	101.5	Harrison,Matt, Tex	3.71
Hughes,Phil, NYY	5.41	Scherzer,Max, Det	44.9	Wilson,C.J., LAA	101.2	Romero,Ricky, Tor	3.72

Quality Starts		Batters Faced		Innings Pitched		Most Pitches in a Game	
Price,David, TB	25	Verlander,Justin, Det	956	Verlander,Justin, Det	238.1	Verlander,Justin, Det	132
Verlander,Justin, Det	25	Shields,James, TB	944	Hernandez,Felix, Sea	232.0	Verlander,Justin, Det	131
Peavy,Jake, CWS	23	Hernandez,Felix, Sea	939	Shields,James, TB	227.2	Hernandez,Felix, Sea	128
Vargas,Jason, Sea	22	Masterson,Justin, Cle	906	Kuroda,Hiroki, NYY	219.2	Lowe,Derek, Cle-NYY	127
Hernandez,Felix, Sea	21	Kuroda,Hiroki, NYY	891	Peavy,Jake, CWS	219.0	Verlander,Justin, Det	127
Weaver,Jered, LAA	21	Vargas,Jason, Sea	887	Vargas,Jason, Sea	217.1	Beckett,Josh, Bos	126
Wilson,C.J., LAA	21	Peavy,Jake, CWS	882	Harrison,Matt, Tex	213.1	Haren,Dan, LAA	126
5 tied with	20	Harrison,Matt, Tex	876	Price,David, TB	211.0	Hernandez,Felix, Sea	126
		Lester,Jon, Bos	876	Masterson,Justin, Cle	206.1	4 tied with	125
		Wilson,C.J., LAA	865	Lester,Jon, Bos	205.1		

Stolen Bases Allowed		Caught Stealing Off		Stolen Base Pct Allowed (minimum 162 IP)		Pickoffs	
Jimenez,Ubaldo, Cle	32	Wilson,C.J., LAA	12	Harrison,Matt, Tex	25.0	Romero,Ricky, Tor	8
Masterson,Justin, Cle	25	Milone,Tommy, Oak	10	Milone,Tommy, Oak	44.4	Blackley,Travis, Oak	7
Darvish,Yu, Tex	23	Price,David, TB	10	Mendoza,Luis, KC	50.0	Milone,Tommy, Oak	6
Wilson,C.J., LAA	22	Romero,Ricky, Tor	10	Price,David, TB	52.4	Sale,Chris, CWS	6
Parker,Jarrod, Oak	21	Sale,Chris, CWS	10	Peavy,Jake, CWS	52.9	Holland,Derek, Tex	5
Feldman,Scott, Tex	20	Scherzer,Max, Det	9	Weaver,Jered, LAA	52.9	Wilson,C.J., LAA	5
Cobb,Alex, TB	19	Chen,Bruce, KC	8	Romero,Ricky, Tor	56.5	Chen,Bruce, KC	4
Doubront,Felix, Bos	19	Kuroda,Hiroki, NYY	8	Hughes,Phil, NYY	57.1	Morales,Franklin, Bos	4
Moore,Matt, TB	19	Peavy,Jake, CWS	8	Sale,Chris, CWS	58.3	11 tied with	3
4 tied with	18	Weaver,Jered, LAA	8	2 tied with	62.5		

2012 American League Pitching Leaders

Strikeouts Per 9 IP
(minimum 162 IP)

Scherzer,Max, Det	11.08
Darvish,Yu, Tex	10.40
Verlander,Justin, Det	9.03
Sale,Chris, CWS	9.00
Moore,Matt, TB	8.88
Sabathia,CC, NYY	8.87
Shields,James, TB	8.82
Price,David, TB	8.74
Hernandez,Felix, Sea	8.65
Nova,Ivan, NYY	8.08

Opp On-Base Percentage
(minimum 162 IP)

Weaver,Jered, LAA	.265
Verlander,Justin, Det	.270
Peavy,Jake, CWS	.284
Price,David, TB	.284
Sabathia,CC, NYY	.285
Sale,Chris, CWS	.291
Vargas,Jason, Sea	.293
Shields,James, TB	.295
Hernandez,Felix, Sea	.296
Kuroda,Hiroki, NYY	.299

Opp Slugging Average
(minimum 162 IP)

Price,David, TB	.318
Verlander,Justin, Det	.331
Hernandez,Felix, Sea	.333
Weaver,Jered, LAA	.340
Darvish,Yu, Tex	.346
Parker,Jarrod, Oak	.358
Wilson,C.J., LAA	.361
Sale,Chris, CWS	.370
Moore,Matt, TB	.380
Sabathia,CC, NYY	.381

Opponent OPS
(minimum 162 IP)

Verlander,Justin, Det	.601
Price,David, TB	.602
Weaver,Jered, LAA	.605
Hernandez,Felix, Sea	.629
Darvish,Yu, Tex	.659
Sale,Chris, CWS	.660
Sabathia,CC, NYY	.666
Parker,Jarrod, Oak	.670
Peavy,Jake, CWS	.671
Shields,James, TB	.678

Home Runs Per Nine IP
(minimum 162 IP)

Hernandez,Felix, Sea	0.54
Parker,Jarrod, Oak	0.55
Darvish,Yu, Tex	0.66
Price,David, TB	0.68
Verlander,Justin, Det	0.72
Masterson,Justin, Cle	0.79
Mendoza,Luis, KC	0.81
Porcello,Rick, Det	0.82
Wilson,C.J., LAA	0.85
Diamond,Scott, Min	0.88

Batting Average vs. LHB
(minimum 125 BF)

Balfour,Grant, Oak	.157
Davis,Wade, TB	.161
Rodney,Fernando, TB	.166
Cook,Ryan, Oak	.171
Peralta,Joel, TB	.173
Perez,Chris, Cle	.181
Blevins,Jerry, Oak	.182
Morrow,Brandon, Tor	.188
Holland,Greg, KC	.194
Drabek,Kyle, Tor	.199

Batting Average vs. RHB
(minimum 225 BF)

Scherzer,Max, Det	.201
Darvish,Yu, Tex	.207
Peavy,Jake, CWS	.210
Santana,Ervin, LAA	.213
Fister,Doug, Det	.220
Verlander,Justin, Det	.222
Floyd,Gavin, CWS	.226
Hernandez,Felix, Sea	.231
Price,David, TB	.232
Masterson,Justin, Cle	.232

Opp BA w/ RISP
(minimum 125 BF)

Sale,Chris, CWS	.169
Verlander,Justin, Det	.200
Vargas,Jason, Sea	.214
Parker,Jarrod, Oak	.215
Darvish,Yu, Tex	.222
Hellickson,Jeremy, TB	.226
Harrison,Matt, Tex	.227
Hughes,Phil, NYY	.227
Hernandez,Felix, Sea	.231
Floyd,Gavin, CWS	.232

OBP vs. Leadoff Hitter
(minimum 150 BF)

Colon,Bartolo, Oak	.236
Weaver,Jered, LAA	.255
Harrison,Matt, Tex	.266
Shields,James, TB	.275
Alvarez,Henderson, Tor	.277
Buchholz,Clay, Bos	.277
Fister,Doug, Det	.278
Peavy,Jake, CWS	.279
Santana,Ervin, LAA	.281
Price,David, TB	.281

Strikeouts / Walks Ratio
(minimum 162 IP)

Sabathia,CC, NYY	4.48
Verlander,Justin, Det	3.98
Hernandez,Felix, Sea	3.98
Peavy,Jake, CWS	3.96
Scherzer,Max, Det	3.85
Shields,James, TB	3.85
Milone,Tommy, Oak	3.81
Sale,Chris, CWS	3.77
Haren,Dan, LAA	3.74
Hughes,Phil, NYY	3.59

Highest GB/FB Ratio
(minimum 162 IP)

Porcello,Rick, Det	2.36
Alvarez,Henderson, Tor	2.34
Masterson,Justin, Cle	2.23
Diamond,Scott, Min	2.09
Romero,Ricky, Tor	2.03
Price,David, TB	1.97
Mendoza,Luis, KC	1.92
Shields,James, TB	1.81
Kuroda,Hiroki, NYY	1.77
Hernandez,Felix, Sea	1.71

Lowest GB/FB Ratio
(minimum 162 IP)

Hughes,Phil, NYY	0.68
Chen,Bruce, KC	0.73
Peavy,Jake, CWS	0.82
Weaver,Jered, LAA	0.84
Moore,Matt, TB	0.87
Scherzer,Max, Det	0.88
Chen,Wei-Yin, Bal	0.88
Vargas,Jason, Sea	0.99
Haren,Dan, LAA	1.00
Jimenez,Ubaldo, Cle	1.00

Sacrifice Flies Allowed

Masterson,Justin, Cle	11
Buchholz,Clay, Bos	9
Beckett,Josh, Bos	8
Chen,Wei-Yin, Bal	8
Haren,Dan, LAA	8
Liriano,Francisco, Min-CWS	8
Parker,Jarrod, Oak	8
5 tied with	7

Sacrifice Hits Allowed

Haren,Dan, LAA	7
Kuroda,Hiroki, NYY	7
Parker,Jarrod, Oak	7
Romero,Ricky, Tor	7
Masterson,Justin, Cle	6
Millwood,Kevin, Sea	6
10 tied with	5

GIDP Induced

Alvarez,Henderson, Tor	30
Buchholz,Clay, Bos	27
Diamond,Scott, Min	27
Harrison,Matt, Tex	27
Lester,Jon, Bos	27
Masterson,Justin, Cle	26
Hernandez,Felix, Sea	23
Kuroda,Hiroki, NYY	23
Lowe,Derek, Cle-NYY	23
Wilson,C.J., LAA	23

GIDP Per Nine IP
(minimum 162 IP)

Alvarez,Henderson, Tor	1.44
Diamond,Scott, Min	1.41
Buchholz,Clay, Bos	1.28
Mendoza,Luis, KC	1.19
Lester,Jon, Bos	1.18
Floyd,Gavin, CWS	1.18
Harrison,Matt, Tex	1.14
Masterson,Justin, Cle	1.13
Romero,Ricky, Tor	1.09
Porcello,Rick, Det	1.07

2012 American League Pitching Leaders

Saves		Blown Saves		Save Pct (minimum 20 Save Ops)		Save Opportunities	
Johnson,Jim, Bal	51	Aceves,Alfredo, Bos	8	Rodney,Fernando, TB	96.0	Johnson,Jim, Bal	54
Rodney,Fernando, TB	48	Cook,Ryan, Oak	7	Johnson,Jim, Bal	94.4	Rodney,Fernando, TB	50
Soriano,Rafael, NYY	42	Strop,Pedro, Bal	7	Nathan,Joe, Tex	92.5	Soriano,Rafael, NYY	46
Perez,Chris, Cle	39	Crow,Aaron, KC	6	Balfour,Grant, Oak	92.3	Perez,Chris, Cle	43
Nathan,Joe, Tex	37	League,Brandon, Sea	6	Soriano,Rafael, NYY	91.3	Nathan,Joe, Tex	40
Valverde,Jose, Det	35	Isringhausen,Jason, LAA	5	Perez,Chris, Cle	90.7	Valverde,Jose, Det	40
Reed,Addison, CWS	29	Valverde,Jose, Det	5	Frieri,Ernesto, LAA	88.5	Wilhelmsen,Tom, Sea	34
Wilhelmsen,Tom, Sea	29	Wilhelmsen,Tom, Sea	5	Janssen,Casey, Tor	88.0	Aceves,Alfredo, Bos	33
Aceves,Alfredo, Bos	25	13 tied with	4	Reed,Addison, CWS	87.9	Reed,Addison, CWS	33
Balfour,Grant, Oak	24			Valverde,Jose, Det	87.5	Broxton,Jonathan, KC	27

Easy Saves		Regular Saves		Tough Saves		Holds Adjusted Saves % (minimum 20 Save Ops)	
Rodney,Fernando, TB	34	Johnson,Jim, Bal	18	Frieri,Ernesto, LAA	3	Rodney,Fernando, TB	96.0
Johnson,Jim, Bal	33	Nathan,Joe, Tex	15	Reed,Addison, CWS	3	Balfour,Grant, Oak	95.1
Perez,Chris, Cle	28	Soriano,Rafael, NYY	13	Rodney,Fernando, TB	3	Johnson,Jim, Bal	94.4
Valverde,Jose, Det	27	Perez,Chris, Cle	11	Soriano,Rafael, NYY	3	Nathan,Joe, Tex	92.5
Soriano,Rafael, NYY	26	Reed,Addison, CWS	11	Wilhelmsen,Tom, Sea	2	Soriano,Rafael, NYY	92.0
Nathan,Joe, Tex	22	Rodney,Fernando, TB	11	14 tied with	1	Perez,Chris, Cle	90.7
Balfour,Grant, Oak	18	Aceves,Alfredo, Bos	10			Frieri,Ernesto, LAA	90.6
Wilhelmsen,Tom, Sea	18	Broxton,Jonathan, KC	10			Reed,Addison, CWS	89.2
Reed,Addison, CWS	15	Janssen,Casey, Tor	10			Janssen,Casey, Tor	88.5
Aceves,Alfredo, Bos	14	Wilhelmsen,Tom, Sea	9			Wilhelmsen,Tom, Sea	87.8

Relief Wins		Relief Losses		Relief Games		Holds	
Jones,Nate, CWS	8	Aceves,Alfredo, Bos	10	Logan,Boone, NYY	80	Peralta,Joel, TB	37
Holland,Greg, KC	7	Thornton,Matt, CWS	10	Peralta,Joel, TB	77	Pestano,Vinnie, Cle	36
Logan,Boone, NYY	7	Robertson,David, NYY	7	Herrera,Kelvin, KC	76	Benoit,Joaquin, Det	30
O'Day,Darren, Bal	7	Farnsworth,Kyle, TB	6	Rodney,Fernando, TB	76	Robertson,David, NYY	30
Smith,Joe, Cle	7	Peralta,Joel, TB	6	Balfour,Grant, Oak	75	Adams,Mike, Tex	27
Cook,Ryan, Oak	6	Ayala,Luis, Bal	5	Thornton,Matt, CWS	74	Thornton,Matt, CWS	26
Gray,Jeff, Min	6	Cordero,Francisco, Tor	5	Benoit,Joaquin, Det	73	Downs,Scott, LAA	25
Ross,Robbie, Tex	6	League,Brandon, Sea	5	Crow,Aaron, KC	73	Strop,Pedro, Bal	24
9 tied with	5	Nathan,Joe, Tex	5	Wilhelmsen,Tom, Sea	73	Logan,Boone, NYY	23
		Villarreal,Brayan, Det	5	2 tied with	72	Padilla,Vicente, Bos	23

Relief Innings		Inherited Runners Scrd % (minimum 30 IR)		Relief Opp On Base Pct (minimum 50 IP)		Relief Opp Slugging Avg (minimum 50 IP)	
Herrera,Kelvin, KC	84.1	Eppley,Cody, NYY	11.9	McGee,Jake, TB	.213	Rodney,Fernando, TB	.198
Aceves,Alfredo, Bos	84.0	Rapada,Clay, NYY	12.3	Rodney,Fernando, TB	.219	McGee,Jake, TB	.239
Wilhelmsen,Tom, Sea	79.1	O'Day,Darren, Bal	14.0	Janssen,Casey, Tor	.241	Balfour,Grant, Oak	.253
Ayala,Luis, Bal	75.0	Padilla,Vicente, Bos	14.7	Balfour,Grant, Oak	.242	Cook,Ryan, Oak	.261
Balfour,Grant, Oak	74.2	Miller,Andrew, Bos	15.2	Peralta,Joel, TB	.254	Frieri,Ernesto, LAA	.269
Rodney,Fernando, TB	74.2	Duensing,Brian, Min	15.6	O'Day,Darren, Bal	.254	Strop,Pedro, Bal	.283
Cook,Ryan, Oak	73.1	Luetge,Lucas, Sea	16.0	Burton,Jared, Min	.255	Johnson,Jim, Bal	.284
Swarzak,Anthony, Min	73.1	Gray,Jeff, Min	18.8	Cook,Ryan, Oak	.256	Atchison,Scott, Bos	.293
Burnett,Alex, Min	71.2	Smith,Joe, Cle	21.3	Atchison,Scott, Bos	.256	Oliver,Darren, Tor	.294
Jones,Nate, CWS	71.2	Ross,Robbie, Tex	22.2	Frieri,Ernesto, LAA	.261	Burton,Jared, Min	.294

2012 American League Pitching Leaders

Relief Opp BA Vs LHB	
(minimum 50 AB)	
Frieri,Ernesto, LAA	.069
Miller,Jim, Oak	.136
Furbush,Charlie, Sea	.147
Miller,Andrew, Bos	.149
Balfour,Grant, Oak	.157
Davis,Wade, TB	.161
Rodney,Fernando, TB	.166
Jones,Nate, CWS	.170
Cook,Ryan, Oak	.171
Walden,Jordan, LAA	.171

Relief Opp BA Vs RHB	
(minimum 50 AB)	
Neshek,Pat, Oak	.094
McGee,Jake, TB	.098
Uehara,Koji, Tex	.125
Crain,Jesse, CWS	.129
Ramos,Cesar, TB	.140
Burton,Jared, Min	.154
Kirkman,Michael, Tex	.160
Cook,Ryan, Oak	.162
Balfour,Grant, Oak	.163
Pestano,Vinnie, Cle	.168

Relief Opp Batting Average	
(minimum 50 IP)	
Frieri,Ernesto, LAA	.140
Balfour,Grant, Oak	.160
Cook,Ryan, Oak	.166
Rodney,Fernando, TB	.167
McGee,Jake, TB	.168
Burton,Jared, Min	.186
Davis,Wade, TB	.189
Delabar,Steve, Sea-Tor	.193
Janssen,Casey, Tor	.195
2 tied with	.200

Relief Earned Run Average	
(minimum 50 IP)	
Rodney,Fernando, TB	0.60
Atchison,Scott, Bos	1.58
McGee,Jake, TB	1.95
Oliver,Darren, Tor	2.07
Cook,Ryan, Oak	2.09
Burton,Jared, Min	2.18
Ross,Robbie, Tex	2.22
Soriano,Rafael, NYY	2.26
O'Day,Darren, Bal	2.28
Frieri,Ernesto, LAA	2.32

Rel OBP 1st Batter Faced	
(minimum 40 BF)	
Miller,Andrew, Bos	.151
Burton,Jared, Min	.156
Dotel,Octavio, Det	.175
McGee,Jake, TB	.203
Janssen,Casey, Tor	.210
Johnson,Jim, Bal	.211
Nathan,Joe, Tex	.212
Crow,Aaron, KC	.219
Smith,Joe, Cle	.225
Robertson,David, NYY	.231

Rel Opp BA w/ Runners On	
(minimum 50 IP)	
Frieri,Ernesto, LAA	.091
Rodney,Fernando, TB	.131
Soriano,Rafael, NYY	.155
Blevins,Jerry, Oak	.160
Balfour,Grant, Oak	.168
Burton,Jared, Min	.173
Cook,Ryan, Oak	.178
Delabar,Steve, Sea-Tor	.180
Villarreal,Brayan, Det	.186
Oliver,Darren, Tor	.190

Relief Opp BA w/ RISP	
(minimum 50 IP)	
Frieri,Ernesto, LAA	.043
Santiago,Hector, CWS	.091
Soriano,Rafael, NYY	.113
Padilla,Vicente, Bos	.136
Rodney,Fernando, TB	.136
Coleman,Louis, KC	.140
Perez,Chris, Cle	.146
Cook,Ryan, Oak	.151
Villarreal,Brayan, Det	.163
3 tied with	.167

Fastest Avg Fastball-Relief	
(minimum 50 IP)	
Herrera,Kelvin, KC	98.5
Jones,Nate, CWS	97.6
Villarreal,Brayan, Det	97.1
Ogando,Alexi, Tex	97.0
Strop,Pedro, Bal	96.9
Wilhelmsen,Tom, Sea	96.3
Rodney,Fernando, TB	96.1
Holland,Greg, KC	96.1
McGee,Jake, TB	95.7
Rogers,Esmil, Cle	95.5

Fastest Average Fastball	
(minimum 162 IP)	
Price,David, TB	95.5
Moore,Matt, TB	94.4
Verlander,Justin, Det	94.3
Scherzer,Max, Det	94.2
Alvarez,Henderson, Tor	93.3
Nova,Ivan, NYY	93.0
Holland,Derek, Tex	93.0
Darvish,Yu, Tex	92.8
Hochevar,Luke, KC	92.6
Lester,Jon, Bos	92.6

Slowest Average Fastball	
(minimum 162 IP)	
Chen,Bruce, KC	86.3
Milone,Tommy, Oak	87.7
Weaver,Jered, LAA	87.8
Vargas,Jason, Sea	88.0
Haren,Dan, LAA	88.5
Diamond,Scott, Min	89.4
Peavy,Jake, CWS	90.8
Chen,Wei-Yin, Bal	91.0
Romero,Ricky, Tor	91.2
Hellickson,Jeremy, TB	91.4

Pitches 100+ Velocity	
Herrera,Kelvin, KC	162
Verlander,Justin, Det	44
Capps,Carter, Sea	43
Jones,Nate, CWS	33
Rodney,Fernando, TB	10
Ogando,Alexi, Tex	7
Pryor,Stephen, Sea	4
Villarreal,Brayan, Det	4
Scheppers,Tanner, Tex	2
7 tied with	1

Pitches 95+ Velocity	
Price,David, TB	1586
Moore,Matt, TB	975
Verlander,Justin, Det	957
Scherzer,Max, Det	869
Rogers,Esmil, Cle	829
Herrera,Kelvin, KC	815
Jones,Nate, CWS	773
Villarreal,Brayan, Det	750
Delabar,Steve, Sea-Tor	746
Strop,Pedro, Bal	746

Pitches Less Than 80 MPH	
Chen,Bruce, KC	913
Wolf,Randy, Bal	784
Hellickson,Jeremy, TB	657
Hughes,Phil, NYY	591
Buchholz,Clay, Bos	572
Greinke,Zack, LAA	556
Weaver,Jered, LAA	552
Stults,Eric, CWS	550
Saunders,Joe, Bal	541
Sale,Chris, CWS	521

Lowest % Fastballs	
(minimum 162 IP)	
Shields,James, TB	33.7
Haren,Dan, LAA	40.1
Chen,Bruce, KC	42.1
Buchholz,Clay, Bos	43.8
Floyd,Gavin, CWS	45.3
Romero,Ricky, Tor	45.4
Darvish,Yu, Tex	47.3
Milone,Tommy, Oak	47.6
Kuroda,Hiroki, NYY	50.4
Peavy,Jake, CWS	51.2

Highest % Fastballs	
(minimum 162 IP)	
Masterson,Justin, Cle	80.7
Alvarez,Henderson, Tor	69.2
Holland,Derek, Tex	68.5
Mendoza,Luis, KC	67.5
Porcello,Rick, Det	67.2
Moore,Matt, TB	65.9
Hughes,Phil, NYY	65.4
Chen,Wei-Yin, Bal	65.1
Harrison,Matt, Tex	63.7
Parker,Jarrod, Oak	62.9

Highest % Curveballs	
(minimum 162 IP)	
Diamond,Scott, Min	29.2
Nova,Ivan, NYY	28.8
Mendoza,Luis, KC	22.8
Hochevar,Luke, KC	20.6
Floyd,Gavin, CWS	19.4
Shields,James, TB	18.2
Hughes,Phil, NYY	18.2
Moore,Matt, TB	17.0
Buchholz,Clay, Bos	16.6
Harrison,Matt, Tex	15.1

2012 American League Pitching Leaders

Highest % Changeups
(minimum 162 IP)

Shields,James, TB	28.9
Hellickson,Jeremy, TB	28.3
Vargas,Jason, Sea	26.9
Milone,Tommy, Oak	25.5
Parker,Jarrod, Oak	22.4
Scherzer,Max, Det	19.7
Romero,Ricky, Tor	18.6
Hernandez,Felix, Sea	18.0
Verlander,Justin, Det	17.3
Moore,Matt, TB	17.1

Highest % Sliders
(minimum 162 IP)

Santana,Ervin, LAA	35.3
Kuroda,Hiroki, NYY	30.4
Chen,Bruce, KC	29.9
Sale,Chris, CWS	26.2
Sabathia,CC, NYY	26.0
Scherzer,Max, Det	19.5
Masterson,Justin, Cle	19.3
Jimenez,Ubaldo, Cle	15.8
Porcello,Rick, Det	15.4
Peavy,Jake, CWS	15.1

Balks

Morales,Franklin, Bos	5
Blackley,Travis, Oak	3
17 tied with	2

Strikeout/Hit Ratio
(minimum 50 IP)

Frieri,Ernesto, LAA	3.08
McGee,Jake, TB	2.21
Delabar,Steve, Sea-Tor	2.00
Cook,Ryan, Oak	1.90
Davis,Wade, TB	1.81
Rodney,Fernando, TB	1.77
Balfour,Grant, Oak	1.76
Villarreal,Brayan, Det	1.74
Peralta,Joel, TB	1.71
Collins,Tim, KC	1.69

Opp OPS vs Fastballs
(minimum 251 BF)

Weaver,Jered, LAA	.549
Price,David, TB	.604
Peavy,Jake, CWS	.636
Hernandez,Felix, Sea	.645
Verlander,Justin, Det	.652
Shields,James, TB	.664
Hammel,Jason, Bal	.670
Wilson,C.J., LAA	.684
Sale,Chris, CWS	.688
Morrow,Brandon, Tor	.690

Opp OPS vs Curveballs
(minimum 100 BF)

Verlander,Justin, Det	.439
Fister,Doug, Det	.466
Hernandez,Felix, Sea	.515
Wilson,C.J., LAA	.535
Moore,Matt, TB	.580
Nova,Ivan, NYY	.616
Shields,James, TB	.616
Mendoza,Luis, KC	.642
Buchholz,Clay, Bos	.672
Diamond,Scott, Min	.682

Opp OPS vs Changeups
(minimum 100 BF)

Sabathia,CC, NYY	.442
Sale,Chris, CWS	.487
Vargas,Jason, Sea	.523
Herrera,Kelvin, KC	.529
Chen,Wei-Yin, Bal	.541
Parker,Jarrod, Oak	.541
Price,David, TB	.560
Benoit,Joaquin, Det	.593
Cobb,Alex, TB	.593
Verlander,Justin, Det	.618

Opp OPS vs Sliders
(minimum 64 BF)

Balfour,Grant, Oak	.347
Cook,Ryan, Oak	.355
Strop,Pedro, Bal	.448
Crow,Aaron, KC	.480
O'Day,Darren, Bal	.497
Morrow,Brandon, Tor	.501
Smyly,Drew, Det	.501
Ogando,Alexi, Tex	.513
Darvish,Yu, Tex	.518
Rapada,Clay, NYY	.523

Earned Runs

Hochevar,Luke, KC	118
Romero,Ricky, Tor	116
Masterson,Justin, Cle	113
Lester,Jon, Bos	110
Chen,Bruce, KC	108
Jimenez,Ubaldo, Cle	106
Santana,Ervin, LAA	102
Alvarez,Henderson, Tor	101
Buchholz,Clay, Bos	96
Nova,Ivan, NYY	95

Hits Per Nine Innings
(minimum 162 IP)

Weaver,Jered, LAA	7.01
Verlander,Justin, Det	7.25
Darvish,Yu, Tex	7.34
Price,David, TB	7.38
Sale,Chris, CWS	7.83
Peavy,Jake, CWS	7.85
Moore,Matt, TB	8.02
Wilson,C.J., LAA	8.05
Hernandez,Felix, Sea	8.11
Shields,James, TB	8.22

2012 National League Pitching Leaders

Earned Run Average (minimum 162 IP)		Winning Percentage (minimum 15 Decisions)		Opponent Batting Average (minimum 162 IP)		Baserunners Per 9 IP (minimum 162 IP)	
Kershaw,Clayton, LAD	2.53	Lohse,Kyle, StL	.842	Gonzalez,Gio, Was	.206	Kershaw,Clayton, LAD	9.41
Dickey,R.A., NYM	2.74	Latos,Mat, Cin	.778	Kershaw,Clayton, LAD	.210	Cain,Matt, SF	9.73
Cueto,Johnny, Cin	2.78	Dickey,R.A., NYM	.769	Cain,Matt, SF	.222	Dickey,R.A., NYM	9.82
Cain,Matt, SF	2.79	Cain,Matt, SF	.762	Dickey,R.A., NYM	.226	Lohse,Kyle, StL	9.98
Lohse,Kyle, StL	2.86	Hamels,Cole, Phi	.739	Latos,Mat, Cin	.230	Lee,Cliff, Phi	10.02
Gonzalez,Gio, Was	2.89	Gonzalez,Gio, Was	.724	Minor,Mike, Atl	.232	Hamels,Cole, Phi	10.24
Zimmermann,Jordan, Was	2.94	Lynn,Lance, StL	.720	McDonald,James, Pit	.233	Bumgarner,Madison, SF	10.33
Hamels,Cole, Phi	3.05	Strasburg,Stephen, Was	.714	Bumgarner,Madison, SF	.234	Gonzalez,Gio, Was	10.39
Lee,Cliff, Phi	3.16	Hudson,Tim, Atl	.696	Volquez,Edinson, SD	.236	Latos,Mat, Cin	10.62
Miley,Wade, Ari	3.33	Cueto,Johnny, Cin	.679	Hamels,Cole, Phi	.237	Minor,Mike, Atl	10.64

Games		Games Started		Complete Games		Shutouts	
Belisle,Matt, Col	80	12 tied with	33	Dickey,R.A., NYM	5	Dickey,R.A., NYM	3
Camp,Shawn, ChC	80			Nolasco,Ricky, Mia	3	Cain,Matt, SF	2
Choate,Randy, Mia-LAD	80			Wainwright,Adam, StL	3	Hamels,Cole, Phi	2
Boggs,Mitchell, StL	78			13 tied with	2	Kershaw,Clayton, LAD	2
Rodriguez,Francisco, Mil	78					Nolasco,Ricky, Mia	2
Gregerson,Luke, SD	77					Santana,Johan, NYM	2
Russell,James, ChC	77					Wainwright,Adam, StL	2
Wright,Wesley, Hou	77					20 tied with	1
Ziegler,Brad, Ari	77						
Durbin,Chad, Atl	76						

Wins		Losses		No Decisions		Wild Pitches	
Gonzalez,Gio, Was	21	Lincecum,Tim, SF	15	Latos,Mat, Cin	15	Lincecum,Tim, SF	17
Dickey,R.A., NYM	20	Bedard,Erik, Pit	14	Lee,Cliff, Phi	15	Garcia,Jaime, StL	12
Cueto,Johnny, Cin	19	Johnson,Josh, Mia	14	Lohse,Kyle, StL	14	Axford,John, Mil	10
Lynn,Lance, StL	18	Richard,Clayton, SD	14	Leake,Mike, Cin	13	Burnett,A.J., Pit	10
Hamels,Cole, Phi	17	9 tied with	13	Zimmermann,Jordan, Was	12	Cahill,Trevor, Ari	10
7 tied with	16			6 tied with	11	Gonzalez,Gio, Was	10
						Harrell,Lucas, Hou	10
						Rodriguez,Fernando, Hou	10
						Rodriguez,Henry, Was	10
						Samardzija,Jeff, ChC	10

Strikeouts		Walks Allowed		Intentional Walks Allowed		Hit Batters	
Dickey,R.A., NYM	230	Volquez,Edinson, SD	105	Harang,Aaron, LAD	10	Kennedy,Ian, Ari	14
Kershaw,Clayton, LAD	229	Lincecum,Tim, SF	90	Latos,Mat, Cin	9	Cueto,Johnny, Cin	12
Hamels,Cole, Phi	216	Harang,Aaron, LAD	85	Nolasco,Ricky, Mia	9	Cahill,Trevor, Ari	11
Gonzalez,Gio, Was	207	Gallardo,Yovani, Mil	81	White,Alex, Col	9	Maholm,Paul, ChC-Atl	11
Lee,Cliff, Phi	207	Harrell,Lucas, Hou	78	Dunn,Mike, Mia	8	Lynn,Lance, StL	10
Gallardo,Yovani, Mil	204	Gonzalez,Gio, Was	76	Webb,Ryan, Mia	8	Zambrano,Carlos, Mia	10
Strasburg,Stephen, Was	197	Zambrano,Carlos, Mia	75	9 tied with	7	5 tied with	9
Cain,Matt, SF	193	Cahill,Trevor, Ari	74				
Bumgarner,Madison, SF	191	Hanson,Tommy, Atl	71				
Lincecum,Tim, SF	190	Zito,Barry, SF	70				

2012 National League Pitching Leaders

Runs Allowed

Lincecum,Tim, SF	111
Richard,Clayton, SD	110
Blanton,Joe, Phi-LAD	106
Kennedy,Ian, Ari	101
Nolasco,Ricky, Mia	100
Rodriguez,Wandy, Hou-Pit	99
Bailey,Homer, Cin	97
Leake,Mike, Cin	97
Lyles,Jordan, Hou	97
Wainwright,Adam, StL	96

Hits Allowed

Richard,Clayton, SD	228
Kennedy,Ian, Ari	216
Nolasco,Ricky, Mia	214
Arroyo,Bronson, Cin	209
Blanton,Joe, Phi-LAD	207
Lee,Cliff, Phi	207
Bailey,Homer, Cin	206
Cueto,Johnny, Cin	205
Rodriguez,Wandy, Hou-Pit	205
Leake,Mike, Cin	201

Doubles Allowed

Kennedy,Ian, Ari	50
Leake,Mike, Cin	46
Miley,Wade, Ari	46
Hanson,Tommy, Atl	45
Richard,Clayton, SD	44
Lee,Cliff, Phi	43
Zito,Barry, SF	43
5 tied with	42

Home Runs Allowed

Richard,Clayton, SD	31
Blanton,Joe, Phi-LAD	29
Kennedy,Ian, Ari	28
Hanson,Tommy, Atl	27
7 tied with	26

Run Support Per Nine IP
(minimum 162 IP)

Lynn,Lance, StL	6.70
Gonzalez,Gio, Was	6.68
Zito,Barry, SF	5.96
Miley,Wade, Ari	5.73
McDonald,James, Pit	5.68
Westbrook,Jake, StL	5.41
Hamels,Cole, Phi	5.39
Hudson,Tim, Atl	5.38
Rodriguez,Wandy, Hou-Pit	5.34
Gallardo,Yovani, Mil	5.29

% Pitches In Strike Zone
(minimum 162 IP)

Lee,Cliff, Phi	51.9
Dickey,R.A., NYM	49.3
Rodriguez,Wandy, Hou-Pit	46.6
Burnett,A.J., Pit	46.0
Zimmermann,Jordan, Was	45.6
Richard,Clayton, SD	45.6
Capuano,Chris, LAD	45.6
Nolasco,Ricky, Mia	45.6
Niese,Jon, NYM	45.3
Bumgarner,Madison, SF	45.0

Pitches Per Start
(minimum 30 GS)

Hamels,Cole, Phi	107.0
Gallardo,Yovani, Mil	105.4
Kershaw,Clayton, LAD	105.1
Cain,Matt, SF	104.5
Cueto,Johnny, Cin	104.5
Lee,Cliff, Phi	103.3
Kennedy,Ian, Ari	102.4
Bumgarner,Madison, SF	102.2
Johnson,Josh, Mia	101.5
Dickey,R.A., NYM	101.3

Pitches Per Batter
(minimum 162 IP)

Richard,Clayton, SD	3.48
Hudson,Tim, Atl	3.50
Correia,Kevin, Pit	3.52
Arroyo,Bronson, Cin	3.54
Westbrook,Jake, StL	3.57
Nolasco,Ricky, Mia	3.57
Burnett,A.J., Pit	3.58
Leake,Mike, Cin	3.59
Lohse,Kyle, StL	3.62
Dickey,R.A., NYM	3.62

Quality Starts

Dickey,R.A., NYM	27
Gallardo,Yovani, Mil	25
Kershaw,Clayton, LAD	25
Lohse,Kyle, StL	24
Zimmermann,Jordan, Was	24
Cueto,Johnny, Cin	23
Hamels,Cole, Phi	23
4 tied with	22

Batters Faced

Dickey,R.A., NYM	927
Richard,Clayton, SD	910
Kershaw,Clayton, LAD	901
Kennedy,Ian, Ari	899
Cueto,Johnny, Cin	888
Cain,Matt, SF	876
Rodriguez,Wandy, Hou-Pit	875
Bailey,Homer, Cin	874
Hamels,Cole, Phi	867
Lohse,Kyle, StL	864

Innings Pitched

Dickey,R.A., NYM	233.2
Kershaw,Clayton, LAD	227.2
Cain,Matt, SF	219.1
Richard,Clayton, SD	218.2
Cueto,Johnny, Cin	217.0
Hamels,Cole, Phi	215.1
Lee,Cliff, Phi	211.0
Lohse,Kyle, StL	211.0
Latos,Mat, Cin	209.1
2 tied with	208.1

Most Pitches in a Game

Santana,Johan, NYM	134
Dickey,R.A., NYM	128
Hamels,Cole, Phi	128
Volquez,Edinson, SD	127
Cahill,Trevor, Ari	126
Cain,Matt, SF	125
Zambrano,Carlos, Mia	125
Bumgarner,Madison, SF	123
Jackson,Edwin, Was	123
5 tied with	122

Stolen Bases Allowed

Burnett,A.J., Pit	38
Hanson,Tommy, Atl	31
Bumgarner,Madison, SF	27
Johnson,Josh, Mia	27
Lincecum,Tim, SF	25
Hamels,Cole, Phi	23
Volquez,Edinson, SD	22
Rodriguez,Fernando, Hou	20
Volstad,Chris, ChC	19
Young,Chris, NYM	19

Caught Stealing Off

Kershaw,Clayton, LAD	12
Hamels,Cole, Phi	11
Hanson,Tommy, Atl	11
Bumgarner,Madison, SF	10
Norris,Bud, Hou	10
Volquez,Edinson, SD	10
Cain,Matt, SF	9
Cueto,Johnny, Cin	9
Lynn,Lance, StL	9
Vogelsong,Ryan, SF	9

Stolen Base Pct Allowed
(minimum 162 IP)

Cueto,Johnny, Cin	10.0
Hudson,Tim, Atl	28.6
Miley,Wade, Ari	33.3
Westbrook,Jake, StL	33.3
Kershaw,Clayton, LAD	40.0
Wainwright,Adam, StL	40.0
Lynn,Lance, StL	50.0
Maholm,Paul, ChC-Atl	50.0
Vogelsong,Ryan, SF	52.6
Blanton,Joe, Phi-LAD	53.3

Pickoffs

Kershaw,Clayton, LAD	11
Cueto,Johnny, Cin	10
Buehrle,Mark, Mia	5
Bumgarner,Madison, SF	5
Dickey,R.A., NYM	5
Hamels,Cole, Phi	5
6 tied with	4

2012 National League Pitching Leaders

Strikeouts Per 9 IP
(minimum 162 IP)

Gonzalez, Gio, Was	9.35
Samardzija, Jeff, ChC	9.28
Lynn, Lance, StL	9.21
Lincecum, Tim, SF	9.19
Kershaw, Clayton, LAD	9.05
Hamels, Cole, Phi	9.03
Gallardo, Yovani, Mil	9.00
Dickey, R.A., NYM	8.86
Lee, Cliff, Phi	8.83
Norris, Bud, Hou	8.82

Opp On-Base Percentage
(minimum 162 IP)

Kershaw, Clayton, LAD	.270
Cain, Matt, SF	.274
Lohse, Kyle, StL	.274
Dickey, R.A., NYM	.278
Lee, Cliff, Phi	.278
Gonzalez, Gio, Was	.283
Bumgarner, Madison, SF	.284
Hamels, Cole, Phi	.285
Miley, Wade, Ari	.290
Niese, Jon, NYM	.291

Opp Slugging Average
(minimum 162 IP)

Gonzalez, Gio, Was	.299
Kershaw, Clayton, LAD	.323
Cain, Matt, SF	.361
Burnett, A.J., Pit	.361
Hudson, Tim, Atl	.361
Dickey, R.A., NYM	.362
Volquez, Edinson, SD	.362
Harrell, Lucas, Hou	.363
Johnson, Josh, Mia	.363
Cueto, Johnny, Cin	.366

Opponent OPS
(minimum 162 IP)

Gonzalez, Gio, Was	.582
Kershaw, Clayton, LAD	.593
Cain, Matt, SF	.635
Dickey, R.A., NYM	.640
Lohse, Kyle, StL	.642
Hamels, Cole, Phi	.661
Niese, Jon, NYM	.663
Hudson, Tim, Atl	.666
Cueto, Johnny, Cin	.667
Burnett, A.J., Pit	.668

Home Runs Per Nine IP
(minimum 162 IP)

Gonzalez, Gio, Was	0.41
Hudson, Tim, Atl	0.60
Harrell, Lucas, Hou	0.60
Westbrook, Jake, StL	0.62
Cueto, Johnny, Cin	0.62
Kershaw, Clayton, LAD	0.63
Miley, Wade, Ari	0.65
Johnson, Josh, Mia	0.66
Wainwright, Adam, StL	0.68
Volquez, Edinson, SD	0.69

Batting Average vs. LHB
(minimum 125 BF)

Motte, Jason, StL	.122
Jansen, Kenley, LAD	.147
Beachy, Brandon, Atl	.148
Arredondo, Jose, Cin	.165
Detwiler, Ross, Was	.170
Clippard, Tyler, Was	.170
Kershaw, Clayton, LAD	.181
Wood, Travis, ChC	.195
Dempster, Ryan, ChC	.197
2 tied with	.198

Batting Average vs. RHB
(minimum 225 BF)

Strasburg, Stephen, Was	.185
Cain, Matt, SF	.191
Gonzalez, Gio, Was	.199
Medlen, Kris, Atl	.207
Latos, Mat, Cin	.208
Kershaw, Clayton, LAD	.216
Dickey, R.A., NYM	.218
Cueto, Johnny, Cin	.220
Stammen, Craig, Was	.224
Lohse, Kyle, StL	.226

Opp BA w/ RISP
(minimum 125 BF)

Zimmermann, Jordan, Was	.163
Cain, Matt, SF	.171
Dickey, R.A., NYM	.177
Kershaw, Clayton, LAD	.180
Kendrick, Kyle, Phi	.183
Lohse, Kyle, StL	.184
Gonzalez, Gio, Was	.190
Bumgarner, Madison, SF	.196
Harang, Aaron, LAD	.202
Hamels, Cole, Phi	.207

OBP vs. Leadoff Hitter
(minimum 150 BF)

Cueto, Johnny, Cin	.234
Bailey, Homer, Cin	.236
Arroyo, Bronson, Cin	.244
Strasburg, Stephen, Was	.256
Miley, Wade, Ari	.265
Westbrook, Jake, StL	.267
Lohse, Kyle, StL	.267
Dickey, R.A., NYM	.268
Kershaw, Clayton, LAD	.273
Gonzalez, Gio, Was	.273

Strikeouts / Walks Ratio
(minimum 162 IP)

Lee, Cliff, Phi	7.39
Blanton, Joe, Phi-LAD	4.88
Dickey, R.A., NYM	4.26
Hamels, Cole, Phi	4.15
Bumgarner, Madison, SF	3.90
Miley, Wade, Ari	3.89
Cain, Matt, SF	3.78
Lohse, Kyle, StL	3.76
Arroyo, Bronson, Cin	3.69
Kershaw, Clayton, LAD	3.64

Highest GB/FB Ratio
(minimum 162 IP)

Westbrook, Jake, StL	2.77
Cahill, Trevor, Ari	2.69
Harrell, Lucas, Hou	2.54
Burnett, A.J., Pit	2.35
Hudson, Tim, Atl	2.20
Wainwright, Adam, StL	1.93
Richard, Clayton, SD	1.93
Maholm, Paul, ChC-Atl	1.87
Leake, Mike, Cin	1.84
Volquez, Edinson, SD	1.79

Lowest GB/FB Ratio
(minimum 162 IP)

Minor, Mike, Atl	0.81
Kennedy, Ian, Ari	0.88
Cain, Matt, SF	0.90
Harang, Aaron, LAD	0.94
Norris, Bud, Hou	0.99
McDonald, James, Pit	0.99
Hanson, Tommy, Atl	1.01
Zito, Barry, SF	1.02
Capuano, Chris, LAD	1.03
Arroyo, Bronson, Cin	1.11

Sacrifice Flies Allowed

Harang, Aaron, LAD	10
Harrell, Lucas, Hou	10
Cain, Matt, SF	9
Burnett, A.J., Pit	8
Jackson, Edwin, Was	8
Johnson, Josh, Mia	8
Minor, Mike, Atl	8
Volstad, Chris, ChC	8
Zambrano, Carlos, Mia	8
7 tied with	7

Sacrifice Hits Allowed

Nolasco, Ricky, Mia	19
Kershaw, Clayton, LAD	18
Capuano, Chris, LAD	16
Buehrle, Mark, Mia	14
Correia, Kevin, Pit	14
Kennedy, Ian, Ari	13
Cahill, Trevor, Ari	12
Zito, Barry, SF	12
5 tied with	11

GIDP Induced

Dickey, R.A., NYM	26
Cahill, Trevor, Ari	23
Westbrook, Jake, StL	23
Richard, Clayton, SD	22
Burnett, A.J., Pit	21
Lee, Cliff, Phi	21
Nolasco, Ricky, Mia	21
Ziegler, Brad, Ari	21
Maholm, Paul, ChC-Atl	19
2 tied with	18

GIDP Per Nine IP
(minimum 162 IP)

Westbrook, Jake, StL	1.19
Cahill, Trevor, Ari	1.04
Dickey, R.A., NYM	1.00
Nolasco, Ricky, Mia	0.99
Burnett, A.J., Pit	0.93
Richard, Clayton, SD	0.91
Maholm, Paul, ChC-Atl	0.91
Lee, Cliff, Phi	0.90
Leake, Mike, Cin	0.86
Minor, Mike, Atl	0.85

2012 National League Pitching Leaders

Saves			Blown Saves			Save Pct			Save Opportunities	
						(minimum 20 Save Ops)				
Kimbrel,Craig, Atl	42		Axford,John, Mil	9		Street,Huston, SD	95.8		Motte,Jason, StL	49
Motte,Jason, StL	42		Bell,Heath, Mia	8		Kimbrel,Craig, Atl	93.3		Kimbrel,Craig, Atl	45
Chapman,Aroldis, Cin	38		Belisle,Matt, Col	7		Myers,Brett, Hou	90.5		Axford,John, Mil	44
Papelbon,Jonathan, Phi	38		Betancourt,Rafael, Col	7		Papelbon,Jonathan, Phi	90.5		Chapman,Aroldis, Cin	43
Hanrahan,Joel, Pit	36		Jansen,Kenley, LAD	7		Hanrahan,Joel, Pit	90.0		Papelbon,Jonathan, Phi	42
Axford,John, Mil	35		Motte,Jason, StL	7		Francisco,Frank, NYM	88.5		Hanrahan,Joel, Pit	40
Clippard,Tyler, Was	32		Rodriguez,Francisco, Mil	7		Chapman,Aroldis, Cin	88.4		Betancourt,Rafael, Col	38
Putz,J.J., Ari	32		Casilla,Santiago, SF	6		Marmol,Carlos, ChC	87.0		Clippard,Tyler, Was	37
Betancourt,Rafael, Col	31		Hernandez,David, Ari	6		Clippard,Tyler, Was	86.5		Putz,J.J., Ari	37
2 tied with	25		Mujica,Edward, Mia-StL	6		Putz,J.J., Ari	86.5		Jansen,Kenley, LAD	32

Easy Saves			Regular Saves			Tough Saves			Holds Adjusted Saves %	
									(minimum 20 Save Ops)	
Motte,Jason, StL	30		Kimbrel,Craig, Atl	15		Motte,Jason, StL	6		Street,Huston, SD	95.8
Clippard,Tyler, Was	26		Chapman,Aroldis, Cin	13		Hensley,Clay, SF	3		Kimbrel,Craig, Atl	93.3
Kimbrel,Craig, Atl	26		Hanrahan,Joel, Pit	13		Burnett,Sean, Was	2		Myers,Brett, Hou	90.5
Chapman,Aroldis, Cin	23		Papelbon,Jonathan, Phi	13		Chapman,Aroldis, Cin	2		Papelbon,Jonathan, Phi	90.5
Hanrahan,Joel, Pit	23		Axford,John, Mil	12		Cishek,Steve, Mia	2		Clippard,Tyler, Was	90.0
Papelbon,Jonathan, Phi	23		Betancourt,Rafael, Col	11		Gregerson,Luke, SD	2		Hanrahan,Joel, Pit	90.0
Putz,J.J., Ari	23		Jansen,Kenley, LAD	11		Lopez,Wilton, Hou	2		Chapman,Aroldis, Cin	89.8
Axford,John, Mil	22		Romo,Sergio, SF	10		Papelbon,Jonathan, Phi	2		Francisco,Frank, NYM	88.9
Betancourt,Rafael, Col	20		Putz,J.J., Ari	9		Street,Huston, SD	2		Marmol,Carlos, ChC	88.0
Casilla,Santiago, SF	18		2 tied with	8		18 tied with	1		Putz,J.J., Ari	86.5

Relief Wins			Relief Losses			Relief Games			Holds	
Belisario,Ronald, LAD	8		Rodriguez,Fernando, Hou	10		Belisle,Matt, Col	80		Boggs,Mitchell, StL	34
Brothers,Rex, Col	8		Axford,John, Mil	8		Camp,Shawn, ChC	80		Grilli,Jason, Pit	32
Casilla,Santiago, SF	7		Belisle,Matt, Col	8		Choate,Randy, Mia-LAD	80		Rodriguez,Francisco, Mil	32
Russell,James, ChC	7		Rauch,Jon, NYM	7		Boggs,Mitchell, StL	78		Burnett,Sean, Was	31
Arredondo,Jose, Cin	6		Rodriguez,Francisco, Mil	7		Rodriguez,Francisco, Mil	78		Mujica,Edward, Mia-StL	30
Loe,Kameron, Mil	6		6 tied with	6		Gregerson,Luke, SD	77		O'Flaherty,Eric, Atl	28
Lopez,Wilton, Hou	6					Russell,James, ChC	77		Bastardo,Antonio, Phi	26
Stammen,Craig, Was	6					Wright,Wesley, Hou	77		Belisle,Matt, Col	26
Ziegler,Brad, Ari	6					Ziegler,Brad, Ari	77		Hernandez,David, Ari	25
17 tied with	5					Durbin,Chad, Atl	76		Gregerson,Luke, SD	24

Relief Innings			Inherited Runners Scrd %			Relief Opp On Base Pct			Relief Opp Slugging Avg	
			(minimum 30 IR)			(minimum 50 IP)			(minimum 50 IP)	
Roenicke,Josh, Col	88.2		Ondrusek,Logan, Cin	9.5		Kimbrel,Craig, Atl	.186		Kimbrel,Craig, Atl	.172
Stammen,Craig, Was	88.1		Brach,Brad, SD	10.9		Chapman,Aroldis, Cin	.225		Chapman,Aroldis, Cin	.226
Belisle,Matt, Col	80.0		Lopez,Javier, SF	13.7		Jansen,Kenley, LAD	.230		Jansen,Kenley, LAD	.274
Ottavino,Adam, Col	79.0		Thatcher,Joe, SD	15.2		Romo,Sergio, SF	.235		Belisario,Ronald, LAD	.278
Camp,Shawn, ChC	77.2		LeCure,Sam, Cin	16.1		Motte,Jason, StL	.245		Hernandez,David, Ari	.282
Hughes,Jared, Pit	75.2		Byrdak,Tim, NYM	17.1		Rauch,Jon, NYM	.250		Ziegler,Brad, Ari	.287
Martinez,Cristhian, Atl	73.2		Boggs,Mitchell, StL	17.6		Hernandez,David, Ari	.263		Romo,Sergio, SF	.290
Resop,Chris, Pit	73.2		Watson,Tony, Pit	18.0		Mujica,Edward, Mia-StL	.268		Boggs,Mitchell, StL	.291
Boggs,Mitchell, StL	73.1		Tolleson,Shawn, LAD	19.4		Putz,J.J., Ari	.269		O'Flaherty,Eric, Atl	.302
Clippard,Tyler, Was	72.2		Ziegler,Brad, Ari	20.4		Lopez,Wilton, Hou	.277		Marshall,Sean, Cin	.308

2012 National League Pitching Leaders

Relief Opp BA Vs LHB
(minimum 50 AB)

Chapman,Aroldis, Cin	.108
O'Flaherty,Eric, Atl	.113
Kimbrel,Craig, Atl	.116
Hoover,J.J., Cin	.120
Motte,Jason, StL	.122
Street,Huston, SD	.127
Hanrahan,Joel, Pit	.135
Lincoln,Brad, Pit	.138
Dolis,Rafael, ChC	.141
Jansen,Kenley, LAD	.147

Relief Opp BA Vs RHB
(minimum 50 AB)

Street,Huston, SD	.132
Kimbrel,Craig, Atl	.136
Belisario,Ronald, LAD	.142
Hernandez,David, Ari	.145
Jansen,Kenley, LAD	.145
Tolleson,Shawn, LAD	.152
Chapman,Aroldis, Cin	.155
Rodriguez,Henry, Was	.158
Valdes,Raul, Phi	.164
Storen,Drew, Was	.164

Relief Opp Batting Average
(minimum 50 IP)

Kimbrel,Craig, Atl	.126
Chapman,Aroldis, Cin	.141
Jansen,Kenley, LAD	.146
Romo,Sergio, SF	.185
Belisario,Ronald, LAD	.187
Hanrahan,Joel, Pit	.187
Hernandez,David, Ari	.190
Motte,Jason, StL	.191
Watson,Tony, Pit	.198
Marmol,Carlos, ChC	.200

Relief Earned Run Average
(minimum 50 IP)

Kimbrel,Craig, Atl	1.01
Chapman,Aroldis, Cin	1.51
O'Flaherty,Eric, Atl	1.73
Romo,Sergio, SF	1.79
Lopez,Wilton, Hou	2.17
Boggs,Mitchell, StL	2.21
Stammen,Craig, Was	2.34
Jansen,Kenley, LAD	2.35
Burnett,Sean, Was	2.38
Gregerson,Luke, SD	2.39

Rel OBP 1st Batter Faced
(minimum 40 BF)

Street,Huston, SD	.175
Chapman,Aroldis, Cin	.176
Romo,Sergio, SF	.188
Boggs,Mitchell, StL	.205
Watson,Tony, Pit	.206
Durbin,Chad, Atl	.213
Betancourt,Rafael, Col	.217
Casilla,Santiago, SF	.219
Rauch,Jon, NYM	.219
2 tied with	.222

Rel Opp BA w/ Runners On
(minimum 50 IP)

Kimbrel,Craig, Atl	.055
Chapman,Aroldis, Cin	.140
Hanrahan,Joel, Pit	.158
Marmol,Carlos, ChC	.161
O'Flaherty,Eric, Atl	.175
Romo,Sergio, SF	.176
Motte,Jason, StL	.177
Clippard,Tyler, Was	.177
Jansen,Kenley, LAD	.181
Gregerson,Luke, SD	.182

Relief Opp BA w/ RISP
(minimum 50 IP)

Kimbrel,Craig, Atl	.030
Grilli,Jason, Pit	.125
Gregerson,Luke, SD	.129
Hanrahan,Joel, Pit	.131
Boggs,Mitchell, StL	.145
Chapman,Aroldis, Cin	.152
Simon,Alfredo, Cin	.160
Mattheus,Ryan, Was	.161
Watson,Tony, Pit	.167
Burnett,Sean, Was	.169

Fastest Avg Fastball-Relief
(minimum 50 IP)

Chapman,Aroldis, Cin	97.7
Kimbrel,Craig, Atl	96.8
Motte,Jason, StL	96.8
Axford,John, Mil	96.2
Hanrahan,Joel, Pit	95.9
Boggs,Mitchell, StL	95.8
Parnell,Bobby, NYM	95.7
Brothers,Rex, Col	95.3
Cruz,Rhiner, Hou	95.0
Hernandez,David, Ari	94.7

Fastest Average Fastball
(minimum 162 IP)

Samardzija,Jeff, ChC	95.0
Zimmermann,Jordan, Was	93.9
Volquez,Edinson, SD	93.6
Jackson,Edwin, Was	93.5
Kershaw,Clayton, LAD	93.2
Gonzalez,Gio, Was	93.1
Lynn,Lance, StL	92.8
Johnson,Josh, Mia	92.8
Detwiler,Ross, Was	92.7
Cueto,Johnny, Cin	92.7

Slowest Average Fastball
(minimum 162 IP)

Dickey,R.A., NYM	83.4
Zito,Barry, SF	83.9
Buehrle,Mark, Mia	85.0
Arroyo,Bronson, Cin	87.2
Maholm,Paul, ChC-Atl	87.4
Capuano,Chris, LAD	88.0
Hudson,Tim, Atl	89.0
Rodriguez,Wandy, Hou-Pit	89.3
Cahill,Trevor, Ari	89.4
Lohse,Kyle, StL	89.5

Pitches 100+ Velocity

Chapman,Aroldis, Cin	242
Cashner,Andrew, SD	104
Rodriguez,Henry, Was	58
Parnell,Bobby, NYM	28
Rosenthal,Trevor, StL	12
Motte,Jason, StL	9
Kimbrel,Craig, Atl	5
Axford,John, Mil	4
3 tied with	1

Pitches 95+ Velocity

Strasburg,Stephen, Was	1368
Eovaldi,Nathan, LAD-Mia	1100
Samardzija,Jeff, ChC	1031
Chapman,Aroldis, Cin	976
Axford,John, Mil	900
Rogers,Esmil, Col	829
Motte,Jason, StL	745
Hanrahan,Joel, Pit	683
Kimbrel,Craig, Atl	608
Parnell,Bobby, NYM	592

Pitches Less Than 80 MPH

Dickey,R.A., NYM	2418
Rodriguez,Wandy, Hou-Pit	1932
Zito,Barry, SF	1452
Arroyo,Bronson, Cin	1372
Buehrle,Mark, Mia	1246
Maholm,Paul, ChC-Atl	1210
Capuano,Chris, LAD	948
Moyer,Jamie, Col	852
Wolf,Randy, Mil	784
Bedard,Erik, Pit	779

Lowest % Fastballs
(minimum 162 IP)

Dickey,R.A., NYM	14.0
Zito,Barry, SF	36.8
Buehrle,Mark, Mia	37.3
Arroyo,Bronson, Cin	38.3
Maholm,Paul, ChC-Atl	41.4
Wainwright,Adam, StL	41.8
Bumgarner,Madison, SF	43.4
Nolasco,Ricky, Mia	44.8
Leake,Mike, Cin	46.3
Hamels,Cole, Phi	46.6

Highest % Fastballs
(minimum 162 IP)

Detwiler,Ross, Was	80.3
Miley,Wade, Ari	72.2
Gonzalez,Gio, Was	70.8
Harrell,Lucas, Hou	70.7
Lynn,Lance, StL	70.4
Kennedy,Ian, Ari	65.9
Cahill,Trevor, Ari	63.0
Zimmermann,Jordan, Was	62.5
Westbrook,Jake, StL	62.3
McDonald,James, Pit	62.2

Highest % Curveballs
(minimum 162 IP)

Burnett,A.J., Pit	34.1
Rodriguez,Wandy, Hou-Pit	30.8
Wainwright,Adam, StL	24.7
Volquez,Edinson, SD	24.6
Gonzalez,Gio, Was	21.0
Zito,Barry, SF	19.9
Niese,Jon, NYM	19.4
Arroyo,Bronson, Cin	18.8
Gallardo,Yovani, Mil	18.5
Vogelsong,Ryan, SF	18.0

2012 National League Pitching Leaders

Highest % Changeups
(minimum 162 IP)

Buehrle,Mark, Mia	27.0
Capuano,Chris, LAD	26.5
Hamels,Cole, Phi	26.3
Volquez,Edinson, SD	25.5
Lincecum,Tim, SF	20.4
Lohse,Kyle, StL	19.2
Cahill,Trevor, Ari	18.5
Blanton,Joe, Phi-LAD	18.4
Cueto,Johnny, Cin	18.0
Richard,Clayton, SD	17.6

Highest % Sliders
(minimum 162 IP)

Bumgarner,Madison, SF	39.0
Norris,Bud, Hou	36.6
Zito,Barry, SF	32.5
Maholm,Paul, ChC-Atl	30.4
Hanson,Tommy, Atl	29.5
Jackson,Edwin, Was	28.2
Latos,Mat, Cin	24.6
Johnson,Josh, Mia	23.9
Zimmermann,Jordan, Was	23.7
Nolasco,Ricky, Mia	23.6

Balks

Kennedy,Ian, Ari	4
Cueto,Johnny, Cin	3
Harrell,Lucas, Hou	3
10 tied with	2

Strikeout/Hit Ratio
(minimum 50 IP)

Kimbrel,Craig, Atl	4.30
Chapman,Aroldis, Cin	3.49
Jansen,Kenley, LAD	3.00
Hernandez,David, Ari	2.04
Bastardo,Antonio, Phi	2.03
Grilli,Jason, Pit	2.00
Marmol,Carlos, ChC	1.80
Motte,Jason, StL	1.76
Romo,Sergio, SF	1.70
Hanrahan,Joel, Pit	1.68

Opp OPS vs Fastballs
(minimum 251 BF)

Belisario,Ronald, LAD	.553
Kershaw,Clayton, LAD	.575
Gonzalez,Gio, Was	.589
Greinke,Zack, Mil	.603
Medlen,Kris, Atl	.617
Lee,Cliff, Phi	.619
Cueto,Johnny, Cin	.637
Billingsley,Chad, LAD	.638
Garza,Matt, ChC	.638
Lohse,Kyle, StL	.639

Opp OPS vs Curveballs
(minimum 100 BF)

Strasburg,Stephen, Was	.467
Gonzalez,Gio, Was	.477
Niese,Jon, NYM	.493
Latos,Mat, Cin	.500
Johnson,Josh, Mia	.528
Burnett,A.J., Pit	.534
Cain,Matt, SF	.551
McDonald,James, Pit	.554
Zito,Barry, SF	.595
Wainwright,Adam, StL	.605

Opp OPS vs Changeups
(minimum 100 BF)

Medlen,Kris, Atl	.296
Clippard,Tyler, Was	.489
Richard,Clayton, SD	.587
Maholm,Paul, ChC-Atl	.596
Gee,Dillon, NYM	.607
Marcum,Shaun, Mil	.617
Sanchez,Anibal, Mia	.620
Capuano,Chris, LAD	.633
Collmenter,Josh, Ari	.634
Volquez,Edinson, SD	.650

Opp OPS vs Sliders
(minimum 64 BF)

Rauch,Jon, NYM	.384
Beachy,Brandon, Atl	.442
Romo,Sergio, SF	.471
Dempster,Ryan, ChC	.479
Kontos,George, SF	.481
Grilli,Jason, Pit	.483
Stammen,Craig, Was	.498
Cain,Matt, SF	.507
Gee,Dillon, NYM	.513
Camp,Shawn, ChC	.524

Earned Runs

Lincecum,Tim, SF	107
Blanton,Joe, Phi-LAD	100
Richard,Clayton, SD	97
Nolasco,Ricky, Mia	95
Kennedy,Ian, Ari	93
Leake,Mike, Cin	91
Wolf,Randy, Mil	90
Hanson,Tommy, Atl	87
Norris,Bud, Hou	87
Wainwright,Adam, StL	87

Hits Per Nine Innings
(minimum 162 IP)

Kershaw,Clayton, LAD	6.72
Gonzalez,Gio, Was	6.73
Cain,Matt, SF	7.26
Dickey,R.A., NYM	7.40
Minor,Mike, Atl	7.58
Latos,Mat, Cin	7.70
McDonald,James, Pit	7.74
Volquez,Edinson, SD	7.88
Bumgarner,Madison, SF	7.91
Hamels,Cole, Phi	7.94

2012 American League Fielding Leaders

2B Pivot %
(minimum 98 G)

Ackley,Dustin, Sea	0.750
Andino,Robert, Bal	0.727
Beckham,Gordon, CWS	0.724
Pedroia,Dustin, Bos	0.721
Kinsler,Ian, Tex	0.709
Johnson,Kelly, Tor	0.676
Kipnis,Jason, Cle	0.646
Weeks,Jemile, Oak	0.631
Cano,Robinson, NYY	0.620
Kendrick,Howie, LAA	0.560

SS Pivot %
(minimum 98 G)

Ryan,Brendan, Sea	0.716
Cabrera,Asdrubal, Cle	0.688
Hardy,J.J., Bal	0.660
Aybar,Erick, LAA	0.653
Peralta,Jhonny, Det	0.644
Escobar,Alcides, KC	0.622
Aviles,Mike, Bos	0.620
Johnson,Elliot, TB	0.595
Jeter,Derek, NYY	0.586
Ramirez,Alexei, CWS	0.573

Highest Pct CS by Catchers
(minimum 600 INN or 50 SBA)

Perez,Salvador, KC	37.5
Wieters,Matt, Bal	36.3
Suzuki,Kurt, Oak	30.2
Olivo,Miguel, Sea	28.8
Molina,Jose, TB	27.8
Avila,Alex, Det	26.2
Wilson,Bobby, LAA	25.0
Santana,Carlos, Cle	24.7
Iannetta,Chris, LAA	22.0
Martin,Russell, NYY	20.3

Lowest Pct CS by Catchers
(minimum 600 INN or 50 SBA)

Mauer,Joe, Min	8.2
Marson,Lou, Cle	13.0
Montero,Jesus, Sea	14.3
Saltalamacchia,J, Bos	15.8
Napoli,Mike, Tex	16.0
Pena,Brayan, KC	16.1
Arencibia,J.P., Tor	18.5
Pierzynski,A.J., CWS	20.0
Martin,Russell, NYY	20.3
Iannetta,Chris, LAA	22.0

2B Double Play %
(minimum 98 G)

Beckham,Gordon, CWS	0.651
Andino,Robert, Bal	0.635
Pedroia,Dustin, Bos	0.635
Ackley,Dustin, Sea	0.604
Kipnis,Jason, Cle	0.575
Kinsler,Ian, Tex	0.566
Johnson,Kelly, Tor	0.556
Weeks,Jemile, Oak	0.518
Cano,Robinson, NYY	0.516
Kendrick,Howie, LAA	0.503

3B Double Play %
(minimum 98 G)

Cabrera,Miguel, Det	0.577
Moustakas,Mike, KC	0.529
Beltre,Adrian, Tex	0.439
Youkilis,Kevin, Bos-CWS	0.439
Callaspo,Alberto, LAA	0.346
Seager,Kyle, Sea	0.333
Lawrie,Brett, Tor	0.328

SS Double Play %
(minimum 98 G)

Ryan,Brendan, Sea	0.686
Aviles,Mike, Bos	0.650
Ramirez,Alexei, CWS	0.628
Cabrera,Asdrubal, Cle	0.618
Hardy,J.J., Bal	0.612
Aybar,Erick, LAA	0.598
Peralta,Jhonny, Det	0.598
Escobar,Yunel, Tor	0.591
Escobar,Alcides, KC	0.587
Johnson,Elliot, TB	0.580

Errors

Cabrera,Asdrubal, Cle	19
Escobar,Alcides, KC	19
Plouffe,Trevor, Min	19
Kinsler,Ian, Tex	18
Rodriguez,Sean, TB	18
Lawrie,Brett, Tor	17
Andrus,Elvis, Tex	16
6 tied with	15

Fielding Errors

Kendrick,Howie, LAA	14
Kinsler,Ian, Tex	13
Betemit,Wilson, Bal	12
Escobar,Alcides, KC	12
Andrus,Elvis, Tex	10
Aviles,Mike, Bos	10
Plouffe,Trevor, Min	10
Fielder,Prince, Det	9
Hannahan,Jack, Cle	9
Seager,Kyle, Sea	9

Throwing Errors

Cabrera,Asdrubal, Cle	12
Rodriguez,Sean, TB	11
Andino,Robert, Bal	9
Dozier,Brian, Min	9
Lawrie,Brett, Tor	9
Plouffe,Trevor, Min	9
Cabrera,Miguel, Det	8
Johnson,Elliot, TB	8
Moustakas,Mike, KC	8
Wieters,Matt, Bal	8

Range Factor for 2B
(minimum 98 games)

Cano,Robinson, NYY	4.82
Johnson,Kelly, Tor	4.82
Beckham,Gordon, CWS	4.75
Kipnis,Jason, Cle	4.73
Andino,Robert, Bal	4.69
Kendrick,Howie, LAA	4.67
Pedroia,Dustin, Bos	4.59
Ackley,Dustin, Sea	4.52
Weeks,Jemile, Oak	4.21
Kinsler,Ian, Tex	4.19

Range Factor for 3B
(minimum 98 games)

Lawrie,Brett, Tor	3.01
Moustakas,Mike, KC	3.01
Callaspo,Alberto, LAA	2.54
Cabrera,Miguel, Det	2.52
Beltre,Adrian, Tex	2.43
Seager,Kyle, Sea	2.42
Youkilis,Kevin, Bos-CWS	2.41

Range Factor for SS
(minimum 98 games)

Cabrera,Asdrubal, Cle	4.90
Escobar,Yunel, Tor	4.84
Hardy,J.J., Bal	4.83
Aviles,Mike, Bos	4.68
Ryan,Brendan, Sea	4.56
Aybar,Erick, LAA	4.47
Andrus,Elvis, Tex	4.37
Ramirez,Alexei, CWS	4.27
Escobar,Alcides, KC	4.24
Peralta,Jhonny, Det	4.14

2012 National League Fielding Leaders

2B Pivot %		SS Pivot %		Highest Pct CS by Catchers		Lowest Pct CS by Catchers	
(minimum 98 G)		(minimum 98 G)		(minimum 600 INN or 50 SBA)		(minimum 600 INN or 50 SBA)	
Barney,Darwin, ChC	0.690	Barmes,Clint, Pit	0.760	Molina,Yadier, StL	45.7	Barajas,Rod, Pit	4.1
Espinosa,Danny, Was	0.677	Crawford,Brandon, SF	0.639	Hanigan,Ryan, Cin	43.3	Baker,John, SD	9.3
Uggla,Dan, Atl	0.673	Tejada,Ruben, NYM	0.623	Montero,Miguel, Ari	34.3	Clevenger,Steve, ChC	11.8
Walker,Neil, Pit	0.611	Desmond,Ian, Was	0.623	Ellis,A.J., LAD	27.5	Flores,Jesus, Was	12.1
Weeks,Rickie, Mil	0.595	Furcal,Rafael, StL	0.597	Rosario,Wilin, Col	27.3	McKenry,Michael, Pit	14.1
Altuve,Jose, Hou	0.590	Reyes,Jose, Mia	0.582	Posey,Buster, SF	26.3	Castro,Jason, Hou	17.4
Hill,Aaron, Ari	0.584	Cozart,Zack, Cin	0.559	Hundley,Nick, SD	26.0	McCann,Brian, Atl	18.3
Ellis,Mark, LAD	0.554	Castro,Starlin, ChC	0.531	Ruiz,Carlos, Phi	24.7	Thole,Josh, NYM	18.6
Murphy,Daniel, NYM	0.550	Cabrera,Everth, SD	0.514	Sanchez,Hector, SF	21.6	Lucroy,Jonathan, Mil	18.6
Phillips,Brandon, Cin	0.534	Rollins,Jimmy, Phi	0.500	2 tied with	20.0	Buck,John, Mia	18.6

2B Double Play %		3B Double Play %		SS Double Play %	
(minimum 98 G)		(minimum 98 G)		(minimum 98 G)	
Barney,Darwin, ChC	0.527	Ramirez,Hanley, Mia-LAD	0.515	Desmond,Ian, Was	0.604
Uggla,Dan, Atl	0.497	Freese,David, StL	0.426	Tejada,Ruben, NYM	0.602
Hill,Aaron, Ari	0.497	Zimmerman,Ryan, Was	0.426	Barmes,Clint, Pit	0.588
Espinosa,Danny, Was	0.485	Alvarez,Pedro, Pit	0.343	Crawford,Brandon, SF	0.586
Phillips,Brandon, Cin	0.475	Wright,David, NYM	0.328	Furcal,Rafael, StL	0.573
Walker,Neil, Pit	0.449	Johnson,Chris, Hou-Ari	0.283	Cozart,Zack, Cin	0.565
Murphy,Daniel, NYM	0.441	Sandoval,Pablo, SF	0.260	Rollins,Jimmy, Phi	0.562
Ellis,Mark, LAD	0.438	Ramirez,Aramis, Mil	0.231	Reyes,Jose, Mia	0.561
Altuve,Jose, Hou	0.426	Headley,Chase, SD	0.228	Castro,Starlin, ChC	0.518
Weeks,Rickie, Mil	0.426	Jones,Chipper, Atl	0.207	Cabrera,Everth, SD	0.373

Errors		Fielding Errors		Throwing Errors	
Alvarez,Pedro, Pit	27	Castro,Starlin, ChC	19	Alvarez,Pedro, Pit	16
Castro,Starlin, ChC	27	Johnson,Chris, Hou-Ari	15	Rosario,Wilin, Col	14
Johnson,Chris, Hou-Ari	19	Wigginton,Ty, Phi	12	Zimmerman,Ryan, Was	12
Zimmerman,Ryan, Was	19	Alvarez,Pedro, Pit	11	Cabrera,Everth, SD	10
Crawford,Brandon, SF	18	Crawford,Brandon, SF	11	Cozart,Zack, Cin	9
Freese,David, StL	18	Descalso,Daniel, StL	11	Castro,Starlin, ChC	8
Gordon,Dee, LAD	18	Freeman,Freddie, Atl	11	Freese,David, StL	8
Reyes,Jose, Mia	18	Gordon,Dee, LAD	11	Pacheco,Jordan, Col	8
3 tied with	16	Weeks,Rickie, Mil	11	Reyes,Jose, Mia	8
		3 tied with	10	Tejada,Ruben, NYM	8

Range Factor for 2B		Range Factor for 3B		Range Factor for SS	
(minimum 98 games)		(minimum 98 games)		(minimum 98 games)	
Barney,Darwin, ChC	5.16	Sandoval,Pablo, SF	2.89	Crawford,Brandon, SF	4.82
Hill,Aaron, Ari	5.06	Headley,Chase, SD	2.67	Castro,Starlin, ChC	4.69
Walker,Neil, Pit	5.01	Freese,David, StL	2.62	Furcal,Rafael, StL	4.54
Scutaro,Marco, Col-SF	5.00	Zimmerman,Ryan, Was	2.53	Cabrera,Everth, SD	4.47
Altuve,Jose, Hou	4.89	Wright,David, NYM	2.50	Cozart,Zack, Cin	4.28
Uggla,Dan, Atl	4.87	Johnson,Chris, Hou-Ari	2.49	Barmes,Clint, Pit	4.24
Ellis,Mark, LAD	4.79	Alvarez,Pedro, Pit	2.38	Tejada,Ruben, NYM	4.14
Phillips,Brandon, Cin	4.55	Jones,Chipper, Atl	2.23	Reyes,Jose, Mia	4.12
Murphy,Daniel, NYM	4.41	Ramirez,Hanley, Mia-LAD	2.15	Rollins,Jimmy, Phi	3.83
Espinosa,Danny, Was	4.39	Ramirez,Aramis, Mil	2.12	Desmond,Ian, Was	3.77

2012 Active Career Batting Leaders

Batting Average
(minimum 1000 PA)

Pujols,Albert	.325
Mauer,Joe	.323
Suzuki,Ichiro	.322
Helton,Todd	.320
Cabrera,Miguel	.318
Votto,Joey	.316
Posey,Buster	.314
Braun,Ryan	.313
Jeter,Derek	.313
Holliday,Matt	.313

On Base Percentage
(minimum 1000 PA)

Helton,Todd	.419
Votto,Joey	.415
Pujols,Albert	.414
Berkman,Lance	.409
Mauer,Joe	.405
Giambi,Jason	.403
Thome,Jim	.402
Jones,Chipper	.401
Johnson,Nick	.399
Abreu,Bobby	.396

Slugging Average
(minimum 1000 PA)

Pujols,Albert	.608
Braun,Ryan	.568
Cabrera,Miguel	.561
Rodriguez,Alex	.560
Thome,Jim	.554
Stanton,Giancarlo	.553
Votto,Joey	.553
Howard,Ryan	.551
Hamilton,Josh	.549
Ortiz,David	.547

Home Runs

Rodriguez,Alex	647
Thome,Jim	612
Pujols,Albert	475
Jones,Chipper	468
Jones,Andruw	434
Giambi,Jason	429
Konerko,Paul	422
Dunn,Adam	406
Ortiz,David	401
Soriano,Alfonso	372

Games

Vizquel,Omar	2968
Jeter,Derek	2585
Thome,Jim	2543
Rodriguez,Alex	2524
Jones,Chipper	2499
Damon,Johnny	2490
Abreu,Bobby	2347
Jones,Andruw	2196
Giambi,Jason	2163
Konerko,Paul	2142

At Bats

Vizquel,Omar	10586
Jeter,Derek	10551
Damon,Johnny	9736
Rodriguez,Alex	9662
Jones,Chipper	8984
Thome,Jim	8422
Abreu,Bobby	8347
Suzuki,Ichiro	8085
Lee,Carlos	7983
Beltre,Adrian	7965

Hits

Jeter,Derek	3304
Rodriguez,Alex	2901
Vizquel,Omar	2877
Damon,Johnny	2769
Jones,Chipper	2726
Suzuki,Ichiro	2606
Abreu,Bobby	2437
Helton,Todd	2420
Thome,Jim	2328
Lee,Carlos	2273

Total Bases

Rodriguez,Alex	5414
Jones,Chipper	4755
Jeter,Derek	4723
Thome,Jim	4667
Damon,Johnny	4214
Pujols,Albert	4206
Helton,Todd	4124
Abreu,Bobby	3981
Lee,Carlos	3854
Konerko,Paul	3851

Doubles

Helton,Todd	570
Abreu,Bobby	565
Jones,Chipper	549
Jeter,Derek	524
Damon,Johnny	522
Rolen,Scott	517
Rodriguez,Alex	512
Pujols,Albert	505
Ortiz,David	482
Lee,Carlos	469

Triples

Crawford,Carl	114
Reyes,Jose	111
Damon,Johnny	109
Rollins,Jimmy	105
Pierre,Juan	92
Suzuki,Ichiro	80
Granderson,Curtis	78
Vizquel,Omar	77
Beltran,Carlos	74
Furcal,Rafael	68

Runs Scored

Rodriguez,Alex	1898
Jeter,Derek	1868
Damon,Johnny	1668
Jones,Chipper	1619
Thome,Jim	1583
Vizquel,Omar	1445
Abreu,Bobby	1441
Pujols,Albert	1376
Helton,Todd	1360
Beltran,Carlos	1267

RBI

Rodriguez,Alex	1950
Thome,Jim	1699
Jones,Chipper	1623
Pujols,Albert	1434
Giambi,Jason	1405
Lee,Carlos	1363
Abreu,Bobby	1349
Helton,Todd	1345
Konerko,Paul	1336
Ortiz,David	1326

Walks

Thome,Jim	1747
Jones,Chipper	1512
Abreu,Bobby	1456
Giambi,Jason	1334
Helton,Todd	1295
Rodriguez,Alex	1217
Dunn,Adam	1170
Berkman,Lance	1163
Jeter,Derek	1039
Vizquel,Omar	1028

Intentional Walks

Pujols,Albert	267
Helton,Todd	184
Jones,Chipper	177
Suzuki,Ichiro	173
Thome,Jim	173
Cabrera,Miguel	161
Berkman,Lance	157
Howard,Ryan	139
Fielder,Prince	133
Ortiz,David	129

Hit By Pitch

Giambi,Jason	175
Rodriguez,Alex	167
Jeter,Derek	163
Utley,Chase	151
Rolen,Scott	127
Johnson,Reed	119
Quentin,Carlos	114
Weeks,Rickie	108
Pierzynski,A.J.	105
Ramirez,Aramis	101

Strikeouts

Thome,Jim	2548
Rodriguez,Alex	2032
Dunn,Adam	2031
Abreu,Bobby	1819
Jones,Andruw	1748
Jeter,Derek	1743
Soriano,Alfonso	1576
Giambi,Jason	1504
Pena,Carlos	1474
Hunter,Torii	1434

2012 Active Career Batting Leaders

Sacrifice Hits		Sacrifice Flies		Stolen Bases		Seasons Played	
Vizquel,Omar	256	Rodriguez,Alex	101	Pierre,Juan	591	Moyer,Jamie	25
Pierre,Juan	161	Lee,Carlos	98	Suzuki,Ichiro	452	Vizquel,Omar	24
Hernandez,Livan	123	Jones,Chipper	97	Crawford,Carl	432	Thome,Jim	22
Oswalt,Roy	105	Vizquel,Omar	94	Reyes,Jose	410	Jones,Chipper	19
Wilson,Jack	104	Rolen,Scott	93	Damon,Johnny	408	Oliver,Darren	19
Jeter,Derek	89	Giambi,Jason	90	Vizquel,Omar	404	Rodriguez,Alex	19
Cairo,Miguel	86	Helton,Todd	88	Rollins,Jimmy	403	6 tied with	18
Dempster,Ryan	85	Abreu,Bobby	83	Abreu,Bobby	399		
Hairston,Jerry	85	Beltran,Carlos	83	Jeter,Derek	348		
Polanco,Placido	83	Konerko,Paul	80	Figgins,Chone	337		

| At Bats Per Home Run | | Grounded Into DP | | Highest SB Success Pct | | Lowest SB Success Pct | |
(minimum 1000 AB)				(minimum 100 SBA)		(minimum 100 SBA)	
Howard,Ryan	13.5	Jeter,Derek	269	Utley,Chase	89.6	DeJesus,David	51.8
Thome,Jim	13.8	Konerko,Paul	263	Beltran,Carlos	86.7	Hall,Bill	60.8
Stanton,Giancarlo	14.2	Jones,Chipper	253	Werth,Jayson	86.7	Kotsay,Mark	61.3
Pujols,Albert	14.6	Pujols,Albert	251	McLouth,Nate	86.1	Pence,Hunter	63.2
Dunn,Adam	14.6	Rodriguez,Alex	235	Bay,Jason	85.2	Berkman,Lance	64.2
Rodriguez,Alex	14.9	Hunter,Torii	219	Kinsler,Ian	83.5	Ramirez,Alexei	66.3
Napoli,Mike	15.5	Young,Michael	215	Rollins,Jimmy	82.9	Carroll,Jamey	67.3
Fielder,Prince	15.8	Vizquel,Omar	207	Venable,Will	82.7	Hart,Corey	67.5
Ortiz,David	16.3	Lee,Carlos	206	Victorino,Shane	82.4	Izturis,Cesar	67.5
Giambi,Jason	16.4	Beltre,Adrian	199	Weeks,Rickie	82.3	Hunter,Torii	67.6

| Strikeouts / Walks Ratio | | At Bats Per GIDP | | OPS | | Secondary Average | |
(minimum 1000 AB)		(minimum 1000 AB)		(minimum 1000 PA)		(minimum 1000 PA)	
Pujols,Albert	.759	Stubbs,Drew	162.8	Pujols,Albert	1.022	Thome,Jim	.487
Hanigan,Ryan	.825	Bourn,Michael	158.7	Votto,Joey	.968	Dunn,Adam	.467
Helton,Todd	.840	Blanco,Gregor	122.6	Helton,Todd	.964	Berkman,Lance	.449
Mauer,Joe	.856	Saunders,Michael	119.9	Cabrera,Miguel	.956	Pujols,Albert	.445
Jones,Chipper	.932	Suzuki,Ichiro	117.2	Thome,Jim	.956	Giambi,Jason	.435
Pedroia,Dustin	.943	Venable,Will	113.0	Berkman,Lance	.953	Howard,Ryan	.422
Keppinger,Jeff	.966	Granderson,Curtis	111.2	Rodriguez,Alex	.945	Rodriguez,Alex	.419
Pierre,Juan	1.002	Drew,Stephen	109.6	Braun,Ryan	.943	Ortiz,David	.419
Callaspo,Alberto	1.022	Bonifacio,Emilio	109.5	Fielder,Prince	.931	Votto,Joey	.417
Vizquel,Omar	1.057	Damon,Johnny	103.6	Jones,Chipper	.930	Fielder,Prince	.414

| Highest Strikeout per PA | | Lowest Strikeout per PA | | Plate Appearances | | At Bats Per RBI | |
(minimum 1000 PA)		(minimum 1000 PA)				(minimum 1000 AB)	
Shoppach,Kelly	.334	Pierre,Juan	.057	Vizquel,Omar	12013	Howard,Ryan	4.4
Reynolds,Mark	.326	Keppinger,Jeff	.064	Jeter,Derek	11895	Pujols,Albert	4.8
Davis,Chris	.310	Polanco,Placido	.068	Rodriguez,Alex	11163	Ortiz,David	4.9
Alvarez,Pedro	.307	Callaspo,Alberto	.086	Damon,Johnny	10917	Rodriguez,Alex	5.0
Saltalamacchia,J	.294	Pedroia,Dustin	.086	Jones,Chipper	10614	Thome,Jim	5.0
Stubbs,Drew	.293	Molina,Yadier	.087	Thome,Jim	10313	Giambi,Jason	5.0
Stanton,Giancarlo	.288	Vizquel,Omar	.090	Abreu,Bobby	9926	Cabrera,Miguel	5.0
Dunn,Adam	.282	Izturis,Cesar	.092	Helton,Todd	9011	Hamilton,Josh	5.1
Howard,Ryan	.278	Suzuki,Ichiro	.093	Lee,Carlos	8787	Teixeira,Mark	5.1
Stewart,Ian	.273	2 tied with	.094	Konerko,Paul	8761	Longoria,Evan	5.2

2012 Active Career Pitching Leaders

Earned Run Average (minimum 750 IP)		Winning Percentage (minimum 100 Decisions)		Opponent Batting Average (minimum 750 IP)		Baserunners Per 9 IP (minimum 750 IP)	
Rivera,Mariano	2.21	Halladay,Roy	.666	Nathan,Joe	.204	Rivera,Mariano	9.31
Kershaw,Clayton	2.79	Weaver,Jered	.662	Rivera,Mariano	.210	Nathan,Joe	10.19
Nathan,Joe	2.87	Verlander,Justin	.656	Kershaw,Clayton	.215	Santana,Johan	10.35
Johnson,Josh	3.15	Hudson,Tim	.654	Wood,Kerry	.217	Kershaw,Clayton	10.39
Wainwright,Adam	3.15	Sabathia,CC	.652	Dotel,Octavio	.217	Hamels,Cole	10.43
Price,David	3.16	Santana,Johan	.641	Young,Chris	.225	Weaver,Jered	10.44
Santana,Johan	3.20	Lester,Jon	.639	Cain,Matt	.227	Halladay,Roy	10.78
Hernandez,Felix	3.22	Pettitte,Andy	.633	Price,David	.227	Cain,Matt	10.81
Weaver,Jered	3.24	Oswalt,Roy	.629	Santana,Johan	.228	Price,David	10.83
Cain,Matt	3.27	Wainwright,Adam	.625	Lincecum,Tim	.228	Haren,Dan	10.86

Games		Games Started		Complete Games		Shutouts	
Rivera,Mariano	1051	Moyer,Jamie	638	Halladay,Roy	66	Halladay,Roy	20
Hawkins,LaTroy	871	Pettitte,Andy	491	Hernandez,Livan	50	Carpenter,Chris	15
Farnsworth,Kyle	810	Hernandez,Livan	474	Sabathia,CC	35	Hudson,Tim	13
Cordero,Francisco	800	Millwood,Kevin	443	Carpenter,Chris	33	Sabathia,CC	12
Dotel,Octavio	752	Suppan,Jeff	417	Moyer,Jamie	33	Lee,Cliff	11
Mota,Guillermo	743	Hudson,Tim	405	Colon,Bartolo	32	Burnett,A.J.	10
Isringhausen,Jason	724	Buehrle,Mark	396	Buehrle,Mark	28	Moyer,Jamie	10
Oliver,Darren	716	Zito,Barry	394	Lee,Cliff	26	Santana,Johan	10
Moyer,Jamie	696	Sabathia,CC	383	Hudson,Tim	25	4 tied with	9
Rodriguez,Francisco	682	2 tied with	377	Pettitte,Andy	25		

Wins		Losses		Innings Pitched		Batters Faced	
Moyer,Jamie	269	Moyer,Jamie	209	Moyer,Jamie	4074.0	Moyer,Jamie	17356
Pettitte,Andy	245	Hernandez,Livan	177	Hernandez,Livan	3189.0	Hernandez,Livan	13816
Halladay,Roy	199	Lowe,Derek	157	Pettitte,Andy	3130.2	Pettitte,Andy	13290
Hudson,Tim	197	Millwood,Kevin	152	Millwood,Kevin	2720.1	Millwood,Kevin	11616
Sabathia,CC	191	Suppan,Jeff	146	Halladay,Roy	2687.1	Lowe,Derek	11301
Hernandez,Livan	178	Pettitte,Andy	142	Hudson,Tim	2682.1	Hudson,Tim	11157
Lowe,Derek	175	Buehrle,Mark	132	Buehrle,Mark	2679.0	Buehrle,Mark	11145
Buehrle,Mark	174	Zito,Barry	132	Lowe,Derek	2658.1	Suppan,Jeff	11139
Colon,Bartolo	171	Dempster,Ryan	124	Sabathia,CC	2564.1	Halladay,Roy	11005
Millwood,Kevin	169	Wright,Jamey	124	Suppan,Jeff	2542.2	Sabathia,CC	10622

Strikeouts		Walks Allowed		Hit Batters		Wild Pitches	
Moyer,Jamie	2441	Moyer,Jamie	1155	Moyer,Jamie	146	Burnett,A.J.	134
Pettitte,Andy	2320	Hernandez,Livan	1066	Wright,Jamey	146	Batista,Miguel	102
Sabathia,CC	2214	Zito,Barry	1004	Padilla,Vicente	109	Lackey,John	97
Millwood,Kevin	2083	Dempster,Ryan	992	Hudson,Tim	108	Garcia,Freddy	94
Halladay,Roy	2066	Pettitte,Andy	983	Burnett,A.J.	107	Suppan,Jeff	89
Santana,Johan	1988	Wright,Jamey	928	Wolf,Randy	102	Hernandez,Felix	85
Hernandez,Livan	1976	Batista,Miguel	899	Zambrano,Carlos	102	Haren,Dan	77
Burnett,A.J.	1971	Zambrano,Carlos	898	Lackey,John	101	Wright,Jamey	77
Dempster,Ryan	1918	Burnett,A.J.	888	Wood,Kerry	99	Hudson,Tim	76
Colon,Bartolo	1833	Suppan,Jeff	871	2 tied with	94	Lincecum,Tim	73

2012 Active Career Pitching Leaders

Saves

Rivera,Mariano	608
Cordero,Francisco	329
Isringhausen,Jason	300
Nathan,Joe	298
Rodriguez,Francisco	294
Valverde,Jose	277
Papelbon,Jonathan	257
Lidge,Brad	225
Fuentes,Brian	204
Street,Huston	201

Save Pct
(minimum 50 Save Ops)

Nathan,Joe	89.5
Rivera,Mariano	89.3
Kimbrel,Craig	89.0
Soria,Joakim	88.9
Valverde,Jose	88.8
Papelbon,Jonathan	88.6
Axford,John	88.3
Feliz,Neftali	88.1
Wilson,Brian	87.2
Bailey,Andrew	87.1

Home Runs Allowed

Moyer,Jamie	522
Hernandez,Livan	362
Suppan,Jeff	337
Buehrle,Mark	300
Millwood,Kevin	296
Colon,Bartolo	294
Lilly,Ted	289
Wolf,Randy	287
Arroyo,Bronson	282
Pettitte,Andy	271

Strikeouts Per 9 IP
(minimum 750 IP)

Dotel,Octavio	10.83
Wood,Kerry	10.32
Lincecum,Tim	9.76
Nathan,Joe	9.51
Kershaw,Clayton	9.29
Scherzer,Max	9.27
Gallardo,Yovani	9.19
Sanchez,Jonathan	9.10
Perez,Oliver	9.07
Liriano,Francisco	9.06

Opp On-Base Percentage
(minimum 750 IP)

Rivera,Mariano	.262
Nathan,Joe	.280
Santana,Johan	.284
Weaver,Jered	.286
Hamels,Cole	.287
Kershaw,Clayton	.288
Haren,Dan	.294
Price,David	.294
Halladay,Roy	.294
Cain,Matt	.295

Opp Slugging Average
(minimum 750 IP)

Rivera,Mariano	.290
Kershaw,Clayton	.319
Nathan,Joe	.336
Johnson,Josh	.348
Lincecum,Tim	.348
Price,David	.351
Isringhausen,Jason	.352
Wilson,C.J.	.353
Hernandez,Felix	.356
Verlander,Justin	.356

Hits Per Nine Innings
(minimum 750 IP)

Nathan,Joe	6.68
Rivera,Mariano	6.94
Kershaw,Clayton	6.98
Wood,Kerry	7.06
Dotel,Octavio	7.18
Cain,Matt	7.49
Young,Chris	7.53
Price,David	7.59
Lincecum,Tim	7.60
Santana,Johan	7.67

Home Runs Per Nine IP
(minimum 750 IP)

Rivera,Mariano	0.48
Johnson,Josh	0.58
Kershaw,Clayton	0.59
Wang,Chien-Ming	0.64
Lincecum,Tim	0.66
Wainwright,Adam	0.66
Billingsley,Chad	0.67
Cordero,Francisco	0.70
Pelfrey,Mike	0.70
Hudson,Tim	0.70

Strikeouts / Walks Ratio
(minimum 750 IP)

Rivera,Mariano	4.04
Haren,Dan	4.01
Hamels,Cole	3.80
Halladay,Roy	3.72
Shields,James	3.68
Lee,Cliff	3.64
Sheets,Ben	3.59
Oswalt,Roy	3.56
Greinke,Zack	3.51
Santana,Johan	3.51

Stolen Base Pct Allowed
(minimum 750 IP)

Cueto,Johnny	33.3
Carpenter,Chris	37.9
Buehrle,Mark	43.2
Zambrano,Carlos	51.5
Kershaw,Clayton	51.9
Duke,Zach	52.3
Colon,Bartolo	52.8
Greinke,Zack	53.5
Santana,Johan	54.7
Saunders,Joe	57.8

GIDP Induced

Pettitte,Andy	346
Moyer,Jamie	333
Lowe,Derek	311
Hernandez,Livan	299
Buehrle,Mark	295
Hudson,Tim	282
Suppan,Jeff	272
Wright,Jamey	260
Halladay,Roy	248
Sabathia,CC	228

GIDP Per Nine IP
(minimum 750 IP)

Cook,Aaron	1.28
Wang,Chien-Ming	1.23
Wright,Jamey	1.23
Westbrook,Jake	1.21
Lannan,John	1.21
Romero,Ricky	1.19
Maholm,Paul	1.15
Hernandez,Roberto	1.14
Wilson,C.J.	1.10
Saunders,Joe	1.08

Complete Game %
(minimum 100 GS)

Halladay,Roy	0.18
Hernandez,Livan	0.11
Carpenter,Chris	0.10
Hernandez,Felix	0.10
Lee,Cliff	0.09
Sabathia,CC	0.09
Shields,James	0.09
Verlander,Justin	0.09
Colon,Bartolo	0.09
Wainwright,Adam	0.07

Quality Start Pct
(minimum 100 GS)

Johnson,Josh	68.8
Weaver,Jered	67.6
Price,David	67.5
Oswalt,Roy	67.2
Lincecum,Tim	67.0
Wainwright,Adam	66.9
Halladay,Roy	66.6
Hernandez,Felix	66.4
Cain,Matt	66.0
Gallardo,Yovani	65.5

Walks Per 9 IP
(minimum 750 IP)

Halladay,Roy	1.86
Haren,Dan	1.89
Buehrle,Mark	2.03
Lee,Cliff	2.04
Rivera,Mariano	2.04
Oswalt,Roy	2.08
Sheets,Ben	2.08
Kuroda,Hiroki	2.10
Nolasco,Ricky	2.10
Shields,James	2.10

Games Finished

Rivera,Mariano	892
Cordero,Francisco	575
Isringhausen,Jason	499
Valverde,Jose	489
Nathan,Joe	470
Rodriguez,Francisco	458
Papelbon,Jonathan	398
Fuentes,Brian	381
Lidge,Brad	368
Street,Huston	348

2012 American League Bill James Leaders

Top Game Scores

Pitcher	Date	Opp	IP	H	R	ER	BB	SO	GS
Hernandez,Felix, Sea	8/15	TB	9.0	0	0	0	0	12	99
Humber,Philip, CWS	4/21	Sea	9.0	0	0	0	0	9	96
Verlander,Justin, Det	5/18	Pit	9.0	1	0	0	2	12	95
Weaver,Jered, LAA	5/2	Min	9.0	0	0	0	1	9	95
Shields,James, TB	10/2	Bal	9.0	2	1	1	0	15	94
Haren,Dan, LAA	5/24	Sea	9.0	4	0	0	0	14	93
Hernandez,Felix, Sea	7/14	Tex	9.0	3	0	0	0	12	93
Shields,James, TB	7/31	Oak	9.0	3	0	0	0	11	92
Hammel,Jason, Bal	6/16	Atl	9.0	1	0	0	2	8	91
Shields,James, TB	9/9	Tex	9.0	2	0	0	0	8	91

Worst Game Scores

Pitcher	Date	Opp	IP	H	R	ER	BB	SO	GS
Lester,Jon, Bos	7/22	Tor	4.0	9	11	11	5	2	-3
Porcello,Rick, Det	4/21	Tex	1.0	10	9	8	1	1	-1
Hochevar,Luke, KC	5/1	Det	4.0	12	9	9	3	2	1
Oswalt,Roy, Tex	7/3	CWS	4.2	13	11	9	1	4	1
Cobb,Alex, TB	8/18	LAA	2.2	12	8	8	0	1	3
Duensing,Brian, Min	8/25	Tex	2.1	10	9	9	1	3	3
Lowe,Derek, Cle	7/20	Bal	3.0	7	9	9	5	0	4
Ross,Tyson, Oak	4/28	Bal	4.0	11	9	9	1	1	4
Drabek,Kyle, Tor	5/27	Tex	3.0	8	9	9	3	1	5
Stewart,Zach, Bos	8/29	LAA	3.0	10	9	9	0	2	5
Vargas,Jason, Sea	6/20	Ari	4.1	9	10	10	2	2	5

Runs Created

Trout,Mike, LAA	127
Encarnacion,Edwin, Tor	124
Cabrera,Miguel, Det	123
Fielder,Prince, Det	116
Cano,Robinson, NYY	110
Beltre,Adrian, Tex	109
Hamilton,Josh, Tex	108
Mauer,Joe, Min	108
Rios,Alex, CWS	103
2 tied with	102

Runs Created Per 27 Outs

Trout,Mike, LAA	8.6
Encarnacion,Edwin, Tor	8.2
Fielder,Prince, Det	7.3
Cabrera,Miguel, Det	7.3
Mauer,Joe, Min	7.2
Beltre,Adrian, Tex	6.8
Hamilton,Josh, Tex	6.8
Murphy,David, Tex	6.7
Gonzalez,Adrian, Bos	6.7
Cespedes,Yoenis, Oak	6.7

Offensive Winning %

Trout,Mike, LAA	.815
Encarnacion,Edwin, Tor	.762
Mauer,Joe, Min	.719
Fielder,Prince, Det	.716
Cabrera,Miguel, Det	.715
Cespedes,Yoenis, Oak	.711
Hunter,Torii, LAA	.693
Zobrist,Ben, TB	.689
Beltre,Adrian, Tex	.680
Cano,Robinson, NYY	.680

Secondary Average
(minimum 502 PA)

Dunn,Adam, CWS	.462
Encarnacion,Edwin, Tor	.456
Trout,Mike, LAA	.445
Willingham,Josh, Min	.416
Hamilton,Josh, Tex	.411
Granderson,Curtis, NYY	.403
Zobrist,Ben, TB	.400
Cabrera,Miguel, Det	.389
Reynolds,Mark, Bal	.370
Fielder,Prince, Det	.363

Isolated Power
(minimum 502 PA)

Hamilton,Josh, Tex	.292
Encarnacion,Edwin, Tor	.277
Cabrera,Miguel, Det	.277
Willingham,Josh, Min	.264
Dunn,Adam, CWS	.263
Granderson,Curtis, NYY	.260
Beltre,Adrian, Tex	.240
Trout,Mike, LAA	.238
Cano,Robinson, NYY	.238
Davis,Chris, Bal	.231

Power / Speed Number
(minimum 502 PA)

Trout,Mike, LAA	37.2
Upton,B.J., TB	29.4
Rios,Alex, CWS	24.0
Jones,Adam, Bal	21.3
Kinsler,Ian, Tex	20.0
Saunders,Michael, Sea	20.0
Encarnacion,Edwin, Tor	19.9
Kipnis,Jason, Cle	19.3
Cespedes,Yoenis, Oak	18.9
Jennings,Desmond, TB	18.3

Speed Scores

Crisp,Coco, Oak	8.24
Revere,Ben, Min	8.16
Ellsbury,Jacoby, Bos	7.74
Jackson,Austin, Det	7.73
Weeks,Jemile, Oak	7.71
Escobar,Alcides, KC	7.47
Granderson,Curtis, NYY	7.43
Aybar,Erick, LAA	7.41
Suzuki,Ichiro, Sea-NYY	7.32
Span,Denard, Min	7.23

Cheap Wins

Buchholz,Clay, Bos	5
Blackburn,Nick, Min	4
11 tied with	3

Tough Losses

Peavy,Jake, CWS	6
Harrison,Matt, Tex	5
Hellickson,Jeremy, TB	5
Kuroda,Hiroki, NYY	5
Santana,Ervin, LAA	5
Wilson,C.J., LAA	5
10 tied with	4

2012 National League Bill James Leaders

Top Game Scores

Pitcher	Date	Opp	IP	H	R	ER	BB	SO	GS
Cain,Matt, SF	6/13	Hou	9.0	0	0	0	0	14	101
Bailey,Homer, Cin	9/28	Pit	9.0	0	0	0	1	10	96
Cain,Matt, SF	4/13	Pit	9.0	1	0	0	0	11	96
Dickey,R.A., NYM	6/18	Bal	9.0	1	0	0	2	13	96
Dickey,R.A., NYM	6/13	TB	9.0	1	1	0	0	12	95
Bumgarner,Madison, SF	6/28	Cin	9.0	1	0	0	2	8	91
Burnett,A.J., Pit	7/31	ChC	9.0	1	0	0	2	8	91
Santana,Johan, NYM	6/1	StL	9.0	0	0	0	5	8	90
Greinke,Zack, Mil	5/9	Cin	8.0	2	0	0	0	11	89
Zambrano,Carlos, Mia	5/7	Hou	9.0	3	0	0	1	9	89

Worst Game Scores

Pitcher	Date	Opp	IP	H	R	ER	BB	SO	GS
Burnett,A.J., Pit	5/2	StL	2.2	12	12	12	1	2	-13
Saunders,Joe, Ari	8/20	Mia	3.2	12	9	9	0	2	3
Jackson,Edwin, Was	9/28	StL	1.1	6	9	8	4	0	4
Norris,Bud, Hou	5/31	Col	1.2	7	9	9	3	2	4
Nolasco,Ricky, Mia	6/20	Bos	3.1	9	9	9	1	1	6
Fiers,Mike, Mil	8/13	Col	2.0	9	8	8	0	1	7
Santana,Johan, NYM	8/11	Atl	1.1	8	8	8	1	2	7
Francis,Jeff, Col	6/9	LAA	3.1	10	8	8	1	1	8
Lilly,Ted, LAD	5/23	Ari	3.1	9	8	8	5	3	8
Zito,Barry, SF	6/19	LAA	3.1	9	8	8	3	1	8

Runs Created

Braun,Ryan, Mil	125
McCutchen,Andrew, Pit	125
Headley,Chase, SD	112
Posey,Buster, SF	111
Wright,David, NYM	105
Bourn,Michael, Atl	102
Hill,Aaron, Ari	101
Holliday,Matt, StL	99
Votto,Joey, Cin	97
2 tied with	96

Runs Created Per 27 Outs

McCutchen,Andrew, Pit	7.9
Posey,Buster, SF	7.8
Braun,Ryan, Mil	7.7
Craig,Allen, StL	6.8
Montero,Miguel, Ari	6.7
Headley,Chase, SD	6.7
Molina,Yadier, StL	6.6
Wright,David, NYM	6.5
Fowler,Dexter, Col	6.4
Jones,Garrett, Pit	6.3

Offensive Winning %

Posey,Buster, SF	.811
McCutchen,Andrew, Pit	.805
Braun,Ryan, Mil	.756
Headley,Chase, SD	.740
Jones,Garrett, Pit	.728
Craig,Allen, StL	.723
Wright,David, NYM	.717
Molina,Yadier, StL	.710
Montero,Miguel, Ari	.701
Ethier,Andre, LAD	.674

Secondary Average

(minimum 502 PA)

Braun,Ryan, Mil	.431
Bruce,Jay, Cin	.389
Headley,Chase, SD	.382
McCutchen,Andrew, Pit	.378
Beltran,Carlos, StL	.369
Kubel,Jason, Ari	.368
LaRoche,Adam, Was	.357
Goldschmidt,Paul, Ari	.356
Gonzalez,Carlos, Col	.353
Davis,Ike, NYM	.353

Isolated Power

(minimum 502 PA)

Braun,Ryan, Mil	.276
Bruce,Jay, Cin	.263
Kubel,Jason, Ari	.253
Jones,Garrett, Pit	.242
Ramirez,Aramis, Mil	.240
LaRoche,Adam, Was	.238
Soriano,Alfonso, ChC	.237
Hart,Corey, Mil	.237
Davis,Ike, NYM	.235
Beltran,Carlos, StL	.227

Power / Speed Number

(minimum 502 PA)

Braun,Ryan, Mil	34.6
Rollins,Jimmy, Phi	26.0
McCutchen,Andrew, Pit	24.3
Heyward,Jason, Atl	23.6
Desmond,Ian, Was	22.8
Ramirez,Hanley, Mia-LAD	22.4
Headley,Chase, SD	22.0
Gonzalez,Carlos, Col	21.0
Harper,Bryce, Was	19.8
Stubbs,Drew, Cin	19.1

Speed Scores

Bourn,Michael, Atl	8.91
Victorino,Shane, Phi-LAD	8.75
Pagan,Angel, SF	8.67
Reyes,Jose, Mia	8.60
Stubbs,Drew, Cin	8.59
Bonifacio,Emilio, Mia	8.38
Maybin,Cameron, SD	8.26
Rollins,Jimmy, Phi	7.52
Fowler,Dexter, Col	7.43
Young,Chris, Ari	7.15

Cheap Wins

Correia,Kevin, Pit	4
Miley,Wade, Ari	4
Nolasco,Ricky, Mia	4
Zito,Barry, SF	4
9 tied with	3

Tough Losses

Johnson,Josh, Mia	7
Samardzija,Jeff, ChC	7
Wood,Travis, ChC	7
Gonzalez,Gio, Was	6
Kershaw,Clayton, LAD	6
7 tied with	5

Additional Bill James Leaders

AL Batters Win Shares (2012)	
Trout,Mike, LAA	38
Cano,Robinson, NYY	34
Cabrera,Miguel, Det	32
Encarnacion,Edwin, Tor	31
Fielder,Prince, Det	27
Zobrist,Ben, TB	27
Hamilton,Josh, Tex	26
Jones,Adam, Bal	26
4 tied with	25

NL Batters Win Shares (2012)	
McCutchen,Andrew, Pit	40
Posey,Buster, SF	38
Headley,Chase, SD	32
Wright,David, NYM	30
Molina,Yadier, StL	29
Bourn,Michael, Atl	28
Braun,Ryan, Mil	28
Pagan,Angel, SF	27
Votto,Joey, Cin	27
Montero,Miguel, Ari	26

AL Pitchers Win Shares (2012)	
Verlander,Justin, Det	23
Price,David, TB	19
Rodney,Fernando, TB	19
Sale,Chris, CWS	19
Harrison,Matt, Tex	18
Johnson,Jim, Bal	17
Peavy,Jake, CWS	17
Kuroda,Hiroki, NYY	16
Weaver,Jered, LAA	16
2 tied with	15

NL Pitchers Win Shares (2012)	
Chapman,Aroldis, Cin	21
Cueto,Johnny, Cin	20
Dickey,R.A., NYM	19
Kershaw,Clayton, LAD	19
Hamels,Cole, Phi	18
Kimbrel,Craig, Atl	18
Medlen,Kris, Atl	18
Gonzalez,Gio, Was	17
4 tied with	16

Batters Win Shares (Career)	
Rodriguez,Alex	471
Jones,Chipper	416
Jeter,Derek	403
Pujols,Albert	398
Thome,Jim	383
Abreu,Bobby	353
Giambi,Jason	322
Helton,Todd	309
Damon,Johnny	307
Berkman,Lance	306

Pitchers Win Shares (Career)	
Rivera,Mariano	257
Moyer,Jamie	225
Halladay,Roy	222
Pettitte,Andy	212
Hudson,Tim	204
Sabathia,CC	194
Buehrle,Mark	188
Lowe,Derek	174
Oswalt,Roy	172
Santana,Johan	171

AL Component ERA (minimum 162 IP)	
Verlander,Justin, Det	2.45
Weaver,Jered, LAA	2.48
Price,David, TB	2.67
Hernandez,Felix, Sea	2.94
Sale,Chris, CWS	3.00
Peavy,Jake, CWS	3.07
Sabathia,CC, NYY	3.10
Parker,Jarrod, Oak	3.24
Shields,James, TB	3.28
Darvish,Yu, Tex	3.31

NL Component ERA (minimum 162 IP)	
Kershaw,Clayton, LAD	2.20
Gonzalez,Gio, Was	2.37
Cain,Matt, SF	2.57
Dickey,R.A., NYM	2.70
Lohse,Kyle, StL	2.72
Bumgarner,Madison, SF	2.95
Hamels,Cole, Phi	2.98
Miley,Wade, Ari	3.05
Latos,Mat, Cin	3.08
Lee,Cliff, Phi	3.11

AL Highest Avg Game Score (minimum 30 GS)	
Verlander,Justin, Det	62.67
Price,David, TB	61.52
Hernandez,Felix, Sea	59.42
Weaver,Jered, LAA	59.17
Peavy,Jake, CWS	57.88
Shields,James, TB	56.97
Kuroda,Hiroki, NYY	55.91
Scherzer,Max, Det	55.56
Harrison,Matt, Tex	54.19
Vargas,Jason, Sea	53.64

AL Lowest Avg Game Score (minimum 30 GS)	
Romero,Ricky, Tor	44.00
Jimenez,Ubaldo, Cle	45.16
Alvarez,Henderson, Tor	45.19
Porcello,Rick, Det	45.42
Hochevar,Luke, KC	45.59
Chen,Bruce, KC	47.06
Masterson,Justin, Cle	47.82
Santana,Ervin, LAA	49.13
Lester,Jon, Bos	49.15
Haren,Dan, LAA	50.00

AL Lowest Offensive Win %	
Escobar,Yunel, Tor	.305
Francoeur,Jeff, KC	.309
Weeks,Jemile, Oak	.340
Peralta,Jhonny, Det	.341
Boesch,Brennan, Det	.350
Beckham,Gordon, CWS	.351
Hardy,J.J., Bal	.359
Young,Delmon, Det	.391
Young,Michael, Tex	.393
Aviles,Mike, Bos	.393

NL Highest Avg Game Score (minimum 30 GS)	
Kershaw,Clayton, LAD	63.00
Dickey,R.A., NYM	62.12
Cain,Matt, SF	60.56
Hamels,Cole, Phi	59.74
Gonzalez,Gio, Was	59.53
Lee,Cliff, Phi	58.93
Cueto,Johnny, Cin	57.45
Bumgarner,Madison, SF	56.97
Lohse,Kyle, StL	56.67
Latos,Mat, Cin	56.15

NL Lowest Avg Game Score (minimum 30 GS)	
Leake,Mike, Cin	48.60
Nolasco,Ricky, Mia	48.81
Lincecum,Tim, SF	48.85
Hanson,Tommy, Atl	49.29
Zito,Barry, SF	49.53
Richard,Clayton, SD	50.33
Blanton,Joe, Phi-LAD	50.43
Harang,Aaron, LAD	51.26
Rodriguez,Wandy, Hou-Pit	51.52
Harrell,Lucas, Hou	51.59

NL Lowest Offensive Win %	
Stubbs,Drew, Cin	.305
Cozart,Zack, Cin	.323
Maybin,Cameron, SD	.425
Barney,Darwin, ChC	.431
Espinosa,Danny, Was	.467
Pacheco,Jordan, Col	.471
Furcal,Rafael, StL	.485
Weeks,Rickie, Mil	.500
Phillips,Brandon, Cin	.520
Victorino,Shane, Phi-LAD	.524

Win Shares

Bill James devised Win Shares as a way to relate a player's individual statistics to the number of wins he contributed to his team. As a single number, Win Shares allows us to easily compare the accomplishments of each player to other players and to compare players across positions.

We credit a team with three Win Shares for each win. If a team wins 100 games, the players on the team will be credited with 300 Win Shares—or 300 thirds-of-a-win. If a team wins 70 games, the players on the team will be credited with 210 Win Shares, and so on.

The following pages contain the sum of a player's Win Shares prior to 2003, followed by his individual season totals from 2003 through 2012. Career totals are also included for each player. Players with zero career Win Shares are no longer shown in this section.

The quality of the team does not affect an individual player's Win Shares. A great player on a bad team will rate just as well as a great player on a good team.

Win Shares are also a great tool for evaluating award voting and Hall of Fame credentials. Generally, 30 Win Shares indicates an MVP-caliber season; 20 Win Shares indicates a season worthy of the Cy Young Award.

Win Shares also adjusts for offensive environment, so it is a great tool to use for looking at the greatest individual seasons in baseball history, as well as the greatest players of all time.

WIN SHARES BY YEAR

Player	<03	03	04	05	06	07	08	09	10	11	12	Career
Aardsma,David			0		4	1	1	16	8		0	30
Abad,Fernando									2	0	0	2
Abreu,Bobby	136	28	33	25	27	18	22	23	20	15	6	353
Abreu,Tony						4	1	1			3	9
Accardo,Jeremy				2	4	14	0	2	0	1	1	24
Aceves,Alfredo							3	7	2	12	6	30
Ackley,Dustin										14	17	31
Acosta,Manny						2	4	1	4	3	0	14
Adams,Matt											1	1
Adams,Mike			5	1	0		6	5	10	12	6	45
Adcock,Nathan										2	3	5
Affeldt,Jeremy	5	12	4	1	3	5	6	10	3	6	5	60
Albaladejo,J						2	1	1	1		0	5
Albers,Matt					0	0	4	2	5	3	6	20
Alburquerque,Al										6	2	8
Allen,Brandon								1	1	3	0	5
Allen,Cody											1	1
Alonso,Yonder									0	4	17	21
Altuve,Jose										2	18	20
Alvarez,Henderson										4	5	9
Alvarez,Pedro									14	3	22	39
Amarista,Alexi										1	6	7
Ambriz,Hector								0		1		1
Anderson,Brett								8	9	4	3	24
Anderson,Bryan									1		1	2
Anderson,Lars									1	0	0	1
Andino,Robert				0	0	0	1	3	0	11	4	19
Andrus,Elvis								17	20	18	23	78
Ankiel,Rick	17	0				8	13	5	4	7	3	57
Aoki,Norichika											15	15
Arencibia,J.P.									1	14	12	27
Arias,Joaquin				1			3	0	1		9	14
Arredondo,Jose							11	1		4	6	22
Arrieta,Jake										5	5	10
Arroyo,Bronson	5	2	11	11	20	11	10	13	14	3	13	113
Asencio,Jairo								0		0	1	1
Atchison,Scott		2	0		2				2	2	6	14
Aumont,Phillippe											2	2
Avery,Xavier											1	1
Avila,Alex								3	7	27	15	52
Avilan,Luis											4	4
Aviles,Mike							17	2	10	5	10	44
Axelrod,Dylan										2	1	3
Axford,John								1	11	15	7	34
Ayala,Luis		11	10	8		4	2	2		5	8	50
Aybar,Erick					1	2	15	20	9	20	16	83
Badenhop,Burke							0	5	4	3	4	16
Bailey,Andrew								17	11	6	0	34
Bailey,Homer						2	0	5	5	5	12	29
Baker,Jeff				1	3	1	7	7	4	3	3	29
Baker,John							9	13	1	0	4	27
Balester,Collin							1	0	2	0	0	3
Balfour,Grant	0	2	3			0	11	5	6	8	15	50
Barajas,Rod	5	5	9	11	7	3	10	12	13	8	6	89
Bard,Daniel								4	11	7	1	23
Barmes,Clint		1	3	9	6	0	12	13	10	10	10	74
Barnes,Brandon											1	1
Barnes,Scott											1	1
Barney,Darwin									1	14	14	29
Bartlett,Jason		0	6	13	16	14	23	16	11	1		100
Barton,Daric						3	9	6	21	4	3	46
Bass,Anthony										5	1	6
Bastardo,Antonio								0	1	10	3	14
Batista,Miguel	32	14	11	8	10	12	0	5	5	4	1	102
Bautista,Jose			0	0	9	12	8	6	34	36	13	118
Baxter,Mike									0	1	7	8
Bay,Jason		5	15	30	21	12	24	29	11	10	1	158
Beachy,Brandon									0	7	9	16
Beato,Pedro										2	1	3
Beavan,Blake										5	5	10
Beckett,Josh	8	11	9	12	11	18	11	16	2	16	7	121

WIN SHARES BY YEAR

Player	<03	03	04	05	06	07	08	09	10	11	12	Career
Beckham,Gordon								12	11	14	13	50
Bedard,Erik	0	6	8	13	17	6	8			6	0	64
Belisario,Ronald								7	3		9	19
Belisle,Matt		0		4	3	5	0	1	11	7	8	39
Beliveau,Jeff										1		1
Bell,Heath			2	0	1	13	6	12	15	11	4	64
Bell,Josh									1	0	0	1
Below,Duane										1	2	3
Belt,Brandon										5	17	22
Beltran,Carlos	72	28	29	21	34	25	29	14	8	26	18	304
Beltre,Adrian	69	13	33	13	17	16	13	10	26	16	25	251
Benoit,Joaquin	3	5	4	6	4	10	2		9	8	7	58
Bergesen,Brad								9	6	0	2	17
Berken,Jason								1	6	1	0	8
Berkman,Lance	72	25	30	20	31	24	36	22	14	30	2	306
Bernadina,Roger							1	0	10	7	10	28
Berry,Quintin											9	9
Betancourt,Rafael		4	5	7	5	16	3	8	8	10	11	77
Betancourt,Yuniesky				3	13	19	8	8	12	11	2	76
Betemit,Wilson	0		1	7	9	8	2	0	12	11	7	57
Bianchi,Jeff											1	1
Billingsley,Chad					6	12	16	9	11	6	8	68
Bixler,Brian							1	0		0	1	2
Blackburn,Nick						0	10	12	3	5	0	30
Blackley,Travis			0			0					5	5
Blackmon,Charlie										1	1	2
Blanco,Gregor							11	0	6		12	29
Blanco,Henry	25	2	5	5	6	0	3	6	3	4	1	60
Blanks,Kyle								5	2	3	0	10
Blanton,Joe			0	13	10	13	7	11	4	1	5	64
Blevins,Jerry						0	3	1	3	2	7	16
Bloomquist,Willie	3	3	2	4	5	2	5	7	3	8	9	51
Blum,Geoff	36	5	3	7	6	9	9	6	7	0		88
Boesch,Brennan									11	12	6	29
Boggs,Mitchell							0	2	4	3	9	18
Bogusevic,Brian									0	4	4	8
Bonifacio,Emilio						1	2	7	5	20	6	41
Bourgeois,Jason							0	0	0	6	1	7
Bourjos,Peter									3	16	5	24
Bourn,Michael					0	4	7	23	18	22	28	102
Bowden,Michael							1	0	0	1	3	5
Boxberger,Brad											2	2
Brach,Brad										0	3	3
Brantley,Michael								3	5	11	18	37
Brantly,Rob											3	3
Braun,Ryan						22	23	36	25	37	28	171
Bray,Bill					3	1	4		1	6	0	15
Breslow,Craig				1	1		6	6	8	3	6	31
Brignac,Reid							0	2	10	4	1	17
Britton,Zach										6	3	9
Brothers,Rex										4	7	11
Brown,Andrew										0	1	1
Brown,Domonic									0	4	5	9
Broxton,Jonathan				0	9	10	10	16	6	0	11	62
Bruce,Jay							7	9	16	22	18	72
Bruney,Brian			2	0	3	2	6	3	0	0	0	16
Buchholz,Clay						3	0	6	18	6	9	42
Buck,John			4	10	8	7	8	6	17	14	9	83
Buck,Travis						10	5	1	0	3	0	19
Buehrle,Mark	39	13	17	22	9	17	16	16	12	15	12	188
Bueno,Francisley								0			2	2
Bumgarner,Madison								1	8	12	11	32
Burckhard,Rob										1		1
Burnett,A.J.	31	0	7	11	9	11	14	12	4	5	11	115
Burnett,Alex									1	1	5	7
Burnett,Sean		2					2	5	7	5	7	28
Burriss,Emmanuel							4	2	0	2	1	9
Burroughs,Sean	3	16	16	6	1					1	0	43
Burton,Jared						5	6	3	1	0	8	23
Butera,Drew									3	3	1	7
Butler,Billy						7	8	18	20	17	21	91
Byrd,Marlon	0	16	5	6	2	13	12	20	19	8	1	102
Byrdak,Tim	0			1	0	4	4	5	3	2	2	21

WIN SHARES BY YEAR												
Player	<03	03	04	05	06	07	08	09	10	11	12	Career
Cabrera,Asdrubal						7	12	18	9	25	19	90
Cabrera,Everth							14	3	0	11		28
Cabrera,Melky				0	13	12	5	14	8	19	25	96
Cabrera,Miguel		12	19	27	33	29	20	25	30	38	32	265
Cahill,Trevor								7	16	9	11	43
Cain,Lorenzo									6	0	7	13
Cain,Matt				5	11	12	14	20	15	15	16	108
Cairo,Miguel	37	3	14	5	5	4	4	0	5	8	1	86
Callaspo,Alberto					1	1	6	17	11	17	15	68
Camp,Shawn			4	0	5	0	3	5	7	4	6	34
Campana,Tony										3	4	7
Cano,Robinson				12	17	21	12	18	34	30	34	178
Canzler,Russ										0	3	3
Capps,Carter											1	1
Capps,Matt				0	7	14	7	2	13	7	4	54
Capuano,Chris		2	4	13	14	5			3	5	9	55
Carlin,Luke						1	0			1	0	2
Carp,Mike								2	0	7	2	11
Carpenter,C (Stl)	43		12	20	19	0	1	21	14	11	1	142
Carpenter,C (Bos)										1	0	1
Carpenter,D (Tor)										2	0	2
Carpenter,D (LAA)											1	1
Carpenter,Matt										0	9	9
Carrasco,D.J.		6	1	4			3	7	4	0	0	25
Carreno,Joel										2	0	2
Carrera,Ezequiel										5	4	9
Carroll,Brett						0	0	5	0	0	0	5
Carroll,Jamey	3	3	6	9	13	5	10	8	14	14	13	98
Carson,Matt								1	1		0	2
Carter,Chris									0	0	8	8
Cashner,Andrew									2	1	2	5
Casilla,Alexi					0	1	9	4	6	7	5	32
Casilla,Santiago			0	0	0	4	3	0	8	8	9	32
Cassevah,Bobby									1	4	0	5
Castillo,Welington									1	0	4	5
Castro,Jason									4		8	12
Castro,Starlin									12	25	23	60
Cecil,Brett								3	10	4	1	18
Cedeno,Ronny				2	5	1	5	7	9	10	4	43
Cedeno,Xavier										0	2	2
Cervelli,Francisco							0	3	7	4	0	14
Cespedes,Yoenis											24	24
Chacin,Jhoulys								0	10	12	4	26
Chamberlain,Joba						5	11	6	5	3	1	31
Chambers,Adron										1	1	2
Chapman,Aroldis									2	4	21	27
Chapman,Jaye											1	1
Chatwood,Tyler										3	3	6
Chavez,Endy	3	9	10	1	13	4	3	3		6	1	53
Chavez,Eric	77	23	18	20	16	6	3	0		6	8	177
Chavez,Jesse							0	4	0	0	0	4
Chen,Bruce	18	0	4	13	0	0		1	9	9	6	60
Chen,Wei-Yin											12	12
Chisenhall,Lonnie										6	4	10
Choate,Randy	5	0	3	0	1	0		5	2	4	4	24
Choo,Shin-Soo				0	4	1	16	23	27	8	25	104
Christian,Justin							1			1	0	2
Chulk,Vinnie		0	4	5	2	5	1	0			0	17
Cingrani,Tony											1	1
Ciriaco,Pedro									1	2	6	9
Cishek,Steve									1	6	10	17
Clement,Jeff						2	3		0		0	5
Clevenger,Steve										0	1	1
Clippard,Tyler						1	1	5	9	13	11	40
Cloyd,Tyler											1	1
Cobb,Alex										3	6	9
Coffey,Todd				3	9	1	1	7	1	5	1	28
Coghlan,Chris							21	8	4	1		34
Coke,Phil							3	5	6	4	3	21
Coleman,Casey									3	0	0	3
Coleman,Louis										5	3	8
Collins,Tim										4	6	10
Collmenter,Josh										10	5	15
Colon,Bartolo	85	17	10	18	1	1	1	2	3	8	9	154
Colon,Roman			2	1	2		3	0			0	8
Colvin,Tyler								0	9	1	13	23
Conger,Hank									1	4	0	5
Conrad,Brooks						0	1	8	2	1		12
Constanza,Jose										3	2	5
Contreras,Jose		7	6	17	13	5	7	4	6	2	0	67
Cook,Aaron	2	3	6	6	12	9	15	11	4	0	1	69
Cook,Ryan										0	14	14
Cooper,David										2	3	5
Corbin,Patrick											4	4
Cordero,Francisco	13	12	17	11	12	12	11	13	10	13	0	124
Corpas,Manuel					3	15	6	1	5		1	31
Corporan,Carlos								0		1	2	3
Correia,Kevin		3	0	2	6	8	0	8	1	4	5	37
Cousins,Scott									1	0	0	1
Cowgill,Collin										2	4	6
Cozart,Zack										1	11	12
Craig,Allen									2	10	20	32
Crain,Jesse			4	10	7	0	5	4	6	10	6	52
Crawford,Brandon										5	13	18
Crawford,Carl	6	13	20	22	21	20	11	19	32	8	3	175
Crisp,Coco	3	8	14	20	9	16	11	4	14	15	18	132
Crow,Aaron										5	6	11
Cruz,Juan	7	0	7	0	6	6	6	2	0	3	2	39
Cruz,Luis							1	1	0		10	12
Cruz,Nelson				0	3	4	7	16	19	16	17	82
Cruz,Tony										2	2	4
Cuddyer,Michael	3	1	10	7	22	16	7	17	15	17	6	121
Cueto,Johnny							6	7	12	12	20	57
Cunningham,Aaron							3	0	3	1	0	7
Damon,Johnny	126	19	26	25	21	15	23	21	13	15	3	307
Danks,John						4	17	16	16	8	1	62
Danks,Jordan											1	1
d'Arnaud,Chase										1	0	1
Darvish,Yu											14	14
Davis,Chris							8	7	1	4	19	39
Davis,Ike									16	6	15	37
Davis,Rajai					0	5	5	13	14	6	11	54
Davis,Wade								2	8	6	7	23
De Aza,Alejandro						1		1	1	9	18	30
De Fratus,Justin										0	1	1
De Jesus,Ivan										0	1	1
de la Rosa,Jorge			0	2	2	3	5	12	8	4	0	36
de la Rosa,Rubby										3	0	3
De Los Santos,F										2	0	2
Deduno,Samuel									0	0	4	4
DeJesus,David		0	9	16	14	15	22	16	11	8	15	126
Del Rosario,Enerio									1	1	0	2
Delabar,Steve										1	4	5
Delgado,Randall										2	3	5
Demel,Sam									1	1	0	2
Dempster,Ryan	34	0	2	14	6	8	18	12	12	5	12	123
Denorfia,Chris				0	2		2	0	10	7	12	33
DeRosa,Mark	14	5	2	4	14	16	23	13	1	3	1	96
Descalso,Daniel									1	10	5	16
Desmond,Ian								2	11	16	18	47
Detwiler,Ross						0		2	0	4	9	15
DeVries,Cole											4	4
DeWitt,Blake							12	0	15	5	0	32
Diamond,Scott										1	11	12
Diaz,Matt		0		2	7	11	1	15	6	2	1	45
Dickerson,Chris							5	7	0	1	1	14
Dickey,R.A.	0	7	4	0	0		3	3	15	11	19	62
Diekman,Jake											1	1
Dillard,Tim								0	0	1	1	2
Dirks,Andy										6	10	16
Dobbs,Greg			1	2	1	7	8	2	1	7	6	35
Dominguez,Matt										0	3	3
Donald,Jason									6	4	0	10
Donaldson,Josh									0		8	8
Doolittle,Sean											5	5
Dotel,Octavio	39	12	14	2	0	3	6	6	6	5	6	99

Player	<03	03	04	05	06	07	08	09	10	11	12	Career
Doubront,Felix									1	0	7	8
Doumit,Ryan				6	2	6	20	4	9	9	10	66
Downs,Darin											2	2
Downs,Matt								1	2	9	1	13
Downs,Scott	3	0	0	5	6	8	11	6	8	10	5	62
Dozier,Brian											4	4
Drabek,Kyle									0	1	2	3
Drew,Stephen					6	16	21	16	20	10	6	95
Duda,Lucas									0	11	13	24
Duensing,Brian							6	13	4	2		25
Duffy,Danny										1	2	3
Duke,Zach				10	10	2	3	12	1	4	2	44
Duncan,Shelley						3	0	0	6	9	3	21
Dunn,Adam	30	13	29	25	18	18	21	24	18	1	13	210
Dunn,Mike								0	2	5	0	7
Durbin,Chad	8	0	1		1	6	8	3	5	1	5	38
Dyson,Jarrod									2	2	8	12
Eaton,Adam											2	2
Edgin,Josh											1	1
Ekstrom,Mike							0	0	1	0		1
Elbert,Scott							0	1	0	4	4	9
Eldred,Brad				1		0			0		0	1
Ellis,A.J.							0	0	4	3	20	27
Ellis,Mark	14	18		21	14	20	13	11	19	9	12	151
Ellsbury,Jacoby					6	16	21	1	34	6		84
Elmore,Jake											1	1
Encarnacion,Edwin				4	14	16	14	6	8	11	31	104
Enright,Barry									6	0	0	6
Eovaldi,Nathan										2	3	5
Eppley,Cody										0	3	3
Escalona,Edgmer								1	3	0		4
Escobar,Alcides							0	4	12	8	14	38
Escobar,Eduardo										0	2	2
Escobar,Yunel					12	13	24	14	20	9		92
Espinosa,Danny									4	22	18	44
Estrada,Marco						0	0	0	4	8		12
Ethier,Andre					11	13	23	21	22	18	22	130
Eveland,Dana				0	0	0	8	0	0	2	1	11
Falu,Irving											3	3
Farnsworth,Kyle	14	7	3	14	5	3	3	2	5	12	1	69
Feldman,Scott				1	3	1	4	14	2	2	4	31
Feliz,Neftali							6	15	12	4		37
Fick,Chuckie											1	1
Field,Tommy									1	0		1
Fielder,Prince				2	16	27	23	36	23	33	27	187
Fien,Casey							0	0		4		4
Fiers,Mike									0	8		8
Fife,Stephen											2	2
Figgins,Chone	0	9	20	22	17	21	12	26	11	1	1	140
Figueroa,Pedro										1		1
Fister,Doug							4	7	18	11	40
Flaherty,Ryan											2	2
Flores,Jesus						6	9	3		1	3	22
Florimon,Pedro										0	1	1
Flowers,Tyler								0	0	3	3	6
Floyd,Gavin			2	0	0	2	15	13	12	11	10	65
Fontenot,Mike				0		5	12	7	7	5	2	38
Ford,Lew		4	21	12	3	2					0	42
Forsythe,Logan										3	8	11
Fowler,Dexter						0	15	13	16	15	59
Francis,Jeff			2	6	13	14	5		4	5	4	53
Francisco,Ben					1	9	10	5	6	2		33
Francisco,Frank			6		0	3	6	9	5	7	2	38
Francisco,Juan							2	0	2	3		7
Francoeur,Jeff				12	15	20	5	9	8	17	6	92
Frandsen,Kevin				0	4	0	1	3			7	15
Frasor,Jason		9	6	4	3	2	10	5	5	2	46
Frazier,Todd										3	13	16
Freeman,Freddie									0	19	18	37
Freese,David							1	8	13	19	41
Friedrich,Christian											2	2
Frieri,Ernesto								0	4	4	11	19
Fuentes,Brian	3	10	2	14	12	10	12	9	9	5	0	86

Player	<03	03	04	05	06	07	08	09	10	11	12	Career
Fukudome,Kosuke							15	17	13	13	0	58
Fuld,Sam					0		4	1	9	3		17
Furbush,Charlie										1	5	6
Furcal,Rafael	46	26	20	26	27	15	8	17	19	7	13	224
Galarraga,Armando						0	13	3	5	0	0	21
Gallardo,Yovani					9	2	10	11	13	16		61
Galvis,Freddy											3	3
Gamel,Mat						0	5	0	0	1		6
Garcia,Avisail											1	1
Garcia,Christian											1	1
Garcia,Freddy	53	8	15	17	14	1	1	4	9	10	3	135
Garcia,Jaime							1		12	7	6	26
Gardner,Brett						3	9	17	16	2		47
Garza,Matt				1	4	12	12	10	10	5		54
Gaudin,Chad		3	1	0	7	9	5	3	2	0	3	33
Gearrin,Cory										0	2	2
Gee,Dillon									3	5	4	12
Gentry,Craig								0	0	5	9	14
Germano,Justin		0		0	4	0		2	0	1		7
Getz,Chris							0	10	4	8	4	26
Giambi,Jason	201	27	8	24	22	6	14	7	6	5	2	322
Giavotella,Johnny										2	1	3
Gillaspie,Conor							0			1	0	1
Gimenez,Chris								1	1	1	3	6
Gimenez,Hector					0				0	1		1
Godfrey,Graham										1	0	1
Goldschmidt,Paul										6	17	23
Gomes,Brandon										3	0	3
Gomes,Jonny		0	0	14	6	8	2	10	18	6	13	77
Gomes,Yan											2	2
Gomez,Carlos					2	13	6	4	7	12	44
Gomez,Jeanmar								2	3	0		5
Gomez,Mauro											3	3
Gonzalez,Adrian			1	1	16	25	24	34	35	27	24	187
Gonzalez,Alberto					0	3	5	2	4	1		15
Gonzalez,Alex	28	20	15	14	10	10		8	19	13	3	140
Gonzalez,Carlos						6	9	25	20	15		75
Gonzalez,E (Hou)		1	0	0	3	5	0	1		0	1	11
Gonzalez,Gio					0	2	15	15	17	49
Gonzalez,Marwin											2	2
Gonzalez,Michael		0	8	6	11	3	3	9	3	2	3	48
Gonzalez,Miguel											10	10
Gordon,Alex					12	15	2	3	24	20	76
Gordon,Dee										6	3	9
Gorzelanny,Tom				0	3	11	0	2	7	4	6	33
Gose,Anthony											4	4
Grandal,Yasmani											11	11
Granderson,Curtis				0	6	20	25	20	20	16	26	21	154
Gray,Jeff							0	1	0	2	2	5
Green,Nick			8	6	2	0		6	0		0	22
Green,Taylor										1	1	2
Greene,Tyler							1	2	3	5		11
Gregerson,Luke								5	9	4	9	27
Gregg,Kevin		2	6	2	4	10	11	7	9	4	2	57
Greinke,Zack		9	3	1	9	15	26	11	10	15	99
Griffin,A.J.											7	7
Grilli,Jason	1		0	1	4	4	7	2		4	6	29
Guerra,Javy										8	5	13
Guerrier,Matt			0	5	5	9	2	11	7	4	1	44
Guthrie,Jeremy			1	0	0	12	13	7	15	8	7	63
Gutierrez,Franklin			0	1	6	5	21	14	4	5	56
Guzman,Jesus								0		13	10	23
Gwynn,Tony				1	3	0	13	6	7	4	34
Hacker,Eric								0		1	0	1
Hafner,Travis	1	7	21	26	24	16	2	8	11	15	3	134
Hagadone,Nick										1	0	1
Hairston,Jerry	31	7	8	9	1	2	12	8	13	10	8	109
Hairston,Scott			3	0	0	7	9	14	5	3	12	53
Hall,Bill	1	3	7	17	20	10	8	4	11	1	0	82
Halladay,Roy	42	23	9	15	20	16	23	21	25	22	6	222
Hamels,Cole					8	15	18	10	16	17	18	102
Hamilton,Josh						11	26	11	30	15	26	119
Hammel,Jason				0	2	3	10	8	5	10	38

482

WIN SHARES BY YEAR

Player	<03	03	04	05	06	07	08	09	10	11	12	Career
Hampson,Justin				0	4	2					1	7
Hand,Brad										1	0	1
Hanigan,Ryan						1	4	8	13	11	18	55
Hannahan,Jack				0	5	5	4			14	8	36
Hanrahan,Joel						2	7	3	7	15	10	44
Hanson,Tommy								10	12	8	6	36
Happ,J.A.						0	2	15	6	1	5	29
Harang,Aaron	4	3	5	11	18	17	6	7	1	8	8	88
Hardy,J.J.				11	3	19	20	6	10	22	20	111
Haren,Dan		1	2	13	14	17	19	20	14	18	6	124
Harper,Bryce											21	21
Harrell,Lucas									1	0	9	10
Harris,Willie	2	2	10	4	1	9	10	9	4	5	0	56
Harrison,Josh										5	4	9
Harrison,Matt							3	1	3	15	18	40
Hart,Corey			0	0	5	21	16	9	18	21	17	107
Harvey,Matt											5	5
Hawkins,LaTroy	37	13	16	5	4	5	6	10	0	6	2	104
Hayes,Brett								0	2	3	1	6
Headley,Chase						0	8	16	15	16	32	87
Hechavarria,Adeiny											3	3
Hefner,Jeremy											1	1
Heisey,Chris									4	8	8	20
Hellickson,Jeremy									3	15	11	29
Helton,Todd	120	35	30	25	21	22	8	23	7	13	5	309
Henderson,Jim											4	4
Hensley,Clay				5	11	0	0		11	1	1	29
Hermida,Jeremy					3	6	13	13	11	4	2	52
Hernandez,David								3	6	10	9	28
Hernandez,Felix				8	8	14	13	26	23	16	15	123
Hernandez,Gorkys											3	3
Hernandez,Livan	50	22	19	13	10	10	3	3	11	5	1	147
Hernandez,Luis							1	1	1	2	0	5
Hernandez,Ramon	41	18	13	10	21	11	11	11	13	10	1	160
Hernandez,Roberto					1	22	3	0	12	2	0	40
Herndon,David									2	3	0	5
Herrera,Elian											4	4
Herrera,Jonathan							1		6	3	3	13
Herrera,Kelvin										0	10	10
Herrmann,Frank									2	2	1	5
Hester,John									1	2	1	4
Heyward,Jason									23	11	22	56
Hicks,Brandon									0	0	1	1
Hill,Aaron				9	14	20	5	25	12	13	25	123
Hill,Koyie		0	1	1		1	0	7	3	1	0	14
Hill,Rich				0	5	13	1	0	1	1	3	24
Hill,Shawn			0		1	6	0	0	2		1	10
Hinshaw,Alex							4	0			1	5
Hinske,Eric	22	12	6	11	7	3	10	5	8	5	0	89
Hochevar,Luke						1	3	1	4	7	1	17
Holland,Derek								2	3	14	8	27
Holland,Greg									0	9	11	20
Holliday,Matt			9	17	19	27	21	25	25	21	21	185
Holt,Brock											3	3
Hoover,J.J.											4	4
Horst,Jeremy										1	4	5
Hosmer,Eric										13	10	23
Hottovy,Tommy										0	1	1
Howard,Ryan			1	10	29	26	24	26	20	21	7	164
Howell,J.P.					1	2	0	11	11	0	3	28
Hudson,Daniel								1	9	16	0	26
Hudson,Orlando	7	17	16	15	20	21	17	20	14	14	3	164
Hudson,Tim	67	23	16	14	7	17	10	4	20	14	12	204
Huff,Aubrey	20	21	20	14	9	12	21	8	28	12	1	166
Huff,David								3	0	1	2	6
Hughes,Jared										0	6	6
Hughes,Luke									0	6	0	6
Hughes,Phil						4	0	10	11	1	9	35
Humber,Philip					0	0	0	0	2	11	1	14
Hundley,Nick							3	10	10	12	2	37
Hunter,Tommy							0	8	10	3	4	25
Hunter,Torii	52	16	13	11	17	22	21	20	23	17	24	236
Hutchison,Drew											3	3

Player	<03	03	04	05	06	07	08	09	10	11	12	Career
Iannetta,Chris					1	5	17	10	3	16	8	60
Ibanez,Raul	27	15	12	17	25	23	21	17	19	12	9	197
Igarashi,Ryota									0	2	0	2
Iglesias,Jose										0	1	1
Infante,Omar	3	3	12	7	5	4	9	7	19	18	14	101
Inge,Brandon	7	4	13	17	17	12	10	13	13	3	10	119
Ishikawa,Travis						1	4	9	4		5	23
Isringhausen,Jason	55	7	15	12	8	12	1	1		4	2	117
Iwakuma,Hisashi											8	8
Izturis,Cesar	8	10	25	6	3	5	9	8	6	1	2	83
Izturis,Maicer			1	6	13	16	11	17	7	13	5	89
Jackson,Austin									18	14	22	54
Jackson,Brett											2	2
Jackson,Edwin		2	0	0	1	2	10	17	9	12	9	62
Jacobs,Mike					5	12	7	14	5	1	1	45
Janish,Paul							1	4	8	3	4	20
Jansen,Kenley									6	6	15	27
Janssen,Casey					4	10		0	5	8	11	38
Jaso,John							0		16	5	21	42
Jay,Jon									8	13	15	36
Jeffress,Jeremy									1	1	0	2
Jenkins,Chad											1	1
Jennings,Dan											2	2
Jennings,Desmond									0	11	13	24
Jepsen,Kevin							0	4	5	0	4	13
Jeter,Derek	175	19	26	26	32	24	18	28	19	13	23	403
Jimenez,Ubaldo					0	4	11	19	22	6	3	65
Johnson,Chris								0	15	8	17	40
Johnson,Dan				9	5	10	1		4	0	2	31
Johnson,Elliot							0			2	10	12
Johnson,Jim					0	0	8	7	3	11	17	46
Johnson,Josh				1	12	0	6	19	16	7	10	71
Johnson,Kelly				9		19	19	6	21	16	14	104
Johnson,Nick	11	14	6	20	25		4	18	2		1	101
Johnson,Reed		11	9	10	16	3	13	3	3	8	8	84
Johnson,Rob						0	0	9	3	3	0	15
Johnson,Steve											5	5
Jones,Adam					1	0	9	13	15	16	26	80
Jones,Andruw	149	23	17	21	22	15	2	6	9	8	4	276
Jones,Chipper	217	26	18	18	22	25	23	20	13	19	15	416
Jones,Garrett						0		10	13	12	23	58
Jones,Nate											9	9
Joyce,Matt							6	1	10	19	13	49
Jurrjens,Jair						2	11	17	4	12	0	46
Ka'aihue,Kila							1		1	0	2	4
Kalish,Ryan									5		1	6
Karstens,Jeff					3	0	1	2	3	9	4	22
Kawasaki,Munenori											2	2
Kearns,Austin	16	12	5	10	17	20	3	2	10	1	5	101
Kelley,Shawn								3	2	2	2	9
Kelly,Don						0		1	5	5	1	12
Kelly,Joe											5	5
Kemp,Matt					3	10	19	26	15	37	21	131
Kendrick,Howie					6	9	15	15	19	18	16	98
Kendrick,Kyle						9	3	2	5	7	8	34
Kennedy,Adam	38	13	13	17	15	2	8	18	7	6	5	142
Kennedy,Ian						2	0	0	11	20	11	44
Keppinger,Jeff			2		1	9	10	5	21	8	14	70
Kershaw,Clayton							5	12	15	23	19	74
Kimbrel,Craig									4	17	18	39
Kinney,Josh					2		1	0		0	1	4
Kinsler,Ian					12	17	24	24	13	22	15	127
Kintzler,Brandon									0	1	2	3
Kipnis,Jason										6	24	30
Kirkman,Michael									2	0	2	4
Kluber,Corey										0	1	1
Konerko,Paul	65	4	20	24	21	16	10	18	29	24	15	246
Kontos,George										0	3	3
Korecky,Bobby							1	0			0	1
Kotchman,Casey			2	4	0	15	14	10	6	17	6	74
Kotsay,Mark	70	13	21	19	11	3	9	4	4	7	3	164
Kottaras,George							0	1	4	4	7	16
Kozma,Pete										1	3	4

Player	<03	03	04	05	06	07	08	09	10	11	12	Career
Kratz,Erik									0	0	7	7
Kubel,Jason			3		1	12	12	19	12	13	13	85
Kuroda,Hiroki							10	5	11	12	16	54
Laffey,Aaron						3	4	5	2	3	3	20
LaHair,Bryan						2				2	6	10
Laird,Brandon										0	1	1
Laird,Gerald		1	3	1	5	10	9	14	6	3	5	57
Langerhans,Ryan	0	0		12	8	5	4	2	2	1	0	34
Lannan,John						2	9	9	4	8	2	34
LaPorta,Matt								3	6	10	0	19
LaRoche,Adam			7	11	16	16	16	17	16	1	22	122
Latos,Mat								1	13	8	16	38
Lawrie,Brett										10	14	24
Layne,Tom											3	3
League,Brandon			1	0	5	0	4	3	8	11	8	40
Leake,Mike									7	9	8	24
LeBlanc,Wade							0	2	6	2	4	14
LeCure,Sam									2	4	5	11
Lee,Carlos	56	20	22	21	22	21	22	18	15	17	15	249
Lee,Cliff	1	3	6	13	10	1	24	17	16	22	14	127
LeMahieu,DJ										0	6	6
Leroux,Chris								0	0	2	0	2
Lester,Jon					5	4	18	17	17	14	8	83
Lewis,Colby	0	1	1	0	0				13	11	8	34
Lewis,Fred					1	5	13	7	10	2	0	38
Liddi,Alex										2	3	5
Lidge,Brad	1	8	22	15	7	10	15	0	8	3	0	89
Lillibridge,Brent							1	1	2	7	1	12
Lilly,Ted	9	10	15	4	11	15	12	14	11	8	3	112
Lincecum,Tim						8	25	22	14	16	0	85
Lincoln,Brad									1	1	6	8
Lind,Adam					3	7	7	21	9	11	9	67
Lindblom,Josh										3	5	8
Lindstrom,Matt						5	6	2	4	5	4	26
Liriano,Francisco				0	16		4	2	14	4	4	44
Lobaton,Jose								0		1	5	6
Loe,Kameron				0	8	2	3	2	5	6	4	30
Logan,Boone					0	3	1	0	4	3	5	16
Lohse,Kyle	14	11	6	10	4	9	12	3	0	9	16	94
Lombardozzi,Steve										0	12	12
Loney,James					3	16	14	18	18	16	5	90
Longoria,Evan							19	24	28	25	14	110
Lopez,Javier		6	0	0	2	4	6	0	6	6	4	34
Lopez,Jose			3	5	16	10	18	12	7	2	3	76
Lopez,Rodrigo	15	2	14	8	4	4		0	3	3	0	53
Lopez,Wilton								0	8	5	9	22
Loup,Aaron											3	3
Loux,Shane	0	0							1	1	0	2
Lowe,Derek	79	12	6	11	15	11	16	7	11	2	4	174
Lowe,Mark					3	0	1	8	1	3	3	19
Lowrie,Jed							7	1	8	5	11	32
Lucroy,Jonathan									4	15	16	35
Ludwick,Ryan		0	6	0	0	10	24	19	17	12	16	104
Luebke,Cory									1	7	2	10
Luetge,Lucas											2	2
Luna,Hector			4	5	9	0	0			0	1	19
Lyles,Jordan										0	1	1
Lynn,Lance										2	11	13
Lyon,Brandon	4	5		0	6	11	6	11	14	0	5	62
MacDougal,Mike	1	9	0	8	5	0	2	5	0	6	0	36
Machado,Manny											7	7
Maholm,Paul				4	7	5	9	8	4	7	11	55
Maier,Mitch						0	1	9	11	3	1	25
Maine,Scott									1	0	1	2
Maldonado,Carlos						0	0		1			1
Maldonado,Martin										0	7	7
Maloney,Matt								1	2	0		3
Manship,Jeff								1	1	0	0	2
Marcum,Shaun				1	3	10	12		14	13	8	61
Markakis,Nick					12	20	23	16	22	19	16	128
Marmol,Carlos					1	11	12	10	16	8	6	64
Maronde,Nick											1	1
Marquis,Jason	12	1	14	12	2	8	8	15	0	6	3	81

Player	<03	03	04	05	06	07	08	09	10	11	12	Career
Marshall,Sean					2	6	4	5	10	11	11	49
Marson,Lou							1	1	5	5	4	16
Marte,Luis										1	2	3
Marte,Starling											5	5
Marte,Victor								0	0		1	1
Martin,Leonys										0	1	1
Martin,Russell					14	22	20	16	9	14	12	107
Martinez,Cristhian								1	1	5	4	11
Martinez,Fernando								0	0	0	2	2
Martinez,J.D.										6	7	13
Martinez,Luis										3	0	3
Martinez,Michael										4	1	5
Masterson,Justin							7	5	5	15	6	38
Mastroianni,Darin										0	5	5
Mather,Joe							4		0	2	2	8
Mathis,Jeff				0	0	2	7	4	3	4	5	25
Matsui,Hideki		19	28	23	6	16	10	18	20	10	0	150
Matsuzaka,Daisuke						12	16	2	7	1	0	38
Mattheus,Ryan										3	7	10
Matusz,Brian								3	10	0	4	17
Mauer,Joe			6	22	30	21	30	32	27	10	25	203
Maxwell,Justin						1			3	2	12	18
Mayberry,John								1	1	11	9	22
Maybin,Cameron						0	3	2	8	17	13	43
Maysonet,Edwin								0	2		2	4
Mazzaro,Vin								2	4	0	1	7
McAllister,Zach										0	4	4
McCann,Brian				6	22	15	18	20	19	23	12	135
McCarthy,Brandon					5	5	3	1	5	11	7	37
McClellan,Kyle							4	6	8	5	0	23
McClendon,Mike									2	2	0	4
McCoy,Mike								0	1	3	1	5
McCutchen,Andrew								18	22	28	40	108
McCutchen,Daniel								2	0	5	0	7
McDonald,Darnell		0				0		1	10	3	1	15
McDonald,James							1	3	4	6	6	20
McDonald,John	5	3	1	4	3	8	1	3	5	6	4	43
McGee,Jake									0	2	8	10
McGehee,Casey							0	17	23	9	5	54
McKenry,Michael									0	2	8	10
McLouth,Nate				1	2	10	24	19	4	9	6	75
McPherson,Kyle											2	2
Medlen,Kris								3	7	0	18	28
Meek,Evan							0	4	9	1	0	14
Mejia,Jenrry									1	0		1
Melancon,Mark								1	2	10	0	13
Mendoza,Luis						2	0	0	0	2	8	12
Mercer,Jordy											2	2
Mesoraco,Devin										1	3	4
Middlebrooks,Will											9	9
Mijares,Jose							1	8	2	1	6	18
Mikolas,Miles											2	2
Miley,Wade										2	14	16
Miller,Andrew					0	2	0	2	0	2	4	10
Miller,Jim							1			1	4	6
Miller,Shelby											2	2
Mills,Brad								0	1	0	1	2
Millwood,Kevin	69	12	5	14	13	5	6	15	5	3	3	150
Milone,Tommy										2	10	12
Minor,Mike									0	3	8	11
Molina,Jose	3	2	6	7	5	4	9	4	4	7	6	57
Molina,Yadier			5	14	9	12	15	20	17	18	29	139
Montero,Jesus										2	10	12
Montero,Miguel					0	3	4	13	9	29	26	84
Moore,Adam								1	3	0	0	4
Moore,Matt										1	8	9
Moore,Scott					1	1	0		1		6	9
Moore,Tyler											6	6
Morales,Franklin						4	0	4	0	3	5	16
Morales,Kendrys					2	2	0	23	8		14	49
Morel,Brent									0	4	1	5
Moreland,Mitch									6	8	9	23
Morgan,Nyjer						4	3	15	9	17	3	51

Player	<03	03	04	05	06	07	08	09	10	11	12	Career
Morneau,Justin		1	9	7	26	18	28	18	17	4	10	138
Morrison,Logan									9	11	4	24
Morrow,Brandon						5	7	4	7	7	10	40
Morse,Michael				5	2	2	0	2	9	25	13	58
Mortensen,Clayton								0	0	3	3	6
Morton,Charlie							0	4	0	8	0	12
Moscoso,Guillermo								1	0	8	2	11
Moseley,Dustin					0	6	0	1	2	4	0	13
Moss,Brandon						1	5	5	0	0	13	24
Mota,Guillermo	10	14	12	3	3	1	4	4	2	4	0	57
Motte,Jason							2	2	6	9	14	33
Moustakas,Mike										4	14	18
Moyer,Jamie	149	18	5	12	10	8	13	6	3		1	225
Moylan,Peter					1	9	1	7	6	1	1	26
Mujica,Edward				1	0	0	4	4	8	7		24
Murphy,Daniel						6	10			14	20	50
Murphy,David				0	5	11	11	15	9	20		71
Murphy,Donnie			0	0		3	1		3	1	2	10
Myers,Brett	3	9	4	14	12	9	7	3	17	6	7	91
Nady,Xavier	0	7	1	8	12	10	20	0	5	4	1	68
Napoli,Mike					10	8	12	10	12	23	12	87
Narveson,Chris					0			2	7	6	0	15
Nathan,Joe	8	11	19	17	20	16	16	16		5	12	140
Nava,Daniel									5		5	10
Navarro,Dioner			0	4	5	6	17	5	2	3	4	46
Navarro,Yamaico									0	2	0	2
Nelson,Chris									0	2	10	12
Neshek,Pat					6	8	1		0	1	3	19
Nicasio,Juan										4	2	6
Nickeas,Mike									0	1	2	3
Niemann,Jeff							0	12	7	7	2	28
Niese,Jon							0	1	6	4	13	24
Nieuwenhuis,Kirk											5	5
Nieves,Wil	1			0	0	1	4	4	2	1	2	15
Nishioka,Tsuyoshi										3	0	3
Nix,Jayson							1	6	6	2	5	20
Nix,Laynce		4	7	4	0	0	0	6	4	7	3	35
Noesi,Hector										2	0	2
Nolasco,Ricky					5	0	14	6	7	5	8	45
Norberto,Jordan									0	0	5	5
Norris,Bud								3	3	7	4	17
Norris,Derek											8	8
Nova,Ivan									2	11	5	18
Nunez,Eduardo									2	8	4	14
O'Day,Darren							2	9	9	0	10	30
O'Flaherty,Eric					0	4	0	4	5	12	8	33
Ogando,Alexi									6	13	7	26
Ohlendorf,Ross						1	0	11	4	0	0	16
Ohman,Will	0			4	5	2	5	0	4	3	0	23
Oliver,Darren	56	10	1		6	5	9	9	6	7	7	116
Oliveros,Lester										1	0	1
Olivo,Miguel	1	8	7	7	13	7	7	9	11	10	4	84
Olmedo,Ray		2	0	1	0	1					0	4
Olson,Garrett						0	1	1	1	1	0	4
Omogrosso,Brian											2	2
Ondrusek,Logan									5	5	5	15
Orr,Pete			3	2	0	1	1			2	2	11
Ortega,Rafael											1	1
Ortiz,David	37	14	24	30	27	27	15	11	18	18	15	236
Oswalt,Roy	35	10	18	21	20	17	16	9	18	7	1	172
Ottavino,Adam									0		5	5
Outman,Josh							1	4		3	0	8
Overbay,Lyle	0	6	17	17	17	6	14	12	15	6	2	112
Owings,Micah						13	2	4	1	5	0	25
Pacheco,Jordan										2	9	11
Padilla,Vicente	23	13	5	6	12	2	8	8	5	1		86
Pagan,Angel					3	5	3	12	23	15	27	88
Palmer,Matt							0	10	1	0	0	11
Papelbon,Jonathan				4	19	15	15	15	10	12	14	104
Paredes,Jimmy										5	0	5
Parker,Jarrod										1	12	13
Parmelee,Chris										6	2	8
Parnell,Bobby							0	2	2	4	8	16

WIN SHARES BY YEAR

Player	<03	03	04	05	06	07	08	09	10	11	12	Career
Parra,Gerardo								9	6	19	9	43
Parra,Manny				2	8	0	2			1		13
Parrino,Andy										1	1	2
Pastornicky,Tyler											3	3
Paterson,Joe										3	0	3
Patton,Troy						1			0	3	7	11
Paul,Xavier								0	0	4	2	6
Pauley,David					0		0		4	7	0	11
Paulino,Felipe							0	0	1	5	4	10
Paulino,Ronny			0	14	10	3	8	8	3	1		47
Pavano,Carl	20	9	19	3		1	1	7	15	9	0	84
Pearce,Steve						2	2	2	1	0	6	13
Peavy,Jake	3	7	15	16	12	21	13	6	6	5	17	121
Pedroia,Dustin					2	18	26	24	12	27	17	126
Peguero,Carlos										2	1	3
Pelfrey,Mike					0	1	12	4	12	3	2	34
Pena,Brayan			0	1	0	0	2	4	5	3		15
Pena,Carlos	14	9	11	7	0	28	22	17	16	18	10	152
Pena,Ramiro								4	3	1	0	8
Pence,Hunter						18	19	17	21	24	18	117
Pennington,Cliff							3	7	19	18	10	57
Penny,Brad	21	10	10	9	11	20	0	7	3	4	0	95
Peralta,Jhonny		5	0	25	15	21	19	10	16	22	12	145
Peralta,Joel			2	5	6	0	0	5	8	6		32
Peralta,Wily											3	3
Perdomo,Luis								1	0		1	2
Perez,Chris							4	3	13	10	8	38
Perez,Juan					0	0				1	0	1
Perez,Luis										2	3	5
Perez,Martin											1	1
Perez,Oliver	4	1	16	2	0	10	8	1	0		3	45
Perez,Rafael					1	9	8	0	6	6	1	31
Perez,Salvador										7	10	17
Perkins,Glen					1	2	7	2	0	8	10	30
Perry,Ryan								4	5	1	0	10
Pestano,Vinnie									0	8	8	16
Petersen,Bryan									0	6	2	8
Petit,Yusmeiro						0	3	3	1		0	7
Pettitte,Andy	110	14	5	21	12	13	10	11	10		6	212
Phelps,Cord										0	1	1
Phelps,David											7	7
Phillips,Brandon	1	4	0	0	14	17	19	19	18	22	20	134
Phillips,Zach										1	0	1
Phipps,Denis											1	1
Pierre,Juan	35	20	22	14	15	12	9	12	14	14	12	179
Pierzynski,A.J.	37	22	12	11	14	8	8	10	12	11	19	164
Pill,Brett										2	1	3
Plouffe,Trevor									0	6	8	14
Podsednik,Scott	1	22	13	12	9	1	2	15	15		3	93
Polanco,Placido	46	18	17	22	14	24	15	21	16	14	5	212
Pollock,A.J.											2	2
Pomeranz,Drew										1	4	5
Pomeranz,Stuart										1		1
Porcello,Rick								13	5	8	7	33
Posey,Buster								0	20	9	38	67
Prado,Martin					2	1	9	12	22	12	23	81
Presley,Alex									0	8	5	13
Price,David							1	6	17	13	19	56
Pridie,Jason								0	0	4	0	4
Pryor,Stephen											1	1
Pujols,Albert	61	41	37	34	37	32	34	39	32	26	25	398
Punto,Nick	0	1	4	6	12	5	10	11	5	8	3	65
Putkonen,Luke											1	1
Putz,J.J.		0	3	5	17	20	5	1	8	13	10	82
Qualls,Chad			4	7	9	9	11	8	0	5	1	54
Quentin,Carlos					5	5	23	8	15	16	11	83
Quintana,Jose											9	9
Quintanilla,Omar				1	0	1	3	1		1	3	10
Quintero,Humberto		0	1	1	0	1	3	4	6	1	3	20
Quiroz,Guillermo			0	0	0	1	1	0	0			2
Raburn,Ryan			0			4	3	9	11	10	1	38
Ramirez,Alexei							18	15	20	20	14	87
Ramirez,Aramis	38	20	19	18	21	21	25	15	13	25	22	237

Player	<03	03	04	05	06	07	08	09	10	11	12	Career
Ramirez,Erasmo											2	2
Ramirez,Hanley				0	25	27	32	34	22	10	17	167
Ramirez,R (NYM)				7	0	9	8	7	7	2		40
Ramos,Cesar								1	0	1	3	5
Ramos,Wilson								3	13	3		19
Ransom,Cody	0	0	2			2	3	1	1	1	6	16
Rapada,Clay						0	2	0	1	1	4	8
Rasmus,Colby								13	17	11	15	56
Rauch,Jon	0		4	2	8	10	9	7	9	4	5	58
Reddick,Josh								0	1	7	16	24
Reed,Addison										0	7	7
Reimold,Nolan								10	0	11	4	25
Repko,Jason				5	4		0	0	2	2	0	13
Resop,Chris				0	1	0	0		2	4	3	10
Revere,Ben									0	9	11	20
Reyes,Jose		12	4	16	28	24	28	5	19	26	23	185
Reynolds,Mark						14	17	20	16	16	12	95
Reynolds,Matt									2	3	4	9
Rhymes,Will									6	1	2	9
Richard,Clayton							0	8	10	2	7	27
Richards,Garrett										0	1	1
Richmond,Scott						1	3		0	0		4
Rios,Alex			7	9	18	22	20	11	18	4	22	131
Rivera,Juan	1	4	12	9	18	1	4	16	10	10	5	90
Rivera,Mariano	110	17	18	19	16	12	20	15	14	14	2	257
Rizzo,Anthony										0	12	12
Roberts,Brian	5	14	16	28	13	22	20	20	7	3	1	149
Roberts,Ryan					0	0	0	8	1	19	9	37
Robertson,David							2	3	4	11	7	27
Robertson,Tyler											1	1
Robinson,Shane							0		0	2		2
Robinson,Trayvon										1	3	4
Rodney,Fernando	0	1		6	8	3	4	10	6	1	19	58
Rodriguez,Alex	220	31	29	34	25	37	23	23	21	14	14	471
Rodriguez,Aneury										0	1	1
Rodriguez,Fernando								0		2	1	3
Rodriguez,F (Mil)	1	9	17	14	17	15	16	10	11	10	5	125
Rodriguez,H (Wsh)								0	1	4	1	6
Rodriguez,Paco											1	1
Rodriguez,Sean							3	0	9	10	8	30
Rodriguez,Wandy				2	2	7	9	16	11	10	9	66
Roenicke,Josh							0	1	0	1	7	9
Rogers,Esmil								0	0	0	4	4
Rogers,Mark									1		3	4
Rolen,Scott	149	24	35	5	21	11	11	17	18	5	8	304
Rollins,Jimmy	38	18	24	21	25	28	24	19	14	25	21	257
Romero,J.C.	16	3	8	5	0	8	7	1	3	1	0	52
Romero,Ricky								10	14	20	2	46
Romine,Andrew									0	0	2	2
Romo,Sergio							4	4	8	9	11	36
Rosales,Adam							0	3	8	0	1	12
Rosario,Wilin										1	9	10
Rosenthal,Trevor											2	2
Ross,Cody		1		0	6	10	16	16	14	14	13	90
Ross,David	1	4	2	3	13	7	5	6	6	7	6	60
Ross,Robbie											8	8
Ross,Tyson									0	3	0	3
Rottino,Vinny				0	0	0				0	2	2
Ruf,Darin											1	1
Ruggiano,Justin					0	1				4	11	16
Ruiz,Carlos					2	13	6	13	19	18	24	95
Runzler,Dan								1	3	0	1	5
Russell,James									1	2	6	9
Rutledge,Josh											6	6
Ryan,Brendan					5	2	14	8	13	11		53
Rzepczynski,Marc								4	2	5	2	13
Sabathia,CC	25	13	11	12	15	24	23	18	20	19	14	194
Saito,Takashi					18	17	9	6	5	4	0	59
Salas,Fernando									1	12	2	15
Sale,Chris									5	11	19	35
Saltalamacchia,J						5	6	6	0	7	8	32
Samardzija,Jeff							3	0	0	7	8	18
Sanches,Brian					0	0	0	6	6	3	0	15

Player	<03	03	04	05	06	07	08	09	10	11	12	Career
Sanchez,Anibal					10	1	0	5	11	10	10	47
Sanchez,Eduardo									5	0		5
Sanchez,Gaby							1	1	17	16	3	38
Sanchez,Hector										0	5	5
Sanchez,Jonathan					2	0	6	7	14	2	0	31
Sandoval,Pablo							6	27	9	23	18	83
Sands,Jerry										0	6	6
Santana,Carlos									7	22	21	50
Santana,Ervin				6	12	3	19	6	14	14	2	76
Santana,Johan	14	16	26	23	24	17	21	14	14		2	171
Santiago,Hector										1	7	8
Santiago,Ramon	4	5	0	0	1	2	6	7	9	5	3	42
Santos,Omir								0	7		0	7
Santos,Sergio								5	12	0		17
Sappelt,Dave										1	3	4
Saunders,Joe				0	4	7	18	11	6	12	8	66
Saunders,Michael								1	6	2	17	26
Savery,Joe										1	0	1
Scahill,Rob											1	1
Schafer,Jordan							2		8	5		15
Schafer,Logan										0	1	1
Scheppers,Tanner											1	1
Scherzer,Max							4	9	13	10	14	50
Schierholtz,Nate						2	3	8	5	13	8	39
Schlereth,Daniel								0	2	4	0	6
Schneider,Brian	10	13	17	16	9	11	10	4	4	2	2	98
Schumaker,Skip			0	0	7	16	18	14	11	7		73
Schwimer,Michael										0	2	2
Scott,Luke				0	11	11	11	14	4	6		68
Scribner,Evan										0	3	3
Scutaro,Marco	0	2	11	11	11	8	15	21	15	11	21	126
Seager,Kyle										3	24	27
Seddon,Chris					0			0		2		2
Segura,Jean											4	4
Sellers,Justin										4	0	4
Shaw,Bryan										3	4	7
Sheets,Ben	14	10	21	11	7	10	15		3		3	94
Sherrill,George		1	2	3	8	7	13	0	3	0		37
Shields,James					6	12	15	11	3	20	12	79
Shoppach,Kelly			0	3	7	14	7	4	4	7		46
Sierra,Moises											1	1
Simmons,Andrelton											8	8
Simon,Alfredo							0	0	4	3	6	13
Sipp,Tony								3	4	7	3	17
Slaten,Doug					1	4	1	0	3	0	1	10
Smith,Joe						3	6	2	3	8	6	28
Smith,Seth						1	3	14	9	13	11	51
Smith,Will											2	2
Smoak,Justin									7	10	9	26
Smyly,Drew											6	6
Snider,Travis							3	4	8	3	5	23
Snyder,Brandon									1	0	1	2
Snyder,Chris			2	4	7	16	15	3	8	5	4	64
Sogard,Eric									0	1	1	2
Solano,Donovan											8	8
Solano,Jhonatan											2	2
Soriano,Alfonso	44	27	16	16	26	20	16	10	15	11	19	220
Soriano,Rafael	1	7	0	1	7	9	2	12	14	4	13	70
Soto,Geovany				0	0	3	21	8	15	10	5	62
Span,Denard							16	21	20	6	15	78
Spence,Josh										2	0	2
Stammen,Craig								3	3	2	9	17
Stanton,Giancarlo									13	19	19	51
Stauffer,Tim				0	1	0		3	9	7	0	20
Stewart,Chris				0	1	0		0	3	2		6
Stewart,Ian						1	9	11	8	1	2	32
Stinson,Josh										0	1	1
Storen,Drew								5	15	5		25
Storey,Mickey											1	1
Straily,Dan											2	2
Strasburg,Stephen									5	2	14	21
Street,Huston				16	14	10	10	15	9	7	9	90
Strop,Pedro								0	0	3	10	13

Player	<03	03	04	05	06	07	08	09	10	11	12	Career
Stubbs,Drew								5	18	13	6	42
Stults,Eric				1	1	2	2			0	7	13
Stutes,Michael										5	0	5
Suppan,Jeff	52	13	9	13	12	9	5	2	3		0	118
Sutton,Drew								3	2	2	4	11
Suzuki,Ichiro	62	23	27	22	24	33	19	28	23	15	11	287
Suzuki,Kurt						7	17	17	10	8	10	69
Swarzak,Anthony								0		4	2	6
Sweeney,Ryan				0	0	12	12	8	7	3		42
Swisher,Nick		1	12	20	18	12	18	22	19	24		146
Tabata,Jose									14	8	6	28
Takahashi,Hisanori									9	5	0	14
Tateyama,Yoshinori										3	0	3
Taylor,Michael										1	0	1
Tazawa,Junichi								0		0	6	6
Teaford,Everett										3	2	5
Teagarden,Taylor							4	3	1	1	2	11
Teixeira,Mark		12	24	33	21	25	28	26	24	22	16	231
Tejada,Ruben									3	11	14	28
Thames,Eric										7	3	10
Thatcher,Joe					2	0	3	5	0		2	12
Thayer,Dale							0	0	0	6		6
Theriot,Ryan				0	6	11	16	17	11	10	7	78
Thole,Josh								2	8	9	4	23
Thomas,Clete							3	7			1	11
Thome,Jim	225	29	20	4	25	21	17	11	14	13	4	383
Thompson,R (Oak)						0	0	1	3	4	0	8
Thornburg,Tyler											1	1
Thornton,Matt			2	1	7	4	10	12	12	5	7	60
Tillman,Chris								2	1	1	8	12
Tolleson,Shawn											2	2
Tolleson,Steve									2	1		3
Tomlin,Josh									4	9	0	13
Torrealba,Yorvit	5	7	4	4	6	6	4	9	12	7	3	67
Torres,Andres	0	0	0	0				8	23	10	10	51
Torres,Carlos								0	0		3	3
Tracy,Chad			11	19	14	6	4	3	2		3	62
Treanor,Matt			1	2	5	6	5	0	3	6	2	30
Triunfel,Carlos											1	1
Trout,Mike										3	38	41
Trumbo,Mark									0	14	19	33
Tulowitzki,Troy					1	24	9	24	25	25	5	113
Turner,Jacob										0	2	2
Turner,Justin								0	0	15	4	19
Uehara,Koji								4	9	8	5	26
Uggla,Dan					23	16	24	18	24	21	23	149
Upton,B.J.			4		2	22	23	13	18	20	17	119
Upton,Justin						1	8	19	14	26	16	84
Uribe,Juan	17	9	18	17	11	13	11	13	16	2	2	129
Utley,Chase		5	8	25	27	28	30	32	25	18	13	211
Valbuena,Luis							1	6	4	0	5	16
Valdes,Raul									2	1	3	6
Valdespin,Jordany											4	4
Valdez,Jose										0	1	1
Valdez,Wilson			1	2		2		1	9	9	2	26
Valencia,Danny									12	10	1	23
Valverde,Jose		11	3	13	4	14	14	11	10	15	11	106
Van Slyke,Scott											1	1
VandenHurk,Rick						0	0	3	0	0	0	3
Vargas,Jason			4	1	0			3	10	8	11	37
Varvaro,Anthony									0	2	0	2
Vasquez,Esmerling								3	1	1	0	5
Veal,Donnie								0			3	3
Velazquez,Gil							0	0		0	1	1
Venable,Will							3	8	15	12	17	55
Venters,Jonny									9	15	5	29
Veras,Jose					1	1	5	2	4	5	6	24
Verlander,Justin				0	15	16	8	21	17	27	23	127
Viciedo,Dayan									3	2	12	17
Victorino,Shane		0		1	11	11	20	22	23	23	17	128
Villanueva,Carlos					4	8	6	2	2	7	6	35
Villarreal,Brayan										0	5	5
Vincent,Nick											3	3

Player	<03	03	04	05	06	07	08	09	10	11	12	Career
Vizquel,Omar	187	5	18	20	20	12	5	6	7	1	1	282
Vogelsong,Ryan	1	0	0	3	0					14	10	28
Volquez,Edinson				0	0	2	16	2	3	0	6	29
Volstad,Chris							7	4	6	2	0	19
Votto,Joey						3	19	24	33	33	27	139
Wade,Cory							7	1		5	0	13
Wainwright,Adam				0	9	13	11	21	20		9	83
Walden,Jordan									2	11	3	16
Waldrop,Kyle										0	2	2
Walker,Neil								0	16	20	21	57
Wallace,Brett									1	4	5	10
Walters,P.J.								0	0	0	1	1
Wang,Chien-Ming				7	16	15	7	0		2	0	47
Watson,Tony										3	5	8
Weaver,Jered					14	12	11	17	19	24	16	113
Webb,Ryan								1	4	4	4	13
Weeks,Jemile										15	7	22
Weeks,Rickie		0		9	10	14	16	7	29	18	14	117
Wells,Casper									4	6	10	20
Wells,Kip	24	15	6	3	0	2	1	2			0	53
Wells,Randy							1	13	9	3	0	26
Wells,Vernon	22	26	13	20	24	15	15	8	21	10	2	176
Werth,Jayson	1	1	11	9		13	17	26	22	17	13	130
Westbrook,Jake	3	6	15	8	13	9	3		9	4	8	78
Wheeler,Dan	2	3	3	10	12	4	12	6	4	3	0	59
White,Alex										1	3	4
Whiteside,Eli		0						3	2	3	0	8
Wieters,Matt								9	12	23	23	67
Wigginton,Ty	3	14	10	4	13	11	14	4	8	4	5	90
Wilhelmsen,Tom										3	13	16
Williams,Jerome		9	7	6	0	0				3	4	29
Willingham,Josh			0	0	14	19	13	11	14	18	22	111
Wilson,Bobby							0	0	3	2	3	8
Wilson,Brian					1	5	9	15	17	9	0	56
Wilson,C.J.				0	3	9	2	11	15	20	9	69
Wilson,Jack	17	12	22	14	12	19	7	9	4	6	1	123
Wise,DeWayne	1	3			0	0	2	2	4	1	6	19
Wolf,Randy	43	12	6	4	2	5	7	14	9	12	2	116
Wood,Kerry	46	18	9	4	2	2	12	6	4	4	0	107
Wood,Travis									6	3	5	14
Worley,Vance									2	11	5	18
Worth,Danny									3	0	2	5
Wright,David			9	26	30	34	27	20	25	14	30	215
Wright,Jamey	41	2	5	4	4	5	3	4	3	6	4	81
Wright,Wesley							3	1	0	1	4	9
Youkilis,Kevin			8	3	22	20	27	28	19	18	11	156
Young,Chris (NYM)			2	10	12	12	5	1	3	3	3	51
Young,Chris (Ari)					2	14	17	8	19	21	9	90
Young,Delmon					2	17	13	7	22	10	7	78
Young,Eric								0	2	4	5	11
Young,Michael	18	22	25	29	26	23	20	17	16	23	9	228
Zagurski,Mike								1	0	0	1	2
Zambrano,Carlos	5	18	20	18	17	16	16	10	11	6	5	142
Ziegler,Brad							12	7	5	6	8	38
Zimmerman,Ryan				2	24	20	9	21	23	15	22	136
Zimmerman,Jordan								3	1	16	10	30
Zito,Barry	49	18	12	13	17	8	5	10	7	0	6	145
Zobrist,Ben					2	1	8	27	21	28	27	114

Instant Replay

Established just before the end of the season in 2008, instant replay has become a big part of baseball. Umpires review disputable home run calls to determine whether the ball left the playing field, was fair or foul, or was interfered with by a fan. Since replay's inception, 34% of the 289 reviewed calls have been overturned.

The chart below summarizes the results. The next few pages provide the details of every instant replay in 2012.

Instant Replay Summary

Season	Instant Replays	Calls Overturned	Percentage
2008	7	2	29%
2009	59	22	37%
2010	69	24	35%
2011	66	17	26%
2012	88	33	38%
Total	289	98	34%

Date	Matchup	Pitcher	Hitter	Inning	Outs	Men On	Score	Initial Ruling	Video Ruling
04/07/2012	NYA@TB	Rapada,Clay	Longoria,Evan	7	0	1_	6-2	HR	GR2B
04/07/2012	BOS@DET	Beckett,Josh	Cabrera,Miguel	5	2	___	5-0	GR2B	HR
04/11/2012	ARI@SD	Luebke,Cory	Bloomquist,Willie	2	2	___	1-0	3B	3B
04/13/2012	MIL@ATL	Jurrjens,Jair	Hart,Corey	6	0	_23	3-8	2B	2B
04/15/2012	TB@BOS	Doubront,Felix	Pena,Carlos	5	1	12_	0-4	Foul	Foul
04/18/2012	CLE@SEA	Vargas,Jason	Cunningham,Aaron	3	0	___	0-3	2B	2B
04/20/2012	NYA@BOS	Nova,Ivan	Ortiz,David	2	0	___	0-3	2B	HR
04/23/2012	PHI@ARI	Kendrick,Kyle	Hill,Aaron	1	0	_2_	0-0	HR	2B
05/02/2012	PIT@STL	Burnett,A.J.	Beltran,Carlos	3	2	12_	9-1	2B	HR
05/04/2012	CIN@PIT	Correia,Kevin	Heisey,Chris	4	2	___	1-0	3B	3B
05/04/2012	TEX@CLE	Lewis,Colby	Hannahan,Jack	3	0	___	2-1	3B	HR
05/05/2012	STL@HOU	Romero,J.C.	Lowrie,Jed	8	1	_2_	6-2	2B	HR
05/05/2012	ATL@COL	Rogers,Esmil	Heyward,Jason	7	0	1_	8-8	Foul	Foul
05/06/2012	CIN@PIT	Morton,Charlie	Stubbs,Drew	3	0	1_	2-0	HR	HR
05/09/2012	COL@SD	Bass,Anthony	Giambi,Jason	4	1	12_	0-2	2B	2B
05/09/2012	COL@SD	Bass,Anthony	Rosario,Wilin	6	2	1_3	2-2	2B	2B
05/09/2012	WAS@PIT	Lincoln,Brad	Desmond,Ian	4	0	___	0-3	FO	FO
05/12/2012	SEA@NYA	Logan,Boone	Carp,Mike	9	1	1_	1-6	HR	2B
05/12/2012	TOR@MIN	Walters,P.J.	Bautista,Jose	6	2	___	1-1	2B	HR
05/14/2012	SD@WAS	Mikolas,Miles	Desmond,Ian	6	1	_23	4-5	2B	2B
05/15/2012	SEA@BOS	Beckett,Josh	Smoak,Justin	2	2	___	0-0	Foul	Foul
05/16/2012	MIN@DET	Porcello,Rick	Willingham,Josh	3	0	___	5-6	2B	2B
05/21/2012	TOR@TB	Drabek,Kyle	Upton,B.J.	1	1	___	0-0	2B	HR
05/24/2012	MIN@CHA	DeVries,Cole	De Aza,Alejandro	5	0	___	4-5	HR	Foul
05/25/2012	PHI@STL	Lee,Cliff	Furcal,Rafael	3	0	___	1-2	HR	HR
05/29/2012	KC@CLE	Masterson,Justin	Moustakas,Mike	2	2	_23	5-2	Foul	Foul
05/29/2012	DET@BOS	Padilla,Vicente	Avila,Alex	8	1	___	3-6	2B	2B
05/30/2012	HOU@COL	Harrell,Lucas	Cuddyer,Michael	1	2	123	0-0	HR	HR
06/02/2012	MIA@PHI	Hamels,Cole	Ramirez,Hanley	4	0	___	0-3	HR	HR
06/02/2012	CIN@HOU	Latos,Mat	Martinez,Fernando	3	2	1_3	3-8	2B	2B
06/05/2012	BAL@BOS	Johnson,Jim	Saltalamacchia,J	9	2	1_	4-6	HR	HR
06/07/2012	ATL@MIA	O'Flaherty,Eric	Stanton,Giancarlo	8	0	___	1-4	2B	HR
06/10/2012	HOU@CHA	Humber,Philip	Maxwell,Justin	5	0	1_	2-3	HR	HR
06/10/2012	OAK@ARI	Doolittle,Sean	Hill,Aaron	8	2	___	4-3	Foul	Foul
06/16/2012	MIL@MIN	Veras,Jose	Mastroianni,Darin	9	1	1_	2-6	Foul	Foul
06/18/2012	TOR@MIL	Coello,Robert	Ramirez,Aramis	7	0	___	6-6	Foul	HR
06/19/2012	TB@WAS	Price,David	Morse,Michael	6	2	1_	2-5	HR	HR
06/19/2012	TEX@SD	Brach,Brad	Beltre,Adrian	7	2	___	6-2	HR	HR
06/26/2012	SD@HOU	Lyles,Jordan	Venable,Will	3	0	___	0-0	3B	HR
06/26/2012	CHA@MIN	Floyd,Gavin	Span,Denard	3	0	___	0-0	Foul	Foul
06/27/2012	STL@MIA	Freeman,Sam	Morrison,Logan	7	1	___	3-3	2B	2B
06/27/2012	CHA@MIN	Gray,Jeff	Pierzynski,A.J.	7	0	___	9-2	3B	3B
06/28/2012	PIT@PHI	Sanches,Brian	Jones,Garrett	8	1	___	5-3	2B	2B
07/05/2012	MIN@DET	Swarzak,Anthony	Young,Delmon	8	1	___	6-3	2B	HR
07/16/2012	CLE@TB	Cobb,Alex	Choo,Shin-Soo	1	0	___	0-0	HR	2B
07/17/2012	NYN@WAS	Clippard,Tyler	Valdespin,Jordany	9	1	12_	0-2	HR	HR
07/20/2012	ATL@WAS	Strasburg,Stephen	Hinske,Eric	6	1	1_	2-9	2B	2B
07/22/2012	CHA@DET	Turner,Jacob	Rios,Alex	6	1	1_	1-6	2B	HR
07/23/2012	MIL@PHI	Wolf,Randy	Howard,Ryan	1	2	___	1-2	2B	HR
07/23/2012	BOS@TEX	Feldman,Scott	Saltalamacchia,J	7	0	___	1-9	2B	2B
07/24/2012	COL@ARI	Roenicke,Josh	Bloomquist,Willie	4	1	_2_	1-1	GR2B	GR2B
07/25/2012	CHN@PIT	Correia,Kevin	DeJesus,David	3	1	___	1-1	GR2B	GR2B
07/27/2012	OAK@BAL	Britton,Zach	Reddick,Josh	5	2	___	5-2	2B	2B
07/27/2012	PIT@HOU	Karstens,Jeff	Francisco,Ben	4	0	___	3-1	HR	HR
08/01/2012	CLE@KC	Mendoza,Luis	Santana,Carlos	4	1	___	0-4	HR	HR
08/01/2012	STL@COL	Pomeranz,Drew	Greene,Tyler	2	1	_2_	2-0	2B	2B
08/04/2012	MIL@STL	Rogers,Mark	Beltran,Carlos	2	0	___	0-1	3B	HR
08/04/2012	PIT@CIN	Leake,Mike	Presley,Alex	3	0	___	1-2	3B	3B
08/07/2012	TEX@BOS	Dempster,Ryan	Middlebrooks,Will	7	2	12_	0-4	HR	HR
08/07/2012	LAA@OAK	Carpenter,David	Norris,Derek	6	2	1_	6-0	2B	HR
08/08/2012	TEX@BOS	Aceves,Alfredo	Cruz,Nelson	9	1	1_	10-9	Foul	Foul
08/09/2012	MIA@NYN	Gaudin,Chad	Torres,Andres	8	0	1_	4-1	3B	3B
08/09/2012	TOR@TB	Janssen,Casey	Longoria,Evan	8	2	1_	6-1	2B	2B
08/12/2012	KC@BAL	Chen,Bruce	Machado,Manny	2	0	1_	0-0	2B	HR
08/12/2012	SD@PIT	Boxberger,Brad	Walker,Neil	7	0	___	10-5	HR	HR
08/15/2012	WAS@SF	Kontos,George	Morse,Michael	5	0	___	4-2	2B	2B
08/16/2012	TB@LAA	Haren,Dan	Zobrist,Ben	2	1	___	0-0	HR	HR
08/16/2012	OAK@KC	Hochevar,Luke	Crisp,Coco	6	2	___	0-0	2B	HR
08/16/2012	TEX@NYA	Holland,Derek	Jones,Andruw	6	2	1_	2-4	HR	HR
08/19/2012	ARI@HOU	Kennedy,Ian	Martinez,Fernando	4	0	___	0-5	HR	2B

Date	Matchup	Pitcher	Hitter	Inning	Outs	Men On	Score	Initial Ruling	Video Ruling
08/24/2012	HOU@NYN	Lyles,Jordan	Wright,David	4	1	___	0-2	HR	HR
08/25/2012	TOR@BAL	Morrow,Brandon	Hardy,J.J.	5	0	1__	2-2	2B	2B
08/26/2012	WAS@PHI	Lee,Cliff	LaRoche,Adam	7	0	_2_	0-4	2B	2B
08/27/2012	CIN@ARI	Skaggs,Tyler	Arroyo,Bronson	6	2	___	2-2	2B	HR
08/28/2012	DET@KC	Holland,Greg	Young,Delmon	9	2	1_3	8-9	Foul	Foul
08/30/2012	CHA@BAL	Quintana,Jose	Reynolds,Mark	3	2	___	4-1	2B	2B
08/31/2012	SF@CHN	Kontos,George	Rizzo,Anthony	5	0	___	5-1	3B	HR
09/01/2012	CHA@DET	Liriano,Francisco	Young,Delmon	5	0	___	2-0	3B	3B
09/06/2012	CHN@WAS	Beliveau,Jeff	LaRoche,Adam	6	1	1__	7-2	HR	HR
09/11/2012	CLE@TEX	Jimenez,Ubaldo	Beltre,Adrian	5	0	___	4-1	2B	HR
09/14/2012	SEA@TEX	Iwakuma,Hisashi	Kinsler,Ian	1	0	___	0-0	2B	HR
09/17/2012	PHI@NYN	Dickey,R.A.	Rollins,Jimmy	5	1	___	1-0	3B	HR
09/22/2012	MIA@NYN	Buehrle,Mark	Hairston,Scott	4	0	___	2-0	2B	HR
09/22/2012	MIA@NYN	Rauch,Jon	Buck,John	9	0	_23	0-4	Foul	HR
09/25/2012	SEA@LAA	Greinke,Zack	Smoak,Justin	4	1	___	0-2	HR	HR
09/29/2012	WAS@STL	Lohse,Kyle	Morse,Michael	1	1	123	0-0	1B	HR
10/02/2012	TEX@OAK	Kirkman,Michael	Crisp,Coco	8	0	___	3-1	Foul	Foul
10/03/2012	SD@MIL	Loe,Kameron	Headley,Chase	5	1	__3	2-6	HR	Foul

The Hall of Fame Monitor

Bill James

What do Evan Longoria, Miguel Cabrera, Adrian Beltre and Alex Rodriguez all have in common?

For the years in which they were born, they are each the leading candidate for the Hall of Fame. The Hall of Fame monitor is in absolutely no sense an effort to say who <u>should</u> go into the Hall of Fame. It is, rather, merely an observation that certain players are making more progress toward the Hall of Fame than are other players.

Players who go into the Hall of Fame tend to do certain things. They tend to hit .300, drive in 100 runs, play in the All Star game, win Gold Gloves, win MVP Awards, lead the league in batting, and play for championship teams. If they are pitchers, they tend to win 20 games, strike out 200 batters, win Cy Young Awards, lead the league in ERA and pile up saves. The more of these types of things a player does, the more likely he is to be elected to the Hall of Fame. We're just trying to keep track of where each player is, as best we can.

The way our system works is, if a player has 100 points that means basically that he's a lock to make the Hall of Fame as long as he hasn't taken steroids and doesn't hang around with Pete Rose. He's a lock for the Hall of Fame based on his performance. The youngest player over 100, by five years, is Albert Pujols. Miguel Cabrera, three years younger than Pujols, is piling up points at a similar pace, although he is not quite to 100 yet.

Many players who do not reach 100 points will nonetheless be selected to the Hall of Fame, but a player who doesn't reach 100 is kind of at the mercy of the voters. He could become a Catfish Hunter, who bursts through the doors of the Hall of Fame like a hurricane, or he could become a Luis Tiant, waiting around and wondering why. If a player concludes his career with less than 70 points, then in general he has little chance of being selected to the Hall of Fame, unless something unusual happens. If he finishes in the range of 70 to 100, like Jason Giambi or Billy Wagner, then he's in the gray area.

It's a complicated system, mathematically, and I'm not going to take the time to explain the details right here. What it is, really, is two systems mashed together and compressed into one. One system measures how the player is doing as a Hall of Fame candidate based on whether he does the things that are characteristic of a Hall of Fame player. . .five points for winning a batting title, two points for playing in the All Star game, etc. The other system measures how he is doing as a Hall of Fame candidate based simply on the quality of his performance. We add the two together and divide by two.

The players here are listed by year of birth. The year 1983 has three very strong Hall of Fame candidates—Miguel Cabrera, Joe Mauer and Ryan Braun. The years 1979-1976, all taken together, don't have a Hall of Fame candidate as strong as any of those three. A striking number of the year-of-birth leaders on these charts have changed in the twelve months since we last updated you. A year ago, Justin Upton was the leading Hall of Fame candidate among those born in 1987; now Upton has been overtaken by Buster Posey. A year ago, the leading candidate born in 1982 was Francisco Rodriguez; now K-Rod has been passed by by Robinson Cano and David Wright. A year ago the leading candidate born in 1981 was Carl Crawford; now Crawford has been leap-frogged by Josh Hamilton and Curtis Granderson. In the year of birth 1979, Ryan Howard has been replaced at the top of the list by Adrian Beltre. In 1978 Jimmy Rollins has pulled ahead of Chase Utley, although the two Philly infielders remain neck-and-neck.

But Jimmy Rollins isn't really competing with Chase Utley for a spot in the Hall of Fame; he is competing with Jimmy Rollins. Rollins has 2,024 career hits, which won't put you in the Hall of Fame. 3,000 hits will put you in the Hall of Fame. A player with 2,024 career hits has basically a one-in-four shot at immortality. At 2,500 hits, it's about 50-50. Rollins is in the zone where every season that he is able to stay healthy and productive moves the odds a little more in his favor.

Leading Hall of Fame Candidates Born in 1992

Player	Points
Bryce Harper	2

Leading Hall of Fame Candidates Born in 1991

Player	Points
Mike Trout	10

Leading Hall of Fame Candidates Born in 1990

Player	Points
Starlin Castro	15
Jose Altuve	3

Leading Hall of Fame Candidates Born in 1989

Player	Points
Giancarlo Stanton	6
Jason Heyward	6
Chris Sale	4
Madison Bumgarner	4
Freddie Freeman	4

Leading Hall of Fame Candidates Born in 1988

Player	Points
Craig Kimbrel	19
Clayton Kershaw	19
Elvis Andrus	15
Neftali Feliz	15
Stephen Strasburg	2
Dustin Ackley	2

Leading Hall of Fame Candidates Born in 1987

Player	Points
Buster Posey	19
Justin Upton	12
Michael Brantley	2
Jemile Weeks	2
Josh Reddick	2
Jeremy Hellickson	2
Daniel Hudson	2
Gerardo Parra	2
Ryan Cook	2
Paul Goldschmidt	2
Lance Lynn	2

Leading Hall of Fame Candidates Born in 1986

Player	Points
Felix Hernandez	24
Andrew McCutchen	18
Billy Butler	14
Pablo Sandoval	13
Matt Wieters	12
Yu Darvish	3

Leading Hall of Fame Candidates Born in 1985

Player	Points
Evan Longoria	21
Carlos Gonzalez	15
David Price	15
Asdrubal Cabrera	13
Gio Gonzalez	11
Chris Perez	11
Adam Jones	10
Yoenis Cespedes	3

Leading Hall of Fame Candidates Born in 1984

Player	Points
Prince Fielder	44
Tim Lincecum	30
Brian McCann	30
Matt Kemp	28
Joakim Soria	25
Troy Tulowitzki	25
Ryan Zimmerman	20
Melky Cabrera	19
Matt Cain	16
B.J. Upton	14
Jon Lester	14

Leading Hall of Fame Candidates Born in 1983

Player	Points
Miguel Cabrera	91
Joe Mauer	66
Ryan Braun	54
Hanley Ramirez	45
Justin Verlander	44
Jose Reyes	42
Dustin Pedroia	40
Joey Votto	34
Nick Markakis	21
Huston Street	20

Leading Hall of Fame Candidates Born in 1982

Player	Points
Robinson Cano	56
David Wright	51
Francisco Rodriguez (Mil)	49
Adrian Gonzalez	45
Yadier Molina	36
Ian Kinsler	28
Brian Wilson	27
Grady Sizemore	23
Jered Weaver	19
Aaron Hill	18
Jhonny Peralta	18

Leading Hall of Fame Candidates Born in 1981	
Player	**Points**
Josh Hamilton	34
Curtis Granderson	32
Carl Crawford	29
Justin Morneau	27
Jake Peavy	21
Brandon Phillips	21
Carlos Zambrano	21
Ben Zobrist	20
Adam Wainwright	16
Alex Rios	16

Leading Hall of Fame Candidates Born in 1978	
Player	**Points**
Jimmy Rollins	59
Chase Utley	56
Aramis Ramirez	47
Victor Martinez	42
Jose Valverde	35
Cliff Lee	33
Vernon Wells	33
Jason Bay	31
Barry Zito	23
Carlos Pena	21

Leading Hall of Fame Candidates Born in 1975	
Player	**Points**
Alex Rodriguez	190
Vladimir Guerrero	108
Scott Rolen	65
David Ortiz	58
Edgar Renteria	54
Francisco Cordero	47
Derek Lee	43
Luis Castillo	36
Tim Hudson	35
Placido Polanco	34

Leading Hall of Fame Candidates Born in 1980	
Player	**Points**
Albert Pujols	158
Mark Teixeira	62
Matt Holliday	50
Jonathan Papelbon	47
CC Sabathia	46
Dan Uggla	29
Jose Bautista	25
Josh Beckett	21
Shane Victorino	20
Nick Swisher	18
Dan Haren	18

Leading Hall of Fame Candidates Born in 1977	
Player	**Points**
Carlos Beltran	68
Andruw Jones	63
Roy Halladay	61
Juan Pierre	36
Rafael Furcal	34
Roy Oswalt	33
J.J. Putz	27
Eric Chavez	26
Brian Roberts	26
Heath Bell	24
Travis Hafner	24

Leading Hall of Fame Candidates Born in 1974	
Player	**Points**
Derek Jeter	162
Miguel Tejada	83
Bobby Abreu	79
Magglio Ordonez	62
Joe Nathan	56
Jason Kendall	55
Hideki Matsui	25
Kevin Millwood	18
R.A. Dickey	9
Jamey Carroll	7

Leading Hall of Fame Candidates Born in 1979	
Player	**Points**
Adrian Beltre	54
Ryan Howard	52
Adam Dunn	48
Johan Santana	45
Mark Buehrle	28
Kevin Youkilis	23
Carlos Ruiz	18
Rafael Soriano	18
Jayson Werth	15
Adam LaRoche	14

Leading Hall of Fame Candidates Born in 1976	
Player	**Points**
Lance Berkman	72
Michael Young	70
Alfonso Soriano	54
Carlos Lee	50
Paul Konerko	50
Troy Glaus	34
Brad Lidge	29
A.J. Pierzynski	25
Aubrey Huff	25
Freddy Garcia	17

Leading Hall of Fame Candidates Born in 1973	
Player	**Points**
Ichiro Suzuki	108
Todd Helton	95
Johnny Damon	56
Bartolo Colon	27
Derek Lowe	26
Octavio Dotel	17
Guillermo Mota	8
Geoff Blum	3

Leading Hall of Fame Candidates Born in **1972**	
Player	Points
Manny Ramirez	125
Chipper Jones	108
Andy Pettitte	53
Jason Isringhausen	46
Garret Anderson	43
Raul Ibanez	26
LaTroy Hawkins	20

Leading Hall of Fame Candidates Born in **1967**	
Player	Points
Trevor Hoffman	112
Omar Vizquel	48

Leading Hall of Fame Candidates Born in **1962**	
Player	Points
Jamie Moyer	28

Leading Hall of Fame Candidates Born in **1971**	
Player	Points
Ivan Rodriguez	111
Billy Wagner	87
Jason Giambi	75
Jorge Posada	64
Jose Contreras	8
Miguel Batista	8

Leading Hall of Fame Candidates Born in **1970**	
Player	Points
Jim Thome	95
Jim Edmonds	64
Takashi Saito	13
Darren Oliver	12

Leading Hall of Fame Candidates Born in **1969**	
Player	Points
Mariano Rivera	154
Ken Griffey Jr.	114

Hey, <u>You</u> Try Finding Something that Rhymes with "Asdrubal"

Bill James

Allow me a moment to blow my own Horn;
Did you hear what we said about Michael Bourn?
We said that he would hit .274,
And that he did hit, neither less nor more.

Jason Heyward, we said, would hit .269
And so he did hit that, right on the line.

Fourteen homers we offered for Jones, Mr. Chipper,
And so he did hit them; my, what a hitter.

An average we offered for one Mr. Kotsay,
.259, as clear as the day,
And he was so nice as to do what we say.

Sixteen homers we said for Cabrera, Asdrubal,
And yes, he did hit them—two, but a Cubal.

We had fourteen homers outlined for Drew Stubbs,
And fourteen he hit, without any flubs.

Michael Morse we projected at .291,
And when the season was wrapped up and done,
Why, that was his average,
Our error was "none".

We had eight home runs for Angel Pagan,
And when he hit "finish", those eight, they were gone;
His ribbies, however, we did miss by juan.

And how did we guess that Jonathan Lucroy
Would hit the twelve homers we had given the boy?
And what can we say about Jack Hanahan?

.244 with four homers; right on, Jack.   Good man.

We had 12 home runs for Will Betemit,
And that was the number that he could not beat.

Jayson Nix' RBI; we foresaw 18;
And he drove in just those,
That we had foreseen.

We drew up the numbers and put in our plan,
41 RBI, for one Denard Span,
And how did we do?
Well. . .the best that we can.
And then 31 for Brendan Ryan,
And how did he do?
Did you think we were lyin?

46 RBI for the A's Coco Crisp,
Didn't miss his output by even a wisp.
And 68 for J. J. Hardy,
68 he produced; let's have a party.

We did not, I admit,
Get everything right,
On Eric Hosmer,
We were none too bright,
On Jason Bartlett,
We did not see the light,
On Brent Morel,
We were flying a kite,
About Marlon Byrd,
Our judgment took flight,
Our guess for one Lind,
Was a bit of a blight,
On Miguel Montero,
We put up a good fight.

But this is the lesson of Player Projection,
We just do it for fun;
Enjoy the Section.

Hitter	Label	G	AB	R	H	2B	3B	HR	RBI	BB	SO	SB	Avg	Slg
Michael Bourn	Projected	152	583	87	160	25	6	3	40	55	127	50	.274	.353
	Actual	155	624	96	171	26	10	9	57	70	155	42	.274	.391
Jason Heyward	Projected	149	540	86	145	31	4	21	74	86	114	14	.269	.457
	Actual	158	587	93	158	30	6	27	82	58	152	21	.269	.479
Chipper Jones	Projected	110	356	53	99	21	1	14	56	57	63	2	.278	.461
	Actual	112	387	58	111	23	0	14	62	57	51	1	.287	.455
Mark Kotsay	Projected	79	166	16	43	9	0	3	18	14	19	1	.259	.367
	Actual	82	143	9	37	8	0	2	14	11	14	0	.259	.357
Asdrubal Cabrera	Projected	143	566	86	158	35	3	16	75	48	105	15	.279	.436
	Actual	143	555	70	150	35	1	16	68	52	99	9	.270	.423
Drew Stubbs	Projected	136	476	75	123	21	3	14	48	52	141	31	.258	.403
	Actual	136	493	75	105	13	2	14	40	42	166	30	.213	.333
Michael Morse	Projected	140	515	68	150	33	1	25	87	38	109	2	.291	.505
	Actual	102	406	53	118	17	1	18	62	16	97	0	.291	.470
Angel Pagan	Projected	136	504	71	140	27	5	8	55	42	78	28	.278	.399
	Actual	154	605	95	174	38	15	8	56	48	97	29	.288	.440
Jonathan Lucroy	Projected	136	478	53	126	24	1	12	64	45	88	3	.264	.393
	Actual	96	316	46	101	17	4	12	58	22	44	4	.320	.513
Jack Hannahan	Projected	81	197	23	48	11	0	4	24	26	47	1	.244	.360
	Actual	105	287	23	70	16	0	4	29	27	63	0	.244	.341
Wilson Betemit	Projected	108	359	43	95	24	1	12	52	37	108	3	.265	.437
	Actual	102	341	41	89	19	0	12	40	31	103	0	.261	.422
Laynce Nix	Projected	121	306	39	76	17	1	14	44	23	81	2	.248	.448
	Actual	70	114	13	28	10	0	3	16	12	42	0	.246	.412
Denard Span	Projected	115	417	64	120	16	5	4	41	45	53	16	.288	.379
	Actual	128	516	71	146	38	4	4	41	47	62	17	.283	.395
Brendan Ryan	Projected	129	401	50	98	18	2	3	31	30	70	11	.244	.322
	Actual	141	407	42	79	19	3	3	31	44	98	11	.194	.278
Coco Crisp	Projected	119	428	62	116	23	3	8	46	39	60	32	.271	.395
	Actual	120	455	68	118	25	7	11	46	45	64	39	.259	.418
J.J. Hardy	Projected	134	503	69	132	26	1	21	68	39	86	0	.262	.443
	Actual	158	663	85	158	30	2	22	68	38	106	0	.238	.389
Eric Hosmer	Projected	153	605	86	188	34	4	23	92	48	87	14	.311	.494
	Actual	152	535	65	124	22	2	14	60	56	95	16	.232	.359
Jason Bartlett	Projected	140	496	66	132	25	3	4	44	44	88	17	.266	.353
	Actual	29	83	8	11	5	0	0	4	12	27	0	.133	.193
Brent Morel	Projected	136	447	53	122	25	2	12	50	25	66	6	.273	.418
	Actual	35	113	14	20	2	0	0	5	7	39	4	.177	.195
Marlon Byrd	Projected	146	556	70	153	33	2	13	66	36	103	5	.275	.412
	Actual	48	143	10	30	2	0	1	9	5	31	0	.210	.245
Adam Lind	Projected	144	557	69	149	32	1	27	94	42	123	1	.268	.474
	Actual	93	321	28	82	14	2	11	45	29	61	0	.255	.414
Miguel Montero	Projected	130	468	60	128	32	1	17	73	47	93	1	.274	.455
	Actual	141	486	65	139	25	2	15	88	73	130	0	.286	.438

2013 Player Projections

Bill James

The poet's claim that we only do projections for fun is somewhat undermined by the fact that professional men rely on us to know what we are guessing about.   A year ago at the winter meetings, the Orioles' Dan Duquette defended his decision to project Chris Davis as a part of the 2012 team by saying "If you take a look at Bill James' projections, they're projecting Davis to slug at .500 next year. Obviously, he'd have to mature and his approach would have to be consistent for him to do that, but he's got that kind of capability."

Well, that created a bit of a ruckus, and some sportswriters, quoting anonymous scouts, were so unkind as to suggest that Duquette was out of his depth as a GM, making personnel decisions based on what he reads in the Bill James Handbook.   What was missed by almost everyone in this controversy was that Chris Davis, in the end, did almost exactly what we had said that he would do, except that he got more playing time than we had projected.   We had projected that he would hit .265 with a .500 slugging percentage and a strikeout/walk ratio of 106 to 27.   In fact, he hit .270 with a .501 slugging percentage—we missed by one point—and a strikeout/walk ratio of 169 to 37.   We did *not* project that he would also pitch two innings and beat the Red Sox, but hey, who didn't?

In science there is what is known as the Observer Effect; also known, or related phenomenon known, as the "Copenhagen Interpretation" or "Schrodinger's Cat".   One changes something by observing it.   We projected Chris Davis to bat 366 times in 2012, which was a lot, considering that he hadn't batted 200 times in a season since 2009.   We believed, however—based on his minor league batting numbers in 2011—that Davis had taken a step forward as a hitter.   What we had failed to allow for was the possibility that somebody would take us seriously.   By projecting his performance, we accidentally involved ourselves in his story, thus helping Davis to get significantly ***more*** at bats than we said he would.

Given the 2012 performance of the Baltimore Orioles Mr. Duquette hardly needs us to defend him.   We're not defending him; we're defending ourselves.   We're serious people.   We're not fortune tellers, and we're not always right, but we're not idiots, either.   We're right about a whole lot of things every year.   We didn't predict that Miggy would hit .330, but we did project that he would hit .329.   We're not apologizing.   We didn't project that Ryan Braun would hit .319 with 112 RBI; we projected that he would hit .317 with 115 RBI. We didn't project that Jay Bruce would have 34 homers and 99 RBI; we projected 32 and 88. We didn't project that Matt Holliday would hit .295 with 27 homers and 102 RBI; we projected that he would hit .307 with 27 homers and 100 RBI. We projected he would get 173 hits and score 98 runs; it was actually 177 hits and 95 Runs scored. That was our 37th most accurate projection of 2012.

We work hard at projecting what players will hit, and, if you compare our projections last year with what the players actually did, you will find that we are essentially right about most players.

Most, but not all, and certainly it would be a sin to overstate our accuracy, so let's deal now with some of the failures. We tend to over-project playing time for young players, and we do that on purpose. We have no way of knowing, in early October, 2012, who will get playing time in the summer of 2013; even the managers and general managers don't know this. Since we don't know, we think it is our responsibility to answer this question: If this young player gets some playing time, how will he do?

For 2013, we've projected a lot of playing time for the Red Sox' Jackie Bradley. It's not that likely that Bradley will actually win a regular job out of spring training. We know this. We're just saying, if he plays, this is how we think he'll play.

Our worst projection for 2012, statistically, was for Francisco Cervelli of the Yankees. We had projected that he would play 92 games, hit .269, and drive in 43 runs. He got one at bat in the major leagues, so whatever we had projected he would do was just totally wrong.

We had projected that Tsuyoshi Nishioka would play 120 games, hit .241 with no homers, 43 RBI and 30 runs scored. Not that we thought that he would be good; we actually thought he would suck, but at least we projected him to play. We did not expect him to pass up his salary for next year, but then, that doesn't happen a lot. Since we projected him to play and he didn't, it's an inaccurate projection. We projected Brandon Allen to hit 22 homers and drive in 70 runs. He got 20 at bats, hit one homer and drove in 3 runs.

Those are bad projections. We had, I would say, about 100 bad projections in this section of the 2012 Handbook. Of our 100 worst projections, 78 were for players who did less than we had projected them to do. Of those 78, at least 60 were for players who did not get the playing time we had projected for them, either because of injuries or because, like Brandon Allen and Tsuyoshi Nishioka, they just really weren't quite good enough to play. We had not predicted that Troy Tulowitzki would miss half of the season with an injury, or that Ryan Howard would, or Evan Longoria, or Jacoby Ellsbury. Our projection for Carl Crawford would actually be uncannily accurate if you just divided everything by five.   Our projection for Franklin Gutierrez would be extremely accurate if you divided it by four.   That happens, and we don't really think that you would hold that against us.

There were a handful of players who *did* get playing time, but who just did not hit the way that we had expected them to hit.   Eric Hosmer is the captain of that team, I suppose, but we had projected Orlando Hudson to hit .263.   He hit .204.   We had projected Geovany Soto to hit .252; he hit .198.   We had projected J. D. Martinez to hit .297; he hit .241.   We had projected Sean Rodriguez to hit .252 with 15 homers; he hit .213 with 6 homers.   We had projected Jemile Weeks to hit .279; he hit .221, and was awful on defense.

We weren't *optimistic* about Endy Chavez or Chone Figgins, but we weren't pessimistic enough.   We thought Logan Morrison would hit .265; he hit .230.   We thought Jose Tabata would hit .283; he hit .243.

That happens, and the opposite happens with essentially the same frequency; there were about 20 players in the majors in 2012—and there will be about 20 in 2013—who just hit much better than we had expected them to hit. We had projected Alex Rios to hit .269 with 15 homers; he hit .304 with 25 homers.   We had projected Andrew McCutchen to hit .277 with 19 homers; he beat that by 50 points and a dozen homers.   We had projected Chase Headley to hit 10 homers and drive in 58 runs; it was actually 31 and 115.   We had projected Wilin Rosario to hit .236 with 13 homers; he hit .260 with 28 homers.   We had projected Carlos Ruiz and Justin Ruggiano to hit in the .270s; they hit well over .300.   We had projected Todd Frazier to hit .248; he hit .273.   We had projected Edwin Encarnacion for 16 homers; he hit 42.

I can live with those, but the one that drives me crazy is Mike Trout.   We had projected Trout, actually, as a very good player; we had projected that he would hit .290 with a .478 slugging percentage, and we had projected his walk rate and his stolen base rate very accurately, and even his runs scored rate.   We had projected him to score runs at a rate that, even though we were 10% low, would still have been enough to lead the league.   The only thing is, we projected him to play only 71 games, thus projected him to hit only 9 home runs and to drive in only 30 runs.

And we should never do that, because that's cheating the reader.   We *knew* that Mike Trout was a terrific young player; we just were afraid to say so because we thought we would look silly, projecting him to steal 45 bases and score 110 runs.   I apologize for that one, because that's what we should never do. We don't always know who is going to play next year; we're not always right about how each player will hit.   But we should never be afraid to say that a young player is going to be a good player.

2013 Hitter Projections

PLAYER			BATTING											BASERUNNING			AVERAGES			
Hitter	Team	Age	G	AB	H	2B	3B	HR	R	RBI	RC	RC27	BB	SO	SB	CS	SB%	Avg	OBP	Slg	OPS
Abreu,Bobby	LAD	39	114	339	87	20	1	8	48	47	48	4.88	54	81	10	4	.71	.257	.360	.392	.753
Ackley,Dustin	Sea	25	151	595	148	28	4	12	82	55	73	4.20	70	108	13	5	.72	.249	.328	.370	.698
Adams,Matt	StL	24	145	503	142	35	0	27	69	89	83	5.94	30	107	3	2	.60	.282	.323	.513	.836
Alonso,Yonder	SD	26	152	557	159	41	1	14	60	73	88	5.72	64	95	5	2	.71	.285	.360	.438	.798
Altuve,Jose	Hou	23	147	551	165	33	4	8	77	42	79	5.16	35	64	30	12	.71	.299	.347	.417	.764
Alvarez,Pedro	Pit	26	147	534	137	29	2	29	70	91	86	5.62	63	165	2	1	.67	.257	.336	.481	.817
Amarista,Alexi	SD	24	77	181	46	10	2	2	22	21	19	3.58	9	23	6	3	.67	.254	.289	.365	.654
Andino,Robert	Bal	29	106	297	72	14	1	5	35	25	31	3.54	23	62	6	3	.67	.242	.299	.347	.646
Andrus,Elvis	Tex	24	156	615	173	26	6	4	94	59	78	4.48	59	89	29	11	.73	.281	.349	.363	.712
Ankiel,Rick	Was	33	103	291	66	16	1	11	36	36	33	3.78	24	91	3	2	.60	.227	.288	.402	.690
Aoki,Norichika	Mil	31	144	409	119	30	2	8	64	40	62	5.41	34	39	22	8	.73	.291	.364	.433	.797
Arenado,Nolan	Col	22	98	356	100	24	1	9	39	40	51	5.18	27	39	0	0	.00	.281	.332	.430	.761
Arencibia,J.P.	Tor	27	116	419	97	24	1	22	51	67	52	4.20	25	111	1	0	1.00	.232	.278	.451	.729
Arias,Joaquin	SF	28	71	148	38	6	1	2	17	14	15	3.51	6	19	3	1	.75	.257	.295	.351	.646
Avery,Xavier	Bal	23	131	396	98	19	3	6	54	29	47	3.98	43	104	26	9	.74	.247	.321	.356	.677
Avila,Alex	Det	26	130	428	115	27	2	15	55	66	71	5.88	69	109	2	1	.67	.269	.373	.446	.819
Aviles,Mike	Bos	32	134	494	132	27	2	13	60	56	60	4.23	22	64	13	7	.65	.267	.300	.409	.709
Aybar,Erick	LAA	29	138	525	146	27	5	7	69	48	65	4.38	28	65	20	7	.74	.278	.321	.389	.709
Barajas,Rod	Pit	37	88	255	55	11	0	10	26	32	25	3.25	17	55	0	0	.00	.216	.278	.376	.654
Barmes,Clint	Pit	34	133	416	97	21	1	9	42	43	40	3.24	25	89	2	2	.50	.233	.286	.353	.640
Barney,Darwin	ChC	27	157	555	149	28	3	5	71	47	61	3.88	31	59	8	3	.73	.268	.311	.357	.667
Barton,Daric	Oak	27	62	154	37	9	1	3	21	16	20	4.41	28	30	2	1	.67	.240	.364	.370	.734
Bautista,Jose	Tor	32	153	544	141	28	1	39	96	99	107	6.84	98	117	7	4	.64	.259	.377	.529	.907
Baxter,Mike	NYM	28	76	163	45	10	1	3	22	20	23	4.98	20	33	4	2	.67	.276	.362	.405	.767
Bay,Jason	NYM	34	133	470	116	23	2	17	69	71	67	4.88	66	128	10	3	.77	.247	.343	.413	.756
Beckham,Gordon	CWS	26	151	512	126	31	1	15	67	62	62	4.14	42	95	5	3	.62	.246	.314	.398	.713
Belt,Brandon	SF	25	155	497	140	32	5	16	64	74	86	6.16	71	122	14	6	.70	.282	.374	.463	.836
Beltran,Carlos	StL	36	145	538	144	32	2	25	81	90	90	5.88	70	113	11	4	.73	.268	.354	.474	.828
Beltre,Adrian	Tex	34	152	591	172	37	1	29	85	97	99	6.13	37	85	2	1	.67	.291	.338	.504	.842
Berkman,Lance	StL	37	134	429	117	26	1	21	66	72	80	6.60	79	92	5	3	.62	.273	.389	.485	.874
Bernadina,Roger	Was	29	118	316	86	15	2	8	43	32	45	4.96	32	66	19	6	.76	.272	.343	.408	.751
Berry,Quintin	Det	28	88	235	58	9	1	2	33	19	27	3.88	26	59	21	4	.84	.247	.330	.319	.649
Betancourt,Yuniesky	KC	31	113	386	100	22	2	9	40	46	43	3.88	14	42	2	2	.50	.259	.287	.396	.683
Betemit,Wilson	Bal	31	123	434	113	28	1	15	51	60	61	4.93	43	132	1	1	.50	.260	.328	.433	.762
Blackmon,Charlie	Col	26	67	186	51	12	1	4	26	22	25	4.71	13	28	7	3	.70	.274	.328	.414	.742
Blanco,Gregor	SF	29	80	183	45	7	1	2	27	14	21	3.85	27	41	11	4	.73	.246	.346	.328	.674
Blanco,Henry	Ari	41	41	124	27	5	0	3	10	12	11	2.95	10	30	1	0	1.00	.218	.276	.331	.607
Bloomquist,Willie	Ari	35	86	334	90	13	2	2	44	23	34	3.52	19	57	10	7	.59	.269	.311	.338	.649
Boesch,Brennan	Det	28	121	391	104	21	2	13	51	53	52	4.66	27	78	5	3	.62	.266	.320	.430	.750
Bogusevic,Brian	Hou	29	124	388	96	19	2	8	51	39	48	4.20	44	91	17	5	.77	.247	.329	.369	.697
Bonifacio,Emilio	Mia	28	153	546	150	20	6	3	74	33	67	4.26	49	104	45	13	.78	.275	.336	.350	.685
Bourjos,Peter	LAA	26	144	572	150	24	11	13	88	57	74	4.46	41	124	24	9	.73	.262	.316	.411	.727
Bourn,Michael	Atl	30	155	609	166	26	7	5	93	46	78	4.44	63	143	44	14	.76	.273	.344	.363	.707
Bradley,Jackie	Bos	23	148	542	140	38	5	13	71	65	80	5.06	77	112	20	9	.69	.258	.351	.419	.769
Brantley,Michael	Cle	26	152	559	156	29	3	7	78	55	73	4.62	54	60	19	8	.70	.279	.344	.379	.723
Brantly,Rob	Mia	23	31	109	31	8	0	2	11	11	15	5.00	8	14	0	0	.00	.284	.333	.413	.746
Braun,Ryan	Mil	29	157	609	191	41	3	36	108	112	130	7.93	59	121	24	8	.75	.314	.382	.568	.950
Brown,Andrew	Col	28	79	265	70	15	1	13	39	43	41	5.41	26	71	2	2	.50	.264	.330	.475	.805
Brown,Domonic	Phi	25	148	533	146	32	4	17	80	77	81	5.35	59	101	12	7	.63	.274	.347	.445	.792
Bruce,Jay	Cin	26	158	581	153	32	4	36	93	98	101	6.06	66	154	9	5	.64	.263	.342	.518	.860
Buck,John	Mia	32	119	383	84	19	1	14	37	50	43	3.74	38	104	0	0	.00	.219	.298	.384	.682
Butera,Drew	Min	29	53	102	20	5	0	1	8	8	7	2.22	7	19	0	0	.00	.196	.261	.275	.536
Butler,Billy	KC	27	161	614	184	43	1	24	78	100	109	6.58	62	101	1	1	.50	.300	.368	.490	.858
Cabrera,Asdrubal	Cle	27	148	582	161	37	2	16	82	73	84	5.13	52	106	12	5	.71	.277	.341	.430	.771
Cabrera,Everth	SD	26	115	403	103	20	4	2	56	29	49	4.14	42	92	40	8	.83	.256	.329	.340	.669
Cabrera,Melky	SF	28	148	600	177	33	5	13	88	75	90	5.45	48	83	14	6	.70	.295	.348	.432	.780
Cabrera,Miguel	Det	30	160	602	199	43	1	38	107	126	146	9.37	80	101	3	2	.60	.331	.413	.595	1.007
Cain,Lorenzo	KC	27	155	597	167	29	6	15	83	71	85	5.06	46	129	24	7	.77	.280	.332	.424	.756
Cairo,Miguel	Cin	39	74	140	34	6	1	2	16	14	14	3.40	8	20	3	1	.75	.243	.298	.343	.641
Callaspo,Alberto	LAA	30	136	451	122	24	2	8	54	48	58	4.54	45	49	4	3	.57	.271	.337	.386	.723
Campana,Tony	ChC	27	82	152	42	5	1	0	22	7	17	3.81	10	32	21	6	.78	.276	.321	.322	.643
Cano,Robinson	NYY	30	161	631	193	47	2	27	100	99	115	6.80	47	91	3	2	.60	.306	.361	.515	.876
Carp,Mike	Sea	27	61	139	35	7	0	5	16	19	18	4.46	14	32	1	1	.50	.252	.329	.410	.739
Carpenter,Matt	StL	27	99	323	93	23	3	8	47	46	52	5.83	37	60	3	2	.60	.288	.365	.452	.817
Carroll,Jamey	Min	39	142	442	119	16	2	1	61	31	49	3.90	50	68	7	4	.64	.269	.349	.321	.670
Carter,Chris	Oak	26	97	327	81	20	1	17	51	56	51	5.35	42	97	4	2	.67	.248	.333	.471	.804
Casilla,Alexi	Min	28	105	287	72	13	2	2	38	24	30	3.55	23	45	17	5	.77	.251	.311	.331	.642
Castillo,Welington	ChC	26	102	333	84	18	0	13	38	48	44	4.59	30	85	0	0	.00	.252	.316	.423	.739
Castro,Jason	Hou	26	121	390	100	21	2	8	50	40	50	4.48	48	76	0	0	.00	.256	.339	.382	.721
Castro,Starlin	ChC	23	158	629	191	35	10	12	83	73	96	5.55	38	86	24	12	.67	.304	.346	.448	.795
Cedeno,Ronny	NYM	30	114	335	85	17	2	5	35	32	37	3.82	24	71	3	2	.60	.254	.306	.361	.667
Cespedes,Yoenis	Oak	27	149	569	169	30	5	28	84	98	105	6.72	53	108	18	6	.75	.297	.364	.515	.879
Chavez,Endy	Bal	35	59	120	30	5	1	1	13	10	12	3.43	6	15	3	1	.75	.250	.286	.333	.619
Chavez,Eric	NYY	35	98	265	67	14	0	10	32	36	36	4.73	28	60	0	0	.00	.253	.324	.419	.743
Chisenhall,Lonnie	Cle	24	148	522	137	31	2	18	75	74	69	4.64	35	94	3	2	.60	.262	.310	.433	.743
Choo,Shin-Soo	Cle	30	154	552	156	35	4	16	80	73	89	5.73	71	137	18	8	.69	.283	.374	.440	.815
Ciriaco,Pedro	Bos	27	95	314	84	14	2	3	37	26	32	3.53	8	53	16	6	.73	.268	.286	.354	.639
Clevenger,Steve	ChC	27	78	226	60	16	1	3	23	26	28	4.39	19	31	1	0	1.00	.265	.322	.385	.707
Colvin,Tyler	Col	27	114	303	77	16	4	12	40	43	40	4.56	17	75	4	2	.67	.254	.296	.452	.748
Constanza,Jose	Atl	29	119	383	109	10	3	1	55	29	45	4.13	35	53	21	9	.70	.285	.344	.334	.679

2013 Hitter Projections

PLAYER			BATTING											BASERUNNING			AVERAGES			
Hitter	Team	Age	G	AB	H	2B	3B	HR	R	RBI	RC	RC27	BB	SO	SB	CS	SB%	Avg	OBP	Slg	OPS
Cooper,David	Tor	26	45	151	42	12	0	4	18	21	22	5.25	14	20	0	0	.00	.278	.343	.437	.780
Cowgill,Collin	Oak	27	52	108	29	6	1	2	15	14	14	4.49	10	20	5	2	.71	.269	.331	.398	.729
Cox,Zack	Mia	24	124	397	98	27	1	10	44	44	45	3.90	22	87	1	1	.50	.247	.286	.395	.682
Cozart,Zack	Cin	27	137	547	142	34	3	15	79	49	70	4.46	37	98	9	3	.75	.260	.308	.415	.723
Craig,Allen	StL	28	139	551	166	37	1	27	87	104	101	6.80	44	96	3	1	.75	.301	.354	.519	.873
Crawford,Brandon	SF	26	143	453	111	24	3	6	50	43	48	3.62	39	92	4	3	.57	.245	.306	.351	.657
Crawford,Carl	LAD	31	153	595	163	25	5	16	83	68	79	4.64	35	115	36	11	.77	.274	.318	.413	.731
Crisp,Coco	Oak	33	132	495	130	26	4	10	72	51	66	4.59	47	72	36	9	.80	.263	.327	.392	.718
Cruz,Luis	LAD	29	115	362	94	24	1	7	37	40	40	3.87	13	42	2	1	.67	.260	.287	.390	.677
Cruz,Nelson	Tex	32	148	562	151	35	1	29	80	94	90	5.63	51	139	11	5	.69	.269	.333	.489	.822
Cruz,Tony	StL	26	68	173	42	10	1	3	17	19	18	3.57	11	30	0	0	.00	.243	.288	.364	.652
Cuddyer,Michael	Col	34	138	526	139	33	3	19	76	77	77	5.12	51	106	8	4	.67	.264	.333	.447	.780
dArnaud,Travis'	Tor	24	125	443	128	30	1	19	66	74	71	5.82	28	98	3	2	.60	.289	.331	.490	.821
Davidson,Matthew	Ari	22	150	546	139	32	1	27	86	83	85	5.39	69	139	4	3	.57	.255	.338	.465	.803
Davis,Chris	Bal	27	138	511	146	31	1	31	79	92	91	6.45	39	150	3	2	.60	.286	.340	.532	.872
Davis,Ike	NYM	26	154	515	137	31	1	31	77	94	93	6.40	69	121	0	0	.00	.266	.354	.511	.865
Davis,Rajai	Tor	32	100	278	72	15	2	3	38	24	31	3.75	18	57	25	9	.74	.259	.313	.360	.673
De Aza,Alejandro	CWS	29	146	587	173	38	5	12	93	60	91	5.54	53	111	28	13	.68	.295	.357	.438	.795
DeJesus,David	ChC	33	144	489	129	26	4	9	68	52	63	4.49	52	86	5	5	.50	.264	.345	.389	.734
Denorfia,Chris	SD	32	129	374	104	19	3	8	51	38	51	4.80	31	54	12	6	.67	.278	.335	.409	.744
Descalso,Daniel	StL	26	121	300	75	16	3	4	38	30	34	3.89	29	53	4	2	.67	.250	.322	.363	.686
Desmond,Ian	Was	27	149	559	156	33	3	18	73	68	81	5.12	36	114	22	8	.73	.279	.326	.445	.772
Dirks,Andy	Det	27	132	484	137	27	3	14	75	58	71	5.26	36	76	10	4	.71	.283	.335	.438	.773
Dobbs,Greg	Mia	34	91	192	50	9	1	4	18	23	22	4.00	11	35	2	1	.67	.260	.304	.380	.684
Dominguez,Matt	Hou	23	147	496	120	28	2	13	52	69	56	3.87	36	69	0	0	.00	.242	.293	.385	.678
Donald,Jason	Cle	28	73	208	54	12	1	4	30	19	26	4.33	18	49	6	2	.75	.260	.325	.385	.709
Donaldson,Josh	Oak	27	133	451	111	27	1	17	60	67	59	4.46	40	92	9	4	.69	.246	.310	.424	.734
Doumit,Ryan	Min	32	126	443	120	29	1	16	51	63	64	5.15	32	88	1	0	1.00	.271	.328	.449	.778
Downs,Matt	Hou	29	74	124	29	7	0	4	15	15	13	3.52	8	24	2	1	.67	.234	.296	.387	.683
Dozier,Brian	Min	26	79	288	73	15	2	5	35	29	32	3.80	18	48	8	4	.67	.253	.300	.372	.671
Drew,Stephen	Oak	30	118	436	110	26	5	11	57	48	58	4.60	46	97	3	2	.60	.252	.325	.411	.736
Duda,Lucas	NYM	27	137	452	121	28	1	18	57	69	72	5.64	58	102	1	1	.50	.268	.356	.454	.810
Duncan,Shelley	Cle	33	81	197	47	11	0	10	27	34	28	4.82	24	46	1	1	.50	.239	.324	.447	.771
Dunn,Adam	CWS	33	153	549	114	25	0	33	76	86	78	4.84	103	213	1	1	.50	.207	.341	.442	.783
Dyson,Jarrod	KC	28	75	175	45	6	2	0	29	10	20	3.88	17	29	18	4	.82	.257	.323	.314	.637
Eaton,Adam	Ari	24	139	529	154	33	5	8	95	42	80	5.36	53	81	36	13	.73	.291	.358	.418	.776
Ellis,A.J.	LAD	32	108	360	94	18	1	7	41	44	49	4.79	58	73	0	0	.00	.261	.368	.375	.743
Ellis,Mark	LAD	36	127	441	111	22	1	8	54	44	49	3.83	36	72	6	3	.67	.252	.317	.361	.677
Ellsbury,Jacoby	Bos	29	152	622	183	35	4	15	100	67	95	5.48	46	88	37	12	.76	.294	.346	.436	.781
Encarnacion,Edwin	Tor	30	150	532	144	31	0	31	82	89	94	6.23	65	94	9	4	.69	.271	.359	.504	.862
Escobar,Alcides	KC	26	152	595	162	26	7	5	74	53	69	4.06	31	91	30	9	.77	.272	.314	.365	.678
Escobar,Yunel	Tor	30	145	544	150	26	1	9	71	55	69	4.52	52	71	5	3	.62	.276	.344	.377	.721
Espinosa,Danny	Was	26	147	553	140	31	3	21	82	66	75	4.63	49	152	19	8	.70	.253	.327	.434	.761
Ethier,Andre	LAD	31	150	566	161	38	2	20	79	85	92	5.88	60	120	2	2	.50	.284	.359	.465	.824
Fielder,Prince	Det	29	161	589	176	34	1	37	95	114	129	8.10	100	106	1	1	.50	.299	.413	.548	.961
Figgins,Chone	Sea	35	55	127	31	5	1	1	16	9	13	3.41	15	27	6	3	.67	.244	.329	.323	.652
Flaherty,Ryan	Bal	26	66	147	35	6	1	6	18	21	18	4.14	11	33	1	1	.50	.238	.300	.415	.715
Flores,Jesus	Was	28	53	113	27	6	0	3	10	15	12	3.63	6	24	0	0	.00	.239	.283	.372	.655
Florimon,Pedro	Min	26	84	280	69	14	2	3	31	27	29	3.49	24	71	9	5	.64	.246	.306	.343	.649
Flowers,Tyler	CWS	27	79	254	60	14	1	13	35	34	38	5.07	36	91	3	1	.75	.236	.338	.453	.791
Forsythe,Logan	SD	26	91	306	81	15	2	5	46	32	40	4.54	38	64	10	4	.71	.265	.352	.376	.727
Fowler,Dexter	Col	27	146	523	143	31	12	10	89	53	84	5.64	77	140	14	7	.67	.273	.369	.436	.805
Francisco,Ben	TB	31	89	193	48	13	0	5	22	21	23	4.07	17	40	3	2	.60	.249	.319	.394	.713
Francisco,Juan	Atl	26	92	235	64	16	1	12	31	41	36	5.44	11	64	1	1	.50	.272	.308	.502	.810
Francoeur,Jeff	KC	29	129	423	110	24	2	13	50	56	53	4.36	26	86	5	3	.62	.260	.314	.418	.732
Frandsen,Kevin	Phi	31	79	254	72	15	1	2	28	23	29	4.10	11	21	2	2	.50	.283	.321	.374	.695
Franklin,Nicholas	Sea	22	147	529	142	33	7	11	62	50	73	4.82	47	120	16	7	.70	.268	.328	.420	.748
Frazier,Todd	Cin	27	105	338	89	23	2	15	46	51	51	5.26	29	78	6	3	.67	.263	.325	.476	.802
Freeman,Freddie	Atl	23	149	553	156	36	1	24	85	95	93	6.06	60	119	3	2	.60	.282	.358	.481	.839
Freese,David	StL	30	144	521	157	29	1	20	72	87	90	6.39	51	115	3	2	.60	.301	.368	.476	.844
Furcal,Rafael	StL	35	127	495	132	23	3	8	72	45	62	4.37	48	65	13	6	.68	.267	.333	.374	.706
Galvis,Freddy	Phi	23	143	465	114	24	3	7	53	44	46	3.36	23	71	11	5	.69	.245	.281	.355	.636
Gamel,Mat	Mil	27	114	442	127	27	2	17	65	72	73	5.97	42	91	6	3	.67	.287	.351	.473	.823
Garcia,Avisail	Det	22	144	504	141	15	4	9	69	44	57	3.96	19	88	19	11	.63	.280	.307	.379	.686
Gardner,Brett	NYY	29	155	498	137	19	7	5	94	41	71	4.92	70	90	44	14	.76	.275	.368	.371	.739
Gentry,Craig	Tex	29	104	246	67	10	2	2	35	23	28	3.96	17	40	14	5	.74	.272	.332	.354	.686
Getz,Chris	KC	29	92	258	69	11	2	1	32	22	29	3.89	21	26	12	5	.71	.267	.327	.337	.665
Giavotella,Johnny	KC	25	128	405	116	24	2	7	55	51	56	4.99	32	55	8	3	.73	.286	.339	.407	.746
Gimenez,Chris	TB	30	68	185	48	9	0	5	24	23	24	4.55	21	42	0	0	.00	.259	.335	.389	.724
Goldschmidt,Paul	Ari	25	153	569	161	39	2	27	105	109	107	6.75	81	137	15	4	.79	.283	.375	.501	.876
Gomes,Jonny	Oak	32	113	322	76	16	1	16	46	49	46	4.82	41	109	4	2	.67	.236	.337	.441	.778
Gomez,Carlos	Mil	27	122	351	88	16	3	11	55	38	43	4.14	21	85	27	7	.79	.251	.302	.407	.710
Gomez,Mauro	Bos	28	94	243	68	17	1	9	36	43	38	5.65	20	57	1	0	1.00	.280	.335	.469	.804
Gonzalez,Adrian	LAD	31	160	624	189	41	1	27	90	107	117	6.98	70	117	1	1	.50	.303	.377	.502	.878
Gonzalez,Carlos	Col	27	145	568	169	36	5	26	98	96	106	6.79	54	127	20	7	.74	.298	.362	.516	.877
Gonzalez,Marwin	Hou	24	78	219	55	13	1	2	21	20	22	3.45	14	28	3	2	.60	.251	.296	.347	.643
Gordon,Alex	KC	29	159	624	177	45	3	19	95	78	103	5.92	77	144	11	5	.69	.284	.366	.457	.823
Gordon,Dee	LAD	25	132	412	109	13	4	1	55	24	42	3.43	23	66	44	15	.75	.265	.307	.323	.629
Gose,Anthony	Tor	22	148	577	146	26	7	9	94	53	72	4.21	60	160	46	14	.77	.253	.324	.369	.694
Grandal,Yasmani	SD	24	120	388	110	24	1	12	59	67	62	5.80	45	74	0	0	.00	.284	.359	.443	.803
Granderson,Curtis	NYY	32	158	587	143	25	6	34	105	86	92	5.33	73	175	13	5	.72	.244	.332	.480	.813

2013 Hitter Projections

Hitter	Team	Age	G	AB	H	2B	3B	HR	R	RBI	RC	RC27	BB	SO	SB	CS	SB%	Avg	OBP	Slg	OPS
Green,Grant	Oak	25	119	465	126	24	2	10	56	52	55	4.12	25	78	11	8	.58	.271	.308	.396	.704
Greene,Tyler	Hou	29	114	339	86	17	2	11	52	35	44	4.43	28	93	17	5	.77	.254	.314	.413	.727
Gutierrez,Franklin	Sea	30	140	487	123	27	1	10	60	49	56	3.95	37	106	12	5	.71	.253	.308	.374	.682
Guzman,Jesus	SD	29	106	300	84	18	1	9	36	44	44	5.22	27	57	4	3	.57	.280	.341	.437	.778
Gwynn,Tony	LAD	30	98	211	52	7	2	1	25	14	21	3.33	19	40	11	5	.69	.246	.312	.313	.624
Gyorko,Jedd	SD	24	145	551	155	29	0	27	79	92	89	5.79	49	106	5	4	.56	.281	.340	.481	.821
Hafner,Travis	Cle	36	100	314	81	17	0	14	40	51	49	5.47	45	74	0	0	.00	.258	.363	.446	.809
Hairston,Jerry	LAD	37	67	183	46	9	0	3	22	18	20	3.77	16	24	2	1	.67	.251	.325	.350	.675
Hairston,Scott	NYM	33	117	304	76	18	1	13	40	40	41	4.63	23	68	5	2	.71	.250	.307	.444	.751
Hamilton,Billy	Cin	22	152	576	166	14	13	4	109	49	90	5.28	77	136	115	33	.78	.288	.372	.378	.751
Hamilton,Josh	Tex	32	147	574	166	35	2	35	96	114	109	6.90	56	144	7	3	.70	.289	.356	.540	.897
Hanigan,Ryan	Cin	32	69	207	57	8	0	3	21	20	27	4.68	28	23	0	0	.00	.275	.367	.357	.725
Hannahan,Jack	Cle	33	90	223	52	13	0	4	23	25	24	3.63	27	57	1	1	.50	.233	.319	.345	.664
Hardy,J.J.	Bal	30	147	578	147	29	1	22	76	71	74	4.46	41	95	0	0	.00	.254	.306	.422	.728
Harper,Bryce	Was	20	154	592	161	31	9	24	105	65	98	5.80	67	119	20	8	.71	.272	.347	.476	.823
Hart,Corey	Mil	31	150	576	156	37	4	27	89	85	92	5.64	48	144	8	4	.67	.271	.334	.490	.824
Hayes,Brett	Mia	29	69	175	39	9	0	3	16	15	15	2.87	9	47	1	0	1.00	.223	.261	.326	.587
Headley,Chase	SD	29	160	608	169	37	2	22	85	88	101	5.91	80	155	14	5	.74	.278	.365	.454	.819
Hechavarria,Adeiny	Tor	24	140	463	120	22	3	6	56	49	49	3.66	25	89	9	5	.64	.259	.299	.359	.657
Heisey,Chris	Cin	28	115	282	76	15	2	11	40	35	40	5.00	19	63	5	2	.71	.270	.327	.454	.781
Helton,Todd	Col	39	105	327	90	20	1	9	44	44	53	5.81	55	60	1	0	1.00	.275	.383	.425	.808
Hernandez,Gorkys	Mia	25	57	117	30	5	1	1	15	10	13	3.76	11	27	6	3	.67	.256	.326	.342	.667
Hernandez,Ramon	Col	37	47	156	39	8	0	5	14	22	19	4.22	11	25	0	0	.00	.250	.316	.397	.713
Herrera,Elian	LAD	28	50	100	27	5	1	1	14	10	13	4.51	10	22	5	2	.71	.270	.342	.370	.712
Herrera,Jonathan	Col	28	109	307	76	10	1	3	37	21	30	3.33	26	42	6	3	.67	.248	.308	.316	.624
Heyward,Jason	Atl	23	158	567	154	32	5	26	92	82	98	6.05	74	129	20	8	.71	.272	.360	.483	.843
Hill,Aaron	Ari	31	153	597	161	37	2	21	83	78	85	5.00	46	86	11	6	.65	.270	.327	.444	.771
Hinske,Eric	Atl	35	97	212	48	12	1	7	25	27	25	3.94	25	64	1	1	.50	.226	.314	.392	.705
Hoes,LJ	Bal	23	147	559	160	26	4	6	77	63	77	4.86	67	83	24	13	.65	.286	.363	.379	.742
Holliday,Matt	StL	33	152	579	174	40	2	27	95	101	113	7.20	71	121	6	3	.67	.301	.385	.516	.902
Hosmer,Eric	KC	23	155	572	158	29	3	20	79	79	88	5.47	56	89	17	4	.81	.276	.342	.442	.784
Howard,Ryan	Phi	33	150	569	143	28	1	36	82	102	95	5.78	75	194	1	1	.50	.251	.344	.494	.837
Hudson,Orlando	CWS	35	91	258	66	12	2	4	32	26	30	4.00	26	50	6	3	.67	.256	.329	.364	.693
Hundley,Nick	SD	29	71	193	45	10	1	5	20	25	21	3.69	16	46	0	0	.00	.233	.299	.373	.672
Hunter,Torii	LAA	37	148	558	151	29	1	19	75	84	79	5.00	49	130	8	4	.67	.271	.336	.428	.764
Iannetta,Chris	LAA	30	110	371	89	19	1	16	49	55	54	4.94	59	99	2	2	.50	.240	.352	.426	.778
Ibanez,Raul	NYY	41	129	412	102	23	1	15	50	62	54	4.51	39	80	2	1	.67	.248	.317	.417	.735
Iglesias,Jose	Bos	23	139	501	120	14	1	2	56	32	41	2.75	30	76	16	6	.73	.240	.285	.283	.569
Infante,Omar	Det	31	142	507	143	25	4	9	60	37	65	4.58	27	63	11	5	.69	.282	.320	.400	.720
Inge,Brandon	Oak	36	93	261	58	11	1	8	29	35	27	3.44	25	78	1	1	.50	.222	.302	.364	.666
Ishikawa,Travis	Mil	29	107	232	60	15	1	6	28	35	31	4.66	24	57	1	1	.50	.259	.333	.409	.743
Izturis,Maicer	LAA	32	101	300	80	17	1	3	39	32	36	4.16	27	40	11	5	.69	.267	.333	.360	.693
Jackson,Austin	Det	26	147	563	165	30	9	12	100	61	90	5.78	60	135	17	7	.71	.293	.363	.442	.805
Jackson,Brett	ChC	24	115	302	73	16	4	11	47	32	43	4.76	39	111	17	6	.74	.242	.328	.430	.759
Janish,Paul	Atl	30	84	208	46	12	0	2	23	16	18	2.87	19	31	1	1	.50	.221	.293	.308	.600
Jaso,John	Sea	29	101	265	69	15	1	6	36	36	38	5.02	41	37	3	1	.75	.260	.364	.392	.756
Jay,Jon	StL	28	142	478	141	26	3	8	68	47	68	5.12	37	70	16	8	.67	.295	.354	.412	.767
Jennings,Desmond	TB	26	141	537	140	27	6	15	96	54	79	5.10	58	111	36	6	.86	.261	.337	.417	.754
Jeter,Derek	NYY	39	124	642	191	28	1	12	97	64	91	5.19	55	96	11	5	.69	.298	.359	.400	.760
Johnson,Chris	Ari	28	129	443	124	26	3	13	49	63	62	5.02	26	106	4	2	.67	.280	.324	.440	.764
Johnson,Elliot	TB	29	104	272	68	12	2	7	33	29	32	3.96	22	70	14	6	.70	.250	.308	.386	.695
Johnson,Kelly	Tor	31	144	511	123	28	3	17	72	59	68	4.50	63	147	12	5	.71	.241	.328	.407	.735
Johnson,Reed	Atl	36	119	283	77	17	1	4	35	27	32	4.00	13	68	2	2	.50	.272	.325	.382	.706
Jones,Adam	Bal	27	158	619	174	33	4	27	90	83	94	5.41	35	125	14	7	.67	.281	.329	.478	.807
Jones,Andruw	NYY	36	99	246	52	10	0	14	33	39	31	4.13	33	74	1	1	.50	.211	.317	.423	.740
Jones,Garrett	Pit	32	140	445	113	27	1	20	57	69	63	4.90	39	100	4	2	.67	.254	.315	.454	.769
Joyce,Matt	TB	28	136	454	118	30	2	20	68	72	73	5.58	62	104	6	4	.60	.260	.354	.467	.821
Kaaihue,Kila'	Oak	29	53	128	31	7	0	6	17	20	20	5.36	21	28	1	0	1.00	.242	.349	.438	.786
Kalish,Ryan	Bos	25	129	409	103	22	1	10	60	48	51	4.24	41	93	21	7	.75	.252	.320	.384	.704
Kearns,Austin	Mia	33	71	148	35	7	0	4	20	17	17	3.88	19	40	1	1	.50	.236	.351	.365	.715
Kelly,Don	Det	33	70	109	26	4	1	2	13	10	11	3.40	9	16	3	1	.75	.239	.303	.349	.651
Kemp,Matt	LAD	28	157	601	179	33	4	31	103	101	113	6.83	59	154	21	8	.72	.298	.363	.521	.884
Kendrick,Howie	LAA	29	153	589	169	39	3	12	73	73	80	4.87	30	119	14	7	.67	.287	.327	.424	.751
Kennedy,Adam	LAD	37	103	258	64	13	1	3	28	24	27	3.58	23	45	5	2	.71	.248	.314	.341	.656
Keppinger,Jeff	TB	33	126	441	128	22	1	7	50	44	58	4.80	32	33	1	1	.50	.290	.342	.392	.735
Kinsler,Ian	Tex	31	153	632	167	39	3	23	110	80	96	5.28	70	86	22	8	.73	.264	.345	.445	.790
Kipnis,Jason	Cle	26	151	594	163	28	5	18	100	83	91	5.40	67	107	28	7	.80	.274	.351	.429	.780
Konerko,Paul	CWS	37	153	572	161	27	0	30	74	92	100	6.33	70	101	0	0	.00	.281	.367	.486	.853
Kotchman,Casey	Cle	30	106	289	75	14	0	7	29	36	35	4.23	24	33	1	1	.50	.260	.329	.381	.710
Kotsay,Mark	SD	37	71	131	33	7	0	2	12	14	14	3.71	11	15	1	0	1.00	.252	.310	.351	.661
Kottaras,George	Oak	30	100	308	74	19	1	13	40	46	46	5.11	49	76	0	0	.00	.240	.345	.435	.780
Kozma,Pete	StL	25	71	197	44	9	1	4	24	19	19	3.19	17	37	3	2	.60	.223	.285	.340	.625
Kratz,Erik	Phi	33	74	274	70	17	0	13	35	43	39	4.95	24	55	1	1	.50	.255	.318	.460	.778
Kubel,Jason	Ari	31	138	495	128	29	2	23	66	85	76	5.37	53	131	1	1	.50	.259	.333	.465	.797
LaHair,Bryan	ChC	30	103	314	84	20	0	14	40	44	49	5.52	32	89	2	1	.67	.268	.335	.465	.800
Laird,Gerald	Det	33	87	263	64	14	1	4	32	25	27	3.51	21	47	1	1	.50	.243	.307	.350	.656
LaPorta,Matt	Cle	28	102	342	86	20	1	14	41	49	48	4.88	33	73	0	0	.00	.251	.321	.439	.760
LaRoche,Adam	Was	33	146	531	136	34	1	26	69	87	83	5.45	61	139	1	1	.50	.256	.334	.471	.805
Lavarnway,Ryan	Bos	25	119	418	109	25	0	16	58	66	61	5.12	47	91	1	1	.50	.261	.335	.435	.771
Lawrie,Brett	Tor	23	155	602	174	36	8	18	96	71	94	5.58	45	105	21	10	.68	.289	.342	.465	.807
Lee,Carlos	Mia	37	144	543	145	29	1	17	58	81	73	4.75	46	52	3	2	.60	.267	.327	.418	.745

2013 Hitter Projections

Hitter	Team	Age	G	AB	H	2B	3B	HR	R	RBI	RC	RC27	BB	SO	SB	CS	SB%	Avg	OBP	Slg	OPS
Lee,Hak-Ju	TB	22	123	381	90	11	6	3	49	26	39	3.41	37	81	21	6	.78	.236	.304	.320	.624
LeMahieu,DJ	Col	24	46	130	38	7	1	1	14	13	17	4.70	8	18	4	2	.67	.292	.333	.385	.718
Lillibridge,Brent	Cle	29	97	192	44	8	1	5	27	18	20	3.40	15	57	12	5	.71	.229	.295	.359	.655
Lind,Adam	Tor	29	141	522	142	30	1	22	60	84	78	5.32	42	114	1	1	.50	.272	.329	.460	.788
Lobaton,Jose	TB	28	91	295	70	17	0	7	29	34	35	4.04	40	72	0	0	.00	.237	.330	.366	.696
Lombardozzi,Steve	Was	24	101	328	96	15	4	4	45	28	44	4.85	20	39	8	4	.67	.293	.339	.399	.738
Loney,James	Bos	29	116	330	92	19	1	7	36	44	45	4.90	28	43	2	1	.67	.279	.337	.406	.743
Longoria,Evan	TB	27	154	578	158	39	1	33	92	112	108	6.64	80	129	6	3	.67	.273	.366	.516	.881
Lopez,Jose	CWS	29	102	317	84	20	0	8	33	41	37	4.11	13	43	1	1	.50	.265	.300	.404	.704
Lowrie,Jed	Hou	29	117	425	111	30	2	15	60	60	65	5.37	53	75	2	1	.67	.261	.344	.447	.792
Lucroy,Jonathan	Mil	27	133	453	130	24	2	14	58	70	69	5.52	39	70	5	2	.71	.287	.346	.442	.788
Ludwick,Ryan	Cin	34	129	425	108	24	1	19	55	71	61	4.99	41	109	1	1	.50	.254	.327	.449	.776
Machado,Manny	Bal	20	141	532	136	30	6	15	68	71	71	4.60	46	93	14	5	.74	.256	.315	.419	.734
Maldonado,Martin	Mil	26	78	245	62	12	0	8	24	33	30	4.24	19	59	1	1	.50	.253	.309	.400	.709
Markakis,Nick	Bal	29	144	573	170	40	2	16	79	78	96	6.16	62	78	5	2	.71	.297	.369	.457	.827
Marson,Lou	Cle	27	80	211	50	11	1	2	27	19	23	3.67	31	45	4	2	.67	.237	.337	.327	.664
Marte,Starling	Pit	24	148	522	155	28	11	15	82	64	81	5.50	29	118	31	16	.66	.297	.336	.479	.815
Martin,Leonys	Tex	25	99	297	85	22	3	7	48	40	44	5.15	24	48	16	10	.62	.286	.340	.451	.791
Martin,Russell	NYY	30	132	462	112	22	0	16	64	60	60	4.41	62	93	8	4	.67	.242	.340	.394	.734
Martinez,Fernando	Hou	24	49	101	26	6	0	3	13	13	12	4.16	6	25	0	0	.00	.257	.318	.406	.724
Martinez,J.D.	Hou	25	124	411	112	22	2	12	47	64	58	5.04	38	86	0	0	.00	.273	.336	.423	.759
Martinez,Michael	Phi	30	55	100	23	4	1	2	11	10	10	3.33	7	14	2	1	.67	.230	.280	.350	.630
Martinez,Victor	Det	34	143	534	162	34	0	16	70	91	90	6.29	54	62	1	0	1.00	.303	.369	.457	.826
Mathis,Jeff	Tor	30	69	154	32	8	0	4	17	17	13	2.75	10	42	1	1	.50	.208	.261	.338	.598
Mauer,Joe	Min	30	142	524	166	34	2	11	81	78	96	6.91	78	74	5	3	.62	.317	.407	.452	.860
Maxwell,Justin	Hou	29	108	316	77	15	2	17	52	47	48	5.09	40	107	14	6	.70	.244	.331	.465	.796
Mayberry,John	Phi	29	110	284	73	17	1	11	37	37	39	4.78	22	63	3	1	.75	.257	.313	.440	.753
Maybin,Cameron	SD	26	149	517	137	23	6	11	80	52	69	4.61	50	121	28	9	.76	.265	.333	.397	.730
McCann,Brian	Atl	29	134	488	130	29	0	23	58	84	78	5.63	57	85	3	2	.60	.266	.347	.467	.814
McCutchen,Andrew	Pit	26	159	598	171	34	6	24	101	81	106	6.31	77	123	22	10	.69	.286	.372	.483	.855
McDonald,John	Ari	38	100	281	65	12	1	5	29	28	25	3.00	14	45	1	1	.50	.231	.270	.335	.605
McGehee,Casey	NYY	30	111	328	82	19	1	9	36	47	40	4.21	28	65	1	1	.50	.250	.311	.396	.707
McKenry,Michael	Pit	28	108	327	78	21	0	11	35	41	42	4.39	36	83	1	0	1.00	.239	.316	.404	.720
McLouth,Nate	Bal	31	126	417	99	22	2	14	64	46	54	4.36	50	84	14	4	.78	.237	.326	.400	.727
Mesoraco,Devin	Cin	25	123	427	109	29	2	16	56	59	62	5.05	44	78	2	1	.67	.255	.326	.445	.771
Middlebrooks,Will	Bos	24	153	537	149	25	1	29	75	99	82	5.44	28	127	11	4	.73	.277	.316	.490	.805
Molina,Jose	TB	38	97	277	62	12	0	6	26	27	25	3.01	20	68	2	1	.67	.224	.281	.332	.613
Molina,Yadier	StL	30	140	507	147	27	0	14	53	70	74	5.27	43	52	8	5	.62	.290	.350	.426	.776
Montero,Jesus	Sea	23	140	534	152	29	1	22	63	82	84	5.72	41	101	0	0	.00	.285	.337	.466	.803
Montero,Miguel	Ari	29	137	496	135	31	1	16	63	79	76	5.47	59	119	0	0	.00	.272	.357	.435	.792
Moore,Scott	Hou	29	81	230	60	14	1	8	29	34	32	4.87	22	53	2	1	.67	.261	.333	.435	.768
Moore,Tyler	Was	26	75	232	60	13	1	13	34	47	36	5.41	18	59	3	1	.75	.259	.315	.491	.806
Morales,Kendrys	LAA	30	137	489	139	29	1	23	63	78	78	5.79	32	97	0	0	.00	.284	.332	.489	.821
Morel,Brent	CWS	26	59	133	33	7	0	2	15	13	13	3.35	8	27	2	1	.67	.248	.296	.346	.642
Moreland,Mitch	Tex	27	115	344	93	21	1	13	45	51	51	5.26	31	65	1	1	.50	.270	.334	.451	.785
Morgan,Nyjer	Mil	32	71	326	87	11	3	2	47	21	35	3.70	23	65	16	7	.70	.267	.329	.337	.666
Morneau,Justin	Min	32	137	516	140	32	1	21	69	89	82	5.67	57	98	1	0	1.00	.271	.348	.459	.808
Morrison,Logan	Mia	25	151	554	142	34	5	23	73	79	87	5.46	74	95	3	2	.60	.256	.347	.460	.807
Morse,Michael	Was	31	134	485	143	29	1	23	64	80	81	6.14	30	105	1	1	.50	.295	.342	.501	.843
Moss,Brandon	Oak	29	144	506	134	33	2	25	73	81	81	5.60	51	132	5	4	.56	.265	.335	.486	.821
Moustakas,Mike	KC	24	156	576	152	39	1	23	75	87	81	4.94	40	105	4	2	.67	.264	.316	.455	.771
Murphy,Daniel	NYM	28	153	552	167	42	3	9	67	72	85	5.68	41	66	9	4	.69	.303	.352	.438	.790
Murphy,David	Tex	31	141	449	126	27	2	13	59	61	68	5.39	47	77	9	5	.64	.281	.350	.437	.787
Murphy,Donnie	Mia	30	69	157	38	10	1	8	20	21	22	4.77	12	37	1	1	.50	.242	.304	.471	.775
Myers,Wil	KC	22	147	564	152	30	4	28	83	89	93	5.81	59	150	8	4	.67	.270	.339	.486	.824
Napoli,Mike	Tex	31	127	440	109	21	1	29	70	75	75	5.86	63	141	3	2	.60	.248	.350	.498	.847
Nava,Daniel	Bos	30	87	256	68	18	1	6	39	35	38	5.20	36	51	3	2	.60	.266	.367	.414	.781
Nelson,Chris	Col	27	104	307	84	18	2	7	40	41	40	4.62	20	63	3	2	.60	.274	.320	.414	.734
Nickeas,Mike	NYM	30	50	102	22	5	0	1	8	9	9	2.93	10	18	0	0	.00	.216	.292	.294	.586
Nieuwenhuis,Kirk	NYM	25	82	251	65	16	1	7	38	27	34	4.68	25	72	5	3	.62	.259	.329	.414	.743
Nix,Jayson	NYY	30	71	169	39	10	0	5	21	18	18	3.55	13	42	4	2	.67	.231	.297	.379	.676
Nix,Laynce	Phi	32	88	174	42	10	1	7	20	24	23	4.53	14	52	1	0	1.00	.241	.298	.431	.729
Norris,Derek	Oak	24	95	292	66	15	1	14	48	46	40	4.54	39	76	9	3	.75	.226	.319	.428	.747
Olivo,Miguel	Sea	34	102	326	75	14	1	12	34	41	32	3.28	12	98	3	3	.50	.230	.262	.390	.651
Olt,Mike	Tex	24	46	160	43	7	0	9	25	34	27	5.95	19	46	2	1	.67	.269	.346	.481	.828
Ortiz,David	Bos	37	147	533	151	37	0	32	89	103	109	7.42	87	105	0	0	.00	.283	.386	.533	.919
Pacheco,Jordan	Col	27	91	281	82	17	1	4	29	33	37	4.79	14	32	3	2	.60	.292	.330	.402	.732
Pagan,Angel	SF	31	147	559	155	32	7	8	80	56	76	4.77	46	90	27	10	.73	.277	.332	.403	.735
Parmelee,Chris	Min	25	64	219	60	14	1	8	29	31	36	5.89	27	45	1	0	1.00	.274	.359	.457	.815
Parra,Gerardo	Ari	26	135	391	111	21	5	7	53	42	55	4.98	34	74	13	7	.65	.284	.346	.417	.763
Parrino,Andy	SD	27	86	286	75	20	1	5	38	32	39	4.76	35	68	5	2	.71	.262	.345	.392	.736
Pastornicky,Tyler	Atl	23	82	238	65	12	2	3	30	23	29	4.26	16	32	8	4	.67	.273	.322	.378	.700
Pearce,Steve	NYY	30	73	169	45	12	1	6	22	25	26	5.41	19	33	2	1	.67	.266	.347	.456	.803
Pedroia,Dustin	Bos	29	156	615	182	45	2	17	96	76	103	6.07	65	67	19	8	.70	.296	.367	.459	.825
Pena,Brayan	KC	31	76	199	52	12	0	3	18	23	22	3.86	12	21	1	1	.50	.261	.307	.367	.673
Pena,Carlos	TB	35	146	478	100	21	1	24	67	75	64	4.39	86	172	2	1	.67	.209	.340	.408	.748
Pence,Hunter	SF	30	154	578	160	31	4	23	80	88	89	5.48	50	126	7	4	.64	.277	.338	.464	.801
Pennington,Cliff	Oak	29	136	442	107	22	3	6	54	38	49	3.74	45	90	18	6	.75	.242	.315	.346	.661
Peralta,Jhonny	Det	31	154	530	140	32	2	16	66	74	73	4.85	49	108	1	1	.50	.264	.329	.423	.751
Perez,Salvador	KC	23	130	498	149	28	1	16	65	70	74	5.51	21	48	0	0	.00	.299	.329	.456	.785
Petersen,Bryan	Mia	27	67	136	36	6	1	2	18	12	16	4.04	13	25	4	3	.57	.265	.338	.368	.705

2013 Hitter Projections

Hitter	Team	Age	G	AB	H	2B	3B	HR	R	RBI	RC	RC27	BB	SO	SB	CS	SB%	Avg	OBP	Slg	OPS
Phillips,Brandon	Cin	32	154	618	171	32	2	20	90	80	85	4.87	39	89	16	7	.70	.277	.327	.432	.759
Pierre,Juan	Phi	35	124	411	116	12	3	1	55	27	45	3.82	25	29	28	11	.72	.282	.336	.333	.669
Pierzynski,A.J.	CWS	36	137	509	137	25	1	17	56	61	65	4.54	24	69	0	0	.00	.269	.310	.422	.732
Plouffe,Trevor	Min	27	121	428	104	25	2	19	60	54	56	4.47	34	87	3	2	.60	.243	.302	.444	.746
Podsednik,Scott	Bos	37	48	118	31	5	1	1	14	8	13	3.76	9	21	6	3	.67	.263	.320	.347	.668
Polanco,Placido	Phi	37	103	337	94	16	1	4	40	31	40	4.26	21	29	1	1	.50	.279	.331	.368	.699
Posey,Buster	SF	26	146	534	173	36	2	24	79	98	113	8.12	65	86	1	1	.50	.324	.400	.534	.934
Prado,Martin	Atl	29	148	574	167	38	3	11	78	63	84	5.29	47	67	10	6	.62	.291	.347	.425	.772
Presley,Alex	Pit	27	96	302	87	14	5	8	43	32	45	5.29	24	52	11	6	.65	.288	.343	.447	.790
Profar,Jurickson	Tex	20	136	569	150	32	6	16	80	67	84	5.14	67	93	20	6	.77	.264	.341	.425	.767
Pujols,Albert	LAA	33	156	606	185	43	0	38	105	117	133	8.14	84	73	9	4	.69	.305	.394	.564	.959
Punto,Nick	LAD	35	89	204	47	9	1	1	25	16	20	3.27	27	44	6	2	.75	.230	.320	.299	.619
Quentin,Carlos	SD	30	127	461	118	30	1	26	72	82	75	5.67	50	79	2	1	.67	.256	.350	.495	.845
Quintanilla,Omar	Bal	31	71	188	47	11	1	4	25	17	22	4.03	15	37	1	1	.50	.250	.309	.383	.692
Quintero,Humberto	KC	33	66	169	40	9	0	2	12	17	14	2.82	5	32	0	0	.00	.237	.267	.325	.592
Raburn,Ryan	Det	32	90	250	61	15	1	8	32	33	30	4.08	20	68	3	2	.60	.244	.305	.408	.713
Ramirez,Alexei	CWS	31	158	599	161	26	2	14	73	75	71	4.14	32	80	15	8	.65	.269	.309	.389	.698
Ramirez,Aramis	Mil	35	150	570	163	38	1	27	81	102	96	6.09	47	86	5	3	.62	.286	.350	.498	.848
Ramirez,Hanley	LAD	29	144	555	156	33	3	22	90	75	91	5.78	59	113	23	10	.70	.281	.356	.470	.827
Ramos,Wilson	Was	25	119	413	111	24	1	13	50	50	57	4.91	33	73	0	0	.00	.269	.324	.426	.751
Ransom,Cody	Ari	37	89	256	59	15	0	11	34	38	32	4.20	27	82	2	1	.67	.230	.306	.418	.724
Rasmus,Colby	Tor	26	149	558	132	29	4	23	87	72	73	4.42	58	145	6	3	.67	.237	.312	.427	.738
Reddick,Josh	Oak	26	156	598	148	33	5	30	90	85	86	4.91	54	125	9	5	.64	.247	.311	.470	.781
Reimold,Nolan	Bal	29	117	377	99	20	1	17	51	54	58	5.37	42	77	7	3	.70	.263	.340	.456	.796
Revere,Ben	Min	25	125	520	150	12	5	0	64	33	60	4.08	31	47	40	12	.77	.288	.331	.331	.662
Reyes,Jose	Mia	30	151	620	183	33	10	11	96	56	96	5.55	53	56	39	13	.75	.295	.352	.434	.786
Reynolds,Mark	Bal	29	155	542	125	28	1	32	85	90	82	5.08	80	201	5	3	.62	.231	.336	.463	.799
Rhymes,Will	TB	30	74	211	57	8	2	2	26	18	25	4.14	19	24	5	3	.62	.270	.333	.355	.689
Rios,Alex	CWS	32	157	596	163	35	3	20	84	78	83	4.89	35	94	20	8	.71	.273	.318	.443	.761
Rivera,Juan	LAD	34	52	167	43	8	0	6	18	26	21	4.37	12	23	1	1	.50	.257	.319	.413	.732
Rizzo,Anthony	ChC	23	157	604	171	40	1	33	86	109	106	6.31	55	126	7	4	.64	.283	.346	.517	.862
Roberts,Brian	Bal	35	63	239	64	17	1	4	33	23	33	4.82	27	41	9	3	.75	.268	.345	.397	.742
Roberts,Ryan	TB	32	126	377	94	20	1	11	51	45	48	4.33	43	73	9	5	.64	.249	.328	.395	.723
Robinson,Trayvon	Sea	25	89	336	85	15	2	9	43	37	42	4.22	33	97	18	8	.69	.253	.320	.390	.710
Rodriguez,Alex	NYY	37	135	518	140	24	0	26	84	91	86	5.87	67	125	10	3	.77	.270	.364	.467	.831
Rodriguez,Sean	TB	28	103	256	63	14	1	8	37	32	33	4.40	25	61	6	2	.75	.246	.328	.402	.730
Rolen,Scott	Cin	38	104	337	85	23	1	9	42	47	43	4.42	31	63	2	1	.67	.252	.324	.407	.731
Rollins,Jimmy	Phi	34	149	594	150	32	4	18	90	63	78	4.50	54	80	25	7	.78	.253	.317	.411	.728
Rosales,Adam	Oak	30	52	129	32	7	1	3	17	15	15	3.98	10	27	1	1	.50	.248	.307	.388	.695
Rosario,Wilin	Col	24	117	414	108	19	1	28	63	68	63	5.30	24	95	3	3	.50	.261	.303	.514	.817
Ross,Cody	Bos	32	137	468	119	30	1	19	63	69	65	4.81	42	121	3	2	.60	.254	.321	.444	.765
Ross,David	Atl	36	93	302	71	16	1	12	31	42	40	4.48	37	101	1	1	.50	.235	.321	.414	.734
Ruggiano,Justin	Mia	31	145	515	143	33	1	19	73	76	79	5.36	48	128	24	11	.69	.278	.339	.456	.796
Ruiz,Carlos	Phi	34	131	443	124	31	1	12	55	62	68	5.51	50	61	3	2	.60	.280	.365	.436	.800
Rutledge,Josh	Col	24	143	512	142	36	6	16	80	62	73	5.07	19	94	18	4	.82	.277	.308	.465	.773
Ryan,Brendan	Sea	31	135	397	90	18	2	3	48	30	35	2.92	34	82	11	5	.69	.227	.296	.305	.601
Saltalamacchia,Jarrod	Bos	28	110	368	88	20	1	19	52	54	51	4.74	36	109	0	0	.00	.239	.309	.454	.762
Sanchez,Gaby	Pit	29	115	354	93	22	0	11	44	49	50	4.94	40	58	3	2	.60	.263	.343	.418	.761
Sanchez,Hector	SF	23	60	142	37	9	0	2	12	20	15	3.71	5	28	0	0	.00	.261	.291	.366	.657
Sandoval,Pablo	SF	26	150	554	165	39	3	22	77	88	98	6.53	49	78	2	1	.67	.298	.356	.498	.854
Sands,Jerry	Bos	25	99	263	69	17	1	13	41	47	41	5.47	26	60	1	1	.50	.262	.329	.483	.812
Santana,Carlos	Cle	27	147	532	139	35	2	25	86	91	96	6.30	103	103	4	3	.57	.261	.383	.476	.859
Santiago,Ramon	Det	33	96	232	55	8	1	3	25	21	21	3.07	18	41	1	1	.50	.237	.306	.319	.625
Saunders,Michael	Sea	26	142	509	122	26	3	17	69	54	64	4.22	51	130	20	7	.74	.240	.309	.403	.712
Schafer,Jordan	Hou	26	118	387	90	16	2	5	51	31	40	3.38	43	101	28	11	.72	.233	.313	.323	.635
Schierholtz,Nate	Phi	29	116	266	71	15	3	7	31	29	36	4.75	19	48	4	2	.67	.267	.321	.425	.745
Schumaker,Skip	StL	33	132	430	119	22	2	3	55	36	52	4.32	38	67	3	2	.60	.277	.337	.358	.695
Scott,Luke	TB	35	89	251	61	16	1	12	32	39	36	4.90	26	64	2	1	.67	.243	.321	.458	.780
Scutaro,Marco	SF	37	149	587	165	31	1	8	82	63	75	4.58	53	58	6	4	.60	.281	.344	.378	.722
Seager,Kyle	Sea	25	155	551	153	38	1	17	65	76	81	5.21	45	90	13	6	.68	.278	.337	.443	.779
Segura,Jean	Mil	23	147	477	139	16	6	6	66	50	65	4.84	35	69	35	11	.76	.291	.340	.388	.728
Shoppach,Kelly	NYM	33	92	249	54	14	0	9	28	32	27	3.60	24	96	1	0	1.00	.217	.306	.382	.688
Simmons,Andrelton	Atl	23	154	522	151	26	5	10	70	62	77	5.32	49	59	18	5	.78	.289	.351	.416	.767
Singleton,Jonathan	Hou	21	142	501	132	28	2	20	86	73	77	5.38	62	142	8	3	.73	.263	.345	.447	.792
Smith,Seth	Oak	30	137	416	108	27	3	15	59	56	62	5.20	47	93	4	2	.67	.260	.339	.447	.786
Smoak,Justin	Sea	26	139	501	117	24	0	19	56	62	64	4.32	66	109	1	1	.50	.234	.324	.395	.719
Snider,Travis	Pit	25	89	284	79	19	1	11	43	45	45	5.63	28	68	5	3	.62	.278	.345	.468	.813
Snyder,Chris	Hou	32	83	233	49	10	0	9	25	33	27	3.82	37	69	0	0	.00	.210	.326	.369	.695
Sogard,Eric	Oak	27	80	272	70	12	2	5	36	26	33	4.14	28	34	11	5	.69	.257	.327	.371	.698
Solano,Donovan	Mia	25	93	295	74	14	2	2	27	24	29	3.38	17	47	6	2	.75	.251	.294	.332	.626
Soriano,Alfonso	ChC	37	144	530	130	32	1	27	67	79	73	4.71	40	142	6	3	.67	.245	.304	.462	.767
Soto,Geovany	Tex	30	109	336	81	20	1	13	41	48	46	4.69	40	87	1	0	1.00	.241	.327	.423	.750
Span,Denard	Min	29	138	538	151	26	6	5	78	50	72	4.74	55	71	19	8	.70	.281	.350	.379	.729
Stanton,Giancarlo	Mia	23	151	522	148	33	3	43	88	103	113	7.79	62	145	6	3	.67	.284	.365	.605	.970
Stewart,Chris	NYY	31	62	135	32	7	0	2	14	13	13	3.25	11	18	1	1	.50	.237	.299	.333	.633
Stewart,Ian	ChC	28	62	143	34	7	1	6	20	20	19	4.49	16	37	1	1	.50	.238	.327	.427	.754
Stubbs,Drew	Cin	28	146	536	132	21	3	16	85	53	68	4.28	54	161	33	9	.79	.246	.319	.386	.705
Sutton,Drew	Pit	30	54	111	29	8	0	2	15	12	15	4.70	13	26	2	1	.67	.261	.344	.387	.731
Suzuki,Ichiro	NYY	39	160	654	192	23	3	7	81	47	82	4.54	35	71	28	8	.78	.294	.331	.370	.701
Suzuki,Kurt	Was	29	120	397	98	21	0	8	43	47	42	3.64	27	61	2	1	.67	.247	.306	.360	.666
Sweeney,Ryan	Bos	28	86	227	62	14	1	2	27	24	28	4.39	20	40	1	1	.50	.273	.335	.370	.705

510

2013 Hitter Projections

PLAYER			BATTING												BASERUNNING			AVERAGES			
Hitter	Team	Age	G	AB	H	2B	3B	HR	R	RBI	RC	RC27	BB	SO	SB	CS	SB%	Avg	OBP	Slg	OPS
Swisher,Nick	NYY	32	149	544	139	33	1	25	82	86	89	5.70	86	143	2	1	.67	.256	.362	.458	.820
Tabata,Jose	Pit	24	102	324	90	19	2	3	47	26	41	4.42	29	48	12	7	.63	.278	.345	.377	.721
Teixeira,Mark	NYY	33	157	598	159	37	1	35	96	115	108	6.38	83	116	2	1	.67	.266	.364	.507	.870
Tejada,Ruben	NYM	23	122	429	119	22	1	2	49	33	49	4.07	34	59	5	3	.62	.277	.338	.347	.685
Thames,Eric	Sea	26	100	329	89	21	3	12	45	43	49	5.26	25	81	3	2	.60	.271	.326	.462	.788
Theriot,Ryan	SF	33	120	397	107	16	1	1	49	31	42	3.69	33	50	11	6	.65	.270	.330	.322	.653
Thole,Josh	NYM	26	105	298	79	18	1	2	24	28	35	4.16	31	38	1	0	1.00	.265	.338	.352	.691
Torrealba,Yorvit	Mil	34	64	152	38	8	0	3	15	16	17	3.84	12	30	1	1	.50	.250	.313	.362	.675
Torres,Andres	NYM	35	119	354	85	20	4	6	50	31	43	4.08	44	92	13	5	.72	.240	.328	.370	.698
Treanor,Matt	LAD	37	60	137	29	4	0	2	13	14	12	2.86	17	30	1	1	.50	.212	.312	.285	.597
Trout,Mike	LAA	21	157	606	197	31	12	30	122	87	143	8.89	73	135	53	9	.85	.325	.402	.564	.966
Trumbo,Mark	LAA	27	147	548	146	28	2	31	71	98	84	5.39	36	130	5	3	.62	.266	.315	.495	.810
Tulowitzki,Troy	Col	28	148	554	165	34	3	28	94	96	106	6.99	62	85	9	5	.64	.298	.372	.522	.893
Turner,Justin	NYM	28	77	169	47	12	0	2	21	18	21	4.44	13	20	2	1	.67	.278	.344	.385	.729
Uggla,Dan	Atl	33	159	588	140	32	1	28	92	87	86	4.97	84	174	3	2	.60	.238	.341	.439	.780
Upton,B.J.	TB	28	155	580	144	34	3	23	88	75	84	4.89	68	167	35	11	.76	.248	.329	.436	.765
Upton,Justin	Ari	25	155	585	169	34	5	25	106	86	105	6.42	70	135	19	9	.68	.289	.372	.492	.864
Uribe,Juan	LAD	34	60	140	32	7	0	4	14	18	14	3.37	10	30	0	0	.00	.229	.294	.364	.658
Utley,Chase	Phi	34	122	464	127	27	2	19	77	70	77	5.89	57	74	13	3	.81	.274	.372	.463	.836
Valbuena,Luis	ChC	27	90	261	66	16	1	7	33	30	34	4.51	29	54	2	1	.67	.253	.330	.402	.732
Valdespin,Jordany	NYM	25	85	264	71	13	1	9	34	32	33	4.25	13	46	16	9	.64	.269	.306	.428	.734
Valdez,Wilson	Cin	35	87	214	51	8	1	1	23	17	18	2.84	13	30	4	2	.67	.238	.282	.299	.581
Valencia,Danny	Bos	28	83	238	61	15	1	6	26	31	28	4.09	14	41	1	1	.50	.256	.298	.403	.701
Venable,Will	SD	30	136	400	102	19	4	11	56	46	53	4.53	37	99	20	6	.77	.255	.324	.445	.729
Viciedo,Dayan	CWS	24	153	516	140	23	0	24	66	77	73	5.03	31	107	1	1	.50	.271	.316	.455	.772
Victorino,Shane	LAD	32	155	572	154	29	7	14	85	59	80	4.87	52	77	29	9	.76	.269	.338	.418	.755
Vitters,Josh	ChC	23	140	487	122	31	1	15	54	66	57	4.01	28	89	7	5	.58	.251	.293	.411	.703
Votto,Joey	Cin	29	156	571	178	46	1	27	93	97	128	8.36	105	105	8	5	.62	.312	.422	.538	.960
Walker,Neil	Pit	27	154	593	163	40	2	17	77	88	86	5.14	54	111	9	5	.64	.275	.337	.435	.773
Wallace,Brett	Hou	26	141	487	129	26	1	16	59	58	66	4.79	39	131	1	0	1.00	.265	.325	.421	.745
Weeks,Jemile	Oak	26	102	343	91	16	5	2	44	28	41	4.13	34	50	14	6	.70	.265	.337	.359	.695
Weeks,Rickie	Mil	30	152	592	147	30	4	23	98	66	85	4.91	74	164	15	5	.75	.248	.345	.429	.774
Wells,Casper	Sea	28	93	233	57	13	2	10	35	31	32	4.67	24	62	3	2	.60	.245	.323	.446	.769
Wells,Vernon	LAA	34	90	266	65	14	1	11	33	36	33	4.23	18	42	4	2	.67	.244	.297	.429	.726
Werth,Jayson	Was	34	153	554	148	32	2	20	83	74	89	5.64	82	142	14	4	.78	.267	.367	.440	.807
Wheeler,Ryan	Ari	24	53	112	32	7	0	3	13	19	16	5.14	8	22	1	1	.50	.286	.333	.429	.762
Wieters,Matt	Bal	27	142	522	137	29	1	22	68	81	79	5.32	59	105	2	1	.67	.262	.341	.448	.789
Wigginton,Ty	Phi	35	105	282	68	14	0	10	32	35	34	4.11	26	65	1	1	.50	.241	.314	.397	.711
Willingham,Josh	Min	34	147	532	132	31	1	30	78	93	87	5.63	75	149	4	2	.67	.248	.354	.479	.833
Wilson,Bobby	LAA	30	65	124	29	7	0	2	11	13	12	3.28	10	21	0	0	.00	.234	.291	.339	.630
Wise,DeWayne	CWS	35	105	254	62	13	2	7	34	26	28	3.70	13	64	12	5	.71	.244	.284	.394	.677
Wright,David	NYM	30	154	582	176	41	2	21	94	100	111	6.97	83	121	16	8	.67	.302	.392	.488	.880
Youkilis,Kevin	CWS	34	135	495	131	32	2	21	83	80	82	5.84	71	119	2	1	.67	.265	.371	.465	.836
Young,Chris	Ari	29	155	571	137	39	2	23	82	75	80	4.71	69	144	17	8	.68	.240	.325	.436	.761
Young,Delmon	Det	27	142	542	151	31	1	17	63	80	72	4.76	24	101	3	2	.60	.279	.315	.434	.749
Young,Eric	Col	28	92	219	60	10	2	2	38	15	29	4.57	23	39	21	6	.78	.274	.348	.365	.714
Young,Michael	Tex	36	153	598	176	33	2	12	79	77	85	5.21	42	83	3	2	.60	.294	.343	.416	.759
Zimmerman,Ryan	Was	28	150	595	171	39	2	25	92	93	103	6.29	64	115	4	2	.67	.287	.359	.486	.844
Zobrist,Ben	TB	32	154	552	146	35	4	18	87	76	89	5.60	89	110	15	7	.68	.264	.369	.440	.809

2013 Pitcher Projections

Bill James

(Disclaimer: Due to an oversight, this article actually compares pitchers not to the projections published here a year ago, but to updated projections published in the spring of 2013. The differences are slight, but. . .sorry)

We project that in 2013 Bronson Arroyo will go 12-12 with a 3.88 ERA. This would be bigger news if Bronson Arroyo didn't go 12-12 with a 3.88 ERA pretty much every year. We project that Justin Verlander will lead the American League in wins and that Clayton Kershaw (Gesundheit) will lead the National League in wins, which, you know. . .it isn't calculated to make news.

"News" is the unexpected; man bites dog. Lion defends lamb from psychotic cow. Minister murders his gay lover. Trailer Court beats up tornado. Congress co-operates. What we're dealing with here is what we would expect to happen. The normal.

Occasionally our projections do make news, but that's an accident. Occasionally we're exactly right, but that's an accident, too. Last year we projected that Derek Lowe would go 9-11, and he did, but that's just an accident. We get about ten won-lost records exactly right each year, but most of those are relievers who we projected to go 3-4. Last year I think we only got four won-lost records exactly right, and two of those were 5-4 and 2-2. The fourth one was Brian Matusz, 6-10.

We miss by one win or one loss on a whole lot of players. Last year we had Rick Porcello at 10-11; he was actually 10-12. We had Verlander down for 18-8; he was 17-8. We had Bud Norris at 7-12, and he was 7-13. We had projected that Sergio Romo would go 4-1 with a 1.67 ERA; it was actually 4-2 with a 1.79 ERA, but, because we didn't know that Brian Wilson would get hurt, we had not projected any saves for him.

Our five worst projections from last season were for Daniel Hudson, Mike Pelfrey, Brian Wilson, Felipe Paulino and Dustin Moseley, all of whom, I think, were injured:

Pitcher	Label	G	GS	IP	H	BB	SO	W	L	Pct	Sv	ERA
Daniel Hudson	Projected	32	32	224	201	58	199	15	10	.600	0	3.29
	Actual	9	9	45	62	12	37	3	2	.600	0	7.35
Mike Pelfrey	Projected	34	32	188	210	65	106	9	12	.429	0	4.40
	Actual	3	3	20	24	4	13	0	0	.000	0	2.29
Brian Wilson	Projected	60	0	61	52	28	65	4	3	.571	40	3.10
	Actual	2	0	2	4	2	2	0	0	.000	1	9.00
Felipe Paulino	Projected	33	24	157	167	67	143	7	11	.389	0	4.59
	Actual	7	7	38	31	15	39	3	1	.750	0	1.67
Dustin Moseley	Projected	21	21	128	145	41	78	5	10	.333	0	4.85
	Actual	1	1	5	5	2	4	0	0	.000	0	9.00

Occasionally we have a bad projection for a player because we have him projected as a starter, but he pitches relief (like Wade Davis in 2012) or vice versa. Occasionally we have a terrible projection (in terms of accuracy) because a pitcher pitches much better than we expected.   Last year we had projected Fernando Rodney to have 1 save, a 4.24 ERA and a strikeout/walk ratio of 47-35; it was actually 48 saves, an 0.60 ERA and a strikeout/walk ratio 76-15.   There are about 20 of those a year in the major leagues; Rodney was the worst one last year. We had Aroldis Chapman projected to make 10 starts and have a 3.39 ERA—which, in retrospect, I don't really understand, since he has never made a start in the major leagues.   Must have been something we read somewhere. We had Wade Miley projected to go 4-5 after a mid-season callup; he was 16-11. We had R. A. Dickey projected to go 11-12 with a 3.93 ERA; that wasn't close. We had Lance Lynn projected into a starter/reliever compromise role, like Aroldis.   We had Kyle Lohse projected to go 9-10 with a 4.02 ERA; he went 16-3 with a 2.86.   We were way too low on Johnny Cueto and Barry Zito.

Cliff Lee had more strikeouts than we projected for him and fewer walks, and we had projected his starts and ERA almost perfectly, but whereas he had projected him to go 16-10, it was actually 6-9.

Fernando Rodney's season was probably not foreseeable, at least until he signed with Tampa Bay, and in failing to anticipate the season that RA Dickey had, we were in company with the rest of the English-speaking, knuckleball-watching world. Our projection for Gio Gonzalez, on the other hand, was a clear and absolute failure on our part, and reflects some serious error in our process. We had Gio Gonzalez projected to go 10-13 with a 4.09 ERA, which is entirely inexplicable since he had won 15 and 16 games the previous two seasons with ERAs barely over 3.00.   There is no reason that we should have made an error of that nature.

But last year we projected that Tony Watson would have an ERA of 3.38, and he did.   Tony Watson, if you are wondering, is a lefty reliever with the Pirates.   We projected that Dana Eveland would have a 4.73 ERA, and he did. We projected that Clayton Kershaw would have 229 strikeouts, and he did.   A blind pig will find a softball once in a while; about as often as he would find an acorn, I guess.

We don't have a perfect process, and what makes it more difficult to build on is that it is not a perfectible process; we're always going to be wrong about players like Rodney, Dickey and Cliff Lee. It's like umpiring; we'll never have perfect umpiring, but we keep working to make it a little bit better. We'll keep working on it, and these are the projections that we have for you for 2013.

2013 Pitcher Projections

Pitcher	Team	Age	G	GS	IP	H	HR	BB	SO	HB	W	L	Pct	Sv	BR/9	ERA
Abad,Fernando	Hou	27	28	12	82	93	11	27	71	2	3	6	.333	0	13.4	4.83
Aceves,Alfredo	Bos	31	62	0	88	79	9	33	67	7	5	5	.500	0	12.2	3.68
Acosta,Manny	NYM	32	54	0	55	52	6	24	49	2	3	3	.500	0	12.8	3.76
Adams,Mike	Tex	34	60	0	55	45	4	15	55	1	4	2	.667	0	10.0	2.45
Affeldt,Jeremy	SF	34	71	0	63	58	4	24	53	3	4	3	.571	0	12.1	3.43
Albers,Matt	Ari	30	64	0	62	62	6	25	47	3	3	4	.429	0	13.1	4.21
Alvarez,Henderson	Tor	23	31	31	186	205	26	48	100	6	8	12	.400	0	12.5	4.40
Ambriz,Hector	Hou	29	35	0	39	44	5	19	31	1	1	3	.250	0	14.8	5.31
Anderson,Brett	Oak	25	29	29	172	171	15	41	134	9	10	9	.526	0	11.6	3.61
Archer,Chris	TB	24	26	26	161	142	11	90	159	9	8	10	.444	0	13.5	3.91
Arredondo,Jose	Cin	29	62	0	58	49	6	32	56	1	3	3	.500	0	12.7	3.72
Arrieta,Jake	Bal	27	35	0	36	35	4	15	30	2	2	2	.500	0	13.0	4.25
Arroyo,Bronson	Cin	36	33	33	218	222	33	43	136	7	12	12	.500	0	11.2	3.88
Atchison,Scott	Bos	37	28	0	34	32	3	6	28	1	2	1	.667	0	10.3	2.91
Avilan,Luis	Atl	23	53	0	58	55	6	25	46	3	3	3	.500	0	12.9	4.03
Axelrod,Dylan	CWS	27	13	5	44	43	3	16	38	2	2	2	.500	0	12.5	3.68
Axford,John	Mil	30	78	0	72	61	5	35	90	1	4	4	.500	45	12.1	3.25
Ayala,Luis	Bal	35	67	0	73	78	7	17	50	5	4	4	.500	0	12.3	3.95
Badenhop,Burke	TB	30	58	0	56	56	4	16	40	3	3	3	.500	0	12.1	3.54
Bailey,Andrew	Bos	29	47	0	48	41	4	16	46	1	3	2	.600	36	10.9	2.81
Bailey,Homer	Cin	27	33	33	210	215	24	54	172	7	12	12	.500	0	11.8	3.86
Baker,Scott	Min	31	28	28	168	172	21	41	137	5	9	10	.474	0	11.7	3.86
Balfour,Grant	Oak	35	75	0	77	53	6	28	83	1	5	3	.625	35	9.6	2.22
Bard,Daniel	Bos	28	66	0	67	54	6	28	67	6	3	4	.429	1	11.8	3.63
Bass,Anthony	SD	25	28	19	132	123	11	48	102	2	8	7	.533	2	11.8	3.61
Bastardo,Antonio	Phi	27	65	0	52	40	6	25	64	2	3	3	.500	2	11.6	3.29
Batista,Miguel	Atl	42	24	2	35	35	4	20	23	2	1	2	.333	0	14.7	4.89
Beachy,Brandon	Atl	26	12	12	70	56	6	23	76	2	5	3	.625	0	10.4	3.09
Beavan,Blake	Sea	24	29	29	180	203	20	31	89	7	8	12	.400	0	12.0	4.10
Beckett,Josh	LAD	33	28	28	174	165	18	51	153	7	13	7	.650	0	11.5	3.26
Bedard,Erik	Pit	34	17	17	95	87	10	40	92	2	5	5	.500	0	12.2	3.79
Belisario,Ronald	LAD	30	75	0	83	71	6	35	68	5	5	4	.556	0	12.0	3.36
Belisle,Matt	Col	33	74	0	70	78	6	15	55	3	4	4	.500	6	12.3	3.99
Bell,Heath	Mia	35	73	0	65	56	4	26	63	1	4	3	.571	9	11.5	3.05
Benoit,Joaquin	Det	35	71	0	72	57	9	21	79	1	5	3	.625	0	9.9	2.75
Bergesen,Brad	Ari	27	32	0	52	58	7	16	28	2	2	3	.400	0	13.2	4.50
Berken,Jason	ChC	29	8	8	45	54	6	15	31	2	2	3	.400	0	14.2	5.20
Betancourt,Rafael	Col	38	61	0	60	52	7	10	65	0	4	3	.571	29	9.3	2.55
Billingsley,Chad	LAD	28	19	19	122	115	9	44	108	5	7	7	.500	0	12.1	3.61
Blackburn,Nick	Min	31	14	14	74	90	10	22	35	2	3	6	.333	0	13.9	5.23
Blackley,Travis	Oak	30	28	14	105	106	12	30	76	5	5	6	.455	0	12.1	3.94
Blanton,Joe	LAD	32	29	29	182	201	24	35	131	4	9	11	.450	0	11.9	4.10
Blevins,Jerry	Oak	29	65	0	63	55	6	24	61	3	4	3	.571	0	11.7	3.43
Boggs,Mitchell	StL	29	75	0	70	71	6	22	51	4	4	4	.500	0	12.5	3.86
Bowden,Michael	ChC	26	44	0	60	55	7	27	50	1	3	4	.429	0	12.4	3.90
Boxberger,Brad	SD	25	38	0	44	33	3	22	60	2	3	2	.600	0	11.7	3.07
Brach,Brad	SD	27	73	0	75	61	7	28	87	2	5	3	.625	0	10.9	3.00
Breslow,Craig	Bos	32	64	0	62	55	5	22	55	2	4	3	.571	0	11.5	3.19
Britton,Zach	Bal	25	19	17	97	98	8	41	72	2	5	6	.455	0	13.1	4.08
Brothers,Rex	Col	25	75	0	76	65	6	41	103	1	5	4	.556	0	12.7	3.55
Broxton,Jonathan	Cin	29	65	0	62	53	3	22	71	2	4	3	.571	20	11.2	2.90
Buchholz,Clay	Bos	28	30	30	205	188	22	72	163	8	12	11	.522	0	11.8	3.64
Buehrle,Mark	Mia	34	31	31	205	218	23	41	106	3	11	12	.478	0	11.5	3.78
Bumgarner,Madison	SF	23	32	32	203	194	17	48	174	6	13	9	.591	0	11.0	3.37
Burnett,A.J.	Pit	36	32	32	209	203	26	76	190	12	11	13	.458	0	12.5	4.05
Burnett,Alex	Min	25	66	0	69	71	5	27	47	5	3	4	.429	0	13.4	4.17
Burnett,Sean	Was	30	67	0	55	54	5	15	40	2	3	3	.500	0	11.6	3.60
Burns,Cory	SD	25	33	0	36	31	1	11	40	1	3	1	.750	0	10.8	2.75
Burton,Jared	Min	32	63	0	62	54	5	18	52	4	4	3	.571	0	11.0	3.05
Cabrera,Alberto	ChC	24	48	0	43	48	4	21	40	2	2	3	.400	0	14.9	5.02
Cahill,Trevor	Ari	25	31	31	202	191	19	76	137	8	12	11	.522	0	12.3	3.79
Cain,Matt	SF	28	33	33	226	188	19	57	188	7	17	8	.680	0	10.0	2.95
Camp,Shawn	ChC	37	79	0	75	80	6	21	50	4	4	5	.444	0	12.6	3.96
Capps,Matt	Min	29	54	0	52	52	6	9	37	2	3	3	.500	18	10.9	3.46
Capuano,Chris	LAD	34	32	32	194	194	25	54	160	5	10	11	.476	0	11.7	3.90
Carpenter,Chris	StL	38	30	30	202	189	14	47	157	8	15	8	.652	0	10.9	3.25
Cashner,Andrew	SD	26	28	28	176	194	15	68	176	7	12	7	.632	0	13.8	3.68
Casilla,Santiago	SF	32	76	0	69	59	6	27	65	3	5	3	.625	1	11.6	3.26
Cecil,Brett	Tor	26	27	27	166	173	20	53	127	5	8	11	.421	0	12.5	4.17
Cedeno,Xavier	Hou	26	60	0	44	46	4	17	36	2	2	3	.400	0	13.3	4.09
Chacin,Jhoulys	Col	25	27	27	163	153	16	72	133	6	9	9	.500	0	12.8	3.92
Chamberlain,Joba	NYY	27	43	0	41	39	4	11	43	2	3	2	.600	0	11.4	3.51
Chapman,Aroldis	Cin	25	63	0	67	44	4	32	98	3	4	3	.571	48	10.6	2.42
Chatwood,Tyler	Col	23	23	23	128	150	12	62	78	4	5	9	.357	0	15.2	5.34
Chen,Bruce	KC	36	32	32	182	190	27	50	128	7	9	11	.450	0	12.2	4.25
Chen,Wei-Yin	Bal	27	31	31	193	186	29	57	154	5	10	11	.476	0	11.6	3.92
Choate,Randy	LAD	37	80	0	38	33	2	18	34	3	2	2	.500	0	12.8	3.55
Cishek,Steve	Mia	27	66	0	62	53	2	26	59	6	4	3	.571	26	12.3	3.05
Clippard,Tyler	Was	28	73	0	74	59	9	27	77	2	5	3	.625	14	10.7	3.04
Cloyd,Tyler	Phi	26	12	12	66	63	8	17	51	3	4	4	.500	0	11.3	3.68

2013 Pitcher Projections

PLAYER			HOW MUCH			WHAT HE WILL GIVE UP					THE RESULTS				
Pitcher	Team	Age	G	GS	IP	H	HR	BB	SO	HB	W	L	Pct	Sv	BR/9	ERA
Cobb,Alex	TB	25	27	27	169	168	12	56	152	8	9	10	.474	0	12.4	3.73
Coke,Phil	Det	30	61	0	44	47	3	16	36	1	2	2	.500	0	13.1	4.09
Coleman,Louis	KC	27	45	0	53	41	6	24	62	2	3	3	.500	0	11.4	3.23
Collins,Tim	KC	23	72	0	61	46	5	33	75	1	4	3	.571	0	11.8	3.25
Collmenter,Josh	Ari	27	25	8	73	69	8	17	56	1	5	3	.625	0	10.7	3.33
Cook,Aaron	Bos	34	20	7	56	65	5	17	24	1	2	4	.333	0	13.3	4.50
Cook,Ryan	Oak	26	73	0	80	59	4	32	81	5	6	3	.667	0	10.8	2.48
Corbin,Patrick	Ari	23	28	26	156	163	15	41	138	8	8	9	.471	0	12.2	3.92
Corpas,Manuel	ChC	30	59	0	59	61	6	19	40	4	3	4	.429	0	12.8	4.12
Correia,Kevin	Pit	32	29	27	176	185	22	49	112	4	9	11	.450	0	12.2	4.09
Crain,Jesse	CWS	31	58	0	57	48	5	26	53	2	3	3	.500	0	12.0	3.32
Crow,Aaron	KC	26	73	0	63	62	7	26	56	2	3	4	.429	0	12.9	4.00
Cruz,Rhiner	Hou	26	51	0	58	58	6	34	50	4	2	4	.333	0	14.9	4.97
Cueto,Johnny	Cin	27	33	33	215	203	20	55	169	13	14	10	.583	0	11.3	3.52
Danks,John	CWS	28	28	28	173	171	20	57	133	5	9	10	.474	0	12.1	3.90
Darvish,Yu	Tex	26	32	32	214	176	16	88	247	11	14	9	.609	0	11.6	3.45
Davis,Wade	TB	27	55	0	69	65	8	26	54	3	4	4	.500	0	12.3	3.78
de la Rosa,Jorge	Col	32	24	24	151	151	19	58	136	6	8	9	.471	0	12.8	4.23
Deduno,Samuel	Min	29	23	23	124	108	8	76	107	10	6	8	.429	0	14.1	4.06
Delabar,Steve	Tor	29	67	0	76	59	8	42	93	6	4	4	.500	0	12.7	3.67
Delgado,Randall	Atl	23	25	25	137	132	15	63	122	5	7	9	.438	0	13.1	4.20
Dempster,Ryan	Tex	36	31	31	190	180	20	66	172	5	11	10	.524	0	11.9	3.74
Detwiler,Ross	Was	27	30	30	183	192	15	61	124	5	10	10	.500	0	12.7	3.98
DeVries,Cole	Min	28	18	18	97	112	14	22	71	3	4	7	.364	0	12.7	4.55
Diamond,Scott	Min	26	30	30	196	221	15	49	130	3	9	13	.409	0	12.5	4.41
Dickey,R.A.	NYM	38	34	34	226	198	21	56	152	9	16	8	.667	0	10.5	3.58
Dolis,Rafael	ChC	25	27	0	32	33	2	17	23	1	1	2	.333	0	14.3	4.50
Dotel,Octavio	Det	39	61	0	65	54	7	18	76	2	5	2	.714	0	10.2	2.77
Doubront,Felix	Bos	25	33	33	202	186	24	74	189	9	12	11	.522	0	12.0	3.70
Downs,Darin	Det	28	26	0	30	31	2	10	27	1	2	2	.500	0	12.6	3.90
Downs,Scott	LAA	37	55	0	39	33	3	13	30	1	3	1	.750	0	10.8	2.77
Drabek,Kyle	Tor	25	12	12	78	80	9	47	55	1	3	6	.333	0	14.8	5.08
Duensing,Brian	Min	30	51	14	128	143	13	36	81	3	6	8	.429	0	12.8	4.29
Duffy,Danny	KC	24	9	9	52	53	6	24	49	2	2	3	.400	0	13.7	4.50
Dunn,Mike	Mia	28	71	0	46	40	4	25	52	1	2	3	.400	0	12.9	3.72
Durbin,Chad	Atl	35	74	0	60	60	8	26	47	3	3	4	.429	0	13.4	4.50
Eovaldi,Nathan	Mia	23	27	27	176	166	11	72	129	5	10	10	.500	0	12.4	3.63
Eppley,Cody	NYY	27	60	0	48	45	3	21	44	1	3	2	.600	0	12.6	3.56
Escalona,Edgmer	Col	26	32	0	35	33	5	12	32	2	2	2	.500	0	12.1	3.86
Estrada,Marco	Mil	29	30	30	181	179	19	46	162	3	11	9	.550	0	11.3	3.63
Familia,Jeurys	NYM	23	28	28	163	167	12	90	148	8	7	11	.389	0	14.6	4.58
Farnsworth,Kyle	TB	37	50	0	40	35	4	14	39	2	2	2	.500	0	11.5	3.15
Feldman,Scott	Tex	30	25	15	101	109	11	27	62	4	5	6	.455	0	12.5	4.19
Fick,Chuckie	Hou	27	31	0	41	40	4	20	30	3	2	3	.400	0	13.8	4.39
Fien,Casey	Min	29	55	0	53	50	8	16	47	1	3	3	.500	0	11.4	3.74
Fiers,Mike	Mil	28	29	29	172	153	17	52	170	6	12	7	.632	0	11.0	3.40
Fife,Stephen	LAD	26	7	7	35	36	3	12	22	2	2	2	.500	0	12.9	4.11
Fister,Doug	Det	29	32	32	212	221	18	43	147	10	13	10	.565	0	11.6	3.69
Floyd,Gavin	CWS	30	29	29	162	163	19	52	127	9	8	10	.444	0	12.4	4.06
Francis,Jeff	Col	32	30	30	164	193	18	36	107	6	8	10	.444	0	12.9	4.55
Francisco,Frank	NYM	33	53	0	51	47	5	22	55	1	3	3	.500	8	12.4	3.71
Frasor,Jason	Tor	35	36	0	33	30	3	15	33	1	2	2	.500	0	12.5	3.82
Friedrich,Christian	Col	25	21	21	127	145	17	40	103	3	6	8	.429	0	13.3	4.82
Frieri,Ernesto	LAA	27	67	0	68	49	6	33	79	5	5	3	.625	36	11.5	3.04
Furbush,Charlie	Sea	27	43	0	37	34	6	13	35	1	2	2	.500	0	11.7	3.89
Galarraga,Armando	Hou	31	8	8	40	40	7	19	27	2	1	3	.250	0	13.7	5.18
Gallardo,Yovani	Mil	27	33	33	208	190	22	76	217	2	13	10	.565	0	11.6	3.59
Garcia,Jaime	StL	26	29	29	180	182	15	47	151	3	12	8	.600	0	11.6	3.60
Garza,Matt	ChC	29	31	31	198	186	22	62	171	7	11	11	.500	0	11.6	3.68
Gaudin,Chad	Mia	30	51	0	67	70	8	25	51	4	3	5	.375	0	13.3	4.43
Gearrin,Cory	Atl	27	38	0	34	30	1	14	35	3	2	2	.500	0	12.4	3.44
Gee,Dillon	NYM	27	8	8	55	55	7	19	43	4	3	3	.500	0	12.8	4.09
Germano,Justin	ChC	30	23	22	119	125	16	24	80	8	6	7	.462	0	11.9	4.01
Gomez,Jeanmar	Cle	25	18	14	72	79	8	25	49	2	3	5	.375	0	13.2	4.63
Gonzalez,Edgar	Hou	30	12	12	68	74	7	18	46	3	3	5	.375	0	12.6	4.10
Gonzalez,Gio	Was	27	32	32	202	172	17	83	204	6	14	8	.636	0	11.6	3.21
Gonzalez,Michael	Was	35	56	0	44	36	4	19	49	1	3	2	.600	0	11.5	3.27
Gonzalez,Miguel	Bal	29	27	27	174	161	19	56	138	11	10	9	.526	0	11.8	3.67
Gorzelanny,Tom	Was	30	43	2	69	68	7	27	57	2	4	4	.500	0	12.7	4.04
Gray,Jeff	Min	31	37	0	42	47	4	18	26	3	2	3	.400	0	14.6	5.14
Gregerson,Luke	SD	29	78	0	74	61	6	23	74	2	5	3	.625	0	10.5	2.68
Gregg,Kevin	Bal	35	34	0	39	37	4	23	36	2	2	3	.400	0	14.3	4.62
Greinke,Zack	LAA	29	34	34	222	214	20	57	209	5	15	10	.600	0	11.2	3.45
Griffin,A.J.	Oak	25	19	19	100	90	11	22	81	4	6	5	.545	0	10.4	3.24
Grilli,Jason	Pit	36	64	0	59	54	5	23	60	3	3	3	.500	0	12.2	3.66
Guerra,Javy	LAD	27	46	0	47	42	2	22	40	1	3	2	.600	0	12.4	3.26
Guthrie,Jeremy	KC	34	33	33	197	203	27	56	118	10	10	12	.455	0	12.3	4.20
Halladay,Roy	Phi	36	32	32	230	219	19	43	189	6	15	11	.577	0	10.5	3.21
Hamels,Cole	Phi	29	31	31	223	197	25	52	211	5	14	10	.583	0	10.3	3.23
Hammel,Jason	Bal	30	28	28	161	169	17	58	122	5	8	10	.444	0	13.0	4.30
Hanrahan,Joel	Pit	31	59	0	57	51	5	26	58	2	3	3	.500	40	12.5	3.63

2013 Pitcher Projections

Pitcher	Team	Age	G	GS	IP	H	HR	BB	SO	HB	W	L	Pct	Sv	BR/9	ERA
Hanson,Tommy	Atl	26	28	28	160	142	18	61	156	7	9	9	.500	0	11.8	3.66
Happ,J.A.	Tor	30	28	28	161	158	20	72	144	3	8	10	.444	0	13.0	4.30
Harang,Aaron	LAD	35	29	29	173	179	21	73	138	4	7	12	.368	0	13.3	4.53
Haren,Dan	LAA	32	34	34	218	211	26	41	186	5	15	9	.625	0	10.6	3.47
Harrell,Lucas	Hou	28	31	31	196	205	13	82	132	4	9	13	.409	0	13.4	4.18
Harrison,Matt	Tex	27	33	33	203	212	20	60	128	2	12	11	.522	0	12.1	3.90
Harvey,Matt	NYM	24	30	30	192	172	15	88	196	10	11	10	.524	0	12.7	3.70
Hawkins,LaTroy	LAA	40	49	0	45	45	4	13	29	1	3	2	.600	0	11.8	3.60
Hefner,Jeremy	NYM	27	30	18	121	129	10	31	79	2	7	7	.500	0	12.0	3.87
Hellickson,Jeremy	TB	26	32	32	187	163	22	65	151	7	11	10	.524	0	11.3	3.51
Henderson,Jim	Mil	30	64	0	56	49	6	28	59	3	3	3	.500	0	12.9	4.02
Hendriks,Liam	Min	24	19	19	113	117	10	30	82	3	6	7	.462	0	11.9	3.82
Hensley,Clay	SF	33	52	0	45	44	4	23	33	2	2	3	.400	0	13.8	4.40
Hernandez,David	Ari	28	71	0	70	60	8	26	75	3	4	3	.571	14	11.4	3.34
Hernandez,Felix	Sea	27	33	33	232	208	17	60	216	8	14	11	.560	0	10.7	3.18
Hernandez,Livan	Mil	38	43	0	65	76	8	17	35	1	3	4	.429	0	13.0	4.57
Hernandez,Roberto	Cle	32	25	25	154	162	16	48	91	9	7	10	.412	0	12.8	4.21
Herrera,Kelvin	KC	23	76	0	90	80	6	22	86	3	6	4	.600	0	10.5	2.80
Herrmann,Frank	Cle	29	29	0	39	43	4	11	28	1	2	2	.500	0	12.7	4.15
Hochevar,Luke	KC	29	31	31	192	204	24	62	137	10	9	13	.409	0	12.9	4.45
Holland,Derek	Tex	26	29	29	187	183	27	58	155	5	10	10	.500	0	11.8	3.99
Holland,Greg	KC	27	70	0	74	61	4	34	88	0	5	3	.625	31	11.6	3.04
Hoover,J.J.	Cin	25	29	0	34	31	2	14	36	1	3	1	.750	1	12.2	2.91
Horst,Jeremy	Phi	27	47	0	48	47	4	21	43	1	2	3	.400	0	12.9	3.94
Howell,J.P.	TB	30	51	0	45	41	6	21	43	3	2	3	.400	0	13.0	4.00
Hudson,Daniel	Ari	26	14	14	85	81	9	21	74	3	5	4	.556	0	11.1	3.49
Hudson,Tim	Atl	37	29	29	193	178	14	54	120	9	12	9	.571	0	11.2	3.36
Huff,David	Cle	28	12	8	53	60	8	15	34	1	2	4	.333	0	12.9	4.75
Hughes,Jared	Pit	27	67	0	76	80	6	25	55	6	4	5	.444	0	13.1	4.14
Hughes,Phil	NYY	27	33	33	201	194	28	54	176	5	12	11	.522	0	11.3	3.76
Humber,Philip	CWS	30	20	20	116	124	18	39	85	5	5	8	.385	0	13.0	4.66
Hunter,Tommy	Bal	26	48	0	50	56	8	10	29	1	2	3	.400	0	12.1	4.50
Isringhausen,Jason	LAA	40	44	0	39	34	4	18	31	1	2	2	.500	0	12.2	3.92
Jackson,Edwin	Was	29	32	32	199	206	22	63	154	4	11	11	.500	0	12.3	3.98
Jansen,Kenley	LAD	25	57	0	58	31	3	23	95	2	4	2	.667	35	8.7	1.55
Janssen,Casey	Tor	31	65	0	68	65	6	14	56	3	4	3	.571	3	10.9	3.18
Jenkins,Chad	Tor	25	25	6	64	76	10	20	37	2	2	5	.286	0	13.8	5.20
Jepsen,Kevin	LAA	28	64	0	64	62	5	22	60	2	4	3	.571	2	12.1	3.52
Jimenez,Ubaldo	Cle	29	29	29	170	158	15	82	151	8	9	10	.474	0	13.1	3.97
Johnson,Jim	Bal	30	71	0	70	69	5	15	47	3	4	3	.571	43	11.2	3.34
Johnson,Josh	Mia	29	31	31	196	176	11	62	166	4	13	9	.591	0	11.1	3.21
Johnson,Steve	Bal	25	39	0	43	41	6	20	39	2	2	3	.400	0	13.2	4.40
Jones,Nate	CWS	27	71	0	80	75	5	37	77	2	4	5	.444	0	12.8	3.71
Karstens,Jeff	Pit	30	24	16	105	111	13	19	67	2	6	6	.500	0	11.3	3.86
Kelley,Shawn	Sea	29	43	0	44	37	5	14	44	1	3	2	.600	0	10.6	3.07
Kelly,Casey	SD	23	22	22	127	139	11	38	105	6	6	8	.429	0	13.0	4.25
Kelly,Joe	StL	25	61	0	67	72	5	23	48	3	4	4	.500	0	13.2	4.16
Kendrick,Kyle	Phi	28	29	29	180	191	22	53	95	8	8	12	.400	0	12.6	4.25
Kennedy,Ian	Ari	28	33	33	214	196	24	57	191	11	13	10	.565	0	11.1	3.49
Kershaw,Clayton	LAD	25	32	32	221	170	14	60	227	4	18	7	.720	0	9.5	2.65
Keuchel,Dallas	Hou	25	21	21	112	123	10	34	60	2	5	8	.385	0	12.8	4.18
Kimbrel,Craig	Atl	25	64	0	65	34	3	22	109	2	5	2	.714	39	8.0	1.38
Kinney,Josh	Sea	34	53	0	51	46	3	18	51	5	3	3	.500	0	12.2	3.35
Kintzler,Brandon	Mil	28	27	0	33	33	2	11	27	1	2	2	.500	0	12.3	3.55
Kirkman,Michael	Tex	26	38	0	43	41	4	24	40	1	2	3	.400	0	13.8	4.40
Kluber,Corey	Cle	27	27	27	159	172	17	65	149	10	7	11	.389	0	14.0	4.75
Kontos,George	SF	28	59	0	57	53	7	17	53	1	4	3	.571	0	11.2	3.47
Kuroda,Hiroki	NYY	38	33	33	212	206	24	50	152	4	13	10	.565	0	11.0	3.73
Lackey,John	Bos	34	33	33	209	208	21	59	163	14	12	12	.500	0	12.1	4.05
Laffey,Aaron	Tor	28	27	11	79	90	8	29	43	4	3	6	.333	0	14.0	4.78
Lannan,John	Was	28	10	10	55	61	5	21	30	2	2	4	.333	0	13.7	4.58
Latos,Mat	Cin	25	33	33	208	177	20	64	194	3	15	8	.652	0	10.6	3.16
Layne,Tom	SD	28	50	0	33	35	3	15	22	2	1	2	.333	0	14.2	4.64
League,Brandon	LAD	30	76	0	77	73	5	28	58	3	4	4	.500	2	12.2	3.51
Leake,Mike	Cin	25	29	29	178	190	26	42	119	5	9	11	.450	0	12.0	4.15
LeBlanc,Wade	Mia	28	47	6	84	84	11	21	63	2	4	5	.444	0	11.5	3.75
LeCure,Sam	Cin	29	49	0	57	56	6	20	50	3	3	3	.500	0	12.5	3.95
Lee,Cliff	Phi	34	32	32	224	217	20	32	193	4	15	10	.600	0	10.2	3.17
Lester,Jon	Bos	29	33	33	211	198	20	75	192	8	12	12	.500	0	12.0	3.71
Lewis,Colby	Tex	33	14	14	88	83	12	19	77	3	6	4	.600	0	10.7	3.58
Lincecum,Tim	SF	29	32	32	197	169	16	87	211	5	13	9	.591	0	11.9	3.47
Lincoln,Brad	Tor	28	60	2	87	91	10	21	69	5	4	5	.444	0	12.1	3.93
Lindblom,Josh	Phi	26	73	0	70	70	7	30	66	5	3	5	.375	0	13.5	4.37
Lindstrom,Matt	Ari	33	53	0	54	57	4	16	44	3	3	3	.500	0	12.7	3.83
Liriano,Francisco	CWS	29	32	28	154	144	15	81	152	7	7	10	.412	0	13.6	4.21
Locke,Jeff	Pit	25	15	12	69	70	7	25	60	4	3	4	.429	0	12.9	4.04
Loe,Kameron	Mil	31	69	0	68	74	7	19	46	2	4	4	.500	0	12.6	4.24
Logan,Boone	NYY	28	82	0	59	58	6	26	60	4	3	4	.429	0	13.4	4.27
Lohse,Kyle	StL	34	32	32	208	215	20	42	130	5	13	10	.565	0	11.3	3.63
Lopez,Javier	SF	35	69	0	38	37	1	16	26	2	2	2	.500	1	13.0	3.55
Lopez,Wilton	Hou	29	66	0	74	81	6	11	52	2	4	4	.500	30	11.4	3.53

2013 Pitcher Projections

PLAYER			HOW MUCH			WHAT HE WILL GIVE UP					THE RESULTS					
Pitcher	Team	Age	G	GS	IP	H	HR	BB	SO	HB	W	L	Pct	Sv	BR/9	ERA
Lowe,Mark	Tex	30	32	0	32	31	4	12	28	0	2	2	.500	0	12.1	3.94
Luebke,Cory	SD	28	24	24	155	129	13	46	140	3	11	6	.647	0	10.3	3.02
Luetge,Lucas	Sea	26	59	0	38	36	2	18	36	1	2	2	.500	0	13.0	3.79
Lyles,Jordan	Hou	22	28	28	163	185	18	46	125	9	6	12	.333	0	13.3	4.64
Lynn,Lance	StL	26	29	29	185	181	16	67	171	8	11	9	.550	0	12.5	3.84
Lyon,Brandon	Tor	33	70	0	62	62	5	21	46	2	3	3	.500	7	12.3	3.63
Madson,Ryan	Phi	32	67	0	66	62	5	17	62	3	4	3	.571	43	11.2	3.41
Maholm,Paul	Atl	31	31	31	198	209	18	58	126	10	10	12	.455	0	12.6	4.00
Marcum,Shaun	Mil	31	32	32	196	182	25	58	161	5	12	10	.545	0	11.2	3.63
Marmol,Carlos	ChC	30	63	0	62	43	4	46	80	6	3	3	.500	32	13.8	3.63
Marquis,Jason	SD	34	22	22	130	143	15	41	75	6	6	9	.400	0	13.2	4.50
Marshall,Sean	Cin	30	73	0	62	58	4	16	57	2	4	3	.571	0	11.0	3.05
Martinez,Cristhian	Atl	31	52	0	71	70	7	17	54	1	4	4	.500	0	11.2	3.30
Masterson,Justin	Cle	28	34	34	204	206	15	79	160	12	10	12	.455	0	13.1	4.01
Matsuzaka,Daisuke	Bos	32	25	25	151	142	18	67	135	8	7	9	.438	0	12.9	4.11
Mattheus,Ryan	Was	29	75	0	78	73	7	26	56	4	5	4	.556	0	11.9	3.46
Matusz,Brian	Bal	26	43	8	69	74	9	28	55	1	3	5	.375	0	13.4	4.70
Mazzaro,Vin	KC	26	22	3	40	44	4	17	30	2	2	3	.400	0	14.2	4.73
McAllister,Zach	Cle	25	28	28	170	190	20	50	134	6	8	11	.421	0	13.0	4.50
McCarthy,Brandon	Oak	29	28	28	182	179	18	35	131	5	11	9	.550	0	10.8	3.46
McDonald,James	Pit	28	31	31	172	159	19	72	153	7	9	10	.474	0	12.5	3.87
McGee,Jake	TB	26	67	0	59	49	5	16	65	1	4	2	.667	0	10.1	2.59
McHugh,Collin	NYM	26	15	8	43	40	4	15	38	3	3	2	.600	0	12.1	3.56
Medlen,Kris	Atl	27	30	30	190	169	14	36	173	4	14	7	.667	0	9.9	2.94
Mejia,Jenrry	NYM	23	10	6	32	34	2	13	21	1	2	2	.500	0	13.5	4.22
Melancon,Mark	Bos	28	47	0	57	54	5	17	54	3	3	3	.500	0	11.7	3.47
Mendoza,Luis	KC	29	32	32	193	216	16	70	109	13	8	13	.381	0	13.9	4.62
Mijares,Jose	SF	28	80	0	56	52	5	24	49	3	3	3	.500	0	12.7	3.86
Mikolas,Miles	SD	24	27	0	40	40	2	15	32	1	2	2	.500	0	12.6	3.60
Miley,Wade	Ari	26	30	30	199	200	17	50	150	3	12	10	.545	0	11.4	3.57
Miller,Andrew	Bos	28	55	0	42	38	4	28	53	2	2	3	.400	0	14.6	4.71
Miller,Jim	Oak	31	29	0	47	45	5	18	45	2	2	3	.400	0	12.4	3.83
Milone,Tommy	Oak	26	29	29	178	186	17	41	152	4	10	10	.500	0	11.7	3.59
Minor,Mike	Atl	25	30	30	189	178	24	61	177	4	11	10	.524	0	11.6	3.76
Moore,Matt	TB	24	32	32	202	160	19	84	232	8	13	10	.565	0	11.2	3.25
Morales,Franklin	Bos	27	38	17	122	111	15	52	107	8	6	7	.462	0	12.6	3.98
Morrow,Brandon	Tor	28	30	30	187	163	19	66	191	7	11	9	.550	0	11.4	3.47
Mortensen,Clayton	Bos	28	36	0	50	52	7	21	37	2	2	3	.400	0	13.5	4.68
Moscoso,Guillermo	Col	29	30	3	59	62	7	19	49	1	3	3	.500	0	12.5	4.12
Motte,Jason	StL	31	70	0	75	59	7	18	85	3	5	3	.625	45	9.6	2.52
Mujica,Edward	StL	29	76	0	72	69	9	13	60	1	5	3	.625	0	10.4	3.13
Myers,Brett	CWS	32	77	0	79	78	10	20	64	2	4	5	.444	0	11.4	3.76
Narveson,Chris	Mil	31	21	21	131	133	16	52	106	3	7	8	.467	0	12.9	4.26
Nathan,Joe	Tex	38	68	0	67	51	7	16	79	2	5	3	.625	37	9.3	2.28
Neshek,Pat	Oak	32	46	0	39	34	5	14	38	1	2	2	.500	0	11.3	3.23
Niemann,Jeff	TB	30	22	22	118	114	14	35	94	5	6	7	.462	0	11.7	3.81
Niese,Jon	NYM	26	29	29	190	202	19	54	153	6	10	11	.476	0	12.4	3.98
Noesi,Hector	Sea	26	28	28	171	183	21	60	128	5	7	12	.368	0	13.1	4.53
Nolasco,Ricky	Mia	30	29	29	194	208	22	43	149	5	9	12	.429	0	11.9	3.94
Norberto,Jordan	Oak	26	28	0	42	35	3	21	42	1	2	2	.500	0	12.2	3.43
Norris,Bud	Hou	28	29	29	173	171	22	69	168	7	7	12	.368	0	12.8	4.27
Nova,Ivan	NYY	26	29	29	179	193	20	60	134	7	9	11	.450	0	13.1	4.42
O'Day,Darren	Bal	30	71	0	73	61	8	16	66	5	5	3	.625	0	10.1	2.71
O'Flaherty,Eric	Atl	28	61	0	57	51	2	18	47	3	4	2	.667	0	11.4	3.00
Ogando,Alexi	Tex	29	61	0	68	57	6	18	60	2	5	2	.714	0	10.2	2.65
Ohlendorf,Ross	SD	30	12	10	61	69	8	23	44	4	2	4	.333	0	14.2	5.16
Oliver,Darren	Tor	42	59	0	55	49	4	14	47	2	4	2	.667	0	10.6	2.95
Omogrosso,Brian	CWS	29	26	0	32	32	3	12	31	1	2	2	.500	0	12.7	3.94
Ondrusek,Logan	Cin	28	55	0	50	47	5	26	35	2	2	3	.400	0	13.5	4.32
Oswalt,Roy	Tex	35	24	24	136	136	13	32	107	5	9	7	.562	0	11.4	3.64
Ottavino,Adam	Col	27	21	9	63	69	7	28	55	3	3	4	.429	0	14.3	5.00
Outman,Josh	Col	28	30	3	35	37	3	18	29	1	2	2	.500	0	14.4	4.63
Padilla,Vicente	Bos	35	52	0	44	46	6	13	34	3	2	3	.400	0	12.7	4.30
Papelbon,Jonathan	Phi	32	67	0	68	55	6	17	81	3	5	3	.625	41	9.9	2.51
Parker,Jarrod	Oak	24	31	31	207	193	12	75	170	9	12	11	.522	0	12.0	3.52
Parnell,Bobby	NYM	28	73	0	73	77	6	26	62	2	4	4	.500	24	12.9	4.07
Parra,Manny	Mil	30	57	0	51	56	5	29	47	1	2	4	.333	0	15.2	5.29
Patton,Troy	Bal	27	41	0	40	42	5	10	27	2	2	2	.500	0	12.2	4.05
Paulino,Felipe	KC	29	16	16	99	103	10	39	91	4	5	6	.455	0	13.3	4.27
Pavano,Carl	Min	37	30	30	184	209	22	30	101	7	9	12	.429	0	12.0	4.11
Peavy,Jake	CWS	32	31	31	211	189	22	47	200	7	14	9	.609	0	10.4	3.20
Penny,Brad	SF	35	28	0	34	39	4	11	19	1	2	2	.500	0	13.5	4.50
Peralta,Joel	TB	37	76	0	71	57	8	18	67	2	5	3	.625	0	9.8	2.66
Peralta,Wily	Mil	24	10	10	56	58	4	30	54	3	3	4	.429	0	14.6	4.66
Perdomo,Luis	Min	29	28	0	33	32	3	15	25	1	2	2	.500	0	13.1	4.09
Perez,Chris	Cle	27	60	0	58	44	6	20	59	4	4	2	.667	41	10.6	2.79
Perez,Martin	Tex	22	17	12	106	118	11	48	81	2	5	7	.417	0	14.3	4.84
Perez,Oliver	Sea	31	41	0	38	38	6	19	35	2	1	3	.250	0	14.0	4.74
Perkins,Glen	Min	30	67	0	72	80	8	19	56	3	3	5	.375	27	12.8	4.38
Pestano,Vinnie	Cle	28	70	0	76	60	6	27	89	3	5	3	.625	25	10.7	2.72
Phelps,David	NYY	26	35	17	124	121	12	42	113	5	7	7	.500	0	12.2	3.70

2013 Pitcher Projections

PLAYER			HOW MUCH			WHAT HE WILL GIVE UP					THE RESULTS					
Pitcher	Team	Age	G	GS	IP	H	HR	BB	SO	HB	W	L	Pct	Sv	BR/9	ERA
Pineda,Michael	Sea	24	29	29	187	158	22	56	183	7	12	9	.571	0	10.6	3.37
Porcello,Rick	Det	24	31	31	178	207	18	45	102	7	9	11	.450	0	13.1	4.50
Price,David	TB	27	32	32	216	183	20	63	202	7	16	9	.640	0	10.5	3.13
Putz,J.J.	Ari	36	61	0	59	47	4	12	65	2	4	2	.667	28	9.3	2.29
Qualls,Chad	Pit	34	54	0	47	50	5	13	35	1	2	3	.400	0	12.3	4.02
Raley,Brooks	ChC	25	10	10	56	65	7	20	37	2	2	4	.333	0	14.0	4.98
Ramirez,Erasmo	Sea	23	24	24	149	155	13	33	111	9	7	9	.438	0	11.9	3.81
Ramirez,Ramon	NYM	31	60	0	62	55	5	31	50	1	4	3	.571	0	12.6	3.48
Rapada,Clay	NYY	32	66	0	35	32	2	14	34	2	2	2	.500	0	12.3	3.34
Rauch,Jon	NYM	34	74	0	59	57	7	13	44	1	4	3	.571	8	10.8	3.36
Reed,Addison	CWS	24	60	0	54	44	5	16	65	2	4	2	.667	32	10.3	2.67
Resop,Chris	Pit	30	61	0	72	70	6	27	65	2	4	4	.500	0	12.4	3.75
Reynolds,Matt	Col	28	68	0	48	48	7	15	48	1	3	3	.500	0	12.0	3.94
Richard,Clayton	SD	29	32	32	212	219	22	52	129	5	12	12	.500	0	11.7	3.78
Richards,Garrett	LAA	25	45	6	70	72	7	29	51	4	4	4	.500	0	13.5	4.37
Rivera,Mariano	NYY	43	64	0	62	47	3	10	59	3	6	1	.857	46	8.7	1.89
Robertson,David	NYY	28	76	0	72	56	4	28	97	2	5	3	.625	5	10.8	2.63
Robertson,Tyler	Min	25	54	0	34	37	4	15	28	1	1	2	.333	0	14.0	4.76
Rodney,Fernando	TB	36	77	0	78	64	5	27	72	5	4	4	.500	47	11.1	2.77
Rodriguez,Aneury	Hou	25	23	7	62	66	8	27	47	2	2	5	.286	0	13.8	4.79
Rodriguez,Fernando	Hou	29	71	0	69	76	8	34	59	3	2	5	.286	0	14.7	5.22
Rodriguez,Francisco	Mil	31	77	0	74	63	6	30	84	1	5	3	.625	0	11.4	3.04
Rodriguez,Wandy	Pit	34	32	32	206	202	22	63	168	6	11	11	.500	0	11.8	3.80
Roenicke,Josh	Col	30	61	0	67	67	6	31	55	3	3	4	.429	6	13.6	4.16
Rogers,Esmil	Cle	27	70	0	84	96	8	34	72	6	3	6	.333	0	14.6	5.04
Rogers,Mark	Mil	27	12	12	70	68	7	40	62	3	3	4	.429	0	14.3	4.63
Romero,Ricky	Tor	28	32	32	185	183	19	89	140	10	8	12	.400	0	13.7	4.43
Romo,Sergio	SF	30	75	0	64	46	5	11	75	3	6	1	.857	16	8.4	1.83
Rosenberg,B.J.	Phi	27	38	2	46	46	6	18	47	3	2	3	.400	0	13.1	4.50
Ross,Tyson	Oak	26	17	8	53	55	4	24	40	2	2	4	.333	0	13.8	4.25
Rusin,Chris	ChC	26	14	14	76	81	8	25	50	4	3	5	.375	0	13.0	4.38
Russell,James	ChC	27	76	0	67	74	11	19	49	2	3	5	.375	0	12.8	4.84
Rzepczynski,Marc	StL	27	67	0	43	42	4	17	40	2	2	2	.500	0	12.8	3.98
Sabathia,CC	NYY	32	34	34	233	216	20	56	211	8	16	10	.615	0	10.8	3.28
Salas,Fernando	StL	28	66	0	60	51	7	22	64	2	4	3	.571	0	11.2	3.30
Sale,Chris	CWS	24	30	30	198	163	20	57	214	6	14	8	.636	0	10.3	3.09
Samardzija,Jeff	ChC	28	30	30	193	177	21	63	169	6	10	11	.476	0	11.5	3.78
Sanchez,Anibal	Det	29	31	31	201	200	18	56	175	6	12	10	.545	0	11.7	3.72
Sanchez,Jonathan	Col	30	16	16	84	75	10	57	84	4	4	5	.444	0	14.6	4.71
Santana,Ervin	LAA	30	31	31	205	198	30	68	161	10	11	11	.500	0	12.1	4.04
Santana,Johan	NYM	34	27	27	185	169	20	61	162	2	11	9	.550	0	11.3	3.50
Santos,Sergio	Tor	29	62	0	64	54	5	32	79	4	4	3	.571	21	12.7	3.52
Saunders,Joe	Bal	32	29	29	189	201	24	50	110	4	9	12	.429	0	12.1	4.10
Scheppers,Tanner	Tex	26	49	0	39	41	3	12	40	3	2	2	.500	0	12.9	4.15
Scherzer,Max	Det	28	31	31	191	180	22	60	198	7	12	9	.571	0	11.6	3.72
Scribner,Evan	Oak	27	41	0	50	43	4	16	51	1	3	2	.600	0	10.8	2.88
Seddon,Chris	Cle	29	34	0	42	45	5	14	30	1	2	3	.400	0	12.9	4.50
Shaw,Bryan	Ari	25	61	0	62	63	4	23	47	5	3	4	.429	0	13.2	4.06
Shields,James	TB	31	32	32	218	212	27	56	191	7	12	12	.500	0	11.4	3.67
Simon,Alfredo	Cin	32	35	0	61	69	8	22	44	3	3	4	.429	1	13.9	5.02
Sipp,Tony	Cle	29	61	0	58	47	9	25	61	1	3	3	.500	0	11.3	3.57
Smith,Joe	Cle	29	74	0	68	58	4	25	55	2	5	3	.625	0	11.2	2.91
Smith,Will	KC	23	22	22	129	152	14	40	90	3	5	9	.357	0	13.6	4.81
Soria,Joakim	KC	29	50	0	50	42	4	14	53	2	4	2	.667	33	10.4	2.70
Soriano,Rafael	NYY	33	68	0	72	54	7	26	75	1	5	3	.625	2	10.1	2.63
Stammen,Craig	Was	29	59	0	90	95	10	32	67	1	4	6	.400	6	12.8	4.30
Storen,Drew	Was	25	61	0	54	44	4	16	50	2	4	2	.667	33	10.3	2.50
Storey,Mickey	Hou	27	50	0	61	58	6	17	59	3	3	3	.500	0	11.5	3.39
Strasburg,Stephen	Was	24	32	32	208	159	14	57	255	4	17	6	.739	0	9.5	2.68
Street,Huston	SD	29	60	0	57	46	6	13	59	1	4	2	.667	44	9.5	2.53
Strop,Pedro	Bal	28	70	0	62	56	2	33	63	3	4	3	.571	0	13.4	3.63
Stults,Eric	SD	33	17	12	78	82	7	23	59	1	4	4	.500	0	12.2	3.92
Swarzak,Anthony	Min	27	40	4	90	104	11	27	57	3	4	6	.400	0	13.4	4.80
Takahashi,Hisanori	Pit	38	51	0	48	44	6	15	43	0	3	2	.600	0	11.1	3.38
Tazawa,Junichi	Bos	27	57	0	65	61	5	19	65	2	4	3	.571	2	11.4	2.49
Teaford,Everett	KC	29	22	4	65	64	9	21	48	2	3	4	.429	0	12.0	3.88
Teheran,Julio	Atl	22	25	25	149	151	15	55	119	10	7	9	.438	0	13.0	4.23
Thayer,Dale	SD	32	71	0	62	60	5	14	52	2	4	3	.571	0	11.0	3.19
Thornton,Matt	CWS	36	71	0	62	54	4	18	65	2	4	3	.571	2	10.7	2.76
Tillman,Chris	Bal	25	31	31	188	191	24	72	155	5	9	12	.429	0	12.8	4.31
Tolleson,Shawn	LAD	25	56	0	52	42	5	20	62	1	4	2	.667	0	10.9	2.94
Torres,Carlos	Col	30	24	0	49	48	4	22	43	2	3	3	.500	0	12.9	4.04
Turner,Jacob	Mia	22	25	25	152	147	16	52	104	5	8	9	.471	0	12.1	3.79
Uehara,Koji	Tex	38	43	0	40	34	5	6	39	0	3	1	.750	4	9.0	2.25
Valdes,Raul	Phi	35	29	0	30	31	4	6	30	1	2	2	.500	0	11.4	3.60
Valverde,Jose	Det	35	73	0	74	58	6	32	73	3	5	3	.625	37	11.3	3.04
Vargas,Jason	Sea	30	31	31	205	206	27	55	135	4	10	13	.435	0	11.6	3.82
Vasquez,Esmerling	Min	29	12	12	63	57	6	33	53	6	3	4	.429	0	13.7	4.14
Venters,Jonny	Atl	28	64	0	63	56	3	30	60	4	4	3	.571	0	12.9	3.57
Veras,Jose	Mil	32	71	0	70	61	6	39	76	3	4	4	.500	0	13.2	3.99
Verlander,Justin	Det	30	33	33	231	195	19	58	220	7	18	8	.692	0	10.1	3.00

2013 Pitcher Projections

PLAYER			HOW MUCH			WHAT HE WILL GIVE UP					THE RESULTS					
Pitcher	Team	Age	G	GS	IP	H	HR	BB	SO	HB	W	L	Pct	Sv	BR/9	ERA
Villanueva,Carlos	Tor	29	24	24	146	139	21	51	127	5	7	9	.438	0	12.0	4.01
Villarreal,Brayan	Det	26	55	0	60	55	6	31	59	5	3	4	.429	0	13.6	4.35
Vincent,Nick	SD	26	42	0	41	38	3	12	40	2	3	1	.750	0	11.4	3.07
Vogelsong,Ryan	SF	35	32	32	185	178	16	66	155	8	11	10	.524	0	12.3	3.75
Volquez,Edinson	SD	29	30	30	165	145	16	90	159	8	9	10	.474	0	13.3	3.98
Volstad,Chris	ChC	26	28	28	155	171	18	53	99	4	6	11	.353	0	13.2	4.59
Wainwright,Adam	StL	31	31	31	203	191	15	53	174	5	14	8	.636	0	11.0	3.33
Walden,Jordan	LAA	25	42	0	36	34	2	16	39	1	2	2	.500	0	12.8	3.75
Waldrop,Kyle	Min	27	27	0	37	42	3	12	20	3	2	3	.400	0	13.9	4.62
Walters,P.J.	Min	28	13	13	68	75	9	25	57	5	3	5	.375	0	13.9	4.90
Watson,Tony	Pit	28	71	0	58	48	6	23	54	2	4	3	.571	0	11.3	3.26
Weaver,Jered	LAA	30	33	33	220	188	23	52	187	3	17	8	.680	0	9.9	3.07
Webb,Ryan	Mia	27	68	0	62	67	4	20	43	2	3	4	.429	0	12.9	4.06
Weiland,Kyle	Hou	26	24	24	129	128	17	60	115	12	5	10	.333	0	14.0	4.74
Westbrook,Jake	StL	35	28	28	173	187	15	58	101	5	9	10	.474	0	13.0	4.21
White,Alex	Col	24	24	24	148	153	18	63	106	7	7	9	.438	0	13.6	4.56
Wilhelmsen,Tom	Sea	29	71	0	78	70	7	31	71	5	4	5	.444	42	12.2	3.58
Williams,Jerome	LAA	31	36	9	118	132	16	29	77	6	6	7	.462	0	12.7	4.58
Wilson,Brian	SF	31	44	0	44	39	2	23	47	1	3	2	.600	37	12.9	3.48
Wilson,C.J.	LAA	32	34	34	198	171	15	82	176	9	13	9	.591	0	11.9	3.45
Wolf,Randy	Bal	36	28	21	137	141	17	45	96	7	6	9	.400	0	12.7	4.27
Wood,Travis	ChC	26	31	31	196	191	22	66	159	9	10	12	.455	0	12.2	3.90
Worley,Vance	Phi	25	20	20	113	118	11	38	91	4	5	7	.417	0	12.7	4.06
Wright,Jamey	LAD	38	74	0	72	74	5	32	47	5	3	5	.375	0	13.9	4.38
Wright,Wesley	Hou	28	75	0	58	55	6	21	52	4	3	4	.429	0	12.4	3.88
Young,Chris	NYM	34	24	24	144	124	16	52	112	3	9	7	.562	0	11.2	3.44
Zagurski,Mike	Ari	30	46	0	37	33	4	19	41	2	2	2	.500	0	13.1	4.14
Zambrano,Carlos	Mia	32	37	10	90	83	8	43	68	5	4	6	.400	0	13.1	4.00
Ziegler,Brad	Ari	33	82	0	76	72	3	25	51	2	5	3	.625	0	11.7	3.08
Zimmermann,Jordan	Was	27	31	31	190	178	18	41	157	8	13	8	.619	0	10.8	3.32
Zito,Barry	SF	35	33	33	192	183	21	75	133	6	11	11	.500	0	12.4	3.94

Career Targets

This section is designed to give probabilities on players achieving important career milestones. The method (formerly under the name of "The Favorite Toy") was developed by Bill James and takes into account a player's age and performance level in predicting the probability that he will accumulate certain career stats. A detailed explanation of how the system works can be found in the glossary.

Congratulations to Miguel Cabrera for winning the first American League Triple Crown since Carl Yastrzemski's 1967 season. Cabrera's league-leading 139 RBI gives him a career total of 1,123, and this season he has picked up 16% in his chances for 2000 career RBI and is now the most likely player in baseball to break Hank Aaron's record of 2,298 runs batted in.

Cabrera's 44 home runs this season—he now has 321 career homers—boosted his chances of reaching 600 homers in his career by 17%, and for the first time has put him on our leaderboard with a 7% chance at breaking Barry Bonds' record.

Lastly, Cabrera's 205 hits this season, which gave him the league lead with a .330 batting average, leaves him as the only player on our list with a chance to break Pete Rose's record for career hits. Cabrera only has a 2% chance, but it's still a chance.

3,000 Hits	
% chance to reach milestone	
Jeter,Derek	done
Rodriguez,Alex	98%
Pujols,Albert	66%
Cabrera,Miguel	58%
Beltre,Adrian	53%
Suzuki,Ichiro	44%
Damon,Johnny	35%
Young,Michael	35%
Cano,Robinson	32%
Reyes,Jose	27%
Castro,Starlin	24%
Butler,Billy	23%
Pierre,Juan	20%
Braun,Ryan	19%
Gonzalez,Adrian	19%
Andrus,Elvis	18%
Fielder,Prince	16%
Rollins,Jimmy	16%
Jones,Adam	13%
Upton,Justin	12%
Lee,Carlos	12%
McCutchen,Andrew	12%
Ramirez,Aramis	12%
Cabrera,Melky	12%
Wright,David	12%
Jones,Chipper	11%
Markakis,Nick	10%
Konerko,Paul	10%
Vizquel,Omar	8%
Zimmerman,Ryan	8%
Young,Delmon	8%
Pedroia,Dustin	7%
Kemp,Matt	6%
Holliday,Matt	5%
Pence,Hunter	5%
Jackson,Austin	4%
Gonzalez,Carlos	4%
Francoeur,Jeff	4%
Rios,Alex	4%
Trout,Mike	4%
Phillips,Brandon	4%
Prado,Martin	3%
Kendrick,Howie	2%
Escobar,Alcides	2%
Bourn,Michael	2%
Cabrera,Asdrubal	2%
Bruce,Jay	1%
Heyward,Jason	< 1%
Gordon,Alex	< 1%
Ramirez,Hanley	< 1%

Career Targets

762 Home Runs
% chance to break record

Pujols,Albert	10%
Cabrera,Miguel	7%
Rodriguez,Alex	< 1%
Stanton,Giancarlo	< 1%

2,298 RBI
% chance to break record

Cabrera,Miguel	19%
Pujols,Albert	11%
Rodriguez,Alex	10%

2,296 Runs Scored
% chance to break record

Rodriguez,Alex	4%
Cabrera,Miguel	4%
Pujols,Albert	3%

4,257 Hits
% chance to break record

Cabrera,Miguel	2%

900 Home Runs
% chance to reach milestone

2,000 RBI
% chance to reach milestone

Rodriguez,Alex	98%
Cabrera,Miguel	43%
Pujols,Albert	43%
Fielder,Prince	11%
Beltre,Adrian	9%
Braun,Ryan	7%
Teixeira,Mark	4%
Cano,Robinson	3%
Gonzalez,Adrian	3%
Butler,Billy	2%

6,857 Total Bases
% chance to break record

Cabrera,Miguel	13%
Pujols,Albert	10%

4,000 Hits
% chance to reach milestone

Cabrera,Miguel	9%
Jeter,Derek	5%
Castro,Starlin	3%

800 Home Runs
% chance to reach milestone

Pujols,Albert	3%
Cabrera,Miguel	2%

600 Home Runs
% chance to reach milestone

Rodriguez,Alex	done
Thome,Jim	done
Pujols,Albert	87%
Cabrera,Miguel	39%
Dunn,Adam	29%
Fielder,Prince	18%
Stanton,Giancarlo	16%
Braun,Ryan	13%
Beltre,Adrian	9%
Teixeira,Mark	8%

793 Doubles
% chance to break record

Pujols,Albert	21%
Cabrera,Miguel	19%
Cano,Robinson	15%
Butler,Billy	3%
Gonzalez,Adrian	1%

Most Likely No-Hitter
% chance to reach milestone

Strasburg,Stephen	27%
Scherzer,Max	24%
Darvish,Yu	20%
Kershaw,Clayton	17%
Gonzalez,Gio	16%
Gallardo,Yovani	14%
Sale,Chris	14%
Moore,Matt	14%
Lynn,Lance	13%
Price,David	13%

700 Home Runs
% chance to reach milestone

Rodriguez,Alex	59%
Pujols,Albert	26%
Cabrera,Miguel	16%
Stanton,Giancarlo	5%
Fielder,Prince	3%
Dunn,Adam	2%
Braun,Ryan	< 1%

500 Home Runs
% chance to reach milestone

Rodriguez,Alex	done
Thome,Jim	done
Pujols,Albert	98%
Dunn,Adam	91%
Cabrera,Miguel	87%
Konerko,Paul	65%
Beltre,Adrian	47%
Fielder,Prince	46%
Teixeira,Mark	44%
Braun,Ryan	34%

1,000 Stolen Bases
% chance to reach milestone

Pitchers on Course for 300 Wins

Bill James

The nature of the battle for 300 Wins is that pitchers take very small steps forward until they have an off year, and then they take a large step back. For several years the two leading candidates for 300 career wins, among active pitchers, have been CC Sabathia and Roy Halladay. Halladay and Sabathia had both taken small steps forward for several years. In 2012 both took steps backward. This makes the prospect of a 300-game winner less immediate than it was a year ago, and frankly, it wasn't all that immediate a year ago.

The #4 candidate from 2011, Cliff Lee, pitched well but won only six games, so that wasn't helpful, either. Lee became the first pitcher ever to strike out 200 batters and win only six games. The previous low was eight. This leaves Justin Verlander, the number three 300-win candidate from a year ago, as the best candidate in the game to win 300 games; appropriate, because he is the best pitcher, but the odds are still 5-3 against his winning 300, and if it happens it is ten years down the road. Halladay, Tim Hudson or Sabathia could win 300 as soon as 2018, but the calendar is catching up with Hudson and Halladay, and Sabathia is, as the sportswriters used to say, carrying around a piano. It appears that it may be a few years before baseball has another 300-game winner, but we survived a 45-year drought without a Triple Crown; we're hardy.

In the chart below "EWL" is "Established Win Level". "Momentum" is a summary of various indicators of the force with which a pitcher is moving forward, including his health record, his age, and other factors.

Pitchers on Course For 300 Wins

Name	2012 Age	R/L	W	L	EWL	Momentum	Chance
Verlander, Justin	29	R	124	65	17.4	.905	37%
Sabathia, CC	31	L	191	102	15.1	.868	36%
Hernandez, Felix	26	R	98	76	13.7	.905	23%
Cain, Matt	27	R	85	78	13.9	.896	18%
Halladay, Roy	35	R	199	100	11.9	.801	15%
Shields, James	30	R	87	73	14.5	.867	12%
Hamels, Cole	28	L	91	60	14.9	.816	6%
Lee, Cliff	33	L	125	78	10.4	.837	5%
Hudson, Tim	36	R	197	104	12.3	.696	5%
Burnett, A.J.	35	R	137	121	13.4	.760	4%
Greinke, Zack	28	R	91	78	14.1	.804	4%
Buehrle, Mark	33	L	174	132	11.3	.732	3%
Arroyo, Bronson	35	R	124	115	10.7	.762	1%
Pettitte, Andy	40	L	245	142	4.8	.677	1%
Millwood, Kevin	37	R	169	152	6.2	.666	<1%
Lohse, Kyle	33	R	118	109	12.4	.691	<1%
Zito, Barry	34	L	160	132	10.3	.664	<1%
Peavy, Jake	31	R	120	93	10.5	.707	<1%
Moyer, Jamie	49	L	269	209	2.6	.568	<1%
Lowe, Derek	39	R	175	157	7.8	.654	<1%
Beckett, Josh	32	R	132	95	8.6	.675	<1%
Colon, Bartolo	39	R	171	122	7.6	.609	<1%

EWL: Established Win Level

Baseball Glossary

% Inherited Scored
The percentage of inherited baserunners a relief pitcher allows to score.

% Pitches Taken
The percentage of pitches that a batter does not swing at out of the total number of pitches thrown to him.

1st Batter Average
The Batting Average that a relief pitcher allows to the first batter he faces when he enters a game.

1st Batter OBP
The On-Base Percentage that a relief pitcher allows to the first batter he faces when he enters a game.

1st to 3rd (Baserunning)
"Moved" is the number of times a runner goes from 1st base to 3rd base on a SINGLE. "Chances" are the number of times a runner is on 1st base and a batter is credited with a SINGLE.

1st to Home (Baserunning)
"Moved" is the number of times a runner goes from 1st base to home on a DOUBLE. "Chances" are the number of times a runner is on 1st base and a batter is credited with a DOUBLE.

2nd to Home (Baserunning)
"Moved" is the number of times a runner goes from 2nd base to home on a SINGLE. "Chances" are the number of times a runner is on 2nd base and a batter is credited with a SINGLE.

Active Career Batting Leaders
A list of batting leaders among active (appearing in the most recent season) players. An active player is eligible when he meets the minimum requirements for the following categories:

> 1,000 At Bats—Batting Average, On-Base Percentage, Slugging Average, At Bats Per HR, At Bats Per GDP, At Bats Per RBI, Strikeout to Walk Ratio
> 100 Stolen Base Attempts—Stolen Base Success Percentage

Active Career Pitching Leaders
A list of pitching leaders among active (appearing in the most recent season) players. An active player is eligible when he meets the minimum requirements for the following categories:

750 Innings Pitched—Earned Run Average, Opponent Batting Average, all "Per 9 Innings" categories, Strikeout to Walk Ratio
250 Games Started—Complete Game Frequency
100 Decisions—Win-Loss Percentage

AVG Allowed ScPos
The Batting Average allowed by a pitcher while pitching with runners in scoring position.

AVG Bases Loaded
The Batting Average of a hitter while batting with the bases loaded.

Base Taken
A player is credited with a Base Taken whenever he moves up a base on a Wild Pitch, Passed Ball, Balk, Sacrifice Fly, or Defensive Indifference.

Batting Average
Hits divided by at bats.

Blown Save
When a relief pitcher enters a game in a Save Situation (see definition for Save Situation) and allows the other team to score the tying or go-ahead run.

Bomb (Intentional Walk)
An Intentional Walk is counted as a "Bomb" if
1) The next batter, after the IBB, does not ground into a double play, and
2) Multiple runs are scored in the inning, after the intentional walk.

BR Gain (Baserunning)
BR Gain (or Loss if a negative number) is the total of all the types of extra baserunning advances minus the (triple) penalty for all the BR Outs compared with what would be expected based on the MLB averages.

BR Outs (Baserunning)
BR Outs include the sum of Outs Advancing, Doubled Offs, and when a runner is tagged out on the bases when another runner moves up on a Wild Pitch, Passed Ball, or scores on a Sacrifice Fly.

BS Win
A Blown Save Win is a "win" credited to a reliever who has blown a save opportunity.

Career Targets
This method, once called the Favorite Toy, is a way to estimate the probability that a player will achieve a specific career goal. In this example, 3,000 hits will be used. The four components of the formula are Needed Hits, Years Remaining, Established Hit Level and Projected Remaining Hits.

Needed Hits. This is the number of Hits (or any statistic) that a player needs to reach a desired goal.

Years Remaining. This is the estimated number of years remaining in the player's career. It is determined using the player's age (on June 30th of the previous year; use 2012 when making the calculation after the 2012 season is complete). The formula is (42 - age) divided by two. This means a player who is 20 years old will have 11 remaining seasons, a player who is 25 years old will have 8.5 remaining seasons and a player who is 35 years old will have 3.5 remaining seasons. If the player is a catcher, then multiply his remaining seasons by .7. The only stipulation is that years remaining must always be greater than or equal to 1.5.

Established Hit Level. The Established Hit Level is a weighted average of the player's hits over the past three seasons. To calculate the Established Hit Level after the 2012 season is complete, add 2010 Hits, (2011 Hits multiplied by two) and (2012 Hits multiplied by three), then divide by six. If the Established Hit Level is less than 75% of the most recent performance (2012 Hits in this case), then the Established Hit Level is equal to .75 times the most recent performance.

Projected Remaining Hits. This is calculated by multiplying Years Remaining by the Established Hit Level.

The probability of achieving the specified goal is found by dividing Projected Remaining Hits by Needed Hits, then subtracting .5. The maximum that any player has of achieving a goal is .97 raised to the power of (Need Hits / Established Hit Level). This prevents the possibility of a player reaching a goal from being higher than 100 percent, which is impossible.

Catcher's ERA
The ERA for a catcher is equal to the ERA of pitchers pitching while the catcher is playing behind the plate. It is calculated exactly like ERA for pitchers. Take the number of earned runs allowed while the catcher is playing, multiply it by 9 and then divide it by the total number of defensive innings that the catcher was behind the plate.

Cheap Win
A starting pitcher who wins the game with a game score under 50 gets credit for a cheap win. See Game Score.

Clean Outing
A Clean Outing is a game in which the reliever is not charged with a run (earned or otherwise) AND does not allow an inherited runner to score.

Cleanup Slugging Average
The Slugging Average of a batter when he bats in the cleanup spot, or fourth, in the batting order.

Close and Late
A situation in a game that is very similar to a Save Situation. The following requirements are necessary for a Close and Late game:
  1. The game is in the seventh inning or later AND

2.The batting team is either leading by one run or tied OR

3.The tying run is on base, at bat, or on deck.

Component ERA (ERC)

A statistic that estimates what a pitcher's ERA should have been, based on his pitching performance. The ERC formula is calculated as follows:

1.Subtract the pitcher's Home Runs Allowed from his Hits Allowed.

2.Multiply Step 1 by 1.255.

3.Multiply his Home Runs Allowed by four.

4.Add Steps 2 and 3 together.

5.Multiply Step 4 by .89.

6.Add his Walks and Hit Batsmen.

7.Multiply Step 6 by .475.

8.Add Steps 5 and 7 together.

This yields the pitcher's total base estimate (PTB), which is:

$$PTB \ = \ 0.89 \times (1.255 \times (H - HR) + 4 \times HR) + 0.475 \times (BB + HB)$$

For those pitchers for whom there is intentional walk data, use this formula instead:

$$PTB \ = \ 0.89 \times (1.255 \times (H - HR) + 4 \times HR) + 0.56 \times (BB + HB - IBB)$$

9.Add Hits and Walks and Hit Batsmen.

10.Multiply Step 9 by PTB.

11.Divide Step 10 by Batters Facing Pitcher. If BFP data is unavailable, approximate it by multiplying Innings Pitched by 2.9, then adding Step 9.

12.Multiply Step 11 by 9.

13.Divide Step 12 by Innings Pitched.

14.Subtract .56 from Step 13.

This is the pitcher's ERC, which is:

$$\frac{(H + BB + HB) \times PTB}{BFP \times IP} \times 9 - 0.56$$

If the result after Step 13 is less than 2.24, adjust the formula as follows:

$$\frac{(H + BB + HB) \times PTB}{BFP \times IP} \times 9 \times 0.75$$

Consecutive Days

A count of how many times the pitcher was used after having pitched on the previous day or (in a few cases) in an earlier game on the same day.

Defensive Runs Saved (Runs Saved, for short) is the innovative metric introduced by John Dewan in *The Fielding Bible—Volume II* and modified in *The Fielding Bible—Volume III*. The Runs Saved value indicates how many runs a player saved or hurt his team in the field compared to the average player at his position. A player of zero Runs Saved is about average; a positive number of runs saved indicates above-average defense, below-average fielders post negative Runs Saved totals. There are seven components of Runs Saved:

Plus Minus Runs Saved (all positions except Catcher)
Adjusted Earned Runs Saved (Catchers)
Stolen Base Runs Saved (Catchers, Pitchers)
Bunt Runs Saved (Corner Infielders, Pitchers, Catchers)
Double Play Runs Saved (Middle Infielders)
Outfield Arm Runs Saved (Outfielders)
Good Play/Misplay Runs Saved (All Positions)

Double Play %
Successful Double Plays divided by the number of Double Play opportunities. This statistic includes both the fielder who started the play and the pivot man.

Double Play Opportunity
A fielder is considered to have a double play opportunity when a ground ball is hit with a runner on first base and less than 2 outs and that fielder is involved in the play. This is used to calculate Double Play % and Pivot %.

Doubled Off
A runner is Doubled Off when he is out for failing to get back to his base before he, or the base, is tagged after a ball hit in the air is caught.

Early Entry
A count of the number of times the reliever entered the game in the sixth inning or earlier.

Earned Run Average
The number of earned runs that a pitcher surrenders per nine innings that he pitches. It is calculated by multiplying the total earned runs allowed by nine and dividing by the total number of innings pitched.

Easy Save
This label is used to separate Saves by difficulty level (Easy or Tough). A Save is considered Easy if the relief pitcher enters the game, pitches one inning or less, and the first batter he faces does not at least represent the tying run.

Fielding Percentage
The percentage of plays a player makes in the field without making an error out of the total number of opportunities. It is calculated by adding (Putouts plus Assists) and dividing by (Putouts plus Assists plus Errors).

Games Finished

The relief pitcher who is in the game for each team when the game ends is credited with a Game Finished.

Game Score

To determine the starting pitcher's Game Score:
Start with 50.
Add 1 point for each out recorded by the starting pitcher.
Add 2 points for each inning the pitcher completes after the fourth inning.
Add 1 point for each strikeout.
Subtract 2 points for each hit allowed.
Subtract 4 points for each earned run allowed.
Subtract 2 points for an unearned run.
Subtract 1 point for each walk.

GDP

Grounded into Double Play

GDP Opportunity

This is a situation where the batter has a chance to ground into a double play. It occurs with at least a runner on first base and less than two outs.

Ground / Fly Ratio (Grd/Fly, GB/FB)

Calculated for both batters and pitchers. For batters, it is the number of groundballs hit divided by the number of flyballs hit. For pitchers, it is exactly the same but uses the number of groundballs and flyballs allowed. Every fair batted ball is included except for bunts and line drives.

Hold

A relief pitcher is given a Hold anytime he enters the game in a Save Situation (see definition for Save Situation), records one out or more, and exits the game without giving up the lead. If the pitcher finishes the game, then he will only earn credit for a Save. He cannot receive credit for both a Hold and a Save.

Holds Adjusted Save Percentage (same as Save/Hold Percentage)

Holds plus Saves divided by Holds plus Saves Opportunities.

Inherited Runner

When a relief pitcher enters the game, any runner who was on base at the time is considered an Inherited Runner.

Isolated Power

Slugging Average minus Batting Average.

K/BB Ratio

Strikeouts divided by Walks.

Leadoff On-Base Percentage
The On-Base Percentage of a batter when he bats leadoff, or first, in the batting order.

Leverage Index
Leverage is the amount of swing in the possible change in win probability, compared to the average swing in all situations. The average swing value, by definition, is indexed to 1.00.

If the score of the game is 12-0 or 14-1 the possible changes in win probability will be very close to negligible. Whether the pitcher gives up a home run or gets a double play ball doesn't really change the outcome of the game. There won't be much swing in either direction for the probability of the win. But in the late innings of a close game, the change in win probability among the various events will have rather wild swings. With a runner on first, two outs, down by one, and in the bottom of the ninth, the game can hinge on one swing of that bat. A home run and an out will both end the game, but with different outcomes for the teams involved. The Leverage Index we use (LI) was developed at the website Tangotiger.net, and compiled at the website Fangraphs.com.

Long Outing
A Long Outing is one in which the starting pitcher throws more than 110 pitches. Prior to 2002, we used 120 pitches as the cutoff in the Manager's Record section.

Long Save
A Long Save is when the pitcher credited with a save pitches more than one inning.

Manufactured Runs
1) A run that scores without a hit, or a run on which the only hit(s) is/are infield hits, is always scored as a Manufactured Run.
2) A run which is driven in by a home run is never scored a Manufactured Run, under any circumstance.
3) A run which is driven in by a double or a triple is scored as a Manufactured Run only if *two* of the four bases result from advancing on one of these four acts: a sacrifice bunt, a stolen base, a hit and run, or a bunt single.
4) Otherwise, a run is considered to be a Manufactured Run if two of the four bases do not result from the runner being forced along by a walk, a hit batsman, or a safe hit reaching the outfield.
5) A forceout or fielder's choice which does not improve the position of the base runners should not be counted as contributing toward a Manufactured Run. Advancing on a forceout or a fielder's choice DOES count toward a manufactured run, if the play is one which improves the position of the baserunners.
6) A base "gained" on a double play does not count as a contribution to a Manufactured Run. A run scored on a double play is a Manufactured Run only if two of the OTHER bases are not attributable to forced advancement.

Not Good Outcome (Intentional Walk)
A Not Good Outcome (NG) for an Intentional Walk occurs when one run scored in the inning after the intentional walk (and the next batter after the intentional walk did not ground into a double play).

Offensive Winning Percentage (OWP)

A player's Offensive Winning Percentage is the winning percentage of a hypothetical team which has an offense consisting of nine of that player, and pitching and defense which is average for the player's league. It is calculated by taking the square of RC/27 (see the definition for Runs Created per 27 Outs), dividing it by the sum of the square of RC/27 and the square of the average runs scored per game in the league.

On-Base Percentage

(Hits plus Walks plus Hit by Pitcher) divided by (At Bats plus Walks plus Hit by Pitcher plus Sacrifice Flies).

$$\frac{H + BB + HBP}{AB + BB + HBP + SF}$$

Opponent Batting Average

Hits Allowed divided by (Batters Faced minus Walks minus Hit Batsmen minus Sacrifice Hits minus Sacrifice Flies minus Catcher's Interference).

$$\frac{H}{BFP - BB - HBP - SH - SF - CI}$$

Opposition OPS

The OPS of the hitters facing the pitcher.

Out Advancing

A runner is out advancing when he is tagged out attempting to score from 2nd base on a single or from 1st base on a double, or attempting to go from 1st base to 3rd base on a single.

PA*

Used in the denominator for the calculation of On-Base Percentage. It is calculated by subtracting (Sacrifice Hits plus Times Reached Base on Defensive Interference) from Plate Appearances (see definition for Plate Appearances).

Park Index

To calculate the park index for home runs in a given ballpark, we take the total home runs of both the home team and its opponents at the ballpark and compare it to the total home runs of the home team and its opponents in other games. We then divide each of those totals by the at-bats in the equivalent situations, so that if there are more at-bats in either situation the index is not skewed. The result is then multiplied by 100 to yield the familiar form.

The park indices for doubles, triples, walks, strikeouts and home runs by lefties and righties are determined like home runs above—relative to at-bats. Indices of at-bats, runs, hits, errors and infield fielding errors (E-Infield) are calculated relative to games. The three batting average indices are calculated as is, since these are already relative to at-bats.

PCS (Pitchers' Caught Stealing)

The number of runners officially scored as Caught Stealing where the pitcher initiated the play. The normal Caught Stealing is when a runner is out attempting to steal a base but the play was initiated by the catcher. PCS plays are often referred to as pickoffs, but differ when the runner breaks towards the next base as opposed to returning to the base he was currently on. Pickoffs occur when the pitcher throws to a base that a runner is leading from, and the runner is out attempting to return to that base. Pickoffs are not an official statistic.

Pitches per PA

The total number of pitches a hitter sees divided by his total Plate Appearances.

Pivot %

Successful Double Plays turned by pivot man divided by the number of Double Play opportunities with that pivot man involved.

Plate Appearances

At Bats plus Total Walks plus Hit By Pitcher plus Sacrifice Hits plus Sacrifice Flies plus Times Reached on Defensive Interference.

Platoon Advantage %

Platoon Advantage % is the percentage of players in the starting lineup who have the platoon advantage (i.e. bats right against a left-handed pitcher or bats left against a right-hander) against the starting pitcher; e.g. if the opposing starting pitcher is right handed and the batting team has six left-handed batters in its lineup, the platoon advantage for that game would be 67%.

Plus/Minus System

The Plus/Minus System is a method for evaluating defensive play on batted balls. It is made possible by a game scoring system in which each batted ball is rated for type (line drive, grounder, etc.), velocity within its type (hard, medium or soft), and location on the field. A player gets credit (a "plus" number) if he makes a play that at least one other player at his position missed during the season and he loses credit (a "minus" number") if he misses a play that at least one player made. The size of the credits are proportional to the percentage of times all players make the play. All plays for each player at his position are summed to get his total plus/minus for the season. A total of zero would be average and any other number would approximate how many plays more or less the player made than the average player at the position for the number of chances the player had to field batted balls.

Power/Speed Number

A single number that reflects a combination of power and speed. To achieve a high Power/Speed Number, a player must score high in both power and speed. To calculate the Power/Speed Number, multiply Home Runs by Stolen Bases by two, and divide by the sum of Home Runs and Stolen Bases.

$$\frac{2 \times HR \times SB}{HR + SB}$$

PPO (Pitcher Pickoff)

The number of baserunners thrown out when a pitcher throws to a base with a leading baserunner, and the runner is tagged out attempting to return to the base. PPO is not an official statistic and does not count toward Caught Stealing totals.

Productive Out

An out made by the batter which moves at least one baserunner up at least one base. See also Unproductive Out.

Quality Start

A game where the starting pitcher pitches for at least six innings and allows no more than three earned runs.

Quality Start Percentage

Quality Starts divided by Games Started (see the definition for Quality Start).

Quick Hooks

Used in the Manager's Record. For Quick Hooks and Slow Hooks a score is calculated for each game that is the sum of the number of Pitches plus 10 times the number of Runs Allowed. The bottom 25% of scores in the league are considered to be Quick Hooks.

Range Factor

The number of Successful Chances (Putouts plus Assists) times nine divided by the number of Defensive Innings Played. The average for a player at each position in 2012:

> Second Base: 4.76
> Third Base: 2.57
> Shortstop: 4.39
> Left Field: 1.99
> Center Field: 2.58
> Right Field: 2.07

RBI %

The percentage of all potential runs driven in by a certain hitter. Simply put, it's RBIs divided by RBI Opportunities. RBI Opportunities are a weighted total for baserunners available to be driven in by the batter. They are defined like so:

1.00 for each runner on third base with less than 2 outs, plus
.70 for each runner on third base with 2 out, plus
.70 for each runner on second base, plus
.40 for each runner on first base, plus
.10 for each bases-empty plate appearance.

Regular Saves

Any save which does not meet the definition either of an Easy Save or a Tough Save is a "Regular" Save.

Run Support Per 9 IP

The total number of runs scored by a pitcher's team while he is in the game multiplied by nine and divided by total Innings Pitched.

Runs Created

"Runs Created" is an estimate of the number of a team's runs which are created by each individual hitter. The Cincinnati Reds scored 820 runs last year, let us say. How many of those were created by Joey Votto? How many by Brandon Phillips? How many by Jay Bruce?

There are many different formulas for estimating runs created. . .did you want the one that involves swinging a dead cat in the cemetery under a full moon? Yeah, I don't blame you. . .worm-eaten persimmons are so hard to find in the modern world.

This is the one we use now; it is complicated enough. First, there is an "A" Factor in the formula, a "B" Factor, and a "C" factor. The "A" Factor, which represents the number of times the hitter is on base, is Hits, Plus Walks, Plus Hit Batsmen, Minus Caught Stealing, Minus Grounded Into Double Play. The "B" Factor, which represents the hitter's ability to advance other runners, is 1.125 times the player's Singles, plus 1.69 times his Doubles, plus 3.02 times his Triples, plus 3.73 times his Home Runs, plus .29 times his Walks and Hit Batsmen, not counting intentional walks, plus .492 times Sacrifice Hits, Sacrifice Flies and Stolen Bases, minus .04 times Strikeouts. The "C" Factor, which represents opportunities, is At Bats, Plus Walks, Plus Hit By Pitch, Plus Sacrifice Hits, Plus Sacrifice Flies.

Having made these initial calculations of the A, B and C factors, we then change the "A" factor to "A plus 2.4 times C".

We change the "B" factor to "B plus 3 times C".

We change the "C" factor to "9 times C".

Multiply A times B, divide by then new C ("9 times C"), and subtract .90 times by the original C.

This is our first, temporary estimate of the player's runs created. We what we have done here is to ask these questions:
>   1. How many runs would a team probably score that consisted of eight "ordinary" type of hitters, plus this particular hitter?
>   2. How many of those runs would be created by the eight ordinary type of hitters?
>   3. What is the difference-and thus, how many runs did our player create?

To estimate this, we have placed our player in the context of eight hitters with a .300 on base percentage (2.4 divided by 8) and a .375 advancement percentage (3 divided by 8). For each trip through the batting order, the eight ordinary-type hitters would produce 9/10 of a run (2.4 times 3, divided by 8). The "9" in the denominator is eight ordinary hitters plus our man. The "-.9" being subtracted at the end is the runs created by the "ordinary" hitters. In essence, we have placed the hitter in a neutral solution, measured the neutral solution without our hitter, measured it with our hitter, and then estimated the contribution of this hitter as being the difference between the two.

We're not quite done. After that, we adjust the player's runs created estimate for his performance in two "run-sensitive" situations. Suppose that a player whose overall batting average is .250 has batted 100 times with runners in scoring position, and has gone 30-for-100. That's five hits better than expected, 30 hits where we would have expected 25. His team will score an extra five runs because he has done that, and so we increase the player's runs created estimate by five runs. If the player has hit poorly with runners in scoring position, we decrease it by the shortfall in the same way.

Suppose that a player has batted 250 times with runners on base, 250 times with the bases empty, and that he has hit 20 home runs overall. We would expect him to have hit 10 with men on base, 10 with the bases empty, right?

Suppose that he didn't. Suppose that he hit 12 with the bases empty, 8 with men on base. His team would score two runs less than expected because he did this, and we would thus penalize him two runs for the shortfall.

This is our second runs created estimate-the player's runs created, adjusted for his batting performance in run-sensitive situations.

Suppose, however, that we figure the runs created for all of the individuals on a team, and we add them up, and it doesn't match the runs actually scored by the team? What if the formulas say that the team should have scored 800 runs, but they actually scored 820?

Then obviously, the formulas missed. We're trying to measure the runs ACTUALLY created by each hitter as best we can, in the real world, not the theoretical impact of some combination of singles, doubles, triples and walks. If the actual number is different than the estimates, we have to adjust the estimates to fit the facts. In this case-820 runs scored with only 800 runs created-we would multiply each runs created estimate by 820/800, or 1.025. Then we round it off to an integer, and that's the player's estimated runs created.

Let go of that cat, Arthur. Heck, the moon isn't full for three weeks, anyway.

Runs Created per 27 Outs (RC/27)
This statistic estimates the number of runs per game that a team made up of nine of the same player would score. To calculate RC/27, multiply Runs Created by league outs per team game, divide the result by outs made by the player (the sum of at bats plus sacrifice hits plus sacrifice flies plus caught stealing plus grounded into double plays, minus hits). The formula written out is:

$$\frac{\frac{RC \times 3 \times LgIP}{2 \times LgG}}{AB - H + SH + SF + CS + GDP}$$

Runs Saved

See Defensive Runs Saved.

Save Opportunities
The sum of Saves and Blown Saves (see Save Situation).

Save/Hold Percentage (same as Holds Adjusted Saves Percentage)
The sum of Saves and Holds, divided by the sum of Saves, Holds, and Blown Saves.

For several years we figured "Save Percentage", which is simply Saves divided by Save Opportunities, and this stat has some currency in the game. But the Save Percentage severely discriminates against middle relievers, who have no real chance to be credited with the Save, since they will be taken out of the game and replaced by the Closer even if they throw 110 miles an hour and strike out everybody they see. Middle relievers typically have Save Percentages of zero, even if they pitch well. The Save/Hold Percentage is a much more realistic evaluation of a pitcher's success in Save situations.

Save Percentage
A pitcher's Saves divided by the total number of Save Situations he faces (see definition for Save Situation).

Save Situation
A relief pitcher is in a Save Situation when he enters the game with his team in the lead, has the opportunity to finish the game, is not the winning pitcher of record at the time, and meets any one of the three following conditions:

> 1. The pitcher's team is leading by no more than three runs and the pitcher has the chance to pitch for at least one inning,
> OR
> 2. The pitcher enters the game with the potential tying run on base, at bat, or on deck,
> OR
> 3. The pitcher pitches three or more effective innings regardless of the lead. The determination of a save in this situation is made by the official scorer.

It is not possible to have more than one save credited to a single team in a game.

SB Gain (Baserunning)
Stolen Base attempts must be successful greater than about two thirds of the time to have a positive result on the number of runs scored. SB gain is therefore the number of bases stolen minus two times the number of caught stealing (SB Gain = SB - 2CS). For example, a runner steals 30 bases and is caught stealing 7 times. His SB Gain would be 30 - 2*7 = +16. Another runner steals 10 bases and is caught stealing 6 times. His SB Gain (actually a loss) would be 10 - 2*6 = -2.

SB Success Percentage
Stolen Bases divided by the number of Stolen Base attempts (Stolen Bases plus Caught Stealing).

$$\frac{SB}{SB + CS}$$

Secondary Average

A number meant to reflect everything else except for batting average. A player will have a high Secondary Average if he hits for power, takes walks and steals bases. It is calculated with the following formula:

$$\frac{TB - H + BB + SB}{AB}$$

Similarity Score

A number which reflects the similarity between two different statistical lines, either for a player or for a team. A score of 1,000 means that the statistical lines are identical.

Slow Hooks

Used in the Manager's Record. For Quick Hooks and Slow Hooks a score is calculated for each game that is the sum of the number of Pitches plus 10 times the number of Runs Allowed. The top 25% of scores in the league are considered to be Slow Hooks.

Slugging Average

Total Bases divided by At Bats.

$$\frac{TB}{AB}$$

Speed Score

Speed score is an estimate of a player's running speed, based on six indicators of running speed found in his batting and fielding records. Those six indicators are stolen base success rate, the frequency of stolen base attempts, triples, grounding into double plays, runs scored as a percentage of times on base, and defensive position and range.

The full process of estimating Speed Scores is long and complex, and can be found on Bill James Online or by contacting Baseball Info Solutions.

Total Bases

Hits plus Doubles plus (2 times Triples) plus (3 times Home Runs).

$$H + 2B + (2 \times 3B) + (3 \times HR)$$

Tough Loss

A starting pitcher who loses the game with a game score over 50 gets credit for a tough loss. See Game Score.

Tough Save

This label is used to separate Saves by difficulty level (Easy or Tough). A Save is considered Tough if the relief pitcher enters the game with the tying run on base.

Unproductive Out
An out made by the batter which is not the third out of an inning, but comes with runners on base which fails to advance any baserunner, or results in a weaker baserunner configuration than before the out. See also Productive Out.

Win Probability
The probability of a team winning the game determined at any time during the game based on the score, inning, outs and base situation.

Winning Percentage
Wins divided by (Wins plus Losses).

Minor League Abbreviation Key

Abbreviation	Team	Level	League	MLB Affiliate	First Year	Last Year
Abrdn	Aberdeen IronBirds	A-	New York-Penn League	Baltimore Orioles	2002	2012
Akron	Akron Aeros	AA	Eastern League	Cleveland Indians	1997	2012
Albq	Albuquerque Isotopes	AAA	Pacific Coast League	Miami Marlins	2003	2008
Albq	Albuquerque Isotopes	AAA	Pacific Coast League	Los Angeles Dodgers	2009	2012
Altna	Altoona Curve	AA	Eastern League	Pittsburgh Pirates	1999	2012
Angels	AZL Angels	R	Arizona League	Los Angeles Angels	2001	2012
Ark	Arkansas Travelers	AA	Texas League	Los Angeles Angels	2001	2012
As	AZL Athletics	R	Arizona League	Oakland Athletics	1988	2012
Ashvll	Asheville Tourists	A	South Atlantic League	Colorado Rockies	1994	2012
Astros	GCL Astros	R	Gulf Coast League	Houston Astros	2009	2012
Auburn	Auburn Doubledays	A-	New York-Penn League	Toronto Blue Jays	2001	2010
Auburn	Auburn Doubledays	A-	New York-Penn League	Washington Nationals	2011	2012
Augsta	Augusta GreenJackets	A	South Atlantic League	San Francisco Giants	2005	2012
Augsta	Augusta Greenjackets	A	South Atlantic League	Boston Red Sox	1999	2004
B Jays	GCL Blue Jays	R	Gulf Coast League	Toronto Blue Jays	2007	2012
Batvia	Batavia Muckdogs	A-	New York-Penn League	Philadelphia Phillies	1998	2006
Batvia	Batavia Muckdogs	A-	New York-Penn League	St Louis Cardinals	2007	2012
Beloit	Beloit Snappers	A	Midwest League	Milwaukee Brewers	1995	2004
Beloit	Beloit Snappers	A	Midwest League	Minnesota Twins	2005	2012
BG	Bowling Green Hot Rods	A	Midwest League	Tampa Bay Rays	2010	2012
BG	Bowling Green Hot Rods	A	South Atlantic League	Tampa Bay Rays	2009	2009
Billings	Billings Mustangs	R+	Pioneer League	Cincinnati Reds	1974	2012
Bklyn	Brooklyn Cyclones	A-	New York-Penn League	New York Mets	2001	2012
Bkrsfld	Bakersfield Blaze	A+	California League	Tampa Bay Rays	2001	2004
Bkrsfld	Bakersfield Blaze	A+	California League	Texas Rangers	2005	2010
Bkrsfld	Bakersfield Blaze	A+	California League	Cincinnati Reds	2011	2012
Bluefld	Bluefield Orioles	R+	Appalachian League	Baltimore Orioles	1963	2010
Bluefld	Bluefield Blue Jays	R+	Appalachian League	Toronto Blue Jays	2011	2012
Bnghtn	Binghamton Mets	AA	Eastern League	New York Mets	1992	2012
Boise	Boise Hawks	A-	Northwest League	Chicago Cubs	2001	2012
Bowie	Bowie Baysox	AA	Eastern League	Baltimore Orioles	1993	2012
Bradtn	Bradenton Marauders	A+	Florida State League	Pittsburgh Pirates	2010	2012
Braves	GCL Braves	R	Gulf Coast League	Atlanta Braves	1976	2012
Brewrs	AZL Brewers	R	Arizona League	Milwaukee Brewers	2001	2012
Brham	Birmingham Barons	AA	Southern League	Chicago White Sox	1986	2012
Bristol	Bristol White Sox	R+	Appalachian League	Chicago White Sox	1995	2012
BrvdCt	Brevard County Manatees	A+	Florida State League	Washington Nationals	2002	2004
BrvdCt	Brevard County Manatees	A+	Florida State League	Milwaukee Brewers	2005	2012
Btl Crk	Battle Creek Yankees	A	Midwest League	New York Yankees	2003	2004
Buffalo	Buffalo Bisons	AAA	International League	New York Mets	2009	2012
Buffalo	Buffalo Bisons	AAA	International League	Cleveland Indians	1995	2008
Burlgtn	Burlington Bees	A	Midwest League	Kansas City Royals	2001	2010
Burlgtn	Burlington Royals	R+	Appalachian League	Kansas City Royals	2007	2012
Burlgtn	Burlington Bees	A	Midwest League	Oakland Athletics	2011	2012
CapeF	Cape Fear Crocs	A	South Atlantic League	Washington Nationals	1997	2000
Cards	GCL Cardinals	R	Gulf Coast League	St Louis Cardinals	2007	2012
Carlina	Carolina Mudcats	AA	Southern League	Cincinnati Reds	2009	2011
Carlina	Carolina Mudcats	AA	Southern League	Colorado Rockies	1999	2002
Carlina	Carolina Mudcats	AA	Southern League	Miami Marlins	2003	2008
Carlina	Carolina Mudcats	A+	Carolina League	Cleveland Indians	2012	2012
Casper	Casper Rockies	R+	Pioneer League	Colorado Rockies	2001	2007
Casper	Casper Ghosts	R+	Pioneer League	Colorado Rockies	2008	2011
Charltt	Charlotte Stone Crabs	A+	Florida State League	Tampa Bay Rays	2009	2012
Charltt	Charlotte Knights	AAA	International League	Chicago White Sox	1999	2012
Chatt	Chattanooga Lookouts	AA	Southern League	Cincinnati Reds	1988	2008
Chatt	Chattanooga Lookouts	AA	Southern League	Los Angeles Dodgers	2009	2012
Clinton	Clinton LumberKings	A	Midwest League	Seattle Mariners	2009	2012
Clinton	Clinton LumberKings	A	Midwest League	Texas Rangers	2003	2008
Clmbs	Columbus Catfish	A	South Atlantic League	Tampa Bay Rays	2007	2008
Clmbs	Columbus Clippers	AAA	International League	Cleveland Indians	2009	2012

Minor League Abbreviation Key

Abbreviation	Team	Level	League	MLB Affiliate	First Year	Last Year
Clmbs	Columbus Catfish	A	South Atlantic League	Los Angeles Dodgers	2004	2006
Clmbs	Columbus Clippers	AAA	International League	New York Yankees	1979	2006
Clrwtr	Clearwater Threshers	A+	Florida State League	Philadelphia Phillies	2004	2012
ColSpr	Colorado Springs Sky Sox	AAA	Pacific Coast League	Colorado Rockies	1993	2012
Conn	Connecticut Defenders	AA	Eastern League	San Francisco Giants	2006	2009
Conn	Connecticut Tigers	A-	New York-Penn League	Detroit Tigers	2010	2012
CpChr	Corpus Christi Hooks	AA	Texas League	Houston Astros	2005	2012
CRpds	Cedar Rapids Kernels	A	Midwest League	Los Angeles Angels	1993	2012
CtnSC	Charleston - SC RiverDogs	A	South Atlantic League	Tampa Bay Rays	1997	2004
CtnSC	Charleston RiverDogs	A	South Atlantic League	New York Yankees	2005	2012
CtnWV	Charleston - WV Alley Cats	A	South Atlantic League	Toronto Blue Jays	2001	2004
Cubs	AZL Cubs	R	Arizona League	Chicago Cubs	1993	2012
Danvle	Danville Braves	R+	Appalachian League	Atlanta Braves	1993	2012
Dayton	Dayton Dragons	A	Midwest League	Cincinnati Reds	2000	2012
DBcks	AZL Diamondbacks	R	Arizona League	Arizona Diamondbacks	2011	2012
Ddgrs	GCL Dodgers	R	Gulf Coast League	Los Angeles Dodgers	2001	2008
Ddgrs	AZL Dodgers	R	Arizona League	Los Angeles Dodgers	2009	2012
Dlmrva	Delmarva Shorebirds	A	South Atlantic League	Baltimore Orioles	1997	2012
Dnedin	Dunedin Blue Jays	A+	Florida State League	Toronto Blue Jays	1990	2012
Drham	Durham Bulls	AAA	International League	Tampa Bay Rays	1998	2012
Dytona	Daytona Cubs	A+	Florida State League	Chicago Cubs	1993	2012
Edmtn	Edmonton Trappers	AAA	Pacific Coast League	Washington Nationals	2003	2004
Edmtn	Edmonton Trappers	AAA	Pacific Coast League	Minnesota Twins	2001	2002
Elizab	Elizabethton Twins	R+	Appalachian League	Minnesota Twins	1974	2012
ElPaso	El Paso Diablos	AA	Texas League	Arizona Diamondbacks	1999	2004
Erie	Erie SeaWolves	AA	Eastern League	Detroit Tigers	2001	2012
Eugene	Eugene Emeralds	A-	Northwest League	San Diego Padres	2001	2012
Everett	Everett AquaSox	A-	Northwest League	Seattle Mariners	1995	2012
Expos	GCL Expos	R	Gulf Coast League	Washington Nationals	1986	2004
Frdrck	Frederick Keys	A+	Carolina League	Baltimore Orioles	1990	2012
Fresno	Fresno Grizzlies	AAA	Pacific Coast League	San Francisco Giants	1998	2012
Frisco	Frisco RoughRiders	AA	Texas League	Texas Rangers	2003	2012
FtMyrs	Fort Myers Miracle	A+	Florida State League	Minnesota Twins	1993	2012
FtWyn	Fort Wayne Wizards	A	Midwest League	San Diego Padres	1999	2008
FtWyn	Fort Wayne TinCaps	A	Midwest League	San Diego Padres	2009	2012
GdJunc	Grand Junction Rockies	R+	Pioneer League	Colorado Rockies	2012	2012
Giants	AZL Giants	R	Arizona League	San Francisco Giants	2000	2012
Gr Falls	Great Falls White Sox	R+	Pioneer League	Chicago White Sox	2003	2007
Gr Falls	Great Falls Voyagers	R+	Pioneer League	Chicago White Sox	2008	2012
Grnsbr	Greensboro Grasshoppers	A	South Atlantic League	Miami Marlins	2005	2012
Grnville	Greeneville Astros	R+	Appalachian League	Houston Astros	2004	2012
Grnville	Greenville Braves	AA	Southern League	Atlanta Braves	1984	2004
Grnville	Greenville Bombers	A	South Atlantic League	Boston Red Sox	2005	2005
Grnville	Greenville Drive	A	South Atlantic League	Boston Red Sox	2006	2012
Gt Lks	Great Lakes Loons	A	Midwest League	Los Angeles Dodgers	2007	2012
Gwnntt	Gwinnett Braves	AAA	International League	Atlanta Braves	2009	2012
Helena	Helena Brewers	R+	Pioneer League	Milwaukee Brewers	2003	2012
Hgrstn	Hagerstown Suns	A	South Atlantic League	Washington Nationals	2007	2012
Hgrstn	Hagerstown Suns	A	South Atlantic League	San Francisco Giants	2001	2004
Hi Dsrt	High Desert Mavericks	A+	California League	Seattle Mariners	2007	2012
Hi Dsrt	High Desert Mavericks	A+	California League	Milwaukee Brewers	2001	2004
Hkry	Hickory Crawdads	A	South Atlantic League	Pittsburgh Pirates	1999	2008
Hkry	Hickory Crawdads	A	South Atlantic League	Texas Rangers	2009	2012
Hntsvl	Huntsville Stars	AA	Southern League	Milwaukee Brewers	1999	2012
Hrsbrg	Harrisburg Senators	AA	Eastern League	Washington Nationals	1991	2012
HudVal	Hudson Valley Renegades	A-	New York-Penn League	Tampa Bay Rays	1997	2012
Idaho	Idaho Falls Padres	R+	Pioneer League	San Diego Padres	1995	2003
Idaho	Idaho Falls Chukars	R+	Pioneer League	Kansas City Royals	2004	2012
Indns	GCL Indians	R	Gulf Coast League	Cleveland Indians	2006	2008
Indns	AZL Indians	R	Arizona League	Cleveland Indians	2009	2012
Indy	Indianapolis Indians	AAA	International League	Pittsburgh Pirates	2005	2012
InldEm	Inland Empire 66ers	A+	California League	Seattle Mariners	2003	2006
InldEm	Inland Empire 66ers	A+	California League	Los Angeles Dodgers	2007	2010

Minor League Abbreviation Key

Abbreviation	Team	Level	League	MLB Affiliate	First Year	Last Year
InldEm	Inland Empire 66ers	A+	California League	Los Angeles Angels	2011	2012
Iowa	Iowa Cubs	AAA	Pacific Coast League	Chicago Cubs	1982	2012
Jacksn	Jackson Generals	AA	Southern League	Seattle Mariners	2011	2012
Jaxnvl	Jacksonville Suns	AA	Southern League	Miami Marlins	2009	2012
Jaxnvl	Jacksonville Suns	AA	Southern League	Los Angeles Dodgers	2001	2008
JhsCty	Johnson City Cardinals	R+	Appalachian League	St Louis Cardinals	1975	2012
Jmstwn	Jamestown Jammers	A-	New York-Penn League	Miami Marlins	2002	2012
Jupiter	Jupiter Hammerheads	A+	Florida State League	Miami Marlins	2002	2012
Kane	Kane County Cougars	A	Midwest League	Oakland Athletics	2003	2010
Kane	Kane County Cougars	A	Midwest League	Kansas City Royals	2011	2012
Knapol	Kannapolis Intimidators	A	South Atlantic League	Chicago White Sox	2001	2012
Kngspt	Kingsport Mets	R+	Appalachian League	New York Mets	1984	2012
Knstn	Kinston Indians	A+	Carolina League	Cleveland Indians	1990	2011
Lakwd	Lakewood BlueClaws	A	South Atlantic League	Philadelphia Phillies	2001	2012
Lancst	Lancaster JetHawks	A+	California League	Houston Astros	2009	2012
Lancst	Lancaster Jethawks	A+	California League	Arizona Diamondbacks	2001	2006
Lansng	Lansing Lugnuts	A	Midwest League	Chicago Cubs	1999	2004
Lk Cty	Lake County Captains	A	South Atlantic League	Cleveland Indians	2003	2009
Lk Cty	Lake County Captains	A	Midwest League	Cleveland Indians	2010	2012
Lk Els	Lake Elsinore Storm	A+	California League	San Diego Padres	2001	2012
Lkland	Lakeland Flying Tigers	A+	Florida State League	Detroit Tigers	1990	2006
Lkland	Lakeland Tigers	A+	Florida State League	Detroit Tigers	2007	2012
Lng Isl	Long Island Ducks	IND	Atlantic League	Independent	2000	2012
Lnsng	Lansing Lugnuts	A	Midwest League	Toronto Blue Jays	2005	2012
Lowell	Lowell Spinners	A-	New York-Penn League	Boston Red Sox	1996	2012
LsVgs	Las Vegas 51s	AAA	Pacific Coast League	Toronto Blue Jays	2009	2012
LsVgs	Las Vegas 51s	AAA	Pacific Coast League	Los Angeles Dodgers	2001	2008
Lsvlle	Louisville Bats	AAA	International League	Cincinnati Reds	2000	2012
LV	Lehigh Valley IronPigs	AAA	International League	Philadelphia Phillies	2008	2012
Lxngtn	Lexington Legends	A	South Atlantic League	Houston Astros	2001	2012
Lynbrg	Lynchburg Hillcats	A+	Carolina League	Pittsburgh Pirates	1995	2009
Lynbrg	Lynchburg Hillcats	A+	Carolina League	Cincinnati Reds	2010	2010
Lynbrg	Lynchburg Hillcats	A+	Carolina League	Atlanta Braves	2011	2012
Macon	Macon Braves	A	South Atlantic League	Atlanta Braves	1991	2002
Mdest	Modesto As'	A+	California League	Oakland Athletics	1990	2004
Mdest	Modesto Nuts	A+	California League	Colorado Rockies	2005	2012
MdHat	Medicine Hat Blue Jays	R+	Pioneer League	Toronto Blue Jays	1978	2002
Mdland	Midland RockHounds	AA	Texas League	Oakland Athletics	1999	2012
Memp	Memphis Redbirds	AAA	Pacific Coast League	St Louis Cardinals	1998	2012
Mets	GCL Mets	R	Gulf Coast League	New York Mets	2004	2011
MhVlly	Mahoning Valley Scrappers	A-	New York-Penn League	Cleveland Indians	1999	2012
Mich	Michigan Battle Cats	A	Midwest League	Houston Astros	1999	2002
Missi	Mississippi Braves	AA	Southern League	Atlanta Braves	2005	2012
Mobile	Mobile BayBears	AA	Southern League	Arizona Diamondbacks	2007	2012
Mont	Montgomery Biscuits	AA	Southern League	Tampa Bay Rays	2004	2012
Mrlns	GCL Marlins	R	Gulf Coast League	Miami Marlins	1992	2012
MrtlBh	Myrtle Beach Pelicans	A+	Carolina League	Atlanta Braves	1999	2010
MrtlBh	Myrtle Beach Pelicans	A+	Carolina League	Texas Rangers	2011	2012
Ms	AZL Mariners	R	Arizona League	Seattle Mariners	1989	2012
Msoula	Missoula Osprey	R+	Pioneer League	Arizona Diamondbacks	1999	2012
Nashv	Nashville Sounds	AAA	Pacific Coast League	Milwaukee Brewers	2005	2012
Nats	GCL Nationals	R	Gulf Coast League	Washington Nationals	2005	2012
NewOr	New Orleans Zephyrs	AAA	Pacific Coast League	New York Mets	2007	2008
NewOr	New Orleans Zephyrs	AAA	Pacific Coast League	Miami Marlins	2009	2012
NewOr	New Orleans Zephyrs	AAA	Pacific Coast League	Houston Astros	1997	2004
NHam	New Hampshire Fisher Cats	AA	Eastern League	Toronto Blue Jays	2004	2012
Norfolk	Norfolk Tides	AAA	International League	New York Mets	1993	2006
Norfolk	Norfolk Tides	AAA	International League	Baltimore Orioles	2007	2012
Nrwich	Norwich Navigators	AA	Eastern League	San Francisco Giants	2003	2005
NWArk	Northwest Arkansas Naturals	AA	Texas League	Kansas City Royals	2008	2012
NwBrit	New Britain Rock Cats	AA	Eastern League	Minnesota Twins	1997	2012
NwHav	New Haven Ravens	AA	Eastern League	Toronto Blue Jays	2003	2003
Ogden	Ogden Raptors	R+	Pioneer League	Los Angeles Dodgers	2003	2012

Minor League Abbreviation Key

Abbreviation	Team	Level	League	MLB Affiliate	First Year	Last Year
OKCity	Oklahoma City RedHawks	AAA	Pacific Coast League	Texas Rangers	2009	2010
OKCity	Oklahoma City RedHawks	AAA	Pacific Coast League	Houston Astros	2011	2012
Okla	Oklahoma RedHawks	AAA	Pacific Coast League	Texas Rangers	1998	2008
Omha	Omaha Royals	AAA	Pacific Coast League	Kansas City Royals	1969	2010
Omha	Omaha Storm Chasers	AAA	Pacific Coast League	Kansas City Royals	2011	2012
Oneont	Oneonta Tigers	A-	New York-Penn League	Detroit Tigers	1999	2009
Orem	Orem Owlz	R+	Pioneer League	Los Angeles Angels	2005	2012
Orioles	GCL Orioles	R	Gulf Coast League	Baltimore Orioles	2007	2012
Padres	AZL Padres	R	Arizona League	San Diego Padres	2004	2012
Penscla	Pensacola Blue Wahoos	AA	Southern League	Cincinnati Reds	2012	2012
Peoria	Peoria Chiefs	A	Midwest League	St Louis Cardinals	1995	2004
Peoria	Peoria Chiefs	A	Midwest League	Chicago Cubs	2005	2012
Phillies	GCL Phillies	R	Gulf Coast League	Philadelphia Phillies	1999	2012
Pirates	GCL Pirates	R	Gulf Coast League	Pittsburgh Pirates	1968	2012
PlmBh	Palm Beach Cardinals	A+	Florida State League	St Louis Cardinals	2003	2012
Portlnd	Portland Beavers	AAA	Pacific Coast League	San Diego Padres	2001	2010
Portlnd	Portland Sea Dogs	AA	Eastern League	Boston Red Sox	2003	2012
Princtn	Princeton Devil Rays	R+	Appalachian League	Tampa Bay Rays	1997	2007
Princtn	Princeton Rays	R+	Appalachian League	Tampa Bay Rays	2008	2012
Provo	Provo Angels	R+	Pioneer League	Los Angeles Angels	2001	2004
Ptomc	Potomac Nationals	A+	Carolina League	Washington Nationals	2005	2012
Ptomc	Potomac Cannons	A+	Carolina League	Cincinnati Reds	2003	2004
Pulaski	Pulaski Blue Jays	R+	Appalachian League	Toronto Blue Jays	2003	2006
Pulaski	Pulaski Mariners	R+	Appalachian League	Seattle Mariners	2008	2012
Pwtckt	Pawtucket Red Sox	AAA	International League	Boston Red Sox	1977	2012
QuadC	Quad City Swing	A	Midwest League	Minnesota Twins	2004	2004
QuadC	Quad City Swing	A	Midwest League	St Louis Cardinals	2005	2007
QuadC	Quad Cities River Bandits	A	Midwest League	St Louis Cardinals	2008	2012
Rays	GCL Rays	R	Gulf Coast League	Tampa Bay Rays	2009	2012
Rchmd	Richmond Flying Squirrels	AA	Eastern League	San Francisco Giants	2010	2012
Rchmd	Richmond Braves	AAA	International League	Atlanta Braves	1966	2008
RCuca	Rancho Cucamonga Quakes	A+	California League	Los Angeles Angels	2001	2010
RCuca	Rancho Cucamonga Quakes	A+	California League	Los Angeles Dodgers	2011	2012
Rdng	Reading Phillies	AA	Eastern League	Philadelphia Phillies	1967	2012
RdRck	Round Rock Express	AAA	Pacific Coast League	Houston Astros	2005	2010
RdRck	Round Rock Express	AA	Texas League	Houston Astros	2000	2004
RdRck	Round Rock Express	AAA	Pacific Coast League	Texas Rangers	2011	2012
Reds	GCL Reds	R	Gulf Coast League	Cincinnati Reds	1999	2009
Reds	AZL Reds	R	Arizona League	Cincinnati Reds	2010	2012
RedSx	GCL Red Sox	R	Gulf Coast League	Boston Red Sox	1989	2012
Reno	Reno Aces	AAA	Pacific Coast League	Arizona Diamondbacks	2009	2012
Rngrs	AZL Rangers	R	Arizona League	Texas Rangers	2003	2012
Roch	Rochester Red Wings	AAA	International League	Minnesota Twins	2003	2012
Rome	Rome Braves	A	South Atlantic League	Atlanta Braves	2003	2012
Royals	AZL Royals	R	Arizona League	Kansas City Royals	2004	2012
Salem	Salem Avalanche	A+	Carolina League	Houston Astros	2003	2008
Salem	Salem Red Sox	A+	Carolina League	Boston Red Sox	2009	2012
Salt Lk	Salt Lake Stingers	AAA	Pacific Coast League	Los Angeles Angels	2001	2005
Salt Lk	Salt Lake Bees	AAA	Pacific Coast League	Los Angeles Angels	2006	2012
Savann	Savannah Sand Gnats	A	South Atlantic League	Washington Nationals	2003	2006
Savann	Savannah Sand Gnats	A	South Atlantic League	New York Mets	2007	2012
Sbend	South Bend Silver Hawks	A	Midwest League	Arizona Diamondbacks	1997	2012
Scrmto	Sacramento River Cats	AAA	Pacific Coast League	Oakland Athletics	2000	2012
SlmKzr	Salem-Keizer Volcanoes	A-	Northwest League	San Francisco Giants	1997	2012
SnAnt	San Antonio Missions	AA	Texas League	Seattle Mariners	2006	2006
SnAnt	San Antonio Missions	AA	Texas League	San Diego Padres	2007	2012
SnJos	San Jose Giants	A+	California League	San Francisco Giants	1990	2012
Spkane	Spokane Indians	A-	Northwest League	Texas Rangers	2003	2012
Sprgfld	Springfield Cardinals	AA	Texas League	St Louis Cardinals	2005	2012
Srsota	Sarasota Reds	A+	Florida State League	Cincinnati Reds	2005	2009
Srsota	Sarasota Red Sox	A+	Florida State League	Boston Red Sox	1995	2004
Stcktn	Stockton Ports	A+	California League	Oakland Athletics	2005	2012
Stcktn	Stockton Ports	A+	California League	Texas Rangers	2003	2004

Minor League Abbreviation Key

Abbreviation	Team	Level	League	MLB Affiliate	First Year	Last Year
StCol	State College Spikes	A-	New York-Penn League	Pittsburgh Pirates	2007	2012
StIsInd	Staten Island Yankees	A-	New York-Penn League	New York Yankees	1999	2012
StLuci	St. Lucie Mets	A+	Florida State League	New York Mets	1990	2012
S-WB	Scranton/Wilkes-Barre Red Barons	AAA	International League	Philadelphia Phillies	1989	2006
S-WB	Scranton/Wilkes-Barre Yankees	AAA	International League	New York Yankees	2007	2012
SWMch	Southwest Michigan Devil Rays	A	Midwest League	Tampa Bay Rays	2005	2006
Syrcse	Syracuse SkyChiefs	AAA	International League	Toronto Blue Jays	1978	2006
Syrcse	Syracuse Chiefs	AAA	International League	Toronto Blue Jays	2007	2008
Syrcse	Syracuse Chiefs	AAA	International League	Washington Nationals	2009	2012
Tacom	Tacoma Rainiers	AAA	Pacific Coast League	Seattle Mariners	1995	2012
Tampa	Tampa Yankees	A+	Florida State League	New York Yankees	1994	2012
Tenn	Tennessee Smokies	AA	Southern League	Chicago Cubs	2007	2012
Tigers	GCL Tigers	R	Gulf Coast League	Detroit Tigers	1995	2012
Toledo	Toledo Mud Hens	AAA	International League	Detroit Tigers	1987	2012
TriCity	Tri-City Dust Devils	A-	Northwest League	Colorado Rockies	2001	2012
TriCity	Tri-City ValleyCats	A-	New York-Penn League	Houston Astros	2002	2012
Trntn	Trenton Thunder	AA	Eastern League	New York Yankees	2003	2012
Trntn	Trenton Thunder	AA	Eastern League	Boston Red Sox	1995	2002
Tucsn	Tucson Padres	AAA	Pacific Coast League	San Diego Padres	2011	2012
Tucsn	Tucson Sidewinders	AAA	Pacific Coast League	Arizona Diamondbacks	1998	2008
Tulsa	Tulsa Drillers	AA	Texas League	Colorado Rockies	2003	2012
Twins	GCL Twins	R	Gulf Coast League	Minnesota Twins	1989	2012
Vancvr	Vancouver Canadians	A-	Northwest League	Oakland Athletics	1999	1999
Vancvr	Vancouver Canadians	A-	Northwest League	Toronto Blue Jays	2011	2012
VeroB	Vero Beach Dodgers	A+	Florida State League	Los Angeles Dodgers	1990	2006
VeroB	Vero Beach Devil Rays	A+	Florida State League	Tampa Bay Rays	2007	2008
Visalia	Visalia Oaks	A+	California League	Colorado Rockies	2003	2004
Visalia	Visalia Rawhide	A+	California League	Arizona Diamondbacks	2007	2012
Vrmnt	Vermont Expos	A-	New York-Penn League	Washington Nationals	1994	2005
Vrmnt	Vermont Lake Monsters	A-	New York-Penn League	Washington Nationals	2006	2010
Vrmnt	Vermont Lake Monsters	A-	New York-Penn League	Oakland Athletics	2011	2012
Wilmg	Wilmington Blue Rocks	A+	Carolina League	Kansas City Royals	2007	2012
WinSa	Winston-Salem Warthogs	A+	Carolina League	Chicago White Sox	1997	2008
WinSa	Winston-Salem Dash	A+	Carolina League	Chicago White Sox	2009	2012
Wisc	Wisconsin Timber Rattlers	A	Midwest League	Seattle Mariners	1995	2008
Wisc	Wisconsin Timber Rattlers	A	Midwest League	Milwaukee Brewers	2009	2012
WMich	West Michigan Whitecaps	A	Midwest League	Detroit Tigers	1997	2012
Wmspt	Williamsport Crosscutters	A-	New York-Penn League	Philadelphia Phillies	2007	2012
Wmspt	Williamsport Crosscutters	A-	New York-Penn League	Pittsburgh Pirates	1999	2006
WTenn	West Tenn Diamond Jaxx	AA	Southern League	Seattle Mariners	2007	2010
WTenn	West Tenn Diamond Jaxx	AA	Southern League	Chicago Cubs	1998	2006
WV	West Virginia Power	A	South Atlantic League	Milwaukee Brewers	2005	2008
WV	West Virginia Power	A	South Atlantic League	Pittsburgh Pirates	2009	2012
Yakima	Yakima Bears	A-	Northwest League	Arizona Diamondbacks	2001	2012
Yanks	GCL Yankees	R	Gulf Coast League	New York Yankees	1984	2012

Baseball Info Solutions

Baseball Info Solutions has been supplying top notch, timely, and in-depth baseball data and analytics to its customers since 2002. BIS collects a statistical snapshot of every important moment of every Major League Baseball game with the most advanced technology, resulting in a database that includes traditional data, pitch-by-pitch data, and defensive positioning data. The company also has the highest quality pitch charting data available anywhere, including pitch type, location, and velocity.

BIS provides data and/or analysis to about half of the 30 Major League Baseball teams as well as media companies, websites, fantasy services, game companies, and private individuals. No request is too big or too small, and every inquiry is answered in a timely and personal manner. We provide the personal touch to meet any customized needs.

Baseball Info Solutions continues to break new ground in data collection and analysis, providing its clients with the latest and greatest baseball information available anywhere. Over the past decade, BIS has specialized in innovative defensive data and analytics that have shifted the landscape of the sabermetric industry.

John Dewan, the principal owner and president of BIS, has been on the cutting edge of baseball analysis for over 25 years. His experience goes all the way back to his days as Executive Director of Project Scoresheet, the Bill James-led effort that pioneered the new wave of baseball statistics that are now common terminology.

The rest of the BIS team includes former scouts and collegiate baseball players as well as research, programming and database management experts. Additionally, BIS recruits and trains the best video scouting talent from across the country, and BIS internships have been the starting point for many successful baseball operations executives.

For data inquiries, job openings, or other information, please contact BIS at:

Baseball Info Solutions
41 S. 2nd Street
Coplay, PA 18037
610-261-2370
www.baseballinfosolutions.com

Acknowledgements

The Bill James Handbook is a complete record of the just-finished season. As such, we have to wait until the season is "in the books" for us to, well, put it in the book. In order to get the book to you on November 1, we rely heavily on a number of people who play vital roles during the intense two-week process.

First of all, there's Bill James. Some people ask us if we at BIS do all the work then simply slap Bill's name on the cover. Nothing could be further from the truth. As I write this, Bill and I are debating exactly how many at-bats to project for certain players who are not and will never be household names.

John and Sue Dewan are majority owners of BIS, with John stepping in as President this year. No matter how many other obligations John has, he always makes enough time to dig through the Handbook in painstaking detail.

Jeff Spoljaric and Andrew Gibson inherited the unenviable task of coordinating and physically producing the Handbook. In their spare time, Jeff is Vice President of Information Technology and Andrew works with him as an IT Associate. Patrick Coyle also lends his expertise to the IT department.

Jon Vrecsics and Jim Swavely coordinate the BIS minor league operation, while Dan Casey, Mike Piekarski, and Todd Radcliffe lead the legion of major league video scouts. All five spend countless hours stat-checking literally every number in this book, twice. If the numbers in this book differ from those published elsewhere, rest assured that these guys have noticed it, dug into it, and concluded that these numbers are the correct ones.

Scott Spratt joined the R&D Department a few weeks ago. We've thrown him right into the fire with this Handbook, and he's handled it like a veteran.

Jim Capuano's job is to take all of the in-depth data and groundbreaking analysis we do at BIS and work with strategic partners to share it with the rest of the world.

Our video scout crew, which seems to get better and better every year, included Zach Anastasi, Brandon Barak, Joel Chavez, Randy Chrisman, Jason Eisele, Josh Flowerman, Adam Hayes, Chris Koller, Alex Lewin, Eric Longenhagen, Matt Marsh, Ryan McCauley, Matt McGrath, Kevin Morrissey, Eric Nehs, Ryan Smith, Michael Syer, and Andy Tworischuk.

Our partners at ACTA Publications include President and Co-Publisher Greg Pierce, along with my fellow Alabamian Amanda Modelski, Tom Wright, Donna Ryding, Mary Eggert, and Isz.

Our friends in the baseball industry have provided countless insights over the years. They include Greg Ambrosius, Andy Andres, David Appelman, Matthew Berry, Jim Callis, Doug Dennis, Jeff Erickson, Peter Gammons, Steve Gardner, Jason Grey, Durward Hamil, Eric Karabell, Peter Kreutzer, Michael Lehrer, Chris Liss, Gene McCaffrey, Deric McKamey, Sig Mejdal, John Menna, Bob Meyerhoff, Mike Murphy, Lawr Michaels, Patrick Newman, Rob Neyer, Alex Patton, Mike Phillips, Scott Pianowski, David Pinto, Joe Posnanski, Nate Ravitz, Hal Richman, Steve Ruskowski, Mike Salfino, Peter Schoenke, Ron Shandler, Joe Sheehan, John Sickels, Mark Simon, Dave Studenmund, Tom Tango, Mark Watson, Rick Wilton, Trace Wood, Don Zminda, Todd Zola

Special thanks to Larry Taylor and Manos Kypar, who sent us suggestions for the Handbook. We liked them so much, we made more work for ourselves just to fit them into the book. Also, a special thank you goes to Steve Ruskowski for his stat-checking assistance.

An extra special thanks goes to Steve Moyer and Rob Burckhard. Both have played vital roles in past Handbooks and at BIS in general but have since parted ways. We appreciate all of your contributions over the years.

Thanks to everyone we haven't had space to mention by name. Lastly, thanks to you the reader.

Ben Jedlovec
Baseball Info Solutions